THE SCHOTTENSTEIN EDITION

סידור

SIDDUR

שמחת יהושע

The ArtScroll Series®

Rabbi Nosson Scherman / Rabbi Meir Zlotowitz
General Editors

A PROJECT OF THE

Mesorah Heritage Foundation

סדור לימות החול

שמחת יהושע

Published by

Mesorah Publications, ltd

*T*his volume is dedicated in honor of
our parents and grandparents

Jerome Schottenstein ז״ל

יעקב מאיר חיים בן אפרים אליעזר הכהן ע״ה

a great and modest leader
who dedicated his attainments
to the benefit of his people,
and who, in the process, made history.

Geraldine Schottenstein Hoffman

whose strength of character,
generous spirit, and devotion to family
earn her the affection of her loved ones
and the admiration of her friends.

Leonard and Heddy Rabe

whose consistent example of quiet spirituality,
of kindness and character,
of integrity and sincerity
make them role models to all who know them.

Jay and Jeanie Schottenstein

Joseph Aaron and Lindsay Brooke

Jacob Meir, Jonah Philip, Emma Blake

Jonathan Richard and Nicole Lauren

Winnie Simone, Teddi Isabella, Allegra Giselle, and Elodie Yael

Jeffrey Adam and Ariella

Jerome Meir

≪ TABLE OF CONTENTS ≫

⋗ The Interlinear Translation — How to Read it

There is a difficulty inherent in any interlinear translation of Hebrew to English: the fact that English and Hebrew are read in opposite directions. ArtScroll has developed a patented system of notations that helps the reader navigate the two languages simultaneously, without confusion.

These notations consist of the following:

1) single arrow notations ⟨ between English phrases direct the reader's eye toward the next English phrase, reading right to left, for example:

$$\text{אַשְׁרֵי יוֹשְׁבֵי בֵיתֶךָ,}$$

《 in Your house, ⟨ are those who dwell ⟨ Praiseworthy

2) Double arrow notations 《 indicate a logical break between phrases, equivalent to a period, semicolon, dash and many commas.

3) Bold double arrow notations **《** indicate the completion of a sentence at the end of a verse.

With these double arrows, the reader need not search for commas, semicolons, and periods. This was done to make the translation as user-friendly as possible; it allows the reader to continue following the Hebrew moving to the left, without the distraction of looking for English punctuation marks on the *right* side of the English words.

The arrows also identify the specific Hebrew word or words that are translated by the English phrase. This is especially useful where two or more Hebrew words are translated as a unit.

For quotations, one further convention was used: Wherever text would normally be set off by quotation marks, the quotation has been set in italics.

ܒ§ Publisher's Preface

In 1984, the publication of the *Complete ArtScroll Siddur* launched what many observers regard as a revolution in the understanding and appreciation of *tefillah*/prayer. Since then, countless people have told us that their discovery of the Siddur marked a turning point in their lives. Its new translation, user-friendly instructions, and inspirational commentary gave them a new appreciation and understanding of prayer.

In 2001, the publication of the Schottenstein Edition Interlinear *Tehillim/ Psalms* inaugurated a new revolution in the comprehension and quality of prayer. The response to the *Tehillim* has been so positive that it was virtually an injunction to publish the other books of prayer in a similar format. The Ashkenaz Shabbos-Festival and Weekday Siddurim followed, and elicited a similar response.

As one user commented, "It made me appreciate more than ever the importance of every single word of the prayers." We are proud, therefore, to inaugurate the same service in *Nusach Sefard*. With this new format, we hope that additional multitudes will pray with a comprehension they have never had before. We are hopeful that אי"ה the publication of these "interlinear" Siddurim will initiate the same sort of awakening in the lives of many people as the original ArtScroll Siddur has achieved for many years.

Why?

A look at a typical page of this Siddur provides the answer. Even someone fluent in Hebrew will often come across an unfamiliar word or phrase. To look at an adjoining column or facing page for the translation will often cause a loss of concentration, and one may find it difficult to return to the exact phrase of the prayer. Next time, the worshiper may well decide to forgo the translation in favor of continuing the prayer without a lapse. The result

is a frequent tug of war between the desire for understanding and the need not to interrupt the recitation, especially if one is praying with the congregation.

This new format provides the best solution yet. It is called "interlinear," a word that may sound cryptic, but whose meaning is immediately obvious when one looks at the page. The translation is directly beneath each word or phrase — not opposite the line, but intermingled with it. Instantly, the worshiper sees the meaning and continues his recitation.

This basic concept was first used in England in 1874. Why has it not become a common feature of the Siddur and *Tehillim?* Because the sentence structure of Hebrew is very different from that of English, and this complicates the task of translation. For example, take the very familiar phrase תְּהִלַּת ה' יְדַבֶּר פִּי, which our *Tehillim* and Siddur translate quite accurately as *May my mouth declare the praise of* HASHEM. But a *literal, word-by-word* translation is *The praise of* HASHEM *will declare my mouth* — accurate, perhaps, but hardly comprehensible. Undoubtedly, the difficulty of making an interlinear translation both accurate and readable led to its disuse. Thus, the editors of this interlinear translation had to be masters of both syntax and meaning, often adding a word here and there in order to do justice both to translation and comprehensibility.

But there is another, more basic, problem — the discrepancy between the Hebrew that reads right to left, and the English that reads left to right. The eye is confused, as it were, like an American stepping off a curb in England, and instinctively looking to his left, while traffic speeds toward him from the right. Consequently, a way had to be found to solve the right-left problem. Another glance at a page in this edition will show the solution. After each English word or phrase, there is a barely obtrusive arrow, which directs the eye in the direction of the Hebrew. We have tested this device, and found that it solves the problem to an amazing degree. These arrows keep the reader's eye moving in the direction of the Hebrew without interfering with his reading of the English. To indicate a comma or pause, there is a double arrow, and to indicate a period at the end of a verse, the double arrow is bold. A patent is pending on this revolutionary new graphics icon, which was developed in conjunction with RABBI BENYAMIN GOHARI, whose efforts we gratefully acknowledge.

At the bottom of the page, the commentary elucidates the intent of the more difficult phrases and, where the syntax remains difficult after the interlinear translation, the commentary gives a flowing English rendering.

This new Interlinear Series is dedicated by **JAY AND JEANIE SCHOTTEN-STEIN.** The Schottensteins are familiar to Jews worldwide as the Patrons of the Hebrew and English editions of ArtScroll's Schottenstein Edition of the Babylonian Talmud. With this new series, they extend their vision beyond the Torah study of multitudes to the quality of prayer of *Klal Yisrael*. The three pillars of the universe are Torah, service, and kind deeds (*Avos* 1:2). With this new initiative, Jay and Jeanie strengthen all three pillars: The Schottenstein Talmud, among their other benefactions, is raising Torah study to a new plateau; the generosity of the extended Schottenstein family has been legendary for generations; and now, with the Interlinear Series, prayerful service of God will be elevated for countless thousands of people.

This Interlinear Siddur follows the SEIF EDITION TRANSLITERATED SIDDUR, which is of enormous benefit to people who find it difficult to read Hebrew. HESHE and HARRIET SEIF are good friends and distinguished supporters of worthy causes, here and in Israel.

◆§ **Contents** The Siddur includes translations and commentaries on all the standard prayers and weekday Torah readings. As much as possible, the services for each day are self-contained, so that the reader will be spared the annoying chore of turning back and forth. The Overview provides a perspective on prayer and the three daily prayers.

◆§ **Translation** The translation strives to balance the lofty beauty of the heavily nuanced text with a readily understood English rendering. Obviously, the word-by-word nature of this work constrains the fluidity of the language, but yet it does flow. Occasionally, we rely on the commentary to clarify the meaning of the text.

◆§ **Commentary** The commentary has two goals: to explain the difficult passages and to involve the reader in the spiritual and inspirational experience of prayer. We have avoided purely technical or grammatical comments. Unattributed comments are sometimes the author's own, but usually distill the general trend of standard commentaries.

◆§ **Laws and Instructions** Clear instructions are provided throughout. More complex or lengthy halachos are discussed in the "Laws" section at the end of the Siddur. This section includes general halachos that are relevant to the weekday prayer service. Throughout the Siddur, we refer to these laws by paragraph (§) number.

◆§ **Layout and Typography** Though this Siddur's interlinear system sets it apart dramatically from others, it fundamentally maintains the pattern of the ArtScroll Siddur, which has been greatly praised for its ease of use and clarity of layout. This Siddur, with its clear instructions, copious subtitles, and precise page headings, was designed to make the service easy for everyone to follow. Paragraphs begin with bold-type words to facilitate finding the individual *tefillos;* portions said aloud by the *chazzan* are indicated by either the symbol ❖ or the word *chazzan.* An asterisk (*) after a word indicates that the word or phrase is treated in the commentary. Numbered footnotes give the Scriptural sources of countless verses that have been melded into the prayers, as well as variant readings. A footnote beginning "Cf." indicates that the Scriptural source is paraphrased.

◆§ **Hebrew Grammar** As a general rule in the Hebrew language, the accent is on the last syllable. Where it is on an earlier syllable, it is indicated with a *messeg,* a vertical line below the accented letter: שִׁירוּ. In the case of the *Shema* and the Song at the Sea, which are printed with the cantillation [*trop*], the accent follows the *trop.* שְׁוָא נָע [*sh'va na]* is indicated by a hyphen mark above the letter: בְּרֵכוּ, except for a *sh'va* on the first letter of a word, which is always a *sh'va na.* In identifying a *sh'va na,* we have followed the rules of the Vilna Gaon and Rabbi Yaakov Emden.

◆§ Acknowledgments

Supervising and editing the entire project was RABBI MENACHEM DAVIS, who brought uncommon skills to this very difficult task, and accomplished it brilliantly. He is sensitive to the subtleties and nuances of both the Hebrew and English languages and has the ability to discover ways of converting even complex syntactical constructions into the interlinear word-by-word format. With exemplary dedication he has produced an edifying work to enhance the ability of our people to communicate with the One Above. RABBI YAAKOV BLINDER provided valuable research and prepared preliminary drafts of much of the translation. His diligent efforts were essential to the timely publication of the Siddur.

We are grateful to REB NOACH DEAR and REB ZECHARIAH FRUCHTHANDLER, who suggested how valuable this format would be. We acknowledge several of the scholars who contributed to previous editions of the ArtScroll Siddur. RABBI AVIE GOLD is the source of much of the material, and his

meticulous reading and suggestions enrich every page. His is a unique blend of knowledge, skill, and dedication. RABBI HERSH GOLDWURM זצ"ל had compiled the "Laws," reviewed most of the instructions, and re-searched the accuracy of the text. His contribution to ArtScroll was great and his loss is sorely felt.

Indispensable to this volume were the earlier works of RABBI AVROHOM CHAIM FEUER, the author of the classic ArtScroll *Tehillim,* and RABBI HILLEL DANZIGER, who adapted Rabbi Feuer's work to produce the one-volume ArtScroll *Tehillim.* We are grateful also to the scholars and editors in Israel and America for their valuable research and comments.

The design of the page was a challenge even for our cherished friend and colleague REB SHEAH BRANDER, the acknowledged genius in this demanding field. His achievement in this work is truly extraordinary.

MRS. LEA BRAFMAN, is our dedicated and outstandingly competent comptroller.

SHMUEL BLITZ, director of our Jerusalem office, provided indispensible assistance in coordinating the editorial process.

We are grateful also to RABBI MOSHE ROSENBLUM for reviewing the Hebrew text and *nikkud,* to RABBI LIPA ZICHERMAN for reviewing and verify-ing the accuracy of the *Nusach Sefard* text, to MRS. JUDI DICK and MRS. MINDY STERN, who reviewed the manuscript and made valuable comments and suggestions; to MRS. FAYGIE WEINBAUM for her proofreading; and to MRS. CHUMIE LIPSCHITZ, MRS. RUCHY REIFER, and MISS LIBBY ZWEIG who assisted in the typesetting.

We are confident that the new interlinear format will be a great boon for countless people and we look forward to the publication of forthcoming works in this new series. Prayer, in the words of the Sages, is the "service of the heart," and hearts overflowing with devotion to God long to couple their service with the comprehension of the mind. This volume will help sincere people achieve that goal, and for being able to help accomplish that, we are grateful to the One Who listens to the prayers of His people.

Rabbi Meir Zlotowitz   Rabbi Nosson Scherman

Teves 5763 / December 2002
Brooklyn, N.Y.

✑ Editor's Preface

K*oheles* said, טובים השנים מן האחד, *two are better than one*. It does not take the wisdom of the wisest man to know that. Obviously, Solomon describes a situation where the result is *greater* than the sum of the individual efforts or capabilities. The word for this is synergy.

Being a part of the ArtScroll family for over two years, and looking back at what I have assisted in producing, I observe that synergy does not even tell a fraction of the ArtScroll story. If someone had told me that in less than two years I would produce four major works, one on *Tehillim* and three Siddurim, I would have thought they were irrational or delusional. Yet that reality is part of the ArtScroll synergy. I alone would not have conceived of the interlinear project, would not have undertaken the intensive effort required, and — were the first two conditions somehow met — I could not have completed four such projects in that time on my own. In fact I could not have accomplished what has been produced without being inside the ArtScroll intellectual pressure cooker. Scholars such as RABBI NOSSON SCHERMAN, who is renowned for his eloquence and depth in expressing so many of the ideas of the ArtScroll oeuvre, and who was always available for consultation; RABBI MENACHEM SILBER, whose encyclopedic knowledge was readily proffered, and who provided access to critical volumes from his personal library; RABBI AVIE GOLD, whose knowledge and sage advice on intricate topics of *Piyut* and *Nusach* parallel his inspiring dedication to his research; and RABBI MOSHE ROSENBLUM, a consummate scholar of Hebrew, *Mikrah* and *Parshanus* — all contributed to the interlinear project in those subtle ways that drive one's efforts.

RABBI SHEAH BRANDER is often commended for his design skill and layout expertise. As an outsider I did not appreciate the ingenuity and total dedication needed to produce an interlinear Siddur, an exceptional vehicle for prayer. The myriad subtleties that make the Siddur pleasant to use and

enable it to enhance one's prayers are daunting. Someone once defined the hallmark of a work of genius as being obvious in retrospect but impossible to arrive at in prospect. Reb Sheah's work is that of genius.

The vision and energy behind the unique ArtScroll synergy is RABBI MEIR ZLOTOWITZ. Without his prodding I certainly would not have worked as hard, and also not as well. Reb Meir has been involved not only in the broad outlines of the interlinear project, but in the intricate details as well. As one of the reviewers of *Tehillim* and the Siddurim, he contributed to the clarity of language and beauty of the page, significantly enriching these works. May he succeed in envisioning and incubating many more projects — to enlighten and inspire.

I express a special appreciation to RABBI YAAKOV BLINDER who has worked closely with me on the Siddurim. I benefited from his prodigious knowledge and hope Hashem will allow us to continue our collaboration.

I am grateful for the inspiration and enthusiasm of my wife Edna. Without her vision and encouragement, I would never have dreamed of working at ArtScroll. May Hashem grant that we be *zocheh* together to enjoy the further growth in Torah and *yiras Shamayim* of our children and grandchildren.

The Schottenstein Interlinear Series has served as a unifier. My mother and mother-in-law have voiced their appreciation for the enhancement to their prayers; even scholars in yeshivos have written to express their enthusiasm. I am overwhelmed by the positive response to the works thus far published. In these grim times, when our People are more dependent than ever on prayer, I am humbled that I may have facilitated their efforts at communicating with the Creator, by making the original words of the Prophets and Sages directly accessible to all.

Menachem Davis

Teves 5763 / December 2002

An Overview / Prayer, a Timeless Need

When we think of the word "prayer" we think of our needs and requests, and the litany is endless: "Heal me." "Enlighten me." "Enrich me." "Redeem me." "Glorify me." "Forgive me."

Perhaps our concept of prayer has been all wrong. As children we would ask God to grant our wishes, just as we asked our parents to take us places and to buy us toys. "Please, Father, take me to . . .!" "Please, Mother, buy me that . . .!" "Please, God, give me this . . .!" Rather than fall into the modern trap of insisting that man can control so much of his life and environment that he need not pray, let us examine what prayer really is and always was. When we are done, we will realize that the commandment to pray is no less binding today than ever, and that our need for its benefits is perhaps greater than ever.

AS A SYNONYM FOR A HUMAN BEING, the Mishnah (*Bava Kamma* 2a) uses the name מַבְעֶה [*mav'eh*], an unfamiliar word that the Talmud (ibid. 3b) derives from the root בעה, *to pray*. In other words,

Man's Essence

the Talmud defines man as "the creature that prays." Furthermore, the Talmud teaches that even נֶפֶשׁ, *the life-sustaining soul,* is synonymous with prayer (*Berachos* 5b). Strange. Such definitions appear fitting for intensely spiritual, observant people — but what of someone whose observance is casual, or a nonbeliever? The Talmud's teaching applies even to such people. How, then, is prayer so central to their lives?

What is man but his soul, for his soul and intelligence are what make him "man" rather than simply a higher order of beast. And what is man's soul but his innermost longing, whatever matters to him most? As the Sages pithily expressed it, a burglar prays for God's help as he prepares to enter the home of his victim (*Berachos* 63b in *Ein Yaakov*). Incongruous, is it not, that on the threshold of a sin that may result in violence, even murder, the thief asks for the help of the One Who commands him to desist? Yes, but because his most sincere desire is to commit his crime undetected, his *soul* cries out for success. Wherever one puts his faith is a form of prayer, whether or not that word is in his vocabulary (*Michtav MeEliyahu*).

Prayer, then, is not a list of requests. It is an introspective process, a clarifying, refining process of discovering what one is, what he should be, and how to achieve the transformation. Indeed, the commandment to pray is expressed by the Torah as a service of the *heart,* not of the mouth (*Taanis* 2a).

XXI / **AN OVERVIEW** — PRAYER, A TIMELESS NEED

To the extent that we improve ourselves with prayer, we become capable of absorbing God's blessings, but the blessings depend on each person's mission. One man's task may be to act as God's treasurer, to amass wealth and distribute it for worthy causes, or to set an example of how to remain uncorrupted by riches. Another's mission may call for modest or reduced circumstances. Meyer Amshel Rothschild became rich because his mission was to be the banker of monarchs and the patron of paupers; and Rabbi Zusha of Anipoli remained destitute because his mission was to subsist on a crust of bread and bowl of beans, and joyously say that he never experienced a bad day in his life! Each recited the prayer for prosperity in *Shemoneh Esrei* and each was answered — in the manner that was best for him. But the reasons for these differences between people and nations are not apparent to human intelligence. Nor do we discern the hand of God in the complexities of everyday life.

In this welter of contradictions, man needs all his inner strength as a Jew and bearer of the Torah to ward off the attacks on his faith. We may enter adulthood with the idealism of youth and a faith ingrained by parents and teachers, but life chips away incessantly at them. In the eloquent words of *R' Samson Raphael Hirsch* (*Horeb*): Life often robs you of the power and strength its circumstances make necessary, for it tends to remove truth from you and to offer falsehood; it forces you to surrender where your task is to conquer.

Modern society has learned that people "burn out" if they never withdraw to relax and regain perspective and inner strength. What makes us think we can fight the moral war demanded by God without removing ourselves from the trenches every now and then to regain our perspective on the purpose and strategy of the battle?

ITS HEBREW NAME IS תְּפִלָּה, *TEFILLAH,* a word that gives us an insight into the Torah's concept of prayer. The root of *tefillah* is פלל, to *judge,* to

Prayer's Function
differentiate, to *clarify,* to *decide.* In life, we constantly sort out evidence from rumor, valid options from wild speculations, fact from fancy. The exercise of such judgment is called פְּלִילָה. Indeed, the word פְּלִילִים (from פלל) is used for a court of law (*Exodus* 21:22), and what is the function of a court if not to sift evidence and make a decision? A logical extension of פלל is the related root פלה, meaning a clear separation between two things. Thus, prayer is the soul's yearning to define what truly matters and to ignore the trivialities that often masquerade as essential (*Siddur Avodas HaLev*).

People always question the need for prayer: Does not God know our requirements without being reminded? Of course He does, He knows them better than we do. If prayer were intended only to inform God of our

desires and deficiencies, it would be unnecessary. Its true purpose is to raise the level of the supplicants by helping them develop *true* perceptions of life so that they can become worthy of His blessing.

This is the function of the evaluating, decision-making process of תְּפִלָּה, *prayer*. The Hebrew verb for praying is מִתְפַּלֵל; it is a reflexive word, meaning that the subject acts upon himself. Prayer is a process of *self*-evaluation, *self*-judgment; a process of removing oneself from the *tumult* of life to a little corner of truth and refastening the bonds that tie one to the *purpose* of life.

THE TALMUD RELATES THAT when R' Yishmael *Kohen Gadol* (High Priest) was in the Holy of Holies on Yom Kippur, God asked him for a blessing. He

God's Need   replied: May it be Your will that Your mercy conquer Your anger, that Your mercy overshadow Your Attributes, that You behave toward Your children with the Attribute of Mercy, and that for their sake You go beyond the boundary of judgment (*Berachos* 7a).

This passage is astounding both for what it says and for what it does not. Why did God need R' Yishmael's blessing? Why didn't R' Yishmael comply by blessing God? How does a request that God treat Israel kindly constitute a blessing of God? What do we give God when we bless Him?

Rashba (*Teshuvos* 5:51) derives the word בְּרָכָה, *blessing,* from בְּרֵיכָה, *spring.* A spring flows constantly and its waters increase. When we bless God, we are proclaiming our hope for an increase — but of what? God Himself is infinite, without beginning or end; we cannot and dare not suggest that He can grow beyond what He is.

While it is true that man cannot grasp God's essence even to the minutest degree, we nevertheless can perceive Him as He relates to us. The prosperous society "sees" Him as the Beneficent God; the afflicted individual smarts at His judgment; the Torah scholar thrills to His wisdom. Or man can be so nasty and brutish as to think that power comes only from the barrel of a gun and prosperity from the blades of a harvester.

God's degree of revelation in the universe is in proportion to Israel's spiritual capacity to receive it. When Israel was at its zenith, God revealed Himself on Mount Sinai in unprecedented splendor; when Israel sank into exile and spiritual confusion, He was so concealed that Israel wondered whether it was still His Nation (see *Overview* to ArtScroll *Megillas Esther*). God desires man's perception of Him to deepen and the degree of His revelation to increase. Since this is His wish, He is pleased — *blessed* — when man makes it possible for this to happen. Accordingly, whenever a Jew prays or blesses God, he plays a part in carrying out His wish to display His Presence in the world's affairs.

In this sense, R' Yishmael *Kohen Gadol* gave God the ultimate blessing.

The outcome of a successful prayer is to permit God to come closer to Israel, to restrain His anger and show His mercy, to respond to Israel's attempts to serve and sanctify Him by allowing His love to quash His Attribute of Judgment. R' Yishmael wished for the desired result of the prayers — the *increase* of God's Presence. Thus, his was the perfect blessing (*Nefesh HaChaim*).

TEFILLAH IS A UNIQUELY HUMAN FUNCTION, because it blends man's intelligence and imagination with his ability to put concepts into words. The

Spoken Prayer faculty of intelligent speech, more than any other, sets man apart from animals. The Torah tells us that God breathed life into Adam and man became נֶפֶשׁ חַיָּה, *a living being* (*Genesis* 2:7). *Onkelos* renders: *man became* רוּחַ מְמַלְּלָא, *a speaking spirit*. *Onkelos* seems to equate speech with life. Clearly there is more to the soul than the power of speech, but it is through speech that man can praise God, articulate the wisdom of His Torah, and unite with others to create a phalanx of servants dedicated to doing God's will.

Since, as we have seen above, prayer is the innermost longing of the soul, it must be expressed in the form that is most representative of the human soul, intelligent speech. That *tefillah* requires clear enunciation of the words is derived from the prayer of Hannah (*I Samuel* 1:15). The Sages regard her outpouring of distress and devotion as the very epitome of the grandeur of prayer. She poured out her heart silently — her voice was not heard by others, but her lips moved. It is true that the prayers preceding *Shemoneh Esrei* — prayers that help man elevate himself to the level at which he can pour out his soul directly to God — may be said loudly, because most people better arouse themselves to devotion and concentration by praying aloud. *Shemoneh Esrei,* however, is man's intimate heart-talk with God, it *must* be silent; nevertheless, as Hannah's example showed, even a silent prayer must be spoken, for the spoken word is symbolic of the most elevated facet of man's soul (see also *Nesivos Olam*).

From the authorship of *Shemoneh Esrei,* we can draw an important conclusion about its significance. It is not a particularly long prayer — only eighteen blessings in its original formulation with a nineteenth added later (see comm. to בִּרְכַּת הַמִּינִים, p. 154) — and only several hundred words altogether. Nor is its subject matter mysterious; it was couched in very lean and simple Hebrew so that its content could be mastered easily (*Rabbeinu Bachya, Deuteronomy* 11:13). Nevertheless it had to be composed by one of the most august bodies in history, the אַנְשֵׁי כְּנֶסֶת הַגְּדֹלָה, *Men of the Great Assembly,* that led Israel at the start of the Second Temple era, and consisted of one hundred-twenty great elders, among them many prophets. Surely Israel possessed large numbers of inspired poets and

writers. Couldn't some of them have been commissioned to compose the necessary prayers? Did the entire leadership of the nation have to take the task upon itself?

Obviously it did. Every word and syllable has a thousand effects in ways we cannot imagine. Even the mystical interpretations of *Arizal,* who made known many of the Kabbalistic intentions that are contained within the text of the *tefillah,* barely scratched the surface of the meanings intended by the Men of the Great Assembly. Every word of *Shemoneh Esrei* is essential, separately and in the context of the entire prayer. The text was so profound and its effects so metaphysical and extraordinary, that it could not be entrusted to poets, only to prophets. Let us try to understand why.

THAT PRAYER IS SOUL-TALK, THAT IT REPRESENTS man at the summit of his aspirations for holiness, helps us understand why the language of prayer

The Holy Tongue
is Hebrew. It is true that the Sages allow prayer in any language (*Sotah* 33a), but this is not a blanket permission, nor does it equate Hebrew, the Holy Tongue, with other languages. The halachic authorities frown upon prayer in other languages (see *Mishnah Berurah* and *Aruch HaShulchan* to *Orach Chaim* Chs. 62 and 101). *Ramban* (*Exodus* 30:13) shows that Hebrew is the language God used in creating the universe and the language of prophecy; that, he explains, is why it is called the Holy Tongue. That alone helps explain why the prayers have greater sanctity if they are uttered in Hebrew. The commentators note that no translation can capture all the nuances of the prayers, or the prophetic words of God or the sacred compositions of the Men of the Great Assembly and their sublime successors down the ages.

But there is more. If one prays in a language other than Hebrew, he does not fulfill his obligation unless he understands whatever he says, but if he prays in Hebrew, he fulfills his obligation even if he does not understand (see *Beur Halachah, Orach Chaim* 62). Why? Clearly, לָשׁוֹן הַקֹּדֶשׁ, the Holy Tongue, has virtues beyond the obvious one that it was the original language of the prayers.

Rabbi Dov Ber, the Maggid of Mezritch, writes: It is known in Kabbalistic literature that the letters of the *Aleph-Beis* were created first of all. Thereafter, by means of the letters, the Holy One, Blessed is He, created all the worlds. This thought is hidden in the first phrase in the Torah, בְּרֵאשִׁית בָּרָא אֱלֹהִים אֵת, *In the beginning God created* אֵת — that is, God's first act of creation was to create the letters from א to ת (*Or Torah*).

The twenty-two sacred letters are profound, primal, spiritual forces. They are, in effect, the raw materials of creation. When God combined them into words, phrases, commands, they brought about creation,

translating His will into reality. There is an analogy in the physical realm: one combination of hydrogen and oxygen produces water, while another produces hydrogen peroxide. So it is with all the elements and their infinite possible combinations. Similarly, there is a Divine science in the Hebrew alphabet. *Sefer Yetzirah* ["The Book of Creation"], the early Kabbalistic work ascribed to the patriarch Abraham, describes how the sacred letters were used as the agency of creation. The letters can be arranged in countless combinations, by changing their order within words and interchanging letters in line with the rules of various Kabbalistic letter-systems. Each rearrangement results in a new blend of the cosmic spiritual forces represented by the letters.

This explains why Adam's first demonstration of greatness came when God asked him to give names to all the creatures of the new universe. When Adam said that an ox should be called שׁוֹר and an eagle נֶשֶׁר, he was saying that the spiritual forces expressed by those letters — in the formula signified by those unique arrangements of letters and vowels — were translated by God into the nerve, sinew, skin, size, shape, and strength of a sturdy ox or a soaring eagle. When the verse tells us that whatever name Adam conferred, *that remained its name* (*Genesis* 2:1), we are told that the spiritual forces that Adam identified remain active for all time. The same spiritual forces that God translated into an ox-שׁוֹר at the dawn of creation remain the essence of an ox-שׁוֹר for all time (*Tanya, Shaar HaYichud V'HaEmunah*).

The Men of the Great Assembly had the ability to combine letters, verses, and ideas in ways that unlock the gates of heaven. Their composition of the *tefillah* is tantamount to an act of creation, which is why it is so important not to deviate from their language and formulation. This is not to denigrate the importance of comprehension and emotional involvement. Prayer in the language one understands is sanctioned by the Sages themselves, and surely, a well-understood prayer is immeasurably more worthy than one that is merely mouthed as a string of uncomprehended sounds. Nevertheless, this does not detract a whit from the importance of praying in the Holy Tongue; it merely points up the responsibility to understand the prayers in their original, holiest form.

WHEN R' YISHMAEL *KOHEN GADOL* BLESSED GOD, it was with the request that the entire nation of Israel enjoy Heavenly mercy. The plural nature of his

Plural Prayer prayer is reflected in all our supplications, primarily in *Shemoneh Esrei*, which pleads for everyone, not merely for the individual who prays and his loved ones.

R' Yishmael knew that *God* is blessed when His people are secure, because then all humanity can come to recognize that in the service of

God lies success. Conversely, when Israel's condition is reduced, God's Name is desecrated. If our intention in praying for Israel's greater benefit is to bring about a sanctification of God's Name, then our *tefillah* is worthy of those who composed it — and of Him to Whom it is directed.

Even personal prayers for our own needs are not necessarily selfish in nature. God feels the distress of every individual. *Midrash Tanchuma* (*Acharei*) teaches: Every salvation that comes upon even an individual Jew is also the salvation of the Holy One, Blessed is He, for it is written (*Psalms* 91:15,16) עִמּוֹ אָנֹכִי בְצָרָה . . . וְאַרְאֵהוּ בִּישׁוּעָתִי, [God says,] *"I am with him in his distress . . . I will show him My salvation."* Israel says . . . "If You respond to us, the salvation will be Your own." If a Jew has in mind when he prays for wealth that God suffers along with him when he finds it hard to pay his bills and clothe his child, then the plea for himself becomes a plea for God Himself, as it were.

We are at our noblest when we pray in the plural, because only by pleading for the greater good of all Israel and all of the world can we fully achieve God's purpose of allowing His beneficence to flow upon all of His creation. Even when we have crying personal needs, we subsume them in the general need. Our hearts may break because of our own poverty or illness, but we want *all* Israel to prosper and be restored to good health. And if we *must* pray for ourselves, let us strive to do so in the hope that our benefit will rebound to God's glory, not our own. None of this is intended to denigrate the prayer of the lone individual thinking of his wife, his child, his bills, himself. Someone standing on a lower rung of the ladder to heaven need not be ashamed because the goal seems so lofty. Instead let him be proud and grateful that he has left the enticing, binding pull of earthly power and set his sights upward.

Does modern man have less need to pray because he has gained so much control over his environment? No, just the opposite. *Because* man has become so powerful, he can — and does — fail to realize that he is strong only because God has made him so, and that he is no less dependent on the One Above than were his humblest ancestors, scratching at rocky soil with a wooden plow. Prayer is God's gift to help us mine nuggets of truth so that we can understand ourselves and our role, and thereby allow Him to carry out His desire to bless man. Let us bless God as R' Yishmael *Kohen Gadol* did — by creating the conditions for Him to shower His blessings on His creatures.

The Three Daily Prayers

אָמַר ר׳ יוֹסֵי בְּרַבִּי חֲנִינָא, תְּפִלּוֹת אָבוֹת תִּקְּנוּם.
ר׳ יְהוֹשֻׁעַ בֶּן לֵוִי אָמַר, תְּפִלּוֹת נֶגֶד תְּמִידִים תִּקְּנוּם

R' Yose son of R' Chanina said: The Patriarchs established the [three daily] prayers. R' Yehoshua ben Levi said: [The Sages] established the prayers to correspond to the daily continual offerings (Berachos 26b).

I. Patriarchs and Offerings

In ascribing the daily prayers either to the Patriarchs or to the nation's need for a counterpart to the Temple offerings, the Sages do not mean to imply that the *concept* of prayer originated with the Patriarchs or with the אַנְשֵׁי כְנֶסֶת הַגְּדֹלָה, *Men of the Great Assembly,* who led the nation after the Babylonian Exile. Prayers were recited long before the birth of Abraham; the Midrash is replete with the prayers of all the generations, and it is axiomatic that such righteous people as Adam and Noah, along with countless others, must have prayed. Rather, R' Yose and R' Yehoshua are discussing the *symbolism* of the prayers: according to R' Yose, each of the daily *Shemoneh Esrei* prayers symbolizes one of the Patriarchs; while according to R' Yehoshua, it symbolizes a segment of the daily Temple service.

The simplest function of man's prayer is for him to acknowledge that all of creation is dependent on and stems from God. Logic and experience dictate that every effect has a cause and every offspring a parent. We can trace them all as far back as history and intelligence allow us, but when we can go no further we face the quintessential reality — only God is timeless and independent. He preceded all and created all; He sustains all and is the only Source of blessing. By our prayers we acknowledge this, for the entire catalogue of human needs are included in them — and they are directed only to Him. This realization is symbolized by both the Patriarchs and the offerings.

Before the Patriarchs there was spiritual desolation and darkness; they brought Torah and light. They were a new birth of man, a new mode of existence. Therefore *only* they are called אָבוֹת, *Fathers* of Israel — not Adam and not Noah, even though they are as much our biological ancestors as Abraham. Because the Patriarchs became a new spiritual beginning of Israel, and therefore of mankind, they are regarded as the "first cause" after whom Israel must pattern its prayers.

The offerings symbolize that man returns all his material possessions and his very life to God. The sanctified animal is man's property; the Temple service symbolizes that all parts of man's body and even his soul are offered to God. No undertaking is more vital to man's performance of his duties as God's servant and surrogate on earth. This function, too, is symbolized by the three prayers of the day (*Maharal*).

II. Three Periods of the Day

SUNRISE AND SUNSET AFFECT MAN'S EMOTIONS in opposite ways. Sunrise begins a day of new activity: new potential, new opportunity. Nature smiles as
Fact and Faith it springs to life and invites man to take up his tasks and win new triumphs. At sunset, however, darkness occupies the earth, and man, his energy depleted, prepares to entrust his soul and fate to God's protection as he sleeps. Night and day have become the most common metaphors for physical and spiritual conditions. "Day" represents success and optimism; "night" represents failure and foreboding.

An essential part of the morning and evening services illustrates this contrast. At both services it is required that reference be made to the Exodus (*Berachos* 12b), although the paragraphs in which this is done are not identical.

The prayer of the morning is described by the term חַסְדֶּךָ, *Your kindness;* it refers *only* to the Exodus, an event that has already taken place and that demonstrated that God's kindness is beyond belief and without limit. The prayer of the evening, however, is described as אֱמוּנָתֶךָ, *your faith;* it refers primarily to the future redemption and calls upon Israel to have "faith" in something it has not yet witnessed but must believe will happen: that God will redeem His chosen ones in the future just as He has saved them from every exile and persecution, from Egyptian times onward.

Kabbalistic literature notes a further insight in the above citation. Day is the time of God's מִדַּת הַחֶסֶד, *Attribute of Kindness,* the time when He showers the world with His generosity, but night is the time of His מִדַּת הַדִּין, *Attribute of Judgment,* when man is exposed unprotected to the harshness of the elements and to the consequences of his deeds; it is the time when his salvation lies in the אֱמוּנָה, *faith,* that ultimately God will display His mercy, just as night is followed by dawn.

Thus, we have seen the symbolism of the morning and evening prayers: to ask for God's exercise of kindness and for His protection against judgment. But what of *Minchah,* the afternoon prayer? The lives of the three Patriarchs and their relationship to the three prayers show the way to an answer.

ABRAHAM'S LIFE WAS LIKE THE RISING SUN. From the time he first accepted God's calling and migrated to Canaan, he grew in prestige, power and

The Patriarchs Pray

spiritual success. Even the Hittites addressed him respectfully as *a prince of God* (*Genesis* 23:6). He was neither envied nor hated, despite being an alien who had surpassed his hosts. But Isaac's life was different. With his very birth came fulfillment of the prophecy that Abraham's *offspring shall be aliens in a land not their own* (*Genesis* 15:13, see *Rashi*). Abraham's sun began to set, and Isaac experienced resentment in situations almost exactly like those where Abraham had found goodwill. Finally, with Jacob, night fell. From Esau to Laban, to strife among his sons, to exile in Egypt, Jacob's life was filled with travail and foreboding. Each Patriarch was uniquely associated with a prayer that best corresponded to the path of his life (see *Maharsha, Berachos* 26b). The *Zohar* points out that Abraham's life represented a gift of God's kindness: חֶסֶד לְאַבְרָהָם . . . תִּתֵּן, *give . . . kindness to Abraham* (*Micah* 7:20). But Isaac and Jacob experienced a descent from kindness to judgment. It would seem that Jacob's treatment was the harshest of all, but the *Zohar* explains that the opposite is true. Isaac was born in the house of Abraham where he began life hearing plaudits from Canaan and basking in Abraham's glory; to plunge from such heights to the relative ignominy of his later life is a burden far more severe than that borne by Jacob, who began life in the shadows. Despite the almost uninterrupted ordeals of his life, near the end Jacob speaks of *God Who shepherds me from my youth until this day* and *the angel who redeems me from all evil* (*Genesis* 48:15-16). There is a ray of light in Jacob's closing days that is absent in Isaac's. Isaac dies while it is still twilight, so to speak, but ahead of him is total darkness. Jacob dies in the dead of night, but he sees new generations growing up and he foresees the dawn of the Exodus and the revelation at Sinai.

ISAAC'S FORTUNES WERE SYMBOLIZED BY the sinking sun, the time of day when, the Sages say, the world is subject to דִּינָא קַשְׁיָא, *harsh judgment.*

Harsh and Mild Judgments

The structure of *Minchah* is illustrative of this aspect of the day, for *Minchah* consists of little more than *Shemoneh Esrei,* the introspective prayer of spiritual self-appraisal and withdrawal from the temptation and delusion of life (see following Section).

But Jacob approached God in the evening (*Berachos* 26b), and the place where he prayed was Mount Moriah, where Isaac had been spared at the *Akeidah* and where the future Temple would be built. As Jacob slept, God watched over him and when he awoke he realized that he was at the site of the future House of God. There he had a revelation of angels and a

promise of Divine protection — and all this spiritual elevation and tempo-
ral assurance came at a time when he was fleeing from the death threat of
Esau to a tenuous refuge with the scheming, larcenous Laban. Jacob's was
the prayer of night, but it was a night that looked to a dawn of unprecedented brilliance.

The *Zohar* calls evening a time of דִּינָא רַפְיָא, *mild judgment*. The morning
of Abraham is the time of חֶסֶד, *kindness;* the afternoon of Isaac is the time
of דִּין, *judgment;* the night of Jacob is a combination of both. At a time
when God's creatures are too weak to bear the harshness of absolute
judgment, God softens the judgment with kindness. This combination of
judgment and kindness is called רַחֲמִים, *mercy.*

Thus, the Jew begins his day with gratitude for God's kindness [חֶסֶד],
ends it by standing in judgment for his deeds [דִּין], and spends his darkest
period comforted by the faith that God's mercy [רַחֲמִים] will not let him
falter, that it will buoy him until morning comes once more (*R' Munk*).

III. The Daily Sacrifices

ACCORDING TO R' YEHOSHUA BEN LEVI'S VIEW, the *tefillos* correspond to the
daily sacrifices. Each morning and each evening, a sheep was offered

**Potential and
Accomplishment**
as a communal burnt-offering. Every member of
the nation shared in the offering by virtue of the
annual half-shekel head tax, from whose pro-
ceeds all communal offerings were brought. These daily offerings were
brought every day, even on the Sabbath, festivals and Yom Kippur, to
symbolize Israel's awareness that the entire universe is always on God's
Altar, as it were, and that without God's continuous attention and mercy
there could be no universe. It is a reciprocal process: God gives life and
man devotes his life to God.

These two offerings represent Israel's ceding of all its productive capacities to God. Daytime is the period most symbolic of This World, man's
time of vigor and activity; consequently, it is vital for him to acknowledge
the world's true Sovereign, both at the beginning and end of his day.

The first appearance of the sun is the birth of a new day, a new period
of accomplishment. The productive hours of the day end when the sun
goes down; that is the time when man takes inventory and feels satisfaction at his day's achievements. Those are the times when man should
ascribe both his potential and his accomplishment to God.

But the night is more obviously God's, and this is reflected in the fact
that no offerings are prescribed for the nighttime, when man is clearly
passive and dependent on God to renew his strength for another day of

activity. Only one sacrificial service remains for the night. In the event that limbs or other sacrificial parts had not been burned during the day, they could be placed on the Altar all night. This symbolizes that even when it is clear beyond question that God is King, man must make an additional effort to consecrate everything to Him, even the relatively minor remainders of the day's accomplishments. Thus, *Shacharis* corresponds to the offering that dedicates to God the incoming day's potential; *Minchah* corresponds to the offering that acknowledges Him as Master of everything done; and *Maariv* proclaims that even when man is inactive, we declare His absolute Oneness and uncontested sovereignty.

וַיֹּאמֶר אֱלֹהִים לְיִשְׂרָאֵל בְּמַרְאֹת הַלַּיְלָה, *And God spoke to Israel in visions of the night* (*Genesis* 46:2).

ISRAEL IN EXILE IS LIKENED TO JACOB WHO SPENT so much of his life as a wanderer and an exile. But Jacob is the Patriarch of Torah, too, and that
Outgrowths of Day allegiance to Torah has been and remains our guarantor against the savage blows of so many centuries without the Temple.

We do not find God speaking to Abraham or Isaac in a vision of the night, only to Jacob. At that moment, Jacob was poised to leave the Promised Land to begin a long, long Egyptian exile. Jacob was afraid, and well he might be, because by the time the exile ended his children would have fallen to the forty-ninth level of impurity where they were barely distinguishable from the Egyptians.

The night when hope was enveloped in darkness was about to begin, so God came to Jacob *in visions of the night* to show him that even though Jews might be exiled from their Land, they could never be exiled from their God. גָּלוּ לְבָבֶל שְׁכִינָה עִמָּהֶם, *When they were exiled to Babylon, the Divine Presence was with them* (*Megillah* 29a). Therefore, Jacob, the Patriarch of exile, originated *Maariv,* to show his children that exile-evening may be epilogue to one day, but it is prologue to another, even better one.

The Evening Service represents the burning of the offerings in the Temple, a service that could be concluded at night only if the rest of the service had been done during the previous day. This is the eternal lesson that, by continuing our loyalty to Torah — which began in the golden, daylight eras of our history — we maintain our bond with God no matter how dark the night (*Meshech Chochmah*).

Nosson Scherman

Chanukah 5763
December 2002

✦§ The Names of God

In this work, the Four-Letter Name of God is translated "Hashem," the pronunciation traditionally used for the Name to avoid pronouncing it unnecessarily. This pronunciation should be used when studying the meanings of the prayers. However, if one prays in English, he should say "God" or he should pronounce the Name in the proper Hebrew way — *Adōnoy* — in accord with the ruling of most halachic authorities. One does not fulfill his obligation by saying "Lord."

The Four-Letter Name of Hashem [יְ-ה-וֹ-ה] indicates that God is timeless and infinite, since the letters of this Name are those of the words הָיָה הוֶֹה וְיִהְיֶה, *He was, He is, and He will be*. This Name is *never* pronounced as it is spelled.

During prayer, or when a blessing is recited, or when Torah verses are read, the Four-Letter Name should be pronounced as if it were spelled אֲדֹנָי, *Adōnoy*, the Name that identifies God as the Master of All. At other times, it should be pronounced הַשֵּׁם, *Hashem*, literally, "the Name."

According to the *Shulchan Aruch*, one should have both meanings — the Master of All and the Timeless, Infinite One — in mind when reciting the Four-Letter Name during prayer (*Orach Chaim* Ch. 5). According to the *Vilna Gaon*, however, one need have in mind only the meaning of the Name as it is pronounced — the Master of All (ibid.).

When the Name is spelled אֲדֹנָי in the prayer or verse, all agree that one should have in mind that God is the Master of All.

The Name אֱלֹהִים, *Elōhim, God*, refers to Him as the One Who is all-powerful and Who is in direct overlordship of the universe (ibid.). This is also used as a generic name for the angels, a court, rulers, and even idols. However, when the term אֱלֹהִים is used for the God of Israel, it means the One Omniscient God, Who is uniquely identified with His Chosen People.

✦§ Pronouncing the Names of God

The following table gives the pronunciations of the Name when it appears with a prefix. In all these cases, the accent is on the last syllable (*noy*). The only prefixes that might appear before the Name are the letters משה וכלב (and ד, in Aramaic). The first two letters (שמ) do not absorb the "ah" sound under the first letter of the Name, while all the other letters (הוכלב,ד) do, as follows:

בַּי-ה-וֹ-ה	— *Ba-dōnoy*	כַּי-ה-וֹ-ה	— *Ka-dōnoy*
דַּי-ה-וֹ-ה	— *Da-dōnoy*	לַי-ה-וֹ-ה	— *La-dōnoy*
הַי-ה-וֹ-ה	— *Ha-dōnoy*	מֵי-ה-וֹ-ה	— *May-adōnoy*
וַי-ה-וֹ-ה	— *Va-dōnoy*	שֶׁי-ה-וֹ-ה	— *She-adōnoy*

Sometimes the Name appears with the vowelization יְ-הֹ-וִ-ה. This version of the Name is pronounced as if it were spelled אֱלֹהִים, *Elōhim*, the Name that refers to God as the One Who is all-powerful. When it appears with a prefix לֵי-הֹ-וִ-ה, it is pronounced *Lay-lōhim*. We have translated this Name as *Hashem/Elohim* to indicate that it refers to the aspects inherent in each of those Names.

סידור

SIDDUR

שבחי הודו ישורון

❧ UPON ARISING / הַשְׁכָּמַת הַבּוֹקֶר ❧

A JEW SHOULD WAKE UP WITH GRATITUDE TO GOD FOR HAVING RESTORED HIS FACULTIES,
AND WITH A LIONLIKE RESOLVE TO SERVE HIS CREATOR. HE SHOULD IMMEDIATELY DECLARE:

מוֹדֶה אֲנִי* לְפָנֶיךָ, מֶלֶךְ חַי וְקַיָּם, שֶׁהֶחֱזַרְתָּ

⟨ for You have ⟨⟨ and ⟨ living ⟨ King, ⟨⟨ before You, ⟨   I give thanks*
returned   eternal,

בִּי נִשְׁמָתִי בְּחֶמְלָה – רַבָּה אֱמוּנָתֶךָ.

⟨⟨ is Your faithfulness! ⟨ – abundant ⟨⟨ with compassion ⟨ my soul ⟨ within me

WASH THE HANDS ACCORDING TO THE RITUAL PROCEDURE: PICK UP THE VESSEL OF WATER WITH
THE RIGHT HAND, PASS IT TO THE LEFT, AND POUR OVER THE RIGHT. THEN WITH THE RIGHT HAND
POUR OVER THE LEFT. FOLLOW THIS PROCEDURE UNTIL WATER HAS BEEN POURED OVER EACH HAND
THREE TIMES. THEN, RECITE:

רֵאשִׁית חָכְמָה יִרְאַת יהוה, שֵׂכֶל טוֹב

⟨ good understanding ⟨⟨ of Hashem, ⟨ is the fear ⟨ of wisdom ⟨   The beginning
[is given]

לְכָל עֹשֵׂיהֶם, תְּהִלָּתוֹ עֹמֶדֶת לָעַד.¹ בָּרוּךְ שֵׁם

⟨ is the ⟨ Blessed ⟨⟨ forever. ⟨ endures ⟨ His praise ⟨⟨ their ⟨ to all
Name   practitioners;

כְּבוֹד מַלְכוּתוֹ לְעוֹלָם וָעֶד.² תּוֹרָה צִוָּה לָנוּ

⟨ to ⟨ that was ⟨ The Torah ⟨⟨ and ever. ⟨ for ever ⟨   kingdom ⟨ of His
us commanded   glorious

מֹשֶׁה, מוֹרָשָׁה קְהִלַּת יַעֲקֹב.³ שְׁמַע בְּנִי מוּסַר

⟨ the ⟨ my ⟨ Hear, ⟨⟨ of Jacob. ⟨ of the ⟨ is the ⟨⟨ by Moses,
discipline child,   Congregation   heritage

אָבִיךָ, וְאַל תִּטּוֹשׁ תּוֹרַת אִמֶּךָ.⁴ תּוֹרָה תְהֵא

⟨ should ⟨ The Torah ⟨⟨ of your ⟨ the teaching ⟨ forsake ⟨ and ⟨⟨ of your
be   mother.   do not   father,

אֱמוּנָתִי, וְאֵל שַׁדַּי בְּעֶזְרָתִי. וְאַתֶּם הַדְּבֵקִים

⟨ who cling ⟨ And you ⟨⟨ [should] assist me. ⟨ and El Shaddai ⟨⟨ my faith,

---

(1) *Psalms* 111:10. (2) See *Pesachim* 56a. (3) *Deuteronomy* 33:4. (4) *Proverbs* 1:8.

מוֹדֶה אֲנִי ❧— *I give thanks.* As soon as a Jew wakes up in the morning and opens his eyes, he thanks God for restoring his faculties. Then, he acknowledges that God did so in the expectation that he will serve Him, and that God is abundantly faithful to reward those who do so.

בַּיהוה אֱלֹהֵיכֶם, חַיִּים כֻּלְּכֶם הַיּוֹם.¹ לִישׁוּעָתְךָ

‹ For Your   ‹‹ today. ‹ — all of you — ‹ you are ‹   your God, ‹ to Hᴀsʜᴇᴍ,
salvation   alive

קִוִּיתִי יהוה.²

‹‹ Hᴀsʜᴇᴍ. ‹ I do yearn,

✦ DONNING THE TZITZIS / לְבִישַׁת צִיצִית ✦

HOLD THE *TALLIS KATTAN* IN READINESS TO PUT ON, INSPECT THE *TZITZIS*,
AND RECITE THE BLESSING. THEN DON THE *TALLIS KATTAN* AND KISS THE *TZITZIS*.
ONE WHO WEARS A *TALLIS* FOR *SHACHARIS* DOES NOT RECITE THIS BLESSING (SEE COMMENTARY).

בָּרוּךְ אַתָּה יהוה אֱלֹהֵינוּ מֶלֶךְ הָעוֹלָם,

‹‹ of the universe, ‹ King ‹ our God, ‹ Hᴀsʜᴇᴍ, ‹ are You, ‹ Blessed

אֲשֶׁר קִדְּשָׁנוּ בְּמִצְוֹתָיו, וְצִוָּנוּ עַל מִצְוַת צִיצִת.

‹‹ of *tzitzis.* ‹ the com- ‹ regard- ‹ and com- ‹ with His ‹ has sanctified ‹ Who
          mandment   ing   manded us commandments,   us

יְהִי רָצוֹן מִלְּפָנֶיךָ, יהוה אֱלֹהַי וֵאלֹהֵי אֲבוֹתַי, שֶׁתְּהֵא

‹ that it ‹‹ of my ‹ and the ‹ my God ‹ Hᴀsʜᴇᴍ, ‹‹ before You, ‹ the will ‹ May
should be forefathers, God   it be

חֲשׁוּבָה מִצְוַת צִיצִת לְפָנֶיךָ, כְּאִלּוּ קִיַּמְתִּיהָ בְּכָל פְּרָטֶיהָ

‹ its aspects, ‹ in all ‹ I had ‹ as if ‹ before ‹‹ of ‹ — the com- ‹‹ considered
              fulfilled it   You *tzitzis* — mandment

וְדִקְדּוּקֶיהָ וְכַוָּנוֹתֶיהָ, וְתַרְיַ"ג מִצְוֹת הַתְּלוּיִם בָּהּ. אָמֵן סֶלָה.

‹‹ *Selah.* ‹ Amen, ‹‹ upon ‹ that are ‹ command- ‹ as well ‹‹ and its ‹ its details
            it. dependent ments as the 613 intentions,

(1) *Deuteronomy* 4:4. (2) *Genesis* 49:18.

✦ לְבִישַׁת צִיצִית / DONNING THE TZITZIS ✦

Since *tzitzis* need not be worn at night, the commandment of *tzitzis* [*Numbers* 15:38] is classified as a time-related commandment and, as such, is not required of women. It may be fulfilled in two ways: by means of the *tallis kattan* (lit. small garment), popularly known simply as "the *tzitzis*," which is worn throughout the day, usually under the shirt; and by means of the familiar large *tallis*, commonly known simply as "the *tallis*," which is worn during *Shacharis*. Among Sephardic Jews and Jews of German extraction, the *tallis* is worn even by children, but in most Ashkenazic congregations

it is worn during prayer only by one who is or has been married. Although, strictly speaking, one should recite the appropriate blessings over each garment upon donning it, the custom is that one who wears a *tallis* at *Shacharis* does not recite the blessing עַל מִצְוַת צִיצִית, *regarding the commandment of tzitzis*, when donning the *tallis kattan*. Instead, before donning the large *tallis* he has in mind that the blessing לְהִתְעַטֵּף בַּצִיצִת, *to wrap ourselves in tzitzis*, should apply to both garments.

Before donning his *tallis* or *tallis kattan*, one must untangle the fringes and examine them carefully to be sure that none of the strings have

⤜{ DONNING THE TALLIS / עטיפת טלית }⤛

BEFORE DONNING THE *TALLIS*, INSPECT THE *TZITZIS* WHILE RECITING THESE VERSES:

בָּרְכִי נַפְשִׁי* אֶת יהוה, יהוה אֱלֹהַי

⟨ my God, ⟨ HASHEM, ⟪ HASHEM; ⟨ O my soul,* ⟨ Bless,

גָּדַלְתָּ מְּאֹד, הוֹד וְהָדָר לָבָשְׁתָּ. עֹטֶה אוֹר

⟨ light ⟨ donning ⟪ You have worn; ⟨ and majesty ⟨ glory ⟪ You are very great;

כַּשַּׂלְמָה, נוֹטֶה שָׁמַיִם כַּיְרִיעָה.¹

⟪ like a curtain. ⟨ the heavens ⟨ stretching out ⟪ as a garment,

MANY RECITE THE FOLLOWING DECLARATION OF INTENT BEFORE DONNING THE *TALLIS*:

לְשֵׁם יִחוּד* קֻדְשָׁא בְּרִיךְ הוּא וּשְׁכִינְתֵּהּ, בִּדְחִילוּ וּרְחִימוּ

⟨ and love, ⟨ in fear ⟪ and His Presence, ⟪ is He, ⟨ Blessed ⟪ of the Holy One, ⟨ of the unification* ⟨ For the sake

לְיַחֵד שֵׁם* י״ה בּו״ה בְּיִחוּדָא שְׁלִים, בְּשֵׁם כָּל יִשְׂרָאֵל.

⟪ Israel. ⟨ of all ⟨ in the name ⟪ that is complete, ⟨ in unity ⟨ with Yud-Vav-Kei ⟨ Yud-Kei ⟨ the Name* ⟨ to unify

הֲרֵינִי* מִתְעַטֵּף גּוּפִי בַּצִּיצִת, כֵּן תִּתְעַטֵּף נִשְׁמָתִי וּרְמַ״ח

⟨ and my 248 ⟪ my soul, ⟨ may be wrapped ⟨ so ⟪ in tzitzis; ⟨ my body ⟨ to wrap ⟨ I am ready*

---

(1) *Psalms* 104:1-2.

torn. It is especially important to check the places where the strings are looped through the holes in the corners of the garment, for if even one of the strings is torn there, the *tzitzis* are invalid and the garment may not be worn.

⤜{ DONNING THE TALLIS / עטיפת טלית }⤛

בָּרְכִי נַפְשִׁי‎ — *Bless, O my soul . . .* These two verses describe God figuratively as donning garments of majesty and light. Because the *tallis* symbolizes the splendor of God's commandments, we liken our wearing of it to wrapping ourselves in God's glory and brilliance. Similarly, the Kabbalistic references in the following לְשֵׁם יִחוּד prayer associate the *tallis* with protection, elevation, and illumination.

לְשֵׁם יִחוּד . . . הֲרֵינִי‎ — *For the sake of the unification . . . I am ready.* This preliminary formulation serves two purposes. It is a statement of intent that the act about to be per-

formed is to fulfill the Torah's commandment. The second purpose, indicated by the mystical references, is a prayer that the Kabbalistic spiritual qualities of the commandment be realized. Some authorities omit the sentence beginning לְשֵׁם יִחוּד and start the supplication from הֲרֵינִי. Others omit the entire prayer, but all agree that one should have intent to fulfill the *mitzvah*.

לְיַחֵד שֵׁם . . .‎ — *To unify the Name . . .* The first half of the Divine Name, formed of the letters *yud* and *hei*, symbolizes the Attribute of (Strict) Justice, while the second half, formed of the letters *vav* and *hei*, symbolizes the Attribute of Mercy. The blend of both Attributes leads to His desired goal for Creation. Since these letters form the sacred Four-Letter Name that is not to be uttered as it is spelled, and since many commentators maintain that this prohibition

אֵבָרַי וּשְׁסָ"ה גִידַי* בְּאוֹר הַצִיצַת הָעוֹלָה תַּרְיַ"ג. וּכְשֵׁם

⟨ And just ⟨⟨ of 613. ⟨ which has the numerical value ⟨⟨ of *tzitzis*, ⟨ in the illumination ⟨⟨ sinews* ⟨ and my 365 ⟨ organs

שֶׁאֲנִי מִתְכַּסֶּה בְּטַלִּית בָּעוֹלָם הַזֶּה, כַּךְ אֶזְכֶּה לַחֲלוּקָא

⟨ the garb ⟨ may I merit ⟨ so ⟨⟨ in This World, ⟨ in a *tallis* ⟨ wrap myself ⟨ as I

דְרַבָּנָן וּלְטַלִּית נָאֶה לָעוֹלָם הַבָּא בְּגַן עֵדֶן. וְעַל יְדֵי

⟨ means ⟨ And ⟨⟨ of Eden. ⟨ in the Garden ⟨ to Come, ⟨ in the World ⟨ and a beautiful *tallis* ⟨ of the rabbis by

מִצְוַת צִיצַת תִּנָּצֵל נַפְשִׁי וְרוּחִי וְנִשְׁמָתִי וּתְפִלָּתִי מִן

⟨ from ⟨⟨ and my prayer be, ⟨ my soul, ⟨ my spirit, ⟨⟨ my life force, ⟨ rescued ⟨⟨ of *tzitzis*, ⟨ of the commandment

הַחִיצוֹנִים. וְהַטַּלִּית יִפְרוֹשׂ כְּנָפָיו עֲלֵיהֶם וְיַצִּילֵם כְּנֶשֶׁר

⟨ like an eagle ⟨⟨ and rescue them, ⟨ over them ⟨ its wings ⟨ spread ⟨ May the *tallis* ⟨⟨ the external forces.

יָעִיר קִנּוֹ, עַל גּוֹזָלָיו יְרַחֵף.¹ וּתְהֵא חֲשׁוּבָה מִצְוַת צִיצַת

⟨⟨ of *tzitzis* – ⟨ – the commandment ⟨ considered ⟨ May it be ⟨⟨ hovering. ⟨ its eaglets ⟨ over ⟨⟨ its nest, ⟨ arousing

לִפְנֵי הַקָּדוֹשׁ בָּרוּךְ הוּא כְּאִלּוּ קִיַּמְתִּיהָ בְּכָל פְּרָטֶיהָ

⟨ its aspects, ⟨ in all ⟨ I had fulfilled it ⟨ as if ⟨⟨ is He, ⟨ Blessed ⟨⟨ the Holy One, ⟨ before

וְדִקְדּוּקֶיהָ וְכַוָּנוֹתֶיהָ וְתַרְיַ"ג מִצְוֹת הַתְּלוּיִם בָּהּ. אָמֵן סֶלָה.

⟨⟨ *Selah*. ⟨ Amen, ⟨⟨ upon it. ⟨ that are dependent ⟨ commandments ⟨ as well as ⟨⟨ and its 613 ⟨ intentions, ⟨ its details,

UNFOLD THE *TALLIS*, HOLD IT IN READINESS TO WRAP AROUND YOURSELF, AND RECITE THE FOLLOWING BLESSING:

בָּרוּךְ אַתָּה יהוה אֱלֹהֵינוּ מֶלֶךְ הָעוֹלָם,

⟨⟨ of the universe, ⟨ King ⟨ our God, ⟨ HASHEM, ⟨ are You, ⟨ Blessed

אֲשֶׁר קִדְּשָׁנוּ בְּמִצְוֹתָיו, וְצִוָּנוּ לְהִתְעַטֵּף בַּצִיצַת.

⟨⟨ in *tzitzis*. ⟨ to wrap ourselves ⟨ and commanded us ⟨ with His commandments, ⟨ has sanctified us ⟨ Who

(1) *Deuteronomy* 32:11.

extends even to uttering the four letters of the Name consecutively, the commonly used pronunciation of these letters in the לְשֵׁם יִחוּד prayer is *Yud-Kei b'Vav Kei.*

גִידַי וּשְׁסָ"ה אֵבָרַי ח אַבְרֵי וּרְמַ"ח — *My 248 organs and my 365 sinews.* The Sages' computation of the important organs, 248, is equal to the number of positive commandments, while the 365 sinews

equal the number of negative commandments. This symbolizes the principle that man was created to perform God's will. The total number of sinews and organs in man, and the total number of Divine commandments, are each 613, a number symbolized by the commandment of צִיצִית, *tzitzis* [צ=90; י=10; צ=90; י=10; ת=400, totaling 600; the 5 knots and 8 threads of each

WRAP THE *TALLIS* AROUND YOUR HEAD AND BODY, THEN RECITE:

מַה יָּקָר חַסְדְּךָ אֱלֹהִים, וּבְנֵי אָדָם בְּצֵל

‹ in the ‹ Mankind ‹‹ O God! ‹ is Your ‹ precious ‹ How
shelter   kindness,

כְּנָפֶיךָ יֶחֱסָיוּן. יִרְוְיֻן מִדֶּשֶׁן בֵּיתֶךָ, וְנַחַל עֲדָנֶיךָ

‹ of Your ‹ and from ‹ of Your ‹ from the ‹ They will ‹‹ takes refuge. ‹ of Your
delights   the stream   House,   abundance   be sated   wings

תַשְׁקֵם. כִּי עִמְּךָ מְקוֹר חַיִּים, בְּאוֹרְךָ נִרְאֶה

‹ may we ‹ by Your ‹‹ of life; ‹ is the ‹ with You ‹ For ‹‹ You give
see   light   source   them to drink.

אוֹר. מְשֹׁךְ חַסְדְּךָ לְיֹדְעֶיךָ, וְצִדְקָתְךָ לְיִשְׁרֵי לֵב.[1]

‹‹ of ‹ to the ‹ and Your ‹‹ to those who ‹ Your ‹ Extend ‹‹ light.
heart.   upright   charity   know You,   kindness

❧ סדר הנחת תפילין / PUTTING ON TEFILLIN ❧

לְשֵׁם יִחוּד* קֻדְשָׁא בְּרִיךְ הוּא וּשְׁכִינְתֵּהּ, בִּדְחִילוּ וּרְחִימוּ,

‹‹ and love, ‹ in fear ‹‹ and His ‹‹ is He, ‹ Blessed ‹‹ of the ‹ of the ‹ For the
      Presence,   Holy One,   unification*   sake

לְיַחֵד שֵׁם י״ה בּו״ה בְּיִחוּדָא שְׁלִים, בְּשֵׁם כָּל יִשְׂרָאֵל.

‹‹ Israel. ‹ of all ‹ in the ‹‹ that is ‹ in unity ‹ with ‹ Yud- ‹ the ‹ to
     name   complete,   Vav-Kei   Kei   Name   unify

---

(1) *Psalms* 36:8-11.

fringe make up the other 13]. Thus, by wrapping our bodies in the *tallis*, we dedicate ourselves totally to the task of serving God.

Additionally, as mentioned later in this prayer, the *tallis* represents the concept that God protects those who serve Him.

❧ הֲנָחַת תְּפִלִּין / PUTTING ON TEFILLIN ❧

לְשֵׁם יִחוּד ❧ — *For the sake of the unification.* In its broad outline, this introductory supplication serves the same dual purpose as the לְשֵׁם יִחוּד for *tzitzis*. Four separate Scriptural passages command Israel to put on *tefillin;* all four are mentioned here and the parchments inserted into the *tefillin* contain these passages. Much of the language of this prayer is drawn from *Ramban* to *Exodus* 13:16, who explains that the arm-*tefillin* represents God's strength and our

resolve to submit our hearts and power to Him. The head-*tefillin* represents our resolve to dedicate the seat of our intellect to Him.

Tefillin are described as an אוֹת, *a sign,* of the covenant between God and Israel (*Exodus* 13:9,16; *Deuteronomy* 4:8, 11:18) — a measure of their profound significance.

Since *tefillin* are not worn on the Sabbath, festivals, or at night, it is a time-related commandment and therefore is not incumbent upon women.

Nowhere does the Scriptural *mitzvah* of *tefillin* specify that it should be worn only during prayer. Indeed, throughout the generations, righteous people wore *tefillin* all day, except when they were engaged in activities unbecoming to the sanctity of *tefillin.*

הִנְנִי מְכַוֵּן בַּהֲנָחַת תְּפִלִּין לְקַיֵּם מִצְוַת בּוֹרְאִי, שֶׁצִּוָּנוּ

Behold, I intend, in putting on tefillin, to fulfill the commandment of my Creator, Who commanded us

לְהָנִיחַ תְּפִלִּין, כַּכָּתוּב בְּתוֹרָתוֹ: וּקְשַׁרְתָּם לְאוֹת עַל יָדֶךְ,

to put on tefillin, as is written in His Torah: Bind them as a sign upon your arm,

וְהָיוּ לְטֹטָפֹת בֵּין עֵינֶיךָ.¹ וְהֵם אַרְבַּע פַּרְשִׁיּוֹת אֵלּוּ —

and they shall be tefillin between your eyes. They [consist of] these four portions —

שְׁמַע, וְהָיָה אִם שָׁמֹעַ, קַדֶּשׁ, וְהָיָה כִּי יְבִאֲךָ — שֶׁיֵּשׁ

[1] Shema; [2] And it will be, if you will hearken; [3] Sanctify; [4] and it will be, when He shall bring you — which contain

בָּהֶם יִחוּדוֹ וְאַחְדּוּתוֹ יִתְבָּרַךְ שְׁמוֹ בָּעוֹלָם; וְשֶׁנִּזְכּוֹר נִסִּים

in them His Oneness and His Unity — blessed is His Name, in the universe; and [the idea that] we should recall miracles

וְנִפְלָאוֹת שֶׁעָשָׂה עִמָּנוּ בְּהוֹצִיאָנוּ מִמִּצְרָיִם; וַאֲשֶׁר לוֹ

and wonders that He did for us when He took us out from Egypt, and [the idea that] He has

הַכֹּחַ וְהַמֶּמְשָׁלָה בָּעֶלְיוֹנִים וּבַתַּחְתּוֹנִים לַעֲשׂוֹת בָּהֶם כִּרְצוֹנוֹ.

the strength and dominion over the upper realms and the lower realms to do with them as He wishes.

וְצִוָּנוּ לְהָנִיחַ עַל הַיָּד, לְזִכְרוֹן זְרוֹעַ הַנְּטוּיָה, וְשֶׁהִיא נֶגֶד

He commanded us [the tefillin] to put upon the arm as a reminder of the outstretched arm [of the Exodus], and because it is opposite

הַלֵּב, לְשַׁעְבֵּד בָּזֶה תַּאֲוֹת וּמַחְשְׁבוֹת לִבֵּנוּ לַעֲבוֹדָתוֹ, יִתְבָּרַךְ

the heart, subjugating thereby the passions and thoughts of our heart to His service — blessed

שְׁמוֹ. וְעַל הָרֹאשׁ נֶגֶד הַמֹּחַ, שֶׁהַנְּשָׁמָה שֶׁבְּמוֹחִי, עִם

is His Name; and upon the head, opposite the brain, so that the soul that is in my brain, together with

שְׁאָר חוּשַׁי וְכֹחוֹתַי, כֻּלָּם יִהְיוּ מְשֻׁעְבָּדִים לַעֲבוֹדָתוֹ, יִתְבָּרַךְ

the rest of my senses and faculties, all may be subjugated to His service — blessed

---

(1) *Deuteronomy* 6:8.

However, the halachah requires that one maintain intellectual and bodily purity while wearing *tefillin*, a task that is by no means easy. Consequently, the custom was adopted that *tefillin* be worn only during *Shacharis*. The Sages teach that a man who recites the *Shema* and *Shemoneh Esrei* but does not wear *tefillin* is like one who bears false witness against himself (*Berachos* 14b). This is because *tefillin* and those two prayers are all symbolic of man's total submission to God. Thus, to utter the prayers without *tefillin* subtly implies a lack of suffi-

שְׁמוֹ. וּמִשֶּׁפַע מִצְוַת תְּפִלִּין יִתְמַשֵּׁךְ עָלַי לִהְיוֹת לִי

‹ so that I ‹‹ onto ‹ be ‹ of *tefillin* ‹ of the com- ‹ May some of the ‹‹ is His
may have   me,   extended   mandment   [spiritual] emanations   Name.

חַיִּים אֲרוּכִים, וְשֶׁפַע קְדֶשׁ, וּמַחֲשָׁבוֹת קְדוֹשׁוֹת בְּלִי הַרְהוּר

‹ thoughts ‹ without ‹ and holy thoughts, ‹ of ‹ with ‹ a long life,
holiness, emanations

חֵטְא וְעָוֹן כְּלָל; וְשֶׁלֹּא יְפַתֵּנוּ וְלֹא יִתְגָּרֶה בָּנוּ יֵצֶר הָרָע,

‹‹ – the Evil ‹‹ against ‹ incite ‹ nor ‹ lure us ‹ so that ‹‹ at all; ‹ or ‹ of sin
Inclination –   us   it not   iniquity

וְיַנִּיחֵנוּ לַעֲבֹד אֶת יהוה כַּאֲשֶׁר עִם לְבָבֵנוּ. וִיהִי רָצוֹן מִלְּפָנֶיךָ,

‹‹ before ‹ the will ‹ May ‹‹ our hearts ‹ it is ‹ as ‹ HASHEM ‹ to serve ‹ but rather
You,   it be   [to do].   in   allow us

יהוה אֱלֹהֵינוּ וֵאלֹהֵי אֲבוֹתֵינוּ, שֶׁתְּהֵא חֲשׁוּבָה מִצְוַת הֲנָחַת

‹ of put- ‹ – the com- ‹‹ considered ‹ that it be ‹‹ of our ‹ and the ‹ our God ‹ HASHEM,
ting on   mandment   forefathers,   God

תְּפִלִּין לִפְנֵי הַקָּדוֹשׁ בָּרוּךְ הוּא, כְּאִלּוּ קִיַּמְתִּיהָ בְּכָל פְּרָטֶיהָ

‹ its ‹ in all ‹ I had ‹ as if ‹‹ is He, ‹ Blessed ‹‹ the Holy ‹ before ‹‹ *tefillin* –
aspects,   fulfilled it   One,

וְדִקְדוּקֶיהָ וְכַוָּנוֹתֶיהָ, וְתַרְיַ"ג מִצְוֹת הַתְּלוּיִם בָּהּ. אָמֵן סֶלָה.

‹‹ *Selah.* ‹ Amen, ‹‹ upon ‹ that are ‹ command- ‹ as well as ‹‹ and its ‹ its details,
it.   dependent   ments   the 613   intentions,

STAND WHILE PUTTING ON *TEFILLIN*.
PLACE THE ARM-*TEFILLIN* UPON THE LEFT BICEPS (OR THE RIGHT BICEPS OF ONE WHO WRITES LEFT-HANDED), HOLD IT IN PLACE READY FOR TIGHTENING, THEN RECITE THE BLESSING:

בָּרוּךְ אַתָּה יהוה אֱלֹהֵינוּ מֶלֶךְ הָעוֹלָם, אֲשֶׁר

‹ Who ‹‹ of the universe, ‹ King ‹ our God, ‹ HASHEM, ‹ are You, ‹ Blessed

קִדְּשָׁנוּ בְּמִצְוֹתָיו, וְצִוָּנוּ לְהָנִיחַ תְּפִלִּין.

‹‹ *tefillin.* ‹ to put on ‹ and has com- ‹ with His ‹ has
manded us   commandments   sanctified us

TIGHTEN THE ARM-*TEFILLIN* AND WRAP THE STRAP SEVEN TIMES AROUND THE ARM.
WITHOUT ANY INTERRUPTION WHATSOEVER, PUT THE HEAD-*TEFILLIN* IN PLACE,
ABOVE THE HAIRLINE AND OPPOSITE THE SPACE BETWEEN THE EYES.
BEFORE TIGHTENING THE HEAD-*TEFILLIN* RECITE THE FOLLOWING BLESSING:

בָּרוּךְ אַתָּה יהוה אֱלֹהֵינוּ מֶלֶךְ הָעוֹלָם, אֲשֶׁר

‹ Who ‹‹ of the universe, ‹ King ‹ our God, ‹ HASHEM, ‹ are You, ‹ Blessed

קִדְּשָׁנוּ בְּמִצְוֹתָיו, וְצִוָּנוּ עַל מִצְוַת תְּפִלִּין.

‹‹ of *tefillin.* ‹ the ‹ regarding ‹ and has com- ‹ with His ‹ has
commandment   manded us   commandments   sanctified us

TIGHTEN THE HEAD-*TEFILLIN* AND RECITE:

בָּרוּךְ שֵׁם* כְּבוֹד מַלְכוּתוֹ לְעוֹלָם וָעֶד.

《 and ever. 〈　for ever　〈 kingdom 〈 of His glorious 〈 is the Name* 〈 Blessed

AFTER THE HEAD-*TEFILLIN* IS SECURELY IN PLACE, RECITE:

וּמֵחָכְמָתְךָ, אֵל עֶלְיוֹן, תַּאֲצִיל עָלַי; וּמִבִּינָתְךָ

〈 and from Your 《 me; 〈 may You 《 the 〈 God, 〈 From Your wisdom,
understanding　　　　imbue　Most High,

תְּבִינֵנִי; וּבְחַסְדְּךָ תַּגְדִּיל עָלַי; וּבִגְבוּרָתְךָ

〈 and with 〈 with me; 〈 deal greatly 〈 and with 《 grant me
Your power　　　　　　　　　Your kindness　understanding;

תַּצְמִית אֹיְבַי וְקָמָי. וְשֶׁמֶן הַטּוֹב תָּרִיק עַל

〈 upon 〈 pour out 〈　The fine oil 《 and those who 〈 my foes 〈 cut down
　　　　　　　　　　　　　　rise against me.

שִׁבְעָה קְנֵי הַמְּנוֹרָה, לְהַשְׁפִּיעַ טוּבְךָ לִבְרִיּוֹתֶיךָ.

《 to Your 〈 Your 〈 to cause to 《 of the 〈 branches 〈 the seven
creations.　goodness　emanate　Menorah,

פּוֹתֵחַ אֶת יָדֶךָ, וּמַשְׂבִּיעַ לְכָל חַי רָצוֹן.[1]

《 [with its] desire. 〈 living thing 〈 every 〈 and satisfy 〈 Your hand 〈 You open

**WRAP THE STRAP AROUND THE MIDDLE FINGER AND HAND ACCORDING TO YOUR CUSTOM.
WHILE DOING THIS, RECITE:**

וְאֵרַשְׂתִּיךְ לִי* לְעוֹלָם, וְאֵרַשְׂתִּיךְ לִי

〈 to Me 〈 and I will betroth you 《 forever; 〈 to Me* 〈 I will betroth you

בְּצֶדֶק וּבְמִשְׁפָּט וּבְחֶסֶד וּבְרַחֲמִים. וְאֵרַשְׂתִּיךְ

〈 and I will 《 and with mercy; 〈 with kindness, 〈 with justice, 〈 with
betroth you　　　　　　　　　　　　　　righteousness,

לִי בָּאֱמוּנָה, וְיָדַעַתְּ אֶת יהוה.[2]

《 HASHEM. 〈 and you shall know 〈 with fidelity, 〈 to Me

---

(1) *Psalms* 145:16. (2) *Hosea* 2:21-22.

cient submission (R' Yonah, ibid.).

שֵׁם בָּרוּךְ §⊷ — *Blessed is the Name.* See commentary on page 133.

לִי וְאֵרַשְׂתִּיךְ §⊷ — *I will betroth you to Me.* God

declares that Israel remains His betrothed for all eternity. This is symbolized by the wrapping of the *tefillin* strap around the fingers in the manner of a groom putting the betrothal ring on his bride's finger.

IT IS PROPER, WHILE WEARING *TEFILLIN*, TO RECITE THE FOUR SCRIPTURAL PASSAGES THAT ARE CONTAINED IN THE *TEFILLIN*. TWO OF THEM — וְהָיָה אִם שָׁמֹעַ AND שְׁמַע — WILL BE RECITED LATER AS PART OF *KRIAS SHEMA* (P. 132). THE OTHER TWO PASSAGES, GIVEN BELOW, ARE RECITED EITHER AFTER PUTTING ON THE *TEFILLIN*, OR BEFORE REMOVING THEM.

——— *Exodus* 13:1-10 / שמות יג:א-י ———

וַיְדַבֵּר יהוה* אֶל מֹשֶׁה לֵּאמֹר: קַדֶּשׁ לִי כָל

⟨ every ⟨ to Me ⟨ Sanctify ⟪ saying: ⟨ Moses, ⟨ to ⟨ HASHEM spoke*

בְּכוֹר,* פֶּטֶר כָּל רֶחֶם בִּבְנֵי יִשְׂרָאֵל בָּאָדָם

⟨ of man ⟪ of Israel, ⟨ among the ⟨ womb ⟨ of ⟨ – the first ⟪ firstborn*
                      Children   every   issue

וּבַבְּהֵמָה,* לִי הוּא. וַיֹּאמֶר מֹשֶׁה אֶל הָעָם:

⟪ the people: ⟨ to ⟨ Moses said ⟪ is Mine. ⟪ and of beast;*

זָכוֹר אֶת הַיּוֹם הַזֶּה אֲשֶׁר יְצָאתֶם מִמִּצְרַיִם

⟨ from Egypt, ⟨ you departed ⟨ on which ⟨ this day ⟨ Remember

מִבֵּית עֲבָדִים, כִּי בְּחֹזֶק יָד הוֹצִיא יהוה אֶתְכֶם

⟨ HASHEM took you out ⟨ hand ⟨ with a strong ⟨ for ⟪ of bondage, ⟨ from the house

מִזֶּה, וְלֹא יֵאָכֵל חָמֵץ. הַיּוֹם אַתֶּם יֹצְאִים,

⟪ are leaving, ⟨ you ⟨ Today ⟪ [therefore] *chametz* may not be eaten. ⟪ from here,

בְּחֹדֶשׁ הָאָבִיב.* וְהָיָה כִי יְבִיאֲךָ יהוה אֶל אֶרֶץ

⟨ the land ⟨ to ⟨ HASHEM will bring you ⟨ when ⟨ And it ⟪ of springtime.* ⟨ in the month
                            shall be,

וַיְדַבֵּר ה׳ ﬔ — *Hashem spoke.* God spoke these words to Moses immediately after the death of the Egyptian firstborns and the Exodus of the Jewish people from Egypt. The portion commands Israel forever to commemorate the Exodus in the form of specific commandments.

קַדֶּשׁ לִי כָל בְּכוֹר — *Sanctify to Me every firstborn.* Obviously, the sanctification of firstborn Jews is in commemoration of the fact that when God slew the Egyptian firstborn, He spared those of Israel. Although these firstborn are redeemed at the age of thirty days (*Numbers* 18:16), this commandment always keeps fresh in the Jewish mind that God has first claim, as it were, on its firstborn. In another sense, this unique sanctity of the first involves not only people, but firstborn domestic animals, first fruits, first crops and the various tithes. All of them are dedicated in one

way or another to God's service. This particular chapter discusses human and animal firstborn; the others are discussed elsewhere in the Torah.

וּבַבְּהֵמָה — *And of beast.* Firstborn male cattle, sheep and goats are given to the *Kohen* to be offered on the Altar. But if the firstborn animal has a physical blemish that renders it invalid as an offering, it becomes the personal property of the *Kohen* to use as he wishes.

בְּחֹדֶשׁ הָאָבִיב — *In the month of springtime.* This phrase ordains that Pesach, the festival of the Exodus, always occurs in springtime. Since twelve ordinary lunar months have only 354 days, a thirteenth month is added to the Hebrew calendar seven times in every nineteen-year cycle to ensure that Pesach will indeed fall in the spring. [The workings of the calendar are discussed at length in ArtScroll *Bircas HaChammah*

הַכְּנַעֲנִי וְהַחִתִּי וְהָאֱמֹרִי וְהַחִוִּי וְהַיְבוּסִי אֲשֶׁר

⟨ which ⟨ and the ⟨ the ⟨ the Amorites, ⟨ the Hittites, ⟨ of the
Jebusites, Hivvites Canaanites,

נִשְׁבַּע לַאֲבֹתֶיךָ לָתֶת לָךְ, אֶרֶץ זָבַת חָלָב וּדְבָשׁ,

《 and ⟨ with ⟨ flowing ⟨ – a land 《 you ⟨ to give ⟨ to your ⟨ He
honey – milk forefathers swore

וְעָבַדְתָּ אֶת הָעֲבֹדָה הַזֹּאת בַּחֹדֶשׁ הַזֶּה. שִׁבְעַת

⟨ Seven 《 in this month. ⟨ this service ⟨ you shall perform

יָמִים תֹּאכַל מַצֹּת,* וּבַיּוֹם הַשְּׁבִיעִי חַג* לַיהוה.

《 to HASHEM. ⟨ is a festival* ⟨ and on the seventh day 《 matzos,* ⟨ you shall eat ⟨ days

מַצּוֹת יֵאָכֵל אֵת שִׁבְעַת הַיָּמִים, וְלֹא יֵרָאֶה לְךָ

⟨ in your ⟨ be seen ⟨ there 《 days; ⟨ these seven ⟨ shall be ⟨ Matzos
possession may not eaten

חָמֵץ,* וְלֹא יֵרָאֶה לְךָ שְׂאֹר, בְּכָל גְּבֻלֶךָ. וְהִגַּדְתָּ

⟨ And you 《 your ⟨ in all 《 leaven, ⟨ in your ⟨ may there ⟨ nor 《 chametz,*
shall tell borders. possession be seen

לְבִנְךָ בַּיּוֹם הַהוּא לֵאמֹר: בַּעֲבוּר זֶה* עָשָׂה יהוה

⟨ that HASHEM acted ⟨ of this* ⟨ It is because 《 saying: ⟨ on that day, ⟨ your son

לִי בְּצֵאתִי מִמִּצְרָיִם. וְהָיָה לְךָ לְאוֹת עַל יָדְךָ,*

《 your ⟨ on ⟨ a sign ⟨ for you ⟨ And [it] 《 Egypt. ⟨ when I left ⟨ on my
arm,* shall be behalf

---

and *Mishnah Rosh Hashanah*.] The relationship between spring and the Exodus symbolizes the idea that the Jewish people always remain fresh and filled with the potential for growth.

שִׁבְעַת יָמִים תֹּאכַל מַצֹּת — *Seven days you shall eat matzos.* The absolute requirement that one eat *matzah* applies only to the *Seder* night. This verse means that if one wishes to eat "bread" at any time during Pesach, it must be *matzah*. The prohibition of *chametz*, however, applies throughout the festival.

וּבַיּוֹם הַשְּׁבִיעִי חַג — *And on the seventh day is a festival.* The seventh day is a *Yom Tov* on which labor is forbidden. Outside of *Eretz Yisrael*, an eighth day is added to Pesach.

לֹא יֵרָאֶה לְךָ חָמֵץ — *There may not be seen in your*

possession *chametz.* This verse is the basis for the prohibition against keeping or owning *chametz* during Pesach. Among the familiar observances resulting from this commandment is the sale of *chametz* to a non-Jew.

בַּעֲבוּר זֶה — *It is because of this.* Tell your children that we were redeemed from Egypt because we were ready to observe God's commandments. In the Haggadah this verse is the answer to the wicked son who questions the purpose of fulfilling the commandments. He is told, "It is because of this that Hashem acted on **my** behalf . . ., to remove me from Egypt; had you, the wicked son, been there, you would not have been redeemed."

לְאוֹת עַל יָדְךָ — *A sign on your arm.* As expressed in the לְשֵׁם יִחוּד prayer, the placement of *tefillin*

וּלְזִכָּרוֹן בֵּין עֵינֶיךָ, לְמַעַן תִּהְיֶה תּוֹרַת יהוה בְּפִיךָ,

‹ in your ‹ mouth;   the Torah of HASHEM should be   ‹ so that ›‹ your eyes, ‹ between ‹ and a reminder

כִּי בְּיָד חֲזָקָה הוֹצִאֲךָ יהוה מִמִּצְרָיִם. וְשָׁמַרְתָּ

‹ And you shall observe   from Egypt. ‹ HASHEM took you out ‹ with a strong hand ‹ for

אֶת הַחֻקָּה הַזֹּאת לְמוֹעֲדָהּ, מִיָּמִים יָמִימָה.

‹ to year. ‹ from year ‹ at its designated time, ‹ this decree

— שמות יג:יא-טז / *Exodus* 13:11-16 —

וְהָיָה כִּי יְבִאֲךָ יהוה* אֶל אֶרֶץ הַכְּנַעֲנִי,

‹ of the Canaanites, ‹ the land ‹ to ‹ HASHEM will bring you* ‹ when ‹ And it shall be,

כַּאֲשֶׁר נִשְׁבַּע לְךָ וְלַאֲבֹתֶיךָ, וּנְתָנָהּ לָךְ.

‹ to you, ‹ and He will have given it ‹ and to your forefathers, ‹ to you ‹ He swore ‹ as

וְהַעֲבַרְתָּ כָל פֶּטֶר רֶחֶם לַיהוה, וְכָל פֶּטֶר שֶׁגֶר

‹ that is delivered ‹ first issue ‹ and every ‹ to HASHEM, ‹ of the womb ‹ first issue ‹ every ‹ that you shall set aside

בְּהֵמָה אֲשֶׁר יִהְיֶה לְךָ הַזְּכָרִים לַיהוה. וְכָל

‹ And every ›‹ are for HASHEM.‹ the males ‹ to you, ‹ belongs ‹ that ‹ by livestock

פֶּטֶר חֲמֹר תִּפְדֶּה בְשֶׂה,* וְאִם לֹא תִפְדֶּה

‹ redeem [it] ‹ you do not ‹ and if ›‹ with a lamb or kid;* ‹ you shall redeem ‹ of a donkey ‹ first issue

---

symbolizes that we subjugate our physical strength, the arm, and our soul and intellect, the head, to the service of God.

וְהָיָה כִּי יְבִאֲךָ ה' — *And it shall be, when Hashem will bring you.* The Talmud (*Bechoros* 4b-5a) explains in two ways: either the consecration of the firstborn would affect only those born after the Jewish nation was brought into *Eretz Yisrael;* or the nation would earn its right to the Holy Land in the merit of sanctifying the firstborn.

וְכָל פֶּטֶר חֲמֹר תִּפְדֶּה בְשֶׂה — *Every first issue of a donkey you shall redeem with a lamb or kid.* In Hebrew, the word שֶׂה refers to the young of both sheep and goats (as, for example, in *Genesis*

30:32, *Numbers* 15:11, and *Deuteronomy* 14:4). There is no equivalent word in English, therefore we translate שֶׂה as *lamb or kid.*

The donkey is the only nonkosher animal that has the privileged status of the firstborn. Although the Talmud (*Bechoros* 5b) refers to this as a decree, it also offers the reason that this commandment is a memorial of the Exodus when the Jews left Egypt with countless donkeys laden with riches of the land. *Rashi* suggests also that the donkey recalls the plagues on the Egyptians who were likened to donkeys (*Ezekiel* 23:20).

Since a donkey cannot be consecrated as an offering, it is redeemed with a lamb or kid, which

וַעֲרַפְתּוֹ, וְכֹל בְּכוֹר אָדָם בְּבָנֶיךָ תִּפְדֶּה. וְהָיָה

‹ And it ‹‹ you must ‹ among ‹ of man ‹ firstborn ‹ And ‹‹ you shall break its
shall be, redeem. your sons every neck from the back.

כִּי יִשְׁאָלְךָ בִנְךָ מָחָר לֵאמֹר: מַה זֹּאת,* וְאָמַרְתָּ

‹ You shall ‹‹ is this?* ‹ What ‹‹ saying, ‹ in the ‹ your son will ‹ when
say future, ask you

אֵלָיו: בְּחֹזֶק יָד הוֹצִיאָנוּ יהוה מִמִּצְרַיִם מִבֵּית

‹ from the ‹ from Egypt, ‹ Hashem took us out ‹ hand ‹ With a ‹‹ to him,
house strong

עֲבָדִים. וַיְהִי כִּי הִקְשָׁה פַרְעֹה לְשַׁלְּחֵנוּ,

‹‹ to send us out, ‹ Pharaoh stubbornly refused ‹ when ‹‹ And it ‹‹ of bondage.
happened,

וַיַּהֲרֹג יהוה כָּל בְּכוֹר בְּאֶרֶץ מִצְרַיִם, מִבְּכֹר

‹ from the ‹‹ of Egypt, ‹ in the land ‹ the ‹ all ‹ that Hashem killed
firstborn firstborn

אָדָם וְעַד בְּכוֹר בְּהֵמָה, עַל כֵּן אֲנִי זֹבֵחַ לַיהוה

‹ to Hashem ‹ sacrifice ‹ I ‹ this ‹ For ‹‹ of beast. ‹ the ‹ down to ‹ of man
reason firstborn

כָּל פֶּטֶר רֶחֶם הַזְּכָרִים, וְכָל בְּכוֹר בָּנַי אֶפְדֶּה.

‹‹ I redeem. ‹ of my ‹ the ‹ and all ‹‹ that are males, ‹ of the ‹ first ‹ all
sons firstborn womb issue

וְהָיָה לְאוֹת עַל יָדְכָה, וּלְטוֹטָפֹת* בֵּין עֵינֶיךָ, כִּי

‹ for ‹‹ your ‹ between ‹ and tefillin* ‹ your arm ‹ upon ‹ a sign ‹ And it
eyes; shall be

בְּחֹזֶק יָד הוֹצִיאָנוּ יהוה מִמִּצְרַיִם.

‹‹ from Egypt. ‹ Hashem took us out ‹ hand ‹ with a
strong

becomes the private property of a *Kohen*, while the donkey may be used unrestrictedly by its owner. Should the Israelite owner refuse to redeem his donkey, he is denied its use: He must put it to death immediately by administering a blow with an axe to the back of the neck.

מַה זֹאת — *What is this?* In the Haggadah, this

question is ascribed to the simple child, who wishes to learn but is incapable of adequately analyzing the *Seder* service.

טוֹטָפֹת — *Tefillin.* Many interpretations are given for this untranslatable word; all agree, however, that it refers to the head-*tefillin*. See the commentary on page 134.

⚜ INTRODUCTORY PRAYER / תפלה קודם התפלה ⚜

SOME RECITE THE FOLLOWING DEEPLY MYSTICAL SELECTION (FROM *TIKKUNEI ZOHAR*),
AND יְדִיד נֶפֶשׁ, *BELOVED OF THE SOUL*, AT THIS POINT.

פָּתַח אֵלִיָּהוּ וְאָמַר: רִבּוֹן עָלְמִין, אַנְתְּ הוּא חַד, וְלָא

‹ but ‹‹ a ‹ Who ‹ it is ‹‹ of the ‹ Master ‹‹ and said: ‹ Elijah began speaking
not Unity, are You universe,

בְחוּשְׁבָּן. אַנְתְּ הוּא עִלָּאָה עַל כָּל עִלָּאִין, סְתִימָא עַל כָּל

‹ all ‹ than ‹ more ‹‹ supreme ‹ all ‹ over ‹ supreme ‹ Who ‹ it is ‹‹ in the sense of
hidden ones, are You disparate parts;

סְתִימִין. לֵית מַחֲשָׁבָה תְּפִיסָא בָךְ כְּלָל. אַנְתְּ הוּא דְאַפֵּיקַת

‹ brought ‹ Who ‹ It is ‹‹ at all. ‹ of ‹ can have any ‹ intelligence ‹ no ‹‹ hidden ones;
forth You You perception

עֲשַׂר תִּקּוּנִין, וְקָרֵינַן לְהוֹן עֲשַׂר סְפִירָן,[1] לְאַנְהָגָא בְהוֹן עָלְמִין

‹ worlds ‹ through ‹ to direct ‹ *Sefiros* – ‹ the ‹ them ‹ – we ‹‹ emanations ‹ ten
them *Ten* call

סְתִימִין דְּלָא אִתְגַּלְיָן, וְעָלְמִין דְּאִתְגַּלְיָן. וּבְהוֹן אִתְכַּסִּיאַת

‹ You conceal ‹ Through ‹‹ that are ‹ and ‹‹ revealed, ‹ not ‹ that are
Yourself them revealed. worlds hidden,

מִבְּנֵי נָשָׁא, וְאַנְתְּ הוּא דְקָשִׁיר לוֹן, וּמְיַחֵד לוֹן, וּבְגִין דְּאַנְתְּ

‹ You ‹ and ‹‹ them; ‹ and ‹ them ‹ connects ‹ Who ‹ but it ‹‹ from human
because unites is You beings,

מִלְּגָאו, כָּל מַאן דְּאַפְרִישׁ חַד מִן חַבְרֵיהּ מֵאִלֵּין עֲשַׂר

‹ Ten ‹ of these ‹ another ‹ from ‹ one ‹ who seeks ‹ anyone ‹‹ are within
one to separate them,

סְפִירָן, אִתְחֲשֵׁב לֵיהּ כְּאִלּוּ אַפְרִישׁ בָּךְ. וְאִלֵּין עֲשַׂר סְפִירָן[1]

‹‹ *Sefiros* ‹ Ten ‹ These ‹‹ within ‹ he had caused ‹ as if ‹ is regarded ‹‹ *Sefiros*
You. a separation

אִנּוּן אָזְלִין כְּסִדְרָן, חַד אָרִיךְ וְחַד קָצִיר וְחַד בֵּינוּנִי. וְאַנְתְּ

‹ It is ‹‹ mediating ‹ and ‹‹ short, ‹ one ‹ long, ‹ one ‹‹ according to ‹ proceed ‹ – they
You [between them]. one their [fixed] order:

הוּא דְּאַנְהִיג לוֹן, וְלֵית מַאן דְּאַנְהִיג לָךְ, לָא לְעֵלָּא וְלָא

‹ not ‹ above, ‹ not ‹‹ You ‹ that directs ‹ any- ‹ but there ‹‹ them, ‹ direct ‹ Who
thing is not

לְתַתָּא וְלָא מִכָּל סִטְרָא. לְבוּשִׁין תְּקִינַת לוֹן דְּמִנַּיְהוּ פָּרְחִין

‹ fly ‹ from ‹‹ for ‹ You made ‹ *Garments* ‹‹ side. ‹ from ‹ and ‹ below,
which them, any not

---

(1) See *Bamidbar Rabbah* 14:12.

נִשְׁמָתִין לִבְנֵי נָשָׁא. וְכַמָּה גוּפִין תְּקִינַת לוֹן, דְּאִתְקְרִיאוּ גוּפִין

❬ bodies ❭ ❬ which are called ❭ ❬❬ for them, ❭ ❬ You have ❭ ❬ bodies ❭ ❬ And ❭ ❬❬ to human ❭ ❬ do the souls
made   many   beings.

לְגַבֵּי לְבוּשִׁין דִּמְכַסְיָן עֲלֵיהוֹן. וְאִתְקְרִיאוּ בְּתִקּוּנָא דָא.   חֶסֶד

❬ Chesed ❬❬ in this ❭ by ❭ They are ❬❬ over them. ❬ that cover ❭ to the ❬ only
[Kindness]   way: convention   called   garments   relative

דְּרוֹעָא יְמִינָא, גְּבוּרָה דִּרוֹעָא שְׂמָאלָא, תִּפְאֶרֶת גּוּפָא,   נֶצַח

❬ Netzach ❬❬ is the ❭ Tiferes ❭ ❬❬ is the left arm; ❭ Gevurah ❬❬ is the right arm;
[Eternity;   torso;   [Splendor]   [Power]
Triumph]

וְהוֹד תְּרֵין שׁוֹקִין, יְסוֹד סִיּוּמָא דְגוּפָא אוֹת בְּרִית קֹדֶשׁ,

❬❬ of the sacred ❬ [which is] ❬❬ of the ❭ is the end ❬ Yesod ❬❬ thighs; ❭ are the ❬ and Hod
covenant;   the symbol   torso,   [Foundation]   two   [Glory]

מַלְכוּת פֶּה תּוֹרָה שֶׁבְּעַל פֶּה קְרִינָן לָהּ. חָכְמָה מוֹחָא אִיהִי

❬ which ❬ is the ❬ Chochmah ❬❬ to it. ❬ we refer ❬ [which] as the Oral Torah ❬❬ is the ❬ Malchus
is   brain,   [Wisdom]   mouth,   [Kingship]

מַחֲשָׁבָה מִלְּגָאו, בִּינָה לִבָּא וּבָהּ הַלֵּב מֵבִין – וְעַל אִלֵּין

❬ these ❬ – and ❬❬ that ❬ is the ❬ within ❬ is the ❬ Binah ❬❬ that is ❬ thought
regarding understands heart which heart [insight, internal;
                                             understanding]

תְּרֵין כְּתִיב: הַנִּסְתָּרֹת לַיהוה אֱלֹהֵינוּ,¹ – כֶּתֶר עֶלְיוֹן אִיהוּ

❬ is ❬ Keser Elyon [the ❬❬ our God – ❬ belong to ❬ The hidden ❬❬ is ❬ [last] two
Supreme Crown]   HASHEM   mysteries   written: [Sefiros]

כֶּתֶר מַלְכוּת, וַעֲלֵהּ אִתְּמַר: מַגִּיד מֵרֵאשִׁית אַחֲרִית,² וְאִיהוּ

❬ and ❬❬ the ❬ from the ❬ He Who ❬❬ is said: ❬ and con- ❬ of kingship, ❬ the
this is outcome, beginning foretells   cerning it   crown

קַרְקַפְתָּא דִתְפִלֵּי מִלְּגָאו אִיהוּ יו״ד ה״א וא״ו ה״א דְאִיהוּ³

❬ which is ❬❬ Kei, ❬ Vav ❬ Kei ❬ Yud ❬❬ is [the ❬ Within ❬❬ of the ❬ the outer
Four-Letter [the tefillin] tefillin. cover
[the Name]:

אֹרַח אֲצִילוּת. אִיהוּ שַׁקְיוּ דְאִילָנָא בִּדְרוֹעוֹי וְעַנְפוֹי, כְּמַיָּא

❬ like ❬❬ and ❬ with its arms ❬ the tree of ❬ irrigates ❬ This ❬❬ of Atzilus [spir- ❬ the
water   branches,   the Sefiros   [Name] itual emanation]. path

דְאַשְׁקֵי לְאִילָנָא וְאִתְרַבֵּי בְּהַהוּא שַׁקְיוּ. רִבּוֹן הָעוֹלָמִים, אַנְתְּ

❬ You ❬❬ of the ❬ O ❬❬ irrigation. ❬ through ❬ that then ❬ a tree ❬ that
universe,   Master   that   grows   irrigates

---

(1) *Deuteronomy* 29:28. (2) *Isaiah* 46:10. (3) When fully spelled out, יו״ד, ה״א, וא״ו, ה״א have the numerical value forty-five, representing the Name of forty-five.

הוּא עִלַּת הָעִלּוֹת, וְסִבַּת הַסִּבּוֹת, דְּאַשְׁקֵי לְאִילָנָא בְּהַהוּא

‹ through ‹ the tree ‹ Who ‹‹ of [all] ‹ and ‹ of [all] ‹ the ‹ are
that   irrigates   reasons, Reason causes, Cause

נְבִיעוּ. וְהַהוּא נְבִיעוּ אִיהוּ כְּנִשְׁמָתָא לְגוּפָא, דְּאִיהוּ חַיִּים

‹ [gives] ‹ in that it ‹‹ to the ‹ like the soul ‹ – it is ‹‹ spring ‹ That ‹‹ spring.
life   body,

לְגוּפָא. וּבָךְ לֵית דִּמְיוֹן וְלֵית דְּיוּקְנָא מִכָּל מַה דִּלְגָאו וּלְבַר.

‹‹ or ‹ [either] ‹ to anything ‹ likeness ‹ and ‹ similar ‹ there is ‹ [However,] ‹‹ to the
without. within   there is no   nothing   in You   body.

וּבְרֵאת שְׁמַיָּא וְאַרְעָא, וְאַפֵּיקַת מִנְּהוֹן שִׁמְשָׁא וְסִיהֲרָא וְכוֹכְבַיָּא

‹ the stars, ‹ the moon, ‹ the sun, ‹ from them ‹ and drew ‹ and earth, ‹ heaven ‹ You
[the heavens] forth   created

וּמַזָּלַיָּא. וּבְאַרְעָא, אִילָנִין וּדְשָׁאִין, וְגִנְתָא דְּעֵדֶן וְעִשְׂבִּין וְחֵיוָן

‹ beasts, ‹ grasses, ‹‹ of ‹ the ‹‹ and the ‹ – [You ‹‹ And on ‹‹ and the
Eden, Garden vegetation, drew forth] earth constellations.
the trees,

וּבְעִירִין וְעוֹפִין וְנוּנִין, וּבְנֵי נָשָׁא, לְאִשְׁתְּמוֹדַע בְּהוֹן עִלָּאִין,

‹‹ the ‹ through [the ‹ to make known ‹‹ and human ‹ fish, ‹ birds, ‹ cattle,
upper contemplation   beings,
realms; of] them,

וְאֵיךְ יִתְנַהֲגוּן בְּהוֹן עִלָּאִין וְתַתָּאִין, וְאֵיךְ אִשְׁתְּמוֹדְעָן

‹‹ [Your actions] ‹ and ‹‹ and the ‹ – [the func- ‹‹ [is dependent] ‹ their ‹ and
can be discerned how   lower tioning] of the on them [men] functioning how
[realm]; upper [realm]

מֵעִלָּאֵי וְתַתָּאֵי, וְלֵית דְּיָדַע בָּךְ כְּלָל. וּבַר מִנָּךְ לֵית יְחוּדָא

‹ unifying ‹ there ‹ You ‹ Without ‹‹ at all. ‹ You ‹ can ‹ – but ‹‹ and the ‹ from the
force   is no   know   no one lower ones upper realms

בְּעִלָּאֵי וְתַתָּאֵי, וְאַנְתְּ אִשְׁתְּמוֹדַע עִלַּת עַל כֹּלָּא, וְאָדוֹן

‹ and the ‹‹ all ‹ above ‹ as the ‹ are known ‹ and ‹‹ and the ‹ in the
Lord   Cause   You   lower realm, upper realm

עַל כֹּלָּא. וְכָל סְפִירָן, כָּל חַד אִית לֵיהּ שֵׁם יְדִיעַ וּבְהוֹן

‹ and with ‹‹ which is ‹ name ‹ its ‹ has ‹ one ‹ each ‹ the ‹ [Regarding] ‹‹ all. ‹ over
those names specific;   Sefiros, all

אִתְקְרִיאוּ מַלְאָכַיָּא. וְאַנְתְּ לֵית לָךְ שֵׁם יְדִיעַ, דְּאַנְתְּ הוּא

‹ for Your ‹‹ that is ‹ a ‹ do not have ‹ but You ‹‹ the angels; ‹ are identified
essence   specific, Name

מְמַלֵּא כָּל שְׁמָהָן. וְאַנְתְּ הוּא שְׁלִימוּ דְּכֻלְּהוּ. וְכַד אַנְתְּ תִּסְתַּלֵּק

‹ withdraw ‹ You ‹ When ‹‹ to them ‹ perfection ‹ Who ‹ It is You ‹‹ names. ‹ all ‹ saturates
all.   give

מִנְּהוֹן, אִשְׁתְּאָרוּ כֻּלְּהוּ שְׁמָהָן כְּגוּפָא בְּלָא נִשְׁמָתָא. אַנְתְּ חַכִּים,

are — You — a soul. — without — is like — their names — of all — what remains — from them, — wise,

וְלָא בְּחָכְמָה יְדִיעָא. אַנְתְּ הוּא מֵבִין, וְלָא מִבִּינָה יְדִיעָא.

that is definable. — a type of understanding — but — understanding — are — You — that is definable; — a wisdom — but without

לֵית לָךְ אֲתַר יְדִיעָא. אֶלָּא לְאִשְׁתְּמוֹדְעָא תּוּקְפָּךְ וְחֵילָךְ

and organized force; — Your power — to make known — [Your purpose is] only — that is identifiable. — location — You have no

לִבְנֵי נָשָׁא, וּלְאַחֲזָאָה לוֹן אֵיךְ אִתְנַהֵג עָלְמָא בְּדִינָא וּבְרַחֲמֵי,

and with mercy — is with judgment — of the world — the direction — how — them — to show — to human beings

דְּאִינּוּן צֶדֶק וּמִשְׁפָּט, כְּפוּם עוֹבְדֵיהוֹן דִּבְנֵי נָשָׁא. דִּין אִיהוּ

is — Judgment — of human beings — the deeds — according to — and justice — righteousness — which are

גְּבוּרָה, מִשְׁפָּט עַמּוּדָא דְּאֶמְצָעִיתָא, צֶדֶק מַלְכוּתָא קַדִּישָׁא,

that is Holy; — is the Kingship — righteousness — that is in the middle; — is the column — justice — Gevurah;

מֹאזְנֵי צֶדֶק תְּרֵין סַמְכֵי קְשׁוֹט, הִין צֶדֶק אוֹת בְּרִית קֹדֶשׁ.

that is sacred. — of the covenant — is the symbol — of righteousness — the measure — of truth; — supports — are — of justice — the two — the scales

כֹּלָּא לְאַחֲזָאָה אֵיךְ אִתְנַהֵג עָלְמָא, אֲבָל לָאו דְּאִית לָךְ

that You have — not — but — the world is conducted, — how — is to demonstrate — All this

צֶדֶק יְדִיעָא דְּאִיהוּ דִין, וְלָאו מִשְׁפָּט יְדִיעָא דְּאִיהוּ רַחֲמֵי,

mercy, — which is — that is knowable [to man], — a justice — nor — judgment; — which is — that is knowable [to man], — a righteousness

וְלָא מִכָּל אִלֵּין מִדּוֹת כְּלָל. בָּרוּךְ יהוה לְעוֹלָם, אָמֵן וְאָמֵן.¹

and Amen. — Amen — forever, — is — Blessed — at all. — attributes — of — any — nor — these — HASHEM

יְדִיד נֶפֶשׁ אָב הָרַחֲמָן, מְשֹׁךְ עַבְדָּךְ אֶל רְצוֹנֶךָ,

Your will. — to — Your servant — draw — Who is compassionate, — Father — of the — Beloved soul,

---

(1) *Psalms* 89:53.

ंיְדִיד נֶפֶשׁ **Yedid Nefesh**.
The composer, R' Eliezer Azikri, was one of the great Kabbalists and halachists of the 16th century in *Eretz Yisrael*, whose major work was *Sefer Charedim*. A central theme of his moral and liturgical writings was the intense love one must feel for God. This theme is readily apparent in *Yedid Nefesh*.

יָרוּץ עַבְדְּךָ כְּמוֹ אַיָּל, יִשְׁתַּחֲוֶה אֶל מוּל הֲדָרֶךָ,

May Your servant run ⟩ like ⟩ a deer ⟩⟩ to bow ⟩ toward ⟩ Your majesty. ⟩⟩

יֶעֱרַב לוֹ יְדִידוֹתֶיךָ, מִנֹּפֶת צוּף וְכָל טָעַם.

It will be ⟩ to ⟩⟩ him ⟩ — Your friendship — ⟩⟩ sweeter ⟩ than the dripping ⟩ of the honeycomb ⟩ and all ⟩ flavors. ⟩⟩

הָדוּר נָאֶה זִיו הָעוֹלָם, נַפְשִׁי חוֹלַת אַהֲבָתֶךָ,

Majestic One, ⟩ Pleasant One, ⟩ Radiance ⟩ of the universe! ⟩⟩ My soul ⟩ pines ⟩ for Your love. ⟩⟩

אָנָּא אֵל נָא רְפָא נָא לָהּ, בְּהַרְאוֹת לָהּ נֹעַם זִיוֶךָ,[1]

Please, O God, ⟩ please, ⟩ heal ⟩ it now, ⟩ by showing ⟩ it ⟩ the pleasantness ⟩ of Your radiance. ⟩⟩

אָז תִּתְחַזֵּק וְתִתְרַפֵּא, וְהָיְתָה לָהּ שִׂמְחַת עוֹלָם.

Then ⟩ it will be strengthened ⟩ and be healed, ⟩⟩ and it will have ⟩ gladness ⟩ eternally. ⟩⟩

וָתִיק, יֶהֱמוּ נָא רַחֲמֶיךָ, וְחוּסָה נָּא עַל בֵּן אֲהוּבֶךָ,

Faithful One, ⟩ may Your mercy please be aroused ⟩⟩ and take pity, ⟩ please, ⟩ on ⟩ Your beloved son. ⟩⟩

כִּי זֶה כַּמָּה נִכְסֹף נִכְסַפְתִּי

For ⟩ now ⟩ it is a long time ⟩ that I have yearned intensely ⟩

לִרְאוֹת (מְהֵרָה) בְּתִפְאֶרֶת עֻזֶּךָ,

to see ⟩ (speedily) ⟩ the splendor ⟩ of Your strength. ⟩⟩

אֵלֶּה חָמְדָה לִבִּי, וְחוּסָה נָא וְאַל תִּתְעַלָּם.

These ⟩ has my heart ⟩⟩ desired, ⟩ so take pity, ⟩ please, ⟩ and ⟩ do not conceal Yourself. ⟩⟩

הִגָּלֵה נָא וּפְרֹשׂ חֲבִיבִי עָלַי אֶת סֻכַּת שְׁלוֹמֶךָ,

Be ⟩ revealed, ⟩ please, ⟩ and ⟩ spread, ⟩ my Beloved, ⟩ upon ⟩ me ⟩ the shelter ⟩ of Your peace. ⟩⟩

תָּאִיר אֶרֶץ מִכְּבוֹדֶךָ, נָגִילָה וְנִשְׂמְחָה בָּךְ,

Illuminate ⟩ the ⟩ world ⟩ with Your glory, ⟩⟩ that we may rejoice ⟩ and be glad ⟩ with You. ⟩⟩

מַהֵר אֱהֹב כִּי בָא מוֹעֵד, וְחָנֵּנוּ כִּימֵי עוֹלָם.

Hasten, ⟩ show [Your] love, ⟩ for ⟩ has the time come, ⟩⟩ and show us grace ⟩ as in days ⟩ of old. ⟩⟩

---

(1) *Numbers* 12:13.

RECITE THE FOLLOWING VERSES UPON ENTERING THE SYNAGOGUE:

מַה טֹּבוּ אֹהָלֶיךָ* יַעֲקֹב, מִשְׁכְּנֹתֶיךָ יִשְׂרָאֵל.¹

《 O Israel. 〈 your dwelling places, 《 O Jacob, 〈 are your tents,* 〈 goodly 〈 How

וַאֲנִי בְּרֹב חַסְדְּךָ אָבוֹא בֵיתֶךָ, אֶשְׁתַּחֲוֶה

〈 I will prostrate myself 《 Your house; 〈 will I enter 〈 of Your kindness 〈 through the abundance 〈 As for me,

אֶל הֵיכַל קָדְשְׁךָ בְּיִרְאָתֶךָ.² יהוה, אָהַבְתִּי

〈 I love 〈 HASHEM, 《 in awe of You. 〈 of Your Holiness 〈 the Sanctuary 〈 toward

מְעוֹן בֵּיתֶךָ, וּמְקוֹם מִשְׁכַּן כְּבוֹדֶךָ.³ וַאֲנִי

〈 I 《 of Your glory. 〈 of the residence 〈 and the place 〈 of Your House, 〈 the shelter

אֶשְׁתַּחֲוֶה וְאֶכְרָעָה, אֶבְרְכָה לִפְנֵי יהוה עֹשִׂי.⁴

《 my Maker. 〈 HASHEM 〈 before 〈 I shall kneel 《 and bow, 〈 shall prostrate myself

וַאֲנִי, תְפִלָּתִי לְךָ יהוה עֵת רָצוֹן, אֱלֹהִים בְּרָב

〈 in the abundance 〈 O God, 《 that is 〈 be at a time 〈 HASHEM, 〈 to You, 〈 may my prayer 《 As for me,

חַסְדֶּךָ, עֲנֵנִי בֶּאֱמֶת יִשְׁעֶךָ.⁵

《 of Your salvation. 〈 with the truth 〈 answer me 〈 of Your kindness,

אֲדוֹן עוֹלָם* אֲשֶׁר מָלַךְ בְּטֶרֶם כָּל־יְצִיר נִבְרָא.

《 was created. 〈 form 〈 any 〈 before 〈 reigned 〈 Who 〈 of the universe* 〈 Master

---

(1) *Numbers* 24:5. (2) *Psalms* 5:8. (3) 26:8. (4) Cf. 95:6. (5) 69:14.

מַה טֹּבוּ אֹהָלֶיךָ — *How goodly are your tents.* The Sages interpret this praise of Israel as a reference to its "tents of learning and prayer." In a deeper sense, the Jewish home achieves its highest level when it incorporates the values of the synagogue and study hall. This collection of verses expresses love and reverence for the synagogue that, in the absence of the Holy Temple, is *the place of the residence of God's glory* among Israel.

אֲדוֹן עוֹלָם — *Master of the universe.* Alternatively *Master eternal.* This inspiring song of praise is attributed to R' Shlomo ibn Gabirol, one of the greatest early *paytanim* [liturgical poets], who flourished in the 11th century. The daily prayer service is inaugurated with the

לְעֵת נַעֲשָׂה בְחֶפְצוֹ כֹּל, אֲזַי מֶלֶךְ שְׁמוֹ נִקְרָא.

« was ‹ His ‹ as ‹ then « all ‹ when His will created ‹ At the
proclaimed. Name "King" things, time

וְאַחֲרֵי כִּכְלוֹת הַכֹּל, לְבַדּוֹ יִמְלוֹךְ נוֹרָא.

« – the Awe- « will reign ‹ He alone « of all, ‹ the end ‹ After
some One.

וְהוּא הָיָה וְהוּא הֹוֶה, וְהוּא יִהְיֶה בְּתִפְאָרָה.

« in splendor. ‹ Who shall ‹ and He « Who is, ‹ and He « Who was, ‹ It is He
remain

וְהוּא אֶחָד וְאֵין שֵׁנִי לְהַמְשִׁיל לוֹ לְהַחְבִּירָה.

« or to be His equal. ‹ to ‹ to compare ‹ second ‹ and there ‹ is One ‹ He
Him is no

בְּלִי רֵאשִׁית בְּלִי תַכְלִית, וְלוֹ הָעֹז וְהַמִּשְׂרָה.

« and the ‹ is the ‹ – His « conclusion, ‹ without « beginning, ‹ Without
dominion. power

וְהוּא אֵלִי וְחַי גֹּאֲלִי, וְצוּר חֶבְלִי בְּעֵת צָרָה.

« of ‹ in a time ‹ [from] my ‹ a Rock « Redeemer, ‹ my « my ‹ He is
distress. pain [to save] living God,

וְהוּא נִסִּי וּמָנוֹס לִי, מְנָת כּוֹסִי בְּיוֹם אֶקְרָא.

« I call. ‹ on ‹ of ‹ the « for ‹ a refuge « my ‹ He is
the day my cup portion me, banner,

בְּיָדוֹ אַפְקִיד רוּחִי בְּעֵת אִישַׁן וְאָעִירָה.

« – and I « I go to ‹ when ‹ my spirit ‹ I shall entrust ‹ Into
shall awaken! sleep His hand

וְעִם רוּחִי גְּוִיָּתִי, יְהוה לִי וְלֹא אִירָא.

« I shall not fear. « is ‹ Hashem « my body ‹ my spirit ‹ With
with me, shall remain;

Name אָדוֹן to recall the merit of Abraham, the first one to address God with this title [*Genesis* 15:2] (*Etz Yosef*), and the one who instituted the morning prayers [*Berachos* 26b] (*Vilna Gaon*).

The song emphasizes that God is timeless, infinite and omnipotent. Mankind can offer Him only one thing: to proclaim Him as King by doing His will and praising Him. Despite God's greatness, however, He involves Himself with man's personal needs in time of pain and distress. The prayer concludes on the inspiring note that, lofty though He is, *Hashem is with me, I shall not fear.*

יִגְדַּל* אֱלֹהִים חַי וְיִשְׁתַּבַּח, נִמְצָא וְאֵין עֵת

⟨ time ⟨ and there ⟨ He ⟪ and may He ⟨ Who ⟨ God ⟨ Exalted be*
limitation is no exists, be praised. lives,

אֶל מְצִיאוּתוֹ.* אֶחָד וְאֵין יָחִיד כְּיִחוּדוֹ, נֶעְלָם

⟨ [He is] ⟪ like His ⟨ unity ⟨ and there ⟪ He is ⟪ His existence.* ⟨ for
inscrutable Oneness. is no One,

וְגַם אֵין סוֹף לְאַחְדּוּתוֹ. אֵין לוֹ דְּמוּת הַגּוּף

⟪ of a ⟨ semblance ⟨ He has no ⟪ to His Oneness. ⟨ limit ⟨ there ⟨ and
body, is no indeed

וְאֵינוֹ גוּף,* לֹא נַעֲרוֹךְ אֵלָיו* קְדֻשָּׁתוֹ. קַדְמוֹן

⟨ He ⟪ [in] His Holiness. ⟨ to Him* ⟨ can we ⟨ nor ⟪ corporeal,* ⟨ nor
preceded compare is He

לְכָל דָּבָר אֲשֶׁר נִבְרָא, רִאשׁוֹן וְאֵין רֵאשִׁית

⟨ precedes ⟨ and ⟨ – the First, ⟪ was ⟨ that ⟨ entity ⟨ every
nothing created

לְרֵאשִׁיתוֹ. הִנּוֹ אֲדוֹן עוֹלָם,* לְכָל נוֹצָר יוֹרֶה

⟨ He ⟨ creature ⟨ to ⟪ of the ⟨ Master ⟨ He is ⟪ His precedence.
teaches every universe,*

גְּדֻלָּתוֹ וּמַלְכוּתוֹ. שֶׁפַע נְבוּאָתוֹ* נְתָנוֹ, אֶל אַנְשֵׁי

⟨ the ⟨ to ⟨ did He ⟨ of His ⟨ The ⟪ and His ⟨ His
people grant prophecy* abundance sovereignty. greatness

⚜ **יִגְדַּל** — *Exalted be.* This song of uncertain authorship summarizes the "Thirteen Principles of Faith" expounded by *Rambam* [Maimonides] in his *Commentary to Mishnah, Sanhedrin,* Ch. 10, and stated succinctly in the renowned *Ani Maamin* prayer. They comprise the basic principles that every Jew is required to believe. In *Rambam's* view, to deny any of them constitutes heresy.

וְאֵין עֵת אֶל מְצִיאוּתוֹ — *And there is no time limitation for His existence.* If God's existence were timebound, it would be no different in kind from that of any living, but not eternal, being. *Rambam* comments that the principle of God's timelessness, with neither beginning nor end, implies that He cannot be dependent in any way on any other being: The timebound is inherently inferior to the timeless. Nothing can exist without God, but He depends on no one and on nothing.

וְאֵינוֹ גוּף — *Nor is He corporeal.* God has no physicality, not even that of invisible, intangible angels.

אֵלָיו — *To Him.* We cannot express God's Holiness through comparison with any physical body.

הִנּוֹ אֲדוֹן עוֹלָם — *He is Master of the universe.* Because He is absolute Master, there is nothing else to which prayers may be directed.

שֶׁפַע נְבוּאָתוֹ — *The abundance of His prophecy.* Judaism depends on the principle that God, through His prophets, revealed His will to Israel.

סְגֻלָּתוֹ וְתִפְאַרְתּוֹ. לֹא קָם בְּיִשְׂרָאֵל כְּמֹשֶׁה*

‹ [anyone] ‹ in Israel ‹ arise ‹ There ≪ and of His ‹ of His
like Moses*   did not   splendor.   choosing

עוֹד, נָבִיא¹ וּמַבִּיט אֶת תְּמוּנָתוֹ.² תּוֹרַת אֱמֶת*

‹ of truth* ‹ A Torah ≪ His image. ‹ who ‹ – a ≪ ever
           gazes at   prophet   again

נָתַן לְעַמּוֹ אֵל, עַל יַד נְבִיאוֹ נֶאֱמַן בֵּיתוֹ.³ לֹא

‹ Never ≪ of His ‹ the most ‹ of His ‹ means ‹ by ≪ – did ‹ to His ‹ He
   household. trusted   prophet,   God –   people   gave

יַחֲלִיף הָאֵל וְלֹא יָמִיר דָּתוֹ, לְעוֹלָמִים לְזוּלָתוֹ.

≪ for any ‹ for all eternity, ≪ His law, ‹ will He ‹ nor ‹ will God amend
other one.   exchange

צוֹפֶה וְיוֹדֵעַ סְתָרֵינוּ, מַבִּיט לְסוֹף דָּבָר בְּקַדְמָתוֹ.

≪ at its ‹ of a ‹ the ‹ He ≪ our secrets, ‹ and ‹ He
inception.   matter   outcome perceives   knows scrutinizes

גּוֹמֵל לְאִישׁ חֶסֶד כְּמִפְעָלוֹ, נוֹתֵן לְרָשָׁע רָע

‹ evil ‹ to the ‹ He ≪ according to ‹ with ‹ man ‹ He
   wicked one   assigns   his deed;   kindness   recompenses

כְּרִשְׁעָתוֹ. יִשְׁלַח לְקֵץ הַיָּמִין מְשִׁיחֵנוּ, לִפְדּוֹת

‹ to redeem ≪ our Messiah, ‹ of Days ‹ at the ‹ He will ≪ according to
                End   send   his wickedness.

מְחַכֵּי קֵץ יְשׁוּעָתוֹ. מֵתִים יְחַיֶּה אֵל בְּרֹב חַסְדּוֹ,

≪ of His ‹ in the ‹ will God revive ‹ The dead ≪ salvation. ‹ His ‹ those
kindness, abundance   final longing for

בָּרוּךְ עֲדֵי עַד שֵׁם תְּהִלָּתוֹ.

≪ of His praise. ‹ is the ‹ and ‹ for ever ‹ blessed
           Name   ever

---

(1) Cf. *Deuteronomy* 34:10. (2) Cf. *Numbers* 12:8. (3) Cf. 12:7.

כְּמֹשֶׁה — *[Anyone] like Moses.* It is imperative to acknowledge that Moses' prophecy is unparalleled; otherwise another "prophet" could conceivably challenge or amend it, thus questioning the authenticity of the Torah.

תּוֹרַת אֱמֶת — *A Torah of truth.* God gave Moses not only the Written Law, but the Oral Law as well. Neither is complete without the other, and *Torah of truth* is a term that includes both.

⭒ MORNING BLESSINGS / בִּרְכוֹת הַשַּׁחַר ⭒

ALTHOUGH MANY AUTHORITIES HOLD THAT THE BLESSING עַל נְטִילַת יָדַיִם SHOULD BE RECITED IMMEDIATELY AFTER THE RITUAL WASHING OF THE HANDS UPON ARISING, OTHERS CUSTOMARILY RECITE IT HERE. SIMILARLY, SOME RECITE אֲשֶׁר יָצַר IMMEDIATELY AFTER RELIEVING THEMSELVES IN THE MORNING, WHILE OTHERS RECITE IT HERE.

בָּרוּךְ אַתָּה יהוה אֱלֹהֵינוּ מֶלֶךְ הָעוֹלָם,
‹ of the universe, ‹ King ‹ our God, ‹ HASHEM, ‹ are You, ‹ Blessed

אֲשֶׁר קִדְּשָׁנוּ בְּמִצְוֹתָיו, וְצִוָּנוּ עַל נְטִילַת יָדָיִם.*
‹ the hands.* ‹ washing ‹ regarding ‹ and has commanded us ‹ with His commandments ‹ has sanctified ‹ Who us

בָּרוּךְ אַתָּה יהוה אֱלֹהֵינוּ מֶלֶךְ הָעוֹלָם,
‹ of the universe, ‹ King ‹ our God, ‹ HASHEM, ‹ are You, ‹ Blessed

אֲשֶׁר יָצַר אֶת הָאָדָם בְּחָכְמָה,* וּבָרָא בוֹ
‹ within him ‹ and created ‹ with wisdom,* ‹ man ‹ fashioned ‹ Who

נְקָבִים נְקָבִים, חֲלוּלִים חֲלוּלִים.* גָּלוּי וְיָדוּעַ
‹ and known ‹ It is obvious ‹ and all manner of cavities.* ‹ all manner of openings*

לִפְנֵי כִסֵּא כְבוֹדֶךָ, שֶׁאִם יִפָּתֵחַ אֶחָד מֵהֶם, אוֹ
‹ or ‹ of them ‹ [even] one ‹ there would be ruptured ‹ that if ‹ of Your glory, ‹ the throne ‹ before

יִסָּתֵם אֶחָד מֵהֶם, אִי אֶפְשָׁר לְהִתְקַיֵּם וְלַעֲמוֹד
‹ and to stand ‹ to survive ‹ be possible ‹ it would not ‹ of them, ‹ [even] one ‹ would be blocked

לְפָנֶיךָ אֲפִילוּ שָׁעָה אֶחָת. בָּרוּךְ אַתָּה יהוה,
‹ HASHEM, ‹ are You, ‹ Blessed ‹ one hour. ‹ for even ‹ before You,

רוֹפֵא כָל בָּשָׂר וּמַפְלִיא לַעֲשׂוֹת.
‹ in His acts. ‹ and is wondrous ‹ flesh, ‹ all ‹ Who heals

עַל נְטִילַת יָדַיִם — *Regarding washing the hands.* Blessings are generally recited in conjunction with the acts to which they apply. Nevertheless, some postpone the blessings עַל נְטִילַת יָדַיִם, for washing the hands, and אֲשֶׁר יָצַר, for relieving oneself, so that they will be recited as part of *Shacharis* (see *Mishnah Berurah* 4:4, 6:9).

אֲשֶׁר יָצַר אֶת הָאָדָם בְּחָכְמָה — *Who fashioned man with wisdom.* This phrase has two meanings: (a) When God created man, He gave him the gift of wisdom; and (b) God used wisdom when He created man, as is demonstrated in the precise balance of his organs and functions.

נְקָבִים, חֲלוּלִים — *Openings and . . . cavities.* The mouth, nostrils, and other orifices are the

AT THIS POINT, SOME RECITE אלהי נשמה, "MY GOD, THE SOUL ..." (P. 27).

BLESSINGS OF THE TORAH / ברכות התורה

IT IS FORBIDDEN TO STUDY OR RECITE TORAH PASSAGES BEFORE RECITING THE FOLLOWING BLESSINGS. HOWEVER, THESE BLESSINGS NEED NOT BE REPEATED IF ONE STUDIES AT VARIOUS TIMES OF THE DAY.

בָּרוּךְ אַתָּה יהוה אֱלֹהֵינוּ מֶלֶךְ הָעוֹלָם, אֲשֶׁר
Blessed ⟨ are You, ⟨ HASHEM, ⟨ our God, ⟨ King ⟨ of the universe, ⟨ Who ⟩⟩

קִדְּשָׁנוּ בְּמִצְוֹתָיו, וְצִוָּנוּ לַעֲסוֹק בְּדִבְרֵי תוֹרָה.
has ⟨ with His ⟨ and com- ⟨ to engross ⟨ in the ⟨ of Torah. ⟩⟩
sanctified us   commandments   manded us   ourselves   words

וְהַעֲרֶב נָא יהוה אֱלֹהֵינוּ אֶת דִּבְרֵי תוֹרָתְךָ
Sweeten, ⟨ please, ⟨ HASHEM, ⟨ our God, ⟩⟩ the words ⟨ of Your Torah ⟨

בְּפִינוּ וּבְפִיּוֹת עַמְּךָ בֵּית יִשְׂרָאֵל. וְנִהְיֶה אֲנַחְנוּ
in our ⟨ in the ⟨ of Your ⟨ the ⟨ of Israel, ⟩⟩ that we ⟩⟩ — we ⟨
mouth   mouths   people,   House   may be

וְצֶאֱצָאֵינוּ (וְצֶאֱצָאֵי צֶאֱצָאֵינוּ) וְצֶאֱצָאֵי עַמְּךָ
and our offspring ⟨ (and the ⟨ of our ⟨ and the ⟨ of Your ⟨
                    offspring   offspring)   offspring   people,

בֵּית יִשְׂרָאֵל, כֻּלָּנוּ יוֹדְעֵי שְׁמֶךָ וְלוֹמְדֵי תוֹרָתֶךָ
the ⟨ of Israel ⟩⟩ — all ⟨ who ⟨ Your ⟨ and study ⟨ Your Torah ⟨
House   of us   know   Name

לִשְׁמָהּ.* בָּרוּךְ אַתָּה יהוה, הַמְלַמֵּד תּוֹרָה
for its own sake.* ⟩⟩ Blessed ⟨ are You, ⟨ HASHEM, ⟩⟩ Who teaches ⟨ Torah ⟨

לְעַמּוֹ יִשְׂרָאֵל.
to His people ⟨ Israel. ⟩⟩

---

openings that lead in and out of the body. The cavities are the inner hollows that contain such organs as the lungs, heart, stomach, and brain.

⟨⟨ ברכות התורה / BLESSINGS OF THE TORAH ⟩⟩

As stated explicitly in the Talmudic selection [אֵלוּ דְבָרִים] at the conclusion of these blessings, Torah study is the paramount commandment. Without it, man cannot know God's will; with it, he can penetrate the wisdom of the Creator

Himself. Each part of the blessings expresses a different idea. אֲשֶׁר קִדְּשָׁנוּ, Who has sanctified us, applies to the commandments; וְהַעֲרֶב, Sweeten, is a prayer; אֲשֶׁר בָּחַר בָּנוּ, Who selected us, is an expression of gratitude for the gift of the Torah.

לִשְׁמָהּ — For its own sake. May we study Torah for no other reason than to know it and become imbued with its wisdom.

בָּרוּךְ אַתָּה יהוה אֱלֹהֵינוּ מֶלֶךְ הָעוֹלָם, אֲשֶׁר

⟨ Who ⟨⟨ of the ⟨ King ⟨ our God, ⟨ Hashem, ⟨ are You, ⟨ Blessed
universe,

בָּחַר בָּנוּ מִכָּל הָעַמִּים וְנָתַן לָנוּ אֶת תּוֹרָתוֹ.

⟨⟨ His Torah. ⟨ us ⟨ and gave ⟨ the peoples ⟨ from all ⟨ us ⟨ selected

בָּרוּךְ אַתָּה יהוה, נוֹתֵן הַתּוֹרָה.

⟨⟨ of the Torah. ⟨ Giver ⟨⟨ Hashem, ⟨ are You, ⟨ Blessed

וַיְדַבֵּר יהוה אֶל מֹשֶׁה לֵּאמֹר. דַּבֵּר אֶל

⟨ to ⟨ Speak ⟨⟨ saying, ⟨ Moses ⟨ to ⟨ Hashem spoke

אַהֲרֹן וְאֶל בָּנָיו לֵאמֹר, כֹּה תְבָרְכוּ אֶת בְּנֵי

⟨ the Children ⟨ shall you bless ⟨ 'So ⟨⟨ saying: ⟨ his sons ⟨ and to ⟨ Aaron

יִשְׂרָאֵל, אָמוֹר לָהֶם. יְבָרֶכְךָ יהוה וְיִשְׁמְרֶךָ.

⟨⟨ and ⟨ "May Hashem ⟨⟨ to them: ⟨ saying ⟨⟨ of Israel,
safeguard you. bless you

יָאֵר יהוה פָּנָיו אֵלֶיךָ וִיחֻנֶּךָּ. יִשָּׂא יהוה פָּנָיו

⟨ His coun- ⟨ May Hashem ⟨⟨ and be gra- ⟨ for ⟨ His coun- ⟨ May Hashem
tenance turn cious to you. you tenance illuminate

אֵלֶיךָ, וְיָשֵׂם לְךָ שָׁלוֹם. וְשָׂמוּ אֶת שְׁמִי עַל

⟨ upon ⟨ My Name ⟨ Let them ⟨⟨ peace."' ⟨ for ⟨ and ⟨ to you
place you establish

בְּנֵי יִשְׂרָאֵל, וַאֲנִי אֲבָרְכֵם.¹

⟨⟨ shall bless them. ⟨ and I ⟨⟨ of Israel, ⟨ the
Children

(1) *Numbers* 6:22-27.

◆§ Selections from the Written and Oral Torah

A *mitzvah* must be performed immediately after a blessing is recited for it. Having recited the blessings for the study of Torah, we immediately recite selections from both the Written and Oral Torah. First we recite the Scriptural verses of the Priestly Blessings, then a Talmudic selection from the Mishnah (*Pe'ah* 1:1) and Gemara (*Shabbos* 127a). The Talmudic selection discusses the reward for various commandments and concludes with the declaration that Torah study is equivalent to them all, an appropriate addendum to the Blessings of the Torah.

אֵלּוּ דְבָרִים שֶׁאֵין לָהֶם שִׁעוּר:* הַפֵּאָה וְהַבִּכּוּרִים

‹ the first-fruit ‹ the corner of a ‹‹ prescribed ‹ that have no ‹ are the ‹ These
offering, field [which must measure:* precepts
be left for the poor],

וְהָרֵאָיוֹן* וּגְמִילוּת חֲסָדִים וְתַלְמוּד תּוֹרָה.¹

‹‹ of Torah. ‹ and study ‹ of kindness ‹ the bestowal ‹ the pilgrimage,*

אֵלּוּ דְבָרִים שֶׁאָדָם אוֹכֵל פֵּרוֹתֵיהֶם בָּעוֹלָם הַזֶּה

‹‹ in This World, ‹ their fruits ‹ enjoys ‹ of which ‹ are the ‹ These
a person precepts

וְהַקֶּרֶן קַיֶּמֶת לוֹ לָעוֹלָם הַבָּא.* וְאֵלּוּ הֵן: כִּבּוּד

‹ honoring ‹‹ are ‹ These ‹‹ to ‹ in the ‹ for ‹ remains ‹ but whose
they: Come.* World him intact principal

אָב וָאֵם, וּגְמִילוּת חֲסָדִים, וְהַשְׁכָּמַת בֵּית

‹ at the ‹ early ‹‹ of kindness, ‹ the bestowal ‹‹ and ‹ [one's]
house attendance mother, father

הַמִּדְרָשׁ שַׁחֲרִית וְעַרְבִית, וְהַכְנָסַת אוֹרְחִים,

‹‹ to guests, ‹ hospitality ‹‹ and evening, ‹ morning ‹ of study

וּבִקּוּר חוֹלִים, וְהַכְנָסַת כַּלָּה, וּלְוָיַת הַמֵּת, וְעִיּוּן

‹ absorption ‹‹ the dead, ‹ escorting ‹‹ a bride, ‹ providing for ‹‹ the sick, ‹ visiting

תְּפִלָּה, וַהֲבָאַת שָׁלוֹם בֵּין אָדָם לַחֲבֵרוֹ וּבֵין אִישׁ

‹ a man ‹ and ‹ and his ‹ man ‹ between ‹ peace ‹ bringing ‹‹ in prayer,
between fellow,

לְאִשְׁתּוֹ – וְתַלְמוּד תּוֹרָה כְּנֶגֶד כֻּלָּם.²

‹‹ to them all. ‹ is equivalent ‹ of Torah ‹ – and the study ‹‹ and his wife

---

(1) Mishnah *Pe'ah* 1:1. (2) Tractate *Shabbos* 127a.

אֵלּוּ דְבָרִים שֶׁאֵין לָהֶם שִׁעוּר — *These are the precepts that have no prescribed measure.* The Torah does not prescribe the specific amount required in the performance of the following commandments (*Rav*).

וְהָרֵאָיוֹן — *The pilgrimage.* Though the Torah ordains that a Jew visit the Temple on each of the three Festivals (Pesach, Shavuos, and Succos), one may visit as often as he wishes. Alternatively, there is no set amount for the value of the offering [עוֹלַת רְאִיָּה] that one must bring at such times.

וְהַקֶּרֶן קַיֶּמֶת לוֹ לָעוֹלָם הַבָּא — *But whose principal remains intact for him in the World to Come.* Though one is rewarded for these *mitzvos* in This World, his reward in the World to Come is not diminished.

אֱלֹהַי, נְשָׁמָה* שֶׁנָּתַתָּ בִּי טְהוֹרָה הִיא. אַתָּה

‹ You ‹‹ is pure. ‹ within ‹ that You ‹ the soul* ‹‹ My God,
             me   placed

בְרָאתָהּ, אַתָּה יְצַרְתָּהּ, אַתָּה נְפַחְתָּהּ בִּי, וְאַתָּה

‹ You ‹‹ into me,‹ breathed it ‹ You ‹ fashioned it, ‹ You ‹ created it,

מְשַׁמְּרָהּ בְּקִרְבִּי, וְאַתָּה עָתִיד לִטְּלָהּ מִמֶּנִּי,

‹ from me ‹ take it ‹ will eventually‹ and You ‹ within me, ‹ safeguard it

וּלְהַחֲזִירָהּ בִּי לֶעָתִיד לָבֹא. כָּל זְמַן שֶׁהַנְּשָׁמָה

‹ that the soul ‹ the time ‹ All ‹‹ to Come. ‹ in the Time ‹ to me ‹ and restore it

בְּקִרְבִּי, מוֹדֶה אֲנִי לְפָנֶיךָ, יהוה אֱלֹהַי וֵאלֹהֵי

‹ and the God ‹ my God ‹ HASHEM, ‹ before You, ‹ I give thanks ‹‹ is within me,

אֲבוֹתַי, רִבּוֹן כָּל הַמַּעֲשִׂים, אֲדוֹן כָּל הַנְּשָׁמוֹת.

‹‹ souls. ‹ of all ‹ Lord ‹‹ works, ‹ of all ‹ Master ‹‹ of my
                  forefathers,

בָּרוּךְ אַתָּה יהוה, הַמַּחֲזִיר נְשָׁמוֹת לִפְגָרִים מֵתִים.

‹‹ that are ‹ to the ‹ souls ‹ Who restores ‹‹ HASHEM, ‹ are You, ‹ Blessed
  dead.   bodies

THE *CHAZZAN* RECITES THE FOLLOWING BLESSINGS ALOUD, AND THE CONGREGATION RESPONDS
אָמֵן TO EACH BLESSING. NEVERTHELESS, EACH PERSON MUST RECITE THESE BLESSINGS FOR HIMSELF.

בָּרוּךְ* אַתָּה יהוה אֱלֹהֵינוּ מֶלֶךְ הָעוֹלָם, אֲשֶׁר

‹ Who ‹‹ of the universe, ‹ King ‹ our God, ‹ HASHEM, ‹ are You, ‹ Blessed*

נָתַן לַשֶּׂכְוִי בִינָה*[1] לְהַבְחִין בֵּין יוֹם וּבֵין לַיְלָה.

‹‹ and night. ‹ day ‹ between ‹ to distinguish ‹ understanding* ‹ the heart ‹ gave

---

(1) Cf. *Job* 38:36.

אֱלֹהַי, נְשָׁמָה — *My God, the soul. . .* This prayerful blessing is an expression of gratitude to God for restoring our vitality in the morning with a soul of pure, celestial origin, and for maintaining us in life and in health.

בָּרוּךְ . . . אֲשֶׁר נָתַן לַשֶּׂכְוִי בִינָה — *Blessed . . . Who gave the heart understanding.* The word שֶׂכְוִי means both *heart* and *rooster.* In the context of this blessing, both meanings are implied: The rooster crows, but man's heart reacts and under-

stands how to deal with new situations (*Rosh*).

This series of fifteen blessings is based on *Berachos* 60b, where the Sages teach that as one experiences the phenomena of the new day, he should bless God for providing them. Some of the phenomena are not obvious from the text of the blessing. Among them are: sitting up and stretching [*releases the bound*]; getting out of bed [*straightens the bent*]; standing on the floor [*spreads out the earth . . .*]; donning shoes which

בָּרוּךְ אַתָּה יהוה אֱלֹהֵינוּ מֶלֶךְ הָעוֹלָם,

‹ of the universe, ‹ King ‹ our God, ‹ Hashem, ‹ are You, ‹ Blessed

שֶׁלֹּא עָשַׂנִי גּוֹי.*

‹ a gentile.* ‹ make me ‹ Who did not

בָּרוּךְ אַתָּה יהוה אֱלֹהֵינוּ מֶלֶךְ הָעוֹלָם,

‹ of the universe, ‹ King ‹ our God, ‹ Hashem, ‹ are You, ‹ Blessed

שֶׁלֹּא עָשַׂנִי עָבֶד.*

‹ a slave.* ‹ make me ‹ Who did not

בָּרוּךְ אַתָּה יהוה אֱלֹהֵינוּ מֶלֶךְ הָעוֹלָם,

‹ of the universe, ‹ King ‹ our God, ‹ Hashem, ‹ are You, ‹ Blessed

WOMEN SAY: | **MEN SAY:**

שֶׁעָשַׂנִי כִּרְצוֹנוֹ. | שֶׁלֹּא עָשַׂנִי אִשָּׁה.*

‹ according ‹ Who made me | ‹ a woman.* ‹ make me ‹ Who did not
to His will. |

בָּרוּךְ אַתָּה יהוה אֱלֹהֵינוּ מֶלֶךְ הָעוֹלָם,

‹ of the universe, ‹ King ‹ our God, ‹ Hashem, ‹ are You, ‹ Blessed

פּוֹקֵחַ עִוְרִים.¹

‹ to the blind. ‹ Who gives sight

(1) Psalms 146:8.

symbolizes man's ability to go on his way comfortably [provided me with all my needs]; setting out on one's destination [establishes . . . footsteps]; fastening one's clothing [girds Israel . . .]; putting on a hat, which symbolizes the Jew's reminder that Someone is above him [crowns Israel . . .]; feeling the passing of nighttime exhaustion [gives . . . strength and removes sleep . . .].

Arizal teaches that each day a righteous person should endeavor to respond to a minimum of ninety blessings, four times Kedushah (the verse קָדוֹשׁ קָדוֹשׁ קָדוֹשׁ, Holy, Holy, Holy . . .), ten times Kaddish, and to recite no fewer than one hundred blessings. These figures are alluded to by the letters of the word צַדִּיק, righteous one, which have the numerical equivalents of 90, 4, 10, and

100 respectively. To assure ninety Amen responses, some people recite these fifteen blessings aloud for one another.

שֶׁלֹּא עָשַׂנִי גּוֹי . . . עָבֶד . . . אִשָּׁה — Who did not make me a gentile . . . a slave . . . a woman. The Torah assigns missions to respective groups of people. Within Israel, for example, the Davidic family, Kohanim, and Levites are set apart by virtue of their particular callings, in addition to their shared mission as Jews. All such missions carry extra responsibilities and call for the performance of the mitzvos associated with them. We thank God, therefore, for the challenge of improving His universe in accordance with His will. Male, free Jews have responsibilities and duties not shared by others. For this, they express gratitude that, unlike women, they were not

בָּרוּךְ אַתָּה יהוה אֱלֹהֵינוּ מֶלֶךְ הָעוֹלָם,

Blessed ‹ are You, ‹ HASHEM, ‹ our God, ‹ King ‹ of the universe, «

מַלְבִּישׁ עֲרֻמִּים.

Who clothes ‹ the naked. «

בָּרוּךְ אַתָּה יהוה אֱלֹהֵינוּ מֶלֶךְ הָעוֹלָם,

Blessed ‹ are You, ‹ HASHEM, ‹ our God, ‹ King ‹ of the universe, «

מַתִּיר אֲסוּרִים.¹

Who releases ‹ the bound. «

בָּרוּךְ אַתָּה יהוה אֱלֹהֵינוּ מֶלֶךְ הָעוֹלָם,

Blessed ‹ are You, ‹ HASHEM, ‹ our God, ‹ King ‹ of the universe, «

זוֹקֵף כְּפוּפִים.²

Who straightens ‹ the bent. «

בָּרוּךְ אַתָּה יהוה אֱלֹהֵינוּ מֶלֶךְ הָעוֹלָם,

Blessed ‹ are You, ‹ HASHEM, ‹ our God, ‹ King ‹ of the universe, «

רוֹקַע הָאָרֶץ עַל הַמָּיִם.*³

Who spreads out ‹ the earth ‹ upon ‹ the waters.* «

בָּרוּךְ אַתָּה יהוה אֱלֹהֵינוּ מֶלֶךְ הָעוֹלָם,

Blessed ‹ are You, ‹ HASHEM, ‹ our God, ‹ King ‹ of the universe, «

הַמֵּכִין מִצְעֲדֵי גָבֶר.⁴

Who establishes ‹ the footsteps ‹ of man. «

---

(1) *Psalms* 146:7. (2) 146:8. (3) Cf. 136:6. (4) Cf. 37:23.

---

freed from the obligation to perform the time-related commandments. This follows the Talmudic dictum that an obligatory performance of a commandment is superior to a voluntary one, because it is human nature to resist obligations [גָּדוֹל הַמְצֻוֶּה וְעוֹשֶׂה מִמִּי שֶׁאֵינוֹ מְצֻוֶּה וְעוֹשֶׂה]. Women, on the other hand, both historically and because of their nature, are the guardians of tradition, the molders of character, children, and family. Furthermore, women have often been the protectors of Judaism when the impetuosity and aggressiveness of the male nature led the men astray. The classic precedent was in the Wilderness when the men — not the women — worshiped the Golden Calf. Thus, though women were not given the privilege of the challenge assigned to men, they are created closer to God's ideal of perfection. They express their gratitude in the blessing שֶׁעָשַׂנִי כִּרְצוֹנוֹ, *Who made me according to His will* (R' Munk).

רוֹקַע הָאָרֶץ עַל הַמָּיִם — *Who spreads out the earth upon the waters.* By nature, water spreads and floods everything in its path, while earth tends to sink beneath the surface of the water. God

בָּרוּךְ אַתָּה יהוה אֱלֹהֵינוּ מֶלֶךְ הָעוֹלָם,

Blessed ‹ are You, ‹ HASHEM, ‹ our God, ‹ King ‹ of the universe, «

שֶׁעָשָׂה לִי כָּל צָרְכִּי.

Who has provided ‹ me ‹ with all ‹ my needs. «

בָּרוּךְ אַתָּה יהוה אֱלֹהֵינוּ מֶלֶךְ הָעוֹלָם,

Blessed ‹ are You, ‹ HASHEM, ‹ our God, ‹ King ‹ of the universe, «

אוֹזֵר יִשְׂרָאֵל בִּגְבוּרָה.

Who girds ‹ Israel ‹ with strength. «

בָּרוּךְ אַתָּה יהוה אֱלֹהֵינוּ מֶלֶךְ הָעוֹלָם,

Blessed ‹ are You, ‹ HASHEM, ‹ our God, ‹ King ‹ of the universe, «

עוֹטֵר יִשְׂרָאֵל בְּתִפְאָרָה.

Who crowns ‹ Israel ‹ with splendor. «

בָּרוּךְ אַתָּה יהוה אֱלֹהֵינוּ מֶלֶךְ הָעוֹלָם,

Blessed ‹ are You, ‹ HASHEM, ‹ our God, ‹ King ‹ of the universe, «

הַנּוֹתֵן לַיָּעֵף כֹּחַ.[1]

Who gives ‹ to the weary ‹ strength. «

ALTHOUGH MANY *SIDDURIM* BEGIN A NEW PARAGRAPH AT וִיהִי רָצוֹן,
THE FOLLOWING IS ONE LONG BLESSING THAT ENDS AT לְעַמּוֹ יִשְׂרָאֵל.

בָּרוּךְ אַתָּה יהוה אֱלֹהֵינוּ מֶלֶךְ הָעוֹלָם,

Blessed ‹ are You, ‹ HASHEM, ‹ our God, ‹ King ‹ of the universe, «

הַמַּעֲבִיר שֵׁנָה מֵעֵינַי וּתְנוּמָה מֵעַפְעַפָּי. וִיהִי

Who removes ‹ sleep ‹ from my eyes ‹ and slumber ‹ from my eyelids. « And may it be ‹

רָצוֹן מִלְּפָנֶיךָ,* יהוה אֱלֹהֵינוּ וֵאלֹהֵי אֲבוֹתֵינוּ,

the will ‹ before You,* « HASHEM, ‹ our God ‹ and the God ‹ of our forefathers, «

(1) Cf. *Isaiah* 40:29.

formed the earth so that it remains always in place (*Radak*).

וִיהִי רָצוֹן מִלְּפָנֶיךָ — *And may it be the will before You.* As is common in prayers, we call upon God

שֶׁתַּרְגִּילֵנוּ בְּתוֹרָתֶךָ וְדַבְּקֵנוּ בְּמִצְוֹתֶיךָ, וְאַל

⟨ and ⟨⟨ to Your ⟨ and attach us ⟨ to [study] ⟨ that You
do not commandments; Your Torah accustom us

תְּבִיאֵנוּ לֹא לִידֵי חֵטְא, וְלֹא לִידֵי עֲבֵרָה וְעָוֹן,

⟨ and sin, ⟨ of trans- ⟨ into the ⟨ nor ⟨ of inadver- ⟨ into the ⟨ neither ⟨ bring us
gression influence tent sin influence

וְלֹא לִידֵי נִסָּיוֹן, וְלֹא לִידֵי בִזָּיוֹן, וְאַל יִשְׁלֹט

⟨ dominate ⟨ And ⟨⟨ of scorn. ⟨ into the ⟨ nor ⟨ of ⟨ into the ⟨ nor
let not influence temptation, influence

בָּנוּ יֵצֶר הָרָע. וְהַרְחִיקֵנוּ מֵאָדָם רָע וּמֵחָבֵר

⟨ and from a ⟨ who is ⟨ from a ⟨ Distance us ⟨⟨ for Evil. ⟨ the ⟨ over
companion evil person Inclination us

רָע. וְדַבְּקֵנוּ בְּיֵצֶר הַטּוֹב וּבְמַעֲשִׂים טוֹבִים, וְכוֹף

⟨ And ⟨⟨ that are ⟨ and to deeds ⟨ for Good ⟨ to the ⟨ and ⟨⟨ who
compel good. Inclination attach us is evil,

אֶת יִצְרֵנוּ לְהִשְׁתַּעְבֶּד לָךְ. וּתְנֵנוּ הַיּוֹם וּבְכָל

⟨ and ⟨ today ⟨ Allow us ⟨⟨ to You. ⟨ to be subservient ⟨ our [Evil]
every to elicit Inclination

יוֹם לְחֵן וּלְחֶסֶד וּלְרַחֲמִים בְּעֵינֶיךָ וּבְעֵינֵי כָל

⟨ of ⟨ and in ⟨ in Your eyes ⟨ and mercy ⟨ kindness, ⟨ grace, ⟨ day
all the eyes

רוֹאֵינוּ, וְתִגְמְלֵנוּ חֲסָדִים טוֹבִים. בָּרוּךְ אַתָּה

⟨ are You, ⟨ Blessed ⟨⟨ that are ⟨ kindnesses ⟨ and bestow ⟨⟨ who see us,
beneficent. upon us

יהוה, הַגּוֹמֵל חֲסָדִים טוֹבִים לְעַמּוֹ יִשְׂרָאֵל.

⟨⟨ Israel. ⟨ to His ⟨ that are ⟨ kindnesses ⟨ Who ⟨⟨ HASHEM,
people beneficent bestows

as *the God of our forefathers*, because we wish to identify with the merit of our righteous forebears (*Etz Yosef*).

When a person starts off well, his chances for future success are enhanced immeasurably.

Having thanked God for giving us new life, health, and vigor at the start of a new day, we pray that He provide us the circumstances in which we may serve Him and that He remove impediments to His service (*Siach Yitzchak*).

יְהִי רָצוֹן* מִלְּפָנֶיךָ, יהוה אֱלֹהַי וֵאלֹהֵי

‹ and the God ‹ my God ‹ Hashem, ‹‹ before You, ‹ the will* ‹ May it be

אֲבוֹתַי, שֶׁתַּצִּילֵנִי הַיּוֹם וּבְכָל יוֹם מֵעַזֵּי פָנִים

‹ from those who are brazen-faced ‹ day ‹ and every ‹ today ‹ that You rescue me ‹‹ of my forefathers,

וּמֵעַזּוּת פָּנִים, מֵאָדָם רָע, מִיֵּצֶר רָע, וּמֵחָבֵר

‹ from a companion ‹ that is evil, ‹ from an inclination ‹ who is evil, ‹ from a person ‹‹ and from brazen-facedness,

רָע, וּמִשָּׁכֵן רָע, וּמִפֶּגַע רָע, מֵעַיִן הָרָע, מִלָּשׁוֹן

‹ from speech ‹ that is evil, ‹ from an eye ‹ that is evil, ‹ from a mishap ‹ who is evil, ‹ from a neighbor ‹ who is evil,

הָרָע, מִמַּלְשִׁינוּת, מֵעֵדוּת שֶׁקֶר, מִשִּׂנְאַת

‹ from the hatred ‹ that is false, ‹ from testimony ‹ from informers, ‹ that is evil,

הַבְּרִיּוֹת, מֵעֲלִילָה, מִמִּיתָה מְשׁוּנָה, מֵחֳלָיִים

‹ from illnesses ‹ that is unnatural, ‹ from death ‹ from libel, ‹ of people,

רָעִים, מִמִּקְרִים רָעִים, וּמִשָּׂטָן הַמַּשְׁחִית, מִדִּין

‹ from legal proceedings ‹‹ which is destructive, ‹ and from a spiritual impediment ‹ that are harmful, ‹ from occurrences ‹ that are harmful,

קָשֶׁה וּמִבַּעַל דִּין קָשֶׁה, בֵּין שֶׁהוּא בֶן בְּרִית,*

‹ of the covenant* ‹ member ‹ he ‹ whether ‹‹ who is harsh, ‹ and from a litigant ‹ that are harsh,

וּבֵין שֶׁאֵינוֹ בֶן בְּרִית, וּמִדִּינָהּ שֶׁל גֵּיהִנֹּם.

‹‹ Gehinnom. ‹ of ‹ and from the judgment ‹‹ of the covenant, ‹ member ‹ a ‹ he is not ‹ or whether

---

ּ⊷ יְהִי רָצוֹן — *May it be the will.* This personal prayer was recited by Rabbi Yehudah HaNasi every day after *Shacharis* (Berachos 16b). It is a prayer for protection in day-to-day dealings with one's fellow men. Explicit mention is made here of dealings with brazen-faced people who deny us the respect due us, and also the possibility that we ourselves might sin against others through our lack of consideration of the respect due to them. During the recitation of this prayer, one may add his personal requests for God's help during the day (*Tur*).

בֶּן בְּרִית — *A member of the covenant*, Abraham's covenant of circumcision, the symbol of Israel's bond with God.

THE AKEIDAH / עקדה

אֱלֹהֵינוּ וֵאלֹהֵי אֲבוֹתֵינוּ, זָכְרֵנוּ בְּזִכָּרוֹן טוֹב לְפָנֶיךָ,

《 before 〈 that is 〈 with a 〈 remember《 of our 〈 and the God 〈 Our God
You,   favorable   memory   us   forefathers,

וּפָקְדֵנוּ בִּפְקֻדַּת יְשׁוּעָה וְרַחֲמִים מִשְּׁמֵי שְׁמֵי קֶדֶם. וּזְכָר

〈Remem-《primeval. 〈 of 〈 from the 〈 and mercy 〈 of 〈 with a 〈 and
ber   heavens   loftiest   salvation   recollection   recall us

לָנוּ יהוה אֱלֹהֵינוּ אַהֲבַת הַקַּדְמוֹנִים אַבְרָהָם יִצְחָק

〈 Isaac, 〈 Abraham, 〈 of the Patriarchs, 〈 the love 《 our 〈 – O《on our
                      God –   HASHEM,   behalf

וְיִשְׂרָאֵל עֲבָדֶיךָ, אֶת הַבְּרִית וְאֶת הַחֶסֶד וְאֶת הַשְּׁבוּעָה

〈 and the oath 〈 the kindness 〈 the covenant, 《Your servants, 〈 and Israel,

שֶׁנִּשְׁבַּעְתָּ לְאַבְרָהָם אָבִינוּ בְּהַר הַמּוֹרִיָּה, וְאֶת הָעֲקֵדָה

〈 and the Akeidah, 《 Moriah, 〈 at Mount 〈 our father 〈 to Abraham 〈 that You swore

שֶׁעָקַד אֶת יִצְחָק בְּנוֹ עַל גַּבֵּי הַמִּזְבֵּחַ, כַּכָּתוּב בְּתוֹרָתֶךָ:

《 in Your 〈 as it is 《 of the altar, 〈 top 〈 on 〈 his son 〈 Isaac 〈 when he
Torah: written   bound

——— בראשית כב:א-יט / *Genesis 22:1-19* ———

וַיְהִי אַחַר הַדְּבָרִים הָאֵלֶּה, וְהָאֱלֹהִים נִסָּה

〈 tested 〈 that God 〈 these things 〈 after 〈 And it happened

אֶת אַבְרָהָם, וַיֹּאמֶר אֵלָיו, אַבְרָהָם, וַיֹּאמֶר

〈 and he replied, 《 Abraham, 〈 to him, 〈 He said 《 Abraham.

הִנֵּנִי. וַיֹּאמֶר, קַח נָא אֶת בִּנְךָ, אֶת יְחִידְךָ, אֲשֶׁר

〈 whom 〈 your only one, 〈 your son, 〈please, 〈Take, 〈And He said, 《Here I am.

⁜ עֲקֵדָה / THE AKEIDAH ⁜

The *Akeidah* is the story of the most difficult challenge to Abraham's faith in God: He was commanded to sacrifice Isaac, his beloved son and sole heir, to God. Father and son jointly demonstrated their total devotion, whereupon God ordered Abraham to release Isaac. The Kabbalistic masters, from *Zohar* to *Arizal*, have stressed the great importance of the daily recitation of the *Akeidah*. In response to their writings, the *Akeidah* has been incorporated into the great majority of *siddurim*, although it is not recited in all congregations. In some, it is recited individually rather than as part of the public morning service. The *Zohar* records that this recitation of Abraham's and Isaac's readiness to put love of God ahead of life itself is a source of Heavenly mercy whenever Jewish lives are threatened. *Avodas HaKodesh* comments that the *Akeidah* should inspire us to attain greater love of God, and to follow the example of Abraham and Isaac. *Arizal* teaches that the recitation brings atonement to someone who repents sincerely, for he identifies himself with these two Patriarchs who placed loyalty to God above all other considerations.

אָהַבְתָּ, אֶת יִצְחָק, וְלֶךְ לְךָ אֶל אֶרֶץ הַמֹּרִיָה,
‹‹ of Moriah; ‹ the Land ‹ to ‹ yourself ‹ and get ‹‹ — Isaac — ‹‹ you love

וְהַעֲלֵהוּ שָׁם לְעֹלָה עַל אַחַד הֶהָרִים אֲשֶׁר אֹמַר
‹ I shall ‹ which ‹ of the ‹ one ‹ upon ‹‹ as an ‹ there ‹ bring him up
indicate   mountains   offering,

אֵלֶיךָ. וַיַּשְׁכֵּם אַבְרָהָם בַּבֹּקֶר,* וַיַּחֲבֹשׁ אֶת חֲמֹרוֹ,
‹‹ his donkey; ‹ and he ‹‹ in the ‹ Abraham rose early ‹‹ to you.
                saddled   morning,*

וַיִּקַּח אֶת שְׁנֵי נְעָרָיו* אִתּוֹ, וְאֵת יִצְחָק בְּנוֹ,
‹‹ his son. ‹ and Isaac, ‹‹ with him, ‹ young men* ‹ his two ‹ he took

וַיְבַקַּע עֲצֵי עֹלָה, וַיָּקָם וַיֵּלֶךְ אֶל הַמָּקוֹם
‹ the place ‹ toward ‹ and went ‹ and rose ‹‹ for the offering, ‹ wood ‹ He split

אֲשֶׁר אָמַר לוֹ הָאֱלֹהִים. בַּיּוֹם הַשְּׁלִישִׁי,
‹ On the third day ‹‹ God indicated to him. ‹ which

וַיִּשָּׂא אַבְרָהָם אֶת עֵינָיו, וַיַּרְא אֶת הַמָּקוֹם
‹ the place ‹ and perceived ‹‹ his eyes, ‹ Abraham raised

מֵרָחֹק. וַיֹּאמֶר אַבְרָהָם אֶל נְעָרָיו, שְׁבוּ לָכֶם
‹ [by] ‹ Stay ‹‹ his young ‹ to ‹ Abraham said ‹‹ from afar.
yourselves   men,

פֹּה עִם הַחֲמוֹר, וַאֲנִי וְהַנַּעַר נֵלְכָה עַד כֹּה,
‹‹ there; ‹ until ‹ will go ‹ and the lad ‹ [while] I ‹‹ the donkey, ‹ with ‹ here

וְנִשְׁתַּחֲוֶה וְנָשׁוּבָה* אֲלֵיכֶם. וַיִּקַּח אַבְרָהָם
‹ Abraham took ‹‹ to you. ‹ and we will ‹ we will prostrate
                          return*   ourselves

אֶת עֲצֵי הָעֹלָה, וַיָּשֶׂם עַל יִצְחָק בְּנוֹ, וַיִּקַּח בְּיָדוֹ
‹ in his ‹ He took ‹‹ his son. ‹ Isaac, ‹ on ‹ and ‹‹ for the ‹ the wood
hand   placed it   offering,

וַיַּשְׁכֵּם אַבְרָהָם בַּבֹּקֶר — *Abraham rose early in the morning.* He began early, with alacrity, to do God's will, even though he had been commanded to slaughter his beloved Isaac. From this verse the Sages derive that one should perform his religious obligations (e.g., circumcision) as early in

the day as possible (*Pesachim* 4a).

שְׁנֵי נְעָרָיו — *His two young men.* Ishmael, his older son, and Eliezer, his trusted servant.

וְנִשְׁתַּחֲוֶה וְנָשׁוּבָה — *We will prostrate ourselves and we will return.* An unintended prophecy

אֶת הָאֵשׁ וְאֶת הַמַּאֲכֶלֶת, וַיֵּלְכוּ שְׁנֵיהֶם יַחְדָּו.

《 together. 〈 the two of them 〈 and they went, 《 and the knife, 〈 the fire

וַיֹּאמֶר יִצְחָק אֶל אַבְרָהָם אָבִיו, וַיֹּאמֶר, אָבִי,

《 My father! 〈 and he said: 《 his father, 〈 Abraham 〈 to 〈 [Then] Isaac spoke

וַיֹּאמֶר, הִנֶּנִּי בְנִי; וַיֹּאמֶר, הִנֵּה הָאֵשׁ וְהָעֵצִים,

〈 and the wood, 〈 the fire 〈 Here are 〈 And he said, 《 my son. 〈 Here I am, 〈 And he said,

וְאַיֵּה הַשֶּׂה לְעֹלָה. וַיֹּאמֶר אַבְרָהָם, אֱלֹהִים

〈 God 《 Abraham said: 《 for the offering? 〈 is the lamb 〈 but where

יִרְאֶה לּוֹ הַשֶּׂה* לְעֹלָה, בְּנִי, וַיֵּלְכוּ שְׁנֵיהֶם יַחְדָּו.

《 together. 〈 the two of them 〈 And they went, 《 my son. 〈 for the offering, 〈 the lamb* 〈 for 〈 will seek out Himself

וַיָּבֹאוּ אֶל הַמָּקוֹם אֲשֶׁר אָמַר לוֹ הָאֱלֹהִים, וַיִּבֶן

〈 and build 《 God had indicated to him, 〈 which 〈 the place 〈 at 〈 They arrived

שָׁם אַבְרָהָם אֶת הַמִּזְבֵּחַ, וַיַּעֲרֹךְ אֶת הָעֵצִים,

《 the wood; 〈 and arranged 〈 the altar 〈 did Abraham 〈 there

וַיַּעֲקֹד אֶת יִצְחָק בְּנוֹ, וַיָּשֶׂם אֹתוֹ עַל הַמִּזְבֵּחַ

〈 the altar 〈 on 〈 him 〈 and he placed 〈 his son, 〈 Isaac, 〈 he bound

מִמַּעַל לָעֵצִים. וַיִּשְׁלַח אַבְרָהָם אֶת יָדוֹ, וַיִּקַּח

〈 and took 〈 his hand 〈 Abraham stretched out 《 the wood. 〈 atop

אֶת הַמַּאֲכֶלֶת לִשְׁחֹט אֶת בְּנוֹ. וַיִּקְרָא אֵלָיו

〈 to him 〈 And there called 《 his son. 〈 to slaughter 〈 the knife

מַלְאַךְ יהוה מִן הַשָּׁמַיִם, וַיֹּאמֶר, אַבְרָהָם,

〈 Abraham! 〈 and he said, 《 heaven, 〈 from 〈 of HASHEM 〈 an angel

---

came from Abraham's lips. Instead of saying "I will return" — without Isaac — he said "we," for such, indeed, was God's intention.

אֱלֹהִים יִרְאֶה לּוֹ הַשֶּׂה — *God will seek out for Himself the lamb.* The Midrash teaches that

Isaac understood from this reply that he would be the sacrificial "lamb." Nevertheless, though Isaac at the age of 37 was in the prime of life and Abraham was a century his senior, *the two of them went together,* united in their dedication.

אַבְרָהָם, וַיֹּאמֶר, הִנֵּנִי. וַיֹּאמֶר, אַל תִּשְׁלַח יָדְךָ

⟨ your ⟨ stretch out ⟨ Do not ⟪ And he ⟪ Here ⟨ And he ⟪ Abraham!
hand said, I am. said,

אֶל הַנַּעַר, וְאַל תַּעַשׂ לוֹ מְאוּמָה, כִּי עַתָּה

⟨ now ⟨ for ⟪ anything, ⟨ to him ⟨ do ⟨ nor ⟨ the lad ⟨ against

יָדַעְתִּי כִּי יְרֵא אֱלֹהִים אַתָּה, וְלֹא חָשַׂכְתָּ

⟨ withheld ⟨ since you ⟪ are you, ⟨ of God ⟨ a fearer ⟨ that ⟨ I know
have not

אֶת בִּנְךָ אֶת יְחִידְךָ מִמֶּנִּי. וַיִּשָּׂא אַבְרָהָם

⟨ Abraham raised ⟪ from Me. ⟨ your only one, ⟨ your son,

אֶת עֵינָיו וַיַּרְא, וְהִנֵּה אַיִל, אַחַר, נֶאֱחַז בַּסְּבַךְ

⟨ in the ⟨ caught ⟨ —afterwards, ⟪ a ram! ⟨ —behold ⟪ and saw ⟨ his eyes
thicket

בְּקַרְנָיו, וַיֵּלֶךְ אַבְרָהָם וַיִּקַּח אֶת הָאַיִל, וַיַּעֲלֵהוּ

⟨ and brought it ⟨ the ram ⟨ and he took ⟨ Abraham went ⟪ by its horns.

לְעֹלָה תַּחַת בְּנוֹ. וַיִּקְרָא אַבְרָהָם שֵׁם

⟨ the name ⟨ Abraham called ⟪ of his son. ⟨ instead ⟨ as an offering

הַמָּקוֹם הַהוּא יהוה יִרְאֶה,* אֲשֶׁר יֵאָמֵר הַיּוֹם,

⟪ this day: ⟨ it is said ⟨ as ⟪ Yireh,* ⟨ HASHEM ⟨ of that site

בְּהַר יהוה יֵרָאֶה. וַיִּקְרָא מַלְאַךְ יהוה אֶל

⟨ to ⟨ An angel of HASHEM called ⟪ is seen. ⟨ HASHEM ⟨ On the
mountain

אַבְרָהָם שֵׁנִית מִן הַשָּׁמָיִם. וַיֹּאמֶר, בִּי נִשְׁבַּעְתִּי

⟪ I swear ⟨ By ⟨ and he said, ⟪ heaven ⟨ from ⟨ a second ⟨ Abraham
My Self time

נְאֻם יהוה, כִּי יַעַן אֲשֶׁר עָשִׂיתָ אֶת הַדָּבָר הַזֶּה,

⟨ this thing ⟨ you have done ⟨ since ⟨ that ⟪ of ⟨ — the
HASHEM — word

ה' יִרְאֶה — *HASHEM Yireh*, literally, *HASHEM will see*. God will see the mountain where the *Akeidah* took place as the appropriate site for His Temple. Indeed, the *Akeidah* took place on the site of the future Temple (*Onkelos*). Alternatively, God will eternally "see" the *Akeidah* as a source of merit for the offspring of Abraham and Isaac (*Rabbeinu Bachya*).

וְלֹא חָשַׂכְתָּ אֶת בִּנְךָ אֶת יְחִידֶךָ. כִּי בָרֵךְ אֲבָרֶכְךָ,

‹ I shall surely bless you ‹ that ‹‹ your only one, ‹ your son, ‹ withheld ‹ and have not

וְהַרְבָּה אַרְבֶּה אֶת זַרְעֲךָ כְּכוֹכְבֵי הַשָּׁמַיִם,

‹ of the heavens ‹ like the stars ‹ your offspring ‹ and greatly shall I increase

וְכַחוֹל אֲשֶׁר עַל שְׂפַת הַיָּם, וְיִרַשׁ זַרְעֲךָ

‹ will your ‹ and inherit ‹‹ of the sea; ‹ the shore ‹ is on ‹ which ‹ and like the sand
offspring

אֵת שַׁעַר אֹיְבָיו. וְהִתְבָּרְכוּ בְזַרְעֲךָ כֹּל גּוֹיֵי

‹ the ‹ will all ‹ by your ‹ and bless ‹‹ of their ‹ the gates
nations　　offspring　themselves　enemies;

הָאָרֶץ, עֵקֶב אֲשֶׁר שָׁמַעְתָּ בְּקֹלִי. וַיָּשָׁב אַבְרָהָם

‹ Abraham returned ‹‹ to My voice. ‹ you have listened ‹ because ‹‹ of the earth,

אֶל נְעָרָיו, וַיָּקֻמוּ וַיֵּלְכוּ יַחְדָּו אֶל בְּאֵר שָׁבַע,

‹‹ Beer-sheba, ‹ to ‹ together ‹ and went ‹ and they ‹‹ his young ‹ to
rose　　men,

וַיֵּשֶׁב אַבְרָהָם בִּבְאֵר שָׁבַע.

‹‹ at Beer-sheba. ‹ and Abraham stayed

רִבּוֹנוֹ שֶׁל עוֹלָם, כְּמוֹ שֶׁכָּבַשׁ אַבְרָהָם אָבִינוּ אֶת רַחֲמָיו

‹ his mercy ‹ our ‹ did ‹ suppress ‹ Just as ‹‹ the ‹ of ‹ Master
forefather Abraham　　　　universe!

(מֵעַל בֶּן יְחִידוֹ) לַעֲשׂוֹת רְצוֹנְךָ בְּלֵבָב שָׁלֵם, כֵּן יִכְבְּשׁוּ

‹ suppress ‹ so ‹‹ wholeheartedly, ‹ Your will ‹ in order ‹ his only ‹ [his] ‹ (regarding
to do　　　one,)　son,

רַחֲמֶיךָ אֶת כַּעַסְךָ מֵעָלֵינוּ, וְיִגֹּלּוּ רַחֲמֶיךָ עַל מִדּוֹתֶיךָ

‹‹ Your (strict) ‹ may Your ‹ and ‹‹ from ‹ Your anger ‹ may Your
attributes,　mercy overwhelm　upon us,　　　mercy

(וְתִתְכַּנֵּס אִתָּנוּ לִפְנִים מִשּׁוּרַת דִּינֶךָ), וְתִתְנַהֵג עִמָּנוּ, יהוה

‹ — O ‹‹ with us ‹ and conduct ‹‹ of Your ‹ the line ‹ beyond ‹ with us ‹ (and may
Hashem,　　　Yourself　law),　　　You step

אֱלֹהֵינוּ, בְּמִדַּת הַחֶסֶד וּבְמִדַּת הָרַחֲמִים. וּבְטוּבְךָ הַגָּדוֹל,

‹‹ that is ‹ In Your ‹‹ of mercy. ‹ and with the ‹ of ‹ with the ‹‹ our God —
great,　goodness　　　attribute　kindness　attribute

יָשׁוּב חֲרוֹן אַפְּךָ מֵעַמְּךָ וּמֵעִירֶךָ וּמֵאַרְצְךָ וּמִנַּחֲלָתֶךָ. וְקַיֶּם
‹ Fulfill ‹‹ and from ‹ from ‹ from ‹ from Your ‹ wrath ‹ may Your ‹ turn
Your heritage. Your Land, Your City, people, burning away

לָנוּ, יהוה אֱלֹהֵינוּ, אֶת הַדָּבָר שֶׁהִבְטַחְתָּנוּ בְּתוֹרָתֶךָ, עַל יְדֵי
‹ the ‹ by ‹‹ in Your ‹ that You ‹ the ‹ our God, ‹ HASHEM, ‹ for
hand Torah, pledged to us declaration us,

מֹשֶׁה עַבְדֶּךָ, כָּאָמוּר: וְזָכַרְתִּי אֶת בְּרִיתִי יַעֲקוֹב, וְאַף אֶת בְּרִיתִי
‹ My covenant ‹ also ‹‹ with ‹ My covenant ‹ I shall ‹‹ as it ‹ Your ‹ of
Jacob: remember is said: servant, Moses,

יִצְחָק, וְאַף אֶת בְּרִיתִי אַבְרָהָם אֶזְכֹּר, וְהָאָרֶץ אֶזְכֹּר.¹ וְנֶאֱמַר:
‹‹ And it ‹ shall I ‹ and the ‹ shall I ‹ with ‹ My covenant ‹ and ‹‹ with
is said: remember. Land remember; Abraham also Isaac,

וְאַף גַּם זֹאת, בִּהְיוֹתָם בְּאֶרֶץ אֹיְבֵיהֶם, לֹא מְאַסְתִּים וְלֹא
‹ nor ‹ despise ‹ I will ‹‹ of their ‹ in the ‹ when they ‹ this, ‹ all ‹ And
them not enemies, land will be despite

גְעַלְתִּים לְכַלֹּתָם, לְהָפֵר בְּרִיתִי אִתָּם, כִּי אֲנִי יהוה אֱלֹהֵיהֶם.²
‹‹ their God. ‹ HASHEM, ‹ I am ‹ for ‹‹ with ‹ My ‹ to annul ‹‹ to destroy ‹ abhor them
them, covenant them,

וְנֶאֱמַר: וְזָכַרְתִּי לָהֶם בְּרִית רִאשׁוֹנִים, אֲשֶׁר הוֹצֵאתִי אֹתָם
‹ I took them out ‹ that ‹‹ of the ‹ the ‹ for ‹ And I will ‹‹ And it
ancient ones, covenant them remember is said:

מֵאֶרֶץ מִצְרַיִם לְעֵינֵי הַגּוֹיִם, לִהְיוֹת לָהֶם לֵאלֹהִים, אֲנִי יהוה.³
‹‹ am ‹ I ‹‹ a God; ‹ to ‹ to be ‹‹ of the ‹ in the ‹ of Egypt ‹ from
HASHEM. them nations, very sight the land

וְנֶאֱמַר: וְשָׁב יהוה אֱלֹהֶיךָ אֶת שְׁבוּתְךָ וְרִחֲמֶךָ, וְשָׁב
‹ and He ‹‹ and He will ‹ your captivity, ‹ your ‹ will ‹ Then ‹‹ And it
will once have mercy God, HASHEM, bring back is said:
again upon you,

וְקִבֶּצְךָ מִכָּל הָעַמִּים אֲשֶׁר הֱפִיצְךָ יהוה אֱלֹהֶיךָ שָׁמָּה. אִם
‹ If ‹‹ thereto. ‹ HASHEM, your God, scattered you ‹ that ‹ the peoples ‹ from ‹ gather
all you in

יִהְיֶה נִדַּחֲךָ בִּקְצֵה הַשָּׁמָיִם, מִשָּׁם יְקַבֶּצְךָ יהוה אֱלֹהֶיךָ וּמִשָּׁם
‹ and from ‹‹ HASHEM your God, ‹ from ‹‹ of heaven, ‹ at the ‹ your dispersed
there will gather you in, there ends will be

יִקָּחֶךָ.⁴ וְנֶאֱמַר: וֶהֱבִיאֲךָ יהוה אֱלֹהֶיךָ אֶל הָאָרֶץ אֲשֶׁר
‹ that ‹ the Land ‹ to ‹ And HASHEM, your God, will bring you ‹‹ And it ‹‹ He will
is said: take you.

(1) Leviticus 26:42. (2) 26:44. (3) 26:45. (4) Deuteronomy 30:3-4.

יָרְשׁוּ אֲבוֹתֶיךָ, וִירִשְׁתָּהּ, וְהֵיטִבְךָ וְהִרְבְּךָ מֵאֲבוֹתֶיךָ.¹ וְנֶאֱמַר

⟨ And it ⟩ ⟨⟨ than your ⟩ ⟨ and make ⟩ ⟨ He will ⟩ ⟨⟨ and you shall ⟩ ⟨ your forefathers
was said　　forefathers.　you more　do good　possess it;　took possession of
　　　　　　　　　　　　numerous　to you

עַל יְדֵי נְבִיאֶךָ: יהוה חָנֵּנוּ, לְךָ קִוִּינוּ, הֱיֵה זְרֹעָם לַבְּקָרִים, אַף

⟨and ⟨⟨ every ⟩ ⟨ their ⟩ ⟨ Be ⟨⟨ we have ⟩ ⟨ for ⟨⟨ grant us ⟩ ⟨ HASHEM, ⟨⟨ of Your ⟩ ⟨ the ⟨ by
even　morning,　[strong] arm　hoped!　You　favor;　　　prophet:　hand

יְשׁוּעָתֵנוּ בְּעֵת צָרָה.² וְנֶאֱמַר: וְעֵת צָרָה הִיא לְיַעֲקֹב, וּמִמֶּנָּה

⟨ but ⟨⟨ for Jacob, ⟨ it will ⟨ of ⟨ A ⟨⟨ And it ⟨⟨ of ⟩ ⟨ in a ⟨ our salvation
from it　　　　be　distress　time　is said:　distress.　time

יִוָּשֵׁעַ.³ וְנֶאֱמַר: בְּכָל צָרָתָם לוֹ צָר, וּמַלְאַךְ פָּנָיו הוֹשִׁיעָם,

⟨⟨ rescued ⟨ from ⟨ and so ⟨⟨ it was ⟨ to ⟨ their ⟨ In all ⟨ And it ⟨⟨ he will
them.　before Him an angel　troubling, Him　troubles,　　is said:　be saved.

בְּאַהֲבָתוֹ וּבְחֶמְלָתוֹ הוּא גְאָלָם, וַיְנַטְּלֵם וַיְנַשְּׂאֵם כָּל יְמֵי

⟨ the ⟨ all ⟨ and bore ⟨ and lifted ⟨⟨ redeemed ⟨ He ⟨ and with His ⟨ With His love
days　　them　them　them;　　compassion

עוֹלָם.⁴ וְנֶאֱמַר: מִי אֵל כָּמוֹךָ, נֹשֵׂא עָוֹן וְעוֹבֵר עַל פֶּשַׁע

⟨ transgression ⟨ and ⟨ iniquity ⟨ Who ⟨⟨ like You, ⟨ is a ⟨ Who, ⟨⟨ And it ⟨⟨ of the
overlooks　forgives　　God　　is said:　world.

לִשְׁאֵרִית נַחֲלָתוֹ, לֹא הֶחֱזִיק לָעַד אַפּוֹ כִּי חָפֵץ חֶסֶד הוּא.

⟨⟨ He desires kindness. ⟨ for ⟨ His ⟨ forever ⟨ retained ⟨ He has ⟨⟨ of His ⟨ for the
wrath　not　heritage?　remnant

יָשׁוּב יְרַחֲמֵנוּ, יִכְבֹּשׁ עֲוֹנֹתֵינוּ, וְתַשְׁלִיךְ בִּמְצֻלוֹת יָם כָּל

⟨ all ⟨ of the ⟨ into the ⟨ and cast ⟨ our iniquities, ⟨ He will ⟨⟨ be merciful ⟨ He will
sea　depths　　suppress　to us;　again

חַטֹּאתָם. תִּתֵּן אֱמֶת לְיַעֲקֹב, חֶסֶד לְאַבְרָהָם, אֲשֶׁר נִשְׁבַּעְתָּ

⟨ You swore ⟨ as ⟨⟨ to Abraham, ⟨ kindness ⟨⟨ to Jacob, ⟨ truth ⟨ Grant ⟨⟨ their sins.

לַאֲבוֹתֵינוּ מִימֵי קֶדֶם.⁵ וְנֶאֱמַר: וַהֲבִיאוֹתִים אֶל הַר קָדְשִׁי,

⟨⟨ My holy ⟨ to ⟨ And I will ⟨⟨ And it ⟨⟨ of old. ⟨ from ⟨ to our
mountain,　bring them　is said:　days　forefathers

וְשִׂמַּחְתִּים בְּבֵית תְּפִלָּתִי, עוֹלֹתֵיהֶם וְזִבְחֵיהֶם לְרָצוֹן עַל

⟨ on ⟨ will find ⟨ and their feast- ⟨ their elevation- ⟨⟨ of prayer; ⟨ in My ⟨ and I will
favor　offerings　offerings　　house　gladden them

מִזְבְּחִי, כִּי בֵיתִי בֵּית תְּפִלָּה יִקָּרֵא לְכָל הָעַמִּים.⁶

⟨⟨ nations. ⟨ for all ⟨ will be ⟨ of Prayer' ⟨ 'a ⟨ My ⟨ for ⟨⟨ My Altar,
called　House　House

---

(1) Deuteronomy 30:5. (2) Isaiah 33:2. (3) Jeremiah 30:7.
(4) Isaiah 63:9. (5) Micah 7:18-20. (6) Isaiah 56:7.

לְעוֹלָם* יְהֵא אָדָם יְרֵא שָׁמַיִם בְּסֵתֶר וּבַגָּלוּי,*

≪ and in public,* ⟨ [both] in private ⟨ of Heaven, ⟨ be ⟨ a ⟨ should ⟨ Always*
fearing person

וּמוֹדֶה עַל הָאֱמֶת,* וְדוֹבֵר אֱמֶת בִּלְבָבוֹ,*

≪ within his heart,* ⟨ the truth ⟨ speaking ≪ the truth,* ⟨ acknowledging

וְיַשְׁכֵּם וְיֹאמַר:

≪ and proclaim: ⟨ and should arise early

רִבּוֹן כָּל הָעוֹלָמִים* וַאֲדוֹנֵי הָאֲדוֹנִים, לֹא עַל

⟨ because of ⟨ It is not ≪ of [all] lords! ⟨ and Lord ⟨ worlds* ⟨ of all ⟨ Master

צִדְקוֹתֵינוּ אֲנַחְנוּ מַפִּילִים תַּחֲנוּנֵינוּ לְפָנֶיךָ, כִּי

⟨ but ≪ before You, ⟨ our supplications ⟨ cast ⟨ that we ⟨ our righteousness

עַל רַחֲמֶיךָ הָרַבִּים. מָה אָנוּ, מֶה חַיֵּינוּ, מֶה

⟨ What ≪ is our life? ⟨ What ≪ are we? ⟨ What ≪ that is abundant. ⟨ Your mercy ⟨ because of

---

לְעוֹלָם — *Always.* The section beginning here and extending until קָרְבָּנוֹת / *Offerings* is in its totality a profound and succinct summation of basic Jewish faith and loyalty to God. What is more, it is a resounding declaration of joyous pride in our Jewishness, a pride that overcomes all persecutions and that moves us to pray for the time when all will recognize the truth of the Torah's message, and we will proudly proclaim the message that the anti-Semites attempt to silence.

Furthermore, the declarations contained in this section represent the manner in which a Jew should conduct himself *always,* not merely on ceremonial occasions.

יְרֵא שָׁמַיִם בְּסֵתֶר וּבַגָּלוּי — *Fearing of Heaven, [both] in private and in public.* Some people behave piously when in the view of others, but not when their behavior goes unseen. Others are God fearing in private but are embarrassed to do so in public for fear of being labeled as nonconformists. But the Jew must strive to be consistently God fearing, whatever his surroundings.

וּמוֹדֶה עַל הָאֱמֶת — *Acknowledging the truth.* One who seeks the truth is not ashamed to concede his errors. But if he cares more about his reputation than the truth, he will stubbornly persist in falsehood and sin.

וְדוֹבֵר אֱמֶת בִּלְבָבוֹ — *Speaking the truth within his heart.* The Sages cite Rav Safra as the prototype of inner honesty (*Chullin* 94b and *Rashi* to *Makkos* 24a). Once, while he was praying and therefore not permitted to speak, Rav Safra was offered a satisfactory price for something he wished to sell. The buyer did not realize why Rav Safra did not respond, so he kept increasing his bid. When Rav Safra finished his prayers, he insisted on accepting no more than the first offer, because in his heart he had intended to sell for that price.

רִבּוֹן כָּל הָעוֹלָמִים — *Master of all worlds!* We now begin leading up to *Shema,* the affirmation of the Oneness of God and acknowledgment of His absolute mastery. We declare that, given the inherent powerlessness and inadequacy of man, Israel is enormously privileged in having been selected as God's Chosen People. Therefore, we dedicate ourselves to proclaim His Oneness through the *Shema.* After the blessing that follows the *Shema* we pray for Israel's salvation so

חַסְדֵּנוּ, מַה צִּדְקוֹתֵינוּ, מַה יְּשׁוּעָתֵנוּ, מַה כֹּחֵנוּ,

‹‹ is our ‹ What ‹‹ is our ‹ What ‹‹ is our ‹ What ‹‹ is our
strength? salvation? righteousness? kindness?

מַה גְּבוּרָתֵנוּ. מַה נֹּאמַר לְפָנֶיךָ, יהוה אֱלֹהֵינוּ

‹ our God ‹ HASHEM, ‹‹ before You, ‹ can we say ‹ What ‹‹ is our might? ‹ What

וֵאלֹהֵי אֲבוֹתֵינוּ, הֲלֹא כָּל הַגִּבּוֹרִים כְּאַיִן

‹ like nothing ‹ the mighty ‹ all ‹ Are not ‹‹ of our forefathers? ‹ and the God

לְפָנֶיךָ, וְאַנְשֵׁי הַשֵּׁם כְּלֹא הָיוּ, וַחֲכָמִים כִּבְלִי

‹ as if ‹ the wise ‹‹ existed, ‹ as if they ‹ of renown ‹ and people ‹‹ before You,
devoid had never

מַדָּע, וּנְבוֹנִים כִּבְלִי הַשְׂכֵּל. כִּי רוֹב מַעֲשֵׂיהֶם

‹ of their deeds ‹ the ‹ For ‹‹ of ‹ as if ‹ and the ‹‹ of
multitude intelligence? devoid perceptive wisdom

תֹּהוּ, וִימֵי חַיֵּיהֶם הֶבֶל לְפָנֶיךָ, וּמוֹתַר הָאָדָם מִן

‹ over ‹ of man ‹ The ‹‹ before ‹ are ‹ of their ‹ and the ‹ is
preeminence You. worthless lives days useless

הַבְּהֵמָה אָיִן, כִּי הַכֹּל הָבֶל – לְבַד הַנְּשָׁמָה [1]

‹ the soul ‹ – except ‹‹ is ‹ all ‹ for ‹‹ is ‹ beast
for worthless nonexistent,

הַטְּהוֹרָה, שֶׁהִיא עֲתִידָה לִתֵּן דִּין וְחֶשְׁבּוֹן לִפְנֵי

‹ before ‹ and reckoning ‹ justification ‹ to give ‹ destined ‹ that is ‹‹ that is pure,

כִּסֵּא כְבוֹדֶךָ. וְכָל הַגּוֹיִם כְּאַיִן נֶגְדֶּךָ, שֶׁנֶּאֱמַר:

‹‹ as it is said: ‹‹ before ‹ are as if ‹ the ‹ And ‹‹ of Your Glory. ‹ the
You, nonexistent nations all throne

הֵן גּוֹיִם כְּמַר מִדְּלִי, וּכְשַׁחַק מֹאזְנַיִם נֶחְשָׁבוּ,

‹‹ are they ‹ a scale ‹ and like the ‹‹ from a ‹ are like a ‹ the ‹‹ *It is so*
reckoned; *powder rubbed off* bucket, bitter drop nations that*

הֵן אִיִּים כַּדַּק יִטּוֹל. [2]

‹‹ He will ‹ like ‹ the ‹ *it is so*
cast away. dust islands that*

---

(1) *Ecclesiastes* 3:19. (2) *Isaiah* 40:15.

that we may be able to sanctify His Name without hindrance. This prayer was composed by the Talmudic sage Rabbi Yochanan (*Yoma* 87b) for use in the Yom Kippur *viduy* (confession) service.

אֲבָל אֲנַחְנוּ* עַמֶּךָ, בְּנֵי בְרִיתֶךָ, בְּנֵי אַבְרָהָם
‹ of Abraham, ‹ children ‹‹ of Your ‹ members ‹‹ Your ‹ we are* ‹ But
                                  covenant,   people,

אֹהַבְךָ שֶׁנִּשְׁבַּעְתָּ לּוֹ בְּהַר הַמּוֹרִיָּה, זֶרַע יִצְחָק
‹ of Isaac, ‹ the ‹‹ Moriah; ‹ at ‹ to ‹ that You swore ‹‹ Your
            offspring   Mount him   beloved,

יְחִידוֹ שֶׁנֶּעֱקַד עַל גַּבֵּי הַמִּזְבֵּחַ, עֲדַת יַעֲקֹב בִּנְךָ
‹ Your ‹ of Jacob, ‹ the ‹‹ of the altar; ‹ top ‹ on ‹ who was ‹ his
  son,   community   bound   only son,

בְּכוֹרֶךָ, שֶׁמֵּאַהֲבָתְךָ שֶׁאָהַבְתָּ אוֹתוֹ וּמִשִּׂמְחָתְךָ
‹ and the joy ‹ him ‹ with which ‹ who – because of ‹‹ Your
                     You loved   Your love   firstborn,

שֶׁשָּׂמַחְתָּ בּוֹ, קָרָאתָ אֶת שְׁמוֹ יִשְׂרָאֵל וִישֻׁרוּן.*
‹‹ and ‹ Israel ‹ his name ‹ You called ‹‹ in ‹ with which
Jeshurun.*   him – You delighted

לְפִיכָךְ אֲנַחְנוּ חַיָּבִים לְהוֹדוֹת לָךְ, וּלְשַׁבֵּחֲךָ,
‹ to praise You, ‹ You, ‹ to thank ‹ are obliged ‹ we ‹ Therefore,

וּלְפָאֶרְךָ, וּלְבָרֶךְ וּלְקַדֵּשׁ וְלִתֵּן שֶׁבַח וְהוֹדָיָה
‹ and thanks ‹ praise ‹ and to offer ‹ to sanctify, ‹ to bless, ‹‹ to glorify You,

לִשְׁמֶךָ. אַשְׁרֵינוּ,* מַה טּוֹב חֶלְקֵנוּ, וּמַה נָּעִים
‹ pleasant ‹ how ‹ is our portion, ‹ good ‹ how ‹‹ We are fortunate,* ‹‹ to Your Name.

גּוֹרָלֵנוּ, וּמַה יָּפָה יְרֻשָּׁתֵנוּ. ❖ אַשְׁרֵינוּ, כְּשֶׁאָנוּ
‹ for we ‹‹ We are fortunate, ‹‹ our heritage! ‹ beautiful ‹ and how ‹ our lot,

---

§אֲבָל אֲנַחְנוּ — *But we are.* In contrast to the above-described futility of man, we Jews are privileged to carry on the mission of our forefathers. Abraham is described as God's beloved, meaning that he sought always to make God beloved in the eyes of man. God swore to him at Mount Moriah where the *Akeidah* took place and where Isaac demonstrated his own devotion to God. Jacob is called God's firstborn because the Jewish nation, which bears Jacob's name, was given that title by God Himself (*Exodus* 4:22) in verification of the fact that God considered

Jacob, not Esau, to be the legitimate firstborn.

יִשְׂרָאֵל וִישֻׁרוּן — *Israel and Jeshurun.* These two names are descriptive of Jacob's stature. The name יִשְׂרָאֵל (from שְׂרָרָה, *mastery*) means that Jacob *triumphed* over an angel (see *Genesis* 35:10), and יְשֻׁרוּן (from יָשָׁר, *upright, fair*) refers to *dedication to justice* in accordance with God's will.

אַשְׁרֵינוּ — *We are fortunate.* Although, as noted in *Tikkun Tefillah,* this section of the service was compiled during a period of intense persecution, we do not feel downtrodden. To the

מַשְׁכִּימִים וּמַעֲרִיבִים, בְּבָתֵּי כְנֵסִיּוֹת וּבְבָתֵּי

‹ and in the halls ‹ in the synagogues ‹‹ and stay late, ‹ come early

מִדְרָשׁוֹת, וּמְיַחֲדִים שִׁמְךָ בְּכָל יוֹם תָּמִיד,

‹‹ continually, ‹ day ‹ each ‹ Your Name ‹ and unify ‹‹ of study,

וְאוֹמְרִים פַּעֲמַיִם בְּאַהֲבָה:

‹‹ with love: ‹ twice [a day] ‹ and proclaim

שְׁמַע l יִשְׂרָאֵל,* יהוה l אֱלֹהֵינוּ, יהוה l אֶחָד:[1]

‹‹ the One ‹ HASHEM ‹‹ is our God, ‹ HASHEM ‹‹ O Israel:* ‹ Hear,
[and Only].   is

IN AN UNDERTONE:

בָּרוּךְ שֵׁם כְּבוֹד מַלְכוּתוֹ לְעוֹלָם וָעֶד.[2]

‹‹ and ever. ‹ for ever ‹ kingdom ‹ of His glorious ‹ is the Name ‹ Blessed

SOME CONGREGATIONS COMPLETE THE FIRST CHAPTER OF THE *SHEMA* (THE FOLLOWING PARA-
GRAPH — *DEUTERONOMY* 6:5-9) HERE, ALTHOUGH MOST OMIT IT. HOWEVER IF YOU FEAR THAT
YOU WILL NOT RECITE THE FULL *SHEMA* LATER IN *SHACHARIS* BEFORE THE PRESCRIBED TIME HAS
ELAPSED (SEE *LAWS* §17), COMPLETE ALL THREE PARAGRAPHS OF *SHEMA* (P. 132) HERE.

וְאָהַבְתָּ אֵת l יהוה l אֱלֹהֶיךָ, בְּכָל-לְבָבְךָ,

‹ your heart, ‹ with all ‹ your God, ‹ HASHEM, ‹ You shall love

וּבְכָל-נַפְשְׁךָ, וּבְכָל-מְאֹדֶךָ: וְהָיוּ הַדְּבָרִים הָאֵלֶּה,

‹ — these matters ‹‹ They ‹‹ your ‹ and with ‹ your soul, ‹ with all
should be   resources.   all

אֲשֶׁר l אָנֹכִי מְצַוְּךָ הַיּוֹם, עַל-לְבָבֶךָ: וְשִׁנַּנְתָּם

‹ Teach them ‹‹ your heart. ‹ upon ‹‹ today — ‹ command ‹ I ‹ that
thoroughly   you

---

(1) *Deuteronomy* 6:4. (2) See *Pesachim* 56a.

contrary, we are fortunate to be God's Chosen People and proud to proclaim His Oneness.

שְׁמַע יִשְׂרָאֵל *— Hear, O Israel.* During the middle of the 5th century the Persian king, Yezdegerd II, forbade the Jews to observe the Sabbath and to recite the *Shema*. His purpose was to eradicate belief in Hashem as the Creator (which is symbolized by the Sabbath) and in His Oneness, as it is proclaimed in the *Shema*. To insure that the *Shema* would not be read in defiance of his decree, the king stationed guards in the synagogue for the first quarter of the day, when the *Shema* must be read. To counteract his design, the Sages instituted two recitations of the first verse of *Shema*: the one here, which was to be recited at home, and another one as part of the Sabbath *Kedushah* of *Mussaf*. Although these services contain only the first verse of the *Shema*, this is sufficient to fulfill the *Shema* obligation in cases of extreme emergency (*Berachos* 13b). Even when, in response to the prayers of the Sages, Yezdegerd was killed

לְבָנֶיךָ, וְדִבַּרְתָּ בָּם בְּשִׁבְתְּךָ בְּבֵיתֶךָ, וּבְלֶכְתְּךָ

> while you walk ‹ in your home, ‹ while you sit ‹ of them ‹ and speak ‹ to your children

בַדֶּרֶךְ, וּבְשָׁכְבְּךָ וּבְקוּמֶךָ: וּקְשַׁרְתָּם לְאוֹת

> as a sign ‹ Bind them ‹‹ and when you arise. ‹ when you lie down, ‹ on the way,

עַל־יָדֶךָ, וְהָיוּ לְטֹטָפֹת בֵּין עֵינֶיךָ: וּכְתַבְתָּם

> And write them ‹‹ your eyes. ‹ between ‹ tefillin ‹ and they shall be ‹ your arm ‹ upon

עַל־מְזֻזוֹת בֵּיתֶךָ וּבִשְׁעָרֶיךָ:

> ‹‹ and upon your gates. ‹ of your house ‹ the doorposts ‹ on

אַתָּה הוּא* עַד שֶׁלֹּא נִבְרָא הָעוֹלָם, אַתָּה

> You are ‹‹ the world was created. ‹ before ‹ the One Who [existed]* ‹ You are

הוּא מִשֶּׁנִּבְרָא הָעוֹלָם, אַתָּה הוּא בָּעוֹלָם הַזֶּה,

> in This World, ‹ the One Who [exists] ‹ You are ‹‹ after the world was created. ‹ the One Who [exists]

וְאַתָּה הוּא לְעוֹלָם הַבָּא. ❖ קַדֵּשׁ אֶת שִׁמְךָ עַל

> through ‹ Your Name ‹ Sanctify ‹‹ to Come. ‹ in the World ‹ the One Who [will exist] are ‹ and You

מַקְדִּישֵׁי שְׁמֶךָ,* וְקַדֵּשׁ אֶת שִׁמְךָ בְּעוֹלָמֶךָ.

> ‹‹ in Your universe. ‹ Your Name ‹ and sanctify ‹‹ Your Name,* ‹ those who sanctify

וּבִישׁוּעָתְךָ תָּרִים וְתַגְבִּיהַ קַרְנֵנוּ לְמַעְלָה,

> ‹‹ up high, ‹ our pride ‹ and raise ‹ may You exalt ‹ Through Your salvation

---

and his decree was rescinded, the two *Shema* recitations remained part of the regular ritual, and the one that had been recited at home was included in this part of the synagogue service.

§•❧ **אַתָּה הוּא** — *You are the One Who [existed].* This phrase and the ones that follow express the idea that God is eternal and unchanging, unaffected by time or place.

קַדֵּשׁ אֶת שְׁמְךָ עַל מַקְדִּישֵׁי שְׁמֶךָ — *Sanctify Your Name through those who sanctify Your Name.* When originally composed, this referred to the Jewish martyrs who had sanctified the Name through unyielding loyalty. In later times, it came to refer also to those who cling to the commandments despite hardship and temptation.

וְהוֹשִׁיעֵנוּ בְּקָרוֹב לְמַעַן שְׁמֶךָ. בָּרוּךְ הַמְקַדֵּשׁ
‹ is He Who ‹ Blessed ≪ of Your ‹ for the ‹ soon ‹ and save us
sanctifies   Name.   sake

שְׁמוֹ בָּרַבִּים.*
≪ among the ‹ His
multitudes.* Name

אַתָּה הוּא יהוה אֱלֹהֵינוּ, בַּשָּׁמַיִם וּבָאָרֶץ
‹ and on earth ‹ in heaven ‹ our God, ‹ HASHEM, ‹ the One Who is ‹ You are

וּבִשְׁמֵי הַשָּׁמַיִם הָעֶלְיוֹנִים. אֱמֶת, אַתָּה הוּא
‹ the One ‹ [that] You ‹ It is true, ≪ on high. ‹ and in the loftiest heavens
Who is   are

רִאשׁוֹן* וְאַתָּה הוּא אַחֲרוֹן,* וּמִבַּלְעָדֶיךָ אֵין
‹ there ‹ and other than You ≪ the Last,* ‹ the One ‹ and You ‹ the First*
is no   Who is   are

אֱלֹהִים. קַבֵּץ נְפוּצוֹת קֹוֶיךָ מֵאַרְבַּע כַּנְפוֹת
‹ corners ‹ from the four ‹ who yearn ‹ the dispersed ‹ Gather ≪ God.
for You,   ones   in

הָאָרֶץ. יַכִּירוּ וְיֵדְעוּ כָּל בָּאֵי עוֹלָם כִּי אַתָּה הוּא
‹ the One ‹ You ‹ that ≪ [into] the ‹ who ‹ – all ≪ and ‹ May they ≪ of the
Who is   are   world – come   know   recognize   earth.

הָאֱלֹהִים לְבַדֶּךָ, עֶלְיוֹן לְכֹל מַמְלְכוֹת הָאָרֶץ.
≪ of the earth. ‹ the kingdoms ‹ over all ‹ supreme ≪ alone, ‹ God

אַתָּה עָשִׂיתָ אֶת הַשָּׁמַיִם וְאֶת הָאָרֶץ, אֶת הַיָּם,
‹ the sea, ‹ and the earth, ‹ the heavens, ‹ made ‹ You

וְאֶת כָּל אֲשֶׁר בָּם. וּמִי בְּכָל מַעֲשֵׂה יָדֶיךָ
≪ of Your ‹ the work ‹ among all ‹ Who is ≪ in them. ‹ that is ‹ and all
hands   there

---

(1) *Jeremiah* 14:22. (2) Cf. *Isaiah* 44:6. (3) Cf. 11:12. (4) *II Kings* 19:15. (5) Cf. *Nehemiah* 9:6.

הַמְקַדֵּשׁ שְׁמוֹ בָּרַבִּים — *He Who sanctifies His Name among the multitudes.* May the time come when no Jew need ever fear to express his Jewishness openly.

רִאשׁוֹן ... אַחֲרוֹן — *The First ... the Last.* This means that God preexisted and will survive everything — not that He had a beginning or will have an end, for God is infinite and timeless.

בָּעֶלְיוֹנִים אוֹ בַתַּחְתּוֹנִים שֶׁיֹּאמַר לְךָ, מַה תַּעֲשֶׂה
‹ are You   ‹ What   ‹ to   ‹ who can say   ‹‹ those below —   ‹ or   ‹ — those above
  doing   You,

וּמַה תִּפְעָל. אָבִינוּ שֶׁבַּשָּׁמַיִם, חַי וְקַיָּם, עֲשֵׂה
‹ perform ‹‹   and   ‹ living ‹‹   Who is in   ‹   Our ‹‹   are You   ‹ and
          enduring,   Heaven,   Father   accomplishing?   what

עִמָּנוּ צְדָקָה וָחֶסֶד בַּעֲבוּר שִׁמְךָ הַגָּדוֹל הַגִּבּוֹר
‹ mighty, ‹   that is   ‹ of Your ‹ for the sake ‹   and   ‹ charity   ‹ for us
          great,   Name   kindness

וְהַנּוֹרָא שֶׁנִּקְרָא עָלֵינוּ,[1] וְקַיֶּם לָנוּ יהוה אֱלֹהֵינוּ
‹‹ our God,   ‹ HASHEM, ‹‹ for   ‹ Fulfill   ‹‹ upon us.   ‹ that has been ‹   and
                          us,   proclaimed   awesome,

אֶת הַדָּבָר שֶׁהִבְטַחְתָּנוּ עַל יְדֵי צְפַנְיָה חוֹזָךְ,
‹‹ Your   ‹ of Zephaniah ‹   the   ‹   by   ‹ that You pledged to us   ‹   the declaration
  seer,   hand

כָּאָמוּר: בָּעֵת הַהִיא אָבִיא אֶתְכֶם, וּבָעֵת קַבְּצִי
‹ I will   ‹   and at   ‹ you [in]   ‹ I will bring   ‹   At that time   ‹‹ as it is said:
  gather   [that] time

אֶתְכֶם, כִּי אֶתֵּן אֶתְכֶם לְשֵׁם וְלִתְהִלָּה בְּכֹל
‹ among ‹   and praise   ‹   for   ‹   you   ‹ I will   ‹ for ‹‹ you [in],
  all   renown   designate

עַמֵּי הָאָרֶץ, בְּשׁוּבִי אֶת שְׁבוּתֵיכֶם לְעֵינֵיכֶם,
‹‹ before your   ‹   your captivity,   ‹   when I ‹‹ of the earth,   ‹   the
  own eyes,   bring back   peoples

אָמַר יהוה.[2]
‹‹ HASHEM.   ‹ said

---

(1) Cf. *Jeremiah* 14:9. (2) *Zephaniah* 3:20.

⊰ קָרְבָּנוֹת / OFFERINGS ⊱

From the beginning of its existence as a nation, Israel *saw* — whether it understood why or how — that the sacrificial service effected a closeness to God and the manifestation of His Presence. The offerings represented the Jew's submission to God of his self and his resources.

Abraham asked God how Israel would achieve forgiveness when the Temple would lie in ruins and they could no longer bring offerings.

God replied, "When Israel recites the Scriptural order of the offerings, I will consider it as if they had brought the offerings and I will forgive their sins" (*Megillah* 31a; *Taanis* 27b).

﴾ קרבנות / OFFERINGS ﴿

הכיור / THE LAVER

וַיְדַבֵּר יהוה אֶל מֹשֶׁה לֵאמֹר. וְעָשִׂיתָ כִּיּוֹר

⟨ a laver ⟨ You shall make ⟪ saying: ⟨ Moses, ⟨ to ⟨ HASHEM spoke

נְחֹשֶׁת, וְכַנּוֹ נְחֹשֶׁת, לְרָחְצָה, וְנָתַתָּ אֹתוֹ בֵּין

⟨ between ⟨ it ⟨ and you ⟪ for washing; ⟨ of copper, ⟨ and its ⟨ of copper,
shall place   base

אֹהֶל מוֹעֵד וּבֵין הַמִּזְבֵּחַ, וְנָתַתָּ שָׁמָּה מָיִם. וְרָחֲצוּ

⟪ They shall ⟪ water. ⟨ there ⟨ and you ⟪ and the Altar, ⟨ of ⟨ the Tent
wash   shall put   Appointment

אַהֲרֹן וּבָנָיו מִמֶּנּוּ, אֶת יְדֵיהֶם וְאֶת רַגְלֵיהֶם.

⟪   and their feet. ⟨   their hands   ⟨ from ⟪ and his ⟨ — Aaron
                                                              [the laver]   sons —

בְּבֹאָם אֶל אֹהֶל מוֹעֵד יִרְחֲצוּ מַיִם וְלֹא יָמֻתוּ,*

⟪ perish,* ⟨ so that ⟨ with ⟨ they shall ⟨ of ⟨ the Tent ⟨ into ⟨ When
            they not   water   wash   Appointment   they enter

אוֹ בְגִשְׁתָּם אֶל הַמִּזְבֵּחַ לְשָׁרֵת לְהַקְטִיר אִשֶּׁה

⟨ a fire- ⟨ to burn ⟪ to serve, ⟨ the Altar ⟨ to ⟨ when they ⟨ or
offering   approach

Rav Yitzchak said: The Torah writes זֹאת תּוֹרַת הַחַטָּאת, this is the Torah [teaching] of the sin-offering (Leviticus 6:18), to imply that whoever involves himself in the study of the sin-offering is regarded as if he had actually brought a sin-offering (Menachos 110a).

In the inspiring words of R' Samson R. Hirsch (Horeb §624): "The Temple has fallen, the Altar has disappeared, the harps of the singers are heard no more, but their spirit has become the heritage of Israel; it still infuses the word which alone survives as an expression of the inward Divine service."

The section dealing with the קָרְבָּנוֹת, offerings, logically follows the previous prayer, אַתָּה הוּא, which expresses longing for Israel's redemption. Since the offerings require the existence of the Holy Temple as the spiritual center of the nation, we pray that God gather us in from our dispersion. Then, our message will become a truly universal one, for God will have set us up "for renown and praise among all the peoples of the earth."

The offerings whose laws are about to be recited are all communal ones; the Sages chose them because they illustrate our wish that Israel become united as a single nation in God's service.

⋙ הַכִּיּוֹר / The Laver

Before the Kohanim could begin the Temple service, they had to take sanctified water and pour it over their hands and feet. This water was drawn from the כִּיּוֹר, laver, a large copper basin in the Temple Courtyard. In preparation for our "verbal sacrificial service" therefore, we "wash" ourselves with water from the laver, as it were.

וְלֹא יָמֻתוּ — So that they not perish. The offense of performing the service without washing did not incur a court-imposed death penalty, but the violator made himself liable to a punishment from Heaven for his display of contempt.

לַיהוה. וְרָחֲצוּ יְדֵיהֶם וְרַגְלֵיהֶם וְלֹא יָמֻתוּ,

‹‹ perish; ‹ so that ‹ and their feet ‹ their hands ‹ They shall ‹‹ to Hashem.
they not　　　　　　　　　　　　　　　　　　wash

וְהָיְתָה לָהֶם חָק עוֹלָם, לוֹ וּלְזַרְעוֹ לְדֹרֹתָם.¹

‹‹ throughout their ‹ and for his ‹ for ‹‹ that is ‹ a ‹ for them ‹ and this
generations.　offspring　　him　eternal　decree　　　　　shall be

THE TAKING OF ASHES / תרומת הדשן

וַיְדַבֵּר יהוה אֶל מֹשֶׁה לֵּאמֹר. צַו אֶת אַהֲרֹן

‹　　Aaron　‹ Command ‹‹ saying: ‹ Moses ‹ to ‹　Hashem spoke

וְאֶת בָּנָיו לֵאמֹר, זֹאת תּוֹרַת הָעֹלָה, הִוא

‹— it is ‹‹ of the elevation- ‹ is the ‹ This ‹‹ saying: ‹ and his sons,
offering　teaching

הָעֹלָה* עַל מוֹקְדָה עַל הַמִּזְבֵּחַ כָּל הַלַּיְלָה* עַד

‹ until ‹ night* ‹ all ‹ the Altar ‹ on ‹ the pyre ‹ [that ‹the elevation-
stays] on　offering*

הַבֹּקֶר, וְאֵשׁ הַמִּזְבֵּחַ תּוּקַד בּוֹ. וְלָבַשׁ הַכֹּהֵן מִדּוֹ

‹ his ‹ shall the ‹ Don ‹‹ on it. ‹ shall be ‹ of the Altar ‹ and the ‹‹ morning,
garment Kohen　　　　　kept burning　　　　fire

בַד,* וּמִכְנְסֵי בַד יִלְבַּשׁ עַל בְּשָׂרוֹ, וְהֵרִים

‹ He is to lift up ‹‹ his flesh. ‹ upon ‹ shall he don ‹ of linen ‹ and breeches ‹‹ of linen,*

---

(1) *Exodus* 30:17-21.

⊷§ תְּרוּמַת הַדֶּשֶׁן / The Taking of Ashes

These verses are recited here because they concern the first service of the day: to remove a small portion of the ashes from the previous day's offerings. It was performed first thing in the morning, before the *tamid*, daily continual-offering, was brought. In addition, the passage contains three references to fire on the Altar: (a) עַל מוֹקְדָה, *on the pyre*; (b) וְאֵשׁ הַמִּזְבֵּחַ, *the fire of the Altar*; (c) וְהָאֵשׁ עַל הַמִּזְבֵּחַ, *the fire on the Altar*. This teaches that three fires were kept burning on the Altar (*Yoma* 45a). They were: מַעֲרָכָה גְדוֹלָה, *the large pyre*, upon which the offerings were burned; מַעֲרָכָה שְׁנִיָה שֶׁל קְטֹרֶת, *the secondary pyre for the incense*, from which glowing coals were taken and brought into the

Sanctuary for the morning and afternoon incense service; and מַעֲרָכָה לְקִיּוּם הָאֵשׁ, *the pyre for perpetuation of the flame*, which was kept burning at all times in the event either of the other fires became extinguished.

הוּא הָעֹלָה . . . כָּל הַלַּיְלָה — *It is the elevation-offering . . . all night.* Although it was preferable to burn all offerings during the day, it was permitted to place them on the fires all night, provided the service of their blood was completed during the day.

מִדּוֹ בַד — *His garment of linen.* The *Kohen* must wear his full priestly raiment; like all Temple services, this one may not be performed if the *Kohen* is lacking even one of the prescribed garments (described in *Exodus* Ch. 28).

עַל   הָעֹלָה אֶת הָאֵשׁ תֹּאכַל אֲשֶׁר אֶת הַדֶּשֶׁן*

‹ upon ‹ of the elevation-offering ‹ the fire consumed ‹ that ‹   the ashes*

הַמִּזְבֵּחַ, וְשָׂמוֹ אֵצֶל הַמִּזְבֵּחַ. וּפָשַׁט אֶת בְּגָדָיו,*

‹ his garments* ‹ Then he 《 the Altar. ‹ next to ‹ and he ‹ the Altar,
shall remove   shall place it

וְלָבַשׁ בְּגָדִים אֲחֵרִים, וְהוֹצִיא אֶת הַדֶּשֶׁן אֶל

‹ to ‹ the ashes ‹ then he shall remove 《 other garments; ‹ and don

מִחוּץ לַמַּחֲנֶה, אֶל מָקוֹם טָהוֹר. וְהָאֵשׁ עַל

‹ on ‹ The fire 《 which is pure. ‹ a place ‹ to 《 of the camp, ‹ the outside

הַמִּזְבֵּחַ תּוּקַד בּוֹ, לֹא תִכְבֶּה, וּבִעֵר עָלֶיהָ

‹ on it ‹ and burn 《   be ‹ it may 《 on it; ‹ shall be ‹ the Altar
                extinguished;   not   kept burning

הַכֹּהֵן עֵצִים בַּבֹּקֶר בַּבֹּקֶר,* וְעָרַךְ עָלֶיהָ הָעֹלָה,*

《the elevation- ‹ upon it ‹ He is to   《   each and every ‹ wood ‹ shall the
  offering*   prepare   morning.*   *Kohen*

וְהִקְטִיר עָלֶיהָ חֶלְבֵי הַשְּׁלָמִים.* אֵשׁ תָּמִיד

‹ that is ‹ A fire 《 of the peace-offering.* ‹ the fats ‹ upon it ‹ and burn
permanent

תּוּקַד עַל הַמִּזְבֵּחַ, לֹא תִכְבֶּה.¹

《 be extinguished. ‹ it may not 《 the Altar; ‹ on ‹ shall be kept
burning

---

(1) *Leviticus* 6:1-6.

וְהֵרִים אֶת הַדֶּשֶׁן — *He is to lift up the ashes.* He is to take glowing ashes from the burnt flesh of offerings, not from wood ashes. The portion taken for this service need be no larger than a handful and it is placed on the floor of the Courtyard, to the east of the ramp leading up to the Altar (the ramp is on the south side of the Altar). This removal of ashes is a required part of the daily morning service, whether or not the Altar had to be cleaned of excess ashes.

וּפָשַׁט אֶת בְּגָדָיו — *Then he shall remove his garments.* Unlike the previous verse that dis-cusses a daily *mitzvah*, this verse discusses the cleaning of the Altar, which was done whenever the accumulation of ashes atop the Altar interfered with the service, but need not be done daily. The ashes were removed and taken to a designated place outside of Jerusalem; in the Wilderness, they were taken to a place outside the Israelite camp. In speaking of ''removal'' of the priestly garments the verse advises that the *Kohen* should wear less expensive or well-worn priestly garments when performing this service because the ashes would soil his clothing: ''The outfit one wears while cooking his master's meal, one should not wear while filling his master's goblet'' (*Yoma* 23a).

עֵצִים בַּבֹּקֶר בַּבֹּקֶר — *Wood each and every morning.* Wood must be placed on the Altar fire every morning.

הָעֹלָה . . . הַשְּׁלָמִים — *The elevation-offering . . . the peace-offering.* The morning continual

THE TAMID-OFFERING / קרבן התמיד

SOME HOLD THAT THE FOLLOWING (UNTIL קְטֹרֶת/INCENSE) SHOULD BE RECITED WHILE STANDING.
SOME OMIT THE FOLLOWING PARAGRAPH ON THE SABBATH AND ON FESTIVALS.

יְהִי רָצוֹן מִלְּפָנֶיךָ,* יהוה אֱלֹהֵינוּ וֵאלֹהֵי אֲבוֹתֵינוּ,

May it be ‹ the will ‹ before You,* ‹ HASHEM, ‹‹ our God ‹ and the God ‹ of our forefathers,

שֶׁתְּרַחֵם עָלֵינוּ וְתִמְחַל לָנוּ עַל כָּל חַטֹּאתֵינוּ, וּתְכַפֵּר לָנוּ

that You have mercy ‹ on us ‹ and pardon ‹‹ us ‹ for ‹ all ‹‹ our inadvertent sins, ‹ atone ‹‹ for us ‹

עַל כָּל עֲוֹנוֹתֵינוּ, וְתִסְלַח לָנוּ עַל כָּל פְּשָׁעֵינוּ, וְשֶׁיִּבָּנֶה

for ‹ all ‹ our iniquities, ‹‹ our ‹ and forgive ‹‹ us ‹ for ‹ all ‹ our willful sins; ‹ and that rebuilt should be

בֵּית הַמִּקְדָּשׁ בִּמְהֵרָה בְיָמֵינוּ, וְנַקְרִיב לְפָנֶיךָ קָרְבַּן הַתָּמִיד

the Holy Temple ‹ speedily, ‹ in our days, ‹‹ so that we may offer ‹ before You ‹ the ‹ offering ‹‹ that is continual,

שֶׁיְּכַפֵּר בַּעֲדֵנוּ, כְּמוֹ שֶׁכָּתַבְתָּ עָלֵינוּ בְּתוֹרָתֶךָ עַל יְדֵי מֹשֶׁה

that it may atone ‹ for us, ‹‹ as ‹ You have written ‹ for us ‹ in Your Torah, ‹‹ by ‹ the hand ‹ of Moses,

עַבְדֶּךָ, מִפִּי כְבוֹדֶךָ, כָּאָמוּר:

Your ‹‹ servant, ‹ from Your glorious mouth, ‹‹ as it is said:

וַיְדַבֵּר יהוה* אֶל מֹשֶׁה לֵּאמֹר. צַו אֶת בְּנֵי

HASHEM spoke* ‹ to ‹ Moses, ‹ saying: ‹‹ Command ‹ the Children

יִשְׂרָאֵל וְאָמַרְתָּ אֲלֵהֶם, אֶת קָרְבָּנִי לַחְמִי*

of Israel ‹ and tell ‹ them: ‹‹ My offering, ‹‹ My food* ‹

---

elevation-offering had to go on the Altar before any other offerings; similarly, the last offering of the day was the afternoon continual offering.

קָרְבַּן הַתָּמִיד / The Tamid Offering

יְהִי רָצוֹן מִלְּפָנֶיךָ — *May it be the will before You.* We are about to begin "offering" our communal sacrifices, as it were. Before doing so, we recite a brief prayer that God end the exile and make it possible for us to bring the true offerings, not just the recitations that take their place.

וַיְדַבֵּר ה' . . . קָרְבָּנִי לַחְמִי — *HASHEM spoke . . . My offering, My food.* The offering referred to here is the עֹלַת תָּמִיד, *continual elevation-*

offering or *tamid.* The offering is called תָּמִיד, *continual,* because it is brought regularly, day in and day out; it is a communal offering purchased with the annual half-*shekel* contributions, collected especially for this purpose. The offering is called *food* in the figurative sense, referring to the parts that are burned on the Altar. The aroma that is *satisfying* does not refer to the aroma *per se,* for just as God does not require our "food," He does not benefit from the scent of burning flesh. Rather, the aroma of the burning offering is pleasing to God because it represents the culmination of our performance of His will. In the words of the Sages, God is pleased, שֶׁאָמַרְתִּי וְנַעֲשָׂה רְצוֹנִי, *for I have spoken,*

לְאִשַּׁי, רֵיחַ נִיחֹחִי, תִּשְׁמְרוּ לְהַקְרִיב לִי

‹ Me ‹ to offer ‹ you are to be ⟪ that is ‹ My aroma ⟪ for My fires,
scrupulous satisfying,

בְּמוֹעֲדוֹ. וְאָמַרְתָּ לָהֶם, זֶה הָאִשֶּׁה אֲשֶׁר תַּקְרִיבוּ

‹ you are ‹ that ‹ the fire- ‹ This ⟪ them: ‹ And you are ⟪ in its
to offer offering is to tell appointed time.

לַיהוה, כְּבָשִׂים בְּנֵי שָׁנָה תְמִימִם, שְׁנַיִם לַיּוֹם,

‹ daily, ‹ two ‹ unblemished, ‹ first year, ‹ in their ‹ male lambs, ⟪ to Hashem:

עֹלָה תָמִיד. אֶת הַכֶּבֶשׂ אֶחָד תַּעֲשֶׂה בַבֹּקֶר,

⟪ in the ‹ you shall ‹ The one lamb ⟪ that is ‹ an elevation-
morning, do continual. offering

וְאֵת הַכֶּבֶשׂ הַשֵּׁנִי תַּעֲשֶׂה בֵּין הָעַרְבָּיִם.

⟪ in the afternoon; ‹ you shall do ‹ that is second ‹ and the lamb

וַעֲשִׂירִית הָאֵיפָה סֹלֶת לְמִנְחָה,* בְּלוּלָה בְשֶׁמֶן

‹ with oil ‹ mixed ⟪ for a meal- ‹ of fine ‹ of an *ephah* ‹ with a tenth
offering,* flour

כָּתִית רְבִיעִת הַהִין. עֹלַת תָּמִיד, הָעֲשֻׂיָה בְּהַר

‹ at ‹ that was done ⟪ that is ‹ It is the ⟪ of a hin. ‹ a quarter ‹ from
Mount continual, elevation- crushed
offering [olives]

סִינַי, לְרֵיחַ נִיחֹחַ, אִשֶּׁה לַיהוה. וְנִסְכּוֹ רְבִיעִת

‹ is a quarter ‹ And its ⟪ to Hashem. ‹ a fire- ⟪ that is ‹ for an ⟪ Sinai,
libation offering satisfying, aroma

הַהִין לַכֶּבֶשׂ הָאֶחָד, בַּקֹּדֶשׁ הַסֵּךְ נֶסֶךְ שֵׁכָר

‹ of fermen- ‹ a ‹ pour ‹ on the Holy ⟪ for each lamb, ‹ of a hin
ted wine libation [Altar]

---

and My will has been done.

סֹלֶת לְמִנְחָה — *Of fine flour for a meal-offering.*
Every elevation- and peace-offering, communal
or private, is accompanied by a meal-offering,
which is burned completely on the Altar, and a
libation of wine, which is poured onto the Altar.
The wine is called נְסָכִים and the meal-offering,

which consists of fine flour mixed with olive oil,
is called מִנְחַת נְסָכִים. The amount of flour, oil,
and wine depends on the species of the animal.
For sheep — the animal used for the *tamid* —
the amounts are a tenth-*ephah* (approximately
4½ lbs.) of flour, and a quarter-*hin* (approx. 30
fl. oz.) each of oil and wine. A table of the

לַיהוה. וְאֵת הַכֶּבֶשׂ הַשֵּׁנִי תַּעֲשֶׂה בֵּין הָעַרְבָּיִם,

》 in the afternoon; 〈 you are 〈 that is 〈 And the lamb 》 to Hᴀsʜᴇᴍ.
to do second

כְּמִנְחַת הַבֹּקֶר וּכְנִסְכּוֹ תַּעֲשֶׂה, אִשֵּׁה רֵיחַ נִיחֹחַ

〈 that is 〈 for an 〈 a fire- 》 shall you 〈 and like its 〈 of the 〈 like the
satisfying aroma offering do, libation morning meal-offering

לַיהוה.¹

》 to Hᴀsʜᴇᴍ.

וְשָׁחַט אֹתוֹ עַל יֶרֶךְ הַמִּזְבֵּחַ צָפֹנָה לִפְנֵי יהוה,

》 Hᴀsʜᴇᴍ, 〈 before 》 on the 〈 of the Altar 〈 the side 〈 on 〈 it 〈 He is to
north, slaughter

וְזָרְקוּ בְּנֵי אַהֲרֹן הַכֹּהֲנִים אֶת דָּמוֹ עַל הַמִּזְבֵּחַ

〈 the Altar, 〈 upon 〈 its blood 》 the Kohanim — 〈 — the sons 》 and they
of Aaron shall throw

סָבִיב.*²

》 all around.*

יְהִי רָצוֹן מִלְּפָנֶיךָ, יהוה אֱלֹהֵינוּ וֵאלֹהֵי אֲבוֹתֵינוּ, שֶׁתְּהֵא

》 that 》 of our 〈 and the 〈 our God 〈 Hᴀsʜᴇᴍ, 》 before You, 〈 the will 》 May
it be forefathers, God it be

אֲמִירָה זוֹ חֲשׁוּבָה וּמְקֻבֶּלֶת וּמְרֻצָּה לְפָנֶיךָ כְּאִלּוּ הִקְרַבְנוּ

〈 we had 〈 as if 》 before You 〈 and 〈 and 〈 worthy 》 – this recital –
offered favorable acceptable,

קָרְבַּן הַתָּמִיד בְּמוֹעֲדוֹ וּבִמְקוֹמוֹ וּכְהִלְכָתוֹ.

》 and according to 〈 in its place, 〈 in its set time, 〈 the continual offering
its requirement.

---

(1) Numbers 28:1-8. (2) Leviticus 1:11.

amounts needed for other species may be found on p. 65.

סָבִיב — All around. Immediately after slaughter, the blood which spurted from the tamid was received in a sacred vessel by a Kohen and

dashed on the northeast and southwest corners of the Altar. This is called "all around" because blood thrown at a corner would spread out to the two adjacent sides, so that all four sides of the Altar would receive some blood.

﴾ INCENSE / קְטֹרֶת ﴿

אַתָּה הוּא יהוה אֱלֹהֵינוּ שֶׁהִקְטִירוּ אֲבוֹתֵינוּ לְפָנֶיךָ

❮ before You ❮ that our forefathers burned ❮❮ our God, ❮ HASHEM, ❮❮ the One, ❮ You are

אֶת קְטֹרֶת הַסַּמִּים בִּזְמַן שֶׁבֵּית הַמִּקְדָּשׁ הָיָה קַיָּם, כַּאֲשֶׁר

❮ as ❮❮ standing, ❮ was ❮ when the Holy Temple ❮ in the ❮ spices ❮ the incense
time

צִוִּיתָ אוֹתָם עַל יְדֵי מֹשֶׁה נְבִיאֶךָ, כַּכָּתוּב בְּתוֹרָתֶךָ:

❮❮ in Your Torah: ❮ as is written ❮ Your ❮ of ❮ the ❮ by ❮ them ❮ You com-
prophet, Moses hand manded

וַיֹּאמֶר יהוה אֶל מֹשֶׁה, קַח לְךָ סַמִּים,* נָטָף

❮ —stacte, ❮❮ spices* ❮ [for] Take ❮❮ Moses: ❮ to ❮ HASHEM said
yourself

וּשְׁחֵלֶת וְחֶלְבְּנָה, סַמִּים וּלְבֹנָה זַכָּה, בַּד בְּבַד

❮ of equal weight ❮❮ that is ❮ and ❮ spices ❮❮ and galbanum — ❮ onycha,
pure; frankincense

﴾ קְטֹרֶת / INCENSE ﴿

Incense, blended according to a strictly pre-scribed formula, was burned in the Temple on the Golden Altar, morning and evening. The Golden Altar was located inside the Temple building. It was much smaller than the stone Altar used for offerings, which in the Tabernacle was covered with copper plates, and was located in the Court-yard. *Arizal* writes that the careful recitation of this section helps bring one to repentance. *R' Hirsch* comments that the incense symbolized Is-rael's duty to make all its actions pleasing to God.

According to *Zohar*, the chapter and laws of קְטֹרֶת should be recited here "in order to remove impurity from the world prior to the prayers [the complete *Shacharis* service] that take the place of offerings." In response to the *Zohar's* dictum, it has become customary to include קְטֹרֶת in this part of the service. Interestingly, the halachah also called for the recitation of קְטֹרֶת after *Shacharis* every day, following the Psalm of the Day, a practice still followed in *Nusach Sefard*. *Rama*, however, notes that since it is important to enunciate each of the ingredients and measure-ments carefully and clearly, because the recitation

takes the place of the actual mixture which, as we shall see below, had to be precise, and since working people, under the stress of hurrying to earn their livelihood, often tend to slur or omit words in the last part of *Shacharis*, *Nusach Ashkenaz* omits the קְטֹרֶת at the end of *Shacharis*. Nevertheless, it is retained here because people who come to the synagogue early enough can recite it properly. On the Sabbath and Festivals, however, קְטֹרֶת is indeed recited after *Mussaf* because on those days people have the time and peace of mind to recite the passages carefully (*Orach Chaim* 132:2).

וַיֹּאמֶר ה' אֶל מֹשֶׁה קַח לְךָ סַמִּים — *HASHEM said to Moses: Take [for] yourself spices.* As enumerated below in the Talmudic passage beginning תָּנוּ רַבָּנָן, *Taught did the Rabbis*, eleven different spices were used in the incense mixture, but only four of them — stacte, onycha, galbanum, and frankincense — are named in the Scriptural verse. The identity of the other spices is part of the Oral Law. That there are a total of eleven spices is derived from this verse in the following manner: סַמִּים, *spices*, is plural, yielding two kinds; then three spices are named, for a total of five; the word

יִהְיֶה.* וְעָשִׂיתָ אֹתָהּ קְטֹרֶת, רֹקַח, מַעֲשֵׂה רוֹקֵחַ,

《 of a 〈 the 〈 a spice- 〈 into 〈 it 〈 You shall 《 shall
perfumer, handiwork compound, incense, make they be.*

מְמֻלָּח, טָהוֹר, קֹדֶשׁ. וְשָׁחַקְתָּ* מִמֶּנָּה* הָדֵק,

《 finely 〈 some of it* 〈 You shall grind* 《 and holy. 〈 pure 〈 thoroughly
mixed,

וְנָתַתָּה מִמֶּנָּה* לִפְנֵי הָעֵדֻת בְּאֹהֶל מוֹעֵד אֲשֶׁר

〈 where 《 of 〈 in the Tent 〈 the 〈 before 〈 some of it* 〈 and you
Appointment, Testimony shall place

אִוָּעֵד לְךָ שָׁמָּה, קֹדֶשׁ קָדָשִׁים תִּהְיֶה לָכֶם.[1]

《 for you. 〈 it shall be 〈 of holies 〈 holy 《 there; 〈 you 〈 I shall designate
a time to meet

וְנֶאֱמַר: וְהִקְטִיר עָלָיו אַהֲרֹן קְטֹרֶת סַמִּים,

《 spices, 〈 the incense 〈 shall Aaron, 〈 upon it 〈 Burn 《 It is also
written:

בַּבֹּקֶר בַּבֹּקֶר בְּהֵיטִיבוֹ אֶת הַנֵּרֹת* יַקְטִירֶנָּה.

《 he is to burn it. 〈 the lamps* 〈 when he prepares 〈 each and every morning

וּבְהַעֲלֹת אַהֲרֹן אֶת הַנֵּרֹת בֵּין הָעַרְבַּיִם

〈 in the afternoon, 〈 the lamps 〈 And when Aaron ignites

יַקְטִירֶנָּה, קְטֹרֶת תָּמִיד לִפְנֵי יהוה לְדֹרֹתֵיכֶם.[2]

《 throughout your 〈 Hashem, 〈 before 〈 that is 〈 an incense 《 he is to burn it,
generations. continual

---

(1) *Exodus* 30:34-36. (2) 30:7-8.

סַמִּים appears again implying the addition of another group of five (equivalent to the five given above). Finally *frankincense* is added, for a total of eleven.

The exact translations of the spices are not known with absolute certainty.

בַּד בְּבַד יִהְיֶה — *Of equal weight shall they be.* The four spices given by name are of equal weight. The other seven, however, were different from these four, as will be seen from the Talmudic passage that follows.

וְשָׁחַקְתָּ — *You shall grind.* The incense must be pulverized into a fine powder.

מִמֶּנָּה . . . מִמֶּנָּה — *Some of it . . . some of it.* The repetition alludes to the special Yom Kippur incense service, when the incense is reground and the *Kohen Gadol* [High Priest] takes it into the Holy of Holies, the only time of the year when a human being enters that most sacred place. On all other days, incense is burned twice a day in the Sanctuary.

בְּהֵיטִיבוֹ אֶת הַנֵּרֹת — *When he prepares the lamps.* The *Kohen* prepares the lamps of the Menorah every morning, before the incense is burned.

——— כריתות ו., ירושלמי יומא ד:ה / Talmud, *Kereisos* 6a, *Yerushalmi Yoma* 4:5 ———

תָּנוּ רַבָּנָן,* פִּטוּם הַקְּטֹרֶת כֵּיצַד. שְׁלֹשׁ מֵאוֹת

וְשִׁשִּׁים וּשְׁמוֹנָה מָנִים* הָיוּ בָהּ. שְׁלֹשׁ מֵאוֹת

וְשִׁשִּׁים וַחֲמִשָּׁה כְּמִנְיַן יְמוֹת הַחַמָּה – מָנֶה לְכָל

יוֹם, פְּרַס בְּשַׁחֲרִית וּפְרַס בֵּין הָעַרְבָּיִם;

וּשְׁלֹשָׁה מָנִים יְתֵרִים,* שֶׁמֵּהֶם מַכְנִיס כֹּהֵן גָּדוֹל

מְלֹא חָפְנָיו בְּיוֹם הַכִּפּוּרִים. וּמַחֲזִירָן לְמַכְתֶּשֶׁת

בְּעֶרֶב יוֹם הַכִּפּוּרִים, וְשׁוֹחֲקָן יָפֶה יָפֶה כְּדֵי

שֶׁתְּהֵא דַקָּה מִן הַדַּקָּה. וְאַחַד עָשָׂר סַמָּנִים הָיוּ

בָהּ, וְאֵלּוּ הֵן: (א) הַצֳּרִי, (ב) וְהַצִּפֹּרֶן, (ג) הַחֶלְבְּנָה,

(ד) וְהַלְּבוֹנָה, מִשְׁקַל שִׁבְעִים שִׁבְעִים מָנֶה; (ה) מוֹר,

---

◆§ תָּנוּ רַבָּנָן — *Taught did the Rabbis.* This passage explains how the incense mixture was prepared and it gives the names and amounts that are not specified in Scripture.

מָנִים — *Maneh.* A *maneh* is approximately equal to twenty ounces.

וּשְׁלֹשָׁה מָנִים יְתֵרִים — *And three maneh extra.* In addition to the regular incense service, on Yom Kippur there was a special service that was performed in the Holy of Holies. Three *maneh* were taken before Yom Kippur and ground again to make them extra fine. The *Kohen Gadol* filled both hands with that incense, and used it for the special Yom Kippur service.

(ו) וּקְצִיעָה, (ז) שִׁבֹּלֶת נֵרְדְּ, (ח) וְכַרְכֹּם, מִשְׁקָל
‹ weighing ‹ saffron, ‹ spikenard, ‹ cassia,

שִׁשָּׁה עָשָׂר שִׁשָּׁה עָשָׂר מָנֶה; (ט) הַקֹּשְׁטְ
‹ costus, ‹ maneh; ‹ each sixteen

שְׁנֵים עָשָׂר, (י) וְקִלּוּפָה שְׁלֹשָׁה, (יא) וְקִנָּמוֹן
‹ and cinnamon ‹ three; ‹ aromatic bark, ‹ twelve [maneh];

תִּשְׁעָה. בֹּרִית כַּרְשִׁינָה תִּשְׁעָה קַבִּין,* יֵין
‹ wine ‹ kav;* ‹ nine ‹ of Carshina ‹ [Additionally,] lye ‹ nine.

קַפְרִיסִין סְאִין* תְּלָתָא וְקַבִּין תְּלָתָא, וְאִם
‹ – if ‹ and three kav ‹ three se'ah* ‹ of Cyprus

אֵין לוֹ יֵין קַפְרִיסִין, מֵבִיא חֲמַר חִוַּרְיָן עַתִּיק,
‹ that is old – ‹ that is white ‹ wine ‹ he brings ‹ of Cyprus, ‹ wine ‹ he has no

מֶלַח סְדוֹמִית רֹבַע; מַעֲלֶה עָשָׁן* כָּל שֶׁהוּא.
‹ a minute amount. ‹ and maaleh ashan * ‹ a quarter[-kav], ‹ of Sodom, ‹ salt

רַבִּי נָתָן הַבַּבְלִי אוֹמֵר: אַף כִּפַּת הַיַּרְדֵּן
‹ of the Jordan ‹ amber ‹ Also ‹ says: ‹ the Babylonian ‹ Nassan ‹ Rabbi

כָּל שֶׁהוּא. וְאִם נָתַן בָּהּ דְּבַשׁ, פְּסָלָהּ. וְאִם
‹ And if ‹ he invali- ‹ fruit- ‹ in it ‹ he ‹ If ‹ a minute amount.
   dated it.   honey,   placed

חִסַּר* אַחַת מִכָּל סַמָּנֶיהָ, חַיָּב מִיתָה.
‹ to the death ‹ he is ‹ its spices, ‹ of all ‹ any one ‹ he left out*
   penalty.   liable

קַבִּין . . . סְאִין — *Kav . . . se'ah.* A *kav* contains a volume of approximately forty fluid ounces (but see p. 64). A *se'ah* is equal to six *kav.*

מַעֲלֶה עָשָׁן — *Maaleh ashan* [lit. *a smoke-raising herb*]. As implied by its name, the addition of this herb caused the smoke of the incense to ascend straight as a pillar.

וְאִם חִסֵּר — *And if he left out.* If he used either more or less than the prescribed amount of any ingredient, he is liable to death at the hands of Heaven (*Etz Yosef*). According to *Rashi* (*Kereisos* 6b) this liability applies only to the annual Yom Kippur service performed in the Holy of Holies, because the *Kohen Gadol* is considered to have made a בִּיאָה רֵיקָנִית, *an empty-handed coming,* since he did not have the proper mixture. *Rambam,* however, applies this ruling to the whole year (*Hil. Klei HaMikdash* 2:8) because it is regarded as קְטֹרֶת זָרָה, *strange* [unauthorized] *incense.*

רַבָּן שִׁמְעוֹן בֶּן גַּמְלִיאֵל אוֹמֵר: הַצֳּרִי אֵינוֹ

‹ is nothing ‹ Stacte ‹‹ says: ‹ Gamliel ‹ ben ‹ Shimon ‹ Rabban

אֶלָּא שְׂרָף הַנּוֹטֵף מֵעֲצֵי הַקְּטָף. בְּרִית כַּרְשִׁינָה

‹ of Carshina, ‹ Lye ‹‹ of balsam. ‹ from trees ‹ that drips ‹ the sap ‹ but

לָמָה הִיא בָאָה, כְּדֵי לְיַפּוֹת בָּהּ אֶת הַצִּפֹּרֶן,

‹‹ the onycha, ‹ with it ‹ to refine ‹ In order ‹‹ brought? ‹ is it ‹ why

כְּדֵי שֶׁתְּהֵא נָאָה. יֵין קַפְרִיסִין לָמָה הוּא בָא,

‹‹ brought? ‹ is it ‹ why ‹ of Cyprus, ‹ Wine ‹‹ pleasing. ‹ that it should be ‹ In order

כְּדֵי לִשְׁרוֹת בּוֹ אֶת הַצִּפֹּרֶן, כְּדֵי שֶׁתְּהֵא עַזָּה.

‹‹ pungent. ‹ that it should be ‹ In order ‹ the onycha, ‹ in it ‹ to soak ‹ In order

וַהֲלֹא מֵי רַגְלַיִם יָפִין לָהּ, אֶלָּא שֶׁאֵין מַכְנִיסִין

‹ bring ‹ they do not ‹ Nevertheless ‹‹ for that? ‹ more suitable ‹ urine ‹ But is not

מֵי רַגְלַיִם בַּמִּקְדָּשׁ מִפְּנֵי הַכָּבוֹד.

‹‹ respect. ‹ out of ‹ into the Temple ‹ urine

תַּנְיָא, רַבִּי נָתָן אוֹמֵר: כְּשֶׁהוּא שׁוֹחֵק, אוֹמֵר,

‹‹ [the one in charge] would say, ‹ would grind [the incense], ‹ As he ‹‹ says: ‹ Nassan ‹ Rabbi ‹‹ It is taught:

הָדֵק הֵיטֵב, הֵיטֵב הָדֵק, מִפְּנֵי שֶׁהַקּוֹל יָפֶה

‹ is beneficial ‹ the sound ‹ because ‹‹ grind, ‹ thoroughly ‹ thoroughly, ‹ Grind

לַבְּשָׂמִים. פִּטְּמָהּ לַחֲצָאִין,* כְּשֵׁרָה; לִשְׁלִישׁ

‹ but as to a third ‹‹ it was fit for use, ‹ in half-quantities,* ‹ If one mixed it ‹‹ for the spices.

פִּטְּמָהּ לַחֲצָאִין — *If one mixed it in half-quantities.* Instead of mixing 368 *maneh* as was customarily done, someone mixed only 184 *maneh*. Since the manner of compounding was transmitted orally, the question arose whether it was forbidden to prepare spice-mixtures totaling *less* than the usual 368 *maneh*. Rabbi Nassan stated that he had learned that it *was* permitted to make mixtures containing exactly half the usual amount, but he did not know whether mixtures smaller than this were also permitted. To this, Rabbi Yehudah replied that any amount, even a one-day supply, was acceptable, provided the ingredients were in the correct proportion.

וְלִרְבִיעַ, לֹא שָׁמָעְנוּ. אָמַר רַבִּי יְהוּדָה: זֶה

‹ This is ‹‹ Yehudah: ‹ Rabbi ‹ Said ‹‹ — we have not heard [the law]. ‹‹ or a quarter

הַכְּלָל – אִם כְּמִדָּתָהּ, כְּשֵׁרָה לַחֲצָאִין; וְאִם

‹ But if ‹‹ [even] in half ‹ it is fit ‹‹ in its proper ‹ If ‹‹ the general rule:
the full amount.   for use   proportion,

חִסַּר אַחַת מִכָּל סַמָּנֶיהָ, חַיָּב מִיתָה.

‹‹ to the death penalty. ‹ he is liable ‹ its spices, ‹ of all ‹ any one ‹ he left out

תַּנְיָא, בַּר קַפָּרָא אוֹמֵר: אַחַת לְשִׁשִּׁים אוֹ

‹ or ‹ every sixty ‹ Once ‹‹ says: ‹ Kappara ‹ Bar ‹‹ It is taught:

לְשִׁבְעִים שָׁנָה* הָיְתָה בָּאָה שֶׁל שִׁירַיִם

‹‹ — the accumulated ‹‹ reach ‹ it would ‹ years,* ‹ seventy
leftovers —

לַחֲצָאִין. וְעוֹד תָּנֵי בַּר קַפָּרָא: אִלּוּ הָיָה נוֹתֵן

‹ put ‹ one had ‹ If ‹‹ Kappara: ‹ Bar ‹ taught ‹ Further- ‹‹ half the
more   yearly quantity.

בָּהּ קוֹרְטוֹב שֶׁל דְּבַשׁ,* אֵין אָדָם יָכוֹל לַעֲמֹד

‹ withstood ‹ could have ‹ person ‹ no ‹‹ fruit-honey,* ‹ of ‹ a kortov ‹ into it

מִפְּנֵי רֵיחָהּ. וְלָמָּה אֵין מְעָרְבִין בָּהּ דְּבַשׁ,

‹‹ fruit-honey? ‹ into it ‹ mix ‹ did they not ‹ Why ‹‹ its scent.

מִפְּנֵי שֶׁהַתּוֹרָה אָמְרָה: כִּי כָל שְׂאֹר וְכָל דְּבַשׁ

‹ fruit-honey, ‹ or any ‹ leaven ‹ any ‹ For ‹‹ said: ‹ the Torah ‹ Because

לֹא תַקְטִירוּ מִמֶּנּוּ אִשֶּׁה לַיהוה.¹

‹‹ to HASHEM. ‹ a fire-offering ‹ from them ‹ you are not to burn

---

(1) *Leviticus* 2:11.

אַחַת לְשִׁשִּׁים אוֹ לְשִׁבְעִים שָׁנָה — *Once every sixty or seventy years.* We learned earlier that three *maneh* were set aside from which the *Kohen Gadol* filled his hands on Yom Kippur. A quantity (depending on the size of the *Kohen Gadol's* hands) of this mixture was unused, and was set aside. Over many years, enough of this leftover incense had accumulated to provide 184 *maneh*, or a half-year supply of incense. When

that happened, only half the usual mixture had to be made for the coming year.

קוֹרְטוֹב שֶׁל דְּבַשׁ — *A kortov of fruit-honey.* Honey or any other fruit juice or produce would have made the scent overpowering, but the Torah forbids the use of fruit products in the incense (*Rashi* to *Leviticus* 2:11; see *Mishneh L'Melech* to *Hil. Issurei Mizbe'ach* 5:1).

A *kortov* equals ¹⁄₂₅₆ of a *kav*, or approxi-

RECITE THREE TIMES:

יהוה צְבָאוֹת עִמָּנוּ,* מִשְׂגָּב לָנוּ אֱלֹהֵי יַעֲקֹב,

HASHEM, ⟨ Master ⟨ is with us,* ⟨ a ⟨ for us ⟨ is the ⟨ of Jacob, ⟨
of Legions, stronghold God

סֶלָה.¹

⟨ Selah!

RECITE THREE TIMES:

יהוה צְבָאוֹת, אַשְׁרֵי אָדָם בֹּטֵחַ בָּךְ.²

HASHEM, ⟨ Master of ⟨ praiseworthy ⟨ is the ⟨ who ⟨ in You. ⟨
Legions, man trusts

RECITE THREE TIMES:

יהוה הוֹשִׁיעָה, הַמֶּלֶךְ יַעֲנֵנוּ בְיוֹם קָרְאֵנוּ.³

HASHEM, ⟨ save! ⟨ May the King ⟨ answer us ⟨ on the day ⟨ we call! ⟨

אַתָּה סֵתֶר לִי, מִצַּר תִּצְּרֵנִי, רָנֵּי פַלֵּט,

You are ⟨ a shelter ⟨ for me; ⟨ from ⟨ You preserve ⟨ with ⟨ of
distress me; glad song rescue,

תְּסוֹבְבֵנִי, סֶלָה.⁴ וְעָרְבָה לַיהוה מִנְחַת יְהוּדָה

You envelop me, ⟨ Selah! ⟨ And pleasing ⟨ to HASHEM ⟨ let be the ⟨ of Judah ⟨
offering

וִירוּשָׁלָיִם, כִּימֵי עוֹלָם וּכְשָׁנִים קַדְמֹנִיּוֹת.⁵

and Jerusalem, ⟨ as in days ⟨ of old ⟨ and in years ⟨ gone by. ⟨

---

(1) *Psalms* 46:8. (2) 84:13. (3) 20:10. (4) 32:7. (5) *Malachi* 3:4.

mately ¹⁄₂₀ of a fluid ounce. Here it is used to mean a minimal amount, a drop.

‎ה׳ צְבָאוֹת עִמָּנוּ — *H ASHEM, Master of Legions, is with us.* Yerushalmi Berachos 5:1 cites Rabbi Yochanan who says of the first two verses, "One should never let them depart from his mouth." Therefore, they have been introduced into the daily prayers at several points. *Arizal* teaches that they should be repeated three times after each mention of קְטֹרֶת, *incense*, which is why they are inserted here and when קְטֹרֶת is again recited after the morning prayers.

The first verse proclaims the principle of הַשְׁגָּחָה פְּרָטִית, *individual Providence*, while the second declares the praise of one who trusts in

God. *Iyun Tefillah* points to two events that show how הַשְׁגָּחָה פְּרָטִית and total trust in God played important roles in shaping Rabbi Yochanan's life and lifestyle. Once, Rabbi Yochanan and his colleague Ilfa were so poverty stricken that they had no choice but to leave the study hall to seek their fortune. On the way, Rabbi Yochanan — but not Ilfa — heard one angel say to another that the two former students deserved to die because "they forsake the eternal life and go to engage in a temporary life." Since Ilfa did not hear the message, Rabbi Yochanan understood that it was directed not at Ilfa but at himself. He returned to the yeshiva and became the outstanding sage of his time (*Taanis* 21a). Thus, Rabbi Yochanan's

Talmud, Yoma 33a / יומא לג.

אַבַּיֵי הֲוָה מְסַדֵּר* סֵדֶר הַמַּעֲרָכָה מִשְּׁמָא דִגְמָרָא
« the ‹ based on ‹ of the Altar ‹ the ‹ list* ‹ would ‹ Abaye
tradition, service, order

וְאַלִּבָּא דְאַבָּא שָׁאוּל: מַעֲרָכָה גְדוֹלָה* קוֹדֶמֶת
‹ precedes ‹ The [arrangement ‹‹ with Abba Shaul: ‹ and in
of the] large pyre* accordance

לְמַעֲרָכָה שְׁנִיָּה* שֶׁל קְטֹרֶת; וּמַעֲרָכָה שְׁנִיָּה שֶׁל
‹ of ‹ the secondary pyre ‹‹ the incense- ‹ of ‹ that of the
offering; secondary pyre*

קְטֹרֶת קוֹדֶמֶת לְסִדּוּר שְׁנֵי גִזְרֵי עֵצִים;* וְסִדּוּר
‹ the ‹‹ of wood;* ‹ logs ‹ of two the ‹ precedes ‹ the incense-
placement placement offering

שְׁנֵי גִזְרֵי עֵצִים קוֹדֶם לְדִשּׁוּן מִזְבֵּחַ הַפְּנִימִי;*
‹‹ that is ‹ from the ‹ the removal ‹ precedes ‹ of wood ‹ logs ‹ of two
inside;* Altar of ashes

life was changed by a particular incident of individual Providence.

As an elderly man, Rabbi Yochanan, who had become wealthy notwithstanding his Torah study, pointed out to Rabbi Chiya bar Abba many valuable properties that he had sold in order to enable him not to interrupt his Torah study. Rabbi Chiya wept at the thought that Rabbi Yochanan had left nothing for his own old age. Rabbi Yochanan replied, "Chiya, my son, do you think so little of what I have done? I have sold a material thing, that was presented after six days, as it says (Exodus 20:11): For in six days HASHEM made heaven and earth. But the Torah was given after forty days [of God's instruction to Moses] as it says (ibid. 34:28): And [Moses] was there with HASHEM for forty days." It was because of such commitment that Rabbi Yochanan was regarded by his generation as the very symbol of dedication to Torah study and faith that God would provide for his material needs (Shir HaShirim Rabbah to 8:7). As a man of such faith, Rabbi Yochanan personifies the verse . . . praiseworthy is the man who trusts in You.

◆§ אַבַּיֵי הֲוָה מְסַדֵּר — Abaye would list. To

conclude the description of the daily Temple service, we recite its full order as transmitted by Abaye. Although he lived several generations after the Destruction, he taught the order, as it had been transmitted orally, in the name of Abba Shaul, a Mishnaic sage (tanna) who lived in the time of Rabbi Meir. For the convenience of the reader we will define the less familiar terms:

מַעֲרָכָה גְדוֹלָה — The large pyre. At the center of the Altar, a large pyre was arranged upon which the offerings were burned.

מַעֲרָכָה שְׁנִיָּה — The secondary pyre. Near the southwest corner of the Altar, a smaller pyre was maintained, from which glowing coals were taken into the Sanctuary for the burning of the morning and afternoon incense service.

סִדּוּר שְׁנֵי גִזְרֵי עֵצִים — The placement of two logs of wood. Two large sections of wood were placed on the large pyre every morning. More wood could be added during the day, as needed.

מִזְבֵּחַ הַפְּנִימִי — The Altar that is inside. Made of wood plated with gold and much smaller than the Outer Altar (one cubit across versus thirty-two), the Inner Altar was used on a daily basis but only for incense.

וְדִשּׁוּן מִזְבֵּחַ הַפְּנִימִי קוֹדֵם לַהֲטָבַת חָמֵשׁ נֵרוֹת;*

‹‹ lamps [of ‹ of the ‹ the cleaning ‹ precedes ‹ that is inside ‹ from ‹ the removal
the Menorah];* five the Altar of ashes

וַהֲטָבַת חָמֵשׁ נֵרוֹת קוֹדֶמֶת לְדַם הַתָּמִיד;*

‹‹ of the continual- ‹ the [throwing ‹ precedes ‹ lamps ‹ of the five ‹ the cleaning
offering;* of the] blood

וְדַם הַתָּמִיד קוֹדֵם לַהֲטָבַת שְׁתֵּי נֵרוֹת; וַהֲטָבַת

‹ the cleaning ‹‹ lamps; ‹ of the ‹ the cleaning ‹ precedes ‹ of the continual- ‹ the
[other] two offering blood

שְׁתֵּי נֵרוֹת קוֹדֶמֶת לִקְטֹרֶת; וּקְטֹרֶת קוֹדֶמֶת

‹ precedes ‹ the incense ‹ the incense; ‹ precedes ‹ lamps ‹ of the two

לְאֵבָרִים;* וְאֵבָרִים לְמִנְחָה;* וּמִנְחָה לַחֲבִתִּין;*

‹‹ [precedes] ‹ the meal- ‹‹ [precedes] the ‹ the [burning of ‹‹ the [burning of
the pan-cakes;* offering meal-offering;* the] limbs the] limbs
[of the *tamid*];*

וַחֲבִתִּין לִנְסָכִין;* וּנְסָכִין לְמוּסָפִין;* וּמוּסָפִין

‹ the *mussaf*- ‹‹ [precede] the ‹ the wine- ‹‹ [precede] the ‹ the pan-cakes
offering *mussaf*-offering;* libations wine-libations;*

לְבָזִיכִין;* וּבָזִיכִין קוֹדְמִין לְתָמִיד שֶׁל

‹ of ‹ the continual- ‹ precede ‹ the bowls ‹‹ [precedes] the bowls
offering [of frankincense];*

בֵּין הָעַרְבָּיִם, שֶׁנֶּאֱמַר: וְעָרַךְ עָלֶיהָ הָעֹלָה,

‹ the elevation- ‹ upon it ‹ And he is ‹‹ for it is said: ‹‹ the afternoon,
offering to arrange

לַהֲטָבַת חָמֵשׁ נֵרוֹת — *The cleaning of the five lamps [of the Menorah]*. The Temple Menorah had seven lamps. Scriptural exegesis teaches that the lamps, which had burned all night, are cleaned in two stages, first five and then the remaining two.

דַּם הַתָּמִיד — *The [throwing of the] blood of the continual-offering*. The slaughter had taken place before the cleaning of the lamps.

אֵבָרִים —*The [burning of the]limbs [of the tamid]*, the continual-offering.

מִנְחָה —*The meal-offering*, that accompanied the *tamid*.

חֲבִתִּין — *The pan-cakes*. The *Kohen Gadol* was required to bring a meal-offering every day, half in the morning and half in the afternoon. It was baked in a low, flat pan called a מַחֲבַת, hence the name חֲבִתִּין is related to [מַחֲבַת] מִנְחַת חֲבִתִּין.

נְסָכִין — *The wine-libations*, that accompanied the *tamid*.

מוּסָפִין — *The mussaf-offering*, on the Sabbath, Festivals, and Rosh Chodesh.

בָּזִיכִין —*The bowls [of frankincense]*. Two bowls of לְבוֹנָה, *frankincense*, were placed with the showbread every Sabbath. The bread was eaten by the *Kohanim* and the incense was burned on

וְהִקְטִיר עָלֶיהָ חֶלְבֵי הַשְּׁלָמִים. עָלֶיהָ הַשְׁלֵם*[1]

⟨ you are to ⟨ "upon it" ⟪ of the peace- ⟨ the fats ⟨ upon it ⟨ and burn
complete*   offerings;

כָּל הַקָּרְבָּנוֹת כֻּלָּם.

⟪ in their ⟨ the [day's] ⟨ all
entirety.   offerings

אָנָּא בְּכֹחַ* גְּדֻלַּת יְמִינְךָ תַּתִּיר צְרוּרָה.*

אב"ג ית"ץ   ⟨ the bundled ⟨ untie ⟨ of Your ⟨ of the ⟨ With the ⟪ We beg
[sins].*   right hand, greatness strength* You!

קַבֵּל רִנַּת עַמְּךָ שַׂגְּבֵנוּ טַהֲרֵנוּ נוֹרָא.

קר"ע שט"ן   ⟨ O Awesome ⟨ purify us, ⟨ strengthen ⟪ of Your ⟨ the ⟨ Accept
One.   us,   people; prayer

נָא גִבּוֹר דּוֹרְשֵׁי יִחוּדְךָ* כְּבָבַת שָׁמְרֵם.

נג"ד יכ"ש   ⟨ guard them. ⟨ like the pupil ⟪ Your ⟨ – those ⟪ O Strong ⟨ Please,
of an eye   Oneness,* who foster   One

בָּרְכֵם טַהֲרֵם רַחֲמֵם צִדְקָתְךָ* תָּמִיד גָּמְלֵם.

בט"ר צת"ג   ⟪ recompense ⟨ always ⟨ may Your ⟪ show them ⟨ purify ⟨ Bless
them.   righteousness mercy;* them, them,

חֲסִין קָדוֹשׁ בְּרוֹב טוּבְךָ נַהֵל עֲדָתֶךָ.

חק"ב טנ"ע   ⟪ Your ⟨ guide ⟨ of Your ⟨ with the ⟪ Holy ⟨ Powerful
congregation.   goodness abundance One, One,

---

(1) *Leviticus* 6:5.

the Altar after the showbread was removed from the Table on the following Sabbath.

הַשְּׁלָמִים. עָלֶיהָ הַשְׁלֵם — *Of the peace-offerings; "upon it"* (the elevation-offering) *you are to complete.* The Sages expound the word הַשְּׁלָמִים, *the peace-offering,* here as if vowelized הַשְׁלֵמִים, from the root שלם in *hifil,* which means completions, thus meaning that all the services of the day should be completed after the morning *tamid,* and before the afternoon *tamid.*

אָנָּא בְּכֹחַ ❧— *We beg You! With the strength* ... This prayer — ascribed to the *tanna* Rabbi Nechunia ben Hakanah — has profound mystical significance. It contains forty-two words, the initials of which form the secret forty-two-letter Name of God. Moreover, the six initials of each of its seven verses form Divine Names. Traditionally, they are indicated in small type at the end of each line. The Kabbalists teach that each line

should be divided into phrases of two words each, but our translation follows the division indicated by a simple reading of the phrases.

This prayer is inserted at this point because it is an eloquent plea that God save Israel from exile. After having recited the order of the Temple service, it is a most fitting time for us to pray for the redemption (*Seder HaYom*).

תַּתִּיר צְרוּרָה — *Untie the bundled [sins].* The accumulated sins of Israel are bound together like a barrier that prevents our prayers from ascending to the Heavenly Throne. We ask God to remove this obstacle (*Iyun Tefillah*).

דּוֹרְשֵׁי יִחוּדְךָ — *Those who foster Your Oneness.* The acknowledgment of God's Oneness is paramount. As the nation that accepts this obligation upon itself, Israel pleads for God's protection (*Iyun Tefillah*).

רַחֲמֵם — *Show them mercy.* According to some

יָחִיד גֵּאֶה לְעַמְּךָ פְּנֵה זוֹכְרֵי קְדֻשָּׁתֶךָ.

‹‹ Your holiness. ‹ those who ‹‹ turn, ‹ to Your ‹ Exalted ‹ Unique
proclaim   people   One,   One,

שַׁוְעָתֵנוּ קַבֵּל וּשְׁמַע צַעֲקָתֵנוּ יוֹדֵעַ תַּעֲלֻמוֹת.

‹‹ of mysteries. ‹ O Knower ‹‹ our cry, ‹ and hear ‹‹ accept, ‹ Our entreaty

בָּרוּךְ שֵׁם כְּבוֹד מַלְכוּתוֹ לְעוֹלָם וָעֶד.

‹‹ and ever. ‹ for ever ‹ kingdom ‹ of His ‹ is the ‹ Blessed
                                      glorious Name

רִבּוֹן הָעוֹלָמִים,* אַתָּה צִוִּיתָנוּ לְהַקְרִיב קָרְבַּן הַתָּמִיד

‹ the continual-offering ‹ to bring ‹ commanded us ‹ You ‹‹ of the worlds,* ‹ Master

בְּמוֹעֲדוֹ, וְלִהְיוֹת כֹּהֲנִים בַּעֲבוֹדָתָם, וּלְוִיִּם בְּדוּכָנָם, וְיִשְׂרָאֵל

‹ and ‹‹ on their ‹ Levites ‹‹ at their assigned ‹ Kohanim ‹ and that ‹‹ at its
Israelites platform,   service,   there be   set time,

בְּמַעֲמָדָם. וְעַתָּה בַּעֲוֹנוֹתֵינוּ חָרַב בֵּית הַמִּקְדָּשׁ וּבָטֵל

‹ and dis- ‹ was the Holy ‹ destroyed ‹‹ through our sins, ‹ But now, ‹‹ at their station.
continued   Temple,

הַתָּמִיד, וְאֵין לָנוּ לֹא כֹהֵן בַּעֲבוֹדָתוֹ, וְלֹא לֵוִי בְּדוּכָנוּ, וְלֹא

‹ nor ‹ on his ‹ Levite ‹ nor ‹ at his service, ‹ Kohen ‹ and we have ‹‹ was the continual-
        platform,   neither   offering;

יִשְׂרָאֵל בְּמַעֲמָדוֹ.* וְאַתָּה אָמַרְתָּ: וּנְשַׁלְּמָה פָרִים שְׂפָתֵינוּ.¹

‹‹ with our lips. ‹ for the ‹ Let us ‹‹ said: ‹ But You ‹‹ at his station.* ‹ Israelite
            bulls   compensate

לָכֵן יְהִי רָצוֹן מִלְּפָנֶיךָ, יהוה אֱלֹהֵינוּ וֵאלֹהֵי אֲבוֹתֵינוּ,

‹‹ of our ‹ and the ‹ our God ‹ HASHEM, ‹‹ before You, ‹ the will ‹ may ‹ There-
forefathers, God   it be   fore,

שֶׁיְּהֵא שִׂיחַ שִׂפְתוֹתֵינוּ חָשׁוּב וּמְקֻבָּל וּמְרֻצֶּה לְפָנֶיךָ, כְּאִלּוּ

‹ as if ‹‹ before ‹ and ‹ acceptable, ‹ worthy, ‹‹ of our lips — ‹ – the ‹‹ that it
        You,   favorable   prayer   be

הִקְרַבְנוּ קָרְבַּן הַתָּמִיד בְּמוֹעֲדוֹ, וְעָמַדְנוּ עַל מַעֲמָדוֹ.

‹‹ its station. ‹ at ‹ and we ‹‹ at its set ‹ the continual-offering ‹ we had
                    had stood   time   brought

---

(1) *Hosea* 14:3.

versions, this phrase reads רַחֲמֵי צִדְקָתֶךְ, *the
mercy of Your righteousness.*

רִבּוֹן הָעוֹלָמִים ‹§ — *Master of the worlds.* We
pray that our recitation of the morning service
be accepted in place of the Temple service that
we are unable to perform. As we say further in

this prayer, "*Let us compensate for the bulls with
our lips.*"

לֹא כֹהֵן בַּעֲבוֹדָתוֹ, וְלֹא לֵוִי בְּדוּכָנוּ, וְלֹא יִשְׂרָאֵל בְּמַעֲמָדוֹ
— *Neither Kohen at his service, nor Levite on his
platform, nor Israelite at his station.* All three
categories of Jews were represented in the daily

ON ROSH CHODESH ADD THE FOLLOWING PARAGRAPH:

וּבְרָאשֵׁי חָדְשֵׁיכֶם תַּקְרִיבוּ עֹלָה לַיהוה, פָּרִים בְּנֵי

On the first [day] / of your months / you shall bring / an elevation-offering / to HASHEM: / bulls, / young ones

בָקָר שְׁנַיִם, וְאַיִל אֶחָד, כְּבָשִׂים בְּנֵי שָׁנָה שִׁבְעָה, תְּמִימִם.

of the herd / – two; / one ram, / male / lambs / in / their year / first, / – seven, / unblemished.

וּשְׁלֹשָׁה עֶשְׂרֹנִים סֹלֶת מִנְחָה בְּלוּלָה בַשֶּׁמֶן לַפָּר הָאֶחָד,

And three / tenths [of an ephah] / of fine flour / for a meal-offering / mixed / with [olive] oil / for each bull;

וּשְׁנֵי עֶשְׂרֹנִים סֹלֶת מִנְחָה בְּלוּלָה בַשֶּׁמֶן לָאַיִל הָאֶחָד.

and two / tenths [of an ephah] / of fine flour / for a meal-offering / mixed / with [olive] oil / for the single ram.

וְעִשָּׂרֹן עִשָּׂרוֹן, סֹלֶת מִנְחָה בְּלוּלָה בַשֶּׁמֶן לַכֶּבֶשׂ הָאֶחָד,

And a tenth [of an ephah] each / of fine flour / for a meal-offering / mixed / with [olive] oil / for each lamb

עֹלָה רֵיחַ נִיחֹחַ, אִשֶּׁה לַיהוה. וְנִסְכֵּיהֶם – חֲצִי הַהִין

an elevation-offering, / that is / a satisfying, aroma / a fire-offering / to HASHEM. / And their libations / – a half / of a hin

יִהְיֶה לַפָּר, וּשְׁלִישִׁת הַהִין לָאַיִל, וּרְבִיעִת הַהִין לַכֶּבֶשׂ –

shall be / for a bull, / a third / of a hin / for the ram, / and a quarter / of a hin / for a lamb –

יָיִן; זֹאת עֹלַת חֹדֶשׁ בְּחָדְשׁוֹ לְחָדְשֵׁי הַשָּׁנָה. וּשְׂעִיר עִזִּים

– of wine. / This / is / the elevation-offering / month / upon its renewal, / for the months / of the year. / And a / male / of the goats

אֶחָד לְחַטָּאת לַיהוה, עַל עֹלַת הַתָּמִיד יֵעָשֶׂה, וְנִסְכּוֹ.¹

– one, / for a sin-offering / to HASHEM, / in addition to / the continual elevation-offering / shall it be made, / and its libation.

(1) *Numbers* 28:11-15.

communal service. The *Kohanim* performed the service, Levites stood on a platform to sing the psalm of the day (see p. 232), and the rest of the nation had delegates who recited special prayers and Scriptural passages.

◆§ Mussaf / Additional Offerings

On the Sabbath, Festivals, and Rosh Chodesh, the *mussaf* (additional) offerings are brought in addition to the regular *tamid*-offering. As noted above, all elevation- and peace-offerings are ac-

Animal offering	Volume of Meal			Volume of Wine-Libation		
	Biblical	eggs	fluid oz.	Biblical	eggs	fluid oz.
פַּר, *Bull*	3 tenth-*ephahs*	129.6	220.3	$\frac{1}{2}$ *hin*	36	61.2
אַיִל, *Ram*	2 tenth-*ephahs*	86.4	146.9	$\frac{1}{3}$ *hin*	24	40.8
כֶּבֶשׂ, *Yearling Lamb*	1 tenth-*ephah*	43.2	73.4	$\frac{1}{4}$ *hin*	18	30.6

——— Mishnah, *Zevachim* Chapter 5 / משנה, זבחים פרק ה ———

[א] אֵיזֶהוּ מְקוֹמָן* שֶׁל זְבָחִים. קָדְשֵׁי קָדָשִׁים*

| ‹‹ of the holy offerings,* ‹ The holiest ‹‹ the offerings? ‹ of ‹ the location* ‹ What is [1] |

שְׁחִיטָתָן בַּצָּפוֹן.* פַּר וְשָׂעִיר שֶׁל יוֹם הַכִּפּוּרִים

‹‹ Yom Kippur ‹ of ‹ and the he-goat ‹ The bull ‹‹ is in the north.* ‹ their slaughter

שְׁחִיטָתָן בַּצָּפוֹן, וְקִבּוּל דָּמָן בִּכְלִי שָׁרֵת בַּצָּפוֹן.

‹‹ is in the north. ‹ of service ‹ in a vessel ‹ of their blood ‹ and the reception ‹ is in the north ‹ – their slaughter

וְדָמָן טָעוּן הַזָּיָה עַל בֵּין הַבַּדִּים,* וְעַל הַפָּרֹכֶת,*

‹‹ the Curtain [of the Holy of Holies]* ‹ and toward ‹‹ the poles [of the Holy Ark],* ‹ the area between ‹ upon ‹ sprinkling ‹ requires ‹ Their blood

---

companied by meal-offerings [consisting of meal mixed with olive oil] and wine-libations. The amount of oil used for each meal-offering is the same as the amount of wine used for the libation.

It should be noted that the Talmud gives the various measurements in terms of the volume of an average egg. We base our conversions on the minimal authoritative opinion, which estimates the volume of the Talmudic "egg" at 1.7 fluid ounces. Other authoritative estimates range to as much as twice this figure.

אֵיזֶהוּ מְקוֹמָן / **What Is the Location**

The Talmud (*Kiddushin* 30a) teaches that one should study Scripture, Mishnah [the compilation of laws], and Gemara [the explanation of the laws] every day. In fulfillment of that injunction, the Sages instituted that passages from each of these three categories be included here. Since Scriptural passages regarding the Temple offerings are part of the service in any case, they chose a chapter of the Mishnah on the same subject. Chapter 5 of *Zevachim* was chosen for three reasons: (a) It discusses all the sacrifices; (b) it is the only chapter in the Mishnah in which there is no halachic dispute; and (c) its text is of very ancient origin, possibly even from the days of Moses.

1. אֵיזֶהוּ מְקוֹמָן — *What is the location* ... in the Courtyard where various categories of animal offerings were slaughtered and the part of the

Altar upon which their blood was placed.

קָדְשֵׁי קָדָשִׁים — *The holiest of the holy offerings.* This refers to sin- [חַטָּאוֹת], guilt- [אֲשָׁמוֹת], elevation- [עוֹלוֹת], and communal peace- [זִבְחֵי שַׁלְמֵי צִבּוּר] offerings. They have stricter laws than individual peace- [שְׁלָמִים] and thanksgiv- ing- [תּוֹדָה] offerings [see below, 6-8], which are called "offerings of holiness of a lesser degree" [קָדָשִׁים קַלִּים]. Among the stricter laws involving the holiest of the holy offerings are that they must be eaten in, and may not be removed from, the Temple Courtyard; and that anyone who makes personal use of the parts to be burned on the Altar [מוֹעֵל בְּהֶקְדֵּשׁ], even before their blood is sprinkled, must undergo a procedure of atonement. Offerings of a lesser degree of holiness, on the other hand, may be eaten and taken anywhere within the walls of Jerusalem, and one who makes personal use of the parts to be burned on the Altar requires atonement only if he does so after the blood has been sprinkled.

בַּצָּפוֹן — *In the north* of the Altar.

עַל בֵּין הַבַּדִּים — *Upon the area between the poles [of the Holy Ark].* On Yom Kippur, the *Kohen Gadol* brought blood into the Holy of Holies and sprinkled part of it toward the Holy Ark, between the two poles of the Ark that extended from either side of it toward the Sanctuary.

וְעַל הַפָּרֹכֶת — *And toward the Curtain,* that

וְעַל מִזְבַּח הַזָּהָב.* מַתָּנָה אַחַת מֵהֶן מְעַכֶּבֶת.

《 prevents 〈 of 〈 [The omission of even] 《 of gold.* 〈 the Altar 〈 and
[atonement]. these one application [of blood] upon

שִׁיְרֵי הַדָּם הָיָה שׁוֹפֵךְ עַל יְסוֹד מַעֲרָבִי שֶׁל

〈 of 〈 the western base 〈 onto 〈 pour 〈 he would 〈 blood 〈 The leftover

מִזְבֵּחַ הַחִיצוֹן; אִם לֹא נָתַן, לֹא עִכֵּב.

《 he has not prevented 《 but if he did not apply [the 《 outside; 〈 the Altar
[atonement]. leftover blood to the base],

[כב] **פָּרִים** הַנִּשְׂרָפִים* וּשְׂעִירִים הַנִּשְׂרָפִים*

《 that are completely 〈 and he-goats 〈 that are completely 〈 The bulls [2]
burned* burned*

שְׁחִיטָתָן בַּצָּפוֹן, וְקִבּוּל דָּמָן בִּכְלֵי שָׁרֵת בַּצָּפוֹן.

《 is in the 〈 of 〈 in a 〈 of their 〈 and the 〈 is in the 〈 —their slaughter
north. service vessel blood reception north,

וְדָמָן טָעוּן הַזָּיָה עַל הַפָּרֹכֶת וְעַל מִזְבַּח הַזָּהָב.

《 of Gold. 〈 the Altar 〈 and 〈 the Curtain 〈 toward 〈 sprinkling 〈 requires 〈 Their
upon blood

מַתָּנָה אַחַת מֵהֶן מְעַכֶּבֶת. שִׁיְרֵי הַדָּם הָיָה שׁוֹפֵךְ

〈 pour 〈 he 〈 blood 〈 The 《 prevents 〈 of 〈 [The omission of even]
would leftover [atonement]. them one application [of blood]

עַל יְסוֹד מַעֲרָבִי שֶׁל מִזְבֵּחַ הַחִיצוֹן; אִם לֹא נָתַן,

《 but if he did not 《 outside; 〈 the Altar 〈 of 〈 the western base 〈 onto
apply [the leftover
blood to the base],

---

separated the Holy of Holies from the Sanctuary. Toward this Curtain, too, the *Kohen Gadol* sprinkled the blood.

מִזְבַּח הַזָּהָב — *The Altar of gold*, upon which the incense was burned every day. See above p. 53.

2. פָּרִים הַנִּשְׂרָפִים — *The bulls that are completely burned.* Certain parts (see *Leviticus* 4:8-12) of the animal are placed upon the Altar-pyre to be consumed by the fire. The remainder of the animal is burned outside of Jerusalem (see below).

With the exception of the Yom Kippur sacrifices, only two kinds of bull offerings are completely burned, no part of them being eaten by the *Kohanim*. They are (a) פַּר הֶעְלֵם דָּבָר שֶׁל צִבּוּר, the bull brought if the Sanhedrin (highest court) erred in a halachic ruling, and, as a result of following that ruling, most of the people violated a commandment for which, if the sin had been committed intentionally, the penalty would be כָּרֵת, *spiritual excision;* (b) פַּר כֹּהֵן מָשִׁיחַ, the bull brought by the *Kohen Gadol* if he made an erroneous halachic decision regarding the above type of sin and he himself acted on this ruling.

שְׂעִירִים הַנִּשְׂרָפִים — *He-goats that are completely*

לֹא עִכֵּב. אֵלּוּ וָאֵלּוּ נִשְׂרָפִין בְּבֵית הַדֶּשֶׁן.*

he has not prevented [atonement]. Both these and those [the Yom Kippur offerings] are burned in the place where the Altar ashes [are deposited].*

[ג] **חַטֹּאת** הַצִּבּוּר וְהַיָּחִיד* — אֵלּוּ הֵן

[3] Sin-offerings of the community and of the individual* — these are

חַטֹּאת הַצִּבּוּר: שְׂעִירֵי רָאשֵׁי חֳדָשִׁים וְשֶׁל

the sin-offerings of the community: the he-goats of Rosh Chodesh and of

מוֹעֲדוֹת — שְׁחִיטָתָן בַּצָּפוֹן, וְקִבּוּל דָּמָן בִּכְלִי

the Festivals — their slaughter is in the north, and the reception of their blood in a vessel

שָׁרֵת בַּצָּפוֹן. וְדָמָן טָעוּן אַרְבַּע מַתָּנוֹת עַל

of service is in the north. Their blood requires four applications, on [one]

אַרְבַּע קְרָנוֹת. כֵּיצַד, עָלָה בַכֶּבֶשׁ, וּפָנָה לַסּוֹבֵב*

[each of] the four corners [of the Altar]. How is it done? [The Kohen] ascended the ramp, turned to the surrounding ledge*

וּבָא לוֹ לְקֶרֶן דְּרוֹמִית מִזְרָחִית, מִזְרָחִית

and arrived at the corner which is south-east, east,

צְפוֹנִית, צְפוֹנִית מַעֲרָבִית, מַעֲרָבִית דְּרוֹמִית.

north [corner], the north-west [corner], west [corner], and the west-south [corner].

---

burned. If the Sanhedrin erroneously permitted an act that was a violation of the laws against idol worship, and a majority of the community followed their ruling, their atonement consists of a communal sin-offering — a he-goat that is completely burned.

נִשְׂרָפִין בְּבֵית הַדֶּשֶׁן — *Are burned in the place where the Altar ashes [are deposited].* The excess ashes from the Altar were removed whenever necessary to a ritually clean place outside of Jerusalem. The offerings mentioned in this mishnah and also the offerings of Yom Kippur were burned in that place.

3. חַטֹּאת הַצִּבּוּר וְהַיָּחִיד — *Sin-offerings of the community and of the individual.* Before giving the laws of sin-offerings, the mishnah lists the kinds of communal sin-offerings that fall under this category. The listing is necessary, because the earlier mishnahs, too, have discussed communal sin-offerings, but they fell under the special category of offerings that were completely burned.

וּפָנָה לַסּוֹבֵב — *Turned to the surrounding ledge.* The Altar was ten cubits high. Six cubits above

שִׁיֵרֵי הַדָּם הָיָה שׁוֹפֵךְ עַל יְסוֹד דְּרוֹמִי. וְנֶאֱכָלִין

‹ They are eaten ‹‹ the southern base. ‹ onto ‹ pour ‹ he would ‹ blood ‹ The leftover

לִפְנִים מִן הַקְּלָעִים,* לִזְכְרֵי כְהֻנָּה, בְּכָל מַאֲכָל,

‹‹ of preparation, ‹ in any manner ‹‹ of the priesthood, ‹ by males ‹‹ the [Courtyard] curtains,* ‹ of ‹ inside

לְיוֹם וָלַיְלָה, עַד חֲצוֹת.*

‹‹ midnight.* ‹ until ‹ and on the [following] night ‹ on the day [of offering]

SOME ADD THE FOLLOWING:

יְהִי רָצוֹן מִלְּפָנֶיךָ, יהוה אֱלֹהֵינוּ וֵאלֹהֵי אֲבוֹתֵינוּ, אִם נִתְחַיַּבְתִּי

‹ I am obligated to bring ‹ that ‹‹ of our forefathers, ‹ and the God ‹ our God ‹ HASHEM, ‹‹ before You, ‹ the ‹ May it be will

חַטָּאת שֶׁתְּהֵא אֲמִירָה זוֹ מְרוּצָה לְפָנֶיךָ כְּאִלּוּ הִקְרַבְתִּי חַטָּאת.

‹‹ a sin-offering. ‹ I have brought ‹ as if ‹‹ before You, ‹ accepted ‹‹ favorably ‹ – this recitation – ‹ that it should be ‹‹ a sin-offering,

[ד] **הָעוֹלָה** קֹדֶשׁ קָדָשִׁים. שְׁחִיטָתָהּ בַּצָּפוֹן,

‹ is in the north ‹ Its slaughter ‹‹ of the holy offerings. ‹ is among the holiest ‹ The elevation-offering ‹ [4]

וְקִבּוּל דָּמָהּ בִּכְלִי שָׁרֵת בַּצָּפוֹן. וְדָמָהּ טָעוּן שְׁתֵּי

‹ two ‹ requires ‹ Its blood ‹‹ is in the north. ‹ of service ‹ in a vessel ‹ of its blood ‹ and the reception

---

the ground, a one-cubit-wide ledge went completely around the Altar. The walls ascended another three cubits to the Altar top upon which the pyres (see p. 48) burned. In the square cubit located at each corner of the Altar top, the walls rose an additional cubit. These four protrusions were called קַרְנוֹת הַמִּזְבֵּחַ, *the "corners" of the Altar*. The blood of the sin-offerings was placed on these "corners" or the area below them, on the upper half of the Altar. In order to reach this area, the *Kohen* walked around the Altar on the surrounding ledge, with the utensil containing the blood. He stopped at each corner of the Altar, dipped his right index finger into the utensil containing the blood, deposited the blood, and would then go on to the next corner.

וְנֶאֱכָלִין לִפְנִים מִן הַקְּלָעִים — *They are eaten inside of the [Courtyard] curtains*. After the specified fats are removed to be burned on the Altar, the flesh of the sin-offerings is distributed to be eaten by male *Kohanim*. It could be prepared and eaten only within the Temple Courtyard. The term "curtains" is borrowed from the period in the Wilderness, when the Tabernacle Courtyard was enclosed not by walls, but by curtains.

עַד חֲצוֹת — *Until midnight*. A sin-offering could be eaten for the remainder of the day on which it was sacrificed and for the following evening. Under Scriptural law it could be eaten until dawn, but the Sages imposed a deadline of midnight to prevent a transgression.

מַתָּנוֹת שֶׁהֵן אַרְבַּע;* וּטְעוּנָה הַפְּשֵׁט* וְנִתּוּחַ,*

<< and dis- < flaying* < It requires << that are equivalent < applications
memberment,*   to four.*

וְכָלִיל לָאִשִּׁים.

<< by the fire. < and it is entirely
consumed

SOME ADD THE FOLLOWING:

יְהִי רָצוֹן, כְּאִלּוּ הִקְרַבְתִּי עוֹלָה.

<< an elevation < I have < as if < [Your] < May
offering.   brought   will   it be

[ה] זִבְחֵי שַׁלְמֵי צִבּוּר* וַאֲשָׁמוֹת,* אֵלּוּ הֵן

< are <— these << and guilt- < of the < of peace- < Sacrifices [5]
offerings* community* offerings

אֲשָׁמוֹת: אֲשַׁם גְּזֵלוֹת,* אֲשַׁם מְעִילוֹת,* אֲשַׁם

< the guilt- << for misuse of < the guilt- << for < the guilt- << the guilt-
offering   sacred objects*   offering   thefts,* offering   offerings:

שִׁפְחָה חֲרוּפָה,* אֲשַׁם נָזִיר,* אֲשַׁם מְצוֹרָע,*

<< of a metzora,* < the guilt- << of a < the guilt- << who was < [for violating]
offering   Nazirite,* offering   betrothed,*   a maidservant

---

4. שְׁתֵּי מַתָּנוֹת שֶׁהֵן אַרְבַּע — *Two applications that are equivalent to four.* As explained above in the chapter of the *tamid*, p. 50, blood was thrown from the service-vessel at the northeast and the southwest corners of the Altar. The blood would spread out to the two adjacent walls. Thus, the two applications of blood would result in blood on all four walls of the Altar.

הַפְּשֵׁט — *Flaying.* The hide of offerings of greater holiness (other than those discussed in mishnah 2) was removed and given to the *Kohanim.*

וְנִתּוּחַ — *And dismemberment.* The elevation-offering was cut up in a prescribed way; only then was it completely burned.

5. זִבְחֵי שַׁלְמֵי צִבּוּר — *Sacrifices of peace-offerings of the community.* The only such offerings are the two sheep that are brought in addition to the Shavuos *mussaf*-offering [Leviticus 23:19]. The other communal offerings are either sin- or elevation-offerings.

אֲשָׁמוֹת — *Guilt-offerings.* There are six kinds of

guilt-offerings, all of which are listed in this mishnah. They are:

(a) אֲשַׁם גְּזֵלוֹת — *... for thefts.* If someone owed money — whether a loan, a theft, an article held in safekeeping, or whatever — and intentionally swore falsely that he did not owe it, he is required to bring a guilt-offering as an atonement. See *Leviticus* 5:20-26.

(b) אֲשַׁם מְעִילוֹת — *... for misuse of sacred objects.* If someone unintentionally used objects belonging to the Sanctuary for his personal benefit he must atone by bringing a guilt-offering. See ibid. 5:14-16.

(c) אֲשַׁם שִׁפְחָה חֲרוּפָה — *... [for violating] a maidservant who was betrothed.* The woman involved was a non-Jewish slave who had been owned by two Jewish partners. One of the partners freed her, thus making her half free and half slave. But since a freed non-Jewish slave has the same status as a proselyte, this half-free maidservant is half Jewish and half non-Jewish and is forbidden to marry either a

אָשָׁם תָּלוּי.* שְׁחִיטָתָן בַּצָּפוֹן, וְקִבּוּל דָּמָן בִּכְלִי

⟨ in a ⟨ of their ⟨ and the ⟨ is in the ⟨ — their slaughter ⟨⟨ in case ⟨ and the guilt-
vessel　blood　reception　north　　　　　　　　　of doubt*　offering

שָׁרֵת בַּצָּפוֹן, וְדָמָן טָעוּן שְׁתֵּי מַתָּנוֹת שֶׁהֵן

⟨ that are ⟨ applications ⟨ two ⟨ requires ⟨ Their ⟨⟨ is in the ⟨ of service
equivalent to　　　　　　　　　　blood　　north.

אַרְבַּע. וְנֶאֱכָלִין לִפְנִים מִן הַקְּלָעִים לִזְכְרֵי

⟨ by males ⟨⟨ the [Courtyard] ⟨ of ⟨ inside ⟨ They are eaten ⟨⟨ four.
curtains,

כְהֻנָּה, בְּכָל מַאֲכָל, לְיוֹם וָלַיְלָה, עַד חֲצוֹת.

⟨⟨ midnight. ⟨ until ⟨ and on the ⟨ on the day ⟨⟨ of ⟨ in any ⟨⟨ of the
[following] night　[of offering]　preparation,　manner　priesthood,

SOME ADD THE FOLLOWING:

יְהִי רָצוֹן מִלְּפָנֶיךָ, יהוה אֱלֹהֵינוּ וֵאלֹהֵי אֲבוֹתֵינוּ, אִם נִתְחַיַּבְתִּי

⟨ I am obli- ⟨ that ⟨⟨ of our ⟨ and the ⟨ our God ⟨ HASHEM, ⟨⟨ before You, ⟨ the ⟨ May
gated to bring　if　forefathers,　God　　　　　　　　　　　　　will　it be

אָשָׁם שֶׁתְּהֵא אֲמִירָה זוֹ מְרוּצָה לְפָנֶיךָ כְּאִלּוּ הִקְרַבְתִּי אָשָׁם.

⟨⟨ a guilt- ⟨ I have ⟨ as if ⟨⟨ before ⟨ accepted ⟨⟨ – this ⟨ that it ⟨ a guilt-
offering.　brought　　　　　You,　favorably　recitation –　should be　offering,

[ו] הַתּוֹדָה* וְאֵיל נָזִיר* קָדְשִׁים קַלִּים.*

⟨⟨ of a lesser ⟨ are offerings ⟨ of a ⟨ and the ⟨ The thanksgiving- [6]
degree.*　of holiness　Nazirite*　ram　offering*

non-Jew or a Jew. She is, however, permitted to a Jewish indentured servant [עֶבֶד עִבְרִי], who is permitted to both a Jewish woman and a non-Jewish maidservant. If she became betrothed to a Jewish indentured servant and then had relations with another man, the adulterer must bring a guilt-offering in atonement.

(d) אֲשַׁם נָזִיר — . . . of a Nazirite, who became טָמֵא, ritually contaminated, through contact with a corpse. See Numbers 6:9-12.

(e) אֲשַׁם מְצוֹרָע — . . . of a metzora. One afflicted by the leprouslike disease described in Leviticus (Ch. 13) regains his complete ritual purity upon bringing a series of offerings after he is cured. The guilt-offering is brought on the eighth day after he is pronounced cured. See Leviticus 14:10-12.

(f) אֲשָׁם תָּלוּי — . . . in case of doubt. This is the only guilt-offering not prescribed for a specific offense or phenomenon. It is required whenever there is a question of whether one has become liable to bring a חַטָּאת, sin-offering. As long as such a doubt exists, the possible transgressor can protect himself from punishment by bringing a guilt-offering. However, if and when it becomes established that the offense was indeed committed, he must bring his sin-offering. See Leviticus 5:17-19.

6. הַתּוֹדָה — The thanksgiving-offering. This offering is brought by someone who survives major danger or illness. See ibid. 7:12.

אֵיל נָזִיר — Ram of a Nazirite, which is brought when a Nazirite completes his period of abstinence. See Numbers 6:13-21.

קָדְשִׁים קַלִּים — Offerings of holiness of a lesser

שְׁחִיטָתָן בְּכָל מָקוֹם בָּעֲזָרָה, וְדָמָן טָעוּן שְׁתֵּי

‹ two ‹ requires ‹ and their blood ‹ in the Courtyard, ‹ place ‹ is in any ‹ Their slaughter

מַתָּנוֹת שֶׁהֵן אַרְבַּע. וְנֶאֱכָלִין בְּכָל הָעִיר, לְכָל

‹ by any ‹‹ the City [of Jerusalem] ‹ throughout ‹ They are eaten ‹‹ that are equivalent to four. ‹ applications

אָדָם, בְּכָל מַאֲכָל, לְיוֹם וָלַיְלָה, עַד חֲצוֹת.

‹‹ midnight. ‹ until ‹ and on the [following] night ‹ on the day [of offering] ‹‹ of ‹ in any manner ‹‹ person,

הַמּוּרָם מֵהֶם* כַּיּוֹצֵא בָהֶם, אֶלָּא שֶׁהַמּוּרָם

‹ the separated portion ‹ except that ‹‹ like ‹ is to be treated ‹ from them* ‹ The [priestly] portion separated

נֶאֱכָל לַכֹּהֲנִים, לִנְשֵׁיהֶם וְלִבְנֵיהֶם וּלְעַבְדֵיהֶם.

‹‹ and by their slaves. ‹ by their children, ‹ by their wives, ‹ [only] by the Kohanim, ‹ may be eaten

SOME ADD THE FOLLOWING:

יְהִי רָצוֹן, כְּאִלּוּ הִקְרַבְתִּי תוֹדָה.

‹‹ a thanksgiving-offering. ‹ I have brought ‹ as if ‹ [Your] will ‹ May it be

[ז] **שְׁלָמִים*** קָדָשִׁים קַלִּים. שְׁחִיטָתָן בְּכָל

‹ is in any ‹ Their slaughter ‹‹ of a lesser degree. ‹ are offerings of holiness ‹ The peace-offerings* [7]

מָקוֹם בָּעֲזָרָה, וְדָמָן טָעוּן שְׁתֵּי מַתָּנוֹת שֶׁהֵן

‹ that are equivalent to ‹ applications ‹ two ‹ requires ‹ and their blood ‹‹ in the Courtyard, ‹ place

אַרְבַּע. וְנֶאֱכָלִין בְּכָל הָעִיר, לְכָל אָדָם, בְּכָל

‹ in any manner ‹‹ person, ‹ by any ‹‹ the City [of Jerusalem] ‹ throughout ‹ They are eaten ‹‹ four.

---

degree. Their greater leniency is obvious from a comparison of the laws in this mishnah with those above.

הַמּוּרָם מֵהֶם — *The [priestly] portion separated from them.* In the case of most "offerings of lesser holiness," the *Kohen's* portion consists of

the breast and right thigh before they are cooked. In the case of the Nazirite's ram, he also receives the cooked right foreleg.

7. שְׁלָמִים — *Peace-offerings.* The peace-offerings may be eaten for *two* days and the intervening night, while thanksgiving-offerings

מַאֲכָל, לִשְׁנֵי יָמִים וְלַיְלָה אֶחָד. הַמּוּרָם מֵהֶם

of preparation, · for two · days · and the one [intervening] night. · The [priestly] portion separated · from them

כַּיּוֹצֵא בָהֶם, אֶלָּא שֶׁהַמּוּרָם נֶאֱכָל לַכֹּהֲנִים,

is to be treated · like them, · except that · the separated portion · may be · eaten · [only] by the Kohanim,

לִנְשֵׁיהֶם וְלִבְנֵיהֶם וּלְעַבְדֵיהֶם.

by their wives, · by their children, · and by their slaves.

SOME ADD THE FOLLOWING:

יְהִי רָצוֹן, כְּאִלּוּ הִקְרַבְתִּי שְׁלָמִים.

May it be · [Your] will · as if · I have brought · a peace-offering.

[ח] הַבְּכוֹר וְהַמַּעֲשֵׂר וְהַפֶּסַח קָדָשִׁים

[8] The firstborn, · the tithe of animals, · and the pesach-offering · are offerings of holiness

קַלִּים. שְׁחִיטָתָן בְּכָל מָקוֹם בָּעֲזָרָה, וְדָמָן טָעוּן

of a lesser degree: · Their slaughter · is in any · place · in the Courtyard, · and their blood · requires

מַתָּנָה אֶחָת,* וּבִלְבַד שֶׁיִּתֵּן כְּנֶגֶד הַיְסוֹד. שָׁנָה

a single application,* · provided · he applies it · above · the base. · They differ

בַּאֲכִילָתָן: הַבְּכוֹר נֶאֱכָל לַכֹּהֲנִים, וְהַמַּעֲשֵׂר

in their consumption: · The firstborn · is eaten · by Kohanim, · and the tithe

לְכָל אָדָם. וְנֶאֱכָלִין בְּכָל הָעִיר, בְּכָל מַאֲכָל,

by any · person. · They are eaten · throughout · the City [of Jerusalem] · in any manner · of preparation,

---

(mishnah 6) are eaten for only one day and the night that follows.

8. וְדָמָן טָעוּן מַתָּנָה אֶחָת — *Their blood requires a single application.* Unlike all the offerings mentioned above, the offerings mentioned in this mishnah do not require multiple applica-

tions of blood. The יְסוֹד, *base*, is a part of the Altar, one cubit high and one cubit wide, that juts out along the entire lengths of the west and north walls, but is only one cubit long along the lengths of the south and east walls. The blood may be applied only to a part of the Altar wall

לִשְׁנֵי יָמִים וְלַיְלָה אֶחָד. הַפֶּסַח* אֵינוֹ נֶאֱכָל

‹ eaten   ‹ is not   ‹ The *pesach*-offering*   «   and the one [intervening] night.   ‹ days   ‹ for two

אֶלָּא בַלַּיְלָה, וְאֵינוֹ נֶאֱכָל אֶלָּא עַד חֲצוֹת, וְאֵינוֹ

‹ and is not« midnight, ‹ until ‹ except ‹ eaten ‹ and is not « at night, ‹ except

נֶאֱכָל אֶלָּא לִמְנוּיָו,* וְאֵינוֹ נֶאֱכָל אֶלָּא צָלִי.

«roasted. ‹ except ‹ and is not eaten [in any « by those ‹ except ‹ eaten
manner of preparation] registered for it;*

—— *Baraisa DeR' Yishmael* – Introduction to *Sifra* / ברייתא דר' ישמעאל–ספרא, פתיחה ——

רַבִּי יִשְׁמָעֵאל אוֹמֵר: בִּשְׁלֹשׁ עֶשְׂרֵה מִדּוֹת

‹ rules   ‹ Through thirteen   «   says: ‹   Rabbi Yishmael

that is directly above the base.

הַפֶּסַח ... לִמְנוּיָו — *The pesach-offering ... by those registered for it.* Those who eat from a particular *pesach*-offering must have reserved their share in it prior to its slaughter. [See *Exodus* 12:4.] With regard to all other offerings, any qualified person may partake of the flesh.

רַבִּי יִשְׁמָעֵאל / Rabbi Yishmael

As noted above, the Sages prefaced *Shacharis* with selections from Scripture, Mishnah, and Gemara. As used in the Talmud, Mishnah means a listing of laws and Gemara means the logic behind and the application of the laws. As a selection from Gemara, the Sages chose one that presents the thirteen methods used in Scriptural interpretation. This passage is a *baraisa* [literally, *outside*], meaning that it is one of the countless Talmudic teachings that was "left out" of the Mishnah when that basic compendium of laws was formulated. Though not part of the Mishnah, the *baraisos* are authoritative and are cited by the Gemara consistently. Unlike most *baraisos* which are statements of law, this one is a basic introduction to an understanding of the derivation of the laws. It shows us how the very brief statements of the Torah can be "mined" to reveal a host of principles and teachings. This is why such use of these thirteen rules is called דְּרַשׁ, which

implies *investigation* and *seeking out*; we seek to elicit principles and laws from the sometimes cryptic words of the Torah.

This particular *baraisa* is the introduction to *Sifra*, a Midrashic work that exhaustively interprets the Book of *Leviticus*. Since most of *Sifra* is of a halachic nature, it was natural that it be introduced with a listing of the principles of halachic interpretation. And since *Sifra* deals mainly with the Temple service, this *baraisa* is particularly apt for this section of *Shacharis*.

◆§ The Oral Law

The Torah was composed by God according to the rules of logic and textual analysis contained in Rabbi Yishmael's *baraisa*. (These rules are also known as hermeneutic principles.) The oral tradition governs the way in which these rules are applied and we have no authority to use them in a manner that contradicts or is not sanctioned by the Oral Law. Thus, when we speak of Rabbinic exegesis, or the way in which the Torah is expounded, we do not speak of the invention of new laws, but of the means by which the Oral Law was implied in the Torah itself. It should also be noted that the great majority of the laws were handed down for many centuries from teacher to student, and they were well known without a need to search for their Scriptural sources. Consequently, in the

הַתּוֹרָה נִדְרֶשֶׁת בָּהֶן. (א) מִקַּל וָחֹמֶר;

‹ the Torah ‹ is elucidated ‹‹ thereby: ‹‹ (1) through a conclusion inferred from a lenient law to a strict one;

(ב) וּמִגְּזֵרָה שָׁוָה; (ג) מִבִּנְיַן אָב מִכָּתוּב אֶחָד,

‹‹ (2) through tradition that similar words in different contexts are meant to create a connection between the two topics; ‹‹ (3) through [establishing] a general principle from one passage

וּמִבִּנְיַן אָב מִשְּׁנֵי כְתוּבִים; (ד) מִכְּלָל וּפְרָט;

and through establishing a general principle from two passages; ‹‹ (4) through a generalization [limited by] a specification;

Talmudic era when the Sages attempted to set forth the Scriptural derivation of such well-known laws as the use of an *esrog* or the law that an eye for an eye refers to monetary compensation, there were disputes concerning the exact Scriptural interpretations although the laws were familiar.

◈§ The Thirteen Rules

The following is a brief explanation with illustrations of the Thirteen Rules by means of which the Torah is expounded:

(1) קַל וָחֹמֶר. Logic dictates that if a lenient case has a stringency, the same stringency applies to a stricter case. Another way of putting it is that laws can be derived from less obvious situations and applied to more obvious ones. For example, if it is forbidden to pluck an apple from a tree on *Festivals* (when food may be prepared by means that may be prohibited on the Sabbath), surely plucking is forbidden on the *Sabbath*. Conversely, if it is permitted to slice vegetables on the Sabbath, it is surely permitted on Festivals.

(2) גְּזֵרָה שָׁוָה. In strictly limited cases, the Sinaitic tradition teaches that two independent laws or cases are meant to shed light upon one another. The indication that the two laws are complementary can be seen in two ways: (a) The same or similar words appear in both cases, e.g., the word בְּמוֹעֲדוֹ, *in its proper time* (*Numbers* 28:2), is understood to indicate that the daily offering must be brought even on the Sabbath. Similarly, the same word in the context of the *pesach*-offering (ibid. 9:2) should be interpreted to mean that it is offered even if its appointed day, too, falls on the Sabbath (*Pesachim* 66a). (b)

When two different topics are placed next to one another (this is also called הֶיקֵּשׁ, *comparison*), e.g., many laws regarding technical processes of divorce and betrothal are derived from one another because Scripture (*Deuteronomy* 24:2) mentions divorce and betrothal in the same phrase by saying וְיָצְאָה... וְהָיְתָה לְאִישׁ אַחֵר, *she shall depart* [through divorce] ... *and become betrothed to another man*. This juxtaposition implies that the two changes of marital status are accomplished through similar legal processes (*Kiddushin* 5a).

(3) בִּנְיַן אָב... A general principle derived from one passage is applied to all cases that logically appear to be similar. This rule is also known as a מַה מָּצִינוּ, lit. *"what do we find?"* For example, since the Torah specifies that one may not marry even his maternal half-sister, this בִּנְיַן אָב dictates that the prohibition against marrying one's father's sister applies equally to his father's maternal half-sister (*Yevamos* 54b). The same rule applies when two different passages shed light on one another. Similar situations may be derived from the combination of the two passages.

(4) כְּלָל וּפְרָט. When a generality is followed by a specification, the law is applied only to the specification. For example, in listing the animals from which sacrificial offerings may be brought, the Torah says: *From the* [*domestic*] *animals, from the cattle and sheep/goats* (*Leviticus* 1:2). This rule teaches that no animals but cattle and sheep/goats may be used. In such cases the generality [i.e., domestic animals] is mentioned only to teach that no part of the

(ה) וּמִפְּרָט וּכְלָל;   (ו) כְּלָל וּפְרָט וּכְלָל, אִי אַתָּה דָן

⟨ — you may not ⟨⟨ (6) through a generalization [fol- ⟨⟨ (5) through a specification
infer [anything]   lowed by] a specification [followed   [broadened by]
                     by another] generalization   a generalization;

אֶלָּא כְּעֵין הַפְּרָט;   (ז) מִכְּלָל שֶׁהוּא צָרִיךְ לִפְרָט,

⟨⟨   (7) through a generalization that requires   ⟨⟨   except that which is similar
           a specification [to clarify its meaning];   to the specification;

וּמִפְּרָט שֶׁהוּא צָרִיךְ לִכְלָל;   (ח) כָּל דָּבָר שֶׁהָיָה

⟨ (8) any item that was included   ⟨⟨   or a specification that requires a generalization
                                              [to clarify its meaning];

בִּכְלָל וְיָצָא מִן הַכְּלָל לְלַמֵּד, לֹא לְלַמֵּד עַל

⟨ — it is not to teach   ⟨⟨ but was then singled out from the general- ⟨⟨ in a general-
only about   ization in order to teach something   ization,

עַצְמוֹ יָצָא, אֶלָּא לְלַמֵּד עַל הַכְּלָל כֻּלּוֹ יָצָא;

⟨⟨   but to apply its teaching to the generalization   ⟨⟨   itself that it was
           in its entirety that it was singled out;   singled out,

---

general group is included in the law except for the specified items.

(5) פְּרָט וּכְלָל. This is the reverse of the above case. In describing the obligation to return lost objects, the Torah says that one should return: *His donkey . . . his garment . . . any lost object* (*Deuteronomy* 22:3). The concluding generality teaches that there are *no* exceptions to this rule.

(6) . . . כְּלָל וּפְרָט וּכְלָל. The difference between this rule and כְּלָל וּפְרָט (rule 4) is that here the Scriptural phrase is concluded by a general statement. The two general statements imply that everything is included while the specific items in the middle imply that only they are meant. The apparent contradiction is resolved this way: Everything *is* included, provided it is essentially similar to the items specified. For example, in the verse imposing a fine on a thief, there are two general terms — *for any matter of dishonesty* and *for any lost item* — implying that the thief is liable no matter what he has taken. However, sandwiched between these general terms, a number of specific items are mentioned: *an ox . . . or a garment* (*Exodus* 22:8). This teaches that the fine applies to any movable object that has intrinsic value, but *not*

to real estate, which is not movable, or to contracts, which testify to a debt, but have no intrinsic value (*Bava Metzia* 57b).

(7) . . . כְּלָל שֶׁהוּא צָרִיךְ לִפְרָט. This rule tells us that the principles of פְּרָט וּכְלָל and כְּלָל וּפְרָט (numbers 4 and 5 above) do not apply in cases where the introductory general statement or specification requires further clarification for its meaning to be clear. For example, the Torah commands that after slaughtering fowl or nondomesticated kosher animals, וְכִסָּהוּ בֶּעָפָר, *he is to cover [its blood] with earth* (*Leviticus* 17:13). The generalization *to cover* requires clarification because it could be taken to mean that it can be poured into an enclosed pot or covered with wood. Therefore, *with earth* is needed to indicate that the covering must be a soft substance that can easily mix with the blood. Accordingly, it is not a "specification" in the sense of principle 4, but a clarification (*Chullin* 88b).

(8) . . . כָּל דָּבָר שֶׁהָיָה בִּכְלָל וְיָצָא . . . לְלַמֵּד. This principle is best explained by an example. The Torah (*Leviticus* 7:19) forbids the eating of sacrificial meat by anyone who is טָמֵא, *ritually contaminated*. The very next verse singles out

(ט) כָּל דָּבָר שֶׁהָיָה בִכְלָל וְיָצָא לִטְעוֹן טוֹעַן אֶחָד

> but was then singled out to discuss «« (9) any item that was included
a provision of one kind　　　　　　　　　　　　　in a generalization,

שֶׁהוּא כְעִנְיָנוֹ, יָצָא לְהָקֵל וְלֹא לְהַחֲמִיר;

«« was singled out to be more lenient «« that is similar to the
and not to be more stringent;　　　　　　　　　　　　general category,

(י) כָּל דָּבָר שֶׁהָיָה בִכְלָל וְיָצָא לִטְעוֹן טְעַן אַחֵר

> but was then singled out to discuss «« (10) any item that was included
a provision of a different kind,　　　　　　　　　in a general statement,

שֶׁלֹּא כְעִנְיָנוֹ, יָצָא לְהָקֵל וּלְהַחֲמִיר;

«« was singled out both to be «« that is not similar to
more lenient and more stringent;　　　　　　　the general category,

(יא) כָּל דָּבָר שֶׁהָיָה בִכְלָל וְיָצָא לִדּוֹן בַּדָּבָר הֶחָדָשׁ,

«« but was then singled out «« (11) any item that was included
to be treated as a new case,　　　　　　　　in a generalization,

אִי אַתָּה יָכוֹל לְהַחֲזִירוֹ לִכְלָלוֹ, עַד שֶׁיַּחֲזִירֶנּוּ

> unless it is returned «« you are not permitted to return it
to its general statement

---

the שְׁלָמִים, *peace-offering*, and states that a contaminated person who eats of it is liable to כָּרֵת,
spiritual excision. This principle teaches that the
peace-offering is not an exception to the general
rule; rather, the punishment specified for the
peace-offering applies to all offerings.

(9) ... כְּעִנְיָנוֹ ... לִטְעוֹן וְיָצָא ... Again, this
principle requires an example. In imposing the
death penalty on a murderer (*Leviticus* 24:21), the
Torah does not differentiate between premedi-
tated and careless murders. Then the Torah
describes a person who chops wood carelessly
with the result that someone is killed by a flying
piece of wood. Although this case would seem to
require the death penalty discussed earlier, the
Torah requires such a murderer to go into exile.
This principle teaches that he has been singled
out for *lenient* treatment, meaning that his exile is
instead of the death penalty, not in *addition* to it.

(10) ... כְּעִנְיָנוֹ שֶׁלֹּא ... לִטְעוֹן וְיָצָא ... After
describing the laws regulating a Jewish indentured servant (עֶבֶד עִבְרִי) who goes free after six

years of service (*Exodus* 21:1-6), the Torah turns
to a Jewish indentured maidservant — who
should have been included with her male counterpart. Instead, the Torah says of her that her
avenues of going free are entirely unlike those of
the male. This has lenient applications, for she
may go free even before six years of service (upon
the onset of puberty or the death of her master),
and it also has a stringent application, for her
master can betroth her against her will to himself
or to his son (see *Exodus* 21:7-11).

(11) ... לִדּוֹן וְיָצָא ... A *Kohen's* entire family is
permitted to eat *terumah* [the priestly tithe], but
if his daughter marries a non-*Kohen*, she may no
longer eat *terumah* (*Leviticus* 22:11,12). What if
she is widowed or divorced without children and
returns to her father's household? Since marriage
had removed her from the permitted status of the
rest of the family, she would not have been
permitted to eat *terumah* again unless the Torah
had specifically returned her to the family group
(which it did, ibid. 22:13).

הַכָּתוּב לִכְלָלוֹ בְּפֵרוּשׁ; ❖ (יב) דָּבָר הַלָּמֵד מֵעִנְיָנוֹ,

‹‹ (12) a matter elucidated from its context,　‹‹ by Scripture to its generalization explicitly;

וְדָבָר הַלָּמֵד מִסּוֹפוֹ; (יג) וְכֵן שְׁנֵי כְתוּבִים

‹　(13) similarly, two passages　　‹‹　　or a matter elucidated from the passage following it;

הַמַּכְחִישִׁים זֶה אֶת זֶה, עַד שֶׁיָּבוֹא

‹ [cannot be resolved] ‹‹　　　　that contradict one another,
until there comes

הַכָּתוּב הַשְּׁלִישִׁי וְיַכְרִיעַ בֵּינֵיהֶם.

‹‹ and reconciles between them. ‹　　　a third passage

יְהִי רָצוֹן* מִלְּפָנֶיךָ, יהוה אֱלֹהֵינוּ וֵאלֹהֵי

‹ and the God ‹ our God ‹ Hashem, ‹‹ before You, ‹　the will* ‹ May it be

אֲבוֹתֵינוּ, שֶׁיִּבָּנֶה בֵּית הַמִּקְדָּשׁ בִּמְהֵרָה בְיָמֵינוּ,

‹‹ in our days. ‹ speedily ‹ shall the Holy Temple be, ‹ that rebuilt ‹‹ of our forefathers,

וְתֵן חֶלְקֵנוּ בְּתוֹרָתֶךָ.[1] וְשָׁם נַעֲבָדְךָ בְּיִרְאָה כִּימֵי

‹ as in ‹‹ with ‹ may we ‹ and ‹‹ be in Your ‹ our ‹ Grant
days　reverence　serve You　there　　Torah,　portion　that

עוֹלָם וּכְשָׁנִים קַדְמוֹנִיּוֹת.[2]

‹‹ gone by. ‹ and as in years ‹ of old

---

(1) *Ethics of the Fathers* 5:24. (2) *Malachi* 3:4.

(12) דָּבָר הַלָּמֵד מֵעִנְיָנוֹ. In the Ten Commandments, the Torah commands, "*You shall not steal.*" The Sages derive from the context that the theft in question must be a capital offense since the injunction against stealing is preceded by the commandments not to kill and not to commit adultery with a married woman, which are both capital offenses. The only theft for which someone can receive the death penalty is kidnaping a fellow Jew and treating him as a slave. Thus, *You shall not steal* refers to kidnaping.

דָּבָר הַלָּמֵד מִסּוֹפוֹ. Another form of contextual clarification is that which is found in *Leviticus* 14:34,35. First the Torah teaches that a house with a "leprouslike" spot must be torn down. From the end of the passage — which describes the cleansing of the stone, wood, and mortar of the house — we derive that this law applies only to houses made of stone, wood, and mortar.

(13) . . . שְׁנֵי כְתוּבִים. Two verses may seem to be contradictory, until a third verse explains that each of the two has its own application. After being commanded to remove Isaac from the altar, Abraham asked God to explain two contradictory verses. First God said that Isaac would be the forefather of Israel (*Genesis* 21:12) and then He commanded that Abraham slaughter him (ibid. 22:2). God explained that the wording of the command was to *place Isaac on the altar*, but not to *slaughter* him on it (*Midrash* to ibid. v. 12). Thus, there is no contradiction.

§ יְהִי רָצוֹן — *May it be the will.* Having

THE RABBIS' KADDISH / קדיש דרבנן

IN THE PRESENCE OF A *MINYAN*, MOURNERS RECITE קַדִּישׁ דְּרַבָּנָן, THE RABBIS' *KADDISH*.
SEE *LAWS* §121-122. [A TRANSLITERATION OF THIS *KADDISH* APPEARS ON PAGE 880.]

יִתְגַּדַּל וְיִתְקַדַּשׁ שְׁמֵהּ רַבָּא.* (.Cong – אָמֵן.*) בְּעָלְמָא דִי בְרָא

⟨ He ⟨ that ⟨ in the ⟨⟨ (Amen.*) ⟨⟨ that is ⟨ may His ⟨ and be ⟨ Grow exalted
created world great!* – Name sanctified

כִרְעוּתֵהּ,* וְיַמְלִיךְ מַלְכוּתֵהּ, וְיַצְמַח פֻּרְקָנֵהּ וִיקָרֵב מְשִׁיחֵהּ.

⟨⟨ His ⟨ and bring ⟨ His ⟨ and cause ⟨ to His ⟨ and may He ⟨⟨ according
Messiah, near salvation, to sprout kingship, give reign to His will,*

(.Cong – אָמֵן.) בְּחַיֵּיכוֹן* וּבְיוֹמֵיכוֹן וּבְחַיֵּי דְכָל בֵּית יִשְׂרָאֵל,

⟨⟨ of Israel, ⟨ Family ⟨ of the ⟨ and in the ⟨ and in ⟨ in your ⟨⟨ (Amen.)
entire lifetimes your days, lifetimes*

בַּעֲגָלָא וּבִזְמַן קָרִיב.* וְאִמְרוּ: אָמֵן.

⟨⟨ Amen. ⟨ Now ⟨⟨ that comes ⟨ and at ⟨ swiftly
respond: soon.* a time

---

substituted the laws of the offerings for the actual Temple service, we pray that we may soon be able to offer them in the rebuilt Temple.

קַדִּישׁ דְּרַבָּנָן / The Rabbis' Kaddish ⧉

"Whenever ten or more Israelites engage in the study of the Oral Law — for example, Mishnah, Halachah, and even Midrash or Aggadah — one of them recites the Rabbis' *Kaddish* [upon conclusion of the study]" (*Rambam, Nusach HaKaddish*). Many commentators maintain that it is recited only after Midrashic material or Scriptural exegesis. *Magen Avraham*, therefore, rules that unless Scriptural verses have been expounded upon, as in the above section of *Shacharis*, a brief Aggadic passage should be taught after halachic study in order that this *Kaddish* may be recited. It has become customary in most communities for this *Kaddish* to be recited by mourners.

[A full commentary and Overview appear in the ArtScroll *Kaddish*.]

יִתְגַּדַּל וְיִתְקַדַּשׁ שְׁמֵהּ רַבָּא — *Grow exalted and be sanctified may His Name that is great!* The ultimate sanctification of God's Name will come when Israel is redeemed; in this sense *Kaddish* is a plea for the final Redemption. It is also an expression of Israel's mission to bring recognition of His sovereignty primarily upon the community as a whole, and *Kaddish* is therefore recited only in the presence of a *minyan* [a quorum of ten males over *bar mitzvah*] (R' Munk).

אָמֵן — *Amen.* The word אָמֵן, *Amen*, is the congregant's affirmation that he believes in what the reader has just said. It is derived from the same root as אֱמוּנָה, *faithfulness* (Tur, Orach Chaim 124). Additionally, it stands for אֵל מֶלֶךְ נֶאֱמָן, *God, the King Who is trustworthy* (Shabbos 119b).

בְּעָלְמָא דִי בְרָא כִרְעוּתֵהּ — *In the world that He created according to His will.* God had His concept of a perfect world before He began creation. Then He began to create in accordance with His prior will (Ran). Or it refers to the *future.* Only then will mankind function in accordance with God's original intention (R' Yehudah ben Yakar).

בְּחַיֵּיכוֹן — *In your lifetimes.* The one reciting the *Kaddish* expresses the hope that his fellow congregants may all live to witness the Redemption of Israel and the sanctification of God's Name (Abudraham).

בַּעֲגָלָא וּבִזְמַן קָרִיב — *Swiftly and at a time that comes soon.* May the travail preceding the Messianic epoch be over *swiftly* and not be drawn out; and may it begin very soon (Aruch HaShulchan).

CONGREGATION RESPONDS:

אָמֵן. יְהֵא שְׁמֵהּ רַבָּא* מְבָרַךְ לְעָלַם וּלְעָלְמֵי עָלְמַיָּא.

《 and for all eternity. 〈 forever 〈 be blessed 〈 that is great* 〈 His Name 〈 May 《 Amen.

MOURNER CONTINUES:

יְהֵא שְׁמֵהּ רַבָּא מְבָרַךְ לְעָלַם וּלְעָלְמֵי עָלְמַיָּא. יִתְבָּרַךְ*

〈 Blessed,* 《 and for all eternity. 〈 forever 〈 be blessed 〈 that is great 〈 His Name 〈 May

וְיִשְׁתַּבַּח וְיִתְפָּאַר וְיִתְרוֹמַם וְיִתְנַשֵּׂא וְיִתְהַדָּר וְיִתְעַלֶּה

〈 elevated, 〈 honored, 〈 upraised, 〈 exalted, 〈 glorified, 〈 praised,

וְיִתְהַלָּל שְׁמֵהּ דְּקֻדְשָׁא בְּרִיךְ הוּא (.Cong— בְּרִיךְ הוּא) —

《 is He) 〈 (Blessed 《 is He 〈 Blessed 〈 of the Holy One, 〈 be the Name 〈 and lauded

ROSH HASHANAH TO YOM KIPPUR SUBSTITUTE:

°לְעֵלָּא מִן כָּל [°לְעֵלָּא (וּ)לְעֵלָּא* מִכָּל] בִּרְכָתָא*

〈 blessing* 〈 any 〈 exceedingly beyond* 〈 any 〈 beyond

וְשִׁירָתָא תֻּשְׁבְּחָתָא וְנֶחֱמָתָא דַּאֲמִירָן בְּעָלְמָא.

《 in the world. 〈 that are uttered 〈 and consolation 〈 praise 《 and song,

וְאִמְרוּ: אָמֵן. (.Cong–אָמֵן.)

《 (Amen.) 《 Amen. 〈 Now respond:

יְהֵא שְׁמֵהּ רַבָּא — *May His Name that is great* ... The Talmud stresses in several places that the response, יְהֵא שְׁמֵהּ רַבָּא, *May His Name that is great* ..., has an enormous cosmic effect. Indeed, the halachah states that an opportunity to respond to *Kaddish* takes precedence over an opportunity to respond to any other prayer, even *Kedushah* and *Borchu*. Consequently, if *Kaddish* is about to be recited in one room and *Kedushah* in another, one should go to hear *Kaddish* (*Mishnah Berurah* 56:6).

The Talmud (*Shabbos* 19b) teaches that one must respond יְהֵא שְׁמֵהּ רַבָּא ''with all his power,'' meaning his total concentration (*Rashi, Tosafos*). Though it is preferable to raise one's voice when saying it, one should not say it so loudly that he will invite ridicule (*R' Yonah*). And it must be enunciated clearly (*Maharal*).

יִתְבָּרַךְ — *Blessed.* This begins a series of praises that continue the central theme of *Kaddish:* In time to come God's greatness will be acknowl-

edged by all of mankind (*Emek Berachah*).

לְעֵלָּא מִן כָּל בִּרְכָתָא — *Beyond any blessing.* No words or ideas can praise God adequately.

לְעֵלָּא וּלְעֵלָּא — *Exceedingly beyond* [lit. *beyond and beyond*]. During עֲשֶׂרֶת יְמֵי תְּשׁוּבָה, *the Ten Days of Repentance* [from Rosh Hashanah to Yom Kippur], the word לְעֵלָּא is repeated to stress that God's majesty is even more pronounced during this period of judgment than it is all year round. The two words מִן כָּל are contracted into the single word מִכָּל. This is done to keep the total number of words in this section of *Kaddish* at twenty-eight, the number of human experiences listed in *Ecclesiastes* 3:2-8: *A time to be born and a time to die . . . a time for war and a time for peace.* The underlying theme is that in every stage of life and every form of existence, man must search for the way to utilize it to serve God.

[In some congregations the conjunctive וּ, *and*, is omitted and the phrase reads לְעֵלָּא לְעֵלָּא.]

עַל יִשְׂרָאֵל וְעַל רַבָּנָן,* וְעַל תַּלְמִידֵיהוֹן וְעַל כָּל
‹ all ‹ and upon ‹ their disciples ‹ upon ‹ the teachers,* ‹ upon ‹ Israel, ‹ Upon

תַּלְמִידֵי תַלְמִידֵיהוֹן, וְעַל כָּל מָאן דְּעָסְקִין בְּאוֹרַיְתָא,
‹ in the study ‹ who engage ‹ those ‹ all ‹ and ‹‹ of their ‹ the
of Torah,   upon   disciples,   disciples

דִּי בְאַתְרָא¹ הָדֵין וְדִי בְכָל אֲתַר וַאֲתַר.* יְהֵא לְהוֹן
‹ for ‹ may ‹‹ other place;* ‹ in any ‹ or who ‹ in this place ‹ who
them   there be   are   are

וּלְכוֹן* שְׁלָמָא רַבָּא, חִנָּא וְחִסְדָּא וְרַחֲמִין,* וְחַיִּין
‹ life ‹‹ and mercy,* ‹ kindness, ‹ grace, ‹ that is ‹ peace ‹ and for
                     abundant,   you*

אֲרִיכִין, וּמְזוֹנֵי רְוִיחֵי, וּפֻרְקָנָא מִן קֳדָם אֲבוּהוֹן דִּי
‹ Who ‹ their ‹ before ‹ from ‹‹ and ‹ that is ‹ nourish- ‹ that is
is   Father   salvation   ample,   ment   long,

בִשְׁמַיָּא* (וְאַרְעָא). וְאִמְרוּ: אָמֵן. (אָמֵן. – Cong.)
‹‹ (Amen.)   ‹‹ Amen. ‹ Now respond: ‹‹ (and on earth).‹ in Heaven*

יְהֵא שְׁלָמָא רַבָּא מִן שְׁמַיָּא, וְחַיִּים טוֹבִים עָלֵינוּ וְעַל כָּל
‹ all ‹ and ‹ upon us ‹‹ that is ‹ and life ‹‹ Heaven, ‹ from ‹ that is ‹ peace ‹ May
     upon   good,   abundant   there be

---

(1) In *Eretz Yisrael* add קַדִּישָׁא, *holy*.

עַל יִשְׂרָאֵל וְעַל רַבָּנָן —*Upon Israel, (and) upon the teachers*. It is because of this section that this *Kaddish* is called the Rabbis' *Kaddish*. Though this is a prayer for the benefit of the Torah community, it begins with mention of Israel. Any prayer for Torah scholars is a prayer for the nation, because Israel's welfare depends on Torah study (*R' Hirsch*).

וְדִי בְכָל אֲתַר וַאֲתַר — *Or who are in any other place*. The reference to all the various places implies that every town and neighborhood, individually, benefits from those who study Torah within it.

יְהֵא לְהוֹן וּלְכוֹן — *May there be for them and for you*. The blessing is extended not only to the Torah teachers and their students, but to all the people present in their congregation.

חִנָּא וְחִסְדָּא וְרַחֲמִין — *Grace, kindness, and mercy*. These terms are often used synonymously, but when they are used together we must assume that they have distinct meanings.

Some interpretations are as follows:

❑ These terms refer to how God views us: The most deserving people are nourished through God's חִנָּא, *grace*, while at the other extreme, even the least worthy are recipients of רַחֲמִין, *mercy*, because He displays compassion to every living thing. Those in between are provided for through חִסְדָּא, *kindness* (*R' Hirsch*).

❑ Or, these are characteristics that *we* hope to have: חִנָּא, *grace*, is the quality that makes a person beloved by others; חִסְדָּא, *kindness*, refers to a generous, considerate human being who is kind to others, even the undeserving; רַחֲמִין, *mercy*, is the quality of compassion by which one withholds punishment even when a wrong-doer has earned it (*Siach Yitzchak*).

אֲבוּהוֹן דִּי בִשְׁמַיָּא — *Their Father Who is in Heaven*. The word וְאַרְעָא, *and on earth*, is an addition which, although rejected by some commentators, is used in many congregations.

יִשְׂרָאֵל. וְאִמְרוּ: אָמֵן. (.Cong – אָמֵן.)
《 (Amen.)   《 Amen. 〈 Now respond: 《 Israel.

**BOW; TAKE THREE STEPS BACK: BOW LEFT AND SAY . . . עֹשֶׂה שָׁלוֹם, "HE WHO MAKES PEACE . . ."; BOW
RIGHT AND SAY . . . הוּא, "MAY HE . . ."; BOW FORWARD AND SAY . . . וְעַל כָּל יִשְׂרָאֵל, "AND UPON
ALL ISRAEL . . ." REMAIN IN PLACE FOR A FEW MOMENTS, THEN TAKE THREE STEPS FORWARD.**

עֹשֶׂה °שָׁלוֹם בִּמְרוֹמָיו, הוּא בְּרַחֲמָיו יַעֲשֶׂה שָׁלוֹם עָלֵינוּ,
〈 upon us, 〈 peace 〈 make 〈 in His 〈 may 《 in His heights, 〈 peace 〈 He Who
                              compassion He   makes

וְעַל כָּל יִשְׂרָאֵל. וְאִמְרוּ: אָמֵן. (.Cong – אָמֵן.)
《 (Amen.)   《 Amen. 〈 Now respond: 《 Israel. 〈 all 〈 and upon

FROM ROSH HASHANAH TO YOM KIPPUR SOME SAY:
°הַשָּׁלוֹם
〈 the peace

SOME CONGREGATIONS RECITE מִזְמוֹר לְדָוִד, PSALM 15, AT THIS POINT.

———————— Psalm 15 / תהלים טו ————————

מִזְמוֹר לְדָוִד; יהוה מִי יָגוּר בְּאָהֳלֶךָ, מִי יִשְׁכֹּן
〈 may 〈 Who 《 in Your Tent? 〈 may 〈 who 〈 HASHEM, 《 by David. 〈 A psalm
dwell   sojourn

בְּהַר קָדְשֶׁךָ. הוֹלֵךְ תָּמִים וּפֹעֵל צֶדֶק, וְדֹבֵר אֱמֶת בִּלְבָבוֹ.
《 from his 〈 the 〈 and 《 what 〈 and 《 in perfect 〈 One who 《 on Your Holy
heart.   truth speaks is right, does innocence, walks   Mountain?

לֹא רָגַל עַל לְשֹׁנוֹ, לֹא עָשָׂה לְרֵעֵהוּ רָעָה, וְחֶרְפָּה לֹא נָשָׂא
〈 he has 〈 and 《 evil, 〈 to his 〈 who has 《 his 〈 on 〈 slander 〈 Who
not cast disgrace   fellow not done tongue,   has no

עַל קְרֹבוֹ. נִבְזֶה בְּעֵינָיו נִמְאָס, וְאֶת יִרְאֵי יהוה יְכַבֵּד,
《 he 〈 HASHEM 〈 but those 《 is 〈 in his 〈 A contemp- 《 his 〈 upon
honors;   who fear repulsive, eyes tible person close one.

נִשְׁבַּע לְהָרַע וְלֹא יָמִר. כַּסְפּוֹ לֹא נָתַן בְּנֶשֶׁךְ, וְשֹׁחַד
〈 and a 《 with 〈 he does 〈 His 《 retracting. 〈 without 〈 to his 〈 one who
bribe interest, not lend money   detriment can swear

עַל נָקִי לֹא לָקָח; עֹשֵׂה אֵלֶּה לֹא יִמּוֹט לְעוֹלָם.
《 forever. 〈 falter 〈 will not 〈 of these 〈 The doer 《 he does not take. 〈 the innocent 〈 against

---

ה׳ מִי יָגוּר / Psalm 15 ◆§

Maharshal writes that it was his practice to
recite out loud the עֲשֶׂרֶת הַדִּבְּרוֹת, *the Ten
Commandments*, before *Pesukei D'Zimrah*,
since בָּרוּךְ שֶׁאָמַר, *Blessed is He Who spoke*,
corresponds to the ten utterances with which
God created the world, which, in turn, corre-

spond to the Ten Commandments. In order to
circumvent the *Arizal's* objection to that recita-
tion, *Ohr HaYashar* instituted the recitation of
Psalm 15, which corresponds to the Ten
Commandments, as explained in the *Midrash
HaNe'elam (Zohar Chadash, Vayeitzei)*. See
Likutei Maharich.

SOME CONGREGATIONS RECITE יְדִיד נֶפֶשׁ, *YEDID NEFESH*, AT THIS POINT.

יְדִיד **נֶפֶשׁ** אָב הָרַחֲמָן, מְשׁךְ עַבְדְּךָ אֶל רְצוֹנֶךָ,

Beloved ‹ of the soul, ‹ Father ‹ Who is compassionate, ‹ draw ‹ Your servant ‹ to ‹ Your will.

יָרוּץ עַבְדְּךָ כְּמוֹ אַיָּל, יִשְׁתַּחֲוֶה אֶל מוּל הֲדָרֶךָ,

May Your servant run ‹ like ‹ a deer ‹ to bow ‹ toward ‹ Your majesty.

יֶעֱרַב לוֹ יְדִידוֹתֶיךָ, מִנְּפֶת צוּף וְכָל טָעַם.

It will be ‹ to ‹ him ‹ sweeter ‹ Your friendship — ‹ than the ‹ dripping ‹ honeycomb ‹ and all ‹ of the flavors.

הָדוּר נָאֶה זִיו הָעוֹלָם, נַפְשִׁי חוֹלַת אַהֲבָתֶךָ,

Majestic One, ‹ Pleasant One, ‹ Radiance ‹ of the universe! ‹ My soul ‹ pines ‹ for Your love.

אָנָּא אֵל נָא רְפָא נָא לָהּ, בְּהַרְאוֹת לָהּ נֹעַם זִיוֶךָ,

O Please, ‹ God, ‹ please, ‹ heal ‹ it now, ‹ by showing ‹ it ‹ the ‹ pleasantness ‹ of Your radiance.

אָז תִּתְחַזֵּק וְתִתְרַפֵּא, וְהָיְתָה לָהּ שִׂמְחַת עוֹלָם.

Then ‹ it will be strengthened ‹ and be healed, ‹ and it will have ‹ gladness ‹ eternally.

וָתִיק, יֶהֱמוּ נָא רַחֲמֶיךָ, וְחוּסָה נָּא עַל בֵּן אֲהוּבֶךָ,

Faithful One, ‹ may Your mercy please be aroused ‹ and take pity, ‹ please, ‹ on ‹ Your beloved son.

כִּי זֶה כַּמָּה נִכְסֹף נִכְסַפְתִּי

For ‹ now ‹ it is a long time ‹ that I have yearned intensely

לִרְאוֹת (מְהֵרָה) בְּתִפְאֶרֶת עֻזֶּךָ,

to see ‹ (speedily) ‹ the splendor ‹ of Your strength.

אֵלֶּה חָמְדָה לִבִּי, וְחוּסָה נָא וְאַל תִּתְעַלָּם.

These ‹ has my heart desired, ‹ so take pity, ‹ please, ‹ and ‹ do not ‹ conceal Yourself.

הִגָּלֵה נָא וּפְרֹשׂ חֲבִיבִי עָלַי אֶת סֻכַּת שְׁלוֹמֶךָ,

Be revealed, ‹ please, ‹ and ‹ spread, ‹ my Beloved, ‹ upon ‹ me ‹ the shelter ‹ of Your peace.

תָּאִיר אֶרֶץ מִכְּבוֹדֶךָ, נָגִילָה וְנִשְׂמְחָה בָּךְ,

Illuminate ‹ the ‹ world ‹ with Your glory, ‹ that we may ‹ rejoice ‹ and be glad ‹ with You.

מַהֵר אֱהֹב כִּי בָא מוֹעֵד, וְחָנֵּנוּ כִּימֵי עוֹלָם.

Hasten, ‹ show [Your] love, ‹ for ‹ has the ‹ come ‹ time, ‹ and show ‹ us grace ‹ as in ‹ days ‹ of old.

FOR HOSHANA RABBAH, SEE *THE INTERLINEAR SIDDUR FOR THE SABBATH AND FESTIVALS.*

SEE *LAWS* §30 FOR INSTRUCTIONS FOR LATECOMERS.

⊰‖ PESUKEI D'ZIMRAH / פסוקי דזמרה ‖⊱

—————— *I Chronicles* 16:8-36 / דברי הימים א טז:ח-לו ——————

הוֹדוּ לַיהוה* קִרְאוּ בִשְׁמוֹ,* הוֹדִיעוּ בָעַמִּים

⟨ among the ⟨ make known ⟨⟨ His Name,* ⟨ declare ⟨ to HASHEM,* ⟨ Give thanks
peoples

⊰‖ פְּסוּקֵי דְזִמְרָה / PESUKEI D'ZIMRAH ‖⊱

The Sages taught that one should set forth the praises of God before making requests of Him (*Berachos* 32a). In this section of *Shacharis*, we concentrate on God's revelation in nature and history — on how His glory can be seen in Creation and in the unfolding of events. Accordingly פְּסוּקֵי דְזִמְרָה means *Verses of Praise*. However, many commentators relate the word זְמְרָה to the verb תִזְמֹר, *prune* (*Leviticus* 25:4). In this view, we now recite "Verses of Pruning," which are designed "to cut away" the mental and spiritual hindrances to proper prayer. Thus, by focusing on God's glory all around us, we prepare ourselves for the *Shema* and *Shemoneh Esrei*, when we accept Him as our King and pray for the needs of the Jewish people.

Because it is a separate section of *Shacharis* with a purpose all its own, *Pesukei D'Zimrah* is introduced with a blessing [בָּרוּךְ שֶׁאָמַר] and concluded with a blessing [יִשְׁתַּבַּח]. In this way, it is similar to *Hallel*, which is a complete unit and is therefore introduced by, and concluded with, a blessing. Accordingly, the verses of הוֹדוּ, *Give thanks*, should properly follow שֶׁאָמַר בָּרוּךְ, as they indeed do in *Nusach Ashkenaz*. Nevertheless, *Nusach Sefard* places הוֹדוּ before בָּרוּךְ שֶׁאָמַר in closer proximity to the *Korbanos* section of *Shacharis*, as is explained below.

⊰§ הוֹדוּ לַה' — *Give thanks to HASHEM*. The first twenty-nine verses of this lengthy prayer form a jubilant song that David taught Assaf and his colleagues. Assaf and his family were musicians and psalmists whose own compositions are included in the Book of *Psalms*. This song was intended by David to be sung when the Holy Ark was brought to Jerusalem.

According to *Seder Olam*, during the last forty-three years before Solomon inaugurated the Temple, the first fifteen of these verses were sung in the Tabernacle every day during the morning *tamid*-offering service, and the last fourteen were sung during the afternoon *tamid* service. With very minor changes, these verses are also found in *Psalms* 105:1-15, 96:2-13, and 106:47-48. [Incidentally, it is because these verses were recited during the sacrificial service that the *Nusach Sefard* ritual places הוֹדוּ before *Pesukei D'Zimrah*. Given the fact that these verses relate to the offerings, they should be recited immediately after the *Korbanos* section of *Shacharis*. *Nusach Ashkenaz*, however, does not make this change, because the verses speak of *general* praise, and thus are similar to the rest of *Pesukei D'Zimrah* (see *Beis Yosef*, *Orach Chaim* 50).]

In its entirety this song calls upon Israel to maintain its faith in God and its confidence that He will bring it salvation from exile and persecution. The first fifteen verses refer to the miracles of past salvations and how our Patriarchs had complete faith in God even though they had nothing to go by but His covenant and oath. The second group of fourteen verses begins שִׁירוּ לַה', *Sing to HASHEM, everyone on earth*. It refers to the song of gratitude that everyone will sing in Messianic times. Thus, this section parallels the theme of the morning *Shema* blessings (p. 123) in which we emphasize the redemption of the past, while the second section parallels the evening *Shema* blessings (p. 406) in which we stress the redemption of the future.

The third section of this prayer continues with a collection of verses. It is discussed on p. 87, s.v. רוֹמְמוּ.

קִרְאוּ בִשְׁמוֹ — *Declare His Name*. Whatever you accomplish, ascribe it to God's help, and let even the gentile nations know that God's guiding hand is everywhere (*Vilna Gaon*).

עֲלִילוֹתָיו. שִׁירוּ לוֹ, זַמְּרוּ לוֹ, שִׂיחוּ בְּכָל

‹ of all ‹ speak ‹‹ to Him, ‹ make music ‹‹ to Him, ‹ Sing ‹‹ His actions.

נִפְלְאֹתָיו. הִתְהַלְלוּ בְּשֵׁם קָדְשׁוֹ, יִשְׂמַח לֵב

‹ the heart ‹ glad will be ‹‹ of His Holiness, ‹ in the Name ‹ Glory ‹‹ His wonders.

מְבַקְשֵׁי יהוה. דִּרְשׁוּ יהוה וְעֻזּוֹ, בַּקְּשׁוּ פָנָיו

‹ His Presence ‹ seek ‹‹ and His might, ‹ HASHEM ‹ Search out ‹‹ HASHEM. ‹ of those who seek

תָּמִיד. זִכְרוּ נִפְלְאֹתָיו אֲשֶׁר עָשָׂה, מֹפְתָיו

‹ His marvels ‹‹ He performed, ‹ that ‹ His wonders ‹ Remember ‹‹ always.

וּמִשְׁפְּטֵי פִיהוּ. זֶרַע יִשְׂרָאֵל עַבְדּוֹ, בְּנֵי יַעֲקֹב

‹ of Jacob, ‹ children ‹‹ His servant, ‹ of Israel, ‹ O seed ‹‹ of His mouth. ‹ and the judgments

בְּחִירָיו. הוּא יהוה אֱלֹהֵינוּ, בְּכָל הָאָרֶץ

‹ the earth ‹ over all ‹‹ our God, ‹ HASHEM, ‹ He is ‹‹ His chosen ones.

מִשְׁפָּטָיו. זִכְרוּ לְעוֹלָם בְּרִיתוֹ, דָּבָר צִוָּה לְאֶלֶף

‹ for a thousand ‹ He com-manded ‹ — the Word ‹‹ His covenant ‹ forever ‹ Remember ‹‹ are His judgments.

דּוֹר.* אֲשֶׁר כָּרַת אֶת אַבְרָהָם, וּשְׁבוּעָתוֹ

‹ and His oath ‹‹ with Abraham ‹ He made ‹ — that ‹‹ generations*

לְיִצְחָק. וַיַּעֲמִידֶהָ לְיַעֲקֹב לְחֹק, לְיִשְׂרָאֵל בְּרִית

‹ as a covenant ‹ for Israel ‹‹ as a statute, ‹ for Jacob ‹ Then He established it ‹‹ to Isaac.

עוֹלָם. לֵאמֹר, לְךָ אֶתֵּן אֶרֶץ כְּנָעַן, חֶבֶל

‹ the lot ‹ of Canaan, ‹ the Land ‹ I shall give ‹ To you ‹ saying, ‹‹ everlasting,

נַחֲלַתְכֶם. בִּהְיוֹתְכֶם מְתֵי מִסְפָּר, כִּמְעַט וְגָרִים

‹ dwelling ‹ hardly ‹‹ in number, ‹ but few ‹ When you were ‹‹ of your inheritance.

לְאֶלֶף דּוֹר — *For a thousand generations.* God's word — His covenant with Israel — lasts for a *thousand generations,* a poetic expression meaning forever. He sealed His covenant with Abraham, designated Isaac as Abraham's successor, and then chose Jacob over Esau, thus making Israel His chosen people everlastingly (*Tzilosa D'Avraham*).

בָּהּ. וַיִּתְהַלְּכוּ מִגּוֹי אֶל גּוֹי, וּמִמַּמְלָכָה אֶל

‹ to ‹ from one kingdom ‹ nation, ‹ to ‹ from nation ‹ and they wandered ‹‹ there;

עַם אַחֵר. לֹא הִנִּיחַ לְאִישׁ לְעָשְׁקָם, וַיּוֹכַח

‹ and He rebuked ‹‹ to rob them, ‹ any man ‹ — He did not allow ‹‹ another people.

עֲלֵיהֶם מְלָכִים. אַל תִּגְּעוּ בִמְשִׁיחָי, וּבִנְבִיאַי

‹ and to My ‹ My anointed ‹ Dare not touch ‹‹ kings: ‹ for their sake
prophets　　ones,

אַל תָּרֵעוּ. שִׁירוּ לַיהוה* כָּל הָאָרֶץ, בַּשְּׂרוּ מִיּוֹם

‹ from day ‹ announce ‹‹ on earth, ‹ everyone ‹ to Hashem,* ‹ Sing ‹‹ harm. ‹ do no

אֶל יוֹם יְשׁוּעָתוֹ. סַפְּרוּ בַגּוֹיִם אֶת כְּבוֹדוֹ, בְּכָל

‹ among ‹‹ His glory, ‹ among the ‹ Relate ‹‹ His salvation. ‹ day ‹ to
all　　　　　nations

הָעַמִּים נִפְלְאוֹתָיו. כִּי גָדוֹל יהוה וּמְהֻלָּל מְאֹד,

‹‹ exceedingly, ‹ and lauded ‹ is Hashem ‹ great ‹ That ‹‹ His wonders: ‹ peoples

וְנוֹרָא הוּא עַל כָּל אֱלֹהִים. ❖ כִּי כָּל אֱלֹהֵי

‹ the gods ‹ all ‹ For ‹‹ powers. ‹ all ‹ above ‹ is He ‹ and awesome

הָעַמִּים אֱלִילִים, וַיהוה (PAUSE) שָׁמַיִם עָשָׂה.*

‹‹ did make!* ‹ heaven ‹ — but Hashem ‹‹ are worthless ‹ of the peoples

הוֹד וְהָדָר לְפָנָיו, עֹז וְחֶדְוָה בִּמְקֹמוֹ. הָבוּ

‹ Render ‹‹ are in ‹ and delight ‹ might ‹‹ are before ‹ and ‹ Glory
His place.　　　　Him,　majesty

שִׁירוּ לַה׳ — *Sing to Hashem.* As is stated repeatedly in *Prophets*, in Messianic times all nations will follow Israel's lead in recognizing and serving God. The fourteen verses beginning here allude to those days. However, David also referred to a salvation that occurred in his own lifetime. The Philistines had captured the Holy Ark and destroyed the Tabernacle at Shiloh. But the presence of the Ark in the Philistine cities brought plagues upon them. Recognizing the hand of God in their suffering, the Philistines returned the Ark with a gift of tribute to God. The same will happen in future times when Israel's oppressors will recognize God's majesty.

וַה׳ שָׁמַיִם עָשָׂה — *But Hashem heaven did make.* After having proclaimed that the gods of the nations are vain and useless *nothings*, David made this logical argument: The most prominent and seemingly powerful idols were the heavenly bodies — but since *Hashem made heaven*, how can anyone justify worshiping His creations in preference to Him? (*Radak*).

It is important to pause between אֱלִילִים, *worthless* [the idols], and וַה׳, *but* [lit. *and*] Hashem. If the two words are read together, it could ח״ו be understood to mean: *all of the gods . . . are worthless and Hashem*, as if to say that He is like them.

לַיהוה מִשְׁפְּחוֹת עַמִּים, הָבוּ לַיהוה כָּבוֹד וָעֹז.

    《 and ❬ honor ❬ unto ❬ render《 of the ❬ O families ❬ unto
    might.   Hashem   peoples,   Hashem,

הָבוּ לַיהוה כָּבוֹד שְׁמוֹ, שְׂאוּ מִנְחָה וּבְאוּ לְפָנָיו,

    《 before ❬ and ❬ an offering ❬ raise《 [worthy of] ❬ honor ❬ to Hashem ❬ Render
    Him;   come   up   His Name,

הִשְׁתַּחֲווּ לַיהוה בְּהַדְרַת קֹדֶשׁ. חִילוּ מִלְּפָנָיו

    ❬ before ❬ Tremble《 of His ❬ in the beauty ❬ before ❬ bow down
    Him,   holy place.   Hashem

כָּל הָאָרֶץ, אַף תִּכּוֹן תֵּבֵל בַּל תִּמּוֹט.* יִשְׂמְחוּ

    ❬ Glad   《 topple.* ❬ so that ❬ is the ❬ firmly ❬ indeed,《 on earth, ❬ everyone
    will be   it cannot world established

הַשָּׁמַיִם וְתָגֵל הָאָרֶץ, וְיֹאמְרוּ בַגּוֹיִם, יהוה

    ❬ Hashem ❬ among the ❬ and they ❬ the earth ❬ and ❬ the heavens
    nations,   will say   rejoice will

מָלָךְ. יִרְעַם הַיָּם וּמְלֹאוֹ, יַעֲלֹץ הַשָּׂדֶה וְכָל אֲשֶׁר

    ❬ that is ❬ and ❬ the field ❬ exult will《 and its ❬ the ❬ Roar《 has
    everything   fullness; sea   will   reigned!

בּוֹ. אָז יְרַנְּנוּ עֲצֵי הַיָּעַר, מִלְּפְנֵי יהוה, כִּי בָא

    ❬ He will ❬ for ❬ Hashem, ❬ before《 of the ❬ the trees ❬ sing ❬ Then《 in it.
    have arrived   forest   joyously will

לִשְׁפּוֹט אֶת הָאָרֶץ. הוֹדוּ לַיהוה כִּי טוֹב, כִּי

    ❬ for《 He is ❬ for ❬ to Hashem, ❬ Give《 the earth. ❬ to judge
    good,   thanks

לְעוֹלָם חַסְדּוֹ. וְאִמְרוּ הוֹשִׁיעֵנוּ אֱלֹהֵי יִשְׁעֵנוּ,

    《 of our ❬ O God ❬ Save us, ❬ And say,《 is His ❬ enduring
    salvation,   kindness!   forever

וְקַבְּצֵנוּ וְהַצִּילֵנוּ מִן הַגּוֹיִם, לְהֹדוֹת לְשֵׁם קָדְשֶׁךָ,

    ❬ of Your ❬ the Name ❬ to thank《 among ❬ from ❬ and rescue us ❬ and gather us
    Holiness,   the nations,

תֵּבֵל בַּל תִּמּוֹט — *The world so that it cannot topple.* Though the turbulent history of war and conflict often makes it seem as though man will destroy his planet, the climax of history will be the peace and fulfillment of Messianic times. God has ordained that the world will survive (*Radak*).

לְהִשְׁתַּבֵּחַ בִּתְהִלָּתֶךָ. בָּרוּךְ יהוה אֱלֹהֵי יִשְׂרָאֵל
⟨ of Israel, ⟨ the God ⟨ is HASHEM, ⟨ Blessed ⟨⟨ in Your praise! ⟨ and to glory

מִן הָעוֹלָם וְעַד הָעֹלָם, וַיֹּאמְרוּ כָל הָעָם, אָמֵן,
⟨ Amen ⟨⟨ the ⟨ – all ⟨⟨ and let ⟨ the World ⟨ to ⟨ [This] World ⟨ from
people – them say [to Come],

וְהַלֵּל לַיהוה. ❖ רוֹמְמוּ יהוה אֱלֹהֵינוּ* וְהִשְׁתַּחֲווּ
⟨ and bow down ⟨ our God,* ⟨ HASHEM, ⟨ Exalt ⟨⟨ to HASHEM! ⟨ and praise

לַהֲדֹם רַגְלָיו, קָדוֹשׁ הוּא.[1] רוֹמְמוּ יהוה אֱלֹהֵינוּ
⟨ our God, ⟨ HASHEM, ⟨ Exalt ⟨⟨ is He! ⟨ holy ⟨⟨ at His footstool;

וְהִשְׁתַּחֲווּ לְהַר קָדְשׁוֹ, כִּי קָדוֹשׁ יהוה אֱלֹהֵינוּ.[2]
⟨⟨ our God. ⟨ is HASHEM, ⟨ holy ⟨ for ⟨⟨ of His ⟨ at the ⟨ and bow down
Holiness; Mount

וְהוּא רַחוּם יְכַפֵּר עָוֹן וְלֹא יַשְׁחִית, וְהִרְבָּה
⟨ frequently ⟨⟨ destroy; ⟨ and does ⟨ of ⟨ is ⟨ the Merciful ⟨ Neverthe-
not iniquity forgiving One, less, He,

לְהָשִׁיב אַפּוֹ, וְלֹא יָעִיר כָּל חֲמָתוֹ.[3] אַתָּה יהוה,
⟨ HASHEM, ⟨ You, ⟨⟨ His entire ⟨ arousing ⟨ not ⟨⟨ His ⟨ He
wrath. anger, withdraws

לֹא תִכְלָא רַחֲמֶיךָ מִמֶּנִּי, חַסְדְּךָ וַאֲמִתְּךָ תָּמִיד
⟨ always ⟨ and Your ⟨ may Your ⟨⟨ from me; ⟨ Your mercy ⟨ withhold ⟨ do not
truth kindness

---

(1) *Psalms* 99:5. (2) 99:9. (3) 78:38.

רוֹמְמוּ ה' אֱלֹהֵינוּ — *Exalt* HASHEM, *our God . . .*
From this point until its end, the prayer contains
a collection of verses from throughout *Psalms*,
which Rabbi Profiat Duran, a refugee from the
Spanish massacres of 1391, describes as פְּסוּקֵי
דְרַחֲמֵי, *Verses of Mercy*, because they are
effective in beseeching God for mercy. Accordingly, they were adopted in the prayers for an
end to exile and dispersion.

From *Etz Yosef*, *World of Prayer* and others,
the following progression of thought emerges
from these verses. Even if הֲדֹם רַגְלָיו, *His*
footstool, the Temple, has been destroyed, God

heeds our prayers recited at הַר קָדְשׁוֹ, *the Mount*
of His Holiness. But the millions of Jews who
cannot come to the Temple Mount need not fear
that their prayers are in vain because God is
always merciful and ready to withdraw His
anger in the face of sincere prayer. Though
Israel may have suffered grievously in the many
places of its dispersion, God avenges it and helps
those who call upon Him.

The term God's "footstool" refers to the place
on earth where He rests His glory, as we find in
Isaiah 66:1: *So says* HASHEM, *"The heaven is My*
throne and the earth is My footstool."

1. יִצְּרוּנִי. זְכֹר רַחֲמֶיךָ יהוה וַחֲסָדֶיךָ, כִּי מֵעוֹלָם

> protect me. » Remember < Your mercies, < HASHEM, < and Your kindnesses, < for < eternal <

2. הֵמָּה. תְּנוּ עֹז לֵאלֹהִים, עַל יִשְׂרָאֵל גַּאֲוָתוֹ,

> are they. » Acknowledge < [invincible] might < to God; < upon < Israel < is His grandeur »

וְעֻזּוֹ בַּשְּׁחָקִים. נוֹרָא אֱלֹהִים מִמִּקְדָּשֶׁיךָ, אֵל

> — as His might » is in the skies. » You are awesome, < O God, < from Your Sanctuaries; < God <

יִשְׂרָאֵל הוּא נֹתֵן עֹז וְתַעֲצֻמוֹת לָעָם, בָּרוּךְ

> of Israel » He — it is < Who grants < might < and power < to the people; < blessed <

3. אֱלֹהִים. אֵל נְקָמוֹת יהוה, אֵל נְקָמוֹת הוֹפִיעַ.

> is God. » O God < of vengeance, < HASHEM; < O God < of vengeance, < appear! «

4. הִנָּשֵׂא שֹׁפֵט הָאָרֶץ, הָשֵׁב גְּמוּל עַל גֵּאִים.

> Arise, < O Judge « of the earth, < render < retribution < to < the haughty. «

5. לַיהוה הַיְשׁוּעָה, עַל עַמְּךָ בִרְכָתֶךָ סֶּלָה.

> To HASHEM < is Salvation, « upon < Your people < is Your blessing, « Selah. «

❖ יהוה צְבָאוֹת עִמָּנוּ, מִשְׂגָּב לָנוּ אֱלֹהֵי יַעֲקֹב

> HASHEM, < Master of Legions, < is with us, « a stronghold < for us < is the God < of Jacob, «

6. סֶלָה. יהוה צְבָאוֹת, אַשְׁרֵי אָדָם בֹּטֵחַ בָּךְ. יהוה

> Selah. « HASHEM, < Master of Legions, < praiseworthy < is the man < who trusts < in You. « HASHEM, <

8. הוֹשִׁיעָה, הַמֶּלֶךְ יַעֲנֵנוּ בְיוֹם קָרְאֵנוּ. הוֹשִׁיעָה

> save! « May the King < answer us < on the day < we call. « Save <

אֶת עַמֶּךָ, וּבָרֵךְ אֶת נַחֲלָתֶךָ, וּרְעֵם וְנַשְּׂאֵם

> Your nation, < and bless < tend them « Your inheritance; < and raise them up <

---

(1) Psalms 40:12. (2) 25:6. (3) 68:35-36. (4) 94:1-2. (5) 3:9. (6) 46:8. (7) 84:13. (8) 20:10.

עַד הָעוֹלָם. ¹נַפְשֵׁנוּ חִכְּתָה לַיהוה, עֶזְרֵנוּ וּמָגִנֵּנוּ

forever. Our soul longed for Hashem; our help and our shield

הוּא. כִּי בוֹ יִשְׂמַח לִבֵּנוּ, כִּי בְשֵׁם קָדְשׁוֹ בָטָחְנוּ.

is He. For Him will be gladdened our hearts; for in His Holiness Name we trusted.

²יְהִי חַסְדְּךָ יהוה עָלֵינוּ, כַּאֲשֶׁר יִחַלְנוּ לָךְ.

May Your kindness, Hashem, be upon us, just as we awaited You.

³הַרְאֵנוּ יהוה חַסְדֶּךָ, וְיֶשְׁעֲךָ תִּתֶּן לָנוּ קוּמָה

Show us, Hashem, Your kindness, and Your salvation grant us. Arise!

עֶזְרָתָה לָּנוּ, וּפְדֵנוּ לְמַעַן חַסְדֶּךָ. ⁴אָנֹכִי יהוה

Assist us! And redeem us for the sake of Your kindness! I am Hashem,

אֱלֹהֶיךָ הַמַּעַלְךָ מֵאֶרֶץ מִצְרָיִם, הַרְחֶב פִּיךָ

your God, Who raised you from the land of Egypt. Open wide your mouth

וַאֲמַלְאֵהוּ. ⁵אַשְׁרֵי הָעָם שֶׁכָּכָה לּוֹ, אַשְׁרֵי

and I will fill it. Praiseworthy is the people that such is their lot; praiseworthy

הָעָם שֶׁיהוה אֱלֹהָיו. ❖ ⁶וַאֲנִי בְּחַסְדְּךָ בָטָחְתִּי,

is the people that Hashem is their God. But as for me, in Your kindness I trust;

יָגֵל לִבִּי בִּישׁוּעָתֶךָ, אָשִׁירָה לַיהוה, כִּי גָמַל

my heart will exult in Your salvation. I will sing to Hashem, for He has dealt kindly

⁷עָלָי.

with me.

---

(1) *Psalms* 28:9. (2) 33:20-22. (3) 85:8.
(4) 44:27. (5) 81:11. (6) 144:15. (7) 13:6.

─────── Psalm 30 / תהלים ל ───────

מִזְמוֹר שִׁיר חֲנֻכַּת הַבַּיִת* לְדָוִד. אֲרוֹמִמְךָ יהוה

〈 HASHEM, 〈   I will   〈〈 by David. 〈 of the 〈 for the 〈 a song 〈 A psalm,
exalt You,   Temple,* inauguration

כִּי דִלִּיתָנִי, וְלֹא שִׂמַּחְתָּ אֹיְבַי לִי. יהוה אֱלֹהָי,

〈 my God, 〈 HASHEM, 〈〈 over 〈 let my foes rejoice 〈 and not 〈 You have 〈 for
         me.   drawn me up,

שִׁוַּעְתִּי אֵלֶיךָ וַתִּרְפָּאֵנִי. יהוה, הֶעֱלִיתָ מִן שְׁאוֹל

〈 the lower 〈 from 〈 You have 〈 HASHEM, 〈〈 and You 〈 to You 〈 I cried out
world   raised up   healed me.

נַפְשִׁי,* חִיִּיתַנִי מִיָּרְדִי בוֹר. זַמְּרוּ לַיהוה חֲסִידָיו,

〈 His devout 〈 to HASHEM, 〈 Sing 〈〈 to the 〈 from my 〈 You have 〈〈 my soul;*
ones,   grave. descent preserved me

וְהוֹדוּ לְזֵכֶר קָדְשׁוֹ. כִּי רֶגַע בְּאַפּוֹ, חַיִּים בִּרְצוֹנוֹ;

〈〈 results from 〈 life 〈〈 His anger 〈 but a 〈 For 〈〈 to His holy Name. 〈 and give
His favor.   endures; moment   thanks

מִזְמוֹר שִׁיר / Psalm 30 ◆§

This psalm was introduced into the morning prayers during the 17th century. Apparently, it was decided to include it in *Shacharis* because it was sung to inaugurate the morning Temple service, and thus is an appropriate prelude to the prayers that take the place of that service (*Tikkun Tefillah*). It is also a fitting conclusion to the Scriptural and Talmudical passages regarding the offerings. Additionally, מִזְמוֹר שִׁיר is an appropriate introduction to the morning psalms of praise because of its emphasis on our faith that God can rescue us from even the most hopeless situations (*R' Munk*).

חֲנֻכַּת הַבַּיִת — *The inauguration of the Temple.* How is this psalm, which deals only with David's illness, related to the dedication of the Temple? *Radak* explains that Solomon's eventual inauguration of the Temple represented David's vindication against the taunts and charges of his enemies. His offspring could not have gained the privilege of building the Temple if David had been a sinner.

R' Reuven Margulies suggests that the psalm

was composed in response to the events described in *II Samuel* Ch. 24. God decreed a plague in punishment for David conducting a census of the people. The plague was halted when David accepted the responsibility: *"Behold I have sinned ... but these sheep — what have they done? Let Your hand be against me and my father's family"* (ibid. v. 17). At that moment the prophet Gad directed David to build an altar on the exact site of the future Temple. *I Chronicles* (21:26) states that Hashem sent fire from Heaven upon the altar that David made, thus "inaugurating" the Temple To Be. [See *Abarbanel* to *Samuel*.]

ה' הֶעֱלִיתָ מִן שְׁאוֹל נַפְשִׁי — *HASHEM, You have raised up from the lower world my soul.* R' Yerucham Levovitz notes that David speaks as if he had already died and descended to the "lower world," where sinners are punished after death. From this we learn that one can suffer the anguish of purgatory even while alive! As the Talmud (*Nedarim* 22a) teaches: "Whoever becomes angry is subjected to all types of *Gehinnom.*" The flames of frustration, anguish,

בָּעֶרֶב יָלִין בֶּכִי וְלַבְּקֶר רִנָּה. וַאֲנִי אָמַרְתִּי

‹ In the evening ‹ one lies down ‹ weeping, ‹‹ but with dawn ‹‹ – a cry of joy! ‹ I ‹ had said

בְשַׁלְוִי, בַּל אֶמּוֹט לְעוֹלָם. יהוה, בִּרְצוֹנְךָ

‹‹ in my serenity, ‹ I would not falter, ‹ ever. ‹‹ But, HASHEM, ‹ [it is only] through Your favor

הֶעֱמַדְתָּה לְהַרְרִי עֹז, הִסְתַּרְתָּ פָנֶיךָ הָיִיתִי

‹ that You supported ‹ my greatness ‹‹ to be mighty; ‹ when You concealed ‹ Your face, ‹ I was

נִבְהָל. אֵלֶיךָ יהוה אֶקְרָא, וְאֶל אֲדֹנָי אֶתְחַנָּן.

‹‹ confounded. ‹ To You, ‹ HASHEM, ‹ I would call ‹ and to ‹ the Lord ‹ I would appeal.

מַה בֶּצַע בְּדָמִי, בְּרִדְתִּי אֶל שָׁחַת; הֲיוֹדְךָ עָפָר,*

‹ What is there ‹ gain ‹ in my death, ‹ in my descent ‹ to ‹‹ the Pit? ‹‹ Will the dust acknowledge You?*

הֲיַגִּיד אֲמִתֶּךָ. שְׁמַע יהוה וְחָנֵּנִי, יהוה הֱיֵה

‹ Will it declare ‹‹ Your truth? ‹ Hear, ‹ O HASHEM, ‹ and favor me; ‹‹ HASHEM, ‹ be

עֹזֵר לִי. ❖ הָפַכְתָּ מִסְפְּדִי לְמָחוֹל לִי, פִּתַּחְתָּ שַׂקִּי

‹‹ my Helper! ‹ You have transformed ‹ my lament ‹ into dancing ‹‹ for me, ‹ You undid ‹ my sackcloth

וַתְּאַזְּרֵנִי שִׂמְחָה. לְמַעַן יְזַמֶּרְךָ כָבוֹד וְלֹא יִדֹּם,

‹ and You girded me ‹ with gladness. ‹‹ So that ‹ sing to You ‹ [might] my soul ‹ and not ‹‹ be silenced,

יהוה אֱלֹהַי לְעוֹלָם אוֹדֶךָּ.

‹ HASHEM, ‹ my God, ‹ forever ‹‹ will I thank You.

---

and melancholy are the equivalent of the fires of *Gehinnom*. Throughout the Book of *Psalms*, most references to "falling into the lower world" refer to this type of emotional inferno.

הֲיוֹדְךָ עָפָר — *Will the dust acknowledge You?* Though the soul continues in the afterlife, it has lost the opportunity to spread knowledge of God among men.

THE FOLLOWING PARAGRAPH IS RECITED WHILE STANDING.

יְהוה מֶלֶךְ,¹ יהוה מָלָךְ,² יהוה יִמְלֹךְ לְעֹלָם וָעֶד.³

‹ Hashem ‹ reigns, ›› Hashem ‹ has ›› Hashem ‹ shall ‹ for ever ›› and
reigned, reign ever.

יהוה מֶלֶךְ, יהוה מָלָךְ, יהוה יִמְלֹךְ לְעֹלָם וָעֶד.

‹ Hashem ‹ reigns, ›› Hashem ‹ has ›› Hashem ‹ shall ‹ for ever ›› and
reigned, reign ever.

וְהָיָה יהוה לְמֶלֶךְ עַל כָּל הָאָרֶץ, בַּיּוֹם הַהוּא יִהְיֶה

‹Then will ›› Hashem ‹ be King ‹ over ‹ all ›› the world ‹ — on that day ‹ shall

יהוה אֶחָד וּשְׁמוֹ אֶחָד.⁴

‹ Hashem ‹ be One ‹ and His ›› be One.
Name

הוֹשִׁיעֵנוּ יהוה אֱלֹהֵינוּ, וְקַבְּצֵנוּ מִן הַגּוֹיִם, לְהוֹדוֹת

‹ Save us ‹ Hashem, ‹ our God, ‹ and ‹ from ›› among ‹ to thank
gather us the nations,

לְשֵׁם קָדְשֶׁךָ, לְהִשְׁתַּבֵּחַ בִּתְהִלָּתֶךָ. ❖ בָּרוּךְ יהוה אֱלֹהֵי

‹ the ‹ of Your ‹ and to glory ›› in Your praise! ‹ Blessed ‹ is ‹ the
Holiness, Name Hashem, God

יִשְׂרָאֵל מִן הָעוֹלָם וְעַד הָעוֹלָם, וְאָמַר כָּל הָעָם:

‹ of Israel, ‹ from ‹ [This] ‹ to ›› the World ›› and let ‹ — all ›› the
World [to Come], them say people —

אָמֵן, הַלְלוּיָהּ.⁵ כֹּל הַנְּשָׁמָה תְּהַלֵּל יָהּ, הַלְלוּיָהּ.⁶

›› Amen! ›› Halleluyah! ‹ Let all ‹ souls ‹ praise ‹ God, ›› Halleluyah!

—— תהלים סז / Psalm 67 ——

לַמְנַצֵּחַ בִּנְגִינֹת מִזְמוֹר שִׁיר. אֱלֹהִים יְחָנֵּנוּ וִיבָרְכֵנוּ,

‹ For the ‹ with the ‹ a psalm, ‹ a song. ›› May God ‹ favor ›› and bless
conductor *neginos,* us, us

יָאֵר פָּנָיו אִתָּנוּ סֶלָה. לָדַעַת בָּאָרֶץ דַּרְכֶּךָ, בְּכָל

‹ may He ‹ His coun- ‹ with ›› Selah. ‹ To make ‹ on earth ‹ Your ›› among
illuminate tenance us, known way, all

(1) *Psalms* 10:16. (2) 93:1 et al. (3) *Exodus* 15:18.
(4) *Zechariah* 14:9. (5) *Psalms* 106:47-48. (6) 150:6.

גּוֹיִם יְשׁוּעָתֶךָ. יוֹדֽוּךָ עַמִּים, אֱלֹהִים, יוֹדֽוּךָ עַמִּים

《 will the 〈 acknowl- 《 O God; 〈 will the 〈 Acknowl- 《 Your 〈 nations
peoples edge You　　　　　　 peoples, edge You salvation.

כֻּלָּם. יִשְׂמְחוּ וִירַנְּנוּ לְאֻמִּים, כִּי תִשְׁפֹּט עַמִּים

〈 the 〈 You will 〈 because 《 regimes, 〈 and singing 〈 Glad 《 – all of
peoples judge　　　　　　 for joy will be　　 will be them.

מִישֹׁר, וּלְאֻמִּים בָּאָרֶץ תַּנְחֵם סֶלָה. יוֹדֽוּךָ עַמִּים,

〈 will the 〈 Acknowl- 《 Selah. 《 [with fairness] 〈 on earth 〈 and the 《 fairly
peoples, edge You　　　　　 You will guide,　　　　 regimes

אֱלֹהִים; יוֹדֽוּךָ עַמִּים כֻּלָּם. אֶרֶץ נָתְנָה יְבוּלָהּ,

《 its 〈 will then 〈 The 《 – all of 《 will the 〈 acknowl- 《 O God;
produce; have yielded earth them. peoples edge You

יְבָרְכֵֽנוּ אֱלֹהִים אֱלֹהֵֽינוּ. יְבָרְכֵֽנוּ אֱלֹהִים, וְיִירְאוּ

〈 and may 《 May God bless us, 《 – our God. 《 may God bless us
they fear

אוֹתוֹ כָּל אַפְסֵי אָרֶץ.

《 of the earth. 〈 the ends 〈 – all 《 Him

◄§ Permitted Responses During *Pesukei D'Zimrah*

From this point until after the completion of the silent *Shemoneh Esrei,* conversation is forbidden. From בָּרוּךְ שֶׁאָמַר, *Blessed is He Who spoke,* until יִשְׁתַּבַּח, *Praised* (p. 119), certain congregational and individual responses [e.g., בָּרוּךְ הוּא וּבָרוּךְ שְׁמוֹ and בָּרִיךְ הוּא] are omitted. The following responses, however, should be made: אָמֵן, *Amen,* after any blessing; *Kaddish; Borchu; Kedushah;* and the Rabbis' *Modim.* Additionally, one should join the congregation in reciting the first verse of the *Shema* and בָּרוּךְ שֵׁם, and may recite the אֲשֶׁר יָצַר blessing if he had to relieve himself during *Pesukei D'Zimrah.*

If one is in the middle of reciting *Pesukei D'Zimrah* and the congregation has already reached the Torah reading, it is preferable that he not be called to the Torah. However, if (a) one is the only *Kohen* or Levite present, or (b) the *gabbai* inadvertently called him to the Torah, then he may recite the blessings and even read the portion softly along with the Torah reader.

If after reciting בָּרוּךְ שֶׁאָמַר one realizes that he has forgotten to recite the morning Blessings of the Torah (p. 24), he should pause to recite them and their accompanying verses. Likewise, if he fears that he will not reach the *Shema* before the prescribed time, he should recite all three paragraphs of *Shema.*

On days that *Hallel* (p. 502) is recited in its abridged form, if one is between בָּרוּךְ שֶׁאָמַר and יִשְׁתַּבַּח when the congregation begins *Hallel,* one should pause, recite the verses of *Hallel* with the congregation (but not the blessings that precede and follow it), then return to where he left off.

In all cases of permitted responses it is preferable to respond between psalms, whenever possible. Thus, for example, if one realizes that the congregation is approaching *Kedushah,* he should not begin a new psalm, but should wait for the congregation to recite *Kedushah,* then continue his prayers.

The responses permitted above do not apply during the final blessings of בָּרוּךְ שֶׁאָמַר [בָּרוּךְ אַתָּה ה' מֶלֶךְ מְהֻלָּל בַּתִּשְׁבָּחוֹת] and יִשְׁתַּבַּח [בָּרוּךְ אַתָּה ה' from the words 'ה אַתָּה בָּרוּךְ], *Blessed are You, Hashem,* until the blessing's conclusion] where no interruptions are permitted.

(See also *Laws* §33-38.)

SOME RECITE THIS SHORT KABBALISTIC DECLARATION OF INTENT BEFORE RECITING בָּרוּךְ שֶׁאָמַר, *BLESSED IS HE WHO SPOKE*:

הֲרֵינִי מְזַמֵּן אֶת פִּי לְהוֹדוֹת וּלְהַלֵּל וּלְשַׁבֵּחַ אֶת בּוֹרְאִי. לְשֵׁם יְחוּד קֻדְשָׁא

‹‹ of the ‹ of the ‹ For the ‹‹ my Creator. ‹ and to ‹ to laud, ‹ to thank, ‹ my ‹ prepare ‹ I now
Holy unifica- sake praise mouth
One, tion

בְּרִיךְ הוּא וּשְׁכִינְתֵּיהּ עַל יְדֵי הַהוּא טָמִיר וְנֶעְלָם, בְּשֵׁם כָּל יִשְׂרָאֵל.

‹‹ Israel. ‹ of ‹–[I pray] ‹‹ and Who is ‹ Who is ‹ Him ‹ through ‹ and His ‹‹ is He, ‹ Blessed
all in the name inscrutable hidden Presence,

STAND WHILE RECITING בָּרוּךְ שֶׁאָמַר, *BLESSED IS HE WHO SPOKE*. DURING ITS RECITATION, HOLD THE TWO FRONT *TZITZIS* OF THE *TALLIS* (OR *TALLIS KATTAN*) IN THE RIGHT HAND, AND AT ITS CONCLUSION KISS THE *TZITZIS* AND RELEASE THEM. CONVERSATION IS FORBIDDEN FROM THIS POINT UNTIL AFTER *SHEMONEH ESREI*, EXCEPT FOR CERTAIN PRAYER RESPONSES (SEE BOX, PAGE 93 AND *LAWS* §33-38).

בָּרוּךְ שֶׁאָמַר וְהָיָה הָעוֹלָם,* בָּרוּךְ הוּא.

‹‹ is He. ‹ — blessed ‹‹ and the world ‹ He Who spoke, ‹ Blessed is
came into being*

בָּרוּךְ אוֹמֵר וְעֹשֶׂה,* בָּרוּךְ גּוֹזֵר וּמְקַיֵּם, בָּרוּךְ

‹ blessed ‹‹ and Who ‹ is He Who ‹ blessed ‹‹ and Who ‹ is He Who ‹ Blessed
fulfills; decrees does;* speaks

עֹשֶׂה בְרֵאשִׁית, בָּרוּךְ מְרַחֵם עַל הָאָרֶץ,*

‹‹ the earth;* ‹ on ‹ is He Who ‹ blessed ‹‹ Creation; ‹ is He Who
has mercy maintains

בָּרוּךְ שֶׁאָמַר / **Baruch She'amar** ⏵

The commentators record an ancient tradition that this prayer was transcribed by the Men of the Great Assembly approximately 2400 years ago from a script that fell from heaven. The prayer contains 87 words, equal to the numerical value of פָּז, *finest gold*. This alludes to the verse (*Song of Songs* 5:11): רֹאשׁוֹ כֶּתֶם פָּז, *His opening words* [i.e., the introductory words of *Pesukei D'Zimrah*] were finest gold.

In recognition of its lofty status, one must stand when reciting *Baruch She'amar*. Kabbalists teach that one should hold his two front *tzitzis* during *Baruch She'amar* and kiss them upon concluding the prayer. Mystically, this signifies that *Baruch She'amar* has an effect on ''the higher regions.''

Baruch She'amar begins with a series of phrases in which we bless seven aspects of God. The view of *Rabbi David Hoffmann*, cited and expounded in *World of Prayer*, asserts that these

seven ideas are all implied by the Four-Letter Name, י-ה-ו-ה. That Name contains the letters of הָיָה הֹוֶה יִהְיֶה, *He was, He is, He will be*. It is the Name that symbolizes God's eternity, His mastery of all situations, and the fact that He brought everything into being and will carry out His will and word. The seven ideas expressed by this Name are:

(1) שֶׁאָמַר וְהָיָה הָעוֹלָם — *He Who spoke, and the world came into being*. God is the Creator Who brought all of Creation into being and maintains it [עֹשֶׂה בְרֵאשִׁית] with no more than His word.

(2) אוֹמֵר וְעֹשֶׂה — *He Who speaks and Who does*. God brings His promise into being even when people no longer seem to deserve His generosity. Conversely, גּוֹזֵר וּמְקַיֵּם, He *decrees and fulfills*; when He warns of punishment, the sinner cannot escape unless he repents sincerely.

(3) מְרַחֵם עַל הָאָרֶץ — *He Who has mercy on the earth*. The Four-Letter Name also refers to Him as the merciful God, Who has compassion on the

בָּרוּךְ מְרַחֵם עַל הַבְּרִיּוֹת, בָּרוּךְ מְשַׁלֵּם שָׂכָר

‹ a ‹ is He Who ‹ blessed ‹‹ the creatures; ‹ on ‹ is He Who ‹ blessed
reward   gives   has mercy

טוֹב לִירֵאָיו,* בָּרוּךְ חַי לָעַד וְקַיָּם לָנֶצַח,*

‹‹ to ‹ and Who ‹ forever ‹ is He ‹ blessed ‹‹ to those who ‹ that is
eternity;* endures   Who lives   fear Him;*   good

בָּרוּךְ פּוֹדֶה וּמַצִּיל,* בָּרוּךְ שְׁמוֹ.* בָּרוּךְ אַתָּה

‹ are You, ‹ Blessed ‹‹ is His ‹ – blessed ‹‹ and Who ‹ is He Who ‹ blessed
Name!*   rescues*   redeems

יהוה אֱלֹהֵינוּ מֶלֶךְ הָעוֹלָם, הָאֵל אָב הָרַחֲמָן*

‹‹ Who is ‹ Father ‹‹ the God, ‹‹ of the ‹ King ‹ our God, ‹ HASHEM,
merciful,*   universe,

הַמְהֻלָּל בְּפֶה עַמּוֹ,* מְשֻׁבָּח וּמְפֹאָר בִּלְשׁוֹן

‹ by the ‹ and glorified ‹ praised ‹‹ of His ‹ by the ‹ Who is lauded
tongue   people,* mouth

חֲסִידָיו וַעֲבָדָיו.* וּבְשִׁירֵי* דָוִד עַבְדֶּךָ נְהַלֶּלְךָ

‹ we shall ‹ Your ‹ of David ‹ And through ‹‹ and His ‹ of His
laud You, servant   the psalms* servants.* devout ones

---

earth and all its בְּרִיּוֹת, creatures.

(4) מְשַׁלֵּם שָׂכָר טוֹב לִירֵאָיו — He Who gives a reward that is good to those who fear Him. His reward may not be dispensed in This World, but it will surely be dispensed in the World to Come. Whatever the case, no good deed goes unrewarded.

(5) חַי לָעַד וְקַיָּם לָנֶצַח — He Who lives forever and Who endures to eternity. Not only is God's existence infinite and eternal, He lives forever, in the sense that He continues to involve Himself in the affairs of the universe.

(6) פּוֹדֶה וּמַצִּיל — He Who redeems people from moral decline and Who rescues them from physical danger. The classic example of this is the Redemption from Egypt, when God took a degraded, powerless rabble and transformed it into a great nation.

(7) בָּרוּךְ שְׁמוֹ — Blessed is His Name! The Name by which we call God can in no way express His true essence. Nevertheless, in His kindness to man, He allows us to glimpse some of His properties and express them in a Name.

הָאֵל אָב הָרַחֲמָן — The God, Father Who is merciful. We bless God with awareness that He is both all-powerful [אֵל] and filled with mercy, like a father whose behavior is a constant expression of mercy, even when he must be harsh (Siach Yitzchak).

בְּפֶה עַמּוֹ — By the mouth of His people. The Kabbalists comment that בְּפֶה has the numerical value of 87, and alludes to the number of words in this prayer. Magen Avraham and Mishnah Berurah (51:1) favor the usage of this word. Nevertheless, some commentators feel that the word בְּפִי, which has the same meaning, is the preferred grammatical form.

חֲסִידָיו וַעֲבָדָיו — His devout ones and His servants. We would not dare to compose praises on our own, for we are totally inadequate to evaluate God. We praise Him with the words of the great and holy people of the past (Etz Yosef).

וּבְשִׁירֵי ... חֵי הָעוֹלָמִים — And through the psalms ... Life-giver of the worlds. Etz Yosef explains that each phrase previews a different part of the prayer service that follows: וּבְשִׁירֵי

יהוה אֱלֹהֵינוּ בִּשְׁבָחוֹת וּבִזְמִרוֹת, וּנְגַדֶּלְךָ
‹ we shall exalt You, ‹‹ and songs, ‹ with praises ‹ our God ‹ HASHEM,

וּנְשַׁבֵּחֲךָ וּנְפָאֶרְךָ וְנַמְלִיכְךָ וְנַזְכִּיר שִׁמְךָ, מַלְכֵּנוּ
‹ our King, ‹‹ Your Name, ‹ and mention ‹ proclaim Your reign, ‹ glorify You, ‹ praise You,

אֱלֹהֵינוּ. ⬦ יָחִיד, חֵי הָעוֹלָמִים,* מֶלֶךְ מְשֻׁבָּח
‹ [that] praised ‹‹ King, ‹‹ of the worlds,* ‹ Life-giver ‹ O Unique One, ‹‹ our God.

וּמְפֹאָר עֲדֵי עַד שְׁמוֹ הַגָּדוֹל. בָּרוּךְ אַתָּה יהוה,
‹‹ HASHEM, ‹ are You, ‹ Blessed ‹‹ that is great. ‹ is His Name, ‹ eternally ‹ and glorified

מֶלֶךְ מְהֻלָּל בַּתִּשְׁבָּחוֹת. (אָמֵן.) —Cong.)
‹‹ (Amen.) ‹‹ with praises. ‹ Who is lauded ‹ the King

**IN MOST CONGREGATIONS מִזְמוֹר לְתוֹדָה (PSALM 100) IS RECITED WHILE STANDING.
IT IS OMITTED ON EREV YOM KIPPUR, EREV PESACH, AND CHOL HAMOED PESACH.**

מִזְמוֹר לְתוֹדָה; הָרִיעוּ לַיהוה כָּל הָאָרֶץ.
‹‹ the earth. ‹ all ‹ to HASHEM, ‹ call out ‹‹ of thanksgiving, ‹ A psalm

עִבְדוּ אֶת יהוה בְּשִׂמְחָה,* בֹּאוּ לְפָנָיו בִּרְנָנָה.
‹‹ with joyous song. ‹ before Him ‹ come ‹‹ with gladness,* ‹ HASHEM ‹ Serve

דְּעוּ כִּי יהוה הוּא אֱלֹהִים; הוּא עָשָׂנוּ, וְלוֹ
‹ and His ‹ made us ‹ He ‹‹ is God; ‹ He ‹ HASHEM, ‹ that ‹ Know

---

נְהַלֶּלְךָ דָוִד עַבְדְּךָ, *And through the psalms of David Your servant we shall laud You*, refers to בִּשְׁבָחוֹת; הוֹדוּ לַה', *with praises*, refers to מִזְמוֹר לְתוֹדָה; וּבִזְמִרוֹת, *and songs*, are the psalms that compose the heart of *Pesukei D'Zimrah*; וּנְגַדֶּלְךָ, *we shall exalt You*, refers to אָז יָשִׁיר, where mention is made of God's יַד הַגְּדֹלָה; וּנְשַׁבֵּחֲךָ, *we shall praise You*, refers to יִשְׁתַּבַּח; וּנְפָאֶרְךָ, *we shall glorify You*, refers to the first of the blessings of *Shema*, where we say יוֹצֵר אוֹר; וְנַזְכִּיר שִׁמְךָ, *mention Your Name*, refers to the second of the blessings of *Shema*, where we say שִׁמְךָ; וְנַמְלִיכְךָ, *proclaim Your reign*, refers to the acceptance of God's absolute

sovereignty (קַבָּלַת עוֹל מַלְכוּת שָׁמַיִם) in *Shema*; and finally, חֵי הָעוֹלָמִים, *Life-giver of the worlds*, alludes, through the numerical value of חַי, to the *Shemoneh Esrei*, the eighteen blessings.

עִבְדוּ אֶת ה' בְּשִׂמְחָה — *Serve HASHEM with gladness.* But in *Psalms* 2:11 we are told to *serve HASHEM with awe.* How can we reconcile gladness with awe for God? To feel fear, respect, and awe for God is essential to spiritual growth. Once a person realizes that his fear is the beginning of a process that leads to personal greatness and bliss, even the difficulties along the way can be accepted with gladness (*Ikkarim*).

אֲנַחְנוּ, עַמּוֹ וְצֹאן מַרְעִיתוֹ. בֹּאוּ שְׁעָרָיו בְּתוֹדָה,

⟨ with ⟨ His gates ⟨ Enter ⟪ of His pasture. ⟨ and the ⟨ His ⟪ are we,
thanksgiving,　　　　　　　　　　　　　　sheep　people

חֲצֵרֹתָיו בִּתְהִלָּה; הוֹדוּ לוֹ, בָּרְכוּ שְׁמוֹ. ∴ כִּי טוֹב

⟨ good ⟨ For　⟪ His ⟨ bless ⟨ to ⟨ give ⟪ with praise; ⟨ His courtyards
　　　　　　　Name.　　　　Him, thanks

יהוה, לְעוֹלָם חַסְדּוֹ, וְעַד דֹּר וָדֹר אֱמוּנָתוֹ.

⟪　is His　⟨ to gen- ⟨ gener- ⟨ and ⟪　is His　⟨ enduring ⟪ is Hashem,
faithfulness.　eration　ation　from　kindness,　forever

THE FOLLOWING PRAYER SHOULD BE RECITED WITH SPECIAL INTENSITY.

יְהִי כְבוֹד יהוה* לְעוֹלָם, יִשְׂמַח יהוה

⟨ let Hashem rejoice ⟨ endure forever, ⟨ of Hashem* ⟨ the glory ⟨ May

בְּמַעֲשָׂיו.[1] יְהִי שֵׁם יהוה מְבֹרָךְ מֵעַתָּה וְעַד

⟨ until ⟨ from this time ⟨ be blessed ⟨ of Hashem ⟨ the Name ⟨ Let ⟪ in His works.

עוֹלָם. מִמִּזְרַח שֶׁמֶשׁ עַד מְבוֹאוֹ, מְהֻלָּל שֵׁם

⟨ is the Name ⟨ praised ⟪ its setting, ⟨ to ⟨ of the sun ⟨ From the rising ⟪ eternity.

יהוה. רָם עַל כָּל גּוֹיִם יהוה, עַל הַשָּׁמַיִם

⟨ the heavens ⟨ above ⟪ is Hashem, ⟨ nations ⟨ all ⟨ above ⟨ High ⟪ of Hashem.

כְּבוֹדוֹ.[2] יהוה שִׁמְךָ* לְעוֹלָם, יהוה זִכְרְךָ* לְדֹר

⟨ from ⟨ Your mem- ⟨ Hashem, ⟪ forever, ⟨ Your ⟨ Hashem, ⟪ is His glory.
generation　orial is*　　　　　　　　Name is*

(1) *Psalms* 104:31. (2) 113:2-4.

❧ יְהִי כְבוֹד ה' — *May the glory of* Hashem. This
is a collection of verses, primarily from *Psalms*,
that revolves around two themes: the sovereignty of God and the role of Israel. Central to
tefillah and to the purpose of creation is מַלְכוּת
שָׁמַיִם, *the Kingship of Heaven*, which means
that every being exists as part of God's plan and
is dedicated to His service. This idea is found in
nature itself, for, as David says lyrically, man
attains awareness of God when he contemplates
the beauty and perfection of the universe. The
Sages chose *Psalms* 104:31 to begin this prayer
because it was the praise proclaimed by an angel
when the newly created plant world developed

according to God's wishes (*Chullin* 60a). In
other words, the "glory" of God is revealed on
earth when His will is done. Most of this prayer
deals with this concept of God's glory and
Kingship. The last five verses speak of God's
selection of the Jewish people and pleads for His
mercy and attentiveness to their prayers (see
World of Prayer).

שִׁמְךָ . . . זִכְרְךָ — *Your Name is . . . Your memorial
is.* The *Name* of God represents what He truly is
and implies a thorough understanding of His
actions and the reasons for them. But because
man's limited intelligence cannot reach this
level of understanding, we do not pronounce

וָדֹר. ¹ יהוה בַּשָּׁמַיִם הֵכִין כִּסְאוֹ, וּמַלְכוּתוֹ בַּכֹּל

⟨ over all ⟨ and His ⟪ His ⟨ has ⟨ in heaven ⟨ HASHEM ⟪ to gen-
kingdom throne, established eration.

מָשָׁלָה. ² יִשְׂמְחוּ הַשָּׁמַיִם וְתָגֵל הָאָרֶץ,* וְיֹאמְרוּ

⟨ and they ⟪ the earth,* ⟨ and rejoice ⟨ the heavens ⟨ Glad will be ⟪ does reign.
will proclaim will

בַּגּוֹיִם יהוה מָלָךְ. ³ יהוה מֶלֶךְ,*⁴ יהוה מָלָךְ,⁵

⟪ has ⟨ HASHEM ⟪ reigns,* ⟨ HASHEM ⟨ has ⟨ HASHEM ⟨ among the
reigned, reigned! nations,

יהוה יִמְלֹךְ לְעֹלָם וָעֶד. ⁶ יהוה מֶלֶךְ עוֹלָם וָעֶד,

⟪ and ever, ⟨ for ever ⟨ is King ⟨ HASHEM ⟪ and ever. ⟨ for ever ⟨ shall reign ⟨ HASHEM

אָבְדוּ גוֹיִם* מֵאַרְצוֹ. ⁷ יהוה הֵפִיר עֲצַת גּוֹיִם, הֵנִיא

⟨ He ⟪ of ⟨ the ⟨ annuls ⟨ HASHEM ⟪ from His ⟨ [then] the nations
thwarts nations; counsel earth. will have vanished*

מַחְשְׁבוֹת עַמִּים. ⁸ רַבּוֹת מַחֲשָׁבוֹת בְּלֶב אִישׁ,

⟪ of ⟨ that are ⟨ are the designs ⟨ Many ⟪ of peoples. ⟨ the designs
man, in the heart

וַעֲצַת יהוה הִיא תָקוּם. ⁹ עֲצַת יהוה לְעוֹלָם

⟨ forever ⟨ of ⟨ The ⟪ will prevail. ⟨ — only ⟪ of HASHEM ⟨ but the
HASHEM counsel it counsel

תַּעֲמֹד, מַחְשְׁבוֹת לִבּוֹ לְדֹר וָדֹר. ¹⁰ כִּי הוּא אָמַר

⟨ spoke ⟨ He ⟨ For ⟪ to gen- ⟨ from gen- ⟨ of His ⟨ the designs ⟪ will endure,
eration. eration heart

---

(1) *Psalms* 135:13. (2) *103:19.* (3) *I Chronicles* 16:31. (4) *Psalms* 10:16. (5) *93:1 et al.*
(6) *Exodus* 15:18. (7) *Psalms* 10:16. (8) *33:10.* (9) *Proverbs* 19:21. (10) *Psalms* 33:11.

the Name י־ה־ו־ה as it is spelled; thereby we symbolize our inability to know God as He truly is. In this sense, the pronunciation HASHEM is God's *memorial* (see *Pesachim* 50a).

יִשְׂמְחוּ הַשָּׁמַיִם וְתָגֵל הָאָרֶץ — *Glad will be the heavens and rejoice will the earth.* The celestial and terrestrial parts of Creation serve God. They will truly rejoice when all nations, too, acknowledge that HASHEM has reigned.

ה׳ מֶלֶךְ — *HASHEM reigns . . .* This is one of the most familiar verses in the entire liturgy, but, surprisingly enough, it is not found in Scripture. Rather, each phrase comes from a different part of Scripture. In combination, the three phrases express the eternity of God's reign.

אָבְדוּ גוֹיִם — *[Then] the nations will have vanished.* The verse refers only to the *evil* people among the nations, for their deeds prevent others from acknowledging God (*Rashi, Radak*).

וַיְהִי, הוּא צִוָּה וַיַּעֲמֹד.¹ כִּי בָחַר יהוה בְּצִיּוֹן,

‹‹ Zion; ‹ HASHEM has chosen ‹ For ‹‹ and it ‹ com- ‹ He ‹‹ and it came
endured. manded to be;

אִוָּהּ לְמוֹשָׁב לוֹ.² כִּי יַעֲקֹב בָּחַר לוֹ יָהּ, יִשְׂרָאֵל

‹ Israel ‹‹ by ‹ for His ‹ was ‹ Jacob ‹ For ‹‹ for ‹ for a ‹ He has
God, own selected Him. habitation desired it

לִסְגֻלָּתוֹ.³ כִּי לֹא יִטֹּשׁ יהוה עַמּוֹ, וְנַחֲלָתוֹ

‹ and His ‹‹ His people, ‹ will HASHEM ‹ forsake not ‹ Because ‹‹ as His treasure.
heritage

לֹא יַעֲזֹב.⁴ ❖ וְהוּא רַחוּם יְכַפֵּר עָוֹן וְלֹא יַשְׁחִית,

‹‹ destroy; ‹ and ‹ of ‹ is ‹ the Merci- ‹ Neverthe- ‹‹ He will not
does not iniquity forgiving ful One, less, He, abandon.

וְהִרְבָּה לְהָשִׁיב אַפּוֹ, וְלֹא יָעִיר כָּל חֲמָתוֹ.⁵

‹‹ His entire wrath. ‹ arousing ‹ not ‹‹ His anger, ‹ He withdraws ‹ frequently

יהוה הוֹשִׁיעָה, הַמֶּלֶךְ יַעֲנֵנוּ בְיוֹם קָרְאֵנוּ.⁶

‹‹ we call. ‹ on the day ‹ answer us ‹ May the King ‹‹ save! ‹ HASHEM,

אַשְׁרֵי יוֹשְׁבֵי בֵיתֶךָ, עוֹד יְהַלְלוּךָ סֶּלָה.⁷ אַשְׁרֵי

‹ Praise- ‹ Selah. ‹‹ they will ‹ continually ‹‹ in Your ‹ are those ‹ Praiseworthy
worthy praise You, house, who dwell

הָעָם שֶׁכָּכָה לּוֹ, אַשְׁרֵי הָעָם שֶׁיהוה אֱלֹהָיו.⁸

‹‹ is their ‹ that HASHEM ‹ is the ‹ praise- ‹‹ is ‹ that such ‹ is the
God. people worthy their lot; people

_____

(1) *Psalms* 33:9. (2) 132:13. (3) 135:4. (4) 94:14. (5) 78:38. (6) 20:10. (7) 84:5. (8) 144:15.

אַשְׁרֵי‎ / Ashrei

The Talmud (*Berachos* 4b) teaches that the Sages assured a share in the World to Come to anyone who recites *Ashrei* properly three times a day. It has this special status because no other psalm possesses both of these virtues: (a) Beginning with the word אֲרוֹמִמְךָ (the first substantive word of the psalm), the initials of the psalm's respective verses follow the order of the *aleph-beis*; and (b) it contains the inspiring and reassuring testimony to God's mercy, פּוֹתֵחַ אֶת יָדֶךָ ..., *You open Your hand* ... As *Zohar* teaches, the recitation of this verse is not considered a *request* that God open His hand

for us; rather it is purely a recitation of praise.

Psalm 145 begins with the verse תְּהִלָּה לְדָוִד; the two preliminary verses, each beginning with the word אַשְׁרֵי, are affixed to תְּהִלָּה לְדָוִד for two reasons: (a) By expressing the idea that those who dwell in God's house of prayer and service are praiseworthy, these verses set the stage for the succeeding psalms of praise, for we, the praiseworthy ones, are about to laud the God in Whose house we dwell; and (b) the word אַשְׁרֵי is found three times in these verses. This alludes to the Talmudic dictum that one who recites Psalm 145 three times a day is assured of a share in the World to Come; thus, those who

תהלים קמה / Psalm 145

תְּהִלָּה לְדָוִד; אֲרוֹמִמְךָ* אֱלוֹהַי הַמֶּלֶךְ, וַאֲבָרְכָה

‹ A psalm of praise ›› by David: ‹ I will exalt You,* ‹ my God, ‹ the King, ›› and I will bless

שִׁמְךָ לְעוֹלָם וָעֶד. בְּכָל יוֹם אֲבָרְכֶךָּ,* וַאֲהַלְלָה

‹ Your Name ‹ for ever ›› and ever. ‹ Every ‹ day ›› I will bless You,* ‹ and I will laud

שִׁמְךָ לְעוֹלָם וָעֶד. גָּדוֹל יהוה וּמְהֻלָּל מְאֹד,

‹ Your Name ‹ for ever ›› and ever. ‹ Great ‹ is Hashem, ‹ and lauded ›› exceedingly,

וְלִגְדֻלָּתוֹ אֵין חֵקֶר.* דּוֹר לְדוֹר יְשַׁבַּח מַעֲשֶׂיךָ,

‹ and His greatness ‹ is beyond investigation.* ›› Generation ‹ to ‹ generation ‹ will praise ›› Your actions,

וּגְבוּרֹתֶיךָ יַגִּידוּ. הֲדַר כְּבוֹד הוֹדֶךָ וְדִבְרֵי

and Your mighty deeds ‹ they will recount. ›› The splendrous ‹ glory ‹ of Your majesty ‹ and Your deeds

נִפְלְאֹתֶיךָ אָשִׂיחָה. וֶעֱזוּז נוֹרְאֹתֶיךָ יֹאמֵרוּ,

‹ that are wondrous ‹ I shall discuss. ›› And of the might ‹ of Your awesome deeds ‹ they will speak, ››

וּגְדוּלָּתְךָ אֲסַפְּרֶנָּה. זֵכֶר רַב טוּבְךָ יַבִּיעוּ,

‹ and Your greatness ‹ I shall relate. ›› A recollection ‹ of Your abundant goodness ‹ they will utter, ››

וְצִדְקָתְךָ יְרַנֵּנוּ. חַנּוּן וְרַחוּם* יהוה, אֶרֶךְ אַפַּיִם

and of Your righteousness ‹ they will sing joyfully. ›› Gracious ‹ and merciful* ‹ is Hashem, ‹ slow ‹ to anger,

---

do so are indeed אַשְׁרֵי, *praiseworthy.*

תְּהִלָּה . . . אֲרוֹמִמְךָ — *A psalm . . . I will exalt You.* Beginning with the word אֲרוֹמִמְךָ, the initial words of the respective verses follow the order of the *aleph-beis.* According to *Abudraham* the *aleph-beis* structure symbolizes that we praise God with every sound available to the organs of speech. *Midrash Tadshei* records that the Psalmists and Sages used the *aleph-beis* formula in chapters that they wanted people to follow more readily or to memorize easily.

בְּכָל יוֹם אֲבָרְכֶךָּ — *Every day I will bless You.* True, no mortal can pretend to know God's essence, but each of us *is* equipped to appreciate life, health, sustenance, sunshine, rainfall, and so on. For these and their daily renewal, we give daily blessings (*Siach Yitzchak*).

וְלִגְדֻלָּתוֹ אֵין חֵקֶר — *And His greatness is beyond investigation.* Much though we may try, we can understand neither God's essence nor His ways through human analysis, for He is infinite. We *must* rely on the traditions that have come to us from earlier generations, as the next verse suggests (*Rama*).

חַנּוּן וְרַחוּם — *Gracious and merciful.* Because God is *merciful,* He is אֶרֶךְ אַפַּיִם, *slow to anger,* so

וּגְדָל חָסֶד. **טוֹב** יהוה לַכֹּל, וְרַחֲמָיו עַל כָּל

‹ all ‹ are on ‹ His mercies ‹‹ to all; ‹ HASHEM is good ‹‹ in [bestowing] ‹ and great and kindness.

מַעֲשָׂיו. **יוֹדוּךָ** יהוה כָּל מַעֲשֶׂיךָ, וַחֲסִידֶיךָ

‹ and Your devout ones ‹‹ Your creations, ‹ — all ‹‹ HASHEM ‹ They thank You, ‹‹ His creations.

יְבָרְכוּכָה. **כְּבוֹד** מַלְכוּתְךָ יֹאמֵרוּ, וּגְבוּרָתְךָ

‹ and of Your power ‹‹ they will speak, ‹ of Your kingdom ‹ Of the glory ‹‹ will bless You.

יְדַבֵּרוּ. **לְהוֹדִיעַ** לִבְנֵי הָאָדָם גְּבוּרֹתָיו, וּכְבוֹד

‹ and of the glorious ‹‹ of His mighty deeds, ‹ mankind ‹ To inform ‹‹ they will declare.

הֲדַר מַלְכוּתוֹ. **מַלְכוּתְךָ** מַלְכוּת כָּל עֹלָמִים,

‹‹ eternities, ‹ [spanning] all ‹ is a kingdom ‹ Your kingdom ‹‹ of His kingdom. ‹ splendor

וּמֶמְשַׁלְתְּךָ בְּכָל דּוֹר וָדֹר. **סוֹמֵךְ** יהוה* לְכָל

‹ all ‹ HASHEM supports* ‹‹ after generation. ‹ generation ‹ is ‹ and Your dominion throughout

הַנֹּפְלִים, וְזוֹקֵף לְכָל הַכְּפוּפִים. **עֵינֵי** כֹל אֵלֶיךָ

‹ to You ‹ of all ‹ The eyes ‹‹ those who are bent. ‹ all ‹ and straightens ‹‹ those who are fallen,

יְשַׂבֵּרוּ,* **וְאַתָּה** נוֹתֵן לָהֶם אֶת אָכְלָם בְּעִתּוֹ.

‹‹ in its proper time. ‹ their food ‹ them ‹ give ‹ and You ‹‹ do look with hope,*

---

that punishment, although deserved, is delayed as long as possible to allow time for repentance. And because He is *gracious*, He is גְּדָל חָסֶד, *great in bestowing kindness* (Siach Yitzchak).

סוֹמֵךְ ה׳ — *HASHEM supports.* No verse in *Ashrei* begins with a נ, because in the context of this verse that speaks of God supporting the fallen, the letter נ can be taken as an allusion to נְפִילָה, Israel's future *downfall*, ח״ו, and the Psalmist refused to suggest such tragedy. Nevertheless, knowing that downfalls would take place, the Psalmist comforted Israel by saying *Hashem supports all the fallen ones.* Even when a

dreaded downfall happens, the people can look forward to His support (*Berachos* 4b). *Maharsha* comments that by omitting a direct mention of downfall, the Psalmist implies that even when Israel *does* suffer reverses, those reverses will never be final. Rather, as the next verse declares, God will support the fallen.

עֵינֵי כֹל אֵלֶיךָ יְשַׂבֵּרוּ — *The eyes of all do look to You with hope.* Even animals instinctively rely upon God for their sustenance [how much more so should man recognize the beneficence of his Maker!] (*Radak*).

CONCENTRATE INTENTLY WHILE RECITING THE VERSE פּוֹתֵחַ, *YOU OPEN* ...
IT IS CUSTOMARY TO TOUCH THE ARM-*TEFILLIN* WHILE SAYING THE FIRST HALF OF THE VERSE,
AND THE HEAD-*TEFILLIN* WHILE SAYING THE SECOND.

פּוֹתֵחַ* אֶת יָדֶךָ, וּמַשְׂבִּיעַ לְכָל חַי רָצוֹן.
You open* ⟨ Your hand, ⟩⟨ and satisfy ⟨ every ⟩ living ⟨ [with its] ⟩⟩
thing desire.

צַדִּיק* יהוה בְּכָל דְּרָכָיו, וְחָסִיד* בְּכָל מַעֲשָׂיו.
Righteous* ⟨ is ⟨ in all ⟨ and ⟨⟨ His ways, ⟨ and ⟩ in all ⟨ His deeds. ⟩⟩
HASHEM magnanimous*

קָרוֹב יהוה לְכָל קֹרְאָיו, לְכֹל אֲשֶׁר יִקְרָאֻהוּ
Close ⟨ is HASHEM ⟨ to all ⟩⟩ who call upon Him, ⟨ to all ⟨ who ⟨ call upon Him ⟩

בֶּאֱמֶת. **רְצוֹן** יְרֵאָיו יַעֲשֶׂה, וְאֶת שַׁוְעָתָם יִשְׁמַע
sincerely. ⟩⟩ The will ⟨ of those who ⟨⟨ He will do; ⟨ and their cry ⟨ He will ⟩
fear Him hear,

וְיוֹשִׁיעֵם. **שׁוֹמֵר** יהוה אֶת כָּל אֹהֲבָיו, וְאֵת כָּל
and He will save them. ⟩⟩ HASHEM protects ⟨ all ⟩⟨ who love Him; ⟨ but all ⟩

הָרְשָׁעִים יַשְׁמִיד. ❖ **תְּהִלַּת** יהוה יְדַבֶּר פִּי, וִיבָרֵךְ
the wicked ⟨ He will ⟨⟨ The ⟨ praise ⟨ of ⟨⟨ He will ⟨ and ⟩
destroy. HASHEM declare, mouth may my bless

כָּל בָּשָׂר שֵׁם קָדְשׁוֹ לְעוֹלָם וָעֶד. וַאֲנַחְנוּ נְבָרֵךְ*
may ⟨ flesh ⟨ the ⟨ Name ⟨ of His ⟨ for ever ⟨ and ⟩⟩ But we ⟨ will bless* ⟩
all Holiness for ever.

יָהּ מֵעַתָּה וְעַד עוֹלָם; הַלְלוּיָהּ.* ¹
God ⟨ from this time ⟨ until ⟨ eternity. ⟩⟩ Halleluyah!* ⟩⟩

---

(1) *Psalms* 115:18.

פּוֹתֵחַ — *You open.* When reciting this verse, one must have in mind the meaning of the words because this declaration of God's universal goodness is one of the two reasons the Sages required the thrice-daily recitation of this psalm. One who forgot to concentrate on the meaning must recite the verse again (*Tur* and *Shulchan Aruch* 51:7). This verse should be recited with great joy at the knowledge that God cares for every creature (*Yesod V'Shoresh HaAvodah*).

צַדִּיק ... חָסִיד — *Righteous ... magnanimous.*

God's ways are just and *righteous*, meaning that He judges people only according to their deeds. Nevertheless, even when justice calls for harsh punishment, He is *magnanimous* in softening the blow, for He is merciful (*Vilna Gaon*).

וַאֲנַחְנוּ נְבָרֵךְ — *But we will bless.* This verse is appended to *Ashrei* for, having recited *Ashrei* which holds an assurance of the World to Come, we express the hope that we will bless God *forever* — that is, in both worlds (*Levush*).

הַלְלוּיָהּ — *Halleluyah.* This word is composed of

— תהלים קמו / Psalm 146 —

הַלְלוּיָהּ; הַלְלִי נַפְשִׁי אֶת יהוה.* אֲהַלְלָה

⟨ I will praise ⟨⟨ HASHEM!* ⟨ O my soul ⟨ Praise ⟨⟨ Halleluyah!

יהוה בְּחַיָּי, אֲזַמְּרָה לֵאלֹהַי בְּעוֹדִי. אַל תִּבְטְחוּ

⟨ Do not rely ⟨⟨ while I exist. ⟨ to my God ⟨ I will make music ⟨⟨ while I live, ⟨ HASHEM

בִנְדִיבִים, בְּבֶן אָדָם* שֶׁאֵין לוֹ תְשׁוּעָה. תֵּצֵא

⟨ When depart ⟨⟨ salvation. ⟨ for he holds no ⟨ [nor] on a human being,* ⟨⟨ on nobles,

רוּחוֹ יָשֻׁב לְאַדְמָתוֹ, בַּיּוֹם הַהוּא אָבְדוּ עֶשְׁתֹּנֹתָיו.

⟨⟨ do all his plans. ⟨ perish ⟨ on that day ⟨⟨ to his earth, ⟨ he returns ⟨ does his spirit,

אַשְׁרֵי שֶׁאֵל יַעֲקֹב בְּעֶזְרוֹ, שִׂבְרוֹ עַל יהוה אֱלֹהָיו.

⟨⟨ his God. ⟨ HASHEM, ⟨ is in ⟨ whose hope ⟨⟨ is his help, ⟨ of Jacob ⟨ whom the God ⟨ Praiseworthy is he

עֹשֶׂה שָׁמַיִם וָאָרֶץ,* אֶת הַיָּם וְאֶת כָּל אֲשֶׁר בָּם;

⟨⟨ is in them; ⟨ that ⟨ and all ⟨ the sea ⟨ and earth,* ⟨ of heaven ⟨ [He is] the Maker

הַשֹּׁמֵר אֱמֶת לְעוֹלָם. עֹשֶׂה מִשְׁפָּט לַעֲשׁוּקִים,

⟨⟨ for the exploited; ⟨ justice ⟨ He does ⟨⟨ forever. ⟨ truth ⟨ He safeguards

נֹתֵן לֶחֶם לָרְעֵבִים; יהוה מַתִּיר אֲסוּרִים. יהוה

⟨ HASHEM ⟨⟨ the bound; ⟨ releases ⟨ HASHEM ⟨⟨ to the hungry. ⟨ bread ⟨ He gives

---

two words: הַלְלוּ, *praise*, and יָהּ, *God.* הַלְלוּ denotes crying out in exultation, while the unique meaning implied by the Name יָהּ means "the One Who is forever." The Psalmist addresses everyone: Use your energy to be *excited* over God — and only God — and nothing else (*R' Avigdor Miller*).

Psalm 146 / הַלְלוּיָהּ הַלְלִי נַפְשִׁי אֶת ה׳ ﬞ

Radak interprets this psalm as a hymn of encouragement for Jews in exile. The Psalmist begins by insisting that he will praise God as long as he lives and warning his fellow Jews not to rely on human beings. After praising God as the One

Who cares for the underprivileged and oppressed, he concludes that God will reign forever — despite the current ascendancy of our enemies.

בְּבֶן אָדָם — *[Nor] on a human being.* When rulers help Israel, it is because God has influenced them to do so. So it will be when the nations seem to have a hand in the Messianic redemptions (*Radak*).

עֹשֶׂה שָׁמַיִם וָאָרֶץ — *[He is] the Maker of heaven and earth.* Unlike kings and rulers whose powers are limited in both time and space, God is everywhere and is all powerful (*Yerushalmi Berachos* 9:1).

פֹּקֵחַ עִוְרִים, יהוה זֹקֵף כְּפוּפִים; יהוה אֹהֵב

< loves   « HASHEM «   the bent; < straightens < HASHEM « to the blind; < gives sight

צַדִּיקִים. יהוה שֹׁמֵר אֶת גֵּרִים,* יָתוֹם וְאַלְמָנָה

< and widow < orphan «   strangers,* < protects < HASHEM « the righteous.

יְעוֹדֵד; וְדֶרֶךְ רְשָׁעִים יְעַוֵּת. ❖ יִמְלֹךְ יהוה

< HASHEM shall reign « He contorts. < of the wicked < but the way « He encourages;

לְעוֹלָם, אֱלֹהַיִךְ צִיּוֹן לְדֹר וָדֹר; הַלְלוּיָהּ.

« Halleluyah! «   to < from < O Zion, < your God, « forever;
                   generation, generation

──────── תהלים קמז / Psalm 147 ────────

הַלְלוּיָהּ; כִּי טוֹב* זַמְּרָה אֱלֹהֵינוּ, כִּי

< for « to our God, < to make music < it is good* < For «   Halleluyah!

נָעִים נָאוָה תְהִלָּה. בּוֹנֵה יְרוּשָׁלַיִם יהוה, נִדְחֵי

< the « is < of Jerusalem < The « is praise. < and < pleasant
outcasts HASHEM;   Builder   befitting

יִשְׂרָאֵל יְכַנֵּס. הָרוֹפֵא לִשְׁבוּרֵי לֵב, וּמְחַבֵּשׁ

< and the One « of the brokenhearted, <   He is « He will < of Israel
Who bandages   the Healer   gather in.

לְעַצְּבוֹתָם. מוֹנֶה מִסְפָּר לַכּוֹכָבִים,* לְכֻלָּם

< to all of them « of the stars,* < the number < He counts « their sorrows.

שֵׁמוֹת יִקְרָא. גָּדוֹל אֲדוֹנֵינוּ וְרַב כֹּחַ, לִתְבוּנָתוֹ

< His « in < and < is our Lord < Great « He assigns. < names
understanding   strength; abundant

גֵּרִים אֶת שֹׁמֵר ה׳ — *HASHEM protects strangers.*
God is the Protector of all weak and defenseless
strangers, whether uprooted Jews or gentile
converts (*Radak*).

Psalm 147 / הַלְלוּיָהּ כִּי טוֹב⦾
Continuing the theme of redemption, this
psalm places its primary focus on Jerusalem, the
center from which holiness, redemption, and
Torah will emanate. In this sense, Jerusalem
cannot be considered rebuilt until the Redemption, because the city's spiritual grandeur
cannot be recaptured by mere architecture and

growing numbers of people.

לַכּוֹכָבִים מִסְפָּר מוֹנֶה — *He counts the number of
the stars.* Having given the assurance that God
will rebuild Jerusalem and gather in Israel in joy,
the Psalmist goes on to illustrate God's ability to
do so. The next series of verses catalogue His
might, compassion, and attention to individual
needs.

The stars number in the billions, but God is
aware of each one and gives it a "name" that
denotes its purpose in the universe. Thus,
nothing goes unnoticed or unprovided for.

אֵין מִסְפָּר. מְעוֹדֵד עֲנָוִים יהוה, מַשְׁפִּיל

⟨ He lowers ⟨⟨ does Hashem; ⟨ the humble ⟨ Encourage ⟨⟨ calculation. ⟨ is beyond

רְשָׁעִים עֲדֵי אָרֶץ. עֱנוּ לַיהוה בְּתוֹדָה, זַמְּרוּ

⟨ sing ⟨⟨ with thanks, ⟨ to Hashem ⟨ Call out ⟨⟨ the ground. ⟨ to ⟨ the wicked

לֵאלֹהֵינוּ בְכִנּוֹר. הַמְכַסֶּה שָׁמַיִם בְּעָבִים, הַמֵּכִין

⟨ Who ⟨⟨ with clouds, ⟨ the ⟨ It is He ⟨⟨ with the ⟨ to our God
prepares / heavens / Who covers / harp.

לָאָרֶץ מָטָר; הַמַּצְמִיחַ הָרִים חָצִיר. נוֹתֵן

⟨ He gives ⟨⟨ grass. ⟨ [on] the mountains ⟨ Who makes sprout ⟨⟨ rain, ⟨ for the earth

לִבְהֵמָה לַחְמָהּ, לִבְנֵי עֹרֵב אֲשֶׁר יִקְרָאוּ. לֹא

⟨ Not ⟨⟨ cry out. ⟨ that ⟨ ravens ⟨ to young ⟨⟨ its food, ⟨ to an animal

בִגְבוּרַת הַסּוּס* יֶחְפָּץ, לֹא בְשׁוֹקֵי הָאִישׁ*

⟨ of man* ⟨ the thighs ⟨ and not ⟨⟨ does He desire, ⟨ of the horse* ⟨ the strength

יִרְצֶה. רוֹצֶה יהוה אֶת יְרֵאָיו, אֶת הַמְיַחֲלִים

⟨ those who yearn ⟨⟨ those who fear Him, ⟨ Hashem desires ⟨⟨ does He favor.

לְחַסְדּוֹ. שַׁבְּחִי יְרוּשָׁלַיִם אֶת יהוה; הַלְלִי

⟨ laud ⟨⟨ Hashem, ⟨ O Jerusalem ⟨ Praise ⟨⟨ for His kindness.

אֱלֹהַיִךְ, צִיּוֹן. כִּי חִזַּק בְּרִיחֵי* שְׁעָרָיִךְ, בֵּרַךְ

⟨ and [He ⟨⟨ of your gates, ⟨ the bars* ⟨ He has ⟨ For ⟨⟨ O Zion. ⟨ your God,
has] blessed / strengthened

בָּנַיִךְ בְּקִרְבֵּךְ. הַשָּׂם גְּבוּלֵךְ שָׁלוֹם, חֵלֶב חִטִּים*

⟨ wheat* ⟨ [and with] ⟨⟨ peaceful, ⟨ your ⟨ [It is He] ⟨⟨ in your ⟨ your
the choicest / borders / Who makes / midst. / children

יַשְׂבִּיעֵךְ. הַשֹּׁלֵחַ אִמְרָתוֹ אָרֶץ, עַד מְהֵרָה יָרוּץ

⟨ runs ⟨ swiftly ⟨⟨ earthward; ⟨ His ⟨ [It is He] Who ⟨⟨ He satiates
utterance / dispatches / you.

בִּגְבוּרַת הַסּוּס . . . בְּשׁוֹקֵי הָאִישׁ — *The strength of the horse . . . the thighs of man.* The earlier verses spoke of God's compassion for helpless creatures. Now the Psalmist says in contrast, God is unimpressed with powerful battle horses or with the skill of the rider who controls the horse with his thighs (*Radak; Ibn Ezra*).

כִּי חִזַּק בְּרִיחֵי — *For He has strengthened the bars.* The verse is figurative. The Jerusalem of the future will not need bars on its gates. The people will feel secure because God will protect their city (*Radak*).

חֵלֶב חִטִּים — *The choicest wheat.* Wheat is a symbol of prosperity and, therefore, it is an

דְּבָרוֹ. הַנֹּתֵן שֶׁלֶג כַּצָּמֶר, כְּפוֹר כָּאֵפֶר יְפַזֵּר.

《 He scatters. 〈 like ashes 〈 frost 《 like fleece, 〈 snow 〈 [It is He] 《 His word. Who gives

מַשְׁלִיךְ קַרְחוֹ כְפִתִּים, לִפְנֵי קָרָתוֹ מִי יַעֲמֹד.

《 can stand? 〈 who 〈 His cold 〈 — before 《 like crumbs 〈 His ice 〈 He hurls

יִשְׁלַח דְּבָרוֹ וְיַמְסֵם,* יַשֵּׁב רוּחוֹ יִזְּלוּ מָיִם. ❖ מַגִּיד

〈 He relates 《 the waters 〈 His 〈 He 《 and it 〈 His 〈 He issues
flow. wind, blows melts them;* command

דְּבָרָיו לְיַעֲקֹב,* חֻקָּיו וּמִשְׁפָּטָיו לְיִשְׂרָאֵל.

《 to Israel. 〈 and judgments 〈 His statutes 《 to Jacob,* 〈 His words

לֹא עָשָׂה כֵן לְכָל גּוֹי, וּמִשְׁפָּטִים בַּל יְדָעוּם;

《 —they know 《 such judgments 《 nation; 〈 for any 〈 so 〈 He did not do
them not, other

הַלְלוּיָהּ.

《 Halleluyah!

──────── תהלים קמח / Psalm 148 ────────

הַלְלוּיָהּ; הַלְלוּ אֶת יהוה* מִן הַשָּׁמַיִם,*

《 the heavens;* 〈 from 〈 HASHEM* 〈 Praise 《 Halleluyah!

הַלְלוּהוּ בַּמְּרוֹמִים. הַלְלוּהוּ כָל מַלְאָכָיו,*

《 His angels;* 〈 all 〈 Praise Him, 《 in the heights: 〈 praise Him

omen of peace, because prosperous people are less contentious (*Berachos* 57a).

יִשְׁלַח דְּבָרוֹ וְיַמְסֵם — *He issues His command and it melts them.* The Psalmist had spoken of the many solid forms of moisture: snow, frost, ice — but at God's command, everything melts and flows like water. The Jew should emulate nature by conforming to the will of God (*R' Hirsch*).

מַגִּיד דְּבָרָיו לְיַעֲקֹב — *He relates His words to Jacob.* God gave *His words,* the Torah, to *Jacob,* — the entire Jewish nation — even those who are not capable of understanding its intricacies and mysteries. But to *Israel* — the greatest members of the nation — He made known the many variations and shadings of wisdom to be found within His statutes and judgments (*Zohar*).

Lest you wonder at the many centuries that

have gone by without the redemption of Jerusalem and Israel, do not forget that the Torah itself — the very purpose of Creation — was not given to man until 2448 years after Creation. That God sees fit to delay is not cause for despair (*Siach Yitzchak*).

הַלְלוּיָהּ הַלְלוּ אֶת ה' / Psalm 148

Only after the Temple and Jerusalem are built will all the universe join in joyous songs of praise to God. Zion is the meeting point of heaven and earth, as it were, because it is from there that God's heavenly blessings emanate to the rest of the universe.

הַלְלוּ . . . מִן הַשָּׁמַיִם — *Praise . . . from the heavens.* The Psalmist begins by calling upon the heavenly beings to praise God, and then he directs his call to earthly beings. God's praises echo

הַלְלוּהוּ כָּל צְבָאָיו.* הַלְלוּהוּ שֶׁמֶשׁ וְיָרֵחַ,
‹ and moon; ‹ sun ‹ Praise Him, « His legions.* ‹ all ‹ praise Him,

הַלְלוּהוּ כָּל כּוֹכְבֵי אוֹר. הַלְלוּהוּ שְׁמֵי הַשָּׁמָיִם,
« the loftiest heavens, ‹ Praise Him, « that are bright. ‹ stars ‹ all ‹ praise Him,

וְהַמַּיִם אֲשֶׁר מֵעַל הַשָּׁמָיִם. יְהַלְלוּ אֶת שֵׁם
‹ the Name ‹ Let them praise « the heavens. ‹ above ‹ that are ‹ and the waters

יהוה, כִּי הוּא צִוָּה וְנִבְרָאוּ. וַיַּעֲמִידֵם לָעַד
‹ for ever ‹ And He « and they ‹ commanded ‹ He ‹ for « of Hashem,
established them were created.

לְעוֹלָם, חָק נָתַן* וְלֹא יַעֲבוֹר. הַלְלוּ אֶת יהוה
‹ Hashem ‹ Praise « be broken. ‹ that ‹ He ‹ a decree « and ever,
will not issued*

מִן הָאָרֶץ, תַּנִּינִים וְכָל תְּהֹמוֹת. אֵשׁ וּבָרָד,
‹ and hail, Fire « [watery] depths. ‹ and all ‹ sea giants « the earth: ‹ from

שֶׁלֶג וְקִיטוֹר, רוּחַ סְעָרָה עֹשָׂה דְבָרוֹ. הֶהָרִים
‹ the mountains « His word; ‹ fulfilling ‹ of the storm ‹ the wind « and vapor, ‹ snow

וְכָל גְּבָעוֹת, עֵץ פְּרִי וְכָל אֲרָזִים. הַחַיָּה וְכָל
‹ and all ‹ beasts « cedars; ‹ and all ‹ yielding fruit ‹ trees « hills; ‹ and all

בְּהֵמָה, רֶמֶשׂ וְצִפּוֹר כָּנָף. מַלְכֵי אֶרֶץ וְכָל
‹ and all ‹ of the earth ‹ kings « with wings; ‹ and birds ‹ crawling things « cattle,

לְאֻמִּים, שָׂרִים וְכָל שֹׁפְטֵי אָרֶץ. בַּחוּרִים וְגַם
‹ and also ‹ young men « on earth; ‹ judges ‹ and all ‹ princes « regimes,

בְּתוּלוֹת,* זְקֵנִים עִם נְעָרִים. יְהַלְלוּ אֶת שֵׁם
‹ the Name ‹ Let them praise « youths. ‹ together with ‹ old men ‹ maidens,*

from the heavens and descend to earth, where the devout echo the heavenly songs with their own praises (Sforno).

מַלְאָכָיו ... צְבָאָיו — *His angels ... His legions.* The *angels* are spiritual beings without physical form while the *legions* are the heavenly bodies, which are so numerous that they are likened to legions (Radak).

חָק נָתַן — *A decree He issued.* God ordained that the sun shine by day and the moon by night, and this *decree* can never be violated (Rashi).

בַּחוּרִים וְגַם בְּתוּלוֹת — *Young men and also maidens.* The use here of the word וְגַם, *and also,* is noteworthy. The Psalmist does not say that young men *and* women will be together, because such mingling would be immodest.

יְהוָה, כִּי נִשְׂגָּב שְׁמוֹ לְבַדּוֹ; הוֹדוֹ עַל אֶרֶץ

‹ earth ‹ is above ‹ His glory ‹‹ alone; ‹ is His Name ‹ exalted ‹ for ‹ of Hashem,

וְשָׁמָיִם. וַיָּרֶם קֶרֶן לְעַמּוֹ, תְּהִלָּה לְכָל חֲסִידָיו,

‹‹ His devout ‹ for all ‹ [causing] ‹‹ of His ‹ the pride ‹ He has ‹‹ and heaven.
ones,   praise   nation,   exalted

לִבְנֵי יִשְׂרָאֵל עַם קְרֹבוֹ; הַלְלוּיָהּ.

‹‹ Halleluyah! ‹‹ with whom ‹ the ‹ of Israel, ‹ for the
       He is intimate, people   Children

—— Psalm 149 / תהלים קמט ——

הַלְלוּיָהּ; שִׁירוּ לַיהוָה* שִׁיר חָדָשׁ, תְּהִלָּתוֹ

‹ His praise ‹‹ that is new; ‹ a song ‹ to Hashem* ‹ Sing ‹‹ Halleluyah!

בִּקְהַל חֲסִידִים. יִשְׂמַח יִשְׂרָאֵל בְּעֹשָׂיו,* בְּנֵי

‹ let the ‹‹ in its Maker;* ‹ Let Israel rejoice ‹‹ of the devout. ‹ is in the
Children   congregation

צִיּוֹן* יָגִילוּ בְמַלְכָּם. יְהַלְלוּ שְׁמוֹ בְמָחוֹל, בְּתֹף

‹ with ‹‹ with dancing; ‹ His ‹ Let them ‹‹ in their King. ‹ rejoice ‹ of Zion*
drums   Name   praise

וְכִנּוֹר יְזַמְּרוּ לוֹ. כִּי רוֹצֶה יְהוָה בְּעַמּוֹ,* יְפָאֵר

‹ He adorns ‹‹ His people;* ‹ Hashem desires ‹ For ‹‹ to ‹ let them ‹ and harp
                       Him. make music

עֲנָוִים בִּישׁוּעָה. יַעְלְזוּ חֲסִידִים בְּכָבוֹד, יְרַנְּנוּ עַל

‹ upon ‹ let them ‹‹ in glory, ‹ let the devout ‹ Exult ‹‹ with salvation. ‹ the humble
sing joyously

Only later, when he speaks of old men and youths, does the Psalmist say עִם, *with* — that they will be *together* (*Sefer Chassidim*).

Psalm 149 / הַלְלוּיָהּ שִׁירוּ לַה׳ ‎־‎

In every generation, God confronts us with new challenges and problems, yet He provides us with the opportunity to solve them. Thus, our songs of praise never grow stale, because they are always infused with new meaning. But the greatest, newest song of all will spring from Israel's lips when history reaches its climax with the arrival of the Messiah.

בְּעֹשָׂיו — *In its Maker*. Although God made *all* nations, only Israel is His Chosen People (*Sforno*).

בְּנֵי צִיּוֹן — *The Children of Zion*. The future holiness of Zion — the place from which the Torah's teachings will emanate — will be of a higher order than anything we now know. The Jews who benefit from this spiritual aura will be called *the Children of Zion*.

כִּי רוֹצֶה ה׳ בְּעַמּוֹ — *For Hashem desires His people*. God looks forward to Israel's praises (*Radak*).

מִשְׁכְּבוֹתָם.* רוֹמְמוֹת אֵל בִּגְרוֹנָם,* וְחֶרֶב פִּיפִיּוֹת

<< double edged, < and a sword, << are in their throats,* < of God < The lofty praises << their beds.*

בְּיָדָם. לַעֲשׂוֹת נְקָמָה בַּגּוֹיִם, תּוֹכֵחוֹת* בַּלְאֻמִּים.

<< among the regimes; < rebukes* << among the nations, < vengeance < — to execute << is in their hand

לֶאְסֹר מַלְכֵיהֶם בְּזִקִּים, וְנִכְבְּדֵיהֶם בְּכַבְלֵי

< with shackles < and their nobles << with chains, < their kings < to bind

בַרְזֶל. לַעֲשׂוֹת בָּהֶם מִשְׁפָּט כָּתוּב,* הָדָר הוּא

< it will be < [That judgment day,] a splendor < that was written.* << the judgment < upon them < to execute << of iron;

לְכָל חֲסִידָיו; הַלְלוּיָהּ.

<< Halleluyah! < His devout ones, < for all

——— Psalm 150 / תהלים קן ———

הַלְלוּיָהּ; הַלְלוּ אֵל* בְּקָדְשׁוֹ, הַלְלוּהוּ בִּרְקִיעַ

< in the firmament < praise Him << in His Sanctuary; < God* < Praise << Halleluyah!

עֻזּוֹ. הַלְלוּהוּ בִגְבוּרֹתָיו, הַלְלוּהוּ כְּרֹב גֻּדְלוֹ.

<< of His greatness. < as befits the abundance < praise Him << for His mighty acts; < Praise Him << of His power.

הַלְלוּהוּ בְּתֵקַע שׁוֹפָר, הַלְלוּהוּ בְּנֵבֶל וְכִנּוֹר.

<< and harp. < with lyre < praise Him << of the shofar; < with the blast < Praise Him

---

עַל מִשְׁכְּבוֹתָם — *Upon their beds.* The righteous will thank God for allowing them to go to bed without fear of danger and attack (*Etz Yosef*).

רוֹמְמוֹת אֵל בִּגְרוֹנָם — *The lofty praises of God are in their throats.* Though Israel goes into battle holding its *double-edged sword,* it knows that its victory depends on the help of God to Whom it sings praises (*Rashi; Radak*). The expression *in their throats* symbolizes that the prayers are not merely mouthed, but are deeply felt (*Radak*).

תּוֹכֵחוֹת — *Rebukes.* Though Israel is forced to wage battle against its enemies, its primary goal is that the other nations accept moral rebuke.

לַעֲשׂוֹת בָּהֶם מִשְׁפָּט כָּתוּב — *To execute upon them*

the judgment that was written. The future judgment upon the nations has been written in the *Prophets.* The execution of that judgment will bring the reign of justice to earth, and that will be the *splendor* — the pride and vindication — of the righteous who have always lived justly.

הַלְלוּיָהּ הַלְלוּ אֵל / **Psalm 150**

This final psalm of the Book of *Psalms* sums up man's task by saying that he must enrich his spiritual self by recognizing God's greatness and by praising Him. The Psalmist's lengthy list of musical instruments reflects the full spectrum of human emotions and spiritual potential, all of which can be aroused by music.

הַלְלוּהוּ בְתֹף וּמָחוֹל, הַלְלוּהוּ בְּמִנִּים וְעֻגָב.

‹ and flute. ‹ with organ ‹ praise Him ‹‹ and dance; ‹ with drum ‹ Praise Him

הַלְלוּהוּ בְצִלְצְלֵי שֶׁמַע, הַלְלוּהוּ בְּצִלְצְלֵי

‹ with trumpets ‹ praise Him ‹ clanging; ‹ with cymbals ‹ Praise Him

תְרוּעָה. ❖ כֹּל הַנְּשָׁמָה תְּהַלֵּל* יָהּ; הַלְלוּיָהּ.*

‹‹ Halleluyah!* ‹‹ God, ‹ praise* ‹ souls ‹ Let all ‹‹ resounding.

כֹּל הַנְּשָׁמָה תְּהַלֵּל יָהּ; הַלְלוּיָהּ.

‹‹ Halleluyah! ‹‹ God, ‹ praise ‹ souls ‹ Let all

בָּרוּךְ יהוה לְעוֹלָם,* אָמֵן וְאָמֵן.*[1] בָּרוּךְ יהוה

‹ is Hashem ‹ Blessed ‹‹ and Amen.* ‹ Amen ‹‹ forever*, ‹ is Hashem ‹ Blessed

מִצִּיּוֹן, שֹׁכֵן יְרוּשָׁלָיִם, הַלְלוּיָהּ.[2] בָּרוּךְ יהוה

‹ is Hashem ‹ Blessed ‹‹ Halleluyah! ‹‹ in Jerusalem, ‹ He Who ‹‹ from Zion,
dwells

אֱלֹהִים אֱלֹהֵי יִשְׂרָאֵל, עֹשֵׂה נִפְלָאוֹת לְבַדּוֹ.

‹‹ by Himself. ‹ wondrous things ‹ Who does ‹‹ of Israel, ‹ the God ‹ God,

❖ וּבָרוּךְ שֵׁם כְּבוֹדוֹ לְעוֹלָם, וְיִמָּלֵא כְבוֹדוֹ

‹ may His glory ‹ and fill ‹‹ forever; ‹ of His glory ‹ is the Name ‹ Blessed

אֶת כָּל הָאָרֶץ, אָמֵן וְאָמֵן.[3]

‹‹ and Amen. ‹ Amen ‹‹ the earth. ‹ all

---

(1) Psalms 89:53. (2) 135:21. (3) 72:18-19.

כֹּל הַנְּשָׁמָה תְּהַלֵּל — *Let all souls praise.* Far greater than the most sublime instrumental songs of praise is the song of the human soul. God's greatest praise is the soul that utilizes its full potential in His service (*Radak*).

Having now concluded the six psalms that are the main part of *Pesukei D'Zimrah*, we repeat the last verse to signify that this section has come to an end (*Abudraham*).

הַלְלוּיָהּ — *Halleluyah.* The root הלל, *praise,* appears thirteen times in this psalm, an allusion to God's Thirteen Attributes of Mercy [not counting the repetition of the last verse, since in *Psalms* it is not repeated] (*Radak*).

בָּרוּךְ ה' לְעוֹלָם ❧ — *Blessed is Hashem forever.* This collection of verses, each of which begins with the word בָּרוּךְ, is in the nature of a blessing after the six psalms that, as noted above, are the very essence of *Pesukei D'Zimrah* (*Etz Yosef*). The term בָּרוּךְ, which refers to God as the Source of all blessing, is particularly relevant to the just concluded psalms, since they describe God's kindness, power, and future redemption (*R' Munk*).

אָמֵן וְאָמֵן — *Amen and Amen.* The repetition is meant to reemphasize the statement. Responding "Amen" can have three connotations (*Shevuos* 29b): (a) to accept a vow upon oneself, (b) to

ONE MUST STAND FROM וַיְבָרֶךְ דָּוִיד UNTIL AFTER THE PHRASE אַתָּה הוּא ה' הָאֱלֹהִים;
HOWEVER, THERE IS A GENERALLY ACCEPTED CUSTOM TO REMAIN STANDING
UNTIL AFTER בָּרְכוּ (P. 123).

——————— *I Chronicles* 29:10-13 / דברי הימים א כט:י-יג ———————

וַיְבָרֶךְ דָּוִיד* אֶת יהוה לְעֵינֵי כָּל הַקָּהָל,

⟨ the ⟨ of all ⟨ in the sight ⟨   HASHEM   ⟨   And David blessed*
congregation.

וַיֹּאמֶר דָּוִיד: בָּרוּךְ אַתָּה יהוה אֱלֹהֵי יִשְׂרָאֵל

⟨ of Israel ⟨ the God ⟨ HASHEM, ⟨ are You, ⟨ Blessed ⟨⟨   David said:

אָבִינוּ,* מֵעוֹלָם וְעַד עוֹלָם. לְךָ יהוה הַגְּדֻלָּה*

⟨ is the ⟨ HASHEM, ⟨ Yours, ⟨⟨ the World ⟨ to ⟨ from [This] ⟨⟨ our
greatness,*   [to Come].   World   forefather,*

וְהַגְּבוּרָה וְהַתִּפְאֶרֶת וְהַנֵּצַח וְהַהוֹד, כִּי כֹל

⟨ every- ⟨ for ⟨⟨ and the majesty; ⟨ the triumph, ⟨ the glory, ⟨ the strength,
thing

בַּשָּׁמַיִם וּבָאָרֶץ; לְךָ יהוה הַמַּמְלָכָה וְהַמִּתְנַשֵּׂא

⟨ and the ⟨ is the kingdom, ⟨ HASHEM, ⟨ Yours, ⟨⟨ and on earth ⟨ in heaven
sovereignty   [is Yours];

IT IS CUSTOMARY TO SET ASIDE SOMETHING FOR CHARITY WHILE RECITING וְהָעֹשֶׁר וְהַכָּבוֹד מִלְּפָנֶיךָ.

לְכֹל לְרֹאשׁ. וְהָעֹשֶׁר וְהַכָּבוֹד מִלְּפָנֶיךָ, וְאַתָּה

⟨ and You ⟨⟨ [come] from ⟨ and honor ⟨ Wealth ⟨⟨ leader. ⟨ over
before You   every

acknowledge the truth of a statement, and (c) to
express the hope that a statement come true. In
our prayers, any or all are expressed by Amen,
depending on the context (*Iyun Tefillah*).

וַיְבָרֶךְ דָּוִיד — *And David blessed.* The
following selections from the praises of David,
Nehemiah, and Moses, in that order, are
appended to *Pesukei D'Zimrah* because the
fifteen terms of praise found in *Yishtabach* are
based on these selections (*Abudraham*).

The first four verses of this prayer were
uttered by David at one of the supreme
moments of his life: Although he had been
denied Divine permission to build the Holy
Temple, he had assembled the necessary contributions and materials so that his heir, Solomon,
would be prepared to build upon assuming the

throne. In the presence of the assembled
congregation, he thanked and blessed God for
having allowed him to set aside resources for the
Divine service (*I Chronicles* 29:10-13). For this
reason, many adopted the custom of setting
aside something for charity at this point.

יִשְׂרָאֵל אָבִינוּ — *Israel our forefather.* David
mentioned only Israel/Jacob, because he was the
first to make a vow to contribute tithes for a
holy cause as a source of merit in a time of
distress (*Genesis* 28:20), an example followed by
David (*Bereishis Rabbah* 70:1); and also because
it was Jacob who first spoke of the Holy Temple
(*Radak*) and designated Mount Moriah as its
site [see ArtScroll *Bereishis* 28:16-19].

לְךָ ה' הַגְּדֻלָּה — *Yours, HASHEM, is the greatness.*
In his moment of public glory, David scrupu-

מוֹשֵׁל בַּכֹּל, וּבְיָדְךָ כֹּחַ וּגְבוּרָה, וּבְיָדְךָ לְגַדֵּל

⟨ to make ⟨ and it is in ⟪ and strength ⟨ is power ⟨ in Your ⟪ over ⟨ rule
great Your hand hand everything;

וּלְחַזֵּק לַכֹּל. וְעַתָּה אֱלֹהֵינוּ מוֹדִים אֲנַחְנוּ

⟨ we thank ⟪ our God, ⟨ So now, ⟪ anyone. ⟨ or to strengthen

לָךְ, וּמְהַלְלִים לְשֵׁם תִּפְאַרְתֶּךָ.

⟪ of Your splendor. ⟨ the Name ⟨ and we praise ⟪ You

─────── Nehemiah 9:5-11 / נחמיה ט:ה-יא ───────

וִיבָרְכוּ שֵׁם כְּבוֹדֶךָ וּמְרוֹמַם עַל כָּל בְּרָכָה

⟨ blessing ⟨ every ⟨ above ⟨ that is exalted ⟨ of Your ⟨ the ⟨ Let them
glory Name bless

וּתְהִלָּה. אַתָּה הוּא יהוה לְבַדֶּךָ,* אַתָּה עָשִׂיתָ

⟨ have made ⟨ You ⟪ alone.* ⟨ HASHEM, ⟨ Who are ⟨ It is You ⟪ and praise.

אֶת הַשָּׁמַיִם, שְׁמֵי הַשָּׁמַיִם* וְכָל צְבָאָם, הָאָרֶץ

⟨ the earth ⟨ their legions, ⟨ and all ⟨ the loftiest heavens* ⟪ the heavens,

וְכָל אֲשֶׁר עָלֶיהָ, הַיַּמִּים וְכָל אֲשֶׁר בָּהֶם, וְאַתָּה

⟨ and You ⟪ in them; ⟨ that is ⟨ and ⟨ the seas ⟪ upon it, ⟨ that is ⟨ and
everything everything

מְחַיֶּה אֶת כֻּלָּם,* וּצְבָא הַשָּׁמַיִם לְךָ מִשְׁתַּחֲוִים.*

⟪ do bow.* ⟨ to You ⟨ of heaven ⟨ and the legions ⟨ to all of them;* ⟨ give life

---

lously made clear that his every achievement was made possible by God and that it was meant to be utilized in His service. Lest anyone think that his attainments are to his *own* credit, David proclaims that God is Master of everything in heaven and earth and — because He has *sovereignty over every leader* — He decrees who shall attain a high position and who shall be toppled.

אַתָּה הוּא ה׳ לְבַדֶּךָ — *It is You Who are* H*ASHEM, alone.* The next six verses were recited by the people, led by Ezra, Nehemiah, and the most distinguished Levites the day after Shemini Atzeres, when the newly arrived Jews had completed their first festival season in Jerusalem after returning from their Babylonian exile.

They gathered in devotion and repentance and echoed the resolve voiced by David nearly 500 years earlier.

שְׁמֵי הַשָּׁמַיִם — *The loftiest heavens.* This refers either to the highest spiritual spheres or to the farthest reaches of space.

וְאַתָּה מְחַיֶּה אֶת כֻּלָּם — *And You give life to all of them.* Even inanimate objects have "life" in the sense that they have whatever conditions are necessary for their continued existence (*Iyun Tefillah*).

לְךָ מִשְׁתַּחֲוִים — *To You do bow.* Despite their awesome size and power over other parts of the universe, the heavenly bodies *bow* in the sense that they exist totally to serve God (*Iyun Tefillah*).

❖ אַתָּה הוּא יהוה הָאֱלֹהִים אֲשֶׁר בָּחַרְתָּ
‹ selected ‹ [You] Who ‹‹ the God, ‹ Hashem ‹ Who are ‹ It is You

בְּאַבְרָם,* וְהוֹצֵאתוֹ מֵאוּר כַּשְׂדִּים, וְשַׂמְתָּ שְּׁמוֹ
‹ his ‹ and ‹‹ of Ur Kasdim ‹ brought him out ‹‹ Abram,*
name designated

אַבְרָהָם.* וּמָצָאתָ אֶת לְבָבוֹ נֶאֱמָן לְפָנֶיךָ —
‹‹ before You ‹ faithful ‹ his heart ‹ You found ‹‹ Abraham.*

וְכָרוֹת* עִמּוֹ הַבְּרִית לָתֵת אֶת אֶרֶץ הַכְּנַעֲנִי
‹ of the ‹ the land ‹ to give ‹ the covenant ‹ with ‹ — and You
Canaanite, him established*

הַחִתִּי הָאֱמֹרִי וְהַפְּרִזִּי וְהַיְבוּסִי וְהַגִּרְגָּשִׁי, לָתֵת
‹ — to ‹‹ and the ‹ the Jebusite, ‹ the Perizzite, ‹ the Amorite, ‹ the Hittite,
give [it] Girgashite

לְזַרְעוֹ, וַתָּקֶם אֶת דְּבָרֶיךָ, כִּי צַדִּיק אָתָּה.*
‹‹ are You.* ‹ righteous ‹ for ‹ Your word, ‹ and You upheld ‹‹ to his offspring;

וַתֵּרֶא אֶת עֳנִי אֲבֹתֵינוּ בְּמִצְרָיִם, וְאֶת זַעֲקָתָם
‹ and their outcry ‹‹ in Egypt, ‹ of our forefathers ‹ the suffering ‹ You observed

---

אֲשֶׁר בָּחַרְתָּ בְּאַבְרָם — *Who selected Abram.* After cataloguing the endless array of Creation and its components, we acknowledge that of them all, God chose Abraham and his offspring as His chosen ones — an astonishing testimony to the Patriarch and the nation he founded (*Siach Yitzchak*).

וְשַׂמְתָּ שְּׁמוֹ אַבְרָהָם — *And designated his name Abraham.* The change of name signified that Abram's mission had been changed and elevated. His original name was a contracted version of אַב אֲרָם, *father of Aram*, because he had been a spiritual father of his native Aram. The additional ה implies that he had become אַב הֲמוֹן גּוֹיִם, *father of a multitude of nations*, marking him as the spiritual mentor of all mankind (see *Genesis* 17:4-5).

וְכָרוֹת ⁓ — *And You established . . .* We have followed the virtually universal practice that *siddurim* begin a paragraph with וְכָרוֹת. However in the Book of *Nehemiah*, this is not the

beginning of a new verse, but a continuation of the above; namely, that in reward for Abraham's faithfulness, God made a covenant with him.

In many congregations, the section beginning with וְכָרוֹת is chanted aloud when a circumcision is to be performed in the synagogue, because the circumcision sealed the covenant of which Abraham's new name was a part. There are varying customs regarding reciting this section at a circumcision. In most of these congregations it is said by the *mohel*, in some by the rabbi. In some, all the verses from וְכָרוֹת until (but not including) יִשְׁתַּבַּח are recited responsively, with the *mohel* reciting the first aloud, the congregation the next, and so on. In some congregations, the *mohel* recites aloud only the verses from וְכָרוֹת until בְּמַיִם עַזִּים.

כִּי צַדִּיק אָתָּה — *For righteous are You.* God keeps His word even when Israel, on its own merits, is unworthy of the gift (*Iyun Tefillah*).

שָׁמַעְתָּ עַל יַם סוּף. וַתִּתֵּן אֹתֹת וּמֹפְתִים*
‹ and wonders* › signs ‹ You imposed ≪ of Reeds. ‹ the Sea ‹ at ‹ You heard

בְּפַרְעֹה וּבְכָל עֲבָדָיו וּבְכָל עַם אַרְצוֹ, כִּי יָדַעְתָּ
‹ You ‹ for ≪ of his ‹ the ‹ and upon ‹ his ‹ and upon ‹ upon Pharaoh
knew   land,   people   all   servants,   all

כִּי הֵזִידוּ* עֲלֵיהֶם, וַתַּעַשׂ לְךָ שֵׁם כְּהַיּוֹם הַזֶּה.*
≪ as [clear as] this ‹ a ‹ for ‹ and You ≪ against ‹ they sinned ‹ that
[very] day.*   name Yourself   made   them;   flagrantly*

❖ וְהַיָּם בָּקַעְתָּ לִפְנֵיהֶם, וַיַּעַבְרוּ בְתוֹךְ הַיָּם
‹ of the Sea ‹ in the midst ‹ and they crossed ≪ before them, ‹ You split ‹ The Sea

בַּיַּבָּשָׁה, וְאֶת רֹדְפֵיהֶם הִשְׁלַכְתָּ בִמְצוֹלֹת, כְּמוֹ
‹ like ‹ into the depths, ‹ You hurled ‹ but their pursuers ≪ on dry land;

אֶבֶן בְּמַיִם עַזִּים.
≪ that are turbulent. ‹ into waters, ‹ a stone

THE SONG AT THE SEA / שירת הים
—— Exodus 14:30-15:19 / שמות יד:ל-טו:יט ——

וַיּוֹשַׁע יהוה* בַּיּוֹם הַהוּא אֶת־יִשְׂרָאֵל מִיַּד
‹ from the hand ‹ Israel ‹ on that day, ‹ Hashem saved*

אֹתֹת וּמֹפְתִים — *Signs and wonders. Signs* are miracles that were foretold by a prophet; *wonders* occur without prior announcement (*Rambam*).

כִּי הֵזִידוּ — *That they sinned flagrantly* (lit. *willfully*). The Egyptians sinned against the Jews by mistreating and enslaving them. Had the servitude not been so harsh and hateful, the Egyptians would not have suffered such devastation.

כְּהַיּוֹם הַזֶּה — *As [clear as] this [very] day.* The miracles of the Exodus were witnessed by the public and were thus indisputable (*Etz Yosef*).

שִׁירַת הַיָּם / The Song at the Sea

The early commentators note that the miracles of the Exodus, beginning with the Ten Plagues, illustrated that God controls all facets of nature. Thus, they remained the testimony to God as the all-powerful Creator: No human being saw the Creation of the universe, but millions of Jews witnessed the Exodus. The climax of those mirac-

ulous events was the Splitting of the Sea; as the Passover Haggadah relates, the miracles at the Sea were many times as great as those that took place in Egypt itself. That event was celebrated by Moses and the entire nation in the glorious Song of the Sea, a combination of praise and faith that fits in with the theme of *Pesukei D'Zimrah.*

We have included the cantillation symbols [*trop*] for the convenience of those who recite the Song in the manner it is read from the Torah. Additionally, we have inserted commas for those unfamiliar with this notation. The basis for reciting the Song with this cantillation is found in Kabbalistic literature, which attaches great importance to the joyful, musical recitation of the Song, as if one were standing at the seashore witnessing the miracle. The *Zohar* states that one who recites the Song with the proper intent will merit to sing the praises of future miracles.

וַיּוֹשַׁע ה' — *Hashem saved.* The Torah sums

מִצְרַיִם, וַיַּרְא יִשְׂרָאֵל אֶת־מִצְרַיִם מֵת עַל־

‹ on ‹ dead ‹ the Egyptians ‹ and Israel saw ≪ of Egypt,

שְׂפַת הַיָּם: ❖ וַיַּרְא יִשְׂרָאֵל אֶת־הַיָּד הַגְּדֹלָה

‹ that is great, ‹ the hand, ‹ And Israel saw ≪ of the sea. ‹ the shore

אֲשֶׁר עָשָׂה יהוה בְּמִצְרַיִם, וַיִּירְאוּ* הָעָם

‹ did the people ‹ and fear* ≪ upon Egypt, ‹ HASHEM inflicted ‹ that

אֶת־יהוה, וַיַּאֲמִינוּ* בַּיהוה וּבְמשֶׁה עַבְדּוֹ:

≪ His servant. ‹ and in Moses, ‹ in HASHEM ‹ and they had faith* ‹ HASHEM,

אָז יָשִׁיר־ ❖ משֶׁה וּבְנֵי יִשְׂרָאֵל

‹ of Israel ‹ and the Children ‹ did Moses ‹ choose to sing* ‹ Then

אֶת־הַשִּׁירָה הַזֹּאת לַיהוה, וַיֹּאמְרוּ לֵאמֹר,

≪ saying [the ‹ and they said, ≪ to HASHEM, ‹ this song
following]:

אָשִׁירָה לַיהוה כִּי־גָאֹה גָּאָה, סוּס וְרֹכְבוֹ רָמָה

‹ He ‹ with its ‹ the ≪ [above] the ‹ He is ‹ for ‹ to HASHEM ‹ I shall sing
hurled rider horse arrogant, exalted

בַיָּם: עָזִּי וְזִמְרָת יָהּ* וַיְהִי־לִי לִישׁוּעָה, זֶה אֵלִי*

‹ is my ‹ This ≪ a salvation. ‹ for ‹ and He ≪ is ‹ and my ‹ My ≪ into
God,*   me was God,* praise might the sea.

up the miracles at the Sea as a prelude to Moses' song.

וַיִּירְאוּ . . . וַיַּאֲמִינוּ — *And fear . . . and they had faith.* The fact that God has the power to perform miracles is unimportant; the Creator of the universe has no difficulty in halting the flow of a Sea. What *did* matter was the effect the miracle had on Israel. The people felt a new and higher degree of *fear*, in the sense of awe and reverence. And their *faith* increased immeasurably, for they had seen that, through His prophet, God promised salvation from danger and had indeed saved them.

אָז יָשִׁיר ‏⧉ — *Then choose to sing.* Rather than שָׁר, *sang*, the Torah uses the verb יָשִׁיר, literally *will* sing. In the simple sense, the verse means

that upon seeing the miracle the people decided that they *would* sing. Midrashically, the verb implies the principle that God will bring the dead back to life in Messianic times — and then they *will* sing God's praises once again (*Rashi*).

עָזִּי וְזִמְרָת יָהּ — *My might and my praise is God.* The translation follows *Targum Onkelos*. According to *Rashi* the phrase is translated: *God's might and His cutting away [of the enemy] was a salvation for me.*

זֶה אֵלִי — *This is my God.* So obvious was God's presence that the Jews could point to it, as it were, and say, "This is my God." As the Sages put it: "A maidservant at the sea saw more than the prophet Yechezkel [saw in the heavenly prophecy]" (*Rashi*).

וְאַנְוֵהוּ,* אֱלֹהֵי אָבִי וַאֲרֹמְמֶנְהוּ: יהוה אִישׁ

‹ is ‹ HASHEM ≪ and I will exalt Him. ‹ of my ‹ the God ≪ and I will build
Master   father,   Him a Sanctuary;*

מִלְחָמָה, יהוה שְׁמוֹ:* מַרְכְּבֹת פַּרְעֹה וְחֵילוֹ

‹ and his ‹ of Pharaoh ‹ The chariots ≪ is His ‹ HASHEM ‹ of war,
army   Name.*

יָרָה בַיָּם, וּמִבְחַר שָׁלִשָׁיו טֻבְּעוּ בְיַם־סוּף:

≪ of ‹ in the ‹ were ‹ of his officers ‹ and the pick ≪ into the ‹ He
Reeds.   Sea   mired   sea;   hurled

תְּהֹמֹת יְכַסְיֻמוּ, יָרְדוּ בִמְצוֹלֹת כְּמוֹ־אָבֶן:

≪ stone. ‹ like ‹ into the depths ‹ they descended ≪ covered them; ‹ Deep waters

יְמִינְךָ* יהוה נֶאְדָּרִי בַּכֹּחַ, יְמִינְךָ יהוה תִּרְעַץ

‹ smashes ‹ HASHEM, ‹ Your right ≪ with ‹ is adorned ‹ HASHEM, ‹ Your right
hand,   strength;   hand,*

אוֹיֵב: וּבְרֹב גְּאוֹנְךָ תַּהֲרֹס קָמֶיךָ, תְּשַׁלַּח חֲרֹנְךָ

‹ Your ‹ You dispatch ≪ Your ‹ You shatter ‹ grandeur ‹ In Your ≪ the
wrath,   opponents;   abundant   enemy.

יֹאכְלֵמוֹ כַּקַּשׁ: וּבְרוּחַ אַפֶּיךָ נֶעֶרְמוּ מַיִם, נִצְּבוּ

‹ stand up ≪ were the ‹ heaped ≪ from Your ‹ At a blast ≪ like straw. ‹ it consumes
straight   waters;   up   nostrils,   them

כְמוֹ־נֵד נֹזְלִים, קָפְאוּ תְהֹמֹת בְּלֶב־יָם:

≪ of the ‹ in the ‹ were the ‹ congealed ≪ did the running ‹ a wall ‹ as
sea.   heart   deep waters   water,

וְאַנְוֵהוּ — And I will build Him a Sanctuary. The root of the word is נָוֶה, abode. An alternative interpretation based on the same root: I will make myself into a Godly sanctuary (Rashi) — to remake oneself in God's image, emulating His attributes, is to build the greatest of all sanctuaries.

Another translation is I will beautify or glorify Him [based on the root נאה, fitting, beautiful]. The Sages teach that this should be done by performing the commandments in a beautiful manner, by having beautiful tefillin, a beautiful succah, a beautiful esrog, and so on (Shabbos 133b).

ה' שְׁמוֹ — HASHEM is His Name. Alternatively, Through HASHEM His Name. Mortal kings require legions and armaments, but God overcomes His enemies with nothing more than His Name. Moreover, this Name of mercy applies to Him even when He is forced to vanquish the wicked (Rashi).

יְמִינְךָ — Your right hand. Of course God has no "hand" or any other physical characteristic. All the many Scriptural references to physicality are allegorical. The right hand symbolizes power; God's wrath is described as a blast from His nostrils, because angry people tend to snort.

אָמַר אוֹיֵב,* אֶרְדֹּף אַשִּׂיג אֲחַלֵּק שָׁלָל,

« plunder; ‹ I will divide ‹ I will overtake, ‹ I will pursue, «　The enemy declared:*

תִּמְלָאֵמוֹ נַפְשִׁי, אָרִיק חַרְבִּי, תּוֹרִישֵׁמוֹ יָדִי:

«will my ‹ impoverish　« my sword, ‹ I will　« will my ‹　satisfied
hand.　them　　unsheathe　desires be;　with them

נָשַׁפְתָּ בְרוּחֲךָ כִּסָּמוֹ יָם, צָלֲלוּ כַּעוֹפֶרֶת בְּמַיִם,

‹ in the ‹　like lead　‹ sink « did ‹ enshroud « with Your ‹ You blew
waters　　　　the sea;　them　　wind;

אַדִּירִים: מִי־כָמֹכָה בָּאֵלִם יהוה, מִי כָּמֹכָה

‹ is like You, ‹ Who « HASHEM! ‹ among the ‹ is like You ‹ Who «　did the
heavenly powers,　　　　mighty ones.

נֶאְדָּר בַּקֹּדֶשׁ, נוֹרָא תְהִלֹּת עֹשֵׂה פֶלֶא: נָטִיתָ

‹ You « wonders! ‹ doing　« [beyond] ‹ awesome « in holiness, ‹ mighty
stretched out　　　　　　praise,

יְמִינְךָ, תִּבְלָעֵמוֹ אָרֶץ: נָחִיתָ בְחַסְדְּךָ עַם־זוּ

‹ this people ‹　in Your　‹ You guided « did the ‹ swallow them «　Your
kindness　　　earth.　　　　right hand;

גָּאָלְתָּ, נֵהַלְתָּ בְעָזְּךָ אֶל־נְוֵה קָדְשֶׁךָ:* שָׁמְעוּ

‹ Hear　«　of Your　‹ the　‹ to ‹ with Your ‹ You led　« that You
holiness.*　abode　　might　[them]　redeemed;

עַמִּים יִרְגָּזוּן, חִיל אָחַז יֹשְׁבֵי פְּלָשֶׁת:* אָז נִבְהֲלוּ

‹ were ‹ Then « of Philistia.* ‹　the　‹ gripped ‹ terror « they were « did
confounded　　　　dwellers　　　　　agitated;　peoples;

אַלּוּפֵי אֱדוֹם,* אֵילֵי מוֹאָב יֹאחֲזֵמוֹ רָעַד, נָמֹגוּ

‹ dissolved « did　‹ – grip them « of Moab ‹　the　« of Edom,* ‹　the
trembling;　　　　　　powers　　　　chieftains

אָמַר אוֹיֵב — *The enemy declared.* In order to coax his people to join him in pursuit of the Jews, Pharaoh (*the enemy*) spoke confidently of his ability to overtake and plunder them.

נְוֵה קָדְשֶׁךָ — *The abode of Your holiness,* the Holy Temple. Although the Temple would not be built for over 400 years, prophetic song combines the past with the future, because in the Divine perception they are interrelated.

פְּלָשֶׁת...אֱדוֹם... —*Philistia...Edom...*Not all the nations were of equal status. Philistia and Canaan rightly feared conquest because their lands comprised *Eretz Yisrael,* while Edom and Moab would not be attacked by Israel. They did not fear losing their land, but they feared retribution because they did not and would not show compassion for Jewish suffering (*Rashi*).

כָּל יֹשְׁבֵי כְנָעַן: תִּפֹּל עֲלֵיהֶם אֵימָתָה וָפַחַד,

and terror, ‹ may fear ‹ upon them ‹ Fall ≪ of Canaan. ‹ the dwellers ‹ were all

בִּגְדֹל זְרוֹעֲךָ יִדְּמוּ כָּאָבֶן, עַד־יַעֲבֹר עַמְּךָ* יהוה,

HASHEM, ‹ do Your ‹ pass ‹ until ≪ as stone; ‹ may they ‹ of Your ‹ at the
people,* through be still arm greatness

עַד־יַעֲבֹר עַם־זוּ קָנִיתָ: תְּבִאֵמוֹ* וְתִטָּעֵמוֹ בְּהַר

on the ‹ and implant ‹ You shall ≪ that You ‹ do this ‹ pass ‹ until
mount them bring them* have acquired. people through

נַחֲלָתְךָ, מָכוֹן לְשִׁבְתְּךָ פָּעַלְתָּ יהוה, מִקְּדָשׁ

the ≪ HASHEM: ‹ which You ‹ of Your ‹ the ≪ of Your
Sanctuary, have made, dwelling-place, foundation heritage,

אֲדֹנָי כּוֹנְנוּ יָדֶיךָ: יהוה ׀ יִמְלֹךְ* לְעֹלָם וָעֶד:

≪ and ‹ for ever ‹ shall reign* ‹ HASHEM ‹ that Your hands ‹ my Lord,
ever. established.

יהוה ׀ יִמְלֹךְ לְעֹלָם וָעֶד: (יהוה מַלְכוּתֵהּ קָאֵם

‹ stands ‹ — His kingdom ≪ HASHEM ≪ and ever. ‹ for ever ‹ shall reign ‹ HASHEM

לְעָלַם וּלְעָלְמֵי עָלְמַיָּא.) כִּי בָא סוּס פַּרְעֹה

‹ of ‹ did the ‹ come ‹ When ≪ and to all eternity. ‹ forever
Pharaoh cavalry

בְּרִכְבּוֹ וּבְפָרָשָׁיו בַּיָּם, וַיָּשֶׁב יהוה עֲלֵהֶם אֶת־מֵי

‹ the waters ‹ upon them ‹ did ‹ and turn ≪ into ‹ and horsemen ‹ with his
HASHEM back the sea, chariots

הַיָּם וּבְנֵי יִשְׂרָאֵל הָלְכוּ בַיַּבָּשָׁה בְּתוֹךְ הַיָּם:

≪ the sea. ‹ amid ‹ on the ‹ walked ‹ of Israel ‹ the ≪ of
dry bed Children the sea,

עַד יַעֲבֹר עַמְּךָ — *Until pass through do Your people.* This phrase continues the previous idea: The terror of the nations would continue until Israel crossed into *Eretz Yisrael.* The term *pass through* is used twice: once in reference to the crossing of the Jordan and once in reference to the waters of the Arnon, on the border of Israel and Moab [see *Numbers* 21:13-20] (*Rashi*).

תְּבִאֵמוֹ — *You shall bring them.* Moses unknow-

ingly prophesied that he would not enter into the Land, for he said, "You shall bring *them,*" and not "You shall bring *us*" (*Rashi*).

ה׳ יִמְלֹךְ — *HASHEM shall reign.* This verse is repeated to signify that it is the climax of the Song — that God's sovereignty shall be recognized forever. Most congregations follow the *Arizal,* who taught that the Aramaic *Targum* of this verse should also be recited.

❖ כִּי לַיהוה הַמְּלוּכָה,* וּמֹשֵׁל* בַּגּוֹיִם.¹ וְעָלוּ

‹ Ascend ‹‹ the nations. ‹ and He rules* ‹‹ the kingship* ‹ to HASHEM belongs ‹ For

מוֹשִׁעִים* בְּהַר צִיּוֹן, לִשְׁפֹּט אֶת הַר עֵשָׂו,

‹‹ of Esau, ‹ the mountain ‹ to judge ‹ Zion ‹ up Mount ‹ will the saviors*

וְהָיְתָה לַיהוה הַמְּלוּכָה.² וְהָיָה יהוה לְמֶלֶךְ*

‹ be King* ‹ HASHEM ‹ Then will ‹‹ the kingship. ‹ and to HASHEM will be

עַל כָּל הָאָרֶץ, בַּיּוֹם הַהוּא יִהְיֶה יהוה אֶחָד

‹ be One ‹ HASHEM ‹ shall ‹ — on that day ‹‹ the world ‹ all ‹ over

וּשְׁמוֹ אֶחָד.*³ (וּבְתוֹרָתְךָ כָּתוּב לֵאמֹר: שְׁמַע

‹ Hear ‹‹ saying: ‹ it is written, ‹ (And in Your Torah ‹‹ be One.* ‹ and His Name

יִשְׂרָאֵל, יהוה אֱלֹהֵינוּ, יהוה אֶחָד.⁴)

‹‹ the One [and Only].) ‹ HASHEM is ‹‹ is our God, ‹ HASHEM ‹ O Israel:

**STAND WHILE RECITING יִשְׁתַּבַּח . . . THE FIFTEEN EXPRESSIONS OF PRAISE – בְּרָכוֹת . . . שִׁיר וּשְׁבָחָה
וְהוֹדָאוֹת – SHOULD BE RECITED WITHOUT PAUSE, BUT NOT NECESSARILY IN ONE BREATH.**

יִשְׁתַּבַּח שִׁמְךָ לָעַד, מַלְכֵּנוּ, הָאֵל הַמֶּלֶךְ

‹ the King ‹ the God, ‹‹ our King, ‹‹ forever, ‹ may Your ‹ Praised
                                          Name be

---

(1) *Psalms* 22:29. (2) *Obadiah* 1:21. (3) *Zechariah* 14:9. (4) *Deuteronomy* 6:4.

. . . כִּי לַהֹ׳ הַמְּלוּכָה — *For to HASHEM belongs the kingship* . . . These added verses are appropriate to the climactic verse that God will reign forever.

מוֹשִׁעִים — *The saviors.* Those who will in the future lead Israel out of exile will come to Mount Zion from which they will complete the conquest of the archenemy, Esau, whose descendants are responsible for the current exile (*Rashi*).

וּמֹשֵׁל . . . לְמֶלֶךְ — *And He rules . . . be King.* The term מוֹשֵׁל, *ruler,* refers to one who forces his subjects to obey him, while מֶלֶךְ, *king,* is one who is willingly accepted. Now God is *King* over Israel alone because only Israel acknowledges His sovereignty with love, but He *rules* the nations despite their refusing to accept Him as their God. In the future, however, all nations will proclaim Him as their King (*Vilna Gaon*).

יִהְיֶה הֹ׳ אֶחָד וּשְׁמוֹ אֶחָד — *Shall HASHEM be One and His Name be One.* But does He not have One

Name today? Rabbi Nachman bar Yitzchak taught: The world of the future will be unlike the world of today. In the world of today God's Name is spelled one way and pronounced differently, whereas in the world of the future all will be One — the spelling and pronunciation will both be י-ה-ר-ה (*Pesachim* 50a). This means that since we fail to perceive God's nature as it is expressed in the true pronunciation of His Name, we may not utter it. But in the future, there will be no contradiction between perception and reality.

⋙ יִשְׁתַּבַּח / **Yishtabach**

As noted in the commentary on page 83, the יִשְׁתַּבַּח prayer concludes *Pesukei D'Zimrah.* There are fifteen expressions of praise in the first half of the paragraph. Fifteen is also the numerical value of the Divine Name יָה, the letters used by God to create heaven and earth. This number alludes to the fifteen שִׁיר הַמַּעֲלוֹת, *Songs of*

הַגָּדוֹל וְהַקָּדוֹשׁ, בַּשָּׁמַיִם וּבָאָרֶץ. כִּי לְךָ נָאֶה,

‹‹ are fitting, ‹ to You ‹ Because ‹‹ and on earth. ‹ in heaven ‹‹ and Who is holy, ‹ Who is great

יהוה אֱלֹהֵינוּ וֵאלֹהֵי אֲבוֹתֵינוּ, שִׁיר וּשְׁבָחָה,

‹ and praise, ‹ song ‹‹ of our forefathers, ‹ and the God ‹ our God ‹ Hashem,

הַלֵּל וְזִמְרָה, עֹז וּמֶמְשָׁלָה, נֶצַח גְּדֻלָּה וּגְבוּרָה,

‹ and strength, ‹ greatness, ‹ triumph, ‹ and dominion, ‹ power ‹ and hymns, ‹ lauding

תְּהִלָּה וְתִפְאֶרֶת, קְדֻשָׁה וּמַלְכוּת, בְּרָכוֹת

‹ blessings ‹ and sovereignty, ‹ holiness ‹ and glory, ‹ praise

וְהוֹדָאוֹת לְשִׁמְךָ הַגָּדוֹל וְהַקָּדוֹשׁ, וּמֵעוֹלָם וְעַד

‹ to ‹ and from [This] World ‹ and holy; ‹ that is great ‹ to Your Name ‹ and thanksgivings

עוֹלָם אַתָּה אֵל. ❖ בָּרוּךְ אַתָּה יהוה, אֵל מֶלֶךְ

‹ King ‹ God, ‹‹ Hashem, ‹ are You, ‹ Blessed ‹‹ God. ‹ You are ‹‹ the World [to Come]

גָּדוֹל וּמְהֻלָּל בַּתִּשְׁבָּחוֹת,* אֵל הַהוֹדָאוֹת,

‹‹ of thanksgivings, ‹ God ‹‹ through praises,* ‹ and lauded ‹ [Who is] exalted

אֲדוֹן הַנִּפְלָאוֹת, בּוֹרֵא כָּל הַנְּשָׁמוֹת, רִבּוֹן כָּל

‹ of all ‹ Master ‹‹ souls, ‹ of all ‹ Creator ‹‹ of wonders, ‹ Master

הַמַּעֲשִׂים, הַבּוֹחֵר בְּשִׁירֵי זִמְרָה,* מֶלֶךְ יָחִיד

‹ Unique One, ‹ – King, ‹‹ that are melodious,* ‹ songs [of praise] ‹ Who chooses ‹‹ deeds,

אֵל חֵי הָעוֹלָמִים.*   (אָמֵן. –Cong.)

‹‹ of the worlds.* ‹ Life-giver ‹ God,   ‹‹ (Amen.)

Ascents [Psalms 120-134], composed by David.

גָּדוֹל וּמְהֻלָּל בַּתִּשְׁבָּחוֹת — *Exalted and lauded through praises.* God does not require our praises in order to be exalted, for His infinite greatness is beyond our capacity to comprehend, much less express. Rather, it is His will that we have the privilege of exalting Him, despite our inability to do so adequately. This is the implication of *Who chooses songs [of praise] that are melodious;* we praise Him because He wishes us to do so.

הַבּוֹחֵר בְּשִׁירֵי זִמְרָה — *Who chooses songs [of praise] that are melodious. Rabbi Simchah Bunim of P'shis'cha interpreted homiletically that the word שִׁירֵי can be translated remnants (from שִׁירַיִם, leftovers). God wishes to see how much of the lofty sentiments of our prayers remain with us after we close our siddur. Thus, He chooses what is left over* after the Songs of Praise have been uttered.

חֵי הָעוֹלָמִים — *Life-giver of the worlds.* This

FROM ROSH HASHANAH UNTIL YOM KIPPUR MANY CONGREGATIONS RECITE THE FOLLOWING (PSALM 130). THE ARK IS OPENED. EACH VERSE IS RECITED ALOUD BY THE *CHAZZAN*, THEN REPEATED BY THE CONGREGATION.

שִׁיר הַמַּעֲלוֹת;* מִמַּעֲמַקִּים קְרָאתִיךָ, יהוה. אֲדֹנָי,

⟨ O Lord, ⟪ HASHEM. ⟨ I called You, ⟨ From the depths ⟪ of ascents.* ⟨ A song

שִׁמְעָה בְקוֹלִי,* תִּהְיֶינָה אָזְנֶיךָ קַשֻּׁבוֹת לְקוֹל תַּחֲנוּנָי.

⟪ of my pleas. ⟨ to the sound ⟨ attentive ⟪ — Your ⟪ may they be ⟪ my voice;* ⟨ hear
                                    ears —

אִם עֲוֹנוֹת תִּשְׁמָר, יָהּ;* אֲדֹנָי, מִי יַעֲמֹד. כִּי עִמְּךָ

⟨ with You ⟨ For ⟪ could ⟨ who ⟨ O Lord, ⟪ O ⟨ You preserve, ⟨ iniquities ⟨ If
                   survive?   God,*

הַסְּלִיחָה, לְמַעַן תִּוָּרֵא. קִוִּיתִי יהוה, קִוְּתָה נַפְשִׁי,*

⟪ did my ⟨ placed ⟪ in HASHEM, ⟨ I placed ⟪ You may ⟨ so that ⟪ is forgiveness,
  soul,* hope   my hope   be feared.

וְלִדְבָרוֹ הוֹחָלְתִּי. נַפְשִׁי לַאדֹנָי, מִשֹּׁמְרִים לַבֹּקֶר,*

⟪ for the ⟨ among those ⟪ [yearns] ⟨ My soul ⟪ I yearned. ⟨ and for
  dawn,*   longing   for the Lord,   His word

שֹׁמְרִים לַבֹּקֶר. יַחֵל יִשְׂרָאֵל אֶל יהוה; כִּי עִם יהוה

⟨ HASHEM ⟨ with ⟨ for ⟪ HASHEM, ⟨ for ⟨ shall Israel ⟨ Yearn ⟪ for the ⟨ those
                                                                dawn.   longing

הַחֶסֶד, וְהַרְבֵּה עִמּוֹ פְדוּת. וְהוּא יִפְדֶּה אֶת יִשְׂרָאֵל,

⟨ Israel ⟨ shall ⟨ And He ⟪ is ⟨ with ⟨ and ⟪ is
          redeem   redemption. Him abundant kindness,

מִכֹּל עֲוֹנוֹתָיו.

⟪ its iniquities. ⟨ from all

THE ARK IS CLOSED.

essential principle of Jewish belief reiterates that Creation is an ongoing process — God created and continues to create. Because He gives life constantly, our thanks and praise should be likewise constant (*R' Munk*).

שִׁיר הַמַּעֲלוֹת — *A song of ascents.* The contents of the psalm are clearly suited to this period, since it speaks of supplication for forgiveness and of reliance on God as the sole Source of kindness and redemption. It is one of the fifteen Songs of Ascents that symbolize the fifteen steps leading up to the Sanctuary and also the rungs of man's spiritual ladder of fulfillment.

אֲדֹנָי שִׁמְעָה בְקוֹלִי — *O Lord, hear my voice.* Although I am extremely distant from You, and I have sunk to the most remote depths, please hear my voice (*Ibn Ezra*).

When a supplicant has the presence of mind to articulate his requests, he need not shout. But when misery robs him of his equanimity, he cries out in anguish (*Pri Tzaddik*).

אִם עֲוֹנוֹת תִּשְׁמָר יָהּ — *If iniquities You preserve, O God.* We cannot deny that we have sinned abundantly, but if God preserves our sins and refuses to forgive them unless we are totally deserving, we could not survive (*Ibn Ezra*).

קִוִּיתִי ה' קִוְּתָה נַפְשִׁי — *I placed my hope in HASHEM, placed hope did my soul.* My body put confidence in Hashem for physical security in this world, and *my soul placed hope* in Him to merit the glory and spiritual bliss of the World to Come (*Radak*).

נַפְשִׁי לַאדֹנָי מִשֹּׁמְרִים לַבֹּקֶר — *My soul [yearns] for the Lord, among those longing for the dawn.* I am

THE *CHAZZAN* RECITES חֲצִי קַדִּישׁ, HALF-*KADDISH*.

יִתְגַּדַּל וְיִתְקַדַּשׁ שְׁמֵהּ רַבָּא. (.קong. –אָמֵן) בְּעָלְמָא דִּי בְרָא
⟨ He ⟨ that ⟨ in the ⟨⟨ (Amen.) ⟨⟨ that is ⟨ may His⟨ and be ⟨ Grow exalted
created world great! — Name sanctified

כִרְעוּתֵהּ, וְיַמְלִיךְ מַלְכוּתֵהּ, וְיַצְמַח פֻּרְקָנֵהּ וִיקָרֵב מְשִׁיחֵהּ.
⟨⟨ His ⟨ and bring ⟨ His ⟨ and cause ⟨ to His ⟨ and may He ⟨⟨ according
Messiah, near salvation, to sprout kingship, give reign to His will,

(.Cong– אָמֵן.) בְּחַיֵּיכוֹן וּבְיוֹמֵיכוֹן וּבְחַיֵּי דְכָל בֵּית יִשְׂרָאֵל,
⟨⟨ of Israel, ⟨ Family ⟨ of the ⟨ and in the ⟨ and in ⟨ in your ⟨⟨ (Amen.)
entire lifetimes your days, lifetimes

בַּעֲגָלָא וּבִזְמַן קָרִיב. וְאִמְרוּ: אָמֵן.
⟨⟨ Amen. ⟨ Now ⟨⟨ that comes ⟨ and at ⟨ swiftly
respond: soon. a time

CONGREGATION RESPONDS:

אָמֵן. יְהֵא שְׁמֵהּ רַבָּא מְבָרַךְ לְעָלַם וּלְעָלְמֵי עָלְמַיָּא.
⟨⟨ and for all eternity. ⟨ forever ⟨ be blessed ⟨ that is ⟨ His ⟨ May ⟨⟨ Amen.
great Name

CHAZZAN CONTINUES:

יְהֵא שְׁמֵהּ רַבָּא מְבָרַךְ לְעָלַם וּלְעָלְמֵי עָלְמַיָּא. יִתְבָּרַךְ
⟨ Blessed, ⟨⟨ and for all eternity. ⟨ forever ⟨ be ⟨ that ⟨ His ⟨ May
blessed is great Name

וְיִשְׁתַּבַּח וְיִתְפָּאַר וְיִתְרוֹמַם וְיִתְנַשֵּׂא וְיִתְהַדָּר וְיִתְעַלֶּה
⟨ elevated, ⟨ honored, ⟨ upraised, ⟨ exalted, ⟨ glorified, ⟨ praised,

וְיִתְהַלָּל שְׁמֵהּ דְּקֻדְשָׁא בְּרִיךְ הוּא (.Cong– בְּרִיךְ הוּא) —
⟨⟨ is He) ⟨ (Blessed ⟨⟨ is He ⟨ Blessed ⟨ of the ⟨ be the ⟨ and lauded
Holy One, Name

ROSH HASHANAH TO YOM KIPPUR SUBSTITUTE:

°לְעֵלָּא מִן כָּל [°לְעֵלָּא (וּ)לְעֵלָּא מִכָּל] בִּרְכָתָא
⟨ blessing ⟨ any ⟨ exceedingly beyond ⟨ any ⟨ beyond

וְשִׁירָתָא, תֻּשְׁבְּחָתָא וְנֶחֱמָתָא דַּאֲמִירָן בְּעָלְמָא.
⟨⟨ in the world. ⟨ that are uttered ⟨ and consolation ⟨ praise ⟨⟨ and song,

וְאִמְרוּ: אָמֵן. (.Cong– אָמֵן.)
⟨⟨ (Amen.) ⟨⟨ Amen. ⟨ Now
respond:

---

among those who constantly look out for the first signs of the dawn of redemption. The phrase שֹׁמְרִים לַבֹּקֶר is repeated for emphasis: I have not been discouraged by hopeful signs which proved to be unfounded. Rather, I persistently watched for the morning, time and time again (*Rashi*).

THE *CHAZZAN* SUMMONS THE CONGREGATION TO JOIN IN THE FORTHCOMING PRAYERS,
BOWING AT בָּרְכוּ AND STRAIGHTENING UP AT ה'.

בָּרְכוּ אֶת יהוה הַמְבֹרָךְ.

《 the blessed One. 〈 HASHEM, 〈 Bless

THE CONGREGATION, FOLLOWED BY *CHAZZAN*, RESPONDS,
BOWING AT בָּרוּךְ AND STRAIGHTENING UP AT ה'.

בָּרוּךְ יהוה הַמְבֹרָךְ לְעוֹלָם וָעֶד.

《 and 〈 for ever 〈 the blessed 〈 HASHEM, 〈 Blessed is
ever.   One,

BLESSINGS OF THE SHEMA / בִּרְכוֹת קְרִיאַת שְׁמַע

IT IS PREFERABLE THAT ONE SIT WHILE RECITING THE FOLLOWING SERIES OF PRAYERS — PARTIC-
ULARLY THE *KEDUSHAH* VERSES, קָדוֹשׁ קָדוֹשׁ קָדוֹשׁ AND בָּרוּךְ כְּבוֹד – UNTIL *SHEMONEH ESREI*.

TOUCH THE ARM-*TEFILLIN* AT יוֹצֵר אוֹר AND THE HEAD-*TEFILLIN* AT וּבוֹרֵא חֹשֶׁךְ.

בָּרוּךְ אַתָּה יהוה אֱלֹהֵינוּ מֶלֶךְ הָעוֹלָם, יוֹצֵר

〈 Who 《 of the 〈 king 〈 our God, 〈 HASHEM, 〈 are You, 〈 Blessed
forms universe,

אוֹר וּבוֹרֵא חֹשֶׁךְ,* עֹשֶׂה שָׁלוֹם וּבוֹרֵא אֶת הַכֹּל.¹

《 all.   〈 and 〈 peace 〈 Who 《 darkness,* 〈 and 〈 light
creates makes creates

---

(1) Cf. *Isaiah* 45:7.

בִּרְכוֹת קְרִיאַת שְׁמַע /
Blessings of the Shema

The third section of *Shacharis* is about to begin. Its central feature is the *Shema*, whose recitation is required by the Torah and which is the basic acceptance of God's sovereignty and Oneness. The *Shema* is accompanied by three blessings (two before and one after), in which we express God's mastery over nature, pray for intellectual and moral attainment through the study of Torah, and describe God's role in the flow of history (*R' Munk*).

יוֹצֵר אוֹר וּבוֹרֵא חֹשֶׁךְ — *Who forms light and creates darkness.* Since the beginning of time, the term "light" has symbolized renewal of life, wisdom, happiness — all the things associated with goodness. "Darkness," however, is associated with suffering, failure, and death. The philosophers of idolatry claimed that the "good" god who creates light cannot be the "bad" one

who creates darkness. Therefore, they reasoned, there must be at least two gods. In modern times, the same argument is presented in different terms: How can there be a God if He allows bad things to happen? This blessing refutes the argument that anything people find unpleasant either is not an act of God or proves that He lacks power. To the contrary, we believe unequivocally that God is One; what appears to our limited human intelligence to be contradictory or evil is in actuality part of the plan of the One Merciful God, despite our failure to understand it.

The "light" of this blessing refers not merely to the newly dawned day, but to the physical forces of Creation itself. Light is the energy-giving, life-giving force of the universe, and, in the words of the Psalmist (19:2): *The heavens declare the glory of God*, by functioning harmoniously and efficiently in accordance with His will (*R' Munk*).

הַמֵּאִיר לָאָרֶץ וְלַדָּרִים* עָלֶיהָ בְּרַחֲמִים,

‹‹ with compassion, ‹ upon it, ‹ and those who dwell* ‹ the earth ‹ He Who illuminates

וּבְטוּבוֹ מְחַדֵּשׁ בְּכָל יוֹם תָּמִיד מַעֲשֵׂה

‹ the work ‹‹ perpetually — ‹ day, ‹ — every ‹ He renews ‹ and in His goodness

בְרֵאשִׁית. מָה רַבּוּ מַעֲשֶׂיךָ* יהוה, כֻּלָּם בְּחָכְמָה

‹ with wisdom ‹ all of ‹‹ Hashem; ‹ are Your ‹ abundant ‹ How ‹‹ of Creation.
them works,*

עָשִׂיתָ, מָלְאָה הָאָרֶץ קִנְיָנֶךָ.¹ הַמֶּלֶךְ הַמְרוֹמָם

‹ Who was ‹ [You are] ‹‹ with Your ‹ is the earth ‹ full ‹‹ You made;
exalted the King possessions.

לְבַדּוֹ מֵאָז, הַמְשֻׁבָּח וְהַמְפֹאָר וְהַמִּתְנַשֵּׂא

‹ and upraised ‹ glorified, ‹ Who is praised, ‹ from before ‹ in solitude
Creation,

מִימוֹת עוֹלָם. אֱלֹהֵי עוֹלָם, בְּרַחֲמֶיךָ הָרַבִּים

‹ that is ‹ with Your ‹‹ of eternity, ‹ God ‹‹ of old. ‹ since days
abundant compassion

(1) Psalms 104:24.

◆§ הַמֵּאִיר לָאָרֶץ וְלַדָּרִים §◆ — He Who illuminates the earth and those who dwell. The earth's dwellers enjoy the light, but so does the earth itself, because sunlight makes vegetation possible.

מָה רַבּוּ מַעֲשֶׂיךָ — How abundant are Your works.

This refers to the heavenly bodies and other major forces in Creation. Homiletically, the Talmud (Chullin 127a) interprets, how diverse are Your works; some can live only on land, others only in the sea, and so on.

◆§ **Interruptions During Blessings of the Shema**

As a general rule, no אָמֵן, Amen, or other prayer response may be recited between Borchu and Shemoneh Esrei, but there are exceptions. The main exception is "between chapters" [בֵּין הַפְּרָקִים] of the Shema Blessings — i.e., after each of the blessings, and between the three chapters of Shema. At those points, אָמֵן (but not בָּרוּךְ הוּא וּבָרוּךְ שְׁמוֹ) may be responded to every blessing. Some responses, however, are so important that they are permitted at any point in the Shema blessings. They are:

(a) In Kaddish, עָלְמַיָּא . . . רַבָּא שְׁמֵהּ יְהֵא אָמֵן and the אָמֵן after דַּאֲמִירָן בְּעָלְמָא;

(b) the response to בָּרְכוּ (even of one called to the Torah); and

(c) during the chazzan's repetition of Shemoneh Esrei —

1) in Kedushah, the verses קָדוֹשׁ, קָדוֹשׁ, קָדוֹשׁ and מִמְּקוֹמוֹ ה' כְּבוֹד בָּרוּךְ . . . כָּבוֹד;

2) the אָמֵן after שׁוֹמֵעַ תְּפִלָּה, הָאֵל הַקָּדוֹשׁ; and

3) the three words מוֹדִים אֲנַחְנוּ לָךְ.

During the recital of the two verses שְׁמַע and בָּרוּךְ שֵׁם, absolutely no interruptions are permitted. (See also laws §39-43.)

רַחֵם עָלֵינוּ, אָדוֹן עֻזֵנוּ, צוּר מִשְׂגַּבֵּנוּ, מָגֵן

⟨ O ⟨ stronghold, ⟨ our ⟨ of our ⟨ O Master ⟨⟨ on us; ⟨ have
Shield   rocklike power,   compassion

יִשְׁעֵנוּ, מִשְׂגָּב בַּעֲדֵנוּ. אֵל בָּרוּךְ* גְּדוֹל דֵּעָה,

⟨⟨ in ⟨ Who is ⟨ The blessed God,* ⟨⟨ for us. ⟨ Who is a ⟨ of our
knowledge, great   stronghold   salvation,

הֵכִין וּפָעַל זָהֲרֵי חַמָּה, טוֹב יָצַר כָּבוֹד לִשְׁמוֹ,

⟨⟨ for His ⟨ provides ⟨ that ⟨ the ⟨⟨ of the ⟨ the rays ⟨ and ⟨ prepared
Name.   honor   which He Beneficent   sun;   produced
                        fashioned One,

מְאוֹרוֹת נָתַן סְבִיבוֹת עֻזּוֹ, פִּנּוֹת צְבָאָיו קְדוֹשִׁים

⟨ holy ones ⟨⟨ of His ⟨ The ⟨⟨ His ⟨ all around ⟨ did He ⟨ Luminaries
              legions, leaders power.   place

רוֹמְמֵי שַׁדַּי, תָּמִיד מְסַפְּרִים כְּבוֹד אֵל וּקְדֻשָׁתוֹ.

⟨⟨ and His ⟨ of ⟨ the honor ⟨ relate ⟨ constantly ⟨⟨ the ⟨ who exalt
sanctity. God   Almighty,

תִּתְבָּרַךְ יהוה אֱלֹהֵינוּ בַּשָּׁמַיִם מִמַּעַל וְעַל

⟨ and on ⟨ above ⟨ in the heavens ⟨ our God, ⟨ HASHEM, ⟨ May You be
                                                              blessed,

הָאָרֶץ מִתָּחַת, עַל כָּל שֶׁבַח מַעֲשֵׂה יָדֶיךָ, וְעַל

⟨ and ⟨⟨ of Your ⟨ work ⟨ the ⟨ all ⟨ for ⟨⟨ below, ⟨ the earth
for   hands,   excellent

מְאוֹרֵי אוֹר שֶׁעָשִׂיתָ, הֵמָּה יְפָאֲרוּךָ, סֶּלָה.

⟨⟨ forever. ⟨ glorify You, ⟨ may they ⟨⟨ that You ⟨ of light ⟨ the
                                     have formed,   luminaries

תִּתְבָּרַךְ* לָנֶצַח, צוּרֵנוּ מַלְכֵּנוּ וְגֹאֲלֵנוּ, בּוֹרֵא

⟨ Creator ⟨⟨ and our ⟨ our King ⟨ our Rock, ⟨ eternally, ⟨ May You be blessed*
            Redeemer,

אֵל בָּרוּךְ — *The blessed God.* From here until
תָּמִיד, the words follow the order of the
aleph-beis. This use of the *aleph-beis* acrostic
conveys the idea that we praise God with every
available sound, and that His greatness is
absolutely complete and harmonious.

תִּתְבָּרַךְ ◆§ — *May You be blessed.* The previous

paragraph expressed man's praise of God. Now
we turn to the angels' praise of Him. Since there
have been people who worshiped the heavenly
bodies as independent gods, we now cite the
prayers of the heavenly legions, for they know
that the sun and the moon are but God's
creatures and servants.

קְדוֹשִׁים. יִשְׁתַּבַּח שִׁמְךָ לָעַד מַלְכֵּנוּ, יוֹצֵר

‹ O Fashioner ‹‹ our King, ‹ forever, ‹ may Your Name be praised ‹‹ of holy ones;

מְשָׁרְתִים, וַאֲשֶׁר מְשָׁרְתָיו כֻּלָּם עוֹמְדִים בְּרוּם

‹ at the ‹ stand ‹ all ‹ ministering ‹ and ‹‹ of ministering
summit   angels; Whose   angels;

עוֹלָם, וּמַשְׁמִיעִים בְּיִרְאָה יַחַד בְּקוֹל דִּבְרֵי

‹ the words ‹‹ loudly, ‹ together, ‹‹ with awe, ‹ and proclaim ‹ of the universe

אֱלֹהִים חַיִּים וּמֶלֶךְ עוֹלָם.¹ כֻּלָּם אֲהוּבִים, כֻּלָּם

‹ they ‹‹ beloved; ‹ They ‹‹ of the ‹ and King ‹ of the living God
are all   are all   universe.

בְּרוּרִים, כֻּלָּם גִּבּוֹרִים, כֻּלָּם קְדוֹשִׁים, וְכֻלָּם

‹ and they all ‹‹ holy; ‹ they are all ‹‹ mighty; ‹ they are all ‹‹ flawless;

עֹשִׂים בְּאֵימָה וּבְיִרְאָה רְצוֹן קוֹנֵיהֶם.* ❖ וְכֻלָּם

‹ And they all ‹‹ of their Maker.* ‹ the will ‹ and reverence ‹ with trepidation ‹ do

פּוֹתְחִים אֶת פִּיהֶם בִּקְדֻשָּׁה וּבְטָהֳרָה, בְּשִׁירָה

‹ with song ‹‹ and in purity, ‹ in holiness ‹ their mouth ‹ open

וּבְזִמְרָה, וּמְבָרְכִין וּמְשַׁבְּחִין וּמְפָאֲרִין וּמַעֲרִיצִין

‹ revere, ‹ glorify, ‹ praise, ‹ and bless, ‹‹ and with hymn,

וּמַקְדִּישִׁין וּמַמְלִיכִין —

‹‹ and declare the kingship ‹ sanctify

אֶת שֵׁם הָאֵל הַמֶּלֶךְ הַגָּדוֹל הַגִּבּוֹר וְהַנּוֹרָא,

‹‹ and Who is ‹ Who is ‹ Who is great, ‹ the King ‹ of God, ‹ of the Name
awesome;   mighty

---

(1) Cf. *Jeremiah* 10:10.

רְצוֹן קוֹנֵיהֶם — *The will of their Maker.* Although most texts published in modern times read קוֹנָם, *their Maker,* based on the ruling of *Vilna Gaon* and the *Baal HaTanya,* virtually all of the old texts read קוֹנֵיהֶם, which is preferred by most halachic authorities (see *Ba'er Hetev* and *Shaarei Teshuvah* 59:1). The objection to the original text is that קוֹנֵיהֶם, with a *yud,* would normally be translated in the plural, *Makers,* implying ח"ו that there is more than one God. The commentators deal with the translation in two ways: The "plural" means that each of the myriad angels individually serves its Maker, thus the plural refers to the angels, not God (*Maharal*); God is frequently described in the plural to indicate respect, as in אֱלֹהִים חַיִּים (*Shaarei Teshuvah*).

קָדוֹשׁ הוּא. ❖ וְכֻלָּם מְקַבְּלִים* עֲלֵיהֶם עַל [1]

‹ holy ‹ is He. « Then they all ‹ accept* ‹ upon themselves ‹ the yoke

מַלְכוּת שָׁמַיִם זֶה מִזֶּה,* וְנוֹתְנִים בְּאַהֲבָה רְשׁוּת

of the sovereignty ‹ of heaven, «‹ one ‹ from the other,* « and grant, ‹ lovingly, ‹ permission

זֶה לָזֶה, לְהַקְדִּישׁ לְיוֹצְרָם, בְּנַחַת רוּחַ בְּשָׂפָה

‹ one ‹ to « to sanctify ‹ the One Who formed them, « the calmness ‹ with « of spirit, ‹ with articulation

בְּרוּרָה וּבִנְעִימָה. קְדֻשָּׁה כֻלָּם כְּאֶחָד עוֹנִים

‹ that is clear, « and with sweet melody. « Sanctification ‹ all of them ‹ as one ‹ proclaim

בְּאֵימָה וְאוֹמְרִים בְּיִרְאָה:

« with reverence: ‹ and say ‹ with trepidation,

CONGREGATION RECITES ALOUD WITH THE *CHAZZAN*:

קָדוֹשׁ קָדוֹשׁ קָדוֹשׁ* יהוה צְבָאוֹת,*

« Master of Legions;* ‹ is HASHEM, ‹ holy* ‹ holy, ‹ Holy,

מְלֹא כָל הָאָרֶץ כְּבוֹדוֹ. [2]

« with His glory. ‹ world ‹ is the whole ‹ filled

❖ וְהָאוֹפַנִּים* וְחַיּוֹת הַקֹּדֶשׁ בְּרַעַשׁ גָּדוֹל

‹ with great noise, « and the holy *Chayos*, ‹ Then the *Ofanim**

---

(1) Cf. *Deuteronomy* 10:17; *Psalms* 99:3. (2) *Isaiah* 6:3.

וְכֻלָּם מְקַבְּלִים . . . זֶה מִזֶּה — *Then they all accept . . . one from the other.* Tanna deVei Eliyahu contrasts the behavior of the angels with that of human beings. Unlike people whose competitive jealousies cause them to thwart and outdo one another, the angels urge one another to take the initiative in serving and praising God. Conflict is the foe of perfection, harmony is its ally.

קָדוֹשׁ קָדוֹשׁ קָדוֹשׁ ⁊§ — *Holy, holy, holy.* Targum Yonasan (*Isaiah* 6:3) renders: *Holy* in the most exalted heaven, the abode of His presence; *holy* on earth, product of His strength; *holy* for ever and ever is HASHEM, Master of Legions . . .

כָּבוֹד refers to the glory of God that is present *within* the material world; it is the degree of

Godliness that man is capable of perceiving even within Creation. קָדוֹשׁ, on the other hand, refers to God's essence, which is beyond all comprehension.

צְבָאוֹת — *Master of Legions.* Although it is commonly translated simply as *hosts* or *legions*, the word צְבָאוֹת is a Name of God (see *Shevuos* 35a), which means that He is the *Master* of all the heavenly hosts. The word צָבָא is used to refer to an organized, disciplined group. Thus, an army is called צָבָא. In the context of this Divine Name, it refers to the idea that the infinite heavenly bodies are organized according to God's will to do His service.

וְהָאוֹפַנִּים — *Then the Ofanim.* The varieties of

מִתְנַשְּׂאִים לְעֻמַּת שְׂרָפִים, לְעֻמָּתָם מְשַׁבְּחִים
< they offer praise < facing them << the *Seraphim;* < toward < raise themselves

וְאוֹמְרִים:
<< and proclaim:

CONGREGATION RECITES ALOUD WITH THE *CHAZZAN*:

בָּרוּךְ* כְּבוֹד יהוה מִמְּקוֹמוֹ.*[1]
<< from His place.* < of Hashem < is the glory < Blessed*

לָאֵל* בָּרוּךְ* נְעִימוֹת יִתֵּנוּ. לַמֶּלֶךְ* אֵל חַי
< living < the < to the King,* << do they < sweet < Who is < To the God*
　　　　　God,　　　　　　　offer;　melodies　blessed*

וְקַיָּם, זְמִרוֹת יֹאמֵרוּ וְתִשְׁבָּחוֹת יַשְׁמִיעוּ. כִּי
< For << do they < and praises < do they sing < hymns < and
　　　　proclaim.　　　　　　　　　　　　　　　enduring,

הוּא לְבַדּוֹ מָרוֹם וְקָדוֹשׁ, פּוֹעֵל גְּבוּרוֹת, עֹשֶׂה
< makes << mighty < performs << and holy – < Who is << alone < He
　　　　deeds,　　　　　　　　　　exalted

---

(1) *Ezekiel* 3:12.

angels are not translated since we lack the vocabulary to define them. *Rambam* (*Yesodei HaTorah* 2:7) notes that there are ten levels of angels. Their names are *Chayos, Ofanim, Er'eilim, Chashmalim, Seraphim, Melachim, Elohim, B'nei Elohim, Cherubim,* and *Ishim.*

בָּרוּךְ ... מִמְּקוֹמוֹ — *Blessed ... from His place.* "Place" refers to a particular position or level of eminence. For example, we say that a person "takes his father's place." But in the case of God, all we can do is bless His eminence as *we* perceive it coming to us *from* His place. In other words, we see Him in His role as Sustainer, Healer, Judge, Life-giver and so on, but we do not know what He really is. Though the angels have a better knowledge of God than do people, they too have no comprehension of His true essence (*Nefesh HaChaim*).

לָאֵל בָּרוּךְ — *To the God Who is blessed.*

Earlier in this *Shema* blessing (p. 125), we recited a twenty-two-word *aleph-beis* acrostic that began with this same expression: אֵל בָּרוּךְ, *the God Who is blessed.* Now, in keeping with the general principle regarding a long blessing, we conclude it by returning to the theme with which the blessing began. Thus, we return to the theme of *the God Who is blessed,* Whom we gratefully praise for His works of Creation in general and the heavenly luminaries in particular — upon which we will conclude by blessing Him as יוֹצֵר הַמְּאוֹרוֹת, [God] *Who fashions the luminaries.*

לָאֵל ... לַמֶּלֶךְ — *To the God ... to the King.* The commentators differ regarding the vocalization of these two words. Many hold that they are read לַאֵל and לַמֶּלֶךְ. We have followed the version preferred by *Arizal,* but every congregation should maintain its custom.

חֲדָשׁוֹת, בַּעַל מִלְחָמוֹת, זוֹרֵעַ צְדָקוֹת,* מַצְמִיחַ

‹ brings about ‹‹ kindnesses,* ‹ sows ‹‹ of wars, ‹ is Master ‹‹ new things, the sprouting

יְשׁוּעוֹת, בּוֹרֵא רְפוּאוֹת, נוֹרָא תְהִלּוֹת, אֲדוֹן

‹ is the ‹‹ beyond ‹ is ‹‹ cures, ‹ creates ‹‹ of salvations, Master praise, awesome

הַנִּפְלָאוֹת. הַמְחַדֵּשׁ בְּטוּבוֹ בְּכָל יוֹם תָּמִיד

‹ perpetually, ‹ day, ‹ every ‹ in His goodness ‹ Who renews ‹ of wonders,

מַעֲשֵׂה בְרֵאשִׁית. כָּאָמוּר: לְעֹשֵׂה אוֹרִים גְּדֹלִים,

‹‹ the great luminaries, ‹ [Give thanks] to ‹‹ As it is said: ‹‹ of Creation. ‹ the work Him Who makes

כִּי לְעוֹלָם חַסְדּוֹ.¹ (וְהִתְקִין מְאוֹרוֹת מְשַׂמֵּחַ

‹ [to] gladden ‹ luminaries ‹ (He established ‹‹ is His ‹ enduring ‹ for kindness. forever

עוֹלָמוֹ אֲשֶׁר בָּרָא.) ❖ אוֹר חָדָשׁ* עַל צִיּוֹן

‹ Zion ‹ on ‹ A new light* ‹‹ He created.) ‹ which ‹ His world

תָּאִיר, וְנִזְכֶּה כֻלָּנוּ בִּמְהֵרָה לְאוֹרוֹ. בָּרוּךְ

‹ Blessed ‹‹ [to benefit ‹ speedily, ‹ all of us, ‹ and may ‹‹ may You from] its light. we merit, shine,

אַתָּה יהוה, יוֹצֵר הַמְּאוֹרוֹת. (אָמֵן.)

‹‹ (Amen.) –Cong.) ‹‹ the luminaries. ‹ Who ‹‹ HASHEM, ‹ are You, fashions

אַהֲבַת עוֹלָם* אֲהַבְתָּנוּ יהוה אֱלֹהֵינוּ, חֶמְלָה

‹ with a ‹‹ our God; ‹ HASHEM, ‹ have You ‹ that is ‹ [With] a love compassion loved us, eternal*

---

(1) *Psalms* 136:7.

זוֹרֵעַ צְדָקוֹת — *Sows kindnesses.* God does not merely reward man for his good deeds; He rewards him even for the chain reaction that results from human kindness. Thus, an act of kindness is like a seed that can produce luxuriant vegetation (*Etz Yosef*).

אוֹר חָדָשׁ — *A new light.* The *new* light is actually a return of the original brilliance of Creation.

That light was concealed for the enjoyment of the righteous in the Messianic era. May it soon shine upon Zion (*Yaavetz*).

אַהֲבַת עוֹלָם — *[With] a love that is eternal.* Up to now, we have blessed God for having created the luminaries, but there is a light even greater than that of the brightest stars and the sun — the light of the Torah. Now, in this second blessing

גְדוֹלָה וִיתֵרָה חָמַלְתָּ עָלֵינוּ. אָבִינוּ מַלְכֵּנוּ, בַּעֲבוּר

‹ for the sake ‹ « our King, ‹ Our Father, « to us. ‹ have You shown ‹ and exceeding compassion ‹ that is great

שִׁמְךָ הַגָּדוֹל, וּבַעֲבוּר אֲבוֹתֵינוּ שֶׁבָּטְחוּ בְךָ,

‹ in You ‹ who trusted ‹ of our forefathers ‹ and for the sake « that is great, ‹ of Your Name

וַתְּלַמְּדֵם חֻקֵּי חַיִּים, לַעֲשׂוֹת רְצוֹנְךָ בְּלֵבָב שָׁלֵם,

« wholeheartedly, ‹ Your will ‹ to do « of life, ‹ the decrees ‹ and to whom You taught

כֵּן תְּחָנֵּנוּ וּתְלַמְּדֵנוּ. אָבִינוּ אָב הָרַחֲמָן הַמְרַחֵם,

« [and] Who acts mercifully, ‹ Who is merciful ‹ Father « Our Father, « and teach us. ‹ may You be ‹ so gracious to us

רַחֵם עָלֵינוּ, וְתֵן בְּלִבֵּנוּ בִּינָה, לְהָבִין וּלְהַשְׂכִּיל,

‹ and to comprehend, ‹ to understand ‹ under-standing, ‹ in our hearts ‹ and instill « upon us, ‹ have mercy

לִשְׁמוֹעַ לִלְמוֹד וּלְלַמֵּד, לִשְׁמֹר וְלַעֲשׂוֹת וּלְקַיֵּם

‹ and to fulfill ‹ to perform, ‹ to observe, ‹ to teach, ‹ to learn, ‹ to listen,

אֶת כָּל דִּבְרֵי תַלְמוּד תּוֹרָתֶךָ בְּאַהֲבָה. וְהָאֵר

‹ Enlighten « with love. ‹ of Your Torah ‹ of the teaching ‹ the words ‹ all

עֵינֵינוּ בְּתוֹרָתֶךָ, וְדַבֵּק לִבֵּנוּ בְּמִצְוֹתֶיךָ, וְיַחֵד

‹ and unify « to Your commandments, ‹ our hearts ‹ attach « in Your Torah, ‹ our eyes

לְבָבֵנוּ* לְאַהֲבָה וּלְיִרְאָה אֶת שְׁמֶךָ,¹ לְמַעַן לֹא

‹ we not ‹ so that « Your Name, ‹ and to fear ‹ to love ‹ our hearts*

נֵבוֹשׁ* וְלֹא נִכָּלֵם וְלֹא נִכָּשֵׁל לְעוֹלָם וָעֶד.* כִּי

‹ for « and ever;* ‹ for ever ‹ stumble ‹ nor ‹ be humiliated, ‹ nor ‹ be ashamed,*

(1) Cf. *Psalms* 86:11.

---

before *Shema*, we thank God for the Torah and pray that He grant us the wisdom to understand it properly (*Yaavetz; R' Munk*).

וְיַחֵד לְבָבֵנוּ — *And unify our hearts.* Man's desires and needs propel him in many directions. We ask

God to unify our emotions and wishes to serve Him in love and fear.

לְמַעַן לֹא נֵבוֹשׁ . . . לְעוֹלָם וָעֶד — *So that we not be ashamed . . . for ever and ever.* Inner shame is what one feels deep within himself when he

בְּשֵׁם קָדְשְׁךָ הַגָּדוֹל הַגִּבּוֹר וְהַנּוֹרָא בָּטָחְנוּ, נָגִילָה

‹ — may ‹‹ ‹‹ do we trust ‹ and awesome ‹ mighty, ‹ that is great, ‹ of Your ‹ in the
we exult   holiness   Name

וְנִשְׂמְחָה בִּישׁוּעָתֶךָ. וְרַחֲמֶיךָ, יהוה אֱלֹהֵינוּ,

‹‹ our God, ‹ HASHEM, ‹ May Your compassion, ‹‹ in Your salvation. ‹ and rejoice

וַחֲסָדֶיךָ הָרַבִּים, אַל יַעַזְבוּנוּ נֶצַח סֶלָה וָעֶד.

‹‹ and ‹ for ever ‹ eternally, ‹ forsake us ‹ not ‹‹ that is ‹ and Your
ever.   abundant,   kindness

AT THIS POINT, GATHER THE FOUR *TZITZIS* BETWEEN THE FOURTH AND FIFTH FINGERS OF THE LEFT HAND. HOLD THE *TZITZIS* IN THIS MANNER THROUGHOUT THE *SHEMA*.

מַהֵר וְהָבֵא עָלֵינוּ בְּרָכָה וְשָׁלוֹם מְהֵרָה מֵאַרְבַּע

‹ from the four ‹ speedily, ‹ and peace, ‹ blessing ‹ us ‹ and bring ‹ Hurry

כַּנְפוֹת (כָּל) הָאָרֶץ, וּשְׁבוֹר עוֹל הַגּוֹיִם מֵעַל

‹ from ‹ of the ‹ the yoke ‹ break ‹‹ the world; ‹ (all) ‹ corners of
upon   nations

צַוָּארֵנוּ, וְתוֹלִיכֵנוּ מְהֵרָה קוֹמְמִיוּת לְאַרְצֵנוּ. כִּי

‹ For ‹‹ to our land. ‹ with upright pride ‹ speedily, ‹ and lead us, ‹‹ our necks,

אֵל פּוֹעֵל יְשׁוּעוֹת אָתָּה, וּבָנוּ בָחַרְתָּ מִכָּל עַם

‹ peoples ‹ from ‹ You have ‹ and us ‹‹ are You, ‹ salvations, ‹ Who ‹ the
among all   chosen   performs   God

וְלָשׁוֹן. ❖ וְקֵרַבְתָּנוּ מַלְכֵּנוּ לְשִׁמְךָ הַגָּדוֹל סֶלָה

‹ forever ‹ that is great ‹ to Your ‹ our King, ‹ And You have ‹‹ and
Name   brought us close,   tongues.

בֶּאֱמֶת בְּאַהֲבָה, לְהוֹדוֹת לְךָ וּלְיַחֶדְךָ בְּאַהֲבָה,

‹‹ with love, ‹ and proclaim ‹ to ‹ to offer ‹‹ in love, ‹ in truth,
Your Oneness   You,   thanks

וּלְאַהֲבָה אֶת שְׁמֶךָ. בָּרוּךְ אַתָּה יהוה, הַבּוֹחֵר

‹ Who chooses ‹‹ HASHEM, ‹ are You, ‹ Blessed ‹‹ Your Name. ‹ and to love

(אָמֵן. —Cong.)   בְּעַמּוֹ יִשְׂרָאֵל בְּאַהֲבָה.

‹‹ (Amen.)   ‹‹ with love. ‹ Israel ‹ His people

---

knows he has done wrong — even though the people around him may sing his praises. The cost of such shame is borne primarily in the World to

Come, where it can diminish one's eternal bliss or even destroy it entirely. Therefore we pray that our eternity not be marred by inner shame.

THE SHEMA / שמע

IMMEDIATELY BEFORE ITS RECITATION CONCENTRATE ON FULFILLING THE POSITIVE COMMANDMENT OF RECITING THE *SHEMA*. IT IS IMPORTANT TO ENUNCIATE EACH WORD CLEARLY AND NOT TO RUN WORDS TOGETHER. FOR THIS REASON, VERTICAL LINES HAVE BEEN PLACED BETWEEN TWO WORDS THAT ARE NOT SEPARATED BY A COMMA OR A HYPHEN AND ARE PRONE TO BEING SLURRED INTO ONE.

WHEN PRAYING WITHOUT A *MINYAN*, BEGIN WITH THE FOLLOWING THREE-WORD FORMULA:

אֵל מֶלֶךְ נֶאֱמָן.*

❰❰ Who is trustworthy.* ❰ King ❰ God,

RECITE THE FIRST VERSE ALOUD, WITH THE RIGHT HAND COVERING THE EYES, AND CONCENTRATE INTENSELY UPON ACCEPTING GOD'S ABSOLUTE SOVEREIGNTY.

שְׁמַע | יִשְׂרָאֵל,* יהוה | אֱלֹהֵינוּ, יהוה | אֶחָד:*¹

❰❰ the One ❰ HASHEM ❰❰ is our God, ❰ HASHEM ❰❰ O Israel:* ❰ Hear,
[and Only].*   is

IN AN UNDERTONE:

בָּרוּךְ שֵׁם* כְּבוֹד מַלְכוּתוֹ לְעוֹלָם וָעֶד.²

❰❰ and ever. ❰ for ever ❰ kingdom ❰ of His glorious ❰ is the Name* ❰ Blessed

---

(1) *Deuteronomy* 6:4. (2) See *Pesachim* 56a.

❧ שְׁמַע / THE SHEMA ❧

The recitation of the three paragraphs of *Shema* is required by the Torah, and one must have in mind that he is about to fulfill this commandment. Although one should try to concentrate on the meaning of all three paragraphs, one must concentrate at least on the meaning of the first verse (שְׁמַע) and the second verse (בָּרוּךְ שֵׁם) because the recitation of *Shema* represents fulfillment of the paramount commandment of acceptance of God's absolute sovereignty (קַבָּלַת עוֹל מַלְכוּת שָׁמַיִם). By declaring that God is One, Unique, and Indivisible, we subordinate every facet of our personalities, possessions — our very lives — to His will.

A summary of the laws of the *Shema* appears in *Laws* §46-60. For a full commentary and Overview, see ArtScroll *Shema Yisrael*.

In the שְׁמַע we have included the cantillation symbols (*trop*) for the convenience of those who recite שְׁמַע in the manner it is read from the Torah. Additionally, to enable those unfamiliar with this notation to group the words properly, commas have been inserted.

❧ אֵל מֶלֶךְ נֶאֱמָן — *God, King Who is trustworthy.* The Sages teach that there are both 248 organs in the human body and 248 positive

commandments. This parallel number symbolizes that the purpose of physical existence is to obey the precepts of the Torah. The total number of words in the three paragraphs of *Shema* is 245. The Sages wished to convey the above symbolism in the recitation of the *Shema*, so they added three words to it. If a *minyan* is present, the congregation listens to the *chazzan's* repetition aloud of the three words ה׳ אֱלֹהֵיכֶם אֱמֶת. If there is no *minyan* the three words אֵל מֶלֶךְ נֶאֱמָן are recited before *Shema* is begun. These words were chosen because their initials spell אָמֵן [literally, *it is true*], thus testifying to our belief in the truths we are about to recite.

The three words of the verse mean: He is אֵל, God, the All-powerful source of all mercy; He is the מֶלֶךְ, King, Who rules, leads, and exercises supervision over all; and He is נֶאֱמָן, trustworthy, fair, apportioning no more suffering nor less good than one deserves (*Anaf Yosef*).

❧ שְׁמַע יִשְׂרָאֵל — *Hear, O Israel.* Although the commentators find many layers of profound meaning in this seminal verse, one should bear in mind at least the following points during its recitation:

❏ At this point in history, HASHEM is only

WHILE RECITING THE FIRST PARAGRAPH (*DEUTERONOMY* 6:5-9), CONCENTRATE ON
ACCEPTING THE COMMANDMENT TO LOVE GOD.

וְאָהַבְתָּ* ‹ אֵת ׀ יהוה ׀ אֱלֹהֶיךָ, בְּכָל־לְבָבְךָ,
‹your heart,‹ with all ‹ your God, ‹ HASHEM, ‹ You shall love*

וּבְכָל־נַפְשְׁךָ, וּבְכָל־מְאֹדֶךָ: וְהָיוּ הַדְּבָרִים הָאֵלֶּה,
‹ — these matters ‹‹ They ‹‹ your ‹ and with ‹ your soul, ‹ with all
should be resources. all

אֲשֶׁר ׀ אָנֹכִי מְצַוְּךָ הַיּוֹם,* עַל־לְבָבֶךָ: וְשִׁנַּנְתָּם
‹ Teach them ‹‹ your heart. ‹ upon ‹‹ today* — ‹ command ‹ I ‹ that
thoroughly   you

אֱלֹהֵינוּ, *our God*, for He is not acknowledged universally. Ultimately, however, all will recognize Him as ה' אֶחָד, *the One and Only God* (*Rashi; Aruch HaShulchan* 61:4).

❑ ה' — *HASHEM.* God is the Eternal One, Who was, is, and always will be [הָיָה הֹוֶה וְיִהְיֶה], and He is אָדוֹן, *Master,* of all.

❑ אֱלֹהֵינוּ — *Our God.* He is All-Powerful (*Orach Chaim* 5).

◆§ אֶחָד — *The One [and Only].* The word has two connotations: (a) There is no God other than HASHEM (*Rashbam*); and, (b) though we perceive God in many roles — kind, angry, merciful, wise, judgmental, and so on — these different attributes are not contradictory, even though human intelligence does not comprehend their harmony.

In saying the word אֶחָד, *the One and Only,* draw out the second syllable (חָ) a bit and emphasize the final consonant (ד). While drawing out the ח — a letter with the numerical value of eight — bear in mind that God is Master of the earth and the seven heavens. While clearly enunciating the final ד — which has the numerical value of four — bear in mind that God is Master in all four directions, meaning everywhere.

◆§ **The enlarged ע and ד**

In Torah scrolls, the letters ע of שְׁמַע and ד of אֶחָד are enlarged. Together they form the word עֵד, *witness,* alluding to the thought that every Jew, by pronouncing the *Shema,* bears witness to HASHEM's unity and declares it to all the world (*Rokeach; Kol Bo; Abudraham*).

◆§ בָּרוּךְ שֵׁם — *Blessed is the Name.* This verse is

recited in an undertone because:

(a) At Jacob's deathbed his children affirmed their loyalty to God by proclaiming the verse *Shema* ["Israel" in that context refers to Jacob]. Jacob responded: *"Blessed is the Name . . ."* The Sages taught: Should we say these words in our prayers because Jacob said them? Yes. But, on the other hand, Moses did not transmit them to us, for they are not found in the Torah. Therefore, let us say them softly (*Pesachim* 56a).

(b) Moses heard this beautiful prayer from the angels, and taught it to Israel. We dare not say it aloud, because we are sinful and therefore unworthy of using an angelic formula. On Yom Kippur, however, when Israel elevates itself to the sin-free level of angels, we do proclaim it loudly (*Devarim Rabbah* 2:36).

◆§ וְאָהַבְתָּ — *You shall love.* One should learn to fulfill the commandments out of love, rather than fear — and certainly not out of habit. The Mishnah (*Berachos* 9:5) explains that one should serve God with all his emotions and desires (*with all your heart*), even to the point of giving up his life for God (*with all your soul*), and even at the cost of his wealth (*with all your resources*).

אֲשֶׁר אָנֹכִי מְצַוְּךָ הַיּוֹם — *That I command you today.* Although the Torah was given thousands of years ago, we are not to regard the commandments as an ancient rite that we follow out of loyalty and habit. Rather, we are to regard them with as much freshness and enthusiasm as if God had given them this very day (*Sifre*).

לְבָנֶיךָ, וְדִבַּרְתָּ בָּם בְּשִׁבְתְּךָ בְּבֵיתֶךָ, וּבְלֶכְתְּךָ

‹ while you walk ‹ in your home, ‹ while you sit ‹ of ‹ and speak ‹ to your
them children

TOUCH THE ARM-*TEFILLIN* AT "… וּקְשַׁרְתָּם" AND THE HEAD-*TEFILLIN* AT "… וְהָיוּ לְטֹטָפֹת".

בַדֶּרֶךְ, וּבְשָׁכְבְּךָ וּבְקוּמֶךָ: וּקְשַׁרְתָּם* לְאוֹת |

‹ as a sign ‹ Bind them* « and when ‹ when you ‹ on the way,
you arise. lie down,

עַל־יָדֶךָ, וְהָיוּ לְטֹטָפֹת* בֵּין | עֵינֶיךָ:* וּכְתַבְתָּם |

‹ And write them « your eyes.* ‹ between ‹ *tefillin** ‹ and they ‹ your arm ‹ upon
shall be

עַל־מְזֻזוֹת בֵּיתֶךָ וּבִשְׁעָרֶיךָ:

« and upon your gates. ‹ of your house ‹ the doorposts ‹ on

**WHILE RECITING THE SECOND PARAGRAPH (*DEUTERONOMY* 11:13-21), CONCENTRATE ON
ACCEPTING ALL THE COMMANDMENTS AND ON THE CONCEPT OF REWARD AND PUNISHMENT.**

וְהָיָה,* אִם־שָׁמֹעַ תִּשְׁמְעוּ אֶל־מִצְוֺתַי אֲשֶׁר |

‹ that ‹ My ‹ to ‹ you continually hearken ‹ that if ‹ And it will be*
commandments

אָנֹכִי מְצַוֶּה | אֶתְכֶם הַיּוֹם, לְאַהֲבָה אֶת־יְהֹוה

‹ HASHEM, ‹ to love « today, ‹ you ‹ command ‹ I

אֱלֹהֵיכֶם וּלְעָבְדוֹ, בְּכָל־לְבַבְכֶם וּבְכָל־נַפְשְׁכֶם:

« your soul ‹ and with all ‹ your heart ‹ with all « and to serve Him, ‹ your God,

וְנָתַתִּי מְטַר־אַרְצְכֶם בְּעִתּוֹ, יוֹרֶה וּמַלְקוֹשׁ,

« and the late ‹ the « in its proper ‹ for your land ‹ rain ‹ — then I
rain, early rain time, will provide

וּקְשַׁרְתָּם — *Bind them. Tefillin,* on the arm next
to the heart, and on the head, consecrate one's
physical, emotional, and intellectual capacities
to God's service (*Ramban*). The *mezuzah* on the
doorpost consecrates one's home to Him.

לְטֹטָפֹת — *Tefillin.* The etymology of the word
טֹטָפֹת is obscure. The translation *tefillin* follows
Onkelos. Rashi quotes the Talmudic derivation
(*Sanhedrin* 4b) that the word is a compound of
foreign words that combine to mean four, referring to the four compartments of the head-*tefillin*.

Ramban explains the words as *an ornament.*

בֵּין עֵינֶיךָ — *Between your eyes.* This expression
in Scripture means above the hairline, above the
center point *between the eyes.* See *Menachos*
37a,b.

וְהָיָה § — *And it will be.* This paragraph of
Shema specifies the duty to perform מִצְוֺתַי, *My
commandments,* and teaches that when the
nation is righteous, it will be rewarded with
success and prosperity. When it sins, it will
experience poverty and exile.

וְאָסַפְתָּ דְגָנֶךָ וְתִירֹשְׁךָ וְיִצְהָרֶךָ: וְנָתַתִּי | עֵשֶׂב |
‹ grass ‹ I will provide « and your oil. ‹ your wine, ‹ your grain, ‹ that you may gather in

בְּשָׂדְךָ לִבְהֶמְתֶּךָ, וְאָכַלְתָּ וְשָׂבָעְתָּ: הִשָּׁמְרוּ*
‹ Beware* « and be satisfied. ‹ and you will eat « for your cattle, ‹ in your field

לָכֶם פֶּן־יִפְתֶּה* לְבַבְכֶם, וְסַרְתֶּם וַעֲבַדְתֶּם |
‹ and serve ‹ and you turn astray « be your heart, ‹ seduced* ‹ lest ‹ for yourselves

אֱלֹהִים | אֲחֵרִים וְהִשְׁתַּחֲוִיתֶם לָהֶם:* וְחָרָה |
‹ Then shall blaze « to them.* ‹ and bow ‹ of others ‹ gods

אַף־יהוה בָּכֶם, וְעָצַר | אֶת־הַשָּׁמַיִם וְלֹא־יִהְיֶה
‹ so that there will not be ‹ the heaven ‹ He will restrain « against you. ‹ of ‹ the HASHEM wrath

מָטָר,* וְהָאֲדָמָה לֹא תִתֵּן אֶת־יְבוּלָהּ, וַאֲבַדְתֶּם* |
‹ And you will be banished* ‹ its produce. ‹ will not yield ‹ and the ground « rain,*

מְהֵרָה מֵעַל הָאָרֶץ הַטֹּבָה | אֲשֶׁר | יהוה נֹתֵן
‹ gives ‹ HASHEM ‹ which ‹ the good land ‹ from upon ‹ swiftly

לָכֶם: וְשַׂמְתֶּם אֶת־דְּבָרַי | אֵלֶּה עַל־לְבַבְכֶם
‹ your heart ‹ upon ‹ these words of Mine ‹ Place « you.

TOUCH THE ARM-*TEFILLIN* AT "...וּקְשַׁרְתֶּם" AND THE HEAD-*TEFILLIN* AT "...וְהָיוּ לְטוֹטָפֹת".

וְעַל־נַפְשְׁכֶם, וּקְשַׁרְתֶּם | אֹתָם | לְאוֹת | עַל־
‹ upon ‹ for a sign ‹ them ‹ bind « your soul; ‹ and upon

יֶדְכֶם, וְהָיוּ לְטוֹטָפֹת בֵּין | עֵינֵיכֶם: וְלִמַּדְתֶּם |
‹ Teach « your eyes. ‹ between ‹ *tefillin* ‹ and they « your arm shall be

וְאָכַלְתָּ וְשָׂבָעְתָּ. הִשָּׁמְרוּ — *And you will eat and be satisfied. Beware* ... Prosperity is often the greatest challenge to religious devotion (*Rashi*).

יִפְתֶּה...וְהִשְׁתַּחֲוִיתֶם לָהֶם — *Seduced...and bow to them,* to strange gods. A seemingly minor surrender to temptation can be the beginning of a course that will end in idolatry (*Rashi*).

וְלֹא יִהְיֶה מָטָר...וַאֲבַדְתֶּם — *So that there will not be rain ... And you will be banished.* First will come famine. If that does not bring repentance, exile will follow (*Vilna Gaon*).

אֹתָם* ׀ אֶת־בְּנֵיכֶם לְדַבֵּר בָּם, בְּשִׁבְתְּךָ* בְּבֵיתֶךָ,
‹ in your home, ‹ while you sit* ‹‹ them, ‹ to discuss ‹ to your children, ‹ them*

וּבְלֶכְתְּךָ בַדֶּרֶךְ, וּבְשָׁכְבְּךָ וּבְקוּמֶךָ: וּכְתַבְתָּם ׀
‹ And write them ‹‹ and when you arise. ‹ when you lie down, ‹‹ on the way, ‹ while you walk

עַל־מְזוּזוֹת בֵּיתֶךָ וּבִשְׁעָרֶיךָ: לְמַעַן ׀ יִרְבּוּ ׀
‹ to prolong ‹ In order ‹‹ and upon your gates. ‹ of your house ‹ the doorposts ‹ on

יְמֵיכֶם וִימֵי בְנֵיכֶם עַל הָאֲדָמָה ׀ אֲשֶׁר
‹ that ‹ the land ‹ upon ‹ of your children ‹ and the days ‹ your days

נִשְׁבַּע ׀ יהוה ׀ לַאֲבֹתֵיכֶם לָתֵת לָהֶם, כִּימֵי
‹ like the days ‹‹ them, ‹ to give ‹ to your ancestors ‹ HASHEM swore

הַשָּׁמַיִם ׀ עַל־הָאָרֶץ:*
‹‹ the earth.* ‹ on ‹ of the heaven

BEFORE RECITING THIS PARAGRAPH, THE *TZITZIS*, WHICH HAVE BEEN HELD IN THE LEFT HAND, ARE TAKEN IN THE RIGHT HAND ALSO. THE *TZITZIS* ARE KISSED AT EACH MENTION OF *TZITZIS*, AND AT THE END OF THE PARAGRAPH, AND ARE PASSED BEFORE THE EYES AT וּרְאִיתֶם אֹתוֹ, *"THAT YOU MAY SEE IT."*

Numbers 15:37-41

וַיֹּאמֶר ׀ יהוה* ׀ אֶל־מֹשֶׁה לֵּאמֹר: דַּבֵּר ׀
‹ Speak ‹‹ saying: ‹ Moses, ‹ to ‹ HASHEM said*

אֶל־בְּנֵי ׀ יִשְׂרָאֵל וְאָמַרְתָּ אֲלֵהֶם, וְעָשׂוּ לָהֶם
‹ for them- selves ‹ that they are to make ‹ to them ‹ and say ‹ of Israel ‹ the ‹ to Children

---

בְּשִׁבְתְּךָ ... אֹתָם וְלִמַּדְתֶּם — *Teach them ... while you sit.* In giving the command to educate children in the Torah, the verse speaks in the plural (וְלִמַּדְתֶּם), while the other words in the verse (בְּשִׁבְתְּךָ and so on) are in the singular. This alludes to a *communal* responsibility for the Torah education of children (*Iyun Tefillah*).

כִּימֵי הַשָּׁמַיִם עַל הָאָרֶץ — *Like the days of the heaven on the earth.* Eretz Yisrael is the eternal heritage of the Jewish people, just as heaven will always remain above the earth. Alternatively, just as heaven showers blessings upon the earth in the form of life-giving rain, so too Israel will be blessed in the Land God has sworn to it.

וַיֹּאמֶר ה' — *HASHEM said.* The recitation of the third paragraph of *Shema* fulfills the commandment to recall the Exodus every day. By liberating Israel from Egypt, God laid claim to the nation's eternal allegiance. No Jew is free to exempt himself from that obligation (*Rashi*).

עַל־ וּנְתָנוּ ׀ לְדֹרֹתָם בְּגְדֵיהֶם עַל־כַּנְפֵי צִיצִת*
‹ upon ‹ And they ‹‹ throughout ‹ of their ‹ the ‹ on ‹ tzitzis*
are to place their generations. garments, corners

צִיצִת, לָכֶם וְהָיָה תְּכֵלֶת:* פְּתִיל הַכָּנָף צִיצִת
‹‹ tzitzis, ‹ for you ‹ And it shall ‹‹ of techeiles.* ‹ a thread ‹ of the ‹ the tzitzis
constitute corner

׀ כָּל־מִצְוֹת אֶת־ וּזְכַרְתֶּם אֹתוֹ וּרְאִיתֶם
‹ all the commandments ‹ that and remember ‹ it ‹ that you may see

אַחֲרֵי ׀ וְלֹא־תָתוּרוּ* אֹתָם, וַעֲשִׂיתֶם יְהוָה
‹ after ‹ explore* ‹ and not ‹‹ them, ‹ and perform ‹ of Hashem

׀ זֹנִים אַתֶּם־אֲשֶׁר עֵינֵיכֶם ׀ וְאַחֲרֵי לְבַבְכֶם
‹ stray ‹ you ‹ which ‹ your eyes ‹ and after ‹ your heart

אֶת־כָּל־ ׀ וַעֲשִׂיתֶם תִּזְכְּרוּ לְמַעַן אַחֲרֵיהֶם:
‹ all ‹ and perform ‹ you may remember ‹ so that ‹‹ after them;

לֵאלֹהֵיכֶם: קְדֹשִׁים וִהְיִיתֶם מִצְוֹתָי,
‹‹ to your God. ‹ holy ‹ and be ‹ My commandments,

CONCENTRATE ON FULFILLING THE COMMANDMENT TO REMEMBER THE EXODUS FROM EGYPT.

אֶתְכֶם ׀ הוֹצֵאתִי אֲשֶׁר אֱלֹהֵיכֶם ׀ יְהוָה אֲנִי
‹ you ‹ has removed ‹ Who ‹ your God, ‹ Hashem, ‹ I am

׀ אֲנִי לֵאלֹהִים, לָכֶם לִהְיוֹת מִצְרַיִם מֵאֶרֶץ
‹ I am ‹‹ a God; ‹ to you ‹ to be ‹ of Egypt ‹ from the land

— אֱמֶת:* אֱלֹהֵיכֶם ׀ יהוה
‹‹ — It is true...* ‹‹ your God. ‹ Hashem

צִיצִת — *Tzitzis. Rashi* offers two explanations for the term *tzitzis* or tassels: either because of the threads that hang down — the term *tzitzis* meaning *curls* or *locks* as in *Ezekiel* 7:3; or because of the command associated with them: *that you may see it* — the term *tzitzis*, according to this interpretation, derived from the verb צִיץ, *gaze*, as in *Song of Songs* 2:9, with the noun denoting "an object to be gazed at."

פְּתִיל תְּכֵלֶת — *A thread of techeiles. Techeiles* is wool dyed sky-blue with the secretion of an amphibian, the *chilazon.* For many centuries the identity of the animal has been unknown. Even in the absence of the *techeiles* thread, however, the commandment of *tzitzis* remains binding (*Menachos* 38a).

וְלֹא תָתוּרוּ — *And not explore.* The eye sees, then the heart covets, then the body sins (*Rashi*).

אֱמֶת — *True.* Although this word belongs to the next paragraph, it is appended to the

CHAZZAN REPEATS:

יהוה אֱלֹהֵיכֶם אֱמֶת,

‹ is true, ‹ your God, ‹ HASHEM,

וְיַצִּיב* וְנָכוֹן וְקַיָּם וְיָשָׁר וְנֶאֱמָן וְאָהוּב

‹ beloved, ‹ faithful, ‹ fair, ‹ and enduring, ‹ established ‹ and certain,*

וְחָבִיב וְנֶחְמָד וְנָעִים וְנוֹרָא וְאַדִּיר וּמְתֻקָּן

‹ correct, ‹ powerful, ‹ awesome, ‹ pleasant, ‹ desirable, ‹ cherished,

וּמְקֻבָּל וְטוֹב וְיָפֶה הַדָּבָר הַזֶּה עָלֵינוּ לְעוֹלָם

‹ for ever ‹ to us ‹ is this affirmation ‹ and beautiful ‹ good, ‹ accepted,

וָעֶד. אֱמֶת אֱלֹהֵי עוֹלָם מַלְכֵּנוּ צוּר יַעֲקֹב,

‹ of Jacob ‹ the Rock ‹ is our King; ‹ of the universe ‹ the God ‹ True — ‹ and ever.

מָגֵן יִשְׁעֵנוּ, לְדֹר וָדֹר הוּא קַיָּם, וּשְׁמוֹ קַיָּם,

‹ endures ‹ and His Name ‹ endures ‹ He ‹ after generation ‹ Generation ‹ of our salvation. ‹ is the Shield

וְכִסְאוֹ נָכוֹן, וּמַלְכוּתוֹ וֶאֱמוּנָתוֹ לָעַד קַיָּמֶת.

‹ endure. ‹ forever ‹ and faithfulness ‹ His sovereignty ‹ is well established; ‹ and His Throne

וּדְבָרָיו חָיִים וְקַיָּמִים, נֶאֱמָנִים וְנֶחֱמָדִים לָעַד

‹ forever ‹ and desirable ‹ faithful ‹ and enduring, ‹ are living ‹ His words

AT THIS POINT THE *TZITZIS* ARE KISSED AND RELEASED.

conclusion of the previous one.

One may not interrupt between the last words of the *Shema* and אֱמֶת, so that we declare, as did the prophet [*Jeremiah* 10:10], וַה׳ אֱלֹהִים אֱמֶת, *HASHEM, God, is true* (*Berachos* 14a).

אֱמֶת . . . וְיַצִּיב ‹§ — *True . . . and certain.* This paragraph begins the third and final blessing of the *Shema*, which ends with גָּאַל יִשְׂרָאֵל, *Who redeemed Israel.* Like אֱמֶת וֶאֱמוּנָה, *True and faithful*, its counterpart in the Evening Service, this blessing continues our fulfillment of the requirement to recall the Exodus, morning and evening.

As the Sages teach (*Berachos* 12a), whoever omits either the morning or evening blessing has not properly discharged his obligation of reciting the *Shema* and its attendant prayers. Although both the morning and evening blessings of redemption refer to the Exodus, there is a basic difference between them. The Talmud (ibid.) teaches that the formulation of these blessings is based on the verse לְהַגִּיד בַּבֹּקֶר חַסְדֶּךָ וֶאֱמוּנָתְךָ בַּלֵּילוֹת, *to relate Your kindness in the dawn and Your faithfulness in the nights* (*Psalms* 92:3). This implies that in the morning we express gratitude for already existing *kind-*

וּלְעוֹלְמֵי עוֹלָמִים. ❖ עַל אֲבוֹתֵינוּ וְעָלֵינוּ, עַל

‹ for ‹‹ and for us, ‹ our forefathers ‹ for ‹‹ and to all eternity;

בָּנֵינוּ וְעַל דּוֹרוֹתֵינוּ, וְעַל כָּל דּוֹרוֹת זֶרַע

‹ of the ‹ the ‹ all ‹ and ‹‹ our generations, ‹ and ‹ our
offspring generations for children

יִשְׂרָאֵל עֲבָדֶיךָ.

‹‹ [who are] Your servants. ‹‹ of Israel,

עַל הָרִאשׁוֹנִים וְעַל הָאַחֲרוֹנִים, דָּבָר טוֹב

‹ is ‹ the ‹ the later ‹ and for ‹ the earlier generations ‹ For
good matter generations,

וְקַיָּם לְעוֹלָם וָעֶד, אֱמֶת וֶאֱמוּנָה חֹק וְלֹא יַעֲבֹר.

‹‹ be ‹ that ‹ a ‹ and faithful, ‹ it is ‹‹ and ‹ for ever ‹ and
breached: cannot decree true ever; enduring

אֱמֶת שָׁאַתָּה הוּא יהוה אֱלֹהֵינוּ וֵאלֹהֵי אֲבוֹתֵינוּ,

‹‹ of our ‹ and the ‹ our God ‹ HASHEM, ‹ that You are ‹ It is true
forefathers, God

❖ מַלְכֵּנוּ מֶלֶךְ אֲבוֹתֵינוּ, גֹּאֲלֵנוּ גֹּאֵל אֲבוֹתֵינוּ,

‹‹ of our ‹ the ‹ our ‹‹ of our ‹ and the ‹ our King
forefathers, Redeemer Redeemer, forefathers, King

יוֹצְרֵנוּ צוּר יְשׁוּעָתֵנוּ, פּוֹדֵנוּ וּמַצִּילֵנוּ מֵעוֹלָם

‹ — always ‹‹ and our ‹ our ‹‹ of our salvation; ‹ the ‹ our
Rescuer Liberator Rock Molder,

הוּא שְׁמֶךָ, וְאֵין לָנוּ עוֹד אֱלֹהִים זוּלָתֶךָ, סֶלָה.

‹‹ forever. ‹ but You, ‹ God ‹ other ‹ And we ‹‹ been Your ‹ has this
have no Name.

---

ness, while in the evening we express our *faith* in something that has not yet taken place.

As *Rashi* and *Tosafos* explain, the morning blessing of אֱמֶת וְיַצִּיב concentrates on God's *kindness* in having redeemed us from Egypt, while אֱמֶת וֶאֱמוּנָה, which is recited at *night*, is based on the theme of our *faith* that God will redeem us in the future, just as He did at the time of the Exodus.

Including the word אֱמֶת, *true*, there are sixteen adjectives describing הַדָּבָר הַזֶּה, *this affirmation,* i.e. the total message contained in the sixteen verses of the first two paragraphs of the *Shema* (including בָּרוּךְ שֵׁם). Thus, it is as if we affirm each verse with an adjective acknowledging its truth. *Etz Yosef* and others show how each adjective is suited to the verse it affirms.

עֶזְרַת אֲבוֹתֵינוּ* אַתָּה הוּא מֵעוֹלָם, מָגֵן

‹ Shield ‹‹ always, ‹ You have been ‹ of our forefathers* ‹ The help

וּמוֹשִׁיעַ לָהֶם וְלִבְנֵיהֶם אַחֲרֵיהֶם בְּכָל דּוֹר וָדוֹר.

‹‹ generation. ‹ in every ‹ after them ‹ and for their ‹ for ‹ and Savior
children them

בְּרוּם עוֹלָם מוֹשָׁבֶךָ, וּמִשְׁפָּטֶיךָ וְצִדְקָתְךָ עַד

‹ extend ‹ and Your ‹ and Your justice ‹ is Your ‹ of the ‹ At the
to righteousness dwelling, universe zenith

אַפְסֵי אָרֶץ. אֱמֶת אַשְׁרֵי אִישׁ שֶׁיִּשְׁמַע לְמִצְוֹתֶיךָ,

‹ Your ‹ who obeys ‹ is the ‹ that ‹ It is ‹‹ of the ‹ the ends
commandments, person praiseworthy true earth.

וְתוֹרָתְךָ וּדְבָרְךָ יָשִׂים עַל לִבּוֹ. אֱמֶת אַתָּה הוּא

‹ that You are ‹ It is true ‹‹ his heart. ‹ upon ‹ places ‹ and Your word ‹ and Your teaching

אָדוֹן לְעַמֶּךָ, וּמֶלֶךְ גִּבּוֹר לָרִיב רִיבָם לְאָבוֹת

‹ for the ‹ their ‹ to ‹ and a mighty King ‹ for Your ‹ the
fathers cause champion people Master

וּבָנִים. אֱמֶת אַתָּה הוּא רִאשׁוֹן וְאַתָּה הוּא

‹ and that You are ‹ the First ‹ that You are ‹ It is true ‹‹ and the sons.

אַחֲרוֹן, וּמִבַּלְעָדֶיךָ אֵין לָנוּ מֶלֶךְ¹ גּוֹאֵל וּמוֹשִׁיעַ.

‹‹ or savior. ‹ redeemer, ‹ king, ‹ we have no ‹ and other than You ‹‹ the Last,

אֱמֶת מִמִּצְרַיִם גְּאַלְתָּנוּ יהוה אֱלֹהֵינוּ, וּמִבֵּית

‹ and from ‹‹ our God, ‹ HASHEM, ‹ You ‹ that from Egypt ‹ It is true
the house redeemed us,

עֲבָדִים פְּדִיתָנוּ. כָּל בְּכוֹרֵיהֶם הָרָגְתָּ, וּבְכוֹרְךָ

‹ but Your ‹‹ You slew, ‹ their firstborn ‹ All ‹‹ You liberated ‹ of slavery
firstborn, us.

יִשְׂרָאֵל גָּאָלְתָּ, וְיַם סוּף לָהֶם בָּקַעְתָּ, וְזֵדִים

‹ the willful ‹‹ You split; ‹ for them ‹ of ‹ the ‹‹ You ‹ Israel,
sinners Reeds Sea redeemed;

(1) Cf. *Isaiah* 44:6.

עֶזְרַת אֲבוֹתֵינוּ — *The help of our forefathers.* This passage elaborates upon the Exodus within the context of God's eternal supervision of Israel and mastery over its destiny.

טִבַּעְתָּ, וִידִידִים הֶעֱבַרְתָּ, וַיְכַסּוּ מַיִם צָרֵיהֶם,

‹‹ their foes; ‹ and the water covered ‹‹ You brought across; ‹ the dear ones ‹‹ You drowned;

אֶחָד מֵהֶם לֹא נוֹתָר.¹ עַל זֹאת שִׁבְּחוּ אֲהוּבִים

‹ the beloved ones praised ‹ this, ‹ For ‹‹ left. ‹ was not ‹ of them ‹ even one

וְרוֹמְמוּ לָאֵל, וְנָתְנוּ יְדִידִים זְמִרוֹת שִׁירוֹת

‹ songs, ‹ hymns, ‹ the dear ones offered ‹‹ God; ‹ and exalted

וְתִשְׁבָּחוֹת, בְּרָכוֹת וְהוֹדָאוֹת, לְמֶלֶךְ אֵל חַי

‹ Who is living ‹ the God ‹ to the King, ‹ and thanksgivings ‹ blessings ‹ praises,

וְקַיָּם, רָם וְנִשָּׂא, גָּדוֹל וְנוֹרָא, מַשְׁפִּיל גֵּאִים עֲדֵי

‹ to ‹ the haughty ‹ Who humbles ‹‹ and awesome, ‹ great ‹ and uplifted, ‹ exalted ‹ and enduring,

אָרֶץ, וּמַגְבִּיהַּ שְׁפָלִים עֲדֵי מָרוֹם, מוֹצִיא

‹ frees ‹‹ the heights, ‹ to ‹ the lowly ‹ and lifts ‹‹ the ground,

אֲסִירִים, וּפוֹדֶה עֲנָוִים, וְעוֹזֵר דַּלִּים, וְעוֹנֶה לְעַמּוֹ

‹ to His people, ‹ and Who responds ‹‹ the poor, ‹ and helps ‹ the humble, ‹ liberates ‹ the captive,

יִשְׂרָאֵל בְּעֵת שַׁוְּעָם אֵלָיו.²

‹‹ to Him. ‹ they cry out ‹ at the time ‹ Israel,

**RISE FOR *SHEMONEH ESREI*. SOME TAKE THREE STEPS BACKWARD AT THIS POINT;
OTHERS DO SO BEFORE צוּר יִשְׂרָאֵל.**

❖ תְּהִלּוֹת לְאֵל עֶלְיוֹן גּוֹאֲלָם, בָּרוּךְ הוּא וּמְבֹרָךְ.

‹‹ Who is blessed — ‹ One ‹ – the ‹‹ their ‹ the Most blessed Redeemer ‹ to God ‹ Praises High,

מֹשֶׁה וּבְנֵי יִשְׂרָאֵל לְךָ עָנוּ שִׁירָה בְּשִׂמְחָה רַבָּה

‹ with great joy ‹ a song ‹ proclaimed ‹ to You ‹ of Israel ‹ and the Children ‹ Moses

וְאָמְרוּ כֻלָּם:

‹‹ unanimously: ‹ and said

---

(1) *Psalms* 106:11. (2) Cf. 22:25; 28:2; 31:23.

מִי כָמְכָה בָּאֵלִם יהוה, מִי כָּמְכָה נֶאְדָּר

⟨ mighty ⟨ is like You, ⟨ Who ⟪ HASHEM! ⟨ among the ⟨ is like You ⟨ Who
heavenly powers,

בַּקֹּדֶשׁ, נוֹרָא תְהִלּת, עֹשֵׂה פֶלֶא.¹

⟪ wonders! ⟨ doing ⟪ [beyond] praise, ⟨ awesome ⟪ in holiness,

❖ שִׁירָה חֲדָשָׁה שִׁבְּחוּ גְאוּלִים לְשִׁמְךָ הַגָּדוֹל

⟨ Your great Name ⟨ the redeemed ones praised ⟨ [With] a new song

עַל שְׂפַת הַיָּם, יַחַד כֻּלָּם הוֹדוּ וְהִמְלִיכוּ וְאָמְרוּ:

⟪ and said: ⟨ acknowledged ⟨ gave ⟨ all of ⟨ together ⟪ of the ⟨ the shore ⟨ at
Your sovereignty, thanks, them Sea;

יהוה יִמְלֹךְ לְעֹלָם וָעֶד.²

⟪ and ever! ⟨ for ever ⟨ shall reign ⟨ HASHEM

IT IS FORBIDDEN TO INTERRUPT OR PAUSE BETWEEN גָּאַל יִשְׂרָאֵל **AND** SHEMONEH ESREI,
EVEN FOR KADDISH, KEDUSHAH, BORCHU **OR AMEN.**

❖ צוּר יִשְׂרָאֵל,* קוּמָה בְּעֶזְרַת יִשְׂרָאֵל, וּפְדֵה

⟪ and liberate, ⟨ of Israel ⟨ to the aid ⟨ arise ⟨ of Israel,* ⟨ Rock

כִנְאֻמֶךָ יְהוּדָה וְיִשְׂרָאֵל. וְנֶאֱמַר: גֹּאֲלֵנוּ יהוה

⟨ HASHEM, ⟪ Our ⟪ And it is said: ⟪ and Israel. ⟨ Judah ⟪ as You
Redeemer, pledged,

צְבָאוֹת שְׁמוֹ, קְדוֹשׁ יִשְׂרָאֵל.³ בָּרוּךְ אַתָּה יהוה,

⟪ HASHEM, ⟨ are You, ⟨ Blessed ⟪ of Israel. ⟨ the Holy ⟪ is His ⟨ Master of
One Name, Legions

גָּאַל יִשְׂרָאֵל.*

⟪ Israel.* ⟨ Who
redeemed

---

(1) Exodus 15:11. (2) 15:18. (3) Isaiah 47:4.

◄§ צוּר יִשְׂרָאֵל — Rock of Israel. Since the end of
Shema, we have concentrated on an elaboration
of the miracles of the Exodus. We do not lose
sight, however, of our faith that there is another,
greater redemption yet to come. Thus we
conclude with a plea that God rise up again to
redeem Israel from this exile as He did in ancient
Egypt.

גָּאַל יִשְׂרָאֵל — Who redeemed Israel. The text of
the blessing is in keeping with the Talmudic
dictum that prayer — Shemoneh Esrei — should
immediately follow mention of God's redemption of Israel. Only after we have set forth our
faith in God as our Redeemer may we begin
Shemoneh Esrei, in which we pray to Him for
our personal and national needs (R' S.R. Hirsch).

֞SHEMONEH ESREI / עמידה – שמונה עשרה ֞

HAVING TAKEN THREE STEPS BACKWARD, TAKE THREE STEPS FORWARD. REMAIN STANDING WITH FEET TOGETHER WHILE RECITING *SHEMONEH ESREI*. RECITE IT WITH QUIET DEVOTION AND WITHOUT ANY INTERRUPTION. ALTHOUGH IT SHOULD NOT BE AUDIBLE TO OTHERS, ONE MUST PRAY LOUDLY ENOUGH TO HEAR HIMSELF. SEE *LAWS* §§44-45;61-95 FOR A BRIEF SUMMARY OF ITS LAWS, INCLUDING HOW TO RECTIFY THE OMISSION OF PHRASES THAT ARE ADDED AT PARTICULAR TIMES OF THE YEAR.

אֲדֹנָי, שְׂפָתַי תִּפְתָּח,* וּפִי יַגִּיד תְּהִלָּתֶךָ.[1]

《 Your praise. 《 may 《 that my 《《 open,* 《 my lips 《 O Lord, declare mouth

PATRIARCHS / אבות

BEND THE KNEES AT בָּרוּךְ, *BLESSED*; BOW AT אַתָּה, *YOU*; STRAIGHTEN UP AT ה', *HASHEM*.

בָּרוּךְ אַתָּה* יהוה אֱלֹהֵינוּ וֵאלֹהֵי אֲבוֹתֵינוּ,*

《《 of our forefathers,* 《 and the God 《 our God 《 HASHEM, 《 are You,* 《 Blessed

---

(1) *Psalms* 51:17.

שְׁמוֹנֶה עֶשְׂרֵה / SHEMONEH ESREI ֞

The Talmud refers to *Shemoneh Esrei* simply as תְּפִלָּה, *The Prayer*, for in *Shemoneh Esrei* we formulate our needs and ask God to fulfill them. The three daily *Shemoneh Esrei* prayers were instituted by the Patriarchs and they are in place of the daily Temple offerings (*Berachos* 26b).

Shemoneh Esrei means eighteen, and, indeed, the original *Shemoneh Esrei* consisted of eighteen blessings. The requirement that there be precisely eighteen was based on various Scriptural supports (*Megillah* 17b). The text of the individual blessings was composed by the Men of the Great Assembly at the beginning of the Second Temple period and it was put into its current form under Rabban Gamliel II after the Destruction, over four centuries later (ibid.). A nineteenth blessing was added later (see commentary to וְלַמַּלְשִׁינִים, p. 154), but the name *Shemoneh Esrei* was left unchanged. The *Zohar* refers to the *Shemoneh Esrei* as *Amidah* ["standing prayer"] and the two names are used interchangeably.

Shemoneh Esrei has three sections: (a) In the first three blessings, the supplicant pays homage to God, like a servant praising his master before he presumes to make a request; (b) the middle section of thirteen blessings contains the supplicant's requests; (c) in the last three blessings, he takes leave, expressing gratitude and confidence in his Master's graciousness (*Berachos* 34a).

Even the middle section is not merely a catalogue of selfish requests. In each blessing, we first acknowledge God's mastery, and only then make the request. Thus, each blessing is an affirmation of God's power (*Vilna Gaon*).

אֲדֹנָי שְׂפָתַי תִּפְתָּח — *O Lord, my lips open* . . . Man's mind and heart may be ready for prayer, but he needs God's help to express himself properly (*Abudraham*). Alternatively, שְׂפָתַי, *my lips*, can mean *my boundaries*. Thus we ask God to free us from our limitations so that we can praise Him properly (*Ramban*).

אֲבוֹת / Patriarchs

The first blessing of *Shemoneh Esrei* is known as אֲבוֹת, *Patriarchs*, because it recalls the greatness of our forefathers in whose merit God pledged to help Israel throughout history, even if we are unworthy.

בָּרוּךְ אַתָּה — *Blessed are You.* [Since God is perfect by definition, what benefit can man's blessing confer upon Him?]

— This is a declaration of fact: God *is* blessed in the sense that He is perfect and complete (*Sefer HaChinuch* 430).

— God is the *Source* of inexhaustible blessing, and He has created the world in order to do good to His creatures. Since this is His will, we pray for the Redemption, when man will be worthy of His utmost blessing (*Rashba; R' Bachya*).

אֱלֹהֵינוּ וֵאלֹהֵי אֲבוֹתֵינוּ — *Our God and the God of our forefathers.* First we call Him *our God*

אֱלֹהֵי אַבְרָהָם, אֱלֹהֵי יִצְחָק, וֵאלֹהֵי יַעֲקֹב,

‹‹ of Jacob; ‹ and God ‹ of Isaac, ‹ God ‹ of Abraham, ‹ God

הָאֵל הַגָּדוֹל הַגִּבּוֹר וְהַנּוֹרָא, אֵל עֶלְיוֹן,* גּוֹמֵל

‹ Who ‹‹ the ‹ God, ‹‹ and awesome; ‹ mighty, ‹ [Who is] ‹ God
bestows Most High,* great,

חֲסָדִים טוֹבִים וְקוֹנֵה הַכֹּל,* וְזוֹכֵר חַסְדֵי אָבוֹת,

‹‹ of the ‹ the ‹ Who ‹‹ everything,* ‹ and ‹ [that are] ‹ kindnesses
Patriarchs, kindnesses recalls creates beneficent

וּמֵבִיא גוֹאֵל* לִבְנֵי בְנֵיהֶם, לְמַעַן שְׁמוֹ בְּאַהֲבָה.

‹‹ with love. ‹ of His ‹ for the ‹‹ of their ‹ to the ‹ a ‹ and brings
Name, sake children, children Redeemer*

FROM ROSH HASHANAH TO YOM KIPPUR ADD:

זָכְרֵנוּ לְחַיִּים,* מֶלֶךְ חָפֵץ בַּחַיִּים,

‹‹ life, ‹ Who desires ‹ O King ‹ for life,* ‹ Remember us

וְכָתְבֵנוּ בְּסֵפֶר הַחַיִּים, לְמַעַנְךָ אֱלֹהִים חַיִּים.

‹‹ O Living God. ‹— for Your sake, ‹‹ of Life ‹ in the Book ‹ and inscribe us

[IF FORGOTTEN, DO NOT REPEAT SHEMONEH ESREI. SEE LAWS §61.]

BEND THE KNEES AT בָּרוּךְ, BLESSED; BOW AT אַתָּה, YOU; STRAIGHTEN UP AT ה', HASHEM.

מֶלֶךְ עוֹזֵר וּמוֹשִׁיעַ וּמָגֵן.* בָּרוּךְ אַתָּה יהוה,

‹‹ HASHEM, ‹ are You, ‹ Blessed ‹‹ and Shield.* ‹ Savior, ‹ Helper, ‹ O King,

---

because we are obligated to serve Him and know Him to the limit of *our* capacity. But there is much about His ways that we cannot understand. In response to such doubts we proclaim that He is *the God of our forefathers*, and we have trust in the tradition they transmitted (*Dover Shalom*).

אֵל עֶלְיוֹן — *God, the Most High*. The word עֶלְיוֹן, *most high*, means that God is so exalted that He is far beyond the comprehension of even the holiest angels. We can understand Him only superficially, by studying His deeds — that He *bestows kindnesses that are beneficent* (*Siach Yitzchak*).

וְקוֹנֵה הַכֹּל — *And creates everything*. The translation is based on the consensus of commentators, both here and to *Genesis* 14:19. Some translate *the Owner of everything*. Either way,

the sense of the phrase is that God is Master of all creation.

וּמֵבִיא גוֹאֵל — *And brings a Redeemer*. The phrase is in present tense. Every event, no matter how dreadful it may seem, is a step toward the Ultimate Redemption by the Messiah (*Siach Yitzchak*).

זָכְרֵנוּ לְחַיִּים — *Remember us for life*. During the Ten Days of Repentance, our prayers stress our pleas for life. But we request the sort of life that God considers meaningful — לְמַעַנְךָ, *for Your sake* (*Sefer HaChaim*).

עוֹזֵר וּמוֹשִׁיעַ וּמָגֵן — *Helper, Savior, and Shield*. God "helps" [עוֹזֵר] those who try to help themselves; He "saves" [מוֹשִׁיעַ] even without the victim's participation; and "shields" [מָגֵן] to prevent danger from approaching (*Iyun Tefillah*). Alternately, *Bnei Yisas'char* comments that עוֹזֵר

מָגֵן אַבְרָהָם.*

《 of Abraham.* 〈 Shield

גבורות / GOD'S MIGHT

אַתָּה גִּבּוֹר לְעוֹלָם אֲדֹנָי, מְחַיֵּה מֵתִים*

〈 of the dead* 〈 the Revivifier 《 O Lord, 〈 eternally, 〈 mighty 〈 You are

אַתָּה, רַב לְהוֹשִׁיעַ.

《 able to save, 〈 abundantly 《 are You;

BETWEEN SHEMINI ATZERES AND PESACH:

מַשִּׁיב הָרוּחַ וּמוֹרִיד הַגֶּשֶׁם* [נ״א הַגָּשֶׁם].

《 the rain.* 〈 and brings down 〈 Who makes the wind blow

FROM PESACH THROUGH SUCCOS:

מוֹרִיד הַטָּל

《 the dew. 〈 Who brings down

—— **[IF FORGOTTEN, SEE LAWS §68-74.]** ——

מְכַלְכֵּל חַיִּים בְּחֶסֶד, מְחַיֵּה מֵתִים בְּרַחֲמִים

〈 with mercy 〈 the dead 〈 Who revivifies 《 with kindness, 〈 the living 〈 Who sustains

רַבִּים,* סוֹמֵךְ נוֹפְלִים, וְרוֹפֵא חוֹלִים, וּמַתִּיר

〈 Who releases 《 the sick, 〈 Who heals 《 the fallen, 〈 Who supports 《 abundant,*

refers to the help that God provides without any prayer on the part of the victim, while מוֹשִׁיעַ refers to God's response to a prayer.

מָגֵן אַבְרָהָם — *Shield of Abraham.* God preserves the spark of Abraham within every Jew, no matter how far he may have strayed (*Chiddushei HaRim*).

גבורות / God's Might ⇐

מְחַיֵּה מֵתִים — *The Revivifier of the dead.* The concept that God restores life is found three times in this section, alluding to the three kinds of revivification: man's awakening every morning after deathlike slumber; the rain that has the life-sustaining quality of causing vegetation to grow; and the literal revivification of the dead that will take place in the Messianic age (*Abudraham*).

מַשִּׁיב הָרוּחַ וּמוֹרִיד הַגֶּשֶׁם — *Who makes the wind blow and brings down the rain.* Rather than a request for wind and rain (which is made in a

later blessing), this is a praise of the One Whose life-giving power includes rule over the elements that make vegetation possible.

If this phrase is recited during the months from Pesach to Shemini Atzeres when excessive wind and rain are a curse, *Shemoneh Esrei* must be repeated. However, if the phrase concerning dew is recited during the wintry months, *Shemoneh Esrei* need not be repeated. Even though the full extent of God's power over wind and rain was omitted, the phrase for dew has at least partially set forth His control over precipitation. This is sufficient, after the fact, to validate the *Shemoneh Esrei*. See *Laws* §70-75.

בְּרַחֲמִים רַבִּים — *With mercy abundant.* The living are sustained with kindness, but the dead require *abundant mercy*, because the living can earn sustenance through prayer and repentance, but the dead cannot help themselves (*Iyun Tefillah*).

אֲסוּרִים, וּמְקַיֵּם אֱמוּנָתוֹ לִישֵׁנֵי עָפָר. מִי

‹ Who ‹‹ in the dust. ‹ to those asleep ‹ His faith ‹ and Who maintains ‹‹ the confined,

כָּמוֹךָ בַּעַל גְּבוּרוֹת, וּמִי דוֹמֶה לָּךְ, מֶלֶךְ

‹ O King ‹‹ to You, ‹ is comparable ‹ and who ‹‹ of mighty deeds, ‹ O Master ‹ is like You,

מֵמִית וּמְחַיֶּה וּמַצְמִיחַ יְשׁוּעָה.*

‹‹ salvation!* ‹ and makes sprout ‹ and restores life ‹ Who causes death

FROM ROSH HASHANAH TO YOM KIPPUR ADD:

מִי כָמוֹךָ אָב הָרַחֲמָן, זוֹכֵר יְצוּרָיו לְחַיִּים בְּרַחֲמִים.

‹‹ with mercy! ‹‹ for life, ‹ His creatures ‹ Who recalls ‹ Who is Merciful, ‹ Father ‹ is like You, ‹ Who

[IF FORGOTTEN, DO NOT REPEAT SHEMONEH ESREI. SEE LAWS §61.]

וְנֶאֱמָן אַתָּה לְהַחֲיוֹת מֵתִים. בָּרוּךְ אַתָּה

‹ are You, ‹ Blessed ‹‹ the dead. ‹ to revivify ‹ are You ‹ And faithful

יהוה, מְחַיֵּה הַמֵּתִים.

‹‹ the dead. ‹ Who revivifies ‹‹ HASHEM,

DURING THE CHAZZAN'S REPETITION, KEDUSHAH IS RECITED HERE.
DURING THE SILENT SHEMONEH ESREI, CONTINUE אַתָּה קָדוֹשׁ, YOU ARE HOLY (P. 148).

KEDUSHAH* / קְדוּשָׁה*

STAND WITH FEET TOGETHER AND AVOID ANY INTERRUPTIONS.
RISE ON TOES WHEN SAYING קָדוֹשׁ, קָדוֹשׁ, קָדוֹשׁ — HOLY, HOLY, HOLY;
בָּרוּךְ — BLESSED (OF כְּבוֹד בָּרוּךְ); AND יִמְלֹךְ — HASHEM SHALL REIGN.

CONGREGATION, THEN CHAZZAN:

נַקְדִּישָׁךְ וְנַעֲרִיצָךְ, כְּנֹעַם שִׂיחַ סוֹד שַׂרְפֵי קֹדֶשׁ,

‹ of the holy Seraphim ‹ of the assemblage ‹ speech ‹ in the manner of the pleasant ‹ and we shall revere You ‹ We shall sanctify You

קְדֻשָׁה / **Kedushah** — וּמַצְמִיחַ יְשׁוּעָה *And makes sprout salvation.*
Good deeds are like seeds that are planted and produce crops. People can merit revivification because of the good their children do or through beneficial outcomes of undertakings they initiated in their lifetimes (Siach Yitzchak).

Kedushah / קְדֻשָׁה
Kedushah, Sanctification, expresses the concept that God is exalted above and separated from the limitations of material existence. When a minyan (quorum of ten men) is present, it becomes the representative of the nation and

הַמְשַׁלְּשִׁים לְךָ קְדֻשָׁה, כַּכָּתוּב עַל יַד נְבִיאֶךָ, וְקָרָא זֶה

‹ And one [angel] ‹‹ Your ‹ by ‹ as it is ‹‹ Holy, ‹ to ‹ who recite
would call prophet, written You three times

אֶל זֶה וְאָמַר:

‹‹ and say: ‹ an- ‹ to
other

ALL:

קָדוֹשׁ קָדוֹשׁ קָדוֹשׁ* יהוה צְבָאוֹת, מְלֹא כָל הָאָרֶץ

‹ world ‹ is the ‹ filled ‹‹ Master of ‹ is HASHEM, ‹ holy* ‹ holy, ‹ Holy,
whole Legions;

כְּבוֹדוֹ.*[1] ❖ לְעֻמָּתָם מְשַׁבְּחִים וְאוֹמְרִים:

‹‹ and proclaim: ‹ they offer praise ‹ Facing them ‹‹ with
His glory.*

ALL:

בָּרוּךְ כְּבוֹד יהוה, מִמְּקוֹמוֹ.*[2] ❖ וּבְדִבְרֵי קָדְשְׁךָ כָּתוּב

‹ it is ‹ that are ‹ And in Your ‹‹ from His place.* ‹ of HASHEM ‹ is the ‹ Blessed
written holy Writings glory

לֵאמֹר:

‹‹ saying:

ALL:

יִמְלֹךְ יהוה* לְעוֹלָם, אֱלֹהַיִךְ צִיּוֹן לְדֹר וָדֹר, הַלְלוּיָהּ.[3]

‹‹ Halleluyah! ‹‹ to ‹ from ‹ O Zion, ‹ your God, ‹‹ forever; ‹ HASHEM shall reign*
generation, generation

---

(1) Isaiah 6:3. (2) Ezekiel 3:12. (3) Psalms 146:10.

---

echoes the angels who sing God's praises by proclaiming His holiness and glory. We emulate them by reciting Kedushah, a prayer based on that of the angels themselves, and by standing with feet together, in the manner of the angels (Ezekiel 1:7). When reciting the words — קָדוֹשׁ קָדוֹשׁ קָדוֹשׁ (of בָּרוּךְ כְּבוֹד); and יִמְלֹךְ — we rise up on our toes to symbolize that we seek to break loose from the bonds of earth and unite our service with that of the angels.

Based on the teachings of Arizal, everyone recites the entire Kedushah, even those parts labeled "Chazzan." Many congregations, however, follow the custom recorded in Shulchan Aruch (Ch. 125) that only verses labeled "All" are recited by everyone. Each congregation, of course, should maintain its own custom.

קָדוֹשׁ קָדוֹשׁ קָדוֹשׁ — Holy, holy, holy. God is holy with relation to the spiritual world, holy with relation to the physical world, and holy with relation to the World to Come (Targum Yonasan).

מְלֹא כָל הָאָרֶץ כְּבוֹדוֹ — Filled is the whole world with His glory. Man can bring God's holiness — awesome though it is — to earth, by fulfilling the Torah's commandments (Zohar).

מִמְּקוֹמוֹ — From His place. See commentary on p. 128.

יִמְלֹךְ ה' — HASHEM shall reign. The Sages inserted this verse into Kedushah because they wanted all prayers to include an implied or direct plea for the rebuilding of Zion [Jerusalem] (Abudraham).

HOLINESS OF GOD'S NAME / קדושת השם

אַתָּה קָדוֹשׁ וְשִׁמְךָ
⟨ You ⟨ are holy ⟨ and Your Name ⟩

קָדוֹשׁ,*   וּקְדוֹשִׁים*
⟨ is holy,*   ⟨⟨ and holy ones*

בְּכָל יוֹם יְהַלְלוּךָ
⟨ every ⟨ day ⟨ praise You,

סֶלָה, כִּי אֵל מֶלֶךְ
⟨⟨ forever, ⟨ for, ⟨ O God, ⟨ a King,

גָּדוֹל וְקָדוֹשׁ אָתָּה.
⟨ great ⟨ and holy ⟨⟨ are You.

בָּרוּךְ אַתָּה יהוה,
⟨ Blessed ⟨ are You, ⟨⟨ HASHEM,

°הָאֵל הַקָּדוֹשׁ.*
⟨ the God ⟨⟨ Who is holy.*

IN SOME CONGREGATIONS THE *CHAZZAN* SUBSTITUTES אַתָּה קָדוֹשׁ FOR לְדוֹר וָדוֹר IN HIS REPETITION:

לְדוֹר וָדוֹר נַגִּיד גָּדְלֶךָ וּלְנֵצַח
⟨ From gen-eration ⟨ to gen-eration ⟨ we shall ⟨ relate ⟨⟨ Your greatness ⟨ and for all

נְצָחִים קְדֻשָּׁתְךָ נַקְדִּישׁ,
⟨ eternity ⟨ Your holiness ⟨⟨ shall we sanctify.

וְשִׁבְחֲךָ אֱלֹהֵינוּ מִפִּינוּ לֹא
⟨ Your praise, ⟨⟨ our God, ⟨ from our mouth ⟨ shall ⟨ not

יָמוּשׁ לְעוֹלָם וָעֶד, כִּי אֵל מֶלֶךְ
⟨ leave ⟨ for ever ⟨ and ever, ⟨⟨ for, ⟨ O God, ⟨ a King,

גָּדוֹל וְקָדוֹשׁ אָתָּה. בָּרוּךְ אַתָּה
⟨ great ⟨ and holy ⟨⟨ are You. ⟨ Blessed ⟨ are You.

יהוה, °הָאֵל הַקָּדוֹשׁ.
⟨⟨ HASHEM, ⟨ the God ⟨⟨ Who is holy.

FROM ROSH HASHANAH TO YOM KIPPUR SUBSTITUTE:

°הַמֶּלֶךְ הַקָּדוֹשׁ.
⟨⟨ Who is holy. ⟨ the King

[IF FORGOTTEN, REPEAT *SHEMONEH ESREI.* SEE LAWS §62-63.]

INSIGHT / בינה

אַתָּה חוֹנֵן לְאָדָם דַּעַת,* וּמְלַמֵּד לֶאֱנוֹשׁ
⟨ You ⟨ graciously endow ⟨ man ⟨⟨ with knowledge* ⟨ and teach ⟨⟨ to a [frail] mortal

---

קְדוּשַׁת הַשֵּׁם / Holiness of God's Name

אַתָּה קָדוֹשׁ וְשִׁמְךָ קָדוֹשׁ — *You are holy and Your Name is holy.* God's "Name" refers to the manner in which we perceive His actions.

וּקְדוֹשִׁים — *And holy ones.* The term may refer to the angels (*Iyun Tefillah*) or, as most commentators agree, to Israel (*Abudraham*). *Ramban* measures human holiness by how well a person controls his permissible desires. Someone who indulges his lusts and passions without directly violating the law is described as a נָבָל בִּרְשׁוּת הַתּוֹרָה, *degenerate with the Torah's permission.*

הָאֵל/הַמֶּלֶךְ הַקָּדוֹשׁ — *The God/King Who is holy.* The Name אֵל, *God,* connotes mercy. During the Ten Days of Repentance when God sits on His Throne of Judgment, as it were, the term מֶלֶךְ, *King,* which connotes strict judgment, is more appropriate. Thus, although we plead for mercy, we acknowledge His majesty.

בִּינָה / Insight

אַתָּה חוֹנֵן לְאָדָם דַּעַת — *You graciously endow man with knowledge.* [This blessing begins the middle section of the *Shemoneh Esrei,* in which man makes his requests of God. The first plea is

בְּינָה. חָנֵּנוּ מֵאִתְּךָ חָכְמָה בִּינָה וָדֵעַת.

‹ and   ‹ insight,   ‹ [with]   ‹ from   ‹ Endow us ‹ insight.
knowledge.   wisdom,   Yourself   graciously

בָּרוּךְ אַתָּה יהוה, חוֹנֵן הַדָּעַת.

‹ of wisdom. ‹ gracious Giver ‹ Hashem, ‹ are You, ‹ Blessed

REPENTANCE / תשובה

הֲשִׁיבֵנוּ אָבִינוּ* לְתוֹרָתֶךָ, וְקָרְבֵנוּ מַלְכֵּנוּ

‹ our King, ‹ and bring us near, ‹ to Your Torah, ‹ our Father,* ‹   Bring us back,

לַעֲבוֹדָתֶךָ, וְהַחֲזִירֵנוּ* בִּתְשׁוּבָה שְׁלֵמָה לְפָנֶיךָ.

‹ before   ‹   in complete repentance,   ‹ and influence us ‹ to Your service,
You.   to return*

בָּרוּךְ אַתָּה יהוה, הָרוֹצֶה בִּתְשׁוּבָה.

‹   repentance. ‹ Who desires ‹ Hashem, ‹ are You, ‹ Blessed

FORGIVENESS / סליחה

STRIKE THE LEFT SIDE OF THE CHEST WITH THE RIGHT FIST
WHILE RECITING THE WORDS חָטָאנוּ, SINNED, AND פָשָׁעְנוּ, WILLFULLY SINNED.

סְלַח* לָנוּ אָבִינוּ כִּי חָטָאנוּ, מְחַל* לָנוּ מַלְכֵּנוּ

‹ our King, ‹ us, ‹ pardon* ‹ we have sinned; ‹ for ‹ our Father, ‹ us, ‹   Forgive*

כִּי פָשָׁעְנוּ, כִּי אֵל טוֹב וְסַלָּח אָתָּה. בָּרוּךְ

‹ Blessed ‹ are You. ‹ and ‹ Who is ‹ the God ‹ for ‹ we have ‹ for
                forgiving   good   willfully sinned;

אַתָּה יהוה, חַנּוּן הַמַּרְבֶּה לִסְלוֹחַ.

‹   forgives. ‹ Who ‹ the gracious ‹ Hashem, ‹ are You,
            abundantly   One

---

for wisdom and knowledge — because man's intelligence is his primary characteristic, the one that sets him apart from animals] (*Vilna Gaon*).

תְּשׁוּבָה / Repentance

אָבִינוּ — *Our Father.* Only in this prayer for repentance, and in the next one, for forgiveness, do we refer to God as *our Father.* A father has the responsibility to teach his son the proper way to live — but even if a son has rebelled and become estranged, the father's compassion will assert itself if his son repents and seeks for-giveness (*Etz Yosef*).

וְהַחֲזִירֵנוּ — *And influence us to return.* God never *compels* anyone to repent, but if a person makes a sincere beginning, God will make his way easier.

סְלִיחָה / Forgiveness

סְלַח ... מְחַל — *Forgive ... pardon.* סְלִיחָה, forgiveness, means not even harboring resent-ment or ill-will, while מְחִילָה, *pardon,* means only forgoing the right to punish for a wrong (*Abudraham*).

REDEMPTION / גְּאֻלָּה

רְאֵה נָא בְעָנְיֵנוּ,* וְרִיבָה רִיבֵנוּ, וּגְאָלֵנוּ¹ גְּאֻלָּה

‹ with a ‹ and ‹‹ our ‹ champion ‹‹ our ‹ please, ‹ Behold,
redemption redeem us cause, affliction,*

שְׁלֵמָה מְהֵרָה לְמַעַן שְׁמֶךָ,* כִּי אֵל גּוֹאֵל חָזָק

‹ Who is ‹ a ‹ O ‹ for, ‹‹ Your ‹ for the ‹ speedily ‹ that is
powerful Redeemer God, Name,* sake of complete,

אָתָּה. בָּרוּךְ אַתָּה יהוה, גּוֹאֵל יִשְׂרָאֵל.

‹‹ of Israel. ‹ Redeemer ‹‹ HASHEM, ‹ are You, ‹ Blessed ‹‹ are You.

ON A FAST DAY, THE *CHAZZAN* RECITES עֲנֵנוּ, *ANSWER US*, AT THIS POINT. SEE *LAWS* §84-86.

עֲנֵנוּ יהוה עֲנֵנוּ, בְּיוֹם צוֹם תַּעֲנִיתֵנוּ, כִּי בְצָרָה גְדוֹלָה

‹ in great distress ‹ for ‹‹ of our public ‹ on ‹‹ answer ‹ HASHEM, ‹ Answer
gathering for fasting, this day us, us,

אֲנָחְנוּ. אַל תֵּפֶן אֶל רִשְׁעֵנוּ, וְאַל תַּסְתֵּר פָּנֶיךָ מִמֶּנּוּ, וְאַל

‹ and ‹‹ from ‹ Your ‹ hide ‹ do ‹‹ our ‹ to ‹ pay ‹ Do ‹‹ are we.
do not us, Face not wickedness, attention not

תִּתְעַלַּם מִתְּחִנָּתֵנוּ. הֱיֵה נָא קָרוֹב לְשַׁוְעָתֵנוּ, יְהִי נָא חַסְדְּךָ

‹ Your ‹ please let ‹‹ to our outcry; ‹ near ‹ Please be ‹‹ our supplication. ‹ ignore
kindness

לְנַחֲמֵנוּ, טֶרֶם נִקְרָא אֵלֶיךָ עֲנֵנוּ, כַּדָּבָר שֶׁנֶּאֱמַר: וְהָיָה טֶרֶם

‹ [that] ‹ And it ‹‹ is said: ‹ as it ‹‹ answer ‹ to You ‹ we call ‹— before ‹‹ comfort us
before will be us,

יִקְרָאוּ וַאֲנִי אֶעֱנֶה, עוֹד הֵם מְדַבְּרִים וַאֲנִי אֶשְׁמָע.² כִּי אַתָּה

‹ You, ‹ For ‹‹ will hear. ‹ I ‹ [yet] speak, ‹ they ‹ [that] ‹‹ will ‹ I ‹ they call,
while answer;

יהוה הָעוֹנֶה בְּעֵת צָרָה, פּוֹדֶה וּמַצִּיל בְּכָל עֵת צָרָה

‹ of ‹ time ‹ in ‹ and ‹ Who ‹‹ of ‹ in time ‹ are the One ‹ HASHEM,
distress every rescues redeems distress, Who responds

וְצוּקָה. בָּרוּךְ אַתָּה יהוה, הָעוֹנֶה לְעַמּוֹ יִשְׂרָאֵל בְּעֵת צָרָה.

‹‹ of ‹ in time ‹ Israel, ‹ to His ‹ Who ‹‹ HASHEM, ‹ are ‹ Blessed ‹‹ and
distress. people, responds You, woe.

---

(1) Cf. *Psalms* 119: 153-154. (2) *Isaiah* 65:24.

גְּאוּלָה / Redemption

רְאֵה נָא בְעָנְיֵנוּ — *Behold, please, our affliction.* Though Israel's suffering results from its own sins, our enemies cannot claim that they merely do God's work, since Israel suffers much more than necessary at their hands (*Etz Yosef*).

לְמַעַן שְׁמֶךָ — *For the sake of Your Name.* Israel's suffering is a reflection on our God, and therefore, a desecration of His Name (*Etz Yosef*).

עֲנֵנוּ / Fast Day Prayer

On a fast day, the *chazzan* recites this prayer in his repetition as a separate blessing at this point,

HEALTH AND HEALING / רְפוּאָה

רְפָאֵנוּ יהוה וְנֵרָפֵא,* הוֹשִׁיעֵנוּ וְנִוָּשֵׁעָה, כִּי

⟨ for ⟨⟨ – then we ⟨⟨ save us ⟨⟨ – then we will ⟨⟨ Hashem ⟨ Heal us,
will be saved, be healed;*

תְהִלָּתֵנוּ אָתָּה, ¹ וְהַעֲלֵה

⟨ Bring ⟨⟨ is You. ⟨ the One we praise

RECITE ONE OF THE ALTERNATE VERSIONS:

רְפוּאָה שְׁלֵמָה	אֲרוּכָה וּמַרְפֵּא לְכָל תַּחֲלוּאֵינוּ
⟨ that is complete ⟨ healing	⟨ of our illnesses, ⟨ to all ⟨ and healing ⟨ cure
לְכָל מַכּוֹתֵינוּ,	וּלְכָל מַכְאוֹבֵינוּ וּלְכָל מַכּוֹתֵינוּ,
⟨⟨ our ailments, ⟨ for all	⟨⟨ of our ailments,⟨ and to all⟨ of our pains, ⟨ and to all

°°כִּי אֵל מֶלֶךְ רוֹפֵא נֶאֱמָן וְרַחֲמָן אָתָּה.

⟨⟨ are You. ⟨ and compassionate ⟨ Who is faithful ⟨ Healer ⟨ [and] King, ⟨ O God, ⟨ for

בָּרוּךְ אַתָּה יהוה, רוֹפֵא חוֹלֵי עַמּוֹ יִשְׂרָאֵל.

⟨⟨ Israel. ⟨ of His people ⟨ the sick ⟨ Who heals ⟨⟨ Hashem, ⟨ are You, ⟨ Blessed

°°AT THIS POINT ONE MAY INSERT A PRAYER FOR ONE WHO IS ILL:

יְהִי רָצוֹן מִלְּפָנֶיךָ, יהוה אֱלֹהַי וֵאלֹהֵי אֲבוֹתַי, שֶׁתִּשְׁלַח מְהֵרָה

⟨ quickly ⟨ that ⟨⟨ of my ⟨ and the ⟨ my ⟨ Hashem, ⟨⟨ before You,⟨ the ⟨ May
You send forefathers, God God will it be

רְפוּאָה שְׁלֵמָה מִן הַשָּׁמַיִם, רְפוּאַת הַנֶּפֶשׁ וּרְפוּאַת הַגּוּף

⟨⟨ of the ⟨ and a ⟨ of the ⟨ a healing ⟨⟨ heaven, ⟨ from ⟨⟨ which is ⟨ a healing
body healing spirit complete,

FOR A FEMALE FOR A MALE

לַחוֹלָה / לַחוֹלֶה (SICK ONE'S NAME) בֶּן / בַּת (MOTHER'S NAME) בְּתוֹךְ שְׁאָר

⟨ the other ⟨ among ⟨ daughter of / son of ⟨ to the sick one

חוֹלֵי יִשְׂרָאֵל.

⟨⟨ of Israel. ⟨ sick ones

CONTINUE ... כִּי אֵל

---

(1) Cf. *Jeremiah* 17:14.

as long as a full *minyan* of ten is completing the fast (some require only seven, see *Laws* §84-86). If fewer are fasting, or if the *chazzan* forgot to recite עֲנֵנוּ in its proper place, he incorporates it into the *Acceptance of Prayer* blessing (p. 157), and omits the concluding blessing of עֲנֵנוּ.

The individual does not recite עֲנֵנוּ at *Shacharis* at all lest he become ill and not complete the fast.

רְפוּאָה / **Health and Healing**

רְפָאֵנוּ ה' וְנֵרָפֵא — *Heal us, Hashem — then we will be healed.* Only if God *Himself* undertakes to cure the patient — not through an agent, angelic or human — can we be confident that it will not be a temporary or a partial measure: *then we will be healed* (*Etz Yosef* from *Zohar*).

YEAR OF PROSPERITY / ברכת השנים

וְתֵן בְּרָכָה, *GIVE A BLESSING*, IS RECITED FROM CHOL HAMOED PESACH THROUGH *MINCHAH* OF DECEMBER 4TH (OR 5TH IN THE YEAR BEFORE A CIVIL LEAP YEAR); **וְתֵן טַל וּמָטָר לִבְרָכָה**, *GIVE DEW AND RAIN FOR A BLESSING*, IS RECITED FROM *MAARIV* OF DECEMBER 4TH (OR 5TH) UNTIL PESACH. [IF THE WRONG PHRASE WAS RECITED AND FOR THE PRACTICE IN *ERETZ YISRAEL*, SEE LAWS §75-83.]

SOME CONGREGATIONS SUBSTITUTE THE PARAGRAPH **בָּרְכֵנוּ** FOR **בָּרֵךְ עָלֵינוּ**, FROM PESACH THROUGH DECEMBER 4TH (OR 5TH).

בָּרֵךְ עָלֵינוּ* יהוה אֱלֹהֵינוּ

‹ Bless   ‹ on our   ≪ —O   ‹ our God— ≪
behalf*   HASHEM,

אֶת הַשָּׁנָה הַזֹּאת וְאֶת כָּל

this year   ≪ and ‹ all ‹

מִינֵי תְבוּאָתָהּ לְטוֹבָה, וְתֵן

‹ of the   ‹ of its crops   ‹ for goodness; ≪ and give

WINTER	SUMMER
טַל וּמָטָר לִבְרָכָה	**בְּרָכָה**
‹ for a blessing ‹ and rain ‹ dew	‹ a blessing

עַל פְּנֵי הָאֲדָמָה, וְשַׂבְּעֵנוּ

‹ and satisfy us ≪ of the earth; ‹ the face ‹ on

מִטּוּבָהּ, וּבָרֵךְ שְׁנָתֵנוּ

‹ our year ‹ and bless ≪ from its bounty;

כַּשָּׁנִים הַטּוֹבוֹת לִבְרָכָה,

≪ for blessing. ‹ that were good, ‹ like the years

כִּי אֵל טוֹב וּמֵטִיב אָתָּה,

≪ are You, ‹ and beneficent ‹ good ‹ O God, ‹ For

וּמְבָרֵךְ הַשָּׁנִים. בָּרוּךְ אַתָּה

‹ are You, ‹ Blessed ≪ the years. ‹ the One Who blesses

יהוה, מְבָרֵךְ הַשָּׁנִים.

≪ the years. ‹ Who blesses ≪ HASHEM,

בָּרְכֵנוּ, יהוה אֱלֹהֵינוּ,

≪ Bless us, ‹ —O ‹ our God— ≪
HASHEM,

בְּכָל מַעֲשֵׂה יָדֵינוּ,

≪ of our hands, ‹ the work ‹ in all

וּבָרֵךְ שְׁנָתֵנוּ בְּטַלְלֵי

‹ with the ‹ our year ‹ and bless dews

רָצוֹן בְּרָכָה וּנְדָבָה.

≪ and ‹ blessing, ‹ of favor, generosity.

וּתְהִי אַחֲרִיתָהּ חַיִּים

‹ for life, ‹ its end be ‹ And may

וְשָׂבָע וְשָׁלוֹם, כַּשָּׁנִים

‹ like the ≪ and ‹ satisfaction, years peace,

הַטּוֹבוֹת לִבְרָכָה. כִּי

≪ For ≪ — for a ≪ that were blessing. good

אֵל טוֹב וּמֵטִיב אָתָּה

≪ are ‹ and ‹ good ‹ O You, beneficent God,

וּמְבָרֵךְ הַשָּׁנִים. בָּרוּךְ

≪ Blessed ≪ the years. ‹ the One Who blesses

אַתָּה יהוה, מְבָרֵךְ

‹ Who blesses ≪ HASHEM, ‹ are You,

הַשָּׁנִים.

≪ the years.

⇜ בִּרְכַּת הַשָּׁנִים / Year of Prosperity

בָּרֵךְ עָלֵינוּ — *Bless on our behalf.* We request a blessing on our general business activities and then proceed to ask for abundant crops. Even in bad times some people prosper, and even in good times some farms and businesses fail. We

INGATHERING OF EXILES / קיבוץ גליות

תְּקַע בְּשׁוֹפָר גָּדוֹל* ¹ לְחֵרוּתֵנוּ, וְשָׂא נֵס ² לְקַבֵּץ

⟨ to gather ⟨ a banner ⟨ raise ⟪ for our freedom, ⟨ the great *shofar** ⟨ Sound

גָּלֻיּוֹתֵינוּ, וְקַבְּצֵנוּ יַחַד מְהֵרָה מֵאַרְבַּע כַּנְפוֹת

⟨ corners ⟨ from the four ⟨ speedily, ⟨ together, ⟨ and gather us ⟪ our exiles,

הָאָרֶץ לְאַרְצֵנוּ. בָּרוּךְ אַתָּה יהוה, ³ מְקַבֵּץ נִדְחֵי

⟨ the dispersed ⟨ Who gathers in ⟪ Hashem, ⟨ are You, ⟨ Blessed ⟪ to our Land. ⟨ of the earth

עַמּוֹ יִשְׂרָאֵל.

⟪ Israel. ⟨ of His people

RESTORATION OF JUSTICE / דין

הָשִׁיבָה שׁוֹפְטֵינוּ* כְּבָרִאשׁוֹנָה, וְיוֹעֲצֵינוּ

⟨ and our counselors ⟨ as [they were] in earliest times ⟨ our judges * ⟨ Restore

כְּבַתְּחִלָּה, ⁴ וְהָסֵר מִמֶּנּוּ יָגוֹן וַאֲנָחָה, וּמְלוֹךְ

⟨ and reign ⟪ and groan; ⟨ sorrow ⟨ from us ⟨ remove ⟪ as at the beginning;

עָלֵינוּ מְהֵרָה אַתָּה יהוה לְבַדְּךָ בְּחֶסֶד

⟨ with kindness ⟪ alone — ⟨ Hashem, ⟨ — You, ⟪ speedily ⟨ over us,

וּבְרַחֲמִים, וְצַדְּקֵנוּ בְּצֶדֶק וּבְמִשְׁפָּט. בָּרוּךְ אַתָּה

⟨ are You, ⟨ Blessed ⟪ and through judgment. ⟨ through righteousness ⟨ and justify us ⟪ and compassion,

---

(1) Cf. *Isaiah* 27:13. (2) Cf. 11:12, 18:3, 62:10; see 66:20. (3) Cf. 11:12. (4) Cf. 1:26.

ask not only for general prosperity, but that we be allowed to share in it (*R' S.R. Hirsch*).

⋙ **קיבוץ גָּלִיּוֹת / Ingathering of Exiles**

תְּקַע בְּשׁוֹפָר גָּדוֹל — *Sound the great shofar.* There are three differences between this prayer for redemption and the earlier one of גְּאוּלָה, *Redemption:* (a) The earlier blessing refers to God's *daily* help in all sorts of crises and suffering, while this one refers to the *future* Redemption from exile; (b) the earlier blessing refers only to *physical* salvation, while this one

is a plea for *spiritual* deliverance; (c) this one specifies not only freedom from oppression, but the ingathering of all exiles to *Eretz Yisrael.*

⋙ **דין / Restoration of Justice**

הָשִׁיבָה שׁוֹפְטֵינוּ — *Restore our judges.* When Elijah heralds the Messiah's coming, he will first reestablish the Sanhedrin, and then the Redemption will begin. A secondary theme of this prayer is the wish that God help all Jewish judges rule wisely and justly (*Yaaros D'vash*).

יְהֹוה, °מֶלֶךְ אוֹהֵב צְדָקָה וּמִשְׁפָּט.

‹‹ and judgment. ‹ righteousness ‹ Who loves ‹ the King ‹‹ HASHEM,

FROM ROSH HASHANAH TO YOM KIPPUR SUBSTITUTE:

°הַמֶּלֶךְ הַמִּשְׁפָּט.

‹‹ of Judgment. ‹ the King

[IF FORGOTTEN, DO NOT REPEAT SHEMONEH ESREI. SEE LAWS §64.]

AGAINST HERETICS / בִּרְכַּת הַמִּינִים

וְלַמַּלְשִׁינִים* אַל תְּהִי תִקְוָה, וְכָל הַמִּינִים

‹ the heretics ‹ and all ‹‹ hope; ‹ let there not be ‹ And for slanderers*

כְּרֶגַע יֹאבֵדוּ, וְכָל אוֹיְבֵי עַמְּךָ מְהֵרָה יִכָּרֵתוּ,

‹‹ may they be cut down. ‹ speedily ‹ of Your people ‹ the enemies ‹ and all ‹‹ may they perish; ‹ in an instant

וְהַזֵּדִים מְהֵרָה תְעַקֵּר וּתְשַׁבֵּר וּתְמַגֵּר וּתְכַלֵּם

‹ destroy them, ‹‹ cast down; ‹ smash, ‹ uproot, ‹ – may You speedily ‹‹ The willful sinners

וְתַשְׁפִּילֵם וְתַכְנִיעֵם בִּמְהֵרָה בְיָמֵינוּ. בָּרוּךְ

‹ Blessed ‹‹ in our days. ‹ speedily ‹ and humble them ‹ pull them down,

אַתָּה יְהֹוה, שׁוֹבֵר אוֹיְבִים וּמַכְנִיעַ זֵדִים.

‹‹ willful sinners. ‹ and humbles ‹ enemies ‹ Who breaks ‹‹ HASHEM, ‹ are You,

THE RIGHTEOUS / צַדִּיקִים

עַל הַצַּדִּיקִים* וְעַל הַחֲסִידִים, וְעַל זִקְנֵי

‹ the elders ‹ on ‹‹ the devout, ‹ on ‹ the righteous,* ‹ On

בִּרְכַּת הַמִּינִים / Against Heretics

וְלַמַּלְשִׁינִים — *And for slanderers.* This blessing was not part of the original eighteen blessings; it was instituted in Yavneh, during the tenure of Rabban Gamliel II as *Nasi* of Israel, some time after the destruction of the Second Temple. The blessing was composed in response to the threats of heretical Jewish sects such as the Sadducees, Boethusians, Essenes, and the early Christians, who tried to lead Jews astray through example and persuasion, and used their political power to oppress observant Jews and to slander them to the anti-Semitic Roman government.

In this atmosphere, Rabban Gamliel composed a prayer against the heretics and slanderers, and incorporated it in the *Shemoneh Esrei* to make the populace aware of the danger (*Rambam*).

Despite the disappearance from within Israel of the particular sects against whom it was directed, it is still relevant, because there are always nonbelievers and heretics who endanger the spiritual continuity of Israel (*Yaaros D'vash*).

צַדִּיקִים / The Righteous

The righteous, devout, elders, and scholars are the leaders of the nation. Because the nation needs them, the Sages instituted a special prayer

שְׁאֵרִית עַמְּךָ בֵּית יִשְׂרָאֵל, וְעַל פְּלֵיטַת בֵּית

‹ of the ‹ the remnant ‹ on ‹‹ of Israel, ‹ the ‹ of Your ‹ of the
academy   Family people,   remainder

סוֹפְרֵיהֶם, וְעַל גֵּרֵי הַצֶּדֶק וְעָלֵינוּ, יֶהֱמוּ נָא

‹ — please may ‹‹ and on ‹ who are ‹ the ‹ on ‹‹ of their scholars,
aroused be   ourselves   righteous converts

רַחֲמֶיךָ יהוה אֱלֹהֵינוּ, וְתֵן שָׂכָר טוֹב לְכָל

‹ to all ‹ which ‹ a ‹ and ‹‹ our God, ‹ HASHEM, ‹ Your
is good   reward give   compassion,

הַבּוֹטְחִים בְּשִׁמְךָ בֶּאֱמֶת, וְשִׂים חֶלְקֵנוּ עִמָּהֶם,

‹‹ with them, ‹ our lot ‹ Put ‹‹ in sincerity. ‹ in Your Name ‹ who believe

וּלְעוֹלָם לֹא נֵבוֹשׁ* כִּי בְךָ בָּטָחְנוּ.[1] וְעַל חַסְדְּךָ

‹ Your ‹ and ‹‹ we trust, ‹ in ‹ for ‹ feel ‹ we ‹ and forever
kindness upon   You   ashamed,* will not

הַגָּדוֹל בֶּאֱמֶת (וּבְתָמִים) נִשְׁעָנֵּנוּ. בָּרוּךְ אַתָּה

‹ are You, ‹ Blessed ‹‹ do we rely. ‹ (and in perfection) ‹ in sincerity ‹‹ that is great,

יהוה, מִשְׁעָן וּמִבְטָח לַצַּדִּיקִים.

‹‹ of the righteous. ‹ and Assurance ‹ Mainstay ‹‹ HASHEM,

REBUILDING JERUSALEM / בנין ירושלים

וְלִירוּשָׁלַיִם* עִירְךָ בְּרַחֲמִים תָּשׁוּב, וְתִשְׁכּוֹן

‹ and may ‹‹ may You ‹ in compassion ‹ Your City, ‹ And to Jerusalem,*
You rest   return,

בְּתוֹכָהּ כַּאֲשֶׁר דִּבַּרְתָּ, וּבְנֵה אוֹתָהּ בְּקָרוֹב

‹ soon ‹ it ‹ May You ‹‹ You have ‹ as ‹ within it,
rebuild   spoken.

---

(1) Cf. *Psalms* 25:2.

for their welfare (R' *Yehudah ben Yakar*).

וּלְעוֹלָם לֹא נֵבוֹשׁ — *And forever we will not feel
ashamed.* One who puts his faith in people feels
ashamed for he has been shown to be helpless on
his own. But he is not ashamed to have trusted in
God, as no one can succeed without His help
(*Dover Shalom*).

בנין ירושלים / **Rebuilding Jerusalem** §◄

וְלִירוּשָׁלַיִם — *And to Jerusalem.* After having
sought God's blessing on Israel's leaders and
righteous people, we seek His blessing for the
Holy City. No blessing is complete until the seat
of holiness, Jerusalem, is rebuilt in all its
grandeur (*Iyun Tefillah*).

בִּימֵינוּ בִּנְיַן עוֹלָם, וְכִסֵּא דָוִד עַבְדְּךָ* מְהֵרָה
‹ speedily, ‹ Your servant,* ‹ of David, ‹ and the throne ‹‹ that is eternal, ‹ as a structure ‹ in our days

לְתוֹכָהּ תָּכִין. בָּרוּךְ אַתָּה יהוה, בּוֹנֵה יְרוּשָׁלָיִם.
‹‹ of Jerusalem. ‹ Builder ‹‹ HASHEM, ‹ are You, ‹ Blessed ‹‹ may You ‹ within it establish.

מלכות בית דוד / DAVIDIC REIGN

אֶת צֶמַח דָּוִד* עַבְדְּךָ מְהֵרָה תַצְמִיחַ, וְקַרְנוֹ
‹ and his pride ‹‹ may You cause to flourish, ‹ speedily, ‹‹ Your servant, ‹ of David,* ‹ offspring ‹ The

תָּרוּם בִּישׁוּעָתֶךָ, כִּי לִישׁוּעָתְךָ קִוִּינוּ כָּל הַיּוֹם
‹ all day long ‹ we hope ‹ for Your salvation ‹ because ‹‹ through Your salvation, ‹ may You exalt

(וּמְצַפִּים לִישׁוּעָה). בָּרוּךְ אַתָּה יהוה, מַצְמִיחַ
‹ Who causes to flourish ‹‹ HASHEM, ‹ are You, ‹ Blessed ‹‹ for salvation). ‹ (and await eagerly

קֶרֶן יְשׁוּעָה.
‹‹ of salvation. ‹ the pride

קבלת תפלה / ACCEPTANCE OF PRAYER

אָב הָרַחֲמָן שְׁמַע קוֹלֵנוּ, יהוה אֱלֹהֵינוּ
‹ our God, ‹ HASHEM, ‹‹ our voice, ‹ hear ‹ Who is merciful, ‹ Father

חוּס וְרַחֵם עָלֵינוּ, וְקַבֵּל בְּרַחֲמִים וּבְרָצוֹן
‹ and with favor ‹ with compassion ‹ and accept ‹‹ on us, ‹ and have compassion ‹ have pity

---

וְכִסֵּא דָוִד עַבְדְּךָ — *And the throne of David, Your servant.* Jerusalem cannot be considered rebuilt unless a worthy descendant of David is seated on the throne (R' Yitzchak Zev Soloveitchik).

❧ מלכות בית דוד / **Davidic Reign**

אֶת צֶמַח דָּוִד — *The offspring of David.* Zechariah (6:12) teaches that Messiah's name will be צֶמַח, *Tzemach,* literally, the *sprouting* or *flourishing* of a plant. This indicates that the normal process of redemption is like the barely perceptible daily growth of a plant (*Iyun Tefillah*).

In the previous blessing the mention of David indicates that the realization of Jerusalem's potential depends on the Davidic heir. Here we are taught that the ultimate salvation of the Jewish people is possible only through the Davidic Messiah.

❧ קַבָּלַת תְּפִלָּה / **Acceptance of Prayer**

[In the middle section of *Shemoneh Esrei* we have asked God to grant our specific needs. We now close the section with a general plea that He take note of our call and grant our requests.]

אֶת תְּפִלָּתֵנוּ, כִּי אֵל שׁוֹמֵעַ תְּפִלּוֹת וְתַחֲנוּנִים

⟨ and supplications ⟨ prayers ⟨ Who hears ⟨ God ⟨ for ⟪ our prayer,

אָתָּה. וּמִלְּפָנֶיךָ מַלְכֵּנוּ, רֵיקָם אַל תְּשִׁיבֵנוּ,

⟪ turn us away. ⟨ do not ⟨ empty-handed ⟪ our King, ⟨ From before Yourself, ⟪ are You.

חָנֵּנוּ וַעֲנֵנוּ וּשְׁמַע תְּפִלָּתֵנוּ,°°

⟪ our prayer, ⟨ and hear ⟨ answer us, ⟨ Be gracious with us,

**°°DURING THE SILENT *SHEMONEH ESREI* ONE MAY INSERT
THE FOLLOWING PERSONAL PRAYER FOR FORGIVENESS:**

אָנָּא יהוה, חָטָאתִי עָוִיתִי וּפָשַׁעְתִּי לְפָנֶיךָ, מִיּוֹם הֱיוֹתִי

⟨ I have ⟨ from ⟨ before ⟨ and willfully ⟨ been ⟨ I have ⟨ HASHEM, ⟨ Please,
existed the day You, sinned iniquitous, sinned,

עַל הָאֲדָמָה עַד הַיּוֹם הַזֶּה (וּבִפְרָט בַּחֵטְא . . .). אָנָּא

⟨Please, ⟪with the sin of . . . ⟨ and especially ⟪ this very day ⟨ until ⟨ earth ⟨ on

יהוה, עֲשֵׂה לְמַעַן שִׁמְךָ הַגָּדוֹל, וּתְכַפֶּר לִי עַל חֲטָאַי

⟨ my inad- ⟨ for ⟨ to ⟨ and grant ⟪ which is ⟨ of Your ⟨ for the ⟨ act ⟨ HASHEM,
vertent sins, me atonement great Name sake

וַעֲוֹנַי וּפְשָׁעַי שֶׁחָטָאתִי וְשֶׁעָוִיתִי וְשֶׁפָּשַׁעְתִּי לְפָנֶיךָ,

⟪ before ⟨ and sinned ⟨ been ⟨ [through which] ⟨ and my ⟨ my in-
You, willfully iniquitous, I have sinned, willful sins iquities,

מִנְּעוּרַי עַד הַיּוֹם הַזֶּה. וּתְמַלֵּא כָּל הַשֵּׁמוֹת שֶׁפָּגַמְתִּי

⟨ that I have ⟨ the [Holy] ⟨ all ⟨ And make ⟪ this very day. ⟨ until ⟨ from
blemished Names whole my youth

CONTINUE . . . כִּי אַתָּה (P. 158)

בְּשִׁמְךָ הַגָּדוֹל.

⟪ that is ⟨ within
great. Your Name

**°°DURING THE SILENT *SHEMONEH ESREI* ONE MAY INSERT
THE FOLLOWING PERSONAL PRAYER FOR LIVELIHOOD:**

אַתָּה הוּא יהוה הָאֱלֹהִים, הַזָּן וּמְפַרְנֵס וּמְכַלְכֵּל

⟪ and supports, ⟨ sustains, ⟨ Who nourishes, ⟨ the God ⟨ HASHEM, ⟨ Who are ⟨ It is You

מְקַרְנֵי רְאֵמִים עַד בֵּיצֵי כִנִּים. הַטְרִיפֵנִי לֶחֶם חֻקִּי,¹ וְהַמְצֵא

⟨ provide ⟨allotted ⟨ with the ⟨ Supply me ⟪ of lice. ⟨ the ⟨ to ⟨ of re'eimim ⟨ from the
to me; bread eggs horns

---

(1) *Proverbs* 30:8.

לִי וּלְכָל בְּנֵי בֵיתִי מְזוֹנוֹתַי קוֹדֶם שֶׁאֶצְטָרֵךְ לָהֶם, בְּנַחַת

⟨ in ⟪ for it; ⟨ I have need ⟨ before ⟨ my food, ⟨⟨ of my ⟨ members ⟨ and ⟨ for
contentment   household,   for all   me

וְלֹא בְצַעַר, בְּהֶתֵּר וְלֹא בְאִסּוּר, בְּכָבוֹד וְלֹא בְבִזָּיוֹן,

⟪ in ⟨ but ⟨ in a forbidden ⟨ but ⟨ in a permissible ⟪ in pain, ⟨ but
disgrace,   not   manner,   not   manner   not

לְחַיִּים וּלְשָׁלוֹם, מִשֶּׁפַע בְּרָכָה וְהַצְלָחָה, וּמִשֶּׁפַע בְּרָכָה

⟨ of the ⟨ and from ⟪ and success ⟨ of ⟨ from the ⟨⟨ and for ⟨ for life
spring   the flow   blessing   flow   peace;

עֶלְיוֹנָה, כְּדֵי שֶׁאוּכַל לַעֲשׂוֹת רְצוֹנֶךָ וְלַעֲסוֹק בְּתוֹרָתֶךְ

⟨ in Your Torah ⟨ and engage ⟪ Your will ⟨ to do ⟨ I be enabled ⟨ so that ⟪ On High,

וּלְקַיֵּם מִצְוֹתֶיךָ. וְאַל תַּצְרִיכֵנִי לִידֵי מַתְּנַת בָּשָׂר וָדָם. וִיקֻיַּם

⟨ and may ⟨ and ⟨ of ⟨ of the gifts ⟨ make me ⟨ Do ⟪ Your com- ⟨ and fulfill
there be   blood; ⟨ flesh ⟨ of the hands   needful   not   mandments.
fulfilled

בִּי מִקְרָא שֶׁכָּתוּב: פּוֹתֵחַ אֶת יָדֶךָ, וּמַשְׂבִּיעַ לְכָל חַי

⟨ living ⟨ every ⟨ and satisfy ⟪ Your hand, ⟨ You open ⟪ that states, ⟨ the verse ⟨ in
thing   me

רָצוֹן.¹ וְכָתוּב: הַשְׁלֵךְ עַל יהוה יְהָבְךָ וְהוּא יְכַלְכְּלֶךָ.²

⟪ will ⟨ and He ⟨ Your ⟨ HASHEM ⟨ upon ⟨ Cast ⟨ and that ⟪ [with its]
sustain you.   burden   states,   desire,

CONTINUE . . . כִּי אַתָּה (BELOW)

כִּי אַתָּה שׁוֹמֵעַ תְּפִלַּת כָּל פֶּה, עַמְּךָ יִשְׂרָאֵל

⟨ Israel ⟨ [the prayer] of ⟪ mouth, ⟨ of ⟨ the prayer ⟨ hear ⟨ You ⟨ for
Your people   every

בְּרַחֲמִים. בָּרוּךְ אַתָּה יהוה, שׁוֹמֵעַ תְּפִלָּה.

⟪ prayer. ⟨ Who hears ⟪ HASHEM, ⟨ are You, ⟨ Blessed ⟪ with compassion.

TEMPLE SERVICE / עֲבוֹדָה

רְצֵה* יהוה אֱלֹהֵינוּ בְּעַמְּךָ יִשְׂרָאֵל, וְלִתְפִלָּתָם

⟨ and toward ⟨ Israel, ⟨ toward ⟪ our God, ⟨ HASHEM, ⟪ Be
their prayer   Your people   favorable,*

---

(1) *Psalms* 145:16. (2) 55:23.

עֲבוֹדָה / Temple Service
רְצֵה — *Be favorable.* This begins the final section of *Shemoneh Esrei*. Like a servant who is grateful for having had the opportunity to express himself before his master, we thank God for having been attentive to our prayers.

שָׁעֵה, וְהָשֵׁב אֶת הָעֲבוֹדָה* לִדְבִיר בֵּיתֶךָ. וְאִשֵּׁי

‹ The fire- ‹‹ of Your ‹ to the Holy ‹ the service * ‹ and restore ‹‹ turn,
offerings   Temple.   of Holies

יִשְׂרָאֵל* וּתְפִלָּתָם מְהֵרָה בְּאַהֲבָה תְקַבֵּל בְּרָצוֹן,

‹‹ favorably, ‹ accept ‹ with love ‹ speedily, ‹ and their prayer, ‹ of Israel*

וּתְהִי לְרָצוֹן תָּמִיד עֲבוֹדַת יִשְׂרָאֵל עַמֶּךָ.

‹‹ Your people. ‹ of Israel ‹ the service ‹ always ‹ to Your favor ‹ and may it be

ON ROSH CHODESH AND CHOL HAMOED ADD THE FOLLOWING.
[IF FORGOTTEN, REPEAT *SHEMONEH ESREI*. SEE *LAWS* §88.]
(DURING THE *CHAZZAN'S* REPETITION, THE CONGREGATION RESPONDS אָמֵן, AMEN, AS INDICATED.)

אֱלֹהֵינוּ וֵאלֹהֵי אֲבוֹתֵינוּ, יַעֲלֶה, וְיָבֹא, וְיַגִּיעַ, וְיֵרָאֶה,

‹ be noted, ‹ reach, ‹ come, ‹ may ‹‹ of our ‹ and the ‹ Our God
there rise,   forefathers,   God

וְיֵרָצֶה, וְיִשָּׁמַע, וְיִפָּקֵד, וְיִזָּכֵר זִכְרוֹנֵנוּ וּפִקְדוֹנֵנוּ, וְזִכְרוֹן

‹ the ‹‹ and ‹ – the ‹‹ and be ‹ be ‹ be heard, ‹ be
remem- consideration remembrance remembered considered,   favored,
brance of us;   of us

אֲבוֹתֵינוּ, וְזִכְרוֹן מָשִׁיחַ בֶּן דָּוִד עַבְדֶּךָ, וְזִכְרוֹן יְרוּשָׁלַיִם

‹ of Jerusalem, ‹ the ‹‹ Your ‹ of ‹ son ‹ of ‹ the ‹‹ of our
remembrance servant; David,   Messiah, remembrance forefathers;

עִיר קָדְשֶׁךָ, וְזִכְרוֹן כָּל עַמְּךָ בֵּית יִשְׂרָאֵל לְפָנֶיךָ, לִפְלֵיטָה

‹ for ‹ before ‹‹ of ‹ the ‹ of Your ‹ and the ‹‹ of Your ‹ the
deliverance,   You   Israel – Family entire people remembrance Holiness;   City

לְטוֹבָה לְחֵן וּלְחֶסֶד וּלְרַחֲמִים, לְחַיִּים (טוֹבִים) וּלְשָׁלוֹם, בְּיוֹם

‹ on the ‹‹ and for ‹ (that is ‹ for life ‹ and for ‹ for ‹ for ‹ for
day of   peace,   good),   compassion, kindness, grace, goodness,

---

הָעֲבוֹדָה — *The service.* As we conclude *She-moneh Esrei*, which is our substitute for the Temple's sacrificial service, we ask that the *true* service be restored to the Temple (*Etz Yosef*).

וְאִשֵּׁי יִשְׂרָאֵל — *The fire-offerings of Israel.* Since the Temple is not standing, this phrase is taken in an allegorical sense. It refers to: the souls and the deeds of the righteous, which are as pleasing as offerings; Jewish prayers that are like sacrificial offerings; or the altar fires and offerings of the Messianic era. Some repunctuate the blessing to read: *... and restore the service ... and the fire-offerings of Israel. Their prayer, speedily, with love accept favorably ...*

יַעֲלֶה וְיָבֹא / **Festival Prayer**

On Rosh Chodesh and Festivals, we add this prayer that God remember us for good and blessing. The logical place for this prayer is the רְצֵה blessing, which asks for a return of the service to the Temple, where Rosh Chodesh and the Festivals will be marked by special offerings. This call for a remembrance specifically on these days is based on *Numbers* 10:10 (*Levush, Orach Chaim* 487).

This prayer contains eight words [... יַעֲלֶה וְיִזָּכֵר] expressing one general theme — that our remembrance rise before God and be favorably received. *Rabbi S.R. Hirsch* offers the following

ON SUCCOS:

חַג הַסֻּכּוֹת הַזֶּה.
‹‹ this Festival of Succos.

ON PESACH:

חַג הַמַּצּוֹת הַזֶּה.
‹‹ this Festival of Matzos.

ON ROSH CHODESH:

רֹאשׁ הַחֹדֶשׁ הַזֶּה.
‹‹ this New Moon.

זָכְרֵנוּ יהוה אֱלֹהֵינוּ בּוֹ לְטוֹבָה (.אָמֵן–.Cong), וּפָקְדֵנוּ בוֹ
‹ on ‹ consider ‹‹ (Amen;) ‹‹ for ‹ on ‹ our God, ‹ HASHEM, ‹ Remember
it us goodness; it us

לִבְרָכָה (.אָמֵן–.Cong), וְהוֹשִׁיעֵנוּ בוֹ לְחַיִּים טוֹבִים (.אָמֵן–.Cong).
‹‹(Amen.) ‹‹ that is good. ‹ for life ‹ on it ‹ and save us ‹‹ (Amen;) ‹‹ for blessing;

וּבִדְבַר יְשׁוּעָה וְרַחֲמִים, חוּס וְחָנֵּנוּ וְרַחֵם עָלֵינוּ וְהוֹשִׁיעֵנוּ,
‹‹ and save ‹ with ‹ and be com- ‹ be ‹ have ‹‹ and ‹ of ‹ In the
us, passionate gracious, pity, compassion, salvation matter

כִּי אֵלֶיךָ עֵינֵינוּ, כִּי אֵל מֶלֶךְ חַנּוּן וְרַחוּם אָתָּה.[1]
‹‹ are ‹ and com- ‹ Who is ‹ King, ‹ God, ‹ because, ‹‹ are our ‹ to You ‹ for
You. passionate gracious eyes [turned],

וְתֶחֱזֶינָה עֵינֵינוּ* בְּשׁוּבְךָ לְצִיּוֹן בְּרַחֲמִים.
‹‹ in compassion. ‹ to Zion ‹ Your return ‹ may our eyes* ‹ Witness

בָּרוּךְ אַתָּה יהוה, הַמַּחֲזִיר שְׁכִינָתוֹ לְצִיּוֹן.
‹‹ to Zion. ‹ His Presence ‹ Who restores ‹‹ HASHEM, ‹ are You, ‹ Blessed

THANKSGIVING [MODIM] / הוֹדָאָה

BOW AT מוֹדִים, WE THANK; STRAIGHTEN UP AT ה', HASHEM. IN HIS REPETITION THE CHAZZAN
RECITES THE ENTIRE מוֹדִים ALOUD, WHILE THE CONGREGATION RECITES מוֹדִים דְּרַבָּנָן (P. 162) SOFTLY.

מוֹדִים אֲנַחְנוּ לָךְ, שָׁאַתָּה הוּא יהוה
‹ HASHEM, ‹ Who are ‹ for it is You ‹‹ You, ‹ We thank

אֱלֹהֵינוּ וֵאלֹהֵי אֲבוֹתֵינוּ לְעוֹלָם וָעֶד. צוּרֵנוּ,
‹ our Rock, ‹‹ and ever; ‹ for ever ‹ of our forefathers, ‹ and the God ‹ our God

(1) Cf. Nehemiah 9:31.

interpretations of the eight expressions: May our personal behavior and fortune *rise* [יַעֲלֶה] above ordinary human existence; and *come* [וְיָבֹא] before God to merit His interest; may nothing prevent them from *reaching* [וְיַגִּיעַ] God and gaining His acceptance; may they be *noted* [וְיֵרָאֶה] in the best possible light; may they be worthy of God's *favor* [וְיֵרָצֶה]; may God *hear of* [וְיִשָּׁמַע] the impact these remembrances have on

our lives; may God *consider* [וְיִפָּקֵד] our needs; and may He *remember* [וְיִזָּכֵר] us and our relationship to Him.

וְתֶחֱזֶינָה עֵינֵינוּ — *Witness may our eyes.* One does not see the splendor of the miracles bringing about his salvation unless he is personally worthy. Therefore, we pray that *we* may be worthy to witness the return to Zion with our own eyes (*Yaaros D'vash*).

צוּר חַיֵּינוּ,* מָגֵן יִשְׁעֵנוּ אַתָּה הוּא לְדוֹר וָדוֹר.

‹‹ to gen- ‹ from gen- ‹ are ‹ [is what] ‹‹ of our ‹ Shield ‹‹ of our ‹ the
eration. eration You salvation, lives,* Rock

נוֹדֶה לְּךָ* וּנְסַפֵּר תְּהִלָּתֶךָ[1] עַל חַיֵּינוּ*

‹ our lives* ‹ for ‹‹ Your praise, ‹ and relate ‹ You * ‹ We shall thank

הַמְּסוּרִים בְּיָדֶךָ, וְעַל נִשְׁמוֹתֵינוּ הַפְּקוּדוֹת

‹ that are entrusted ‹ our souls ‹ and for ‹‹ into Your hands, ‹ that are committed

לָךְ,* וְעַל נִסֶּיךָ* שֶׁבְּכָל יוֹם עִמָּנוּ, וְעַל

‹ and for ‹‹ are with us; ‹ day ‹ that every ‹ Your miracles* ‹ and for ‹‹ to You;*

נִפְלְאוֹתֶיךָ* וְטוֹבוֹתֶיךָ שֶׁבְּכָל עֵת, עֶרֶב וָבֹקֶר

‹ morning, ‹ – evening, ‹‹ times ‹ that are at all ‹ and favors ‹ Your wonders*

וְצָהֳרָיִם. הַטּוֹב כִּי לֹא כָלוּ רַחֲמֶיךָ, וְהַמְרַחֵם

‹ and the Com-passionate One, ‹‹ are Your compassions, ‹ exhausted ‹ never ‹ for ‹ The Bene-ficent One, ‹‹ and afternoon.

כִּי לֹא תַמּוּ חֲסָדֶיךָ,[2] כִּי מֵעוֹלָם קִוִּינוּ לָךְ.

‹‹ in You. ‹ have we put our hope ‹ always ‹ – for ‹‹ are Your kindnesses ‹ ended ‹ never ‹ for

(1) Cf. *Psalms* 79:13. (2) Cf. *Lamentations* 3:22.

הוֹדָאָה / Thanksgiving [Modim]

צוּר חַיֵּינוּ — *Rock of our lives.* Our parents are the "rocks" from whom our bodies are hewn, but from You we receive life itself (*Etz Yosef*).

נוֹדֶה לְּךָ — *We shall thank You.* Having begun the blessing by describing God's greatness and our relationship to Him, we now specify those things for which we thank Him.

עַל חַיֵּינוּ — *For our lives.* Lest anyone think that he is master over his own life, we acknowledge that every breath and heartbeat is a direct result of God's mercy (*Olas Tamid*).

נִשְׁמוֹתֵינוּ הַפְּקוּדוֹת לָךְ — *Our souls that are entrusted to You.* The word נְשָׁמָה, *neshamah,*

refers to the higher soul that provides man his holiness, as opposed to the lower soul that merely sustains him. During slumber, this *neshamah* leaves the body and is, so to speak, entrusted to God's safekeeping, to be returned to man in the morning (*Derech Hashem*).

נִסֶּיךָ ... נִפְלְאוֹתֶיךָ — *Your miracles ... Your wonders.* Miracles are the extraordinary events acknowledged by everyone to be the results of God's intervention. *Wonders* are the familiar things that we do not regard as miracles because we have grown accustomed to them, such as breathing, raining, and growing. We thank God for both *miracles* and *wonders,* because we recognize that He is their Creator (*Etz Yosef*).

מודים דרבנן / MODIM OF THE RABBIS

מוֹדִים אֲנַחְנוּ לָךְ, שָׁאַתָּה הוּא יהוה אֱלֹהֵינוּ וֵאלֹהֵי

‹ and the God ‹ our God ‹ Hashem, ‹ Who are ‹ for it is You ‹‹ You, ‹   We thank

אֲבוֹתֵינוּ, אֱלֹהֵי כָל בָּשָׂר, יוֹצְרֵנוּ, יוֹצֵר בְּרֵאשִׁית.* בְּרָכוֹת

‹ Blessings ‹‹   of the   ‹   the   ‹   our   ‹‹ flesh, ‹ of all ‹ the God ‹‹   of our
        universe.*   Molder   Molder,   forefathers,

וְהוֹדָאוֹת לְשִׁמְךָ הַגָּדוֹל וְהַקָּדוֹשׁ, עַל שֶׁהֶחֱיִיתָנוּ וְקִיַּמְתָּנוּ.

‹‹ and You have ‹ You have ‹ for ‹‹ and that ‹ that is ‹ [are due] to ‹ and thanks
    sustained us.   given us life   is holy,   great   Your Name

כֵּן תְּחַיֵּנוּ וּתְקַיְּמֵנוּ, וְתֶאֱסוֹף גָּלֻיּוֹתֵינוּ לְחַצְרוֹת קָדְשֶׁךָ,

‹‹ of Your ‹   to the   ‹ our exiles ‹ and gather ‹‹   and   ‹ may You continue ‹ So
  Sanctuary,   Courtyards   sustain us,   to give us life

לִשְׁמוֹר חֻקֶּיךָ וְלַעֲשׂוֹת רְצוֹנֶךָ, וּלְעָבְדְּךָ בְּלֵבָב שָׁלֵם,

‹‹ wholeheartedly. ‹   and to   ‹‹ Your will, ‹   to do   ‹‹   Your   ‹ to observe
            serve You   decrees,

עַל שֶׁאֲנַחְנוּ מוֹדִים לָךְ. בָּרוּךְ אֵל הַהוֹדָאוֹת.

‹‹ of thanksgivings. ‹ is the ‹ Blessed ‹‹ You. ‹ to thank ‹ [inspiring] ‹ [We thank
        God   us   You] for

**ON CHANUKAH AND PURIM ADD THE FOLLOWING [IF FORGOTTEN,
DO NOT REPEAT SHEMONEH ESREI; SEE LAWS §89]:**

(וְ)עַל הַנִּסִּים,* וְעַל הַפֻּרְקָן, וְעַל הַגְּבוּרוֹת, וְעַל

‹ and for ‹ the mighty deeds, ‹ and for ‹ the salvation, ‹ and for ‹ the miracles,* ‹ (And) for

הַתְּשׁוּעוֹת, וְעַל הַנִּפְלָאוֹת, וְעַל הַנֶּחָמוֹת, וְעַל הַמִּלְחָמוֹת,

‹ the battles ‹ and for ‹ the consolations, ‹ and for ‹ the wonders, ‹ and for ‹   the victories,

שֶׁעָשִׂיתָ לַאֲבוֹתֵינוּ בַּיָּמִים הָהֵם בַּזְּמַן הַזֶּה.*

‹‹ at this time:* ‹ in those days, ‹‹   for our   ‹ which You
                forefathers   performed

מוֹדִים דְּרַבָּנָן / **Modim of the Rabbis**

When the *chazzan* bows and recites *Modim* in the manner of a slave accepting the total authority of his master, each congregant must also make his own declaration of submission (*Abudraham*). The Talmud (*Sotah* 40a and *Yerushalmi* 1:8) cites the personal declarations used by a number of rabbis, and concludes that the proper custom is to recite them all. This collection of prayers was thus given the name *Modim of the Rabbis*.

יוֹצֵר בְּרֵאשִׁית — *The Molder of the universe.* Although the literal meaning of בְּרֵאשִׁית is *the beginning*, it is used to mean the entire universe that was set in motion when God uttered the

first statement of Creation (*Iyun Tefillah*).

עַל הַנִּסִּים / **Chanukah — Purim**

The declaration of gratitude for the miracles of Chanukah and Purim is inserted in this section of *Shemoneh Esrei* that is likewise devoted to expressions of thankfulness.

(וְ)עַל הַנִּסִּים — *(And) for the miracles.* Most of the early sources omit the conjunctive prefix וְ, *and.* Nevertheless, since this declaration continues the recitation of God's beneficence for which we give thanks, *Mishnah Berurah* 682 maintains that it should be said.

בַּיָּמִים הָהֵם בַּזְּמַן הַזֶּה — *In those days, at this time.* The miracles occurred in days of yore during

ON CHANUKAH:

בִּימֵי מַתִּתְיָהוּ בֶּן יוֹחָנָן כֹּהֵן גָּדוֹל חַשְׁמוֹנַאי וּבָנָיו,

‹ and his ‹‹   the   ‹ the High Priest, ‹   of ‹ the ‹‹   of   ‹ In the
sons,   Hasmonean,   Yochanan, son   Mattisyahu,   days

כְּשֶׁעָמְדָה מַלְכוּת יָוָן הָרְשָׁעָה עַל עַמְּךָ יִשְׂרָאֵל, לְהַשְׁכִּיחָם

‹   to make   ‹‹ Israel, ‹ Your ‹ against ‹‹ – which was ‹‹ of ‹ did the ‹ when rise up
them forget   people   wicked – Greece kingdom

תּוֹרָתֶךָ, וּלְהַעֲבִירָם מֵחֻקֵּי רְצוֹנֶךָ.* וְאַתָּה בְּרַחֲמֶיךָ

‹ in Your mercy ‹ But You ‹‹ of Your Will.* ‹ from the ‹ and to compel ‹‹   Your
                                          statutes   them to stray   Torah

הָרַבִּים, עָמַדְתָּ לָהֶם בְּעֵת צָרָתָם, רַבְתָּ אֶת רִיבָם, דַּנְתָּ

‹ judged ‹ their cause, ‹   You   ‹‹ of their ‹ in the ‹ for ‹ stood up ‹‹ which is
              championed   distress.   time   them   abundant

אֶת דִּינָם, נָקַמְתָּ אֶת נִקְמָתָם.¹ מָסַרְתָּ גִבּוֹרִים בְּיַד חַלָּשִׁים,

‹‹ of the ‹ into the ‹ the strong ‹   You   ‹‹ their wrong. ‹ and You ‹‹ their claim,
weak,   hands   delivered   avenged

וְרַבִּים בְּיַד מְעַטִּים, וּטְמֵאִים* בְּיַד טְהוֹרִים, וּרְשָׁעִים* בְּיַד

‹ into the ‹ the wicked* ‹‹ of the pure, ‹ into the ‹ the impure* ‹‹ of the few, ‹ into the ‹   the
hands   hands   hands many

צַדִּיקִים, וְזֵדִים* בְּיַד עוֹסְקֵי תוֹרָתֶךָ. וּלְךָ עָשִׂיתָ שֵׁם גָּדוֹל

‹ that ‹   a   ‹ You ‹ For ‹‹ of Your ‹ of the ‹ into the ‹ and the ‹‹   of the
is great Name made Yourself   Torah.   diligent   hands   willful   righteous,
                                        students   sinners*

---

(1) Cf. *Jeremiah* 51:36.

this season — Chanukah during Kislev, and Purim during Adar. According to this view, we praise God in this prayer only for the miracles He performed for our ancestors (*Etz Yosef*).

Levush, however, holds that this phrase contains a double measure of praise: for the miracles performed in ancient days (*in those days*) and also for the countless hidden miracles that are constantly performed every day (*at this time*) to sustain life and health, both for the individual and for the nation.

There is a particular significance to the date of a miracle, because God visits the holy emanations of each miracle upon Israel annually on the date it occurred. (See *Overview*, ArtScroll edition of *Lamentations*.)

חֲנוּכָּה / Chanukah ⦿

לְהַשְׁכִּיחָם תּוֹרָתֶךָ וּלְהַעֲבִירָם מֵחֻקֵּי רְצוֹנֶךָ — *To make them forget Your Torah and to compel them to*

stray from the statutes of Your Will. The Syrian-Greeks knew that the basis of the Jewish religion is the study of Torah; if Torah study were neglected, then the decline of ritual observance would be inevitable and swift. Therefore, they concentrated first on causing Torah to be forgotten, knowing that the deterioration of observance would soon follow (*R' Hirsch*).

טְמֵאִים...רְשָׁעִים...זֵדִים — *Impure...wicked... willful sinners.* The wicked people in this passage were not the Syrian-Greeks, but their Jewish collaborators. They were טְמֵאִים, *impure*, preferring the immorality of the Greeks to the moral purity of the Jews; רְשָׁעִים, *wicked*, in their lowly lack of restraint in contrast to the Jewish requirement that one stop to consider every act in the light of the Law; and זֵדִים, *willful sinners*, in their drive to eradicate the study of the Torah (*R' Hirsch*).

וְקָדוֹשׁ בְּעוֹלָמֶךָ, וּלְעַמְּךָ יִשְׂרָאֵל עָשִׂיתָ תְּשׁוּעָה גְדוֹלָה[1]

‹ of great ‹ a victory ‹ You ‹ Israel ‹ and for ⟪ in Your ‹ and holy
magnitude   performed   Your people   world,

וּפֻרְקָן כְּהַיּוֹם הַזֶּה.* וְאַחַר כֵּן* בָּאוּ בָנֶיךָ לִדְבִיר בֵּיתֶךָ,

⟪ of Your ‹ to the Holy ‹ Your ‹ came ‹ Thereafter,* ⟪ as this very day.* ‹ and a
House,   of Holies   children   salvation

וּפִנּוּ אֶת הֵיכָלֶךָ, וְטִהֲרוּ אֶת מִקְדָּשֶׁךָ, וְהִדְלִיקוּ נֵרוֹת

‹ lights ‹ and kindled ⟪ the site of Your Holiness ‹ purified ⟪ Your Temple, ‹ cleansed

בְּחַצְרוֹת קָדְשֶׁךָ, וְקָבְעוּ שְׁמוֹנַת יְמֵי חֲנֻכָּה אֵלּוּ,

⟪ – these – ⟪ of ‹ days ‹ the eight ‹ and they ⟪ of Your ‹ in the
  Chanukah   established   Sanctuary;   Courtyards

לְהוֹדוֹת וּלְהַלֵּל לְשִׁמְךָ הַגָּדוֹל.

⟪ that is great. ‹ to Your ‹ and praise ‹ to express
   Name   thanks

ON PURIM:

בִּימֵי מָרְדְּכַי וְאֶסְתֵּר בְּשׁוּשַׁן הַבִּירָה, כְּשֶׁעָמַד עֲלֵיהֶם*

‹ against ‹ when ⟪ the capital, ‹ in ‹ and ‹ of ‹ In the
them*   rise up   Shushan,   Esther,   Mordechai   days

הָמָן הָרָשָׁע, בִּקֵּשׁ לְהַשְׁמִיד לַהֲרֹג וּלְאַבֵּד אֶת כָּל הַיְּהוּדִים,

‹ the Jews, ‹ all ‹ and to ‹ to slay, ‹ to destroy, ‹ and he ⟪ the ‹ did
   exterminate   sought   wicked, Haman,

מִנַּעַר וְעַד זָקֵן, טַף וְנָשִׁים בְּיוֹם אֶחָד, בִּשְׁלוֹשָׁה עָשָׂר

‹ on the thirteenth [day] ‹ on the same day, ⟪ and ‹ infants ⟪ old, ‹ to ‹ from
   women,   young

לְחֹדֶשׁ שְׁנֵים עָשָׂר, הוּא חֹדֶשׁ אֲדָר, וּשְׁלָלָם לָבוֹז.[2]

⟪ to be ‹ and their ⟪ of Adar, ‹ the ‹ which ⟪ of the twelfth month,
plundered. possessions   month   is

וְאַתָּה בְּרַחֲמֶיךָ הָרַבִּים הֵפַרְתָּ אֶת עֲצָתוֹ, וְקִלְקַלְתָּ

‹ and ⟪ his counsel ‹ nullified ⟪ which is ‹ in Your ‹ But You,
frustrated   abundant,   mercy

---

(1) Cf. *I Samuel* 19:5. (2) *Esther* 3:13.

כְּהַיּוֹם הַזֶּה — *As this very day.* This is an expression used in Scripture to indicate unquestionable clarity: The miracle was as great and as obvious as this very day. [Cf. *Genesis* 25:31, 50:20; *Nehemiah* 9:10.]

וְאַחַר כֵּן — *Thereafter.* By their actions after the success of their revolt, the Jews proved that they were interested not in military victory, nor in political power, but in undisturbed service of God (*Chofetz Chaim*).

⊰ פורים / Purim

כְּשֶׁעָמַד עֲלֵיהֶם —*When rise up against them.* The paragraph describing the miracle of Purim is briefer than that describing Chanukah. The danger of Purim was straightforward — the extermination of the nation — and requires no

אֶת מַחֲשַׁבְתּוֹ, וַהֲשֵׁבוֹתָ לּוֹ גְּמוּלוֹ בְרֹאשׁוֹ,* וְתָלוּ אוֹתוֹ

‹ him ‹ and they ‹‹ upon his ‹ his ‹ to ‹ and ‹‹ his intention
hanged   own head,* recompense him returned

וְאֶת בָּנָיו עַל הָעֵץ.

‹‹ the gallows. ‹ on ‹ and his sons

וְעַל כֻּלָּם יִתְבָּרַךְ וְיִתְרוֹמַם וְיִתְנַשֵּׂא שִׁמְךָ

‹ may Your ‹ and upraised ‹ and exalted, ‹ blessed, ‹ all these, ‹ For
Name be,

מַלְכֵּנוּ תָּמִיד לְעוֹלָם וָעֶד.

‹‹ and ever. ‹ for ever ‹ continually, ‹‹ our King,

FROM ROSH HASHANAH TO YOM KIPPUR ADD:

וּכְתוֹב לְחַיִּים טוֹבִים כָּל בְּנֵי בְרִיתֶךָ.

‹‹ of Your ‹ the ‹ all ‹ that is ‹ for a life ‹ And
covenant. members   good   inscribe

[IF FORGOTTEN, DO NOT REPEAT SHEMONEH ESREI. SEE LAWS §61.]

BEND THE KNEES AT בָּרוּךְ, BLESSED; BOW AT אַתָּה, YOU; STRAIGHTEN UP AT ה', HASHEM.

וְכֹל הַחַיִּים* יוֹדוּךָ סֶּלָה, וִיהַלְלוּ וִיבָרְכוּ

‹ and bless ‹ — and praise ‹‹ forever! ‹ will gratefully ‹ alive* ‹ Everything
acknowledge You,

אֶת שִׁמְךָ הַגָּדוֹל, בֶּאֱמֶת לְעוֹלָם, כִּי טוֹב, הָאֵל

‹ O God ‹‹ it is good. ‹ for ‹ forever, ‹ sincerely, ‹‹ that is great, ‹ Your Name

יְשׁוּעָתֵנוּ וְעֶזְרָתֵנוּ סֶלָה, הָאֵל הַטּוֹב. בָּרוּךְ

‹ Blessed ‹‹ Who is beneficent. ‹ the God ‹‹ forever, ‹ and of our help, ‹ of our salvation

אַתָּה יהוה, הַטּוֹב שִׁמְךָ וּלְךָ נָאֶה לְהוֹדוֹת.

‹‹ to give ‹ it is ‹ and ‹ is Your ‹ The ‹‹ HASHEM, ‹ are You,
thanks. fitting to You Name, Beneficent One

---

elaboration. The peril of Chanukah was more subtle. It involved assimilation and impurity. Many are unaware of the dangerous aspects of an assault on our spirituality. They only perceive danger when it is blatantly physical in nature. Therefore, the Chanukah miracle requires a more detailed explanation (R' Hirsch).

וַהֲשֵׁבוֹתָ לּוֹ גְמוּלוֹ בְרֹאשׁוֹ — *And returned to him his recompense upon his own head.* All Haman's

plans boomeranged! The gallows he prepared for Mordechai was used for him; the day he designated for the murder of the Jews became the day on which they rose up against their enemies. His primary anger was against the Jewish children, but his own children hung from the gallows he built for Mordechai (*Etz Yosef*).

•§ וְכֹל הַחַיִּים — *Everything alive.* This prayer refers specifically to the universal praise that

THE *CHAZZAN* RECITES בִּרְכַּת כֹּהֲנִים DURING HIS REPETITION EXCEPT IN A HOUSE OF MOURNING. THE *CHAZZAN* FACES RIGHT AT וְיִשְׁמְרֶךָ; FACES LEFT AT וִיחֻנֶּךָּ וְאֵלֶיךָ; FACES THE ARK FOR THE REST OF THE BLESSINGS.

אֱלֹהֵינוּ וֵאלֹהֵי אֲבוֹתֵינוּ, בָּרְכֵנוּ בַבְּרָכָה הַמְשֻׁלֶּשֶׁת, בַּתּוֹרָה,

‹ [that is] in ‹‹ of three ‹ with the ‹ bless us ‹‹ of our ‹ and ‹ Our God
the Torah   verses,   blessing   forefathers, the God

הַכְּתוּבָה עַל יְדֵי מֹשֶׁה עַבְדֶּךָ, הָאֲמוּרָה מִפִּי אַהֲרֹן וּבָנָיו,

‹ and his ‹ of ‹ from the ‹ that was ‹‹ Your ‹ of ‹ the ‹ by ‹ that was
sons,   Aaron   mouth   said   servant,   Moses,   hand   written

כֹּהֲנִים עַם קְדוֹשֶׁךָ, כָּאָמוּר:

‹‹ as it is ‹ Your holy ‹‹ the
said: people,   Kohanim,

(*.כֵּן יְהִי רָצוֹן – Cong.)   יְבָרֶכְךָ יהוה, וְיִשְׁמְרֶךָ.

‹‹ His will.* ‹ be ‹ May so   ‹‹ and safeguard you. ‹ May HASHEM bless you

(.כֵּן יְהִי רָצוֹן – Cong.)   יָאֵר יהוה פָּנָיו אֵלֶיךָ וִיחֻנֶּךָּ.

‹‹ His will. ‹ be ‹ May so   ‹‹ and be ‹ for you ‹ His ‹ May HASHEM
                           gracious to you.   countenance illuminate

(.כֵּן יְהִי רָצוֹן – Cong.)¹ יִשָּׂא יהוה פָּנָיו אֵלֶיךָ וְיָשֵׂם לְךָ שָׁלוֹם.

‹‹ His will. ‹ be ‹ May so   ‹‹ peace. ‹ for ‹ and ‹ to you ‹ His ‹ May HASHEM
                       you establish   countenance turn

SOME CONGREGATIONS RECITE THE FOLLOWING WHILE THE *CHAZZAN* RECITES שִׂים שָׁלוֹם:

אַדִּיר בַּמָּרוֹם, שׁוֹכֵן בִּגְבוּרָה, אַתָּה שָׁלוֹם וְשִׁמְךָ שָׁלוֹם.²

‹‹ is Peace! ‹ and Your ‹ are ‹ You ‹‹ in power! ‹ Who ‹ on high, ‹ Mighty One
Name   Peace   dwells

יְהִי רָצוֹן שֶׁתָּשִׂים עָלֵינוּ וְעַל כָּל עַמְּךָ בֵּית יִשְׂרָאֵל חַיִּים

‹ life ‹‹ of Israel, ‹ the ‹ of Your ‹ all ‹ and ‹ upon us ‹ that You ‹ [Your] will ‹ May
House people,   upon   place   it be

וּבְרָכָה לְמִשְׁמֶרֶת שָׁלוֹם.

‹‹ of peace. ‹ for a safeguard ‹ and blessing

---

(1) *Numbers* 6:24-26. (2) Cf. *Judges* 6:24 and *Shabbos* 10b.

will emerge with the restoration of the Divine service in the rebuilt Temple.

בִּרְכַּת כֹּהֲנִים §⊷ — The Priestly Blessing

God commanded Aaron and his descendants to bless the Jewish people by pronouncing the blessings listed in the Torah (*Numbers* 6:22-27). Although originally the *Kohanim* pronounced these blessings every day, a centuries-old custom has developed that they do so only in *Mussaf* on Festivals, when the Jewish people still feel the joy that should accompany these blessings. Only in parts of *Eretz Yisrael* and in

some Sephardic communities has the practice of daily recitation been retained. Where the *Kohanim* do not bless the nation every day, this prayer is recited by the *chazzan* at *Shacharis*, *Mussaf*, and the *Minchah* of fast days. It contains the text of the Priestly Blessings and a prayer that God fulfill it upon us.

כֵּן יְהִי רָצוֹן — *May so be His will.* In many congregations there is a custom to add each phrase בְּזְכוּת אַבְרָהָם, *in the merit of Abraham,* בְּזְכוּת יִצְחָק, *in the merit of Isaac,* and בְּזְכוּת יַעֲקֹב, *in the merit of Jacob,* after the response כֵּן יְהִי רָצוֹן fol-

PEACE / שלום

שִׂים שָׁלוֹם, טוֹבָה, וּבְרָכָה, חַיִּים, חֵן, וָחֶסֶד

⟨ kindness, ⟨ gracious- ⟨ life, ⟨ blessing, ⟨ goodness, ⟨ peace, ⟨ Establish
ness,

וְרַחֲמִים* עָלֵינוּ וְעַל כָּל יִשְׂרָאֵל עַמֶּךָ. בָּרְכֵנוּ

⟨ Bless us, ⟪ Your ⟨ of Israel ⟨ all ⟨ and ⟨ upon us ⟨ and
people. upon compassion*

אָבִינוּ, כֻּלָּנוּ כְּאֶחָד בְּאוֹר פָּנֶיךָ, כִּי בְאוֹר

⟨ with the ⟨ for ⟪ of Your ⟨ with the ⟪ as one, ⟨ all of us ⟪ our Father,
light countenance, light

פָּנֶיךָ נָתַתָּ לָּנוּ, יהוה אֱלֹהֵינוּ, תּוֹרַת חַיִּים

⟨ of life ⟨ the Torah ⟪ our God, ⟨ HASHEM, ⟨ us, ⟨ You gave ⟨ of Your
countenance

וְאַהֲבַת חֶסֶד,* וּצְדָקָה, וּבְרָכָה, וְרַחֲמִים, וְחַיִּים,

⟨ life, ⟨ compassion, ⟨ blessing, ⟨ righteousness, ⟨ of ⟨ and a love
kindness,*

וְשָׁלוֹם. וְטוֹב יִהְיֶה בְּעֵינֶיךָ לְבָרְכֵנוּ וּלְבָרֵךְ

⟨ and to bless ⟨ to bless us ⟨ in Your eyes ⟨ may it be ⟨ And good ⟪ and peace.

אֶת כָּל עַמְּךָ יִשְׂרָאֵל בְּכָל עֵת וּבְכָל שָׁעָה

⟨ hour ⟨ and at every ⟨ time ⟨ at every ⟨ Israel ⟨ of Your people ⟨ all

בִּשְׁלוֹמֶךָ, (בְּרוֹב עוֹז וְשָׁלוֹם).

⟪ and peace). ⟨ strength ⟨ (with ⟪ with Your peace,
abundant

---

lowing each verse of the Priestly Blessings. The linkage of the three blessings to the three Patriarchs is explained by R' Yehudah ben Yakar.

שלום / Peace

The text of שִׂים שָׁלוֹם contains allusions to the Priestly Blessing, and the six forms of goodness listed here — peace, goodness, blessing, graciousness, kindness, and compassion — allude to the six blessings of *Bircas Kohanim* (Etz Yosef).

חֵן וָחֶסֶד וְרַחֲמִים — *Graciousness, kindness, and compassion.* Man goes through stages of devel-

opment in life. When he is growing and improving, he is the recipient of God's חֵן, *graciousness.* In his period of maturity, when an individual may not improve, but continues the accomplishments of his more fruitful period, God grants him חֶסֶד, *kindness.* Sometimes he declines or does not deserve God's help — but even then God shows רַחֲמִים, *compassion* (Ikkarim).

וְאַהֲבַת חֶסֶד — *And a love of kindness.* God is not content if we merely act kindly toward others. He wants us to *love* kindness. That which some-

FROM ROSH HASHANAH TO YOM KIPPUR ADD THE FOLLOWING:

בְּסֵפֶר חַיִּים בְּרָכָה וְשָׁלוֹם, וּפַרְנָסָה טוֹבָה, וּגְזֵרוֹת טוֹבוֹת,

》that are 〈 and 〈 that is 〈 and 〈 and 〈 blessing, 〈 of life, 〈 In the
good, decrees good, livelihood peace, book

יְשׁוּעוֹת וְנֶחָמוֹת, נִזָּכֵר וְנִכָּתֵב לְפָנֶיךָ, אֲנַחְנוּ וְכָל עַמְּךָ

〈 and Your 〈 – we 》 before 〈 and may we 〈 may we be 》 and 〈 salvations
entire people You be inscribed remembered consolations,

בֵּית יִשְׂרָאֵל, לְחַיִּים טוֹבִים וּלְשָׁלוֹם.

》 and for 〈 that is 〈 for a life 〈 of Israel – 〈 the
peace. good Family

[IF FORGOTTEN, DO NOT REPEAT SHEMONEH ESREI. SEE LAWS §61, 65.]

בָּרוּךְ אַתָּה יהוה, הַמְבָרֵךְ אֶת עַמּוֹ יִשְׂרָאֵל

〈 Israel 〈 His people 〈 Who blesses 》 HASHEM, 〈 are You, 〈 Blessed

בַּשָׁלוֹם.

》 with peace.

**ALTHOUGH THE CHAZZAN'S REPETITION ENDS HERE, HE SHOULD ADD
THE NEXT VERSE IN AN UNDERTONE. INDIVIDUALS CONTINUE:**

יִהְיוּ לְרָצוֹן* אִמְרֵי פִי וְהֶגְיוֹן לִבִּי לְפָנֶיךָ,

》 before 》 of my 〈 and the 〈 of my 〈 – the 〈 find favor* 〈 May
You, heart – thoughts mouth expressions they

יהוה צוּרִי וְגֹאֲלִי.¹

》 and my Redeemer. 〈 my Rock 〈 HASHEM,

---

(1) Psalms 19:15.

one loves is never a chore (Chofetz Chaim).

◆§ יִהְיוּ לְרָצוֹן — *May they find favor.* We conclude *Shemoneh Esrei* with this brief request that our prayers find favor before God. Kabbalistic literature attaches great sanctity to this verse and stresses that it be recited slowly and fervently.

Some authorities maintain that since יִהְיוּ לְרָצוֹן closes the *Shemoneh Esrei* prayer, it should be recited before אֱלֹהַי נְצוֹר, which is not an integral part of *Shemoneh Esrei* (see below). Others hold that since the Sages have appended אֱלֹהַי נְצוֹר, *Shemoneh Esrei* ends after אֱלֹהַי נְצוֹר, at which point יִהְיוּ לְרָצוֹן should be said. To accommodate both views, some authorities hold

that יִהְיוּ לְרָצוֹן should be said both before and after אֱלֹהַי נְצוֹר.

◆§ אֱלֹהַי נְצוֹר / **Concluding Prayers**

Many Talmudic Sages composed supplications that they would recite at the conclusion of *Shemoneh Esrei*, some of which are cited in *Berachos* 16b-17a. The prayer now in universal use is based on that of Mar, son of Rabina (ibid. 17a).

While one is reciting אֱלֹהַי נְצוֹר, he may not respond to blessings and the like except for the exceptions given below. In the case of those exceptions, it is preferable to recite יִהְיוּ לְרָצוֹן before responding, but if there is not enough time to do so, the responses should be said

אֱלֹהַי, נְצוֹר לְשׁוֹנִי מֵרָע,* וּשְׂפָתַי מִדַּבֵּר

< from speaking   < and my lips   ≪ from evil*   < my tongue   < guard   < My God,

מִרְמָה,¹ וְלִמְקַלְלַי נַפְשִׁי תִדּוֹם,* וְנַפְשִׁי כֶּעָפָר*

< like dust*   < and let my soul   ≪ be silent;*   < let my soul   < To those who curse me,   ≪ deceitfully.

לַכֹּל תִּהְיֶה. פְּתַח לִבִּי בְּתוֹרָתֶךָ,* וְאַחֲרֵי

< so that to follow   ≪ to Your Torah,*   < my heart   < Open   ≪ be.   < to everyone

מִצְוֹתֶיךָ תִּרְדּוֹף נַפְשִׁי. וְכָל הַקָּמִים וְהַחוֹשְׁבִים

< and who plot   < who rise up   < As for all   ≪ shall my soul pursue.   < Your commandments

עָלַי לְרָעָה, מְהֵרָה הָפֵר עֲצָתָם וְקַלְקֵל

< and disrupt   ≪ their counsel,   < nullify   < speedily   ≪ to do evil,   < against me

מַחֲשַׁבְתָּם.² יְהִי רָצוֹן מִלְּפָנֶיךָ, יהוה אֱלֹהַי

< my God   < HASHEM,   ≪ before You,   < the will   < May it be   ≪ their scheme.

וֵאלֹהֵי אֲבוֹתַי, שֶׁלֹּא תַעֲלֶה קִנְאַת אָדָם עָלַי,

≪ against me,   < of any man   < the jealousy   < be aroused   < that there not   ≪ of my forefathers,   < and the God

---

(1) Cf. *Psalms* 34:14. (2) See *Berachos* 17a.

---

anyway. The responses are: *Borchu*; the Amen after אָמֵן יְהֵא שְׁמֵהּ and שׁוֹמֵעַ תְּפִלָּה and הָאֵל הַקָּדוֹשׁ and רַבָּא and the last Amen of the Half-*Kaddish*; in *Kedushah*, the two verses קָדוֹשׁ and בָּרוּךְ כְּבוֹד; and the three words מוֹדִים אֲנַחְנוּ לָךְ. (See *Orach Chaim* Ch. 122.)

אֱלֹהַי נְצוֹר לְשׁוֹנִי מֵרָע — *My God, guard my tongue from evil.* We pray that God protect us from situations that tempt us to speak ill of others (*Abudraham*).

The Midrash (*Vayikra Rabbah* 33:1) relates that Rabban Shimon ben Gamliel once sent his servant, Tavi, to buy "good food." Tavi, who was famous for his wisdom, brought back a tongue. Thereupon Rabban Shimon sent him to buy some "bad food." Again, he returned with a

tongue. Rabban Shimon asked him to explain how the same food can be both good and bad. Tavi said, "From a tongue can come good or bad. When a tongue speaks *good*, there is nothing better, but when a tongue speaks *ill*, there is nothing worse."

נַפְשִׁי תִדּוֹם . . . כֶּעָפָר — *Let my soul be silent . . . like dust.* We should ignore barbs and insults, because the less a person cares about his prestige, the less he will let selfishness interfere with his service of God and his efforts toward self-improvement (*Ruach Chaim*).

פְּתַח לִבִּי בְּתוֹרָתֶךָ — *Open my heart to Your Torah.* Our goal is to serve God in a positive manner by studying Torah and fulfilling its commandments (*Abudraham*).

וְלֹא קִנֵּאתִי עַל אֲחֵרִים, וְשֶׁלֹּא אֶכְעַס הַיּוֹם,

nor ⟨ my jealousy ⟨ against ⟨ others; ⟨⟨ and that I not ⟨ become angry ⟨ today,

וְשֶׁלֹּא אַכְעִיסֶךָ, וְתַצִּילֵנִי מִיֵּצֶר הָרָע, וְתֵן בְּלִבִּי

and that I not ⟨ anger You. ⟨⟨ Rescue me ⟨ from the Inclination ⟨⟨ for Evil, and ⟨ place ⟨ in my heart

הַכְנָעָה וַעֲנָוָה. מַלְכֵּנוּ וֵאלֹהֵינוּ, יַחֵד שְׁמְךָ

submissiveness ⟨ and humility. ⟨⟨ and our God, ⟨ O our King ⟨⟨ unify ⟨ Your Name

בְּעוֹלָמֶךָ, בְּנֵה עִירְךָ, יַסֵּד בֵּיתֶךָ, וְשַׁכְלֵל הֵיכָלֶךָ,

in Your world; ⟨⟨ rebuild ⟨ Your City, ⟨⟨ lay the foundation ⟨ of Your House, ⟨⟨ perfect ⟨ Your Sanctuary;

וְקַבֵּץ קִבּוּץ גָּלִיּוֹת, וּפְדֵה צֹאנֶךָ, וְשַׂמַּח עֲדָתֶךָ.

gather ⟨ the ingathering ⟨ of the exiles, ⟨⟨ redeem ⟨ Your sheep, ⟨⟨ and gladden ⟨ Your congregation.

עֲשֵׂה לְמַעַן שְׁמֶךָ, עֲשֵׂה לְמַעַן יְמִינֶךָ, עֲשֵׂה

Act ⟨ for the sake ⟨ of Your Name; ⟨⟨ act ⟨ for the sake ⟨ of Your right hand; ⟨⟨ act

לְמַעַן תּוֹרָתֶךָ, עֲשֵׂה לְמַעַן קְדֻשָּׁתֶךָ. לְמַעַן

for the sake ⟨ of Your Torah; ⟨⟨ act ⟨ for the sake ⟨⟨ of Your sanctity. ⟨ In order that

יֵחָלְצוּן יְדִידֶיךָ, הוֹשִׁיעָה יְמִינְךָ וַעֲנֵנִי.[1]

released may be ⟨ Your beloved ones ⟨⟨ — save ⟨ with Your right hand, ⟨ and answer me. ⟨⟨

SOME RECITE VERSES PERTAINING TO THEIR NAMES AT THIS POINT. SEE PAGE 764.

יִהְיוּ לְרָצוֹן אִמְרֵי פִי וְהֶגְיוֹן לִבִּי לְפָנֶיךָ,

May they ⟨ find favor ⟨⟨ — the expressions ⟨ of my mouth ⟨ and the thoughts ⟨ of my heart — ⟨⟨ before You, ⟨⟨

יהוה צוּרִי וְגֹאֲלִי.[2]

HASHEM, ⟨ my Rock ⟨ and my Redeemer. ⟨⟨

---

(1) *Psalms* 60:7; 108:7. (2) 19:15.

◄§ Verses for People's Names

It is a source of merit to recite a Torah verse that represents one's name before reciting the verse יִהְיוּ לְרָצוֹן. The verse should either contain the person's name or else begin and end with the first and last letters of his name (*Kitzur Sh'lah*).

BOW. TAKE THREE STEPS BACK. BOW LEFT AND SAY . . . עֹשֶׂה, *"HE WHO MAKES . . .";* BOW RIGHT AND SAY . . . הוּא, *"MAY HE . . .";* BOW FORWARD AND SAY . . . וְעַל כָּל יִשְׂרָאֵל, *"AND UPON ALL ISRAEL . . . "*

עֹשֶׂה °שָׁלוֹם בִּמְרוֹמָיו,¹ הוּא יַעֲשֶׂה שָׁלוֹם

⟨ peace ⟨ make ⟨ may He ⟨⟨ in His heights, ⟨ peace ⟨ He Who makes

עָלֵינוּ, וְעַל כָּל יִשְׂרָאֵל.² וְאִמְרוּ: אָמֵן.

⟨⟨ Amen. ⟨ Now respond: ⟨⟨ Israel. ⟨ all ⟨ and upon ⟨⟨ upon us,

FROM ROSH HASHANAH TO YOM KIPPUR SOME SAY:

°הַשָּׁלוֹם

⟨ the peace

יְהִי רָצוֹן מִלְּפָנֶיךָ,* יהוה אֱלֹהֵינוּ וֵאלֹהֵי אֲבוֹתֵינוּ,

⟨⟨ of our ⟨ and the ⟨ our God ⟨ Hashem, ⟨⟨ before You,* ⟨ the will ⟨ May
forefathers, God it be

שֶׁיִּבָּנֶה בֵּית הַמִּקְדָּשׁ בִּמְהֵרָה בְיָמֵינוּ, וְתֵן חֶלְקֵנוּ

⟨ our portion ⟨ Grant that ⟨⟨ in our days. ⟨ speedily ⟨ shall the Holy Temple be, ⟨ that rebuilt

בְּתוֹרָתֶךָ.³ וְשָׁם נַעֲבָדְךָ בְּיִרְאָה, כִּימֵי עוֹלָם וּכְשָׁנִים

⟨ and as in ⟨ of old ⟨ as in ⟨⟨ with ⟨ we may ⟨ so that ⟨⟨ be in Your Torah,
years days reverence, serve You there

קַדְמוֹנִיּוֹת. וְעָרְבָה לַיהוה מִנְחַת יְהוּדָה וִירוּשָׁלָֽיִם,

⟨⟨ and Jerusalem, ⟨ of Judah ⟨ let be the offering ⟨ to Hashem ⟨ And pleasing ⟨⟨ gone by.

כִּימֵי עוֹלָם וּכְשָׁנִים קַדְמוֹנִיּוֹת.⁴

⟨⟨ gone by. ⟨ and in years ⟨ of old ⟨ as in days

THE INDIVIDUAL'S RECITATION OF *SHEMONEH ESREI* ENDS HERE. REMAIN STANDING IN PLACE UNTIL THE *CHAZZAN* REACHES *KEDUSHAH* — OR AT LEAST UNTIL THE *CHAZZAN* BEGINS HIS REPETITION — THEN TAKE THREE STEPS FORWARD. THE *CHAZZAN* HIMSELF, OR ONE PRAYING ALONE, SHOULD REMAIN IN PLACE FOR A FEW MOMENTS BEFORE TAKING THREE STEPS FORWARD.

ON PURIM MANY CONGREGATIONS RECITE *KROVETZ* DURING THE *CHAZZAN'S* REPETITION (P. 585).

ON MOST WEEKDAYS *SHACHARIS* CONTINUES WITH *TACHANUN* (P. 172).

FROM ROSH HASHANAH TO YOM KIPPUR CONTINUE WITH *AVINU MALKEINU* (P. 178).

ON FAST DAYS (WITH THE EXCEPTION OF TISHAH B'AV AND THE FAST OF GEDALIAH) *SELICHOS* ARE RECITED EITHER BEFORE *TACHANUN* OR IMMEDIATELY AFTER נְפִילַת אַפַּיִם, *PUTTING DOWN THE HEAD* (P. 176).

ON ROSH CHODESH, CHANUKAH, CHOL HAMOED CONTINUE WITH הַלֵּל (P. 502).

ON PURIM CONTINUE WITH חֲצִי קַדִּישׁ (P. 197) AND THE REMOVAL OF THE TORAH FROM THE ARK, THE TORAH READING (P. 793), AND THE MEGILLAH READING (P. 581).

ON OTHER DAYS WHEN *TACHANUN* IS OMITTED (SEE P. 172 FOR LISTING) THE *CHAZZAN* RECITES חֲצִי קַדִּישׁ (P. 197), INDIVIDUALS GO ON TO אַשְׁרֵי (P. 214).

---

(1) *Job* 25:2. (2) Cf. *Berachos* 16b. (3) *Ethics of the Fathers* 5:24. (4) *Malachi* 3:4.

◈§ יְהִי רָצוֹן מִלְּפָנֶיךָ — *May it be the will before You.* It is appropriate to conclude the *Shemoneh Esrei*, which takes the place of the Temple Service, with this plea (from *Avos* 5:24) that God permit the rebuilding of the Temple so that we can perform the Service in actuality.

⧉ תחנון / TACHANUN ⧉

וידוי / CONFESSION

THE *VIDUI*/CONFESSIONAL IS RECITED WHILE STANDING.

אֱלֹהֵינוּ   וֵאלֹהֵי   אֲבוֹתֵינוּ,   תָּבֹא   לְפָנֶיךָ
⟩ before You ⟨   come   ⟨⟨ of our forefathers, ⟩   and the God   ⟨   Our God

תְּפִלָּתֵנוּ,[1]   וְאַל   תִּתְעַלַּם   מִתְּחִנָּתֵנוּ,[2]   שֶׁאֵין   אָנוּ
⟩ For we are not ⟨⟨ our supplication. ⟨   ignore   ⟩ and do not ⟨⟨ may our prayer,

עַזֵּי   פָנִים   וּקְשֵׁי   עֹרֶף,   לוֹמַר   לְפָנֶיךָ   יהוה   אֱלֹהֵינוּ
⟩ our God ⟨ Hashem, ⟨⟨ before You, ⟨ as to say ⟩ necked ⟨ and stiff- ⟩ faced ⟨ so brazen-

וֵאלֹהֵי   אֲבוֹתֵינוּ,   צַדִּיקִים   אֲנַחְנוּ   וְלֹא   חָטָאנוּ,
⟨⟨ sinned ⟨ and have not ⟨ that we are righteous   ⟨⟨ of our forefathers, ⟩ and the God

אֲבָל   אֲנַחְנוּ   וַאֲבוֹתֵינוּ   חָטָאנוּ.[3]
⟨⟨ have sinned. ⟨ and our forefathers ⟨ we ⟨⟨ — for indeed,

---

(1) Cf. *Psalms* 88:3. (2) Cf. 55:2. (3) Cf. 106:6.

⧉ תַּחֲנוּן / TACHANUN ⧉

The Talmud (*Bava Metzia* 59a) teaches that if one submissively places his head upon his arm in fervent, intense prayer immediately after *Shemoneh Esrei*, his prayer is warmly accepted by God and can achieve great results.

וִדּוּי / Confession

The custom of confessing as a prelude to *Tachanun* is based on the *Zohar*. The confession, beginning with the last phrase of the opening paragraph (אֲבָל אֲנַחְנוּ וַאֲבוֹתֵינוּ חָטָאנוּ, *indeed we and our forefathers have sinned*),

---

⋙ Occasions and Days on Which *Tachanun* Is Omitted

(a) In a house of mourning during the *shivah* period;

(b) in the presence of a bridegroom, from the day of his wedding (If the wedding ceremony will take place after sunset, the day of the wedding also begins at sunset) until after the *Sheva Berachos* week (if both bride and groom have been previously married, the period of celebration extends for only three days including the day of the wedding);

(c) in the synagogue where a circumcision will take place later that day, or in the presence of a primary participant (the father, the *mohel,* or the *sandak*) in a circumcision that will take place later that day;

(d) on the Sabbath; Festivals (including Chol HaMoed); Rosh Chodesh; the entire month of Nissan; Lag B'Omer; from Rosh Chodesh Sivan until the day after Shavuos (some congregations do not resume *Tachanun* until 14 Sivan); Tishah B'Av; 15 Av; between Yom Kippur and the day after Succos (some congregations do not resume until 2 Cheshvan); Chanukah; Tu B'Shevat; Purim and Shushan Purim (in a leap year this applies also to 14-15 Adar I); or at *Minchah* of the day preceding any of the days listed above;

(e) on Erev Rosh Hashanah and Erev Yom Kippur (but at *Minchah* on the day preceding these days *Tachanun* is said);

(f) in some congregations, it is omitted on Pesach Sheni (14 Iyar) and in some congregations outside Israel it is also not said on 15 Iyar. However, it is said at *Minchah* on 13 Iyar.

STRIKE THE LEFT SIDE OF THE CHEST WITH THE RIGHT FIST WHILE RECITING
EACH OF THE SINS OF THE FOLLOWING CONFESSIONAL LITANY:

אָשַׁמְנוּ, בָּגַדְנוּ, גָּזַלְנוּ, דִּבַּרְנוּ דְפִי. הֶעֱוִינוּ,

《 We have com- 《 slander. 《 we have   《 we have   《 we have   《   We have
mitted iniquity;   spoken   robbed;   betrayed;   been guilty;

וְהִרְשַׁעְנוּ, זַדְנוּ, חָמַסְנוּ, טָפַלְנוּ שֶׁקֶר. יָעַצְנוּ רָע,

《 that 《 We have 《 false 《 we have 《 we have 《 we have 《 we have
is bad;   given   accusations. made   extorted;   sinned   committed
          advice   willfully;   wickedness;

כִּזַּבְנוּ, לַצְנוּ, מָרַדְנוּ, נִאַצְנוּ, סָרַרְנוּ, עָוִינוּ,

《 we have 《 we have 《 we have pro- 《 we have 《 we have 《 we have been
been iniquitous; strayed; voked [God's anger]; rebelled;   scorned;   deceitful;

פָּשַׁעְנוּ, צָרַרְנוּ, קִשִּׁינוּ עֹרֶף. רָשַׁעְנוּ, שִׁחַתְנוּ,

《 we have   《 We have   《 our 《 we have 《 we have caused 《 we have sinned
been corrupt; been wicked;   necks. stiffened   distress;   rebelliously;

תִּעַבְנוּ, תָּעִינוּ, תִּעְתָּעְנוּ.*

《   we have   《 we have 《 we have commit-
        scoffed.*   gone astray; ted abominations;

סַרְנוּ מִמִּצְוֹתֶיךָ וּמִמִּשְׁפָּטֶיךָ הַטּוֹבִים, וְלֹא

《 and it 《   that are   《   and from   《 from Your 《 We have
was not   good,   Your laws   commandments turned away

שָׁוָה לָנוּ.¹ וְאַתָּה צַדִּיק עַל כָּל הַבָּא עָלֵינוּ, כִּי

《 for 《 upon 《 that has 《 all 《 in 《 are 《 And You 《 for 《 worth-
        us,   come   righteous   us.   while

אֱמֶת עָשִׂיתָ וַאֲנַחְנוּ הִרְשָׁעְנוּ.²

《 have acted wickedly. 《 while we 《 have You acted, 《 truthfully

---

(1) Cf. *Job* 33:27. (2) *Nehemiah* 9:33.

should be said while one stands with head and body slightly bowed, portraying contrition and submission. It is customary to strike oneself lightly opposite the heart with the right fist while saying each individual expression of sin. This act symbolizes that sin is caused by the desires of the heart and that the beginning of repentance is the resolve to curb one's passions

(*Matnos Kehunah* to *Koheles Rabbah* Ch. 7).

The confession is formulated in the plural because the Jewish people are like a single body and each of us is like one of its organs. We are responsible for one another, for the good or evil of every Jew affects us all.

תִּעְתָּעְנוּ — *We have scoffed.* This translation follows *II Chronicles* 36:16: וּמִתַּעְתְּעִים בִּנְבִאָיו,

אֵל אֶרֶךְ אַפַּיִם אַתָּה, וּבַעַל הָרַחֲמִים נִקְרֵאתָ,

⟨ are You ⟨ of Mercy ⟨ and ⟨ are You, ⟨ to anger, ⟨ Who ⟨ God,
called;   Master   is slow

וְדֶרֶךְ תְּשׁוּבָה הוֹרֵיתָ. גְּדֻלַּת רַחֲמֶיךָ וַחֲסָדֶיךָ,

⟨ and Your ⟨ of Your ⟨ The ⟨ have You ⟨ of ⟨ and
kindness   mercy   greatness   taught.   repentance   the way

תִּזְכּוֹר הַיּוֹם וּבְכָל יוֹם לְזֶרַע יְדִידֶיךָ. תֵּפֶן אֵלֵינוּ

⟨ to us ⟨ Turn ⟨ of Your ⟨ for the ⟨ day, ⟨ and ⟨ this ⟨ may You
           beloved ones. offspring   every   day   remember,

בְּרַחֲמִים, כִּי אַתָּה הוּא בַּעַל הָרַחֲמִים. בְּתַחֲנוּן

⟨ With ⟨ of Mercy. ⟨ the ⟨ are ⟨ You ⟨ for ⟨ in mercy,
supplication   Master

וּבִתְפִלָּה פָּנֶיךָ נְקַדֵּם, כְּהוֹדַעְתָּ לֶעָנָיו מִקֶּדֶם.

⟨ in ancient ⟨ to the ⟨ in the manner ⟨ we ⟨ Your ⟨ and prayer
times.   humble one   that You   approach, Presence
        [Moses]   made known

מֵחֲרוֹן אַפְּךָ שׁוּב, כְּמוֹ בְּתוֹרָתְךָ כָּתוּב.[1] וּבְצֵל

⟨ In the ⟨ it is ⟨ in Your Torah ⟨ as ⟨ turn ⟨ of Your ⟨ From the
shadow   written.   back,   anger   fierceness

כְּנָפֶיךָ נֶחֱסֶה וְנִתְלוֹנָן, כְּיוֹם וַיֵּרֶד יהוה בֶּעָנָן.[2]

⟨ in a ⟨ when HASHEM ⟨ as on ⟨ and may ⟨ may we ⟨ of Your
cloud.   descended   the day   we dwell,   find shelter   wings

❖ תַּעֲבוֹר עַל פֶּשַׁע וְתִמְחֶה אָשָׁם, כְּיוֹם וַיִּתְיַצֵּב

⟨ when He ⟨ as on ⟨ guilt, ⟨ and erase ⟨ sin ⟨ Overlook
[God] stood   the day

---

(1) Cf. *Exodus* 32:12. (2) 34:5.

and [they] scoffed at His prophets. The disrespect for Torah scholars was identified by the Sages as the final sin that led to the destruction of the first Temple (*Etz Yosef*; see also *Targum Yonasan* to *Genesis* 27:12, מְגַחֵךְ, *one who laughs or scoffs*). Alternatively, *Chayei Adam* suggests *You have let us go astray*.

אֵל אֶרֶךְ אַפַּיִם וי״ג מִדּוֹת הָרַחֲמִים ⟨⟨

God Who Is Slow to Anger
The Thirteen Attributes of Mercy

The *Zohar* teaches that the Thirteen Attributes of Mercy should always be recited with *Tachanun*. The paragraph אֵל אֶרֶךְ אַפַּיִם introduces the Thirteen Attributes.

The verse of the Thirteen Attributes may be

עִמּוֹ שָׁם.¹ תַּאֲזִין שַׁוְעָתֵנוּ וְתַקְשִׁיב מֶנּוּ מַאֲמַר,

《 [our] 〈 from 〈 and hear 〈 to our cry 〈 Give 《 there. 〈 with him
declaration,   us   heed   [Moses]

כְּיוֹם וַיִּקְרָא בְּשֵׁם יהוה,¹ וְשָׁם נֶאֱמַר:

《 it was said: 〈 and there 《 of 〈 with the 〈 when He 〈 as on
                                         HASHEM,   Name   called out   the day

CONGREGATION AND *CHAZZAN* RECITE LOUDLY AND IN UNISON:

וַיַּעֲבֹר יהוה עַל פָּנָיו וַיִּקְרָא:

《 and 《 his [Moses'] 〈 before 〈 And HASHEM passed
proclaimed: face,

יהוה, יהוה, אֵל, רַחוּם, וְחַנּוּן, אֶרֶךְ אַפַּיִם,

〈 to anger, 〈 Slow 《 and 〈 Compas- 〈 God, 〈 HASHEM, 〈 HASHEM,
                          Gracious,   sionate

וְרַב חֶסֶד, וֶאֱמֶת, נֹצֵר חֶסֶד לָאֲלָפִים, נֹשֵׂא

〈 Forgiver 《 for thousands 〈 of 〈 Preserver 《 and Truth, 〈 in 〈 and
          [of generations], kindness   Kindness Abundant

עָוֹן, וָפֶשַׁע, וְחַטָּאָה, וְנַקֵּה.² וְסָלַחְתָּ לַעֲוֹנֵנוּ

〈 our 〈 May You 《 and Who 〈 and inadvertent 〈 willful sin, 〈 of
iniquities   forgive   absolves.   sin,   iniquity,

וּלְחַטָּאתֵנוּ וּנְחַלְתָּנוּ.³ סְלַח לָנוּ אָבִינוּ כִּי

〈 for 《 our Father, 〈 us, 〈 Forgive 《 and make us 《 and our sins,
                                              Your heritage.

חָטָאנוּ, מְחַל לָנוּ מַלְכֵּנוּ כִּי פָשָׁעְנוּ.⁴ כִּי אַתָּה

〈 You, 〈 For 《 we have 〈 for 《 our King, 〈 us, 〈 pardon 《 we have
              willfully sinned.   sinned;

אֲדֹנָי טוֹב וְסַלָּח, וְרַב חֶסֶד לְכָל קֹרְאֶיךָ.⁵

《 who call 〈 to all 〈 in 〈 and 《 and 〈 are 〈 O Lord,
upon You.   kindness abundant forgiving, good

---

(1) *Exodus* 34:5. (2) 34:6-7. (3) 34:9. (4) From the weekday *Shemoneh Esrei*. (5) *Psalms* 86:5.

said only in the presence of a *minyan*. If there is no *minyan*, it may be recited not in the form of a prayer, but in the manner of reading from the Torah, that is, with the musical cantillation (*trop*) of the Torah reading (*Orach Chaim* 565:5).

PUTTING DOWN THE HEAD / נְפִילַת אַפַּיִם

THE FOLLOWING (UNTIL נַפְשִׁי רָגַע) SHOULD PREFERABLY BE RECITED WHILE ONE IS SEATED. IF A
TORAH SCROLL IS PRESENT, ONE SHOULD REST HIS HEAD ON HIS ARM (SEE COMMENTARY). MANY
OMIT THE VERSE וַיֹּאמֶר דָּוִד, AND DAVID SAID . . ., AND BEGIN WITH רַחוּם וְחַנּוּן, O MERCIFUL . . .

וַיֹּאמֶר דָּוִד* אֶל גָּד, צַר לִי מְאֹד, נִפְּלָה נָא

‹ now ‹ Let us ‹‹ exceed- ‹ am I ‹ Dis- to Gad, ‹ And David said*
      fall   ingly.   tressed

בְיַד יהוה, כִּי רַבִּים רַחֲמָיו, וּבְיַד אָדָם אַל אֶפְּלָה.¹

‹‹ let me not fall. ‹ but into human ‹‹ are His ‹ abundant ‹ for ‹‹ of ‹ into the
              hands   mercies,   HASHEM, hand

רַחוּם וְחַנּוּן* חָטָאתִי לְפָנֶיךָ. יהוה מָלֵא

‹ Who ‹ HASHEM, ‹‹ before You. ‹ I have ‹ and gracious ‹ O merciful
is full   sinned   One,*

רַחֲמִים, רַחֵם עָלַי וְקַבֵּל תַּחֲנוּנָי.

‹‹ my supplications. ‹ and accept ‹ on me ‹ have mercy ‹‹ of mercy,

——— Psalms 6:2-11 / תהלים ו:ב-יא ———

יהוה, אַל בְּאַפְּךָ* תוֹכִיחֵנִי, וְאַל בַּחֲמָתְךָ תִיסְּרֵנִי.

‹‹ chastise me. ‹ in Your wrath ‹ nor ‹ rebuke me, ‹ in Your anger* ‹ do not ‹ HASHEM,

---

(1) *II Samuel* 24:14.

נְפִילַת אַפַּיִם / Putting Down the Head

The act of נְפִילַת אַפַּיִם, *putting down the head*,
"burying" one's face in submissive supplication,
is based on the actions of Moses, Aaron, and
Joshua, who cast themselves down before God in
times of stress (*Numbers* 16:22; *Joshua* 7:6).

This portion of *Tachanun* is recited with the
head down and resting on the left arm, preferably in a sitting position. One wearing *tefillin* on
the left arm rests his head on his right arm out of
respect for the *tefillin*. The head should not rest
on the bare arm; rather, the arm should be
covered with a sleeve, *tallis*, or even a cloth. This
posture is an indication of the feelings of despair
and guilt that combine with the undying hope
that God's mercy will rescue the supplicant no
matter how hopeless his plight. Since Joshua cast
himself down in the presence of the Holy Ark,
the act of falling on the face is done only in the
presence of a Torah scroll — an Ark containing a
Torah scroll. If a Torah is not present, *Tachanun*

is recited with the head held erect.

וַיֹּאמֶר דָּוִד — *And David said.* King David
had sinned by taking a census of the Jews in a
manner forbidden by the Torah (see *Exodus*
30:12). God, through the agency of the prophet
Gad, gave King David a choice of three calamities, one of which he and his people would have
to suffer in atonement for his sin: seven years of
hunger; three months of defeat in battle; or a
three-day death plague. David chose the last
because that one would be inflicted directly by
God, Whose mercy is ever present even when His
wrath is aroused. His choice proved wise when
God mercifully halted the plague after a duration
of only half a day. Similarly, in *Tachanun*, we
cast ourselves upon God's compassion.

רַחוּם וְחַנּוּן — *O merciful and gracious One.* This
verse is not of Scriptural origin. It is based on the
dictum that God tempers the judgment of someone who confesses that he has sinned (*Etz Yosef*).

ה׳ אל באפך — *HASHEM, do not in Your anger.*

חָנֵּנִי יהוה כִּי אֻמְלַל אָנִי, רְפָאֵנִי יהוה כִּי

‹ for ‹ HASHEM, ‹ heal me, ‹‹ am I; ‹ feeble ‹ for ‹ HASHEM, ‹ Favor me,

נִבְהֲלוּ עֲצָמָי. וְנַפְשִׁי נִבְהֲלָה מְאֹד, וְאַתָּה יהוה

‹ HASHEM, ‹ and You, ‹‹ utterly, ‹ is terrified ‹ My soul ‹‹ do my ‹ shudder
                                                                bones.   with terror

עַד מָתָי.* שׁוּבָה יהוה חַלְּצָה נַפְשִׁי, הוֹשִׁיעֵנִי

‹ save me ‹‹ my soul; ‹ release ‹ HASHEM, ‹ Desist, ‹‹ when?* ‹ until

לְמַעַן חַסְדֶּךָ. כִּי אֵין בַּמָּוֶת זִכְרֶךָ, בִּשְׁאוֹל מִי

‹ who ‹ in the grave ‹‹ is there ‹ in death ‹ not ‹ For ‹‹ Your ‹ as befits
                              mention of You;   kindness.

יוֹדֶה לָּךְ. יָגַעְתִּי בְּאַנְחָתִי, אַשְׂחֶה בְכָל לַיְלָה

‹ night ‹ every ‹ I drench ‹‹ with my sigh; ‹ I am wearied ‹‹ You? ‹ will praise

מִטָּתִי, בְּדִמְעָתִי עַרְשִׂי אַמְסֶה. עָשְׁשָׁה   מִכַּעַס

‹ because of anger ‹ Dimmed ‹‹ I soak. ‹ my couch ‹ with my tears ‹‹ my bed;

עֵינִי, עָתְקָה בְּכָל צוֹרְרָי. סוּרוּ מִמֶּנִּי כָּל פֹּעֲלֵי

‹ doers ‹ all ‹ from me, ‹ Depart ‹‹ my tormentors. ‹ by all ‹ aged ‹ is my eye,

אָוֶן, כִּי שָׁמַע יהוה קוֹל בִּכְיִי. שָׁמַע יהוה

‹ HASHEM has heard ‹‹ of my weeping. ‹ the sound ‹ HASHEM has heard ‹ for ‹‹ of evil,

תְּחִנָּתִי, יהוה תְּפִלָּתִי יִקָּח. יֵבֹשׁוּ וְיִבָּהֲלוּ מְאֹד

‹ utterly, ‹ and ‹ Let them ‹‹ will ‹ my prayer ‹ HASHEM ‹‹ my plea,
           confounded be shamed   accept.

כָּל אֹיְבָי, יָשֻׁבוּ יֵבֹשׁוּ רָגַע.

‹‹ in an ‹ and be ‹ may they ‹‹ my ‹ all
        instant. shamed   regret   enemies;

ON MONDAY AND THURSDAY, CONTINUE וְהוּא רַחוּם, *HE, THE MERCIFUL ONE* . . . (P. 182).
ON OTHER DAYS CONTINUE שׁוֹמֵר יִשְׂרָאֵל, *O GUARDIAN OF ISRAEL* . . . (P. 194).
BETWEEN ROSH HASHANAH AND YOM KIPPUR (AND IN MANY COMMUNITIES ON FAST DAYS)
אָבִינוּ מַלְכֵּנוּ, *AVINU MALKEINU* (P. 178) IS RECITED.

David composed this psalm when he was sick and in pain. He intended his prayer for every person in distress, and particularly for Israel when it suffered oppression and deprivation.

Even if he must be punished for his deeds,

David pleaded, let God do so gradually, but not *in anger*, for then it would be beyond human endurance (*Radak*).

עַד מָתָי — *Until when?* How long will You watch my suffering and not cure me?

﷽ אבינו מלכנו / AVINU MALKEINU ﷽

FROM ROSH HASHANAH TO YOM KIPPUR [AND IN MANY COMMUNITIES ON FAST DAYS], אָבִֽינוּ מַלְכֵּֽנוּ
IS RECITED AFTER *SHEMONEH ESREI* OF BOTH *SHACHARIS* AND *MINCHAH* [EXCEPT ON THOSE DAYS ON
WHICH *TACHANUN* IS OMITTED (SEE BOX, P. 172); WHEN *EREV YOM KIPPUR* FALLS ON A FRIDAY,
HOWEVER, אָבִֽינוּ מַלְכֵּֽנוּ IS RECITED DURING *SHACHARIS*, EVEN THOUGH *TACHANUN* IS OMITTED].

WHEN THERE IS A *BRIS MILAH*, EVEN THOUGH *TACHANUN* IS NOT SAID, *AVINU MALKEINU* IS SAID.

THE DOORS OF THE ARK ARE KEPT OPEN WHILE אָבִֽינוּ מַלְכֵּֽנוּ IS RECITED. [AS THE ARK IS OPENED,
SOME SAY THE WORDS: פְּתַח שַׁעֲרֵי שָׁמַֽיִם לִתְפִלָּתֵֽנוּ, *OPEN THE GATES OF HEAVEN TO OUR PRAYER*.]

ACCORDING TO MANY AUTHIORITIES, אָבִֽינוּ מַלְכֵּֽנוּ MAY BE RECITED WITHOUT A *MINYAN*.

אָבִֽינוּ מַלְכֵּֽנוּ, חָטָֽאנוּ לְפָנֶֽיךָ.
❰❰ before You. ❰ we have sinned ❰ our King, ❰ Our Father,

אָבִֽינוּ מַלְכֵּֽנוּ, אֵין לָֽנוּ מֶֽלֶךְ אֶלָּא אָֽתָּה.
❰❰ You. ❰ other than ❰ King ❰ we have no ❰ our King, ❰ Our Father,

אָבִֽינוּ מַלְכֵּֽנוּ, עֲשֵׂה עִמָּֽנוּ לְמַֽעַן שְׁמֶֽךָ.
❰❰ of Your ❰ for the ❰ with us ❰ deal ❰ our King, ❰ Our Father,
Name. sake [kindly]

ON FAST DAYS:	ROSH HASHANAH TO YOM KIPPUR:
אָבִֽינוּ מַלְכֵּֽנוּ, בָּרֵךְ עָלֵֽינוּ	אָבִֽינוּ מַלְכֵּֽנוּ, חַדֵּשׁ עָלֵֽינוּ
❰ upon us ❰ bestow ❰ our King, ❰ Our Father, blessing	❰ upon ❰ inaugurate ❰ our King, ❰ Our Father, us
שָׁנָה טוֹבָה.	שָׁנָה טוֹבָה.
❰❰ that is good. ❰ for a year	❰❰ that is good. ❰ a year

אָבִֽינוּ מַלְכֵּֽנוּ, בַּטֵּל מֵעָלֵֽינוּ כָּל גְּזֵרוֹת קָשׁוֹת.
❰❰ that are harsh. ❰ decrees ❰ all ❰ from upon us ❰ nullify ❰ our King, ❰ Our Father,

אָבִֽינוּ מַלְכֵּֽנוּ, בַּטֵּל מַחְשְׁבוֹת שׂוֹנְאֵֽינוּ.
❰❰ of those who hate us. ❰ the thoughts ❰ nullify ❰ our King, ❰ Our Father,

אָבִֽינוּ מַלְכֵּֽנוּ, הָפֵר עֲצַת אוֹיְבֵֽינוּ.
❰❰ of our enemies. ❰ the counsel ❰ thwart ❰ our King, ❰ Our Father,

אָבִֽינוּ מַלְכֵּֽנוּ, כַּלֵּה כָּל צַר וּמַשְׂטִין מֵעָלֵֽינוּ.
❰❰ from upon us. ❰ and adversary ❰ foe ❰ every ❰ annihilate ❰ our King, ❰ Our Father,

---

﷽ אָבִֽינוּ מַלְכֵּֽנוּ / AVINU MALKEINU ﷽

Avinu Malkeinu combines pleas for our personal and national needs with expressions of repentance. This prayer is based on an incident related in the Talmud (*Taanis* 25b). During a drought, a day of public fast and prayer was proclaimed, but no rain fell. Then Rabbi Akiva recited five brief supplications, each beginning *Our Father, our King*, and it began to rain.

Over time brief prayers with this beginning were added, expanding Rabbi Akiva's five supplications to more than forty; in the Sephardic rite, to more than fifty. The introductory formula expresses our dual relationship to God: because He created and loves us, He is our merciful *Father*; because it is our duty to serve Him, He is our *King*.

אָבִֽינוּ מַלְכֵּֽנוּ, סְתוֹם פִּיּוֹת מַשְׂטִינֵֽנוּ וּמְקַטְרִיגֵֽנוּ.
⟪ and accusers. ⟨ of our adversaries ⟨ the mouths ⟨ seal ⟨ our King, ⟨ Our Father,

אָבִֽינוּ מַלְכֵּֽנוּ, כַּלֵּה דֶּֽבֶר וְחֶֽרֶב וְרָעָב וּשְׁבִי וּמַשְׁחִית
⟨ destruction, ⟨ captivity, ⟨ famine, ⟨ sword, ⟨ pestilence, ⟨ exterminate ⟨ our King, ⟨ Our Father,

וְעָוֹן וּשְׁמַד מִבְּנֵי בְרִיתֶֽךָ.
⟪ of Your ⟨ from the ⟨ and forced ⟨ iniquity,
covenant. members conversion

אָבִֽינוּ מַלְכֵּֽנוּ, מְנַע מַגֵּפָה מִנַּחֲלָתֶֽךָ.
⟪ from Your heritage. ⟨ the plague ⟨ withhold ⟨ our King, ⟨ Our Father,

אָבִֽינוּ מַלְכֵּֽנוּ, סְלַח וּמְחַל לְכָל עֲוֹנוֹתֵֽינוּ.
⟪ our iniquities. ⟨ all ⟨ and pardon ⟨ forgive ⟨ our King, ⟨ Our Father,

אָבִֽינוּ מַלְכֵּֽנוּ, מְחֵה וְהַעֲבֵר פְּשָׁעֵֽינוּ וְחַטֹּאתֵֽינוּ מִנֶּֽגֶד עֵינֶֽיךָ.
⟪ Your ⟨ from ⟨ and our ⟨ our willful ⟨ and ⟨ wipe ⟨ our King, ⟨ Our
eyes. before inadvertent sins sins remove away Father,

אָבִֽינוּ מַלְכֵּֽנוּ, מְחוֹק בְּרַחֲמֶֽיךָ הָרַבִּים כָּל שִׁטְרֵי חוֹבוֹתֵֽינוּ.
⟪ of our guilt. ⟨ records ⟨ all ⟨ that is ⟨ through Your ⟨ erase ⟨ our King, ⟨ Our
abundant compassion Father,

EACH OF THE NEXT NINE VERSES IS RECITED BY *CHAZZAN*, THEN CONGREGATION.

אָבִֽינוּ מַלְכֵּֽנוּ, הַחֲזִירֵֽנוּ בִּתְשׁוּבָה שְׁלֵמָה לְפָנֶֽיךָ.
⟪ before You. ⟨ that is complete ⟨ in repentance ⟨ cause us to return ⟨ our King, ⟨ Our Father,

אָבִֽינוּ מַלְכֵּֽנוּ, שְׁלַח רְפוּאָה שְׁלֵמָה לְחוֹלֵי עַמֶּֽךָ.
⟪ of Your people. ⟨ to the sick ⟨ that is complete ⟨ recovery ⟨ send ⟨ our King, ⟨ Our Father,

אָבִֽינוּ מַלְכֵּֽנוּ, קְרַע רֹֽועַ גְּזַר דִּינֵֽנוּ.
⟪ of our ⟨ of the ⟨ the evil ⟨ tear up ⟨ our King, ⟨ Our Father,
judgment. decree

אָבִֽינוּ מַלְכֵּֽנוּ, זָכְרֵֽנוּ בְּזִכָּרוֹן טוֹב לְפָנֶֽיךָ.
⟪ before You. ⟨ that is ⟨ with a ⟨ recall us ⟨ our King, ⟨ Our Father,
favorable memory

ON FAST DAYS (EXCEPT THE FAST OF GEDALIAH):	ROSH HASHANAH TO YOM KIPPUR:
אָבִֽינוּ מַלְכֵּֽנוּ, זָכְרֵֽנוּ	אָבִֽינוּ מַלְכֵּֽנוּ, כָּתְבֵֽנוּ
⟨ remember us ⟨ our King, ⟨ Our Father,	⟨ inscribe us ⟨ our King, ⟨ Our Father,
לְחַיִּים טוֹבִים.	בְּסֵֽפֶר חַיִּים טוֹבִים.
⟪ that is good. ⟨ for life	⟪ that is good. ⟨ of life ⟨ in the book
אָבִֽינוּ מַלְכֵּֽנוּ, זָכְרֵֽנוּ	אָבִֽינוּ מַלְכֵּֽנוּ, כָּתְבֵֽנוּ
⟨ remember us ⟨ our King, ⟨ Our Father,	⟨ inscribe us ⟨ our King, ⟨ Our Father,
לִגְאֻלָּה וִישׁוּעָה.	בְּסֵֽפֶר גְּאֻלָּה וִישׁוּעָה.
⟪ and salvation. ⟨ for redemption	⟪ and salvation. ⟨ of redemption ⟨ in the book

<table>
<tr><td align="center">ON FAST DAYS:</td><td align="center">ROSH HASHANAH TO YOM KIPPUR:</td></tr>
</table>

ON FAST DAYS:

אָבִינוּ מַלְכֵּנוּ, זָכְרֵנוּ
⟨ remember us ⟨ our King, ⟨ Our Father,

לְפַרְנָסָה וּלְכַלְכָּלָה.
« and support. ⟨ for sustenance

אָבִינוּ מַלְכֵּנוּ, זָכְרֵנוּ
⟨ remember us ⟨ our King, ⟨ Our Father,

לִזְכִיּוֹת.
« for merits.

אָבִינוּ מַלְכֵּנוּ, זָכְרֵנוּ
⟨ remember us ⟨ our King, ⟨ Our Father,

לִסְלִיחָה וּמְחִילָה.
« and pardon. ⟨ for forgiveness

ROSH HASHANAH TO YOM KIPPUR:

אָבִינוּ מַלְכֵּנוּ, כָּתְבֵנוּ
⟨ inscribe us ⟨ our King, ⟨ Our Father,

בְּסֵפֶר פַּרְנָסָה וְכַלְכָּלָה.
« and support. ⟨ of sustenance ⟨ in the book

אָבִינוּ מַלְכֵּנוּ, כָּתְבֵנוּ
⟨ inscribe us ⟨ our King, ⟨ Our Father,

בְּסֵפֶר זְכֻיּוֹת.
« of merits. ⟨ in the book

אָבִינוּ מַלְכֵּנוּ, כָּתְבֵנוּ
⟨ inscribe us ⟨ our King, ⟨ Our Father,

בְּסֵפֶר סְלִיחָה וּמְחִילָה.
« and pardon. ⟨ of forgiveness ⟨ in the book

END OF RESPONSIVE READING. ALL CONTINUE:

אָבִינוּ מַלְכֵּנוּ, הַצְמַח לָנוּ יְשׁוּעָה בְּקָרוֹב.
« soon. ⟨ salvation ⟨ for us ⟨ make sprout ⟨ our King, ⟨ Our Father,

אָבִינוּ מַלְכֵּנוּ, הָרֵם קֶרֶן יִשְׂרָאֵל עַמֶּךָ.
« Your people. ⟨ of Israel, ⟨ the pride ⟨ raise high ⟨ our King, ⟨ Our Father,

אָבִינוּ מַלְכֵּנוּ, הָרֵם קֶרֶן מְשִׁיחֶךָ.
« of Your Anointed. ⟨ the pride ⟨ raise high ⟨ our King, ⟨ Our Father,

אָבִינוּ מַלְכֵּנוּ, מַלֵּא יָדֵינוּ מִבִּרְכוֹתֶיךָ.
« from Your blessings. ⟨ our hands ⟨ fill ⟨ our King, ⟨ Our Father,

אָבִינוּ מַלְכֵּנוּ, מַלֵּא אֲסָמֵינוּ שָׂבָע.
« with abundance. ⟨ our storehouses ⟨ fill ⟨ our King, ⟨ Our Father,

אָבִינוּ מַלְכֵּנוּ, שְׁמַע קוֹלֵנוּ, חוּס וְרַחֵם עָלֵינוּ.
« on us. ⟨ and have mercy ⟨ have pity ⟨ our voice, ⟨ hear ⟨ our King, ⟨ Our Father,

אָבִינוּ מַלְכֵּנוּ, קַבֵּל בְּרַחֲמִים וּבְרָצוֹן אֶת תְּפִלָּתֵנוּ.
« our prayer. ⟨ and favor ⟨ with compassion ⟨ accept ⟨ our King, ⟨ Our Father,

אָבִינוּ מַלְכֵּנוּ, פְּתַח שַׁעֲרֵי שָׁמַיִם לִתְפִלָּתֵנוּ.
« to our prayer. ⟨ of heaven ⟨ the gates ⟨ open ⟨ our King, ⟨ Our Father,

אָבִינוּ מַלְכֵּנוּ, זְכוֹר כִּי עָפָר אֲנָחְנוּ.
« are we. ⟨ dust ⟨ that ⟨ remember ⟨ our King, ⟨ Our Father,

אָבִינוּ מַלְכֵּנוּ, נָא אַל תְּשִׁיבֵנוּ רֵיקָם מִלְּפָנֶיךָ.
« from before ⟨ empty- ⟨ turn us away ⟨ do ⟨ please ⟨ our King, ⟨ Our Father,
You. handed not

אָבִינוּ מַלְכֵּנוּ, תְּהֵא הַשָּׁעָה הַזֹּאת שְׁעַת רַחֲמִים וְעֵת רָצוֹן

Our Father, ⟩ our King, ⟩ may ⟩ this moment ⟩ be a ⟩ of ⟩ of ⟩ and a ⟩ of
moment compassion time favor

מִלְּפָנֶיךָ.

before You. ≪

אָבִינוּ מַלְכֵּנוּ, חֲמוֹל עָלֵינוּ וְעַל עוֹלָלֵינוּ וְטַפֵּנוּ.

Our Father, ⟩ our King, ⟩ take pity ⟩ upon us, ⟩ and upon ⟩ our children ⟩ and our infants. ≪

אָבִינוּ מַלְכֵּנוּ, עֲשֵׂה לְמַעַן הֲרוּגִים עַל שֵׁם קָדְשֶׁךָ.

Our Father, ⟩ our King, ⟩ act ⟩ for the ⟩ of those who ⟩ the ⟩ for ⟩ of Your ≪
sake were murdered Name Holiness.

אָבִינוּ מַלְכֵּנוּ, עֲשֵׂה לְמַעַן טְבוּחִים עַל יִחוּדֶךָ.

Our Father, ⟩ our King, ⟩ act ⟩ for the ⟩ of those who ⟩ for ⟩ Your ≪
sake were slaughtered Oneness.

אָבִינוּ מַלְכֵּנוּ, עֲשֵׂה לְמַעַן בָּאֵי בָאֵשׁ וּבַמַּיִם עַל קִדּוּשׁ שְׁמֶךָ.

Our ⟩ our King, ⟩ act ⟩ for the ⟩ of those ⟩ into ⟩ and ⟩ for ⟩ the sanc- ⟩ of Your ≪
Father, sake who enter fire water tification Name.

אָבִינוּ מַלְכֵּנוּ, נְקוֹם לְעֵינֵינוּ נִקְמַת דַּם עֲבָדֶיךָ הַשָּׁפוּךְ.

Our Father, ⟩ our King, ⟩ avenge ⟩ before ⟩ the ⟩ of the ⟩ of Your ⟩ that was ≪
our eyes revenge blood servants spilled.

אָבִינוּ מַלְכֵּנוּ, עֲשֵׂה לְמַעַנְךָ אִם לֹא לְמַעֲנֵנוּ.

Our King, ⟩ our King, ⟩ act ⟩ for Your sake ⟩ if ⟩ not ⟩ for our sake. ≪

אָבִינוּ מַלְכֵּנוּ, עֲשֵׂה לְמַעַנְךָ וְהוֹשִׁיעֵנוּ.

Our Father, ⟩ our King, ⟩ act ⟩ for Your sake ⟩ and save us. ≪

אָבִינוּ מַלְכֵּנוּ, עֲשֵׂה לְמַעַן רַחֲמֶיךָ הָרַבִּים.

Our Father, ⟩ our King, ⟩ act ⟩ for the ⟩ of Your ⟩ that is ≪
sake compassion abundant.

אָבִינוּ מַלְכֵּנוּ, עֲשֵׂה לְמַעַן שִׁמְךָ הַגָּדוֹל הַגִּבּוֹר וְהַנּוֹרָא,

Our Father, ⟩ our King, ⟩ act ⟩ for the ⟩ of Your ⟩ that is ⟩ mighty, ⟩ and ⟩
sake Name great, awesome

שֶׁנִּקְרָא עָלֵינוּ.

that is proclaimed ⟩ upon us. ≪

❖ אָבִינוּ מַלְכֵּנוּ, חָנֵּנוּ וַעֲנֵנוּ, כִּי אֵין בָּנוּ מַעֲשִׂים, עֲשֵׂה

Our Father, ⟩ our King, ⟩ be gracious ⟩ and ⟩ though ⟩ we have no ⟩ worthy ≪ treat ⟩
with us answer us, deeds;

עִמָּנוּ צְדָקָה וָחֶסֶד וְהוֹשִׁיעֵנוּ.

us ⟩ with charity ⟩ and kindness, ⟩ and save us. ≪

ON MONDAY AND THURSDAY, CONTINUE וְהוּא רַחוּם, *HE, THE MERCIFUL ONE* . . . (P. 182).
ON OTHER DAYS CONTINUE שׁוֹמֵר יִשְׂרָאֵל, *O GUARDIAN OF ISRAEL* . . . (P. 194).
ON DAYS WHEN *TACHANUN* IS NOT RECITED THE *CHAZZAN* RECITES חֲצִי קַדִּישׁ, *HALF KADDISH* (P. 197).

TACHANUN FOR MONDAY AND THURSDAY / תחנון לשני וחמישי

REMAIN STANDING FROM THE BEGINNING OF וְהוּא רַחוּם UNTIL THE END OF *TACHANUN* (P. 197).

וְהוּא רַחוּם* יְכַפֵּר עָוֹן וְלֹא יַשְׁחִית, וְהִרְבָּה

⟨ frequently ⟪ destroy; ⟨ and does ⟨ of ⟨ is ⟨ the Merciful ⟨ He,
not iniquity forgiving One,*

לְהָשִׁיב אַפּוֹ וְלֹא יָעִיר כָּל חֲמָתוֹ.¹ אַתָּה יהוה,

⟨ Hashem, ⟨ You, ⟪ His wrath. ⟨ all of ⟨ arousing ⟨ not ⟪ His anger, ⟨ He withdraws

לֹא תִכְלָא רַחֲמֶיךָ מִמֶּנּוּ, חַסְדְּךָ וַאֲמִתְּךָ תָּמִיד

⟨ always ⟨ and Your ⟨ may Your ⟪ from us; ⟨ Your mercy ⟨ withhold ⟨ do not
truth kindness

יִצְּרוּנוּ.² הוֹשִׁיעֵנוּ יהוה אֱלֹהֵינוּ וְקַבְּצֵנוּ מִן הַגּוֹיִם,

⟪ among ⟨ from ⟨ and gather ⟨ our God, ⟨ Hashem, ⟨ Save us, ⟪ protect us.
the nations, us

לְהוֹדוֹת לְשֵׁם קָדְשֶׁךָ, לְהִשְׁתַּבֵּחַ בִּתְהִלָּתֶךָ.³

⟪ in Your praise. ⟨ and to glory ⟨ of Your holiness, ⟨ the Name ⟨ to thank

(1) *Psalms* 78:38. (2) Cf. 40:12. (3) 106:47.

❧ תַּחֲנוּן לְשֵׁנִי וַחֲמִישִׁי /
Tachanun for Monday and Thursday

On Mondays and Thursdays, the *Tachanun* service is augmented with additional supplications following the *falling on the face*. The choice of these two days for special prayers is based on one of the earliest events in Israel's national history. According to the Midrashic tradition, Moses ascended Mount Sinai to receive the Second Tablets on Thursday, the first day of Elul, and descended forty days later on Monday, Yom Kippur. Since those were days when God accepted Israel's repentance for the sin of the Golden Calf, and demonstrated His love for Israel with the greatest of all gifts — the Torah, in the form of the Second Tablets — Monday and Thursday remain days of Divine mercy (see *Bava Kamma* 82a; *Tos.* s.v. כדי). Ezra instituted that Rabbinical courts should convene on Monday and Thursday, and Kabbalistic literature teaches that on these days the Heavenly Court judges man. Consequently, extra supplications were introduced into the *Tachanun* recited each Monday and Thursday.

These prayers must be said while standing and with great feeling.

Machzor Kol Bo and others record a tradition regarding the authorship of these prayers. Three elders, Rabbi Shmuel, Rabbi Binyamin, and Rabbi Yosef, were set adrift on rudderless boats by the Romans after the destruction of Jerusalem. They landed on a distant shore where they were persecuted by the local ruler. Each of the three composed a prayer requesting the easing of their plight. God heeded their supplications: the ruler died and was succeeded by a benevolent king who treated the three with respect and kindness. Seeing that their prayers had been pleasing to God, they distributed copies of the text to other Jewish communities, which added them to the *Tachanun* of Monday and Thursday.

❧ וְהוּא רַחוּם — *He, the Merciful One.* In a mystical comment on this verse, *Zohar* teaches that God, in His mercy, does not allow the forces of impurity to prevent our prayers from reaching Him. Were they to succeed, we could never hope to attain forgiveness.

אִם עֲוֹנוֹת תִּשְׁמָר* יָהּ, אֲדֹנָי מִי יַעֲמֹד. כִּי עִמְּךָ

‹ with ‹ For « could ‹ who ‹ O « O ‹ You ‹ iniquities ‹ If
You survive? Lord, God, preserve,*

הַסְּלִיחָה, לְמַעַן תִּוָּרֵא.¹ לֹא כַחֲטָאֵינוּ תַּעֲשֶׂה

‹ shall You ‹ according to ‹ Not « You may ‹ so that « is forgiveness,
deal our sins be feared.

לָנוּ, וְלֹא כַעֲוֹנוֹתֵינוּ תִּגְמֹל עָלֵינוּ.² אִם עֲוֹנֵינוּ

‹ our ‹ If « us. ‹ shall You ‹ according to ‹ nor « with
iniquities repay our iniquities us,

עָנוּ בָנוּ, יהוה עֲשֵׂה לְמַעַן שְׁמֶךָ.*³ זְכֹר רַחֲמֶיךָ

‹ Your ‹ Remember « of Your ‹ for the ‹ act ‹ O ‹ against ‹ testify
mercies, Name.* sake HASHEM, us,

יהוה וַחֲסָדֶיךָ, כִּי מֵעוֹלָם הֵמָּה.⁴ יַעֲנֵנוּ יהוה

‹ May HASHEM « are they. ‹ eternal ‹ for ‹ and Your ‹ HASHEM,
answer us kindnesses,

בְּיוֹם צָרָה, יְשַׂגְּבֵנוּ שֵׁם אֱלֹהֵי יַעֲקֹב.⁵ יהוה

‹ HASHEM, « of Jacob. ‹ of the God ‹ by the ‹ may we be made « of ‹ on the
Name impregnable distress; day

הוֹשִׁיעָה, הַמֶּלֶךְ יַעֲנֵנוּ בְיוֹם קָרְאֵנוּ.⁶ אָבִינוּ

‹ Our Father, « we call. ‹ on the day ‹ answer us ‹ May the King « save!

מַלְכֵּנוּ, חָנֵּנוּ וַעֲנֵנוּ, כִּי אֵין בָּנוּ מַעֲשִׂים, עֲשֵׂה

‹ deal « worthy deeds; ‹ we have ‹ though « and ‹ be gracious ‹ our King,
no answer us, with us

עִמָּנוּ צְדָקָה כְּרֹב רַחֲמֶיךָ, וְהוֹשִׁיעֵנוּ לְמַעַן שְׁמֶךָ.

« of Your ‹ for the ‹ and save us « of Your ‹ according to ‹ with ‹ with us
Name. sake mercy, the abundance charity

---

(1) *Psalms* 130:3-4. (2) Cf. 103:10. (3) *Jeremiah* 14:7. (4) *Psalms* 25:6. (5) Cf. 20:2. (6) 20:10.

אִם עֲוֹנוֹת תִּשְׁמָר — *If iniquities You preserve.*
Because of man's human frailties he cannot
survive unless God is willing to overlook his sins
to some degree. The next verse continues that
since we are fully aware that only God — not an
angel or any other power — can forgive, we
stand in awe of Him (*Iyun Tefillah*).

לְמַעַן שְׁמֶךָ — *For the sake of Your Name.* In a
theme repeated often in *Tachanun* and elsewhere, we make the point that if Israel is
permitted to suffer excessively, God's *Own*
Name is desecrated because it appears as
though He is powerless to help His chosen
ones. In pleading for Israel after the sins of

אֲדוֹנֵינוּ אֱלֹהֵינוּ, שְׁמַע קוֹל תַּחֲנוּנֵינוּ, וּזְכָר

‹ recall ‹‹   of our   ‹ the ‹ hear ‹ our God,   ‹ Our Master,
     supplications;   sound

לֶנוּ אֶת בְּרִית אֲבוֹתֵינוּ וְהוֹשִׁיעֵנוּ לְמַעַן שְׁמֶךָ.

‹‹ of Your ‹ for the ‹ and save us ‹‹   of our   ‹ the covenant ‹ for us
Name.   sake   forefathers,

וְעַתָּה, אֲדֹנָי אֱלֹהֵינוּ,* אֲשֶׁר הוֹצֵאתָ אֶת עַמְּךָ

‹ Your people ‹ have taken out ‹ You Who ‹ our God,* ‹ O Lord, ‹ And now,

מֵאֶרֶץ מִצְרַיִם בְּיָד חֲזָקָה וַתַּעַשׂ לְךָ שֵׁם

‹ renown ‹   for   ‹ and made ‹‹ with a strong hand, ‹ of Egypt ‹   from
     Yourself   the land

כְּיוֹם הַזֶּה, חָטָאנוּ רָשָׁעְנוּ. אֲדֹנָי, כְּכָל צִדְקֹתֶיךָ,

‹‹   Your   ‹ in keeping ‹ O Lord, ‹‹ and we have ‹ — we have ‹‹ as [clear as]
righteousness,   with all   acted wickedly.   sinned   this day

יָשָׁב נָא אַפְּךָ וַחֲמָתְךָ מֵעִירְךָ יְרוּשָׁלַיִם הַר

‹ the   ‹ Jerusalem, ‹ from Your ‹ and Your ‹ Your ‹ please, ‹ with-
mountain   City   wrath   anger   draw,

קָדְשֶׁךָ, כִּי בַחֲטָאֵינוּ וּבַעֲוֹנוֹת אֲבֹתֵינוּ, יְרוּשָׁלַיִם

‹ Jerusalem ‹‹   of our   ‹ and because of ‹ because of ‹ for ‹‹ of Your
         ancestors,   the iniquities   our sins   holiness;

וְעַמְּךָ לְחֶרְפָּה לְכָל סְבִיבֹתֵינוּ. וְעַתָּה שְׁמַע

‹ pay heed, ‹ And now, ‹‹ those around us. ‹ of all ‹ have become ‹ and Your
                      the scorn   people

אֱלֹהֵינוּ אֶל תְּפִלַּת עַבְדְּךָ וְאֶל תַּחֲנוּנָיו, וְהָאֵר

‹ and   ‹‹   his   ‹ and to ‹ of Your ‹ the prayer ‹ to   ‹ our God,
shine   supplications,   servant

---

the Golden Calf and the spies, Moses also argued that if Israel were to perish, the Egyptians would claim that it was because God did not intend, or was unable, to bring them into the Land of Israel (*Exodus* 32:12, *Numbers* 14:16).

וְעַתָּה אֲדֹנָי אֱלֹהֵינוּ — *And now, O Lord, our God.* The next five verses are the end of a long, sixteen-verse prayer recited by Daniel (9:4-19).

When Daniel came to fear that the Babylonian exile might never end, he pleaded for God's guidance and help. The prayer had three components that are familiar parts of Jewish supplications: praise of God, confession, and the prayer itself. This paragraph of *Tachanun* is concluded with the last three verses of Daniel's confession. The next paragraph begins with his two verses of prayer.

פָּנֶיךָ עַל מִקְדָּשְׁךָ הַשָּׁמֵם, לְמַעַן אֲדֹנָי.*¹

》 of the Lord.* 〈   for the 〈   which is 〈   Your   〈 upon 〈 Your
sake   desolate,   Sanctuary,   countenance

הַטֵּה אֱלֹהַי אָזְנְךָ* וּשְׁמָע, פְּקַח עֵינֶיךָ וּרְאֵה

〈 and see 〈 Your eyes 〈 open 》 and listen; 〈 Your ear,* 〈 my God, 〈 Incline,

שֹׁמְמֹתֵינוּ, וְהָעִיר אֲשֶׁר נִקְרָא שִׁמְךָ עָלֶיהָ, כִּי

〈 for 》 upon; 〈 Your Name is proclaimed 〈 which 〈 and the city 》 our desolation,

לֹא עַל צִדְקֹתֵינוּ אֲנַחְנוּ מַפִּילִים תַּחֲנוּנֵינוּ

〈 our supplications 〈 cast 〈 do we 〈 of our righteousness 〈 because 〈 not

לְפָנֶיךָ, כִּי עַל רַחֲמֶיךָ הָרַבִּים. אֲדֹנָי שְׁמָעָה,

》 heed; 〈 O Lord, 》 which is 〈 of Your 〈 because 〈 but 》 before You;
abundant.   compassion,

אֲדֹנָי סְלָחָה, אֲדֹנָי הַקְשִׁיבָה, וַעֲשֵׂה, אַל

〈 do not 》 and act, 〈 be attentive 〈 O Lord, 》 forgive; 〈 O Lord,

תְּאַחַר, לְמַעַנְךָ אֱלֹהַי, כִּי שִׁמְךָ נִקְרָא* עַל

〈 upon 〈 is proclaimed* 〈 Your Name 〈 for 》 my God, 〈 for Your sake, 》 delay;

עִירְךָ וְעַל עַמֶּךָ.² אָבִינוּ אָב הָרַחֲמָן,* הַרְאֵנוּ

〈 – show us 》 Who is merciful* 〈 the 〈 Our Father, 》 Your 〈 and 〈 Your
Father   people. upon   City

אוֹת לְטוֹבָה וְקַבֵּץ נְפוּצֹתֵינוּ מֵאַרְבַּע כַּנְפוֹת

〈 corners 〈 from the four 〈 our dispersed ones 〈 and gather in 》 for good, 〈 an omen

---

(1) *Daniel* 9:15-17. (2) 9:18-19.

לְמַעַן אֲדֹנָי — *For the sake of the Lord*. In a
homiletical interpretation the Sages say that this
refers to Abraham, who preached to an un-
knowing world that only Hashem is the true
Lord [אֲדֹנָי]. Thus: "Help us for the sake of the
one who proclaimed You as the Lord" (*Berachos*
7b).

◆§ הַטֵּה אֱלֹהַי אָזְנְךָ — *Incline, my God, Your ear*.
Despite the sins we have just confessed, we
plead with God to heed our call. Even if we are
not deserving, at least let Him help us for the

sake of His Name that is desecrated by the
destruction of His city and the persecution of
His people.

כִּי שִׁמְךָ נִקְרָא — *For Your Name is proclaimed*.
Each nation has an angel appointed to oversee
its fortunes, but God Himself maintains personal dominion over Israel and Jerusalem
(*Tikkunei Zohar*).

הָאָב הָרַחֲמָן — *The Father Who is merciful*. We
do not claim to be worthy, but a father loves his
children even when they stray.

הָאָרֶץ, יַכִּירוּ וְיֵדְעוּ כָּל הַגּוֹיִם, כִּי אַתָּה יהוה
‹ are ‹ You ‹ that ≪ the ‹ – all ≪ and let ‹ let them ≪ of the
HASHEM, nations – them realize recognize world;

אֱלֹהֵינוּ. וְעַתָּה יהוה אָבִינוּ אָתָּה, אֲנַחְנוּ הַחֹמֶר
‹ are the clay ‹ we ≪ are You; ‹ our Father ‹ HASHEM, ‹ And now, ≪ our God.

וְאַתָּה יֹצְרֵנוּ, וּמַעֲשֵׂה יָדְךָ כֻּלָּנוּ. הוֹשִׁיעֵנוּ לְמַעַן
‹ for the ‹ Save us ≪ are we ‹ of Your ‹ and the work ‹ are our ‹ and You
sake all. hands Molder,

שְׁמֶךָ, אָבִינוּ מַלְכֵּנוּ צוּרֵנוּ וְגוֹאֲלֵנוּ. חוּסָה* יהוה
‹ HASHEM, ‹ Have pity,* ≪ and our ‹ our Rock, ‹ our King, ‹ our Father, ≪ of Your
Redeemer. Name,

עַל עַמֶּךָ וְאַל תִּתֵּן נַחֲלָתְךָ לְחֶרְפָּה לִמְשָׁל בָּם
‹ that they be ≪ for scorn, ‹ Your heritage ‹ give ‹ do not ≪ Your ‹ on
ruled over over people;

גּוֹיִם, לָמָּה יֹאמְרוּ בָעַמִּים, אַיֵּה אֱלֹהֵיהֶם.²
≪ is their God? ‹ Where ≪ among the ‹ should ‹ Why ≪ by
peoples, they say nations.

יְדַעְנוּ יהוה כִּי חָטָאנוּ וְאֵין מִי יַעֲמֹד בַּעֲדֵנוּ,
≪ for us; ‹ can ‹ who ‹ and there ‹ we have ‹ that ‹ HASHEM, ‹ We know,
stand up is no one sinned.

אֶלָּא שִׁמְךָ הַגָּדוֹל יַעֲמָד לָנוּ בְּעֵת צָרָה. יְדַעְנוּ
‹ We ≪ of ‹ in time ‹ for us ‹ will ‹ Your great Name ‹ only
know distress. stand up

כִּי אֵין בָּנוּ מַעֲשִׂים, צְדָקָה עֲשֵׂה עִמָּנוּ לְמַעַן
‹ for the ‹ with us ‹ deal ‹ with ≪ any worthy ‹ in us ‹ there ‹ that
sake charity deeds; are not

שְׁמֶךָ. כְּרַחֵם אָב עַל בָּנִים, כֵּן תְּרַחֵם יהוה
‹ HASHEM, ‹ have mercy, ‹ so ≪ his ‹ toward ‹ a father ‹ As merciful ≪ of Your
children, is as Name.

---

(1) *Isaiah* 64:7. (2) *Joel* 2:17.

חוּסָה — *Have pity.* This term expresses the idea that a craftsman always has special regard for the object he has created. Since we are God's handiwork — as the previous verse puts it, we are the clay and He is our Molder — He should not permit His Own product to be destroyed.

עָלֵינוּ,¹ וְהוֹשִׁיעֵנוּ לְמַעַן שְׁמֶךָ. חֲמֹל עַל עַמֶּךָ,

《 Your 〈 on 〈 Have 《 of Your 〈 for the 〈 and save us 《 on us,
people; 　　compassion 　Name. 　　sake

רַחֵם עַל נַחֲלָתֶךָ, חְוּסָה נָא כְּרֹב רַחֲמֶיךָ.

《 of Your 〈 according to 〈 we beg 〈 have 《 Your heritage; 〈 on 〈 have
mercy. 　　the abundance 　You, 　pity, 　　　　　　　　　mercy

חָנֵּנוּ מַלְכֵּנוּ וַעֲנֵנוּ, כִּי לְךָ יהוה הַצְּדָקָה, עֹשֵׂה

〈 You 《 is the 〈 HASHEM, 〈 Yours, 〈 for 《 and 〈 our King, 〈 Be gracious
Who do 　righteousness, 　　　　　　　　　　answer us, 　　　　　with us,

נִפְלָאוֹת בְּכָל עֵת.

《 times. 〈 at all 〈 wonders

הַבֶּט נָא,* רַחֵם נָא, וְהוֹשִׁיעָה נָא צֹאן

〈 the 〈 we beg 〈 and save, 〈 we beg 〈 have 〈 we beg 〈 Look,
flock 　You, 　　　　　　　You, 　mercy, 　　You,*

מַרְעִיתֶךָ, וְאַל יִמְשָׁל בָּנוּ קֶצֶף, כִּי לְךָ יהוה

〈 HASHEM, 〈 Yours, 〈 for 《 by anger, 〈 let us not be dominated 《 of Your pasture;

הַיְשׁוּעָה. בְּךָ תוֹחַלְתֵּנוּ, אֱלְוֹהַּ סְלִיחוֹת, אָנָּא

〈 please, 《 of forgiveness; 〈 O God 〈 is our hope, 〈 In You 《 is salvation.

סְלַח נָא, כִּי אֵל טוֹב וְסַלָּח אָתָּה.²

《 are You. 〈 and 〈 Who is 〈 God 〈 for 《 now, 〈 forgive
forgiving 　good

אָנָּא* מֶלֶךְ חַנּוּן וְרַחוּם,³ זְכֹר וְהַבֶּט לִבְרִית

〈 at the 〈 and look 〈 remember 《 and com- 〈 Who is 〈 O King 〈 Please,*
Covenant 　　　　　　　　passionate, 　gracious

---

(1) Cf. *Psalms* 103:13. (2) Cf. *Nehemiah* 9:31. (3) Alternate text: רַחוּם וְחַנּוּן.

הַבֶּט נָא — *Look, we beg You.* This prayer for
compassion stresses our helplessness and total
dependence on Him. It introduces the concept
that we are the "sheep of God's pasture." Like
sheep we depend totally on the guidance and
protection of our Shepherd.

אָנָּא — *Please.* This supplication emphasizes
the experiences of the Patriarchs, Abraham and
Isaac. It singles out the בְּרִית בֵּין הַבְּתָרִים,
Covenant Between the Parts (*Genesis* Ch. 15),
and the *Akeidah* of Isaac (*Genesis* Ch. 22; see
commentary above, p. 33). In the Covenant, God

בֵּין הַבְּתָרִים, וְתֵרָאֶה לְפָנֶיךָ עֲקֵדַת יָחִיד.*

« of the only [son].* ‹ the binding ‹ before You ‹ may there appear « the Parts; ‹ between

וּלְמַעַן יִשְׂרָאֵל אָבִינוּ, אַל תַּעַזְבֵנוּ אָבִינוּ, וְאַל

‹ do not « our Father; ‹ forsake us, ‹ do not ‹ our father, ‹ of Israel, ‹ And for the sake

תִּטְּשֵׁנוּ מַלְכֵּנוּ, וְאַל תִּשְׁכָּחֵנוּ יוֹצְרֵנוּ, וְאַל תַּעַשׂ

‹ cause ‹ and do not « our Molder; ‹ forget us, ‹ do not « our King; ‹ cast us away,

עִמָּנוּ כָּלָה בְּגָלוּתֵינוּ, כִּי אֵל מֶלֶךְ חַנּוּן וְרַחוּם

‹ and compassionate ‹ Who is gracious ‹ the King, ‹ God, ‹ for « in our exile, ‹ annihilation ‹ our

אָתָּה.¹

« are You.

אֵין כָּמוֹךָ* חַנּוּן וְרַחוּם יהוה אֱלֹהֵינוּ, אֵין

‹ There is none ‹‹ our God. ‹ HASHEM, ‹ and compassionate, ‹ gracious « like You,* ‹ There is none

כָּמוֹךָ אֵל אֶרֶךְ אַפַּיִם וְרַב חֶסֶד וֶאֱמֶת. הוֹשִׁיעֵנוּ

‹ Save us « and truth. ‹ in kindness ‹ and is abundant ‹ to anger ‹ Who is slow ‹ God ‹ like You,

וְרַחֲמֵנוּ בְּרַחֲמֶיךָ הָרַבִּים, מֵרַעַשׁ וּמֵרְגֶז² הַצִּילֵנוּ.

« rescue us. ‹ and trembling ‹ from quaking « that is abundant; ‹ with Your mercy ‹ and be merciful with us

(1) Cf. *Nehemiah* 9:31. (2) Cf. *Job* 39:24, *Ezekiel* 12:18, *Psalms* 77:19.

sealed a treaty with Abraham that his descendants would inherit *Eretz Yisrael* and always be God's nation. The covenant was made in response to Abraham's wish to know how he could be sure that sinfulness or changing conditions would not prevent his offspring from inheriting the Land. Thus, it remains an eternal assurance to Israel, despite exile and oppression.

עֲקֵדַת יָחִיד — *The binding of the only [son].* In commanding Abraham to bind Isaac on the altar, God referred to Isaac as אֶת בִּנְךָ אֶת יְחִידְךָ, *your only son.* The Sages teach that the memory of the *Akeidah* always remains before God as a merit

for Isaac's offspring. Thus, the events mentioned here — the Covenant and the *Akeidah* — have spiritual effects that transcend time and distance. [For commentary and Overviews, see ArtScroll *Bereishis/Genesis*, Ch. 22.]

❧ אֵין כָּמוֹךָ — *There is none like You.* This supplication consists mainly of verses from various parts of Scripture. Their unifying theme is an acknowledgment that we cannot justify our deeds. Nevertheless we have confidence that — against all odds and against our enemies' confident predictions of our doom — God's mercy is constant and He will help us find the way to repentance and forgiveness.

זְכֹר לַעֲבָדֶיךָ לְאַבְרָהָם לְיִצְחָק וּלְיַעֲקֹב, אַל תֵּפֶן

‹ pay ‹ do ‹‹ and Jacob; ‹ Isaac, ‹ Abraham, ‹ Your ‹ Remember
regard　not　　　　　　　　　　　　　　　　　　servants,

אֶל קְשִׁי הָעָם הַזֶּה וְאֶל רִשְׁעוֹ וְאֶל חַטָּאתוֹ.¹ שׁוּב

‹ With- ‹‹ its ‹ and to ‹ its ‹ and to ‹ of this ‹ the ‹ to
draw　sinfulness.　　wickedness　　people　stubbornness

מֵחֲרוֹן אַפֶּךָ וְהִנָּחֵם עַל הָרָעָה לְעַמֶּךָ.² וְהָסֵר

‹ Remove ‹‹ [meant] for ‹ the evil ‹ from ‹ and relent ‹ anger ‹ from Your
Your people.　　　　　　　　　　　　　　　　　flaring

מִמֶּנּוּ מַכַּת הַמָּוֶת כִּי רַחוּם אָתָּה, כִּי כֵן דַּרְכֶּךָ,

‹‹ is Your ‹ such ‹ for ‹‹ are You; ‹ compas- ‹ for ‹‹ that is ‹ the ‹ from us
manner,　　　　　　　sionate　　　deadly,　plague

לַעֲשׂוֹת חֶסֶד חִנָּם בְּכָל דּוֹר וָדוֹר. חוּסָה יהוה

‹ Hashem, ‹ Have ‹‹ after ‹ gener- ‹ through- ‹ un- ‹ kind- ‹ to do
pity,　generation.　ation　out　deserved　ness

עַל עַמֶּךָ וְהַצִּילֵנוּ מִזַּעְמֶךָ, וְהָסֵר מִמֶּנּוּ מַכַּת

‹ the ‹ from us ‹ remove ‹‹ from Your ‹ and ‹‹ Your ‹ upon
plague　　　　　wrath;　rescue us　people,

הַמַּגֵּפָה וּגְזֵרָה קָשָׁה, כִּי אַתָּה שׁוֹמֵר יִשְׂרָאֵל.

‹‹ of Israel. ‹ are the ‹ You ‹ for ‹‹ that are ‹ and decrees ‹ of disease
Guardian　　　　　　harsh,

לְךָ אֲדֹנָי הַצְּדָקָה וְלָנוּ בֹּשֶׁת הַפָּנִים.³ מַה

‹ What ‹‹ facedness. ‹ is shame- ‹ and ours ‹‹ is righteousness, ‹ O Lord, ‹ Yours,

נִתְאוֹנֵן, וּמַה נֹּאמַר, מַה נְּדַבֵּר, וּמַה נִּצְטַדָּק.⁴

‹‹ justification ‹ What ‹ can we ‹ What ‹‹ can ‹ What ‹‹ complaint
can we offer?　declare?　we say?　can we make?

נַחְפְּשָׂה דְרָכֵינוּ וְנַחְקֹרָה, וְנָשׁוּבָה אֵלֶיךָ, כִּי

‹ for ‹‹ to You, ‹ and return ‹ and investigate them, ‹ our ways ‹ Let us examine

יְמִינְךָ פְּשׁוּטָה לְקַבֵּל שָׁבִים. אָנָּא יהוה הוֹשִׁיעָה

‹ save ‹ Hashem, ‹ Please, ‹‹ those who ‹ to accept ‹ is extended ‹ Your right
return.　hand

---

(1) *Deuteronomy* 9:27. (2) *Exodus* 32:12. (3) *Daniel* 9:7.
(4) Cf. *Genesis* 44:16. (5) Cf. *Lamentations* 3:40.

נָא, אָנָּא יהוה הַצְלִיחָה נָא.¹ אָנָּא יהוה עֲנֵנוּ
‹ answer us ‹ Hashem, ‹ Please, « now! ‹ bring success ‹ Hashem, ‹ please, « now;

בְּיוֹם קָרְאֵנוּ.² לְךָ יהוה חִכִּינוּ, לְךָ יהוה קִוִּינוּ,
« we have ‹ Hashem, ‹ for « we have ‹ Hashem, ‹ For « we call. ‹ on the
hoped;   You,   waited;   You,   day

לְךָ יהוה נְיַחֵל. אַל תֶּחֱשֶׁה וּתְעַנֵּנוּ, כִּי נֶאֱמוּ
‹ declared ‹ for « thereby letting ‹ be silent, ‹ Do « we do ‹ Hashem, ‹ for
         us suffer,   not   yearn.   You,

גּוֹיִם, אָבְדָה תִקְוָתָם. כָּל בֶּרֶךְ לְךָ תִכְרַע וְכָל
‹ and « will bend, ‹ to You ‹ knee ‹ Every « is their hope. ‹ Lost « have the
every   nations:

קוֹמָה לְפָנֶיךָ לְבַד תִּשְׁתַּחֲוֶה.
« will bow down. ‹ alone ‹ before You ‹ erect
                                      [spine]

הַפּוֹתֵחַ יָד* בִּתְשׁוּבָה לְקַבֵּל פּוֹשְׁעִים
‹ transgressors ‹ to accept ‹ for repentance, ‹ a hand* ‹ You Who open

וְחַטָּאִים, נִבְהֲלָה נַפְשֵׁנוּ מֵרֹב עִצְּבוֹנֵנוּ, אַל
‹ do not « of our ‹ from the ‹ is our soul ‹ — confounded « and
       depression;   abundance   sinners

תִּשְׁכָּחֵנוּ נֶצַח. קוֹמָה וְהוֹשִׁיעֵנוּ. אַל תִּשְׁפֹּךְ
‹ pour ‹ Do not « and save us. ‹ Arise « eternally. ‹ forget us

חֲרוֹנְךָ עָלֵינוּ, כִּי אֲנַחְנוּ עַמְּךָ בְּנֵי בְרִיתֶךָ. אֵל,
‹ O God, « of Your ‹ the ‹ are Your ‹ we ‹ for « upon us, ‹ Your anger
       covenant. members people,

הַבִּיטָה דַּל כְּבוֹדֵנוּ בַּגּוֹיִם, וְשִׁקְּצוּנוּ כְּטֻמְאַת
‹ like the ‹ and how they are « among ‹ of our ‹ the impov- ‹ look upon
   impurity   repulsed by us   the nations,   honor   erishment

---

(1) *Psalms* 118:25. (2) Cf. 20:10.

הַפּוֹתֵחַ יָד — *You Who open a hand.* Some-times a person has become so sinful that there is no reason to think that he can still repent. Even then, however, there is hope. As the Sages put it, God opens a place for the penitent beneath His Own Heavenly Throne, as it were. The point is that God's mercy exceeds all imaginable boundaries (*Etz Yosef*).

הַנִּדָּה. עַד מָתַי עֻזְּךָ בַּשְּׁבִי,* וְתִפְאַרְתְּךָ בְּיַד צָר.¹

≪ of the ⟨ in the ⟨ and Your ≪ be in ⟨ will Your ⟨ when ⟨ Until ≪ of the
oppressor? hand splendor captivity* strength menstruant.

עוֹרְרָה גְבוּרָתְךָ וְהוֹשִׁיעֵנוּ לְמַעַן שְׁמֶךָ. אַל

⟨ Let ≪ of Your ⟨ for the ⟨ and save us ⟨ Your might ⟨ Arouse
not Name. sake

יִמְעֲטוּ לְפָנֶיךָ תְּלָאוֹתֵינוּ. מַהֵר יְקַדְּמוּנוּ רַחֲמֶיךָ

⟨ may Your ⟨ come ⟨ Swiftly ≪ our travails. ⟨ before ⟨ be considered
mercy toward us You insignificant

בְּעֵת צָרוֹתֵנוּ. לֹא לְמַעֲנֵנוּ, אֶלָּא לְמַעַנְךָ פְּעַל,

≪ act, ⟨ for Your ⟨ but ≪ for our sake, ⟨ Not ≪ of our ⟨ at the
own sake distress. time

וְאַל תַּשְׁחִית אֶת זֵכֶר שְׁאֵרִיתֵנוּ. כִּי לְךָ

⟨ to You ⟨ For ≪ of our remnant. ⟨ the remembrance ⟨ destroy ⟨ and do not

מִיַחֲלוֹת עֵינֵינוּ, כִּי אֵל מֶלֶךְ חַנּוּן וְרַחוּם אָתָּה.

≪ are You. ⟨ and ⟨ gracious ⟨ [and] ⟨ O ⟨ for ≪ do our eyes long,
merciful King, God,

וּזְכוֹר עֵדוּתֵינוּ, בְּכָל יוֹם תָּמִיד אוֹמְרִים פַּעֲמַיִם

⟨ twice ⟨ we recite ⟨ constantly, ⟨ day ⟨ every ≪ our ⟨ And
testimony— remember

בְּאַהֲבָה: שְׁמַע יִשְׂרָאֵל, יהוה אֱלֹהֵינוּ, יהוה אֶחָד.²

≪ the One ⟨ HASHEM ⟨ is our God, ⟨ HASHEM ⟨ O Israel, ⟨ Hear, ≪ with love:
[and Only].

יהוה אֱלֹהֵי יִשְׂרָאֵל,* שׁוּב מֵחֲרוֹן אַפֶּךָ

⟨ anger, ⟨ from Your flaring ⟨ withdraw ≪ of Israel,* ⟨ God ⟨ HASHEM,

וְהִנָּחֵם עַל הָרָעָה לְעַמֶּךָ.³

≪ [meant] for Your people. ⟨ the evil ⟨ from ⟨ and relent

---

(1) Cf. *Psalms* 78:61. (2) *Deuteronomy* 6:4. (3) *Exodus* 32:12.

עַד מָתַי עֻזְּךָ בַּשְּׁבִי —*Until when will Your strength
be in captivity.* This is based on *Psalms* 78:61,
which describes the Philistine capture of the
Holy Ark in the time of Eli and Samuel. In our
context, it refers to the holy places and spiritual

power that seem to have lost their ability to
protect Israel.

ה׳ אֱלֹהֵי יִשְׂרָאֵל ﷾ — *HASHEM, God of Israel.*
According to tradition, this section of *Tachanun*
was composed by King Hezekiah. When

הַבֵּט מִשָּׁמַיִם וּרְאֵה, כִּי הָיִינוּ לַעַג וָקֶלֶס

⟨ and ⟨ an object ⟨ we have ⟨ that ⟨ and see ⟨ from heaven ⟨ Look
derision of scorn become

בַּגּוֹיִם, נֶחְשַׁבְנוּ כְּצֹאן לַטֶּבַח יוּבָל, לַהֲרֹג

⟨ — to be ≪ led ⟨ to slaughter ⟨ as sheep ⟨ we are ≪ among
killed, regarded the nations;

וּלְאַבֵּד וּלְמַכָּה וּלְחֶרְפָּה.¹ וּבְכָל זֹאת שִׁמְךָ לֹא

⟨ we ⟨ Your ⟨ this ⟨ But ≪ and for ⟨ for beating, ≪ and to be
have not Name despite all humiliating. destroyed,

שְׁכַחֲנוּ, נָא אַל תִּשְׁכָּחֵנוּ.

≪ forget us. ⟨ do not ⟨ please ≪ forgotten;

יהוה אֱלֹהֵי יִשְׂרָאֵל, שׁוּב מֵחֲרוֹן אַפֶּךָ

⟨ anger, ⟨ from Your flaring ⟨ withdraw ≪ of Israel, ⟨ God ⟨ HASHEM,

וְהִנָּחֵם עַל הָרָעָה לְעַמֶּךָ.

≪ [meant] for Your people. ⟨ the evil ⟨ from ⟨ and relent

זָרִים אוֹמְרִים אֵין תּוֹחֶלֶת וְתִקְוָה, חֹן אִם

⟨ to the ⟨ Be ≪ nor hope ⟨ expectation ⟨ There ≪ say, ⟨ Foreigners
nation gracious [for them]. is no

לִשְׁמְךָ מְקַוֶּה, טָהוֹר יְשׁוּעָתֵנוּ קָרְבָה, יָגַעְנוּ וְלֹא

⟨ and there ⟨ We are ≪ bring near! ⟨ our salvation ⟨ O Pure ≪ hopes. ⟨ who to
is no exhausted One, Your Name

הוּנַח לָנוּ,² רַחֲמֶיךָ יִכְבְּשׁוּ אֶת כַּעַסְךָ מֵעָלֵינוּ.

≪ against us. ⟨ Your anger ⟨ conquer ⟨ May Your ≪ for us. ⟨ rest
mercy provided

---

(1) Cf. *Psalms* 44:14,23; *Isaiah* 53:7. (2) *Lamentations* 5:5.

Jerusalem was besieged by Sennacherib and the situation seemed hopeless, the righteous king went to the Temple and poured out his heart in this supplication. As its stanzas clearly show, it is an eloquent plea for God's intervention in the face of impending disaster, and thus expresses our hope that God will help Israel today as He did in Hezekiah's time. The commentators note that Hezekiah spelled his name in the initials of the stanzas [קוֹלֵנוּ, חוּסָה, זָרִים, הַבֵּט, י׳], but with the modesty for which he was famous, he put the letters out of order so that it would not be obvious that he was the supplication's author.

Or HaYashar notes that the numerical value of ה׳ אֱלֹהֵי יִשְׂרָאֵל, *God of Israel*, is 613. Hezekiah used this particular salutation because the reminder that Israel observes the 613 commandments is certain to evoke God's compassion.

אָנָּא שׁוּב מֵחֲרוֹנְךָ, וְרַחֵם סְגֻלָּה אֲשֶׁר בָּחָרְתָּ.[1]

❮❮ You have ❮ that ❮ on the treasured ❮ and have ❮ from Your ❮ withdraw ❮ Please,
chosen.　　　　　　nation　　　mercy　　　anger,

יהוה אֱלֹהֵי יִשְׂרָאֵל, שׁוּב מֵחֲרוֹן אַפֶּךָ

❮ anger, ❮ from Your flaring ❮ withdraw ❮❮ of Israel, ❮ God ❮ HASHEM,

וְהִנָּחֵם עַל הָרָעָה לְעַמֶּךָ.

❮❮ [meant] for Your people. ❮ the evil ❮ from ❮ and relent

חוּסָה יהוה עָלֵינוּ בְּרַחֲמֶיךָ, וְאַל תִּתְּנֵנוּ

❮ turn us over ❮ and do not ❮❮ in Your mercy, ❮ on us ❮ HASHEM, ❮ Have pity,

בִּידֵי אַכְזָרִים. לָמָּה יֹאמְרוּ הַגּוֹיִם אַיֵּה נָא

❮ now ❮ Where ❮❮ – the ❮❮ should ❮ Why ❮❮ of those who ❮ into the
　　　　　nations –　　they say　　　　　are cruel.　　　hands

אֱלֹהֵיהֶם,[2] לְמַעַנְךָ עֲשֵׂה עִמָּנוּ חֶסֶד וְאַל תְּאַחַר.[3]

❮❮ delay. ❮ and ❮ with ❮ with us ❮ deal ❮ For Your ❮❮ is their God?
　　　　do not　kindness,　　　　　　　sake,

אָנָּא שׁוּב מֵחֲרוֹנְךָ, וְרַחֵם סְגֻלָּה אֲשֶׁר בָּחָרְתָּ.[1]

❮❮ You have ❮ that ❮ on the treasured ❮ and have ❮ from Your ❮ withdraw ❮ Please,
chosen.　　　　　　nation　　　mercy　　　anger,

יהוה אֱלֹהֵי יִשְׂרָאֵל, שׁוּב מֵחֲרוֹן אַפֶּךָ

❮ anger, ❮ from Your flaring ❮ withdraw ❮❮ of Israel, ❮ God ❮ HASHEM,

וְהִנָּחֵם עַל הָרָעָה לְעַמֶּךָ.

❮❮ [meant] for Your people. ❮ the evil ❮ from ❮ and relent

קוֹלֵנוּ תִשְׁמַע וְתָחֹן, וְאַל תִּטְּשֵׁנוּ בְּיַד

❮ into the ❮ cast us away ❮ and do ❮❮ and accept ❮ hear ❮ Our voice
hand　　　　　　　　not　with grace,

אוֹיְבֵינוּ לִמְחוֹת אֶת שְׁמֵנוּ. זְכֹר אֲשֶׁר נִשְׁבַּעְתָּ

❮ You swore ❮ what ❮ Remember ❮❮ our name. ❮ to blot out ❮ of our enemies,

לַאֲבוֹתֵינוּ: כְּכוֹכְבֵי הַשָּׁמַיִם אַרְבֶּה אֶת זַרְעֲכֶם,[4]

❮❮ your offspring ❮ will I multiply ❮ of the heaven ❮ Like the stars ❮❮ to our forefathers:

---

(1) Cf. *Deuteronomy* 7:6. (2) *Psalms* 115:2. (3) Cf. *Daniel* 9:19. (4) Cf. *Exodus* 32:13.

וְעַתָּה נִשְׁאַרְנוּ מְעַט מֵהַרְבֵּה.¹ וּבְכָל זֹאת
this ⟨ But despite all ⟪ from many. ⟨ few ⟨ we remain ⟨ — but now

שִׁמְךָ לֹא שָׁכָחְנוּ, נָא אַל תִּשְׁכָּחֵנוּ.
⟪ forget us. ⟨ do not ⟨ please ⟪ forgotten; ⟨ we have ⟨ Your
                                      not   Name

יהוה אֱלֹהֵי יִשְׂרָאֵל, שׁוּב מֵחֲרוֹן אַפֶּךָ
⟨ anger, ⟨ from Your flaring ⟨ withdraw ⟪ of Israel, ⟨ God ⟨ HASHEM,

וְהִנָּחֵם עַל הָרָעָה לְעַמֶּךָ.
⟪ [meant] for Your people. ⟨ the evil ⟨ from ⟨ and relent

עָזְרֵנוּ אֱלֹהֵי יִשְׁעֵנוּ עַל דְּבַר כְּבוֹד שְׁמֶךָ,
⟪ of Your ⟨ of the ⟨ the sake ⟨ for ⟨ of our ⟨ O God ⟨ Assist us,
      Name;   glory   salvation,

וְהַצִּילֵנוּ וְכַפֵּר עַל חַטֹּאתֵינוּ לְמַעַן שְׁמֶךָ.²
⟪ of Your ⟨ for the ⟨ our sins ⟨ for ⟨ and grant ⟨ rescue us,
    Name.   sake   atonement

יהוה אֱלֹהֵי יִשְׂרָאֵל, שׁוּב מֵחֲרוֹן אַפֶּךָ
⟨ anger, ⟨ from Your flaring ⟨ withdraw ⟪ of Israel, ⟨ God ⟨ HASHEM,

וְהִנָּחֵם עַל הָרָעָה לְעַמֶּךָ.
⟪ [meant] for Your people. ⟨ the evil ⟨ from ⟨ and relent

ON ALL DAYS, *TACHANUN* CONTINUES HERE.

שׁוֹמֵר יִשְׂרָאֵל,* שְׁמוֹר שְׁאֵרִית יִשְׂרָאֵל, וְאַל
⟨ let not ⟪ of Israel; ⟨ the remnant ⟨ safeguard ⟪ of Israel,* ⟨ O Guardian

יֹאבַד יִשְׂרָאֵל, הָאוֹמְרִים שְׁמַע יִשְׂרָאֵל.
⟪ O Israel. ⟨ Hear ⟨ those who proclaim: ⟪ Israel be destroyed —

---

(1) Cf. *Jeremiah* 42:2. (2) *Psalms* 79:9.

שׁוֹמֵר יִשְׂרָאֵל§ — *O Guardian of Israel.* As noted above, this plea to God as our Guardian enforces the theme that we are helpless and totally dependent on His mercy. However, we do not come to God emptyhanded; each of the paragraphs beginning שׁוֹמֵר, *O Guardian,*

stresses an aspect of Israel's importance to God. Israel deserves God's mercy because: (a) It continues to proclaim its allegiance to God by proclaiming the *Shema;* (b) Israel is unique in that it demonstrates to the world that God is One and Unique; and (c) like the angels,

שׁוֹמֵר גּוֹי אֶחָד, שְׁמוֹר שְׁאֵרִית עַם אֶחָד,

O Guardian of the nation that is unique, safeguard the remnant of the people that is unique;

וְאַל יֹאבַד גּוֹי אֶחָד, הַמְּיַחֲדִים שִׁמְךָ, יהוה

let not be destroyed the nation that is unique, those who proclaim the Oneness of Your Name: HASHEM

אֱלֹהֵינוּ יהוה אֶחָד.

is our God, HASHEM the One [and Only]!

שׁוֹמֵר גּוֹי קָדוֹשׁ, שְׁמוֹר שְׁאֵרִית עַם קָדוֹשׁ,

O Guardian of the nation that is holy, safeguard the remnant of the people that is holy;

וְאַל יֹאבַד גּוֹי קָדוֹשׁ, הַמְּשַׁלְּשִׁים בְּשָׁלֹשׁ

let not be destroyed the nation that is holy, those who proclaim three times the threefold

קְדֻשּׁוֹת לְקָדוֹשׁ.

sanctifications to the Holy One.

מִתְרַצֶּה* בְּרַחֲמִים וּמִתְפַּיֵּס בְּתַחֲנוּנִים,

You Who become favorable* through compassion and Who become conciliatory through supplications,

הִתְרַצֵּה וְהִתְפַּיֵּס לְדוֹר עָנִי, כִּי אֵין עוֹזֵר.

be favorable and be conciliatory to the generation that is poor, for there is no helper.

אָבִינוּ מַלְכֵּנוּ, חָנֵּנוּ וַעֲנֵנוּ, כִּי אֵין בָּנוּ מַעֲשִׂים,

Our Father, our King be gracious with us and answer us, though we have no worthy deeds;

עֲשֵׂה עִמָּנוּ צְדָקָה וָחֶסֶד וְהוֹשִׁיעֵנוּ.

treat us with charity and kindness, and save us.

Israel praises and exalts God with the trebled proclamation of His holiness, Kedushah (see p. 146).

מִתְרַצֶּה — *You Who become favorable.* May we have succeeded through our supplications in arousing God's mercy.

STAND UP AFTER THE WORDS וַאֲנַחְנוּ לֹא נֵדַע UNTIL CONCLUSION OF THE PARAGRAPH.

וַאֲנַחְנוּ לֹא נֵדַע מַה נַּעֲשֶׂה,* כִּי עָלֶיךָ

⟨ upon You ⟨ rather ⟨ we should do,* ⟨ what ⟨ know not ⟨ We

עֵינֵינוּ.¹ זְכֹר רַחֲמֶיךָ יהוה וַחֲסָדֶיךָ, כִּי מֵעוֹלָם

⟨ eternal ⟨ for ⟨ and Your kindnesses, ⟨ HASHEM, ⟨ Your mercies, ⟨ Remember ⟨⟨ are our eyes.

הֵמָּה.² יְהִי חַסְדְּךָ יהוה עָלֵינוּ, כַּאֲשֶׁר יִחַלְנוּ

⟨ we awaited ⟨ just as ⟨⟨ be upon us, ⟨ HASHEM, ⟨ Your kindness, ⟨ May ⟨⟨ are they.

לָךְ.*³ אַל תִּזְכָּר לָנוּ עֲוֹנֹת רִאשֹׁנִים, מַהֵר

⟨ swiftly ⟨⟨ of the ancients; ⟨ the sins ⟨ against us ⟨ recall ⟨ Do not ⟨⟨ You.*

יְקַדְּמוּנוּ רַחֲמֶיךָ, כִּי דַלּוֹנוּ מְאֹד.*⁴ עָזְרֵנוּ בְּשֵׁם

⟨ is through ⟨ Our help ⟨⟨ exceed-ingly.* ⟨ we have become impoverished ⟨ for ⟨⟨ may Your mercies, ⟨ advance to meet us the Name

יהוה, עֹשֵׂה שָׁמַיִם וָאָרֶץ.⁵ חָנֵּנוּ יהוה חָנֵּנוּ, כִּי

⟨ for ⟨⟨ favor us, ⟨ HASHEM, ⟨ Favor us, ⟨⟨ and earth. ⟨ of heaven ⟨ Maker ⟨⟨ of HASHEM,

רַב שָׂבַעְנוּ בוּז.⁶ בְּרֹגֶז רַחֵם תִּזְכּוֹר.⁷ בְּרֹגֶז עֲקֵדָה

⟨ the binding [of Isaac] ⟨⟨ Amid wrath, ⟨⟨ You should remember! ⟨ to be merciful ⟨⟨ Amid wrath, ⟨⟨ with contempt. ⟨ sated ⟨ we are fully

תִּזְכּוֹר. בְּרֹגֶז תְּמִימוּת תִּזְכּוֹר. יהוה הוֹשִׁיעָה,

⟨⟨ save! ⟨ HASHEM, ⟨⟨ You should remember! ⟨ the perfect ones ⟨⟨ Amid wrath, ⟨⟨ You should remember!

---

(1) *II Chronicles* 20:12. (2) *Psalms* 25:6. (3) 33:22. (4) 79:8. (5) 121:2. (6) 123:3. (7) *Habakkuk* 3:2.

וַאֲנַחְנוּ לֹא נֵדַע מַה נַּעֲשֶׂה — *We know not what we should do.* We have prayed in every possible manner — sitting, standing, and casting ourselves down in supplication. Moses, too, prayed in these three postures. Now, we beg of God to help, for "we know not what else we should do." To allude to this concept it is customary to sit while reciting the first three words of this prayer and then to stand (*Abudraham*).

We are like orphaned children who depend totally on their guardian. Similarly, we look to God for His help and mercy, recognizing that only He can rescue us from our plight (*Etz Yosef*). Appropriately, this verse is from the prayer of King Yehoshafat, who prayed for help against an overwhelming invasion.

כַּאֲשֶׁר יִחַלְנוּ לָךְ — *Just as we awaited You.* If we are undeserving, O God, then help us because You will thereby sanctify Your Name (*Alshich*).

כִּי דַלּוֹנוּ מְאֹד — *For we have become impoverished exceedingly.* The prayer concludes with the plea that we have already suffered mightily and that God in His mercy knows that we are helpless without Him.

הַמֶּלֶךְ יַעֲנֵנוּ בְיוֹם קָרְאֵנוּ.¹ כִּי הוּא יָדַע יִצְרֵנוּ,

‹‹ our nature, ‹ knew ‹ He ‹ For ‹‹ we call. ‹ on the day ‹ answer us ‹ May the King

זָכוּר כִּי עָפָר אֲנָחְנוּ.² ❖ עָזְרֵנוּ אֱלֹהֵי יִשְׁעֵנוּ עַל

‹ for ‹ of our salvation, ‹ O God ‹ Assist us, ‹‹ are we. ‹ dust ‹ that ‹ He is mindful

דְּבַר כְּבוֹד שְׁמֶךָ, וְהַצִּילֵנוּ וְכַפֵּר עַל חַטֹּאתֵינוּ

‹ our sins ‹ for ‹ and grant atonement ‹ rescue us ‹‹ of Your Name; ‹ of the glory ‹ the sake

לְמַעַן שְׁמֶךָ.³

‹‹ of Your Name. ‹ for the sake

THE *CHAZZAN* RECITES חֲצִי קַדִּישׁ, HALF-*KADDISH*.

יִתְגַּדַּל וְיִתְקַדַּשׁ שְׁמֵהּ רַבָּא. (אָמֵן. – Cong.) בְּעָלְמָא דִּי בְרָא

‹ He ‹ that ‹ in the world ‹‹ (Amen.) ‹‹ that is ‹ may His ‹ and be ‹ Grow exalted created great! – Name sanctified

כִרְעוּתֵהּ, וְיַמְלִיךְ מַלְכוּתֵהּ, וְיַצְמַח פֻּרְקָנֵהּ וִיקָרֵב מְשִׁיחֵהּ.

‹‹ His Messiah, ‹ and bring near ‹ His salvation, ‹ and cause to sprout ‹ to His kingship, ‹ and may He give reign ‹‹ according to His will,

(אָמֵן. – Cong.) בְּחַיֵּיכוֹן וּבְיוֹמֵיכוֹן וּבְחַיֵּי דְכָל בֵּית יִשְׂרָאֵל,

‹‹ of Israel, ‹ Family ‹ of the entire ‹ and in the lifetime ‹ and in your days, ‹ in your lifetimes ‹‹ (Amen.)

בַּעֲגָלָא וּבִזְמַן קָרִיב. וְאִמְרוּ: אָמֵן.

‹‹ Amen. ‹ Now respond: ‹‹ that comes soon. ‹ and at a time ‹ swiftly

CONGREGATION RESPONDS:

אָמֵן. יְהֵא שְׁמֵהּ רַבָּא מְבָרַךְ לְעָלַם וּלְעָלְמֵי עָלְמַיָּא.

‹‹ and for all eternity. ‹ forever ‹ be blessed ‹ that is great ‹ His Name ‹ May ‹‹ Amen.

CHAZZAN CONTINUES:

יְהֵא שְׁמֵהּ רַבָּא מְבָרַךְ לְעָלַם וּלְעָלְמֵי עָלְמַיָּא. יִתְבָּרַךְ

‹ Blessed, ‹‹ and for all eternity. ‹ forever ‹ be blessed ‹ that is great ‹ His Name ‹ May

וְיִשְׁתַּבַּח וְיִתְפָּאַר וְיִתְרוֹמַם וְיִתְנַשֵּׂא וְיִתְהַדָּר וְיִתְעַלֶּה

‹ elevated, ‹ honored, ‹ upraised, ‹ exalted, ‹ glorified, ‹ praised,

וְיִתְהַלָּל שְׁמֵהּ דְּקֻדְשָׁא בְּרִיךְ הוּא (בְּרִיךְ הוּא – Cong.) —

‹‹ is He) ‹ (Blessed ‹‹ is He ‹ Blessed ‹ of the Holy One, ‹ be the Name ‹ and lauded

---

(1) *Psalms* 20:10. (2) 103:14. (3) 79:9.

ROSH HASHANAH TO YOM KIPPUR SUBSTITUTE:

°לְעֵלָּא מִן כָּל [°לְעֵלָּא (וּ)לְעֵלָּא מִכָּל] בִּרְכָתָא

‹ blessing ‹ any ‹ exceedingly beyond ‹ any ‹ beyond

וְשִׁירָתָא, תֻּשְׁבְּחָתָא וְנֶחֱמָתָא דַּאֲמִירָן בְּעָלְמָא.

« in the world. ‹ that are uttered ‹ and consolation ‹ praise « and song,

וְאִמְרוּ: אָמֵן. (.אָמֵן–Cong.)

« (Amen.) « Amen. ‹ Now respond:

WHEN THE TORAH IS NOT READ, CONTINUE WITH אַשְׁרֵי, ASHREI (P. 214).

﷽ הוצאת ספר תורה ﷽

﷽ REMOVAL OF THE TORAH FROM THE ARK ﷽

THE FOLLOWING SHORT SUPPLICATION IS RECITED, WHILE STANDING ERECT, BEFORE THE TORAH
READING ON MONDAY AND THURSDAY. IT IS OMITTED ON FESTIVALS (INCLUDING CHOL HAMOED),
ROSH CHODESH, EREV PESACH, TISHAH B'AV, (IN SOME CONGREGATIONS, 15 AV,) EREV YOM KIPPUR,
CHANUKAH, PURIM AND SHUSHAN PURIM, THE 14TH AND 15TH OF ADAR I (PURIM KATTAN), AND IN A
HOUSE OF MOURNING.

IN MOST *SIDDURIM* THIS PRAYER APPEARS IN TWO VERSIONS: VERSION A, ASCRIBED TO THE COMMU-
NITIES OF GERMANY, BOHEMIA, AND LESSER POLAND (WESTERN GALICIA); AND VERSION B, TO THE
COMMUNITIES OF GREATER POLAND (POLAND AND LITHUANIA). IN SOME CONGREGATIONS BOTH
VERSIONS ARE RECITED.

VERSION A

אֵל אֶֽרֶךְ אַפַּֽיִם* וְרַב חֶֽסֶד וֶאֱמֶת,¹ אַל בְּאַפְּךָ

‹ in Your ‹ do not « and truth, ‹ in ‹ and ‹ to anger* ‹ slow ‹ O God,
anger　　　　　　　　　　　kindness abundant

תוֹכִיחֵֽנוּ.² חֽוּסָה יהוה עַל עַמֶּֽךָ,³ וְהוֹשִׁיעֵֽנוּ מִכָּל

‹ from all ‹ and save us ‹ Your people, ‹ on ‹ HASHEM, ‹ Have pity, « chastise us.

רָע. חָטָֽאנוּ לְךָ, אָדוֹן; סְלַח נָא כְּרֹב רַחֲמֶֽיךָ, אֵל.

« O ‹ in accordance with ‹ please, ‹ forgive « Master; ‹ against ‹ We have « evil.
God. Your abundant mercy, [us], You, sinned

---

(1) Cf. *Exodus* 34:6. (2) *Psalms* 6:2. (3) *Joel* 2:17.

אֵל אֶֽרֶךְ אַפַּֽיִם — *O God, slow to anger.* As
we prepare for the Torah to be removed from
the Ark, we recognize that we have fallen far
short of the standards it sets for us. Realizing
how unworthy we are to take the Torah into
our hands, we recite the brief prayer אֵל אֶֽרֶךְ
אַפַּֽיִם, *O God, slow to anger,* which is both a
confession and a plea for mercy (R' Hirsch).

The two versions of the prayer differ only
slightly from one another. Version A asks that
we not be chastised as a result of God's anger at
our shortcomings, while version B asks that
God not conceal His face from us, i.e., that He
not make it impossible for us to perceive His
Presence and gain some understanding of His
ways. Some early authorities such as *Kol Bo,*

VERSION B

אֵל אֶרֶךְ אַפַּיִם* וְרַב חֶסֶד וֶאֱמֶת,¹ אַל תַּסְתֵּר
⟨ conceal ⟨ do not ⟨⟨ and truth, ⟨ in ⟨ and ⟨ to anger* ⟨ slow ⟨O God,
kindness abundant

פָּנֶיךָ מִמֶּנּוּ.² חוּסָה יהוה עַל יִשְׂרָאֵל עַמֶּךָ,³
⟨⟨ Your ⟨ Israel, ⟨ on ⟨ HASHEM, ⟨ Have pity, ⟨⟨ from us. ⟨ Your
people, countenance

וְהַצִּילֵנוּ מִכָּל רָע. חָטָאנוּ לָךְ, אָדוֹן; סְלַח נָא
⟨ please, ⟨ forgive ⟨⟨ Master; ⟨ against ⟨ We have ⟨⟨ evil. ⟨ from all ⟨ and rescue us
[us], You, sinned

כְּרֹב רַחֲמֶיךָ, אֵל.
⟨⟨ O God. ⟨ in accordance with
Your abundant mercy,

ALL RISE AND REMAIN STANDING UNTIL THE TORAH IS PLACED ON THE *BIMAH*.
THE ARK IS OPENED. BEFORE THE TORAH IS REMOVED, THE CONGREGATION RECITES:

וַיְהִי בִּנְסֹעַ הָאָרֹן* וַיֹּאמֶר מֹשֶׁה, קוּמָה
⟨ Arise, ⟨⟨ Moses would say: ⟨ would ⟨ that when ⟨ It would be
the Ark* travel

יהוה וְיָפֻצוּ אֹיְבֶיךָ וְיָנֻסוּ מְשַׂנְאֶיךָ מִפָּנֶיךָ.⁴ כִּי
⟨ For ⟨⟨ from ⟨ those who ⟨ Let flee ⟨⟨ be Your foes. ⟨ and let ⟨ HASHEM,
before You. hate You scattered

מִצִּיּוֹן תֵּצֵא תוֹרָה, וּדְבַר יהוה מִירוּשָׁלָיִם.⁵
⟨⟨ from Jerusalem. ⟨ of HASHEM ⟨ and the ⟨⟨ the Torah, ⟨ will come ⟨ from Zion
word forth

בָּרוּךְ שֶׁנָּתַן תּוֹרָה לְעַמּוֹ יִשְׂרָאֵל בִּקְדֻשָּׁתוֹ.
⟨⟨ in His holiness. ⟨ Israel ⟨ to His ⟨ the Torah ⟨ is He Who ⟨ Blessed
people gave

---

(1) Cf. *Exodus* 34:6. (2) Cf. *Psalms* 27:9. (3) Cf. *Joel* 2:17. (4) *Numbers* 10:35. (5) *Isaiah* 2:3.

Abudraham, and *Levush* hold that both versions should be recited, but few congregations follow this practice.

וַיְהִי בִּנְסֹעַ הָאָרֹן — *It would be that when travel would the Ark*. When the Ark is opened we declare, as Moses did when the Ark traveled, that God's word is invincible. Having acknowl-

edged this, we can read from the Torah with the proper awareness. We continue that it is God's will that the Torah's message go forth to the entire world, and by blessing Him for having given us the Torah, we accept our responsibility to carry out its commands and spread its message (*R' Hirsch*).

בְּרִיךְ שְׁמֵהּ* דְּמָרֵא עָלְמָא, בְּרִיךְ כִּתְרָךְ

‹ is Your crown   ‹ blessed   « of the universe;   ‹ of the Master   ‹ is the Name*   ‹ Blessed

וְאַתְרָךְ. יְהֵא רְעוּתָךְ עִם עַמָּךְ יִשְׂרָאֵל לְעָלַם,

« forever,   ‹ Israel   ‹ Your people   ‹ with   ‹ May Your favor be   « and Your place.

וּפֻרְקָן יְמִינָךְ אַחֲזֵי לְעַמָּךְ בְּבֵית מַקְדְּשָׁךְ,

« in Your holy Temple,   ‹ to Your people   ‹ may You display   ‹ of Your right hand   ‹ and the salvation

וּלְאַמְטוּיֵי לָנָא מִטּוּב נְהוֹרָךְ, וּלְקַבֵּל צְלוֹתָנָא

‹ our prayers   ‹ and to accept   « of Your light,   ‹ of the goodness   ‹ to us   ‹ to extend

בְּרַחֲמִין. יְהֵא רַעֲוָא קֳדָמָךְ, דְּתוֹרִיךְ לָן חַיִּין

‹ life   ‹ for us   ‹ that You extend   ‹ before You   ‹ the will   ‹ May it be   « with mercy.

בְּטִיבוּתָא, וְלֶהֱוֵי אֲנָא פְּקִידָא בְּגוֹ צַדִּיקַיָּא,

« the righteous;   ‹ among   ‹ am counted   ‹ I   ‹ and it should be that   « with goodness,

לְמִרְחַם עֲלַי וּלְמִנְטַר יָתִי וְיָת כָּל דִּי לִי,

« is mine   ‹ that   ‹ and all   « me,   ‹ and protect   « on me   ‹ that You have mercy

וְדִי לְעַמָּךְ יִשְׂרָאֵל. אַנְתְּ הוּא זָן לְכֹלָּא,

‹ all   ‹ nourishes   ‹ Who   ‹ It is You   « Israel.   ‹ belongs to   ‹ and Your people [all] that

וּמְפַרְנֵס לְכֹלָּא, אַנְתְּ הוּא שַׁלִּיט עַל כֹּלָּא.

« everything.   ‹ over   ‹ rules   ‹ Who   ‹ it is You   « all;   ‹ and sustains

אַנְתְּ הוּא דְּשַׁלִּיט עַל מַלְכַיָּא, וּמַלְכוּתָא

‹ and kingship   ‹ kings,   ‹ over   ‹ rules   ‹ Who   ‹ It is You

דִּילָךְ הִיא. אֲנָא עַבְדָּא דְּקֻדְשָׁא בְּרִיךְ הוּא,

« is He,   ‹ Blessed   ‹ of the Holy One,   ‹ a servant   ‹ I am   « is Yours.

דְּסָגִידְנָא קַמֵּהּ וּמִקַּמָּא דִּיקַר אוֹרַיְתֵהּ בְּכָל

‹ at all   ‹ of His Torah   ‹ the glory   ‹ and before   ‹ before Him   ‹ and prostrate myself

---

בְּרִיךְ שְׁמֵהּ ‹§ — *Blessed is the Name.* The *Zohar* declares that when the congregation prepares to read from the Torah, the heavenly Gates of Mercy are opened and God's love for Israel is aroused. Therefore, it is an auspicious occasion for the recital of this prayer which asks for God's compassion, pleads that He display His salvation in the rebuilt Holy Temple, declares

עִדָּן וְעִדָּן. לָא עַל אֱנָשׁ רָחִיצְנָא, וְלָא עַל
< on < nor 《 do I put trust, < any man < in < Not 《 times.

בַּר אֱלָהִין סָמִיכְנָא, אֶלָּא בֵּאלָהָא דִשְׁמַיָּא,
< of heaven, < on the God < – only 《 do I rely < any angel

דְּהוּא אֱלָהָא קְשׁוֹט, וְאוֹרַיְתֵהּ קְשׁוֹט, וּנְבִיאְוֹהִי
< Whose prophets 《 is truth, < Whose Torah 《 of truth, < the God < Who is

קְשׁוֹט, וּמַסְגֵּא לְמֶעְבַּד טַבְוָן וּקְשׁוֹט. בֵּהּ אֲנָא
< I < In Him 《 and truth. < with kindness < acts < and Who abundantly 《 are true,

רָחִיץ, וְלִשְׁמֵהּ קַדִּישָׁא יַקִּירָא אֲנָא אֲמַר
< declare < I 《 and glorious – < – holy 《 and to His Name 《 trust,

תֻּשְׁבְּחָן. יְהֵא רַעֲוָא קֳדָמָךְ, דְּתִפְתַּח לִבָּאִי
< my heart < that You open < before You < the will < May it be 《 praises.

בְּאוֹרַיְתָא, (וְתִיהַב לִי בְּנִין דְּכְרִין דְּעָבְדִין
< who carry out < male children < me < (and that You give 《 to the Torah,

רְעוּתָךְ,) וְתַשְׁלִים מִשְׁאֲלִין דְּלִבָּאִי, וְלִבָּא
< and the heart < of my heart < the wishes < and that You fulfill 《 Your will,)

דְכָל עַמָּךְ יִשְׂרָאֵל, לְטַב וּלְחַיִּין וְלִשְׁלָם. (אָמֵן.)[1]
《 (Amen.) 《 and for peace. < for life, < for good, < Israel < Your people < of all

THE *CHAZZAN* TURNS TO THE ARK, BOWS WHILE RAISING THE TORAH, AND RECITES:

גַּדְּלוּ* לַיהוה אִתִּי וּנְרוֹמְמָה שְׁמוֹ יַחְדָּו.[2]
《 in unison. < His < and let us exalt 《 with me, < of HASHEM < Declare the
            Name   greatness*

THE *CHAZZAN* TURNS TO HIS RIGHT AND CARRIES THE TORAH TO THE *BIMAH*,
AS THE CONGREGATION RESPONDS:

לְךָ יהוה הַגְּדֻלָּה* וְהַגְּבוּרָה וְהַתִּפְאֶרֶת
< the glory, < the strength, < is the greatness,* < HASHEM, < Yours,

(1) *Zohar Vayakhel* 206a. (2) *Psalms* 34:4.

our faith in Him and His Torah, and asks that He make us receptive to its wisdom.

◗ גַּדְּלוּ — *Declare the greatness.* Our rejoicing in the Torah manifests itself in praise of its Giver.

The *chazzan* calls upon the congregation to join him in praising God.

◗ לְךָ ה' הַגְּדֻלָּה — *Yours, HASHEM, is the greatness.* This praise was first uttered by David in his

וְהַנֵּצַח וְהַהוֹד כִּי כֹל בַּשָּׁמַיִם וּבָאָרֶץ, לְךָ

the triumph, > and the majesty; >> for > everything > in heaven > and on earth > Yours,>> [is Yours];

יהוה הַמַּמְלָכָה וְהַמִּתְנַשֵּׂא לְכֹל לְרֹאשׁ. רוֹמְמוּ[1]

HASHEM, > is the kingdom, > and the sovereignty > over every > leader. >> Exalt >

יהוה אֱלֹהֵינוּ, וְהִשְׁתַּחֲווּ לַהֲדֹם רַגְלָיו,* קָדוֹשׁ

HASHEM, > our God, > and bow down > at His footstool;* >> holy >

הוּא. רוֹמְמוּ יהוה אֱלֹהֵינוּ, וְהִשְׁתַּחֲווּ לְהַר

is He! >> Exalt > HASHEM, > our God, > and bow down > at the Mount >

קָדְשׁוֹ, כִּי קָדוֹשׁ יהוה אֱלֹהֵינוּ.[2]

of His Holiness; > for > holy > is HASHEM, > our God. >>

AS THE CHAZZAN CARRIES THE TORAH, THE CONGREGATION RECITES:

אַב הָרַחֲמִים הוּא יְרַחֵם עַם עֲמוּסִים,* וְיִזְכֹּר

Father > of compassion! >> May He > have mercy > [on] the nation > that is borne [by Him],* >> and may He remember >

בְּרִית אֵיתָנִים,* וְיַצִּיל נַפְשׁוֹתֵינוּ מִן הַשָּׁעוֹת

the covenant > of the [spiritually] mighty ones.* >> May He rescue > our souls > from > the times >

הָרָעוֹת, וְיִגְעַר בְּיֵצֶר הָרָע מִן הַנְּשׂוּאִים, וְיָחֹן

that are bad, >> and denounce > the Evil Inclination > from > those [harming] those carried by Him, >> grant graciously >

אוֹתָנוּ לִפְלֵיטַת עוֹלָמִים, וִימַלֵּא מִשְׁאֲלוֹתֵינוּ

us > eternal deliverance, >> and fulfill > our requests >

בְּמִדָּה טוֹבָה יְשׁוּעָה וְרַחֲמִים.

in good measure, > with salvation > and mercy. >>

---

(1) *I Chronicles* 29:11. (2) *Psalms* 99:5,9.

ecstasy at seeing how wholeheartedly the people contributed toward the eventual building of the Temple. He ascribed the greatness of that and every other achievement to God's graciousness.

לַהֲדֹם רַגְלָיו — *At His footstool*, the Temple, as if to say that God's Heavenly Presence extends earthward, like a footstool helping support a monarch sitting on his throne. In a further sense,

this represents our resolve to live in such a way that we are worthy of His Presence resting upon us (*R' Hirsch*).

עַם עֲמוּסִים — *The nation that is borne [by Him]*, the nation that God Himself bears as His personal responsibility (*Etz Yosef*).

אֵיתָנִים — *The [spiritually] mighty ones* is a term used often for Abraham, Isaac, and Jacob.

THE *GABBAI* USES THE FOLLOWING FORMULA TO CALL A *KOHEN* TO THE TORAH:

וְתִגָּלֶה וְתֵרָאֶה מַלְכוּתוֹ עָלֵינוּ בִּזְמַן קָרוֹב, וְיָחֹן פְּלֵיטָתֵנוּ

‹ to our ‹ and may He ‹‹ that comes ‹ at a ‹ over us ‹ may His ‹ and become ‹ And be
remnant   be gracious   soon,   time   Kingship   visible   revealed

וּפְלֵיטַת עַמּוֹ בֵּית יִשְׂרָאֵל לְחֵן וּלְחֶסֶד וּלְרַחֲמִים וּלְרָצוֹן.

‹‹ and for ‹ for mercy, ‹ for kindness,‹ for gra- ‹‹ of Israel, ‹ the ‹ of His ‹ and the
favor.   ciousness,   Family people,   remnant

וְנֹאמַר: אָמֵן. הַכֹּל הָבוּ גֹדֶל* לֵאלֹהֵינוּ וּתְנוּ כָבוֹד לַתּוֹרָה.

‹‹ to the ‹ honor ‹ and ‹ to our God ‹ great- ‹ ascribe ‹ Every- ‹‹ Amen. ‹ And let us
Torah.   give   ness*   one   respond:

°כֹּהֵן קְרָב, יַעֲמֹד (NAME) בֶּן (FATHER'S NAME) הַכֹּהֵן.

‹‹ the *Kohen.*   ‹ son of   ‹ Arise, ‹‹ approach! ‹ *Kohen,*

°IF NO *KOHEN* IS PRESENT, THE *GABBAI* SAYS:

אֵין כַּאן כֹּהֵן, יַעֲמֹד (NAME) בֶּן (FATHER'S NAME) יִשְׂרָאֵל (לֵוִי) בִּמְקוֹם כֹּהֵן.

‹‹ of a ‹ in place ‹ (the ‹ the ‹   son of   ‹ Arise ‹‹ Kohen ‹ No
Kohen!   Levite), Israelite   is present.

בָּרוּךְ שֶׁנָּתַן תּוֹרָה לְעַמּוֹ יִשְׂרָאֵל בִּקְדֻשָּׁתוֹ. (תּוֹרַת יהוה

‹ of ‹ (The Torah ‹‹ in His holiness. ‹ Israel ‹ to His ‹ the Torah ‹ is He ‹ Blessed
HASHEM   people   Who gave

תְּמִימָה מְשִׁיבַת נָפֶשׁ, עֵדוּת יהוה נֶאֱמָנָה מַחְכִּימַת פֶּתִי. פִּקּוּדֵי

‹ The ‹‹ the ‹ making wise ‹ is trust- ‹ of ‹ the ‹‹ the ‹ restoring ‹ is perfect,
orders   simple one.   worthy, HASHEM testimony   soul;

יהוה יְשָׁרִים מְשַׂמְּחֵי לֵב, מִצְוַת יהוה בָּרָה מְאִירַת עֵינָיִם.¹ יהוה

‹ HASHEM, ‹‹ the ‹ enlightening ‹ is ‹ of ‹ the ‹‹ the ‹ gladdening ‹ are ‹ of
eyes.   clear, HASHEM command heart;   upright, HASHEM

עֹז לְעַמּוֹ יִתֵּן, יהוה יְבָרֵךְ אֶת עַמּוֹ בַשָּׁלוֹם.² הָאֵל תָּמִים

‹ Perfect ‹ The ‹‹ with peace. ‹ His people ‹ will ‹ HASHEM ‹‹ will ‹ to His ‹ strength
God!   bless   give;   people

דַּרְכּוֹ, אִמְרַת יהוה צְרוּפָה, מָגֵן הוּא לְכֹל הַחֹסִים בּוֹ.³)

‹‹ in Him.) ‹ who take ‹ for all ‹ He is ‹ a shield ‹‹ is flawless; ‹ of ‹ the ‹‹ is His
refuge   HASHEM   utterance   way;

CONGREGATION, THEN *GABBAI*:

וְאַתֶּם הַדְּבֵקִים בַּיהוה אֱלֹהֵיכֶם, חַיִּים כֻּלְּכֶם הַיּוֹם.⁴

‹‹ today. ‹‹ —all of ‹‹ you ‹‹ your God, ‹ to HASHEM, ‹ who cling ‹ And you
you —   are alive

---

(1) *Psalms* 19:8-9. (2) 29:11. (3) *II Samuel* 22:31; cf. *Psalms* 18:31. (4) *Deuteronomy* 4:4.

הַכֹּל הָבוּ גֹדֶל — *Everyone ascribe greatness.* The
gabbai calls upon the congregation to show

honor to God by giving honor to His word — the
Torah — from which we are about to read.

⁂ READING OF THE TORAH / קריאת התורה ⁂

THE READER SHOWS THE *OLEH* (PERSON CALLED TO THE TORAH) THE PLACE IN THE TORAH. THE *OLEH* TOUCHES THE TORAH WITH A CORNER OF HIS *TALLIS*, OR THE BELT OR MANTLE OF THE TORAH, AND KISSES IT. HE THEN BEGINS THE BLESSING, BOWING AT בָּרְכוּ AND STRAIGHTENING UP AT ה'.
SEE LAWS §96-113.

בָּרְכוּ אֶת יהוה* הַמְבֹרָךְ.
《 the blessed One. 〈   HASHEM,*   〈 Bless

CONGREGATION, FOLLOWED BY *OLEH*, RESPONDS, BOWING AT בָּרוּךְ AND STRAIGHTENING UP AT ה'.

בָּרוּךְ יהוה הַמְבֹרָךְ לְעוֹלָם וָעֶד.
《 and ever. 〈   for ever 〈 the blessed One, 〈 is HASHEM, 〈 Blessed

OLEH CONTINUES:

בָּרוּךְ אַתָּה יהוה אֱלֹהֵינוּ מֶלֶךְ הָעוֹלָם, אֲשֶׁר
〈 Who 《 of the universe, 〈 King 〈 our God, 〈 HASHEM, 〈 are You, 〈 Blessed

בָּחַר בָּנוּ מִכָּל הָעַמִּים, וְנָתַן לָנוּ אֶת תּוֹרָתוֹ.
《 His Torah. 〈 us 〈 and gave 〈 the peoples 〈 from all 〈 us 〈 selected

בָּרוּךְ אַתָּה יהוה, נוֹתֵן הַתּוֹרָה.   (אָמֵן. –CONG.)
《 (Amen.)   《 of the Torah. 〈 Giver 《 HASHEM, 〈 are You, 〈 Blessed

AFTER HIS TORAH PORTION HAS BEEN READ, THE *OLEH* RECITES:

בָּרוּךְ אַתָּה יהוה אֱלֹהֵינוּ מֶלֶךְ הָעוֹלָם, אֲשֶׁר
〈 Who 《 of the universe, 〈 King 〈 our God, 〈 HASHEM, 〈 are You, 〈 Blessed

נָתַן לָנוּ תּוֹרַת אֱמֶת, וְחַיֵּי עוֹלָם* נָטַע בְּתוֹכֵנוּ.
《 within us. 〈 He 〈 of 〈 and the 《 of truth, 〈 the Torah 〈 us 〈 gave
implanted eternity* life

בָּרוּךְ אַתָּה יהוה, נוֹתֵן הַתּוֹרָה.   (אָמֵן. –CONG.)
《 (Amen.)   《 of the Torah. 〈 Giver 《 HASHEM, 〈 are You, 〈 Blessed

---

THE TORAH READINGS BEGIN ON PAGE 767.

בָּרְכוּ אֶת ה' — *Bless HASHEM.* This call to the congregation to bless God prior to the Torah reading is based on the practice of Ezra (*Nehemiah* 8:6). Before he read from the Torah to the multitude, he blessed God and they responded in kind. Similarly, the Sages (*Berachos* 21a) derive the Scriptural requirement to recite a blessing before Torah study from the

verse, *When I proclaim the Name of* HASHEM, *ascribe greatness to our God* (*Deuteronomy* 32:3). The implication is that the public study of Torah requires a blessing.

תּוֹרַת אֱמֶת, וְחַיֵּי עוֹלָם — *The Torah of truth, and the life of eternity.* Torah of truth refers to the Written Torah, and *life of eternity* to the Oral Law. The Oral Law is described as *implanted*

THANKSGIVING BLESSING / בִּרְכַּת הַגּוֹמֵל

THE FOLLOWING IS RECITED BY ONE WHO SURVIVED A DANGEROUS SITUATION:

בָּרוּךְ אַתָּה יהוה אֱלֹהֵינוּ מֶלֶךְ הָעוֹלָם, הַגּוֹמֵל לְחַיָּבִים*

⟨ upon the ⟨ Who ⟪ of the ⟨ King ⟨ our God, ⟨HASHEM,⟨are You, ⟨ Blessed
unworthy* bestows universe,

טוֹבוֹת, שֶׁגְּמָלַנִי כָּל טוֹב.

⟪ goodness. ⟨ every ⟨ Who has ⟪ good
bestowed upon me things,

CONGREGATION RESPONDS:

אָמֵן. מִי שֶׁגְּמָלְךָ כָּל טוֹב, הוּא יִגְמָלְךָ כָּל טוֹב, סֶלָה.

⟪ for- ⟨ good- ⟨ every ⟨ [continue ⟨— may ⟪ good- ⟨ every ⟨ Who has ⟨ He ⟪ Amen.
ever. ness to] bestow He ness bestowed
upon you upon you

BAR MITZVAH BLESSING / בָּרוּךְ שֶׁפְּטָרַנִי

AFTER A BAR MITZVAH BOY COMPLETES HIS FIRST ALIYAH, HIS FATHER RECITES:

בָּרוּךְ (אַתָּה יהוה אֱלֹהֵינוּ מֶלֶךְ הָעוֹלָם,) שֶׁפְּטָרַנִי

⟨Who has removed ⟪ of the ⟨ King ⟨ our God, ⟨ HASHEM, ⟨ (are You, ⟨ Blessed [is
my responsibility universe,) the One,]

מֵעָנְשׁוֹ* שֶׁלָּזֶה.

⟪ due this ⟨ for the
[boy]. punishment*

---

within us, because Jews constantly expand their Torah knowledge through their personal study and analysis (*Tur Orach Chaim* 139).

בִּרְכַּת הַגּוֹמֵל / Thanksgiving Blessing

When the Temple stood, a person who had been spared from a life-threatening situation would bring a thanksgiving offering. Now, the obligation to thank God is discharged by reciting the thanksgiving blessing during the Torah reading, within three days of the event, if possible. It is customary, but not required, that the person reciting the blessing be called for an *aliyah*. The types of events that require one to recite the blessing are derived from Psalm 107. They are: (a) completion of a sea journey; (b) completion of a hazardous land journey; (c) recovery from a major illness; (d) release from captivity. By extension, however, the blessing should be recited whenever someone has been spared from a life-threatening situation (*Orach Chaim* 219:9).

לְחַיָּבִים — *Upon the unworthy* (lit. *guilty*). The term is used in recognition of the fact that the grateful person may not have been worthy of Divine protection. Thus, if danger was a natural result of his ordeal, it is an act of God's generosity that saved him.

בָּרוּךְ שֶׁפְּטָרַנִי / Bar Mitzvah Blessing

Midrash Rabbah to *Genesis* 25:27 teaches that this blessing is to be said by a father when his son becomes a *bar mitzvah*. Since the calling to the Torah is symbolic of religious adulthood, the father recites the blessing after his son has said the blessing following his *aliyah*. Although in most congregations the blessing is recited in abbreviated form (omitting the parenthesized phrase), many major Rabbinic authorities, with the concurrence of the *Vilna Gaon*, rule that the blessing should be recited in its full form.

שֶׁפְּטָרַנִי מֵעָנְשׁוֹ — *Who has removed my responsibility for the punishment.* There are two interpretations of the punishment: (a) Until the *bar mitzvah*, the father was responsible for his

מי שברך ליולדת בת (וקריאת שם)

PRAYER FOR MOTHER AND HER NEWBORN DAUGHTER

THE BRACKETED PASSAGE IS INCLUDED ONLY AT THE NAMING OF THE BABY.

מִי שֶׁבֵּרַךְ אֲבוֹתֵינוּ אַבְרָהָם יִצְחָק וְיַעֲקֹב, הוּא יְבָרֵךְ

‹ bless ‹— may ‹‹ and Jacob ‹ Isaac, ‹ Abraham, ‹ our forefathers, ‹ Who blessed ‹ The One
He

אֶת הָאִשָּׁה הַיּוֹלֶדֶת (NEW MOTHER'S NAME) בַּת (HER FATHER'S NAME)

‹ daughter of ‹ who has given birth, ‹ the woman

וְאֶת בִּתָּהּ הַנּוֹלְדָה לָהּ בְּמַזָּל טוֹב, [וְיִקָּרֵא שְׁמָהּ בְּיִשְׂרָאֵל

‹ in Israel: ‹‹ and let her name be called ‹‹ at an auspicious time, ‹ to her ‹ who was born ‹ and her daughter

(BABY'S NAME) בַּת (BABY'S FATHER'S NAME)] בַּעֲבוּר שֶׁבַּעְלָהּ וְאָבִיהָ

‹ [the infant's] father, ‹ her husband, ‹ because ‹ daughter of

יִתֵּן לִצְדָקָה. בִּשְׂכַר זֶה יִזְכּוּ לְגַדְּלָהּ (לְתוֹרָה) לְחֻפָּה

‹ to marriage ‹ (to Torah,) ‹ to raise her ‹ may they merit ‹ for this, ‹ In reward ‹‹ to charity [on their behalf]. ‹ will contribute

וּלְמַעֲשִׂים טוֹבִים. וְנֹאמַר: אָמֵן. — Cong.) אָמֵן.)

‹‹ (Amen.) ‹‹ Amen. ‹ Now let us respond: ‹‹ and to good deeds.

מי שברך ליולדת בן

PRAYER FOR MOTHER AND HER NEWBORN SON

מִי שֶׁבֵּרַךְ אֲבוֹתֵינוּ אַבְרָהָם יִצְחָק וְיַעֲקֹב, הוּא יְבָרֵךְ

‹ bless ‹— may ‹‹ and Jacob ‹ Isaac, ‹ Abraham, ‹ our forefathers, ‹ Who blessed ‹ The One
He

אֶת הָאִשָּׁה הַיּוֹלֶדֶת (NEW MOTHER'S NAME) בַּת (HER FATHER'S NAME)

‹ daughter of ‹ who has given birth, ‹ the woman

וְאֶת בְּנָהּ הַנּוֹלָד לָהּ בְּמַזָּל טוֹב, בַּעֲבוּר שֶׁבַּעְלָהּ וְאָבִיו

‹ [the infant's] father, ‹ her husband, ‹ because ‹‹ at an auspicious time, ‹ to her ‹ who was born ‹ and her son

יִתֵּן לִצְדָקָה. בִּשְׂכַר זֶה יִזְכּוּ (לְהַכְנִיסוֹ בִּבְרִיתוֹ שֶׁל

‹ of ‹ to the covenant ‹ (to bring him in ‹ may they merit ‹ for this, ‹ In reward ‹‹ to charity [on their behalf]. ‹ will contribute

---

child's actions and could be punished if they were deficient; or, (b) until the *bar mitzvah*, the child could have suffered for the failures of his parents. According to the second interpretation, the father is grateful that his own sins will no longer harm his child (*Magen Avraham* 225).

אַבְרָהָם אָבִינוּ בְּעִתּוֹ וּבִזְמַנּוֹ וּ . . .) לְגַדְּלוֹ לְתוֹרָה וּלְחֻפָּה

‹ to   ‹ to Torah, ‹ to raise ‹   and) ‹‹ in its proper time, ‹ our ‹ Abraham,
marriage,   him   forefather,

(אָמֵן.) –Cong.)   וּלְמַעֲשִׂים טוֹבִים. וְנֹאמַר: אָמֵן.

‹‹ (Amen.)   ‹‹ Amen. ‹‹ Now let ‹‹   and to good deeds,
                                       us respond:

מִי שֶׁבֵּרַךְ לְחוֹלֶה (זָכָר) / PRAYER FOR A SICK MAN

מִי שֶׁבֵּרַךְ אֲבוֹתֵינוּ אַבְרָהָם יִצְחָק וְיַעֲקֹב, מֹשֶׁה אַהֲרֹן

‹ Aaron, ‹ Moses, ‹   and   ‹ Isaac, ‹ Abraham, ‹   our   ‹ Who blessed ‹ The
                   Jacob,   forefathers,   One

דָּוִד וּשְׁלֹמֹה, הוּא יְבָרֵךְ וִירַפֵּא אֶת הַחוֹלֶה (PATIENT'S NAME) בֶּן

‹ son of   ‹ the sick person ‹ and heal ‹ bless ‹– may ‹‹ and   ‹ David,
                                                        He   Solomon

בַּעֲבוּר שֶׁ (SUPPLICANT'S NAME)°° (MOTHER'S NAME) יִתֵּן לִצְדָקָה בַּעֲבוּרוֹ.

‹‹ on his ‹ to charity ‹ will   ‹ because
   behalf.   contribute

––––––––––– MANY CONGREGATIONS SUBSTITUTE: –––––––––––

°°בַּעֲבוּר שֶׁכָּל הַקָּהָל מִתְפַּלְּלִים בַּעֲבוּרוֹ.

‹‹ for him. ‹ is praying ‹ congregation ‹ the entire ‹ because

בִּשְׂכַר זֶה, הַקָּדוֹשׁ בָּרוּךְ הוּא יִמָּלֵא רַחֲמִים עָלָיו,

‹ for him ‹   with   ‹ – may He ‹‹ is He ‹ Blessed ‹ the Holy ‹ for ‹ In reward
              compassion be filled   One,   this,

לְהַחֲלִימוֹ וּלְרַפֹּאתוֹ וּלְהַחֲזִיקוֹ וּלְהַחֲיוֹתוֹ, וְיִשְׁלַח לוֹ מְהֵרָה

‹ speedily ‹ him ‹ And may ‹‹   and to   ‹ to strengthen ‹ to heal him, ‹ to restore
             He send   revivify him.   him,   his health,

רְפוּאָה שְׁלֵמָה מִן הַשָּׁמַיִם, לִרְמַ"ח אֵבָרָיו, וּשְׁסָ"ה גִּידָיו,

‹‹ sinews, ‹ and 365 ‹ organs ‹ for his 248 ‹‹ heaven ‹ from ‹ a complete recovery

בְּתוֹךְ שְׁאָר חוֹלֵי יִשְׂרָאֵל, רְפוּאַת הַנֶּפֶשׁ, וּרְפוּאַת הַגּוּף,

‹‹ of the ‹ and a ‹ of the spirit ‹ a recovery ‹‹ of Israel, ‹ sick ‹ the other ‹ among
 body,   recovery   people

הַשְׁתָּא, בַּעֲגָלָא וּבִזְמַן קָרִיב. וְנֹאמַר: אָמֵן. (–CONG.) אָמֵן.)

‹‹ (Amen.)   ‹‹ Amen. ‹ Now let ‹‹ that comes ‹ and at ‹ swiftly, ‹ now,
                      us respond: soon.   a time

מי שברך לחולה (נקבה) / PREAYER FOR A SICK WOMAN

מִי שֶׁבֵּרַךְ אֲבוֹתֵינוּ אַבְרָהָם יִצְחָק וְיַעֲקֹב, מֹשֶׁה אַהֲרֹן
‹ Aaron, ‹ Moses, ‹ and ‹ Isaac, ‹ Abraham, ‹ our ‹ Who blessed ‹ The
Jacob, forefathers, One

דָּוִד וּשְׁלֹמֹה, הוּא יְבָרֵךְ וִירַפֵּא אֶת הַחוֹלָה (PATIENT'S NAME) בַּת
‹ daughter ‹ the sick person ‹ and heal ‹ bless ‹– may ‹‹ and ‹ David,
of He Solomon

°°בַּעֲבוּר שֶׁ(SUPPLICANT'S NAME) יִתֵּן לִצְדָקָה בַּעֲבוּרָה. (MOTHER'S NAME)
‹‹ on her ‹ to charity ‹ will ‹ because
behalf. contribute

——— MANY CONGREGATIONS SUBSTITUTE: ———

°°בַּעֲבוּר שֶׁכָּל הַקָּהָל מִתְפַּלְלִים בַּעֲבוּרָה.
‹‹ for her. ‹ is praying ‹ congregation ‹ the entire ‹ because

בִּשְׂכַר זֶה, הַקָּדוֹשׁ בָּרוּךְ הוּא יִמָּלֵא רַחֲמִים עָלֶיהָ,
‹ for her ‹ with ‹ – may He ‹‹ is He ‹ Blessed ‹ the Holy ‹ for ‹ In reward
compassion be filled One, this,

לְהַחְלִימָה וּלְרַפֹּאתָהּ וּלְהַחֲזִיקָהּ וּלְהַחֲיוֹתָהּ, וְיִשְׁלַח לָהּ
‹ her ‹ And may ‹‹ and to ‹ to strengthen ‹ to heal her, ‹ to restore
He send revivify her. her, her health,

מְהֵרָה רְפוּאָה שְׁלֵמָה מִן הַשָּׁמַיִם, לְכָל אֵבָרֶיהָ, וּלְכָל גִּידֶיהָ,
‹‹ sinews, ‹ and ‹ organs ‹ for ‹‹ heaven ‹ from ‹ a complete recovery ‹ speedily
all her all her

בְּתוֹךְ שְׁאָר חוֹלֵי יִשְׂרָאֵל, רְפוּאַת הַנֶּפֶשׁ, וּרְפוּאַת הַגּוּף,
‹‹ of the ‹ and a ‹ of the spirit ‹ a recovery ‹‹ of Israel, ‹ sick ‹ the other ‹ among
body, recovery people

הַשְׁתָּא, בַּעֲגָלָא וּבִזְמַן קָרִיב. וְנֹאמַר: אָמֵן. (–CONG. אָמֵן.)
‹‹ (Amen.) ‹‹ Amen. ‹ Now let ‹‹ that comes ‹ and at ‹ swiftly, ‹ now,
us respond: soon. a time

IN MANY CONGREGATIONS THE *GABBAI* RECITES THE FOLLOWING PRAYER FOR THOSE WHO
PASSED AWAY DURING THE YEAR AND, IN MANY CONGREGATIONS, FOR THOSE WHOSE *YAHRZEIT*
FALLS DURING THE COMING WEEK:

FOR A MAN:

אֵל מָלֵא רַחֲמִים, שׁוֹכֵן בַּמְּרוֹמִים, הַמְצֵא מְנוּחָה נְכוֹנָה עַל
‹ on ‹ that is ‹ rest ‹ grant ‹‹ on High, ‹ Who ‹ of mercy, ‹ full ‹ O
proper dwells God,

כַּנְפֵי הַשְּׁכִינָה, בְּמַעֲלוֹת קְדוֹשִׁים וּטְהוֹרִים, כְּזֹהַר הָרָקִיעַ
‹ of the ‹ who like ‹‹ and pure ‹ of the holy ‹ in the lofty ‹‹ of the Divine ‹ the
firmament the glow ones, levels Presence, wings

מַזְהִירִים, אֶת נִשְׁמַת (NAME OF THE DECEASED) בֶּן (FATHER'S NAME) שֶׁהָלַךְ

‹ who went on   ‹ son of   ‹ — for the soul of ‹‹   shine

לְעוֹלָמוֹ, בַּעֲבוּר שֶׁ(NAME OF SUPPLICANT) יִתֵּן צְדָקָה בְּעַד הַזְכָּרַת

‹ the   ‹ for ‹ to charity ‹ will   ‹ because, ‹‹   to his
remembrance   contribute   world,

נִשְׁמָתוֹ, בְּגַן עֵדֶן תְּהֵא מְנוּחָתוֹ, לָכֵן בַּעַל הָרַחֲמִים

‹ of mercy ‹ may the ‹ There- ‹‹ his resting ‹ should ‹ of Eden ‹ In the ‹‹   of his
              Master   fore   place.   be   Garden   soul.

יַסְתִּירֵהוּ בְּסֵתֶר כְּנָפָיו לְעוֹלָמִים, וְיִצְרוֹר בִּצְרוֹר הַחַיִּים

‹ of Life ‹ in the Bond ‹ and may ‹‹ for eternity; ‹ of His ‹ in the ‹ shelter him
              He bind   wings   shelter

אֶת נִשְׁמָתוֹ, יהוה הוּא נַחֲלָתוֹ, וְיָנוּחַ בְּשָׁלוֹם עַל מִשְׁכָּבוֹ.

‹‹ his resting ‹ in ‹ in peace ‹ and may ‹‹ his heritage, ‹ is ‹ Hashem ‹‹   his soul.
   place.   he repose

(אָמֵן. –Cong.)   וְנֹאמַר: אָמֵן.

‹‹ (Amen.)   ‹‹ Amen. ‹‹ Now let us respond:

FOR A WOMAN:

אֵל מָלֵא רַחֲמִים, שׁוֹכֵן בַּמְּרוֹמִים, הַמְצֵא מְנוּחָה נְכוֹנָה עַל

‹ on ‹ that is ‹   rest   ‹ grant ‹‹   on High,   ‹ Who ‹ of mercy, ‹ full ‹ O
        proper   dwells   God,

כַּנְפֵי הַשְּׁכִינָה, בְּמַעֲלוֹת קְדוֹשִׁים וּטְהוֹרִים, כְּזֹהַר הָרָקִיעַ

‹ of the ‹ who like ‹‹ and pure ‹ of the holy ‹ in the lofty ‹‹ of the Divine ‹ the
firmament the glow   ones,   levels   Presence,   wings

מַזְהִירִים, אֶת נִשְׁמַת (NAME OF THE DECEASED) בַּת (FATHER'S NAME) שֶׁהָלְכָה

‹ who went on   ‹ daughter of   ‹ — for the soul of ‹‹   shine

לְעוֹלָמָהּ, בַּעֲבוּר שֶׁ(NAME OF SUPPLICANT) יִתֵּן צְדָקָה בְּעַד הַזְכָּרַת

‹ the   ‹ for ‹ to charity ‹ will   ‹ because, ‹‹   to her
remembrance   contribute   world,

נִשְׁמָתָהּ, בְּגַן עֵדֶן תְּהֵא מְנוּחָתָהּ, לָכֵן בַּעַל הָרַחֲמִים

‹ of mercy ‹ may the ‹ There- ‹‹ her resting ‹ should ‹ of Eden ‹ In the ‹‹   of her
              Master   fore   place.   be   Garden   soul.

יַסְתִּירֶהָ בְּסֵתֶר כְּנָפָיו לְעוֹלָמִים, וְיִצְרוֹר בִּצְרוֹר הַחַיִּים

‹ of Life ‹ in the Bond ‹ and may ‹‹ for eternity; ‹ of His ‹ in the ‹ shelter her
              He bind   wings   shelter

אֶת נִשְׁמָתָהּ, יהוה הוּא נַחֲלָתָהּ, וְתָנוּחַ בְּשָׁלוֹם עַל מִשְׁכָּבָהּ.

‹‹ her resting ‹ in ‹ in peace ‹ and may ‹‹ her heritage, ‹ is ‹ Hashem ‹‹   her soul.
   place.   she repose

(אָמֵן. –Cong.)   וְנֹאמַר: אָמֵן.

‹‹ (Amen.)   ‹‹ Amen. ‹‹ Now let us respond:

HALF-*KADDISH* / חֲצִי קַדִּישׁ

**WHEN THE TORAH READING HAS BEEN COMPLETED,
THE READER RECITES חֲצִי קַדִּישׁ, HALF-*KADDISH*.**

יִתְגַּדַּל וְיִתְקַדַּשׁ שְׁמֵהּ רַבָּא. (.Cong –אָמֵן.) בְּעָלְמָא דִּי בְרָא

‹ He ‹ that ‹ in the   (Amen.)   ‹ that is ‹ may His‹ and be ‹ Grow exalted
created   world   great! —   Name   sanctified

כִרְעוּתֵהּ, וְיַמְלִיךְ מַלְכוּתֵהּ, וְיַצְמַח פֻּרְקָנֵהּ וִיקָרֵב מְשִׁיחֵהּ.

‹‹ His ‹ and bring ‹ His ‹ and cause ‹ to His ‹ and may He ‹‹ according
Messiah,   near   salvation,   to sprout   kingship,   give reign   to His will,

(.Cong –אָמֵן.) בְּחַיֵּיכוֹן וּבְיוֹמֵיכוֹן וּבְחַיֵּי דְכָל בֵּית יִשְׂרָאֵל,

‹‹ of Israel, ‹ Family ‹ of the ‹ and in the ‹ and in ‹ in your ‹‹ (Amen.)
entire   lifetimes   your days,   lifetimes

בַּעֲגָלָא וּבִזְמַן קָרִיב. וְאִמְרוּ: אָמֵן.

‹‹ Amen. ‹ Now ‹‹ that comes ‹ and at ‹ swiftly
respond: soon.   a time

CONGREGATION RESPONDS:

אָמֵן. יְהֵא שְׁמֵהּ רַבָּא מְבָרַךְ לְעָלַם וּלְעָלְמֵי עָלְמַיָּא.

‹‹ and for all eternity. ‹ forever ‹ be blessed ‹ that is great ‹ His Name ‹ May ‹‹ Amen.

CHAZZAN CONTINUES:

יְהֵא שְׁמֵהּ רַבָּא מְבָרַךְ לְעָלַם וּלְעָלְמֵי עָלְמַיָּא. יִתְבָּרַךְ

‹ Blessed, ‹‹ and for all eternity. ‹ forever ‹ be ‹ that ‹ His ‹ May
blessed   is great   Name

וְיִשְׁתַּבַּח וְיִתְפָּאַר וְיִתְרוֹמַם וְיִתְנַשֵּׂא וְיִתְהַדָּר וְיִתְעַלֶּה

‹ elevated, ‹ honored, ‹ upraised, ‹ exalted, ‹ glorified, ‹ praised,

וְיִתְהַלָּל שְׁמֵהּ דְּקֻדְשָׁא בְּרִיךְ הוּא (.Cong –בְּרִיךְ הוּא) —

‹‹ is He) ‹ (Blessed ‹‹ is He ‹ Blessed ‹ of the ‹ be the ‹ and lauded
Holy One,   Name

ROSH HASHANAH TO YOM KIPPUR SUBSTITUTE:

°לְעֵלָּא מִן כָּל [°לְעֵלָּא (וּ)לְעֵלָּא מִכָּל] בִּרְכָתָא

‹ blessing   ‹ any   ‹ exceedingly beyond   ‹ any   ‹ beyond

וְשִׁירָתָא, תֻּשְׁבְּחָתָא וְנֶחֱמָתָא דַּאֲמִירָן בְּעָלְמָא.

‹‹ in the world. ‹ that are uttered ‹ and consolation ‹ praise ‹‹ and song,

וְאִמְרוּ: אָמֵן. (.Cong –אָמֵן.)

‹‹ (Amen.)   ‹‹ Amen. ‹ Now respond:

◄§ חֲצִי קַדִּישׁ — *Half-Kaddish.* Half-*Kaddish* is
recited after the Torah reading is completed to
signify that this unit of the service is over.
However, when the Torah reading immedi-

ately precedes *Shemoneh Esrei,* as when the
Torah is read at *Minchah,* the Half-*Kaddish*
is recited after the Torah is returned to the
Ark.

HAGBAHAH AND GELILAH / הגבהה וגלילה

ALL STAND. THE TORAH IS RAISED FOR ALL TO SEE.
EACH PERSON LOOKS AT THE TORAH AND RECITES ALOUD:

[יהוה אֱלֹהֵינוּ אֱמֶת, מֹשֶׁה אֱמֶת, וְתוֹרָתוֹ

⟨ and his Torah ⟨⟨ is true; ⟨ Moses ⟨⟨ is true; ⟨ our God, ⟨ [Hashem,

אֱמֶת.] וְזֹאת הַתּוֹרָה* אֲשֶׁר שָׂם מֹשֶׁה לִפְנֵי

⟨ before ⟨ Moses placed ⟨ that ⟨ is the Torah* ⟨ This ⟨⟨ is true.]

בְּנֵי יִשְׂרָאֵל,¹ עַל פִּי יהוה בְּיַד מֹשֶׁה.²

⟨⟨ of Moses. ⟨ through the hand ⟨ of Hashem, ⟨ the word ⟨ according to ⟨⟨ of Israel, ⟨ the Children

SOME ADD:

עֵץ חַיִּים* הִיא לַמַּחֲזִיקִים בָּהּ, וְתֹמְכֶיהָ מְאֻשָּׁר.*³

⟨⟨ are praiseworthy.* ⟨ and its supporters ⟨⟨ it, ⟨ for those who grasp ⟨ is it ⟨ of life* ⟨ A tree

דְּרָכֶיהָ דַרְכֵי נֹעַם, וְכָל נְתִיבוֹתֶיהָ שָׁלוֹם.⁴ אֹרֶךְ יָמִים

⟨ of days ⟨ Length ⟨⟨ are peace. ⟨ its paths ⟨ and all ⟨⟨ of pleasantness, ⟨ are ways ⟨ Its ways

בִּימִינָהּ, בִּשְׂמֹאלָהּ עֹשֶׁר וְכָבוֹד.⁵ יהוה חָפֵץ לְמַעַן

⟨ for the sake ⟨⟨ desired, ⟨ Hashem ⟨⟨ and honor. ⟨ are wealth ⟨ at its left ⟨⟨ are at its right;

צִדְקוֹ, יַגְדִּיל תּוֹרָה* וְיַאְדִּיר.⁶

⟨⟨ and [make it] glorious. ⟨ the Torah* ⟨ that He ⟨⟨ make great ⟨ of [Israel's] righteousness,

(1) Deuteronomy 4:44. (2) Numbers 9:23. (3) Proverbs 3:18. (4) 3:17. (5) 3:16. (6) Isaiah 42:21.

וְזֹאת הַתּוֹרָה § — This is the Torah. As everyone looks at the words and columns of the unrolled Torah Scroll held aloft, they declare the cardinal tenet of faith that the Torah now in our hands is the same one that God transmitted to Moses.

עֵץ חַיִּים — A tree of life. The soil gives of its strength and substance to the tree that is planted in it. In this manner the soil ennobles its own substance by having it absorbed into the life and growth of the tree so that the latter blossoms and bears fruit. What is true of the soil is true also of those who cling to the Torah and let it be their guide. By dedicating all their energies and substance to the spirit of this Law and to the power of the will of God as revealed in its words, they grow and their talents unfold, they are ennobled and refined and bear ripe fruit, and this fruit is none other than חַיִּים, life, for only the Divine ideal, translated into living reality in this manner, can be true life (R' Hirsch).

וְתֹמְכֶיהָ מְאֻשָּׁר – And its supporters are praiseworthy. תֹמְכֶיהָ is in the plural, while מְאֻשָּׁר is in the singular. This indicates that if the many pool their energies for the sake of the preservation and upholding of the Torah, then these many will be welded into one united group through their common striving on behalf of the Torah (R' Hirsch).

יַגְדִּיל תּוֹרָה — That He make great the Torah. Israel's suffering in exile was ordained by God

ON PURIM AND TISHAH B'AV THE TORAH IS RETURNED AT THIS POINT (TURN TO P. 225), FOLLOWED BY THE *MEGILLAH* ON PURIM AND THE RECITATION OF *KINNOS* ON TISHAH B'AV.

ON MONDAY AND THURSDAY, THE *CHAZZAN* RECITES THE FOLLOWING PRAYER ALOUD. IT IS OMITTED ON DAYS WHEN *TACHANUN* IS NOT RECITED.

יְהִי רָצוֹן* מִלְּפְנֵי אָבִינוּ שֶׁבַּשָּׁמַיִם, לְכוֹנֵן אֶת בֵּית

May it be ‹ the will* ‹ before ‹ our Father ‹ Who is in heaven, ‹ to establish ‹ to ‹ the House ‹

חַיֵּינוּ,* וּלְהָשִׁיב אֶת שְׁכִינָתוֹ בְּתוֹכֵנוּ, בִּמְהֵרָה בְיָמֵינוּ.

of our lives* ‹ and to return ‹ His Presence ‹ into our midst, ‹ speedily, ‹ in our days ‹

וְנֹאמַר: אָמֵן. (אָמֵן.–Cong.)

‹ — and let us say: ‹ Amen. ‹ (Amen.)

יְהִי רָצוֹן מִלְּפְנֵי אָבִינוּ שֶׁבַּשָּׁמַיִם, לְרַחֵם עָלֵינוּ

May it be ‹ the will ‹ before ‹ our Father ‹ Who is in heaven, ‹ to have mercy ‹ upon us ‹

וְעַל פְּלֵיטָתֵנוּ,* וְלִמְנֹעַ מַשְׁחִית וּמַגֵּפָה מֵעָלֵינוּ וּמֵעַל

and upon ‹ our remnant,* ‹ and to keep away ‹ destruction ‹ and disease ‹ from upon us ‹ from upon ‹ and from upon ‹

כָּל עַמּוֹ בֵּית יִשְׂרָאֵל. וְנֹאמַר: אָמֵן. (אָמֵן.–Cong.)

all ‹ of His people, ‹ the House ‹ of Israel. ‹ — and let us say: ‹ Amen. ‹ (Amen.)

יְהִי רָצוֹן מִלְּפְנֵי אָבִינוּ שֶׁבַּשָּׁמַיִם, לְקַיֵּם בָּנוּ חַכְמֵי

May it be ‹ the will ‹ before ‹ our Father ‹ Who is in heaven, ‹ to preserve ‹ among us ‹ the sages ‹

to cleanse them of their sins, just as the Torah was given to them for that purpose (*Kara*).

יְהִי רָצוֹן ‹§ — *May it be the will.* This very ancient series of prayers dates from the days of Rav Amram Gaon (9th century), whose *siddur* prescribed that it be recited after the Torah reading on Monday and Thursday. Apparently, the merit of communal Torah reading makes the time most fitting to beseech God for the fulfillment of His people's yearnings.

בֵּית חַיֵּינוּ — *The House of our lives.* The Temple

is a primary factor in Jewish life because it is there that the Presence of God will rest. Consequently, it will give strength and meaning to Jewish spiritual life.

וְעַל פְּלֵיטָתֵנוּ — *And upon our remnant.* In the literal sense, this phrase refers to the many remnants of our people that escaped the countless pogroms, persecutions, expulsions, and slaughters of Jewish history. In the broader sense, it refers to the exiled nation that still survives the Destruction of the Temple and the dispersion of its people.

יִשְׂרָאֵל,* הֵם וּנְשֵׁיהֶם וּבְנֵיהֶם וּבְנוֹתֵיהֶם וְתַלְמִידֵיהֶם
‹ their disciples, ‹ their daughters, ‹ their sons, ‹ their wives, ‹ – them, ‹‹ of Israel*

וְתַלְמִידֵי תַלְמִידֵיהֶם, בְּכָל מְקוֹמוֹת מוֹשְׁבוֹתֵיהֶם.
‹‹ of their dwelling ‹ the places ‹ in all ‹ of their disciples, ‹ and the disciples

וְנֹאמַר: אָמֵן.
‹‹ Amen. ‹‹ – and let us say:

(אָמֵן.–Cong.)
‹‹ (Amen.)

יְהִי רָצוֹן מִלְפְנֵי אָבִינוּ שֶׁבַּשָׁמַיִם, שֶׁנִּשְׁמַע
‹ that we may hear ‹‹ Who is in heaven, ‹ our Father ‹ before ‹ the will ‹‹ May it be

וְנִתְבַּשֵׂר בְּשׂוֹרוֹת טוֹבוֹת, יְשׁוּעוֹת וְנֶחָמוֹת, וִיקַבֵּץ
‹ and that ‹‹ and ‹ salvations, ‹ of good tidings, ‹ and be informed
He gather in   consolations,

נִדָּחֵינוּ מֵאַרְבַּע כַּנְפוֹת הָאָרֶץ. וְנֹאמַר: אָמֵן.
‹‹ Amen. ‹‹ – and let ‹‹ of the earth ‹ corners ‹ from ‹ our dispersed
              us say: the four   ones

(אָמֵן.–Cong.)
‹‹ (Amen.)

THE ENTIRE CONGREGATION, FOLLOWED BY THE *CHAZZAN*, RECITES THE NEXT STANZA ALOUD:

אַחֵינוּ* כָּל בֵּית יִשְׂרָאֵל, הַנְּתוּנִים בְּצָרָה וּבְשִׁבְיָה,
‹‹ and ‹ in distress ‹ who are ‹‹ of Israel, ‹ House ‹ the ‹ Our
captivity,   found   entire   brothers,*

הָעוֹמְדִים בֵּין בַּיָּם וּבֵין בַּיַּבָּשָׁה, הַמָּקוֹם יְרַחֵם
‹ have ‹ – may the Omni- ‹‹ on land ‹ or ‹ at sea ‹ whether ‹ who are
mercy   present One   whether   situated

עֲלֵיהֶם וְיוֹצִיאֵם מִצָּרָה לִרְוָחָה, וּמֵאֲפֵלָה לְאוֹרָה,
‹ to light, ‹ from darkness ‹ to relief, ‹ from distress ‹ and remove them ‹‹ on them

וּמִשִׁעְבּוּד לִגְאֻלָּה, הַשְׁתָּא בַּעֲגָלָא וּבִזְמַן קָרִיב.
‹‹ that comes ‹ and at ‹ speedily, ‹ now, ‹‹ to redemption, ‹ from subjugation
soon   a time

וְנֹאמַר: אָמֵן.
‹‹ Amen. ‹‹ – and let us say:

(אָמֵן.–Cong.)
‹‹ (Amen.)

חַכְמֵי יִשְׂרָאֵל — *The sages of Israel.* Singled out in this prayer are the Torah sages, for Israel was, is, and will be a nation only by virtue of the Torah.

אֲחֵינוּ §◉ — *Our brothers.* This brief plea for God's mercy on all suffering Jews is often recited communally when prayers are offered for Jews who are in danger.

❧ אשרי – ובא לציון / ASHREI – UVA L'TZION ❧

THIS CONCLUDING SECTION OF *SHACHARIS* IS RECITED EVERY WEEKDAY.

אַשְׁרֵי יוֹשְׁבֵי בֵיתֶךָ, עוֹד יְהַלְלוּךָ סֶּלָה.¹ אַשְׁרֵי

‹ Praise- ‹‹ *Selah.* ‹‹ they will ‹ continually ‹‹ in Your ‹ are those ‹ Praiseworthy
worthy   praise You,   house,   who dwell

²הָעָם שֶׁכָּכָה לוֹ, אַשְׁרֵי הָעָם שֶׁיהוה אֱלֹהָיו.

‹‹ is their ‹ that HASHEM ‹ is the ‹ praise- ‹‹ is ‹ that such ‹ is the
God.   people   worthy   their lot;   people

——— *Psalm* 145 / תהלים קמה ———

תְּהִלָּה לְדָוִד; אֲרוֹמִמְךָ אֱלוֹהַי הַמֶּלֶךְ, וַאֲבָרְכָה

‹ and I will ‹‹ the King, ‹ my God ‹ I will exalt ‹‹ by David: ‹ A psalm
bless   You,   of praise

שִׁמְךָ לְעוֹלָם וָעֶד. בְּכָל יוֹם אֲבָרְכֶךָּ, וַאֲהַלְלָה

‹ and I will laud ‹‹ I will bless ‹ day ‹ Every ‹‹ and ‹ for ever ‹ Your
You,   ever.   Name

שִׁמְךָ לְעוֹלָם וָעֶד. גָּדוֹל יהוה וּמְהֻלָּל מְאֹד,

‹‹ exceed- ‹ and lauded ‹ is ‹ Great ‹‹ and ever. ‹ for ever ‹ Your
ingly,   HASHEM   Name

וְלִגְדֻלָּתוֹ אֵין חֵקֶר. דּוֹר לְדוֹר יְשַׁבַּח מַעֲשֶׂיךָ,

‹‹ Your actions, ‹ will praise ‹ to ‹ Generation ‹‹ is beyond ‹ and His
         generation   investigation.   greatness

וּגְבוּרֹתֶיךָ יַגִּידוּ. הֲדַר כְּבוֹד הוֹדֶךָ וְדִבְרֵי

‹ and Your ‹ of Your ‹ glory ‹ The ‹‹ they will ‹ and Your
deeds   majesty   splendrous   recount.   mighty deeds

נִפְלְאֹתֶיךָ אָשִׂיחָה. וֶעֱזוּז נוֹרְאֹתֶיךָ יֹאמֵרוּ,

‹‹ they ‹ of Your ‹ And of ‹‹ I shall discuss. ‹ that are wondrous
will speak,   awesome deeds   the might

---

(1) *Psalms* 84:5. (2) 144:15.

❧ אַשְׁרֵי – וּבָא לְצִיּוֹן / Ashrei – Uva L'Tzion

With *Shemoneh Esrei* and *Tachanun*, both the *Shacharis* service and we who have recited it reached the climax of spiritual elevation. Now, we return to the everyday life with which we will grapple for the rest of the day.

Ashrei is the perfect symbol of this transition, because it praises not only God's Omnipotence, but also His closeness and compassion for all creatures. Most importantly, it contains the critical verse, *You open Your hand, and satisfy the desire of every living thing*, which, the

וּגְדֻלָּתְךָ אֲסַפְּרֶנָּה. זֵכֶר רַב טוּבְךָ יַבִּיעוּ,

‹ they will utter, ‹ of Your abundant goodness ‹ A recollection ‹‹ I shall relate. ‹ and Your greatness

וְצִדְקָתְךָ יְרַנְּנוּ. חַנּוּן וְרַחוּם יהוה, אֶרֶךְ אַפַּיִם

‹ to anger, ‹ slow ‹‹ is HASHEM, ‹ and merciful ‹ Gracious ‹‹ they will sing joyfully. ‹ and of Your righteousness

וּגְדָל חָסֶד. טוֹב יהוה לַכֹּל, וְרַחֲמָיו עַל כָּל

‹ all ‹ are on ‹ His mercies ‹‹ to all; ‹ HASHEM is good ‹‹ in [bestowing] ‹ and great kindness.

מַעֲשָׂיו. יוֹדוּךָ יהוה כָּל מַעֲשֶׂיךָ, וַחֲסִידֶיךָ

‹ and Your devout ones ‹‹ Your creations, ‹ – all ‹ HASHEM ‹ They will thank You, ‹‹ His creations.

יְבָרְכוּכָה. כְּבוֹד מַלְכוּתְךָ יֹאמֵרוּ, וּגְבוּרָתְךָ

‹ and of Your power ‹‹ they will speak, ‹ of Your kingdom ‹ Of the glory ‹‹ will bless You.

יְדַבֵּרוּ. לְהוֹדִיעַ לִבְנֵי הָאָדָם גְּבוּרֹתָיו, וּכְבוֹד

‹ and of the glorious ‹‹ of His mighty deeds, ‹ mankind ‹ To inform ‹‹ they will declare.

הֲדַר מַלְכוּתוֹ. מַלְכוּתְךָ מַלְכוּת כָּל עֹלָמִים,

‹‹ eternities, ‹ [spanning] all ‹ is a kingdom ‹ Your kingdom ‹‹ of His kingdom. ‹ splendor

וּמֶמְשַׁלְתְּךָ בְּכָל דּוֹר וָדֹר. סוֹמֵךְ יהוה לְכָל

‹ all ‹ HASHEM supports ‹‹ after generation. ‹ generation ‹ is throughout ‹ and Your dominion

הַנֹּפְלִים, וְזוֹקֵף לְכָל הַכְּפוּפִים. עֵינֵי כֹל אֵלֶיךָ

‹ to You ‹ of all ‹ The eyes ‹‹ those who are bent. ‹ all ‹ and straightens ‹‹ those who are fallen,

יְשַׂבֵּרוּ, וְאַתָּה נוֹתֵן לָהֶם אֶת אָכְלָם בְּעִתּוֹ.

‹‹ in its proper time. ‹ their food ‹ them ‹ give ‹ and You ‹‹ do look with hope,

---

Sages teach, is the reason *Ashrei* is recited three times daily. The *Zohar* teaches that the *Ashrei* of *Pesukei D'Zimrah* is meant as praise of God rather than a plea for mercy and sustenance.

The *Ashrei* we are about to recite now, however, is our plea that God provide our needs, coming as it does after the prayers of *Shemoneh Esrei*. Only now, after the praise and

CONCENTRATE INTENTLY WHILE RECITING THE VERSE פּוֹתֵחַ, *YOU OPEN . . .*

פּוֹתֵחַ אֶת יָדֶךָ, וּמַשְׂבִּיעַ לְכָל חַי רָצוֹן. צַדִּיק

⟨ Righteous ⟨⟨ [with its] ⟨ living ⟨ every ⟨ and satisfy ⟨⟨ Your hand, ⟨ You open
desire. thing

יהוה בְּכָל דְּרָכָיו, וְחָסִיד בְּכָל מַעֲשָׂיו.

⟨⟨ His deeds. ⟨ in all ⟨ and magnanimous ⟨⟨ His ways, ⟨ in all ⟨ is Hashem

קָרוֹב יהוה לְכָל קֹרְאָיו, לְכֹל אֲשֶׁר יִקְרָאֻהוּ

⟨ call upon Him ⟨ who ⟨ to all ⟨⟨ who call ⟨ to all ⟨ is Hashem ⟨ Close
upon Him,

בֶאֱמֶת. רְצוֹן יְרֵאָיו יַעֲשֶׂה, וְאֶת שַׁוְעָתָם יִשְׁמַע

⟨ He will ⟨ and their cry ⟨⟨ He will do; ⟨ of those who ⟨ The will ⟨⟨ sincerely.
hear, fear Him

וְיוֹשִׁיעֵם. שׁוֹמֵר יהוה אֶת כָּל אֹהֲבָיו, וְאֵת כָּל

⟨ but all ⟨⟨ who love Him; ⟨ all ⟨ Hashem protects ⟨⟨ and He will save them.

הָרְשָׁעִים יַשְׁמִיד. ❖ תְּהִלַּת יהוה יְדַבֶּר פִּי, וִיבָרֵךְ

⟨ and bless ⟨⟨ may my ⟨ of ⟨ The ⟨⟨ He will ⟨ the wicked
mouth declare, Hashem praise destroy.

כָּל בָּשָׂר שֵׁם קָדְשׁוֹ לְעוֹלָם וָעֶד. וַאֲנַחְנוּ נְבָרֵךְ

⟨ will bless ⟨ But we ⟨⟨ and ⟨ for ever ⟨ of His ⟨ the ⟨ flesh ⟨ may
ever. Holiness Name all

יָהּ מֵעַתָּה וְעַד עוֹלָם; הַלְלוּיָהּ.[1]

⟨⟨ Halleluyah! ⟨⟨ eternity. ⟨ until ⟨ from this time ⟨ God

——————— תהלים כ / Psalm 20 ———————

לַמְנַצֵּחַ* מִזְמוֹר לְדָוִד. יַעַנְךָ יהוה בְּיוֹם

⟨ on the day ⟨ May Hashem answer you ⟨⟨ by David. ⟨ a psalm ⟨ For the conductor,*

---

(1) *Psalms* 115:18.

exaltation of *Shemoneh Esrei*, may we pray for ourselves *(World of Prayer)*. [A commentary to *Ashrei* appears on pages 99-103.]

  ◈§ לַמְנַצֵּחַ — *For the conductor.* The *Vilna Gaon* comments that this psalm contains seventy words, alluding to the seventy-year exile before

◈§ **Occasions and Days on Which לַמְנַצֵּחַ (Psalm 20) Is Omitted**

(a) In a house of mourning during the *shivah* period;

(b) on Rosh Chodesh, Erev Pesach, Chol HaMoed, Tishah B'Av, Erev Yom Kippur, Chanukah, Purim and Shushan Purim, and the 14th and 15th of Adar I (Purim Kattan).

צָרָה;* יְשַׂגֶּבְךָ שֵׁם אֱלֹהֵי יַעֲקֹב.* יִשְׁלַח עֶזְרְךָ

distress;* may you be made impregnable by the Name of the God of Jacob.* May He dispatch your help

מִקְדָשׁ,* וּמִצִּיּוֹן יִסְעָדֶךָּ. יִזְכֹּר כָּל מִנְחֹתֶיךָ,*

from the Sanctuary,* and from Zion may He support you. May He remember all your offerings,*

וְעוֹלָתְךָ יְדַשְּׁנֶה* סֶלָה. יִתֶּן לְךָ כִלְבָבֶךָ, וְכָל

and your burnt-offerings, may He accept with favor* Selah. May He grant you as your heart [desires], and every

עֲצָתְךָ יְמַלֵּא. נְרַנְּנָה בִּישׁוּעָתֶךָ, וּבְשֵׁם אֱלֹהֵינוּ

plan of yours may He fulfill. May we sing for joy at your salvation, and in the Name of our God

נִדְגֹּל; יְמַלֵּא יהוה כָּל מִשְׁאֲלוֹתֶיךָ. עַתָּה יָדַעְתִּי*

raise our banner; may HASHEM fulfill all your requests. Now I know*

כִּי הוֹשִׁיעַ יהוה מְשִׁיחוֹ; יַעֲנֵהוּ מִשְּׁמֵי קָדְשׁוֹ,

that HASHEM has saved His Anointed one; He will answer him from His sacred heaven,

---

the construction of the Second Temple. Since this psalm alludes to the period before the construction of an earlier Temple, it was inserted into the daily prayers to symbolize the period before the building of the Third and final Temple. This period is called by the Sages חֶבְלֵי מָשִׁחַ, the *birthpangs of the Messiah.* Just as labor pains grow more severe as the time of birth approaches, so the trials of the exile will intensify before the coming of Messiah. Therefore, the psalm was inserted into the daily prayers to beseech God for help in time of distress. Because of its somber nature, the psalm is omitted on festive days.

בְּיוֹם צָרָה — *On the day of distress;* before it is too late (*Malbim*).

אֱלֹהֵי יַעֲקֹב — *The God of Jacob.* Of all the Partriachs, Jacob had the hardest life — the threats from Esau, exile under Laban and Pharaoh, the death of Rachel, the kidnaping of Dinah, the loss of Joseph — but God protected

him. Therefore, in time of distress we call upon *Jacob's God* (*Kad HaKemach*).

יִשְׁלַח עֶזְרְךָ מִקְדָש — *May He dispatch your help from the Sanctuary,* from the Holy of Holies inside the Temple where the Holy Ark rests and where God's spirit dwells. From there will go forth Divine aid in battle (*Radak*). We pray that our aid come from the Sanctuary, based in holiness, and not from unholy sources such as the hands of gentile kings and armies which may fight on our side. It is the holiness of the Jewish people themselves, their sacred deeds and words, that is their main ally in battle.

מִנְחֹתֶיךָ — *Your offerings,* Israel's offerings in the Temple (*Ibn Ezra*); or the prayers offered in time of danger (*Rashi*).

יְדַשְּׁנֶה — *May He accept with favor,* lit. *burn to ashes* (*Radak*).

עַתָּה יָדַעְתִּי — *Now I know.* After God grants salvation, I will know that He is the Source of help and triumph (*Radak*).

בִּגְבוּרוֹת יֵשַׁע יְמִינוֹ. אֵלֶּה בָרֶכֶב וְאֵלֶּה

< and some < with chariots, < Some ≪ of His right arm. < victories < with the omnipotent

בַסּוּסִים, וַאֲנַחְנוּ בְּשֵׁם יהוה אֱלֹהֵינוּ נַזְכִּיר.

≪ call out. < our God, < of HASHEM, < in the Name < but we, ≪ with horses;

הֵמָּה* כָּרְעוּ וְנָפָלוּ, וַאֲנַחְנוּ קַמְנוּ וַנִּתְעוֹדָד.

≪ and were invigorated. < arose < but we ≪ and fell, < dropped to < They*
their knees

❖ יהוה הוֹשִׁיעָה, הַמֶּלֶךְ יַעֲנֵנוּ בְיוֹם קָרְאֵנוּ.

≪ we call. < on the day < answer us < May the King ≪ save! < HASHEM

THE PRIMARY PART OF **וּבָא לְצִיּוֹן** IS THE *KEDUSHAH* RECITED BY THE ANGELS. THESE VERSES ARE PRESENTED IN BOLD TYPE AND IT IS PREFERABLE THAT THE CONGREGATION RECITE THEM ALOUD WITH THE *CHAZZAN*. HOWEVER, THE INTERPRETIVE TRANSLATION IN ARAMAIC (WHICH FOLLOWS THE VERSES IN BOLD TYPE) SHOULD BE RECITED SOFTLY.

וּבָא לְצִיּוֹן גּוֹאֵל,* וּלְשָׁבֵי פֶשַׁע בְּיַעֲקֹב,

≪ among Jacob < from willful sin < and to those who repent ≪ shall a redeemer,* < to Zion < Come

נְאֻם יהוה.

≪ of HASHEM. < — the words

הֵמָּה — *They.* Our seemingly invincible enemies fell in defeat, but we, who had been losing, arose and overwhelmed them when we called out in God's Name (*Radak*).

⧉ וּבָא לְצִיּוֹן / **Uva L'Tzion**

The most important part of the וּבָא לְצִיּוֹן prayer is the recitation in unison of the angel's praises of God. The Talmud refers to this part of the prayer as קְדֻשָּׁה דְסִדְרָא, *The Order of Kedushah.*

The Talmud (*Sotah* 49a) declares that since the destruction of the Temple, even the physical beauty and pleasures of the world began deteriorating. If so, by what merit does the world endure? Rava teaches, because of *The Order of Kedushah* that is contained in the prayer *Uva L'Tzion,* and the recitation of *Kaddish* following the public study of Torah. *Rashi* explains that after the Destruction, the primary focus of holiness in the universe is Torah study. In *Uva L'Tzion,* the Talmudic Sages combined the Scriptural verses containing the angels' praises of God with the interpretive translation of *Yonasan ben Uziel.* Thus, this prayer constitutes Torah study and, because it is placed toward the end of the service, when even latecomers are present in the synagogue, it involves the entire congregation in Torah study. This emphasis on Torah study is further stressed by the latter part of *Uva L'Tzion* which lauds the study and observance of the Torah. The *Kaddish* recited after public Torah study is a further affirmation of the Torah's central role in Jewish existence.

R' Yaakov Emden explains the significance of *Uva L'Tzion* differently. Since the Destruction, we lack the Temple service as a means to assure acceptance of Israel's prayers. But God does not spurn the prayers of those who repent, nor is the merit of Torah study diminished. Thus, at the conclusion of *Shacharis,* the Sages inserted *Uva L'Tzion,* which begins with a prophetic assurance to penitents and contains Torah study revolving around the sublime angelic praise: *Holy, Holy, Holy.*

וּבָא לְצִיּוֹן גּוֹאֵל — *Come to Zion shall a redeemer.*

IN A HOUSE OF MOURNING AND ON TISHAH B'AV THE FOLLOWING VERSE IS OMITTED:

וַאֲנִי, זֹאת בְּרִיתִי* אוֹתָם, אָמַר יהוה, רוּחִי אֲשֶׁר

‹ that ‹ My spirit ‹‹ Hashem: ‹ said ‹‹ with them, ‹ is My ‹ this ‹‹ And as
covenant* for Me,

עָלֶיךָ, וּדְבָרַי אֲשֶׁר שַׂמְתִּי בְּפִיךָ, לֹא יָמוּשׁוּ

‹ be ‹ shall ‹ in your ‹ I have ‹ that ‹ and My ‹ is upon
withdrawn not mouth placed words you

מִפִּיךָ וּמִפִּי זַרְעֲךָ* וּמִפִּי זֶרַע זַרְעֲךָ, אָמַר

‹ said ‹‹ of your ‹ of the ‹ [nor] from ‹‹ of your ‹ [nor] from ‹‹ from your
offspring, offspring the mouth offspring,* the mouth mouth,

יהוה, מֵעַתָּה וְעַד עוֹלָם.¹

‹‹ eternity. ‹ until ‹ from this time ‹‹ Hashem,

❖ וְאַתָּה קָדוֹשׁ יוֹשֵׁב תְּהִלּוֹת יִשְׂרָאֵל.*² וְקָרָא זֶה

‹ And one [angel] ‹‹ of Israel.* ‹ upon the ‹ enthroned ‹‹ the Holy ‹ Yet You are
will call praises One,

אֶל זֶה וְאָמַר: קָדוֹשׁ קָדוֹשׁ קָדוֹשׁ יהוה צְבָאוֹת,

‹‹ Master of Legions, ‹ is Hashem, ‹ holy ‹ holy, ‹ Holy, ‹‹ and say: ‹ another ‹ to

מְלֹא כָל הָאָרֶץ כְּבוֹדוֹ.³ וּמְקַבְּלִין דֵּין מִן דֵּין

‹ the ‹ from ‹ one ‹ And they receive ‹‹ [with] His ‹ world ‹ is the ‹ filled
other [permission] glory. whole

---

(1) *Isaiah* 59:20-21. (2) *Psalms* 22:4. (3) *Isaiah* 6:3.

God pledges that Messiah will come to redeem the City of Zion and the people of Israel. Not only those who remained righteous throughout the ordeal of exile will be saved, but even those who had been sinners will join in the glorious future, provided they return to the ways of God (*Etz Yosef*).

זֹאת בְּרִיתִי — *This is My covenant.* God affirms that His covenant with Israel will always remain in force: that His *spirit* [of prophecy] and the *words* [of His Torah] will remain with Israel forever (*Metzudos*).

מִפִּיךָ וּמִפִּי זַרְעֲךָ... — *From your mouth, [nor] from the mouth of your offspring ...* — Three generations are mentioned here. This is a Divine assurance that if a family produces three con-

secutive generations of profound Torah scholars, the blessing of Torah knowledge *shall not be withdrawn* from its posterity (*Bava Metzia* 85a). In a broader sense, we see the fulfillment of this blessing in the miracle that Torah greatness has remained with Israel throughout centuries of exile and flight from country to country and from continent to continent (*Siach Yitzchak*).

יוֹשֵׁב תְּהִלּוֹת יִשְׂרָאֵל — *Enthroned upon the praises of Israel.* Although God is praised by myriad angels, He values the praises of Israel above all; as the Sages teach (*Chullin* 90b), the angels are not permitted to sing their praises above until the Jewish people sing theirs below (*Abudraham*).

וְאָמְרִין: קַדִּישׁ בִּשְׁמֵי מְרוֹמָא עִלָּאָה בֵּית
‹ the abode ‹ on high, ‹ in the lofty heavens ‹ Holy ‹‹ and say:

שְׁכִינְתֵּהּ, קַדִּישׁ עַל אַרְעָא עוֹבַד גְּבוּרְתֵּהּ, קַדִּישׁ
‹ holy ‹‹ of His might; ‹ the product ‹ earth, ‹ on ‹ holy ‹‹ of His Presence;

לְעָלַם וּלְעָלְמֵי עָלְמַיָּא, יהוה צְבָאוֹת, מַלְיָא
‹ filled ‹‹ Master of Legions; ‹ is HASHEM, ‹ and to all eternity ‹ forever

כָּל אַרְעָא זִיו יְקָרֵהּ.¹ ❖ וַתִּשָּׂאֵנִי רוּחַ,* וָאֶשְׁמַע
‹ and I heard ‹‹ A wind lifted me,* ‹‹ of His glory. ‹ with the radiance ‹ world ‹ is the whole

אַחֲרַי קוֹל רַעַשׁ גָּדוֹל: בָּרוּךְ כְּבוֹד יהוה
‹ of HASHEM ‹ is the glory ‹ Blessed ‹‹ of a great noise: ‹ the sound ‹ behind me

מִמְּקוֹמוֹ.² וּנְטָלַתְנִי רוּחָא, וְשִׁמְעֵת בַּתְרַי קָל
‹ the sound ‹ behind me ‹ and I heard ‹ A wind lifted me, ‹‹ from His place.

זִיעַ סַגִּיא דִּמְשַׁבְּחִין וְאָמְרִין: בְּרִיךְ יְקָרָא דַיהוה
‹ of HASHEM ‹ is the glory ‹ Blessed ‹‹ and saying: ‹ of those who were praising ‹ that was great ‹ of noise

מֵאֲתַר בֵּית שְׁכִינְתֵּהּ.³ יהוה יִמְלֹךְ לְעָלַם וָעֶד.⁴
‹‹ and ever. ‹ for ever ‹ shall reign ‹ HASHEM ‹‹ of His Presence. ‹ of the abode ‹ from the place

יהוה מַלְכוּתֵהּ קָאֵם לְעָלַם וּלְעָלְמֵי עָלְמַיָּא.⁵
‹‹ and to all eternity. ‹ forever ‹ stands ‹ – His kingdom ‹‹ HASHEM

יהוה אֱלֹהֵי אַבְרָהָם יִצְחָק וְיִשְׂרָאֵל אֲבֹתֵינוּ,
‹ our forefathers, ‹ and Israel, ‹ Isaac, ‹ of Abraham, ‹ God ‹ HASHEM,

שָׁמְרָה זֹּאת* לְעוֹלָם, לְיֵצֶר מַחְשְׁבוֹת לְבַב
‹ of the heart ‹ of the thoughts ‹ as the product ‹ forever ‹ this* ‹ may You safeguard

(1) *Targum Yonasan.* (2) *Ezekiel* 3:12. (3) *Targum Yonasan.* (4) *Exodus* 15:18. (5) *Targum Onkelos.*

וַתִּשָּׂאֵנִי רוּחַ — *A wind lifted me.* These words were uttered by the prophet Yechezkel, who had just been commanded to undertake a difficult mission on behalf of the exiled Jews. God sent a wind to lift him and transport him to Babylon, and as he was lifted, Yechezkel heard the song of the angels. This suggests that the person who ignores his own convenience in order to serve God can expect to climb spiritual heights beyond his normal capacity.

שָׁמְרָה זֹּאת — *May You safeguard this.* May God help us remain with the above fervent declara-

עַמֶּךָ, וְהָכֵן לְבָבָם אֵלֶיךָ.[1] וְהוּא רַחוּם, יְכַפֵּר עָוֹן

⟨ of ⟨ is for- ⟨ the Merciful ⟨ And ⟪ to You. ⟨ their ⟨ and may ⟪ of Your
iniquity giving One, He, heart You direct people,

וְלֹא יַשְׁחִית, וְהִרְבָּה לְהָשִׁיב אַפּוֹ, וְלֹא יָעִיר

⟨ arousing ⟨ not ⟪ His anger, ⟨ He withdraws ⟨ frequently ⟪ destroy; ⟨ and does not

כָּל חֲמָתוֹ.[2] כִּי אַתָּה אֲדֹנָי טוֹב וְסַלָּח, וְרַב חֶסֶד

⟨ kind ⟨ and ⟪ and ⟨ are ⟨ O Master, ⟨ You, ⟨ For ⟪ of His ⟨ all
abundantly forgiving, good wrath.

לְכָל קֹרְאֶיךָ.[3] צִדְקָתְךָ צֶדֶק לְעוֹלָם,* וְתוֹרָתְךָ

⟨ and Your ⟪ everlasting,* ⟨ is a ⟨ Your ⟪ who call ⟨ to all
Torah righteousness righteousness upon You.

אֱמֶת.[4] תִּתֵּן אֱמֶת לְיַעֲקֹב,* חֶסֶד לְאַבְרָהָם,

⟪ to Abraham, ⟨ kindness ⟪ to Jacob,* ⟨ truth ⟨ Grant ⟪ is truth.

אֲשֶׁר נִשְׁבַּעְתָּ לַאֲבֹתֵינוּ מִימֵי קֶדֶם.[5] בָּרוּךְ אֲדֹנָי,

⟪ is the ⟨ Blessed ⟪ of old. ⟨ from ⟨ to our forefathers ⟨ You swore ⟨ as
Lord; days

יוֹם יוֹם יַעֲמָס לָנוּ,* הָאֵל יְשׁוּעָתֵנוּ סֶלָה.[6] יהוה

⟨ HASHEM, ⟪ Selah. ⟪ of our salvation, ⟨ the God ⟪ He loads us up ⟨ by day ⟨ day
[with blessings],*

צְבָאוֹת עִמָּנוּ, מִשְׂגָּב לָנוּ אֱלֹהֵי יַעֲקֹב סֶלָה.[7]

⟪ Selah. ⟪ of Jacob, ⟨ is the God ⟨ for us ⟨ a Stronghold ⟪ is with us, ⟨ Master of Legions,

יהוה צְבָאוֹת, אַשְׁרֵי אָדָם בֹּטֵחַ בָּךְ.[8] יהוה

⟨ HASHEM, ⟪ in You. ⟨ who trusts ⟨ is the man ⟨ praiseworthy ⟨ Master of Legions, ⟨ HASHEM,

---

(1) *I Chronicles* 29:18. (2) *Psalms* 78:38. (3) 86:5. (4) 119:142.
(5) *Micah* 7:20. (6) *Psalms* 68:20. (7) 46:8. (8) 84:13.

tion of His holiness and kingship (*Abudraham*).

צִדְקָתְךָ צֶדֶק לְעוֹלָם — *Your righteousness is a righteousness everlasting.* People question the ways of God because they do not see the righteous rewarded nor the wicked punished. But this question is a product of shortsightedness. God's justice is not measured in months or years. His reward lasts forever, so it does not matter if it is delayed during the temporary stay of our bodies on earth (*Siach Yitzchak*).

תִּתֵּן אֱמֶת לְיַעֲקֹב — *Grant truth to Jacob.* Even if we are undeserving of Your salvation, nevertheless, fulfill Your promise to the Patriarchs that You will help their offspring. Thus, You will establish Your attribute of truth, the attribute symbolized by Jacob (*Etz Yosef*).

יַעֲמָס לָנוּ — *He loads us up [with blessings].* God gives us the daily responsibility to perform countless commandments (*Targum*) because He desires to load us up with blessings (*Radak*).

הוֹשִׁיעָה, הַמֶּלֶךְ יַעֲנֵנוּ בְיוֹם קָרְאֵנוּ.¹ בָּרוּךְ הוּא

‹ is He, ‹ Blessed ≪ we call. ‹ on the day ‹ answer us ‹ May the King ≪ save!

אֱלֹהֵינוּ שֶׁבְּרָאָנוּ לִכְבוֹדוֹ, וְהִבְדִּילָנוּ מִן הַתּוֹעִים,

≪ those who ‹ from ‹ and separated ≪ for His glory, ‹ Who created us ‹ our God,
go astray,   us

וְנָתַן לָנוּ תּוֹרַת אֱמֶת, וְחַיֵּי עוֹלָם נָטַע בְּתוֹכֵנוּ.

≪ within us. ‹ implanted ‹ eternal ‹ and life ≪ of truth, ‹ the Torah ‹ us ‹ and gave

הוּא יִפְתַּח לִבֵּנוּ* בְּתוֹרָתוֹ, וְיָשֵׂם בְּלִבֵּנוּ אַהֲבָתוֹ

‹ with love ‹ our heart ‹ and ≪ to His Torah ‹ our heart* ‹ open ‹ May He
of Him   imbue

וְיִרְאָתוֹ וְלַעֲשׂוֹת רְצוֹנוֹ וּלְעָבְדוֹ בְּלֵבָב שָׁלֵם,

≪ that is ‹ with a heart ‹ and to serve ‹ His will ‹ and [the desire] ‹ and awe
whole,   Him   to do   of Him

לְמַעַן לֹא נִיגַע לָרִיק, וְלֹא נֵלֵד לַבֶּהָלָה.²

≪ for futility. ‹ produce ‹ nor ‹ in vain ‹ we do not toil ‹ so that

יְהִי רָצוֹן מִלְפָנֶיךָ, יהוה אֱלֹהֵינוּ וֵאלֹהֵי

‹ and the God ‹ our God ‹ Hashem, ≪ before You, ‹ the will ‹ May it be

אֲבוֹתֵינוּ, שֶׁנִּשְׁמֹר חֻקֶּיךָ בָּעוֹלָם הַזֶּה, וְנִזְכֶּה

‹ and that ‹ in This World, ‹ Your ‹ that we ≪ of our
we merit   decrees   observe   forefathers,

וְנִחְיֶה וְנִרְאֶה וְנִירַשׁ טוֹבָה וּבְרָכָה לִשְׁנֵי

‹ in the years ‹ and blessing ‹ goodness ‹ and we inherit ‹ and we see ‹ that we live

יְמוֹת הַמָּשִׁיחַ וּלְחַיֵּי הָעוֹלָם הַבָּא. לְמַעַן

‹ So that ≪ to Come. ‹ of the World ‹ and for the life ‹ of Messianic times

יְזַמֶּרְךָ כָבוֹד וְלֹא יִדֹּם, יהוה אֱלֹהַי לְעוֹלָם

‹ forever ‹ my God, ‹ Hashem, ≪ be silenced; ‹ and not ‹ [might] my soul, ‹ sing to You

---

(1) *Psalms* 20:10. (2) Cf. *Isaiah* 65:23.

הוּא יִפְתַּח לִבֵּנוּ — *May He open our heart.* This verse contains a major principle of the nature of Torah study. Though it is a rigorous and demanding intellectual pursuit, it cannot be mastered without pure motives, faith and love of God, and Divine help. If someone studies Torah only for the sake of the prestige it will give him to outwit less-accomplished scholars, he will not succeed: his struggle for knowledge *will be in vain.* Or if someone has attained Torah knowl-

אוֹדֶךָ. ¹בָּרוּךְ הַגֶּבֶר אֲשֶׁר יִבְטַח בַּיהוה,* וְהָיָה

⟨then will ⟨⟨ in HASHEM,* ⟨ trusts ⟨ who ⟨ is the man ⟨ Blessed ⟨⟨ will I thank You.

יהוה מִבְטַחוֹ. ²בִּטְחוּ בַיהוה עֲדֵי עַד, כִּי בְּיָהּ

⟨ in God, ⟨ for ⟨⟨ forever, ⟨ in HASHEM ⟨ Trust ⟨⟨ his security. ⟨ HASHEM be

יהוה צוּר עוֹלָמִים. ❖ ³וְיִבְטְחוּ בְךָ יוֹדְעֵי שְׁמֶךָ,

⟨⟨ Your ⟨ those who ⟨⟨ in ⟨ And they ⟨⟨ of the worlds. ⟨ is the ⟨ HASHEM,
Name, know You, will trust strength

כִּי לֹא עָזַבְתָּ דֹרְשֶׁיךָ, יהוה. ⁴יהוה חָפֵץ לְמַעַן

⟨ for the ⟨ desired, ⟨ HASHEM ⟨⟨ HASHEM. ⟨ those who ⟨ You have not ⟨ for
sake seek You, forsaken

צִדְקוֹ, יַגְדִּיל תּוֹרָה וְיַאְדִּיר. ⁵

⟨⟨ and glorious. ⟨ to make the ⟨ of [Israel's]
Torah great righteousness,

SOME CONGREGATIONS CONCLUDE:

⁶יהוה אֲדוֹנֵינוּ, מָה אַדִּיר שִׁמְךָ בְּכָל הָאָרֶץ.

⟨⟨ the earth. ⟨⟨ throughout ⟨ is Your Name ⟨ mighty ⟨ how ⟨⟨ our Master, ⟨ HASHEM,

⁷חִזְקוּ וְיַאֲמֵץ לְבַבְכֶם, כָּל הַמְיַחֲלִים לַיהוה.

⟨⟨ for HASHEM. ⟨ who wait ⟨ all ⟨⟨ in your ⟨ and He will ⟨ Be
longingly hearts, instill courage strong,

ON ROSH CHODESH AND CHOL HAMOED THE TORAH IS RETURNED TO THE ARK AT THIS POINT
(P. 225) AND THE *CHAZZAN* RECITES HALF-*KADDISH* (P. 210), WHICH IS FOLLOWED BY THE *MUSSAF
SHEMONEH ESREI* (FOR ROSH CHODESH, P. 517; FOR CHOL HAMOED, P. 532).

THE *CHAZZAN* RECITES קַדִּישׁ שָׁלֵם, FULL *KADDISH*.

יִתְגַּדַּל וְיִתְקַדַּשׁ שְׁמֵהּ רַבָּא. (Cong. – אָמֵן.) בְּעָלְמָא דִּי בְרָא

⟨ He ⟨ that ⟨ in the ⟨⟨ (Amen.) ⟨⟨ that is ⟨ may His ⟨ and be ⟨ Grow exalted
created world great! — Name sanctified

כִרְעוּתֵהּ, וְיַמְלִיךְ מַלְכוּתֵהּ, וְיַצְמַח פֻּרְקָנֵהּ וִיקָרֵב מְשִׁיחֵהּ.

⟨⟨ His ⟨ and bring ⟨ His ⟨ and cause ⟨ to His ⟨ and may He ⟨⟨ according
Messiah, near salvation, to sprout kingship, give reign to His will,

---

(1) *Psalms* 30:13. (2) *Jeremiah* 17:7. (3) *Isaiah* 26:4.
(4) *Psalms* 9:11. (5) *Isaiah* 42:21. (6) *Psalms* 8:2. (7) 31:25.

---

edge in a commendable way, but later discards
his faith, he will have lost the merit of his study
— and will have *produced for futility* (Vilna
Gaon).

אֲשֶׁר יִבְטַח בַּה׳ — *Who trusts in* HASHEM. In direct
proportion to the extent that someone trusts in
God, God *will be his security* (Chiddushei
HaRim).

(Cong. – אָמֵן.) בְּחַיֵּיכוֹן וּבְיוֹמֵיכוֹן וּבְחַיֵּי דְכָל בֵּית יִשְׂרָאֵל,

(Amen.) in your lifetimes and in your days, and in the lifetimes of the entire Family of Israel,

בַּעֲגָלָא וּבִזְמַן קָרִיב. וְאִמְרוּ: אָמֵן.

swiftly and at a time that comes soon. Now respond: Amen.

CONGREGATION RESPONDS:

אָמֵן. יְהֵא שְׁמֵהּ רַבָּא מְבָרַךְ לְעָלַם וּלְעָלְמֵי עָלְמַיָּא.

Amen. May His Name that is great be blessed forever and for all eternity.

CHAZZAN CONTINUES:

יְהֵא שְׁמֵהּ רַבָּא מְבָרַךְ לְעָלַם וּלְעָלְמֵי עָלְמַיָּא. יִתְבָּרַךְ

May His Name that is great be blessed forever and for all eternity. Blessed,

וְיִשְׁתַּבַּח וְיִתְפָּאַר וְיִתְרוֹמַם וְיִתְנַשֵּׂא וְיִתְהַדָּר וְיִתְעַלֶּה

praised, honored, exalted, upraised, glorified, elevated,

וְיִתְהַלָּל שְׁמֵהּ דְּקֻדְשָׁא בְּרִיךְ הוּא (Cong. – בְּרִיךְ הוּא) –

and lauded be the Name of the Holy One, Blessed is He (Blessed is He) –

ROSH HASHANAH TO YOM KIPPUR SUBSTITUTE:

°לְעֵלָּא מִן כָּל [°לְעֵלָּא (וּ)לְעֵלָּא מִכָּל] בִּרְכָתָא

beyond any exceedingly beyond any blessing

וְשִׁירָתָא, תֻּשְׁבְּחָתָא וְנֶחֱמָתָא דַּאֲמִירָן בְּעָלְמָא.

and song, praise and consolation that are uttered in the world.

וְאִמְרוּ: אָמֵן. (Cong. – אָמֵן.)

Now respond: Amen. (Amen.)

CONGREGATION:

(קַבֵּל בְּרַחֲמִים וּבְרָצוֹן אֶת תְּפִלָּתֵנוּ.)

(Accept with mercy and with favor our prayers.)

CHAZZAN CONTINUES:

תִּתְקַבֵּל צְלוֹתְהוֹן וּבָעוּתְהוֹן דְּכָל (בֵּית) יִשְׂרָאֵל

May accepted be the prayers and supplications of the entire (Family of) Israel

קֳדָם אֲבוּהוֹן דִּי בִשְׁמַיָּא. וְאִמְרוּ: אָמֵן. (Cong. – אָמֵן.)

before their Father Who is in Heaven. Now respond: Amen. (Amen.)

CONGREGATION:

(יְהִי שֵׁם יהוה מְבֹרָךְ מֵעַתָּה וְעַד עוֹלָם.[1])

(Let the Name of Hashem be blessed from this time until eternity.)

---

(1) *Psalms* 113:2.

CHAZZAN CONTINUES:

יְהֵא שְׁלָמָא רַבָּא מִן שְׁמַיָּא, וְחַיִּים טוֹבִים עָלֵינוּ וְעַל כָּל
⟨ all ⟨ and ⟨ upon us ⟨ that is ⟪ and life ⟪ Heaven, ⟨ from ⟨ that is ⟨ peace ⟨ May
          upon   good,   abundant   there be

יִשְׂרָאֵל. וְאִמְרוּ: אָמֵן. (.Cong – אָמֵן.)
          ⟪ (Amen.)   ⟪ Amen. ⟨ Now respond: ⟪ Israel.

CONGREGATION:

(עֶזְרִי מֵעִם יהוה, עֹשֵׂה שָׁמַיִם וָאָרֶץ.[1])
⟪ and earth.) ⟨ of heaven ⟨ Maker ⟪ HASHEM, ⟨ is from ⟨ (My help

BOW; TAKE THREE STEPS BACK: BOW LEFT AND SAY . . . עֹשֶׂה שָׁלוֹם, *"HE WHO MAKES PEACE . . .";* BOW
RIGHT AND SAY . . . הוּא, *"MAY HE . . .";* BOW FORWARD AND SAY . . . וְעַל כָּל יִשְׂרָאֵל, *"AND UPON
ALL ISRAEL . . ."* REMAIN IN PLACE FOR A FEW MOMENTS, THEN TAKE THREE STEPS FORWARD.

עֹשֶׂה °שָׁלוֹם בִּמְרוֹמָיו, הוּא יַעֲשֶׂה שָׁלוֹם עָלֵינוּ, וְעַל
⟨ and ⟨ upon us, ⟨ peace ⟨ make ⟨ may He ⟪ in His heights, ⟨ peace ⟨ He Who
   upon   makes

כָּל יִשְׂרָאֵל. וְאִמְרוּ: אָמֵן. (.Cong – אָמֵן.)
          ⟪ (Amen.)   ⟪ Amen. ⟨ Now respond: ⟪ Israel. ⟨ all

FROM ROSH HASHANAH TO YOM KIPPUR SOME SAY:
°הַשָּׁלוֹם
⟨ the peace

RETURNING THE TORAH / הכנסת ספר תורה

ALL RISE AND REMAIN STANDING UNTIL THE TORAH IS RETURNED TO THE ARK.
THE *CHAZZAN* TAKES THE TORAH IN HIS RIGHT ARM AND RECITES:

יְהַלְלוּ אֶת שֵׁם יהוה, כִּי נִשְׂגָּב שְׁמוֹ לְבַדּוֹ –
⟪ alone; ⟨ is His Name ⟨ exalted ⟨ for ⟨ of HASHEM, ⟨ the Name ⟨ Let them praise

CONGREGATION RESPONDS:

– הוֹדוֹ עַל אֶרֶץ וְשָׁמָיִם. וַיָּרֶם קֶרֶן לְעַמּוֹ, תְּהִלָּה
⟨ [causing] ⟪ of His ⟨ the ⟨ He has ⟪ and ⟨ earth ⟨ is ⟨ His
   praise   people, pride exalted   heaven.   above glory

לְכָל חֲסִידָיו, לִבְנֵי יִשְׂרָאֵל עַם קְרֹבוֹ, הַלְלוּיָהּ.[2]
⟪ Halleluyah! ⟪ with whom ⟨ the ⟨ of Israel, ⟨ for the ⟪ His devout ⟨ for all
              He is intimate. people   Children   ones,

——— תהלים כד / Psalm 24 ———

לְדָוִד מִזְמוֹר; לַיהוה הָאָרֶץ וּמְלוֹאָהּ, תֵּבֵל
⟨ the inha- ⟪ and its ⟨ is the earth ⟨ HASHEM's ⟪ a psalm. ⟨ By David,
  bited land fullness,

---

(1) *Psalms* 121:2. (2) 148:13-14.

וְיֹשְׁבֵי בָהּ. כִּי הוּא עַל יַמִּים יְסָדָהּ, וְעַל נְהָרוֹת

‹ rivers ‹ and ‹ founded it, ‹ seas ‹ upon ‹ He ‹ For « in it. ‹ and those
who dwell
upon

יְכוֹנְנֶהָ. מִי יַעֲלֶה בְהַר יהוה, וּמִי יָקוּם בִּמְקוֹם

‹ in the place ‹ may ‹ and « of ‹ the ‹ may ‹ Who « established it.
stand who HASHEM, mountain ascend

קָדְשׁוֹ. נְקִי כַפַּיִם וּבַר לֵבָב; אֲשֶׁר לֹא נָשָׂא

‹ sworn ‹ has not ‹ who « heart; ‹ and pure ‹ hands ‹ One « of His
with clean sanctity?

לַשָּׁוְא נַפְשִׁי, וְלֹא נִשְׁבַּע לְמִרְמָה. יִשָּׂא בְרָכָה

‹ a blessing ‹ He will « deceitfully. ‹ sworn ‹ and « by My ‹ in vain
receive has not soul,

מֵאֵת יהוה, וּצְדָקָה מֵאֱלֹהֵי יִשְׁעוֹ. זֶה דּוֹר

‹ the ‹ This « of his ‹ from the ‹ and just « HASHEM ‹ from
generation is salvation. God kindness

דֹּרְשָׁיו, מְבַקְשֵׁי פָנֶיךָ יַעֲקֹב סֶלָה. שְׂאוּ שְׁעָרִים

‹ O gates, ‹ Raise « Selah. « [the nation « Your ‹ those who « of those who
up, of] Jacob, Presence — strive for seek Him,

רָאשֵׁיכֶם, וְהִנָּשְׂאוּ פִּתְחֵי עוֹלָם, וְיָבוֹא מֶלֶךְ

‹ — the « so that He ‹ [you] everlasting ‹ and be uplifted, « your heads,
King may enter entrances,

הַכָּבוֹד. מִי זֶה מֶלֶךְ הַכָּבוֹד, יהוה עִזּוּז וְגִבּוֹר,

« and the ‹ the ‹ HASHEM, « of Glory? ‹ King ‹ is ‹ Who « of Glory.
strong; mighty this

יהוה גִּבּוֹר מִלְחָמָה. שְׂאוּ שְׁעָרִים רָאשֵׁיכֶם, וּשְׂאוּ

‹ and « your heads, ‹ O gates, ‹ Raise « in battle. ‹ the ‹ HASHEM,
raise up, up, strong

פִּתְחֵי עוֹלָם, וְיָבֹא מֶלֶךְ הַכָּבוֹד. מִי הוּא זֶה מֶלֶךְ

‹ King ‹ this ‹ is He, ‹ Who « of Glory. ‹ — the « so that He ‹ [you] everlasting
King may enter entrances,

הַכָּבוֹד, יהוה צְבָאוֹת הוּא מֶלֶךְ הַכָּבוֹד סֶלָה.

« Selah! « of Glory, ‹ the King ‹ He is ‹ Master ‹ HASHEM, « of Glory?
of Legions,

AS THE TORAH IS PLACED INTO THE ARK, THE FOLLOWING VERSES ARE RECITED:

וּבְנֻחֹה יֹאמַר,* שׁוּבָה יהוה רִבְבוֹת אַלְפֵי

‹ thousands ‹ to the ‹ Hashem, ‹ Return, ‹‹ he would ‹ And when
                myriad   say:*   it rested

יִשְׂרָאֵל. קוּמָה יהוה לִמְנוּחָתֶךָ, אַתָּה וַאֲרוֹן

‹ and the ‹ You ‹‹ to Your ‹ Hashem, ‹ Arise ‹‹ of Israel.
   Ark   resting place,

עֻזֶּךָ. כֹּהֲנֶיךָ יִלְבְּשׁוּ צֶדֶק, וַחֲסִידֶיךָ יְרַנֵּנוּ.

‹‹ will sing ‹ and Your ‹‹ in ‹ be clothed ‹ Let Your ‹‹ of Your
  joyously.   devout ones righteousness,   Kohanim   strength.

בַּעֲבוּר דָּוִד עַבְדֶּךָ, אַל תָּשֵׁב פְּנֵי מְשִׁיחֶךָ. כִּי

‹ For ‹‹ of Your ‹ the ‹ turn not away ‹‹ Your ‹ of ‹ For the
        anointed.   face   servant, David, sake

לֶקַח טוֹב נָתַתִּי לָכֶם, תּוֹרָתִי אַל תַּעֲזֹבוּ. ❖ עֵץ

‹ A tree ‹‹ forsake. ‹ do not ‹ My Torah ‹‹ you; ‹ have I given ‹ a good teaching

חַיִּים הִיא לַמַּחֲזִיקִים בָּהּ, וְתֹמְכֶיהָ מְאֻשָּׁר.

‹‹ are praise- ‹ and its ‹‹ it, ‹ for those who grasp ‹ it is ‹ of life
   worthy.   supporters

דְּרָכֶיהָ דַרְכֵי נֹעַם, וְכָל נְתִיבֹתֶיהָ שָׁלוֹם.

‹‹ are peace. ‹ its paths ‹ and all ‹‹ of pleasantness, ‹ are ways ‹ Its ways

הֲשִׁיבֵנוּ יהוה אֵלֶיךָ וְנָשׁוּבָה, חַדֵּשׁ יָמֵינוּ כְּקֶדֶם.

‹‹ as of old. ‹ our days ‹ renew ‹‹ and we ‹ to You, ‹ Hashem, ‹ Bring us
                              shall return,   back,

ON ROSH CHODESH AND CHOL HAMOED THE *CHAZZAN* RECITES HALF-*KADDISH* (P. 210), FOLLOWED BY THE *MUSSAF SHEMONEH ESREI* (FOR ROSH CHODESH, P. 517; FOR CHOL HAMOED, P. 532). ON PURIM THE *MEGILLAH* IS READ (SEE P. 581). ON TISHAH B'AV, *KINNOS* ARE RECITED.

(1) *Numbers* 10:36. (2) *Psalms* 132:8-10. (3) *Proverbs* 4:2. (4) 3:18. (5) 3:17. (6) *Lamentations* 5:21.

§ וּבְנֻחֹה יֹאמַר — *And when it rested he would say.* This is the companion verse to וַיְהִי בִּנְסֹעַ הָאָרֹן, *When the Ark would travel,* above (p. 199), which Moses said when the Ark began to journey. When it came to rest, he expressed his hope that God's Presence would find comfortable repose among the multitudes of the Jewish people; in other words, that Israel should be worthy of being host to God's holiness.

The rest of this paragraph is a selection of verses from Scripture on the themes of a resting place for God's Law, the greatness of the Torah, and the hope that God will see fit to draw us closer to His service.

IN MANY CONGREGATIONS, THE FOLLOWING PSALMS AND VERSES ARE RECITED BEFORE THE SONG
OF THE DAY. ON DAYS WHEN *TACHANUN* IS OMITTED (SEE P. 172) PSALM 86 IS OMITTED BUT THE
TWO FOLLOWING PARAGRAPHS, בֵּית יַעֲקֹב, "O HOUSE OF JACOB," AND PSALM 124 ARE RECITED.
HOWEVER, ON DAYS WHEN EVEN אֵל אֶרֶךְ אַפַּיִם, "O GOD, SLOW TO ANGER," WOULD BE OMITTED
(SEE P. 198), SHACHARIS CONTINUES WITH THE SONG OF THE DAY (P. 232).

— תהלים פח / Psalm 86 —

תְּפִלָּה לְדָוִד; הַטֵּה יהוה אָזְנְךָ עֲנֵנִי, כִּי עָנִי וְאֶבְיוֹן

‹ and ‹ poor ‹ for ‹‹ answer ‹ Your ‹ HASHEM, ‹ incline, ‹‹ by ‹ A prayer
destitute me, ear, David;

אָנִי. שָׁמְרָה נַפְשִׁי כִּי חָסִיד אָנִי;* הוֹשַׁע עַבְדְּךָ, אַתָּה

‹ — O ‹‹ Your ‹ save ‹‹ am I;* ‹ devout ‹ for ‹ my soul, ‹ Guard ‹‹ am I.
You, servant

אֱלֹהַי, הַבּוֹטֵחַ אֵלֶיךָ. חָנֵּנִי אֲדֹנָי, כִּי אֵלֶיךָ אֶקְרָא כָּל

‹ all ‹ do I call ‹ to You ‹ for ‹‹ O Lord, ‹ Show ‹‹ You. ‹ who trusts ‹‹ my God —
me favor,

הַיּוֹם. שַׂמֵּחַ נֶפֶשׁ עַבְדֶּךָ, כִּי אֵלֶיךָ אֲדֹנָי נַפְשִׁי אֶשָּׂא.

‹‹ I lift ‹ my soul ‹ O Lord, ‹ to You, ‹ for ‹‹ of Your ‹ the ‹ Gladden ‹‹ day
up. servant, soul long.

כִּי אַתָּה אֲדֹנָי טוֹב וְסַלָּח, וְרַב חֶסֶד לְכָל קֹרְאֶיךָ.

‹‹ who call ‹ to all ‹ kind ‹ and ‹‹ and ‹ are ‹ O Lord, ‹ You, ‹ For
upon You. abundantly forgiving, good

הַאֲזִינָה יהוה תְּפִלָּתִי,* וְהַקְשִׁיבָה בְּקוֹל תַּחֲנוּנוֹתָי.*

‹‹ of my ‹ the sound ‹ and heed ‹‹ to my prayer,* ‹ HASHEM, ‹ Give ear,
supplications.*

תְּפִלָּה לְדָוִד / Psalm 86

The custom of reciting Psalm 86 is mentioned
by several early authorities such as *HaManhig,
Tur,* and *Abudraham,* and it was incorporated
into the daily *Shacharis* by *Seder HaYom* and
Arizal. This psalm has a dual purpose: It is a
prayer that God help us not to transgress His
will during the long day of working for a livelihood and the often trying task of interacting
with other people; toward this end, the psalm
contains the verse: *Teach me, HASHEM, Your
way, that I may walk in Your truth* (Abudraham). Also, this is a request that God accept the
pleas of *Tachanun* and the latter section of
Shacharis; thus, it contains the verses: *Give ear,
HASHEM, to my prayers, and heed the sound of
my supplications. On the day of my distress I
call upon You, for You will answer me* (Vaya'as
Avraham). Because the latter verse speaks of *the
day of my distress,* this psalm is omitted on
festive days when *Tachanun* is not said.

שָׁמְרָה נַפְשִׁי כִּי חָסִיד אָנִי — *Guard my soul, for
devout am I.* Do not look askance at David's
apparent self-glorification, for he truly was
exceptionally pious. His devotion to God was
quite extraordinary; although he occasionally
erred, his heart remained upright, and he immediately repented of his sins. His enemies made
every effort to harm him, yet David sought their
welfare; they rejoiced at his failures, yet he was
gladdened by their moments of success. David
confronted his enemies with the claim that he
was a devout person only so that they might
learn from his example, not because he sought
personal glory (Radak).

A חָסִיד, *devout person,* is one who selflessly
neglects his own welfare and devotes himself to
the needs of others. He does not seek his own
advantage but seeks to guarantee the rights of
his fellow man (R' Hirsch).

תְּפִלָּתִי . . . תַּחֲנוּנוֹתָי — *My prayer . . . my supplications.* תְּפִלָּה, *prayer,* is an outpouring of the

בְּיוֹם צָרָתִי אֶקְרָאֶךָ כִּי תַעֲנֵנִי. אֵין כָּמוֹךָ בָאֱלֹהִים,*

‹ among the ‹ like You ‹ There is « You will ‹ for « I call ‹ of my ‹ On the
  powers,*   none   answer me.   upon You, distress   day

אֲדֹנָי, וְאֵין כְּמַעֲשֶׂיךָ. כָּל גּוֹיִם אֲשֶׁר עָשִׂיתָ יָבוֹאוּ

‹ will come ‹ You have ‹ that ‹ the ‹ All « like Your ‹ and there « O Lord,
            made   nations   works.   is nothing

וְיִשְׁתַּחֲווּ לְפָנֶיךָ, אֲדֹנָי; וִיכַבְּדוּ לִשְׁמֶךָ. כִּי גָדוֹל אַתָּה

‹ are You ‹ great ‹ For « to Your ‹ and will « O Lord, ‹ before ‹ and bow
                        Name.   give glory   You,   down

וְעֹשֵׂה נִפְלָאוֹת, אַתָּה אֱלֹהִים לְבַדֶּךָ. הוֹרֵנִי יהוה דַּרְכֶּךָ,

« Your ‹ O ‹ Teach « alone. ‹ O God, ‹ You, « of wonders; ‹ and a
  way, HASHEM, me,   worker

אֲהַלֵּךְ בַּאֲמִתֶּךָ, יַחֵד לְבָבִי לְיִרְאָה שְׁמֶךָ. אוֹדְךָ אֲדֹנָי

‹ O Lord, ‹ I will « Your ‹ to fear ‹ my ‹ unite « in Your ‹ [so that]
          thank You, Name.   heart   truth;   I may walk

אֱלֹהַי בְּכָל לְבָבִי, וַאֲכַבְּדָה שְׁמְךָ לְעוֹלָם. כִּי חַסְדְּךָ גָּדוֹל

‹ is great ‹ Your ‹ For « forever. ‹ to Your ‹ and I will « my heart, ‹ with all ‹ my God,
           kindness   Name   give honor

עָלָי,* וְהִצַּלְתָּ נַפְשִׁי מִשְּׁאוֹל תַּחְתִּיָּה. אֱלֹהִים, זֵדִים קָמוּ

‹ have ‹ trans- ‹ O God, « at its ‹ from ‹ my soul ‹ and You « toward
arisen gressors   deepest. the grave   have rescued me,*

עָלָי, וַעֲדַת עָרִיצִים בִּקְשׁוּ נַפְשִׁי; וְלֹא שָׂמוּךָ לְנֶגְדָּם.

« in front of ‹ and they have « my soul; ‹ has ‹ of ruthless ‹ and a « against
  themselves.   not set You   sought   men   company   me,

וְאַתָּה אֲדֹנָי אֵל רַחוּם וְחַנּוּן, אֶרֶךְ אַפַּיִם וְרַב חֶסֶד

‹ in ‹ Abundant ‹ to ‹ Slow « and Com- ‹ the ‹ are ‹ O Lord, ‹ But You,
Kindness   Anger,   passionate, Merciful God

---

soul which yearns to be released from the narrow confines of the flesh, so that it may soar heavenward to its Divine source; while תְּחִנָּה, supplication, is a plea that God fulfill man's bodily needs. Once one gains Divine attention through prayer for spiritual liberation, God becomes receptive to all his wishes — even to requests for the fulfillment of mundane needs.

בֵּאלֹהִים — Among the powers. This refers to the celestial powers, such as the angels (Targum), or to the luminaries, the sun, moon, and stars. The idolaters who worship these forces imagine that they have independent strength. Indeed, the Almighty did invest these forces and bodies

with the ability to influence events, but they are merely God's agents and have no power to act on their own (Radak).

כִּי חַסְדְּךָ גָדוֹל עָלָי — For Your kindness is great toward me. There is a human tendency to beg for help in times of distress, but not to remember the rescuer after the passage of time. Often we discover that after God has lifted a man from the depths of despair, he fails to show appreciation. As he becomes increasingly successful, this man views past help as less and less significant. We, however, declare that the more God's kindness comes toward us, the greater God's goodness appears to be (Tehillos Hashem).

וֶאֱמֶת. פְּנֵה אֵלַי וְחָנֵּנִי; תְּנָה עֻזְּךָ לְעַבְדֶּךָ,* וְהוֹשִׁיעָה

and Truth. Turn to me and show me favor; give Your strength to Your servant, and save*

לְבֶן אֲמָתֶךָ.* עֲשֵׂה עִמִּי אוֹת לְטוֹבָה; וְיִרְאוּ שֹׂנְאַי וְיֵבְשׁוּ,

the son of Your handmaid.* Display for me a sign for good; so that my enemies see it and be ashamed,

כִּי אַתָּה יהוה עֲזַרְתַּנִי וְנִחַמְתָּנִי.

for You, HASHEM, will have helped me and consoled me.

בֵּית יַעֲקֹב,* לְכוּ וְנֵלְכָה בְּאוֹר יהוה.¹ כִּי כָּל הָעַמִּים

O House of Jacob:* Come, let us walk by the light of HASHEM. For all the peoples

יֵלְכוּ אִישׁ בְּשֵׁם אֱלֹהָיו, וַאֲנַחְנוּ נֵלֵךְ בְּשֵׁם יהוה אֱלֹהֵינוּ

will go forth, each man in the name of his god, but we shall go forth in the Name of HASHEM, our God

לְעוֹלָם וָעֶד.² יְהִי יהוה אֱלֹהֵינוּ עִמָּנוּ, כַּאֲשֶׁר הָיָה עִם

for ever and ever. May HASHEM, our God, be with us, as He was with

אֲבוֹתֵינוּ, אַל יַעַזְבֵנוּ וְאַל יִטְּשֵׁנוּ. לְהַטּוֹת לְבָבֵנוּ אֵלָיו,

our forefathers; may He not abandon us nor forsake us. [But rather] turn our hearts to Him,

לָלֶכֶת בְּכָל דְּרָכָיו, וְלִשְׁמֹר מִצְוֹתָיו וְחֻקָּיו וּמִשְׁפָּטָיו,

to walk in all His ways, and to observe His commandments, His decrees, and His statutes,

אֲשֶׁר צִוָּה אֶת אֲבֹתֵינוּ. וְיִהְיוּ דְבָרַי אֵלֶּה, אֲשֶׁר הִתְחַנַּנְתִּי

that He commanded our forefathers. May they be — these words of mine, which I have supplicated

---

(1) *Isaiah* 2:5. (2) *Micah* 4:5.

תְּנָה עֻזְּךָ לְעַבְדֶּךָ — *Give Your strength to Your servant.* Intensify Your concern for me and provide me with heightened intellectual capacity and superior physical strength so that I may overcome my enemies (*Meiri*).

וְהוֹשִׁיעָה לְבֶן אֲמָתֶךָ — *And save the son of Your handmaid.* Judaism teaches that man has free will and is responsible for his actions and decisions. Nevertheless, a person's ancestry and upbringing have an important effect on his character and ideas; a mother's influence is particularly significant in this respect. We identify ourselves as both עַבְדֶּךָ, *Your servant,* and בֶּן

אֲמָתֶךָ, *the son of Your handmaid,* implying: I am Your servant of my own free will, yet my development was influenced by the fact that my mother was Your devoted handmaid (*Radak*).

בֵּית יַעֲקֹב / O House of Jacob

The following verses are reminders to us that, although we are concluding our prayers and embarking on a day of business or labor, we should bear in mind the constant responsibility that all our activities be consonant with the teachings of the Torah. The last four verses in this section are taken from the beautiful prayer of Solomon when he inaugu-

לִפְנֵי יהוה, קְרֹבִים אֶל יהוה אֱלֹהֵינוּ יוֹמָם וְלָיְלָה, לַעֲשׂוֹת

‹ that He ‹‹ and by ‹ by day ‹ our God, ‹ Hashem, ‹ to ‹ near ‹‹ Hashem – ‹ before
perform　　　night,

מִשְׁפַּט עַבְדּוֹ, וּמִשְׁפַּט עַמּוֹ יִשְׂרָאֵל, דְּבַר יוֹם בְּיוֹמוֹ. לְמַעַן

‹ so that ‹‹ in its ‹ each day's ‹ Israel, ‹ for His ‹ and justice ‹‹ for His ‹ justice
day;　　need　　　　　　people　　　　　servant,

דַּעַת כָּל עַמֵּי הָאָרֶץ, כִּי יהוה הוּא הָאֱלֹהִים, אֵין עוֹד.¹

‹‹ [and] there is ‹ God, ‹ is ‹ Hashem ‹ that ‹‹ of the ‹ the ‹ – all ‹ they shall
no other.　　　　　　　　　　　　earth – peoples　　know

──────── Psalm 124 / תהלים קכד ────────

שִׁיר הַמַּעֲלוֹת לְדָוִד; לוּלֵי יהוה שֶׁהָיָה לָנוּ, יֹאמַר

‹ – declare ‹ with ‹ been ‹ Hashem ‹ Had not ‹‹ by ‹ of ascents, ‹ A song
it　　us　　　　　　　　　　David.

נָא יִשְׂרָאֵל.* לוּלֵי יהוה שֶׁהָיָה לָנוּ, בְּקוּם עָלֵינוּ אָדָם.

‹‹ did ‹ against ‹ when ‹‹ with ‹ been ‹ Hashem ‹ Had ‹‹ [should] ‹ now
men,　　us　　rose up　　us　　　　　　　not　　Israel!*

אֲזַי חַיִּים בְּלָעוּנוּ, בַּחֲרוֹת אַפָּם בָּנוּ. אֲזַי הַמַּיִם שְׁטָפוּנוּ,

‹‹ would have ‹ the ‹ Then ‹‹ against ‹ did their ‹ when ‹‹ they would ‹ alive ‹ then
inundated us; waters　　　us.　　anger　　flare up have swallowed us,

נַחְלָה עָבַר עַל נַפְשֵׁנוּ. אֲזַי עָבַר עַל נַפְשֵׁנוּ, הַמַּיִם

‹ – the ‹‹ our soul ‹ across ‹ they would ‹ Then ‹‹ our soul. ‹ across ‹ would have ‹ the
waters　　　　　　have surged　　　　　　　　　surged　current

הַזֵּידוֹנִים. בָּרוּךְ יהוה, שֶׁלֹּא נְתָנָנוּ טֶרֶף לְשִׁנֵּיהֶם. נַפְשֵׁנוּ

‹ Our soul ‹‹ for their teeth. ‹ as prey ‹ present ‹ Who ‹‹ is ‹ Blessed ‹‹ that are
us　　did not Hashem,　　　　　　treacherous.

כְּצִפּוֹר נִמְלְטָה מִפַּח יוֹקְשִׁים; הַפַּח נִשְׁבַּר וַאֲנַחְנוּ

‹ and we ‹ broke ‹ the snare ‹‹ of the hunters; ‹ from the snare ‹ escaped ‹ is like a bird

נִמְלָטְנוּ. עֶזְרֵנוּ בְּשֵׁם יהוה, עֹשֵׂה שָׁמַיִם וָאָרֶץ.

‹‹ and earth. ‹ of heaven ‹ Maker ‹‹ of ‹ is through ‹ Our help ‹‹ escaped.
Hashem,　the Name

───────────────
(1) I Kings 8:57-60.

rated the Temple. It combines the pleas that God
help us during the day and that He accept our
just-concluded prayers.

שִׁיר הַמַּעֲלוֹת / Psalm 124 ◆⑤

This psalm is recited at this point because it
proclaims our faith that we survive only because
of God's constant safekeeping. Secure in this
faith, we can go out to face the challenges of a

livelihood and a hostile world.

לוּלֵי ה׳ שֶׁהָיָה לָנוּ יֹאמַר נָא יִשְׂרָאֵל — *Had not
Hashem been with us — declare it now [should]
Israel!* Let us now declare that had He not
appeared as Hashem, in His aspect as the Dis-
penser of Kindness, and offered compassionate
protection, Israel could not have endured the
terrible exile (Sforno).

﹩ SONG OF THE DAY / שיר של יום ﹩

A DIFFERENT PSALM IS ASSIGNED AS THE שִׁיר שֶׁל יוֹם, *SONG OF THE DAY*, FOR EACH DAY OF THE WEEK.

SUNDAY

הַיּוֹם יוֹם רִאשׁוֹן בַּשַּׁבָּת, שֶׁבּוֹ הָיוּ הַלְוִיִּם אוֹמְרִים בְּבֵית הַמִּקְדָּשׁ:

《 in the Holy Temple: 〈 recite 〈 the Levites 〈 on 〈 of the 〈 is the first day 〈 Today
would which week,

─────── תהלים כד / Psalm 24 ───────

לְדָוִד מִזְמוֹר; לַיהוה הָאָרֶץ* וּמְלוֹאָהּ, תֵּבֵל וְיֹשְׁבֵי בָהּ.

《 in 〈 and those 〈 the inhab- 《 and its 〈 is the 〈 HASHEM's 《 a psalm. 〈 By David,
it. who dwell ited land fullness, earth*

כִּי הוּא עַל יַמִּים יְסָדָהּ,* וְעַל נְהָרוֹת יְכוֹנְנֶהָ. מִי יַעֲלֶה*

〈 may 〈 Who 《 established 〈 rivers 〈 and 〈 founded it,* 〈 seas 〈 upon 〈 He 〈 For
ascend* it. upon

בְהַר יהוה, וּמִי יָקוּם בִּמְקוֹם קָדְשׁוֹ. נְקִי כַפַּיִם* וּבַר לֵבָב;

《 heart; 〈 and 〈 One 《 of His 〈 in the place 〈 may 〈 and 《 of 〈 the
pure with clean sanctity? stand who HASHEM, mountain

אֲשֶׁר לֹא נָשָׂא לַשָּׁוְא נַפְשִׁי, וְלֹא נִשְׁבַּע לְמִרְמָה. יִשָּׂא

〈 He will 《 deceitfully. 〈 sworn 〈 and 《 [by] My 〈 in vain 〈 sworn 〈 has 〈 who
receive has not soul, not

﹩ שִׁיר שֶׁל יוֹם / SONG OF THE DAY ﹩

As part of the morning Temple service, the Levites chanted a psalm that was suited to the significance of that particular day of the week (*Tamid* 7:4). As a memorial to the Temple, these psalms have been incorporated into *Shacharis*. The Talmud (*Rosh Hashanah* 31a) explains how each psalm was appropriate to its respective day; we will note these reasons in the commentary. The introductory sentence, *"Today is the first day of the Sabbath . . . ,"* helps fulfill the Torah's command to remember the Sabbath always. By counting the days of the week with reference to the forthcoming Sabbath we tie our existence to the Sabbath. This is in sharp contrast to the non-Jewish custom of assigning names to the days in commemoration of events or gods, such as Sunday for the sun, Monday for the moon, and so on (*Ramban, Exodus* 20:8).

﹩ יוֹם רִאשׁוֹן / The First Day

The first day's psalm teaches that everything belongs to God, because on the first day of Creation, God was the sole existence — even the angels had not yet been created. He took possession of His newly created world with the intention of ceding it to man (*Rosh Hashanah* 31a).

לַה׳ הָאָרֶץ — *HASHEM's is the earth.* Since the world belongs to God, anyone who derives pleasure from His world without reciting the proper blessing expressing thanks to the Owner is regarded as a thief (*Berachos* 35a).

כִּי הוּא עַל יַמִּים יְסָדָהּ — *For He upon seas founded it.* The entire planet was covered with water until God commanded it to gather in seas and rivers, thereby exposing the dry land (*Ibn Ezra*).

מִי יַעֲלֶה . . . — *Who may ascend . . . ?* God's most intense Presence is in the Temple, so those who wish to draw near and to perceive His splendor must be especially worthy (*Rashi*). By extension, one who wishes to enjoy spiritual elevation must refine his behavior.

נְקִי כַפַּיִם — *One with clean hands.* This verse

בְּרָכָה* מֵאֵת יהוה, וּצְדָקָה מֵאֱלֹהֵי יִשְׁעוֹ. זֶה דּוֹר דֹּרְשָׁיו,

‹‹ of those ‹ the gen- ‹ This ‹‹ of his ‹ from the ‹ and just ‹‹ HASHEM ‹ from ‹ a
who seek eration is salvation. God kindness blessing*
Him,

מְבַקְשֵׁי פָנֶיךָ יַעֲקֹב סֶלָה. שְׂאוּ שְׁעָרִים* רָאשֵׁיכֶם,

‹‹ your heads, ‹ O gates,* ‹ Raise ‹‹ Selah. ‹‹ [the nation ‹‹ Your ‹ those who
up, of] Jacob, Presence— strive for

וְהִנָּשְׂאוּ פִּתְחֵי עוֹלָם,* וְיָבוֹא מֶלֶךְ הַכָּבוֹד.* מִי זֶה מֶלֶךְ

‹ King ‹ is ‹ Who ‹‹ of Glory.* ‹ — the ‹‹ so that He ‹ [you] everlasting ‹ and be
this King may enter entrances,* uplifted,

הַכָּבוֹד, יהוה עִזּוּז וְגִבּוֹר, יהוה גִּבּוֹר מִלְחָמָה. ✧ שְׂאוּ שְׁעָרִים

‹ O gates, ‹ Raise ‹ in battle. ‹ the ‹ HASHEM, ‹‹ and the ‹ the ‹ HASHEM, ‹‹ of Glory?
up, strong strong; mighty

רָאשֵׁיכֶם, וּשְׂאוּ פִּתְחֵי עוֹלָם, וְיָבֹא מֶלֶךְ הַכָּבוֹד. מִי הוּא

‹ is He, ‹ Who ‹‹ of Glory. ‹ — the ‹‹ so that He ‹ [you] everlasting ‹ and ‹‹ your heads,
King may enter entrances, raise up,

זֶה מֶלֶךְ הַכָּבוֹד, יהוה צְבָאוֹת הוּא מֶלֶךְ הַכָּבוֹד סֶלָה.

‹‹ Selah! ‹‹ of Glory, ‹ the ‹ He is ‹ Master ‹ HASHEM, ‹‹ of Glory? ‹ King ‹ this
King of Legions,

MANY CONGREGATIONS CONTINUE WITH הוֹשִׁיעֵנוּ, SAVE US (P. 242).
IN THE PRESENCE OF A MINYAN, MOURNERS RECITE קַדִּישׁ יָתוֹם, THE MOURNER'S KADDISH (P. 243).

MONDAY

הַיּוֹם יוֹם שֵׁנִי בַּשַּׁבָּת, שֶׁבּוֹ הָיוּ הַלְוִיִּם אוֹמְרִים בְּבֵית הַמִּקְדָּשׁ:

‹‹ in the Holy Temple: ‹ recite ‹ the Levites ‹ on ‹ of the ‹ is the second ‹ Today
would which week, day

———— Psalm 48 / תהלים מח ————

שִׁיר מִזְמוֹר לִבְנֵי קֹרַח. גָּדוֹל יהוה וּמְהֻלָּל מְאֹד,

‹ and much praised, ‹ is HASHEM ‹ Great ‹‹ of Korah. ‹ by the sons ‹ a psalm, ‹ A song,

---

answers the previous question. To "ascend," one
must have hands clean from dishonest gain, he
must be honest in his dealings with man, and
reverent in his attitude toward God.

יִשָּׂא בְרָכָה — He will receive a blessing. Because
he honors God's Name in heart and behavior,
such a person earns God's blessing, kindness,
and salvation (R' Hirsch).

שְׂאוּ שְׁעָרִים — Raise up, O gates. When Solomon
sought to bring the Ark into the Temple, the
gates remained shut despite all his pleas, until he
prayed that God open the gates in the merit of
David, who made all the preparations for the

building of the Temple. Thus, this verse alludes
to Solomon's future prayer (Shabbos 30a). The
plea to the gate is repeated later to allude to the
Ark's reentry when the Third Temple will be
built (Ibn Ezra).

פִּתְחֵי עוֹלָם — [You] everlasting entrances. The
holiness of the Temple gates is eternal.

מֶלֶךְ הַכָּבוֹד — The King of Glory. God is given
this title because He gives glory to those who
revere Him (Midrash).

יוֹם שֵׁנִי / The Second Day

On this day, God separated between the

בְּעִיר אֱלֹהֵינוּ, הַר קָדְשׁוֹ. יְפֵה נוֹף, מְשׂוֹשׂ כָּל הָאָרֶץ,*

the earth,* « of all ‹ joy ‹ of ‹ fairest « of His Holiness, ‹ Mount ‹ of our God, ‹ in the City

הַר צִיּוֹן* יַרְכְּתֵי צָפוֹן,* קִרְיַת מֶלֶךְ רָב. אֱלֹהִים

God ‹ of the great king. « of the City ‹ [by] the northern side* ‹ Zion,* ‹ Mount

בְּאַרְמְנוֹתֶיהָ נוֹדַע לְמִשְׂגָּב. כִּי הִנֵּה הַמְּלָכִים נוֹעֲדוּ,*

assembled,* « the kings ‹ behold ‹ For « as the Stronghold. ‹ is known ‹ in the city's palaces

עָבְרוּ יַחְדָּו. הֵמָּה רָאוּ כֵּן תָּמָהוּ, נִבְהֲלוּ נֶחְפָּזוּ. רְעָדָה

Trembling « and fled ‹ they were ‹ « were ‹ and ‹ saw ‹ They « together. ‹ they came in haste. confounded astounded, indeed

אֲחָזָתַם שָׁם, חִיל כַּיּוֹלֵדָה. בְּרוּחַ קָדִים תְּשַׁבֵּר אֳנִיּוֹת

the ships ‹ You ‹ from ‹ With « like a woman ‹ convulsions « there, ‹ gripped them smashed the east a wind in birth travail.

תַּרְשִׁישׁ.* כַּאֲשֶׁר שָׁמַעְנוּ* כֵּן רָאִינוּ בְּעִיר יהוה צְבָאוֹת,

Master ‹ of ‹ in the « we saw ‹ so ‹ we heard,* ‹ As « of Tarshish.* of Legions, Hashem, City

בְּעִיר אֱלֹהֵינוּ, אֱלֹהִים יְכוֹנְנֶהָ עַד עוֹלָם סֶלָה. דִּמִּינוּ

We ‹ « Selah! « eternity, ‹ to ‹ establish it ‹ may God « of our God, ‹ in the City hoped,

אֱלֹהִים חַסְדֶּךָ, בְּקֶרֶב הֵיכָלֶךָ. כְּשִׁמְךָ אֱלֹהִים, כֵּן

so ‹ O God, ‹ Like Your Name, « of Your Sanctuary. ‹ in the midst ‹ for Your kindness ‹ O God,

---

heavenly and earthly components of the universe and ruled over both. Nevertheless, the psalm specifies Jerusalem because the seat of His holiness is Jerusalem (*Rosh Hashanah* 31a). *Resisei Laylah* comments that this day's separation between heaven and earth initiated the eternal strife between the spiritual and the physical. This is why the Levites chose a psalm composed by the sons of Korach, the man who instigated a quarrel against Moses.

מְשׂוֹשׂ כָּל הָאָרֶץ — *Joy of all the earth*. This title was given to Jerusalem because the Holy City gave joy to the troubled, who gained atonement through the Temple service, and because the spiritual uplift of its holiness eased distress (*Rashi*).

הַר צִיּוֹן — *Mount Zion*. The word Zion comes from צִיּוּן, *a monument*. The site of God's

Sanctuary remains an eternal memorial to truth and sanctity (*R' Hirsch*).

יַרְכְּתֵי צָפוֹן — *The northern side*. Mount Zion was north of the City of David, the *great king* (*Radak*). The source of joy was the northern part of the Temple Courtyard, because atonement offerings were slaughtered there (*Rashi*).

הַמְּלָכִים נוֹעֲדוּ — *The kings assembled*. When kings assembled at various times to attack Jerusalem, they saw that God was its *Stronghold*. Seeing His miracles (next verse) they were astounded and fled (*Radak*).

אֳנִיּוֹת תַּרְשִׁישׁ — *The ships of Tarshish*. A sea near Africa, Tarshish represents invading fleets that were dispatched against *Eretz Yisrael*.

כַּאֲשֶׁר שָׁמַעְנוּ — *As we heard* from our ancestors about God's miraculous salvations, so too here we ourselves witnessed similar wonders (*Rashi*).

תְּהִלָּתְךָ עַל קַצְוֵי אֶרֶץ; צֶדֶק מָלְאָה יְמִינֶךָ. יִשְׂמַח הַר

‹ Mount ‹ May glad- ❮ Your ‹ fills ‹ Righteous- ❮ of the ‹ the ‹ to ❮ is Your
dened be right hand. ness earth. ends praise:

צִיּוֹן, תָּגֵלְנָה בְּנוֹת יְהוּדָה, לְמַעַן מִשְׁפָּטֶיךָ. סֹבּוּ צִיּוֹן

‹ Zion ‹ Walk ❮ of Your ‹ because ❮ of Judah, ‹ the ‹ rejoice ❮ Zion,
about judgments. daughters

וְהַקִּיפוּהָ, סִפְרוּ מִגְדָּלֶיהָ. ❖ שִׁיתוּ לִבְּכֶם לְחֵילָה, פַּסְּגוּ

‹ raise up ❮ her ‹ in your ‹ Mark ❮ her towers. ‹ count ❮ and encircle
ramparts, hearts well her,

אַרְמְנוֹתֶיהָ, לְמַעַן תְּסַפְּרוּ לְדוֹר אַחֲרוֹן. כִּי זֶה אֱלֹהִים

‹ is God, ‹ this ‹ For ❮ to the succeeding ‹ you may ‹ that ❮ her palaces,
generation. recount it

אֱלֹהֵינוּ עוֹלָם וָעֶד, הוּא יְנַהֲגֵנוּ עַל־מוּת.*

❮ eternally.* ‹ will guide us ‹ He ❮ and ever, ‹ for ever ‹ our God,

MANY CONGREGATIONS CONTINUE WITH הוֹשִׁיעֵנוּ, *SAVE US* (P. 242).
IN THE PRESENCE OF A *MINYAN*, MOURNERS RECITE קַדִּישׁ יָתוֹם, *THE MOURNER'S KADDISH* (P. 243).

TUESDAY

הַיּוֹם יוֹם שְׁלִישִׁי בַּשַּׁבָּת, שֶׁבּוֹ הָיוּ הַלְוִיִּם אוֹמְרִים בְּבֵית הַמִּקְדָּשׁ:

❮ in the Holy Temple: ‹ recite ‹ the Levites ‹ on ‹ of the ‹ is the third ‹ Today
would which week, day

——— תהלים פב / Psalm 82 ———

מִזְמוֹר לְאָסָף; אֱלֹהִים נִצָּב בַּעֲדַת אֵל,* בְּקֶרֶב

‹ in the ❮ in the Divine ‹ stands ‹ God ❮ by Asaph: ‹ A psalm
midst assembly,*

עַל־מוּת — *Eternally.* This is rendered as two words: God will guide us *beyond death;* through His guidance, only Israel from among the nations attains immortality (*R' Hirsch*). Alternatively, *like children.* The two words are rendered as one: עֲלָמוּת, *youth.* God will guide us like a father caring for his young (*Targum; Rashi*); or He will preserve the enthusiasm and vigor of our youth (*Meiri*).

יוֹם שְׁלִישִׁי / The Third Day

On the third day, God caused the dry land to become visible and fit for habitation. He did so in order that man follow the Torah's laws and deal justly with other people. Therefore the psalm speaks of justice (*Rosh Hashanah* 31a).

Maharsha explains that the theme of this psalm — the maintenance of equity and justice — is a prerequisite for the continued existence of the world that was revealed on the third day. But this message is not limited only to courts. In his own personal life, every Jew is a judge, for his opinions and decisions about people can affect their lives in a thousand different ways.

בַּעֲדַת אֵל — *In the Divine assembly.* Judges who seek truth and justice are the Divine *assembly,* because they represent God's justice on earth. As a result of their sincerity, God Himself penetrates into their hearts — בְּקֶרֶב אֱלֹהִים, *in the midst of judges* — to insure that they reach a just verdict (*Alshich*).

אֱלֹהִים יִשְׁפֹּט. עַד מָתַי* תִּשְׁפְּטוּ עָוֶל, וּפְנֵי רְשָׁעִים

> of the ⟨ and the ⟨ lawlessly ⟨ will you ⟨ when* ⟨ Until ⟨⟨ shall He ⟨ of judges
> wicked   presence   judge.   judge.

תִּשְׂאוּ סֶלָה. שִׁפְטוּ דָל וְיָתוֹם, עָנִי וָרָשׁ הַצְדִּיקוּ.

> ⟨⟨ vindicate. ⟨ and ⟨ the ⟨⟨ and the ⟨ for the ⟨ Dispense ⟨⟨ Selah? ⟨⟨ will you
>   impoverished poor   orphan;   needy   justice   favor,

פַּלְּטוּ דַל וְאֶבְיוֹן, מִיַּד רְשָׁעִים הַצִּילוּ. לֹא יָדְעוּ*

> ⟨ They do ⟨⟨ deliver them. ⟨ of the wicked ⟨ and from ⟨⟨ and ⟨ the ⟨ Rescue
> not know*   the hand   destitute,   needy

וְלֹא יָבִינוּ, בַּחֲשֵׁכָה יִתְהַלָּכוּ; יִמּוֹטוּ כָּל מוֹסְדֵי אָרֶץ.

> ⟨⟨ of the ⟨ the ⟨ do all ⟨ collapse ⟨⟨ they walk; ⟨ in darkness ⟨⟨ do they ⟨ nor
> earth. foundations   understand,

אֲנִי אָמַרְתִּי אֱלֹהִים אַתֶּם, וּבְנֵי עֶלְיוֹן כֻּלְּכֶם. אָכֵן כְּאָדָם

> ⟨ like men ⟨ But ⟨⟨ are you all. ⟨ of the ⟨ sons ⟨⟨ are you, ⟨ Angelic ⟨ said, ⟨ I
>   Most High

תְּמוּתוּן, וּכְאַחַד הַשָּׂרִים תִּפֹּלוּ. ❖ קוּמָה אֱלֹהִים* שָׁפְטָה

> ⟨ judge ⟨ O God,* ⟨ Arise, ⟨⟨ you shall fall. ⟨ of the princes ⟨ and like one ⟨⟨ you shall die,

הָאָרֶץ, כִּי אַתָּה תִנְחַל בְּכָל הַגּוֹיִם.

> ⟨⟨ the nations. ⟨ of all ⟨ allot the portion ⟨ You ⟨ for ⟨⟨ the earth,

MANY CONGREGATIONS CONTINUE WITH הוֹשִׁיעֵנוּ, *SAVE US* (P. 242).
IN THE PRESENCE OF A *MINYAN,* MOURNERS RECITE קַדִּישׁ יָתוֹם, *THE MOURNER'S KADDISH* (P. 243).

WEDNESDAY

הַיּוֹם יוֹם רְבִיעִי בַּשַּׁבָּת, שֶׁבּוֹ הָיוּ הַלְוִיִּם אוֹמְרִים בְּבֵית הַמִּקְדָּשׁ:

> ⟨⟨ in the Holy Temple: ⟨ recite ⟨ the Levites ⟨ on ⟨ of the ⟨ is the fourth ⟨ Today
>   would   which   week,   day

——— Psalms 94:1-95:3 / תהלים צד:א-צה:ג ———

אֵל נְקָמוֹת יהוה, אֵל נְקָמוֹת הוֹפִיעַ. הִנָּשֵׂא שֹׁפֵט

> ⟨ O ⟨ Arise, ⟨⟨ appear! ⟨ of ⟨ O ⟨⟨ HASHEM; ⟨ of vengeance, ⟨ O God
> Judge   vengeance,   God

עַד מָתַי — *Until when . . . ?* The next three verses are directed to judges who fail to carry out their responsibilities. Included in this exhortation is the clear message that judges should take the initiative in seeking out and correcting injustice.

לֹא יָדְעוּ — *They do not know.* The Psalmist exclaims that many judges are unaware of their awesome responsibility; they walk in darkness, blinded by prejudice and selfishness.

קוּמָה אֱלֹהִים — *Arise, O God.* Since human judges are corrupt, *You* must see to it that justice prevails in the world.

יוֹם רְבִיעִי / **The Fourth Day**

On the fourth day, God created the sun, moon, and stars, but instead of recognizing them as God's servants, man eventually came to regard the luminaries as independent gods that should be worshiped. Because of this idolatry,

הָאָרֶץ, הָשֵׁב גְּמוּל עַל גֵּאִים. עַד מָתַי רְשָׁעִים, יהוה,

‹‹ O ‹ will the ‹ when ‹ Until ‹‹ the ‹ to ‹ retribution ‹ render ‹‹ of the
HASHEM, wicked, haughty. earth,

עַד מָתַי רְשָׁעִים יַעֲלֹזוּ. יַבִּיעוּ יְדַבְּרוּ עָתָק, יִתְאַמְּרוּ

‹ they glorify ‹‹ malicious ‹ they utter ‹ They speak ‹‹ exult? ‹ will the ‹ when ‹ until
themselves, falsehood, freely, wicked

כָּל פֹּעֲלֵי אָוֶן. עַמְּךָ יהוה יְדַכְּאוּ, וְנַחֲלָתְךָ יְעַנּוּ. אַלְמָנָה

‹ The widow ‹‹ they ‹ and Your ‹‹ they ‹ HASHEM, ‹ Your ‹‹ of ‹ doers ‹ all
afflict. heritage crush, people, evil.

וְגֵר יַהֲרֹגוּ, וִיתוֹמִים יְרַצֵּחוּ. וַיֹּאמְרוּ: לֹא יִרְאֶה יָּהּ,*

‹‹ will ‹ See not : ‹ And they say, ‹‹ they ‹ and the ‹‹ they ‹ and the
God,* murder. orphans slay, stranger

וְלֹא יָבִין אֱלֹהֵי יַעֲקֹב. בִּינוּ* בֹּעֲרִים בָּעָם, וּכְסִילִים מָתַי

‹ when ‹ and you ‹‹ among ‹ you ‹ Under- ‹‹ of Jacob. ‹ will ‹ understand not
fools, the people; boors stand,* the God

תַּשְׂכִּילוּ. הֲנֹטַע אֹזֶן הֲלֹא יִשְׁמָע, אִם יֹצֵר עַיִן הֲלֹא

‹ not ‹ the ‹ He Who ‹ Will ‹‹ will He not hear? ‹ the ‹ The One ‹‹ will you gain
eye fashions ear, Who implants wisdom?

יַבִּיט. הֲיֹסֵר גּוֹיִם הֲלֹא יוֹכִיחַ, הַמְלַמֵּד אָדָם דָּעַת.

‹‹ knowledge. ‹ man ‹ It is He Who ‹‹ will He not punish? ‹ nations, ‹ He Who ‹‹ see?
teaches chastises

יהוה יֹדֵעַ מַחְשְׁבוֹת אָדָם, כִּי הֵמָּה הָבֶל. אַשְׁרֵי הַגֶּבֶר*

‹ is the ‹ Praiseworthy ‹‹ futile. ‹ they are ‹ that ‹‹ of man, ‹ the thoughts ‹ knows ‹ HASHEM
man*

אֲשֶׁר תְּיַסְּרֶנּוּ יָּהּ, וּמִתּוֹרָתְךָ תְלַמְּדֶנּוּ. לְהַשְׁקִיט לוֹ*

‹ to ‹ to give rest ‹‹ You teach him, ‹ and [whom] ‹‹ God disciplines, ‹ whom
him* from Your Torah

God showed Himself to be, as this psalm describes Him, the *God of vengeance,* for despite his seemingly limitless patience and mercy, He does not forever tolerate evil.

וַיֹּאמְרוּ לֹא יִרְאֶה יָּהּ — *And they say, "See not will God . . ."* or *"God will not see . . ."* When the Temple was destroyed, it was as if God's power had been diminished and His Four-letter Name abbreviated to the two letters of יָּהּ (*Eruvin* 18b). This gives evildoers the pretext to claim that God was detached from the world and unable to see the wickedness being done on earth (*Zera Yaakov*).

בִּינוּ — *Understand.* If only the boors would

realize that God cannot be fooled or ignored! (*Radak*).

אַשְׁרֵי הַגֶּבֶר — *Praiseworthy is the man.* The wicked ask why the righteous suffer, if God truly controls everything. The Psalmist answers that God afflicts the righteous only when it is to their benefit, to correct them, to make them realize the futility of physical pleasures, or to atone for their sins (*Radak; Meiri*).

לְהַשְׁקִיט לוֹ — *To give rest to him.* The suffering of good people on earth spares them from the far worse *days of evil* in Gehinnom; thus they will rest while evil is purged from the world and *dug for the wicked is a pit* (*Rashi*).

מִימֵי רָע, עַד יִכָּרֶה לָרָשָׁע שָׁחַת. כִּי לֹא יִטֹּשׁ יהוה

‹ will ‹ forsake not ‹ Because ❭❭ is a pit. ‹ for the ‹ dug ‹ while ❭❭ of ‹ from
HASHEM   wicked   evil,   the days

עַמּוֹ, וְנַחֲלָתוֹ* לֹא יַעֲזֹב. כִּי עַד צֶדֶק יָשׁוּב מִשְׁפָּט,*

❭❭ shall justice revert,* ‹ righteousness ‹ to ‹ For ❭❭ He will not ‹ and His ❭❭ His
                      abandon.   heritage*   people,

וְאַחֲרָיו כָּל יִשְׁרֵי לֵב. מִי יָקוּם לִי עִם מְרֵעִים, מִי

‹ Who ❭❭ evildoers? ‹ against ‹ for ‹ will ‹ Who ❭❭ heart. ‹ of upright ‹ will ‹ and
       me   rise up   be all   following it

יִתְיַצֵּב לִי עִם פֹּעֲלֵי אָוֶן. לוּלֵי יהוה עֶזְרָתָה לִּי, כִּמְעַט

‹ in a ❭❭ to ‹ been a help ‹ Had HASHEM not ❭❭ of ‹ the ‹ against ‹ for ‹ will stand
  moment   me,   evil?   doers   me   up

שָׁכְנָה דוּמָה נַפְשִׁי. אִם אָמַרְתִּי מָטָה רַגְלִי,* חַסְדְּךָ

‹ Your ❭❭ My foot falters,* ‹ I said, ‹ If ❭❭ my soul. ‹ in the ‹ would
kindness,   silent grave have dwelt

יהוה יִסְעָדֵנִי. בְּרֹב שַׂרְעַפַּי בְּקִרְבִּי, תַּנְחוּמֶיךָ יְשַׁעַשְׁעוּ

‹ cheered ‹ Your comforts ❭❭ within me, ‹ were my ‹ When ❭❭ supported ‹ HASHEM,
                forebodings abundant   me.

נַפְשִׁי. הַיְחָבְרְךָ כִּסֵּא הַוּוֹת, יֹצֵר עָמָל עֲלֵי חֹק. יָגוֹדּוּ

‹ They join ❭❭ a ‹ into ‹ evil ‹ – those ‹ of ‹ – the ❭❭ Can it be asso- ❭❭ my
together statute?   who fashion destruction? throne   ciated with You   soul.

עַל נֶפֶשׁ צַדִּיק, וְדָם נָקִי יַרְשִׁיעוּ. וַיְהִי יהוה לִי

‹ for ‹ Then HASHEM ❭❭ they ‹ that is ‹ and the ❭❭ of the ‹ the soul ‹ against
‹ me   became   condemn. innocent blood   righteous,

לְמִשְׂגָּב, וֵאלֹהַי לְצוּר מַחְסִי. וַיָּשֶׁב עֲלֵיהֶם אֶת אוֹנָם,

❭❭ their own ‹ upon them ‹ He turned ❭❭ of my ‹ the Rock ‹ and my ❭❭ a stronghold,
violence,   refuge.   God,

וּבְרָעָתָם יַצְמִיתֵם; יַצְמִיתֵם יהוה אֱלֹהֵינוּ. ❖ לְכוּ נְרַנְּנָה*

‹ Let us sing ‹ Come! ❭❭ our God. ‹ will ‹ cut them off ❭❭ He will cut ‹ and with their
joyfully*   HASHEM,   them off;   own evil

לַיהוה, נָרִיעָה לְצוּר יִשְׁעֵנוּ. נְקַדְּמָה פָנָיו בְּתוֹדָה, בִּזְמִרוֹת

‹ with ❭❭ with ‹ Him ‹ Let us greet ❭❭ of our ‹ to the ‹ let us call ❭❭ to HASHEM,
praiseful songs thanksgiving,   salvation. Rock   out

וְנַחֲלָתוֹ — *His heritage.* Even in exile, Israel knows it will survive, because it is God's *heritage* (Radak).

כִּי עַד צֶדֶק יָשׁוּב מִשְׁפָּט — *For to righteousness shall justice revert.* For the good person who has sinned, God's punishment will cause him to repent (Rashi).

מָטָה רַגְלִי — *"My foot falters."* When Israel fears it will falter, God's goodness supports it (Radak).

לְכוּ נְרַנְּנָה — *Come! Let us sing joyfully.* The next three verses are not part of the psalm of the day,

נָרִיעַ לוֹ. כִּי אֵל גָּדוֹל יהוה, וּמֶלֶךְ גָּדוֹל עַל כָּל אֱלֹהִים.

《 heavenly 〈 all 〈 above 〈 and a great King **《** is Hᴀsʜᴇᴍ, 〈 a great God 〈 For**《** to 〈 let us
powers.   Him. call out

MANY CONGREGATIONS CONTINUE WITH **הוֹשִׁיעֵנוּ**, SAVE US (P. 242).
IN THE PRESENCE OF A MINYAN, MOURNERS RECITE **קַדִּישׁ יָתוֹם**, THE MOURNER'S KADDISH (P. 243).

THURSDAY

הַיּוֹם יוֹם חֲמִישִׁי בַּשַּׁבָּת, שֶׁבּוֹ הָיוּ הַלְוִיִּם אוֹמְרִים בְּבֵית הַמִּקְדָּשׁ:

《 in the Holy Temple: 〈 recite 〈 the Levites 〈 on 〈 of the 〈 is the fifth day 〈 Today
                         would   which   week,

——————— Psalm 81 / תהלים פא ———————

לַמְנַצֵּחַ עַל הַגִּתִּית* לְאָסָף. הַרְנִינוּ לֵאלֹהִים עוּזֵּנוּ,

《our strength, 〈 to God 〈 Sing joyously **《** by Asaph. 〈 the gittis,* 〈 on 〈 For the conductor,

הָרִיעוּ לֵאלֹהֵי יַעֲקֹב. שְׂאוּ זִמְרָה וּתְנוּ תֹף, כִּנּוֹר נָעִים

〈 the sweet harp 〈 the 〈 and 〈 a song 〈 Raise up **《** of Jacob. 〈 to the God 〈 call out
                  drum,   sound

עִם נָבֶל. תִּקְעוּ בַחֹדֶשׁ שׁוֹפָר,* בַּכֵּסֶה לְיוֹם חַגֵּנוּ.

《 of our 〈 for the 〈 at the time **《** the shofar,* 〈 at the moon's 〈 Blow **《** the lyre. 〈 with
festivals. day   appointed   renewal

כִּי חֹק לְיִשְׂרָאֵל הוּא, מִשְׁפָּט לֵאלֹהֵי יַעֲקֹב. עֵדוּת

〈 As a **《** of Jacob. 〈 for the God 〈 a judgment **《** is it, 〈 for Israel 〈 a 〈 Because
testimony   [day]   decree

בִּיהוֹסֵף שָׂמוֹ,* בְּצֵאתוֹ עַל אֶרֶץ מִצְרָיִם, שְׂפַת

〈 a language **《** of Egypt, 〈 the land 〈 over 〈 when He went out 〈 He appointed it* 〈 for Joseph

and are not recited in all congregations. They
are the opening verses of the next psalm and are
recited because of their inspiring message that is
an apt climax to the song of the day.

יוֹם חֲמִישִׁי / The Fifth Day

On the fifth day of Creation, God made the
birds and the fish, which bring joy to the world.
Upon observing the broad variety of colorful
birds and fish, man is awed by the enormous
scope of God's creative ability, and is stirred to
praise Him with song (Rosh Hashanah 31a).

הַגִּתִּית — The gittis. A musical instrument named
after the town of Gath, where it was made
(Rashi).

תִּקְעוּ בַחֹדֶשׁ שׁוֹפָר — Blow at the moon's renewal
the shofar. The moon's renewal is a poetic term
for the first day of the lunar month, when the

moon becomes visible again. This verse refers to
Rosh Hashanah, which occurs on the first day of
Tishrei, and is when the shofar is blown.

עֵדוּת בִּיהוֹסֵף שָׂמוֹ — As a testimony for Joseph He
appointed it. The entire verse is based on the life
of Joseph. The Talmud (Rosh Hashanah 10b)
teaches that Joseph was released from prison and
appointed viceroy of Egypt on Rosh Hashanah.
In honor of that event, God ordained the mitzvah
of shofar on Rosh Hashanah as a testimony, or a
reminder of Joseph's freedom.

Joseph's name, usually spelled יוֹסֵף, appears
here with an extra letter, יְהוֹסֵף. The Talmud here
explains that because Joseph sanctified God's
Name by refusing the temptation of his master's
wife, God inserted a letter of His own Name —
the letter ה — into Joseph's (Sotah 12a).

לֹא יָדַעְתִּי אֶשְׁמָע.* הֲסִירוֹתִי* מִסֵּבֶל שִׁכְמוֹ, כַּפָּיו

⟨ unknown to me ⟨ I heard.* ≪ [Says God:] I removed* ⟨ from the burden ⟨ his shoulder, ⟨ his hands

מִדּוּד תַּעֲבֹרְנָה. בַּצָּרָה קָרֵאתָ וָאֲחַלְּצֶךָּ, אֶעֶנְךָ בְּסֵתֶר

⟨ from the kettle ⟨ passed. ≪ In distress ⟨ you called out, ≪ and I released you; ≪ I answered you, ≪ [when you called] privately,

רָעַם, אֶבְחָנְךָ עַל מֵי מְרִיבָה* סֶלָה. שְׁמַע עַמִּי וְאָעִידָה

⟨ with a thunderous reply. ≪ I tested you ⟨ at the ⟨ Waters ⟨ of Strife.* ⟨ Selah. ≪ Listen, ⟨ My people, ⟨ and I will attest

בָּךְ, יִשְׂרָאֵל אִם תִּשְׁמַע לִי. לֹא יִהְיֶה בְךָ אֵל זָר,

⟨ to you; O Israel, ⟨ if you would but listen ⟨ to Me. ≪ There shall not be ⟨ within you ⟨ [any] strange god, ≪

וְלֹא תִשְׁתַּחֲוֶה לְאֵל נֵכָר. אָנֹכִי יהוה אֱלֹהֶיךָ הַמַּעַלְךָ

⟨ nor ⟨ shall you bow ⟨ before an alien god. ≪ I am ⟨ HASHEM, ⟨ your God, ⟨ Who raised you

מֵאֶרֶץ מִצְרָיִם, הַרְחֶב פִּיךָ* וַאֲמַלְאֵהוּ. וְלֹא שָׁמַע עַמִּי

⟨ from the land ⟨ of Egypt. ⟨ Open wide ⟨ your mouth* ⟨ and I will fill it. ≪ But listen not ⟨ did My people

לְקוֹלִי, וְיִשְׂרָאֵל לֹא אָבָה לִי. וָאֲשַׁלְּחֵהוּ בִּשְׁרִירוּת

≪ to My voice; ⟨ Israel ⟨ did not ⟨ desire ≪ Me. ⟨ So I let them pursue ⟨ the fantasies

לִבָּם, יֵלְכוּ בְּמוֹעֲצוֹתֵיהֶם. לוּ עַמִּי שֹׁמֵעַ לִי, יִשְׂרָאֵל

⟨ of their heart, ≪ that they might follow ⟨ their own counsels. ⟨ If only ⟨ My people ⟨ would heed ≪ Me, ⟨ Israel [if only]

בִּדְרָכַי יְהַלֵּכוּ. כִּמְעַט אוֹיְבֵיהֶם אַכְנִיעַ, וְעַל צָרֵיהֶם

⟨ in My ways ≪ would walk. ⟨ In an instant ⟨ their foes ⟨ I would subdue, ⟨ and against ⟨ their tormentors

אָשִׁיב יָדִי. מְשַׂנְאֵי יהוה יְכַחֲשׁוּ לוֹ,* וִיהִי עִתָּם לְעוֹלָם.

⟨ I would turn ⟨ My hand. ≪ Those who hate ⟨ HASHEM ⟨ would lie to him;* ≪ but their time would be ⟨ forever.

שְׁפַת לֹא יָדַעְתִּי אֶשְׁמָע — *A language unknown to me I heard.* In order to qualify as a ruler under Egyptian law, Joseph had to know all the languages of the world — a requirement that was fulfilled when the angel Gabriel taught them to him (Rashi).

הֲסִירוֹתִי — *I removed.* On the same day, God freed Joseph from his menial prison tasks of carrying burdens and doing kitchen chores (Rashi).

מֵי מְרִיבָה — *The Waters of Strife*, when Israel had no water and engaged in "strife" against Moses.

See Numbers 20:1-13.

הַרְחֶב פִּיךָ — *Open wide your mouth*, with requests, and I will fulfill them. God urges Israel to ask all that its heart desires (Ibn Ezra). By asking God for *everything* that he needs, a person demonstrates his belief that God's power and generosity know no bounds (Taanis 3:6).

מְשַׂנְאֵי ה' יְכַחֲשׁוּ לוֹ — *Those who hate HASHEM* (Israel's enemies, because Israel's enemies are God's enemies as well) *would lie to him* (Israel). They deny that they ever harmed Israel (Radak).

וַיַּאֲכִילֵהוּ* מֵחֵלֶב חִטָּה; וּמִצּוּר, דְּבַשׁ אַשְׂבִּיעֶךָ. ❖

《 I would sate you. 〈 with 《 and from 《 wheat, 〈 with the 〈 And He would
honey   a rock,   choicest   feed him*

MANY CONGREGATIONS CONTINUE WITH הוֹשִׁיעֵנוּ, *SAVE US* (P. 242).
IN THE PRESENCE OF A *MINYAN*, MOURNERS RECITE קַדִּישׁ יָתוֹם, *THE MOURNER'S KADDISH* (P. 243).

FRIDAY

הַיּוֹם יוֹם שִׁשִּׁי בַּשַּׁבָּת, שֶׁבּוֹ הָיוּ הַלְוִיִם אוֹמְרִים בְּבֵית הַמִּקְדָּשׁ:

《 in the Holy Temple: 〈 recite 〈 the Levites 〈 on 〈 of the 〈 is the sixth day 〈 Today
would   which   week,

——— Psalm 93 / תהלים צג ———

יהוה מָלָךְ גֵּאוּת לָבֵשׁ,* לָבֵשׁ יהוה עֹז הִתְאַזָּר, אַף

〈 in- 《 and [with 〈 strength 〈 has 〈 donned 《 has He 〈 grandeur 《 has 〈 HASHEM
deed strength] He   HASHEM   donned;*   reigned,
girded Himself;

תִּכּוֹן תֵּבֵל בַּל תִּמּוֹט. נָכוֹן כִּסְאֲךָ מֵאָז, מֵעוֹלָם אָתָּה.

《 are You. 〈 eternal 《 from 〈 is Your 〈 Established 《 topple. 〈 that it 〈 is the 〈 firmed
of old;   throne   should not world

נָשְׂאוּ נְהָרוֹת, יהוה, נָשְׂאוּ נְהָרוֹת קוֹלָם;* יִשְׂאוּ נְהָרוֹת

〈 [like] 〈 they 《 their 〈 [like] 〈 they 《 O 〈 [like] 〈 They
rivers   shall raise voice;* rivers raised HASHEM, rivers, raised

דָּכְיָם. מִקֹּלוֹת מַיִם רַבִּים, אַדִּירִים מִשְׁבְּרֵי יָם, אַדִּיר

〈 mighty 《 of the 〈 than the 〈 mightier 《 of many waters, 〈 More than 《 their de-
sea,   waves   the roars   structiveness.

וַיַּאֲכִילֵהוּ — *He would feed him.* In the Wilderness, God provided Israel with manna that was finer than *the choicest wheat* and provided them with honey-sweet water *from a rock (Ibn Ezra).*

יוֹם שִׁשִּׁי ⁧⁑⁩ / The Sixth Day

Because it describes God in His full grandeur and power as He was when He completed the six days of Creation, and because it describes Him as "donning" grandeur and "girding" Himself like one dressing in his Sabbath finery, this psalm was designated as the song of Friday, when the footsteps of the approaching Sabbath can be heard (*Rosh Hashanah* 31a; *R' Yaakov Emden*).

גֵּאוּת לָבֵשׁ — *Grandeur has He donned.* The concept of *grandeur* represents God's revelation as the dominant force before whom the mighti-

est natural forces yield. In man, grandeur — or arrogance — is a contemptible trait, because man's power is limited at best. But to God, *grandeur* is becoming because all forces owe their existence to Him, while He is dependent on nothing (*Midrash Shocher Tov*).

God "dons" grandeur. It is similar to a person donning a garment; our knowledge of him is shaped by the contours and quality of the garment, but the garment is hardly his essence. No matter how much of God's greatness we think we understand, our puny intellect grasps but the minutest fraction of His infinite greatness. He does us the favor of allowing mankind this degree of insight so that we can aspire to the privilege of praising Him.

נָשְׂאוּ נְהָרוֹת קוֹלָם — *They raised [like] rivers their voice.* The enemies of Israel will roar

בַּמָּרוֹם יהוה. ❖ עֵדֹתֶיךָ* נֶאֶמְנוּ מְאֹד לְבֵיתְךָ נַאֲוָה קֹדֶשׁ,

‹‹ the Sacred ‹ about Your ‹ are exceedingly ‹ Your ‹‹ are You ‹ on high,
Dwelling; House, trustworthy testimonies* HASHEM.

יהוה, לְאֹרֶךְ יָמִים.*

‹‹ days.* ‹ may it be ‹ O
for lengthy HASHEM,

MANY CONGREGATIONS CONTINUE WITH הוֹשִׁיעֵנוּ, SAVE US (BELOW).
IN THE PRESENCE OF A MINYAN, MOURNERS RECITE קַדִּישׁ יָתוֹם, THE MOURNER'S KADDISH (P. 243).

ON ALL DAYS:

IN MANY CONGREGATIONS THE FOLLOWING VERSES ARE ADDED:

הוֹשִׁיעֵנוּ יהוה אֱלֹהֵינוּ, וְקַבְּצֵנוּ מִן הַגּוֹיִם, לְהֹדוֹת

‹ to thank ‹‹ among ‹ from ‹ and gather ‹ our God, ‹ HASHEM, ‹ Save us,
the nations, us

לְשֵׁם קָדְשֶׁךָ, לְהִשְׁתַּבֵּחַ בִּתְהִלָּתֶךָ. בָּרוּךְ יהוה אֱלֹהֵי

‹ the ‹‹ is ‹ Blessed ‹‹ in Your praise! ‹ and to glory ‹ of Your ‹‹ the Name
God HASHEM, holiness,

יִשְׂרָאֵל, מִן הָעוֹלָם וְעַד הָעוֹלָם, וְאָמַר כָּל הָעָם: אָמֵן,

‹‹ Amen! ‹‹ the ‹ — all ‹‹ and let ‹‹ The World ‹ to ‹ [This] ‹ from ‹ of Israel,
people — them say [to Come], World

הַלְלוּיָהּ.[1] בָּרוּךְ יהוה מִצִּיּוֹן, שֹׁכֵן יְרוּשָׁלָיִם, הַלְלוּיָהּ.

‹‹ Halleluyah! ‹‹ in Jerusalem, ‹ He Who ‹ from Zion, ‹‹ is ‹ Blessed ‹‹ Halleluyah!
dwells HASHEM

בָּרוּךְ יהוה אֱלֹהִים אֱלֹהֵי יִשְׂרָאֵל, עֹשֵׂה נִפְלָאוֹת לְבַדּוֹ.

‹‹ by ‹ wondrous ‹ Who ‹‹ of Israel, ‹ the God ‹ God, ‹ is ‹ Blessed
Himself. things does HASHEM,

❖ וּבָרוּךְ שֵׁם כְּבוֹדוֹ לְעוֹלָם, וְיִמָּלֵא כְבוֹדוֹ אֶת כָּל הָאָרֶץ,

‹‹ the earth, ‹ all ‹ may His ‹ and fill ‹‹ forever, ‹ of His ‹ is the ‹ Blessed
glory glory Name

אָמֵן וְאָמֵן.[3]

‹‹ and Amen. ‹ Amen

---

(1) *Psalms* 106:47-48. (2) 135:21. (3) 72:18-19.

against Israel like raging rivers at flood stage (*Radak*).

The repetition of the phrase represents the destruction of the two Temples (*Etz Yosef*).

עֵדֹתֶיךָ — *Your testimonies.* The assurances of Your prophets regarding the eventual rebuilding

of the Temple (*Rashi*).

ה׳ לְאֹרֶךְ יָמִים — *O HASHEM, may it be for lengthy days.* The psalm closes with a plea that when the *trustworthy* prophecies about the Third Temple are fulfilled, may it stand for *lengthy days*, a Scriptural idiom meaning forever (*Radak*).

MOURNER'S KADDISH / קַדִּישׁ יָתוֹם

IN THE PRESENCE OF A *MINYAN*, MOURNERS RECITE קַדִּישׁ יָתוֹם, THE MOURNER'S *KADDISH*.
[A TRANSLITERATION OF THIS *KADDISH* APPEARS ON PAGE 879.]

יִתְגַּדַּל וְיִתְקַדַּשׁ שְׁמֵהּ רַבָּא. (אָמֵן. – Cong.) בְּעָלְמָא דִּי בְרָא

⟨ He ⟨ that ⟨   in the   ⟨⟨   (Amen.)   ⟨⟨ that is ⟨ may His ⟨ and be ⟨ Grow exalted
created   world   great! —   Name   sanctified

כִרְעוּתֵהּ, וְיַמְלִיךְ מַלְכוּתֵהּ, וְיַצְמַח פֻּרְקָנֵהּ וִיקָרֵב מְשִׁיחֵהּ.

⟨⟨ His   ⟨ and bring ⟨   His   ⟨ and cause ⟨   to His   ⟨ and may He ⟨ according
Messiah,   near   salvation, to sprout   kingship,   give reign   to His will,

אָמֵן.) בְּחַיֵּיכוֹן וּבְיוֹמֵיכוֹן וּבְחַיֵּי דְכָל בֵּית יִשְׂרָאֵל, – Cong.)

⟨⟨ of Israel, ⟨ Family ⟨ of the ⟨ and in the ⟨   and in   ⟨ in your ⟨⟨ (Amen.)
entire   lifetimes   your days,   lifetimes

בַּעֲגָלָא וּבִזְמַן קָרִיב. וְאִמְרוּ: אָמֵן.

⟨⟨ Amen. ⟨ Now ⟨⟨ that comes ⟨ and at ⟨   swiftly
respond: soon.   a time

CONGREGATION RESPONDS:

אָמֵן. יְהֵא שְׁמֵהּ רַבָּא מְבָרַךְ לְעָלַם וּלְעָלְמֵי עָלְמַיָּא.

⟨⟨   and for all eternity. ⟨ forever ⟨ be blessed ⟨ that is great ⟨ His Name ⟨ May ⟨⟨ Amen.

MOURNER CONTINUES:

יְהֵא שְׁמֵהּ רַבָּא מְבָרַךְ לְעָלַם וּלְעָלְמֵי עָלְמַיָּא. יִתְבָּרַךְ

⟨ Blessed, ⟨⟨   and for all eternity. ⟨ forever ⟨   be   ⟨ that ⟨ His ⟨ May
blessed   is great Name

וְיִשְׁתַּבַּח וְיִתְפָּאַר וְיִתְרוֹמַם וְיִתְנַשֵּׂא וְיִתְהַדָּר וְיִתְעַלֶּה

⟨ elevated, ⟨ honored, ⟨ upraised, ⟨ exalted, ⟨ glorified, ⟨ praised,

וְיִתְהַלָּל שְׁמֵהּ דְּקֻדְשָׁא בְּרִיךְ הוּא (בְּרִיךְ הוּא) – Cong.) –

⟨⟨ is He) ⟨ (Blessed ⟨⟨ is He ⟨ Blessed ⟨ of the Holy One, ⟨ be the Name ⟨ and lauded

ROSH HASHANAH TO YOM KIPPUR SUBSTITUTE:

°לְעֵלָּא מִן כָּל [°לְעֵלָּא (וּ)לְעֵלָּא מִכָּל] בִּרְכָתָא

⟨ blessing ⟨   any   ⟨   exceedingly beyond   ⟨   any   ⟨ beyond

וְשִׁירָתָא, תֻּשְׁבְּחָתָא וְנֶחֱמָתָא דַּאֲמִירָן בְּעָלְמָא.

⟨⟨ in the world. ⟨ that are uttered ⟨ and consolation ⟨   praise   ⟨⟨ and song,

וְאִמְרוּ: אָמֵן. (אָמֵן. – Cong.)

⟨⟨ (Amen.)   ⟨⟨ Amen. ⟨ Now respond:

◄§ קַדִּישׁ יָתוֹם / Mourner's Kaddish

For the eleven months following the death
of a parent and on the *yahrzeit*, or anniversary
of the death, a son is obligated to recite
Kaddish as a source of merit for the soul of the

departed. For commentary see "The Rabbis'
Kaddish," p. 78. A discussion of the concept
and basis underlying the recitation of the
Mourner's *Kaddish* appears in the ArtScroll
Kaddish.

יְהֵא שְׁלָמָא רַבָּא מִן שְׁמַיָּא, וְחַיִּים טוֹבִים עָלֵינוּ וְעַל כָּל
‹ all ‹ and ‹ upon us ‹‹ that is ‹ and life ‹‹ Heaven, ‹ from ‹ that is ‹ peace ‹ May
upon   good,   abundant   there be

יִשְׂרָאֵל. וְאִמְרוּ: אָמֵן. (.אָמֵן – Cong.)
‹‹ (Amen.)   ‹‹ Amen. ‹ Now respond: ‹‹ Israel.

**BOW; TAKE THREE STEPS BACK: BOW LEFT AND SAY ... עֹשֶׂה שָׁלוֹם, *"HE WHO MAKES PEACE ..."*; BOW
RIGHT AND SAY ... הוּא, *"MAY HE ..."*; BOW FORWARD AND SAY ... וְעַל כָּל יִשְׂרָאֵל, *"AND UPON
ALL ISRAEL ..."* REMAIN IN PLACE FOR A FEW MOMENTS, THEN TAKE THREE STEPS FORWARD.**

עֹשֶׂה °שָׁלוֹם בִּמְרוֹמָיו, הוּא יַעֲשֶׂה שָׁלוֹם עָלֵינוּ, וְעַל
‹ and upon ‹ upon us, ‹ peace ‹ make ‹ may He ‹‹ in His heights, ‹ peace ‹ He Who makes

כָּל יִשְׂרָאֵל. וְאִמְרוּ: אָמֵן. (.אָמֵן – Cong.)
‹‹ (Amen.)   ‹‹ Amen. ‹ Now respond: ‹‹ Israel. ‹ all

FROM ROSH HASHANAH TO YOM KIPPUR SOME SAY:
°הַשָּׁלוֹם
‹ the peace

MANY CONGREGATIONS RECITE PSALM 104 ON ROSH CHODESH AT THIS POINT.

──── תהלים קד / Psalm 104 ────

בָּרְכִי נַפְשִׁי אֶת יהוה;* יהוה אֱלֹהַי, גָּדַלְתָּ מְאֹד,*
‹‹ You are very great;* ‹ my God, ‹ HASHEM, ‹‹ HASHEM.* ‹ O my soul, ‹ Bless,

הוֹד וְהָדָר לָבָשְׁתָּ. עֹטֶה אוֹר כַּשַּׂלְמָה, נוֹטֶה שָׁמַיִם
‹ the ‹ stretching ‹ as a garment, ‹ light ‹ donning ‹‹ You have ‹ and ‹ majesty
heavens out   worn;   splendor

כַּיְרִיעָה. הַמְקָרֶה בַמַּיִם עֲלִיּוֹתָיו; הַשָּׂם עָבִים רְכוּבוֹ,
‹‹ as His ‹ clouds ‹ He Who ‹‹ His upper ‹ with ‹ He Who roofs ‹‹ like a
chariot;   sets   chambers;   water   curtain.

הַמְהַלֵּךְ עַל כַּנְפֵי רוּחַ. עֹשֶׂה מַלְאָכָיו רוּחוֹת, מְשָׁרְתָיו
‹ His ‹‹ the winds, ‹ His ‹ He ‹‹ of wind. ‹ wings ‹ on ‹ He Who
attendants   messengers makes   walks

∾§ Rosh Chodesh / Psalm 104

This psalm is recited as the Song of the Day for Rosh Chodesh, the New Moon, because the Psalmist alludes to the New Moon in the verse: *He made the moon for festivals (Tur).*

These words are not merely an allusion to the new month. Rather, they set the tone of this entire composition, whose main theme is God's complete mastery over every aspect of Creation. Throughout the monthly lunar cycle, the size of the moon visibly waxes and wanes, to demonstrate dramatically that God has total mastery over His creations. No other natural phenomenon conveys this message as vividly and forcefully as the moon's cycle. Thus, the theme of the New Moon complements the theme of this entire hymn of praise to the Master of Creation.

בָּרְכִי נַפְשִׁי אֶת ה' — *Bless, O my soul, HASHEM.* By calling upon his soul to bless God, the Psalmist suggests that the human soul is God's great gift to man; man, in effect, thanks God for the ability to reason, articulate, and rise to spiritual heights.

ה' אֱלֹהַי גָּדַלְתָּ מְאֹד — *HASHEM, my God, You are*

אֵשׁ לֹהֵט. יָסַד אֶרֶץ עַל מְכוֹנֶיהָ, בַּל תִּמּוֹט עוֹלָם

⟨ for ever ⟩ topple ⟨ that ⟪ its ⟨ upon ⟨ the earth ⟩ He ⟪ flaming. ⟨ the
it not foundations, established fire,

וָעֶד. תְּהוֹם כַּלְּבוּשׁ כִּסִּיתוֹ, עַל הָרִים יַעַמְדוּ מָיִם. מִן

⟨ From ⟪ water. ⟨ would ⟨ the ⟨ upon ⟨ You ⟪ as with ⟪ The ⟪ and
stand mountains covered it; a garment watery deep, ever.

גַּעֲרָתְךָ יְנוּסוּן,* מִן קוֹל רַעַמְךָ יֵחָפֵזוּן. יַעֲלוּ הָרִים,

⟨ mountains, ⟨ They ⟪ they ⟨ of Your ⟨ the ⟨ from ⟪ they flee;* ⟨ Your
ascend rush away. thunder sound rebuke

יֵרְדוּ בְקָעוֹת, אֶל מְקוֹם זֶה יָסַדְתָּ לָהֶם. גְּבוּל שַׂמְתָּ

⟨ You set, ⟨ A ⟪ for ⟨ foundation ⟨ whose ⟨ the special ⟨ to ⟪ to valleys, ⟨ they
boundary them. You laid place descend

בַּל יַעֲבֹרוּן, בַּל יְשׁוּבוּן לְכַסּוֹת הָאָרֶץ. הַמְשַׁלֵּחַ מַעְיָנִים

⟨ the springs ⟨ He sends ⟪ the earth. ⟨ to cover ⟨ they cannot ⟪ they cannot
return overstep,

בַּנְּחָלִים,* בֵּין הָרִים יְהַלֵּכוּן. יַשְׁקוּ כָּל חַיְתוֹ שָׂדָי,

⟪ of the ⟨ beast ⟨ every ⟨ They ⟪ they flow. ⟨ mountains ⟨ between ⟪ into the
field, water streams,*

יִשְׁבְּרוּ פְרָאִים צְמָאָם. עֲלֵיהֶם עוֹף הַשָּׁמַיִם יִשְׁכּוֹן,

⟪ dwell, ⟨ of the heaven ⟨ birds ⟨ Near them ⟪ thirst. ⟨ the wild ⟨ they
creatures' quench

מִבֵּין עֳפָאִים יִתְּנוּ קוֹל. מַשְׁקֶה הָרִים מֵעֲלִיּוֹתָיו, מִפְּרִי

⟨ from ⟪ from His upper ⟨ the ⟨ He waters ⟪ song. ⟨ they ⟨ the ⟨ from
the fruit chambers, mountains give forth branches among

מַעֲשֶׂיךָ תִּשְׂבַּע הָאָרֶץ. מַצְמִיחַ חָצִיר לַבְּהֵמָה,* וְעֵשֶׂב

⟨ and ⟪ for the ⟨ vegetation ⟨ He causes ⟨ is the ⟨ sated ⟨ of Your
plants animal,* to sprout earth. works,

לַעֲבֹדַת הָאָדָם; לְהוֹצִיא לֶחֶם מִן הָאָרֶץ. וְיַיִן יְשַׂמַּח

⟨ that ⟨ and ⟪ the earth; ⟨ from ⟨ bread ⟨ to bring forth ⟨ of man, ⟨ through
gladdens wine the labor

---

very great. We cannot define the extent of God's greatness; we say only that God is very great. Man can merely *begin* a recital of God's truly innumerable blessings (*Ibn Ezra*).

מִן גַּעֲרָתְךָ יְנוּסוּן — *From Your rebuke they flee.* At the beginning of Creation, water covered the entire surface of the earth. When God called out יִקָּווּ הַמַּיִם, *Let the waters gather* (*Genesis* 1:9), they all fled from where they were spread out and consolidated into seas and oceans (*Rashi*).

הַמְשַׁלֵּחַ מַעְיָנִים בַּנְּחָלִים — *He sends the springs*

into the streams. The Psalmist describes poetically how God instituted a natural system whereby the earth would be watered to provide for people and vegetation.

... מַצְמִיחַ חָצִיר לַבְּהֵמָה — *He causes to sprout vegetation for the animal* ... For animals, which cannot engage in agriculture, God causes vegetation to sprout. Man, however, must labor to earn his daily bread. Before he can partake of food, he must first sow, thresh, knead, and bake his bread (*R' Yosef Titzak;* see *Pesachim* 118a).

לְבַב אֱנוֹשׁ,* לְהַצְהִיל פָּנִים מִשָּׁמֶן, וְלֶחֶם לְבַב אֱנוֹשׁ

the heart ‹ of man ‹ and bread ‹ from oil, « the face ‹ to make glow « of man,* ‹ the heart [through which]

יִסְעָד. יִשְׂבְּעוּ עֲצֵי יהוה, אַרְזֵי לְבָנוֹן אֲשֶׁר נָטָע.

is sustained. « He has planted. ‹ that ‹ of Lebanon ‹ the cedars « of ‹ are the ‹ trees « HASHEM, ‹ Sated «

אֲשֶׁר שָׁם צִפֳּרִים יְקַנֵּנוּ, חֲסִידָה בְּרוֹשִׁים בֵּיתָהּ.

is its home. « — among the cypresses ‹ the stork « the birds ‹ nest, ‹ there ‹ That «

הָרִים הַגְּבֹהִים לַיְּעֵלִים, סְלָעִים מַחְסֶה לַשְׁפַנִּים. עָשָׂה

He made ‹ for the gophers. « as refuge ‹ rocks « for the wild goats, ‹ High mountains «

יָרֵחַ לְמוֹעֲדִים,* שֶׁמֶשׁ יָדַע מְבוֹאוֹ. תָּשֶׁת חֹשֶׁךְ וִיהִי

and it is ‹ darkness ‹ You make « its destination. ‹ knows ‹ the sun « for Festivals,* ‹ the moon

לָיְלָה, בּוֹ תִרְמֹשׂ כָּל חַיְתוֹ יָעַר. הַכְּפִירִים שֹׁאֲגִים

roar ‹ The young lions « of the forest. ‹ beast ‹ every ‹ stirs ‹ in « night, which

לַטָּרֶף, וּלְבַקֵּשׁ מֵאֵל אָכְלָם. תִּזְרַח הַשֶּׁמֶשׁ יֵאָסֵפוּן,

and they are gathered in, ‹ does the sun ‹ Rise « their food. ‹ from God ‹ and to seek « after their prey,

וְאֶל מְעוֹנֹתָם יִרְבָּצוּן. יֵצֵא אָדָם לְפָעֳלוֹ, וְלַעֲבֹדָתוֹ עֲדֵי

until ‹ and to his labor « to his work, ‹ Man goes forth « they crouch. ‹ their dens ‹ and in

עָרֶב. מָה רַבּוּ מַעֲשֶׂיךָ יהוה,* כֻּלָּם בְּחָכְמָה עָשִׂיתָ,*

You made;* ‹ with wisdom ‹ all of them « HASHEM;* ‹ are Your ‹ abundant ‹ How « evening.

מָלְאָה הָאָרֶץ קִנְיָנֶךָ.* זֶה הַיָּם, גָּדוֹל וּרְחַב יָדָיִם; שָׁם

there « measure; ‹ and of broad ‹ great ‹ the sea, ‹ This « with Your possessions.* ‹ is the earth ‹ full

---

וְיַיִן יְשַׂמַּח לְבַב אֱנוֹשׁ — *And wine that gladdens the heart of man.* God creates the grapes from which wine is pressed. When drunk in sensible proportions, wine gladdens the heart and drives away melancholy. It heightens the intellect and even prepares the mind for prophecy (*Radak*).

עָשָׂה יָרֵחַ לְמוֹעֲדִים — *He made the moon for Festivals.* The moon and its cycles were made to facilitate the lunar calendar, upon which the Torah bases the dating of the Festivals.

מָה רַבּוּ מַעֲשֶׂיךָ ה׳ — *How abundant are Your works, HASHEM.* רַבּוּ, *how abundant,* has both a quantitative meaning, *how numerous,* and a qualitative meaning, *how great* (*Radak*).

כֻּלָּם בְּחָכְמָה עָשִׂיתָ — *All of them with wisdom You made.* No creature evolved by chance; every one was designed by God in His *wisdom* and demonstrates His omnipotence (*Sforno*).

מָלְאָה הָאָרֶץ קִנְיָנֶךָ — *Full is the earth with Your possessions.* God did not allow even a single inch to go to waste. Every spot is full of wondrous creations which testify to Hashem's absolute

רֶמֶשׂ וְאֵין מִסְפָּר, חַיּוֹת קְטַנּוֹת עִם גְּדֹלוֹת. שָׁם אֳנִיּוֹת

‹ ships ‹ There ≪ great. ‹ as ‹ small ‹ creatures ≪ number, ‹ are ‹ creeping
well as   without things

יְהַלֵּכוּן, לִוְיָתָן זֶה יָצַרְתָּ לְשַׂחֶק בּוֹ. כֻּלָּם אֵלֶיךָ

‹ to You ‹ All of them ≪ with. ‹ to sport ‹ You fashioned ‹ this Leviathan ≪ travel,

יְשַׂבֵּרוּן, לָתֵת אָכְלָם בְּעִתּוֹ. תִּתֵּן לָהֶם, יִלְקֹטוּן; תִּפְתַּח

‹ You ≪ they gather ‹ to them, ‹ You ≪ in its ‹ their ‹ to ≪ look with
open   it in;   give proper time. food provide hope,

יָדְךָ, יִשְׂבְּעוּן טוֹב. תַּסְתִּיר פָּנֶיךָ, יִבָּהֵלוּן; תֹּסֵף רוּחָם,

‹ their ‹ when You ≪ they are ‹ Your face, ‹ When You ≪ with ‹ they are ‹ Your
spirit, retrieve   terrified;   hide   good. sated   hand,

יִגְוָעוּן, וְאֶל עֲפָרָם יְשׁוּבוּן. תְּשַׁלַּח רוּחֲךָ יִבָּרֵאוּן,*

≪ they are ‹ Your ‹ When You ≪ they return. ‹ their dust ‹ and to ≪ they
created,*   breath,   send forth   perish,

וּתְחַדֵּשׁ פְּנֵי אֲדָמָה. יְהִי כְבוֹד יהוה לְעוֹלָם, יִשְׂמַח יהוה

‹ let HASHEM ≪ endure ‹ of ‹ the glory ‹ May ≪ of the ‹ the ‹ and You
  rejoice   forever; HASHEM   earth. surface renew

בְּמַעֲשָׂיו. הַמַּבִּיט לָאָרֶץ וַתִּרְעָד, יִגַּע בֶּהָרִים וְיֶעֱשָׁנוּ.

≪ and they ‹ the ‹ He ≪ and it ‹ toward ‹ He looks ≪ in His works.
  smoke.   mountains touches trembles; the earth

אָשִׁירָה לַיהוה בְּחַיָּי, אֲזַמְּרָה לֵאלֹהַי בְּעוֹדִי. יֶעֱרַב עָלָיו

‹ to ‹ Sweet ≪ while ‹ to my ‹ I will sing ≪ while ‹ to HASHEM ‹ I will sing
Him   I endure. God praises   I live;

שִׂיחִי, אָנֹכִי אֶשְׂמַח בַּיהוה. ✶ יִתַּמּוּ חַטָּאִים מִן הָאָרֶץ,

≪ the ‹ from ‹ will sinners ‹ Perish ≪ in HASHEM. ‹ will rejoice ‹ — I ≪ may my
  earth,   words be

וּרְשָׁעִים עוֹד אֵינָם,* בָּרְכִי נַפְשִׁי אֶת יהוה; הַלְלוּיָהּ.

≪ Halleluyah! ≪ HASHEM. ‹ O my soul, ‹ Bless, ≪ will ‹ more ‹ and the
                                            not be;*   wicked

IN THE PRESENCE OF A *MINYAN*, MOURNERS RECITE קַדִּישׁ יָתוֹם, *THE MOURNER'S KADDISH* (P. 243).
THE SERVICE CONTINUES WITH וַיְהִי בִּנְסֹעַ – THE REMOVAL OF THE TORAH FROM THE ARK (P. 199).

mastery over the world (*Radak*).

תְּשַׁלַּח רוּחֲךָ יִבָּרֵאוּן — *When You send forth Your breath, they are created.* When man dies, God snatches the breath of life from him, but He will return it at the time of תְּחִיַּת הַמֵּתִים, *the revivification of the dead.* Then the dead bodies will be re-created, and their souls restored (*Radak*).

יִתַּמּוּ חַטָּאִים מִן הָאָרֶץ וּרְשָׁעִים עוֹד אֵינָם — *Perish*

will sinners from the earth, and the wicked more will not be or *the wicked will be no more.* The Hebrew word for *sinner* has two forms: חוֹטְאִים and חַטָּאִים. The latter form may be homiletically interpreted as חֲטָאִים, *sins.* Thus, the Talmud (*Berachos* 10a) teaches that when sin will cease to be perpetrated, the wicked will be no more, for then everyone will be righteous.

קַוֵּה אֶל יהוה,* חֲזַק וְיַאֲמֵץ לִבֶּךָ, וְקַוֵּה אֶל

⟨ and place your ⟨⟨ in your ⟨ and He will ⟨ strengthen ⟨⟨ HASHEM;* ⟨ Place your hope in
hope in heart, instill courage yourself

יהוה.¹ אֵין קָדוֹשׁ כַּיהוה, כִּי אֵין בִּלְתֶּךָ, וְאֵין

⟨ and there ⟨⟨ besides ⟨ there is ⟨ for ⟨⟨ as HASHEM, ⟨ as holy ⟨ There is ⟨⟨ HASHEM.
is no You, none none

צוּר כֵּאלֹהֵינוּ.² כִּי מִי אֱלוֹהַּ מִבַּלְעֲדֵי יהוה, וּמִי

⟨ and ⟨⟨ HASHEM, ⟨ besides ⟨ God ⟨ who is ⟨ For ⟨⟨ like our God. ⟨ Rock
who is

צוּר זוּלָתִי אֱלֹהֵינוּ.³

⟨⟨ our God? ⟨ except for ⟨ a Rock

אֵין* כֵּאלֹהֵינוּ,* אֵין כַּאדוֹנֵינוּ, אֵין כְּמַלְכֵּנוּ,

⟨⟨ like our ⟨ there is ⟨⟨ like our ⟨ there is ⟨⟨ like our God;* ⟨ There is
King; none Master; none none*

אֵין כְּמוֹשִׁיעֵנוּ. מִי* כֵאלֹהֵינוּ, מִי כַאדוֹנֵינוּ, מִי

⟨ Who ⟨⟨ is like our ⟨ Who ⟨⟨ is like* our God? ⟨ Who ⟨⟨ like our Savior. ⟨ there is
Master? none

---

(1) Psalms 27:14. (2) I Samuel 2:2. (3) Psalms 18:32.

קַוֵּה אֶל ה׳ — *Place your hope in* HASHEM. The three introductory verses express the idea that our hopes go out to God because there is none like Him, the same concept that is set forth in אֵין כֵּאלֹהֵינוּ. There is further significance in the first verse, because the repetition of the word קַוֵּה, *hope*, teaches that if someone prays and is not granted his request, he should pray again (*Berachos* 32b). Since, as noted below, אֵין כֵּאלֹהֵינוּ is tantamount to a repetition of the requests of *Shemoneh Esrei*, it is as if we are expressing our hope in God by praying again.

אֵין כֵּאלֹהֵינוּ — *There is none like our God.* This declaration of faith was a response to a particular need of Sabbaths and Festivals. The Sages teach that men should strive to recite one hundred blessings every day. On weekdays, the bulk of this total is accounted for by the three-times-a-day recitation of *Shemoneh Esrei*, which contains nineteen blessings. On the Sabbath and Festivals, however, each *Shemoneh Esrei* contains only seven blessings. One means of filling this gap is the recitation of אֵין כֵּאלֹהֵינוּ, because each declaration of faith — *there is none like our God. . .who is like our God*, etc. — is regarded as a blessing of sorts. Furthermore, the initial letters of the words אֵין, מִי, and נוֹדֶה spell אָמֵן, a further allusion to the concept of blessing. Thus the recitation of this paragraph is equivalent to twenty blessings (*Kol Bo*).

Nevertheless, in *Nusach Sefard*, this hymn is recited every day, in accordance with the view of many authorities, among them *Rambam*, *Tur*, and *Arizal*. The twelve praises, *There is none . . ., Who is . . .,* and so on, are symbolic of the original twelve middle blessings of the *Shemoneh Esrei*, in which we acknowledge God as the sole Power Who can grant our requests.

Nusach Ashkenaz, which omits the *Ketores/* Incense passages on weekdays, also omits אֵין כֵּאלֹהֵינוּ. *Nusach Sefard*, which includes the *Ketores* passage, prefaces it with אֵין כֵּאלֹהֵינוּ even on weekdays.

אֵין . . . מִי — *There is none . . . Who is like?* First

נוֹדֶה לֵאלֹהֵינוּ. נוֹדֶה כְמוֹשִׁיעֵנוּ, מִי כְמַלְכֵּנוּ,
‹ let us   ‹‹ our God;   ‹ Let us   ‹‹ is like our Savior? ‹ Who ‹‹ is like our
thank   thank   King?

בָּרוּךְ לְמוֹשִׁיעֵנוּ. נוֹדֶה לְמַלְכֵּנוּ, נוֹדֶה לַאדוֹנֵינוּ,
‹ Blessed ‹‹ our Savior. ‹ let us thank ‹‹ our King; ‹ let us thank ‹‹ our Master;

בָּרוּךְ מַלְכֵּנוּ, בָּרוּךְ אֲדוֹנֵינוּ, בָּרוּךְ אֱלֹהֵינוּ,
‹ blessed ‹‹ is our King; ‹ blessed ‹‹ is our Master; ‹ blessed ‹‹ is our God;

אַתָּה הוּא אֱלֹהֵינוּ. אַתָּה הוּא מוֹשִׁיעֵנוּ.
‹ Who are ‹ it is You ‹‹ our God; ‹ Who are ‹ It is You ‹‹ is our Savior.

אַתָּה הוּא מַלְכֵּנוּ, אַתָּה הוּא מוֹשִׁיעֵנוּ. אֲדוֹנֵינוּ,
‹‹ our Savior. ‹ Who are ‹ it is You ‹‹ our King; ‹ Who are ‹‹ it is You ‹‹ our Master;

אַתָּה תָקוּם תְּרַחֵם צִיּוֹן, כִּי אַתָּה תוֹשִׁיעֵנוּ.
‹ for ‹‹ to Zion, ‹ and show mercy ‹ will arise ‹ You ‹‹ will save us. ‹ You

עֵת לְחֶנְנָהּ כִּי בָא מוֹעֵד.¹
‹‹ the appointed time ‹ for ‹‹ to favor ‹ [there
will have come.   her,   will come]
                                                          the time

——— Talmud, *Kereisos* 6a / ‏כריתות ו. ———

פִּטּוּם הַקְּטֹרֶת:* (א) הַצֳּרִי, (ב) וְהַצִּפֹּרֶן, (ג) הַחֶלְבְּנָה,*
‹ galbanum,* ‹ onycha, ‹ stacte, ‹‹ of the incense mix- ‹ The
                                          ture* [consisted of]: formulation

(ד) וְהַלְּבוֹנָה, מִשְׁקַל שִׁבְעִים שִׁבְעִים מָנֶה; (ה) מוֹר,
‹ myrrh, ‹‹ *maneh;* ‹ each seventy ‹ weighing ‹‹ and frankincense,

(1) *Psalms* 102:14.

we declare unequivocally our recognition that nothing compares to our God. Then we ask the rhetorical question: Can anyone or anything compare to Him?

פִּטּוּם הַקְּטֹרֶת **§** — *The formulation of the incense mixture.* The *Zohar*, followed by others, writes that the *Ketores* passages should be recited at the conclusion of *Shacharis*. *Tur* (*Orach Chaim* 132) rules that this course should be adopted. Since the morning prayer is in place of the תָּמִיד שֶׁל שַׁחַר, *morning continual offering,*

it is logical that the service be concluded with the incense offering as it was in the Temple. It should be noted that we cannot be certain of the exact translation of the spices included in the incense. For commentary and discussion, see pp. 53-59.

הַחֶלְבְּנָה — *Galbanum.* The Talmud (*Kerisus* 6b) notes that galbanum has a foul odor, yet is included in the incense mixture to teach that all Jews, even the sinners of Israel, should be welcomed to participate in the service of God.

(ו) וּקְצִיעָה, (ז) שִׁבֹּלֶת נֵרְדְּ, (ח) וְכַרְכֹּם, מִשְׁקַל
‹‹ weighing ‹‹ saffron, ‹ spikenard, ‹ cassia,

שִׁשָּׁה עָשָׂר שִׁשָּׁה עָשָׂר מָנֶה; (ט) הַקֹּשְׁטְ
‹ costus, ‹‹ maneh; ‹ each sixteen

שְׁנֵים עָשָׂר, (י) וְקִלּוּפָה שְׁלֹשָׁה, (יא) וְקִנָּמוֹן
‹ and cinnamon ‹‹ three; ‹ aromatic bark, ‹‹ twelve [maneh];

תִּשְׁעָה. בֹּרִית כַּרְשִׁינָה תִּשְׁעָה קַבִּין, יֵין
‹ wine ‹‹ kav; ‹ nine ‹ of Carshina ‹ [Additionally,] lye ‹‹ nine.

קַפְרִיסִין סְאִין תְּלָתָא וְקַבִּין תְּלָתָא, וְאִם
‹ — if ‹‹ and three kav ‹ three se'ah ‹ of Cyprus

אֵין לוֹ יֵין קַפְרִיסִין, מֵבִיא חֲמַר חִוַּרְיָן עַתִּיק,
‹‹ that is old – ‹ that is white ‹ wine ‹ he brings ‹‹ of Cyprus, ‹ wine ‹ he has no

מֶלַח סְדוֹמִית רֹבַע הַקַּב; מַעֲלֶה עָשָׁן
‹ and maaleh ashan ‹‹ of a kav; ‹ a quarter ‹ of Sodom, ‹ salt

כָּל שֶׁהוּא. רַבִּי נָתָן הַבַּבְלִי אוֹמֵר: אַף כִּפַּת
‹ amber ‹ Also ‹‹ says: ‹ the Babylonian ‹ Nassan ‹ Rabbi ‹‹ a minute amount.

הַיַּרְדֵּן כָּל שֶׁהוּא. וְאִם נָתַן בָּהּ דְּבַשׁ, פְּסָלָהּ.
‹‹ he invali- ‹‹ fruit- ‹ in it ‹ he ‹ If ‹‹ a minute amount. ‹ of the Jordan
dated it. honey, placed

וְאִם חִסַּר אַחַת מִכָּל סַמָּנֶיהָ, חַיָּב מִיתָה.
‹‹ to the death ‹ he is ‹ its spices, ‹ of all ‹ any one ‹ he left out ‹ And if
penalty. liable

רַבָּן שִׁמְעוֹן בֶּן גַּמְלִיאֵל אוֹמֵר: הַצֳּרִי אֵינוֹ
‹ is nothing ‹ Stacte ‹‹ says: ‹ Gamliel ‹ ben ‹ Shimon ‹ Rabban

אֶלָּא שְׂרָף הַנּוֹטֵף מֵעֲצֵי הַקְּטָף. בֹּרִית כַּרְשִׁינָה
‹ of Carshina ‹ Lye ‹‹ of balsam. ‹ from trees ‹ that drips ‹ the sap ‹ but
[is used]

שֶׁשָּׁפִין בָּהּ אֶת הַצִּפֹּרֶן כְּדֵי שֶׁתְּהֵא נָאָה; יֵין
‹ Wine ‹‹ pleasing. ‹ that it ‹ in order ‹‹ the onycha, ‹ with it ‹ because
should be they bleach

קַפְרִיסִין שֶׁשּׁוֹרִין בּוֹ אֶת הַצִּפֹּרֶן כְּדֵי שֶׁתְּהֵא

‹ that it ‹ in order ‹‹ the onycha ‹ in it ‹ because they ‹ of Cyprus
should be   soak   [is used]

עַזָּה; וַהֲלֹא מֵי רַגְלַיִם יָפִין לָהּ, אֶלָּא שֶׁאֵין

‹ they do ‹ never- ‹‹ for that, ‹ is more ‹ urine ‹ Even ‹‹ pungent.
not   theless   suitable   though

מַכְנִיסִין מֵי רַגְלַיִם בָּעֲזָרָה מִפְּנֵי הַכָּבוֹד.

‹‹ respect. ‹ out of ‹ into the Temple ‹ urine ‹ bring

תַּנְיָא, רַבִּי נָתָן אוֹמֵר: כְּשֶׁהוּא שׁוֹחֵק, אוֹמֵר

‹‹ [the one ‹ would grind ‹ As he ‹‹ says: ‹ Nassan ‹ Rabbi ‹‹ It is taught:
in charge] [the incense],   would say,

הָדֵק הֵיטֵב, הֵיטֵב הָדֵק, מִפְּנֵי שֶׁהַקּוֹל יָפֶה

‹ is beneficial ‹ the sound ‹ because ‹‹ grind, ‹ thoroughly ‹ thoroughly, ‹ Grind

לַבְּשָׂמִים. פִּטְּמָהּ לַחֲצָאִין, כְּשֵׁרָה; לִשְׁלִישׁ

‹ but as to a third ‹‹ it was fit for use, ‹ in half-quantities, ‹ If one mixed it ‹‹ for the spices.

וְלִרְבִיעַ, לֹא שָׁמַעְנוּ. אָמַר רַבִּי יְהוּדָה: זֶה

‹ This is ‹‹ Yehudah: ‹ Rabbi ‹ Said ‹‹ — we have not heard [the law]. ‹‹ or a quarter

הַכְּלָל — אִם כְּמִדָּתָהּ, כְּשֵׁרָה לַחֲצָאִין; וְאִם

‹ But if ‹‹ [even] in half ‹ it is fit ‹‹ in its proper ‹ If ‹‹ the general rule:
the full amount. for use   proportion,

חִסַּר אַחַת מִכָּל סַמָּנֶיהָ, חַיָּב מִיתָה.

‹‹ to the death penalty. ‹ he is liable ‹ its spices, ‹ of all ‹ any one ‹ he left out

תַּנְיָא, בַּר קַפָּרָא אוֹמֵר: אַחַת לְשִׁשִּׁים אוֹ

‹ or ‹ every sixty ‹ Once ‹‹ says: ‹ Kappara ‹ Bar ‹‹ It is taught:

לְשִׁבְעִים שָׁנָה הָיְתָה בָאָה שֶׁל שִׁירַיִם

‹‹ — the accumulated ‹‹ reach ‹ it would ‹ years, ‹ seventy
leftovers —

לַחֲצָאִין. וְעוֹד תָּנֵי בַּר קַפָּרָא: אִלּוּ הָיָה נוֹתֵן

‹ put ‹ one had ‹ If ‹‹ Kappara: ‹ Bar ‹ taught ‹ Further- ‹‹ half the
more yearly quantity.

בָּהּ קוֹרְטוֹב שֶׁל דְּבַשׁ, אֵין אָדָם יָכוֹל לַעֲמֹד
‹ withstood ‹ could have ‹ person ‹ no ‹‹ fruit-honey, ‹ of ‹ a kortov ‹ into it

מִפְּנֵי רֵיחָהּ. וְלָמָּה אֵין מְעָרְבִין בָּהּ דְּבַשׁ,
‹‹ fruit-honey? ‹ into it ‹ mix ‹ did they not ‹ Why ‹‹ its scent.

מִפְּנֵי שֶׁהַתּוֹרָה אָמְרָה: כִּי כָל שְׂאֹר וְכָל דְּבַשׁ
‹ fruit-honey, ‹ or any ‹ leaven ‹ any ‹ For ‹‹ said: ‹ the Torah ‹ Because

לֹא תַקְטִירוּ מִמֶּנּוּ אִשֶּׁה לַיהוה.¹
‹‹ to Hashem. ‹ a fire-offering ‹ from them ‹ you are not to burn

RECITE THREE TIMES:

יהוה צְבָאוֹת עִמָּנוּ, מִשְׂגָּב לָנוּ אֱלֹהֵי יַעֲקֹב,
‹‹ of Jacob, ‹ is the God ‹ for us ‹ a stronghold ‹‹ is with us, ‹ Master of Legions, ‹ Hashem,

סֶלָה.²
‹‹ Selah!

RECITE THREE TIMES:

יהוה צְבָאוֹת, אַשְׁרֵי אָדָם בֹּטֵחַ בָּךְ.³
‹‹ in You. ‹ who trusts ‹ is the man ‹ praiseworthy ‹ Master of Legions, ‹ Hashem,

RECITE THREE TIMES:

יהוה הוֹשִׁיעָה, הַמֶּלֶךְ יַעֲנֵנוּ בְיוֹם קָרְאֵנוּ.⁴
‹‹ we call! ‹ on the day ‹ answer us ‹ May the King ‹‹ save! ‹ Hashem,

אַתָּה סֵתֶר לִי, מִצַּר תִּצְּרֵנִי, רָנֵּי פַלֵּט,
‹ of rescue, ‹ with glad song ‹‹ You preserve me; ‹ from distress ‹‹ for me; ‹ a shelter ‹ You are

תְּסוֹבְבֵנִי, סֶלָה.⁵ וְעָרְבָה לַיהוה מִנְחַת יְהוּדָה
‹ of Judah ‹ let be the offering ‹ to Hashem ‹ And pleasing ‹‹ Selah! ‹‹ You envelop me,

וִירוּשָׁלָיִם, כִּימֵי עוֹלָם וּכְשָׁנִים קַדְמֹנִיּוֹת.⁶
‹‹ gone by. ‹ and in years ‹ of old ‹ as in days ‹‹ and Jerusalem,

(1) Leviticus 2:11. (2) Psalms 46:8. (3) 84:13. (4) 20:10. (5) 32:7. (6) Malachi 3:4.

─────── Talmud, *Niddah* 73a / נדה עג. ───────

תָּנָא דְּבֵי אֵלִיָּהוּ:* כָּל הַשּׁוֹנֶה הֲלָכוֹת בְּכָל

‹ every ‹ Torah laws ‹ who studies ‹ Anyone ‹‹ of Elijah:* ‹ the Taught
Academy

יוֹם, מֻבְטָח לוֹ שֶׁהוּא בֶּן עוֹלָם הַבָּא, שֶׁנֶּאֱמַר:

‹‹ as it is said, ‹‹ to Come, ‹ in the ‹ will be a ‹ that he ‹ to ‹ — it is assured ‹‹ day
World participant him

הֲלִיכוֹת עוֹלָם לוֹ,¹ אַל תִּקְרֵי* הֲלִיכוֹת, אֶלָּא

‹ but: ‹ ways, ‹ read:* ‹ — do not ‹‹ are His ‹ of the world ‹ The ways

הֲלָכוֹת.*

‹‹ laws. *

─────── Talmud, *Berachos* 64a / ברכות סד. ───────

אָמַר רַבִּי אֶלְעָזָר* אָמַר רַבִּי חֲנִינָא:

‹‹ Chanina: ‹ Rabbi ‹ in the ‹ Elazar* ‹ Rabbi ‹ Said
name of

תַּלְמִידֵי חֲכָמִים מַרְבִּים שָׁלוֹם בָּעוֹלָם, שֶׁנֶּאֱמַר:

‹‹ as it is said: ‹‹ in the world, ‹ peace ‹ increase ‹ Torah scholars

וְכָל בָּנַיִךְ לִמּוּדֵי יהוה, וְרַב שְׁלוֹם בָּנָיִךְ,² אַל

‹ Do ‹‹ will your ‹ peace ‹ and ‹ of ‹ will be ‹ your ‹ And all
not children have. abundant HASHEM, students children

תִּקְרֵי בָּנָיִךְ אֶלָּא בּוֹנָיִךְ. ❖ שָׁלוֹם רָב לְאֹהֲבֵי

‹ to those ‹ There is abundant ‹‹ your ‹ but ‹ your ‹ read
who love peace builders. children,

───

(1) *Habakkuk* 3:6. (2) *Isaiah* 54:13.

───

◈ תָּנָא דְּבֵי אֵלִיָּהוּ — *Taught the Academy of Elijah.* This homiletical teaching likens the ways of the world to the laws that govern a Jew's life on earth. Only by studying, knowing and practicing the laws of the Torah can a Jew assure himself of ultimate success.

אַל תִּקְרֵי — *Do not read.* The intention is not to change the accepted reading of Scripture. Whenever such a statement appears in Rabbinic literature it means that the verse contains an allusion in addition to its literal meaning, *as if it were pronounced differently.*

הֲלָכוֹת — *Laws.* According to this homiletical teaching, the verse reads, *[One who studies] laws — the world is his.*

◈ אָמַר רַבִּי אֶלְעָזָר — *Said Rabbi Elazar.* This famous teaching is the concluding statement of tractate *Berachos.* Maharsha there, in a comment that applies here as well, explains that the tractate deals with prayers and blessings that

תוֹרָתֶךָ, וְאֵין לָמוֹ מִכְשׁוֹל.¹ יְהִי שָׁלוֹם בְּחֵילֵךְ,

‹‹ within your ‹ peace ‹ May ‹‹ a stumbling ‹ for ‹ and there ‹ Your Torah,
wall, there be block. them is not

שַׁלְוָה בְּאַרְמְנוֹתָיִךְ. לְמַעַן אַחַי וְרֵעָי, אֲדַבְּרָה נָּא

‹ I shall speak ‹‹ and my ‹ of my ‹ For the ‹‹ within your ‹ serenity
comrades brethren sake palaces.

שָׁלוֹם בָּךְ. לְמַעַן בֵּית יהוה אֱלֹהֵינוּ, אֲבַקְשָׁה

‹ I will request ‹‹ our God, ‹ of ‹ of the ‹ For the ‹‹ in your ‹ [of]
HASHEM, House sake midst. peace

טוֹב לָךְ.² יהוה עֹז לְעַמּוֹ יִתֵּן, יהוה יְבָרֵךְ

‹ will bless ‹ HASHEM ‹ will give, ‹ to His nation ‹ strength ‹ HASHEM, ‹‹ for you. ‹ good

אֶת עַמּוֹ בַשָּׁלוֹם.³

‹‹ with peace. ‹ His nation

THE RABBIS' KADDISH / קדיש דרבנן

IN THE PRESENCE OF A *MINYAN*, MOURNERS RECITE קַדִּיש דְּרַבָּנָן, THE RABBIS' *KADDISH*.
[A TRANSLITERATION OF THIS *KADDISH* APPEARS ON PAGE 880.]

יִתְגַּדַּל וְיִתְקַדַּשׁ שְׁמֵהּ רַבָּא. (–Cong. אָמֵן.) בְּעָלְמָא דִּי בְרָא

‹ He ‹ that ‹ in the ‹‹ (Amen.) ‹‹ that is ‹ may His ‹ and be ‹ Grow exalted
created world great! — Name sanctified

כִרְעוּתֵהּ, וְיַמְלִיךְ מַלְכוּתֵהּ, וְיַצְמַח פֻּרְקָנֵהּ וִיקָרֵב מְשִׁיחֵהּ.

‹‹ His ‹ and bring ‹ His ‹ and cause ‹ to His ‹ and may He ‹‹ according
Messiah, near salvation, to sprout kingship, give reign to His will,

(–Cong. אָמֵן.) בְּחַיֵּיכוֹן וּבְיוֹמֵיכוֹן וּבְחַיֵּי דְכָל בֵּית יִשְׂרָאֵל,

‹‹ of Israel, ‹ Family ‹ of the ‹ and in the ‹ and in ‹ in your ‹‹ (Amen.)
entire lifetimes lifetimes your days, lifetimes

בַּעֲגָלָא וּבִזְמַן קָרִיב. וְאִמְרוּ: אָמֵן.

‹‹ Amen. ‹ Now ‹‹ that comes ‹ and at ‹ swiftly
respond: soon. a time

CONGREGATION RESPONDS:

אָמֵן. יְהֵא שְׁמֵהּ רַבָּא מְבָרַךְ לְעָלַם וּלְעָלְמֵי עָלְמַיָּא.

‹‹ and for all eternity. ‹ forever ‹ be ‹ that is ‹ His ‹ May ‹‹ Amen.
blessed great Name

---

(1) *Psalms* 119:165. (2) 122:7-9. (3) 29:11.

had been instituted by the Sages. The reason
they promulgated these expressions of devotion

was to increase the harmony in the universe
between man and his Maker.

MOURNER CONTINUES:

יְהֵא שְׁמֵהּ רַבָּא מְבָרַךְ לְעָלַם וּלְעָלְמֵי עָלְמַיָּא. יִתְבָּרַךְ
‹ Blessed, ‹‹ and for all eternity. ‹ forever ‹ be ‹ that ‹ His ‹ May
blessed is great Name

וְיִשְׁתַּבַּח וְיִתְפָּאַר וְיִתְרוֹמַם וְיִתְנַשֵּׂא וְיִתְהַדָּר וְיִתְעַלֶּה
‹ elevated, ‹ honored, ‹ upraised, ‹ exalted, ‹ glorified, ‹ praised,

וְיִתְהַלָּל שְׁמֵהּ דְּקֻדְשָׁא בְּרִיךְ הוּא (.Cong–בְּרִיךְ הוּא) —
‹‹ is He) ‹ (Blessed ‹‹ is He ‹ Blessed ‹ of the Holy One, ‹ be the Name ‹ and lauded

ROSH HASHANAH TO YOM KIPPUR SUBSTITUTE:

°לְעֵלָּא מִן כָּל [°לְעֵלָּא (וּ)לְעֵלָּא מִכָּל] בִּרְכָתָא
‹ blessing ‹ any ‹ exceedingly beyond ‹ any ‹ beyond

וְשִׁירָתָא תֻּשְׁבְּחָתָא וְנֶחֱמָתָא דַּאֲמִירָן בְּעָלְמָא.
‹‹ in the world. ‹ that are uttered ‹ and consolation ‹ praise ‹‹ and song,

וְאִמְרוּ: אָמֵן. (אָמֵן–Cong.)
‹‹ (Amen.) ‹‹ Amen. ‹ Now respond:

עַל יִשְׂרָאֵל וְעַל רַבָּנָן, וְעַל תַּלְמִידֵיהוֹן וְעַל כָּל
‹ all ‹ and upon ‹ their disciples ‹ upon ‹ the teachers, ‹ upon ‹ Israel, ‹ Upon

תַּלְמִידֵי תַלְמִידֵיהוֹן, וְעַל כָּל מָאן דְּעָסְקִין בְּאוֹרַיְתָא,
‹ in the study ‹ who engage ‹ those ‹ all ‹ and ‹‹ of their ‹ the
of Torah, upon disciples, disciples

דִּי בְאַתְרָא¹ הָדֵין וְדִי בְּכָל אֲתַר וַאֲתַר. יְהֵא לְהוֹן
‹ for ‹ may ‹‹ other place; ‹ in any ‹ or who ‹ in this place ‹ who
them there be are are

וּלְכוֹן שְׁלָמָא רַבָּא, חִנָּא וְחִסְדָּא וְרַחֲמִין, וְחַיִּין
‹ life ‹‹ and mercy, ‹ kindness, ‹ grace, ‹ that is abundant, ‹ peace ‹ and for you

אֲרִיכִין, וּמְזוֹנֵי רְוִיחֵי, וּפֻרְקָנָא מִן קֳדָם אֲבוּהוֹן דִּי
‹ Who ‹ their ‹ before ‹ from ‹‹ and ‹ that is ‹ nourish- ‹ that is
is Father salvation ample, ment long,

בִּשְׁמַיָּא (וְאַרְעָא). וְאִמְרוּ: אָמֵן. (אָמֵן – Cong.)
‹‹ (Amen.) ‹‹ Amen. ‹ Now respond: ‹‹ (and on earth). ‹ in Heaven

יְהֵא שְׁלָמָא רַבָּא מִן שְׁמַיָּא, וְחַיִּים טוֹבִים עָלֵינוּ וְעַל כָּל
‹ all ‹ and ‹ upon us ‹‹ that is ‹ and life ‹‹ Heaven, ‹ from ‹ that is ‹ peace ‹ May
upon good, abundant there be

יִשְׂרָאֵל. וְאִמְרוּ: אָמֵן. (אָמֵן – Cong.)
‹‹ (Amen.) ‹‹ Amen. ‹ Now respond: ‹‹ Israel.

(1) In *Eretz Yisrael* add קַדִּישָׁא, *holy.*

BOW; TAKE THREE STEPS BACK: BOW LEFT AND SAY . . . עֹשֶׂה שָׁלוֹם, *"HE WHO MAKES PEACE . . .";* **BOW RIGHT AND SAY . . . הוּא,** *"MAY HE . . .";* **BOW FORWARD AND SAY . . . וְעַל כָּל יִשְׂרָאֵל,** *"AND UPON ALL ISRAEL . . ."* **REMAIN IN PLACE FOR A FEW MOMENTS, THEN TAKE THREE STEPS FORWARD.**

עֹשֶׂה °שָׁלוֹם בִּמְרוֹמָיו, הוּא בְּרַחֲמָיו יַעֲשֶׂה שָׁלוֹם עָלֵינוּ,
⟨ upon us, ⟨ peace ⟨ make ⟨ in His ⟨ may ⟪ in His heights, ⟨ peace ⟨ He Who
                         compassion   He   makes

וְעַל כָּל יִשְׂרָאֵל. וְאִמְרוּ: אָמֵן. (.Cong – אָמֵן.)
⟪ (Amen.)   ⟪ Amen. ⟨ Now ⟪ Israel. ⟨ all ⟨ and
                          respond: upon

FROM ROSH HASHANAH TO YOM KIPPUR SOME SAY:

°הַשָׁלוֹם
⟨ the peace

ALEINU / עלינו

STAND WHILE RECITING עָלֵינוּ, *"IT IS OUR DUTY . . ."*

עָלֵינוּ* לְשַׁבֵּחַ לַאֲדוֹן הַכֹּל, לָתֵת גְּדֻלָּה
⟨ greatness ⟨ to ascribe ⟪ of all, ⟨ the Master ⟨ to praise ⟨ It is our duty*

לְיוֹצֵר בְּרֵאשִׁית, שֶׁלֹא עָשָׂנוּ כְּגוֹיֵי הָאֲרָצוֹת, וְלֹא
⟨ and ⟪ of the lands, ⟨ like the ⟨ for He has not ⟪ of primeval ⟨ to the
has not   nations   made us   creation,   Molder

שָׂמָנוּ כְּמִשְׁפְּחוֹת הָאֲדָמָה. שֶׁלֹא שָׂם חֶלְקֵנוּ*
⟨ our portion* ⟨assigned ⟨ for He ⟪ of the earth; ⟨ like the families ⟨established
                        has not   us

עָלֵינוּ / Aleinu ⁓

According to many early sources, among them a Geonic responsum attributed to *Rav Hai Gaon, Rokeach,* and *Kol Bo,* this declaration of faith and dedication was composed by Joshua after he led Israel across the Jordan. During the Talmudic era it was part of the Rosh Hashanah *Mussaf* service, and at some point during medieval times it became part of the daily service.

Bach (Orach Chaim 133) explains that *Aleinu* was added to the daily prayers to instill faith in the Oneness of God's kingship, and the conviction that He will one day *remove detestable idolatry from the earth . . . ,* thus preventing Jews from being tempted to follow the beliefs and lifestyles of the nations among whom they dwell (see *Iyun Tefillah* and *Emek Berachah*).

As we can surmise from its authorship and its placement at the conclusion of every service, its significance is profound. Its first paragraph [עָלֵינוּ] proclaims the difference between Israel's concept of God and that of the other nations. The second paragraph [וְעַל כֵּן] expresses our confidence that all humanity will eventually recognize His sovereignty and declare its obedience to His commandments. It should be clear, however, that this does not imply a belief or even a hope that they will convert to Judaism. Rather, they will accept Him as *the only God* and obey the universal Noahide laws that are incumbent upon all nations (R' Hirsch).

עָלֵינוּ — *It is our duty.* Lit. It is upon us.

חֶלְקֵנוּ . . . וְגוֹרָלֵנוּ — *Our portion . . . our lot.* God does not punish gentile nations until they have

כָּהֶם, וְגוֹרָלֵנוּ* כְּכָל הֲמוֹנָם. (שֶׁהֵם מִשְׁתַּחֲוִים*

< bow* < (For they « their < like all < nor our lot* < like
multitudes. theirs

לְהֶבֶל וָרִיק, וּמִתְפַּלְלִים אֶל אֵל לֹא יוֹשִׁיעַ.)[1]

« save.) < who < a god < to < and pray < and < to vanity
does not emptiness

BOW WHILE RECITING וַאֲנַחְנוּ כּוֹרְעִים וּמִשְׁתַּחֲוִים, *"BUT WE BEND OUR KNEES, BOW."*

וַאֲנַחְנוּ כּוֹרְעִים וּמִשְׁתַּחֲוִים וּמוֹדִים, לִפְנֵי

< before « and acknowledge < bow, < bend our knees, < But we
our thanks,

מֶלֶךְ מַלְכֵי הַמְּלָכִים הַקָּדוֹשׁ בָּרוּךְ הוּא.

« He. < Blessed is < the Holy One, « of kings, < over kings < the King

שֶׁהוּא נוֹטֶה שָׁמַיִם וְיֹסֵד אָרֶץ,[2] וּמוֹשַׁב

< the seat « earth's < and < heaven < stretches out < He
foundation; establishes

יְקָרוֹ בַּשָּׁמַיִם מִמַּעַל, וּשְׁכִינַת עֻזּוֹ בְּגָבְהֵי

< is in the < of His < and the « above, < is in the heavens < of His
loftiest power Presence homage

מְרוֹמִים. הוּא אֱלֹהֵינוּ, אֵין עוֹד. אֱמֶת מַלְכֵּנוּ,

< is our King, < True « other. < and there < our God < He is « heights.
is none

(1) *Isaiah* 45:20. (2) 51:13.

reached the full quota of sin, beyond which He no longer extends mercy. Then He brings retribution upon them, often destroying them totally. Such powerful ancient empires as Egypt, Persia, Greece, Rome, and Carthage have ceased to exist or become insignificant. God does not act this way with regard to Israel, however. The world survives whether or not there is a Roman Empire, but the world could not survive without Israel. Therefore, God punishes Israel in stages, so that it will never be destroyed (*Siach Yitzchak*).

... שֶׁהֵם מִשְׁתַּחֲוִים — *For they bow* ... The inclusion of this verse restores the original version of *Aleinu*. In the year 1400, a baptized Jew, seeking to prove his loyalty to the Church, spread the slander that this passage was a slur on Christianity. He "proved" his contention by the coincidence that the numerical value of וָרִיק, *emptiness*, is 316, the same as יֵשׁוּ, the Hebrew name of their messiah. The charge was refuted time and again, particularly by the 17th-century scholar, Menasseh ben Israel. Church insistence and repeated persecutions, backed up by governmental enforcement, caused the line to be deleted from most Ashkenazic *siddurim*. Many congregations have not yet reinstated it to the *Aleinu* prayer. However, prominent authorities, among them Rabbi Yehoshua Leib Diskin, insist that *Aleinu* be recited in its original form (*World of Prayer; Siach Yitzchak*).

אֶפֶס זוּלָתוֹ, כַּכָּתוּב בְּתוֹרָתוֹ: וְיָדַעְתָּ הַיּוֹם
‹ this day ‹ You are to know ‹‹ in His Torah: ‹ as it is written ‹‹ beside Him, ‹ there is nothing

וַהֲשֵׁבֹתָ אֶל לְבָבֶךָ,* כִּי יהוה הוּא הָאֱלֹהִים
‹‹ the God ‹ He is ‹ HASHEM ‹ that ‹‹ your heart,* ‹ to ‹ and take

בַּשָּׁמַיִם מִמַּעַל וְעַל הָאָרֶץ מִתָּחַת, אֵין עוֹד.¹
‹‹ other. ‹ there is none ‹‹ below — ‹ the earth ‹ and on ‹ above ‹ — in heaven

וְעַל כֵּן נְקַוֶּה לְךָ* יהוה אֱלֹהֵינוּ לִרְאוֹת
‹ that we may see ‹‹ our God, ‹ HASHEM, ‹ in You,* ‹ we put our hope ‹ And therefore

מְהֵרָה בְּתִפְאֶרֶת עֻזֶּךָ, לְהַעֲבִיר גִּלּוּלִים מִן
‹ from ‹ detestable idolatry ‹ to remove ‹‹ of Your might, ‹ the splendor ‹ very soon

הָאָרֶץ, וְהָאֱלִילִים כָּרוֹת יִכָּרֵתוּן, לְתַקֵּן
‹ to perfect ‹‹ will be utterly cut off, ‹ and false gods ‹‹ the earth,

עוֹלָם בְּמַלְכוּת שַׁדַּי. וְכָל בְּנֵי בָשָׂר יִקְרְאוּ
‹ will call ‹ humanity ‹ Then all ‹‹ of the Almighty. ‹ through the sovereignty ‹ the universe

בִשְׁמֶךָ, לְהַפְנוֹת אֵלֶיךָ כָּל רִשְׁעֵי אָרֶץ.
‹‹ of the earth. ‹ the wicked ‹ all ‹ toward You ‹ to turn ‹‹ upon Your Name,

יַכִּירוּ וְיֵדְעוּ כָּל יוֹשְׁבֵי תֵבֵל, כִּי לְךָ תִּכְרַע
‹ should bend ‹ to You ‹ that ‹‹ of the world — ‹ the inhabitants ‹ — all ‹‹ and know ‹ May they recognize

(1) Deuteronomy 4:39.

וְיָדַעְתָּ הַיּוֹם וַהֲשֵׁבֹתָ אֶל לְבָבֶךָ — *You are to know this day and take to your heart.* The masters of Mussar explain that an abstract belief in God does not suffice to make people observe the mitzvos as they should. After obtaining knowledge we must take it to heart; that is, develop a sincere commitment to act upon the knowledge.

וְעַל כֵּן נְקַוֶּה לְךָ — *And therefore we put our hope in You.* Having expressed our determination to affirm God's Kingship and to serve Him, we now pray for the conditions that will best enable us to do so. Specifically, we ask that He

remove all vestiges of idolatry from the world and thereby perfect the universe through the Almighty's sovereignty. In this context, "idolatry" refers not merely to the worship of statues and supernatural forces, but to all creeds that are alien to the Torah. These include faith in nature, excess zeal to amass money or power, and every explanation of events that ignores the guiding hand of God in worldly affairs. When this happens, as the last two-thirds of the prayer declares exultantly, all the world will accept God's reign and will serve Him.

כָּל בֶּרֶךְ, תִּשָּׁבַע כָּל לָשׁוֹן, לְפָנֶיךָ יהוה 1.

‹ HASHEM, ‹ Before You, « tongue. ‹ every ‹ should swear « knee, ‹ every

אֱלֹהֵינוּ יִכְרְעוּ וְיִפֹּלוּ, וְלִכְבוֹד שִׁמְךָ יְקָר

‹ homage ‹ of Your ‹ and to « and cast ‹ they will bend ‹ our God,
Name the glory themselves down, their knees

יִתֵּנוּ. וִיקַבְּלוּ כֻלָּם אֶת עוֹל מַלְכוּתֶךָ, וְתִמְלֹךְ

‹ that You «‹ of Your kingship, ‹ the yoke ‹ will all ‹ and accept «‹ they will
may reign offer,

עֲלֵיהֶם מְהֵרָה לְעוֹלָם וָעֶד. כִּי הַמַּלְכוּת

‹ the kingdom ‹ For « and ever. ‹ for ever ‹ very soon ‹ over them

שֶׁלְּךָ הִיא וּלְעוֹלְמֵי עַד תִּמְלוֹךְ בְּכָבוֹד, כַּכָּתוּב

‹ as it is written «‹ in glory, ‹ You will reign ‹ and ever ‹ and for ever «‹ is Yours,

בְּתוֹרָתֶךָ: יהוה יִמְלֹךְ לְעֹלָם וָעֶד. 2 ∴ וְנֶאֱמַר:

«‹ And it is said: « and ever. ‹ for ever ‹ shall reign ‹ HASHEM «‹ in Your Torah:

וְהָיָה יהוה לְמֶלֶךְ עַל כָּל הָאָרֶץ, בַּיּוֹם הַהוּא

‹ — on that day «‹ the world ‹ all ‹ over ‹ be King ‹ HASHEM ‹ Then will

יִהְיֶה יהוה אֶחָד וּשְׁמוֹ אֶחָד. 3.

« be One. ‹ and His Name ‹ be One ‹ HASHEM ‹ shall

SOME CONGREGATIONS RECITE THE FOLLOWING AFTER עָלֵינוּ, ALEINU:

אַל תִּירָא מִפַּחַד פִּתְאֹם, וּמִשֹּׁאַת רְשָׁעִים כִּי

‹ when ‹ of the ‹ nor the «‹ [that comes] ‹ terror ‹ Do not fear
wicked holocaust suddenly,

תָבֹא. 4 עֻצוּ עֵצָה וְתֻפָר, דַּבְּרוּ דָבָר וְלֹא יָקוּם, כִּי

‹ for «‹ stand, ‹ and it ‹ your ‹ speak «‹ and it will ‹ a ‹ Plan « it
shall not speech be annulled; conspiracy comes.

עִמָּנוּ אֵל. 5 וְעַד זִקְנָה אֲנִי הוּא, וְעַד שֵׂיבָה אֲנִי

‹ I ‹ [your] ‹ and «‹ I remain ‹ [your] ‹ Even « is ‹ with
elder years, even till unchanged; old age, till God. us

אֶסְבֹּל, אֲנִי עָשִׂיתִי וַאֲנִי אֶשָּׂא, וַאֲנִי אֶסְבֹּל וַאֲמַלֵּט. 6.

« and rescue ‹ shall ‹ I «‹ shall ‹ and I ‹ created ‹ I «‹ shall carry
[you]. carry [you] bear [you]; [you] [you].

(1) Cf. *Isaiah* 45:23. (2) *Exodus* 15:18. (3) *Zechariah* 14:9. (4) *Proverbs* 3:25. (5) *Isaiah* 8:10. (6) 46:4.

MOURNER'S KADDISH / קדיש יתום

IN THE PRESENCE OF A *MINYAN*, MOURNERS RECITE קדיש יתום, THE MOURNER'S *KADDISH*.
[A TRANSLITERATION OF THIS *KADDISH* APPEARS ON PAGE 879.]

יִתְגַּדַּל וְיִתְקַדַּשׁ שְׁמֵהּ רַבָּא. (-Cong. אָמֵן.) בְּעָלְמָא דִּי בְרָא
‹ He ‹ that ‹ in the ‹‹   (Amen.)   ‹ that is ‹ may His‹ and be ‹ Grow exalted
created   world   great! —   Name   sanctified

כִרְעוּתֵהּ, וְיַמְלִיךְ מַלְכוּתֵהּ, וְיַצְמַח פֻּרְקָנֵהּ וִיקָרֵב מְשִׁיחֵהּ.
‹‹ His ‹ and bring ‹ His ‹ and cause ‹ to His ‹ and may He ‹‹ according
Messiah,   near   salvation,   to sprout   kingship,   give reign   to His will,

(-Cong. אָמֵן.) בְּחַיֵּיכוֹן וּבְיוֹמֵיכוֹן וּבְחַיֵּי דְכָל בֵּית יִשְׂרָאֵל,
‹‹ of Israel, ‹ Family ‹ of the ‹ and in the ‹ and in ‹ in your ‹‹ (Amen.)
entire   lifetimes   your days,   lifetimes

בַּעֲגָלָא וּבִזְמַן קָרִיב. וְאִמְרוּ: אָמֵן.
‹‹ Amen. ‹ Now ‹‹ that comes ‹ and at ‹ swiftly
respond: soon.   a time

CONGREGATION RESPONDS:

אָמֵן. יְהֵא שְׁמֵהּ רַבָּא מְבָרַךְ לְעָלַם וּלְעָלְמֵי עָלְמַיָּא.
‹‹ and for all eternity. ‹ forever ‹ be blessed ‹ that is great ‹ His Name ‹ May ‹‹ Amen.

MOURNER CONTINUES:

יְהֵא שְׁמֵהּ רַבָּא מְבָרַךְ לְעָלַם וּלְעָלְמֵי עָלְמַיָּא. יִתְבָּרַךְ
‹ Blessed, ‹‹ and for all eternity. ‹ forever ‹ be blessed ‹ that is great ‹ His Name ‹ May

וְיִשְׁתַּבַּח וְיִתְפָּאַר וְיִתְרוֹמַם וְיִתְנַשֵּׂא וְיִתְהַדָּר וְיִתְעַלֶּה
‹ elevated, ‹ honored, ‹ upraised, ‹ exalted, ‹ glorified, ‹ praised,

וְיִתְהַלָּל שְׁמֵהּ דְּקֻדְשָׁא בְּרִיךְ הוּא (-Cong. בְּרִיךְ הוּא) —
‹‹ is He) ‹ (Blessed ‹‹ is He ‹ Blessed ‹ of the Holy One, ‹ be the Name ‹ and lauded

ROSH HASHANAH TO YOM KIPPUR SUBSTITUTE:

°לְעֵלָּא מִן כָּל [°לְעֵלָּא (וּ)לְעֵלָּא מִכָּל] בִּרְכָתָא
‹ blessing ‹ any ‹ exceedingly beyond ‹ any ‹ beyond

וְשִׁירָתָא, תֻּשְׁבְּחָתָא וְנֶחֱמָתָא דַּאֲמִירָן בְּעָלְמָא.
‹‹ in the world. ‹ that are uttered ‹ and consolation ‹ praise ‹‹ and song,

וְאִמְרוּ: אָמֵן. (-Cong. אָמֵן.)
‹‹ (Amen.)   ‹‹ Amen. ‹ Now respond:

יְהֵא שְׁלָמָא רַבָּא מִן שְׁמַיָּא, וְחַיִּים טוֹבִים עָלֵינוּ וְעַל כָּל
‹ all ‹ and ‹ upon us ‹‹ that is ‹ and life ‹‹ Heaven, ‹ from ‹ that is ‹ peace ‹ May
upon   good,   abundant   there be

יִשְׂרָאֵל. וְאִמְרוּ: אָמֵן. (-Cong. אָמֵן.)
‹‹ (Amen.)   ‹‹ Amen. ‹ Now respond: ‹‹ Israel.

BOW; TAKE THREE STEPS BACK: BOW LEFT AND SAY . . . **עֹשֶׂה שָׁלוֹם**, *"HE WHO MAKES PEACE . . .";* BOW
RIGHT AND SAY . . . **הוּא**, *"MAY HE . . .";* BOW FORWARD AND SAY . . . **וְעַל כָּל יִשְׂרָאֵל**, *"AND UPON
ALL ISRAEL . . ."* REMAIN IN PLACE FOR A FEW MOMENTS, THEN TAKE THREE STEPS FORWARD.

עֹשֶׂה °שָׁלוֹם בִּמְרוֹמָיו, הוּא יַעֲשֶׂה שָׁלוֹם עָלֵינוּ, וְעַל
⟨ and upon ⟨ upon us, ⟨ peace ⟨ make ⟨ may He ⟨⟨ in His heights, ⟨ peace ⟨ He Who makes

כָּל יִשְׂרָאֵל. וְאִמְרוּ: אָמֵן. (Cong. – אָמֵן.)
⟨⟨ (Amen.) ⟨⟨ Amen. ⟨ Now respond: ⟨⟨ Israel. ⟨ all

FROM ROSH HASHANAH TO YOM KIPPUR SOME SAY:

°הַשָּׁלוֹם
⟨ the peace

ON CHANUKAH, MANY RECITE PSALM 30, **מִזְמוֹר שִׁיר חֲנֻכַּת הַבַּיִת** (P. 90) HERE.

FROM ROSH CHODESH ELUL THRU SHEMINI ATZERES, PSALM 27 IS RECITED HERE. DURING
THE MONTH OF ELUL (EXCEPT ON EREV ROSH HASHANAH) THE *SHOFAR* IS SOUNDED HERE.

——— Psalm 27 / תהלים כז ———

לְדָוִד; יהוה אוֹרִי* וְיִשְׁעִי, מִמִּי אִירָא; יהוה מָעוֹז
⟨ the ⟨ HASHEM ⟨⟨ shall I ⟨ whom ⟨⟨ and my ⟨ is my ⟨ HASHEM ⟨⟨ By David.
strength is fear? salvation, light*

חַיַּי, מִמִּי אֶפְחָד. בִּקְרֹב עָלַי מְרֵעִים לֶאֱכֹל אֶת בְּשָׂרִי;
⟨⟨ my flesh ⟨ to devour ⟨ evildoers ⟨ against ⟨ When ⟨⟨ shall I ⟨ whom ⟨⟨ of my
me there would dread? life,
approach

צָרַי וְאֹיְבַי לִי, הֵמָּה כָשְׁלוּ וְנָפָלוּ. אִם תַּחֲנֶה עָלַי
⟨ against ⟨ there would ⟨ Even ⟨⟨ and fall. ⟨ stumble ⟨ it is they ⟨⟨ against ⟨ and my ⟨ – my
me encamp if who me – foes tormentors

מַחֲנֶה, לֹא יִירָא לִבִּי; אִם תָּקוּם עָלַי מִלְחָמָה, בְּזֹאת
⟨ in this ⟨ a war, ⟨ against ⟨ there ⟨ even ⟨⟨ my heart would ⟨ an army,
me would arise if not fear;

⁜ The Shofar

On the first day of Elul, Moses ascended
Mount Sinai to begin a sojourn of forty days
and nights during which he would receive the
second Tablets of the Law. This signified that
God had forgiven Israel for the sin of the
Golden Calf, which had caused Moses to break
the first Tablets. When Moses went up to the
mountain, the *shofar* was sounded in the camp
to serve as a warning that the people should not
lose their spirit of repentance. We maintain this
tradition by sounding the *shofar* on each day of
Elul, except Erev Rosh Hashanah, as a call to
repentance.

⁜ Psalm 27 / לְדָוִד ה' אוֹרִי ⁜

אוֹרִי ה' — *HASHEM is my light.* The custom to
recite this psalm during the period of repentance is based on the Midrash. It expounds:
HASHEM is my light, on Rosh Hashanah; *and my
salvation*, on Yom Kippur; *He will hide me in
His shelter* (below), an allusion to Succos. The
implication is that on Rosh Hashanah God
helps us see the light and this enables us to
repent; on Yom Kippur He provides us salvation by forgiving our sins. Once we are
forgiven, He shelters us from all foes and
dangers, just as He sheltered our ancestors in the
Wilderness. Because of this allusion to the

אֲנִי בוֹטֵחַ.* אַחַת שָׁאַלְתִּי מֵאֵת יהוה,* אוֹתָהּ אֲבַקֵּשׁ;

‹‹ I shall seek: ‹ that ‹ HASHEM,* ‹ of ‹ I asked ‹ One thing ‹‹ trust.* ‹ I

שִׁבְתִּי בְּבֵית יהוה כָּל יְמֵי חַיַּי, לַחֲזוֹת בְּנֹעַם יהוה,

‹ of HASHEM ‹ the delight ‹ to behold ‹‹ of my life, ‹ the days ‹ all ‹ of ‹ in the HASHEM ‹ House ‹ [Would that] I dwell

וּלְבַקֵּר בְּהֵיכָלוֹ. כִּי יִצְפְּנֵנִי בְּסֻכֹּה* בְּיוֹם רָעָה; יַסְתִּרֵנִי

‹ He will conceal me ‹‹ of evil; ‹ on the day ‹ in His Shelter* ‹ He will hide me ‹ Indeed, ‹‹ in His Sanctuary. ‹ and to contemplate

בְּסֵתֶר אָהֳלוֹ, בְּצוּר יְרוֹמְמֵנִי. וְעַתָּה יָרוּם רֹאשִׁי עַל

‹ above ‹ is my head ‹ is my ‹ elevated ‹ Now ‹‹ He will lift me ‹ upon a rock ‹‹ of His ‹ in the Tent; concealment

אֹיְבַי סְבִיבוֹתַי, וְאֶזְבְּחָה בְאָהֳלוֹ זִבְחֵי תְרוּעָה;

‹‹ accompanied by joyous song; ‹ offerings ‹ in His Tent ‹ and I will slaughter ‹ around me, ‹ my enemies

אָשִׁירָה וַאֲזַמְּרָה לַיהוה. שְׁמַע יהוה קוֹלִי אֶקְרָא,*

‹‹ when I call,* ‹ my voice ‹ HASHEM, ‹ Hear, ‹‹ to HASHEM. ‹ and chant praise ‹ I will sing

וְחָנֵּנִי וַעֲנֵנִי. לְךָ אָמַר לִבִּי: בַּקְּשׁוּ פָנָי,* אֶת פָּנֶיךָ יהוה

‹ HASHEM, ‹ Your Presence, ‹‹ My Presence.* ‹ Seek ‹ my heart has said, ‹ On Your ‹‹ and behalf, answer me. ‹ show me favor

---

preparation for repentance and its aftermath, the custom was adopted to recite this psalm during the entire repentance period from Rosh Chodesh Elul through Shemini Atzeres.

בְּזֹאת אֲנִי בוֹטֵחַ — *In this I trust.* I trust in the motto expressed in the opening verse, HASHEM *is my light and my salvation, whom shall I fear?* (Rashi; Radak).

According to *Ibn Ezra* and *Sforno,* the reason for this trust is expressed in the following verses: I trust in God because I have always requested only spiritual success, and never anything vain and worthless.

אַחַת שָׁאַלְתִּי מֵאֵת ה' — *One thing I asked of* HASHEM. Man's desires always change. Each moment breeds new whims and fresh requests, but I have had only one desire ... and what is more: אוֹתָהּ אֲבַקֵּשׁ, *that I shall* [continue to] *seek,* because this request embodies all of my desires: to serve God and understand His ways (Malbim).

בְּסֻכֹּה — *In His shelter.* The spelling of this word is בְּסֻכֹּה, *in a shelter,* but it is pronounced בְּסֻכּוֹ, *in His shelter.* David declares: "Often, when I am in danger, a *shelter* seems to appear as if by chance. I am not misled. I know that God Himself has provided this salvation and that it is *His* shelter" (R' A. Ch. Feuer).

שְׁמַע ה' קוֹלִי אֶקְרָא — *Hear,* HASHEM, *my voice when I call.* Previously David had discussed his wars against human armies. In such battles, he is confident of Divine salvation. Now he turns his attention to the most difficult struggle of all, the struggle against the Evil Inclination (Otzar Nechmad).

לְךָ אָמַר לִבִּי בַּקְּשׁוּ פָנָי — *On Your behalf, my heart has said, "Seek My Presence"* (lit. *My Face*). In expressing the desire to seek God's Presence, my own heart spoke as if it were God's emissary. It is He Who implants in the Jew's heart the noble aspiration that he wishes to dwell in the House of God all his life.

אֲבַקֵּשׁ. אַל תַּסְתֵּר פָּנֶיךָ מִמֶּנִּי, אַל תַּט בְּאַף עַבְדֶּךָ;

‹‹ Your ‹ in ‹ repel ‹ do ‹‹ from me, ‹ Your ‹ conceal ‹ Do ‹‹ do I seek.
servant. anger not Presence not

עֶזְרָתִי הָיִיתָ, אַל תִּטְּשֵׁנִי וְאַל תַּעַזְבֵנִי, אֱלֹהֵי יִשְׁעִי.

‹‹ of my ‹ O God ‹ forsake me, ‹ and ‹ abandon ‹ do ‹‹ You have ‹ My
salvation. do not me, not been, Helper

כִּי אָבִי וְאִמִּי עֲזָבוּנִי,* וַיהוה יַאַסְפֵנִי. הוֹרֵנִי יהוה

‹ HASHEM, ‹ Teach ‹‹ will gather ‹ HASHEM ‹‹ have ‹ and my ‹ my ‹ Though
me, me in. forsaken me,* mother father

דַּרְכֶּךָ; וּנְחֵנִי בְּאֹרַח מִישׁוֹר, לְמַעַן שׁוֹרְרָי.* אַל תִּתְּנֵנִי

‹ deliver ‹ Do ‹‹ my watchful ‹ because ‹ of integrity, ‹ on the ‹ and ‹‹ Your way;
me not foes.* of path lead me

בְּנֶפֶשׁ צָרָי, כִּי קָמוּ בִי עֵדֵי שֶׁקֶר, וִיפֵחַ חָמָס.

‹‹ violence. ‹ and those ‹ false ‹ against ‹ there ‹ for ‹‹ of my ‹ to the
who breathe witnesses me have arisen tormentors, wishes

❖ לוּלֵא הֶאֱמַנְתִּי* לִרְאוֹת בְּטוּב יהוה בְּאֶרֶץ חַיִּים.*

‹‹ of life!* ‹ in the land ‹ of ‹ the ‹ that I ‹ Had I not trusted*
HASHEM goodness would see

קַוֵּה אֶל יהוה; חֲזַק וְיַאֲמֵץ לִבֶּךָ,* וְקַוֵּה אֶל יהוה.

‹‹ HASHEM. ‹ and place ‹‹ in your ‹ and He will ‹ strengthen ‹‹ HASHEM;* ‹ Place your
your hope in heart,* instill courage yourself hope in

IN THE PRESENCE OF A *MINYAN*, MOURNERS RECITE
קַדִּישׁ יָתוֹם, *THE MOURNER'S KADDISH* (PAGE 260).

כִּי אָבִי וְאִמִּי עֲזָבוּנִי — *Though my father and my mother have forsaken me.* After my youth and adolescence, they sent me out on my own (*Sforno*).

לְמַעַן שׁוֹרְרָי — *Because of my watchful foes,* i.e., in order to frustrate my enemies who enviously and maliciously seek out my flaws and scrutinize my ways [from שׁוּר, *to stare*] (*Radak*).

לוּלֵא הֶאֱמַנְתִּי — *Had I not trusted ...!* The meaning of this exclamation is implied: If not for my faith, such false witnesses would have destroyed me long ago. I never stopped believing, so I ignored them and continued to serve God with devotion (*Rashi; Radak*).

בְּאֶרֶץ חַיִּים — *In the land of life.* A reference to the World to Come (*Berachos* 4a).

קַוֵּה אֶל ה׳ — *Place your hope in HASHEM.* Because of my boundless faith in HASHEM I hope for His aid at all times and pay no heed to my enemies (*Radak*).

חֲזַק וְיַאֲמֵץ לִבֶּךָ — *Strengthen yourself and He will instill courage in your heart.* Just as someone trying to purify himself is given assistance (*Yoma* 38b), so too someone trying to strengthen his faith is helped by God (*Alshich*).

Malbim observes that hoping for God's help is vastly different than hoping for the aid of man. Heartache and disillusionment are the lot of one who is dependent on people. Not so with regard to God. Placing one's hope in Him is exhilarating, and brings renewed strength.

IN A HOUSE OF MOURNING, PSALM 49 IS RECITED AFTER *SHACHARIS* AND *MINCHAH.*
(SOME SUBSTITUTE PSALM 16 (P. 809) ON DAYS WHEN *TACHANUN* IS NOT RECITED.)

—— Psalm 49 / תהלים מט ——

לַמְנַצֵּחַ לִבְנֵי קֹרַח מִזְמוֹר. שִׁמְעוּ זֹאת כָּל הָעַמִּים,
For the conductor, ≫ by the ⟨ sons ⟨ of ⟨ a psalm. ≫ Hear ⟨ this ⟨ all ⟨ you ≫ peoples,
Korah,

הַאֲזִינוּ כָּל יֹשְׁבֵי חָלֶד. גַּם בְּנֵי אָדָם, גַּם בְּנֵי אִישׁ;
give ear ⟨ all ⟨ you ⟨ of decaying ≫ even ⟨ sons ⟨ of Adam, ⟨ even ⟨ sons ≫ of man;
dwellers   earth;

יַחַד עָשִׁיר וְאֶבְיוֹן.* פִּי יְדַבֵּר חָכְמוֹת, וְהָגוּת לִבִּי
≫ together ⟨ rich – ⟨ and poor.* ≫ My ⟨ will speak ⟨ wisdom, ≫ and the ⟨ of my
mouth   meditations heart

תְבוּנוֹת. אַטֶּה לְמָשָׁל אָזְנִי, אֶפְתַּח בְּכִנּוֹר חִידָתִי.
≫ are insightful. I will ⟨ to the ⟨ my ear; ≫ I will ⟨ with a ⟨ my riddle. ≫
incline parable solve harp

לָמָה אִירָא* בִּימֵי רָע, עֲוֹן עֲקֵבַי יְסוּבֵּנִי. הַבֹּטְחִים
Why ⟩ should I ⟨ in days ⟨ of evil, ⟨ [when] the ⟨ that I trod ⟨ will sur- ≫ Those who ⟩
be fearful*   injunctions upon round me? rely

עַל חֵילָם, וּבְרֹב עָשְׁרָם יִתְהַלָּלוּ. אָח לֹא פָדֹה יִפְדֶּה
on ⟨ their ⟨ their ⟨ and of their ⟨ they are ≫ [yet] –⟩ cannot ⟨ be redeemed ⟩
possessions, great wealth boastful, a brother in any way

אִישׁ, לֹא יִתֵּן לֵאלֹהִים כָּפְרוֹ. וְיֵקַר פִּדְיוֹן נַפְשָׁם,
by a ≫ he cannot ⟨ to God ⟨ his ≫ Too ⟨ costly ⟨ is the ⟨ of their ⟩
man, give ransom. redemption soul

וְחָדַל לְעוֹלָם. וִיחִי עוֹד לָנֶצַח, לֹא יִרְאֶה הַשָּׁחַת.
and ⟨ forever. ≫ Can one ⟨ until ⟨ eternity, ≫ never ⟨ to see ⟨ the pit? ≫
unattainable live

כִּי יִרְאֶה חֲכָמִים יָמוּתוּ, יַחַד כְּסִיל וָבַעַר יֹאבֵדוּ,
Though ⟩ he sees ⟨ that wise men ⟨ die, ≫ that ⟨ the ⟨ and ⟨ perish ⟩
together foolish boorish

⧫§ A House of Mourning / Psalm 49

Recognizing their father's greed for wealth as the root of his downfall, the righteous sons of Korah composed this psalm teaching that man should use his sojourn on earth to enhance his spiritual development so that he will be better prepared for the World to Come. This concept is a source of comfort for those who have lost a close relative.

יַחַד עָשִׁיר וְאֶבְיוֹן — *Together — rich and poor.*

Both are obsessed with money: The rich man wants more and the poor man thinks it will solve all his problems (*Or Olam*).

לָמָה אִירָא ... — *Why should I be fearful ...?* Why does a person misuse his limited time in this world? It will only cause him pain and anguish *in days of evil* — at the end of his sojourn in life, when he will have to give an accounting for *the injunctions that* he *trod upon* which *will surround* him.

וְעָזְבוּ לַאֲחֵרִים חֵילָם. קִרְבָּם בָּתֵּימוֹ לְעוֹלָם, מִשְׁכְּנֹתָם

< their < are forever, < their < [nevertheless,] < their < to others < and leave
dwellings   houses   in their   possessions,
    imagination

לְדוֹר וָדֹר; קָרְאוּ בִשְׁמוֹתָם עֲלֵי אֲדָמוֹת. וְאָדָם

< But as < the lands. < throughout < their names < they have < after gen- < for gen-
for man: proclaimed   eration;   eration

בִּיקָר בַּל יָלִין, נִמְשַׁל כַּבְּהֵמוֹת נִדְמוּ. זֶה דַרְכָּם

< is their < This < that are < to the animals < he is < he shall not < In glory
way,   silenced.   likened   repose;

כֵּסֶל לָמוֹ, וְאַחֲרֵיהֶם בְּפִיהֶם יִרְצוּ סֶלָה. כַּצֹּאן לִשְׁאוֹל

< for the < Like < Selah! < speak < their < yet of their < is < folly
Lower World sheep,   soothingly, mouths   destiny   theirs,

שַׁתּוּ, מָוֶת יִרְעֵם; וַיִּרְדּוּ בָם יְשָׁרִים לַבֹּקֶר, וְצוּרָם

< their form < at < shall the < them < and < shall con- < death < they are
daybreak;   upright   dominate sume them;   destined,

לְבַלּוֹת שְׁאוֹל מִזְּבֻל לוֹ. אַךְ אֱלֹהִים יִפְדֶּה נַפְשִׁי

< my soul < will < God < But < [each] from < in the grave, < is doomed
redeem   his dwelling.   to rot

מִיַּד שְׁאוֹל, כִּי יִקָּחֵנִי סֶלָה. אַל תִּירָא כִּי יַעֲשִׁר

< becomes < when < Fear not < Selah! < He will < for < of the Lower < from
wealthy   take me,   World,   the hand

אִישׁ, כִּי יִרְבֶּה כְּבוֹד בֵּיתוֹ. כִּי לֹא בְמוֹתוֹ יִקַּח הַכֹּל,

< at all, < will < upon < nothing < For < of his < the < he < when < does
he take his death   house. glory increases   man,

לֹא יֵרֵד אַחֲרָיו כְּבוֹדוֹ. כִּי נַפְשׁוֹ בְּחַיָּיו יְבָרֵךְ,

< he may < in his < himself < Though < will his < after him < descend not
bless, lifetime   glory.

וְיוֹדֻךָ כִּי תֵיטִיב לָךְ. תָּבוֹא עַד דּוֹר אֲבוֹתָיו, עַד

< unto < of its < the < to < It shall < yourself. < you < if < others will
fathers; generation   come   improve   praise you

נֵצַח לֹא יִרְאוּ אוֹר. ❖ אָדָם בִּיקָר וְלֹא יָבִין, נִמְשַׁל

< he is < but [if he] < is < Man < light. < they shall not see < eternity
likened understands not, glorious

כַּבְּהֵמוֹת נִדְמוּ.

< that are < to the animals
without speech.

IN THE PRESENCE OF A *MINYAN*, MOURNERS RECITE קַדִּישׁ יָתוֹם (PAGE 260).

ﬥ READINGS FOLLOWING SHACHARIS / הוספות ﬤ
THE SIX REMEMBRANCES / שש זכירות

REMEMBRANCE OF THE EXODUS FROM EGYPT / זְכִירַת יְצִיאַת מִצְרַיִם

—————— Deuteronomy 16:3 / דברים טז:ג ——————

לְמַעַן תִּזְכֹּר אֶת יוֹם צֵאתְךָ מֵאֶרֶץ מִצְרַיִם כֹּל יְמֵי חַיֶּיךָ.

In order that / you may remember / the day / of your departure / from / of Egypt / all / the days / the / of your life.

REMEMBRANCE OF RECEIVING THE TORAH AT MOUNT SINAI / זְכִירַת מַעֲמַד הַר סִינַי

—————— Deuteronomy 4:9-10 / דברים ד:ט-י ——————

רַק הִשָּׁמֶר לְךָ וּשְׁמֹר נַפְשְׁךָ מְאֹד, פֶּן תִּשְׁכַּח אֶת הַדְּבָרִים

Only / beware / for / yourself / and / beware / for your soul / especially, / lest / you forget / the things

אֲשֶׁר רָאוּ עֵינֶיךָ, וּפֶן יָסוּרוּ מִלְּבָבְךָ כֹּל יְמֵי חַיֶּיךָ, וְהוֹדַעְתָּם

that / your eyes / have seen, / and lest / they be removed / from your heart / all / the days / of your life. / And you are to make them known

לְבָנֶיךָ וְלִבְנֵי בָנֶיךָ. יוֹם אֲשֶׁר עָמַדְתָּ לִפְנֵי יהוה אֱלֹהֶיךָ

to your children / and to the children / of your children / — the day / that / you stood / before / HASHEM, / your God,

בְּחֹרֵב.

at Sinai.

REMEMBRANCE OF AMALEK'S ATTACK / זְכִירַת מַעֲשֵׂה עֲמָלֵק

—————— Deuteronomy 25:17-19 / דברים כה:יז-יט ——————

זָכוֹר אֵת אֲשֶׁר עָשָׂה לְךָ עֲמָלֵק, בַּדֶּרֶךְ בְּצֵאתְכֶם מִמִּצְרָיִם.

Remember / what / Amalek did to you / on the way, / as you were leaving / from Egypt.

אֲשֶׁר קָרְךָ בַּדֶּרֶךְ, וַיְזַנֵּב בְּךָ כָּל הַנֶּחֱשָׁלִים אַחֲרֶיךָ, וְאַתָּה עָיֵף

How / he happened / upon you / on the way / and he killed / among / you / all / the weaklings / at your rear, / while / you were faint

---

⋖§ The Six Remembrances

The Torah commands that six events be remembered always. Consequently, some authorities maintain that the verses containing these commandments should be recited daily.

The Exodus. Even though the Exodus is mentioned in the *Shema* of *Shacharis* and *Maariv*, it is so essential to Israel's mission that it is recalled yet again. That God once redeemed Israel from degrading slavery inspires us with confidence in the future Redemption.

Receiving the Torah at Sinai. Israel's redemption — its very existence — is based on the mission entrusted to us when God presented us with the Torah, represented by the Ten Commandments, at Sinai. If we are not the nation of Torah, we are nothing.

Amalek's attack. Amalek's ability to attack Israel was a consequence of Israel's failure to study the Torah with sufficient zeal (*Tanchuma, Beshalach*). Thus the episode of Amalek cautions us to hold the Torah dear. Also, the fate of

וְיָגֵעַ, וְלֹא יָרֵא אֱלֹהִים. וְהָיָה בְּהָנִיחַ יהוה אֱלֹהֶיךָ לְךָ מִכָּל־

⟨ from ⟨ that when Hashem, your God, ⟨ It shall ⟪ God. ⟨ and he did ⟪ and
all   lets you rest   be   not fear   exhausted,

אֹיְבֶיךָ מִסָּבִיב, בָּאָרֶץ אֲשֶׁר יהוה אֱלֹהֶיךָ נֹתֵן לְךָ נַחֲלָה

⟨ as an in-⟨ to ⟨ gives ⟨ your God, ⟨ Hashem, ⟨ that ⟨ in the land ⟪ all around, ⟨ your
heritance you   enemies

לְרִשְׁתָּהּ, תִּמְחֶה אֶת זֵכֶר עֲמָלֵק מִתַּחַת הַשָּׁמָיִם, לֹא תִּשְׁכָּח.

⟪ forget. ⟨ Do ⟪ the heavens. ⟨ from ⟨ of Amalek ⟨ the ⟨ you are ⟪ to take pos-
not   beneath   memory   to erase   session of it;

זְכִירַת מַעֲשֵׂה הָעֵגֶל / REMEMBRANCE OF THE GOLDEN CALF

——— Deuteronomy 9:7 / דברים ט:ז ———

זְכֹר, אַל תִּשְׁכַּח, אֵת אֲשֶׁר הִקְצַפְתָּ אֶת יהוה אֱלֹהֶיךָ,

⟨ your God, ⟨ Hashem, ⟨ you angered ⟨ that ⟨ forget, ⟨ do not ⟨ Remember,

בַּמִּדְבָּר.

⟪ in the Wilderness.

זְכִירַת מִרְיָם / REMEMBRANCE OF MIRIAM

——— Deuteronomy 24:9 / דברים כד:ט ———

זָכוֹר אֵת אֲשֶׁר עָשָׂה יהוה אֱלֹהֶיךָ לְמִרְיָם, בַּדֶּרֶךְ

⟨ on the way ⟪ to Miriam, ⟨ Hashem, your God, did ⟨ which ⟨ that ⟨ Remember

בְּצֵאתְכֶם מִמִּצְרָיִם.

⟪ from Egypt. ⟨ when you were leaving

זְכִירַת הַשַּׁבָּת / REMEMBRANCE OF THE SABBATH

——— Exodus 20:8 / שמות כ:ח ———

זָכוֹר אֶת יוֹם הַשַּׁבָּת לְקַדְּשׁוֹ.

⟪ to sanctify it. ⟨ of the Sabbath ⟨ the day ⟨ Remember

Amalek — total extinction — reminds us that evil has no future.

The Golden Calf. One of the most dismal episodes in Jewish history, the Golden Calf, caused Israel to fall from the spiritual pedestal it had ascended upon receiving the Ten Commandments — and it caused Moses to shatter the Tablets themselves. The lesson that remained was that we must have faith in God's promise and never deviate from His Torah, even if we think that we have found a better way to serve Him.

Miriam. Miriam criticized her brother Moses, on the grounds that he did not live with his wife. She failed to consider that a man of Moses'

humility and unselfishness would not have done so unless he had been commanded always to hold himself in readiness for prophecy, a status that required abstinence. Miriam was punished with *tzara'as*, a disease similar to leprosy, and was healed because of Moses' prayers. This teaches us never to slander another person.

The Sabbath. By refraining from work on the Seventh Day, the day that God rested upon the completion of Creation, the Jew offers enduring testimony that God created the world. Throughout the week, we remember the Sabbath by directing our purchases and preparations toward its honor.

﴾ שלשה עשר עקרים ﴿
﴾ THE THIRTEEN PRINCIPLES OF FAITH ﴿

1/א

אֲנִי מַאֲמִין בֶּאֱמוּנָה שְׁלֵמָה, שֶׁהַבּוֹרֵא יִתְבָּרַךְ שְׁמוֹ

His 〈 – blessed 〈〈 that the 〈 that is 〈 with faith 〈 believe 〈 I
Name –   be   Creator   complete

הוּא בוֹרֵא וּמַנְהִיג לְכָל הַבְּרוּאִים, וְהוּא לְבַדּוֹ עָשָׂה

〈 made, 〈 alone 〈 and [that] He 〈〈 that were created, 〈 all 〈 and guides 〈 creates 〈 He

וְעוֹשֶׂה וְיַעֲשֶׂה לְכָל הַמַּעֲשִׂים.

〈〈 that is made. 〈 everything 〈 and will make 〈 makes,

2/ב

אֲנִי מַאֲמִין בֶּאֱמוּנָה שְׁלֵמָה, שֶׁהַבּוֹרֵא יִתְבָּרַךְ שְׁמוֹ

His 〈 – blessed 〈〈 that the 〈 that is 〈 with faith 〈 believe 〈 I
Name –   be   Creator   complete

הוּא יָחִיד וְאֵין יְחִידוּת כָּמוֹהוּ בְּשׁוּם פָּנִים, וְהוּא

〈 and [that] He 〈〈 way, 〈 in any 〈 like Him 〈 uniqueness 〈 and there is no 〈 is unique 〈 He

לְבַדּוֹ אֱלֹהֵינוּ, הָיָה הֹוֶה וְיִהְיֶה.

〈〈 and Who [always] will be. 〈 Who is, 〈 Who was, 〈 is our God, 〈 alone

3/ג

אֲנִי מַאֲמִין בֶּאֱמוּנָה שְׁלֵמָה, שֶׁהַבּוֹרֵא יִתְבָּרַךְ שְׁמוֹ אֵינוֹ

〈 is 〈〈 His 〈 – blessed 〈〈 that the 〈 that is 〈 with faith 〈 believe 〈 I
not   Name –   be   Creator   complete

﴾ שְׁלֹשָׁה עָשָׂר עִקְרִים /

The Thirteen Principles of Faith

Historically, Judaism never separated belief from performance. In the Torah, the commandment to believe in God is not stated differently than the commandment to lend money to a fellow Jew in need, or to refrain from eating non-kosher food. However, philosophical speculation and dogmas of faith became prevalent among other religions and, in time, began to influence a number of Jews. To counteract this trend, medieval Rabbinical authorities felt the need to define the principles of Judaism. The "Thirteen Principles of Faith" are based upon the formulation of *Rambam* [Maimonides] in his *Commentary to the Mishnah* (*Sanhedrin*, Ch. 10) and have achieved virtually universal acceptance.

It is commendable to recite these principles every day after *Shacharis*. As *Rambam* himself writes, one does not become imbued with them from a perfunctory reading. One must constantly review and study them.

The Thirteen Principles fall into three general categories: (a) the nature of belief in God; (b) the authenticity of the Torah, its validity and immutability; and (c) man's responsibility and ultimate reward.

(A) The Nature of Belief in God

1. *God's Existence.* There is no partnership in Creation. God is the sole Creator and the universe continues to exist only because He wills it so. He could exist if everything else were to come to an end, but it is inconceivable that there could be any form of existence independent of Him.

2. *God is a complete and total Unity.* He is not a collection of limbs and organs, as are man and animals. He cannot be split as can a rock or

גוּף, וְלֹא יַשִּׂיגוּהוּ מַשִּׂיגֵי הַגּוּף, וְאֵין לוֹ שׁוּם דִּמְיוֹן כְּלָל.

《 what- 〈 compar- 〈 any 〈 and that there 《 that are 〈 to phe- 〈 subject 〈 and is 〈 physical
soever. ison is not to Him physical, nomena not

ד/4

אֲנִי מַאֲמִין בֶּאֱמוּנָה שְׁלֵמָה, שֶׁהַבּוֹרֵא יִתְבָּרַךְ שְׁמוֹ

《 His 〈 – blessed 《 that the 〈 that is 〈 with faith 〈 believe 〈 I
Name – be Creator complete

הוּא רִאשׁוֹן וְהוּא אַחֲרוֹן.

《 is the very last. 〈 and He 〈 is the very first 〈 He

ה/5

אֲנִי מַאֲמִין בֶּאֱמוּנָה שְׁלֵמָה, שֶׁהַבּוֹרֵא יִתְבָּרַךְ שְׁמוֹ

《 His 〈 – blessed 《 that the 〈 that is 〈 with faith 〈 believe 〈 I
Name – be Creator complete

לוֹ לְבַדּוֹ רָאוּי לְהִתְפַּלֵּל, וְאֵין לְזוּלָתוֹ רָאוּי לְהִתְפַּלֵּל.

《 to pray. 〈 is it proper 〈 and to no other 〈 to pray 〈 is it proper 〈 alone 〈 to Him

ו/6

אֲנִי מַאֲמִין בֶּאֱמוּנָה שְׁלֵמָה, שֶׁכָּל דִּבְרֵי נְבִיאִים אֱמֶת.

《 are 〈 of the 〈 the 〈 that 〈 that is 〈 with faith 〈 believe 〈 I
true. prophets words all complete

ז/7

אֲנִי מַאֲמִין בֶּאֱמוּנָה שְׁלֵמָה, שֶׁנְּבוּאַת מֹשֶׁה רַבֵּנוּ

《 our 〈 of 〈 that the 〈 that is 〈 with faith 〈 believe 〈 I
teacher Moses prophecy complete

---

divided into component elements as can everything in Creation. This is the concept expressed in the first verse of *Shema*.

3. *God is not physical.* He is totally unaffected by material conditions or the laws of nature and physics. The Torah speaks of God's "eyes," "hands," of God "moving" or "resting," "sitting" or "standing" and so forth only to help man grasp the concepts being conveyed.

4. *God is eternal and the First Source.* Everything in the created universe has a moment when it came into existence; by definition nothing created can be infinite. God transcends time, however, because time itself is His creation.

5. *Prayers should be directed to God.* It is tempting to beseech the angels or such mighty forces as the sun and the constellations, because God has entrusted them with carrying out His will. However, this is illusory. None of them have any power independent of what God assigns them. Therefore, prayers should be directed only toward God Himself.

(B) Authenticity of the Torah

6. *God communicates with man.* In order for man to carry out his Divinely ordained mission, he must know what it is. Prophecy is the means by which God communicates His wishes to man. It is a gift that man can attain upon reaching heights of self-perfection.

7. *Moses' prophecy is unique.* Moses' prophecy is not only true, but of a quality unapproached by that of any other prophet before or since. It is essential that his prophecy be unrivaled so that no later "prophet" could ever claim that he had received a "Torah" that was superior to that of Moses.

עָלָיו הַשָּׁלוֹם הָיְתָה אֲמִתִּית, וְשֶׁהוּא הָיָה אָב לַנְּבִיאִים,

‹‹ of the ‹ the ‹ was ‹ and that ‹‹ true, ‹ was ‹‹ — peace be
prophets, father   he   upon him —

לַקּוֹדְמִים לְפָנָיו וְלַבָּאִים אַחֲרָיו.

‹‹ after him. ‹ and those ‹ him ‹ [both] those
who came   who preceded

ח/8

אֲנִי מַאֲמִין בֶּאֱמוּנָה שְׁלֵמָה, שֶׁכָּל הַתּוֹרָה הַמְּצוּיָה

‹ that is ‹ Torah ‹ that the ‹ that is ‹ with faith ‹ believe ‹ I
found   entire   complete

עַתָּה בְּיָדֵינוּ הִיא הַנְּתוּנָה לְמֹשֶׁה רַבֵּנוּ עָלָיו הַשָּׁלוֹם.

‹‹ — peace be ‹‹ our ‹ to ‹ the [same] one ‹ is ‹ in our ‹ now
upon him. teacher Moses   that was given   hands

ט/9

אֲנִי מַאֲמִין בֶּאֱמוּנָה שְׁלֵמָה, שֶׁזֹּאת הַתּוֹרָה לֹא תְהֵא

‹ be ‹ will not ‹ Torah ‹ that this ‹ that is complete ‹ with faith ‹ believe ‹ I

מֻחְלֶפֶת וְלֹא תְהֵא תּוֹרָה אַחֶרֶת מֵאֵת הַבּוֹרֵא יִתְבָּרַךְ שְׁמוֹ.

‹‹ His ‹ — blessed ‹‹ the ‹ from ‹ another Torah ‹ will ‹ nor ‹‹ exchanged,
Name. be Creator   there be

י/10

אֲנִי מַאֲמִין בֶּאֱמוּנָה שְׁלֵמָה, שֶׁהַבּוֹרֵא יִתְבָּרַךְ שְׁמוֹ

‹‹ His ‹ — blessed ‹‹ that the ‹ that is ‹ with faith ‹ believe ‹ I
Name — be Creator complete

יוֹדֵעַ כָּל מַעֲשֵׂה בְנֵי אָדָם וְכָל מַחְשְׁבוֹתָם, שֶׁנֶּאֱמַר: הַיֹּצֵר

‹ He Who ‹ as it is said, ‹ their thoughts, ‹ and ‹ of human ‹ the deeds ‹ all ‹ knows
fashions   all   beings

יַחַד לִבָּם, הַמֵּבִין אֶל כָּל מַעֲשֵׂיהֶם.[1]

‹‹ their deeds. ‹ all ‹ Who ‹‹ their ‹ together
comprehends hearts,

---

(1) Psalms 33:15.

8. *The entire Torah is God given.* Every word in the Torah was dictated to Moses by God. In *Rambam's* classic formulation, all the verses of the Torah have equal sanctity, and there is no difference between [the apparently trivial verses:] *and the children of Ham were Cush and Mizrayim,* and *his wife's name was Mehitabel . . .* and [the awesomely important verses:] *I am HASHEM, your God,* and *Hear, O Israel.* Moreover, the same applies to the Oral Law that elucidates the Torah. All was given by God to Moses.

9. *The Torah is unchangeable.* Since both the Written and Oral Law were God given, they cannot be improved upon in any manner.

(C) Man's Responsibility and Ultimate Reward

10. *God knows man's thoughts and deeds.* Man's individual deeds are important to God and so are the hopes and thoughts that motivate him. God is aware of everything man thinks and does.

יא/11

אֲנִי מַאֲמִין בֶּאֱמוּנָה שְׁלֵמָה, שֶׁהַבּוֹרֵא יִתְבָּרַךְ שְׁמוֹ

‹‹ His ‹ – blessed ‹‹ that the ‹ that is ‹ with faith ‹ believe ‹ I
Name – 　　be 　　　Creator 　　complete

גוֹמֵל טוֹב לְשׁוֹמְרֵי מִצְוֹתָיו וּמַעֲנִישׁ לְעוֹבְרֵי מִצְוֹתָיו.

‹‹ His com- ‹ those who ‹ and ‹‹ His com- ‹ those who ‹ with ‹ rewards
mandments. violate 　　punishes mandments, observe 　　good

יב/12

אֲנִי מַאֲמִין בֶּאֱמוּנָה שְׁלֵמָה, בְּבִיאַת הַמָּשִׁיחַ, וְאַף עַל פִּי

‹ and even ‹‹ of the ‹ in the ‹ that is ‹ with faith ‹ believe ‹ I
though 　Messiah, coming 　complete

שֶׁיִּתְמַהְמֵהַּ, עִם כָּל זֶה אֲחַכֶּה לּוֹ בְּכָל יוֹם שֶׁיָּבוֹא.[1]

‹‹ [certain] that ‹‹ day, ‹ every ‹ him ‹ I await ‹‹ that – ‹ all ‹ – with ‹‹ he may delay
he will come.

יג/13

אֲנִי מַאֲמִין בֶּאֱמוּנָה שְׁלֵמָה, שֶׁתִּהְיֶה תְּחִיַּת הַמֵּתִים

‹ of the ‹ a revi- ‹ that there ‹ that is ‹ with faith ‹ believe ‹ I
dead 　vification will be 　complete

בְּעֵת שֶׁיַּעֲלֶה רָצוֹן מֵאֵת הַבּוֹרֵא יִתְבָּרַךְ שְׁמוֹ וְיִתְעַלֶּה זִכְרוֹ

‹‹ His ‹ and exalted ‹ His ‹ – blessed ‹‹ the ‹ from ‹ the will ‹ there ‹ when-
mention – 　be 　　Name 　be 　Creator 　[for it] 　arises 　ever

לָעַד וּלְנֵצַח נְצָחִים.

‹‹ and for all eternity. ‹ forever

לִישׁוּעָתְךָ קִוִּיתִי יהוה. קִוִּיתִי יהוה לִישׁוּעָתְךָ.[2] יהוה לִישׁוּעָתְךָ קִוִּיתִי

‹‹ I do ‹ for Your ‹ HASHEM, ‹‹ for Your ‹ HASHEM, ‹ I do ‹‹ HASHEM. ‹ I do ‹ For Your
yearn. salvation 　　salvation. 　　yearn, 　　yearn, 　salvation

לְפוּרְקָנָךְ סַבָּרִית יהוה.[3] סַבָּרִית יהוה לְפוּרְקָנָךְ. יהוה לְפוּרְקָנָךְ סַבָּרִית.

‹‹ I do ‹ for Your ‹ HASHEM, ‹‹ for Your ‹ HASHEM, ‹ I do ‹‹ HASHEM. ‹ I do ‹ For Your
yearn. salvation 　　salvation. 　　yearn, 　　yearn, 　salvation

---

(1) Cf. *Habakkuk* 2:3. (2) *Genesis* 49:18. (3) *Targum Onkelos*.

11. *Reward and punishment.* No one acts in a vacuum and no deed goes unrewarded or unpunished. This includes the dictum that one cannot cancel out a bad deed with a good one. Each is treated independently.

12. *The Messiah will come.* We are to conduct our lives according to the Torah and remain faithful that the Messiah will come at the time deemed by

God to be proper. This faith includes the principle that only the Davidic dynasty will provide the Messianic king.

13. *The dead will live again* in the Messianic era, when the world will attain a new spiritual and physical level of perfection. Those who have not been found unworthy to enter this exalted era will live again and enjoy it.

❧ THE TEN COMMANDMENTS / עשרת הדברות ❧

——————— Exodus 20:1-14 / שמות כ:א-יד ———————

וַיְדַבֵּר אֱלֹהִים אֵת כָּל הַדְּבָרִים הָאֵלֶּה לֵאמֹר.

《 saying: 〈 these statements, 〈 all 〈 God spoke

1/א

אָנֹכִי יהוה אֱלֹהֶיךָ, אֲשֶׁר הוֹצֵאתִיךָ מֵאֶרֶץ מִצְרַיִם מִבֵּית עֲבָדִים.

《 of 〈 from the 〈 of Egypt, 〈 of the 〈 has taken 〈 Who 〈 your 〈 Hashem, 〈 I am
slavery. house   land   you out   God,

2/ב

לֹא יִהְיֶה לְךָ אֱלֹהִים אֲחֵרִים עַל פָּנָי. לֹא תַעֲשֶׂה לְךָ

〈 for 〈 You shall 《 My 〈 in 〈 of others 〈 the gods 〈 to 〈 be 〈 There
yourself not make   presence.   you   shall not

פֶסֶל וְכָל תְּמוּנָה אֲשֶׁר בַּשָּׁמַיִם מִמַּעַל, וַאֲשֶׁר בָּאָרֶץ מִתָּחַת,

《 below, 〈 on the 〈 or that 《 above, 〈 in the 〈 of that 〈 likeness 〈 nor 《 a carved
earth   which is   heavens which is   any   image,

וַאֲשֶׁר בַּמַּיִם מִתַּחַת לָאָרֶץ. לֹא תִשְׁתַּחֲוֶה לָהֶם וְלֹא תָעָבְדֵם,

《 worship 〈 nor 〈 to 〈 You shall not 《 the earth. 〈 beneath 〈 in the 〈 or that
them,   them prostrate yourself   water   which is

כִּי אָנֹכִי יהוה אֱלֹהֶיךָ, אֵל קַנָּא, פֹּקֵד עֲוֹן אָבֹת עַל בָּנִים,

〈 children, 〈 upon 〈 of 〈 the 〈 Who 《 Who is 〈 a 〈 your God, 〈 Hashem, 〈 I am 〈 for
fathers sin visits jealous, God

עַל שִׁלֵּשִׁים, וְעַל רִבֵּעִים לְשֹׂנְאָי. וְעֹשֶׂה חֶסֶד לַאֲלָפִים,

〈 for thousands 〈 with 〈 but Who 《 for My 〈 the fourth 〈 and 〈 the third 〈 upon
[of generations] kindness acts enemies; [generation], upon [generation],

לְאֹהֲבַי, וּלְשֹׁמְרֵי מִצְוֹתָי.

《 My com- 〈 and those 〈 to those
mandments. who observe who love Me

3/ג

לֹא תִשָּׂא אֶת שֵׁם יהוה אֱלֹהֶיךָ לַשָּׁוְא, כִּי לֹא יְנַקֶּה יהוה,

〈 Hashem will not absolve 〈 for 《 in vain, 〈 your God, 〈 of Hashem, 〈 the Name 〈 You shall not take

אֵת אֲשֶׁר יִשָּׂא אֶת שְׁמוֹ לַשָּׁוְא.

《 in vain. 〈 His Name 〈 takes 〈 who 〈 anyone

❧ עֲשֶׂרֶת הַדִּבְּרוֹת / The Ten Commandments
During the Temple era, the Ten Commandments were recited as a part of the *Shema* service
each morning. Later, certain heretics denied the
validity of the rest of the Torah, but accepted
only the Ten Commandments as the word of
God. To prove their point, they cited the fact
that the Ten Commandments were recited each
day, while the rest of the Torah was not. To
counteract their claims, the Talmudic Sages
(*Berachos* 12a) removed the Ten Commandments from the formal public prayer service and
forbade their reinsertion into the service or their
recitation in any public forum (except when

ד/4

זָכוֹר אֶת יוֹם הַשַּׁבָּת לְקַדְּשׁוֹ. שֵׁשֶׁת יָמִים תַּעֲבֹד וְעָשִׂיתָ

⟨ and do ⟨ shall you labor ⟨ days ⟨ Six ⟪ to sanctify it. ⟨ of the Sabbath ⟨ the day ⟨ Remember

כָּל מְלַאכְתֶּךָ. וְיוֹם הַשְּׁבִיעִי שַׁבָּת לַיהוה אֱלֹהֶיךָ, לֹא תַעֲשֶׂה

⟨ You may not do ⟪ your God. ⟨ to ⟨ is the ⟨ but the Seventh Day ⟪ your work; ⟨ all
HASHEM, Sabbath

כָּל מְלָאכָה, אַתָּה וּבִנְךָ וּבִתֶּךָ, עַבְדְּךָ וַאֲמָתְךָ וּבְהֶמְתֶּךָ, וְגֵרְךָ

⟨ and your ⟨ your ⟨ and your ⟨ your ⟨ and your ⟨ your ⟨ – you, ⟪ work ⟨ any
convert animal, maidservant, slave daughter, son

אֲשֶׁר בִּשְׁעָרֶיךָ. כִּי שֵׁשֶׁת יָמִים עָשָׂה יהוה אֶת הַשָּׁמַיִם וְאֶת

⟨ and ⟨ the heavens ⟨ HASHEM made ⟨ days ⟨ in six ⟨ For ⟪ within your gates. ⟨ who is

הָאָרֶץ, אֶת הַיָּם וְאֶת כָּל אֲשֶׁר בָּם, וַיָּנַח בַּיּוֹם הַשְּׁבִיעִי,

⟪ on the Seventh Day. ⟨ and He ⟪ is in ⟨ that ⟨ all ⟨ and ⟨ the sea ⟪ the earth,
rested them,

עַל כֵּן בֵּרַךְ יהוה אֶת יוֹם הַשַּׁבָּת וַיְקַדְּשֵׁהוּ.

⟪ and sanctified it. ⟨ of the Sabbath ⟨ the day ⟨ HASHEM blessed ⟨ this [reason] ⟨ For

ה/5

כַּבֵּד אֶת אָבִיךָ וְאֶת אִמֶּךָ, לְמַעַן יַאֲרִכוּן יָמֶיךָ עַל הָאֲדָמָה

⟨ the land ⟨ upon ⟨ your days will be ⟨ so that ⟪ your ⟨ and ⟨ your father ⟨ Honor
lengthened mother,

אֲשֶׁר יהוה אֱלֹהֶיךָ נֹתֵן לָךְ.

⟪ you. ⟨ gives ⟨ your God, ⟨ HASHEM, ⟨ that

ח/8　　　　　　　**ז/7**　　　　　　　**ו/6**

לֹא תִגְנֹב,　　　　　לֹא תִנְאָף,　　　　　לֹא תִרְצַח,

⟪ you shall not steal;　　⟪ you shall not commit adultery;　　⟪ You shall not kill;

ט/9

לֹא תַעֲנֶה בְרֵעֲךָ עֵד שָׁקֶר.

⟪ false witness. ⟨ against your fellow ⟨ you shall not bear

י/10

לֹא תַחְמֹד בֵּית רֵעֶךָ, לֹא תַחְמֹד אֵשֶׁת רֵעֶךָ, וְעַבְדּוֹ וַאֲמָתוֹ

⟨ his maid-servant, ⟨ his slave, ⟪ of your fellow, ⟨ the wife ⟨ you shall not covet ⟪ of your fellow; ⟨ the house ⟨ You shall not covet

וְשׁוֹרוֹ וַחֲמֹרוֹ, וְכֹל אֲשֶׁר לְרֵעֶךָ.

⟪ belongs to your fellow. ⟨ that ⟨ [nor] anything ⟨ his donkey, ⟨ his ox,

---

they appear in the course of the regular Torah readings). Moreover, even an individual may not recite them as a part of the formal service. Nevertheless, an individual may (and, according to some authorities, should) recite them either before or after his regular prayers.

❧ CHAPTER OF REPENTANCE / פרשת התשובה ❧

**R' ELIEZER OF METZ IN HIS *SEFER YEREIM* (13TH CENTURY) RECOMMENDS
THE DAILY RECITATION OF THIS CHAPTER.**

—— *Deuteronomy* 30:1-10 / דברים ל:א-י ——

וְהָיָה כִי יָבְאוּ עָלֶיךָ כָּל הַדְּבָרִים הָאֵלֶּה, הַבְּרָכָה וְהַקְּלָלָה

⟨ and the ⟨ – the ⟨⟨ these things ⟨ all ⟨ upon ⟨ there will ⟨ that ⟨ It will be
curse   blessing   you   come   when

אֲשֶׁר נָתַתִּי לְפָנֶיךָ, וַהֲשֵׁבֹתָ אֶל לְבָבֶךָ, בְּכָל הַגּוֹיִם אֲשֶׁר

⟨ that ⟨ the ⟨ among ⟨ your heart ⟨ to ⟨ then you ⟨⟨ before ⟨ I have ⟨ that
nations   all   will take it   you —   presented

הִדִּיחֲךָ יהוה אֱלֹהֶיךָ שָׁמָּה. וְשַׁבְתָּ עַד יהוה אֱלֹהֶיךָ, וְשָׁמַעְתָּ

⟨ and you ⟨ your God, ⟨ HASHEM, ⟨ unto ⟨ and you ⟨ thereto; ⟨ HASHEM, your God,
will listen   will return   dispersed you

בְקֹלוֹ, כְּכֹל אֲשֶׁר אָנֹכִי מְצַוְּךָ הַיּוֹם, אַתָּה וּבָנֶיךָ, בְּכָל לְבָבְךָ

⟨ your ⟨ with ⟨⟨ and your ⟨ – you ⟨ today ⟨ command ⟨ I ⟨ that ⟨ according to ⟨⟨ to His
heart   all   children —   you   everything   voice,

וּבְכָל נַפְשֶׁךָ. וְשָׁב יהוה אֱלֹהֶיךָ אֶת שְׁבוּתְךָ וְרִחֲמֶךָ, וְשָׁב

⟨ and He ⟨⟨ and He will ⟨ your captivity, ⟨ Then HASHEM, your God, ⟨⟨ your ⟨ and
will once   have mercy   will bring back   soul.   with all
again   upon you,

וְקִבֶּצְךָ מִכָּל הָעַמִּים, אֲשֶׁר הֱפִיצְךָ יהוה אֱלֹהֶיךָ שָׁמָּה. אִם

⟨ If ⟨⟨ thereto. ⟨ HASHEM, your God, scattered you ⟨ that ⟨ the peoples ⟨ from all ⟨ gather you in

יִהְיֶה נִדַּחֲךָ בִּקְצֵה הַשָּׁמָיִם, מִשָּׁם יְקַבֶּצְךָ יהוה אֱלֹהֶיךָ וּמִשָּׁם

⟨ and from ⟨⟨ HASHEM, your God, ⟨ from ⟨⟨ of heaven, ⟨ at the ⟨ your dispersed
there   will gather you in,   there   ends   will be

יִקָּחֶךָ. וֶהֱבִיאֲךָ יהוה אֱלֹהֶיךָ אֶל הָאָרֶץ אֲשֶׁר יָרְשׁוּ אֲבֹתֶיךָ

⟨ your forefathers ⟨ that ⟨ the Land ⟨ to ⟨ And HASHEM, your God, ⟨⟨ He will
took possession of   will bring you   take you.

וִירִשְׁתָּהּ, וְהֵיטִבְךָ וְהִרְבְּךָ מֵאֲבֹתֶיךָ. וּמָל יהוה אֱלֹהֶיךָ

⟨ HASHEM, your God, ⟨⟨ than your ⟨ and make you ⟨ He will do ⟨⟨ and you shall
will circumcise   forefathers. more numerous good to you   possess it;

אֶת לְבָבְךָ וְאֶת לְבַב זַרְעֶךָ, לְאַהֲבָה אֶת יהוה אֱלֹהֶיךָ בְּכָל

⟨ with ⟨ your God, ⟨ HASHEM, ⟨ to love ⟨⟨ of your ⟨ and the heart ⟨ your heart
all   offspring,

לְבָבְךָ וּבְכָל נַפְשֶׁךָ, לְמַעַן חַיֶּיךָ. וְנָתַן יהוה אֱלֹהֶיךָ אֵת כָּל

⟨ all ⟨ HASHEM, your God, ⟨⟨ you may ⟨ so that ⟨ your soul, ⟨ and ⟨ your
          will place   live.   with all   heart

הָאָלוֹת הָאֵלֶּה, עַל אֹיְבֶיךָ וְעַל שֹׂנְאֶיךָ אֲשֶׁר רְדָפְוּךָ. וְאַתָּה

< You « have <– those « those who < and < your < upon < these curses
pursued you. who hate you upon enemies

תָשׁוּב, וְשָׁמַעְתָּ בְּקוֹל יהוה, וְעָשִׂיתָ אֶת כָּל מִצְוֹתָיו אֲשֶׁר

< that < His com- < all < and you « of < to the < and you < shall
mandments shall perform HASHEM, voice shall listen return

אָנֹכִי מְצַוְּךָ הַיּוֹם. וְהוֹתִירְךָ יהוה אֱלֹהֶיךָ בְּכֹל מַעֲשֵׂה יָדֶךָ,

« of your < the < in all < HASHEM, your God, « today. < command < I
hands, work will make you abundant you

בִּפְרִי בִטְנְךָ וּבִפְרִי בְהֶמְתְּךָ וּבִפְרִי אַדְמָתְךָ לְטֹבָה, כִּי

< for « for good, < of your < and in < of your < in the < of your < in the
Land the fruit animals, fruit womb, fruit

יָשׁוּב יהוה לָשׂוּשׂ עָלֶיךָ לְטוֹב, כַּאֲשֶׁר שָׂשׂ עַל אֲבֹתֶיךָ. כִּי

< when « your < over < He < as « for good, < over < to < HASHEM will
forefathers, rejoiced you rejoice return

תִשְׁמַע בְּקוֹל יהוה אֱלֹהֶיךָ, לִשְׁמֹר מִצְוֹתָיו וְחֻקֹּתָיו הַכְּתוּבָה

< that are < and His < His com- < to « your God, < of < to the < you will
written decrees mandments observe HASHEM, voice listen

בְּסֵפֶר הַתּוֹרָה הַזֶּה, כִּי תָשׁוּב אֶל יהוה אֱלֹהֶיךָ בְּכָל לְבָבְךָ

< your < with < your God, < HASHEM, < to < you < when « in this Book of the Torah,
heart all return

וּבְכָל נַפְשֶׁךָ.

« your < and
soul. with all

MANY RECITE THE FOLLOWING SUPPLICATORY PARAGRAPH AFTER פָּרָשַׁת הַתְּשׁוּבָה,
THE CHAPTER OF REPENTANCE. IT IS OMITTED ON THE SABBATH AND FESTIVALS.

יְהִי רָצוֹן מִלְּפָנֶיךָ, יהוה אֱלֹהַי וֵאלֹהֵי אֲבוֹתַי, שֶׁתַּחְתּוֹר

< that You dig « of my < and the < my God < HASHEM, « before < the will < May
forefathers, God You, it be

חֲתִירָה מִתַּחַת כִּסֵּא כְבוֹדֶךָ, לְהַחֲזִיר בִּתְשׁוּבָה שְׁלֵמָה לְכָל

< all < in complete < to bring « of Your < the < beneath < a tunnel
repentance back Glory, Throne

פּוֹשְׁעֵי עַמְּךָ בֵּית יִשְׂרָאֵל. וּבִכְלָלָם תַּחֲזִירֵנִי בִּתְשׁוּבָה שְׁלֵמָה

< in complete < bring me < And along « of Israel. < the < of Your < the
repentance back with them, House people, evildoers

לְפָנֶיךָ, כִּי יְמִינְךָ פְּשׁוּטָה לְקַבֵּל שָׁבִים, וְרוֹצֶה אַתָּה בִּתְשׁוּבָה.

« repentance. < and You desire < penitents < to < is < Your right < for « before
accept outstretched hand You,

אָמֵן, סֶלָה.

« Selah. « Amen.

❧ CHAPTER OF REVERENCE FOR GOD / פרשת היראה ❧

R' ELIEZER OF METZ IN HIS *SEFER YEREIM* (13TH CENTURY) RECOMMENDS
THE DAILY RECITATION OF THIS CHAPTER.

—— *Deuteronomy* 10:12-11:9 / דברים י:יב-יא:ט ——

וְעַתָּה יִשְׂרָאֵל, מָה יהוה אֱלֹהֶיךָ שֹׁאֵל מֵעִמָּךְ, כִּי אִם
‹ Only 《 of you? ‹ ask ‹ your God, ‹ [does] ‹ what ‹ Israel, ‹ And now, HASHEM,

לְיִרְאָה אֶת יהוה אֱלֹהֶיךָ, לָלֶכֶת בְּכָל דְּרָכָיו, וּלְאַהֲבָה אֹתוֹ,
《《 Him, ‹ and to love ‹ His ways ‹ in all ‹ to go 《 your God, ‹ HASHEM, ‹ to fear

וְלַעֲבֹד אֶת יהוה אֱלֹהֶיךָ בְּכָל לְבָבְךָ וּבְכָל נַפְשֶׁךָ. לִשְׁמֹר
‹ to 《 your ‹ and ‹ your ‹ with all ‹ your God, ‹ HASHEM, ‹ and to
observe　soul,　with all　heart　　　　　　　　　　　　　　　　　serve

אֶת מִצְוֹת יהוה וְאֶת חֻקֹּתָיו, אֲשֶׁר אָנֹכִי מְצַוְּךָ הַיּוֹם, לְטוֹב
‹ as a 《 today, ‹ command ‹ I ‹ which 《 and His decrees, ‹ of ‹ the
benefit　　　　　　you　　　　　　　　　　　　　HASHEM　commandments

לָךְ. הֵן לַיהוה אֱלֹהֶיךָ הַשָּׁמַיִם וּשְׁמֵי הַשָּׁמַיִם, הָאָרֶץ וְכָל
‹ and ‹ the ‹ and highest heaven, ‹ are the ‹ your God, ‹ to ‹ Behold, 《 for
everything　earth　　　　　　　　　　heaven　　　　　HASHEM,　　　　　you.

אֲשֶׁר בָּהּ. רַק בַּאֲבֹתֶיךָ חָשַׁק יהוה לְאַהֲבָה אוֹתָם, וַיִּבְחַר
‹ and He 《 them, ‹ to love ‹ did HASHEM ‹ your ‹ Only 《 is in it. ‹ that
chose　　　　　　　cherish,　forefathers

בְּזַרְעָם אַחֲרֵיהֶם, בָּכֶם, מִכָּל הָעַמִּים, כַּיּוֹם הַזֶּה. וּמַלְתֶּם
‹ You shall 《 as [clear as] 《 the peoples, ‹ from 《 – you – 《 after them ‹ their
cut away　this very day.　　　　　　among all　　　　　　　　　　offspring

אֵת עָרְלַת לְבַבְכֶם, וְעָרְפְּכֶם לֹא תַקְשׁוּ עוֹד. כִּי יהוה
‹ HASHEM, 《 For 《 any ‹ you shall not 《 and your 《 of your ‹ the barrier
　　　　　　longer.　stiffen　　　neck　　　　heart,

אֱלֹהֵיכֶם הוּא אֱלֹהֵי הָאֱלֹהִים וַאֲדֹנֵי הָאֲדֹנִים, הָאֵל הַגָּדֹל
‹ Who is ‹ the 《 of the lords, ‹ and ‹ of the powers ‹ is the ‹ – He 《 your God
great,　God　　　　　　the Lord　　　　　　　　　God

הַגִּבֹּר וְהַנּוֹרָא, אֲשֶׁר לֹא יִשָּׂא פָנִים וְלֹא יִקַּח שֹׁחַד. עֹשֶׂה
‹ He car- 《 a bribe. ‹ accept ‹ and ‹ show favor ‹ does ‹ Who 《 and Who ‹ Who is
ries out　　　　does not　　　　　　not　　　is awesome,　mighty,

מִשְׁפַּט יָתוֹם וְאַלְמָנָה, וְאֹהֵב גֵּר לָתֶת לוֹ לֶחֶם וְשִׂמְלָה.
《 and ‹ bread ‹ him ‹ giving ‹ the ‹ and loves 《 and the ‹ of the ‹ the
clothing.　　　　　　　stranger,　　　widow,　orphan　judgment

וַאֲהַבְתֶּם אֶת הַגֵּר, כִּי גֵרִים הֱיִיתֶם בְּאֶרֶץ מִצְרָיִם. אֶת יהוה
‹ HASHEM, 《 of Egypt. ‹ in the land ‹ were you ‹ strangers ‹ for 《 the stranger, ‹ You shall love

אֱלֹהֶיךָ תִּירָא, אֹתוֹ תַעֲבֹד, וּבוֹ תִדְבָּק, וּבִשְׁמוֹ תִּשָּׁבֵעַ. הוּא

⟨ He ⟨⟨ shall you ⟨ and by ⟨⟨ shall you ⟨ to ⟨⟨ shall ⟨ Him ⟨⟨ shall you ⟨ your God,
  swear. His Name   cling,   Him you serve,   fear,

תְהִלָּתְךָ וְהוּא אֱלֹהֶיךָ, אֲשֶׁר עָשָׂה אִתְּךָ אֶת הַגְּדֹלֹת

⟨ the great   ⟨ for you ⟨ did   ⟨ Who ⟨⟨ is your God, ⟨ and He ⟨ is your praise

וְאֶת הַנּוֹרָאֹת הָאֵלֶּה, אֲשֶׁר רָאוּ עֵינֶיךָ. בְּשִׁבְעִים נֶפֶשׁ   יָרְדוּ

⟨ descended ⟨ souls ⟨ With   ⟨⟨ your eyes saw. ⟨ which ⟨ [things] that ⟨ and the awesome
             seventy   are these

אֲבֹתֶיךָ מִצְרַיְמָה, וְעַתָּה שָׂמְךָ יהוה אֱלֹהֶיךָ כְּכוֹכְבֵי הַשָּׁמַיִם

⟨ of heaven ⟨ like the ⟨   HASHEM, your God,   ⟨ and now ⟨⟨ to Egypt, ⟨   your
         stars   has made you   forefathers

לָרֹב. וְאָהַבְתָּ אֵת יהוה אֱלֹהֶיךָ, וְשָׁמַרְתָּ מִשְׁמַרְתּוֹ וְחֻקֹּתָיו

⟨ His   ⟨ His charge, ⟨ and you ⟨ your God, ⟨ HASHEM, ⟨ You shall ⟨⟨ in abun-
decrees,   shall observe   love   dance.

וּמִשְׁפָּטָיו וּמִצְוֹתָיו כָּל הַיָּמִים. וִידַעְתֶּם הַיּוֹם, כִּי לֹא אֶת

⟨ with ⟨ it is ⟨ that ⟨ today ⟨ You should ⟨⟨ the days. ⟨ all ⟨ and His com- ⟨   His
  not   know   mandments, ordinances,

בְּנֵיכֶם אֲשֶׁר לֹא יָדְעוּ וַאֲשֶׁר לֹא רָאוּ אֶת מוּסַר יהוה

⟨ of   ⟨ the discipline   ⟨ see ⟨ did not ⟨ and who ⟨ know ⟨ did not ⟨ – who ⟨⟨ your
HASHEM,   children

אֱלֹהֵיכֶם, אֶת גָּדְלוֹ, אֶת יָדוֹ הַחֲזָקָה וּזְרֹעוֹ הַנְּטוּיָה.

⟨⟨ that is   ⟨ and His ⟨   that is   ⟨ His hand ⟨ His greatness, ⟨⟨ your God,
outstretched, arm   strong,

וְאֶת אֹתֹתָיו וְאֶת מַעֲשָׂיו אֲשֶׁר עָשָׂה בְּתוֹךְ מִצְרָיִם, לְפַרְעֹה

⟨ to Pharaoh, ⟨⟨ of Egypt, ⟨ in the ⟨ He ⟨ that ⟨ and His deeds ⟨   His signs
                   midst performed

מֶלֶךְ מִצְרַיִם וּלְכָל אַרְצוֹ. וַאֲשֶׁר עָשָׂה לְחֵיל מִצְרַיִם לְסוּסָיו

⟨ to its ⟨⟨ of Egypt, ⟨ to the ⟨ He did ⟨ and ⟨⟨ his land; ⟨ and to ⟨ of Egypt, ⟨ king
horses   army   what   all

וּלְרִכְבּוֹ, אֲשֶׁר הֵצִיף אֶת מֵי יַם סוּף עַל פְּנֵיהֶם בְּרָדְפָם

⟨ when they ⟨ them   ⟨ over ⟨ of ⟨ of the ⟨ the waters ⟨ He   ⟨ how ⟨⟨ and its
chased   Reeds Sea   swept   chariots,

אַחֲרֵיכֶם, וַיְאַבְּדֵם יהוה עַד הַיּוֹם הַזֶּה. וַאֲשֶׁר עָשָׂה לָכֶם

⟨ for ⟨ He did ⟨ and ⟨⟨ this very day; ⟨ until ⟨ and HASHEM   ⟨⟨ after you,
you   what   destroyed them

בַּמִּדְבָּר, עַד בֹּאֲכֶם עַד הַמָּקוֹם הַזֶּה. וַאֲשֶׁר עָשָׂה לְדָתָן

⟨ to ⟨ He did ⟨ and ⟨⟨   this place; ⟨ to ⟨ you ⟨ until ⟨⟨ in the
Dathan   what   came   Wilderness,

וְלַאֲבִירָם בְּנֵי אֱלִיאָב בֶּן רְאוּבֵן, אֲשֶׁר פָּצְתָה הָאָרֶץ אֶת פִּיהָ,

‹ its mouth ‹ the earth opened wide ‹ that ‹‹ of Reuben, ‹ son ‹ of Eliab ‹ the ‹ and Abiram, sons

וַתִּבְלָעֵם וְאֶת בָּתֵּיהֶם וְאֶת אָהֳלֵיהֶם, וְאֵת כָּל הַיְקוּם אֲשֶׁר

‹ that ‹ the ‹ and all ‹ and their tents ‹ and their ‹and swallowed were possessions households them

בְּרַגְלֵיהֶם, בְּקֶרֶב כָּל יִשְׂרָאֵל. כִּי עֵינֵיכֶם הָרֹאֹת אֶת כָּל

‹ all ‹ that see ‹ it is your ‹ — rather, ‹‹ Israel ‹ of all ‹ in the ‹ at their own eyes midst feet,

מַעֲשֵׂה יהוה הַגָּדֹל, אֲשֶׁר עָשָׂה. וּשְׁמַרְתֶּם אֶת כָּל הַמִּצְוָה

‹ command- ‹ the entire ‹ So you shall ‹‹ He did. ‹ which ‹ that is ‹ of ‹ the work ment observe great, HASHEM

אֲשֶׁר אָנֹכִי מְצַוְּךָ הַיּוֹם, לְמַעַן תֶּחֶזְקוּ וּבָאתֶם וִירִשְׁתֶּם

‹ and you ‹ and you ‹ you will ‹ so that ‹‹ today, ‹ command ‹ I ‹ that will possess will come be strong, you

אֶת הָאָרֶץ אֲשֶׁר אַתֶּם עֹבְרִים שָׁמָּה לְרִשְׁתָּהּ. וּלְמַעַן תַּאֲרִיכוּ

‹ you will ‹ and so ‹‹ to possess ‹ thereto, ‹ are crossing ‹ you ‹ which ‹ the Land, prolong that it, over

יָמִים עַל הָאֲדָמָה אֲשֶׁר נִשְׁבַּע יהוה לַאֲבֹתֵיכֶם לָתֵת לָהֶם

‹ to ‹ to give ‹ to your ‹ HASHEM swore ‹ that ‹ the Land ‹ on ‹ your days them forefathers

וּלְזַרְעָם, אֶרֶץ זָבַת חָלָב וּדְבָשׁ.

‹‹ and ‹ with ‹ flowing ‹ — a ‹‹ and to their honey. milk land offspring

MANY RECITE THE FOLLOWING SUPPLICATORY PARAGRAPH AFTER פָּרָשַׁת הַיִּרְאָה,
THE CHAPTER OF REVERENCE. **IT IS OMITTED ON THE SABBATH AND FESTIVALS.**

יְהִי רָצוֹן מִלְּפָנֶיךָ, יהוה אֱלֹהַי וֵאלֹהֵי אֲבוֹתַי, שֶׁתִּטַּע

‹ that You ‹‹ of my ‹ and ‹ my God ‹ HASHEM, ‹‹ before You, ‹ the will ‹ May implant forefathers the God it be

אַהֲבָתְךָ וְיִרְאָתְךָ בְּלִבִּי וּבְלֵב כָּל יִשְׂרָאֵל עַמֶּךָ, לְיִרְאָה

‹ to ‹‹ your ‹ Israel ‹ of all ‹ and in ‹ in my ‹ and Your ‹ Your love revere people, the heart heart reverence

אֶת שִׁמְךָ הַגָּדוֹל הַגִּבּוֹר וְהַנּוֹרָא, בְּכָל לְבָבֵנוּ וּבְכָל נַפְשֵׁנוּ,

‹‹ our soul ‹ and ‹ our ‹ with all ‹‹ and that is ‹ that is ‹ that is ‹ Your Name with all heart awesome, mighty, great

יִרְאַת הָרוֹמְמוּת שֶׁל אֵין סוֹף, בָּרוּךְ וְיִתְעַלֶּה שְׁמְךָ, כִּי גָדוֹל

‹ great ‹ for ‹‹ be Your ‹ and uplifted ‹ blessed ‹‹ the Infinite ‹ of ‹ for the ‹ — a Name, One, exaltedness reverence

אַתָּה וְנוֹרָא שְׁמֶךָ. אָמֵן, סֶלָה.

‹‹ Selah. ‹‹ Amen. ‹‹ is Your ‹ and ‹ are You Name. awesome

﷽ **THE CHAPTER OF MANNA / פָּרָשַׁת הַמָּן** ﷽

THE COMMENTATORS CITE THE *YERUSHALMI* THAT ONE WHO RECITES THIS CHAPTER EVERY DAY IS
ASSURED THAT HIS FOOD WILL NOT BE LACKING. *LEVUSH* EXPLAINS THAT THIS CHAPTER TEACHES
THAT GOD PROVIDES EACH DAY'S SUSTENANCE — JUST AS HE PROVIDED THE MANNA EACH DAY IN
THE WILDERNESS.

MANY RECITE THE FOLLOWING SUPPLICATORY PARAGRAPH BEFORE **פָּרָשַׁת הַמָּן**,
THE CHAPTER OF MANNA. IT IS OMITTED ON THE SABBATH AND FESTIVALS.

יְהִי רָצוֹן מִלְּפָנֶיךָ, יהוה אֱלֹהֵינוּ וֵאלֹהֵי אֲבוֹתֵינוּ, שֶׁתַּזְמִין

May it be / the will / before You, / HASHEM, / our God / and / of our / that you / forefathers, the God / provide

פַּרְנָסָה לְכָל עַמְּךָ בֵּית יִשְׂרָאֵל, וּפַרְנָסָתִי וּפַרְנָסַת אַנְשֵׁי בֵיתִי

a livelihood / all / people, / House / of Your / the / of / my livelihood / and the / — and my / of my household members livelihood

בִּכְלָלָם, בְּנַחַת וְלֹא בְצַעַר, בְּכָבוֹד וְלֹא בְבִזּוּי, בְּהֶתֵּר וְלֹא

included with them — / with / and / with / and / with / and / in a permissible / not / ease / not / honor / not / disgrace, / manner, in a permissible / pain, manner

בְאִסּוּר — כְּדֵי שֶׁנּוּכַל לַעֲבֹד עֲבֹדָתֶךָ וְלִלְמוֹד תוֹרָתֶךָ — כְּמוֹ

in a forbidden / so / we will / to / Your / and study / Your Torah, / just as / manner, / that / be able / perform / service,

שֶׁזַּנְתָּ לַאֲבוֹתֵינוּ מָן בַּמִּדְבָּר, בְּאֶרֶץ צִיָּה וַעֲרָבָה.

You / our / manna / in the / with / in a land / arid / and / nourished / forefathers / Wilderness, / desolate.

——— *Exodus 16:4-36 / שמות טז:ד-לו* ———

וַיֹּאמֶר יהוה אֶל מֹשֶׁה, הִנְנִי מַמְטִיר לָכֶם לֶחֶם מִן הַשָּׁמָיִם,

HASHEM said / to / Moses, / Behold, / I shall / for you / food / from / heaven; / rain down

וְיָצָא הָעָם וְלָקְטוּ דְּבַר יוֹם בְּיוֹמוֹ, לְמַעַן אֲנַסֶּנּוּ הֲיֵלֵךְ

let the people / and pick / the / of each / on its / so that / I can test / whether they / go out / portion / day / day, / them, / will follow

בְּתוֹרָתִי אִם לֹא. וְהָיָה בַּיּוֹם הַשִּׁשִּׁי, וְהֵכִינוּ אֵת אֲשֶׁר יָבִיאוּ,

My teaching / or / not. / And it / on the sixth day / [when] they / what / they / shall be / prepare / bring,

וְהָיָה מִשְׁנֶה עַל אֲשֶׁר יִלְקְטוּ יוֹם יוֹם. וַיֹּאמֶר מֹשֶׁה וְאַהֲרֹן אֶל

that it / double / over / what / they pick / every day. / Moses and Aaron said / to / will be

כָּל בְּנֵי יִשְׂרָאֵל, עֶרֶב וִידַעְתֶּם כִּי יהוה הוֹצִיא אֶתְכֶם

all / the / Children / of Israel, / In the / you shall / that / HASHEM / took you out / evening, / know

מֵאֶרֶץ מִצְרָיִם. וּבֹקֶר וּרְאִיתֶם אֶת כְּבוֹד יהוה, בְּשָׁמְעוֹ

the land / of Egypt. / And in the / you will see / the glory / of / HASHEM, / when / morning / HASHEM, / He hears

אֶת תְּלֻנֹּתֵיכֶם עַל יהוה, וְנַחְנוּ מָה, כִּי תַלִּינוּ עָלֵינוּ.

against — you should — that — nothing — — for — HASHEM — against — your complaints
us. incite complaints we are

וַיֹּאמֶר מֹשֶׁה, בְּתֵת יהוה לָכֶם בָּעֶרֶב בָּשָׂר לֶאֱכֹל וְלֶחֶם

and bread — to eat, — meat — in the evening — you — When HASHEM gives — — Moses said,

בַּבֹּקֶר לִשְׂבֹּעַ, בִּשְׁמֹעַ יהוה אֶת תְּלֻנֹּתֵיכֶם אֲשֶׁר אַתֶּם

you — that — your complaints — as HASHEM hears — for satiety, — in the morning

מַלִּינִם עָלָיו, וְנַחְנוּ מָה, לֹא עָלֵינוּ תְלֻנֹּתֵיכֶם, כִּי עַל יהוה.

HASHEM! — against — but — are your — against — not — nothing – — — for — against — incite
complaints, us we are Him

וַיֹּאמֶר מֹשֶׁה אֶל אַהֲרֹן, אֱמֹר אֶל כָּל עֲדַת בְּנֵי יִשְׂרָאֵל, קִרְבוּ

'Draw — of Israel: — of the — assem- — the — to — Say — Aaron, — to — Moses said
near Children bly entire

לִפְנֵי יהוה, כִּי שָׁמַע אֵת תְּלֻנֹּתֵיכֶם. וַיְהִי כְּדַבֵּר אַהֲרֹן אֶל כָּל

the — to — when Aaron — And it — your complaints.' — He has — for — HASHEM, — before
entire spoke happened heard

עֲדַת בְּנֵי יִשְׂרָאֵל, וַיִּפְנוּ אֶל הַמִּדְבָּר, וְהִנֵּה כְּבוֹד יהוה נִרְאָה

was — of — the — and — the — toward — they — of Israel, — of the — assem-
seen HASHEM glory behold, Wilderness, turned Children bly

בֶּעָנָן. וַיְדַבֵּר יהוה אֶל מֹשֶׁה לֵּאמֹר. שָׁמַעְתִּי אֶת תְּלוּנֹת בְּנֵי

of the — the — I have — saying, — Moses, — to — HASHEM spoke — in a
Children complaints heard cloud.

יִשְׂרָאֵל, דַּבֵּר אֲלֵהֶם לֵאמֹר, בֵּין הָעַרְבַּיִם תֹּאכְלוּ בָשָׂר,

meat — you shall eat — 'In the afternoon — saying: — to them, — Speak — of Israel.

וּבַבֹּקֶר תִּשְׂבְּעוּ לָחֶם, וִידַעְתֶּם כִּי אֲנִי יהוה אֱלֹהֵיכֶם. וַיְהִי

And it — your God.' — HASHEM, — I am — that — and you — with — you shall — and in the
happened shall know bread, be sated morning

בָעֶרֶב, וַתַּעַל הַשְּׂלָו וַתְּכַס אֶת הַמַּחֲנֶה, וּבַבֹּקֶר הָיְתָה שִׁכְבַת

a layer — there — and in the — the camp, — and — that the quail — in the
was morning covered went up evening

הַטַּל סָבִיב לַמַּחֲנֶה. וַתַּעַל שִׁכְבַת הַטָּל, וְהִנֵּה עַל פְּנֵי הַמִּדְבָּר

of the — the — upon — and — of dew, — did — Evaporate — the camp. — surround- — of
Wilderness surface behold, the layer ing dew

דַּק מְחֻסְפָּס, דַּק כַּכְּפֹר עַל הָאָרֶץ. וַיִּרְאוּ בְנֵי יִשְׂרָאֵל, וַיֹּאמְרוּ

and — The Children of Israel saw, — the — upon — like – thin — exposed — was some-
they said earth. frost thing thin

אִישׁ אֶל אָחִיו, מָן הוּא, כִּי לֹא יָדְעוּ מַה הוּא, וַיֹּאמֶר מֹשֶׁה

Moses said — it was. — what — they did — for — is it? — What — another, — to — one
not know

אֲלֵהֶם, הוּא הַלֶּחֶם אֲשֶׁר נָתַן יהוה לָכֶם לְאָכְלָה. זֶה הַדָּבָר

‹ is the ‹ This ≪ to eat. ‹ you ‹ Hashem ‹ that ‹ is the food ‹ This ≪ to them,
thing · has given

אֲשֶׁר צִוָּה יהוה, לִקְטוּ מִמֶּנּוּ אִישׁ לְפִי אָכְלוֹ, עֹמֶר לַגֻּלְגֹּלֶת,

≪ per ‹ an ≪ to what ‹ accor- ‹ for each ‹ from ‹ 'Gather ‹ Hashem has ‹ that
person; · omer · he eats, · ding · man · it,· commanded:

מִסְפַּר נַפְשֹׁתֵיכֶם, אִישׁ לַאֲשֶׁר בְּאָהֳלוֹ תִּקָּחוּ. וַיַּעֲשׂוּ כֵן בְּנֵי

‹ – the ≪ so ‹ They did≪ shall ‹ is in ‹ for ‹ each ‹ of your ‹ according to
Children · you take.' · his tent · whomever · man · people, · the number

יִשְׂרָאֵל, וַיִּלְקְטוּ הַמַּרְבֶּה וְהַמַּמְעִיט. וַיָּמֹדּוּ בָעֹמֶר, וְלֹא

‹ and ≪ in an ‹ And they ≪ and he who ‹ he who ‹ and they ≪ of Israel –
no · omer, · measured · took less. · took more, · gathered,

הֶעְדִּיף הַמַּרְבֶּה, וְהַמַּמְעִיט לֹא הֶחְסִיר, אִישׁ לְפִי אָכְלוֹ

‹ what ‹ according ‹ everyone≪ lacking; ‹ was ‹ and the one who ≪ the one who ‹ extra had
he eats · to · not · had taken less · had taken more,

לָקָטוּ. וַיֹּאמֶר מֹשֶׁה אֲלֵהֶם, אִישׁ אַל יוֹתֵר מִמֶּנּוּ עַד בֹּקֶר.

≪morning. ‹ until ‹ of it ‹ leave ‹ shall ‹ Each ≪ to them, ‹ Moses said ≪ had they
· over · not · person· gathered.

וְלֹא שָׁמְעוּ אֶל מֹשֶׁה, וַיּוֹתִרוּ אֲנָשִׁים מִמֶּנּוּ עַד בֹּקֶר וַיָּרֻם

‹ and it be- ≪ morn- ‹ until ‹ from it ‹ and some people ≪ Moses, ‹ to ‹ But they did
came infested · ing, · left over· not listen

תּוֹלָעִים וַיִּבְאַשׁ, וַיִּקְצֹף עֲלֵהֶם מֹשֶׁה. וַיִּלְקְטוּ אֹתוֹ בַּבֹּקֶר

‹ morning ‹ it ‹ They ≪ was ‹ at them ‹ and angry≪ and it stank; ‹ with worms
· gathered · Moses.

בַּבֹּקֶר, אִישׁ כְּפִי אָכְלוֹ, וְחַם הַשֶּׁמֶשׁ וְנָמָס. וַיְהִי בַּיּוֹם הַשִּׁשִּׁי,

‹ on the sixth day ‹ It ≪ it ‹ of the ‹ and in ≪ to what ‹ accor- ‹ every ≪ by
· happened · melted. · sun · the heat · he eats, · ding · man · morning,

לָקְטוּ לֶחֶם מִשְׁנֶה, שְׁנֵי הָעֹמֶר לָאֶחָד, וַיָּבֹאוּ כָּל נְשִׂיאֵי

‹ the ‹ – all ≪ and they ≪ for each ‹ omers ‹ two ≪ that was ‹ food ‹ that they
princes · came · one; · double, · gathered

הָעֵדָה, וַיַּגִּידוּ לְמֹשֶׁה. וַיֹּאמֶר אֲלֵהֶם, הוּא אֲשֶׁר דִּבֶּר יהוה,

≪ Hashem had ‹ is what ‹ This ≪ to them, ‹ He said ≪ Moses. ‹ and they ≪ of the
spoken; · told · assembly –

שַׁבָּתוֹן שַׁבַּת קֹדֶשׁ לַיהוה מָחָר, אֵת אֲשֶׁר תֹּאפוּ אֵפוּ,

≪ bake, ‹ you wish ‹ which ‹ That ≪ is ‹ for ‹ of ‹ a ‹ a rest day,
to bake, · tomorrow. · Hashem, · holiness · Sabbath

וְאֵת אֲשֶׁר תְּבַשְּׁלוּ בַּשֵּׁלוּ, וְאֵת כָּל הָעֹדֵף הַנִּיחוּ לָכֶם

‹ for ‹ put ‹ that is ‹ and all ≪ cook; ‹ you wish ‹ which ‹ and that
yourselves · away · left over, · to cook,

לְמִשְׁמֶרֶת עַד הַבְּקֶר. וַיַּנִּיחוּ אֹתוֹ עַד הַבְּקֶר כַּאֲשֶׁר
as ⟨ morning, ⟨ until ⟨ They put it away ⟪ the morning. ⟨ until ⟨ for safekeeping

צִוָּה מֹשֶׁה, וְלֹא הִבְאִישׁ, וְרִמָּה לֹא הָיְתָה בּוֹ. וַיֹּאמֶר מֹשֶׁה,
⟪ Moses said, ⟪ in it. ⟨ was not ⟨ and ⟨ stink ⟨ and it ⟪ Moses had
            infestation   did not   commanded;

אִכְלֻהוּ הַיּוֹם, כִּי שַׁבָּת הַיּוֹם לַיהוה, הַיּוֹם לֹא תִמְצָאֻהוּ
find it ⟨ you ⟨ today ⟪ for HASHEM; ⟨ today ⟨ it is a ⟨ for ⟨ today, ⟨ Eat it
will not   Sabbath

בַּשָּׂדֶה. שֵׁשֶׁת יָמִים תִּלְקְטֻהוּ, וּבַיּוֹם הַשְּׁבִיעִי שַׁבָּת, לֹא יִהְיֶה
be ⟨ there ⟪ —a ⟪ but on the Seventh Day ⟨ shall you ⟨ days ⟨ Six ⟪ in the
[any] will not Sabbath—   gather it,   field.

בּוֹ. וַיְהִי בַּיּוֹם הַשְּׁבִיעִי, יָצְאוּ מִן הָעָם לִלְקֹט, וְלֹא מָצָאוּ.
⟪ find. ⟨ and they ⟪ to gather, ⟨ the ⟨ from ⟨ [some] ⟪ on the Seventh Day, ⟨ It ⟪ on
did not   people   went out   happened it.

וַיֹּאמֶר יהוה אֶל מֹשֶׁה, עַד אָנָה מֵאַנְתֶּם לִשְׁמֹר מִצְוֹתַי
⟨ My com- ⟨ to ⟨ will you ⟨ when ⟨ Until ⟪ Moses, ⟨ to ⟨ HASHEM said
mandments observe   all refuse

וְתוֹרֹתָי. רְאוּ כִּי יהוה נָתַן לָכֶם הַשַּׁבָּת, עַל כֵּן הוּא נֹתֵן לָכֶם
⟨ you ⟨ gives ⟨ He ⟨ therefore, ⟪ the ⟨ you ⟨ has ⟨ HASHEM ⟨ that ⟨ See ⟪ and My
                 Sabbath;   given   teachings?

בַּיּוֹם הַשִּׁשִּׁי לֶחֶם יוֹמָיִם, שְׁבוּ אִישׁ תַּחְתָּיו, אַל יֵצֵא אִישׁ
⟨ any ⟨ go ⟨ let ⟪ in his ⟨—each ⟪ You should ⟪ for ⟨ food ⟨ on the sixth day
man out not place;   man— remain two days.

מִמְּקֹמוֹ בַּיּוֹם הַשְּׁבִיעִי. וַיִּשְׁבְּתוּ הָעָם בַּיּוֹם הַשְּׁבִיעִי. וַיִּקְרְאוּ
⟪ They ⟪ on the Seventh Day. ⟨ did the ⟨ Rest ⟪ on the Seventh Day. ⟨ from his
called   people   place

בֵית יִשְׂרָאֵל אֶת שְׁמוֹ מָן, וְהוּא כְּזֶרַע גַּד לָבָן, וְטַעְמוֹ
⟨ and its ⟪ [but] ⟨ of co- ⟨ was like ⟨ It ⟪ manna. ⟨ its name ⟪ of Israel — ⟨ — the
taste   white, riander, the seed   House

כְּצַפִּיחִת בִּדְבָשׁ. וַיֹּאמֶר מֹשֶׁה, זֶה הַדָּבָר אֲשֶׁר צִוָּה יהוה,
⟪ HASHEM has ⟨ that ⟨ is the ⟨ This ⟪ Moses said, ⟪ [fried] ⟨ was like
commanded: thing   in honey.   a cake

מְלֹא הָעֹמֶר מִמֶּנּוּ לְמִשְׁמֶרֶת לְדֹרֹתֵיכֶם, לְמַעַן יִרְאוּ
⟨ they ⟨ so that ⟪ for your ⟨ [shall be] for a ⟨ of it ⟨ An omer-full
will see   generations, safeguarded treasure

אֶת הַלֶּחֶם אֲשֶׁר הֶאֱכַלְתִּי אֶתְכֶם בַּמִּדְבָּר בְּהוֹצִיאִי אֶתְכֶם
⟨ when I took you out ⟨ in the Wilderness ⟨ you ⟨ I fed ⟨ that ⟨ the food

מֵאֶרֶץ מִצְרָיִם. וַיֹּאמֶר מֹשֶׁה אֶל אַהֲרֹן, קַח צִנְצֶנֶת אַחַת וְתֶן
⟨ and put ⟨ one jar ⟨ Take ⟪ Aaron, ⟨ to ⟨ Moses said ⟪ of Egypt. ⟨ from the land

שָׁמָּה מְלֹא הָעֹמֶר מָן, וְהַנַּח אֹתוֹ לִפְנֵי יהוה, לְמִשְׁמֶרֶת

⟨ as a safeguarded ⟨ HASHEM ⟨ before ⟨ it ⟨ and place ⟨⟨ of ⟨ an omer-full ⟨ there
treasure   manna,

לְדֹרֹתֵיכֶם. כַּאֲשֶׁר צִוָּה יהוה אֶל מֹשֶׁה, וַיַּנִּיחֵהוּ אַהֲרֹן לִפְנֵי

⟨ before ⟨ Aaron placed it ⟨⟨ Moses, ⟨ to ⟨ HASHEM ⟨ As ⟨⟨ for your
                                                    commanded   generations.

הָעֵדֻת לְמִשְׁמָרֶת. וּבְנֵי יִשְׂרָאֵל אָכְלוּ אֶת הַמָּן אַרְבָּעִים

⟨ for forty ⟨ the manna ⟨ ate ⟨ of Israel ⟨ The ⟨⟨ as a safeguarded ⟨ the [Ark of]
                                                    Children   treasure.   Testimony

שָׁנָה, עַד בֹּאָם אֶל אֶרֶץ נוֹשָׁבֶת, אֶת הַמָּן אָכְלוּ עַד בֹּאָם

⟨ they ⟨ until ⟨ they ⟨ the manna ⟨⟨ that was ⟨ a land ⟨ to ⟨ they ⟨ until ⟨⟨ years,
came   ate   inhabited;   came

אֶל קְצֵה אֶרֶץ כְּנָעַן. וְהָעֹמֶר עֲשִׂרִית הָאֵיפָה הוּא.

⟨⟨ it is. ⟨ of an ephah ⟨ — a tenth ⟨⟨ The omer ⟨⟨ of ⟨ of the ⟨ the ⟨ to
                                                            Canaan.   land   border

⁂ PRAYER FOR LIVELIHOOD / תפלה על פרנסה ⁂

[THIS PRAYER IS NOT RECITED ON THE SABBATH AND FESTIVALS.]

אַתָּה הוּא יהוה לְבַדֶּךָ, אַתָּה עָשִׂיתָ אֶת הַשָּׁמַיִם

⟨ the heavens, ⟨ have made ⟨ You ⟨⟨ alone. ⟨ HASHEM, ⟨ Who are ⟨ It is You

וּשְׁמֵי הַשָּׁמַיִם, הָאָרֶץ וְכָל אֲשֶׁר עָלֶיהָ, הַיַּמִּים וְכָל אֲשֶׁר

⟨ that is ⟨ and ⟨ the seas ⟨⟨ upon it, ⟨ that is ⟨ and ⟨ the earth ⟨ the loftiest heavens,
everything   everything

בָּהֶם, וְאַתָּה מְחַיֶּה אֶת כֻּלָּם.[1] וְאַתָּה הוּא שֶׁעָשִׂיתָ נִסִּים

⟨ miracles ⟨ performed ⟨ Who ⟨ It is You ⟨⟨ to all of them. ⟨ give life ⟨ and You ⟨⟨ in them;

וְנִפְלָאוֹת גְּדוֹלוֹת תָּמִיד עִם אֲבוֹתֵינוּ. גַּם בַּמִּדְבָּר הִמְטַרְתָּ

⟨ You rained ⟨ in the ⟨ Also ⟨⟨ our ⟨ for ⟨ always, ⟨ and great wonders,
down   Wilderness   forefathers.

לָהֶם לֶחֶם מִן הַשָּׁמַיִם,[2] וּמִצּוּר הַחַלָּמִישׁ, הוֹצֵאתָ לָהֶם מַיִם,[3]

⟨⟨ water, ⟨ for ⟨ You brought ⟨ of flint ⟨ and from ⟨⟨ heaven, ⟨ from ⟨ food ⟨ for
                them   forth   the rock   them

וְגַם נָתַתָּ לָהֶם כָּל צָרְכֵיהֶם, וְשִׂמְלֹתָם לֹא בָלְתָה מֵעֲלֵיהֶם.[4]

⟨⟨ upon them. ⟨ wear out ⟨ did ⟨ and their ⟨⟨ their needs, ⟨ all ⟨ for ⟨ You ⟨ and
                        not   clothing   them provided also

כֵּן בְּרַחֲמֶיךָ הָרַבִּים וּבַחֲסָדֶיךָ הָעֲצוּמִים, תְּזוּנֵנוּ וּתְפַרְנְסֵנוּ

⟨ sustain us, ⟨ nourish ⟨⟨ that is ⟨ and in Your ⟨ that is ⟨ in Your ⟨ So
                        us,   powerful,   kindness   abundant   mercy   too,

---

(1) Cf. *Nehemiah* 9:6. (2) Cf. *Exodus* 16:4. (3) Cf. *Deuteronomy* 8:15. (4) Cf. 8:4.

וּתְכַלְכְּלֵנוּ וְתַסְפִּיק כָּל צָרְכֵנוּ, וְצָרְכֵי עַמְּךָ בֵּית יִשְׂרָאֵל

‹ of Israel, ‹ the ‹ of Your ‹ and the ‹ our ‹ all ‹ and supply ‹‹ support us,
House people, needs needs

הַמְרֻבִּים, בְּמִלּוּי וּבְרֶוַח, בְּלִי טֹרַח וְעָמָל גָּדוֹל, מִתַּחַת

‹ coming ‹‹ or great toil, ‹ travail ‹ without ‹ and plenty, ‹ with ‹‹ which are ‹‹ abundant,
from fullness

יָדְךָ הַנְּקִיָּה, וְלֹא מִתַּחַת יְדֵי בָשָׂר וָדָם.

‹‹ and ‹ [of man,] ‹ the ‹ coming ‹ and ‹‹ Your pure hand,
blood. of flesh hands from not

יְהִי רָצוֹן מִלְּפָנֶיךָ, יהוה אֱלֹהַי וֵאלֹהֵי אֲבוֹתַי, שֶׁתָּכִין לִי

‹ for ‹ that you ‹‹ of my ‹ and ‹ my ‹ HASHEM, ‹‹ before You, ‹ the will ‹ May
me prepare forefathers, the God God it be

וּלְאַנְשֵׁי בֵיתִי כָּל מַחְסוֹרֵנוּ, וְתַזְמִין לָנוּ כָּל צָרְכֵנוּ. לְכָל יוֹם

‹ day ‹ for ‹‹ our ‹ all ‹ for ‹ and make ‹ that we lack ‹ all ‹ of my ‹ and for the
every needs, us ready household members

וָיוֹם מֵחַיֵּינוּ דֵי מַחְסוֹרֵנוּ, וּלְכָל שָׁעָה וְשָׁעָה מִשְּׁעוֹתֵינוּ דֵי

‹ suffi- ‹ of our hours, ‹ after ‹ hour ‹ and for ‹‹ for our needs, ‹ suffi- ‹ of our ‹ after
cient hour every cient lives, day

סִפּוּקֵנוּ, וּלְכָל עֶצֶם מֵעֲצָמֵינוּ דֵי מִחְיָתֵנוּ, כְּיָדְךָ הַטּוֹבָה

‹ that is ‹ in accordance ‹‹ nourish- ‹ suffi- ‹ of our bones ‹ bone ‹ and for ‹‹ supply,
benevolent with Your hand ment, cient every

וְהָרְחָבָה, וְלֹא כְּמְעוּט מִפְעָלֵינוּ, וְקֹצֶר חֲסָדֵינוּ, וּמִזְּעֵיר

‹ or from ‹ kindness ‹ the ‹ of our deeds, ‹ according to the ‹ and ‹‹ and
the paucity due us, limited meagerness not generous,

גְּמוּלוֹתֵינוּ. וְיִהְיוּ מְזוֹנוֹתַי, וּמְזוֹנוֹת אַנְשֵׁי בֵיתִי וְזַרְעִי וְזֶרַע

‹ and the ‹ my ‹‹ of my ‹ of the ‹ and the ‹ my ‹ May it ‹‹ of the payment
children offspring household, members nourishment nourishment be that we deserve.

זַרְעִי, מְסוּרִים בְּיָדְךָ, וְלֹא בְּיַד בָּשָׂר וָדָם.

‹‹ and ‹ [of man] ‹ to the ‹ and ‹ to Your ‹ are ‹ of my
blood. of flesh hand not hand committed offspring

✤ תפלה אחר התפלה – בקר וערב ✤

✤ AFTER PRAYER SERVICES — MORNING AND EVENING ✤

יְהִי יהוה אֱלֹהֵינוּ עִמָּנוּ, כַּאֲשֶׁר הָיָה עִם אֲבֹתֵינוּ, אַל יַעַזְבֵנוּ

‹ may He not ‹‹ our ‹ with ‹ He ‹ as ‹‹ be ‹ our God, ‹ HASHEM, ‹ May
abandon us forefathers; was with us,

וְאַל יִטְּשֵׁנוּ. לְהַטּוֹת לְבָבֵנוּ אֵלָיו, לָלֶכֶת בְּכָל דְּרָכָיו, וְלִשְׁמֹר

‹ and to ‹‹ His ways, ‹ in all ‹ to walk ‹‹ to Him, ‹ our ‹ To turn ‹‹ forsake us. ‹ nor
observe hearts

מִצְוֹתָיו וְחֻקָּיו וּמִשְׁפָּטָיו, אֲשֶׁר צִוָּה אֶת אֲבֹתֵינוּ. וְיִהְיוּ

דְבָרַי אֵלֶּה, אֲשֶׁר הִתְחַנַּנְתִּי לִפְנֵי יהוה, קְרֹבִים אֶל יהוה

אֱלֹהֵינוּ יוֹמָם וָלַיְלָה, לַעֲשׂוֹת מִשְׁפַּט עַבְדּוֹ, וּמִשְׁפַּט עַמּוֹ

יִשְׂרָאֵל, דְּבַר יוֹם בְּיוֹמוֹ. לְמַעַן דַּעַת כָּל עַמֵּי הָאָרֶץ, כִּי יהוה

הוּא הָאֱלֹהִים, אֵין עוֹד.[1] יהוה, נְחֵנִי בְצִדְקָתֶךָ לְמַעַן שׁוֹרְרָי,

הַיְשַׁר לְפָנַי דַּרְכֶּךָ.[2] וַאֲנִי בְּתֻמִּי אֵלֵךְ, פְּדֵנִי וְחָנֵּנִי.[3] פְּנֵה אֵלַי

וְחָנֵּנִי, כִּי יָחִיד וְעָנִי אָנִי.[4] רַגְלִי עָמְדָה בְמִישׁוֹר, בְּמַקְהֵלִים

אֲבָרֵךְ יהוה.[5] יהוה שֹׁמְרִי, יהוה צִלִּי עַל יַד יְמִינִי.[6] עֶזְרִי מֵעִם

יהוה, עֹשֵׂה שָׁמַיִם וָאָרֶץ.[7] יהוה יִשְׁמָר צֵאתִי וּבוֹאִי, לְחַיִּים

וּלְשָׁלוֹם, מֵעַתָּה וְעַד עוֹלָם.[8] הַשְׁקִיפָה מִמְּעוֹן קָדְשְׁךָ, מִן

הַשָּׁמַיִם, וּבָרֵךְ אֶת עַמְּךָ אֶת יִשְׂרָאֵל, וְאֵת הָאֲדָמָה אֲשֶׁר

נָתַתָּה לָנוּ, כַּאֲשֶׁר נִשְׁבַּעְתָּ לַאֲבֹתֵינוּ, אֶרֶץ זָבַת חָלָב וּדְבָשׁ.[9]

---

(1) *I Kings* 8:57-60. (2) *Psalms* 5:9. (3) 26:11. (4) 25:16. (5) 26:12.
(6) Cf. 121:5. (7) 121:2. (8) Cf. 121:8. (9) *Deuteronomy* 26:15.

אֵל הַכָּבוֹד, אֶתֵּן לָךְ שִׁיר וְהַלֵּל, וְאֶעֱבוֹד לָךְ יוֹם וָלֵיל.

O God ⟨ of glory, ⟨ I will ⟨ with ⟨ You ⟨ and ⟨ and ⟨ You ⟨ and I ⟨ day ⟨ and
present   song   praise,   will serve   night.

בָּרוּךְ יָחִיד וּמְיוּחָד, הָיָה הֹוֶה וְיִהְיֶה, יהוה אֱלֹהֵי

Blessed ⟨ is He Who ⟨ and Who ⟨ Who ⟨ Who ⟨ and Who ⟨ HASHEM, ⟨ God, ⟨ the
is one   is unique;   was,   is,   will be;   God

יִשְׂרָאֵל, מֶלֶךְ מַלְכֵי הַמְּלָכִים הַקָּדוֹשׁ בָּרוּךְ הוּא. הוּא

of Israel, ⟨ the King ⟨ over kings ⟨ of kings, ⟨ the Holy One, ⟨ Blessed ⟨ is He. ⟨ He

אֱלֹהִים חַיִּים, מֶלֶךְ חַי וְקַיָּם לָעַד וּלְעוֹלְמֵי עַד. בָּרוּךְ שֵׁם

is the living God, ⟨ the ⟨ Who ⟨ and ⟨ forever ⟨ and for ⟨ and ⟨ Blessed ⟨ is the
King   is alive   enduring   all eternity.   Name

כְּבוֹד מַלְכוּתוֹ לְעוֹלָם וָעֶד. לִישׁוּעָתְךָ קִוִּיתִי יהוה.[1] כִּי כָל

of His ⟨ Kingdom ⟨ for ever ⟨ and ⟨ For Your ⟨ I do ⟨ HASHEM.[1] ⟨ For ⟨ all
glorious   ever.   salvation   yearn,

הָעַמִּים יֵלְכוּ אִישׁ בְּשֵׁם אֱלֹהָיו, וַאֲנִי אֵלֵךְ בְּשֵׁם יהוה

the peoples ⟨ walk, ⟨ each ⟨ in the ⟨ of his god; ⟨ but as ⟨ I will ⟨ in the ⟨ of
man   name   for me,   walk   Name   HASHEM,

אֱלֹהִים חַיִּים וּמֶלֶךְ עוֹלָם.[2] עֶזְרִי מֵעִם יהוה, עֹשֵׂה שָׁמַיִם

the living God ⟨ and ⟨ King ⟨ of the ⟨ My ⟨ is from ⟨ HASHEM, ⟨ Maker ⟨ of
universe.   help   heaven

וָאָרֶץ.[3] יהוה יִמְלֹךְ לְעֹלָם וָעֶד.[4]

and ⟨ HASHEM ⟨ shall ⟨ for ever ⟨ and
earth.   reign   ever.

--- Psalm 67 / תהלים סז ---

לַמְנַצֵּחַ בִּנְגִינֹת מִזְמוֹר שִׁיר. אֱלֹהִים יְחָנֵּנוּ וִיבָרְכֵנוּ, יָאֵר

For the ⟨ with the ⟨ a psalm, ⟨ a ⟨ May God ⟨ favor ⟨ and bless ⟨ may He
conductor   neginos,   song.   us,   us,   illuminate

פָּנָיו אִתָּנוּ סֶלָה. לָדַעַת בָּאָרֶץ דַּרְכֶּךָ, בְּכָל גּוֹיִם יְשׁוּעָתֶךָ.

His coun- ⟨ with ⟨ Selah. ⟨ To make ⟨ on earth ⟨ Your ⟨ among ⟨ nations ⟨ Your
tenance   us,   known   way,   all   salvation.

יוֹדוּךָ עַמִּים, אֱלֹהִים; יוֹדוּךָ עַמִּים כֻּלָּם. יִשְׂמְחוּ וִירַנְּנוּ

Acknowledge ⟨ the ⟨ O God; ⟨ acknowledge ⟨ the ⟨ all of ⟨ Glad ⟨ and singing
You   peoples,   You   peoples   them.   will be   for joy will be

לְאֻמִּים, כִּי תִשְׁפֹּט עַמִּים מִישֹׁר, וּלְאֻמִּים בָּאָרֶץ תַּנְחֵם

regimes, ⟨ because ⟨ You will ⟨ the ⟨ fairly ⟨ and the ⟨ on ⟨ [with fairness]
  judge   peoples   regimes   earth   You will guide,

---

(1) *Genesis* 49:18. (2) Cf. *Micah* 4:5. (3) *Psalms* 121:2. (4) *Exodus* 15:18.

סֶלָה. יוֹדוּךָ עַמִּים, אֱלֹהִים; יוֹדוּךָ עַמִּים כֻּלָּם. אֶרֶץ

‹ The ‹‹ – all ‹‹ will the ‹ acknowledge ‹‹ O God; ‹ will the ‹ Acknowledge ‹‹ Selah.
earth of them. peoples You peoples, You

נָתְנָה יְבוּלָהּ, יְבָרְכֵנוּ אֱלֹהִים אֱלֹהֵינוּ. יְבָרְכֵנוּ אֱלֹהִים,

‹‹ May God bless us, ‹‹ – our God. ‹‹ may God bless us ‹‹ its ‹ will then
produce; have yielded

וְיִירְאוּ אוֹתוֹ כָּל אַפְסֵי אָרֶץ.

‹‹ of the earth. ‹ the ends ‹ – all ‹‹ Him ‹ and may
they fear

SOME RECITE *ADON OLAM* (P. 19) **AT THIS POINT.**

תְּפִלָּה כְּשֶׁיּוֹצֵא מִבֵּית הַכְּנֶסֶת

PRAYER UPON LEAVING THE SYNAGOGUE

SIT BRIEFLY AND RECITE:

אַךְ צַדִּיקִים יוֹדוּ לִשְׁמֶךָ, יֵשְׁבוּ יְשָׁרִים אֶת פָּנֶיךָ.[1]

‹‹ in Your ‹ will the ‹ dwell ‹‹ to Your ‹ will give ‹ the ‹ Only
presence. upright Name; thanks righteous

STAND AND SAY:

כִּי כָּל הָעַמִּים יֵלְכוּ אִישׁ בְּשֵׁם אֱלֹהָיו, וַאֲנִי אֵלֵךְ בְּשֵׁם

‹ in the ‹ I will ‹ but as ‹‹ of his ‹ in the ‹ each ‹‹ walk, ‹ the ‹ all ‹ For
Name walk for me, god; name man peoples

יהוה אֱלֹהִים חַיִּים וּמֶלֶךְ עוֹלָם.[2] עֶזְרִי מֵעִם יהוה, עֹשֵׂה

‹ Maker ‹‹ HASHEM, ‹ is ‹ My ‹‹ of the ‹ and ‹ the living God ‹ of
from help universe. King HASHEM,

שָׁמַיִם וָאָרֶץ.[3] יהוה יִמְלֹךְ לְעֹלָם וָעֶד.[4]

‹‹ and ever. ‹ for ever ‹ shall reign ‹ HASHEM ‹‹ and earth. ‹ of heaven

**THEN WALK BACKWARDS, RESPECTFULLY, TO THE EXIT, AS IF TAKING LEAVE OF A KING.
AT THE DOOR, BOW TOWARD THE ARK AND RECITE:**

יהוה, נְחֵנִי בְצִדְקָתֶךָ לְמַעַן שׁוֹרְרָי, הַיְשַׁר לְפָנַי דַּרְכֶּךָ.[5]

‹‹ Your ‹ before ‹ make ‹‹ my watchful ‹ because ‹ in Your ‹ guide ‹ HASHEM,
way. me straight enemies; of righteousness, me

UPON LEAVING RECITE:

גָּד גְּדוּד יְגוּדֶנּוּ, וְהוּא יָגֻד עָקֵב.[6] וַיְהִי דָוִד לְכָל דְּרָכָיו

‹ his ‹ in all ‹ David was ‹‹ on [its] ‹ will troop ‹ and he ‹ will troop ‹ a troop ‹ [From]
ways tracks [safely]. back forth, Gad

מַשְׂכִּיל, וַיהוה עִמּוֹ.[7] וְנֹחַ מָצָא חֵן בְּעֵינֵי יהוה.[8]

‹‹ of HASHEM. ‹ in the ‹ favor ‹ found ‹ And ‹‹ was with ‹ and ‹‹ successful;
eyes Noah him. HASHEM

---

(1) *Psalms* 140:14. (2) Cf. *Micah* 4:5. (3) *Psalms* 121:2. (4) *Exodus* 15:18.
(5) *Psalms* 5:9. (6) *Genesis* 49:19. (7) *I Samuel* 18:14. (8) *Genesis* 6:8.

ONE WHO WILL ENGAGE IN COMMERCE RECITES:

עֶזְרִי מֵעִם יהוה, עֹשֵׂה שָׁמַיִם וָאָרֶץ.¹ הַשְׁלֵךְ עַל יהוה יְהָבְךָ

< your < HASHEM < upon < Cast 《 and < of < Maker 《 HASHEM, < is < My help
burden   earth.   heaven   from

וְהוּא יְכַלְכְּלֶךָ.² שְׁמָר תָּם וּרְאֵה יָשָׁר, כִּי אַחֲרִית לְאִישׁ

< for the < there is a < for 《 the < and < the < Guard 《 will sustain < and He
man   destiny   upright,   watch   perfect   you.

שָׁלוֹם.⁴ בְּטַח בַּיהוה וַעֲשֵׂה טוֹב, שְׁכָן אֶרֶץ וּרְעֵה אֱמוּנָה.

《 with < and nourish < in the < dwell 《 good; < and do < in HASHEM < Trust 《 of peace.
faithfulness.   [yourself]   land

הִנֵּה אֵל יְשׁוּעָתִי, אֶבְטַח וְלֹא אֶפְחָד, כִּי עָזִּי וְזִמְרָת יָהּ יהוה,

《 HASHEM, < is < and my < my < For 《 fear. < and < I shall < is my < God < Behold,
       God,   praise might   not   trust   salvation;

וַיְהִי לִי לִישׁוּעָה.⁵ אֲנִי רוֹצֶה לֵילֵךְ הַיּוֹם לַעֲשׂוֹת מַשָּׂא וּמַתָּן

《 and < trading < to engage in < today < to go < wish < I 《 a salvation. < for < and
dealing,   me He was

בִּרְשׁוּת הַשֵּׁם יִתְבָּרֵךְ וּלְמַעַן שְׁמוֹ, וְלָשֵׂא וְלִתֵּן בָּאֱמוּנָה.

《 faithfully. < and < and to 《 of His < and for < may He be < of < with the
        deal   trade   Name,   the sake blessed, HASHEM, permission

רִבּוֹנוֹ שֶׁל עוֹלָם, בְּדִבְרֵי קָדְשְׁךָ כָּתוּב לֵאמֹר: וְהַבּוֹטֵחַ בַּיהוה

< in < One who < saying: < it is < in Your holy writings < the < of < O
HASHEM,   trusts   written,   Universe,   Master

חֶסֶד יְסוֹבְבֶנּוּ.⁶ וּכְתִיב: וְאַתָּה מְחַיֶּה אֶת כֻּלָּם.⁷ יהוה אֱלֹהִים

< God < HASHEM, 《 to them all. < give life < You 《 And it is 《 surrounds < kindness
                               written: him.

אֱמֶת,⁸ תֵּן בְּרָכָה וְהַצְלָחָה בְּכָל מַעֲשֵׂה יָדַי, כִּי בָטַחְתִּי בָךְ,

《 in < I trust < for 《 of my < the work < in all < and success < blessing < grant 《 of truth,
You,   hands,

שֶׁעַל יְדֵי מַשָּׂא וּמַתָּן וַעֲסָקִים שֶׁלִּי, תִּשְׁלַח לִי בְּרָכָה, כְּדֵי

< so 《 a < me < You will < that < and < and < the < that through
that   blessing,   send   I do,   activities dealing, trading

שֶׁאוּכַל לְפַרְנֵס אֶת עַצְמִי וּבְנֵי בֵיתִי, בְּנַחַת וְלֹא בְצַעַר,

《 in pain, < and < in < of my < and the < myself < to < I will be
          not tranquility household members   support   able

---

(1) *Psalms* 121:2. (2) 55:23. (3) 37:37. (4) 37:3. (5) *Isaiah* 12:2.
(6) *Psalms* 32:10. (7) *Nehemiah* 9:6. (8) Cf. *Jeremiah* 10:10.

בְּהֶתֵּר וְלֹא בְאִסּוּר, לְחַיִּים וּלְשָׁלוֹם. וִיקֻיַּם בִּי מִקְרָא

⟨ the ⟨ in me ⟨ May there ⟪ and for ⟨ for life ⟪ in a ⟨ and ⟨ in a
verse   be fulfilled   peace.   forbidden not permissible
                                       manner,   manner

שֶׁכָּתוּב: הַשְׁלֵךְ עַל יהוה יְהָבְךָ, וְהוּא יְכַלְכְּלֶךָ.¹ אָמֵן.

⟪ Amen. ⟪ will sustain ⟨ and He ⟨ your ⟨ HASHEM ⟨ upon ⟨ Cast ⟪ that is
           you.   burden   written:

⊰{ תפלה כשנכנס ויוצא מבית המדרש }⊱
⊰{ PRAYERS ON ENTERING AND LEAVING THE STUDY HALL }⊱

ON ENTERING THE *BEIS HAMIDRASH,* **OR ON BEGINNING TO STUDY TORAH, EVEN ALONE,
ONE RECITES THE FOLLOWING PRAYER:**

יְהִי רָצוֹן מִלְּפָנֶיךָ, יהוה אֱלֹהַי וֵאלֹהֵי אֲבוֹתַי, שֶׁלֹּא יֶאֱרַע

⟨ occur ⟨ that ⟪ of my ⟨ and God ⟨ my ⟨ HASHEM, ⟪ before ⟨ the will ⟨ May
        there not forefathers,   God   You,   it be

דְּבַר תַּקָלָה עַל יָדִי, וְלֹא אֶכָּשֵׁל בִּדְבַר הֲלָכָה וְיִשְׂמְחוּ בִּי

⟨ over ⟨ and [lead to] ⟪ of law, ⟪ in a ⟨ And let me ⟪ of ⟨ because ⟨ that leads ⟨ any
me   the rejoicing   matter   not stumble   me.   to a mishap matter

חֲבֵרַי. שֶׁלֹּא אוֹמַר עַל טָמֵא טָהוֹר וְלֹא עַל טָהוֹר טָמֵא,

⟪ that it is ⟨ [some- ⟨ of ⟨ and ⟪ that it ⟨ [something] ⟨ of ⟨ Let me not say ⟪ of my
impure;   thing] pure   not   is pure, that is impure   colleagues.

וְלֹא עַל מֻתָּר אָסוּר וְלֹא עַל אָסוּר מֻתָּר, וְלֹא יִכָּשְׁלוּ

⟨ stumble ⟨ Not ⟪ that it is ⟨ [something] ⟨ on ⟨ nor ⟪ that it is ⟨ [something] ⟨ on ⟨ nor
                  permitted.   forbidden   forbidden,   permitted

חֲבֵרַי בִּדְבַר הֲלָכָה וְאֶשְׂמַח בָּהֶם. כִּי יהוה יִתֵּן חָכְמָה,

⟪ wisdom; ⟨ grants ⟨ HASHEM ⟨ For ⟪ over ⟨ that [might lead] ⟨ of law ⟨ in a ⟨ should my
                                them. me to rejoice   matter   colleagues

מִפִּיו דַּעַת וּתְבוּנָה.² גַּל עֵינַי וְאַבִּיטָה נִפְלָאוֹת מִתּוֹרָתֶךָ.³

⟪ from Your ⟨ wonders ⟨ that I may ⟨ my ⟨ Unveil ⟪ and under- ⟨ [come] ⟨ from His
  Torah.   perceive   eyes   standing. knowledge mouth

---

(1) *Psalms* 55:23. (2) *Proverbs* 2:6. (3) *Psalms* 119:18.

⊰§ תפלה כשנכנס ויוצא מבית המדרש / **Prayer on Entering and Leaving the Study Hall**

The Talmud (*Berachos* 28b) presents the reciting of these two prayers as the practice of the *tanna* R' Nechunya ben Hakanah.

However, the *Rambam* (*Commentary to the Mishnah*) infers that they are obligatory for everyone. This is also the ruling of the *Tur* and the *Shulchan Aruch* (O.C. 110:8). The *Ritva*, though, states that these prayers are optional.

ON LEAVING THE *BEIS HAMIDRASH*, OR, IF ONE IS STUDYING TORAH ALL DAY,
WHEN HE STOPS HIS STUDIES AT NIGHT, ONE RECITES THE FOLLOWING PRAYER:

מוֹדֶה אֲנִי לְפָנֶיךָ יהוה אֱלֹהַי, שֶׁשַּׂמְתָּ חֶלְקִי מִיּוֹשְׁבֵי בֵית

⟨in the⟩ ⟨with those⟩ my ⟨ that You ⟨⟨ my ⟨ Hashem, ⟨ before ⟨ I give thanks
House who dwell portion have placed God, You,

הַמִּדְרָשׁ, וְלֹא שַׂמְתָּ חֶלְקִי מִיּוֹשְׁבֵי קְרָנוֹת, שֶׁאֲנִי מַשְׁכִּים וְהֵם

⟨ and ⟨ arise early ⟨ For I ⟨⟨ [idly] in ⟨ with those ⟨ my ⟨ and You did ⟨ of Study,
they the corners. who sit portion not place

מַשְׁכִּימִים, אֲנִי מַשְׁכִּים לְדִבְרֵי תוֹרָה, וְהֵם מַשְׁכִּימִים

⟨ arise early ⟨ and they ⟨⟨ of Torah, ⟨ for matters ⟨ arise early ⟨ I ⟨⟨ arise early;

לִדְבָרִים בְּטֵלִים, אֲנִי עָמֵל וְהֵם עֲמֵלִים, אֲנִי עָמֵל וּמְקַבֵּל

⟨ and receive ⟨ toil ⟨ I ⟨⟨ toil; ⟨ and they ⟨ toil ⟨ I ⟨⟨ of idleness. ⟨ for matters

שָׂכָר וְהֵם עֲמֵלִים וְאֵינָם מְקַבְּלִים שָׂכָר,* אֲנִי רָץ וְהֵם רָצִים,

⟨⟨ run; ⟨ and ⟨ run ⟨ I ⟨⟨ a reward.* ⟨ receive ⟨ and do not ⟨ toil ⟨ and ⟨⟨ a
they they reward,

אֲנִי רָץ לְחַיֵּי הָעוֹלָם הַבָּא, וְהֵם רָצִים לִבְאֵר שַׁחַת, שֶׁנֶּאֱמַר:

⟨⟨ As is said: ⟨⟨ of ⟨ to the pit ⟨ run ⟨ and ⟨⟨ to ⟨ of the ⟨ to the ⟨ run ⟨ I
destruction. they Come, World life

וְאַתָּה אֱלֹהִים תּוֹרִידֵם לִבְאֵר שַׁחַת, אַנְשֵׁי דָמִים וּמִרְמָה לֹא

⟨ shall ⟨ and ⟨ of blood- ⟨ men ⟨⟨ of ⟨ into the ⟨ You will ⟨ O God, ⟨ And You,
not deceit shed destruction; well lower them

יֶחֱצוּ יְמֵיהֶם, וַאֲנִי אֶבְטַח בָּךְ.[1]

⟨⟨ in ⟨ I will trust ⟨ but as ⟨⟨ their ⟨ live
You. for me, days; out half

---

(1) *Psalms* 55:24.

וְאֵינָם מְקַבְּלִים שָׂכָר — *And do not receive a reward.* The *Chofetz Chaim* (quoted in *Chofetz Chaim al HaTorah, Bechukosai*) asks: Doesn't everyone who works receive pay for his work? The answer, claims the *Chofetz Chaim*, lies in the word *toil*. If a tailor, for example, toils long hours but does not complete the suit he is working on, he has no claim for payment. However, if a Torah student toils hard, but does not succeed in fully understanding the subject he was studying, he still will be rewarded for his toil.

❧ BLESSING AFTER MEALS / ברכת המזון ❧

IT IS CUSTOMARY TO RECITE PSALM 137 BEFORE *BIRCAS HAMAZON* ON THE WEEKDAYS.

עַל נַהֲרוֹת בָּבֶל, שָׁם יָשַׁבְנוּ, גַּם בָּכִינוּ, בְּזָכְרֵנוּ

⟨ when we ⟨⟨ we wept ⟨ and ⟨ we sat ⟨ there ⟨ of ⟨ the rivers ⟨ By
remembered also Babylon,

אֶת צִיּוֹן. עַל עֲרָבִים בְּתוֹכָהּ, תָּלִינוּ כִּנֹּרוֹתֵינוּ. כִּי שָׁם

⟨ there ⟨ For ⟨⟨ our lyres. ⟨ we hung ⟨ within it ⟨ the willows ⟨ On ⟨⟨ Zion.

שְׁאֵלוּנוּ שׁוֹבֵינוּ דִּבְרֵי שִׁיר וְתוֹלָלֵינוּ שִׂמְחָה שִׁירוּ לָנוּ

⟨ for ⟨ Sing ⟨⟨ joyous ⟨ with our lyres ⟨ of ⟨ words ⟨ did our ⟨ request
us music: [playing] song, captors from us

מִשִּׁיר צִיּוֹן. אֵיךְ נָשִׁיר אֶת שִׁיר יהוה, עַל אַדְמַת נֵכָר.

⟨⟨ of an ⟨ the soil ⟨ upon ⟨ of ⟨ the song ⟨ can we ⟨ How ⟨⟨ of ⟨ from
alien [god]? HASHEM sing Zion! the songs

אִם אֶשְׁכָּחֵךְ יְרוּשָׁלָיִם, תִּשְׁכַּח יְמִינִי. תִּדְבַּק לְשׁוֹנִי

⟨ let my ⟨ Adhere ⟨⟨ let my right ⟨ [then] forget ⟨⟨ O Jerusalem, ⟨ I forget you, ⟨ If
tongue hand [its skill].

לְחִכִּי, אִם לֹא אֶזְכְּרֵכִי; אִם לֹא אַעֲלֶה אֶת יְרוּשָׁלַיִם

⟨ Jerusalem ⟨ I fail to elevate ⟨ if ⟨⟨ I fail to remember you, ⟨ if ⟨ to my palate,

עַל רֹאשׁ שִׂמְחָתִי. זְכֹר יהוה לִבְנֵי אֱדוֹם אֵת יוֹם

⟨ the day ⟨ [to repay] the ⟨ HASHEM, ⟨ Remember, ⟨⟨ of my joys. ⟨ the ⟨ above
offspring of Edom, foremost

יְרוּשָׁלָיִם; הָאֹמְרִים עָרוּ עָרוּ, עַד הַיְסוֹד בָּהּ. בַּת בָּבֶל

⟨ of ⟨ O ⟨⟨ of it. ⟨ the very ⟨ to ⟨ Destroy! ⟨ Destroy! ⟨⟨ [to repay] ⟨ of Jerusalem;
Babylon daughter foundation those who say,

הַשְּׁדוּדָה, אַשְׁרֵי שֶׁיְשַׁלֶּם לָךְ אֶת גְּמוּלֵךְ שֶׁגָּמַלְתְּ לָנוּ.

⟨⟨ us. ⟨ for how ⟨ your recompense ⟨ you ⟨ is the one ⟨ praise- ⟨⟨ who has
you treated who repays worthy been violated,

אַשְׁרֵי שֶׁיֹּאחֵז וְנִפֵּץ אֶת עֹלָלַיִךְ אֶל הַסָּלַע.

⟨⟨ the rock. ⟨ against ⟨ your infants ⟨ and dash ⟨ the one who ⟨ Praiseworthy
will clutch will be

❧ ברכת הַמָּזוֹן / BLESSING AFTER MEALS ❧

The commandment to thank God after a meal is of Scriptural origin: וְאָכַלְתָּ וְשָׂבָעְתָּ וּבֵרַכְתָּ אֶת ה׳ אֱלֹהֶיךָ עַל הָאָרֶץ הַטֹּבָה אֲשֶׁר נָתַן לָךְ, *And you shall eat and you shall be satisfied and you shall bless HASHEM, your God, for the good Land that He gave you* (Deuteronomy 8:10). As the verse indicates, the Scriptural requirement applies only when one has eaten his fill — *you shall eat and you shall be satisfied.* From earliest times, however, the Jewish people have undertaken to express their gratitude to God even after a modest meal, provided one had eaten at least as much bread as the volume of an olive [כְּזַיִת].

IT IS CUSTOMARY TO RECITE PSALM 126 BEFORE *BIRCAS HAMAZON* ON THE SABBATH AND FESTIVALS, ON DAYS WHEN *TACHANUN* IS NOT SAID, AND AT FESTIVE MEALS SUCH AS A WEDDING, A *BRIS*, OR A *PIDYON HABEN*.

שִׁיר הַמַּעֲלוֹת; בְּשׁוּב יהוה אֶת שִׁיבַת צִיּוֹן, הָיִינוּ

‹ we will be ‹‹ of ‹ captivity ‹ the ‹ When HASHEM ‹‹ of ascents. ‹ A song
Zion, will return

כְּחֹלְמִים. אָז יִמָּלֵא שְׂחוֹק פִּינוּ, וּלְשׁוֹנֵנוּ רִנָּה; אָז

‹Then ‹‹ with ‹ and our ‹‹ our ‹ with ‹ filled ‹ Then ‹‹ like dreamers.
glad song. tongue mouth, laughter will be

יֹאמְרוּ בַגּוֹיִם: הִגְדִּיל יהוה לַעֲשׂוֹת עִם אֵלֶּה. הִגְדִּיל

‹ Greatly ‹‹ these. ‹ with ‹ done ‹ has HASHEM ‹ Greatly ‹‹ among the ‹ will they
nations, declare

יהוה לַעֲשׂוֹת עִמָּנוּ, הָיִינוּ שְׂמֵחִים. שׁוּבָה יהוה

‹ O HASHEM, ‹ Return, ‹‹ gladdened. ‹ we were ‹‹ with us, ‹ done ‹ has HASHEM

אֶת שְׁבִיתֵנוּ, כַּאֲפִיקִים בַּנֶּגֶב. הַזֹּרְעִים בְּדִמְעָה, בְּרִנָּה

‹ with ‹‹ tearfully, ‹ Those ‹‹ in the ‹ like springs ‹‹ our captivity,
glad song who sow desert.

יִקְצֹרוּ. הָלוֹךְ יֵלֵךְ וּבָכֹה נֹשֵׂא מֶשֶׁךְ הַזָּרַע; בֹּא יָבֹא

‹ he will ‹ but ‹‹ of ‹ the ‹ does he ‹‹ weeping, ‹ he ‹ Walk on, ‹‹ will reap.
return return seeds, measure who carries walks

בְּרִנָּה, נֹשֵׂא אֲלֻמֹּתָיו.

‹‹ of his sheaves. ‹ a bearer ‹‹ in exultation,

There are several opinions regarding the modern equivalent of this Talmudic measurement; they range from one, to one and four-fifths fluid ounces.

The first to compose a text for Blessing After Meals was Moses, whose text is still recited as the first blessing. Although Moses' blessing was composed in gratitude for the *manna* in the Wilderness, it makes no mention of the *manna*. It is equally noteworthy that the commandment of Blessing After Meals (cited above) was given in the context of a general exhortation to Israel that they remember the heavenly food with which God nourished them in the Wilderness. The message seems obvious: When we thank God for giving us food, we are recognizing that there is no intrinsic difference between the *manna* and the livelihood one wrests from the earth through sweat and hard toil; both are gifts from heaven.

שִׁיר הַמַּעֲלוֹת / Psalm 126

This is one of the fifteen psalms (*Psalms* 120-134) known as the *Songs of Ascents*. The "*ascents*" correspond to the fifteen steps leading to the inner courtyard of the Temple. As the procession ascended into the holy area with water for the special service of Succos, the Levites would stand on the steps singing each of the fifteen psalms in turn.

The commentators note that all fifteen psalms refer to Jewish prayers that we may "*ascend*" from exile and return to *Eretz Yisrael* and a rebuilt Temple. R' S. R. *Hirsch* comments that they are like a spiritual ladder of fifteen steps, designed to help a Jew climb out of the misery of oppressive circumstances.

הִנְנִי מוּכָן וּמְזוּמָן לְקַיֵּם מִצְוַת עֲשֵׂה שֶׁל בִּרְכַּת הַמָּזוֹן,

‹‹ Meals, ‹ Blessing ‹ of ‹ the positive ‹ to ‹ and ‹ am ‹ I now
After   commandment   perform ready prepared

שֶׁנֶּאֱמַר: וְאָכַלְתָּ וְשָׂבָעְתָּ, וּבֵרַכְתָּ אֶת יהוה אֱלֹהֶיךָ, עַל

‹ for ‹‹ your God, ‹ HASHEM, ‹ and you ‹ and you shall ‹ And you ‹ for it is said:
                                    shall bless   be satisfied   shall eat

הָאָרֶץ הַטֹּבָה אֲשֶׁר נָתַן לָךְ. ¹ לְשֵׁם יִחוּד קוּדְשָׁא בְּרִיךְ

‹ Blessed ‹‹ of the ‹ of the ‹ For the ‹‹ you. ‹ He gave ‹ which ‹ that is good ‹ the Land
         Holy One, unification   sake

הוּא וּשְׁכִינְתֵּיהּ בִּדְחִילוּ וּרְחִימוּ עַל יְדֵי הַהוּא טָמִיר

‹ Who is ‹ Him ‹ through ‹ and in love, ‹ in awe ‹‹ and His ‹‹ is He,
hidden   Presence,

וְנֶעְלָם בְּשֵׁם כָּל יִשְׂרָאֵל. וִיהִי נֹעַם אֲדֹנָי אֱלֹהֵינוּ

‹ our God, ‹ of the ‹ the ‹ May ‹‹ Israel. ‹ of all ‹ – [I pray] ‹‹ and Who is
        Lord, pleasantness   in the name   inscrutable

עָלֵינוּ וּמַעֲשֵׂה יָדֵינוּ כּוֹנְנָה עָלֵינוּ וּמַעֲשֵׂה יָדֵינוּ כּוֹנְנֵהוּ. ²

‹‹ establish ‹ of our ‹ the work ‹‹ for us; ‹ establish ‹ of our ‹ the work ‹‹ be
it.   hands   hands   upon us;

ZIMUN/INVITATION / זימון

IF THREE OR MORE MALES, AGED THIRTEEN OR OLDER, PARTICIPATE IN A MEAL, A LEADER IS APPOINTED
TO FORMALLY INVITE THE OTHERS TO JOIN HIM IN THE RECITATION OF *BIRCAS HAMAZON.*
WHEN *ZIMUN* IS RECITED, IT IS PREFERABLE FOR THE LEADER TO HOLD A CUP OF WINE (O.C. 182).
(ON CERTAIN OCCASIONS A SPECIAL *ZIMUN* IS RECITED: FOR *SHEVA BERACHOS* SEE PAGE 318;
FOR THE CIRCUMCISION FEAST SEE PAGE 332.) THE REGULAR *ZIMUN* FOLLOWS.

רַבּוֹתַי מִיר וֶועלֶן בֶּענְטְשֶׁען [רַבּוֹתַי נְבָרֵךְ]. – Leader

‹‹ [let us bless. ‹ Gentlemen,] ‹‹ bless. ‹ let us ‹ Gentlemen,

יְהִי שֵׁם יהוה מְבֹרָךְ מֵעַתָּה וְעַד עוֹלָם. ³ – Others

‹‹ eternity. ‹ until ‹ from this time ‹ be blessed ‹ of HASHEM ‹ the Name ‹ Let

יְהִי שֵׁם יהוה מְבֹרָךְ* מֵעַתָּה וְעַד עוֹלָם. ³ – Leader

‹‹ eternity. ‹ until ‹ from this time ‹ be blessed* ‹ of HASHEM ‹ the Name ‹ Let

---

(1) *Deuteronomy* 8:10. (2) *Psalms* 90:17. (3) 113:2.

⋄§ זימון / Zimun (Invitation)

The word *zimun* connotes both *invitation* and *presentation.* When three or more people eat together, one *invites* the others to respond to his praise of God; and all of them jointly are required to *present themselves* as a group to come together in praise of God (based on

Berachos 49b).

יְהִי שֵׁם ה׳ מְבֹרָךְ — *Let the Name of HASHEM be blessed.* The leader, too, repeats the blessings because it would be improper and even sacrilegious for him to ask others to bless God while he, being part of the group, refrains from joining them (*Rashba*).

IF TEN MEN JOIN IN THE *ZIMUN*, AMONG WHOM AT LEAST SEVEN ATE BREAD,
ADD GOD'S NAME (IN PARENTHESES).

בִּרְשׁוּת* מָרָנָן וְרַבָּנָן וְרַבּוֹתַי, נְבָרֵךְ (אֱלֹהֵינוּ)

⟨ (our God,) ⟨ let us bless* ⟨ and ⟨ and ⟨ of the distin- ⟨ With the
[Him,] gentlemen, rabbis guished people permission*

שֶׁאָכַלְנוּ מִשֶּׁלוֹ.

≪ of what ⟨ for we
is His. have eaten.

בָּרוּךְ (אֱלֹהֵינוּ) שֶׁאָכַלְנוּ מִשֶּׁלוֹ וּבְטוּבוֹ חָיִינוּ. — Others

≪ we ⟨ and through ⟨ of what ⟨ for we ⟨ (our God,) ⟨ Blessed
live. His goodness is His have eaten is [He,]

THOSE WHO HAVE NOT EATEN RESPOND:

בָּרוּךְ (אֱלֹהֵינוּ) וּמְבֹרָךְ שְׁמוֹ תָּמִיד לְעוֹלָם וָעֶד.

≪ and ⟨ for ever ⟨ continuously, ⟨ is His ⟨ and ⟨ (our God,) ⟨ Blessed
ever. Name blessed is [He,]

בָּרוּךְ (אֱלֹהֵינוּ) שֶׁאָכַלְנוּ מִשֶּׁלוֹ וּבְטוּבוֹ חָיִינוּ. — Leader

≪ we ⟨ and through ⟨ of what ⟨ for we ⟨ (our God,) ⟨ Blessed
live. His goodness is His have eaten is [He,]

(בָּרוּךְ הוּא וּבָרוּךְ שְׁמוֹ.)

≪ is His Name.) ⟨ and Blessed ⟨ is He ⟨ (Blessed

THE *ZIMUN* LEADER RECITES THE BLESSING AFTER MEALS (AT LEAST THE FIRST BLESSING AND THE
CONCLUSION OF THE OTHERS) ALOUD. ASIDE FROM RESPONDING AMEN AT THE CONCLUSION OF
EACH BLESSING, IT IS FORBIDDEN TO INTERRUPT THE BLESSING AFTER MEALS FOR ANY RESPONSE
OTHER THAN THOSE PERMITTED DURING THE *SHEMA*.

FIRST BLESSING: FOR THE NOURISHMENT / הברכה הראשונה – ברכת הזן

בָּרוּךְ אַתָּה יהוה אֱלֹהֵינוּ מֶלֶךְ הָעוֹלָם,

≪ of the universe, ⟨ King ⟨ our God, ⟨ HASHEM, ⟨ are You, ⟨ Blessed

---

בִּרְשׁוּת — *With the permission.* Since one of the group assumes the privilege of leading them all in the recitation, he requests their permission.

נְבָרֵךְ — *Let us bless.* A commandment done by an individual cannot be compared to one done by a group. When three recite *Bircas HaMazon* together, they say נְבָרֵךְ, *let us bless*; ten men say, נְבָרֵךְ אֱלֹהֵינוּ, *let us bless our God* ... (*Berachos* 49b; see also *Rashi, Leviticus* 26:8). When many people unite to do God's will, each individual in the group reaches a far higher level than he would have had he acted alone, no matter how meritoriously he had acted (*Chofetz Chaim*).

⧉ הַבְּרָכָה הָרִאשׁוֹנָה – בִּרְכַּת הַזָּן /
First Blessing: For the Nourishment

Bircas HaMazon comprises four blessings, of which the first three are Scripturally ordained and the fourth was instituted by the Sages. The first blessing was, as noted above, composed by Moses in gratitude for the manna with which God sustained Israel daily in the Wilderness (*Berachos* 48b). For that reason it precedes נוֹדֶה, *the Blessing for the Land*, even though it might seem more logical to thank God first for the land that produces food (*Bayis Chadash*).

הַזָּן אֶת הָעוֹלָם כֻּלּוֹ, בְּטוּבוֹ, בְּחֵן בְּחֶסֶד

‹ with kindness, ‹ — with grace, ≪ in His goodness ‹ all of it, ‹ the world, ‹ Who nourishes

וּבְרַחֲמִים, הוּא נוֹתֵן לֶחֶם לְכָל בָּשָׂר, כִּי

‹ for ≪ flesh, ‹ to all ‹ food ‹ gives ‹ He ≪ and with compassion.

לְעוֹלָם חַסְדּוֹ.¹ וּבְטוּבוֹ הַגָּדוֹל, תָּמִיד לֹא

‹ never ‹ that is great, ‹ And through His goodness ≪ is His kindness. ‹ forever

חָסַר לָנוּ, וְאַל יֶחְסַר לָנוּ* מָזוֹן לְעוֹלָם וָעֶד.

≪ and ever. ‹ for ever ‹ nourishment, ‹ may we lack,* ‹ and never ‹ have we lacked,

בַּעֲבוּר שְׁמוֹ הַגָּדוֹל,* כִּי הוּא אֵל זָן וּמְפַרְנֵס*

‹ and sustains* ‹ Who nourishes ‹ is ‹ He ‹ because ≪ that is great,* ‹ of His Name ‹ For the sake

לַכֹּל, וּמֵטִיב* לַכֹּל, וּמֵכִין מָזוֹן לְכָל בְּרִיּוֹתָיו

‹ of His creatures ‹ for all ‹ nourishment ‹ and He ≪ all, ‹ and benefits* ‹ all,
prepares

אֲשֶׁר בָּרָא. כָּאָמוּר: פּוֹתֵחַ אֶת יָדֶךָ, וּמַשְׂבִּיעַ

‹ and satisfy ≪ Your hand, ‹ You open ≪ As it is said, ≪ He has created. ‹ which

לְכָל חַי רָצוֹן.² ❖ בָּרוּךְ אַתָּה יהוה, הַזָּן

‹ Who nourishes ≪ HASHEM, ‹ are You, ‹ Blessed ≪ [with its] desire. ‹ living thing ‹ every

(אָמֵן.) — Others)

≪ (Amen.)

אֶת הַכֹּל.

≪ all.

(1) *Psalms* 136:25. (2) 145:16.

תָּמִיד לֹא חָסַר לָנוּ וְאַל יֶחְסַר לָנוּ — *Never have we lacked, and never may we lack.* The subject of the sentence is מָזוֹן, *nourishment,* and the verse expresses the prayer that just as food was never lacking in the Wilderness, may it never be lacking in the future (*Etz Yosef*).

בַּעֲבוּר שְׁמוֹ הַגָּדוֹל — *For the sake of His Name that is great.* We declare that the motive for our request for eternally abundant food is but for

the sake of *His Name that is great* so that we may be better able to serve Him; and we bless Him *because...*

זָן וּמְפַרְנֵס ... וּמֵטִיב — *Who nourishes and sustains...benefits.* זָן, *nourishes,* refers to food; מְפַרְנֵס, *sustains,* refers to clothing; מֵטִיב, *bene-fits,* refers to shelter. In conjunction, the three phrases enumerate the basic needs of life, all of which are provided by God (*Etz Yosef*).

SECOND BLESSING: FOR THE LAND / בִּרְכַּת הָאָרֶץ – הַבְּרָכָה הַשְּׁנִיָּה

נוֹדֶה לְךָ יהוה אֱלֹהֵינוּ, עַל שֶׁהִנְחַלְתָּ
We thank › You, ‹ HASHEM, ‹ our God, ‹ because ‹ You have given as a heritage

לַאֲבוֹתֵינוּ* אֶרֶץ חֶמְדָּה טוֹבָה וּרְחָבָה.* וְעַל
to our forefathers* › a Land, ‹ desirable, ‹ good, ‹ and spacious;* ‹ because

שֶׁהוֹצֵאתָנוּ יהוה אֱלֹהֵינוּ מֵאֶרֶץ מִצְרַיִם,
You brought us out, › HASHEM, ‹ our God, ‹ from the land ‹ of Egypt

וּפְדִיתָנוּ מִבֵּית עֲבָדִים, וְעַל בְּרִיתְךָ שֶׁחָתַמְתָּ
and You redeemed us › from the house ‹ of bondage; ‹ for ‹ Your covenant ‹ which You sealed

בִּבְשָׂרֵנוּ,* וְעַל תּוֹרָתְךָ שֶׁלִּמַּדְתָּנוּ, וְעַל חֻקֶּיךָ
in our flesh;* › Your Torah ‹ for ‹ which You taught us ‹ and for ‹ Your statutes

שֶׁהוֹדַעְתָּנוּ, וְעַל חַיִּים חֵן וָחֶסֶד שֶׁחוֹנַנְתָּנוּ,
which You made known to us; › for ‹ life, ‹ grace, ‹ and lovingkindness ‹ which You granted us;

וְעַל אֲכִילַת מָזוֹן שָׁאַתָּה זָן וּמְפַרְנֵס אוֹתָנוּ
and for › [our] eating ‹ of the food ‹ with which You ‹ nourish ‹ and sustain ‹ us

תָּמִיד, בְּכָל יוֹם וּבְכָל עֵת וּבְכָל שָׁעָה.
constantly, › every ‹ day, ‹ in every ‹ time, ‹ and in every ‹ hour.

/ הַבְּרָכָה הַשְּׁנִיָּה – בִּרְכַּת הָאָרֶץ
Second Blessing: For the Land

The second blessing was also ordained by the Torah [*Deut.* 8:10, see *Overview* to ArtScroll *Bircas HaMazon*] and formulated by Joshua (*Berachos* 48a). He saw how deeply Moses desired to enter *Eretz Yisrael*, and how eager the Patriarchs were to be buried there. When Joshua was privileged to enter *Eretz Yisrael*, he composed this blessing in honor of the Land (*Shibbolei HaLeket*).

The blessing begins and ends with thanks. The expression of gratitude refers to each of the enumerated items: the Land, the Exodus, the covenant, the Torah, the statutes, life, grace, kindness, and food.

שֶׁהִנְחַלְתָּ לַאֲבוֹתֵינוּ — *You have given as a heritage to our forefathers.* Eretz Yisrael is referred to as נַחֲלָה, *a heritage,* implying that it remains eternally our inheritance. Thus, the long exile means only that God has denied us access in punishment for our sins, not that it has ceased to be ours.

חֶמְדָּה טוֹבָה וּרְחָבָה — *Desirable, good, and spacious.* Whoever does not say that the Land is *desirable, good, and spacious* has not properly fulfilled his obligation [of *Bircas HaMazon*] (*Berachos* 48b), because once the Torah required that the Land be mentioned, the Sages decreed that its praises should likewise be enumerated (*Talmidei R' Yonah*).

וְעַל בְּרִיתְךָ שֶׁחָתַמְתָּ בִּבְשָׂרֵנוּ — *For Your covenant*

ON CHANUKAH AND PURIM ADD THE FOLLOWING.

(וּ)עַל הַנִּסִּים, וְעַל הַפֻּרְקָן, וְעַל הַגְּבוּרוֹת, וְעַל

< and for < the mighty deeds, < and for < the salvation, < and for < the miracles, < (And) for

הַתְּשׁוּעוֹת, וְעַל הַנִּפְלָאוֹת, וְעַל הַנֶּחָמוֹת, וְעַל הַמִּלְחָמוֹת,

< the battles < and for < the consolations, < and for < the wonders, < and for < the victories,

שֶׁעָשִׂיתָ לַאֲבוֹתֵינוּ בַּיָּמִים הָהֵם בַּזְּמַן הַזֶּה.

« at this time: < in those days, « for our < that You
forefathers performed

ON CHANUKAH:

בִּימֵי מַתִּתְיָהוּ בֶּן יוֹחָנָן כֹּהֵן גָּדוֹל חַשְׁמוֹנָאִי וּבָנָיו,

« and his « the < the High Priest, < of < the « of < In the
sons, Hasmonean, Yochanan, son Mattisyahu, days

כְּשֶׁעָמְדָה מַלְכוּת יָוָן הָרְשָׁעָה עַל עַמְּךָ יִשְׂרָאֵל, לְהַשְׁכִּיחָם

< to make « Israel, < Your < against «—which was « of < did the < when rise up
them forget people wicked— Greece kingdom

תּוֹרָתֶךָ, וּלְהַעֲבִירָם מֵחֻקֵּי רְצוֹנֶךָ. וְאַתָּה בְּרַחֲמֶיךָ

< in Your < But You « of Your Will. < from the < and to compel « Your
compassion statutes them to stray Torah

הָרַבִּים, עָמַדְתָּ לָהֶם בְּעֵת צָרָתָם, רַבְתָּ אֶת רִיבָם, דַּנְתָּ

< judged < their cause, < You « of their < in the < for < stood up « which is
championed distress. time them abundant

אֶת דִּינָם, נָקַמְתָּ אֶת נִקְמָתָם.[1] מָסַרְתָּ גִבּוֹרִים בְּיַד חַלָּשִׁים,

« of the < into the < the strong < You « their wrong. < and You « their claim,
weak, hands delivered avenged

וְרַבִּים בְּיַד מְעַטִּים, וּטְמֵאִים בְּיַד טְהוֹרִים, וּרְשָׁעִים בְּיַד

< into the < the wicked « of the pure, < into the < the impure « of the few, < into the < the
hands hands many

צַדִּיקִים, וְזֵדִים בְּיַד עוֹסְקֵי תוֹרָתֶךָ. וּלְךָ עָשִׂיתָ שֵׁם גָּדוֹל

< that < a < You < For « of Your < of the < into the < and the « of the
is great Name made Yourself Torah. diligent hands willful righteous,
students sinners

וְקָדוֹשׁ בְּעוֹלָמֶךָ, וּלְעַמְּךָ יִשְׂרָאֵל עָשִׂיתָ תְּשׁוּעָה גְדוֹלָה[2]

< of great < a victory < You < Israel < and for « in Your < and holy
magnitude performed Your people world,

---

(1) Cf. *Jeremiah* 51:36. (2) Cf. *I Samuel* 19:5.

which You sealed in our flesh. The reference is to circumcision, of which the Sages required mention in the blessing of the Land (*Berachos* 48b) because the Land was promised to Abraham in

the merit of circumcision (*Genesis* 17:7-8).

Women are not subject to the commandments of circumcision and Torah study. Nevertheless, women do say, *For Your covenant which You*

וּפֻרְקָן כְּהַיּוֹם הַזֶּה. וְאַחַר כֵּן בָּאוּ בָנֶיךָ לִדְבִיר בֵּיתֶךָ,

< of Your < to the Holy < Your < came < Thereafter, ≪ as this very day. < and a
House, of Holies children   salvation

וּפִנּוּ אֶת הֵיכָלֶךָ, וְטִהֲרוּ אֶת מִקְדָּשֶׁךָ, וְהִדְלִיקוּ נֵרוֹת

< lights < and kindled ≪ Your holy site, < purified ≪ Your Temple, < cleansed

בְּחַצְרוֹת קָדְשֶׁךָ, וְקָבְעוּ שְׁמוֹנַת יְמֵי חֲנֻכָּה אֵלּוּ,

≪—these— ≪ of < days < the eight < and they < of Your < in the
Chanukah   established Sanctuary; Courtyards

לְהוֹדוֹת וּלְהַלֵּל לְשִׁמְךָ הַגָּדוֹל.

≪ that is great. < to Your < and praise < to express
Name   thanks

ON PURIM:

בִּימֵי מָרְדְּכַי וְאֶסְתֵּר בְּשׁוּשַׁן הַבִּירָה, כְּשֶׁעָמַד עֲלֵיהֶם

< against < when ≪ the capital, < in < and < of < In the
them   rise up   Shushan, Esther, Mordechai days

הָמָן הָרָשָׁע, בִּקֵּשׁ לְהַשְׁמִיד לַהֲרֹג וּלְאַבֵּד אֶת כָּל הַיְּהוּדִים,

< the Jews, < all < and to < to slay, < to destroy, < he ≪ the < did
exterminate   sought   wicked, Haman,

מִנַּעַר וְעַד זָקֵן, טַף וְנָשִׁים בְּיוֹם אֶחָד, בִּשְׁלוֹשָׁה עָשָׂר

< on the thirteenth [day] < on the same day, ≪ and < infants ≪ old, < to < from
women,   young

לְחֹדֶשׁ שְׁנֵים עָשָׂר, הוּא חֹדֶשׁ אֲדָר, וּשְׁלָלָם לָבוֹז.¹

≪ to be < and their ≪ of Adar, < the < which ≪ twelve < of month
plundered. possessions   month   is

וְאַתָּה בְּרַחֲמֶיךָ הָרַבִּים הֵפַרְתָּ אֶת עֲצָתוֹ, וְקִלְקַלְתָּ

< and ≪ his counsel, < nullified ≪ which is < in Your mercy < But You,
frustrated   abundant,

אֶת מַחֲשַׁבְתּוֹ, וַהֲשֵׁבוֹתָ לוֹ גְּמוּלוֹ בְּרֹאשׁוֹ, וְתָלוּ אוֹתוֹ

< him < and they ≪ upon his < his < to < and ≪ his intention,
hanged   own head, recompense him returned

וְאֶת בָּנָיו עַל הָעֵץ.

≪ the gallows. < on < and his sons

---

(1) *Esther* 3:13.

sealed in our flesh; for Your Torah which You taught us. Magen Avraham explains that since women do not require circumcision, they are considered as equivalent to circumcised men in this regard; and since women must study the laws of those commandments that are applicable to them, they have a share in the study of Torah.

וְעַל הַכֹּל, יהוה אֱלֹהֵינוּ, אֲנַחְנוּ מוֹדִים לָךְ

⟨ You ⟨ thank ⟨ we ⟨ our God, ⟨ HASHEM, ⟨ everything, ⟨ For

וּמְבָרְכִים אוֹתָךְ, יִתְבָּרַךְ שִׁמְךָ בְּפִי כָּל חַי

⟨ the ⟨ of ⟨ by the ⟨ may Your ⟨ Blessed ⟨ You. ⟨ and bless
living, all mouth Name be

תָּמִיד לְעוֹלָם וָעֶד. כַּכָּתוּב, וְאָכַלְתָּ וְשָׂבָעְתָּ,

⟨ and you shall ⟨ And you ⟨ As it is ⟨ and ever. ⟨ for ever ⟨ continuously
be satisfied shall eat written:

וּבֵרַכְתָּ אֶת יהוה אֱלֹהֶיךָ, עַל הָאָרֶץ הַטֹּבָה

⟨ that is ⟨ the Land ⟨ for ⟨ your God, ⟨ HASHEM, ⟨ and you
good shall bless

אֲשֶׁר נָתַן לָךְ.¹ ❖ בָּרוּךְ אַתָּה יהוה, עַל הָאָרֶץ

⟨ the Land ⟨ for ⟨ HASHEM, ⟨ are You, ⟨ Blessed ⟨ you. ⟨ He gave ⟨ which

וְעַל הַמָּזוֹן. (אָמֵן – Others)

⟨ (Amen.) ⟨ the nourishment. ⟨ and for

THIRD BLESSING: FOR JERUSALEM / הַבְּרָכָה הַשְּׁלִישִׁית – בּוֹנֵה יְרוּשָׁלַיִם

רַחֵם נָא יהוה אֱלֹהֵינוּ עַל יִשְׂרָאֵל עַמֶּךָ,

⟨ Your people; ⟨ Israel ⟨ on ⟨ our God, ⟨ HASHEM, ⟨ we beg You ⟨ Have mercy,

וְעַל יְרוּשָׁלַיִם עִירֶךָ, וְעַל צִיּוֹן מִשְׁכַּן כְּבוֹדֶךָ,

⟨ of Your ⟨ the resting ⟨ Zion, ⟨ on ⟨ Your City; ⟨ Jerusalem, ⟨ on
Glory; place

---

(1) *Deuteronomy* 8:10.

◆§ הַבְּרָכָה הַשְּׁלִישִׁית – בּוֹנֵה יְרוּשָׁלַיִם / **Third Blessing: For Jerusalem**

This blessing is the final one required by the Torah. It was composed by David and Solomon.

David, who conquered Jerusalem, referred to *Israel, Your people,* and *Jerusalem, Your City.* After the Temple was built, Solomon added, *the House, great and holy* (*Berachos* 48b).

◆§ If One Forgot to Recite עַל הַנִּסִּים on Chanukah and Purim

If one realized his error before reaching the Name HASHEM at the end of this blessing (בָּרוּךְ אַתָּה ה', *Blessed are You, HASHEM*) he should go back to עַל הַנִּסִּים and continue from there.

If he has already recited the phrase בָּרוּךְ אַתָּה ה', *Blessed are You, HASHEM,* he continues to recite *Bircas HaMazon* until reaching the series of seasonal prayers which begin הָרַחֲמָן, *The compassionate One* (p. 308), and rectifies the omission as indicated there. If the omission is not discovered until after that point, nothing need be done.

וְעַל מַלְכוּת בֵּית דָּוִד מְשִׁיחֶךָ,* וְעַל הַבַּיִת

‹ the ‹ and on ‹‹ Your anointed;* ‹ of David, ‹ of the ‹ on the monarchy
House, House

הַגָּדוֹל וְהַקָּדוֹשׁ שֶׁנִּקְרָא שִׁמְךָ עָלָיו. אֱלֹהֵינוּ

‹ Our God, ‹‹ upon which Your Name is called. ‹ and holy, ‹ great

אָבִינוּ, רְעֵנוּ זוּנֵנוּ פַּרְנְסֵנוּ וְכַלְכְּלֵנוּ וְהַרְוִיחֵנוּ,

‹ relieve us, ‹ support us, ‹ sustain us, ‹ nourish ‹ — tend ‹‹ our Father
us, us,

וְהַרְוַח לָנוּ יהוה אֱלֹהֵינוּ מְהֵרָה מִכָּל

‹ from all ‹ speedily, ‹ our God, ‹ HASHEM, ‹ to us, ‹ and
grant relief

צָרוֹתֵינוּ. וְנָא אַל תַּצְרִיכֵנוּ* יהוה אֱלֹהֵינוּ,

‹‹ our God — ‹ — HASHEM, ‹‹ make us dependent* ‹ do not ‹ Please, ‹‹ our troubles.

לֹא לִידֵי מַתְּנַת בָּשָׂר וָדָם,* וְלֹא לִידֵי

‹ upon ‹ nor ‹ and blood* ‹ of flesh ‹ the gifts ‹ upon ‹ neither

הַלְוָאָתָם, כִּי אִם לְיָדְךָ הַמְּלֵאָה הַפְּתוּחָה

‹ open, ‹ that is full, ‹ upon Your Hand ‹ but only ‹‹ their loans,

הַקְּדוֹשָׁה וְהָרְחָבָה, שֶׁלֹּא נֵבוֹשׁ וְלֹא נִכָּלֵם

‹ be humiliated ‹ nor ‹ be ashamed ‹ that we not ‹‹ and generous, ‹ holy,

לְעוֹלָם וָעֶד.

‹‹ and ever. ‹ for ever

As composed by David and Solomon, the blessing was a prayer that God maintain the tranquility of the Land. Following the destruction and exile, the blessing was changed to embody a prayer for the return of the Land, the Temple, and the Davidic dynasty. Before David's conquest of Jerusalem, the blessing had yet another form (*Tur*), a request for God's mercy upon the nation (*Aruch HaShulchan*).

וְעַל מַלְכוּת בֵּית דָּוִד מְשִׁיחֶךָ — *On the monarchy of the house of David, Your anointed.* It is mandatory that the monarchy of David's dynasty be mentioned in this blessing. Whoever has not mentioned it has not fulfilled his obligation

(*Berachos* 49a), because it was David who sanctified Jerusalem (*Rashi*), and because the consolation for the exile will not be complete until David's kingdom is restored (*Rambam*).

וְנָא אַל תַּצְרִיכֵנוּ . . . לִידֵי מַתְּנַת בָּשָׂר וָדָם — *Please, do not make us dependent . . . upon the gifts of flesh and blood,* do not make us dependent upon others. The firm believer knows that God's blessing will come inevitably without requiring him to beg for favors. Therefore, if one feels compelled by the need to seek the help of others, his faith can be eroded. Thus we pray to God not to test us in this manner (*Olas Tamid*).

ON THE SABBATH ADD THE FOLLOWING. [IF FORGOTTEN, SEE BELOW.]

רְצֵה וְהַחֲלִיצֵנוּ יהוה אֱלֹהֵינוּ בְּמִצְוֹתֶיךָ, וּבְמִצְוַת

⟨ and through the ⟨ through Your ⟨ our God, ⟨ HASHEM, ⟨ to give us rest, ⟨ May it be
commandment commandments pleasing to You

יוֹם הַשְּׁבִיעִי הַשַּׁבָּת הַגָּדוֹל וְהַקָּדוֹשׁ הַזֶּה, כִּי יוֹם זֶה

⟨ this day, ⟨ For ⟨⟨ – this ⟨⟨ and holy ⟨ that is great ⟨ the ⟨ of the
one. Sabbath Seventh Day,

גָּדוֹל וְקָדוֹשׁ הוּא לְפָנֶיךָ, לִשְׁבָּת בּוֹ וְלָנוּחַ בּוֹ בְּאַהֲבָה

⟨⟨ in love, ⟨ on it, ⟨ and to ⟨ on it ⟨ to cease ⟨⟨ before ⟨ it is ⟨ and holy ⟨ great
rest work You,

כְּמִצְוַת רְצוֹנֶךָ, וּבִרְצוֹנְךָ הָנִיחַ לָנוּ יהוה אֱלֹהֵינוּ,

⟨⟨ our God, ⟨ HASHEM, ⟨⟨ to us, ⟨ grant rest ⟨ And through ⟨⟨ by Your will. ⟨ as ordained
Your will,

שֶׁלֹּא תְהֵא צָרָה וְיָגוֹן וַאֲנָחָה בְּיוֹם מְנוּחָתֵנוּ, וְהַרְאֵנוּ

⟨ And ⟨⟨ of our rest. ⟨ on this ⟨ or lament ⟨ grief, ⟨ any ⟨ be ⟨ that there
show us, day distress, should not

יהוה אֱלֹהֵינוּ בְּנֶחָמַת צִיּוֹן עִירֶךָ, וּבְבִנְיַן יְרוּשָׁלַיִם

⟨ of Jerusalem, ⟨ and the ⟨⟨ Your City, ⟨ of Zion, ⟨ the ⟨ our God, ⟨ HASHEM,
rebuilding consolation

עִיר קָדְשֶׁךָ, כִּי אַתָּה הוּא בַּעַל הַיְשׁוּעוֹת וּבַעַל הַנֶּחָמוֹת.

⟨⟨ of ⟨ and ⟨ of salvations ⟨ Master ⟨ Who ⟨ it is ⟨ for ⟨⟨ of Your ⟨ City
consolations. Master are You holiness,

⤐§ If One Omitted יַעֲלֶה וְיָבֹא or רְצֵה

(a) If he realizes his omission after having recited the blessing of בּוֹנֵה, Who rebuilds, he makes up for the omission by reciting the appropriate Compensatory Blessing (pp. 310-312).

(b) If he realizes his omission after having recited the first six words of the fourth blessing, he may still switch immediately into the Compensatory Blessing since the words בָּרוּךְ אַתָּה . . . הָעוֹלָם are identical in both blessings. (However, the Compensatory Blessing need not be recited after the third Sabbath meal if *Bircas HaMazon* is recited after sunset.)

(c) If the omission is discovered after having recited the word הָאֵל, *the Almighty,* of the fourth blessing, it is too late for the Compensatory Blessing to be recited. In that case:

(i) On the Sabbath and on a Festival day, at the first two meals *Bircas HaMazon* must be repeated in its entirety; at the third meal, nothing need be done.

(ii) On Rosh Chodesh and on Chol HaMoed, nothing need be done except if the day fell on the Sabbath and רְצֵה, *Retzei,* was omitted. In that case, at the first two meals *Bircas HaMazon* must be repeated. But if רְצֵה was recited and יַעֲלֶה וְיָבֹא was omitted, nothing need be done.

ON ROSH CHODESH, CHOL HAMOED, AND FESTIVALS ADD. [IF FORGOTTEN, SEE P. 301.]

אֱלֹהֵינוּ וֵאלֹהֵי אֲבוֹתֵינוּ, יַעֲלֶה, וְיָבֹא, וְיַגִּיעַ, וְיֵרָאֶה,

⟨ be noted, ⟨ reach, ⟨ come, ⟨ may ⟪ of our ⟨ and the ⟨ Our God
there rise, forefathers, God

וְיֵרָצֶה, וְיִשָּׁמַע, וְיִפָּקֵד, וְיִזָּכֵר זִכְרוֹנֵנוּ וּפִקְדוֹנֵנוּ, וְזִכְרוֹן

⟨ the ⟪ and ⟨ – the ⟪ and be ⟨ be ⟨ be heard, ⟨ be
remem- consideration remembrance remembered considered, favored,
brance of us; of us

אֲבוֹתֵינוּ, וְזִכְרוֹן מָשִׁיחַ בֶּן דָּוִד עַבְדֶּךָ, וְזִכְרוֹן יְרוּשָׁלַיִם

⟨ of Jerusalem, ⟨ the ⟪ Your ⟨ of ⟨ son ⟨ of ⟨ the ⟪ of our
remembrance servant; David, Messiah, remembrance forefathers;

עִיר קָדְשֶׁךָ, וְזִכְרוֹן כָּל עַמְּךָ בֵּית יִשְׂרָאֵל לְפָנֶיךָ, לִפְלֵיטָה

⟨ for ⟨ before ⟪ of ⟨ the ⟨ of Your ⟨ and the ⟪ of Your ⟨ the
deliverance, You Israel – Family entire people remembrance holiness; City

לְטוֹבָה לְחֵן וּלְחֶסֶד וּלְרַחֲמִים, לְחַיִּים (טוֹבִים) וּלְשָׁלוֹם בְּיוֹם

⟨ on the ⟪ and for ⟨ (that is ⟨ for life ⟨ and for ⟨ for ⟨ for ⟨ for
day of peace, good), compassion, kindness, grace, goodness,

SHAVUOS:	PESACH:	ROSH CHODESH:
חַג הַשָּׁבֻעוֹת	חַג הַמַּצּוֹת	רֹאשׁ הַחֹדֶשׁ
⟪ of Shavuos ⟨ the Festival	⟪ of Matzos ⟨ the Festival	⟪ Moon ⟨ the New

SHEMINI ATZERES / SIMCHAS TORAH:	SUCCOS:	ROSH HASHANAH:
שְׁמִינִי עֲצֶרֶת הַחַג	חַג הַסֻּכּוֹת	הַזִּכָּרוֹן
⟪ Festival ⟨ the Shemini Atzeres	⟪ of Succos ⟨ the Festival	⟪ Remembrance

הַזֶּה. זָכְרֵנוּ יהוה אֱלֹהֵינוּ בּוֹ לְטוֹבָה, וּפָקְדֵנוּ בוֹ לִבְרָכָה,

⟪ for ⟨ on ⟨ consider ⟪ for ⟨ on ⟨ our God, ⟨ HASHEM, ⟨ Remember ⟪ – this.
blessing; it us goodness; it us

וְהוֹשִׁיעֵנוּ בוֹ לְחַיִּים טוֹבִים. וּבִדְבַר יְשׁוּעָה וְרַחֲמִים, חוּס

⟨ have ⟪ and com- ⟨ of ⟨ In the ⟪ that is ⟨ for life ⟨ on it ⟨ and save us
pity, passion, salvation matter good.

וְחָנֵּנוּ וְרַחֵם עָלֵינוּ וְהוֹשִׁיעֵנוּ, כִּי אֵלֶיךָ עֵינֵינוּ, כִּי אֵל

⟨ God, ⟨ be- ⟪ are our eyes ⟨ to ⟨ for ⟪ and save us, ⟨ with us, ⟨ and be com- ⟨ be
cause, [turned], You passionate gracious,

מֶלֶךְ חַנּוּן וְרַחוּם אָתָּה.[1]

⟪ are You. ⟨ and com- ⟨ Who is ⟨ King,
passionate gracious

(1) Cf. Nehemiah 9:31.

וּבְנֵה ✦ יְרוּשָׁלַיִם* עִיר הַקֹּדֶשׁ בִּמְהֵרָה
‹ soon ‹ of holiness, ‹ the City ‹ Jerusalem,* ‹ Rebuild

בְיָמֵינוּ. בָּרוּךְ אַתָּה יהוה, בּוֹנֵה בְרַחֲמָיו
‹ in His mercy ‹ Who rebuilds ≪ Hashem, ‹ are You, ‹ Blessed ≪ in our days.

(אָמֵן. – Others) יְרוּשָׁלָיִם. אָמֵן.*
≪ (Amen.) ≪ Amen.* ≪ Jerusalem.

[WHEN REQUIRED, THE COMPENSATORY BLESSING (PP. 310-312) IS RECITED HERE.]

FOURTH BLESSING: GOD'S GOODNESS / הַבְּרָכָה הָרְבִיעִית – הַטּוֹב וְהַמֵּטִיב

בָּרוּךְ אַתָּה יהוה אֱלֹהֵינוּ מֶלֶךְ הָעוֹלָם,
≪ of the universe, ‹ King ‹ our God, ‹ Hashem, ‹ are You, ‹ Blessed

הָאֵל אָבִינוּ מַלְכֵּנוּ אַדִּירֵנוּ בּוֹרְאֵנוּ גּוֹאֲלֵנוּ
‹ our Redeemer, ‹ our Creator, ‹ our Sovereign, ‹ our King, ‹ our Father, ‹ the Almighty,

יוֹצְרֵנוּ קְדוֹשֵׁנוּ קְדוֹשׁ יַעֲקֹב, רוֹעֵנוּ רוֹעֵה
‹ the ‹ our ≪ of Jacob, ‹ Holy One ‹ our Holy One, ‹ our Maker,
Shepherd Shepherd,

יִשְׂרָאֵל, הַמֶּלֶךְ הַטּוֹב וְהַמֵּטִיב לַכֹּל, שֶׁבְּכָל
‹ For, every ≪ for all. ‹ and Who does good ‹ Who is good ‹ the King ≪ of Israel,

יוֹם וָיוֹם* הוּא הֵטִיב, הוּא מֵטִיב, הוּא יֵיטִיב
‹ will do good ‹ and He ‹ does good, ‹ He ‹ did good, ‹ He ‹ after day* ‹ day

וּבְנֵה יְרוּשָׁלַיִם — *Rebuild Jerusalem.* This concludes the third blessing, and returns to the theme with which the blessing began — a plea for God's mercy on Jerusalem (*Pesachim* 104a).

אָמֵן — *Amen.* This blessing is unique in that one responds "Amen" after his own blessing. This unusual formula serves as a demarcation between the first three blessings, which are ordained by the Torah, and the next blessing, which is Rabbinic in origin (*Berachos* 45b; *Rambam; Tur*). Since the word Amen is not part of the actual blessing, there should be a slight pause before it is said.

הַבְּרָכָה הָרְבִיעִית – הַטּוֹב וְהַמֵּטִיב /
Fourth Blessing: For God's Goodness

The essence of this blessing is the phrase הַטּוֹב וְהַמֵּטִיב, *Who is good and Who does good.* The court of Rabban Gamliel the Elder in Yavneh composed this blessing in gratitude to God for preserving the bodies of the victims of the Roman massacre at Beitar, and for eventually allowing them to be brought to burial (*Berachos* 48b).

שֶׁבְּכָל יוֹם וָיוֹם — *For, every day after day.* It is insufficient to thank God for His graciousness to *past* generations. We must be conscious of the fact that His goodness and bounty occur constantly.

לָנוּ. הוּא גְמָלָנוּ הוּא גּוֹמְלֵנוּ הוּא יִגְמְלֵנוּ

to us. ‹ He ‹ was bountiful with us, ‹ He ‹ is bountiful with us, ‹ and He ‹ will be bountiful with us

לָעַד, לְחֵן וּלְחֶסֶד וּלְרַחֲמִים, וּלְרֶוַח הַצָּלָה

forever ‹ with — grace ‹ and with kindness ‹ and with compassion, ‹ with relief, ‹ rescue,

וְהַצְלָחָה, בְּרָכָה וִישׁוּעָה נֶחָמָה פַּרְנָסָה

success, ‹ blessing, ‹ salvation, ‹ consolation, ‹ sustenance,

וְכַלְכָּלָה ❖ וְרַחֲמִים וְחַיִּים וְשָׁלוֹם וְכָל טוֹב,

support, ‹ compassion, ‹ life, ‹ peace, ‹ and all good;

וּמִכָּל טוּב לְעוֹלָם אַל יְחַסְּרֵנוּ.* (אָמֵן. — Others)

and of all ‹ good things ‹ may He forever ‹ not ‹ deprive us.* ‹ (Amen.)

THE LEADER MAY PUT DOWN THE CUP OF WINE AT THIS POINT.

הָרַחֲמָן* הוּא יִמְלוֹךְ עָלֵינוּ לְעוֹלָם וָעֶד.

The compassionate One!* ‹ May He ‹ reign ‹ over us ‹ for ever ‹ and ever.

הָרַחֲמָן הוּא יִתְבָּרַךְ בַּשָּׁמַיִם וּבָאָרֶץ. הָרַחֲמָן

The compassionate One! ‹ May He ‹ be blessed ‹ in heaven ‹ and on earth. ‹ The compassionate One!

הוּא יִשְׁתַּבַּח לְדוֹר דּוֹרִים, וְיִתְפָּאַר בָּנוּ

May He ‹ be praised ‹ generation ‹ after generation; ‹ may He be glorified ‹ through us

לָעַד וּלְנֵצַח נְצָחִים, וְיִתְהַדַּר בָּנוּ לָעַד

forever ‹ and to the ultimate time, ‹ and be honored ‹ through us ‹ forever

וּלְעוֹלְמֵי עוֹלָמִים. הָרַחֲמָן הוּא יְפַרְנְסֵנוּ

and for all eternity. ‹ The compassionate One! ‹ May He ‹ sustain us

---

לְעוֹלָם אַל יְחַסְּרֵנוּ — *May He forever not deprive us.* This concludes the fourth blessing. Unlike the other blessings of *Bircas HaMazon*, this one does not conclude with a brief blessing summing up the theme of the section. As noted above, the essential text of the blessing consists of the two words — הַטּוֹב וְהַמֵּטִיב, *Who is good and Who does good* — and it is therefore similar to the short blessings recited before performing a commandment or partaking of food. The addition to the text of considerable outpourings of gratitude does not alter the fact that the brief text does not require a double blessing (*Rashi* to *Berachos* 49a).

◆§ הָרַחֲמָן — *The compassionate One!* After completing the four blessings of *Bircas HaMazon* we recite a selection of brief prayers for God's compassion (*Aruch HaShulchan*).

בִּכְבוֹד. הָרַחֲמָן הוּא יִשְׁבּוֹר עֻלֵּנוּ מֵעַל צַוָּארֵנוּ,

‹‹ our necks ‹ from ‹ our yoke ‹ break ‹ May He ‹ The compas- ‹‹ in honor.
[of oppression] sionate One!

וְהוּא יוֹלִיכֵנוּ קוֹמְמִיּוּת לְאַרְצֵנוּ. הָרַחֲמָן הוּא

‹ May ‹ The compas- ‹‹ to our Land. ‹ erect ‹ guide us ‹ and may
He sionate One! He

יִשְׁלַח לָנוּ בְּרָכָה מְרֻבָּה בַּבַּיִת הַזֶּה, וְעַל

‹ and upon ‹‹ to this house ‹ that is abundant ‹ blessing ‹ us ‹ send

שֻׁלְחָן זֶה שֶׁאָכַלְנוּ עָלָיו. הָרַחֲמָן הוּא יִשְׁלַח

‹ send ‹ May He ‹ The compas- ‹‹ on it. ‹ that we ‹ this table
sionate One! have eaten

לָנוּ אֶת אֵלִיָּהוּ הַנָּבִיא זָכוּר לַטּוֹב, וִיבַשֶּׂר

‹ to ‹‹ for ‹ — who is ‹‹ the ‹ Elijah ‹ us
proclaim good — remembered Prophet

לָנוּ* בְּשׂוֹרוֹת טוֹבוֹת יְשׁוּעוֹת וְנֶחָמוֹת.

‹‹ and consolations. ‹ salvations, ‹‹ that are good, ‹ tidings ‹ to us*

THE FOLLOWING IS A BLESSING THAT A GUEST RECITES FOR HIS HOST.

יְהִי רָצוֹן שֶׁלֹּא יֵבוֹשׁ וְלֹא יִכָּלֵם בַּעַל הַבַּיִת הַזֶּה,

‹‹ of this house — ‹ — the ‹‹ be ‹ nor ‹ be ‹ that ‹ [God's] ‹ May
master humiliated ashamed he not will it be

לֹא בָּעוֹלָם הַזֶּה וְלֹא בָּעוֹלָם הַבָּא, וְיַצְלִיחַ בְּכָל

‹ in all ‹ May he be ‹‹ to Come. ‹ in the World ‹ nor ‹ in This World ‹ not
successful

נְכָסָיו,* וְיִהְיוּ נְכָסָיו מֻצְלָחִים וּקְרוֹבִים לָעִיר,* וְאַל

‹ May ‹‹ at ‹ and [con- ‹ successful ‹ May his dealings ‹‹ his
there not hand.* veniently] close be dealings.*

יִשְׁלוֹט שָׂטָן בְּמַעֲשֵׂה יָדָיו, וְאַל יִזְדַּקֵּק לְפָנָיו שׁוּם

‹ any ‹ to him ‹ attach ‹ and may ‹‹ of his ‹ over ‹ any evil ‹ be in
itself there not hands, the work impediment control

דְּבַר חֵטְא וְהִרְהוּר עָוֹן, מֵעַתָּה וְעַד עוֹלָם.¹

‹‹ eternity. ‹ until ‹ from this ‹‹ of sin ‹ or thought ‹ of ‹ matter
time transgression

(1) *Orach Chaim* 201; see *Berachos* 46a.

וִיבַשֵּׂר לָנוּ — *To proclaim to us.* Elijah will proclaim the news of the arrival of Messiah [*Malachi* 3:23] (*Iyun Tefillah*).

נְכָסָיו — *His dealings.* Lit. *his possessions.*
וּקְרוֹבִים לָעִיר — *And close at hand.* Lit. *and close to the city.*

GUESTS RECITE THE FOLLOWING (CHILDREN AT THEIR PARENTS'
TABLE INCLUDE THE APPLICABLE WORDS IN PARENTHESES):

הָרַחֲמָן הוּא יְבָרֵךְ

‹ bless ‹ May He ‹ The compassionate One!

אֶת (אָבִי מוֹרִי) בַּעַל הַבַּיִת הַזֶּה,

‹ of this house, ‹ the master (‹ my teacher ‹ my father,)

וְאֶת (אִמִּי מוֹרָתִי) בַּעֲלַת הַבַּיִת הַזֶּה,

« of this house ‹ the lady (‹ my teacher ‹ my mother,) ‹ and

אוֹתָם וְאֶת בֵּיתָם וְאֶת זַרְעָם וְאֶת כָּל אֲשֶׁר לָהֶם.

« is theirs. ‹ that ‹ all ‹ and ‹ their family, ‹ their house, ‹ — them,

AT ONE'S OWN TABLE (INCLUDE THE APPLICABLE WORDS IN PARENTHESES):

הָרַחֲמָן הוּא יְבָרֵךְ אוֹתִי

‹ me ‹ bless ‹ May He ‹ The compassionate One!

(וְאֶת אִשְׁתִּי / וְאֶת בַּעְלִי. וְאֶת זַרְעִי)

(‹ and my children ‹ my husband ‹ and / ‹ my wife ‹ and)

וְאֶת כָּל אֲשֶׁר לִי.

« is mine. ‹ that ‹ all ‹ and

ALL CONTINUE:

אוֹתָנוּ וְאֶת כָּל אֲשֶׁר לָנוּ, כְּמוֹ שֶׁנִּתְבָּרְכוּ

‹ blessed were ‹ — just as « is ours ‹ that ‹ all ‹ and « Us

אֲבוֹתֵינוּ אַבְרָהָם יִצְחָק וְיַעֲקֹב בַּכֹּל מִכֹּל

‹ from ‹ in « and ‹ Isaac, ‹ Abraham, ‹ our forefathers, everything, everything, Jacob —

כֹּל,*₁ כֵּן יְבָרֵךְ אוֹתָנוּ כֻּלָּנוּ יַחַד בִּבְרָכָה

‹ with a ‹ together, ‹ all of us, ‹ us, ‹ may He ‹ So « with blessing bless everything.*

שְׁלֵמָה, וְנֹאמַר, אָמֵן.

« Amen! ‹ And let us say: « that is perfect.

(1) Cf. *Genesis* 24:1; 27:33; 33:11.

בַּכֹּל מִכֹּל כֹּל — *In everything, from everything, with everything.* The three expressions, each indicating that no necessary measure of good-ness was lacking, are used by the Torah refer-ring respectively to the three Patriarchs.

בַּמָּרוֹם יְלַמְּדוּ עֲלֵיהֶם* וְעָלֵינוּ* זְכוּת,

⟨ merit ⟨⟨ and upon us,* ⟨ upon them* ⟨⟨ may there be pleaded ⟨ On high,

שֶׁתְּהֵא לְמִשְׁמֶרֶת שָׁלוֹם.* וְנִשָּׂא בְרָכָה

⟨ a blessing ⟨ May we receive ⟨⟨ of peace.* ⟨ for a safeguard ⟨ that may serve

מֵאֵת יהוה, וּצְדָקָה מֵאֱלֹהֵי יִשְׁעֵנוּ, וְנִמְצָא

⟨ and may ⟨⟨ of our salvation, ⟨ from the God ⟨ and kindness ⟨⟨ from HASHEM, we find that is just

חֵן וְשֵׂכֶל טוֹב בְּעֵינֵי אֱלֹהִים וְאָדָם.¹

⟨⟨ and man. ⟨ of God ⟨ in the eyes ⟨ and good understanding ⟨ favor

---

AT A CIRCUMCISION FEAST CONTINUE WITH הָרַחֲמָן, *THE COMPASSIONATE ONE,* ON PAGE 334.

IF ANY OF THE FOLLOWING VERSES WAS OMITTED, *BIRCAS HAMAZON* NEED NOT BE REPEATED.

ON THE SABBATH ADD:

הָרַחֲמָן הוּא יַנְחִילֵנוּ יוֹם שֶׁכֻּלוֹ שַׁבָּת*

⟨ a Sabbath* ⟨ which will be completely ⟨ the day ⟨ cause us to inherit ⟨ May He ⟨ The compassionate One!

וּמְנוּחָה לְחַיֵּי הָעוֹלָמִים.

⟨⟨ that is eternal. ⟨ for life ⟨ and a rest day

ON ROSH CHODESH ADD:

הָרַחֲמָן הוּא יְחַדֵּשׁ עָלֵינוּ אֶת הַחֹדֶשׁ הַזֶּה לְטוֹבָה וְלִבְרָכָה.

⟨⟨ and for blessing. ⟨ for goodness ⟨ this month ⟨ upon us ⟨ inaugurate ⟨ May He ⟨ The compassionate One!

ON FESTIVALS ADD:

הָרַחֲמָן הוּא יַנְחִילֵנוּ יוֹם שֶׁכֻּלוֹ טוֹב.

⟨⟨ good. ⟨ which is completely ⟨ the day ⟨ cause us to inherit ⟨ May He ⟨ The compassionate One!

ON ROSH HASHANAH ADD:

הָרַחֲמָן הוּא יְחַדֵּשׁ עָלֵינוּ אֶת הַשָּׁנָה הַזֹּאת לְטוֹבָה וְלִבְרָכָה.

⟨⟨ and for blessing. ⟨ for goodness ⟨ this year ⟨ upon us ⟨ inaugurate ⟨ May He ⟨ The compassionate One!

---

(1) Cf. *Proverbs* 3:4.

עֲלֵיהֶם — *Upon them,* the master and mistress of the home, or any others who were mentioned in the preceding prayer.

וְעָלֵינוּ — *And upon us,* all gathered around the table. [When one eats alone this term refers to the people who were previously specified and to the Jewish people in general.]

לְמִשְׁמֶרֶת שָׁלוֹם — *For a safeguard of peace,* to assure that the home will be peaceful.

יוֹם שֶׁכֻּלוֹ שַׁבָּת — *The day which will be completely a Sabbath,* an allusion to the World to Come after the final Redemption.

ON SUCCOS ADD:

הָרַחֲמָן הוּא יָקִים לָנוּ אֶת סֻכַּת דָּוִיד הַנֹּפֶלֶת.[1]

》 which is fallen. 〈 of David, 〈 the booth 〈 for us 〈 erect 〈 May He 〈 The compassionate One!

ON CHANUKAH AND PURIM, IF AL HANISSIM WAS NOT RECITED IN ITS PROPER PLACE, ADD:

הָרַחֲמָן הוּא יַעֲשֶׂה לָנוּ נִסִּים וְנִפְלָאוֹת

〈 and wonders 〈 miracles 〈 for us 〈 perform 〈 May He 〈 The compassionate One!

כַּאֲשֶׁר עָשָׂה לַאֲבוֹתֵינוּ בַּיָּמִים הָהֵם בַּזְּמַן הַזֶּה.

》 at this time. 〈 in those days, 〈 for our forefathers 〈 He performed 〈 as

ON CHANUKAH CONTINUE בִּימֵי — IN THE DAYS OF . . . (P. 297).
ON PURIM CONTINUE בִּימֵי — IN THE DAYS OF . . . (P. 298).

הָרַחֲמָן הוּא יְזַכֵּנוּ לִימוֹת הַמָּשִׁיחַ וּלְחַיֵּי

〈 and of the life 〈 of Messiah 〈 of the days 〈 make us worthy 〈 May He 〈 The compassionate One!

DAYS MUSSAF IS RECITED: / WEEKDAYS:

הָעוֹלָם הַבָּא. [מַגְדִּיל*] / מִגְדּוֹל* יְשׁוּעוֹת מַלְכּוֹ

〈 to His king 〈 salvations 〈 He Who is a tower* of / He Who magnifies* 》 to Come. 〈 of the World

וְעֹשֶׂה חֶסֶד לִמְשִׁיחוֹ לְדָוִד וּלְזַרְעוֹ עַד עוֹלָם.[2]

》 forever. 〈 and to his offspring 〈 to David 〈 to His anointed, 〈 kindness 〈 and does

עֹשֶׂה שָׁלוֹם בִּמְרוֹמָיו,*[3] הוּא יַעֲשֶׂה שָׁלוֹם

〈 peace 〈 make 〈 may He 》 in His heights,* 〈 peace 〈 He Who makes

עָלֵינוּ וְעַל כָּל יִשְׂרָאֵל.[4] וְאִמְרוּ, אָמֵן.

》 Amen! 〈 Now respond: 《 Israel. 〈 all 〈 and upon 》 upon us

---

(1) Cf. *Amos* 9:11. (2) *Psalms* 18:51, *II Samuel* 22:51. (3) *Job* 25:2. (4) Cf. *Berachos* 16b.

מִגְדּוֹל/מַגְדִּיל — *He Who magnifies/is a tower.* Both verses were written by King David and, in the context of *Bircas HaMazon*, king refers to King Messiah. The phrase from *Psalms* [מַגְדִּיל] was chosen for weekdays because it was written before David became king. David composed the phrase from *Samuel* [מִגְדּוֹל] when he was

at the peak of his greatness, and it is therefore more suited to the Sabbath and Festivals (*Etz Yosef*).

עֹשֶׂה שָׁלוֹם בִּמְרוֹמָיו — *He Who makes peace in His heights.* Even the heavenly beings require God to make peace among them, how much more so fractious man! (*Etz Yosef*).

יְראוּ אֶת יהוה* קְדֹשָׁיו, כִּי אֵין מַחְסוֹר

‹ deprivation ‹ there is no ‹ for « O [you] His holy ones, ‹ HASHEM,* ‹ Fear

לִירֵאָיו. כְּפִירִים רָשׁוּ וְרָעֵבוּ, וְדֹרְשֵׁי יהוה

‹ HASHEM ‹ but those who seek ‹ and hunger, ‹ may want ‹ Young lions « for His reverent ones.

לֹא יַחְסְרוּ כָל טוֹב. הוֹדוּ לַיהוה כִּי טוֹב,

‹ He is good, ‹ for ‹ to HASHEM ‹ Give thanks « good. ‹ any ‹ lack ‹ will not

כִּי לְעוֹלָם חַסְדּוֹ. פּוֹתֵחַ אֶת יָדֶךָ, וּמַשְׂבִּיעַ

‹ and satisfy « Your hand, ‹ You open « is His kindness. ‹ enduring forever ‹ for

לְכָל חַי רָצוֹן. בָּרוּךְ הַגֶּבֶר אֲשֶׁר יִבְטַח

‹ trusts ‹ who ‹ is the man ‹ Blessed « [with its] desire. ‹ living thing ‹ every

בַּיהוה, וְהָיָה יהוה מִבְטַחוֹ.* נַעַר הָיִיתִי גַם

‹ and also ‹ I have been ‹ A youth « his security.* ‹ then HASHEM will be « in HASHEM;

זָקַנְתִּי, וְלֹא רָאִיתִי צַדִּיק נֶעֱזָב, וְזַרְעוֹ

‹ nor his children « forsaken, ‹ a righteous man ‹ but I have not seen « I have aged;

מְבַקֵּשׁ לָחֶם.* יהוה עֹז לְעַמּוֹ יִתֵּן, יהוה

‹ HASHEM « will give; ‹ to His people ‹ strength ‹ HASHEM « for bread.* ‹ begging

---

(1) *Psalms* 34:10-11. (2) 136:1 et al. (3) 145:16. (4) *Jeremiah* 17:7. (5) *Psalms* 37:25.

יְראוּ אֶת ה׳ — *Fear HASHEM.* Those who fear God are content, even if they are lacking in material possessions. But the wicked are never satisfied; whatever they have only whets their appetite for more (*Anaf Yosef*).

אֲשֶׁר יִבְטַח בַּה׳ וְהָיָה ה׳ מִבְטַחוֹ — *Who trusts in HASHEM; then HASHEM will be his security.* God will be a bastion of trust to a man in direct proportion to the amount of trust he places in God (*Chiddushei HaRim*).

צַדִּיק נֶעֱזָב וְזַרְעוֹ מְבַקֵּשׁ לָחֶם — *A righteous man forsaken, nor his children begging for bread.* A righteous man may suffer misfortune, but God will surely have mercy on His children (*Radak; Malbim*). I have never seen a righteous man consider himself forsaken even if his children must beg for bread. Whatever his lot in life, he trusts that God brings it upon him for a constructive and merciful purpose (*Anaf Yosef*).

יְבָרֵךְ אֶת עַמּוֹ בַשָּׁלוֹם.*1

》 with peace.* 〈 His people 〈 will bless

FOR *SHEVA BERACHOS* CONTINUE ON PAGE 319.

**WHEN THE LEADER SAID THE BLESSING AFTER MEALS WITH A CUP OF WINE,
HE LIFTS THE CUP AND RECITES THE FOLLOWING BLESSING:**

בָּרוּךְ אַתָּה יהוה אֱלֹהֵינוּ מֶלֶךְ הָעוֹלָם,

》 of the 〈 King 〈 our God, 〈 HASHEM, 〈 are You, 〈 Blessed
universe,

(אָמֵן. – All respond)

》 (Amen.)

בּוֹרֵא פְּרִי הַגָּפֶן.

》 of the 〈 the fruit 〈 Who
vine. creates

⊰{ COMPENSATORY BLESSINGS / ברכות למי ששכח }⊱

SEE BELOW AND ON PAGE 301 FOR INSTANCES WHEN COMPENSATORY BLESSINGS MUST BE RECITED.
WHEN THE COMPENSATORY BLESSING IS RECITED AT THE FIRST OR SECOND SABBATH OR FESTIVAL
MEAL, ONE CONCLUDES WITH ... בָּרוּךְ אַתָּה ה' מְקַדֵּשׁ. AT THE THIRD MEAL THIS CLOSING BLESSING
IS NOT RECITED. AFTER THE APPROPRIATE BLESSING, CONTINUE WITH THE FOURTH BLESSING,
הַטּוֹב וְהַמֵּטִיב, GOD'S GOODNESS (P. 303).

IF ONE FORGOT רְצֵה ON THE SABBATH:

בָּרוּךְ אַתָּה יהוה אֱלֹהֵינוּ מֶלֶךְ הָעוֹלָם, אֲשֶׁר נָתַן שַׁבָּתוֹת

〈 Sabbaths 〈 gave 〈 Who 》 of the universe, 〈 King 〈 our God, 〈 HASHEM, 〈 are You, 〈 Blessed

לִמְנוּחָה לְעַמּוֹ יִשְׂרָאֵל בְּאַהֲבָה, לְאוֹת וְלִבְרִית. בָּרוּךְ אַתָּה

〈 are You, 〈 Blessed 》 and for a covenant. 〈 for a sign 》 with love, 〈 Israel 〈 to His people 〈 for rest

יהוה, מְקַדֵּשׁ הַשַּׁבָּת.

》 the Sabbath. 〈 Who sanctifies 》 HASHEM,

IF ONE FORGOT יַעֲלֶה וְיָבֹא ON ROSH CHODESH:

בָּרוּךְ אַתָּה יהוה אֱלֹהֵינוּ מֶלֶךְ הָעוֹלָם, אֲשֶׁר נָתַן רָאשֵׁי חֳדָשִׁים

〈 Moons 〈 New 〈 gave 〈 Who 》 of the universe, 〈 King 〈 our God, 〈 HASHEM, 〈 are You, 〈 Blessed

לְעַמּוֹ יִשְׂרָאֵל לְזִכָּרוֹן.

》 as a 〈 Israel 〈 to His
remembrance. people

---

(1) *Psalms* 29:11.

בְּשָׁלוֹם — *With peace.* Rabbi Shimon ben Chalafta said: "The Holy One, Blessed is He, could find no container which would hold Israel's blessings as well as peace would, as it says: *HASHEM to His people will give strength, HASHEM will bless His people with peace"* (Uktzin 3:12).

IF ONE FORGOT BOTH רְצֵה AND יַעֲלֶה וְיָבֹא ON ROSH CHODESH THAT FALLS ON THE SABBATH:

בָּרוּךְ אַתָּה יהוה אֱלֹהֵינוּ מֶלֶךְ הָעוֹלָם, אֲשֶׁר נָתַן שַׁבָּתוֹת
⟨ Sabbaths ⟨ gave ⟨ Who ⟨⟨ of the universe, ⟨ King ⟨ our God, ⟨ Hashem, ⟨ are You, ⟨ Blessed

לִמְנוּחָה לְעַמּוֹ יִשְׂרָאֵל בְּאַהֲבָה, לְאוֹת וְלִבְרִית, וְרָאשֵׁי חֳדָשִׁים
⟨ Moons ⟨ and New ⟨⟨ and for a covenant, ⟨ for a sign ⟨⟨ with love, ⟨ Israel ⟨ to His people ⟨ for rest

לְזִכָּרוֹן. בָּרוּךְ אַתָּה יהוה, מְקַדֵּשׁ הַשַּׁבָּת וְיִשְׂרָאֵל וְרָאשֵׁי חֳדָשִׁים.
⟪ Moons. ⟨ and New ⟨ Israel, ⟨ the Sabbath, ⟨ Who re-sanctifies ⟨ Hashem, ⟨ are You, ⟨ Blessed ⟪ for a remembrance.

IF ONE FORGOT יַעֲלֶה וְיָבֹא ON A FESTIVAL:

בָּרוּךְ אַתָּה יהוה אֱלֹהֵינוּ מֶלֶךְ הָעוֹלָם, אֲשֶׁר נָתַן יָמִים טוֹבִים
⟨ Festivals ⟨ gave ⟨ Who ⟨ of the universe, ⟨ King ⟨ our God, ⟨ Hashem, ⟨ are You, ⟨ Blessed

לְעַמּוֹ יִשְׂרָאֵל לְשָׂשׂוֹן וּלְשִׂמְחָה, אֶת יוֹם
⟨ — the day of [the] ⟨ and gladness ⟨ for happiness ⟨ Israel ⟨ to His people

SHEMINI ATZERES/SIMCHAS TORAH	SUCCOS	SHAVUOS	PESACH
שְׁמִינִי עֲצֶרֶת הֶחָג	חַג הַסֻּכּוֹת	חַג הַשָּׁבֻעוֹת	חַג הַמַּצּוֹת
⟪ Festival ⟨ Shemini Atzeres	⟪ Festival of Succos	⟪ Festival of Shavuos	⟪ Festival of Matzos

הַזֶּה. בָּרוּךְ אַתָּה יהוה, מְקַדֵּשׁ יִשְׂרָאֵל וְהַזְּמַנִּים.
⟪ and the [festive] seasons. ⟨ Israel ⟨ Who sanctifies ⟪ Hashem, ⟨ are You, ⟨ Blessed ⟪ — this.

IF ONE FORGOT BOTH רְצֵה AND יַעֲלֶה וְיָבֹא ON A FESTIVAL THAT FALLS ON THE SABBATH:

בָּרוּךְ אַתָּה יהוה אֱלֹהֵינוּ מֶלֶךְ הָעוֹלָם, אֲשֶׁר נָתַן שַׁבָּתוֹת
⟨ Sabbaths ⟨ gave ⟨ Who ⟨⟨ of the universe, ⟨ King ⟨ our God, ⟨ Hashem, ⟨ are You, ⟨ Blessed

לִמְנוּחָה לְעַמּוֹ יִשְׂרָאֵל בְּאַהֲבָה, לְאוֹת וְלִבְרִית, וְיָמִים טוֹבִים
⟨ and Festivals ⟨⟨ and a covenant, ⟨ for a sign ⟨⟨ with love, ⟨ Israel ⟨ to His people ⟨ for rest

לְשָׂשׂוֹן וּלְשִׂמְחָה, אֶת יוֹם
⟨ — the day of [the] ⟪ and gladness ⟨ for happiness

SHEMINI ATZERES/SIMCHAS TORAH	SUCCOS	SHAVUOS	PESACH
שְׁמִינִי עֲצֶרֶת הֶחָג	חַג הַסֻּכּוֹת	חַג הַשָּׁבֻעוֹת	חַג הַמַּצּוֹת
⟪ Festival ⟨ Shemini Atzeres	⟪ Festival of Succos	⟪ Festival of Shavuos	⟪ Festival of Matzos

הַזֶּה. בָּרוּךְ אַתָּה יהוה, מְקַדֵּשׁ הַשַּׁבָּת וְיִשְׂרָאֵל וְהַזְּמַנִּים.
⟪ and the [festive] seasons. ⟨ Israel, ⟨ the Sabbath, ⟨ Who sanctifies ⟨ Hashem, ⟨ are You, ⟨ Blessed ⟪ — this.

IF ONE FORGOT יַעֲלֶה וְיָבֹא ON CHOL HAMOED:

בָּרוּךְ אַתָּה יהוה אֱלֹהֵינוּ מֶלֶךְ הָעוֹלָם, אֲשֶׁר נָתַן מוֹעֲדִים לְעַמּוֹ
⟨ to His people ⟨ appointed Festivals ⟨ gave ⟨ Who ⟪ of the universe, ⟨ King ⟨ our God, ⟨ Hashem, ⟨ are You, ⟨ Blessed

יִשְׂרָאֵל לְשָׁשׂוֹן וּלְשִׂמְחָה, אֶת יוֹם
‹ the day of ‹‹ and gladness, ‹ for happiness ‹ Israel

ON SUCCOS: | **ON PESACH:**

חַג הַסֻּכּוֹת הַזֶּה. | חַג הַמַּצּוֹת הַזֶּה.
‹‹ this Festival of Succos. | ‹‹ this Festival of Matzos.

IF ONE FORGOT BOTH רְצֵה AND יַעֲלֶה וְיָבֹא ON THE SABBATH OF CHOL HAMOED:

בָּרוּךְ אַתָּה יהוה אֱלֹהֵינוּ מֶלֶךְ הָעוֹלָם, אֲשֶׁר נָתַן שַׁבָּתוֹת
‹ Sabbaths ‹ gave ‹ Who ‹‹ of the universe, ‹ King ‹ our God, ‹ Hashem, ‹ are You, ‹ Blessed

לִמְנוּחָה לְעַמּוֹ יִשְׂרָאֵל בְּאַהֲבָה, לְאוֹת וְלִבְרִית, וּמוֹעֲדִים לְשָׂשׂוֹן
‹ for ‹ and appointed ‹ and a ‹ for a sign ‹‹ with love, ‹ Israel ‹ to His ‹ for rest
happiness   Festivals   covenant,   people

וּלְשִׂמְחָה – אֶת יוֹם
‹ – the day of ‹‹ and gladness

ON SUCCOS: | **ON PESACH:**

חַג הַסֻּכּוֹת הַזֶּה. | חַג הַמַּצּוֹת הַזֶּה.
‹‹ this Festival of Succos. | ‹‹ this Festival of Matzos.

בָּרוּךְ אַתָּה יהוה, מְקַדֵּשׁ הַשַּׁבָּת וְיִשְׂרָאֵל וְהַזְּמַנִּים.
‹‹ and the [festive] seasons. ‹ Israel, ‹ the Sabbath, ‹ Who sanctifies ‹‹ Hashem, ‹ are You, ‹ Blessed

IF ONE FORGOT יַעֲלֶה וְיָבֹא ON ROSH HASHANAH:

בָּרוּךְ אַתָּה יהוה אֱלֹהֵינוּ מֶלֶךְ הָעוֹלָם, אֲשֶׁר נָתַן יָמִים טוֹבִים
‹ Festivals ‹ gave ‹ Who ‹‹ of the universe, ‹ King ‹ our God, ‹ Hashem, ‹ are You, ‹ Blessed

לְעַמּוֹ יִשְׂרָאֵל, אֶת יוֹם הַזִּכָּרוֹן הַזֶּה. בָּרוּךְ אַתָּה יהוה, מְקַדֵּשׁ
‹ Who ‹‹ Hashem, ‹ are You, ‹ Blessed ‹‹ – this day of Remembrance. ‹‹ Israel ‹ to His people
sanctifies

יִשְׂרָאֵל וְיוֹם הַזִּכָּרוֹן.
‹‹ of Remembrance. ‹ and the day ‹ Israel

IF ONE FORGOT BOTH יַעֲלֶה וְיָבֹא AND רְצֵה ON ROSH HASHANAH THAT FALLS ON THE SABBATH:

בָּרוּךְ אַתָּה יהוה אֱלֹהֵינוּ מֶלֶךְ הָעוֹלָם, אֲשֶׁר נָתַן שַׁבָּתוֹת
‹ Sabbaths ‹ gave ‹ Who ‹‹ of the universe, ‹ King ‹ our God, ‹ Hashem, ‹ are You, ‹ Blessed

לִמְנוּחָה לְעַמּוֹ יִשְׂרָאֵל בְּאַהֲבָה, לְאוֹת וְלִבְרִית, וְיָמִים טוֹבִים
‹ and Festivals ‹‹ and a covenant, ‹ for a sign ‹‹ with love, ‹ Israel ‹ to His people ‹ for rest

לְיִשְׂרָאֵל, אֶת יוֹם הַזִּכָּרוֹן הַזֶּה. בָּרוּךְ אַתָּה יהוה, מְקַדֵּשׁ
‹ Who ‹‹ Hashem, ‹ are You, ‹ Blessed ‹‹ – this day of Remembrance. ‹‹ to Israel
sanctifies

הַשַּׁבָּת וְיִשְׂרָאֵל וְיוֹם הַזִּכָּרוֹן.
‹‹ of Remembrance. ‹ and the day ‹ Israel, ‹ the Sabbath,

⁜ BLESSINGS AFTER OTHER FOODS / ברכות אחרונות ⁑

THE THREE-FACETED BLESSING / מעין שלש

THE FOLLOWING BLESSING IS RECITED AFTER PARTAKING OF: (A) GRAIN PRODUCTS (OTHER THAN BREAD OR MATZAH) MADE FROM WHEAT, BARLEY, RYE, OATS, OR SPELT; (B) GRAPE WINE OR GRAPE JUICE; (C) GRAPES, FIGS, POMEGRANATES, OLIVES, OR DATES. (IF FOODS FROM TWO OR THREE OF THESE GROUPS WERE EATEN, THEN THE INSERTIONS FOR EACH GROUP ARE CONNECTED WITH THE CONJUNCTIVE וֹ, THUS וְעַל. THE ORDER IN SUCH A CASE IS GRAIN, WINE, FRUIT.)

בָּרוּךְ אַתָּה יהוה אֱלֹהֵינוּ מֶלֶךְ הָעוֹלָם, עַל

Blessed ⟩ are You, ⟩ HASHEM, ⟩ our God, ⟩ King ⟩ of the universe, ⟩ for

AFTER FRUITS:	AFTER WINE:	AFTER GRAIN PRODUCTS:
[וְעַל] הָעֵץ וְעַל	[וְעַל] הַגֶּפֶן וְעַל	הַמִּחְיָה* וְעַל
[and for] ⟩ the tree ⟩ and for	[and for] ⟩ the vine ⟩ and for	the nourishment* ⟩ and for
פְּרִי הָעֵץ,	פְּרִי הַגֶּפֶן,	הַכַּלְכָּלָה,
the fruit ⟩ of the tree,	the fruit ⟩ of the vine	the sustenance

וְעַל תְּנוּבַת הַשָּׂדֶה, וְעַל אֶרֶץ חֶמְדָּה* טוֹבָה וּרְחָבָה,

and for ⟩ the produce ⟩ of the field; ⟩ for ⟩ the Land ⟩ – desirable,* ⟩ good, ⟩ and spacious –

שֶׁרָצִיתָ וְהִנְחַלְתָּ לַאֲבוֹתֵינוּ, לֶאֱכֹל מִפִּרְיָהּ וְלִשְׂבּוֹעַ

that You desired ⟩ to give as a heritage ⟩ to our forefathers, ⟩ to eat ⟩ of its fruit ⟩ and to be satisfied

מִטּוּבָהּ. רַחֵם נָא* יהוה אֱלֹהֵינוּ עַל יִשְׂרָאֵל עַמֶּךָ,

with its goodness. ⟩ Have mercy, ⟩ we beg You,* ⟩ HASHEM, ⟩ our God, ⟩ on ⟩ Israel ⟩ Your people;

מעין שלש / The Three-Faceted Blessing

The Sages instituted a special blessing of thanks to be recited after partaking of the Seven Species for which the Torah praises *Eretz Yisrael* (Deuteronomy 8:8). This blessing is known as בְּרָכָה אַחַת מֵעֵין שָׁלֹשׁ — literally, a single blessing that is an abridgment of three — because it summarizes the Scripturally ordained blessings of *Bircas HaMazon*. Actually, the fourth blessing, too, is included (see commentary further), but the title does not allude to it because the fourth blessing is Rabbinic in origin.

הַמִּחְיָה — *Nourishment.* This is the generic term referring to all foods made from the five species of grain: wheat, barley, rye, oats, and spelt. The

word מָזוֹן is a synonym for מִחְיָה, but the Sages preferred not to use the more familiar מָזוֹן because, had they done so, the concluding blessing would have been עַל הָאָרֶץ וְעַל הַמָּזוֹן, *for the Land and the nourishment,* precisely the concluding words of the second blessing of *Bircas HaMazon.* Instead they preferred to make this blessing distinct from any other (*Vaya'as Avraham*).

וְעַל אֶרֶץ חֶמְדָּה — *For the Land – desirable.* This begins the second section of the blessing. It parallels the second blessing of *Bircas HaMazon* in thanking God for *Eretz Yisrael.*

רַחֵם נָא — *Have mercy, we beg You.* This begins the third section of the blessing, paralleling the third blessing of *Bircas HaMazon.*

וְעַל יְרוּשָׁלַיִם עִירֶךָ, וְעַל צִיּוֹן מִשְׁכַּן כְּבוֹדֶךָ, וְעַל מִזְבְּחֶךָ

on ⟨ Jerusalem, ⟨ Your City; ⟨ on ⟨ Zion, ⟨ the resting ⟨ of Your ⟨⟨ on ⟨ Your Altar,
place ⟨ glory;

וְעַל הֵיכָלֶךָ. וּבְנֵה יְרוּשָׁלַיִם עִיר הַקֹּדֶשׁ בִּמְהֵרָה בְּיָמֵינוּ,

and ⟨ Your ⟨⟨ Rebuild ⟨ Jerusalem, ⟨ the City ⟨ of ⟨ speedily ⟨ in our
on Temple. holiness, days.

וְהַעֲלֵנוּ לְתוֹכָהּ, וְשַׂמְּחֵנוּ בְּבִנְיָנָהּ, וְנֹאכַל מִפִּרְיָהּ, וְנִשְׂבַּע

Bring us up ⟨ into it ⟨ and gladden ⟨ in its ⟨⟨ let us eat ⟨ from its ⟨ and let us
us rebuilding; fruit be satisfied

מִטּוּבָהּ, וּנְבָרֶכְךָ עָלֶיהָ בִּקְדֻשָּׁה וּבְטָהֳרָה.

with its ⟨⟨ and let us ⟨ upon it ⟨ in holiness ⟨ and purity.
goodness, bless You

ON THE SABBATH:

וּרְצֵה וְהַחֲלִיצֵנוּ בְּיוֹם הַשַּׁבָּת הַזֶּה.

And may it be ⟨ to give us rest ⟨ on this Sabbath day. ⟨⟨
pleasing to You

ON ROSH CHODESH:

וְזָכְרֵנוּ לְטוֹבָה בְּיוֹם רֹאשׁ הַחֹדֶשׁ הַזֶּה.

And ⟨ remember us ⟨ for ⟨ on the ⟨ of this New Moon. ⟨⟨
goodness day

ON PESACH:

וְשַׂמְּחֵנוּ בְּיוֹם חַג הַמַּצּוֹת הַזֶּה.

And ⟨ on the ⟨ of this Festival of Matzos. ⟨⟨
gladden us day

ON SHAVUOS:

וְשַׂמְּחֵנוּ בְּיוֹם חַג הַשָּׁבֻעוֹת הַזֶּה.

And ⟨ on the ⟨ of this Festival of Shavuos. ⟨⟨
gladden us day

ON ROSH HASHANAH:

וְזָכְרֵנוּ לְטוֹבָה בְּיוֹם הַזִּכָּרוֹן הַזֶּה.

And ⟨ for ⟨ on this Day of Remembrance. ⟨⟨
remember us goodness

ON SUCCOS:

וְשַׂמְּחֵנוּ בְּיוֹם חַג הַסֻּכּוֹת הַזֶּה.

And ⟨ on the ⟨ of this Festival of Succos. ⟨⟨
gladden us day

ON SHEMINI ATZERES / SIMCHAS TORAH:

וְשַׂמְּחֵנוּ בְּיוֹם שְׁמִינִי עֲצֶרֶת הַחַג הַזֶּה.

And ⟨ on the ⟨ of Shemini Atzeres ⟨ this Festival. ⟨⟨
gladden us day

כִּי אַתָּה* יהוה טוֹב וּמֵטִיב לַכֹּל,* וְנוֹדֶה לְּךָ עַל הָאָרֶץ וְעַל

⟨ and ⟨ the Land ⟨ for ⟨ You ⟨ and we ⟪ to all,* ⟨ and do ⟨ are ⟨ HASHEM, ⟨ You,* ⟨ For
for   thank   good   good

AFTER FRUITS:	AFTER WINE:	AFTER GRAIN PRODUCTS:
[וְעַל] הַפֵּרוֹת.°°	¹°[וְעַל] פְּרִי הַגָּפֶן.	הַמִּחְיָה (וְעַל הַכַּלְכָּלָה).
⟪ the fruit. ⟨ [and for]	⟪ of the ⟨ the ⟨ [and for] vine. fruit	⟪ the nourishment.

בָּרוּךְ אַתָּה יהוה, עַל הָאָרֶץ וְעַל

⟨ and for ⟨ the Land ⟨ for ⟪ HASHEM, ⟨ are You, ⟨ Blessed

[וְעַל] הַפֵּרוֹת.°°	¹°[וְעַל] פְּרִי הַגָּפֶן.	הַמִּחְיָה (וְעַל הַכַּלְכָּלָה).
⟪ the fruit. ⟨ [and for]	⟪ of the ⟨ the ⟨ [and for] vine. fruit	⟪ the ⟨ (and ⟨ the sustenance). for nourishment

°ON WINE FROM *ERETZ YISRAEL*, SUBSTITUTE גַּפְנָהּ, *OF ITS VINE*, FOR הַגֶּפֶן, *OF THE VINE*.
°°ON FRUIT FROM *ERETZ YISRAEL*, SUBSTITUTE פֵּרוֹתֶיהָ, *ITS FRUIT*, FOR הַפֵּרוֹת, *THE FRUIT*.

BOREI NEFASHOS / בּוֹרֵא נְפָשׁוֹת

AFTER EATING OR DRINKING ANY FOOD TO WHICH NEITHER *BIRCAS HAMAZON* NOR THE
THREE-FACETED BLESSING APPLIES, SUCH AS FRUITS OTHER THAN THE ABOVE, VEGETABLES, OR
BEVERAGES OTHER THAN WINE, RECITE:

בָּרוּךְ אַתָּה יהוה אֱלֹהֵינוּ מֶלֶךְ הָעוֹלָם, בּוֹרֵא נְפָשׁוֹת רַבּוֹת

⟨ numerous ⟨ Who ⟪ of the ⟨ King ⟨ our God, ⟨ HASHEM, ⟨ are You, ⟨ Blessed
living things   creates   universe,

וְחֶסְרוֹנָן, עַל כָּל מַה שֶּׁבָּרָאתָ (SOME SUBSTITUTE – שֶׁבָּרָא) לְהַחֲיוֹת בָּהֶם

⟨ with which to ⟨ (He has ⟨ You have ⟨ that ⟨ all ⟨ for ⟪ with their
sustain   created)   created   deficiencies;

נֶפֶשׁ כָּל חָי. בָּרוּךְ חֵי הָעוֹלָמִים.*

⟪ of the worlds.* ⟨ the ⟨ Blessed ⟪ being. ⟨ of ⟨ the life
                  Life-giver is He,   every

---

(1) When the blessing includes fruit, say הַגֶּפֶן.

אַתָּה... טוֹב וּמֵטִיב לַכֹּל — *You ... are good and do
good to all.* This section of the blessing parallels
the Rabbinically instituted fourth blessing of
Bircas HaMazon.

◆§ בּוֹרֵא נְפָשׁוֹת / **Borei Nefashos**

This blessing, like *Bircas HaMazon,* thanks
God not only for His grace to humans, but to all
living things (*Iyun Tefillah*).

חֵי הָעוֹלָמִים — *The Life-giver of the worlds.* This
phrase is based on *Daniel* 12:7 where God is
described as the One Who gives life to the entire
universe. Daniel used the singular חֵי הָעוֹלָם, referring to God as the *Provider of Life to This
World.* The plural form of our blessing describes
God as the Life-giver of both This World and the
World to Come (*Abudraham*).

⊰{ THE MARRIAGE SERVICE / סדר אירוסין ונישואין }⊱

WHEN THE GROOM REACHES THE *CHUPAH*, THE *CHAZZAN* SINGS:

בָּרוּךְ הַבָּא. מִי אַדִּיר עַל הַכֹּל, מִי בָּרוּךְ עַל הַכֹּל, מִי

⟨ He ⟪ all, ⟨ above ⟨ is ⟨ He ⟪ all, ⟨ above ⟨ is ⟨ He ⟪ is he who ⟨ Blessed
Who blessed Who powerful Who has come!

גָּדוֹל עַל הַכֹּל, מִי דָגוּל עַל הַכֹּל, הוּא יְבָרֵךְ אֶת הֶחָתָן

⟨ the groom ⟨ — may He bless ⟪ all ⟨ above ⟨ is pre- ⟨ He ⟪ all, ⟨ above ⟨ is
eminent Who great

וְאֶת הַכַּלָּה.

⟪ and the bride.

AS THE BRIDE APPROACHES THE *CHUPAH*, THE GROOM SHOULD TAKE A STEP OR TWO FORWARD IN GREETING. SHE THEN CIRCLES THE GROOM, ACCORDING TO THE CUSTOM, AND THE *CHAZZAN* SINGS:

בְּרוּכָה הַבָּאָה. מִי בֶן* שִׂיחַ שׁוֹשַׁן חוֹחִים,* אַהֲבַת כַּלָּה

⟨ of a ⟨ the love ⟪ among ⟨ of the ⟨ the ⟨ under- ⟨ He ⟨ is she who ⟨ Blessed
bride, the thorns,* rose speech stands* Who has come!

מְשׂוֹשׂ דּוֹדִים, הוּא יְבָרֵךְ אֶת הֶחָתָן וְאֶת הַכַּלָּה.

⟪ and the bride. ⟨ the groom ⟨ bless ⟨ — may ⟪ of the ⟨ who is
He beloved ones the joy

It was a condition of Creation that man and woman join together as a single unit in loyalty and devotion to one another (see *Genesis* 2:24). The Talmud sees the relationship between man and wife as the habitat for God's Own Presence. The name for man, אִישׁ, contains the letter י, while the name for woman, אִשָּׁה, contains the letter ה. These two letters spell one of God's Names; thus, when man and wife come together in harmony and purity, when they are devoted to one another in the shared responsibility of carrying out the duties prescribed for them by God and his Torah, they jointly become a resting place on earth for God's majesty (*Sotah* 17a).

Indeed, one of the Talmud's most frequently used terms for the betrothal ceremony, קִדּוּשִׁין, *kiddushin*, is indicative of this sanctity. The literal translation of *kiddushin* is consecration. When a Jewish groom places a ring on his bride's finger and recites הֲרֵי אַתְּ מְקֻדֶּשֶׁת לִי, *behold you are consecrated to me . . .*, his words put their future relationship on a higher plane, one that aspires to holiness and achievement in the service of God Himself (see *Kiddushin* 2b).

The wedding ceremony consists of two separate parts. The first is *kiddushin*, also known as *erusin*. It takes effect when the bride accepts the ring from her groom. When *kiddushin/erusin* is accomplished, the couple is considered to be married to the extent that their relationship can be severed only by means of divorce or death. However, the couple may not live together until the next ceremony takes place. That ceremony is נִשּׂוּאִין, *nisu'in*, or marriage, also known as *chupah* or canopy, because it commonly takes place under a canopy held aloft on four posts.

The canopy signifies the new household being formed by the union of the new couple, and the recitation of the blessings under the canopy consecrates the new relationship.

Before the *chupah* part of the service takes place, the *kesubah* is read aloud. The *kesubah* is the halachically required marriage contract that spells out the obligations of a man to his wife during the marriage and provides for the wife's support if the marriage ends in death or divorce.

⊰§ מִי בֶן — *He Who understands.* God understands the idealism and purity upon which a Jewish home is built, as is expressed further.

שִׂיחַ שׁוֹשַׁן חוֹחִים — *The speech of the rose among the thorns.* The allusion to Israel as a rose among thorns appears in *Shir HaShirim* (2:2). The Midrash interprets the "rose" as an allusion to the

317 / THE MARRIAGE SERVICE

THE *MESADER KIDDUSHIN* HOLDS A CUP OF WINE AND RECITES:

בָּרוּךְ אַתָּה יהוה אֱלֹהֵינוּ מֶלֶךְ הָעוֹלָם, בּוֹרֵא פְּרִי הַגָּפֶן.

Blessed are You, Hashem, our God, King of the universe, Who creates the fruit of the vine.

(אָמֵן. – All respond)

(Amen.)

בָּרוּךְ אַתָּה יהוה אֱלֹהֵינוּ מֶלֶךְ הָעוֹלָם, אֲשֶׁר קִדְּשָׁנוּ

Blessed are You, Hashem, our God, King of the universe, Who has sanctified us

בְּמִצְוֹתָיו, וְצִוָּנוּ עַל הָעֲרָיוֹת,* וְאָסַר לָנוּ אֶת הָאֲרוּסוֹת,

with His commandments, and has commanded us regarding forbidden unions;* Who forbade to us betrothed women,

וְהִתִּיר לָנוּ אֶת הַנְּשׂוּאוֹת לָנוּ עַל יְדֵי חֻפָּה וְקִדּוּשִׁין. בָּרוּךְ

and permitted to us women who are married to us through canopy and consecration. Blessed

אַתָּה יהוה, מְקַדֵּשׁ עַמּוֹ יִשְׂרָאֵל עַל יְדֵי חֻפָּה וְקִדּוּשִׁין.

are You, Hashem, Who sanctified His people Israel through canopy and consecration.

(אָמֵן. – All respond)

(Amen.)

THE GROOM AND BRIDE EACH DRINK FROM THE WINE. THE GROOM THEN HOLDS
HIS RING READY TO PLACE ON THE BRIDE'S RIGHT INDEX FINGER AND SAYS TO HER:

הֲרֵי אַתְּ מְקֻדֶּשֶׁת לִי, בְּטַבַּעַת זוֹ,* כְּדַת מֹשֶׁה וְיִשְׂרָאֵל.

Behold, you are consecrated to me by means of this ring,* according to the ritual of Moses and Israel.

Jewish wife who scrupulously observes the laws of family purity. Also, it refers to the *mesader kiddushin*, who is thoroughly conversant with the laws and procedures of the marriage ceremony. Thus, this brief song that is chanted just before the marriage ceremony is in praise of two of the participants: the bride whose idealism and loyalty to halachah will maintain the purity of the family, and the *mesader kiddushin* whose knowledge of the law assures that the ceremony will be performed properly.

וְצִוָּנוּ עַל הָעֲרָיוֹת — *And has commanded us regarding forbidden unions.* Although this blessing begins with the formula usually reserved for blessings over *mitzvos* [. . . אֲשֶׁר קִדְּשָׁנוּ בְּמִצְוֹתָיו, *Who has sanctified us with His commandments* . . .] *Rosh* (*Kesubos* §12) explains that this blessing is totally unrelated to the commandment of

פְּרוּ וּרְבוּ, *be fruitful and multiply.* Rather, it falls under the category of blessings of praise; we thank and praise God for elevating the Jewish people by giving us a unique moral standard that specifies whom we may and may not marry.

בְּטַבַּעַת זוֹ — *By means of this ring.* Any object of value worth at least a *perutah* effects *kiddushin*. Then why was a ring chosen for this purpose?

— So that a Jewish woman can always wear something that recalls the moment when she and her husband consecrated, and embarked on, their new life together (*Chinuch*).

— Just as a ring is round and therefore without end, so may the blessings and joy of the new couple be endless (*Dover Shalom*).

— Just as a ring resembles a link in a chain, so may this new family become a link in the eternal chain of the Jewish heritage.

AFTER THE RING IS PLACED ON THE BRIDE'S FINGER, THE *KESUBAH* (MARRIAGE CONTRACT) IS READ ALOUD AND HANDED TO THE GROOM WHO PRESENTS IT TO THE BRIDE. THEN A SECOND CUP OF WINE IS POURED AND SEVEN BLESSINGS (שֶׁבַע בְּרָכוֹת) ARE RECITED ALOUD. FIRST THE BLESSING OVER WINE IS RECITED AND THEN BLESSINGS 1-6 ON PP. 319-321. THE HONOR OF RECITING THESE SEVEN BLESSINGS MAY BE DIVIDED AMONG SEVERAL PEOPLE. AFTER THE BLESSINGS BOTH GROOM AND BRIDE DRINK FROM THE WINE. THE GROOM THEN SMASHES A GLASS WITH HIS RIGHT FOOT TO SYMBOLIZE THAT UNTIL THE TEMPLE IS REBUILT OUR JOY CANNOT BE COMPLETE. THIS ACT CONCLUDES THE PUBLIC MARRIAGE SERVICE. THEN THE GROOM AND BRIDE MUST SPEND SOME TIME TOGETHER IN A COMPLETELY PRIVATE ROOM.

❧ SHEVA BERACHOS / שבע ברכות ❧

WHEN *SHEVA BERACHOS* ARE RECITED, THE LEADER RECITES THE FOLLOWING *ZIMUN*, WITH A CUP OF WINE IN HAND.

Leader — רַבּוֹתַי מִיר וֶעלֶן בֶּענטְשֶׁען [רַבּוֹתַי נְבָרֵךְ].

Gentlemen, ⟩ let us ⟩ bless. ⟩⟨ [Gentlemen,] ⟩ [let us bless.] ⟩⟨

Others — יְהִי שֵׁם יהוה מְבֹרָךְ מֵעַתָּה וְעַד עוֹלָם.[1]

Let ⟩ the ⟩ Name ⟩ of ⟩ be ⟩ from ⟩ until ⟩ eternity. ⟩⟨
HASHEM blessed this time

Leader — יְהִי שֵׁם יהוה מְבֹרָךְ מֵעַתָּה וְעַד עוֹלָם.[1]

Let ⟩ the ⟩ Name ⟩ of ⟩ be ⟩ from ⟩ until ⟩ eternity. ⟩⟨
HASHEM blessed this time

IN MANY CONGREGATIONS THE FOLLOWING IS NOT RECITED ON THE SABBATH:

Leader — דְּוַי הָסֵר* וְגַם חָרוֹן, וְאָז אִלֵּם בְּשִׁיר יָרוֹן,*

Pain ⟩ banish* ⟩ and also ⟩ wrath, ⟩ and then ⟩⟨ the mute ⟩ in song ⟨ will exult.* ⟩⟨

נַחֵנוּ בְמַעְגְּלֵי צֶדֶק,[2] שְׁעֵה בִּרְכַּת בְּנֵי אַהֲרֹן.*

Guide ⟩ in the paths ⟩ of ⟩ righteousness, ⟨ heed ⟩⟨ the ⟩ blessing ⟩ of the ⟩ children ⟩ of ⟨ Aaron.* ⟩⟨

(1) *Psalms* 113:2. (2) Cf. 23:3.

❧ שֶׁבַע בְּרָכוֹת / SHEVA BERACHOS ❧

The number seven in Jewish thought denotes completion — seven days in the week, seven years in the Sabbatical Year cycle, seven days to inaugurate the Tabernacle, etc. Thus we find that both Jacob and Samson celebrated their marriages for seven days (*Genesis* 29:27; *Rashi*; *Judges* 14:17). Accordingly, if either the bride or groom has never been married, their joy is complete and they celebrate it for seven full days.

The seven days (one day if both groom and bride were previously married) beginning with the wedding day are known as the week of *Sheva Berachos* [lit. *Seven Blessings*]. During this period, the seven blessings recited under the marriage canopy are repeated after each meal attended by the newly married couple, if certain other conditions are met: (a) a *minyan* is present at the meal; (b) at least one person is present who

did not participate in any of the couple's earlier meals. However, a newcomer is not required on the Sabbath or on a Festival.

❧ Zimun for Sheva Berachos

דְּוַי הָסֵר — *Pain banish.* The first letters of each phrase spell דּוֹנַשׁ. Donash ben Labrat, composer of this brief poem, was a 10th-century pioneer Hebrew grammarian, frequently cited by *Rashi*.

אִלֵּם בְּשִׁיר יָרוֹן—*The mute in song will exult.* This is based on the prophecy of *Isaiah* (35:6) that all handicaps will be healed in the World to Come.

בִּרְכַּת בְּנֵי אַהֲרֹן — *The blessing of the children of Aaron.* Most commentators agree that this was the original text. The blessing referred to is *Bircas Kohanim*, the Priestly Blessing.

Some texts were later changed to בְּנֵי יְשֻׁרוּן, *the children of Jeshurun* (a synonym for Israel), with the blessing referring to *Bircas HaMazon*,

בִּרְשׁוּת מָרָנָן וְרַבָּנָן וְרַבּוֹתַי, נְבָרֵךְ אֱלֹהֵינוּ שֶׁהַשִּׂמְחָה – Leader
‹ for this ‹ our God, ‹ let us ‹‹ and ‹ and ‹ of the distin- ‹ With the
celebration bless gentlemen, rabbis guished people permission

בִּמְעוֹנוֹ,* (וּ)שֶׁאָכַלְנוּ מִשֶּׁלוֹ.
‹‹ of what is His. ‹ (and) we have eaten ‹ is in His abode*

בָּרוּךְ אֱלֹהֵינוּ שֶׁהַשִּׂמְחָה בִּמְעוֹנוֹ, (וּ)שֶׁאָכַלְנוּ מִשֶּׁלוֹ – Others
‹ of what ‹ (and) ‹ is in ‹ for this ‹ is our God, ‹ Blessed
is His we have eaten His abode celebration

וּבְטוּבוֹ חָיִינוּ.
‹‹ we live. ‹ and through
His goodness

בָּרוּךְ אֱלֹהֵינוּ שֶׁהַשִּׂמְחָה בִּמְעוֹנוֹ, (וּ)שֶׁאָכַלְנוּ מִשֶּׁלוֹ – Leader
‹ of what ‹ (and) ‹ is in ‹ for this ‹ is our God, ‹ Blessed
is His we have eaten His abode celebration

וּבְטוּבוֹ חָיִינוּ.
‹‹ we live. ‹ and through
His goodness

(בָּרוּךְ הוּא וּבָרוּךְ שְׁמוֹ.)
‹‹ is His Name.) ‹ and Blessed ‹ is He ‹ (Blessed

CONTINUE WITH *BIRCAS HAMAZON* (P. 294).

AFTER *BIRCAS HAMAZON* A SECOND CUP IS POURED AND THE FOLLOWING SEVEN BLESSINGS ARE RE-
CITED. THE FIRST SIX MAY ALL BE RECITED BY ONE PERSON OR DISTRIBUTED AMONG SEVERAL PEOPLE.
WHOEVER RECITES A BLESSING HOLDS THE SECOND CUP AS HE RECITES.

1. **בָּרוּךְ** אַתָּה יהוה אֱלֹהֵינוּ מֶלֶךְ הָעוֹלָם, שֶׁהַכֹּל בָּרָא
‹ Who has created ‹‹ of the ‹ King ‹ our God, ‹ HASHEM, ‹ are You, ‹ Blessed
everything universe,

לִכְבוֹדוֹ.*
‹‹ for His glory.*

(אָמֵן.) – All respond)
‹‹ (Amen.)

2. **בָּרוּךְ** אַתָּה יהוה אֱלֹהֵינוּ מֶלֶךְ הָעוֹלָם, יוֹצֵר
‹ Who fashioned ‹‹ of the universe, ‹ King ‹ our God, ‹ HASHEM, ‹ are You, ‹ Blessed

הָאָדָם.*
‹‹ the Man.*

(אָמֵן.) – All respond)
‹‹ (Amen.)

which is recited by all Jews (see *Taz, Even HaEzer* 62, and *Sheirusa Ditzlosa*).

Some say both: בִּרְכַּת יְשׁוּרוּן כְּבִרְכַּת בְּנֵי אַהֲרֹן, *[Heed] the blessing of Jeshurun as if it were the blessing of the children of Aaron.*

שֶׁהַשִּׂמְחָה בִּמְעוֹנוֹ — *For this celebration is in His abode.* The unmixed joy with which we celebrate the marriage is a gift of God, because there is no sadness before Him; only joy (*Etz Yosef*).

1. שֶׁהַכֹּל בָּרָא לִכְבוֹדוֹ — *Who has created every-*

thing for His glory. This blessing does not deal directly with marriage. It was instituted in honor of the guests who gathered to celebrate the marriage, for they emulate God Himself, Who served as a member of the wedding party in the Garden of Eden when Adam married Eve (*Rashi, Kesubos* 8a).

2. יוֹצֵר הָאָדָם — *Who fashioned the Man.* This blessing refers to the creation of Adam, the first human being, and constitutes an introduction to

3. **בָּרוּךְ** אַתָּה יהוה אֱלֹהֵינוּ מֶלֶךְ הָעוֹלָם, אֲשֶׁר

Blessed / are You, / HASHEM, / our God, / King / of the universe, / Who

יָצַר אֶת הָאָדָם בְּצַלְמוֹ,* בְּצֶלֶם דְּמוּת תַּבְנִיתוֹ,* וְהִתְקִין

fashioned / the Man / in His image,* / in the image / of the / semblance / likeness, / of his / and prepared

לוֹ מִמֶּנּוּ* בִּנְיַן עֲדֵי עַד.* בָּרוּךְ אַתָּה יהוה, יוֹצֵר

for / him / — from / himself* — / a / building / for eternity.* / Blessed / are You, / HASHEM, / Who fashioned

הָאָדָם.

the Man.

(אָמֵן. — All respond)

(Amen.)

4. **שׂוֹשׂ** תָּשִׂישׂ* וְתָגֵל הָעֲקָרָה,* בְּקִבּוּץ בָּנֶיהָ לְתוֹכָהּ

May she rejoice intensely* / and exult / — the barren one* — / through the ingathering / of her children / amidst her

בְּשִׂמְחָה. בָּרוּךְ אַתָּה יהוה, מְשַׂמֵּחַ צִיּוֹן בְּבָנֶיהָ.*

in gladness. / Blessed / are You, / HASHEM, / Who gladdens / Zion / through her children.*

(אָמֵן. — All respond)

(Amen.)

5. **שַׂמֵּחַ** תְּשַׂמַּח* רֵעִים הָאֲהוּבִים,* כְּשַׂמֵּחֲךָ יְצִירְךָ*

Gladden intensely* / the companions / who are / beloved,* / as You gladdened / Your creation*

---

the next blessing, which thanks God for the creation of males and females (*Rashi*).

3. בְּצַלְמוֹ — *In His image.* The commentators generally agree that the Divine *image* refers to wisdom, intelligence, and free will (see ArtScroll *Genesis* 1:26).

בְּצֶלֶם דְּמוּת תַּבְנִיתוֹ — *In the image of the semblance of his likeness.* The translation spells the word *his* with a lower case "h" following *Abudraham* who interprets the phrase as referring to the human body. Thus, we are thanking God for providing man with a body that serves as host to the soul and as a tool for the performance of commandments.

וְהִתְקִין לוֹ מִמֶּנּוּ — *And prepared for him — from himself.* Eve was created from *Adam himself,* from a part of Adam's body.

בִּנְיַן עֲדֵי עַד — *A building for eternity.* Eve is called a *building* following the verse (*Genesis* 2:22) that narrates her creation (*Rashi*). The resultant human couple was to reproduce and populate the earth forever (*Avodas Yisrael*).

4. שׂוֹשׂ תָּשִׂישׂ — *May she rejoice intensely.* The repetition of the Hebrew verb form indicates intensity and continuity. The same is true of the next blessing. Thus we pray that the joy and gladness of both Jerusalem and the new couple will be intense and never-ending.

הָעֲקָרָה — *The barren one,* Jerusalem, whose future joy is likened by the prophets to the joy of bride and groom (see *Isaiah* 62:5).

מְשַׂמֵּחַ צִיּוֹן בְּבָנֶיהָ — *Who gladdens Zion through her children.* How will God comfort Jerusalem? — By gathering her children to her in happiness (*Tanchuma; Abudraham*).

5. שַׂמֵּחַ תְּשַׂמַּח — *Gladden intensely.* May God bring joy to the newly joined lives of the bride and groom (*Etz Yosef*).

רֵעִים הָאֲהוּבִים — *The companions who are beloved;* the bride and groom who, through marriage, become loving companions to one another (*Avodas Yisrael*).

יְצִירְךָ — *Your creation,* Adam, whose lonely life was gladdened when Eve was formed and

בְּגַן עֵדֶן מִקֶּדֶם.* בָּרוּךְ אַתָּה יהוה, מְשַׂמֵּחַ חָתָן וְכַלָּה.*

‹‹ and ‹ groom ‹ Who ‹‹ HASHEM, ‹ are You, ‹ Blessed ‹‹ from days ‹ of ‹ in the
bride.* gladdens of old.* Eden Garden

(אָמֵן.) – All respond)
‹‹ (Amen.)

6. בָּרוּךְ אַתָּה יהוה אֱלֹהֵינוּ מֶלֶךְ הָעוֹלָם, אֲשֶׁר בָּרָא

‹ created ‹ Who ‹‹ of the universe, ‹ King ‹ our God, ‹ HASHEM, ‹ are You, ‹ Blessed

שָׂשׂוֹן* וְשִׂמְחָה, חָתָן וְכַלָּה, גִּילָה רִנָּה, דִּיצָה וְחֶדְוָה,

‹ delight, ‹ pleasure, ‹glad song,‹ rejoicing,‹‹ and bride, ‹ groom ‹‹ and gladness, ‹ joy*

אַהֲבָה וְאַחֲוָה, וְשָׁלוֹם וְרֵעוּת.* מְהֵרָה יהוה אֱלֹהֵינוּ

‹ our God, ‹ HASHEM, ‹ Soon, ‹‹ and companionship.* ‹ peace, ‹ brotherhood, ‹ love,

יִשָּׁמַע בְּעָרֵי יְהוּדָה וּבְחֻצוֹת יְרוּשָׁלָיִם, קוֹל שָׂשׂוֹן וְקוֹל

‹ and the ‹ of joy ‹ the ‹‹ of Jerusalem, ‹ and in the ‹ of Judah ‹ in the ‹ let there
sound sound streets cities be heard

שִׂמְחָה, קוֹל חָתָן וְקוֹל כַּלָּה,¹ קוֹל מִצְהֲלוֹת חֲתָנִים

‹ of grooms ‹ of the jubilance ‹ the ‹‹ of the ‹ and the ‹ of the ‹ the ‹‹ of gladness,
sound bride, voice groom voice

מֵחֻפָּתָם, וּנְעָרִים מִמִּשְׁתֵּה נְגִינָתָם. בָּרוּךְ אַתָּה

‹ are You, ‹ Blessed ‹‹ of song. ‹ from their feasts ‹ and of youths ‹ from their canopies

יהוה, מְשַׂמֵּחַ חָתָן עִם הַכַּלָּה.

‹‹ the bride. ‹ with ‹ the groom ‹ Who gladdens ‹ HASHEM,

(אָמֵן.) – All respond)
‹‹ (Amen.)

THE LEADER OF *BIRCAS HAMAZON* RECITES THE SEVENTH BLESSING WHILE HOLDING THE FIRST CUP:

7. בָּרוּךְ אַתָּה יהוה אֱלֹהֵינוּ מֶלֶךְ הָעוֹלָם, בּוֹרֵא

‹ Who creates ‹‹ of the universe, ‹ King ‹ our God, ‹ HASHEM, ‹ are You, ‹ Blessed

(אָמֵן.) – All respond)   פְּרִי הַגָּפֶן.
‹‹ (Amen.)   ‹‹ of the vine. ‹ the fruit

THE LEADER DRINKS SOME OF THE WINE FROM HIS CUP (IN MANY COMMUNITIES, THE PERSON WHO RECITED THE LAST BLESSING ALSO RECITES A BLESSING ON WINE, QUIETLY, AND DRINKS FROM THE SECOND CUP); THEN WINE FROM THE TWO CUPS IS MIXED TOGETHER AND ONE CUP IS GIVEN TO THE GROOM AND THE OTHER TO THE BRIDE. IT IS LAUDABLE FOR THOSE PRESENT TO DRINK A BIT OF WINE FROM THE כּוֹס שֶׁל בְּרָכָה, *CUP OF BLESSING*, SINCE IT WAS USED IN THE PERFORMANCE OF A MITZVAH.

---

(1) Cf. *Jeremiah* 33:10-11.

brought to him (*Avodas Yisrael*).

מִקֶּדֶם — *From days of old.* This follows the theme of this blessing, which asks that the newlyweds be granted the bliss of Adam and Eve.

מְשַׂמֵּחַ חָתָן וְכַלָּה — *Who gladdens groom and bride*, individually, for each must be the recipient of God's blessing. The following blessing

reads חָתָן עִם הַכַּלָּה, *the groom "with" the bride,* an expression of thanks for the joy of the couple.

6. שָׂשׂוֹן . . . וְרֵעוּת — *Joy . . . and companionship.* There are ten expressions of joy in this blessing; they allude to the ten canopies which, according to the Talmud (*Bava Basra* 75a), God erected for Adam and Eve in the Garden of Eden.

❧ CIRCUMCISION / ברית מילה ❧

WHEN THE INFANT IS BROUGHT IN, THE ENTIRE ASSEMBLAGE GREETS HIM:

בָּרוּךְ הַבָּא!*

《 is he who arrives!* 〈 Blessed

THE *MOHEL* (IN SOME CONGREGATIONS, ALL THOSE PRESENT) THEN RECITES:

וַיְדַבֵּר יהוה אֶל מֹשֶׁה לֵּאמֹר. פִּינְחָס* בֶּן אֶלְעָזָר בֶּן אַהֲרֹן

〈 of 〈 son 〈 of Elazar 〈 son 〈 Phinehas,* 《 saying: 〈 Moses, 〈 to 〈 HASHEM spoke
Aaron

הַכֹּהֵן הֵשִׁיב אֶת חֲמָתִי מֵעַל בְּנֵי יִשְׂרָאֵל, בְּקַנְאוֹ אֶת קִנְאָתִי

〈 My 〈 when he 《 of Israel, 〈 the 〈 from 〈 My wrath 〈 turned 《 the
vengeance zealously avenged   Children upon   back   Kohen,

בְּתוֹכָם, וְלֹא כִלִּיתִי אֶת בְּנֵי יִשְׂרָאֵל בְּקַנְאָתִי. לָכֵן אֱמֹר,

《 say, 〈 There- 《 in My 〈 of Israel 〈 the 〈 so that I did 〈 among
fore   jealousy.   Children   not consume   them,

הִנְנִי נֹתֵן לוֹ אֶת בְּרִיתִי שָׁלוֹם.¹

《 of peace. 〈 My covenant 〈 him 〈 giving 〈 Behold!
I am

---

(1) *Numbers* 25:10-12.

❧ בְּרִית מִילָה / CIRCUMCISION ❧

The commandment of מִילָה (*milah*), circumcision, was given to Abraham when he was 99 years old. As indicated by the Torah (*Genesis* Ch. 17) and expounded by the Sages and commentators, circumcision signifies perfection, the indelible mark of the Jew as God's servant, and the covenant between God and the Jewish people. Only after Abraham's circumcision could he and Sarah have a son and begin the building of the Jewish nation. In later centuries, the entire nation circumcised itself prior to the Exodus from Egypt, and those born during the forty-year sojourn in the Wilderness were circumcised upon entering *Eretz Yisrael* under Joshua's leadership. Clearly, circumcision is crucial to Israel's very existence as a nation.

The Talmud (*Shabbos* 130a) teaches that every commandment originally accepted with joy is still performed with joy — and *milah* is the prime example of such a commandment. The joy with which parents bring their newborn sons into the "Covenant of Abraham" remains a universal expression of devotion to their Jewish heritage. Although parents ordinarily would never dream of inflicting pain on and drawing blood from their child, they celebrate his *milah* with a festival air because they are conferring upon him the seal of Jewish eternity as God's chosen people.

❧ בָּרוּךְ הַבָּא — *Blessed is he who arrives!* In addition to its simple meaning as a greeting to the baby, this is an allusion to the circumcision itself, since the numerical value of the word הַבָּא is eight, the day when circumcision is performed (*Abudraham*).

פִּינְחָס — *Phinehas.* Circumcision is associated with the prophet Elijah. As we shall see below, Elijah complained to God that the Jewish people were not sufficiently zealous in observing the *mitzvah* of *milah.* Since there is an opinion that Elijah and Phinehas are one and the same (see *Bava Metzia* 114b, *Rashi* s.v. לאו), it is customary to recite this passage which: (a) states the Divine assurance that the zealousness of Phinehas/Elijah was for the benefit of Israel; and (b) contains God's pledge that Phinehas would be given the *covenant* (an allusion to the circumcision covenant) of peace.

TWO SEATS ARE PREPARED, ONE UPON WHICH THE *SANDAK* WILL SIT AS HE HOLDS THE BABY DURING THE CIRCUMCISION. THE SECOND IS PREPARED FOR אֵלִיָּהוּ הַנָּבִיא, *ELIJAH THE PROPHET*. THE BABY IS FIRST PLACED UPON THE כִּסֵּא שֶׁל אֵלִיָּהוּ, *THRONE OF ELIJAH*, BY THE FATHER OR ONE OF THE PROMINENT GUESTS, WHEREUPON THE *MOHEL* SAYS:

זֶה הַכִּסֵּא שֶׁל אֵלִיָּהוּ* הַנָּבִיא, זָכוּר לַטּוֹב.

》for the 〈 who is 》 the 〈 Elijah* 〈 of 〈 the 〈 This is
good.   remembered   prophet,   Throne

THE *MOHEL* THEN SAYS:

לִישׁוּעָתְךָ* קִוִּיתִי יהוה.¹ שִׂבַּרְתִּי לִישׁוּעָתְךָ יהוה,

》O HASHEM,〈 for Your salvation, 〈 I hoped 》 HASHEM. 〈 I do yearn, 〈 For Your salvation*

וּמִצְוֹתֶיךָ עָשִׂיתִי.² אֵלִיָּהוּ מַלְאַךְ הַבְּרִית,* הִנֵּה שֶׁלְּךָ לְפָנֶיךָ,

》 is now 〈yours 〈behold 》 of the 〈messenger 〈 O Elijah,》I performed. 〈 and your
before you;   covenant,*   commandments

עֲמוֹד עַל יְמִינִי וְסָמְכֵנִי.* שִׂבַּרְתִּי לִישׁוּעָתְךָ יהוה. שָׂשׂ אָנֹכִי

〈 do 〈 Rejoice》 O 〈 for Your 〈 I hoped》 and assist me. 〈 my 〈 at 〈 stand
 I   HASHEM. salvation,   right

עַל אִמְרָתֶךָ, כְּמוֹצֵא שָׁלָל רָב.³ שָׁלוֹם רָב לְאֹהֲבֵי תוֹרָתֶךָ,

》 Your 〈 to those 〈 There is 》abundant spoils. 〈 like one 》 Your word, 〈 over
 Torah,   who love abundant peace   who finds

וְאֵין לָמוֹ מִכְשׁוֹל.⁴ אַשְׁרֵי תִּבְחַר* וּתְקָרֵב, יִשְׁכֹּן חֲצֵרֶיךָ —

》 in Your 〈 to dwell 〈 and whom 〈 is the one 〈 Praise-》 a stumbling 〈 for 〈 and
courts;   You draw   whom You   worthy   block.   them there
                  near   choose*   is not

(1) *Genesis* 49:18. (2) *Psalms* 119:166. (3) 119:162. (4) 119:165.

◆§ זֶה הַכִּסֵּא שֶׁל אֵלִיָּהוּ — *This is the Throne of Elijah.* The custom of setting aside a chair — preferably a handsome one — as the "Throne of Elijah" is based on a passage in *Pirkei deR' Eliezer* (Ch. 29). After fleeing from the wrath of King Ahab, Elijah declared to God that he had zealously defended the Divine honor against sinners who neglected His בְּרִית, *covenant*, a reference to Israel's neglect of circumcision (*I Kings* 19:10). God replied, "By your life, henceforth Jews will perform circumcision only when you see it with your own eyes." Some commentators see this pledge as a reward for Elijah's zeal, while others see it as a rebuke that implied he was wrong in blaming the whole nation for the neglect of some sinners (*Derishah, Yoreh Deah* 265). Whatever the interpretation, the Sages instituted the ritual of placing the infant on the Throne of Elijah, who, as מַלְאַךְ הַבְּרִית, *messenger of the covenant* (see below), attends every circumcision.

◆§ לִישׁוּעָתְךָ — *For Your salvation.* These verses, all but one of Scriptural origin, express our total reliance on God for our needs and salvation, and our joy in serving Him through the performance of His commandments.

אֵלִיָּהוּ מַלְאַךְ הַבְּרִית — *O Elijah, messenger of the covenant.* The term מַלְאַךְ הַבְּרִית, *messenger of the covenant,* is found in *Malachi* 3:1, where *Radak* explains that it refers to Elijah, who will come to herald the Redemption. It can also be translated *angel of the covenant,* because Elijah has the status of an angel.

וְסָמְכֵנִי — *And assist me.* As the one with responsibility to oversee the performance of circumcision, Elijah is asked to stand close to and assist the *mohel.* Immediately after this declaration, the *mohel* repeats his hope for God's salvation, to stress that he prays only to God, not to Elijah (*Iyun Tefillah*).

אַשְׁרֵי תִּבְחַר — *Praiseworthy is the one whom*

ALL PRESENT RESPOND

נִשְׂבְּעָה בְּטוּב בֵּיתֶךָ, קְדֹשׁ הֵיכָלֶךָ.¹

of Your 《 the holiest 《 of Your 《 with the 《 may we be
Sanctuary.   part   House,   goodness   sated

WHEN THE *MOHEL* IS READY TO PERFORM THE CIRCUMCISION, THE BABY'S FATHER SAYS:

הִנְנִי מוּכָן וּמְזֻמָּן לְקַיֵּם מִצְוַת עֲשֵׂה שֶׁצִּוַּנִי הַבּוֹרֵא

– the 《 that He has 《 the positive 《 to 《 and 《 prepared 《 Behold,
Creator, commanded me commandment perform ready   I am

יִתְבָּרַךְ, לָמוּל אֶת בְּנִי.

《 my son. 《 to 《 may He be
            circumcise Blessed –

**IN SOME CONGREGATIONS AT THIS POINT THE FATHER VERBALLY APPOINTS
THE *MOHEL* AS HIS AGENT TO PERFORM THE CIRCUMCISION ON HIS SON.
THE *MOHEL* THEN TAKES THE INFANT AND PROCLAIMS JOYOUSLY:**

אָמַר הַקָּדוֹשׁ בָּרוּךְ הוּא* לְאַבְרָהָם אָבִינוּ, הִתְהַלֵּךְ לְפָנַי

before 《 Walk 《 our 《 to Abraham, 《 is He,* 《 Blessed 《 the Holy 《 Said
Me   forefather,   One,

וֶהְיֵה תָמִים.² הִנְנִי מוּכָן וּמְזֻמָּן לְקַיֵּם מִצְוַת עֲשֵׂה שֶׁצִּוָּנוּ

《 that He has 《 the positive 《 to 《 and 《 prepared 《 Behold, 《 perfect. 《 and be
commanded us commandment perform ready   I am

הַבּוֹרֵא יִתְבָּרַךְ, לָמוּל.

《 to 《 may He be 《 – the
        circumcise. Blessed –   Creator,

**THE BABY IS PLACED ON THE *SANDAK'S* KNEES.
JUST BEFORE PERFORMING THE CIRCUMCISION, THE *MOHEL* RECITES:**

בָּרוּךְ* אַתָּה יהוה אֱלֹהֵינוּ מֶלֶךְ הָעוֹלָם, אֲשֶׁר קִדְּשָׁנוּ

has sancti- 《 Who 《 of the 《 King 《 our God, 《 HASHEM, 《 are You, 《 Blessed*
fied us   universe,

בְּמִצְוֺתָיו, וְצִוָּנוּ עַל הַמִּילָה.   (אָמֵן. – All respond)

《 circumcision. 《 regarding 《 and has com- 《 with His com-   《 (Amen.)
                              manded us   mandments,

---

(1) *Psalms* 65:5. (2) *Genesis* 17:1.

You choose. God picked Israel to be His chosen people, and the choice is expressed by sealing Israel's flesh with the mark of the covenant (*Iyun Tefillah*).

אָמַר הַקָּדוֹשׁ בָּרוּךְ הוּא — *Said the Holy One, Blessed is He.* God said to Abraham just before giving him the commandment of *milah*, implying that only through this *mitzvah* can a Jew attain perfection.

◆§ בָּרוּךְ — *Blessed.* The two blessings signify

two aspects of the *mitzvah*: that the organ of desire be controlled and that the child become worthy to enter the spiritual realm represented by the covenant made between God and Abraham (*Dover Shalom*).

As noted in *Yoreh Deah* 265:7, the authorities differ on the question of whether the father should recite שֶׁהֶחֱיָנוּ, *Who has kept us alive . . .* The prevailing custom in most communities is not to recite it since the joy of the occasion is

AS THE *MOHEL* PERFORMS THE CIRCUMCISION,
THE FATHER (OR, IF THE FATHER IS NOT PRESENT, THE *SANDAK*) RECITES:

בָּרוּךְ אַתָּה יהוה אֱלֹהֵינוּ מֶלֶךְ הָעוֹלָם, אֲשֶׁר קִדְּשָׁנוּ

⟨ has sancti- ⟨ Who ⟨⟨ of the ⟨ King ⟨ our God, ⟨ HASHEM, ⟨ are You, ⟨ Blessed
fied us　　　　　　universe,

בְּמִצְוֹתָיו, וְצִוָּנוּ לְהַכְנִיסוֹ בִּבְרִיתוֹ שֶׁל אַבְרָהָם אָבִינוּ.

⟨⟨ our ⟨ Abraham, ⟨ of ⟨ into the ⟨ to bring ⟨ and has com- ⟨ with His com-
forefather.　　　　　　covenant　　him　　manded us　　mandments,

ALL RESPOND, LOUDLY AND JOYFULLY:

אָמֵן. כְּשֵׁם שֶׁנִּכְנַס לַבְּרִית,* כֵּן יִכָּנֵס

⟨ may he ⟨ so ⟨⟨ into the ⟨ he has ⟨ Just as ⟨⟨ Amen.
enter　　　　covenant,*　entered

לְתוֹרָה וּלְחֻפָּה וּלְמַעֲשִׂים טוֹבִים.

⟨⟨ that are ⟨ and [the perform- ⟨ the marriage ⟨ into the [study
good.　　ance of] deeds　canopy,　of] Torah,

AFTER THE CIRCUMCISION, THE BABY IS HELD BY ONE OF THE PROMINENT GUESTS WHILE THE FOLLOWING PRAYERS (INCLUDING THE GIVING OF THE NAME) ARE RECITED. THE HONOR OF RECITING THE BLESSINGS AND OF GIVING THE NAME MAY BE GIVEN TO ONE PERSON, OR TWO. SIMILARLY, TWO PEOPLE MAY HOLD THE BABY, ONE DURING THE BLESSINGS, AND ONE FOR THE NAMING.

A CUP OF WINE IS FILLED AND HELD IN THE RIGHT HAND BY THE MAN RECITING THE BLESSINGS.

בָּרוּךְ אַתָּה יהוה אֱלֹהֵינוּ מֶלֶךְ הָעוֹלָם, בּוֹרֵא פְּרִי הַגָּפֶן.

⟨⟨ of the ⟨ the ⟨ Who ⟨⟨ of the ⟨ King ⟨ our God, ⟨ HASHEM, ⟨ are You, ⟨ Blessed
vine.　fruit　creates　　universe,

אָמֵן. – All respond)
⟨⟨ (Amen.)

בָּרוּךְ אַתָּה יהוה אֱלֹהֵינוּ מֶלֶךְ הָעוֹלָם, אֲשֶׁר קִדַּשׁ

⟨ sanctified ⟨ Who ⟨⟨ of the ⟨ King ⟨ our God, ⟨ HASHEM, ⟨ are You, ⟨ Blessed
universe,

muted because of the pain inflicted upon the infant.

כְּשֵׁם שֶׁנִּכְנַס לַבְּרִית — *Just as he has entered into the covenant.* The assembled guests proclaim their joy that a new member has been added to the covenant of Abraham. Simultaneously they offer their blessing that he may live a life of happiness and spiritual fulfillment. *Abudraham* notes that this blessing involves the father's responsibilities to his son: just as he has carried out his duty to circumcise, so may he carry out his duties to teach him Torah, arrange his marriage, and train him in the performance of good deeds.

Why are these three blessings listed in this order?

— *Abudraham* notes that the order is chronological. First, he studies Torah. Then, as the Mishnah (*Avos* 5:25) prescribes, comes marriage at age 18; finally, since the Heavenly Court withholds punishment until age 20, comes the time when a failure to do good deeds is no longer tolerated.

— Torah study begins in early childhood. Even when one is so burdened with family responsibility that time for study is lacking, he must still perform good deeds (cf. *Dover Shalom*).

יְדִיד מִבֶּטֶן,* וְחֹק בִּשְׁאֵרוֹ שָׂם, וְצֶאֱצָאָיו חָתַם בְּאוֹת

⟨ the beloved one ⟩ ⟨ from the womb* ⟩ ⟨ and [the mark of] the decree [of circumcision] ⟩ ⟨ in his flesh ⟩ ⟨ placed, ⟩ ⟨ and his offspring ⟩ ⟨ sealed ⟩ ⟨ with the sign

בְּרִית קֹדֶשׁ. עַל כֵּן בִּשְׂכַר זֹאת,* אֵל חַי, חֶלְקֵנוּ צוּרֵנוּ,

⟨ of the holy covenant. ⟩ ⟨ Therefore, ⟩ ⟨ as reward ⟩ ⟨ for this* ⟩ ⟨ — O Living God, ⟩ ⟨ our Portion, ⟩ ⟨ our Rock —

צַוֵּה* לְהַצִּיל יְדִידוּת שְׁאֵרֵנוּ מִשַּׁחַת,* לְמַעַן בְּרִיתוֹ אֲשֶׁר

⟨ may You command* ⟩ ⟨ to rescue ⟩ ⟨ the beloved [soul] ⟩ ⟨ [within] our flesh ⟩ ⟨ from destruction,* ⟩ ⟨ for the sake ⟩ ⟨ of His covenant ⟩ ⟨ that

שָׂם בִּבְשָׂרֵנוּ. בָּרוּךְ אַתָּה יהוה, כּוֹרֵת הַבְּרִית. (All respond—אָמֵן.)

⟨ He has placed ⟩ ⟨ in our flesh. ⟩ ⟨ Blessed ⟩ ⟨ are You, ⟩ ⟨ HASHEM, ⟩ ⟨ Who establishes ⟩ ⟨ the covenant. ⟩ ⟨ (Amen.)

GIVING THE NAME / קריאת השם

UPON REACHING THE WORDS IN BOLD TYPE, THE READER PAUSES WHILE ALL PRESENT RECITE THEM ALOUD; HE THEN REPEATS THEM AND CONTINUES:

אֱלֹהֵינוּ וֵאלֹהֵי אֲבוֹתֵינוּ, קַיֵּם אֶת הַיֶּלֶד הַזֶּה לְאָבִיו

⟨ Our God ⟩ ⟨ and the God ⟩ ⟨ of our forefathers, ⟩ ⟨ preserve ⟩ ⟨ this child ⟩ ⟨ for his father

וּלְאִמּוֹ, וְיִקָּרֵא שְׁמוֹ בְּיִשְׂרָאֵל (BABY'S HEBREW NAME) בֶּן (BABY'S FATHER'S HEBREW NAME).

⟨ and for his mother, ⟩ ⟨ and may his name be called ⟩ ⟨ in Israel ⟩ ⟨ (BABY'S HEBREW NAME) ⟩ ⟨ son of ⟩ ⟨ (BABY'S FATHER'S HEBREW NAME).

אֲשֶׁר קִדֵּשׁ יְדִיד מִבֶּטֶן — *Who sanctified the beloved one from the womb.* There are several interpretations of this phrase. Primary among them are:

❏ The *beloved one* is Isaac, the first person to be sanctified from the womb, in the sense that he was conceived after the commandment of circumcision was given. He and *his offspring* throughout the generations have in their flesh the *mark of the decree*, which is the sign of the holy covenant (*Rashi, Shabbos* 137b).

❏ The blessing tells how God put His seal, circumcision, in all the generations of the Jewish people. It started with Abraham, God's *beloved*, for whose righteousness God longed when he was still in the womb; continued with Isaac, in whose flesh *the mark of the decree was placed*; and then went on to Isaac's offspring, Jacob and his descendants (*Rabbeinu Tam* ibid., and *Menachos* 53a).

בִּשְׂכַר זֹאת — *As reward for this,* for circumcis-ing ourselves.

צַוֵּה — *May You command.* This is a prayer that God preserve the souls of the circumcised, as noted below. Some *siddurim* read in the past tense: צִוִּיתָ, *You commanded.*

יְדִידוּת שְׁאֵרֵנוּ מִשַּׁחַת — *The beloved [soul] [within] our flesh from destruction.* In the merit of circumcising our flesh, may our soul be spared the destructive suffering of *Gehinnom*. As the Sages teach (*Eruvin* 19a), Abraham saved his circumcised offspring from *Gehinnom*.

⌘ קריאת השם / **Giving the Name**

The custom of naming a boy at his circumcision is based on the fact that God gave Abram the name Abraham in conjunction with the *mitzvah*, commandment, of *milah*, and that Moses' parents gave him the Hebrew name Yekusiel at the time of his *milah* (*Pirkei deR' Eliezer*). At the time of the *bris*, the infant enters

יִשְׂמַח הָאָב בְּיוֹצֵא חֲלָצָיו, וְתָגֵל אִמּוֹ בִּפְרִי בִטְנָהּ. כַּכָּתוּב:

May the father rejoice ‹ in the issue ‹ of his loins, ‹ and may his mother exult ‹ in the fruit ‹ of her womb, ‹ as it is written:

יִשְׂמַח אָבִיךָ וְאִמֶּךָ, וְתָגֵל יוֹלַדְתֶּךָ.¹ וְנֶאֱמַר: וָאֶעֱבֹר עָלַיִךְ

Rejoice ‹ may your father ‹ and ‹ mother ‹ and ‹ may she who gave birth to you. ‹ And it is said: ‹ Then I passed ‹ by you

וָאֶרְאֵךְ מִתְבּוֹסֶסֶת בְּדָמָיִךְ, וָאֹמַר לָךְ בְּדָמַיִךְ חֲיִי, וָאֹמַר לָךְ

and I saw you ‹ wallowing ‹ in your blood, ‹ and I said ‹ to you: ‹ 'In your blood, ‹ live!' ‹ and I said ‹ to you:

בְּדָמַיִךְ חֲיִי.*² וְנֶאֱמַר: זָכַר לְעוֹלָם בְּרִיתוֹ, דָּבָר צִוָּה לְאֶלֶף

'In your blood, ‹ live!' ‹ And it is said: ‹ He remembered ‹ forever ‹ His covenant ‹ — the Word ‹ He commanded ‹ for a thousand*

דּוֹר. אֲשֶׁר כָּרַת אֶת אַבְרָהָם, וּשְׁבוּעָתוֹ לְיִשְׂחָק. וַיַּעֲמִידֶהָ

generations — ‹ that ‹ He made ‹ with ‹ Abraham, ‹ and His vow ‹ to Isaac. ‹ Then He established it

לְיַעֲקֹב לְחֹק, לְיִשְׂרָאֵל בְּרִית עוֹלָם.³ וְנֶאֱמַר. וַיָּמָל אַבְרָהָם

for Jacob ‹ as a statute, ‹ for Israel ‹ as a covenant ‹ everlasting.³ ‹ And it is said: ‹ Abraham circumcised

אֶת יִצְחָק בְּנוֹ, בֶּן שְׁמֹנַת יָמִים, כַּאֲשֶׁר צִוָּה אֹתוֹ אֱלֹהִים.⁴

Isaac ‹ his son ‹ at the age ‹ of eight ‹ days, ‹ as ‹ God had commanded him.⁴

הוֹדוּ לַיהוה* כִּי טוֹב, כִּי לְעוֹלָם חַסְדּוֹ. הוֹדוּ לַיהוה כִּי טוֹב,⁵

Give thanks ‹ to HASHEM ‹ for ‹ He is good; ‹ for ‹ enduring ‹ is His kindness! ‹ Give thanks ‹ to HASHEM ‹ for ‹ He is good;*

(1) *Proverbs* 23:25. (2) *Ezekiel* 16:6. (3) *Psalms* 105:8-10. (4) *Genesis* 21:4. (5) *Psalms* 118:1, et al.

the covenant of Israel, and it is then appropriate to give him the name that expresses his sanctity, because the spiritual destiny of a person is contained in his name.

Among Ashkenazic Jews, it is customary to name a child after a deceased forebear or spiritual leader to whom the family has had ties. Thereby it is hoped that the infant will benefit from the merit of the deceased and also carry on his good works (*Dover Shalom*). [This subject is discussed in detail in the ArtScroll *Bris Milah*.]

וָאֹמַר לָךְ בְּדָמַיִךְ חֲיִי — *And I said to you: 'In your blood, live!'* This verse is an allusion to the time in Egypt just before the Exodus when Israel was commanded to circumcise its males and to bring the *pesach* offering. In the merit of these two commandments, both involving blood, the nation would earn redemption and eternal life as God's chosen people (*Sifre; Targum* to *Ezekiel* 16:6). *Milah* on the Jew's body marks him as God's servant, while the *pesach* offering symbolizes that he is ready to actively carry out God's will (*Gur Aryeh, Exodus* 12:6). [See ArtScroll *Ezekiel* for a further discussion of the subject.]

The congregation recites this statement aloud two times, symbolizing life in both worlds. Each time, the *mohel* dips his finger into the wine and puts a drop into the infant's mouth, symbolizing the commandments of *milah* and *pesach* that bring life to the Jewish people (*Tur, Yoreh Deah* 265).

הוֹדוּ לַה' — *Give thanks to* HASHEM. When Yocheved gave birth to Moses, she saw that he

כִּי לְעוֹלָם חַסְדּוֹ. (BABY'S HEBREW NAME) בֶּן (FATHER'S HEBREW NAME)

for ⟩ forever ⟨ enduring ⟩ is His ⟨⟨   son of   ⟨⟨
kindness!

זֶה הַקָּטָן גָּדוֹל יִהְיֶה.

this ⟩ little ⟨ great ⟩ may he ⟨⟨
one —   become.

כְּשֵׁם שֶׁנִּכְנַס לַבְּרִית, כֵּן יִכָּנֵס

Just as ⟩ he has ⟨ into the ⟨⟨ so ⟩ may he ⟨
entered covenant, enter

לְתוֹרָה, וּלְחֻפָּה, וּלְמַעֲשִׂים טוֹבִים.

into the ⟩ the ⟨ and [the ⟩ ⟨⟨ that are
[study of] marriage performance good.
Torah, canopy, of] deeds

THE ONE WHO RECITED THE BLESSINGS DRINKS SOME WINE.
THE *MOHEL* BLESSES THE CHILD:

מִי שֶׁבֵּרַךְ אֲבוֹתֵינוּ אַבְרָהָם יִצְחָק וְיַעֲקֹב, הוּא יְבָרֵךְ

bless ⟩ may ⟨ ⟨⟨ and Jacob, ⟨ Isaac, ⟨ Abraham, ⟨ our ⟨ Who blessed ⟨ He
He forefathers,

אֶת הַיֶּלֶד רַךְ הַנִּמּוֹל (BABY'S HEBREW NAME) בֶּן* (FATHER'S HEBREW NAME),

⟨⟨ [just] cir- ⟨ — tender,⟨⟨ the child   son of*   ⟨⟨
cumcised —

וְיִשְׁלַח לוֹ* רְפוּאָה שְׁלֵמָה, בַּעֲבוּר שֶׁנִּכְנַס לַבְּרִית. וּכְשֵׁם

Just as ⟩ into the ⟨ he has ⟨ because ⟨⟨ a complete recovery, ⟨ him* ⟨ and may
covenant. entered He send

שֶׁנִּכְנַס לַבְּרִית כֵּן יִכָּנֵס לְתוֹרָה, וּלְחֻפָּה, וּלְמַעֲשִׂים

he has ⟩ into the ⟨ so ⟨⟨ may he ⟨ into the ⟨ the marriage ⟨ and [the ⟨
entered covenant, enter [study of] canopy, performance
Torah, of] deeds

טוֹבִים. וְנֹאמַר: אָמֵן. (אָמֵן.–All respond)

that are ⟨⟨ And let ⟨ Amen. ⟨⟨   (Amen.) ⟨⟨
good. us say,

---

was טוֹב, *good* (*Exodus* 2:2), which the Talmud (*Sotah* 12a) understands to mean that he was born circumcised. Thus, we praise God for being *good*, meaning that He has now enabled the newborn infant to attain the degree of goodness symbolized by *milah* (*HaManhig*).

בֶּן — *Son of.* Although it is customary when reciting prayers for the sick to use the name of the patient's mother, here the father's name is

used, since we do not consider being circumcised an illness. Rather, the intent of the prayer is that the child not become ill as a result of the surgery of the *bris*. Therefore this text is also appropriate for the Sabbath (*Shaar HaKollel, Seder HaMilah,* 9, at end of *Shulchan Aruch HaRav*).

וְיִשְׁלַח לוֹ — *And may He send him.* Some add וּלְאִמּוֹ, *and to his mother* (baby's mother's He-

THE *MOHEL* AND FATHER THEN RECITE THE FOLLOWING PRAYER:

רַבּוֹנוֹ שֶׁל עוֹלָם, יְהִי רָצוֹן מִלְּפָנֶיךָ, שֶׁיְּהֵא חָשׁוּב וּמְרֻצֶּה

⟨ desired, ⟨ worthy, ⟨ that it be ⟨ before You, ⟨ the ⟨⟨ the ⟨ of ⟨ Master
will it be universe,

וּמְקֻבָּל לְפָנֶיךָ, כְּאִלּוּ הִקְרַבְתִּיהוּ לִפְנֵי כִסֵּא כְבוֹדֶךָ. וְאַתָּה,

⟨ and may ⟨⟨ of Your ⟨ the ⟨ before ⟨ I had offered him ⟨ as if ⟨ before You ⟨ and
You, Glory, Throne accepted

בְּרַחֲמֶיךָ הָרַבִּים, שְׁלַח עַל יְדֵי מַלְאָכֶיךָ הַקְּדוֹשִׁים נְשָׁמָה

⟨ a soul ⟨⟨ that are holy, ⟨ Your angels ⟨ through ⟨ send ⟨ that is ⟨ in Your mercy
abundant,

קְדוֹשָׁה וּטְהוֹרָה

and pure ⟨ that is holy

FATHER SAYS: | **MOHEL SAYS:**

(BABY'S HEBREW NAME) לִבְנִי | (FATHER'S HEBREW NAME) בֶּן (BABY'S HEBREW NAME) לְ

⟨ to my son, | ⟨ son of ⟨ to

הַנִּמּוֹל עַתָּה לִשְׁמְךָ הַגָּדוֹל, וְשֶׁיִּהְיֶה לִבּוֹ פָּתוּחַ כְּפִתְחוֹ

⟨ as the ⟨ [as] ⟨ and may ⟨⟨ that is ⟨ for the ⟨ now ⟨ who
entrance open his heart be great, sake of has been
Your Name circumcised

שֶׁל אוֹלָם, בְּתוֹרָתְךָ הַקְּדוֹשָׁה, לִלְמֹד וּלְלַמֵּד, לִשְׁמֹר

⟨ to ⟨ and to teach, ⟨ to learn ⟨⟨ to Your holy Torah, ⟨⟨ of the Temple,
observe

וְלַעֲשׂוֹת. וְתֶן לוֹ אֲרִיכוּת יָמִים וְשָׁנִים, חַיִּים שֶׁל יִרְאַת

⟨ fear ⟨ of ⟨ a life ⟨⟨ and years, ⟨ of days ⟨ length ⟨ him ⟨ Give ⟨⟨ and to
perform.

חֵטְא, חַיִּים שֶׁל עֹשֶׁר וְכָבוֹד, חַיִּים שֶׁתְּמַלֵּא מִשְׁאֲלוֹת לִבּוֹ

⟨ of his ⟨ all the ⟨ in which ⟨ a life ⟨⟨ and ⟨ wealth ⟨ of ⟨ a life ⟨⟨ of sin,
heart wishes You fulfill honor,

לְטוֹבָה. אָמֵן, וְכֵן יְהִי רָצוֹן.

⟨⟨ [Your] will. ⟨ be ⟨ – may ⟨⟨ Amen ⟨⟨ for good.
such

**CONGREGATION RECITES עָלֵינוּ (P. 256), FOLLOWED BY THE MOURNER'S KADDISH.
A FESTIVE MEAL FOLLOWS.**

---

brew name), בַּת, *daughter of* (her father's Hebrew name). [Here as well we use the father's
name, since childbirth is not considered an ill-

ness. However, if the delivery was by Cae-
sarean section, or if complications are present,
her mother's name should be used.]

YOM L'YABASHAH / יום ליבשה

THIS LITURGICAL POEM, COMPOSED BY THE 12TH-CENTURY *PAYTAN* RABBI YEHUDAH HALEVI,
IS CUSTOMARILY SUNG AT THE CIRCUMCISION FEAST.
THE INITIAL LETTERS OF THE STANZAS FORM THE AUTHOR'S NAME.

יום לְיַבָּשָׁה נֶהֶפְכוּ מְצוּלִים,* שִׁירָה חֲדָשָׁה שִׁבְּחוּ גְאוּלִים.

The day [on which] land into dry were transformed the deep waters, [with] a new song the redeemed ones praised [Your Name].

הִטְבַּעְתָּ בְתַרְמִית רַגְלֵי בַת עֲנָמִית,* וּפַעֲמֵי שׁוּלַמִּית*

You caused to sink — because of her deceitfulness — the feet of the daughter of the Anamite; but the footsteps of the Shulamite*

יָפוּ בַנְּעָלִים. שִׁירָה חֲדָשָׁה שִׁבְּחוּ גְאוּלִים.

remained beautiful in shoes. [With] a new song the redeemed ones praised.

וְכָל רוֹאֵי יְשׁוּרוּן,* בְּבֵית הוֹדִי יְשׁוֹרְרוּן, אֵין כָּאֵל יְשׁוּרוּן,

All those who see Jeshurun, in My Majestic Home will sing: There is none like God, O Jeshurun*

וְאוֹיְבֵינוּ פְלִילִים. שִׁירָה חֲדָשָׁה שִׁבְּחוּ גְאוּלִים.

— even our enemies will so judge. [With] a new song the redeemed ones praised.

דְּגָלַי כֵּן תָּרִים,* עַל הַנִּשְׁאָרִים, וּתְלַקֵּט נִפְזָרִים, כִּמְלַקֵּט

My banners may You indeed raise over those who remain [in exile]; and gather the scattered ones, as one gathers*

שִׁבֳּלִים. שִׁירָה חֲדָשָׁה שִׁבְּחוּ גְאוּלִים.

stalks of grain. [With] a new song the redeemed ones praised.

הַבָּאִים עִמָּךְ,* בִּבְרִית חוֹתָמָךְ, וּמִבֶּטֶן לִשְׁמָךְ, הֵמָּה נִמוֹלִים.

Those who come with You into the covenant of Your seal, and [directly] from the womb for Your Name's sake they are circumcised.*

---

(1) Cf. *Psalms* 66:6. (2) Cf. *Song of Songs* 7:1-2. (3) *Deuteronomy* 33:26.
(4) 32:31. (5) *Isaiah* 17:5. (6) Cf. *Genesis* 34:22.

יום לְיַבָּשָׁה נֶהֶפְכוּ מְצוּלִים — *The day [on which] into dry land were transformed the deep waters.* The reference is to the seventh day of Pesach, when the sea split for the benefit of the Jewish people. Not only the Sea of Reeds, but all concentrations of water split; therefore, the *zemer* uses the plural מְצוּלִים, *deep waters.*

עֲנָמִית — *Anamite.* Egypt is entitled Anamite because Anamim was a son of Mitzraim, the progenitor of Egypt (*Genesis* 10:13).

וּפַעֲמֵי שׁוּלַמִּית — *But the footsteps of the Shulamite,* Israel. The footsteps of Israel that are beautifully shod refers to the loyalty of the Jewish people in going to Jerusalem three times a year for the pilgrimage festivals (*Sotah* 49b).

יְשׁוּרוּן — *Jeshurun.* A title representing Israel in its state of righteousness and spiritual exaltation, from יָשָׁר, *upright.*

דְּגָלַי כֵּן תָּרִים — *My banners may You indeed raise.* A prayer that God gather up the scattered survivors of our people wherever they are and bring them together as a farmer collects stalks during the harvest.

הַבָּאִים עִמָּךְ — *Those who come with You.* The Jewish people approach God with the mark of

שִׁירָה חֲדָשָׁה שִׁבְּחוּ גְאוּלִים.
« the redeemed ones praised. ‹ [With] a new song

הַרְאֵה אוֹתוֹתָם,* לְכָל רוֹאֵי אוֹתָם, וְעַל כַּנְפֵי כְסוּתָם, יַעֲשׂוּ
‹ they will ‹ of their ‹ the ‹ and on « them, ‹ who see ‹ to all ‹ their signs* ‹ Display
make / garments / corners

גְּדִילִים.*1
« fringes.*

שִׁירָה חֲדָשָׁה שִׁבְּחוּ גְאוּלִים.
« the redeemed ones praised. ‹ [With] a new song

לְמִי זֹאת* נִרְשֶׁמֶת, הַכֶּר נָא דְּבַר אֱמֶת, לְמִי הַחוֹתֶמֶת,
‹ is the seal ‹ Whose « of truth: ‹ this ‹ please, ‹ Recognize, « marked? ‹ is ‹ For
matter / this* / Whom

וּלְמִי הַפְּתִילִים.2
« are the threads? ‹ and whose

שִׁירָה חֲדָשָׁה שִׁבְּחוּ גְאוּלִים.
« the redeemed ones praised. ‹ [With] a new song

וְשׁוּב שֵׁנִית לְקַדְּשָׁהּ,* וְאַל תּוֹסִיף לְגָרְשָׁהּ, וְהַעֲלֵה אוֹר
‹ the ‹ raise « to drive ‹ continue ‹ and ‹ and betroth ‹ once ‹ Return
light / her away; / do not / her,* / again

שִׁמְשָׁהּ, וְנֵסוּ הַצְּלָלִים.3
« the shadows. ‹ and let flee ‹ of her sun

שִׁירָה חֲדָשָׁה שִׁבְּחוּ גְאוּלִים.
« the redeemed ones praised. ‹ [With] a new song

יְדִידִים רוֹמְמוּךְ, בְּשִׁירָה קִדְּמוּךְ, מִי כָמְכָה, יהוה, בָּאֵלִים.4
« among the ‹ HASHEM, ‹ is like You, ‹ Who « they ‹ with song « exalted You; ‹ The beloved
mighty ones! / approached You: / ones

שִׁירָה חֲדָשָׁה שִׁבְּחוּ גְאוּלִים.
« the redeemed ones praised. ‹ [With] a new song

בִּגְלַל אָבוֹת תּוֹשִׁיעַ בָּנִים, וְתָבִיא גְאֻלָּה לִבְנֵי בְנֵיהֶם.
« of their ‹ to the ‹ redemption ‹ and bring « the ‹ save ‹ of the ‹ For the
children. / children / offspring, / forefathers / sake

---

(1) Cf. *Deuteronomy* 22:12. (2) Cf. *Genesis* 38:25. (3) *Song of Songs* 2:17, 4:6. (4) Cf. *Exodus* 15:11.

the covenant sealed into their flesh. From early infancy, almost as soon as he emerges from his mother's womb, a Jewish boy is circumcised. This stanza, which calls for God's mercy in the merit of *milah*, is the reason this *zemer* is sung at the circumcision feast.

הַרְאֵה אוֹתוֹתָם — *Display their signs.* The Divine Presence resting upon the Jewish people is the *sign* that they are God's people (see *Deuteronomy* 28:10).

יַעֲשׂוּ גְדִילִים — *They will make fringes.* Tzitzis are like the insignia of a royal servant.

לְמִי זֹאת — *For Whom is this.* This stanza proclaims that Israel's loyalty to God is plain to all. What other nation observes the Torah's commandments? What other nation has the signet, the seal of circumcision, and the threads of *tzitzis*?

וְשׁוּב שֵׁנִית לְקַדְּשָׁה — *Return once again and betroth her.* May God renew His ties to Israel by bringing her back into His "home" and never again exiling her. May He show her the bright sun of redemption and banish the shadows of exile.

זימון לסעודת הברית / ZIMUN FOR THE CIRCUMCISION FEAST

THIS *ZIMUN* IS RECITED BY THE LEADER HOLDING A CUP OF WINE:

Leader – רַבּוֹתַי מִיר וֶועלֶען בֶּענְטְשֶׁען [רַבּוֹתַי נְבָרֵךְ].

≪ [let us bless. ⟨ Gentlemen,] ≪ bless. ⟨ we wish to ⟨ Gentlemen,

Others – יְהִי שֵׁם יהוה מְבֹרָךְ מֵעַתָּה וְעַד עוֹלָם.[1]

≪ eternity. ⟨ until ⟨ from ⟨ be ⟨ of ⟨ the ⟨ Let
this time blessed HASHEM Name

Leader – יְהִי שֵׁם יהוה מְבֹרָךְ מֵעַתָּה וְעַד עוֹלָם.[1]

≪ eternity. ⟨ until ⟨ from ⟨ be ⟨ of ⟨ the ⟨ Let
this time blessed HASHEM Name

נוֹדֶה לְשִׁמְךָ* בְּתוֹךְ אֱמוּנַי,* בְּרוּכִים אַתֶּם לַיהוה.

≪ to HASHEM. ⟨ are you ⟨ blessed ≪ my ⟨ among ⟨ to Your ⟨ We give
faithful;* Name* thanks

Others – נוֹדֶה לְשִׁמְךָ בְּתוֹךְ אֱמוּנַי, בְּרוּכִים אַתֶּם לַיהוה.

≪ to HASHEM. ⟨ are you ⟨ blessed ≪ my ⟨ among ⟨ to Your ⟨ We give
faithful; Name thanks

Leader – בִּרְשׁוּת אֵל אָיוֹם וְנוֹרָא, מִשְׂגָּב לְעִתּוֹת בַּצָּרָה,

≪ of ⟨ in times ⟨ the ≪ and ⟨ — fearful ≪ of the ⟨ With the
trouble, Refuge awesome, Almighty permission

אֵל נֶאְזָר בִּגְבוּרָה, אַדִּיר בַּמָּרוֹם יהוה.

≪ HASHEM. ≪ on high — ⟨ the ≪ with ⟨ girded ⟨ the
Mighty strength, Almighty

Others – נוֹדֶה לְשִׁמְךָ בְּתוֹךְ אֱמוּנַי, בְּרוּכִים אַתֶּם לַיהוה.

≪ to HASHEM. ⟨ are you ⟨ blessed ≪ my ⟨ among ⟨ to Your ⟨ We give
faithful; Name thanks

Leader – בִּרְשׁוּת הַתּוֹרָה הַקְּדוֹשָׁה, טְהוֹרָה הִיא וְגַם פְּרוּשָׁה,

≪ explicit, ⟨ and also ⟨ it is ⟨ pure ≪ of the holy Torah, ⟨ With the
permission

צִוָּה לָנוּ מוֹרָשָׁה,* מֹשֶׁה עֶבֶד יהוה.*

≪ of HASHEM.* ⟨ servant ⟨ [by] Moses, ≪ as a heritage,* ⟨ to us ⟨ commanded

---

(1) *Psalms* 113:2.

⧏ Bircas HaMazon for Bris Milah

נוֹדֶה לְשִׁמְךָ — *We give thanks to Your Name.* There are indications that this song was recited by Polish Jews following *all* festive meals. With the passage of time, the custom was discontinued except at circumcisions [possibly because circumcisions, as the Sages teach (*Shabbos* 130a), have always been celebrated with great joy].

אֱמוּנַי — *My faithful.* The one who leads the group in *Bircas HaMazon* refers to his companions as *faithful*, people whose faith is in God.

מוֹרָשָׁה — *Heritage.* The Torah is the *heritage* of Israel. As such we are not free to neglect it or cede it to any other nation.

עֶבֶד ה׳ — *Servant* (lit. *slave*) *of Hashem.* A slave is totally the property of his master. He has neither personality nor initiative of his own. Moses is honored with this title because he was

– Others   נוֹדֶה לְשִׁמְךָ בְּתוֹךְ אֱמוּנַי, בְּרוּכִים אַתֶּם לַיהוה.

to Hashem. ⟨ are you ⟨ blessed ⟨⟨ my ⟨ among ⟨ to Your ⟨ We give
faithful;   Name   thanks

– Leader   בִּרְשׁוּת הַכֹּהֲנִים הַלְוִיִּם, אֶקְרָא לֵאלֹהֵי הָעִבְרִיִּים,

of the ⟨ upon ⟨ I call ⟨⟨ [from] the ⟨ of the ⟨ With the
Hebrews,   the God   tribe of Levi, *Kohanim*   permission

אֲהוֹדֶנּוּ בְּכָל אִיִּים,* אֲבָרְכָה אֶת יהוה.

to Hashem. ⟨ I will give ⟨⟨ islands,* ⟨ unto all ⟨ I will
blessing   thank Him

– Others   נוֹדֶה לְשִׁמְךָ בְּתוֹךְ אֱמוּנַי, בְּרוּכִים אַתֶּם לַיהוה.

to Hashem. ⟨ are you ⟨ blessed ⟨⟨ my ⟨ among ⟨ to Your ⟨ We give
faithful;   Name   thanks

– Leader   בִּרְשׁוּת מָרָנָן וְרַבָּנָן וְרַבּוֹתַי, אֶפְתְּחָה בְּשִׁיר פִּי וּשְׂפָתַי,

and my ⟨ my ⟨ in song ⟨ I open ⟨⟨ and ⟨ and ⟨ of the distin- ⟨ With the
lips,   mouth   gentlemen, rabbis guished people, permission

וְתֹאמַרְנָה עַצְמוֹתַי, בָּרוּךְ הַבָּא בְּשֵׁם יהוה.

of Hashem. ⟨ in the ⟨ is he who ⟨ Blessed ⟨⟨ shall my ⟨ and proclaim
Name   comes   bones,

– Others   נוֹדֶה לְשִׁמְךָ בְּתוֹךְ אֱמוּנַי, בְּרוּכִים אַתֶּם לַיהוה.

to Hashem. ⟨ are you ⟨ blessed ⟨⟨ my ⟨ among ⟨ to Your ⟨ We give
faithful;   Name   thanks

**IF TEN MEN JOIN IN THE *ZIMUN*, AMONG WHOM AT LEAST SEVEN ATE BREAD,
ADD GOD'S NAME (IN PARENTHESES).**

– Leader   בִּרְשׁוּת מָרָנָן וְרַבָּנָן וְרַבּוֹתַי,

and gentlemen, ⟨ and ⟨ of the distin- ⟨ With the
rabbis guished people, permission

נְבָרֵךְ (אֱלֹהֵינוּ) שֶׁאָכַלְנוּ מִשֶּׁלוֹ.

of what is His. ⟨ for we have eaten ⟨ (our God) ⟨ let us bless [Him,]

– Others   בָּרוּךְ (אֱלֹהֵינוּ) שֶׁאָכַלְנוּ מִשֶּׁלוֹ, וּבְטוּבוֹ חָיִינוּ.

we live. ⟨ and through ⟨ of what ⟨ for we ⟨ (our God,) ⟨ Blessed
His goodness   is His   have eaten   is [He,]

– Leader   בָּרוּךְ (אֱלֹהֵינוּ) שֶׁאָכַלְנוּ מִשֶּׁלוֹ, וּבְטוּבוֹ חָיִינוּ.

we live. ⟨ and through ⟨ of what ⟨ for we ⟨ (our God,) ⟨ Blessed
His goodness   is His   have eaten   is [He,]

(בָּרוּךְ הוּא וּבָרוּךְ שְׁמוֹ.)

is His Name.) ⟨ and Blessed ⟨ is He ⟨ (Blessed

**CONTINUE WITH BIRCAS HAMAZON, *BLESSING AFTER MEALS* (P. 294),
UNTIL בְּעֵינֵי אֱלֹהִים וְאָדָם, *IN THE EYES OF GOD AND MAN* (P. 307).**

---

completely devoted to the will of God.
אִיִּים — *Islands.* The expression *islands* is used
to indicate that the praise of God will be so

universal that even the isolated inhabitants of
far-flung islands will praise Him (see *Isaiah*
42:10 and *Malbim* there).

A DESIGNATED PERSON (OR PERSONS) RECITES THE FOLLOWING PRAYERS ALOUD.
SOMEONE OTHER THAN THE FATHER SHOULD RECITE THE FOLLOWING STANZA:

הָרַחֲמָן הוּא יְבָרֵךְ אֲבִי הַיֶּלֶד וְאִמּוֹ, וְיִזְכּוּ לְגַדְּלוֹ

⟨ to raise ⟨ and may ⟨⟨ and [the ⟨ of the ⟨ the ⟨ bless ⟨ May ⟨ The compassion-
him, they merit child's] mother; child father He ate One!

וּלְחַנְּכוֹ וּלְחַכְּמוֹ,* מִיּוֹם הַשְּׁמִינִי וָהָלְאָה יֵרָצֶה דָמוֹ,*

⟨⟨ may his blood ⟨ onward ⟨ from the eighth day ⟨ and to make ⟨ to educate
find favor,* him wise;* him,

וִיהִי יהוה אֱלֹהָיו עִמּוֹ. (אָמֵן.—All respond)

⟨⟨ be with him. ⟨ his God, ⟨ HASHEM, ⟨ and may ⟨⟨ (Amen.)

SOMEONE OTHER THAN THE *SANDAK* SHOULD RECITE THE FOLLOWING STANZA:

הָרַחֲמָן הוּא יְבָרֵךְ בַּעַל בְּרִית הַמִּילָה,* אֲשֶׁר שָׂשׂ

⟨ was ⟨ who ⟨⟨ of ⟨ of the ⟨ the ⟨ bless ⟨ May ⟨ The compassion-
joyful circumcision,* covenant master He ate One!

לַעֲשׂוֹת צֶדֶק בְּגִילָה, וִישַׁלֵּם פָּעֳלוֹ וּמַשְׂכֻּרְתּוֹ כְּפוּלָה,*

⟨⟨ be doubled,* ⟨ and his ⟨⟨ for his ⟨ May he be ⟨⟨ with ⟨ righteous- ⟨ to do
recompense deed, rewarded rejoicing. ness

וְיִתְּנֵהוּ לְמַעְלָה לְמָעְלָה. (אָמֵן.—All respond)

⟨⟨ and higher. ⟨ higher ⟨ and may He ⟨⟨ (Amen.)
place him

הָרַחֲמָן הוּא יְבָרֵךְ רַךְ הַנִּמּוֹל לִשְׁמוֹנָה, וְיִהְיוּ יָדָיו וְלִבּוֹ*

⟨ and ⟨ his ⟨ and ⟨⟨ on the ⟨ who was ⟨ the ⟨ bless ⟨ May ⟨ The compassion-
his heart* strength may eighth day circumcised tender one He ate One!

לָאֵל אֱמוּנָה, וְיִזְכֶּה לִרְאוֹת פְּנֵי הַשְּׁכִינָה,* שָׁלֹשׁ פְּעָמִים

⟨ times ⟨ three ⟨⟨ the Divine Presence,* ⟨ to perceive ⟨ and may ⟨⟨ be faithful to God,
he merit

הָרַחֲמָן / The Compassionate One!

לְגַדְּלוֹ וּלְחַנְּכוֹ וּלְחַכְּמוֹ — *To raise him, to educate him, and to make him wise.* "To raise him" physically by providing for his needs; "to educate him" by teaching him proper behavior and his obligations to God and people; "to make him wise" by teaching him the Torah.

מִיּוֹם הַשְּׁמִינִי וָהָלְאָה יֵרָצֶה דָמוֹ — *From the eighth day onward may his blood find favor.* Animals are acceptable for Temple offerings from the eighth day after birth. Thus, the blessing is that the eight-day-old infant be beloved to God from this eighth day of his life as if he were a holy offering.

בַּעַל בְּרִית הַמִּילָה — *The master of the covenant of circumcision.* This phrase refers to the *sandak*,

the one who held the infant while the circumcision was performed (*Maharil*).

וּמַשְׂכֻּרְתּוֹ כְּפוּלָה — *And his recompense be doubled.* He has participated in the physical act of circumcision, and he has done it joyfully. For each — the precept and the joy — he earns recompense (*Dover Shalom*).

יָדָיו וְלִבּוֹ — *His strength* (lit. *his hands*) *and his heart.* May he devote all his physical and intellectual abilities to God's service.

פְּנֵי הַשְּׁכִינָה — *The Divine Presence.* The juxtaposition of circumcision with God's Presence is based on an account in the *Zohar* which relates that God's Presence once departed from the Jews because an uncircumcised person mingled with them (*R' Reuven Margulies*).

בְּשָׁנָה.*
《 a year.*

(אָמֵן.–All respond)
《(Amen.)

SOMEONE OTHER THAN THE *MOHEL* SHOULD RECITE THE FOLLOWING STANZA:

הָרַחֲמָן הוּא יְבָרֵךְ הַמָּל בְּשַׂר הָעָרְלָה, וּפָרַע וּמָצַץ
〈 and 〈 and 《 that was 〈 the 〈 the one who 〈 bless 〈 May 〈 The compassion-
drew uncovered uncut, flesh circumcised He ate One!

דְּמֵי הַמִּילָה, אִישׁ הַיָּרֵא וְרַךְ הַלֵּבָב עֲבוֹדָתוֹ פְּסוּלָה,
《 is unfit 〈 his service 〈 and faint hearted, 〈 who is 〈 A person 《 of the 〈 the
fearful circumcision. bloods

(וְ)אִם שָׁלֹשׁ אֵלֶּה* לֹא יַעֲשֶׂה לָהּ.
《upon it. 〈 he does not perform 〈 these three [acts]* 〈 — (and) if

(אָמֵן.–All respond)
《(Amen.)

הָרַחֲמָן הוּא יִשְׁלַח לָנוּ מְשִׁיחוֹ הוֹלֵךְ תָּמִים, בִּזְכוּת
〈 in the 《 with 〈 who goes 〈 His 〈 us 〈 send 〈 May 〈 The compassion-
merit wholesomeness, anointed He ate One!

חָתָן* לַמּוּלוֹת דָּמִים, לְבַשֵּׂר בְּשׂוֹרוֹת טוֹבוֹת וְנִחוּמִים,
《 and 〈 good tidings 〈 to proclaim《 [is] 〈 [who] for the sake 〈 of the
consolations, bloodied, of circumcision groom*

לְעַם אֶחָד מְפֻזָּר וּמְפֹרָד בֵּין הָעַמִּים.
《 the nations. 〈 among 〈 and splintered 〈 dispersed 〈 to the one nation

(אָמֵן.–All respond)
《(Amen.)

הָרַחֲמָן הוּא יִשְׁלַח לָנוּ כֹּהֵן צֶדֶק* אֲשֶׁר לֻקַּח לְעֵילוֹם,*
《 into hiding,*〈 was 〈 who 〈 the righteous 〈 us 〈 send 〈 May 〈 The compassion-
taken *Kohen* He ate One!

עַד הוּכַן כִּסְאוֹ כַּשֶּׁמֶשׁ וְיַהֲלוֹם, וַיָּלֶט פָּנָיו בְּאַדַּרְתּוֹ*
〈 with his 〈 his face 〈 he who 《 and 〈 [as bright] 〈 is His 〈 established 〈 until
cloak* covered diamond – as sun throne

וַיִּגְלוֹם, בְּרִיתִי הָיְתָה אִתּוֹ הַחַיִּים וְהַשָּׁלוֹם. (אָמֵן.–All respond)
《(Amen.)   《 and for peace. 〈 for life 〈 with him 〈 was 〈 My 《 and enwrapped
covenant himself,

ON WEEKDAYS CONTINUE הָרַחֲמָן הוּא יְזַכֵּנוּ, *THE COMPASSIONATE ONE! MAY HE MAKE US WOR-THY . . . , P. 308. (ON THE SABBATH AND FESTIVALS, CONTINUE WITH THE APPROPRIATE PRAYER, P. 307.)*

שָׁלֹשׁ פְּעָמִים בַּשָּׁנָה — *Three times a year*, on Pe-sach, Shavuos, and Succos, when Jews perceive the Presence of God in the Temple (*Deut.* 16:16).

שָׁלֹשׁ אֵלֶּה — *These three [acts]*. The three essen-tial parts of the mitzvah: מִילָה, *circumcision*; פְּרִיעָה, *uncovering*; and מְצִיצָה, *drawing*.

חָתָן — *Groom*. The word חָתָן, *groom*, in Hebrew refers to any honored person, whether it is a bridegroom or the infant being circumcised.

כֹּהֵן צֶדֶק — *The righteous Kohen* is the prophet

Elijah who will herald the coming of the Messiah (*Dover Shalom*).

לְעֵילוֹם — *Into hiding*. Elijah was swept up to heaven while still alive (see *II Kings* 2:1), to re-main concealed until the coming of the Messiah. Then Elijah will be revealed as if on a throne.

וַיָּלֶט פָּנָיו בְּאַדַּרְתּוֹ — *He who covered his face with his cloak*. When Elijah fled from the death threat of Ahab and Jezebel and hid in a cave, God came to him and he covered his face (*I Kings* 19:13).

REDEMPTION OF THE FIRSTBORN / פדיון הבן

THE FATHER AND THE *KOHEN* STAND. HOLDING HIS CHILD, THE FATHER DECLARES TO THE *KOHEN*:

זֶה בְּנִי בְכוֹרִי,* הוּא פֶּטֶר רֶחֶם לְאִמּוֹ. וְהַקָּדוֹשׁ בָּרוּךְ הוּא

⟨ is ⟨ Blessed ⟨ and the ⟨⟨ of his ⟨ of the ⟨ the first ⟨ he is ⟨⟨ my ⟨ my ⟨ This is
He,   Holy One,   mother,   womb   issue   firstborn;*   son,

צִוָּה לִפְדּוֹתוֹ. שֶׁנֶּאֱמַר: וּפְדוּיָו מִבֶּן חֹדֶשׁ תִּפְדֶּה, בְּעֶרְכְּךָ,

⟨⟨ according ⟨⟨ shall you ⟨ of one ⟨ from ⟨⟨ And those ⟨⟨ as it is ⟨⟨ to redeem ⟨ has com-
to your   redeem,   month   the age   who are to   said: him,   manded
valuation —   be redeemed,

כֶּסֶף חֲמֵשֶׁת שְׁקָלִים בְּשֶׁקֶל הַקֹּדֶשׁ עֶשְׂרִים גֵּרָה הוּא.¹ וְנֶאֱמַר:

⟨ And it ⟨⟨ it is. ⟨ gerah ⟨ twenty ⟨⟨ of the ⟨ in the ⟨ shekels ⟨ of five ⟨ the
is said: Sanctuary,   shekel   silver

קַדֶּשׁ לִי כָל בְּכוֹר פֶּטֶר כָּל רֶחֶם בִּבְנֵי יִשְׂרָאֵל, בָּאָדָם

⟨ [both] ⟨⟨ of Israel, ⟨ among the ⟨ womb ⟨ of ⟨ the first ⟨ firstborn, ⟨ every ⟨ for ⟨ Sanctify
of man   Children   every   issue   Me

וּבַבְּהֵמָה, לִי הוּא.²

⟨⟨ it is. ⟨ Mine ⟨ and of beast,

THE *KOHEN* ASKS:

מַאי בָּעִית טְפֵי,* לִיתֵּן לִי בִּנְךָ בְכוֹרְךָ שֶׁהוּא פֶּטֶר רֶחֶם

⟨ of the ⟨ the first ⟨ who is ⟨ your ⟨ your ⟨ to ⟨ to give ⟨⟨ more:* ⟨ do you ⟨ Which
womb   issue   firstborn   son,   me   want

---

(1) *Numbers* 18:16. (2) *Exodus* 13:2.

פדיון הבן / REDEMPTION OF THE FIRSTBORN

When a male baby who was his mother's first conception becomes a month old, his father must redeem him by giving five silver *shekels* to a *Kohen*. It is commonly accepted that five silver dollars are adequate for the performance of this *mitzvah* although some authorities hold that the silver dollar is less than the *shekel* and so seven silver dollars should be used. Like the marriage and circumcision ceremonies, the redemption is celebrated with a festive meal. The ceremony is customarily performed as soon as the guests are seated and have made the *Hamotzi* blessing over bread. Thereupon the baby is brought to the place where the father and the *Kohen* are seated. To show love for the *mitzvah*, the baby is usually brought on a silver tray bedecked with jewelry.

In declaring that firstborn males must be redeemed, the Torah teaches that God laid claim to all firstborn Jews at the time that He slew all the firstborn Egyptians in the last of the Ten Plagues. *Sefer HaChinuch* (Mitzvah 18) explains that this *mitzvah* teaches man to dedicate his very first achievements to God. Although firstborn children, like first fruits, are the culmination of much yearning, labor, and sacrifice, and it is human nature to want them for oneself, the Torah wants us to recognize that they are a gift from God and should be dedicated to His service. Thus, man *redeems* his firstborn.

§ **זֶה בְּנִי בְכוֹרִי** — *This is my son, my firstborn.* The dialogue between the father and the *Kohen* is not an integral part of the *mitzvah* and indeed, the text varies from community to community. The purpose of the conversation is simply to establish that the infant is a firstborn and that the father and *Kohen* are empowered to carry out the redemption.

§ **מַאי בָּעִית טְפֵי** — *Which do you want more.* Despite the implication that the father has the choice of leaving his son with the *Kohen* if he

לְאִמּוֹ, אוֹ בָעִית לִפְדוֹתוֹ בְּעַד חָמֵשׁ סְלָעִים כִּדְמְחַיַּבְתְּ

⟨ as you are ⟨ *shekels* ⟨ five ⟨ for ⟨ to redeem ⟨ do you ⟨ or ⟨⟨ of his
required to do him want mother,

מִדְּאוֹרַיְתָא?

⟨⟨ by the Torah?

THE FATHER REPLIES:

חָפֵץ אֲנִי לִפְדּוֹת אֶת בְּנִי, וְהֵילָךְ דְּמֵי פִּדְיוֹנוֹ כִּדְמְחַיַּבְנָא

⟨ as I am ⟨ of his ⟨ with ⟨ I present ⟨⟨ my son. ⟨ to redeem ⟨ I wish
required to do redemption the cost you

מִדְּאוֹרַיְתָא.

⟨⟨ by the Torah.

**WITH THE REDEMPTION MONEY IN HAND,
THE FATHER RECITES THE FOLLOWING BLESSINGS:**

בָּרוּךְ אַתָּה יהוה אֱלֹהֵינוּ מֶלֶךְ הָעוֹלָם, אֲשֶׁר קִדְּשָׁנוּ

⟨ sanctified ⟨ Who ⟨⟨ of the ⟨ King ⟨ our God, ⟨ HASHEM, ⟨ are You, ⟨ Blessed
us has universe,

בְּמִצְוֹתָיו, וְצִוָּנוּ עַל פִּדְיוֹן הַבֵּן. (אָמֵן.–All respond)

⟨⟨ of a son. ⟨ the ⟨ regarding ⟨ and has ⟨ with His com- ⟨⟨ (Amen.)
redemption commanded us mandments

בָּרוּךְ אַתָּה יהוה אֱלֹהֵינוּ מֶלֶךְ הָעוֹלָם, שֶׁהֶחֱיָנוּ וְקִיְּמָנוּ

⟨ and has ⟨ Who has kept ⟨⟨ of the ⟨ King ⟨ our God, ⟨ HASHEM, ⟨ are You, ⟨ Blessed
sustained us, us alive, universe,

וְהִגִּיעָנוּ לַזְּמַן הַזֶּה. (אָמֵן.–All respond)

⟨⟨ to this season. ⟨ and has ⟨⟨ (Amen.)
brought us

**THE *KOHEN* ACCEPTS THE MONEY, AND, WHILE SWINGING IT IN A CIRCULAR MOTION
OVER THE INFANT'S HEAD, HE SAYS:**

זֶה תַּחַת זֶה.* זֶה חִלּוּף זֶה. זֶה מָחוּל* עַל זֶה. וְיִכָּנֵס זֶה הַבֵּן

⟨ May this ⟨⟨ that. ⟨ through ⟨ re- ⟨ this ⟨⟨ for ⟨ in ⟨ this ⟨⟨ of ⟨ instead ⟨ This
son enter deemed* is that; exchange is that;* is

prefers not to part with five *shekels*, this is not
so. First, the Torah *requires* the father to redeem
his son; second, the child is not the property of
the *Kohen* and is not taken from his parents
even if the father refuses to redeem him. Rather
this question is so framed in order to increase the
father's love for his son and the *mitzvah* of
redeeming him. One must also recognize that
during many periods, five silver *shekels* was an

enormous sum for most people (*Chut HaShani*).

זֶה תַּחַת זֶה — *This is instead of that.* The *Kohen*
signifies his acceptance of the redemption,
which frees the infant of all future obligations
regarding this *mitzvah*.

מָחוּל — *Redeemed.* This translation is supported by the text מְחוּלָל found in the *Rashba*
(*Responsum* 200).

לְחַיִּים, לְתוֹרָה וּלְיִרְאַת שָׁמֶיִם. יְהִי רָצוֹן שֶׁכְּשֵׁם שֶׁנִּכְנַס

⟨ he has ⟨ that just as ⟨ [Your] ⟨ May ⟪ of ⟨ and into fear ⟨ into Torah, ⟨ into life,
entered   will   it be   Heaven.

לְפִדְיוֹן כֵּן יִכָּנֵס לְתוֹרָה וּלְחֻפָּה וּלְמַעֲשִׂים טוֹבִים. אָמֵן.

⟪ Amen. ⟪ that are ⟨ and [the ⟨ the marriage ⟨ into the ⟨ may ⟨ so ⟪ into this re-
   good.   performance   canopy,   [study of]   he enter   demption,
       of] deeds   Torah,

THE *KOHEN* STANDS, PLACES HIS RIGHT HAND ON THE INFANT'S HEAD AND BLESSES HIM:

יְשִׂמְךָ אֱלֹהִים כְּאֶפְרַיִם וְכִמְנַשֶּׁה.* יְבָרֶכְךָ יהוה* וְיִשְׁמְרֶךָ.

⟪ and safe- ⟨ May HASHEM ⟪ and like ⟨ like Ephraim ⟨ May God make you
guard you.   bless you*   Menashe.*

יָאֵר יהוה פָּנָיו אֵלֶיךָ וִיחֻנֶּךָּ. יִשָּׂא יהוה פָּנָיו אֵלֶיךָ, וְיָשֵׂם

⟨ and ⟨ to ⟨ His ⟨ May HASHEM ⟪ and be gra- ⟨ for ⟨ His ⟨ May HASHEM
establish   you   countenance   turn   cious to you.   you   countenance   illuminate

לְךָ שָׁלוֹם. כִּי אֹרֶךְ יָמִים וּשְׁנוֹת חַיִּים וְשָׁלוֹם יוֹסִיפוּ

⟨ shall they ⟨ and ⟨ of life, ⟨ and years ⟨ of days, ⟨ length ⟨ For ⟪ peace. ⟨ for
[the Torah and   peace   you
commandments]
increase

לָךְ. יהוה יִשְׁמָרְךָ מִכָּל רָע, יִשְׁמֹר אֶת נַפְשֶׁךָ.

⟪ your soul. ⟨ He will ⟪ evil; ⟨ from ⟨ will protect ⟨ HASHEM ⟪ for
         guard   every   you   you.

**THE *KOHEN* HANDS THE INFANT TO THE FATHER;
THEN THE *KOHEN* TAKES A CUP OF WINE AND RECITES:**

בָּרוּךְ אַתָּה יהוה אֱלֹהֵינוּ מֶלֶךְ הָעוֹלָם, בּוֹרֵא פְּרִי הַגָּפֶן.

⟪ of the ⟨ the ⟨ Who ⟪ of the ⟨ King ⟨ our God, ⟨ HASHEM, ⟨ are You, ⟨ Blessed
vine.   fruit   creates   universe,

(אָמֵן.–All respond)
⟪ (Amen.)

**THE FESTIVE MEAL IN CELEBRATION OF THE *MITZVAH* CONTINUES,
FOLLOWED BY *BIRCAS HAMAZON*, P. 292.**

---

(1) *Genesis* 48:20. (2) *Numbers* 6:24-26. (3) *Proverbs* 3:2. (4) *Psalms* 121:7.

~§ יְשִׂמְךָ אֱלֹהִים כְּאֶפְרַיִם וְכִמְנַשֶּׁה — *May God make you like Ephraim and like Menashe.* This is the blessing that the Patriarch Jacob conferred upon his grandchildren, the two sons of Joseph and the first Jews born and raised in exile. They grew to be sources of pride to the Patriarch, despite having been raised in Pharaoh's court at a time when there was no Jewish religious life in

Egypt except for that within the intimacy of their own family.

~§ יְבָרֶכְךָ ה' — *May HASHEM bless you.* These verses form the Priestly Blessings (see p. 166). The priests were designated as the instruments through which God allows His blessing to rest upon Israel.

❧ WAYFARER'S PRAYER / תפלת הדרך ❧

**ONE SETTING OUT ON A JOURNEY RECITES THE FOLLOWING PRAYER
ONCE HE LEAVES THE CITY LIMITS.**

יְהִי רָצוֹן מִלְּפָנֶיךָ, יהוה אֱלֹהֵינוּ וֵאלֹהֵי אֲבוֹתֵינוּ,

May ⟨ it be ⟩ the will ⟨ before You, ⟩⟩ HASHEM, ⟨ our God ⟩ and the God ⟨ of our forefathers, ⟩⟩

שֶׁתּוֹלִיכֵנוּ לְשָׁלוֹם,* וְתַצְעִידֵנוּ לְשָׁלוֹם, וְתַדְרִיכֵנוּ לְשָׁלוֹם,

that You lead us ⟨ toward peace,* ⟩⟩ emplace ⟨ toward our footsteps ⟨ peace, ⟩⟩ guide us ⟨ toward peace, ⟩⟩

וְתַגִּיעֵנוּ לִמְחוֹז חֶפְצֵנוּ לְחַיִּים וּלְשִׂמְחָה וּלְשָׁלוֹם,*

and make ⟨ the ⟨ we desire ⟩⟩ for life, ⟨⟨ for gladness, ⟨ and for us reach ⟨ destination ⟩ peace,* ⟩⟩

ONE PLANNING TO RETURN THE SAME DAY ADDS:

[וְתַחֲזִירֵנוּ לְבֵיתֵנוּ לְשָׁלוֹם,] וְתַצִּילֵנוּ מִכַּף כָּל אוֹיֵב

and return us ⟨ to our homes ⟩⟩ in peace. ⟨ May You rescue us ⟨ from ⟨ the hand ⟩ of ⟨ every ⟨ foe,

וְאוֹרֵב וְלִסְטִים וְחַיּוֹת רָעוֹת בַּדֶּרֶךְ,* וּמִכָּל מִינֵי

ambush, ⟨ bandits, ⟨ and ⟨ animals ⟨ that are ⟨ along ⟩⟩ and ⟨ manner ⟨ harmful ⟩ the way,* ⟩⟩ from all

---

❧ תְּפִלַּת הַדֶּרֶךְ / WAYFARER'S PRAYER ❧

Someone who sets out on a journey must pray that he arrive safely (*Berachos* 29b). This applies even if there is no reason to expect danger, provided that the distance will be at least one *parsah* (approx. 3 miles). The prayer should be recited as soon as one has gone about 140 feet past the last house of his town. In the event the entire journey will be less than one *parsah*, the prayer may be recited, but the concluding blessing (בָּרוּךְ אַתָּה ה' שׁוֹמֵעַ תְּפִלָּה, *Blessed are You, HASHEM, Who hears prayer*) should be omitted. The prayer is recited once each day, even though the journey will be interrupted by rest, work, sightseeing, etc. However, if one's journey has ended, and he subsequently decides to embark on another journey on the same day, the Wayfarer's Prayer should be recited a second time. On a journey that will last for many days, the prayer is recited once each day.

It is preferable to recite a blessing before reciting the prayer so that it will be both preceded as well as concluded by blessings. Customarily this is done by consuming some food or drink and saying the final blessing. It is suggested that one eat a food that requires the final מֵעֵין שָׁלֹשׁ, *Three-faceted*, blessing and not בּוֹרֵא נְפָשׁוֹת, *Borei Nefashos*.

Although it is preferable to interrupt one's travel and to stand while reciting the prayer, this need not be done if it is difficult.

שֶׁתּוֹלִיכֵנוּ לְשָׁלוֹם — *That You lead us toward peace.* In connection with this prayer, the Talmud (*Berachos* 30a) stresses that it be said in the plural. Whenever one unites himself with the needs of others, he increases the chance that his prayer will be heard.

לְחַיִּים וּלְשִׂמְחָה וּלְשָׁלוֹם — *For life, for gladness, and for peace.* Though we have prayed that we reach our destination, that is hardly enough. We reemphasize that whatever our goals in life, they are worthwhile only if reaching them does not come at the cost of life, gladness, and peace.

וְחַיּוֹת רָעוֹת בַּדֶּרֶךְ — *And animals that are harm-*

פָּרְעָנִיּוֹת הַמִּתְרַגְּשׁוֹת לָבוֹא לָעוֹלָם. וְתִשְׁלַח בְּרָכָה

‹ blessing ‹ May You send «« to the world. ‹ to come ‹ that assemble ‹ of misfortunes

בְּכָל מַעֲשֵׂה יָדֵינוּ, וְתִתְּנֵנוּ לְחֵן וּלְחֶסֶד וּלְרַחֲמִים

‹ and compassion ‹ kindness, ‹ grace, ‹ and grant us ‹ of our hands, ‹ the work ‹ in all

בְּעֵינֶיךָ וּבְעֵינֵי כָל רוֹאֵינוּ, וְתִשְׁמַע קוֹל תַּחֲנוּנֵינוּ, כִּי

‹ because «« of our supplication, ‹ the sound ‹ May You hear «« who ‹ of all ‹ and in the eyes ‹ in Your eyes

אֵל שׁוֹמֵעַ תְּפִלָּה וְתַחֲנוּן אָתָּה. בָּרוּךְ אַתָּה יהוה,

«« HASHEM, ‹ are You, ‹ Blessed «« are You. ‹ and supplication ‹ prayer ‹ Who hears ‹ a God

שׁוֹמֵעַ תְּפִלָּה.

«« prayer. ‹ Who hears

EACH OF THE FOLLOWING PARAGRAPHS IS RECITED THREE TIMES:

וְיַעֲקֹב הָלַךְ לְדַרְכּוֹ,* וַיִּפְגְּעוּ בוֹ מַלְאֲכֵי אֱלֹהִים.

«« of God. ‹ did angels ‹ and encountered «« on his way* ‹ went ‹ Jacob

וַיֹּאמֶר יַעֲקֹב כַּאֲשֶׁר רָאָם, מַחֲנֵה אֱלֹהִים זֶה, וַיִּקְרָא

‹ So he called «« is ‹ that is this. ‹ A camp «« he saw ‹ when ‹ Jacob said

שֵׁם הַמָּקוֹם הַהוּא מַחֲנָיִם.*¹

«« Machanayim.* ‹ of that place ‹ the name

---

(1) *Genesis* 32:2-3.

ful along the way. Even in societies where bandits and wild animals do not exist, these terms are relevant because they refer figuratively to all the problems and perils that are associated with travel. The Sages teach that a person's sins are more likely to be recalled against him when he is traveling.

וְיַעֲקֹב הָלַךְ לְדַרְכּוֹ§ — *Jacob went on his way.* At this point it is customary to add various Scriptural selections that embody either prayers or assurances that God will assist wayfarers. The first two verses tell of Jacob travel-

ing from the house of Laban back to *Eretz Yisrael.* As he entered the Land, he was met by angels who were sent to assist and protect him.

מַחֲנָיִם — *Machanayim.* The name Machanayim, literally "two camps," refers to Jacob's own entourage and that of the angels. *Ramban* explains that Jacob intended to equate the two camps, the human one and the angelic one. Since both were composed of dedicated servants of God, they were of comparable caliber. This is fitting for the Wayfarer's Prayer be-

הַמַּלְאָךְ הַגֹּאֵל אֹתִי מִכָּל רָע יְבָרֵךְ אֶת הַנְּעָרִים,

‹‹ the lads, ‹ bless ‹ evil ‹ from all ‹ me ‹ who redeems ‹ May the angel

וְיִקָּרֵא בָהֶם שְׁמִי, וְשֵׁם אֲבֹתַי אַבְרָהָם וְיִצְחָק, וְיִדְגּוּ

‹ and like fish may they proliferate ‹‹ and Isaac, ‹ Abraham ‹ of my forefathers ‹ and the names ‹‹ may my name be, ‹ upon them ‹ and declared

לָרֹב בְּקֶרֶב הָאָרֶץ.¹

‹‹ the land. ‹ within ‹ abundantly

לִישׁוּעָתְךָ* קִוִּיתִי יהוה. (קִוִּיתִי יהוה לִישׁוּעָתְךָ. יהוה

‹ Hashem, ‹‹ for Your salvation. ‹ Hashem, ‹ (I do yearn, ‹‹ Hashem. ‹ I do yearn, ‹ For Your salvation*

לִישׁוּעָתְךָ קִוִּיתִי.)

‹‹ I do yearn.) ‹ for Your salvation

הִנֵּה אָנֹכִי שֹׁלֵחַ מַלְאָךְ* לְפָנֶיךָ לִשְׁמָרְךָ בַּדָּרֶךְ, וְלַהֲבִיאֲךָ

‹ and to bring you ‹‹ on the way, ‹ to protect you ‹ before you ‹ an angel* ‹ am sending ‹ I ‹ Indeed

אֶל הַמָּקוֹם אֲשֶׁר הֲכִנֹתִי.³

‹‹ I have prepared. ‹ that ‹ the place ‹ to

יהוה עֹז לְעַמּוֹ יִתֵּן, יהוה יְבָרֵךְ אֶת עַמּוֹ בַשָּׁלוֹם.*⁴

‹‹ with peace.* ‹ His nation ‹ will bless ‹ Hashem ‹‹ will give, ‹ to His nation ‹ strength ‹ Hashem,

---

(1) *Genesis* 48:16. (2) *49:18.* (3) *Exodus* 23:20. (4) *Psalms* 29:11.

cause, as many commentators teach, one should repent before setting out on a journey. If this is done, then the traveler may indeed be likened to an angel.

לִישׁוּעָתְךָ — *For Your salvation.* In Jacob's deathbed blessing to his children, he prophetically quoted this brief prayer that Samson would later utter when he was a blinded, degraded captive of the Philistines (*Rashi*). The Kabbalists find in these three words mystical combinations of letters that provide salvation

against enemies (*R' Bachya*). Thus, this prayer applies to the perils of the way as well.

הִנֵּה אָנֹכִי שֹׁלֵחַ מַלְאָךְ — *Indeed I am sending an angel.* God gave this assurance to Moses as the Jewish people were about to embark from Mount Sinai to *Eretz Yisrael.*

ה' יְבָרֵךְ אֶת עַמּוֹ בַשָּׁלוֹם — *Hashem will bless His nation with peace.* The Wayfarer's Prayer makes constant reference to peace, which the Sages describe as the only vessel that can contain blessings (*Uktzin* 3:12).

⛥ BLESSINGS FOR ENJOYMENT / ברכות הנהנין ⛥

BLESSINGS BEFORE FOOD OR DRINK / ברכות קודם האכילה והשתיה

UPON WASHING THE HANDS BEFORE EATING BREAD:

בָּרוּךְ אַתָּה יהוה אֱלֹהֵינוּ מֶלֶךְ הָעוֹלָם, אֲשֶׁר קִדְּשָׁנוּ

‹ has sanctified us ‹ Who ‹ of the universe, ‹‹ ‹ King ‹ our God, ‹ Hashem, ‹ are You, ‹ Blessed

בְּמִצְוֹתָיו, וְצִוָּנוּ עַל נְטִילַת יָדָיִם.

‹‹ the hands. ‹ washing ‹ regarding ‹ and has commanded us ‹ with His commandments,

BEFORE EATING BREAD:

בָּרוּךְ אַתָּה יהוה אֱלֹהֵינוּ מֶלֶךְ הָעוֹלָם, הַמּוֹצִיא לֶחֶם

‹ bread ‹ Who brings forth ‹‹ of the universe, ‹ King ‹ our God, ‹ Hashem, ‹ are You, ‹ Blessed

מִן הָאָרֶץ.

‹‹ the earth. ‹ from

BEFORE EATING PRODUCTS OF WHEAT, BARLEY, RYE, OATS OR SPELT (AND RICE, ACCORDING TO MANY OPINIONS):

בָּרוּךְ אַתָּה יהוה אֱלֹהֵינוּ מֶלֶךְ הָעוֹלָם, בּוֹרֵא מִינֵי מְזוֹנוֹת.

‹‹ of nourishment. ‹ species ‹ Who creates ‹‹ of the universe, ‹ King ‹ our God, ‹ Hashem, ‹ are You, ‹ Blessed

BEFORE DRINKING GRAPE WINE OR GRAPE JUICE:

בָּרוּךְ אַתָּה יהוה אֱלֹהֵינוּ מֶלֶךְ הָעוֹלָם, בּוֹרֵא פְּרִי הַגָּפֶן.

‹‹ of the vine. ‹ the fruit ‹ Who creates ‹‹ of the universe, ‹ King ‹ our God, ‹ Hashem, ‹ are You, ‹ Blessed

BEFORE EATING TREE-GROWN FRUIT:

בָּרוּךְ אַתָּה יהוה אֱלֹהֵינוּ מֶלֶךְ הָעוֹלָם, בּוֹרֵא פְּרִי הָעֵץ.

‹‹ of the tree. ‹ the fruit ‹ Who creates ‹‹ of the universe, ‹ King ‹ our God, ‹ Hashem, ‹ are You, ‹ Blessed

BEFORE EATING PRODUCE THAT GREW DIRECTLY FROM THE EARTH:

בָּרוּךְ אַתָּה יהוה אֱלֹהֵינוּ מֶלֶךְ הָעוֹלָם, בּוֹרֵא פְּרִי הָאֲדָמָה.

‹‹ of the ground. ‹ the fruit ‹ Who creates ‹‹ of the universe, ‹ King ‹ our God, ‹ Hashem, ‹ are You, ‹ Blessed

---

⛥ Blessings

Ideally, every act and pleasure should be undertaken with an awareness that it is God Who is being served and He Who dispenses to us our needs and desires. In order to help inculcate this awareness in the Jewish people, the Sages, from the time of Ezra and his court, composed the various blessings and ordained the occasions upon which they must be recited. The very fact that the day is filled with events that require blessings provides constant inspiration. The thinking person finds himself drawn ever closer to the loving God by the awareness that every delicious morsel and soothing drink affords him a fresh opportunity to recognize and thank the Giver of all. In the words of the Talmud, who-

BEFORE EATING OR DRINKING ANY OTHER FOODS:

בָּרוּךְ אַתָּה יהוה אֱלֹהֵינוּ מֶלֶךְ הָעוֹלָם, שֶׁהַכֹּל נִהְיָה

⟨ came ⟨ that ⟨⟨ of the ⟨ King ⟨ our God, ⟨ HASHEM, ⟨ are You, ⟨ Blessed
to be everything universe,

בִּדְבָרוֹ.

⟨⟨ through
His word.

BLESSINGS OVER FRAGRANCE / ברכות הריח

UPON ENTERING A PERFUMERY OR UPON SMELLING FRAGRANCES OF (A) NONVEGETABLE ORIGIN (E.G., MUSK); (B) UNDETERMINED ORIGIN; OR (C) A BLEND OF SPICES OF DIFFERENT ORIGINS:

בָּרוּךְ אַתָּה יהוה אֱלֹהֵינוּ מֶלֶךְ הָעוֹלָם, בּוֹרֵא מִינֵי בְשָׂמִים.

⟨⟨ of ⟨ species ⟨ Who ⟨⟨ of the ⟨ King ⟨ our God, ⟨ HASHEM, ⟨ are You, ⟨ Blessed
fragrance. creates universe,

UPON SMELLING FRAGRANT SHRUBS AND TREES OR THEIR FLOWERS (E.G., ROSES):

בָּרוּךְ אַתָּה יהוה אֱלֹהֵינוּ מֶלֶךְ הָעוֹלָם, בּוֹרֵא עֲצֵי בְשָׂמִים.

⟨⟨ that are ⟨ trees ⟨ Who ⟨⟨ of the ⟨ King ⟨ our God, ⟨ HASHEM, ⟨ are You, ⟨ Blessed
fragrant. creates universe,

UPON SMELLING FRAGRANT HERBS, GRASSES OR FLOWERS:

בָּרוּךְ אַתָּה יהוה אֱלֹהֵינוּ מֶלֶךְ הָעוֹלָם, בּוֹרֵא עִשְׂבֵי

⟨ herbage ⟨ Who ⟨⟨ of the ⟨ King ⟨ our God, ⟨ HASHEM, ⟨ are You, ⟨ Blessed
creates universe,

בְשָׂמִים.

⟨⟨ that is fragrant.

UPON SMELLING FRAGRANT EDIBLE FRUIT OR NUTS:

בָּרוּךְ אַתָּה יהוה אֱלֹהֵינוּ מֶלֶךְ הָעוֹלָם, הַנּוֹתֵן רֵיחַ טוֹב

⟨ a good ⟨ Who ⟨⟨ of the ⟨ King ⟨ our God, ⟨ HASHEM, ⟨ are You, ⟨ Blessed
aroma places universe,

בַּפֵּרוֹת.

⟨⟨ into fruits.

---

ever enjoys this world's pleasures without reciting a blessing is tantamount to one who steals from God (*Berachos* 35a).

There are three other categories of blessings: 1. בִּרְכוֹת הַנֶּהֱנִין, *blessings for enjoyment*, which apply when one has physical pleasure such as eating and drinking; 2. בִּרְכוֹת הַמִּצְוֹת, *blessings for the performance of the commandments*, such as those recited upon putting on *tefillin* or lighting the Sabbath candles; and 3. בִּרְכוֹת הַהוֹדָאָה, *blessings of praise and gratitude*, like those recited upon witnessing natural phenomena (p. 347-348), the blessings in *Shemoneh Esrei* and other prayers, and the blessings for heavenly benefits that do not involve physical pleasure (pp. 348-350), such as the שֶׁהֶחֱיָנוּ blessing that is recited upon various occasions when one feels great joy at having lived to see a particular event (*Rambam, Hil. Berachos* 1:2-4).

◄§ BLESSINGS OVER MITZVOS / ברכות המצוות §►

UPON AFFIXING A *MEZUZAH* TO THE DOORPOST:

בָּרוּךְ אַתָּה יהוה אֱלֹהֵינוּ מֶלֶךְ הָעוֹלָם, אֲשֶׁר קִדְּשָׁנוּ

⟨ has   ⟨ Who   ⟨⟨ of the   ⟨ King   ⟨ our God,   ⟨ Hashem,   ⟨ are You,   ⟨ Blessed
sanctified us   universe,

בְּמִצְוֹתָיו, וְצִוָּנוּ לִקְבֹּעַ מְזוּזָה.

《 a mezuzah.   ⟨ to affix   ⟨ and has   ⟨ with His com-
commanded us   mandments,

UPON BUILDING A PROTECTIVE RAILING AROUND ONE'S ROOF:

בָּרוּךְ אַתָּה יהוה אֱלֹהֵינוּ מֶלֶךְ הָעוֹלָם, אֲשֶׁר קִדְּשָׁנוּ

⟨ has   ⟨ Who   ⟨⟨ of the   ⟨ King   ⟨ our God,   ⟨ Hashem,   ⟨ are You,   ⟨ Blessed
sanctified us   universe,

בְּמִצְוֹתָיו, וְצִוָּנוּ לַעֲשׂוֹת מַעֲקֶה.

《 a parapet.   ⟨ to construct   ⟨ and has   ⟨ with His com-
commanded us   mandments,

UPON IMMERSING IN A *MIKVEH* METAL OR GLASS UTENSILS (USED FOR THE PREPARATION OR SERVING OF FOOD OR DRINK) THAT HAVE BEEN MADE BY OR PURCHASED FROM A GENTILE (IF THERE IS DOUBT WHETHER IT BELONGED TO A GENTILE, OR IF THE UTENSIL IS MADE OF ALUMINUM, IMMERSE THE UTENSIL WITHOUT A BLESSING):

בָּרוּךְ אַתָּה יהוה אֱלֹהֵינוּ מֶלֶךְ הָעוֹלָם, אֲשֶׁר קִדְּשָׁנוּ

⟨ has   ⟨ Who   ⟨⟨ of the   ⟨ King   ⟨ our God,   ⟨ Hashem,   ⟨ are You,   ⟨ Blessed
sanctified us   universe,

ONE UTENSIL: **MULTIPLE UTENSILS:**

בְּמִצְוֹתָיו, וְצִוָּנוּ עַל טְבִילַת כֵּלִים. / כֶּלִי.

《 of a   /   《 of   ⟨ the   ⟨ regarding   ⟨ and has   ⟨ with His com-
vessel.   vessels.   immersion   commanded us   mandments,

AN OLIVE-SIZE PIECE OF DOUGH CALLED *CHALLAH* MUST BE SEPARATED AND BURNED FROM EACH BATCH OF DOUGH THAT IS AT LEAST 2 POUNDS 10 OUNCES. REGARDING THE AMOUNT OF DOUGH REQUIRED FOR THE RECITATION OF THE BLESSING, OPINIONS VARY FROM 3 LBS. 10.7 OZ. – 4 LBS. 15.2 OZ.

בָּרוּךְ אַתָּה יהוה אֱלֹהֵינוּ מֶלֶךְ הָעוֹלָם, אֲשֶׁר קִדְּשָׁנוּ

⟨ has   ⟨ Who   ⟨⟨ of the   ⟨ King   ⟨ our God,   ⟨ Hashem,   ⟨ are You,   ⟨ Blessed
sanctified us   universe,

בְּמִצְוֹתָיו, וְצִוָּנוּ לְהַפְרִישׁ חַלָּה מִן הָעִסָּה.

《 the dough.   ⟨ from   ⟨ challah   ⟨ to separate   ⟨ and has   ⟨ with His com-
commanded us   mandments,

◄§ הַפְרָשַׁת תְּרוּמוֹת וּמַעְשְׂרוֹת / Separation of Terumah and Maaser

Grains, fruits, and vegetables that grew in the halachic boundaries of *Eretz Yisrael* may not be eaten (in any form) until תְּרוּמָה (*terumah*), *the Priestly share*, תְּרוּמַת מַעֲשֵׂר, *the Priestly tithe*, and the various forms of מַעֲשֵׂר (*maaser*), *tithes* [for the Levites, the poor, and the portion that was to be eaten in Jerusalem in Temple times], are separated from them. The Levite tithe was separated every year; the tithe for the poor in the third and sixth years; and the second tithe, that

הפרשת תרומות ומעשרות
SEPARATION OF *TERUMAH* AND TITHES FROM FOODS GROWN IN *ERETZ YISRAEL*

SEE THE COMMENTARY FOR A BRIEF INTRODUCTION TO THIS REQUIREMENT. ONE PUTS SLIGHTLY MORE THAN ONE PERCENT OF THE FOOD ASIDE. THEN, IF THE TITHES HAVE DEFINITELY NOT BEEN TAKEN AS YET (*TEVEL*), HE RECITES THE FOLLOWING BLESSING AND DECLARATION. BUT IF THEIR STATUS IS DOUBTFUL (*DEMAI*), THE BLESSING IS OMITTED, BUT THE DECLARATION IS RECITED.

בָּרוּךְ אַתָּה יהוה אֱלֹהֵינוּ מֶלֶךְ הָעוֹלָם, אֲשֶׁר קִדְּשָׁנוּ
Blessed ⟩ are You, ⟩ HASHEM, ⟩ our God, ⟩ King ⟩ of the universe, ⟩ Who ⟩ has sanctified us

בְּמִצְוֹתָיו, וְצִוָּנוּ לְהַפְרִישׁ תְּרוּמוֹת וּמַעֲשֵׂרוֹת.
with His commandments, ⟩ and has commanded us ⟩ to separate ⟩ *terumos* ⟩ and tithes.

IF PRODUCE FROM MORE THAN ONE SPECIES IS BEING PREPARED, THEN THE ADDITIONS IN PARENTHESES SHOULD BE ADDED.

מַה שֶׁהוּא יוֹתֵר מֵאֶחָד מִמֵּאָה מִן הַכֹּל שֶׁיֵּשׁ כַּאן, הֲרֵי
That part [of the portion set aside] ⟩ which ⟩ is ⟩ more ⟩ than one ⟩ percent ⟩ of ⟩ every-thing ⟩ that is ⟩ here, ⟩ is hereby declared

הוּא תְּרוּמָה גְדוֹלָה בַּצַּד הָעֶלְיוֹן (כָּל מִין עַל מִינוֹ). וְהָאֶחָד
to be ⟩ *terumah,* the priestly share, ⟩ at the top side [of the portion] ⟩ for ⟩ species ⟩ (each ⟩ species ⟩ its own ⟩ The one

מִמֵּאָה שֶׁנִּשְׁאַר כַּאן, עִם תִּשְׁעָה חֲלָקִים כָּמוֹהוּ, בַּצַּד הָעֶלְיוֹן
percent ⟩ remaining ⟩ here, ⟩ together with ⟩ nine ⟩ portions ⟩ of equal size ⟩ at the top side

שֶׁל הַפֵּרוֹת הַלָּלוּ, הֲרֵי הֵם מַעֲשֵׂר רִאשׁוֹן (כָּל מִין עַל מִינוֹ).
of ⟩ this produce, ⟩ are ⟩ to be declared ⟩ the first [Levite] tithe ⟩ (each ⟩ species ⟩ for ⟩ species ⟩ its own.

אוֹתוֹ הָאֶחָד מִמֵּאָה שֶׁעֲשִׂיתִיו מַעֲשֵׂר רִאשׁוֹן, הֲרֵי הוּא
That ⟩ one ⟩ percent ⟩ that I have made ⟩ the first tithe ⟩ is hereby declared ⟩ to be

---

was to be eaten in Jerusalem, was taken in the first, second, fourth, and fifth years. If the tithes have definitely not been taken as yet, the food is known as *tevel* and a blessing is made when the tithes are separated. If their status is doubtful, they are known as *demai* and tithes are separated, but without a blessing. In either case the declaration beginning מַה שֶּׁהוּא, *that part which is*, should be recited. Moreover, this declaration must be understood by the person separating the *terumah* and tithes, and should therefore be recited in a language that he understands.

These laws are complex and one going to *Eretz Yisrael* or eating produce that grew there should become familiar with them. Here, we offer only the texts that must be recited when the tithes are separated. Especially with regard to the redemption of a quantity of מַעֲשֵׂר שֵׁנִי, *the second tithe*, that is worth less than a *perutah*, consult a competent halachic authority.

The bit of food that was set aside may not be eaten nor may it be thrown away in a disrespectful manner. It should be buried or put aside to decompose naturally, or, if there is concern for a violation of the law, it should be carefully wrapped and then it may be thrown away. Liquids should be poured into the drain in the sink, and any containers rinsed out.

תְּרוּמַת מַעֲשֵׂר (כָּל מִין עַל מִינוֹ). עוֹד תִּשְׁעָה חֲלָקִים כָּאֵלֶּה
like ⟨ portions ⟨ nine ⟨ An ⟪ its own ⟨ for ⟨ spe- ⟨(each⟪ the *terumah* of the
these   additional species).   cies   tithe, (the priestly tithe)

בְּצַד הַתַּחְתּוֹן שֶׁל הַפֵּרוֹת, הֲרֵי הֵם מַעֲשֵׂר שֵׁנִי (כָּל מִין עַל
for ⟨ spe- ⟨(each⟪ the second tithe, ⟨ to be ⟨ are ⟨ the produce ⟨ of ⟨ at the bottom side
cies   declared

מִינוֹ), וְאִם הֵם חַיָּבִים בְּמַעֲשֵׂר עָנִי – הֲרֵי הֵם מַעֲשֵׂר עָנִי
⟪ the tithe of ⟨ let [the bottom ⟨ the tithe of the poor ⟨ must ⟨ this ⟨ but if ⟪ its own
the poor   nine portions] be [separated from it],   have [produce]   species,)

(כָּל מִין עַל מִינוֹ).
⟪ its own species). ⟨ for ⟨ species ⟨(each

IF THE SECOND TITHE HAD DEFINITELY NOT BEEN SEPARATED AS YET, IT MUST BE REDEEMED AND THE FOLLOWING BLESSING AND DECLARATION ARE RECITED. IF THERE IS DOUBT AS TO WHETHER THE SECOND TITHE HAS BEEN REDEEMED, THE BLESSING IS OMITTED, BUT THE DECLARATION IS RECITED.

בָּרוּךְ אַתָּה יהוה אֱלֹהֵינוּ מֶלֶךְ הָעוֹלָם, אֲשֶׁר קִדְּשָׁנוּ
has ⟨ Who ⟪ of the ⟨ King ⟨ our God, ⟨ HASHEM, ⟨ are You, ⟨ Blessed
sanctified us   universe,

בְּמִצְוֹתָיו, וְצִוָּנוּ עַל פִּדְיוֹן מַעֲשֵׂר שֵׁנִי.
⟪ the second tithe. ⟨ to redeem ⟨ and has ⟨ with His com-
commanded us mandments,

מַעֲשֵׂר שֵׁנִי זֶה, הוּא וְחֻמְשׁוֹ, הֲרֵי הוּא מְחֻלָּל עַל
⟨ onto ⟨ redeemed ⟨ to be ⟨ are ⟪ and its ⟨ it ⟪   This second tithe,
declared   extra fifth,

פְּרוּטָה אַחַת מִן הַמַּטְבֵּעַ שֶׁיִּחַדְתִּי לִפְדְיוֹן מַעֲשֵׂר שֵׁנִי. אוֹתוֹ
⟨ That ⟪ of the second ⟨ for the ⟨ that I have ⟨ the coin ⟨ of ⟨ one *perutah*
tithe.   redemption set aside

שֶׁאֵינוֹ שָׁוֶה פְרוּטָה, הֲרֵי הוּא מְחֻלָּל בְּשָׁוְיוֹ.
⟪ for its ⟨ redeemed ⟨ to be ⟨ is ⟪ a *perutah* ⟨ worth ⟨ which
value.   declared   is not

FRUIT FROM THE FOURTH YEAR AFTER A TREE WAS PLANTED HAS SANCTITY SIMILAR TO MAASER SHENI, THE SECOND TITHE, AND MUST BE SIMILARLY REDEEMED. IF THE FOURTH-YEAR FRUIT HAS DEFINITELY NOT BEEN REDEEMED, THE FOLLOWING BLESSING AND DECLARATION ARE RECITED (OVER FRUIT GROWN IN ISRAEL). IF THERE IS DOUBT WHETHER IT IS FOURTH-YEAR FRUIT OR WHETHER IT HAS BEEN REDEEMED, OR THE FRUIT GREW OUT OF ISRAEL, THE BLESSING IS OMITTED, BUT THE DECLARATION IS RECITED.

בָּרוּךְ אַתָּה יהוה אֱלֹהֵינוּ מֶלֶךְ הָעוֹלָם, אֲשֶׁר קִדְּשָׁנוּ
has ⟨ Who ⟪ of the ⟨ King ⟨ our God, ⟨ HASHEM, ⟨ are You, ⟨ Blessed
sanctified us   universe,

בְּמִצְוֹתָיו, וְצִוָּנוּ עַל פִּדְיוֹן רְבָעִי.
⟪ fourth-year fruit. ⟨ to redeem ⟨ and has ⟨ with His com-
commanded us mandments,

אִם הַפֵּירוֹת רְבָעִי, הוּא וְחֻמְשׁוֹ הֲרֵי הוּא מְחֻלָּל עַל
⟨onto ⟨redeemed ⟨to be⟨ are ⟨ and its ⟨ it ⟪is fourth-⟨ the fruit ⟨ If
declared extra fifth year fruit,

פְּרוּטָה אַחַת מִן הַמַּטְבֵּעַ שֶׁיִּחַדְתִּי לִפְדְיוֹן מַעֲשֵׂר שֵׁנִי וּרְבָעִי.
⟪and fourth-⟨ of the second ⟨ for the ⟨ that I have ⟨ the coin ⟨ of ⟨ one perutah
year fruit. tithe redemption set aside

ברכות הודאה
BLESSINGS OF PRAISE AND GRATITUDE

BLESSINGS OVER PHENOMENA AND EVENTS / ברכות הראיה והשמיעה

THE FIRST THREE BLESSINGS OF THIS SECTION MAY BE RECITED ONLY ONCE EACH DAY, UNLESS THE SKIES HAVE CLEARED COMPLETELY AND THEN THE CLOUDS RETURNED. EXCEPT AS OTHERWISE INDICATED, THE REMAINING BLESSINGS ARE RECITED ONLY IF THIRTY DAYS HAVE ELAPSED SINCE THE PHENOMENON WAS LAST SEEN. IF UNSURE WHETHER TO RECITE ONE OF THE BLESSINGS IN THIS SECTION ON A PARTICULAR OCCASION, RECITE THE BLESSING BUT OMIT THE OPENING CLAUSE, בָּרוּךְ . . . הָעוֹלָם, BLESSED . . . UNIVERSE, AND SUBSTITUTE, בָּרוּךְ, BLESSED IS HE.

UPON SEEING LIGHTNING:

בָּרוּךְ אַתָּה יהוה אֱלֹהֵינוּ מֶלֶךְ הָעוֹלָם, עֹשֶׂה מַעֲשֵׂה
⟨the work ⟨ Who ⟪ of the ⟨ King ⟨ our God, ⟨HASHEM,⟨ are You, ⟨ Blessed
does universe,

בְּרֵאשִׁית.
⟪ of Creation.

UPON HEARING THUNDER:

בָּרוּךְ אַתָּה יהוה אֱלֹהֵינוּ מֶלֶךְ הָעוֹלָם, שֶׁכֹּחוֹ וּגְבוּרָתוֹ
⟨ and His ⟨ for His ⟪ of the ⟨ King ⟨ our God, ⟨HASHEM,⟨ are You, ⟨ Blessed
power strength universe,

מָלֵא עוֹלָם.
⟪ the universe. ⟨ fill

UPON SEEING A RAINBOW IN THE SKY:

בָּרוּךְ אַתָּה יהוה אֱלֹהֵינוּ מֶלֶךְ הָעוֹלָם, זוֹכֵר הַבְּרִית,
⟪ the ⟨ Who ⟪ of the ⟨ King ⟨ our God, ⟨HASHEM,⟨ are You, ⟨ Blessed
covenant, remembers universe,

וְנֶאֱמָן בִּבְרִיתוֹ, וְקַיָּם בְּמַאֲמָרוֹ.
⟪ His word. ⟨ and Who ⟪ in His ⟨ Who is
fulfills covenant, trustworthy

UPON EXPERIENCING AN EARTHQUAKE, OR SEEING A COMET, EXCEPTIONALLY LOFTY MOUNTAINS, OR EXCEPTIONALLY LARGE RIVERS (IN THEIR NATURAL COURSE):

בָּרוּךְ אַתָּה יהוה אֱלֹהֵינוּ מֶלֶךְ הָעוֹלָם, עֹשֶׂה מַעֲשֵׂה
⟨the work ⟨Who does ⟪ of the universe, ⟨ King ⟨ our God, ⟨HASHEM,⟨ are You, ⟨ Blessed

בְּרֵאשִׁית.
⟪ of Creation.

UPON SEEING THE OCEAN (SOME INCLUDE THE MEDITERRANEAN SEA):

שֶׁעָשָׂה הָעוֹלָם, מֶלֶךְ אֱלֹהֵינוּ יהוה אַתָּה **בָּרוּךְ**
‹Who made ‹‹ of the universe, ‹ King ‹ our God, ‹ HASHEM, ‹ are You, ‹ Blessed

אֶת הַיָּם הַגָּדוֹל.
‹‹   the great sea.

UPON SEEING EXCEPTIONALLY BEAUTIFUL PEOPLE, TREES OR FIELDS
(MANY OMIT THE WORDS IN PARENTHESES):

לוֹ שֶׁכָּכָה הָעוֹלָם,) מֶלֶךְ אֱלֹהֵינוּ יהוה (אַתָּה **בָּרוּךְ**
‹ He has ‹ that such ‹‹ of the universe,) ‹ King ‹ our God, ‹ HASHEM, ‹ (are You, ‹ Blessed

בְּעוֹלָמוֹ.
‹‹ in His universe.

UPON SEEING EXCEPTIONALLY STRANGE-LOOKING PEOPLE OR ANIMALS:

מְשַׁנֶּה הַבְּרִיּוֹת. הָעוֹלָם, מֶלֶךְ אֱלֹהֵינוּ יהוה אַתָּה **בָּרוּךְ**
‹‹ the ‹ Who ‹‹ of the ‹ King ‹ our God, ‹ HASHEM, ‹ are You, ‹ Blessed
creatures. differentiates universe,

UPON SEEING FRUIT TREES IN BLOOM DURING THE SPRING
(THIS BLESSING MAY BE RECITED ONLY ONCE EACH YEAR):

שֶׁלֹּא חִסַּר בְּעוֹלָמוֹ הָעוֹלָם, מֶלֶךְ אֱלֹהֵינוּ יהוה אַתָּה **בָּרוּךְ**
‹ from His ‹ withhold ‹ Who ‹‹ of the ‹ King ‹ our God, ‹ HASHEM, ‹ are You, ‹ Blessed
universe   did not   universe,

בָּהֶם לֵהָנוֹת טוֹבִים, וְאִילָנוֹת טוֹבוֹת בְּרִיּוֹת בּוֹ וּבָרָא דָּבָר,
‹ with ‹ to cause ‹‹ that are ‹ and trees ‹ that are ‹ creatures ‹ in it ‹ and He ‹‹ anything,
them   pleasure   good,   good   created

בְּנֵי אָדָם.
‹‹ for mankind.

UPON SEEING AN OUTSTANDING TORAH SCHOLAR:

מֵחָכְמָתוֹ שֶׁחָלַק הָעוֹלָם, מֶלֶךְ אֱלֹהֵינוּ יהוה אַתָּה **בָּרוּךְ**
‹ of His ‹ Who has ‹‹ of the ‹ King ‹ our God, ‹ HASHEM, ‹ are You, ‹ Blessed
knowledge apportioned universe,

לִירֵאָיו.
‹‹ to those who
fear Him.

UPON SEEING AN OUTSTANDING SECULAR SCHOLAR:

מֵחָכְמָתוֹ שֶׁנָּתַן הָעוֹלָם, מֶלֶךְ אֱלֹהֵינוּ יהוה אַתָּה **בָּרוּךְ**
‹ of His ‹ Who has ‹‹ of the ‹ King ‹ our God, ‹ HASHEM, ‹ are You, ‹ Blessed
knowledge given universe,

לְבָשָׂר וָדָם.
‹‹ to mortals.

UPON SEEING A GENTILE KING WHO RULES LAWFULLY, BUT WHO CANNOT BE OVERRULED, AND WHO HAS THE POWER OF LIFE AND DEATH, THE FOLLOWING IS RECITED. REGARDING MODERN-DAY ELECTED RULERS, MOST AUTHORITIES SUGGEST THAT ONE OMIT THE OPENING CLAUSE, . . . בָּרוּךְ הָעוֹלָם, *BLESSED . . . UNIVERSE*, AND SUBSTITUTE, בָּרוּךְ, *BLESSED IS HE.*

בָּרוּךְ אַתָּה יהוה אֱלֹהֵינוּ מֶלֶךְ הָעוֹלָם, שֶׁנָּתַן מִכְּבוֹדוֹ

Blessed ⟨ are You, ⟨ HASHEM, ⟨ our God, ⟨ King ⟨ of the universe, ⟨⟨ Who has given ⟨ of His glory

לְבָשָׂר וָדָם.

⟨⟨ to mortals.

UPON SEEING 600,000 OR MORE JEWS TOGETHER:

בָּרוּךְ אַתָּה יהוה אֱלֹהֵינוּ מֶלֶךְ הָעוֹלָם, חֲכַם הָרָזִים.

Blessed ⟨ are You, ⟨ HASHEM, ⟨ our God, ⟨ King ⟨ of the universe, ⟨⟨ Knower ⟨ ⟨⟨ of secrets.

UPON ONE'S FIRST MEETING WITH A FRIEND WHO HAS RECOVERED FROM A LIFE-THREATENING ILLNESS:

בְּרִיךְ רַחֲמָנָא מַלְכָּא דְעָלְמָא, דִּי יְהָבָךְ לָן וְלָא יְהָבָךְ

Blessed ⟨ is the Merciful One, ⟨ King ⟨ of the universe, ⟨⟨ Who ⟨ has given you ⟨ to us, ⟨ and has not ⟨ given you

לְעַפְרָא.

⟨⟨ to the dust.

UPON SEEING A DESTROYED SYNAGOGUE:

בָּרוּךְ אַתָּה יהוה אֱלֹהֵינוּ מֶלֶךְ הָעוֹלָם, דַּיַּן הָאֱמֶת.

Blessed ⟨ are You, ⟨ HASHEM, ⟨ our God, ⟨ King ⟨ of the universe, ⟨⟨ the Judge ⟨ Who is true.

UPON SEEING A DESTROYED SYNAGOGUE THAT HAS BEEN RESTORED TO ITS PREVIOUS GRANDEUR (MANY OMIT THE WORDS IN PARENTHESES):

בָּרוּךְ (אַתָּה יהוה אֱלֹהֵינוּ מֶלֶךְ הָעוֹלָם), מַצִּיב גְּבוּל

Blessed ⟨ (are You, ⟨ HASHEM, ⟨ our God, ⟨ King ⟨ of the universe,) ⟨⟨ Who establishes ⟨ the boundary

אַלְמָנָה.[1]

⟨⟨ of a widow.

UPON SEEING A PLACE WHERE ONE HAD EARLIER EXPERIENCED A MIRACLE THAT SAVED HIM FROM IMMINENT DANGER (ONE WHO EXPERIENCED SUCH SALVATION IN MORE THAN ONE PLACE DURING HIS LIFETIME MUST APPEND A ROSTER OF THE OTHER PLACES TO THE END OF THE BLESSING):

בָּרוּךְ אַתָּה יהוה אֱלֹהֵינוּ מֶלֶךְ הָעוֹלָם, שֶׁעָשָׂה לִי

Blessed ⟨ are You, ⟨ HASHEM, ⟨ our God, ⟨ King ⟨ of the universe, ⟨⟨ Who performed ⟨ for me

נֵס בַּמָּקוֹם הַזֶּה (וּבְ...).

⟨ a miracle ⟨ at this place ⟨ (and at . . .). ⟨⟨

---

(1) Cf. *Proverbs* 15:25.

UPON SEEING A PLACE WHERE ONE'S PARENTS, ANCESTORS, TORAH TEACHER, OR THE NATION AS A WHOLE WAS MIRACULOUSLY SAVED FROM IMMINENT DANGER:

בָּרוּךְ אַתָּה יהוה אֱלֹהֵינוּ מֶלֶךְ הָעוֹלָם, שֶׁעָשָׂה

‹ Who performed ‹‹ of the universe, ‹ King ‹ our God, ‹ HASHEM, ‹ are You, ‹ Blessed

THE NATION	ONE'S TEACHER	ONE'S FOREBEARS	ONE'S MOTHER	ONE'S FATHER
לַאֲבוֹתֵינוּ	לְרַבִּי	לַאֲבוֹתַי	לְאִמִּי	לְאָבִי
‹ for our ancestors	‹ for my teacher	‹ for my ancestors	‹ for my mother	‹ for my father

נֵס בַּמָּקוֹם הַזֶּה.

‹‹   at this place. ‹ a miracle

VARIOUS BLESSINGS / ברכות שונות

UPON (A) EATING SEASONAL FRUITS OF A NEW SEASON FOR THE FIRST TIME; (B) PURCHASING A NEW GARMENT OF SIGNIFICANT VALUE TO THE WEARER (E.G., A SUIT OR DRESS); (C) PERFORMANCE OF A SEASONAL *MITZVAH*; OR (D) DERIVING SIGNIFICANT BENEFIT FROM AN EVENT (IF OTHERS ALSO BENE-FIT, THE BLESSING הַטּוֹב וְהַמֵּטִיב, *WHO IS GOOD AND DOES GOOD* — SEE BELOW — IS SUBSTITUTED):

בָּרוּךְ אַתָּה יהוה אֱלֹהֵינוּ מֶלֶךְ הָעוֹלָם, שֶׁהֶחֱיָנוּ וְקִיְּמָנוּ

‹ and has ‹ Who has kept ‹‹ of the ‹ King ‹ our God, ‹ HASHEM, ‹ are You, ‹ Blessed
sustained us, us alive, universe,

וְהִגִּיעָנוּ לַזְּמַן הַזֶּה.

‹‹ to this season. ‹ and has brought us

UPON HEARING UNUSUALLY GOOD NEWS THAT BENEFITS BOTH ONESELF AND OTHERS:

בָּרוּךְ אַתָּה יהוה אֱלֹהֵינוּ מֶלֶךְ הָעוֹלָם, הַטּוֹב וְהַמֵּטִיב.

‹‹ and Who ‹ Who is ‹‹ of the ‹ King ‹ our God, ‹ HASHEM, ‹ are You, ‹ Blessed
does good. good universe,

UPON HEARING UNUSUALLY BAD NEWS:

בָּרוּךְ אַתָּה יהוה אֱלֹהֵינוּ מֶלֶךְ הָעוֹלָם, דַּיַּן הָאֱמֶת.

‹‹ Who is ‹ the ‹‹ of the ‹ King ‹ our God, ‹ HASHEM, ‹ are You, ‹ Blessed
true. Judge universe,

UPON DONNING A NEW GARMENT OF SIGNIFICANT VALUE TO THE WEARER (E.G., A NEW SUIT OR DRESS):

בָּרוּךְ אַתָּה יהוה אֱלֹהֵינוּ מֶלֶךְ הָעוֹלָם, מַלְבִּישׁ עֲרֻמִּים.

‹‹ the naked. ‹‹ Who clothes ‹ of the universe, ‹ King ‹ our God, ‹ HASHEM, ‹ are You, ‹ Blessed

For the blessings recited . . . at a *bris milah* (circumcision), see p. 322.
at a *pidyon haben* (redemption of the firstborn), see p. 336.
at a wedding ceremony and a *sheva berachos,* see pp. 316-321.
when kindling the Chanukah menorah, see p. 577.
when reading the *Megillah,* see p. 581.
after using the bathroom, see p. 23.
upon visiting a cemetery, see p. 606.
upon taking the *lulav* and *esrog,* see p. 499.
upon sitting down to a meal in the *succah,* see p. 560.

❖ WEEKDAY MINCHAH / מִנְחָה לְחוֹל ❖

MANY CONGREGATIONS BEGIN *MINCHAH* WITH THE RECITATION OF *KORBANOS* [OFFERINGS]
AND *KETORES* [INCENSE]. SOME CONGREGATIONS BEGIN *MINCHAH* WITH אַשְׁרֵי (PAGE 360).

OFFERINGS / קָרְבָּנוֹת

THE LAVER / הַכִּיּוֹר

וַיְדַבֵּר יהוה אֶל מֹשֶׁה לֵּאמֹר. וְעָשִׂיתָ כִּיּוֹר
⟨ a laver ⟨ You shall make ⟨⟨ saying: ⟨ Moses, ⟨ to ⟨ HASHEM spoke

נְחֹשֶׁת, וְכַנּוֹ נְחֹשֶׁת, לְרָחְצָה, וְנָתַתָּ אֹתוֹ בֵּין
⟨ between ⟨ it ⟨ and you ⟨⟨ for washing; ⟨ of copper, ⟨ and its ⟨ of copper,
shall place base

אֹהֶל מוֹעֵד וּבֵין הַמִּזְבֵּחַ, וְנָתַתָּ שָׁמָּה מָיִם. וְרָחֲצוּ
⟨⟨ They shall ⟨⟨ water. ⟨ there ⟨ and you ⟨⟨ and the Altar, ⟨ of ⟨ the Tent
wash shall put Appointment

אַהֲרֹן וּבָנָיו מִמֶּנּוּ, אֶת יְדֵיהֶם וְאֶת רַגְלֵיהֶם.
⟨⟨ and their feet. ⟨ their hands ⟨ from ⟨⟨ and his ⟨ — Aaron
[the laver] sons —

בְּבֹאָם אֶל אֹהֶל מוֹעֵד יִרְחֲצוּ מַיִם וְלֹא יָמֻתוּ,
⟨⟨ perish, ⟨ so that ⟨ with ⟨ they shall ⟨ of ⟨ the Tent ⟨ into ⟨ When
they not water wash Appointment they enter

אוֹ בְגִשְׁתָּם אֶל הַמִּזְבֵּחַ לְשָׁרֵת לְהַקְטִיר אִשֶּׁה
⟨ a fire- ⟨ to burn ⟨⟨ to serve, ⟨ the Altar ⟨ to ⟨ when they ⟨ or
offering approach

לַיהוה. וְרָחֲצוּ יְדֵיהֶם וְרַגְלֵיהֶם וְלֹא יָמֻתוּ,
⟨⟨ perish; ⟨ so that ⟨ and their feet ⟨ their hands ⟨ They shall ⟨⟨ to HASHEM.
they not wash

וְהָיְתָה לָהֶם חָק עוֹלָם, לוֹ וּלְזַרְעוֹ לְדֹרֹתָם.¹
⟨⟨ throughout their ⟨ and for his ⟨ for ⟨⟨ that is ⟨ a ⟨ for them ⟨ and this
generations. offspring him eternal decree shall be

---

(1) *Exodus* 30:17-21.

❖ מִנְחָה לְחוֹל / **WEEKDAY MINCHAH** ❖

Minchah corresponds to the *tamid*, the daily afternoon offering in the Temple (*Berachos* 26b), so it is recited only when it was permissible to offer the *tamid*: from one half hour after

midday until evening. The preferable time, however, is not before three and a half variable hours after midday (*Orach Chaim* 233:1). A variable hour is one-twelfth of the time from sunrise to sunset.

THE TAMID-OFFERING / קרבן התמיד

SOME HOLD THAT THE FOLLOWING (UNTIL קטרת/INCENSE) SHOULD BE RECITED WHILE STANDING.

יְהִי רָצוֹן מִלְּפָנֶיךָ, יהוה אֱלֹהֵינוּ וֵאלֹהֵי אֲבוֹתֵינוּ,

May it be ⟨ the will ⟩ before You ⟨ Hashem, ⟩ our God ⟨ and the God ⟨ of our forefathers,

שֶׁתְּרַחֵם עָלֵינוּ וְתִמְחָל לָנוּ עַל כָּל חַטֹּאתֵינוּ, וּתְכַפֶּר לָנוּ

that You have mercy ⟨ on us ⟩ and pardon ⟨ for ⟩ us ⟨ all ⟩ our errors, ⟩ atone ⟨ for us

עַל כָּל עֲוֺנוֹתֵינוּ, וְתִסְלַח לָנוּ עַל כָּל פְּשָׁעֵינוּ, וְשֶׁיִּבָּנֶה

for ⟨ all ⟩ our iniquities, ⟨ and forgive ⟨ us ⟩ for ⟨ all ⟩ our willful sins; ⟩ and that re-built should be

בֵּית הַמִּקְדָּשׁ בִּמְהֵרָה בְיָמֵינוּ, וְנַקְרִיב לְפָנֶיךָ קָרְבַּן הַתָּמִיד

the Holy Temple ⟨ speedily, ⟨ in our days, ⟩ so that we may offer ⟨ before You ⟨ the ⟨ offering ⟨ that is continual,

שֶׁיְּכַפֵּר בַּעֲדֵנוּ, כְּמוֹ שֶׁכָּתַבְתָּ עָלֵינוּ בְּתוֹרָתֶךָ עַל יְדֵי מֹשֶׁה

that it may atone ⟨ for us, ⟨ as ⟨ You have written ⟨ for us ⟨ in Your Torah, ⟩ by ⟨ the hand ⟨ of Moses,

עַבְדֶּךָ, מִפִּי כְבוֹדֶךָ, כָּאָמוּר:

Your servant, ⟩ from Your glorious mouth, ⟨ as it is said:

וַיְדַבֵּר יהוה אֶל מֹשֶׁה לֵּאמֹר. צַו אֶת בְּנֵי

Hashem spoke ⟩ to ⟨ Moses, ⟨ saying: ⟩ Command ⟨ the Children

יִשְׂרָאֵל וְאָמַרְתָּ אֲלֵהֶם, אֶת קָרְבָּנִי לַחְמִי

of Israel ⟨ and tell ⟨ them: ⟩ My offering, ⟨ My food

לְאִשַּׁי, רֵיחַ נִיחֹחִי, תִּשְׁמְרוּ לְהַקְרִיב לִי

for My fires, ⟨ My aroma ⟨ that is satisfying, ⟩ you are to be scrupulous ⟨ to offer ⟨ Me

בְּמוֹעֲדוֹ. וְאָמַרְתָּ לָהֶם, זֶה הָאִשֶּׁה אֲשֶׁר תַּקְרִיבוּ

in its appointed time. ⟩ And you are to tell ⟨ them: ⟩ This ⟨ is the fire-offering ⟨ that ⟨ you are to offer

לַיהוה, כְּבָשִׂים בְּנֵי שָׁנָה תְמִימִם, שְׁנַיִם לַיּוֹם,

to Hashem: ⟩ male lambs, ⟨ in their first year, ⟨ unblemished, ⟨ two ⟨ daily,

עֹלָה תָמִיד. אֶת הַכֶּבֶשׂ אֶחָד תַּעֲשֶׂה בַבֹּקֶר,

an elevation-offering ⟨ that is continual. ⟩ The one lamb ⟨ you shall do ⟨ in the morning,

וְאֵת הַכֶּבֶשׂ הַשֵּׁנִי תַּעֲשֶׂה בֵּין הָעַרְבָּיִם.

and the lamb ⟨ that is second ⟨ you shall do ⟨ ⟪ in the afternoon;

וַעֲשִׂירִית הָאֵיפָה סֹלֶת לְמִנְחָה, בְּלוּלָה בְּשֶׁמֶן

with a tenth ⟨ of an *ephah* ⟨ of fine ⟨ for a meal- ⟪ mixed ⟨ with oil ⟨
flour   offering,

כָּתִית רְבִיעִת הַהִין. עֹלַת תָּמִיד, הָעֲשֻׂיָה בְּהַר

from ⟨ a quarter ⟨ of a *hin*. ⟪ It is the ⟨ that is ⟨ continual, elevation- ⟪ that was done ⟨ at
crushed   satisfying,   offering   Mount
[olives]

סִינַי, לְרֵיחַ נִיחֹחַ, אִשֶּׁה לַיהוה. וְנִסְכּוֹ רְבִיעִת

Sinai, ⟪ aroma ⟨ that is ⟪ a fire- ⟨ to HASHEM. ⟪ And its ⟨ is a quarter
satisfying,   offering   libation

הַהִין לַכֶּבֶשׂ הָאֶחָד, בַּקֹּדֶשׁ הַסֵּךְ נֶסֶךְ שֵׁכָר

of a *hin* ⟨ for each lamb, ⟨ on the Holy ⟨ to be ⟪ a ⟨ of fermen-
[Altar]   libation poured,   ted wine

לַיהוה. וְאֵת הַכֶּבֶשׂ הַשֵּׁנִי תַּעֲשֶׂה בֵּין הָעַרְבָּיִם,

to HASHEM. ⟪ And the lamb ⟨ that is ⟨ you are ⟨ ⟪ in the afternoon;
second   to do

כְּמִנְחַת הַבֹּקֶר וּכְנִסְכּוֹ תַּעֲשֶׂה, אִשֵּׁה רֵיחַ נִיחֹחַ

like the ⟨ of the ⟨ and its ⟨ shall you ⟪ a fire- ⟨ for an ⟨ that is
meal-offering morning   libation   do,   offering aroma   satisfying

לַיהוה.[1]

⟪ to HASHEM.

וְשָׁחַט אֹתוֹ עַל יֶרֶךְ הַמִּזְבֵּחַ צָפֹנָה לִפְנֵי יהוה,

He is to ⟨ it ⟨ on ⟨ the side ⟨ of the Altar ⟨ on the ⟨ before ⟨ HASHEM,
slaughter   north,

וְזָרְקוּ בְּנֵי אַהֲרֹן הַכֹּהֲנִים אֶת דָּמוֹ עַל הַמִּזְבֵּחַ

⟪ and they ⟨ — the sons ⟨ ⟪ the *Kohanim* — ⟨ its blood ⟨ upon ⟨ the Altar,
shall throw of Aaron

סָבִיב.[2]

⟪ all around.

---

(1) *Numbers* 28:1-8. (2) *Leviticus* 1:11.

יְהִי רָצוֹן מִלְּפָנֶיךָ, יהוה אֱלֹהֵינוּ וֵאלֹהֵי אֲבוֹתֵינוּ, שֶׁתְּהֵא

⟨ that ⟨ of our ⟨ and the ⟨ our God ⟨ Hashem, ⟨ before You, ⟨ the will ⟨ May
it be   forefathers,   God   it be

אֲמִירָה זוּ חֲשׁוּבָה וּמְקֻבֶּלֶת וּמְרֻצָּה לְפָנֶיךָ כְּאִלּוּ הִקְרַבְנוּ

⟨ we had ⟨ as if ⟨ before You ⟨ and ⟨ and ⟨ worthy ⟨ — this recital —
offered   favorable   acceptable,

קָרְבַּן הַתָּמִיד בְּמוֹעֲדוֹ וּבִמְקוֹמוֹ וּכְהִלְכָתוֹ.

⟨ and according to ⟨ in its place, ⟨ in its set time, ⟨ the continual offering
its requirement.

קטרת / INCENSE

אַתָּה הוּא יהוה אֱלֹהֵינוּ שֶׁהִקְטִירוּ אֲבוֹתֵינוּ לְפָנֶיךָ

⟨ before You ⟨ that our forefathers burned ⟨ our God, ⟨ Hashem, ⟨ the One, ⟨ You are

אֶת קְטֹרֶת הַסַּמִּים בִּזְמַן שֶׁבֵּית הַמִּקְדָּשׁ הָיָה קַיָּם, כַּאֲשֶׁר

⟨ as ⟨ standing, ⟨ was ⟨ when the Holy Temple ⟨ in the time ⟨ spices ⟨ the incense

צִוִּיתָ אוֹתָם עַל יְדֵי מֹשֶׁה נְבִיאֶךָ, כַּכָּתוּב בְּתוֹרָתֶךָ:

⟨ in Your Torah: ⟨ as is written ⟨ Your ⟨ of ⟨ the ⟨ by ⟨ them ⟨ You com-
prophet, Moses   hand   manded

וַיֹּאמֶר יהוה אֶל מֹשֶׁה, קַח לְךָ סַמִּים, נָטָף

⟨ —stacte, ⟨ spices ⟨ [for] ⟨ Take ⟨ Moses: ⟨ to ⟨ Hashem said
yourself

וּשְׁחֵלֶת וְחֶלְבְּנָה, סַמִּים וּלְבֹנָה זַכָּה, בַּד בְּבַד

⟨ of equal weight ⟨ that is ⟨ and ⟨ spices ⟨ and galbanum — ⟨ onycha,
pure;   frankincense

יִהְיֶה. וְעָשִׂיתָ אֹתָהּ קְטֹרֶת, רֹקַח, מַעֲשֵׂה רוֹקֵחַ,

⟨ of a ⟨ the ⟨ a spice- ⟨ into ⟨ it ⟨ You shall ⟨ shall
perfumer, handiwork compound, incense,   make   they be.

מְמֻלָּח, טָהוֹר, קֹדֶשׁ. וְשָׁחַקְתָּ מִמֶּנָּה הָדֵק,

⟨ finely ⟨ some of it ⟨ You shall grind ⟨ and holy. ⟨ pure ⟨ thoroughly mixed,

וְנָתַתָּה מִמֶּנָּה לִפְנֵי הָעֵדֻת בְּאֹהֶל מוֹעֵד אֲשֶׁר

⟨ where ⟨ of ⟨ in the Tent ⟨ the ⟨ before ⟨ some of it ⟨ and you
Appointment,   Testimony   shall place

אִוָּעֵד לְךָ שָׁמָּה, קֹדֶשׁ קָדָשִׁים תִּהְיֶה

⟨ it shall be ⟨ of holies ⟨ holy ⟨ there; ⟨ you ⟨ I shall designate
a time to meet

לָכֶם. וְנֶאֱמַר: וְהִקְטִיר עָלָיו אַהֲרֹן קְטֹרֶת סַמִּים,¹

‹ spices, ‹ the incense ‹ shall Burn Aaron, ‹ upon it ‹ Burn ≪ It is also written: ≪ for you.

בַּבֹּקֶר בַּבֹּקֶר בְּהֵיטִיבוֹ אֶת הַנֵּרֹת יַקְטִירֶנָּה.

≪ he is to burn it. ‹ the lamps ‹ when he prepares ‹ each and every morning

וּבְהַעֲלֹת אַהֲרֹן אֶת הַנֵּרֹת בֵּין הָעַרְבַּיִם,

‹ in the afternoon, ‹ the lamps ‹ And when Aaron ignites

יַקְטִירֶנָּה, קְטֹרֶת תָּמִיד לִפְנֵי יהוה לְדֹרֹתֵיכֶם.²

≪ throughout your generations. ‹ HASHEM, ‹ before ‹ that is continual ‹ an incense ≪ he is to burn it,

———— Talmud, *Kereisos* 6a, *Yerushalmi Yoma* 4:5 / כריתות ו., ירושלמי יומא ד:ה ————

תָּנוּ רַבָּנָן, פִּטּוּם הַקְּטֹרֶת כֵּיצַד. שְׁלֹשׁ מֵאוֹת

‹ hundred ‹ Three ≪ how is it done? ≪ of the incense ‹ The mixture, formulation ≪ did the Rabbis: ‹ Taught

וְשִׁשִּׁים וּשְׁמוֹנָה מָנִים הָיוּ בָהּ. שְׁלֹשׁ מֵאוֹת

‹ hundred ‹ three ≪ in it: ‹ were ‹ *maneh* ‹ eight ‹ sixty-

וְשִׁשִּׁים וַחֲמִשָּׁה כְּמִנְיַן יְמוֹת הַחַמָּה – מָנֶה לְכָל

‹ for each ‹ – a *maneh* ≪ of the solar [year] ‹ of days ‹ corresponding to the number ‹ five ‹ sixty-

יוֹם, פְּרַס בְּשַׁחֲרִית וּפְרַס בֵּין הָעַרְבַּיִם;

≪ in the afternoon; ‹ and half ‹ in the morning ‹ half ≪ day,

וּשְׁלֹשָׁה מָנִים יְתֵרִים, שֶׁמֵּהֶם מַכְנִיס כֹּהֵן גָּדוֹל

≪ the *Kohen Gadol,* ≪ would bring, ‹ from which ≪ extra, ‹ *maneh* ‹ and three

מְלֹא חָפְנָיו בְּיוֹם הַכִּפֻּרִים. וּמַחֲזִירָן לַמַּכְתֶּשֶׁת

‹ to the mortar ‹ He would return them ≪ [into the Holy of Holies] ‹ his hands ‹ the amount that fills

בְּעֶרֶב יוֹם הַכִּפֻּרִים, וְשׁוֹחֲקָן יָפֶה יָפֶה כְּדֵי

‹ so that ≪ very thoroughly ‹ and grind them ≪ Yom Kippur, ‹ on the day before

————————
(1) *Exodus* 30:34-36. (2) 30:7-8.

שֶׁתְּהֵא דַקָּה מִן הַדַּקָּה. וְאַחַד עָשָׂר סַמָּנִים הָיוּ
‹ were ‹ kinds of spices ‹ Eleven   « the fine. ‹ of ‹ the finest ‹ it would be

בָּהּ, וְאֵלּוּ הֵן: (א) הַצֳּרִי, (ב) וְהַצִּפֹּרֶן, (ג) הַחֶלְבְּנָה,
‹ galbanum,   ‹ onycha,   ‹ stacte, « are they: ‹ and these ‹ in it,

(ד) וְהַלְּבוֹנָה, מִשְׁקַל שִׁבְעִים שִׁבְעִים מָנֶה; (ה) מוֹר,
‹ myrrh, « maneh; ‹   each seventy   ‹ weighing « and frankincense,

(ו) וּקְצִיעָה, (ז) שִׁבֹּלֶת נֵרְדְּ, (ח) וְכַרְכֹּם, מִשְׁקַל
« weighing « saffron,   ‹ spikenard,   ‹ cassia,

שִׁשָּׁה עָשָׂר שִׁשָּׁה עָשָׂר מָנֶה; (ט) הַקֹּשְׁטְ
‹ costus,   « maneh; ‹   each sixteen

שְׁנֵים עָשָׂר, (י) וְקִלּוּפָה שְׁלֹשָׁה, (יא) וְקִנָּמוֹן
‹ and cinnamon « three; ‹ aromatic bark, « twelve [maneh];

תִּשְׁעָה. בֹּרִית כַּרְשִׁינָה תִּשְׁעָה קַבִּין, יֵין
‹ wine « kav; ‹ nine ‹ of Carshina ‹ [Additionally,] lye « nine.

קַפְרִיסִין סְאִין תְּלָתָא וְקַבִּין תְּלָתָא, וְאִם
‹ — if « and three kav ‹ three se'ah ‹ of Cyprus

אֵין לוֹ יֵין קַפְרִיסִין, מֵבִיא חֲמַר חִוַּרְיָן עַתִּיק,
« that is old — ‹ that is white ‹ wine ‹ he brings « of Cyprus, ‹ wine ‹ he has no

מֶלַח סְדוֹמִית רֹבַע; מַעֲלֵה עָשָׁן כָּל שֶׁהוּא.
« a minute amount. ‹ and maaleh ashan « a quarter[-kav], ‹ of Sodom, ‹ salt

רַבִּי נָתָן הַבַּבְלִי אוֹמֵר: אַף כִּפַּת הַיַּרְדֵּן
‹ of the Jordan ‹ amber ‹ Also « says: ‹ the Babylonian ‹ Nassan ‹ Rabbi

כָּל שֶׁהוּא. וְאִם נָתַן בָּהּ דְּבַשׁ, פְּסָלָהּ. וְאִם
‹ And if « he invalidated it. « fruit-honey, ‹ in it ‹ he placed ‹ If « a minute amount.

חִסַּר אַחַת מִכָּל סַמָּנֶיהָ, חַיָּב מִיתָה.
« to the death penalty. ‹ he is liable ‹ its spices, ‹ of all ‹ any one ‹ he left out

רַבָּן שִׁמְעוֹן בֶּן גַּמְלִיאֵל אוֹמֵר: הַצֳּרִי אֵינוֹ
‹ is nothing ‹ Stacte « says: ‹ Gamliel ‹ ben ‹ Shimon ‹ Rabban

אֶלָּא שְׂרָף הַנּוֹטֵף מֵעֲצֵי הַקְּטָף. בְּרִית כַּרְשִׁינָה

‹ of Carshina, ‹ Lye ≫ of balsam. ‹ from trees ‹ that drips ‹ the sap ‹ but

לָמָה הִיא בָאָה, כְּדֵי לְיַפּוֹת בָּה אֶת הַצִּפֹּרֶן,

≪ the onycha, ‹ with it ‹ to refine ‹ In order ≪ brought? ‹ is it ‹ why

כְּדֵי שֶׁתְּהֵא נָאָה. יֵין קַפְרִיסִין לָמָה הוּא בָא,

≪ brought? ‹ is it ‹ why ‹ of Cyprus, ‹ Wine ≪ pleasing. ‹ that it should be ‹ in order

כְּדֵי לִשְׁרוֹת בּוֹ אֶת הַצִּפֹּרֶן, כְּדֵי שֶׁתְּהֵא עַזָּה.

≪ pungent. ‹ that it ‹ in order ‹ the onycha, ‹ in it ‹ to soak ‹ In order
should be

וַהֲלֹא מֵי רַגְלַיִם יָפִין לָהּ, אֶלָּא שֶׁאֵין מַכְנִיסִין

‹ bring ‹ they ‹ Never- ≪ for that? ‹ more ‹ urine ‹ But is not
do not theless suitable

מֵי רַגְלַיִם בַּמִּקְדָּשׁ מִפְּנֵי הַכָּבוֹד.

≪ respect. ‹ out of ‹ into the Temple ‹ urine

תַּנְיָא, רַבִּי נָתָן אוֹמֵר: כְּשֶׁהוּא שׁוֹחֵק, אוֹמֵר,

≪ [the one ‹ would grind ‹ As he ≪ says: ‹ Nassan ‹ Rabbi ≪ It is taught:
in charge] [the incense],
would say,

הָדֵק הֵיטֵב, הֵיטֵב הָדֵק, מִפְּנֵי שֶׁהַקּוֹל יָפֶה

‹ is beneficial ‹ the sound ‹ because ≪ grind, ‹ thoroughly ‹ thoroughly, ‹ Grind

לַבְּשָׂמִים. פִּטְּמָהּ לַחֲצָאִין, כְּשֵׁרָה; לִשְׁלִישׁ

‹ but as to ≪ it was fit ‹ in half-quantities, ‹ If one mixed it ≪ for the spices.
a third for use,

וְלִרְבִיעַ, לֹא שָׁמָעְנוּ. אָמַר רַבִּי יְהוּדָה: זֶה

‹ This is ≪ Yehudah: ‹ Rabbi ‹ Said ≪ — we have not heard [the law]. ≪ or a quarter

הַכְּלָל – אִם כְּמִדָּתָהּ, כְּשֵׁרָה לַחֲצָאִין; וְאִם

‹ But if ≪ [even] in half ‹ it is fit ≪ in its proper ‹ If ≪ the general rule:
the full amount. for use proportion,

חִסַּר אַחַת מִכָּל סַמָּנֶיהָ, חַיָּב מִיתָה.

≪ to the death penalty. ‹ he is liable ‹ its spices, ‹ of all ‹ any one ‹ he left out

תַּנְיָא, בַּר קַפָּרָא אוֹמֵר: אַחַת לְשִׁשִּׁים אוֹ

‹ or ‹ every sixty ‹ Once ‹‹ says: ‹ Kappara ‹ Bar ‹‹ It is taught:

לְשִׁבְעִים שָׁנָה הָיְתָה בָאָה שֶׁל שִׁירַיִם

‹‹ — the accumulated ‹‹ reach ‹ it would ‹ years, ‹ seventy
leftovers —

לַחֲצָאִין. וְעוֹד תָּנֵי בַּר קַפָּרָא: אִלּוּ הָיָה נוֹתֵן

‹ put ‹ one had ‹ If ‹‹ Kappara: ‹ Bar ‹ taught ‹ Further- ‹‹ half the yearly
more   quantity.

בָּהּ קוֹרְטוֹב שֶׁל דְּבַשׁ, אֵין אָדָם יָכוֹל לַעֲמֹד

‹ withstood ‹ could have ‹ person ‹ no ‹‹ fruit-honey, ‹ of ‹ a kortov ‹ into it

מִפְּנֵי רֵיחָהּ. וְלָמָּה אֵין מְעָרְבִין בָּהּ דְּבַשׁ,

‹‹ fruit-honey? ‹ into it ‹ mix ‹ did they not ‹ Why ‹‹ its scent.

מִפְּנֵי שֶׁהַתּוֹרָה אָמְרָה: כִּי כָל שְׂאֹר וְכָל דְּבַשׁ

‹ fruit-honey, ‹ or any ‹ leaven ‹ any ‹ For ‹‹ said: ‹ the Torah ‹ Because

לֹא תַקְטִירוּ מִמֶּנּוּ אִשֶּׁה לַיהוה.¹

‹‹ to Hashem. ‹ a fire-offering ‹ from them ‹ you are not to burn

RECITE THREE TIMES:

יהוה צְבָאוֹת עִמָּנוּ, מִשְׂגָּב לָנוּ אֱלֹהֵי יַעֲקֹב,

‹‹ of Jacob, ‹ is the ‹ for us ‹ a ‹‹ is with us, ‹ Master ‹ Hashem,
God   stronghold   of Legions,

סֶלָה.²

‹‹ Selah!

RECITE THREE TIMES:

יהוה צְבָאוֹת, אַשְׁרֵי אָדָם בֹּטֵחַ בָּךְ.³

‹‹ in You. ‹ who ‹ is the ‹ praiseworthy ‹ Master of ‹ Hashem,
trusts   man   Legions,

RECITE THREE TIMES:

יהוה הוֹשִׁיעָה, הַמֶּלֶךְ יַעֲנֵנוּ בְיוֹם קָרְאֵנוּ.⁴

‹‹ we call! ‹ on the day ‹ answer us ‹ May the King ‹‹ save! ‹ Hashem,

---

(1) *Leviticus* 2:11. (2) *Psalms* 46:8. (3) 84:13. (4) 20:10.

אַתָּה סֵתֶר לִי, מִצַּר תִּצְּרֵנִי, רָנֵּי פַלֵּט,
‹ of ‹ with ≪ You preserve ‹ from ≪ for me; ‹ a shelter ‹ You are
rescue, glad song   me;   distress

תְּסוֹבְבֵנִי, סֶלָה.¹ וְעָרְבָה לַיהוה מִנְחַת יְהוּדָה
‹ of Judah ‹ let be the ‹ to Hashem ‹ And pleasing ≪ Selah! ≪ You envelop me,
offering

וִירוּשָׁלָיִם, כִּימֵי עוֹלָם וּכְשָׁנִים קַדְמֹנִיּוֹת.²
≪   gone by. ‹ and in years ‹ of old ‹ as in days ≪ and Jerusalem,

אָנָּא בְכֹחַ גְּדֻלַּת יְמִינְךָ תַּתִּיר צְרוּרָה.   אב״ג ית״ץ
≪ the bundled ‹ untie ‹ of Your ‹ of the ‹ With the ≪ We beg
[sins].   right hand, greatness strength You!

קַבֵּל רִנַּת עַמְּךָ שַׂגְּבֵנוּ טַהֲרֵנוּ נוֹרָא.   קר״ע שט״ן
≪ O Awesome ‹ purify us, ‹ strengthen ≪ of Your ‹ the ‹ Accept
One.   us,   people; prayer

נָא גִבּוֹר דּוֹרְשֵׁי יִחוּדְךָ כְּבָבַת שָׁמְרֵם.   נג״ד יכ״ש
≪ guard them. ‹ like the pupil ≪ Your ‹ – those ≪ O Strong ‹ Please,
of an eye Oneness, who foster One

בָּרְכֵם טַהֲרֵם רַחֲמֵם צִדְקָתְךָ³ תָּמִיד גָּמְלֵם.   בט״ר צת״ג
≪ recompense ‹ always ‹ may Your ≪ show them ‹ purify ‹ Bless
them.   righteousness mercy, them, them,

חֲסִין קָדוֹשׁ בְּרוֹב טוּבְךָ נַהֵל עֲדָתֶךָ.   חק״ב טנ״ע
≪   Your ‹ guide ‹ of Your ‹ with the ≪ Holy ‹ Powerful
congregation. goodness abundance One, One,

יָחִיד גֵּאֶה לְעַמְּךָ פְּנֵה זוֹכְרֵי קְדֻשָּׁתֶךָ.   יג״ל פז״ק
≪ Your holiness. ‹ those who ≪ turn, ‹ to Your ‹ Exalted ‹ Unique
proclaim   people One, One,

שַׁוְעָתֵנוּ קַבֵּל וּשְׁמַע צַעֲקָתֵנוּ יוֹדֵעַ תַּעֲלֻמוֹת.   שק״ו צי״ת
≪ of mysteries. ‹ O Knower ≪ our cry, ‹ and hear ≪ accept, ‹ Our entreaty

בָּרוּךְ שֵׁם כְּבוֹד מַלְכוּתוֹ לְעוֹלָם וָעֶד.
≪ and ever. ‹ for ever ‹ kingdom ‹ of His ‹ is the ‹ Blessed
glorious Name

---

(1) *Psalms* 32:7. (2) *Malachi* 3:4. (3) Alternatively: רַחֲמֵי צִדְקָתֶךָ, *the mercy of Your righteousness.*

ASHREI / אשרי

אַשְׁרֵי יוֹשְׁבֵי בֵיתֶךָ, עוֹד יְהַלְלוּךָ סֶּלָה. אַשְׁרֵי [1]

‹ Praise-worthy ‹‹ Selah. ‹‹ they will ‹ continually ‹‹ in Your ‹ are those ‹ Praiseworthy
praise You, house, who dwell

הָעָם שֶׁכָּכָה לּוֹ, אַשְׁרֵי הָעָם שֶׁיהוה אֱלֹהָיו. [2]

‹‹ is their ‹ that HASHEM ‹ is the ‹ praise- ‹‹ is ‹ that such ‹ is the
God. people worthy their lot; people

——— Psalm 145 / תהלים קמה ———

תְּהִלָּה לְדָוִד; אֲרוֹמִמְךָ אֱלוֹהַי הַמֶּלֶךְ, וַאֲבָרְכָה

‹ and I will ‹‹ the King, ‹ my God ‹ I will exalt ‹‹ by David: ‹ A psalm
bless You, of praise

שִׁמְךָ לְעוֹלָם וָעֶד. בְּכָל יוֹם אֲבָרְכֶךָּ, וַאֲהַלְלָה

‹ and I will laud ‹‹ I will bless You, ‹ day ‹ Every ‹‹ and ever. ‹ for ever ‹ Your Name

שִׁמְךָ לְעוֹלָם וָעֶד. גָּדוֹל יהוה וּמְהֻלָּל מְאֹד,

‹‹ exceedingly, ‹ and lauded ‹ is HASHEM ‹ Great ‹‹ and ever. ‹ for ever ‹ Your Name

וְלִגְדֻלָּתוֹ אֵין חֵקֶר. דּוֹר לְדוֹר יְשַׁבַּח מַעֲשֶׂיךָ,

‹‹ Your actions, ‹ will praise ‹ to ‹ Generation ‹‹ is beyond ‹ and His
generation investigation. greatness

וּגְבוּרוֹתֶיךָ יַגִּידוּ. הֲדַר כְּבוֹד הוֹדֶךָ וְדִבְרֵי

‹ and Your ‹ of Your ‹ glory ‹ The ‹‹ they will ‹ and Your
deeds majesty splendorous recount. mighty deeds

נִפְלְאֹתֶיךָ אָשִׂיחָה. וֶעֱזוּז נוֹרְאֹתֶיךָ יֹאמֵרוּ,

‹‹ they ‹ of Your ‹ And of ‹‹ I shall discuss. ‹ that are wondrous
will speak, awesome deeds the might

וּגְדוּלָּתְךָ אֲסַפְּרֶנָּה. זֵכֶר רַב טוּבְךָ יַבִּיעוּ,

‹‹ they ‹ of Your abundant ‹ A ‹‹ I shall relate. ‹ and Your
will utter, goodness recollection greatness

וְצִדְקָתְךָ יְרַנֵּנוּ. חַנּוּן וְרַחוּם יהוה, אֶרֶךְ אַפַּיִם

‹ to anger, ‹ slow ‹‹ is ‹ and ‹ Gracious ‹‹ they will ‹ and of Your
HASHEM, merciful sing joyfully. righteousness

---

(1) *Psalms* 84:5. (2) 144:15.

וּגְדָל חָסֶד. **טוֹב** יהוה לַכֹּל, וְרַחֲמָיו עַל כָּל

‹ all ‹ are on ‹ His mercies ‹‹ to all; ‹ HASHEM is good ‹‹ in [bestowing] ‹ and
kindness. great

מַעֲשָׂיו. **יוֹדֽוּךָ** יהוה כָּל מַעֲשֶׂיךָ, וַחֲסִידֶיךָ

‹ and Your ‹‹ Your creations, ‹ — all ‹‹ HASHEM ‹ They will ‹‹ His creations.
devout ones thank You,

יְבָרְכֽוּכָה. **כְּבוֹד** מַלְכוּתְךָ יֹאמֵֽרוּ, וּגְבוּרָתְךָ

‹ and of Your ‹‹ they will speak, ‹ of Your kingdom ‹ Of the glory ‹‹ will bless You.
power

יְדַבֵּֽרוּ. **לְהוֹדִֽיעַ** לִבְנֵי הָאָדָם גְּבוּרֹתָיו, וּכְבוֹד

‹ and of the ‹‹ of His ‹ mankind ‹ To inform ‹‹ they will
glorious mighty deeds, declare.

הֲדַר מַלְכוּתוֹ. **מַלְכוּתְךָ** מַלְכוּת כָּל עֹלָמִים,

‹‹ eternities, ‹ [spanning] ‹ is a kingdom ‹ Your kingdom ‹ of His kingdom. ‹ splendor
all

וּמֶמְשַׁלְתְּךָ בְּכָל דּוֹר וָדֹר. **סוֹמֵךְ** יהוה לְכָל

‹ all ‹ HASHEM supports ‹‹ after ‹ generation ‹ is ‹ and Your dominion
generation. throughout

הַנֹּפְלִים, וְזוֹקֵף לְכָל הַכְּפוּפִים. **עֵינֵי** כֹל אֵלֶֽיךָ

‹ to You ‹ of all ‹ The eyes ‹‹ those who ‹ all ‹ and ‹‹ those who are
are bent. straightens fallen,

יְשַׂבֵּֽרוּ, וְאַתָּה נוֹתֵן לָהֶם אֶת אָכְלָם בְּעִתּוֹ.

‹‹ in its ‹ their food ‹ them ‹ give ‹ and You ‹‹ do look
proper time. with hope,

CONCENTRATE INTENTLY WHILE RECITING THE VERSE **פּוֹתֵחַ**, YOU OPEN . . .

פּוֹתֵֽחַ אֶת יָדֶֽךָ, וּמַשְׂבִּֽיעַ לְכָל חַי רָצוֹן. **צַדִּיק**

‹ Righteous ‹‹ [with its] ‹ living ‹ every ‹ and satisfy ‹‹ Your hand, ‹ You open
desire. thing

יהוה בְּכָל דְּרָכָיו, וְחָסִיד בְּכָל מַעֲשָׂיו.

‹‹ His deeds. ‹ in all ‹ and magnanimous ‹‹ His ways, ‹ in all ‹ is HASHEM

קָרוֹב יהוה לְכָל קֹרְאָיו, לְכֹל אֲשֶׁר יִקְרָאֻֽהוּ

‹ call upon Him ‹ who ‹ to all ‹‹ who call ‹ to all ‹ is HASHEM ‹ Close
upon Him,

בֶּאֱמֶת. רְצוֹן יְרֵאָיו יַעֲשֶׂה, וְאֶת שַׁוְעָתָם יִשְׁמַע

‹ He will hear, ‹ and their cry ≪ He will do; ‹ of those who fear Him ≪ The will ≪ sincerely.

וְיוֹשִׁיעֵם. שׁוֹמֵר יהוה אֶת כָּל אֹהֲבָיו, וְאֵת כָּל

‹ but all ≪ who love Him; ‹ all ‹ HASHEM protects ≪ and He will save them.

הָרְשָׁעִים יַשְׁמִיד. ❖ תְּהִלַּת יהוה יְדַבֶּר פִּי, וִיבָרֵךְ

‹ and bless ≪ may my mouth declare, ‹ HASHEM ‹ of ‹ The praise ≪ He will destroy. ‹ the wicked

כָּל בָּשָׂר שֵׁם קָדְשׁוֹ לְעוֹלָם וָעֶד. וַאֲנַחְנוּ

‹ But we ≪ and ever. ‹ for ever ‹ of His Holiness ‹ the Name ‹ flesh ‹ may all

נְבָרֵךְ יָהּ מֵעַתָּה וְעַד עוֹלָם; הַלְלוּיָהּ.¹

≪ Halleluyah! ≪ eternity. ‹ until ‹ from this time ‹ God ‹ will bless

---

ON PUBLIC FAST DAYS:

ASHREI AND HALF-KADDISH ARE RECITED. IF SEVEN MEMBERS OF THE MINYAN ARE FASTING, THE TORAH, AND HAFTARAH, ARE READ (SEE P. 199). THE READINGS ARE ON P. 793. ON TISHAH B'AV, TALLIS AND TEFILLIN ARE WORN, AND PASSAGES OMITTED FROM SHACHARIS ARE RECITED.

THE CHAZZAN RECITES חֲצִי קַדִּישׁ, HALF-KADDISH.

יִתְגַּדַּל וְיִתְקַדַּשׁ שְׁמֵהּ רַבָּא. (–Cong. אָמֵן.) בְּעָלְמָא דִי בְרָא

‹ He created ‹ that ‹ in the world ≪ (Amen.) ≪ that is ‹ may His Name ‹ great! — Name ‹ and be sanctified ‹ Grow exalted

כִרְעוּתֵהּ, וְיַמְלִיךְ מַלְכוּתֵהּ, וְיַצְמַח פֻּרְקָנֵהּ וִיקָרֵב מְשִׁיחֵהּ.

≪ His Messiah, ‹ and bring near ‹ His salvation, ‹ and cause to sprout ‹ to His kingship, ‹ and may He give reign ≪ according to His will,

(–Cong. אָמֵן.) בְּחַיֵּיכוֹן וּבְיוֹמֵיכוֹן וּבְחַיֵּי דְכָל בֵּית יִשְׂרָאֵל,

≪ of Israel, ‹ Family ‹ of the entire ‹ and in the lifetimes ‹ and in your days, ‹ in your lifetimes (Amen.)

בַּעֲגָלָא וּבִזְמַן קָרִיב. וְאִמְרוּ: אָמֵן.

≪ Amen. ‹ Now respond: ≪ that comes soon. ‹ and at a time ‹ swiftly

CONGREGATION RESPONDS:

אָמֵן. יְהֵא שְׁמֵהּ רַבָּא מְבָרַךְ לְעָלַם וּלְעָלְמֵי עָלְמַיָּא.

≪ and for all eternity. ‹ forever ‹ be blessed ‹ that is great ‹ His Name ‹ May ≪ Amen.

CHAZZAN CONTINUES:

יְהֵא שְׁמֵהּ רַבָּא מְבָרַךְ לְעָלַם וּלְעָלְמֵי עָלְמַיָּא. יִתְבָּרַךְ

‹ Blessed, ≪ and for all eternity. ‹ forever ‹ be blessed ‹ that is great ‹ His Name ‹ May

---

(1) Psalms 115:18.

וְיִשְׁתַּבַּח וְיִתְפָּאַר וְיִתְרוֹמַם וְיִתְנַשֵּׂא וְיִתְהַדָּר וְיִתְעַלֶּה
‹ elevated, ‹ honored, ‹ upraised, ‹ exalted, ‹ glorified, ‹ praised,

וְיִתְהַלָּל שְׁמֵהּ דְּקֻדְשָׁא בְּרִיךְ הוּא (.Cong – בְּרִיךְ הוּא) —
‹‹ is He) (Blessed ‹‹ is He ‹ Blessed ‹ of the ‹ be the ‹ and lauded
　　　　　　　　　　　　　　　　　　　Holy One,　Name

ROSH HASHANAH TO YOM KIPPUR SUBSTITUTE:

°לְעֵלָּא מִן כָּל [°לְעֵלָּא (וּ)לְעֵלָּא מִכָּל] בִּרְכָתָא
‹ blessing ‹ any　exceedingly beyond　　　‹ any ‹ beyond

וְשִׁירָתָא, תֻּשְׁבְּחָתָא וְנֶחֱמָתָא דַּאֲמִירָן בְּעָלְמָא.
‹‹ in the world. ‹ that are uttered ‹ and consolation ‹ praise ‹‹ and song,

וְאִמְרוּ: אָמֵן. (אָמֵן –Cong.)
‹‹ (Amen.) ‹‹ Amen. ‹ Now respond:

﷽ SHEMONEH ESREI / עמידה – שמונה עשרה

TAKE THREE STEPS BACKWARD, THEN THREE STEPS FORWARD. REMAIN STANDING WITH FEET
TOGETHER WHILE RECITING SHEMONEH ESREI. RECITE IT WITH QUIET DEVOTION AND WITHOUT
ANY INTERRUPTION. ALTHOUGH IT SHOULD NOT BE AUDIBLE TO OTHERS, ONE MUST PRAY LOUDLY
ENOUGH TO HEAR HIMSELF. SEE LAWS §44-45; 61-95 FOR A BRIEF SUMMARY OF ITS LAWS INCLUDING
HOW TO RECTIFY THE OMISSION OF PHRASES THAT ARE ADDED AT PARTICULAR TIMES OF THE YEAR.

כִּי שֵׁם יהוה אֶקְרָא, הָבוּ גֹדֶל לֵאלֹהֵינוּ.¹
‹‹ to our God. ‹ greatness ‹ ascribe ‹‹ I call out, ‹ of ‹ the ‹ When
　　　　　　　　　　　　　　　　　HASHEM　Name

אֲדֹנָי שְׂפָתַי תִּפְתָּח, וּפִי יַגִּיד תְּהִלָּתֶךָ.²
‹‹ Your praise. ‹ may ‹ that my ‹‹ open, ‹ my lips ‹ O Lord,
　　　　　　　declare　mouth

PATRIARCHS / אבות

BEND THE KNEES AT בָּרוּךְ, BLESSED; BOW AT אַתָּה, YOU; STRAIGHTEN UP AT ה', HASHEM.

בָּרוּךְ אַתָּה יהוה אֱלֹהֵינוּ וֵאלֹהֵי אֲבוֹתֵינוּ,
‹‹ of our forefathers, ‹ and the God ‹ our God ‹ HASHEM, ‹ are You, ‹ Blessed

אֱלֹהֵי אַבְרָהָם, אֱלֹהֵי יִצְחָק, וֵאלֹהֵי יַעֲקֹב,
‹‹ of Jacob; ‹ and God ‹ of Isaac, ‹ God ‹ of Abraham, ‹ God

הָאֵל הַגָּדוֹל הַגִּבּוֹר וְהַנּוֹרָא, אֵל עֶלְיוֹן, גּוֹמֵל
‹ Who ‹‹ the ‹ God, ‹‹ and awesome; ‹ mighty, ‹ [Who is] ‹ God
bestows　Most High,　　　　　　　　　　　　great,

---

(1) Deuteronomy 32:3. (2) Psalms 51:17.

חֲסָדִים טוֹבִים וְקוֹנֵה הַכֹּל, וְזוֹכֵר חַסְדֵי אָבוֹת,

‹‹ of the ‹ the ‹ Who ‹‹ everything, ‹ and ‹ [that are] ‹ kindnesses
Patriarchs kindnesses recalls   creates beneficent

וּמֵבִיא גוֹאֵל לִבְנֵי בְנֵיהֶם, לְמַעַן שְׁמוֹ בְּאַהֲבָה.

‹‹ with love. ‹ of His ‹ for the ‹‹ of their ‹ to the ‹ a ‹ and brings
     Name, sake children children Redeemer

FROM ROSH HASHANAH TO YOM KIPPUR ADD:

זָכְרֵנוּ לְחַיִּים, מֶלֶךְ חָפֵץ בַּחַיִּים,

‹‹ life, ‹ Who desires ‹ O King ‹ for life, ‹ Remember us

וְכָתְבֵנוּ בְּסֵפֶר הַחַיִּים, לְמַעַנְךָ אֱלֹהִים חַיִּים.

‹‹ O Living God. ‹— for Your sake, ‹‹ of Life ‹ in the Book ‹ and inscribe us

[IF FORGOTTEN, DO NOT REPEAT *SHEMONEH ESREI*. SEE LAWS §61.]

BEND THE KNEES AT בָּרוּךְ, *BLESSED*; BOW AT אַתָּה, *YOU*; STRAIGHTEN UP AT ה', *HASHEM.*

מֶלֶךְ עוֹזֵר וּמוֹשִׁיעַ וּמָגֵן. בָּרוּךְ אַתָּה יהוה,

‹‹ HASHEM, ‹ are You, ‹ Blessed ‹‹ and Shield. ‹ Savior, ‹ Helper, ‹ O King,

מָגֵן אַבְרָהָם.

‹‹ of Abraham. ‹ Shield

GOD'S MIGHT / גבורות

אַתָּה גִּבּוֹר לְעוֹלָם אֲדֹנָי, מְחַיֵּה מֵתִים

‹ of the dead ‹ the Revivifier ‹‹ O Lord, ‹ eternally, ‹ mighty ‹ You are

אַתָּה, רַב לְהוֹשִׁיעַ.

‹‹ able to save, ‹ abundantly ‹‹ are You;

BETWEEN SHEMINI ATZERES AND PESACH:	FROM PESACH THROUGH SUCCOS:
מַשִּׁיב הָרוּחַ וּמוֹרִיד הַגֶּשֶׁם [נ"א הַגָּשֶׁם].	מוֹרִיד הַטָּל
‹‹ the rain. ‹ and ‹ Who makes ‹ brings down the wind blow	‹‹ the ‹ Who ‹ dew. brings down

——— [IF FORGOTTEN, SEE *LAWS* §68-74.] ———

מְכַלְכֵּל חַיִּים בְּחֶסֶד, מְחַיֵּה מֵתִים בְּרַחֲמִים

‹ with mercy ‹ the dead ‹ Who revivifies ‹‹ with kindness, ‹ the living ‹ Who sustains

רַבִּים, סוֹמֵךְ נוֹפְלִים, וְרוֹפֵא חוֹלִים, וּמַתִּיר

‹ Who releases ‹‹ the sick, ‹ Who heals ‹‹ the fallen, ‹ Who supports ‹‹ abundant,

אֲסוּרִים, וּמְקַיֵּם אֱמוּנָתוֹ לִישֵׁנֵי עָפָר. מִי

‹ Who ‹‹ in the dust. ‹ to those asleep ‹ His faith ‹ and Who maintains ‹‹ the confined,

כָמוֹךָ בַּעַל גְּבוּרוֹת, וּמִי דּוֹמֶה לָּךְ, מֶלֶךְ

‹ O King ‹‹ to You, ‹ is comparable ‹ and who ‹‹ of mighty deeds, ‹ O Master ‹ is like You,

מֵמִית וּמְחַיֶּה וּמַצְמִיחַ יְשׁוּעָה.

‹‹ salvation! ‹ and makes sprout ‹ and restores life ‹ Who causes death

FROM ROSH HASHANAH TO YOM KIPPUR ADD:

מִי כָמוֹךָ אַב הָרַחֲמָן, זוֹכֵר יְצוּרָיו לְחַיִּים בְּרַחֲמִים.

‹‹ with mercy! ‹‹ for life, ‹ His creatures ‹ Who recalls ‹‹ Who is Merciful, ‹ Father ‹ is like ‹ Who You,

[IF FORGOTTEN, DO NOT REPEAT SHEMONEH ESREI. SEE LAWS §61.]

וְנֶאֱמָן אַתָּה לְהַחֲיוֹת מֵתִים. בָּרוּךְ אַתָּה

‹ are You, ‹ Blessed ‹‹ the dead. ‹ to revivify ‹ are You ‹ And faithful

יהוה, מְחַיֵּה הַמֵּתִים.

‹‹ the dead. ‹ Who revivifies ‹‹ HASHEM,

DURING THE *CHAZZAN'S* REPETITION, *KEDUSHAH* IS RECITED HERE.
DURING THE SILENT *SHEMONEH ESREI*, CONTINUE אַתָּה קָדוֹשׁ, *YOU ARE HOLY* (P. 366).

KEDUSHAH / קדושה

STAND WITH FEET TOGETHER AND AVOID ANY INTERRUPTIONS. RISE ON TOES WHEN SAYING קָדוֹשׁ,
קָדוֹשׁ, קָדוֹשׁ – *HOLY, HOLY, HOLY;* בָּרוּךְ – *BLESSED;* AND יִמְלֹךְ – *HASHEM SHALL REIGN.*
CONGREGATION, THEN *CHAZZAN:*

נַקְדִּישָׁךְ וְנַעֲרִיצָךְ, כְּנֹעַם שִׂיחַ סוֹד שַׂרְפֵי קֹדֶשׁ,

‹ of the holy Seraphim ‹ of the assemblage ‹ speech ‹ in the manner of the pleasant ‹ and we shall revere You ‹ We shall sanctify You

הַמְשַׁלְּשִׁים לְךָ קְדֻשָּׁה, כַּכָּתוּב עַל יַד נְבִיאֶךָ, וְקָרָא זֶה

‹ And one [angel] would call ‹‹ Your prophet, ‹ by ‹ as it is written ‹‹ Holy, ‹ to You ‹ who recite three times

אֶל זֶה וְאָמַר:

‹‹ and say: ‹ another ‹ to

ALL:

קָדוֹשׁ קָדוֹשׁ קָדוֹשׁ יהוה צְבָאוֹת, מְלֹא כָל הָאָרֶץ כְּבוֹדוֹ.[1]

‹‹ with His glory. ‹ world ‹ is the whole ‹ filled ‹‹ Master of Legions; ‹ is HASHEM, ‹ holy ‹ holy, ‹ Holy,

(1) *Isaiah* 6:3.

❖ לְעֻמָּתָם מְשַׁבְּחִים וְאוֹמְרִים:

《 and proclaim: 〈 they offer praise 〈 Facing them

ALL:

כָּתוּב 〈 קָדְשְׁךָ 〈 וּבְדִבְרֵי ❖ 1. מִמְּקוֹמוֹ. יהוה, כְּבוֹד בָּרוּךְ

〈 it is 〈 that are 〈 And in Your ❖ 《 from 〈 of Hashem 〈 is the 〈 Blessed
written holy Writings His place. glory

לֵאמֹר:

《 saying:

ALL:

2.הַלְלוּיָהּ. וָדֹר, לְדֹר צִיּוֹן אֱלֹהַיִךְ לְעוֹלָם, יהוה יִמְלֹךְ

《 Halleluyah! 《 to 〈 from 〈 O Zion, 〈 your God, 《 forever; 〈 Hashem shall reign
generation, generation

קְדוּשַׁת הַשֵׁם / HOLINESS OF GOD'S NAME

(left column)	(right column)
IN SOME CONGREGATIONS THE CHAZZAN SUBSTITUTES אַתָּה קָדוֹשׁ FOR לְדוֹר וָדוֹר IN HIS REPETITION:	וְשִׁמְךָ קָדוֹשׁ **אַתָּה**
	〈 and Your 〈 are holy 〈 You
	Name

וּלְנֵצַח גָּדְלְךָ נַגִּיד וָדוֹר לְדוֹר

〈 and for 《 Your 〈 we shall 〈 to gen- 〈 From gen-
all greatness relate eration eration

בְּכָל וּקְדוֹשִׁים קָדוֹשׁ,

〈 every 〈 and holy ones 《 is holy,

נַקְדִּישׁ, קְדֻשָּׁתְךָ נְצָחִים

《 shall we sanctify. 〈 Your holiness 〈 eternity

כִּי סֶּלָה, יְהַלְלוּךָ יוֹם

〈 for, 《 forever, 〈 praise You, 〈 day

לֹא מִפִּינוּ אֱלֹהֵינוּ וְשִׁבְחֲךָ

〈 shall 〈 from our 〈 our God, 〈 Your praise,
not mouth

וְקָדוֹשׁ גָּדוֹל מֶלֶךְ אֵל

〈 and holy 〈 great 〈 a King, 〈 O God,

מֶלֶךְ אֵל כִּי וָעֶד, לְעוֹלָם יָמוּשׁ

〈 a 〈 O 〈 for, 〈 and 〈 for ever 〈 leave
King, God, ever,

אָתָּה בָּרוּךְ אָתָּה.

〈 are You, 〈 Blessed 《 are You.

אַתָּה בָּרוּךְ אַתָּה. וְקָדוֹשׁ גָּדוֹל

〈 are You, 〈 Blessed 《 are You. 〈 and holy 〈 great

הַקָּדוֹשׁ. הָאֵל °יהוה,

《 Who is holy. 〈 the God 《 Hashem,

הַקָּדוֹשׁ. הָאֵל °יהוה,

《 Who is holy. 〈 the God 《 Hashem,

FROM ROSH HASHANAH TO YOM KIPPUR SUBSTITUTE:

הַקָּדוֹשׁ. הַמֶּלֶךְ°

《 Who is holy. 〈 the King

[IF FORGOTTEN, REPEAT SHEMONEH ESREI. SEE LAWS §62-63.]

(1) Ezekiel 3:12. (2) Psalms 146:10.

INSIGHT / בינה

אַתָּה חוֹנֵן לְאָדָם דַּעַת, וּמְלַמֵּד לֶאֱנוֹשׁ בִּינָה.

insight. ‹ to a [frail] mortal ‹ and teach ≪ with ‹ man ‹ graciously endow ‹ You

חָנֵּנוּ מֵאִתְּךָ חָכְמָה בִּינָה וָדָעַת. בָּרוּךְ אַתָּה

‹ are You, ‹ Blessed ≪ and knowledge. ‹ insight, ‹ [with] wisdom, ‹ from Yourself ‹ Endow us graciously

יהוה, חוֹנֵן הַדָּעַת.

≪ of wisdom. ‹ gracious Giver ‹ HASHEM,

REPENTANCE / תשובה

הֲשִׁיבֵנוּ אָבִינוּ לְתוֹרָתֶךָ, וְקָרְבֵנוּ מַלְכֵּנוּ

‹ our King, ‹ and bring us near, ≪ to Your Torah, ‹ our Father, ‹ Bring us back,

לַעֲבוֹדָתֶךָ, וְהַחֲזִירֵנוּ בִּתְשׁוּבָה שְׁלֵמָה לְפָנֶיךָ.

≪ before You. ‹ in complete repentance, ‹ and influence us to return ≪ to Your service,

בָּרוּךְ אַתָּה יהוה, הָרוֹצֶה בִּתְשׁוּבָה.

≪ repentance. ‹ Who desires ≪ HASHEM, ‹ are You, ‹ Blessed

FORGIVENESS / סליחה

STRIKE THE LEFT SIDE OF THE CHEST WITH THE RIGHT FIST
WHILE RECITING THE WORDS חָטָאנוּ, SINNED, AND פָּשָׁעְנוּ, WILLFULLY SINNED.

סְלַח לָנוּ אָבִינוּ כִּי חָטָאנוּ, מְחַל לָנוּ מַלְכֵּנוּ

‹ our King, ‹ us, ‹ pardon ≪ we have sinned; ‹ for ‹ our Father, ‹ us, ‹ Forgive

כִּי פָשָׁעְנוּ, כִּי אֵל טוֹב וְסַלָּח אָתָּה. בָּרוּךְ

‹ Blessed ≪ are You. ‹ and forgiving ‹ Who is good ‹ the God ‹ for ≪ we have willfully sinned;

אַתָּה יהוה, חַנּוּן הַמַּרְבֶּה לִסְלוֹחַ.

≪ forgives. ‹ Who abundantly ‹ the gracious One ≪ HASHEM, ‹ are You,

גאולה / REDEMPTION

רְאֵה נָא בְעָנְיֵנוּ, וְרִיבָה רִיבֵנוּ, וּגְאָלֵנוּ¹ גְאֻלָּה

⟨ Behold, ⟩ please, ⟨ our ⟩⟩ champion ⟨ our ⟩⟩ and ⟨ with a
affliction, cause, redeem us redemption

שְׁלֵמָה מְהֵרָה לְמַעַן שְׁמֶךָ, כִּי אֵל גּוֹאֵל חָזָק

that is ⟨ speedily ⟨ for the ⟨⟨ Your ⟨ for, ⟨ a ⟨ Who is
complete, sake of Name, God, Redeemer powerful

אָתָּה. בָּרוּךְ אַתָּה יהוה, גּוֹאֵל יִשְׂרָאֵל.

⟨⟨ are You. ⟨ Blessed ⟨ are You, ⟨⟨ Hashem, ⟨ Redeemer ⟨ of Israel.

ON A FAST DAY, THE CHAZZAN RECITES עֲנֵנוּ, ANSWER US, AT THIS POINT. SEE LAWS §84-86.

עֲנֵנוּ יהוה עֲנֵנוּ, בְּיוֹם צוֹם תַּעֲנִיתֵנוּ, כִּי בְצָרָה גְדוֹלָה

⟨ Answer ⟨ Hashem, ⟨⟨ answer ⟨⟨ on ⟨ of our public ⟨⟨ for ⟨ in great distress
us, us, this day gathering for fasting,

אֲנָחְנוּ. אַל תֵּפֶן אֶל רִשְׁעֵנוּ, וְאַל תַּסְתֵּר פָּנֶיךָ מִמֶּנוּ, וְאַל

⟨⟨ are we. ⟨ Do ⟨ pay ⟨ to ⟨⟨ our ⟨ do ⟨ hide ⟨⟨ do ⟨ Your ⟨ from ⟨⟨ and
not attention not wickedness, not Face us, do not

תִּתְעַלַּם מִתְּחִנָּתֵנוּ. הֱיֵה נָא קָרוֹב לְשַׁוְעָתֵנוּ, יְהִי נָא חַסְדְּךָ

⟨ ignore ⟨ our supplication. ⟨ Please be ⟨ near ⟨ to our outcry; ⟨⟨ please let ⟨ Your
kindness

לְנַחֲמֵנוּ, טֶרֶם נִקְרָא אֵלֶיךָ עֲנֵנוּ, כַּדָּבָר שֶׁנֶּאֱמַר: וְהָיָה טֶרֶם

⟨ comfort us ⟨⟨ before ⟨— we call ⟨ to You ⟨⟨ answer ⟨ as it ⟨ is said: ⟨⟨ And it ⟨ [that]
us, will be before

יִקְרָאוּ וַאֲנִי אֶעֱנֶה, עוֹד הֵם מְדַבְּרִים וַאֲנִי אֶשְׁמָע.² כִּי אַתָּה

⟨ they call, ⟨ I ⟨ will ⟨ [that] they ⟨ [yet] speak, ⟨ I ⟨⟨ will hear. ⟨ For ⟨ You,
answer; while

יהוה הָעוֹנֶה בְּעֵת צָרָה, פּוֹדֶה וּמַצִּיל בְּכָל עֵת צָרָה

⟨ Hashem, ⟨ are the One ⟨ in time ⟨⟨ of ⟨ Who ⟨ and ⟨ in ⟨ time ⟨ of
Who responds distress, redeems rescues every distress

וְצוּקָה. בָּרוּךְ אַתָּה יהוה, הָעוֹנֶה לְעַמּוֹ יִשְׂרָאֵל בְּעֵת

⟨⟨ and woe. ⟨ Blessed ⟨ are You, ⟨⟨ Hashem, ⟨ Who ⟨ to His ⟨ Israel, ⟨ in time
responds people,

צָרָה.

⟨⟨ of
distress.

---

(1) Cf. *Psalms* 119:153-154. (2) *Isaiah* 65:24.

HEALTH AND HEALING / רפואה

רְפָאֵנוּ יהוה וְנֵרָפֵא, הוֹשִׁיעֵנוּ וְנִוָּשֵׁעָה, כִּי
⟨ for ⟨⟨ — then we ⟨⟨ save us ⟨⟨ — then we ⟨⟨ HASHEM ⟨   Heal us,
will be saved,   will be healed;

תְהִלָּתֵנוּ אָתָּה,¹ וְהַעֲלֵה
⟨   Bring   ⟨⟨ is You. ⟨ the One we praise

RECITE ONE OF THE ALTERNATE VERSIONS:

רְפוּאָה שְׁלֵמָה	אֲרוּכָה וּמַרְפֵּא לְכָל תַּחֲלוּאֵינוּ
⟨ that is ⟨ healing complete	⟨ of our illnesses, ⟨ to all ⟨ and healing ⟨ cure
לְכָל מַכּוֹתֵינוּ,	וּלְכָל מַכְאוֹבֵינוּ וּלְכָל מַכּוֹתֵינוּ,
⟨⟨ our ailments, ⟨ for all	⟨⟨ of our ⟨ and to all ⟨ of our pains, ⟨ and to all ailments,

°°כִּי אֵל מֶלֶךְ רוֹפֵא נֶאֱמָן וְרַחֲמָן אָתָּה. בָּרוּךְ
⟨ Blessed ⟨⟨ are You.⟨   and   ⟨ Who is ⟨ Healer ⟨ [and] ⟨ O ⟨ for
compassionate faithful   King, God,

אַתָּה יהוה, רוֹפֵא חוֹלֵי עַמּוֹ יִשְׂרָאֵל.
⟨⟨ Israel. ⟨ of His ⟨ the sick ⟨ Who ⟨⟨ HASHEM, ⟨ are You,
people   heals

°°AT THIS POINT ONE MAY INSERT A PRAYER FOR ONE WHO IS ILL:

יְהִי רָצוֹן מִלְּפָנֶיךָ, יהוה אֱלֹהַי וֵאלֹהֵי אֲבוֹתַי, שֶׁתִּשְׁלַח מְהֵרָה
⟨ quickly ⟨ that ⟨⟨ of my ⟨ and the ⟨ my ⟨ HASHEM, ⟨⟨ before You, ⟨ the ⟨ May
You send forefathers, God God   will it be

רְפוּאָה שְׁלֵמָה מִן הַשָּׁמַיִם, רְפוּאַת הַנֶּפֶשׁ וּרְפוּאַת הַגּוּף
⟨⟨ of the ⟨ and a ⟨ of the ⟨ a healing ⟨⟨ heaven, ⟨ from ⟨⟨ which is ⟨ a healing
body healing spirit   complete,

FOR A FEMALE FOR A MALE

לַחוֹלֶה / לַחוֹלָה (MOTHER'S NAME) בֶּן / בַּת (SICK ONE'S NAME) בְּתוֹךְ שְׁאָר
⟨ the other ⟨ among ⟨ daughter of / son of ⟨ to the sick one

חוֹלֵי יִשְׂרָאֵל.
⟨⟨ of Israel. ⟨ sick ones

CONTINUE . . . כִּי אֵל (ABOVE)

(1) Cf. *Jeremiah* 17:14.

YEAR OF PROSPERITY / ברכת השנים

וְתֵן בְּרָכָה, *GIVE A BLESSING*, IS RECITED FROM CHOL HAMOED PESACH THROUGH *MINCHAH* OF DECEMBER 4TH (OR 5TH IN THE YEAR BEFORE A CIVIL LEAP YEAR); וְתֵן טַל וּמָטָר לִבְרָכָה, *GIVE DEW AND RAIN FOR A BLESSING*, IS RECITED FROM *MAARIV* OF DECEMBER 4TH (OR 5TH) UNTIL PESACH. [IF THE WRONG PHRASE WAS RECITED AND FOR THE PRACTICE IN ERETZ YISRAEL, SEE *LAWS* §75-83.]

SOME CONGREGATIONS SUBSTITUTE THE PARAGRAPH בָּרְכֵנוּ FOR בָּרֵךְ עָלֵינוּ, FROM PESACH THROUGH DECEMBER 4TH (OR 5TH).

בָּרֵךְ עָלֵינוּ יהוה אֱלֹהֵינוּ
Bless ⟨ on our ⟨ —O ⟨ our God —⟩⟩
behalf HASHEM,

אֶת הַשָּׁנָה הַזֹּאת וְאֶת כָּל
this year ⟨⟨ and ⟨ all ⟩

מִינֵי תְבוּאָתָהּ לְטוֹבָה, וְתֵן
of the ⟨ of its crops ⟨ for goodness; ⟨⟨ and ⟩
kinds give

	SUMMER	WINTER
טַל וּמָטָר לִבְרָכָה	בְּרָכָה
dew ⟩ and rain ⟩ for a blessing	a blessing ⟩

עַל פְּנֵי הָאֲדָמָה, וְשַׂבְּעֵנוּ
on ⟩ the face ⟨ of the earth; ⟨⟨ and satisfy us ⟩

מִטּוּבָהּ, וּבָרֵךְ שְׁנָתֵנוּ
from its bounty; ⟨⟨ and bless ⟨ our year ⟩

כַּשָּׁנִים הַטּוֹבוֹת לִבְרָכָה,
like the years ⟨ that were good, ⟨ for blessing. ⟨⟨

כִּי אֵל טוֹב וּמֵטִיב אָתָּה,
For ⟨ O God, ⟨ good ⟨ and ⟨⟨ are You,
beneficent

וּמְבָרֵךְ הַשָּׁנִים. בָּרוּךְ אַתָּה
the One ⟨ the years. ⟨⟨ Blessed ⟨ are You, ⟩
Who blesses

יהוה, מְבָרֵךְ הַשָּׁנִים.
HASHEM, ⟨⟨ Who blesses ⟨ the years. ⟨⟨

בָּרְכֵנוּ, יהוה אֱלֹהֵינוּ,
Bless us, ⟨ —O ⟨ our God —⟩⟩
HASHEM,

בְּכָל מַעֲשֵׂה יָדֵינוּ,
in all ⟨ the work ⟨ of our hands, ⟩

וּבָרֵךְ שְׁנָתֵנוּ בְּטַלְלֵי
and bless ⟨ our year ⟨ with the ⟩
dews

רָצוֹן בְּרָכָה וּנְדָבָה.
of favor. ⟨ blessing, ⟨ and ⟩⟨
generosity.

וּתְהִי אַחֲרִיתָהּ חַיִּים
And may ⟨ its end be ⟨ for life, ⟩

וְשֹׂבַע וְשָׁלוֹם, כַּשָּׁנִים
satisfaction, ⟨ and ⟨⟨ like the ⟩
peace, years

הַטּוֹבוֹת לִבְרָכָה. כִּי
that were ⟨⟨ —for a ⟨⟨ For ⟨⟨
good blessing.

אֵל טוֹב וּמֵטִיב אָתָּה
O ⟨ good ⟨ and ⟨⟨ are
God, beneficent You,

וּמְבָרֵךְ הַשָּׁנִים. בָּרוּךְ
the One ⟨ the years. ⟨⟨ Blessed ⟨⟨
Who blesses

אַתָּה יהוה, מְבָרֵךְ
are You, ⟨ HASHEM, ⟨⟨ Who blesses ⟩

הַשָּׁנִים.
the years. ⟨⟨

INGATHERING OF EXILES / קיבוץ גליות

תְּקַע בְּשׁוֹפָר גָּדוֹל[1] לְחֵרוּתֵנוּ, וְשָׂא נֵס[2] לְקַבֵּץ
⟨ to gather ⟨ a banner ⟨ raise   ⟨⟨ for our freedom, ⟨   the great *shofar*   ⟨   Sound

גָּלֻיּוֹתֵינוּ, וְקַבְּצֵנוּ יַחַד מְהֵרָה מֵאַרְבַּע כַּנְפוֹת
⟨ corners   ⟨ from the four   ⟨ speedily, ⟨ together, ⟨ and gather us ⟨⟨   our exiles,

הָאָרֶץ לְאַרְצֵנוּ[3] בָּרוּךְ אַתָּה יהוה, מְקַבֵּץ נִדְחֵי
⟨ the   ⟨ Who   ⟨⟨ HASHEM, ⟨ are You, ⟨ Blessed   ⟨⟨ to our Land. ⟨ of the earth
dispersed gathers in

עַמּוֹ יִשְׂרָאֵל.
⟨⟨   Israel. ⟨ of His people

RESTORATION OF JUSTICE / דין

הָשִׁיבָה שׁוֹפְטֵינוּ כְּבָרִאשׁוֹנָה, וְיוֹעֲצֵינוּ
⟨   and our   ⟨   as [they were]   ⟨   our judges   ⟨   Restore
counselors   in earliest times

כְּבַתְּחִלָּה,[4] וְהָסֵר מִמֶּנּוּ יָגוֹן וַאֲנָחָה, וּמְלוֹךְ
⟨ and reign   ⟨⟨ and groan; ⟨ sorrow ⟨ from us   ⟨ remove ⟨⟨ as at the beginning;

עָלֵינוּ מְהֵרָה אַתָּה יהוה לְבַדְּךָ בְּחֶסֶד
⟨ with kindness ⟨⟨ alone — ⟨   HASHEM, ⟨ – You, ⟨⟨ speedily ⟨ over us,

וּבְרַחֲמִים, וְצַדְּקֵנוּ בְּצֶדֶק וּבְמִשְׁפָּט. בָּרוּךְ אַתָּה
⟨ are You, ⟨ Blessed ⟨⟨ and through ⟨   through   ⟨ and justify ⟨⟨ and compassion,
judgment.   righteousness   us

יהוה, °מֶלֶךְ אוֹהֵב צְדָקָה וּמִשְׁפָּט.
⟨⟨ and judgment. ⟨ righteousness ⟨ Who loves ⟨ the King ⟨⟨ HASHEM,

FROM ROSH HASHANAH TO YOM KIPPUR SUBSTITUTE:

°הַמֶּלֶךְ הַמִּשְׁפָּט.
⟨⟨ of Judgment. ⟨ the King

[IF FORGOTTEN, DO NOT REPEAT *SHEMONEH ESREI*. SEE *LAWS* §64.]

AGAINST HERETICS / ברכת המינים

וְלַמַּלְשִׁינִים אַל תְּהִי תִקְוָה, וְכָל הַמִּינִים
⟨ the heretics ⟨ and all ⟨⟨   hope; ⟨ let there not be ⟨   And for slanderers

---

(1) Cf. *Isaiah* 27:13. (2) Cf. 11:12, 18:3, 62:10; see 66:20. (3) Cf. 11:12. (4) Cf. 1:26.

כְּרֶגַע יֹאבֵדוּ, וְכָל אוֹיְבֵי עַמְּךָ מְהֵרָה יִכָּרֵתוּ,
《 may they 〈 speedily 〈 of Your 〈 the 〈 and all 《 may they 〈 in an
be cut down. people enemies perish; instant

וְהַזֵּדִים מְהֵרָה תְעַקֵּר וּתְשַׁבֵּר וּתְמַגֵּר וּתְכַלֵּם
〈 destroy 《 cast down; 〈 smash, 〈 uproot, 〈 — may You 《 The willful
them, speedily sinners

וּתַשְׁפִּילֵם וְתַכְנִיעֵם בִּמְהֵרָה בְיָמֵינוּ. בָּרוּךְ
〈 Blessed 《 in our days. 〈 speedily 〈 and humble them 〈 pull them down,

אַתָּה יהוה, שׁוֹבֵר אוֹיְבִים וּמַכְנִיעַ זֵדִים.
《 willful sinners. 〈 and humbles 〈 enemies 〈 Who breaks 《 HASHEM, 〈 are You,

THE RIGHTEOUS / צדיקים

עַל הַצַּדִּיקִים וְעַל הַחֲסִידִים, וְעַל זִקְנֵי
〈 the elders 〈 on 《 the devout, 〈 on 〈 the righteous, 〈 On

שְׁאֵרִית עַמְּךָ בֵּית יִשְׂרָאֵל, וְעַל פְּלֵיטַת בֵּית
〈 of the 〈 the remnant 〈 on 《 of Israel, 〈 the 〈 of Your 〈 of the
academy Family people, remainder

סוֹפְרֵיהֶם, וְעַל גֵּרֵי הַצֶּדֶק וְעָלֵינוּ, יֶהֱמוּ נָא
〈 — please may 《 and on 〈 who are 〈 the 〈 on 《 of their scholars,
aroused be ourselves righteous converts

רַחֲמֶיךָ יהוה אֱלֹהֵינוּ, וְתֵן שָׂכָר טוֹב לְכָל
〈 to all 〈 which is good 〈 a reward 〈 and give 《 our God, 〈 HASHEM, 〈 Your compassion,

הַבּוֹטְחִים בְּשִׁמְךָ בֶּאֱמֶת, וְשִׂים חֶלְקֵנוּ עִמָּהֶם,
《 with them, 〈 our lot 〈 Put 《 in sincerity. 〈 in Your Name 〈 who believe

וּלְעוֹלָם לֹא נֵבוֹשׁ כִּי בְךָ בָּטָחְנוּ.[1] וְעַל חַסְדְּךָ
〈 Your 〈 and 《 we trust, 〈 in 〈 for 〈 feel 〈 we 〈 and forever
kindness upon You ashamed, will not

הַגָּדוֹל בֶּאֱמֶת (וּבְתָמִים) נִשְׁעָנְנוּ. בָּרוּךְ אַתָּה
〈 are You, 〈 Blessed 《 do we rely. 〈 (and in perfection) 〈 in sincerity 《 that is great,

יהוה, מִשְׁעָן וּמִבְטָח לַצַּדִּיקִים.
《 of the righteous. 〈 and Assurance 〈 Mainstay 《 HASHEM,

---

(1) Cf. *Psalms* 25:2.

REBUILDING JERUSALEM / בִּנְיַן יְרוּשָׁלַיִם

וְלִירוּשָׁלַיִם עִירְךָ בְּרַחֲמִים תָּשׁוּב, וְתִשְׁכּוֹן
⟨ and may ⟨⟨ may You ⟨ in compassion ⟨ Your City, ⟨ And to Jerusalem,
You rest return,

בְּתוֹכָהּ כַּאֲשֶׁר דִּבַּרְתָּ, וּבְנֵה אוֹתָהּ בְּקָרוֹב
⟨ soon ⟨ it ⟨ May You rebuild ⟨⟨ You have spoken. ⟨ as ⟨ within it,

בְּיָמֵינוּ בִּנְיַן עוֹלָם, וְכִסֵּא דָוִד עַבְדְּךָ מְהֵרָה
⟨ speedily, ⟨ Your ⟨ of David, ⟨ and the ⟨⟨ that is ⟨ as a ⟨ in our days
servant, throne eternal, structure

לְתוֹכָהּ תָּכִין. °°בָּרוּךְ אַתָּה יהוה, בּוֹנֵה יְרוּשָׁלָיִם.
⟨⟨ of Jerusalem. ⟨ Builder ⟨⟨ HASHEM, ⟨ are You, ⟨ Blessed ⟨⟨ may You ⟨ within it
establish.

°° **DURING** *MINCHAH* **OF TISHAH B'AV SUBSTITUTE THE FOLLOWING CONCLUSION.**
[IF FORGOTTEN, DO NOT REPEAT *SHEMONEH ESREI;* **SEE** *LAWS* §87.]

נַחֵם יהוה אֱלֹהֵינוּ אֶת אֲבֵלֵי צִיּוֹן, וְאֶת אֲבֵלֵי
⟨ and the mourners ⟨ of Zion ⟨ the mourners ⟨ our God, ⟨ O HASHEM, ⟨ Console

יְרוּשָׁלָיִם, וְאֶת הָעִיר הָאֲבֵלָה וְהַחֲרֵבָה וְהַבְּזוּיָה וְהַשּׁוֹמֵמָה.
⟨⟨ and that is ⟨ that is ⟨ that is ⟨ that is ⟨ and the City ⟨⟨ of Jerusalem,
desolate: scorned, ruined, mournful,

הָאֲבֵלָה מִבְּלִי בָנֶיהָ, וְהַחֲרֵבָה מִמְּעוֹנוֹתֶיהָ, וְהַבְּזוּיָה
⟨ scorned ⟨⟨ without her abodes, ⟨ ruined ⟨⟨ her children, ⟨ without ⟨ mournful

מִכְּבוֹדָהּ, וְהַשּׁוֹמֵמָה מֵאֵין יוֹשֵׁב. וְהִיא יוֹשֶׁבֶת וְרֹאשָׁהּ
⟨ with head ⟨ sits ⟨ She ⟨⟨ inhabitant. ⟨ without ⟨ and desolate ⟨⟨ without her glory,

חָפוּי כְּאִשָּׁה עֲקָרָה שֶׁלֹּא יָלָדָה. וַיְבַלְּעוּהָ לִגְיוֹנוֹת,
⟨ have legions, ⟨ Devoured her ⟨⟨ gave ⟨ who ⟨ who is ⟨ like a ⟨ that is
birth. never barren woman covered

וַיִּירָשׁוּהָ עוֹבְדֵי זָרִים, וַיַּטִּילוּ אֶת עַמְּךָ יִשְׂרָאֵל לֶחָרֶב,
⟨ to the ⟨ Israel ⟨ Your people ⟨ they ⟨⟨ have idolaters; ⟨ and
sword have cast conquered her

וַיַּהַרְגוּ בְזָדוֹן חֲסִידֵי עֶלְיוֹן. עַל כֵּן צִיּוֹן בְּמַר תִּבְכֶּה,
⟨ weeps ⟨ bitterly ⟨ Zion ⟨ Therefore, ⟨⟨ of the ⟨ the devout ⟨ wantonly ⟨ and
Supreme One. servants murdered

וִירוּשָׁלַיִם תִּתֵּן קוֹלָהּ. לִבִּי לִבִּי עַל חַלְלֵיהֶם, מֵעַי
⟨ My ⟨⟨ their slain! ⟨ [it aches] ⟨⟨ my ⟨ My ⟨⟨ her ⟨ raises ⟨ and Jerusalem
innards, for heart, heart, voice.

מֵעַי עַל חַלָלֵיהֶם, כִּי אַתָּה יהוה בָּאֵשׁ הִצַּתָּהּ, וּבָאֵשׁ

< and with << You con- < with fire < HASHEM, < You < For << their slain! < [they] << my
fire   sumed her,   ache] for innards,

אַתָּה עָתִיד לִבְנוֹתָהּ, כָּאָמוּר: וַאֲנִי אֶהְיֶה לָהּ, נְאֻם

< — the << for her < will be < I << as it is said: < rebuild her, < in the < You will
words   future

יהוה, חוֹמַת אֵשׁ סָבִיב, וּלְכָבוֹד אֶהְיֶה בְתוֹכָהּ.¹ בָּרוּךְ

< Blessed << in her < will I be < and << surrounding, < of fire < a wall << of
           midst.   glorious   HASHEM —

אַתָּה יהוה, מְנַחֵם צִיּוֹן וּבוֹנֵה יְרוּשָׁלָיִם.

<< Jerusalem. < and < Zion < Who << HASHEM, < are You,
       rebuilds   consoles

CONTINUE . . . אֶת צֶמַח (BELOW)

מלכות בית דוד / DAVIDIC REIGN

אֶת צֶמַח דָּוִד עַבְדְּךָ מְהֵרָה תַצְמִיחַ, וְקַרְנוֹ

< and his << may You cause < speedily, << Your < of David, < offspring < The
pride   to flourish,   servant,

תָּרוּם בִּישׁוּעָתֶךָ, כִּי לִישׁוּעָתְךָ קִוִּינוּ כָּל הַיּוֹם

< all day long < we hope < for Your < because << through Your < may You
                         salvation,   salvation,   exalt

(וּמְצַפִּים לִישׁוּעָה). בָּרוּךְ אַתָּה יהוה, מַצְמִיחַ

< Who causes << HASHEM, < are You, < Blessed << for salvation). < (and await eagerly
to flourish

קֶרֶן יְשׁוּעָה.

<< of salvation. < the pride

קבלת תפלה / ACCEPTANCE OF PRAYER

אָב הָרַחֲמָן שְׁמַע קוֹלֵנוּ, יהוה אֱלֹהֵינוּ

< our God, < HASHEM, << our voice, < hear < Who is merciful, < Father

חוּס וְרַחֵם עָלֵינוּ, וְקַבֵּל בְּרַחֲמִים וּבְרָצוֹן

< and with < with < and << on us, < and have < have
favor   compassion accept   compassion pity

(1) Zechariah 2:9.

אֶת תְּפִלָּתֵנוּ, כִּי אֵל שׁוֹמֵעַ תְּפִלּוֹת וְתַחֲנוּנִים

⟨ and supplications ⟨ prayers ⟨ Who hears ⟨ God ⟨ for ⟨⟨ our prayer,

אָתָּה. וּמִלְּפָנֶיךָ מַלְכֵּנוּ, רֵיקָם אַל תְּשִׁיבֵנוּ,

⟨⟨ turn us away. ⟨ do not ⟨ empty-handed ⟨⟨ our King, ⟨ From before Yourself, ⟨⟨ are You.

חָנֵּנוּ וַעֲנֵנוּ וּשְׁמַע תְּפִלָּתֵנוּ,°°

⟨⟨ our prayer, ⟨ and hear ⟨ answer us, ⟨ Be gracious with us,

---

°°ON A FAST DAY, ONE WHO IS FASTING ADDS THE FOLLOWING.
[IF FORGOTTEN, DO NOT REPEAT *SHEMONEH ESREI*. SEE LAWS §84-86.]

עֲנֵנוּ יהוה עֲנֵנוּ, בְּיוֹם צוֹם תַּעֲנִיתֵנוּ, כִּי בְצָרָה גְדוֹלָה

⟨ in great distress ⟨ for ⟨⟨ of our public gathering for fasting, ⟨ on this day ⟨⟨ answer us, ⟨ Hashem, ⟨ Answer us,

אֲנָחְנוּ. אַל תֵּפֶן אֶל רִשְׁעֵנוּ, וְאַל תַּסְתֵּר פָּנֶיךָ מִמֶּנּוּ, וְאַל

⟨ and do not ⟨⟨ from us, ⟨ Your Face ⟨ hide ⟨ do not ⟨⟨ our wickedness, ⟨ to ⟨ pay attention ⟨ Do not ⟨⟨ are we.

תִּתְעַלַּם מִתְּחִנָּתֵנוּ. הֱיֵה נָא קָרוֹב לְשַׁוְעָתֵנוּ, יְהִי נָא חַסְדְּךָ

⟨ Your kindness ⟨ please let ⟨⟨ to our outcry; ⟨ near ⟨ Please be ⟨⟨ our supplication. ⟨ ignore

לְנַחֲמֵנוּ, טֶרֶם נִקְרָא אֵלֶיךָ עֲנֵנוּ, כַּדָּבָר שֶׁנֶּאֱמַר: וְהָיָה טֶרֶם

⟨ [that] before ⟨ And it will be ⟨⟨ is said: ⟨ as it ⟨⟨ answer us, ⟨ to You ⟨ we call ⟨ — before ⟨⟨ comfort us

יִקְרָאוּ וַאֲנִי אֶעֱנֶה, עוֹד הֵם מְדַבְּרִים וַאֲנִי אֶשְׁמָע.¹ כִּי אַתָּה

⟨ You, ⟨ For ⟨⟨ will hear. ⟨ I ⟨ [yet] speak, ⟨ they ⟨ [that] ⟨⟨ will answer; ⟨ I ⟨ they call,

יהוה הָעוֹנֶה בְּעֵת צָרָה, פּוֹדֶה וּמַצִּיל בְּכָל עֵת צָרָה

⟨ of distress ⟨ time ⟨ in every ⟨ and rescues ⟨ Who redeems ⟨⟨ of distress, ⟨ in time ⟨ are the One Who responds ⟨ Hashem,

וְצוּקָה.

⟨⟨ and woe.

CONTINUE . . . כִּי אַתָּה (P. 377)

---

(1) *Isaiah* 65:24.

°°DURING THE SILENT *SHEMONEH ESREI* ONE MAY INSERT
THE FOLLOWING PERSONAL PRAYER FOR FORGIVENESS:

אָנָּא יהוה, חָטָאתִי עָוִיתִי וּפָשַׁעְתִּי לְפָנֶיךָ, מִיּוֹם הֱיוֹתִי

⟨ Please, ⟨ HASHEM, ⟨ I have ⟨ been ⟨ and willfully ⟨⟨ before ⟨ from ⟨ I have
     sinned,   iniquitous,   sinned,   You,   the day   existed

עַל הָאֲדָמָה עַד הַיּוֹם הַזֶּה (וּבִפְרָט בַּחֵטְא . . .). אָנָּא

⟨ on ⟨ earth ⟨ until ⟨ this very day ⟨⟨ and especially ⟨ with the sin of . . . ⟨⟨ ⟨Please,

יהוה, עֲשֵׂה לְמַעַן שִׁמְךָ הַגָּדוֹל, וּתְכַפֵּר לִי עַל חֲטָאַי

⟨ HASHEM, ⟨ act ⟨ for the ⟨ of Your ⟨ which is ⟨⟨ and grant ⟨ to ⟨ for ⟨ my inad-
     sake   Name   great   atonement   me   vertent sins,

וַעֲוֹנִי וּפְשָׁעַי שֶׁחָטָאתִי וְשֶׁעָוִיתִי וְשֶׁפָּשַׁעְתִּי לְפָנֶיךָ,

⟨ my in- ⟨ and my ⟨ [through which] ⟨ been ⟨ and sinned ⟨ ⟨⟨ before
  iquities,   willful sins,   I have sinned,   iniquitous,   willfully   You,

מִנְּעוּרַי עַד הַיּוֹם הַזֶּה. וּתְמַלֵּא כָּל הַשֵּׁמוֹת שֶׁפָּגַמְתִּי

⟨ from ⟨ until ⟨ this very day. ⟨⟨ And make ⟨ all ⟨ the [Holy] ⟨ that I have
  my youth   whole   Names   blemished

בְּשִׁמְךָ הַגָּדוֹל.

CONTINUE . . . כִּי אַתָּה (P. 377)

⟨⟨ which is ⟨ within
  great.   Your Name

°°DURING THE SILENT *SHEMONEH ESREI* ONE MAY INSERT
THE FOLLOWING PERSONAL PRAYER FOR LIVELIHOOD:

אַתָּה הוּא יהוה הָאֱלֹהִים, הַזָּן וּמְפַרְנֵס וּמְכַלְכֵּל

⟨⟨ and ⟨ sustains, ⟨ Who ⟨ the God ⟨ HASHEM, ⟨ Who are ⟨ It is You
  supports,   nourishes,

מִקַּרְנֵי רְאֵמִים עַד בֵּיצֵי כִנִּים. הַטְרִיפֵנִי לֶחֶם חֻקִּי[1], וְהַמְצֵא

⟨ provide ⟨⟨ allotted ⟨ with the ⟨ Supply me ⟨⟨ of lice. ⟨ the ⟨ to ⟨ of *re'eimim* ⟨ from the
     to me;   bread   eggs   horns

לִי וּלְכָל בְּנֵי בֵיתִי מְזוֹנוֹתַי קוֹדֶם שֶׁאֶצְטָרֵךְ לָהֶם, בְּנַחַת

⟨ in ⟨⟨ for it; ⟨ I have need ⟨ before ⟨ my food, ⟨⟨ of my ⟨ members ⟨ and ⟨ for
  contentment   household,   for all   me

וְלֹא בְצַעַר, בְּהֶתֵּר וְלֹא בְאִסּוּר, בְּכָבוֹד וְלֹא בְּבִזָּיוֹן,

⟨⟨ in ⟨ but ⟨ in honor ⟨⟨ in a forbidden ⟨ but ⟨ in a permissible ⟨⟨ in pain, ⟨ but
  disgrace,   not   manner   not   manner   not

לְחַיִּים וּלְשָׁלוֹם, מִשֶּׁפַע בְּרָכָה וְהַצְלָחָה, וּמִשֶּׁפַע בְּרָכָה

⟨ of the ⟨ and from ⟨⟨ and success ⟨ of ⟨ from the ⟨ and for ⟨ for life
  spring   the flow   blessing   flow   peace,

_____

(1) *Proverbs* 30:8.

עֶלְיוֹנָה, כְּדֵי שֶׁאוּכַל לַעֲשׂוֹת רְצוֹנֶךָ וְלַעֲסוֹק בְּתוֹרָתֶךָ

‹ in Your Torah ‹ and engage ‹‹ Your will ‹ to do ‹ I be enabled ‹ so that ‹‹ On High,

וּלְקַיֵּם מִצְוֹתֶיךָ. וְאַל תַּצְרִיכֵנִי לִידֵי מַתְּנַת בָּשָׂר וָדָם. וִיקֻיַּם

‹ and may there be fulfilled ‹‹ and ‹ of ‹ of the gifts of the hands ‹ make me needful ‹ Do not ‹‹ Your commandments. ‹ and fulfill

blood; flesh

בִּי מִקְרָא שֶׁכָּתוּב: פּוֹתֵחַ אֶת יָדֶךָ, וּמַשְׂבִּיעַ לְכָל חַי

‹ living thing ‹ every ‹ and satisfy ‹‹ Your hand, ‹ You open ‹‹ that states, ‹ the verse ‹ in me

רָצוֹן.¹ וְכָתוּב: הַשְׁלֵךְ עַל יהוה יְהָבְךָ וְהוּא יְכַלְכְּלֶךָ.²

‹‹ will ‹ and He ‹ Your burden ‹ HASHEM ‹ upon ‹ Cast ‹ and that ‹‹ [with its] desire,

sustain you.   states,

CONTINUE ... **כִּי אַתָּה** (BELOW)

כִּי אַתָּה שׁוֹמֵעַ תְּפִלַּת כָּל פֶּה, עַמְּךָ יִשְׂרָאֵל

‹ Israel ‹ [the prayer] of Your people ‹‹ mouth, ‹ of ‹ every ‹ the prayer ‹ hear ‹ You ‹ for

בְּרַחֲמִים. בָּרוּךְ אַתָּה יהוה, שׁוֹמֵעַ תְּפִלָּה.

‹‹ prayer. ‹ Who hears ‹‹ HASHEM, ‹ are You, ‹ Blessed ‹‹ with compassion.

TEMPLE SERVICE / עֲבוֹדָה

רְצֵה יהוה אֱלֹהֵינוּ בְּעַמְּךָ יִשְׂרָאֵל, וְלִתְפִלָּתָם

‹ and toward their prayer ‹ Israel, ‹ toward Your people ‹‹ our God, ‹ HASHEM, ‹‹ Be favorable,

שְׁעֵה, וְהָשֵׁב אֶת הָעֲבוֹדָה לִדְבִיר בֵּיתֶךָ. וְאִשֵּׁי

‹ The fire-offerings ‹‹ of Your Temple. ‹ to the Holy of Holies ‹ the service ‹ and restore ‹‹ turn,

יִשְׂרָאֵל וּתְפִלָּתָם מְהֵרָה בְּאַהֲבָה תְקַבֵּל בְּרָצוֹן,

‹‹ favorably, ‹ accept ‹ with love ‹ speedily, ‹ and their prayer, ‹ of Israel

וּתְהִי לְרָצוֹן תָּמִיד עֲבוֹדַת יִשְׂרָאֵל עַמֶּךָ.

‹‹ Your people. ‹ of Israel ‹ the service ‹ always ‹ to Your favor ‹ and may it be

(1) *Psalms* 145:16. (2) 55:23.

ON ROSH CHODESH AND CHOL HAMOED ADD THE FOLLOWING.
[IF FORGOTTEN, REPEAT *SHEMONEH ESREI*. SEE *LAWS* §88.]
(DURING THE *CHAZZAN'S* REPETITION, THE CONGREGATION RESPONDS אָמֵן, *AMEN*, AS INDICATED.)

אֱלֹהֵינוּ וֵאלֹהֵי אֲבוֹתֵינוּ, יַעֲלֶה, וְיָבֹא, וְיַגִּיעַ, וְיֵרָאֶה,

‹ be noted, ‹ reach, ‹ come, ‹ may ‹‹ of our ‹ and the God ‹ Our God
there rise,   forefathers,

וְיֵרָצֶה, וְיִשָּׁמַע, וְיִפָּקֵד, וְיִזָּכֵר זִכְרוֹנֵנוּ וּפִקְדוֹנֵנוּ, וְזִכְרוֹן

‹ the ‹‹ and ‹ – the ‹‹ and be ‹ be ‹ be heard, ‹ be
remem- consideration remembrance remembered considered,   favored,
brance   of us;   of us

אֲבוֹתֵינוּ, וְזִכְרוֹן מָשִׁיחַ בֶּן דָּוִד עַבְדֶּךָ, וְזִכְרוֹן יְרוּשָׁלַיִם

‹ of Jerusalem, ‹ the ‹‹ Your ‹ of ‹ son ‹ of ‹ the ‹‹ of our
          remembrance servant; David,   Messiah, remembrance forefathers;

עִיר קָדְשֶׁךָ, וְזִכְרוֹן כָּל עַמְּךָ בֵּית יִשְׂרָאֵל לְפָנֶיךָ, לִפְלֵיטָה

‹ for ‹ before ‹‹ of ‹ the ‹ of Your ‹ and the ‹‹ of Your ‹ the
deliverance, You Israel – Family entire people remembrance Holiness; City

לְטוֹבָה לְחֵן וּלְחֶסֶד וּלְרַחֲמִים, לְחַיִּים (טוֹבִים) וּלְשָׁלוֹם, בְּיוֹם

‹ on the ‹‹ and for ‹ (that is ‹ for life ‹ and for ‹ for ‹ for ‹ for
day of   peace,   good),   compassion, kindness, grace, goodness,

ON SUCCOS:	ON PESACH:	ON ROSH CHODESH:
חַג הַסֻּכּוֹת הַזֶּה.	חַג הַמַּצּוֹת הַזֶּה.	רֹאשׁ הַחֹדֶשׁ הַזֶּה.
‹‹ this Festival of Succos.	‹‹ this Festival of Matzos.	‹‹ this New Moon.

זָכְרֵנוּ יהוה אֱלֹהֵינוּ בּוֹ לְטוֹבָה (אָמֵן. –Cong.), וּפָקְדֵנוּ בוֹ

‹ on ‹ consider ‹‹ (Amen;) ‹‹ for ‹ on ‹ our God, ‹ Hashem, ‹ Remember
it   us   goodness; it   us

לִבְרָכָה (אָמֵן. –Cong.), וְהוֹשִׁיעֵנוּ בוֹ לְחַיִּים טוֹבִים (אָמֵן. –Cong.).

‹‹ (Amen.) ‹‹ that is good. ‹ for life ‹ on it ‹ and save us ‹‹ (Amen;) ‹‹ for blessing;

וּבִדְבַר יְשׁוּעָה וְרַחֲמִים, חוּס וְחָנֵּנוּ וְרַחֵם עָלֵינוּ

‹ with us, ‹ and be ‹ be ‹ have pity, ‹‹ and ‹ of ‹ In the
compassionate gracious,   compassion, salvation matter

וְהוֹשִׁיעֵנוּ, כִּי אֵלֶיךָ עֵינֵינוּ, כִּי אֵל מֶלֶךְ חַנּוּן וְרַחוּם

‹ and com- ‹ Who is ‹ King, ‹ God, ‹ because, ‹‹ are our ‹ to You ‹ for ‹‹ and save us,
passionate gracious   eyes [turned],

אָתָּה.[1]

‹‹ are You.

---

(1) Cf. *Nehemiah* 9:31.

וְתֶחֱזֶינָה עֵינֵינוּ בְּשׁוּבְךָ לְצִיּוֹן בְּרַחֲמִים.

《 in compassion. 〈 to Zion 〈 Your return 〈 may our eyes 〈 Witness

בָּרוּךְ אַתָּה יהוה, הַמַּחֲזִיר שְׁכִינָתוֹ לְצִיּוֹן.

《 to Zion. 〈 His Presence 〈 Who restores 《 Hashem, 〈 are You, 〈 Blessed

THANKSGIVING [MODIM] / הודאה

BOW AT מוֹדִים, *WE THANK*; STRAIGHTEN UP AT ה', *HASHEM*. IN HIS REPETITION THE *CHAZZAN*
RECITES THE ENTIRE מוֹדִים ALOUD, WHILE THE CONGREGATION RECITES מוֹדִים דְּרַבָּנָן (P. 380) SOFTLY.

מוֹדִים אֲנַחְנוּ לָךְ, שָׁאַתָּה הוּא יהוה

〈 Hashem, 〈 Who are 〈 for it is You 《 You, 〈   We thank

אֱלֹהֵינוּ וֵאלֹהֵי אֲבוֹתֵינוּ לְעוֹלָם וָעֶד. צוּרֵנוּ,

〈 our Rock, 《 and ever; 〈 for ever 〈 of our forefathers, 〈 and the God 〈   our God

צוּר חַיֵּינוּ, מָגֵן יִשְׁעֵנוּ אַתָּה הוּא לְדוֹר וָדוֹר.

《 to gen- 〈 from gen- 〈 are 〈 [is what] 《 of our 〈 Shield 《 of our 〈 the
eration.   eration   You   salvation,   lives,   Rock

נוֹדֶה לְּךָ וּנְסַפֵּר תְּהִלָּתֶךָ[1] עַל חַיֵּינוּ

〈 our lives 〈 for 《 Your praise, 〈 and relate 〈 You 〈 We shall thank

הַמְּסוּרִים בְּיָדֶךָ, וְעַל נִשְׁמוֹתֵינוּ הַפְּקוּדוֹת

〈 that are 〈 that are 〈 our souls 〈 and for 《 into Your 〈 that are
 entrusted   hands,   committed

לָךְ, וְעַל נִסֶּיךָ שֶׁבְּכָל יוֹם עִמָּנוּ, וְעַל

〈 and for 《 are with us; 〈 day 〈 that every 〈 Your miracles 〈 and for 《 to You;

נִפְלְאוֹתֶיךָ וְטוֹבוֹתֶיךָ שֶׁבְּכָל עֵת, עֶרֶב וָבֹקֶר

〈 morning, 〈 – evening, 《 times 〈 that are at all 〈 and favors 〈 Your wonders

וְצָהֳרָיִם. הַטּוֹב כִּי לֹא כָלוּ רַחֲמֶיךָ, וְהַמְרַחֵם

〈 and the Com- 《 are Your 〈 exhausted 〈 never 〈 for 〈 The Bene- 《 and afternoon.
 passionate One, compassions,   ficent One,

כִּי לֹא תַמּוּ חֲסָדֶיךָ,[2] כִּי מֵעוֹלָם קִוִּינוּ לָךְ.

《 in You. 〈 have we 〈 always 〈 – for 《 are Your 〈 ended 〈 never 〈 for
          put our hope   kindnesses

---

(1) Cf. *Psalms* 79:13. (2) Cf. *Lamentations* 3:22.

מודים דרבנן / MODIM OF THE RABBIS

מוֹדִים אֲנַחְנוּ לָךְ, שָׁאַתָּה הוּא יהוה אֱלֹהֵינוּ וֵאלֹהֵי

‹ and the God ‹ our God ‹ HASHEM, ‹ Who are ‹ for it is You ‹‹ You, ‹   We thank

אֲבוֹתֵינוּ, אֱלֹהֵי כָל בָּשָׂר, יוֹצְרֵנוּ, יוֹצֵר בְּרֵאשִׁית. בְּרָכוֹת

‹ Blessings ‹‹ of the ‹ the ‹ our ‹‹ flesh, ‹ of all ‹ the God ‹ of our
universe. Molder Molder,   forefathers,

וְהוֹדָאוֹת לְשִׁמְךָ הַגָּדוֹל וְהַקָּדוֹשׁ, עַל שֶׁהֶחֱיִיתָנוּ וְקִיַּמְתָּנוּ.

‹‹ and You have ‹ You have ‹ for ‹‹ and that ‹ that is ‹ [are due] to ‹ and thanks
sustained us. given us life is holy, great Your Name

כֵּן תְּחַיֵּנוּ וּתְקַיְּמֵנוּ, וְתֶאֱסוֹף גָּלֻיּוֹתֵינוּ לְחַצְרוֹת קָדְשֶׁךָ,

‹‹ of Your ‹ to the ‹ our exiles ‹ and gather ‹‹ and ‹ may You continue ‹ So
Sanctuary, Courtyards sustain us, to give us life

לִשְׁמוֹר חֻקֶּיךָ וְלַעֲשׂוֹת רְצוֹנֶךָ, וּלְעָבְדְּךָ בְּלֵבָב שָׁלֵם,

‹‹ wholeheartedly. ‹ and to ‹‹ Your will, ‹ to do ‹‹ Your ‹ to observe
serve You decrees,

עַל שֶׁאֲנַחְנוּ מוֹדִים לָךְ. בָּרוּךְ אֵל הַהוֹדָאוֹת.

‹‹ of thanksgivings. ‹ is the ‹ Blessed ‹‹ You. ‹ to thank ‹ [inspiring] ‹ [We thank
God us You] for

ON CHANUKAH AND PURIM ADD THE FOLLOWING [IF FORGOTTEN, DO NOT REPEAT *SHEMONEH ESREI*; SEE LAWS §89]:

וְעַל הַנִּסִּים, וְעַל הַפֻּרְקָן, וְעַל הַגְּבוּרוֹת, וְעַל

‹ and for ‹ the mighty deeds, ‹ and for ‹ the salvation, ‹ and for ‹ the miracles, ‹ And for

הַתְּשׁוּעוֹת, וְעַל הַנִּפְלָאוֹת, וְעַל הַנֶּחָמוֹת, וְעַל הַמִּלְחָמוֹת,

‹ the battles ‹ and for ‹ the consolations, ‹ and for ‹ the wonders, ‹ and for ‹ the victories,

שֶׁעָשִׂיתָ לַאֲבוֹתֵינוּ בַּיָּמִים הָהֵם בַּזְּמַן הַזֶּה.

‹‹ at this time: ‹ in those days, ‹‹ for our ‹ which You
forefathers performed

ON CHANUKAH:

בִּימֵי מַתִּתְיָהוּ בֶּן יוֹחָנָן כֹּהֵן גָּדוֹל חַשְׁמוֹנָאִי וּבָנָיו,

‹‹ and his ‹‹ the ‹ the High Priest, ‹ of ‹ the ‹‹ of ‹ In the
sons, Hasmonean, Yochanan, son Mattisyahu, days

כְּשֶׁעָמְדָה מַלְכוּת יָוָן הָרְשָׁעָה עַל עַמְּךָ יִשְׂרָאֵל, לְהַשְׁכִּיחָם

‹ to make ‹‹ Israel, ‹ Your ‹ against ‹‹ —which was ‹‹ of ‹ did the ‹ when rise up
them forget people wicked— Greece kingdom

תּוֹרָתֶךָ, וּלְהַעֲבִירָם מֵחֻקֵּי רְצוֹנֶךָ. וְאַתָּה בְּרַחֲמֶיךָ

‹ in Your mercy ‹ But You ‹‹ of Your Will. ‹ from the ‹ and to compel ‹‹ Your
statutes them to stray Torah

הָרַבִּים, עָמַדְתָּ לָהֶם בְּעֵת צָרָתָם, רַבְתָּ אֶת רִיבָם, דַּנְתָּ

which is abundant ‹ stood up ‹ for ‹ them ‹ in the time ‹ of their distress. ‹ You championed ‹ of their ‹ their cause, ‹ judged

אֶת דִּינָם, נָקַמְתָּ אֶת נִקְמָתָם.¹ מָסַרְתָּ גִבּוֹרִים בְּיַד חַלָּשִׁים,

into the hands ‹ the strong ‹ You delivered ‹ their wrong. ‹ and You avenged ‹ their claim, ‹ of the weak,

וְרַבִּים בְּיַד מְעַטִּים, וּטְמֵאִים בְּיַד טְהוֹרִים, וּרְשָׁעִים בְּיַד

into the hands ‹ the wicked ‹ of the pure, ‹ into the hands ‹ the impure ‹ of the few, ‹ into the hands ‹ the many

צַדִּיקִים, וְזֵדִים בְּיַד עוֹסְקֵי תוֹרָתֶךָ. וּלְךָ עָשִׂיתָ שֵׁם גָּדוֹל

of the ‹ and the ‹ into the hands ‹ of Your ‹ For ‹ You ‹ made ‹ a ‹ that ‹ righteous, ‹ willful sinners ‹ diligent students ‹ Torah. ‹ Yourself ‹ Name ‹ is great

וְקָדוֹשׁ בְּעוֹלָמֶךָ, וּלְעַמְּךָ יִשְׂרָאֵל עָשִׂיתָ תְּשׁוּעָה גְדוֹלָה²

of great magnitude ‹ a victory ‹ You performed ‹ Israel ‹ and for Your people ‹ in Your world, ‹ and holy

וּפֻרְקָן כְּהַיּוֹם הַזֶּה. וְאַחַר כֵּן בָּאוּ בָנֶיךָ לִדְבִיר בֵּיתֶךָ,

of Your ‹ to the Holy ‹ Your ‹ came ‹ Thereafter, ‹ as this very day. ‹ and a House, ‹ of Holies ‹ children ‹ salvation

וּפִנּוּ אֶת הֵיכָלֶךָ, וְטִהֲרוּ אֶת מִקְדָּשֶׁךָ, וְהִדְלִיקוּ נֵרוֹת

lights ‹ and kindled ‹ the site of Your Holiness ‹ purified ‹ Your Temple, ‹ cleansed

בְּחַצְרוֹת קָדְשֶׁךָ, וְקָבְעוּ שְׁמוֹנַת יְמֵי חֲנֻכָּה אֵלּוּ,

—these— ‹ of ‹ days ‹ the eight ‹ and they established ‹ of Your Sanctuary; ‹ in the Courtyards ‹ Chanukah

לְהוֹדוֹת וּלְהַלֵּל לְשִׁמְךָ הַגָּדוֹל.

that is great. ‹ to Your Name ‹ and praise ‹ to express thanks

ON PURIM:

בִּימֵי מָרְדְּכַי וְאֶסְתֵּר בְּשׁוּשַׁן הַבִּירָה, כְּשֶׁעָמַד עֲלֵיהֶם

against them ‹ when rise up ‹ the capital, ‹ in Shushan, ‹ and Esther, ‹ of Mordechai ‹ In the days

הָמָן הָרָשָׁע, בִּקֵּשׁ לְהַשְׁמִיד לַהֲרֹג וּלְאַבֵּד אֶת כָּל הַיְּהוּדִים,

the Jews, ‹ all ‹ and to exterminate ‹ to slay, ‹ to destroy, ‹ and he sought ‹ the wicked, ‹ did Haman,

מִנַּעַר וְעַד זָקֵן, טַף וְנָשִׁים בְּיוֹם אֶחָד, בִּשְׁלוֹשָׁה עָשָׂר

on the thirteenth [day] ‹ on the same day, ‹ and women, ‹ infants ‹ old, ‹ to ‹ from young

---

(1) Cf. *Jeremiah* 51:36. (2) Cf. *I Samuel* 19:5.

לְחֹדֶשׁ שְׁנֵים עָשָׂר, הוּא חֹדֶשׁ אֲדָר, וּשְׁלָלָם לָבוֹז.[1]

‹‹ to be ‹ and their ‹‹ of Adar, ‹ the ‹ which ‹‹ of the twelfth month,
plundered. possessions month is

וְאַתָּה בְּרַחֲמֶיךָ הָרַבִּים הֵפַרְתָּ אֶת עֲצָתוֹ, וְקִלְקַלְתָּ

‹ and ‹‹ his counsel ‹ nullified ‹‹ which is ‹ in Your ‹ But You,
frustrated abundant, mercy

אֶת מַחֲשַׁבְתּוֹ, וַהֲשֵׁבוֹתָ לּוֹ גְּמוּלוֹ בְּרֹאשׁוֹ, וְתָלוּ אוֹתוֹ

‹ him ‹ and they ‹‹ upon his ‹ his ‹ to ‹ and ‹‹ his intention
hanged own head, recompense him returned

וְאֶת בָּנָיו עַל הָעֵץ.

‹‹ the gallows. ‹ on ‹ and his sons

וְעַל כֻּלָּם יִתְבָּרַךְ וְיִתְרוֹמַם וְיִתְנַשֵּׂא שִׁמְךָ

‹ may Your ‹ and upraised ‹ and exalted, ‹ blessed, ‹ all these, ‹ For
Name be,

מַלְכֵּנוּ תָּמִיד לְעוֹלָם וָעֶד.

‹‹ and ever. ‹ for ever ‹ continually, ‹‹ our King,

FROM ROSH HASHANAH TO YOM KIPPUR ADD:

וּכְתוֹב לְחַיִּים טוֹבִים כָּל בְּנֵי בְרִיתֶךָ.

‹‹ of Your ‹ the ‹ all ‹ that is ‹ for a life ‹ And
covenant. members good inscribe

[IF FORGOTTEN, DO NOT REPEAT SHEMONEH ESREI. SEE LAWS §61.]

BEND THE KNEES AT בָּרוּךְ, *BLESSED*; **BOW AT** אַתָּה, *YOU*; **STRAIGHTEN UP AT** ה', *HASHEM.*

וְכֹל הַחַיִּים יוֹדוּךָ סֶּלָה, וִיהַלְלוּ וִיבָרְכוּ

‹ and bless ‹ — and praise ‹‹ forever! ‹ will gratefully ‹ alive ‹ Everything
acknowledge You,

אֶת שִׁמְךָ הַגָּדוֹל, בֶּאֱמֶת לְעוֹלָם, כִּי טוֹב. הָאֵל

‹ O God ‹‹ it is good. ‹ for ‹ forever, ‹ sincerely, ‹‹ that is great, ‹ Your Name

יְשׁוּעָתֵנוּ וְעֶזְרָתֵנוּ סֶלָה, הָאֵל הַטוֹב. בָּרוּךְ

‹ Blessed ‹‹ Who is beneficent. ‹ the God ‹‹ forever, ‹ and of our help, ‹ of our salvation

אַתָּה יהוה, הַטוֹב שִׁמְךָ וּלְךָ נָאֶה לְהוֹדוֹת.

‹‹ to give ‹ it is ‹ and ‹ is Your ‹ The ‹‹ HASHEM, ‹ are You,
thanks. fitting to You Name, *Beneficent One*

(1) *Esther* 3:13.

ON PUBLIC FAST DAYS AT *MINCHAH*: THE *CHAZZAN* RECITES בִּרְכַּת כֹּהֲנִים DURING HIS REPETI-
TION EXCEPT IN A HOUSE OF MOURNING. THE *CHAZZAN* FACES RIGHT AT וְיִשְׁמְרֶךָ; FACES LEFT AT
פָּנָיו אֵלֶיךָ וִיחֻנֶּךָ; FACES THE ARK FOR THE REST OF THE BLESSINGS.

אֱלֹהֵינוּ וֵאלֹהֵי אֲבוֹתֵינוּ, בָּרְכֵנוּ בַבְּרָכָה הַמְשֻׁלֶּשֶׁת, בַּתּוֹרָה

‹ [that is] in ‹‹ of three ‹ with the ‹ bless us ‹‹ of our ‹ and ‹ Our God
the Torah   verses   blessing   forefathers, the God

הַכְּתוּבָה עַל יְדֵי מֹשֶׁה עַבְדֶּךָ, הָאֲמוּרָה מִפִּי אַהֲרֹן וּבָנָיו,

‹ and his ‹ of ‹ from the ‹ that was ‹‹ Your ‹ of ‹ the ‹ by ‹ that was
sons,   Aaron   mouth   said   servant, Moses, hand   written

כֹּהֲנִים עַם קְדוֹשֶׁךָ, כָּאָמוּר:

‹‹ as it is ‹ Your holy ‹‹ the
said: people,   Kohanim,

יְבָרֶכְךָ יהוה, וְיִשְׁמְרֶךָ. (כֵּן יְהִי רָצוֹן. – Cong.)

‹‹ His will. ‹ be ‹ May so   ‹‹ and safeguard you. ‹ May HASHEM bless you

יָאֵר יהוה פָּנָיו אֵלֶיךָ וִיחֻנֶּךָ. (כֵּן יְהִי רָצוֹן. – Cong.)

‹‹ His will. ‹ be ‹ May so   ‹‹ and be ‹ for you ‹ His ‹ May HASHEM
                              gracious to you.   countenance illuminate

יִשָּׂא יהוה פָּנָיו אֵלֶיךָ וְיָשֵׂם לְךָ שָׁלוֹם.[1] (כֵּן יְהִי רָצוֹן. – Cong.)

‹‹ His will. ‹ be ‹ May so   ‹‹ peace. ‹ for ‹ and ‹ to you ‹ His ‹ May HASHEM
                              you establish   countenance turn

SOME CONGREGATIONS RECITE THE FOLLOWING WHILE THE *CHAZZAN* RECITES שִׂים שָׁלוֹם:

אַדִּיר בַּמָּרוֹם, שׁוֹכֵן בִּגְבוּרָה, אַתָּה שָׁלוֹם וְשִׁמְךָ שָׁלוֹם.[2]

‹‹ is Peace! ‹ and Your ‹ are ‹ You ‹‹ in power! ‹ Who ‹ on high, ‹ Mighty One
Name   peace   dwells

יְהִי רָצוֹן שֶׁתָּשִׂים עָלֵינוּ וְעַל כָּל עַמְּךָ בֵּית יִשְׂרָאֵל חַיִּים

‹ life ‹‹ of Israel, ‹ the ‹ of Your ‹ all ‹ and ‹ upon us ‹ that You ‹ [Your] will ‹ May
House   people,   upon   place   it be

וּבְרָכָה לְמִשְׁמֶרֶת שָׁלוֹם.

‹‹ of peace. ‹ for a safeguard ‹ and blessing

PEACE / שָׁלוֹם

שִׂים שָׁלוֹם, טוֹבָה, וּבְרָכָה, חַיִּים, חֵן,

‹ graciousness, ‹ life, ‹ blessing, ‹ goodness, ‹ peace, ‹ Establish

וָחֶסֶד וְרַחֲמִים עָלֵינוּ וְעַל כָּל יִשְׂרָאֵל עַמֶּךָ.

‹‹ Your ‹ of Israel ‹ all ‹ and ‹ upon us ‹ and compassion ‹ kindness,
people.

---

(1) *Numbers* 6:24-26. (2) Cf. *Judges* 6:24 and *Shabbos* 10b.

בָּרְכֵנוּ אָבִינוּ, כֻּלָּנוּ כְּאֶחָד בְּאוֹר פָּנֶיךָ, כִּי בְאוֹר
‹ with the ‹ for ‹‹ of Your ‹ with the ‹‹ as one, ‹ all of us ‹‹ our ‹ Bless us,
light   countenance, light   Father,

פָּנֶיךָ נָתַתָּ לָּנוּ, יהוה אֱלֹהֵינוּ, תּוֹרַת חַיִּים
‹ of life ‹ the Torah ‹‹ our God, ‹ HASHEM, ‹ us, ‹ You ‹ of Your
                                                        gave   countenance

וְאַהֲבַת חֶסֶד, וּצְדָקָה, וּבְרָכָה, וְרַחֲמִים, וְחַיִּים,
‹ life, ‹ compassion, ‹ blessing, ‹ righteousness, ‹ of ‹ and a love
                                                  kindness,

וְשָׁלוֹם. וְטוֹב יִהְיֶה בְּעֵינֶיךָ לְבָרְכֵנוּ וּלְבָרֵךְ
‹ and to bless ‹ to bless us ‹ in Your eyes ‹ may it be ‹ And good ‹‹ and peace.

אֶת כָּל עַמְּךָ יִשְׂרָאֵל בְּכָל עֵת וּבְכָל שָׁעָה
‹ hour ‹ and at ‹ time ‹ at every ‹ Israel ‹ of Your ‹ all
        every   people

בִּשְׁלוֹמֶךָ, (בְּרוֹב עוֹז וְשָׁלוֹם).
‹‹ and peace). ‹ strength ‹ (with ‹‹ with Your peace,
                           abundant

FROM ROSH HASHANAH TO YOM KIPPUR ADD THE FOLLOWING:

בְּסֵפֶר חַיִּים בְּרָכָה וְשָׁלוֹם, וּפַרְנָסָה טוֹבָה, וּגְזֵרוֹת טוֹבוֹת,
‹‹ that are ‹ and ‹ that is ‹ and ‹ and ‹ blessing, ‹ of life, ‹ In the
good,   decrees good, livelihood peace,   book

יְשׁוּעוֹת וְנֶחָמוֹת, נִזָּכֵר וְנִכָּתֵב לְפָנֶיךָ, אֲנַחְנוּ וְכָל עַמְּךָ
‹ and Your ‹ — we ‹‹ before ‹ and may we ‹ may we be ‹‹ and ‹ salvations,
entire people   You   be inscribed remembered consolations,

בֵּית יִשְׂרָאֵל, לְחַיִּים טוֹבִים וּלְשָׁלוֹם.
‹‹ and for ‹ that is ‹ for a life ‹‹ of Israel — ‹ the
peace.   good   Family

[IF FORGOTTEN, DO NOT REPEAT SHEMONEH ESREI. SEE LAWS §61, 65.]

בָּרוּךְ אַתָּה יהוה, הַמְּבָרֵךְ אֶת עַמּוֹ יִשְׂרָאֵל
‹ Israel ‹ His people ‹ Who blesses ‹‹ HASHEM, ‹ are You, ‹ Blessed

בַּשָּׁלוֹם.
‹‹ with peace.

ALTHOUGH THE *CHAZZAN'S* REPETITION ENDS HERE, HE SHOULD ADD
THE NEXT VERSE IN AN UNDERTONE. INDIVIDUALS CONTINUE:

יִהְיוּ לְרָצוֹן אִמְרֵי פִי וְהֶגְיוֹן לִבִּי לְפָנֶיךָ, יהוה צוּרִי וְגֹאֲלִי.¹

《 and my 〈 my 〈 Hashem, 《 before 《 of my 〈 and the 〈 of my 〈 — the 〈 find 〈 May
Redeemer. Rock You, heart — thoughts mouth expressions favor they

אֱלֹהַי, נְצוֹר לְשׁוֹנִי מֵרָע, וּשְׂפָתַי מִדַּבֵּר

〈 from 〈 and my lips 《 from evil 〈 my tongue 〈 guard 〈 My God,
speaking

מִרְמָה, וְלִמְקַלְלַי נַפְשִׁי תִדּוֹם, וְנַפְשִׁי כֶּעָפָר²

〈 like dust 〈 and let 《 be silent; 〈 let my 〈 To those who 《 deceitfully.
my soul soul curse me,

לַכֹּל תִּהְיֶה. פְּתַח לִבִּי בְּתוֹרָתֶךָ, וְאַחֲרֵי

〈 so that 《 to Your Torah, 〈 my heart 〈 Open 《 be. 〈 to
to follow everyone

מִצְוֹתֶיךָ תִּרְדּוֹף נַפְשִׁי. וְכָל הַקָּמִים וְהַחוֹשְׁבִים

〈 and who plot 〈 who rise up 〈 As for all 《 shall my soul 〈 Your com-
pursue. mandments

עָלַי לְרָעָה, מְהֵרָה הָפֵר עֲצָתָם וְקַלְקֵל

〈 and 《 their counsel, 〈 nullify 〈 speedily 《 to do evil, 〈 against
disrupt me

מַחֲשַׁבְתָּם. יְהִי רָצוֹן מִלְּפָנֶיךָ, יהוה אֱלֹהַי³

〈 my God 〈 Hashem, 《 before You, 〈 the will 〈 May it be 《 their scheme.

וֵאלֹהֵי אֲבוֹתַי, שֶׁלֹּא תַעֲלֶה קִנְאַת אָדָם עָלַי,

《 against 〈 of any 〈 the 〈 be aroused 〈 that there 《 of my 〈 and the God
me, man jealousy not forefathers,

וְלֹא קִנְאָתִי עַל אֲחֵרִים, וְשֶׁלֹּא אֶכְעַס הַיּוֹם,

〈 today, 〈 become 〈 and that 《 others; 〈 against 〈 my 〈 nor
angry I not jealousy

וְשֶׁלֹּא אַכְעִיסֶךָ, וְתַצִּילֵנִי מִיֵּצֶר הָרָע, וְתֵן בְּלִבִּי

〈 in my 〈 and 《 for Evil, 〈 from the 〈 Rescue me 《 anger You. 〈 and that
heart place Inclination I not

(1) *Psalms* 19:15. (2) Cf. 34:14. (3) See *Berachos* 17a.

הַכְנָעָה וַעֲנָוָה. מַלְכֵּנוּ וֵאלֹהֵינוּ, יַחֵד שִׁמְךָ

⟨ Your Name ⟨ unify ⟪ and our God, ⟨ O our King ⟪ and humility. ⟨ submissiveness

בְּעוֹלָמֶךָ, בְּנֵה עִירְךָ, יַסֵּד בֵּיתֶךָ, וְשַׁכְלֵל הֵיכָלֶךָ,

⟪ Your ⟨ perfect ⟪ of Your ⟨ lay the ⟪ Your ⟨ rebuild ⟪ in Your world;
Sanctuary;   House, foundation City,

וְקַבֵּץ קִבּוּץ גָּלִיּוֹת, וּפְדֵה צֹאנֶךָ, וְשַׂמֵּחַ עֲדָתֶךָ.

⟪ Your ⟨ and gladden ⟪ Your ⟨ redeem ⟪ of the ⟨ the ⟨ gather
congregation.   sheep,   exiles, ingathering

עֲשֵׂה לְמַעַן שְׁמֶךָ, עֲשֵׂה לְמַעַן יְמִינֶךָ, עֲשֵׂה

⟨ act ⟪ of Your ⟨ for the sake ⟨ act ⟪ of Your ⟨ for the sake ⟨ Act
right hand; Name;

לְמַעַן תּוֹרָתֶךָ, עֲשֵׂה לְמַעַן קְדֻשָּׁתֶךָ. לְמַעַן

⟨ In order ⟪ of Your sanctity. ⟨ for the ⟨ act ⟪ of Your Torah; ⟨ for the
that sake sake

יֵחָלְצוּן יְדִידֶיךָ, הוֹשִׁיעָה יְמִינְךָ וַעֲנֵנִי.[1]

⟪ and answer ⟨ with Your ⟨ — save ⟪ Your ⟨ released
me. right hand, beloved ones may be

SOME RECITE VERSES PERTAINING TO THEIR NAMES AT THIS POINT. SEE PAGE 764.

AN INDIVIDUAL WHO WISHES TO ACCEPT A FAST UPON HIMSELF RECITES THE FOLLOWING
DECLARATION AT THIS POINT DURING *MINCHAH* (OR LATER WHILE IT IS STILL DAYTIME) ON THE
DAY BEFORE THE FAST:

רִבּוֹן כָּל הָעוֹלָמִים, הֲרֵי אֲנִי לְפָנֶיךָ בְּתַעֲנִית נְדָבָה

⟨ that is ⟨ [to accept] ⟨ [come] ⟨ I ⟨ behold, ⟪ the worlds, ⟨ of all ⟨ Master
voluntary a fast before You

לְמָחָר. יְהִי רָצוֹן מִלְּפָנֶיךָ, יהוה אֱלֹהַי וֵאלֹהֵי אֲבוֹתַי,

⟪ of my ⟨ and the ⟨ my God ⟨ Hashem, ⟪ before You, ⟨ the will ⟨ May ⟪ for
forefathers, God it be tomorrow.

שֶׁתְּקַבְּלֵנִי בְּאַהֲבָה וּבְרָצוֹן, וְתָבֹא לְפָנֶיךָ תְּפִלָּתִי,

⟪ shall my ⟨ before You ⟨ that come ⟪ and favor; ⟨ with love ⟨ that You
prayer; accept me

וְתַעֲנֶה עֲתִירָתִי בְּרַחֲמֶיךָ הָרַבִּים. כִּי אַתָּה שׁוֹמֵעַ

⟨ hear ⟨ You ⟨ For ⟪ that is ⟨ in Your mercy ⟨ my entreaty ⟨ and that
abundant. You answer

תְּפִלַּת כָּל פֶּה.

⟪ mouth. ⟨ of every ⟨ the prayer

---

(1) *Psalms* 60:7; 108:7.

AT MINCHAH ON THE AFTERNOON OF AN INDIVIDUAL'S FAST, HE RECITES THE FOLLOWING:

רִבּוֹן כָּל הָעוֹלָמִים, גָּלוּי וְיָדוּעַ לְפָנֶיךָ, בִּזְמַן שֶׁבֵּית הַמִּקְדָּשׁ

‹ when the ‹ that in ‹‹ before ‹ and ‹ it is ‹‹ the worlds, ‹ of all ‹ Master
Holy Temple   the time   You   known revealed

קַיָּם אָדָם חוֹטֵא וּמֵבִיא קָרְבָּן, וְאֵין מַקְרִיבִים מִמֶּנּוּ

‹ of it [on ‹ was offered ‹ Although ‹‹ an ‹ he ‹‹ sinned, ‹ if ‹‹ existed,
the Altar]   nothing   offering.   brought   someone

אֶלָּא חֶלְבּוֹ וְדָמוֹ, וְאַתָּה בְּרַחֲמֶיךָ הָרַבִּים מְכַפֵּר. וְעַכְשָׁו

‹ Now ‹‹ would grant ‹ that is ‹ in Your mercy ‹‹ yet You ‹‹ and its ‹ for its fat ‹ except
atonement. abundant   blood,

יָשַׁבְתִּי בְתַעֲנִית, וְנִתְמַעֵט חֶלְבִּי וְדָמִי. יְהִי רָצוֹן מִלְּפָנֶיךָ,

‹‹ before ‹ the will ‹ May ‹‹ and my ‹ has my ‹‹ and ‹‹ in a fast ‹ I have
You,   it be own blood. own fat diminished   engaged

שֶׁיִּהְא מְעוּט חֶלְבִּי וְדָמִי שֶׁנִּתְמַעֵט הַיּוֹם, כְּאִלּוּ הִקְרַבְתִּיו

‹ I had ‹ as if ‹‹ today, ‹ that was ‹ and my ‹ of my ‹ the ‹ that
offered it   diminished blood fat, diminution [considered]
                                    should be

לְפָנֶיךָ עַל גַּב הַמִּזְבֵּחַ, וְתִרְצֵנִי.

‹‹ and may You ‹‹ of the Altar, ‹ top ‹ on ‹ before
show me favor.   You

יִהְיוּ לְרָצוֹן אִמְרֵי פִי וְהֶגְיוֹן לִבִּי לְפָנֶיךָ,

‹‹ before ‹‹ of my ‹ and the ‹ of my ‹ – the ‹‹ find favor ‹ May they
You,   heart –   thoughts mouth expressions

יהוה צוּרִי וְגֹאֲלִי.[1]

‹‹ and my Redeemer. ‹ my Rock ‹ HASHEM,

**BOW. TAKE THREE STEPS BACK. BOW LEFT AND SAY . . . עֹשֶׂה, "HE WHO MAKES . . ."; BOW RIGHT AND
SAY . . . הוּא, "MAY HE . . ."; BOW FORWARD AND SAY . . . וְעַל כָּל יִשְׂרָאֵל, "AND UPON ALL ISRAEL . . ."**

עֹשֶׂה °שָׁלוֹם בִּמְרוֹמָיו,[2] הוּא יַעֲשֶׂה שָׁלוֹם

‹ peace ‹ make ‹ may He ‹‹ in His heights, ‹ peace ‹ He Who makes

עָלֵינוּ, וְעַל כָּל יִשְׂרָאֵל.[3] וְאִמְרוּ: אָמֵן.

‹‹ Amen. ‹ Now respond: ‹‹ Israel. ‹ all ‹ and upon ‹‹ upon us,

FROM ROSH HASHANAH TO YOM KIPPUR SOME SAY:

°הַשָּׁלוֹם

‹ the peace

---

(1) *Psalms* 19:15. (2) *Job* 25:2. (3) Cf. *Berachos* 16b.

יְהִי רָצוֹן מִלְּפָנֶיךָ, יהוה אֱלֹהֵינוּ וֵאלֹהֵי

‹ and the God ‹   our God   ‹ HASHEM,   « before You,   ‹   the will   « May it be

אֲבוֹתֵינוּ, שֶׁיִּבָּנֶה בֵּית הַמִּקְדָּשׁ בִּמְהֵרָה בְיָמֵינוּ,

« in our days. ‹   speedily   ‹ shall the Holy Temple be, ‹ that rebuilt « of our forefathers,

וְתֵן חֶלְקֵנוּ בְּתוֹרָתֶךָ.¹ וְשָׁם נַעֲבָדְךָ בְּיִרְאָה,

«with reverence, ‹ we may serve You ‹ so that there «be in Your Torah, ‹our portion ‹Grant that

כִּימֵי עוֹלָם וּכְשָׁנִים קַדְמוֹנִיּוֹת. וְעָרְבָה לַיהוה מִנְחַת

‹ let be   ‹   to   ‹ And pleasing «   gone by.   ‹   and as in   ‹ of old   ‹ as in
the offering   HASHEM   years   days

יְהוּדָה וִירוּשָׁלָיִם, כִּימֵי עוֹלָם וּכְשָׁנִים קַדְמוֹנִיּוֹת.²

«   gone by.   ‹ and in years   ‹ of old   ‹ as in days « and Jerusalem, ‹ of Judah

THE INDIVIDUAL'S RECITATION OF *SHEMONEH ESREI* ENDS HERE. REMAIN STANDING IN PLACE UNTIL
THE *CHAZZAN* REACHES *KEDUSHAH* — OR AT LEAST UNTIL THE *CHAZZAN* BEGINS HIS REPETITION —
THEN TAKE THREE STEPS FORWARD. THE *CHAZZAN* HIMSELF, OR ONE PRAYING ALONE, SHOULD
REMAIN IN PLACE FOR A FEW MOMENTS BEFORE TAKING THREE STEPS FORWARD.

IN MOST *NUSACH SEFARD* CONGREGATIONS, *TACHANUN* IS NOT RECITED AT *MINCHAH.* THE *CHAZZAN*
RECITES קַדִּישׁ שָׁלֵם, *THE FULL KADDISH* (P. 393), INDIVIDUALS GO ON TO עָלֵינוּ, *ALEINU* (P. 395).
HOWEVER SOME CONGREGATIONS RECITE *TACHANUN* (SEE PAGE 172 FOR DAYS WHEN
TACHANUN IS OMITTED) BUT OMIT IT IF *MINCHAH* BEGINS LATE IN THE DAY.

BETWEEN ROSH HASHANAH AND YOM KIPPUR (AND ON FAST DAYS, IN MANY CONGREGATIONS)
אָבִינוּ מַלְכֵּנוּ (P. 178) IS RECITED AT THIS POINT. HOWEVER, MOST CONGREGATIONS THAT RECITE
TACHANUN AS WELL, INSERT אָבִינוּ מַלְכֵּנוּ BEFORE שׁוֹמֵר יִשְׂרָאֵל (P. 392).

תחנון / TACHANUN

THE *VIDUI*/CONFESSIONAL (UNTIL THE END OF P. 390) IS RECITED WHILE STANDING.

אֱלֹהֵינוּ וֵאלֹהֵי אֲבוֹתֵינוּ, תָּבֹא לְפָנֶיךָ תְּפִלָּתֵנוּ, וְאַל³

‹ and «   may our   ‹ before ‹ come «   of our   ‹ and the   ‹   Our God
do not   prayer,   You   forefathers,   God

תִּתְעַלַּם מִתְּחִנָּתֵנוּ,⁴ שֶׁאֵין אָנוּ עַזֵּי פָנִים וּקְשֵׁי עֹרֶף,

‹ necked ‹ and stiff- ‹ faced ‹ so brazen- ‹ For we are not « our supplication. ‹ ignore

לוֹמַר לְפָנֶיךָ יהוה אֱלֹהֵינוּ וֵאלֹהֵי אֲבוֹתֵינוּ, צַדִּיקִים

‹   that   «   of our   « and the   ‹ our God ‹ HASHEM ‹ before You, ‹ as to say
righteous   forefathers,   God

אֲנַחְנוּ וְלֹא חָטָאנוּ, אֲבָל אֲנַחְנוּ וַאֲבוֹתֵינוּ חָטָאנוּ.⁵

«   have   ‹ and our   ‹   we   « – for « sinned ‹ and have ‹ are we
sinned.   forefathers   indeed,   not

---

(1) *Ethics of the Fathers* 5:24. (2) *Malachi* 3:4. (3) Cf. *Psalms* 88:3. (4) Cf. 55:2. (5) Cf. 106:6.

⧫ Tachanun

Although the *Shulchan Aruch, Arizal, Sh'lah,*
and virtually all early authorities include *Tacha-*

nun in the *Minchah* service, most *Nusach Sefard*
congregations, especially chassidic ones, have
come to omit it. *Darkei Chaim V'Shalom* explains

**STRIKE THE LEFT SIDE OF THE CHEST WITH THE RIGHT FIST WHILE RECITING
EACH OF THE SINS OF THE FOLLOWING CONFESSIONAL LITANY:**

אָשַׁמְנוּ, בָּגַדְנוּ, גָּזַלְנוּ, דִּבַּרְנוּ דְפִי. הֶעֱוִינוּ, וְהִרְשַׁעְנוּ,

《 we have 《 We have 《 slander. 〈 we have 《 we have 《 we have 《 We have
committed committed spoken robbed; betrayed; been guilty;
wickedness; iniquity;

זַדְנוּ, חָמַסְנוּ, טָפַלְנוּ שֶׁקֶר. יָעַצְנוּ רָע, כִּזַּבְנוּ, לַצְנוּ,

《 we have 《 we have 《 that 〈 We have 《 false 〈 we have 《 we have 《 we have
scorned; been is bad; given accusations. made extorted; sinned
deceitful; advice willfully;

מָרַדְנוּ, נִאַצְנוּ, סָרַרְנוּ, עָוִינוּ, פָּשַׁעְנוּ, צָרַרְנוּ, קִשִּׁינוּ

〈 we have 《 we have 《 we have 《 we have 《 we have 《 we have 《 we have
stiffened caused sinned been strayed; provoked rebelled;
distress; rebelliously; iniquitous; [God's anger];

עֹרֶף. רָשַׁעְנוּ, שִׁחַתְנוּ, תִּעַבְנוּ, תָּעִינוּ, תִּעְתָּעְנוּ.

《 we have 《 we have 《 we have commit- 《 we have 《 We have 《 our
scoffed. gone astray; ted abominations; been corrupt; been wicked; necks.

סַרְנוּ מִמִּצְוֹתֶיךָ וּמִמִּשְׁפָּטֶיךָ הַטּוֹבִים, וְלֹא שָׁוָה לָנוּ.[1]

《 for 〈 worth- 〈 and it 《 that are 〈 and from 〈 from Your 〈 We have
us. while was not good, Your laws commandments turned away

וְאַתָּה צַדִּיק עַל כָּל הַבָּא עָלֵינוּ, כִּי אֱמֶת עָשִׂיתָ וַאֲנַחְנוּ

〈 while we 《 have 〈 truthfully 〈 for 《 upon 〈 that has 〈 all 〈 in 〈 are 〈 And You
You acted, us, come righteous

הִרְשָׁעְנוּ.[2]

《 have acted wickedly.

ONE PRAYING WITHOUT A *MINYAN* OMITS FROM HERE UNTIL THE END OF PAGE 390.

אֵל אֶרֶךְ אַפַּיִם אַתָּה, וּבַעַל הָרַחֲמִים נִקְרֵאתָ, וְדֶרֶךְ

〈 and 《 are You 〈 of Mercy 〈 and 《 are You, 〈 to anger, 〈 Who 〈 God,
the way called; Master is slow

תְּשׁוּבָה הוֹרֵיתָ. גְּדֻלַּת רַחֲמֶיךָ וַחֲסָדֶיךָ, תִּזְכּוֹר הַיּוֹם

〈 this 〈 may You 〈 and Your 〈 of Your 〈 The 《 have You 〈 of
day remember, kindness mercy greatness taught. repentance

וּבְכָל יוֹם לְזֶרַע יְדִידֶיךָ. תֵּפֶן אֵלֵינוּ בְּרַחֲמִים, כִּי אַתָּה

〈 You 〈 for 《 in mercy, 〈 to us 〈 Turn 《 of Your 〈 for the 《 day, 〈 and
beloved ones. offspring every

(1) Cf. *Job* 33:27. (2) *Nehemiah* 9:33.

---

that this omission originated from the fact that *Minchah* is usually recited at the very end of the day, with the result that *Tachanun* would be recited after *twilight*, a time when it is improper to say *Tachanun* (*Tzilosa D'Avraham*). Commentary appears on pages 172-177, 194-196.

הוּא בַּעַל הָרַחֲמִים. בְּתַחֲנוּן וּבִתְפִלָּה פָּנֶיךָ נְקַדֵּם,
the ⟨ are ⟨ the ⟨ of Mercy. ⟨⟨ With ⟨ and prayer ⟨⟨ Your ⟨ we
Master ⟨ approach, Presence ⟨ supplication

כְּהוֹדַעְתָּ לֶעָנָיו מִקֶּדֶם. מֵחֲרוֹן אַפְּךָ שׁוּב, כְּמוֹ
as ⟨⟨ turn ⟨ of Your ⟨ From the ⟨⟨ in ancient ⟨ to the humble ⟨ in the manner that
back, ⟨ anger ⟨ fierceness ⟨ times. ⟨ one [Moses] ⟨ You made known

בְּתוֹרָתְךָ כָּתוּב.[1] וּבְצֵל כְּנָפֶיךָ נֶחֱסֶה וְנִתְלוֹנָן, כְּיוֹם
as on ⟨⟨ and may ⟨ may we ⟨ of Your ⟨ In the ⟨⟨ it is ⟨ in Your Torah
the day ⟨ we dwell, ⟨ find shelter ⟨ wings ⟨ shadow ⟨ written.

וַיֵּרֶד יהוה בֶּעָנָן.[2] ❖ תַּעֲבוֹר עַל פֶּשַׁע וְתִמְחֶה אָשָׁם,
⟨⟨ guilt, ⟨ and erase ⟨ sin ⟨ Overlook ⟨⟨ in a cloud. ⟨ when HASHEM descended

כְּיוֹם וַיִּתְיַצֵּב עִמּוֹ שָׁם.[2] תַּאֲזִין שַׁוְעָתֵנוּ וְתַקְשִׁיב מֶנּוּ
from ⟨ and hear ⟨ to our cry ⟨ Give ⟨⟨ there. ⟨ with him ⟨ when He ⟨ as on
us ⟨ heed ⟨ [Moses] ⟨ [God] stood ⟨ the day

מַאֲמַר, כְּיוֹם וַיִּקְרָא בְשֵׁם יהוה,[2] וְשָׁם נֶאֱמַר:
⟨⟨ it was said: ⟨ and there ⟨⟨ of ⟨ with the ⟨ when He ⟨ as on ⟨⟨ [our]
⟨ HASHEM, ⟨ Name ⟨ called out ⟨ the day ⟨ declaration,

CONGREGATION AND *CHAZZAN* RECITE LOUDLY AND IN UNISON:

וַיַּעֲבֹר יהוה עַל פָּנָיו וַיִּקְרָא:
⟨⟨ and ⟨⟨ his [Moses'] ⟨ before ⟨ And HASHEM passed
proclaimed: ⟨ face,

יהוה, יהוה, אֵל, רַחוּם, וְחַנּוּן, אֶרֶךְ אַפַּיִם, וְרַב חֶסֶד,
⟨ in ⟨ and ⟨ to anger, ⟨ Slow ⟨⟨ and ⟨ Compas- ⟨ God, ⟨ HASHEM, ⟨ HASHEM,
Kindness Abundant ⟨ Gracious, ⟨ sionate

וֶאֱמֶת, נֹצֵר חֶסֶד לָאֲלָפִים, נֹשֵׂא עָוֹן, וָפֶשַׁע, וְחַטָּאָה,
⟨ and inadvertent ⟨ willful ⟨ of ⟨ Forgiver ⟨⟨ for thousands ⟨ of ⟨ Preserver ⟨⟨ and
sin, ⟨ sin, ⟨ iniquity, ⟨ [of generations], ⟨ kindness ⟨ Truth,

וְנַקֵּה.[3] וְסָלַחְתָּ לַעֲוֹנֵנוּ וּלְחַטָּאתֵנוּ וּנְחַלְתָּנוּ.[4] סְלַח לָנוּ
us, ⟨ Forgive ⟨⟨ and make us ⟨⟨ and our sins, ⟨ our ⟨ May You ⟨⟨ and Who
⟨ Your heritage. ⟨ iniquities ⟨ forgive ⟨ absolves.

אָבִינוּ כִּי חָטָאנוּ, מְחַל לָנוּ מַלְכֵּנוּ כִּי פָשָׁעְנוּ. כִּי
⟨ For ⟨⟨ we have ⟨ for ⟨⟨ our King, ⟨ us, ⟨ pardon ⟨⟨ we have ⟨ for ⟨⟨ our Father,
willfully sinned. ⟨ sinned;

אַתָּה אֲדֹנָי טוֹב וְסַלָּח, וְרַב חֶסֶד לְכָל קֹרְאֶיךָ.[6]
⟨⟨ who call ⟨ to all ⟨ in ⟨ and ⟨⟨ and ⟨ are ⟨ O Lord, ⟨ You,
upon You. ⟨ kindness abundant ⟨ forgiving, ⟨ good

---

(1) Cf. *Exodus* 32:12. (2) 34:5. (3) 34:6-7. (4) 34:9. (5) Weekday *Shemoneh Esrei*. (6) *Psalms* 86:5.

THE FOLLOWING (UNTIL יָבְשׁוּ רָגַע) SHOULD PREFERABLY BE RECITED WHILE ONE IS SEATED. IF A
TORAH SCROLL IS PRESENT, ONE SHOULD REST HIS HEAD ON HIS ARM. MANY OMIT THE VERSE
וַיֹּאמֶר דָּוִד, *AND DAVID SAID* . . ., AND BEGIN WITH רַחוּם וְחַנּוּן, *O MERCIFUL* . . .

וַיֹּאמֶר דָּוִד אֶל גָּד, צַר לִי מְאֹד, נִפְּלָה נָּא בְיַד יהוה, כִּי

〈 for 〈 of 〈 into the 〈 now 〈 Let us 《 exceed- 〈 am I 〈 Dis- 〈 Gad, 〈 to 〈 And David said
HASHEM, hand   fall   ingly.   tressed

רַבִּים רַחֲמָיו, וּבְיַד אָדָם אַל אֶפְּלָה.¹ **רַחוּם וְחַנּוּן** חָטָאתִי

〈 I have 〈 and gra- 〈 O 《 let me not fall. 〈 but into human 《 are His 〈 abundant
sinned   cious One, merciful   hands   mercies,

לְפָנֶיךָ. יהוה מָלֵא רַחֲמִים, רַחֵם עָלַי וְקַבֵּל תַּחֲנוּנָי.

《 my 〈 and 〈 on me 〈 have 《 of mercy, 〈 Who is 〈 HASHEM, 《 before You.
supplications. accept   mercy   full

——— תהלים ו:ב-יא / *Psalms 6:2-11* ———

יהוה, אַל בְּאַפְּךָ תוֹכִיחֵנִי, וְאַל בַּחֲמָתְךָ תְיַסְּרֵנִי. חָנֵּנִי

〈 Favor 《 chastise me. 〈 in Your 〈 nor 〈 rebuke me, 〈 in Your 〈 do not 〈 HASHEM,
me,   wrath   anger

יהוה כִּי אֻמְלַל אָנִי, רְפָאֵנִי יהוה כִּי נִבְהֲלוּ עֲצָמָי. וְנַפְשִׁי

〈 My soul 《 do my 〈 shudder 〈 for 〈 HASHEM, 〈 heal me, 《 am I; 〈 feeble 〈 for 〈 HASHEM,
          bones. with terror,

נִבְהֲלָה מְאֹד, וְאַתָּה יהוה עַד מָתָי. שׁוּבָה יהוה חַלְּצָה

〈 release 〈 HASHEM, 〈 Desist, 《 when? 〈 until 〈 HASHEM, 〈 and You, 《 utterly, 〈 is terrified

נַפְשִׁי, הוֹשִׁיעֵנִי לְמַעַן חַסְדֶּךָ. כִּי אֵין בַּמָּוֶת זִכְרֶךָ,

《 is there 〈 in death 〈 not 〈 For 《 Your 〈 as befits 〈 save me 《 my soul;
mention of You!   kindness.

בִּשְׁאוֹל מִי יוֹדֶה לָּךְ. יָגַעְתִּי בְּאַנְחָתִי, אַשְׂחֶה בְכָל לַיְלָה

〈 night 〈 every 〈 I drench 《 with my sigh; 〈 I am 《 You? 〈 will 〈 who 〈 in the
                                            wearied   praise   grave

מִטָּתִי, בְּדִמְעָתִי עַרְשִׂי אַמְסֶה. עָשְׁשָׁה מִכַּעַס עֵינִי,

〈 is my eye, 〈 because of anger 〈 Dimmed 《 I soak. 〈 my couch 〈 with my tears 《 my bed;

עָתְקָה בְּכָל צוֹרְרָי. סוּרוּ מִמֶּנִּי כָּל פֹּעֲלֵי אָוֶן, כִּי

〈 for 《 of evil, 〈 doers 〈 all 〈 from me, 〈 Depart 《 my tormentors. 〈 by all 〈 aged

שָׁמַע יהוה קוֹל בִּכְיִי. שָׁמַע יהוה תְּחִנָּתִי, יהוה תְּפִלָּתִי

〈 my prayer 〈 HASHEM 《 my plea, 〈 HASHEM has heard 《 of my 〈 the 〈 HASHEM has heard
                                          weeping. sound

יִקָּח. יֵבֹשׁוּ וְיִבָּהֲלוּ מְאֹד כָּל אֹיְבָי, יָשֻׁבוּ יֵבֹשׁוּ רָגַע.

《 in an 〈 and be 〈 may they 《 my 〈 all 〈 utterly, 〈 and 〈 Let them 《 will
instant. shamed   regret   enemies;   be shamed accept.

---

(1) *II Samuel* 24:14.

ON DAYS THAT אָבִינוּ מַלְכֵּנוּ, *AVINU MALKEINU* (P. 178) IS RECITED, SOME INSERT IT AT THIS POINT.

THE FOLLOWING IS RECITED WHILE SITTING ERECT.

שׁוֹמֵר יִשְׂרָאֵל, שְׁמוֹר שְׁאֵרִית יִשְׂרָאֵל, וְאַל יֹאבַד

O Guardian ⟨ of Israel, ⟩ safeguard ⟨ the remnant ⟩ of Israel; ⟨ let it not be destroyed

יִשְׂרָאֵל, הָאוֹמְרִים שְׁמַע יִשְׂרָאֵל.

– Israel ⟨ those who proclaim: ⟩ Hear ⟨ O Israel.

שׁוֹמֵר גּוֹי אֶחָד, שְׁמוֹר שְׁאֵרִית עַם אֶחָד, וְאַל יֹאבַד

O Guardian ⟨ of the ⟩ nation that is ⟨ unique, ⟩ safeguard ⟨ the remnant ⟩ of the ⟩ people that is ⟨ unique; ⟨ let not ⟩ be destroyed

גּוֹי אֶחָד, הַמְיַחֲדִים שִׁמְךָ, יהוה אֱלֹהֵינוּ יהוה אֶחָד.

the ⟨ nation that is ⟩ unique, ⟨ those who proclaim ⟩ of Your Name: the Oneness ⟨ HASHEM ⟩ is our God, ⟨ HASHEM ⟩ the One [and Only]!

שׁוֹמֵר גּוֹי קָדוֹשׁ, שְׁמוֹר שְׁאֵרִית עַם קָדוֹשׁ, וְאַל

O Guardian ⟨ of the ⟩ nation that is ⟨ holy, ⟩ safeguard ⟨ the remnant ⟩ of the ⟩ people that is ⟨ holy; ⟨ let not

יֹאבַד גּוֹי קָדוֹשׁ, הַמְשַׁלְּשִׁים בְּשָׁלֹשׁ קְדֻשּׁוֹת לְקָדוֹשׁ.

be destroyed ⟨ the ⟩ nation that is ⟨ holy, ⟩ those who proclaim ⟨ the threefold ⟩ three times ⟨ sanctifications ⟨ to the Holy One.

מִתְרַצֶּה בְּרַחֲמִים וּמִתְפַּיֵּס בְּתַחֲנוּנִים, הִתְרַצֵּה

You Who become favorable ⟨ through compassion ⟩ and Who become conciliatory ⟨ through supplications, ⟨ be favorable

וְהִתְפַּיֵּס לְדוֹר עָנִי, כִּי אֵין עוֹזֵר. אָבִינוּ מַלְכֵּנוּ, חָנֵּנוּ

and be conciliatory ⟨ to the ⟩ generation that is ⟨ poor, ⟨ for ⟩ there is no ⟩ helper. ⟨ Our Father, ⟨ our King ⟩ be gracious with us

וַעֲנֵנוּ, כִּי אֵין בָּנוּ מַעֲשִׂים, עֲשֵׂה עִמָּנוּ צְדָקָה וָחֶסֶד

and answer us, ⟨ though ⟨ we have no ⟨ worthy deeds; ⟨ treat ⟨ us ⟨ with charity ⟨ and kindness,

וְהוֹשִׁיעֵנוּ.

and save us. ⟩

STAND UP AFTER THE WORDS וַאֲנַחְנוּ לֹא נֵדַע, UNTIL THE CONCLUSION OF THE PARAGRAPH.

וַאֲנַחְנוּ לֹא נֵדַע מַה נַּעֲשֶׂה, כִּי עָלֶיךָ עֵינֵינוּ.[1] זְכֹר

We ⟨ know not ⟨ what ⟨ we should do, ⟨ rather ⟨ upon ⟨ You ⟨ are our eyes. ⟩ Remember

(1) *II Chronicles* 20:12.

רַחֲמֶיךָ יהוה וַחֲסָדֶיךָ, כִּי מֵעוֹלָם הֵמָּה.¹ יְהִי חַסְדְּךָ

〈 Your kindness 〈 May 《 are they. 〈 eternal 〈 for 〈 and Your HASHEM, 〈 Your
kindnesses, mercies,

יהוה עָלֵינוּ, כַּאֲשֶׁר יִחַלְנוּ לָךְ.² אַל תִּזְכָּר לָנוּ עֲוֹנוֹת

〈 the sins 〈 against us 〈 recall 〈 Do not 《 You. 〈 we awaited 〈 just as 《 be upon 《 HASHEM,

רִאשׁוֹנִים, מַהֵר יְקַדְּמוּנוּ רַחֲמֶיךָ, כִּי דַלּוֹנוּ מְאֹד.³

《 exceed-ingly. 〈 we have become impoverished 〈 for 《 may Your mercies, 〈 advance to meet us 〈 swiftly 《 of the ancients;

עָזְרֵנוּ בְּשֵׁם יהוה, עֹשֵׂה שָׁמַיִם וָאָרֶץ.⁴ חָנֵּנוּ יהוה חָנֵּנוּ,

《 favor us, 〈 HASHEM, 〈 Favor 《 and earth. 〈 of heaven 〈 Maker 《 of HASHEM, the Name 〈 is through 〈 Our help

כִּי רַב שָׂבַעְנוּ בוּז.⁵ בְּרֹגֶז רַחֵם תִּזְכּוֹר.⁶ בְּרֹגֶז עֲקֵדָה

〈 the binding [of Isaac] 《 Amid wrath, 《 You should remember! 〈 to be 《 Amid wrath, 《 with 〈 sated 〈 we are for fully 〈 contempt.

תִּזְכּוֹר. בְּרֹגֶז תְּמִימוּת תִּזְכּוֹר. יהוה הוֹשִׁיעָה, הַמֶּלֶךְ

〈 May the King 《 save! 〈 HASHEM, 《 You should remember! 〈 the perfect ones 《 Amid wrath, 《 You should remember!

יַעֲנֵנוּ בְיוֹם קָרְאֵנוּ.⁷ כִּי הוּא יָדַע יִצְרֵנוּ, זָכוּר כִּי עָפָר

〈 dust 〈 that 〈 He is 《 our nature, 〈 knew 〈 He 〈 For 《 we call. 〈 on the day 〈 answer us mindful

אֲנָחְנוּ. ❖⁸ עָזְרֵנוּ אֱלֹהֵי יִשְׁעֵנוּ עַל דְּבַר כְּבוֹד שְׁמֶךָ,

《 of Your Name; 〈 of the glory 〈 the sake 〈 for 〈 of our salvation, 〈 O God 〈 Assist us, 《 are we.

וְהַצִּילֵנוּ וְכַפֵּר עַל חַטֹּאתֵינוּ לְמַעַן שְׁמֶךָ.⁹

《 of Your Name. 〈 for the sake 〈 our sins 〈 for 〈 and grant atonement 〈 rescue us

THE *CHAZZAN* **RECITES** קַדִּישׁ שָׁלֵם, **THE FULL** *KADDISH*.

יִתְגַּדַּל וְיִתְקַדַּשׁ שְׁמֵהּ רַבָּא. (.אָמֵן – .Cong) בְּעָלְמָא דִּי בְרָא

〈 He 〈 that 〈 in the world 《 (Amen.) 《 that is 〈 may His Name 〈 and be sanctified 〈 Grow exalted created

כִרְעוּתֵהּ, וְיַמְלִיךְ מַלְכוּתֵהּ, וְיַצְמַח פֻּרְקָנֵהּ וִיקָרֵב מְשִׁיחֵהּ.

《 His Messiah, 〈 and bring near 〈 His salvation, 〈 and cause to sprout 〈 to His kingship, 〈 and may He give reign 《 according to His will,

(.אָמֵן – .Cong) בְּחַיֵּיכוֹן וּבְיוֹמֵיכוֹן וּבְחַיֵּי דְכָל בֵּית יִשְׂרָאֵל,

《 of Israel, 〈 Family 〈 of the entire 〈 and in the lifetime 〈 and in your days, 〈 in your lifetimes 《 (Amen.)

---

(1) *Psalms* 25:6. (2) 33:22. (3) 79:8. (4) 121:2. (5) 123:3.
(6) *Habakkuk* 3:2. (7) *Psalms* 20:10. (8) 103:14. (9) 79:9.

בַּעֲגָלָא וּבִזְמַן קָרִיב. וְאִמְרוּ: אָמֵן.

‹‹ Amen. ‹ Now ‹‹ that ‹ and at ‹ swiftly
respond: comes soon. a time

CONGREGATION RESPONDS:

אָמֵן. יְהֵא שְׁמֵהּ רַבָּא מְבָרַךְ לְעָלַם וּלְעָלְמֵי עָלְמַיָּא.

‹‹ and for all eternity. ‹ forever ‹ be blessed ‹ that is great ‹ His Name ‹ May ‹‹ Amen.

CHAZZAN CONTINUES:

יְהֵא שְׁמֵהּ רַבָּא מְבָרַךְ לְעָלַם וּלְעָלְמֵי עָלְמַיָּא. יִתְבָּרַךְ

‹ Blessed, ‹‹ and for all eternity. ‹ forever ‹ be blessed ‹ that is great ‹ His Name ‹ May

וְיִשְׁתַּבַּח וְיִתְפָּאַר וְיִתְרוֹמַם וְיִתְנַשֵּׂא וְיִתְהַדָּר וְיִתְעַלֶּה

‹ elevated, ‹ honored, ‹ upraised, ‹ exalted, ‹ glorified, ‹ praised,

וְיִתְהַלָּל שְׁמֵהּ דְּקֻדְשָׁא בְּרִיךְ הוּא (.Cong – בְּרִיךְ הוּא) —

‹‹ is He) ‹ (Blessed ‹‹ is He ‹ Blessed ‹ of the Holy One, ‹ be the Name ‹ and lauded

ROSH HASHANAH TO YOM KIPPUR SUBSTITUTE:

°לְעֵלָּא מִן כָּל [°לְעֵלָּא (וּ)לְעֵלָּא מִכָּל] בִּרְכָתָא

‹ blessing ‹ any ‹ exceedingly beyond ‹ any ‹ beyond

וְשִׁירָתָא, תֻּשְׁבְּחָתָא וְנֶחֱמָתָא דַּאֲמִירָן בְּעָלְמָא.

‹‹ in the world. ‹ that are uttered ‹ and consolation ‹ praise ‹‹ and song,

וְאִמְרוּ: אָמֵן. (.Cong – אָמֵן.)

‹‹ (Amen.) ‹‹ Amen. ‹ Now respond:

CONGREGATION:

(קַבֵּל בְּרַחֲמִים וּבְרָצוֹן אֶת תְּפִלָּתֵנוּ.)

‹‹ our prayers.) ‹ and with favor ‹ with mercy ‹ (Accept

CHAZZAN CONTINUES:

תִּתְקַבֵּל צְלוֹתְהוֹן וּבָעוּתְהוֹן דְּכָל בֵּית יִשְׂרָאֵל

‹ Israel ‹ Family of ‹ of the entire ‹ and supplications ‹ the prayers ‹ May accepted be

קֳדָם אֲבוּהוֹן דִּי בִשְׁמַיָּא. וְאִמְרוּ: אָמֵן. (.Cong – אָמֵן.)

‹‹ (Amen.) ‹‹ Amen. ‹ Now respond: ‹‹ is in Heaven. ‹ Who ‹ their Father ‹ before

CONGREGATION:

(יְהִי שֵׁם יהוה מְבֹרָךְ מֵעַתָּה וְעַד עוֹלָם.[1])

‹‹ eternity.) ‹ until ‹ from this ‹ be ‹ of ‹ the ‹ (Let
time blessed HASHEM Name

CHAZZAN CONTINUES:

יְהֵא שְׁלָמָא רַבָּא מִן שְׁמַיָּא, וְחַיִּים טוֹבִים עָלֵינוּ וְעַל כָּל

‹ all ‹ and ‹ upon us ‹‹ that is ‹ and life ‹‹ Heaven, ‹ from ‹ that is ‹ peace ‹ May
upon good, abundant there be

(1) *Psalms* 113:2.

יִשְׂרָאֵל. וְאִמְרוּ: אָמֵן. (.Cong – אָמֵן.)

《 (Amen.)   《 Amen. ⟨ Now respond: 《 Israel.

CONGREGATION:

(עֶזְרִי מֵעִם יהוה, עֹשֵׂה שָׁמַיִם וָאָרֶץ.[1])

《 and earth.) ⟨ of heaven ⟨ Maker 《 HASHEM, ⟨ is from ⟨ (My help

BOW; TAKE THREE STEPS BACK: BOW LEFT AND SAY . . . **עֹשֶׂה שָׁלוֹם**, *"HE WHO MAKES PEACE . . ."*; BOW
RIGHT AND SAY . . . **הוּא**, *"MAY HE . . ."*; BOW FORWARD AND SAY . . . **וְעַל כָּל יִשְׂרָאֵל**, *"AND UPON
ALL ISRAEL . . ."* REMAIN IN PLACE FOR A FEW MOMENTS, THEN TAKE THREE STEPS FORWARD.

עֹשֶׂה °שָׁלוֹם בִּמְרוֹמָיו, הוּא יַעֲשֶׂה שָׁלוֹם עָלֵינוּ, וְעַל

⟨ and upon ⟨ upon us, ⟨ peace ⟨ make ⟨ may He 《 in His heights, ⟨ peace ⟨ He Who makes

כָּל יִשְׂרָאֵל. וְאִמְרוּ: אָמֵן. (.Cong – אָמֵן.)

《 (Amen.)   《 Amen. ⟨ Now respond: 《 Israel. ⟨ all

FROM ROSH HASHANAH TO YOM KIPPUR SOME SAY:

°הַשָּׁלוֹם

⟨ the peace

ALEINU / עלינו

STAND WHILE RECITING עָלֵינוּ, *"IT IS OUR DUTY . . ."*

עָלֵינוּ לְשַׁבֵּחַ לַאֲדוֹן הַכֹּל, לָתֵת גְּדֻלָּה

⟨ greatness ⟨ to ascribe 《 of all, ⟨ the Master ⟨ to praise ⟨ It is our duty

לְיוֹצֵר בְּרֵאשִׁית, שֶׁלֹּא עָשָׂנוּ כְּגוֹיֵי הָאֲרָצוֹת, וְלֹא

⟨ and 《 of the lands, ⟨ like the ⟨ for He has not 《 of primeval ⟨ to the
has not   nations   made us   creation,   Molder

שָׂמָנוּ כְּמִשְׁפְּחוֹת הָאֲדָמָה. שֶׁלֹּא שָׂם חֶלְקֵנוּ

⟨ our portion ⟨ assigned ⟨ for He has not 《 of the earth; ⟨ like the families ⟨ established us

כָּהֶם, וְגוֹרָלֵנוּ כְּכָל הֲמוֹנָם. (שֶׁהֵם מִשְׁתַּחֲוִים

⟨ bow ⟨ (For they 《 their multitudes. ⟨ like all ⟨ nor our lot ⟨ like theirs

לְהֶבֶל וָרִיק, וּמִתְפַּלְּלִים אֶל אֵל לֹא יוֹשִׁיעַ.[2])

《 save.) ⟨ who ⟨ a god ⟨ to ⟨ and pray ⟨ and ⟨ to vanity
does not   emptiness

BOW WHILE RECITING וַאֲנַחְנוּ כּוֹרְעִים וּמִשְׁתַּחֲוִים, *"BUT WE BEND OUR KNEES, BOW."*

וַאֲנַחְנוּ כּוֹרְעִים וּמִשְׁתַּחֲוִים וּמוֹדִים, לִפְנֵי

⟨ before 《 and acknowledge ⟨ bow, ⟨ bend our knees, ⟨ But we
our thanks,

(1) *Psalms* 121:2. (2) *Isaiah* 45:20.

מֶלֶךְ מַלְכֵי הַמְּלָכִים הַקָּדוֹשׁ בָּרוּךְ הוּא. שֶׁהוּא

‹ He ‹‹ He. ‹ Blessed is ‹ the Holy One, ‹‹ of kings, ‹ over kings ‹ the King

נוֹטֶה שָׁמַיִם וְיֹסֵד אָרֶץ,¹ וּמוֹשַׁב יְקָרוֹ בַּשָּׁמַיִם

‹ is in the ‹ of His ‹ the seat ‹‹ earth's ‹ and ‹ heaven ‹ stretches
heavens   homage   foundation; establishes   out

מִמַּעַל, וּשְׁכִינַת עֻזּוֹ בְּגָבְהֵי מְרוֹמִים. הוּא

‹ He is ‹‹ heights. ‹ is in the loftiest ‹ of His power ‹ and the Presence ‹‹ above,

אֱלֹהֵינוּ, אֵין עוֹד. אֱמֶת מַלְכֵּנוּ, אֶפֶס זוּלָתוֹ,

‹‹ beside ‹ there is ‹ is our King, ‹ True ‹‹ other. ‹ and there ‹ our God
Him,   nothing   is none

כַּכָּתוּב בְּתוֹרָתוֹ: וְיָדַעְתָּ הַיּוֹם וַהֲשֵׁבֹתָ אֶל

‹ to ‹ and take ‹ this day ‹ You are to know ‹‹ in His Torah: ‹ as it is written

לְבָבֶךָ, כִּי יהוה הוּא הָאֱלֹהִים בַּשָּׁמַיִם מִמַּעַל

‹ above ‹ — in heaven ‹‹ the God ‹ He is ‹ Hashem ‹ that ‹‹ your heart,

וְעַל הָאָרֶץ מִתָּחַת, אֵין עוֹד.²

‹‹ other. ‹ there is none ‹‹ below — ‹ the earth ‹ and on

וְעַל כֵּן נְקַוֶּה לְּךָ יהוה אֱלֹהֵינוּ לִרְאוֹת

‹ that we ‹‹ our God, ‹ Hashem, ‹ in You, ‹ we put ‹ And therefore
may see   our hope

מְהֵרָה בְּתִפְאֶרֶת עֻזֶּךָ, לְהַעֲבִיר גִּלּוּלִים מִן

‹ from ‹ detestable idolatry ‹ to remove ‹‹ of Your might, ‹ the splendor ‹ very soon

הָאָרֶץ, וְהָאֱלִילִים כָּרוֹת יִכָּרֵתוּן, לְתַקֵּן

‹ to perfect ‹‹ will be utterly cut off, ‹ and false gods ‹‹ the earth,

עוֹלָם בְּמַלְכוּת שַׁדַּי. וְכָל בְּנֵי בָשָׂר יִקְרָאוּ

‹ will call ‹ humanity ‹ Then all ‹‹ of the ‹ through the ‹ the
              Almighty.   sovereignty   universe

בִשְׁמֶךָ, לְהַפְנוֹת אֵלֶיךָ כָּל רִשְׁעֵי אָרֶץ.

‹‹ of the earth. ‹ the wicked ‹ all ‹ toward You ‹ to turn ‹‹ upon Your Name,

---

(1) *Isaiah* 51:13. (2) *Deuteronomy* 4:39.

יַכִּירוּ וְיֵדְעוּ כָּל יוֹשְׁבֵי תֵבֵל, כִּי לְךָ תִּכְרַע

‹ should bend ‹ to You ‹ that ‹‹ of the world — ‹ the inhabitants ‹ — all ‹‹ and know ‹ May they recognize

כָּל בֶּרֶךְ, תִּשָּׁבַע כָּל לָשׁוֹן.¹ לְפָנֶיךָ יהוה

‹ HASHEM, ‹ Before You, ‹‹ tongue. ‹ every ‹ should swear ‹‹ knee, ‹ every

אֱלֹהֵינוּ יִכְרְעוּ וְיִפְּלוּ, וְלִכְבוֹד שִׁמְךָ יְקָר

‹ homage ‹ of Your Name ‹ and to the glory ‹‹ and cast themselves down, ‹ they will bend their knees ‹ our God,

יִתֵּנוּ. וִיקַבְּלוּ כֻלָּם אֶת עוֹל מַלְכוּתֶךָ, וְתִמְלֹךְ

‹ that You may reign ‹‹ of Your kingship, ‹ the yoke ‹ will all ‹ and accept ‹‹ they will offer,

עֲלֵיהֶם מְהֵרָה לְעוֹלָם וָעֶד. כִּי הַמַּלְכוּת

‹ the kingdom ‹ For ‹‹ and ever. ‹ for ever ‹ very soon ‹ over them

שֶׁלְּךָ הִיא וּלְעוֹלְמֵי עַד תִּמְלוֹךְ בְּכָבוֹד, כַּכָּתוּב

‹ as it is written ‹‹ in glory, ‹ You will reign ‹ and ever ‹ and for ever ‹‹ is Yours,

בְּתוֹרָתֶךָ: יהוה יִמְלֹךְ לְעֹלָם וָעֶד.² ❖ וְנֶאֱמַר:

‹‹ And it is said: ‹‹ and ever. ‹ for ever ‹ shall reign ‹ HASHEM ‹‹ in Your Torah:

וְהָיָה יהוה לְמֶלֶךְ עַל כָּל הָאָרֶץ, בַּיּוֹם הַהוּא

‹ — on that day ‹‹ the world ‹ all ‹ over ‹ be King ‹ HASHEM ‹ Then will

יִהְיֶה יהוה אֶחָד וּשְׁמוֹ אֶחָד.³

‹‹ be One. ‹ and His Name ‹ be One ‹ HASHEM ‹ shall

SOME CONGREGATIONS RECITE THE FOLLOWING AFTER עָלֵינוּ, ALEINU:

אַל תִּירָא מִפַּחַד פִּתְאֹם, וּמִשֹּׁאַת רְשָׁעִים כִּי

‹ when ‹ of the wicked ‹ nor the holocaust ‹‹ [that comes] suddenly, ‹ terror ‹ Do not fear

תָבֹא.⁴ עֻצוּ עֵצָה וְתֻפָר, דַּבְּרוּ דָבָר וְלֹא יָקוּם, כִּי

‹ for ‹‹ stand, ‹ and it shall not ‹ your speech ‹ speak ‹‹ and it will be annulled; ‹ a conspiracy ‹ Plan ‹‹ it comes.

עִמָּנוּ אֵל.⁵ וְעַד זִקְנָה אֲנִי הוּא, וְעַד שֵׂיבָה אֲנִי

‹ I ‹ [your] elder years, ‹ and even till ‹‹ I remain unchanged; ‹ [your] old age, ‹ Even ‹‹ is ‹ with us

(1) Cf. *Isaiah* 45:23. (2) *Exodus* 15:18. (3) *Zechariah* 14:9. (4) *Proverbs* 3:25. (5) *Isaiah* 8:10.

אֶסְבֹּל, אֲנִי עָשִׂיתִי וַאֲנִי אֶשָּׂא, וַאֲנִי אֶסְבֹּל וַאֲמַלֵּט.[1]

≪ and rescue ⟨ shall ⟨ I ≪ shall ⟨ and I ⟨ created ⟨ I ≪ shall carry
[you]. carry [you] bear [you]; [you] [you].

MOURNER'S KADDISH / קדיש יתום

IN THE PRESENCE OF A *MINYAN*, MOURNERS RECITE קַדִּישׁ יָתוֹם, THE MOURNER'S *KADDISH*.
[A TRANSLITERATION OF THIS *KADDISH* APPEARS ON PAGE 879.]

יִתְגַּדַּל וְיִתְקַדַּשׁ שְׁמֵהּ רַבָּא. (–Cong. אָמֵן.) בְּעָלְמָא דִּי בְרָא

⟨ He ⟨ that ⟨ in the ≪ (Amen.) ≪ that is ⟨ may His ⟨ and be ⟨ Grow exalted
created world great! – Name sanctified

כִרְעוּתֵהּ, וְיַמְלִיךְ מַלְכוּתֵהּ, וְיַצְמַח פֻּרְקָנֵהּ וִיקָרֵב מְשִׁיחֵהּ.

≪ His ⟨ and bring ⟨ His ⟨ and cause ⟨ to His ⟨ and may He ≪ according
Messiah, near salvation, to sprout kingship, give reign to His will,

(–Cong. אָמֵן.) בְּחַיֵּיכוֹן וּבְיוֹמֵיכוֹן וּבְחַיֵּי דְכָל בֵּית יִשְׂרָאֵל,

≪ of Israel, ⟨ Family ⟨ of the ⟨ and in the ⟨ and in ⟨ in your ≪ (Amen.)
entire lifetimes your days, lifetimes

בַּעֲגָלָא וּבִזְמַן קָרִיב. וְאִמְרוּ: אָמֵן.

≪ Amen. ⟨ Now ≪ that ⟨ and at ⟨ swiftly
respond: comes soon. a time

CONGREGATION RESPONDS:

אָמֵן. יְהֵא שְׁמֵהּ רַבָּא מְבָרַךְ לְעָלַם וּלְעָלְמֵי עָלְמַיָּא.

≪ and for all eternity. ⟨ forever ⟨ be blessed ⟨ that is great ⟨ His Name ⟨ May ≪ Amen.

MOURNER CONTINUES:

יְהֵא שְׁמֵהּ רַבָּא מְבָרַךְ לְעָלַם וּלְעָלְמֵי עָלְמַיָּא. יִתְבָּרַךְ

⟨ Blessed, ≪ and for all eternity. ⟨ forever ⟨ be blessed ⟨ that is great ⟨ His Name ⟨ May

וְיִשְׁתַּבַּח וְיִתְפָּאַר וְיִתְרוֹמַם וְיִתְנַשֵּׂא וְיִתְהַדָּר וְיִתְעַלֶּה

⟨ elevated, ⟨ honored, ⟨ upraised, ⟨ exalted, ⟨ glorified, ⟨ praised,

וְיִתְהַלָּל שְׁמֵהּ דְּקֻדְשָׁא בְּרִיךְ הוּא (–Cong. בְּרִיךְ הוּא) –

≪ is He) ⟨ (Blessed ≪ is He ⟨ Blessed ⟨ of the Holy One, ⟨ be the Name ⟨ and lauded

ROSH HASHANAH TO YOM KIPPUR SUBSTITUTE:

°לְעֵלָּא מִן כָּל [°לְעֵלָּא (וּ)לְעֵלָּא מִכָּל] בִּרְכָתָא

⟨ blessing ⟨ any ⟨ exceedingly beyond ⟨ any ⟨ beyond

וְשִׁירָתָא, תֻּשְׁבְּחָתָא וְנֶחֱמָתָא דַּאֲמִירָן בְּעָלְמָא.

≪ in the world. ⟨ that are uttered ⟨ and consolation ⟨ praise ≪ and song,

וְאִמְרוּ: אָמֵן. (–Cong. אָמֵן.)

≪ (Amen.) ≪ Amen. ⟨ Now respond:

(1) *Isaiah* 46:4.

יְהֵא שְׁלָמָא רַבָּא מִן שְׁמַיָּא, וְחַיִּים טוֹבִים עָלֵינוּ וְעַל כָּל

⟨ all ⟨ and ⟨ upon us ⟪ that is ⟨ and life ⟪ Heaven, ⟨ from ⟨ that is ⟨ peace ⟨ May
upon   good,   abundant   there be

יִשְׂרָאֵל. וְאִמְרוּ: אָמֵן. (.Cong – אָמֵן.)

⟪ (Amen.)   ⟪ Amen. ⟨ Now respond: ⟪ Israel.

BOW; TAKE THREE STEPS BACK: BOW LEFT AND SAY . . . עֹשֶׂה שָׁלוֹם, "HE WHO MAKES PEACE . . ."; BOW RIGHT AND SAY . . . הוּא, "MAY HE . . ."; BOW FORWARD AND SAY . . . וְעַל כָּל יִשְׂרָאֵל, "AND UPON ALL ISRAEL . . ." REMAIN IN PLACE FOR A FEW MOMENTS, THEN TAKE THREE STEPS FORWARD.

עֹשֶׂה °שָׁלוֹם בִּמְרוֹמָיו, הוּא יַעֲשֶׂה שָׁלוֹם עָלֵינוּ, וְעַל

⟨ and upon ⟨ upon us, ⟨ peace ⟨ make ⟨ may He ⟪ in His heights, ⟨ peace ⟨ He Who makes

כָּל יִשְׂרָאֵל. וְאִמְרוּ: אָמֵן. (.Cong – אָמֵן.)

⟪ (Amen.)   ⟪ Amen. ⟨ Now respond: ⟪ Israel. ⟨ all

FROM ROSH HASHANAH TO YOM KIPPUR SOME SAY:
°הַשָּׁלוֹם
⟨ the peace

FROM ROSH CHODESH ELUL THRU SHEMINI ATZERES, PSALM 27 IS RECITED AFTER MINCHAH.

———— תהלים כז / Psalm 27 ————

לְדָוִד; יהוה אוֹרִי וְיִשְׁעִי, מִמִּי אִירָא; יהוה מָעוֹז

⟨ the ⟨ Hashem ⟪ shall I ⟨ whom ⟨ and my ⟨ is my ⟨ Hashem ⟪ By David.
strength is   fear?   salvation, light

חַיַּי, מִמִּי אֶפְחָד. בִּקְרֹב עָלַי מְרֵעִים לֶאֱכֹל אֶת בְּשָׂרִי;

⟪ my flesh ⟨ to devour ⟨ evildoers ⟨ against ⟨ When ⟪ shall I ⟨ whom ⟪ of my
me   there would dread?   life,
approach

צָרַי וְאֹיְבַי לִי, הֵמָּה כָשְׁלוּ וְנָפָלוּ. אִם תַּחֲנֶה עָלַי

⟨ against ⟨ there would ⟨ Even ⟪ and fall. ⟨ stumble ⟨ it is they ⟪ against ⟨ and my ⟨ — my
me   encamp   if   who   me — foes tormentors

מַחֲנֶה, לֹא יִירָא לִבִּי; אִם תָּקוּם עָלַי מִלְחָמָה, בְּזֹאת

⟨ in this ⟨ a war, ⟨ against ⟨ there ⟨ even ⟪ my heart would ⟨ an army,
me would arise if   not fear;

אֲנִי בוֹטֵחַ. אַחַת שָׁאַלְתִּי מֵאֵת יהוה, אוֹתָהּ אֲבַקֵּשׁ;

⟪ I shall ⟨ that ⟨ Hashem, ⟨ of ⟨ I asked ⟨ One ⟪ trust. ⟨ I
seek: thing

שִׁבְתִּי בְּבֵית יהוה כָּל יְמֵי חַיַּי, לַחֲזוֹת בְּנֹעַם יהוה,

⟨ of ⟨ the ⟨ to behold ⟪ of my ⟨ the ⟨ all ⟨ of ⟨ in the ⟨ [Would that]
Hashem delight   life, days   Hashem House I dwell

וְלַבַּקֵּר בְּהֵיכָלוֹ. כִּי יִצְפְּנֵנִי בְּסֻכֹּה בְּיוֹם רָעָה; יַסְתִּרֵנִי

and to contemplate | in His Sanctuary. | Indeed, | He will hide me | in His Shelter | on the day | of evil; | He will conceal me

בְּסֵתֶר אָהֳלוֹ, בְּצוּר יְרוֹמְמֵנִי. וְעַתָּה יָרוּם רֹאשִׁי עַל

in the concealment | of His Tent; | upon | a rock | He will lift me. | Now | is elevated | is my head | above

אֹיְבַי סְבִיבוֹתַי, וְאֶזְבְּחָה בְאָהֳלוֹ זִבְחֵי תְרוּעָה;

my enemies | around me, | and I will slaughter | in His Tent | offerings | accompanied by joyous song;

אָשִׁירָה וַאֲזַמְּרָה לַיהוה. שְׁמַע יהוה קוֹלִי אֶקְרָא,

I will sing | and chant praise | to Hashem. | Hear, | Hashem, | my voice | when I call,

וְחָנֵּנִי וַעֲנֵנִי. לְךָ אָמַר לִבִּי: בַּקְּשׁוּ פָנָי, אֶת פָּנֶיךָ יהוה

show me favor | answer me. | On Your behalf, | and | My heart has said, | Seek | My Presence. | Your Presence, | Hashem,

אֲבַקֵּשׁ. אַל תַּסְתֵּר פָּנֶיךָ מִמֶּנִּי, אַל תַּט בְּאַף עַבְדֶּךָ;

do I seek. | Do not | conceal | Your Presence | from me, | do not | repel | in anger | Your servant.

עֶזְרָתִי הָיִיתָ, אַל תִּטְּשֵׁנִי וְאַל תַּעַזְבֵנִי, אֱלֹהֵי יִשְׁעִי.

My Helper | You have been, | do not | abandon me, | and | do not | forsake me, | O God | of my salvation.

כִּי אָבִי וְאִמִּי עֲזָבוּנִי, וַיהוה יַאַסְפֵנִי. הוֹרֵנִי יהוה

Though | my father | and my mother | have forsaken me, | Hashem | will gather me in. | Teach me, | Hashem,

דַּרְכֶּךָ; וּנְחֵנִי בְּאֹרַח מִישׁוֹר, לְמַעַן שׁוֹרְרָי. אַל תִּתְּנֵנִי

Your way; | and lead me | on the path | of integrity, | because of | my watchful foes. | Do not | deliver me

בְּנֶפֶשׁ צָרָי, כִּי קָמוּ בִי עֵדֵי שֶׁקֶר, וִיפֵחַ חָמָס.

to the wishes | of my tormentors, | for | there have arisen | against me | false | witnesses | and those who breathe | violence.

❖ לוּלֵא הֶאֱמַנְתִּי לִרְאוֹת בְּטוּב יהוה בְּאֶרֶץ חַיִּים.

Had I not trusted | that I | would see | the | goodness | of Hashem | in the land | of life!

קַוֵּה אֶל יהוה; חֲזַק וְיַאֲמֵץ לִבֶּךָ, וְקַוֵּה אֶל יהוה.

Place your hope in | Hashem; | strengthen | yourself | and He will instill courage | in your heart, | and place your hope in | Hashem.

IN THE PRESENCE OF A *MINYAN*, MOURNERS RECITE קַדִּישׁ יָתוֹם (PAGE 398).

IN A HOUSE OF MOURNING, PSALM 49 IS RECITED AFTER *MINCHAH*.
(SOME SUBSTITUTE PSALM 16 (P. 809) ON DAYS WHEN *TACHANUN* IS NOT RECITED.)

——— תהלים מט / Psalm 49 ———

לַמְנַצֵּחַ לִבְנֵי קֹרַח מִזְמוֹר. שִׁמְעוּ זֹאת כָּל הָעַמִּים,

‹‹ you ‹ all ‹ this ‹ Hear ‹‹ a psalm. ‹ of ‹ by the ‹ For the
peoples, Korah, sons conductor,

הַאֲזִינוּ כָּל יֹשְׁבֵי חָלֶד. גַּם בְּנֵי אָדָם, גַּם בְּנֵי אִישׁ;

‹‹ of ‹ sons ‹ even ‹ of Adam, ‹ sons ‹ even ‹‹ of decaying ‹ you ‹ all ‹ give ear
man; earth; dwellers

יַחַד עָשִׁיר וְאֶבְיוֹן. פִּי יְדַבֵּר חָכְמוֹת, וְהָגוּת לִבִּי

‹ of my ‹ and the ‹‹ wisdom, ‹ will speak ‹ My ‹‹ and poor. ‹ – rich ‹‹ together
heart meditations mouth

תְבוּנוֹת. אַטֶּה לְמָשָׁל אָזְנִי, אֶפְתַּח בְּכִנּוֹר חִידָתִי.

‹‹ my riddle. ‹ with a ‹ I will ‹‹ my ear; ‹ to the ‹ I will ‹‹ are insightful.
harp solve parable incline

לָמָּה אִירָא בִּימֵי רָע, עֲוֹן עֲקֵבַי יְסוּבֵּנִי. הַבֹּטְחִים

‹ Those who ‹‹ will ‹ that I trod ‹ [when] ‹ of evil, ‹ in days ‹ should I ‹ Why
rely surround upon the be fearful
me? injunctions

עַל חֵילָם, וּבְרֹב עָשְׁרָם יִתְהַלָּלוּ. אָח לֹא פָדֹה יִפְדֶּה

‹ be redeemed ‹ cannot ‹ – [yet] ‹‹ they are ‹ and of their ‹‹ their ‹ on
in any way a brother boastful, great wealth possessions,

אִישׁ, לֹא יִתֵּן לֵאלֹהִים כָּפְרוֹ. וְיֵקַר פִּדְיוֹן נַפְשָׁם,

‹ of their ‹ is the ‹ Too ‹‹ his ‹ to God ‹ he cannot ‹‹ by a
soul redemption costly ransom. give man,

וְחָדַל לְעוֹלָם. וִיחִי עוֹד לָנֶצַח, לֹא יִרְאֶה הַשָּׁחַת.

‹‹ the pit? ‹ to see ‹ never ‹‹ eternity, ‹ until ‹ Can one ‹‹ forever. ‹ and
live unattainable

כִּי יִרְאֶה חֲכָמִים יָמוּתוּ, יַחַד כְּסִיל וָבַעַר יֹאבֵדוּ,

‹ perish ‹ and ‹ the ‹ that ‹‹ die, ‹ that wise men ‹ he sees ‹ Though
boorish foolish together

וְעָזְבוּ לַאֲחֵרִים חֵילָם. קִרְבָּם בָּתֵּימוֹ לְעוֹלָם, מִשְׁכְּנֹתָם

‹ their ‹‹ are forever, ‹ their ‹ [nevertheless,] ‹‹ their ‹ to others ‹ and leave
dwellings houses in their possessions,
imagination

לְדוֹר וָדֹר; קָרְאוּ בִשְׁמוֹתָם עֲלֵי אֲדָמוֹת. וְאָדָם

⟨ But as ⟩ ⟪ the lands. ⟨ throughout ⟨ their names ⟨ they have ⟪ after gen- ⟨ for gen-
for man: proclaimed   eration;   eration

בִּיקָר בַּל יָלִין, נִמְשַׁל כַּבְּהֵמוֹת נִדְמוּ. זֶה דַרְכָּם

⟪ is their ⟨ This ⟪ that are ⟨ to the animals ⟨ he is ⟪ he shall not ⟨ In glory
way,   silenced.   likened   repose;

כֶּסֶל לָמוֹ, וְאַחֲרֵיהֶם בְּפִיהֶם יִרְצוּ סֶלָה. כַּצֹאן לִשְׁאוֹל

⟨ for the ⟨ Like ⟪ Selah! ⟪ speak ⟨ their ⟨ yet of their ⟨ is ⟨ folly
Lower World   sheep,   soothingly,   mouths   destiny   theirs,

שַׁתּוּ, מָוֶת יִרְעֵם; וַיִּרְדּוּ בָם יְשָׁרִים לַבֹּקֶר, וְצוּרָם

⟨ their form ⟪ at ⟨ shall the ⟨ them ⟨ and ⟪ shall ⟨ death ⟪ they are
daybreak;   upright   dominate   consume   destined,
  them;

לְבַלּוֹת שְׁאוֹל מִזְּבֻל לוֹ. אַךְ אֱלֹהִים יִפְדֶּה נַפְשִׁי מִיַּד

⟨ from ⟨ my ⟨ will ⟨ God ⟨ But ⟪ [each] from ⟨ in the grave, ⟨ is doomed
the hand soul redeem   his dwelling.   to rot

שְׁאוֹל, כִּי יִקָּחֵנִי סֶלָה. אַל תִּירָא כִּי יַעֲשִׁר אִישׁ, כִּי

⟨ when ⟪ a man becomes ⟨ when ⟨ Fear not ⟪ Selah! ⟪ He will ⟪ for ⟨ of the
wealthy,   take me,   Lower
  World,

יִרְבֶּה כְּבוֹד בֵּיתוֹ. כִּי לֹא בְמוֹתוֹ יִקַּח הַכֹּל, לֹא יֵרֵד

⟨ descend not ⟪ at all, ⟨ will ⟨ upon ⟨ nothing ⟨ For ⟪ of his ⟨ the ⟨ he
he take his death   house.   glory   increases

אַחֲרָיו כְּבוֹדוֹ. כִּי נַפְשׁוֹ בְּחַיָּיו יְבָרֵךְ, וְיוֹדֻךָ כִּי תֵיטִיב

⟨ you ⟨ if ⟨ others ⟪ he may ⟨ in his ⟨ himself ⟨ Though ⟪ will his ⟨ after him
improve   will praise   bless,   lifetime   glory.
  you

לָךְ. תָּבוֹא עַד דּוֹר אֲבוֹתָיו, עַד נֵצַח לֹא יִרְאוּ אוֹר.

⟪ light. ⟨ they shall ⟨ eternity ⟨ unto ⟪ of its ⟨ the ⟨ to ⟨ It shall ⟪ yourself.
not see   fathers;   generation   come

❖ אָדָם בִּיקָר וְלֹא יָבִין, נִמְשַׁל כַּבְּהֵמוֹת נִדְמוּ.

⟪ that are ⟨ to the animals ⟨ he is ⟨ but [if he] ⟨ is ⟨ Man
without   likened   understands   glorious
speech.   not,

IN THE PRESENCE OF A *MINYAN*, MOURNERS RECITE קַדִּישׁ יָתוֹם (PAGE 398).

IN THE SYNAGOGUE, CHANUKAH LIGHTS ARE KINDLED BEFORE *MAARIV*;
ON THE CONCLUSION OF THE SABBATH BEFORE *ALEINU* (SEE P. 577).

﴾ WEEKDAY MAARIV / מעריב לחול ﴿

THE FOLLOWING VERSES ARE OMITTED ON THE CONCLUSION OF THE SABBATH AND FESTIVALS
(AND, IN SOME CONGREGATIONS, ON CHOL HAMOED).
ON THOSE DAYS *MAARIV* BEGINS WITH וְהוּא רַחוּם, *HE, THE MERCIFUL ONE* (P. 406).

שִׁיר הַמַּעֲלוֹת;* הִנֵּה בָּרְכוּ אֶת יהוה כָּל עַבְדֵי יהוה,

⟨ of ⟨ you ⟨ all ⟨ HASHEM, ⟨ bless ⟨ Behold, ⟪ of ascents.* ⟨ A song
HASHEM, servants

הָעֹמְדִים בְּבֵית יהוה בַּלֵּילוֹת.* שְׂאוּ יְדֵכֶם קֹדֶשׁ, וּבָרְכוּ

⟨ and ⟨ in the ⟨ your ⟨ Lift ⟪ in the ⟨ of ⟨ in the ⟨ who stand
bless   Sanctuary   hands   nights.*   HASHEM   House

אֶת יהוה. יְבָרֶכְךָ יהוה מִצִּיּוֹן, עֹשֵׂה שָׁמַיִם וָאָרֶץ.¹

⟪ and earth. ⟨ of heaven ⟨ Maker ⟪ from Zion, ⟨ May HASHEM bless you ⟪ HASHEM.

(1) *Psalms* 134.

⌁§ Laws of *Maariv*

As a general rule, no אָמֵן, *Amen,* or other prayer response may be recited between *Borchu* and *Shemoneh Esrei,* but there are exceptions. The main exception is "between chapters" [בֵּין הַפְּרָקִים] of the *Shema Blessings* — after each of the blessings, and between the three chapters of *Shema.* At those points, every אָמֵן (but not בָּרוּךְ הוּא וּבָרוּךְ שְׁמוֹ) may be said.

Some responses, however, are so important that they are permitted at any point in the *Shema* blessings. They are: (a) In *Kaddish,* עָלְמַיָּא . . . שְׁמֵהּ רַבָּא and the אָמֵן after יְהֵא and the אָמֵן after דַּאֲמִירָן בְּעָלְמָא; and (b) the response to בָּרְכוּ.

No interruptions whatever are permitted during the two verses of שְׁמַע and בָּרוּךְ שֵׁם.

The ideal time for *Maariv* is after dark. However, if one will not have a *minyan* later, he may recite *Maariv* as much as one and a quarter hours before sunset, in which case he must repeat the three chapters of *Shema* after dark (see *Laws* §25-26).

◊ מַעֲרִיב / THE EVENING SERVICE ◊

Maariv also has its basis in the Temple service. In the Temple, sacrifices were not offered in the evening, but any sacrificial parts that had not been burned during the day would be placed on the Altar and burned at night. This explains why *Maariv* began as a voluntary service; unlike *Shacharis* and *Minchah,* which took the place of the required *tamid* offerings, the evening service on the Altar was not always needed. During Talmudic times, the universal consensus of Jewry adopted *Maariv* as an obligatory service like *Shacharis* and *Minchah.*

⌁§ שִׁיר הַמַּעֲלוֹת / A Song of Ascents

The *Nusach Sefard* custom of reciting these verses, which refer to the service of God at

night, is based on *Shiltei Gibborim* to *Berachos* 8a, who writes that one should study Torah before the evening *Shema.* The one exception is the *Maariv* at the beginning and end of the Sabbath and Festivals. Presumably the reason for the omission then is because the time before *Maariv* is devoted to Torah study, prayers, or *zemiros.* Some hold that if *Maariv* is recited immediately after *Minchah,* it is not necessary to recite these verses because the prayers of *Minchah* serve the purpose of Torah verses before *Maariv.* It is customary, however, to recite שִׁיר הַמַּעֲלוֹת, even if *Maariv* follows immediately after *Minchah.*

הָעֹמְדִים בְּבֵית ה׳ בַּלֵּילוֹת — *Who stand in the House of* HASHEM *in the nights.* The genuine servant of

RECITE THREE TIMES:

יהוה צְבָאוֹת עִמָּנוּ, מִשְׂגָּב לָנוּ אֱלֹהֵי יַעֲקֹב, סֶלָה.¹

《 Selah! 《 of Jacob, 〈 is the 〈 for us 〈 a 〈《 is with us, 〈 Master of 〈 HASHEM,
God stronghold Legions,

RECITE THREE TIMES:

יהוה צְבָאוֹת, אַשְׁרֵי אָדָם בֹּטֵחַ בָּךְ.²

《 in You. 〈 who 〈 is the 〈 praiseworthy 〈 Master of 〈 HASHEM,
trusts man Legions,

RECITE THREE TIMES:

יהוה הוֹשִׁיעָה, הַמֶּלֶךְ יַעֲנֵנוּ בְיוֹם קָרְאֵנוּ.³

《 we call! 〈 on the day 〈 answer us 〈 May the King 《 save! 〈 HASHEM,

הוֹשִׁיעָה אֶת עַמֶּךָ, וּבָרֵךְ אֶת נַחֲלָתֶךָ, וּרְעֵם וְנַשְּׂאֵם

〈 and raise 〈 tend 《 Your inheritance; 〈 and 〈 Your nation, 〈 Save
them up them bless

עַד הָעוֹלָם.⁴ מִי יִתֵּן מִצִּיּוֹן יְשׁוּעַת יִשְׂרָאֵל, בְּשׁוּב יהוה

〈 When HASHEM 《 of Israel! 〈 the 〈 out of 〈 If only He 《 forever.
restores salvation Zion would grant

שְׁבוּת עַמּוֹ, יָגֵל יַעֲקֹב יִשְׂמַח יִשְׂרָאֵל.⁵ בְּשָׁלוֹם יַחְדָּו

〈 in 〈 In peace, 《 Israel will rejoice. 《 Jacob will exult, 《 of His 〈 the
harmony, people, captivity

אֶשְׁכְּבָה וְאִישָׁן, כִּי אַתָּה יהוה לְבָדָד, לָבֶטַח תּוֹשִׁיבֵנִי.⁶

《 will make 〈 securely 〈 HASHEM alone, 〈 You, 〈 for 《 and I sleep, 〈 I lie down
me dwell.

יוֹמָם יְצַוֶּה יהוה חַסְדּוֹ, וּבַלַּיְלָה שִׁירֹה עִמִּי,* תְּפִלָּה

〈 – a 《 is with 〈 His resting 〈 even by 《 His loving- 〈 HASHEM will 〈 In the
prayer me* place night kindness; command day

לְאֵל חַיָּי.⁷ ❖ וּתְשׁוּעַת צַדִּיקִים מֵיהוה, מָעוּזָּם בְּעֵת צָרָה.

《 of 〈 in 〈 their 《 is from 〈 of the 〈 And the 《 of my 〈 to the
distress. time might HASHEM, righteous salvation life! God

(1) *Psalms* 46:8. (2) 84:13. (3) 20:10. (4) 28:9. (5) 14:7. (6) 4:9. (7) 42:9.

Hashem never abandons his post. Even at night, in times of adversity and gloom, he remains on guard at his post (*Malbim*).

The Talmud (*Menachos* 110a) says that this stich refers to the dedicated Torah scholars who arise to study in the middle of the night. God deems their self-sacrifice equal to service in His Holy Temple.

וּבַלַּיְלָה שִׁירֹה עִמִּי — *Even by night His resting place is with me.* Even in the dark night of exile, God is with me. שיר here means *encampment*, as in the Aramaic שרא, *he camped*] (*Rashi*). Others render: *His song is with me* (*Ibn Ezra; Radak*).

וַיַּעְזְרֵם יהוה וַיְפַלְּטֵם, יְפַלְּטֵם מֵרְשָׁעִים וְיוֹשִׁיעֵם, כִּי

⟨ for ⟨⟨ and He will ⟨ from the ⟨ He will cause ⟨⟨ and caused ⟨ Hashem helped them,
save them, wicked them to escape them to escape;

חָסוּ בוֹ.¹

⟨⟨ in ⟨ they took
Him. refuge

THE CHAZZAN RECITES חֲצִי קַדִּישׁ, HALF-KADDISH.

יִתְגַּדַּל וְיִתְקַדַּשׁ שְׁמֵהּ רַבָּא. (–אָמֵן.) בְּעָלְמָא דִּי בְרָא

⟨ He ⟨ that ⟨ in the ⟨⟨ (Amen.) ⟨⟨ that is ⟨ may His ⟨ and be ⟨ Grow exalted
created world great! – Name sanctified

כִרְעוּתֵהּ, וְיַמְלִיךְ מַלְכוּתֵהּ, וְיַצְמַח פֻּרְקָנֵהּ וִיקָרֵב מְשִׁיחֵהּ.

⟨⟨ His ⟨ and bring ⟨ His ⟨ and cause ⟨ to His ⟨ and may He ⟨⟨ according
Messiah, near salvation, to sprout kingship, give reign to His will,

(–אָמֵן.) בְּחַיֵּיכוֹן וּבְיוֹמֵיכוֹן וּבְחַיֵּי דְכָל בֵּית יִשְׂרָאֵל,

⟨⟨ of Israel, ⟨ Family ⟨ of the ⟨ and in the ⟨ and in ⟨ in your ⟨⟨ (Amen.)
entire lifetimes your days, lifetimes

בַּעֲגָלָא וּבִזְמַן קָרִיב. וְאִמְרוּ: אָמֵן.

⟨⟨ Amen. ⟨ Now ⟨⟨ that ⟨ and at ⟨ swiftly
respond: comes soon. a time

CONGREGATION RESPONDS:

אָמֵן. יְהֵא שְׁמֵהּ רַבָּא מְבָרַךְ לְעָלַם וּלְעָלְמֵי עָלְמַיָּא.

⟨⟨ and for all eternity. ⟨ forever ⟨ be blessed ⟨ that is great ⟨ His Name ⟨ May ⟨⟨ Amen.

CHAZZAN CONTINUES:

יְהֵא שְׁמֵהּ רַבָּא מְבָרַךְ לְעָלַם וּלְעָלְמֵי עָלְמַיָּא. יִתְבָּרַךְ

⟨ Blessed, ⟨⟨ and for all eternity. ⟨ forever ⟨ be blessed ⟨ that is great ⟨ His Name ⟨ May

וְיִשְׁתַּבַּח וְיִתְפָּאַר וְיִתְרוֹמַם וְיִתְנַשֵּׂא וְיִתְהַדָּר וְיִתְעַלֶּה

⟨ elevated, ⟨ honored, ⟨ upraised, ⟨ exalted, ⟨ glorified, ⟨ praised,

וְיִתְהַלָּל שְׁמֵהּ דְּקֻדְשָׁא בְּרִיךְ הוּא (–בְּרִיךְ הוּא) –

⟨⟨ is He) ⟨ (Blessed ⟨⟨ is He ⟨ Blessed ⟨ of the Holy One, ⟨ be the Name ⟨ and lauded

ROSH HASHANAH TO YOM KIPPUR SUBSTITUTE:

°לְעֵלָּא מִן כָּל [°לְעֵלָּא (וּ)לְעֵלָּא מִכָּל] בִּרְכָתָא

⟨ blessing ⟨ any ⟨ exceedingly beyond ⟨ any ⟨ beyond

וְשִׁירָתָא, תֻּשְׁבְּחָתָא וְנֶחֱמָתָא דַּאֲמִירָן בְּעָלְמָא.

⟨⟨ in the world. ⟨ that are uttered ⟨ and consolation ⟨ praise ⟨⟨ and song,

וְאִמְרוּ: אָמֵן. (–אָמֵן.)

⟨⟨ (Amen.) ⟨⟨ Amen. ⟨ Now respond:

---

(1) *Psalms* 37:39-40.

CONGREGATION AND _CHAZZAN_:

וְהוּא רַחוּם* יְכַפֵּר עָוֹן וְלֹא יַשְׁחִית,

‹‹ destroy; ‹ and ‹ of ‹ is ‹ the Merciful ‹ He,
    does not iniquity forgiving One,*

וְהִרְבָּה לְהָשִׁיב אַפּוֹ, וְלֹא יָעִיר כָּל חֲמָתוֹ.[1]

‹‹ His wrath. ‹ all ‹ arousing ‹ not ‹‹ His anger, ‹ He withdraws ‹ frequently

❖ יהוה הוֹשִׁיעָה, הַמֶּלֶךְ יַעֲנֵנוּ בְיוֹם קָרְאֵנוּ.[2]

‹‹ we call. ‹ on the day ‹ answer us ‹ May the King ‹‹ save! ‹ HASHEM,

**THE _CHAZZAN_ SUMMONS THE CONGREGATION TO JOIN IN THE FORTHCOMING PRAYERS,
BOWING AT בָּרְכוּ AND STRAIGHTENING UP AT 'ה.**

בָּרְכוּ* אֶת יהוה הַמְבֹרָךְ.

‹‹ the blessed One. ‹ HASHEM, ‹ Bless*

**THE CONGREGATION, FOLLOWED BY _CHAZZAN_, RESPONDS,
BOWING AT בָּרוּךְ AND STRAIGHTENING UP AT 'ה.**

בָּרוּךְ יהוה הַמְבֹרָךְ* לְעוֹלָם וָעֶד.

‹‹ and ever. ‹ for ever ‹ the blessed One,* ‹ HASHEM, ‹ Blessed is

---

(1) _Psalms_ 78:38. (2) 20:10.

וְהוּא רַחוּם ❧ — _He, the Merciful One._ The night represents darkness, judgment, and suffering. Therefore the custom developed to recite this verse that calls upon God's mercy. This particular verse is especially apt because it contains thirteen words, alluding to God's Thirteen Attributes of Mercy (_Tola'as Yaakov_).

בָּרְכוּ ❧ — _Bless. Borchu_ is recited only in the presence of a _minyan_, a quorum of ten adult males. The _chazzan_ summons the congregation to proclaim its blessing of God and to join in the forthcoming prayers. As the _Zohar_ puts it: All sacred acts require summoning.

With relation to God, the term _bless_ cannot mean that we add anything to His powers or possessions. Rather it constitutes our declaration that He is the _source_ of all blessing (_Kad HaKemach_). Furthermore, it represents our dedication to allow His will to be fulfilled by our obedience to His commandments. Thus, in a sense we _do_ confer something upon Him, for it is in our power to accomplish His goals for man (_R' Hirsch_). [See Overview for a discussion of these concepts.]

בָּרוּךְ ה' הַמְבֹרָךְ ... — _Blessed is HASHEM, the blessed One._ With or without our _human_ acknowledgment, God is constantly "blessed" by all aspects of Creation — from the spiritual beings above to the humblest pebble — through the fact that they function in accordance with His will (_Kad HaKemach; Kol Bo_).

The _chazzan_ must not let it appear as though he excludes himself from the obligation to bless God. Therefore, when the congregation has concluded its response, he repeats it (_Tur_).

בְּרְכוֹת קְרִיאַת שְׁמַע ❧ /
Blessings of the Shema

The nighttime Blessings of the _Shema_ are similar in theme to those of the morning, except that there are three in the morning and four in the evening. The total of seven is based on the verse (_Psalms_ 119:164): _Seven times a day I praise You_ (_Berachos_ 11a, _Rashi_). Of the evening blessings, the first describes God's control over nature, the seasons, and the cycles of light. The second blessing speaks of God's gift of the Torah, the very essence of Israel's survival. The third refers

ברכות קריאת שמע / BLESSINGS OF THE SHEMA

בָּרוּךְ אַתָּה* יהוה אֱלֹהֵינוּ מֶלֶךְ הָעוֹלָם, אֲשֶׁר
⟨ Who ⟪of the universe, ⟨ King ⟨ our God, ⟨ HASHEM, ⟨ are You,* ⟨ Blessed

בִּדְבָרוֹ* מַעֲרִיב עֲרָבִים, בְּחָכְמָה פּוֹתֵחַ שְׁעָרִים,*
⟨ gates,* ⟨ opens ⟨ with wisdom ⟪ evenings, ⟨ brings on ⟨ by His word*

וּבִתְבוּנָה מְשַׁנֶּה עִתִּים,* וּמַחֲלִיף אֶת הַזְּמַנִּים,
⟪ the seasons, ⟨ changes ⟪ periods,* ⟨ alters ⟨ with understanding

וּמְסַדֵּר אֶת הַכּוֹכָבִים בְּמִשְׁמְרוֹתֵיהֶם בָּרָקִיעַ
⟨ in the heavens ⟨ in their constellations ⟨ the stars ⟨ and orders

כִּרְצוֹנוֹ. בּוֹרֵא יוֹם וָלָיְלָה, גּוֹלֵל אוֹר מִפְּנֵי חֹשֶׁךְ
⟨ darkness ⟨ before ⟨ light ⟨ rolling away ⟨ and night, ⟨ day ⟨ He creates ⟪ as He wills.

וְחֹשֶׁךְ מִפְּנֵי אוֹר. וּמַעֲבִיר יוֹם וּמֵבִיא לָיְלָה,
⟪ night, ⟨ and brings ⟨ day ⟨ He removes ⟪ light. ⟨ before ⟨ and darkness

וּמַבְדִּיל בֵּין יוֹם וּבֵין לָיְלָה, יהוה צְבָאוֹת* שְׁמוֹ.
⟪ is His ⟨ Master ⟨— HASHEM, ⟪ night ⟨ and ⟨ day ⟨ between ⟨ and
Name. of Legions,* between separates

❖ אֵל חַי וְקַיָּם, תָּמִיד יִמְלוֹךְ עָלֵינוּ, לְעוֹלָם וָעֶד.
⟪ and ⟨ for ever ⟨ over us, ⟨ may ⟨ continually ⟪ and ⟨ the ⟨ God,
ever. He reign enduring, living

בָּרוּךְ אַתָּה יהוה, הַמַּעֲרִיב עֲרָבִים. (Cong. – אָמֵן.)
⟪ (Amen.) ⟪ evenings. ⟨ Who brings on ⟪ HASHEM, ⟨ are You, ⟨ Blessed

---

to the Exodus, but with emphasis on the future Redemption. The fourth, which the Talmud describes as an extension of the theme of redemption, stresses God's protection of His people from the terrors and dangers of night and slumber.

בָּרוּךְ אַתָּה... אֲשֶׁר בִּדְבָרוֹ — *Blessed are You... Who by His word.* The command of God created day just as it created night, for every moment of the day and night has a purpose in God's plan. This recognition of God's ever-present will is especially important at night, which represents the period of fear, failure, and exile (R' Hirsch).

פּוֹתֵחַ שְׁעָרִים — *Opens gates.* A figurative refer-

ence to the "gates" which "open" to release the light of the morning sun and "close" upon it in the evening — as if the sun were brought out at dawn and put to rest at dusk (*Iyun Tefillah*).

וּבִתְבוּנָה מְשַׁנֶּה עִתִּים — *With understanding alters periods.* With deep understanding of the needs of a particular time segment, God varies weather conditions from day to day and from hour to hour (*Siach Yitzchak*).

ה' צְבָאוֹת — *HASHEM, Master of Legions.* He takes the infinite number of forces and conditions that form the universe and harmonizes them to perform His will (R' Hirsch).

אַהֲבַת עוֹלָם*

אַהֲבַת עוֹלָם* בֵּית יִשְׂרָאֵל עַמְּךָ אָהָבְתָּ.
[With] a love « that is eternal,* « the « of Israel, « Your « have
Family people, You loved.

תּוֹרָה וּמִצְוֹת, חֻקִּים וּמִשְׁפָּטִים, אוֹתָנוּ לִמַּדְתָּ.
« Torah and commandments, « decrees « and ordinances « have You taught us.

עַל כֵּן יהוה אֱלֹהֵינוּ, בְּשָׁכְבֵנוּ וּבְקוּמֵנוּ נָשִׂיחַ
« Therefore, « HASHEM, « our God, « upon our « and upon our « we will
retiring arising, discuss

בְּחֻקֶּיךָ, וְנִשְׂמַח* בְּדִבְרֵי תַלְמוּד תּוֹרָתֶךָ,
« Your decrees, and we will « with « of the study « of Your
rejoice* the words Torah

וּבְמִצְוֹתֶיךָ לְעוֹלָם וָעֶד. ❖ כִּי הֵם חַיֵּינוּ, וְאֹרֶךְ
and with Your « For « they « are our life « and the
commandments length
for ever « and ever. « for ever

יָמֵינוּ,* וּבָהֶם נֶהְגֶּה יוֹמָם וָלָיְלָה. וְאַהֲבָתְךָ, אַל
of our « and about « day « we will « and night. « Your love « do not
days* them meditate

תָּסִיר מִמֶּנּוּ לְעוֹלָמִים. בָּרוּךְ אַתָּה יהוה, אוֹהֵב
remove « from us « forever. « Blessed « are You, « HASHEM, « Who loves

עַמּוֹ יִשְׂרָאֵל.
« His people « Israel.

אָמֵן.) –Cong.)
« (Amen.)

---

§אַהֲבַת עוֹלָם — *[With] a love that is eternal.* Like the blessing immediately before the morning *Shema*, this blessing is an ecstatic expression of gratitude to God for the gift of Torah. Only after acknowledging our dependence on, and love for, the Torah, can we go on to express our undivided loyalty and dedication to ה' אֶחָד, *HASHEM, the One and Only God,* Who gave us this most precious gift.

The blessing begins with an expression of an axiom of Jewish existence: God loves us. The fact that He chose to give us His Torah proves that it is the vehicle for our national fulfillment. Therefore we dedicate ourselves to study it — constantly, joyously, and devotedly *(Siach Yitzchak).*

וְנִשְׂמַח — *And we will rejoice.* Torah study must be seen not as a chore, but as a source of joy. A mourner, for example, is forbidden to study Torah except for tragic passages or relevant laws, because normal study would gladden him at a time when he is required to feel grief over his loss.

כִּי הֵם חַיֵּינוּ וְאֹרֶךְ יָמֵינוּ — *For they are our life and the length of our days.* The word life means different things to different people. The Torah teaches us that the only *true* life is one in the service of God, one that is dedicated to the study of Torah and the performance of *mitzvos.* When a person lives such a life, he is assured that a natural consequence of his efforts is אֹרֶךְ יָמִים, *lengthy days,* of eternal blessing and joy in the World to Come *(Or HaChaim).*

THE SHEMA / שמע

IMMEDIATELY BEFORE ITS RECITATION CONCENTRATE ON FULFILLING THE POSITIVE COMMANDMENT
OF RECITING THE *SHEMA* TWICE DAILY.
IT IS IMPORTANT TO ENUNCIATE EACH WORD CLEARLY AND NOT TO RUN WORDS TOGETHER.
FOR THIS REASON, VERTICAL LINES HAVE BEEN PLACED BETWEEN TWO WORDS THAT ARE NOT
SEPARATED BY A COMMA OR A DASH AND ARE APT TO BE SLURRED INTO ONE.

WHEN PRAYING WITHOUT A *MINYAN*, BEGIN WITH THE FOLLOWING THREE-WORD FORMULA:

אֵל מֶלֶךְ נֶאֱמָן.

《 Who is trustworthy. 〈 King 〈 God,

RECITE THE FIRST VERSE ALOUD, WITH THE RIGHT HAND COVERING THE EYES,
AND CONCENTRATE INTENSELY UPON ACCEPTING GOD'S ABSOLUTE SOVEREIGNTY.

שְׁמַע | יִשְׂרָאֵל, יְהוָה | אֱלֹהֵינוּ, יְהוָה | אֶחָד:¹

《 the One 〈 HASHEM 《 is our God, 〈 HASHEM 《 O Israel: 〈 Hear,
[and Only].　　　　is

IN AN UNDERTONE:

בָּרוּךְ שֵׁם כְּבוֹד מַלְכוּתוֹ לְעוֹלָם וָעֶד.²

《 and ever. 〈 for ever 〈 kingdom 〈 of His glorious 〈 is the Name 〈 Blessed

WHILE RECITING THE FIRST PARAGRAPH (*DEUTERONOMY 6:5-9*), CONCENTRATE ON
ACCEPTING THE COMMANDMENT TO LOVE GOD.

וְאָהַבְתָּ אֵת | יהוה | אֱלֹהֶיךָ, בְּכָל-לְבָבְךָ,

〈your heart, 〈 with all 〈 your God, 〈 HASHEM, 〈 You shall love

וּבְכָל-נַפְשְׁךָ, וּבְכָל-מְאֹדֶךָ: וְהָיוּ הַדְּבָרִים הָאֵלֶּה,

〈 — these matters 《 They 《 your 〈 and with 〈 your soul, 〈 with all
　　　　　　　　should be　resources.　　all

אֲשֶׁר | אָנֹכִי מְצַוְּךָ הַיּוֹם, עַל-לְבָבֶךָ: וְשִׁנַּנְתָּם

〈 Teach them 《 your heart. 〈 upon 《 today — 〈 command 〈 I 〈 that
　thoroughly　　　　　　　　　　　　　　　　you

---

(1) *Deuteronomy* 6:4. (2) See *Pesachim* 56a.

שְׁמַע / THE SHEMA ⊱

The recitation of the three paragraphs of
Shema is required by the Torah, and one must
have in mind that he is about to fulfill this
commandment. Although one should try to concentrate on the meaning of all three paragraphs,
one must concentrate at least on the meaning of
the first verse (שְׁמַע) and the second verse (בָּרוּךְ
שֵׁם) because the recitation of *Shema* represents
fulfillment of the paramount commandment
of acceptance of God's absolute sovereignty
(קַבָּלַת עוֹל מַלְכוּת שָׁמַיִם). By declaring that God is

One, Unique, and Indivisible, we subordinate
every facet of our personalities, possessions —
our very lives — to His will.

A summary of the laws of the *Shema* appears
in *Laws* §46-60. For a full commentary and Overview, see ArtScroll *Shema Yisrael* and pages
132-137 above. In the שְׁמַע we have included the
cantillation symbols (*trop*) for the convenience
of those who recite שְׁמַע in the manner it is read
from the Torah. Nevertheless, to enable those
unfamiliar with this notation to group the words
properly, commas have been inserted.

לְבָנֶיךָ, וְדִבַּרְתָּ בָּם בְּשִׁבְתְּךָ בְּבֵיתֶךָ, וּבְלֶכְתְּךָ
while you walk ⟨ in your home, ⟨ while you sit ⟨ of ⟨ and speak ⟨ to your
them children

בַדֶּרֶךְ, וּבְשָׁכְבְּךָ וּבְקוּמֶךָ: וּקְשַׁרְתָּם לְאוֹת ׀
as a sign ⟨ Bind them ⟪ and when ⟨ when you ⟨ on the way,
you arise. lie down,

עַל־יָדֶךָ, וְהָיוּ לְטֹטָפֹת בֵּין ׀ עֵינֶיךָ: וּכְתַבְתָּם ׀
And write them ⟪ your eyes. ⟨ between ⟨ tefillin ⟨ and they shall be ⟨ your arm ⟨ upon

עַל־מְזֻזוֹת בֵּיתֶךָ וּבִשְׁעָרֶיךָ:
⟪ and upon your gates. ⟨ of your house ⟨ the doorposts ⟨ on

WHILE RECITING THE SECOND PARAGRAPH (*DEUTERONOMY*** 11:13-21), CONCENTRATE ON
ACCEPTING ALL THE COMMANDMENTS AND ON THE CONCEPT OF REWARD AND PUNISHMENT.**

וְהָיָה, אִם־שָׁמֹעַ תִּשְׁמְעוּ אֶל־מִצְוֹתַי, אֲשֶׁר ׀
that ⟨ My commandments ⟨ to ⟨ you continually hearken ⟨ that if ⟨ And it will be

אָנֹכִי מְצַוֶּה ׀ אֶתְכֶם הַיּוֹם, לְאַהֲבָה אֶת־יהוה ׀
Hashem, ⟨ to love ⟪ today, ⟨ you ⟨ command ⟨ I

אֱלֹהֵיכֶם וּלְעָבְדוֹ, בְּכָל־לְבַבְכֶם וּבְכָל־נַפְשְׁכֶם:
⟪ your soul ⟨ and with all ⟨ your heart ⟨ with all ⟪ and to serve Him, ⟨ your God,

וְנָתַתִּי מְטַר־אַרְצְכֶם בְּעִתּוֹ, יוֹרֶה וּמַלְקוֹשׁ,
⟪ and the late ⟨ the ⟪ in its proper ⟨ for your land ⟨ rain ⟨ — then I
rain, early rain time, will provide

וְאָסַפְתָּ דְגָנֶךָ וְתִירֹשְׁךָ וְיִצְהָרֶךָ: וְנָתַתִּי ׀ עֵשֶׂב ׀
grass ⟨ I will ⟪ and your oil. ⟨ your wine, ⟨ your ⟨ that you
provide grain, may gather in

בְּשָׂדְךָ לִבְהֶמְתֶּךָ, וְאָכַלְתָּ וְשָׂבָעְתָּ: הִשָּׁמְרוּ לָכֶם
for ⟨ Beware ⟪ and be ⟨ and you ⟪ for your cattle, ⟨ in your field
yourselves satisfied. will eat

פֶּן־יִפְתֶּה לְבַבְכֶם, וְסַרְתֶּם וַעֲבַדְתֶּם ׀ אֱלֹהִים ׀
gods ⟨ and serve ⟨ and you turn astray ⟪ be your heart, ⟨ seduced ⟨ lest

אֲחֵרִים וְהִשְׁתַּחֲוִיתֶם לָהֶם: וְחָרָה ׀ אַף־יהוה
of ⟨ the ⟨ Then shall ⟪ to them. ⟨ and bow ⟨ of others
Hashem wrath blaze

בָּכֶם, וְעָצַר ׀ אֶת־הַשָּׁמַ֫יִם, וְלֹא־יִהְיֶ֫ה מָטָ֫ר,

<< rain, < so that there will not be < the heaven < He will restrain << against you.

וְהָ֣אֲדָמָה לֹא תִתֵּן אֶת־יְבוּלָ֫הּ, וַאֲבַדְתֶּם ׀ מְהֵרָ֫ה

< swiftly < And you will be banished << its produce. < will not yield < and the ground

מֵעַל֙ הָאָ֫רֶץ הַטֹּבָ֫ה ׀ אֲשֶׁר ׀ יהוה נֹתֵן לָכֶֽם:

<< you. < gives < Hashem < which < the good land < from upon

וְשַׂמְתֶּם֙ ׀ אֶת־דְּבָרַי ׀ אֵ֫לֶּה עַל־לְבַבְכֶם וְעַל־

< and upon < your heart < upon < these words of Mine < Place

נַפְשְׁכֶם, וּקְשַׁרְתֶּ֫ם ׀ אֹתָם֙ ׀ לְאוֹת֙ ׀ עַל־יֶדְכֶ֫ם,

<< your arm < upon < for a sign < them < bind << your soul;

וְהָי֣וּ לְטוֹטָפֹת֙ בֵּין ׀ עֵינֵיכֶ֫ם: וְלִמַּדְתֶּ֫ם ׀ אֹתָ֫ם ׀

< them < Teach << your eyes. < between < tefillin < and they shall be

אֶת־בְּנֵיכֶם לְדַבֵּר בָּם, בְּשִׁבְתְּךָ֙ בְּבֵיתֶ֫ךָ, וּבְלֶכְתְּךָ֣

< while you walk < in your home, < while you sit << them, < to discuss < to your children,

בַדֶּ֫רֶךְ, וּֽבְשָׁכְבְּךָ֖ וּבְקוּמֶֽךָ: וּכְתַבְתָּ֫ם ׀ עַל־מְזוּז֖וֹת

< the doorposts < on < And write << and when < when you << on the

 them   you arise.   lie down,   way,

בֵּיתֶ֫ךָ וּבִשְׁעָרֶֽיךָ: לְמַ֫עַן ׀ יִרְבּ֫וּ ׀ יְמֵיכֶם֙ ׀ וִימֵ֫י

< and the days < your days < to prolong < In order << and upon your gates. < of your house

בְּנֵיכֶם עַל הָֽאֲדָמָ֫ה ׀ אֲשֶׁר ׀ נִשְׁבַּ֫ע ׀ יהוה

< Hashem swore < that < the land < upon < of your children

לַאֲבֹֽתֵיכֶם לָתֵת לָהֶם, כִּימֵי הַשָּׁמַ֫יִם ׀ עַל־הָאָֽרֶץ:

<< the earth. < on < of the heaven < like the days << them, < to give < to your ancestors

Numbers 15:37-41

וַיֹּ֫אמֶר ׀ יהוה ׀ אֶל־מֹשֶׁה ׀ לֵּאמֹ֫ר: דַּבֵּ֫ר ׀

< Speak << saying: < Moses, < to < Hashem said

אֶל־בְּנֵ֫י ׀ יִשְׂרָאֵל֙ ׀ וְאָמַרְתָּ֫ אֲלֵהֶ֫ם, וְעָשׂ֫וּ לָהֶם

< for them- < that they < to them < and say < of Israel < the < to

 selves   are to make   Children

צִיצִת עַל־כַּנְפֵי בִגְדֵיהֶם לְדֹרֹתָם, וְנָתְנוּ ‏ עַל־
< upon   < And they << throughout   < of their   < the   < on < tzitzis
          are to place their generations. garments, corners

צִיצִת הַכָּנָף פְּתִיל תְּכֵלֶת: וְהָיָה לָכֶם לְצִיצִת,
<< tzitzis, < for you < And it shall << of techeiles. < a thread < of the < the tzitzis
                        constitute   corner

וּרְאִיתֶם ‏ אֹתוֹ ‏ וּזְכַרְתֶּם ‏ אֶת־כָּל־מִצְוֹת ‏
< all the commandments < and remember < it   < that you may see

יהוה וַעֲשִׂיתֶם ‏ אֹתָם, וְלֹא־תָתוּרוּ ‏ אַחֲרֵי
< after   < explore < and not << them,   < and perform < of HASHEM

לְבַבְכֶם וְאַחֲרֵי ‏ עֵינֵיכֶם אֲשֶׁר־אַתֶּם זֹנִים ‏
< stray < you < which < your eyes   < and after < your heart

אַחֲרֵיהֶם: לְמַעַן תִּזְכְּרוּ וַעֲשִׂיתֶם ‏ אֶת־כָּל־
< all   < and perform < you may remember < so that << after them;

מִצְוֹתָי, וִהְיִיתֶם קְדֹשִׁים לֵאלֹהֵיכֶם:
<< to your God.   < holy   < and be < My commandments,

CONCENTRATE ON FULFILLING THE COMMANDMENT TO REMEMBER THE EXODUS FROM EGYPT.

אֲנִי יהוה ‏ אֱלֹהֵיכֶם אֲשֶׁר הוֹצֵאתִי ‏ אֶתְכֶם ‏
< you   < has removed < Who   < your God,   < HASHEM, < I am

מֵאֶרֶץ מִצְרַיִם לִהְיוֹת לָכֶם לֵאלֹהִים, אֲנִי ‏
< I am << a God;   < to you < to be   < of Egypt < from the land

יהוה ‏ אֱלֹהֵיכֶם: אֱמֶת —
<< — It is true... << your God,   < HASHEM

CHAZZAN REPEATS:

יהוה אֱלֹהֵיכֶם אֱמֶת,*
<< is true,* < your God, < HASHEM,

אֱמֶת ⁊ — *True.* Although this word belongs to the next paragraph, it is appended to the conclusion of the previous one.

One may not interrupt between the last words of the *Shema* and אֱמֶת, so that we declare, as did the prophet [*Jeremiah* 10:10], וַה' אֱלֹהִים אֱמֶת, HASHEM, God, is true (*Berachos* 14a).

וֶאֱמוּנָה* כָּל זֹאת, וְקַיָּם עָלֵינוּ, כִּי הוּא

⟨ He ⟨ that ⟨⟨ for us ⟨ and it is firmly ⟨ this, ⟨ is all ⟨ and faithful*
established

יהוה אֱלֹהֵינוּ וְאֵין זוּלָתוֹ, וַאֲנַחְנוּ יִשְׂרָאֵל עַמּוֹ.

⟨⟨ His ⟨ Israel, ⟨ and we are ⟨⟨ but Him, ⟨ and there ⟨⟨ our God, ⟨ is HASHEM
people. is none

הַפּוֹדֵנוּ מִיַּד מְלָכִים, מַלְכֵּנוּ הַגּוֹאֲלֵנוּ מִכַּף כָּל

⟨ of all ⟨ from ⟨ Who delivers us ⟨ our King ⟨⟨ of kings, ⟨ from the ⟨ He is the One
the hand power Who redeems us

הֶעָרִיצִים. הָאֵל הַנִּפְרָע לָנוּ מִצָּרֵינוּ,* וְהַמְשַׁלֵּם

⟨ and Who ⟨⟨ from our foes* ⟨ for us ⟨ Who exacts ⟨ He is ⟨⟨ the cruel tyrants.
repays vengeance the God

גְּמוּל לְכָל אֹיְבֵי נַפְשֵׁנוּ.* הָעֹשֶׂה גְדֹלוֹת עַד אֵין

⟨ that are ⟨ great deeds ⟨ Who ⟨⟨ of our soul;* ⟨ the ⟨ upon ⟨ just
beyond performs enemies all retribution

חֵקֶר, נִסִּים וְנִפְלָאוֹת עַד אֵין מִסְפָּר.¹ הַשָּׂם נַפְשֵׁנוּ

⟨ our soul ⟨ Who set ⟨⟨ number. ⟨ that are ⟨ and wonders ⟨ miracles ⟨⟨ compre-
beyond hension,

---

(1) *Job* 9:10.

❖ אֱמֶת וֶאֱמוּנָה — *True and faithful.* The morning
blessing of אֱמֶת וְיַצִּיב, *True and certain*, concentrates on God's kindness in having redeemed us
from Egypt, while אֱמֶת וֶאֱמוּנָה, *True and faithful*,
recited at night, symbolizes exile and stresses our
faith that God will redeem us from this exile just
as He did at the Exodus (*Berachos* 12a; *Rashi* and
Tosafos).

Alternatively, the faithfulness of the nights
refers to man's confidence that God will return
his soul in the morning, refreshed and rested after
a night of sleep (*Talmidei R' Yonah*; *Tos.*,
Berachos 12a; *Rashi* in *Pardes*).

Chiddushei HaRim explains that אֱמֶת, *truth*,
refers to something that we know to be true,
either because our senses tell us so or because we
have conclusive evidence. אֱמוּנָה, *faith*, refers to
something that we *believe*, even though we have
no proof that it happened. We know the Exodus
to be *true*, because it was witnessed by millions of
people, but the future Redemption is not yet an

accomplished fact. Nevertheless we have a perfect *faith* that God will bring it about, as He
promised through the prophets. This is just as
real for us as our *faith* in another phenomenon
that has not yet taken place — that we will wake
up from our sleep tomorrow morning.

מִצָּרֵינוּ . . . אֹיְבֵי נַפְשֵׁנוּ — *From our foes . . . enemies
of our soul.* The term *foe* [צָר] refers to one who
actually causes harm, while *enemy* [אוֹיֵב] is one
who hates and encourages harm, even though he
has not done anything actively (*Malbim* to *Isaiah*
59:18). Later a third kind of enemy is mentioned:
שׂוֹנֵא, *one who hates.* A שׂוֹנֵא does nothing against
the object of his hate; he merely rejoices at his
suffering and downfall (*Siach Yitzchak*).

The expression *enemies of our soul* implies
that their enmity is directed against Israel's spiritual essence. They do not desire the physical
destruction of the Jewish people, but they cannot
abide Israel's loyalty to the Torah (*Siach
Yitzchak*).

בַּחַיִּים,* וְלֹא נָתַן לַמּוֹט רַגְלֵנוּ.¹ הַמַּדְרִיכֵנוּ עַל

‹ upon ‹　　Who led us　《 our foot. ‹ to falter ‹ allow ‹ and did not 《　in life*

בָּמוֹת אוֹיְבֵינוּ, וַיָּרֶם קַרְנֵנוּ עַל כָּל שׂנְאֵינוּ.

《 who hate us; ‹　all　‹ above ‹ our pride ‹ and raised 《 of our enemies ‹ the heights

הָעֹשֶׂה לָנוּ נִסִּים וּנְקָמָה בְּפַרְעֹה, אוֹתוֹת

‹　signs　　《 upon Pharaoh; ‹ and vengeance ‹ miracles ‹ for us ‹ Who wrought

וּמוֹפְתִים בְּאַדְמַת בְּנֵי חָם. הַמַּכֶּה בְעֶבְרָתוֹ כָּל

‹ all ‹　in His anger ‹ Who struck 《 of ‹ of the ‹ in the land ‹ and wonders
　　　　　　　　　　　　　　　　　　　Ham; offspring

בְּכוֹרֵי מִצְרָיִם, וַיּוֹצֵא אֶת עַמּוֹ יִשְׂרָאֵל מִתּוֹכָם

‹ from their midst ‹　Israel　‹ His people ‹ and removed 《 of Egypt, ‹ the firstborn

לְחֵרוּת עוֹלָם. הַמַּעֲבִיר בָּנָיו בֵּין גִּזְרֵי יַם סוּף,

《 of ‹ of the ‹ the ‹ through ‹ His ‹ Who brought 《 everlasting; ‹ to freedom
Reeds,　Sea　split parts　　　children

אֶת רוֹדְפֵיהֶם וְאֶת שׂנְאֵיהֶם בִּתְהוֹמוֹת טִבַּע.

《 He sank. ‹ into the depths ‹　　and those　　　‹　　[while] those
　　　　　　　　　　　　　　　　who hated them,　　　　　who pursued them

וְרָאוּ בָנָיו גְּבוּרָתוֹ, שִׁבְּחוּ וְהוֹדוּ לִשְׁמוֹ. ❖ וּמַלְכוּתוֹ

‹　And His　《 to His ‹ and gave ‹ they ‹ His ‹ When His children ‹ And His
　Kingship　　Name.　thanks　praised　power,　perceived　　Kingship

בְּרָצוֹן קִבְּלוּ עֲלֵיהֶם. מֹשֶׁה וּבְנֵי יִשְׂרָאֵל לְךָ

‹ to ‹　of Israel　‹ and the ‹ Moses 《　upon ‹　they ‹ willingly
You　　　　　　Children　　themselves;　accepted

עָנוּ שִׁירָה בְּשִׂמְחָה רַבָּה וְאָמְרוּ כֻלָּם:

《 unanimously: ‹ and said ‹　　with great gladness　‹ in song ‹ exclaimed

מִי כָמֹכָה בָּאֵלִם יהוה, מִי כָּמֹכָה נֶאְדָּר

‹　mighty　‹ is like You, ‹ Who 《 Hashem! ‹　among the ‹ is like You ‹ Who
　　　　　　　　　　　　　　　　　heavenly powers,

---

(1) *Psalms* 66:9.

הַשָּׁם נַפְשֵׁנוּ בַּחַיִּים —*Who set our soul in life.* A reference to the night in Egypt when all firstborn non-Jewish males died, but Jewish souls were protected (*Abudraham*). This also implies God's protection from the murderous designs of our enemies in all generations (*Siach Yitzchak*).

בְּקֹדֶשׁ, נוֹרָא תְהִלֹּת,* עֹשֵׂה פֶלֶא.[1]

《 wonders! 〈 doing 《《 [beyond] praise,* 〈 awesome 《《 in holiness,

מַלְכוּתְךָ רָאוּ בָנֶיךָ* בּוֹקֵעַ יָם לִפְנֵי מֹשֶׁה,

《《 Moses; 〈 before 〈 the 〈 as You 《《 did Your children 〈 Your Majesty
      Sea split   behold,*

זֶה אֵלִי[2] עָנוּ וְאָמְרוּ:

《《 then 《《 they 《《 my God! 〈 This is
they said: exclaimed;

יהוה יִמְלֹךְ לְעֹלָם וָעֶד.[3]

《《 and ever! 〈 for ever 〈 shall reign 〈 HASHEM

וְנֶאֱמַר: כִּי פָדָה יהוה אֶת יַעֲקֹב,* וּגְאָלוֹ מִיַּד

〈 from 〈 and delivered 〈 Jacob* 〈 HASHEM has 〈 For 〈 And it is
the hand him   redeemed   further said:

חָזָק מִמֶּנּוּ. בָּרוּךְ אַתָּה יהוה, גָּאַל יִשְׂרָאֵל.[4]

《《 Israel. 〈 Who 《《 HASHEM, 〈 are You, 〈 Blessed 《《 than he. 〈 of one
   redeemed   mightier

אָמֵן.) – Cong.)

《《 (Amen.)

הַשְׁכִּיבֵנוּ* יהוה אֱלֹהֵינוּ לְשָׁלוֹם, וְהַעֲמִידֵנוּ

〈 and raise us up, 《《 in peace, 〈 our God, 〈 HASHEM, 〈 Lay us down to sleep,*

---

(1) Exodus 15:11. (2) 15:2. (3) 15:18. (4) Jeremiah 31:10.

נוֹרָא תְהִלֹּת — *Awesome [beyond] praise*. We are too terrified to attempt a complete assessment of His greatness, because whatever we say is insufficient (*Rashi*).

Rambam comments that it is impossible for people to praise God adequately; the only way to laud Him is by simply recounting His awe-inspiring deeds. Thus he would render this phrase: [God's] *awesomeness constitutes His praises*.

מַלְכוּתְךָ רָאוּ בָנֶיךָ — *Your Majesty did Your children behold*. As the Sages taught: A maidservant saw more [of God's majesty and holiness] at the Sea than did even Ezekiel in his prophecies! (*Etz Yosef*).

כִּי פָדָה ה' אֶת יַעֲקֹב — *For HASHEM has redeemed Jacob*. Jacob/Israel was the Patriarch who solidified the Jewish destiny. It was he who faced more dangerous, hostile situations than did either Abraham or Isaac (*Acharis Shalom*).

This blessing should be said with intense joy in the confident knowledge that God is our past and future Redeemer (*Yesod V'Shoresh HaAvodah*).

הַשְׁכִּיבֵנוּ — *Lay us down to sleep*. The Talmud (*Berachos* 4a) describes this blessing as an extension of the previous blessing of redemption [גְאוּלָה אֲרִיכְתָּא]. Whereas the theme of the earlier blessing was God's redemption of Israel from Egypt [and the allusion to the future redemption], this one describes Him as our Savior from

מַלְכֵּנוּ לְחַיִּים טוֹבִים וּלְשָׁלוֹם. וּפְרוֹשׂ עָלֵינוּ
‹ over us ‹ Spread ‹‹ and for peace. ‹ that is good ‹ for life ‹ our King,

סֻכַּת שְׁלוֹמֶךָ, וְתַקְּנֵנוּ בְּעֵצָה טוֹבָה* מִלְּפָנֶיךָ,
‹‹ from before You, ‹ that is good* ‹ with counsel ‹ Set us aright ‹‹ of Your peace. ‹ the shelter

וְהוֹשִׁיעֵנוּ מְהֵרָה לְמַעַן שְׁמֶךָ. וְהָגֵן בַּעֲדֵנוּ,
‹‹ us; ‹ Shield ‹‹ of Your Name. ‹ for the sake ‹ speedily ‹ and save us

וְהָסֵר מֵעָלֵינוּ אוֹיֵב, דֶּבֶר, וְחֶרֶב, וְרָעָב, וְיָגוֹן,
‹‹ and woe; ‹ famine, ‹ sword, ‹ plague, ‹ foe, ‹ from us ‹ remove

וְהָסֵר שָׂטָן מִלְּפָנֵינוּ וּמֵאַחֲרֵינוּ,* וּבְצֵל כְּנָפֶיךָ*
‹ of Your wings* ‹ and in the shadow ‹ and from behind us,* ‹ from before us ‹ spiritual impediment ‹ and remove

תַּסְתִּירֵנוּ,¹ כִּי אֵל שׁוֹמְרֵנוּ וּמַצִּילֵנוּ אָתָּה, כִּי
‹ for ‹‹ are You; ‹ and rescues us ‹ Who protects ‹ God ‹ For ‹‹ shelter us.

אֵל מֶלֶךְ חַנּוּן וְרַחוּם אָתָּה.² וּשְׁמוֹר צֵאתֵנוּ
‹ our going ‹ Safeguard ‹‹ are You. ‹ and Compassionate ‹ Gracious ‹ King, ‹ God,

וּבוֹאֵנוּ, לְחַיִּים וּלְשָׁלוֹם מֵעַתָּה וְעַד עוֹלָם.³
‹‹ eternity. ‹ and for all ‹ from now ‹ and for peace ‹ for life ‹ and our coming

בָּרוּךְ אַתָּה יהוה, שׁוֹמֵר עַמּוֹ יִשְׂרָאֵל לָעַד.
‹‹ forever. ‹ Israel ‹ His people ‹ Who safeguards ‹‹ Hashem, ‹ are You, ‹ Blessed

(אָמֵן. – Cong.)
‹‹ (Amen.)

---

(1) Cf. *Psalms* 17:8. (2) Cf. *Nehemiah* 9:31. (3) Cf. *Psalms* 121:8.

the dangers and afflictions associated with the terrors of night, literally and figuratively (*Seder HaYom*).

וְתַקְּנֵנוּ בְּעֵצָה טוֹבָה — *Set us aright with counsel that is good.* Help us plan well at night for the activity of the next day, and let the relaxation of the night give us a clearer perspective for the deliberations of the day (R' Hirsch).

מִלְּפָנֵינוּ וּמֵאַחֲרֵינוּ — *From before us and from behind us.* Protect us from spiritual harm in the future [*before us*] and from the consequences of what has already occurred [*behind us*] (R' Hirsch).

וּבְצֵל כְּנָפֶיךָ — *And in the shadow of Your wings.* *Psalms* 91:4 likens God's protection to the wings of a mother bird sheltering her young.

FOR INSTANCES WHEN THE FOLLOWING PRAYER (UNTIL HALF-*KADDISH*) IS OMITTED, SEE COMMENTARY.

בָּרוּךְ יהוה לְעוֹלָם,* אָמֵן וְאָמֵן.¹ בָּרוּךְ יהוה

⟨ is Hashem ⟨ Blessed ⟨⟨ and Amen. ⟨ Amen ⟨⟨ forever,* ⟨ is Hashem ⟨ Blessed

מִצִּיּוֹן, שֹׁכֵן יְרוּשָׁלָיִם, הַלְלוּיָהּ.² בָּרוּךְ יהוה

⟨ is Hashem, ⟨ Blessed ⟨⟨ Halleluyah! ⟨⟨ in Jerusalem, ⟨ He Who dwells ⟨⟨ from Zion,

אֱלֹהִים אֱלֹהֵי יִשְׂרָאֵל, עֹשֵׂה נִפְלָאוֹת לְבַדּוֹ.

⟨⟨ by Himself. ⟨ wondrous things ⟨ Who does ⟨⟨ of Israel, ⟨ the God ⟨ God,

וּבָרוּךְ שֵׁם כְּבוֹדוֹ לְעוֹלָם, וְיִמָּלֵא כְבוֹדוֹ

⟨ may His glory ⟨ and fill ⟨⟨ forever; ⟨ of His glory ⟨ is the Name ⟨ Blessed

אֶת כָּל הָאָרֶץ, אָמֵן וְאָמֵן.³ יְהִי כְבוֹד יהוה

⟨ of Hashem ⟨ the glory ⟨ May ⟨⟨ and Amen. ⟨ Amen ⟨⟨ the earth. ⟨ all

לְעוֹלָם, יִשְׂמַח יהוה בְּמַעֲשָׂיו.⁴ יְהִי שֵׁם יהוה

⟨ of Hashem ⟨ the Name ⟨ Let ⟨⟨ in His works. ⟨ let Hashem rejoice ⟨⟨ endure forever;

מְבֹרָךְ מֵעַתָּה וְעַד עוֹלָם.⁵ כִּי לֹא יִטֹּשׁ יהוה

⟨ Hashem will not forsake ⟨ For ⟨⟨ eternity. ⟨ until ⟨ from this time ⟨ be blessed

אֶת עַמּוֹ בַּעֲבוּר שְׁמוֹ הַגָּדוֹל, כִּי הוֹאִיל יהוה

⟨ Hashem has vowed ⟨ for ⟨⟨ that is great, ⟨ of His Name, ⟨ for the sake ⟨⟨ His people

לַעֲשׂוֹת אֶתְכֶם לוֹ לְעָם.⁶ וַיַּרְא כָּל הָעָם

⟨ the people ⟨ did all ⟨ See ⟨⟨ a people. ⟨ for Him ⟨ you ⟨ to make

(1) *Psalms* 89:53. (2) 135:21. (3) 72:18-19. (4) 104:31. (5) 113:2. (6) *I Samuel* 12:22.

➳ בָּרוּךְ ה' לְעוֹלָם — *Blessed is Hashem forever.* The following collection of Scriptural verses was introduced during the Geonic era. At that time most people gathered in the fields for prayers (apparently on the way from their farms to their homes). In order to shorten the service so that it could be completed before dark, this collection of verses was substituted for *Shemoneh Esrei*, which would be recited later by each individual in the safety of his home. Another version has it that these verses were added in order to allow latecomers time to catch up to the congregation. Whichever the reason, it was retained even after the practice of praying in the fields was discontinued.

Since they took the place of *Shemoneh Esrei*

in the communal service, the verses of בָּרוּךְ ה' were selected so as to contain the name Hashem nineteen times, paralleling the blessings of *Shemoneh Esrei*. The theme of this prayer is redemption, because it follows the *Shema* blessings of redemption.

Since בָּרוּךְ ה' was instituted originally for the benefit of working people, it was never recited on days when work is forbidden. Therefore it is always omitted from the *Maariv* of the Sabbath and Festivals. While most congregations recite these verses on all other evenings, there are some that also omit it from the *Maariv* immediately after the Sabbath and Festivals and during Chol HaMoed. According to some customs, it is omitted entirely nowadays.

וַיִּפְּלוּ עַל פְּנֵיהֶם, וַיֹּאמְרוּ, יהוה הוּא הָאֱלֹהִים,

‹‹ is the God! ‹ — He ‹ Hashem ‹‹ and they said, ‹‹ their faces ‹ on ‹ and they fell

יהוה הוּא הָאֱלֹהִים.[1] וְהָיָה יהוה לְמֶלֶךְ עַל כָּל

‹ all ‹ over ‹ be King ‹ Hashem ‹ Then will ‹‹ is the God! ‹ — He ‹ Hashem

הָאָרֶץ, בַּיּוֹם הַהוּא יִהְיֶה יהוה אֶחָד וּשְׁמוֹ אֶחָד.[2]

‹‹ be One. ‹ and His Name ‹ be One ‹ Hashem ‹ shall ‹ — on that day ‹‹ the world

יְהִי חַסְדְּךָ יהוה עָלֵינוּ, כַּאֲשֶׁר יִחַלְנוּ לָךְ.[3]

‹‹ You. ‹ we awaited ‹ just as ‹‹ be upon us, ‹ Hashem, ‹ Your kindness, ‹ May

הוֹשִׁיעֵנוּ יהוה אֱלֹהֵינוּ, וְקַבְּצֵנוּ מִן הַגּוֹיִם,

‹‹ among the ‹ from ‹ and gather us ‹ our God, ‹ Hashem, ‹ Save us

nations,

לְהוֹדוֹת לְשֵׁם קָדְשֶׁךָ, לְהִשְׁתַּבֵּחַ בִּתְהִלָּתֶךָ.[4] כָּל

‹ All ‹‹ in Your praise! ‹ and to glory ‹ of Your Holiness ‹ the Name ‹ to thank

גּוֹיִם אֲשֶׁר עָשִׂיתָ יָבוֹאוּ וְיִשְׁתַּחֲווּ לְפָנֶיךָ אֲדֹנָי,

‹‹ O Lord, ‹ before You, ‹ and bow down ‹ will come ‹ You have made ‹ that ‹ the nations

וִיכַבְּדוּ לִשְׁמֶךָ. כִּי גָדוֹל אַתָּה וְעֹשֵׂה נִפְלָאוֹת,

‹‹ wonders, ‹ and You work ‹ are You ‹ great ‹ For ‹‹ to Your Name. ‹ and they will
give glory

אַתָּה אֱלֹהִים לְבַדֶּךָ.[5] וַאֲנַחְנוּ עַמְּךָ וְצֹאן

‹ and the sheep ‹ Your people ‹‹ As for us, ‹‹ alone. ‹ O God ‹ You

מַרְעִיתֶךָ, נוֹדֶה לְּךָ לְעוֹלָם, לְדוֹר וָדֹר נְסַפֵּר

‹ we shall ‹ after ‹ for ‹‹ forever; ‹ You ‹ we shall ‹‹ of Your pasture,
relate   generation generation   thank

תְּהִלָּתֶךָ.[6] בָּרוּךְ יהוה בַּיּוֹם. בָּרוּךְ יהוה בַּלָּיְלָה.

‹‹ by night; ‹ is Hashem ‹ blessed ‹‹ by day; ‹ is Hashem ‹ Blessed ‹‹ Your praise.

בָּרוּךְ יהוה בְּשָׁכְבֵנוּ. בָּרוּךְ יהוה בְּקוּמֵנוּ.

‹‹ when we arise. ‹ is Hashem ‹ Blessed ‹‹ when we retire; ‹ is Hashem ‹ blessed

כִּי בְיָדְךָ נַפְשׁוֹת הַחַיִּים וְהַמֵּתִים. אֲשֶׁר

‹ That ‹‹ and of the dead. ‹ of the living ‹ are the souls ‹ in Your hand ‹ For

(1) *I Kings* 18:39. (2) *Zechariah* 14:9. (3) *Psalms* 33:22. (4) 106:47. (5) 86:9-10. (6) 79:13.

בְּיָדוֹ נֶפֶשׁ כָּל חָי, וְרוּחַ כָּל בְּשַׂר אִישׁ.¹ בְּיָדְךָ

‹ In Your hand ‹ mankind. ‹ of all ‹ and the spirit ‹ the living ‹ of all ‹ is the soul ‹ in His hand

אַפְקִיד רוּחִי, פָּדִיתָה אוֹתִי, יהוה אֵל אֱמֶת.²

« of truth. ‹ God ‹ O Hashem, ‹ me, ‹ You redeemed « my spirit; ‹ I shall entrust

אֱלֹהֵינוּ שֶׁבַּשָּׁמַיִם, יַחֵד שְׁמְךָ, וְקַיֵּם מַלְכוּתְךָ

‹ Your kingdom ‹ establish « to Your Name; ‹ bring unity « Who is in heaven, ‹ Our God,

תָּמִיד, וּמְלוֹךְ עָלֵינוּ לְעוֹלָם וָעֶד.

« and ever. ‹ for ever ‹ over us ‹ and reign « forever

יִרְאוּ עֵינֵינוּ וְיִשְׂמַח לִבֵּנוּ וְתָגֵל נַפְשֵׁנוּ

« may our soul ‹ and exult « may our heart, ‹ rejoice « may our eyes, ‹ See

בִּישׁוּעָתְךָ בֶּאֱמֶת, בֶּאֱמֹר לְצִיּוֹן מָלַךְ מָלַךְ אֱלֹהָיִךְ³

« has Your God . ‹ Reigned « to Zion, ‹ when it is told « in truth, ‹ in Your salvation

יהוה מֶלֶךְ,⁴ יהוה מָלָךְ,⁵ יהוה יִמְלוֹךְ לְעוֹלָם

‹ for ever ‹ shall reign ‹ Hashem « has reigned, ‹ Hashem « reigns, ‹ Hashem

וָעֶד.❖ ⁶ כִּי הַמַּלְכוּת שֶׁלְּךָ הִיא, וּלְעוֹלְמֵי עַד

‹ and ever ‹ and for ever « is Yours ‹ the kingdom ‹ For « and ever.

תִּמְלוֹךְ בְּכָבוֹד, כִּי אֵין לָנוּ מֶלֶךְ אֶלָּא אָתָּה.

« You. ‹ except for ‹ King ‹ we have no ‹ for « in glory, ‹ You will reign

בָּרוּךְ אַתָּה יהוה, הַמֶּלֶךְ בִּכְבוֹדוֹ תָּמִיד יִמְלוֹךְ

‹ will reign ‹ always ‹ Who in His glory ‹ the King « Hashem, ‹ are You, ‹ Blessed

עָלֵינוּ לְעוֹלָם וָעֶד, וְעַל כָּל מַעֲשָׂיו. (אָמֵן. – Cong.)

« (Amen.) « His creation. ‹ all ‹ and over ‹ and ever, ‹ for ever ‹ over us

THE *CHAZZAN* RECITES חֲצִי קַדִּיש, HALF-*KADDISH*.

יִתְגַּדַּל וְיִתְקַדַּשׁ שְׁמֵהּ רַבָּא. (אָמֵן. – Cong.) בְּעָלְמָא דִּי בְרָא

‹ He ‹ that ‹ in the world « (Amen.) « that is ‹ may His ‹ and be ‹ Grow exalted
created ‹ great! — ‹ Name ‹ sanctified

כִרְעוּתֵהּ, וְיַמְלִיךְ מַלְכוּתֵהּ, וְיַצְמַח פֻּרְקָנֵהּ וִיקָרֵב מְשִׁיחֵהּ.

« His Messiah, ‹ and bring near ‹ His salvation, ‹ and cause to sprout ‹ to His kingship, ‹ and may He give reign « according to His will,

(1) *Job* 12:10. (2) *Psalms* 31:6. (3) Cf. *Isaiah* 52:7. (4) *Psalms* 10:16. (5) 93:1 et al. (6) *Exodus* 15:18.

(.אָמֵן –) Cong. בְּחַיֵּיכוֹן וּבְיוֹמֵיכוֹן וּבְחַיֵּי דְכָל בֵּית יִשְׂרָאֵל,
《 of Israel, 〈 Family 〈 of the 〈 and in the 〈 and in 〈 in your 《 (Amen.)
entire   lifetimes   your days,   lifetimes

בַּעֲגָלָא וּבִזְמַן קָרִיב. וְאִמְרוּ: אָמֵן.
《 Amen. 〈 Now 《 that 〈 and at 〈 swiftly
respond: comes soon. a time

CONGREGATION RESPONDS:

אָמֵן. יְהֵא שְׁמֵהּ רַבָּא מְבָרַךְ לְעָלַם וּלְעָלְמֵי עָלְמַיָּא.
《 and for all eternity. 〈 forever 〈 be blessed 〈 that is great 〈 His Name 〈 May 《 Amen.

CHAZZAN CONTINUES:

יְהֵא שְׁמֵהּ רַבָּא מְבָרַךְ לְעָלַם וּלְעָלְמֵי עָלְמַיָּא. יִתְבָּרַךְ
〈 Blessed, 《   and for all eternity. 〈 forever 〈 be blessed 〈 that is great 〈 His Name 〈 May

וְיִשְׁתַּבַּח וְיִתְפָּאַר וְיִתְרוֹמַם וְיִתְנַשֵּׂא וְיִתְהַדָּר וְיִתְעַלֶּה
〈 elevated, 〈 honored, 〈 upraised, 〈 exalted, 〈 glorified, 〈 praised,

וְיִתְהַלָּל שְׁמֵהּ דְּקֻדְשָׁא בְּרִיךְ הוּא (.בְּרִיךְ הוּא –) Cong. –
《 is He) 〈 (Blessed 《 is He 〈 Blessed 〈 of the Holy One, 〈 be the Name 〈 and lauded

ROSH HASHANAH TO YOM KIPPUR SUBSTITUTE:

°לְעֵלָּא מִן כָּל [°לְעֵלָּא (וּ)לְעֵלָּא מִכָּל] בִּרְכָתָא
〈 blessing 〈 any 〈 exceedingly beyond 〈 any 〈 beyond

וְשִׁירָתָא, תֻּשְׁבְּחָתָא וְנֶחֱמָתָא דַּאֲמִירָן בְּעָלְמָא.
《 in the world. 〈 that are uttered 〈 and consolation 〈 praise 《 and song,

וְאִמְרוּ: אָמֵן. (.אָמֵן –) Cong.
《 (Amen.) 《 Amen. 〈 Now respond:

❧ SHEMONEH ESREI / עמידה – שמונה עשרה ❧

TAKE THREE STEPS BACKWARD, THEN THREE STEPS FORWARD. REMAIN STANDING WITH FEET
TOGETHER WHILE RECITING *SHEMONEH ESREI*. RECITE IT WITH QUIET DEVOTION AND WITHOUT
ANY INTERRUPTION. ALTHOUGH IT SHOULD NOT BE AUDIBLE TO OTHERS, ONE MUST PRAY LOUDLY
ENOUGH TO HEAR HIMSELF. SEE *LAWS* §44-45; 61-95 FOR A BRIEF SUMMARY OF ITS LAWS INCLUDING
HOW TO RECTIFY THE OMISSION OF PHRASES THAT ARE ADDED AT PARTICULAR TIMES OF THE YEAR.

אֲדֹנָי שְׂפָתַי תִּפְתָּח, וּפִי יַגִּיד תְּהִלָּתֶךָ.[1]
《 Your praise. 〈 may 〈 that my 《 open, 〈 my lips 〈 O Lord,
declare mouth

PATRIARCHS / אבות

BEND THE KNEES AT בָּרוּךְ, *BLESSED;* BOW AT אַתָּה, *YOU;* STRAIGHTEN UP AT ה', *HASHEM.*

בָּרוּךְ אַתָּה יהוה אֱלֹהֵינוּ וֵאלֹהֵי אֲבוֹתֵינוּ,
《of our forefathers, 〈 and the God 〈 our God 〈 HASHEM, 〈 are You, 〈 Blessed

---

(1) *Psalms* 51:17.

אֱלֹהֵי אַבְרָהָם, אֱלֹהֵי יִצְחָק, וֵאלֹהֵי יַעֲקֹב,

《 of Jacob; 〈 and God 〈 of Isaac, 〈 God 〈 of Abraham, 〈 God

הָאֵל הַגָּדוֹל הַגִּבּוֹר וְהַנּוֹרָא, אֵל עֶלְיוֹן, גּוֹמֵל

〈 Who 《 the 〈 God, 《 and awesome; 〈 mighty, 〈 [Who is] 〈 God
bestows Most High,
great,

חֲסָדִים טוֹבִים וְקוֹנֵה הַכֹּל, וְזוֹכֵר חַסְדֵי אָבוֹת,

《 of the 〈 the 〈 Who 《 everything, 〈 and 〈 [that are] 〈 kindnesses
Patriarchs, kindnesses recalls creates beneficent

וּמֵבִיא גוֹאֵל לִבְנֵי בְנֵיהֶם, לְמַעַן שְׁמוֹ בְּאַהֲבָה.

《 with love. 〈 of His 〈 for the 《 of their 〈 to the 〈 a 〈 and brings
Name, sake children, children Redeemer

BEND THE KNEES AT בָּרוּךְ, *BLESSED*; BOW AT אַתָּה, *YOU*; STRAIGHTEN UP AT ה', *HASHEM*.

מֶלֶךְ עוֹזֵר וּמוֹשִׁיעַ וּמָגֵן. בָּרוּךְ אַתָּה יהוה,

《 HASHEM, 〈 are You, 〈 Blessed 《 and Shield. 〈 Savior, 〈 Helper, 〈 O King,

מָגֵן אַבְרָהָם.

《 of Abraham. 〈 Shield

GOD'S MIGHT / גְּבוּרוֹת

אַתָּה גִּבּוֹר לְעוֹלָם אֲדֹנָי, מְחַיֶּה מֵתִים

〈 of the dead 〈 the Revivifier 《 O Lord, 〈 eternally, 〈 mighty 〈 You are

אַתָּה, רַב לְהוֹשִׁיעַ.

《 able to save, 〈 abundantly 《 are You;

BETWEEN SHEMINI ATZERES AND PESACH:	FROM PESACH THROUGH SUCCOS:
מַשִּׁיב הָרוּחַ וּמוֹרִיד הַגֶּשֶׁם [נ"א הַגָּשֶׁם].	מוֹרִיד הַטָּל
《 the rain. 〈 and 〈 Who makes brings down the wind blow	《 the 〈 Who dew. brings down

───── [IF FORGOTTEN, SEE *LAWS* §68-74.] ─────

מְכַלְכֵּל חַיִּים בְּחֶסֶד, מְחַיֵּה מֵתִים בְּרַחֲמִים

‹ with mercy ‹ the dead ‹ Who ≪ with ‹ the living ‹ Who sustains
revivifies kindness,

רַבִּים, סוֹמֵךְ נוֹפְלִים, וְרוֹפֵא חוֹלִים, וּמַתִּיר

‹ Who ≪ the sick, ‹ Who heals ≪ the fallen, ‹ Who ≪ abundant,
releases supports

אֲסוּרִים, וּמְקַיֵּם אֱמוּנָתוֹ לִישֵׁנֵי עָפָר. מִי

‹ Who ≪ in the ‹ to those ‹ His faith ‹ and Who ≪ the confined,
dust. asleep maintains

כָמוֹךָ בַּעַל גְּבוּרוֹת, וּמִי דוֹמֶה לָּךְ, מֶלֶךְ

‹ O King ≪ to You, ‹ is ‹ and ≪ of mighty ‹ O ‹ is like
comparable who deeds, Master You,

מֵמִית וּמְחַיֶּה וּמַצְמִיחַ יְשׁוּעָה.

≪ salvation! ‹ and makes ‹ and restores ‹ Who causes
sprout life death

FROM ROSH HASHANAH TO YOM KIPPUR ADD:

מִי כָמוֹךָ אָב הָרַחֲמָן, זוֹכֵר יְצוּרָיו לְחַיִּים בְּרַחֲמִים.

≪ with mercy! ≪ for life, ‹ His ‹ Who ≪ Who is ‹ Father ‹ is like ‹ Who
creatures recalls Merciful, You,

[IF FORGOTTEN, DO NOT REPEAT SHEMONEH ESREI. SEE LAWS §61.]

וְנֶאֱמָן אַתָּה לְהַחֲיוֹת מֵתִים. בָּרוּךְ אַתָּה

‹ are You, ‹ Blessed ≪ the dead. ‹ to revivify ‹ are You ‹ And faithful

יהוה, מְחַיֵּה הַמֵּתִים.

≪ the dead. ‹ Who revivifies ≪ HASHEM,

HOLINESS OF GOD'S NAME / קְדוּשַׁת הַשֵּׁם

אַתָּה קָדוֹשׁ וְשִׁמְךָ קָדוֹשׁ, וּקְדוֹשִׁים בְּכָל יוֹם

‹ day ‹ every ‹ and holy ones ≪ is holy, ‹ and Your ‹ are holy ‹ You
Name

יְהַלְלוּךָ סֶּלָה, כִּי אֵל מֶלֶךְ גָּדוֹל וְקָדוֹשׁ אָתָּה.

≪ are You. ‹ and holy ‹ great ‹ a King, ≪ O God, ‹ for, ≪ forever, ‹ praise You,

בָּרוּךְ אַתָּה יהוה, °הָאֵל הַקָּדוֹשׁ.

《 Who is holy. ⟨ the God 《 Hashem, ⟨ are You, ⟨ Blessed

FROM ROSH HASHANAH TO YOM KIPPUR SUBSTITUTE:

°הַמֶּלֶךְ הַקָּדוֹשׁ.

《 Who is holy. ⟨ the King

[IF FORGOTTEN, REPEAT SHEMONEH ESREI. SEE LAWS §62-63.]

INSIGHT / בינה

אַתָּה חוֹנֵן לְאָדָם דַּעַת, וּמְלַמֵּד לֶאֱנוֹשׁ בִּינָה.

《 insight. ⟨ to a [frail] ⟨ and teach 《 with ⟨ man ⟨ graciously ⟨ You
                    mortal   knowledge   endow

**AT THE CONCLUSION OF THE SABBATH AND OF FESTIVALS, EVEN FROM YOM TOV
TO CHOL CHAMOED, ADD [IF FORGOTTEN, SEE LAWS §66]:**

אַתָּה חוֹנַנְתָּנוּ לְמַדַּע תּוֹרָתֶךָ, וַתְּלַמְּדֵנוּ לַעֲשׂוֹת

⟨ to perform ⟨ and You have ⟨ Your ⟨ [with the intelligence ⟨ have graciously ⟨ You
             taught us   Torah,   needed] to study   endowed us

חֻקֵּי רְצוֹנֶךָ. וַתַּבְדֵּל יהוה אֱלֹהֵינוּ בֵּין קֹדֶשׁ לְחוֹל,

《 and the ⟨ the ⟨ between 《 our God, ⟨ Hashem, 《 You have 《 of Your ⟨ the
  secular, sacred   distinguished,   will.   decrees

בֵּין אוֹר לְחוֹשֶׁךְ, בֵּין יִשְׂרָאֵל לָעַמִּים, בֵּין יוֹם הַשְּׁבִיעִי

⟨ the Seventh ⟨ between 《 and the ⟨ Israel ⟨ between 《 and ⟨ light ⟨ between
  Day   peoples,   darkness,

לְשֵׁשֶׁת יְמֵי הַמַּעֲשֶׂה. אָבִינוּ מַלְכֵּנוּ, הָחֵל עָלֵינוּ הַיָּמִים

⟨ the days ⟨ for us ⟨ begin ⟨ our King, ⟨ Our Father, 《 of work. ⟨ days ⟨ and the six

הַבָּאִים לִקְרָאתֵנוּ לְשָׁלוֹם חֲשׂוּכִים מִכָּל חֵטְא

《 sin, ⟨ of all ⟨ devoid 《 for peace, ⟨ that are approaching us

וּמְנֻקִּים מִכָּל עָוֹן וּמְדֻבָּקִים בְּיִרְאָתֶךָ. וְ . . .

《 And . . . 《 to fearing You. ⟨ and devoted ⟨ iniquity ⟨ of all ⟨ cleansed

חָנֵּנוּ מֵאִתְּךָ חָכְמָה בִּינָה וָדָעַת. בָּרוּךְ אַתָּה

⟨ are You, ⟨ Blessed 《 and ⟨ insight, ⟨ [with] ⟨ from ⟨ Endow us
           knowledge.   wisdom,   Yourself graciously

יהוה, חוֹנֵן הַדָּעַת.

《 of wisdom. ⟨ gracious 《 Hashem,
              Giver

REPENTANCE / תשובה

הֲשִׁיבֵֽנוּ אָבִֽינוּ לְתוֹרָתֶֽךָ, וְקָרְבֵֽנוּ מַלְכֵּֽנוּ
‹ our King, ‹ and bring ‹‹ to Your Torah, ‹ our Father, ‹ Bring us back,
us near,

לַעֲבוֹדָתֶֽךָ, וְהַחֲזִירֵֽנוּ בִּתְשׁוּבָה שְׁלֵמָה לְפָנֶֽיךָ.
‹‹ before ‹ in complete repentance, ‹ and influence us ‹‹ to Your service,
You.   to return

בָּרוּךְ אַתָּה יהוה, הָרוֹצֶה בִּתְשׁוּבָה.
‹‹ repentance. ‹ Who desires ‹‹ Hashem, ‹ are You, ‹ Blessed

FORGIVENESS / סליחה

STRIKE THE LEFT SIDE OF THE CHEST WITH THE RIGHT FIST
WHILE RECITING THE WORDS חָטָֽאנוּ, *SINNED,* AND פָשָֽׁעְנוּ, *WILLFULLY SINNED.*

סְלַח לָֽנוּ אָבִֽינוּ כִּי חָטָֽאנוּ, מְחַל לָֽנוּ מַלְכֵּֽנוּ
‹ our King, ‹ us, ‹ pardon ‹‹ we have sinned; ‹ for ‹ our Father, ‹ us, ‹ Forgive

כִּי פָשָֽׁעְנוּ, כִּי אֵל טוֹב וְסַלָּח אָֽתָּה. בָּרוּךְ
‹ Blessed ‹‹ are You. ‹ and ‹ Who is ‹ the God ‹ for ‹‹ we have ‹ for
forgiving   good   willfully sinned;

אַתָּה יהוה, חַנּוּן הַמַּרְבֶּה לִסְלֽוֹחַ.
‹‹ forgives. ‹ Who ‹ the gracious ‹‹ Hashem, ‹ are You,
abundantly   One

REDEMPTION / גאולה

רְאֵה נָא בְעָנְיֵֽנוּ, וְרִיבָה רִיבֵֽנוּ, וּגְאָלֵֽנוּ גְּאֻלָּה[1]
‹ with a ‹ and ‹‹ our ‹ champion ‹ our ‹ please, ‹ Behold,
redemption redeem us   cause,   affliction,

שְׁלֵמָה מְהֵרָה לְמַֽעַן שְׁמֶֽךָ, כִּי אֵל גּוֹאֵל חָזָק
‹ Who is ‹ a ‹ O ‹ for, ‹‹ Your ‹ for the ‹ speedily ‹ that is
powerful Redeemer God,   Name,   sake of   complete,

אָֽתָּה. בָּרוּךְ אַתָּה יהוה, גּוֹאֵל יִשְׂרָאֵל.
‹‹ of Israel. ‹ Redeemer ‹‹ Hashem, ‹ are You, ‹ Blessed ‹‹ are You.

---

(1) Cf. *Psalms* 119:153-154.

HEALTH AND HEALING / רְפוּאָה

רְפָאֵנוּ יהוה וְנֵרָפֵא, הוֹשִׁיעֵנוּ וְנִוָּשֵׁעָה, כִּי

⟨ for ⟩ ⟨ — then we will be saved, ⟩ ⟨ save us ⟩ ⟨ — then we will be healed; ⟩ ⟨ HASHEM ⟩ Heal us,

תְהִלָּתֵנוּ אָתָּה,¹ וְהַעֲלֵה

⟨ Bring ⟩ ⟨ is You. ⟨ the One we praise

RECITE ONE OF THE ALTERNATE VERSIONS:

רְפוּאָה שְׁלֵמָה ⎸ אֲרוּכָה וּמַרְפֵּא לְכָל תַּחֲלוּאֵינוּ

⟨ that is complete ⟩ ⟨ healing ⟩ ⎸ ⟨ of our illnesses, ⟨ to all ⟨ and healing ⟨ cure

לְכָל מַכּוֹתֵינוּ, ⎸ וּלְכָל מַכְאוֹבֵינוּ וּלְכָל מַכּוֹתֵינוּ,

⟨⟨ our ailments, ⟨ for all ⎸ ⟨⟨ of our ailments, ⟨ and to all ⟨ of our pains, ⟨ and to all

°°כִּי אֵל מֶלֶךְ רוֹפֵא נֶאֱמָן וְרַחֲמָן אָתָּה. בָּרוּךְ

⟨ Blessed ⟨⟨ are You. ⟨ and compassionate ⟨ Who is faithful ⟨ Healer ⟨ [and] ⟨ O King, ⟨ God, ⟨ for

אַתָּה יהוה, רוֹפֵא חוֹלֵי עַמּוֹ יִשְׂרָאֵל.

⟨⟨ Israel. ⟨ of His people ⟨ the sick ⟨ Who heals ⟨⟨ HASHEM, ⟨ are You,

---

°°AT THIS POINT ONE MAY INSERT A PRAYER FOR ONE WHO IS ILL:

יְהִי רָצוֹן מִלְּפָנֶיךָ, יהוה אֱלֹהַי וֵאלֹהֵי אֲבוֹתַי, שֶׁתִּשְׁלַח מְהֵרָה

⟨ quickly ⟨ that You send ⟨⟨ of my forefathers, ⟨ and the God ⟨ my God ⟨ HASHEM, ⟨⟨ before You, ⟨ the will ⟨ May it be

רְפוּאָה שְׁלֵמָה מִן הַשָּׁמַיִם, רְפוּאַת הַנֶּפֶשׁ וּרְפוּאַת הַגּוּף

⟨⟨ of the body ⟨ and a healing ⟨ of the spirit ⟨ a healing ⟨⟨ heaven, ⟨ from ⟨⟨ which is ⟨ a healing complete,

FOR A FEMALE / FOR A MALE

שְׁאָר בְּתוֹךְ (MOTHER'S NAME) בֶּן / בַּת (SICK ONE'S NAME) לַחוֹלֶה / לַחוֹלָה

⟨ the other ⟨ among ⟨ daughter of / son of ⟨ ⟨ to the sick one

חוֹלֵי יִשְׂרָאֵל.

⟨⟨ of Israel. ⟨ sick ones

CONTINUE . . . כִּי אֵל (ABOVE)

---

(1) Cf. *Jeremiah* 17:14.

YEAR OF PROSPERITY / בּרכת השנים

וְתֵן בְּרָכָה, *GIVE A BLESSING,* IS RECITED FROM CHOL HAMOED PESACH THROUGH *MINCHAH* OF DECEMBER 4TH (OR 5TH IN THE YEAR BEFORE A CIVIL LEAP YEAR); וְתֵן טַל וּמָטָר לִבְרָכָה, *GIVE DEW AND RAIN FOR A BLESSING,* IS RECITED FROM *MAARIV* OF DECEMBER 4TH (OR 5TH) UNTIL PESACH. [IF THE WRONG PHRASE WAS RECITED AND FOR THE PRACTICE IN ERETZ YISRAEL, SEE *LAWS* §75-83.]

בָּרֵךְ עָלֵינוּ יהוה אֱלֹהֵינוּ
〈 our God — 〈 — O 《 on our 〈 Bless
HASHEM,   behalf

אֶת הַשָּׁנָה הַזֹּאת וְאֶת כָּל
〈 all 〈 and 《 this year

מִינֵי תְבוּאָתָהּ לְטוֹבָה, וְתֵן
〈 and 《 for goodness; 〈 of its crops 〈 of the kinds
give

WINTER	SUMMER
טַל וּמָטָר לִבְרָכָה	בְּרָכָה
〈 for a blessing 〈 and rain 〈 dew	〈 a blessing

עַל פְּנֵי הָאֲדָמָה, וְשַׂבְּעֵנוּ
〈 and satisfy us 《 of the earth; 〈 the face 〈 on

מִטּוּבָהּ, וּבָרֵךְ שְׁנָתֵנוּ
〈 our year 〈 and bless 《 from its bounty;

כַּשָּׁנִים הַטּוֹבוֹת לִבְרָכָה,
《 for blessing. 〈 that were good, 〈 like the years

כִּי אֵל טוֹב וּמֵטִיב אַתָּה,
《 are You, 〈 and 〈 good 〈 O God, 〈 For
beneficent

וּמְבָרֵךְ הַשָּׁנִים. בָּרוּךְ אַתָּה
〈 are You, 〈 Blessed 《 the years. 〈 the One
Who blesses

יהוה, מְבָרֵךְ הַשָּׁנִים.
《 the years. 〈 Who blesses 《 HASHEM,

SOME CONGREGATIONS SUBSTITUTE THE PARAGRAPH בָּרְכֵנוּ FOR בָּרֵךְ עָלֵינוּ, FROM PESACH THROUGH DECEMBER 4TH (OR 5TH).

בָּרְכֵנוּ, יהוה אֱלֹהֵינוּ,
〈 our God — 〈 — O 《 Bless us,
HASHEM,

בְּכָל מַעֲשֵׂה יָדֵינוּ,
《 of our hands, 〈 the work 〈 in all

וּבָרֵךְ שְׁנָתֵנוּ בְּטַלְלֵי
〈 with the 〈 our year 〈 and bless
dews

רָצוֹן בְּרָכָה וּנְדָבָה.
《 and 〈 blessing, 〈 of favor,
generosity.

וּתְהִי אַחֲרִיתָהּ חַיִּים
〈 for life, 〈 its end be 〈 And may

וְשֶׂבַע וְשָׁלוֹם, כַּשָּׁנִים
〈 like the 《 and 〈 satisfaction,
years peace,

הַטּוֹבוֹת לִבְרָכָה. כִּי
《 For 《 — for a 《 that were
blessing. good

אֵל טוֹב וּמֵטִיב אַתָּה
《 are 〈 and 〈 good 〈 O
You, beneficent God,

וּמְבָרֵךְ הַשָּׁנִים. בָּרוּךְ
《 Blessed 《 the years. 〈 the One
Who blesses

אַתָּה יהוה, מְבָרֵךְ
〈 Who blesses 《 HASHEM, 〈 are You,

הַשָּׁנִים.
《 the years.

INGATHERING OF EXILES / קיבוץ גליות

תְּקַע בְּשׁוֹפָר גָּדוֹל[1] לְחֵרוּתֵנוּ, וְשָׂא נֵס[2] לְקַבֵּץ

< to gather < a banner < raise 《 for our freedom, < the great *shofar* < Sound

גָּלֻיּוֹתֵינוּ, וְקַבְּצֵנוּ יַחַד מְהֵרָה מֵאַרְבַּע כַּנְפוֹת

< corners < from the four < speedily, < together, < and gather us 《 our exiles,

הָאָרֶץ לְאַרְצֵנוּ.[3] בָּרוּךְ אַתָּה יהוה, מְקַבֵּץ נִדְחֵי

< the < Who 《 Hashem, < are You, < Blessed 《 to our Land. < of the earth
　dispersed　gathers in

עַמּוֹ יִשְׂרָאֵל.

《 Israel. < of His people

RESTORATION OF JUSTICE / דין

הָשִׁיבָה שׁוֹפְטֵינוּ כְּבָרִאשׁוֹנָה, וְיוֹעֲצֵינוּ

< and our < as [they were] < our judges < Restore
　counselors　in earliest times

כְּבַתְּחִלָּה,[4] וְהָסֵר מִמֶּנּוּ יָגוֹן וַאֲנָחָה, וּמְלוֹךְ

< and reign 《 and groan; < sorrow < from us < remove 《 as at the beginning;

עָלֵינוּ מְהֵרָה אַתָּה יהוה לְבַדְּךָ בְּחֶסֶד

< with kindness 《 alone — < Hashem, < — You, 《 speedily < over us,

וּבְרַחֲמִים, וְצַדְּקֵנוּ בְּצֶדֶק וּבְמִשְׁפָּט. בָּרוּךְ אַתָּה

< are You, < Blessed 《 and through < through < and justify 《 and compassion,
　　judgment.　righteousness　us

יהוה, °מֶלֶךְ אוֹהֵב צְדָקָה וּמִשְׁפָּט.

《 and judgment. < righteousness < Who loves < the King 《 Hashem,

FROM ROSH HASHANAH TO YOM KIPPUR SUBSTITUTE:

°הַמֶּלֶךְ הַמִּשְׁפָּט.

《 of Judgment. < the King

[IF FORGOTTEN, DO NOT REPEAT SHEMONEH ESREI. SEE LAWS §64.]

AGAINST HERETICS / ברכת המינים

וְלַמַּלְשִׁינִים אַל תְּהִי תִקְוָה, וְכָל הַמִּינִים

< the heretics < and all 《 hope; < let there not be < And for slanderers

---

(1) Cf. *Isaiah* 27:13. (2) Cf. 11:12, 18:3, 62:10; see 66:20. (3) Cf. 11:12. (4) Cf. 1:26.

כְּרֶגַע יֹאבֵדוּ, וְכָל אוֹיְבֵי עַמְּךָ מְהֵרָה יִכָּרֵתוּ,

in an instant ‹ may they perish; ‹‹ and all ‹ the ‹ enemies ‹ of Your people ‹ speedily ‹ may they be cut down. ‹‹

וְהַזֵּדִים מְהֵרָה תְעַקֵּר וּתְשַׁבֵּר וּתְמַגֵּר וּתְכַלֵּם

The willful sinners ‹‹ — may You speedily ‹ uproot, ‹ smash, ‹ cast down; ‹‹ destroy them, ‹

וּתְשַׁפִּילֵם וְתַכְנִיעֵם בִּמְהֵרָה בְיָמֵינוּ. בָּרוּךְ

pull them down, ‹ and humble them ‹ speedily ‹ in our days. ‹‹ Blessed ‹

אַתָּה יהוה, שׁוֹבֵר אוֹיְבִים וּמַכְנִיעַ זֵדִים.

are You, ‹ HASHEM, ‹ Who breaks ‹‹ enemies ‹ and humbles ‹ willful sinners. ‹‹

THE RIGHTEOUS / צדיקים

עַל הַצַּדִּיקִים וְעַל הַחֲסִידִים, וְעַל זִקְנֵי

On ‹ the righteous, ‹ on ‹‹ the devout, ‹ on ‹‹ the elders ‹

שְׁאֵרִית עַמְּךָ בֵּית יִשְׂרָאֵל, וְעַל פְּלֵיטַת בֵּית

of the remainder ‹ of Your people, ‹ the Family ‹‹ of Israel, ‹ on ‹ the remnant ‹ of the academy

סוֹפְרֵיהֶם, וְעַל גֵּרֵי הַצֶּדֶק וְעָלֵינוּ, יֶהֱמוּ נָא

of their scholars, ‹‹ on ‹ the ‹ converts who are righteous ‹ and on ourselves ‹‹ — please may aroused be ‹

רַחֲמֶיךָ יהוה אֱלֹהֵינוּ, וְתֵן שָׂכָר טוֹב לְכָל

Your compassion, ‹ HASHEM, ‹‹ our God, ‹ and give ‹ a reward ‹ which is good ‹ to all ‹

הַבּוֹטְחִים בְּשִׁמְךָ בֶּאֱמֶת, וְשִׂים חֶלְקֵנוּ עִמָּהֶם,

who believe ‹ in Your Name ‹ in sincerity. ‹‹ Put ‹ our lot ‹ with them, ‹‹

וּלְעוֹלָם לֹא נֵבוֹשׁ כִּי בְךָ בָּטָחְנוּ.¹ וְעַל חַסְדְּךָ

and forever ‹ we ‹ will not feel ‹ for ‹ in You ‹ we trust, ‹‹ and ‹ upon ‹ Your kindness ‹

הַגָּדוֹל בֶּאֱמֶת (וּבְתָמִים) נִשְׁעָנּוּ. בָּרוּךְ אַתָּה

that is great, ‹‹ in sincerity ‹ (and in perfection) ‹ do we rely. ‹‹ Blessed ‹ are You, ‹

יהוה, מִשְׁעָן וּמִבְטָח לַצַּדִּיקִים.

HASHEM, ‹‹ Mainstay ‹ and Assurance ‹ of the righteous. ‹‹

(1) Cf. *Psalms* 25:2.

REBUILDING JERUSALEM / בנין ירושלים

וְלִירוּשָׁלַיִם עִירְךָ בְּרַחֲמִים תָּשׁוּב, וְתִשְׁכּוֹן

‹ and may ‹‹ may You ‹ in compassion ‹ Your City, ‹ And to Jerusalem,
You rest　　return,

בְּתוֹכָהּ כַּאֲשֶׁר דִּבַּרְתָּ, וּבְנֵה אוֹתָהּ בְּקָרוֹב

‹ soon ‹ it ‹ May You rebuild ‹‹ You have spoken. ‹ as ‹ within it,

בְּיָמֵינוּ בִּנְיַן עוֹלָם, וְכִסֵּא דָוִד עַבְדְּךָ מְהֵרָה

‹ speedily, ‹ Your ‹ of David, ‹ and the ‹‹ that is ‹ as a ‹ in our days
　　　servant,　　throne　　eternal,　structure

לְתוֹכָהּ תָּכִין. בָּרוּךְ אַתָּה יהוה, בּוֹנֵה יְרוּשָׁלָיִם.

‹‹ of Jerusalem. ‹ Builder ‹‹ HASHEM, ‹ are You, ‹ Blessed ‹‹ may You ‹ within it
　　　　　　　　　　　　　　　　　　　　　　establish.

DAVIDIC REIGN / מלכות בית דוד

אֶת צֶמַח דָּוִד עַבְדְּךָ מְהֵרָה תַצְמִיחַ, וְקַרְנוֹ

‹ and his ‹‹ may You cause ‹ speedily, ‹‹ Your ‹ of David, ‹ offspring ‹ The
pride　to flourish,　　　　　　servant,

תָּרוּם בִּישׁוּעָתֶךָ, כִּי לִישׁוּעָתְךָ קִוִּינוּ כָּל הַיּוֹם

‹ all day long ‹ we hope ‹ for Your ‹ because ‹‹ through Your ‹ may You
　　　　　　　salvation　　　　　salvation,　exalt

(וּמְצַפִּים לִישׁוּעָה). בָּרוּךְ אַתָּה יהוה, מַצְמִיחַ

‹ Who causes ‹‹ HASHEM, ‹ are You, ‹ Blessed ‹‹ for salvation). ‹ (and await eagerly
to flourish

קֶרֶן יְשׁוּעָה.

‹‹ of salvation. ‹ the pride

ACCEPTANCE OF PRAYER / קבלת תפלה

אָב הָרַחֲמָן שְׁמַע קוֹלֵנוּ, יהוה אֱלֹהֵינוּ

‹ our God, ‹ HASHEM, ‹‹ our voice, ‹ hear ‹ Who is merciful, ‹ Father

חוּס וְרַחֵם עָלֵינוּ, וְקַבֵּל בְּרַחֲמִים וּבְרָצוֹן

‹ and with ‹ with ‹ and ‹‹ on us, ‹ and have ‹ have
favor　compassion　accept　　　compassion　pity

אֶת תְּפִלָּתֵנוּ, כִּי אֵל שׁוֹמֵעַ תְּפִלּוֹת וְתַחֲנוּנִים

‹ and supplications ‹ prayers ‹ Who hears ‹ God ‹ for ‹‹ our prayer,

אָתָּה. וּמִלְּפָנֶיךָ מַלְכֵּנוּ, רֵיקָם אַל תְּשִׁיבֵנוּ,

《 turn us away. 〈 do not 〈 empty- 《 our King, 〈 From before 《 are You.
handed   Yourself,

°° חָנֵּנוּ וַעֲנֵנוּ וּשְׁמַע תְּפִלָּתֵנוּ,

《 our prayer, 〈 and hear 〈 answer 〈 Be gracious
us,   with us,

**°°ONE MAY INSERT THE FOLLOWING PERSONAL PRAYER FOR FORGIVENESS
AT THIS POINT:**

אָנָּא יהוה, חָטָאתִי עָוִיתִי וּפָשַׁעְתִּי לְפָנֶיךָ, מִיּוֹם הֱיוֹתִי

〈 I have 〈 from 《 before 〈 and willfully 〈 been 〈 I have 〈 HASHEM, 〈 Please,
existed   the day   You,   sinned   iniquitous,   sinned,

עַל הָאֲדָמָה עַד הַיּוֹם הַזֶּה (וּבִפְרָט בַּחֵטְא . . .). אָנָּא

〈Please, 《 with the sin of . . . 〈 and especially 《 this very day 〈 until 〈 earth 〈 on

יהוה, עֲשֵׂה לְמַעַן שִׁמְךָ הַגָּדוֹל, וּתְכַפֶּר לִי עַל חֲטָאַי

〈 my inad- 〈 for 〈 to 〈 and grant 《 which is 〈 of Your 〈 for the 〈 act 〈 HASHEM,
vertent sins,   me   atonement   great   Name   sake

וַעֲוֹנַי וּפְשָׁעַי שֶׁחָטָאתִי וְשֶׁעָוִיתִי וְשֶׁפָּשַׁעְתִּי לְפָנֶיךָ,

《 before 〈 and sinned 〈 been 〈 [through which] 〈 and my 〈 my in-
You,   willfully   iniquitous,   I have sinned,   willful sins   iquities,

מִנְּעוּרַי עַד הַיּוֹם הַזֶּה. וּתְמַלֵּא כָּל הַשֵּׁמוֹת שֶׁפָּגַמְתִּי

〈 that I have 〈 the [Holy] 〈 all 〈 And make 《 this very day. 〈 until 〈 from
blemished   Names   whole   my youth

בְּשִׁמְךָ הַגָּדוֹל.

CONTINUE . . . כִּי אַתָּה (P. 431)

《 which is 〈 within
great.   Your Name

**°°ONE MAY INSERT THE FOLLOWING PERSONAL PRAYER FOR LIVELIHOOD
AT THIS POINT:**

אַתָּה הוּא יהוה הָאֱלֹהִים, הַזָּן וּמְפַרְנֵס וּמְכַלְכֵּל

《 and 〈 sustains, 〈 Who 〈 the God 〈 HASHEM, 〈 Who are 〈 It is You
supports,   nourishes,

מִקַּרְנֵי רְאֵמִים עַד בֵּיצֵי כִנִּים. הַטְרִיפֵנִי לֶחֶם חֻקִּי,¹ וְהַמְצֵא

〈 provide 《 allotted 〈 with the 〈 Supply me 《 of lice. 〈 the 〈 to 〈 of re'eimim 〈 from the
to me;   bread   eggs   horns

לִי וּלְכָל בְּנֵי בֵיתִי מְזוֹנוֹתַי קֹדֶם שֶׁאֶצְטָרֵךְ לָהֶם, בְּנַחַת

〈 in 《 for it; 〈 I have need 〈 before 〈 my food, 《 of my 〈 members 〈 and 〈 for
contentment   household,   for all   me

---

(1) *Proverbs* 30:8.

וְלֹא בְצַעַר, בְּהֶתֵּר וְלֹא בְאִסּוּר, בְּכָבוֹד וְלֹא בְּבִזָּיוֹן,

in disgrace, but not / in honor / in a forbidden manner, / but not / in a permissible manner / in pain, / but not

לְחַיִּים וּלְשָׁלוֹם, מִשֶּׁפַע בְּרָכָה וְהַצְלָחָה, וּמִשֶּׁפַע בְּרָכָה

of the spring / and from the flow / and success / of / from the blessing / flow / and for peace; / for life

עֶלְיוֹנָה, כְּדֵי שֶׁאוּכַל לַעֲשׂוֹת רְצוֹנֶךָ וְלַעֲסוֹק בְּתוֹרָתֶךָ

in Your Torah / and engage / Your will / to do / I be enabled / so that / On High,

וּלְקַיֵּם מִצְוֹתֶיךָ. וְאַל תַּצְרִיכֵנִי לִידֵי מַתְּנַת בָּשָׂר וָדָם. וִיְקֻיַּם

and may there be fulfilled / and / of / of the gifts / make me / Do / Your com- / and fulfill / blood; / flesh / of the hands / needful / not / mandments.

בִּי מִקְרָא שֶׁכָּתוּב: פּוֹתֵחַ אֶת יָדֶךָ, וּמַשְׂבִּיעַ לְכָל חַי

living thing / every / and satisfy / Your hand, / You open / that states, / the verse / in me

רָצוֹן. וְכָתוּב: הַשְׁלֵךְ עַל יהוה יְהָבְךָ וְהוּא יְכַלְכְּלֶךָ.²

will sustain you. / and He / Your / HASHEM / upon / Cast / and that / [with its] / states, / desire,

CONTINUE ... כִּי אַתָּה (BELOW)

כִּי אַתָּה שׁוֹמֵעַ תְּפִלַּת כָּל פֶּה, עַמְּךָ יִשְׂרָאֵל

Israel / [the prayer] of Your people / mouth, / of every / the prayer / hear / You / for

בְּרַחֲמִים. בָּרוּךְ אַתָּה יהוה, שׁוֹמֵעַ תְּפִלָּה.

prayer. / Who hears / HASHEM, / are You, / Blessed / with compassion.

TEMPLE SERVICE / עבודה

רְצֵה יהוה אֱלֹהֵינוּ בְּעַמְּךָ יִשְׂרָאֵל, וְלִתְפִלָּתָם

and toward their prayer / Israel, / toward / our God, / HASHEM, / Be favorable,

שְׁעֵה, וְהָשֵׁב אֶת הָעֲבוֹדָה לִדְבִיר בֵּיתֶךָ. וְאִשֵּׁי

The fire-offerings / of Your Temple. / to the Holy of Holies / the service / and restore / turn,

(1) *Psalms* 145:16. (2) 55:23.

יִשְׂרָאֵל וּתְפִלָּתָם מְהֵרָה בְּאַהֲבָה תְקַבֵּל בְּרָצוֹן,

favorably, ⟨ accept ⟨ with love ⟨ speedily, ⟨ and their prayer, ⟨ of Israel

וּתְהִי לְרָצוֹן תָּמִיד עֲבוֹדַת יִשְׂרָאֵל עַמֶּךָ.

Your people. ⟨ of Israel ⟨ the service ⟨ always ⟨ to Your favor ⟨ and may it be

---

ON ROSH CHODESH AND CHOL HAMOED ADD THE FOLLOWING.
[IF FORGOTTEN, REPEAT SHEMONEH ESREI EXCEPT AT MAARIV OF ROSH CHODESH. SEE LAWS §88.]

אֱלֹהֵינוּ וֵאלֹהֵי אֲבוֹתֵינוּ, יַעֲלֶה, וְיָבֹא, וְיַגִּיעַ, וְיֵרָאֶה,

⟨ be noted, ⟨ reach, ⟨ come, ⟨ may there rise, **of our forefathers,** ⟨ and the God ⟨ Our God

וְיֵרָצֶה, וְיִשָּׁמַע, וְיִפָּקֵד, וְיִזָּכֵר זִכְרוֹנֵנוּ וּפִקְדוֹנֵנוּ, וְזִכְרוֹן

⟨ the — and — the and be be ⟨ be heard, be
remem- consideration remembrance remembered considered, favored,
brance of us; of us

אֲבוֹתֵינוּ, וְזִכְרוֹן מָשִׁיחַ בֶּן דָּוִד עַבְדֶּךָ, וְזִכְרוֹן יְרוּשָׁלַיִם

⟨ of Jerusalem, ⟨ the Your ⟨ of ⟨ son of ⟨ the of our
remembrance servant; David, Messiah, remembrance forefathers;

עִיר קָדְשֶׁךָ, וְזִכְרוֹן כָּל עַמְּךָ בֵּית יִשְׂרָאֵל לְפָנֶיךָ, לִפְלֵיטָה

⟨ for ⟨ before of ⟨ the ⟨ of Your and the of Your ⟨ the
deliverance, You Israel — Family entire people remembrance Holiness; City

לְטוֹבָה לְחֵן וּלְחֶסֶד וּלְרַחֲמִים, לְחַיִּים (טוֹבִים) וּלְשָׁלוֹם, בְּיוֹם

⟨ on the and for ⟨ (that is ⟨ for life ⟨ and for ⟨ for ⟨ for ⟨ for
day of peace, good), compassion, kindness, grace, goodness,

ON SUCCOS:	ON PESACH:	ON ROSH CHODESH:
חַג הַסֻּכּוֹת הַזֶּה.	חַג הַמַּצּוֹת הַזֶּה.	רֹאשׁ הַחֹדֶשׁ הַזֶּה.
this Festival of Succos.	**this Festival of Matzos.**	**this New Moon.**

זָכְרֵנוּ יהוה אֱלֹהֵינוּ בּוֹ לְטוֹבָה, וּפָקְדֵנוּ בוֹ לִבְרָכָה,

for ⟨ on ⟨ consider for ⟨ on ⟨ our God, ⟨ HASHEM, ⟨ Remember
blessing; it us goodness; it us

וְהוֹשִׁיעֵנוּ בוֹ לְחַיִּים טוֹבִים. וּבִדְבַר יְשׁוּעָה וְרַחֲמִים, חוּס

⟨ have and ⟨ of ⟨ In the that is good. ⟨ for life ⟨ on it ⟨ and save us
pity, compassion, salvation matter

וְחָנֵּנוּ וְרַחֵם עָלֵינוּ וְהוֹשִׁיעֵנוּ, כִּי אֵלֶיךָ עֵינֵינוּ, כִּי

⟨ be- are our eyes ⟨ to You ⟨ for and save us, ⟨ with us, ⟨ and be com- be
cause, [turned], passionate gracious,

אֵל מֶלֶךְ חַנּוּן וְרַחוּם אָתָּה.[1]

are You. ⟨ and com- ⟨ Who is ⟨ King, ⟨ God,
passionate gracious

---

(1) Cf. *Nehemiah* 9:31.

וְתֶחֱזֶינָה עֵינֵינוּ בְּשׁוּבְךָ לְצִיּוֹן בְּרַחֲמִים.

‹ in compassion. ‹ to Zion ‹ Your return ‹ may our eyes ‹ Witness

בָּרוּךְ אַתָּה יהוה, הַמַּחֲזִיר שְׁכִינָתוֹ לְצִיּוֹן.

‹ to Zion. ‹ His Presence ‹ Who restores ‹ Hashem, ‹ are You, ‹ Blessed

THANKSGIVING [MODIM] / הודאה

BOW AT מודים, *WE THANK;* STRAIGHTEN UP AT ה', *HASHEM.*

מוֹדִים אֲנַחְנוּ לָךְ, שָׁאַתָּה הוּא יהוה

‹ Hashem, ‹ Who are ‹ for it is You ‹ You, ‹ We thank

אֱלֹהֵינוּ וֵאלֹהֵי אֲבוֹתֵינוּ לְעוֹלָם וָעֶד. צוּרֵנוּ,

‹ our Rock, ‹ and ever; ‹ for ever ‹ of our forefathers, ‹ and the God ‹ our God

צוּר חַיֵּינוּ, מָגֵן יִשְׁעֵנוּ אַתָּה הוּא לְדוֹר וָדוֹר.

‹ to gen- ‹ from gen- ‹ are ‹ [is what] ‹ of our ‹ Shield ‹ of our ‹ the
eration. eration You salvation, lives, Rock

נוֹדֶה לְּךָ וּנְסַפֵּר תְּהִלָּתֶךָ[1] עַל חַיֵּינוּ

‹ our lives ‹ for ‹ Your praise, ‹ and relate ‹ You ‹ We shall thank

הַמְּסוּרִים בְּיָדֶךָ, וְעַל נִשְׁמוֹתֵינוּ הַפְּקוּדוֹת

‹ that are ‹ our souls ‹ and for ‹ into Your ‹ that are
entrusted hands, committed

לָךְ, וְעַל נִסֶּיךָ שֶׁבְּכָל יוֹם עִמָּנוּ, וְעַל

‹ and for ‹ are with us; ‹ day ‹ that every ‹ Your miracles ‹ and for ‹ to You;

נִפְלְאוֹתֶיךָ וְטוֹבוֹתֶיךָ שֶׁבְּכָל עֵת, עֶרֶב וָבֹקֶר

‹ morning, ‹ —evening, ‹ times ‹ that are at all ‹ and favors ‹ Your wonders

וְצָהֳרָיִם. הַטּוֹב כִּי לֹא כָלוּ רַחֲמֶיךָ, וְהַמְרַחֵם

‹ and the Com- ‹ are Your ‹ exhausted ‹ never ‹ for ‹ The Bene- ‹ and afternoon.
passionate One, compassions, ficent One,

כִּי לֹא תַמּוּ חֲסָדֶיךָ,[2] כִּי מֵעוֹלָם קִוִּינוּ לָךְ.

‹ in You. ‹ have we ‹ always ‹ — for ‹ are Your ‹ ended ‹ never ‹ for
put our hope kindnesses

---

(1) Cf. *Psalms* 79:13. (2) Cf. *Lamentations* 3:22.

**ON CHANUKAH AND PURIM ADD THE FOLLOWING [IF FORGOTTEN,
DO NOT REPEAT SHEMONEH ESREI; SEE LAWS §89]:**

וְעַל הַנִּסִּים, וְעַל הַפֻּרְקָן, וְעַל הַגְּבוּרוֹת, וְעַל

‹ and for ‹ the mighty deeds, ‹ and for ‹ the salvation, ‹ and for ‹ the miracles, ‹ And for

הַתְּשׁוּעוֹת, וְעַל הַנִּפְלָאוֹת, וְעַל הַנֶּחָמוֹת, וְעַל הַמִּלְחָמוֹת,

‹ the battles ‹ and for ‹ the consolations, ‹ and for ‹ the wonders, ‹ and for ‹ the victories,

שֶׁעָשִׂיתָ לַאֲבוֹתֵינוּ בַּיָּמִים הָהֵם בַּזְּמַן הַזֶּה.

« at this time: ‹ in those days, « for our ‹ which You
                forefathers   performed

ON CHANUKAH:

בִּימֵי מַתִּתְיָהוּ בֶּן יוֹחָנָן כֹּהֵן גָּדוֹל חַשְׁמוֹנָאִי וּבָנָיו,

« and his « the ‹ the High Priest, ‹ of ‹ the « of ‹ In the
sons, Hasmonean,   Yochanan, son Mattisyahu, days

כְּשֶׁעָמְדָה מַלְכוּת יָוָן הָרְשָׁעָה עַל עַמְּךָ יִשְׂרָאֵל, לְהַשְׁכִּיחָם

‹ to make « Israel, ‹ Your ‹ against « —which was ‹ of ‹ did the ‹ when rise up
them forget   people   wicked— Greece kingdom

תּוֹרָתֶךָ, וּלְהַעֲבִירָם מֵחֻקֵּי רְצוֹנֶךָ. וְאַתָּה בְּרַחֲמֶיךָ

‹ in Your mercy ‹ But You « of Your Will. ‹ from the ‹ and to compel « Your
                   statutes   them to stray   Torah

הָרַבִּים, עָמַדְתָּ לָהֶם בְּעֵת צָרָתָם, רַבְתָּ אֶת רִיבָם, דַּנְתָּ

‹ judged ‹ their cause, ‹ You « of their ‹ in the ‹ for ‹ stood up « which is
           championed distress. time them   abundant

אֶת דִּינָם, נָקַמְתָּ אֶת נִקְמָתָם.[1] מָסַרְתָּ גִבּוֹרִים בְּיַד חַלָּשִׁים,

« of the ‹ into the ‹ the strong ‹ You « their wrong. ‹ and You « their claim,
weak, hands   delivered   avenged

וְרַבִּים בְּיַד מְעַטִּים, וּטְמֵאִים בְּיַד טְהוֹרִים, וּרְשָׁעִים בְּיַד

‹ into the ‹ the wicked « of the pure, ‹ into the ‹ the impure « of the few, ‹ into the ‹ the
hands   hands   hands many

צַדִּיקִים, וְזֵדִים בְּיַד עוֹסְקֵי תוֹרָתֶךָ. וּלְךָ עָשִׂיתָ שֵׁם גָּדוֹל

‹ that ‹ a ‹ You ‹ For « of Your ‹ of the ‹ into the ‹ and the « of the
is great Name made Yourself Torah. diligent hands willful righteous,
           students   sinners

וְקָדוֹשׁ בְּעוֹלָמֶךָ, וּלְעַמְּךָ יִשְׂרָאֵל עָשִׂיתָ תְּשׁוּעָה גְדוֹלָה[2]

‹ of great ‹ a victory ‹ You ‹ Israel ‹ and for « in Your ‹ and holy
magnitude   performed   Your people world,

וּפֻרְקָן כְּהַיּוֹם הַזֶּה. וְאַחַר כֵּן בָּאוּ בָנֶיךָ לִדְבִיר בֵּיתֶךָ,

« of Your ‹ to the Holy ‹ Your ‹ came ‹ Thereafter, « as this very day. ‹ and a
House, of Holies children   salvation

---

(1) Cf. *Jeremiah* 51:36. (2) Cf. *I Samuel* 19:5.

וּפִנּוּ אֶת הֵיכָלֶךָ, וְטִהֲרוּ אֶת מִקְדָּשֶׁךָ, וְהִדְלִיקוּ נֵרוֹת
⟨ lights ⟨ and kindled ⟪   the site of   ⟨ purified ⟪ Your Temple, ⟨ cleansed
                                    Your Holiness

בְּחַצְרוֹת קָדְשֶׁךָ, וְקָבְעוּ שְׁמוֹנַת יְמֵי חֲנֻכָּה אֵלּוּ,
⟪—these—⟪ of ⟨ days ⟨ the eight ⟨ and they ⟪ of Your ⟨   in the
        Chanukah   established Sanctuary;   Courtyards

לְהוֹדוֹת וּלְהַלֵּל לְשִׁמְךָ הַגָּדוֹל.
⟪ that is ⟨ to Your ⟨ and praise ⟨ to express
  great.   Name   thanks

ON PURIM:

בִּימֵי מָרְדְּכַי וְאֶסְתֵּר בְּשׁוּשַׁן הַבִּירָה, כְּשֶׁעָמַד עֲלֵיהֶם
⟨ against ⟨ when ⟪ the capital, ⟨ in ⟨ and ⟨ of ⟨ In the
  them   rise up   Shushan, Esther, Mordechai days

הָמָן הָרָשָׁע, בִּקֵּשׁ לְהַשְׁמִיד לַהֲרֹג וּלְאַבֵּד אֶת כָּל הַיְּהוּדִים,
⟨ the Jews, ⟨ all ⟨ and to ⟨ to slay, ⟨ to destroy, ⟨ and he ⟪ the ⟨ did
                    exterminate   sought wicked, Haman,

מִנַּעַר וְעַד זָקֵן, טַף וְנָשִׁים בְּיוֹם אֶחָד, בִּשְׁלוֹשָׁה עָשָׂר
⟨ on the thirteenth [day] ⟨ on the same day, ⟪ and ⟨ infants ⟪ old, ⟨ to ⟨ from
                                             women,   young

לְחֹדֶשׁ שְׁנֵים עָשָׂר, הוּא חֹדֶשׁ אֲדָר, וּשְׁלָלָם לָבוֹז.¹
⟪ to be ⟨ and their ⟪ of Adar, ⟨ the ⟨ which ⟪   of the twelfth month,
plundered. possessions   month   is

וְאַתָּה בְּרַחֲמֶיךָ הָרַבִּים הֵפַרְתָּ אֶת עֲצָתוֹ, וְקִלְקַלְתָּ
⟨ and ⟪ his counsel ⟨ nullified ⟪ which is ⟨ in Your ⟨ But You,
frustrated   abundant, mercy

אֶת מַחֲשַׁבְתּוֹ, וַהֲשֵׁבוֹתָ לּוֹ גְּמוּלוֹ בְּרֹאשׁוֹ, וְתָלוּ אוֹתוֹ
⟨ him ⟨ and they ⟪ upon his ⟨ his ⟨ to ⟨ and ⟪ his intention
       hanged   own head, recompense him returned

וְאֶת בָּנָיו עַל הָעֵץ.
⟪ the gallows. ⟨ on ⟨ and his sons

וְעַל כֻּלָּם יִתְבָּרַךְ וְיִתְרוֹמַם וְיִתְנַשֵּׂא שִׁמְךָ
⟨ may Your ⟨ and upraised ⟨ and exalted, ⟨ blessed, ⟨ all these, ⟨ For
  Name be,

מַלְכֵּנוּ תָּמִיד לְעוֹלָם וָעֶד.
⟪ and ever. ⟨ for ever ⟨ continually, ⟪ our King,

---

(1) *Esther* 3:13.

FROM ROSH HASHANAH TO YOM KIPPUR ADD:

וּכְתוֹב לְחַיִּים טוֹבִים כָּל בְּנֵי בְרִיתֶךָ.

≪ of Your ⟨ the ⟨ all ⟨ that is ⟨ for a life ⟨ And
covenant. members good inscribe

[IF FORGOTTEN, DO NOT REPEAT SHEMONEH ESREI. SEE LAWS §61.]

BEND THE KNEES AT בָּרוּךְ, BLESSED; BOW AT אַתָּה, YOU; STRAIGHTEN UP AT ה', HASHEM.

וְכֹל הַחַיִּים יוֹדוּךָ סֶּלָה, וִיהַלְלוּ וִיבָרְכוּ

⟨ and bless ⟨ – and praise ≪ forever! ⟨ will gratefully ⟨ alive ⟨ Everything
acknowledge You,

אֶת שִׁמְךָ הַגָּדוֹל, בֶּאֱמֶת לְעוֹלָם, כִּי טוֹב. הָאֵל

⟨ O God ≪ it is good. ⟨ for ⟨ forever, ⟨ sincerely, ≪ that is great, ⟨ Your Name

יְשׁוּעָתֵנוּ וְעֶזְרָתֵנוּ סֶלָה, הָאֵל הַטּוֹב. בָּרוּךְ

⟨ Blessed ≪ Who is beneficent. ⟨ the God ≪ forever, ⟨ and of our help, ⟨ of our salvation

אַתָּה יהוה, הַטּוֹב שִׁמְךָ וּלְךָ נָאֶה לְהוֹדוֹת.

≪ to give ⟨ it is ⟨ and ⟨ is Your ⟨ The ≪ HASHEM, ⟨ are You,
thanks. fitting to You Name, Beneficent One

PEACE / שלום

SOME CONGREGATIONS RECITE שִׂים שָׁלוֹם, ESTABLISH PEACE...,
OTHERS RECITE שָׁלוֹם רָב, PEACE, ABUNDANT.... SEE COMMENTARY.

שָׁלוֹם רָב עַל ⟨ upon ≪ abundant, ≪ Peace,	שִׂים שָׁלוֹם, טוֹבָה, וּבְרָכָה, ⟨ blessing, ⟨ goodness, ⟨ peace, ⟨ Establish
יִשְׂרָאֵל עַמְּךָ ⟨ Your people ⟨ Israel	חַיִּים, חֵן, וָחֶסֶד וְרַחֲמִים ⟨ and compassion ⟨ kindness, ⟨ graciousness, ⟨ life,
תָּשִׂים לְעוֹלָם, ≪ forever, ⟨ establish	עָלֵינוּ וְעַל כָּל יִשְׂרָאֵל עַמֶּךָ. ≪ Your people. ⟨ of Israel ⟨ all ⟨ and upon ⟨ upon us
כִּי אַתָּה הוּא ⟨ Who are ⟨ it is You ⟨ for	בָּרְכֵנוּ אָבִינוּ, כֻּלָּנוּ כְּאֶחָד, ≪ as one, ⟨ all of us ≪ our Father, ⟨ Bless us,

שִׂים שָׁלוֹם / The Peace Blessing – שָׁלוֹם רָב

The text of שָׁלוֹם שִׂים contains allusions to the Priestly Blessings (see p. 167). Since the Priestly Blessings are pronounced only at *Shacharis*, at *Mussaf*, and [on fast days] at *Minchah*, many congregations recite שִׂים שָׁלוֹם only at these

three services, but not at *Maariv*, when שָׁלוֹם רָב is substituted. However, other congregations follow *Arizal*, *Rabbi Yaakov Emden*, and other authorities, who rule that there is no reason to differentiate between prayers, and שִׂים שָׁלוֹם should be recited at all times, including *Maariv*.

בְּאוֹר פָּנֶיךָ, כִּי בְאוֹר פָּנֶיךָ
with the light of Your countenance, for with the light of Your countenance

נָתַתָּ לָּנוּ, יהוה אֱלֹהֵינוּ, תּוֹרַת
You gave us, Hashem, our God, the Torah

חַיִּים וְאַהֲבַת חֶסֶד, וּצְדָקָה,
of life and a love of kindness, righteousness,

וּבְרָכָה, וְרַחֲמִים, וְחַיִּים,
blessing, compassion, life,

וְשָׁלוֹם. וְטוֹב יִהְיֶה בְּעֵינֶיךָ
and peace. And good may it be in Your eyes

לְבָרְכֵנוּ וּלְבָרֵךְ אֶת כָּל עַמְּךָ
to bless us and to bless all Your people

יִשְׂרָאֵל בְּכָל עֵת וּבְכָל שָׁעָה
Israel at every time and at every hour

בִּשְׁלוֹמֶךָ, (בְּרֹב עֹז וְשָׁלוֹם).
with Your peace, (with abundant strength and peace).

מֶלֶךְ אָדוֹן לְכָל
King, Master of all

הַשָּׁלוֹם. וְטוֹב
peace. And good

יִהְיֶה בְּעֵינֶיךָ
may it be in Your eyes

לְבָרְכֵנוּ וּלְבָרֵךְ
to bless us and to bless

אֶת כָּל עַמְּךָ
all of Your people

יִשְׂרָאֵל בְּכָל
Israel at every

עֵת וּבְכָל שָׁעָה
time and at every hour

בִּשְׁלוֹמֶךָ.
with Your peace.

FROM ROSH HASHANAH TO YOM KIPPUR ADD THE FOLLOWING:

בְּסֵפֶר חַיִּים בְּרָכָה וְשָׁלוֹם, וּפַרְנָסָה טוֹבָה, וּגְזֵרוֹת טוֹבוֹת,
In the book of life, blessing, and peace, and good livelihood, and good decrees that are,

יְשׁוּעוֹת וְנֶחָמוֹת, נִזָּכֵר וְנִכָּתֵב לְפָנֶיךָ, אֲנַחְנוּ וְכָל עַמְּךָ
salvations, and consolations, may we be remembered and may we be inscribed before You — we and Your entire people

בֵּית יִשְׂרָאֵל, לְחַיִּים טוֹבִים וּלְשָׁלוֹם.
the Family of Israel — for a life that is good and for peace.

[IF FORGOTTEN, DO NOT REPEAT SHEMONEH ESREI. SEE LAWS §61, 65.]

בָּרוּךְ אַתָּה יהוה, הַמְּבָרֵךְ אֶת עַמּוֹ יִשְׂרָאֵל

‹ Israel ‹ His people ‹ Who blesses ‹‹ Hashem, ‹ are You, ‹ Blessed

בַּשָּׁלוֹם.

‹‹ with peace.

יִהְיוּ לְרָצוֹן אִמְרֵי פִי וְהֶגְיוֹן לִבִּי לְפָנֶיךָ,

‹‹ before You, ‹‹ of my heart — ‹ and the thoughts ‹ of my mouth ‹ — the expressions ‹‹ find favor ‹ May they

יהוה צוּרִי וְגֹאֲלִי.[1]

‹‹ and my Redeemer. ‹ my Rock ‹ Hashem,

אֱלֹהַי, נְצוֹר לְשׁוֹנִי מֵרָע, וּשְׂפָתַי מִדַּבֵּר

‹ from speaking ‹ and my lips ‹‹ from evil ‹ my tongue ‹ guard ‹ My God,

מִרְמָה,[2] וְלִמְקַלְלַי נַפְשִׁי תִדּוֹם, וְנַפְשִׁי כֶּעָפָר

‹ like dust ‹ and let my soul ‹‹ be silent; ‹ let my soul ‹ To those who curse me, ‹‹ deceitfully.

לַכֹּל תִּהְיֶה. פְּתַח לִבִּי בְּתוֹרָתֶךָ, וְאַחֲרֵי

‹ so that to follow ‹‹ to Your Torah, ‹ my heart ‹ Open ‹‹ be. ‹ to everyone

מִצְוֹתֶיךָ תִּרְדּוֹף נַפְשִׁי. וְכָל הַקָּמִים וְהַחוֹשְׁבִים

‹ and who plot ‹ who rise up ‹ As for all ‹‹ shall my soul pursue. ‹ Your commandments

עָלַי לְרָעָה, מְהֵרָה הָפֵר עֲצָתָם וְקַלְקֵל

‹ and disrupt ‹‹ their counsel, ‹ nullify ‹ speedily ‹‹ to do evil, ‹ against me

מַחֲשַׁבְתָּם.[3] יְהִי רָצוֹן מִלְּפָנֶיךָ, יהוה אֱלֹהַי

‹ my God ‹ Hashem, ‹‹ before You, ‹ the will ‹ May it be ‹‹ their scheme.

וֵאלֹהֵי אֲבוֹתַי, שֶׁלֹּא תַעֲלֶה קִנְאַת אָדָם עָלַי,

‹‹ against me, ‹ of any man ‹ the jealousy ‹ be aroused ‹ that there not ‹‹ of my forefathers, ‹ and the God

---

(1) *Psalms* 19:15. (2) Cf. 34:14. (3) See *Berachos* 17a.

וְלֹא קִנֵּאתִי עַל אֲחֵרִים, וְשֶׁלֹּא אֶכְעֹס הַיּוֹם,

⟨ today, ⟨ become ⟨ and that ⟪ others; ⟨ against ⟨ my ⟨ nor
             angry   I not   jealousy

וְשֶׁלֹּא אַכְעִיסֶךָ, וְתַצִּילֵנִי מִיֵּצֶר הָרָע, וְתֵן בְּלִבִּי

⟨ in my ⟨ and ⟪ for Evil, ⟨ from the ⟨ Rescue me ⟪ anger You. ⟨ and that
  heart   place   Inclination   I not

הַכְנָעָה וַעֲנָוָה. מַלְכֵּנוּ וֵאלֹהֵינוּ, יַחֵד שִׁמְךָ

⟨ Your ⟨ unify ⟪ and our God, ⟨ O, our King ⟪ and ⟨ submissive-
  Name   humility.   ness

בְּעוֹלָמֶךָ, בְּנֵה עִירְךָ, יַסֵּד בֵּיתֶךָ, וְשַׁכְלֵל הֵיכָלֶךָ,

⟪ Your ⟨ perfect ⟪ of Your ⟨ lay the ⟪ Your ⟨ rebuild ⟪ in Your world;
  Sanctuary;   House, foundation City,

וְקַבֵּץ קִבּוּץ גָּלֻיּוֹת, וּפְדֵה צֹאנֶךָ, וְשַׂמַּח עֲדָתֶךָ.

⟪ Your ⟨ and gladden ⟪ Your ⟨ redeem ⟪ of the ⟨ the ⟨ gather
  congregation.   sheep,   exiles, ingathering

עֲשֵׂה לְמַעַן שְׁמֶךָ, עֲשֵׂה לְמַעַן יְמִינֶךָ, עֲשֵׂה

⟨ act ⟪ of Your ⟨ for the sake ⟨ act ⟪ of Your ⟨ for the sake ⟨ Act
        right hand;   Name;

לְמַעַן תּוֹרָתֶךָ, עֲשֵׂה לְמַעַן קְדֻשָּׁתֶךָ. לְמַעַן

⟨ In order ⟪ of Your sanctity. ⟨ for the ⟨ act ⟪ of Your Torah; ⟨ for the
  that   sake   sake

יֵחָלְצוּן יְדִידֶיךָ, הוֹשִׁיעָה יְמִינְךָ וַעֲנֵנִי.[1]

⟪ and answer ⟨ with Your ⟨ — save ⟪ Your ⟨ released
  me.   right hand,   beloved ones   may be

SOME RECITE VERSES PERTAINING TO THEIR NAMES AT THIS POINT. SEE PAGE 764.

יִהְיוּ לְרָצוֹן אִמְרֵי פִי וְהֶגְיוֹן לִבִּי לְפָנֶיךָ,

⟪ before ⟪ of my ⟨ and the ⟨ of my ⟨ — the ⟪ find favor ⟨ May they
  You,   heart — thoughts   mouth expressions

יהוה צוּרִי וְגֹאֲלִי.[2]

⟪ and my ⟨ my Rock ⟨ HASHEM,
  Redeemer.

---

(1) *Psalms* 60:7; 108:7. (2) 19:15.

**BOW. TAKE THREE STEPS BACK. BOW LEFT AND SAY . . . עֹשֶׂה, *"HE WHO MAKES . . ."*; BOW RIGHT AND SAY . . . הוּא, *"MAY HE . . ."*; BOW FORWARD AND SAY . . . וְעַל כָּל יִשְׂרָאֵל, *"AND UPON ALL ISRAEL . . ."*

עֹשֶׂה °שָׁלוֹם בִּמְרוֹמָיו, הוּא יַעֲשֶׂה שָׁלוֹם
⟨ peace ⟨ make ⟨ may He ⟨⟨ in His heights, ⟨ peace ⟨ He Who makes

עָלֵינוּ, וְעַל כָּל יִשְׂרָאֵל. וְאִמְרוּ: אָמֵן.
⟨⟨ Amen. ⟨ Now respond: ⟨⟨ Israel. ⟨ all ⟨ and upon ⟨⟨ upon us,

FROM ROSH HASHANAH TO YOM KIPPUR SOME SAY:

°הַשָּׁלוֹם
⟨ the peace

יְהִי רָצוֹן מִלְּפָנֶיךָ, יהוה אֱלֹהֵינוּ וֵאלֹהֵי
⟨ and the God ⟨ our God ⟨ Hashem, ⟨⟨ before You, ⟨ the will ⟨ May it be

אֲבוֹתֵינוּ, שֶׁיִּבָּנֶה בֵּית הַמִּקְדָּשׁ בִּמְהֵרָה בְיָמֵינוּ,
⟨⟨ in our days. ⟨ speedily ⟨ shall the Holy Temple be, ⟨ that rebuilt ⟨⟨ of our forefathers,

וְתֵן חֶלְקֵנוּ בְּתוֹרָתֶךָ. וְשָׁם נַעֲבָדְךָ בְּיִרְאָה, כִּימֵי
⟨ as in ⟨⟨ with ⟨ we may ⟨ so that ⟨⟨ be in Your Torah, ⟨ our portion ⟨ Grant
days reverence, serve You there that

עוֹלָם וּכְשָׁנִים קַדְמוֹנִיּוֹת. וְעָרְבָה לַיהוה מִנְחַת
⟨ let be ⟨ to ⟨ And pleasing ⟨⟨ gone by. ⟨ and as in ⟨ of old
the offering Hashem years

יְהוּדָה וִירוּשָׁלָיִם, כִּימֵי עוֹלָם וּכְשָׁנִים קַדְמוֹנִיּוֹת.
⟨⟨ gone by. ⟨ and in years ⟨ of old ⟨ as in days ⟨⟨ and Jerusalem, ⟨ of Judah

SHEMONEH ESREI ENDS HERE.
STAND IN PLACE FOR A FEW MOMENTS THEN TAKE THREE STEPS FORWARD.

ON REGULAR WEEKNIGHTS THE SERVICE CONTINUES WITH THE FULL *KADDISH* (BELOW).

AT THE CONCLUSION OF THE SABBATH (EXCEPT ON PURIM AND TISHAH B'AV, AND EXCEPT WHEN A FESTIVAL [OR EREV PESACH] WILL OCCUR BEFORE THE COMING SABBATH) CONTINUE ON P. 476.

THE *CHAZZAN* RECITES קַדִּישׁ שָׁלֵם, FULL *KADDISH*.

יִתְגַּדַּל וְיִתְקַדַּשׁ שְׁמֵהּ רַבָּא. (Cong. – אָמֵן.) בְּעָלְמָא דִּי בְרָא
⟨ He ⟨ that ⟨ in the ⟨⟨ (Amen.) ⟨⟨ that is ⟨ may His ⟨ and be ⟨ Grow exalted
created world great! — Name sanctified

כִרְעוּתֵהּ, וְיַמְלִיךְ מַלְכוּתֵהּ, וְיַצְמַח פֻּרְקָנֵהּ וִיקָרֵב מְשִׁיחֵהּ.
⟨⟨ His ⟨ and bring ⟨ His ⟨ and cause ⟨ to His ⟨ and may He ⟨⟨ according
Messiah, near salvation, to sprout kingship, give reign to His will,

(1) *Job* 25:2. (2) Cf. *Berachos* 16b. (3) *Ethics of the Fathers* 5:24. (4) *Malachi* 3:4.

(–אָמֵן.) בְּחַיֵּיכוֹן וּבְיוֹמֵיכוֹן וּבְחַיֵּי דְכָל בֵּית יִשְׂרָאֵל, (Cong.)
of Israel, ⟨ Family ⟨ of the ⟨ and in the ⟨ and in ⟨ in your ⟨⟨ (Amen.)
entire lifetimes your days, lifetimes

בַּעֲגָלָא וּבִזְמַן קָרִיב. וְאִמְרוּ: אָמֵן.
⟨⟨ Amen. ⟨ Now ⟨⟨ that ⟨ and at ⟨ swiftly
respond: comes soon. a time

CONGREGATION RESPONDS:

אָמֵן. יְהֵא שְׁמֵהּ רַבָּא מְבָרַךְ לְעָלַם וּלְעָלְמֵי עָלְמַיָּא.
⟨⟨ and for all eternity. ⟨ forever ⟨ be blessed ⟨ that is great ⟨ His Name ⟨ May ⟨⟨ Amen.

CHAZZAN CONTINUES:

יְהֵא שְׁמֵהּ רַבָּא מְבָרַךְ לְעָלַם וּלְעָלְמֵי עָלְמַיָּא. יִתְבָּרַךְ
⟨ Blessed, ⟨⟨ and for all eternity. ⟨ forever ⟨ be blessed ⟨ that is great ⟨ His Name ⟨ May

וְיִשְׁתַּבַּח וְיִתְפָּאַר וְיִתְרוֹמַם וְיִתְנַשֵּׂא וְיִתְהַדָּר וְיִתְעַלֶּה
⟨ elevated, ⟨ honored, ⟨ upraised, ⟨ exalted, ⟨ glorified, ⟨ praised,

וְיִתְהַלָּל שְׁמֵהּ דְּקֻדְשָׁא בְּרִיךְ הוּא (–בְּרִיךְ הוּא) –
⟨⟨ is He) ⟨ (Blessed ⟨⟨ is He ⟨ Blessed ⟨ of the Holy One, ⟨ be the Name ⟨ and lauded

ROSH HASHANAH TO YOM KIPPUR SUBSTITUTE:

°לְעֵלָּא מִן כָּל [°לְעֵלָּא (וּ)לְעֵלָּא מִכָּל] בִּרְכָתָא
⟨ blessing ⟨ any ⟨ exceedingly beyond ⟨ any ⟨ beyond

וְשִׁירָתָא, תֻּשְׁבְּחָתָא וְנֶחֱמָתָא דַּאֲמִירָן בְּעָלְמָא.
⟨⟨ in the world. ⟨ that are uttered ⟨ and consolation ⟨ praise ⟨⟨ and song,

וְאִמְרוּ: אָמֵן. (–אָמֵן.) (Cong.)
⟨⟨ (Amen.) ⟨⟨ Amen. ⟨ Now respond:

CONGREGATION:

(קַבֵּל בְּרַחֲמִים וּבְרָצוֹן אֶת תְּפִלָּתֵנוּ.)
⟨⟨ our prayers.) ⟨ and with favor ⟨ with mercy ⟨ (Accept

CHAZZAN CONTINUES:

תִּתְקַבֵּל צְלוֹתְהוֹן וּבָעוּתְהוֹן דְּכָל בֵּית יִשְׂרָאֵל
⟨ Israel ⟨ Family of ⟨ of the entire ⟨ and supplications ⟨ the prayers ⟨ May accepted be

קֳדָם אֲבוּהוֹן דִּי בִשְׁמַיָּא. וְאִמְרוּ: אָמֵן. (Cong.) – אָמֵן.
⟨⟨ (Amen.) ⟨⟨ Amen. ⟨ Now respond:⟨⟨ is in Heaven.⟨ Who ⟨ their Father ⟨ before

CONGREGATION:

(יְהִי שֵׁם יהוה מְבֹרָךְ מֵעַתָּה וְעַד עוֹלָם.[1])
⟨⟨ eternity.) ⟨ until ⟨ from this ⟨ be ⟨ of ⟨ the ⟨ (Let
time blessed HASHEM Name

(1) *Psalms* 113:2.

CHAZZAN CONTINUES:

יְהֵא שְׁלָמָא רַבָּא מִן שְׁמַיָּא, וְחַיִּים טוֹבִים עָלֵינוּ וְעַל כָּל

‹ all ‹ and ‹ upon us ‹‹ that is ‹ and life ‹‹ Heaven, ‹ from ‹ that is ‹ peace ‹ May
upon good, abundant there be

יִשְׂרָאֵל. וְאִמְרוּ: אָמֵן. (.Cong – אָמֵן.)

‹‹ (Amen.) ‹‹ Amen. ‹ Now respond: ‹‹ Israel.

CONGREGATION:

(עֶזְרִי מֵעִם יהוה, עֹשֵׂה שָׁמַיִם וָאָרֶץ.[1])

‹‹ and earth.) ‹ of heaven ‹ Maker ‹‹ HASHEM, ‹ is from ‹ (My help

BOW; TAKE THREE STEPS BACK: BOW LEFT AND SAY . . . **עֹשֶׂה שָׁלוֹם**, *"HE WHO MAKES PEACE . . .";* BOW
RIGHT AND SAY . . . **הוּא**, *"MAY HE . . .";* BOW FORWARD AND SAY . . . **וְעַל כָּל יִשְׂרָאֵל**, *"AND UPON
ALL ISRAEL . . ."* REMAIN IN PLACE FOR A FEW MOMENTS, THEN TAKE THREE STEPS FORWARD.

עֹשֶׂה °שָׁלוֹם בִּמְרוֹמָיו, הוּא יַעֲשֶׂה שָׁלוֹם עָלֵינוּ, וְעַל

‹ and ‹ upon us, ‹ peace ‹ make ‹ may He ‹‹ in His heights, ‹ peace ‹ He Who
upon makes

כָּל יִשְׂרָאֵל. וְאִמְרוּ: אָמֵן. (.Cong – אָמֵן.)

‹‹ (Amen.) ‹‹ Amen. ‹ Now respond: ‹‹ Israel. ‹ all

FROM ROSH HASHANAH TO YOM KIPPUR SOME SAY:

°הַשָּׁלוֹם

‹ the peace

BETWEEN PESACH AND SHAVUOS, THE *OMER* IS COUNTED (P. 447).
[SOME COUNT AFTER *ALEINU* AND *KADDISH*.]

ON PURIM THE *MEGILLAH* IS READ (P. 581); ON TISHAH B'AV *EICHAH* IS READ.
ON WEEKNIGHTS, BOTH ARE FOLLOWED BY **וְאַתָּה קָדוֹשׁ** (P. 479) AND THE SERVICE
CONTINUES THERE. IF PURIM OCCURS ON *MOTZA'EI SHABBOS*, CONTINUE **וִיהִי נֹעַם** (P. 477).

ALEINU / עלינו

STAND WHILE RECITING **עָלֵינוּ**, *"IT IS OUR DUTY . . ."*

עָלֵינוּ לְשַׁבֵּחַ לַאֲדוֹן הַכֹּל, לָתֵת גְּדֻלָּה

‹ greatness ‹ to ascribe ‹‹ of all, ‹ the Master ‹ to praise ‹ It is our duty

לְיוֹצֵר בְּרֵאשִׁית, שֶׁלֹּא עָשָׂנוּ כְּגוֹיֵי הָאֲרָצוֹת, וְלֹא

‹ and ‹‹ of the lands, ‹ like the ‹ for He has not ‹‹ of primeval ‹ to the
has not nations made us creation, Molder

שָׂמָנוּ כְּמִשְׁפְּחוֹת הָאֲדָמָה. שֶׁלֹּא שָׂם שָׁם חֶלְקֵנוּ

‹ our ‹ assigned ‹ for He ‹‹ of the earth; ‹ like the families ‹ established
portion has not us

_____

(1) *Psalms* 121:2.

כָּהֶם, וְגוֹרָלֵנוּ כְּכָל הֲמוֹנָם. (שֶׁהֵם מִשְׁתַּחֲוִים

like theirs ⟨ nor our lot ⟨ like all ⟨ their multitudes. ⟨⟨ (For they ⟨ bow ⟨

לְהֶבֶל וָרִיק, וּמִתְפַּלְּלִים אֶל אֵל לֹא יוֹשִׁיעַ.[1])

to vanity ⟨ and ⟨ emptiness ⟨ and pray ⟨ to ⟨ a god ⟨ who does not ⟨ save.) ⟨⟨

BOW WHILE RECITING וַאֲנַחְנוּ כּוֹרְעִים וּמִשְׁתַּחֲוִים, "BUT WE BEND OUR KNEES, BOW."

וַאֲנַחְנוּ כּוֹרְעִים וּמִשְׁתַּחֲוִים וּמוֹדִים, לִפְנֵי

before ⟨ and acknowledge our thanks, ⟨⟨ bow, ⟨ bend our knees, ⟨ But we ⟨

מֶלֶךְ מַלְכֵי הַמְּלָכִים הַקָּדוֹשׁ בָּרוּךְ הוּא. שֶׁהוּא

He ⟨ He. ⟨⟨ Blessed is ⟨ the Holy One, ⟨ of kings, ⟨⟨ over kings ⟨ the King ⟨

נוֹטֶה שָׁמַיִם וְיֹסֵד אָרֶץ,[2] וּמוֹשַׁב יְקָרוֹ בַּשָּׁמַיִם

is in the heavens ⟨ of His homage ⟨ the seat ⟨⟨ earth's foundation; ⟨ and establishes ⟨ heaven ⟨ stretches out ⟨

מִמַּעַל, וּשְׁכִינַת עֻזּוֹ בְּגָבְהֵי מְרוֹמִים. הוּא

He is ⟨⟨ heights. ⟨ is in the loftiest ⟨ of His power ⟨ and the Presence ⟨⟨ above, ⟨

אֱלֹהֵינוּ, אֵין עוֹד. אֱמֶת מַלְכֵּנוּ, אֶפֶס זוּלָתוֹ,

beside Him, ⟨⟨ there is nothing ⟨ is our King, ⟨ True ⟨⟨ other. ⟨ and there is none ⟨ our God ⟨

כַּכָּתוּב בְּתוֹרָתוֹ: וְיָדַעְתָּ הַיּוֹם וַהֲשֵׁבֹתָ אֶל

to ⟨ and take ⟨ this day ⟨ You are to know ⟨⟨ in His Torah: ⟨ as it is written ⟨

לְבָבֶךָ, כִּי יהוה הוּא הָאֱלֹהִים בַּשָּׁמַיִם מִמַּעַל

above ⟨ – in heaven ⟨⟨ the God ⟨ He is ⟨ HASHEM ⟨ that ⟨⟨ your heart, ⟨

וְעַל הָאָרֶץ מִתָּחַת, אֵין עוֹד.[3]

other. ⟨ there is none ⟨⟨ below – ⟨ the earth ⟨ and on ⟨

(1) Isaiah 45:20. (2) 51:13. (3) Deuteronomy 4:39.

וְעַל כֵּן נְקַוֶּה לְּךָ יהוה אֱלֹהֵינוּ לִרְאוֹת
And therefore ⟩ we put ⟩ in You, ⟩ Hashem, ⟩ our God, ⟩ that we
our hope   may see

מְהֵרָה בְּתִפְאֶרֶת עֻזֶּךָ, לְהַעֲבִיר גִּלּוּלִים מִן
very soon ⟩ the splendor ⟩ of Your ⟩ to remove ⟩ detestable ⟩ from
might,   idolatry

הָאָרֶץ, וְהָאֱלִילִים כָּרוֹת יִכָּרֵתוּן, לְתַקֵּן
the earth, ⟩ and false gods ⟩ will be utterly cut off, ⟩ to perfect

עוֹלָם בְּמַלְכוּת שַׁדַּי. וְכָל בְּנֵי בָשָׂר יִקְרְאוּ
the ⟩ through the ⟩ of the ⟩ Then all ⟩ humanity ⟩ will call
universe   sovereignty   Almighty.

בִשְׁמֶךָ, לְהַפְנוֹת אֵלֶיךָ כָּל רִשְׁעֵי אָרֶץ.
upon Your ⟩ to turn ⟩ toward You ⟩ all ⟩ the wicked ⟩ of the
Name,   earth.

יַכִּירוּ וְיֵדְעוּ כָּל יוֹשְׁבֵי תֵבֵל, כִּי לְךָ תִּכְרַע
May they ⟩ and know ⟩ all — ⟩ the ⟩ of the ⟩ that ⟩ to You ⟩ should
recognize   inhabitants world —   bend

כָּל בֶּרֶךְ, תִּשָּׁבַע כָּל לָשׁוֹן.¹ לְפָנֶיךָ יהוה
every ⟩ knee, ⟩ should swear ⟩ every ⟩ tongue. ⟩ Before You, ⟩ Hashem,

אֱלֹהֵינוּ יִכְרְעוּ וְיִפֹּלוּ, וְלִכְבוֹד שִׁמְךָ יְקָר
our God, ⟩ they will bend ⟩ and cast ⟩ and to ⟩ of Your ⟩ homage
their knees themselves down, the glory   Name

יִתֵּנוּ. וִיקַבְּלוּ כֻלָּם אֶת עוֹל מַלְכוּתֶךָ, וְתִמְלֹךְ
they will ⟩ and accept ⟩ will all ⟩ the yoke ⟩ of Your kingship, ⟩ that You
offer,   may reign

עֲלֵיהֶם מְהֵרָה לְעוֹלָם וָעֶד. כִּי הַמַּלְכוּת
over them ⟩ very soon ⟩ for ever ⟩ and ever. ⟩ For ⟩ the kingdom

שֶׁלְּךָ הִיא וּלְעוֹלְמֵי עַד תִּמְלוֹךְ בְּכָבוֹד, כַּכָּתוּב
is Yours, ⟩ and for ever ⟩ and ⟩ You will ⟩ in glory, ⟩ as it is
ever   reign   written

_____

(1) Cf. *Isaiah* 45:23.

בְּתוֹרָתֶךָ: יהוה יִמְלֹךְ לְעֹלָם וָעֶד.¹ ❖ וְנֶאֱמַר:

》And it is said: 《 and ever. 〈 for ever 〈 shall reign 〈 HASHEM 《 in Your Torah:

וְהָיָה יהוה לְמֶלֶךְ עַל כָּל הָאָרֶץ, בַּיּוֹם הַהוּא

〈 — on that day 《 the world 〈 all 〈 over 〈 be King 〈 HASHEM 〈 Then will

יִהְיֶה יהוה אֶחָד וּשְׁמוֹ אֶחָד.²

《 be One. 〈 and His 〈 be One 〈 HASHEM 〈 shall
Name

SOME CONGREGATIONS RECITE THE FOLLOWING AFTER עָלֵינוּ, *ALEINU*:

אַל תִּירָא מִפַּחַד פִּתְאֹם, וּמִשֹּׁאַת רְשָׁעִים כִּי

〈 when 〈 of the 〈 nor the 《 [that comes] 〈 terror 〈 Do not fear
     wicked   holocaust   suddenly,

תָבֹא.³ עֻצוּ עֵצָה וְתֻפָר, דַּבְּרוּ דָבָר וְלֹא יָקוּם, כִּי

〈 for 《 stand, 〈 and it 〈 your 〈 speak 《 and it will 〈 a 〈 Plan 《 it
       shall not speech   be annulled; conspiracy   comes.

עִמָּנוּ אֵל.⁴ וְעַד זִקְנָה אֲנִי הוּא, וְעַד שֵׂיבָה אֲנִי

〈 I 〈 [your] 〈 and 《 I remain 〈 [your] 〈 Even 《 is 〈 with
elder years, even till   unchanged;   old age,   till   God.   us

אֶסְבֹּל, אֲנִי עָשִׂיתִי וַאֲנִי אֶשָּׂא, וַאֲנִי אֶסְבֹּל וַאֲמַלֵּט.⁵

《 and rescue 〈 shall 〈 I 《 shall 〈 and I 〈 created 〈 I 《 shall carry
[you].   carry [you]   bear [you];   [you]   [you].

MOURNER'S KADDISH / קדיש יתום

IN THE PRESENCE OF A *MINYAN*, MOURNERS RECITE קַדִּיש יָתוֹם, THE MOURNER'S *KADDISH*.
[A TRANSLITERATION OF THIS *KADDISH* APPEARS ON PAGE 879.]

יִתְגַּדַּל וְיִתְקַדַּשׁ שְׁמֵהּ רַבָּא. (אָמֵן. – Cong.) בְּעָלְמָא דִּי בְרָא

〈 He 〈 that 〈 in the 《 (Amen.) 《 that is 〈 may His 〈 and be 〈 Grow exalted
created   world   great! — Name sanctified

כִרְעוּתֵהּ, וְיַמְלִיךְ מַלְכוּתֵהּ, וְיַצְמַח פֻּרְקָנֵהּ וִיקָרֵב מְשִׁיחֵהּ.

《 His 〈 and bring 〈 His 〈 and cause 〈 to His 〈 and may He 《 according
Messiah, near   salvation, to sprout kingship, give reign   to His will,

(Cong. – אָמֵן.) בְּחַיֵּיכוֹן וּבְיוֹמֵיכוֹן וּבְחַיֵּי דְכָל בֵּית יִשְׂרָאֵל,

《 of Israel, 〈 Family 〈 of the 〈 and in the 〈 and in 〈 in your 《 (Amen.)
     entire lifetimes   your days,   lifetimes

---

(1) *Exodus* 15:18. (2) *Zechariah* 14:9. (3) *Proverbs* 3:25. (4) *Isaiah* 8:10. (5) 46:4.

בַּעֲגָלָא וּבִזְמַן קָרִיב. וְאִמְרוּ: אָמֵן.

‹‹ Amen. ‹ Now ‹‹ that ‹ and at ‹ swiftly
respond: comes soon. a time

CONGREGATION RESPONDS:

אָמֵן. יְהֵא שְׁמֵהּ רַבָּא מְבָרַךְ לְעָלַם וּלְעָלְמֵי עָלְמַיָּא.

‹‹ and for all eternity. ‹ forever ‹ be blessed ‹ that is great ‹ His Name ‹ May ‹‹ Amen.

MOURNER CONTINUES:

יְהֵא שְׁמֵהּ רַבָּא מְבָרַךְ לְעָלַם וּלְעָלְמֵי עָלְמַיָּא. יִתְבָּרַךְ

‹ Blessed, ‹‹ and for all eternity. ‹ forever ‹ be blessed ‹ that is great ‹ His Name ‹ May

וְיִשְׁתַּבַּח וְיִתְפָּאַר וְיִתְרוֹמַם וְיִתְנַשֵּׂא וְיִתְהַדָּר וְיִתְעַלֶּה

‹ elevated, ‹ honored, ‹ upraised, ‹ exalted, ‹ glorified, ‹ praised,

וְיִתְהַלָּל שְׁמֵהּ דְּקֻדְשָׁא בְּרִיךְ הוּא (.Cong –בְּרִיךְ הוּא) —

‹‹ is He) ‹ (Blessed ‹‹ is He Blessed ‹ of the ‹ be the ‹ and lauded
Holy One, Name

ROSH HASHANAH TO YOM KIPPUR SUBSTITUTE:

°לְעֵלָּא מִן כָּל [°לְעֵלָּא (וּ)לְעֵלָּא מִכָּל] בִּרְכָתָא

‹ blessing ‹ any ‹ exceedingly beyond ‹ any ‹ beyond

וְשִׁירָתָא, תֻּשְׁבְּחָתָא וְנֶחֱמָתָא דַּאֲמִירָן בְּעָלְמָא.

‹‹ in the world. ‹ that are uttered ‹ and consolation ‹ praise ‹‹ and song,

וְאִמְרוּ: אָמֵן. (.Cong–אָמֵן.)

‹‹ (Amen.) ‹‹ Amen. ‹ Now respond:

יְהֵא שְׁלָמָא רַבָּא מִן שְׁמַיָּא, וְחַיִּים טוֹבִים עָלֵינוּ וְעַל כָּל

‹ all ‹ and ‹ upon us ‹ that is ‹ and life ‹‹ Heaven, ‹ from ‹ that is ‹ peace ‹ May
upon good, abundant there be

יִשְׂרָאֵל. וְאִמְרוּ: אָמֵן. (.Cong – אָמֵן.)

‹‹ (Amen.) ‹‹ Amen. ‹ Now respond: ‹‹ Israel.

**BOW; TAKE THREE STEPS BACK: BOW LEFT AND SAY . . . עֹשֶׂה שָׁלוֹם, *"HE WHO MAKES PEACE . . .";* BOW
RIGHT AND SAY . . . הוּא, *"MAY HE . . .";* BOW FORWARD AND SAY . . . וְעַל כָּל יִשְׂרָאֵל, *"AND UPON
ALL ISRAEL . . ."* REMAIN IN PLACE FOR A FEW MOMENTS, THEN TAKE THREE STEPS FORWARD.**

עֹשֶׂה °שָׁלוֹם בִּמְרוֹמָיו, הוּא יַעֲשֶׂה שָׁלוֹם עָלֵינוּ, וְעַל

‹ and upon ‹ upon us, ‹ peace ‹ make ‹ may He ‹‹ in His heights, ‹ peace ‹ He Who makes

כָּל יִשְׂרָאֵל. וְאִמְרוּ: אָמֵן. (.Cong – אָמֵן.)

‹‹ (Amen.) ‹‹ Amen. ‹ Now respond: ‹‹ Israel. ‹ all

FROM ROSH HASHANAH TO YOM KIPPUR SOME SAY:

°הַשָּׁלוֹם

‹ the peace

⇥ **COUNTING OF THE OMER / ספירת העומר** ⇤

THE *OMER* IS COUNTED FROM THE SECOND NIGHT OF PESACH UNTIL THE NIGHT BEFORE SHAVUOS.
EVEN ONE PRAYING WITHOUT A *MINYAN* RECITES THE ENTIRE *OMER* SERVICE.
IN SOME CONGREGATIONS, THE FOLLOWING PRAYER PRECEDES THE COUNTING OF THE *OMER*.

לְשֵׁם יִחוּד קֻדְשָׁא בְּרִיךְ הוּא וּשְׁכִינְתֵּיהּ, בִּדְחִילוּ

⟨ in fear　⟨⟨ and His Presence, ⟨ is He, ⟨ Blessed ⟨⟨ of the ⟨ of the ⟨ For the
　　　　　　　　　　　　　　　　　　　　　Holy One, unification sake

וּרְחִימוּ לְיַחֵד שֵׁם יוּ"ד הֵ"א בְּוָא"ו הֵ"א בְּיִחוּדָא

⟨ in unity　⟨ with *Vav-Kei*　⟨ *Yud-Kei*　⟨⟨ the Name ⟨ to unify ⟨ and love

שְׁלִים, בְּשֵׁם כָּל יִשְׂרָאֵל. הִנְנִי מוּכָן וּמְזֻמָּן לְקַיֵּם

⟨ to ⟨ and ⟨ prepared ⟨ Behold ⟨⟨ Israel. ⟨ of all ⟨ in the ⟨⟨ that is
perform ready 　　　　I am 　　　　　　　　　name 　　　perfect,

מִצְוַת עֲשֵׂה שֶׁל סְפִירַת הָעוֹמֶר, כְּמוֹ שֶׁכָּתוּב בַּתּוֹרָה:

⟨⟨ in the ⟨ it is ⟨ as ⟨⟨ the *Omer*, ⟨ counting ⟨ of ⟨ the positive
Torah: written 　　　　　　　　　　　　　commandment

וּסְפַרְתֶּם לָכֶם מִמָּחֳרַת הַשַּׁבָּת, מִיּוֹם הֲבִיאֲכֶם אֶת

⟨ the ⟨ you brought ⟨ from ⟨⟨ of the ⟨ from the ⟨ for ⟨ You are to
　　　　　　　the day 　rest day, 　morrow 　yourselves 　count

⇥ ספירת הָעוֹמֶר /
Counting of the Omer

The Torah commands that from the second day of Pesach — the day the *Omer*-offering of new barley is brought in the Temple — forty-nine days are to be counted, and the festival of Shavuos celebrated on the fiftieth day. This period is called *Sefiras HaOmer*, the Counting of the Omer. The *Sefirah* count also recalls an earlier event. During the seven weeks following the Exodus, our ancestors prepared themselves for receiving the Torah at Mount Sinai. This responsibility to prepare oneself to receive the Torah is present every year, as we relive the Exodus from bondage and materialism, and strive to be worthy of the gift of Torah. In ancient times, the *Sefirah* period was a time of rejoicing. Now it is observed as a time of semimourning because of several reasons: the absence of the Temple; the death of R' Akiva's 24,000 students during thirty-three days of the *Sefirah;* and a series of bloody massacres of Jewish communities during the Crusades.

⇥ **A Summary of Laws of *Sefirah***

The *Omer* is counted, while standing, after nightfall. Before reciting the blessing, one should be careful *not* to say "Today is the —————th day." If he did so, for example, in response to someone who asked which day it is, he *should* count formally; however, he may not recite the blessing, since he has already counted that day. Where there are days and weeks, this does not apply unless he also mentioned the week. In both cases, he may recite the blessing on succeeding nights.

If one forgets to count at night, he counts during the day *without* a blessing, but may recite the blessing on succeeding nights. But if one forgot to count throughout the day, he counts without a blessing on succeeding nights.

עֹמֶר הַתְּנוּפָה, שֶׁבַע שַׁבָּתוֹת תְּמִימֹת תִּהְיֶינָה. עַד

⟨ until ⟪ they should be — ⟨ that are complete ⟨ weeks ⟨ — seven ⟪ that is waved ⟨ Omer-offering

מִמָּחֳרַת הַשַּׁבָּת הַשְּׁבִיעִת תִּסְפְּרוּ חֲמִשִּׁים יוֹם,

⟨ days, ⟨ fifty ⟨ you are to count ⟨ of the seventh week ⟨ the morrow

וְהִקְרַבְתֶּם מִנְחָה חֲדָשָׁה לַיהוה.¹ וִיהִי נֹעַם אֲדֹנָי

⟨ of the Lord, ⟨ the pleasantness ⟨ May ⟪ to Hashem. ⟪ that is new, ⟪ a meal-offering, ⟨ and then offer

אֱלֹהֵינוּ עָלֵינוּ, וּמַעֲשֵׂה יָדֵינוּ כּוֹנְנָה עָלֵינוּ, וּמַעֲשֵׂה

⟨ the work ⟪ for us; ⟨ establish ⟨ of our hands ⟨ the work ⟪ be upon us; ⟨ our God,

יָדֵינוּ כּוֹנְנֵהוּ.²

⟪ establish it. ⟨ of our hands,

THE *CHAZZAN*, FOLLOWED BY THE CONGREGATION, RECITES THE BLESSING AND COUNTS.

בָּרוּךְ אַתָּה יהוה אֱלֹהֵינוּ מֶלֶךְ הָעוֹלָם,

⟪ of the universe, ⟨ King ⟨ our God, ⟨ Hashem, ⟨ are You, ⟨ Blessed

אֲשֶׁר קִדְּשָׁנוּ בְּמִצְוֹתָיו וְצִוָּנוּ עַל סְפִירַת

⟨ the counting ⟨ regarding ⟨ and has commanded us ⟨ with His commandments ⟨ has sanctified us ⟨ Who

הָעוֹמֶר.   (אָמֵן. – Cong.)

⟪ of the Omer.   ⟪ (Amen.)

INSERT THE APPROPRIATE DAY'S COUNT. SEE CHART ON PP. 452-453.

הָרַחֲמָן הוּא יַחֲזִיר לָנוּ עֲבוֹדַת בֵּית הַמִּקְדָּשׁ

⟨ of the Temple ⟨ the service ⟨ for us ⟨ return ⟨ May He ⟪ The Compassionate One!

לִמְקוֹמָהּ, בִּמְהֵרָה בְיָמֵינוּ. אָמֵן סֶלָה.

⟪ Selah! ⟪ Amen, ⟪ in our days. ⟨ speedily ⟨ to its place,

(1) *Leviticus* 23:15-16. (2) *Psalms* 90:17.

—— Psalm 67 / תהלים סז ——

לַמְנַצֵּחַ בִּנְגִינֹת מִזְמוֹר שִׁיר. אֱלֹהִים יְחָנֵּנוּ

〈 favor us 〈 May God 《 a song. 〈 a psalm, 〈 with the 〈 For the
neginos, conductor

וִיבָרְכֵנוּ, יָאֵר פָּנָיו אִתָּנוּ סֶלָה. לָדַעַת בָּאָרֶץ

〈 on earth 〈 To make 《 Selah. 《 with us, 〈 His 〈 may He 《 and bless us,
known countenance illuminate

דַּרְכֶּךָ, בְּכָל גּוֹיִם יְשׁוּעָתֶךָ. יוֹדוּךָ עַמִּים,

〈 will the 〈 Acknowledge 《 Your salvation. 〈 nations 〈 among all 《 Your way,
peoples, You

אֱלֹהִים; יוֹדוּךָ עַמִּים כֻּלָּם. יִשְׂמְחוּ וִירַנְּנוּ

〈 and singing 〈 Glad will be 《 – all of 《 will the 〈 acknowledge 《 O God;
for joy will be them. peoples You

לְאֻמִּים, כִּי תִשְׁפֹּט עַמִּים מִישֹׁר, וּלְאֻמִּים

〈 and the 《 fairly 〈 the peoples 〈 You will 〈 because 《 regimes,
regimes judge

בָּאָרֶץ תַּנְחֵם סֶלָה. יוֹדוּךָ עַמִּים, אֱלֹהִים;

《 O God; 〈 will the 〈 Acknowledge 《 Selah. 《 [with fairness] 〈 on earth
peoples, You You will guide,

יוֹדוּךָ עַמִּים כֻּלָּם. אֶרֶץ נָתְנָה יְבוּלָהּ,

《 its produce; 〈 will then 〈 The earth 《 – all of 《 will the 〈 acknowledge
have yielded them. peoples You

יְבָרְכֵנוּ אֱלֹהִים אֱלֹהֵינוּ. יְבָרְכֵנוּ אֱלֹהִים,

《 May God bless us, 《 – our God. 《 may God bless us

וְיִירְאוּ אוֹתוֹ כָּל אַפְסֵי אָרֶץ.

《 of the 〈 the ends 〈 – all 《 Him 〈 and may
earth. they fear

אָנָּא בְּכֹחַ גְּדֻלַּת יְמִינְךָ תַּתִּיר צְרוּרָה.

אב"ג ית"ץ

《 the bundled 〈 untie 〈 of Your 〈 of the 〈 With the 《 We beg
[sins]. right hand, greatness strength You!

קַבֵּל רִנַּת עַמְּךָ שַׂגְּבֵנוּ טַהֲרֵנוּ נוֹרָא.

קר"ע שט"ן

《 O Awesome 〈 purify us, 〈 strengthen 《 of Your 《 the 〈 Accept
One. us, people; prayer

נָא גִבּוֹר דּוֹרְשֵׁי יְחוּדְךָ כְּבָבַת שָׁמְרֵם.

נג"ד יכ"ש

» guard them. ‹ like the pupil » Your ‹ – those » O Strong ‹ Please,
of an eye Oneness, who foster One

בָּרְכֵם טַהֲרֵם רַחֲמֵם צִדְקָתְךָ¹ תָּמִיד גָּמְלֵם.

בט"ר צת"ג

» recompense ‹ always ‹ may Your » show them ‹ purify ‹ Bless them,
them. righteousness mercy; them,

חֲסִין קָדוֹשׁ בְּרוֹב טוּבְךָ נַהֵל עֲדָתֶךָ.

חק"ב טנ"ע

» Your ‹ guide ‹ of Your ‹ with the » Holy ‹ Powerful
congregation. goodness abundance One, One,

יָחִיד גֵּאֶה לְעַמְּךָ פְּנֵה זוֹכְרֵי קְדֻשָּׁתֶךָ.

יג"ל פז"ק

» Your holiness. ‹ those who » turn, ‹ to Your ‹ Exalted ‹ Unique
proclaim people One, One,

שַׁוְעָתֵנוּ קַבֵּל וּשְׁמַע צַעֲקָתֵנוּ יוֹדֵעַ תַּעֲלֻמוֹת.

שק"ו צי"ת

» of mysteries. ‹ O » our cry, ‹ and hear ‹ accept, » Our
Knower entreaty

בָּרוּךְ שֵׁם כְּבוֹד מַלְכוּתוֹ לְעוֹלָם וָעֶד.

» and ever. ‹ for ever ‹ kingdom ‹ of His ‹ is the ‹ Blessed
glorious Name

רִבּוֹנוֹ שֶׁל עוֹלָם, אַתָּה צִוִּיתָנוּ עַל יְדֵי מֹשֶׁה עַבְדֶּךָ

« Your ‹ Moses, ‹ through ‹ commanded » You » the ‹ of Master
servant, us universe,

לִסְפּוֹר סְפִירַת הָעוֹמֶר, כְּדֵי לְטַהֲרֵנוּ מִקְּלִפּוֹתֵינוּ

‹ from our ‹ to purify us ‹ in order » of the Omer, ‹ the Counting ‹ to count
encrustations of evil

וּמִטֻּמְאוֹתֵינוּ, כְּמוֹ שֶׁכָּתַבְתָּ בְּתוֹרָתֶךָ: וּסְפַרְתֶּם

‹ You are to count » in Your Torah: ‹ You have written ‹ as » and from our tumah-
contaminations,

לָכֶם מִמָּחֳרַת הַשַּׁבָּת מִיּוֹם הֲבִיאֲכֶם אֶת עֹמֶר

‹ Omer- ‹ the ‹ you brought ‹ from » of the ‹ from the ‹ for
offering the day rest day, morrow yourselves

הַתְּנוּפָה, שֶׁבַע שַׁבָּתוֹת תְּמִימֹת תִּהְיֶינָה. עַד מִמָּחֳרַת

‹ the morrow ‹ until » they ‹ that are ‹ weeks ‹ – seven » that is waved
should be – complete

הַשַּׁבָּת הַשְּׁבִיעִת תִּסְפְּרוּ חֲמִשִּׁים יוֹם.² כְּדֵי שֶׁיִּטָּהֲרוּ

‹ cleansed ‹ so that » days, ‹ fifty ‹ you are to ‹ of the seventh week
should be count

(1) Alternatively: רַחֲמֵי צִדְקָתְךָ, the mercy of Your righteousness. (2) Leviticus 23:15-16.

נַפְשׁוֹת עַמְּךָ יִשְׂרָאֵל מִזֻּהֲמָתָם. וּבְכֵן יְהִי רָצוֹן מִלְּפָנֶיךָ,

⟨⟨ before You, ⟨ the ⟨ may ⟨ Therefore, ⟨⟨ of their ⟨ Israel ⟨ of Your ⟨ the souls
will it be contamination. people

יהוה אֱלֹהֵינוּ וֵאלֹהֵי אֲבוֹתֵינוּ, שֶׁבִּזְכוּת סְפִירַת

⟨ of the ⟨ that in the merit ⟨⟨ of our forefathers, ⟨ and the God ⟨ our God ⟨ HASHEM,
Counting

הָעוֹמֶר שֶׁסָּפַרְתִּי הַיּוֹם, יְתֻקַּן מַה שֶּׁפָּגַמְתִּי בִּסְפִירָה*

⟨ in the ⟨ blemish I ⟨ whatever ⟨ may there ⟨⟨ today, ⟨ that I have ⟨ of the
Sefirah* have caused be corrected counted Omer

(INSERT THE APPROPRIATE SEFIRAH; SEE CHART ON PP. 452-453.)

וְאֶטְהַר וְאֶתְקַדֵּשׁ בִּקְדֻשָּׁה שֶׁל מַעְלָה, וְעַל יְדֵי זֶה

⟨ this, ⟨ and ⟨⟨ Above, ⟨ of ⟨ with the ⟨ and may I be ⟨ May I be
through holiness sanctified cleansed

יֻשְׁפַּע שֶׁפַע רַב בְּכָל הָעוֹלָמוֹת. וּלְתַקֵּן אֶת נַפְשׁוֹתֵינוּ,

⟨ our lives, ⟨ And may ⟨⟨ the worlds. ⟨ in all ⟨ that is ⟨ a ⟨ may
it correct abundant bounty there flow

וְרוּחוֹתֵינוּ, וְנִשְׁמוֹתֵינוּ, מִכָּל סִיג וּפְגָם, וּלְטַהֲרֵנוּ

⟨ may it purify us ⟨⟨ and blemish; ⟨ sediment ⟨ from all ⟨ and our souls ⟨ our spirits,

וּלְקַדְּשֵׁנוּ בִּקְדֻשָּׁתְךָ הָעֶלְיוֹנָה. אָמֵן סֶלָה.

⟨⟨ Selah! ⟨⟨ Amen, ⟨⟨ that is exalted. ⟨ with Your ⟨ and may it
holiness sanctify us

IN SOME CONGREGATIONS, MOURNERS RECITE THE MOURNER'S KADDISH (P. 445), FOLLOWED BY ALEINU (P. 442) [IF NOT RECITED BEFORE THE OMER]. IN OTHERS, ALEINU IS RECITED IMMEDIATELY.

בִּסְפִירָה — *In the Sefirah.* While man can have no conception of God's essence, for His true being is beyond human intelligence, we can perceive Him in the various ways in which He seems to behave toward us, such as mercy, power, judgment, etc.

The writings of Kabbalah refer to these ways through which God interacts with the Creation as the seven *Sefiros*, translated as *Emanations*. The order of the *Sefiros* is as follows:

1) חֶסֶד — *Lovingkindness*
2) גְּבוּרָה — *Power*
3) תִּפְאֶרֶת — *Splendor*
4) נֶצַח — *Eternity*
5) הוֹד — *Glory*
6) יְסוֹד — *Foundation*
7) מַלְכוּת — *Kingship*

Each one of the *Sefiros* also combines with the others; e.g. . . . . חֶסֶד שֶׁבְּחֶסֶד, חֶסֶד שֶׁבִּגְבוּרָה,

resulting in a total of forty-nine Emanations. The masters of Kabbalah taught that the seven weeks of *Sefirah* (which in its plain meaning is translated *counting*) correspond to these *Sefiros*/Emanations, beginning with חֶסֶד שֶׁבְּחֶסֶד on the first day and concluding with מַלְכוּת שֶׁבְּמַלְכוּת on the forty-ninth.

The *Sefiros* exist in man's personal world as well. A Jew is commanded to emulate the ways of his Creator and that includes developing himself in these forty-nine ways. For example, when a person's sense of responsibility motivates him to organize charity projects, his actions are illustrative of חֶסֶד שֶׁבִּגְבוּרָה, *kindness within strength.* One who fails in this area has shown himself lacking in this particular trait. On each day of the *Sefirah* period, one should strive to develop in himself that day's emanation-trait (ArtScroll *Lag BaOmer*).

SEFIRAH	COUNT	DAY
חֶסֶד שֶׁבְּחֶסֶד	הַיּוֹם יוֹם אֶחָד לָעוֹמֶר	1
גְּבוּרָה שֶׁבְּחֶסֶד	הַיּוֹם שְׁנֵי יָמִים לָעוֹמֶר	2
תִּפְאֶרֶת שֶׁבְּחֶסֶד	הַיּוֹם שְׁלֹשָׁה יָמִים לָעוֹמֶר	3
נֶצַח שֶׁבְּחֶסֶד	הַיּוֹם אַרְבָּעָה יָמִים לָעוֹמֶר	4
הוֹד שֶׁבְּחֶסֶד	הַיּוֹם חֲמִשָּׁה יָמִים לָעוֹמֶר	5
יְסוֹד שֶׁבְּחֶסֶד	הַיּוֹם שִׁשָּׁה יָמִים לָעוֹמֶר	6
מַלְכוּת שֶׁבְּחֶסֶד	הַיּוֹם שִׁבְעָה יָמִים, שֶׁהֵם שָׁבוּעַ אֶחָד, לָעוֹמֶר	7
חֶסֶד שֶׁבִּגְבוּרָה	הַיּוֹם שְׁמוֹנָה יָמִים, שֶׁהֵם שָׁבוּעַ אֶחָד וְיוֹם אֶחָד, לָעוֹמֶר	8
גְּבוּרָה שֶׁבִּגְבוּרָה	הַיּוֹם תִּשְׁעָה יָמִים, שֶׁהֵם שָׁבוּעַ אֶחָד וּשְׁנֵי יָמִים, לָעוֹמֶר	9
תִּפְאֶרֶת שֶׁבִּגְבוּרָה	הַיּוֹם עֲשָׂרָה יָמִים, שֶׁהֵם שָׁבוּעַ אֶחָד וּשְׁלֹשָׁה יָמִים, לָעוֹמֶר	10
נֶצַח שֶׁבִּגְבוּרָה	הַיּוֹם אַחַד עָשָׂר יוֹם, שֶׁהֵם שָׁבוּעַ אֶחָד וְאַרְבָּעָה יָמִים, לָעוֹמֶר	11
הוֹד שֶׁבִּגְבוּרָה	הַיּוֹם שְׁנֵים עָשָׂר יוֹם, שֶׁהֵם שָׁבוּעַ אֶחָד וַחֲמִשָּׁה יָמִים, לָעוֹמֶר	12
יְסוֹד שֶׁבִּגְבוּרָה	הַיּוֹם שְׁלֹשָׁה עָשָׂר יוֹם, שֶׁהֵם שָׁבוּעַ אֶחָד וְשִׁשָּׁה יָמִים, לָעוֹמֶר	13
מַלְכוּת שֶׁבִּגְבוּרָה	הַיּוֹם אַרְבָּעָה עָשָׂר יוֹם, שֶׁהֵם שְׁנֵי שָׁבוּעוֹת, לָעוֹמֶר	14
חֶסֶד שֶׁבְּתִפְאֶרֶת	הַיּוֹם חֲמִשָּׁה עָשָׂר יוֹם, שֶׁהֵם שְׁנֵי שָׁבוּעוֹת וְיוֹם אֶחָד, לָעוֹמֶר	15
גְּבוּרָה שֶׁבְּתִפְאֶרֶת	הַיּוֹם שִׁשָּׁה עָשָׂר יוֹם, שֶׁהֵם שְׁנֵי שָׁבוּעוֹת וּשְׁנֵי יָמִים, לָעוֹמֶר	16
תִּפְאֶרֶת שֶׁבְּתִפְאֶרֶת	הַיּוֹם שִׁבְעָה עָשָׂר יוֹם, שֶׁהֵם שְׁנֵי שָׁבוּעוֹת וּשְׁלֹשָׁה יָמִים, לָעוֹמֶר	17
נֶצַח שֶׁבְּתִפְאֶרֶת	הַיּוֹם שְׁמוֹנָה עָשָׂר יוֹם, שֶׁהֵם שְׁנֵי שָׁבוּעוֹת וְאַרְבָּעָה יָמִים, לָעוֹמֶר	18
הוֹד שֶׁבְּתִפְאֶרֶת	הַיּוֹם תִּשְׁעָה עָשָׂר יוֹם, שֶׁהֵם שְׁנֵי שָׁבוּעוֹת וַחֲמִשָּׁה יָמִים, לָעוֹמֶר	19
יְסוֹד שֶׁבְּתִפְאֶרֶת	הַיּוֹם עֶשְׂרִים יוֹם, שֶׁהֵם שְׁנֵי שָׁבוּעוֹת וְשִׁשָּׁה יָמִים, לָעוֹמֶר	20
מַלְכוּת שֶׁבְּתִפְאֶרֶת	הַיּוֹם אֶחָד וְעֶשְׂרִים יוֹם, שֶׁהֵם שְׁלֹשָׁה שָׁבוּעוֹת, לָעוֹמֶר	21
חֶסֶד שֶׁבְּנֶצַח	הַיּוֹם שְׁנַיִם וְעֶשְׂרִים יוֹם, שֶׁהֵם שְׁלֹשָׁה שָׁבוּעוֹת וְיוֹם אֶחָד, לָעוֹמֶר	22
גְּבוּרָה שֶׁבְּנֶצַח	הַיּוֹם שְׁלֹשָׁה וְעֶשְׂרִים יוֹם, שֶׁהֵם שְׁלֹשָׁה שָׁבוּעוֹת וּשְׁנֵי יָמִים, לָעוֹמֶר	23
תִּפְאֶרֶת שֶׁבְּנֶצַח	הַיּוֹם אַרְבָּעָה וְעֶשְׂרִים יוֹם, שֶׁהֵם שְׁלֹשָׁה שָׁבוּעוֹת וּשְׁלֹשָׁה יָמִים, לָעוֹמֶר	24
נֶצַח שֶׁבְּנֶצַח	הַיּוֹם חֲמִשָּׁה וְעֶשְׂרִים יוֹם, שֶׁהֵם שְׁלֹשָׁה שָׁבוּעוֹת וְאַרְבָּעָה יָמִים, לָעוֹמֶר	25
הוֹד שֶׁבְּנֶצַח	הַיּוֹם שִׁשָּׁה וְעֶשְׂרִים יוֹם, שֶׁהֵם שְׁלֹשָׁה שָׁבוּעוֹת וַחֲמִשָּׁה יָמִים, לָעוֹמֶר	26
יְסוֹד שֶׁבְּנֶצַח	הַיּוֹם שִׁבְעָה וְעֶשְׂרִים יוֹם, שֶׁהֵם שְׁלֹשָׁה שָׁבוּעוֹת וְשִׁשָּׁה יָמִים, לָעוֹמֶר	27
מַלְכוּת שֶׁבְּנֶצַח	הַיּוֹם שְׁמוֹנָה וְעֶשְׂרִים יוֹם, שֶׁהֵם אַרְבָּעָה שָׁבוּעוֹת, לָעוֹמֶר	28
חֶסֶד שֶׁבְּהוֹד	הַיּוֹם תִּשְׁעָה וְעֶשְׂרִים יוֹם, שֶׁהֵם אַרְבָּעָה שָׁבוּעוֹת וְיוֹם אֶחָד, לָעוֹמֶר	29
גְּבוּרָה שֶׁבְּהוֹד	הַיּוֹם שְׁלֹשִׁים יוֹם, שֶׁהֵם אַרְבָּעָה שָׁבוּעוֹת וּשְׁנֵי יָמִים, לָעוֹמֶר	30
תִּפְאֶרֶת שֶׁבְּהוֹד	הַיּוֹם אֶחָד וּשְׁלֹשִׁים יוֹם, שֶׁהֵם אַרְבָּעָה שָׁבוּעוֹת וּשְׁלֹשָׁה יָמִים, לָעוֹמֶר	31
נֶצַח שֶׁבְּהוֹד	הַיּוֹם שְׁנַיִם וּשְׁלֹשִׁים יוֹם, שֶׁהֵם אַרְבָּעָה שָׁבוּעוֹת וְאַרְבָּעָה יָמִים, לָעוֹמֶר	32
הוֹד שֶׁבְּהוֹד	הַיּוֹם שְׁלֹשָׁה וּשְׁלֹשִׁים יוֹם, שֶׁהֵם אַרְבָּעָה שָׁבוּעוֹת וַחֲמִשָּׁה יָמִים, לָעוֹמֶר	33
יְסוֹד שֶׁבְּהוֹד	הַיּוֹם אַרְבָּעָה וּשְׁלֹשִׁים יוֹם, שֶׁהֵם אַרְבָּעָה שָׁבוּעוֹת וְשִׁשָּׁה יָמִים, לָעוֹמֶר	34
מַלְכוּת שֶׁבְּהוֹד	הַיּוֹם חֲמִשָּׁה וּשְׁלֹשִׁים יוֹם, שֶׁהֵם חֲמִשָּׁה שָׁבוּעוֹת, לָעוֹמֶר	35
חֶסֶד שֶׁבִּיסוֹד	הַיּוֹם שִׁשָּׁה וּשְׁלֹשִׁים יוֹם, שֶׁהֵם חֲמִשָּׁה שָׁבוּעוֹת וְיוֹם אֶחָד, לָעוֹמֶר	36
גְּבוּרָה שֶׁבִּיסוֹד	הַיּוֹם שִׁבְעָה וּשְׁלֹשִׁים יוֹם, שֶׁהֵם חֲמִשָּׁה שָׁבוּעוֹת וּשְׁנֵי יָמִים, לָעוֹמֶר	37
תִּפְאֶרֶת שֶׁבִּיסוֹד	הַיּוֹם שְׁמוֹנָה וּשְׁלֹשִׁים יוֹם, שֶׁהֵם חֲמִשָּׁה שָׁבוּעוֹת וּשְׁלֹשָׁה יָמִים, לָעוֹמֶר	38
נֶצַח שֶׁבִּיסוֹד	הַיּוֹם תִּשְׁעָה וּשְׁלֹשִׁים יוֹם, שֶׁהֵם חֲמִשָּׁה שָׁבוּעוֹת וְאַרְבָּעָה יָמִים, לָעוֹמֶר	39
הוֹד שֶׁבִּיסוֹד	הַיּוֹם אַרְבָּעִים יוֹם, שֶׁהֵם חֲמִשָּׁה שָׁבוּעוֹת וַחֲמִשָּׁה יָמִים, לָעוֹמֶר	40
יְסוֹד שֶׁבִּיסוֹד	הַיּוֹם אֶחָד וְאַרְבָּעִים יוֹם, שֶׁהֵם חֲמִשָּׁה שָׁבוּעוֹת וְשִׁשָּׁה יָמִים, לָעוֹמֶר	41
מַלְכוּת שֶׁבִּיסוֹד	הַיּוֹם שְׁנַיִם וְאַרְבָּעִים יוֹם, שֶׁהֵם שִׁשָּׁה שָׁבוּעוֹת, לָעוֹמֶר	42
חֶסֶד שֶׁבְּמַלְכוּת	הַיּוֹם שְׁלֹשָׁה וְאַרְבָּעִים יוֹם, שֶׁהֵם שִׁשָּׁה שָׁבוּעוֹת וְיוֹם אֶחָד, לָעוֹמֶר	43
גְּבוּרָה שֶׁבְּמַלְכוּת	הַיּוֹם אַרְבָּעָה וְאַרְבָּעִים יוֹם, שֶׁהֵם שִׁשָּׁה שָׁבוּעוֹת וּשְׁנֵי יָמִים, לָעוֹמֶר	44
תִּפְאֶרֶת שֶׁבְּמַלְכוּת	הַיּוֹם חֲמִשָּׁה וְאַרְבָּעִים יוֹם, שֶׁהֵם שִׁשָּׁה שָׁבוּעוֹת וּשְׁלֹשָׁה יָמִים, לָעוֹמֶר	45
נֶצַח שֶׁבְּמַלְכוּת	הַיּוֹם שִׁשָּׁה וְאַרְבָּעִים יוֹם, שֶׁהֵם שִׁשָּׁה שָׁבוּעוֹת וְאַרְבָּעָה יָמִים, לָעוֹמֶר	46
הוֹד שֶׁבְּמַלְכוּת	הַיּוֹם שִׁבְעָה וְאַרְבָּעִים יוֹם, שֶׁהֵם שִׁשָּׁה שָׁבוּעוֹת וַחֲמִשָּׁה יָמִים, לָעוֹמֶר	47
יְסוֹד שֶׁבְּמַלְכוּת	הַיּוֹם שְׁמוֹנָה וְאַרְבָּעִים יוֹם, שֶׁהֵם שִׁשָּׁה שָׁבוּעוֹת וְשִׁשָּׁה יָמִים, לָעוֹמֶר	48
מַלְכוּת שֶׁבְּמַלְכוּת	הַיּוֹם תִּשְׁעָה וְאַרְבָּעִים יוֹם, שֶׁהֵם שִׁבְעָה שָׁבוּעוֹת, לָעוֹמֶר.	49

DAY	COUNT
1	TODAY IS ONE DAY OF THE *OMER*.
2	TODAY IS TWO DAYS OF THE *OMER*.
3	TODAY IS THREE DAYS OF THE *OMER*.
4	TODAY IS FOUR DAYS OF THE *OMER*.
5	TODAY IS FIVE DAYS OF THE *OMER*.
6	TODAY IS SIX DAYS OF THE *OMER*.
7	TODAY IS SEVEN DAYS, WHICH ARE ONE WEEK OF THE *OMER*.
8	TODAY IS EIGHT DAYS, WHICH ARE ONE WEEK AND ONE DAY OF THE *OMER*.
9	TODAY IS NINE DAYS, WHICH ARE ONE WEEK AND TWO DAYS OF THE *OMER*.
10	TODAY IS TEN DAYS, WHICH ARE ONE WEEK AND THREE DAYS OF THE *OMER*.
11	TODAY IS ELEVEN DAYS, WHICH ARE ONE WEEK AND FOUR DAYS OF THE *OMER*.
12	TODAY IS TWELVE DAYS, WHICH ARE ONE WEEK AND FIVE DAYS OF THE *OMER*.
13	TODAY IS THIRTEEN DAYS, WHICH ARE ONE WEEK AND SIX DAYS OF THE *OMER*.
14	TODAY IS FOURTEEN DAYS, WHICH ARE TWO WEEKS OF THE *OMER*.
15	TODAY IS FIFTEEN DAYS, WHICH ARE TWO WEEKS AND ONE DAY OF THE *OMER*.
16	TODAY IS SIXTEEN DAYS, WHICH ARE TWO WEEKS AND TWO DAYS OF THE *OMER*.
17	TODAY IS SEVENTEEN DAYS, WHICH ARE TWO WEEKS AND THREE DAYS OF THE *OMER*.
18	TODAY IS EIGHTEEN DAYS, WHICH ARE TWO WEEKS AND FOUR DAYS OF THE *OMER*.
19	TODAY IS NINETEEN DAYS, WHICH ARE TWO WEEKS AND FIVE DAYS OF THE *OMER*.
20	TODAY IS TWENTY DAYS, WHICH ARE TWO WEEKS AND SIX DAYS OF THE *OMER*.
21	TODAY IS TWENTY-ONE DAYS, WHICH ARE THREE WEEKS OF THE *OMER*.
22	TODAY IS TWENTY-TWO DAYS, WHICH ARE THREE WEEKS AND ONE DAY OF THE *OMER*.
23	TODAY IS TWENTY-THREE DAYS, WHICH ARE THREE WEEKS AND TWO DAYS OF THE *OMER*.
24	TODAY IS TWENTY-FOUR DAYS, WHICH ARE THREE WEEKS AND THREE DAYS OF THE *OMER*.
25	TODAY IS TWENTY-FIVE DAYS, WHICH ARE THREE WEEKS AND FOUR DAYS OF THE *OMER*.
26	TODAY IS TWENTY-SIX DAYS, WHICH ARE THREE WEEKS AND FIVE DAYS OF THE *OMER*.
27	TODAY IS TWENTY-SEVEN DAYS, WHICH ARE THREE WEEKS AND SIX DAYS OF THE *OMER*.
28	TODAY IS TWENTY-EIGHT DAYS, WHICH ARE FOUR WEEKS OF THE *OMER*.
29	TODAY IS TWENTY-NINE DAYS, WHICH ARE FOUR WEEKS AND ONE DAY OF THE *OMER*.
30	TODAY IS THIRTY DAYS, WHICH ARE FOUR WEEKS AND TWO DAYS OF THE *OMER*.
31	TODAY IS THIRTY-ONE DAYS, WHICH ARE FOUR WEEKS AND THREE DAYS OF THE *OMER*.
32	TODAY IS THIRTY-TWO DAYS, WHICH ARE FOUR WEEKS AND FOUR DAYS OF THE *OMER*.
33	TODAY IS THIRTY-THREE DAYS, WHICH ARE FOUR WEEKS AND FIVE DAYS OF THE *OMER*.
34	TODAY IS THIRTY-FOUR DAYS, WHICH ARE FOUR WEEKS AND SIX DAYS OF THE *OMER*.
35	TODAY IS THIRTY-FIVE DAYS, WHICH ARE FIVE WEEKS OF THE *OMER*.
36	TODAY IS THIRTY-SIX DAYS, WHICH ARE FIVE WEEKS AND ONE DAY OF THE *OMER*.
37	TODAY IS THIRTY-SEVEN DAYS, WHICH ARE FIVE WEEKS AND TWO DAYS OF THE *OMER*.
38	TODAY IS THIRTY-EIGHT DAYS, WHICH ARE FIVE WEEKS AND THREE DAYS OF THE *OMER*.
39	TODAY IS THIRTY-NINE DAYS, WHICH ARE FIVE WEEKS AND FOUR DAYS OF THE *OMER*.
40	TODAY IS FORTY DAYS, WHICH ARE FIVE WEEKS AND FIVE DAYS OF THE *OMER*.
41	TODAY IS FORTY-ONE DAYS, WHICH ARE FIVE WEEKS AND SIX DAYS OF THE *OMER*.
42	TODAY IS FORTY-TWO DAYS, WHICH ARE SIX WEEKS OF THE *OMER*.
43	TODAY IS FORTY-THREE DAYS, WHICH ARE SIX WEEKS AND ONE DAY OF THE *OMER*.
44	TODAY IS FORTY-FOUR DAYS, WHICH ARE SIX WEEKS AND TWO DAYS OF THE *OMER*.
45	TODAY IS FORTY-FIVE DAYS, WHICH ARE SIX WEEKS AND THREE DAYS OF THE *OMER*.
46	TODAY IS FORTY-SIX DAYS, WHICH ARE SIX WEEKS AND FOUR DAYS OF THE *OMER*.
47	TODAY IS FORTY-SEVEN DAYS, WHICH ARE SIX WEEKS AND FIVE DAYS OF THE *OMER*.
48	TODAY IS FORTY-EIGHT DAYS, WHICH ARE SIX WEEKS AND SIX DAYS OF THE *OMER*.
49	TODAY IS FORTY-NINE DAYS, WHICH ARE SEVEN WEEKS OF THE *OMER*.

❧{ KIDDUSH LEVANAH / קידוש לבנה }❧

——— תהלים קמח:א-י / Psalm 148:1-6 ———

הַלְלוּיָהּ; הַלְלוּ אֶת יהוה מִן הַשָּׁמַיִם,*
« the heavens;* ‹ from ‹ HASHEM ‹ Praise « Halleluyah!

הַלְלוּהוּ בַּמְּרוֹמִים. הַלְלוּהוּ כָל מַלְאָכָיו,
« His angels; ‹ all ‹ Praise Him, « in the heights. ‹ praise Him

הַלְלוּהוּ כָל צְבָאָיו. הַלְלוּהוּ שֶׁמֶשׁ וְיָרֵחַ,
« and moon; ‹ sun ‹ Praise Him, « His legions. ‹ all ‹ praise Him,

הַלְלוּהוּ כָל כּוֹכְבֵי אוֹר. הַלְלוּהוּ שְׁמֵי הַשָּׁמַיִם,
« of the ‹ the most ‹ Praise Him, « that ‹ stars ‹ all ‹ praise Him,
heavens   exalted   are bright.

קִדּוּשׁ לְבָנָה ❧ / Sanctification of the Moon

The Sanctification of the Moon [Kiddush Levanah] should not be confused with the Sanhedrin's קִדּוּשׁ הַחֹדֶשׁ, Sanctification of the Month, by which the court pronounced the appropriate day as the beginning of a new month. That proclamation was the sole province of the court and affected the calendar; the Sanctification of the Moon — not the month — has no calendrical significance.

There are two bases for this ritual. Rabbi Yochanan taught that one who blesses the new moon in its proper time is regarded like one who greets the Shechinah [God's Presence] (Sanhedrin 42a). This is because the way we recognize the existence of God is through His miracles and revelations to Israel. In nature it is seen through the orderly functioning of the enormously complex heavenly bodies. We may note that as science discovers more and more of the vastness of the universe, the presence of a Creator becomes more and more obvious to one who wishes to see; indeed, to deny Him is ludicrous. This phenomenon is most apparent in the cycles of the moon, because its changes are more visible than those of any other body. Thus, when we greet the moon, we greet its Maker and Guide (Rabbeinu Yonah, Berachos 4).

The second aspect of the prayer is its significance for the history of Israel. Just as the moon is reborn after a period of decline and total disappearance, so too, Israel's decline will end and its light will once again blaze to fullness. As an example, the Midrash (Shemos Rabbah 15) states that when Israel is worthy of God's favor it is like the waxing moon, but when it is not worthy, it is like the waning moon. In this vein, ancient Israel's rise and fall paralleled the phases of the moon. There were fifteen generations from Abraham to Solomon, during which Israel rose to the zenith of its greatness. The decline began during Solomon's reign; there were fifteen generations from then (including Solomon) to the reign of Zedekiah, when the First Temple was destroyed. This corresponds to the twenty-nine-day cycle of the moon.

Because the moon is such a significant allusion to God as the Creator and to Israel's rebirth, Kiddush Levanah should be recited joyously, preferably at the conclusion of the Sabbath while people are still dressed in their finest clothes. Conversely, it is not recited on the Sabbath or a Festival (except under unusual circumstances), because we do not set two different causes for joy in competition with one another (World of Prayer). It is also customary to defer Kiddush Levanah until after Tishah B'Av and Yom Kippur because the sadness of Av and the dread of the Days of Judgment are inappropriate to the joy required during Kiddush Levanah.

הַלְלוּיָהּ הַלְלוּ אֶת ה׳ מִן הַשָּׁמַיִם — Halleluyah! Praise HASHEM from the heavens. The first six

וְהַמַּיִם אֲשֶׁר מֵעַל הַשָּׁמָיִם. יְהַלְלוּ אֶת שֵׁם

the Name ⟨ Let them ⟪ the heavens. ⟨ above ⟨ that are ⟨ and the
praise waters

יהוה, כִּי הוּא צִוָּה וְנִבְרָאוּ. וַיַּעֲמִידֵם לָעַד

for ever ⟨ And He ⟪ and they ⟨ commanded ⟨ He ⟨ for ⟪ of
established them were created. HASHEM,

לְעוֹלָם, חָק נָתַן וְלֹא יַעֲבוֹר.

⟪ change. ⟨ that ⟨ He ⟨ a ⟪ and ever,
will not issued decree

MANY RECITE THE FOLLOWING DECLARATION OF INTENT:

הֲרֵינִי מוּכָן וּמְזֻמָּן לְקַיֵּם הַמִּצְוָה לְקַדֵּשׁ הַלְּבָנָה.

⟪ the moon. ⟨ to sanctify ⟨ the ⟨ to ⟨ and ⟨ prepared ⟨ I am
commandment perform ready hereby

לְשֵׁם יְחוּד קֻדְשָׁא בְּרִיךְ הוּא וּשְׁכִינְתֵּיה עַל יְדֵי הַהוּא

Him ⟨ through ⟨ and His ⟨ is He, ⟨ Blessed ⟪ of the Holy ⟨ of the ⟨ For the
Presence, One, unification sake

טָמִיר וְנֶעְלָם, בְּשֵׁם כָּל יִשְׂרָאֵל.

⟪ Israel. ⟨ of all ⟨ [I pray] in ⟨ and Who is ⟨ Who is
the name inscrutable hidden

verses of Psalm 148 describe how the heavens praise God, and they are therefore used as the preface to *Kiddush Levanah*. The rest of the psalm, however, deals with man's praise of God.

◆§ Laws of *Kiddush Levanah*

It is preferable that *Kiddush Levanah* be recited: (a) standing under the open sky; (b) with a *minyan*; (c) at the departure of the Sabbath. When these optimal conditions are not feasible, they may be waived (e.g., a shut-in may recite *Kiddush Levanah* indoors if he can see the moon through a window or door; one who cannot join a *minyan* may say it himself — see below; if the sky is cloudy at the departure of the Sabbath, *Kiddush Levanah* may be recited on another night of the week).

The earliest time for reciting *Kiddush Levanah* is 72 hours after the *molad* (first appearance of the new moon), although some authorities would delay its recitation until seven full days after the *molad*.

The latest time for *Kiddush Levanah* is midmonth, 14 days, 18 hours and 22 minutes (some authorities extend this limit to 15 full days) after the *molad*.

Kiddush Levanah should not be recited on a Sabbath or a Festival unless it is the last remaining night before the midmonth deadline.

If one cannot recite *Kiddush Levanah* with a *minyan* he should try to do so in the presence of at least three others with whom to exchange the *Shalom Aleichem* greeting. If this, too, is not possible, one may recite *Kiddush Levanah* by himself. During Tishrei, *Kiddush Levanah* is generally postponed until after Yom Kippur; during Av, until after Tishah B'Av.

ONE SHOULD LOOK AT THE MOON BEFORE RECITING THIS BLESSING.

בָּרוּךְ* אַתָּה יהוה אֱלֹהֵינוּ מֶלֶךְ הָעוֹלָם, אֲשֶׁר

‹ Who ‹‹ of the universe, ‹ King ‹ our God, ‹ Hashem, ‹ are You, ‹ Blessed*

בְּמַאֲמָרוֹ בָּרָא* שְׁחָקִים, וּבְרוּחַ פִּיו כָּל צְבָאָם.

‹‹ their legion. ‹ all ‹ of His mouth ‹ and with the breath ‹‹ the heavens, ‹ created* ‹ with His utterance

חֹק וּזְמַן נָתַן לָהֶם שֶׁלֹּא יְשַׁנּוּ אֶת תַּפְקִידָם.

‹‹ their assigned task. ‹ alter ‹ that they not ‹‹ them, ‹ did He give ‹ and a schedule ‹ A rule

שָׂשִׂים וּשְׂמֵחִים לַעֲשׂוֹת רְצוֹן קוֹנָם, פּוֹעֵל אֱמֶת

‹ truth, ‹ the One Who does ‹‹ of their Creator, ‹ the will ‹ to perform ‹ and happy ‹ They are joyous

שֶׁפְּעֻלָּתוֹ אֱמֶת. וְלַלְּבָנָה אָמַר שֶׁתִּתְחַדֵּשׁ, עֲטֶרֶת

‹ as a crown ‹ that it should renew itself, ‹ He said ‹ To the moon ‹‹ is truth. ‹ Whose deed

תִּפְאֶרֶת לַעֲמוּסֵי בָטֶן, שֶׁהֵם עֲתִידִים לְהִתְחַדֵּשׁ

‹ to renew themselves ‹ are destined ‹ those who ‹‹ from the womb, ‹ for those borne [by Him] ‹ of splendor

כְּמוֹתָהּ,* וּלְפָאֵר לְיוֹצְרָם עַל שֵׁם כְּבוֹד

‹ of His glorious ‹ the sake ‹ for ‹ their Molder, ‹ and to glorify ‹‹ like it,* ‹ kingdom. [row order: כְּבוֹד שֵׁם עַל]

מַלְכוּתוֹ. בָּרוּךְ אַתָּה יהוה, מְחַדֵּשׁ חֳדָשִׁים.

‹‹ the months. ‹ Who renews ‹‹ Hashem, ‹ are You, ‹ Blessed ‹‹ kingdom.

RECITE THREE TIMES:

בָּרוּךְ יוֹצְרֵךְ,* בָּרוּךְ עוֹשֵׂךְ, בָּרוּךְ קוֹנֵךְ,

‹‹ is your Owner; ‹ blessed ‹‹ is your Maker; ‹ blessed ‹‹ is your Molder;* ‹ Blessed

---

בָּרוּךְ ... בְּמַאֲמָרוֹ בָּרָא אֲשֶׁר — *Blessed ... Who with His utterance created.* God created heaven and its infinite bodies with nothing more than His word. The very existence of so many galaxies and solar systems testifies undeniably to Creation because so huge and complex a universe could not have come about by chance.

לְהִתְחַדֵּשׁ כְּמוֹתָהּ — *To renew themselves like it.* The majesty of the Jewish people will be re-

newed, and the nation will render praise to God and the glories of His kingdom. Alternatively, this refers to the dead who will be revivified after the Redemption (*Re'ah*).

בָּרוּךְ יוֹצְרֵךְ — *Blessed is your Molder.* The initials of these four titles of God spell יַעֲקֹב, *Jacob.* Just as the moon is called הַמָּאוֹר הַקָּטֹן, *the smaller luminary (Genesis* 1:16), in relation to the sun, so Jacob was called בֶּנָהּ הַקָּטֹן, *her younger* [lit.,

בָּרוּךְ **בּוֹרְאָךְ.**

》 is your Creator. 〈 blessed

RECITE THREE TIMES. RISE ON THE TOES AS IF IN DANCE:

כְּשֵׁם שֶׁאֲנִי רוֹקֵד* כְּנֶגְדֵּךְ וְאֵינִי יָכוֹל לִנְגּוֹעַ

〈 to touch 〈 able 〈 but I am not 〈 opposite you, 〈 dance* 〈 as I 〈 Just

בָּךְ, כַּךְ לֹא יוּכְלוּ כָּל אוֹיְבַי לִנְגּוֹעַ בִּי לְרָעָה.

》 for evil. 〈 me 〈 to touch 》–all my enemies– 》 may they not be able 〈 so 》 you,

RECITE THREE TIMES:

תִּפֹּל עֲלֵיהֶם אֵימָתָה וָפַחַד, בִּגְדֹל זְרוֹעֲךָ

〈 of Your 〈 at the 〈 and fear; 〈 terror 〈 upon them 〈 Let there fall
   arm, 　greatness

יִדְּמוּ כָּאֶבֶן.¹

》 as stone. 〈 let them be still

RECITE THREE TIMES:

כָּאֶבֶן יִדְּמוּ* זְרוֹעֲךָ בִּגְדֹל וָפַחַד אֵימָתָה

〈 and terror 〈 fear 》 greatness; 〈 at Your arm's 〈 let them be still,* 〈 As stone

עֲלֵיהֶם תִּפֹּל.

》 let there fall. 〈 upon them

RECITE THREE TIMES:

דָּוִד מֶלֶךְ יִשְׂרָאֵל* חַי וְקַיָּם.

》 and endures. 〈 lives 〈 of Israel,* 〈 king 〈 David,

---

(1) *Exodus* 15:16.

smaller] son (*Genesis* 27:15,42), because he was the younger of Rebecca's twin sons. This alludes to the concept, derived by *Vayikra Rabbah* 36 from *Isaiah* 43:1, that God created the universe for the sake of Jacob and his offspring (*Sh'lah*).

This verse and the following ones are repeated three times to give special emphasis to their message.

כְּשֵׁם שֶׁאֲנִי רוֹקֵד — *Just as I dance*. Often in Scripture, a prophecy is accompanied by a physical act. This has the effect of making the prophecy irreversible. Here too, we, in a symbolic way, exert ourselves to touch the moon while remaining on earth, and we pray that, in

like fashion, the exertions of our enemies against us will be of no avail. Thus, we reinforce the point by a physical act (*Dover Shalom*).

כָּאֶבֶן יִדְּמוּ — *As stone let them be still.* We now repeat the previous verse, but we reverse the order of the words. This reversal implies that the natural order of nature, too, may sometimes be reversed. In other words, God will sometimes protect us through the natural order of events; at other times He will perform open miracles to thwart those who seek our harm (*World of Prayer*).

דָּוִד מֶלֶךְ יִשְׂרָאֵל — *David, king of Israel.* As noted above, the phases of the moon allude to the

THE PERSON WHO WAS GREETED RESPONDS: **EXTEND GREETINGS THREE TIMES:**

עֲלֵיכֶם שָׁלוֹם.   שָׁלוֹם עֲלֵיכֶם.*

‹‹ peace. ‹ Upon you,   ‹‹ upon you.* ‹ Peace

RECITE THREE TIMES:

סִמָּן טוֹב וּמַזָּל טוֹב יְהֵא לָנוּ וּלְכָל יִשְׂרָאֵל. אָמֵן.

‹‹ Amen. ‹‹ Israel. ‹ and ‹ for us ‹ may ‹‹ that is ‹ and ‹ that is ‹ A sign
for all   there be good, fortune good

קוֹל דּוֹדִי הִנֵּה זֶה בָּא מְדַלֵּג עַל הֶהָרִים

‹‹ the ‹ over ‹ leaping ‹‹ came ‹ it ‹ indeed, ‹‹ of my ‹ The voice
mountains, [suddenly], beloved,

מְקַפֵּץ עַל הַגְּבָעוֹת. דּוֹמֶה דוֹדִי לִצְבִי אוֹ

‹ or ‹ to a gazelle ‹ is my ‹ Comparable ‹‹ the hills. ‹ over ‹ skipping
beloved

לְעֹפֶר הָאַיָּלִים, הִנֵּה זֶה עוֹמֵד אַחַר כָּתְלֵנוּ,

‹‹ our wall, ‹ behind ‹ was standing ‹ He ‹ Indeed, ‹‹ of the deer. ‹ to a young one

מַשְׁגִּיחַ מִן הַחַלֹּנוֹת, מֵצִיץ מִן הַחֲרַכִּים.[1]

‹‹ the lattices. ‹ through ‹ peering ‹‹ the windows, ‹ through ‹ observing

──────── תהלים קכא / Psalm 121 ────────

שִׁיר לַמַּעֲלוֹת; אֶשָּׂא עֵינַי אֶל הֶהָרִים, מֵאַיִן

‹ from ‹‹ the ‹ to ‹ my eyes ‹ I raise ‹‹ to the ascents. ‹ A song
whence mountains;

יָבֹא עֶזְרִי. עֶזְרִי מֵעִם יהוה, עֹשֵׂה שָׁמַיִם וָאָרֶץ.

‹‹ and earth. ‹ of heaven ‹ Maker ‹‹ Hashem, ‹ is from ‹ My help ‹‹ my help? ‹ will
come

---

(1) *Song of Songs* 2:8-9.

Davidic dynasty. Thus, we include this confident expression of faith that David's reign endures and will shine again. This verse was composed by Rabbi Yehudah HaNasi (*Rosh Chodesh* 25a).

שָׁלוֹם עֲלֵיכֶם — *Peace upon you*. Various reasons are given for the inclusion of this greeting in *Kiddush Levanah*.

❏ Having greeted the *Shechinah*, we joyously bestow the blessing of peace upon one another (*Levush*).

❏ After cursing our enemies, we make clear that we wish no ill to our brethren (*Mateh Moshe*).

❏ At the beginning of Creation, as recorded in the Talmud (*Chullin* 60b), the sun and moon were of equal size. When the moon complained that two kings cannot wear the same crown, i.e., it should be larger than the sun, the moon was made smaller. Nevertheless, the sun continues to shine its brilliant light upon the moon, thus delivering a message to

אַל יִתֵּן לַמּוֹט רַגְלֶךָ, אַל יָנוּם שֹׁמְרֶךָ. הִנֵּה לֹא

⟨ [He] ⟩ ⟨ It is so, ⟫ will your ⟨ not slumber ⟫ of your ⟨ the ⟨ He will not
neither that   Guardian.   foot;   faltering   allow

יָנוּם וְלֹא יִישָׁן, שׁוֹמֵר יִשְׂרָאֵל. יהוה שֹׁמְרֶךָ,

⟫is your Guardian; ⟨ Hashem ⟫of Israel. ⟨ — the Guardian⟫ sleeps ⟨ nor ⟨ slumbers

יהוה צִלְּךָ עַל יַד יְמִינֶךָ. יוֹמָם הַשֶּׁמֶשׁ לֹא

⟨ will not ⟨ the sun ⟨ By day ⟫ your right hand. ⟨ at ⟨ is your ⟨ Hashem
protective Shade

יַכֶּכָּה, וְיָרֵחַ בַּלָּיְלָה. יהוה יִשְׁמָרְךָ מִכָּל רָע,

⟫evil; ⟨ from ⟨ will protect ⟨ Hashem ⟫ by night. ⟨ nor the ⟫ harm you,
every   you   moon

יִשְׁמֹר אֶת נַפְשֶׁךָ. יהוה יִשְׁמָר צֵאתְךָ וּבוֹאֶךָ,

⟨ and your ⟨ your ⟨ will ⟨ Hashem ⟫ your soul. ⟨ He will
arrival,   departure safeguard   safeguard

מֵעַתָּה וְעַד עוֹלָם.

⟫ eternity. ⟨ until ⟨ from this time

—————— תהלים קנ / Psalm 150 ——————

הַלְלוּיָהּ; הַלְלוּ אֵל בְּקָדְשׁוֹ, הַלְלוּהוּ בִּרְקִיעַ

⟨ in the ⟨ praise Him ⟫ in His ⟨ God ⟨ Praise ⟫ Halleluyah!
firmament   Sanctuary;

עֻזּוֹ. הַלְלוּהוּ בִגְבוּרֹתָיו, הַלְלוּהוּ כְּרֹב גֻּדְלוֹ.

⟫ of His ⟨ as befits the ⟨ praise Him ⟫ for His mighty acts; ⟨ Praise Him ⟫ of His
greatness. abundance   power.

הַלְלוּהוּ בְּתֵקַע שׁוֹפָר, הַלְלוּהוּ בְּנֵבֶל וְכִנּוֹר.

⟫ and harp. ⟨ with lyre ⟨ praise Him ⟫ of the shofar; ⟨ with the blast ⟨ Praise Him

הַלְלוּהוּ בְּתֹף וּמָחוֹל, הַלְלוּהוּ בְּמִנִּים וְעֻגָב.

⟫ and flute. ⟨ with organ ⟨ praise Him ⟫ and dance; ⟨ with drum ⟨ Praise Him

הַלְלוּהוּ בְצִלְצְלֵי שָׁמַע, הַלְלוּהוּ בְּצִלְצְלֵי

⟨ with trumpets ⟨ praise Him ⟨ clanging; ⟨ with cymbals ⟨ Praise Him

man not to harbor a grudge against others
who have wronged him. We express this

resolve by wishing peace upon our fellow
Jews (Anaf Yosef).

תְּרוּעָה. כֹּל הַנְּשָׁמָה תְּהַלֵּל יָהּ; הַלְלוּיָהּ.
‹‹ Halleluyah! ‹‹ God, ‹ praise ‹ souls ‹ Let all ‹‹ resounding.

תָּנָא דְּבֵי רַבִּי יִשְׁמָעֵאל: אִלְמָלֵי לֹא זָכוּ
‹ not privileged ‹ If it had been ‹‹ Yishmael: ‹ of ‹ by the ‹ It was
that Rabbi Academy taught

יִשְׂרָאֵל אֶלָּא לְהַקְבִּיל פְּנֵי אֲבִיהֶם שֶׁבַּשָּׁמַיִם
‹ in Heaven ‹ of their Father ‹ the ‹ [the mitzvah] ‹ except ‹ was Israel
Countenance of greeting for

פַּעַם אַחַת בַּחֹדֶשׁ, דַּיָּם. אָמַר אַבַּיֵּי: הִלְכָּךְ
‹ Therefore ‹‹ Abaye: ‹ Said ‹‹ it would have ‹ in a month, ‹ once
sufficed them.

צָרִיךְ לְמֵימְרָא מְעֻמָּד.¹ מִי זֹאת עֹלָה מִן
‹ from ‹ who rises ‹ is this ‹ Who ‹‹ while standing. ‹ to recite it ‹ it is necessary

הַמִּדְבָּר מִתְרַפֶּקֶת עַל דּוֹדָהּ.²
‹‹ her Beloved? ‹ to ‹ clinging ‹‹ the desert,

וִיהִי רָצוֹן מִלְפָנֶיךָ, יהוה אֱלֹהַי וֵאלֹהֵי אֲבוֹתַי,
‹‹ of my ‹ and the God ‹ my God ‹ Hashem, ‹‹ before You, ‹ the will ‹ May it be
forefathers,

לְמַלֹּאת פְּגִימַת הַלְּבָנָה, וְלֹא יִהְיֶה בָּהּ שׁוּם
‹ any ‹ in it ‹ be ‹ that there not ‹‹ of the moon, ‹ the flaw ‹ to fill

מִעוּט, וִיהִי אוֹר הַלְּבָנָה כְּאוֹר הַחַמָּה, וּכְאוֹר
‹ and like ‹‹ of the sun ‹ be like ‹ of the moon ‹ And may the ‹‹ diminution.
the light the light light

שִׁבְעַת יְמֵי בְרֵאשִׁית,³ כְּמוֹ שֶׁהָיְתָה קוֹדֶם
‹ before ‹ it was ‹ as ‹‹ of Creation, ‹ days ‹ of the seven

מִעוּטָהּ, שֶׁנֶּאֱמַר: אֶת שְׁנֵי הַמְּאֹרֹת הַגְּדֹלִים.⁴
‹‹ that are great. ‹ luminaries ‹ The two ‹‹ as it is said: ‹‹ its diminishment,

וְיִתְקַיֵּם בָּנוּ מִקְרָא שֶׁכָּתוּב: וּבִקְשׁוּ אֶת יהוה
‹ Hashem, ‹ They shall seek ‹‹ that is written: ‹ the verse ‹ with us ‹ And may
there be fulfilled

(1) Sanhedrin 42a (see Rashi). (2) Song of Songs 8:5. (3) Cf. Isaiah 30:26. (4) Genesis 1:16.

אֱלֹהֵיהֶם, וְאֵת דָּוִיד מַלְכָּם.¹ אָמֵן.

‹‹ Amen. ‹‹ their king. ‹ and David, ‹ their God,

——— תהלים סז / Psalm 67 ———

לַמְנַצֵּחַ בִּנְגִינֹת מִזְמוֹר שִׁיר. אֱלֹהִים יְחָנֵּנוּ

‹ favor us ‹ May God ‹‹ a song. ‹ a psalm, ‹ with the *neginos,* ‹ For the conductor

וִיבָרְכֵנוּ, יָאֵר פָּנָיו אִתָּנוּ סֶלָה. לָדַעַת בָּאָרֶץ

‹ on earth ‹ To make known ‹‹ Selah. ‹‹ with us, ‹ His countenance ‹ may He illuminate ‹‹ and bless us,

דַּרְכֶּךָ, בְּכָל גּוֹיִם יְשׁוּעָתֶךָ. יוֹדוּךָ עַמִּים, אֱלֹהִים;

‹‹ O God; ‹ will the peoples, ‹ Acknowledge You ‹‹ Your salvation. ‹ nations ‹ among all ‹‹ Your way,

יוֹדוּךָ עַמִּים כֻּלָּם. יִשְׂמְחוּ וִירַנְּנוּ לְאֻמִּים, כִּי

‹ because ‹‹ regimes, ‹ and singing for joy will be ‹ Glad will be ‹‹ — all of them. ‹‹ will the peoples ‹ acknowledge You

תִשְׁפֹּט עַמִּים מִישֹׁר, וּלְאֻמִּים בָּאָרֶץ תַּנְחֵם

‹‹ [with fairness] You will guide, ‹ on earth ‹ and the regimes ‹‹ fairly ‹ the peoples ‹ You will judge

סֶלָה. יוֹדוּךָ עַמִּים, אֱלֹהִים; יוֹדוּךָ עַמִּים

‹‹ will the peoples ‹ acknowledge You ‹‹ O God; ‹ will the peoples, ‹ Acknowledge You ‹‹ Selah.

כֻּלָּם. אֶרֶץ נָתְנָה יְבוּלָהּ, יְבָרְכֵנוּ אֱלֹהִים

‹‹ may God bless us ‹‹ its produce; ‹ will then have yielded ‹ The earth ‹‹ — all of them.

אֱלֹהֵינוּ. יְבָרְכֵנוּ אֱלֹהִים, וְיִירְאוּ אוֹתוֹ כָּל

‹ — all ‹‹ Him ‹ and may they fear ‹‹ May God bless us, ‹‹ — our God.

אַפְסֵי אָרֶץ.

‹‹ of the earth. ‹ the ends

IN MOST CONGREGATIONS, עָלֵינוּ, *ALEINU* (PAGE 442), FOLLOWED BY THE MOURNER'S *KADDISH* (PAGE 445), IS REPEATED AT THIS POINT.

---

(1) *Hosea* 3:5.

❧ קריאת שמע על המטה / THE BEDTIME SHEMA ❧

רִבּוֹנוֹ שֶׁל עוֹלָם, הֲרֵינִי מוֹחֵל לְכָל מִי שֶׁהִכְעִיס
⟨ angered ⟨ who ⟨ anyone ⟨ forgive ⟨ I hereby ⟨⟨ the universe, ⟨ of ⟨ Master

וְהִקְנִיט אוֹתִי, אוֹ שֶׁחָטָא כְּנֶגְדִּי – בֵּין בְּגוּפִי, בֵּין
⟨ whether ⟨ against ⟨ – whether ⟨⟨ against me ⟨ who sinned ⟨ or ⟨ me ⟨ or
my body, antagonized

בְּמָמוֹנִי, בֵּין בִּכְבוֹדִי, בֵּין בְּכָל אֲשֶׁר לִי; בֵּין בְּאוֹנֶס,
⟨ [he did so] ⟨ whether ⟨⟨ mine; ⟨ that ⟨ against ⟨ or ⟨ against ⟨ whether ⟨ against
accidentally, is anything whether my honor my property,

בֵּין בְּרָצוֹן, בֵּין בְּשׁוֹגֵג, בֵּין בְּמֵזִיד; בֵּין בְּדִבּוּר, בֵּין
⟨ whether ⟨ through ⟨ whether ⟨⟨ purposely; ⟨ or ⟨ carelessly, ⟨ whether ⟨ willfully, ⟨ whether
speech, whether

בְּמַעֲשֶׂה, בֵּין בְּמַחֲשָׁבָה, בֵּין בְּהִרְהוּר; בֵּין בְּגִלְגּוּל זֶה,
⟨ in this ⟨ whether ⟨⟨ with fleeting ⟨ or ⟨ in deliberation, ⟨ whether ⟨ through deed,
transmigration thought; whether

בֵּין בְּגִלְגּוּל אַחֵר – לְכָל בַּר יִשְׂרָאֵל, וְלֹא יֵעָנֵשׁ שׁוּם
⟨ any ⟨ be ⟨ May not ⟨⟨ Jew. ⟨ [I forgive] ⟨⟨ in another ⟨ or
punished every transmigration; whether

אָדָם בִּסְבָתִי. יְהִי רָצוֹן מִלְּפָנֶיךָ, יהוה אֱלֹהַי וֵאלֹהֵי
⟨ and the ⟨ my God ⟨ HASHEM, ⟨⟨ before You, ⟨ the will ⟨ May ⟨⟨ because of ⟨ person
God it be me.

אֲבוֹתַי, שֶׁלֹּא אֶחֱטָא עוֹד, וְלֹא אֶחֱזוֹר בָּהֶם, וְלֹא
⟨ and that ⟨⟨ to ⟨ and that I not return ⟨⟨ anymore, ⟨ sin ⟨ that I not ⟨⟨ of my
never them, forefathers,

אָשׁוּב עוֹד לְהַכְעִיסֶךָ, וְלֹא אֶעֱשֶׂה הָרַע בְּעֵינֶיךָ.
⟨⟨ in Your eyes. ⟨ what is evil ⟨ and that I not do ⟨⟨ anger You, ⟨ shall I again

◁§ The Bedtime Shema

The recital of the *Shema* immediately before retiring is understood to be a protection against the dangers of the night (*Berachos* 5a).

The essence of the *Shema* is the *HaMapil* benediction and the first section of the *Shema*. The recital of the other psalms and verses are of ancient origin — many of the sources can be traced to the Talmud and the earliest halachic treatises such as *Kol Bo* (*Eliyah Rabbah*).

A full treatment of the Bedtime *Shema* appears

in the ArtScroll edition of *Shema*.

◁§ רִבּוֹנוֹ שֶׁל עוֹלָם / Master of the Universe

Before retiring for the evening it is proper for one to examine his deeds of that day; should one recall an improper deed he should pray for forgiveness and undertake to correct his ways. It is also proper for one to forgive those who have wronged him. In the merit of this, one will be granted long life (*Mishnah Berurah* 239 1:9). Accordingly, many recite this prayer before beginning the *Shema*.

וּמַה שֶּׁחָטָאתִי לְפָנֶיךָ מָחוֹק בְּרַחֲמֶיךָ הָרַבִּים, אֲבָל
‹ but ‹‹ that are ‹ in Your ‹ may You ‹ before ‹ sins I have done ‹ What-
abundant, mercies erase You, ever

לֹא עַל יְדֵי יִסּוּרִים וָחֳלָיִים רָעִים. יִהְיוּ לְרָצוֹן אִמְרֵי
‹—the ex- ‹‹ find ‹ May ‹‹ that ‹ or ‹ suffering ‹ through ‹ not
pressions favor they are bad. illnesses

פִי וְהֶגְיוֹן לִבִּי לְפָנֶיךָ, יהוה צוּרִי וְגֹאֲלִי.¹
‹‹ and my ‹ my ‹ HASHEM, ‹‹ before ‹‹ of my ‹ and the ‹ of my
Redeemer. Rock You, heart— thoughts mouth

ברכת המפיל / HAMAPIL

בָּרוּךְ אַתָּה יהוה אֱלֹהֵינוּ מֶלֶךְ הָעוֹלָם,
‹‹ of the universe, ‹ King ‹ our God, ‹ HASHEM, ‹ are You, ‹ Blessed

הַמַּפִּיל חֶבְלֵי שֵׁנָה עַל עֵינָי, וּתְנוּמָה עַל
‹ upon ‹ and slumber ‹ my eyes ‹ upon ‹ of sleep ‹ the bonds ‹ Who casts

עַפְעַפָּי,* וּמֵאִיר לְאִישׁוֹן בַּת עָיִן.* וִיהִי רָצוֹן
‹ the will ‹ May ‹‹ of the eye.* ‹ the pupil ‹ and Who ‹ my eyelids,*
it be illuminates

מִלְּפָנֶיךָ, יהוה אֱלֹהַי וֵאלֹהֵי אֲבוֹתַי, שֶׁתַּשְׁכִּיבֵנִי
‹ that You lay me ‹‹ of my ‹ and the ‹ my God ‹ HASHEM, ‹‹ before You,
down to sleep forefathers, God

---

(1) *Psalms* 19:15.

הַמַּפִּיל / HaMapil

There is a difference of opinion regarding the sequence of the prayers. Most *siddurim* — this volume included — place the *HaMapil* benediction first and then the *Shema*. This follows the order recorded by *Rambam* (*Hilchos Tefillah* 7:1). According to *Shulchan Aruch*, however, since *HaMapil* refers directly to the onset of slumber it should be recited as close as possible to the moment of sleep, at the very end of the *Shema* service (*Orach Chaim* 239:1, apparently following the Talmud, *Berachos* 60b).

It is not proper to eat, drink, or talk after reciting the הַמַּפִּיל benediction; one should go to sleep immediately thereafter. One who cannot fall asleep should repeat the passages of the *Shema* and Psalms until sleep overtakes him (*Derech HaChaim; Aruch HaShulchan*).

הַמַּפִּיל חֶבְלֵי שֵׁנָה עַל עֵינָי וּתְנוּמָה עַל עַפְעַפָּי — *Who casts the bonds of sleep upon my eyes and slumber upon my eyelids.* This directly corresponds to the benediction recited in the morning: הַמַּעֲבִיר שֵׁנָה מֵעֵינָי וּתְנוּמָה מֵעַפְעַפָּי, *Who removes sleep from my eyes, and slumber from my eyelids.* There we thank God for returning us to active living; here we thank Him for the gift of sleep (*World of Prayer*).

The expression *bonds of sleep* figuratively depicts the whole body as being securely bound by sleep. Others render חֶבְלֵי שֵׁנָה as "portion" of sleep (see *Deut.* 32:9; *Chizkuni; Abudraham*).

וּמֵאִיר לְאִישׁוֹן בַּת עָיִן — *And Who illuminates the pupil of the eye.* When one craves sleep, the pupils of his eyes are figuratively darkened; when one has slept and is fully rested, his eyes are "brightened" (*Abudraham*).

לְשָׁלוֹם וְתַעֲמִידֵנִי לְחַיִּים טוֹבִים וּלְשָׁלוֹם. וְתֵן

‹ Grant that » and for that peace. ‹ that is good ‹ for life ‹ and raise me up ‹ in peace

חֶלְקִי בְּתוֹרָתֶךָ, וְתַרְגִּילֵנִי לִדְבַר מִצְוָה, וְאַל

‹ and do not « of mitzvos; ‹ with matters ‹ Accustom me [to be occupied] » be in Your Torah. ‹ my portion

תַּרְגִּילֵנִי לִדְבַר עֲבֵרָה, וְאַל תְּבִיאֵנִי לֹא לִידֵי

‹ into the influence ‹ neither ‹ bring me ‹ and » do not of transgressions; matters ‹ with ‹ accustom me [to be occupied]

חֵטְא, וְלֹא לִידֵי נִסָּיוֹן, וְלֹא לִידֵי בִזָּיוֹן, וְיִשְׁלוֹט

‹ And allow to dominate » of scorn. ‹ into the influence ‹ nor ‹ of temp-tation, ‹ into the influence ‹ nor ‹ of error,

בִּי יֵצֶר טוֹב, וְאַל יִשְׁלוֹט בִּי יֵצֶר הָרָע, וְתַצִּילֵנִי

‹ Rescue me » for the Evil Inclination. ‹ over me ‹ allow to dominate ‹ and ‹ for the Good Inclination, ‹ over me

מִשָּׁטָן וּמִפֶּגַע רָע וּמֵחֳלָיִים רָעִים. וְאַל יְבַהֲלוּנִי

‹ May I not be confounded « that are serious. ‹ and from illnesses ‹ that is evil, ‹ from a mishap ‹ from a spiritual impediment,

רַעְיוֹנַי,* וַחֲלוֹמוֹת רָעִים, וְהִרְהוּרִים רָעִים. וּתְהֵא

‹ may » that are bad; ‹ and fleeting thoughts ‹ that are bad, ‹ dreams ‹ by my ideas,*

מִטָּתִי שְׁלֵמָה לְפָנֶיךָ. וְהָאֵר עֵינַי פֶּן אִישַׁן הַמָּוֶת.*¹

« the [sleep of] death.* ‹ I sleep ‹ lest ‹ my eyes ‹ and may You illuminate « before You, ‹ be perfect ‹ my offspring

בָּרוּךְ אַתָּה יהוה, הַמֵּאִיר לָעוֹלָם כֻּלּוֹ בִּכְבוֹדוֹ.

« with His glory. ‹ the entire world ‹ Who illuminates « HASHEM, ‹ are You, ‹ Blessed

(1) Cf. Psalms 13:4.

וְאַל יְבַהֲלוּנִי רַעְיוֹנַי — *May I not be confounded by my ideas.* May the ideas and fantasies that we nurse in our wakeful hours not produce disturbing nightmares or immoral dreams. Such dreams menace the purity of our thoughts and feelings even during our waking hours (*World of Prayer*).

וְהָאֵר עֵינַי פֶּן אִישַׁן הַמָּוֶת — *And may You illuminate my eyes lest I sleep the [sleep of] death.* When asleep we are in a state related to death and utter darkness, but God guards our souls, as it were. We now beseech Him to return us to a state of vigorous sparkling light on the morrow lest our slumber become the sleep of death.

THE SHEMA / שמע

ADD THIS PHRASE WHEN ALL THREE PARAGRAPHS OF THE SHEMA ARE RECITED:

אֵל מֶלֶךְ נֶאֱמָן.*

≪ Who is trustworthy.* ‹ King ‹ God,

RECITE THE FIRST VERSE ALOUD, WITH THE RIGHT HAND COVERING THE EYES, AND CONCENTRATE INTENSELY UPON ACCEPTING GOD'S ABSOLUTE SOVEREIGNTY.

שְׁמַע | יִשְׂרָאֵל, יהוה | אֱלֹהֵינוּ, יהוה | אֶחָד:¹

≪ the One ‹ HASHEM ≪ is our God, ‹ HASHEM ≪ O Israel: ‹ Hear,
[and Only]. is

IN AN UNDERTONE:

בָּרוּךְ שֵׁם כְּבוֹד מַלְכוּתוֹ לְעוֹלָם וָעֶד.²

≪ and ever. ‹ for ever ‹ kingdom ‹ of His glorious ‹ is the Name ‹ Blessed

WHILE RECITING THE FOLLOWING PARAGRAPH (DEUTERONOMY 6:5-9), CONCENTRATE ON ACCEPTING THE COMMANDMENT TO LOVE GOD.

וְאָהַבְתָּ אֵת | יהוה | אֱלֹהֶיךָ, בְּכָל-לְבָבְךָ,

‹ your heart, ‹ with all ‹ your God, ‹ HASHEM, ‹ You shall love

וּבְכָל-נַפְשְׁךָ, וּבְכָל-מְאֹדֶךָ: וְהָיוּ הַדְּבָרִים הָאֵלֶּה,

‹ — these matters ≪ They ≪ your ‹ and with ‹ your soul, ‹ with all
should be resources. all

אֲשֶׁר | אָנֹכִי מְצַוְּךָ הַיּוֹם, עַל-לְבָבֶךָ: וְשִׁנַּנְתָּם

‹ Teach them ≪ your heart. ‹ upon ≪ today — ‹ command ‹ I ‹ that
thoroughly you

לְבָנֶיךָ, וְדִבַּרְתָּ בָּם בְּשִׁבְתְּךָ בְּבֵיתֶךָ, וּבְלֶכְתְּךָ

‹ while you ‹ in your home, ‹ while you sit ‹ of ‹ and speak ‹ to your
walk them children

בַדֶּרֶךְ, וּבְשָׁכְבְּךָ וּבְקוּמֶךָ: וּקְשַׁרְתָּם לְאוֹת |

‹ as a sign ‹ Bind them ≪ and when ‹ when you ‹ on the way,
you arise. lie down,

---

(1) Deuteronomy 6:4. (2) See Pesachim 56a.

שְׁמַע / Shema

The halachah mandates that only the first paragraph of *Shema* must be recited at bedtime. However, one who recited *Maariv* before the stars were out should recite all three paragraphs again (*Aruch HaShulchan*, O.C. 239; see *Abudraham*; Rashi, *Berachos* 2a). *Magen Avra-*

ham (O.C. 239:1) suggests, however, that it is desirable to recite all three paragraphs in any case.

אֵל מֶלֶךְ נֶאֱמָן — *God, King Who is trustworthy.* This phrase is recited when all three paragraphs of the *Shema* are recited (*Machatzis HaShekel*).

עַל־יָדֶךָ, וְהָיוּ לְטֹטָפֹת בֵּין ׀ עֵינֶיךָ: וּכְתַבְתָּם ׀

And write them ≫ your eyes. ⟨ between ⟨ tefillin ⟨ and they ⟨ your ⟨ upon
shall be arm

עַל־מְזֻזוֹת בֵּיתֶךָ וּבִשְׁעָרֶיךָ:

≫ and upon your ⟨ of your ⟨ the ⟨ on
gates. house doorposts

וִיהִי נֹעַם אֲדֹנָי אֱלֹהֵינוּ עָלֵינוּ; וּמַעֲשֵׂה יָדֵינוּ

⟨ of our ⟨ the work ≫ be upon ⟨ our God, ⟨ of ⟨ the ⟨ May
hands, us; the Lord, pleasantness

כּוֹנְנָה עָלֵינוּ, וּמַעֲשֵׂה יָדֵינוּ כּוֹנְנֵהוּ.¹

≫ establish it. ⟨ of our hands, ⟨ the work ≫ for us; ⟨ establish

— תהלים צא / Psalm 91 —

יֹשֵׁב בְּסֵתֶר עֶלְיוֹן, בְּצֵל שַׁדַּי יִתְלוֹנָן.

≫ he shall ⟨ of the ⟨ in the [protec- ≪ of the ⟨ in the refuge ⟨ Whoever
dwell. Almighty tive] shade Most High, sits

אֹמַר לַיהוה: מַחְסִי וּמְצוּדָתִי, אֱלֹהַי אֶבְטַח

⟨ I will trust ⟨ my God, ≪ and my ⟨ [He is] ⟨ of Hashem, ⟨ I will say
fortress, my refuge

בּוֹ. כִּי הוּא יַצִּילְךָ מִפַּח יָקוּשׁ, מִדֶּבֶר הַוּוֹת.

≪ that is ⟨ from ≪ that ⟨ from ⟨ will deliver ⟨ He ⟨ For ≪ in
devastating. pestilence entraps, the snare you Him.

בְּאֶבְרָתוֹ יָסֶךְ לָךְ, וְתַחַת כְּנָפָיו תֶּחְסֶה; צִנָּה

⟨ [His] ≪ you will ⟨ His wings ⟨ and ≪ you, ⟨ He will ⟨ With His wing
shield find refuge; beneath cover

וְסֹחֵרָה אֲמִתּוֹ. לֹא תִירָא מִפַּחַד לָיְלָה, מֵחֵץ

⟨ [nor] ≪ of night; ⟨ the terror ⟨ You shall not fear ≪ are His ⟨ and armor
the arrow truth.

יָעוּף יוֹמָם. מִדֶּבֶר בָּאֹפֶל יַהֲלֹךְ, מִקֶּטֶב יָשׁוּד

⟨ who lays ⟨ [nor] the ≪ walks; ⟨ that in gloom ⟨ [nor] the ≪ by day; ⟨ that flies
waste destroyer pestilence

(1) *Psalms* 90:17.

צָהֳרָיִם. יִפֹּל מִצִּדְּךָ אֶלֶף, וּרְבָבָה מִימִינֶךָ, אֵלֶיךָ

at noon. ❰❰ Fall ❰ at your ❰❰ may a ❰ and a ❰❰ at your ❰ but to
victim side thousand myriad right hand, you

לֹא יִגָּשׁ. רַק בְּעֵינֶיךָ תַבִּיט, וְשִׁלֻּמַת רְשָׁעִים

it shall not ❰❰ Merely ❰ with your ❰ will you ❰❰ and the ❰ of the
approach. eyes peer, retribution wicked

תִּרְאֶה. כִּי אַתָּה יהוה מַחְסִי, עֶלְיוֹן שַׂמְתָּ

will you see. ❰❰ Because ❰ You, ❰ Hashem, ❰ are my ❰❰ [in] the ❰ have you
[you said], refuge, Most High made

מְעוֹנֶךָ. לֹא תְאֻנֶּה אֵלֶיךָ רָעָה, וְנֶגַע לֹא יִקְרַב

the abode ❰❰ Not ❰ befall ❰ you ❰ will evil, ❰❰ will ❰ and a ❰ will not
of your trust. plague come near

בְּאָהֳלֶךָ. כִּי מַלְאָכָיו יְצַוֶּה לָךְ, לִשְׁמָרְךָ בְּכָל

your tent. ❰❰ For ❰ His angels ❰ He will ❰❰ for you, ❰ to protect you ❰ in all
command

דְּרָכֶיךָ. עַל כַּפַּיִם יִשָּׂאוּנְךָ, פֶּן תִּגֹּף בָּאֶבֶן רַגְלֶךָ.

your ways. ❰❰ On ❰ [their] ❰ lest ❰❰ they will ❰ you ❰ against ❰ your
palms carry you, strike a stone foot. ❰❰

כִּי עַל שַׁחַל וָפֶתֶן תִּדְרֹךְ, תִּרְמֹס כְּפִיר וְתַנִּין.

Upon ❰ the lion ❰ and the ❰❰ you will ❰ you will ❰ the young ❰ the ❰❰ Because ❰
viper tread; trample lion serpent.

בִּי חָשַׁק וַאֲפַלְּטֵהוּ, אֲשַׂגְּבֵהוּ כִּי יָדַע שְׁמִי. יִקְרָאֵנִי

for ❰ he has ❰ yearned ❰ and I will ❰❰ and I will ❰ for ❰ he ❰ My ❰❰ He will call ❰
Me deliver him; elevate him knows Name. upon Me

וְאֶעֱנֵהוּ, עִמּוֹ אָנֹכִי בְצָרָה; אֲחַלְּצֵהוּ וַאֲכַבְּדֵהוּ.

and I will ❰❰ and I will ❰ [together] ❰ am I ❰❰ in distress; ❰ I will release ❰ and I will bring
answer him, with him him him honor. ❰❰

אֹרֶךְ יָמִים אַשְׂבִּיעֵהוּ, וְאַרְאֵהוּ בִּישׁוּעָתִי.

With long ❰ life ❰ will I satisfy him, ❰❰ and I will show him ❰ My salvation. ❰❰

אֹרֶךְ יָמִים אַשְׂבִּיעֵהוּ, וְאַרְאֵהוּ בִּישׁוּעָתִי.

With long ❰ life ❰ will I satisfy him, ❰❰ and I will show him ❰ My salvation. ❰❰

תהלים ג:ב-ט / Psalm 3:2-9

יהוה, מָה רַבּוּ צָרָי, רַבִּים קָמִים עָלָי.

HASHEM, ‹ how ‹ numerous ‹ are my ‹ Many ‹ rise up ‹ against me! tormentors!

רַבִּים אֹמְרִים לְנַפְשִׁי, אֵין יְשׁוּעָתָה לוֹ בֵאלֹהִים

Many ‹ say ‹ of my soul, ‹ There ‹ salvation ‹ for ‹ from God, is no him

סֶלָה. וְאַתָּה יהוה מָגֵן בַּעֲדִי, כְּבוֹדִי וּמֵרִים

Selah! ‹ But You, ‹ HASHEM, ‹ are a ‹ for me, ‹ for my ‹ and the One shield soul, Who raises

רֹאשִׁי. קוֹלִי אֶל יהוה אֶקְרָא, וַיַּעֲנֵנִי* מֵהַר קָדְשׁוֹ

my head. ‹ With my ‹ to ‹ HASHEM ‹ I call out, ‹ and He ‹ from His holy voice answers me* mountain,

סֶלָה. אֲנִי שָׁכַבְתִּי וָאִישָׁנָה, הֱקִיצוֹתִי,* כִּי יהוה

Selah. ‹ I ‹ lay down ‹ and I slept; ‹ yet I awoke,* ‹ for ‹ HASHEM

יִסְמְכֵנִי. לֹא אִירָא מֵרִבְבוֹת עָם, אֲשֶׁר סָבִיב

supports me. ‹ I fear not ‹ the myriads ‹ of people ‹ that ‹ all around

שָׁתוּ עָלָי. קוּמָה יהוה, הוֹשִׁיעֵנִי אֱלֹהַי, כִּי הִכִּיתָ

are ‹ against ‹ Rise up, ‹ HASHEM; ‹ save me, ‹ my God, ‹ for ‹ You deployed me. struck

אֶת כָּל אֹיְבַי לֶחִי, שִׁנֵּי רְשָׁעִים שִׁבַּרְתָּ.

all ‹ of my ‹ on the ‹ The ‹ of the wicked ‹ You broke. enemies cheek. teeth

לַיהוה הַיְשׁוּעָה, עַל עַמְּךָ בִרְכָתֶךָ* סֶלָה.

To HASHEM ‹ is salvation; ‹ upon ‹ Your people ‹ is Your blessing,* ‹ Selah.

Psalm 3 / ה׳ מָה רַבּוּ צָרָי

This psalm was composed by David when he perceived through Divine inspiration that his salvation was forthcoming. Verse 6 — *I lay down and I slept; yet I awoke, for HASHEM supports me* — makes this psalm especially appropriate for the night.

וַיַּעֲנֵנִי — *And He answers me* (lit. *He did answer me*). The word literally is in past tense. David

had such great confidence in God's response that whenever he prayed he was sure that his plea would be fulfilled. It was as if God had *already* answered his request (*Radak*).

הֱקִיצוֹתִי — *Yet I awoke.* From my worries I awoke triumphantly, filled with faith that God would support me (*Rashi*).

עַל עַמְּךָ בִרְכָתֶךָ — *Upon Your people is* (their duty is) *Your blessing.* Your people are obliged

הַשְׁכִּיבֵנוּ יהוה אֱלֹהֵינוּ לְשָׁלוֹם, וְהַעֲמִידֵנוּ

⟨ and raise us up, ⟨⟨ in peace, ⟨ our God, ⟨ HASHEM, ⟨ Lay us down to sleep,

מַלְכֵּנוּ לְחַיִּים טוֹבִים וּלְשָׁלוֹם. וּפְרוֹשׂ עָלֵינוּ

⟨ over us ⟨ Spread ⟨⟨ and for peace. ⟨ that is good ⟨ for life ⟨ our King,

סֻכַּת שְׁלוֹמֶךָ, וְתַקְּנֵנוּ בְּעֵצָה טוֹבָה מִלְּפָנֶיךָ,

⟨⟨ from before You, ⟨ that is good ⟨ with counsel ⟨ Set us aright ⟨⟨ of Your peace. ⟨ the shelter

וְהוֹשִׁיעֵנוּ מְהֵרָה לְמַעַן שְׁמֶךָ. וְהָגֵן בַּעֲדֵנוּ,

⟨⟨ us; ⟨ Shield ⟨⟨ of Your Name. ⟨ for the sake ⟨ speedily ⟨ and save us

וְהָסֵר מֵעָלֵינוּ אוֹיֵב, דֶּבֶר, וְחֶרֶב, וְרָעָב, וְיָגוֹן,

⟨⟨ and sorrow; ⟨ famine, ⟨ sword, ⟨ plague, ⟨ foe, ⟨ from us ⟨ remove

וְהָסֵר שָׂטָן מִלְּפָנֵינוּ וּמֵאַחֲרֵינוּ, וּבְצֵל כְּנָפֶיךָ

⟨ of Your wings ⟨ and in the shadow ⟨⟨ and from behind us, ⟨ from before us ⟨ spiritual impediment ⟨ and remove

תַּסְתִּירֵנוּ,[1] כִּי אֵל שׁוֹמְרֵנוּ וּמַצִּילֵנוּ אָתָּה, כִּי

⟨ for ⟨⟨ are You; ⟨ and rescues us ⟨ Who protects ⟨ God ⟨ For ⟨⟨ shelter us.

אֵל מֶלֶךְ חַנּוּן וְרַחוּם אָתָּה.[2] וּשְׁמוֹר צֵאתֵנוּ

⟨ our going ⟨ Safeguard ⟨⟨ are You. ⟨ and Compassionate ⟨ Gracious ⟨ King, ⟨ God,

וּבוֹאֵנוּ, לְחַיִּים וּלְשָׁלוֹם מֵעַתָּה וְעַד עוֹלָם.[3]

⟨⟨ eternity. ⟨ until ⟨ from now ⟨ and for peace ⟨ for life ⟨ and our coming

בָּרוּךְ יהוה בַּיּוֹם, בָּרוּךְ יהוה בַּלַּיְלָה, בָּרוּךְ

⟨ blessed ⟨⟨ by night; ⟨ is HASHEM ⟨ blessed ⟨⟨ by day; ⟨ is HASHEM ⟨ Blessed

---

(1) Cf. *Psalms* 17:8. (2) Cf. *Nehemiah* 9:31. (3) Cf. *Psalms* 121:8.

to bless You and to offer thanks for Your salvation (*Rashi*). [God derives strength, so to speak, from the blessings and prayers of man. Man's appreciation of God's control of human events influences His guidance of the universe.]

יהוה בְּשָׁכְבֵנוּ, בָּרוּךְ יהוה בְּקוּמֵנוּ. כִּי בְיָדְךָ

⟨ in Your ⟨ For ⟪ when we ⟨ is ⟨ blessed ⟪ when we retire; ⟨ is
hand arise. HASHEM HASHEM

נַפְשׁוֹת הַחַיִּים וְהַמֵּתִים. אֲשֶׁר בְּיָדוֹ נֶפֶשׁ כָּל

⟨ of all ⟨ is the ⟨ in His ⟨ that ⟪ and of the dead; ⟨ of the living ⟨ are the
soul hand souls

חַי, וְרוּחַ כָּל בְּשַׂר אִישׁ. בְּיָדְךָ אַפְקִיד רוּחִי,

⟪ my spirit; ⟨ I shall ⟨ In Your ⟪ mankind. ⟨ of all ⟨ and the ⟪ the
entrust hand spirit living,

פָּדִיתָה אוֹתִי, יהוה אֵל אֱמֶת. אֱלֹהֵינוּ

⟨ Our God, ⟪ of truth. ⟨ God ⟨ O HASHEM, ⟨ me, ⟨ You redeemed

שֶׁבַּשָּׁמַיִם, יַחֵד שִׁמְךָ וְקַיֵּם מַלְכוּתְךָ תָּמִיד,

⟪ forever ⟨ Your kingdom ⟨ establish ⟪ to Your ⟨ bring ⟪ Who is in heaven,
Name; unity

וּמְלוֹךְ עָלֵינוּ לְעוֹלָם וָעֶד.

⟪ and ever. ⟨ for ever ⟨ over us ⟨ and reign

יִרְאוּ עֵינֵינוּ וְיִשְׂמַח לִבֵּנוּ וְתָגֵל נַפְשֵׁנוּ

⟪ may our ⟨ and rejoice ⟪ may our ⟨ and be ⟪ may our eyes, ⟨ See
soul heart, gladdened

בִּישׁוּעָתְךָ בֶּאֱמֶת, בֶּאֱמֹר לְצִיּוֹן מָלַךְ אֱלֹהָיִךְ.

⟪ has Your ⟨ Reigned ⟪ to Zion, ⟨ when it ⟪ in truth, ⟨ in Your salvation
God. is told

יהוה מֶלֶךְ, יהוה מָלָךְ, יהוה יִמְלֹךְ לְעֹלָם

⟨ for ever ⟨ shall reign ⟨ HASHEM ⟪ has reigned, ⟨ HASHEM ⟪ reigns, ⟨ HASHEM

וָעֶד. כִּי הַמַּלְכוּת שֶׁלְּךָ הִיא, וּלְעוֹלְמֵי עַד

⟨ and ⟨ and for ever ⟪ is Yours ⟨ the kingdom ⟨ For ⟪ and
ever ever.

תִּמְלוֹךְ בְּכָבוֹד, כִּי אֵין לָנוּ מֶלֶךְ אֶלָּא אָתָּה.

⟪ You. ⟨ except for ⟨ King ⟨ we have no ⟨ for ⟪ in glory, ⟨ You will reign

(1) *Job* 12:10. (2) *Psalms* 31:6. (3) Cf. *Isaiah* 52:7.
(4) *Psalms* 10:16. (5) 93:1 et al. (6) *Exodus* 15:18.

הַמַּלְאָךְ* הַגֹּאֵל אֹתִי מִכָּל רָע יְבָרֵךְ

‹ bless ‹ evil ‹ from all ‹ me ‹ who redeems ‹ May the angel*

אֶת הַנְּעָרִים, וְיִקָּרֵא בָהֶם שְׁמִי,* וְשֵׁם אֲבֹתַי

‹ of my ‹ and the ‹‹ may my ‹ upon ‹ and ‹‹ the lads,
forefathers names name be,* them declared

אַבְרָהָם וְיִצְחָק, וְיִדְגּוּ לָרֹב* בְּקֶרֶב הָאָרֶץ.¹

‹‹ the land. ‹ within ‹ abundantly* ‹ and like fish may ‹‹ and Isaac, ‹ Abraham
they proliferate

וַיֹּאמֶר, אִם שָׁמוֹעַ תִּשְׁמַע* לְקוֹל יהוה

‹ of HASHEM, ‹ the voice ‹ you diligently heed* ‹ If ‹‹ He said:

אֱלֹהֶיךָ, וְהַיָּשָׁר בְּעֵינָיו תַּעֲשֶׂה, וְהַאֲזַנְתָּ

‹ and you listen ‹‹ you do, ‹ in His eyes ‹ and that ‹‹ your God,
closely which is proper

לְמִצְוֹתָיו, וְשָׁמַרְתָּ כָּל חֻקָּיו, כָּל הַמַּחֲלָה

‹ malady ‹ the ‹‹ His decrees, ‹ all ‹ and you ‹‹ to His
entire observe commandments

אֲשֶׁר שַׂמְתִּי בְמִצְרַיִם* לֹא אָשִׂים עָלֶיךָ, כִּי

‹ for ‹‹ upon you, ‹ I will not inflict ‹ upon Egypt* ‹ I inflicted ‹ that

אֲנִי יהוה רֹפְאֶךָ.²

‹‹ your Healer. ‹ HASHEM ‹ I am

---

(1) *Genesis* 48:16. (2) *Exodus* 15:26.

הַמַּלְאָךְ — *May the angel.* The following passages are a collection of Scriptural verses discussing God's "mercy." This first verse, *May the angel who redeems*, etc., was Jacob's blessing to his grandsons Ephraim and Menashe (*Genesis* 48:16). The prayer is directed not to the angel, who has no power except as an agent of God, but to God Who dispatched the angel.

וְיִקָּרֵא בָהֶם שְׁמִי — *And declared upon them may my name be.* May they constantly strive to such heights that they will be worthy to have their names coupled with those of the Patriarchs (R' *Avraham ben HaRambam*).

וְיִדְגּוּ לָרֹב — *And like fish may they proliferate* abundantly. R' Hirsch explains that just as fish enjoy contentment hidden from the gaze of human beings, so Jews who live in the sphere assigned them by God will have a degree of serenity and happiness far beyond the comprehension of those around them.

וַיֹּאמֶר אִם שָׁמוֹעַ תִּשְׁמַע — *He said, "If you diligently heed."* This passage forms the basis for the Talmudic statement [*Berachos* 5a] that Torah study, no less than the reading of the *Shema*, wards off danger (*World of Prayer*).

כָּל הַמַּחֲלָה אֲשֶׁר שַׂמְתִּי בְמִצְרַיִם — *The entire malady* (the plagues) *that I inflicted upon Egypt.* If the Jews remain faithful, they will be spared physical affliction (*Ramban*).

וַיֹּאמֶר יהוה אֶל הַשָּׂטָן,* יִגְעַר יהוה בְּךָ

‹ O you, ‹ shall ‹ Denounce ‹ the Satan,* ‹ to ‹ HASHEM said
HASHEM

הַשָּׂטָן, וְיִגְעַר יהוה בְּךָ הַבֹּחֵר בִּירוּשָׁלָיִם,

‹‹ Jerusalem. ‹ [HASHEM] ‹‹ O you, ‹ shall ‹ and denounce ‹‹ Satan,
Who chooses HASHEM, again

הֲלוֹא זֶה אוּד מֻצָּל מֵאֵשׁ.¹

‹‹ from a fire? ‹ rescued ‹ a firebrand ‹ this [man] ‹ Is not

הִנֵּה מִטָּתוֹ* שֶׁלִּשְׁלֹמֹה, שִׁשִּׁים גִּבֹּרִים סָבִיב

‹ encircle ‹ mighty ones ‹ Sixty ‹‹ of Shlomo! ‹ The couch* ‹ Indeed!

לָהּ, מִגִּבֹּרֵי יִשְׂרָאֵל. כֻּלָּם אֲחֻזֵי חֶרֶב, מְלֻמְּדֵי

‹ learned ‹‹ the ‹ gripping ‹ All ‹‹ of Israel. ‹ of the ‹ it,
sword, mighty ones

מִלְחָמָה, אִישׁ חַרְבּוֹ עַל יְרֵכוֹ מִפַּחַד בַּלֵּילוֹת.²

‹‹ in the ‹ from terror ‹ his ‹ on ‹ with his ‹ each ‹ in warfare,
nights. thigh, sword

RECITE THREE TIMES:

יְבָרֶכְךָ יהוה,* וְיִשְׁמְרֶךָ. יָאֵר יהוה פָּנָיו אֵלֶיךָ,

‹ for you ‹ His ‹ May HASHEM ‹‹ and ‹ May HASHEM bless you*
countenance illuminate safeguard you.

וִיחֻנֶּךָּ. יִשָּׂא יהוה פָּנָיו אֵלֶיךָ, וְיָשֵׂם לְךָ שָׁלוֹם.³

‹‹ peace. ‹ for you ‹ and ‹ to you ‹ His ‹ May HASHEM ‹‹ and be gra-
establish countenance turn cious to you.

---

(1) *Zechariah* 3:2. (2) *Song of Songs* 3:7-8. (3) *Numbers* 6:24-26.

₪§ וַיֹּאמֶר ה' אֶל הַשָּׂטָן — *HASHEM said to the Satan.* Satan had accused the High Priest Joshua of being overly permissive with his sinful children and of hindering the rebuilding of the Temple. Thereupon God — Who chose Jerusalem — rebuked Satan, reminding him that Joshua had been Divinely vindicated inasmuch as he had been miraculously spared from the fires of Nebuchadnezzar. This metaphor also applies to the Jewish nation as a whole. It, too, is like a *firebrand rescued from a fire,* for it has suffered

from the fires of exile and endured them.

הִנֵּה מִטָּתוֹ — *Indeed! The couch.* This passage refers allegorically to the Jewish people symbolized by the sixty myriads (the 600,000 battleworthy males) who emerged from Egypt. See *Commentary* in the ArtScroll edition of *Shir HaShirim* for the full interpretation.

§₪ יְבָרֶכְךָ ה' — *May HASHEM bless you.* The blessing contains sixty letters; this has significant Kabbalistic meaning as it parallels the sixty myriads of the previous passage.

RECITE THREE TIMES:

הִנֵּה לֹא יָנוּם וְלֹא יִישָׁן,* שׁוֹמֵר יִשְׂרָאֵל.¹

It is so, / [He] / neither / slumbers / nor / sleeps* / – the Guardian / of Israel. ≫

RECITE THREE TIMES:

לִישׁוּעָתְךָ קִוִּיתִי יהוה,* קִוִּיתִי יהוה

For Your salvation / I do yearn, ≫ / HASHEM.* / I do yearn, / HASHEM, ≫

לִישׁוּעָתְךָ. יהוה לִישׁוּעָתְךָ קִוִּיתִי.

for Your salvation. ≫ HASHEM, / for Your salvation / I do yearn. ≫

RECITE THREE TIMES:

בְּשֵׁם יהוה* אֱלֹהֵי יִשְׂרָאֵל, מִימִינִי מִיכָאֵל,

In the Name / of HASHEM,* / God / of Israel: / at my right ≫ / may Michael be, ≫

וּמִשְּׂמֹאלִי גַּבְרִיאֵל, וּמִלְּפָנַי אוּרִיאֵל, וּמֵאַחוֹרַי

at my left / Gabriel, / before me ≫ / Uriel, / and behind me ≫

רְפָאֵל, וְעַל רֹאשִׁי שְׁכִינַת אֵל.

Raphael; / and above ≫ / my head / the Presence / of God. ≫

———— תהלים קכח / Psalm 128 ————

שִׁיר הַמַּעֲלוֹת; אַשְׁרֵי כָּל יְרֵא יהוה,

A song / of ascents. / Praiseworthy ≫ / is each / who fears / person / HASHEM, ≫

הַהֹלֵךְ בִּדְרָכָיו. יְגִיעַ כַּפֶּיךָ כִּי תֹאכֵל, אַשְׁרֶיךָ

who walks / in His ways. ≫ / The labor / of your hands / when – / – you eat ≫ / you are praiseworthy,

_____

(1) *Psalms* 121:4. (2) *Genesis* 49:18.

_____

⤶§ **הִנֵּה לֹא יָנוּם וְלֹא יִישָׁן** — *It is so, that [He] neither slumbers nor sleeps.* And therefore you will be able to sleep peacefully without fear of harm (*R' Hirsch*).

⤶§ **לִישׁוּעָתְךָ קִוִּיתִי ה'...** — *For Your salvation I do yearn, HASHEM* . . . The Kabbalists find in this three-word prayer mystical combinations of letters spelling the Divine Name that provides salvation from enemies. In order to arrive at the combination of letters yielding this Name,

the three words of this prayer must be recited in three different orders (*R' Bachya*).

⤶§ **בְּשֵׁם ה'** — *In the Name of HASHEM.* God's angels surround you at His command: Michael, performing His unique miracles; Gabriel, the emissary of His almighty power; Uriel, who bears the light of God before you; Raphael, who brings you healing from Him. Above your head is the Presence of God Himself (*R' Hirsch*).

וְטוֹב לָךְ. אֶשְׁתְּךָ כְּגֶפֶן פֹּרִיָּה בְּיַרְכְּתֵי בֵיתֶךָ;

‹‹ of your ‹ in the inner ‹ fruitful, ‹ will be like ‹ Your wife ‹‹ with ‹ and it
home; chambers a vine, you. is well

בָּנֶיךָ כִּשְׁתִלֵי זֵיתִים סָבִיב לְשֻׁלְחָנֶךָ. הִנֵּה כִי כֵן

‹ thus ‹ for ‹ Indeed, ‹‹ your table. ‹ surrounding ‹ of olive ‹ will be ‹ your
trees like shoots children

יְבֹרַךְ גָּבֶר יְרֵא יהוה. יְבָרֶכְךָ יהוה מִצִּיּוֹן, וּרְאֵה

‹ and may ‹‹ from Zion, ‹ May HASHEM bless you ‹‹ HASHEM. ‹ who ‹ the ‹ is blessed
you gaze fears man

בְּטוּב יְרוּשָׁלָיִם כֹּל יְמֵי חַיֶּיךָ. וּרְאֵה בָנִים

‹ children ‹ And may ‹‹ of your ‹ the ‹ all of Jerusalem ‹ upon the
you see life. days goodness

לְבָנֶיךָ, שָׁלוֹם עַל יִשְׂרָאֵל.

‹‹ Israel. ‹ upon ‹ peace ‹‹ [born] to
your children,

RECITE THREE TIMES:

רִגְזוּ וְאַל תֶּחֱטָאוּ,* אִמְרוּ בִלְבַבְכֶם עַל

‹ while ‹ in your hearts ‹ reflect ‹‹ and do not sin;* ‹ Tremble
on

מִשְׁכַּבְכֶם, וְדֹמּוּ סֶלָה.[1]

‹‹ Selah. ‹‹ and be ‹ your beds,
utterly silent,

---

(1) *Psalms* 4:5.

רִגְזוּ וְאַל תֶּחֱטָאוּ ﬠﬧ — *Tremble and do not sin.*
This verse exhorts Israel to tremble so greatly at
the thought of sin that the very idea of transgression becomes disturbing and traumatic
(*Shaarei Teshuvah*).

The Talmud (*Berachos* 5a) interprets this
verse homiletically: A person should constantly
provoke his יֵצֶר טוֹב, *good inclination*, to
battle against his יֵצֶר הָרָע, *evil inclination*, as
it says, רִגְזוּ וְאַל תֶּחֱטָאוּ, literally, *provoke* or
agitate and do not sin. If he succeeds in defeat-

ing the evil inclination, all is well. If not, he
should engage in Torah study, as it says,
אִמְרוּ בִלְבַבְכֶם, *reflect in your hearts.* If he is
victorious, all is well. If not, he should recite
the portion of *Shema* [whereby one accepts
the yoke of God's sovereignty] when he lies
down to sleep, as it says, עַל מִשְׁכַּבְכֶם, *while on
your beds.* If he conquers, all is well. If not, he
should remind himself of the awesome day of
death, as it says, וְדֹמּוּ סֶלָה, *and be utterly silent,
Selah.*

אֲדוֹן עוֹלָם* אֲשֶׁר מָלַךְ בְּטֶרֶם כָּל־יְצִיר

⟨ form ⟨ any ⟨ before ⟨ reigned ⟨ Who ⟨ of the universe* ⟨ Master

נִבְרָא. לְעֵת נַעֲשָׂה בְחֶפְצוֹ כֹּל, אֲזַי מֶלֶךְ שְׁמוֹ

⟨His Name⟨as "King"⟨ then⟨⟨ all things,⟨ when His will created ⟨At the time ⟨⟨was created.

נִקְרָא. וְאַחֲרֵי כִּכְלוֹת הַכֹּל, לְבַדּוֹ יִמְלוֹךְ נוֹרָא.

⟨⟨—the Awe-⟨⟨will reign ⟨ He ⟨⟨ of all, ⟨ the end ⟨ After ⟨⟨ was
some One.   alone   proclaimed.

וְהוּא הָיָה וְהוּא הֹוֶה, וְהוּא יִהְיֶה בְּתִפְאָרָה.

⟨⟨ in splendor. ⟨ Who shall ⟨ and He ⟨⟨ Who is ⟨ and He ⟨⟨Who was ⟨ It is He
remain

וְהוּא אֶחָד וְאֵין שֵׁנִי לְהַמְשִׁיל לוֹ לְהַחְבִּירָה.

⟨⟨ or to be His equal. ⟨ to ⟨ to compare ⟨ second ⟨ and there ⟨ is One ⟨ He
Him   is no

בְּלִי רֵאשִׁית בְּלִי תַכְלִית, וְלוֹ הָעֹז וְהַמִּשְׂרָה.

⟨⟨ and the ⟨ is the ⟨ — His ⟨⟨ conclusion, ⟨ without ⟨⟨ beginning, ⟨ Without
dominion.   power

וְהוּא אֵלִי וְחַי גֹּאֲלִי, וְצוּר חֶבְלִי בְּעֵת צָרָה.

⟨⟨ of ⟨ in a time ⟨ from my ⟨ a Rock ⟨⟨ Redeemer, ⟨ my ⟨⟨ my ⟨ He is
distress.   pain   [to save me]   living   God,

וְהוּא נִסִּי וּמָנוֹס לִי, מְנָת כּוֹסִי בְּיוֹם אֶקְרָא.

⟨⟨ I call. ⟨ on ⟨ of ⟨ the ⟨⟨ for ⟨ a refuge ⟨⟨ my ⟨ He is
the day   my cup   portion   me,   banner,

בְּיָדוֹ אַפְקִיד רוּחִי בְּעֵת אִישָׁן וְאָעִירָה.

⟨⟨ — and I ⟨⟨ I go to ⟨ when ⟨ my spirit ⟨ I shall entrust ⟨ Into
shall awaken!   sleep   His hand

וְעִם רוּחִי גְּוִיָּתִי, יהוה לִי וְלֹא אִירָא.

⟨⟨ I shall not fear. ⟨⟨ is ⟨ HASHEM ⟨⟨ my body ⟨ my spirit ⟨ With
with me,   shall remain;

◆§ **אֲדוֹן עוֹלָם** — *Master of the universe.* Alternatively, *Master eternal.* This inspiring song of praise is attributed to R' Shlomo ibn Gabirol, who flourished in the 11th century. He was one of the greatest early *paytanim* [liturgical poets]. The song emphasizes that God is timeless, infinite and omnipotent. Mankind can offer Him only one thing: to proclaim Him as King, by doing His will and praising Him. Despite God's greatness, however, He involves Himself with man's personal needs in time of pain and distress. The prayer concludes on the inspiring note that, lofty though He is, *HASHEM is with me, I shall not fear.*

❧ סדר מוצאי שבת ❧
❧ SABBATH CONCLUSION ❧

THE REGULAR WEEKDAY *MAARIV* IS RECITED UNTIL THE END OF *SHEMONEH ESREI*,
PAGES 406-440, THEN THE SERVICE CONTINUES BELOW.
HOWEVER, IF A FESTIVAL (OR EREV PESACH) FALLS BEFORE THE COMING SABBATH,
THE *CHAZZAN* RECITES THE FULL *KADDISH* (P. 440) AND THE SERVICE CONTINUES THERE.

THE *CHAZZAN* RECITES חֲצִי קַדִּישׁ, HALF-*KADDISH*.

יִתְגַּדַּל וְיִתְקַדַּשׁ שְׁמֵהּ רַבָּא. (.Cong – אָמֵן) בְּעָלְמָא דִּי בְרָא
Grow exalted ⟩ that ⟩ He ⟩ in the ⟩ ⟨⟨ (Amen.) ⟩⟩ ⟨⟨ that is ⟩ may His ⟩ and be ⟩ ⟨ Grow exalted
created world great! – Name sanctified

כִרְעוּתֵהּ, וְיַמְלִיךְ מַלְכוּתֵהּ, וְיַצְמַח פֻּרְקָנֵהּ וִיקָרֵב מְשִׁיחֵהּ.
⟨⟨ His ⟩ and bring ⟩ His ⟩ and cause ⟩ to His ⟩ and may He ⟨⟨ according
Messiah, near salvation, to sprout kingship, give reign to His will,

(.Cong – אָמֵן) בְּחַיֵּיכוֹן וּבְיוֹמֵיכוֹן וּבְחַיֵּי דְכָל בֵּית יִשְׂרָאֵל,
⟨⟨ of Israel, ⟩ Family ⟩ of the ⟩ and in the ⟩ and in ⟩ in your ⟨⟨ (Amen.)
entire lifetimes your days, lifetimes

בַּעֲגָלָא וּבִזְמַן קָרִיב. וְאִמְרוּ: אָמֵן.
⟨⟨ Amen. ⟩ Now ⟩⟩ that ⟩ and at ⟩ swiftly
respond: comes soon. a time

CONGREGATION RESPONDS:

אָמֵן. יְהֵא שְׁמֵהּ רַבָּא מְבָרַךְ לְעָלַם וּלְעָלְמֵי עָלְמַיָּא.
⟨⟨ and for all eternity. ⟩ forever ⟩ be blessed ⟩ that is great ⟩ His Name ⟩ May ⟨⟨ Amen.

CHAZZAN CONTINUES:

יְהֵא שְׁמֵהּ רַבָּא מְבָרַךְ לְעָלַם וּלְעָלְמֵי עָלְמַיָּא. יִתְבָּרַךְ
⟨ Blessed, ⟨⟨ and for all eternity. ⟩ forever ⟩ be blessed ⟩ that is great ⟩ His Name ⟩ May

וְיִשְׁתַּבַּח וְיִתְפָּאַר וְיִתְרוֹמַם וְיִתְנַשֵּׂא וְיִתְהַדָּר וְיִתְעַלֶּה
⟨ elevated, ⟩ honored, ⟩ upraised, ⟩ exalted, ⟩ glorified, ⟩ praised,

וְיִתְהַלָּל שְׁמֵהּ דְּקֻדְשָׁא בְּרִיךְ הוּא (.Cong – בְּרִיךְ הוּא) –
⟨⟨ is He) ⟩ (Blessed ⟨⟨ is He ⟩ Blessed ⟩ of the Holy One, ⟩ be the Name ⟩ and lauded

ROSH HASHANAH TO YOM KIPPUR SUBSTITUTE:

°לְעֵלָּא מִן כָּל [°לְעֵלָּא (וּ)לְעֵלָּא מִכָּל] בִּרְכָתָא
⟨ blessing ⟩ any ⟩ exceedingly beyond ⟩ any ⟩ beyond

וְשִׁירָתָא, תֻּשְׁבְּחָתָא וְנֶחֱמָתָא דַּאֲמִירָן בְּעָלְמָא.
⟨⟨ in the world. ⟩ that are uttered ⟩ and consolation ⟩ praise ⟨⟨ and song,

וְאִמְרוּ: אָמֵן. (.Cong – אָמֵן)
⟨⟨ (Amen.) ⟨⟨ Amen. ⟩ Now respond:

וִיהִי נֹעַם אֲדֹנָי אֱלֹהֵינוּ עָלֵינוּ; וּמַעֲשֵׂה יָדֵינוּ

⟨ of our ⟨ the work ⟪ be upon ⟨ our God, ⟨ of the ⟨ the ⟨ May
hands, us; Lord, pleasantness

כּוֹנְנָה עָלֵינוּ, וּמַעֲשֵׂה יָדֵינוּ כּוֹנְנֵהוּ.¹

⟪ establish it. ⟨ of our hands, ⟨ the work ⟨ for us; ⟨ establish

———— תהלים צא / Psalm 91 ————

יֹשֵׁב בְּסֵתֶר עֶלְיוֹן, בְּצֵל שַׁדַּי יִתְלוֹנָן. אֹמַר

⟨ I will ⟪ he shall ⟨ of the ⟨ in the [protec- ⟪ of the ⟨ in the ⟨ Whoever
say dwell. Almighty tive] shade Most High, refuge sits

לַיהוה: מַחְסִי וּמְצוּדָתִי, אֱלֹהַי אֶבְטַח בּוֹ. כִּי

⟨ For ⟪ in Him . ⟨ I will trust ⟨ my God, ⟪ and my fortress, ⟨ [He is] my refuge ⟨ of HASHEM,

הוּא יַצִּילְךָ מִפַּח יָקוּשׁ, מִדֶּבֶר הַוּוֹת. בְּאֶבְרָתוֹ

⟨ With His ⟪ that is ⟨ from ⟪ that ⟨ from ⟨ will deliver ⟨ He
wing devastating. pestilence entraps, the snare you

יָסֶךְ לָךְ, וְתַחַת כְּנָפָיו תֶּחְסֶה; צִנָּה וְסֹחֵרָה

⟨ and armor ⟨ His ⟪ you will ⟨ His wings ⟨ and ⟪ you, ⟨ He will
shield be protected; beneath cover

אֲמִתּוֹ. לֹא תִירָא מִפַּחַד לָיְלָה, מֵחֵץ יָעוּף יוֹמָם.

⟪ by day; ⟨ that ⟨ [nor] of ⟪ of night; ⟨ the terror ⟨ You shall not fear ⟪ is His
flies the arrow truth.

מִדֶּבֶר בָּאֹפֶל יַהֲלֹךְ, מִקֶּטֶב יָשׁוּד צָהֳרָיִם. יִפֹּל

⟨ Fall ⟪ at noon. ⟨ who lays ⟨ [nor] the ⟪ walks; ⟨ that in ⟨ [nor] the
victim waste destroyer gloom pestilence

(1) *Psalms* 90:17.

◄§ Maariv at the Conclusion of the Sabbath

After *Shemoneh Esrei*, two additional prayers are recited: וַיְהִי נֹעַם and וְאַתָּה קָדוֹשׁ, both of which set the tone for the transition from the Sabbath to the weekdays.

The verse וִיהִי נֹעַם contains two aspects of our concept of blessing. On the one hand, we ask that God give us the satisfaction of "pleasantness in our handiwork," meaning that we have the freedom to be productive. On the other hand, we ask God Himself to "establish our handiwork," meaning that we give up our

independence to the will and law of God. We ask that this declaration become the framework of the workweek that now begins — may we be free to enjoy our handiwork, but may it always be done according to the laws of the Torah.

We then go on to Psalm 91, another psalm composed by Moses. The Talmud (*Shavuos* 150) calls it שִׁיר שֶׁל פְּגָעִים, *Song of Afflictions*, because it expresses prayerful confidence that God will protect us from the dangers and afflictions of life. *Tur* (*Orach Chaim* 294) calls it

מִצִּדְּךָ אֶלֶף, וּרְבָבָה מִימִינֶךָ, אֵלֶיךָ לֹא יִגָּשׁ. רַק

‹ Merely ‹‹ it shall not ‹ but to ‹‹ at your ‹ and a ‹‹ may a ‹ at your
approach. you right hand, myriad thousand side

בְּעֵינֶיךָ תַבִּיט, וְשִׁלֻּמַת רְשָׁעִים תִּרְאֶה. כִּי אַתָּה

‹ You, ‹ Because ‹‹ will you ‹ of the ‹ and the ‹‹ will you ‹ with your
[you said], see. wicked retribution peer, eyes

יהוה מַחְסִי, עֶלְיוֹן שַׂמְתָּ מְעוֹנֶךָ. לֹא תְאֻנֶּה

‹ befall ‹ Not ‹‹ the abode ‹ have you ‹ [in] the ‹‹ are my ‹ HASHEM,
of your trust. made Most High refuge,

אֵלֶיךָ רָעָה, וְנֶגַע לֹא יִקְרַב בְּאָהֳלֶךָ. כִּי

‹ For ‹‹ your tent. ‹ will not come near ‹ and a plague ‹‹ will evil, ‹ you

מַלְאָכָיו יְצַוֶּה לָךְ, לִשְׁמָרְךָ בְּכָל דְּרָכֶיךָ. עַל

‹ On ‹‹ your ways. ‹ in all ‹ to protect you ‹‹ for you, ‹ He will charge ‹ His angels

כַּפַּיִם יִשָּׂאוּנְךָ, פֶּן תִּגֹּף בָּאֶבֶן רַגְלֶךָ. עַל שַׁחַל

‹ the lion ‹ Upon ‹‹ your ‹ against ‹ you ‹ lest ‹‹ they will ‹ [their]
foot. a stone strike carry you, palms

וָפֶתֶן תִּדְרֹךְ, תִּרְמֹס כְּפִיר וְתַנִּין. כִּי בִי חָשַׁק

‹ he has ‹ for ‹ Because ‹‹ and the ‹ the young ‹ you will ‹‹ you will ‹ and the
yearned Me serpent. lion trample tread; viper

וַאֲפַלְּטֵהוּ, אֲשַׂגְּבֵהוּ כִּי יָדַע שְׁמִי. יִקְרָאֵנִי

‹ He will call ‹‹ My ‹ he ‹ for ‹ I will ‹‹ and I will
upon Me Name. knows elevate him deliver him;

וְאֶעֱנֵהוּ, עִמּוֹ אָנֹכִי בְצָרָה; אֲחַלְּצֵהוּ וַאֲכַבְּדֵהוּ.

‹‹ and I will bring ‹ I will release ‹‹ in distress; ‹ am I ‹ [together] ‹‹ and I will
him honor. him with him answer him,

אֹרֶךְ יָמִים אַשְׂבִּיעֵהוּ, וְאַרְאֵהוּ בִּישׁוּעָתִי.

‹‹ My salvation. ‹ and I will show him ‹‹ will I satisfy him, ‹ life ‹ With long

אֹרֶךְ יָמִים אַשְׂבִּיעֵהוּ, וְאַרְאֵהוּ בִּישׁוּעָתִי.

‹‹ My salvation. ‹ and I will show him ‹‹ will I satisfy him, ‹ life ‹ With long

---

מִזְמוֹר שֶׁל בְּרָכָה, *Psalm of Blessing*, a more positive way of expressing the same idea. As the
protective holiness of the Sabbath leaves us, we
ask God to continue to extend His protection

over us throughout the workweek.

Abudraham notes that Psalm 91 contains 124
words and that a repetition of the psalm would
yield 248 words, a number equivalent to the

**THE VERSES IN BOLD TYPE ARE THE *KEDUSHAH* RECITED BY THE ANGELS.
IT IS PREFERABLE THAT THE CONGREGATION RECITE THEM ALOUD WITH THE *CHAZZAN*.**

וְאַתָּה קָדוֹשׁ יוֹשֵׁב תְּהִלּוֹת יִשְׂרָאֵל.¹ וְקָרָא זֶה

‹ And one ‹‹ of Israel. ‹ upon the ‹ enthroned ‹‹ the Holy ‹ Yet You are
[angel] will call   praises   One,

אֶל זֶה וְאָמַר: קָדוֹשׁ קָדוֹשׁ קָדוֹשׁ יהוה

‹ is HASHEM, ‹ holy ‹ holy, ‹ Holy, ‹‹ and say: ‹ another ‹ to

צְבָאוֹת, מְלֹא כָל הָאָרֶץ כְּבוֹדוֹ.² וּמְקַבְּלִין דֵּין

‹ one ‹ And they receive ‹‹ [with] His ‹ world ‹ is the ‹ filled ‹‹ Master of
    [permission]   glory.   whole   Legions,

מִן דֵּין וְאָמְרִין: קַדִּישׁ בִּשְׁמֵי מְרוֹמָא עִלָּאָה בֵּית

‹ the ‹ on high, ‹ in the lofty heavens ‹ Holy ‹‹ and say: ‹ the ‹ from
abode   other

שְׁכִינְתֵּהּ, קַדִּישׁ עַל אַרְעָא עוֹבַד גְּבוּרְתֵּהּ, קַדִּישׁ

‹ holy ‹‹ of His might; ‹ the product ‹ earth, ‹ on ‹ holy ‹‹ of His Presence;

לְעָלַם וּלְעָלְמֵי עָלְמַיָּא, יהוה צְבָאוֹת, מַלְיָא

‹ filled ‹‹ Master of Legions; ‹ is HASHEM, ‹ and to all eternity ‹ forever

כָל אַרְעָא זִיו יְקָרֵהּ.✧ וַתִּשָּׂאֵנִי רוּחַ, וָאֶשְׁמַע³

‹ and I heard ‹‹ A wind lifted me, ‹‹ of His ‹ with the ‹ world ‹ is the
    glory.   radiance   whole

אַחֲרַי קוֹל רַעַשׁ גָּדוֹל: בָּרוּךְ כְּבוֹד יהוה

‹ of ‹ is the ‹ Blessed ‹‹ of a great noise: ‹ the ‹ behind me
HASHEM   glory   sound

---

(1) *Psalms* 22:4. (2) *Isaiah* 6:3. (3) *Targum Yonasan.*

organs and limbs of the body, thus symbolizing God's protection of every part of those who serve Him. Rather than trouble the congregation to repeat the psalm, it has become customary to repeat the last verse אֶרֶךְ יָמִים, *With long life*.

וְאַתָּה קָדוֹשׁ § / Yet You Are the Holy One

Having requested God's blessings during the forthcoming week, we now ask that the Sabbath holiness remain with us, and afford us spiritual protection throughout the week, even though the day itself is departing. Therefore we recite the verses that proclaim God's holiness on earth as well as in heaven. Then we go on to acknowledge that we were created to glorify Him and we pray that we be capable of absorbing the teachings of the Torah. For commentary see pages 218-223.

Since these prayers refer to the six days of labor, they are not recited if a Festival (Pesach, Shavuos, Rosh Hashanah, Yom Kippur, Succos) will occur during the coming week. In that case, the holiness of the Festival suffices to infuse the week with the sanctity for which we long.

מִמְּקוֹמוֹ.¹ וּנְטָלַתְנִי רוּחָא, וְשִׁמְעֵת בַּתְרַי קָל
‹ the sound ‹ behind me ‹ and I heard ‹ A wind lifted me, « from His place.

זִיעַ סַגִּיא דִּמְשַׁבְּחִין וְאָמְרִין: בְּרִיךְ יְקָרָא דַיהוה
‹ of HASHEM ‹ is the honor ‹ Blessed ‹ and saying: of those who were praising ‹ of the great noise

מֵאֲתַר בֵּית שְׁכִינְתֵּהּ.² יהוה יִמְלֹךְ לְעֹלָם וָעֶד.³
« and ever. ‹ for ever ‹ shall reign ‹ HASHEM « of His Presence. ‹ of the abode ‹ from the place

יהוה מַלְכוּתֵהּ קָאֵם לְעָלַם וּלְעָלְמֵי עָלְמַיָּא.⁴
« and to all eternity. ‹ forever ‹ stands ‹ — His kingdom « HASHEM

יהוה אֱלֹהֵי אַבְרָהָם יִצְחָק וְיִשְׂרָאֵל אֲבֹתֵינוּ,
‹ our forefathers, ‹ and Israel, ‹ Isaac ‹ of Abraham, ‹ God ‹ HASHEM,

שָׁמְרָה זֹּאת לְעוֹלָם, לְיֵצֶר מַחְשְׁבוֹת לְבַב
‹ of the heart ‹ of the thoughts ‹ as the product ‹ forever ‹ this ‹ may You preserve

עַמֶּךָ, וְהָכֵן לְבָבָם אֵלֶיךָ.⁵ וְהוּא רַחוּם, יְכַפֵּר עָוֹן
‹ of ‹ is for-giving ‹ the Merciful One, ‹ And He, « to You. ‹ their heart ‹ and may You direct « of Your people, iniquity

וְלֹא יַשְׁחִית, וְהִרְבָּה לְהָשִׁיב אַפּוֹ, וְלֹא יָעִיר
‹ arousing ‹ not « His anger, ‹ He withdraws ‹ frequently « destroy; ‹ and does not

כָּל חֲמָתוֹ.⁶ כִּי אַתָּה אֲדֹנָי טוֹב וְסַלָּח, וְרַב חֶסֶד
‹ kind ‹ and abundantly ‹ and forgiving, « are ‹ O Lord, ‹ You, ‹ For « of His wrath. ‹ all good

לְכָל קֹרְאֶיךָ.⁷ צִדְקָתְךָ צֶדֶק לְעוֹלָם, וְתוֹרָתְךָ
‹ and Your Torah « everlasting, ‹ is a righteousness ‹ Your righteousness « who call upon You. ‹ to all

אֱמֶת.⁸ תִּתֵּן אֱמֶת לְיַעֲקֹב, חֶסֶד לְאַבְרָהָם,
« to Abraham, ‹ kindness « to Jacob, ‹ truth ‹ Grant « is truth.

(1) Ezekiel 3:12. (2) Targum Yonasan. (3) Exodus 15:18. (4) Targum Onkelos.
(5) I Chronicles 29:18. (6) Psalms 78:38. (7) 86:5. (8) 119:142.

אֲשֶׁר נִשְׁבַּעְתָּ לַאֲבֹתֵינוּ מִימֵי קֶדֶם. בָּרוּךְ אֲדֹנָי,¹

‹ is the ‹ Blessed ‹‹ of old. ‹ from ‹ to our forefathers ‹ You swore ‹ as
Lord; days

יוֹם יוֹם יַעֲמָס לָנוּ, הָאֵל יְשׁוּעָתֵנוּ סֶלָה. יהוה²

‹ Hashem, ‹‹ Selah. ‹‹ of our salvation, ‹ the God ‹‹ He loads us up ‹ by day ‹ day
[with blessings],

צְבָאוֹת עִמָּנוּ, מִשְׂגָּב לָנוּ אֱלֹהֵי יַעֲקֹב סֶלָה.³

‹‹ Selah. ‹‹ of Jacob, ‹ is the God ‹ for us ‹ a stronghold ‹‹ is with us, ‹ Master of
Legions,

יהוה צְבָאוֹת, אַשְׁרֵי אָדָם בֹּטֵחַ בָּךְ.⁴ יהוה

‹ Hashem, ‹‹ in You. ‹ who ‹ is the man ‹ praiseworthy ‹ Master of ‹ Hashem,
trusts Legions,

הוֹשִׁיעָה, הַמֶּלֶךְ יַעֲנֵנוּ בְיוֹם קָרְאֵנוּ.⁵ בָּרוּךְ הוּא

‹ is He, ‹ Blessed ‹‹ we call. ‹ on the day ‹ answer ‹ May the ‹‹ save!
us King

אֱלֹהֵינוּ שֶׁבְּרָאָנוּ לִכְבוֹדוֹ, וְהִבְדִּילָנוּ מִן הַתּוֹעִים,

‹‹ those who ‹ from ‹ and separated ‹‹ for His glory, ‹ Who created us ‹ our God,
stray, us

וְנָתַן לָנוּ תּוֹרַת אֱמֶת, וְחַיֵּי עוֹלָם נָטַע בְּתוֹכֵנוּ.

‹‹ within us. ‹ implanted ‹ eternal ‹ and life ‹‹ of truth, ‹ the Torah ‹ us ‹ and gave

הוּא יִפְתַּח לִבֵּנוּ בְּתוֹרָתוֹ, וְיָשֵׂם בְּלִבֵּנוּ אַהֲבָתוֹ

‹ with love ‹ our heart ‹ and ‹‹ to His Torah ‹ our heart ‹ open ‹ May He
of Him imbue

וְיִרְאָתוֹ וְלַעֲשׂוֹת רְצוֹנוֹ וּלְעָבְדוֹ בְּלֵבָב שָׁלֵם,

‹‹ that is ‹ with a heart ‹ and to serve ‹ His will ‹ and [the will] ‹ and awe
whole, Him to do of Him

לְמַעַן לֹא נִיגַע לָרִיק, וְלֹא נֵלֵד לַבֶּהָלָה.⁶

‹‹ for futility. ‹ produce ‹ nor ‹ in vain ‹ toil ‹ we do not ‹ so that

יְהִי רָצוֹן מִלְּפָנֶיךָ, יהוה אֱלֹהֵינוּ וֵאלֹהֵי

‹ and the God ‹ our God ‹ Hashem, ‹‹ before You, ‹ the will ‹ May it be

(1) *Micah* 7:20. (2) *Psalms* 68:20. (3) 46:8. (4) 84:13. (5) 20:10. (6) Cf. *Isaiah* 65:23.

אֲבוֹתֵֽינוּ, שֶׁנִּשְׁמֹר חֻקֶּֽיךָ בָּעוֹלָם הַזֶּה, וְנִזְכֶּה

⟨ and that we merit   ⟨ in This World,   ⟨ Your decrees   ⟨ that we observe   ⟪ of our forefathers,

וְנִחְיֶה וְנִרְאֶה וְנִירַשׁ טוֹבָה וּבְרָכָה לִשְׁנֵי

⟨ in the years   ⟨ and blessing   ⟨ goodness   ⟨ and we inherit   ⟨ and we see   ⟨ that we live

יְמוֹת הַמָּשִׁיחַ וּלְחַיֵּי הָעוֹלָם הַבָּא. לְמַֽעַן

⟨ So that   ⟪ to Come.   ⟨ of the World   ⟨ and for the life   of Messianic times

יְזַמֶּרְךָ כָבוֹד וְלֹא יִדֹּם, יהוה אֱלֹהַי לְעוֹלָם

⟨ forever   ⟨ my God,   ⟨ Hashem,   ⟪ be silenced;   ⟨ and not   ⟨ [might] my soul,   ⟨ sing to You

אוֹדֶֽךָּ.[1] בָּרוּךְ הַגֶּֽבֶר אֲשֶׁר יִבְטַח בַּיהוה, וְהָיָה

⟨ then will   ⟨ in Hashem,   ⟨ trusts   ⟨ who   ⟨ is the man   ⟨ Blessed   ⟪ will I thank You.

יהוה מִבְטַחוֹ.[2] בִּטְחוּ בַיהוה עֲדֵי עַד, כִּי בְּיָהּ

⟨ in God,   ⟨ for   ⟪ forever,   ⟨ in Hashem   ⟨ Trust   ⟪ his security.   ⟨ Hashem be

יהוה צוּר עוֹלָמִים.[3] ❖ וְיִבְטְחוּ בְךָ יוֹדְעֵי שְׁמֶֽךָ,

⟪ Your Name,   ⟨ those who know   ⟪ in You,   ⟨ And they will trust   ⟪ of the worlds.   ⟨ is the strength   ⟨ Hashem,

כִּי לֹא עָזַֽבְתָּ דֹּרְשֶֽׁיךָ, יהוה.[4] יהוה חָפֵץ לְמַֽעַן

⟨ for the sake   ⟨ desired,   ⟨ Hashem   ⟪ Hashem.   ⟨ those who seek You,   ⟨ You have not forsaken   ⟨ for

צִדְקוֹ, יַגְדִּיל תּוֹרָה וְיַאְדִּיר.[5]

⟪ and glorious.   ⟨ to make the Torah great   ⟨ of [Israel's] righteousness,

SOME CONGREGATIONS CONCLUDE:

יהוה אֲדוֹנֵֽינוּ, מָה אַדִּיר שִׁמְךָ בְּכָל הָאָֽרֶץ.[6]

⟪ the earth.   ⟨ throughout   ⟨ is Your Name   ⟨ mighty   ⟨ how   ⟪ our Master,   ⟨ Hashem,

חִזְקוּ וְיַאֲמֵץ לְבַבְכֶם, כָּל הַמְיַחֲלִים לַיהוה.[7]

⟪ for Hashem.   ⟨ who wait longingly   ⟨ all   ⟪ in Your hearts,   ⟨ and He will instill courage   ⟨ Be strong,

(1) *Psalms* 30:13. (2) *Jeremiah* 17:7. (3) *Isaiah* 26:4.
(4) *Psalms* 9:11. (5) *Isaiah* 42:21. (6) *Psalms* 8:2. (7) 31:25.

THE *CHAZZAN* RECITES קַדִּישׁ שָׁלֵם, THE FULL *KADDISH*.

יִתְגַּדַּל וְיִתְקַדַּשׁ שְׁמֵהּ רַבָּא. (אָמֵן.) בְּעָלְמָא דִּי בְרָא

‹ He ‹ that ‹ in the ‹‹ (Amen.) ‹‹ that is ‹ may His‹ and be ‹ Grow exalted
created world great! — Name sanctified

כִרְעוּתֵהּ, וְיַמְלִיךְ מַלְכוּתֵהּ, וְיַצְמַח פֻּרְקָנֵהּ וִיקָרֵב מְשִׁיחֵהּ.

‹‹ His ‹ and bring ‹ His ‹ and cause ‹ to His ‹ and may He ‹‹ according
Messiah, near salvation, to sprout kingship, give reign to His will,

(אָמֵן.) בְּחַיֵּיכוֹן וּבְיוֹמֵיכוֹן וּבְחַיֵּי דְכָל בֵּית יִשְׂרָאֵל,

‹‹ of Israel, ‹ Family ‹ of the ‹ and in the ‹ and in ‹ in your ‹‹ (Amen.)
entire lifetimes your days, lifetimes

בַּעֲגָלָא וּבִזְמַן קָרִיב. וְאִמְרוּ: אָמֵן.

‹‹ Amen. ‹ Now ‹‹ that ‹ and at ‹ swiftly
respond: comes soon. a time

CONGREGATION RESPONDS:

אָמֵן. יְהֵא שְׁמֵהּ רַבָּא מְבָרַךְ לְעָלַם וּלְעָלְמֵי עָלְמַיָּא.

‹‹ and for all eternity. ‹ forever ‹ be blessed ‹ that is great‹ His Name ‹ May ‹‹ Amen.

CHAZZAN CONTINUES:

יְהֵא שְׁמֵהּ רַבָּא מְבָרַךְ לְעָלַם וּלְעָלְמֵי עָלְמַיָּא. יִתְבָּרַךְ

‹ Blessed, ‹‹ and for all eternity. ‹ forever ‹ be blessed ‹ that is great ‹ His Name ‹ May

וְיִשְׁתַּבַּח וְיִתְפָּאַר וְיִתְרוֹמַם וְיִתְנַשֵּׂא וְיִתְהַדָּר וְיִתְעַלֶּה

‹ elevated, ‹ honored, ‹ upraised, ‹ exalted, ‹ glorified, ‹ praised,

וְיִתְהַלָּל שְׁמֵהּ דְּקֻדְשָׁא בְּרִיךְ הוּא (בְּרִיךְ הוּא) —

‹‹ is He) ‹ (Blessed ‹‹ is He ‹ Blessed ‹ of the Holy One, ‹ be the Name ‹ and lauded

ROSH HASHANAH TO YOM KIPPUR SUBSTITUTE:

°לְעֵלָּא מִן כָּל [°לְעֵלָּא (וּ)לְעֵלָּא מִכָּל] בִּרְכָתָא

‹ blessing ‹ any ‹ exceedingly beyond ‹ any ‹ beyond

וְשִׁירָתָא, תֻּשְׁבְּחָתָא וְנֶחֱמָתָא דַּאֲמִירָן בְּעָלְמָא.

‹‹ in the world. ‹ that are uttered ‹ and consolation ‹ praise ‹‹ and song,

וְאִמְרוּ: אָמֵן. (אָמֵן.)

‹‹ (Amen.) ‹‹ Amen. ‹ Now respond:

CONGREGATION:

(קַבֵּל בְּרַחֲמִים וּבְרָצוֹן אֶת תְּפִלָּתֵנוּ.)

‹‹ our prayers.) ‹ and with favor ‹ with mercy ‹ (Accept

CHAZZAN CONTINUES:

תִּתְקַבֵּל צְלוֹתְהוֹן וּבָעוּתְהוֹן דְּכָל בֵּית יִשְׂרָאֵל

‹ Israel ‹ Family of ‹ of the entire ‹ and supplications ‹ the prayers ‹ May accepted be

קֳדָם אֲבוּהוֹן דִּי בִשְׁמַיָּא. וְאִמְרוּ: אָמֵן. (Cong. – אָמֵן.)

‹ (Amen.) › ‹ Amen. ‹ Now respond: ‹ is in Heaven. ‹ Who ‹ their Father ‹ before

CONGREGATION:

(יְהִי שֵׁם יהוה מְבֹרָךְ מֵעַתָּה וְעַד עוֹלָם.[1])

‹ eternity.) ‹ until ‹ from this ‹ be ‹ of ‹ the ‹ (Let
                  time   blessed HASHEM Name

CHAZZAN CONTINUES:

יְהֵא שְׁלָמָא רַבָּא מִן שְׁמַיָּא, וְחַיִּים טוֹבִים עָלֵינוּ וְעַל כָּל

‹ all ‹ and ‹ upon us ‹ that is ‹ and life ‹ Heaven, ‹ from ‹ that is ‹ peace ‹ May
 upon   good,   abundant   there be

יִשְׂרָאֵל. וְאִמְרוּ: אָמֵן. (Cong. – אָמֵן.)

‹ (Amen.) › ‹ Amen. ‹ Now respond: ‹ Israel.

CONGREGATION:

(עֶזְרִי מֵעִם יהוה, עֹשֵׂה שָׁמַיִם וָאָרֶץ.[2])

‹ and earth.) ‹ of heaven ‹ Maker ‹ HASHEM, ‹ is from ‹ (My help

BOW; TAKE THREE STEPS BACK: BOW LEFT AND SAY . . . **עֹשֶׂה שָׁלוֹם**, *"HE WHO MAKES PEACE . . .";* BOW
RIGHT AND SAY . . . **הוּא**, *"MAY HE . . .";* BOW FORWARD AND SAY . . . **וְעַל כָּל יִשְׂרָאֵל**, *"AND UPON
ALL ISRAEL . . ."* REMAIN IN PLACE FOR A FEW MOMENTS, THEN TAKE THREE STEPS FORWARD.

עֹשֶׂה °שָׁלוֹם בִּמְרוֹמָיו, הוּא יַעֲשֶׂה שָׁלוֹם עָלֵינוּ, וְעַל

‹ and ‹ upon us, ‹ peace ‹ make ‹ may He ‹ in His heights, ‹ peace ‹ He Who
 upon   makes

כָּל יִשְׂרָאֵל. וְאִמְרוּ: אָמֵן. (Cong. – אָמֵן.)

‹ (Amen.) › ‹ Amen. ‹ Now respond: ‹ Israel. ‹ all

FROM ROSH HASHANAH TO YOM KIPPUR SOME SAY:

°הַשָׁלוֹם

‹ the peace

DURING CHANUKAH THE SYNAGOGUE *MENORAH* IS LIT AT THIS POINT (P. 557).
BETWEEN PESACH AND SHAVUOS, THE *OMER* IS COUNTED (P. 447).

CONTINUE WITH *ALEINU* (P. 442).

---

(1) *Psalms* 113:2. (2) 121:2.

פְּסוּקֵי בְּרָכָה ⇦/Verses of Blessing

After *Maariv*, the collection of Scriptural
passages is recited. In most *Nusach Sefard* congregations it is customary for individuals to recite them at home after *Havdalah*. This collection is primarily an anthology of blessings,
beginning with that given by Isaac to Jacob. By
reciting them now, on the threshold of a new
week, we invoke God's blessing on the labor of
the coming six days.
Siddur Avodas Yisrael divides the Scriptural

selections into seven topics: (1) בְּרָכָה, *blessing;*
(2) גְּאוּלָה, *redemption;* (3) יְשׁוּעָה, *salvation;*
(4) דַּעַת ה׳, *knowledge of God;* (5) פִּדְיוֹם, *rescue;*
(6) הֲפוּךְ צָרָה, *transformation of distress to relief;*
and (7) שָׁלוֹם, *peace.* He notes also that the order
of the verses as they are quoted here does not
always follow the order in which they appear
in the Torah. This is simply because in וְיִתֶּן לְךָ
they are placed in logical sequence according
to topics, as is evident when one follows the
text.

485 / SABBATH CONCLUSION

VERSES OF BLESSING / פסוקי ברכה

וְיִתֶּן לְךָ* הָאֱלֹהִים מִטַּל הַשָּׁמַיִם וּמִשְׁמַנֵּי

‹ and of the fatness ‹ of the heavens ‹ of the dew ‹‹ may God, ‹ to you* ‹ And give

הָאָרֶץ, וְרֹב דָּגָן וְתִירֹשׁ. יַעַבְדוּךָ עַמִּים, וְיִשְׁתַּחֲווּ

‹ and bow down ‹‹ will ‹ Serve you ‹‹ and wine. ‹ grain ‹ and ‹‹ of the earth,
peoples, abundant

לְךָ לְאֻמִּים, הֱוֵה גְבִיר לְאַחֶיךָ, וְיִשְׁתַּחֲווּ לְךָ בְּנֵי

‹ will ‹ to you ‹ and bow down ‹‹ to your ‹ a lord ‹ be ‹‹ will nations; ‹ to you
the sons kinsmen,

אִמֶּךָ, אֹרְרֶיךָ אָרוּר, וּמְבָרֲכֶיךָ בָּרוּךְ.¹ וְאֵל שַׁדַּי

‹‹ And El Shaddai ‹‹ be ‹ and they who ‹‹ be cursed, ‹ [may] they ‹‹ of your
blessed. bless you who curse you mother;

יְבָרֵךְ אֹתְךָ* וְיַפְרְךָ וְיַרְבֶּךָ, וְהָיִיתָ לִקְהַל עַמִּים.

‹‹ of ‹ a ‹ and may ‹‹ and make ‹ make you ‹‹ you,* ‹ may He
peoples. congregation you be you numerous, fruitful bless

וְיִתֶּן לְךָ אֶת בִּרְכַּת אַבְרָהָם, לְךָ וּלְזַרְעֲךָ אִתָּךְ,

‹‹ with ‹ and to your ‹ to you ‹‹ of Abraham, ‹ the blessing ‹ you ‹ May He
you, offspring grant

לְרִשְׁתְּךָ אֶת אֶרֶץ מְגֻרֶיךָ, אֲשֶׁר נָתַן אֱלֹהִים

‹ God granted ‹ which ‹ of your ‹ the land ‹ that you may
sojournings, possess

לְאַבְרָהָם.² מֵאֵל אָבִיךָ וְיַעְזְרֶךָ, וְאֵת שַׁדַּי וִיבָרֲכֶךָ,

‹‹ and He will ‹ Shaddai ‹ and ‹‹ and He will ‹ of your ‹ [It is] from ‹‹ to Abraham.
bless you with help you, father the God

בִּרְכֹת שָׁמַיִם מֵעָל, בִּרְכֹת תְּהוֹם רֹבֶצֶת תָּחַת,

‹‹ below, ‹ crouching ‹ of the deep ‹ blessings ‹‹ from above, ‹ of heaven ‹ – blessings

---

(1) *Genesis* 27:28-29. (2) 28:3-4.

וְיִתֶּן לְךָ — *And give to you.* The first
verses comprise the blessing given by Isaac to
Jacob at the time that Jacob posed as Esau.

וְאֵל שַׁדַּי יְבָרֵךְ אֹתְךָ — *And El Shaddai may He
bless you.* The name *El Shaddai* has been translated the *All-Sufficient One* or the *Almighty*. It
refers to the aspect of God that determines how

much or how little blessing a person needs, how
much suffering he can endure and so on. God
determines what is דַּי, *enough*, and has the absolute power to ensure that only this and neither more nor less comes into being.

This verse and the next one are the blessing
given by Isaac to Jacob just before Jacob was

בִּרְכֹת שָׁדַיִם וָרָחַם. בִּרְכֹת אָבִיךָ* גָּבְרוּ עַל
⟨ beyond ⟨ exceeded ⟨ of your father* ⟨ The blessings ⟪ and womb. ⟨ of the bosom ⟨ blessings

בִּרְכֹת הוֹרַי, עַד תַּאֲוַת גִּבְעֹת עוֹלָם, תִּהְיֶיןָ
⟨ let them be ⟪ of the world; ⟨ of the hills ⟨ the bounds ⟨ to ⟪ of my parents, ⟨ the blessings

לְרֹאשׁ יוֹסֵף, וּלְקָדְקֹד נְזִיר אֶחָיו. ¹ וַאֲהֵבְךָ* וּבֵרַכְךָ
⟨ and He will bless you, ⟨ And He will love you,* ⟪ from his brothers. ⟨ of the one separated ⟨ and upon the head ⟪ of Joseph, ⟨ upon the head

וְהִרְבֶּךָ, וּבֵרַךְ פְּרִי בִטְנְךָ וּפְרִי אַדְמָתֶךָ, דְּגָנְךָ
⟨ your grain, ⟨ of your land, ⟨ and the fruit ⟨ of your womb ⟨ the fruit ⟨ He will bless ⟪ and He will make you numerous;

וְתִירֹשְׁךָ וְיִצְהָרֶךָ, שְׁגַר אֲלָפֶיךָ וְעַשְׁתְּרֹת צֹאנֶךָ,
⟪ of your sheep, ⟨ and the flocks ⟨ of your cattle ⟨ the offspring ⟪ and your oil, ⟨ your wine,

עַל הָאֲדָמָה אֲשֶׁר נִשְׁבַּע לַאֲבֹתֶיךָ לָתֶת לָךְ. בָּרוּךְ
⟨ Blessed ⟪ to you. ⟨ to give ⟨ to your forefathers ⟨ He swore ⟨ that ⟨ the land ⟨ on

תִּהְיֶה מִכָּל הָעַמִּים, לֹא יִהְיֶה בְךָ עָקָר וַעֲקָרָה,
⟨ or barren woman, ⟨ a barren man ⟨ among you ⟨ there shall not be ⟪ peoples; ⟨ of all ⟨ shall you be

וּבִבְהֶמְתֶּךָ. וְהֵסִיר יהוה מִמְּךָ כָּל חֳלִי, וְכָל
⟨ and all ⟪ illness; ⟨ all ⟨ from you ⟨ HASHEM will remove ⟪ nor among your cattle.

מַדְוֵי מִצְרַיִם הָרָעִים אֲשֶׁר יָדַעְתָּ, לֹא יְשִׂימָם
⟨ place them ⟨ – He will not ⟪ you knew ⟨ that ⟨ the bad maladies of Egypt

בָּךְ, וּנְתָנָם בְּכָל שֹׂנְאֶיךָ. ²
⟪ your enemies. ⟨ upon all ⟨ but He will set them ⟪ upon you,

---

(1) *Genesis* 49:25-26. (2) *Deuteronomy* 7:13-15.

sent to Paddan Aram to escape the murderous wrath of Esau and to find a wife for himself.

בִּרְכֹת אָבִיךָ — *The blessings of your father*. This verse is the climax of Jacob's blessing to Joseph, who earned the distinction of primacy among his brothers. Although all of Jacob's blessings had awesome significance, that given to Joseph is cited here because Jacob described it as sur-

passing all others in that he wanted it to be unbounded by any limits.

וַאֲהֵבְךָ — *And He will love you*. In the last weeks of Moses' life, he exhorted and taught, warned and blessed. The verses from here to the end of the paragraph are but one of many blessings Moses pronounced as the Divine reward for Israel's loyalty to God and His commandments.

הַ**מַּלְאָךְ*** הַגֹּאֵל אֹתִי מִכָּל רָע יְבָרֵךְ

‹— may he bless ‹‹ evil ‹ from all ‹ me ‹ who redeems ‹ The angel*

אֶת הַנְּעָרִים וְיִקָּרֵא בָהֶם שְׁמִי, וְשֵׁם אֲבֹתַי

‹ of my forefathers, ‹ and the names ‹‹ may my name be, ‹ upon them ‹ and declared ‹‹ the lads;

אַבְרָהָם וְיִצְחָק, וְיִדְגּוּ לָרֹב בְּקֶרֶב הָאָרֶץ.¹

‹‹ the land. ‹ within ‹ abundantly ‹— and like fish may ‹‹ and Isaac ‹ Abraham
they proliferate

יהוה אֱלֹהֵיכֶם הִרְבָּה אֶתְכֶם, וְהִנְּכֶם הַיּוֹם כְּכוֹכְבֵי

‹ like the stars ‹ today ‹ and here you are ‹ has made you numerous, ‹ your God, ‹ HASHEM,

הַשָּׁמַיִם לָרֹב. יהוה אֱלֹהֵי אֲבוֹתֵכֶם יֹסֵף עֲלֵיכֶם

‹ you ‹ increase ‹ of your forefathers, ‹ the God ‹ May ‹‹ in ‹ of heaven
HASHEM, abundance.

כָּכֶם אֶלֶף פְּעָמִים, וִיבָרֵךְ אֶתְכֶם כַּאֲשֶׁר דִּבֶּר לָכֶם.²

‹‹ to you. ‹ He spoke ‹ as ‹ you ‹ and bless ‹‹ times, ‹ a thousand ‹ [more] than you are

בָּרוּךְ אַתָּה בָּעִיר,* וּבָרוּךְ אַתָּה בַּשָּׂדֶה. בָּרוּךְ

‹ Blessed ‹‹ in the field. ‹ are you ‹ blessed ‹‹ in the city;* ‹ are you ‹ Blessed

אַתָּה בְּבֹאֶךָ, וּבָרוּךְ אַתָּה בְּצֵאתֶךָ. בָּרוּךְ טַנְאֲךָ

‹ is your fruit basket ‹ Blessed ‹‹ upon your departure. ‹ are you ‹ blessed ‹‹ upon your arrival; ‹ are you

וּמִשְׁאַרְתֶּךָ. בָּרוּךְ פְּרִי בִטְנְךָ וּפְרִי אַדְמָתְךָ וּפְרִי

‹ and the fruit ‹ of your land, ‹ the fruit ‹ of your womb, ‹ is the fruit ‹ Blessed ‹‹ and your kneading trough.

---

(1) *Genesis* 48:16. (2) *Deuteronomy* 1:10-11.

◆§ הַמַּלְאָךְ — *The angel*. This paragraph is devoted to blessings given by aged leaders who took pride in the growth of a young and thriving new generation. The first verse has become one of the classic blessings conferred upon children. It was given by Jacob on his deathbed to Menashe and Ephraim, the Egypt-born children of Joseph. The last two verses, beginning ה׳ אֱלֹהֵיכֶם, HASHEM, *your God*, were Moses' proud description of the nation that he had led out of Egypt and his blessing that their future greatness should dwarf anything that had happened in the past.

◆§ בָּרוּךְ אַתָּה בָּעִיר — *Blessed are you in the city*. Moses pronounced this stirring series of blessings upon his people, telling them that if they observed the Torah, there would be no area of their lives that would be untouched by God's generosity. These blessings were the introduction to Moses' תּוֹכָחָה, *chastisement*, in which he warned the people of the woes that would befall them if they neglected the Torah.

בְּהֶמְתֶּךָ, שְׁגַר אֲלָפֶיךָ וְעַשְׁתְּרוֹת צֹאנֶךָ.[1] יְצַו יהוה

HASHEM will command ‹ of your sheep. ‹ and the flocks ‹ of your cattle ‹ the ‹ of your animal, offspring

אִתָּךְ אֶת הַבְּרָכָה בַּאֲסָמֶיךָ וּבְכֹל מִשְׁלַח יָדֶךָ,

your hand, ‹ to which you set ‹ and in everything ‹ in your storehouses ‹ the blessing to accompany you,

וּבֵרַכְךָ בָּאָרֶץ אֲשֶׁר יהוה אֱלֹהֶיךָ נֹתֵן לָךְ.

you. ‹ gives ‹ your God, ‹ HASHEM, ‹ that ‹ in the land ‹ and He will bless you

יִפְתַּח יהוה לְךָ אֶת אוֹצָרוֹ הַטּוֹב, אֶת הַשָּׁמַיִם,

– the heavens – ‹ of goodness ‹ His storehouse ‹ for you ‹ HASHEM will open

לָתֵת מְטַר אַרְצְךָ בְּעִתּוֹ, וּלְבָרֵךְ אֵת כָּל מַעֲשֵׂה

the work ‹ all ‹ and to bless ‹ in its time, ‹ of your land ‹ the rain ‹ to grant

יָדֶךָ, וְהִלְוִיתָ גּוֹיִם רַבִּים, וְאַתָּה לֹא תִלְוֶה.[2] כִּי

For ‹ borrow. ‹ will not ‹ but you ‹ to many nations, ‹ and you will lend ‹ of your hands;

יהוה אֱלֹהֶיךָ בֵּרַכְךָ* כַּאֲשֶׁר דִּבֶּר לָךְ, וְהַעֲבַטְתָּ

and you will lend ‹ to you; ‹ He spoke ‹ as ‹ will have blessed you* ‹ your God, ‹ HASHEM,

גּוֹיִם רַבִּים, וְאַתָּה לֹא תַעֲבֹט, וּמָשַׁלְתָּ

and you will dominate ‹ borrow; ‹ will not ‹ but you ‹ to many nations,

בְּגוֹיִם רַבִּים, וּבְךָ לֹא יִמְשֹׁלוּ.[3] אַשְׁרֶיךָ יִשְׂרָאֵל,*

O Israel;* ‹ Praiseworthy are you, ‹ dominate. ‹ they will not ‹ but over you ‹ many nations,

---

(1) *Deuteronomy* 28:3,6,5,4. (2) 28:8,12. (3) 15:6.

This long blessing seems to be entirely material in nature, without mention of spiritual growth. This is one of the great miracles of creation. We would expect people to attain spiritual riches in return for spiritual service of God; the Torah has no need to mention that. But it is miraculous and inspiring that in return for the study of Torah and the performance of *mitzvos*, God promises His people health, wealth, and physical security (*Ramban*).

כִּי ה' אֱלֹהֶיךָ בֵּרַכְךָ — *For HASHEM, your God, will have blessed you.* This verse, from a different part of *Deuteronomy*, is inserted here because it is very similar to the one just cited. The term וְהַעֲבַטְתָּ, *you will lend*, comes from the word עֲבֹט, *collateral.* Although it is similar in meaning to תִלְוֶה, *may you lend*, it is a stronger term because it implies a continuing moral and legal obligation.

אַשְׁרֶיךָ יִשְׂרָאֵל — *Praiseworthy are you, O Israel.* These two verses are Moses' last words to his people. Though they had tried him sorely during the forty years in the Wilderness and though their provocation had caused him to be

מִי כָמְוֹךָ, עַם נוֹשַׁע בַּיהוה, מָגֵן עֶזְרֶךָ, וַאֲשֶׁר
< and Who << of your   < Who is << by God, < saved <– a people << is like < who
          help,   the Shield   you?

חֶרֶב גַּאֲוָתֶךָ, וְיִכָּחֲשׁוּ אֹיְבֶיךָ לָךְ, וְאַתָּה עַל
< upon < but you << with you, < will your   < False << of your < is the
                              enemies be   grandeur.   Sword

בָּמוֹתֵימוֹ תִדְרֹךְ.¹
<< will trample. < their heights

REDEMPTION / גְּאוּלָה

מָחִיתִי* כָעָב פְּשָׁעֶיךָ וְכֶעָנָן חַטֹּאתֶיךָ, שׁוּבָה
< return << your < and like a < your willful < like a < I have wiped
       transgressions;   cloud   sins,   thick mist   away*

אֵלַי כִּי גְאַלְתִּיךָ. רָנּוּ שָׁמַיִם, כִּי עָשָׂה יהוה, הָרִיעוּ
< shout for << HASHEM has done < for < O heaven, < Sing << I have < for < to Me,
    joy,   [wonders];   gladly, redeemed you!

תַּחְתִּיּוֹת אָרֶץ, פִּצְחוּ הָרִים רִנָּה, יַעַר וְכָל עֵץ בּוֹ,
<<within < the < and [and] the<< in glad < O < break out, << of the < O depths
   it,   trees all forest   song, mountains,   earth;

כִּי גָאַל יהוה יַעֲקֹב וּבְיִשְׂרָאֵל יִתְפָּאָר.² גֹּאֲלֵנוּ
<< Our << He will glory. < and in Israel << Jacob < HASHEM has redeemed < for
Redeemer

יהוה צְבָאוֹת שְׁמוֹ, קְדוֹשׁ יִשְׂרָאֵל.³
<< of Israel. < [is] the Holy < is His < Master of < – HASHEM,
                One   Name –   Legions,

SALVATION / יְשׁוּעָה

יִשְׂרָאֵל נוֹשַׁע* בַּיהוה תְּשׁוּעַת עוֹלָמִים,
<< everlasting; < [with] a salvation < by God < is saved* < Israel

(1) *Deuteronomy* 33:29. (2) *Isaiah* 44:22-23. (3) 47:4.

denied the privilege of ever entering *Eretz Yis-rael*, Moses' life came to its end amid expressed feelings of love and praise of the nation that meant more to him than life and glory.

◆§ מָחִיתִי — *I have wiped away.* The section of redemption makes clear that the basis of redemption is repentance and a return to God,

which brings forgiveness of sin.

◆§ יִשְׂרָאֵל נוֹשַׁע — *Israel is saved.* The first few verses of salvation provide an interesting insight into the nature of exile from which Israel is to be saved. Each of the first three verses promises that Israel will no longer be ashamed.

לֹא תֵבֹשׁוּ וְלֹא תִכָּלְמוּ* עַד עוֹלְמֵי עַד.¹ וַאֲכַלְתֶּם

⟨ You will eat, ⟩⟩   ⟨ and ever. ⟩ ⟨ for ever ⟩ ⟨ humiliated* ⟩ ⟨ nor ⟩ ⟨ you will not be shamed

אָכוֹל וְשָׂבוֹעַ, וְהִלַּלְתֶּם אֶת שֵׁם יהוה אֱלֹהֵיכֶם,

⟨⟨ your God, ⟩ ⟨ of Hashem, ⟩ ⟨ the Name ⟩ ⟨ and you will praise ⟩ ⟨ and being satisfied, ⟩ ⟨ eating

אֲשֶׁר עָשָׂה עִמָּכֶם לְהַפְלִיא, וְלֹא יֵבֹשׁוּ עַמִּי לְעוֹלָם.

⟨⟨ ever. ⟩ ⟨ will My ⟩ ⟨ shamed ⟩ ⟨ and not ⟩⟩ ⟨ wondrously, ⟩ ⟨ with you ⟩ ⟨ has done ⟩ ⟨ Who
     people be

וִידַעְתֶּם כִּי בְקֶרֶב יִשְׂרָאֵל אָנִי, וַאֲנִי יהוה אֱלֹהֵיכֶם,

⟨ your God ⟩ ⟨ am ⟩ ⟨ and ⟩⟩ ⟨ am I, ⟩ ⟨ of Israel ⟩ ⟨ in the ⟩ ⟨ that ⟩ ⟨ And you
     Hashem, ⟨ that I ⟩   midst   will know

וְאֵין עוֹד, וְלֹא יֵבֹשׁוּ עַמִּי לְעוֹלָם.² כִּי בְשִׂמְחָה

⟨ in gladness ⟩ ⟨ For ⟩⟩ ⟨ ever. ⟩ ⟨ will My ⟩ ⟨ shamed ⟩ ⟨ and not ⟩⟩ ⟨ other; ⟩ ⟨ and there
     people be   is no

תֵצֵאוּ וּבְשָׁלוֹם תּוּבָלוּן, הֶהָרִים וְהַגְּבָעוֹת יִפְצְחוּ

⟨ will ⟩ ⟨ and the hills ⟩ ⟨ the mountains ⟩⟩ ⟨ you will ⟩ ⟨ and in peace ⟩ ⟨ you will
break out   be brought;   go out,

לִפְנֵיכֶם רִנָּה, וְכָל עֲצֵי הַשָּׂדֶה יִמְחֲאוּ כָף.³ הִנֵּה

⟨ Behold, ⟩⟩ ⟨ hands. ⟩ ⟨ will clap ⟩ ⟨ of the field ⟩ ⟨ the trees ⟩ ⟨ and all ⟩⟩ ⟨ in glad song, ⟩ ⟨ before you

אֵל יְשׁוּעָתִי, אֶבְטַח וְלֹא אֶפְחָד, כִּי עָזִּי וְזִמְרָת

⟨ and my praise ⟩ ⟨ my might ⟩ ⟨ For ⟩⟩ ⟨ fear. ⟩ ⟨ and not ⟩ ⟨ I shall trust ⟩⟩ ⟨ is my salvation; ⟩ ⟨ God

יָהּ יהוה וַיְהִי לִי לִישׁוּעָה. וּשְׁאַבְתֶּם מַיִם בְּשָׂשׂוֹן,

⟨ in joy, ⟩ ⟨ water ⟩ ⟨ You will draw ⟩⟩ ⟨ a salvation. ⟩ ⟨ for ⟩ ⟨ and ⟩⟩ ⟨ Hashem, ⟩ ⟨ is
     me   He was   God,

מִמַּעַיְנֵי הַיְשׁוּעָה. וַאֲמַרְתֶּם בַּיּוֹם הַהוּא, הוֹדוּ

⟨ Give thanks ⟩⟩ ⟨ on that day, ⟩ ⟨ And you will say ⟩⟩ ⟨ of salvation. ⟩ ⟨ from the springs

לַיהוה קִרְאוּ בִשְׁמוֹ, הוֹדִיעוּ בָעַמִּים עֲלִילֹתָיו,

⟨⟨ His acts; ⟩ ⟨ among the peoples ⟩ ⟨ make known ⟩ ⟨ His Name, ⟩ ⟨ declare ⟩ ⟨ to Hashem,

---

(1) Isaiah 45:17. (2) Joel 2:26-27. (3) Isaiah 55:12.

לֹא תֵבשׁוּ וְלֹא תִכָּלְמוּ — *You will not be shamed nor humiliated*. These two terms refer respectively to the shame that is felt inwardly and the humiliation that is inflicted publicly by others. In exile, Israel suffers from both. The outer humiliation is obvious, the inner shame is caused by becoming subject to more powerful nations and by being forced to adopt alien cultures and values. With the salvation of redemption and the resultant sovereignty of God's will, Israel will feel joy and pride.

הַזְכִּירוּ כִּי נִשְׂגָּב שְׁמוֹ. זַמְּרוּ יהוה כִּי גֵאוּת עָשָׂה,

‹‹ has He ‹ with ‹ for ‹ to Hashem ‹ Make ‹‹ is His ‹ exalted ‹ that ‹ declare
acted; grandeur music Name.

מוֹדַעַת זֹאת בְּכָל הָאָרֶץ. צַהֲלִי וָרֹנִּי יוֹשֶׁבֶת צִיּוֹן,

‹‹ of ‹ O inhabitant ‹ and sing ‹ Exult ‹‹ the world. ‹ throughout ‹ this is known
Zion, for joy, all

כִּי גָדוֹל בְּקִרְבֵּךְ קְדוֹשׁ יִשְׂרָאֵל.¹ וְאָמַר

‹ And [His nation] ‹‹ of Israel. ‹ is the Holy ‹ in your midst ‹ great ‹ for
will say One

בַּיּוֹם הַהוּא, הִנֵּה אֱלֹהֵינוּ זֶה, קִוִּינוּ לוֹ וְיוֹשִׁיעֵנוּ,

‹‹ that He would ‹ for ‹ we have ‹‹ this is our God; ‹ Behold, ‹‹ on that day:
save us. Him, hoped

זֶה יהוה קִוִּינוּ לוֹ, נָגִילָה וְנִשְׂמְחָה בִּישׁוּעָתוֹ.²

‹‹ at His salvation. ‹ and be gladdened ‹ we shall ‹‹ for ‹ we have ‹‹ is Hashem; ‹ This
rejoice Him; hoped

KNOWLEDGE OF GOD / דעת ה'

בֵּית יַעֲקֹב,* לְכוּ וְנֵלְכָה בְּאוֹר יהוה.³ וְהָיָה

‹ It shall be ‹‹ of Hashem. ‹ by the light ‹ let us go ‹ —come, ‹ of Jacob* ‹ O House

אֱמוּנַת עִתֶּיךָ חֹסֶן יְשׁוּעֹת חָכְמַת וָדַעַת, יִרְאַת

‹ Fear ‹‹ and wisdom. ‹ —through ‹ of [your] ‹ the strength ‹ of your ‹ the stability
knowledge salvations times,

יהוה הִיא אוֹצָרוֹ.⁴ וַיְהִי דָוִד לְכָל דְּרָכָיו מַשְׂכִּיל,

‹‹ successful, ‹ his ways ‹ in all ‹ And David was ‹‹ is one's ‹ —that ‹ of Hashem
treasure.

וַיהוה עִמּוֹ.⁵

‹‹ was with him. ‹ and Hashem

---

(1) *Isaiah* 12:2-6. (2) 25:9. (3) 2:5. (4) 33:6. (5) *I Samuel* 18:14.

בֵּית יַעֲקֹב — *O House of Jacob.* These three verses provide a definition of the salvation of which we have just spoken: Salvation is meaningless unless it includes knowledge of God's Torah. This concept is expressed in the Talmudic dictum that there is no truly free person except for one who occupies himself with the Torah. As the second of these verses teaches, one's treasure is knowledge, wisdom, and fear of God, and as the third verse teaches, success comes through God's help. A further allusion to the necessity of Torah knowledge is the passage in *Shabbos* 31a that expounds the second verse as symbolic of the Six Orders of the Mishnah. Thus, the first verse refers to the Written Torah, the second to the Oral Law, and the third expresses the assurance that knowledge of the Torah is the key to success.

RESCUE / פדיום

פָּדָה* בְּשָׁלוֹם נַפְשִׁי מִקְּרָב לִי, כִּי בְרַבִּים הָיוּ

‹ were ‹ with ‹ even ‹‹ against ‹ from ‹ my soul, ‹ in peace ‹ He redeemed*
my enemies many though, me, battles

עִמָּדִי. [1] וַיֹּאמֶר הָעָם אֶל שָׁאוּל, הֲיוֹנָתָן יָמוּת

‹‹ die, ‹ Shall Jonathan ‹‹ Saul: ‹ to ‹ The people said ‹‹ against me.

אֲשֶׁר עָשָׂה הַיְשׁוּעָה הַגְּדוֹלָה הַזֹּאת בְּיִשְׂרָאֵל,

‹‹ for Israel? ‹ this great salvation ‹ performed ‹ who

חָלִילָה, חַי יהוה, אִם יִפֹּל מִשַּׂעֲרַת רֹאשׁוֹ

‹ of his head ‹ any of the hair ‹ there falls ‹ if ‹‹ As HASHEM lives, ‹ In no way!

אַרְצָה, כִּי עִם אֱלֹהִים עָשָׂה הַיּוֹם הַזֶּה,

‹‹ this day! ‹ has he acted ‹ God ‹ with ‹ For ‹‹ to the ground. . .!

וַיִּפְדּוּ הָעָם אֶת יוֹנָתָן וְלֹא מֵת. [2] וּפְדוּיֵי יהוה יְשֻׁבוּן,

‹‹ will ‹ by ‹ Those ‹‹ die. ‹ and he ‹ Jonathan ‹ And the people
return, HASHEM redeemed did not redeemed

וּבָאוּ צִיּוֹן בְּרִנָּה, וְשִׂמְחַת עוֹלָם עַל רֹאשָׁם,

‹‹ on their heads; ‹ that is eternal ‹ with gladness ‹‹ with glad song, ‹ to Zion ‹ and will come

שָׂשׂוֹן וְשִׂמְחָה יַשִּׂיגוּ וְנָסוּ יָגוֹן וַאֲנָחָה. [3]

‹‹ and sighing. ‹ will sorrow ‹ and flee ‹‹ will they attain, ‹ and gladness ‹ joy

TRANSFORMATION OF DISTRESS TO RELIEF / הפוך צרה

הָפַכְתָּ מִסְפְּדִי לְמָחוֹל לִי, פִּתַּחְתָּ שַׂקִּי,

‹ my sackcloth ‹‹ You undid ‹‹ for me; ‹ into dancing ‹ my lament ‹ You have transformed

וַתְּאַזְּרֵנִי שִׂמְחָה. [4] וְלֹא אָבָה יהוה אֱלֹהֶיךָ לִשְׁמֹעַ

‹ to pay heed ‹‹ your God — ‹ — HASHEM, ‹‹ He did not consent ‹‹ with gladness. ‹ and You
girded me

---

(1) *Psalms* 55:19. (2) *I Samuel* 14:45. (3) *Isaiah* 35:10. (4) *Psalms* 30:12.

◆§ **פָּדָה** — *He redeemed.* The Talmud (*Berachos* 55b) teaches that one who has had a disturbing dream and is depressed by it should come before three people and tell them he has had such a dream. They reply with the wish that God change the implication of the dream from bad to good. Then they recite these nine verses that express the prayer that the dream's evil omen be transformed to the good, that the dreamer be rescued from distress, and that he know only peace. In the context of the conclusion of the Sabbath, we change the order of the three sections. Since there is now no actual distress, we begin with the verses of rescue, asking God to save us from events during the week that would challenge the spiritual elevation we absorbed during the Sabbath.

אֶל בִּלְעָם, וַיַּהֲפֹךְ יהוה אֱלֹהֶיךָ לְךָ אֶת הַקְּלָלָה

‹ the curse ‹ for you ‹ your God, ‹ did HASHEM, ‹ and transform ‹‹ Balaam, ‹ to

לִבְרָכָה, כִּי אֲהֵבְךָ יהוה אֱלֹהֶיךָ.¹ אָז תִּשְׂמַח

‹ gladdened ‹ Then ‹‹ your God. ‹ does HASHEM, ‹ love you ‹ for ‹‹ to blessing,

בְּתוּלָה בְּמָחוֹל, וּבַחֻרִים וּזְקֵנִים יַחְדָּו, וְהָפַכְתִּי

‹ and I shall ‹‹ together ‹ and elders ‹ and young men ‹‹ in a dance, ‹ will the maiden be
transform [will rejoice];

אֶבְלָם לְשָׂשׂוֹן, וְנִחַמְתִּים וְשִׂמַּחְתִּים מִיגוֹנָם.²

‹‹ from their sorrow. ‹ and gladden them ‹ and I shall console ‹‹ to joy, ‹ their mourning
them

PEACE / שלום

בּוֹרֵא נִיב שְׂפָתָיִם, שָׁלוֹם שָׁלוֹם לָרָחוֹק

‹ for far ‹ peace, ‹ Peace, ‹‹ of the lips: ‹ the speech ‹ I [will] create

וְלַקָּרוֹב, אָמַר יהוה וּרְפָאתִיו.³ וְרוּחַ לָבְשָׁה

‹ clothed ‹ A spirit ‹‹ and I shall heal him. ‹‹ HASHEM, ‹ says ‹ and for near,

אֶת עֲמָשַׂי, רֹאשׁ הַשָּׁלִישִׁים, לְךָ דָוִיד וְעִמְּךָ

‹ and [we] ‹ David, ‹ [and he said:] ‹‹ of the officers, ‹ head ‹‹ Amasai,
are with you, [We] are yours,

בֶן יִשַׁי שָׁלוֹם, שָׁלוֹם לְךָ, וְשָׁלוֹם לְעֹזְרֶךָ, כִּי עֲזָרְךָ

‹ assist ‹ for ‹‹ unto those ‹ and peace ‹‹ unto ‹ Peace ‹‹ Peace! ‹‹ of Jesse! ‹ son
you who assist you, you,

אֱלֹהֶיךָ, וַיְקַבְּלֵם דָוִיד וַיִּתְּנֵם בְּרָאשֵׁי הַגְּדוּד.⁴

‹‹ of troops. ‹ as heads ‹ and appointed them ‹ David accepted them ‹‹ does your God!

וַאֲמַרְתֶּם, כֹּה לֶחָי, וְאַתָּה שָׁלוֹם וּבֵיתְךָ שָׁלוֹם

‹‹ may there ‹ for your ‹‹ may there ‹ for you ‹‹ may it be as ‹ So ‹‹ And you shall say:
be peace. household be peace, long as you live;

וְכֹל אֲשֶׁר לְךָ שָׁלוֹם.⁵ יהוה עֹז לְעַמּוֹ יִתֵּן, יהוה

‹ HASHEM ‹‹ will ‹ to His ‹ strength ‹ HASHEM ‹‹ may there ‹ is yours ‹ that ‹ and for all
give; nation be peace!

יְבָרֵךְ אֶת עַמּוֹ בַשָּׁלוֹם.⁶

‹‹ with peace. ‹ His nation ‹ will bless

---

(1) *Deuteronomy* 23:6. (2) *Jeremiah* 31:12. (3) *Isaiah* 57:19.
(4) *I Chronicles* 12:19. (5) *I Samuel* 25:6. (6) *Psalms* 29:11.

Talmud, Tractate *Megillah* 31a / מסכת מגילה לא.

אָמַר רַבִּי יוֹחָנָן:* בְּכָל מָקוֹם שֶׁאַתָּה מוֹצֵא
< find < where you < place < In every << Yochanan:* < Rabbi < Said

גְּדֻלָּתוֹ שֶׁל הַקָּדוֹשׁ בָּרוּךְ הוּא, שָׁם אַתָּה מוֹצֵא
< find < you < there << is He, < Blessed < the Holy One, < of < [mention of] the greatness

עַנְוְתָנוּתוֹ. דָּבָר זֶה כָּתוּב בַּתּוֹרָה, וְשָׁנוּי בַּנְּבִיאִים,
<< in the Prophets, < repeated << in the Torah, < is written < This idea << His humility.

וּמְשֻׁלָּשׁ בַּכְּתוּבִים. כָּתוּב בַּתּוֹרָה: כִּי יהוה
< HASHEM, < For << in the Torah: < It is written << in the Writings. < and [stated] a third time

אֱלֹהֵיכֶם הוּא אֱלֹהֵי הָאֱלֹהִים וַאֲדֹנֵי הָאֲדֹנִים,
<< of masters, < and the Master < of heavenly forces < is the God < He < your God,

הָאֵל הַגָּדֹל הַגִּבֹּר וְהַנּוֹרָא אֲשֶׁר לֹא יִשָּׂא פָנִים
< show favoritism < does not < Who << and awesome, < mighty, < Who is great, < the God

וְלֹא יִקַּח שֹׁחַד.[1] וּכְתִיב בַּתְרֵהּ: עֹשֶׂה מִשְׁפַּט יָתוֹם
< of the orphan < the justice < He performs << after that: < And it is written < any bribe. < accept < and does not

וְאַלְמָנָה, וְאֹהֵב גֵּר לָתֶת לוֹ לֶחֶם וְשִׂמְלָה.[2] שָׁנוּי
< It is repeated << and clothing. < food < him < to give < the < and loves << and the widow, stranger,

בַּנְּבִיאִים, דִּכְתִיב: כִּי כֹה אָמַר רָם וְנִשָּׂא שֹׁכֵן עַד
<< in the Prophets, < for it is written: << for- ever, < abides < and uplifted < the exalted < [One], < says < so < For <<

וְקָדוֹשׁ שְׁמוֹ, מָרוֹם וְקָדוֹשׁ אֶשְׁכּוֹן, וְאֶת דַּכָּא וּשְׁפַל
< and < the lowly < — but I < I abide << and holiness < 'In < and Whose despondent am with exaltedness Name is holy:

(1) *Deuteronomy* 10:17. (2) 10:18.

╣◄ אָמַר רַבִּי יוֹחָנָן — *Said Rabbi Yochanan.* This Talmudic passage provides perspective for the coming week in the following ways:

❑ Rabbi Yochanan's teaching gives us confidence to pray. People have a fear, a sense of inadequacy to pray to God: What are we and who are we that we ask God to take notice of us? Rabbi Yochanan replies with a host of Scriptural pas-

sages teaching that even when God's grandeur is most apparent, He reveals His humility, meaning that He is concerned with the needs and fears of even the humblest man (*Avodas Yisrael*).

❑ Judaism teaches that a Jew should always seek to emulate God's compassion, generosity, and other traits. Consequently, as we leave the rarefied spiritual atmosphere of the Sabbath,

רוּחַ, לְהַחֲיוֹת רוּחַ שְׁפָלִים וּלְהַחֲיוֹת לֵב נִדְכָּאִים.¹

of spirit, ⟪ to revive ⟨ the spirit ⟨ of the lowly ⟪ and to revive ⟨ the ⟩ of the heart despondent.'

מְשֻׁלָּשׁ בַּכְּתוּבִים, דִּכְתִיב: שִׁירוּ לֵאלֹהִים, זַמְּרוּ

And it is stated ⟨ in the Writings, ⟪ for it is written: ⟪ Sing ⟨ to God, ⟨ make a third time music

שְׁמוֹ, סֹלּוּ לָרֹכֵב בָּעֲרָבוֹת, בְּיָהּ שְׁמוֹ, וְעִלְזוּ לְפָנָיו.²

[to] His ⟪ extol ⟨ the One ⟨ upon the highest ⟪ with ⟨ His ⟪ and exult ⟨ before Name; Who rides heavens, Yah Name, Him.

וּכְתִיב בַּתְרֵהּ: אֲבִי יְתוֹמִים וְדַיַּן אַלְמָנוֹת,

And it is written ⟨ after that: ⟪ The Father ⟨ of orphans ⟨ and Defender ⟨ of widows

אֱלֹהִים בִּמְעוֹן קָדְשׁוֹ.³

is God ⟨ in the abode ⟨ ⟪ of His holiness.

יְהִי יהוה אֱלֹהֵינוּ עִמָּנוּ כַּאֲשֶׁר הָיָה עִם אֲבוֹתֵינוּ,

May ⟨ HASHEM, our God, ⟪ be with us, ⟨ as ⟪ He was ⟨ with ⟨ our forefathers;

אַל יַעַזְבֵנוּ וְאַל יִטְּשֵׁנוּ.⁴ וְאַתֶּם הַדְּבֵקִים בַּיהוה

to HASHEM, ⟨ who cling ⟨ You ⟪ forsake us. ⟨ nor ⟨ abandon us ⟨ may He not

אֱלֹהֵיכֶם, חַיִּים כֻּלְּכֶם הַיּוֹם.⁵ כִּי נִחַם יהוה צִיּוֹן,

⟪ Zion; ⟨ HASHEM will comfort ⟨ For ⟪ today. ⟨ all of you, ⟨ are alive, ⟪ your God,

נִחַם כָּל חָרְבֹתֶיהָ, וַיָּשֶׂם מִדְבָּרָהּ כְּעֵדֶן וְעַרְבָתָהּ

He will ⟨ all ⟨ her ruins. ⟪ He will ⟨ her wilderness ⟨ like ⟨ and her comfort make Eden wasteland

כְּגַן יהוה, שָׂשׂוֹן וְשִׂמְחָה יִמָּצֵא בָהּ, תּוֹדָה וְקוֹל

like a ⟨ of HASHEM. ⟪ Joy ⟨ and gladness ⟨ will be found ⟪ there, ⟨ thanks- ⟨ and the garden giving sound

זִמְרָה.⁷ יהוה חָפֵץ לְמַעַן צִדְקוֹ, יַגְדִּיל תּוֹרָה וְיַאְדִּיר.⁶

⟪ of music. ⟨ HASHEM ⟨ desired, ⟨ for the ⟨ of [Israel's] ⟨ to make the ⟨ and glorious. Torah great righteousness, sake

(1) *Isaiah* 57:15. (2) *Psalms* 68:5. (3) 68:6. (4) *I Kings* 8:57.
(5) *Deuteronomy* 4:4. (6) *Isaiah* 51:3. (7) 42:21.

we are reminded that God remains near to those who are weak. This encourages us in our own lives and provides both an inspiration and a warning: an inspiring call to the privileged that they be concerned with the weak — as God is; and a warning not to take advantage of the defenseless, for God is the Father of orphans and the Defender of widows (*World of Prayer*).

—— תהלים קכח / Psalm 128 ——

שִׁיר הַמַּעֲלוֹת;* אַשְׁרֵי כָּל יְרֵא יהוה, הַהֹלֵךְ
‹ who walks ‹‹ HASHEM, ‹ who ‹ is each ‹ Praise- ‹‹ of ascents.* ‹ A song
fears person worthy

בִּדְרָכָיו. יְגִיעַ כַּפֶּיךָ כִּי תֹאכֵל, אַשְׁרֶיךָ וְטוֹב לָךְ.
‹‹ with ‹ and it ‹ you are ‹‹ you eat — ‹—when ‹‹ of your ‹ The ‹‹ in His ways.
you. is well praiseworthy, hands, labor

אֶשְׁתְּךָ כְּגֶפֶן פֹּרִיָּה בְּיַרְכְּתֵי בֵיתֶךָ; בָּנֶיךָ כִּשְׁתִלֵי
‹ will be ‹ your ‹‹ of your ‹ in the inner ‹ fruitful, ‹ will be like ‹ Your wife
like shoots children home; chambers a vine,

זֵיתִים סָבִיב לְשֻׁלְחָנֶךָ. הִנֵּה כִי כֵן יְבֹרַךְ גָּבֶר יְרֵא
‹ who ‹ the man ‹ is blessed ‹ so ‹ for ‹ Behold, ‹‹ your table. ‹ surrounding ‹ of olive
fears trees

יהוה. יְבָרֶכְךָ יהוה מִצִּיּוֹן, וּרְאֵה בְּטוֹב יְרוּשָׁלָיִם
‹ of Jerusalem, ‹ upon the ‹ and may ‹‹ from Zion, ‹ May HASHEM bless you ‹‹ HASHEM.
goodness you gaze

כֹּל יְמֵי חַיֶּיךָ. וּרְאֵה בָנִים לְבָנֶיךָ, שָׁלוֹם עַל
‹ upon ‹ peace ‹‹ [born] to ‹ children ‹ And may ‹‹ of your life. ‹ the days ‹ all
your children, you see

יִשְׂרָאֵל.
‹‹ Israel.

❧ HAVDALAH / הבדלה ⁂

AT THE CONCLUSION OF THE SABBATH BEGIN HERE:

הִנֵּה אֵל יְשׁוּעָתִי אֶבְטַח וְלֹא אֶפְחָד, כִּי עָזִּי
‹ my ‹ For ‹‹ fear. ‹ and not ‹ I shall trust ‹‹ is my ‹ God ‹ Behold,
might salvation;

וְזִמְרָת יָהּ יהוה, וַיְהִי לִי לִישׁוּעָה. וּשְׁאַבְתֶּם
‹ You will draw ‹‹ a salvation. ‹ for me ‹ and ‹‹ HASHEM, ‹ is ‹ and my
He was God, praise

❧ שִׁיר הַמַּעֲלוֹת — *A song of ascents.* This psalm, which extols the economic and family life of one who fears God, is recited here as an exhortation to honesty and compassion during the ensuing week (*Avodas Yisrael*).

The Talmud (*Berachos* 8a) expounds this psalm to teach that one who enjoys the fruits of his own labor is assured of God's blessing in This World as well as in the World to Come.

מַיִם בְּשָׂשׂוֹן, מִמַּעַיְנֵי הַיְשׁוּעָה. לַיהוה
⟨ To Hashem ⟩ ≪ of salvation. ⟨ from the springs ⟨ in joy, ⟨ water

הַיְשׁוּעָה, עַל עַמְּךָ בִרְכָתֶךָ סֶּלָה. יהוה
⟨ Hashem, ≪ Selah. ≪ is Your ⟨ Your ⟨ upon ≪ is salvation,
blessing, people

צְבָאוֹת עִמָּנוּ, מִשְׂגָּב לָנוּ אֱלֹהֵי יַעֲקֹב סֶלָה.
≪ Selah. ≪ of Jacob, ⟨ is the God ⟨ for us ⟨ a stronghold ≪ is with us, ⟨ Master
of Legions,

יהוה צְבָאוֹת, אַשְׁרֵי אָדָם בֹּטֵחַ בָּךְ. יהוה
⟨ Hashem, ≪ in You. ⟨ who ⟨ is the ⟨ praiseworthy ⟨ Master ⟨ Hashem,
trusts man of Legions,

הוֹשִׁיעָה, הַמֶּלֶךְ יַעֲנֵנוּ בְיוֹם קָרְאֵנוּ. לַיְּהוּדִים
⟨ For the Jews ≪ we call. ⟨ on the ⟨ answer ⟨ May the ≪ save!
day us King

הָיְתָה אוֹרָה וְשִׂמְחָה, וְשָׂשֹׂן וִיקָר, כֵּן תִּהְיֶה
⟨ may it be ⟨ So ≪ and honor. ⟨ joy ⟨ gladness, ⟨ light, ⟨ there was

לָּנוּ. כּוֹס יְשׁוּעוֹת אֶשָּׂא, וּבְשֵׁם יהוה אֶקְרָא.
≪ I will ⟨ of Hashem ⟨ and the ≪ I will raise, ⟨ of salvations ⟨ The cup ≪ for us!
invoke. Name

THE FOLLOWING IS RECITED AT THE CONCLUSION OF THE SABBATH AND OF FESTIVALS:

סַבְרִי מָרָנָן וְרַבָּנָן וְרַבּוֹתַי:
≪ and ⟨ and ⟨ distinguished ⟨ By your
gentlemen: rabbis people leave,

בָּרוּךְ אַתָּה יהוה אֱלֹהֵינוּ מֶלֶךְ הָעוֹלָם,
≪ of the ⟨ King ⟨ our God, ⟨ Hashem, ⟨ are You, ⟨ Blessed
universe,

(אָמֵן. – All respond)
≪ (Amen.)

בּוֹרֵא פְּרִי הַגָּפֶן.
≪ of the ⟨ the ⟨ Who
vine. fruit creates

---

(1) *Isaiah* 12:2-3. (2) *Psalms* 3:9. (3) 46:12. (4) 84:13.
(5) 20:10. (6) *Esther* 8:16. (7) *Psalms* 116:13.

**THE FOLLOWING TWO BLESSINGS ARE RECITED
AT THE CONCLUSION OF THE SABBATH ONLY:**

AFTER THE FOLLOWING BLESSING SMELL THE SPICES:

בָּרוּךְ אַתָּה יהוה אֱלֹהֵינוּ מֶלֶךְ הָעוֹלָם,
Blessed ⟨ are You, ⟨ HASHEM, ⟨ our God, ⟨ King ⟨ of the universe, ⟩⟩

בּוֹרֵא מִינֵי בְשָׂמִים. (אָמֵן. – All respond)
Who creates ⟨ species ⟨ of fragrance. ⟩⟩   (Amen.) ⟩⟩

AFTER THE FOLLOWING BLESSING HOLD FINGERS UP TO THE FLAME TO SEE THE REFLECTED LIGHT:

בָּרוּךְ אַתָּה יהוה אֱלֹהֵינוּ מֶלֶךְ הָעוֹלָם,
Blessed ⟨ are You, ⟨ HASHEM, ⟨ our God, ⟨ King ⟨ of the universe, ⟩⟩

בּוֹרֵא מְאוֹרֵי הָאֵשׁ. (אָמֵן. – All respond)
Who creates illuminations ⟨ the ⟨ of fire. ⟩⟩   (Amen.) ⟩⟩

THE FOLLOWING IS RECITED AT THE CONCLUSION OF THE SABBATH AND OF FESTIVALS:

בָּרוּךְ אַתָּה יהוה אֱלֹהֵינוּ מֶלֶךְ הָעוֹלָם,
Blessed ⟨ are You, ⟨ HASHEM, ⟨ our God, ⟨ King ⟨ of the universe, ⟩⟩

הַמַּבְדִּיל בֵּין קֹדֶשׁ לְחוֹל, בֵּין אוֹר לְחְשֶׁךְ,
Who distinguishes ⟨ between ⟨ the sacred ⟨ and the secular, ⟨ between ⟨ light ⟨ and darkness, ⟩⟩

בֵּין יִשְׂרָאֵל לָעַמִּים, בֵּין יוֹם הַשְּׁבִיעִי
between ⟨ Israel ⟨ and the nations, ⟩⟩ between ⟨ the Seventh Day ⟨

לְשֵׁשֶׁת יְמֵי הַמַּעֲשֶׂה. בָּרוּךְ אַתָּה יהוה,
and the six ⟨ days ⟨ of labor. ⟩⟩ Blessed ⟨ are You, ⟨ HASHEM, ⟩⟩

הַמַּבְדִּיל בֵּין קֹדֶשׁ לְחוֹל. (אָמֵן. – All respond)
Who distinguishes ⟨ between ⟨ sacred ⟨ and secular. ⟩⟩ (Amen.) ⟩⟩

**THE ONE WHO RECITED *HAVDALAH*, OR SOMEONE ELSE PRESENT FOR *HAVDALAH*, SHOULD DRINK
MOST OF THE WINE FROM THE CUP, THEN EXTINGUISH THE FLAME BY POURING LEFTOVER WINE OVER
IT INTO A DISH. IT IS CUSTOMARY TO DIP THE FINGERS INTO THE WINE-DISH AND TOUCH THE
EYELIDS AND INNER POCKETS WITH THEM. THIS SYMBOLIZES THAT THE "LIGHT OF THE MITZVAH"
WILL GUIDE US AND INVOKE BLESSING FOR THE COMING WEEK.**

﴾ THE FOUR SPECIES / נְטִילַת לוּלָב ﴿

MANY RECITE THE FOLLOWING DECLARATION OF INTENT BEFORE TAKING THE FOUR SPECIES:

יְהִי רָצוֹן* מִלְּפָנֶיךָ, יהוה אֱלֹהַי וֵאלֹהֵי אֲבוֹתַי, בִּפְרִי

⟨ [that] ⟨⟨ of my ⟨ and the ⟨ my God ⟨ Hᴀsʜᴇᴍ, ⟨⟨ before You, ⟨ the will* ⟨ May
through forefathers, God it be
the fruit

עֵץ הָדָר,* וְכַפּוֹת תְּמָרִים,* וַעֲנַף עֵץ עָבוֹת,* וְעַרְבֵי נָחַל,*

⟨⟨ of the ⟨ and the ⟨⟨ of the ⟨ the ⟨⟨ of the ⟨ the ⟨⟨ of the
brook willows myrtle tree,* twigs date-palm,* branches esrog tree,*

אוֹתִיּוֹת שִׁמְךָ הַמְּיֻחָד* תְּקָרֵב אֶחָד אֶל אֶחָד, וְהָיוּ לַאֲחָדִים

⟨ united ⟨ that they ⟨ the ⟨ to ⟨ one ⟨ may You ⟨⟨ of Your unified ⟨ – the letters
may become other, draw close Name* –

בְּיָדִי, וְלֵידַע אֵיךְ שִׁמְךָ נִקְרָא עָלַי, וְיִירְאוּ מִגֶּשֶׁת אֵלָי.

⟨⟨ me. ⟨ of ⟨ and that ⟨⟨ upon ⟨ is called ⟨ Your ⟨ how ⟨ and that [I] ⟨⟨ in my
approaching [evil forces] me, Name might know hand;
may be fearful

וּבְנַעֲנוּעִי אוֹתָם תַּשְׁפִּיעַ שֶׁפַע בְּרָכוֹת מִדַּעַת עֶלְיוֹן לְנָוֶה

⟨ to the ⟨ of the ⟨ from the ⟨ of ⟨ an out- ⟨ may You ⟨ them, ⟨ And when
abode Most High wisdom blessings pouring cause to flow I wave

---

(1) Cf. *Leviticus* 23:40.

﴾ נְטִילַת לוּלָב / THE FOUR SPECIES ﴿

The Torah commands the taking of the Four Species on Succos and concludes: *You shall be joyous before* HASHEM . . . (*Leviticus* 23:40). The Midrash explains the connection between this *mitzvah* and joyousness:

In earlier days if a litigant's claim before the royal court was decided in his favor, he would receive a spear from the king. When he left the palace holding the king's spear aloft, all knew that he had been victorious in his suit. Similarly, during the Days of Awe, the Jewish people were on trial before the Heavenly Court. On Succos, "the season of joy," we celebrate our happiness that God has accepted our repentance — a confidence symbolized by the *lulav* held aloft.

יְהִי רָצוֹן ﬩ – *May it be the will.* This prayer, as well as many others that are replete with Kabbalistic implications, was introduced by the 17th-century master of Kabbalah, R' Nassan of Hanover, and first appeared in his *Shaarei Tzion* (Prague, 5422/1662).

בִּפְרִי עֵץ הָדָר — *Through the fruit of the esrog* (lit. *beautiful*) *tree.* The Torah does not specify the *esrog* by name, but uses this descriptive phrase. *Targum* renders הָדָר, *beautiful,* as אֶתְרוֹגִין, *esrogin.*

וְכַפּוֹת תְּמָרִים — *The branches of the date-palm [the lulav].* In the Scriptural verse, the terms for *esrog* and *lulav* are not connected by the conjunctive ו, *and.* However, conjunctions do connect terms for *lulav, hadasim* (myrtle), and *aravos* (willow). From this it is derived that the species be held in two groups: the *esrog* by itself; and a bundle containing the *lulav, hadasim,* and *aravos* (*Succah* 24b).

וַעֲנַף עֵץ עָבוֹת — *The twigs of the myrtle tree [hadasim].* Literally, עֵץ עָבוֹת means a *thick* or *braided* tree. The Talmud (*Succah* 32b) understands this to refer to a species whose leaf coverage is thick, completely covering the twig, and whose leaves overlap each other, as if they were braided — and identify it as the *myrtle.*

אוֹתִיּוֹת שִׁמְךָ הַמְּיֻחָד — *The letters of Your unified Name.* Kabbalah teaches that each of the Four

אַפִּרְיוֹן, לִמְכוֹן בֵּית אֱלֹהֵינוּ. וּתְהֵא חֲשׁוּבָה לְפָנֶיךָ מִצְוַת

‹ – the ‹‹ before ‹ reckoned ‹ And may ‹‹ of our ‹ of the ‹ to the ‹‹ of the
mitzvah You it be God. House foundation Tabernacle,

אַרְבָּעָה מִינִים אֵלוּ, כְּאִלּוּ קִיַּמְתִּיהָ בְּכָל פְּרָטוֹתֶיהָ וְשָׁרְשֶׁיהָ

‹‹ and its ‹ its particulars ‹ with ‹ I had ‹ as if ‹‹ of these Four Species —
roots, all fulfilled it

וְתַרְיַ"ג מִצְוֹת הַתְּלוּיִים בָּהּ. כִּי כַוָּנָתִי לְיַחֵדָא שְׁמָא דְקֻדְשָׁא

‹ of the ‹ the ‹ is to unify ‹ my ‹ For ‹‹ upon ‹ that are ‹ mitzvos ‹ and [with]
Holy One, Name intention it. dependent the 613

בְּרִיךְ הוּא וּשְׁכִינְתֵּהּ, בִּדְחִילוּ וּרְחִימוּ, לְיַחֵד שֵׁם י"ה בּוָ"ה

‹ with ‹ Yud- ‹ the ‹ to unify ‹‹ and in ‹ in awe ‹‹ and His ‹ is He, ‹ Blessed
Vav-Kei Kei Name love, Presence,

בְּיִחוּדָא שְׁלִים, בְּשֵׁם כָּל יִשְׂרָאֵל. אָמֵן. בָּרוּךְ יהוה לְעוֹלָם,

‹‹ forever, ‹ is ‹ Blessed ‹‹ Amen. ‹ Israel; ‹ of all ‹ in the ‹‹ in perfect unity,
HASHEM name

אָמֵן, וְאָמֵן.[1]

‹‹ and Amen. ‹ Amen

---

(1) *Psalms* 89:53.

Species is identified with another of the letters of the Four-Letter Name of God. Rabbi Michael Ber Weissmandl (in *Toras Chemed*) adduces a complex series of calculations to prove that the *aravos, lulav, hadasim,* and *esrog* correspond, in that order, with the four letters of the Name.

◆§ Laws of the Four Species

If at all possible one should not eat or drink before taking the Species.

Most *siddurim* place the blessings of the Four Species just before *Hallel,* in accordance with the ruling of *Shulchan Aruch* (644:1) that the Species be taken between *Shemoneh Esrei* and *Hallel.* However, many follow *Arizal's* view that these blessings should be recited in the *succah* and, therefore, recite them before entering the synagogue for *Shacharis.*

The שֶׁהֶחֱיָנוּ blessing is recited on the first day that the Four Species are taken. Thus, if the first day of Succos coincides with the Sabbath, this blessing is recited on Sunday. Additionally, if one was unable to take the Four Species on the first day of Succos, he recites this blessing the first time he is able to, regardless of which day of Succos it is. [A full exposition of the significance and laws of the *mitzvah* may be found in the ArtScroll *Succos — Its Significance, Laws, and Prayers.*]

In addition to holding the Four Species together — which is sufficient for performance of the commandment — one should also perform נַעֲנוּעִים, the *waving* (or *shaking*), of the Species in six directions — the four points of the compass, up and down. It is preferable that one face east while waving the Species. The sequence followed in most *Nusach Sefard* congregations is that of the *Arizal*: right (south), left (north), straight ahead (east), up, down, and back (west).

The generally followed manner of waving is to stretch out the arms and shake strongly enough to rustle the *lulav's* leaves, and then to draw the Species close to the chest and shake again. This is repeated three times in each direction (*Rama, Orach Chaim* 651:9).

The Species are also held during the recitation of *Hallel* and *Hoshanos.* During certain verses of *Hallel,* they are waved again in the manner described above. Although one should follow the custom of his own congregation, the customary rule is to wave the Species when the verses הוֹדוּ לַהּ' כִּי טוֹב and אָנָּא ה' הוֹשִׁיעָה נָּא are recited (ibid. 651:8).

THE FOUR SPECIES — *LULAV, HADASIM, ARAVOS, ESROG* — ARE TAKEN IN HAND EVERY DAY OF SUCCOS, THROUGH HOSHANA RABBAH, EXCEPT ON THE SABBATH. THE *LULAV-* BUNDLE IS PICKED UP WITH THE RIGHT HAND, THEN THE *ESROG (PITAM* FACING DOWN) WITH THE LEFT. AFTER THE BLESSINGS ARE RECITED, THE *ESROG* IS TURNED OVER AND THE FOUR SPECIES ARE WAVED IN THE SIX DIRECTIONS. (SEE *LAWS* ON PAGE 500.)

בָּרוּךְ אַתָּה יהוה אֱלֹהֵינוּ מֶלֶךְ הָעוֹלָם,

Blessed ‹ are You, ‹ HASHEM, ‹ our God, ‹ King ‹ of the universe,

אֲשֶׁר קִדְּשָׁנוּ בְּמִצְוֹתָיו, וְצִוָּנוּ עַל נְטִילַת

Who ‹ has ‹ with His ‹ and has ‹ concerning ‹ the taking
sanctified us commandments commanded us

לוּלָב.*

‹‹ of a palm branch.*

THE FOLLOWING BLESSING IS ADDED ONLY ON THE FIRST DAY THAT THE FOUR SPECIES ARE TAKEN.

בָּרוּךְ אַתָּה יהוה אֱלֹהֵינוּ מֶלֶךְ הָעוֹלָם,

Blessed ‹ are You, ‹ HASHEM, ‹ our God, ‹ King ‹ of the universe,

שֶׁהֶחֱיָנוּ וְקִיְּמָנוּ וְהִגִּיעָנוּ לַזְּמַן הַזֶּה.

Who has ‹ sustained ‹ and brought us ‹ to this season.
kept us alive, us,

עַל נְטִילַת לוּלָב §ֵּ — *Concerning the taking of a palm branch.* The Talmud (*Succah* 37b) explains that only the *lulav* is mentioned in the benediction since the date-palm tree, of which the *lulav* is a branch, is taller than any of the other species.

§ֵּ **Hallel**

The prophets ordained that the six psalms of *Hallel* [literally *praise*] be recited on each Festival, and also to commemorate times of national deliverance from peril. Moreover, before David redacted and incorporated these psalms into the Book of *Psalms*, *Hallel* was already known to the nation: Moses and Israel recited it after being saved from the Egyptians at the sea; Joshua, after defeating the kings of Canaan; Deborah and Barak, after defeating Sisera; Hezekiah, after defeating Sennacherib; Chananyah, Mishael, and Azariah, after being saved from the evil Nebuchadnezzar; and Mordechai and Esther, after the defeat of the wicked Haman (*Pesachim* 117a).

These psalms were singled out as the unit of praise because they contain five fundamental themes of Jewish faith: the Exodus, the Splitting of the Sea, the Giving of the Torah at Sinai, the future Resurrection of the Dead, and the coming of the Messiah (ibid. 118a).

Hallel is omitted on Rosh Hashanah and Yom Kippur because they are days of judgment and it is inappropriate to sing joyful praises on days when our very survival is being weighed on the scales of judgment. It is omitted on Purim, because, despite the miracle of the day, the Jewish people remained in exile as servants of Ahasuerus, and thus the deliverance was not complete. On Chanukah, however, not only was the military victory more complete, the *Hallel* also commemorates the miracle of the lights, which marked the rededication of the Temple.

❧ HALLEL / הלל ❧

HALLEL IS RECITED AFTER THE SHEMONEH ESREI OF SHACHARIS ON CHOL HAMOED, CHANUKAH, AND ROSH CHODESH. ON ROSH CHODESH (EXCEPT ON ROSH CHODESH TEVES) AND ON CHOL HAMOED PESACH, TWO PARAGRAPHS (AS INDICATED IN THE TEXT) ARE OMITTED.

THOSE WHO WEAR TEFILLIN ON CHOL HAMOED, REMOVE THEM BEFORE HALLEL.
[HOWEVER ON THE FIRST DAY OF CHOL HAMOED PESACH, MANY PEOPLE DO NOT REMOVE THE TEFILLIN UNTIL AFTER THE TORAH READING, SINCE THE READING MENTIONS TEFILLIN.]

THE CHAZZAN RECITES THE BLESSING. THE CONGREGATION, AFTER RESPONDING AMEN, REPEATS IT, AND CONTINUES WITH THE FIRST PSALM:

בָּרוּךְ אַתָּה יהוה אֱלֹהֵינוּ מֶלֶךְ הָעוֹלָם, אֲשֶׁר
⟨ Who ⟨⟨ of the universe, ⟨ King ⟨ our God, ⟨ HASHEM, ⟨ are You, ⟨ Blessed

קִדְּשָׁנוּ בְּמִצְוֹתָיו, וְצִוָּנוּ לִקְרוֹא אֶת הַהַלֵּל.
≪ the Hallel. ⟨ to recite ⟨ and has ⟨ with His ⟨ has
commanded us commandments sanctified us

אָמֵן.) —Cong.)
≪ (Amen.)

—————— Psalm 113 / תהלים קיג ——————

הַלְלוּיָהּ; הַלְלוּ עַבְדֵי יהוה,* הַלְלוּ אֶת שֵׁם
⟨ Name ⟨ the ⟨ praise ≪ of HASHEM;* ⟨ you servants ⟨ Give praise, ≪ Halleluyah!

יהוה. יְהִי שֵׁם יהוה מְבֹרָךְ מֵעַתָּה וְעַד עוֹלָם.
≪ eternity. ⟨ until ⟨ from this ⟨ be blessed ⟨ of ⟨ the ⟨ Let ≪ of
time HASHEM Name HASHEM!

מִמִּזְרַח שֶׁמֶשׁ עַד מְבוֹאוֹ, מְהֻלָּל שֵׁם יהוה.
≪ of HASHEM. ⟨ is the Name ⟨ praised ≪ its setting, ⟨ to ⟨ of the sun ⟨ From the rising

רָם עַל כָּל גּוֹיִם יהוה, עַל הַשָּׁמַיִם כְּבוֹדוֹ. מִי
⟨ Who ≪ is His glory. ⟨ the heavens ⟨ above ≪ is HASHEM, ⟨ nations ⟨ all ⟨ above ⟨ High

כַּיהוה אֱלֹהֵינוּ, הַמַּגְבִּיהִי לָשָׁבֶת. הַמַּשְׁפִּילִי
⟨ — yet deigns ≪ is enthroned ⟨ Who on high ≪ our God, ⟨ is like HASHEM,

לִרְאוֹת, בַּשָּׁמַיִם וּבָאָרֶץ.* ❖ מְקִימִי מֵעָפָר דָּל,
≪ the ⟨ from the ⟨ He raises ≪ and the earth?* ⟨ upon the ⟨ to look
needy, dust heavens

❧ **הַלְלוּיָהּ הַלְלוּ עַבְדֵי ה׳** — Halleluyah! Give praise, you servants of HASHEM. Only after their liberation from Pharaoh's bondage could the Jews be the servants of HASHEM.

הַמַּשְׁפִּילִי לִרְאוֹת בַּשָּׁמַיִם וּבָאָרֶץ — Yet deigns to look (lit. bends down low to see) upon the heavens and the earth? This is the challenging and exciting aspect of God's relationship to

מֵאַשְׁפֹּת יָרִים אֶבְיוֹן. לְהוֹשִׁיבִי עִם נְדִיבִים,

《 nobles, 〈 with 〈 to seat them 《 the 〈 He lifts 〈 from the
destitute, trash heaps

עִם נְדִיבֵי עַמּוֹ. מוֹשִׁיבִי עֲקֶרֶת הַבַּיִת,* אֵם

〈 into a 〈 of the house* 〈 the barren 〈 He transforms 《 of His 〈 the nobles 〈 with
mother woman people.

הַבָּנִים שְׂמֵחָה; הַלְלוּיָהּ.

《 Halleluyah! 《 who is joyous. 〈 of children

———— Psalm 114 / תהלים קיד ————

בְּצֵאת יִשְׂרָאֵל מִמִּצְרָיִם,* בֵּית יַעֲקֹב

〈 of Jacob 〈 the household 《 of Egypt,* 〈 When Israel went out

מֵעַם לֹעֵז.* הָיְתָה יְהוּדָה לְקָדְשׁוֹ,* יִשְׂרָאֵל

〈 Israel 《 His sanctuary,* 〈 Judah became 《 of alien 〈 from a
tongue,* people

מַמְשְׁלוֹתָיו. הַיָּם רָאָה וַיָּנֹס, הַיַּרְדֵּן יִסֹּב

〈 turned 〈 the Jordan 《 and fled; 〈 saw 〈 The sea 《 His dominions.

לְאָחוֹר. הֶהָרִים רָקְדוּ כְאֵילִים,* גְּבָעוֹת כִּבְנֵי

〈 like young 〈 the hills 《 like rams;* 〈 skipped 〈 The mountains 《 backward.

צֹאן. ❖ מַה לְּךָ הַיָּם כִּי תָנוּס, הַיַּרְדֵּן תִּסֹּב

〈 that you turn 〈 O Jordan, 《 you flee? 〈 that 〈 O sea, 〈 ails you, 〈 What 《 lambs.

man: as we act toward God, so does He respond to us. If we ignore His presence, He withdraws high *above the heavens;* but if we welcome His proximity, He lovingly involves Himself in every phase of our lives (*R' A.C. Feuer*).

מוֹשִׁיבִי עֲקֶרֶת הַבַּיִת — *He transforms the barren woman of the house.* The Creator exercises complete control over nature. This control is vividly demonstrated when God wondrously transforms a barren woman into a mother (*Radak*).

בְּצֵאת יִשְׂרָאֵל מִמִּצְרָיִם ❧ — *When Israel went out of Egypt.* The second chapter of *Hallel* continues the theme of the first chapter, which praises God for raising up the needy and destitute. Israel were thus elevated when they left Egypt and risked their lives by entering the Sea at God's command.

בֵּית יַעֲקֹב מֵעַם לֹעֵז — *The household of Jacob from a people of alien tongue.* Even the Jews who were forced to communicate with the Egyptians in the language of the land did so only under duress. Among themselves, however, they spoke only the Holy Tongue and regarded Egyptian as a foreign language.

הָיְתָה יְהוּדָה לְקָדְשׁוֹ — *Judah became His sanctuary.* God singled out the tribe of Judah to be the family of royalty, because they sanctified God's Name at the Sea of Reeds. Led by their prince, Nachshon ben Aminadav, this tribe was the first to leap into the threatening waters (*Rosh*).

הֶהָרִים רָקְדוּ כְאֵילִים — *The mountains skipped like rams.* When Israel received the Torah, Sinai and the neighboring mountains and hills shook and trembled at the manifestation of God's

לְאָחוֹר. הֶהָרִים תִּרְקְדוּ כְאֵילִים, גְּבָעוֹת כִּבְנֵי

‹ like young ‹ O hills, ‹‹ like rams? ‹ that you skip ‹ O mountains, ‹‹ backward?

צֹאן. מִלִּפְנֵי אָדוֹן חוּלִי אָרֶץ, מִלִּפְנֵי אֱלוֹהַּ

‹ of the God ‹ before the presence ‹‹ did the earth, ‹ tremble ‹ of the Lord ‹ Before the Presence ‹‹ lambs?

יַעֲקֹב. הַהֹפְכִי הַצּוּר אֲגַם מָיִם,* חַלָּמִישׁ

‹ the flint ‹‹ of water,* ‹ into a pond ‹ the rock ‹ Who turns ‹‹ of Jacob,

לְמַעְיְנוֹ מָיִם.

‹‹ of water. ‹ into a flowing fountain

ON ROSH CHODESH (EXCEPT ON ROSH CHODESH TEVES) AND ON THE LAST SIX DAYS OF PESACH THE FOLLOWING PARAGRAPH IS OMITTED.

——— Psalm 115:1-11 / תהלים קטו:א-יא ———

לֹא לָנוּ,* יהוה, לֹא לָנוּ; כִּי לְשִׁמְךָ תֵּן

‹ give ‹ for Your Name's sake ‹ but ‹‹ for our sake, ‹ not ‹ Hashem, ‹ for our sake,* ‹ Not

Presence and the thunder and lightning that accompanied it.

הַהֹפְכִי הַצּוּר אֲגַם מָיִם — Who turns the rock into a pond of water. When the Jews thirsted for water in the Wilderness, God instructed Moses (Exodus 17:6), "You shall smite the rock and water shall come out of it, so that the people may drink."

◄§ Abridged Hallel / Pesach and Rosh Chodesh

The Talmud (Arachin 10b) teaches that a Festival day whose mussaf-offering is different from that of the previous day is cause for the recitation of the full Hallel, as each new offering is an indication of a new spiritual manifestation. On Succos, when each of the eight days has a different mussaf-offering (Numbers 29:12-34), the full Hallel is recited each day. On the other hand, the mussaf-offering on Pesach is identical every day; consequently only the "abridged" or "half" Hallel is recited on the last six days.

Another reason the shorter version of Hallel is recited during the latter days of Pesach is that the Jewish people did not attain their full level of holiness until they accepted the Torah on Shavuos. To signify this lack of completion without the Torah, we abbreviate Hallel (Sh'lah).

The prophets did not ordain that Hallel be recited on Rosh Chodesh because it is neither a Festival nor a day on which a miracle occurred (Arachin 10b).

Nevertheless, the custom developed — first in Babylonia and later in Eretz Yisrael — to recite the abridged version on Rosh Chodesh (Taanis 28b). Hallel alludes to the kingship of David and, as noted in the commentary to Kiddush Levanah (p. 454), Rosh Chodesh recalls the renewal of the Davidic dynasty. Nevertheless, in order to demonstrate that the Hallel of Rosh Chodesh is not of the same status as that of the Festivals, the abridged version is recited.

In the abridged form, the first eleven verses of both Psalm 115 [לֹא לָנוּ] and Psalm 116 [אָהַבְתִּי] are omitted. Since their general themes are repeated in their second halves [זְכָרֵנוּ ה' and מָה אָשִׁיב], nothing essential is lost by their omission (Eliyah Rabbah).

◄§ לֹא לָנוּ — Not for our sake. The preceding psalm depicts the awe inspired by God's miracles. Here the Psalmist describes the after-

כְּבוֹד* עַל חַסְדְּךָ עַל אֲמִתֶּךָ. לָמָּה יֹאמְרוּ

‹‹ should ‹ Why ‹‹ Your truth! ‹ [and] ‹ Your ‹ for ‹ glory*
they say for kindness

הַגּוֹיִם, אַיֵּה נָא אֱלֹהֵיהֶם. וֵאלֹהֵינוּ בַשָּׁמָיִם,

‹‹ is in the heavens; ‹ Our God ‹‹ is their God? ‹ now ‹ Where ‹‹ — the nations,

כֹּל אֲשֶׁר חָפֵץ עָשָׂה. עֲצַבֵּיהֶם כֶּסֶף וְזָהָב,

‹‹ and gold, ‹ are silver ‹ Their idols ‹‹ He does! ‹ He pleases ‹ whatever

מַעֲשֵׂה יְדֵי אָדָם. פֶּה לָהֶם וְלֹא יְדַבֵּרוּ,*

‹‹ speak;* ‹ but cannot ‹ they have, ‹ A mouth ‹‹ of man. ‹ of the hands ‹ the work

עֵינַיִם לָהֶם וְלֹא יִרְאוּ. אָזְנַיִם לָהֶם וְלֹא

‹ but cannot ‹ they have, ‹ ears ‹‹ see; ‹ but cannot ‹ they have, ‹ eyes

יִשְׁמָעוּ, אַף לָהֶם וְלֹא יְרִיחוּן. יְדֵיהֶם

‹‹ Their hands ‹‹ smell. ‹ but cannot ‹ they have, ‹ a nose ‹‹ hear;

וְלֹא יְמִישׁוּן, רַגְלֵיהֶם וְלֹא יְהַלֵּכוּ, לֹא יֶהְגּוּ

‹ they cannot ‹‹ — they cannot walk; ‹‹ their feet ‹‹ — they cannot feel;
utter [a sound]

בִּגְרוֹנָם. כְּמוֹהֶם יִהְיוּ עֹשֵׂיהֶם, כֹּל אֲשֶׁר בֹּטֵחַ

‹ trust ‹ who ‹ all ‹‹ those who ‹ should ‹ Like them ‹‹ from their
make them, become throat.

בָּהֶם. ❖ יִשְׂרָאֵל בְּטַח בַּיהוה,* עֶזְרָם וּמָגִנָּם הוּא.*

‹‹ is He!* ‹ and their ‹ their help ‹‹ in Hashem;* ‹ trust ‹ O Israel, ‹‹ in them!
shield

math of that inspiration. Although Israel remained imbued with faith, our oppressors soon began to scoff, "Where is your God?" We pray that God will intervene again in the affairs of man, not for our sake, but for His.

לֹא לָנוּ ה׳ . . . כִּי לְשִׁמְךָ תֵּן כָּבוֹד — *Not for our sake, Hashem . . . but for Your Name's sake give glory.* We beg You to redeem us, not because we are personally worthy, nor because of the merit of our forefathers (*Iyun Tefillah*). Rather, we urgently strive to protect Your glorious Name, so that no one can deny Your mastery and dominion (*Radak*).

פֶּה לָהֶם וְלֹא יְדַבֵּרוּ — *A mouth they have, but cannot speak.* These illustrations emphasize the total impotence of man-made idols, which even lack the senses that ordinary men possess.

יִשְׂרָאֵל בְּטַח בַּה׳ — *O Israel, trust in Hashem.* The psalm now contrasts the Children of Israel, who trust in God alone, with those described in the previous verse, who trust in the lifeless and helpless idols (*Ibn Ezra*).

The Psalmist speaks of three kinds of Jews, each with a different motive for serving God. Some cling to God simply because they feel that He is their Father, and they are His devoted sons.

בֵּית אַהֲרֹן בִּטְחוּ בַיהוה, עֶזְרָם וּמָגִנָּם הוּא.*

‹ is He!* ‹ and their ‹ their help ‹‹ in Hashem; ‹ trust ‹ of Aaron, ‹ House
shield

יִרְאֵי יהוה בִּטְחוּ בַיהוה, עֶזְרָם וּמָגִנָּם הוּא.*

‹ is He!* ‹ and their ‹ their help ‹‹ in Hashem; ‹ trust ‹ Hashem, ‹ You
shield who fear

—— Psalm 115:12-18 / תהלים קטו:יב-יח ——

יהוה זְכָרָנוּ יְבָרֵךְ;* יְבָרֵךְ אֶת בֵּית יִשְׂרָאֵל,

‹‹ of Israel, ‹ the House ‹ He will ‹‹ will ‹ Who has ‹ Hashem
bless bless:* remembered us

יְבָרֵךְ אֶת בֵּית אַהֲרֹן. יְבָרֵךְ יִרְאֵי יהוה,

‹‹ Hashem, ‹ those ‹ He will ‹‹ of Aaron. ‹ the House ‹ He will
who fear bless bless

הַקְּטַנִּים עִם הַגְּדֹלִים. יֹסֵף יהוה עֲלֵיכֶם,

‹‹ upon you, ‹ May Hashem increase ‹‹ the great. ‹ as well as ‹ the small

עֲלֵיכֶם וְעַל בְּנֵיכֶם.* בְּרוּכִים אַתֶּם לַיהוה,

‹‹ by Hashem, ‹ are you ‹ Blessed ‹‹ your children!* ‹ and upon ‹ upon you

עֹשֵׂה שָׁמַיִם וָאָרֶץ. ❖ הַשָּׁמַיִם שָׁמַיִם לַיהוה,

‹‹ are for ‹ the heavens ‹ As for ‹‹ and earth. ‹ of heaven ‹ Maker
Hashem; the heavens,

וְהָאָרֶץ נָתַן לִבְנֵי אָדָם.* לֹא הַמֵּתִים

‹ [can] the dead ‹ Neither ‹‹ to mankind.* ‹ He has given ‹ but the earth

These are called יִשְׂרָאֵל, Israel, God's chosen, beloved nation. The second group serves God out of love. They resemble the *House of Aaron,* the *Kohanim*-priests who never betrayed God and were therefore designated to stand in His presence, in the Temple, for all time. Finally, *you who fear Hashem* refers to a third group of Jews, who serve God out of fear and awe (*Maharal*).

עֶזְרָם וּמָגִנָּם הוּא — *Their help and their shield is He!* This is thrice repeated. Since each successive group possesses a different level of faith, it deserves a totally different degree of Divine protection. Thus God's response to each group is mentioned separately.

◆§ ה׳ זְכָרָנוּ יְבָרֵךְ — *Hashem Who has remem-*

bered us will bless. The Psalmist expresses confidence that just as God has blessed His people in the past, so will He bless them in the future.

יֹסֵף ה׳ עֲלֵיכֶם, עֲלֵיכֶם וְעַל בְּנֵיכֶם — *May Hashem increase upon you, upon you and upon your children!* The true nature of בְּרָכָה, *blessing,* means increase and abundance (*Ibn Ezra*).

Abarbanel explains that the Psalmist foresaw that Israel would suffer from attrition in exile and they would fear eventual extinction. Therefore, he offers the assurance that, at the advent of Messiah, their number will increase dramatically.

הַשָּׁמַיִם שָׁמַיִם לַה׳ וְהָאָרֶץ נָתַן לִבְנֵי אָדָם — *As for the heavens, the heavens are for Hashem; but the*

יְהַלְלוּ יָהּ,* וְלֹא כָּל יֹרְדֵי דוּמָה. וַאֲנַחְנוּ
‹ But we ‹‹ silence. ‹ who descend into ‹ any ‹ nor ‹‹ God,* ‹ praise

נְבָרֵךְ יָהּ מֵעַתָּה וְעַד עוֹלָם; הַלְלוּיָהּ.
‹‹ Halleluyah! ‹‹ eternity. ‹ until ‹ from this time ‹ God ‹ will bless

ON ROSH CHODESH (EXCEPT ON ROSH CHODESH TEVES) AND ON THE LAST SIX DAYS OF PESACH THE FOLLOWING PARAGRAPH IS OMITTED.

—— Psalm 116:1-11 / תהלים קטז:א-יא ——

אָהַבְתִּי* כִּי יִשְׁמַע יהוה, אֶת קוֹלִי תַּחֲנוּנָי.
‹‹ my ‹ my voice, ‹ Hashem hears ‹ for ‹ I love [Him],*
supplications.

כִּי הִטָּה אָזְנוֹ לִי, וּבְיָמַי אֶקְרָא. אֲפָפוּנִי חֶבְלֵי
‹ have the ‹ Encircled ‹‹ shall I call. ‹ so in ‹‹ to me, ‹ His ear ‹ He has ‹ As
pains me my days inclined

מָוֶת,* וּמְצָרֵי שְׁאוֹל מְצָאוּנִי; צָרָה וְיָגוֹן אֶמְצָא.
‹‹ I would ‹ and grief ‹ distress ‹‹ have found ‹ of the grave ‹ and the ‹‹ of
find. me; confines death;*

earth He has given to mankind. Since the heavens remain under God's firm control, all celestial bodies are compelled to act in accordance with His will without freedom of choice. On earth, however, man was granted the freedom to determine his own actions and beliefs (Maharit).

Many commentators explain this verse homiletically. Man need not perfect heaven because it is already dedicated to the holiness of God. But the earth is man's province. We are bidden to perfect it and transform its material nature into something spiritual. Indeed, we were created to make the earth heavenlike.

לֹא הַמֵּתִים יְהַלְלוּ יָהּ — Neither [can] the dead praise God. The people who fail to recognize God's omnipresence and influence over the world resemble the dead, who are insensitive to all external stimuli and who are oblivious to reality (R' Azariah Figo). However, the souls of the righteous continue to praise God even after they depart from their bodies (Ibn Ezra).

A dried-out, bleached, or brittle lulav is invalid for use during the Festival of Succos, because the lulav symbolizes the human spine,

which enables man to lead an active life. Thus the lulav must be fresh and supple, for the dead cannot praise God (Yalkut Shimoni 873).

אָהַבְתִּי §— I love [Him]. The Psalmist foresaw that Israel would feel completely alone in exile. The nations would taunt them, "Your prayers and pleas are worthless, because God has turned a deaf ear to you." Therefore, he composed this psalm to encourage the downcast exiles with the assurance that indeed: HASHEM hears my voice, my supplications.

The Talmud (Rosh Hashanah 16b-17a) explains that this psalm describes the day of Final Judgment at the time of תְּחִיַּת הַמֵּתִים, the Revivification of the Dead. The average person, who is neither completely righteous nor completely wicked, will be saved from Gehinnom because God will hear his cries, and He will forgive him. In gratitude, he will sing, "I love Him, for HASHEM hears my voice, my supplications."

חֶבְלֵי מָוֶת — The pains of death. This is an apt description of the exile, when Israel is surrounded by violent enemies who seek to kill them (Abarbanel).

וּבְשֵׁם יהוה אֶקְרָא: אָנָּה יהוה מַלְּטָה נַפְשִׁי.

« my soul. ⟨ save ⟨ HASHEM, ⟨ Please, « I would ⟨ of HASHEM ⟨ [Then] the Name
invoke,

חַנּוּן יהוה וְצַדִּיק, וֵאלֹהֵינוּ מְרַחֵם. שֹׁמֵר

⟨ Protector « is merciful. ⟨ our God « and righteous, ⟨ is HASHEM ⟨ Gracious

פְּתָאִים יהוה, דַּלּוֹתִי וְלִי יְהוֹשִׁיעַ. שׁוּבִי נַפְשִׁי

⟨ my soul, ⟨ Return, « He saved. ⟨ but me ⟨ I was « is ⟨ of the simple
brought low, HASHEM;

לִמְנוּחָיְכִי,* כִּי יהוה גָּמַל עָלָיְכִי. כִּי חִלַּצְתָּ

⟨ You have ⟨ For « you. ⟨ has ⟨ HASHEM ⟨ for « to your rest;*
delivered rewarded

נַפְשִׁי מִמָּוֶת; אֶת עֵינִי מִן דִּמְעָה, אֶת רַגְלִי

⟨ my feet « tears, ⟨ from ⟨ my eyes « from death, ⟨ my soul

מִדֶּחִי. ❖ אֶתְהַלֵּךְ לִפְנֵי יהוה, בְּאַרְצוֹת הַחַיִּים.*

« of the living.* ⟨ in the lands ⟨ HASHEM ⟨ before ⟨ I shall walk « from stumbling.

הֶאֱמַנְתִּי כִּי אֲדַבֵּר, אֲנִי עָנִיתִי מְאֹד. אֲנִי

⟨ I « exceedingly. ⟨ suffer ⟨ I « I say, ⟨ although ⟨ I have kept faith

אָמַרְתִּי בְחָפְזִי, כָּל הָאָדָם כֹּזֵב.*

« is deceitful.* ⟨ mankind ⟨ All « in my haste, ⟨ said

──── Psalm 116:12-19 / תהלים קטז:יב-יט ────

מָה אָשִׁיב לַיהוה,* כָּל תַּגְמוּלוֹהִי עָלָי.

« on me? ⟨ the kindnesses He ⟨ for all « HASHEM* ⟨ can I repay ⟨ How
has bestowed

שׁוּבִי נַפְשִׁי לִמְנוּחָיְכִי — *Return, my soul, to your rest.* When misery and persecution upset me, I told my soul that it would find peace and comfort only if it would *return* to God (*Radak*).

אֶתְהַלֵּךְ לִפְנֵי ה' בְּאַרְצוֹת הַחַיִּים — *I shall walk before HASHEM in the lands of the living.* How I yearn to return to *Eretz Yisrael* where the very air makes men healthy and robust and the holy atmosphere grants the mind renewed vitality and alertness! (*Radak*). Eretz Yisrael is identified as the *land of the living* because the dead are destined to be resurrected there.

אֲנִי אָמַרְתִּי בְחָפְזִי כָּל הָאָדָם כֹּזֵב — *I said in my haste, "All mankind is deceitful."* This bitter comment was originally uttered by David when the people of Zif betrayed his hiding place to King Saul [see *I Samuel 23:19-29*] (*Rashi*). It is also a reference to the bleak, dismal exile [for the exile discourages the Jews and leads them to the hasty, premature conclusion that all the prophets' promises concerning redemption were *deceitful*] (*Abarbanel*).

מָה אָשִׁיב לַה' — *How can I repay HASHEM?* What gift can I give to the King Who owns

כּוֹס יְשׁוּעוֹת אֶשָּׂא,* וּבְשֵׁם יהוה אֶקְרָא.

‹ The cup ‹ of salvations ‹ I will raise* ‹ and the ‹ of ‹ I will
Name HASHEM invoke.

נְדָרַי לַיהוה אֲשַׁלֵּם,* נֶגְדָה נָא לְכָל עַמּוֹ.

‹ My vows ‹ to HASHEM ‹ I will pay,* ‹ in the ‹ now, ‹ of His ‹ people.
presence, entire

יָקָר בְּעֵינֵי יהוה, הַמָּוְתָה לַחֲסִידָיו. אָנָּה יהוה

‹ Difficult ‹ in the ‹ of ‹ is the death ‹ of His ‹ Please, ‹ HASHEM,
eyes HASHEM devout ones.

כִּי אֲנִי עַבְדֶּךָ; אֲנִי עַבְדְּךָ בֶּן אֲמָתֶךָ,* פִּתַּחְתָּ

‹ for ‹ I am ‹ Your ‹ I am ‹ Your ‹ son ‹ of Your ‹ You have
servant, servant, handmaiden;* released

לְמוֹסֵרָי. ❖ לְךָ אֶזְבַּח זֶבַח תּוֹדָה, וּבְשֵׁם יהוה

‹ my bonds. ‹ To You ‹ I will ‹ an ‹ of ‹ and the ‹ of
sacrifice offering thanksgiving, Name HASHEM

אֶקְרָא. נְדָרַי לַיהוה אֲשַׁלֵּם, נֶגְדָה נָא לְכָל

‹ I will invoke. ‹ My vows ‹ to HASHEM ‹ I will pay, ‹ in the ‹ now, ‹ of His
presence, entire

עַמּוֹ. בְּחַצְרוֹת בֵּית יהוה, בְּתוֹכֵכִי יְרוּשָׁלָיִם;

‹ people, ‹ in the Courtyards ‹ of the ‹ of HASHEM, ‹ in your midst, ‹ O Jerusalem.
House

הַלְלוּיָהּ.

‹ Halleluyah!

---

everything? (*Ibn Ezra*). How can I possibly repay His acts of kindness, for they are too numerous to recount? (*Radak*). How can I even approach Him? He is eternal and I am finite; He is the highest, and I am the lowest! (*Ibn Yachya*).

כּוֹס יְשׁוּעוֹת אֶשָּׂא — *The cup of salvations I will raise.* This refers to the wine libations that will accompany the thanksgiving offerings of the returning exiles (*Rashi*).

נְדָרַי לַה׳ אֲשַׁלֵּם — *My vows to HASHEM I will pay.* As I was fleeing and wandering in exile, I

vowed that if God would return me safely to *Eretz Yisrael*, I would render thanksgiving offerings to His Name; now I will make good on my vows (*Radak*).

אֲנִי עַבְדְּךָ בֶּן אֲמָתֶךָ — *I am Your servant, son of Your handmaiden.* The slave who is born to a *handmaiden* is far more submissive than a slave who was born free (*Rashi*). The former serves his master instinctively and as a matter of course, whereas the latter serves him only in response to external threats (*Sforno*).

—— Psalm 117 / תהלים קיז ——

הַלְלוּ אֶת יהוה,* כָּל גּוֹיִם;* שַׁבְּחוּהוּ כָּל

‹ all ‹ extol Him, « nations;* ‹ all ‹ HASHEM,* ‹ Praise

הָאֻמִּים.* כִּי גָבַר עָלֵינוּ חַסְדּוֹ,* וֶאֱמֶת יהוה

‹ of ‹ and « has His ‹ us ‹ overwhelmed ‹ For « the states!*
HASHEM   the truth   kindness,*

לְעוֹלָם; הַלְלוּיָהּ.

« Halleluyah! « is eternal.

EACH OF THE FOLLOWING FOUR VERSES IS RECITED ALOUD BY THE CHAZZAN.
AFTER EACH VERSE, THE CONGREGATION RESPONDS: הוֹדוּ לַה' כִּי טוֹב כִּי לְעוֹלָם חַסְדּוֹ,
AND THEN RECITES THE NEXT VERSE.

> ON SUCCOS THE FOUR SPECIES ARE WAVED THE FIRST TIME THE VERSE הוֹדוּ לַה' IS RECITED, AS
> FOLLOWS: THREE TIMES TO THE RIGHT AT הוֹדוּ; THREE TIMES TO THE LEFT AT כִּי; THREE TIMES
> STRAIGHT AHEAD AT טוֹב; THREE TIMES UP AT כִּי; THREE TIMES DOWN AT לְעוֹלָם; AND THREE
> TIMES BACK AT חַסְדּוֹ.

—— Psalm 118 / תהלים קיח ——

הוֹדוּ לַיהוה כִּי טוֹב,*

« He is good;* ‹ for ‹ to HASHEM ‹ Give thanks

כִּי לְעוֹלָם חַסְדּוֹ.

« is His ‹ enduring ‹ for
kindness!   forever

יֹאמַר נָא יִשְׂרָאֵל,

«   Let Israel say now,

כִּי לְעוֹלָם חַסְדּוֹ.

« is His ‹ enduring ‹ For
kindness!   forever

יֹאמְרוּ נָא בֵית אַהֲרֹן,

« of ‹ – the « now ‹ Let them
Aaron — House   say

כִּי לְעוֹלָם חַסְדּוֹ.

« is His ‹ enduring ‹ For
kindness!   forever

הַלְלוּ אֶת ה' — *Praise HASHEM.* This psalm, containing only two verses, is the shortest chapter in all of Scripture. *Radak* explains that its brevity symbolizes the simplicity of the world order which will prevail after the advent of the Messiah.

גּוֹיִם . . . הָאֻמִּים — *Nations . . . the states.* הָאֻמִּים, *the states,* is written with the definite article, whereas גּוֹיִם, *nations,* is written without it. This teaches that הָאֻמִּים refers to large nations that are well known and powerful; whereas גּוֹיִם refers even to insignificant, backward nations that have no prominence (*Iyun Tefillah*).

כִּי גָבַר עָלֵינוּ חַסְדּוֹ — *For overwhelmed us has His kindness.* Why should non-Jewish peoples and nations praise God for overwhelming Israel with Divine kindness? Israel will merit God's kindness because of the extraordinary service they rendered to Him. Recognizing Israel's distinction, the nations will consider it a privilege to become subservient to God's chosen ones, and will praise Him for His kindness to the Jews (*Yaavetz HaDoresh*).

הוֹדוּ לַה' כִּי טוֹב — *Give thanks to HASHEM for He is good.* This is a general expression of thanksgiving to God. No matter what occurs,

כִּי לְעוֹלָם חַסְדּוֹ.   יֹאמְרוּ נָא יִרְאֵי יהוה,

《 is His < enduring < For   《 HASHEM — < – those 《 now < Let them
kindness! forever   who fear say

מִן הַמֵּצַר* קָרָאתִי יָּה, עָנָנִי בַמֶּרְחָב יָה.

《 did < with < answer 《 God; < did I call < the straits* < From
God. expansiveness me upon

יהוה לִי לֹא אִירָא, מַה יַּעֲשֶׂה לִי אָדָם.

《 can man affect me? < how 《 I have no fear; < is with me, < HASHEM

יהוה לִי בְּעֶזְרָי,* וַאֲנִי אֶרְאֶה בְשֹׂנְאָי.

《 my foes. < can face < therefore I 《 through my < is with < HASHEM
helpers;* me

טוֹב לַחֲסוֹת בַּיהוה, מִבְּטֹחַ בָּאָדָם.* טוֹב

< It is better 《 on man.* < than to rely 《 in HASHEM < to take refuge < It is better

לַחֲסוֹת בַּיהוה, מִבְּטֹחַ בִּנְדִיבִים. כָּל גּוֹיִם

< the nations < All 《 on nobles. < than to rely 《 in HASHEM < to take refuge

סְבָבוּנִי, בְּשֵׁם יהוה כִּי אֲמִילַם. סַבּוּנִי גַם

< also < They 《 I cut them < that < of HASHEM < it is in 《 surround me;
encircle me, down! the Name

סְבָבוּנִי, בְּשֵׁם יהוה כִּי אֲמִילַם. סַבּוּנִי כִדְבֹרִים,

《 like bees, < They 《 I cut them < that < of < it is in 《 they surround
encircle me down! HASHEM, the Name me;

דֹּעֲכוּ כְּאֵשׁ קוֹצִים; בְּשֵׁם יהוה כִּי אֲמִילַם.

《 I cut them < that < of < it is in 《 of thorns; < as a fire < but they are
down! HASHEM, the Name extinguished

God is always good and everything He does is for the best, even though this may not be readily apparent to man (*Abarbanel*).

מִן הַמֵּצַר ֶּ — *From the straits.* This psalm expresses gratitude and confidence. Just as David himself was catapulted from his personal straits to a reign marked by accomplishment and glory, so too Israel can look forward to Divine redemption from the straits of exile and oppression.

ה' לִי בְּעֶזְרָי — *HASHEM is with me through my helpers.* I have many helpers, but I place my trust in them only because HASHEM is with them. If my helpers were not granted strength by God, their assistance would be futile (*Ibn Ezra; Radak*).

טוב לַחֲסוֹת בַּה׳ מִבְּטֹחַ בָּאָדָם — *It is better to take refuge in HASHEM than to rely on man.* חָסְיוֹן, *taking refuge,* denotes absolute confidence even though no guarantees have been given; בְּטָחוֹן, *reliance,* however, presupposes a promise of protection. The Psalmist says that it is far better to put one's trust in God's protection, even without

דָּחֹה דְּחִיתַנִי לִנְפֹּל, וַיהוה עֲזָרָנִי.* עָזִּי וְזִמְרָת
‹ and my ‹ My ‹‹ assisted ‹ but HASHEM ‹‹ that I ‹ You pushed me hard
praise might me.* might fall,

יָהּ, וַיְהִי לִי לִישׁוּעָה. קוֹל רִנָּה וִישׁוּעָה
‹ and salvation ‹ of rejoicing ‹ The sound ‹‹ a salvation. ‹ for me ‹ and He was ‹‹ is God,

בְּאָהֳלֵי צַדִּיקִים,* יְמִין יהוה עֹשָׂה חָיִל.
‹‹ [deeds of] valor. ‹ does ‹ of HASHEM ‹ The right hand ‹‹ of the righteous,* ‹ is in the tents

יְמִין יהוה רוֹמֵמָה, יְמִין יהוה עֹשָׂה חָיִל.
‹‹ [deeds of] ‹ does ‹ of HASHEM ‹ the ‹‹ is raised ‹ of HASHEM ‹ The right
valor. right hand triumphantly; hand

לֹא אָמוּת כִּי אֶחְיֶה, וַאֲסַפֵּר מַעֲשֵׂי יָהּ.*
‹‹ of God.* ‹ the deeds ‹ and relate ‹‹ I shall live ‹ But ‹ I shall not die!

יַסֹּר יִסְּרַנִּי יָּהּ, וְלַמָּוֶת לֹא נְתָנָנִי.* פִּתְחוּ לִי
‹ for ‹ Open ‹‹ He did not ‹ but to death ‹‹ has ‹ Chastened me
me give me over.* God, exceedingly

שַׁעֲרֵי צֶדֶק, אָבֹא בָם אוֹדֶה יָהּ. זֶה הַשַּׁעַר
‹ the gate ‹ This is ‹‹ God. ‹ and ‹ them ‹ I will ‹‹ of ‹ the gates
thank enter righteousness;

לַיהוה, צַדִּיקִים יָבֹאוּ בוֹ.* אוֹדְךָ* כִּי עֲנִיתָנִי,
‹‹ You have ‹ for ‹ I thank You*‹‹ through ‹ shall ‹ the righteous ‹‹ of HASHEM;
answered me it.* enter

a pledge from Him, than to rely on the most profuse assurances of human beings (R' Bachya; Vilna Gaon).

דָּחֹה דְּחִיתַנִי לִנְפֹּל וַה' עֲזָרָנִי — *You pushed me hard that I might fall, but HASHEM assisted me.* In the preceding verses, the Psalmist speaks of his enemy indirectly; now, however, he addresses the foe directly.

קוֹל רִנָּה וִישׁוּעָה בְּאָהֳלֵי צַדִּיקִים — *The sound of rejoicing and salvation is in the tents of the righteous.* When God's right hand does valiantly for the sake of His chosen people, then the righteous will respond by filling their tents with sounds of rejoicing over this salvation (Radak).

לֹא אָמוּת כִּי אֶחְיֶה וַאֲסַפֵּר מַעֲשֵׂי יָהּ — *I shall not die! But I shall live and relate the deeds of God.* I will

survive the assassination attempts of my enemies and live to recount the deeds of God, Who saved me from my foes (Radak).

יַסֹּר יִסְּרַנִּי יָּהּ וְלַמָּוֶת לֹא נְתָנָנִי — *Chastened me exceedingly has God, but to death He did not give me over.* Throughout the duration of the exile, I survived because whatever suffering God decreed was only to atone for my sins (Rashi).

זֶה הַשַּׁעַר לַה' צַדִּיקִים יָבֹאוּ בוֹ — *This is the gate of HASHEM; the righteous shall enter through it.* This refers to the gate of the Temple. When the exile is over, the righteous will enter through this gate, and they will thank God for answering their plea for redemption (Targum; Rashi).

◆§ Repetition of Verses

אוֹדְךָ — *I thank You.* From this point until the

וַתְּהִי, עֲנִיתָנִי כִּי אוֹדְךָ. לִישׁוּעָה. לִי וַתְּהִי

‹ and ‹‹ You have ‹ for ‹ I thank ‹‹ a salvation. ‹ for ‹ and
[You have] answered me You me [You have]
become become

הָיְתָה הַבּוֹנִים, מָאֲסוּ אֶבֶן לִישׁוּעָה. לִי

‹ has become ‹ by the builders ‹ despised ‹ The stone ‹‹ a salvation. ‹ for me

הָיְתָה הַבּוֹנִים, מָאֲסוּ אֶבֶן פִּנָּה.* לְרֹאשׁ

‹ has become ‹ by the builders ‹ despised ‹ The stone ‹‹ the cornerstone.*

הִיא זֹאת, הָיְתָה יהוה מֵאֵת פִּנָּה. לְרֹאשׁ

‹ it ‹‹ this; ‹ emanated ‹ HASHEM ‹ From ‹‹ the cornerstone.

הִיא זֹאת, הָיְתָה יהוה מֵאֵת נִפְלָאת בְּעֵינֵינוּ.*

‹ it ‹‹ this; ‹ emanated ‹ HASHEM ‹ From ‹‹ in our eyes.* ‹ is wondrous

נָגִילָה יהוה, עָשָׂה הַיּוֹם זֶה. בְּעֵינֵינוּ נִפְלָאת

‹ let us rejoice ‹‹ HASHEM has made; ‹ is the day ‹ This ‹‹ in our eyes. ‹ is wondrous

---

end of the Scriptural part of *Hallel* — the nine verses until יְהַלְלוּךְ — each verse is recited twice.

Up until this point, this entire psalm, which begins with הוֹדוּ לַה׳, *Give thanks to* HASHEM, follows a pattern, namely, that each new theme is repeated in the next verse or two in the same or slightly different words. Therefore the custom was introduced to follow through on this repetition by repeating the rest of the verses as well (*Rashi* to *Succah* 38a).

Another reason for repeating these verses is based upon the Talmud (*Pesachim* 119a) which relates that these verses were recited in a responsive dialogue between Samuel, Jesse, David, and David's brothers when the prophet announced that the young shepherd would be the future king of Israel. To honor these distinguished personages, we repeat each one's statement, as if it were a full chapter.

אֶבֶן מָאֲסוּ הַבּוֹנִים הָיְתָה לְרֹאשׁ פִּנָּה — *The stone despised by the builders has become the cornerstone.* This verse refers to David, who was rejected by his own father and brothers (*Targum*). When the prophet Samuel announced that one of Jesse's sons was to be

anointed king, no one even thought of summoning David, who was tending the sheep [see *I Samuel* 16:4-13].

Israel too is called אֶבֶן, *stone* (*Genesis* 49:24), for Israel is the cornerstone of God's design for the world. The world endures only by virtue of Israel's observance of God's laws, a fact that has influenced all nations to appreciate and accept certain aspects of God's commands. If not for the order and meaning that Israel has brought to the world, it would long ago have sunk into chaos. But the builders, the rulers of the nations, despised the Jews, claiming that they were parasites who made no contribution to the common good. When the dawn of redemption arrives, however, all nations will realize that Israel is indeed the cornerstone of the world (*Radak*).

מֵאֵת ה׳ הָיְתָה זֹּאת הִיא נִפְלָאת בְּעֵינֵינוּ — *From* HASHEM *emanated this; it is wondrous in our eyes.* When David was crowned, all were amazed. But David said, "This is even more surprising and wondrous to me than it is to anyone else!"

Similarly, when Israel is catapulted to glory and tranquility in the future, the nations who

וְנִשְׂמְחָה בוֹ. זֶה הַיּוֹם עָשָׂה יהוה, נָגִילָה
⟨ let us ⟩ ⟨⟨ HASHEM has made; ⟨ is the day ⟨ This ⟨⟨ on it. ⟨ and be glad
rejoice

וְנִשְׂמְחָה בוֹ.
⟨⟨ on it. ⟨ and be glad

THE NEXT FOUR LINES ARE RECITED RESPONSIVELY, *CHAZZAN*, THEN CONGREGATION.

ON SUCCOS THE FOUR SPECIES ARE WAVED: THREE TIMES TO THE RIGHT AND THREE TIMES TO THE LEFT AT אָנָּא; THREE TIMES STRAIGHT AHEAD AND THREE TIMES UP AT הוֹשִׁיעָה; THREE TIMES DOWN AND THREE TIMES BACK AT נָא.

אָנָּא יהוה, הוֹשִׁיעָה נָּא.
⟨⟨ now! ⟨ save ⟨ HASHEM, ⟨ Please,

אָנָּא יהוה, הוֹשִׁיעָה נָּא.
⟨⟨ now! ⟨ save ⟨ HASHEM, ⟨ Please,

אָנָּא יהוה, הַצְלִיחָה נָא.
⟨⟨ now! ⟨ bring success ⟨ HASHEM, ⟨ Please,

אָנָּא יהוה, הַצְלִיחָה נָא.
⟨⟨ now! ⟨ bring success ⟨ HASHEM, ⟨ Please,

בָּרוּךְ הַבָּא בְּשֵׁם יהוה, בֵּרַכְנוּכֶם מִבֵּית
⟨ from the ⟨ we bless you ⟨⟨ of HASHEM; ⟨ in the ⟨ is he who ⟨ Blessed
House   Name   comes

יהוה. בָּרוּךְ הַבָּא בְּשֵׁם יהוה, בֵּרַכְנוּכֶם מִבֵּית
⟨ from the ⟨ we bless you ⟨⟨ of HASHEM; ⟨ in the ⟨ is he who ⟨ Blessed ⟨⟨ of
House   Name   comes   HASHEM.

יהוה. אֵל יהוה וַיָּאֶר לָנוּ, אִסְרוּ חַג בַּעֲבֹתִים*
⟨ with cords* ⟨ the festival ⟨ bind ⟨ for us; ⟨ He ⟨⟨ is ⟨ The ⟨⟨ of
                [offering]   illuminated HASHEM. Almighty HASHEM.

persecuted the Jews will ask in surprise, "Aren't these the very Jews who were once despised and afflicted?"

The Jews will respond, "We are even more amazed than you are, for only we know the depths of degradation we suffered!"

Then a Heavenly voice will proclaim, "This has emanated from HASHEM!"

אסרו חג בעבתים — *Bind the festival [offering] with cords.* The four corners of the Altar symbolize the four corners of the earth. The word קָרְבָּן, *offering*, literally means a vehicle for

עַד קַרְנוֹת הַמִּזְבֵּחַ. אֵל יהוה וַיָּאֶר לָנוּ, אִסְרוּ

⟨ bind ⟨⟨ for us; ⟨ He ⟨⟨ is ⟨ The ⟨⟨ of the Altar. ⟨ the corners ⟨⟨ until
illuminated   HASHEM. Almighty

חַג בַּעֲבֹתִים עַד קַרְנוֹת הַמִּזְבֵּחַ. אֵלִי אַתָּה

⟨ You are, ⟨ My God ⟨⟨ of the Altar. ⟨ the corners ⟨ until ⟨ with cords ⟨ the festival
[offering]

וְאוֹדֶךָּ, אֱלֹהַי אֲרוֹמְמֶךָּ. אֵלִי אַתָּה וְאוֹדֶךָּ,

⟨⟨ and I will ⟨ You are, ⟨ My God ⟨⟨ I will exalt You. ⟨ my God, ⟨⟨ and I will
thank You;   thank You;

אֱלֹהַי אֲרוֹמְמֶךָּ.

⟨⟨ I will exalt You. ⟨ my God,

ON SUCCOS THE FOUR SPECIES ARE WAVED THE FIRST TIME THE VERSE הוֹדוּ לַה' IS RECITED, AS
FOLLOWS: THREE TIMES TO THE RIGHT AT הוֹדוּ; THREE TIMES TO THE LEFT AT כִּי; THREE TIMES
STRAIGHT AHEAD AT טוֹב; THREE TIMES UP AT כִּי; THREE TIMES DOWN AT לְעוֹלָם; AND THREE
TIMES BACK AT חַסְדּוֹ.

הוֹדוּ לַיהוה כִּי טוֹב, כִּי לְעוֹלָם חַסְדּוֹ.

⟨⟨ is His ⟨ enduring ⟨ for ⟨⟨ He is ⟨ for ⟨ to HASHEM, ⟨ Give
kindness.   forever   good;   thanks

הוֹדוּ לַיהוה כִּי טוֹב, כִּי לְעוֹלָם חַסְדּוֹ.

⟨⟨ is His ⟨ enduring ⟨ for ⟨⟨ He is ⟨ for ⟨ to HASHEM, ⟨ Give
kindness.   forever   good;   thanks

יְהַלְלוּךָ* יהוה אֱלֹהֵינוּ (עַל) כָּל מַעֲשֶׂיךָ,*

⟨⟨ of Your ⟨ — all ⟨ (for) ⟨⟨ our God ⟨ HASHEM, ⟨⟨ They shall
works.*   praise You,*

---

coming close [קֵרוּב] to God, and this closeness is
the purpose of creation. In the future, life will be
a constant חַג, *festival*, of rejoicing in God's
service. As long as man is far from the Altar (far
from God), the festive spirit remains dormant
within him — bound up with cords. But in the
environs of the Altar, man escapes these bonds
and attains a lofty spirit of total festive
celebration.

❧ יְהַלְלוּךָ . . . כָּל מַעֲשֶׂיךָ — *They shall praise
You . . . all of Your works.* This paragraph is not

part of *Psalms*, but is a concluding blessing that
sums up the broad theme of *Hallel* — that Israel
and the entire universe will join in praising God.
They shall praise You . . . all Your works means
that in the perfect world of the future, the entire
universe, including the broad variety of human
beings, will function harmoniously according
to God's will. This is the highest form of praise,
for without it all the beautiful spoken and sung
words and songs of praise are insincere and
meaningless.

וַחֲסִידֶיךָ צַדִּיקִים* עוֹשֵׂי רְצוֹנֶךָ,* וְכָל עַמְּךָ בֵּית

‹ the ‹ of Your ‹ and ≪ Your will,* ‹ who do ‹ the righteous,* ‹ And Your
House people, all devout ones,

יִשְׂרָאֵל בְּרִנָּה יוֹדוּ וִיבָרְכוּ וִישַׁבְּחוּ וִיפָאֲרוּ

‹ glorify, ‹ praise, ‹ bless, ‹ will thank, ‹ with glad song ≪ of Israel,

וִישׁוֹרְרוּ וִירוֹמְמוּ וְיַעֲרִיצוּ וְיַקְדִּישׁוּ וְיַמְלִיכוּ

‹ and proclaim the ‹ sanctify, ‹ extol, ‹ exalt, ‹ sing about,
sovereignty of

אֶת שִׁמְךָ מַלְכֵּנוּ תָּמִיד. ❖ כִּי לְךָ טוֹב לְהוֹדוֹת

≪ to give ‹ it is ‹ to You ‹ For ≪ continuously. ‹ our King, ‹ Your Name,
thanks, good

וּלְשִׁמְךָ נָאֶה לְזַמֵּר, כִּי מֵעוֹלָם וְעַד עוֹלָם אַתָּה

‹ You ‹ the World ‹ to ‹ from [This] ‹ for ≪ to sing ‹ it is ‹ and unto
[to Come] World praises, proper Your Name

אֵל. בָּרוּךְ אַתָּה יהוה, מֶלֶךְ מְהֻלָּל בַּתִּשְׁבָּחוֹת.

≪ with praises. ‹ Who is lauded ‹ the King ≪ HASHEM, ‹ are You, ‹ Blessed ≪ are God.

אָמֵן.) –Cong.)

≪ (Amen.)

ON ROSH CHODESH MANY RECITE THE FOLLOWING VERSE AFTER HALLEL:

וְאַבְרָהָם זָקֵן בָּא בַּיָּמִים, וַיהוה בֵּרַךְ אֶת אַבְרָהָם בַּכֹּל.¹

≪ with ‹ Abraham ‹ had ‹ and ≪ in years, ‹ well ‹ was ‹ Now Abraham
everything. blessed HASHEM on old,

ON DAYS THAT MUSSAF IS RECITED, THE CHAZZAN RECITES THE FULL KADDISH (P. 223),
AND THE SERVICE CONTINUES WITH THE SONG OF THE DAY (P. 232).
ON DAYS THAT MUSSAF IS NOT RECITED, THE CHAZZAN RECITES HALF-KADDISH (P. 197),
AND THE SERVICE CONTINUES WITH THE REMOVAL OF THE TORAH FROM THE ARK (P. 199).
ON SUCCOS CONTINUE WITH THE HOSHANA SERVICE (P. 552).

(1) Genesis 24:1.

וַחֲסִידֶיךָ צַדִּיקִים — And Your devout ones, the righteous. The word חָסִיד, devout one, refers to one who serves God beyond the minimum requirement of the halachah. These people serve as an example for the righteous people, who fulfill all the requirements of the Law, and for the masses of Israel, whose goal is to serve God, even though they may not equal the spiritual accomplishments of the devout and the righteous.

עוֹשֵׂי רְצוֹנֶךָ — Who do Your will. In an inspiring homiletical interpretation, Yismach Yisrael interprets that the good deeds of the righteous can remake God's will, as it were. In other words, when Jews serve Him properly, God responds by lavishing kindness and a sense of fulfillment upon the world. Then, Hallel will become not only a song of thanksgiving for the miracles of the past, but also a song of praise for the longed-for redemption.

◈⟊ MUSSAF OF ROSH CHODESH / מוסף לראש חדש ⟊◈

TEFILLIN MUST BE REMOVED BEFORE MUSSAF. (IT IS PREFERABLE THAT THEY BE REMOVED AFTER KADDISH.) THIS SHOULD BE DONE QUICKLY AND THE TEFILLIN SHOULD NOT BE ROLLED UP IN ORDER NOT TO CAUSE UNDUE DELAY BETWEEN KADDISH AND MUSSAF. SINCE THE MINYAN SHOULD BEGIN SHEMONEH ESREI TOGETHER, IT IS ADVISABLE THAT SOMEONE SIGNAL THE CONGREGATION TO BEGIN THE SILENT SHEMONEH ESREI IN UNISON.

TAKE THREE STEPS BACKWARD, THEN THREE STEPS FORWARD. REMAIN STANDING WITH FEET TOGETHER WHILE RECITING SHEMONEH ESREI. RECITE IT WITH QUIET DEVOTION AND WITHOUT ANY INTER-RUPTION. ALTHOUGH IT SHOULD NOT BE AUDIBLE TO OTHERS, ONE MUST PRAY LOUDLY ENOUGH TO HEAR HIMSELF. SEE LAWS §44-45; 68-74; 89-95 FOR A BRIEF SUMMARY OF ITS LAWS INCLUDING HOW TO RECTIFY THE OMISSION OF PHRASES THAT ARE ADDED AT PARTICULAR TIMES OF THE YEAR.

כִּי שֵׁם יהוה אֶקְרָא, הָבוּ גֹדֶל לֵאלֹהֵינוּ.¹

≪ to our God. ⟨ greatness ⟨ ascribe ≪ I call out, ⟨ of ⟨ the ⟨ When
HASHEM Name

אֲדֹנָי שְׂפָתַי תִּפְתָּח, וּפִי יַגִּיד תְּהִלָּתֶךָ.²

≪ Your praise. ⟨ may ⟨ that my ≪ open, ⟨ my lips ⟨ O Lord,
declare mouth

PATRIARCHS / אבות

BEND THE KNEES AT בָּרוּךְ, BLESSED; BOW AT אַתָּה, YOU; STRAIGHTEN UP AT ה', HASHEM.

בָּרוּךְ אַתָּה יהוה אֱלֹהֵינוּ וֵאלֹהֵי אֲבוֹתֵינוּ,

≪ of our forefathers, ⟨ and the God ⟨ our God ⟨ HASHEM, ⟨ are You, ⟨ Blessed

אֱלֹהֵי אַבְרָהָם, אֱלֹהֵי יִצְחָק, וֵאלֹהֵי יַעֲקֹב,

≪ of Jacob; ⟨ and God ⟨ of Isaac, ⟨ God ⟨ of Abraham, ⟨ God

הָאֵל הַגָּדוֹל הַגִּבּוֹר וְהַנּוֹרָא, אֵל עֶלְיוֹן, גּוֹמֵל

⟨ Who ≪ the ⟨ God, ≪ and awesome; ⟨ mighty, ⟨ [Who is] ⟨ God
bestows Most High, great,

חֲסָדִים טוֹבִים וְקוֹנֵה הַכֹּל, וְזוֹכֵר חַסְדֵי אָבוֹת,

≪ of the ⟨ the ⟨ Who ≪ everything, ⟨ and ⟨ [that are] ⟨ kindnesses
Patriarchs, kindnesses recalls creates beneficent

וּמֵבִיא גוֹאֵל לִבְנֵי בְנֵיהֶם, לְמַעַן שְׁמוֹ בְּאַהֲבָה.

≪ with love. ⟨ of His ⟨ for the ≪ of their ⟨ to the ⟨ a ⟨ and brings
Name, sake children, children Redeemer

---

(1) Deuteronomy 32:3. (2) Psalms 51:17.

◈⟊ Mussaf

This Mussaf [lit. additional] prayer com-memorates the communal offering that was brought on Rosh Chodesh (Numbers 28:11-15).

Commentary to the beginning of Shemoneh Esrei may be found on pp. 143-148.

Such authors as Sh'lah and Yesod V'Shoresh HaAvodah attach special importance to the

BEND THE KNEES AT בָּרוּךְ, *BLESSED;* **BOW AT** אַתָּה, *YOU;* **STRAIGHTEN UP AT** ה', *HASHEM.*

מֶלֶךְ עוֹזֵר וּמוֹשִׁיעַ וּמָגֵן. בָּרוּךְ אַתָּה יהוה,
《 HASHEM, 〈 are You, 〈 Blessed 《 and Shield. 〈 Savior, 〈 Helper, 〈 O King,

מָגֵן אַבְרָהָם.
《 of Abraham. 〈 Shield

GOD'S MIGHT / גבורות

אַתָּה גִּבּוֹר לְעוֹלָם אֲדֹנָי, מְחַיֵּה מֵתִים
〈 of the dead 〈 the Revivifier 《 O Lord, 〈 eternally, 〈 mighty 〈 You are

אַתָּה, רַב לְהוֹשִׁיעַ.
《 able to save, 〈 abundantly 《 are You;

ROSH CHODESH CHESHVAN—
ROSH CHODESH NISSAN:

ROSH CHODESH IYAR—
ROSH CHODESH ELUL:

מַשִּׁיב הָרוּחַ וּמוֹרִיד הַגֶּשֶׁם [נ"א הַגָּשֶׁם].
《 the rain. 〈 and 〈 Who makes
brings down the wind blow

מוֹרִיד הַטָּל
《 the 〈 Who
dew. brings down

―――――― **[IF FORGOTTEN, SEE** *LAWS* **§68-74.]** ――――――

מְכַלְכֵּל חַיִּים בְּחֶסֶד, מְחַיֵּה מֵתִים בְּרַחֲמִים
〈 with mercy 〈 the dead 〈 Who revivifies 《 with kindness, 〈 the living 〈 Who sustains

רַבִּים, סוֹמֵךְ נוֹפְלִים, וְרוֹפֵא חוֹלִים, וּמַתִּיר
〈 Who releases 《 the sick, 〈 Who heals 《 the fallen, 〈 Who supports 《 abundant,

אֲסוּרִים, וּמְקַיֵּם אֱמוּנָתוֹ לִישֵׁנֵי עָפָר. מִי כָמוֹךְ
〈 is like 〈 Who 《 in the 〈 to those 〈 His faith 〈 and Who 《 the confined,
You, dust. asleep maintains

בַּעַל גְּבוּרוֹת, וּמִי דּוֹמֶה לָּךְ, מֶלֶךְ מֵמִית וּמְחַיֵּה
〈 and 〈 Who causes 〈 O King 《 to You, 〈 is 〈 and 〈 of mighty 〈 O
restores life death comparable who deeds, Master

וּמַצְמִיחַ יְשׁוּעָה. וְנֶאֱמָן אַתָּה לְהַחֲיוֹת מֵתִים.
《 the dead. 〈 to revivify 〈 are You 〈 And faithful 《 salvation! 〈 and makes sprout

בָּרוּךְ אַתָּה יהוה, מְחַיֵּה הַמֵּתִים.
《 the dead. 〈 Who revivifies 《 HASHEM, 〈 are You, 〈 Blessed

need for repentance and intense concentration during *Mussaf.* As the text of *Mussaf* says,

Rosh Chodesh is a זְמַן כַּפָּרָה, *time of atonement.* The fact that the prayer commemorates a Tem-

DURING THE *CHAZZAN'S* REPETITION, *KEDUSHAH* IS RECITED HERE.

KEDUSHAH / קדושה

STAND WITH FEET TOGETHER AND AVOID ANY INTERRUPTIONS. RISE ON TOES WHEN SAYING קָדוֹשׁ,
קָדוֹשׁ, קָדוֹשׁ – *HOLY, HOLY, HOLY;* בָּרוּךְ – *BLESSED;* AND יִמְלֹךְ – *HASHEM SHALL REIGN.*

CONGREGATION, THEN *CHAZZAN:*

כֶּתֶר יִתְּנוּ לְךָ יהוה אֱלֹהֵינוּ, מַלְאָכִים הֲמוֹנֵי מַעְלָה,

‹‹ of above ‹ the ‹ — the angels, ‹‹ our God ‹ HASHEM, ‹ You, ‹ they ‹ A crown
multitudes will give

עִם עַמְּךָ יִשְׂרָאֵל, קְבוּצֵי מַטָּה.

‹‹ below. ‹ assembled ‹‹ Israel, ‹ Your ‹ together
people with

CONGREGATION, THEN *CHAZZAN:*

יַחַד כֻּלָּם קְדֻשָׁה לְךָ יְשַׁלֵּשׁוּ, כַּדָּבָר הָאָמוּר עַל יַד

‹ by ‹ spoken ‹ as the ‹‹ will recite ‹ to ‹ Holy, ‹‹ all of ‹ Together,
statement three times You them

נְבִיאֶךָ, וְקָרָא זֶה אֶל זֶה וְאָמַר:

‹‹ and say: ‹ another ‹ to ‹ And one ‹‹ Your
would call prophet,

ALL:

קָדוֹשׁ קָדוֹשׁ קָדוֹשׁ יהוה צְבָאוֹת, מְלֹא כָל הָאָרֶץ כְּבוֹדוֹ.[1]

‹‹ with ‹ world ‹ is the ‹ filled ‹‹ Master of ‹ is HASHEM, ‹ holy ‹ holy, ‹ Holy,
His glory. whole Legions;

❖ לְעֻמָּתָם מְשַׁבְּחִים וְאוֹמְרִים:

‹‹ and proclaim: ‹ they offer praise ‹ Facing them

ALL:

בָּרוּךְ כְּבוֹד יהוה, מִמְּקוֹמוֹ.[2] ❖ וּבְדִבְרֵי קָדְשְׁךָ כָּתוּב

‹ it is ‹ that are ‹ And in Your ‹‹ from ‹ of HASHEM ‹ is the ‹ Blessed
written holy Writings His place. glory

לֵאמֹר:

‹‹ saying:

ALL:

יִמְלֹךְ יהוה לְעוֹלָם, אֱלֹהַיִךְ צִיּוֹן לְדֹר וָדֹר, הַלְלוּיָהּ.[3]

‹‹ Halleluyah! ‹‹ to ‹ from ‹ O Zion, ‹ your God, ‹‹ forever; ‹ HASHEM shall reign
generation, generation

(1) *Isaiah* 6:3. (2) *Ezekiel* 3:12. (3) *Psalms* 146:10.

ple offering that we cannot now offer makes it incumbent upon us that we plead fervently for God's mercy and an end of the exile. The com- mentators add that a *Shemoneh Esrei* can hardly take the place of an offering unless it is prayed with sincere devotion.

HOLINESS OF GOD'S NAME / קדושת השם

אַתָּה קָדוֹשׁ וְשִׁמְךָ
⟨ and Your ⟨ are holy ⟨ You
Name

קָדוֹשׁ, וּקְדוֹשִׁים בְּכָל
⟨ every ⟨ and holy ones ⟨⟨ is holy,

יוֹם יְהַלְלוּךָ סֶּלָה, כִּי
⟨ for, ⟨⟨ forever, ⟨ praise You, ⟨ day

אֵל מֶלֶךְ גָּדוֹל וְקָדוֹשׁ
⟨ and holy ⟨ great ⟨ a King, ⟨ O God,

אָתָּה. בָּרוּךְ אַתָּה
⟨ are You, ⟨ Blessed ⟨⟨ are You.

יהוה, הָאֵל הַקָּדוֹשׁ.
⟨⟨ Who is holy. ⟨ the God ⟨⟨ Hashem,

IN SOME CONGREGATIONS THE *CHAZZAN*
SUBSTITUTES אַתָּה קָדוֹשׁ FOR לְדוֹר וָדוֹר
IN HIS REPETITION:

לְדוֹר וָדוֹר נַגִּיד גָּדְלָךְ וּלְנֵצַח
⟨ and for ⟨⟨ Your ⟨ we shall ⟨ to gen- ⟨ From gen-
all greatness relate eration eration

נְצָחִים קְדֻשָּׁתְךָ נַקְדִּישׁ,
⟨⟨ shall we sanctify. ⟨ Your holiness ⟨ eternity

וְשִׁבְחֲךָ אֱלֹהֵינוּ מִפִּינוּ לֹא
⟨ shall ⟨ from our ⟨ our God, ⟨ Your praise,
not mouth

יָמוּשׁ לְעוֹלָם וָעֶד, כִּי אֵל מֶלֶךְ
⟨ a ⟨ O ⟨ for, ⟨⟨ and ⟨ for ever ⟨ leave
King, God, ever,

גָּדוֹל וְקָדוֹשׁ אָתָּה. בָּרוּךְ אַתָּה
⟨ are You, ⟨ Blessed ⟨⟨ are You. ⟨ and holy ⟨ great

יהוה, הָאֵל הַקָּדוֹשׁ.
⟨⟨ Who is holy. ⟨ the God ⟨⟨ Hashem,

HOLINESS OF THE DAY / קדושת היום

רָאשֵׁי חֳדָשִׁים לְעַמְּךָ נָתַתָּ,* זְמַן כַּפָּרָה*
⟨ of ⟨ a time ⟨⟨ You have ⟨ to Your ⟨ Moons ⟨ New
atonement* given,* people

לְכָל תּוֹלְדוֹתָם,* בִּהְיוֹתָם מַקְרִיבִים לְפָנֶיךָ זִבְחֵי
⟨ offerings ⟨ before ⟨ sacrifice ⟨ when they ⟨⟨ their offspring,* ⟨ for all
You would

---

§ רָאשֵׁי חֳדָשִׁים לְעַמְּךָ נָתַתָּ — *New Moons to Your people You have given.* The first commandment given to the Jewish nation as a whole was that of proclaiming the start of each new month (*Exodus* 12:2). This *mitzvah* gave the Jewish people, through its courts, the authority to determine the calendar. It also provides an insight into the nature of the people: like the moon, the Jewish nation can become great and then seem to disappear, but it always renews itself; and by means of regulating the calendar, the Jewish nation constantly renews its consciousness of God's control over the universe. [See also com-

mentary to *Kiddush Levanah* (p. 454).]

זְמַן כַּפָּרָה — *A time of atonement.* The offerings of Rosh Chodesh — and the prayers that take their place in the absence of the Temple — atone for unintentional contamination of the Temple and its offerings [טֻמְאַת מִקְדָּשׁ וְקָדָשָׁיו] (*Shevuos* 2b); for sins that can bring epidemics, specifically diphtheria, upon children (*Daas Zekeinim* to *Numbers* 28:9); and for general sins that prevent the coming of Messiah (*Iyun Tefillah*).

לְכָל תּוֹלְדוֹתָם — *For all their offspring,* the Jewish people, the offspring of the nation to whom the Rosh Chodesh commandment was originally

רָצוֹן, וּשְׂעִירֵי חַטָּאת* לְכַפֵּר בַּעֲדָם. זִכָּרוֹן

‹ As a remembrance   « on their behalf.   ‹ to atone   ‹ of sin-offerings*   ‹ and goats   « for favor,

לְכֻלָּם יִהְיוּ, וּתְשׁוּעַת נַפְשָׁם* מִיַּד שׂוֹנֵא. מִזְבֵּחַ

‹ An Altar   « of the enemy.   ‹ from the hand   ‹ for their soul*   ‹ and as a salvation   « they would serve,   ‹ for them all

חָדָשׁ בְּצִיּוֹן תָּכִין, וְעוֹלַת רֹאשׁ חֹדֶשׁ נַעֲלֶה

‹ may we bring up   ‹ Moon   ‹ of the New   ‹ and the elevation-offering   « may You establish,   ‹ in Zion   ‹ that is new

עָלָיו, וּשְׂעִירֵי עִזִּים נַעֲשֶׂה בְרָצוֹן.* וּבַעֲבוֹדַת

‹ In the service   « with favor.*   ‹ may we prepare   ‹ and he-goats   « upon it,

בֵּית הַמִּקְדָּשׁ נִשְׂמַח כֻּלָּנוּ, וּבְשִׁירֵי דָוִד עַבְדֶּךָ

‹ Your servant   ‹ of David   ‹ as well as in the songs   « all together,   ‹ may we rejoice   ‹ of the Holy Temple

הַנִּשְׁמָעִים בְּעִירֶךָ, הָאֲמוּרִים לִפְנֵי מִזְבְּחֶךָ.

« Your Altar.   ‹ before   ‹ when they are recited   « in Your City,   ‹ that are heard

אַהֲבַת עוֹלָם תָּבִיא לָהֶם, וּבְרִית אָבוֹת לַבָּנִים

‹ upon the children   ‹ of the forefathers   ‹ and the covenant   « them,   ‹ may You bring   ‹ that is eternal   ‹ A love

תִּזְכּוֹר. יְהִי רָצוֹן מִלְּפָנֶיךָ, יהוה אֱלֹהֵינוּ וֵאלֹהֵי

‹ and the God   ‹ our God   ‹ HASHEM,   « before You,   ‹ the will   ‹ May it be   « may You recall.

---

given. Additionally it refers to the children who are spared from serious illness by the offerings and prayers of the day (see above comment). In a novel comment, *Kuzari* writes that this refers to the month's offspring, the events that will take place during the ensuing month.

זִבְחֵי רָצוֹן וּשְׂעִירֵי חַטָּאת — *Offerings for favor, and goats of sin-offerings.* The *Mussaf*, or additional offering, of Rosh Chodesh is enumerated later in the *Shemoneh Esrei*. It includes several animals as elevation-offerings which are intended to gain God's favor, and a goat as a sin-offering, which atones for sin.

זִכָּרוֹן לְכֻלָּם יִהְיוּ וּתְשׁוּעַת נַפְשָׁם — *As a remembrance for them all they would serve, and as a salvation for their soul.* The Torah describes the offerings of the Festivals and Rosh Chodesh as Israel's ''remembrance'' before God (*Numbers* 10:10). It is axiomatic that Israel's devotion to God's service brings salvation from human and spiritual enemies.

וּשְׂעִירֵי עִזִּים נַעֲשֶׂה בְרָצוֹן — *And he-goats may we prepare with favor.* The prescribed communal sin-offerings are brought even when no sins have been committed. At such longed-for times, these offerings are sources of spiritual elevation.

אֲבוֹתֵינוּ, שֶׁתַּעֲלֵנוּ בְשִׂמְחָה לְאַרְצֵנוּ, וְתִטָּעֵנוּ

‹ and that You ‹‹ to our land, ‹ joyfully ‹ that You ‹‹ of our
imbed us   bring us up   forefathers,

בִּגְבוּלֵנוּ. וַהֲבִיאֵנוּ לְצִיּוֹן עִירְךָ בְּרִנָּה, וְלִירוּשָׁלַיִם

‹ to Jerusalem, ‹‹ in glad ‹ Your ‹ to Zion, ‹ May You ‹‹ in our borders.
                    song,   City,   bring us

בֵּית מִקְדָּשְׁךָ בְּשִׂמְחַת עוֹלָם. וְשָׁם נַעֲשֶׂה

‹ we shall ‹ There ‹‹ that is ‹ in rejoicing ‹ Your Holy Temple,
perform   eternal.

לְפָנֶיךָ אֶת קָרְבְּנוֹת חוֹבוֹתֵינוּ, תְּמִידִים

‹ the continual ‹‹ that are our ‹ the offerings ‹ before You
offerings   obligation,

כְּסִדְרָם, וּמוּסָפִים כְּהִלְכָתָם, וְאֶת מוּסַף יוֹם

‹ of the ‹ And the additional ‹‹ according to ‹ and the additional ‹‹ according to
day   offering   their law.   offerings   their order,

רֹאשׁ הַחֹדֶשׁ הַזֶּה נַעֲשֶׂה וְנַקְרִיב לְפָנֶיךָ בְּאַהֲבָה

‹ with love ‹ before You ‹ and we ‹ we shall ‹ of this New Moon
                          shall bring perform

כְּמִצְוַת רְצוֹנֶךָ, כְּמוֹ שֶׁכָּתַבְתָּ עָלֵינוּ בְּתוֹרָתֶךָ,

‹‹ in Your Torah, ‹ for us ‹ You have ‹ as ‹‹ of Your ‹ according to
                            written   will,   the commandment

עַל יְדֵי מֹשֶׁה עַבְדֶּךָ, מִפִּי כְבוֹדֶךָ, כָּאָמוּר:

‹‹ as it is said: ‹‹ of Your ‹ from the ‹ Your ‹ Moses ‹ through
                    glory,   statement   servant,

וּבְרָאשֵׁי חָדְשֵׁיכֶם* תַּקְרִיבוּ עֹלָה לַיהוה,

‹‹ to ‹ an elevation- ‹ you are to ‹ of your months* ‹ And on the first
HASHEM: offering   bring

פָּרִים בְּנֵי בָקָר שְׁנַיִם, וְאַיִל אֶחָד, כְּבָשִׂים

‹ male lambs ‹‹ one ram; ‹‹ two; ‹ young bulls,

Here, we express the hope that in the Temple of the future, sin-offerings will come only for that purpose (Maharit Algazi).

וּבְרָאשֵׁי חָדְשֵׁיכֶם — *And on the first of your months.* The New Moons are described as

"yours" because the authority to proclaim them is vested in Israel through its rabbinical courts. As is done in every *Mussaf Shemoneh Esrei*, the special offering of the day is set forth, including its animals, meal-offerings, and drink-offerings.

בְּנֵי שָׁנָה שִׁבְעָה, תְּמִימִם. וּמִנְחָתָם וְנִסְכֵּיהֶם¹

‹ and their wine-libations ‹ And their meal-offerings » unblemished. ‹ seven ‹ in their first year

כְּמִדְבָּר, שְׁלֹשָׁה עֶשְׂרֹנִים לַפָּר, וּשְׁנֵי עֶשְׂרֹנִים

‹ tenth-*ephahs* ‹ two » for each bull; ‹ tenth-*ephahs* ‹ three » as specified:

לָאַיִל, וְעִשָּׂרוֹן לַכֶּבֶשׂ, וְיַיִן כְּנִסְכּוֹ, וְשָׂעִיר

‹ A he-goat » for its wine-libation. ‹ and wine » for each lamb; ‹ one tenth-*ephah* » for the ram;

לְכַפֵּר, וּשְׁנֵי תְמִידִים כְּהִלְכָתָם.²

» according to their law. ‹ continual daily offerings ‹ and two ‹ for atonement

DURING THE *CHAZZAN'S* REPETITION, THE CONGREGATION RESPONDS אָמֵן, AS INDICATED.

אֱלֹהֵינוּ* וֵאלֹהֵי אֲבוֹתֵינוּ, חַדֵּשׁ עָלֵינוּ

‹ for us ‹ inaugurate » of our forefathers, ‹ and the God ‹ Our God*

אֶת הַחֹדֶשׁ הַזֶּה לְטוֹבָה וְלִבְרָכָה (אָמֵן),

» (Amen,) » and for blessing, ‹ — for good » this month

לְשָׂשׂוֹן וּלְשִׂמְחָה (אָמֵן), לִישׁוּעָה וּלְנֶחָמָה (אָמֵן),

» (Amen,) » and for consolation, ‹ for salvation » (Amen,) » and for gladness, ‹ for joy

לְפַרְנָסָה וּלְכַלְכָּלָה (אָמֵן), לְחַיִּים טוֹבִים וּלְשָׁלוֹם

» and for peace, ‹ that is good ‹ for life » (Amen,) ‹ and for support ‹ for sustenance

(אָמֵן), לִמְחִילַת חֵטְא וְלִסְלִיחַת עָוֹן (אָמֵן)

» (Amen,) » of iniquity, ‹ and for forgiveness ‹ of sin ‹ for pardon » (Amen,)

DURING A JEWISH LEAP YEAR, ADD:

[וּלְכַפָּרַת פָּשַׁע (אָמֵן].] וִיהִי הַחֹדֶשׁ הַזֶּה סוֹף

‹ the end » — this month — » May it be » (Amen.) » of willful sin. ‹ and for atonement

---

(1) *Numbers* 28:11. (2) Cf. 28:12-15.

אֱלֹהֵינוּ ◆§ — *Our God.* Having set forth the characteristics and the service of Rosh Chodesh, we conclude with a final plea that God fill the new month with every form of happiness and blessing. Since the year has twelve months, we specify twelve types of blessing. They are grouped in six pairs and the congregation answers Amen after each of them. [In a Jewish leap year, which has a thirteenth month, a thirteenth term of blessing is added: וּלְכַפָּרַת פָּשַׁע, *and for atonement of willful sin.* Most congregations recite the additional phrase only

וְקֵץ לְכָל צָרוֹתֵינוּ, תְּחִלָּה וָרֹאשׁ לְפִדְיוֹן נַפְשֵׁנוּ.

‹‹ of our soul. ‹ for the redemption ‹ and the beginning ‹ the start ‹‹ our troubles, ‹ of ‹ and the termination all

כִּי בְעַמְּךָ יִשְׂרָאֵל בָּחַרְתָּ מִכָּל הָאֻמּוֹת,*

‹‹ the nations,* ‹ from all ‹‹ You have chosen ‹ Israel ‹ Your people ‹ For

וְחֻקֵּי רָאשֵׁי חֳדָשִׁים לָהֶם קָבָעְתָּ. בָּרוּךְ אַתָּה

‹ are You, ‹ Blessed ‹‹ You have set forth. ‹ for them ‹ Moons ‹ of the New ‹ and the decrees

יהוה, מְקַדֵּשׁ יִשְׂרָאֵל וְרָאשֵׁי חֳדָשִׁים.*

‹‹ Moons.* ‹ and the New ‹ Israel ‹ Who sanctifies ‹‹ Hashem,

TEMPLE SERVICE / עבודה

רְצֵה יהוה אֱלֹהֵינוּ בְּעַמְּךָ יִשְׂרָאֵל, וְלִתְפִלָּתָם

‹ and toward their prayer ‹ Israel, ‹ toward Your people ‹‹ our God, ‹ Hashem, ‹‹ Be favorable,

שְׁעֵה, וְהָשֵׁב אֶת הָעֲבוֹדָה לִדְבִיר בֵּיתֶךָ. וְאִשֵּׁי

‹ The fire-offerings ‹‹ of Your Temple. ‹ to the Holy of Holies ‹ the service ‹ and restore ‹‹ turn,

יִשְׂרָאֵל וּתְפִלָּתָם מְהֵרָה בְּאַהֲבָה תְקַבֵּל בְּרָצוֹן,

‹‹ favorably, ‹ accept ‹ with love ‹ speedily, ‹ and their prayer, ‹ of Israel

וּתְהִי לְרָצוֹן תָּמִיד עֲבוֹדַת יִשְׂרָאֵל עַמֶּךָ.

‹‹ Your people. ‹ of Israel ‹ the service ‹ always ‹ to Your favor ‹ and may it be

until the Second Adar, the extra month, while some recite it throughout the leap year.]

בָּחַרְתָּ מִכָּל הָאֻמּוֹת — *You have chosen (Israel) from all the nations.* Unlike most nations, we calculate our calendar by the moon as well as the sun. Israel is likened to the moon in several ways. Like the moon, we are assured of a return to our past glory even after periods of utter decline. Additionally, unlike the sun that sets at night, the moon is in the sky by day as well as at night. Thus, even though our glow is sometimes not noticeable, it is like that of the moon when the sun holds sway; it is

present nonetheless (R' Yaakov Emden).

מְקַדֵּשׁ יִשְׂרָאֵל וְרָאשֵׁי חֳדָשִׁים — *Who sanctifies Israel and the New Moons.* Israel is mentioned before the New Moons because the sanctity of the new moon depends on the prior sanctification of the Jewish people and the declaration issued by its court. In the blessing of the Sabbath (מְקַדֵּשׁ הַשַּׁבָּת, *Who sanctifies the Sabbath*), however, Israel is not mentioned in the blessing of sanctification because the holiness of the Sabbath preceded and is independent of the existence of the Jewish people.

וְתֶחֱזֶינָה עֵינֵינוּ בְּשׁוּבְךָ לְצִיּוֹן בְּרַחֲמִים.

《 in compassion. **〈** to Zion **〈** Your return **〈** may our eyes **〈** Witness

בָּרוּךְ אַתָּה יהוה, הַמַּחֲזִיר שְׁכִינָתוֹ לְצִיּוֹן.

《 to Zion. **〈** His Presence **〈** Who restores **《** Hashem, **〈** are You, **〈** Blessed

THANKSGIVING [MODIM] / הודאה

BOW AT מוֹדִים, *WE THANK;* STRAIGHTEN UP AT 'ה, *HASHEM.* IN HIS REPETITION THE *CHAZZAN* RECITES THE ENTIRE מוֹדִים ALOUD, WHILE THE CONGREGATION RECITES מוֹדִים דְּרַבָּנָן (P. 526) SOFTLY.

מוֹדִים אֲנַחְנוּ לָךְ, שָׁאַתָּה הוּא יהוה

〈 Hashem, **〈** Who are **〈** for it is You **《** You, **〈** We thank

אֱלֹהֵינוּ וֵאלֹהֵי אֲבוֹתֵינוּ לְעוֹלָם וָעֶד. צוּרֵנוּ,

〈 our Rock, **《** and ever; **〈** for ever **〈** of our forefathers, **〈** and the God **〈** our God

צוּר חַיֵּינוּ, מָגֵן יִשְׁעֵנוּ אַתָּה הוּא לְדוֹר וָדוֹר.

《 to gen- **〈** from gen- **〈** are **〈** [is what] **《** of our **〈** Shield **《** of our **〈** the
eration. eration You salvation, lives, Rock

נוֹדֶה לְּךָ וּנְסַפֵּר תְּהִלָּתֶךָ¹ עַל חַיֵּינוּ

〈 our lives **〈** for **《** Your praise, **〈** and relate **〈** You **〈** We shall thank

הַמְּסוּרִים בְּיָדֶךָ, וְעַל נִשְׁמוֹתֵינוּ הַפְּקוּדוֹת

〈 that are **〈** our souls **〈** and for **《** into Your **〈** that are
entrusted hands, committed

לָךְ, וְעַל נִסֶּיךָ שֶׁבְּכָל יוֹם עִמָּנוּ, וְעַל

〈 and for **《** are with us; **〈** day **〈** that every **〈** Your miracles **〈** and for **《** to You;

נִפְלְאוֹתֶיךָ וְטוֹבוֹתֶיךָ שֶׁבְּכָל עֵת, עֶרֶב וָבְקֶר

〈 morning, **〈**—evening, **《** times **〈** that are at all **〈** and favors **〈** Your wonders

וְצָהֳרָיִם. הַטּוֹב כִּי לֹא כָלוּ רַחֲמֶיךָ, וְהַמְרַחֵם

〈 and the Com- **《** are Your **〈** exhausted **〈** never **〈** for **〈** The Bene- **《** and afternoon.
passionate One, compassions, ficent One,

כִּי לֹא תַמּוּ חֲסָדֶיךָ,² כִּי מֵעוֹלָם קִוִּינוּ לָךְ.

《 in You. **〈** have we **〈** always **〈**—for **《** are Your **〈** ended **〈** never **〈** for
put our hope kindnesses

---

(1) Cf. *Psalms* 79:13. (2) Cf. *Lamentations* 3:22.

MODIM OF THE RABBIS / מוֹדִים דְּרַבָּנָן

מוֹדִים אֲנַחְנוּ לָךְ, שָׁאַתָּה הוּא יהוה אֱלֹהֵינוּ וֵאלֹהֵי
‹ and the God ‹ our God ‹ HASHEM, ‹ Who are ‹ for it is You ‹‹ You, ‹   We thank

אֲבוֹתֵינוּ, אֱלֹהֵי כָל בָּשָׂר, יוֹצְרֵנוּ, יוֹצֵר בְּרֵאשִׁית. בְּרָכוֹת
‹ Blessings ‹‹ of the ‹ the ‹ our ‹‹ flesh, ‹ of all ‹ the God ‹‹ of our
universe. Molder Molder, forefathers,

וְהוֹדָאוֹת לְשִׁמְךָ הַגָּדוֹל וְהַקָּדוֹשׁ, עַל שֶׁהֶחֱיִיתָנוּ וְקִיַּמְתָּנוּ.
‹‹ and You have ‹ You have ‹ for ‹‹ and that ‹ that is ‹ [are due] to ‹ and thanks
sustained us. given us life is holy, great Your Name

כֵּן תְּחַיֵּנוּ וּתְקַיְּמֵנוּ, וְתֶאֱסוֹף גָּלֻיוֹתֵינוּ לְחַצְרוֹת קָדְשֶׁךָ,
‹‹ of Your ‹ to the ‹ our exiles ‹ and gather ‹‹ and ‹ may You continue ‹ So
Sanctuary, Courtyards sustain us, to give us life

לִשְׁמוֹר חֻקֶּיךָ וְלַעֲשׂוֹת רְצוֹנֶךָ, וּלְעָבְדְּךָ בְּלֵבָב שָׁלֵם,
‹‹ wholeheartedly. ‹ and to ‹‹ Your will, ‹ to do ‹‹ Your ‹ to observe
serve You decrees,

עַל שֶׁאֲנַחְנוּ מוֹדִים לָךְ. בָּרוּךְ אֵל הַהוֹדָאוֹת.
‹‹ of thanksgivings. ‹ is the ‹ Blessed ‹‹ You. ‹ to thank ‹ [inspiring] ‹ [We thank
God us You] for

ON CHANUKAH ADD THE FOLLOWING [IF FORGOTTEN, DO NOT REPEAT *SHEMONEH ESREI*; SEE LAWS §89]:

וְעַל הַנִּסִּים, וְעַל הַפֻּרְקָן, וְעַל הַגְּבוּרוֹת, וְעַל
‹ and for ‹ the mighty deeds, ‹ and for ‹ the salvation, ‹ and for ‹ the miracles, ‹ And for

הַתְּשׁוּעוֹת, וְעַל הַנִּפְלָאוֹת, וְעַל הַנֶּחָמוֹת, וְעַל הַמִּלְחָמוֹת,
‹ the battles ‹ and for ‹ the consolations, ‹ and for ‹ the wonders, ‹ and for ‹ the victories,

שֶׁעָשִׂיתָ לַאֲבוֹתֵינוּ בַּיָּמִים הָהֵם בַּזְּמַן הַזֶּה.
‹‹ at this time: ‹ in those days, ‹‹ for our ‹ which You
forefathers performed

בִּימֵי מַתִּתְיָהוּ בֶּן יוֹחָנָן כֹּהֵן גָּדוֹל חַשְׁמוֹנָאִי וּבָנָיו,
‹‹ and his ‹‹ the ‹ the High Priest, ‹ of ‹ the ‹‹ of ‹ In the
sons, Hasmonean, Yochanan, son Mattisyahu, days

כְּשֶׁעָמְדָה מַלְכוּת יָוָן הָרְשָׁעָה עַל עַמְּךָ יִשְׂרָאֵל, לְהַשְׁכִּיחָם
‹ to make ‹‹ Israel, ‹ Your ‹ against ‹‹ —which was ‹‹ of ‹ did the ‹ when rise up
them forget people wicked— Greece kingdom

תּוֹרָתֶךָ, וּלְהַעֲבִירָם מֵחֻקֵּי רְצוֹנֶךָ. וְאַתָּה בְּרַחֲמֶיךָ
‹ in Your mercy ‹ But You ‹‹ of Your Will. ‹ from the ‹ and to compel ‹‹ Your
statutes them to stray Torah

הָרַבִּים, עָמַדְתָּ לָהֶם בְּעֵת צָרָתָם, רַבְתָּ אֶת רִיבָם, דַּנְתָּ
‹ judged ‹ their cause, ‹ You ‹‹ of their ‹ in the ‹ for ‹ stood up ‹‹ which is
championed distress. time them abundant

אֶת דִּינָם, נָקַמְתָּ אֶת נִקְמָתָם.¹ מָסַרְתָּ גִבּוֹרִים בְּיַד חַלָּשִׁים,
‹‹ of the ‹ into the ‹ the strong ‹ You ‹‹ their wrong. ‹ and You ‹‹ their claim,
weak, hands delivered avenged

וְרַבִּים בְּיַד מְעַטִּים, וּטְמֵאִים בְּיַד טְהוֹרִים, וּרְשָׁעִים בְּיַד
‹ into the ‹ the wicked ‹‹ of the pure, ‹ into the ‹ the impure ‹‹ of the few, ‹ into the ‹ the
hands hands hands many

צַדִּיקִים, וְזֵדִים בְּיַד עוֹסְקֵי תוֹרָתֶךָ. וּלְךָ עָשִׂיתָ שֵׁם גָּדוֹל
‹ that ‹ a ‹ You ‹ For ‹‹ of Your ‹ of the ‹ into the ‹ and the ‹‹ of the
is great Name made Yourself Torah. diligent hands willful righteous,
students sinners

וְקָדוֹשׁ בְּעוֹלָמֶךָ, וּלְעַמְּךָ יִשְׂרָאֵל עָשִׂיתָ תְּשׁוּעָה גְדוֹלָה²
‹ of great ‹ a victory ‹ You ‹ Israel ‹ and for ‹‹ in Your ‹ and holy
magnitude performed Your people world,

וּפֻרְקָן כְּהַיּוֹם הַזֶּה. וְאַחַר כֵּן בָּאוּ בָנֶיךָ לִדְבִיר בֵּיתֶךָ,
‹‹ of Your ‹ to the Holy ‹ Your ‹ came ‹ Thereafter, ‹‹ as this very day. ‹ and a
House, of Holies children salvation

וּפִנּוּ אֶת הֵיכָלֶךָ, וְטִהֲרוּ אֶת מִקְדָּשֶׁךָ, וְהִדְלִיקוּ נֵרוֹת
‹ lights ‹ and kindled ‹‹ the site of Your Holiness ‹ purified ‹‹ Your Temple, ‹ cleansed

בְּחַצְרוֹת קָדְשֶׁךָ, וְקָבְעוּ שְׁמוֹנַת יְמֵי חֲנֻכָּה אֵלּוּ,
‹‹ — these — ‹‹ of ‹ days ‹ the eight ‹ and they ‹‹ of Your ‹ in the
Chanukah established Sanctuary; Courtyards

לְהוֹדוֹת וּלְהַלֵּל לְשִׁמְךָ הַגָּדוֹל.
‹‹ that is great. ‹ to Your ‹ and praise ‹ to express
Name thanks

וְעַל כֻּלָּם יִתְבָּרַךְ וְיִתְרוֹמַם וְיִתְנַשֵּׂא שִׁמְךָ
‹ may Your ‹ and upraised ‹ and exalted, ‹ blessed, ‹ all these, ‹ For
Name be,

מַלְכֵּנוּ תָּמִיד לְעוֹלָם וָעֶד.
‹‹ and ever. ‹ for ever ‹ continually, ‹‹ our King,

BEND THE KNEES AT בָּרוּךְ, BLESSED; BOW AT אַתָּה, YOU; STRAIGHTEN UP AT ה', HASHEM.

וְכֹל הַחַיִּים יוֹדוּךָ סֶּלָה, וִיהַלְלוּ וִיבָרְכוּ
‹ and bless ‹ — and praise ‹‹ forever! ‹ will gratefully ‹ alive ‹ Everything
acknowledge You,

אֶת שִׁמְךָ הַגָּדוֹל, בֶּאֱמֶת לְעוֹלָם, כִּי טוֹב, הָאֵל
‹ O God ‹‹ it is good. ‹ for ‹ forever, ‹ sincerely, ‹‹ that is great, ‹ Your Name

---

(1) Cf. Jeremiah 51:36. (2) Cf. I Samuel 19:5.

יְשׁוּעָתֵנוּ וְעֶזְרָתֵנוּ סֶלָה, הָאֵל הַטּוֹב. בָּרוּךְ

⟨Blessed ⟪ Who is beneficent. ⟨ the God ⟪ forever, ⟨ and of our help, ⟨ of our salvation

אַתָּה יהוה, הַטּוֹב שִׁמְךָ וּלְךָ נָאֶה לְהוֹדוֹת.

⟪ to give ⟨ it is ⟨ and ⟨ is Your ⟨ The ⟪ Hashem, ⟨ are You,
thanks.   fitting   to You   Name,   Beneficent One

THE *CHAZZAN* RECITES בִּרְכַּת כֹּהֲנִים DURING HIS REPETITION EXCEPT IN A HOUSE OF MOURNING.
THE *CHAZZAN* FACES RIGHT AT וְיִשְׁמְרֶךָ; FACES LEFT AT וִיחֻנֶּךָּ פָּנָיו אֵלֶיךָ; FACES THE ARK FOR THE
REST OF THE BLESSINGS.

אֱלֹהֵינוּ וֵאלֹהֵי אֲבוֹתֵינוּ, בָּרְכֵנוּ בַבְּרָכָה הַמְשֻׁלֶּשֶׁת, בַּתּוֹרָה

⟨ [that is] in ⟨ of three ⟨ with the ⟨ bless us ⟪ of our ⟨ and ⟨ Our God
the Torah   verses,   blessing   forefathers,   the God

הַכְּתוּבָה עַל יְדֵי מֹשֶׁה עַבְדֶּךָ, הָאֲמוּרָה מִפִּי אַהֲרֹן וּבָנָיו,

⟨ and his ⟨ of ⟨ from the ⟨ that was ⟪ Your ⟨ of ⟨ the ⟨ by ⟨ that was
sons,   Aaron   mouth   said   servant,   Moses,   hand   written

כֹּהֲנִים עַם קְדוֹשֶׁךָ, כָּאָמוּר:

⟪ as it is said: ⟨ Your holy people, ⟪ the *Kohanim*,

יְבָרֶכְךָ יהוה, וְיִשְׁמְרֶךָ.   (Cong. — כֵּן יְהִי רָצוֹן.)

⟪ His will. ⟨ be ⟨ May so   ⟪ and safeguard you. ⟨ May Hashem bless you

יָאֵר יהוה פָּנָיו אֵלֶיךָ וִיחֻנֶּךָּ.   (Cong. — כֵּן יְהִי רָצוֹן.)

⟪ His will. ⟨ be ⟨ May so   ⟪ and be ⟨ for you ⟨ His ⟨ May Hashem
gracious to you.   countenance   illuminate

יִשָּׂא יהוה פָּנָיו אֵלֶיךָ וְיָשֵׂם לְךָ שָׁלוֹם.[1]   (Cong. — כֵּן יְהִי רָצוֹן.)

⟪ His will. ⟨ be ⟨ May so   ⟪ peace. ⟨ for ⟨ and ⟨ to you ⟨ His ⟨ May Hashem
you establish   countenance   turn

SOME CONGREGATIONS RECITE THE FOLLOWING WHILE THE *CHAZZAN* RECITES שִׂים שָׁלוֹם:

אַדִּיר בַּמָּרוֹם, שׁוֹכֵן בִּגְבוּרָה, אַתָּה שָׁלוֹם וְשִׁמְךָ שָׁלוֹם.[2]

⟪ is Peace! ⟨ and Your ⟨ are ⟨ You ⟪ in power! ⟨ Who ⟨ on high, ⟨ Mighty One
Name   peace   dwells

יְהִי רָצוֹן שֶׁתָּשִׂים עָלֵינוּ וְעַל כָּל עַמְּךָ בֵּית יִשְׂרָאֵל חַיִּים

⟨ life ⟪ of Israel, ⟨ the ⟨ of Your ⟨ all ⟨ and ⟨ upon us ⟨ that You ⟨ [Your] will ⟨ May
House   people,   upon   place   it be

וּבְרָכָה לְמִשְׁמֶרֶת שָׁלוֹם.

⟪ of peace. ⟨ for a safeguard ⟨ and blessing

שלום / PEACE

שִׂים שָׁלוֹם, טוֹבָה, וּבְרָכָה, חַיִּים, חֵן,

⟨ graciousness, ⟨ life, ⟨ blessing, ⟨ goodness, ⟨ peace, ⟨ Establish

(1) *Numbers* 6:24-26. (2) Cf. *Judges* 6:24 and *Shabbos* 10b.

וָחֶסֶד וְרַחֲמִים עָלֵינוּ וְעַל כָּל יִשְׂרָאֵל עַמֶּךָ.
‹‹ Your people. ‹ of Israel ‹ all ‹ and upon ‹ upon us ‹ and compassion ‹ kindness,

בָּרְכֵנוּ אָבִינוּ, כֻּלָּנוּ כְּאֶחָד, בְּאוֹר פָּנֶיךָ, כִּי בְאוֹר
‹ with the ‹ for ‹‹ of Your ‹ with the ‹‹ as one, ‹ all of us ‹‹ our ‹ Bless us,
light   countenance, light   Father,

פָּנֶיךָ נָתַתָּ לָנוּ, יהוה אֱלֹהֵינוּ, תּוֹרַת חַיִּים
‹ of life ‹ the Torah ‹‹ our God, ‹ HASHEM, ‹ us, ‹ You ‹ of Your
                                                  gave   countenance

וְאַהֲבַת חֶסֶד, וּצְדָקָה, וּבְרָכָה, וְרַחֲמִים, וְחַיִּים,
‹ life, ‹ compassion, ‹ blessing, ‹ righteousness, ‹ of kindness, ‹ and a love

וְשָׁלוֹם. וְטוֹב יִהְיֶה בְּעֵינֶיךָ לְבָרְכֵנוּ וּלְבָרֵךְ
‹ and to bless ‹ to bless us ‹ in Your eyes ‹ may it be ‹ And good ‹‹ and peace.

אֶת כָּל עַמְּךָ יִשְׂרָאֵל בְּכָל עֵת וּבְכָל שָׁעָה
‹ hour ‹ and at every ‹ time ‹ at every ‹ Israel ‹ of Your people ‹ all

בִּשְׁלוֹמֶךָ, (בְּרוֹב עוֹז וְשָׁלוֹם). בָּרוּךְ אַתָּה
‹ are You, ‹ Blessed ‹‹ and peace). ‹ strength ‹ (with abundant ‹‹ with Your peace,

יהוה, הַמְבָרֵךְ אֶת עַמּוֹ יִשְׂרָאֵל בַּשָּׁלוֹם.
‹‹ with peace. ‹ Israel ‹ His people ‹ Who blesses ‹‹ HASHEM,

**ALTHOUGH THE *CHAZZAN'S* REPETITION ENDS HERE, HE SHOULD ADD
THE NEXT VERSE IN AN UNDERTONE. INDIVIDUALS CONTINUE:**

יִהְיוּ לְרָצוֹן אִמְרֵי פִי וְהֶגְיוֹן לִבִּי לְפָנֶיךָ, יהוה צוּרִי וְגֹאֲלִי.[1]
‹‹ and my ‹ my ‹ HASHEM, ‹‹ before ‹‹ of my ‹ and the ‹ of my ‹ — the ‹ find ‹ May
Redeemer. Rock   You,   heart — thoughts mouth expressions favor they

אֱלֹהַי, נְצוֹר לְשׁוֹנִי מֵרָע, וּשְׂפָתַי מִדַּבֵּר
‹ from speaking ‹ and my lips ‹‹ from evil ‹ my tongue ‹ guard ‹ My God,

מִרְמָה, וְלִמְקַלְלַי נַפְשִׁי תִדּוֹם, וְנַפְשִׁי כֶּעָפָר[2]
‹ like dust ‹ and let ‹‹ be silent; ‹ let my ‹ To those who ‹‹ deceitfully.
           my soul   soul   curse me,

לַכֹּל תִּהְיֶה. פְּתַח לִבִּי בְּתוֹרָתֶךָ, וְאַחֲרֵי
‹ so that to follow ‹‹ to Your Torah, ‹ my heart ‹ Open ‹‹ be. ‹ to everyone

---

(1) *Psalms* 19:15. (2) Cf. 34:14.

מִצְוֹתֶיךָ   תִּרְדּוֹף נַפְשִׁי.   וְכָל הַקָּמִים וְהַחוֹשְׁבִים

and who plot ⟨ who rise up ⟨ As for all ⟩ shall my soul pursue. ⟨ Your commandments

עָלַי לְרָעָה, מְהֵרָה הָפֵר עֲצָתָם וְקַלְקֵל

and disrupt ⟨ their counsel, ⟨ nullify ⟨ speedily ⟨ to do evil, ⟨ against me

מַחֲשַׁבְתָּם. יְהִי רָצוֹן מִלְּפָנֶיךָ, יהוה אֱלֹהַי

my God ⟨ HASHEM, ⟨ before You, ⟨ the will ⟨ May it be ⟨ their scheme.

וֵאלֹהֵי אֲבוֹתַי, שֶׁלֹּא תַעֲלֶה קִנְאַת אָדָם עָלַי,

against ⟨ of any ⟨ the ⟨ be aroused ⟨ that there ⟨ of my ⟨ and the God
me, man jealousy not forefathers,

וְלֹא קִנְאָתִי עַל אֲחֵרִים, וְשֶׁלֹּא אֶכְעַס הַיּוֹם,

today, ⟨ become angry ⟨ and that I not ⟨ others; ⟨ against ⟨ my jealousy ⟨ nor

וְשֶׁלֹּא אַכְעִיסֶךָ, וְתַצִּילֵנִי מִיֵּצֶר הָרָע, וְתֵן בְּלִבִּי

in my ⟨ and ⟨ for Evil, ⟨ from the ⟨ Rescue me ⟨ anger You. ⟨ and that
heart place Inclination I not

הַכְנָעָה וַעֲנָוָה. מַלְכֵּנוּ וֵאלֹהֵינוּ, יַחֵד שְׁמֶךָ

Your Name ⟨ unify ⟨ and our God, ⟨ O our King ⟨ and humility. ⟨ submissiveness

בְּעוֹלָמֶךָ, בְּנֵה עִירְךָ, יַסֵּד בֵּיתֶךָ, וְשַׁכְלֵל הֵיכָלֶךָ,

Your ⟨ perfect ⟨ of Your ⟨ lay the ⟨ Your ⟨ rebuild ⟨ in Your world;
Sanctuary; House, foundation City,

וְקַבֵּץ קִבּוּץ גָּלֻיּוֹת, וּפְדֵה צֹאנֶךָ, וְשַׂמַּח עֲדָתֶךָ.

Your ⟨ and gladden ⟨ Your ⟨ redeem ⟨ of the ⟨ the ⟨ gather
congregation. sheep, exiles, ingathering

עֲשֵׂה לְמַעַן שְׁמֶךָ, עֲשֵׂה לְמַעַן יְמִינֶךָ,

of Your ⟨ for the sake ⟨ act ⟨ of Your Name; ⟨ for the sake ⟨ Act
right hand;

עֲשֵׂה לְמַעַן תּוֹרָתֶךָ, עֲשֵׂה לְמַעַן קְדֻשָּׁתֶךָ.

of Your sanctity. ⟨ for the sake ⟨ act ⟨ of Your Torah; ⟨ for the sake ⟨ act

לְמַעַן יֵחָלְצוּן יְדִידֶיךָ, הוֹשִׁיעָה יְמִינְךָ וַעֲנֵנִי.

and answer ⟨ with Your ⟨ — save ⟨ Your ⟨ released ⟨ In order
me. right hand, beloved ones may be that

(1) See *Berachos* 17a. (2) *Psalms* 60:7; 108:7.

SOME RECITE VERSES PERTAINING TO THEIR NAMES HERE. SEE PAGE 764.

יִהְיוּ לְרָצוֹן אִמְרֵי פִי וְהֶגְיוֹן לִבִּי לְפָנֶיךָ,

〈〈 before 〈〈 of my 〈 and the 〈 of my 〈 – the 〈〈 find favor 〈 May they
You, heart — thoughts mouth expressions

יהוה צוּרִי וְגֹאֲלִי.¹

〈〈 and my Redeemer. 〈 my Rock 〈 HASHEM,

BOW. TAKE THREE STEPS BACK. BOW LEFT AND SAY . . . עֹשֶׂה, *"HE WHO MAKES . . ."*; BOW RIGHT AND
SAY . . . הוּא, *"MAY HE . . ."*; BOW FORWARD AND SAY . . . וְעַל כָּל יִשְׂרָאֵל, *"AND UPON ALL ISRAEL . . ."*

עֹשֶׂה שָׁלוֹם בִּמְרוֹמָיו,² הוּא יַעֲשֶׂה שָׁלוֹם

〈 peace 〈 make 〈 may He 〈〈 in His heights, 〈 peace 〈 He Who makes

עָלֵינוּ, וְעַל כָּל יִשְׂרָאֵל.³ וְאִמְרוּ: אָמֵן.

〈〈 Amen. 〈 Now respond:〈〈 Israel. 〈 all 〈 and upon 〈〈 upon us,

יְהִי רָצוֹן מִלְּפָנֶיךָ, יהוה אֱלֹהֵינוּ וֵאלֹהֵי

〈 and the God 〈 our God 〈 HASHEM, 〈〈 before You, 〈 the will 〈 May it be

אֲבוֹתֵינוּ, שֶׁיִּבָּנֶה בֵּית הַמִּקְדָּשׁ בִּמְהֵרָה בְיָמֵינוּ, וְתֵן

〈 Grant 〈〈 in 〈 speedily 〈 shall the 〈 that rebuilt 〈〈 of our
that our days. Holy Temple be, forefathers,

חֶלְקֵנוּ בְּתוֹרָתֶךָ.⁴ וְשָׁם נַעֲבָדְךָ בְּיִרְאָה, כִּימֵי עוֹלָם

〈 of old 〈 as in 〈〈 with 〈 we may 〈 so that 〈 be in Your 〈 our portion
days reverence, serve You there Torah,

וּכְשָׁנִים קַדְמוֹנִיּוֹת. וְעָרְבָה לַיהוה מִנְחַת יְהוּדָה

〈 of Judah 〈 let be the 〈 to HASHEM 〈 And pleasing 〈〈 gone by. 〈 and as in years
offering

וִירוּשָׁלָיִם, כִּימֵי עוֹלָם וּכְשָׁנִים קַדְמוֹנִיּוֹת.⁵

〈〈 gone by. 〈 and in years 〈 of old 〈 as in days 〈〈 and Jerusalem,

THE INDIVIDUAL'S RECITATION OF *SHEMONEH ESREI* ENDS HERE. REMAIN STANDING IN PLACE UNTIL
THE *CHAZZAN* REACHES *KEDUSHAH* — OR AT LEAST UNTIL THE *CHAZZAN* BEGINS HIS REPETITION —
THEN TAKE THREE STEPS FORWARD. THE *CHAZZAN* HIMSELF, OR ONE PRAYING ALONE, SHOULD
REMAIN IN PLACE FOR A FEW MOMENTS BEFORE TAKING THREE STEPS FORWARD.

THE *CHAZZAN* RECITES קַדִּישׁ שָׁלֵם, THE FULL *KADDISH* (P. 223).
THE SERVICE CONTINUES WITH קַוֵּה אֶל ה', *PLACE YOUR HOPE IN HASHEM* (P. 248).

(1) *Psalms* 19:15. (2) *Job* 25:2. (3) Cf. *Berachos* 16b. (4) *Ethics of the Fathers* 5:24. (5) *Malachi* 3:4.

מוסף לחול המועד
MUSSAF FOR CHOL HAMOED

FOR HOSHANA RABBAH, SEE *THE INTERLINEAR SIDDUR FOR THE SABBATH AND FESTIVALS.*

TAKE THREE STEPS BACKWARD, THEN THREE STEPS FORWARD. REMAIN STANDING WITH FEET TOGETHER WHILE RECITING *SHEMONEH ESREI.* RECITE IT WITH QUIET DEVOTION AND WITHOUT ANY INTERRUPTION. ALTHOUGH IT SHOULD NOT BE AUDIBLE TO OTHERS, ONE MUST PRAY LOUDLY ENOUGH TO HEAR HIMSELF. SEE *LAWS* §44-45; 90-95 FOR A BRIEF SUMMARY OF ITS LAWS.

כִּי שֵׁם יהוה אֶקְרָא, הָבוּ גְדֶל לֵאלֹהֵינוּ.¹

‹ to our God. ‹ greatness ‹ ascribe ‹‹ I call out, ‹ of HASHEM ‹ the Name ‹ When

אֲדֹנָי שְׂפָתַי תִּפְתָּח, וּפִי יַגִּיד תְּהִלָּתֶךָ.²

‹‹ Your praise. ‹ may ‹ that my ‹‹ open, ‹ my lips ‹ O Lord,
declare mouth

PATRIARCHS / אבות

BEND THE KNEES AT בָּרוּךְ, *BLESSED*; BOW AT אַתָּה, *YOU*; STRAIGHTEN UP AT ה', *HASHEM.*

בָּרוּךְ אַתָּה יהוה אֱלֹהֵינוּ וֵאלֹהֵי אֲבוֹתֵינוּ,

‹‹ of our forefathers, ‹ and the God ‹ our God ‹ HASHEM, ‹ are You, ‹ Blessed

אֱלֹהֵי אַבְרָהָם, אֱלֹהֵי יִצְחָק, וֵאלֹהֵי יַעֲקֹב, הָאֵל

‹ God ‹‹ of Jacob; ‹ and God ‹ of Isaac, ‹ God ‹ of Abraham, ‹ God

הַגָּדוֹל הַגִּבּוֹר וְהַנּוֹרָא, אֵל עֶלְיוֹן, גּוֹמֵל

‹ Who bestows ‹‹ the Most High, ‹ God, ‹‹ and awesome; ‹ mighty, ‹ [Who is] great,

חֲסָדִים טוֹבִים וְקוֹנֵה הַכֹּל, וְזוֹכֵר חַסְדֵי אָבוֹת,

‹‹ of the ‹ the ‹ Who ‹‹ everything, ‹ and ‹ [that are] ‹ kindnesses
Patriarchs, kindnesses recalls creates beneficent

וּמֵבִיא גוֹאֵל לִבְנֵי בְנֵיהֶם, לְמַעַן שְׁמוֹ בְּאַהֲבָה.

‹‹ with love. ‹ of His ‹ for the ‹‹ of their ‹ to the ‹ a ‹ and brings
Name, sake children, children Redeemer

---

(1) *Deuteronomy* 32:3. (2) *Psalms* 51:17.

מוסף לחול המועד / MUSSAF FOR CHOL HAMOED

The *Shemoneh Esrei* of *Mussaf* corresponds to the *mussaf-*, or additional-, offerings of the Festivals, Rosh Chodesh, and the Sabbath. Thus, it is natural that these offerings be enumerated in the *Shemoneh Esrei* of *Mussaf.*

The necessity of enumerating the offerings of each day is the focus of a halachic dispute between the *Rishonim* (medieval rabbinic authorities). In detailing the various offerings of each day, we follow the view of *Rabbeinu Tam* (*Rosh Hashanah* 35a). However, if one omitted the description of the offering, or recited the wrong day's offering, and has already

BEND THE KNEES AT בָּרוּךְ, *BLESSED;* BOW AT אַתָּה, *YOU;* STRAIGHTEN UP AT ה', *HASHEM.*

מֶלֶךְ עוֹזֵר וּמוֹשִׁיעַ וּמָגֵן. בָּרוּךְ אַתָּה יהוה,

≪ HASHEM, ⟨ are You, ⟨ Blessed ≪ and Shield. ⟨ Savior, ⟨ Helper, ⟨ O King,

מָגֵן אַבְרָהָם.

≪ of Abraham. ⟨ Shield

GOD'S MIGHT / גבורות

אַתָּה גִּבּוֹר לְעוֹלָם אֲדֹנָי, מְחַיֵּה מֵתִים אַתָּה,

≪ are You; ⟨ of the dead ⟨ the Revivifier ≪ O Lord, ⟨ eternally, ⟨ mighty ⟨ You are

רַב לְהוֹשִׁיעַ, מוֹרִיד הַטָּל. מְכַלְכֵּל חַיִּים בְּחֶסֶד,

≪ with ⟨ the ⟨ Who sustains ≪ the ⟨ Who makes ≪ able to save, ⟨ abun-
kindness, living dew. descend dantly

מְחַיֵּה מֵתִים בְּרַחֲמִים רַבִּים, סוֹמֵךְ נוֹפְלִים,

≪ the fallen, ⟨ Who ≪ abundant, ⟨ with mercy ⟨ the dead ⟨ Who
supports revivifies

וְרוֹפֵא חוֹלִים, וּמַתִּיר אֲסוּרִים, וּמְקַיֵּם אֱמוּנָתוֹ

⟨ His faith ⟨ and Who ≪ the confined, ⟨ Who ≪ the sick, ⟨ Who heals
maintains releases

לִישֵׁנֵי עָפָר. מִי כָמוֹךְ בַּעַל גְּבוּרוֹת, וּמִי דוֹמֶה

⟨ is com- ⟨ and ≪ of mighty ⟨ O Master ⟨ is like ⟨ Who ≪ in the ⟨ to those
parable who deeds, You, dust. asleep

לָךְ, מֶלֶךְ מֵמִית וּמְחַיֵּה וּמַצְמִיחַ יְשׁוּעָה. וְנֶאֱמָן

⟨ And ≪ salvation! ⟨ and makes ⟨ and restores ⟨ Who causes ⟨ O ≪ to
faithful sprout life death King You,

אַתָּה לְהַחֲיוֹת מֵתִים. בָּרוּךְ אַתָּה יהוה,

≪ HASHEM, ⟨ are You, ⟨ Blessed ≪ the dead. ⟨ to revivify ⟨ are You

מְחַיֵּה הַמֵּתִים.

≪ the dead. ⟨ Who revivifies

---

completed the blessing . . . *Who sanctifies Israel and the seasons,* he may complete *Shemoneh Esrei* and is not required to rectify his error (*Mishnah Berurah* 488:13). This accords with *Rashi's* view that it is sufficient merely to recite the general statement, ''נַעֲשֶׂה וְנַקְרִיב . . . בְּתוֹרָתֶךְ,

we will perform and offer before You with love, according to the commandment of Your will, as You have written for us in Your Torah,'' and the offerings need not be enumerated.

The commentary for the first section of *Shemoneh Esrei* may be found on pp. 143-148.

DURING THE *CHAZZAN'S* REPETITION, *KEDUSHAH* IS RECITED HERE.

קְדוּשָׁה / KEDUSHAH

STAND WITH FEET TOGETHER AND AVOID ANY INTERRUPTIONS. RISE ON TOES WHEN SAYING קָדוֹשׁ,
קָדוֹשׁ, קָדוֹשׁ – *HOLY, HOLY, HOLY;* בָּרוּךְ – *BLESSED;* AND יִמְלֹךְ – *HASHEM SHALL REIGN.*

CONGREGATION, THEN *CHAZZAN:*

כֶּתֶר יִתְּנוּ לְךָ יהוה אֱלֹהֵינוּ, מַלְאָכִים הֲמוֹנֵי מַעְלָה,

עִם עַמְּךָ יִשְׂרָאֵל, קְבוּצֵי מַטָּה.

CONGREGATION, THEN *CHAZZAN:*

יַחַד כֻּלָּם קְדֻשָּׁה לְךָ יְשַׁלֵּשׁוּ, כַּדָּבָר הָאָמוּר עַל יַד

נְבִיאֶךָ, וְקָרָא זֶה אֶל זֶה וְאָמַר:

ALL:

קָדוֹשׁ קָדוֹשׁ קָדוֹשׁ יהוה צְבָאוֹת, מְלֹא כָל הָאָרֶץ כְּבוֹדוֹ.[1]

❖ לְעֻמָּתָם מְשַׁבְּחִים וְאוֹמְרִים:

ALL:

בָּרוּךְ כְּבוֹד יהוה, מִמְּקוֹמוֹ.[2] ❖ וּבְדִבְרֵי קָדְשְׁךָ כָּתוּב

לֵאמֹר:

ALL:

יִמְלֹךְ יהוה לְעוֹלָם, אֱלֹהַיִךְ צִיּוֹן לְדֹר וָדֹר, הַלְלוּיָהּ.[3]

(1) *Isaiah* 6:3. (2) *Ezekiel* 3:12. (3) *Psalms* 146:10.

HOLINESS OF GOD'S NAME / קְדוּשַׁת הַשֵּׁם

אַתָּה קָדוֹשׁ וְשִׁמְךָ
‹ and Your ‹ are holy ‹ You
Name

קָדוֹשׁ, וּקְדוֹשִׁים בְּכָל
‹ every ‹ and holy ones ≪ is holy,

יוֹם יְהַלְלוּךָ סֶּלָה, כִּי
‹ for, ≪ forever, ‹ praise You, ‹ day

אֵל מֶלֶךְ גָּדוֹל וְקָדוֹשׁ
‹ and holy ‹ great ‹ a King, ‹ O God,

אָתָּה. בָּרוּךְ אַתָּה
‹ are You, ‹ Blessed ≪ are You.

יהוה, הָאֵל הַקָּדוֹשׁ.
≪ Who is holy. ‹ the God ≪ HASHEM,

IN SOME CONGREGATIONS THE *CHAZZAN*
SUBSTITUTES אַתָּה קָדוֹשׁ FOR לְדוֹר וָדוֹר
IN HIS REPETITION:

לְדוֹר וָדוֹר נַגִּיד גָּדְלָךְ וּלְנֵצַח
‹ and for ≪ Your ‹ we shall ‹ to gen- ‹ From gen-
all greatness relate eration eration

נְצָחִים קְדֻשָּׁתְךָ נַקְדִּישׁ,
≪ shall we sanctify. ‹ Your holiness ‹ eternity

וְשִׁבְחֲךָ אֱלֹהֵינוּ מִפִּינוּ לֹא
‹ shall ‹ from our ≪ our God, ‹ Your praise,
not mouth

יָמוּשׁ לְעוֹלָם וָעֶד, כִּי אֵל מֶלֶךְ
‹ a ‹ O ‹ for, ≪ and ‹ for ever ‹ leave
King, God, ever,

גָּדוֹל וְקָדוֹשׁ אָתָּה. בָּרוּךְ אַתָּה
‹ are You, ‹ Blessed ≪ are You. ‹ and holy ‹ great

יהוה, הָאֵל הַקָּדוֹשׁ.
≪ Who is holy. ‹ the God ≪ HASHEM,

HOLINESS OF THE DAY / קְדוּשַׁת הַיּוֹם

אַתָּה בְחַרְתָּנוּ מִכָּל הָעַמִּים, אָהַבְתָּ אוֹתָנוּ,
‹ us ‹ You loved ≪ the peoples; ‹ from all ‹ have chosen us ‹ You

וְרָצִיתָ בָּנוּ, וְרוֹמַמְתָּנוּ מִכָּל הַלְּשׁוֹנוֹת, וְקִדַּשְׁתָּנוּ
‹ and You ≪ the tongues; ‹ above ‹ You exalted us ≪ in us; ‹ and found
sanctified us all favor

בְּמִצְוֹתֶיךָ, וְקֵרַבְתָּנוּ מַלְכֵּנוּ לַעֲבוֹדָתֶךָ, וְשִׁמְךָ
≪ and Your ≪ to Your service, ‹ our King, ‹ You drew ≪ with Your
Name, us close, commandments.

הַגָּדוֹל וְהַקָּדוֹשׁ עָלֵינוּ קָרָאתָ.
≪ did You proclaim. ‹ upon us ≪ and holy, ‹ great

וַתִּתֶּן לָנוּ יהוה אֱלֹהֵינוּ בְּאַהֲבָה מוֹעֲדִים
‹ appointed Festivals ≪ with love, ‹ our God, ‹ HASHEM, ‹ us, ‹ And You gave

לְשִׂמְחָה, חַגִּים וּזְמַנִּים לְשָׂשׂוֹן, אֶת יוֹם
‹ the day ≪ for joy, ‹ and seasons ‹ Festivals ≪ for gladness,

ON SUCCOS:

חַג הַסֻּכּוֹת הַזֶּה,
‹‹ of this Festival of Succos,

זְמַן שִׂמְחָתֵנוּ
‹‹ of our gladness ‹ the time

ON PESACH:

חַג הַמַּצּוֹת הַזֶּה,
‹‹ of this Festival of Matzos,

זְמַן חֵרוּתֵנוּ
‹‹ of our freedom ‹ the time

מִקְרָא קֹדֶשׁ, זֵכֶר לִיצִיאַת מִצְרָיִם.
‹‹ from Egypt. ‹ of the Exodus ‹ a commemoration ‹ a holy convocation,

וּמִפְּנֵי חֲטָאֵינוּ* גָּלִינוּ מֵאַרְצֵנוּ,* וְנִתְרַחַקְנוּ
‹ and we have been sent far away ‹‹ from our Land,* ‹ we have been exiled ‹ of our sins* ‹ But because

מֵעַל אַדְמָתֵנוּ.* וְאֵין אֲנַחְנוּ יְכוֹלִים לַעֲלוֹת
‹ to ascend, ‹ able ‹ and we are not ‹‹ our soil,* ‹ from upon

וְלֵרָאוֹת וּלְהִשְׁתַּחֲוֹת לְפָנֶיךָ, וְלַעֲשׂוֹת חוֹבוֹתֵינוּ
‹ our obligations ‹ and to perform ‹‹ before You, ‹ and to prostrate ourselves ‹ to appear,

בְּבֵית בְּחִירָתֶךָ, בַּבַּיִת הַגָּדוֹל וְהַקָּדוֹשׁ
‹ and holy, ‹ that is great ‹ in the House ‹‹ You have chosen, ‹ in the House

שֶׁנִּקְרָא שִׁמְךָ עָלָיו, מִפְּנֵי הַיָּד שֶׁנִּשְׁתַּלְּחָה
‹ that was sent forth ‹ of the hand ‹ because ‹‹ upon which Your Name was proclaimed,

בְּמִקְדָּשֶׁךָ. יְהִי רָצוֹן מִלְּפָנֶיךָ, יהוה אֱלֹהֵינוּ
‹ our God ‹ HASHEM, ‹‹ before You, ‹ the will ‹ May it be ‹‹ against Your Sanctuary.

§ **וּמִפְּנֵי חֲטָאֵינוּ** — *But because of our sins*. This is a cardinal principle of Jewish faith. History is not haphazard; Israel's exile and centuries-long distress is a result of its sins. It is axiomatic, therefore, that only repentance can reverse this process.

מֵאַרְצֵנוּ . . . מֵעַל אַדְמָתֵנוּ — *From our Land . . . from upon our soil*. The term אֶרֶץ, *Land*, refers to the entire country from which the nation as a whole was exiled; אֲדָמָה, *soil*, refers to the individual parcels of land. These two conditions involve halachic differences. Some commandments, such as the laws of the Jubilee Year and the laws of Jewish indentured servants, cannot be observed unless the nation as a whole lives in *Eretz Yisrael*. Other commandments, such as those relating to tithes and the use of fruits during a tree's first four years, are observed by Jewish landowners in *Eretz Yisrael* even if the country is under foreign rule. We now say that the exile has deprived all or most of our people of these two categories of commandments. Then, we go on to mention a third category that we are deprived of in exile — the performance of the Temple service.

וֵאלֹהֵי אֲבוֹתֵינוּ, מֶֽלֶךְ רַחֲמָן, שֶׁתָּשׁוּב וּתְרַחֵם
‹ be com- ‹ that You ‹‹ Who is ‹ O King ‹‹ of our ‹ and the God
passionate once again merciful, forefathers,

עָלֵֽינוּ וְעַל מִקְדָּשְׁךָ בְּרַחֲמֶֽיךָ הָרַבִּים, וְתִבְנֵֽהוּ
‹ and rebuild it ‹‹ in Your abundant mercy, ‹ Your Sanctuary ‹ and ‹ toward us
toward

מְהֵרָה וּתְגַדֵּל כְּבוֹדוֹ.* אָבִֽינוּ מַלְכֵּֽנוּ, גַּלֵּה כְּבוֹד
‹ the glory ‹ reveal ‹‹ our King, ‹ Our Father, ‹‹ its glory.* ‹ and increase ‹ soon

מַלְכוּתְךָ עָלֵֽינוּ מְהֵרָה, וְהוֹפַע וְהִנָּשֵׂא עָלֵֽינוּ
‹ over us ‹ and be uplifted ‹ appear ‹‹ speedily; ‹ upon us, ‹ of Your Kingship

לְעֵינֵי כָּל חָי. וְקָרֵב פְּזוּרֵֽינוּ מִבֵּין הַגּוֹיִם,
‹‹ the ‹ from ‹ our scattered ‹ Draw in ‹‹ the ‹ of all ‹ before
nations, among ones living. the eyes

וּנְפוּצוֹתֵֽינוּ כַּנֵּס מִיַּרְכְּתֵי אָֽרֶץ. וַהֲבִיאֵֽנוּ לְצִיּוֹן
‹ to Zion, ‹ Bring us ‹‹ of the ‹ from the ends ‹ gather in ‹ and our
earth. dispersed ones

עִירְךָ בְּרִנָּה, וְלִירוּשָׁלַֽיִם בֵּית מִקְדָּשְׁךָ בְּשִׂמְחַת
‹ with ‹ of Your ‹ the site ‹ and to Jerusalem, ‹‹ in glad ‹ Your City,
gladness Sanctuary, song,

עוֹלָם. וְשָׁם נַעֲשֶׂה לְפָנֶֽיךָ אֶת קָרְבְּנוֹת חוֹבוֹתֵֽינוּ,
‹‹ of our ‹ the offerings ‹ before You ‹ we will ‹ There ‹‹ that is
obligations perform eternal.

תְּמִידִים כְּסִדְרָם, וּמוּסָפִים כְּהִלְכָתָם. וְאֶת מוּסַף
‹ And the ‹‹ according to ‹ and the ‹ according to ‹ — the continual-
additional-offering their laws. additional-offerings their order offerings

---

וְתִבְנֵֽהוּ מְהֵרָה וּתְגַדֵּל כְּבוֹדוֹ — *And rebuild it soon and increase its glory.* Eretz Yisrael and the Temple are more than geographical or architectural concepts. There is a spiritual Presence that complements the material locations on earth. When Israel sinned, the spiritual Presence withdrew because it could not tolerate the proximity of sinners. Consequently, the Jewish people were exiled from the Land that they had contaminated spiritually. Conversely, the return of the Jews to the Land is incomplete unless we can also bring about the return of the Divine holiness to the Land and to the Temple Mount. Thus we now pray that God rebuild the Temple in the sense that He return His Presence to *Eretz Yisrael*, a condition that can come about only when God's sovereignty is accepted by all, and the Jewish people are returned to their Land. Then will come the fulfillment of our longing — that we will merit to serve God in His Temple as He ordained in the Torah (*Sh'lah*)

ON PESACH:

יוֹם חַג הַמַּצּוֹת הַזֶּה,

of this Festival of Matzos, ‹ of the day

ON SUCCOS:

יוֹם חַג הַסֻּכּוֹת הַזֶּה,

of this Festival of Succos, ‹ of the day

נַעֲשֶׂה וְנַקְרִיב לְפָנֶיךָ בְּאַהֲבָה כְּמִצְוַת רְצוֹנֶךָ,

of Your will, ‹ according to the commandment ‹‹ with love, ‹ before You ‹ and offer ‹ we will perform

כְּמוֹ שֶׁכָּתַבְתָּ עָלֵינוּ בְּתוֹרָתֶךָ, עַל יְדֵי מֹשֶׁה

of Moses, ‹ the hand ‹ through ‹ in Your Torah, ‹ for us ‹ You have written ‹ as

עַבְדֶּךָ, מִפִּי כְבוֹדֶךָ כָּאָמוּר:

‹‹ as it is said: ‹ from Your glorious mouth, ‹‹ Your servant,

---

ON CHOL HAMOED PESACH

וְהִקְרַבְתֶּם אִשֶּׁה עֹלָה לַיהוה, פָּרִים בְּנֵי בָקָר

‹ young bulls, ‹‹ to HASHEM: ‹ an elevation-offering ‹ a fire-offering, ‹ You shall offer

שְׁנַיִם, וְאַיִל אֶחָד, וְשִׁבְעָה כְבָשִׂים בְּנֵי שָׁנָה,

‹‹ in their first year; ‹ male lambs ‹ and seven ‹‹ one ram ‹‹ two,

תְּמִימִם יִהְיוּ לָכֶם. וּמִנְחָתָם וְנִסְכֵּיהֶם כְּמְדֻבָּר,¹

‹‹ were as mentioned [in the Torah]: ‹ and their wine-libations ‹ And their meal-offerings ‹‹ for you. ‹ shall they be ‹ unblemished

שְׁלֹשָׁה עֶשְׂרֹנִים לַפָּר, וּשְׁנֵי עֶשְׂרֹנִים לָאַיִל,

‹‹ for each ram, ‹ tenth-ephah ‹ two ‹‹ for each bull, ‹ tenth-ephah ‹ three

וְעִשָּׂרוֹן לַכֶּבֶשׂ, וְיַיִן כְּנִסְכּוֹ. וְשָׂעִיר לְכַפֵּר,

‹‹ for atonement, ‹ a he-goat ‹‹ according to its libation requirement, ‹ and wine ‹‹ for each lamb, ‹ one tenth-ephah

וּשְׁנֵי תְמִידִים כְּהִלְכָתָם.

‹‹ according to their law. ‹ continual offerings ‹ and two

CONTINUE ON PAGE 543.

(1) *Numbers* 28:19.

ON THE FIRST DAY OF CHOL HAMOED SUCCOS

וּבַיּוֹם הַשֵּׁנִי, פָּרִים בְּנֵי בָקָר שְׁנֵים עָשָׂר, אֵילִם

⟨ rams, ⟨⟨ twelve, ⟨ young bulls, ⟨⟨ And on the second day:

שְׁנָיִם, כְּבָשִׂים בְּנֵי שָׁנָה אַרְבָּעָה עָשָׂר, תְּמִימִם.[1]

⟨⟨ unblemished. ⟨⟨ fourteen, ⟨ in their first year, ⟨ male lambs ⟨⟨ two,

וּמִנְחָתָם וְנִסְכֵּיהֶם כַּמְדֻבָּר, שְׁלֹשָׁה עֶשְׂרֹנִים

⟨ tenth-*ephah* ⟨ three ⟨⟨ were as mentioned ⟨ and their wine- ⟨ And their meal-
[in the Torah]: libations offerings

לַפָּר, וּשְׁנֵי עֶשְׂרֹנִים לָאָיִל, וְעִשָּׂרוֹן לַכֶּבֶשׂ, וְיָיִן

⟨ and ⟨⟨ for each ⟨ one tenth- ⟨⟨ for each ⟨ tenth-*ephah* ⟨ two ⟨⟨ for each
wine lamb, *ephah* ram, bull,

כְּנִסְכּוֹ. וְשָׂעִיר לְכַפֵּר, וּשְׁנֵי תְמִידִים כְּהִלְכָתָם.

⟨⟨ according ⟨ continual- ⟨ and two ⟨⟨ for ⟨ a he-goat ⟨⟨ according
to their law. offerings atonement, to its libation
requirement,

וּבַיּוֹם הַשְּׁלִישִׁי, פָּרִים עַשְׁתֵּי עָשָׂר, אֵילִם

⟨ rams, ⟨⟨ eleven, ⟨ bulls, ⟨⟨ And on the third day:

שְׁנָיִם, כְּבָשִׂים בְּנֵי שָׁנָה אַרְבָּעָה עָשָׂר, תְּמִימִם.[2]

⟨⟨ unblemished. ⟨⟨ fourteen, ⟨ in their first year, ⟨ male lambs ⟨⟨ two,

וּמִנְחָתָם וְנִסְכֵּיהֶם כַּמְדֻבָּר, שְׁלֹשָׁה עֶשְׂרֹנִים

⟨ tenth-*ephah* ⟨ three ⟨⟨ were as mentioned ⟨ and their wine- ⟨ And their meal-
[in the Torah]: libations offerings

לַפָּר, וּשְׁנֵי עֶשְׂרֹנִים לָאָיִל, וְעִשָּׂרוֹן לַכֶּבֶשׂ, וְיָיִן

⟨ and ⟨⟨ for each ⟨ one tenth- ⟨⟨ for each ⟨ tenth-*ephah* ⟨ two ⟨⟨ for each
wine lamb, *ephah* ram, bull,

כְּנִסְכּוֹ. וְשָׂעִיר לְכַפֵּר, וּשְׁנֵי תְמִידִים כְּהִלְכָתָם.

⟨⟨ according ⟨ continual ⟨ and two ⟨⟨ for ⟨ a he-goat ⟨⟨ according
to their law. offerings atonement, to its libation
requirement,

CONTINUE ON PAGE 543.

(1) *Numbers* 29:17. (2) 29:20.

ON THE SECOND DAY OF CHOL HAMOED SUCCOS

וּבַיּוֹם הַשְּׁלִישִׁי, פָּרִים עַשְׁתֵּי עָשָׂר, אֵילִם
And on the third day: bulls, eleven, rams,

שְׁנָיִם, כְּבָשִׂים בְּנֵי שָׁנָה אַרְבָּעָה עָשָׂר, תְּמִימִם.[1]
two, male lambs in their first year, fourteen, unblemished.

וּמִנְחָתָם וְנִסְכֵּיהֶם כְּמִדְבָּר, שְׁלֹשָׁה עֶשְׂרֹנִים
And their meal-offerings and their wine-libations were as mentioned [in the Torah]: three tenth-*ephah*

לַפָּר, וּשְׁנֵי עֶשְׂרֹנִים לָאָיִל, וְעִשָּׂרוֹן לַכֶּבֶשׂ, וְיַיִן
for each bull, two tenth-*ephah* for each ram, one tenth-*ephah* for each lamb, and wine

כְּנִסְכּוֹ. וְשָׂעִיר לְכַפֵּר, וּשְׁנֵי תְמִידִים כְּהִלְכָתָם.
according to its libation requirement, a he-goat for atonement, and two continual-offerings according to their law.

וּבַיּוֹם הָרְבִיעִי פָּרִים עֲשָׂרָה, אֵילִם שְׁנָיִם,
And on the fourth day: bulls, ten, rams, two,

כְּבָשִׂים בְּנֵי שָׁנָה אַרְבָּעָה עָשָׂר, תְּמִימִם.[2]
male lambs in their first year, fourteen, unblemished.

וּמִנְחָתָם וְנִסְכֵּיהֶם כְּמִדְבָּר, שְׁלֹשָׁה עֶשְׂרֹנִים
And their meal-offerings and their wine-libations were as mentioned [in the Torah]: three tenth-*ephah*

לַפָּר, וּשְׁנֵי עֶשְׂרֹנִים לָאָיִל, וְעִשָּׂרוֹן לַכֶּבֶשׂ, וְיַיִן
for each bull, two tenth-*ephah* for each ram, one tenth-*ephah* for each lamb, and wine

כְּנִסְכּוֹ. וְשָׂעִיר לְכַפֵּר, וּשְׁנֵי תְמִידִים כְּהִלְכָתָם.
according to its libation requirement, a he-goat for atonement, and two continual-offerings according to their law.

CONTINUE ON PAGE 543.

(1) *Numbers* 29:20. (2) 29:23.

ON THE THIRD DAY OF CHOL HAMOED SUCCOS

וּבַיּוֹם הָרְבִיעִי פָּרִים עֲשָׂרָה, אֵילִם שְׁנַיִם,
«< two, ‹ rams, «< ten, ‹ bulls, «< And on the fourth day:

כְּבָשִׂים בְּנֵי שָׁנָה אַרְבָּעָה עָשָׂר, תְּמִימִם.¹
«< unblemished. «< fourteen, ‹ in their first year, ‹ male lambs

וּמִנְחָתָם וְנִסְכֵּיהֶם כִּמְדֻבָּר, שְׁלֹשָׁה עֶשְׂרֹנִים
‹ tenth-ephah ‹ three «< were as mentioned ‹ and their wine- ‹ And their meal-
[in the Torah]: libations offerings

לַפָּר, וּשְׁנֵי עֶשְׂרֹנִים לָאָיִל, וְעִשָּׂרוֹן לַכֶּבֶשׂ, וְיָיִן
‹ and «< for each ‹ one tenth- «< for each ‹ tenth-ephah ‹ two «< for each
wine lamb, ephah ram, bull,

כְּנִסְכּוֹ. וְשָׂעִיר לְכַפֵּר, וּשְׁנֵי תְמִידִים כְּהִלְכָתָם.
«< according ‹ continual- ‹ and two «< for ‹ a he-goat «< according
to their law. offerings atonement, to its libation
requirement,

וּבַיּוֹם הַחֲמִישִׁי, פָּרִים תִּשְׁעָה, אֵילִם שְׁנַיִם,
«< two, ‹ rams, «< nine, ‹ bulls, «< And on the fifth day:

כְּבָשִׂים בְּנֵי שָׁנָה אַרְבָּעָה עָשָׂר, תְּמִימִם.²
«< unblemished. «< fourteen, ‹ in their first year, ‹ male lambs

וּמִנְחָתָם וְנִסְכֵּיהֶם כִּמְדֻבָּר, שְׁלֹשָׁה עֶשְׂרֹנִים
‹ tenth-ephah ‹ three «< were as mentioned ‹ and their wine- ‹ And their meal-
[in the Torah]: libations offerings

לַפָּר, וּשְׁנֵי עֶשְׂרֹנִים לָאָיִל, וְעִשָּׂרוֹן לַכֶּבֶשׂ, וְיָיִן
‹ and «< for each ‹ one tenth- «< for each ‹ tenth-ephah ‹ two «< for each
wine lamb, ephah ram, bull,

כְּנִסְכּוֹ. וְשָׂעִיר לְכַפֵּר, וּשְׁנֵי תְמִידִים כְּהִלְכָתָם.
«< according ‹ continual- ‹ and two «< for ‹ a he-goat «< according
to their law. offerings atonement, to its libation
requirement,

CONTINUE ON PAGE 543.

(1) *Numbers* 29:23. (2) 29:26.

ON THE FOURTH DAY OF CHOL HAMOED SUCCOS

וּבַיּוֹם הַחֲמִישִׁי פָּרִים תִּשְׁעָה, אֵילִם שְׁנָיִם,

And on the fifth day: ›› bulls, ‹ nine, ›› rams, ‹ two, ››

כְּבָשִׂים בְּנֵי שָׁנָה אַרְבָּעָה עָשָׂר, תְּמִימִם.[1]

male lambs ‹ in their first year, ‹ fourteen, ›› unblemished. ‹‹

וּמִנְחָתָם וְנִסְכֵּיהֶם כַּמְדֻבָּר, שְׁלֹשָׁה עֶשְׂרֹנִים

And their meal- ‹ and their wine- ‹ were as mentioned ›› three ‹ tenth-*ephah* ‹
offerings libations [in the Torah]:

לַפָּר, וּשְׁנֵי עֶשְׂרֹנִים לָאָיִל, וְעִשָּׂרוֹן לַכֶּבֶשׂ, וְיַיִן

for each ›› tenth-*ephah* ‹ for each ›› one tenth- ‹ for each ›› and ‹
bull, ram, *ephah* lamb, wine

כְּנִסְכּוֹ. וְשָׂעִיר לְכַפֵּר, וּשְׁנֵי תְמִידִים כְּהִלְכָתָם.

according ›› a he-goat ‹ for ›› and two ‹ continual- ‹ according ››
to its libation atonement, offerings to their law.
requirement,

וּבַיּוֹם הַשִּׁשִּׁי, פָּרִים שְׁמֹנָה, אֵילִם שְׁנָיִם,

And on the sixth day: ›› bulls, ‹ eight, ›› rams, ‹ two, ››

כְּבָשִׂים בְּנֵי שָׁנָה אַרְבָּעָה עָשָׂר, תְּמִימִם.[2]

male lambs ‹ in their first year, ‹ fourteen, ›› unblemished. ‹‹

וּמִנְחָתָם וְנִסְכֵּיהֶם כַּמְדֻבָּר, שְׁלֹשָׁה עֶשְׂרֹנִים

And their meal- ‹ and their wine- ‹ were as mentioned ›› three ‹ tenth-*ephah* ‹
offerings libations [in the Torah]:

לַפָּר, וּשְׁנֵי עֶשְׂרֹנִים לָאָיִל, וְעִשָּׂרוֹן לַכֶּבֶשׂ, וְיַיִן

for each ›› tenth-*ephah* ‹ for each ›› one tenth- ‹ for each ›› and ‹
bull, ram, *ephah* lamb, wine

כְּנִסְכּוֹ. וְשָׂעִיר לְכַפֵּר, וּשְׁנֵי תְמִידִים כְּהִלְכָתָם.

according ›› a he-goat ‹ for ›› and two ‹ continual- ‹ according ››
to its libation atonement, offerings to their law.
requirement,

CONTINUE ON PAGE 543.

---

(1) *Numbers* 29:26. (2) 29:29.

ON ALL DAYS CONTINUE HERE:

אֱלֹהֵינוּ* וֵאלֹהֵי אֲבוֹתֵינוּ, מֶלֶךְ רַחֲמָן רַחֵם

< have < Who is < O King < of our < and < Our God*
mercy merciful,   forefathers, the God

עָלֵינוּ, טוֹב וּמֵטִיב* הִדָּרֶשׁ לָנוּ. שׁוּבָה אֵלֵינוּ

< to us < Return << by us. < let Yourself < and beneficent < O << on us;
be sought out One,* good

בַּהֲמוֹן רַחֲמֶיךָ,¹ בִּגְלַל אָבוֹת שֶׁעָשׂוּ רְצוֹנֶךָ. בְּנֵה

< Rebuild << Your will. < who did < of the < for the << of Your mercy, < in the
forefathers sake yearning

בֵיתְךָ כְּבַתְּחִלָּה, וְכוֹנֵן מִקְדָּשְׁךָ עַל מְכוֹנוֹ,

<< its prepared < on < Your Sanctuary < and << as it was at first, < Your
site; establish House

וְהַרְאֵנוּ בְּבִנְיָנוֹ, וְשַׂמְּחֵנוּ בְּתִקּוּנוֹ. וְהָשֵׁב כֹּהֲנִים

< the < Restore << in its < and gladden us < its rebuilding < show us
Kohanim restoration.

לַעֲבוֹדָתָם, וּלְוִיִּם לְשִׁירָם וּלְזִמְרָם, וְהָשֵׁב

< and << and their music; < to their song < and the << to their service
restore Levites

יִשְׂרָאֵל לִנְוֵיהֶם. וְשָׁם נַעֲלֶה וְנֵרָאֶה* וְנִשְׁתַּחֲוֶה

< and prostrate < and appear* < we will < And << to their < Israel
ourselves ascend there dwellings.

לְפָנֶיךָ, בְּשָׁלֹשׁ פַּעֲמֵי רְגָלֵינוּ, כַּכָּתוּב בְּתוֹרָתֶךָ:

<< in Your Torah: < as it is << of our < occasions < on the << before
written pilgrimage, three You,

---

(1) Cf. *Isaiah* 63:15.

אֱלֹהֵינוּ . . . טוֹב וּמֵטִיב §— *Our God . . . O good and beneficent One.* With regard to human beings, someone may be good, but not have the resources to benefit others. On the other hand, someone may benefit others by helping them do good deeds, but for himself he may prefer to indulge his sinful nature. God, however, is perfect — He is both good and beneficent (*Iyun Tefillah*).

וְשָׁם נַעֲלֶה וְנֵרָאֶה — *And there we will ascend and appear.* Having been returned to *Eretz Yisrael*, we will be able to fulfill the commandment of going up to the Temple to appear before God.

שָׁלוֹשׁ פְּעָמִים בַּשָּׁנָה, יֵרָאֶה כָל זְכוּרְךָ אֶת פְּנֵי

< before the « your < all « shall there < a year < times < Three
Presence males appear

יהוה אֱלֹהֶיךָ, בַּמָּקוֹם אֲשֶׁר יִבְחָר, בְּחַג הַמַּצּוֹת,

« of Matzos, < on the « He will < that < in the place < your God, < of
Festival choose; HASHEM,

וּבְחַג הַשָּׁבֻעוֹת, וּבְחַג הַסֻּכּוֹת, וְלֹא יֵרָאֶה

< and they shall « of Succos; < and on « of Shavuos, < on the
not appear the Festival Festival

אֶת פְּנֵי יהוה רֵיקָם.* אִישׁ כְּמַתְּנַת יָדוֹ, כְּבִרְכַּת

< according to « of his < according < Every « empty < of HASHEM < before the
the blessing hand, to the gift man handed.* Presence

יהוה אֱלֹהֶיךָ, אֲשֶׁר נָתַן לָךְ.¹

« you. < He gave < that < your God, < of HASHEM,

וְהַשִּׂיאֵנוּ* יהוה אֱלֹהֵינוּ אֶת בִּרְכַּת מוֹעֲדֶיךָ

< of Your < the blessing < our God, < HASHEM, < Bestow upon us,*
appointed
Festivals

לְחַיִּים וּלְשָׁלוֹם, לְשִׂמְחָה וּלְשָׂשׂוֹן, כַּאֲשֶׁר

< as « and for joy, < for gladness « and for peace, < for life

רָצִיתָ* וְאָמַרְתָּ לְבָרְכֵנוּ. קַדְּשֵׁנוּ בְּמִצְוֹתֶיךָ

< with Your < Sanctify us « to bless us. < and promised < You
commandments desired*

וְתֵן חֶלְקֵנוּ בְּתוֹרָתֶךָ, שַׂבְּעֵנוּ מִטּוּבֶךָ וְשַׂמַּח

< and < from Your < satisfy us « be in Your < our < and grant
gladden goodness Torah; portion that

---

(1) Deuteronomy 16:16-17.

רֵיקָם — *Empty handed*. During the pilgrimages, each Jew must offer elevation-offerings and peace-offerings in honor of the Festivals. However, though one may not come empty handed — without offerings — he should give only as much as he can afford, but not more, *according to the gift of his hand*, depending on

the extent of God's blessing (*Rashi*).

וְהַשִּׂיאֵנוּ — *Bestow upon us*. In concluding the central portion of the *Shemoneh Esrei*, we ask God to give all the joyous blessings of the day and season.

כַּאֲשֶׁר רָצִיתָ — *As You desired*. God wishes to bless and help His people; it remains for us to be

נַפְשֵׁנוּ בִּישׁוּעָתֶךָ, וְטַהֵר לִבֵּנוּ לְעָבְדְּךָ בֶּאֱמֶת.

》 sincerely. 〈 to serve You 〈 our heart 〈 and purify 〈 with Your salvation, 〈 our souls

וְהַנְחִילֵנוּ יהוה אֱלֹהֵינוּ בְּשִׂמְחָה וּבְשָׂשׂוֹן מוֹעֲדֵי

〈 the appoin- 》 and with 〈 — with 》 our God 〈 HASHEM, 》 And give us
ted Festivals joy — gladness as a heritage,

קָדְשֶׁךָ, וְיִשְׂמְחוּ בְךָ יִשְׂרָאֵל מְקַדְּשֵׁי שְׁמֶךָ.

》 of Your 〈 the sanctifiers 〈 — Israel 》 in You 〈 and may 》 of Your
Name. they rejoice holiness,

בָּרוּךְ אַתָּה יהוה, מְקַדֵּשׁ יִשְׂרָאֵל וְהַזְּמַנִּים.*

》 and the [festive] 〈 Israel 〈 Who 》 HASHEM, 〈 are You, 〈 Blessed
seasons.* sanctifies

TEMPLE SERVICE / עבודה

רְצֵה יהוה אֱלֹהֵינוּ בְּעַמְּךָ יִשְׂרָאֵל, וְלִתְפִלָּתָם

〈 and toward 〈 Israel, 〈 toward 》 our God, 〈 HASHEM, 》 Be
their prayer Your people favorable,

שְׁעֵה, וְהָשֵׁב אֶת הָעֲבוֹדָה לִדְבִיר בֵּיתֶךָ. וְאִשֵּׁי

〈 The fire- 》 of Your 〈 to the Holy 〈 the service 〈 and restore 》 turn,
offerings Temple. of Holies

יִשְׂרָאֵל וּתְפִלָּתָם מְהֵרָה בְּאַהֲבָה תְקַבֵּל בְּרָצוֹן,

》 favorably, 〈 accept 〈 with love 〈 speedily, 〈 and their 〈 of Israel
prayer,

וּתְהִי לְרָצוֹן תָּמִיד עֲבוֹדַת יִשְׂרָאֵל עַמֶּךָ.

》 Your 〈 of Israel 〈 the service 〈 always 〈 to Your 〈 and may
people. favor it be

וְתֶחֱזֶינָה עֵינֵינוּ בְּשׁוּבְךָ לְצִיּוֹן בְּרַחֲמִים.

》 in compassion. 〈 to Zion 〈 Your return 〈 may our eyes 〈 Witness

worthy of His blessings.

מְקַדֵּשׁ יִשְׂרָאֵל וְהַזְּמַנִּים — *Who sanctifies Israel and the [festive] seasons.* The use of the word זְמַנִּים, *[festive] seasons,* rather than the Scriptural term מוֹעֲדִים, *appointed Festivals,* alludes

to a special feature of the Jewish calendar. The Torah ordains that Pesach must fall in the springtime, thus the court must take the זְמַנִּים, *seasons,* into account in formulating the calendar (R' Bachya).

בָּרוּךְ אַתָּה יהוה, הַמַּחֲזִיר שְׁכִינָתוֹ לְצִיּוֹן.

Blessed ‹ are You, ‹ Hashem, ‹‹ Who restores ‹ His Presence ‹ to Zion. ‹‹

THANKSGIVING [MODIM] / הודאה

BOW AT מוֹדִים, WE THANK; STRAIGHTEN UP AT ה', HASHEM. IN HIS REPETITION THE CHAZZAN RECITES THE ENTIRE מוֹדִים ALOUD, WHILE THE CONGREGATION RECITES מוֹדִים דְּרַבָּנָן (P. 547) SOFTLY.

מוֹדִים אֲנַחְנוּ לָךְ, שָׁאַתָּה הוּא יהוה

We thank ‹ You, ‹‹ for it is You ‹ Who are ‹ Hashem, ‹

אֱלֹהֵינוּ וֵאלֹהֵי אֲבוֹתֵינוּ לְעוֹלָם וָעֶד. צוּרֵנוּ,

our God ‹ and the God ‹ of our forefathers, ‹ for ever ‹ and ever; ‹‹ our Rock, ‹

צוּר חַיֵּינוּ, מָגֵן יִשְׁעֵנוּ אַתָּה הוּא לְדוֹר

the Rock ‹ of our lives, ‹‹ Shield ‹‹ of our salvation, ‹ [is what] You ‹‹ are ‹ from generation ‹

וָדוֹר. נוֹדֶה לְךָ וּנְסַפֵּר תְּהִלָּתֶךָ[1] עַל חַיֵּינוּ

to generation. ‹‹ We shall thank ‹ You ‹ and relate ‹ Your praise, ‹‹ for ‹ our lives ‹

הַמְּסוּרִים בְּיָדֶךָ, וְעַל נִשְׁמוֹתֵינוּ הַפְּקוּדוֹת

that are committed ‹ into Your hands, ‹‹ and for ‹ our souls ‹ that are entrusted ‹

לָךְ, וְעַל נִסֶּיךָ שֶׁבְּכָל יוֹם עִמָּנוּ, וְעַל

to You; ‹‹ and for ‹ Your miracles ‹ that every ‹ day ‹‹ are with us; ‹‹ and for ‹

נִפְלְאוֹתֶיךָ וְטוֹבוֹתֶיךָ שֶׁבְּכָל עֵת, עֶרֶב וָבֹקֶר

Your wonders ‹ and favors ‹ that are at all ‹‹ times ‹ that are at all ‹ —evening, ‹ morning, ‹

וְצָהֳרָיִם. הַטּוֹב כִּי לֹא כָלוּ רַחֲמֶיךָ, וְהַמְרַחֵם

and afternoon. ‹‹ The Beneficent One, ‹ for ‹ never ‹ exhausted ‹ are Your compassions, ‹‹ and the Compassionate One,

כִּי לֹא תַמּוּ חֲסָדֶיךָ,[2] כִּי מֵעוֹלָם קִוִּינוּ לָךְ.

for ‹ never ‹ ended ‹ are Your kindnesses ‹‹ — for ‹ always ‹ have we put our hope ‹ in You. ‹‹

(1) Cf. *Psalms* 79:13. (2) Cf. *Lamentations* 3:22.

מודים דרבנן / MODIM OF THE RABBIS

מוֹדִים אֲנַחְנוּ לָךְ, שָׁאַתָּה הוּא יהוה אֱלֹהֵינוּ וֵאלֹהֵי
‹ and the ‹ our God ‹ Hashem, ‹ Who ‹ for it is ‹‹ You, ‹ We thank
God are You

אֲבוֹתֵינוּ, אֱלֹהֵי כָל בָּשָׂר, יוֹצְרֵנוּ, יוֹצֵר בְּרֵאשִׁית. בְּרָכוֹת
‹ Blessings ‹‹ of the ‹ the ‹ our ‹‹ flesh, ‹ of all ‹ the God ‹‹ of our
universe. Molder Molder, forefathers,

וְהוֹדָאוֹת לְשִׁמְךָ הַגָּדוֹל וְהַקָּדוֹשׁ, עַל שֶׁהֶחֱיִיתָנוּ וְקִיַּמְתָּנוּ.
‹‹ and You have ‹ You have ‹ for ‹‹ and that ‹ that is ‹ [are due] to ‹ and thanks
sustained us. given us life is holy, great Your Name

כֵּן תְּחַיֵּנוּ וּתְקַיְּמֵנוּ, וְתֶאֱסוֹף גָּלֻיּוֹתֵינוּ לְחַצְרוֹת קָדְשֶׁךָ,
‹‹ of Your ‹ to the ‹ our exiles ‹ and gather ‹‹ and ‹ may You continue ‹ So
Sanctuary, Courtyards sustain us, to give us life

לִשְׁמוֹר חֻקֶּיךָ וְלַעֲשׂוֹת רְצוֹנֶךָ, וּלְעָבְדְּךָ בְּלֵבָב שָׁלֵם,
‹‹ wholeheartedly. ‹ and to ‹‹ Your will, ‹ to do ‹‹ Your ‹ to observe
serve You decrees,

עַל שֶׁאֲנַחְנוּ מוֹדִים לָךְ. בָּרוּךְ אֵל הַהוֹדָאוֹת.
‹‹ of thanksgivings. ‹ is the ‹ Blessed ‹‹ You. ‹ to thank ‹‹ [inspiring] ‹ [We thank
God us You] for

וְעַל כֻּלָּם יִתְבָּרַךְ וְיִתְרוֹמַם וְיִתְנַשֵּׂא שִׁמְךָ
‹ may Your ‹ and upraised ‹ and exalted, ‹ blessed, ‹ all these, ‹ For
Name be,

מַלְכֵּנוּ תָּמִיד לְעוֹלָם וָעֶד.
‹‹ and ever. ‹ for ever ‹ continually, ‹‹ our King,

BEND THE KNEES AT בָּרוּךְ, BLESSED; BOW AT אַתָּה, YOU; STRAIGHTEN UP AT ה', HASHEM.

וְכֹל הַחַיִּים יוֹדוּךָ סֶּלָה, וִיהַלְלוּ וִיבָרְכוּ
‹ and bless ‹ — and praise ‹‹ forever! ‹ will gratefully ‹ alive ‹ Everything
acknowledge You,

אֶת שִׁמְךָ הַגָּדוֹל, בֶּאֱמֶת לְעוֹלָם, כִּי טוֹב. הָאֵל
‹ O God ‹‹ it is good. ‹ for ‹ forever, ‹ sincerely, ‹‹ that is great, ‹ Your Name

יְשׁוּעָתֵנוּ וְעֶזְרָתֵנוּ סֶלָה, הָאֵל הַטּוֹב. בָּרוּךְ
‹ Blessed ‹‹ Who is beneficent. ‹ the God ‹‹ forever, ‹ and of our help, ‹ of our salvation

אַתָּה יהוה, הַטּוֹב שִׁמְךָ וּלְךָ נָאֶה לְהוֹדוֹת.
‹‹ to give ‹ it is ‹ and ‹ is Your ‹ The ‹‹ Hashem, ‹ are You,
thanks. fitting to You Name, Beneficent One

THE *CHAZZAN* RECITES בִּרְכַּת כֹּהֲנִים DURING HIS REPETITION EXCEPT IN A HOUSE OF MOURNING.
THE *CHAZZAN* FACES RIGHT AT וְיִשְׁמְרֶךָ; FACES LEFT AT אֵלֶיךָ וִיחֻנֶּךָּ; FACES THE ARK FOR THE
REST OF THE BLESSINGS.

אֱלֹהֵינוּ וֵאלֹהֵי אֲבוֹתֵינוּ, בָּרְכֵנוּ בַבְּרָכָה הַמְשֻׁלֶּשֶׁת, בַּתּוֹרָה
⟨ [that is] in ≪ of three ⟨ with the ⟨ bless us ≪ of our ⟨ and ⟨ Our God
the Torah   verses   blessing   forefathers, the God

הַכְּתוּבָה עַל יְדֵי מֹשֶׁה עַבְדֶּךָ, הָאֲמוּרָה מִפִּי אַהֲרֹן וּבָנָיו,
⟨ and his ⟨ of ⟨ from the ⟨ that was ≪ Your ⟨ of ⟨ the ⟨ by ⟨ that was
sons,   Aaron mouth   said   servant, Moses, hand   written

כֹּהֲנִים עַם קְדוֹשֶׁךָ, כָּאָמוּר:
≪ as it is said: ⟨ Your holy ⟨ the
               people,   Kohanim,

יְבָרֶכְךָ יהוה, וְיִשְׁמְרֶךָ.   (.כֵּן יְהִי רָצוֹן – Cong.)
≪ and safeguard you. ⟨ May HASHEM bless you   ≪ His will. ⟨ be ⟨ May so

יָאֵר יהוה פָּנָיו אֵלֶיךָ וִיחֻנֶּךָּ.   (.כֵּן יְהִי רָצוֹן – Cong.)
≪ and be ⟨ for you ⟨ His ⟨ May HASHEM   ≪ His will. ⟨ be ⟨ May so
gracious to you.   countenance illuminate

יִשָּׂא יהוה פָּנָיו אֵלֶיךָ וְיָשֵׂם לְךָ שָׁלוֹם.[1] (.כֵּן יְהִי רָצוֹן – Cong.)
≪ peace. ⟨ for ⟨ and ⟨ to you ⟨ His ⟨ May HASHEM   ≪ His will. ⟨ be ⟨ May so
you establish   countenance turn

SOME CONGREGATIONS RECITE THE FOLLOWING WHILE THE *CHAZZAN* RECITES שִׂים שָׁלוֹם:

אַדִּיר בַּמָּרוֹם, שׁוֹכֵן בִּגְבוּרָה, אַתָּה שָׁלוֹם וְשִׁמְךָ שָׁלוֹם.[2]
≪ is Peace! ⟨ and Your ⟨ are ⟨ You ≪ in power! ⟨ Who ⟨ on high, ⟨ Mighty One
              Name   peace   dwells

יְהִי רָצוֹן שֶׁתָּשִׂים עָלֵינוּ וְעַל כָּל עַמְּךָ בֵּית יִשְׂרָאֵל חַיִּים
⟨ life ≪ of Israel, ⟨ the ⟨ of Your ⟨ all ⟨ and ⟨ upon us ⟨ that You ⟨ [Your] will ⟨ May
              House people,   upon   place   it be

וּבְרָכָה לְמִשְׁמֶרֶת שָׁלוֹם.
≪ of peace. ⟨ for a safeguard ⟨ and blessing

PEACE / שָׁלוֹם

שִׂים שָׁלוֹם, טוֹבָה, וּבְרָכָה, חַיִּים, חֵן,
⟨ graciousness, ⟨ life, ⟨ blessing, ⟨ goodness, ⟨ peace, ⟨ Establish

וָחֶסֶד וְרַחֲמִים עָלֵינוּ וְעַל כָּל יִשְׂרָאֵל עַמֶּךָ.
≪ Your ⟨ of Israel ⟨ all ⟨ and ⟨ upon us ⟨ and ⟨ kindness,
people.   upon   compassion

---

(1) *Numbers* 6:24-26. (2) Cf. *Judges* 6:24 and *Shabbos* 10b.

בָּרְכֵנוּ אָבִינוּ, כֻּלָּנוּ כְּאֶחָד, בְּאוֹר פָּנֶיךָ, כִּי בְאוֹר
⟨ with the ⟨ for ⟪ of Your ⟨ with the ⟪ as one, ⟨ all of us ⟪ our ⟨ Bless us,
light   countenance, light   Father,

פָּנֶיךָ נָתַתָּ לָּנוּ, יהוה אֱלֹהֵינוּ, תּוֹרַת חַיִּים
⟨ of life ⟨ the Torah ⟪ our God, ⟨ Hashem, ⟨ us, ⟨ You ⟨ of Your
                                              gave countenance

וְאַהֲבַת חֶסֶד, וּצְדָקָה, וּבְרָכָה, וְרַחֲמִים, וְחַיִּים,
⟨ life, ⟨ compassion, ⟨ blessing, ⟨ righteousness, ⟨ of kindness, ⟨ and a love

וְשָׁלוֹם. וְטוֹב יִהְיֶה בְּעֵינֶיךָ לְבָרְכֵנוּ וּלְבָרֵךְ
⟨ and to bless ⟨ to bless us ⟨ in Your eyes ⟨ may it be ⟨ And good ⟪ and peace.

אֶת כָּל עַמְּךָ יִשְׂרָאֵל בְּכָל עֵת וּבְכָל שָׁעָה
⟨ hour ⟨ and at every ⟨ time ⟨ at every ⟨ Israel ⟨ of Your people ⟨ all

בִּשְׁלוֹמֶךָ, (בְּרוֹב עוֹז וְשָׁלוֹם). בָּרוּךְ אַתָּה
⟨ are You, ⟨ Blessed ⟪ and peace). ⟨ strength ⟨ (with abundant ⟪ with Your peace,

יהוה, הַמְּבָרֵךְ אֶת עַמּוֹ יִשְׂרָאֵל בַּשָּׁלוֹם.
⟪ with peace. ⟨ Israel ⟨ His people ⟨ Who blesses ⟪ Hashem,

**ALTHOUGH THE *CHAZZAN'S* REPETITION ENDS HERE, HE SHOULD ADD
THE NEXT VERSE IN AN UNDERTONE. INDIVIDUALS CONTINUE:**

יִהְיוּ לְרָצוֹן אִמְרֵי פִי וְהֶגְיוֹן לִבִּי לְפָנֶיךָ, יהוה צוּרִי וְגֹאֲלִי.[1]
⟪ and my ⟨ my ⟨ Hashem, ⟪ before ⟪ of my ⟨ and the ⟨ of my ⟨ — the ⟪ find ⟨ May
Redeemer. Rock   You,   heart — thoughts mouth expressions favor they

אֱלֹהַי, נְצוֹר לְשׁוֹנִי מֵרָע, וּשְׂפָתַי מִדַּבֵּר
⟨ from ⟨ and my lips ⟪ from evil ⟨ my tongue ⟨ guard ⟨ My God,
speaking

מִרְמָה, וְלִמְקַלְלַי נַפְשִׁי תִדּוֹם, וְנַפְשִׁי כֶּעָפָר[2]
⟨ like dust ⟨ and let ⟪ be silent; ⟨ let my ⟨ To those who ⟪ deceitfully.
            my soul   soul   curse me,

לַכֹּל תִּהְיֶה. פְּתַח לִבִּי בְּתוֹרָתֶךָ, וְאַחֲרֵי
⟨ so that to ⟪ to Your Torah, ⟨ my heart ⟨ Open ⟪ be. ⟨ to
follow   everyone

---

(1) *Psalms* 19:15. (2) Cf. 34:14.

מִצְוֹתֶיךָ תִּרְדּוֹף נַפְשִׁי. וְכָל הַקָּמִים וְהַחוֹשְׁבִים

‹ and who plot ‹ who rise up ‹ As for all ≪ shall my soul pursue. ‹ Your commandments

עָלַי לְרָעָה, מְהֵרָה הָפֵר עֲצָתָם וְקַלְקֵל

‹ and disrupt ≪ their counsel, ‹ nullify ‹ speedily ≪ to do evil, ‹ against me

מַחֲשַׁבְתָּם. [1] יְהִי רָצוֹן מִלְּפָנֶיךָ, יהוה אֱלֹהַי

‹ my God ‹ HASHEM, ≪ before You, ‹ the will ‹ May it be ≪ their scheme.

וֵאלֹהֵי אֲבוֹתַי, שֶׁלֹּא תַעֲלֶה קִנְאַת אָדָם עָלַי,

≪ against ‹ of any ‹ the ‹ be aroused ‹ that there ≪ of my ‹ and the God
me, man jealousy not forefathers,

וְלֹא קִנְאָתִי עַל אֲחֵרִים, וְשֶׁלֹּא אֶכְעַס הַיּוֹם,

‹ today, ‹ become angry ‹ and that I not ≪ others; ‹ against ‹ my jealousy ‹ nor

וְשֶׁלֹּא אַכְעִיסֶךָ, וְתַצִּילֵנִי מִיֵּצֶר הָרָע, וְתֶן בְּלִבִּי

‹ in my ‹ and ‹ for Evil, ‹ from the ‹ Rescue me ≪ anger You. ‹ and that
heart place Inclination I not

הַכְנָעָה וַעֲנָוָה. מַלְכֵּנוּ וֵאלֹהֵינוּ, יַחֵד שִׁמְךָ

‹ Your Name ‹ unify ≪ and our God, ‹ O our King ≪ and humility. ‹ submissiveness

בְּעוֹלָמֶךָ, בְּנֵה עִירְךָ, יַסֵּד בֵּיתֶךָ, וְשַׁכְלֵל הֵיכָלֶךָ,

≪ Your ‹ perfect ≪ of Your ‹ lay the ≪ Your ‹ rebuild ≪ in Your world;
Sanctuary; House, foundation City,

וְקַבֵּץ קִבּוּץ גָּלֻיּוֹת, וּפְדֵה צֹאנֶךָ, וְשַׂמֵּחַ עֲדָתֶךָ.

≪ Your ‹ and gladden ≪ Your ‹ redeem ≪ of the ‹ the ‹ gather
congregation. sheep, exiles, ingathering

עֲשֵׂה לְמַעַן שְׁמֶךָ, עֲשֵׂה לְמַעַן יְמִינֶךָ,

≪ of Your ‹ for the sake ‹ act ≪ of Your Name; ‹ for the sake ‹ Act
right hand;

עֲשֵׂה לְמַעַן תּוֹרָתֶךָ, עֲשֵׂה לְמַעַן קְדֻשָּׁתֶךָ.

≪ of Your sanctity. ‹ for the sake ‹ act ≪ of Your Torah; ‹ for the sake ‹ act

לְמַעַן יֵחָלְצוּן יְדִידֶיךָ, הוֹשִׁיעָה יְמִינְךָ וַעֲנֵנִי. [2]

≪ and answer ‹ with Your ‹ — save ≪ Your ‹ released ‹ In order
me. right hand, beloved ones may be that

---

(1) See *Berachos* 17a. (2) *Psalms* 60:7; 108:7.

SOME RECITE VERSES PERTAINING TO THEIR NAMES HERE. SEE PAGE 764.

יִהְיוּ לְרָצוֹן אִמְרֵי פִי וְהֶגְיוֹן לִבִּי לְפָנֶיךָ,

《 before 〈 of my 〈 and the 〈 of my 〈 — the 《 find favor 〈 May they
You, heart — thoughts mouth expressions

יהוה צוּרִי וְגֹאֲלִי.¹

《 and my Redeemer. 〈 my Rock 〈 HASHEM,

BOW. TAKE THREE STEPS BACK. BOW LEFT AND SAY . . . עֹשֶׂה, "HE WHO MAKES . . ."; BOW RIGHT AND
SAY . . . הוּא, "MAY HE . . ."; BOW FORWARD AND SAY . . . וְעַל כָּל יִשְׂרָאֵל, "AND UPON ALL ISRAEL . . . "

עֹשֶׂה שָׁלוֹם בִּמְרוֹמָיו,² הוּא יַעֲשֶׂה שָׁלוֹם

〈 peace 〈 make 〈 may He 《 in His heights, 〈 peace 〈 He Who makes

עָלֵינוּ, וְעַל כָּל יִשְׂרָאֵל. וְאִמְרוּ: אָמֵן.³

《 Amen. 〈 Now respond: 《 Israel. 〈 all 〈 and upon 《 upon us,

יְהִי רָצוֹן מִלְּפָנֶיךָ, יהוה אֱלֹהֵינוּ וֵאלֹהֵי

〈 and the God 〈 our God 〈 HASHEM, 《 before You, 〈 the will 〈 May it be

אֲבוֹתֵינוּ, שֶׁיִּבָּנֶה בֵּית הַמִּקְדָּשׁ בִּמְהֵרָה בְיָמֵינוּ, וְתֵן

〈 Grant 《 in 〈 speedily 〈 shall the 〈 that rebuilt 《 of our
that our days. Holy Temple be, forefathers,

חֶלְקֵנוּ בְּתוֹרָתֶךָ.⁴ וְשָׁם נַעֲבָדְךָ בְּיִרְאָה, כִּימֵי עוֹלָם

〈 of old 〈 as in 《 with 〈 we may 〈 so that 《 be in Your 〈 our portion
days reverence, serve You there Torah,

וּכְשָׁנִים קַדְמוֹנִיּוֹת. וְעָרְבָה לַיהוה מִנְחַת יְהוּדָה

〈 of Judah 〈 let be the 〈 to HASHEM 〈 And pleasing 《 gone by. 〈 and as in years
offering

וִירוּשָׁלָיִם, כִּימֵי עוֹלָם וּכְשָׁנִים קַדְמוֹנִיּוֹת.⁵

《 gone by. 〈 and in years 〈 of old 〈 as in days 《 and Jerusalem,

THE INDIVIDUAL'S RECITATION OF SHEMONEH ESREI ENDS HERE. REMAIN STANDING IN PLACE UNTIL
THE CHAZZAN REACHES KEDUSHAH — OR AT LEAST UNTIL THE CHAZZAN BEGINS HIS REPETITION —
THEN TAKE THREE STEPS FORWARD. THE CHAZZAN HIMSELF, OR ONE PRAYING ALONE, SHOULD
REMAIN IN PLACE FOR A FEW MOMENTS BEFORE TAKING THREE STEPS FORWARD.

THE CHAZZAN RECITES קַדִּישׁ שָׁלֵם, THE FULL KADDISH (P. 223).
THE SERVICE CONTINUES WITH קַוֵּה אֶל ה', PLACE YOUR HOPE IN HASHEM (P. 248).

(1) Cf. Psalms 19:15. (2) Job 25:2. (3) Cf. Berachos 16b. (4) Ethics of the Fathers 5:24. (5) Malachi 3:4.

‡ HOSHANOS / הושענות ‡

FOR HOSHANA RABBAH, SEE *THE INTERLINEAR SIDDUR FOR THE SABBATH AND FESTIVALS.*

EACH DAY'S *HOSHANA* SERVICE BEGINS WITH THE FOLLOWING INTRODUCTORY STANZA
CHANTED RESPONSIVELY — *CHAZZAN*, THEN CONGREGATION:

הוֹשַׁעְנָא.   הוֹשַׁעְנָא,* לְמַעַנְךָ אֱלֹהֵינוּ,
《 Please save!   《 our God! 《 — for Your sake, 《 Please save*

הוֹשַׁעְנָא.   הוֹשַׁעְנָא, לְמַעַנְךָ בּוֹרְאֵנוּ,
《 Please save!   《 our Creator! 《 — for Your sake, 《 Please save

הוֹשַׁעְנָא.   הוֹשַׁעְנָא, לְמַעַנְךָ גּוֹאֲלֵנוּ,
《 Please save!   《 our Redeemer! 《 — for Your sake, 《 Please save

הוֹשַׁעְנָא.   הוֹשַׁעְנָא, לְמַעַנְךָ דּוֹרְשֵׁנוּ,
《 Please save!   《 the One Who seeks us! 《 — for Your sake, 《 Please save

FOUNDATION STONE / אבן שתיה

אֶבֶן שְׁתִיָּה.* בֵּית הַבְּחִירָה. גֹּרֶן אָרְנָן. דְּבִיר הַמֻּצְנָע.
《 the hidden Sanctuary; 《 the [site of] 《 the chosen Temple; 《 [Please save]
Ornan's granary;   the foundation stone;*

הַר הַמּוֹרִיָּה. וְהַר יֵרָאֶה. זְבוּל תִּפְאַרְתֶּךָ. חָנָה דָוִד.
《 the [place where] 《 of Your 《 the 《 and Mount 《 Moriah, 《 Mount
David encamped;   Splendor;   residence   He-is-Seen;

טוֹב הַלְּבָנוֹן. יְפֵה נוֹף מְשׂוֹשׂ כָּל הָאָרֶץ. כְּלִילַת יֹפִי. לִינַת
《 the 《 the perfection 《 the earth; 《 of all 《 joy 《 of 《 the 《 the goodness
lodging   of beauty;   sites, fairest   of Lebanon;

הַצֶּדֶק. מָכוֹן לְשִׁבְתֶּךָ. נָוֵה שַׁאֲנָן. סֻכַּת שָׁלֵם. עֲלִיַּת
《 the pilgri- 《 of 《 the 《 of 《 the 《 for Your 《 the 《 of
mage site   Salem; Tabernacle tranquility; abode   dwelling; foundation righteousness;

👈 הושענות / Hoshanos

[The commentary below is abridged from the ArtScroll *Hoshanos*, by Rabbi Avie Gold.]

👈 הושַׁעְנָא — *Please save.* This word is compounded of the words הוֹשַׁע, *save*, and נָא, *please.* Indeed, many *siddurim* give it as two words. נָא may also be translated *now*; thus, הוֹשַׁעְנָא would mean *save now.*

In the introductory stanza each verse begins and ends with the word הוֹשַׁעְנָא. Although it does not appear in the *siddurim*, most congregations add the word הוֹשַׁעְנָא, *please save*, to each

phrase of each *Hoshana*, either:
— before it (הוֹשַׁעְנָא לְמַעַן אֲמִתָּךְ);
— after it (לְמַעַן אֲמִתָּךְ הוֹשַׁעְנָא);
— or both (הוֹשַׁעְנָא לְמַעַן אֲמִתָּךְ הוֹשַׁעְנָא).

👈 אֶבֶן שְׁתִיָּה / Foundation Stone

Each phrase of this prayer alludes to either the Holy Temple or to the city of Jerusalem. We ask God to please redeem the *Beis HaMikdash* from its present desolation and desecration; from the wild foxes that prowl over it [see *Lamentations* 5:18] (*Beis Avraham*); that it may be rebuilt, speedily in our days (*Shaar HaShamayim*).

ON EACH DAY OF SUCCOS: Immediately after *Hallel,* special prayers called *Hoshanos* are recited. The Ark is opened and a Torah scroll is removed and carried to the *bimah* where one member of the congregation holds it. The Ark remains open and the Torah is held at the *bimah* until the conclusion of the *Hoshana* service. The *lulav* and *esrog* are held during the entire service.

Four introductory stiches are recited responsively — *chazzan,* then congregation — each day. Upon completing the introductory verses the *chazzan* leads all males who are carrying a *lulav* and *esrog* around the *bimah* as he reads the day's *Hoshana* [see below] responsively with the congregation. He should time his steps to complete the circuit as he recites the last verse of the *Hoshana.*

Two factors determine which *Hoshana* is recited: (a) the day of the week; and (b) the day of the month. The accompanying diagrams record the four calendrical possibilities for the Festival of Succos, and the *Hoshana* recited in each case.

IF THE FIRST DAY OF SUCCOS FALLS ON MONDAY

S	M	T	W	T	F	S
14	15 FIRST DAY SUCCOS	16 SECOND DAY SUCCOS	17 אערוך שועי P. 556	18 אום אני חומה P. 554	19 אל למושעות P. 557	20 SHABBOS CHOL HAMOED

IF THE FIRST DAY OF SUCCOS FALLS ON TUESDAY

S	M	T	W	T	F	S
13	14	15 FIRST DAY SUCCOS	16 SECOND DAY SUCCOS	17 אערוך שועי P. 556	18 * אל למושעות P. 557	19 SHABBOS CHOL HAMOED
20 אדון המושיע P. 555	21 HOSHANA RABBAH	22	23	24	25	26

* Some congregations substitute אֹם אֲנִי חֹמָה (p. 554).

IF THE FIRST DAY OF SUCCOS FALLS ON THURSDAY

S	M	T	W	T	F	S
11	12	13	14	15 FIRST DAY SUCCOS	16 SECOND DAY SUCCOS	17 SHABBOS CHOL HAMOED
18 אערוך שועי P. 556	19 אל למושעות P. 557	20 אדון המושיע P. 555	21 HOSHANA RABBAH	22	23	24

IF THE FIRST DAY OF SUCCOS FALLS ON THE SABBATH

S	M	T	W	T	F	S
9	10	11	12	13	14	15 FIRST DAY SUCCOS
16 SECOND DAY SUCCOS	17 אערוך שועי P. 556	18 אבן שתיה P. 552	19 אל למושעות P. 557	20 אדון המושיע P. 555	21 HOSHANA RABBAH	22

שְׁבָטִים. פִּנַּת יְקְרַת. צִיּוֹן הַמְּצֻיֶּנֶת. קֹדֶשׁ הַקֳּדָשִׁים.

‹‹ of Holies; ‹ the Holy ‹‹ that is distinguished; ‹ Zion ‹‹ that is precious; ‹ the cornerstone ‹‹ of the tribes;

רָצוּף אַהֲבָה. שְׁכִינַת כְּבוֹדֶךָ. תֵּל תַּלְפִּיּוֹת.

‹‹ of Talpios. ‹ the hill ‹‹ of Your Honor; ‹ the resting place ‹‹ with love; ‹ the [place] decked

CONTINUE אֲנִי וָהוֹ (P. 558).

NATION [THAT DECLARES,] "I AM A WALL!" / אוֹם אֲנִי חוֹמָה

אוֹם אֲנִי חוֹמָה.*[1] בָּרָה כַּחַמָּה. גּוֹלָה וְסוּרָה. דָּמְתָה

‹ likened ‹‹ and displaced; ‹ – yet exiled ‹‹ as the sun ‹ Brilliant ‹‹ [that declares,] I am a wall!* ‹ [Please save] the nation

לְתָמָר. הַהֲרוּגָה עָלֶיךָ. וְנֶחְשֶׁבֶת כְּצֹאן טִבְחָה. זְרוּיָה

‹ although scattered ‹‹ for slaughter; ‹ like sheep ‹ and considered ‹‹ for Your sake, ‹ yet killed ‹‹ to a palm tree

בֵּין מַכְעִיסֶיהָ. חֲבוּקָה וּדְבוּקָה בָּךְ. טוֹעֶנֶת עֻלָּךְ. יְחִידָה

‹ – unique ‹‹ Your yoke ‹ bearing ‹‹ to You, ‹ and clings ‹‹ she hugs ‹ those who taunt her, ‹ among

לְיַחֲדָךְ. כְּבוּשָׁה בַּגּוֹלָה. לוֹמֶדֶת יִרְאָתָךְ. מְרוּטַת לֶחִי.

‹‹ in the cheek, ‹ Plucked ‹‹ to fear You. ‹ she learns ‹ in exile, ‹ While vanquished ‹‹ in declaring Your Oneness.

נְתוּנָה לְמַכִּים. סוֹבֶלֶת סִבְלָךְ. עֲנִיָּה סֹעֲרָה. פְּדוּיַת

‹ she was redeemed ‹‹ and storm-tossed, ‹ Afflicted ‹‹ Your burden. ‹ she carries ‹‹ to assaulters, ‹ given over

טוֹבִיָּה. צֹאן קָדָשִׁים. קְהִלּוֹת יַעֲקֹב. רְשׁוּמִים בִּשְׁמֶךָ.

‹‹ with Your Name, ‹ inscribed ‹ of Jacob, ‹ congregations ‹ Sacred sheep, ‹‹ by Tobias (Moses).

שׁוֹאֲגִים הוֹשַׁעְנָא. תְּמוּכִים עָלֶיךָ.

‹‹ upon You! ‹ – they rely ‹ Please save us! ‹ they cry,

CONTINUE אֲנִי וָהוֹ (P. 558).

(1) Cf. *Song of Songs* 8:9-10.

אוֹם אֲנִי חוֹמָה / Nation [That Declares,] *I Am a Wall*

Many metaphors are used in Scripture and Rabbinic writing to describe the nation of Israel. During the third *hakafah*-circuit, which corresponds to the Patriarch Jacob (Israel), from whom the nation derived its name, an alphabetical catalogue of such metaphors is chanted in prayer for the nation's redemption and salvation (*Bnei Yisas'char*).

Most of the epithets in this *Hoshana* are particularly applicable to Israel during its decline and exile. Material poverty is juxtaposed with spiritual wealth as the *paytan* paints a word picture depicting Israel's unwavering faith.

אֲדוֹן הַמּוֹשִׁיעַ / LORD WHO SAVES

אֲדוֹן הַמּוֹשִׁיעַ.* בִּלְתְּךָ אֵין לְהוֹשִׁיעַ. גִּבּוֹר וְרַב

⟨ and ⟨ powerful ⟨⟨ [able] to save; ⟨ there is ⟨ other than ⟨ Who saves;* ⟨ [Please save]
abundantly   no one   You   O Lord

לְהוֹשִׁיעַ. דַּלּוֹתִי וְלִי יְהוֹשִׁיעַ. הָאֵל הַמּוֹשִׁיעַ. וּמַצִּיל

⟨ He ⟨⟨ Who is the ⟨ the God ⟨⟨ He saved; ⟨ but ⟨ I was ⟨⟨ [able] to save;
rescues   Savior;   me   brought low,

וּמוֹשִׁיעַ. זוֹעֲקֶיךָ תּוֹשִׁיעַ. חוֹכֶיךָ הוֹשִׁיעַ. טְלָאֶיךָ תַּשְׂבִּיעַ.

⟨⟨ grant ⟨ to Your ⟨⟨ save; ⟨ those who ⟨⟨ You will ⟨ those who ⟨⟨ and saves;
satiation; lambs   yearn for You   save;   cry out to You

יְבוּל לְהַשְׁפִּיעַ. כָּל שִׂיחַ תַּדְשֵׁא וְתוֹשִׁיעַ. לַגַּיְא

⟨ the ⟨⟨ and save; ⟨ cause to ⟨ [kinds of] ⟨ all ⟨⟨ cause an ⟨ of crops
valleys   sprout   trees   abundance;

בַּל תַּרְשִׁיעַ. מִגְדִּים תַּמְתִּיק וְתוֹשִׁיעַ. נְשִׂיאִים לְהַסִּיעַ.

⟨⟨ let [the wind] ⟨ the soaring ⟨⟨ and save; ⟨ sweeten ⟨ the luscious ⟨⟨ do not condemn
transport;   clouds   fruit   [because of man];

שְׂעִירִים לְהָנִיעַ. עֲנָנִים מִלְּהַמְנִיעַ. פּוֹתֵחַ יָד וּמַשְׂבִּיעַ.

⟨⟨ and satisfy; ⟨ Your ⟨ You open ⟨⟨ from holding ⟨ [prevent] ⟨⟨ be ⟨ let the stormy
hand   back;   the clouds   conveyed;   winds

צְמֵאֶיךָ תַּשְׂבִּיעַ. קוֹרְאֶיךָ תּוֹשִׁיעַ. רְחוּמֶיךָ תּוֹשִׁיעַ.

⟨⟨ save; ⟨ Your beloved ⟨⟨ save; ⟨ those who ⟨⟨ satisfy; ⟨ those who
ones   call out to You   thirst for You

שׁוֹחֲרֶיךָ הוֹשִׁיעַ. תְּמִימֶיךָ תּוֹשִׁיעַ.

⟨⟨ save. ⟨ Your wholesome ⟨⟨ save; ⟨ those who
ones   seek You

CONTINUE אֲנִי וָהוֹ (P. 558).

אֲדוֹן הַמּוֹשִׁיעַ/Lord Who Saves

Every part of Creation may be assigned to one of four categories of existence. In ascending spiritual order they are: דּוֹמֵם, *mineral* [lit. *silent*]; צוֹמֵחַ, *vegetable* [lit. *sprouting*]; חַי, *animal* [lit. *living*]; and מְדַבֵּר, *human* [lit. *speaking*].

In the Divine plan for the world, each member of one realm is capable of becoming elevated to a higher one. Indeed, this is the purpose of its existence. The minerals in the soil, water, and air are absorbed by plants, which, in turn, serve as food for the animals. Finally, these become the fare of man. Scripture alludes to this system of elevation: *And I shall give grass [vegetable] in your field*

[mineral] for your cattle [animal] and you [man] shall eat and be sated (Deuteronomy 11:15).

But this process of uplifting certainly does not end with man. Man must raise himself from the evil which fills his heart. The last words of the above verse, *and you shall eat and be sated*, also appear as the opening of another verse which continues: *and you shall bless* HASHEM, *your God*. Recitation of a blessing is the fulfillment of a *mitzvah*, and, as Kabbalah teaches, while study of Torah provides the soul's sustenance, the performance of *mitzvos* supplies its raiment. Man must use the baser elements of creation in the fulfillment of *mitzvos*, but he needs guidance to use them wisely.

אֶעֱרוֹךְ שׁוּעִי / I SHALL ARRANGE MY PRAYER

אֶעֱרוֹךְ שׁוּעִי.* בְּבֵית שַׁוְעִי. גִּלִּיתִי בַצּוֹם פְּשָׁעִי.

‹‹ my ‹ on the ‹ I have ‹‹ of my ‹ in the ‹‹ my prayer,* ‹ [Please save]
transgression; fast day, revealed, prayer; house   I shall arrange

דְּרַשְׁתִּיךָ בּוֹ לְהוֹשִׁיעִי. הַקְשִׁיבָה לְקוֹל שַׁוְעִי. וְקוּמָה

‹ and arise ‹‹ of my ‹ to the ‹ hearken ‹‹ for [You] to ‹ on that ‹ I sought
prayer, voice save me; [day] You

וְהוֹשִׁיעִי. זְכוֹר וְרַחֵם מוֹשִׁיעִי. חַי כֵּן תְּשַׁעְשְׁעִי. טוֹב

‹ O Bene- ‹ as [I requested] ‹ O Living ‹‹ my Savior; ‹ and be ‹ remember ‹‹ and save
volent One, grant me joy; God, merciful, me;

בְּאַנֶק שְׁעִי. יָחִישׁ מוֹשִׁיעִי. כַּלֵּה מַרְשִׁיעִי. לְבַל עוֹד

‹ any ‹ so that ‹‹ my accuser, ‹ destroy ‹ [the arrival of]] may He ‹‹ turn; ‹ to my
longer You will not my savior; hasten sigh

תַּרְשִׁיעִי. מַהֵר אֱלֹהֵי יִשְׁעִי. נֶצַח לְהוֹשִׁיעִי. שָׂא נָא עֲוֹן

‹ the ‹ pardon, ‹‹ to save me; ‹ eternally ‹‹ of my ‹ God ‹ hasten, ‹‹ find me
iniquity please, salvation, guilty;

רִשְׁעִי. עֲבוֹר עַל פְּשָׁעִי. פְּנֵה נָא לְהוֹשִׁיעִי. צוּר צַדִּיק

‹ Righteous ‹ O ‹‹ to save me; ‹ please, ‹ turn, ‹‹ my ‹ commute ‹‹ of my
One, Rock, transgression; wickedness;

מוֹשִׁיעִי. קַבֵּל נָא שַׁוְעִי. רוֹמֵם קֶרֶן יִשְׁעִי. שַׁדַּי מוֹשִׁיעִי.

‹‹ my ‹ O ‹‹ of my ‹ O [God,] ‹ raise ‹‹ my ‹ please, ‹ accept, ‹‹ my Savior,
Savior, Almighty, salvation; Horn me up, prayer;

תּוֹפִיעַ וְתוֹשִׁיעִי.

‹‹ and save me. ‹ appear

CONTINUE אֲנִי וָהוֹ (PAGE 558).

אֶעֱרוֹךְ שׁוּעִי ⇐ / I Shall Arrange My Prayer
One must always anticipate troublesome situations and pray for salvation before oppressive times arrive (Sanhedrin 44b). When is the opportune time for such prayer? Seek HASHEM when He may be found; call to Him when He is near (Isaiah 55:6). The Talmud asks, "When may He be found? When is He near?" and answers, "During the Ten Days [of Awe] beginning with Rosh Hashanah and culminating with Yom Kippur" (Rosh Hashanah 18a).

Now Israel prays that God recall its repentance during the period when God called for it. In response to my having revealed my transgression before You on Yom Kippur, may You pardon the iniquity of my wickedness and commute my transgression. Just as I sought You on that day, for salvation, You, in turn, arise . . . remember and be merciful, my Savior. Because this Hoshana refers to Yom Kippur it is recited on the third day of Succos [unless that day is the Sabbath], the same day of the week as Yom Kippur.

O GOD! BRING ABOUT SALVATIONS / אֵל לְמוֹשָׁעוֹת

אֵל לְמוֹשָׁעוֹת.* בְּאַרְבַּע שְׁבֻעוֹת.* גְּשִׁים בְּשַׁוְעוֹת.

‹‹ with pleas; ‹ of those ‹‹ oaths* ‹ because of ‹‹ Bring about ‹ [Please save]
who approach   the four   salvations,*   O God!

דּוֹפְקֵי עָרֶךְ הוֹגֵי שַׁעֲשׁוּעוֹת. וְחִידֹתָם.

‹ and in its ‹‹ upon the beloved ‹ who ‹‹ prayers; ‹ where ‹ who knock
mysteries   Torah   meditate   arranged are [on the doors]

מִשְׁתַּעְשְׁעוֹת. זֹעֲקִים לְהַשְׁעוֹת. חוֹכֵי יְשׁוּעוֹת. טְפוּלִים

‹ who cling ‹‹ [Your] ‹ who ‹ to get Your ‹ who cry out ‹‹ take joy;
salvations; await attention;

בָּךְ שָׁעוֹת. יוֹדְעֵי בִין שָׁעוֹת. כּוֹרְעֶיךָ בְּשַׁוְעוֹת.

‹‹ as they ‹ who bow ‹ of the ‹ the ‹ who ‹‹ turning their ‹ to
pray,   down to You hours; wisdom understand attention [to You]; You,

לְהָבִין שְׁמוּעוֹת. מִפִּיךְ נִשְׁמָעוֹת. נוֹתֵן תְּשׁוּעוֹת. סְפוּרוֹת

‹As [our fathers] ‹‹ of ‹ O ‹‹ were heard, ‹ that from ‹‹ the lessons ‹ to
recounted   salvations. Granter   Your mouth   understand

מַשְׁמָעוֹת. עֵדוּת מַשְׁמִיעוֹת. פּוֹעֵל יְשׁוּעוֹת. צַדִּיק

‹[send the Messiah] ‹‹ of ‹ O Worker ‹‹ they make ‹ the ‹‹ [so] have we
who is *righteous* salvations,   heard.   Testimony   heard,

נוֹשָׁעוֹת.¹ קִרְיַת תְּשׁוּעוֹת. רֶגֶשׁ תְּשָׁאוֹת. שָׁלֹשׁ

‹ [during] ‹‹ tumultuous, ‹ with ‹‹ of salvations, ‹ for the ‹‹ *and victorious*,
the three   masses   city

שָׁעוֹת. תָּחִישׁ לִתְשׁוּעוֹת.

‹‹ of salvations. ‹ hasten ‹‹ hours [of prayer
the time   each day];

CONTINUE אֲנִי וָהוֹ (PAGE 558).

---

(1) Cf. *Zechariah* 9:9.

אֵל לְמוֹשָׁעוֹת /
O God! Bring About Salvations

Although the Psalmist (68:21) uses the phrase אֵל לְמוֹשָׁעוֹת, *God of salvations*, while contrasting God's salvation of Israel with His destruction of its enemies, here it is used to introduce a description of the Jews' clinging to God, and their observance of His *mitzvos*, despite their exile.

בְּאַרְבַּע שְׁבֻעוֹת — *Because of the four oaths.* God made the Jewish people swear with four oaths that they would not attempt to force the Final Redemption on their own. Therefore, under constant persecution in exile, we pray to God to *bring about salvations.*

AFTER EACH DAY'S *HAKAFAH*-CIRCUIT CONTINUE:

אֲנִי וָהוּ הוֹשִׁיעָה נָּא.*

≪ now.* ⟨ bring salvation ⟨ VAHO, ⟨ ANI

AS YOU SAVED THE MIGHTY ONES / כהושעת אלים

כְּהוֹשַׁעְתָּ אֵלִים* בְּלוּד עִמָּךְ, בְּצֵאתְךָ לְיֵשַׁע עַמָּךְ,

≪ Your ⟨ to save ⟨ when You ⟨ along with ⟨ in Lud ⟨ the mighty ⟨ As You saved
nation   went forth Yourself, (Egypt) ones* [Israel]

כֵּן הוֹשַׁעְנָא.

≪ save now. ⟨ – so

כְּהוֹשַׁעְתָּ גוֹי וֵאלֹהִים, דְּרוּשִׁים לְיֵשַׁע אֱלֹהִים,¹

≪ of God ⟨ the ⟨ who required ≪ and God, ⟨ the ⟨ As You saved
salvation   nation

כֵּן הוֹשַׁעְנָא.

≪ save now. ⟨ – so

כְּהוֹשַׁעְתָּ הֲמוֹן צְבָאוֹת, וְעִמָּם מַלְאֲכֵי צְבָאוֹת,

≪ hosts of angels ⟨ and with ≪ of hosts ⟨ the ⟨ As You saved
them [of Israel], multitudes

כֵּן הוֹשַׁעְנָא.

≪ save now. ⟨ – so

כְּהוֹשַׁעְתָּ זַכִּים מִבֵּית עֲבָדִים, חַנּוּן בְּיָדָם מַעֲבִידִים,

≪ was enslaved ⟨ by their ⟨ [as if even] the ≪ of ⟨ from the ⟨ the pure ⟨ As You saved
hands Gracious One, slavery, house ones

כֵּן הוֹשַׁעְנָא.

≪ save now. ⟨ – so

(1) Cf. *II Samuel* 7:23.

אֲנִי וָהוּ הוֹשִׁיעָה נָּא — *ANI VAHO, bring salvation now.* According to Rabbi Yehudah, אֲנִי וָהוּ הוֹשִׁיעָה נָּא was the prayer recited by the *Kohanim* as they circled the Altar in the Temple on Succos. אֲנִי וָהוּ are part of a mystical, Seventy-two-Letter Name of God. These particular parts of the Name were used to allude to the idea that both I (אֲנִי) and He (הוּא), as it were, are awaiting to be redeemed from exile, as the verse says, עִמּוֹ אָנֹכִי בְצָרָה, *I (God) am together with him (Israel) in distress* (*Psalms* 91:15)

(*Succah* 45a, *Rashi* and *Tosafos* ad loc.). This idea is the central theme of this *Hoshana*, כְּהוֹשַׁעְתָּ.

כְּהוֹשַׁעְתָּ אֵלִים /
As You Saved the Mighty Ones

This *Hoshana*, which is recited after each day's circuit [except on the Sabbath], contains various poetical allusions to the Exodus from Egypt and other incidents of God's salvation of Israel, and beseeches that we be granted similar salvation.

כְּהוֹשַׁעְתָּ טְבוּעִים בְּצוּל גְּזָרִים, יְקָרְךָ עִמָּם מַעֲבִירִים,

As You saved / those [threatened with] sinking / in the depths / of the split waters, / as Your splendor / with them / they carried across

כֵּן הוֹשַׁעְנָא.

— so / — save now.

כְּהוֹשַׁעְתָּ כַּנָּה מְשׁוֹרֶרֶת וַיִּוָּשַׁע,[1] לְגוֹחָהּ[2] מְצֻיֶּנֶת

As You saved / the fundamental nation / which sang, / And He delivered; / regarding Him Who drew them forth / it is punctuated,

וַיִּוָּשַׁע,

And He was delivered

כֵּן הוֹשַׁעְנָא.

— so / — save now.

כְּהוֹשַׁעְתָּ מַאֲמַר וְהוֹצֵאתִי אֶתְכֶם, נָקוּב[3] וְהוֹצֵאתִי

As You saved / with the declaration, / I shall bring forth / you, / which can be pronounced, / I shall be brought forth

אֶתְכֶם,

with you

כֵּן הוֹשַׁעְנָא.

— so / — save now.

כְּהוֹשַׁעְתָּ סוֹבְבֵי מִזְבֵּחַ, עוֹמְסֵי עֲרָבָה לְהַקִּיף מִזְבֵּחַ,

As You saved / those who went around / the Altar, / who carried / the willow / to encircle / the Altar

כֵּן הוֹשַׁעְנָא.

— so / — save now.

כְּהוֹשַׁעְתָּ פִּלְאֵי אָרוֹן כְּהֻפְשַׁע,

As You saved / the Ark of the Wondrous Name, / [captured] as a result of sin;

צַעַר פְּלֶשֶׁת בַּחֲרוֹן אַף וְנוֹשַׁע,

it brought suffering / upon Philistia / with flaring anger, / and it was saved

כֵּן הוֹשַׁעְנָא.

— so / — save now.

כְּהוֹשַׁעְתָּ קְהִלּוֹת בָּבֶלָה שִׁלַּחְתָּ, רַחוּם לְמַעֲנָם שֻׁלָּחְתָּ,

As You saved / the congregations / which to Babylon / You had sent; / O Merciful One, / for their sake / You were also sent there

כֵּן הוֹשַׁעְנָא.

— so / — save now.

כְּהוֹשַׁעְתָּ שְׁבוּת שִׁבְטֵי יַעֲקֹב,

As You saved / the captivity / of the tribes / of Jacob,

תָּשׁוּב וְתָשִׁיב שְׁבוּת אָהֳלֵי יַעֲקֹב,

return Yourself / and restore / the captivity / of the tents / of Jacob;

וְהוֹשִׁיעָה נָּא.

and bring salvation / now.

(1) Exodus 14:30. (2) Cf. Psalms 22:10. (3) Exodus 6:6.

כְּהוֹשַׁעְתָּ שׁוֹמְרֵי מִצְוֹת, וְחוֹכֵי יְשׁוּעוֹת, אֵל לְמוֹשָׁעוֹת,

⟨ bring about ⟨ O ⟨ for salvation, ⟨ and those ⟨⟨ the ⟨ those who ⟨ As You saved
salvations,   God   who hoped   mitzvos,   observed

וְהוֹשִׁיעָה נָא.

⟨⟨ now. ⟨ and bring salvation

אָנִי וָהוֹ הוֹשִׁיעָה נָא.

⟨⟨   now. ⟨ bring salvation ⟨ VAHO, ⟨ ANI

הוֹשִׁיעָה אֶת עַמֶּךָ, וּבָרֵךְ אֶת נַחֲלָתֶךָ, וּרְעֵם וְנַשְּׂאֵם

⟨ and raise ⟨ tend ⟨⟨ Your inheritance; ⟨ and bless ⟨ Your nation, ⟨ Save
them up   them

עַד הָעוֹלָם.[1] וְיִהְיוּ דְבָרַי אֵלֶּה אֲשֶׁר הִתְחַנַּנְתִּי לִפְנֵי

⟨ before ⟨ I have ⟨ which ⟨ – these words ⟨⟨ May they ⟨⟨ forever.
supplicated   of mine,   be

יְהוֹה, קְרֹבִים אֶל יְהוֹה אֱלֹהֵינוּ יוֹמָם וָלַיְלָה, לַעֲשׂוֹת

⟨that He perform⟨ and by night; ⟨ by day ⟨ our God, ⟨ HASHEM, ⟨ to ⟨ near ⟨⟨ HASHEM –

מִשְׁפַּט עַבְדּוֹ וּמִשְׁפַּט עַמּוֹ יִשְׂרָאֵל, דְּבַר יוֹם בְּיוֹמוֹ.

⟨⟨ in its ⟨ each day's need ⟨ Israel, ⟨ for His ⟨ and justice ⟨ for His ⟨ justice
day;   people,   servant

לְמַעַן דַּעַת כָּל עַמֵּי הָאָרֶץ, כִּי יְהוֹה הוּא הָאֱלֹהִים,

⟨⟨ God, ⟨ is ⟨ HASHEM ⟨that ⟨⟨ of the ⟨ the ⟨ – all ⟨⟨ they shall ⟨ so that
     earth –   peoples   know

אֵין עוֹד.[2]

⟨⟨ [and] there is no other.

THE TORAH SCROLL IS RETURNED TO THE ARK.
THE *CHAZZAN* RECITES קַדִּישׁ שָׁלֵם, THE FULL *KADDISH* (P. 223).
THE SERVICE CONTINUES WITH שִׁיר שֶׁל יוֹם, *SONG OF THE DAY* (PP. 232-242)
AND וַיְהִי בִּנְסֹעַ, *IT WOULD BE THAT WHEN TRAVEL . . .* (P. 199).

❧ BLESSING IN THE SUCCAH / ברכת ישיבת הסוכה ❧
UPON SITTING DOWN TO A MEAL IN THE SUCCAH, THE FOLLOWING BLESSING IS RECITED:

בָּרוּךְ אַתָּה יְהוֹה אֱלֹהֵינוּ מֶלֶךְ הָעוֹלָם, אֲשֶׁר קִדְּשָׁנוּ

⟨ has ⟨ Who ⟨⟨ of the ⟨ King ⟨ our God, ⟨ HASHEM, ⟨ are You, ⟨ Blessed
sanctified us   universe,

בְּמִצְוֹתָיו וְצִוָּנוּ לֵישֵׁב בַּסֻּכָּה.

⟨⟨ in the *succah*. ⟨ to dwell ⟨ and has ⟨ with His com-
     commanded us   mandments

(1) *Psalms* 28:9. (2) *I Kings* 8:59-60.

❧ ANNULMENT OF VOWS / סדר התרת נדרים ❧

IT IS MERITORIOUS TO ANNUL VOWS ON THE MORNING BEFORE ROSH HASHANAH (SEE COMMENTARY). THE THREE "JUDGES" SIT WHLE THE PETITIONER SEEKING ANNULMENT STANDS BEFORE THEM AND STATES:

שִׁמְעוּ נָא רַבּוֹתַי, דַּיָּנִים מוּמְחִים. כָּל נֶדֶר אוֹ שְׁבוּעָה אוֹ

⟨ or ⟨ oath ⟨ or ⟨ vow ⟨ Any ⟨⟨ expert judges: ⟨ my ⟨ if you ⟨ Hear,
masters, please,

אִסּוּר אוֹ קוֹנָם אוֹ חֵרֶם שֶׁנָּדַרְתִּי אוֹ נִשְׁבַּעְתִּי בְּהָקִיץ אוֹ

⟨ or ⟨ while ⟨ I swore ⟨ or ⟨ that I vowed ⟨⟨ ban; ⟨ or ⟨ [vow adopted ⟨ or ⟨ prohi-
awake   using the term]   bition,
                                   konam

בַחֲלוֹם, אוֹ נִשְׁבַּעְתִּי בִּשְׁמוֹת הַקְּדוֹשִׁים שֶׁאֵינָם נִמְחָקִים,

⟨⟨ be erased, ⟨ that may not ⟨ using [one of God's] ⟨ that I swore ⟨ or ⟨⟨ in a dream;
                       Holy Names

וּבְשֵׁם הוי"ה בָּרוּךְ הוּא, וְכָל מִינֵי נְזִירוּת שֶׁקִּבַּלְתִּי עָלַי,

⟨ upon ⟨ that I ⟨ of nezirus ⟨ forms ⟨ or ⟨⟨ is He; ⟨ Blessed ⟨ Hashem, ⟨ or using
myself,   accepted   any   the Name

חוּץ מִנְּזִירוּת שִׁמְשׁוֹן, וְכָל שׁוּם אִסּוּר, וַאֲפִלּוּ אִסּוּר הֲנָאָה

⟨ to derive ⟨ a pro- ⟨ even ⟨ prohibition at all, ⟨ or any ⟨⟨ of ⟨ the ⟨ except
benefit   hibition   Samson;   nezirus

שֶׁאָסַרְתִּי עָלַי אוֹ עַל אֲחֵרִים, בְּכָל לָשׁוֹן שֶׁל אִסּוּר, בֵּין

⟨ whether ⟨⟨ prohi- ⟨ of ⟨ expression ⟨ with ⟨ others ⟨ upon ⟨ or ⟨ upon ⟨ that I imposed
bition,   any   myself

בְּלָשׁוֹן אִסּוּר אוֹ חֵרֶם אוֹ קוֹנָם, וְכָל שׁוּם קַבָּלָה אֲפִילוּ שֶׁל

⟨ relating ⟨ – even ⟨⟨ commitment ⟨ or ⟨⟨ konam; ⟨ or ⟨ ban ⟨ or ⟨ prohibition ⟨ with
to   at all   any   the term

מִצְוָה שֶׁקִּבַּלְתִּי עָלַי בֵּין בִּלְשׁוֹן נֶדֶר, בֵּין בִּלְשׁוֹן נְדָבָה,

⟨⟨ [denoting] a ⟨ with an ⟨ wheth- ⟨⟨ [denoting] ⟨ with an ⟨ wheth- ⟨⟨ upon ⟨ that I ⟨⟨ [performing]
specific gift, expression er   a vow, expression er   myself, accepted a mitzvah –

בֵּין בִּלְשׁוֹן שְׁבוּעָה, בֵּין בִּלְשׁוֹן נְזִירוּת, בֵּין בְּכָל לָשׁוֹן, וְגַם

⟨ as ⟨⟨ expres- ⟨ with any ⟨ wheth- ⟨⟨ [denoting] ⟨ with an ⟨ wheth- ⟨⟨ [denoting] ⟨ with an ⟨ wheth-
well as sion,   [other]   er   nezirus, expression er   an oath, expression er

---

❧ הַתָּרַת נְדָרִים / ANNULMENT OF VOWS ❧

The Torah permits people to accept upon themselves personal obligations and prohibitions, and it gives an owner the right to forbid others to benefit from his property. Such undertakings, known as שְׁבוּעוֹת וּנְדָרִים, *oaths and vows*, must be carried out and have the force of a positive commandment, כְּכָל הַיֹּצֵא מִפִּיו יַעֲשֶׂה, *he shall do whatever he has uttered*, and their violation carries the penalty of a negative commandment, לֹא יַחֵל דְּבָרוֹ, *he shall not desecrate his word* (Numbers 30:3). So serious are these matters that they are the primary subject of three tractates: *Nedarim, Nazir, and Shevuos.*

That a person's freely chosen wishes can have the force of Torah law is a striking indication of the sanctity that God attaches to a person's word. Consequently, it is considered a fearsome sin for one to violate his vows and oaths, and the Sages regard it as an extremely serious matter for one to approach the Days of Judgment with such a transgression in hand.

However, the Torah provides a means for one

הַנַּעֲשָׂה בִּתְקִיעַת כָּף, בֵּין כָּל נֶדֶר, וּבֵין כָּל נְדָבָה, וּבֵין שׁוּם

מִנְהַג שֶׁל מִצְוָה שֶׁנָּהַגְתִּי אֶת עַצְמִי, וְכָל מוֹצָא שְׂפָתַי שֶׁיָּצָא

מִפִּי, אוֹ שֶׁנָּדַרְתִּי וְגָמַרְתִּי בְּלִבִּי לַעֲשׂוֹת שׁוּם מִצְוָה

מֵהַמִּצְוֹת, אוֹ אֵיזֶה הַנְהָגָה טוֹבָה אוֹ אֵיזֶה דָבָר טוֹב, שֶׁנָּהַגְתִּי

שָׁלֹשׁ פְּעָמִים, וְלֹא הִתְנֵיתִי שֶׁיְּהֵא בְּלִי נֶדֶר, הֵן דָּבָר

שֶׁעָשִׂיתִי, הֵן עַל עַצְמִי, הֵן עַל אֲחֵרִים, הֵן אוֹתָן הַיְּדוּעִים לִי,

הֵן אוֹתָן שֶׁכְּבָר שָׁכַחְתִּי, בְּכֻלְּהוֹן אִתְחֲרַטְנָא בְהוֹן מֵעִקָּרָא,

וְשׁוֹאֵל וּמְבַקֵּשׁ אֲנִי מִמַּעֲלַתְכֶם הַתָּרָה עֲלֵיהֶם. כִּי יָרֵאתִי

פֶּן אֶכָּשֵׁל וְנִלְכַּדְתִּי, חַס וְשָׁלוֹם, בַּעֲוֹן נְדָרִים וּשְׁבוּעוֹת

וּנְזִירוּת וַחֲרָמוֹת וְאִסּוּרִין וְקוֹנָמוֹת וְהַסְכָּמוֹת. וְאֵין אֲנִי תוֹהֵא

חַס וְשָׁלוֹם, עַל קִיּוּם הַמַּעֲשִׂים הַטּוֹבִים הָהֵם שֶׁעָשִׂיתִי. רַק

In order to free oneself of the sin of such violations before being judged on Rosh Hashanah and Yom Kippur, the halachic authorities urge that one convene a court of at least three people — preferably ten — and seek release from his vows and oaths. However, as the declaration makes clear, this annulment applies only to vows for which the *halachah* permits annulment and for which there is a halachically acceptable reason for doing so. Likewise, annulment is valid only if the vows

to release himself from such obligations. A "court" composed of three knowledgeable people has the authority to decide that the oath or vow was undertaken under a mistaken impression and they may annul the obligation retroactively. [This is an oversimplified explanation of the process of annulment, but the key is that the court has retroactive powers.] One of the pleas that one can make to the court is that he regrets ever having undertaken the obligation as a vow or oath.

אֲנִי מִתְחָרֵט עַל קַבָּלַת הָעִנְיָנִים בִּלְשׁוֹן נֶדֶר אוֹ שְׁבוּעָה אוֹ

‹ I ‹ regret ‹ having accepted ‹ those ‹ with an ‹ of a ‹ or ‹ of an oath ‹ or ‹ matters vow expression

נְזִירוּת אוֹ אִסוּר אוֹ חֵרֶם אוֹ קוֹנָם אוֹ הַסְכָּמָה אוֹ קַבָּלָה בְּלֵב,

‹‹ in my ‹ of ac- ‹ or ‹ of an ‹ or ‹ of a ‹ or ‹ of a ban ‹ or ‹ of a ‹ or ‹ of nezirus heart, ceptance agreement konam prohibition

וּמִתְחָרֵט אֲנִי עַל זֶה שֶׁלֹּא אָמַרְתִּי, הִנְנִי עוֹשֶׂה דָבָר זֶה בְּלִי

‹ without ‹ this act ‹ doing ‹ I am ‹‹ that I did not say, ‹ the ‹ for ‹ and I have regret hereby fact

נֶדֶר וּשְׁבוּעָה וּנְזִירוּת וְחֵרֶם וְאִסוּר וְקוֹנָם וְקַבָּלָה בְּלֵב.

‹‹ in my ‹ or ‹ konam, ‹ prohibition, ‹ ban, ‹ nezirus, ‹ an oath, ‹ [the force heart. acceptance of] a vow,

לָכֵן אֲנִי שׁוֹאֵל הַתָּרָה בְּכֻלְּהוֹן. אֲנִי מִתְחָרֵט עַל כָּל הַנִּזְכָּר,

‹‹ the afore- ‹ all ‹ regret ‹ I ‹‹ for them all. ‹ annulment ‹ request ‹ I ‹ There- mentioned, fore,

בֵּין אִם הָיוּ הַמַּעֲשִׂים מֵהַדְּבָרִים הַנּוֹגְעִים בְּמָמוֹן, בֵּין

‹ whether ‹‹ to money, ‹ relating ‹ of matters ‹ these acts were ‹ if ‹ whether

מֵהַדְּבָרִים הַנּוֹגְעִים בְּגוּף, בֵּין מֵהַדְּבָרִים הַנּוֹגְעִים אֶל

‹ to ‹ relating ‹ of matters ‹ or whether ‹‹ to the body, ‹ relating ‹ of matters

הַנְּשָׁמָה. בְּכֻלְּהוֹן אֲנִי מִתְחָרֵט עַל לְשׁוֹן נֶדֶר וּשְׁבוּעָה וּנְזִירוּת

‹ nezirus, ‹ oath, ‹ of vow, ‹ [using] the ‹ regret ‹ I ‹‹ Regarding ‹‹ the soul. terminology them all,

וְאִסוּר וְחֵרֶם וְקוֹנָם וְקַבָּלָה בְּלֵב. וְהִנֵּה מִצַּד הַדִּין, הַמִּתְחָרֵט

‹ one who ‹ to the ‹ according ‹ Now, ‹‹ in the ‹ and ‹ konam ‹ ban, ‹ prohibition, regrets law, heart. acceptance

וְהַמְבַקֵּשׁ הַתָּרָה צָרִיךְ לִפְרוֹט הַנֶּדֶר, אַךְ דְּעוּ נָא רַבּוֹתַי,

‹‹ my ‹ please, ‹ be ‹ How- ‹‹ the vow. ‹ specify ‹ must ‹ annulment ‹ and who seeks masters, informed, ever,

כִּי אִי אֶפְשָׁר לְפוֹרְטָם כִּי רַבִּים הֵם. וְאֵין אֲנִי מְבַקֵּשׁ

‹ seek ‹ And I do not ‹‹ are they. ‹ many ‹ for ‹ to specify them, ‹ possible ‹ it is not ‹ that

הַתָּרָה עַל אוֹתָם הַנְּדָרִים שֶׁאֵין לְהַתִּיר אוֹתָם. עַל כֵּן

‹ Therefore, ‹‹ them. ‹ annul ‹ that one may not ‹ vows ‹ those ‹ for ‹ annulment

יִהְיוּ נָא בְּעֵינֵיכֶם כְּאִלּוּ הָיִיתִי פוֹרְטָם.

‹‹ specified them. ‹ I had ‹ as if ‹ in your view ‹ please, ‹ may they be,

involve just oneself. If, however, the vows were adopted for the sake of, or involve, someone else, they cannot be annulled without the consent of the other party.

A second aspect of the Annulment of Vows is the concluding declaration, in which one makes the legal declaration that his future undertakings should not have the force of a vow or oath. While this does not free him from the obligation to keep his word, it does remove the severity of sin that attaches to formally proclaimed vows and oaths.

THE JUDGES REPEAT THREE TIMES:

הַכֹּל יִהְיוּ מֻתָּרִים לָךְ, הַכֹּל מְחוּלִים לָךְ, הַכֹּל שְׁרוּיִם לָךְ,

All of them shall be annulled ≪ for ≫ all of them, shall be forgiven ≪ for ≫ you, all of them shall be canceled ≪ for ≫ you.

אֵין כַּאן לֹא נֶדֶר וְלֹא שְׁבוּעָה וְלֹא נְזִירוּת וְלֹא חֵרֶם וְלֹא

There is ≪ now ≫ neither ≪ vow, ≫ nor ≪ oath, ≫ nor ≪ nezirus, ≫ nor ≪ ban, ≫ nor

אִסוּר וְלֹא קוֹנָם וְלֹא נִדּוּי וְלֹא שַׁמְתָּא וְלֹא אָרוּר.

prohibition, ≫ nor ≪ konam, ≫ nor ≪ ostracism, ≫ nor ≪ excommunication, ≫ nor ≪ curse.

אֲבָל יֵשׁ כַּאן מְחִילָה וּסְלִיחָה וְכַפָּרָה. וּכְשֵׁם שֶׁמַּתִּירִים

Rather, ≫ there ≪ now ≫ is ≪ pardon, ≫ forgiveness, ≫ and ≪ atonement. ≫ And just ≪ as we annul [them]

בְּבֵית דִּין שֶׁל מַטָּה, כַּךְ יִהְיוּ מֻתָּרִים בְּבֵית דִּין שֶׁל מַעְלָה.

in the justice court of of [earth] below, ≫ so ≪ may they be ≪ annulled ≫ in the justice court of of [Heaven] above.

THE PETITIONER MAKES THE FOLLOWING DECLARATION:

הֲרֵי אֲנִי מוֹסֵר מוֹדָעָה לִפְנֵיכֶם, וַאֲנִי מְבַטֵּל מִכַּאן וּלְהַבָּא

Behold, ≫ I am ≪ presenting ≫ a declaration of cancellation ≪ before you, ≫ [by which] I ≪ cancel ≫ from this time onward

כָּל הַנְּדָרִים וְכָל שְׁבוּעוֹת וּנְזִירוּת וְאִסּוּרִין וְקוֹנָמוֹת וַחֲרָמוֹת

all ≪ the vows ≫ and all ≪ oaths, ≫ nezirus, ≫ prohibitions, ≫ konams, ≫ bans,

וְהַסְכָּמוֹת וְקַבָּלָה בְּלֵב שֶׁאֲקַבֵּל עָלַי בְּעַצְמִי, הֵן בְּהָקִיץ, הֵן

agreements, ≫ and ≪ acceptance ≫ of the ≪ that I will ≫ upon ≪ on my ≫ both ≪ while ≪ as accept myself own, awake well as

בַּחֲלוֹם, חוּץ מִנִּדְרֵי תַעֲנִית בִּשְׁעַת מִנְחָה. וּבְאִם שֶׁאֶשְׁכַּח

in a dream, ≫ except ≪ for vows ≫ to fast ≪ [undertaken] ≫ of ≪ In case ≪ I forget Minchah. at the time

לִתְנַאי מוֹדָעָה הַזֹּאת, וְאֶדּוֹר מֵהַיּוֹם עוֹד, מֵעַתָּה אֲנִי

the ≫ condition ≪ declaration [of cancellation], ≫ [set forth] in this ≪ and I make ≫ from ≪ onward, ≫ from this ≪ I this day moment

מִתְחָרֵט עֲלֵיהֶם, וּמַתְנֶה עֲלֵיהֶם, שֶׁיִּהְיוּ כֻלָּן בְּטֵלִין וּמְבֻטָּלִין,

regret ≫ them ≪ and ≫ regarding ≪ that they ≫ all of ≪ null ≫ and void, regarding them, shall be, them,

לֹא שְׁרִירִין וְלֹא קַיָּמִין, וְלֹא יְהוֹן חָלִין כְּלָל וּכְלָל. בְּכֻלָּן

without ≫ effect ≫ and ≪ validity, ≫ and they ≪ take effect ≫ at all. ≫ Regarding without shall not them all,

אִתְחֲרַטְנָא בְּהוֹן מֵעַתָּה וְעַד עוֹלָם.

I regret ≫ them ≪ from this time ≫ until ≪ eternity.

﷽{ KAPAROS / סדר כפרות ﷽

TAKE THE CHICKEN [OR MONEY] IN THE RIGHT HAND (SOME SAY נֶפֶשׁ תַּחַת נֶפֶשׁ, *A LIFE FOR A LIFE*, AS THEY DO SO), AND RECITE THE FOLLOWING PARAGRAPH. THEN — WHILE RECITING THE APPROPRIATE PARAGRAPH ON THE NEXT PAGE — CIRCLE THE CHICKEN OR THE MONEY AROUND THE HEAD (SOME DO THIS THREE TIMES). FOLLOW THIS PROCEDURE THREE TIMES.

[ALTERNATIVELY, RECITE THE FOLLOWING PARAGRAPH THREE TIMES. THEN — WHILE CIRCLING THE CHICKEN OR THE MONEY AROUND THE HEAD — RECITE THE APPROPRIATE PARAGRAPH ON THE NEXT PAGE THREE TIMES.]

בְּנֵי אָדָם יֹשְׁבֵי חְשֶׁךְ וְצַלְמָוֶת, אֲסִירֵי עֳנִי וּבַרְזֶל. יוֹצִיאֵם

‹ He takes ≪ and ‹ in ‹ [those] ≪ and the shadow ‹ in ‹ those ‹ of ‹ Children
them out   iron. affliction shackled   of death,   darkness who sat man,

מֵחְשֶׁךְ וְצַלְמָוֶת, וּמוֹסְרוֹתֵיהֶם יְנַתֵּק. אֱוִלִים מִדֶּרֶךְ פִּשְׁעָם,

≪ that is ‹ because of ‹ Fools, ≪ breaks ‹ and their ≪ and the shadow ‹ of
sinful   their path   open.   shackles   of death,   darkness

וּמֵעֲוֹנֹתֵיהֶם יִתְעַנּוּ. כָּל אֹכֶל תְּתַעֵב נַפְשָׁם, וַיַּגִּיעוּ עַד שַׁעֲרֵי

‹ the ‹ until ‹ and they ≪ did their ‹ abhor ‹ food ‹ All ≪ were ‹ and because of
portals   reached   soul,   afflicted.   their iniquities,

מָוֶת. וַיִּזְעֲקוּ אֶל יהוה בַּצַּר לָהֶם, מִמְּצֻקוֹתֵיהֶם יוֹשִׁיעֵם.

≪ He saves ‹ from their straits ≪ in their distress; ‹ HASHEM ‹ to ‹ Then they ≪ of
them.   cried out   death.

יִשְׁלַח דְּבָרוֹ וְיִרְפָּאֵם, וִימַלֵּט מִשְּׁחִיתוֹתָם. יוֹדוּ לַיהוה חַסְדּוֹ,

≪ for His ‹ to ‹ Let them ≪ their ‹ and lets ≪ and cures ‹ His ‹ He
kindness, HASHEM give thanks destruction. them escape them, word dispatches

וְנִפְלְאוֹתָיו לִבְנֵי אָדָם.[1] אִם יֵשׁ עָלָיו מַלְאָךְ מֵלִיץ אֶחָד מִנִּי

‹ out ‹ — [even] ≪ to ‹ an angel ‹ for ‹ there ‹ If ≪ of ‹ to the ‹ and for His
of   one defend him   him   is   man.   children   wonders

אָלֶף, לְהַגִּיד לְאָדָם יָשְׁרוֹ. וַיְחֻנֶּנּוּ וַיֹּאמֶר, פְּדָעֵהוּ מֵרֶדֶת

‹ from ‹ Redeem ≪ and ‹ [God] will be ≪ his up- ‹ for a ‹ to ≪ a thou-
descending him   say,   gracious to him rightness, man   declare sand —

שַׁחַת, מָצָאתִי כֹפֶר.[2]

≪ atonement ‹ I have ≪ to the Pit;
[for him].   found

---

(1) *Psalms* 107:10,14,17-21. (2) *Job* 33:23-24.

﷽{ ATONEMENT / כַּפָּרוֹת ﷽

There is an ancient custom to take a white rooster for males and a white hen for females on the day before Yom Kippur and perform the *Kaparos* [Atonement] ritual. Money may be substituted for the fowl, and the ritual may be performed before Erev Yom Kippur if necessary. It is most important to realize, however, that the atonement results from giving the bird (or its value) to the poor. Only that, as part of repentance, gives meaning to the ceremony. Some use a different chicken for each person,

RECITE THE APPLICABLE PARAGRAPH THREE TIMES. [WHEN MONEY IS USED,
SUBSTITUTE THE BRACKETED WORD/PHRASE FOR THE WORD/PHRASE PRECEDING IT.]
EACH TIME THE PARAGRAPH IS RECITED THE BIRD OR MONEY IS CIRCLED AROUND THE HEAD.

A MAN PERFORMING THE RITUAL FOR HIMSELF:

זֶה חֲלִיפָתִי, זֶה תְּמוּרָתִי, זֶה כַּפָּרָתִי. זֶה הַתַּרְנְגוֹל יֵלֵךְ לְמִיתָה

‹ to [its] ‹ will ‹ rooster ‹This 《 is my ‹ this ‹ is my ‹ this ‹ is my ‹ This
death, go atonement. substitute, exchange,

[זֶה הַכֶּסֶף יֵלֵךְ לִצְדָקָה], וַאֲנִי אֶכָּנֵס וְאֵלֵךְ לְחַיִּים טוֹבִים

‹ that is ‹ to a life ‹ and go ‹ will ‹ while 《 to charity], ‹will go ‹money ‹ [this
good enter I

אֲרוּכִים וּלְשָׁלוֹם.

《 and ‹ and long,
to peace.

TWO OR MORE MEN PERFORMING THE RITUAL FOR THEMSELVES:

זֶה חֲלִיפָתֵנוּ, זֶה תְּמוּרָתֵנוּ, זֶה כַּפָּרָתֵנוּ. זֶה הַתַּרְנְגוֹל יֵלֵךְ

‹ will ‹ rooster ‹This 《 is our ‹ this ‹ is our ‹ this ‹ is our ‹ This
go atonement. substitute, exchange,

לְמִיתָה [זֶה הַכֶּסֶף יֵלֵךְ לִצְדָקָה], וַאֲנַחְנוּ נִכָּנֵס וְנֵלֵךְ לְחַיִּים

‹ to a life ‹ and go ‹ will ‹ while 《 to charity], ‹will go ‹money ‹ [this ‹ to [its]
enter we death,

טוֹבִים אֲרוּכִים וּלְשָׁלוֹם.

《 and ‹ and long, ‹ that is
to peace. good

ONE PERFORMING THE RITUAL FOR A MAN:

זֶה חֲלִיפָתְךָ, זֶה תְּמוּרָתְךָ, זֶה כַּפָּרָתְךָ. זֶה הַתַּרְנְגוֹל יֵלֵךְ

‹ will ‹ rooster ‹This 《 is your ‹ this ‹ is your ‹ this ‹ is your ‹ This
go atonement substitute, exchange,

לְמִיתָה [זֶה הַכֶּסֶף יֵלֵךְ לִצְדָקָה], וְאַתָּה תִּכָּנֵס וְתֵלֵךְ לְחַיִּים

‹ to a life ‹ and go ‹ will ‹ while 《 to charity], ‹will go ‹money ‹ [this ‹ to [its]
enter you death,

טוֹבִים אֲרוּכִים וּלְשָׁלוֹם.

《 and ‹ and long, ‹ that is
to peace. good

---

while others use a single rooster for many men
or a single hen for many women.

A pregnant woman customarily takes both
a hen and a rooster, a hen for herself and a
possible daughter, and a rooster in case she is

carrying a male. Those who use a separate bird
for each person take three birds for a pregnant
woman, two hens, one for herself and one in
case she is carrying a female, and a rooster in
case she is carrying a male.

ONE PERFORMING THE RITUAL FOR TWO OR MORE MEN:

זֶה חֲלִיפַתְכֶם, זֶה תְּמוּרַתְכֶם, זֶה כַּפָּרַתְכֶם. זֶה הַתַּרְנְגוֹל

יֵלֵךְ לְמִיתָה [זֶה הַכֶּסֶף יֵלֵךְ לִצְדָקָה], וְאַתֶּם תִּכָּנְסוּ וְתֵלְכוּ

לְחַיִּים טוֹבִים אֲרוּכִים וּלְשָׁלוֹם.

A WOMAN PERFORMING THE RITUAL FOR HERSELF:

זֹאת [זֶה] חֲלִיפָתִי, זֹאת [זֶה] תְּמוּרָתִי, זֹאת [זֶה] כַּפָּרָתִי.

זֹאת הַתַּרְנְגֹלֶת תֵּלֵךְ לְמִיתָה [זֶה הַכֶּסֶף יֵלֵךְ לִצְדָקָה], וַאֲנִי

אֶכָּנֵס וְאֵלֵךְ לְחַיִּים טוֹבִים אֲרוּכִים וּלְשָׁלוֹם.

TWO OR MORE WOMEN PERFORMING THE RITUAL FOR THEMSELVES:

זֹאת [זֶה] חֲלִיפָתֵנוּ, זֹאת [זֶה] תְּמוּרָתֵנוּ, זֹאת [זֶה] כַּפָּרָתֵנוּ.

זֹאת הַתַּרְנְגֹלֶת תֵּלֵךְ לְמִיתָה [זֶה הַכֶּסֶף יֵלֵךְ לִצְדָקָה], וַאֲנַחְנוּ

נִכָּנֵס וְנֵלֵךְ לְחַיִּים טוֹבִים אֲרוּכִים וּלְשָׁלוֹם.

ONE PERFORMING THE RITUAL FOR A WOMAN:

זֹאת [זֶה] חֲלִיפָתֵךְ, זֹאת [זֶה] תְּמוּרָתֵךְ, זֹאת [זֶה] כַּפָּרָתֵךְ.

זֹאת הַתַּרְנְגֹלֶת תֵּלֵךְ לְמִיתָה [זֶה הַכֶּסֶף יֵלֵךְ לִצְדָקָה], וְאַתְּ

תִּכָּנֵסִי וְתֵלְכִי לְחַיִּים טוֹבִים אֲרוּכִים וּלְשָׁלוֹם.

⟪ and   ⟨ and long, ⟨ that is ⟨ to a life ⟨ and ⟨ will
to peace.   good   go   enter

ONE PERFORMING THE RITUAL FOR TWO OR MORE WOMEN:

זֹאת [זֶה] חֲלִיפַתְכֶן, זֹאת [זֶה] תְּמוּרַתְכֶן, זֹאת [זֶה] כַּפָּרַתְכֶן.

⟪ is your ⟨ [this ⟨ this ⟨ is your ⟨ [this ⟨ this ⟨ is your ⟨ [this ⟨ This
atonement.   substitute,   exchange,

זֹאת הַתַּרְנְגֹלֶת תֵּלֵךְ לְמִיתָה [זֶה הַכֶּסֶף יֵלֵךְ לִצְדָקָה], וְאַתֶּן

⟨ while ⟪ to charity], ⟨will go ⟨money ⟨[this ⟨ to [its] ⟨ will go ⟨ hen ⟨ This
you   death,

תִּכָּנֵסְנָה וְתֵלַכְנָה לְחַיִּים טוֹבִים אֲרוּכִים וּלְשָׁלוֹם.

⟪ and   ⟨ and long, ⟨ that is ⟨ to a life ⟨ and go ⟨ will enter
to peace.   good

A PREGNANT WOMAN PERFORMING THE RITUAL FOR HERSELF:

אֵלּוּ חֲלִיפוֹתֵינוּ [זֶה חֲלִיפָתֵנוּ], אֵלּוּ תְּמוּרוֹתֵינוּ [זֶה תְּמוּרָתֵנוּ],

⟨ is our ⟨ [this ⟨ are our ⟨ these ⟨ is our ⟨ [this ⟨ are our ⟨ These
substitute]   substitutes,   exchange]   exchanges,

אֵלּוּ כַּפָּרוֹתֵינוּ [זֶה כַּפָּרָתֵנוּ]. אֵלּוּ הַתַּרְנְגוֹלִים יֵלְכוּ לְמִיתָה

⟨ to [their] ⟨ will go ⟨ chickens ⟨These ⟪ is our ⟨ [this ⟨ are our ⟨ these
death,   atonement]   atonements.

[זֶה הַכֶּסֶף יֵלֵךְ לִצְדָקָה], וַאֲנַחְנוּ נִכָּנֵס וְנֵלֵךְ לְחַיִּים טוֹבִים

⟨ that is ⟨ to a life ⟨ and go ⟨ will ⟨ while we ⟪ to charity], ⟨will go ⟨money ⟨ [this
good   enter

אֲרוּכִים וּלְשָׁלוֹם.

⟪ and to peace. ⟨ and long,

ONE PERFORMING THE RITUAL FOR A PREGNANT WOMAN:

אֵלּוּ חֲלִיפוֹתֵיכֶם [זֶה חֲלִיפָתְכֶם], אֵלּוּ תְּמוּרוֹתֵיכֶם

⟨ are your substitutes, ⟨ these ⟨ is your exchange] ⟨ [this ⟨ are your exchanges, ⟨ These

[זֶה תְּמוּרַתְכֶם], אֵלּוּ כַּפָּרוֹתֵיכֶם [זֶה כַּפָּרַתְכֶם]. אֵלּוּ הַתַּרְנְגוֹלִים

⟨ chickens ⟨These ⟪ is your ⟨[this ⟪ are your ⟨ these ⟨ is your ⟨ [this
atonement]   atonements.   substitute]

יֵלְכוּ לְמִיתָה [זֶה הַכֶּסֶף יֵלֵךְ לִצְדָקָה], וְאַתֶּם תִּכָּנְסוּ וְתֵלְכוּ

⟨ and go ⟨ will enter ⟨ while ⟪ to charity], ⟨will go ⟨money ⟨[this ⟨ to [their] ⟨ will go
you   death,

לְחַיִּים טוֹבִים אֲרוּכִים וּלְשָׁלוֹם.

⟪ and   ⟨ and long, ⟨ that is ⟨ to a life
to peace.   good

﴾מנחה לערב יום כפור ﴿

﴾MINCHAH OF EREV YOM KIPPUR ﴿

AT THE *MINCHAH* SERVICE OF EREV YOM KIPPUR THE REGULAR SILENT *SHEMONEH ESREI* (PP. 363-385) IS RECITED. BEFORE נְצוֹר אֱלֹהַי, THE FOLLOWING וִדּוּי, *CONFESSION*, IS THEN RECITED. THE *CHAZZAN* DOES NOT REPEAT THE CONFESSION DURING HIS REPETITION OF *SHEMONEH ESREI*. A FULL COMMENTARY OF THIS BASIC COMPONENT OF THE YOM KIPPUR REPENTANCE LITURGY MAY BE FOUND IN THE ARTSCROLL *MACHZOR*.

אֱלֹהֵינוּ וֵאלֹהֵי אֲבוֹתֵינוּ, תָּבֹא לְפָנֶיךָ תְּפִלָּתֵנוּ,[1] וְאַל

⟨ and ⟨⟨ may our ⟨ before ⟨ come ⟨⟨ of our ⟨ and ⟨ Our God
do not   prayer,   You   forefathers,   the God

תִּתְעַלַּם מִתְּחִנָּתֵנוּ,[2] שֶׁאֵין אָנוּ עַזֵּי פָנִים וּקְשֵׁי עֹרֶף, לוֹמַר

⟨ as to ⟨ necked ⟨ and ⟨ faced ⟨ so ⟨ For we are ⟨⟨ our ⟨ ignore
say   stiff   brazen   not   supplication.

לְפָנֶיךָ יהוה אֱלֹהֵינוּ וֵאלֹהֵי אֲבוֹתֵינוּ, צַדִּיקִים אֲנַחְנוּ וְלֹא

⟨ and ⟨ that we are ⟨⟨ of our ⟨ and ⟨ our God, ⟨ HASHEM, ⟨⟨ before
have not   righteous   forefathers,   the God   You,

חָטָאנוּ, אֲבָל אֲנַחְנוּ וַאֲבוֹתֵינוּ חָטָאנוּ.[3]

⟨⟨ have sinned. ⟨ and our ⟨ we ⟨⟨ – for ⟨⟨ sinned
        forefathers   indeed,

STRIKE THE LEFT SIDE OF THE CHEST WITH THE RIGHT FIST WHILE RECITING EACH OF THE SINS OF THE FOLLOWING CONFESSIONAL LITANY:

אָשַׁמְנוּ, בָּגַדְנוּ, גָּזַלְנוּ, דִּבַּרְנוּ דְפִי. הֶעֱוִינוּ, וְהִרְשַׁעְנוּ,

⟨⟨ we have ⟨⟨ We have ⟨⟨ slander. ⟨ we have ⟨⟨ we have ⟨⟨ we have ⟨⟨ We have
committed   committed   spoken   robbed;   betrayed;   been guilty;
wickedness;   iniquity;

זַדְנוּ, חָמַסְנוּ, טָפַלְנוּ שֶׁקֶר. יָעַצְנוּ רָע, כִּזַּבְנוּ, לַצְנוּ,

⟨⟨ we have ⟨⟨ we have ⟨⟨ that ⟨ We have ⟨⟨ false ⟨ we have ⟨⟨ we have ⟨⟨ we have
scorned;   been   is bad;   given   accusations.   made   extorted;   sinned
      deceitful;   advice   willfully;

מָרַדְנוּ, נִאַצְנוּ, סָרַרְנוּ, עָוִינוּ, פָּשַׁעְנוּ, צָרַרְנוּ, קִשִּׁינוּ עֹרֶף.

⟨⟨ our ⟨ we have ⟨⟨ we have ⟨⟨ we have ⟨⟨ we have ⟨⟨ we have ⟨⟨ we have ⟨⟨ we have
necks.   stiffened   caused   sinned   been   strayed;   provoked   rebelled;
          distress;   rebelliously;   iniquitous;   [God's anger];

רָשַׁעְנוּ, שִׁחַתְנוּ, תִּעַבְנוּ, תָּעִינוּ, תִּעְתָּעְנוּ.

⟨⟨ we have ⟨⟨ we have ⟨⟨ we have ⟨⟨ we have ⟨⟨ We have
scoffed.   gone astray;   committed   been corrupt;   been wicked;
                    abominations;

---

(1) Cf. *Psalms* 88:3. (2) Cf. 55:2. (3) Cf. 106:6; *Jeremiah* 3:25.

﴾ MINCHAH EREV YOM KIPPUR ﴿

As found several times in the Torah and as codified by *Rambam* in the Laws of Repen-

tance, the confession of sins is an essential part of repentance. It is human nature for people to rationalize their shortcomings in their own

סָרְנוּ מִמִּצְוֹתֶיךָ וּמִמִּשְׁפָּטֶיךָ הַטּוֹבִים, וְלֹא שָׁוָה לָנוּ.[1]

‹ for ‹ worth- ‹ and it ‹ that are ‹ and from ‹ from Your ‹ We have
us. while was not good, Your laws commandments turned away

וְאַתָּה צַדִּיק עַל כָּל הַבָּא עָלֵינוּ, כִּי אֱמֶת עָשִׂיתָ וַאֲנַחְנוּ

‹ while ‹ have ‹ truthfully ‹ for ‹ upon ‹ that has ‹ all ‹ in ‹ are ‹ And You
we You acted, us, come righteous

הִרְשָׁעְנוּ.[2]

‹ have acted
wickedly.

מַה נֹּאמַר לְפָנֶיךָ יוֹשֵׁב מָרוֹם, וּמַה נְּסַפֵּר לְפָנֶיךָ שׁוֹכֵן

‹ Who ‹ before ‹ can we ‹ and ‹ on high, ‹ Who ‹ before You, ‹ can we ‹ What
abides You, relate what dwells say

שְׁחָקִים, הֲלֹא כָּל הַנִּסְתָּרוֹת וְהַנִּגְלוֹת אַתָּה יוֹדֵעַ.

‹ know. ‹ You ‹ and revealed ‹ hidden things ‹ all ‹ For ‹ in the highest
things indeed, heavens?

אַתָּה יוֹדֵעַ רָזֵי עוֹלָם, וְתַעֲלוּמוֹת סִתְרֵי כָּל חָי. אַתָּה

‹ You ‹ the ‹ of ‹ of the ‹ and the ‹ of the ‹ the ‹ know ‹ You
living. all hidden things mysteries universe, secrets

חֹפֵשׂ כָּל חַדְרֵי בָטֶן,[3] וּבוֹחֵן כְּלָיוֹת וָלֵב. אֵין דָּבָר נֶעְלָם

‹ is ‹ item ‹ No ‹ and ‹ his ‹ and ‹ of [man's] ‹ the ‹ all ‹ probe
hidden thoughts examine innermost chambers
feelings. parts

מִמֶּךָּ, וְאֵין נִסְתָּר מִנֶּגֶד עֵינֶיךָ. וּבְכֵן יְהִי רָצוֹן מִלְּפָנֶיךָ, יהוה

‹ HASHEM, ‹ before ‹ the ‹ may ‹ And so, ‹ Your ‹ from ‹ is con- ‹ and ‹ from
You, will it be eyes. before cealed nothing You

אֱלֹהֵינוּ וֵאלֹהֵי אֲבוֹתֵינוּ, שֶׁתְּכַפֵּר לָנוּ עַל כָּל חַטֹּאתֵינוּ,

‹ our uninten- ‹ all ‹ for ‹ to us ‹ that You grant ‹ of our ‹ and ‹ our God
tional sins, atonement forefathers, the God

וְתִסְלַח לָנוּ עַל כָּל עֲוֹנוֹתֵינוּ, וְתִמְחָל לָנוּ עַל כָּל פְּשָׁעֵינוּ.

‹ our rebel- ‹ all ‹ for ‹ us ‹ and ‹ our inten- ‹ all ‹ for ‹ us ‹ and forgive
lious sins. pardon tional sins,

---

(1) Cf. *Job* 33:27. (2) *Nehemiah* 9:33. (3) *Proverbs* 20:27. (4) *Jeremiah* 11:20.

minds as unavoidable or even to define them as virtues. As long as one refuses to acknowledge his wrongdoing, he cannot repent sincerely. So important is the confession, not only to the process of repentance but also to the Jew's chance to survive the Heavenly judgment, that the Sages ordained that the confession be recited the afternoon before Yom Kippur, lest illness or death prevent someone from praying on Yom Kippur itself.

The confession includes a very wide range of sins, far more than any individual could have committed. This is because it contains not only the sins of the individual supplicant, but also

**STRIKE THE LEFT SIDE OF THE CHEST WITH THE RIGHT FIST
EACH TIME THE WORD שֶׁחָטָאנוּ, *WE HAVE SINNED*, IS SAID.**

עַל חֵטְא שֶׁחָטָאנוּ לְפָנֶיךָ בְּאֹנֶס וּבְרָצוֹן,

‹‹ and
willingly, ‹ under
duress ‹ before
You ‹ that we have
sinned ‹ the sin ‹ For

וְעַל חֵטְא שֶׁחָטָאנוּ לְפָנֶיךָ בְּאִמּוּץ הַלֵּב.[1]

‹‹ of the
heart; ‹ through
hardness ‹ before
You ‹ that we have
sinned ‹ the sin ‹ and
for

עַל חֵטְא שֶׁחָטָאנוּ לְפָנֶיךָ בִּבְלִי דָעַת,

‹‹ knowledge, ‹ without ‹ before
You ‹ that we have
sinned ‹ the sin ‹ for

וְעַל חֵטְא שֶׁחָטָאנוּ לְפָנֶיךָ בְּבִטוּי שְׂפָתָיִם.[2]

‹‹ of the lips; ‹ with the
utterance ‹ before
You ‹ that we have
sinned ‹ the sin ‹ and
for

עַל חֵטְא שֶׁחָטָאנוּ לְפָנֶיךָ בְּגִלּוּי עֲרָיוֹת,

‹‹ through sexual
immorality, ‹ before
You ‹ that we have
sinned ‹ the sin ‹ for

וְעַל חֵטְא שֶׁחָטָאנוּ לְפָנֶיךָ בַּגָּלוּי וּבַסָּתֶר.

‹‹ or in private; ‹ in public ‹ before
You ‹ that we have
sinned ‹ the sin ‹ and
for

עַל חֵטְא שֶׁחָטָאנוּ לְפָנֶיךָ בְּדַעַת וּבְמִרְמָה,

‹‹ and with
deceit, ‹ with
knowledge ‹ before
You ‹ that we have
sinned ‹ the sin ‹ for

וְעַל חֵטְא שֶׁחָטָאנוּ לְפָנֶיךָ בְּדִבּוּר פֶּה.

‹‹ of the
mouth; [harsh] speech ‹ through ‹ before
You ‹ that we have
sinned ‹ the sin ‹ and
for

עַל חֵטְא שֶׁחָטָאנוּ לְפָנֶיךָ בְּהוֹנָאַת רֵעַ,

‹‹ a friend, ‹ through
wronging ‹ before
You ‹ that we have
sinned ‹ the sin ‹ for

(1) Cf. *Deuteronomy* 15:7. (2) Cf. *Leviticus* 5:4.

those of the entire Jewish people. It is axiomatic that had the nation as a whole repented sufficiently, the Final Redemption would already have come. Thus, we share responsibility not only for our own sins, but for those of the past. Furthermore, the principle that all Jews are responsible for one another means that we are all partners in the failures of our brethren.

Despite the wide range of sins enumerated in this long confession, there are many individual sins that are not specified. The confession should be seen not as a complete and exhaustive list of all possible sins, but as a list of categories and causes. For example, the sins of "showing contempt for parents and teachers" and of "foolish speech" are the direct cause of many other misdeeds. Seen in this light, the confession is a means of introspective soul-searching to discover the shortcomings of our personality as well as to identify individual sins.

וְעַל חֵטְא שֶׁחָטָאנוּ לְפָנֶיךָ בְּהַרְהוֹר הַלֵּב.

‹‹ of the ‹ through inner ‹ before ‹ that we have ‹ the sin ‹ and
heart;   thoughts   You   sinned   for

עַל חֵטְא שֶׁחָטָאנוּ לְפָנֶיךָ בּוְעִידַת זְנוּת,

‹‹ for ‹ in a ‹ before ‹ that we have ‹ the sin ‹ for
lewdness,   gathering   You   sinned

וְעַל חֵטְא שֶׁחָטָאנוּ לְפָנֶיךָ בְּוִדּוּי פֶּה.

‹‹ of the ‹ through ‹ before ‹ that we have ‹ the sin ‹ and
mouth;   [insincere]   You   sinned   for
     confession

עַל חֵטְא שֶׁחָטָאנוּ לְפָנֶיךָ בְּזִלְזוּל הוֹרִים וּמוֹרִים,

‹‹ and ‹ for ‹ by showing ‹ before ‹ that we have ‹ the sin ‹ for
teachers,   parents   contempt   You   sinned

וְעַל חֵטְא שֶׁחָטָאנוּ לְפָנֶיךָ בְּזָדוֹן וּבִשְׁגָגָה.

‹‹ and ‹ willfully ‹ before ‹ that we have ‹ the sin ‹ and
inadvertently;   You   sinned   for

עַל חֵטְא שֶׁחָטָאנוּ לְפָנֶיךָ בְּחוֹזֶק יָד,

‹‹ by exercising ‹ before ‹ that we have ‹ the sin ‹ for
coercive power,   You   sinned

וְעַל חֵטְא שֶׁחָטָאנוּ לְפָנֶיךָ בְּחִלּוּל הַשֵּׁם.

‹‹ of [Your] ‹ through ‹ before ‹ that we have ‹ the sin ‹ and
Name;   desecration   You   sinned   for

עַל חֵטְא שֶׁחָטָאנוּ לְפָנֶיךָ בְּטֻמְאַת שְׂפָתָיִם,

‹‹ of the lips, ‹ through ‹ before ‹ that we have ‹ the sin ‹ for
   defilement   You   sinned

וְעַל חֵטְא שֶׁחָטָאנוּ לְפָנֶיךָ בְּטִפְּשׁוּת פֶּה.

‹‹ of the ‹ through foolish ‹ before ‹ that we have ‹ the sin ‹ and
mouth;   [speech]   You   sinned   for

עַל חֵטְא שֶׁחָטָאנוּ לְפָנֶיךָ בְּיֵצֶר הָרָע,

‹‹ for Evil, ‹ with the ‹ before ‹ that we have ‹ the sin ‹ for
Inclination   You   sinned

וְעַל חֵטְא שֶׁחָטָאנוּ לְפָנֶיךָ בְּיוֹדְעִים וּבְלֹא יוֹדְעִים.

‹‹ become ‹ and against ‹ against those ‹ before ‹ that we have ‹ the sin ‹ and
aware of it;   those who   who became   You   sinned   for
   did not   aware of it

וְעַל כֻּלָּם, אֱלוֹהַּ סְלִיחוֹת, סְלַח לָנוּ, מְחַל לָנוּ, כַּפֶּר לָנוּ.

‹‹ to ‹ grant ‹ us, ‹ pardon ‹ us, ‹ forgive ‹‹ of ‹ O God ‹‹ all ‹ for
us. atonement   forgiveness,   these,

עַל חֵטְא שֶׁחָטָאנוּ לְפָנֶיךָ בְּכַחַשׁ וּבְכָזָב,

《 and untrust- 〈 through 〈 before 〈 that we have 〈 the sin 〈 For
worthiness,　denial　You　sinned

וְעַל חֵטְא שֶׁחָטָאנוּ לְפָנֶיךָ בְּכַפַּת שֹׁחַד.[1]

《 in 〈 with a hand 〈 before 〈 that we have 〈 the sin 〈 and
bribery;　involved　You　sinned　for

עַל חֵטְא שֶׁחָטָאנוּ לְפָנֶיךָ בְּלָצוֹן,

《 through 〈 before 〈 that we have 〈 the sin 〈 for
scoffing,　You　sinned

וְעַל חֵטְא שֶׁחָטָאנוּ לְפָנֶיךָ בְּלָשׁוֹן הָרָע.

《 that is 〈 through 〈 before 〈 that we have 〈 the sin 〈 and
evil;　talk　You　sinned　for

עַל חֵטְא שֶׁחָטָאנוּ לְפָנֶיךָ בְּמַשָּׂא וּבְמַתָּן,

《 in business dealings, 〈 before 〈 that we have 〈 the sin 〈 for
You　sinned

וְעַל חֵטְא שֶׁחָטָאנוּ לְפָנֶיךָ בְּמַאֲכָל וּבְמִשְׁתֶּה.

《 and with drink; 〈 with food 〈 before 〈 that we have 〈 the sin 〈 and
You　sinned　for

עַל חֵטְא שֶׁחָטָאנוּ לְפָנֶיךָ בְּנֶשֶׁךְ וּבְמַרְבִּית,[2]

《 and usury, 〈 through 〈 before 〈 that we have 〈 the sin 〈 for
interest　You　sinned

וְעַל חֵטְא שֶׁחָטָאנוּ לְפָנֶיךָ בִּנְטִיַּת גָּרוֹן.[3]

《 the neck [in 〈 through 〈 before 〈 that we have 〈 the sin 〈 and
haughtiness]; extending　You　sinned　for

עַל חֵטְא שֶׁחָטָאנוּ לְפָנֶיךָ בְּשִׂיחַ שִׂפְתוֹתֵינוּ,

《 of our lips 〈 with the 〈 before 〈 that we have 〈 the sin 〈 for
[without thought],　speech　You　sinned

וְעַל חֵטְא שֶׁחָטָאנוּ לְפָנֶיךָ בְּשִׂקּוּר עָיִן.[3]

《 eyes; 〈 with prying 〈 before 〈 that we have 〈 the sin 〈 and
You　sinned　for

עַל חֵטְא שֶׁחָטָאנוּ לְפָנֶיךָ בְּעֵינַיִם רָמוֹת,[4]

《 that are 〈 with eyes 〈 before 〈 that we have 〈 the sin 〈 for
haughty,　You　sinned

וְעַל חֵטְא שֶׁחָטָאנוּ לְפָנֶיךָ בְּעַזּוּת מֵצַח.

《 facedness; 〈 with 〈 before 〈 that we have 〈 the sin 〈 and
brazen-　You　sinned　for

וְעַל כֻּלָּם, אֱלוֹהַּ סְלִיחוֹת, סְלַח לָנוּ, מְחַל לָנוּ, כַּפֶּר לָנוּ.

《 to 〈 grant 〈 us, 〈 pardon 〈 us, 〈 forgive 《 of 〈 O God 《 all 〈 for
us. atonement　forgiveness,　these,

(1) Cf. *Isaiah* 33:15; see also *Proverbs* 21:14. (2) *Leviticus* 25:37. (3) Cf. *Isaiah* 3:16. (4) Cf. *Psalms* 18:28.

574 / ערב יום כפור

עַל חֵטְא שֶׁחָטָאנוּ לְפָנֶיךָ בִּפְרִיקַת עֹל,

<< the yoke [of < in throwing < before < that we have < the sin < For
Your *mitzvos*], off You sinned

וְעַל חֵטְא שֶׁחָטָאנוּ לְפָנֶיךָ בִּפְלִילוּת.

<< in judgment; < before < that we have < the sin < and
You sinned for

עַל חֵטְא שֶׁחָטָאנוּ לְפָנֶיךָ בִּצְדִיַּת רֵעַ,[1]

<< a friend, < through < before < that we have < the sin < for
entrapping You sinned

וְעַל חֵטְא שֶׁחָטָאנוּ לְפָנֶיךָ בְּצָרוּת עָיִן.

<< eye; < through a < before < that we have < the sin < and
begrudging You sinned for

עַל חֵטְא שֶׁחָטָאנוּ לְפָנֶיךָ בְּקַלּוּת רֹאשׁ,

<< headedness, < through < before < that we have < the sin < for
light- You sinned

וְעַל חֵטְא שֶׁחָטָאנוּ לְפָנֶיךָ בְּקַשְׁיוּת עֹרֶף.[2]

<< necked < with stiff- < before < that we have < the sin < and
obstinacy; You sinned for

עַל חֵטְא שֶׁחָטָאנוּ לְפָנֶיךָ בְּרִיצַת רַגְלַיִם לְהָרַע,[3]

<< to do evil, < of our legs < with the < before < that we have < the sin < for
running You sinned

וְעַל חֵטְא שֶׁחָטָאנוּ לְפָנֶיךָ בִּרְכִילוּת.[4]

<< by gossip- < before < that we have < the sin < and
mongering; You sinned for

עַל חֵטְא שֶׁחָטָאנוּ לְפָנֶיךָ בִּשְׁבוּעַת שָׁוְא,

<< in vain, < through [taking] < before < that we have < the sin < for
an oath You sinned

וְעַל חֵטְא שֶׁחָטָאנוּ לְפָנֶיךָ בְּשִׂנְאַת חִנָּם.

<< without < through < before < that we have < the sin < and
cause; hatred You sinned for

עַל חֵטְא שֶׁחָטָאנוּ לְפָנֶיךָ בִּתְשׂוּמֶת יָד,[5]

<< in our < in [defaulting < before < that we have < the sin < for
hand, on a loan] placed You sinned

וְעַל חֵטְא שֶׁחָטָאנוּ לְפָנֶיךָ בְּתִמְהוֹן לֵבָב.[6]

<< of the < through < before < that we have < the sin < and
heart; confusion You sinned for

(1) Cf. *Exodus* 21:13. (2) Cf. *Jeremiah* 19:15. (3) Cf. *Isaiah* 59:7.
(4) Cf. *Leviticus* 19:16. (5) 5:21. (6) *Deuteronomy* 28:28.

וְעַל כֻּלָּם, אֱלוֹהַּ סְלִיחוֹת, סְלַח לָנוּ, מְחַל לָנוּ, כַּפֶּר לָנוּ.

For / all / these, / O God / of forgiveness, / forgive / us, / pardon / us, / grant / us atonement.

וְעַל חֲטָאִים שֶׁאָנוּ חַיָּבִים עֲלֵיהֶם עוֹלָה.

And for / the sins / that we / are obligated / because of them / an elevation-offering;

וְעַל חֲטָאִים שֶׁאָנוּ חַיָּבִים עֲלֵיהֶם חַטָּאת.

And for / the sins / that we / are obligated / because of them / a sin-offering;

וְעַל חֲטָאִים שֶׁאָנוּ חַיָּבִים עֲלֵיהֶם קָרְבָּן עוֹלֶה וְיוֹרֵד.

And for / the sins / that we / are obligated / because of them / a [sin-]offering / that is variable;

וְעַל חֲטָאִים שֶׁאָנוּ חַיָּבִים עֲלֵיהֶם אָשָׁם וַדַּאי וְתָלוּי.

And for / the sins / that we / are obligated / because of them / a guilt-offering / for a definite / or a possible sin;

וְעַל חֲטָאִים שֶׁאָנוּ חַיָּבִים עֲלֵיהֶם מַכַּת מַרְדּוּת.

And for / the sins / that we / are obligated / because of them / lashes / for rebelliousness;

וְעַל חֲטָאִים שֶׁאָנוּ חַיָּבִים עֲלֵיהֶם מַלְקוּת אַרְבָּעִים.

And for / the sins / that we / are obligated / because of them / forty lashes [less one];

וְעַל חֲטָאִים שֶׁאָנוּ חַיָּבִים עֲלֵיהֶם מִיתָה בִּידֵי שָׁמָיִם.

And for / the sins / that we / are obligated / because of them / death / at the hands / of the Heavenly Court;

וְעַל חֲטָאִים שֶׁאָנוּ חַיָּבִים עֲלֵיהֶם כָּרֵת וַעֲרִירִי.

And for / the sins / that we / are obligated / because of them / spiritual excision / and childlessness;

וְעַל חֲטָאִים שֶׁאָנוּ חַיָּבִים עֲלֵיהֶם אַרְבַּע מִיתוֹת בֵּית דִּין —

And for / the sins / that we / are obligated / because of them / the four / death penalties / of the [earthly] court / of justice

סְקִילָה, שְׂרֵפָה, הֶרֶג, וְחֶנֶק.

— stoning, / burning, / beheading, / and strangling;

עַל מִצְוַת עֲשֵׂה וְעַל מִצְוַת לֹא תַעֲשֶׂה, בֵּין שֶׁיֵּשׁ בָּהּ

for / [violation of] a positive commandment / and for / [violation of] a negative commandment, / whether / it has

קוּם עֲשֵׂה, וּבֵין שֶׁאֵין בָּהּ קוּם עֲשֵׂה. אֶת הַגְּלוּיִם לָנוּ

a [remedy] through performing a positive act; / or / whether / it does not have / a [remedy] through performing a positive act; / those that are revealed / to us

וְאֶת שֶׁאֵינָם גְּלוּיִם לָנוּ, אֶת הַגְּלוּיִם לָנוּ, כְּבָר אֲמַרְנוּם לְפָנֶיךָ,

וְהוֹדִינוּ לְךָ עֲלֵיהֶם, וְאֶת שֶׁאֵינָם גְּלוּיִם לָנוּ, לְפָנֶיךָ הֵם גְּלוּיִם

וִידוּעִים, כַּדָּבָר שֶׁנֶּאֱמַר, הַנִּסְתָּרֹת לַיהוה אֱלֹהֵינוּ, וְהַנִּגְלֹת

לָנוּ וּלְבָנֵינוּ עַד עוֹלָם, לַעֲשׂוֹת אֶת כָּל דִּבְרֵי הַתּוֹרָה הַזֹּאת.[1]

כִּי אַתָּה סָלְחָן לְיִשְׂרָאֵל וּמָחֳלָן לְשִׁבְטֵי יְשֻׁרוּן בְּכָל דּוֹר

וָדוֹר, וּמִבַּלְעָדֶיךָ אֵין לָנוּ מֶלֶךְ מוֹחֵל וְסוֹלֵחַ אֶלָּא אַתָּה.

אֱלֹהַי, עַד שֶׁלֹּא נוֹצַרְתִּי אֵינִי כְדַאי, וְעַכְשָׁו שֶׁנּוֹצַרְתִּי

כְּאִלּוּ לֹא נוֹצַרְתִּי, עָפָר אֲנִי בְּחַיַּי, קַל וָחֹמֶר בְּמִיתָתִי. הֲרֵי[2]

אֲנִי לְפָנֶיךָ כִּכְלִי מָלֵא בוּשָׁה וּכְלִמָּה. יְהִי רָצוֹן מִלְּפָנֶיךָ, יהוה

אֱלֹהַי וֵאלֹהֵי אֲבוֹתַי, שֶׁלֹּא אֶחֱטָא עוֹד, וּמַה שֶּׁחָטָאתִי

לְפָנֶיךָ מְחוֹק בְּרַחֲמֶיךָ הָרַבִּים, אֲבָל לֹא עַל יְדֵי יִסּוּרִים

וָחֳלָיִם רָעִים.

RETURN TO אֱלֹהַי נְצוֹר (P. 385) FOR THE CONCLUSION OF SHEMONEH ESREI.

(1) *Deuteronomy* 29:28. (2) Cf. *Genesis* 3:19.

הדלקת הנרות לחנוכה

KINDLING THE CHANUKAH MENORAH

ALL THREE BLESSINGS ARE PRONOUNCED BEFORE KINDLING THE CHANUKAH *MENORAH* FOR THE FIRST TIME. ON ALL SUBSEQUENT NIGHTS, THE THIRD BLESSING, שֶׁהֶחֱיָנוּ, IS OMITTED.

בָּרוּךְ אַתָּה יהוה אֱלֹהֵינוּ מֶלֶךְ הָעוֹלָם, אֲשֶׁר קִדְּשָׁנוּ

Blessed ⟨ are You, ⟨ HASHEM, ⟨ our God, ⟨ King ⟨ of the universe, ⟨⟨ Who ⟨ has sanctified us

בְּמִצְוֹתָיו, וְצִוָּנוּ לְהַדְלִיק נֵר (שֶׁל) חֲנֻכָּה.

with His commandments, and has commanded us ⟨⟨ to kindle ⟨ the light ⟨ of ⟨⟨ Chanukah.

בָּרוּךְ אַתָּה יהוה אֱלֹהֵינוּ מֶלֶךְ הָעוֹלָם, שֶׁעָשָׂה נִסִּים

Blessed ⟨ are You, ⟨ HASHEM, ⟨ our God, ⟨ King ⟨ of the universe, ⟨⟨ Who wrought ⟨ miracles

לַאֲבוֹתֵינוּ, בַּיָּמִים הָהֵם בַּזְּמַן הַזֶּה.

for our forefathers, ⟨ in those days ⟨ at this season. ⟨⟨

בָּרוּךְ אַתָּה יהוה אֱלֹהֵינוּ מֶלֶךְ הָעוֹלָם, שֶׁהֶחֱיָנוּ

Blessed ⟨ are You, ⟨ HASHEM, ⟨ our God, ⟨ King ⟨ of the universe, ⟨⟨ Who has kept us alive,

וְקִיְּמָנוּ וְהִגִּיעָנוּ לַזְּמַן הַזֶּה.

and has sustained us ⟨ and has brought us ⟨ to this season. ⟨⟨

ON THE FIRST NIGHT, THE LIGHT TO THE EXTREME RIGHT IS KINDLED. ON EACH SUBSEQUENT NIGHT, A NEW LIGHT IS ADDED TO THE LEFT OF THE PREVIOUS NIGHT'S LIGHTS. THE NEW LIGHT IS ALWAYS KINDLED FIRST, THE ONE TO ITS RIGHT SECOND, AND SO ON. AFTER ONE LIGHT HAS BEEN KINDLED, הַנֵּרוֹת הַלָּלוּ IS RECITED. THE ADDITIONAL LIGHTS ARE KINDLED DURING ITS RECITATION.

הַנֵּרוֹת הַלָּלוּ אָנוּ מַדְלִיקִין עַל הַנִּסִּים וְעַל הַנִּפְלָאוֹת,*

These lights ⟨ we ⟨ kindle ⟨ for ⟨ the miracles, ⟨ for ⟨ the wonders,* ⟨

וְעַל הַתְּשׁוּעוֹת וְעַל הַנֶּחָמוֹת וְעַל הַמִּלְחָמוֹת, שֶׁעָשִׂיתָ

for ⟨ the salvations, ⟨ and for ⟨ the consolations, ⟨ and for ⟨ the battles ⟨ which You performed

לַאֲבוֹתֵינוּ בַּיָּמִים הָהֵם בַּזְּמַן הַזֶּה, עַל יְדֵי כֹּהֲנֶיךָ

for our forefathers ⟨ in those days ⟨ at this season, ⟨ through ⟨ the hands ⟨ of Your priests

---

הַנֵּרוֹת הַלָּלוּ / HaNeiros HaLalu

[See ArtScroll *Chanukah* for full commentary.]

עַל הַנִּסִּים וְעַל הַנִּפְלָאוֹת — *For the miracles, for the wonders.* The word נִסִּים, *miracles*, refers to the obvious acts of intervention by His Divine Providence. This word can also mean *banners* or *signposts*, for God's miracles are meant to be signposts and symbols that stand out to teach and guide us.

הַקְּדוֹשִׁים. וְכָל שְׁמוֹנַת יְמֵי חֲנֻכָּה, הַנֵּרוֹת הַלָּלוּ
‹ these lights ‹ of Chanukah ‹ days ‹ eight ‹ All ≪ who are holy.

קְדֶשׁ הֵם. וְאֵין לָנוּ רְשׁוּת לְהִשְׁתַּמֵּשׁ בָּהֶם,* אֶלָּא
‹ but ‹ of them,* ‹ to make [personal] use ‹ permission ‹ and we do not have≪ are sacred,

לִרְאוֹתָם בִּלְבָד, כְּדֵי לְהוֹדוֹת וּלְהַלֵּל לְשִׁמְךָ הַגָּדוֹל*
‹ to Your great Name* ‹ and praise ‹ to express ‹ – in ≪ only ‹ to look at
                     thanks   order   them

עַל נִסֶּיךָ וְעַל נִפְלְאוֹתֶיךָ וְעַל יְשׁוּעָתֶךָ.
≪ Your salvation. ‹ and for ‹ Your wonders, ‹ for ≪ Your miracles, ‹ for

AFTER THE LIGHTS HAVE BEEN KINDLED, *MAOZ TZUR* IS CHANTED:

מָעוֹז צוּר יְשׁוּעָתִי,* לְךָ נָאֶה לְשַׁבֵּחַ,
≪ to praise. ‹ it is proper ‹ to You ≪ of my salvation,* ‹ Rock ‹ O Stronghold,

תִּכּוֹן בֵּית תְּפִלָּתִי, וְשָׁם תּוֹדָה נְזַבֵּחַ,
≪ we will ‹ a thanksgiving- ‹ and ≪ of my ‹ the ‹ Restore
bring.   offering   there   Prayer   House

לְעֵת תָּכִין מַטְבֵּחַ, מִצָּר הַמְנַבֵּחַ,
≪ who is ‹ of the ‹ the ‹ when You ‹ At the
bellowing,   foe   slaughter   will prepare   time

The term נִפְלָאוֹת, *wonders*, describes these extraordinary occurrences in terms of their independence from the regular order of things (*R' Hirsch*).

וְאֵין לָנוּ רְשׁוּת לְהִשְׁתַּמֵּשׁ בָּהֶם — *And we do not have permission to make [personal] use of them.* It is forbidden to use the Chanukah lights for any personal purpose — such as reading or doing work by their illumination — "lest one slight the *mitzvos*" (*Shabbos* 21b). The prohibition against enjoying the lights makes it manifestly clear to all that they were kindled for the sole purpose of commemorating the miracle.

In compliance with the prohibition against enjoying the lights, we light a *shamash* [lit. *servant*] flame, which is not holy, so that any incidental pleasure that comes from the lights can be considered as coming from the *shamash*.

כְּדֵי לְהוֹדוֹת וּלְהַלֵּל לְשִׁמְךָ הַגָּדוֹל — *In order to express thanks and praise to Your great Name.* By refraining from utilizing the Chanukah lights for anything but the *mitzvah* itself, and contemplating them while they burn, we make it apparent to all that our intent is to publicize the miracle

and to praise God's great Name in acknowledgment of His great miracles.

§ **מָעוֹז צוּר/Maoz Tzur.** Following the kindling of the lights and recital of *HaNeiros HaLalu* it is customary to recite the following *zemer*.

The author's name, Mordechai [מָרְדְּכַי], appears in the acrostic of the initial letters of the first five stanzas. It was apparently composed in the mid-13th century.

In the *zemer* the *paytan* [liturgical poet] recalls various periods that the Jewish people endured, praises God for redeeming us from each of them, and prays for the restoration of the Temple and for the dawn of the Messianic Redemption.

Shem MiShmuel notes that each of the earlier periods of servitude — the Egyptian bondage and the Babylonian, Persian, and Greek exiles — served to prepare the nation for the tribulations it would encounter in the subsequent exiles.

מָעוֹז צוּר יְשׁוּעָתִי — *O Stronghold, Rock of my salvation.* This opening stanza is a plea for the reestablishment of the Temple, our House of Prayer; the rededication of the Altar; and the

אָז אֶגְמוֹר בְּשִׁיר מִזְמוֹר חֲנֻכַּת הַמִּזְבֵּחַ.

《 of the Altar. 〈 the dedication 〈 a hymn, 〈 with a song, 〈 I shall complete, 〈 then

רָעוֹת שָׂבְעָה נַפְשִׁי,* בְּיָגוֹן כֹּחִי כָּלָה,

《 did he consume. 〈 my strength 〈 with grief 《 was my soul sated,* 〈 With troubles

חַיַּי מֵרְרוּ בְקְשִׁי, בְּשִׁעְבּוּד מַלְכוּת עֶגְלָה,

《 [compared 〈 of the 〈 with the 〈 with 〈 they 〈 My
to] a calf. kingdom bondage hardship, embittered life

וּבְיָדוֹ הַגְּדוֹלָה הוֹצִיא אֶת הַסְּגֻלָּה,

《 the treasured [nation]. 〈 He took out 〈 But with His great power

חֵיל פַּרְעֹה וְכָל זַרְעוֹ יָרְדוּ כְּאֶבֶן בִּמְצוּלָה.

《 into the deep. 〈 like a 〈 went 〈 his 〈 and 〈 of 〈 The
stone, down, offspring all Pharaoh army

דְּבִיר קָדְשׁוֹ* הֱבִיאַנִי, וְגַם שָׁם לֹא שָׁקַטְתִּי,

《 rest. 〈 I did 〈 there 〈 But 《 He brought 〈 of His 〈 [To] the
not also me. holiness* Abode

וּבָא נוֹגֵשׂ וְהִגְלַנִי, כִּי זָרִים עָבַדְתִּי,

《 I served. 〈 foreign 〈 because 《 and 〈 an 〈 For along
[gods] exiled me, oppressor came

וְיֵין רַעַל מָסַכְתִּי, כִּמְעַט שֶׁעָבַרְתִּי,

《 did I perish. 〈 almost 《 I mixed 〈 of bewil- 〈 The
[and drank]; derment wine

קֵץ בָּבֶל, זְרֻבָּבֶל, לְקֵץ שִׁבְעִים נוֹשַׁעְתִּי,

《 I was saved. 〈 of seventy 〈 at the 《 Zerubabel 〈 of [the exile 〈 At the
[years] end [came]; in] Babylonia, end

כְּרוֹת קוֹמַת בְּרוֹשׁ,* בִּקֵּשׁ אֲגָגִי בֶּן הַמְּדָתָא,

《 of 〈 the 〈 [Haman] 〈 sought 《 of the 〈 the lofty 〈 To sever
Hammedatha, son the Agagite, cypress,* height

וְנִהְיְתָה לוֹ לְפַח וּלְמוֹקֵשׁ, וְגַאֲוָתוֹ נִשְׁבָּתָה,

《 was stilled. 〈 and his 《 and a stum- 〈 a snare 〈 for 〈 but it
arrogance bling block, him became

---

renewal of the services there.

רָעוֹת שָׂבְעָה נַפְשִׁי — *With troubles was my soul sated*, during the bondage in Egypt. Scripture (*Jeremiah* 46:20) describes the Egyptians as עֶגְלָה, יְפֵה פִיָּה, *a very fair calf*.

דְּבִיר קָדְשׁוֹ — *[To] the Abode of His holiness*, the Holy of Holies in King Solomon's Temple. The oppressor is Babylonia, who exiled the nation from its land when Israel served foreign gods.

כְּרוֹת קוֹמַת בְּרוֹשׁ — *To sever the lofty height of the cypress*. The Talmud (*Megillah* 10b) expounds on an obscure prophecy of *Isaiah* (55:13): *In place of the thornbush shall come up the cypress* — the prickly, useless "thornbush" is Haman who attempted to destroy Mordechai, the stately "cypress." But Haman's own sinister plans ensnared him and he was hanged on the gallows he had prepared for Mordechai; his name and his sons

רֹאשׁ יְמִינִי נִשֵּׂאתָ, וְאוֹיֵב שְׁמוֹ מָחִיתָ,

⟨ You blotted ⟨ – his ⟪ while ⟨ You ⟨ of the Benjaminite ⟨ The
out, name the enemy lifted, [Mordechai] head

רֹב בָּנָיו וְקִנְיָנָיו, עַל הָעֵץ תָּלִיתָ.

⟪ You hanged ⟨ the ⟨ upon ⟪ and his ⟨ prog- ⟨ [with] his
[him]. gallows possessions— eny numerous

יְוָנִים* נִקְבְּצוּ עָלַי, אֲזַי בִּימֵי חַשְׁמַנִּים,

⟪ of the noble ones ⟨ in the ⟨ then, ⟪ against ⟨ gathered ⟨ The
[the Hasmoneans]. days me, Greeks*

וּפָרְצוּ חוֹמוֹת מִגְדָּלַי וְטִמְּאוּ כָּל הַשְּׁמָנִים,

⟪ the oils. ⟨ all ⟨ and defiled ⟨ of my ⟨ the walls ⟨ They
towers breached

וּמִנּוֹתַר קַנְקַנִּים נַעֲשָׂה נֵס לַשּׁוֹשַׁנִּים,

⟪ for the roses ⟨ a miracle was ⟨ of the ⟨ But from the
[Israel]. wrought flasks one remnant

בְּנֵי בִינָה, יְמֵי שְׁמוֹנָה קָבְעוּ שִׁיר וּרְנָנִים.

⟪ and ⟨ for ⟨ they ⟨ – eight days ⟪ of ⟨ Men
jubilation. song established insight

חֲשׂוֹף זְרוֹעַ קָדְשֶׁךָ,* וְקָרֵב קֵץ הַיְשׁוּעָה,

⟪ salvation. ⟨ the final ⟨ and hasten ⟨ Your holy arm* ⟨ Bare

נְקֹם נִקְמַת דַּם עֲבָדֶיךָ מֵאֻמָּה הָרְשָׁעָה,

⟪ that is wicked. ⟨ from the ⟨ of Your ⟨ the ⟨ Avenge
nation servants blood vengeance

כִּי אָרְכָה לָּנוּ הַיְשׁוּעָה, וְאֵין קֵץ לִימֵי הָרָעָה,

⟪ of evil. ⟨ to the ⟨ end ⟨ and ⟪ is salvation, ⟨ for us ⟨ long ⟨ For
days there is no delayed

דְּחֵה אַדְמוֹן בְּצֵל צַלְמוֹן, הָקֵם לָנוּ רוֹעִים שִׁבְעָה.

⟪ the seven shepherds. ⟨ for us ⟨ establish ⟪ to the nethermost ⟨ the Red ⟨ Repel
shadow; One

---

and possessions were destroyed (R' Hirsch)..

יְוָנִים — *The Greeks.* This refers to the Syrian-Greeks, especially Antiochus IV Epiphanes, the monarch who attempted to Hellenize [impose Greek culture on] *Eretz Yisrael* through force.

חֲשׂוֹף זְרוֹעַ קָדְשֶׁךָ — *Bare Your holy arm.* This final stanza is generally regarded to be a later addition [about 1500] by a different author. The initial letters of the first three words form the acrostic חֲזַק, *be strong.* Since it contains a strong

plea for Divine vengeance against Israel's foes, this stanza was subject to much censorship by Christian authorities. Accordingly, some *siddurim* have replaced certain stiches with others less offensive to the censors. The *Red One* refers to Esau/Edom, whose descendants brought the current exile. The *seven shepherds* (*Micah* 5:4) who will conquer Israel's oppressors are David, Adam, Seth, Methuselah, Abraham, Jacob, and Moses (*Succah* 52b).

≫{ קריאת המגילה }≪
≫{ READING OF THE MEGILLAH }≪

BEFORE READING *MEGILLAS ESTHER* ON PURIM [BOTH AT NIGHT AND AGAIN IN THE MORNING], THE READER RECITES THE FOLLOWING THREE BLESSINGS. THE CONGREGATION SHOULD ANSWER AMEN ONLY [NOT בָּרוּךְ הוּא וּבָרוּךְ שְׁמוֹ] AFTER EACH BLESSING, AND HAVE IN MIND THAT THEY THEREBY FULFILL THE OBLIGATION OF RECITING THE BLESSINGS THEMSELVES. DURING THE MORNING READING, THEY SHOULD ALSO HAVE IN MIND THAT THE THIRD BLESSING APPLIES TO THE OTHER MITZVOS OF PURIM — *SHALACH MANOS*, GIFTS TO THE POOR, AND THE FESTIVE PURIM MEAL — AS WELL AS TO THE *MEGILLAH* READING.

[THESE BLESSINGS ARE RECITED WHETHER OR NOT A *MINYAN* IS PRESENT.]

בָּרוּךְ אַתָּה יהוה אֱלֹהֵינוּ מֶלֶךְ הָעוֹלָם, אֲשֶׁר קִדְּשָׁנוּ

Blessed ‹ are You, ‹ HASHEM, ‹ our God, ‹ King ‹‹ of the universe, ‹ Who ‹ has sanctified us

בְּמִצְוֹתָיו, וְצִוָּנוּ עַל מִקְרָא מְגִלָּה. (אָמֵן. – Cong.)

‹‹ with His commandments, ‹‹ and has commanded us ‹ concerning ‹ the reading ‹ of the Megillah. ‹‹ (Amen.)

בָּרוּךְ אַתָּה יהוה אֱלֹהֵינוּ מֶלֶךְ הָעוֹלָם, שֶׁעָשָׂה נִסִּים

Blessed ‹ are You, ‹ HASHEM, ‹ our God, ‹ King ‹‹ of the universe, ‹ Who ‹ wrought miracles

לַאֲבוֹתֵינוּ, בַּיָּמִים הָהֵם, בַּזְּמַן הַזֶּה. (אָמֵן. – Cong.)

‹‹ for our forefathers, ‹ in those days ‹ at this season. ‹‹ (Amen.)

בָּרוּךְ אַתָּה יהוה אֱלֹהֵינוּ מֶלֶךְ הָעוֹלָם, שֶׁהֶחֱיָנוּ

Blessed ‹ are You, ‹ HASHEM, ‹ our God, ‹ King ‹‹ of the universe, ‹‹ Who has kept us alive,

וְקִיְּמָנוּ וְהִגִּיעָנוּ לַזְּמַן הַזֶּה. (אָמֵן. – Cong.)

‹ and has sustained us ‹ and has brought us ‹ to this season. ‹‹ (Amen.)

[THE *MEGILLAH* IS READ.]

AFTER THE *MEGILLAH* READING, EACH MEMBER OF THE CONGREGATION RECITES THE FOLLOWING BLESSING. [THIS BLESSING IS NOT RECITED UNLESS A *MINYAN* IS PRESENT FOR THE READING.]
IN SOME CONGREGATIONS THE READER RECITES THE BLESSING
AND THE CONGREGATION RESPONDS *AMEN*.

בָּרוּךְ אַתָּה יהוה אֱלֹהֵינוּ מֶלֶךְ הָעוֹלָם, (הָאֵל) הָרָב

Blessed ‹ are You, ‹ HASHEM, ‹ our God, ‹ King ‹‹ of the universe, ‹ (the God) ‹ Who takes up

אֶת רִיבֵנוּ, וְהַדָּן אֶת דִּינֵנוּ, וְהַנּוֹקֵם אֶת נִקְמָתֵנוּ,

‹‹ our grievances, ‹‹ judges ‹ the ‹‹ our claims, ‹ avenges ‹‹ our vengeance,

וְהַמְשַׁלֵּם גְּמוּל לְכָל אֹיְבֵי נַפְשֵׁנוּ, וְהַנִּפְרָע לָנוּ מִצָּרֵינוּ.

‹ and Who pays ‹ just ‹ to all ‹‹ the ‹ soul, ‹‹ of our ‹ and Who ‹ on our ‹‹ from our retribution enemies exacts payment behalf foes.

בָּרוּךְ אַתָּה יהוה, הַנִּפְרָע לְעַמּוֹ יִשְׂרָאֵל מִכָּל צָרֵיהֶם,

《 their foes, 〈 from all 〈 Israel, 〈 on behalf of His people 〈 Who exacts payment 〈 HASHEM, 〈 are You, 〈 Blessed

הָאֵל הַמּוֹשִׁיעַ.

《 Who brings salvation. 〈 the God

AFTER THE NIGHTTIME *MEGILLAH* READING, THE FOLLOWING TWO PARAGRAPHS ARE RECITED. AFTER THE DAYTIME READING, ONLY שׁוֹשַׁנַּת יַעֲקֹב (P. 584) IS RECITED.

אֲשֶׁר הֵנִיא עֲצַת גּוֹיִם וַיָּפֶר מַחְשְׁבוֹת עֲרוּמִים.

《 of the cunning, 〈 the designs 〈 and annulled 〈 of the nations 〈 the counsel 〈 foiled 〈 Who

בְּקוּם עָלֵינוּ אָדָם רָשָׁע, נֵצֶר זָדוֹן מִזֶּרַע עֲמָלֵק.

《 of Amalek. 〈 from the offspring 〈 of wickedness 〈 an offshoot 《 a wicked man, 〈 against us 〈 when there arose

גָּאָה בְעָשְׁרוֹ וְכָרָה לוֹ בּוֹר, וּגְדֻלָּתוֹ יָקְשָׁה לּוֹ לָכֶד.

《 a trap. 〈 for him 〈 set 〈 and his very greatness 《 a pit, 〈 for himself 〈 and dug 〈 with his wealth 〈 He was haughty

דִּמָּה בְנַפְשׁוֹ לִלְכֹּד, וְנִלְכַּד,

《 but he [himself] was trapped; 《 to trap, 〈 in his soul 〈 He thought

בִּקֵּשׁ לְהַשְׁמִיד, וְנִשְׁמַד מְהֵרָה.

《 swiftly. 〈 but he [himself] was destroyed 〈 to destroy, 〈 he sought

הָמָן הוֹדִיעַ אֵיבַת אֲבוֹתָיו, וְעוֹרֵר שִׂנְאַת אַחִים לַבָּנִים.

《 upon the children. 〈 the brotherly hate [of Esau] 〈 and aroused 《 of his forebears, 〈 the enmity 〈 made known 〈 Haman

וְלֹא זָכַר רַחֲמֵי שָׁאוּל, כִּי בְחֶמְלָתוֹ עַל אֲגָג נוֹלַד אוֹיֵב.

《 that the foe was born. 〈 Agag 〈 on his pity 〈 it was through 〈 for 《 of Saul, 〈 the compassion 〈 He did not remember

זָמַם רָשָׁע לְהַכְרִית צַדִּיק, וְנִלְכַּד טָמֵא בִּידֵי טָהוֹר.

《 of the pure one. 〈 in the hands 〈 was the impure one 〈 but trapped 《 the righteous one, 〈 to cut off 〈 did the wicked one 〈 Conspire

חֶסֶד גָּבַר עַל שִׁגְגַת אָב,

《 of the father [Saul], 〈 the error 〈 over 〈 prevailed 〈 Kindness [of Mordechai to Esther]

וְרָשָׁע הוֹסִיף חֵטְא עַל חֲטָאָיו.

《 [Agag's] sins. 〈 upon 〈 sins 〈 added 〈 but the wicked [Haman]

טָמַן בְּלִבּוֹ מַחְשְׁבוֹת עֲרוּמָיו, וַיִּתְמַכֵּר לַעֲשׂוֹת רָעָה.

》 evil. 〈 to doing 〈 and devoted 《 of cunning, 〈 his thoughts 〈 in his 〈 He hid
himself　　　　　　　　　　　　　　　　　　　　　　　　　heart

יָדוֹ שָׁלַח בִּקְדוֹשֵׁי אֵל, כַּסְפּוֹ נָתַן לְהַכְרִית זִכְרָם.

》 their 〈 to destroy 〈 he gave 〈 his 》 of God, 〈 against the 〈 he stretched 〈 His
memory.　　　　　　　　　money　　　holy ones　　　out　　　hand

בִּרְאוֹת מָרְדְּכַי כִּי יָצָא קֶצֶף, וְדָתֵי הָמָן נִתְּנוּ בְשׁוּשָׁן.

》 in 〈 were 〈 of 〈 and the 《 had the 〈 com- 〈 that 〈 When Mordechai saw
Shushan,　issued　Haman　decrees　wrath,　menced

לָבַשׁ שַׂק וְקָשַׁר מִסְפֵּד, וְגָזַר צוֹם, וַיֵּשֶׁב עַל הָאֵפֶר.

》 ashes, 〈 upon 〈 and sat 〈 a fast 〈 and 》 in 〈 and bound 〈 sack- 〈 he
[saying]:　　　　　　　　　decreed　mourning,　himself　cloth　donned

מִי זֶה יַעֲמֹד לְכַפֵּר שְׁגָגָה, וְלִמְחֹל חַטָּאת עֲוֹן אֲבוֹתֵינוּ.

》 of our 〈 [and] the 〈 for the 〈 to gain 》 for errors, 〈 to atone 〈 that can 〈 is it 〈 Who
ancestors? transgressions sinfulness forgiveness　　　　　　　　　　　　　arise

נֵץ פֶּרַח מֵלּוּלָב, הֵן הֲדַסָּה עָמְדָה לְעוֹרֵר יְשֵׁנִים.

》 the sleeping. 〈 to awaken 〈 rose up 〈 Hadassah 〈 behold, 》 from a 〈 bloomed 〈 A
palm branch;　　　　　　　　　　　　　　　　　　　　　　　blossom

סָרִיסֶיהָ הִבְהִילוּ לְהָמָן, לְהַשְׁקוֹתוֹ יֵין חֲמַת תַּנִּינִים.

》 of serpents. 〈 of the 〈 wine 〈 to make him 》 to Haman, 〈 hastened 〈 Her servants
venom　　　　　drink

עָמַד בְּעָשְׁרוֹ וְנָפַל בְּרִשְׁעוֹ, עָשָׂה לוֹ עֵץ וְנִתְלָה עָלָיו.

》 on it. 〈 and was 〈 gallows, 〈 he built 》 through his 〈 and fell 〈 through 〈 He rose
himself hanged　　　　　　　wickedness;　　　his wealth,

פִּיהֶם פָּתְחוּ, כָּל יוֹשְׁבֵי תֵבֵל, כִּי פוּר הָמָן נֶהְפַּךְ לְפוּרֵנוּ.

》 our Purim 〈 turned 〈 of 〈 the 〈 for 》 of the 〈 the 〈 – did 》 they opened 〈 Their
[holiday].　into　Haman　lottery　earth – inhabitants　all　[in praise] mouths

צַדִּיק נֶחֱלַץ מִיַּד רָשָׁע, אוֹיֵב נִתַּן תַּחַת נַפְשׁוֹ.

》 of the life 〈 in place 〈 was 〈 the foe 》 of the 〈 from 〈 was 〈 The
[of the　　given over　　wicked;　the hand　rescued　righteous
righteous one].　　　　　　　　　　　　　　　　man

קִיְּמוּ עֲלֵיהֶם לַעֲשׂוֹת פּוּרִים,

》 Purim, 〈 to celebrate 〈 upon 〈 They
themselves undertook

וְלִשְׂמֹחַ בְּכָל שָׁנָה וְשָׁנָה.

》 after year. 〈 year 〈 every 〈 to rejoice

רָאִיתָ אֶת תְּפִלַּת מָרְדְּכַי וְאֶסְתֵּר,

《 and Esther; 〈 of Mordechai 〈 the prayer 〈 You noted

הָמָן וּבָנָיו עַל הָעֵץ תָּלִיתָ.

《 You hung. 〈 the tree 〈 upon 〈 and his sons 〈 Haman

THE FOLLOWING IS RECITED AFTER BOTH *MEGILLAH* READINGS.

שׁוֹשַׁנַּת יַעֲקֹב צָהֲלָה וְשָׂמֵחָה,

《 and glad, 〈 was cheerful 〈 [that is] Jacob 〈 The rose

בִּרְאוֹתָם יַחַד תְּכֵלֶת מָרְדְּכָי.

《 of Mordechai. 〈 the royal blue [robes] 〈 together 〈 when they saw

תְּשׁוּעָתָם הָיִיתָ לָנֶצַח, וְתִקְוָתָם בְּכָל דּוֹר וָדוֹר.

《 after generation — 〈 genera-tion 〈 through-out 〈 and their hope 〈 eternally, 〈 You have been 〈 Their salvation

לְהוֹדִיעַ, שֶׁכָּל קֹוֶיךָ לֹא יֵבְשׁוּ,

《 be shamed; 〈 will not 〈 those who put their hope in You 〈 that all 〈 to make known

וְלֹא יִכָּלְמוּ לָנֶצַח כָּל הַחוֹסִים בָּךְ.

《 in You. 〈 who take refuge 〈 – all those 〈 ever 〈 and they will not be humiliated

אָרוּר הָמָן, אֲשֶׁר בִּקֵּשׁ לְאַבְּדִי, בָּרוּךְ מָרְדְּכַי הַיְּהוּדִי.

《 the Jew. 〈 be Mordechai 〈 blessed 《 to destroy me; 〈 sought 〈 who 〈 be Haman, 〈 Accursed

אֲרוּרָה זֶרֶשׁ, אֵשֶׁת מַפְחִידִי, בְּרוּכָה אֶסְתֵּר בַּעֲדִי.

《 who shielded me. 〈 be Esther, 〈 blessed 《 of my terrorizer; 〈 the wife 〈 be Zeresh, 〈 Accursed

אֲרוּרִים כָּל הָרְשָׁעִים, בְּרוּכִים כָּל הַצַּדִּיקִים.

《 the righteous. 〈 be all 〈 blessed 《 the wicked, 〈 be all 〈 Accursed

וְגַם חַרְבוֹנָה זָכוּר לַטוֹב.

《 for good. 〈 be 〈 may 〈 And also, 〈 remembered Charvonah

ON SATURDAY EVENING, *MAARIV* CONTINUES WITH ויהי נועם (P. 477).
AFTER THE READING ON A WEEKNIGHT, *MAARIV* CONTINUES WITH וְאַתָּה קָדוֹשׁ (P. 479),
THE FULL *KADDISH* WITHOUT תִּתְקַבֵּל, עָלֵינוּ (P. 442) AND THE MOURNER'S *KADDISH*.
AFTER THE MORNING READING, *SHACHARIS* CONTINUES WITH אַשְׁרֵי-וּבָא לְצִיּוֹן (P. 214).

❧ KROVETZ FOR PURIM / קרובץ לפורים ❧

MANY CONGREGATIONS RECITE *KROVETZ* DURING THE *CHAZZAN'S* REPETITION
OF *SHEMONEH ESREI* ON THE MORNING OF PURIM. SEE COMMENTARY.
THE *CHAZZAN* BEGINS HIS REPETITION (P. 143) AND CONTINUES THROUGH וּמוֹשִׁיעַ וּמָגֵן.
THEN ALL RECITE:

וַיֶּאֱהַב אָמֵן¹ יְתוֹמַת הֵגֵן,

》 who was 〈 the orphan 〈 The adoptive father
worthy.   girl [Esther]   [Mordechai] loved

אֲמָנָה שִׁבְעִים וְחָמֵשׁ² בַּעֲדָהּ לְהָגֵן,*

》 a 〈 was for her 〈 five 〈 at seventy- 〈 The faith
protection.*   [displayed by Abraham]

אָז מֵאָז כְּחָז יוֹדֵעַ נַגֵּן,

《 to play 〈 [did David,] 〈 when 〈 long 〈Then,
music,   who knew   foresee   ago,

אַרְיֵה*³ בֶּן זְאֵב*⁴ לְיֵשַׁע הוֹגֵן,

《 who would 〈 [would arise] 〈 of the wolf 〈 [also] a 《 that [Morde-
be worthy;   as a savior   [Benjamin],*   descend-   chai], the lion
    ant   [Judah],*

---

(1) *Esther* 2:7. (2) *Genesis* 12:4. (3) 49:9. (4) 49:27.

❧ KROVETZ FOR PURIM ❧

The title *Krovetz*, קרוֹבֵץ, is the initials of קוֹל רִנָּה וִישׁוּעָה בְּאָהֳלֵי צַדִּיקִים, *The sound of rejoicing and salvation is in the tents of the righteous* (Psalms 118:15, Bais Yosef, Orach Chaim 68). The term *Krovetz* or alternatively קְרוֹבוֹת, *Krovos*, refers generally to *piyutim* recited during the repetition of the *Shemoneh Esrei*.

The *Krovetz* is recited during *Shacharis* on Purim. It consists of poetic stanzas that are inserted just before the conclusion of the blessings of *Shemoneh Esrei* during the *chazzan's* repetition. The only blessing where this is not done is אֶת צֶמַח דָּוִד, *The offspring of . . . David*, since the composer of the *Krovetz* follows the practice referred to in the *Talmud Yerushalmi* of combining the two blessings בּוֹנֶה יְרוּשָׁלָיִם, *Who rebuilds Jerusalem*, and אֶת צֶמַח דָּוִד, *The offspring of David*, into one blessing (Tosafos Rid, Taanis 13b). The eighteen stanzas of the liturgy begin, respectively, with the words of the Book of *Esther* that tell of Esther's rise to power: וַיֶּאֱהַב הַמֶּלֶךְ אֶת אֶסְתֵּר מִכָּל הַנָּשִׁים וַתִּשָּׂא חֵן וָחֶסֶד לְפָנָיו מִכָּל הַבְּתוּלוֹת וַיָּשֶׂם כֶּתֶר מַלְכוּת בְּרֹאשָׁהּ וַיַּמְלִיכֶהָ תַּחַת וַשְׁתִּי, *The king loved Esther more than all the women, and she won more of his*

grace and favor than all the other maidens; so he set the royal crown upon her head, and made her queen in place of Vashti (Esther 2:17). The initial word is followed by a fivefold repetition of the *aleph-beis*.

The final line of each stanza begins with a word from a second key verse from the Book of *Esther:* וּמָרְדְּכַי יָצָא מִלִּפְנֵי הַמֶּלֶךְ בִּלְבוּשׁ מַלְכוּת תְּכֵלֶת וָחוּר וַעֲטֶרֶת זָהָב גְּדוֹלָה וְתַכְרִיךְ בּוּץ וְאַרְגָּמָן וְהָעִיר שׁוּשָׁן צָהֲלָה וְשָׂמֵחָה, *Mordechai left the king's presence clad in royal apparel of blue and white with a large gold crown and a robe of fine linen and purple; then the city of Shushan was cheerful and glad* (8:15).

The word following these second key words from the above verse begins with an initial of the composer's name אֶלְעָזָר בְּירַבִּי קִילִיר חֲזַק. All of these letters and words appear in bold type.

בַּעֲדָהּ לְהָגֵן — *Was for her a protection*. According to one view in the Midrash (*Genesis Rabbah* 39:13), Esther was 75 years old when she married Ahasuerus, just as Abraham was 75 when he left his father's home.

אַרְיֵה . . . זְאֵב — *Lion . . . wolf.* Mordechai is referred to as both a Judean and a Benjaminite (Esther 2:5; Megillah 12b).

אָץ לְהַזְכִּיר אוֹתוֹ מְנַגֵּן,* וּמָרְדְּכַי אִמַּץ בְּאֶלֶף הַמָּגֵן.*[1]

》 shields* 〈 by the 〈 was 〈 And 》 did the 〈 him [to 〈 to 〈 hurried
[promised thousand strength- Mordechai musician be spared] mention
Abraham]. ened [David].*

CHAZZAN CONCLUDES THE BLESSING:

(אָמֵן. – Cong.)   בָּרוּךְ אַתָּה יהוה, מָגֵן אַבְרָהָם.

》 (Amen.)   》 of Abraham. 〈 Shield 》 HASHEM, 〈 are You, 〈 Blessed

CHAZZAN CONTINUES FROM אַתָּה גִּבּוֹר THROUGH לְהַחֲיוֹת מֵתִים. THEN ALL RECITE:

הַמֶּלֶךְ בְּכֵס יָהּ[2] חַק לְזֶרַע כֹּה יִהְיֶה,[3]

》 [who are described as,] So 〈 for [Abraham's] 〈 decreed 〈 of 〈 by the 〈 The King
[innumerable] shall they be! descendants, God, throne [HASHEM],

בָּקָמִים כָּל נֶשֶׁם לֹא תְחַיֶּה,[4]

》 allow to live! 〈 do not 〈 living 〈 Any 》 about [Amalek]
being who rises
against them:

בֶּן בְּכוֹרַת[5] חַל דְּבַר אֶהְיֶה,[6] בְּקוֹץ אֲשֶׁר נִכְמַר וַיְחַיֶּה,[7]

》 and 〈 he 〈 whom 〈 with the 》 of God, 〈 the 〈 dese- 〈 [But Saul,] the de-
spared. pitied thorn [Agag], word crated scendant of Becorah

בְּכֵן צִפְעוֹ* צָץ לְצִדִּים[8] שֶׁיִּהְיֶה,

》 to become [a thorn] 〈 sprouted, 〈 his offspring 〈 By
in our side, [Haman]* this

יָצָא לְמָרְרוּ מוֹר בִּגְשָׁמִים מְחַיֶּה.

》 [with the help] of the One Who 》 did Mor- 》 to embitter 〈 until he
through the rains, revivifies [the dead]. [dechai], him, went forth

CHAZZAN CONCLUDES THE BLESSING:

(אָמֵן. – Cong.)   בָּרוּךְ אַתָּה יהוה, מְחַיֶּה הַמֵּתִים.

》 (Amen.)   》 the dead. 〈 Who revivifies 》 HASHEM, 〈 are You, 〈 Blessed

KEDUSHAH (P. 146) IS RECITED AT THIS POINT.

---

(1) Cf. *Song of Songs* 4:4. (2) Cf. *Exodus* 17:16. (3) Cf. *Genesis* 15:5. (4) *Deuteronomy* 20:16. (5) *I Samuel* 9:1. (6) *Exodus* 3:14. (7) Cf. *I Samuel* 15:9. (8) *Judges* 2:3.

לְהַזְכִּיר אוֹתוֹ מְנַגֵּן — *To mention him [to be spared] did the musician [David].* David, "the sweet singer of Israel," would not let the traitor Shimi be harmed because Mordechai was destined to descend from him (*II Samuel* 19:23, *Megillah* 12b).

בְּאֶלֶף הַמָּגֵן — *By the thousand shields.* The Midrash (*Song of Songs Rabbah* 4:4) relates that God reassured Abraham that while for him He was like a single shield, for his descendants He will be like a thousand shields. Others see this as referring to the thousand men from Benjamin who accompanied Shimi when he came to David to beg for his life (*Avodas Yisrael*).

צִפְעוֹ — *His offspring [Haman].* Alternatively *his snake.* During the one night that Saul kept him alive, Agag sired a son from whom Haman descended (*Pesichta Esther Rabbah* 7).

CHAZZAN CONTINUES FROM קדּוֹשׁ אַתָּה OR לְדוֹר וָדוֹר THROUGH אַתָּה THROUGH וְקָדוֹשׁ. THEN ALL RECITE:

אֶת אֶסְתֵּר גַּל מִמַּסְתִּיר¹ לְגוֹאֵל, גּוֹי כְּנוֹאָשׁ מִלְהִגָּאֵל,²

» of being 〈 that had 〈 of the 〈 to be a 〈 from 〈 [God] 〈 Esther
redeemed. despaired nation redeemer concealment revealed

גּוֹזֵר אִם אֵין לְאִישׁ גּוֹאֵל,³ גָּלַף מִיָּשְׁפֶה⁴* תַּבְנִית הַגּוֹאֵל,

» of a 〈 the form 〈 from 〈 fashioned 〈 redeemer [he 〈 a person 〈 If 〈 The One
redeemer. yashfeh* will ultimately has no Who
be released], decreed:

גָּשׁ כְּאָח לְצָרָה⁵ לְצַחֲצֵחַ הַגּוֹאֵל,⁶*

» the filth 〈 to polish away 〈 in [times 〈 as a 〈 [Mordechai]
[of sin].* of] distress, brother approached

מִלְפְנֵי* עִיר וְקַדִּישׁ⁷ לְהַקְדִּישׁ אָאֵל.⁸

» will I begin. 〈 to sanctify 〈 the holy angels, 〈 Even
[God's Name] before*

CHAZZAN CONCLUDES THE BLESSING:

בָּרוּךְ אַתָּה יהוה, הָאֵל הַקָּדוֹשׁ. (אָמֵן. – Cong.)

» (Amen.) » Who is holy. 〈 the God 〈 HASHEM, 〈 are You, 〈 Blessed

CHAZZAN CONTINUES FROM אַתָּה חוֹנֵן THROUGH בִּינָה וָדָעַת. THEN ALL RECITE:

מִכָּל דּוֹרוֹ בֵּן לְהִתְבּוֹנֵן, דַּעַת מֵאֵיזֶה חֵטְא צָג צָר שׁוֹנֵן,⁹

» with a 〈 the 〈 stood 〈 sin 〈 for 〈 to 〈 to under- 〈 [Mordechai] 〈 his gen- 〈 Of all
sharpened foe erect which ascertain stand, gave thought eration,
[tongue].

דּבְרַת אָב כְּזָכַר אוֹנֵן, דַּלְתֵי צוּר כְּנֶסָה דָּפַק וְחָנֵן,

» and he 〈 he 〈 – the syn- 〈 of the 〈 At the 〈 he became 〈 when he 〈 of his an- 〈 The
suppli- knocked, agogue– Rock doors distressed. recalled, cestor [Saul matter
cated. [God] sparing Agag],

דְּגָלִים לְשַׁלֵּשׁ תַּעַן וּלְחַנֵּן, הַמֶּלֶךְ זַעֲקָם בֵּן דֵּעָה חוֹנֵן.

» grants 〈 – He 〈 under- 〈 their cry 〈 the King 〈 and to 〈 to 〈 [he decreed] 〈 On [Israel,
graciously. Who stood supplicate; fast, for three encamped
wisdom days by] banners,

---

(1) Cf. *Deuteronomy* 31:18; *Chullin* 139b. (2) Cf. *Pesichta Rabbasi* 33:9; *Megillah* 12a.
(3) *Numbers* 5:8; cf. *Leviticus* 25:26-28. (4) Cf. *Exodus* 28:20. (5) Cf. *Proverbs* 17:17.
(6) Cf. *Malachi* 1:7; *Zephaniah* 3:1. (7) *Daniel* 4:10,20. (8) Cf. *Exodus* 2:21. (9) Cf. *Psalms* 64:4.

מִיָּשְׁפֶה — *From yashfeh.* Mordechai was from Benjamin whose stone in the *Choshen* was *yashfeh* (*Shemos Rabbah* 38:9).

הַגּוֹאֵל — *The filth [of sin].* The Talmud (*Megillah* 12a) explains that the Jews were threatened in punishment for two sins: for eating from the feast of Ahasuerus and for

bowing down to the idol of Nebuchadnezzar. The fast decreed by Esther (4:16) atoned for one and Mordechai's refusal to bow down to Haman atoned for the other.

מִלְפְנֵי — *Even before.* Israel hastens to sanctify God's Name even before the angels do so (*Chullin* 91b).

CHAZZAN CONCLUDES THE BLESSING:

בָּרוּךְ אַתָּה יהוה, חוֹנֵן הַדָּעַת. (Cong. – אָמֵן.)

《 (Amen.) 《 of Wisdom. 〈 gracious Giver 《 HASHEM, 〈 are You, 〈 Blessed

CHAZZAN CONTINUES FROM בִּתְשׁוּבָה שְׁלֵמָה לְפָנֶיךָ THROUGH הֲשִׁיבֵנוּ. THEN ALL RECITE:

הַנָּשִׁים הַהֲגוּנוֹת לְכֵס יְשִׁיבָה, הוּכְרְעוּ וּסְעָרָה בָּם נָשָׁבָה,

《 raged; 〈 against 〈 and the storm 《 were 〈 to sit on the 〈 who were 〈 [All] the
them [of Ahasuerus' deemed [queen's] throne eligible women
anger] ugly,

הֲדַסָּה זֹאת כְּגַע לָה תוֹר¹ וּמַחֲשָׁבָה,

《 and [the king's] 〈 turn 〈 her 〈 when 《 [but] this
consideration, came Hadassah,

הֻלְלָה לְכָל רוֹאֶיהָ וְעֵזֶר לוֹ² שִׁוָּה,

《 he made 〈 for 〈 and a 《 who saw 〈 by all 〈 was
her. himself helpmate her, praised

הֻדַּר יְמִינִי לְשׁוֹבֵב שׁוֹבֵבָה, ³ בִּלְבוּשׁ רַצּוֹת רוֹצֶה בִּתְשׁוּבָה.

《 repentance. 〈 the One 〈 [of sack- with 《 the way- 〈 [and sought] 《 was the 〈 Honored
Who cloth] for garments ward one to bring to Benjaminite
desires appeasing [Israel], repentance [Mordechai],

CHAZZAN CONCLUDES THE BLESSING:

בָּרוּךְ אַתָּה יהוה, הָרוֹצֶה בִּתְשׁוּבָה. (Cong. – אָמֵן.)

《 (Amen.) 《 repentance. 〈 Who desires 《 HASHEM, 〈 are You, 〈 Blessed

CHAZZAN CONTINUES FROM וְסָלַח אַתָּה THROUGH סְלַח לָנוּ. THEN ALL RECITE:

וַתִּשָּׂא וַתָּבֹא בֵאלֹהַּ, וְלֹא יָדְעָה כִּי זֹאת עָשָׂתָה יַד אֱלֹהַּ,

《 of 〈 by the 〈 had been 〈 this [set 〈 that 〈 she did 《 with [faith 〈 and came 〈 She raised up
God, hand done of events] not realize in] God; [to the king] [her eyes]

וַיְּבְעַר חָנֵף בְּכָל גְּבוּל לִשְׁלוֹחַ, ⁴

《 to send [for *all* 〈 his 〈 through- 《 was the 〈 foolish
the beautiful boundaries out hypocritical
women]. [Ahasuerus],

וּבְהַגִּיעַ תוֹר¹ בִּנְיַן לִצְלוֹחַ, וּבַת אֲבִיחַיִל לָבְשָׁה צְלוֹחַ,*

《 success.* 〈 donned 〈 [Esther,] the daughter 《 to 〈 for the building 〈 the 〈 When
of Abihail, flourish, [of the Temple] time came

מַלְכוּת בָּהּ רִבָּה מַרְבֶּה לִסְלוֹחַ.

《 pardons. 〈 — He Who 《 He granted 〈 to 〈 Sovereignty
abundantly abundantly her

---

(1) Cf. *Esther* 2:15. (2) Cf. *Genesis* 2:18. (3) Cf. *Jeremiah* 3:14; *Isaiah* 49:5. (4) Cf. *Megillah* 12b.

וּבַת אֲבִיחַיִל לָבְשָׁה צְלוֹחַ — *[Esther,] the daughter of Abihail, donned success.* Esther was the mother of King Darius who authorized the construction of the Second Temple, after Ahasuerus had ordered the rebuilding halted (*Ezra* 4:6, 23-24).

CHAZZAN CONCLUDES THE BLESSING:

בָּרוּךְ אַתָּה יהוה, חַנּוּן הַמַּרְבֶּה לִסְלוֹחַ. (Cong. – אָמֵן.)

《 (Amen.)　　《 forgives. 〈 Who 〈 the gracious 《 HASHEM, 〈 are You, 〈 Blessed
　　　　　　　　　　　　abundantly　　One,

CHAZZAN CONTINUES FROM רְאֵה THROUGH אַתָּה חֲזַק. גּוֹאֵל. THEN ALL RECITE:

חֵן זֻבְּדָה[1] מֵהַרְרֵי אֵל,[2] זְכוּתָה עִמְעַם בְּיַד בֶּן אֲבִיאֵל,[3]

《 of Abiel. 〈 the de-　〈 [with] 〈 united 〈 her merit 《 [by the merit] of 〈 was 〈 With
　　　　scendant　that of　　　　　　the mighty mountains [Esther] grace
　　　　[Mordechai,]　　　　　　　[the Patriarchs];　apportioned

זֹאת בְּבוֹאָהּ הֲלוֹם נָשְׂאָה עֵין לָאֵל,

《 to God, 〈 her 〈 she raised 《 there [at 〈 when she 〈 [With]
[in prayer]:　eyes　　Ahasuerus' palace], arrived　this,

זָכְרָה נָא לִי צִדְקַת הַרְרֵי אֵל,

《 of the mighty mountains 〈 the 〈 for 〈 please, 〈 Recall,
[the Patriarchs].　righteousness　me

זֶה[4] הֵכִינָה לְאוֹת לְתִקּוּן אֲרִיאֵל,

《 of Ariel 〈 of the 〈 as a 〈 established 〈 This One
[the Temple]. rebuilding symbol [Esther] [God]

תְּכֵלֶת יָדָהּ עָשׂוּת לִגְאוּלֵי אֵל.

《 by God. 〈 for those 《 made, 〈 her 〈 The techeiles
　redeemed　　　　　hands [for the Temple]

CHAZZAN CONCLUDES THE BLESSING:

בָּרוּךְ אַתָּה יהוה, גּוֹאֵל יִשְׂרָאֵל. (Cong. – אָמֵן.)

《 (Amen.)　　《 of Israel. 〈 Redeemer 《 HASHEM, 〈 are You, 〈 Blessed

CHAZZAN CONTINUES FROM רְפָאֵנוּ THROUGH אַתָּה וְרַחֲמָן נֶאֱמָן. רוֹפֵא. THEN ALL RECITE:

וְחֶסֶד חִסְּדָהּ חָסִיד הַמְּחוֹלְלִי, חוּר וְכַרְפַּס[5] וְכֶתֶם וַחֲלִי,[6]

《 and 〈 and gold 《 fine 《 [draping her] 〈 Who 〈 – the Kind 《 He granted 〈 And
jewelry.　　cotton,　in white linen, created me –　One,　her　kindness

חִילָה רוֹץ רֹאשׁ פֶּתֶן מִגַּחֲלִי,

《 [to stop him] 《 of the 〈 the 〈 to crush 〈 He
from pouring burn-　viper　head　　strengthened
ing coals on me,　[Haman],　　　her

חֲרוֹן בּוֹ לְשַׁלֵּחַ[7] עוֹד מִלְּאַבְּלִי,[8] חִלַּת פְּנֵי אֱלֹהִים יהוה חֵילִי,[9]

《 my 〈 HASHEM, 〈 God, 〈 before 〈 She 《 to con- 〈 so that he no 《 to 〈 upon 〈 [God's]
Strength,　　　　　　supplicated sume me. longer be able send,　him　wrath

וְחוּר רַב חִתְּלִי[10] רוֹפֵא חוּלִי.

《 of disease. 〈 – the 《 He 〈 that is 〈 and with
Healer　healed me　great　freedom

(1) Cf. *Genesis* 30:20. (2) *Psalms* 36:7. (3) *I Samuel* 9:1. (4) *Exodus* 15:2. (5) Cf. *Esther* 1:6.
(6) Cf. *Proverbs* 25:12. (7) Cf. *Psalms* 78:49. (8) Cf. *Exodus* 3:2. (9) *Habakkuk* 3:19. (10) *Ezekiel* 16:4.

CHAZZAN CONCLUDES THE BLESSING:

בָּרוּךְ אַתָּה יהוה, רוֹפֵא חוֹלֵי עַמּוֹ יִשְׂרָאֵל.   (Cong. – אָמֵן.)

《 of Israel. 《 of His 《 the sick 《 Who 《《 HASHEM, 《 are 《 Blessed 《《 (Amen.)
people heals You,

CHAZZAN CONTINUES FROM בָּרֵךְ עָלֵינוּ THROUGH וּמְבָרֵךְ הַשָּׁנִים. THEN ALL RECITE:

לְפָנָיו טֶבַע הוֹד אַבְרֵךְ,[1] טָבוּעַ הָיָה וּמוּכָן לְהָאָרֶךְ,

《 to remedy 《 and 《 [so on Mordechai] 《《 for Avrech 《 glory 《 [God] 《 [Long] before
[Israel's troubles]. prepared it was stamped [Joseph]; imprinted [Mordechai],

טָמְנָה וְסִתְּרָה מִפְּרוֹעַ יָרֵךְ,* טָמֵא כְּהִגְרַל גַּפְנָה לְהַבְרֵךְ,*

《 to be 《 to her 《《 became 《 But when the 《《 her 《 not 《 and 《 [Esther]
grafted,* vine her lot, impure one thigh.* revealing concealed, was hidden
[Ahasuerus]

טוֹב פֵּץ לָהּ קוּמִי אוֹרִי כִּי בָא אוֹרֵךְ,[2]

《 your light has come; 《 for 《 and 《 Rise 《《 to 《 declared 《 the Bene-
shine, her: volent One

וַעֲטֶרֶת בִּשְׁנַת טוֹבָתֵךְ[3] בְּגֶשֶׁם אֲבָרֵךְ.*[4]

《《 I will bless.* 《 with rain 《《 of your 《 of the year 《 and the
goodness, crown

CHAZZAN CONCLUDES THE BLESSING:

בָּרוּךְ אַתָּה יהוה, מְבָרֵךְ הַשָּׁנִים.   (Cong. – אָמֵן.)

《 the years. 《 Who blesses 《《 HASHEM, 《 are You, 《 Blessed 《《 (Amen.)

CHAZZAN CONTINUES FROM תְּקַע בְּשׁוֹפָר THROUGH לְאַרְצֵנוּ מֵאַרְבַּע כַּנְפוֹת הָאָרֶץ. THEN ALL RECITE:

מִכָּל יוֹדְעֵי דָת שִׂפַּתֵּי מַרְבֵּעַ,[5]

《《 sitting [before 《 [when] 《 the 《 who 《 More
the Sanhedrin], in rows Torah, know than all

יְקַר יְמִינִי בְּדָת יָמִין[6] רוֹבֵעַ,

《《 disseminated. 《《 – given by 《《 [who] 《《 the 《 [God]
God's right the Law Benjaminite honored
hand – [Mordechai],

יְפִי עֲדִי עֲדָיִים[7] מְשַׁבֵּעַ, יָצָא מְלֻבָּשׁ עַל יַד קוֹבֵעַ,[8]

《《 – [Mordechai,] the one 《《 bedecked 《 he went 《 in settings 《 of 《 of the 《 In the
who gathered together forth [of gold] ornaments select beauty
[much Torah knowledge].

---

(1) Genesis 41:43. (2) Isaiah 60:1. (3) Cf. Psalms 65:12. (4) Cf. Haggai 2:19.
(5) Cf. Genesis 49:14. (6) Cf. Deuteronomy 33:2. (7) Cf. Ezekiel 16:7. (8) Cf. Proverbs 13:11.

מִפְּרוֹעַ יָרֵךְ ... לְהַבְרֵךְ — *Not revealing her thigh ... grafted.* Targum Sheni (2:8) relates that Mordechai attempted to hide Esther from the emissaries of the king so that she would avoid *revealing her thigh* — marrying Ahasuerus. When her lot was determined in heaven that she must *graft her vine* to the impure king —

another metaphor for marriage — God comforted her that the light of Israel's redemption would come through her, as would the resumption of the building of the Temple.

אֲבָרֵךְ — *I will bless.* Haggai (2:19) describes that in the first year after the building of the Temple is resumed there will be a bountiful crop.

יָרַשׁ מַתַּן שְׁאֵלוֹת יַעְבֵּץ, זָהָב יִמֵּן לֶאֱסוֹף* נִדָּחִים מְקַבֵּץ.

≫ He 〈[He Who] 〈 to 〈 He 〈 Gold ≪ of Jabez. 〈 of the requests 〈 the gift 〈 He
gathers in. the dis- collect* induced [for Torah inherited
persed ones [Haman] knowledge]

CHAZZAN CONCLUDES THE BLESSING:

(אָמֵן. – Cong.) בָּרוּךְ אַתָּה יהוה, מְקַבֵּץ נִדְחֵי עַמּוֹ יִשְׂרָאֵל.

≪ (Amen.) ≫ Israel. 〈 of His 〈 the 〈 Who ≪ HASHEM, 〈 are You, 〈 Blessed
people dispersed gathers in

CHAZZAN CONTINUES FROM הַשִּׁיבָה שׁוֹפְטֵינוּ *THROUGH* בְּצֶדֶק וּבְמִשְׁפָּט. *THEN ALL RECITE:*

הַבְּתוּלוֹת כְּהִקָּבֵץ שֵׁנִית² בְּמַאֲהַב,*

≪ because of 〈 a second 〈 – when they 〈 The maidens
[Ahasuerus'] love,* time, were gathered

בְּכְבוּדָּה בַּת מֶלֶךְ³ הַשְּׁלִיכָה יָהַב,⁴

≪ her burden, 〈 cast 〈 of a king 〈 daughter 〈 the
[upon God] [Saul] honorable

כִּי צַדִּיק יהוה צְדָקוֹת אָהֵב,⁵

≪ He loves. 〈 and those of 〈 is 〈 righteous 〈 for
righteous deeds HASHEM,

כָּמַס דוֹב⁶ רִשְׁפֵּי לַהַב,⁷ מַלְהִיב לְלַהֵב,

≫ would be 〈 [in order that] the ≪ of flaming 〈 coals 〈 The bear [Ahasuerus]
ignited. igniter [Haman] [love for Esther], harbored

בָּרָה שׁוּחָה⁸ לָעַד לְחוּמוֹ⁹ לְהַבְהֵב,¹⁰

≪ is to burn 〈 his flesh 〈 – for ≪ a pit 〈 He dug
[in Gehinnom]. eternity [for Israel]

גְדוּלָה* קָפַץ¹¹ בְּדִין מִשְׁפָּט אָהֵב.

≪ loves. 〈 – He Who ≪ the attribute 〈 He closed 〈 With His
judgment of Strict up great [attribute
Justice of Mercy]*

CHAZZAN CONCLUDES THE BLESSING:

(אָמֵן. – Cong.) בָּרוּךְ אַתָּה יהוה, מֶלֶךְ אוֹהֵב צְדָקָה וּמִשְׁפָּט.

≪ (Amen.) ≫ and judgment. 〈 righteousness 〈 Who loves 〈 the King ≪ HASHEM, 〈 are You, 〈 Blessed

---

(1) Cf. *I Chronicles* 4:10; *Temurah* 16a. (2) Cf. *Esther* 2:19. (3) *Psalms* 45:14. (4) Cf. 55:23. (5) 11:7.
(6) Cf. *Daniel* 7:5; *Megillah* 11a. (7) Cf. *Song of Songs* 8:6. (8) Cf. *Psalms* 119:85. (9) Cf. *Zephaniah* 1:17.
(10) Cf. *Hosea* 8:13; *Proverbs* 30:15. (11) Cf. *Deuteronomy* 15:7; *Psalms* 77:10.

לֶאֱסוֹף — *To collect.* The great wealth amassed by Haman was given to Esther and Mordechai. See *Esther* 5:11 and 8:1-2. See also *Megillah* 10b and *Midrash Tehillim* 22:32.

כְּהִקָּבֵץ שֵׁנִית בְּמַאֲהַב — *When they were gathered a second time because of [Ahasuerus'] love.* When Esther refused to reveal her nationality,

Ahasuerus, because of his love for Esther, renewed the gathering of maidens in the hope that Esther would be jealous of his interest in them and divulge her secret (*Megillah* 13a).

גְדוּלָה — *With His great [attribute of Mercy].* God's attribute of beneficence is greater than His attribute of harsh retribution (*Yoma* 76a).

CHAZZAN CONTINUES FROM וְלַמַּלְשִׁינִים THROUGH בִּמְהֵרָה בְיָמֵינוּ. THEN ALL RECITE:

וַיִּשֶּׁם לַיְלָה וּתְנוּמָה הַמְנִיעַ,

≪ He kept from him [Ahasuerus]; ≺ but sleep ≺ the night, ≺[God] brought

לֵיל אֲשֶׁר תַּנִּין¹ וְיָרֵב² הֵנִיעַ,*³

≪ He made ≺ and Jareb ≺ the crocodile ≺ on ≺ on the
    tremble.* [Sennacherib] [Pharaoh] which same night

לַדּוֹרוֹת אוֹתוֹ הִצְנִיעַ, לִהְיוֹת לִפְלְאוֹ צָנוּעַ,

≪ hidden ≺ for His ≺ to be ≪ He ≺ it [Pesach ≺ For future
    away. miracles preserved, night] generations

לָכַד זֵד יָהִיר וּבְאַשְׁמוּרוֹ הִכְנִיעַ,

≪ He defeated ≺ and during [this ≪ who was ≺ the sinner ≺ He
    him. night's] last watch arrogant, [Haman] captured

וְתַכְרִיךְ יְחוּמָיו⁴ שַׂח זֵדִים מַכְנִיעַ.

≪ — He Who humbles ≪ He brought ≺ of his ≺ The whole
    willful sinners. down offspring gang

CHAZZAN CONCLUDES THE BLESSING:

בָּרוּךְ אַתָּה יהוה, שׁוֹבֵר אֹיְבִים וּמַכְנִיעַ זֵדִים. (אָמֵן – Cong.)

≪ (Amen.) ≪ willful ≺ and ≺ enemies ≺ Who ≪ HASHEM, ≺ are ≺ Blessed
    sinners. humbles breaks You,

CHAZZAN CONTINUES FROM נִשְׁעַנְנוּ THROUGH עַל הַצַּדִּיקִים. THEN ALL RECITE:

כֶּתֶר מְלוּכָה מֵאָז הָיָה מִבְטָח,*

≪ promised [to ≺ was ≺ long ≺ of kingship ≺ The
    Benjamin];* ago crown

מֵאֵלָיו* הָיָה לְהִנָּתֵן לְבַת הַבְטָח,

≪ to whom it ≺ to the ≺ to have ≺ it was ≺ on its
    was promised. daughter been given own*

מְלָכוֹת כִּשְׂרוּהָ מַרְאָם הוּטַח,⁵

≪ were covered over ≺ – their ≪ when they ≪ The queens,
    [in embarrassment], faces saw her

מְטוֹבַת זִיו הוֹד מִבְטָח, מֵרֹאשׁ עַד עֵקֶב לִבָּהּ בָּטַח,

≪ trusted ≺ her ≺ end ≺ to ≺ From ≪ of that ≺ of the ≺ of the ≺ from the
    [in God], heart beginning promise. glory splendor goodness

---

(1) Cf. *Ezekiel* 29:3. (2) Cf. *Hosea* 5:13, 10:6. (3) Cf. *Exodus* 20:15, *Rashi*.
(4) Cf. *Psalms* 51:7. (5) Cf. *Isaiah* 44:18.

תַּנִּין וְיָרֵב הֵנִיעַ — *The crocodile [Pharaoh] and Jareb [Sennacherib] He made tremble.* Ahasuerus' sleep was disturbed on the night of Pesach, the night that saw the downfall of Pharaoh and Sennacherib.

מֵאָז הָיָה מִבְטָח — *Long ago was promised [to Benjamin].* Before the birth of Benjamin, God promised Jacob that *kings* would issue from him. Since only Benjamin was yet to be born, that promise required that at least two monarchs would come from Benjamin. The first was Saul and the second was to be Esther.

מֵאֵלָיו — *On its own.* Even without Ahasuerus, Esther was assured of wearing the crown.

בּוּץ לְהַאֲמִירָה¹ בְּמָעֹוז וּמִבְטָח.

《 and Assurance. 〈 with [the 《 distinguishing 〈 with linen
help of her] herself, robes
Stronghold [of royalty]

CHAZZAN CONCLUDES THE BLESSING:

(אָמֵן.) – Cong.)   בָּרוּךְ אַתָּה יהוה, מִשְׁעָן וּמִבְטָח לַצַּדִּיקִים.

《 (Amen.)   《 of the righteous. 〈and Assurance 〈 Mainstay 《 HASHEM, 〈 are You, 〈 Blessed

CHAZZAN CONTINUES FROM וְלִירוּשָׁלַיִם THROUGH תָּכִין לְתוֹכָהּ. THEN ALL RECITE:

מַלְכוּת נֶחְפְּזָה כְּחָזוּ רְבִיד,

《 the royal 〈 when 〈 was 〈 The
necklace they saw startled kingdom

נָבָל, נָתוּן עַל יְדִיד,² מִיַּד מַעֲבִיד,

《 of the 〈 by the 〈 the beloved 〈 upon 〈 placed 〈 of the
sovereign. hand one degenerate
[Mordechai], one [Haman]

נִשְּׂאוּ מֵעַל כֹּל³ וְטַרְחוּ הִכְבִּיד, נִינָיו כִּתְרְזוּ לְהַאֲבִיד,

《 were to be 〈 expelled 〈 [now even] 《 he made 〈 and his 〈 everyone 〈 above 〈 [For] he
discarded. like dung, his children, difficult burden had elevated
[for them]; [Haman]

נְשׂוּאֵי רֶחֶם⁴ זֶבֶד טוֹב הִזְבִּיד,⁵

《 [God] granted 〈 – a good portion 《 from the 〈 [But] those
[them]; [Haman's wealth] womb borne
[Israel] [by God]

וְאַרְגָּמָן יִמְּנָם⁶ לְכוֹנֵן עִיר דָּוִד.*

《 of 〈 the City 〈 to 《 He 〈 with purple
David.* reestablish provided garb [symbol
them, of royalty]

CHAZZAN CONCLUDES THE BLESSING:

(אָמֵן.) – Cong.)   בָּרוּךְ אַתָּה יהוה, בּוֹנֵה יְרוּשָׁלָיִם.

《 (Amen.)   《 of Jerusalem. 〈 Builder 《 HASHEM, 〈 are You, 〈 Blessed

CHAZZAN CONTINUES WITH THE ENTIRE BLESSING OF אֶת צֶמַח, AND
FROM אָב הָרַחֲמָן שְׁמַע קוֹלֵנוּ THROUGH בְּרַחֲמִים יִשְׂרָאֵל. THEN ALL RECITE:

בְּרֹאשָׁהּ שִׂים זֵר אֲשֶׁר הִפְלָא,*

《 [fitted] 〈 which 〈 [by the] 〈 she was 〈 On her
wondrously.* crown, designated head

---

(1) Cf. *Deuteronomy* 26:17,18. (2) Cf. 33:12. (3) Cf. *Esther* 3:1.
(4) Cf. *Isaiah* 46:3. (5) Cf. *Genesis* 30:20. (6) Cf. *Daniel* 1:5.

לְכוֹנֵן עִיר דָּוִד – *To reestablish the City of David.*
This conclusion is appropriate to both of the
blessings — for rebuilding Jerusalem and for the
Davidic Reign — that are combined in the

Jerusalem Talmud, as mentioned above in the
introduction to *Krovetz (Ron Shir VeShevach).*
זֵר אֲשֶׁר הִפְלָא – *[By the] crown which [fitted]*
wondrously. The Talmud (*Avodah Zarah* 44a)

סֻגַּת שׁוֹשָׁן¹ עָלוֹת מִשְׁפָּלָה,

from ‹ rose ‹ with ‹ [Israel,
degradation. up roses described
as] hedged

שִׂיחַת רְדוּמִים עָלוֹת מִמַּכְפֵּלָה,

from Machpelah; ‹ arose ‹ of the ‹ The prayer
slumbering
[Patriarchs]

שֵׂעִיר וְאֶת שְׂרִידָיו² לְשַׁחַת הִפִּילָה,

did it cast down. ‹ to oblivion ‹ and his successors ‹ Seir

סְגוּרֵי כֶלֶא³ הֵפֶן מֵאֲפֵלָה,

from darkness, ‹ [God] ‹ in the prison ‹ Those
removed [of exile] detained

וְהָעִיר רוֹן כָּפֵלָה⁴ לְשׁוֹמֵעַ תְּפִלָּה.

prayer. ‹ to the One ‹ doubled ‹ glad ‹ and the city
Who hears songs of [Shushan]

CHAZZAN CONCLUDES THE BLESSING:

(אָמֵן. – Cong.)   בָּרוּךְ אַתָּה יהוה, שׁוֹמֵעַ תְּפִלָּה.

(Amen.)   prayer. ‹ Who hears ‹ HASHEM, ‹ are You, ‹ Blessed

CHAZZAN CONTINUES FROM רְצֵה THROUGH בְּרַחֲמִים לְצִיּוֹן בְּשׁוּבְךָ. THEN ALL RECITE:

וַיַּמְלִיכֶהָ עָזוּר לְאוֹם מוֹרָאָה,⁵

that was seen ‹ the ‹ to aid ‹ [God] made her
as filthy. nation [Esther] queen

עֲצוּרָה הָיְתָה לָכֵן מֵעֵת נִבְרָאָה,

she was ‹ from ‹ for that ‹ was she ‹ Safe-
created. the time [purpose] guarded

עֲמִיתָהּ הִפְגִּיעַ בַּעֲדָהּ קְרִיאָה,

calling out ‹ on her ‹ appealed ‹ Her companion
[to God], behalf, [Mordechai]

עַד עֵת בֹּא דְבָרוֹ אֲשֶׁר רָאָה,*

he had seen ‹ that ‹ of his ‹ of the ‹ the ‹ until
[in a dream].* vision fulfillment time

(1) Cf. *Song of Songs* 7:3. (2) Cf. *Obadiah* 1:18.
(3) Cf. *Isaiah* 42:7. (4) Cf. *Esther* 8:15. (5) Cf. *Zephaniah* 3:1.

relates that a sign of the worthiness for kingship of the House of David is that the crown would fit perfectly. The same sign applied to Esther, whose crown miraculously fitted perfectly.

דְּבָרוֹ אֲשֶׁר רָאָה — *Of his vision that he had seen [in a dream].* The Midrash (*Esther Rabbah* 8:5) relates that ten years earlier, Mordechai saw a vision in a dream that symbolically foretold the

עֲנוּתָם¹ לַחוֹזִים* שַׁדַּי הֶרְאָה,*

⟨⟨ had shown* ⟨ the Almighty ⟨ to the prophets* ⟨ Their outcry

שׁוֹשַׁן חוֹחִים² לְעׇבְדוֹ בְּיִרְאָה.*

⟨⟨ with awe.* ⟨ serving ⟨⟨ [even] among ⟨ – [Israel,
Him   thorns,   remains]
                                 a rose

CHAZZAN CONCLUDES THE BLESSING:

(אָמֵן – Cong.) בָּרוּךְ אַתָּה יהוה, הַמַּחֲזִיר שְׁכִינָתוֹ לְצִיּוֹן.

⟨⟨ (Amen.)   ⟨⟨ to Zion. ⟨ His Presence ⟨ Who restores ⟨⟨ HASHEM, ⟨ are You, ⟨ Blessed

CHAZZAN CONTINUES FROM מוֹדִים THROUGH וְעֶזְרָתֵנוּ סֶלָה הָאֵ־ל הַטּוֹב. THEN ALL RECITE:

תַּחַת פִּלְפּוּל יַגִּיעַ לֶקַח טוֹב,³

⟨⟨ in the goodly ⟨ and ⟨ of [Mordechai's] ⟨ Because
gift [Torah],   toil   expounding

פְּעֻלַּת צַדִּיק פָּעֳלָם לַטוֹב,

⟨⟨ are for ⟨ whose ⟨ of [any] ⟨ and, like
the good,   actions   righteous man,   the deeds

פְּאֵר אוֹמֵר אֲשֶׁר הוּא טוֹב,

⟨⟨ good, ⟨ was ⟨ which ⟨ of his ⟨ through the
                prayer,   splendor

פּוּר הָפַךְ לְמִשְׁתֶּה וְיוֹם טוֹב,

⟨⟨ and a holiday. ⟨ into a ⟨ was ⟨ [the day of
              feast   changed   Haman's] lot

פְּדוּת כֵּן תָּחִישׁ⁴ לְהָהָר הַטּוֹב,⁵

⟨⟨ for the goodly ⟨ may You ⟨ simi- ⟨ Redemp-
[Temple] Mount,   hasten   larly   tion

צְהָלָה וְזִמְרָה לְהוֹדוֹת לְאֵל טוֹב.

⟨⟨ to the ⟨ give thanks ⟨ and ⟨ [where we will]
benevolent God.   song   with exultation

CHAZZAN CONCLUDES THE BLESSING:

(אָמֵן – Cong.) בָּרוּךְ אַתָּה יהוה, הַטּוֹב שִׁמְךָ וּלְךָ נָאֶה לְהוֹדוֹת.

⟨⟨ (Amen.)   ⟨⟨ to give ⟨ it is ⟨ and ⟨ is Your ⟨ The Bene- ⟨⟨ HASHEM, ⟨ are ⟨ Blessed
thanks.   fitting   to You   Name,   ficent One   You,

---

(1) Cf. *Psalms* 22:25. (2) Cf. *Song of Songs* 2:2.
(3) *Proverbs* 4:2. (4) Cf. *Isaiah* 60:22. (5) *Deuteronomy* 3:25.

---

events that were unfolding.

הֶרְאָה ... לַחוֹזִים – *To the prophets ... had shown.* According to various Midrashic sources, Abraham, Jacob, Moses, and Samuel were shown prophetically the events at the time of Mordechai and Esther. (For a list of sources, see

Ron Shir VeShevach).

לְעׇבְדוֹ בְּיִרְאָה – *Serving him with awe.* These words refer to the conclusion of this blessing that we say only when the *Kohanim* bless the people — שֶׁאוֹתְךָ לְבַדְּךָ בְּיִרְאָה נַעֲבוֹד, *for You alone with awe do we serve.* In *Eretz Yisrael* in the

CHAZZAN CONTINUES FROM אֱלֹהֵינוּ וֵאלֹהֵי אֲבוֹתֵינוּ THROUGH בִּשְׁלוֹמֶךָ. THEN ALL RECITE:

וָשְׁתִּי צוֹאֲנָה*¹ לְמַעֲרָכוֹת, קְצִינוּת כְּהִכְתָּרָה מִמַּלְכוֹת,

≪ above all ‹ she had ‹ though with ≪ to judgment, ‹ was taken ‹ Vashti
other queens. been crowned high rank amid commotion*

רַגְלֵי אַיֶּלֶת בָּמוֹת* דּוֹרְכוֹת,²

≪ strode, ‹ to the ‹ of the doe ‹ The feet
heights* [Esther]

שִׁבְעִים יְמֵי צָר* עֲלוֹת לָהּ אֲרוּכוֹת,³

≪ a cure. ‹ through ‹ should be ‹ of ‹ [so that for
her, provided, distress* Israel's] seventy
days

תָּקְפָה⁴ עִם דּוֹד לְעֵינֶיהָ בְּרֵכוֹת,⁵

≪ are like ‹ for [the Jewish ‹ her uncle ‹ together ‹ She decreed with
pools. people], [Mordechai], with full authority [the
whose eyes observance of Purim],

וְשִׂמְחָה קוֹל נִשְׁמַע מֵחֲרַכּוֹת,*⁶

≪ from the windows ‹ that was ‹ was the ‹ Of
[of heaven],* heard sound rejoicing

וְדוֹבֵר שָׁלוֹם מִמְּעוֹן הַבְּרָכוֹת.

≪ of blessings. ‹ from the ‹ of peace ‹ and from Him
Abode Who speaks

CHAZZAN CONCLUDES THE BLESSING:

בָּרוּךְ אַתָּה יהוה, הַמְבָרֵךְ אֶת עַמּוֹ יִשְׂרָאֵל בַּשָּׁלוֹם. (אָמֵן.–Cong.)

≪ (Amen.) ≪ with peace. ‹ Israel ‹ His people ‹ Who blesses ≪HASHEM,‹ are You,‹ Blessed

(יִהְיוּ לְרָצוֹן אִמְרֵי פִי וְהֶגְיוֹן לִבִּי לְפָנֶיךָ, יהוה צוּרִי וְגֹאֲלִי.⁷)

≪ and my ‹ my ‹ HASHEM, ≪ before ≪ of my ‹ and the ‹ of my ‹ – the ≪ find ‹ (May
Redeemer.) Rock You, heart – thoughts mouth expressions favor they

CHAZZAN RECITES HALF-KADDISH (P. 197) AND THE SERVICE CONTINUES WITH THE TORAH READING.

---

(1) Cf. *Isaiah* 9:4. (2) Cf. *Habakkuk* 3:19. (3) Cf. *Jeremiah* 33:6.
(4) Cf. *Esther* 9:29. (5) Cf. *Song of Songs* 7:5. (6) 2:9. (7) *Psalms* 19:15.

---

time of R' Elazar HaKalir this was the standard conclusion of the blessing (*Iyun Tefillah*).

צוֹאֲנָה — *Was taken amid commotion.* This translation follows *Iyun Tefillah* who combines three separate allusions in the word צוֹאֲנָה. First is the root יָצָא meaning that Vashti was taken out. Then he follows the *Kol Bo* who equates the word with סֹאן (*Isaiah* 9:4), that *Rashi* explains as the tumult of a victory celebration. Finally, the word סֹאן is interpreted by the Talmud (*Sotah* 8b) as a measure — a *se'ah* — alluding to Vashti being punished measure for measure (*Megillah* 12b).

בָּמוֹת — *To the heights.* Vashti had to be removed since the time had come for Esther to ascend, and one reign does not impinge on its successor (*Iyun Tefillah*).

שִׁבְעִים יְמֵי צָר — *Seventy days of distress.* Seventy days elapsed from the thirteenth of Nissan, when Haman's genocidal decree was sent out, until the twenty-third of Sivan when Mordechai's revised letters were sent.

מֵחֲרַכּוֹת — *From the windows [of heaven].* The heavenly court ratified the Purim festival that was decreed by the earthly court (*Megillah* 7a).

❧ בַּר יוֹחָאי / BAR YOCHAI ❧

בַּר יוֹחָאי נִמְשַׁחְתָּ אַשְׁרֶיךָ, שֶׁמֶן שָׂשׂוֹן מֵחֲבֵרֶיךָ.[1]

≫ more than 〈 of joy 〈 [with] ≪ — you are ≫ You were ≪ Bar Yochai!
your peers. oil fortunate — anointed

בַּר יוֹחָאי שֶׁמֶן מִשְׁחַת קֹדֶשׁ, נִמְשַׁחְתָּ מִמִּדַּת הַקֹּדֶשׁ,

≫ that is holy. 〈 from the 〈 were you 〈 things 〈 of 〈 With oil ≪ Bar Yochai!
measure anointed holy anointing

נָשָׂאתָ צִיץ נֵזֶר הַקֹּדֶשׁ,[2] חָבוּשׁ עַל רֹאשְׁךָ פְּאֵרֶךָ.[3]

≫ is your glory. 〈 upon your head 〈 worn ≪ of holiness, 〈 a 〈 the 〈 You bore
crown headplate,

בַּר יוֹחָאי נִמְשַׁחְתָּ אַשְׁרֶיךָ, שֶׁמֶן שָׂשׂוֹן מֵחֲבֵרֶיךָ.

≫ more than 〈 of joy 〈 [with] ≪ — you are ≪ You were ≪ Bar Yochai!
your peers. oil fortunate — anointed

בַּר יוֹחָאי מוֹשַׁב טוֹב יָשַׁבְתָּ, יוֹם נַסְתָּ יוֹם אֲשֶׁר בָּרַחְתָּ,

≪ you fled; 〈 that 〈 the 〈 you 〈 on the ≪ did you 〈 that is 〈 In a ≪ Bar Yochai!
day ran, day settle, good dwelling

בִּמְעָרַת צוּרִים[4] שֶׁעָמַדְתָּ,[5] שָׁם קָנִיתָ הוֹדְךָ וַהֲדָרֶךָ.[6]

≫ and your 〈 your 〈 you 〈 there ≪ where you 〈 of the 〈 in the cave
splendor. majesty acquired stopped — rocks

בַּר יוֹחָאי נִמְשַׁחְתָּ אַשְׁרֶיךָ, שֶׁמֶן שָׂשׂוֹן מֵחֲבֵרֶיךָ.

≫ more than 〈 of joy 〈 [with] ≪ — you are ≪ You were ≪ Bar Yochai!
your peers. oil fortunate — anointed

בַּר יוֹחָאי עֲצֵי שִׁטִּים עוֹמְדִים,[7] לִמּוּדֵי יהוה הֵם לוֹמְדִים,

≪ study; 〈 they 〈 of God 〈 the ≪ standing 〈 of acacia 〈 Like ≪ Bar Yochai!
teaching erect, trees wood

אוֹר מֻפְלָא אוֹר הַיְּקוֹד הֵם יוֹקְדִים,[8] הֲלֹא הֵמָּה יוֹרוּךָ[9] מוֹרֶיךָ.

≪ — your ≪ teach 〈 — will they not 〈 ignite 〈 that 〈 of the 〈 is the 〈 that is 〈 a
teachers. you they blazing fire light wondrous light

בַּר יוֹחָאי נִמְשַׁחְתָּ אַשְׁרֶיךָ, שֶׁמֶן שָׂשׂוֹן מֵחֲבֵרֶיךָ.

≫ more than 〈 of joy 〈 [with] ≪ — you are ≪ You were ≪ Bar Yochai!
your peers. oil fortunate — anointed

---

(1) *Psalms* 45:8. (2) *Exodus* 39:30. (3) Cf. *Ezekiel* 24:17. (4) Cf. *Isaiah* 2:19.
(5) Cf. *Shabbos* 33b. (6) *Psalms* 45:4. (7) *Exodus* 26:15. (8) Cf. *Isaiah* 10:16. (9) Cf. *Job* 8:10.

❧ בַּר יוֹחָאי / Bar Yochai

This famous *zemer* was composed by *Rabbi Shimon ibn Lavi* — whose name is formed by the acrostic — in honor of the *tanna*, R' Shimon bar Yochai, author of the *Zohar*. A phrase-by-phrase commentary can be found in the ArtScroll *Zemiros*.

It is sung on *Lag B'Omer* in most communities; some sing it on Sabbaths of the *Sefirah* period.

בר יוחאי / 598

בַּר יוֹחָאי וְלִשְׂדֵה תַפּוּחִים* עָלִיתָ, לִלְקוֹט בּוֹ מֶרְקָחִים,

≫ Bar Yochai! ⟨ To the Field ⟨ of Apples* ⟨ you ascended, ≫ to gather ⟨ there ⟨ confections: ≫

סוֹד תּוֹרָה בְּצִיצִים וּפְרָחִים,¹ נַעֲשֶׂה אָדָם² נֶאֱמַר בַּעֲבוּרֶךָ.

⟨ The ⟨ mystery ⟨ of Torah ⟨ with ⟨ blossoms ⟨ and flowers – ≫ Let us create ⟨ man ⟨ was said ⟨ for your sake. ≫

בַּר יוֹחָאי נִמְשַׁחְתָּ אַשְׁרֶיךָ, שֶׁמֶן שָׂשׂוֹן מֵחֲבֵרֶיךָ.

≫ Bar Yochai! ⟨ You were anointed ≫ – you are ⟨ fortunate – ≫ [with] oil ⟨ of joy ⟨ more than your peers. ≫

בַּר יוֹחָאי נֶאֱזַרְתָּ בִּגְבוּרָה,³ וּבְמִלְחֶמֶת אֵשׁ דַּת הַשַּׁעְרָה,*⁴

≫ Bar Yochai! ⟨ You were girded ⟨ with strength, ≫ and in the war ⟨ of the fiery Torah ⟨ up to the gate;* ≫

וְחֶרֶב הוֹצֵאתָ מִתַּעְרָהּ,⁵ שָׁלַפְתָּ נֶגֶד צוֹרְרֶיךָ.

⟨ a sword ⟨ You ⟨ unsheathed ⟨ from its scabbard, ≫ drew it ⟨ you ⟨ against ⟨ your enemies. ≫

בַּר יוֹחָאי נִמְשַׁחְתָּ אַשְׁרֶיךָ, שֶׁמֶן שָׂשׂוֹן מֵחֲבֵרֶיךָ.

≫ Bar Yochai! ⟨ You were anointed ≫ – you are ⟨ fortunate – ≫ [with] oil ⟨ of joy ⟨ more than your peers. ≫

בַּר יוֹחָאי לִמְקוֹם אַבְנֵי שַׁיִשׁ⁶ הִגַּעְתָּ,* וּפְנֵי אַרְיֵה⁷ לַיִשׁ,

≫ Bar Yochai! ⟨ To the place ⟨ of ⟨ stones ⟨ of marble ≫ you arrived,* ⟨ before ⟨ a lion – ≫ a huge lion. ≫

גַּם גֻּלַּת כּוֹתֶרֶת⁸ עַל עַיִשׁ*⁹ תָּשׁוּרִי, וּמִי יְשׁוּרֶךָ.

⟨ Even ⟨ a ⟨ rounded ⟨ crown ⟨ upon a constellation's star ≫ you perceived ⟨ who ⟨ but – ≫ can perceive you? ≫

---

(1) Cf. *Shabbos* 145b. (2) *Genesis* 1:26. (3) Cf. *Psalms* 65:7. (4) Cf. *Isaiah* 28:6. (5) Cf. *Ezekiel* 21:8. (6) Cf. *Chagigah* 14b. (7) *Ezekiel* 1:10. (8) Cf. *I Kings* 7:41. (9) *Job* 38:32, see *Rashi*.

וְלִשְׂדֵה תַפּוּחִים —*To the Field of Apples.* In Kabbalistic terminology, the *Field of Apples* refers to a degree of holiness as exalted as that of the Garden of Eden before Adam's sin.

וּבְמִלְחֶמֶת אֵשׁ דַּת הַשַּׁעְרָה — *And in the war of the fiery Torah up to the gate.* The שַׁעַר הָעִיר, *gate of the city*, is an expression frequently used in Scripture to denote the meeting place of the sages or the court. It was in the gatherings of the greatest scholars that R' Shimon distinguished himself as an outstanding warrior in the battle for Torah.

לִמְקוֹם אַבְנֵי שַׁיִשׁ הִגַּעְתָּ — *To the place of stones of marble you arrived.* The reference is to *Chagi-gah* 14b, where R' Akiva, the teacher of R' Shimon, speaks of sparkling marble in Paradise. The reference was not understood, for only one who had been there, as was R' Akiva, could conceive of it. To R' Shimon, however, the mystery was revealed.

עַל עַיִשׁ — *Upon a constellation's star.* The Talmud (*Berachos* 59a) relates that God stopped the floodwaters in Noah's time by taking two stars from עַיִשׁ to seal the hole in the heavens. Such action was not necessary in the time of R' Shimon. During his time no rainbow appeared in the skies, attesting to the absence of even a threat of a flood.

בַּר יוֹחָאי נִמְשַׁחְתָּ אַשְׁרֶיךָ, שֶׁמֶן שָׂשׂוֹן מֵחֲבֵרֶיךָ.

‹‹ more than ‹ of joy ‹ [with] ‹‹ – you are ‹‹ You were ‹‹ Bar Yochai!
your peers.　　　　　 oil　　 fortunate –　 anointed

בַּר יוֹחָאי בִּקְדֶשׁ הַקֳּדָשִׁים,* קַו יָרֹק* מְחַדֵּשׁ חֲדָשִׁים,

‹‹　 new　　 ‹ creates ‹ of ‹ a ‹‹ of Holies,* ‹ In the ‹‹　 Bar Yochai!
conceptions:　　　　　 green* line　　　　 Holy

שֶׁבַע שַׁבָּתוֹת סוֹד חֲמִשִׁים, קָשַׁרְתָּ קִשְׁרֵי שִׁי"ן קְשָׁרֶיךָ.*

‹‹ [as] Your ‹ of Shin ‹ the knots ‹ you ‹‹ of the fifty ‹ are the ‹ weeks ‹ Seven
bonds.* [on tefillin]　　　　 bound　 [levels];　 secret

בַּר יוֹחָאי נִמְשַׁחְתָּ אַשְׁרֶיךָ, שֶׁמֶן שָׂשׂוֹן מֵחֲבֵרֶיךָ.

‹‹ more than ‹ of joy ‹ [with] ‹‹ – you are ‹‹ You were ‹‹ Bar Yochai!
your peers.　　　　　 oil　　 fortunate –　 anointed

בַּר יוֹחָאי יוּ"ד חָכְמָה קְדוּמָה,*

‹‹ primordial,* ‹ of ‹ The ‹‹ Bar Yochai!
　　　　 wisdom　 yud

הִשְׁקַפְתָּ לִכְבוּדָה פְּנִימָה,[1]

‹‹　 that is　 ‹ into its honor ‹ you gazed
innermost,

ל"ב נְתִיבוֹת[2] רֵאשִׁית תְּרוּמָה,

‹‹　 tithe,　 ‹ of the ‹ paths ‹ the
　　　 very first　　　 thirty-two

אַתְּ כְּרוּב מִמְשַׁח[3] זִיו אוֹרֶךָ.

‹‹ of your ‹ with ‹ anointed ‹ like a ‹ you
illumination. the glow　　　 cherub　 are

בַּר יוֹחָאי נִמְשַׁחְתָּ אַשְׁרֶיךָ, שֶׁמֶן שָׂשׂוֹן מֵחֲבֵרֶיךָ.

‹‹ more than ‹ of joy ‹ [with] ‹‹ – you are ‹‹ You were ‹‹ Bar Yochai!
your peers.　　　　　 oil　　 fortunate –　 anointed

---

(1) Cf. *Psalms* 45:14. (2) Cf. *Sefer HaYetzirah* 1:1. (3) *Ezekiel* 28:14.

בְּקֹדֶשׁ הַקֳּדָשִׁים — *In the Holy of Holies.* A person's בִּינָה, *understanding*, is his personal Holy of Holies, for without it, his inspirational flashes of wisdom come to naught or they can be developed grotesquely.

קַו יָרֹק — *A line of green.* The development of wisdom through understanding and application is called a *line*: the flash of חָכְמָה, *wisdom*, is likened to a "point" until it is utilized and developed. As it spreads out into development

and application, it is likened to a spreading line in the color of growing, life-supporting vegetation.

קְשָׁרֶיךָ — *[As] Your bonds.* The *tefillin* are bound upon the heads of Jews and, as the Sages explain, the nations will fear Israel when they perceive that God's will, as it were, is bound around the heads of the Jews.

יוּ"ד חָכְמָה קְדוּמָה — *The yud of wisdom primordial.* The letter י, *yud*, because it is tiny, like

בַּר יוֹחָאי אוֹר מִפְלָא רוּם מַעֲלָה,

⟪ Bar Yochai! ⟩ At a ⟨ that is ⟩ in lofty ⟨ heights
wondrous
light

יָרֵאתָ מִלְּהַבִּיט כִּי רַב לָה

⟨ you ⟨ to gaze, ⟪ for ⟨ great ⟩ is its
feared

תַּעֲלוּמָה, וְאֵין קוֹרֵא לָה, נַמְתָּ עַיִן לֹא תְשׁוּרֶךָ.

⟪ Hiddenness; ⟪ Naught ⟩ does ⟨ You ⟪ her. ⟨ that ⟨ could ⟨ glimpse
one call declared an eye not You.

בַּר יוֹחָאי נִמְשַׁחְתָּ אַשְׁרֶיךָ, שֶׁמֶן שָׂשׂוֹן מֵחֲבֵרֶיךָ.

⟪ Bar Yochai! ⟪ You were ⟪ – you are ⟪ [with] ⟨ of joy ⟪ more than
anointed fortunate – oil your peers.

בַּר יוֹחָאי אַשְׁרֵי יוֹלַדְתֶּךָ,

⟪ Bar Yochai! ⟪ Fortunate ⟨ is she who
bore you,

אַשְׁרֵי הָעָם הֵם לוֹמְדֶיךָ,

⟨ fortunate ⟨ is the ⟨ who are ⟨ who learn
people the ones from you.

וְאַשְׁרֵי הָעוֹמְדִים עַל סוֹדֶךָ,

⟨ And ⟨ fortunate ⟨ are those who ⟪ your mystery,
fully comprehend

לְבוּשֵׁי חֹשֶׁן תֻּמֶּיךָ וְאוּרֶיךָ.[1]

⟨ garbed ⟨ in the ⟨ and Your ⟨ and
priestly [Ineffable Name] ⟪ enlightening.
breastplate that is complete

בַּר יוֹחָאי נִמְשַׁחְתָּ אַשְׁרֶיךָ, שֶׁמֶן שָׂשׂוֹן מֵחֲבֵרֶיךָ.

⟪ Bar Yochai! ⟪ You were ⟪ – you are ⟪ [with] ⟨ of joy ⟪ more than
anointed fortunate – oil your peers.

---

(1) *Deuteronomy* 33:8.

a point, represents the first spark of wisdom. All knowledge begins with an idea — a "spark" or a "point" — which must then be broadened, deepened, and applied. It is the earliest of all emanations because it is the closest to God's Own wisdom.

❧ AMELIORATION OF A DREAM / הטבת חלום ❧

ONE WHO HAS HAD A DISTURBING DREAM SHOULD PERFORM THE FOLLOWING RITUAL THE NEXT MORNING TOGETHER WITH THREE GOOD FRIENDS.

THE THREE FRIENDS RECITE SEVEN TIMES IN UNISON:

הֲלוֹא לֵאלֹהִים פִּתְרֹנִים, סַפְּרוּ נָא לִי.[1]

》 to me. 〈 please, 〈 Relate 》the interpretations 〈 to God 〈 Are not
it, [of dreams]?

THE DREAMER RECITES SEVEN TIMES:

חֶלְמָא טָבָא חֲזָאִי.

》 I have seen. 〈 that is good 〈 A dream

THE THREE FRIENDS RECITE SEVEN TIMES IN UNISON:

חֶלְמָא טָבָא חֲזֵית. טָבָא הוּא וְטָבָא לֶהֱוֵי. רַחֲמָנָא לְשַׁוְּיֵהּ

〈 establish 〈 May the 》 it should 〈 and 》 it is, 〈 Good 》 You have 〈 that is 〈 A dream
it Merciful One be. good seen. good

לְטַב. שְׁבַע זִמְנִין לִגְזְרוּ עֲלֵהּ מִן שְׁמַיָּא דִּי לֶהֱוֵי טָבָא, וְיֶהֱוֵי

〈 and 〈 good, 〈 it 〈 that 〈 heaven 〈 from 〈 about 〈 may they 〈 times 〈 Seven 》 for
may it be should be it decree good.

טָבָא. טָבָא הוּא וְטָבָא לֶהֱוֵי.

》 it 〈 and 》 it is, 〈 Good 》 good.
should be. good

VERSES OF TRANSFORMATION OF DISTRESS TO RELIEF / פסוקים של הפוך צרה

THE DREAMER RECITES:

הָפַכְתָּ מִסְפְּדִי לְמָחוֹל לִי, פִּתַּחְתָּ שַׂקִּי, וַתְּאַזְּרֵנִי שִׂמְחָה.[2]

》 with 〈 and You 〈 my 〈 You 》 for 〈 into 〈 my 〈 You have
gladness. girded me sackcloth undid me; dancing lament transformed

THE THREE FRIENDS RECITE IN UNISON:

אָז תִּשְׂמַח בְּתוּלָה בְּמָחוֹל, וּבַחֻרִים וּזְקֵנִים יַחְדָּו, וְהָפַכְתִּי

〈 and I shall 》 together 〈 and 〈 and young 》 in a dance, 〈 will the 〈 gladdened 〈 Then
transform [will rejoice]; elders men maiden be

אֶבְלָם לְשָׂשׂוֹן, וְנִחַמְתִּים וְשִׂמַּחְתִּים מִיגוֹנָם. וְלֹא אָבָה[3]

》 He did 》 from their 〈 and gladden 〈 and I shall 》 to joy, 〈 their
not consent sorrow. them console them mourning

יְהוָה אֱלֹהֶיךָ לִשְׁמֹעַ אֶל בִּלְעָם, וַיַּהֲפֹךְ יְהוָה אֱלֹהֶיךָ לְּךָ

〈 for 〈 your God, 〈 did 〈 and 〈 Balaam, 〈 to 〈 to pay 》 your 〈 —HASHEM,
you HASHEM, transform heed God —

אֶת הַקְּלָלָה לִבְרָכָה, כִּי אֲהֵבְךָ יְהוָה אֱלֹהֶיךָ.[4]

》 your God. 〈 does HASHEM, 〈 love you 〈 for 》 to blessing, 〈 the curse

---

(1) *Genesis* 40:8. (2) *Psalms* 30:12. (3) *Jeremiah* 31:12. (4) *Deuteronomy* 23:6.

VERSES OF RESCUE / פסוקים של פדיום

THE DREAMER RECITES:

פָּדָה בְשָׁלוֹם נַפְשִׁי מִקְּרָב לִי, כִּי בְרַבִּים הָיוּ עִמָּדִי.¹

against	were my	with	even	against	from	my	in peace	He
me.	enemies	many	though,	me,	battles	soul		redeemed

THE THREE FRIENDS RECITE IN UNISON:

וַיֹּאמֶר הָעָם אֶל שָׁאוּל, הֲיוֹנָתָן יָמוּת אֲשֶׁר עָשָׂה

| performed | who | die, | Shall Jonathan | Saul: | to | | The people said |

הַיְשׁוּעָה הַגְּדוֹלָה הַזֹּאת בְּיִשְׂרָאֵל, חָלִילָה, חַי־יהוה, אִם יִפֹּל

| there falls | if | As HASHEM lives, | In no way! | for Israel? | this great salvation |

מִשַּׂעֲרַת רֹאשׁוֹ אַרְצָה, כִּי עִם אֱלֹהִים עָשָׂה הַיּוֹם הַזֶּה,

| this day! | has he acted | God | with | For | to the ground...! | of his head | any of the hair |

וַיִּפְדּוּ הָעָם אֶת יוֹנָתָן וְלֹא מֵת.² וּפְדוּיֵי יהוה יְשֻׁבוּן, וּבָאוּ צִיּוֹן

| to Zion | and will come | will return, | by HASHEM | Those | die. | and he did not | Jonathan | And the people redeemed |

בְרִנָּה, וְשִׂמְחַת עוֹלָם עַל רֹאשָׁם, שָׂשׂוֹן וְשִׂמְחָה יַשִּׂיגוּ וְנָסוּ

| and flee | will they attain, | and gladness | joy | on their heads; | that is eternal | with gladness | with glad song, |

יָגוֹן וַאֲנָחָה.³

| and sighing. | will sorrow |

VERSES OF PEACE / פסוקים של שלום

THE DREAMER RECITES:

בּוֹרֵא נִיב שְׂפָתָיִם, שָׁלוֹם שָׁלוֹם לָרָחוֹק וְלַקָּרוֹב, אָמַר

| says | and for near, | for far | peace, | Peace, | of the lips: | the speech | I [will] create |

יהוה וּרְפָאתִיו.⁴

| and I shall heal him. | HASHEM, |

THE THREE FRIENDS RECITE IN UNISON:

וְרוּחַ לָבְשָׁה אֶת עֲמָשַׂי רֹאשׁ הַשָּׁלִישִׁים, לְךָ דָוִיד וְעִמְּךָ

| and [we] are with you, | David, | [and he said:] | of the officers, | head | Amasai, | clothed | A spirit [We] are yours, |

בֶן יִשַׁי, שָׁלוֹם שָׁלוֹם לְךָ, וְשָׁלוֹם לְעֹזְרֶךָ, כִּי עֲזָרְךָ אֱלֹהֶיךָ,

| does your God! | assist you | for | unto those who assist you, | and peace | unto you, | Peace | Peace! | of | son Jesse! |

וַיְקַבְּלֵם דָּוִיד וַיִּתְּנֵם בְּרָאשֵׁי הַגְּדוּד.⁵ וַאֲמַרְתֶּם, כֹּה לֶחָי, וְאַתָּה

| for you | So may it be as long as you live; | And you shall say: | of troops. | as heads | and appointed them | David accepted them |

(1) Psalms 55:19. (2) I Samuel 14:45. (3) Isaiah 35:10. (4) 57:19. (5) I Chronicles 12:19.

שָׁלוֹם וּבֵיתְךָ שָׁלוֹם וְכֹל אֲשֶׁר לְךָ שָׁלוֹם. יהוה עֹז לְעַמּוֹ[1]

⟨to His ⟨strength ⟨HASHEM ⟪may there ⟨is yours ⟨that ⟨and ⟪may there ⟨for your ⟪may there
nation be peace! for all be peace, household be peace,

יִתֵּן, יהוה יְבָרֵךְ אֶת עַמּוֹ בַשָּׁלוֹם.[2]

⟪ with peace. ⟨ His nation ⟨will bless ⟨HASHEM ⟪will give;

THE DREAMER RECITES THREE TIMES:

יהוה, שָׁמַעְתִּי שִׁמְעֲךָ יָרֵאתִי.[3]

⟪ I was frightened. ⟨Your report; ⟨ I heard ⟨ HASHEM,

THE THREE FRIENDS RECITE THREE TIMES IN UNISON:

יהוה, פָּעָלְךָ בְּקֶרֶב שָׁנִים חַיֵּיהוּ,

⟪ keep him ⟪ [these] ⟨ – during ⟪ the one ⟪ HASHEM,
alive; years – You made

בְּקֶרֶב שָׁנִים תּוֹדִיעַ, בְּרֹגֶז רַחֵם תִּזְכּוֹר.[3]

⟪ You will ⟨ to be ⟨In the midst ⟪ make it ⟨ [these] ⟨ during
remember. merciful of rage, known: years

THE DREAMER RECITES THREE TIMES:

שִׁיר לַמַּעֲלוֹת, אֶשָּׂא עֵינַי אֶל הֶהָרִים,

⟪ the mountains ⟨ to ⟨ my ⟨ I raise ⟪ to the ⟨A song
eyes ascents.

מֵאַיִן יָבֹא עֶזְרִי. עֶזְרִי מֵעִם יהוה, עֹשֵׂה שָׁמַיִם וָאָרֶץ.[4]

⟪ and earth. ⟨of heaven ⟨Maker ⟪ HASHEM, ⟨is from ⟨ My ⟪ my ⟨ will ⟨ from
help help? come whence

THE THREE FRIENDS RECITE THREE TIMES IN UNISON:

אַל יִתֵּן לַמּוֹט רַגְלֶךָ, אַל יָנוּם שֹׁמְרֶךָ. הִנֵּה לֹא יָנוּם וְלֹא

⟨nor ⟨ slumbers ⟨ [He] ⟨ It is so, ⟪ will your ⟨ not slumber ⟪ of your ⟨ the ⟨ He will
neither that Guardian. foot; faltering not allow

יִישָׁן, שׁוֹמֵר יִשְׂרָאֵל. יהוה שֹׁמְרֶךָ, יהוה צִלְּךָ עַל יַד יְמִינֶךָ.

⟪ your ⟨ at ⟨is your ⟨HASHEM ⟪ is your ⟨HASHEM ⟪ of Israel. ⟨ – the ⟪ sleeps
right hand. protective Guardian; Guardian
Shade

יוֹמָם הַשֶּׁמֶשׁ לֹא יַכֶּכָּה וְיָרֵחַ בַּלָּיְלָה. יהוה יִשְׁמָרְךָ מִכָּל רָע,

⟪ evil;⟨ from ⟨ will ⟨ HASHEM ⟪ by night. ⟨ nor the ⟪ harm ⟨ will ⟨ the sun ⟨ By day
every protect you moon you, not

יִשְׁמֹר אֶת נַפְשֶׁךָ. יהוה יִשְׁמָר צֵאתְךָ וּבוֹאֶךָ, מֵעַתָּה וְעַד

⟨ until ⟨ from this ⟨ and your ⟨ your ⟨ will ⟨ HASHEM ⟪ your soul. ⟨ He will
time arrival, departure guard guard

עוֹלָם.[5]

⟪ eternity.

---

(1) *I Samuel* 25:6. (2) *Psalms* 29:11. (3) *Habakkuk* 3:2. (4) *Psalms* 121:1-2. (5) 121:3-8.

THE DREAMER RECITES THREE TIMES:

וַיְדַבֵּר יהוה אֶל מֹשֶׁה לֵּאמֹר. דַּבֵּר אֶל אַהֲרֹן וְאֶל בָּנָיו

⟨his sons, ⟨and to ⟨Aaron ⟨to ⟨Speak ⟨⟨saying: ⟨Moses, ⟨to ⟨ HASHEM spoke

לֵאמֹר, כֹּה תְבָרְכוּ אֶת בְּנֵי יִשְׂרָאֵל, אָמוֹר לָהֶם.[1]

⟨⟨to them: ⟨ say ⟨⟨of Israel; ⟨the Children ⟨shall you bless ⟨So ⟨⟨ saying:

THE THREE FRIENDS RECITE THREE TIMES IN UNISON:

יְבָרֶכְךָ יהוה וְיִשְׁמְרֶךָ. יָאֵר יהוה פָּנָיו אֵלֶיךָ וִיחֻנֶּךָּ. יִשָּׂא יהוה

⟨May HASHEM ⟨⟨and be ⟨for you ⟨His ⟨May HASHEM ⟨⟨and safe- ⟨ May HASHEM
turn gracious countenance illuminate guard you. bless you
to you.

פָּנָיו אֵלֶיךָ, וְיָשֵׂם לְךָ שָׁלוֹם. וְשָׂמוּ אֶת שְׁמִי עַל בְּנֵי

⟨the ⟨upon ⟨ My Name ⟨And they ⟨⟨ peace. ⟨for ⟨ and ⟨to you ⟨ His
Children shall place you establish countenance

יִשְׂרָאֵל, וַאֲנִי אֲבָרְכֵם.[2]

⟨⟨will bless them. ⟨and I ⟨⟨ of Israel,

THE DREAMER RECITES THREE TIMES:

תּוֹדִיעֵנִי אֹרַח חַיִּים.[3]

⟨⟨of life, ⟨the path ⟨May You make
known to me

THE THREE FRIENDS RECITE THREE TIMES IN UNISON:

שֹׂבַע שְׂמָחוֹת אֶת פָּנֶיךָ, נְעִמוֹת בִּימִינְךָ נֶצַח.[3]

⟨⟨for eternity. ⟨that are in ⟨the delights ⟨⟨ in Your ⟨ of joys ⟨the fullness
Your right hand Presence;

THE THREE FRIENDS RECITE IN UNISON:

לֵךְ בְּשִׂמְחָה אֱכֹל לַחְמֶךָ, וּשְׁתֵה בְלֶב טוֹב יֵינֶךָ, כִּי כְבָר

⟨already ⟨for ⟨⟨your ⟨with a glad ⟨ and ⟨⟨ your ⟨ eat ⟨with joy ⟨⟨Go,
wine, heart drink bread,

רָצָה הָאֱלֹהִים אֶת מַעֲשֶׂיךָ.[4]

⟨⟨ your deeds. ⟨ has God ⟨accepted
with favor

THE DREAMER SETS ASIDE SEVERAL COINS FOR CHARITY AND THREE FRIENDS RECITE IN UNISON:

וּתְשׁוּבָה וּתְפִלָּה וּצְדָקָה מַעֲבִירִין אֶת רֹעַ הַגְּזֵרָה.[5] וְשָׁלוֹם

⟨ And ⟨⟨ of the ⟨ the evil ⟨ remove ⟨ and ⟨and prayer ⟨ And
peace decree. charity repentance

אָמֵן.) – Other(s)) עָלֵינוּ וְעַל כָּל יִשְׂרָאֵל, אָמֵן.

⟨⟨(Amen.) ⟨⟨ Amen. ⟨⟨ Israel, ⟨ all ⟨ and ⟨be upon
upon us

---

(1) *Numbers* 6:22-23. (2) 6:24-27. (3) *Psalms* 16:11. (4) Cf. *Ecclesiastes* 9:7. (5) *U'Nesaneh Tokef.*

﷽ DEATHBED CONFESSION / וידוי של שכיב מרע ﷽

THE FOLLOWING CONFESSION IS RECITED BY OR WITH A PERSON NEAR DEATH, HEAVEN FORBID.

מוֹדֶה אֲנִי לְפָנֶיךָ, יהוה אֱלֹהַי וֵאלֹהֵי אֲבוֹתַי, שֶׁרְפוּאָתִי

❬ that my ❬❬   of my ❬ and the ❬   my ❬ Hashem, ❬❬ before ❬   I acknowledge
recovery   forefathers,   God   God   You,

וּמִיתָתִי בְּיָדֶךָ. יְהִי רָצוֹן מִלְּפָנֶיךָ שֶׁתִּרְפָּאֵנִי רְפוּאָה שְׁלֵמָה,

❬❬ that is ❬ with a ❬   that You ❬   from ❬   the ❬ May ❬❬ are in ❬ and my
complete,   healing   heal me   before You   will   it be   Your hands.   death

וְאִם אָמוּת, תְּהֵא מִיתָתִי כַּפָּרָה עַל כָּל חֲטָאִים עֲווֹנוֹת

❬ the ❬ the uninten- ❬ all ❬ for ❬   an   ❬ may my death be ❬❬ I die, ❬ but if
iniquities,   tional sins,   atonement

וּפְשָׁעִים שֶׁחָטָאתִי וְשֶׁעָוֵיתִי וְשֶׁפָּשַׁעְתִּי לְפָנֶיךָ. וְתֵן חֶלְקִי

❬ my ❬ May ❬❬ before ❬   and ❬ committed, ❬ that I have ❬ and the
share   You grant   You.   transgressed   sinned,   willful sins

בְּגַן עֵדֶן, וְזַכֵּנִי לְעוֹלָם הַבָּא הַצָּפוּן לַצַּדִּיקִים.

❬❬ for the ❬ that is ❬ to ❬ to [enter] ❬ and privi- ❬❬ of ❬ in the
righteous.   hidden away   Come   the World   lege me   Eden,   Garden

﷽ FUNERAL SERVICES / הלוית המת ﷽

THE MOURNERS RECITE THE FOLLOWING BLESSING WHEN THEY RIP THEIR OUTER GARMENTS.

בָּרוּךְ אַתָּה יהוה אֱלֹהֵינוּ מֶלֶךְ הָעוֹלָם, דַּיַּן הָאֱמֶת.*

❬❬ Who ❬ the ❬❬ of the ❬ King ❬ our God, ❬ Hashem, ❬ are You, ❬ Blessed
is true.*   Judge   universe,

וידוי שֶׁל שְׁכִיב מְרַע / DEATHBED CONFESSION ﷽

If a sick person is near death, Heaven forbid, someone should recite the following confession with him. However, it is required that this be done in such a way that his morale not be broken, because this may even hasten death. He should be told, "Many have confessed and did not die and many who did not confess died anyway. In reward for your having confessed, may you live, but everyone who confesses has a share in the World to Come." If the patient cannot speak, he should confess in his heart. One who is unsophisticated should not be asked to confess because it may break his spirit and cause him to weep.

The text here contains the minimum confession as recorded in *Shulchan Aruch* (*Yoreh De'ah* 337:2); if one wishes, he may add the text of the Yom Kippur confession (p. 569).

הַלְוָיַת הַמֵּת / FUNERAL SERVICES ﷽

The ritual of burial combines grief with conso-

lation, mourning with acceptance. The grief and mourning aspects are obvious: the tearful eulogies, ripping of garments, the restrictive laws of the various periods of mourning. The consolation and acceptance are reflected in the prayers and blessings of this difficult period. For one theme runs through them all: God judges righteously. His righteousness was the controlling factor in the sunshine of life, health, growth, and happiness. It is no less so in the somber days of illness, suffering, and death. And His righteousness provides the ultimate consolation that the souls of the departed live on in a better place and will return to reborn bodies after the final Redemption when the dead are revivified.

דַּיַּן הָאֱמֶת — *The Judge Who is true.* Truth is the very seal of God (*Shabbos* 55a) and as such it characterizes His every deed. In acknowledging God's judgment as a manifestation of truth, we proclaim that even the Divine deeds that we

**THOSE WHO HAVE NOT SEEN A JEWISH CEMETERY FOR THIRTY DAYS
RECITE THE FOLLOWING BLESSING WHEN COMING THERE.**

בָּרוּךְ אַתָּה יהוה אֱלֹהֵינוּ מֶלֶךְ הָעוֹלָם, אֲשֶׁר יָצַר* אֶתְכֶם
‹ you ‹fashioned*‹ Who ‹‹ of the ‹ King ‹ our ‹HASHEM,‹are You, ‹ Blessed
[dead souls]   universe,   God,

בַּדִּין,* וְזָן וְכִלְכֵּל אֶתְכֶם בַּדִּין, וְהֵמִית אֶתְכֶם בַּדִּין, וְיוֹדֵעַ
‹ and ‹‹ with ‹ put you to death ‹‹ with ‹ you ‹ and ‹nourished‹‹ with
knows justice,   justice,   sustained   justice,*

מִסְפַּר כֻּלְּכֶם בַּדִּין,* וְהוּא עָתִיד לְהַחֲיוֹתְכֶם וּלְקַיֵּם אֶתְכֶם
‹ you ‹ and ‹ revivify ‹ will ‹and He ‹‹ with ‹ of all of you ‹ the sum
preserve   hereafter   justice,* [dead souls]   total

בַּדִּין. בָּרוּךְ אַתָּה יהוה, מְחַיֵּה הַמֵּתִים.
‹‹ the dead. ‹ Who ‹‹ HASHEM, ‹ are ‹ Blessed ‹‹ with
revivifies   You,   judgment.

אַתָּה גִבּוֹר לְעוֹלָם* אֲדֹנָי, מְחַיֵּה מֵתִים אַתָּה, רַב לְהוֹשִׁיעַ.
‹‹ able ‹ abundantly ‹‹ are ‹ of the ‹ the ‹‹ O Lord, ‹ eternally,* ‹ mighty ‹ You are
to save;   You;   dead Revivifier

מְכַלְכֵּל חַיִּים בְּחֶסֶד, מְחַיֵּה מֵתִים בְּרַחֲמִים רַבִּים, סוֹמֵךְ
‹ Who ‹‹ abundant, ‹ with mercy ‹ the ‹ Who ‹‹ with ‹ the ‹ Who
supports   dead revivifies kindness, living sustains

נוֹפְלִים, וְרוֹפֵא חוֹלִים, וּמַתִּיר אֲסוּרִים, וּמְקַיֵּם אֱמוּנָתוֹ לִישֵׁנֵי
‹ to those ‹ His faith ‹ and Who ‹‹ the ‹ Who ‹‹ the sick, ‹ Who ‹‹ the fallen,
asleep   maintains confined, releases   heals

find hardest to understand are no different at their source than the acts of mercy and kindness that we so crave. Indeed, the Talmud teaches that in time to come people will be privileged to understand God's ways more clearly, and the blessing in times of tragedy, as in times of good fortune, will be הַטּוֹב וְהַמֵּטִיב, *Who is good and Who does good*, in recognition that all God's deeds are equally merciful.

§ בָּרוּךְ. . .אֲשֶׁר יָצַר — *Blessed . . . Who fashioned.* This blessing is not part of the burial service per se. It is recited by anyone who sees Jewish graves for the first time in thirty or more days. Death is a shattering and moving experience. When a month has gone by, the impact lessens and a new visit to a cemetery becomes a new emotional experience. We respond by acknowledging anew the sentiments expressed in this prayer. [Authorities differ regarding the frequency with which this blessing is recited.

Some maintain that it may not be recited more than once in thirty days, even when different cemeteries are visited. Others hold that the blessing is recited whenever the particular graves have not been seen during the past thirty days (see *Mishnah Berurah* 224:17).]

אֲשֶׁר יָצַר אֶתְכֶם בַּדִּין — *Who fashioned you [dead souls] with justice.* The implication is that "justice" in this context refers not to reward and punishment, because we speak here of justice with regard to the fashioning of the newborn. Rather, the term justice refers to God's total plan for Creation.

וְיוֹדֵעַ מִסְפַּר כֻּלְּכֶם בַּדִּין — *And knows the sum total of all of you [dead souls] with justice.* The souls of the departed remain important to God. He keeps account of them and waits for the day when the dead will be brought back to life.

אַתָּה גִבּוֹר לְעוֹלָם — *You are mighty eternally.* From this point to its end, the prayer is taken

עָפָר. מִי כָמְוֹךָ בַּעַל גְּבוּרוֹת, וּמִי דּוֹמֶה לָךְ, מֶלֶךְ מֵמִית

⟨ Who causes ⟨ O ⟨⟨ to ⟨ is ⟨ and ⟨⟨ of mighty ⟨ O ⟨ is like ⟨ Who ⟨⟨ in the
death   King   You, comparable who   deeds,   Master   You,   dust.

וּמְחַיֶּה וּמַצְמִיחַ יְשׁוּעָה. וְנֶאֱמָן אַתָּה לְהַחֲיוֹת מֵתִים.

⟨⟨ the dead. ⟨ to revivify ⟨ are ⟨ And ⟨⟨ salvation! ⟨ and makes ⟨ and restores
  You   faithful   sprout   life

ACCEPTANCE OF JUDGMENT / צדוק הדין

**WHEN THE DECEASED IS BROUGHT TO THE CEMETERY, THE FOLLOWING IS RECITED.
HOWEVER, IT IS OMITTED ON DAYS THAT _TACHANUN_ (P. 172) IS NOT RECITED.**

הַצוּר תָּמִים פָּעֳלוֹ,* כִּי כָל דְּרָכָיו מִשְׁפָּט, אֵל אֱמוּנָה

⟨ of faith ⟨ a God ⟨⟨ are justice; ⟨ His ⟨ all ⟨ for ⟨⟨ is His ⟨ — perfect ⟨⟨ The Rock
  ways   work,*

וְאֵין עָוֶל, צַדִּיק וְיָשָׁר הוּא.[1]

⟨⟨ is He. ⟨ and fair ⟨ righteous ⟨⟨ iniquity, ⟨ without

הַצוּר תָּמִים בְּכָל פְּעַל, מִי יֹאמַר לוֹ מַה תִּפְעָל,* הַשַּׁלִּיט

⟨ He rules ⟨⟨ are You ⟨ What ⟨ to ⟨ can say ⟨ Who ⟨⟨ act. ⟨ in ⟨ — perfect ⟨⟨ The Rock
  doing?*   Him,   every

בְּמַטָּה וּבְמַעַל, מֵמִית וּמְחַיֶּה,* מוֹרִיד שְׁאוֹל וַיָּעַל.[2]

⟨⟨ and ⟨ to the ⟨ lowers ⟨⟨ and ⟨ causes ⟨⟨ and ⟨ below
  raises up.   grave   restores life,* death   above,

הַצוּר תָּמִים בְּכָל מַעֲשֶׂה, מִי יֹאמַר אֵלָיו מַה תַּעֲשֶׂה,

⟨⟨ are You ⟨ What ⟨⟨ to ⟨ can say ⟨ Who ⟨⟨ deed. ⟨ in every ⟨ — perfect ⟨⟨ The Rock
  doing?   Him,

(1) _Deuteronomy_ 32:4. (2) _I Samuel_ 2:6.

from the portion of _Shemoneh Esrei_ (p. 145) that describes God as the Giver of life.

צדוק הדין / Acceptance of Judgment ❧

הַצוּר תָּמִים פָּעֳלוֹ — _The Rock — perfect is His work._ In this moving prayer, the mourners declare their acceptance of the Divine judgment and also plead with God to be merciful to the living. As noted elsewhere, the word צור has the dual connotation of _Rock_, in the sense that God is impregnable and unchanging, and _Molder_ (from צָיָר, _one who fashions_), in the sense that He is the Creator Who molds people and events to suit His purposes. In this prayer, as in many others, both connotations are equally appropriate.

His work is תָּמִים, _perfect_, meaning that

the totality of His deeds forms a harmonious whole. Man's intelligence is incapable of comprehending how all the pieces of God's puzzle fit together, but we have faith that this is so.

מִי יֹאמַר לוֹ מַה תִּפְעָל — _Who can say to Him, "What are You doing?"_ The first step in learning to accept's God's justice is to recognize that we have no power to question His ways.

מֵמִית וּמְחַיֶּה — _Causes death and restores life._ Life and death are in God's hands, but death is not eternal; it is a principle of our faith that God will revivify the dead. Having said that He is a _God of faith_ Who carries out His word, we console ourselves with the knowledge that death is not eternal.

הָאוֹמֵר וְעֹשֶׂה, חֶסֶד חִנָּם לָנוּ תַעֲשֶׂה, וּבִזְכוּת הַנֶּעֱקַד

O He Who says — and does, — kindness — that is undeserved — do for us. — In the merit — of [Isaac] who was bound

כְּשֶׂה,* הַקְשִׁיבָה וַעֲשֵׂה.

like a lamb,* — hearken — and act.

צַדִּיק בְּכָל דְּרָכָיו הַצוּר תָּמִים, אֶרֶךְ אַפַּיִם וּמָלֵא רַחֲמִים,

Righteous — in all — His ways, — O Rock — Who is perfect — slow — to anger — and full of mercy —

חֲמָל נָא וְחוּס נָא עַל אָבוֹת וּבָנִים, כִּי לְךָ אֲדוֹן הַסְּלִיחוֹת

please have compassion — please — and take pity — on — parents — and children, — for — Yours, — O Master, — are forgiveness

וְהָרַחֲמִים.

and mercy.

צַדִּיק אַתָּה יהוה לְהָמִית וּלְהַחֲיוֹת, אֲשֶׁר בְּיָדְךָ פִּקְדוֹן כָּל

Righteous — are You, — HASHEM, — to put to death — and to restore to life, — for — in Your hand — is the safekeeping — of all

רוּחוֹת, חָלִילָה לְךָ זִכְרוֹנֵנוּ לִמְחוֹת,* וְיִהְיוּ נָא עֵינֶיךָ בְּרַחֲמִים

spirits. — It would be sacrilegious — for You — our memory — to erase.* — May — now — Your eyes be — mercifully

עָלֵינוּ פְּקוּחוֹת, כִּי לְךָ אֲדוֹן הָרַחֲמִים וְהַסְּלִיחוֹת.¹

toward us — attentive, — for — Yours, — O Master, — are mercy — and forgiveness.

אָדָם אִם בֶּן שָׁנָה יִהְיֶה,* אוֹ אֶלֶף שָׁנִים יִחְיֶה, מַה יִּתְרוֹן

A man, — whether — one year old — he should be,* — or — a thousand — years — he should live, — what — is the advantage

לוֹ, כְּלֹא הָיָה יִהְיֶה, בָּרוּךְ דַּיַּן הָאֱמֶת, מֵמִית וּמְחַיֶּה.

for him? — As if he had never been — shall he be. — Blessed — is the true Judge, — Who causes death — and restores life.

---

(1) Cf. *II Chronicles* 6:40.

וּבִזְכוּת הַנֶּעֱקַד כְּשֶׂה — *In the merit of [Isaac] who was bound like a lamb.* Isaac was ready to let himself be slaughtered if such was God's will. In the merit of the trait of acceptance of God's will that our people has inherited from him, may God answer our prayers.

חֲלִילָה לְךָ זִכְרוֹנֵנוּ לִמְחוֹת — *It would be sacrilegious for You our memory to erase.* In a paraphrase of Abraham's prayer for the sinful people of Sodom and its surrounding cities (*Genesis* 18:25), we beg God to have mercy on His people.

אָדָם אִם בֶּן שָׁנָה יִהְיֶה — *A man, whether one year old he should be.* No matter how long man lives and how much wealth and fame he amasses, he leaves earth with none of it. The only thing that matters is the degree to which he recognizes and serves God.

וּמְשׁוֹטֵט הַכֹּל בְּעֵינוֹ וּמְשַׁלֵּם — *He scans everything with His eye, and He recompenses.* God sees all that man does, and rewards and punishes justly. Consequently we must accept His judgment.

בָּרוּךְ הוּא כִּי אֱמֶת דִּינוֹ, וּמְשׁוֹטֵט הַכֹּל בְּעֵינוֹ, וּמְשַׁלֵּם*[1]

⟨ and He ⟨⟨ with ⟨ everything ⟨ He scans ⟨⟨ is His ⟨ true ⟨ for ⟨ is He, ⟨ Blessed
recompenses* His eye, judgment,

לָאָדָם חֶשְׁבּוֹנוֹ וְדִינוֹ, וְהַכֹּל לִשְׁמוֹ הוֹדָיָה יִתֵּנוּ.

⟨⟨ shall ⟨ acknowledg- ⟨ to His ⟨ And ⟨⟨ and his ⟨ according to ⟨ man
give. ment Name everyone just sentence. his account

יָדַעְנוּ יהוה כִּי צֶדֶק מִשְׁפָּטֶךָ, תִּצְדַּק בְּדָבְרֶךָ וְתִזְכֶּה

⟨ and ⟨ when You ⟨ You are ⟨⟨ is Your ⟨ righteous ⟨ that ⟨ HASHEM, ⟨ We know,
faultless speak justified judgment;

בְּשָׁפְטֶךָ,[2] וְאֵין לְהַרְהֵר אַחַר מִדַּת שָׁפְטֶךָ, צַדִּיק אַתָּה

⟨ are ⟨ Righteous ⟨⟨ of Your ⟨ the ⟨ about ⟨ have ⟨ One ⟨⟨ when You
You, judgment. quality questions cannot judge.

יהוה וְיָשָׁר מִשְׁפָּטֶיךָ.[3]

⟨⟨ are Your judgments. ⟨ and fair ⟨⟨ HASHEM,

דַּיַּן אֱמֶת, שׁוֹפֵט צֶדֶק וֶאֱמֶת, בָּרוּךְ דַּיַּן הָאֱמֶת, שֶׁכָּל

⟨ for all ⟨⟨ Who is ⟨ is the ⟨ blessed ⟨⟨ and truth; ⟨ with ⟨ Who ⟨ Who is ⟨ O
true, Judge righteousness judges true, Judge

מִשְׁפָּטָיו צֶדֶק וֶאֱמֶת.

⟨⟨ and true. ⟨ are ⟨ His
righteous judgments

נֶפֶשׁ כָּל חַי בְּיָדֶךָ, צֶדֶק מָלְאָה יְמִינְךָ וְיָדֶךָ, רַחֵם עַל[5]

⟨ on ⟨ Have ⟨⟨ and Your ⟨ Your ⟨ are ⟨ with ⟨⟨ are in ⟨ the ⟨ of ⟨ The
mercy [chastising [saving] filled righteous- Your living all souls
left] hand. right hand ness hand;

פְּלֵיטַת צֹאן יָדֶךָ, וְתֹאמַר לַמַּלְאָךְ הֶרֶף יָדֶךָ.[6]

⟨⟨ your ⟨ Hold ⟨ to the Angel ⟨ and say ⟨ of Your ⟨ of the ⟨ the
hand! back [of Death], hand, flock remnant

גְּדֹל הָעֵצָה וְרַב הָעֲלִילִיָּה, אֲשֶׁר עֵינֶיךָ פְקֻחוֹת עַל כָּל

⟨ all ⟨ toward ⟨ are ⟨ Your ⟨ that ⟨⟨ in deed, ⟨ and ⟨ in counsel ⟨ Great
attentive eyes mighty

דַּרְכֵי בְּנֵי אָדָם, לָתֵת לְאִישׁ כִּדְרָכָיו וְכִפְרִי מַעֲלָלָיו.[7]

⟨⟨ of his ⟨ and according to ⟨ according ⟨ each ⟨ to give ⟨ of mankind, ⟨ the
deeds. the consequences to his ways man ways

לְהַגִּיד כִּי יָשָׁר יהוה, צוּרִי וְלֹא עַוְלָתָה בּוֹ.[8]

⟨⟨ in Him. ⟨ wrong ⟨ there is no ⟨ My Rock, ⟨⟨ HASHEM is just. ⟨ that ⟨ To declare

(1) Cf. *II Chronicles* 16:9; *Zechariah* 4:10. (2) Cf. *Psalms* 51:6. (3) 119:137. (4) Cf. *Job* 12:10.
(5) Cf. *Psalms* 48:11. (6) Cf. *II Samuel* 24:16. (7) *Jeremiah* 32:19. (8) *Psalms* 92:16.

יהוה נָתַן, וַיהוה לָקָח, יְהִי שֵׁם יהוה מְבֹרָךְ.[1]

‹‹ be blessed. ‹ of ‹ the ‹ let ‹‹ took ‹ and ‹ gave ‹ HASHEM
HASHEM Name away; HASHEM

וְהוּא רַחוּם, יְכַפֵּר עָוֹן וְלֹא יַשְׁחִית, וְהִרְבָּה לְהָשִׁיב

‹ He ‹ frequently ‹‹ destroy; ‹ and ‹ of ‹ is ‹ the Merciful ‹ He,
withdraws does not iniquity forgiving One,

אַפּוֹ, וְלֹא יָעִיר כָּל חֲמָתוֹ.[2]

‹‹ His entire wrath. ‹ arousing ‹ not ‹‹ His anger,

KADDISH AFTER A BURIAL / קדיש אחר הקבורה

ON DAYS THAT *TACHANUN* IS NOT RECITED THE REGULAR MOURNER'S *KADDISH* IS RECITED.

יִתְגַּדַּל וְיִתְקַדַּשׁ שְׁמֵהּ רַבָּא. (.CONG – אָמֵן.) בְּעָלְמָא דִּי הוּא

‹ which ‹ in the world ‹ (Amen.) ‹‹ that is ‹ may His ‹ and be ‹ Grow
great! — Name sanctified exalted

עָתִיד לְאִתְחַדָּתָא,[3] וּלְאַחֲיָאָה מֵתַיָּא, וּלְאַסָּקָא יָתְהוֹן לְחַיֵּי

‹ to life ‹ them ‹ and will ‹ the dead ‹ and [in which ‹ be renewed, ‹ will
elevate God will] revivify hereafter

עָלְמָא, וּלְמִבְנֵא קַרְתָּא דִירוּשְׁלֵם, וּלְשַׁכְלֵל הֵיכְלֵהּ בְּגַוַּהּ,

‹‹ within ‹ His ‹ and establish ‹ of Jerusalem ‹ the city ‹ and will ‹‹ that is
it, Temple rebuild eternal,

וּלְמֶעֱקַר פּוּלְחָנָא נֻכְרָאָה מֵאַרְעָא, וְלַאֲתָבָא פּוּלְחָנָא דִשְׁמַיָּא

‹ of Heaven ‹ the service ‹ and will ‹‹ from ‹ foreign ‹ worship ‹ and will
return the earth, [to God] uproot

לְאַתְרֵהּ, וְיַמְלִיךְ קֻדְשָׁא בְּרִיךְ הוּא בְּמַלְכוּתֵהּ וִיקָרֵהּ, וְיַצְמַח

‹ and cause ‹ and His ‹ in His ‹‹ is ‹ Blessed ‹‹ will the ‹ and then ‹‹ to its place
to sprout honor, sovereignty He, Holy One, reign

פֻּרְקָנֵהּ וִיקָרֵב מְשִׁיחֵהּ. (.CONG – אָמֵן.) בְּחַיֵּיכוֹן וּבְיוֹמֵיכוֹן

‹ and in ‹ in your ‹ (Amen.) ‹‹ His ‹ and bring ‹ His
your days, lifetimes Messiah, near salvation,

וּבְחַיֵּי דְכָל בֵּית יִשְׂרָאֵל, בַּעֲגָלָא וּבִזְמַן קָרִיב. וְאִמְרוּ: אָמֵן.

‹‹ Amen. ‹ Now ‹‹ that comes ‹ and at ‹ swiftly ‹ of Israel, ‹ Family ‹ of the ‹ and in the
respond: soon. a time entire lifetimes

---

(1) *Job* 1:21. (2) *Psalms* 78:38. (3) *Deuteronomy* 32:12, Onkelos.

קַדִּישׁ אַחַר הַקְּבוּרָה / KADDISH AFTER BURIAL
More directly than any other text of *Kaddish*, this one refers to the state of perfection which will come with the Redemption and the End of Days. The first such blessing to be mentioned in

this special addition to *Kaddish* is the Divine promise that God will restore life to the dead. It goes on to list other Divine gifts that will shower upon earth during that period of spiritual benef-icence. There can be no greater consolation at a

CONGREGATION RESPONDS:

אָמֵן. יְהֵא שְׁמֵהּ רַבָּא מְבָרַךְ לְעָלַם וּלְעָלְמֵי עָלְמַיָּא.

《 and for all eternity. ‹ forever ‹ be blessed‹ that is great ‹ His Name ‹ May 《‹Amen.

MOURNER CONTINUES:

יְהֵא שְׁמֵהּ רַבָּא מְבָרַךְ לְעָלַם וּלְעָלְמֵי עָלְמַיָּא. יִתְבָּרַךְ

‹ Blessed, 《   and for all eternity. ‹ forever ‹ be blessed ‹ that is great ‹ His Name ‹ May

וְיִשְׁתַּבַּח וְיִתְפָּאַר וְיִתְרוֹמַם וְיִתְנַשֵּׂא וְיִתְהַדָּר וְיִתְעַלֶּה

‹ elevated, ‹ honored, ‹ upraised, ‹ exalted, ‹ glorified, ‹ praised,

וְיִתְהַלָּל שְׁמֵהּ דְּקֻדְשָׁא בְּרִיךְ הוּא (.Cong – בְּרִיךְ הוּא) —

《‹ is He) ‹ (Blessed   《‹ is He ‹ Blessed ‹ of the ‹ be the ‹ and lauded
                                                    Holy One, Name

ROSH HASHANAH TO YOM KIPPUR SUBSTITUTE:

°לְעֵלָּא מִן כָּל [°לְעֵלָּא (וּ)לְעֵלָּא מִכָּל] בִּרְכָתָא

‹ blessing   ‹ any ‹ exceedingly beyond   ‹ any ‹ beyond

וְשִׁירָתָא, תֻּשְׁבְּחָתָא וְנֶחֱמָתָא דַּאֲמִירָן בְּעָלְמָא.

《‹ in the world. ‹ that are uttered ‹ and consolation ‹ praise 《 and song,

וְאִמְרוּ: אָמֵן. (.Cong– אָמֵן.)

《 (Amen.)   《 Amen. ‹ Now respond:

יְהֵא שְׁלָמָא רַבָּא מִן שְׁמַיָּא, וְחַיִּים טוֹבִים עָלֵינוּ וְעַל כָּל

‹ all ‹ and ‹ upon us 《 that ‹ and 《 Heaven, ‹ from ‹ that is ‹ peace ‹ May
       upon   is good, life   abundant   there be

יִשְׂרָאֵל. וְאִמְרוּ: אָמֵן. (.Cong – אָמֵן.)

《 (Amen.)   《 Amen. ‹ Now respond: 《 Israel.

**BOW; TAKE THREE STEPS BACK: BOW LEFT AND SAY ... עֹשֶׂה שָׁלוֹם, *"HE WHO MAKES PEACE..."*;
BOW RIGHT AND SAY ... הוּא, *"MAY HE..."*; BOW FORWARD AND SAY ... וְעַל כָּל יִשְׂרָאֵל, *"AND
UPON ALL ISRAEL..."* REMAIN IN PLACE FOR A FEW MOMENTS, THEN TAKE THREE STEPS FORWARD.**

עֹשֶׂה °שָׁלוֹם בִּמְרוֹמָיו, הוּא יַעֲשֶׂה שָׁלוֹם עָלֵינוּ, וְעַל

‹ and ‹ upon us, ‹ peace ‹ make ‹ may He 《 in His heights, ‹ peace ‹ He Who
 upon   makes

כָּל יִשְׂרָאֵל. וְאִמְרוּ: אָמֵן. (.Cong – אָמֵן.)

《 (Amen.)   《 Amen. ‹ Now respond: 《 Israel. ‹ all

FROM ROSH HASHANAH TO YOM KIPPUR SOME SAY:

°הַשָּׁלוֹם

‹ the peace

---

burial than to recall God's guarantee that the
dead will live again, and that life has meaning
and purpose that survive an essentially temporary death.

THOSE PRESENT AT THE BURIAL FORM TWO ROWS THROUGH WHICH THE MOURNERS WALK.
AS THE MOURNERS PASS THEM, THOSE FORMING THE ROWS RECITE THE TRADITIONAL PRAYER
OF CONSOLATION.

הַמָּקוֹם* יְנַחֵם אֶתְכֶם¹ בְּתוֹךְ שְׁאָר אֲבֵלֵי צִיּוֹן וִירוּשָׁלָיִם.

≪ and   ⟨ of ⟨ mourners ⟨ the   ⟨ among ⟨ you   ⟨ — may He ≪   The
Jerusalem.   Zion   other   console   Omnipresent*

AS THE PARTICIPANTS LEAVE THE CEMETERY, THEY TEAR OUT SOME BLADES OF GRASS
AND TOSS THEM OVER THEIR RIGHT SHOULDERS AS THEY RECITE:

וְיָצִיצוּ* מֵעִיר כְּעֵשֶׂב הָאָרֶץ.² זָכוּר כִּי עָפָר אֲנָחְנוּ.³

≪ are we. ⟨ dust ⟨ that ⟨ He is ≪ of the   ⟨ like the ⟨ from   ⟨ May [people]
         mindful   earth.   grass   the city   blossom*

AFTER LEAVING THE CEMETERY, ONE WASHES HIS HANDS RITUALLY AND RECITES:

בִּלַּע הַמָּוֶת* לָנֶצַח, וּמָחָה אֲדֹנָי יֱהוִֹה דִּמְעָה מֵעַל כָּל

⟨ every ⟨ from ⟨ tears   ⟨ and may the Lord HASHEM/ELOHIM ≪ forever, ⟨ death* ⟨ May He
        wipe away   swallow up

פָּנִים, וְחֶרְפַּת עַמּוֹ יָסִיר מֵעַל כָּל הָאָרֶץ, כִּי יהוה דִּבֵּר.⁴

≪ has ⟨ HASHEM ⟨ for ≪ the land, ⟨ all ⟨ from ⟨ He will ⟨ of His ⟨ and the   ≪ face,
spoken.   remove   people   shame

---

(1) For one mourner אוֹתְךָ, you. (2) *Psalms* 72:16. (3) 103:14. (4) *Isaiah* 25:8.

See ArtScroll's *The Kaddish Prayer* for commentary on the text and for an alternate version of the first sentence.

⇐§ הַמָּקוֹם — *The Omnipresent.* At the climax of the burial service, those who have come to share the mourners' grief, and to render the final honor to the departed, form two rows and express their prayerful wish that the mourners be consoled. This is an expression of Jewish brotherhood, symbolized by the mourners walking through the midst of their brethren and by the prayer that includes all those who mourn the national tragedy of Zion and Jerusalem in the category of those who have just become bereaved.

⇐§ וְיָצִיצוּ — *May [people] blossom.* This verse concludes the portrayal given in Psalm 72 of the happy and blessed life that flourishes under the wise leadership of a God-inspired leader. The idea is that God provides the necessary elements for a successful human society just as He provides all the nutrients needed for vegetable life. By throwing grass over our shoulders as we depart the burial field and return to the land of the living, we symbolize our faith in God's benevolent providence for society (R' Hirsch).

⇐§ בִּלַּע הַמָּוֶת — *May He swallow up death.* The ritual cleansing of the hands symbolizes our resolve to improve ourselves and our lives, and put thoughts of death and decay behind us. To express this idea, we recite the verse that prophesies the end of death, tears, and scorn.

◄§ / MISHNAYOS STUDY ►§

It is customary to study Mishnayos as a source of merit for the souls of the departed. An allusion to this custom is found in the letters of the Hebrew word מִשְׁנָה, Mishnah, which — as Arizal and Sh'lah point out — can be rearranged to form the word נְשָׁמָה, neshamah, soul.

Four periods are set aside for the study of Mishnayos as a merit for the departed: (a) the *shivah,* seven-day mourning period, during which time those visiting the mourners study aloud usually between *Minchah* and *Maariv* [the mourners themselves are prohibited from most areas of Torah study on their own during this period]; (b) the remainder of the *sheloshim* (or thirty-day period commencing from the burial),

❧ לימוד משניות לזכר הנפטרים ❧
❧ MISHNAYOS STUDY IN MEMORY OF THE DECEASED ❧

—————— *Mikvaos* Chapter 7 / מקואות פרק ז ——————

[א] יֵשׁ מַעֲלִין אֶת הַמְּקְוֶה* וְלֹא פוֹסְלִין, פּוֹסְלִין וְלֹא

| and | [others] | invalidate | and | a *mikveh,** | that can | There are | [1] |
| do not invalidate [a mikveh] | [it]; | | [certainly] do not | | complete | [substances] | |

YAD AVRAHAM

during which time the mourners themselves also study either on their own or by taking part in group study and discussion; (c) during the entire first year, until the first *yahrzeit*, anniversary of death [as recorded in the Jewish calendar]; and (d) each year on the *yahrzeit*.

Although any section of the six orders of Mishnah may be studied for this purpose, there are two primary traditions. One custom is to study a group of chapters, the initial letters of which form the name of the deceased. Thus if the deceased's name was מֹשֶׁה, first a chapter beginning with the letter מ would be studied, then a chapter beginning with שׁ, followed by a chapter beginning with ה (many sets of Mishnah have an alphabetical listing of chapters to facilitate such study).

Another tradition calls for the study of *Seder Taharos*. Two chapters of *Taharos* are preferred: (a) Chapter 24 of tractate *Keilim*, because each mishnah in it concludes with the word טָהוֹר, *pure*; and (b) Chapter 7 of tractate *Mikvaos* — according to R' Yitzchak Isaac of Komarna's Mishnah commentary — because the initial letters of its final four mishnayos spell the word נְשָׁמָה, *neshamah*, soul. Since the second custom has gained widespread acceptance, we include it below. Some study the entire chapter while others study only the last four mishnayos.

[A full treatment of these and all relevant mishnayos may be found in the ArtScroll Mishnah with the *Yad Avraham* commentary.]

❧ Mikvaos / Chapter 7

A מִקְוֶה, *mikveh* [pl. *mikvaos*], is a body of water used for the cleansing of the *tamei*, ritually unclean person or object. Among the require-

ments that must be met for a body of water to be a valid *mikveh* is that it contain at least forty *se'ah* — approximately 200 gallons — of water. Additionally, the initial forty *se'ah* must be (a) *mechubarin*, or "attached" (a body of water attached to the ground), and not (b) *she'uvin*, "drawn" (water that has been drawn, carried or merely stored in a utensil or other container).

On a Scriptural level, once a body of water contains more than half the required volume of *mechubarin* (i.e., more than twenty *se'ah*), then even if *she'uvin* are added to bring the volume to forty *se'ah*, the body constitutes a valid *mikveh*. However, the Sages decreed that *she'uvin* may not be used to complete the forty *se'ah*. Moreover, they decreed that if even three לֹג, *log* (approximately 36 fluid ounces), of *she'uvin* fall or are poured into a body of less than forty *se'ah* of *mechubarin*, the body is permanently invalidated and may never be used as a *mikveh* even if enough water is later added to it to bring it up to the required forty *se'ah*. The first five mishnayos discuss various details and ramifications of this rabbinic decree.

1. There are three categories of substances which differ in the way they affect the validity of a *mikveh*:

יֵשׁ מַעֲלִין אֶת הַמְּקְוֶה... — *There are [substances] that can complete a mikveh*... The substances in this category (enumerated below) can be used to complete the minimum forty *se'ah* volume of a body of water which already contains more than twenty *se'ah* of *mechubarin*. Since they can even validate a *mikveh*, it is obvious that three *log* of any of these substances do not invalidate a body which contains less than forty *se'ah*.

מַעֲלִין,* לֹא מַעֲלִין וְלֹא פוֹסְלִין.* אֵלּוּ מַעֲלִין וְלֹא פוֹסְלִין:*
《invalidate:* 〈 and 〈 complete 〈 These   《 invalidate 〈 nor 〈 complete 〈 [others] 《complete
        do not   [substances]   [it].*   neither   [it];*

הַשֶּׁלֶג, וְהַבָּרָד, וְהַכְּפוֹר, וְהַגְּלִיד, וְהַמֶּלַח, וְהַטִּיט הַנָּרוֹק.*
《 that can 〈 and mud 〈   salt,   〈   ice,   〈   frost,   〈   hail,   〈   snow,
be poured.*

אָמַר רַבִּי עֲקִיבָא:* הָיָה רַבִּי יִשְׁמָעֵאל דָּן כְּנֶגְדִי לוֹמַר: הַשֶּׁלֶג
〈 Snow 《 saying: 〈 with 〈 would 〈 Yishmael 〈 that 〈 It used 《 Akiva:* 〈 Rabbi 〈 Said
                            me,   argue   Rabbi   to be

אֵינוֹ מַעֲלֶה אֶת הַמִּקְוֶה. וְהֵעִידוּ אַנְשֵׁי מֵידְבָא*   מִשְּׁמוֹ,
〈 in his [Rabbi 〈 of Meidva* 〈   did   〈 But testify 〈   a mikveh.   〈 complete 〈 cannot
Yishmael's] name   the men

שֶׁאָמַר לָהֶם: צְאוּ וְהָבִיאוּ שֶׁלֶג וַעֲשׂוּ מִקְוֶה בַּתְּחִלָּה. רַבִּי
〈 Rabbi 《 from the 〈 a mikveh 〈 and 〈 snow 〈 and bring 〈 Go out 《 to them, 〈 that he
           beginning.   make   said

יד אברהם

פוֹסְלִין וְלֹא מַעֲלִין — [Others] invalidate [a mikveh] and do not complete [it]. If three log of any of the substances in this category (enumerated in mishnah 2) fall into a body of less than forty se'ah, they invalidate that body from ever becoming a mikveh. Additionally, if a mikveh lacks less than three log to complete the forty se'ah minimum, these substances cannot be used to make up the difference [although being less than three log, they would not invalidate the mikveh].

לֹא מַעֲלִין וְלֹא פוֹסְלִין — [Others] neither complete nor invalidate [it]. If an amount of less than three log is necessary to complete the forty se'ah, and that amount of one of the substances in this category (enumerated in mishnah 2) falls in, the body is not considered a valid mikveh. Nevertheless, if the body is missing more than three log of mechubarin, and three log of these substances fall in, the body does not become invalidated. It may still become a mikveh if the proper amount of mechubarin is subsequently added.

אֵלּוּ מַעֲלִין וְלֹא פוֹסְלִין — These [substances] complete and do not invalidate. The mishnah now lists the substances of the first category. The principle underlying this category is that these substances are legally considered water with regard to completing the Scriptural requirement

that a mikveh contain at least forty se'ah. However, they are not considered water with regard to the disqualification of she'uvin for completing a mikveh.

וְהַטִּיט הַנָּרוֹק — Mud that can be poured. Although it is considered water with regard to completing a mikveh which has more than twenty se'ah of proper water, it is not classified as water with regard to the disqualification of she'uvin; thicker mud certainly does not invalidate in this respect.

אָמַר רַבִּי עֲקִיבָא . . . וְהֵעִידוּ אַנְשֵׁי מֵידְבָא . . . — Said Rabbi Akiva . . . But testify did the men of Meidva . . . The people of Meidva testified that only for the sake of discussion and debate did Rabbi Yishmael disagree with Rabbi Akiva regarding the status of snow. In actual practice, however, Rabbi Yishmael likewise ruled that snow can complete a mikveh. Indeed, not only did Rabbi Yishmael permit snow to be used to complete the minimum volume of forty se'ah, he also permitted snow — even snow that had been contained in a utensil — to make up the entire forty se'ah (from the beginning).

Moreover, the term snow refers to all the forms of frozen water listed in the mishnah. This is the view accepted as halachah. [However, according to most authorities, immersion

יוֹחָנָן בֶּן נוּרִי אוֹמֵר: אֶבֶן הַבָּרָד כְּמַיִם.*

‹ Yochanan ‹ ben› ‹ Nuri › ‹ says: › ‹ Stones › ‹ of hail › ‹ are like water.*

כֵּיצַד מַעֲלִין וְלֹא פוֹסְלִין? מִקְוֶה שֶׁיֶּשׁ בּוֹ אַרְבָּעִים סְאָה חָסֵר

‹ How ‹ that they ‹ and ‹ invalidate? ‹ A ‹ that ‹ in ‹ forty ‹ se'ah ‹ minus
is it ‹ do not complete ‹ mikveh ‹ it has

אַחַת, נָפַל מֵהֶם סְאָה לְתוֹכוֹ, וְהֶעֱלָהוּ, נִמְצְאוּ – מַעֲלִין

‹ one, ‹ there fell ‹ of these ‹ se'ah ‹ a ‹ from one ‹ and ‹ into it, ‹ it has completed it [the mikveh]. ‹ It is thus found ‹ that they complete

וְלֹא פוֹסְלִין.*

‹ but do not ‹ invalidate.*

[ב] אֵלוּ פוֹסְלִין וְלֹא מַעֲלִין:* הַמַּיִם* בֵּין טְמֵאִים* בֵּין

[2] ‹ These [substances] ‹ invalidate ‹ [a mikveh] ‹ and ‹ complete [it]: ‹ [drawn] water,* ‹ whether ‹ [ritually] contaminated ‹ or

טְהוֹרִים,* וּמֵי כְבָשִׁים, וּמֵי שְׁלָקוֹת, וְהַתֶּמֶד* עַד שֶׁלֹּא

‹ uncontaminated;* ‹ water ‹ in which [fruits or vegetables] have been soaked, ‹ water ‹ in which [fruits and vegetables] have been cooked; ‹ and marc-wine* ‹ as long as ‹ it has not

הֶחֱמִיץ. כֵּיצַד פוֹסְלִין וְלֹא מַעֲלִין? מִקְוֶה שֶׁיֶּשׁ בּוֹ אַרְבָּעִים

‹ fermented. ‹ How ‹ is it ‹ that they ‹ and ‹ complete? ‹ A ‹ that ‹ in it ‹ forty
‹ invalidate ‹ do not ‹ mikveh ‹ has

סְאָה חָסֵר קוֹרְטוֹב,* וְנָפַל מֵהֶן קוֹרְטוֹב לְתוֹכוֹ –

‹ se'ah ‹ minus ‹ one kortov,* ‹ and ‹ from these [substances] ‹ a kortov ‹ into it,
there fell

YAD AVRAHAM

may not take place until the snow melts.]

אֶבֶן הַבָּרָד כְּמַיִם — *Stones of hail are like water*, regarding the disqualification of *she'uvin*. This view is not accepted by the halachah.

נִמְצְאוּ – מַעֲלִין וְלֹא פוֹסְלִין — *It is thus found that they complete but do not invalidate*. Even if the additional *se'ah* is of *she'uvin*, it completes the *mikveh*. Since a *se'ah* (which contains twenty-four *log*) of *she'uvin* does not disqualify the *mechubarin*, it is obvious that a mere three *log* of *she'uvin* cannot invalidate them.

2. The mishnah now enumerates the substances in the second category mentioned in the previous mishnah. These substances are considered as water in all respects. Thus, if they are *she'uvin*, they cannot be used to complete a *mikveh*; moreover, three *log* invalidate the *mechubarin* of an incomplete *mikveh*.

הַמַּיִם — *[Drawn] water*, *she'uvin*.

בֵּין טְמֵאִים בֵּין טְהוֹרִים — *Whether [ritually] contaminated or uncontaminated.* This phrase is included in the mishnah because there are certain areas of *tumah*-contamination in which the rules applying to contaminated and non-contaminated water differ.

וְהַתֶּמֶד — *Marc-wine*, wine made by soaking the residue of the wine press (skins, pulp, pips) in water. Before fermentation, this liquid is still considered water; after fermentation (see below) it is considered wine.

קוֹרְטוֹב — *Kortov.* The smallest unit of liquid measure, equal to $\frac{1}{64}$ of a *log*.

לֹא הֶעֱלָהוּ;* פּוֹסְלוֹ בִּשְׁלֹשָׁה לְגִין.

« *log*. ‹ with three ‹ They invalidate it ‹« it has not completed [the *mikveh*].*

אֲבָל שְׁאָר הַמַּשְׁקִין,* וּמֵי פֵרוֹת, וְהַצִּיר, וְהַמֻּרְיָס, וְהַתֶּמֶד

‹ and marc-wine ‹ fish sauce,* ‹ fish juice, ‹ fruit juices, ‹ liquids,* ‹ other ‹ But

מִשֶּׁהֶחֱמִיץ — פְּעָמִים מַעֲלִין* וּפְעָמִים שֶׁאֵינָן מַעֲלִין.* כֵּיצַד?

‹« How so? ‹« complete it.* ‹ do not ‹ and ‹ complete [a *mikveh*]* ‹ sometimes ‹« that has fermented,

מִקְוֶה שֶׁיֵּשׁ בּוֹ אַרְבָּעִים סְאָה חָסֵר אַחַת, נָפַל לְתוֹכוֹ סְאָה

‹ a *se'ah* ‹ into it ‹ and there fell ‹« one, ‹ minus ‹ *se'ah* ‹ forty ‹ in it ‹ that has ‹ A *mikveh*

מֵהֶם — לֹא הֶעֱלָהוּ. הָיוּ בּוֹ אַרְבָּעִים סְאָה, נָתַן סְאָה

‹ a *se'ah* [of these substances], ‹ and he put in ‹ *se'ah*, ‹ forty ‹ in it ‹ If there were ‹« it has not completed [it]. ‹ from these [substances],

וְנָטַל סְאָה,* הֲרֵי זֶה כָּשֵׁר.*

‹« valid.* ‹ this [remains] ‹ a *se'ah*,* ‹ and then removed

יד אברהם

לֹא הֶעֱלָהוּ — *It has not completed [the mikveh].* An incomplete *mikveh* can never be completed with *she'uvin*, no matter how minute the amount.

אֲבָל שְׁאָר הַמַּשְׁקִין — *But other liquids.* The mishnah now turns to the third category mentioned in the previous mishnah. This category includes seven substances that are classified (*Machshirim* 6:4) by the halachic term מַשְׁקֶה, *liquid*: (a) dew, (b) water, (c) grape wine, (d) olive oil, (e) blood, (f) milk, and (g) bee honey. Since dew and water were included in the first two categories, for they are forms of water and subject to the disqualification of *she'uvin*, the mishnah's phrase *other liquids* refers to the remaining five.

וְהַצִּיר וְהַמֻּרְיָס — *Fish juice, fish sauce.* The first refers to the watery liquid that oozes from salted or marinated fish; the second is the oil or fat of marinated fish that is used as a sauce.

פְּעָמִים מַעֲלִין — *Sometimes complete [a mikveh].* Even though they are not classified as water.

וּפְעָמִים שֶׁאֵינָן מַעֲלִין — *And sometimes do not complete it.* Nevertheless, they do not invalidate it either.

הָיוּ בּוֹ אַרְבָּעִים סְאָה נָתַן סְאָה וְנָטַל סְאָה — *If there were in it forty se'ah, and he put in a se'ah [of these substances], and then removed a se'ah.* A *se'ah* of these substances was added to a valid *mikveh* of exactly forty *se'ah*, bringing its volume to forty-one *se'ah*. Then a *se'ah* of the combined liquid was removed from the *mikveh*, bringing the volume back to forty *se'ah*. Although the removed *se'ah* contains approximately forty parts water and one part other liquid, and the total volume of water remaining in the *mikveh* is less than the required forty *se'ah*, nevertheless the *mikveh* remains valid.

הֲרֵי זֶה כָּשֵׁר — *This [remains] valid.* The process can be repeated several times and the *mikveh* will remain valid, but only if we can be certain that more than twenty *se'ah* of water remain in the *mikveh*.

3. Besides by the addition of *she'uvin*, the waters of a *mikveh* may become invalidated by שִׁנּוּי מַרְאֶה, *a change of color*. Unlike the disqualification of *she'uvin*, which only invalidates an incomplete *mikveh*, change of color can invalidate even a complete *mikveh*.

[ג] הֵדִיחַ בּוֹ סַלֵּי זֵיתִים וְסַלֵּי עֲנָבִים,* וְשִׁנּוּ אֶת מַרְאָיו

⟨ its color, ⟨ and they ⟨⟨ of grapes,* ⟨ or ⟨ of ⟨ baskets ⟨ in it [a valid ⟨ If one [3]
　　　　　changed　　　　　　　baskets　olives　　　　　　mikveh]　　rinsed

— כָּשֵׁר.* רַבִּי יוֹסֵי אוֹמֵר: מֵי הַצֶּבַע* פּוֹסְלִין אוֹתוֹ בִּשְׁלֹשָׁה

⟨ if there are ⟨　it [a　⟨ invalidates ⟨　Dye-water*　⟨⟨ says: ⟨ Yose ⟨ Rabbi ⟨⟨　it is
　three　mikveh]　　　　　　　　　　　　　　　　　　　　　　　　valid.*

לֻגִּין, וְאֵינָן פּוֹסְלִין אוֹתוֹ בְּשִׁנּוּי מַרְאֶה.

⟨⟨ of color. ⟨ by change ⟨ it ⟨ invalidate ⟨ but does not ⟨⟨ log,

נָפַל לְתוֹכוֹ יַיִן וּמֹחַל,* וְשִׁנּוּ אֶת מַרְאָיו — פָּסוּל.* כֵּיצַד

⟨ How ⟨⟨　it is　⟨　its color, ⟨ and they ⟨⟨ or olive- ⟨ wine ⟨ into it ⟨ If there
　　　invalid.*　　　　　　changed　sap,*　　　　[the mikveh]　fell

יַעֲשֶׂה?* יַמְתִּין לוֹ עַד שֶׁיֵּרְדוּ גְשָׁמִים,* וְיַחְזְרוּ מַרְאֵיהֶן

⟨　of its　⟨ [causes] the ⟨ of the rains* ⟨ the falling ⟨ until ⟨ He should wait ⟨⟨ should one
　color　reverting　　　　　　　　　　　　　　　　　　　　　　　　　　act?*

לְמַרְאֵה הַמַּיִם. הָיוּ בּוֹ אַרְבָּעִים סְאָה,* מְמַלֵּא בְּכָתֵף וְנוֹתֵן

⟨ and ⟨ [carry it] ⟨ he may ⟨ se'ah,* ⟨　forty　⟨ in it ⟨ If there ⟨⟨ of ⟨ to the color
place it　on his　draw　　　　　　　　　[the　[already]　water.
　　　shoulder,　[water],　　　　　　mikveh]　were

לְתוֹכוֹ, עַד שֶׁיַּחְזְרוּ מַרְאֵיהֶן לְמַרְאֵה הַמַּיִם.

⟨⟨ of water. ⟨ to the color ⟨　its color reverts　⟨ until ⟨⟨ into [the
　　　　　　　　　　　　　　　　　　　　　　　　mikveh],

YAD AVRAHAM

הֵדִיחַ בּוֹ סַלֵּי זֵתִים וְסַלֵּי עֲנָבִים ... כָּשֵׁר — *If one rinsed in it [a valid mikveh] baskets of olive or baskets of grapes...it is valid.* The disqualification of change of color applies only if the substances from which that color derives is actually present in the *mikveh*. But the baskets that are rinsed in the *mikveh* do not contain the olives or grapes, only stains from them. This residue is not significant enough to invalidate the *mikveh*.

מֵי הַצֶּבַע — *Dye-water.* This refers to water in which dyestuffs have been soaked, thereby imparting their color to the water, and then removed. Since the dyestuffs are not present when the dye-water falls into the *mikveh*, the *mikveh* is not invalidated by change of color. Moreover, the dye-water retains the status of water insofar as the disqualification of the *she'uvin* is concerned, and it therefore invalidates the *mikveh* if it contains three *log* of *she'uvin*. This view is accepted as halachah.

מֹחַל — *Olive-sap,* a dark watery liquid that oozes out of ripe olives.

פָּסוּל — *It is invalid.* Since the color is an intrinsic part of the wine or olive-water, the presence of that liquid in the discolored *mikveh* invalidates the *mikveh*.

כֵּיצַד יַעֲשֶׂה — *How should one act?* How can the disqualification be removed from (a) the discolored *mechubarin* in an incomplete *mikveh*? and (b) a discolored complete *mikveh*?

גְשָׁמִים — *Rains.* For an incomplete *mikveh* one may not use *she'uvin* to restore the original color, for three *log* would invalidate the water. Therefore, one must wait for natural water (rain) to sufficiently dilute the colored water so that it reverts to the appearance of water.

הָיוּ בּוֹ אַרְבָּעִים סְאָה — *If there [already] were in it [the mikveh] forty se'ah* it does not become invalid by the addition of *she'uvin.* Therefore, one may add any kind of water to it in order to dilute the color.

[ד] נָפַל לְתוֹכוֹ יַיִן אוֹ מֹחַל, וְשָׁנוּ מִקְצָת מַרְאָיו: אִם אֵין

‹ there ‹ if ‹‹ of the ‹ part ‹ and they ‹ olive ‹ or‹ wine ‹ into it ‹ If there   [4]
are not [mikveh's] color, changed sap [a mikveh], fell

בּוֹ מַרְאֵה מַיִם אַרְבָּעִים סְאָה, הֲרֵי זֶה לֹא יִטְבֹּל בּוֹ.*

‹‹ in it.* ‹— one may ‹‹ [in] this ‹ then ‹ [of its] ‹ in forty ‹ of water ‹ the ‹ in it [the
not immerse [mikveh] se'ah, color mikveh]

[ה] שְׁלֹשָׁה לֻגִּין מַיִם, וְנָפַל לְתוֹכָן קוֹרְטוֹב יַיִן, וַהֲרֵי

‹ and ‹‹ of wine, ‹ a kortov ‹ into it ‹ and ‹‹ of [drawn] ‹ log ‹ If there   [5]
now there fell water, are three

מַרְאֵיהֶן כְּמַרְאֵה הַיַּיִן,* וְנָפְלוּ לַמִּקְוֶה — לֹא פְסָלוּהוּ.

‹‹ invalidate ‹ they ‹ into a ‹ and [the ‹‹ of ‹ is like the ‹ its [the water's]
it. did not mikveh, three log] fell wine,* color color

שְׁלֹשָׁה לֻגִּין מַיִם חָסֵר קוֹרְטוֹב, וְנָפַל לְתוֹכָן קוֹרְטוֹב חָלָב,

‹‹ of milk, ‹ a kortov ‹ into it ‹ and ‹‹ a kortov, ‹ minus ‹ of ‹ log ‹ If there
there fell water are three

וַהֲרֵי מַרְאֵיהֶן כְּמַרְאֵה הַמַּיִם,* וְנָפְלוּ לַמִּקְוֶה — לֹא פְסָלוּהוּ.

‹‹ invalidate ‹ they ‹ into a ‹ and [the ‹‹ of ‹ is [still] like ‹ their [the three ‹ and
it. did not mikveh, three log] fell water,* the color log's] color now

רַבִּי יוֹחָנָן בֶּן נוּרִי אוֹמֵר: הַכֹּל הוֹלֵךְ אַחַר הַמַּרְאֶה.*

‹‹ the color.* ‹ according to ‹ goes ‹ Everything ‹‹ says: ‹ Nuri ‹ ben ‹ Yochanan ‹ Rabbi

[ו] מִקְוֶה שֶׁיֵּשׁ בּוֹ אַרְבָּעִים סְאָה מְכֻוָּנוֹת, יָרְדוּ שְׁנַיִם

‹ two ‹ and there ‹‹ exactly, ‹ se'ah ‹ forty ‹ in it ‹ that has ‹ A mikveh   [6]
[people] went down

וְטָבְלוּ זֶה אַחַר זֶה — הָרִאשׁוֹן טָהוֹר, וְהַשֵּׁנִי טָמֵא.* רַבִּי

‹ Rabbi ‹‹ [remains] ‹ but the ‹ is ‹ the first ‹‹ the ‹ after ‹ one ‹‹ and immersed
impure.* second purified, other, [in it],

יד אברהם

4. This mishnah begins with the letter נ of נְשָׁמָה.
לֹא יִטְבֹּל בּוֹ — One may not immerse in it, even in the part that has not been discolored (since that part by itself does not contain the required forty se'ah). If one does immerse in this mikveh, his immersion is invalid.

5. This mishnah begins with the letter ש of נְשָׁמָה.
כְּמַרְאֵה הַיַּיִן — Like the color of wine. Since the three log have taken on the color of wine, they are no longer considered water, and are not subject to the disqualification of she'uvin. Thus, they do not invalidate the mechubarin of an incomplete mikveh.
כְּמַרְאֵה הַמַּיִם — Like the color of water. Although

the three log appear to be all water, since they in fact are not, only the actual water in them is subject to the disqualification of she'uvin, but not the milk. [A drop of milk is not sufficient to discolor water, whereas a drop of wine is.]

הַכֹּל הוֹלֵךְ אַחַר הַמַּרְאֶה — Everything goes according to the color. Wine-colored water is considered as wine and is not subject to the disqualification of she'uvin. Water-colored milk is considered as water and is subject to the she'uvin disqualification. This view is not accepted as halachah.

6. The mishnah begins with the letter מ of נְשָׁמָה.
וְהַשֵּׁנִי טָמֵא — But the second [remains] impure.

יְהוּדָה אוֹמֵר: אִם הָיוּ רַגְלָיו שֶׁל רִאשׁוֹן נוֹגְעוֹת בַּמַּיִם,* אַף
⟨ even ⟪ the ⟨ were [still] ⟨ the first ⟨ of ⟨ that the ⟨ it ⟨ If ⟪ says: ⟨ Yehudah
　　water,*　touching　　　　　　　　　　　feet　was

הַשֵּׁנִי טָהוֹר. הִטְבִּיל בּוֹ אֶת הַסָּגוֹס* וְהֶעֱלָהוּ, מִקְצָתוֹ
⟨ [as long as] ⟪ and lifted ⟨ a thick cloth* ⟨ in it [such ⟨ If one ⟪ is ⟨ the
part of it　　it up,　　　　　　　a mikveh]　immersed　purified.　second

נוֹגֵעַ בַּמַּיִם — טָהוֹר.
⟪ [one who immerses ⟪ the ⟨ [still]
himself] is purified.　water,　touches

הַכַּר וְהַכֶּסֶת שֶׁל עוֹר,* כֵּיוָן שֶׁהִגְבִּיהַּ שִׂפְתוֹתֵיהֶם מִן הַמַּיִם
⟪ the ⟨ out ⟨ their edges ⟨ he lifts ⟨ as ⟪ leather,* ⟨ of ⟨ or a ⟨ [Regarding]
water,　of　　　　　　　　soon as　　　　　　　cushion　a mattress

— הַמַּיִם שֶׁבְּתוֹכָן שְׁאוּבִין. כֵּיצַד יַעֲשֶׂה? מַטְבִּילָן וּמַעֲלֶה
⟨ and ⟨ He should ⟪ should one act ⟨ How ⟪ [become] ⟨ within them ⟨ the water
remove　immerse　[not to disqualify　　she'uvin [drawn].
　　　them　the mikveh]?

אוֹתָן דֶּרֶךְ שׁוּלֵיהֶם.*
⟪ their bottoms ⟨ by ⟨ them
[held upward].*

YAD AVRAHAM

When the first person stepped out of the mikveh, a small amount of mikveh water remained on his body. Thus the mikveh, which originally contained exactly forty se'ah, was incomplete when the second person immersed.

אִם הָיוּ רַגְלָיו שֶׁל רִאשׁוֹן נוֹגְעוֹת בַּמַּיִם — If it was that the feet of the first were [still] touching the water when the second immersed himself. Rabbi Yehudah applies the halachic principle of גּוּד אַחִית, gud achis [lit. extend downward; this principle allows us to view certain types of objects suspended above a surface as extending down to that surface. It is applied primarily to suspended partitions in regard to the law of Sabbath], to the water on the first person's body. Thus, the mikveh is considered full, despite the fact that part of the forty se'ah has been removed. This view is not accepted as halachah.

סָגוֹס — A thick cloth. According to some commentaries, this rule is a continuation of Rabbi Yehudah's opinion and is also based on the principle of gud achis. Thus, this view is also rejected by halachah. Other commentaries maintain that this ruling is not based on gud achis for, unlike the water on a person's body,

the water absorbed by the thick cloth has not been completely removed from the larger body of water. Consequently the person who immersed in this mikveh before the cloth was fully removed is cleansed. According to this interpretation, this view is accepted as halachah.

הַכַּר וְהַכֶּסֶת שֶׁל עוֹר — A mattress or a cushion of leather. These are leather sacks, open on one side, that are filled with stuffing when they are used. If one of these sacks is immersed in the mikveh and removed open side up, the water that has entered the sack becomes she'uvin. Since the mikveh in question originally contained exactly forty se'ah, if the she'uvin were poured back into the mikveh, it would become permanently invalid.

דֶּרֶךְ שׁוּלֵיהֶם — By their bottoms [held upward]. Water that enters the immersed cushion will remain in the mikveh and will not be lifted out with the cushion. Thus the water will not become she'uvin. Nevertheless, since some small amount of water must adhere to the leather and be removed from the mikveh, the mikveh is no longer valid until its minimum volume is restored.

[ז] **הִטְבִּיל** בּוֹ אֶת הַמִּטָּה,* אַף עַל פִּי שֶׁרַגְלֶיהָ שׁוֹקְעוֹת

‹ sink ‹ its legs ‹ even if ‹‹ a bed,* ‹ in it ‹ If one immersed [7]

בְּטִיט הֶעָבֶה — טְהוֹרָה, מִפְּנֵי שֶׁהַמַּיִם מְקַדְּמִין.*

‹‹ comes first.* ‹ the water ‹ because ‹‹ it is purified, ‹ that is thick, ‹ into mud

מִקְוֶה שֶׁמֵּימָיו מְרֻדָּדִין,* כּוֹבֵשׁ* אֲפִילוּ חֲבִילֵי עֵצִים,

‹‹ of wood, ‹ bundles ‹ — even ‹‹ one may press down ‹‹ is shallow,* ‹ whose ‹ [In] a
                       [material* on one side   water   mikveh
                       of the mikveh]

אֲפִילוּ חֲבִילֵי קָנִים,* כְּדֵי שֶׁיִּתְפְּחוּ הַמַּיִם, וְיוֹרֵד וְטוֹבֵל.

‹‹ and ‹ and he may ‹‹ the water [level] ‹ so ‹‹ of reeds* — ‹ bundles ‹ even
immerse. then go down   should rise,   that

מַחַט* שֶׁהִיא נְתוּנָה עַל מַעֲלוֹת הַמְּעָרָה,* הָיָה מוֹלִיךְ

‹ moving ‹ — if ‹‹ of the cave* [with ‹ the steps ‹ on ‹ was placed ‹ that ‹ A needle*
[his hand] one was   a mikveh inside]
forward

וּמֵבִיא בַּמַּיִם, כֵּיוָן שֶׁעָבַר עָלֶיהָ הַגַּל – טְהוֹרָה.

‹‹ it is purified. ‹ a wave, ‹ over it ‹ there ‹ as soon ‹‹ in the water ‹ and
        [the needle] passed   as   [generating waves], back

IF THE MISHNAYOS WERE STUDIED IN THE PRESENCE OF A *MINYAN,* **קַדִּישׁ דְּרַבָּנָן** (P. 78) **IS RECITED.**

יד אברהם

7. This mishnah begins with the letter ה of נְשָׁמָה.

אֶת הַמִּטָּה — *A bed.* The mishnah refers to a high bed with legs that is immersed in a shallow *mikveh*, the bottom of which is covered with thick mud. It is impossible for the entire bed to fit into the *mikveh*'s water at one time unless the legs sink into the mud. But all parts of a utensil must be immersed at the same time if it is to be purified. Thus, the immersion of this bed in a shallow *mikveh* presents a halachic problem.

טְהוֹרָה מִפְּנֵי שֶׁהַמַּיִם מְקַדְּמִין — *It is purified, because the water comes first;* the legs of the bed became wet with *mikveh* water before sinking into the mud. Since the legs are still wet when the topmost part of the bed is immersed, and since that wetness is still connected to the water of the *mikveh*, the immersion is valid.

מִקְוֶה שֶׁמֵּימָיו מְרֻדָּדִין — *A mikveh whose water is shallow,* a body of water that covered a very large area but was too shallow for a person or utensil to be completely submerged at one time.

כּוֹבֵשׁ — *One may press down [material . . .].* Since wood or reeds float and do not raise the level of the *mikveh*, stones may be placed on the bundles

to press them down and hold them in place.

אֲפִילוּ חֲבִילֵי עֵצִים אֲפִילוּ חֲבִילֵי קָנִים — *Even bundles of wood, even bundles of reeds.* Although the bundles may seem to divide the *mikveh* into two bodies, thus invalidating it, since the water can flow freely through the bundles, the water is considered as one body. Obviously stones that sink into the water and raise the water's level may be used for this purpose. However, a partition that divides the pool into two bodies of water would create two incomplete *mikvaos*.

מַחַט — *A needle* became contaminated, but the person who was to immerse it was apprehensive lest it slip from his hand and be lost in the *mikveh*. He therefore placed the needle on the steps leading to a *mikveh*, and swished the water until it passed over the needle. As long as the water did not become detached from the main body, the needle is cleansed.

הַמְּעָרָה — *The cave.* The bodies of water found in many of the caves dotting the Judean hills are often valid *mikvaos* and were frequently used as such in earlier times. Thus a *mikveh* is often referred to as a cave.

תפלה על הנפטר אחר למוד משניות ﴾

﴿ PRAYER AFTER MISHNAH STUDY FOR THE DECEASED ﴾

**IT IS CUSTOMARY TO RECITE THIS PRAYER WHENEVER MISHNAYOS
ARE STUDIED IN MEMORY OF THE DECEASED:**

אָנָּא יהוה מָלֵא רַחֲמִים, אֲשֶׁר בְּיָדְךָ נֶפֶשׁ כָּל חַי, וְרוּחַ כָּל

⟨ of ⟨ and the ⟨⟨ the ⟨ of ⟨ is the ⟨ in Your ⟨ that ⟨ of mercy, ⟨ full ⟨ O ⟨ Please
all spirit living all soul hand HASHEM,

בְּשַׂר אִישׁ.[1] יִהְיֶה נָא לְרָצוֹן לְפָנֶיךָ תּוֹרָתֵנוּ וּתְפִלָּתֵנוּ בַּעֲבוּר

⟨ on behalf ⟨⟨ and our ⟨– our Torah ⟨⟨ before ⟨ favorable ⟨ may they ⟨⟨ mankind,
prayer – study You please be,

נִשְׁמַת [DECEASED'S HEBREW NAME] בֶּן / בַּת [DECEASED'S FATHER'S HEBREW NAME]

⟨ daughter of ⟨ son of
⟨ of the soul

וּגְמוֹל נָא עִמָּהּ בְּחַסְדְּךָ הַגָּדוֹל, לִפְתּוֹחַ לָהּ שַׁעֲרֵי רַחֲמִים

⟨ of mercy ⟨ the gates ⟨ for it ⟨ opening ⟨⟨ which ⟨ according to ⟨ with it ⟨ please, ⟨ and
is great, Your kindness, [the soul] deal,

וָחֶסֶד, וְשַׁעֲרֵי גַּן עֵדֶן.* וּתְקַבֵּל אוֹתָהּ בְּאַהֲבָה וּבְחִבָּה, וְשָׁלַח

⟨ and ⟨⟨ and ⟨ with love ⟨ it ⟨ Accept ⟨⟨ of ⟨ of the ⟨ and the ⟨ and
send affection, Eden.* Garden gates kindness,

לָהּ מַלְאָכֶיךָ הַקְּדוֹשִׁים וְהַטְּהוֹרִים, לְהוֹלִיכָהּ וּלְהוֹשִׁיבָהּ תַּחַת

⟨ under ⟨ and to settle it ⟨ to lead it ⟨⟨ and pure, ⟨ holy ⟨⟨ Your angels, ⟨ to it

עֵץ הַחַיִּים,* אֵצֶל נִשְׁמוֹת הַצַּדִּיקִים וְהַצִּדְקָנִיּוֹת, חֲסִידִים

⟨ devout ⟨⟨ and righteous ⟨ of the ⟨ the souls ⟨ near ⟨⟨ of Life,* ⟨ the
men women, righteous men Tree

וַחֲסִידוֹת, לֵהָנוֹת מִזִּיו שְׁכִינָתֶךָ, וּלְהַשְׂבִּיעָהּ מִטּוּבְךָ הַצָּפוּן

⟨ that is ⟨ from Your ⟨ satiating it ⟨⟨ of Your ⟨ the ⟨ to enjoy ⟨⟨ and devout
hidden away goodness Presence, radiance women,

לַצַּדִּיקִים. וְהַגּוּף יָנוּחַ בַּקֶּבֶר בִּמְנוּחָה נְכוֹנָה, בְּחֶדְוָה וּבְשִׂמְחָה

⟨ with ⟨ with joy, ⟨ that is ⟨ with ⟨ in the ⟨ repose ⟨ May the ⟨⟨ for the
gladness proper, contentment grave body righteous.

---

(1) Cf. *Job* 12:10.

﴿ **תְּפִלָה עַל הַנִּפְטָר** / PRAYER FOR THE DECEASED ﴾

גַּן עֵדֶן — *Garden of Eden.* The term Garden of Eden is widely used in traditional literature to denote the spiritual reward of the righteous in the World to Come. It is not identical to the Garden of Eden mentioned in the Creation as the dwelling place of Adam. As *Ramban* puts it (Comm. to *Genesis* 3:22): "The Garden of Eden is on this earth as is the Tree of Life . . . but just as they are on the earth so do they have their Heavenly counterparts which are called by the same names and which are the foundations of those on earth . . ."

עֵץ הַחַיִּים — *The Tree of Life.* One of the many phases of the Eternal Life; see above, s.v. גַּן עֵדֶן.

וְשָׁלוֹם, כְּדִכְתִיב: יָבוֹא שָׁלוֹם, יָנוּחוּ עַל מִשְׁכְּבוֹתָם, הֹלֵךְ

‹ — he who ‹‹ their repose ‹ in ‹ they ‹‹ in ‹ He will ‹‹ as it is ‹‹ and peace,
walks   will rest   peace,   enter   written:

נְכֹחוֹ.¹ וּכְתִיב: יַעְלְזוּ חֲסִידִים בְּכָבוֹד, יְרַנְּנוּ עַל מִשְׁכְּבוֹתָם.²

‹‹ their beds. ‹ upon ‹ let them ‹‹ in glory, ‹ let the ‹ Exult ‹‹ And it is ‹‹ in his
let them   devout   written: integrity.
sing joyously

וּכְתִיב: אִם תִּשְׁכַּב לֹא תִפְחָד, וְשָׁכַבְתָּ וְעָרְבָה שְׁנָתֶךָ.³

‹‹ your ‹ sweet ‹ when you ‹‹ fear; ‹ you ‹ you lie ‹ If ‹ And it is
sleep.   will be   lie down,   will not   down,   written:

FOR A MALE:

וְתִשְׁמוֹר אוֹתוֹ מֵחִבּוּט הַקֶּבֶר,* וּמֵרִמָּה וְתוֹלֵעָה. וְתִסְלַח

‹ Forgive ‹‹ and maggots. ‹ and from ‹ of the ‹ from the ‹ him ‹ And protect
worms   grave*   tribulations

וְתִמְחוֹל לוֹ עַל כָּל פְּשָׁעָיו, כִּי אָדָם אֵין צַדִּיק בָּאָרֶץ, אֲשֶׁר

‹ who ‹ on earth ‹ so ‹ there is ‹ for ‹‹ his sins, ‹ all ‹ for ‹ him ‹ and pardon
righteous   no person

יַעֲשֶׂה טּוֹב וְלֹא יֶחֱטָא.⁴ וּזְכוֹר לוֹ זְכִיּוֹתָיו וְצִדְקוֹתָיו אֲשֶׁר

‹ that ‹ and the ‹ his merits ‹ for ‹ Remember ‹‹ sins. ‹ and ‹ [only] ‹ does
righteous deeds   him   never   good

עָשָׂה. וְתַשְׁפִּיעַ לוֹ מִנִּשְׁמָתוֹ לְדַשֵּׁן עַצְמוֹתָיו בַּקֶּבֶר מֵרֹב טוֹב

‹good ‹ from the ‹‹ in the ‹ his bones ‹ to keep ‹ from his soul ‹ for ‹ and cause a ‹‹ he per-
abundant   grave,   fresh   him   spiritual flow   formed,

הַצָּפוּן לַצַּדִּיקִים, דִּכְתִיב: מָה רַב טוּבְךָ אֲשֶׁר צָפַנְתָּ

‹ You have ‹ that ‹ is Your ‹ abundant ‹ How ‹‹ as it is ‹‹ for the ‹ that is
hidden away   goodness   written: righteous,   hidden away

לִירֵאֶיךָ.⁵ וּכְתִיב: שֹׁמֵר כָּל עַצְמוֹתָיו, אַחַת מֵהֵנָּה לֹא נִשְׁבָּרָה.⁶

‹‹ broken. ‹ was ‹ of them ‹ even one ‹‹ his bones, ‹ all ‹ He ‹‹ and it is ‹‹ for those who
not   guards   written: fear You,

וְיִשְׁכּוֹן בֶּטַח בָּדָד⁷ וְשַׁאֲנַן מִפַּחַד רָעָה, וְאַל יִרְאֶה פְּנֵי גֵיהִנָּם.*

‹‹ of ‹ the ‹ see ‹ and may ‹‹ of ‹ [free] ‹ and ‹ alone, ‹ secure, ‹ May he
Gehinnom.*   face   he not   evil,   from fear   serene,   rest

---

(1) *Isaiah* 57:2. (2) *Psalms* 149:5. (3) *Proverbs* 3:24. (4) *Ecclesiastes* 7:20.
(5) *Psalms* 31:20. (6) 34:21. (7) Cf. *Deuteronomy* 33:28.

חִבּוּט הַקֶּבֶר — *Tribulations of the grave* (lit. *beating of the grave*), a metaphor for the suffering of the body in its grave. R' Eliyahu de Vidas in his classic *Reishis Chochmah* reproduces a Midrash which describes graphically the pain one may be subjected to in this phase of retribution.

גיהנם — *Gehinnom*, so named after the Valley of Hinnom (*Joshua* 18:16) near Jerusalem. *Gehinnom* is one of the seven names for the place designated for the punishment of sinners (*Eruvin* 19a) and their ultimate rehabilitation and entry into the Garden of Eden.

וְנִשְׁמָתוֹ תְּהֵא צְרוּרָה בִּצְרוֹר הַחַיִּים,*1 וּלְהַחֲיוֹתוֹ בִּתְחִיַּת

⟨ with the ⟨ And [may You] bring ⟩⟩ of Life.* ⟨ in the ⟨ bound ⟨ be ⟨ May his
revivification　him back to life　　　　　　　Bond　　　　　　　　　　soul

הַמֵּתִים עִם כָּל מֵתֵי עַמְּךָ יִשְׂרָאֵל בְּרַחֲמִים. אָמֵן.

⟩⟩ Amen. ⟩⟩ with mercy. ⟨ Israel, ⟨ of Your ⟨ the ⟨ all ⟨ together ⟨ of the
　　　　　　　　　　　　　　　people　deceased　　　　　with　　dead

FOR A FEMALE:

וְתִשְׁמוֹר אוֹתָהּ מֵחִבּוּט הַקֶּבֶר, וּמֵרִמָּה וְתוֹלֵעָה. וְתִסְלַח

⟨ Forgive ⟩⟩ and maggots. ⟨ and from ⟨ of the ⟨ from the ⟨ her ⟨ And protect
　　　　　　　　　　　　worms　grave　tribulations

וְתִמְחוֹל לָהּ עַל כָּל פְּשָׁעֶיהָ, כִּי אָדָם אֵין צַדִּיק בָּאָרֶץ, אֲשֶׁר

⟨ who ⟨ on earth ⟨ so ⟨ there is ⟨ for ⟩⟩ her sins, ⟨ all ⟨ for ⟨ her ⟨ and pardon
　　　　　　　　　　　　righteous　no person

יַעֲשֶׂה טוֹב וְלֹא יֶחֱטָא. וּזְכוֹר לָהּ זְכִיּוֹתֶיהָ וְצִדְקוֹתֶיהָ אֲשֶׁר

⟨ that ⟨ and the ⟨ her merits ⟨ for ⟨ Remember ⟩⟩ sins. ⟨ and ⟨ [only] ⟨ does
　　　righteous deeds　　her　　　　　　　　　never　good

עָשָׂתָה. וְתַשְׁפִּיעַ לָהּ מִנִּשְׁמָתָהּ לְדַשֵּׁן עַצְמוֹתֶיהָ בַּקֶּבֶר מֵרֹב

⟨ from the ⟩⟩ in the ⟨ her bones ⟨ to keep ⟨ from her soul ⟨ for ⟨ and cause a ⟩⟩ she per-
　abundant　grave,　　　　　　　fresh　　　　　　　her　spiritual flow　　formed,

טוּב הַצָּפוּן לַצַּדִּיקִים, דִּכְתִיב: מָה רַב טוּבְךָ אֲשֶׁר צָפַנְתָּ

⟨ You have ⟨ that ⟨ is Your ⟨ abun- ⟨ How ⟩⟩ as it is ⟩⟩ for the ⟨ that is ⟨ good
hidden away　　　goodness　dant　　　written:　　righteous,　hidden away

לִירֵאֶיךָ. וּכְתִיב: שֹׁמֵר כָּל עַצְמֹתָיו, אַחַת מֵהֵנָּה לֹא נִשְׁבָּרָה.

⟩⟩ broken. ⟨ was ⟨ of them ⟨ even one ⟩⟩ his bones, ⟨ all ⟨ He ⟩⟩ and it is ⟨⟨ for those who
　　　not　　　　　　　　　　　　guards　written:　　fear You,

וְתִשְׁכּוֹן בֶּטַח בָּדָד וְשַׁאֲנָן מִפַּחַד רָעָה, וְאַל תִּרְאֶה פְּנֵי גֵיהִנֹּם.

⟩⟩ of ⟨ the ⟨ see ⟨ and may ⟩⟩ of ⟨ [free] ⟨ and ⟨ alone, ⟨ secure, ⟨ May she
Gehinnom. face　she not　evil,　from fear　serene,　　　　rest

וְנִשְׁמָתָהּ תְּהֵא צְרוּרָה בִּצְרוֹר הַחַיִּים, וּלְהַחֲיוֹתָהּ בִּתְחִיַּת

⟨ with the ⟨ And [may You] bring ⟩⟩ of Life. ⟨ in the ⟨ bound ⟨ be ⟨ May her
revivification　her back to life　　　　　Bond　　　　　　　　　soul

הַמֵּתִים עִם כָּל מֵתֵי עַמְּךָ יִשְׂרָאֵל בְּרַחֲמִים. אָמֵן.

⟩⟩ Amen. ⟩⟩ with mercy. ⟨ Israel, ⟨ of Your ⟨ the ⟨ all ⟨ together ⟨ of the
　　　　　　　　　　　　people　deceased　　　　　with　　dead

---

(1) Cf. *I Samuel* 25:29.

צְרוֹר הַחַיִּים — *Bond of Life.* One of the Scriptural
metaphors for the spiritual reward in the World
to Come (see *I Samuel* 25:29).

❧ MOURNING THE DESTRUCTION OF THE TEMPLE ❧

UPON SEEING THE CITIES OF YEHUDAH IN THEIR DESTRUCTION ONE RECITES:

עָרֵי קָדְשְׁךָ הָיוּ מִדְבָּר.¹

》 a wilderness. 〈 became 〈 Your holy cities

UPON SEEING THE CITY OF JERUSALEM IN ITS DESTRUCTION ONE RECITES:

צִיּוֹן מִדְבָּר הָיֶתָה, יְרוּשָׁלַיִם שְׁמָמָה.¹

》 [became] a wasteland. 〈 Jerusalem 》 became; 〈 — a wilderness 》 Zion

כָּלָּה יהוה אֶת חֲמָתוֹ, שָׁפַךְ חֲרוֹן אַפּוֹ, וַיַּצֶּת אֵשׁ בְּצִיּוֹן

〈 in Zion 〈 a fire 〈 He 》 wrath; 〈 His burning 〈 He poured out 》 His fury, 〈 did 〈 Vent HASHEM kindled

וַתֹּאכַל יְסוֹדֹתֶיהָ.²

》 its foundations. 〈 which consumed

UPON SEEING THE TEMPLE IN ITS DESTRUCTION ONE RECITES:

בֵּית קָדְשֵׁנוּ וְתִפְאַרְתֵּנוּ אֲשֶׁר הִלְלוּךָ אֲבֹתֵינוּ, הָיָה לִשְׂרֵפַת

〈 burned 〈 was 》 did our fathers, 〈 praise You 〈 where 》 and our splendor, 〈 of our holiness 〈 The Temple

אֵשׁ, וְכָל מַחֲמַדֵּינוּ הָיָה לְחָרְבָּה.³

》 a ruin. 〈 became 〈 that we desired 〈 and all 》 by fire,

ONE NOW RENDS ONE'S CLOTHING AND THEN CONTINUES:

בָּרוּךְ דַּיַּן הָאֱמֶת, כִּי כָל מִשְׁפָּטָיו צֶדֶק וֶאֱמֶת. הַצּוּר תָּמִים

〈 — perfect 》 The Rock 》 and 〈 are true. 〈 His 〈 all 〈 for 》 Who is true, 〈 is the 〈 Blessed righteous judgments Judge

---

(1) *Isaiah* 64:9. (2) *Lamentations* 4:11. (3) *Isaiah* 64:10.

One who has not seen the site of the cities of Yehudah, or Jerusalem, or the Temple for thirty days is required to perform קְרִיעָה, *rending his upper garment* (O.C. 561). However, most rabbinic authorities today recommend not rending upon seeing the cities of Yehudah. Additionally, many authorities recommend that one should not perform קְרִיעָה on seeing the city of Jerusalem, but only on seeing the site of the Temple (see *Igros Moshe O.C.* vol. 4, 70:11).

Prior to performing קְרִיעָה, the appropriate verses should be recited. If one follows the view that one should only rend on seeing the site of the Temple, all of the verses that are to be said on the city should be combined with the verse for the Temple.

One should stand while performing קְרִיעָה, bowing toward the site of the Temple, crying and lamenting over its destruction. The קְרִיעָה should be performed by hand on the left side of the garment. The current practice is to rend only one's shirt — it is recommended that one remove his jacket before reaching the location where he will be obligated to perform קְרִיעָה.

Seeing the Temple in its destruction: some hold that one should see the ground where the Temple once stood — visible from the east on Har HaZeisim or from Har HaTzofim, or from some of the roofs of the Jewish Quarter. Others indicate that the Dome of the Rock is ample proof of the destruction of the Temple. Others say that seeing the *Kosel HaMaaravi*, the Western Wall, alone is sufficient cause for קְרִיעָה.

פָּעֳלוֹ, כִּי כָל דְּרָכָיו מִשְׁפָּט, אֵל אֱמוּנָה וְאֵין עָוֶל, צַדִּיק וְיָשָׁר

‹ and ‹ right- ‹‹ iniquity, ‹ with- ‹ of faith ‹ a God ‹‹ are ‹ His paths ‹ all ‹ for ‹‹ is His
fair teous out justice; work,

הוּא. וְאַתָּה צַדִּיק עַל כָּל הַבָּא עָלֵינוּ, כִּי אֱמֶת עָשִׂיתָ וַאֲנַחְנוּ

‹ while ‹‹ have You ‹ truth- ‹ for ‹‹ upon ‹ that has ‹ all ‹ in ‹ are ‹ And You ‹‹ is He.
we acted, fully us, come righteous

הִרְשָׁעְנוּ.

‹‹ have acted wickedly.

שַׂמְּחֵנוּ כִּימוֹת עִנִּיתָנוּ, שְׁנוֹת רָאִינוּ רָעָה. יֵרָאֶה אֶל עֲבָדֶיךָ

‹ Your ‹ to ‹ May ‹‹ evil. ‹ [when] ‹ the ‹‹ You ‹ according ‹ Gladden us
servants visible be we saw years afflicted us, to the days

פָּעֳלֶךָ וַהֲדָרְךָ עַל בְּנֵיהֶם.¹

‹‹ upon their ‹ and Your ‹‹ Your
children. majesty deeds,

וִיהִי רָצוֹן מִלְּפָנֶיךָ, שֶׁתְּזַכֵּנוּ בְּרַחֲמֶיךָ הָרַבִּים לִרְאוֹת בִּנְיַן

‹ the ‹ to see ‹‹ that is ‹ in Your ‹‹ that You ‹ before ‹ the will ‹ And
rebuilding abundant, mercy make us worthy, You may it be

הַמִּקְדָּשׁ וִירוּשָׁלַיִם וְעָרֵי יִשְׂרָאֵל וִיהוּדָה, כֵּן יְהִי רָצוֹן אָמֵן.

‹‹ Amen. ‹‹ the ‹ may ‹ So ‹‹ and Judah. ‹ of Israel ‹ and the ‹ Jerusalem, ‹ of the
will. it be Cities Temple,

————————— תהלים עט / Psalm 79 —————————

מִזְמוֹר לְאָסָף; אֱלֹהִים, בָּאוּ גוֹיִם בְּנַחֲלָתֶךָ, טִמְּאוּ אֶת הֵיכַל

‹ the ‹ they have ‹‹ into Your ‹ have the ‹ Entered ‹‹ O God! ‹‹ by Asaph: ‹ A psalm
Sanctuary defiled inheritance, nations

קָדְשֶׁךָ, שָׂמוּ אֶת יְרוּשָׁלַיִם לְעִיִּים. נָתְנוּ אֶת נִבְלַת עֲבָדֶיךָ

‹ of Your ‹ the corpse ‹ They have ‹‹ into heaps ‹ Jerusalem ‹ they have ‹‹ of Your
servants given [of rubble]. turned holiness,

מַאֲכָל לְעוֹף הַשָּׁמַיִם, בְּשַׂר חֲסִידֶיךָ לְחַיְתוֹ אָרֶץ. שָׁפְכוּ דָמָם

‹ their ‹ They ‹‹ of the ‹ to the ‹ of Your ‹ the ‹‹ of the sky, ‹ for the ‹ as food
blood have spilled earth. beasts devout ones flesh birds

כַּמַּיִם, סְבִיבוֹת יְרוּשָׁלַיִם, וְאֵין קוֹבֵר. הָיִינוּ חֶרְפָּה לִשְׁכֵנֵינוּ,

‹ to our ‹ [an object ‹ We ‹‹ who ‹ and there ‹‹ Jerusalem, ‹ all around ‹ like
neighbors, of] disgrace became buries. is none water

לַעַג וָקֶלֶס לִסְבִיבוֹתֵינוּ. עַד מָה יהוה תֶּאֱנַף לָנֶצַח, תִּבְעַר

‹ [until ‹‹ for ‹ will You ‹ Hashem, ‹ when, ‹ Until ‹‹ to those ‹ and ‹ [an
when] will eternity, be angry around us. scorn object of]
it burn mockery

———————————————
(1) *Psalms* 90:15-16.

כְּמוֹ אֵשׁ קִנְאָתֶךָ. שְׁפֹךְ חֲמָתְךָ אֶל הַגּוֹיִם אֲשֶׁר לֹא יְדָעוּךָ;

‹ like ‹ fire ‹‹ Your jealousy? ‹‹ – Your ‹ Pour ‹ Your wrath ‹ upon ‹ the nations ‹ that ‹ do not ‹ recognize You,

וְעַל מַמְלָכוֹת, אֲשֶׁר בְּשִׁמְךָ לֹא קָרָאוּ. כִּי אָכַל אֶת יַעֲקֹב,

‹ and upon ‹ the kingdoms ‹ that ‹ upon Your Name ‹ do not ‹ call. ‹‹ For ‹ they have devoured ‹ Jacob,

וְאֶת נָוֵהוּ הֵשַׁמּוּ. אַל תִּזְכָּר לָנוּ עֲוֹנֹת רִאשֹׁנִים; מַהֵר יְקַדְּמוּנוּ

‹ and His habitation ‹ they have destroyed. ‹‹ Do not ‹ recall ‹ against us ‹ the sins ‹ of the ancients; ‹‹ swiftly ‹ advance to meet us

רַחֲמֶיךָ, כִּי דַלּוֹנוּ מְאֹד. עָזְרֵנוּ אֱלֹהֵי יִשְׁעֵנוּ עַל דְּבַר כְּבוֹד

‹‹ may Your mercies, ‹ for ‹‹ we have become impoverished ‹ exceedingly. ‹‹ Assist us, ‹ O God ‹ of our salvation, ‹ for the sake ‹ of the ‹ the glory

שְׁמֶךָ, וְהַצִּילֵנוּ וְכַפֵּר עַל חַטֹּאתֵינוּ לְמַעַן שְׁמֶךָ. לָמָּה

‹‹ of Your Name, ‹ rescue us ‹ and atone ‹ for ‹ our sins ‹ for the sake ‹ of Your Name. ‹ Why

יֹאמְרוּ הַגּוֹיִם: אַיֵּה אֱלֹהֵיהֶם; יִוָּדַע בַּגּוֹיִם לְעֵינֵינוּ, נִקְמַת דַּם

‹ should the nations say, ‹ Where ‹ is their God? ‹ Let there be known ‹ among ‹ the nations, ‹ before our eyes, ‹ the revenge ‹ for the blood

עֲבָדֶיךָ הַשָּׁפוּךְ. תָּבוֹא לְפָנֶיךָ אֶנְקַת אָסִיר; כְּגֹדֶל זְרוֹעֲךָ,

‹ of Your servants ‹ that was spilled. ‹‹ Let come ‹ before You ‹ the groan ‹ of the prisoner; ‹‹ as [befits] ‹ the greatness ‹ of Your might,

הוֹתֵר בְּנֵי תְמוּתָה. וְהָשֵׁב לִשְׁכֵנֵינוּ שִׁבְעָתַיִם אֶל חֵיקָם,

‹ spare ‹ those condemned ‹ to die. ‹‹ And repay ‹ to our neighbors ‹ sevenfold ‹ into their bosom,

חֶרְפָּתָם אֲשֶׁר חֵרְפוּךָ, אֲדֹנָי. וַאֲנַחְנוּ עַמְּךָ וְצֹאן מַרְעִיתֶךָ,

‹ their disgrace ‹ with ‹ which ‹ they have disgraced You, ‹‹ O Lord. ‹‹ As for us, ‹‹ Your people ‹ and the ‹ sheep ‹ of Your pasture,

נוֹדֶה לְךָ לְעוֹלָם; לְדוֹר וָדֹר נְסַפֵּר תְּהִלָּתֶךָ.

‹‹ we shall thank ‹ You ‹ forever; ‹‹ for ‹ generation ‹ generation ‹ after ‹ we shall relate ‹‹ Your praise.

ON SEEING THE WALLS AROUND THE TEMPLE MOUNT, ESPECIALLY THE *KOSEL HAMAARAVI*, THE WESTERN WALL, AND THE GATE OF MERCY, ONE RECITES:

טָבְעוּ בָאָרֶץ שְׁעָרֶיהָ, אִבַּד וְשִׁבַּר בְּרִיחֶיהָ, מַלְכָּהּ וְשָׂרֶיהָ

‹ Sunk ‹ into the earth ‹ her gates, ‹‹ have her ‹ He has ‹ and ‹ broken destroyed ‹ her bolts; ‹‹ her king ‹ and her officers

בַגּוֹיִם אֵין תּוֹרָה, גַּם נְבִיאֶיהָ לֹא מָצְאוּ חָזוֹן מֵיהוָה.[1]

‹ are among the nations ‹ without ‹ Torah; ‹‹ even ‹ her prophets ‹ did not ‹ find ‹ a vision ‹‹ from Hashem.

---

(1) *Lamentations* 2:9.

﴾ YOM KIPPUR KATAN / יוֹם כִּפּוּר קָטָן ﴿

THE SERVICE IS RECITED AT *MINCHAH*.
THE FIRST PART OF THE SERVICE IS RECITED BEFORE אַשְׁרֵי, *ASHREI*.

———— Psalm 102 / תהלים קב ————

תְּפִלָּה לְעָנִי כִי יַעֲטֹף,* וְלִפְנֵי יהוה יִשְׁפֹּךְ שִׂיחוֹ. יהוה
〈HASHEM, 〈 his sup-〉 he pours 〈 HASHEM 〈 and in 〈 he 〈 when 〈 of the 〈 A prayer
plications: forth front of faints* afflicted man,

שִׁמְעָה תְפִלָּתִי, וְשַׁוְעָתִי אֵלֶיךָ תָבוֹא. אַל תַּסְתֵּר פָּנֶיךָ מִמֶּנִּי
〈 from 〈 Your 〈 hide 〈 Do 〈 let it 〈 —to 〈 and my 〈 my 〈 hear
me face not reach! You cry prayer,

בְּיוֹם צַר לִי; הַטֵּה אֵלַי אָזְנֶךָ, בְּיוֹם אֶקְרָא, מַהֵר עֲנֵנִי. כִּי כָלוּ
〈 con- 〈 For 〈 answer 〈 speedily 〈 that I 〈 on the 〈 Your, 〈 to 〈 incline 〈 of my 〈 on the
sumed me. call, day ear me distress; day

בְעָשָׁן יָמָי, וְעַצְמוֹתַי כְּמוֹקֵד נִחָרוּ. הוּכָּה כָעֵשֶׂב וַיִּבַשׁ לִבִּי, כִּי
〈for 〈 is my 〈 until 〈 like 〈 Smitten 〈 are 〈 as a 〈 and my 〈 are my 〈 in
heart withered grass [by the sun] charred. hearth bones days, smoke

---

﴾ YOM KIPPUR KATAN / יוֹם כִּפּוּר קָטָן ﴿

Longing for the atonement that Israel attained through the sin-offering service of Rosh Chodesh in the *Beis HaMikdash* (see *Numbers* 28:15), the Kabbalists of 16th-century Safed instituted a day of repentance and fasting each Erev Rosh Chodesh. According to the prevailing custom, Yom Kippur Katan [Minor Day of Atonement] is observed on the 29th of most months, but not all. It is omitted on 29 Nissan because we do not fast during that month; on 29 Elul because fasting is prohibited on Erev Rosh Hashanah; in most communities, on 29 Tishrei because we do not fast during Tishrei after Yom Kippur; and on 29 Kislev, for that is the fifth day of Chanukah. It should be noted that although the vast majority of Jews do not fast on these days, many congregations nevertheless observe the day by reciting the Yom Kippur Katan prayer service during *Minchah*. Additionally, many who do not observe Yom Kippur Katan during the rest of the year do observe it on Erev Rosh Chodesh Elul, the month preceding Rosh Hashanah and Yom Kippur. When the day of Rosh Chodesh falls on the Sabbath or Sunday, the observance of Yom Kippur Katan is moved back to the previous Thursday.

תְּפִלָּה לְעָנִי ◈ / Psalm 102

The translation of this psalm follows its context in the Book of *Psalms*. The commentary here will point out alternative interpretations that are particularly relevant to Yom Kippur Katan.

תְּפִלָּה לְעָנִי כִי יַעֲטֹף ... — *A prayer of the afflicted man, when he faints* ... The word יַעֲטֹף, here rendered *he faints*, can also mean *he will wrap himself in a tallis*, as we find in the blessing recited when donning the *tallis*, וְצִוָּנוּ לְהִתְעַטֵּף בַּצִיצִת, *and He has commanded us to wrap ourselves in tzitzis.* Accordingly, the verse may be understood in light of the Talmud's account of Moses' reaction to the nation's sinfulness at the incident of the Golden Calf. Moses feared that their sin was beyond atonement; he thought that his intercession on their behalf would be futile. God then appeared to him as a *chazzan* wrapped in a *tallis* and taught him a special prayer service. He instructed Moses, "Whenever Israel sins, let them follow this prayer service and I will forgive them" (*Rosh Hashanah* 17b). Accordingly, our verse may be explained: *A prayer of a man afflicted [by sin], when he will don a tallis and in front of HASHEM he pours forth His supplication,* that is, the supplication that God taught Moses.

שָׁכַחְתִּי מֵאֲכֹל לַחְמִי.* מִקּוֹל אַנְחָתִי, דָּבְקָה עַצְמִי לִבְשָׂרִי.*

‹‹ to my / ‹ has my / ‹ clung / ‹ of my sigh, / ‹ From the / ‹‹ my / ‹ to eat / ‹ I have
flesh.* / bone / sound / food.* / forgotten

דָּמִיתִי לִקְאַת מִדְבָּר, הָיִיתִי כְּכוֹס חֳרָבוֹת. שָׁקַדְתִּי וָאֶהְיֶה

‹ yet I have / ‹ I have been / ‹‹ of the / ‹ the owl / ‹ I have / ‹‹ of the / ‹ a bird / ‹ I am like
become / diligent, / wasteland, / become like / wilderness;

כְּצִפּוֹר בּוֹדֵד עַל גָּג. כָּל הַיּוֹם חֵרְפוּנִי אוֹיְבָי, מְהוֹלָלַי בִּי

‹ by / ‹‹ those who / ‹‹ do my / ‹ disgrace / ‹ day / ‹ All ‹‹ / a / ‹ upon / ‹ lonely, / ‹‹ like a bird,
me / ridicule me, / enemies; / me / long / rooftop.

נִשְׁבָּעוּ.* כִּי אֵפֶר כַּלֶּחֶם אָכָלְתִּי, וְשִׁקֻּוַי בִּבְכִי מָסָכְתִּי. מִפְּנֵי

‹ because / ‹ have I / ‹ with / ‹ and my / ‹ have I / ‹ like / ‹ ashes / ‹ For ‹‹ they curse.*
of / mixed, / tears / drink / eaten, / bread

זַעַמְךָ וְקִצְפֶּךָ, כִּי נְשָׂאתַנִי וַתַּשְׁלִיכֵנִי. יָמַי כְּצֵל נָטוּי,* וַאֲנִי

‹ and I, / ‹‹ length- / are, like / ‹ My / ‹‹ and hurled / ‹ You have / ‹ for / ‹‹ and Your / ‹ Your
ened,* / a shadow, / days / me down. / raised me high / wrath, / fury

כָּעֵשֶׂב אִיבָשׁ. וְאַתָּה יהוה לְעוֹלָם תֵּשֵׁב, וְזִכְרְךָ לְדֹר וָדֹר.

‹‹ to gen- / ‹ from gen- / ‹ and memory / ‹‹ will be / ‹ forever / ‹ HASHEM, / ‹ But You, / ‹‹ wither / ‹ like grass,
eration. / eration. / of You [endures] / enthroned / away.

אַתָּה תָקוּם תְּרַחֵם צִיּוֹן, כִּי עֵת לְחֶנְנָהּ* כִּי בָא מוֹעֵד. כִּי רָצוּ

‹ cher- / ‹ For ‹‹ the appointed / ‹ for ‹‹ to favor / ‹ [there / ‹ for ‹‹ to / ‹ and show / ‹ will arise / ‹ You
ished / time will / her,* / will come] / Zion, / mercy
have come. / the time

עֲבָדֶיךָ אֶת אֲבָנֶיהָ, וְאֶת עֲפָרָהּ יְחֹנֵנוּ. וְיִירְאוּ גוֹיִם אֶת שֵׁם

‹ the / ‹ will the / ‹ Then / ‹‹ they have / ‹ and her dust / ‹‹ her stones, / ‹ have Your
Name / nations / fear / favored. / servants

יהוה, וְכָל מַלְכֵי הָאָרֶץ אֶת כְּבוֹדֶךָ. כִּי בָנָה יהוה צִיּוֹן, נִרְאָה

‹ He will / ‹‹ Zion, / ‹ HASHEM will / ‹ For ‹‹ / [will fear] / ‹ of the / ‹ the / ‹ and ‹‹ / of
have appeared / have built / Your glory. / earth / kings / all / HASHEM,

---

כִּי שָׁכַחְתִּי מֵאֲכֹל לַחְמִי — For [in my despair] I have forgotten to eat my food. God does not remove the sources of revival. It is the despair of the afflicted person that causes him to neglect drawing upon the available spiritual nourishment that would enable him to bear his troubles bravely (R' S.R. Hirsch). With reference to Yom Kippur Katan this verse may be understood: For I have forgotten [to fulfill Your mitzvos; therefore I am abstaining today] from eating my food.

מִקּוֹל אַנְחָתִי דָּבְקָה עַצְמִי לִבְשָׂרִי — From the sound of my sigh, clung has my bone to my flesh. I have weakened my body by replacing my usual meals with sighing and groaning in prayer.

בִּי נִשְׁבָּעוּ — By me they curse. One who swears, calls upon himself severe punishment should his affirmation be false. In their oaths, Israel's enemies use her severe and well-known suffering as a synonym for punishment, "I should be like Israel if . . ."

יָמַי כְּצֵל נָטוּי — My days are like a shadow, lengthened, just before sunset which will soon disappear altogether. Thus, now, as today's shadows lengthen and the sun is about to set, I stand before You praying for personal and national pardon and an end to our millennia-long exile.

אַתָּה תָקוּם תְּרַחֵם צִיּוֹן — You will arise and show mercy to Zion; for [there will come] the time to favor her. The Midrash teaches: Nothing is more beloved than the Minchah prayer service . . . And what time did King David mean when he said, "My prayer is to You, HASHEM, at a time of

בְּכְבוֹדוֹ. פָּנָה אֶל תְּפִלַּת הָעַרְעָר, וְלֹא בָזָה אֶת תְּפִלָּתָם.

« their prayer. ⟨ have ⟨ and « of each ⟨ the prayer ⟨ to ⟨ He will « in His
despised not desolate one have turned glory.

תִּכָּתֵב זֹאת לְדוֹר אַחֲרוֹן, וְעַם נִבְרָא יְהַלֶּל יָהּ. כִּי הִשְׁקִיף

⟨He gazed ⟨For « God. ⟨ will ⟨ new- ⟨ so that ⟨ for a later ⟨ let this ⟨ Recorded
praise born the people generation, be

מִמְּרוֹם קָדְשׁוֹ, יהוה מִשָּׁמַיִם אֶל אֶרֶץ הִבִּיט. לִשְׁמֹעַ אֶנְקַת

⟨ the ⟨ To hear « looked ⟨ earth ⟨ to ⟨ from ⟨ HASHEM « Sanctuary; ⟨ from His
groaning down: heaven elevated

אָסִיר, לְפַתֵּחַ בְּנֵי תְמוּתָה. לְסַפֵּר בְּצִיּוֹן שֵׁם יהוה, וּתְהִלָּתוֹ

⟨ and His « of ⟨ the ⟨ in Zion ⟨ To « to die. ⟨ those ⟨ to « of the
praise HASHEM, Name declare condemned liberate prisoner;

בִּירוּשָׁלָיִם. בְּהִקָּבֵץ עַמִּים יַחְדָּו, וּמַמְלָכוֹת לַעֲבֹד אֶת יהוה.

« HASHEM. ⟨ [are gathered] ⟨ and « together, ⟨ peoples ⟨ when « in Jerusalem,
to serve kingdoms, gathered are

עִנָּה בַדֶּרֶךְ כֹּחִי, קִצַּר יָמָי. אֹמַר: אֵלִי, אַל תַּעֲלֵנִי בַּחֲצִי

⟨ in the ⟨ remove ⟨ do ⟨ O my ⟨ I say, « my ⟨ He has « my ⟨ through the ⟨ He has
midst me not God, days. shortened strength; wandering afflicted
[of exile]

יָמָי, בְּדוֹר דּוֹרִים שְׁנוֹתֶיךָ. לְפָנִים הָאָרֶץ יָסַדְתָּ, וּמַעֲשֵׂה

⟨ and the ⟨ foundation ⟨ the ⟨ Of old, « do Your ⟨ [endure] through « of my
work You laid, earth's* years. all generations days;*

יָדֶיךָ שָׁמָיִם. הֵמָּה יֹאבֵדוּ, וְאַתָּה תַעֲמֹד; וְכֻלָּם כַּבֶּגֶד

⟨ like a ⟨ all of « will ⟨ but You ⟨ will ⟨ They « is the ⟨ of Your
garment them endure; perish,* heavens.* hands

יִבְלוּ, כַּלְּבוּשׁ תַּחֲלִיפֵם וְיַחֲלֹפוּ. וְאַתָּה הוּא, וּשְׁנוֹתֶיךָ

⟨ and Your « remain ⟨ But You « and they ⟨ You will ⟨ like a cloak « will wear
years the same, will be gone.* exchange them out,

לֹא יִתָּמּוּ. בְּנֵי עֲבָדֶיךָ יִשְׁכּוֹנוּ, וְזַרְעָם לְפָנֶיךָ יִכּוֹן.

« will be ⟨ before ⟨ and their ⟨ shall be ⟨ of Your ⟨ The « will never end.
established. You children settled, servants children

---

favor''? (Psalm 69:14). He meant the time of the Minchah prayer (Aggadas Bereishis 77). Therefore, we, too, recite the Yom Kippur Katan prayers at the time of Minchah.

אַל תַּעֲלֵנִי בַּחֲצִי יָמָי — Do not remove me in the midst of my days. Throughout the exile, Israel says, "O God, do not allow us to be annihilated by our enemy in the middle of our historic experience." The history of Israel is inextricably bound up with God Himself, and of God, it says [below]: But You will endure...and Your years will never end. The children of Your servants shall be set-

tled, and their children before You will be established, eternally, for You are eternal (Rashi).

הָאָרֶץ ... שָׁמַיִם ... יאבדו — The earth ... the heavens ... will perish. Since heaven and earth are only creatures and not creators, they are in a constant state of flux and change and are subject to the ravages of time (Malbim). The most obvious of those never-ending changes are the phases of the moon which is at this moment in its invisible stage, for tonight will be Rosh Chodesh.

כַּלְּבוּשׁ תַּחֲלִיפֵם וְיַחֲלֹפוּ — Like a cloak You will exchange them and they will be gone. As God

IN MOST CONGREGATIONS THE FOLLOWING *PIYUT* IS RECITED RESPONSIVELY AS INDICATED IN THE INSTRUCTIONS BELOW. [IN SOME CONGREGATIONS, EACH STANZA IS CHANTED BY THE *CHAZZAN*, AND THE CONGREGATION THEN RECITES THE REFRAIN BETWEEN STANZAS.]

CHAZZAN, THEN CONGREGATION:

יוֹם זֶה* יְהִי מִשְׁקָל כָּל חַטֹּאתַי בָּטֵל בְּמִעוּטוֹ כִּדְמוּת יָרֵחַ

⟨ of the ⟨ like the ⟨⟨ in its ⟨ be ⟨ my sins ⟨ of all ⟨ the weight ⟨ let ⟨ On this day,*
moon   appearance smallness, nullified

הַיּוֹם,* לְבַד מִסְפַּר זְכֻיּוֹתַי יִרְבֶּה, וְיָצִיץ צִיץ וִיהִי פּוֹרֵחַ.[1]

⟨⟨ in bloom. ⟨ and ⟨ blossoms ⟨ give ⟨⟨ increase, ⟨ of my ⟨ may the ⟨ But ⟨⟨ today.*
be   forth   merits   amount

(יוֹם זֶה . . .)

(On this day . . .)

CONGREGATION, THEN *CHAZZAN*:

וַדַּאי, זְדוֹן לִבִּי אֶצְלוֹ גָלוּי, חוּטֵי עֲוֹנוֹתַי עִם דּוֹק רִשְׁעִי,

⟨⟨ of my ⟨ the ⟨ together ⟨ of my ⟨ — the ⟨⟨ revealed ⟨ is before ⟨ of my ⟨ the ⟨ Certainly
wickedness. cord with   sins   threads   Him   heart   guilt

דִּינִי אֲנִי אֵדַע בָּאֵשׁ קָלוּי, כִּי רַע וּבִישׁ אָרַגְתִּי אֶל פִּשְׁעִי,

⟨⟨ my ⟨ with ⟨ I have ⟨ and evil ⟨ bad- ⟨ for ⟨⟨ I be ⟨ [should be] ⟨ know, ⟨ I ⟨ My
defiance, woven   ness   burned, that in fire   judgment,

הוֹלֵךְ בְּיוֹם וָיוֹם אַחַר בִּצְעִי, מִבֵּית מְקוֹם סֵפֶר תִּינוֹק בּוֹרֵחַ.[2]

⟨⟨ fleeing ⟨ [I was like] ⟨ of ⟨ of the ⟨ from the ⟨⟨ my extorted ⟨ after ⟨ after ⟨ day ⟨ going
[from school]. a child study place house   profit,   day

(יוֹם זֶה . . .)

(On this day . . .)

CONGREGATION, THEN *CHAZZAN*:

אָכֵן בְּחַבְלֵי שָׁוְא עֲוֹן מוֹשֵׁךְ[3] אָחוֹר, לְךָ אֵלִי בָּאתִי נִצָּב,

⟨⟨ to stand ⟨ I have ⟨ my ⟨ Before ⟨⟨ backwards. ⟨ pulls ⟨ iniquity ⟨⟨ of ⟨ with ⟨ Indeed,
come   God,   You,   [us]   falsehood,   ropes

רְפֻאוֹת לְאֶרֶס מַר נָחָשׁ נוֹשֵׁךְ,* שׁוֹאֵל וּמִתְחַנֵּן, נִכְאָב נֶעֱצָב,

⟨⟨ and ⟨ Pained ⟨⟨ and to ⟨ to ⟨⟨ that ⟨ from the ⟨ that is ⟨ for the ⟨ — a cure
saddened,   entreat. request   bites* — serpent   bitter   poison

_____

(1) Cf. *Numbers* 17:23. (2) 10:35, cf. *Ramban*. (3) Cf. *Isaiah* 5:18.

_____

says (*Isaiah* 65:17), "For behold! I am creating new heavens and a new earth ..." (*Metzudas David*).

יוֹם זֶה — *On this day.* This *piyut* was composed by R' Yehudah Aryeh ben Yitzchak de Modena [of 16th-17th-century Venice], who signed his name יְהוּדָה אַרְיֵה מִמּוֹדֵינָא in the acrostic.

הַיּוֹם — *Today.* On the day before Rosh Chodesh we pray that the measure of our sins diminish until it is invisible like today's moon.

נָחָשׁ נוֹשֵׁךְ — *The serpent that bites.* Man's Evil Inclination is often personified as the original serpent that tempted Adam and Eve in the Garden of Eden and induced them to sin.

יוֹשֵׁב בְּעִנּוּיֵי אֶבֶן* מַחְצָב, יָד פֶּה וָעַיִן אֵין לִי טַעַם וָרֵיחַ.

‹‹ or ‹ [nor] a sense ‹‹ I have ‹ and ‹ mouth, ‹ a ‹‹ of the ‹ of the ‹ with the ‹ dwelling
smell. of taste not, eye hand, quarry, stone* afflictions

(יוֹם זֶה . . .)

(On this day . . .)

CONGREGATION, THEN *CHAZZAN*:

הֵן רֹאשׁ חֳדָשִׁים אֶל עַמְּךָ נָתַתָּ,

‹ You have given ‹ Your people ‹ to ‹ Moons ‹ New ‹ Behold,

לִזְמַן כַּפָּרָה עַל כָּל תּוֹלְדוֹתָם,*¹

‹‹ their offspring.* ‹ all ‹ for ‹ of atonement ‹ as a time

מֵאֵת אֲהוּבֶיךָ שׂוֹטֵן הַשְׁבֵּת, עַל כֵּן אֲקַדֶּמְךָ בְּתַחֲנָתָם

‹ with their ‹ I approach ‹ therefore, ‹‹ You ‹ the [words ‹ Your beloved ‹ From
supplications You annulled; of the] Accuser ones,

מִיּוֹם לְפָנָיו בָּא, כִּי אָז* אֵיתָם,²

‹‹ I will be ‹ then* ‹ so ‹‹ that ‹ on the
faultless, that precedes it, day

אָשׁוּב לְאִישׁ תּוֹשָׁב לֹא עוֹד אוֹרֵחַ.*

‹‹ a sojourner.* ‹ longer ‹ and ‹‹ who is a ‹ to being ‹ [and] I will
no resident, a person return

(יוֹם זֶה . . .)

(On this day . . .)

CONGREGATION, THEN *CHAZZAN*:

וּבְרֹב חֲסָדֶיךָ, אַתָּה מַלְכִּי תָּקוּם תְּרַחֵם אֶת צִיּוֹן³ קָדְשֵׁנוּ,

‹‹ our ‹ on Zion, ‹ and have ‹ shall arise ‹ my King, ‹ You, ‹‹ kindness, ‹ With Your
Sanctuary. mercy abundant

דִּירַת מְנוּחָתְךָ שִׂים כָּבוֹד,

‹‹ glory, ‹ give ‹ of Your dwelling ‹ To the abode

כִּי בָהּ נַעֲלֶה עוֹלוֹת רָאשֵׁי חֳדָשֵׁנוּ,

‹‹ Moons. ‹ of our ‹ the burnt- ‹ we will ‹ in it ‹ for
New offerings bring up

---

(1) From *Mussaf Rosh Chodesh.* (2) *Psalms* 19:14. (3) Cf. 102:14.

אֶבֶן — *Stone.* The prophet refers to the tendency to obstinacy as לֵב הָאֶבֶן, *the heart of stone,* and a frame of mind that is receptive to holiness as לֵב בָּשָׂר, *a heart of flesh* (Ezekiel 11:19).

עַל כָּל תּוֹלְדוֹתָם — *For all their offspring.* The burnt-offering of Rosh Chodesh is brought to atone for certain inadvertent improprieties that have taken place during the previous month and of which the perpetrator is totally unaware (see *Rashi* to *Numbers* 28:15). Those incidents are referred to as the תּוֹלְדוֹת, literally *offspring,* of the month (*Beis Yosef* 423 citing *Orchos Chaim* and *R' Yehudah HaLevi*).

אָז — *Then.* I pray for atonement today, the day before Rosh Chodesh, so that I will *then,* on Rosh Chodesh, be unsullied by sin.

תּוֹשָׁב לֹא עוֹד אוֹרֵחַ — *A resident, and no longer a sojourner.* I will devote myself totally to the service of God, and no longer serve Him sporadically.

נָא אֵל שְׁלַח נוֹשֵׂא נֵזֶר* רֹאשֵׁנוּ,

》 of our heads. 〈 the 〈 the one who 〈 send 〈 God, 〈 Please,
crown* will bear
[us]

(יוֹם זֶה . . .)

(On this day . . .)

כִּי שָׁם לְבָבֵנוּ שׁוֹאֵף זוֹרֵחַ.[1]

》 [to behold its] 〈 yearn, 〈 that our 〈 it is 〈 For
radiance. hearts there

WHEN YOM KIPPUR KATTAN IS OBSERVED ON *EREV ROSH CHODESH*, PSALM 20, יַעַנְךָ ה' בְּיוֹם צָרָה
(PAGE 216), IS SAID HERE, AND PSALM 8 IS SAID AT THE END OF THE SERVICE (PAGE 668).

—————— Psalm 8 / תהלים ח ——————

לַמְנַצֵּחַ עַל הַגִּתִּית, מִזְמוֹר לְדָוִד. יהוה אֲדֹנֵינוּ, מָה אַדִּיר

〈 mighty 〈 how 〈our Master, 〈 HASHEM, 〈 by David. 〈 a psalm 〈 the *gittis*, 〈 on 〈 For the conductor,

שִׁמְךָ בְּכָל הָאָרֶץ, אֲשֶׁר תְּנָה הוֹדְךָ עַל הַשָּׁמָיִם. מִפִּי עוֹלְלִים

〈 of 〈 Out of 》the heavens. 〈 on 〈 Your 〈 places 〈 [You] 》 the 〈 through- 〈is Your
babes the mouth majesty Who earth, out Name

וְיֹנְקִים יִסַּדְתָּ עֹז, לְמַעַן צוֹרְרֶיךָ, לְהַשְׁבִּית אוֹיֵב וּמִתְנַקֵּם.

》 and 〈 enemy 〈 to silence 》 Your 〈 because 》 strength, 〈 have You 〈 and
avenger. foes, of established sucklings

כִּי אֶרְאֶה שָׁמֶיךָ מַעֲשֵׂה אֶצְבְּעֹתֶיךָ, יָרֵחַ וְכוֹכָבִים, אֲשֶׁר

〈 that 〈 and the stars 〈 the 》 of Your fingers, 〈 the work 〈 Your 〈 I behold 〈When
moon heavens,

כּוֹנָנְתָּה. מָה אֱנוֹשׁ כִּי תִזְכְּרֶנּוּ, וּבֶן אָדָם כִּי תִפְקְדֶנּוּ.

》You should 〈 that 〈 of [mortal] 〈 and 》 You should 〈 that 〈 [frail] 〈 [I think,] 》 You have
be mindful man the son remember him, man What is set in place.
of him?

וַתְּחַסְּרֵהוּ מְּעַט מֵאֱלֹהִים, וְכָבוֹד וְהָדָר תְּעַטְּרֵהוּ. תַּמְשִׁילֵהוּ

〈 You give him 》 have You 〈 and 〈 and with 》 than the 〈 but 〈 Yet, You have
dominion crowned him. splendor soul angels, slightly, made him less,

בְּמַעֲשֵׂי יָדֶיךָ, כֹּל שַׁתָּה תַחַת רַגְלָיו. צֹנֶה וַאֲלָפִים כֻּלָּם, וְגַם

〈 even 》 all of 〈 and cattle, 〈 sheep 》 his feet: 〈 under 〈 You 〈 every- 》 of Your 〈 over the
them, placed thing hands, work

בַּהֲמוֹת שָׂדָי. צִפּוֹר שָׁמַיִם וּדְגֵי הַיָּם, עֹבֵר אָרְחוֹת יַמִּים.

》 of the 〈 the 〈 for [man even] 》 of 〈 and 〈 of the 〈 the birds 》of the 〈 the beasts
sea. lanes traverses the sea; the fish sky field;

יהוה אֲדֹנֵינוּ, מָה אַדִּיר שִׁמְךָ בְּכָל הָאָרֶץ.

》 the earth! 〈 through- 〈is Your 〈 mighty 〈 how 〈 our 〈 HASHEM,
out Name Master,

---

(1) *Ecclesiastes* 1:5.

נוֹשֵׂא נֵזֶר — *The one who will bear the crown.*
This refers to either the *Mashiach* [the Mes-
siah], who will wear the royal crown, for it is

he who will build the Sanctuary of which we
speak, or to the *Kohen Gadol*, whose forehead
is crowned with the golden *Tzitz* and who will

THE CONGREGATION RECITES THE REGULAR WEEKDAY *MINCHAH* PRAYERS (P. 351).

[IF AT LEAST TEN ARE FASTING, THE TORAH AND *HAFTARAH* ARE READ, FOLLOWING THE ORDER OF PUBLIC FAST DAYS. ONE OF THOSE FASTING SHOULD SERVE AS THE *CHAZZAN*. AS ON OTHER PUBLIC FAST DAYS, THE REPETITION OF *SHEMONEH ESREI* SHOULD INCLUDE עֲנֵנוּ AS AN INDEPENDENT BLESSING BEFORE רְפָאֵנוּ; AND בִּרְכַּת כֹּהֲנִים AND שִׂים שָׁלוֹם SHOULD BE RECITED.]

WHOEVER IS FASTING INCLUDES עֲנֵנוּ BEFORE כִּי אַתָּה שׁוֹמֵעַ.

THE REMAINDER OF THE YOM KIPPUR KATAN SERVICE IS RECITED IMMEDIATELY AFTER THE *CHAZZAN'S* REPETITION, BEFORE HE RECITES THE *KADDISH*.

ALL RECITE:

לְכוּ וְנָשׁוּבָה אֶל יהוה, כִּי הוּא טָרָף וְיִרְפָּאֵנוּ, יַךְ וְיַחְבְּשֵׁנוּ.

‹ and He ‹ He has ‹‹ and He will ‹ has ‹ He ‹ for ‹‹ Hashem, ‹ to ‹ let us return ‹ Come,
will cure / smitten / heal us; / stricken
us. / [us] / [us]

יְחַיֵּנוּ מִיֹּמָיִם, בַּיּוֹם הַשְּׁלִישִׁי יְקִמֵנוּ וְנִחְיֶה לְפָנָיו.¹ כִּי לֹא עַל

‹ be- ‹ not ‹ For ‹‹ before ‹ and we ‹ He will ‹ on the third day ‹‹ after two ‹ He will
cause / Him. / will live / lift us up / days; / revive us

צִדְקֹתֵינוּ אֲנַחְנוּ מַפִּילִים תַּחֲנוּנֵינוּ לְפָנֶיךָ, כִּי עַל רַחֲמֶיךָ

‹ of Your ‹ be- ‹ but ‹‹ before ‹ our ‹ cast ‹ do we ‹ of our
compassion / cause / You; / supplications / righteousness

הָרַבִּים. אֲדֹנָי שְׁמָעָה, אֲדֹנָי סְלָחָה, אֲדֹנָי הַקְשִׁיבָה וַעֲשֵׂה,

‹‹ and ‹ be attentive, ‹ O Lord, ‹‹ forgive; ‹ O Lord, ‹‹ heed; ‹ O Lord, ‹‹ which is
act, / abundant.

אַל תְּאַחַר, לְמַעַנְךָ אֱלֹהַי, כִּי שִׁמְךָ נִקְרָא עַל עִירְךָ וְעַל

‹ and ‹ Your ‹ upon ‹ is ‹ Your ‹ for ‹‹ my God, ‹ for Your ‹‹ delay; ‹ do
upon / city / proclaimed / Name / sake, / not

עַמֶּךָ.*²

‹‹ Your
people.*

THE FOLLOWING VERSE IS RECITED THREE TIMES BY THE *CHAZZAN*, THEN THREE TIMES BY THE CONGREGATION:

הֲשִׁיבֵנוּ יהוה אֵלֶיךָ* וְנָשׁוּבָה, חַדֵּשׁ יָמֵינוּ כְּקֶדֶם.³

‹‹ as of old. ‹ our ‹ renew ‹‹ and we ‹ to ‹‹ Hashem, ‹ Bring us
days / shall return; / You,* / back,

---

(1) *Hosea* 6:1-2. (2) *Daniel* 9:18-19. (3) *Lamentations* 5:21.

lead the services in that Sanctuary.

כִּי שִׁמְךָ נִקְרָא עַל עִירְךָ וְעַל עַמֶּךָ — *For Your Name is proclaimed upon Your city and upon Your people.* Each nation is assigned an angel to oversee its fortunes, but God Himself maintains personal dominion over Israel and Jerusalem

(*Tikkunei Zohar*).

הֲשִׁיבֵנוּ ה' אֵלֶיךָ — *Bring us back, Hashem, to You.* The Jewish soul cries out that it wants to find its way back to the spiritual greatness of yore. If only God would help us begin, we would continue with alacrity.

AN INDIVIDUAL PRAYING WITHOUT A *MINYAN* OMITS THE NEXT TWO PARAGRAPHS,
BEGINNING אֵל מֶלֶךְ, O GOD, KING, AND ה', HASHEM.

אֵל מֶלֶךְ יוֹשֵׁב עַל כִּסֵּא רַחֲמִים, מִתְנַהֵג בַּחֲסִידוּת, מוֹחֵל

O God, ⟩ King ⟩⟩ Who ⟩ on ⟩ the ⟩ of mercy, ⟩⟩ Who acts ⟨ with ⟩⟩ Who ⟨
sits throne kindness, pardons

עֲוֹנוֹת עַמּוֹ, מַעֲבִיר רִאשׁוֹן רִאשׁוֹן,* מַרְבֶּה מְחִילָה לְחַטָּאִים

the sins ⟩ of His ⟩⟩ Who ⟩ [sins] one ⟩⟩ by one,* ⟨ Who abun- ⟩⟩ pardon ⟩ to uninten-
people, removes dantly grants tional sinners

וּסְלִיחָה לַפּוֹשְׁעִים, עֹשֶׂה צְדָקוֹת עִם כָּל בָּשָׂר וָרוּחַ, לֹא

and ⟨ forgiveness ⟩ to willful ⟨ Who ⟩⟩ acts of ⟨ with ⟩ all ⟨ [beings ⟩ and ⟨ — not ⟩⟩
sinners, performs generosity of] flesh spirit

כְּרָעָתָם תִּגְמוֹל. ❖ אֵל הוֹרֵיתָ לָּנוּ לוֹמַר שְׁלֹשׁ עֶשְׂרֵה,

in accord with ⟩ do You repay ⟩⟩ them! ⟨ O ⟨ You ⟩ us ⟨ to recite ⟩ the Thirteen ⟩⟩
their wickedness God, taught [Attributes of Mercy];

וּזְכֹר לָנוּ הַיּוֹם בְּרִית שְׁלֹשׁ עֶשְׂרֵה,* כְּמוֹ שֶׁהוֹדַעְתָּ לֶעָנָיו

remember ⟩ for us ⟩ today ⟨ the ⟨ of [these] Thirteen,* ⟩⟩ as ⟨ You made ⟩ to the
covenant known humble one
[Moses]

מִקֶּדֶם, כְּמוֹ שֶׁכָּתוּב, וַיֵּרֶד יְהוָה בֶּעָנָן וַיִּתְיַצֵּב עִמּוֹ שָׁם,

in ancient ⟩⟩ as ⟨ it is written: ⟩ And HASHEM ⟩⟩ descended ⟨ in a cloud ⟨ and stood ⟩ with ⟨ there, ⟩⟩
times, him

וַיִּקְרָא בְשֵׁם יְהוָה.

and He ⟩ called out ⟨ with the ⟨ of ⟩⟩
Name HASHEM.

CONGREGATION AND *CHAZZAN* RECITE LOUDLY AND IN UNISON:

וַיַּעֲבֹר יְהוָה עַל פָּנָיו וַיִּקְרָא:

And HASHEM passed ⟩ before ⟨ [Moses'] ⟩⟩ and ⟩⟩
face, proclaimed:

⧼ / י"ג מִדּוֹת הָרַחֲמִים

The Thirteen Attributes of Mercy

מַעֲבִיר רִאשׁוֹן רִאשׁוֹן — *Who removes [sins] one by one.* According to the teachings of Beis Hillel [the Academy of Hillel], God, Who is רַב חֶסֶד, *Abundant in Kindness*, מַטֶּה כְלַפֵּי חֶסֶד, *tips [the scales of justice] toward kindness.* The Academy of R' Yishmael explains that God accomplishes this by removing sins one by one, meaning that if one's good deeds are equivalent to his sins, God removes a sin from the balance so that the side of virtue outweighs the side of

sin (*Rashi*). *Rif* interprets that if someone has committed a particular sin for the first time, God holds it in abeyance and does not include it in the calculation, as long as it has not yet become habitual. *Rambam*, based on *Yoma* 86b, writes that the first two sins are removed (*Hil. Teshuvah* 3:5).

בְּרִית שְׁלֹשׁ עֶשְׂרֵה — *The covenant of [these] Thirteen.* R' Yehudah taught that God sealed a covenant with Moses and Israel that the recitation of the Thirteen Attributes would never be in vain (*Rosh Hashanah* 17b).

יהוה, יהוה,* אֵל, רַחוּם, וְחַנּוּן, אֶֽרֶךְ אַפַּֽיִם, וְרַב חֶֽסֶד, וֶאֱמֶת,

⟨⟨ and ⟨ in ⟨ and ⟨ to anger, ⟨ Slow ⟨⟨ and ⟨ Compas- ⟨ God, ⟨ HASHEM,* ⟨ HASHEM,
Truth, Kindness Abundant Gracious, sionate

נֹצֵר חֶֽסֶד לָאֲלָפִים, נֹשֵׂא עָוֹן, וָפֶֽשַׁע, וְחַטָּאָה, וְנַקֵּה.¹

⟨⟨ and Who ⟨ and inad- ⟨ willful ⟨ of ⟨ Forgiver ⟨⟨ for thousands ⟨ of ⟨ Preserver
absolves. vertent sin, sin, iniquity, [of generations], kindness

---

(1) *Exodus* 34:5-7.

ה' ה' — HASHEM, HASHEM. There are various opinions regarding how to enumerate the Thirteen Attributes. We follow the generally accepted view of *Rabbeinu Tam* (*Rosh Hashanah* 17b):

(1) ה' — HASHEM. This Name [containing the letters of הָיָה הֹוֶה יִהְיֶה, *He was, He is, He will be*] designates God as the מְהֻוֶּה, *Prime Cause*, of everything. It is only natural that He wishes to assure the survival of all that He brought into being. Consequently, this Name represents the Attribute of Mercy. In addition, the Name's spelling implies God's timelessness. Though man may sin, he can repent and call upon the timeless God to restore him to his original innocent state. As the Talmud states: אֲנִי הוּא קֹודֶם שֶׁיֶּחֱטָא הָאָדָם, *I am He* [the God of Mercy] *before a person sins*, וַאֲנִי הוּא לְאַחַר שֶׁיֶּחֱטָא הָאָדָם וְיַעֲשֶׂה תְּשׁוּבָה, *and I am He after a person sins and repents* (*Rosh Hashanah* 17b). Based on this dictum, *Rabbeinu Tam* counts the twin use of the Name HASHEM as two attributes. The first is that God is merciful before a person sins, even though He knows that the sin will be committed. And . . .

(2) ה' — HASHEM. God is merciful after the sin has been committed, by granting the sinner time to repent, and by accepting his repentance, though it may be imperfect.

(3) אֵל — *God*. This Name denotes the power of God's mercy, which sometimes surpasses even the compassion indicated by the name HASHEM. He displays this higher degree of mercy to genuinely righteous people who sin, but repent. In return for their previous behavior, God exerts Himself, as it were, to ensure their survival.

(4) רַחוּם — *Compassionate*. In response to pleas for mercy, God eases the suffering of those being punished for their sins. Another manifestation of compassion is that God does not confront deserving people with overpowering temptation.

(5) וְחַנּוּן — *And Gracious*. God is gracious even

to those unworthy of His kindness. Also, if someone finds himself lacking in the willpower to avoid sin and he seeks God's help, he will be given it.

(6) אֶֽרֶךְ אַפַּֽיִם — *Slow to anger*, so that the sinner will have time to repent.

(7) וְרַב חֶֽסֶד — *And Abundant in Kindness*. God shows great kindness to those who lack personal merits. The Talmud teaches, as described above, that God exercises this attribute by removing sins from the scale of justice, thus tilting the scales in favor of merit.

(8) וֶאֱמֶת — *And Truth*. God never reneges; His promise to reward the deserving will be carried out unequivocally.

(9) נֹצֵר חֶֽסֶד לָאֲלָפִים — *Preserver of kindness for thousands [of generations]*. The deeds of the righteous — especially those who serve Him out of intense love — bring benefits to their offspring far into the future.

(10) נֹשֵׂא עָוֹן — *Forgiver of iniquity*. God forgives the intentional sinner, if he repents.

(11) וָפֶֽשַׁע — *[Forgiver of] willful sin*. Even the one who rebels against God and purposely seeks to anger Him is given an opportunity to repent.

(12) וְחַטָּאָה — *And [Forgiver of] inadvertent sin*. God forgives the person who repents of sins committed out of carelessness or apathy. Having already praised God as the Forgiver of intentional sin and rebelliousness, why do we revert to praising Him for this seemingly lesser level of mercy? Because if someone repents out of fear rather than love, his intentional sins are reduced in severity and are treated by God as if they had been done in error. Thus, even after having partially forgiven the intentional sins by reducing their severity, God further forgives those who continue to repent for these lesser sins.

(13) וְנַקֵּה — *And Who absolves*. God wipes away the sins of those who repent sincerely, as if they had never existed.

וְסָלַחְתָּ לַעֲוֹנֵנוּ וּלְחַטָּאתֵנוּ וּנְחַלְתָּנוּ.[1] סְלַח לָנוּ אָבִינוּ כִּי

⟨ for ⟨⟨ our Father, ⟨ us, ⟨ Forgive ⟨⟨ and make us ⟨⟨ and our sins, ⟨ our iniquities ⟨ May You forgive

חָטָאנוּ, מְחַל לָנוּ מַלְכֵּנוּ כִּי פָשָׁעְנוּ.[2] כִּי אַתָּה אֲדֹנָי טוֹב

⟨ are good ⟨ O Lord, ⟨ You, ⟨ For ⟨⟨ we have willfully sinned. ⟨ for ⟨⟨ our King, ⟨ us, ⟨ pardon ⟨⟨ we have sinned.

וְסַלָּח, וְרַב חֶסֶד לְכָל קֹרְאֶיךָ.[3]

⟨⟨ who call upon You. ⟨ to all ⟨ kind ⟨ and ⟨⟨ and abundantly forgiving,

ALL CONTINUE:

אָנָּא יהוה אֱלֹהֵי הַשָּׁמַיִם, תִּכּוֹן תְּפִלָּתֵנוּ קְטֹרֶת לְפָנֶיךָ,[4]

⟨⟨ before You. ⟨ as incense ⟨ should be ⟨ considered ⟨⟨ our prayers ⟨⟨ of Heaven, ⟨ God ⟨ HASHEM, ⟨ Please,

וְתוֹצִיא כָאוֹר צִדְקֵנוּ וּמִשְׁפָּטֵנוּ כַּצָּהֳרָיִם.[5] אֲמָרֵינוּ הַאֲזִינָה

⟨ hear, ⟨ Our words ⟨⟨ like the high noon. ⟨ and our justice ⟨⟨ our righteousness, ⟨ like a light ⟨ Bring forth

יהוה, בִּינָה הֲגִיגֵנוּ,[6] בְּקָרְאֵנוּ עֲנֵנוּ אֱלֹהֵי צִדְקֵנוּ.[7]

⟨⟨ of our vindication. ⟨ O God ⟨ answer ⟨ When we call, ⟨⟨ our thoughts. ⟨ perceive ⟨⟨ HASHEM;

כְּרַחֵם אָב עַל בָּנִים, כֵּן תְּרַחֵם יהוה עָלֵינוּ.[8] לַיהוה

⟨ To HASHEM ⟨⟨ on us. ⟨ HASHEM, ⟨ have mercy, ⟨ so ⟨⟨ his children, ⟨ toward ⟨ a father is ⟨ As merciful as

הַיְשׁוּעָה, עַל עַמְּךָ בִרְכָתֶךָ סֶּלָה.[9] יהוה צְבָאוֹת עִמָּנוּ,

⟨⟨ is with us, ⟨ Master of Legions, ⟨ HASHEM, ⟨⟨ Selah. ⟨ is Your blessing, ⟨ Your people ⟨ upon ⟨⟨ is salvation,

מִשְׂגָּב לָנוּ אֱלֹהֵי יַעֲקֹב סֶלָה.[10] יהוה צְבָאוֹת, אַשְׁרֵי אָדָם

⟨ is the man ⟨ — praise-worthy ⟨⟨ Master of Legions ⟨ HASHEM, ⟨⟨ Selah. ⟨ of Jacob, ⟨ is the God ⟨ for us ⟨ a stronghold

בֹּטֵחַ בָּךְ.[11] יהוה הוֹשִׁיעָה, הַמֶּלֶךְ יַעֲנֵנוּ בְיוֹם קָרְאֵנוּ.[12]

⟨⟨ we call. ⟨ on the day ⟨ answer us ⟨ May the King ⟨⟨ save! ⟨ HASHEM, ⟨⟨ in You. ⟨ who trusts

❖ **סְלַח** נָא לַעֲוֹן הָעָם הַזֶּה כְּגֹדֶל חַסְדֶּךָ, וְכַאֲשֶׁר נָשָׂאתָה

⟨ You have forgiven ⟨ and as ⟨⟨ of Your kindness, ⟨ according to the greatness ⟨ of this people ⟨ the ⟨ please, ⟨ Forgive, iniquity

---

(1) *Exodus* 34:9. (2) From the weekday *Shemoneh Esrei*. (3) *Psalms* 86:5. (4) Cf. 141:2. (5) Cf. 37:6. (6) Cf. 5:2. (7) Cf. 4:2. (8) Cf. 103:13. (9) 3:9. (10) 46:8. (11) 84:13. (12) 20:10.

In the Torah, the verse continues לֹא יְנַקֶּה, *He does not absolve*. The simple interpretation of the verse is that God does not completely erase the sin, but He exacts retribution in minute stages. The Talmud (*Yoma* 86a), however, explains that *He absolves* the sins of those who

לָעָם הַזֶּה מִמִּצְרַיִם וְעַד הֵנָּה,¹ וְשָׁם נֶאֱמַר:

《 it was said: 〈 And there 〈 now. 〈 until 〈 from Egypt 〈 this people

ALL, ALOUD AND IN UNISON:

וַיֹּאמֶר יהוה סָלַחְתִּי כִּדְבָרֶךָ.²

《 according to your word! 〈 I have forgiven 《 And Hashem said:

ALL CONTINUE:

הַטֵּה אֱלֹהַי אָזְנְךָ וּשְׁמָע, פְּקַח עֵינֶיךָ וּרְאֵה שֹׁמְמֹתֵינוּ,

《 our desolation, 〈 and see 〈 Your eyes 〈 open 《 and listen; 〈 Your ear, 〈 my God, 〈 Incline,

וְהָעִיר אֲשֶׁר נִקְרָא שִׁמְךָ עָלֶיהָ, כִּי לֹא עַל צִדְקֹתֵינוּ אֲנַחְנוּ

〈 do we 〈 of our 〈 because 〈 not 〈 for 《 upon; 〈 Your Name is 〈 which 〈 and that
righteousness proclaimed [of] the city

מַפִּילִים תַּחֲנוּנֵינוּ לְפָנֶיךָ, כִּי עַל רַחֲמֶיךָ הָרַבִּים. אֲדֹנָי

〈 O Lord, 《 which is 〈 of Your 〈 because 〈 but 《 before 〈 our 〈 cast
abundant. compassion, You; supplications

שְׁמָעָה, אֲדֹנָי סְלָחָה, אֲדֹנָי הַקְשִׁיבָה, וַעֲשֵׂה אַל תְּאַחַר,

《 delay; 〈 do not 《 and act, 〈 be attentive, 〈 O Lord, 《 forgive; 〈 O Lord, 《 heed;

לְמַעַנְךָ אֱלֹהַי, כִּי שִׁמְךָ נִקְרָא עַל עִירְךָ וְעַל עַמֶּךָ.³

《 Your 〈 and 〈 Your 〈 upon 〈 is 〈 Your 〈 for 《 my God, 〈 for Your
people. upon City proclaimed Name sake,

**IN MOST CONGREGATIONS, THE FOLLOWING *PIYUT* IS RECITED RESPONSIVELY.
THE *CHAZZAN* CHANTS THE FIRST THREE LINES OF EACH STANZA
AND THE CONGREGATION RESPONDS WITH THE FOURTH LINE.**

אֱלֹהֵינוּ וֵאלֹהֵי אֲבוֹתֵינוּ

《 of our fathers: 〈 and God 〈 Our God

מַשְׂאַת כַּפַּי,* מִנְחַת עֶרֶב,⁴ רְצֵה נָא בְכֹשֶׁר,

《 as proper. 〈 please, 〈 accept, 《 of the 〈 as an 〈 of my 〈 The lifting
afternoon, offering hands*

תִּכּוֹן תְּפִלָּתִי קְטֹרֶת לְפָנֶיךָ,⁴ בְּתֹם וּבְיֹשֶׁר,

《 and with 〈 with 〈 before 〈 as 〈 should be 〈 Considered
integrity. sincerity You, incense my prayer

בְּקָרְאִי עֲנֵנִי צוּרִי הַיּוֹם יִפְנֶה,

《 is coming 〈 for the 《 O my 〈 answer 〈 When I
to a close, day Rock, me, call out,

---

(1) *Numbers* 14:19. (2) 14:20. (3) *Daniel* 9:18-19. (4) *Psalms* 141:2.

truly repent; but *He does not absolve* the sins of those who do not repent.

◆§ מַשְׂאַת כַּפַּי — *The lifting of my hands.* This *piyut* was composed by מָרְדְּכַי בַּר שַׁבְּתַי אָרוֹךְ, *Mordechai bar Shabsi Aroch*, as attested to by

the acrostic of the stanzas. We know that he lived sometime before 1234 when *Arugas Ha-Bosem* [which comments on many *piyutim*, including his works] was written. As noted earlier, the Yom Kippur Katan service was

CONG.— **כַּאֲשֶׁר יָבִיאוּ בְנֵי יִשְׂרָאֵל אֶת הַמִּנְחָה.**[*1]

just as — [when] — the — of Israel — « the *minchah*-offering.*
they bring « Children «

רֵיחַ נִיחֹחַ אִמְרֵי פִי, לְפָנֶיךָ צוּר עוֹלָמִים,

Like an satisfying expressions may the that is before O Rock of eternity;
aroma [be] of my mouth You,

**חֶלְבִּי* וְדָמִי הַנִּמְעַט בְּצוֹמִי, תְּמוּר חֲלָבִים וְדָמִים,*

may my may my and my that are being through be in of the fats « and the bloods [of
fat* blood diminished my fast place the Altar offerings].*

קַבֵּל הֶגְיוֹן לִבִּי[2] אֲשֶׁר עָרַכְתִּי הַיּוֹם בַּנְּעִימִים,

Accept the thoughts of my that I have set today « with sweetness,
heart forth

CONG.— **כַּחַטָּאת כָּעֹלָה וְכַמִּנְחָה.**[3]

like the — like the and like the
sin-offering, burnt-offering. *minchah*-offering.

**דְּרשׁ נָא בְיוֹם זֶה[4] דּוֹרְשֶׁיךָ, וְהִדָּרֶשׁ לָהֶם בְּנִיב שְׂפָתָיִם,*[5]

Seek, please, on this day, « those who and respond to them with the of [Your]
seek You, speech lips.*

**שְׁעֵה לְמַעֲמָדָם וְטַהֲרֵם כַּכֶּסֶף מְזֻקָּק שִׁבְעָתָיִם,*[6]

Turn toward their stand « like silver and purify them refined seven times.

וּרְצֵה שִׂיחָתָם כְּשֶׂה אַחַת מִן הַצֹּאן מִן הַמָּאתָיִם,

Be favorable their like a singular from « the flock of two hundred
toward supplications lamb

CONG.— **מִמַּשְׁקֵה יִשְׂרָאֵל לְמִנְחָה.**[7]

of the choicest of Israel « for a *minchah*-offering.
[animals]

כָּלִיל וְעוֹלָה תְּחִנָּתִי תֵּחָשֵׁב, וּמַשְׂטִינַי רִיב תָּרִיב,

Like a burnt- may my be con- « [Against] my a You should
completely offering supplication sidered. adversaries battle fight.
consumed

(1) Isaiah 66:20. (2) Cf. Psalms 19:15. (3) Ezekiel 45:25. (4) Cf. I Kings 22:5.
(5) Cf. Isaiah 57:19. (6) Cf. Psalms 12:7. (7) Ezekiel 45:15.

instituted in the 16th century, at least 300 years after the time of R' Mordechai. In truth, this *piyut* was originally written for Yom Kippur and is still recited during *Minchah* of that day in some congregations.

(הַ)מִּנְחָה — *Minchah*. This word, with or without a prefix, appears as the last word of each stanza and has been left untranslated. Depending on context, it can refer to a meal-offering,

specifically, the one that is part of the afternoon *tamid* [continual] offering; any Altar offering; or a gift of any kind. In some instances it may be understood in more than one way.

חֶלְבִּי...וְדָמִים — *My fat...and the bloods [of the Altar offerings]*. One who is not fasting should omit this line.

בְּנִיב שְׂפָתָיִם — *With the speech of [Your] lips*, by saying סָלַחְתִּי, *I have forgiven* (Etz Yosef).

וְתוֹצִיא כָאוֹר צִדְקֶי,¹ טֶרֶם יָבֹא הַשֶּׁמֶשׁ וְיַעֲרִיב,

« and sets. ‹ the sun descends ‹ before « my ‹ like a ‹ And bring out
righteousness, light

שְׁפֹךְ כַּמַּיִם לִבּוֹ² בִּתְפִלָּתוֹ כָּל אִישׁ,

« man. ‹ is each ‹ in his prayer ‹ his ‹ like ‹ Pouring
heart water out

³מִנְחָה. לַיהוה קָרְבָּנוּ הַמַּקְרִיב וְהִקְרִיב — CONG.

« a minchah - ‹ to ‹ his « — the one «« And he brings
offering. HASHEM, offering who brings —

יְשֻׁרוּן עַמְּךָ יָשִׁיר חַסְדְּךָ בְּטוּב לֶקַח,⁴

« portion. ‹ with a ‹ of Your ‹ sings ‹ Your ‹ Jeshurun
good kindness people

הַטֵּה אֵלָיו אָזְנְךָ וּשְׁמַע, וְעֵינֶיךָ פְּקַח,

« open ‹ and Your eyes « and hear; ‹ Your ear ‹ to them ‹ Incline

⁵וּרְאֵה כִּי טוֹב מִסְתּוֹפֵף בְּשַׁעֲרֵי רַחֲמֶיךָ,

« of Your ‹ of the gates ‹ standing on ‹ they ‹ that ‹ and see
mercy. the threshold favor

⁶מִנְחָה. בְּיָדוֹ הַבָּא מִן וַיִּקַּח — CONG.

« as a minchah - ‹ to their ‹ that ‹ from ‹ And they have
offering. hand which came taken [along],

⁷בְּרֹב רַחֲמֶיךָ אֲמָרַי הַאֲזִינָה יהוה, הֲגִיגִי בִּינָה,

« contemplate. ‹ my « HASHEM; ‹ listen, ‹ to my « mercy, ‹ With Your
thoughts words abundant

אִם נָא מָצָאתִי חֵן בְּעֵינֶיךָ,⁸ אֱלֹהֵי קֶדֶם מְעוֹנָה,⁹

« [Who dwells] in His ‹ primordial ‹ O God « in Your ‹ favor ‹ I have ‹ now ‹ If
Heavenly Abode, eyes, found

וְלָקַחְתָּ מִנְחָתִי מִיָּדִי⁸ אֲשֶׁר הֵבֵאתִי לְךָ בִּתְחִנָּה.

«« in supplication, ‹ You ‹ I have ‹ which ‹ from my ‹ my tribute ‹ then accept
brought hand,

¹⁰וַיְהִי בַּעֲלוֹת הַמִּנְחָה. — CONG.

« of the minchah - ‹ with the ‹ as it was
offering. ascension [in the Temple]

שַׁדַּי לֹא מְצָאנוּךָ שַׂגִּיא כֹחַ¹¹ לָעֵדָה מִקֶּדֶם קָנִיתָ,¹²

« acquired. ‹ that You ‹ to the ‹ in apply- ‹ over- ‹ found ‹ we have ‹ O
long ago Congre- ing Your bearing You to be not Almighty,
gation strength

(1) Cf. *Psalms* 37:6. (2) Cf. *Lamentations* 2:19. (3) *Numbers* 15:4. (4) Cf. *Proverbs* 4:2.
(5) Cf. *Daniel* 9:18. (6) *Genesis* 32:14. (7) Cf. *Psalms* 5:2. (8) *Genesis* 33:10.
(9) Cf. *Deuteronomy* 33:27. (10) *I Kings* 18:36. (11) Cf. *Job* 37:23. (12) Cf. *Psalms* 74:2.

אֶחָד הַמַּרְבֶּה וְאֶחָד הַמַּמְעִיט¹ בְּשׁוּבוֹ נַפְשׁוֹ רָצִית,

Whether ⟩ one's [acts of ⟩ or ⟩ one's [acts of ⟩ if he ⟩⟩ his soul ⟩⟩ You accept
[repentance] are ⟩ whether repentance] are ⟩ repents, ⟩ with favor,
abundant ⟩ are few,

אַךְ יְכַוֵּן לִבּוֹ¹ לְפָנֶיךָ בְּמִנְחָתוֹ בְּעֵת הַקְרֵב אוֹתָהּ –

as long ⟩ he directs ⟩ of his ⟩ before ⟩ in his offering ⟩ at the time ⟩ he brings ⟩⟩ it,
as [the thoughts] heart
You

וְזֹאת תּוֹרַת הַמִּנְחָה². – CONG.

and this ⟩ is the ⟩ of the minchah- ⟩⟩
law offering.

בִּהְיוֹת מִזְבְּחִי וּמִקְדָּשִׁי עַל מְכוֹנוֹ וּגְבוּלוֹ,

When it ⟩ my Altar ⟩ and my ⟩ were ⟩ their ⟩ and their ⟩⟩
was that Temple [proper] place each in boundary,

הָיוּ מְכַפְּרִים עָלֵינוּ בַּשְּׂעִירִים הָעוֹלִים לְגוֹרָלוֹ,*

they would ⟩ atone ⟩ for us ⟩ with goats ⟩ [each] chosen ⟩ for its lot.* ⟩⟩

וְעַתָּה בְּאַשְׁמָתֵנוּ לוּ חָפֵץ יהוה לַהֲמִיתֵנוּ,

But now, ⟩ our guilt, ⟩ because of ⟩ [our consolation ⟩ HASHEM had ⟩ to put us to ⟩⟩
is that] if wanted death,

לֹא לָקַח מִיָּדֵנוּ עֹלָה וּמִנְחָה³. – CONG.

He would ⟩ have ⟩ from our ⟩ [our prayers ⟩ and a ⟩⟩
not accepted hand that replace] a minchah-
burnt-offering. offering.

תַּחֲנוּנִים יְדַבֵּר עַמֹּךְ, יְבַקֵּשׁ סְלִיחָה בְּלֵב מָר,

Supplications ⟩ Your nation ⟩⟩ they ⟩ forgiveness ⟩ with a ⟩ of bitter ⟩⟩
utters; beg heart [remorse].

הִנּוּ מִתְיַצֵּב עַל מָצוֹר וְעוֹמֵד עַל הַמִּשְׁמָר,

Behold, ⟩ they remain ⟩ at ⟩ [their] ⟩ and stand ⟩ on ⟩ guard, ⟩⟩
erect post

מְחַלֶּה פָּנֶיךָ לְעֵת מִנְחַת עֶרֶב וּמְצַפֶּה כֹפֶר,

beseeching ⟩ Your ⟩ at the ⟩ of the ⟩ of the ⟩ and ⟩ atonement, ⟩⟩
Countenance time offering afternoon, seeking

כִּי אָמַר אֲכַבְּרָה פָנָיו בַּמִּנְחָה⁴. – CONG.

for ⟩ they ⟩⟩ we will ⟩ His ⟩ with the ⟩⟩
have said, appease Countenance minchah-offering.

---

(1) Cf. *Talmud, Berachos* 5b; *Menachos* 110a. (2) Cf. *Leviticus* 6:7.
(3) *Judges* 13:23. (4) *Genesis* 32:21.

הָעוֹלִים לְגוֹרָלוֹ — *[Each] chosen for its lot.* On
Yom Kippur, for which this *piyut* was originally intended, two identical goats would be
brought before the Kohen Gadol who would

determine by lots which of the two goats would
be "for HASHEM" and which "for Azazel." The
ritual by which these goats would attain atonement for Israel is described in *Leviticus* 16:7-22.

יְרוּשָׁלַיִם עִירְךָ בְּנֵה וְעָרֶיהָ מִקְצֶה,

《 from one side 〈 and its [sur- 《 build, 〈 Your city, 〈 Jerusalem,
[to the other]. rounding] cities

אֲסוּרִים רְעוּצִים פְּתַח וְלַחָפְשִׁי הוֹצֵא,

《 bring them 〈 and to 《 release, 〈 and the 〈 The
forth. freedom shattered ones imprisoned

וְעָרְבָה לַיהוה מִנְחָתָם כִּימֵי עוֹלָם[1] וּתְשׁוּב וְתִרְצֶה,

《 find favor 〈 and may You 《 of old, 〈 as in 《 may their 〈 to Hashem 〈 And
[in them], once again days offering be, pleasing

עוֹד פְּנוֹת אֶל הַמִּנְחָה.[2] – CONG.

《 [their] 〈 to 〈 turn 〈 to once
minchah-offering. again

וּנְפוּצוֹת יִשְׂרָאֵל לְקַבֵּץ, יָדְךָ שֵׁנִית תּוֹסֵף,[3]

《 should 〈 once 〈 Your 《 to gather 〈 of Israel 〈 The scattered
extend again. more hand in, ones

כְּרוֹעֶה עֶדְרוֹ תִרְעֵם, בְּנָוֶה טוֹב תֶּאֱסֹף,[4]

《 gather 〈 in a good pasture 《 graze 〈 [does with] 〈 As a
[them]. them; his flock, shepherd

וְיָשַׁב מְצָרֵף וְטִהַר אֶת בְּנֵי יִשְׂרָאֵל כַּזָּהָב וְכַכָּסֶף,

《 and like 〈 like gold 〈 of Israel 〈 the Children 〈 and 〈 And a smelter
silver, purify will sit

וְהָיוּ לַיהוה מַגִּישֵׁי מִנְחָה.[5] – CONGREGATION, THEN *CHAZZAN*.

《 of *minchah*- 〈 bringers 〈 unto 〈 and they
offerings. Hashem will be

AN INDIVIDUAL PRAYING WITHOUT A *MINYAN* OMITS THE NEXT TWO PARAGRAPHS,
BEGINNING אֵל מֶלֶךְ, O GOD, KING, AND ה', HASHEM.

אֵל מֶלֶךְ יוֹשֵׁב עַל כִּסֵּא רַחֲמִים, מִתְנַהֵג בַּחֲסִידוּת, מוֹחֵל

〈 Who 《 with 〈 Who acts 《 of mercy, 〈 the 〈 on 〈 Who 〈 King 〈 O God,
pardons kindness, throne sits

עֲוֹנוֹת עַמּוֹ, מַעֲבִיר רִאשׁוֹן רִאשׁוֹן, מַרְבֶּה מְחִילָה לַחַטָּאִים

〈 to uninten- 〈 pardon 〈 Who abun- 《 by one, 〈 [sins] one 〈 Who 《 of His 〈 the sins
tional sinners dantly grants removes people,

וּסְלִיחָה לַפּוֹשְׁעִים, עֹשֶׂה צְדָקוֹת עִם כָּל בָּשָׂר וָרוּחַ, לֹא

〈 – not 《 and 〈 [beings 〈 all 〈 with 〈 acts of 〈 Who 《 to willful 〈 and
spirit of] flesh generosity performs sinners, forgiveness

כְרָעָתָם תִּגְמוֹל. ❖ אֵל הוֹרֵיתָ לָּנוּ לוֹמַר שְׁלֹשׁ עֶשְׂרֵה,

《 the Thirteen 〈 to recite 〈 us 〈 You 〈 O 《 do You repay 〈 in accord with
[Attributes of Mercy]; taught God, them! their wickedness

---

(1) Cf. *Malachi* 3:4. (2) 2:13. (3) Cf. *Isaiah* 11:11. (4) Cf. 40:11. (5) Cf. *Malachi* 3:3.

וּזְכוֹר לָנוּ הַיּוֹם בְּרִית שְׁלֹשׁ עֶשְׂרֵה, כְּמוֹ שֶׁהוֹדַעְתָּ לֶעָנָיו

‹ to the humble one [Moses] ‹ You made known ‹ as ‹‹ of [these] Thirteen, ‹ the covenant ‹ today ‹ for us ‹ remember

מִקֶּדֶם, כְּמוֹ שֶׁכָּתוּב, וַיֵּרֶד יהוה בֶּעָנָן וַיִּתְיַצֵּב עִמּוֹ שָׁם,

‹‹ there, ‹ with him ‹ and stood ‹ in a cloud ‹ And HASHEM descended ‹‹ it is written: ‹ as ‹‹ in ancient times,

וַיִּקְרָא בְשֵׁם יהוה.

‹‹ of HASHEM. ‹ with the Name ‹ and He called out

CONGREGATION AND *CHAZZAN* RECITE LOUDLY AND IN UNISON:

וַיַּעֲבֹר יהוה עַל פָּנָיו וַיִּקְרָא:

‹‹ and proclaimed: ‹‹ [Moses'] face, ‹ before ‹ And HASHEM passed

יהוה, יהוה, אֵל, רַחוּם, וְחַנּוּן, אֶרֶךְ אַפַּיִם, וְרַב חֶסֶד, וֶאֱמֶת,

‹‹ and Truth, ‹ in Kindness ‹ and Abundant ‹ to anger, ‹ Slow ‹‹ and Gracious, ‹ Compassionate ‹ God, ‹ HASHEM, ‹ HASHEM,

נֹצֵר חֶסֶד לָאֲלָפִים, נֹשֵׂא עָוֹן, וָפֶשַׁע, וְחַטָּאָה, וְנַקֵּה.[1]

‹‹ and Who absolves. ‹ and inadvertent sin, ‹ willful sin, ‹ of iniquity, ‹ Forgiver ‹‹ for thousands [of generations], ‹ of kindness ‹ Preserver

וְסָלַחְתָּ לַעֲוֹנֵנוּ וּלְחַטָּאתֵנוּ וּנְחַלְתָּנוּ.[2] סְלַח לָנוּ אָבִינוּ כִּי

‹ for ‹‹ our Father, ‹ us, ‹ Forgive ‹‹ and make us Your heritage. ‹ and our sins, ‹ our iniquities ‹ May You forgive '

חָטָאנוּ, מְחַל לָנוּ מַלְכֵּנוּ כִּי פָשָׁעְנוּ.[3] כִּי אַתָּה אֲדֹנָי טוֹב

‹ are good ‹ O Lord, ‹ You, ‹ For ‹‹ we have willfully sinned. ‹ for ‹‹ our King, ‹ us, ‹ pardon ‹‹ we have sinned;

וְסַלָּח, וְרַב חֶסֶד לְכָל קֹרְאֶיךָ.[4]

‹‹ who call upon You. ‹ to all ‹ kind ‹ and ‹‹ and abundantly forgiving,

ALL CONTINUE:

וּנְשַׁלְּמָה פָרִים שְׂפָתֵינוּ,[5] תִּכּוֹן תְּפִלָּתֵנוּ קְטֹרֶת לְפָנֶיךָ,

‹‹ before You; ‹ as incense ‹ should be our prayer ‹ Considered ‹‹ with our lips. ‹ [for the sacrificial] bulls ‹ Let us substitute

מַשְׂאַת כַּפֵּינוּ מִנְחַת עָרֶב.[6] יִהְיוּ לְרָצוֹן אִמְרֵי פִינוּ וְהֶגְיוֹן

‹ and the thoughts ‹ of our mouth ‹ expressions ‹ find ‹ May ‹‹ of the afternoon. ‹ as an offering ‹ of our hands ‹ the lifting

לִבֵּנוּ לְפָנֶיךָ, יהוה צוּרֵנוּ וְגוֹאֲלֵנוּ.[7]

‹‹ and our Redeemer. ‹ our Rock ‹ HASHEM, ‹‹ before You, ‹‹ of our heart —

---

(1) *Exodus* 34:5-7. (2) 34:9. (3) From the weekday *Shemoneh Esrei.*
(4) *Psalms* 86:5. (5) *Hosea* 14:3. (6) Cf. *Psalms* 141:2. (7) Cf. 19:15.

כְּרַחֵם אָב עַל בָּנִים, כֵּן תְּרַחֵם יהוה עָלֵינוּ.¹ לַיהוה

As merciful / a / father is / toward / his / children, / so / have / Hashem, / mercy, / on us. / To Hashem

הַיְשׁוּעָה, עַל עַמְּךָ בִרְכָתֶךָ סֶּלָה.² יהוה צְבָאוֹת עִמָּנוּ,

is salvation, / upon / Your / people / Your / blessing, / Selah. / Hashem, / Master of / Legions, / is with us,

מִשְׂגָּב לָנוּ אֱלֹהֵי יַעֲקֹב סֶלָה.³ יהוה צְבָאוֹת, אַשְׁרֵי אָדָם

is the / stronghold / for / us / God / of / Jacob, / Selah. / Hashem, / Master of / Legions, / praise-worthy / is the / man

בֹּטֵחַ בָּךְ.⁴ יהוה הוֹשִׁיעָה, הַמֶּלֶךְ יַעֲנֵנוּ בְיוֹם קָרְאֵנוּ.⁵

who / trusts / in / You. / Hashem, / save! / May the / King / answer / us / on the / day / we call.

MANY CONGREGATIONS OMIT THE NEXT TWO PARAGRAPHS, AND CONTINUE
אֱלֹהַי בְּשַׂר עַמְּךָ, MY GOD, THE FLESH OF YOUR PEOPLE (NEXT PAGE).

❖ **סְלַח** נָא לַעֲוֹן הָעָם הַזֶּה כְּגֹדֶל חַסְדֶּךָ, וְכַאֲשֶׁר נָשָׂאתָה

Forgive, / please, / the / iniquity / of this people / according to / the greatness / of Your / kindness, / and as / You have forgiven

לָעָם הַזֶּה מִמִּצְרַיִם וְעַד הֵנָּה,⁶ וְשָׁם נֶאֱמַר:

this people / from Egypt / until / now. / And there / it was said:

ALL, ALOUD AND IN UNISON:

וַיֹּאמֶר יהוה סָלַחְתִּי כִּדְבָרֶךָ.⁷

And Hashem said: / I have forgiven / according to your word!

הַטֵּה אֱלֹהַי אָזְנְךָ וּשְׁמָע, פְּקַח עֵינֶיךָ וּרְאֵה שֹׁמְמֹתֵינוּ,

Incline, / my God, / Your ear, / and listen; / open / Your eyes / and see / our desolation,

וְהָעִיר אֲשֶׁר נִקְרָא שִׁמְךָ עָלֶיהָ, כִּי לֹא עַל צִדְקֹתֵינוּ אֲנַחְנוּ

and [that of] the / city / which / Your Name is / proclaimed / upon; / for / not / because / of our / righteousness / do we

מַפִּילִים תַּחֲנוּנֵינוּ לְפָנֶיךָ, כִּי עַל רַחֲמֶיךָ הָרַבִּים. אֲדֹנָי

cast / our / supplications / before / You; / but / because / of Your / compassion, / which is / abundant. / O Lord,

שְׁמָעָה, אֲדֹנָי סְלָחָה, אֲדֹנָי הַקְשִׁיבָה, וַעֲשֵׂה אַל תְּאַחַר,

heed; / O Lord, / forgive; / O Lord, / be attentive, / and act, / do not / delay;

לְמַעַנְךָ אֱלֹהַי, כִּי שִׁמְךָ נִקְרָא עַל עִירְךָ וְעַל עַמֶּךָ.⁸

for Your / sake, / my God, / for / Your / Name / is / proclaimed / upon / Your / City / and / upon / Your / people.

---

(1) Cf. *Psalms* 103:13. (2) 3:9. (3) 46:8. (4) 84:13. (5) 20:10.
(6) *Numbers* 14:19. (7) 14:20. (8) *Daniel* 9:18-19.

IN MOST CONGREGATIONS, THE FOLLOWING *PIYUT* IS RECITED RESPONSIVELY.

אֱלֹהַי, בְּשַׂר עַמְּךָ* מִפַּחְדְּךָ סָמָר,¹

⟪ became ⟨ from the ⟨ of Your ⟨ the flesh ⟨ My God,
prickly; fear of You people*

וְתָמִיד עוֹמֵד עַל מִשְׁמָר עַד עֵת² מִנְחַת עֶרֶב.

⟪ of the ⟨ of the ⟨ the ⟨until ⟪ guard, ⟨ on ⟨ stand ⟨ they
afternoon, offering time constantly

– CONG. כִּי אָמַר אֲכַפְּרָה פָנָיו בַּמִּנְחָה.³

⟪ with the ⟨ His Coun- ⟨ We will ⟨ they ⟨ for
minchah-offering. tenance appease have said,

לְהַקְשִׁיב לְמַשְׁטִינֵנוּ מָאֵן תְּמָאֵן,

⟪ may You utterly refuse; ⟨ to our Accuser ⟨ To give heed

סָאוֹנוֹ בְרַעַשׁ אַל נָא תְהִי סוֹאֵן,⁴

⟪ [how You] ⟨ be ⟨please, ⟨should ⟪ [over which ⟨ his measure
measure. not, he makes an] [of our sins]
uproar

וְאִם עֲוֹנוֹת תִּשְׁמֹר⁵ הֲלֹא רַבּוּ.

⟪ they would ⟨ surely ⟪ You retain, ⟨ iniquities ⟨ If
be so abundant

–CONG. מֵאֵין עוֹד פְּנוֹת אֶל הַמִּנְחָה.⁶

⟪ [their] ⟨ to ⟨ to turn ⟨ any ⟨ that You
minchah-offering. more would refuse

יִשְׂרָאֵל עַמְּךָ אֲשֶׁר בְּךָ מַאֲמִין,

⟪ has faith, ⟨ in You ⟨which ⟨ Your nation, ⟨ Israel,

אִם בִּשְׂמֹאל דְּחִיתוֹ קָרְבֵהוּ בִימִין,⁷

⟪ with Your ⟨ bring them ⟪ You have pushed ⟨ with Your ⟨ if
right hand. near them away, left hand

בָּא לְשַׁחֵר פָּנֶיךָ.

⟪ Your ⟨ to entreat ⟨ They
Countenance, have come

–CONG. וַיִּקַּח מִן הַבָּא בְיָדוֹ מִנְחָה.⁸

⟪ as a minchah- ⟨ to ⟨ that which ⟨ from ⟨ and they have
offering. their hand, came taken [along],

---

(1) Cf. *Psalms* 119:120. (2) Some *siddurim* have: וּמְצַפֶּה לָעֵת, *and wait for the time*. (3) *Genesis* 32:21.
(4) Cf. *Isaiah* 9:4. (5) *Psalms* 130:3. (6) *Malachi* 2:13. (7) See *Sanhedrin* 107b. (8) *Genesis* 32:14.

אֱלֹהַי בְּשַׂר עַמְּךָ ⁓§ — *My God, the flesh of Your people.* This *piyut* was written by אֱלִיעֶזֶר בְּרַבִּי יִצְחָק הַלֵּוִי, *Eliezer son of R' Yitzchak the Levite,* as attested to in the acrostic of the stanzas. Like מַשְׂאַת כַּפַּי, this *piyut* was originally intended for *Minchah* of Yom Kippur and is recited in some congregations at that service.

עוֹרְכֵי שָׁוְא מְשַׁלְּמֵי פָרִים שְׂפָתוֹתָם,[1]

《 with 〈 for the [sac- 〈 and they 《 their 〈 They
their lips. rificial] bulls substitute prayers, arranged

רְצֵה וְהַשְׁלֵךְ בִּמְצֹלוֹת יָם כָּל חַטֹּאתָם,[2]

《 their sins. 〈 all 〈 of the 〈 into the 〈 and cast 〈 Show
sea depths favor

יֶעֱרַב עָלֶיךָ שִׂיחָתָם וְרִנָּתָם.[3]

《 and song – 〈 – their 《 before 〈 May they
speech You be pleasant

כְּחַטָּאת כְּעֹלָה וּכְמִנְחָה.[4] —CONG.

《 and like the 〈 like the 〈 like the sin-
minchah-offering. burnt-offering. offering,

זֵכֶר פַּר פְּנִים וְשָׂעִיר פְּנִימִי וְחִיצוֹן,*

《 and the [goat] from 〈 of the inner 〈 and the 〈 of the inner 〈 of the 〈 As a re-
outside the Sanctuary,* Sanctuary goat Sanctuary bull membrance

יִהְיוּ נָא אֲמָרֵינוּ לְפָנֶיךָ לְרָצוֹן,[5]

《 favorable. 《 before 〈 – our 《 please 〈 may
You – words they be,

וְתֶעֱרַב מִנְחָתֵנוּ כְּשֶׂה אַחַת מִן הַצֹּאן, מִן הַמָּאתָיִם.

〈 two hundred 〈 of 〈 the flock 〈 from 〈 like a singular 〈 our offering 〈 May
lamb pleasant be

מִמַּשְׁקֵה יִשְׂרָאֵל לְמִנְחָה.[6] —CONG.

《 for a 〈 of Israel 〈 of the choicest
minchah-offering. [animals]

רְאֵה כִּי אָזְלַת יָדֵנוּ[7] וְיוֹשְׁבֵי מָרוֹם שָׁחוּ,

《 are 〈 on 〈 and those who 〈 is our 〈 feeble 〈 that 〈 See
lowered. high [used to] dwell hand

פַּסּוּ אֱמוּנִים[8] וּבְכֵן לָקֵחוּ,

《 they have 〈 and so 《 have the 〈 Vanished
chosen faithful,

---

(1) Cf. *Hosea* 14:3. (2) Cf. *Micah* 7:19. (3) Cf. *Psalms* 104:34. (4) *Ezekiel* 45:25. (5) Cf. *Psalms* 19:15. (6) *Ezekiel* 45:15. (7) Cf. *Deuteronomy* 32:36, with *Ibn Ezra*. (8) Cf. *Psalms* 12:2.

פַּר פְּנִים וְשָׂעִיר פְּנִימִי וְחִיצוֹן — *The bull of the inner Sanctuary and the goat of the inner Sanctuary and the [goat] from outside the Sanctuary.* The Altar service of most offerings included the sprinkling or dabbing of the animals' blood upon the Altar that stood in the Courtyard, outside of the *Beis HaMikdash* proper. However, there are also some offerings of a higher order;

their blood service is performed within the *Beis HaMikdash.* Two such offerings are brought on Yom Kippur — one a bull, the other a goat (see *Leviticus* 16:11-17). Additionally, the *mussaf* offering of each festival, including Yom Kippur, consisted of a number of burnt-offerings accompanied by a goat that was brought as a regular sin-offering (see *Leviticus* 29:11).

כְּבַד פֶּה[1] וַעֲרַל שָׂפָה.[2]

‹‹ lip, ‹ and ‹ mouth ‹ one with
sealed   a heavy

CONG.— וַיִּשְׁלְחוּ בְּנֵי יִשְׂרָאֵל בְּיָדוֹ מִנְחָה.[3]

‹‹ a *minchah*- ‹ in his ‹ of Israel ‹ have the ‹ and sent
offering.   hand   Children

בָּרֵר נִיב שְׂפָתַי[4] כְּשַׁחַר פָּרוּשׂ,[5]

‹‹ spreading; ‹ like the ‹ of my ‹ the ‹ Purify
    dawn   lips   speech

עֲנֵנִי וּרְפָא מִזְבַּחֲךָ הֶהָרוּס,[6]

‹‹ which is ‹ Your Altar ‹ and ‹ answer
ruined.   repair   me

חֶלְקַת לְשׁוֹנִי[7] תֶּעֱרַב כַּשֶּׁמֶן לָרוֹס

‹ to blend ‹ as oil, ‹ be as ‹ of my ‹ May the
     pleasant tongue smoothness

CONG.— אֶת הָעֹלָה וְאֶת הַמִּנְחָה.*[8]

‹‹ and the *minchah*-offering.* ‹ the burnt-offering

בֵּית תְּפִלָּתָם מְקוֹם צָקוּן לַחֲשָׁם,[9]

‹‹ their silent ‹ where they ‹ the ‹ Their house
petitions,   pour out   place   of prayer,

חֲשׁוֹב כְּבִמְקוֹם אֲשֶׁר יְבַשְּׁלוּ שָׁם

‹‹ there ‹ they would cook ‹ that ‹ like the place ‹ consider

הַכֹּהֲנִים אֶת הַחַטָּאת וְאֶת הָאָשָׁם.

‹‹ and the guilt-offering, ‹ the sin-offering ‹‹— the *Kohanim* —

CONG.— וַאֲשֶׁר יֹאפוּ אֶת הַמִּנְחָה.[10]

‹‹ the *minchah*- ‹ they would ‹ and
offering.   bake   where

יְצַוֶּה יהוה חַסְדּוֹ,[11] קוֹמְמִיּוּת הֲשִׁיבֵנִי לְנָוִי,[12]

‹‹ to my ‹ I be returned ‹ that while ‹ His ‹ May HASHEM
abode,   erect   kindness,   command

לְפָאֵר מְקוֹם מִקְדָּשִׁי, לְחַדֵּשׁ הֲדַר זִיוִי,

‹‹ of my ‹ the ‹ to renew ‹‹ of my ‹ the place ‹ to glorify
splendor; glory   Temple,

---

(1) *Exodus* 4:10. (2) 6:12. (3) *Judges* 3:15. (4) Cf. *Isaiah* 57:19. (5) *Joel* 2:2.
(6) Cf. *I Kings* 18:30. (7) Cf. *Proverbs* 6:24. (8) *Exodus* 40:29. (9) Cf. *Isaiah* 26:16.
(10) Cf. *Ezekiel* 46:20. (11) Cf. *Psalms* 42:9. (12) Cf. *Jeremiah* 23:3-4.

אֶת הָעֹלָה וְאֶת הַמִּנְחָה — *The burnt-offering and the minchah-offering.* This reading follows the majority of *siddurim.* Some read, אֶת הַסֹּלֶת וְאֶת הַמִּנְחָה, *the fine flour and the minchah.* That

version is based on the verse, וְשֶׁמֶן שְׁלִישִׁית הַהִין, *and a third of a hin-measure of oil,* לָרֹס אֶת הַסֹּלֶת, *with which to mix the fine flour,* מִנְחָה לַה', *a minchah-offering unto HASHEM* (*Ezekiel* 46:14).

וְיָשַׁב מְצָרֵף וְטִהַר אֶת בְּנֵי לֵוִי,

⟨⟨ of Levi, ⟨ the Children ⟨ and purify ⟨ and a smelter will sit

– CONGREGATION, THEN *CHAZZAN*. — וְהָיוּ לַיהוה מַגִּישֵׁי מִנְחָה.[1]

⟨⟨of *minchah* - ⟨ bringers ⟨ unto ⟨ and they
offerings.   HASHEM   will be

AN INDIVIDUAL PRAYING WITHOUT A *MINYAN* OMITS THE NEXT TWO PARAGRAPHS, BEGINNING אֵל מֶלֶךְ, O GOD, KING, AND ה', HASHEM.

אֵל מֶלֶךְ יוֹשֵׁב עַל כִּסֵּא רַחֲמִים, מִתְנַהֵג בַּחֲסִידוּת, מוֹחֵל

⟨ Who ⟨⟨ with ⟨ Who acts ⟨⟨ of mercy, ⟨ the ⟨ on ⟨ Who ⟨ King ⟨ O God,
pardons   kindness,   throne   sits

עֲוֹנוֹת עַמּוֹ, מַעֲבִיר רִאשׁוֹן רִאשׁוֹן, מַרְבֶּה מְחִילָה לַחַטָּאִים

⟨ to uninten- ⟨ pardon ⟨ Who abun- ⟨⟨ by one, ⟨ [sins] one ⟨ Who ⟨⟨ of His ⟨ the sins
tional sinners   dantly grants   removes   people,

וּסְלִיחָה לַפּוֹשְׁעִים, עֹשֶׂה צְדָקוֹת עִם כָּל בָּשָׂר וָרוּחַ, לֹא

⟨— not ⟨⟨ and ⟨ [beings ⟨ all ⟨ with ⟨ acts of ⟨ Who ⟨⟨ to willful ⟨ and
spirit of] flesh   generosity performs   sinners,   forgiveness

כְרָעָתָם תִּגְמוֹל. ❖ אֵל הוֹרֵיתָ לָּנוּ לוֹמַר שְׁלֹשׁ עֶשְׂרֵה,

⟨⟨ the Thirteen ⟨ to recite ⟨ us ⟨ You ⟨ O ⟨⟨ do You repay ⟨ in accord with
[Attributes of Mercy];   taught   God,   them!   their wickedness

וּזְכוֹר לָנוּ הַיּוֹם בְּרִית שְׁלֹשׁ עֶשְׂרֵה, כְּמוֹ שֶׁהוֹדַעְתָּ לֶעָנָיו

⟨ to the humble ⟨ You made ⟨ as ⟨⟨ of [these] Thirteen, ⟨ the ⟨ today ⟨ for us ⟨ remember
one [Moses] known   covenant

מִקֶּדֶם, כְּמוֹ שֶׁכָּתוּב, וַיֵּרֶד יהוה בֶּעָנָן וַיִּתְיַצֵּב עִמּוֹ שָׁם,

⟨⟨ there, ⟨ with ⟨ and stood ⟨ in a cloud ⟨ And HASHEM ⟨⟨ it is written: ⟨ as ⟨⟨ in ancient
him   descended   times,

וַיִּקְרָא בְשֵׁם יהוה.

⟨⟨ of ⟨ with the ⟨ and He
HASHEM.   Name   called out

CONGREGATION AND *CHAZZAN* RECITE LOUDLY AND IN UNISON:

וַיַּעֲבֹר יהוה עַל פָּנָיו וַיִּקְרָא:

⟨⟨ and ⟨⟨ [Moses'] ⟨ before ⟨ And HASHEM passed
proclaimed: face,

יהוה, יהוה, אֵל, רַחוּם, וְחַנּוּן, אֶרֶךְ אַפַּיִם, וְרַב חֶסֶד, וֶאֱמֶת,

⟨⟨ and ⟨ in ⟨ and ⟨ to anger, ⟨ Slow ⟨⟨ and ⟨ Compas- ⟨ God, ⟨ HASHEM, ⟨ HASHEM,
Truth, Kindness Abundant   Gracious, sionate

נֹצֵר חֶסֶד לָאֲלָפִים, נֹשֵׂא עָוֹן, וָפֶשַׁע, וְחַטָּאָה, וְנַקֵּה.[2]

⟨⟨ and Who ⟨ and inad- ⟨ willful ⟨ of ⟨ Forgiver ⟨⟨ for thousands ⟨ of ⟨ Preserver
absolves.   vertent sin,   sin,   iniquity,   [of generations], kindness

(1) Abridged from *Malachi* 3:3. (2) *Exodus* 34:5-7.

וְסָלַחְתָּ לַעֲוֹנֵנוּ וּלְחַטָּאתֵנוּ וּנְחַלְתָּנוּ.¹ סְלַח לָנוּ אָבִינוּ כִּי

⟨ for ⟨⟨ our ⟨ us, ⟨ Forgive ⟨⟨ and make us ⟨⟨ and our sins, ⟨ our ⟨ May You
Father, Your heritage. iniquities forgive

חָטָאנוּ, מְחַל לָנוּ מַלְכֵּנוּ כִּי פָשָׁעְנוּ.² כִּי אַתָּה אֲדֹנָי טוֹב

⟨ are ⟨ O Lord, ⟨ You, ⟨ For ⟨⟨ we have ⟨ for ⟨⟨ our King, ⟨ us, ⟨ pardon ⟨⟨ we have
good willfully sinned. sinned;

וְסַלָּח, וְרַב חֶסֶד לְכָל קֹרְאֶיךָ.³

⟨⟨ who call ⟨ to all ⟨ kind ⟨ and ⟨⟨ and
upon You. abundantly forgiving,

ALL CONTINUE:

טוֹב יהוה לַכֹּל וְרַחֲמָיו עַל כָּל מַעֲשָׂיו.⁴ טוֹב יהוה לְקֹוָיו,

⟨⟨ to those who ⟨ HASHEM ⟨⟨ His ⟨ all ⟨ are ⟨ His ⟨⟨ to all; ⟨ HASHEM is good
trust in Him, is good creations. on mercies

לְנֶפֶשׁ תִּדְרְשֶׁנּוּ.⁵ טוֹב וְיָחִיל וְדוּמָם לִתְשׁוּעַת יהוה.⁶ טוֹב

⟨ It is ⟨⟨ of HASHEM. ⟨ for the ⟨ silently ⟨ to hope ⟨ It is ⟨⟨ that seeks Him. ⟨ to the
better salvation good soul

לַחֲסוֹת בַּיהוה, מִבְּטֹחַ בָּאָדָם.⁷ טוֹב לַחֲסוֹת בַּיהוה, מִבְּטֹחַ

⟨ than to ⟨ in HASHEM ⟨ to take ⟨ It is ⟨⟨ on man. ⟨ than to ⟨ in HASHEM ⟨ to take
rely refuge better rely refuge

בִּנְדִיבִים.⁸ טוֹב וְיָשָׁר יהוה, עַל כֵּן יוֹרֶה חַטָּאִים בַּדָּרֶךְ.*⁹

⟨⟨ on the way. ⟨ sinners ⟨ He guides ⟨ therefore ⟨⟨ is HASHEM; ⟨ and upright ⟨ Good ⟨⟨ on nobles.

טוֹב יהוה לְמָעוֹז בְּיוֹם צָרָה, וְיוֹדֵעַ חֹסֵי בוֹ.¹⁰ כִּי הוּא יָדַע

⟨ knew ⟨ He ⟨ For ⟨⟨ in ⟨ of those who ⟨ and He is ⟨⟨ of ⟨ on the ⟨ as a ⟨ HASHEM
Him. take refuge mindful distress, day stronghold is good

יִצְרֵנוּ, זָכוּר כִּי עָפָר אֲנָחְנוּ.¹¹ כִּי טוֹב יהוה לְעוֹלָם חַסְדּוֹ,

⟨⟨ His ⟨ forever ⟨⟨ is ⟨ good ⟨ For ⟨⟨ are we. ⟨ dust ⟨ that ⟨ He is ⟨⟨ our
kindness, endures HASHEM, mindful nature;

וְעַד דֹּר וָדֹר אֱמוּנָתוֹ.¹²

⟨⟨ is His ⟨ to gener- ⟨ gener- ⟨ and
faithfulness. ation ation from

כְּרַחֵם אָב עַל בָּנִים, כֵּן תְּרַחֵם יהוה עָלֵינוּ.¹³ לַיהוה

⟨ To ⟨⟨ on us. ⟨ HASHEM, ⟨ have ⟨⟨ his ⟨ toward ⟨ a ⟨ As merciful
HASHEM mercy, children, father is as

---

(1) Exodus 34:9. (2) From the weekday *Shemoneh Esrei*. (3) *Psalms* 86:5. (4) 145:9.
(5) *Lamentations* 3:25. (6) 3:26. (7) *Psalms* 118:8. (8) 118:9. (9) 25:8. (10) *Nahum* 1:7.
(11) *Psalms* 103:14. (12) 100:5. (13) Cf. *Psalms* 103:13.

יוֹרֶה חַטָּאִים בַּדָּרֶךְ — *He guides sinners on the way.* God assists the contrite sinner on the road to repentance (*Radak*). If God takes the trouble to guide even the sinful, then He most certainly guides the righteous (*Makkos* 10b).

הַיְשׁוּעָה, עַל עַמְּךָ בִרְכָתֶךָ סֶּלָה.¹ יהוה צְבָאוֹת עִמָּנוּ,
⟪ is with ⟨ Master of ⟨ Hashem, ⟪ Selah. ⟪ is Your ⟨ Your ⟨ upon ⟪ is salvation,
us, Legions, blessing, people

מִשְׂגָּב לָנוּ אֱלֹהֵי יַעֲקֹב סֶלָה.² יהוה צְבָאוֹת, אַשְׁרֵי אָדָם
⟨ is the ⟨ — praise- ⟪ Master of ⟨ Hashem, ⟪ Selah. ⟪ of ⟨ is the ⟨ for ⟨ a
man worthy Legions Jacob, God us stronghold

בֹּטֵחַ בָּךְ.³ יהוה הוֹשִׁיעָה, הַמֶּלֶךְ יַעֲנֵנוּ בְיוֹם קָרְאֵנוּ.⁴
⟪ we call. ⟨ on the ⟨ answer ⟨ May the ⟪ save! ⟨ Hashem, ⟪ in ⟨ who
day us King You. trusts

MANY CONGREGATIONS OMIT THE NEXT TWO PARAGRAPHS, AND CONTINUE
בַּת עַמִּי, O DAUGHTER OF MY PEOPLE (NEXT PAGE).

❖ **סְלַח** נָא לַעֲוֹן הָעָם הַזֶּה כְּגֹדֶל חַסְדֶּךָ, וְכַאֲשֶׁר נָשָׂאתָה
⟨ You have ⟨ and as ⟪ of Your ⟨ according ⟨ of this people ⟨ the ⟨ please, ⟨ Forgive,
forgiven kindness, to the iniquity
greatness

לָעָם הַזֶּה מִמִּצְרַיִם וְעַד הֵנָּה,⁵ וְשָׁם נֶאֱמַר:
⟪ it was said: ⟨ And there ⟪ now. ⟨ until ⟨ from Egypt ⟨ this people

ALL, ALOUD AND IN UNISON:

וַיֹּאמֶר יהוה סָלַחְתִּי כִּדְבָרֶךָ.⁶
⟪ according to ⟨ I have ⟪ And Hashem said:
your word! forgiven

הַטֵּה אֱלֹהַי אָזְנְךָ וּשְׁמָע, פְּקַח עֵינֶיךָ וּרְאֵה שֹׁמְמֹתֵינוּ,
⟪ our desolation, ⟨ and see ⟨ Your eyes ⟨ open ⟪ and listen; ⟨ Your ear, ⟨ my God, ⟨ Incline,

וְהָעִיר אֲשֶׁר נִקְרָא שִׁמְךָ עָלֶיהָ, כִּי לֹא עַל צִדְקֹתֵינוּ אֲנַחְנוּ
⟨ do we ⟨ of our ⟨ because ⟨ not ⟨ for ⟪ upon; ⟨ Your Name is ⟨ which ⟨ and [that
righteousness proclaimed of] the city

מַפִּילִים תַּחֲנוּנֵינוּ לְפָנֶיךָ, כִּי עַל רַחֲמֶיךָ הָרַבִּים. אֲדֹנָי
⟨ O Lord, ⟪ which is ⟨ of Your ⟨ because ⟨ but ⟪ before ⟨ our ⟨ cast
abundant. compassion, You; supplications

שְׁמָעָה, אֲדֹנָי סְלָחָה, אֲדֹנָי הַקְשִׁיבָה, וַעֲשֵׂה אַל תְּאַחַר,
⟪ delay; ⟨ do not ⟪ and act, ⟨ be attentive, ⟨ O Lord, ⟪ forgive; ⟨ O Lord, ⟪ heed;

לְמַעַנְךָ אֱלֹהַי, כִּי שִׁמְךָ נִקְרָא עַל עִירְךָ וְעַל עַמֶּךָ.⁷
⟪ Your ⟨ and ⟨ Your ⟨ upon ⟨ is ⟨ Your ⟨ for ⟪ my God, ⟨ for Your
people. upon City proclaimed Name sake,

---

(1) *Psalms* 3:9. (2) 46:8. (3) 84:13. (4) 20:10.
(5) *Numbers* 14:19. (6) 14:20. (7) *Daniel* 9:18-19.

IN MOST CONGREGATIONS, THE FOLLOWING *PIYUT* IS RECITED RESPONSIVELY: THE *CHAZZAN* CHANTS EACH STANZA AND THE CONGREGATION RESPONDS WITH THE REFRAIN. IN MANY SYNAGOGUES, THE CONGREGATION RECITES THE REFRAIN ALOUD, AND THE NEXT STANZA SOFTLY; THEN THE *CHAZZAN* REPEATS THE STANZA ALOUD.

בַּת עַמִּי* לֹא תֶחֱשֶׁה, וְלֹא תִשְׁקֹט בְּזַעֲקָה,

≪ in [your] ⟨ be still ⟨ and ≪ be silent, ⟨ do ⟨ of my ⟨ O
outcry! do not not people,* daughter

וּבְמָקוֹם עוֹלָה וְאִשֶּׁה, תָּכִין תַּחַן חוּקָה,

≪ that will be ⟨ a sup- ⟨ prepare ≪ and fire- ⟨ of burnt- ⟨ And in
the standard, plication offerings offerings place

CONG.— לַיהוה מַגִּישֵׁי מִנְחָה בִּצְדָקָה.[1]

≪ in righ- ⟨ of minchah- ⟨ bringers ⟨ [to be]
teousness. offerings unto HASHEM,

נְשִׂיא אֱלֹהִים[2] הַנֶּאֱמָן,[3] רֹאשׁ צוּרִים[4] אֵיתָנַי,[5]

≪ of My mighty ⟨ of the rocklike ⟨ the ≪ the faithful ⟨ of God, ⟨ [Abraham,]
ones, [forebears], first one, prince

הִשְׁכִּים שַׁחַר* וּזְמָן, עֲמוֹד[6] וַעֲרוֹךְ תַּחֲנוּנַי,

≪ My ⟨ and to ⟨ to stand ≪ in timely ⟨ at dawn* ⟨ arose early
supplications; arrange fashion,

בִּמְקוֹם תָּמִיד מִיְמָן,* לְשַׁחֵר עַל קָרְבָּנִי,

≪ My ⟨ with ⟨ to begin ≪ it was ⟨ of the continual- ⟨ in lieu
offerings. the day prepared,* offering

וְכִי הֶאֱמִין בַּיהוה, וַיַּחְשְׁבֶהָ לּוֹ צְדָקָה.[7]

≪ as righteousness. ⟨ to him ⟨ He reckoned it ≪ in HASHEM, ⟨ he trusted ⟨ When

CONG.— לַיהוה מַגִּישֵׁי מִנְחָה בִּצְדָקָה.

≪ in righ- ⟨ of minchah- ⟨ bringers ⟨ [To be]
teousness. offerings unto HASHEM,

---

(1) *Malachi* 3:3. (2) *Genesis* 23:6. (3) *Nehemiah* 9:8. (4) *Numbers* 23:9, *Rashi*.
(5) Cf. *Psalms* 89:1, *Rashi*. (6) Cf. *Genesis* 19:27. (7) 15:6.

⊰§ בַּת עַמִּי — *O daughter of my people.* The *paytan* signed his name, בִּנְיָמִן, *Binyamin*, in the acrostic of the stanzas. Some identify him as R' Binyamin HaRofei of 13th-century Rome, a member of the prominent Anav family, brother of the author of the *Shibbolei HaLeket*.

הִשְׁכִּים שַׁחַר ... בִּמְקוֹם תָּמִיד מִיְמָן — *Arose early at dawn ... in lieu of the continual-offering it was prepared.* The Talmud records two opinions regarding the origin of the three daily prayer services. According to one view, they were instituted by the Patriarchs: Abraham instituted *Shacharis*; Isaac, *Minchah*; and Jacob, *Maariv*. According to the other view, *Shacharis* stands in place of the morning *tamid* or continual-offering; *Minchah* in place of the afternoon *tamid*; and *Maariv* in place of the burning of the fats which had not yet been placed on the Altar during the day (*Berachos* 26b). The *paytan* combines these two opinions as he speaks of Abraham having arisen early to establish the prayer service in lieu of the *tamid*. (See *Overview* p. xxvii ff.)

יְחִידוֹ לְמֵאָה נֶחֱנַן, וְעָקוֹד בְּמִזְבַּח אֲבָנָיו,

His only son [Isaac] ⟩ at [age] one ⟩ hundred ⟩ was granted ⟨⟨ and he ⟩ was bound ⟨ on an altar ⟩ of his stones.

לִפְנוֹת עֶרֶב חָנַן, וְהָאֵל נָשָׂא פָנָיו,

Toward ⟩ evening ⟩ he offered ⟨⟨ and God ⟩ showed him favor; ⟨⟨ supplication,

לְתָמִיד עֶרֶב מְכוֹנָן, לְהִתְרַצּוֹת פְּנֵי אֲדוֹנָיו,

[the prayer] with the continual-offering ⟩ of the afternoon, ⟩ was aligned, ⟨⟨ was ⟩ to appease ⟨ the Coun-tenance ⟩ of his Lord, ⟨⟨

כְּאִישׁ לָקַח מְלֹא חָפְנָיו, קְטֹרֶת סַמִּים דַּקָּה.¹

like the man ⟨ who ⟩ gathered ⟨ his cupped handsful ⟩ of incense- ⟨ spices, ⟩ finely ground. ⟨⟨

 לַיהוה מַגִּישֵׁי מִנְחָה בִּצְדָקָה. —CONG.

[To be] ⟩ unto HASHEM, ⟨ bringers ⟩ of minchah-offerings ⟨ in righ-teousness. ⟨⟨

מְפַלֵּל יוֹשֵׁב אֹהֶל,² הַלָּן בְּמָקוֹם מְשֻׁבָּח,³

[Jacob,] the one who prayed, ⟩ who ⟨ dwelt ⟩ in the tent, ⟨⟨ who slept over ⟩ in the glorious place, ⟨⟨

לְרִבּוּי פְּדָרִים יָהֵל, בְּהִתְקָרֵב בְּבֵית זֶבַח,

like the ⟩ multitudes ⟨ of fats, ⟨⟨ [his prayers] ⟩ shone forth — ⟨⟨ when they were ⟩ offered up [at night] ⟨ in the ⟩ House ⟩ of sacrifice.

וְאִם אֵין קָרְבָּן לִיַחֵל, תְּמוּרָם אֶעֱרָךְ שֶׁבַח,

And if ⟩ there is ⟨ no longer ⟩ an offering ⟩ for which ⟨⟨ to hope, ⟩ in their stead ⟨ I will ⟩ arrange ⟨ praises. ⟨⟨

וְנִבְחַר לַיהוה מִזְבֵּחַ, עֹשֹׂה מִשְׁפָּט וּצְדָקָה.⁴

Even more ⟩ pleasing ⟩ to HASHEM ⟨ than a ⟩ sacrifice ⟨ is doing ⟨ justice ⟩ and righteousness. ⟨⟨

לַיהוה מַגִּישֵׁי מִנְחָה בִּצְדָקָה. —CONG.

[To be] ⟩ unto HASHEM, ⟨ bringers ⟩ of minchah-offerings ⟨ in righ-teousness. ⟨⟨

נֶאֱלַמְתִּי דוּמִיָּה, מֵאֵין עֲבוֹדַת כֹּהֲנִים,

I have ⟩ fallen silent ⟩ and still ⟨ because of ⟩ the absence ⟩ of the service ⟨ of the Kohanim. ⟨⟨

וְאֵיךְ אָשִׁיר בַּשִּׁבְיָה, וְאָסְפוּ לְוִיַּי אֱמוּנִים,

How ⟩ can I ⟩ sing ⟨ while ⟩ in captivity, ⟨⟨ have been ⟩ taken away ⟨ my Levites, ⟩ the faithful ones? ⟨⟨

---

(1) *Leviticus* 16:12. (2) Cf. *Genesis* 25:27. (3) Cf. 28:11, *Rashi*. (4) Cf. *Proverbs* 21:3.

וְעַל כָּל זֹאת אוֹדֶה יָהּ, כִּי הוּא נַעֲלֶה בְדִינִים,

‹ in justice. ‹ is exalted ‹ He ‹ for ‹ to God, ‹ I give thanks ‹ this ‹ all ‹ Despite

לָנוּ בֹּשֶׁת הַפָּנִים, וּלְךָ הַצְּדָקָה,[1]

‹ is the righteousness. ‹ and Yours ‹ facedness ‹ is the shame- ‹ Ours

— CONG. לַיהוה מַגִּישֵׁי מִנְחָה בִּצְדָקָה.

‹ in righ- ‹ of minchah- ‹ bringers ‹ [To be]
teousness. offerings unto HASHEM,

חֵלֶף קָרְבְּנוֹת פֶּדֶר, תְּפִלָּתִי תֵרָאֶה,

‹ be considered, ‹ may my prayer ‹ of fats ‹ of sacrifices ‹ In place

בְּזָכְרִי עַל הַסֵּדֶר, עֲבוֹדַת מְשָׁרְתִים, בָּאֵי

‹ who ‹ of the ministers ‹ the service ‹ to the ‹ according ‹ when I
entered order recall

הֵיכָל חֶדֶר בְּחֶדֶר, וְשָׁמְעוּ מְבַשֵּׂר בְּמַרְאֶה,

‹ in a vision, ‹ the ‹ and who ‹ within ‹ to the ‹ the
prophecy heard a room, room Sanctuary

וְזָרְחָה לָכֶם יְרָאֵי שְׁמִי שֶׁמֶשׁ צְדָקָה,[2]

‹ of righteousness. ‹ the sun ‹ My ‹ who fear ‹ — for ‹ It will shine
Name — you

— CONG., THEN CHAZZAN לַיהוה מַגִּישֵׁי מִנְחָה בִּצְדָקָה.

‹ in righ- ‹ of minchah- ‹ bringers ‹ [To be]
teousness. offerings unto HASHEM,

AN INDIVIDUAL PRAYING WITHOUT A *MINYAN* OMITS THE NEXT TWO PARAGRAPHS,
BEGINNING אֵל מֶלֶךְ, *O GOD, KING,* AND ה', *HASHEM.*

אֵל מֶלֶךְ יוֹשֵׁב עַל כִּסֵּא רַחֲמִים, מִתְנַהֵג בַּחֲסִידוּת, מוֹחֵל

‹ Who ‹ with ‹ Who acts ‹ of mercy, ‹ the ‹ on ‹ Who ‹ King ‹ O God,
pardons kindness, throne sits

עֲוֹנוֹת עַמּוֹ, מַעֲבִיר רִאשׁוֹן רִאשׁוֹן, מַרְבֶּה מְחִילָה לַחַטָּאִים

‹ to uninten- ‹ pardon ‹ Who abun- ‹ by one, ‹ [sins] one ‹ Who ‹ of His ‹ the sins
tional sinners dantly grants removes people,

וּסְלִיחָה לַפּוֹשְׁעִים, עֹשֶׂה צְדָקוֹת עִם כָּל בָּשָׂר וָרוּחַ, לֹא

‹ — not ‹ and ‹ [beings ‹ all ‹ with ‹ acts of ‹ Who ‹ to willful ‹ and
spirit of] flesh generosity performs sinners, forgiveness

כְרָעָתָם תִּגְמוֹל. ❖ אֵל הוֹרֵיתָ לָּנוּ לוֹמַר שְׁלֹשׁ עֶשְׂרֵה,

‹ the Thirteen ‹ to recite ‹ us ‹ You ‹ O ‹ do You repay ‹ in accord with
[Attributes of Mercy]; taught God, them! their wickedness

וּזְכוֹר לָנוּ הַיּוֹם בְּרִית שְׁלֹשׁ עֶשְׂרֵה, כְּמוֹ שֶׁהוֹדַעְתָּ לֶעָנָיו

‹ to the humble ‹ You made ‹ as ‹ of [these] Thirteen, ‹ the ‹ today ‹ for us ‹ remember
one [Moses] known covenant

(1) Cf. *Daniel* 9:7. (2) Cf. *Malachi* 3:20.

מִקֶּדֶם, כְּמוֹ שֶׁכָּתוּב, וַיֵּרֶד יהוה בֶּעָנָן וַיִּתְיַצֵּב עִמּוֹ שָׁם,

‹‹ there, ‹ with him ‹ and stood ‹ in a cloud ‹ And HASHEM descended ‹‹ it is written: ‹ as ‹‹ in ancient times,

וַיִּקְרָא בְשֵׁם יהוה.

‹‹ of ‹ with the HASHEM. ‹ and He Name called out

CONGREGATION AND *CHAZZAN* RECITE LOUDLY AND IN UNISON:

וַיַּעֲבֹר יהוה עַל פָּנָיו וַיִּקְרָא:

‹‹ and proclaimed: ‹‹ [Moses'] face, ‹ before ‹ And HASHEM passed

יהוה, יהוה, אֵל, רַחוּם, וְחַנּוּן, אֶרֶךְ אַפַּיִם, וְרַב חֶסֶד, וֶאֱמֶת,

‹‹ and in Truth, Kindness ‹ Abundant ‹ and ‹ to anger, ‹ Slow ‹ and Compas- Gracious, ‹ God, ‹ HASHEM, ‹ HASHEM, sionate

נֹצֵר חֶסֶד לָאֲלָפִים, נֹשֵׂא עָוֹן, וָפֶשַׁע, וְחַטָּאָה, וְנַקֵּה.[1]

‹‹ and Who and inad- absolves. vertent sin, ‹ willful sin, ‹ of ‹ Forgiver iniquity, ‹‹ for thousands [of generations], ‹ of ‹ Preserver kindness

וְסָלַחְתָּ לַעֲוֹנֵנוּ וּלְחַטָּאתֵנוּ וּנְחַלְתָּנוּ.[2] סְלַח לָנוּ אָבִינוּ כִּי

‹ for ‹‹ our Father, ‹ us, ‹ Forgive ‹‹ and make us Your heritage. ‹‹ and our sins, ‹ our iniquities ‹ May You forgive

חָטָאנוּ, מְחַל לָנוּ מַלְכֵּנוּ כִּי פָשָׁעְנוּ.[3] כִּי אַתָּה אֲדֹנָי טוֹב

‹ are good ‹ O Lord, ‹ You, ‹ For ‹‹ we have willfully sinned. ‹ for ‹‹ our King, ‹ us, ‹ pardon ‹‹ we have sinned;

וְסַלָּח, וְרַב חֶסֶד לְכָל קֹרְאֶיךָ.[4]

‹‹ who call upon You. ‹ to all ‹ kind ‹ and ‹‹ and abundantly forgiving,

ALL CONTINUE. THIS PRAYER IS USUALLY RECITED RESPONSIVELY AS INDICATED:

רַחֲמָנָא* אִדְכַּר לָן קְיָמֵהּ דְּאַבְרָהָם רְחִימָא.

‹‹ the beloved, ‹ [made to] Abraham ‹ the promise ‹ for us ‹ recall ‹ O Compas- sionate One,*

בְּדִיל וְיַעֲבֹר. –CONG.

‹‹ And [HASHEM] passed . . . ‹ for the sake of

רַחֲמָנָא אִדְכַּר לָן קְיָמֵהּ דְּיִצְחָק עֲקִידָא. – CHAZZAN

‹‹ the bound one, ‹ [made to] Isaac ‹ the promise ‹ for us ‹ recall ‹ O Compas- sionate One,

---

(1) *Exodus* 34:5-7. (2) 34:9. (3) From the weekday *Shemoneh Esrei*. (4) *Psalms* 86:5.

§ רַחֲמָנָא — *O Compassionate One.* In this anonymously composed prayer, we ask God, the Compassionate One, to recall the promises He had made to the Patriarchs and the merits of the leaders of Israel throughout the generations.

And He should do so in response to our reciting the Thirteen Attributes of Mercy (*Exodus* 34:6-7) which begin with the words ה' וַיַּעֲבֹר, *And HASHEM passed,* and which we have just recited four times and will soon recite once more.

CONG. – בְּדִיל וַיַּעֲבֹר.
≫ And [HASHEM] ⟨ for the
passed . . . sake of

CHAZZAN – רַחֲמָנָא אִדְכַּר לָן קְיָמֵהּ דְּיַעֲקֹב שְׁלֵימָא.
≫ the perfect ⟨ [made to] ⟨ the ⟨ for us ⟨ recall ⟨ O Compas-
one, Jacob promise sionate One,

CONG. – בְּדִיל וַיַּעֲבֹר.
≫ And [HASHEM] ⟨ for the
passed . . . sake of

CHAZZAN – רַחֲמָנָא אִדְכַּר לָן זְכוּתֵהּ דְּיוֹסֵף צַדִּיקָא.
≫ the righteous ⟨ of ⟨ the ⟨ for us ⟨ recall ⟨ O Compas-
one, Joseph merit sionate One,

CONG. – בְּדִיל וַיַּעֲבֹר.
≫ And [HASHEM] ⟨ for the
passed . . . sake of

CHAZZAN – רַחֲמָנָא אִדְכַּר לָן קְיָמֵהּ דְּמֹשֶׁה נְבִיָּא.
≫ the ⟨ [made to] ⟨ the ⟨ for us ⟨ recall ⟨ O Compas-
prophet, Moses promise sionate One,

CONG. – בְּדִיל וַיַּעֲבֹר.
≫ And [HASHEM] ⟨ for the
passed . . . sake of

CHAZZAN – רַחֲמָנָא אִדְכַּר לָן קְיָמֵהּ דְּאַהֲרֹן כַּהֲנָא.
≫ the ⟨ [made to] ⟨ the ⟨ for us ⟨ recall ⟨ O Compas-
Kohen, Aaron promise sionate One,

CONG. – בְּדִיל וַיַּעֲבֹר.
≫ And [HASHEM] ⟨ for the
passed . . . sake of

CHAZZAN – רַחֲמָנָא אִדְכַּר לָן קַנָּאוּתֵהּ דְּפִינְחָס קַנָּאָה.
≫ the Zealot, ⟨ of Phinehas ⟨ the ⟨ for us ⟨ recall ⟨ O Compas-
zealousness sionate One,

CONG. – בְּדִיל וַיַּעֲבֹר.
≫ And [HASHEM] ⟨ for the
passed . . . sake of

CHAZZAN – רַחֲמָנָא אִדְכַּר לָן קְיָמֵהּ דְּדָוִד מְשִׁיחָא.
≫ the anointed ⟨ [made to] ⟨ the ⟨ for us ⟨ recall ⟨ O Compas-
one, David promise sionate One,

CONG. – בְּדִיל וַיַּעֲבֹר.
≫ And [HASHEM] ⟨ for the
passed . . . sake of

– CHAZZAN – רַחֲמָנָא אִדְכַר לָן צְלוֹתֵיהּ דִּשְׁלֹמֹה מַלְכָּא.

‹‹ the ‹ of ‹ the ‹ for us ‹ recall ‹ O Compas-
king, Solomon prayer sionate One,

– CONG. בְּדִיל וַיַּעֲבֹר.

‹‹ And [HASHEM] ‹ for the
passed . . . sake of

CHAZZAN, THEN CONGREGATION:

רַחֲמָנָא תּוּב מֵרוּגְזָךְ, וְלָא נְהַדַּר רֵיקָם מִן קֳדָמָךְ.

‹‹ before ‹ from ‹ empty- ‹ turn ‹ so that ‹‹ from Your ‹ relent ‹ O Compas-
You. handed back we not anger, sionate One,

**AN INDIVIDUAL PRAYING WITHOUT A MINYAN OMITS THE NEXT TWO PARAGRAPHS,
BEGINNING אֵל מֶלֶךְ, O GOD, KING, AND ה', HASHEM.**

אֵל מֶלֶךְ יוֹשֵׁב עַל כִּסֵּא רַחֲמִים, מִתְנַהֵג בַּחֲסִידוּת, מוֹחֵל

‹ Who ‹‹ with ‹ Who acts ‹‹ of mercy, ‹ the ‹ on ‹ Who ‹ King ‹ O God,
pardons kindness, throne sits

עֲוֹנוֹת עַמּוֹ, מַעֲבִיר רִאשׁוֹן רִאשׁוֹן, מַרְבֶּה מְחִילָה לַחַטָּאִים

‹ to uninten- ‹ pardon ‹ Who abun- ‹ by one, ‹ [sins] one ‹ Who ‹ of His ‹ the sins
tional sinners dantly grants removes people,

וּסְלִיחָה לַפּוֹשְׁעִים, עֹשֶׂה צְדָקוֹת עִם כָּל בָּשָׂר וָרוּחַ, לֹא

‹— not ‹‹ and ‹ [beings ‹ all ‹ with ‹ acts of ‹ Who ‹‹ to willful ‹ and
spirit of] flesh generosity performs sinners, forgiveness

כְרָעָתָם תִּגְמוֹל. ❖ אֵל הוֹרֵיתָ לָּנוּ לוֹמַר שְׁלֹשׁ עֶשְׂרֵה,

‹‹ the Thirteen ‹ to recite ‹ us ‹ You ‹ O ‹‹ do You repay ‹ in accord with
[Attributes of Mercy]; taught God, them! their wickedness

וּזְכוֹר לָנוּ הַיּוֹם בְּרִית שְׁלֹשׁ עֶשְׂרֵה, כְּמוֹ שֶׁהוֹדַעְתָּ לֶעָנָיו

‹ to the humble ‹ You made ‹ as ‹‹ of [these] Thirteen, ‹ the ‹ today ‹ for us ‹ remember
one [Moses] known covenant

מִקֶּדֶם, כְּמוֹ שֶׁכָּתוּב, וַיֵּרֶד יהוה בֶּעָנָן וַיִּתְיַצֵּב עִמּוֹ שָׁם,

‹‹ there, ‹ with ‹ and stood ‹ in a cloud ‹ And HASHEM ‹‹ it is written: ‹ as ‹‹ in ancient
him descended times,

וַיִּקְרָא בְשֵׁם יהוה.

‹‹ of ‹ with the ‹ and He
HASHEM. Name called out

CONGREGATION AND CHAZZAN RECITE LOUDLY AND IN UNISON:

וַיַּעֲבֹר יהוה עַל פָּנָיו וַיִּקְרָא:

‹‹ and ‹‹ [Moses'] ‹ before ‹ And HASHEM passed
proclaimed: face,

יהוה, יהוה, אֵל, רַחוּם, וְחַנּוּן, אֶרֶךְ אַפַּיִם, וְרַב חֶסֶד, וֶאֱמֶת,

‹‹ and ‹ in ‹ and ‹ to anger, ‹ Slow ‹‹ and ‹ Compas- ‹ God, ‹ HASHEM, ‹ HASHEM,
Truth, Kindness Abundant Gracious, sionate

נֹצֵר חֶסֶד לָאֲלָפִים, נֹשֵׂא עָוֹן, וָפֶשַׁע, וְחַטָאָה, וְנַקֵּה.

Preserver ‹ of ‹ kindness ‹ for thousands ‹ Forgiver ‹ of ‹ iniquity, ‹ willful sin, ‹ and inad-vertent sin, ‹ and Who absolves.

וְסָלַחְתָּ לַעֲוֹנֵנוּ וּלְחַטָאתֵנוּ וּנְחַלְתָּנוּ. סְלַח לָנוּ אָבִינוּ כִּי

May You forgive ‹ our iniquities ‹ and our sins, ‹ and make us Your heritage. ‹ Forgive ‹ us, ‹ our Father, ‹ for

חָטָאנוּ, מְחַל לָנוּ מַלְכֵּנוּ כִּי פָשָׁעְנוּ. כִּי אַתָּה אֲדֹנָי טוֹב

we have sinned; ‹ pardon ‹ us, ‹ our King, ‹ for we have willfully sinned. ‹ For ‹ You, ‹ O Lord, ‹ are good

וְסַלָּח, וְרַב חֶסֶד לְכָל קֹרְאֶיךָ.

and abundantly forgiving, ‹ and ‹ kind ‹ to all ‹ who call upon You.

ALL CONTINUE:

אֱלֹהֵינוּ וֵאלֹהֵי אֲבוֹתֵינוּ,

Our God ‹ and God ‹ of our forefathers:

אַל תַּעַשׂ עִמָּנוּ כָּלָה,*[1]

Do ‹ not ‹ carry out ‹ against ‹ us ‹ a complete destruction.*

תֹּאחֵז יָדְךָ בַּמִּשְׁפָּט.[2]

Let Your hand grasp ‹ justice.

בְּבֹא תוֹכֵחָה לְנֶגְדֶּךָ,

When there shall come ‹ [our] ad-monishment ‹ before You,

שְׂמֵנוּ מִסִּפְרְךָ אַל תֶּמַח.[3]

our name ‹ from Your book ‹ do not ‹ erase.

גִּשְׁתְּךָ לַחֲקוֹר מוּסָר,

When You approach ‹ to determine ‹ [our] affliction,

רַחֲמֶיךָ יְקַדְּמוּ רָגְזֶךָ.[4]

may Your mercy ‹ take precedence over ‹ Your wrath.

דַּלּוּת מַעֲשִׂים בְּשׁוּרְךָ,

When the paucity ‹ of [our good] deeds ‹ You see,

קָרֵב צֶדֶק מֵאֵלֶיךָ.

advance ‹ righteous-ness ‹ on Your own.

הוֹרֵנוּ בְּזַעֲקֵנוּ לָךְ,

Teach us ‹ [what to say] ‹ when we cry out to You.

צַו יְשׁוּעָתֵנוּ בְּמַפְגִּיעַ.[5]

Command ‹ our salvation, ‹ when we beseech [You],

וְתָשִׁיב שְׁבוּת אָהֳלֵי תָם,[6]

and return ‹ the ‹ captivity ‹ of the tents ‹ of the whole-some one;

פְּתָחָיו רְאֵה כִּי שָׁמֵמוּ.

his entranceways ‹ see ‹ that ‹ they are in ruins.

---

(1) Cf. *Jeremiah* 5:18. (2) Cf. *Deuteronomy* 32:41. (3) Cf. *Exodus* 32:32-33. (4) Cf. *Habakkuk* 3:2; *Psalms* 79:8. (5) Cf. 44:5; *Job* 36:32. (6) Cf. *Jeremiah* 30:18; *Genesis* 25:27.

אַל תַּעַשׂ עִמָּנוּ כָּלָה ﬥ — *Do not carry out against us a complete destruction.* This un-signed *piyut* appears in the *chazzan's* repetition of the *Mussaf Amidah* on Yom Kippur. Its verses contain an alphabetical acrostic; how-ever, unlike many other *piyutim* that follow the order of the *Aleph-Beis*, this one was composed in accordance with the alphabetic arrangement

זְכוֹר נֶאֱמַת לֹא תִשָּׁכַח ‏ עֵדוּת* מִפִּי זַרְעוֹ.¹

Remem- ‹ Your ‹ It shall ‹ be » – the ‹ from the ‹ of his »
ber utterance, not forgotten Testimony* mouths offspring.

חוֹתָם תְּעוּדָה תַּתִּיר, ‏ סוֹדְךָ שִׂים בִּלְמוּדֶךָ.²

The seal ‹ of the document ‹ unlock; » Your ‹ make ‹ to those who are »
[the Torah] secret accessible Your students.

טַבּוּר* אַגַּן* הַסַּהַר, ‏ נָא אַל יֶחְסַר הַמָּזֶג.*³

The ‹ the drink- ‹ that is » please –› let it ‹ be ‹ the mixed »
center,* ing bowl* moon shaped, not lacking beverage.*

יָה, דַּע אֶת אֲשֶׁר יְדָעוּךָ, ‏ מַגֵּר עַם אֲשֶׁר לֹא יְדָעוּךָ.

O God, ‹ be ‹ with those » crush ‹ the ‹ who ‹ do not ‹ know You, »
intimate who know You; people

כִּי תָשִׁיב לְבִצָּרוֹן, ‏ לְכוּדִים אֲסִירֵי הַתִּקְוָה.*⁴

when ‹ You return ‹ to the fortified » the captured ‹ who are ‹ of hope.* »
[Israel] [Jerusalem], ones prisoners

CONFESSION OF RABBEINU NISSIM / וידוי של רבינו נסים

רִבּוֹנוֹ שֶׁל עוֹלָם, קֹדֶם כָּל דָּבָר, אֵין לִי פֶּה לְהָשִׁיב, וְלֹא

‹ Master ‹ of ‹ the » Before « every- ‹ thing, ‹ [I admit that] ‹ [words] in » to « nor ‹
universe: I have no my mouth, respond, to

מֶצַח לְהָרִים רֹאשׁ, כִּי מִפְּנֵי שֶׁעֲוֹנוֹתַי רַבּוּ מִלִּמְנוֹת, וְחַטֹּאתַי

the ‹ to lift ‹ my » my ‹ but « it is ‹ because » my iniquities ‹ are too ‹ to count, « and my ‹
audacity head, rather many sins

עָצְמוּ מִסַּפֵּר, וּכְמַשָּׂא כָבֵד יִכְבְּדוּ מִמֶּנִּי, מִתְוַדֶּה אֲנִי לְפָנֶיךָ,

are too ‹ to relate, « and, like ‹ that is ‹ they are « for me, ‹ that I confess « before ‹
grave a burden heavy too weighty You,

(1) Cf. *Deuteronomy* 31:21. (2) Cf. *Isaiah* 8:16. (3) *Song of Songs* 7:3. (4) Cf. *Zechariah* 9:12.

---

known as אַ״תְּ בַּ״שׁ, which pairs the letters from opposite ends of the *Aleph-Beis*.

עֵדוּת — *The Testimony.* This term is usually applied to the Tablets of the Ten Commandments (e.g., *Exodus* 32:15), but is used here as a reference to the Torah. King David used it in this manner in the verse, עֵדוּת ה' נֶאֱמָנָה, *the Testimony of HASHEM is trustworthy* (*Psalms* 19:8).

טַבּוּר — *The center,* literally, *the navel.* The *Beis HaMikdash* stood at the center of the spiritual world. It was also the first point on earth to be created.

אַגַּן ... הַמָּזֶג — *The drinking bowl ... the mixed beverage.* The Talmud understands this verse as a reference to the seat of the Sanhedrin in the

Temple complex. The seventy-one justices of the Sanhedrin sat in a semicircle so that each of them could see all of the others during their deliberations (*Sanhedrin* 36b). The beverage in the bowl refers either to the judges who fill the semicircle or to their teachings.

אֲסִירֵי הַתִּקְוָה — *Who are prisoners of hope.* Though Israel is trapped in exile, its people will not abandon their hope in the ultimate Redemption.

⏃ Confession of Rabbeinu Nissim

This confessional supplication is generally ascribed to Rabbeinu Nissim Gaon, who, together with Rabbeinu Chananel, led North African Jewry in the 11th century. However,

יהוה אֱלֹהַי, בִּכְפִיפַת רֹאשׁ, בִּכְפִיפַת קוֹמָה, בִּכְנִיעַת חָיִל,

‹ of [my] capabilities, submission ‹ with full height, ‹ of [my] ‹ with bowing ‹ of [my] head, ‹ with bowing ‹‹ my God, ‹ HASHEM,

בַּחֲלִישַׁת כֹּחַ, בִּשְׁבִירַת לֵב, בִּנְמִיכוּת רוּחַ, בְּקָדָּה, בִּכְרִיעָה,

‹ with kneeling, ‹ with bowing, ‹ with spirit, ‹ with depressed heart, ‹ of [my] ‹ with breaking strength, ‹ of [my] ‹ with weakening

בְּהִשְׁתַּחֲוָיָה, בְּאֵימָה, בִּבְעָתָה, בְּרֶתֶת, בְּזִיעַ, בְּחַלְחוּל,

‹ with terror, ‹ with shuddering, ‹ with quaking, ‹ with trembling, ‹ with fear, ‹ with prostrating,

בְּיִרְאָה, בְּמוֹרָא. אוֹמֵר אֲנִי לְפָנֶיךָ, יהוה אֱלֹהַי, מִקְצָת מַעֲשַׂי

‹ of my deeds ‹ only part ‹ my God, ‹ HASHEM, ‹ before You, ‹ I shall state ‹‹ with awe. ‹ with fright,

הָרָעִים וּמִדְּרָכַי הַמְכֹעָרִים וּמִמַּעֲלָלַי הַמְקֻלְקָלִים. לְאָמְרָם אִי

‹ is not them [all] ‹ To state ‹‹ that are flawed. ‹ and of my actions ‹ that are abhorrent ‹ and of my ways ‹ that are evil

אֶפְשָׁר, לְבָרְרָם אֵין בִּי כֹחַ, לְגַלּוֹתָם לֹא אֶעֱצָר חָיִל, לְדַבְּרָם

‹ to speak of them, ‹‹ the [needed] capabilities; ‹ gather I ‹ to reveal them, ‹‹ the ‹ in I have ‹ to clarify me not ‹‹ possible; strength;

לֹא אֲדָעֵם, לְהַגִּידָם אֵינִי כְדַאי. וְלִתְבּוֹעַ עֲלֵיהֶם סְלִיחָה

‹ forgiveness, ‹ for them ‹ And to demand ‹‹ worthy. ‹ I am not ‹ to relate them, ‹‹ I do not know how;

וּמְחִילָה וְכַפָּרָה, מָה אֲנִי? מֶה חַיַּי? אֲנִי הֶבֶל וָרִיק. אֲנִי רִמָּה

‹ am a worm ‹ I ‹‹ and ‹ I ‹ is my ‹ What ‹‹ am I? ‹— what ‹‹ and ‹ pardon, emptiness; futility life?

וְתוֹלֵעָה.[1] אֲנִי עָפָר וָאֵפֶר.[2] בּוֹשׁ אֲנִי מֵחֲטָאַי. וּמִכְלָם אֲנִי

‹ am I humiliated ‹‹ of my sins; ‹ am I Ashamed ‹‹ and ash. ‹ am dust ‹ I ‹‹ and a maggot;

מִפְּשָׁעַי. אֵין לִי פִּתְחוֹן פֶּה לְהִתְוַדּוֹת לְפָנֶיךָ. גָּדוֹל עֲוֹנִי

‹ is my iniquity ‹ Too great ‹‹ before You. ‹ to confess ‹ my mouth ‹ [right] to open ‹ I have no ‹‹ because of my willful transgressions.

מִנְּשֹׂא.[3] עָצְמוּ פְשָׁעַי מִסַּפֵּר. בֹּשְׁתִּי וְגַם נִכְלַמְתִּי,[4] כַּגַּנָּב

‹ like a burglar ‹‹ humiliated, ‹ and also ‹ I am ashamed ‹‹ to relate. ‹ are my willful transgressions ‹ too grave ‹‹ to bear;

הַנִּמְצָא בַּמַּחְתֶּרֶת.[5]

‹‹ in a break-in. ‹ caught

---

(1) Cf. *Job* 25:6. (2) Cf. *Genesis* 18:27. (3) 4:13. (4) *Jeremiah* 31:18. (5) Cf. *Exodus* 22:1.

some attribute the confession to R' Saadiah Gaon of 10th-century Egypt and Babylonia (Iraq); others, to R' Nissi, who lived in Persia in the 10th century.

רִבּוֹנוֹ שֶׁל עוֹלָם, אִם עָמַדְתִּי לְפָרֵשׁ אֶת חֲטָאַי וּלְבָאֲרָם,

Master ‹ of ‹ the ‹ If ‹‹ I were to ‹ to specify ‹ my sins ‹ and describe ‹ universe: them,

יִכְלֶה הַזְּמַן וְהֵם לֹא יִכְלוּ. עַל אֵיזֶה מֵהֶם אֶתְבַּע, וְעַל אֵיזֶה

time would end ‹ but ‹ they ‹‹ would ‹ end. ‹ would ‹ For ‹‹ which ‹ of ‹‹ can I ‹ For ‹ which not appeal? them

מֵהֶם אֲבַקֵּשׁ, וְעַל אֵיזֶה מֵהֶם אֶתְוַדֶּה. עַל הַכְּלָל אוֹ עַל

of them ‹ can I plead? ‹ For ‹ which ‹ of them ‹‹ For ‹‹ can I confess? ‹ the general ‹ For ‹‹ or ‹ for ‹

הַפְּרָט, עַל הַנִּסְתָּרוֹת אוֹ עַל הַנִּגְלוֹת, עַל הָרִאשׁוֹנוֹת אוֹ עַל

the ‹‹ For ‹ the private ‹ or ‹ for ‹ the public ‹‹ For ‹ the early ones ‹ or ‹ for ‹ particular? ones ones?

הָאַחֲרוֹנוֹת, עַל הַחֲדָשׁוֹת אוֹ עַל הַיְשָׁנוֹת, עַל הַטְּמוּנוֹת אוֹ

the later ones? ‹‹ For ‹ the new ones ‹ or ‹ for ‹ the old ones? ‹‹ For ‹ the hidden ones ‹ or ‹

עַל הַנּוֹדָעוֹת, עַל הַנִּזְכָּרוֹת אוֹ עַל הַנִּשְׁכָּחוֹת מִמֶּנִּי. יוֹדֵעַ אֲנִי

for ‹ the revealed ‹‹ For ‹ those ‹ or ‹ for ‹ those forgotten ‹ by me? ‹‹ I know ‹ ones? remembered

בְּעַצְמִי שֶׁאֵין בִּי לֹא תוֹרָה וְלֹא חָכְמָה, לֹא דַעַת וְלֹא

about ‹ that there ‹ in ‹ neither ‹ Torah ‹ nor ‹‹ wisdom, ‹ neither ‹ knowledge ‹ nor ‹ myself is not me

תְבוּנָה, לֹא צְדָקָה וְלֹא יַשְׁרוּת וְלֹא גְמִילוּת חֲסָדִים. אֲבָל

under- ‹‹ neither ‹ charity ‹ nor ‹ fairness ‹ nor ‹ the ‹ of kind ‹‹ But standing, bestowal deeds. rather,

אֲנִי סָכָל וְלֹא יוֹדֵעַ, בַּעַר וְלֹא מֵבִין, גַּזְלָן וְלֹא נֶאֱמָן, חַיָּב

I ‹ am a ‹ who ‹‹ know, ‹ a boor ‹ who ‹ under- ‹‹ a robber ‹ who ‹‹ trust- ‹ guilty ‹ fool does not does not stand, is not worthy,

וְלֹא זַכַּאי, רָשָׁע וְלֹא צַדִּיק, רַע וְלֹא טוֹב. וְכָל מַעֲשִׂים רָעִים

and ‹ innocent, ‹‹ wicked ‹ and ‹ righteous, ‹‹ evil ‹ and ‹ good, ‹‹ and all ‹ of acts ‹ that not not kinds are evil

עָשִׂיתִי וְגַם עֲבֵרוֹת רָעוֹת עָשִׂיתִי. וְאִם אַתָּה דָן אוֹתִי כְּמַעֲשַׂי,

I have ‹‹ and ‹ trans- ‹ that are ‹ I have ‹‹ If ‹ You ‹ are to ‹ me ‹ according to committed, gressions evil committed. judge my deeds,

אוֹי לִי, וַי לִי, אֲהָהּ עָלַי, אוֹיָה עַל נַפְשִׁי. וְאִם תְּבַקֵּשׁ לְנַקּוֹתִי,

is ‹ woe ‹‹ Alas ‹ for ‹‹ Grief ‹ upon ‹ Woe ‹‹ to ‹ my soul! ‹ If ‹‹ You would ‹ to ‹‹ me! me! me! me! seek cleanse me,

כִּמְטַהֵר וּכְמְצָרֵף כֶּסֶף, לֹא יִשָּׁאֵר מִמֶּנִּי מְאוּמָה, כִּי אֲנִי כְּקַשׁ

like one ‹ and refines ‹‹ silver, ‹ there ‹ be left ‹ of me ‹ anything, ‹‹ for ‹ I ‹ am like who purifies would not straw

לִפְנֵי אֵשׁ, וּכְעֵצִים יְבֵשִׁים לִפְנֵי הָאוֹר, כְּכֶסֶף סִיגִים מְצֻפֶּה

‹ overlaid ‹ with ‹ [like] ‹‹ a flame, ‹ before ‹ that is dry ‹ like wood ‹‹ fire, ‹ before
impurities silver

עַל חֶרֶשׂ,[1] הֶבֶל הַבָּלִים אֵין בּוֹ מַמָּשׁ. בַּמֶּה אֲקַדֵּם[2] אוֹ

‹ or ‹‹ shall I ‹ With ‹ any ‹ in it ‹ that does ‹ of ‹ a ‹‹ earthen- ‹ on
approach [Him]? what substance. not have futilities futility ware,

מָה רְפוּאָה אֲבַקֵּשׁ. כְּבֵן סוֹרֵר וּמוֹרֶה[3] הָיִיתִי, כְּעֶבֶד מוֹרֵד

‹ rebelling ‹ like a ‹‹ have I ‹ and ‹ who is ‹ Like ‹‹ can I seek? ‹ cure ‹ what
slave been, rebellious wayward the son

עַל אֲדוֹנָיו,[4] כְּתַלְמִיד חוֹלֵק עַל רַבּוֹ. אֶת אֲשֶׁר טִהַרְתָּ

‹ You declared ‹ which ‹ That ‹‹ his ‹ with ‹ disputing ‹ like a student ‹‹ his master, ‹ against
pure, teacher.

טִמֵּאתִי, וַאֲשֶׁר טִמֵּאתָ טִהַרְתִּי. אֶת אֲשֶׁר הִתַּרְתָּ אָסַרְתִּי,

‹‹ I forbade, ‹ You ‹ which ‹ that ‹‹ I declared ‹ You declared ‹ and that ‹‹ I declared
permitted, pure; impure, which impure,

וַאֲשֶׁר אָסַרְתָּ הִתַּרְתִּי. אֶת אֲשֶׁר אָהַבְתָּ שָׂנֵאתִי, וַאֲשֶׁר

‹ and that ‹‹ I hated, ‹ You loved, ‹ which ‹ that ‹‹ I permitted; ‹ You forbade, ‹ and that
which

שָׂנֵאתָ אָהַבְתִּי. אֶת אֲשֶׁר הֵקַלְתָּ הֶחֱמַרְתִּי, וַאֲשֶׁר הֶחֱמַרְתָּ

‹ You were ‹ and that ‹‹ I was strict, ‹ You were ‹ about ‹ that ‹‹ I loved; ‹ You hated,
strict, about which lenient, which

הֵקַלְתִּי. אֶת אֲשֶׁר קֵרַבְתָּ רִחַקְתִּי, וַאֲשֶׁר רִחַקְתָּ קֵרַבְתִּי.

‹‹ I drew ‹ You ‹ and that ‹ I distanced ‹ You drew ‹ which ‹ that ‹‹ I was
close. distanced which close, lenient;

אַךְ לֹא לְהַכְעִיסְךָ נִתְכַּוַּנְתִּי. וּבְעַזּוּת מֵצַח בָּאתִי לְבַקֵּשׁ

‹ to beg ‹ I have come ‹ Brazenly ‹‹ did I intend. ‹ to provoke You ‹ not ‹ But

סְלִיחָה מִלְּפָנֶיךָ. שַׂמְתִּי פָנַי כְּכֶלֶב, הֶעֱזְתִּי מֵצַח כְּזוֹנָה,

‹‹ as a ‹ I have been as brazen ‹‹ as a dog, ‹ I have made myself ‹‹ before You. ‹ forgiveness
harlot; [as impudent]

וְנִגַּשְׁתִּי לְפָנֶיךָ בְּבֹשֶׁת פָּנִים. וְכֵן כָּתוּב: וּמֵצַח אִשָּׁה זוֹנָה

‹ who is ‹ of a ‹ The [brazen] ‹‹ it is ‹ And so ‹‹ shamefacedly. ‹ You ‹ and I have
a harlot woman forehead written: approached

הָיָה לָךְ, מֵאַנְתְּ הִכָּלֵם.[5]

‹‹ to feel shame. ‹ you refused ‹ you had;

רִבּוֹנוֹ שֶׁל עוֹלָם, לֹא עַל עַצְמִי בִּלְבַד אֲנִי מִתְפַּלֵּל וּמִתְוַדֶּה,

‹‹ and confess, ‹ pray ‹ that I ‹ alone ‹ myself ‹ for ‹ It is ‹‹ the ‹ of ‹ Master
not universe:

---

(1) *Proverbs* 26:23. (2) *Micah* 6:6. (3) *Deuteronomy* 21:18. (4) Cf. *II Chronicles* 13:6. (5) *Jeremiah* 3:3.

כִּי אִם בַּעֲדִי וּבְעַד קְהָלֶיךָ הָעוֹמְדִים לְפָנֶיךָ. וְאַף עַל פִּי

‹ And even though ‹‹ before You. ‹ that stands ‹ Your ‹ and for ‹ for ‹ rather ‹ but myself

שֶׁאֵינִי רָאוּי וְלֹא זַכַּאי לְהִתְוַדּוֹת עַל עַצְמִי, וְכָל שֶׁכֵּן עַל

‹ for ‹ the more so ‹ and all ‹ myself, ‹ for ‹ to confess ‹ worthy ‹ nor ‹ fitting ‹ I am not

אֲחֵרִים, אֲבָל כִּי דַרְכְּךָ לְהַאֲרִיךְ אַפֶּךָ, וּמִדָּתְךָ לְהַעֲבִיר

‹ to overlook ‹ Your manner ‹ to ‹ since it ‹ never- ‹ theless, ‹ others, ‹‹ anger, ‹ to be slow ‹ Your practice ‹ is indeed

קִצְפֶּךָ, וּמִנְהָגְךָ לְרַחֵם עַל בְּרִיּוֹתֶיךָ, וּבְיוֹתֵר לַשָּׁבִים אֵלֶיךָ

‹ to You ‹ on those who return ‹ —especially ‹‹ Your creations ‹ on ‹ to have mercy ‹ and Your custom ‹ Your wrath,

וּמוֹדִים לְפָנֶיךָ, וְעוֹזְבִים וּמִתְנַחֲמִים עַל פִּשְׁעֵיהֶם, וְלֹא

‹ and do not ‹ their sins, ‹ over ‹ and are remorseful ‹ and who forsake ‹‹ before You, ‹ and confess

מְכַסִּים אוֹתָם. שֶׁכֵּן כָּתוּב: מְכַסֶּה פְּשָׁעָיו לֹא יַצְלִיחַ, וּמוֹדֶה

‹ but he who confesses ‹‹ succeed; will ‹ his sins ‹ He who conceals ‹ is it ‹ For so ‹‹ them. ‹ conceal ‹ will not

וְעוֹזֵב יְרֻחָם.[1] וּמַצִּיל אֶת נַפְשׁוֹ מִדִּינָה שֶׁל גֵּיהִנֹּם.

‹‹ Gehinnom. ‹ of ‹ from the judgment ‹ his soul ‹ And he ‹‹ will be shown mercy. [them] ‹ and forsakes saves

רִבּוֹנוֹ שֶׁל עוֹלָם, מִנְהַג בֵּית דִּינְךָ הַצֶּדֶק לֹא כְמִנְהַג בָּתֵּי דִינִין

‹ of ‹ of ‹ like the ‹ is not ‹ that is ‹ of ‹ of Your ‹ The ‹ the ‹ of ‹ Master justice courts custom righteous justice court custom universe:

שֶׁל בְּנֵי אָדָם. שֶׁמִּדַּת בְּנֵי אָדָם כְּשֶׁהוּא תּוֹבֵעַ אֶת חֲבֵרוֹ

‹ against his fellow ‹ brings a claim ‹ that when one ‹ of humans ‹ For it is the practice ‹‹ humans. ‹ of

בְּמָמוֹן אֶל הַבֵּית דִּין אוֹ אֶל הַשּׁוֹפֵט, אִם יִכְפּוֹר יִנָּצֵל

‹ he will be spared ‹ [the defendant] denies [the claim], ‹ if ‹‹ the judge, ‹ to ‹ or ‹ of ‹ the justice court ‹ to ‹ for money

מִן הַמָּמוֹן, וְאִם יוֹדֶה מִתְחַיֵּב לִתֵּן. וּבֵית דִּינְךָ הַצֶּדֶק לֹא

‹ is not ‹ that is righteous ‹ of justice ‹ But Your court ‹‹ to pay. ‹ he will be liable ‹ he admits it ‹ and if ‹‹ [paying] ‹ from the money;

כֵן הוּא. אֶלָּא אִם יִכְפּוֹר אָדָם, אוֹי לוֹ וְאוֹי לְנַפְשׁוֹ, וְאִם

‹ but if ‹‹ is to his soul; ‹ and ‹ is to woe him ‹ woe ‹ a person denies guilt, ‹ if ‹ Instead, ‹‹ so.

מוֹדֶה וְעוֹזֵב, אַתָּה מְרַחֲמֵהוּ.

‹‹ show him mercy. ‹ You ‹ and forsakes [his sinful behavior], ‹ he confesses

---

(1) *Proverbs* 28:13.

רבּוֹנוֹ שֶׁל עוֹלָם, לוּלֵי חֲטָאֵינוּ וּפְשָׁעֵינוּ, לֹא הָיִינוּ בוֹשִׁים

‹ be ‹ we would not ‹ and our ‹ for our sins ‹ were it ‹‹ the ‹ of ‹ Master
ashamed transgressions not universe:

וְנִכְלָמִים, וְעַל מַה הָיִינוּ מִתְוַדִּים, כִּי אִי אֶפְשָׁר לוֹ לְאָדָם

‹ for a person ‹ possible ‹ it is ‹ For ‹‹ confess? ‹ would ‹ what ‹ –and ‹‹ and
not we for humiliated

לְבַקֵּשׁ עַל חֵטְא, וְהוּא לֹא חָטָא. וְלֹא יִוָּדַע עֹז רַחֲמֶיךָ, אֶלָּא

‹ unless ‹‹ of Your ‹ –the ‹‹ be ‹ And it ‹‹ sin! ‹ did ‹ if he ‹ a sin ‹ for ‹ to seek
mercy– power known would not not [forgiveness]

בְּהַעֲבִירְךָ חַטַּאת יְרֵאֶיךָ. וְלֹא עַל עַצְמִי בִּלְבַד אֲנִי מִתְוַדֶּה,

‹‹ confess, ‹ do I ‹ alone ‹ myself ‹ for ‹ Not ‹‹ of those who ‹ the sins ‹ You overlook
revere You.

כִּי אִם בַּעֲדִי וּבְעַד כָּל קְהָלֶךָ. יְהִי רָצוֹן מִלְּפָנֶיךָ, יהוה

‹ HASHEM, ‹‹ before You, ‹ the will ‹ May ‹‹ of Your ‹ of all ‹ and on ‹ on my ‹ rather ‹ but
it be congregation. behalf behalf

אֱלֹהֵינוּ וֵאלֹהֵי אֲבוֹתֵינוּ, שֶׁתִּסְלַח וְתִמְחָל לָנוּ עַל כָּל

‹ all ‹ for ‹ us ‹ and pardon ‹ that You ‹‹ of our ‹ and the ‹ our God
forgive forefathers, God

עֲוֹנוֹתֵינוּ וּפְשָׁעֵינוּ, וּתְכַפֵּר לָנוּ עַל כָּל חַטֹּאתֵינוּ.

‹‹ our inadvertant ‹ all ‹ for ‹ to us ‹ and grant ‹‹ and our ‹ our willful
sins. atonement rebellious sins, sins

CONFESSION / וידוי

אֱלֹהֵינוּ וֵאלֹהֵי אֲבוֹתֵינוּ, (אָנָּא) תָּבֹא לְפָנֶיךָ תְּפִלָּתֵנוּ,¹ וְאַל

‹ and ‹‹ may our ‹ before ‹ come ‹ (please) ‹‹ of our ‹ and ‹ Our God
do not prayer, You forefathers, the God

תִּתְעַלַּם מִתְּחִנָּתֵנוּ,² שֶׁאֵין אָנוּ עַזֵּי פָנִים וּקְשֵׁי עֹרֶף, לוֹמַר

‹ as to ‹ necked ‹ and stiff- ‹ faced ‹ so ‹ For we are not ‹‹ our ‹ ignore
say brazen- supplication.

לְפָנֶיךָ יהוה אֱלֹהֵינוּ וֵאלֹהֵי אֲבוֹתֵינוּ, צַדִּיקִים אֲנַחְנוּ וְלֹא

‹ and ‹ that we are ‹‹ of our ‹ and ‹ our God, ‹ HASHEM, ‹‹ before
have not righteous forefathers, the God You,

חָטָאנוּ, אֲבָל אֲנַחְנוּ וַאֲבוֹתֵינוּ חָטָאנוּ.³

‹‹ have sinned. ‹ and our ‹ we ‹‹ – for ‹‹ sinned
forefathers indeed,

---

(1) Cf. *Psalms* 88:3. (2) Cf. 55:2. (3) Cf. 106:6.

וידוי / Confession

The confession, beginning with the last phrase of the opening paragraph (אֲנַחְנוּ וַאֲבוֹתֵינוּ חָטָאנוּ, *for indeed, we and our forefathers have sinned*), should be said while standing with one's head

and body slightly bowed to symbolize contrition and submission. It is customary to strike oneself lightly opposite the heart with the right fist while saying each individual expression of sin. This act symbolizes that sin is caused by the

STRIKE THE LEFT SIDE OF THE CHEST WITH THE RIGHT FIST WHILE RECITING EACH OF THE SINS OF THE FOLLOWING CONFESSIONAL LITANY:

אָשַׁמְנוּ, בָּגַדְנוּ, גָּזַלְנוּ, דִּבַּרְנוּ דְפִי. הֶעֱוִינוּ, וְהִרְשַׁעְנוּ,

We have been guilty; We have betrayed; we have robbed; We have slander. We have committed iniquity; we have committed wickedness;

זַדְנוּ, חָמַסְנוּ, טָפַלְנוּ שֶׁקֶר. יָעַצְנוּ רָע, כִּזַּבְנוּ, לַצְנוּ,

we have sinned willfully; we have extorted; we have made false accusations. We have given advice that is bad; we have been deceitful; we have scorned;

מָרַדְנוּ, נִאַצְנוּ, סָרַרְנוּ, עָוִינוּ, פָּשַׁעְנוּ, צָרַרְנוּ, קִשִּׁינוּ עְרֶף.

we have rebelled; we have provoked [God's anger]; we have strayed; we have been iniquitous; we have sinned rebelliously; we have caused distress; we have stiffened our necks.

רָשַׁעְנוּ, שִׁחַתְנוּ, תִּעַבְנוּ, תָּעִינוּ, תִּעְתָּעְנוּ.

We have been wicked; we have been corrupt; we have committed abominations; we have gone astray; we have scoffed.

סַרְנוּ מִמִּצְוֹתֶיךָ וּמִמִּשְׁפָּטֶיךָ הַטּוֹבִים, וְלֹא שָׁוָה לָנוּ.[1] וְאַתָּה

We have turned away from Your commandments and from Your laws that are good, and it was not worth-while for us. And You

צַדִּיק עַל כָּל הַבָּא עָלֵינוּ, כִּי אֱמֶת עָשִׂיתָ וַאֲנַחְנוּ הִרְשַׁעְנוּ.[2]

are righteous in all that has come upon us, for You acted truthfully while we have acted wickedly.

אָשַׁמְנוּ מִכָּל עָם, בּוֹשְׁנוּ מִכָּל דּוֹר, גָּלָה מִמֶּנוּ מָשׂוֹשׂ,

We have become the guiltiest of all peoples; we are more ashamed than all [other] generations; [other] joy has departed from us;

דָּוֶה לִבֵּנוּ בַּחֲטָאֵינוּ, הֻחְבַּל אִוּוּיֵנוּ, וְנִפְרַע פְּאֵרֵנוּ, זְבוּל

our heart has become sickened by our sins; our desirous [treasure] has been ruined, and our splendor destroyed; [God's] abode,

בֵּית מִקְדָּשֵׁנוּ, חָרַב בַּעֲוֹנֵינוּ, טִירָתֵינוּ הָיְתָה לְשַׁמָּה, יְפִי

our Temple, has been destroyed for our iniquities; our Palace has become desolate; the beauty

אַדְמָתֵינוּ לְזָרִים, כֹּחֵנוּ לְנָכְרִים.

of our Land [is given over] to strangers, our power to aliens,

(1) Cf. *Job* 33:27. (2) *Nehemiah* 9:33.

desires of the heart and that the beginning of repentance is the resolve to curb one's passions (*Matnos Kehunah* to *Koheles Rabbah*, Ch. 7).

[Commentary to the *Vidui* service may be found on pp. 172-175 and in the ArtScroll *Yom Kippur Machzor*.]

SOME CONGREGATIONS OMIT THE NEXT THREE PARAGRAPHS AND CONTINUE WITH לְעֵינֵינוּ.

וַעֲדַיִן לֹא שַׁבְנוּ מִטָּעוּתֵנוּ, וְהֵיךְ נָעִיז פָּנֵינוּ וְנַקְשֶׁה עָרְפֵּנוּ,

⟨ and be so stiff-necked ⟨ can we be ⟨ So ⟪ from our ⟨ turned ⟨ we have ⟨ But still
so brazen how waywardness. back not

לוֹמַר לְפָנֶיךָ יהוה אֱלֹהֵינוּ וֵאלֹהֵי אֲבוֹתֵינוּ צַדִּיקִים אֲנַחְנוּ

⟨ are we ⟨ that ⟪ of our ⟨ and the ⟨ our God ⟪ Hashem, ⟨ before ⟨ as to say
righteous forefathers, God You,

וְלֹא חָטָאנוּ, אֲבָל אֲנַחְנוּ וַאֲבוֹתֵינוּ חָטָאנוּ.

⟪ have ⟨ and our ⟨ we ⟨ For in ⟪ sinned? ⟨ and
sinned. forefathers truth, have not

STRIKE THE LEFT SIDE OF THE CHEST WITH THE RIGHT FIST WHILE RECITING
EACH OF THE SINS OF THE FOLLOWING CONFESSIONAL LITANY:

אָשַׁמְנוּ, בָּגַדְנוּ, גָּזַלְנוּ, דִּבַּרְנוּ דְּפִי. הֶעֱוִינוּ, וְהִרְשַׁעְנוּ,

⟪ we have ⟪ We have ⟪ slander. ⟨ we have ⟨ we have ⟪ we have ⟪ We have
committed committed spoken robbed; betrayed; been guilty;
wickedness; iniquity;

זַדְנוּ, חָמַסְנוּ, טָפַלְנוּ שֶׁקֶר. יָעַצְנוּ רָע, כִּזַּבְנוּ, לַצְנוּ,

⟪ we have ⟨ we have ⟪ that ⟨ We have ⟪ false ⟨ we have ⟪ we have ⟪ we have
scorned; been is bad; given accusations. made extorted; sinned
deceitful; advice willfully;

מָרַדְנוּ, נִאַצְנוּ, סָרַרְנוּ, עָוִינוּ, פָּשַׁעְנוּ, צָרַרְנוּ, קִשִּׁינוּ עָרֶף.

⟪ our ⟨ we have ⟪ we have ⟨ we have ⟨ we have ⟪ we have ⟨ we have ⟪ we have
necks. stiffened caused sinned been strayed; provoked rebelled;
distress; rebelliously; iniquitous; [God's anger];

רָשַׁעְנוּ, שִׁחַתְנוּ, תִּעַבְנוּ, תָּעִינוּ, תִּעְתָּעְנוּ.

⟪ we have ⟪ we have ⟪ we have ⟪ we have ⟪ We have
scoffed. gone astray; committed been corrupt; been wicked;
abominations;

סַרְנוּ מִמִּצְוֹתֶיךָ וּמִמִּשְׁפָּטֶיךָ הַטּוֹבִים, וְלֹא שָׁוָה לָנוּ. וְאַתָּה

⟨ And ⟪ for ⟨ worth- ⟨ and it ⟪ that are ⟨ and from ⟨ from Your ⟨ We have
You us. while was not good, Your laws commandments turned away

צַדִּיק עַל כָּל הַבָּא עָלֵינוּ, כִּי אֱמֶת עָשִׂיתָ וַאֲנַחְנוּ הִרְשָׁעְנוּ.

⟪ have acted ⟨ while ⟪ have ⟨ truthfully ⟨ for ⟪ upon ⟨ that has ⟨ all ⟨ in ⟨ are
wickedly. we You acted, us, come righteous

לְעֵינֵינוּ עָשְׁקוּ עֲמָלֵנוּ, מְמֻשָׁךְ וּמְמוֹרָט מִמֶּנּוּ, נָתְנוּ עֻלָּם

⟨ their ⟨ they have ⟪ from us; ⟨ and ⟨ it has been ⟪ [the fruits of] ⟨ they have ⟨ Before our eyes
yoke placed cut off pulled away our labor; stolen

עָלֵינוּ, סָבַלְנוּ עַל שִׁכְמֵנוּ, עֲבָדִים מָשְׁלוּ בָנוּ, פּוֹרֵק אֵין

⟨ there is no one ⟪ over ⟨ have ⟨ slaves ⟪ our ⟨ upon ⟨ we bore ⟪ upon us;
to deliver [us] us; ruled shoulders; [it]

מִיָּדָם, צָרוֹת רַבּוֹת סְבָבוּנוּ, קְרָאנוּךָ יהוה אֱלֹהֵינוּ, רָחַקְתָּ

from their hand; abundant troubles have surrounded us; we called upon You, HASHEM, our God, [but] You have distanced Yourself

מִמֶּנּוּ בַעֲוֹנֵינוּ, שַׁבְנוּ מֵאַחֲרֶיךָ, תָּעִינוּ וְאָבַדְנוּ.

from us because of our iniquities; we have turned away from following after You; we have strayed and we have become lost.

SOME CONGREGATIONS OMIT THE NEXT THREE PARAGRAPHS AND CONTINUE WITH אֵל אֶרֶךְ אַפַּיִם.

וַעֲדַיִן לֹא שַׁבְנוּ מִטָּעוּתֵנוּ, וְהֵיךְ נָעִיז פָּנֵינוּ וְנַקְשֶׁה עָרְפֵּנוּ,

But still we have not turned back from our waywardness. So how can we be so brazen and be so stiff-necked

לוֹמַר לְפָנֶיךָ יהוה אֱלֹהֵינוּ וֵאלֹהֵי אֲבוֹתֵינוּ צַדִּיקִים אֲנַחְנוּ

as to say before You, HASHEM, our God, and the God of our forefathers, that we are righteous

וְלֹא חָטָאנוּ, אֲבָל אֲנַחְנוּ וַאֲבוֹתֵינוּ חָטָאנוּ.

and have not sinned? For in truth, we and our forefathers have sinned.

STRIKE THE LEFT SIDE OF THE CHEST WITH THE RIGHT FIST WHILE RECITING EACH OF THE SINS OF THE FOLLOWING CONFESSIONAL LITANY:

אָשַׁמְנוּ, בָּגַדְנוּ, גָּזַלְנוּ, דִּבַּרְנוּ דְפִי. הֶעֱוִינוּ, וְהִרְשַׁעְנוּ,

We have been guilty; we have betrayed; we have robbed; we have spoken slander. We have committed iniquity; we have committed wickedness;

זַדְנוּ, חָמַסְנוּ, טָפַלְנוּ שֶׁקֶר. יָעַצְנוּ רָע, כִּזַּבְנוּ, לַצְנוּ,

we have sinned willfully; we have extorted; we have made false accusations. We have given bad advice; we have been deceitful; we have scorned;

מָרַדְנוּ, נִאַצְנוּ, סָרַרְנוּ, עָוִינוּ, פָּשַׁעְנוּ, צָרַרְנוּ, קִשִּׁינוּ עֹרֶף.

we have rebelled; we have provoked [God's anger]; we have strayed; we have been iniquitous; we have sinned rebelliously; we have caused distress; we have stiffened our necks.

רָשַׁעְנוּ, שִׁחַתְנוּ, תִּעַבְנוּ, תָּעִינוּ, תִּעְתָּעְנוּ.

We have been wicked; we have been corrupt; we have committed abominations; we have gone astray; we have scoffed.

סַרְנוּ מִמִּצְוֹתֶיךָ וּמִמִּשְׁפָּטֶיךָ הַטּוֹבִים, וְלֹא שָׁוָה לָנוּ. וְאַתָּה

We have turned away from Your commandments and from Your good laws, and it was not worthwhile for us. And You

צַדִּיק עַל כָּל הַבָּא עָלֵינוּ, כִּי אֱמֶת עָשִׂיתָ וַאֲנַחְנוּ הִרְשָׁעְנוּ.

are righteous in all that has come upon us, for You acted truthfully while we have acted wickedly.

ONE PRAYING WITHOUT A *MINYAN* OMITS FROM HERE UNTIL לְכָל קֹרְאָיךָ.

אֵל אֶרֶךְ אַפַּיִם אַתָּה, וּבַעַל הָרַחֲמִים נִקְרֵאתָ, וְדֶרֶךְ

⟨ and ⟨⟨ are You ⟨ of Mercy ⟨ and ⟨⟨ are You, ⟨ to anger, ⟨ Who ⟨ God,
the way   called;   Master   is slow

תְּשׁוּבָה הוֹרֵיתָ. גְּדֻלַּת רַחֲמֶיךָ וַחֲסָדֶיךָ, תִּזְכּוֹר הַיּוֹם וּבְכָל

⟨ and ⟨ this ⟨ may You ⟨ and Your ⟨ of Your ⟨ The ⟨⟨ have You ⟨ of
every day remember, kindness   mercy   greatness taught. repentance

יוֹם לְזֶרַע יְדִידֶיךָ. תֵּפֶן אֵלֵינוּ בְּרַחֲמִים, כִּי אַתָּה הוּא בַּעַל

⟨ the ⟨ are ⟨ You ⟨ for ⟨⟨ in mercy, ⟨ to us ⟨ Turn ⟨⟨ of Your ⟨ for the ⟨⟨ day,
Master   beloved ones. offspring

הָרַחֲמִים. בְּתַחֲנוּן וּבִתְפִלָּה פָּנֶיךָ נְקַדֵּם, כְּהוֹדַעְתָּ לֶעָנָיו

⟨ to the ⟨ in the man- ⟨ we ⟨ Your ⟨ and prayer ⟨ With ⟨⟨ of Mercy.
humble one ner that You approach, Presence   supplication
[Moses]   made known

מִקֶּדֶם. מֵחֲרוֹן אַפְּךָ שׁוּב, כְּמוֹ בְתוֹרָתְךָ כָּתוּב.¹ וּבְצֵל כְּנָפֶיךָ

⟨ of Your ⟨ In the ⟨⟨ it is ⟨ in Your Torah ⟨ as ⟨⟨ turn ⟨ of Your ⟨ From the ⟨⟨ in ancient
wings   shadow   written.   back, anger fierceness   times.

נֶחֱסֶה וְנִתְלוֹנָן, כְּיוֹם וַיֵּרֶד יהוה בֶּעָנָן.² ❖ תַּעֲבוֹר עַל פֶּשַׁע

⟨ sin ⟨ Overlook ⟨⟨ in a ⟨ when HASHEM ⟨ as on ⟨⟨ and may ⟨ may we
cloud.   descended   the day   we dwell, find shelter

וְתִמְחֶה אָשָׁם, כְּיוֹם וַיִּתְיַצֵּב עִמּוֹ שָׁם.² תַּאֲזִין שַׁוְעָתֵנוּ

⟨ to our cry ⟨ Listen ⟨⟨ there. ⟨ with him ⟨ when He ⟨ as on ⟨⟨ guilt, ⟨ and erase
[Moses] [God] stood the day

וְתַקְשִׁיב מֶנּוּ מַאֲמַר, כְּיוֹם וַיִּקְרָא בְשֵׁם יהוה,² וְשָׁם נֶאֱמַר:

⟨⟨ it was ⟨ and ⟨⟨ of ⟨ with the ⟨ when He ⟨ as on ⟨⟨ [our] ⟨ from ⟨ and hear
said: there HASHEM, Name called out the day declaration, us

CONGREGATION AND *CHAZZAN* RECITE LOUDLY AND IN UNISON:

וַיַּעֲבֹר יהוה עַל פָּנָיו וַיִּקְרָא:

⟨⟨ and ⟨⟨ [Moses'] ⟨ before ⟨ And HASHEM passed
proclaimed: face,

יהוה, יהוה, אֵל, רַחוּם, וְחַנּוּן, אֶרֶךְ אַפַּיִם, וְרַב חֶסֶד, וֶאֱמֶת,

⟨⟨ and ⟨ in ⟨ and ⟨ to anger, ⟨ Slow ⟨⟨ and ⟨ Compas- ⟨ God, ⟨ HASHEM, ⟨ HASHEM,
Truth, Kindness Abundant   Gracious, sionate

נֹצֵר חֶסֶד לָאֲלָפִים, נֹשֵׂא עָוֹן, וָפֶשַׁע, וְחַטָּאָה, וְנַקֵּה.³

⟨⟨ and Who ⟨ and inad- ⟨ willful ⟨ of ⟨ Forgiver ⟨⟨ for thousands ⟨ of ⟨ Preserver
absolves. vertent sin, sin, iniquity, [of generations], kindness

וְסָלַחְתָּ לַעֲוֹנֵנוּ וּלְחַטָּאתֵנוּ וּנְחַלְתָּנוּ.⁴ סְלַח לָנוּ אָבִינוּ כִּי

⟨ for ⟨⟨ our ⟨ us, ⟨ Forgive ⟨⟨ and make us ⟨⟨ and our sins, ⟨ our ⟨ May You
Father,   iniquities   Your heritage.   forgive

---

(1) Cf. *Exodus* 32:12. (2) 34:5. (3) 34:6-7. (4) 34:9.

חָטָאנוּ, מְחַל לָנוּ מַלְכֵּנוּ כִּי פָשֶׁעְנוּ.¹ כִּי אַתָּה אֲדֹנָי טוֹב

《 are 《 O Lord, 《 You, 《 For 《《 we have 《 for 《《 our King, 《 us, 《 pardon 《《 we have
good   willfully sinned.   sinned;

וְסַלָּח, וְרַב חֶסֶד לְכָל קֹרְאֶיךָ.²

《《 who call 《 to all 《 kind 《 and 《《 and
upon You.   abundantly forgiving,

THE FOLLOWING VERSES ARE RECITED RESPONSIVELY,
THE *CHAZZAN* FOLLOWED BY THE CONGREGATION:

חָטָאנוּ, צוּרֵנוּ,* סְלַח לָנוּ יוֹצְרֵנוּ.*

《《 our Molder.* 《 us, 《 forgive 《《 our Rock;* 《 We have sinned,

IN SOME CONGREGATIONS THE ARK IS OPENED AT THIS POINT.
CHAZZAN THEN CONGREGATION RECITE LOUDLY AND IN UNISON:

שְׁמַע יִשְׂרָאֵל,* יהוה אֱלֹהֵינוּ, יהוה אֶחָד.³

《《the One [and Only]. 《 HASHEM, 《 is our God, 《 HASHEM 《《 O Israel:* 《 Hear,

CHAZZAN THREE TIMES, THEN CONGREGATION THREE TIMES, LOUDLY AND IN UNISON:

בָּרוּךְ שֵׁם* כְּבוֹד מַלְכוּתוֹ לְעוֹלָם וָעֶד.

《《 and 《 for ever 《 kingdom 《 of His 《 is the 《 Blessed
ever.   glorious Name*

CHAZZAN SEVEN TIMES, THEN CONGREGATION SEVEN TIMES, RECITE LOUDLY AND IN UNISON:

יהוה הוּא הָאֱלֹהִים.*⁴

《《 is God!* 《 — He 《《 HASHEM

CHAZZAN, THEN CONGREGATION:

יהוה מֶלֶךְ,⁵ יהוה מָלָךְ,⁶ יהוה יִמְלֹךְ לְעוֹלָם וָעֶד.⁷

《《 and ever! 《 for ever 《 shall reign 《 HASHEM 《《 has reigned, 《 HASHEM 《《 reigns, 《 HASHEM

THE ARK IS CLOSED.

---

(1) Weekday *Shemoneh Esrei*. (2) *Psalms* 86:5. (3) *Deuteronomy* 6:4.
(4) *I Kings* 18:39. (5) *Psalms* 10:16. (6) 93:1 et al. (7) *Exodus* 15:18.

צוּרֵנוּ ... יוֹצְרֵנוּ — *Our Rock ... our Molder.* A
sin against God is especially serious because it
shows lack of gratefulness to *our Rock* and
Protector. Nevertheless, He knows our human
frailties because He is *our Molder* and Creator.
Therefore, we dare beg forgiveness from Him.

שְׁמַע יִשְׂרָאֵל §• — *Hear, O Israel.* The goal of
Yom Kippur Katan is not simply atonement for
ourselves, but our resolve to use God's mercy
properly. Therefore we end the service with
Israel's historic declaration of loyalty to God.
This verse should be recited loudly and with
the inner resolve that we are ready to give up
our lives, if need be, to sanctify God's Name.

God reckons such sincerity as if we had truly
done so (*Sh'lah*).

בָּרוּךְ שֵׁם §• — *Blessed is the Name.* This
angelic praise is repeated three times to signify
our acknowledgment of God's complete sovereignty — past, present, and future. Thus we
proclaim God's kingdom in the sense of ה' מֶלֶךְ,
ה' מָלָךְ ה' יִמְלוֹךְ לְעֹלָם וָעֶד, *HASHEM reigns,
HASHEM has reigned, HASHEM shall reign for
ever and ever!* which is recited shortly.

ה' הוּא הָאֱלֹהִים §• — *HASHEM — He is God.*
The entire nation called out this acknowledgment of God's sovereignty on Mount Carmel,
after Elijah proved that Ahab's false prophets

ALL CONTINUE:

עֲנֵנוּ אֱלֹהֵי אַבְרָהָם עֲנֵנוּ, עֲנֵנוּ פַּחַד יִצְחָק עֲנֵנוּ, עֲנֵנוּ

⟨ Answer ⟩ answer ⟨ of ⟨ Awesome ⟨ Answer ⟫ answer ⟨ of Abraham, ⟨ God ⟨ Answer
us, us! Isaac, One us, us! us,

אֲבִיר יַעֲקֹב עֲנֵנוּ, עֲנֵנוּ מָגֵן דָּוִד עֲנֵנוּ, עֲנֵנוּ אֱלֹהֵי הַמֶּרְכָּבָה*

⟨ of the ⟨ God ⟨Answer⟫answer ⟨ of ⟨ Shield ⟨ Answer ⟫ answer ⟨ of Jacob, ⟨ Mighty
Chariot,* us, us! David, us, us! One

עֲנֵנוּ, עֲנֵנוּ הָעוֹנֶה בְּעֵת רָצוֹן עֲנֵנוּ, עֲנֵנוּ הָעוֹנֶה בְּעֵת צָרָה

⟨ of ⟨ in time ⟨ You Who ⟨ Answer ⟫ answer ⟨ of ⟨ in time ⟨ You Who ⟨ Answer ⟫ answer
distress, answers us, us! favor, answers us, us!

עֲנֵנוּ, עֲנֵנוּ הָעוֹנֶה בְּעֵת רַחֲמִים עֲנֵנוּ, עֲנֵנוּ רַחוּם וְחַנּוּן עֲנֵנוּ,

⟫ answer ⟨ and ⟨ Merciful ⟨Answer⟫ answer ⟨ of mercy, ⟨ in time ⟨ You Who ⟨ Answer ⟫ answer
us! Gracious us, us! answers us, us!
One,

רַחֲמָנָא עֲנֵינָן, רַחֲמָנָא פְּרוֹק, רַחֲמָנָא אִתְמַלֵּי רַחֲמִין עֲלָן,

⟨ for us ⟨ of com- ⟨ become ⟨ O compas- ⟫ redeem ⟨ O compas- ⟫ answer ⟨ O compas-
passion full sionate One, [us]! sionate One, us! sionate One,

וְעַל כָּל אֱנָשֵׁי בֵיתָנָא, וְעַל כָּל אֲחָנָא בֵּית יִשְׂרָאֵל, וּמֵחֲשׁוֹכָא

⟨ And from ⟫ of Israel! ⟨ the ⟨ our ⟨ all ⟨ and ⟨ of our ⟨ the ⟨ all ⟨ and
darkness House brothers, for household people for

לִנְהוֹרָא אַפֵּקִינָן, בְּדִיל שְׁמָךְ רַבָּא.

⟫ that is ⟨ of Your ⟨ for the ⟨ take us ⟨ to light
great. Name sake out,

WHEN YOM KIPPUR KATAN IS HELD ON EREV ROSH CHODESH, THE *CHAZZAN* RECITES
THE FULL *KADDISH* (PAGE 393), FOLLOWED BY PSALM 8, לַמְנַצֵּחַ עַל הַגִּתִּית (PAGE 632),
AND THE MOURNER'S *KADDISH* (PAGE 398);
FOLLOWED BY עָלֵינוּ (PAGE 395) AND THE MOURNER'S *KADDISH*.

WHEN ROSH CHODESH FALLS ON A SATURDAY OR SUNDAY,
SO THAT YOM KIPPUR KATAN IS HELD ON THE THURSDAY BEFORE,
MINCHAH CONTINUES WITH אָבִינוּ מַלְכֵּנוּ (PAGE 178), AND *TACHANUN* (PAGE 388);
THE *CHAZZAN* RECITES THE FULL *KADDISH* (PAGE 393), FOLLOWED BY PSALM 20,
יַעַנְךָ ה' בְּיוֹם צָרָה (PAGE 216), AND THE MOURNER'S *KADDISH* (PAGE 398);
FOLLOWED BY עָלֵינוּ (PAGE 395) AND THE MOURNER'S *KADDISH*.

had no power (*I Kings* 18:39). It was one of history's greatest public sanctifications of God's Name and faith in His total power. *Arizal* writes that this fervent declaration has enormous effect in the Heavenly spheres and, while reciting it, everyone should dedicate his total loyalty to God.

This proclamation is recited seven times by the *chazzan* and the congregation to symbolize the seven heavens above which God "dwells" (*Tosafos, Berachos* 34a).

אֱלֹהֵי הַמֶּרְכָּבָה — *God of the Chariot.* This is a reference to the Heavenly Throne described in Chapter 1 of *Ezekiel*.

❧{ SELICHOS – סליחות }❧

Rambam (*Hil. Taaniyos* 1:1-4) states that the Torah requires us to assemble, pray, repent, and beg for Heavenly mercy whenever the community is threatened by a natural or man-made calamity. For one to maintain that catastrophe is inevitable or that it can be avoided only by recourse to human remedy is "cruel," for not only will such a course fail to inspire people to improve themselves and thereby merit God's mercy, it will inevitably result in further Divine punishment. One means of bringing about repentance is through fasting, and therefore the Sages ordained that public fasts be proclaimed in times of calamity, as well as permanent fast days to commemorate times of national tragedy.

Within the framework of the *siddur,* this mood of repentance is expressed in *Selichos* (prayers of supplication). They are of ancient origin; several are even mentioned in the mishnayos describing prayers for rain (*Taanis* Ch. 2), but nearly all of them were composed between the 8th and 16th centuries. Several of the *Selichos* are recited not only on a fast day, but also in the *Selichos* that are recited in conjunction with the Days of Awe and the Ten Days of Repentance.

[Note that Tishah B'Av is unique. Since it commemorates the Destruction, an event of overpowering sorrow, it has a prayer order, *Kinnos* (Elegies), all its own.]

The central theme of all the *Selichos,* as well as of the Yom Kippur *Maariv* and *Ne'ilah* services, is the שְׁלֹשׁ עֶשְׂרֵה מִדּוֹת שֶׁל רַחֲמִים, *Thirteen Attributes of Mercy.* This passage appears in the Torah (*Exodus* 34:6-7) at the time when God threatened to do away with the Jewish people after the sin of the Golden Calf. According to R' Yochanan's interpretation (*Rosh Hashanah* 17b), Moses felt that Israel's sin was so grievous that there was no possibility of his intercession on their behalf. Thereupon, God appeared to him in the form of a *chazzan* wrapped in a *tallis* and taught him the Thirteen Attributes, saying, "Anytime that Israel sins, let them perform before Me this procedure and I will forgive them." Thus, this appeal to God's mercy reassures us both that repentance is always possible and that God always awaits our return to Him.

On all the Rabbinically ordained fast days, the *Selichos* follow the same framework: first there is a similar introductory section; this is followed by two supplications recited by the congregation and concluded by the *chazzan,* and a פִּזְמוֹן [*pizmon*], a prayer that is recited responsively; each of these supplications and the *pizmon* are followed by אֵל מֶלֶךְ יוֹשֵׁב and the Thirteen Attributes; and finally another section (pages 684-698) common to all *Selichos,* which includes, among other prayers, an appeal that God recall the merit of the Patriarchs, pleas that He answer us, and a confession of sins.

The *Selichos* for the fast days are found as listed below:

❧ סליחות לשני קמא ❧

❧ SELICHOS — FIRST MONDAY OF BEHAB ❧

SELICHOS ARE RECITED IMMEDIATELY AFTER THE CHAZZAN'S REPETITION OF SHEMONEH ESREI ON THE APPROPRIATE FAST DAYS: THE FASTS OF BEHAB, THE TENTH OF TEVES, THE FAST OF ESTHER AND THE SEVENTEENTH OF TAMMUZ. (ON THE NINTH OF AV, KINNOS ARE RECITED; ON THE FAST OF GEDALIAH, THE SELICHOS OF THE TEN DAYS OF REPENTANCE ARE RECITED.) EVEN THOSE NOT FASTING SHOULD JOIN THE CONGREGATION IN RECITING SELICHOS. THOUGH IT IS PREFERABLE TO STAND DURING SELICHOS, THOSE WHO FIND IT DIFFICULT TO DO SO SHOULD STAND AT LEAST DURING שְׁמַע קוֹלֵנוּ, אֵל מֶלֶךְ, אֵל אֶרֶךְ אַפַּיִם, THE THIRTEEN ATTRIBUTES, AND.

סְלַח לָנוּ אָבִינוּ, כִּי בְרוֹב אִוַּלְתֵּנוּ שָׁגִינוּ,

‹‹ we have ‹ of our ‹ in the ‹ for ‹ our ‹ us, ‹ Forgive
erred; folly abundance Father,

מְחַל לָנוּ מַלְכֵּנוּ, כִּי רַבּוּ עֲוֹנֵינוּ.

‹‹ our ‹ many ‹ for ‹ our King, ‹ us, ‹ pardon
iniquities. are

אֵל אֶרֶךְ אַפַּיִם* אַתָּה, וּבַעַל הָרַחֲמִים נִקְרֵאתָ, וְדֶרֶךְ

‹ and ‹‹ are You ‹ of Mercy ‹ and ‹‹ are You, ‹ to anger,* ‹ Who ‹ God,
the way called; Master is slow

תְּשׁוּבָה הוֹרֵיתָ. גְּדֻלַּת רַחֲמֶיךָ וַחֲסָדֶיךָ, תִּזְכּוֹר הַיּוֹם וּבְכָל

‹ and ‹ this ‹ may You ‹ and Your ‹ of Your ‹ The ‹‹ have You ‹ of
every day remember, kindness mercy greatness taught. repentance

יוֹם לְזֶרַע יְדִידֶיךָ. תֵּפֶן אֵלֵינוּ בְּרַחֲמִים, כִּי אַתָּה הוּא בַּעַל

‹ the ‹ are ‹ You ‹ for ‹‹ in mercy, ‹ to us ‹ Turn ‹‹ of Your ‹ for the ‹‹ day,
Master beloved ones. offspring

הָרַחֲמִים. בְּתַחֲנוּן וּבִתְפִלָּה פָּנֶיךָ נְקַדֵּם, כְּהוֹדַעְתָּ לֶעָנָיו

‹ to the ‹ in the man- ‹‹ we ‹ Your ‹ and prayer ‹ With ‹‹ of Mercy.
humble one ner that You approach, Presence supplication
[Moses] made known

❧ שֵׁנִי קַמָּא / FIRST MONDAY OF BEHAB ❧

The acronym בְּהַ"ב stands for Monday (ב, the second day of the week), Thursday (ה, the fifth day), and Monday. It is an ancient custom going back to Temple times that some people would fast on three days — Monday, Thursday, and Monday — after Pesach and Succos to atone for the possibility that they may have become excessively frivolous and sinned during the long festival of eating and drinking. During Shavuos, which is a one-day festival, there was little chance of such an occurrence, so fasts were not adopted after Shavuos. Since it is not proper to fast unnecessarily during the festive months of Nissan and Tishrei, the fasts were deferred until Iyar and Cheshvan. On the first Sabbath, in these months, a public prayer is recited before Mussaf for the benefit of those who will fast, and on the Monday following that Sabbath, the fasts begin. Monday and Thursday were chosen because they are days of judgment (see p. 182).

❧ אֵל אֶרֶךְ אַפַּיִם /
God, Who is Slow to Anger

After declaring that God's patience with sinful people and His boundless mercy are our primary hope, we beg Him to be as merciful to

מִקֶּדֶם. מֵחֲרוֹן אַפְּךָ שׁוּב, כְּמוֹ בְּתוֹרָתְךָ כָּתוּב.¹ וּבְצֵל כְּנָפֶיךָ

⟨ of Your ⟨ In the ⟪ it is ⟨in Your Torah ⟨ as ⟪ turn ⟨of Your ⟨From the ⟪in ancient
wings   shadow   written.   back, anger fierceness   times.

נֶחֱסֶה וְנִתְלוֹנָן, כְּיוֹם וַיֵּרֶד יהוה בֶּעָנָן. ❖ תַּעֲבוֹר עַל פֶּשַׁע

⟨ sin ⟨   Overlook   ⟪   in a ⟨ when HASHEM ⟨ as on ⟪ and may ⟨ may we
                                 cloud.   descended   the day   we dwell, find shelter

וְתִמְחֶה אָשָׁם, כְּיוֹם וַיִּתְיַצֵּב עִמּוֹ שָׁם.² תַּאֲזִין שַׁוְעָתֵנוּ

⟨ to our cry ⟨   Give   ⟪ there. ⟨ with him ⟨ when He ⟨ as on ⟪ guilt, ⟨ and erase
                  heed   [Moses]   [God] stood   the day

וְתַקְשִׁיב מֶנּוּ מַאֲמָר, כְּיוֹם וַיִּקְרָא בְּשֵׁם יהוה,*² וְשָׁם נֶאֱמַר:

⟪ it was ⟨   and   of ⟨with the ⟨ when He ⟨ as on ⟪ [our] ⟨ from ⟨ and hear
said: there   HASHEM,* Name called out the day declaration, us

CONGREGATION AND CHAZZAN RECITE LOUDLY AND IN UNISON:

וַיַּעֲבֹר יהוה עַל פָּנָיו וַיִּקְרָא:

⟪   and   ⟪ [Moses'] ⟨ before ⟨ And HASHEM passed
proclaimed: face,

יהוה, יהוה, אֵל, רַחוּם, וְחַנּוּן, אֶרֶךְ אַפַּיִם, וְרַב חֶסֶד, וֶאֱמֶת,

⟪ and ⟨   in   ⟨ and ⟨ to anger, ⟨ Slow ⟪ and ⟨Compas- ⟨ God, ⟨ HASHEM, ⟨ HASHEM,
Truth, Kindness Abundant   Gracious, sionate

נֹצֵר חֶסֶד לָאֲלָפִים, נֹשֵׂא עָוֹן, וָפֶשַׁע, וְחַטָּאָה, וְנַקֵּה.³

⟪ and Who ⟨ and inad- ⟨ willful ⟨ of ⟨ Forgiver ⟪ for thousands ⟨ of ⟨ Preserver
absolves. vertent sin, sin,   iniquity,   [of generations], kindness

וְסָלַחְתָּ לַעֲוֹנֵנוּ וּלְחַטָּאתֵנוּ וּנְחַלְתָּנוּ.⁴ סְלַח לָנוּ אָבִינוּ כִּי

⟨ for ⟪ our ⟨ us, ⟨ Forgive ⟪ and make us ⟪ and our sins, ⟨ our ⟨ May You
Father,   Your heritage.   iniquities   forgive

חָטָאנוּ, מְחַל לָנוּ מַלְכֵּנוּ כִּי פָשָׁעְנוּ.⁵ כִּי אַתָּה אֲדֹנָי טוֹב

⟨ are ⟨ O Lord, ⟨ You, ⟨ For ⟪ we have ⟨ for ⟪ our King, ⟨ us, ⟨ pardon ⟪ we have
good   willfully sinned.   sinned;

וְסַלָּח, וְרַב חֶסֶד לְכָל קֹרְאֶיךָ.⁶

⟪ who call ⟨ to all ⟨ kind ⟨ and ⟪ and
upon You.   abundantly forgiving,

---

(1) Cf. *Exodus* 32:12. (2) 34:5. (3) 34:6-7. (4) 34:9. (5) Weekday *Shemoneh Esrei*. (6) *Psalms* 86:5.

us now as He was on the day He taught the
Thirteen Attributes to Moses on Mount Sinai.
On that day, God assured Moses that He would
continue to protect Israel despite the nation's
grievous sin. So may He heed and protect us,
and be merciful to us now.

וַיִּקְרָא בְשֵׁם ה' — *He called out with the Name of*
HASHEM. According to *Mizrachi's* under-

standing of *Rashi* (*Exodus* 34:5), Moses called
out God's Name. However, *Gur Aryeh's* interpretation of *Rashi, Ibn Ezra,* and *Sforno* comment that God called out His Own Name,
teaching Moses the order of the Thirteen Attributes.

For commentary on the Thirteen Attributes
of Mercy turn to page 635.

ALL CONTINUE:

הוֹשִׁיעָה יהוה כִּי גָמַר חָסִיד, כִּי פַסּוּ אֱמוּנִים מִבְּנֵי אָדָם.[1]

‹‹ from mankind. ‹ have truth-ful people ‹ vanished ‹ for ‹‹ is the ‹ gone ‹ for ‹ O ‹ Save, HASHEM, devout one,

לוּלֵי יהוה שֶׁהָיָה לָנוּ, בְּקוּם עָלֵינוּ אָדָם. אֲזַי חַיִּים בְּלָעוּנוּ,

‹‹ they would have swallowed us, ‹ alive ‹ then ‹‹ did men, ‹ against us ‹ when rise up ‹ with us ‹‹ been ‹ HASHEM ‹ Had not

בַּחֲרוֹת אַפָּם בָּנוּ.[2]

‹‹ against us. ‹ did their anger ‹ when flare up

כְּרַחֵם אָב עַל בָּנִים, כֵּן תְּרַחֵם יהוה עָלֵינוּ.[3] לַיהוה

‹ To HASHEM ‹‹ on us. ‹ HASHEM, ‹ have mercy, ‹ so ‹‹ his children, ‹ toward ‹ a father is ‹ As merciful as

הַיְשׁוּעָה, עַל עַמְּךָ בִרְכָתֶךָ סֶּלָה.[4] יהוה צְבָאוֹת עִמָּנוּ,

‹‹ is with us, ‹ Master of Legions, ‹ HASHEM, ‹‹ Selah. ‹‹ is Your blessing, ‹ Your people ‹ upon ‹‹ is salvation,

מִשְׂגָּב לָנוּ אֱלֹהֵי יַעֲקֹב סֶלָה.[5] יהוה צְבָאוֹת, אַשְׁרֵי אָדָם

‹ is the man ‹ — praise-worthy ‹‹ Master of Legions ‹ HASHEM, ‹‹ Selah. ‹‹ of Jacob, ‹ is the God ‹ for us ‹ a stronghold

בֹּטֵחַ בָּךְ.[6] יהוה הוֹשִׁיעָה, הַמֶּלֶךְ יַעֲנֵנוּ בְיוֹם קָרְאֵנוּ.[7]

‹‹ we call. ‹ on the day ‹ answer us ‹ May the King ‹‹ save! ‹ HASHEM, ‹‹ in You. ‹ who trusts

❖ סְלַח נָא לַעֲוֹן הָעָם הַזֶּה כְּגֹדֶל חַסְדֶּךָ, וְכַאֲשֶׁר נָשָׂאתָה

‹ You have forgiven ‹ and as ‹‹ of Your kindness, ‹ according to the greatness ‹ of this people ‹ the iniquity ‹ please, ‹ Forgive,

לָעָם הַזֶּה מִמִּצְרַיִם וְעַד הֵנָּה,[8] וְשָׁם נֶאֱמַר:

‹‹ it was said: ‹ And there ‹‹ now. ‹ until ‹ from Egypt ‹ this people

ALL, ALOUD AND IN UNISON:

וַיֹּאמֶר יהוה סָלַחְתִּי כִּדְבָרֶךָ.[9]

‹‹ according to your word! ‹ I have forgiven ‹‹ And HASHEM said:

ALL CONTINUE:

הַטֵּה אֱלֹהַי אָזְנְךָ וּשְׁמָע, פְּקַח עֵינֶיךָ וּרְאֵה שֹׁמְמֹתֵינוּ,

‹‹ our desolation, ‹ and see ‹ Your eyes ‹ open ‹‹ and listen; ‹ Your ear, ‹ my God, ‹ Incline,

וְהָעִיר אֲשֶׁר נִקְרָא שִׁמְךָ עָלֶיהָ, כִּי לֹא עַל צִדְקֹתֵינוּ אֲנַחְנוּ

‹ do we ‹ of our righteousness ‹ because ‹ not ‹ for ‹‹ upon; ‹ Your Name is proclaimed ‹ which ‹ and [that of] the city

---

(1) Psalms 12:2. (2) 124:2,3. (3) Cf. 103:13. (4) 3:9. (5) 46:8.
(6) 84:13. (7) 20:10. (8) Numbers 14:19. (9) 14:20.

מַפִּילִים תַּחֲנוּנֵינוּ לְפָנֶיךָ, כִּי עַל רַחֲמֶיךָ הָרַבִּים. אֲדֹנָי

‹ O Lord, ‹‹ which is ‹ of Your ‹ because ‹ but ‹‹ before ‹ our ‹ cast
abundant. compassion, You; supplications

שְׁמָעָה, אֲדֹנָי סְלָחָה, אֲדֹנָי הַקְשִׁיבָה, וַעֲשֵׂה אַל תְּאַחַר,

‹‹ delay; ‹ do not ‹‹ and act, ‹ be attentive, ‹ O Lord, ‹‹ forgive; ‹ O Lord, ‹‹ heed;

לְמַעַנְךָ אֱלֹהַי, כִּי שִׁמְךָ נִקְרָא עַל עִירְךָ וְעַל עַמֶּךָ.¹

‹‹ Your ‹ and ‹ Your ‹ upon ‹ is ‹ Your ‹ for ‹‹ my God, ‹ for Your
people. upon City proclaimed Name sake,

אֱלֹהֵינוּ וֵאלֹהֵי אֲבוֹתֵינוּ

‹‹ of our forefathers: ‹ and God ‹ Our God

יִשְׂרָאֵל* עַמְּךָ תְּחִנָּה עוֹרְכִים,

‹‹ they arrange, ‹ [their] sup- ‹ Your ‹ Israel,*
plication people,

שֶׁהֵם מְצֵרִים וּלְהִוָּשֵׁעַ צְרִיכִים,

‹‹ they have need. ‹ and to be saved ‹ are distressed, ‹ for they

צָרֵיהֶם עֲלֵיהֶם עוֹל מַאֲרִיכִים,

‹‹ prolong [their] yoke upon them. ‹ Their foes

כָּל זֹאת הִגִּיעָתַם וְשִׁמְךָ מְבָרְכִים.

‹‹ they bless. ‹ yet Your Name ‹‹ has befallen them, ‹ this ‹ All

חֳלִי וּמַכְאוֹב לְהִכָּתֵב לֹא נִמְסַר,

‹‹ be committed; ‹ cannot ‹ to writing ‹‹ and pain, ‹ The sickness

עֲלוּבִים מִנֹּעַר וּמֵהֶם לֹא הוּסַר,

‹‹ been ‹ [the ‹ and from ‹ from [their] ‹ they are
removed. degradation] them youth, degraded
has never

קָדוֹשׁ, בְּיָדְךָ לִפְתֵחַ מוּסָר,²

‹‹ our bonds, ‹ to break ‹ it is in ‹ O Holy
open Your power One,

כְּאֱמָנוּתְךָ הַנְּקִיָּה וְלֹא כְּאֵמָנוּת בָּשָׂר.

‹‹ of humans. ‹ the practice ‹and unlike ‹‹which is pure, ‹as is Your practice

הַלּוֹבֵשׁ צְדָקָה³ וְלוֹ כַּמְּעִיל עֲטוּיָה,

‹‹ it is draped, ‹ like a ‹ and for ‹‹ righteous- ‹ The One
coat Whom ness, Who dons

---

(1) *Daniel* 9:18-19. (2) Cf. *Job* 12:18. (3) Cf. *Isaiah* 59:17.

◆§ **יִשְׂרָאֵל** — *Israel.* The acrostic spells the author's name, יִצְחָק הַקָּטָן בְּרַבִּי מֵאִיר חֲזַק וֶאֱמָץ, *Yitzchak the Lesser, son of Rabbi Meir be strong and have courage* (France, about 1090-1130).

He was a grandson of Rashi and a brother and colleague of the well-known Tosafists Rashbam and Rabbeinu Tam.

וּמִמַּכָּה עַצְמָהּ מְתַקֵּן רְטִיָּה,[1]

‹‹ its healing ‹ fashions ‹ itself ‹ and Who from
bandage · the wound

קוֹמֵם עֲדָתְךָ מִנְּפִילָתָהּ הַמְּטוּיָה,

‹‹ into the depths, ‹ from its downfall ‹ Your congregation ‹ – raise up

בְּכֹחֲךָ הַגָּדוֹל וּבִזְרוֹעֲךָ הַנְּטוּיָה.[2]

‹‹ that is out- ‹ and with ‹ that is ‹ with Your
stretched. Your arm great strength

טוֹעִים הָאוֹמְרִים נַחֲלָתְךָ לְחַבֵּל,

‹‹ to destroy, ‹ – Your heri- ‹‹ who declare ‹ Mistaken
tage [Israel] [their intention] are they

כְּבוֹדְךָ לְהָמִיר וּבְהֶבֶל לְהִתְהַבֵּל,

‹‹ to become ‹ and with ‹ to [make them] ‹ Your
foolish, foolishness exchange, glory

נְטוֹת מִדְּרָכֶיךָ וְתֹהוּ לְקַבֵּל,

‹‹ to accept, ‹ and non- ‹‹ from Your ‹ to veer
sensical beliefs ways,

וְיִרְאָתְךָ הַקְּדוֹשָׁה לִנְטוֹשׁ וּלְנַבֵּל.

‹‹ and abominate. ‹ to abandon ‹‹ that is holy, ‹ and Your reverence

בְּאַהֲבָתְךָ וּבְחֶמְלָתְךָ[3] מְנַשֵּׂא וּמְנַטֵּל,

‹‹ and bears ‹ You Who ‹ and with Your ‹ With Your
[us], uplifts compassion, love

עֲצַת צוֹרְרֶיךָ תְּסַכֵּל[4] וּמַחְשְׁבוֹתָם תְּבַטֵּל,

‹‹ nullify. ‹ and their intentions ‹‹ confound, ‹ of Your enemies ‹ the plans

רַבָּה מְהוּמָה בֵּינֵיהֶם הַטֵּל,[5]

‹‹ cast, ‹ among them ‹ confusion ‹ Great

וּמַלְאָךְ אַכְזָרִי[6] דּוֹחֶה[7] וּמְטַלְטֵל.

‹‹ and moving them about. ‹ repulsing, ‹ who is cruel, ‹ with an emissary

בַּעֲבוּר כְּבוֹד עַצְמְךָ וְשֵׁם קָדְשְׁךָ הַמְּהֻלָּל,

‹‹ which is ‹ of Your ‹ and that of ‹ of Your own honor ‹ For the
lauded, holiness the Name sake

נוֹרָאוֹת הַפְלֵא לְבַל בַּגּוֹיִם יִתְחַלָּל,

‹‹ be desecrated. ‹ among ‹ so that ‹‹ perform ‹ awesome
the nations It not wondrously, deeds

יוֹעֲצֵיהֶם וְאֵיתָנֵיהֶם תּוֹלִיךְ שׁוֹלָל,[8]

‹‹ to folly, ‹ lead ‹ and strong men ‹ Their advisers

---

(1) Cf. *Jeremiah* 30:17. (2) *Deuteronomy* 9:29. (3) Cf. *Isaiah* 63:9. (4) Cf. *II Samuel* 15:31.
(5) Cf. *Zechariah* 14:13. (6) *Proverbs* 17:11. (7) Cf. *Psalms* 35:5. (8) Cf. *Job* 12:17.

וּבָהֶם תְּעוֹלֵל כַּאֲשֶׁר בִּי הִתְעוֹלָל.[1]

❮❮ they inflicted. ❮ upon me ❮ what ❮ inflict ❮ and upon them

מֵקִים מֵעָפָר דָּל וְאֶבְיוֹן מֵאַשְׁפָּה,[2]

❮❮ from the trash heap, ❮ and the destitute ❮❮ the needy, ❮ from the dust ❮ He Who raises

כְּנִסְתְּךָ אַל תִּתֵּן לְכָלָה וּלְחֶרְפָּה,

❮❮ and disgrace. ❮ to destruction ❮ deliver ❮ do not ❮ Your congregation

אִם בְּפִקּוּדֶיךָ מִתְעַצֶּלֶת וּמַרְפָּה,

❮❮ and indolent, ❮ it is lazy ❮ in [fulfilling] Your commands ❮ If

עַל כָּל פִּשְׁעֶיהָ אַהֲבָתְךָ תְּהֵא מְחַפָּה.[3]

❮❮ cover up. ❮ should ❮ Your love ❮ their sins ❮ all ❮ over

יִתֵּרָה חִבָּתָם[4] לְפָנֶיךָ אֲדוֹנֵי הָאֲדוֹנִים,

❮❮ of lords; ❮ O Lord ❮❮ before You, ❮ is the love of them ❮ Intense

בֵּין כָּךְ וּבֵין כָּךְ קְרוּאִים לְךָ בָּנִים,[5]

❮❮ children. ❮ Your ❮ they are called ❮ that way [sinful] ❮ or whether ❮ this way [virtuous] ❮ whether

רַחֲמֶיךָ יְקַדְּמוּנוּ אֱלֹהֵי עֶלְיוֹנִים וְתַחְתּוֹנִים,

❮❮ and lower realms, ❮ of the upper ❮ O God ❮❮ advance toward us, ❮ May Your mercy

טֶרֶם יִשְׁטְפוּנוּ[6] הַמַּיִם הַזֵּידוֹנִים.[7]

❮❮ that are treacherous. ❮ — the waters ❮ they inundate us ❮ before

חֲפֵצֵי קִרְבָתְךָ[8] עַל כָּל הַבָּאוֹת,[9]

❮❮ befalls [them] — ❮ whatever ❮ of Your nearness ❮ To those who are desirous

הַחִישָׁה לָמוֹ יְשׁוּעוֹת הַנְּבָאוֹת,

❮❮ that were prophesied. ❮ the salvations ❮ for them ❮ hasten

❖ קָדוֹשׁ, עֲשֵׂה עִמָּם לְטוֹבָה אוֹת,[10]

❮❮ sign, ❮ a good ❮ for them ❮ perform ❮ O Holy One,

חָזָק וְאַמִּיץ גּוֹאֲלָם יהוה צְבָאוֹת.[11]

❮❮ Master of Legions. ❮ HASHEM, ❮❮ their Redeemer, ❮❮ and powerful One, ❮ O strong

---

(1) Cf. *Lamentations* 1:22. (2) Cf. *Psalms* 113:7. (3) Cf. *Proverbs* 10:12.
(4) Cf. *Ethics of the Fathers* 3:18. (5) *Kiddushin* 36a. (6) Cf. *Psalms* 124:4. (7) 124:5.
(8) Cf. *Isaiah* 58:2. (9) Cf. *Psalms* 44:18. (10) Cf. 86:17. (11) Cf. *Jeremiah* 50:34.

AN INDIVIDUAL PRAYING WITHOUT A *MINYAN* OMITS THE NEXT TWO PARAGRAPHS,
BEGINNING אֵל מֶלֶךְ, *O GOD, KING*, AND ה', *HASHEM*.

אֵל מֶלֶךְ יוֹשֵׁב* עַל כִּסֵּא רַחֲמִים, מִתְנַהֵג בַּחֲסִידוּת, מוֹחֵל

O God, < King < Who < on < the < of mercy, << Who acts < with < Who
sits* throne kindness, pardons

עֲוֹנוֹת עַמּוֹ, מַעֲבִיר רִאשׁוֹן רִאשׁוֹן, מַרְבֶּה מְחִילָה לַחַטָּאִים

the sins < of His < Who < [sins] one < by one, < Who abun- < pardon < to uninten-
people, removes dantly grants tional sinners

וּסְלִיחָה לַפּוֹשְׁעִים, עֹשֶׂה צְדָקוֹת עִם כָּל בָּשָׂר וָרוּחַ, לֹא

and < to willful < Who < acts of < with < all < [beings < and < — not
forgiveness sinners, performs generosity of] flesh spirit

כְרָעָתָם תִּגְמוֹל. ❖ אֵל הוֹרֵיתָ לָּנוּ לוֹמַר שְׁלֹשׁ עֶשְׂרֵה,

in accord with < do You repay << O < You < us < to recite < the Thirteen
their wickedness them! God, taught [Attributes of Mercy];

וּזְכוֹר לָנוּ הַיּוֹם בְּרִית שְׁלֹשׁ עֶשְׂרֵה, כְּמוֹ שֶׁהוֹדַעְתָּ לֶעָנָיו

remember < for us < today < the < of [these] Thirteen, << as < You made < to the humble
covenant known one [Moses]

מִקֶּדֶם, כְּמוֹ שֶׁכָּתוּב, וַיֵּרֶד יהוה בֶּעָנָן וַיִּתְיַצֵּב עִמּוֹ שָׁם,

in ancient << as << it is written: < And HASHEM << in a cloud < and stood < with < there,
times, descended him

וַיִּקְרָא בְשֵׁם יהוה.

and He < with the < of
called out Name HASHEM.

CONGREGATION AND *CHAZZAN* RECITE LOUDLY AND IN UNISON:

וַיַּעֲבֹר יהוה עַל פָּנָיו וַיִּקְרָא:

And HASHEM passed < before < [Moses'] << and
face, proclaimed:

יהוה, יהוה, אֵל, רַחוּם, וְחַנּוּן, אֶרֶךְ אַפַּיִם, וְרַב חֶסֶד, וֶאֱמֶת,

HASHEM, < HASHEM, < God, < Compas- < and << Slow < to anger, < and < in << and
sionate Gracious, Abundant Kindness Truth,

נֹצֵר חֶסֶד לָאֲלָפִים, נֹשֵׂא עָוֹן, וָפֶשַׁע, וְחַטָּאָה, וְנַקֵּה.

Preserver < of < kindness < for thousands < Forgiver < of < willful < and inad- < and Who
[of generations], iniquity, sin, vertent sin, absolves.

וְסָלַחְתָּ לַעֲוֹנֵנוּ וּלְחַטָּאתֵנוּ וּנְחַלְתָּנוּ. סְלַח לָנוּ אָבִינוּ כִּי

May You < our < and our sins, < and make us << Forgive < us, < our << for
forgive iniquities Your heritage. Father,

☙ אֵל מֶלֶךְ יוֹשֵׁב / **O God, King Who Sits**

God, Who is all-powerful, chooses to exercise mercy even when people are undeserving of it. With infinite kindness He chooses to forgive sins one by one, until a person's merits outnum-ber his wrongs. Since He knows that people are but mortal, He deals kindly with them. As an additional kindness, He taught us the Thirteen Attributes so that we can recite them and gain His forgiveness.

חָטָאנוּ, מְחַל לָנוּ מַלְכֵּנוּ כִּי פָשָׁעְנוּ. כִּי אַתָּה אֲדֹנָי טוֹב

‹ are ‹ O Lord, ‹ You, ‹ For ❰❰ we have ‹ for ❰❰ our King, ‹ us, ‹ pardon ❰❰ we have
good　　　　　　　　　　　　willfully sinned.　　　　　　　　　　　sinned;

וְסַלָּח, וְרַב חֶסֶד לְכָל קֹרְאֶיךָ.

❰❰ who call ‹ to all ‹ kind ‹ and ❰❰ and
upon You.　　　　　　　　abundantly forgiving,

נְשָׂא לְבָבֵנוּ אֶל כַּפָּיִם, אֶל אֵל בַּשָּׁמָיִם.[1] תָּבוֹא לְפָנֶיךָ אֶנְקַת

‹ the ‹ before ‹ Let ❰❰ in heaven. ‹ God ‹ to ‹ our ‹ with ‹ our ‹ We will
groan　You　come　　　　　　　　　　hands　　　hearts　　lift

אָסִיר, כְּגֹדֶל זְרוֹעֲךָ הוֹתֵר בְּנֵי תְמוּתָה.[2] לַאדֹנָי אֱלֹהֵינוּ

‹ our God ‹ To the Lord ❰❰ to die. ‹ those ‹ spare ❰❰ of Your ‹ as [befits] ❰❰ of the
　　　　　　　　　　condemned　　　　　might,　the greatness　prisoner;

הָרַחֲמִים וְהַסְּלִיחוֹת, כִּי מָרַדְנוּ בּוֹ.[3]

❰❰ against ‹ we have ‹ for ❰❰ and the ‹ [belong] the
Him.　rebelled　　　　forgiveness,　compassion

כְּרַחֵם אָב עַל בָּנִים, כֵּן תְּרַחֵם יהוה עָלֵינוּ.[4] לַיהוה

‹ To ❰❰ on us. ‹ HASHEM, ‹ have ‹ so ❰❰ his ‹ toward ‹ a ‹ As merciful
HASHEM　　　　　　　　　mercy,　children,　father is　as

הַיְשׁוּעָה, עַל עַמְּךָ בִרְכָתֶךָ סֶּלָה.[5] יהוה צְבָאוֹת עִמָּנוּ,

❰❰ is with ‹ Master of ‹ HASHEM, ❰❰ Selah. ❰❰ is Your ‹ Your ‹ upon ❰❰ is salvation,
us,　Legions,　　　　　　　　blessing,　people

מִשְׂגָּב לָנוּ אֱלֹהֵי יַעֲקֹב סֶלָה.[6] יהוה צְבָאוֹת, אַשְׁרֵי אָדָם

‹ is the ‹ — praise- ❰❰ Master of ‹ HASHEM, ❰❰ Selah. ‹ of ‹ is the ‹ for ‹ a
man　worthy　Legions　　　　　　　Jacob,　God　us　stronghold

בֹּטֵחַ בָּךְ.[7] יהוה הוֹשִׁיעָה, הַמֶּלֶךְ יַעֲנֵנוּ בְיוֹם קָרְאֵנוּ.[8]

❰❰ we call. ‹ on the ‹ answer ‹ May the ❰❰ save! ‹ HASHEM, ❰❰ in ‹ who
day　us　King　　　　　　　　You.　trusts

אֱלֹהִים בְּיִשְׂרָאֵל גָּדוֹל נוֹדָעְתָּ,[9] אַתָּה יהוה אָבִינוּ אָתָּה.

❰❰ are You. ‹ our ❰❰ are ‹ You ❰❰ are You ‹ to be ‹ in Israel ❰❰ God,
Father　HASHEM;　known.　great

בְּכָל קָרְאֵנוּ אֵלֶיךָ,[10] קָרְבֵנוּ, רָם וְנִשָּׂא אַתָּה בְקִרְבֵּנוּ.

❰❰ in our ‹ are You ‹ and ‹ exalted ❰❰ draw us ❰❰ to You, ‹ we call ‹ When-
midst.　　uplifted　　close;　　　　　　　　ever

גְּמַלְתָּנוּ הַטּוֹבוֹת גַּם בְּחוֹבֵינוּ, לֹא בְּצִדְקוֹתֵינוּ וּבְיֹשֶׁר לְבָבֵנוּ.[11]

❰❰ of our ‹ and the ‹ because of our ‹ not ❰❰ in our guilt, ‹ even ❰❰ good ‹ You have
heart.　uprightness　righteousness　　　　　　　things,　bestowed
upon us

---

(1) *Lamentations* 3:41. (2) *Psalms* 79:11. (3) *Daniel* 9:9. (4) Cf. *Psalms* 103:13. (5) 3:9.
(6) 46:8. (7) 84:13. (8) 20:10. (9) Cf. *Psalms* 76:2. (10) Cf. *Deuteronomy* 4:7. (11) Cf. 9:5.

דּוֹדֵנוּ, גַּם כִּי זְנַחְנוּ, גְּאָלֵנוּ כִּי עֲבָדִים אֲנָחְנוּ.

‹‹ are we. ‹ [Your] ‹ for ‹‹ redeem ‹ we have ‹ if ‹ even ‹‹ Our
servants　　　us,　been forsaken,　　　　Beloved,

הִנֵּנוּ בַּעֲוֹנֵינוּ עַד דַּכָּא,¹ וַתִּקְצַר נֶפֶשׁ לְךָ מְחַכָּה.

‹‹ awaits. ‹ that ‹ is the ‹ filled with ‹ of ‹ at the ‹‹ because of ‹‹ Behold,
for You　soul　anxiety　despair;　point　our sins　we are,

וְאַיֵּה חֲסָדֶיךָ הָרִאשׁוֹנִים עִמָּנוּ, מֵעוֹלָם וְעַד עוֹלָם נֶאֱמָנוּ.

‹‹ were ‹ and ever ‹ which for ‹‹ with us, ‹ of old ‹ are Your ‹ Where
dependable?　ever　　　　　　　　kindnesses

זַעַף נָשָׂא² וַתֵּשׁ כֹּחֵנוּ, יהוה אַל בְּאַפְּךָ תוֹכִיחֵנוּ.³

‹‹ rebuke us. ‹ in your ‹ do ‹ O ‹ is our ‹ and ‹ have ‹ Anger
anger　not HASHEM,　strength;　sapped　we borne,

חַלְחָלוֹת רַבּוֹת בָּלוּ בִשְׂרֵנוּ, נָא אַל בַּחֲמָתְךָ תְיַסְּרֵנוּ.³

‹‹ chastise us. ‹ in Your wrath ‹ do not ‹ please, ‹‹ our flesh; ‹ have withered ‹ Many afflictions

טֹרַח הַצָּרוֹת אֵין לְהַסָּפֵר, אַיֵּה שׁוֹקֵל וְאַיֵּה סוֹפֵר.

‹‹ who can ‹ and where ‹‹ who can ‹ Where ‹‹ be ‹ cannot ‹ of our ‹ The
count it?　is the one　weigh it,　is the one　calculated.　troubles　burden

יָדַעְנוּ רִשְׁעֵנוּ כִּי פָשָׁעְנוּ, כִּי אֱמֶת עָשִׂיתָ וַאֲנַחְנוּ הִרְשָׁעְנוּ.⁴

‹‹ have acted ‹ while we ‹‹ have You ‹ with ‹ for ‹‹ we have ‹ for ‹ our ‹ We
wickedly.　　acted,　truth　sinned,　wickedness,　know

בַּעַס יוּפַר וְחָרוֹן מֶנּוּ יֶחְדָּל, כִּי קָטֹן יַעֲקֹב⁵ וָדָל.

‹‹ and ‹ is ‹ small ‹ for ‹‹ cease, ‹ from ‹ and fury ‹ be ‹ Let
destitute.　Jacob,　　　us　　　　annulled　anger

לַחַץ יוּסַר וְעוֹל מֶנּוּ יֶחְבָּל,⁶ כִּי כָשַׁל כֹּחַ הַסַּבָּל.

‹‹ of the one who ‹ the ‹ failed ‹ for ‹‹ be broken, ‹ from ‹ and let ‹ be re- ‹ Let op-
bears [them].　strength　is　　　us　the yoke　moved,　pression

מְנָת מִדָּתֵנוּ לֹא תַגְבֵּהּ, כִּי נִשְׁאַרְנוּ מְעַט מֵהַרְבֵּה.⁷

‹‹ out of many. ‹ few ‹ we remain ‹ for ‹‹ exact, ‹ do ‹ of measurement ‹ The full
not　[of punishment]　portion

נַחֵם עַל הָרָעָה⁸ לְאֻמָּתֶךָ, מַטֵּה כְּלַפֵּי חֶסֶד⁹ אֲמָנוּתֶךָ.

‹‹ as is Your ‹ kindness ‹ toward ‹ tip [the ‹‹ [decreed] for ‹ the evil ‹ from ‹ Relent
practice.　　　scale]　　Your nation;

סְלָחָה אִם עֲוֹנֵינוּ עָנוּ בָנוּ,¹⁰ עָזְרֵנוּ כִּי עָלֶיךָ נִשְׁעָנוּ.¹¹

‹‹ we depend. ‹ upon You ‹ for ‹‹ help us, ‹ against us, ‹ testify ‹ our sins ‹ if ‹ Forgive [us]

עָרְפֵּנוּ כֹף לְךָ לְהִשְׁתַּעְבֵּד,

‹‹ to be subservient, ‹ to You ‹‹ bend, ‹ Our [stiff] neck

(1) Psalms 90:3. (2) Cf. Micah 7:9. (3) Cf. Psalms 6:2. (4) Nehemiah 9:33.
(5) Cf. Amos 7:2,5. (6) Cf. Isaiah 10:27. (7) Jeremiah 42:2. (8) Cf. Exodus 32:12, Jonah 4:2.
(9) Rosh Hashanah 17a. (10) Jeremiah 14:7. (11) II Chronicles 14:10.

בְּאַהֲבָה וּבְיִרְאָה אוֹתְךָ לַעֲבוֹד וּלְכַבֵּד.[1]

» and honor [You]. ‹ we will serve You ‹ and with reverence ‹ so that with love

פּוֹקְדֶיךָ[2] קִדְּשׁוּ צוֹמוֹת[3] לִקְבּוֹעַ, דַּעְתָּם קְצָרָה צָרְכְּם[4] לִתְבּוֹעַ.

» to ‹ [for them] ‹ is in- » establishing ‹ fasts, ‹ have ‹ Those who
request.   their needs adequate derstanding   [them],   designated   seek You

צְקוֹן[5] לַחֲשָׁם אֵלֶיךָ תָבֹא, חַתֵּל לְאִישׁ אִישׁ נִגְעוֹ וּמַכְאוֹבוֹ.[6]

» and his pain. ‹ his ‹ for each person ‹ heal » come before You; ‹ of their ‹ May the
            wound   whispered outpouring
                                                    [prayer]

קוֹל יַעֲקֹב נוֹהֵם מִתְּהוֹמוֹתֶיךָ, תִּשְׁמַע הַשָּׁמַיִם מְכוֹן שִׁבְתֶּךָ.[7]

» of Your ‹ the » in Heaven, ‹ may You » from Your depths, ‹ groans ‹ of Jacob ‹ The
dwelling.   abode   hear [it]   voice

רוֹדֶה רוֹדְפוֹ[8] בְּאַף תְּכַלֶּה, שְׁנַת שְׁלוּמִים לְרִיב צִיּוֹן[9] תְּגַלֶּה.

» reveal. ‹ of ‹ for the ‹ of retribution ‹ a year » destroy; ‹ —in Your ‹ who ‹ The
         Zion grievance   anger   pursues oppressor

שָׂרִיתָ וְרָדַתָּ מִנֹּעַר קְנוֹתָנוּ, וְאַל תַּשְׁלִיכֵנוּ לְעֵת זִקְנָתֵנוּ.[10]

» of our ‹ in the ‹ cast us off ‹ do not ‹ to acquire ‹ in our youth ‹ and ‹ You saw [our
old age.   time   us;   [to Egypt], descended oppression]

תָּעִינוּ לִשְׂמֹאל וִימִינָךְ תְּקָרְבֵנוּ, כִּכְלוֹת כֹּחֵנוּ אַל תַּעַזְבֵנוּ.[10]

» abandon us. ‹ do ‹ is our ‹ when » draw us ‹ but let Your » to the left ‹ We have
            not   strength,   finished   near;   right hand   [to sin],   strayed

תַּבִּיט וְתָצִיץ וְתַשְׁגִּיחַ לְרַחוּמֶיךָ,

» the recipients of ‹ and oversee ‹ observe, ‹ Look at,
Your mercy;

תִּתְאַזֵּר בַּחֲנִינוֹתֶיךָ, תִּתְלַבֵּשׁ בְּצִדְקוֹתֶיךָ,

» in Your righteousness. ‹ garb Yourself » in Your graciousness; ‹ gird Yourself

❖ תִּתְכַּסֶּה בְּרַחֲמֶיךָ וְתִתְעַטֵּף בַּחֲסִידוּתֶךָ,

» in your [attribute ‹ wrap » in Your [attribute ‹ Clothe
of] kindness,   Yourself   of] mercy;   Yourself

וְתָבֹא לְפָנֶיךָ מִדַּת טוּבְךָ וְעַנְוְתָנוּתֶךָ.[11]

» and humility. ‹ of good- ‹ Your ‹ before ‹ and may
            ness   attribute   You   there come

AN INDIVIDUAL PRAYING WITHOUT A *MINYAN* OMITS THE NEXT TWO PARAGRAPHS,
BEGINNING אֵל מֶלֶךְ, *O GOD, KING,* AND 'ה, *HASHEM.*

אֵל מֶלֶךְ יוֹשֵׁב עַל כִּסֵּא רַחֲמִים, מִתְנַהֵג בַּחֲסִידוּת, מוֹחֵל

‹ Who » with ‹ Who acts » of mercy, ‹ the ‹ on ‹ Who ‹ King ‹ O God,
pardons   kindness,   throne   sits

---

(1) Cf. *Isaiah* 43:23. (2) Cf. 26:16. (3) Cf. *Joel* 1:14, 2:15. (4) Cf. *Berachos* 29b.
(5) Cf. *Isaiah* 26:16. (6) *II Chronicles* 6:29. (7) *I Kings* 8:39, 43.
(8) Cf. *Isaiah* 14:6. (9) 34:8. (10) Cf. *Psalms* 71:9. (11) Cf. *Berachos* 16b.

עֲוֹנוֹת עַמּוֹ, מַעֲבִיר רִאשׁוֹן רִאשׁוֹן, מַרְבֶּה מְחִילָה לַחַטָּאִים

‹ to uninten- ‹ pardon ‹ Who abun- ‹ by one, ‹ [sins] one ‹ Who ‹‹ of His ‹ the sins
tional sinners / dantly grants / / removes / people,

וּסְלִיחָה לַפּוֹשְׁעִים, עֹשֶׂה צְדָקוֹת עִם כָּל בָּשָׂר וָרוּחַ, לֹא

‹ – not ‹‹ and ‹ [beings ‹ all ‹ with ‹ acts of ‹ Who ‹‹ to willful ‹ and
of] flesh / spirit / / generosity / performs / sinners, / forgiveness

כְרָעָתָם תִּגְמוֹל. ❖ אֵל הוֹרֵיתָ לָּנוּ לוֹמַר שְׁלֹשׁ עֶשְׂרֵה,

‹‹ the Thirteen ‹ to recite ‹ us ‹ You ‹ O ‹‹ do You repay ‹ in accord with
[Attributes of Mercy]; / / / taught / God, / them! / their wickedness

וּזְכוֹר לָנוּ הַיּוֹם בְּרִית שְׁלֹשׁ עֶשְׂרֵה, כְּמוֹ שֶׁהוֹדַעְתָּ לֶעָנָיו

‹ to the humble ‹ You made ‹ as ‹‹ of [these] Thirteen, ‹ the ‹ today ‹ for us ‹ remember
one [Moses] / known / / covenant

מִקֶּדֶם, כְּמוֹ שֶׁכָּתוּב, וַיֵּרֶד יהוה בֶּעָנָן וַיִּתְיַצֵּב עִמּוֹ שָׁם,

‹‹ there, ‹ with ‹ and stood ‹ in a cloud ‹ And HASHEM ‹‹ it is written: ‹ as ‹‹ in ancient
him / / descended / times,

וַיִּקְרָא בְשֵׁם יהוה.

‹‹ of ‹ with the ‹ and He
HASHEM. / Name / called out

CONGREGATION AND *CHAZZAN* RECITE LOUDLY AND IN UNISON:

וַיַּעֲבֹר יהוה עַל פָּנָיו וַיִּקְרָא:

‹‹ and ‹‹ [Moses'] ‹ before ‹ And HASHEM passed
proclaimed: / face,

יהוה, יהוה, אֵל, רַחוּם, וְחַנּוּן, אֶרֶךְ אַפַּיִם, וְרַב חֶסֶד, וֶאֱמֶת,

‹‹ and ‹ in ‹ and ‹ to anger, ‹ Slow ‹‹ and ‹ Compas- ‹ God, ‹ HASHEM, ‹ HASHEM,
Truth, Kindness / Abundant / / Gracious, / sionate

נֹצֵר חֶסֶד לָאֲלָפִים, נֹשֵׂא עָוֹן, וָפֶשַׁע, וְחַטָּאָה, וְנַקֵּה.

‹‹ and Who ‹ and inad- ‹ willful ‹ of ‹ Forgiver ‹‹ for thousands ‹ of ‹ Preserver
absolves. / vertent sin, / sin, / iniquity, / / [of generations], / kindness

וְסָלַחְתָּ לַעֲוֹנֵנוּ וּלְחַטָּאתֵנוּ וּנְחַלְתָּנוּ. סְלַח לָנוּ אָבִינוּ כִּי

‹ for ‹‹ our ‹ us, ‹ Forgive ‹‹ and make us ‹‹ and our sins, ‹ our ‹ May You
Father, / / / Your heritage. / / iniquities / forgive

חָטָאנוּ, מְחַל לָנוּ מַלְכֵּנוּ כִּי פָשָׁעְנוּ. כִּי אַתָּה אֲדֹנָי טוֹב

‹ are ‹ O Lord, ‹ You, ‹ For ‹‹ we have ‹ for ‹‹ our King, ‹ us, ‹ pardon ‹‹ we have
good / / / willfully sinned. / / / sinned;

וְסַלָּח, וְרַב חֶסֶד לְכָל קֹרְאֶיךָ.

‹‹ who call ‹ to all ‹ kind ‹ and ‹‹ and
upon You. / / / abundantly forgiving,

THE FOLLOWING PRAYER IS RECITED ALOUD RESPONSIVELY. *CHAZZAN,* THEN CONGREGATION:

מַלְאֲבֵי* רַחֲמִים מְשָׁרְתֵי עֶלְיוֹן,

≪ of the Supreme One, ⟨ servants ⟨ of mercy, ⟨ O angels*

חַלּוּ נָא פְּנֵי אֵל בְּמֵיטַב הִגָּיוֹן,

≪ expression. ⟨ with eloquent ⟨ God ⟨ before ⟨ please, ⟨ entreat,

אוּלַי יָחוֹס עַם עָנִי[1] וְאֶבְיוֹן, אוּלַי יְרַחֵם.

≪ He will ⟨ perhaps ≪ and ⟨ that is ⟨ the ⟨ He will ⟨ Perhaps
have mercy. 　　　　　　 destitute; poor people pity

CONGREGATION, THEN *CHAZZAN:*

אוּלַי יְרַחֵם שְׁאֵרִית יוֹסֵף,

≪ of Joseph, ⟨ on the remnant ⟨ He will have mercy ⟨ Perhaps

שְׁפָלִים וְנִבְזִים פְּשׂוּחֵי[2] שֶׁסֶף,[3]

≪ and ripped, ⟨ torn apart ≪ and disgraced, ⟨ degraded

שְׁבוּיֵי חִנָּם, מְכוּרֵי בְּלֹא בֶסֶף,[4]

≪ money, ⟨ for no ⟨ sold ≪ for naught, ⟨ taken captive

שׁוֹאֲגִים בִּתְפִלָּה וּמְבַקְשִׁים רִשָׁיוֹן,

≪ for approval. ⟨ and pleading ≪ in prayer, ⟨ shouting out

אוּלַי יָחוֹס עַם עָנִי וְאֶבְיוֹן, אוּלַי יְרַחֵם.

≪ He will ⟨ perhaps ≪ and ⟨ that is ⟨ the ⟨ He will ⟨ Perhaps
have mercy. 　　　　　　 destitute; poor people pity

CONGREGATION, THEN *CHAZZAN:*

אוּלַי יְרַחֵם מְעֻנֵּי כֶבֶל,[5]

≪ by chains, ⟨ on those tortured ⟨ He will have mercy ⟨ Perhaps

מְלֻמְּדֵי מַכּוֹת בְּעִנּוּי סֶבֶל,

≪ of suffering; ⟨ with the ⟨ to blows ⟨ accustomed
oppression

מָנוֹד רֹאשׁ נְתוּנִים[6] בְּיוֹשְׁבֵי תֵבֵל,

≪ of the ⟨ among the ⟨ have they ⟨ of heads ⟨ [a cause for]
world, inhabitants been made [in derision] shaking

מָשָׁל בָּעַמִּים[7] בְּקֶצֶף וּבִזָּיוֹן,[8]

≪ and ⟨ with ⟨ among the ⟨ a byword
disgrace. wrath nations, [for contempt]

אוּלַי יָחוֹס עַם עָנִי וְאֶבְיוֹן, אוּלַי יְרַחֵם.

≪ He will ⟨ perhaps ≪ and ⟨ that is ⟨ the ⟨ He will ⟨ Perhaps
have mercy. 　　　　　　 destitute; poor people pity

---

(1) Cf. *Zephaniah* 3:12. (2) Cf. *Lamentations* 3:11. (3) Cf. *I Samuel* 15:33. (4) Cf. *Isaiah* 52:3. (5) Cf. *Psalms* 105:18. (6) Cf. 44:15, 22:8. (7) Cf. 44:15. (8) Cf. *Esther* 1:18.

◉§ מַלְאֲבֵי — *O angels.* The acrostic spells שְׁמוּאֵל כֹּהֵן יְחִי, *Shmuel the Kohen, may he live.*

CONGREGATION, THEN *CHAZZAN:*

אוּלַי יְרַחֵם וְיֵרֶא בָּעֳנִי עַמּוֹ,¹

》 of His 〈 the 〈 and see 〈 He will 〈 Perhaps
people, suffering have mercy

וְיַקְשֵׁב וְיִשְׁמַע הַצָּגִים לְעַמּוֹ,

》 before Him, 〈 those who stand 〈 and hear 〈 and hearken

וְעוֹדִים בְּלַחַשׁ מוּסָר לֱמוֹ,²

》 them, 〈 [when He] 〈 in silent 〈 gathered
chastises prayer

וְעֵינֵיהֶם תּוֹלִים לִמְצוֹא רְצִיּוֹן,

》 favor. 〈 to find 〈 they raise 〈 as their eyes

אוּלַי יָחוֹס עַם עָנִי וְאֶבְיוֹן, אוּלַי יְרַחֵם.

》 He will 〈 perhaps 》 and 〈 that is 〈 the 〈 He will 〈 Perhaps
have mercy. destitute; poor people pity

CONGREGATION, THEN *CHAZZAN:*

אוּלַי יְרַחֵם אוֹמְרֵי סְלַח נָא,

》 please! 〈 Forgive, 〈 on those 〈 He will 〈 Perhaps
who say, have mercy

אוֹמְצֵי שְׁבָחוֹ בְּכָל עֵת וְעוֹנָה,

》 and season, 〈 time 〈 at every 〈 His praise 〈 who strengthen

אֲגוּדִים בַּצָּרָה לִשְׁפּוֹךְ תְּחִנָּה,

》 supplication; 〈 to pour out 〈 in distress 〈 united

אֶת פְּנֵי אֱלֹהֵיהֶם שׁוֹפְכִים לֵב דְּנִיּוֹן,

》 full of anguish. 〈 a heart 〈 they pour out 〈 their God 〈 before

אוּלַי יָחוֹס עַם עָנִי וְאֶבְיוֹן, אוּלַי יְרַחֵם.

》 He will 〈 perhaps 》 and 〈 that is 〈 the 〈 He will 〈 Perhaps
have mercy. destitute; poor people pity

CONGREGATION, THEN *CHAZZAN:*

אוּלַי יְרַחֵם לָקְתָה בְּכִפְלַיִם,³

》 doubly, 〈 on [the nation that] 〈 He will 〈 Perhaps
was punished have mercy

לְעוּטָה אֲרָיוֹת⁴ כְּמוֹ בְּפִי שַׁחֲלִים,⁵

》 of lions 〈 by the 〈 as 〈 by lions 〈 devoured
[Rome], mouth well as [Babylon],

לָקָה וּמִשְׁתַּלֶּמֶת⁶ בַּעֲוֹן שׁוּלָיִם,⁷

》 visible on the bottom 〈 for its 〈 and is repaid 〈 received
of its garments, sins beatings

(1) Cf. *Exodus* 3:7. (2) Cf. *Isaiah* 26:16. (3) Cf. 40:2. (4) Cf. *Tanchuma Vayechi* 14. (5) Cf. *Hosea* 13:7. (6) Cf. *Makkos* 4b. (7) Cf. *Lamentations* 1:9.

לֹא שָׁכְחָה בְּכָל זֹאת מִכְתָּב עוֹז חֶבְיוֹן,¹

《 that was hid- 〈 of [God's] 〈 the 《 this, 〈 despite 《 forgotten, 〈 yet has
den[until Sinai]. might, Scripture all not

אוּלַי יָחוֹס עַם עָנִי וְאֶבְיוֹן, אוּלַי יְרַחֵם.

《 He will 〈 perhaps 《 and 〈 that is 〈 the 〈 He will 〈 Perhaps
have mercy. destitute; poor people pity

CONGREGATION, THEN *CHAZZAN*:

אוּלַי יְרַחֵם כְּבוּשֵׁי פָנִים,

《 their faces 〈 on those 〈 He will 〈 Perhaps
[in shame], who hide have mercy

הַשּׁוֹמְעִים חֶרְפָּתָם וְלֹא מְשִׁיבִים² וְעוֹנִים,

《 or answer. 〈 respond 〈 but 〈 insults directed 〈 who hear
do not at them

נִצְחוֹ מְקַוְּים וּלִישׁוּעוֹ נִשְׁעָנִים,

《 they rely, 〈 and on His 〈 they 〈 For [God's]
salvation hope, triumph

כִּי לֹא כָלוּ רַחֲמָיו³ בְּכִלָּיוֹן,

《 totally. 〈 are His 〈 finished 〈 not 〈 for
mercies

אוּלַי יָחוֹס עַם עָנִי וְאֶבְיוֹן, אוּלַי יְרַחֵם.

《 He will 〈 perhaps 《 and 〈 that is 〈 the 〈 He will 〈 Perhaps
have mercy. destitute; poor people pity

CONGREGATION, THEN *CHAZZAN*:

אוּלַי יְרַחֵם יְחַלֵּץ עָנִי בְּעָנְיוֹ,⁴

《 from its 〈 the afflicted 〈 and set 〈 He will 〈 Perhaps
affliction, [nation] free have mercy

חֲבוּשׁוֹ יַתִּיר מֵאֶרֶץ שִׁבְיוֹ,

《 of its 〈 from the 〈 He shall 〈 His
captivity, land release imprisoned
[nation]

יִגְהֶה מִזּוֹרוֹ⁵ וְיַחֲבוֹשׁ⁶ חָלְיוֹ,

《 its disease, 〈 and curing 〈 its wound 〈 healing

צַעֲקָתוֹ יִשְׁמַע וְיָחִישׁ עֵת פִּדְיוֹן,

《 of 〈 the 〈 and He will 〈 He will 〈 its outcry
redemption. time hasten hear

אוּלַי יָחוֹס עַם עָנִי וְאֶבְיוֹן, אוּלַי יְרַחֵם.

《 He will 〈 perhaps 《 and 〈 that is 〈 the 〈 He will 〈 Perhaps
have mercy. destitute; poor people pity

(1) Cf. *Habakkuk* 3:4. (2) Cf. *Shabbos* 88b. (3) *Lamentations* 3:22.
(4) *Job* 36:15. (5) Cf. *Hosea* 5:13. (6) Cf. *Isaiah* 1:6.

ON ALL DAYS CONTINUE HERE:

**AN INDIVIDUAL PRAYING WITHOUT A *MINYAN* OMITS THE NEXT TWO PARAGRAPHS,
BEGINNING אֵל מֶלֶךְ, O GOD, KING, AND ה', HASHEM.**

אֵל מֶלֶךְ יוֹשֵׁב עַל כִּסֵּא רַחֲמִים, מִתְנַהֵג בַּחֲסִידוּת, מוֹחֵל

⟨ Who ⟨⟨ with ⟨ Who acts ⟨⟨ of mercy, ⟨ the ⟨ on ⟨ Who ⟨ King ⟨ O God,
pardons kindness, throne sits

עֲוֹנוֹת עַמּוֹ, מַעֲבִיר רִאשׁוֹן רִאשׁוֹן, מַרְבֶּה מְחִילָה לַחַטָּאִים

⟨ to uninten- ⟨ pardon ⟨ Who abun- by one, ⟨ [sins] one ⟨ Who ⟨⟨ of His ⟨ the sins
tional sinners dantly grants removes people,

וּסְלִיחָה לַפּוֹשְׁעִים, עֹשֶׂה צְדָקוֹת עִם כָּל בָּשָׂר וָרוּחַ, לֹא

⟨— not ⟨⟨ and ⟨ [beings ⟨ all ⟨ with ⟨ acts of ⟨ Who ⟨⟨ to willful ⟨ and
spirit of] flesh generosity performs sinners, forgiveness

כְּרָעָתָם תִּגְמוֹל. ❖ אֵל הוֹרֵיתָ לָּנוּ לוֹמַר שְׁלֹשׁ עֶשְׂרֵה, וּזְכוֹר

⟨ remember ⟨⟨ the Thirteen ⟨ to recite ⟨ us ⟨ You ⟨ O ⟨⟨ do You repay ⟨ in accord
[Attributes taught God, them! with their
of Mercy]; wickedness

לָּנוּ הַיּוֹם בְּרִית שְׁלֹשׁ עֶשְׂרֵה, כְּמוֹ שֶׁהוֹדַעְתָּ לֶעָנָיו מִקֶּדֶם, כְּמוֹ

⟨ as ⟨⟨ in ancient ⟨ to the humble ⟨ You made ⟨ as ⟨⟨ of [these] Thirteen, ⟨ the ⟨ today ⟨ for
times, one [Moses] known covenant us

שֶׁכָּתוּב, וַיֵּרֶד יהוה בֶּעָנָן וַיִּתְיַצֵּב עִמּוֹ שָׁם, וַיִּקְרָא בְשֵׁם יהוה.

⟨⟨ of ⟨ with the ⟨ and He ⟨⟨ there, ⟨ with ⟨ and stood ⟨ in a ⟨ And HASHEM ⟨⟨ it is written:
HASHEM. Name called out him cloud descended

CONGREGATION AND *CHAZZAN* RECITE LOUDLY AND IN UNISON:

וַיַּעֲבֹר יהוה עַל פָּנָיו וַיִּקְרָא:

⟨⟨ and proclaimed: ⟨⟨ [Moses'] face, ⟨ before ⟨ And HASHEM passed

יהוה, יהוה, אֵל, רַחוּם, וְחַנּוּן, אֶרֶךְ אַפַּיִם, וְרַב חֶסֶד, וֶאֱמֶת,

⟨⟨ and ⟨ in ⟨ and ⟨ to anger, ⟨ Slow ⟨⟨ and ⟨ Compas- ⟨ God, ⟨ HASHEM, ⟨ HASHEM,
Truth, Kindness Abundant Gracious, sionate

נֹצֵר חֶסֶד לָאֲלָפִים, נֹשֵׂא עָוֹן, וָפֶשַׁע, וְחַטָּאָה, וְנַקֵּה.

⟨⟨ and Who ⟨ and inad- ⟨ willful ⟨ of ⟨ Forgiver ⟨⟨ for thousands ⟨ of ⟨ Preserver
absolves. vertent sin, sin, iniquity, [of generations], kindness

וְסָלַחְתָּ לַעֲוֹנֵנוּ וּלְחַטָּאתֵנוּ וּנְחַלְתָּנוּ. סְלַח לָנוּ אָבִינוּ כִּי

⟨ for ⟨⟨ our ⟨ us, ⟨ Forgive ⟨⟨ and make us ⟨⟨ and our sins, ⟨ our ⟨ May You
Father, Your heritage. iniquities forgive '

חָטָאנוּ, מְחַל לָנוּ מַלְכֵּנוּ כִּי פָשָׁעְנוּ. כִּי אַתָּה אֲדֹנָי טוֹב

⟨ are ⟨ O Lord, ⟨ You, ⟨ For ⟨⟨ we have ⟨ for ⟨⟨ our King, ⟨ us, ⟨ pardon ⟨⟨ we have
good willfully sinned. sinned;

וְסַלָּח, וְרַב חֶסֶד לְכָל קֹרְאֶיךָ.

⟨⟨ who call ⟨ to all ⟨ kind ⟨ and ⟨⟨ and
upon You. abundantly forgiving,

זְכֹר רַחֲמֶיךָ יהוה וַחֲסָדֶיךָ, כִּי מֵעוֹלָם הֵמָּה.¹ זָכְרֵנוּ

‹ Remember ‹‹ are ‹ eternal ‹ for ‹‹ and Your ‹ HASHEM, ‹ Your ‹ Remember
us, they. kindnesses, mercies,

יהוה בִּרְצוֹן עַמֶּךָ, פָּקְדֵנוּ בִּישׁוּעָתֶךָ.² זְכֹר עֲדָתְךָ קָנִיתָ

‹ which You ‹ Your ‹ Remem- ‹‹ with Your ‹ recall us ‹‹ to Your ‹ when You ‹ HASHEM,
acquired congregation, ber salvation. people; show favor

קֶדֶם, גָּאַלְתָּ שֵׁבֶט נַחֲלָתֶךָ, הַר צִיּוֹן זֶה שָׁכַנְתָּ בּוֹ.³ זְכֹר

‹ Remem- ‹‹ there. ‹ You ‹ the one ‹ of ‹ the ‹‹ of Your ‹ the ‹ You ‹‹ long
ber, rested Your [where] Zion, Mountain heritage; tribe redeemed ago,
presence

יהוה חִבַּת יְרוּשָׁלָיִם, אַהֲבַת צִיּוֹן אַל תִּשְׁכַּח לָנֶצַח. אַתָּה

‹ You ‹‹ forever. ‹ forget ‹ do ‹ of ‹ the love ‹‹ of Jerusalem; ‹ the ‹ HASHEM,
not Zion affection

תָקוּם תְּרַחֵם צִיּוֹן, כִּי עֵת לְחֶנְנָהּ, כִּי בָא מוֹעֵד.⁴ זְכֹר

‹ Remem- ‹‹ the appointed ‹ for ‹‹ to favor ‹ [there ‹ for ‹‹ to ‹ and show ‹ will arise
ber, time will her, will come] Zion, mercy
have come. the time

יהוה לִבְנֵי אֱדוֹם אֵת יוֹם יְרוּשָׁלָיִם, הָאֹמְרִים עָרוּ עָרוּ

‹ Destroy ‹‹ Destroy! ‹‹ [to repay] ‹ of Jerusalem; ‹ the day ‹ of Edom, ‹ [to repay] ‹ HASHEM,
those who say, the offspring

עַד הַיְסוֹד בָּהּ.⁵ זְכֹר לְאַבְרָהָם לְיִצְחָק וּלְיִשְׂרָאֵל עֲבָדֶיךָ,

‹‹ Your ‹ and for Israel, ‹ for Isaac ‹ for Abraham, ‹ Remem- ‹‹ of it! ‹ the very ‹ to
servants, ber foundation

אֲשֶׁר נִשְׁבַּעְתָּ לָהֶם בָּךְ וַתְּדַבֵּר אֲלֵהֶם, אַרְבֶּה אֶת זַרְעֲכֶם

‹ Your offspring ‹ I shall ‹‹ to them, ‹ and You ‹‹ by Your ‹ to ‹ You swore ‹ that
increase said Being, them

כְּכוֹכְבֵי הַשָּׁמָיִם, וְכָל הָאָרֶץ הַזֹּאת אֲשֶׁר אָמַרְתִּי, אֶתֵּן

‹ I will ‹ I spoke ‹ of which ‹‹ of this land ‹ and all ‹‹ of the ‹ like the stars
give heavens;

לְזַרְעֲכֶם, וְנָחֲלוּ לְעֹלָם.⁶ זְכֹר לַעֲבָדֶיךָ לְאַבְרָהָם לְיִצְחָק

‹ for Isaac ‹ for Abraham, ‹ for Your ‹ Remem- ‹‹ forever. ‹ and they ‹ to your
servants, ber will inherit it offspring,

וּלְיַעֲקֹב, אַל תֵּפֶן אֶל קְשִׁי הָעָם הַזֶּה וְאֶל רִשְׁעוֹ וְאֶל

‹ and ‹‹ its ‹ to ‹‹ of this people, ‹ the stub- ‹ to ‹ pay ‹ do ‹‹ and for
to wickedness, bornness attention not Jacob;

חַטָּאתוֹ.⁷

‹‹ its sinfulness.

(1) *Psalms* 25:6. (2) Cf. 106:4. (3) 74:2. (4) 102:14.
(5) 137:7. (6) *Exodus* 32:13. (7) *Deuteronomy* 9:27.

SELICHOS FOR CHILDREN'S ILLNESS / סליחות לתחלואי ילדים ר״ל

MOST CONGREGATIONS OMIT THE FOLLOWING AND CONTINUE WITH זְכוֹר לָנוּ, PAGE 689.
THESE CONGREGATIONS RECITE THIS SPECIAL PRAYER ONLY IF THERE IS AN ACTUAL EPIDEMIC
AFFLICTING CHILDREN. OTHER CONGREGATIONS RECITE THIS PRAYER ON EVERY FAST DAY.

THE FOLLOWING TWO VERSES ARE RECITED RESPONSIVELY:

אַל נָא תָשֵׁת עָלֵינוּ חַטָּאת, אֲשֶׁר נוֹאַלְנוּ וַאֲשֶׁר חָטָאנוּ.[1]

《 we have 〈 and 〈 we have 〈 that 《 [guilt for 〈 upon us 〈 place 〈 please, 〈 Do
sinned.   that   been foolish   our] sin,   not,

חָטָאנוּ צוּרֵנוּ, סְלַח לָנוּ יוֹצְרֵנוּ.

《 our Molder. 〈 us, 〈 forgive 《 our Rock; 〈 We have sinned,

אֵל נָא רְפָא נָא[2] תַּחֲלוּאֵי גֶפֶן פּוֹרִיָּה,[3]

《 that is 〈 of [Israel, 〈 the 〈 now 〈 cure 〈 please 〈 O
fruitful,   called] the vine   illnesses   God,

בּוֹשָׁה וַחֲפוּרָה וְאָמְלַל פִּרְיָהּ,[4]

《 is its fruit. 〈 and miserable 〈 disgraced, 〈 that shamed,

גְּאָלֶנָּה מִשַּׁחַת וּמִמַּכָּה טְרִיָּה,[5]

《 that is festering. 〈 and from a wound 〈 from ruin 〈 Redeem it

עֲנֵנוּ כְּשֶׁעָנִיתָ לְאַבְרָהָם אָבִינוּ בְּהַר הַמּוֹרִיָּה.

《 Moriah. 〈 on Mount 〈 our father 〈 Abraham 〈 as You answered 〈 Answer us

חָטָאנוּ צוּרֵנוּ, סְלַח לָנוּ יוֹצְרֵנוּ.

《 our Molder. 〈 us, 〈 forgive 《 our Rock; 〈 We have sinned,

דִּגְלֵי עַם פְּדוּיֵי בִזְרוֹעַ חֲשׂוּף,[6]

《 bared 〈 with [God's] 〈 who were 〈 of the 《 The
arm   redeemed   nation,   bannered
                  [camp]

הַצֵּל מִנֶּגֶף וְאַל יִהְיוּ לִשְׁסוּף,

《 torn apart. 〈 become 〈 and let 《 from 〈 — rescue
them not   plague,   [them]

וְתַעֲנֶה קְרִיאָתֵנוּ לְמַעֲשֵׂה יָדֶיךָ תִּכְסוֹף,[7]

《 show yearning 〈 of Your 〈 for the work 《 our call; 〈 Answer
concern.   hands

עֲנֵנוּ כְּשֶׁעָנִיתָ לַאֲבוֹתֵינוּ עַל יַם סוּף.

《 of Reeds. 〈 the Sea 〈 at 〈 our forefathers 〈 as You answered 〈 Answer us

חָטָאנוּ צוּרֵנוּ, סְלַח לָנוּ יוֹצְרֵנוּ.

《 our Molder. 〈 us, 〈 forgive 《 our Rock; 〈 We have sinned,

זְכוּת צוּר חֻצָּב[8] הַיּוֹם לָנוּ תְגַל,

《 reveal. 〈 on our 〈 today 《 from whom 〈 of the rock 〈 The
behalf   [we were] hewn, [Abraham] merit

---

(1) *Numbers* 12:11. (2) 12:13. (3) *Isaiah* 32:12. (4) Cf. *Jeremiah* 15:9.
(5) Cf. *Isaiah* 1:6. (6) Cf. 52:10; *Ezekiel* 4:7. (7) *Job* 14:15. (8) Cf. *Isaiah* 51:1.

חֲשֹׂכֵנוּ מֵאֶנֶף וּנְחֵנוּ בִּישֶׁר מַעְגָּל,[1]

≪ path. ⟨ on a straight ⟨ and guide us ≪ from anger, ⟨ Spare us

טַהֵר טֻמְאָתֵנוּ וְלִמְאוֹר תּוֹרָתְךָ עֵינֵינוּ גַּל,[2]

≪ reveal. ⟨ to our eyes ⟨ of Your Torah ⟨ and the light ≪ our impurity, ⟨ Cleanse

עֲנֵנוּ כְּשֶׁעָנִיתָ לִיהוֹשֻׁעַ בַּגִּלְגָּל.[3]

≪ in Gilgal. ⟨ Joshua ⟨ as You answered ⟨ Answer us

חָטָאנוּ צוּרֵנוּ, סְלַח לָנוּ יוֹצְרֵנוּ.

≪ our Molder. ⟨ us, ⟨ forgive ≪ our Rock; ⟨ We have sinned,

יָהּ רְאֵה דֶּשֶׁן עָקוּד וְהַצְמַח לָנוּ תְרוּפָה,[4]

≪ a cure. ⟨ for ⟨ and cause ≪ of the bound ⟨ the ⟨ see ⟨ O
us to sprout one [Isaac], ashes God,

כַּלֵּה שׁוֹד וָשֶׁבֶר[5] סַעַר וְסוּפָה,[6]

≪ and ⟨ storm ≪ and ⟨ to ⟨ Bring
tempest. destruction, plunder an end

לַמְּדֵנוּ וְחַכְּמֵנוּ אִמְרָתְךָ הַצְּרוּפָה,[7]

≪ which is ⟨ of Your word ⟨ and give us ⟨ Teach us
flawless. the wisdom

עֲנֵנוּ כְּשֶׁעָנִיתָ לִשְׁמוּאֵל בַּמִּצְפָּה.[8]

≪ in Mizpah. ⟨ Samuel ⟨ as You answered ⟨ Answer us

חָטָאנוּ צוּרֵנוּ, סְלַח לָנוּ יוֹצְרֵנוּ.

≪ our Molder. ⟨ us, ⟨ forgive ≪ our Rock; ⟨ We have sinned,

מְתַמֵּם מְרַחֵם[9] שָׁרָשָׁיו אַל תַּקְמֵל,

≪ allow to ⟨ do ⟨— his roots ≪ from the ⟨ The one who
wither. not womb [Jacob] was perfect

נֵקֶנוּ מִכֶּתֶם וָשֶׁמֶץ וְלֹא נֵאָמֵל,

≪ become ⟨ and let ≪ and ⟨ from ⟨ Cleanse
miserable; us not disgrace, stain us

סַעֲדֵנוּ וְנִוָּשֵׁעָה[10] וְאָרְחוֹת חֲסָדֶיךָ[11] נִגָּמֵל,

≪ let us ⟨ of ⟨ and from ≪ so that we ⟨ give us
benefit. kindness Your ways may be saved, support

עֲנֵנוּ כְּשֶׁעָנִיתָ לְאֵלִיָּהוּ בְּהַר הַכַּרְמֶל.[12]

≪ Carmel. ⟨ on Mount ⟨ Elijah ⟨ as You answered ⟨ Answer us

חָטָאנוּ צוּרֵנוּ, סְלַח לָנוּ יוֹצְרֵנוּ.

≪ our Molder. ⟨ us, ⟨ forgive ≪ our Rock; ⟨ We have sinned,

עוֹדְדֵנוּ בְּצֶדֶק מָשׁוּי מִמַּיִם וְכַפֵּר זָדוֹן וּמְשׁוּגָה,

≪ and uninten- ⟨ willful ⟨ and ≪ from the ⟨ of [Moses] ⟨ through the ⟨ Strengthen
tional sin. sin forgive water, who was drawn righteousness us

(1) Cf. *Isaiah* 26:7. (2) Cf. *Psalms* 119:18. (3) Cf. *Joshua* 6:1-20; 7:6-15; 10:12-14. (4) Cf. *Ezekiel* 47:12.
(5) Cf. *Isaiah* 51:19. (6) Cf. *Amos* 1:14. (7) Cf. *Psalms* 119:140. (8) Cf. *I Samuel* 7:9.
(9) Cf. *Bereishis Rabbah* 63:7. (10) Cf. *Psalms* 119:117. (11) Cf. 25:10. (12) Cf. *I Kings* 18:36-38.

פְּדֵנוּ מִמְּהוּמַת מָוֶת[1] וְאָחוֹר בַּל נִסּוֹגָה,[2]

《 retreat. 〈 let us not 〈and backward《《 of death, 〈 from panic 〈 Save us

צַוֵּה יְשׁוּעָתֵנוּ[3] וּבַעֲוֹנוֹתֵינוּ אַל נִתְמוֹגָגָה,[4]

《 dissolve. 〈 let us not 〈 and in our iniquities 《《 our salvation, 〈 Command

עֲנֵנוּ כְּשֶׁעָנִיתָ לְיוֹנָה בִּמְעֵי הַדָּגָה.

《 of the fish. 〈 in the innards 〈 Jonah 〈 as You answered 〈 Answer us

חָטָאנוּ צוּרֵנוּ, סְלַח לָנוּ יוֹצְרֵנוּ.

《 our Molder. 〈 us, 〈 forgive 《《 our Rock; 〈 We have sinned,

קָדְשַׁת אִישׁ חֲסִידֶךָ[5] זְכוֹר לִיפַת פְּעָמַיִם,[6]

《 footsteps. 〈 for the one [Israel] 〈 remem- 〈 of Your devout man 〈 The
having lovely   ber   [Aaron]   holiness

רַחֲמֶיךָ תְּעוֹרֵר כִּי לָקִינוּ בְכִפְלַיִם,[7]

《 doubly. 〈 we have been smitten 〈 for 《《 arouse, 〈 Your mercy

שׁוּבֵנוּ תֹּקֶף לְיִרְאָתֶךָ[8] וְלֹא נֶחֱשֹׁף שׁוּלַיִם,

《 [our sins visible] on the 〈 be 〈 and let 《《 to Your 〈 force- 〈 Return
bottom of our garments.   exposed   not   reverence,   fully   us

עֲנֵנוּ כְּשֶׁעָנִיתָ לְדָוִד וְלִשְׁלֹמֹה בְנוֹ בִּירוּשָׁלָיִם.[9]

《 in Jerusalem. 〈 his son 〈 and Solomon 〈 David 〈 as You answered 〈 Answer us

חָטָאנוּ צוּרֵנוּ, סְלַח לָנוּ יוֹצְרֵנוּ.

《 our Molder. 〈 us, 〈 forgive 《《 our Rock; 〈 We have sinned,

SOME CONGREGATIONS ADD (EITHER ON ALL FAST DAYS, OR ONLY ON THE FAST OF ESTHER):

תַּעֲנֶה לְקוֹרְאֶיךָ, וְהַסְכֵּת מִמְּעוֹנִים,

《 from the 〈 and listen 《《 to those who 〈 (Respond
heavens;   call You,

תִּשְׁמַע שַׁוְעַת צוֹעֲקֶיךָ, שׁוֹמֵעַ אֶל אֶבְיוֹנִים,

《 the destitute. 〈 to 〈 You Who 《《 of those who 〈 the plea 〈 hear
listens   cry out to You,

תְּרַחֵם עַל בָּנֶיךָ, כְּרַחֵם אָב עַל בָּנִים,[10]

《 [his] 〈 for 〈 of a 〈 like the 〈 Your 〈 on 〈 Have
children.   father   mercy   children,   mercy

עֲנֵנוּ כְּשֶׁעָנִיתָ לְמָרְדְּכַי וְאֶסְתֵּר,

《 and Esther, 〈 Mordechai 〈 as You answered 〈 Answer us

וְתָלוּ עַל הָעֵץ חֲמִשִּׁים הָאָב עִם הַבָּנִים.

《 his sons. 〈 with 〈 the father 〈 of fifty 〈 the 〈 on 〈 [allowing]
[Haman]   [cubits]   gallows   them to hang

חָטָאנוּ צוּרֵנוּ, סְלַח לָנוּ יוֹצְרֵנוּ.

《 our Molder. 〈 us, 〈 forgive 《《 our Rock; 〈 We have sinned,

---

(1) Cf. *I Samuel* 5:11. (2) Cf. *Psalms* 44:19. (3) Cf. 44:5. (4) Cf. *Isaiah* 64:6.
(5) Cf. *Deuteronomy* 33:8. (6) Cf. *Song of Songs* 7:2. (7) Cf. *Isaiah* 40:2.
(8) Cf. *Jeremiah* 13:26. (9) Cf. *II Samuel* 7:5-16; 24:25; *I Kings* 9:3. (10) *Psalms* 103:13.

ALL CONTINUE:

זְכוֹר לָנוּ בְּרִית אָבוֹת, כַּאֲשֶׁר אָמַרְתָּ: וְזָכַרְתִּי אֶת בְּרִיתִי

❮ My covenant ❮ And I will ❮ You said: ❮ as ❮❮ of the ❮ the ❮ for ❮ Remember
remember Patriarchs, covenant us

יַעֲקוֹב, וְאַף אֶת בְּרִיתִי יִצְחָק, וְאַף אֶת בְּרִיתִי אַבְרָהָם אֶזְכֹּר,

❮❮ will I ❮ [with] ❮ My covenant ❮ and ❮❮ [with] ❮ My covenant ❮ and ❮❮ [with]
remember; Abraham also Isaac, also Jacob,

וְהָאָרֶץ אֶזְכֹּר.[1] זְכוֹר לָנוּ בְּרִית רִאשׁוֹנִים, כַּאֲשֶׁר אָמַרְתָּ:

❮❮ You said: ❮ as ❮❮ of the ancient ❮ the ❮ for ❮ Remember ❮❮ will I ❮ and the
ones, covenant us remember. Land

וְזָכַרְתִּי לָהֶם בְּרִית רִאשׁוֹנִים, אֲשֶׁר הוֹצֵאתִי אֹתָם מֵאֶרֶץ

❮ from ❮ I took them out ❮ that ❮❮ of the ancient ❮ the ❮ for ❮ And I will
the land ones, covenant them remember

מִצְרַיִם לְעֵינֵי הַגּוֹיִם, לִהְיוֹת לָהֶם לֵאלֹהִים, אֲנִי יהוה.[2] עֲשֵׂה

❮ Do ❮❮ am ❮ I ❮❮ a God; ❮ to ❮ to be ❮❮ of the ❮ in the ❮ of Egypt
HASHEM. them nations, very sight

עִמָּנוּ כְּמָה שֶׁהִבְטַחְתָּנוּ: וְאַף גַּם זֹאת בִּהְיוֹתָם בְּאֶרֶץ

❮ in the ❮ when they ❮❮ this, ❮ all ❮ And ❮❮ You promised us: ❮ as ❮ with us
land will be despite

אֹיְבֵיהֶם, לֹא מְאַסְתִּים וְלֹא גְעַלְתִּים לְכַלֹּתָם לְהָפֵר בְּרִיתִי

❮ My ❮ to annul ❮ to destroy ❮ abhor them ❮ nor ❮ despise them ❮ I will ❮❮ of their
covenant them, not enemies,

אִתָּם, כִּי אֲנִי יהוה אֱלֹהֵיהֶם.[3] הָשֵׁב שְׁבוּתֵנוּ וְרַחֲמֵנוּ, כְּמָה

❮ as ❮❮ and have ❮ our ❮ Bring ❮❮ their God. ❮ HASHEM, ❮ I am ❮ for ❮❮ with
mercy on us, captivity back them,

שֶׁכָּתוּב: וְשָׁב יהוה אֱלֹהֶיךָ אֶת שְׁבוּתְךָ וְרִחֲמֶךָ, וְשָׁב וְקִבֶּצְךָ

❮ gather ❮ and He ❮❮ and He will ❮ your captivity, ❮ your God, ❮ will ❮ Then bring ❮❮ it is
you in will once have mercy HASHEM, back written:
again upon you,

מִכָּל הָעַמִּים אֲשֶׁר הֱפִיצְךָ יהוה אֱלֹהֶיךָ שָׁמָּה.[4] קַבֵּץ נִדָּחֵינוּ,

❮ our dis- ❮ Gather ❮❮ thereto. ❮ HASHEM, your God, scattered you ❮ that ❮ the peoples ❮ from
persed ones all

כְּמָה שֶׁכָּתוּב: אִם יִהְיֶה נִדַּחֲךָ בִּקְצֵה הַשָּׁמָיִם, מִשָּׁם

❮ from ❮❮ of heaven, ❮ at the ends ❮ your dispersed ❮ If ❮ it is written: ❮ as
there will be

יְקַבֶּצְךָ יהוה אֱלֹהֶיךָ, וּמִשָּׁם יִקָּחֶךָ.[5] מָחֵה פְשָׁעֵינוּ כָּעָב

❮ like a ❮ our sins ❮ Wipe ❮❮ He will ❮ and from ❮❮ HASHEM, your God, will gather you in,
mist away take you. there

(1) *Leviticus* 26:42. (2) 26:45. (3) 26:44. (4) *Deuteronomy* 30:3. (5) 30:4.

וְכֶעָנָן, כְּמָה שֶׁכָּתוּב: מָחִיתִי כָעָב פְּשָׁעֶיךָ וְכֶעָנָן חַטֹּאתֶיךָ,

שׁוּבָה אֵלַי כִּי גְאַלְתִּיךָ.¹ מְחֵה פְשָׁעֵינוּ לְמַעַנֶךָ, כַּאֲשֶׁר אָמַרְתָּ:

אָנֹכִי אָנֹכִי הוּא מֹחֶה פְשָׁעֶיךָ לְמַעֲנִי, וְחַטֹּאתֶיךָ לֹא אֶזְכֹּר.²

הַלְבֵּן חֲטָאֵינוּ כַּשֶּׁלֶג וְכַצֶּמֶר, כְּמָה שֶׁכָּתוּב: לְכוּ נָא וְנִוָּכְחָה,

יֹאמַר יְהוָה, אִם יִהְיוּ חֲטָאֵיכֶם כַּשָּׁנִים כַּשֶּׁלֶג יַלְבִּינוּ, אִם

יַאְדִּימוּ כַתּוֹלָע, כַּצֶּמֶר יִהְיוּ.³ זְרוֹק עָלֵינוּ מַיִם טְהוֹרִים

וְטַהֲרֵנוּ, כְּמָה שֶׁכָּתוּב: וְזָרַקְתִּי עֲלֵיכֶם מַיִם טְהוֹרִים וּטְהַרְתֶּם,

מִכֹּל טֻמְאוֹתֵיכֶם וּמִכָּל גִּלּוּלֵיכֶם אֲטַהֵר אֶתְכֶם.⁴ רַחֵם עָלֵינוּ

וְאַל תַּשְׁחִיתֵנוּ, כְּמָה שֶׁכָּתוּב: כִּי אֵל רַחוּם יְהוָה אֱלֹהֶיךָ,

לֹא יַרְפְּךָ וְלֹא יַשְׁחִיתֶךָ, וְלֹא יִשְׁכַּח אֶת בְּרִית אֲבֹתֶיךָ

אֲשֶׁר נִשְׁבַּע לָהֶם.⁵ וּמוֹל אֶת לְבָבֵנוּ לְאַהֲבָה אֶת שְׁמֶךָ, כְּמָה

שֶׁכָּתוּב: וּמָל יהוה אֱלֹהֶיךָ אֶת לְבָבְךָ וְאֶת לְבַב זַרְעֶךָ,

לְאַהֲבָה אֶת יהוה אֱלֹהֶיךָ, בְּכָל לְבָבְךָ וּבְכָל נַפְשְׁךָ, לְמַעַן

---

(1) Isaiah 44:22. (2) 43:25. (3) 1:18. (4) Ezekiel 36:25. (5) Deuteronomy 4:31.

חַיֶּיךָ.¹ הַמָּצֵא לָנוּ בְּבַקָּשָׁתֵנוּ, כְּמָה שֶׁכָּתוּב: וּבִקַּשְׁתֶּם מִשָּׁם

‹ from ‹ And you ‹‹ it is written: ‹ as ‹‹ in our quest, ‹ to us ‹ Be ‹‹ you may
there will seek accessible live.

אֶת יהוה אֱלֹהֶיךָ וּמָצָאתָ, כִּי תִדְרְשֶׁנּוּ בְּכָל לְבָבְךָ וּבְכָל

‹ and ‹ your heart ‹ with ‹ you search ‹ when ‹‹ and you will ‹ your God, ‹ HASHEM,
with all all Him out find [Him],

נַפְשֶׁךָ. ❖² תְּבִיאֵנוּ אֶל הַר קָדְשֶׁךָ, וְשַׂמְּחֵנוּ בְּבֵית תְּפִלָּתֶךָ,

‹‹ of Prayer, ‹ in Your ‹ and gladden ‹ Your holy ‹ to ‹ Bring us ‹‹ your soul.
House us mountain

כְּמָה שֶׁכָּתוּב: וַהֲבִיאוֹתִים אֶל הַר קָדְשִׁי, וְשִׂמַּחְתִּים בְּבֵית

‹ in My ‹ and I will ‹‹ My holy ‹ to ‹ And I will ‹‹ it is written: ‹ as
House gladden them mountain, bring them

תְּפִלָּתִי, עוֹלֹתֵיהֶם וְזִבְחֵיהֶם לְרָצוֹן עַל מִזְבְּחִי, כִּי בֵיתִי

‹ My ‹ for ‹‹ My Altar, ‹ on ‹ will find ‹ and their feast- ‹ their elevation- ‹‹ of Prayer;
house favor offerings offerings

בֵית תְּפִלָּה יִקָּרֵא לְכָל הָעַמִּים.³

‹‹ nations . ‹ for all ‹ will be ‹ of Prayer' ‹ 'a
called House

THE ARK IS OPENED.

שְׁמַע קוֹלֵנוּ יהוה אֱלֹהֵינוּ, חוּס וְרַחֵם עָלֵינוּ, — RESPONSIVELY

‹‹ on us, ‹ and have ‹ have ‹‹ our God; ‹ HASHEM, ‹ our voice, ‹ Hear
compassion pity

וְקַבֵּל בְּרַחֲמִים וּבְרָצוֹן אֶת תְּפִלָּתֵנוּ.⁴

‹‹ our prayer. ‹ and favor ‹ with compassion ‹ and accept

הֲשִׁיבֵנוּ יהוה אֵלֶיךָ וְנָשׁוּבָה, חַדֵּשׁ יָמֵינוּ כְּקֶדֶם.⁵ — RESPONSIVELY

‹‹ as of ‹ our ‹ renew ‹‹ and we shall ‹ to You, ‹ HASHEM, ‹ Bring us
old. days return, back,

אֲמָרֵינוּ הַאֲזִינָה יהוה, בִּינָה הֲגִיגֵנוּ.⁶ — RESPONSIVELY

‹‹ our thoughts. ‹ perceive ‹‹ HASHEM; ‹ hear, ‹ Our words

THE FOLLOWING VERSE IS RECITED IN AN UNDERTONE:

יִהְיוּ לְרָצוֹן אִמְרֵי פִינוּ וְהֶגְיוֹן לִבֵּנוּ לְפָנֶיךָ, יהוה צוּרֵנוּ וְגוֹאֲלֵנוּ.⁷

‹‹ and our ‹ our ‹ HASHEM, ‹‹ before ‹‹ of our ‹ and the ‹ of our ‹ – the ‹‹ find ‹ May
Redeemer. Rock You, heart – thoughts mouth expressions favor they

אַל תַּשְׁלִיכֵנוּ מִלְּפָנֶיךָ, — RESPONSIVELY

‹‹ from Your Presence, ‹ cast us away ‹ Do not

וְרוּחַ קָדְשְׁךָ אַל תִּקַּח מִמֶּנּוּ.⁸

‹‹ from us. ‹ take ‹ do not ‹ of Your Holiness ‹ and the Spirit

---

(1) *Deuteronomy* 30:6. (2) 4:29. (3) *Isaiah* 56:7. (4) From the weekday *Shemoneh Esrei*.
(5) *Lamentations* 5:21. (6) *Psalms* 5:2. (7) Cf. 19:15. (8) 51:13.

– RESPONSIVELY אַל תַּשְׁלִיכֵנוּ לְעֵת זִקְנָה,

⟨ of old age; ⟨ in time ⟨ cast us away ⟨ Do not

כִּכְלוֹת כֹּחֵנוּ אַל תַּעַזְבֵנוּ.¹

《 forsake us not. ⟨ does our strength, ⟨ when fail

אַל תַּעַזְבֵנוּ יהוה, אֱלֹהֵינוּ אַל תִּרְחַק מִמֶּנּוּ.² עֲשֵׂה עִמָּנוּ אוֹת

⟨ a sign ⟨ for us ⟨ Display 《 from us. ⟨ be not distant ⟨ our God, 《 O Hashem; ⟨ Forsake us not,

לְטוֹבָה, וְיִרְאוּ שׂוֹנְאֵינוּ וְיֵבֹשׁוּ, כִּי אַתָּה יהוה עֲזַרְתָּנוּ

⟨ will have ⟨ Hashem, ⟨ You, ⟨ for 《 and be ⟨ may our ⟨ so that 《 for good; helped us — ashamed, — enemies — see it

וְנִחַמְתָּנוּ.³ כִּי לְךָ יהוה הוֹחָלְנוּ, אַתָּה תַעֲנֶה אֲדֹנָי אֱלֹהֵינוּ.⁴

《 our God. ⟨ O Lord, ⟨ will ⟨ You 《 do we wait; ⟨ Hashem, ⟨ for ⟨ Because《 and answer, You, consoled us.

THE ARK IS CLOSED AND EACH INDIVIDUAL CONTINUES UNTIL THE END OF SELICHOS (P. 698).

CONFESSION / וידוי

אֱלֹהֵינוּ וֵאלֹהֵי אֲבוֹתֵינוּ, (אָנָּא) תָּבֹא לְפָנֶיךָ תְּפִלָּתֵנוּ,⁵ וְאַל

⟨ and 《 may our ⟨ before ⟨ come ⟨ (please) 《 of our ⟨ and ⟨ Our God do not — prayer, — You, — forefathers, — the God

תִּתְעַלַּם מִתְּחִנָּתֵנוּ,⁶ שֶׁאֵין אָנוּ עַזֵּי פָנִים וּקְשֵׁי עֹרֶף, לוֹמַר

⟨ as to ⟨ necked ⟨ and stiff- ⟨ faced ⟨ so ⟨ For we are not 《 our ⟨ ignore say brazen- supplication.

לְפָנֶיךָ יהוה אֱלֹהֵינוּ וֵאלֹהֵי אֲבוֹתֵינוּ, צַדִּיקִים אֲנַחְנוּ וְלֹא

⟨ and ⟨ that we are 《 of our ⟨ and ⟨ our God, ⟨ Hashem, 《 before have not righteous forefathers, the God You,

חָטָאנוּ, אֲבָל אֲנַחְנוּ וַאֲבוֹתֵינוּ חָטָאנוּ.⁷

《 have sinned. ⟨ and our forefathers ⟨ we 《 – for indeed, 《 sinned

STRIKE THE LEFT SIDE OF THE CHEST WITH THE RIGHT FIST WHILE RECITING EACH OF THE SINS OF THE FOLLOWING CONFESSIONAL LITANY:

אָשַׁמְנוּ, בָּגַדְנוּ, גָּזַלְנוּ, דִּבַּרְנוּ דֹּפִי. הֶעֱוִינוּ, וְהִרְשַׁעְנוּ,

《 we have 《 We have 《 slander. ⟨ we have 《 we have 《 we have 《 We have committed committed spoken robbed; betrayed; been guilty; wickedness; iniquity;

זַדְנוּ, חָמַסְנוּ, טָפַלְנוּ שֶׁקֶר. יָעַצְנוּ רָע, כִּזַּבְנוּ, לַצְנוּ,

《 we have 《 we have 《 that ⟨ We have 《 false ⟨ we have 《 we have 《 we have scorned; been is bad; given accusations. made extorted; sinned deceitful; advice willfully;

מָרַדְנוּ, נִאַצְנוּ, סָרַרְנוּ, עָוִינוּ, פָּשַׁעְנוּ, צָרַרְנוּ, קִשִּׁינוּ עֹרֶף.

《 our ⟨ we have 《 we have 《 we have 《 we have 《 we have 《 we have 《 we have necks. stiffened caused sinned been strayed; provoked rebelled; distress; rebelliously; iniquitous; [God's anger];

(1) Cf. *Psalms* 71:9. (2) Cf. 38:22. (3) Cf. 86:17. (4) Cf. 38:16. (5) Cf. 88:3. (6) Cf. 55:2. (7) Cf. 106:6.

רָשַׁעְנוּ, שִׁחַתְנוּ, תִּעַבְנוּ, תָּעִינוּ, תִּעְתָּעְנוּ.

‹‹ we have ‹‹ we have ‹‹ we have ‹‹ we have ‹‹ We have
scoffed. gone astray; committed been corrupt; been wicked;
abominations;

סַרְנוּ מִמִּצְוֹתֶיךָ וּמִמִּשְׁפָּטֶיךָ הַטּוֹבִים, וְלֹא שָׁוָה לָנוּ.[1] וְאַתָּה

‹ And ‹‹ for ‹ worth- ‹ and it ‹‹ that are ‹ and from ‹ from Your ‹ We have
You us. while was not good, Your laws commandments turned away

צַדִּיק עַל כָּל הַבָּא עָלֵינוּ, כִּי אֱמֶת עָשִׂיתָ וַאֲנַחְנוּ הִרְשָׁעְנוּ.[2]

‹‹ have acted ‹ while ‹‹ have ‹ truthfully ‹ for ‹‹ upon ‹ that has ‹ all ‹ in ‹ are
wickedly. we You acted, us, come righteous

הִרְשַׁעְנוּ וּפָשַׁעְנוּ, לָכֵן לֹא נוֹשָׁעְנוּ. וְתֵן בְּלִבֵּנוּ לַעֲזוֹב

‹ [the will] ‹ in our ‹ Place ‹‹ been ‹ we ‹ there- ‹‹ and we have ‹ We have acted
to abandon hearts saved. have not fore sinned rebelliously; wickedly

דֶּרֶךְ רֶשַׁע, וְחִישׁ לָנוּ יֶשַׁע, כַּכָּתוּב עַל יַד נְבִיאֶךָ: יַעֲזֹב

‹ Let ‹‹ of Your ‹ the ‹ by ‹ as it is ‹‹ salvation; ‹ to us ‹ and ‹‹ of ‹ the
abandon prophet: hand written hasten wickedness, path

רָשָׁע דַּרְכּוֹ, וְאִישׁ אָוֶן מַחְשְׁבֹתָיו, וְיָשֹׁב אֶל יהוה וִירַחֲמֵהוּ,

‹‹ and He will ‹ HASHEM, ‹ to ‹ and let ‹‹ [abandon] ‹ of ‹ and ‹‹ his ‹ the wicked
have compassion him return his thoughts; iniquity the man way, one
on him,

וְאֶל אֱלֹהֵינוּ כִּי יַרְבֶּה לִסְלוֹחַ.[3]

‹‹ forgiving. ‹ He is abundantly ‹ for ‹ our God, ‹ and to

מָשִׁיחַ צִדְקֶךָ אָמַר לְפָנֶיךָ, שְׁגִיאוֹת מִי יָבִין, מִנִּסְתָּרוֹת

‹ From unper- ‹‹ can ‹ who ‹ Mistakes ‹‹ before You: ‹ said ‹ who is righ- ‹ Your
ceived faults discern? teous [David] anointed one

נַקֵּנִי.[4] נַקֵּנוּ יהוה אֱלֹהֵינוּ מִכָּל פְּשָׁעֵינוּ, וְטַהֲרֵנוּ מִכָּל

‹ of all ‹ and purify us ‹ our sins ‹ of all ‹ our God, ‹ HASHEM, ‹ Cleanse ‹‹ cleanse
us, me.

טֻמְאוֹתֵינוּ, וּזְרוֹק עָלֵינוּ מַיִם טְהוֹרִים וְטַהֲרֵנוּ, כַּכָּתוּב עַל

‹ by ‹ as it is written ‹‹ and purify us, ‹ pure water ‹ upon us ‹ Pour ‹‹ our contaminations.

יַד נְבִיאֶךָ: וְזָרַקְתִּי עֲלֵיכֶם מַיִם טְהוֹרִים וּטְהַרְתֶּם, מִכֹּל

‹ from all ‹‹ and you will ‹ pure water ‹ upon you ‹ I shall pour ‹‹ of Your ‹ the
become pure; prophet: hand

טֻמְאוֹתֵיכֶם וּמִכָּל גִּלּוּלֵיכֶם אֲטַהֵר אֶתְכֶם.[5] עַמְּךָ וְנַחֲלָתְךָ,

‹‹ and Your ‹ Your ‹ you. ‹ I will purify ‹ your ‹ and from ‹ your
heritage, people abominations all contaminations

רְעֵבֵי טוּבְךָ, צְמֵאֵי חַסְדֶּךָ, תְּאֵבֵי יִשְׁעֶךָ, יַכִּירוּ וְיֵדְעוּ כִּי

‹ that ‹ and ‹ –may they ‹‹ for Your ‹ and who ‹‹ for Your ‹ who ‹‹ for Your ‹ who
know recognize salvation long kindness, thirst goodness, hunger

---

(1) Cf. *Job* 33:27. (2) *Nehemiah* 9:33. (3) *Isaiah* 55:7. (4) *Psalms* 19:13. (5) *Ezekiel* 36:25.

לַיהוה אֱלֹהֵינוּ הָרַחֲמִים וְהַסְּלִיחוֹת.

to Hashem, our God, belong mercy and forgiveness.

אֵל רַחוּם שְׁמֶךָ, אֵל חַנּוּן שְׁמֶךָ, בָּנוּ נִקְרָא שְׁמֶךָ, יהוה

Merciful God is Your Name, Gracious God is Your Name, upon us is Your Name proclaimed, Hashem,

עֲשֵׂה לְמַעַן שְׁמֶךָ, עֲשֵׂה לְמַעַן אֲמִתָּךְ, עֲשֵׂה לְמַעַן בְּרִיתָךְ,

Act for the sake of Your Name. Act for the sake of Your truth; Act for the sake of Your covenant;

עֲשֵׂה לְמַעַן גָּדְלְךָ וְתִפְאַרְתָּךְ, עֲשֵׂה לְמַעַן דָּתָךְ, עֲשֵׂה לְמַעַן

Act for the sake of Your greatness and splendor; Act for the sake of Your Law; Act for the sake of

הוֹדָךְ, עֲשֵׂה לְמַעַן וְעוּדָךְ, עֲשֵׂה לְמַעַן זִכְרָךְ, עֲשֵׂה לְמַעַן

Your glory; Act for the sake of Your Meeting House; Act for the sake of Your remembrance; Act for the sake of

חַסְדָּךְ, עֲשֵׂה לְמַעַן טוּבָךְ, עֲשֵׂה לְמַעַן יִחוּדָךְ, עֲשֵׂה לְמַעַן

Your kindness; Act for the sake of Your goodness; Act for the sake of Your Oneness; Act for the sake of

כְּבוֹדָךְ, עֲשֵׂה לְמַעַן לִמּוּדָךְ, עֲשֵׂה לְמַעַן מַלְכוּתָךְ, עֲשֵׂה

Your honor; Act for the sake of Your students; Act for the sake of Your kingship; act

לְמַעַן נִצְחָךְ, עֲשֵׂה לְמַעַן סוֹדָךְ, עֲשֵׂה לְמַעַן עֻזָּךְ, עֲשֵׂה

for the sake of Your eternal [Name]; Act for the sake of Your secret [revealed to those who fear You]; Act for the sake of Your power; act

לְמַעַן פְּאֵרָךְ, עֲשֵׂה לְמַעַן צִדְקָתָךְ, עֲשֵׂה לְמַעַן קְדֻשָּׁתָךְ,

for the sake of Your sanctity; Act for the sake of Your righteousness; Act for the sake of Your glory;

עֲשֵׂה לְמַעַן רַחֲמֶיךָ הָרַבִּים, עֲשֵׂה לְמַעַן שְׁכִינָתָךְ, עֲשֵׂה

Act for the sake of Your mercy that is abundant; Act for the sake of Your Divine Presence; Act

לְמַעַן תְּהִלָּתָךְ, עֲשֵׂה לְמַעַן אוֹהֲבֶיךָ שׁוֹכְנֵי עָפָר, עֲשֵׂה

for the sake of Your praise; Act for the sake of those who loved You who rest in the dust; act

לְמַעַן אַבְרָהָם יִצְחָק וְיַעֲקֹב, עֲשֵׂה לְמַעַן מֹשֶׁה וְאַהֲרֹן,

for the sake of Abraham, Isaac, and Jacob; Act for the sake of Moses and Aaron;

עֲשֵׂה לְמַעַן דָּוִד וּשְׁלֹמֹה, עֲשֵׂה לְמַעַן יְרוּשָׁלַיִם עִיר קָדְשֶׁךָ,

act for the sake of David and Solomon; Act for the sake of Jerusalem, the City of Your holiness;

(1) Cf. *Exodus* 34:6. (2) Cf. *Deuteronomy* 28:10. (3) *Jeremiah* 14:7. (4) Cf. *Exodus* 3:15. (5) *Psalms* 6:5.
(6) Cf. *Isaiah* 54:13. (7) Cf. *Psalms* 25:14. (8) *Isaiah* 26:19. (9) Cf. *Daniel* 9:16,24.

עֲשֵׂה לְמַעַן צִיּוֹן מִשְׁכַּן כְּבוֹדֶךָ,¹ עֲשֵׂה לְמַעַן שְׁמָמוֹת²

‹ the ‹ for the ‹ act ‹‹ of Your ‹ the abode ‹ Zion, ‹ for the ‹ act
desolation   sake of   glory;   sake of

הֵיכָלֶךָ, עֲשֵׂה לְמַעַן הֲרִיסוּת³ מִזְבְּחֶךָ, עֲשֵׂה לְמַעַן הֲרוּגִים

‹ those ‹ for the ‹ act ‹‹ of Your ‹ the ‹ for the ‹ act ‹‹ of Your
killed   sake of   Altar; devastation sake of   Temple;

עַל שֵׁם קָדְשֶׁךָ, עֲשֵׂה לְמַעַן טְבוּחִים עַל יִחוּדֶךָ, עֲשֵׂה

‹ act ‹‹ Your ‹ for ‹ those ‹ for the ‹ act ‹‹ Your holy Name; ‹ for
      Oneness;   slaughtered sake of

לְמַעַן בָּאֵי בָאֵשׁ וּבַמַּיִם עַל קִדּוּשׁ שְׁמֶךָ, עֲשֵׂה לְמַעַן

‹ for the ‹ act ‹‹ of Your ‹ the ‹ for ‹ and water ‹ fire ‹ those who ‹ for the
sake of   Name; sanctification   entered   sake of

יוֹנְקֵי שָׁדַיִם שֶׁלֹּא חָטְאוּ, עֲשֵׂה לְמַעַן גְּמוּלֵי חָלָב שֶׁלֹּא⁵

‹ who ‹ from ‹ the [babies] ‹ for the ‹ act ‹‹ sin; ‹ who ‹ at the ‹ the [infants]
did not milk   weaned   sake of   did not breast sucking

פָּשָׁעוּ, עֲשֵׂה לְמַעַן תִּינוֹקוֹת שֶׁל בֵּית רַבָּן,⁶ עֲשֵׂה לְמַעַנְךָ

‹ for Your ‹ act ‹‹ their teachers' ‹ of ‹ the children ‹ for the ‹ act ‹‹ transgress;
sake   school;   sake of

אִם לֹא לְמַעֲנֵנוּ, עֲשֵׂה לְמַעַנְךָ וְהוֹשִׁיעֵנוּ.

‹‹ and save us. ‹ for Your sake ‹ act ‹‹ for our sake; ‹ not ‹ if

עֲנֵנוּ יהוה עֲנֵנוּ, עֲנֵנוּ אֱלֹהֵינוּ עֲנֵנוּ, עֲנֵנוּ אָבִינוּ⁷ עֲנֵנוּ,

‹‹ answer ‹ our ‹ answer ‹‹ answer ‹ our God, ‹ answer ‹‹ answer ‹ HASHEM, ‹ Answer
us;   Father,   us;   us;   us;   us;   us,

עֲנֵנוּ בּוֹרְאֵנוּ⁸ עֲנֵנוּ, עֲנֵנוּ גוֹאֲלֵנוּ⁹ עֲנֵנוּ, עֲנֵנוּ דוֹרְשֵׁנוּ¹⁰ עֲנֵנוּ,

‹‹ answer ‹ You Who ‹ answer ‹‹ answer ‹ our ‹ answer ‹‹ answer ‹ our Creator, ‹ answer
us; searches us out, us;   us; Redeemer, us;   us;   us,

עֲנֵנוּ הָאֵל הַנֶּאֱמָן¹¹ עֲנֵנוּ, עֲנֵנוּ וָתִיק וְחָסִיד עֲנֵנוּ, עֲנֵנוּ זַךְ

‹ pure ‹ answer ‹‹ answer ‹ and kind ‹ stead- ‹ answer ‹‹ answer ‹ Who is ‹ God ‹ answer
       us;   us;   One,   fast   us;   us;   faithful,   us,

וְיָשָׁר¹² עֲנֵנוּ, עֲנֵנוּ חַי וְקַיָּם¹³ עֲנֵנוּ, עֲנֵנוּ טוֹב וּמֵטִיב¹⁴ עֲנֵנוּ,

‹‹ answer ‹ and ‹ good ‹ answer ‹‹ answer ‹ and ‹ living ‹ answer ‹‹ answer ‹ and
us;   beneficent   us;   us;   enduring   us;   us;   upright
        One,   One,   One,

עֲנֵנוּ יוֹדֵעַ יֵצֶר¹⁵ עֲנֵנוּ, עֲנֵנוּ כּוֹבֵשׁ כְּעָסִים עֲנֵנוּ, עֲנֵנוּ

‹ answer ‹‹ answer ‹ of wrath, ‹ Suppressor ‹ answer ‹ answer ‹ of in- ‹ Knower ‹ answer
us;   us;   us;   us;   clinations,   us,

---

(1) *Psalms* 26:8. (2) Cf. *Jeremiah* 51:26. (3) Cf. *Isaiah* 49:19. (4) *Joel* 2:16.
(5) *Isaiah* 28:9. (6) *Shabbos* 119b. (7) *Isaiah* 64:7. (8) Cf. 43:1. (9) 47:4.
(10) Cf. *Ezekiel* 34:11. (11) *Deuteronomy* 7:9. (12) *Job* 8:6; cf. *Proverbs* 20:11.
(13) Cf. *Daniel* 6:27. (14) Cf. *Psalms* 119:68. (15) Cf. 103:14.

לוֹבֵשׁ צְדָקוֹת¹ עֲנֵנוּ, עֲנֵנוּ מֶלֶךְ מַלְכֵי הַמְּלָכִים² עֲנֵנוּ,

Donner ‹ of righ- ‹ answer ‹ answer ‹ King ‹ over ‹ of kings, ‹ answer
teousness, us; us; kings us;

עֲנֵנוּ **נוֹרָא** וְנִשְׂגָּב³ עֲנֵנוּ, עֲנֵנוּ **סוֹלֵחַ** וּמוֹחֵל עֲנֵנוּ, עֲנֵנוּ

answer ‹ awesome ‹ and powerful ‹ answer ‹‹ answer ‹ You Who ‹ and ‹ answer ‹‹ answer ‹
us, One, us; us; forgives, pardons, us; us,

עוֹנֶה בְּעֵת צָרָה⁴ עֲנֵנוּ, עֲנֵנוּ **פּוֹדֶה** וּמַצִּיל⁵ עֲנֵנוּ, עֲנֵנוּ צַדִּיק

You Who ‹ in time ‹ of ‹ answer ‹‹ answer ‹ Redeemer ‹ and ‹ answer ‹‹ answer ‹ righ-
answers distress, us; us; Rescuer, us; us; teous

וְיָשָׁר⁶ עֲנֵנוּ, עֲנֵנוּ **קָרוֹב** לְקוֹרְאָיו⁷ עֲנֵנוּ, עֲנֵנוּ **קָשֶׁה** לִכְעוֹס⁸

and up- ‹ answer ‹‹ answer ‹ He Who ‹ to those who ‹ answer ‹‹ answer ‹ become ‹
right One, us; us; is close call upon Him, us; us; angry, with difficulty

עֲנֵנוּ, עֲנֵנוּ **רַךְ** לִרְצוֹת⁹ עֲנֵנוּ, עֲנֵנוּ **רַחוּם** וְחַנּוּן¹⁰ עֲנֵנוּ,

answer ‹‹ answer ‹ merciful ‹ You Who ‹ answer ‹‹ answer ‹ and gra- ‹ answer ‹‹ answer ‹
us; us; are easily appeased, us; us; cious One, us;

עֲנֵנוּ **שׁוֹמֵעַ** אֶל אֶבְיוֹנִים¹¹ עֲנֵנוּ, עֲנֵנוּ **תּוֹמֵךְ** תְּמִימִים עֲנֵנוּ,

answer ‹ You Who ‹ the destitute, ‹ answer ‹‹ answer ‹ to ‹ You Who ‹ the ‹ answer ‹‹ answer ‹
us, listens us; us; supports wholesome, us;

עֲנֵנוּ **אֱלֹהֵי** אֲבוֹתֵינוּ עֲנֵנוּ, עֲנֵנוּ **אֱלֹהֵי** אַבְרָהָם¹² עֲנֵנוּ,

answer ‹ God ‹ of our ‹ answer ‹‹ answer ‹ God ‹ of Abraham, ‹ answer ‹‹
us; forefathers, us; us; us;

עֲנֵנוּ **פַּחַד** יִצְחָק¹² עֲנֵנוּ, עֲנֵנוּ **אֲבִיר** יַעֲקֹב¹³ עֲנֵנוּ, עֲנֵנוּ עֶזְרַת

answer ‹ Awesome ‹ of ‹ answer ‹‹ answer ‹ Mighty ‹ of ‹ answer ‹‹ answer ‹ Helper
us, One Isaac, us; us; One Jacob, us; us;

הַשְּׁבָטִים עֲנֵנוּ, עֲנֵנוּ **מִשְׂגַּב** אִמָּהוֹת עֲנֵנוּ, עֲנֵנוּ **עוֹנֶה** בְּעֵת

of the tribes, ‹ answer ‹‹ answer ‹ Stronghold ‹ of the ‹ answer ‹‹ answer ‹ You Who ‹ in a
us, us; Matriarchs, us; us; answers time

רָצוֹן¹⁴ עֲנֵנוּ, עֲנֵנוּ **אֲבִי** יְתוֹמִים¹⁵ עֲנֵנוּ, עֲנֵנוּ **דַּיַּן** אַלְמָנוֹת¹⁵ עֲנֵנוּ.

of favor, ‹ answer ‹‹ answer ‹ Father ‹ of ‹ answer ‹‹ answer ‹ Judge ‹ of ‹ answer ‹‹
us; us; orphans, us; us; widows, us.

מִי שֶׁעָנָה לְאַבְרָהָם אָבִינוּ בְּהַר הַמּוֹרִיָּה¹⁶ הוּא יַעֲנֵנוּ.

He ‹ Who ‹ Abraham ‹ our ‹ on ‹ Moriah ‹‹ may— ‹ answer ‹‹
answered father Mount He us.

מִי שֶׁעָנָה לְיִצְחָק בְּנוֹ כְּשֶׁנֶּעֱקַד עַל גַּבֵּי הַמִּזְבֵּחַ¹⁶ הוּא יַעֲנֵנוּ.

He ‹ Who ‹ Isaac ‹ his ‹ when he ‹ on ‹ top ‹ of the ‹‹ may— ‹ answer ‹‹
answered son was bound altar He us.

---

(1) Cf. *Isaiah* 59:17. (2) *Ethics of the Fathers* 3:1. (3) *Psalms* 47:3, 148:13. (4) Cf. *Isaiah* 49:8; *Psalms* 37:39.
(5) Cf. 34:23,18. (6) *Deuteronomy* 32:4. (7) Cf. *Psalms* 145:18. (8) *Ethics of the Fathers* 5:14.
(9) Cf. 5:14. (10) *Exodus* 34:6. (11) *Psalms* 69:34. (12) *Genesis* 31:42. (13) *Isaiah* 49:26.
(14) Cf. 49:8; *Psalms* 69:14. (15) *Psalms* 68:6. (16) *Genesis* 22:12.

מִי שֶׁעָנָה לְיַעֲקֹב בְּבֵית אֵל[1] הוּא יַעֲנֵנוּ.

He ‹ Who ‹ Jacob ‹ in Beth El ‹‹ He ‹– may answer ‹‹
answered us.

מִי שֶׁעָנָה לְיוֹסֵף בְּבֵית הָאֲסוּרִים[2] הוּא יַעֲנֵנוּ.

He ‹ Who ‹ Joseph ‹ in the prison ‹‹ He ‹– may answer ‹‹
answered us.

מִי שֶׁעָנָה לַאֲבוֹתֵינוּ עַל יַם סוּף[3] הוּא יַעֲנֵנוּ.

He ‹ Who ‹ our forefathers ‹ at ‹ the ‹ of ‹‹ He ‹– may answer ‹‹
answered Sea Reeds us.

מִי שֶׁעָנָה לְמֹשֶׁה בְּחוֹרֵב[4] הוּא יַעֲנֵנוּ.

He ‹ Who ‹ Moses ‹ in Horeb ‹‹ He ‹– may answer ‹‹
answered us.

מִי שֶׁעָנָה לְאַהֲרֹן בַּמַּחְתָּה[5] הוּא יַעֲנֵנוּ.

He ‹ Who ‹ Aaron ‹ with the ‹‹ He ‹– may answer ‹‹
answered fire-pan us.

מִי שֶׁעָנָה לְפִינְחָס בְּקוּמוֹ מִתּוֹךְ הָעֵדָה[6] הוּא יַעֲנֵנוּ.

He ‹ Who ‹ Phinehas ‹ when he ‹ from ‹ the ‹‹ He ‹– may answer ‹‹
answered arose amid congregation us.

מִי שֶׁעָנָה לִיהוֹשֻׁעַ בַּגִּלְגָּל[7] הוּא יַעֲנֵנוּ.

He ‹ Who ‹ Joshua ‹ in Gilgal ‹‹ He ‹– may answer ‹‹
answered us.

מִי שֶׁעָנָה לִשְׁמוּאֵל בַּמִּצְפָּה[8] הוּא יַעֲנֵנוּ.

He ‹ Who ‹ Samuel ‹ in Mizpah ‹‹ He ‹– may answer ‹‹
answered us.

מִי שֶׁעָנָה לְדָוִד וּשְׁלֹמֹה בְנוֹ בִּירוּשָׁלָיִם[9] הוּא יַעֲנֵנוּ.

He ‹ Who ‹ David ‹ and ‹ his son ‹ in Jerusalem ‹‹ He ‹– may answer ‹‹
answered Solomon us.

מִי שֶׁעָנָה לְאֵלִיָּהוּ בְּהַר הַכַּרְמֶל[10] הוּא יַעֲנֵנוּ.

He ‹ Who ‹ Elijah ‹ on ‹ Carmel ‹‹ He ‹– may answer ‹‹
answered Mount us.

מִי שֶׁעָנָה לֶאֱלִישָׁע בִּירִיחוֹ[11] הוּא יַעֲנֵנוּ.

He ‹ Who ‹ Elisha ‹ in Jericho ‹‹ He ‹– may answer ‹‹
answered us.

מִי שֶׁעָנָה לְיוֹנָה בִּמְעֵי הַדָּגָה[12] הוּא יַעֲנֵנוּ.

He ‹ Who ‹ Jonah ‹ in the ‹ of the fish ‹‹ He ‹– may answer ‹‹
answered innards us.

(1) Genesis 35:3. (2) 39:21; 40:41. (3) Exodus 14. (4) 17:6,11; Deuteronomy 9:19.
(5) Numbers 17:11-13. (6) 25:7-13. (7) Joshua 6:1-20; 7:6-15; 10:12-14. (8) I Samuel 7:9.
(9) II Samuel 7:5-16; 21:1,14; 24:25; I Kings 9:3. (10) 18:36-38. (11) II Kings 2:21. (12) Jonah 2:2-11.

מִי שֶׁעָנָה לְחִזְקִיָּהוּ מֶלֶךְ יְהוּדָה בְּחָלְיוֹ[1]   הוּא יַעֲנֵנוּ.

He ‹ Who ‹ answered ‹ Hezekiah, ‹ King ‹ of Judah, ‹ in his illness   may — ‹ answer us. He

מִי שֶׁעָנָה לַחֲנַנְיָה מִישָׁאֵל וַעֲזַרְיָה בְּתוֹךְ כִּבְשַׁן הָאֵשׁ[2]

He ‹ Who ‹ answered ‹ Hananiah, ‹ Mishael ‹ and Azariah ‹ inside ‹ the furnace ‹ of fire

הוּא יַעֲנֵנוּ.

answer — may ‹ us. He

מִי שֶׁעָנָה לְדָנִיֵּאל בְּגוֹב הָאֲרָיוֹת[3]   הוּא יַעֲנֵנוּ.

He ‹ Who ‹ answered ‹ Daniel ‹ in the ‹ of lions den   answer — may ‹ us. He

מִי שֶׁעָנָה לְמָרְדְּכַי וְאֶסְתֵּר בְּשׁוּשַׁן הַבִּירָה[4]   הוּא יַעֲנֵנוּ.

He ‹ Who ‹ answered ‹ Mordechai ‹ and Esther ‹ in Shushan ‹ the capital   answer — may ‹ us. He

מִי שֶׁעָנָה לְעֶזְרָא בַּגּוֹלָה[5]   הוּא יַעֲנֵנוּ.

He ‹ Who ‹ answered ‹ Ezra ‹ in the exile   answer — may ‹ us. He

מִי שֶׁעָנָה לְכָל הַצַּדִּיקִים וְהַחֲסִידִים וְהַתְּמִימִים וְהַיְשָׁרִים

He ‹ Who ‹ answered ‹ all ‹ the righteous, ‹ the devout, ‹ the wholesome ‹ and the upright

הוּא יַעֲנֵנוּ.

answer — may ‹ us. He

רַחֲמָנָא דְּעָנֵי לַעֲנִיֵּי, עֲנֵינָן. רַחֲמָנָא דְּעָנֵי לִתְבִירֵי לִבָּא,

Merciful One ‹ Who ‹ the poor, ‹ answer ‹ Merciful ‹ Who ‹ those of ‹ hearts, answers us! One answers broken

עֲנֵינָן. רַחֲמָנָא דְּעָנֵי לְמַכִּיכֵי רוּחָא, עֲנֵינָן. רַחֲמָנָא עֲנֵינָן.

answer ‹ Merciful ‹ Who ‹ those of ‹ spirit, ‹ answer ‹ Merciful ‹ answer us! One, answers crushed us! One, us!

רַחֲמָנָא חוּס. רַחֲמָנָא פְּרוֹק. רַחֲמָנָא שֵׁזִיב. רַחֲמָנָא רְחַם

Merciful ‹ have ‹ Merciful ‹ redeem! ‹ Merciful ‹ save! ‹ Merciful ‹ have One, pity! One, One, One, mercy

עֲלָן, הַשְׁתָּא בַּעֲגָלָא וּבִזְמַן קָרִיב.

on us ‹ — now, ‹ swiftly, ‹ and at ‹ that comes a time soon.

SHACHARIS CONTINUES WITH TACHANUN, PAGE 172,
OR, IF TACHANUN WAS ALREADY RECITED, AT THE BOTTOM OF PAGE 177.

(1) *II Kings* 20:2-6; *Isaiah* 38:2-8. (2) *Daniel* 3:21-27.
(3) *6:17-23.* (4) *Esther* 8. (5) *Ezra* 8:21-23.

﴾ סליחות לחמישי ﴿

﴾ SELICHOS — THURSDAY OF BEHAB ﴿

ALL BEGIN HERE:

סְלַח לָנוּ אָבִינוּ, כִּי בְרוֹב אִוַּלְתֵּנוּ שָׁגִינוּ,

《 we have 〈 of our folly 〈 in the 〈 for 〈 our 〈 us, 〈 Forgive
erred; abundance Father,

מְחַל לָנוּ מַלְכֵּנוּ, כִּי רַבּוּ עֲוֹנֵינוּ.

《 our iniquities. 〈 many are 〈 for 〈 our King, 〈 us, 〈 pardon

אֵל אֶרֶךְ אַפַּיִם אַתָּה, וּבַעַל הָרַחֲמִים נִקְרֵאתָ, וְדֶרֶךְ

〈 and 《 are You 〈 of Mercy 〈 and 《 are You, 〈 to anger, 〈 Who 〈 God,
the way called; Master is slow

תְּשׁוּבָה הוֹרֵיתָ. גְּדֻלַּת רַחֲמֶיךָ וַחֲסָדֶיךָ, תִּזְכּוֹר הַיּוֹם וּבְכָל

〈 and 〈 this 〈 may You 〈 and Your 〈 of Your 〈 The 《 have You 〈 of
every day remember, kindness mercy greatness taught. repentance

יוֹם לְזֶרַע יְדִידֶיךָ. תֵּפֶן אֵלֵינוּ בְּרַחֲמִים, כִּי אַתָּה הוּא בַּעַל

〈 the 〈 are 〈 You 〈 for 《 in mercy, 〈 to us 《 Turn 《 of Your 〈 for the 《 day,
Master beloved ones. offspring

הָרַחֲמִים. בְּתַחֲנוּן וּבִתְפִלָּה פָּנֶיךָ נְקַדֵּם, כְּהוֹדַעְתָּ לֶעָנָיו

〈 to the 〈 in the man- 《 we 〈 Your 〈 and prayer 〈 With 《 of Mercy.
humble one ner that You approach, Presence supplication
[Moses] made known

מִקֶּדֶם. מֵחֲרוֹן אַפְּךָ שׁוּב, כְּמוֹ בְתוֹרָתְךָ כָּתוּב.[1] וּבְצֵל כְּנָפֶיךָ

〈 of Your 〈 In the 《 it is 〈 in Your Torah 〈 as 《 turn 〈 of Your 〈 From the 《 in ancient
wings shadow written. back, anger fierceness times.

נֶחֱסֶה וְנִתְלוֹנָן, כְּיוֹם וַיֵּרֶד יהוה בֶּעָנָן.[2] ❖ תַּעֲבוֹר עַל פֶּשַׁע

〈 sin 〈 Overlook 《 in a 〈 when HASHEM 〈 as on 《 and may 〈 may we
cloud. descended the day we dwell, find shelter

וְתִמְחֶה אָשָׁם, כְּיוֹם וַיִּתְיַצֵּב עִמּוֹ שָׁם.[2] תַּאֲזִין שַׁוְעָתֵנוּ

〈 to our cry 〈 Give 《 there. 〈 with him 〈 when He 〈 as on 《 guilt, 〈 and erase
heed [Moses] [God] stood the day

וְתַקְשִׁיב מֶנּוּ מַאֲמָר, כְּיוֹם וַיִּקְרָא בְּשֵׁם יהוה,[2] וְשָׁם נֶאֱמַר:

《 it was 〈 and 《 of 〈 with the 〈 when He 〈 as on 《 [our] 〈 from 〈 and hear
said: there HASHEM, Name called out the day declaration, us

CONGREGATION AND CHAZZAN RECITE LOUDLY AND IN UNISON:

וַיַּעֲבֹר יהוה עַל פָּנָיו וַיִּקְרָא:

《 and 《 [Moses'] 〈 before 〈 And HASHEM passed
proclaimed: face,

---

(1) Cf. *Exodus* 32:12. (2) 34:5.

יְהוה, יְהוה, אֵל, רַחוּם, וְחַנּוּן, אֶרֶךְ אַפַּיִם, וְרַב חֶסֶד, וֶאֱמֶת,

Hashem, Hashem, God, Compassionate, and Gracious, Slow to anger, and Abundant Kindness, and Truth,

נֹצֵר חֶסֶד לָאֲלָפִים, נֹשֵׂא עָוֹן, וָפֶשַׁע, וְחַטָּאָה, וְנַקֵּה.[1]

Preserver of kindness for thousands [of generations], Forgiver of iniquity, willful sin, and inadvertent sin, and Who absolves.

וְסָלַחְתָּ לַעֲוֹנֵנוּ וּלְחַטָּאתֵנוּ וּנְחַלְתָּנוּ.[2] סְלַח לָנוּ אָבִינוּ כִּי

May You forgive our iniquities and our sins, and make us Your heritage. Forgive us, our Father, for

חָטָאנוּ, מְחַל לָנוּ מַלְכֵּנוּ כִּי פָשָׁעְנוּ.[3] כִּי אַתָּה אֲדֹנָי טוֹב

we have sinned; pardon us, our King, for we have willfully sinned. For You, O Lord, are good

וְסַלָּח, וְרַב חֶסֶד לְכָל קֹרְאֶיךָ.[4]

and abundantly forgiving, and kind and abundantly forgiving, to all who call upon You.

ALL CONTINUE:

הַאֲזִינָה יהוה תְּפִלָּתֵנוּ, הַקְשִׁיבָה לְקוֹל תַּחֲנוּנוֹתֵינוּ.[5]

Give ear, Hashem, to our prayer, and heed the sound of our supplications.

הַקְשִׁיבָה לְקוֹל שַׁוְעָתֵנוּ מַלְכֵּנוּ וֵאלֹהֵינוּ, כִּי אֵלֶיךָ נִתְפַּלָּל.[6]

Hearken to the sound of our outcry, our King and our God, for to You do we pray.

שְׁמַע יהוה וְחָנֵּנוּ, יהוה הֱיֵה עוֹזֵר לָנוּ.[7]

Hear, O Hashem, and favor us; Hashem, be our helper.

כְּרַחֵם אָב עַל בָּנִים, כֵּן תְּרַחֵם יהוה עָלֵינוּ.[8] לַיהוה

As merciful as a father is toward his children, so have mercy, Hashem, on us. To Hashem

הַיְשׁוּעָה, עַל עַמְּךָ בִרְכָתֶךָ סֶּלָה.[9] יהוה צְבָאוֹת עִמָּנוּ,

is salvation, upon Your people Your blessing, Selah. Hashem, Master of Legions, is with us,

מִשְׂגָּב לָנוּ אֱלֹהֵי יַעֲקֹב סֶלָה.[10] יהוה צְבָאוֹת, אַשְׁרֵי אָדָם

a stronghold for us is the God of Jacob, Selah. Hashem, Master of Legions, praiseworthy is the man

בֹּטֵחַ בָּךְ.[11] יהוה הוֹשִׁיעָה, הַמֶּלֶךְ יַעֲנֵנוּ בְיוֹם קָרְאֵנוּ.[12]

who trusts in You. Hashem, save! May the King answer us on the day we call.

---

(1) Exodus 34:6-7. (2) 34:9. (3) From the weekday Shemoneh Esrei. (4) Psalms 86:5.
(5) Cf. 86:6. (6) Cf. 5:3. (7) Cf. 30:11. (8) Cf. 4:2. (9) 3:9. (10) 46:8. (11) 84:13. (12) 20:10.

❖ **סְלַח** נָא לַעֲוֹן הָעָם הַזֶּה כְּגֹדֶל חַסְדֶּךָ, וְכַאֲשֶׁר נָשָׂאתָה

⟨ You have ⟨ and as ⟨⟨ of Your ⟨ according to ⟨ of this people ⟨ the ⟨ please, ⟨ Forgive,
forgiven   kindness, the greatness   iniquity

לָעָם הַזֶּה מִמִּצְרַיִם וְעַד הֵנָּה,[1] וְשָׁם נֶאֱמַר:

⟨⟨ it was said: ⟨ And there ⟨⟨ now. ⟨ until ⟨ from Egypt ⟨ this people

ALL, ALOUD AND IN UNISON:

וַיֹּאמֶר יהוה סָלַחְתִּי כִּדְבָרֶךָ.[2]

⟨⟨ according to your word! ⟨ I have forgiven ⟨⟨ And HASHEM said:

ALL CONTINUE:

הַטֵּה אֱלֹהַי אָזְנְךָ וּשְׁמָע, פְּקַח עֵינֶיךָ וּרְאֵה שֹׁמְמֹתֵינוּ,

⟨⟨ our desolation, ⟨ and see ⟨ Your eyes ⟨ open ⟨⟨ and listen; ⟨ Your ear, ⟨ my God, ⟨ Incline,

וְהָעִיר אֲשֶׁר נִקְרָא שִׁמְךָ עָלֶיהָ, כִּי לֹא עַל צִדְקֹתֵינוּ אֲנַחְנוּ

⟨ do we ⟨ of our ⟨ because ⟨⟨ not ⟨ for ⟨⟨ upon; ⟨ Your Name is ⟨ which ⟨ and [that
righteousness   proclaimed   of] the city

מַפִּילִים תַּחֲנוּנֵינוּ לְפָנֶיךָ, כִּי עַל רַחֲמֶיךָ הָרַבִּים. אֲדֹנָי

⟨ O Lord, ⟨⟨ which is ⟨ of Your ⟨ because ⟨ but ⟨⟨ before ⟨ our ⟨ cast
abundant. compassion,   You;   supplications

שְׁמָעָה, אֲדֹנָי סְלָחָה, אֲדֹנָי הַקְשִׁיבָה, וַעֲשֵׂה אַל תְּאַחַר,

⟨⟨ delay; ⟨ do not ⟨⟨ and act, ⟨ be attentive, ⟨ O Lord, ⟨⟨ forgive; ⟨ O Lord, ⟨⟨ heed;

לְמַעַנְךָ אֱלֹהַי, כִּי שִׁמְךָ נִקְרָא עַל עִירְךָ וְעַל עַמֶּךָ.[3]

⟨⟨ Your ⟨ and ⟨ Your ⟨ upon ⟨ is ⟨ Your ⟨ for ⟨⟨ my God, ⟨ for Your
people. upon. City   proclaimed Name   sake,

אֱלֹהֵינוּ וֵאלֹהֵי אֲבוֹתֵינוּ

⟨⟨ of our forefathers: ⟨ and the God ⟨ Our God

תַּעֲנִית∗ צִבּוּר קָבְעוּ תִּבְוֹע צְרָכִים,

⟨⟨ for our ⟨ to ⟨ they ⟨ for the entire ⟨ A fast∗
necessities, petition established, community

שׁוּב עָדֶיךָ חַפֵּשׂ וְלַחְקוֹר דְּרָכִים,[4]

⟨⟨ [our] ways ⟨ and ⟨ by ⟨ to You ⟨ to
examining searching   return

רַךְ לִרְצוֹת בִּשְׁלֹשׁ עֶשְׂרֵה עֲרָכִים,

⟨⟨ Attributes ⟨ through the Thirteen ⟨ appeased ⟨ — [You] Who
[of Mercy],   are easily

---

(1) *Numbers* 14:19. (2) 14:20. (3) *Daniel* 9:18-19. (4) Cf. *Lamentations* 3:40.

◈§**תַּעֲנִית** – *A fast.* The verses of this supplication form a reverse alphabetical acrostic from
ת to א. The last ten verses bear the author's sig-

מֵאִיר הַצָּעִיר חֲזַק בְּתוֹרָה וּבְמַעֲשִׂים טוֹבִים, nature,
*Meir, the Younger, may he be strong in Torah
and good deeds.*

קָשֶׁה לִכְעוֹס תֵּת לְאַפֶּיִם אֲרֵכִים.¹

are hard / and Who / to anger, / giving / [Your] / a postponement.
anger

צִדְדֶיךָ מְקֻשָּׁטִים עֵדִים בְּלִי תַּפְשִׁיט,²

roundings / Your sur- / are adorned [with / their orna- / [You] / strip off
Your Attributes], / mentation / should not

פְּאֵר הָרַחֲמִים וְהַסְּלִיחוֹת הוֹד תַּכְשִׁיט,

splendor / – the / of mercy / and / are [like] / adornment.
forgiveness / a glorious

עֵרֶךְ שַׁוְעָתֵנוּ³ לְךָ לְבַד נוֹשִׁיט,

sentation / The pre- / of our / to / alone / we proffer;
supplication / You

סֵדֶר חַיִּים וּפַרְנָסָה לִיצוּרִים תּוֹשִׁיט.

a pattern / of life / and livelihood / to [Your] creations / proffer.

נִסְתְּמָה הַבִּירָה וְנִתְרוֹקַן טְהַר הַשֻּׁלְחָן,

Shut down / was the / and / was the / of [its] Table;
Temple, / emptied / purity

מֵזִין וּמֵזִיחַ סָתַר מֵעֲבַדַת פֻּלְחָן,

worship. / of / nourishment / provider / the [Altar], / and / has been / as a / of
[of sins], / remover / demolished / [place for] / the service

לִשְׁפִיכַת הַנֶּפֶשׁ חָשׁוֹב כְּבַשִׁית זָלְחָן,

flow. / used to / like [libations] / – consider / of my / The
that into the drain / it / soul / outpouring
holes of the Altar

בִּמְעַטֵּר וּמַשְׂבִּיעַ גּוֹאֵל וְרוֹפֵא וְסָלְחָן.⁴

forgives. / and / heals / redeems, / and / [Be for us] the
sustains, / One Who crowns

יָאוֹת לְךָ יַעַן מִמַּנְתָּךְ נִשְׁנֶסֶת,

is girded – / she [Israel] / with Your gift / – because / You / It befits
[Torah]

טוֹב רְוָחֶךָ הֱיוֹת נִזּוֹנֶת וּמִתְפַּרְנֶסֶת,

and sustained, / nourished / she be / of Your / that from
generosity / the goodness

חֵלֶף (לְךָ) שׁוֹאֶלֶת קוֹבֶלֶת וּמִתְנוֹסֶסֶת,

and distinguishes herself [in Your ways]; / and cries out, / she entreats / (to You) / because

זֵכֶר דַּאֲגוֹתֶיהָ לְפָנֶיךָ מְשִׂיחָה וּמַכְנֶסֶת.

and / she / before / of her / the
presents. / expresses / You / worries, / statement

(1) Cf. *Exodus* 34:6. (2) Cf. 33:5. (3) Cf. *Psalms* 5:3-4. (4) Cf. 103:3-5.

וְאֵלֶיךָ הִיא נְשׂוּיָה¹ וּבְךָ חֲסָיָה,

« she takes refuge. ‹ and in You «‹ is lifted, ‹ she ‹ To You

הַוּוֹתֶיהָ הַעֲבֵר² מִי כָמְוֹךָ חֲסִין יָהּ,³

« God? ‹ O ‹ is like ‹ for « remove; ‹ Her
powerful You, who troubles

הֶרֶךְ אֲמָנוּתְךָ בְּחַלְּקְךָ לְלִגְיוֹנְךָ אַפְסַנְיָא,

« their ‹ to Your ‹ to ‹ of Your ‹ [Just as] it is
provisions; legions apportion custom the manner

גְּמוֹל חֶסֶד לַעֲלוּבָה הַלֵּזוּ אַכְסַנְיָא.⁴

« guest ‹ this « upon the ‹ kindness ‹ bestow
[in the body]. [soul] forlorn,

בְּקִיאִים וּמְיֻשָּׁבִים לְרַצּוֹתְךָ בִּדְבָרִים עֲרֵבִים,

«‹ that are ‹ with words ‹ in placating «‹ — and with « Those who
pleasant You composed thoughts are expert

אָפְסוּ פֶּסוּ בְּכֹחָם קַטֵּגוֹר מְעַרְבְּבִים,

« to confound; ‹ the ‹ those who ‹ they have ‹ — they are
Accuser had the ability vanished, no longer,

מְאַהֲבַי לַאֲבִיהֶם שֶׁבַּשָּׁמַיִם זְרִיזִים וּמְעֻרְבָּבִים,

«‹ and pleasing; ‹ were quick ‹ Who is in ‹ to their ‹ those who,
heaven, Father in making
me beloved

יְרֵאָיו נִדְבָּרִים דָּתוֹ שְׁחָרִים וַעֲרָבִים.⁵

« and evening. ‹ morning ‹ His ‹ and ‹ those who
Law discussed feared Him

הִקְדַּשְׁנוּ צוֹם⁶ עוֹלְלִים וְזִקְנֵי אֲסֵפוֹת,⁷

« with their amassed ‹ as well as ‹ for the ‹ a fast ‹ We
knowledge. the elders young ones day, designated

יִשַּׁרְנוּ רִנָּה וּתְפִלָּה⁸ וְשָׁקַדְנוּ סִפּוֹת,⁹

«‹ to your ‹ and we « and prayers, ‹ [our] ‹ We
doorways; hastened cries arranged

חֲשׂוֹךְ לְמַטָּה מֵעָוֹן,¹⁰ וּשְׁלוֹמֵנוּ תִּשְׁפּוֹת,¹¹

« establish. ‹ and our « than our ‹ to less ‹ Withhold
well-being transgressions [Your]
[deserve], retribution]

זְקוֹף דַּל מֵעָפָר וְאֶבְיוֹן מֵאַשְׁפּוֹת.¹²

« from the ‹ and the « from ‹ the ‹ Raise
trash heaps. destitute the dust, needy up

(1) Cf. *Exodus* 19:4. (2) Cf. *Psalms* 57:2. (3) 89:3. (4) Cf. *Vayikra Rabbah* 34:3. (5) Cf. *Malachi* 3:16.
(6) Cf. *Joel* 1:14; 2:15. (7) Cf. *Ecclesiastes* 12:11. (8) Cf. *I Kings* 8:28; *Jeremiah* 7:16; 11:14.
(9) Cf. *Proverbs* 8:34. (10) Cf. *Ezra* 9:13. (11) Cf. *Isaiah* 26:12. (12) Cf. *I Samuel* 2:18; *Psalms* 113:8.

✣ בְּתוֹר הַמַּעֲלָה¹ וּבְמִדּוֹת הֲגוּנוֹת תְּרוּמוֹת,

《《 and lofty, 〈 that are 〈 and with 〈 exalted 〈 On a
           befitting   traits   level

עֲרָבָתֵנוּ² שִׂים לְטוֹב³ יוֹשֵׁב מְרוֹמוֹת,

《《   in the   〈 [You] Who 《《 for the 〈 make 〈 our welfare
    heights.   dwells   best,

וּבְמִקְוֶה טְהָר תָּדִיחַ קַלּוֹת וַחֲמֻרוֹת,

《《 and serious 〈 [both] 〈 cleanse 〈 of pur- 〈 And as in
    [sins],   minor   ification,   a mikveh

מְצוֹא תְפִלָּתֵנוּ חֶסֶד לְאַדֶּרְךָ רוֹמֵמוֹת.

《《   with   〈 that we may 《《 kindness 〈 may our 〈 so that
  exaltation.   glorify You [before You],   prayers   find

AN INDIVIDUAL PRAYING WITHOUT A *MINYAN* OMITS THE NEXT TWO PARAGRAPHS,
BEGINNING אֵל מֶלֶךְ, *O GOD, KING,* AND ה', *HASHEM.*

אֵל מֶלֶךְ יוֹשֵׁב עַל כִּסֵּא רַחֲמִים, מִתְנַהֵג בַּחֲסִידוּת, מוֹחֵל

〈 Who 《《   with   〈 Who acts 〈 of mercy, 〈 the 〈 on 〈 Who 〈 King 〈 O God,
  pardons   kindness,   throne   sits

עֲוֹנוֹת עַמּוֹ, מַעֲבִיר רִאשׁוֹן רִאשׁוֹן, מַרְבֶּה מְחִילָה לַחַטָּאִים

〈 to uninten- 〈 pardon 〈 Who abun- 《《 by one, 〈 [sins] one 〈 Who 《《 of His 〈 the sins
  tional sinners,   dantly grants   removes   people,

וּסְלִיחָה לַפּוֹשְׁעִים, עֹשֶׂה צְדָקוֹת עִם כָּל בָּשָׂר וָרוּחַ, לֹא

〈 — not 《《 and 〈 [beings 〈 all 〈 with 〈 acts of 〈 Who 《《 to willful 〈 and
    spirit   of] flesh   generosity performs   sinners,   forgiveness

כְרָעָתָם תִּגְמוֹל. ✣ אֵל הוֹרֵיתָ לָּנוּ לוֹמַר שְׁלֹשׁ עֶשְׂרֵה,

《《 the Thirteen 〈 to recite 〈 us 〈 You 〈 O 《《 do You repay 〈 in accord with
  [Attributes of Mercy];   taught   God,   them!   their wickedness

וּזְכוֹר לָנוּ הַיּוֹם בְּרִית שְׁלֹשׁ עֶשְׂרֵה, כְּמוֹ שֶׁהוֹדַעְתָּ לֶעָנָיו

〈 to the humble 〈 You made 〈 as 《《 of [these] Thirteen, 〈 the 〈 today 〈 for us 〈 remember
  one [Moses]   known   covenant

מִקֶּדֶם, כְּמוֹ שֶׁכָּתוּב, וַיֵּרֶד יהוה בֶּעָנָן וַיִּתְיַצֵּב עִמּוֹ שָׁם,

《《 there, 〈 with 〈 and stood 〈 in a cloud 〈 And Hashem 《《 it is written: 〈 as 《《 in ancient
    him   descended   times,

וַיִּקְרָא בְשֵׁם יהוה.

《《   of   〈 with the 〈 and He
  Hashem.   Name   called out

CONGREGATION AND *CHAZZAN* RECITE LOUDLY AND IN UNISON:

וַיַּעֲבֹר יהוה עַל פָּנָיו וַיִּקְרָא:

《《   and   《《 [Moses'] 〈 before 〈 And Hashem passed
  proclaimed: face,

---

(1) Cf. *I Chronicles* 17:17. (2) Cf. *I Samuel* 17:18. (3) Cf. *Psalms* 119:122.

יְהוה, יְהוה, אֵל, רַחוּם, וְחַנּוּן, אֶרֶךְ אַפַּיִם, וְרַב חֶסֶד, וֶאֱמֶת,

« and ‹ in ‹ and ‹ to anger, ‹ Slow « and ‹ Compas- ‹ God, ‹ Hashem, ‹ Hashem,
Truth, Kindness Abundant   sionate

נֹצֵר חֶסֶד לָאֲלָפִים, נֹשֵׂא עָוֹן, וָפֶשַׁע, וְחַטָּאָה, וְנַקֵּה.

« and Who ‹ and inad- ‹ willful ‹ of ‹ Forgiver « for thousands ‹ of ‹ Preserver
absolves. vertent sin, sin, iniquity, [of generations], kindness

וְסָלַחְתָּ לַעֲוֹנֵנוּ וּלְחַטָּאתֵנוּ וּנְחַלְתָּנוּ. סְלַח לָנוּ אָבִינוּ כִּי

‹ for « our ‹ us, ‹ Forgive « and make us « and our sins, ‹ our ‹ May You
Father, iniquities forgive
Your heritage.

חָטָאנוּ, מְחַל לָנוּ מַלְכֵּנוּ כִּי פָשָׁעְנוּ. כִּי אַתָּה אֲדֹנָי טוֹב

‹ are ‹ O Lord, ‹ You, ‹ For « we have ‹ for « our King, ‹ us, ‹ pardon « we have
good willfully sinned. sinned;

וְסַלָּח, וְרַב חֶסֶד לְכָל קֹרְאֶיךָ.

« who call ‹ to all ‹ kind ‹ and « and
upon You. abundantly forgiving,

הוֹשִׁיעָה יהוה כִּי גָמַר חָסִיד, כִּי פַסּוּ אֱמוּנִים מִבְּנֵי אָדָם.[1]

« from mankind. ‹ have truth- ‹ vanished ‹ for « is the ‹ gone ‹ for ‹ O ‹ Save,
ful people devout one; Hashem,

כִּי אָדָם אֵין צַדִּיק בָּאָרֶץ, אֲשֶׁר יַעֲשֶׂה טוֹב וְלֹא יֶחֱטָא.[2]

« sins. ‹ and ‹ [only] ‹ he does ‹ that ‹ on earth ‹ who is so ‹ there is no man ‹ For
never good righteous

הוֹשַׁע יהוה אֶת עַמֶּךָ אֶת שְׁאֵרִית יִשְׂרָאֵל. יִשְׂרָאֵל נוֹשַׁע[3]

‹ is saved ‹ Israel « of Israel. ‹ the remnant « Your people, ‹ O Hashem, ‹ Save,

בַּיהוה תְּשׁוּעַת עוֹלָמִים.[4]

« that is eternal. ‹ with a salvation « by Hashem,

כְּרַחֵם אָב עַל בָּנִים, כֵּן תְּרַחֵם יהוה עָלֵינוּ. לַיהוה

‹ To « on us. ‹ Hashem, ‹ have ‹ so « his ‹ toward ‹ a ‹ As merciful
Hashem mercy, children, father is as

הַיְשׁוּעָה, עַל עַמֶּךָ בִרְכָתֶךָ סֶּלָה. יהוה צְבָאוֹת עִמָּנוּ,

« is with ‹ Master of ‹ Hashem, « Selah. « is Your ‹ Your ‹ upon « is salvation,
us, Legions, blessing, people

מִשְׂגָּב לָנוּ אֱלֹהֵי יַעֲקֹב סֶלָה. יהוה צְבָאוֹת, אַשְׁרֵי אָדָם

‹ is the ‹ – praise- « Master of ‹ Hashem, « Selah. « of ‹ is the ‹ for ‹ a
man worthy Legions Jacob, God us stronghold

בֹּטֵחַ בָּךְ. יהוה הוֹשִׁיעָה, הַמֶּלֶךְ יַעֲנֵנוּ בְיוֹם קָרְאֵנוּ.

« we call. ‹ on the day ‹ answer us « May the King « save! ‹ Hashem, « in You. ‹ who trusts

---

(1) *Psalms* 12:2. (2) *Ecclesiastes* 7:20. (3) *Jeremiah* 31:6. (4) *Isaiah* 45:17.

אֱלֹהֵינוּ וֵאלֹהֵי אֲבוֹתֵינוּ

‹‹ of our forefathers: ‹ and the God ‹ Our God

אַנְשֵׁי אֲמָנָה אָבָדוּ, בָּאִים בְּכֹחַ מַעֲשֵׂיהֶם.

‹‹ of their deeds, ‹ in the ‹ — those who ‹‹ are ‹ of ‹ Men
merit would come forth departed faith

גִּבּוֹרִים לַעֲמוֹד בַּפֶּרֶץ,[1] דּוֹחִים אֶת הַגְּזֵרוֹת.

‹‹ harsh decrees. ‹ repulsing ‹ in the breach, ‹ to stand ‹ mighty enough

הָיוּ לָנוּ לְחוֹמָה, וּלְמַחְסֶה בְּיוֹם זַעַם.

‹‹ of wrath, ‹ in the day ‹ and like a refuge ‹‹ like a wall, ‹ for us ‹ They were

זוֹעֲכִים אַף בְּלַחֲשָׁם, חֵמָה עוֹצְרִים בְּשַׁוְעָם.

‹‹ with their ‹ restraining ‹ [His] ‹‹ with their ‹ [God's] ‹ eliminating
supplications. wrath whispered prayers, anger

טֶרֶם קְרָאוּךָ עֲנִיתָם,[2] יוֹדְעִים לַעְתֵּר וּלְרַצֶּךָ.

‹‹ and appease ‹ how to ‹ they knew ‹‹ You answered ‹ they called ‹ Even
You. entreat them; You, before

כְּאָב רִחַמְתָּ לְמַעֲנָם, לֹא הֱשִׁיבוֹתָ פְּנֵיהֶם רֵיקָם.

‹‹ empty- ‹ turn them back ‹ You would ‹‹ for their ‹ You showed ‹ Like a
handed. not sake; compassion father

מֵרוֹב עֲוֹנֵינוּ אֲבַדְנוּם, נֶאֶסְפוּ מֶנּוּ בַּחֲטָאֵינוּ.

‹‹ because of our ‹ from ‹ they were ‹‹ we lost them; ‹ sins ‹ Because of
transgressions. us taken our abundant

סָעוּ הֵמָּה לִמְנוּחוֹת, עָזְבוּ אוֹתָנוּ לַאֲנָחוֹת.

‹‹ to [our] sighs. ‹ us ‹ leaving ‹‹ to [eternal] rest, ‹‹ They departed

פֶּסוּ גוֹדְרֵי פֶרֶץ, צֻמְּתוּ מְשִׁיבֵי חֵמָה.

‹‹ wrath. ‹ are those who ‹ cut off ‹‹ breaches; ‹ are those ‹ Van-
turned back who mended ished

קָמֵי בַּפֶּרֶץ אָיִן, רְאוּיִם לְרַצּוֹתְךָ בְּעֶתֶר.[3]

‹‹ are ‹ in the ‹ Those who ‹‹ with [their] ‹ of appeasing ‹ — those who
gone breach can stand entreaty. You were capable

שְׁטַטְנוּ בְּאַרְבַּע פִּנּוֹת, תְּרוּפָה לֹא מָצָאנוּ.

‹‹ corners ‹ to the ‹ We have been ‹‹ found. ‹ we have ‹ relief
[of the earth]; four dispersed not

❖ שַׁבְנוּ אֵלֶיךָ בְּבֹשֶׁת פָּנִים, לְשַׁחֶרְךָ אֵל[4] בְּעֵת צָרוֹתֵינוּ.

‹‹ of our ‹ in the ‹ God, ‹ to seek You, ‹‹ facedly, ‹ shame- ‹ to You ‹ We have
distress. time returned

**AN INDIVIDUAL PRAYING WITHOUT A *MINYAN* OMITS THE NEXT TWO PARAGRAPHS,
BEGINNING אֵל מֶלֶךְ, *O GOD, KING,* AND ה', *HASHEM.***

(1) Cf. *Ezekiel* 22:30. (2) Cf. *Isaiah* 65:24. (3) Cf. *Yevamos* 64a. (4) Cf. *Psalms* 78:34.

אֵל מֶלֶךְ יוֹשֵׁב עַל כִּסֵּא רַחֲמִים, מִתְנַהֵג בַּחֲסִידוּת, מוֹחֵל

‹ Who ‹‹ with ‹ Who acts ‹‹ of mercy, ‹ the ‹ on ‹ Who ‹ King ‹ O God,
pardons kindness, throne sits

עֲוֹנוֹת עַמּוֹ, מַעֲבִיר רִאשׁוֹן רִאשׁוֹן, מַרְבֶּה מְחִילָה לְחַטָּאִים

‹ to uninten- ‹ pardon ‹ Who abun- ‹‹ by one, ‹ [sins] one ‹ Who ‹‹ of His ‹ the sins
tional sinners dantly grants removes people,

וּסְלִיחָה לַפּוֹשְׁעִים, עֹשֶׂה צְדָקוֹת עִם כָּל בָּשָׂר וָרוּחַ, לֹא

‹— not ‹‹ and ‹ [beings ‹ all ‹ with ‹ acts of ‹ Who ‹‹ to willful ‹ and
spirit of] flesh generosity performs sinners, forgiveness

כְרָעָתָם תִּגְמוֹל. ❖ אֵל הוֹרֵיתָ לָּנוּ לוֹמַר שְׁלֹשׁ עֶשְׂרֵה,

‹‹ the Thirteen ‹ to recite ‹ us ‹ You ‹ O ‹‹ do You repay ‹ in accord with
[Attributes of Mercy]; taught God, them! their wickedness

וּזְכוֹר לָנוּ הַיּוֹם בְּרִית שְׁלֹשׁ עֶשְׂרֵה, כְּמוֹ שֶׁהוֹדַעְתָּ לֶעָנָיו

‹ to the humble ‹ You made ‹ as ‹‹ of [these] Thirteen, ‹ the ‹ today ‹ for us ‹ remember
one [Moses] known covenant

מִקֶּדֶם, כְּמוֹ שֶׁכָּתוּב, וַיֵּרֶד יהוה בֶּעָנָן וַיִּתְיַצֵּב עִמּוֹ שָׁם,

‹‹ there, ‹ with ‹ and stood ‹ in a cloud ‹ And Hashem ‹‹ it is written: ‹ as ‹‹ in ancient
him descended times,

וַיִּקְרָא בְשֵׁם יהוה.

‹‹ of ‹ with the ‹ and He
Hashem. Name called out

CONGREGATION AND *CHAZZAN* **RECITE LOUDLY AND IN UNISON:**

וַיַּעֲבֹר יהוה עַל פָּנָיו וַיִּקְרָא:

‹‹ and ‹ ‹‹ [Moses'] ‹ before ‹ And Hashem passed
proclaimed: face,

יהוה, יהוה, אֵל, רַחוּם, וְחַנּוּן, אֶרֶךְ אַפַּיִם, וְרַב חֶסֶד, וֶאֱמֶת,

‹‹ and ‹ in ‹ and ‹ to anger, ‹ Slow ‹‹ and ‹ Compas- ‹ God, ‹ Hashem, ‹ Hashem,
Truth, Kindness Abundant Gracious, sionate

נֹצֵר חֶסֶד לָאֲלָפִים, נֹשֵׂא עָוֹן, וָפֶשַׁע, וְחַטָּאָה, וְנַקֵּה.

‹‹ and Who ‹ and inad- ‹ willful ‹ of ‹ Forgiver ‹‹ for thousands ‹ of ‹ Preserver
absolves. vertent sin, sin, iniquity, [of generations], kindness

וְסָלַחְתָּ לַעֲוֹנֵנוּ וּלְחַטָּאתֵנוּ וּנְחַלְתָּנוּ. סְלַח לָנוּ אָבִינוּ כִּי

‹ for ‹‹ our ‹ us, ‹ Forgive ‹‹ and make us ‹‹ and our sins, ‹ our ‹ May You
Father, Your heritage. iniquities forgive

חָטָאנוּ, מְחַל לָנוּ מַלְכֵּנוּ כִּי פָשָׁעְנוּ. כִּי אַתָּה אֲדֹנָי טוֹב

‹ are ‹ O Lord, ‹ You, ‹ For ‹‹ we have ‹ for ‹‹ our King, ‹ us, ‹ pardon ‹‹ we have
good willfully sinned. sinned;

וְסַלָּח, וְרַב חֶסֶד לְכָל קֹרְאֶיךָ.

‹‹ who call ‹ to all ‹ kind ‹ and ‹‹ and
upon You. abundantly forgiving,

THE FOLLOWING PRAYER IS RECITED ALOUD RESPONSIVELY.

CHAZZAN, THEN CONGREGATION:

יִשְׂרָאֵל* נוֹשַׁע בַּיהוה¹ תְּשׁוּעַת עוֹלָמִים,²

《 that is 〈 with a 〈 by 〈was saved〈   Israel*
eternal;   salvation   HASHEM

גַּם הַיּוֹם יִוָּשְׁעוּ מִפִּיךָ שׁוֹכֵן מְרוֹמִים,

《 in the 〈 [You] Who 《 by Your 〈 may they 〈 today 〈 also
heights,   dwells   word,   be saved

כִּי אַתָּה רַב סְלִיחוֹת וּבַעַל הָרַחֲמִים.

《 of mercy. 〈 and the 〈 forgiving 〈 are 〈 You 〈 for
Master   abundantly

CONGREGATION, THEN *CHAZZAN:*

שְׁעָרֶיךָ הֵם דוֹפְקִים כַּעֲנִיִּים וְדַלִּים,

《 and the 〈 like the 〈 knock 〈 they 〈 At Your
destitute;   poor   gates

צָקוּן לַחֲשָׁם קְשׁוֹב יָהּ שׁוֹכֵן מְעָלִים,

《 on high, 〈 Who 〈 O 《 hear, 〈 of their 〈 the out-
dwells   God   whispered   pouring
prayers

כִּי אַתָּה רַב סְלִיחוֹת וּבַעַל הָרַחֲמִים.

《 of mercy. 〈 and the 〈 forgiving 〈 are 〈 You 〈 for
Master   abundantly

CONGREGATION, THEN *CHAZZAN:*

פְּחוּדִים הֵם מִכָּל צָרוֹת, מִמְּחָרְפֵיהֶם וּמִלוֹחֲצֵיהֶם,

《   and who 〈 from those who 〈 their 〈 from 〈 are 〈 Frightened
oppress them.   disgrace them   troubles,   all   they

נָא אַל תַּעַזְבֵם יהוה אֱלֹהֵי אֲבוֹתֵיהֶם,

《 of their 〈 the God 〈 O 《 forsake 〈 do 〈 Please
forefathers,   HASHEM,   them,   not

כִּי אַתָּה רַב סְלִיחוֹת וּבַעַל הָרַחֲמִים.

《 of mercy. 〈 and the 〈 forgiving 〈 are 〈 You 〈 for
Master   abundantly

---

(1) Cf. *Deuteronomy* 33:29. (2) *Isaiah* 45:17.

◀§ יִשְׂרָאֵל — *Israel.* The acrostic spells the author's name, שְׁפַטְיָה, *Shephatiah,* a well-known Kabbalist who lived in Oria, Italy. When the Byzantine emperor Basil I issued anti-Jewish decrees (about 873 C.E.), Rabbi Shephatiah traveled to Constantinople in an attempt to convince the emperor to annul his decrees. Although unsuccessful in his overall mission, while he was in Basil's court Rabbi Shephatiah cured a daughter of the emperor who had been "possessed." As a reward, Basil exempted the Jews of Oria, as well

CONGREGATION, THEN *CHAZZAN:*

טוֹבוֹתֶיךָ יְקַדְּמוּ לָהֶם בְּיוֹם תּוֹכֵחָה,

≪ of rebuke, ‹ on the ‹ them ‹ greet ‹ May Your
day   goodness

וּמִתּוֹךְ צָרָה הַמְצִיאֵם פְּדוּת וּרְוָחָה,

≪ and relief, ‹ deliverance ‹ provide ‹ trouble ‹ and out of
for them

כִּי אַתָּה רַב סְלִיחוֹת וּבַעַל הָרַחֲמִים.

≪ of mercy. ‹ and the ‹ forgiving ‹ are ‹ You ‹ for
Master   abundantly

CONGREGATION, THEN *CHAZZAN:*

יִוָּשְׁעוּ לְעֵין כֹּל וְאַל יִמְשְׁלוּ בָם רְשָׁעִים,

≪ the wicked. ‹ over ‹ let ‹ and ‹ of ‹ in the ‹ May they
them   rule   do not everyone, sight be saved

כַּלֵּה שֵׂעִיר וְחוֹתְנוֹ¹ וְיַעֲלוּ לְצִיּוֹן מוֹשִׁיעִים,²

≪ saviors, ‹ to Zion ‹ and let ≪ and his ‹ Seir ‹ Destroy
there   father-in-law [Esau]
go up   [Ishmael],

כִּי אַתָּה רַב סְלִיחוֹת וּבַעַל הָרַחֲמִים.

≪ of mercy. ‹ and the ‹ forgiving ‹ are ‹ You ‹ for
Master   abundantly

CONGREGATION, THEN *CHAZZAN:*

הַקְשִׁיבָה אָדוֹן לְקוֹל שַׁוְעָתָם,

≪ of their ‹ to the ‹ O ‹ Hearken,
outcry,   sound Master,

וְלִמְכוֹן שִׁבְתְּךָ הַשָּׁמַיִם תַּעֲלֶה תְפִלָּתָם,

≪ may their prayer ‹ in the ‹ of Your ‹ and to
ascend,   Heavens dwelling the place

כִּי אַתָּה רַב סְלִיחוֹת וּבַעַל הָרַחֲמִים.

≪ of mercy. ‹ and the ‹ forgiving ‹ are ‹ You ‹ for
Master   abundantly

TURN TO PAGE 684 FOR אֵל מֶלֶךְ, **AND CONTINUE UNTIL THE CONCLUSION OF** *SELICHOS.*

---

(1) Cf. *Genesis* 28:9. (2) Cf. *Obadiah* 1:21.

---

as four other Jewish communities, from his decrees. Both Rabbi Shephatiah and his son and successor, Rabbi Amittai (see p. 712), often allude to the persecutions and forced conversions that Basil inflicted upon the Jews.

﷽ סליחות לשני תנינא ﷽

﷽ SELICHOS — SECOND MONDAY OF BEHAB ﷽

ALL BEGIN HERE:

סְלַח לָנוּ אָבִינוּ, כִּי בְרוֹב אִוַּלְתֵּנוּ שָׁגִינוּ,

‹‹ we have ‹ of our folly ‹ in the ‹ for ‹ our ‹ us, ‹ Forgive
erred;   abundance   Father,

מְחַל לָנוּ מַלְכֵּנוּ, כִּי רַבּוּ עֲוֹנֵינוּ.

‹‹ our iniquities. ‹ many are ‹ for ‹ our King, ‹ us, ‹ pardon

אֵל אֶרֶךְ אַפַּיִם אַתָּה, וּבַעַל הָרַחֲמִים נִקְרֵאתָ, וְדֶרֶךְ

‹ and ‹‹ are You ‹ of Mercy ‹ and ‹‹ are You, ‹ to anger, ‹ Who ‹ God,
the way   called;   Master   is slow

תְּשׁוּבָה הוֹרֵיתָ. גְּדֻלַּת רַחֲמֶיךָ וַחֲסָדֶיךָ, תִּזְכּוֹר הַיּוֹם וּבְכָל

‹ and ‹ this ‹ may You ‹ and Your ‹ of Your ‹ The ‹‹ have You ‹ of
every   day   remember,   kindness   mercy   greatness   taught.   repentance

יוֹם לְזֶרַע יְדִידֶיךָ. תֵּפֶן אֵלֵינוּ בְּרַחֲמִים, כִּי אַתָּה הוּא בַּעַל

‹ the ‹ are ‹ You ‹ for ‹‹ in mercy, ‹ to us ‹ Turn ‹‹ of Your ‹ for the ‹‹ day,
Master   beloved ones. offspring

הָרַחֲמִים. בְּתַחֲנוּן וּבִתְפִלָּה פָּנֶיךָ נְקַדֵּם, כְּהוֹדַעְתָּ לֶעָנָיו

‹ to the ‹ in the man- ‹‹ we ‹ Your ‹ and prayer ‹ With ‹‹ of Mercy.
humble one   ner that You   approach, Presence   supplication
[Moses]   made known

מִקֶּדֶם. מֵחֲרוֹן אַפְּךָ שׁוּב, כְּמוֹ בְתוֹרָתְךָ כָּתוּב.[1] וּבְצֵל כְּנָפֶיךָ

‹ of Your ‹ In the ‹‹ it is ‹ in Your Torah ‹ as ‹‹ turn ‹ of Your ‹ From the ‹‹ in ancient
wings   shadow   written.   back,   anger fierceness   times.

נֶחֱסֶה וְנִתְלוֹנָן, כְּיוֹם וַיֵּרֶד יהוה בֶּעָנָן.[2] ❖ תַּעֲבוֹר עַל פֶּשַׁע

‹ sin ‹ Overlook ‹‹ in a ‹ when Hashem ‹ as on ‹‹ and may ‹ may we
cloud.   descended   the day   we dwell, find shelter

וְתִמְחֶה אָשָׁם, כְּיוֹם וַיִּתְיַצֵּב עִמּוֹ שָׁם.[2] תַּאֲזִין שַׁוְעָתֵנוּ

‹ to our cry ‹ Give ‹‹ there. ‹ with him ‹ when He ‹ as on ‹‹ guilt, ‹ and erase
heed   [Moses]   [God] stood   the day

וְתַקְשִׁיב מֶנּוּ מַאֲמָר, כְּיוֹם וַיִּקְרָא בְשֵׁם יהוה,[2] וְשָׁם נֶאֱמַר:

‹‹ it was ‹ and ‹‹ of ‹ with the ‹ when He ‹ as on ‹‹ [our] ‹ from ‹ and hear
said: there   Hashem, Name   called out the day   declaration,   us

CONGREGATION AND *CHAZZAN* RECITE LOUDLY AND IN UNISON:

וַיַּעֲבֹר יהוה עַל פָּנָיו וַיִּקְרָא:

‹‹ and ‹‹ [Moses'] ‹ before ‹ And Hashem passed
proclaimed: face,

---

(1) Cf. *Exodus* 32:12. (2) 34:5.

יהוה, יהוה, אֵל, רַחוּם, וְחַנּוּן, אֶרֶךְ אַפַּיִם, וְרַב חֶסֶד, וֶאֱמֶת,

‹‹ and ‹ in ‹ and ‹ to anger, ‹ Slow ‹‹ and ‹ Compas- ‹ God, ‹ Hashem, ‹ Hashem,
Truth, Kindness Abundant sionate Gracious,

נֹצֵר חֶסֶד לָאֲלָפִים, נֹשֵׂא עָוֹן, וָפֶשַׁע, וְחַטָּאָה, וְנַקֵּה.[1]

‹‹ and Who ‹ and inad- ‹ willful ‹ of ‹ Forgiver ‹‹ for thousands ‹ of ‹ Preserver
absolves. vertent sin, sin, iniquity, [of generations], kindness

וְסָלַחְתָּ לַעֲוֹנֵנוּ וּלְחַטָּאתֵנוּ וּנְחַלְתָּנוּ.[2] סְלַח לָנוּ אָבִינוּ כִּי

‹ for ‹‹ our ‹ us, ‹ Forgive ‹‹ and our sins, ‹ our ‹ May You
Father, Your heritage. iniquities forgive

חָטָאנוּ, מְחַל לָנוּ מַלְכֵּנוּ כִּי פָשָׁעְנוּ.[3] כִּי אַתָּה אֲדֹנָי טוֹב

‹ are ‹ O Lord, ‹ You, ‹ For ‹‹ we have ‹ for ‹‹ our King, ‹ us, ‹ pardon ‹‹ we have
good willfully sinned. sinned;

וְסַלָּח, וְרַב חֶסֶד לְכָל קֹרְאֶיךָ.[4]

‹‹ who call ‹ to all ‹ kind ‹ and ‹‹ and
upon You. abundantly forgiving,

ALL CONTINUE:

אַל תִּקְצֹף יהוה עַד מְאֹד, וְאַל לָעַד תִּזְכֹּר עָוֹן, הֶן הַבֶּט

‹ see ‹ be- ‹‹ iniquity; ‹ remem- ‹ forever ‹ and ‹‹ exceedingly, ‹ O ‹ be ‹ Do
hold, ber do not Hashem, wrathful, not

נָא עַמְּךָ כֻלָּנוּ. הַעַל אֵלֶּה תִתְאַפַּק יהוה, תֶּחֱשֶׁה

‹ Will You ‹‹ Hashem? ‹ will You restrain ‹ these ‹ Despite ‹‹ are ‹ Your ‹‹ now,
remain silent Yourself, [catastrophes] we all. people

וּתְעַנֵּנוּ עַד מְאֹד.[5] שׁוּבָה יהוה, עַד מָתַי, וְהִנָּחֵם עַל עֲבָדֶיךָ.[6]

‹‹ Your ‹ con- ‹ Relent ‹‹ when ‹ until ‹‹ Hashem; ‹ Return, ‹‹ exceedingly? ‹ and allow
servants. cerning [will You us to suffer
abandon us]?

כְּרַחֵם אָב עַל בָּנִים, כֵּן תְּרַחֵם יהוה עָלֵינוּ.[7] לַיהוה

‹ To ‹‹ on us. ‹ Hashem, ‹ have ‹ so ‹‹ his ‹ toward ‹ a ‹ As merciful
Hashem mercy, children, father is as

הַיְשׁוּעָה, עַל עַמְּךָ בִרְכָתֶךָ סֶּלָה.[8] יהוה צְבָאוֹת עִמָּנוּ,

‹‹ is with ‹ Master of ‹ Hashem, ‹‹ Selah. ‹‹ is Your ‹ Your ‹ upon ‹‹ is salvation,
us, Legions, blessing, people

מִשְׂגָּב לָנוּ אֱלֹהֵי יַעֲקֹב סֶלָה.[9] יהוה צְבָאוֹת, אַשְׁרֵי אָדָם

‹ is the ‹ — praise- ‹‹ Master of ‹ Hashem, ‹‹ Selah. ‹ of ‹ is the ‹ for ‹ a
man worthy Legions Jacob, God us stronghold

בֹּטֵחַ בָּךְ.[11] יהוה הוֹשִׁיעָה, הַמֶּלֶךְ יַעֲנֵנוּ בְיוֹם קָרְאֵנוּ.[10]

‹‹ we call. ‹ on the ‹ answer ‹ May the ‹‹ save! ‹ Hashem, ‹‹ in ‹ who
day us King You. trusts

---

(1) *Exodus* 34:6-7. (2) 34:9. (3) From the weekday *Shemoneh Esrei*. (4) *Psalms* 86:5.
(5) *Isaiah* 64:8,11. (6) *Psalms* 90:13. (7) Cf. 103:13. (8) 3:9. (9) 46:8. (10) 84:13. (11) 20:10.

סְלַח נָא לַעֲוֹן הָעָם הַזֶּה כְּגֹֽדֶל חַסְדֶּֽךָ, וְכַאֲשֶׁר נָשָֽׂאתָה

❬ You have ❬ and as ❮ of Your ❬ according to ❬ of this people ❬ the ❬ please, ❬ Forgive,
forgiven   kindness, the greatness   iniquity

לָעָם הַזֶּה מִמִּצְרַֽיִם וְעַד הֵֽנָּה,¹ וְשָׁם נֶאֱמַר:

❮ it was said: ❬ And there ❮ now. ❬ until ❬ from Egypt ❬ this people

ALL, ALOUD AND IN UNISON:

וַיֹּֽאמֶר יהוה סָלַֽחְתִּי כִּדְבָרֶֽךָ.²

❮ according to your word! ❬ I have forgiven ❮ And HASHEM said:

ALL CONTINUE:

הַטֵּה אֱלֹהַי אָזְנְךָ וּשְׁמָע, פְּקַח עֵינֶֽיךָ וּרְאֵה שֹׁמְמֹתֵֽינוּ,

❮ our desolation, ❬ and see ❬ Your eyes ❬ open ❮ and listen; ❬ Your ear, ❬ my God, ❬ Incline,

וְהָעִיר אֲשֶׁר נִקְרָא שִׁמְךָ עָלֶֽיהָ, כִּי לֹא עַל צִדְקֹתֵֽינוּ אֲנַֽחְנוּ

❬ do we ❬ of our ❬ because ❬ not ❬ for ❮ upon; ❬ Your Name is ❬ which ❬ and [that
righteousness   proclaimed   of] the city

מַפִּילִים תַּחֲנוּנֵֽינוּ לְפָנֶֽיךָ, כִּי עַל רַחֲמֶֽיךָ הָרַבִּים. אֲדֹנָי

❬ O Lord, ❮ which is ❬ of Your ❬ because ❬ but ❮ before ❬ our ❬ cast
abundant.   compassion,   You;   supplications

שְׁמָֽעָה, אֲדֹנָי סְלָֽחָה, אֲדֹנָי הַקְשִֽׁיבָה, וַעֲשֵׂה אַל תְּאַחַר,

❮ delay; ❬ do not ❮ and act, ❬ be attentive, ❬ O Lord, ❬ forgive; ❬ O Lord, ❬ heed;

לְמַעַנְךָ אֱלֹהַי, כִּי שִׁמְךָ נִקְרָא עַל עִירְךָ וְעַל עַמֶּֽךָ.³

❮ Your ❬ and ❬ Your ❬ upon ❬ is ❬ Your ❬ for ❮ my God, ❬ for Your
people.   upon   City   proclaimed Name   sake,

אֱלֹהֵֽינוּ וֵאלֹהֵי אֲבוֹתֵֽינוּ

❮ of our forefathers: ❬ and the God ❬ Our God

אֲפָפֽוּנוּ מַֽיִם* עַד נֶֽפֶשׁ,⁴   בָּֽאנוּ בְּעָמְקֵי מְצוּלָה,⁵

❮ our very ❬ to ❬ have the ❬ Engulfed us   ❮ depths; ❬ into the ❬ we have
soul;   waters,*   deepest   entered

גַּלֵּי יָם עָבְרוּ עָלֵֽינוּ,⁶   דָּכְיוֹת תְּהוֹם כִּסָּֽתְנוּ.

❮ over us; ❬ have ❬ of the ❬ the   ❮ have ❬ of the ❬ the destructive
surged sea waves   covered us.   deep   waves

הוֹדֵֽנוּ נֶהְפַּךְ לְמַשְׁחִית,   וְעוֹד לֹא עָצַֽרְנוּ כֹֽחַ.⁷

❮ into distortion, ❬ was trans- ❬ The majesty   ❮ any ❬ can we ❬ and no
formed   of our   strength; retain   longer
countenance

---

(1) *Numbers* 14:19. (2) 14:20. (3) *Daniel* 9:18-19. (4) Cf. *Jonah* 2:6.
(5) Cf. *Psalms* 69:3. (6) Cf. *Jonah* 2:4. (7) Cf. *Daniel* 10:8.

§⊷ אֲפָפֽוּנוּ מַֽיִם — *Engulfed us have the waters.*   He was the son of and successor to his father,
The *paytan* signed his name אֲמִתַּי, *Amittai*, as   Rabbi Shephatiah (see p. 708), as leader of the
the acrostic of the four stiches of the final verse.   Jewish community in Oria.

זְלַעְפְנוּ עַל חַטאתֵינוּ,
our sins; ⟨ over ⟨ we are gripped with trembling

טְבַסְנוּ עֵצָה מַה לַעֲשׂוֹת,
to do. ⟨ what ⟨ a ⟨ We have consulted to find strategy,

בֻּוֹנַנּוּ בְּלֵב מַחֲשָׁבוֹת,
thoughts, ⟨ in our heart ⟨ we deliberated

מָסֹרֶת בְּיָדֵינוּ מֵאֲבוֹתֵינוּ,
from our forefathers, ⟨ in our hands ⟨ There is a tradition

סוֹתְּרוֹת רוֹעַ גְּזֵרוֹת,[3]
decrees, ⟨ evil ⟨ cancel

פְּצְנוּ בְּהַסְכָּמָה אַחַת,
unanimously, ⟨ in agreement ⟨ We proclaimed

קָדוֹשׁ אוּלַי יַשְׁקִיף,
peer down ⟨ might ⟨ that the [at us], perhaps Holy One

שַׁדַּי, עָשִׂינוּ אֶת שֶׁלָנוּ,
our [part]; ⟨ we have done ⟨ Almighty One,

❖ אַל תֵּשֵׁב עִמָּנוּ בַדִּין,
in ⟨ with us ⟨ sit ⟨ Do judgment; not

תִּיקַר נַפְשֵׁנוּ בְּעֵינֶיךָ,[5]
in Your eyes ⟨ our souls ⟨ May precious be

מְחַל לָנוּ, כַּפֵּר לָנוּ, כְּיוֹם רְדִתְּךָ בֶּעָנָן.
in a cloud. ⟨ when You descended ⟨ as on the day ⟨ for us, ⟨ grant atonement ⟨ us, ⟨ pardon

חֲלְחַלְנוּ עַל רוֹב פְּשָׁעֵינוּ.[1]
of our transgressions. ⟨ the multitude ⟨ over ⟨ we are deeply distressed

יוֹעֵץ בְּקִרְבֵּנוּ אָיִן,
there is none; ⟨ among us – ⟨ A counselor

לְמֵרָחוֹק שְׂאֵת דֵּעָה.[2]
knowledge. ⟨ to bring ⟨ from the distant [past]

נָאָקָה תְּשׁוּבָה וּצְדָקָה,
and charity ⟨ repentance ⟨ that prayer,

עוֹד מֵעַנּוֹת עָם.
to the nation. ⟨ cause suffering ⟨ so that they no longer

צוֹם שֵׁנִי וַחֲמִישִׁי וְשֵׁנִי,
and Monday, ⟨ Thursday ⟨ of Monday, ⟨ the fast

רַחֲמָיו לְקַדֵּם לְרֹגֶז.[4]
over wrath. ⟨ giving precedence ⟨ to His mercy

תַּקִּיף עֲשֵׂה אֶת שֶׁלָךְ.
Yours. ⟨ do ⟨ Powerful One,

מִדֶּבֶר וּמֵחֶרֶב וּמֵרָעָב מַלְּטֵנוּ,
deliver us. ⟨ and from famine ⟨ from the sword ⟨ from plague,

יָהּ סְלַח לָנוּ,
us, ⟨ forgive ⟨ O God,

AN INDIVIDUAL PRAYING WITHOUT A *MINYAN* OMITS THE NEXT TWO PARAGRAPHS, BEGINNING אֵל מֶלֶךְ, *O GOD, KING,* AND ה', *HASHEM*.

אֵל מֶלֶךְ יוֹשֵׁב עַל כִּסֵּא רַחֲמִים, מִתְנַהֵג בַּחֲסִידוּת, מוֹחֵל
Who pardons ⟨ with kindness ⟨ Who acts ⟨ of mercy, ⟨ the throne ⟨ on ⟨ Who sits ⟨ King ⟨ O God,

(1) Cf. *Lamentations* 1:5. (2) Cf. *Job* 36:3. (3) Cf. *Yerushalmi Taanis* 2:1.
(4) Cf. *Habakkuk* 3:2. (5) Cf. *II Kings* 1:14.

עֲוֹנוֹת עַמּוֹ, מַעֲבִיר רִאשׁוֹן רִאשׁוֹן, מַרְבֶּה מְחִילָה לַחַטָּאִים

⟨ to uninten- ⟨ pardon ⟨ Who abun- ⟨ by one, ⟨ [sins] one ⟨ Who ⟨ of His ⟨ the sins
tional sinners   dantly grants   removes   people,

וּסְלִיחָה לַפּוֹשְׁעִים, עֹשֶׂה צְדָקוֹת עִם כָּל בָּשָׂר וָרוּחַ, לֹא

⟨– not ⟨⟨ and ⟨ [beings ⟨ all ⟨ with ⟨ acts of ⟨ Who ⟨⟨ to willful ⟨ and
spirit   of] flesh   generosity performs   sinners,   forgiveness

כְּרָעָתָם תִּגְמוֹל. ❖ אֵל הוֹרֵיתָ לָנוּ לוֹמַר שְׁלֹשׁ עֶשְׂרֵה,

⟨⟨ the Thirteen ⟨ to recite ⟨ us ⟨ You ⟨ O ⟨⟨ do You repay ⟨ in accord with
[Attributes of Mercy];   taught   God,   them!   their wickedness

וּזְכוֹר לָנוּ הַיּוֹם בְּרִית שְׁלֹשׁ עֶשְׂרֵה, כְּמוֹ שֶׁהוֹדַעְתָּ לֶעָנָיו

⟨to the humble ⟨ You made ⟨ as ⟨⟨ of [these] Thirteen, ⟨ the ⟨ today ⟨ for us ⟨ remember
one [Moses]   known   covenant

מִקֶּדֶם, כְּמוֹ שֶׁכָּתוּב, וַיֵּרֶד יהוה בֶּעָנָן וַיִּתְיַצֵּב עִמּוֹ שָׁם,

⟨⟨ there, ⟨ with ⟨ and stood ⟨ in a cloud ⟨ And HASHEM ⟨⟨ it is written: ⟨ as ⟨⟨ in ancient
him   descended   times,

וַיִּקְרָא בְשֵׁם יהוה.

⟨⟨ of ⟨ with the ⟨ and He
HASHEM.   Name   called out

CONGREGATION AND CHAZZAN RECITE LOUDLY AND IN UNISON:

וַיַּעֲבֹר יהוה עַל פָּנָיו וַיִּקְרָא:

⟨⟨ and ⟨⟨ [Moses'] ⟨ before ⟨ And HASHEM passed
proclaimed: face,

יהוה, יהוה, אֵל, רַחוּם, וְחַנּוּן, אֶרֶךְ אַפַּיִם, וְרַב חֶסֶד, וֶאֱמֶת,

⟨⟨ and ⟨ in ⟨ and ⟨ to anger, ⟨ Slow ⟨⟨ and ⟨ Compas- ⟨ God, ⟨ HASHEM, ⟨ HASHEM,
Truth, Kindness Abundant   Gracious, sionate

נֹצֵר חֶסֶד לָאֲלָפִים, נֹשֵׂא עָוֹן, וָפֶשַׁע, וְחַטָּאָה, וְנַקֵּה.

⟨⟨ and Who ⟨ and inad- ⟨ willful ⟨ of ⟨ Forgiver ⟨⟨ for thousands ⟨ of ⟨ Preserver
absolves. vertent sin, sin, iniquity,   [of generations], kindness

וְסָלַחְתָּ לַעֲוֹנֵנוּ וּלְחַטָּאתֵנוּ וּנְחַלְתָּנוּ. סְלַח לָנוּ אָבִינוּ כִּי

⟨ for ⟨⟨ our ⟨ us, ⟨ Forgive ⟨⟨ and make us ⟨ and our sins, ⟨ our ⟨ May You
Father,   iniquities   Your heritage.   forgive

חָטָאנוּ, מְחַל לָנוּ מַלְכֵּנוּ כִּי פָשָׁעְנוּ. כִּי אַתָּה אֲדֹנָי טוֹב

⟨ are ⟨ O Lord, ⟨ You, ⟨ For ⟨⟨ we have ⟨ for ⟨⟨ our King, ⟨ us, ⟨ pardon ⟨⟨ we have
good   willfully sinned.   sinned;

וְסַלָּח, וְרַב חֶסֶד לְכָל קֹרְאֶיךָ.

⟨⟨ who call ⟨ to all ⟨ kind ⟨ and ⟨⟨ and
upon You.   abundantly forgiving,

הַאֲזִינָה יהוה תְּפִלָּתֵנוּ, וְהַקְשִׁיבָה בְּקוֹל תַּחֲנוּנוֹתֵינוּ.[1]

⟨⟨ of our supplications. ⟨ the sound ⟨ and heed ⟨⟨ to our prayer, ⟨ HASHEM, ⟨ Give ear,

---

(1) Cf. *Psalms* 86:6.

שְׁמַע יהוה קוֹלֵנוּ נִקְרָא, חָנֵנוּ וַעֲנֵנוּ. שָׁמְעָה יהוה צֶדֶק,¹

<small>what is / Hashem, / Hear, / and / show us / when / our / Hashem, / Hear,</small>
<small>righteous: / answer us. / favor / we call; / voice</small>

הַקְשִׁיבָה רִנָּתֵנוּ, הַאֲזִינָה תְּפִלָּתֵנוּ.² שְׁמַע יהוה וְחָנֵנוּ, יהוה

<small>Hashem, / and / Hashem, / Hear, / to our / give ear / to our / be attentive</small>
<small>favor us; / prayer. / entreaty;</small>

הֱיֵה עוֹזֵר לָנוּ.³

<small>for us. / a Helper / be</small>

כְּרַחֵם אָב עַל בָּנִים, כֵּן תְּרַחֵם יהוה עָלֵינוּ. לַיהוה

<small>To / on us. / Hashem, / have / so / his / toward / a / As merciful</small>
<small>Hashem / mercy, / children, / father is / as</small>

הַיְשׁוּעָה, עַל עַמְּךָ בִרְכָתֶךָ סֶּלָה. יהוה צְבָאוֹת עִמָּנוּ,

<small>is with / Master of / Hashem, / Selah. / is Your / Your / upon / is salvation,</small>
<small>us, / Legions, / blessing, / people</small>

מִשְׂגָּב לָנוּ אֱלֹהֵי יַעֲקֹב סֶלָה. יהוה צְבָאוֹת, אַשְׁרֵי אָדָם

<small>is the / — praise- / Master of / Hashem, / Selah. / of / is the / for / a</small>
<small>man / worthy / Legions / Jacob, / God / us / stronghold</small>

בֹּטֵחַ בָּךְ. יהוה הוֹשִׁיעָה, הַמֶּלֶךְ יַעֲנֵנוּ בְיוֹם קָרְאֵנוּ.

<small>we call. / on the day / answer us / May the King / save! / Hashem, / in You. / who trusts</small>

אֱלֹהֵינוּ וֵאלֹהֵי אֲבוֹתֵינוּ

<small>of our forefathers: / and the God / Our God</small>

אֲזוֹן תַּחַן וְהַסְכֵּת עֲתִירָה, אַף הָפֵר וְשַׁכֵּךְ עֶבְרָה,

<small>fury. / and calm / annul, / [Your] / entreaty; / and heed / to sup- / Give ear</small>
<small>anger / plication</small>

בָּאֵי לְחַלּוֹתְךָ בְּנֶפֶשׁ מָרָה, בְּשִׁמְךָ הַגָּדוֹל יִמְצְאוּ עֶזְרָה.

<small>help. / may they / that is / — through / that is / with a / to plead / Those</small>
<small>find / Great / Your Name / embittered / soul / with You / who come</small>

גַּעֲיַת נֶאֱנָחִים עֲנוּתָם חֲזֵה, גְּחִינַת קוֹמָתָם אַל תִּבְזֶה,

<small>despise. / do not / of their up- / the bending / observe; / and their / of those / The wail</small>
<small>right bodies / over [in prayer] / affliction, / who groan,</small>

דְּרוֹשׁ עֶלְבּוֹנָם מִצַּר וּבוֹזֶה, דְּרוֹךְ פּוּרָה וְנִצְחָם יִזֶּה.⁴

<small>spurt / and let their / [as] a / trample / and / from [their] / their / Avenge</small>
<small>out. / lifeblood / wine press / [them] / scorner; / oppressor / humiliation</small>

הֲלֹא אַתָּה הָיִיתָ וְהִנֶּךָ, הָיוֹ תִהְיֶה בַּהֲדַר גְּאוֹנֶךָ,

<small>of Your / in the / You shall / and You / have always / that / Is it</small>
<small>majesty. / splendor / always exist / still exist; / existed / You / not so</small>

---

(1) Cf. *Psalms* 27:7. (2) Cf. 17:1. (3) Cf. 30:11. (4) Cf. *Isaiah* 63:3.

וְנֶאֱמַת יִכּוֹן זֶרַע¹ אֱמוּנֶיךָ,   וְהִנָּם כָּלִים מִתִּגְרַת חֲרוֹנֶךָ.²

of Your ‹ from the ‹ devastated ‹ but in fact ‹‹ of Your ‹ the ‹ that ‹ And You
anger. provocation   they are   faithful ones, offspring steadfast declared
                                                 would be

זוֹעֲמוּ בְּעֵוֹנָם וּמִמְּאֲוָיָם נִסָּחוּ,   זוֹרוּ בְּאֲפָסִים וְלֹא נָחוּ,

rested. ‹ and ‹ to the ends ‹ they were ‹‹ they were ‹ and from their ‹‹ because ‹ They have
have not   of the world scattered   torn away; place of delight   of their   become
                                     [the Temple]   straying,   scorned

חֻבְּלָה רוּחָם³ וְלֶעָפָר שָׁחוּ,⁴   חָרְשׁוּ חוֹרְשִׁים וּמַעֲנִית הִמְתִּיחוּ.⁵

they stretched ‹ and their ‹ did the ‹ plowed ‹‹ they are ‹ and to ‹‹ is their ‹ Devastated
out.   furrow   plowers, [over them] prostrated; the dust   spirit,

טָבְעוּ בַבּוֹץ⁶ וְאֵין פּוֹצֶה,   טוֹרְפֵיהֶם שָׁלוּ מִקָּצֶה אֶל קָצֶה,

at every side. ‹ are ‹ Those who ‹‹ to extricate ‹ and there ‹ into the ‹ They
       serene   devour them   [them]. is no one   mire   sank

יוֹם יוֹם לוֹחֲמָם מְנַצֶּה,   יָד פּוֹרְשִׁים מִלַחַץ לֵיצֵא.

to ‹ from ‹‹ [Israel] ‹ while a ‹‹ provoke ‹ their ‹ [after] ‹ Day
escape. oppression extends, [pleading] hand fights, attackers day

כָּלוּ חַיֵּיהֶם בְּיָגוֹן וַאֲנָחָה,⁷   כָּשַׁל רַבָּה⁸ וְעָרְבָה שִׂמְחָה,⁹

is ‹ and ‹ is ‹ faltering ‹ and sighing; ‹ in grief ‹ are their ‹ Con-
gladness. dimmed abundant   lives   sumed

לִישַׁע חוֹכִים וְהִנֵּה צְוָחָה,   לְבָטוּם קָמִים וְכָרוּ שׁוּחָה.¹⁰

a pit. ‹ and dug ‹ did their ‹ made them ‹‹ there is ‹ but ‹‹ they ‹ For
[them] adversaries, distraught   wailing; instead yearn, salvation

מַעֲרִימִים סוֹד¹¹ מִמֶּךָ לְהַדִּיחָם,

to push ‹ from ‹‹ in ‹ They plot
them away; You secret, deviously

מַכְבִּידִים עוֹל¹² לְהַכְשִׁיל כֹּחָם,¹³

their ‹ to cause to ‹ the yoke ‹ they weigh
strength. falter   down

נוֹאֲקִים אֵלֶיךָ בְּהִתְעַטֵּף רוּחָם,¹⁴   נַחַת לִמְצוֹא מִכֹּבֶד טָרְחָם.

of their ‹ from the ‹ to find ‹ relief ‹‹ does their ‹ when grow ‹ To You ‹ They [Israel]
burden. weight   spirit; faint   cry out

שִׂיחַ צָקִים בְּמַעֲמַד צָפוּף,   סְלִיחָה מְבַקְשִׁים בְּקָדְקֹד כָּפוּף,

bowed ‹ with ‹ they seek ‹ forgiveness ‹‹ that is ‹ in an ‹ they pour ‹ Prayers
down. heads   crowded; assembly forth

עוֹשְׁקֵיהֶם הִקְנִיאוּם¹⁵ וּנְתָנוּם לִשְׁסוּף,¹⁶

to slaughter. ‹ and deliver them ‹ provoke them ‹ Their tormentors

---

(1) Cf. *Psalms* 102:29. (2) Cf. 39:11. (3) Cf. *Job* 17:1. (4) Cf. *Psalms* 44:26. (5) Cf. 129:3.
(6) Cf. *Jeremiah* 38:22. (7) Cf. *Psalms* 31:11. (8) Cf. *Jeremiah* 46:16. (9) Cf. *Isaiah* 24:11. (10) *Jeremiah* 18:20.
(11) Cf. *Psalms* 83:4. (12) Cf. *Isaiah* 47:6. (13) Cf. *Lamentations* 1:14. (14) Cf. *Psalms* 142:4.
(15) Cf. *Deuteronomy* 32:21. (16) Original text בְּנֵצֶר נָאֱפוּף, *with the branch of adultery.*

עוֹעִים יִמָּסְכוּ¹ וְיִהְיוּ לִסְפוּף.

❮❮ annihilated! ❮ and may ❮ be poured ❮ [may]
they be　　upon them　insanity

פְּדֵה דְבֵקֶיךָ מֵחֶרֶץ וְכָלוּי,²　　פַּלֵּטַם מִצּוֹרֵר וּתְנֵם לְעֶלְוִי,³

❮❮ supreme. ❮ and make ❮ from ❮ rescue　　❮❮ and ❮ from [evil] ❮ those who ❮ Redeem
them　oppressors　them　　　　destruction; decrees　cling to You

צַוֵּה יְשׁוּעוֹת⁴ מְשַׁחֲרֶיךָ בְּחֶלְוִי,　　צוּר עוֹלָמִים הוֹשִׁיעֵנוּ בְגָלוּי.

❮❮ openly. ❮ save us ❮ of the ❮ O Rock　❮❮ with ❮ for those ❮ salvations ❮ Com-
Universe,　　entreaty;　who seek You　　mand

קַנֵּא וְנוֹקֵם⁵ קַנֵּא לִשְׁמֶךָ,　　קַצֵּץ סַמְלוֹנִים מִצַּוַּאר עַמֶּךָ,

❮❮ of Your ❮ from the ❮ [the enemies'] ❮ cut off　❮❮ for Your ❮ be ❮❮ and avenging ❮ O
people.　neck　yoke　　　　Name;　zealous　One,　zealous

רְאֵה עָמָלֵנוּ⁶ וְשׁוּב מִזַּעְמֶךָ,　　רִיבָה רִיבֵנוּ⁷ מֵעַם חֶרְמֶךָ.⁸

❮❮ [destined] to be ❮ against the ❮ our ❮ champion　❮❮ from Your ❮ and turn ❮❮ our toil, ❮ See
destroyed by You. people [Edom] cause　　anger;　back

שִׁבְעָתַיִם הָשֵׁב לְחֵיק¹⁰ מַאֲנִינָי,⁹　　שַׁכֵּר חִצֶּיךָ מִדָּם¹⁰ מְעַנָּי.

❮❮ of my ❮ with the ❮ Your ❮ intoxicate ❮❮ of those who ❮ to the ❮ repay ❮ Sevenfold
oppressors. blood　arrows　hurt me,　　bosom

❖ תַּטֶּה אָזְנְךָ¹¹ לְקוֹל תַּחֲנוּנַי,　　תִּרְצֵנִי בְּקָרְאִי יְהוָה יְהוָה.

❮❮ HASHEM! ❮ HASHEM, ❮❮ when I ❮ accept me ❮ of my sup- ❮ to the ❮ Your ear ❮ Incline
call out,　favorably　plications;　sound

**AN INDIVIDUAL PRAYING WITHOUT A MINYAN OMITS THE NEXT TWO PARAGRAPHS,
BEGINNING אֵל מֶלֶךְ, O GOD, KING, AND ה', HASHEM.**

אֵל מֶלֶךְ יוֹשֵׁב עַל כִּסֵּא רַחֲמִים, מִתְנַהֵג בַּחֲסִידוּת, מוֹחֵל

❮ Who ❮❮ with ❮ Who acts ❮❮ of mercy, ❮ the ❮ on ❮ Who ❮ King ❮ O God,
pardons　kindness,　　throne　sits

עֲוֹנוֹת עַמּוֹ, מַעֲבִיר רִאשׁוֹן רִאשׁוֹן, מַרְבֶּה מְחִילָה לְחַטָּאִים

❮ to uninten- ❮ pardon ❮ Who abun- ❮ by one, ❮ [sins] one ❮ Who ❮❮ of His ❮ the sins
tional sinners　dantly grants　removes　people,

וּסְלִיחָה לַפּוֹשְׁעִים, עֹשֶׂה צְדָקוֹת עִם כָּל בָּשָׂר וָרוּחַ, לֹא

❮ — not ❮❮ and ❮ [beings ❮ all ❮ with ❮ acts of ❮ Who ❮❮ to willful ❮ and
spirit　of] flesh　generosity performs　sinners,　forgiveness

כְרָעָתָם תִּגְמוֹל. ❖ אֵל הוֹרֵיתָ לָּנוּ לוֹמַר שְׁלֹשׁ עֶשְׂרֵה, וּזְכוֹר

❮ remember ❮❮ the Thirteen ❮ to recite ❮ us ❮ You ❮ O ❮❮ do You ❮ in accord with
[Attributes of Mercy];　taught　God,　repay them! their wickedness

לָנוּ הַיּוֹם בְּרִית שְׁלֹשׁ עֶשְׂרֵה, כְּמוֹ שֶׁהוֹדַעְתָּ לֶעָנָיו מִקֶּדֶם, כְּמוֹ

❮ as ❮❮ in ancient ❮ to the humble ❮ You made ❮ as ❮❮ of [these] Thirteen, ❮ the ❮ today ❮ for us
times,　one [Moses]　known　covenant

---

(1) Cf. *Isaiah* 19:14. (2) Cf. 10:22-23. (3) Cf. *Deuteronomy* 26:19.
(4) *Psalms* 44:5. (5) *Nahum* 1:2. (6) Cf. *Psalms* 25:18. (7) 43:1.
(8) Cf. *Isaiah* 34:5. (9) Cf. *Psalms* 79:12. (10) Cf. *Deuteronomy* 32:42. (11) 86:1.

שֶׁכָּתוּב, וַיֵּרֶד יהוה בֶּעָנָן וַיִּתְיַצֵּב עִמּוֹ שָׁם, וַיִּקְרָא בְשֵׁם יהוה.

《 of 〈 with the 〈 and He 《 there, 〈 with 〈 and stood 〈 in a 〈 And Hashem 《 it is written:
Hashem. Name called out him cloud descended

CONGREGATION AND *CHAZZAN* RECITE LOUDLY AND IN UNISON:

וַיַּעֲבֹר יהוה עַל פָּנָיו וַיִּקְרָא:

《 and proclaimed: 《 [Moses'] face, 〈 before 〈 And Hashem passed

יהוה, יהוה, אֵל, רַחוּם, וְחַנּוּן, אֶרֶךְ אַפַּיִם, וְרַב חֶסֶד, וֶאֱמֶת,

《 and 〈 in 〈 and 〈 to anger, 〈 Slow 《 and 〈 Compas- 〈 God, 〈 Hashem, 〈 Hashem,
Truth, Kindness Abundant Gracious, sionate

נֹצֵר חֶסֶד לָאֲלָפִים, נֹשֵׂא עָוֹן, וָפֶשַׁע, וְחַטָּאָה, וְנַקֵּה.

《 and Who 〈 and inad- 〈 willful 〈 of 〈 Forgiver 《 for thousands 〈 of 〈 Preserver
absolves. vertent sin, sin, iniquity, [of generations], kindness

וְסָלַחְתָּ לַעֲוֹנֵנוּ וּלְחַטָּאתֵנוּ וּנְחַלְתָּנוּ. סְלַח לָנוּ אָבִינוּ כִּי

〈 for 《 our 〈 us, 〈 Forgive 《 and make us 《 and our sins, 〈 our 〈 May You
Father, Your heritage. iniquities forgive

חָטָאנוּ, מְחַל לָנוּ מַלְכֵּנוּ כִּי פָשָׁעְנוּ. כִּי אַתָּה אֲדֹנָי טוֹב

〈 are 〈 O Lord, 〈 You, 〈 For 《 we have 〈 for 《 our King, 〈 us, 〈 pardon 《 we have
good willfully sinned. sinned;

וְסַלָּח, וְרַב חֶסֶד לְכָל קֹרְאֶיךָ.

《 who call 〈 to all 〈 kind 〈 and 〈 and
upon You. abundantly forgiving,

THE FOLLOWING PRAYER IS RECITED ALOUD RESPONSIVELY.
(IN SOME COMMUNITIES *HASHEM, HASHEM* . . . IS SAID AS A REFRAIN.)

CHAZZAN, THEN CONGREGATION:

יהוה יהוה* אֵל, רַחוּם, וְחַנּוּן, אֶרֶךְ אַפַּיִם, וְרַב חֶסֶד,

《 in 〈 and 《 to anger, 〈 Slow 〈 and 《 Compas- 《 God, 《 Hashem,* 《 Hashem,
Kindness Abundant Gracious, sionate

וֶאֱמֶת. נֹצֵר חֶסֶד לָאֲלָפִים, נֹשֵׂא עָוֹן, וָפֶשַׁע, וְחַטָּאָה, וְנַקֵּה.[1]

《 and Who 〈 and inad- 《 willful 《 of 〈 Forgiver 《 for thousands 〈 of 〈 Preserver 《 and
absolves. vertent sin, sin iniquity, [of generations], kindness Truth,

וְסָלַחְתָּ לַעֲוֹנֵנוּ וּלְחַטָּאתֵנוּ וּנְחַלְתָּנוּ.[2]

《 and make us 《 and our sins, 〈 our 〈 May You
Your heritage. iniquities forgive

CONGREGATION, THEN *CHAZZAN*:

אֶזְכְּרָה אֱלֹהִים וְאֶהֱמָיָה,[3] בִּרְאוֹתִי כָּל עִיר עַל תִּלָּהּ בְּנוּיָה,[4]

《 built, 〈 its hilltop 〈 on 〈 city 〈 every 〈 when I see 《 and I shall 〈 O God, 〈 I shall
moan, remember,

---

(1) *Exodus* 34:6-7. (2) 34:9. (3) *Psalms* 77:4. (4) Cf. *Jeremiah* 30:18.

◆§ ה' ה' — *Hashem, Hashem.* The acrostic spells the author's name אמתי. See commentary p. 712.

וְעִיר הָאֱלֹהִים¹ מֻשְׁפֶּלֶת עַד שְׁאוֹל² תַּחְתִּיָה,³

《 that is nethermost. 〈 the depth 〈 to 〈 is lowered 〈 of God 〈 while the City

וּבְכָל זֹאת, אָנוּ לְיָה וְעֵינֵינוּ לְיָה.⁴

《 [look] 〈 and our 〈 are 〈 we 《 this, 〈 But
to God.   eyes   God's   despite all

CONGREGATION, THEN *CHAZZAN:*

מִדַּת הָרַחֲמִים עָלֵינוּ הִתְגַּלְגְּלִי, וְלִפְנֵי קוֹנֵךְ תְּחִנָּתֵנוּ הַפִּילִי,⁵

《 cast; 〈 our 〈 your 〈 and 《 extend, 〈 upon us 〈 of Mercy, 〈 O
supplication Creator before   Attribute

וּבְעַד עַמֵּךְ רַחֲמִים שַׁאֲלִי, כִּי כָל לֵבָב דַּוָּי וְכָל רֹאשׁ לָחֱלָי.⁶

《 is ill. 〈 head 〈 and 〈 is 〈 heart 〈 every 〈 for 《 request, 〈 mercy 《 of your 〈 and on
     every pained   people,   behalf

CONGREGATION, THEN *CHAZZAN:*

תָּמַכְתִּי יְתֵדוֹתַי בִּשְׁלֹשׁ עֶשְׂרֵה תֵבוֹת,

《 words 〈 on the Thirteen 〈 my props 〈 I have
[Attributes],   supported

וּבְשַׁעֲרֵי דְמָעוֹת כִּי לֹא נִשְׁלָבוֹת,⁷

《 closed. 〈 they are 〈 for 〈 of tears 〈 and on
never   [in Heaven],   the gates

לָכֵן שָׁפַכְתִּי שִׂיחַ⁸ פְּנֵי בוֹחֵן לִבּוֹת,⁹

《 hearts. 〈 Him 〈 before 〈 my 〈 I have 〈 Therefore,
Who tests   prayer poured out

בָּטוּחַ אֲנִי בָּאֵלֶּה וּבִזְכוּת שְׁלֹשֶׁת אָבוֹת.

《 Patriarchs. 〈 of the three 〈 and in the merit 〈 in these 〈 do I 〈 Trust

CONGREGATION, THEN *CHAZZAN:*

יְהִי רָצוֹן מִלְּפָנֶיךָ שׁוֹמֵעַ קוֹל בְּכִיּוֹת,¹⁰

《 of weeping, 〈 the 〈 Who 《 before You, 〈 the will 《 May
sound hears   it be

שֶׁתָּשִׂים דִּמְעוֹתֵינוּ בְנֹאדְךָ¹¹ לִהְיוֹת,

《 to remain there. 〈 in Your flask, 〈 our tears 〈 that You place

וְתַצִּילֵנוּ מִכָּל גְּזֵרוֹת אַכְזָרִיּוֹת,

《 that are cruel, 〈 decrees 〈 from all 〈 And [that You]
rescue us

כִּי לְךָ לְבַד עֵינֵינוּ תְלוּיוֹת.

《 fixed. 〈 are our eyes 〈 alone 〈 on You 〈 for

TURN TO PAGE 684 FOR אֵל מֶלֶךְ, AND CONTINUE UNTIL THE CONCLUSION OF *SELICHOS*.

---

(1) *Psalms* 87:3. (2) Cf. *Isaiah* 57:9. (3) Cf. *Deuteronomy* 32:22. (4) Cf. *Succah* 5:4. (5) Cf. *Daniel* 9:18. (6) Cf. *Isaiah* 1:5. (7) Cf. *Berachos* 32b. (8) Cf. *Psalms* 142:3. (9) Cf. 7:10. (10) Cf. 6:9. (11) Cf. 56:9.

﴾ סליחות לעשרה בטבת ﴿

﴾ SELICHOS — TENTH OF TEVES ﴿

ALL BEGIN HERE:

סְלַח לָנוּ אָבִינוּ, כִּי בְרוֹב אִוַּלְתֵּנוּ שָׁגִינוּ,

《 we have 〈 of our folly 〈 in the 〈 for 〈 our 〈 us, 〈 Forgive
erred;   abundance   Father,

מְחַל לָנוּ מַלְכֵּנוּ, כִּי רַבּוּ עֲוֹנֵינוּ.

《 our iniquities. 〈many are 〈 for 〈 our King, 〈 us, 〈 pardon

אֵל אֶרֶךְ אַפַּיִם אַתָּה, וּבַעַל הָרַחֲמִים נִקְרֵאתָ, וְדֶרֶךְ

〈 and 《 are You 〈 of Mercy 〈 and 《 are You, 〈 to anger, 〈 Who 〈 God,
the way   called;   Master   is slow

תְּשׁוּבָה הוֹרֵיתָ. גְּדֻלַּת רַחֲמֶיךָ וַחֲסָדֶיךָ, תִּזְכּוֹר הַיּוֹם וּבְכָל

〈 and 〈 this 〈 may You 〈 and Your 〈 of Your 〈 The 《 have You 〈 of
every   day   remember,   kindness   mercy   greatness   taught.   repentance

יוֹם לְזֶרַע יְדִידֶיךָ. תֵּפֶן אֵלֵינוּ בְּרַחֲמִים, כִּי אַתָּה הוּא בַּעַל

〈 the 〈 are 〈 You 〈 for 《 in mercy, 〈 to us 〈 Turn 《 of Your 〈 for the 《 day,
Master   beloved ones. offspring

הָרַחֲמִים. בְּתַחֲנוּן וּבִתְפִלָּה פָּנֶיךָ נְקַדֵּם, כְּהוֹדַעְתָּ לֶעָנָיו

〈 to the 〈 in the man- 《 we 〈 Your 〈 and prayer 〈 With 《 of Mercy.
humble one   ner that You   approach, Presence   supplication
[Moses]   made known

מִקֶּדֶם. מֵחֲרוֹן אַפְּךָ שׁוּב, כְּמוֹ בְתוֹרָתְךָ כָּתוּב.¹ וּבְצֵל כְּנָפֶיךָ

〈 of Your 〈 In the 《 it is 〈 in Your Torah 〈 as 《 turn 〈 of Your 〈 From the 《 in ancient
wings   shadow   written.   back,   anger   fierceness   times.

נֶחֱסֶה וְנִתְלוֹנָן, כְּיוֹם וַיֵּרֶד יהוה בֶּעָנָן.² ❖ תַּעֲבוֹר עַל פֶּשַׁע

〈 sin 〈 Overlook 《 in a 〈 when HASHEM 〈 as on 《 and may 〈 may we
              cloud.   descended   the day   we dwell, find shelter

וְתִמְחֶה אָשָׁם, כְּיוֹם וַיִּתְיַצֵּב עִמּוֹ שָׁם.² תַּאֲזִין שַׁוְעָתֵנוּ

〈 to our cry 〈 Give 《 there. 〈 with him 〈 when He 〈 as on 《 guilt, 〈 and erase
heed   [Moses]   [God] stood   the day

וְתַקְשִׁיב מֶנּוּ מַאֲמַר, כְּיוֹם וַיִּקְרָא בְשֵׁם יהוה,² וְשָׁם נֶאֱמַר:

《 it was 〈 and 《 of 〈 with the 〈 when He 〈 as on 《 [our] 〈 from 〈 and hear
said: there   HASHEM,   Name   called out   the day   declaration,   us

---

(1) Cf. *Exodus* 32:12. (2) 34:5.

﴾ עֲשָׂרָה בְּטֵבֵת / The Tenth of Teves

    Three tragedies occurred in Teves, but in order to avoid serious hardship on the people, the prophets decreed only one fast day, on the anniversary of the most tragic of the occur-

rences. The three events were:

    8 Teves — On the orders of the Egyptian King Ptolemy II (285-246 B.C.E.), seventy Jewish sages were forced to translate the Torah into Greek. Though miracles guided their work on

CONGREGATION AND *CHAZZAN* RECITE LOUDLY AND IN UNISON:

וַיַּעֲבֹר יהוה עַל פָּנָיו וַיִּקְרָא:

《 and 《《 *[Moses']* 〈 before 〈 And HASHEM passed
proclaimed: face,

יהוה, יהוה, אֵל, רַחוּם, וְחַנּוּן, אֶרֶךְ אַפַּיִם, וְרַב חֶסֶד, וֶאֱמֶת,

《 and 〈 in 〈 and 〈 to anger, 〈 Slow 《《 and 〈 Compas- 〈 God, 〈 HASHEM, 〈 HASHEM,
Truth, Kindness Abundant Gracious, sionate

נֹצֵר חֶסֶד לָאֲלָפִים, נֹשֵׂא עָוֹן, וָפֶשַׁע, וְחַטָּאָה, וְנַקֵּה.[1]

《 and Who 〈 and inad- 〈 willful 〈 of 〈 Forgiver 《《 for thousands 〈 of 〈 Preserver
absolves. vertent sin, sin, iniquity, [of generations], kindness

וְסָלַחְתָּ לַעֲוֹנֵנוּ וּלְחַטָּאתֵנוּ וּנְחַלְתָּנוּ.[2] סְלַח לָנוּ אָבִינוּ כִּי

〈 for 《《 our 〈 us, 〈 Forgive 《《 and make us 《《 and our sins, 〈 our 〈 May You
Father, iniquities forgive

חָטָאנוּ, מְחַל לָנוּ מַלְכֵּנוּ כִּי פָשָׁעְנוּ.[3] כִּי אַתָּה אֲדֹנָי טוֹב

〈 are 〈 O Lord, 〈 You, 〈 For 《《 we have 〈 for 《《 our King, 〈 us, 〈 pardon 《《 we have
good willfully sinned. sinned;

וְסַלָּח, וְרַב חֶסֶד לְכָל קֹרְאֶיךָ.[4]

《《 who call 〈 to all 〈 kind 〈 and 《《 and
upon You. abundantly forgiving,

כִּי עִם יהוה הַחֶסֶד, וְהַרְבֵּה עִמּוֹ פְדוּת.[5] פְּדֵה אֱלֹהִים

〈 O God, 〈 Redeem, 《《 is 〈 with 〈 and 《《 is 〈 HASHEM 〈 with 〈 For
redemption. Him abundant kindness,

אֶת יִשְׂרָאֵל, מִכֹּל צָרוֹתָיו.[6] וְהוּא יִפְדֶּה אֶת יִשְׂרָאֵל, מִכֹּל

〈 from 〈 Israel 〈 shall 〈 And He 《《 its 〈 from all 〈 Israel
all redeem distresses.

עֲוֹנוֹתָיו.[7] פּוֹדֶה יהוה נֶפֶשׁ עֲבָדָיו, וְלֹא יֶאְשְׁמוּ כָּל הַחוֹסִים

〈 those who 〈 – all 《《 and they will not 《《 of His 〈 the 〈 HASHEM redeems 《《 its
take refuge be condemned servants, soul iniquities.

בּוֹ.[8]

《《 in Him.

---

(1) *Exodus* 34:6-7. (2) 34:9. (3) From the weekday *Shemoneh Esrei*.
(4) *Psalms* 86:5. (5) 130:7. (6) 25:22. (7) 130:8. (8) 34:23.

this book, called the Septuagint, the Talmud says "three days of darkness descended on the world," because it was now possible for the unlearned to boast of a superficial, usually erroneous, understanding of the Torah.

9 Teves — Ezra the Scribe and his colleague Nehemiah both died on this date. They led the Jewish people in the rebuilding of the Temple and Jerusalem and forged it into a nation at a time of difficulty and turbulence. The death of Ezra also signified the end of prophecy.

10 Teves — On this fateful day King Nebuchadnezzar began the siege of Jerusalem that resulted in the destruction of the First Temple eighteen months later.

Although the fast's primary focus is on the siege, the other two events are alluded to as well in the *Selichos*.

כְּרַחֵם אָב עַל בָּנִים, כֵּן תְּרַחֵם יהוה עָלֵינוּ.¹ לַיהוה

⟨ To ⟨ on us. ⟨ HASHEM, ⟨ have ⟩ so ⟨⟨ his ⟨ toward ⟨ a ⟨ As merciful
HASHEM   mercy, children, father is as

הַיְשׁוּעָה, עַל עַמְּךָ בִרְכָתֶךָ סֶּלָה.² יהוה צְבָאוֹת עִמָּנוּ,

⟨⟨ is with ⟨ Master of ⟨ HASHEM, ⟨⟨ Selah. ⟨⟨ is Your ⟨ Your ⟨ upon ⟨⟨ is salvation,
us, Legions   blessing, people

מִשְׂגָּב לָנוּ אֱלֹהֵי יַעֲקֹב סֶּלָה.³ יהוה צְבָאוֹת, אַשְׁרֵי אָדָם

⟨ is the ⟨ — praise- ⟨ Master of ⟨ HASHEM, ⟨⟨ Selah. ⟨⟨ of ⟨ is the ⟨ for ⟨ a
man worthy Legions   Jacob, God us stronghold

בֹּטֵחַ בָּךְ.⁴ יהוה הוֹשִׁיעָה, הַמֶּלֶךְ יַעֲנֵנוּ בְיוֹם קָרְאֵנוּ.⁵

⟨⟨ we call. ⟨ on the ⟨ answer ⟨ May the ⟨⟨ save! ⟨ HASHEM, ⟨⟨ in ⟨ who
    day us King   You. trusts

❖ **סְלַח** נָא לַעֲוֹן הָעָם הַזֶּה כְּגֹדֶל חַסְדֶּךָ, וְכַאֲשֶׁר נָשָׂאתָה

⟨ You have ⟨ and as ⟨⟨ of Your ⟨ according to ⟨ of this people ⟨ the ⟨ please, ⟨ Forgive,
forgiven   kindness, the greatness   iniquity

לָעָם הַזֶּה מִמִּצְרַיִם וְעַד הֵנָּה,⁶ וְשָׁם נֶאֱמַר:

⟨⟨ it was said: ⟨ And there ⟨⟨ now. ⟨ until ⟨ from Egypt ⟨ this people

ALL, ALOUD AND IN UNISON:

וַיֹּאמֶר יהוה סָלַחְתִּי כִּדְבָרֶךָ.⁷

⟨⟨ according to ⟨ I have ⟨⟨ And HASHEM said:
your word! forgiven

ALL CONTINUE:

הַטֵּה אֱלֹהַי אָזְנְךָ וּשְׁמָע, פְּקַח עֵינֶיךָ וּרְאֵה שֹׁמְמֹתֵינוּ,

⟨⟨ our desolation, ⟨ and see ⟨ Your eyes ⟨ open ⟨⟨ and listen; ⟨ Your ear, ⟨ my God, ⟨ Incline,

וְהָעִיר אֲשֶׁר נִקְרָא שִׁמְךָ עָלֶיהָ, כִּי לֹא עַל צִדְקֹתֵינוּ אֲנַחְנוּ

⟨ do we ⟨ of our ⟨ because ⟨ not ⟨ for ⟨⟨ upon; ⟨ Your Name is ⟨ which ⟨ and [that
righteousness   proclaimed   of] the city

מַפִּילִים תַּחֲנוּנֵינוּ לְפָנֶיךָ, כִּי עַל רַחֲמֶיךָ הָרַבִּים. אֲדֹנָי

⟨ O Lord, ⟨⟨ which is ⟨ of Your ⟨ because ⟨ but ⟨ before ⟨ our ⟨ cast
abundant. compassion,   You; supplications

שְׁמָעָה, אֲדֹנָי סְלָחָה, אֲדֹנָי הַקְשִׁיבָה, וַעֲשֵׂה אַל תְּאַחַר,

⟨⟨ delay; ⟨ do not ⟨⟨ and act, ⟨ be attentive, ⟨ O Lord, ⟨⟨ forgive; ⟨ O Lord, ⟨⟨ heed;

לְמַעַנְךָ אֱלֹהַי, כִּי שִׁמְךָ נִקְרָא עַל עִירְךָ וְעַל עַמֶּךָ.⁸

⟨⟨ Your ⟨ and ⟨ Your ⟨ upon ⟨ is ⟨ Your ⟨ for ⟨⟨ my God, ⟨ for Your
people. upon City proclaimed Name   sake,

---

(1) Cf. *Psalms* 103:13. (2) 3:9. (3) 46:8. (4) 84:13. (5) 20:10.
(6) *Numbers* 14:19. (7) 14:20. (8) *Daniel* 9:18-19.

אֱלֹהֵינוּ וֵאלֹהֵי אֲבוֹתֵינוּ

《 of our forefathers: 〈 and the God 〈 Our God

אֶזְכְּרָה* מָצוֹק אֲשֶׁר קְרָאָנִי,

《 befell me; 〈 that 〈 the distress 〈 I shall recall*

בִּשָׁלֹשׁ מַכּוֹת בַּחֹדֶשׁ הַזֶּה הִכַּנִי,

《 did He strike me. 〈 in this month 〈 blows 〈 with three

גָּדְעַנִי הֱנִיאַנִי הִכְאַנִי, אַךְ עַתָּה הֶלְאָנִי.[1]

《 He has 〈 now 〈 indeed,《 He grieved 《 He thwarted 《 He cut
wearied me.   me,   me,   me down,

דְּעֲכַנִי בִשְׁמוֹנָה בּוֹ שְׂמָאלִית וִימָנִית,

《 and on 〈 on the left 〈 of [this 〈 on the 〈 He darkened
the right.   month],   eighth   me

הֲלֹא שְׁלָשְׁתָּן קָבַעְתִּי תַעֲנִית,[2]

《 as fasts. 〈 I instituted 〈 the three days 〈 Is it not
[described below] so that

וּמֶלֶךְ יָוָן אִנְּסַנִי לִכְתּוֹב דַּת יְוָנִית,

《 into 〈 the 〈 to 〈 forced 〈 of 〈 The
Greek. Torah translate   me   Greece king

עַל גַּבִּי חָרְשׁוּ חוֹרְשִׁים, הֶאֱרִיכוּ מַעֲנִית.[3]

《 the furrow. 〈 they lengthened 《 the plowers; 〈 plowed 〈 my back 〈 On

זוֹעַמְתִּי בְּתִשְׁעָה בּוֹ בִּכְלִמָּה וָחֶפֶר,

《 and 〈 with 〈 of [this 〈 on the 〈 I was
disgrace; humiliation month]   ninth   scorned

חָשַׁךְ מֵעָלַי מְעִיל הוֹד וָצֶפֶר,

《 and the 〈 of 〈 the 〈 from 〈 [God]
crown. majesty mantle   me   removed

טָרֹף טֹרַף[4] בּוֹ הַנּוֹתֵן אִמְרֵי שֶׁפֶר,[5] הוּא עֶזְרָא הַסּוֹפֵר.

《 the Scribe. 〈 Ezra 〈 — that 《 of beauty 〈 of 〈 was the 〈 on [this 〈 Torn away
is,   [prophecy] sayings   giver   day]

יוֹם עֲשִׂירִי צֻוָּה בֶן בּוּזִי הַחוֹזֶה, כְּתָב לְךָ[6] בְּסֵפֶר הַמַּחֲזֶה,

《 of 〈 in the 〈 for 〈 Record 《 the 《 of [Ezekiel] 〈 command- 《 of the 〈 On the
prophecy   book   yourself   seer: Buzi, the son   ed was   tenth,   day

לְזִכָּרוֹן לְעַם נָמֵס וְנִבְזֶה,[7] אֶת עֶצֶם הַיּוֹם הַזֶּה.[8]

《 of this date. 〈 the essence 《 and dis- 〈 that is 〈 for the 〈 — as a re-
graced — wretched nation membrance

---

(1) *Job* 16:7. (2) Cf. *Orach Chaim* 580:2. (3) Cf. *Psalms* 129:3. (4) *Genesis* 37:33.
(5) 49:21; see *Iyun Tefillah*. (6) *Ezekiel* 24:2. (7) Cf. *I Samuel* 15:9. (8) *Ezekiel* 24:2.

◆§ אֶזְכְּרָה — *I shall recall*. The author signed his name, יוֹסֵף, in the acrostic of the final stanza.

מִנְיַן סֵדֶר חֲדָשִׁים בַּעֲשָׂרָה בּוֹ הָעִיר,

‹‹ [Ezekiel] aroused ‹ in that ‹‹ – in the ‹‹ of the ‹ of the ‹ In the
[lamenting]; [month] tenth one, months order count

נְהִי וִילֵל בְּמוֹ פִי אַפְעִיר,[1]

‹‹ I scream. ‹ with my ‹ and ‹ lament
mouth itself wailing

סֵדֶר פֻּרְעָנִיּוֹת בְּתוֹךְ לְבָבִי יַבְעִיר,

‹‹ burns; ‹ my heart ‹ within ‹ of calamities ‹ The sequence

בְּבֹא אֵלַי הַפָּלִיט לֵאמֹר הֻכְּתָה הָעִיר.[2]

‹‹ The City has been conquered. ‹‹ saying, ‹ did the fugitive ‹ to me ‹ when come

עַל אֵלֶּה עַל פָּנַי אָבָק זֵרִיתִי,[3]

‹‹ I spread; ‹ dust ‹ my ‹ upon ‹‹ these ‹ For
face [tragedies],

פָּצְתִּי עַל אַרְבַּעְתָּן[4] לוּ חֵץ בְּלִבִּי יָרִיתִי,

‹‹ I had ‹ into my ‹ an ‹ If ‹‹ all four ‹ because ‹ I ex-
shot; heart arrow only of them: of claimed,

צָרוֹת עַל אֵלֶּה קֶבֶר לִי כָּרִיתִי,

‹‹ I had dug! ‹ for myself ‹ a grave ‹ [if only] over these misfortunes

צַדִּיק הוּא יהוה כִּי פִּיהוּ מָרִיתִי.[5]

‹‹ I have disobeyed. ‹ His utterance ‹ for ‹‹ HASHEM, ‹ is ‹ Righteous

קָרָאתִי שְׁמְךָ מִתְנַחֵם עַל רָעָתִי,

‹‹ the evil that ‹ over ‹ [You] Who ‹‹ Your ‹ I called out
befalls me; relents Name,

רְאֵה עָנְיִי וּשְׁמַע קוֹל פְּגִיעָתִי,

‹‹ of my prayer. ‹ the sound ‹ and hear ‹‹ my affliction, ‹ see

שְׁמַע תְּחִנָּתִי, חִישׁ נָא יְשׁוּעָתִי,

‹‹ my salvation. ‹ please, ‹ hasten, ‹‹ my supplication; ‹ Hear

אַל תַּעְלֵם אָזְנְךָ לְרַוְחָתִי לְשַׁוְעָתִי.[6]

‹‹ from my cry. ‹‹ from [my ‹ Your ‹ avert ‹ Do
request for] relief, ear not

❖ יֶרַח טֵבֵת מְאֹד לָקִיתִי בּוֹ, וְנִשְׁתַּנּוּ עָלַי סִדְרֵי נְתִיבוֹ,

‹‹ course. ‹ was its ‹ against ‹ And ‹‹ in it. ‹ was I ‹ – exceed- ‹ of ‹ In the
ordinary me, altered, smitten ingly Teves month

סָרַרְתִּי פְּשָׁעָתִי, יְגַלֶּה לִי טוּבוֹ, הָאוֹמֵר לַיָּם עַד פֹּה תָבֹא.[7]

‹‹ may you ‹ here ‹ [Only] ‹ the ‹ – the One ‹‹ His ‹ to ‹ may He ‹‹ I sinned; ‹ I strayed,
come! up to sea: Who tells goodness me [now] reveal

---

(1) Cf. *Psalms* 119:131. (2) Cf. *Ezekiel* 33:21. (3) Cf. *Exodus* 32:20. (4) The translation of the Torah, the death of Ezra and end of prophecy, the beginning of the siege of Jerusalem, and the news of its fall. (5) *Lamentations* 1:18. (6) 3:56. (7) Cf. *Job* 38:11.

**AN INDIVIDUAL PRAYING WITHOUT A *MINYAN* OMITS THE NEXT TWO PARAGRAPHS,
BEGINNING אֵל מֶלֶךְ, *O GOD, KING,* AND 'ה, *HASHEM.***

אֵל מֶלֶךְ יוֹשֵׁב עַל כִּסֵּא רַחֲמִים, מִתְנַהֵג בַּחֲסִידוּת, מוֹחֵל

⟨ Who ⟨⟨ with ⟨ Who acts ⟨⟨ of mercy, ⟨ the ⟨ on ⟨ Who ⟨ King ⟨ O God,
pardons kindness, throne sits

עֲוֹנוֹת עַמּוֹ, מַעֲבִיר רִאשׁוֹן רִאשׁוֹן, מַרְבֶּה מְחִילָה לַחַטָּאִים

⟨ to uninten- ⟨ pardon ⟨ Who abun- ⟨ by one, ⟨ [sins] one ⟨ Who ⟨⟨ of His ⟨ the sins
tional sinners dantly grants removes people,

וּסְלִיחָה לַפּוֹשְׁעִים, עֹשֶׂה צְדָקוֹת עִם כָּל בָּשָׂר וָרוּחַ, לֹא

⟨— not ⟨⟨ and ⟨ [beings ⟨ all ⟨ with ⟨ acts of ⟨ Who ⟨⟨ to willful ⟨ and
spirit of] flesh generosity performs sinners, forgiveness

כְרָעָתָם תִּגְמוֹל. ❖ אֵל הוֹרֵיתָ לָּנוּ לוֹמַר שְׁלֹשׁ עֶשְׂרֵה,

⟨⟨ the Thirteen ⟨ to recite ⟨ us ⟨ You ⟨ O ⟨⟨ do You repay ⟨ in accord with
[Attributes of Mercy]; taught God, them! their wickedness

וּזְכוֹר לָנוּ הַיּוֹם בְּרִית שְׁלֹשׁ עֶשְׂרֵה, כְּמוֹ שֶׁהוֹדַעְתָּ לֶעָנָיו

⟨ to the humble ⟨ You made ⟨ as ⟨⟨ of [these] Thirteen, ⟨ the ⟨ today ⟨ for us ⟨ remember
one [Moses] known covenant

מִקֶּדֶם, כְּמוֹ שֶׁכָּתוּב, וַיֵּרֶד יהוה בֶּעָנָן וַיִּתְיַצֵּב עִמּוֹ שָׁם,

⟨⟨ there, ⟨ with ⟨ and stood ⟨ in a cloud ⟨ And Hashem ⟨⟨ it is written: ⟨ as ⟨⟨ in ancient
him descended times,

וַיִּקְרָא בְשֵׁם יהוה.

⟨⟨ of ⟨ with the ⟨ and He
Hashem. Name called out

CONGREGATION AND *CHAZZAN* RECITE LOUDLY AND IN UNISON:

וַיַּעֲבֹר יהוה עַל פָּנָיו וַיִּקְרָא:

⟨⟨ and ⟨⟨ [Moses'] ⟨ before ⟨ And Hashem passed
proclaimed: face,

יהוה, יהוה, אֵל, רַחוּם, וְחַנּוּן, אֶרֶךְ אַפַּיִם, וְרַב חֶסֶד, וֶאֱמֶת,

⟨⟨ and ⟨ in ⟨ and ⟨ to anger, ⟨ Slow ⟨⟨ and ⟨ Compas- ⟨ God, ⟨ Hashem, ⟨ Hashem,
Truth, Kindness Abundant Gracious, sionate

נֹצֵר חֶסֶד לָאֲלָפִים, נֹשֵׂא עָוֹן, וָפֶשַׁע, וְחַטָּאָה, וְנַקֵּה.

⟨⟨ and Who ⟨ and inad- ⟨ willful ⟨ of ⟨ Forgiver ⟨ for thousands ⟨ of ⟨ Preserver
absolves. vertent sin, sin, iniquity, [of generations], kindness

וְסָלַחְתָּ לַעֲוֹנֵנוּ וּלְחַטָּאתֵנוּ וּנְחַלְתָּנוּ. סְלַח לָנוּ אָבִינוּ כִּי

⟨ for ⟨⟨ our ⟨ us, ⟨ Forgive ⟨⟨ and make us ⟨⟨ and our sins, ⟨ our ⟨ May You
Father, Your heritage. iniquities forgive

חָטָאנוּ, מְחַל לָנוּ מַלְכֵּנוּ כִּי פָשָׁעְנוּ. כִּי אַתָּה אֲדֹנָי טוֹב

⟨ are ⟨ O Lord, ⟨ You, ⟨ For ⟨⟨ we have ⟨ for ⟨⟨ our King, ⟨ us, ⟨ pardon ⟨⟨ we have
good willfully sinned. sinned;

וְסָלַח, וְרַב חֶסֶד לְכָל קֹרְאֶיךָ.

and — and abundantly forgiving, — kind — and — to all — who call upon You.

אֱלֹהִים, בָּאוּ גוֹיִם בְּנַחֲלָתֶךָ, טִמְּאוּ אֶת הֵיכַל קָדְשֶׁךָ,

O God! — Entered have the — nations — into Your inheritance; — they have defiled — the Sanctuary — of Your holiness;

שָׂמוּ אֶת יְרוּשָׁלַיִם לְעִיִּים.[1] אֱלֹהִים, זֵדִים קָמוּ עָלֵינוּ,

they have turned — Jerusalem — into heaps [of rubble]. — O God! — Trans-gressors — have arisen — against us,

וַעֲדַת עָרִיצִים בִּקְשׁוּ נַפְשֵׁנוּ, וְלֹא שָׂמוּךָ לְנֶגְדָּם.[2]

and a company — of ruthless men — has sought — our soul; — and they have not set You — in front of themselves.

כְּרַחֵם אָב עַל בָּנִים, כֵּן תְּרַחֵם יהוה עָלֵינוּ. לַיהוה

As merciful — as — a father is — toward — his children, — so — have mercy, — Hashem, — on us. — To Hashem

הַיְשׁוּעָה, עַל עַמְּךָ בִרְכָתֶךָ סֶּלָה. יהוה צְבָאוֹת עִמָּנוּ,

is salvation, — upon — Your people — Your blessing, — Selah. — Hashem, — Master of Legions, — is with us,

מִשְׂגָּב לָנוּ אֱלֹהֵי יַעֲקֹב סֶּלָה. יהוה צְבָאוֹת, אַשְׁרֵי אָדָם

a stronghold — for us — is the God — of Jacob, — Selah. — Hashem — Master of Legions — praise-worthy — is the man

בֹּטֵחַ בָּךְ. יהוה הוֹשִׁיעָה, הַמֶּלֶךְ יַעֲנֵנוּ בְיוֹם קָרְאֵנוּ.

who trusts — in You. — Hashem, — save! — May the King — answer us — on the day — we call.

אֱלֹהֵינוּ וֵאלֹהֵי אֲבוֹתֵינוּ

Our God — and the God — of our forefathers:

אֶבֶן הָרֹאשָׁה,*[3] לְעִיִּים וְלַחֲרִישָׁה,

The keystone* [the Temple] — has become a heap of rubble, — and a place for plowing,

וְנוֹחֲלֵי מוֹרָשָׁה, מְנוֹד רֹאשׁ בַּלְאֻמִּים.[4]

and the heirs — of the [Torah] heritage — have become — a cause for the shaking — of heads [in conster-nation] — among the nations.

---

(1) *Psalms* 79:1. (2) Cf. 86:14. (3) Cf. *Zechariah* 4:7. (4) *Psalms* 44:15.

∾§ אֶבֶן הָרֹאשָׁה — *The keystone.* The acrostic spells the author's name, אַבְרָהָם בַּר   מְנַחֵם חֲזַק, *Avraham bar Menachem, may he be strong.*

בְּקִרְבִּי לֵב נִכְאָב, נִדְוֶה וְנִדְאָב,

《 and 〈 that is 《 that 〈 is a 〈 Within
anguished. pained aches, heart me

נִשְׁאַרְנוּ כְּאֵין אָב, וְהָיִינוּ כִּיתוֹמִים.¹

《 like orphans. 〈 and we 《 a 〈 as if 〈 We were
became father, without left

רַכָּה וַעֲנֻגָּה,² בַּשׁוֹשַׁנִּים סוּגָה,³

《 hedged 〈 with roselike 《 and 〈 [Israel was]
about; [commandments] delicate, tender

וְעַתָּה הִיא נוּגָה,⁴ מְסוּרָה בְּיַד קָמִים.

《 of her 〈 into the 〈 given over 《 is 〈 she 〈 and now
foes. hand afflicted,

הָיְתָה כְּאַלְמָנָה,⁵ קִרְיָה נֶאֱמָנָה,⁶

《 that was 〈 – the city 《 like a 〈 She
faithful. [Jerusalem] widow became

וְזֶרַע מִי מָנָה,⁷ נִמְכְּרוּ בְּלֹא דָמִים.

《 money. 〈 for no 〈 have been 《 can count 〈 – [that for- 《 And the
sold [them]? – merly,] Who offspring

מְעֻנָּגָה וְרַכָּה,⁸ צָלְחָה לִמְלוּכָה,⁹

《 to sovereignty, 〈 succeeded 〈 and 〈 [Babylon which
tender was] delicate

וּמַעֲנִיתָה אָרְכָה,¹⁰ זֶה כַּמֶּה שָׁנִים וְיָמִים.

《 and days. 〈 years 〈 many 〈 these 〈 she lengthened 〈 and her
[upon me] furrow

בֵּית יַעֲקֹב לִבְזָה, לְלַעַג וּלְעֶזָה,

《 and to 〈 to scorn, 〈 has been 〈 of 〈 The
slander; [relegated] Jacob House
to plunder,

וְהָעִיר הָעַלִּיזָה,¹¹ לְמַטָּעֵי כְרָמִים.¹²

《 vineyards. 〈 has become 《 that was 〈 and the city
a place to plant exuberant [Jerusalem]

רְוִוּיָה תַּרְעֵלָה, בְּיַד בְּנֵי עַוְלָה,

《 of 〈 of 〈 by the 《 with poison, 〈 She is
iniquity people hands drunk

הָרְצוּיָה כְעוֹלָה, וְכִקְטֹרֶת הַסַּמִּים.

《 of spices. 〈 and as 《 as an 〈 – [the city]
the incense elevation- that had been
offering as favored

---

(1) Cf. *Lamentations* 5:3. (2) Cf. *Deuteronomy* 28:56. (3) Cf. *Song of Songs* 7:3.
(4) Cf. *Lamentations* 1:4. (5) 1:1. (6) *Isaiah* 1:21. (7) *Numbers* 23:10. (8) Cf. *Isaiah* 47:1.
(9) Cf. *Ezekiel* 16:13. (10) Cf. *Psalms* 129:3. (11) Cf. *Isaiah* 22:2. (12) *Micah* 1:6.

מָאֲסָה לְזָנוֹחַ, תּוֹרַת אֲבִי זָנוֹחַ,[1]

She disdained ⟩ to forsake ⟩ the Torah ⟩ of [Moses, called] Avi Zanoach,

וְלֹא מָצְאָה מָנוֹחַ, לֵילוֹת וְגַם יָמִים.

so she did not ⟩ find ⟩ any rest, ⟩ by night ⟩ and also ⟩ by day.

נוֹרָא אֵל עֶלְיוֹן, מִמְּךָ יְהִי צִבְיוֹן,

O awesome One, ⟩ God ⟩ the Most High, ⟩ from You ⟩ may there be ⟩ a desire,

לְהָשִׁיב לְרִיב צִיּוֹן, שְׁנַת שִׁלּוּמִים.[2]

to recompense ⟩ the grievance ⟩ of Zion ⟩ with a year ⟩ of retribution.

חַדֵּשׁ יָמֵינוּ כְּקֶדֶם,[3] מְעֹנָה אֱלֹהֵי קֶדֶם,[4]

Renew ⟩ our days ⟩ as of old, ⟩ You Whose dwelling is in heaven, ⟩ God ⟩ of eternity.

וְלַבֵּן כַּצֶּמֶר אָדֹם, וְכַשֶּׁלֶג כְּתָמִים.[5]

Whiten ⟩ like wool, ⟩ the crimson [sins], ⟩ and [whiten] like snow, ⟩ the stains [of sin].

❖ חַזְּקֵנוּ בְּיִרְאָתֶךָ, וּבְקִיּוּם תּוֹרָתֶךָ,

Strengthen us ⟩ in [our] reverence of You ⟩ and in the fulfillment ⟩ of Your Torah.

וּפָקְדֵנוּ בִּישׁוּעָתֶךָ, אֵל מָלֵא רַחֲמִים.

Recall us ⟩ with your salvation, ⟩ O God ⟩ Who is full ⟩ of mercy.

AN INDIVIDUAL PRAYING WITHOUT A *MINYAN* OMITS THE NEXT TWO PARAGRAPHS, BEGINNING אֵל מֶלֶךְ, *O GOD, KING,* AND ה', *HASHEM.*

אֵל מֶלֶךְ יוֹשֵׁב עַל כִּסֵּא רַחֲמִים, מִתְנַהֵג בַּחֲסִידוּת, מוֹחֵל

O God, ⟩ King ⟩ Who sits ⟩ on ⟩ the throne ⟩ of mercy, ⟩ Who acts ⟩ with kindness, ⟩ Who pardons

עֲוֹנוֹת עַמּוֹ, מַעֲבִיר רִאשׁוֹן רִאשׁוֹן, מַרְבֶּה מְחִילָה לַחַטָּאִים

the sins ⟩ of His people, ⟩ Who removes ⟩ [sins] one ⟩ by one, ⟩ Who abundantly grants ⟩ pardon ⟩ to unintentional sinners

וּסְלִיחָה לַפּוֹשְׁעִים, עֹשֶׂה צְדָקוֹת עִם כָּל בָּשָׂר וָרוּחַ, לֹא

and forgiveness ⟩ to willful sinners, ⟩ Who performs ⟩ acts of ⟩ generosity ⟩ with ⟩ all ⟩ [beings of] flesh ⟩ and spirit — not

כְּרָעָתָם תִּגְמוֹל. ❖ אֵל הוֹרֵיתָ לָּנוּ לוֹמַר שְׁלֹשׁ עֶשְׂרֵה, וּזְכוֹר

in accord with ⟩ their wickedness ⟩ do You ⟩ repay them! ⟩ O God, ⟩ You taught ⟩ us ⟩ to recite ⟩ the Thirteen [Attributes of Mercy]; ⟩ remember

---
(1) *I Chronicles* 4:18; *Megillah* 13a. (2) Cf. *Isaiah* 34:8.
(3) *Lamentations* 5:21. (4) *Deuteronomy* 33:27. (5) Cf. *Isaiah* 1:18.

לָנוּ הַיּוֹם בְּרִית שְׁלֹשׁ עֶשְׂרֵה, כְּמוֹ שֶׁהוֹדַעְתָּ לֶעָנָיו מִקֶּדֶם, כְּמוֹ

⟨ as ⟨⟨ in ancient ⟨ to the humble ⟨ You made ⟨ as ⟨⟨ of [these] Thirteen, ⟨ the ⟨ today ⟨ for us
times, one [Moses] known covenant

שֶׁכָּתוּב, וַיֵּרֶד יהוה בֶּעָנָן וַיִּתְיַצֵּב עִמּוֹ שָׁם, וַיִּקְרָא בְשֵׁם יהוה.

⟨⟨ of ⟨ with the ⟨ and He ⟨⟨ there, ⟨ with ⟨ and stood ⟨ in a ⟨ And HASHEM ⟨⟨ it is written:
HASHEM. Name called out him cloud descended

CONGREGATION AND *CHAZZAN* RECITE LOUDLY AND IN UNISON:

וַיַּעֲבֹר יהוה עַל פָּנָיו וַיִּקְרָא:

⟨⟨ and ⟨⟨ [Moses'] ⟨ before ⟨ And HASHEM passed
proclaimed: face,

יהוה, יהוה, אֵל, רַחוּם, וְחַנּוּן, אֶרֶךְ אַפַּיִם, וְרַב חֶסֶד, וֶאֱמֶת,

⟨⟨ and ⟨ in ⟨ and ⟨ to anger, ⟨ Slow ⟨⟨ and ⟨ Compas- ⟨ God, ⟨ HASHEM, ⟨ HASHEM,
Truth, Kindness Abundant Gracious, sionate

נֹצֵר חֶסֶד לָאֲלָפִים, נֹשֵׂא עָוֹן, וָפֶשַׁע, וְחַטָּאָה, וְנַקֵּה.

⟨⟨ and Who ⟨ and inad- ⟨ willful ⟨ of ⟨ Forgiver ⟨⟨ for thousands ⟨ of ⟨ Preserver
absolves. vertent sin, sin, iniquity, [of generations], kindness

וְסָלַחְתָּ לַעֲוֹנֵנוּ וּלְחַטָּאתֵנוּ וּנְחַלְתָּנוּ. סְלַח לָנוּ אָבִינוּ כִּי

⟨ for ⟨⟨ our ⟨ us, ⟨ Forgive ⟨⟨ and make us ⟨⟨ and our sins, ⟨ our ⟨ May You
Father, iniquities Your heritage. forgive

חָטָאנוּ, מְחַל לָנוּ מַלְכֵּנוּ כִּי פָשָׁעְנוּ. כִּי אַתָּה אֲדֹנָי טוֹב

⟨ are ⟨ O Lord, ⟨ You, ⟨ For ⟨⟨ we have ⟨ for ⟨⟨ our King, ⟨ us, ⟨ pardon ⟨⟨ we have
good willfully sinned. sinned;

וְסַלָּח, וְרַב חֶסֶד לְכָל קֹרְאֶיךָ.

⟨⟨ who call ⟨ to all ⟨ kind ⟨ and ⟨⟨ and
upon You. abundantly forgiving,

THE FOLLOWING PRAYER IS RECITED ALOUD RESPONSIVELY.
(IN SOME COMMUNITIES *HASHEM, HASHEM . . .* IS SAID AS A REFRAIN.)

CHAZZAN, THEN CONGREGATION:

אֲבוֹתַי,* כִּי בָטְחוּ, בְּשֵׁם אֱלֹהֵי צוּרִי,

⟨⟨ my Rock, ⟨ of God, ⟨ in the ⟨ they ⟨ when ⟨ My forefathers,*
Name trusted

גָּדְלוּ וְהִצְלֵיחוּ, וְגַם עָשׂוּ פֶרִי,

⟨⟨ fruit. ⟨ pro- ⟨ and ⟨ and succeeded, ⟨ grew
duced also

•§ אֲבוֹתַי — *My forefathers.* The author of this prayer, the Tosafist Rabbi Ephraim of Regensburg, Germany (died 1175), included his grandfather's name, אַבְרָהָם, his father's name, יִצְחָק, and his own name, אֶפְרַיִם, in the acrostic.

וּמֵעַת הֲדֵחוּ, וְהָלְכוּ עִמּוֹ קֶרִי,[1]
≪ with stubborn ⟨ with ⟨ and ⟨ they went ⟨ But from
indifference, Him walked astray the time

הָיוּ הָלוֹךְ וְחָסוֹר עַד הַחֹדֶשׁ הָעֲשִׂירִי.[2]
≪ the tenth month. ⟨ until ⟨ diminishing ⟨ progressively ⟨ they were

CONGREGATION, THEN *CHAZZAN*:

בָּעֲשִׂירִי לַחֹדֶשׁ, סָמַךְ מֶלֶךְ בָּבֶל,[3]
≪ of ⟨ did the ⟨ approach ⟨ of the ⟨ On the tenth
Babylon; king month,

וְצָר עַל עִיר הַקֹּדֶשׁ, וְנִקְרַב רַב הַחוֹבֵל,[4]
≪ destroyer. ⟨ did the ⟨ and draw ≪ the Holy City, ⟨ against ⟨ and he
great near laid siege

נִתַּתִּי הָדֵשׁ, וְעֻנֵּיתִי בַבֶּבֶל,
≪ with ⟨ and was ≪ for ⟨ I was
shackles. tortured trampling, given over

וְהָיָה מִדֵּי חֹדֶשׁ לְאֵבֶל כִּנּוֹרִי.[6]
≪ is my ⟨ into ≪ [this] month ⟨ — when- ≪ So now
harp. mourning [recurs] — ever transformed

CONGREGATION, THEN *CHAZZAN*:

רֵאשִׁית בְּכוּרָה,[7] לְרֵאשִׁית הַחֵרֶם,
≪ for ⟨ became ⟨ of her ⟨ The first
destruction. the first first fruits

שֵׁם אֲחֵרִים הִזְכִּירָה,[8] וְהֶעָוֹן גּוֹרֵם,
≪ that caused ⟨ and it was ≪ she ⟨ of other ⟨ The
[her downfall]. [this] sin mentioned, [gods] names

אֵל לֹא הִכִּירָה, וְשָׁטְפָה בְזֶרֶם,
≪ by the ⟨ so she was ⟨ recognize, ⟨ she ⟨ God
current; swept away did not

צָרָה כְּמַבְכִּירָה,[9] כָּעֵת בַּמָּרוֹם תַּמְרִיא.[10]
≪ soars. ⟨ to the ⟨ [pain] ≪ like at a woman's ⟨ she suffers
heights which now first birth, pain

CONGREGATION, THEN *CHAZZAN*:

הָאֱלֹהִים הֵבִיא, יוֹם רָעָה וּמָצוֹר,
≪ and siege; ⟨ of evil ⟨ a day ⟨ brought ⟨ God

צִוָּה צָרַי סְבִיבַי,[11] עוֹלְלַי לִבְצוֹר,[12]
≪ to harvest ⟨ my ≪ all around ⟨ my ⟨ He com-
gleanings me, enemies manded

---

(1) Cf. *Leviticus* 26:21. (2) *Genesis* 8:5. (3) Cf. *Ezekiel* 24:2. (4) *Jonah* 1:6. (5) *Isaiah* 66:23.
(6) *Job* 30:31. (7) Cf. *Hosea* 9:10. (8) Cf. *Exodus* 23:13. (9) *Jeremiah* 4:31. (10) *Job* 39:18.
(11) Cf. *Lamentations* 1:17. (12) Cf. *Deuteronomy* 24:21; cf. *Micah* 7:1.

יוֹם הֵרֵךְ לְבָבִי, וְאֵין כֹּחַ לַעֲצוֹר,[1]

⟨⟨ to retain, ⟨ strength ⟨ when ⟨⟨ of my ⟨ of the ⟨– the
[I had] no heart, weakening day

וְדַבֵּר אֵל נָבִיא, מְשׁוֹל אֶל בֵּית הַמֶּרִי.[2]

⟨⟨ of rebellion ⟨ the ⟨ for ⟨ Compose ⟨⟨ the prophet ⟨ to ⟨ when
[Israel]. house a parable [Ezekiel]: He said

CONGREGATION, THEN *CHAZZAN:*

מִיּוֹשְׁבֵי שַׁעַר, הֶעֱבִיר אַדֶּרֶת,

⟨⟨ the ⟨ He ⟨ at the gates ⟨ From those
mantle; removed [the Sanhedrin] who sat

חֲמָתוֹ כָּאֵשׁ בָּעַר, וְהֵרִים עֲטֶרֶת,

⟨⟨ the crown. ⟨ and He ⟨ burned ⟨ like fire ⟨ His
took off wrath

וּמִלְּבָנוֹן יַעַר,[3] הִשְׁלִיךְ תִּפְאֶרֶת,[4]

⟨⟨ [His] ⟨ he cast ⟨ forest ⟨ From the
splendor; down [the Temple] Lebanon

וְרוּחַ סוֹעָה וְסָעַר,[5] תְּסַמֵּר שַׂעֲרַת בְּשָׂרִי.[6]

⟨⟨ of my flesh. ⟨ the hair ⟨ made stand ⟨ and a ⟨ that is ⟨ and a
on end tempest violent wind

CONGREGATION, THEN *CHAZZAN:*

יְפֵיפִית נִמְשַׁלְתְּ, וְעַתָּה קְדוֹרַנִּית,

⟨⟨ you are ⟨ but now ⟨⟨ likened, ⟨ You [Israel]
blackened, were to a beauty

בְּעָוֹן כִּי כָשַׁלְתְּ,[7] וְלִבֵּךְ אֲחוֹרַנִּית,

⟨⟨ is turned away. ⟨ and your ⟨⟨ you have ⟨ because
heart stumbled, in sin

זְנָבוּךְ וְנֶחֱשַׁלְתְּ,[8] רִאשׁוֹנָה וּשְׁנִית,

⟨⟨ and then ⟨ in the first ⟨ and you ⟨ They
the second, [exile] were attacked you
weakened from behind

וְהָחְתֵּל לֹא חֻתַּלְתְּ,[9] מְעַט צֳרִי.

⟨⟨ of balm. ⟨ [with even] ⟨ wrapped ⟨ you were ⟨ and with
a bit not a bandage

CONGREGATION, THEN *CHAZZAN:*

צַדִּיק הַצּוּר תָּם, נְשׂוֹא עָוֹן נִלְאָה,

⟨⟨ grew ⟨ iniquity ⟨ of ⟨⟨ Who is ⟨ the ⟨ The Righ-
weary; forgiving perfect, Rock teous One,

(1) Cf. *Daniel* 10:8,16. (2) *Ezekiel* 24:3. (3) Cf. *I Kings* 7:2; *Yoma* 39b. (4) Cf. *Lamentations* 2:1. (5) Cf. *Psalms* 55:9. (6) *Job* 4:15. (7) Cf. *Hosea* 14:2. (8) Cf. *Deuteronomy* 25:18. (9) *Ezekiel* 16:4.

מִכְּרוּב לְמִפְתָּן, לִפְנַת גַּג¹ דָּאָה,²

‹‹ did [His presence] ‹ of the ‹ to the ‹ to the ‹ so from the
fly away,   roof   corner   threshold,   cherub [of the
Holy of Holies]

מֵעֲוֹן הַנִּכְתָּם,³ וְצַעֲקָתָם בָּאָה,⁴

‹‹ reached ‹ and [because] ‹ that had ‹ because
[Him].   the outcry of   become   of the sin
their victims   indelible

רַבָּה רָעָתָם,⁵ כְּעֵץ עָשָׂה פֶּרִי.

‹‹ fruit. ‹ that ‹ like a ‹ was ‹ Abundant
bears   tree   their evil

CONGREGATION, THEN *CHAZZAN:*

חִזֵּק כָּל קָמַי, תּוֹכֵן הָעֲלִילוֹת,⁶

‹‹ of all [man's] ‹— He Who keeps ‹‹ my ‹ all ‹ He has
deeds;   account   adversaries   strengthened

כִּי מָלְאוּ יָמַי, בִּרְוֹעַ מִפְעָלוֹת,

‹‹ actions. ‹ with evil ‹ were ‹ filled ‹ for
my days

וּמִבֹּשֶׁת עֲלוּמַי, שָׁכַחְתִּי⁷ גְמוּלוֹת

‹ the ‹ I forgot ‹ of my ‹ In the
kindnesses   youth   shame

נוֹתֵן לַחְמִי וּמֵימַי, פִּשְׁתִּי וְצַמְרִי.⁸

‹‹ and my ‹ my linen, ‹ my water, ‹ of my ‹ of the
wool.   bread, Provider

CONGREGATION, THEN *CHAZZAN:*

קָמַי פִּיהֶם פָּעֲרוּ,⁹ וְנַחֲלָתִי בִּלֵּעוּ,¹⁰

‹‹ they swal- ‹ and my ‹ they opened ‹ their ‹ My ad-
lowed up;   heritage   wide   mouths   versaries

מְאֹד עָלַי גָּבֵרוּ, וְדָמִי שָׁתוּ וְלָעוּ,¹¹

‹‹ and ‹ they ‹ my ‹‹ they overpowered ‹ exceed-
swallowed.   drank   blood   me;   ingly

נָכְרִים עָלַי צָרוּ, וְאֶת אַחַי הֵרֵעוּ,

‹‹ they ‹ and my ‹‹ besieged me, ‹ Foreign
wronged   brethren   nations

הָאוֹמְרִים עָרוּ עָרוּ,¹² בְּנֵי שֵׂעִיר הַחֹרִי.¹³

‹‹ the Horite ‹ of Seir ‹ [they were] ‹‹ destroy, ‹ Destroy, ‹‹ — [they were]
[Edom].   the offspring   those who said,

---

(1) Cf. *Proverbs* 21:9. (2) See *Rosh Hashanah* 31a. (3) Cf. *Jeremiah* 2:22. (4) Cf. *Genesis* 18:21.
(5) Cf. *Genesis* 6:5. (6) Cf. *I Samuel* 2:3. (7) Cf. *Isaiah* 54:4. (8) Cf. *Hosea* 2:7. (9) Cf. *Isaiah* 5:14.
(10) Cf. *II Samuel* 20:19. (11) Cf. *Obadiah* 1:16. (12) *Psalms* 137:7. (13) *Genesis* 36:20.

CONGREGATION, THEN *CHAZZAN:*

אָמְרוּ לְכוּ נִכַלֵּם, וְנַשְׁבִּיתָה זִכְרָם,[1]

《 their 〈 and 〈 let us 〈 Let us 《 They
memory.   obliterate   destroy them   go,   said,

אֵל קַנָּא וְנוֹקֵם גְּמָלֵם, יִשְׂאוּ אֶת שִׁבְרָם,[2]

《 their destruction. 〈 let them 《 requite 〈 and 〈 Who is 〈 O
bear   them;   avenging, jealous God

כְּמַעֲשֵׂיהֶם שַׁלֵּם, וְיֵבְשׁוּ מִשִּׂבְרָם,[3]

《 of their hope, 〈 and let them 〈 pay 〈 In accordance
be ashamed   [them]   with their deeds

כְּאִישׁ חֲלוֹם חוֹלֵם, שְׁלֹשָׁה סַלֵּי חֹרִי.[4]

《 of wicker. 〈 baskets 〈 of three 〈 who dreamt 〈 like the man
a dream   [Pharaoh's baker]

CONGREGATION, THEN *CHAZZAN:*

פְּצָעַי לֹא רֻכָּכָה, וְחַבּוּרוֹתַי רֶצַח,[5]

《 that were 〈 nor have 〈 been 〈 has 〈 My
murderous;   my wounds   softened,   not   bruise

וְעֵינַי הִכְהֵתָה, צוֹפָה לְדוֹדִי צַח,[6]

《 Who is 〈 for my 〈 looking 〈 has grown 〈 my eye
pure.   Beloved   weak

הַעוֹד לֹא שָׁכָכָה חֲמָתוֹ[7] לָנֶצַח,

《 forever? 〈 is His 〈 assuaged 〈 that 〈 Is it
wrath   not   still so

עַל מֶה עָשָׂה כָּכָה, וּמֶה חָרִי.[8]

《 [this] 〈 and 《 this, 〈 has He 〈 what 〈 For
anger?   why   done   reason

CONGREGATION, THEN *CHAZZAN:*

רַחוּם זֶה אֵלִי, אַל לָעַד תִּזְנַח,

《 abandon 〈 forever 〈 do 《 Who is 〈 the 〈 O Merciful
[us].   not   my God, One   One,

אָרְכוּ יְמֵי אֶבְלִי, וְעוֹד לִבִּי נֶאֱנַח,

《 groans. 〈 my 〈 and 《 of my 〈 are the 〈 Lengthened
heart   still   mourning   days

שׁוּבָה אֶל לְאֹהֱלִי, מְקוֹמְךָ אַל תַּנַּח,[9]

《 forsake. 〈 do not 〈 Your 《 to my 〈 O God, 〈 Return,
place   Tent;

---

(1) Cf. *Deuteronomy* 32:21. (2) Cf. *Genesis* 42:26. (3) Cf. *Psalms* 119:116.
(4) *Genesis* 40:16. (5) Cf. *Isaiah* 1:6. (6) Cf. *Song of Songs* 5:10.
(7) Cf. *Esther* 7:10. (8) Cf. *Deuteronomy* 29:23. (9) *Ecclesiastes* 10:4.

שַׁלֵּם יְמֵי אֶבְלִי,¹ כִּי תָבֹא עַל שְׂכָרִי.²

《 my reward. 〈 to 〈 [You 〈 for 《 of my 〈 the 〈 Terminate
        [give] promised] certainly mourning, days
                        to come

CONGREGATION, THEN *CHAZZAN:*

יהוה מְנָת חֶלְקִי,³ חוּשָׁה לִי לְעֶזְרָה,⁴

《 to assist, 〈 to me 〈 hasten 〈 that is allotted 〈 the 《 HASHEM,
                to me,   Portion

וּפְתַחְתָּ שַׂקִּי, שִׂמְחָה לִי לְאַזְּרָה,⁵

《 to gird me. 〈 [so as] with 〈 my 〈 undo
                gladness   sackcloth,

וְתַגִּיהַּ אֶת חָשְׁכִּי, בְּאוֹרְךָ לְהָאִירָה

〈   by illuminating   〈 my darkness, 〈 Brighten
          with Your light

אֶת נֶשֶׁף חִשְׁקִי,⁷ כִּי אַתָּה נֵרִי.⁶

《 are my 〈 You 〈— for 《 that I 〈 the evening
  lamp.   long for

CONGREGATION, THEN *CHAZZAN:*

מִיָּגוֹן וַאֲנָחָה, פְּדֵה אֵל אֶת נַפְשִׁי,

《 my soul. 〈 O 〈 redeem, 〈 and 〈 From
        God,   sighing sorrow

עֲשֵׂה לְעַמְּךָ הֲנָחָה, מַלְכִּי וּקְדוֹשִׁי,

《 my Holy 〈 my 《 relief, 〈 for Your 〈 Provide
    One.   King,   people

תַּהֲפוֹךְ לָרְוָחָה, אֶת צוֹם הַחֲמִישִׁי,

《 of the fifth 〈 the fast 〈 to well-being 〈 Transform
  [month, Av],

לְשָׂשׂוֹן וּלְשִׂמְחָה, צוֹם הָרְבִיעִי וְצוֹם הָעֲשִׂירִי.⁸

《 of the tenth 〈 and the 〈 of the fourth 〈 the 〈 and 〈 and to joy
  [month,   fast [month,   fast gladness
  Teves].   Tammuz]

TURN TO PAGE 684 FOR אֵל מֶלֶךְ, **AND THE CONCLUSION OF** *SELICHOS.*

(1) Cf. *Isaiah* 60:20. (2) *Genesis* 30:33. (3) *Psalms* 16:5. (4) Cf. *38:23.* (5) Cf. *30:12.*
(6) *II Samuel* 22:29; *Psalms* 18:29. (7) *Isaiah* 21:4. (8) Cf. *Zechariah* 8:19.

﷯ סליחות לתענית אסתר ﷽
﷽ SELICHOS – FAST OF ESTHER ﷽

ALL BEGIN HERE:

סְלַח לָנוּ אָבִינוּ, כִּי בְרוֹב אִוַּלְתֵּנוּ שָׁגִינוּ,

《 we have 《 of our folly 《 in the 《 for 《 our 《 us, 《 Forgive
erred; abundance Father,

מְחַל לָנוּ מַלְכֵּנוּ, כִּי רַבּוּ עֲוֹנֵינוּ.

《 our iniquities. 《 many are 《 for 《 our King, 《 us, 《 pardon

אֵל אֶרֶךְ אַפַּיִם אַתָּה, וּבַעַל הָרַחֲמִים נִקְרֵאתָ, וְדֶרֶךְ

《 and 《《 are You 《 of Mercy 《 and 《《 are You, 《 to anger, 《 Who 《 God,
the way called; Master is slow

תְּשׁוּבָה הוֹרֵיתָ. גְּדֻלַּת רַחֲמֶיךָ וַחֲסָדֶיךָ, תִּזְכּוֹר הַיּוֹם וּבְכָל

《 and 《 this 《 may You 《 and Your 《 of Your 《 The 《《 have You 《 of
every day remember, kindness mercy greatness taught. repentance

יוֹם לְזֶרַע יְדִידֶיךָ. תֵּפֶן אֵלֵינוּ בְּרַחֲמִים, כִּי אַתָּה הוּא בַּעַל

《 the 《 are 《 You 《 for 《《 in mercy, 《 to us 《 Turn 《《 of Your 《 for the 《《 day,
Master beloved ones. offspring

הָרַחֲמִים. בְּתַחֲנוּן וּבִתְפִלָּה פָּנֶיךָ נְקַדֵּם, כְּהוֹדַעְתָּ לֶעָנָיו

《 to the 《 in the man- 《《 we 《 Your 《 and prayer 《 With 《《 of Mercy.
humble one ner that You approach, Presence supplication
[Moses] made known

מִקֶּדֶם. מֵחֲרוֹן אַפְּךָ שׁוּב, כְּמוֹ בְתוֹרָתְךָ כָּתוּב.[1] וּבְצֵל כְּנָפֶיךָ

《 of Your 《 In the 《《 it is 《 in Your Torah 《 as 《《 turn 《 of Your 《 From the 《《 in ancient
wings shadow written. back, anger fierceness times.

נֶחֱסֶה וְנִתְלוֹנָן, כְּיוֹם וַיֵּרֶד יהוה בֶּעָנָן.[2] ❖ תַּעֲבוֹר עַל פֶּשַׁע

《 sin 《 Overlook 《《 in a 《 when HASHEM 《 as on 《《 and may 《 may we
cloud. descended the day we dwell, find shelter

וְתִמְחֶה אָשָׁם, כְּיוֹם וַיִּתְיַצֵּב עִמּוֹ שָׁם.[2] תַּאֲזִין שַׁוְעָתֵנוּ

《 to our cry 《 Give 《《 there. 《 with him 《 when He 《 as on 《《 guilt, 《 and erase
heed [Moses] [God] stood the day

---

(1) Cf. *Exodus* 32:12. (2) 34:5.

﷽ תַּעֲנִית אֶסְתֵּר / The Fast of Esther

Taanis Esther, the Fast of Esther, is unique among the fasts in that it commemorates a triumph instead of a tragedy. The miracle that is commemorated by Purim took place on the thirteenth of Adar, when the Jewish people fought and defeated those who had plotted their extermination. It is a foregone conclusion that our ancestors fasted on that day, because the Jewish people never went to war without fasting and repenting in order to be worthy of God's assistance. The fast was named for Queen Esther because the miracle came about through her and also as a reminder that she requested that the people fast for her when she risked her life to intervene with King Ahasuerus.

וְתַקְשִׁיב מֶנּוּ מַאֲמַר, כְּיוֹם וַיִּקְרָא בְשֵׁם יהוה,¹ וְשָׁם נֶאֱמַר:

and hear ‹ from ‹ [our] ‹‹ as on ‹ when He ‹ with the ‹ of ‹ and ‹‹ it was said: ‹ there HASHEM, Name called out the day declaration, us

CONGREGATION AND CHAZZAN RECITE LOUDLY AND IN UNISON:

וַיַּעֲבֹר יהוה עַל פָּנָיו וַיִּקְרָא:

and ‹‹ and ‹‹ [Moses'] ‹ before ‹ And HASHEM passed proclaimed: face,

יהוה, יהוה, אֵל, רַחוּם, וְחַנּוּן, אֶרֶךְ אַפַּיִם, וְרַב חֶסֶד, וֶאֱמֶת,

and ‹ in ‹ and ‹ to anger, ‹ Slow ‹‹ and ‹ Compas- God, ‹ HASHEM, ‹ HASHEM, Truth, Kindness Abundant Gracious, sionate

נֹצֵר חֶסֶד לָאֲלָפִים, נֹשֵׂא עָוֹן, וָפֶשַׁע, וְחַטָּאָה, וְנַקֵּה.²

and Who ‹ and inad- ‹ willful ‹ of ‹ Forgiver ‹‹ for thousands ‹ of ‹ Preserver absolves. vertent sin, sin, iniquity, [of generations], kindness

וְסָלַחְתָּ לַעֲוֹנֵנוּ וּלְחַטָּאתֵנוּ וּנְחַלְתָּנוּ.³ סְלַח לָנוּ אָבִינוּ כִּי

for ‹‹ our ‹ us, ‹ Forgive ‹‹ and make us ‹‹ and our sins, ‹ our ‹ May You Father, iniquities Your heritage. forgive

חָטָאנוּ, מְחַל לָנוּ מַלְכֵּנוּ כִּי פָשָׁעְנוּ.⁴ כִּי אַתָּה אֲדֹנָי טוֹב

are ‹ O Lord, ‹ You, ‹ For ‹‹ we have ‹ for ‹‹ our King, ‹ us, ‹ pardon ‹‹ we have good willfully sinned. sinned;

וְסַלָּח, וְרַב חֶסֶד לְכָל קֹרְאֶיךָ.⁵

who call ‹ to all ‹ kind ‹ and ‹‹ and upon You. abundantly forgiving,

קַוֵּה קִוֵּינוּ אֶל יהוה, וַיֵּט אֵלֵינוּ וַיִּשְׁמַע שַׁוְעָתֵנוּ.⁶ אַף

Even ‹‹ our cry. ‹ and heard ‹ to us, ‹ He ‹‹ HASHEM, ‹ in ‹ We have placed inclined great hope

אֹרַח מִשְׁפָּטֶיךָ יהוה קִוִּינוּךָ, לְשִׁמְךָ וּלְזִכְרְךָ תַּאֲוַת נָפֶשׁ.⁷

of our ‹ are the ‹ and Your ‹ Your ‹‹ we place ‹ HASHEM, ‹ of Your ‹ [when we are] soul. desire remembrance Name hope in You; judgments, on the path

כְּרַחֵם אָב עַל בָּנִים, כֵּן תְּרַחֵם יהוה עָלֵינוּ.⁸ לַיהוה

To ‹‹ on us. ‹ HASHEM, ‹ have ‹ so ‹‹ his ‹ toward ‹ a ‹ As merciful HASHEM mercy, children, father is as

הַיְשׁוּעָה, עַל עַמְּךָ בִרְכָתֶךָ סֶּלָה.⁹ יהוה צְבָאוֹת עִמָּנוּ,

is with ‹ Master of ‹ HASHEM, ‹‹ Selah. ‹ is Your ‹ Your ‹ upon ‹‹ is salvation, us, Legions, blessing, people

מִשְׂגָּב לָנוּ אֱלֹהֵי יַעֲקֹב סֶלָה.¹⁰ יהוה צְבָאוֹת, אַשְׁרֵי אָדָם

is the ‹ – praise- ‹‹ Master of ‹ HASHEM, ‹‹ Selah. ‹‹ of ‹ is the ‹ for ‹ a man worthy Legions Jacob, God us stronghold

---

(1) *Exodus* 34:5. (2) 34:6-7. (3) 34:9. (4) From the weekday *Shemoneh Esrei.* (5) *Psalms* 86:5.
(6) Cf. 40:2. (7) *Isaiah* 26:8. (8) Cf. *Psalms* 103:13. (9) 3:9. (10) Cf. 46:8.

בְּטֵחַ בָּךְ.¹ יהוה הוֹשִׁיעָה, הַמֶּלֶךְ יַעֲנֵנוּ בְיוֹם קָרְאֵנוּ.²

《 we call. 〈 on the 〈 answer 《 May the 《 save! 〈 HASHEM, 《 in 〈 who
day us King You. trusts

❖ סְלַח נָא לַעֲוֹן הָעָם הַזֶּה כְּגֹדֶל חַסְדֶּךָ, וְכַאֲשֶׁר נָשָׂאתָה

〈 You have 〈 and as 《 of Your 〈 according to 〈 of this people 〈 the 〈 please, 〈 Forgive,
forgiven kindness, the greatness iniquity

לָעָם הַזֶּה מִמִּצְרַיִם וְעַד הֵנָּה,³ וְשָׁם נֶאֱמַר:

《 it was said: 〈 And there 《 now. 〈 until 〈 from Egypt 〈 this people

ALL, ALOUD AND IN UNISON:

וַיֹּאמֶר יהוה סָלַחְתִּי כִּדְבָרֶךָ.⁴

《 according to your word! 〈 I have forgiven 《 And HASHEM said:

ALL CONTINUE:

הַטֵּה אֱלֹהַי אָזְנְךָ וּשְׁמָע, פְּקַח עֵינֶיךָ וּרְאֵה שֹׁמְמֹתֵינוּ,

《 our desolation, 〈 and see 〈 Your eyes 〈 open 《 and listen; 〈 Your ear, 〈 my God, 〈 Incline,

וְהָעִיר אֲשֶׁר נִקְרָא שִׁמְךָ עָלֶיהָ, כִּי לֹא עַל צִדְקֹתֵינוּ אֲנַחְנוּ

〈 do we 〈 of our 〈 because 〈 not 〈 for 《 upon; 〈 Your Name is 〈 which 〈 and [that
righteousness proclaimed of] the city

מַפִּילִים תַּחֲנוּנֵינוּ לְפָנֶיךָ, כִּי עַל רַחֲמֶיךָ הָרַבִּים. אֲדֹנָי

〈 O Lord, 《 which is 〈 of Your 〈 because 〈 but 《 before 〈 our 〈 cast
abundant. compassion, You; supplications

שְׁמָעָה, אֲדֹנָי סְלָחָה, אֲדֹנָי הַקְשִׁיבָה, וַעֲשֵׂה אַל תְּאַחַר,

《 delay; 〈 do not 《 and act, 〈 be attentive, 〈 O Lord, 《 forgive; 〈 O Lord, 《 heed;

לְמַעַנְךָ אֱלֹהַי, כִּי שִׁמְךָ נִקְרָא עַל עִירְךָ וְעַל עַמֶּךָ.⁵

《 Your 〈 and 〈 Your 〈 upon 〈 is 〈 Your 〈 for 《 my God, 〈 for Your
people. upon City proclaimed Name sake,

אֱלֹהֵינוּ וֵאלֹהֵי אֲבוֹתֵינוּ

《 of our forefathers: 〈 and the God 〈 Our God

אָדָם* בְּקוּם עָלֵינוּ,⁶ חֵיל אֲחָזַתְנוּ⁷ לִרְעוֹד,

《 [causing us] 〈 seized us, 〈 fear 《 against us, 〈 rose up 〈 When a man*
to tremble; [Haman]

בְּהִסְתַּפְּחוּ לְמַלְכוּת חָנֵף, כִּמְעַט כָּשַׁלְנוּ לִמְעוֹד,

《 and tottered. 〈 stumbled 〈 we 《 of the hypocri- 〈 the 〈 when he joined
nearly tical [Ahasuerus], kingdom

---

(1) *Psalms* 84:13. (2) 20:10. (3) *Numbers* 14:19. (4) 14:20. (5) *Daniel* 9:18-19.
(6) Cf. *Psalms* 124:2; see *Megillah* 11a. (7) Cf. *Exodus* 15:14.

⏴§ אָדָם — *When a man.* After twenty-two
verses following the *Aleph Beis*, the acrostic
spells מְנַחֵם בְּרַבִּי מָכִיר יִחְיֶה אָמֵן וְאָמֵן, *Menachem,*

son of Rabbi Machir, may he live, Amen and
Amen. Rabbi Menachem (Germany; 11th-12th
cent.) also authored the *Hoshana* prayer for the

גָּמְרוּ לְמָכְרֵנוּ כְּתֵל וְחָרִיץ¹ בְּלִי מִסְעוֹד,

‹ They decided › to sell us ‹ like a hill, › and a ditch, › without ‹ any succor. ❯❯

אָמְרוּ לְכוּ וְנַכְחִידֵם מִגּוֹי, וְלֹא יִזָּכֵר שֵׁם יִשְׂרָאֵל עוֹד².

❯❯ They › said, ‹‹ Come, › let us obliterate › them › from ‹ nationhood, › so that ‹‹ the name › bered › will be ‹ of Israel ‹ any longer. ❯❯

דָּלוּ עֵינַי לַמָּרוֹם³, קְרָאתִיךָ אוֹיְבַי לָקוֹב⁴,

‹ Raised › were my eyes ‹ heavenward; ‹‹ I called upon You, › my enemies ‹ to curse, ❯❯

הַכְרֵת שֵׁם וּשְׁאָר⁵ וּמְחֵה שֵׁם לִרְקוֹב⁶,

‹ to cut off › their › name ‹ and › remnant, ‹‹ and › erase ‹ [their] › name ‹ that it › may rot; ❯❯

וְצַר צוֹרְרַי⁷ בְּנִכְלֵיהֶם אֲשֶׁר נִבְּלוּ לַעֲקוֹב⁸,

‹ and to ‹ those who › oppress me › oppress ‹ with their › conspiracy › that ‹ they have › to deal › conspired › treacherously, ❯❯

וַיֹּאמְרוּ לֹא יִרְאֶה יָּהּ, וְלֹא יָבִין אֱלֹהֵי יַעֲקֹב⁹.

‹ [those] › who say, ‹‹ See not › will › God; ‹‹ will › not › understand ‹ the › God ‹ of Jacob. ❯❯

זְרוּיִם עָנָה וַיֻּגֶּה וְלֹא מִלִּבּוֹ לְכַלּוֹתָם¹⁰,

‹ The scattered › [nation] ‹ He tor- › mented, ‹ afflicted, › and it was not ‹ but ‹ in His › heart ‹ to destroy › them; ❯❯

חָבוּ לִפְנִים¹¹ וְרָדָם בַּהֲסָרַת טַבַּעַת¹² לְהַחֲלוֹתָם,

‹ they › sinned, ‹ outwardly, › and He dis- ‹‹ [only] › ciplined them › through ‹ the removal › of [Ahasuerus'] › ring, ‹ to terrify them. ❯❯

טוֹב דִּבְרוֹ הֵקִים לְעֵינֵי הַגּוֹיִם לְהַעֲלוֹתָם,

‹ But the Bene- › ficent One › His ‹ word › He › kept, ‹ the eyes › before ‹ of the › nations ‹ to elevate them: ❯❯

בְּאֶרֶץ אֹיְבֵיהֶם לֹא מְאַסְתִּים וְלֹא גְעַלְתִּים לְכַלֹּתָם¹³.

‹ In the land › of their enemies ‹ I will not ‹ despise them › nor ‹ abhor them, ‹‹ to destroy them. ❯❯

יָדַע רֶמֶז הַקּוֹרוֹת לְעַם מֵעָפָר¹⁴ וּמֵהֲדַס,

‹ [God] made › an ‹ allusion › of what would ‹ transpire › with the › nation ‹ that is com- › pared to dust ‹ and compared › to myrtles, ❯❯

כָּתַב הַסְתֵּר אַסְתִּיר¹⁶* וּמָר דְּרוֹר¹⁷ מִפַּרְדֵּס,

‹ in writing › [in the Torah] ‹ haster astir ‹ [I will hide]* ‹ and mor deror › [pure myrrh], ‹‹ growing in › an orchard. ❯❯

---

(1) See Megillah 14a. (2) Psalms 83:5. (3) Isaiah 38:14. (4) Cf. Numbers 24:10. (5) Cf. Isaiah 14:22. (6) Cf. Proverbs 10:7. (7) Cf. Exodus 23:22. (8) Cf. Numbers 25:18. (9) Psalms 94:7. (10) Cf. Lamentations 3:33. (11) See Megillah 12a. (12) See 14a. (13) Leviticus 26:44. (14) Cf. Genesis 13:16. (15) See Megillah 13a. (16) Deuteronomy 31:18. (17) Exodus 30:23.

Sabbath of Succos, and אָמַר, I make [myself] bitter, recited on the seventeenth of Tammuz (p. 757).

הַסְתֵּר אַסְתִּיר — Haster astir [I will hide]. The Talmud (Chullin 139b), in a play on words, teaches that there are phrases in the Torah that

לְשַׁבּוֹת הָמָן מִמָּחֳרָת,[1] הֲמִן הָעֵץ הָעֵץ[2] קִנְדָּס,

‖ – [he would hang ‖ [the Torah wrote] ⟨ on the morrow ⟨ Haman ⟨ To eliminate
from] a pole. *hamin ha'etz* [of Pesach],
[from the tree],

תַּחַת הַנַּעֲצוּץ יַעֲלֶה בְרוֹשׁ, וְתַחַת הַסִּרְפָּד יַעֲלֶה הֲדַס.[3]

‖ the myrtle ⟨ will ⟨ of the nettle ⟨ and ‖ a cypress ⟨ will ⟨ of the thorn- ⟨ [Also]
[Esther]. arise [Vashti] instead [Mordechai], arise bush [Haman] Instead

מַקְשִׁיב דְּבַר שֶׁקֶר[4] כָּתַב שִׂטְנָה[5] וָעֶצֶב,

‖ and ⟨ an [edict of] ⟨ wrote ⟨ of falsehood ⟨ to ⟨ He who
suffering. slander [Ahasuerus] words hearkened

נִתְעַטֵּף בְּבִגְדֵי שָׂרָד[6] כְּטָעָה בְּמִנְיַן קֵצֶב,[7]

‖ of the set time ⟨ in the ⟨ when he ⟨ of the ⟨ in the ⟨ He robed
[of redemption]; calculation erred priests garments himself

סָדֵר לְהִשְׁתַּמֵּשׁ בְּשׁוֹנִים[8] כְּלֵי הַמַּחֲצֵב,

‖ of the [Temple, ⟨ vessels ⟨ of the ⟨ to make use ⟨ he arranged
made of] hewn stone, various [a banquet]

וַיָּבוֹא גַם הַשָּׂטָן בְּתוֹכָם לְהִתְיַצֵּב.[9]

‖ to stand. ⟨ among ⟨ did the ⟨ also ⟨ and
them Satan come

עַם הַנִּמְצָאִים בְּשׁוּשָׁן בְּאָכְלָם מִזְבַּח עָכְרָם,

‖ that sullied ⟨ of the ⟨ when they ‖ in Shushan, ⟨ who were ⟨ The [Jewish]
them, feast partook located people

פָּעַר פִּיו[10] לְהַשְׁטִינָם וּלְהַסְגִּירָם בְּיַד נוֹתֵן מִכְרָם,

‖ the price for ⟨ of [Haman] ⟨ into the ⟨ and deliver ⟨ to condemn ⟨ his ⟨ [Satan]
[annihilating] who paid hands them them mouth opened
them. wide

צוּר הִסְכִּים לִכְתּוֹב אִגֶּרֶת לְאַבֵּד שִׂבְרָם,

‖ their hope; ⟨ to destroy ⟨ a ⟨ to have ⟨ consented ⟨ The
document written Rock

אָמַרְתִּי אַפְאֵיהֶם, אַשְׁבִּיתָה מֵאֱנוֹשׁ זִכְרָם.[11]

‖ their ⟨ from ⟨ I will ‖ I would ⟨ I said
memory. man eliminate annihilate them;

---

(1) Cf. *Joshua* 5:12. (2) *Genesis* 3:11. (3) *Isaiah* 55:13; see *Megillah* 10b.
(4) Cf. *Proverbs* 29:12. (5) Cf. *Ezra* 4:6. (6) *Exodus* 31:10. (7) See *Megillah* 11b.
(8) Cf. *Esther* 1:7. (9) *Job* 2:1. (10) Cf. *Isaiah* 5:14. (11) *Deuteronomy* 32:26.

---

both sound like the names of the characters in the Purim story and allude to them. Esther, who reigned in a time when God seemed to forsake Israel, is alluded to when God says הַסְתֵּר אַסְתִּיר, *I will conceal My countenance* (*Deuteronomy* 31:18). Mordechai, who was pure and pleasant,

is alluded to in one of the spices used in the Temple incense, מָר דְּרוֹר, *pure myrrh*, which the *Targum* renders מֵירָא דַכְיָא, *meira dachya* (*Exodus* 30:23). The allusion to Haman who was hung on a gallows is from הֲמִן הָעֵץ, *from this tree* (*Genesis* 3:11).

קְדוֹשִׁים מַלְאֲכֵי הַשָּׁרֵת מַר יִבְכָּיוּן בִּצְעָקָה,[1]

The holy ones — the angels — minister — that bitterly wept with outcry:

רַחוּם הַבֵּט לַבְּרִית וְאַל תָּפֵר לְהַרְחִיקָה,

O Merciful One, look to the covenant, and do not annul [it], to reject it.

שָׁמְעָה מוֹרָשָׁה וַתִּלְבַּשׁ בִּגְדֵי אַלְמָנוּת וּמוּעָקָה,

The Heritage [the Torah] heard and donned garments of widowhood and distress;

וַתָּשֶׂם יָדָהּ עַל רֹאשָׁהּ וַתֵּלֶךְ הָלוֹךְ וְזָעָקָה.[2]

she placed her hand upon her head and went forth, walked as she crying out.

תִּשְׁבִּי שָׁם אֵזוֹר שַׂק בְּמָתְנָיו תַּחְבֹּשֶׁת,

The Tishbite [Elijah] placed a belt of sackcloth upon his loins wrapping it around;

מִהֵר וְהוֹדִיעַ יְשֵׁנֵי מַכְפֵּל אָבוֹת שְׁלֹשֶׁת,

he hurried informed slumber Machpelah the Patriarchs those who in — the three.

נָחַץ לְרוֹעֶה מַה לְּךָ נִרְדָּם לְהִתְעַשֶּׁת,

He rushed to the shepherd [Moses], Why do you sleep and not contemplate [the danger]?

קוּם קְרָא אֶל אֱלֹהֶיךָ, אוּלַי יִתְעַשֵּׁת.[3]

Arise, call out to your God; perhaps He will change His mind!

חוֹתָם טִיט אֲשֶׁר נַעֲשָׂה לְבִלְשָׁן סֵפֶר,[4]

That it was a seal of [only] clay — that [on the decree] — had been made to Bilshan [Mordechai] [Elijah] told.

מִנִּינְוֵה לָמְדוּ לְאַחַר גְּזֵרָה כַּעַס לְהָפֵר,[5]

From Nineveh they learned that [even] after a decree [God's] anger can be annulled.

בֶּן קִישׁ הִקִּישׁ דַּלְתוֹת בֵּית הַסֵּפֶר,

The descendant of Kish — [Mordechai] pounded at the doors of the schoolhouse;

וַיְכַס שַׂק וַיֵּשֶׁב עַל הָאֵפֶר.[6]

he covered himself with sackcloth and sat upon ashes.

רִבֵּץ תִּינוֹקוֹת לְפָנָיו יָמִים שְׁלֹשָׁה צָמִים וּמַכְפָּנִים,

He seated children before him for three days, fasting and famished;

---

(1) Cf. *Isaiah* 33:7. (2) *II Samuel* 13:19. (3) *Jonah* 1:6.
(4) See *Esther Rabbah* 7:18. (5) See *Jonah* 3:10. (6) 3:6.

בְּקוֹל יַעֲקֹב¹ לַחֲלוֹשׁ יְדֵי עַז פָּנִים,

》 with the voice 〈 of 〈 Jacob, 〈 to 〈 weaken 〈 hands 《 of the 〈 the 〈 faced one [Esau, Haman's ancestor]. brazen-

יָדָיו אֱמוּנָה² לָאֵל, הַצִּילֵנִי מֵעֶלְבּוֹנִים,

《 from disgraces, 〈 Rescue me 《 to 〈 faithfully 〈 [He lifted] God: [in prayer] his hands

פֶּן יָבוֹא וְהִכַּנִי אֵם עַל בָּנִים.³

《 children. 〈 with 〈 mother 〈 and strike 〈 he 〈 lest me down, come

מִזֶּה אֵלֶּה וּמִזֶּה אֵלֶּה בְּנֵי אֵיתָנַי וְרַבָּנַי,

《 and my 〈 of my mighty 〈 the 《 were 〈 and on 〈 were these 〈 On this masters; [Patriarchs] children those, that side [children], side

כֻּלָּם צָעֲקוּ וַתַּעַל שַׁוְעָתָם אֶל יהוה.⁴

《 HASHEM. 〈 to 〈 did their prayer 〈 and ascend 《 cried out, 〈 they all

יָהּ לְקוֹל רִנּוּן כְּבוֹא שָׁאַל לְפָנַי,

《 in His inner 〈 asked 《 came 〈 of the 〈 when the 〈 God, chamber, [before Him], shouts sound

וּמֶה קוֹל הַצֹּאן הַזֶּה בְּאָזְנָי.⁵

《 in my ears? 〈 is this sound of sheep 〈 What

רוֹעֶה הֱשִׁיבוֹ הֵם קְטַנֵּי קֹדֶשׁ זֶרַע,

《 offspring; 〈 of the 〈 are the 〈 They 《 answered 〈 The shepherd sacred little ones him, [Moses]

יָהּ הַצֵּל לְקוּחֵי לַמָּוֶת מֵאוֹיֵב הָרַע,

《 who is 〈 from the 《 to [their] 〈 those 〈 rescue 〈 O evil. foe death, being sold God,

חַנּוּן נִכְמְרוּ רַחֲמָיו וַיְבַקֵּשׁ לִבְכּוֹת הַמְּאוֹרָע,⁶

《 over the 〈 to weep 〈 and He 《 was His 〈— aroused 《 The Compas- situation. wished mercy, sionate One

וַיְהִי כִּקְרֹא מֶלֶךְ יִשְׂרָאֵל אֶת הַסֵּפֶר וַיִּקְרָע.⁷

《 he tore [it up]. 《 the document, 〈 of Israel 〈 did the 〈 that when 〈 And so king read it was

יְהוּדִי הוֹקִיעַ יְלָדָיו לְמַטָּה וַאֲבִיהֶם לְמַעְלָה,

《 above; 〈 with their 〈 below 〈 [Haman's] 〈 hanged 〈 Then the Jew father sons [Mordechai]

אִישׁ אִישׁ בְּשָׁלֹשׁ אַמּוֹת וְהָרְבִיעִית אַוֵּיר מְגֻלָּה,⁸

《 left open. 〈 space 《 with the fourth 《 cubits, 〈 [taking up] 〈 each man [cubit], three

---

(1) Cf. *Genesis* 27:11. (2) *Exodus* 17:12. (3) *Genesis* 32:12. (4) Cf. *Exodus* 2:23. (5) *I Samuel* 15:14.
(6) Cf. *Genesis* 43:30. (7) *II Kings* 5:7. (8) See *Targum Yerushalmi, Esther* 9:14.

מִשְׁנֶה¹ נָקָם חָזָה וְשָׂמַח וְשָׂח תְּהִלָּה,

The viceroy [Mordechai], ‹ did see; ‹ the ret-ribution ‹ and he rejoiced ‹ and uttered ‹ praise: ≪

אֹתִי הֵשִׁיב עַל כַּנִּי וְאֹתוֹ תָּלָה.²

Me ‹ He restored ‹ to ‹ my post ‹ on ‹ him ‹ and him ‹ He hanged. ≫

❖ וַתִּכְתֹּב אֶסְתֵּר תֹּקֶף³ לִקְרֹא כְּבַהֲלֵל מְהוֹדִים,⁴

Record ‹ did Esther ‹ the mighty [miracles] ‹ to be read ‹ just as with Hallel ‹ one gives thanks. ≫

מִלְמַעְלָה קִיְּמוּ מַה שֶׁקִּבְּלוּ לְמַטָּה⁵ דוֹדִים,

Up Above ‹ they ratified ‹ what ‹ was adopted ‹ below ‹ by the beloved ones. ≫

נֵס יְנוֹסֵס⁶ לְפַרְסֵם כְּאָז פִּלְאוֹ מַסְהִידִים,

A miracle ‹ may God ‹ may publicize ‹ so that we ‹ just as then ‹ of His won-drous [deeds] ‹ they testified — ≫

בָּעֵת הַזֹּאת רֶוַח וְהַצָּלָה יַעֲמֹד לַיְּהוּדִים.⁷

at this time ‹ relief ‹ and deliverance ‹ will come ‹ to the Jews. ≫

AN INDIVIDUAL PRAYING WITHOUT A *MINYAN* OMITS THE NEXT TWO PARAGRAPHS, BEGINNING אֵל מֶלֶךְ, *O GOD, KING,* AND ה', *HASHEM.*

אֵל מֶלֶךְ יוֹשֵׁב עַל כִּסֵּא רַחֲמִים, מִתְנַהֵג בַּחֲסִידוּת, מוֹחֵל

O God, ‹ King ‹ Who sits ‹ on ‹ the throne ‹ of mercy, ‹ Who acts ‹ with kindness, ‹ Who pardons ≫

עֲווֹנוֹת עַמּוֹ, מַעֲבִיר רִאשׁוֹן רִאשׁוֹן, מַרְבֶּה מְחִילָה לַחַטָּאִים

the sins ‹ of His people, ‹ Who removes ‹ [sins] one ‹ by one, ‹ Who abundantly grants ‹ pardon ‹ to unintentional sinners ≫

וּסְלִיחָה לַפּוֹשְׁעִים, עֹשֶׂה צְדָקוֹת עִם כָּל בָּשָׂר וָרוּחַ, לֹא

and forgiveness ‹ to willful sinners, ≫ ‹ Who ‹ performs ‹ acts of ‹ generosity ‹ with ‹ all ‹ [beings of] flesh ‹ and spirit ‹ — not ≫

כְרָעָתָם תִּגְמוֹל. ❖ אֵל הוֹרֵיתָ לָּנוּ לוֹמַר שְׁלֹשׁ עֶשְׂרֵה,

in accord with ‹ their wickedness ‹ do You repay ≫ ‹ O ‹ God, ‹ You ‹ taught ‹ us ‹ to recite ‹ the Thirteen [Attributes of Mercy]; ≫

וּזְכוֹר לָנוּ הַיּוֹם בְּרִית שְׁלֹשׁ עֶשְׂרֵה, כְּמוֹ שֶׁהוֹדַעְתָּ לֶעָנָיו

remember ‹ for us ‹ today ‹ the covenant ‹ of [these] Thirteen, ‹ as ≫ ‹ You made ‹ known ‹ to the humble one [Moses] ≫

מִקֶּדֶם, כְּמוֹ שֶׁכָּתוּב, וַיֵּרֶד יהוה בֶּעָנָן וַיִּתְיַצֵּב עִמּוֹ שָׁם,

in ancient times, ‹ as ≫ ‹ it is written: ≫ ‹ And HASHEM descended ‹ in a cloud ‹ and stood ‹ with him ‹ there, ≫

וַיִּקְרָא בְּשֵׁם יהוה.

and He called out ‹ the Name ‹ with the ‹ of HASHEM. ≫

(1) *Esther* 10:3. (2) *Genesis* 41:13. (3) Cf. *Esther* 9:29. (4) See *Megillah* 14a.
(5) Cf. *Esther* 9:27; see *Megillah* 7a. (6) Cf. *Psalms* 60:6. (7) *Esther* 4:14.

CONGREGATION AND *CHAZZAN* RECITE LOUDLY AND IN UNISON:

וַיַּעֲבֹר יהוה עַל פָּנָיו וַיִּקְרָא:

《 and   《 [Moses'] 〈 before 〈 And Hashem passed
proclaimed: face,

יהוה, יהוה, אֵל, רַחוּם, וְחַנּוּן, אֶרֶךְ אַפַּיִם, וְרַב חֶסֶד, וֶאֱמֶת,

《 and 〈   in   〈 and 〈 to anger, 〈 Slow 《 and 《 Compas- 〈 God, 〈 Hashem, 〈 Hashem,
Truth, Kindness Abundant   Gracious, sionate

נֹצֵר חֶסֶד לָאֲלָפִים, נֹשֵׂא עָוֹן, וָפֶשַׁע, וְחַטָאָה, וְנַקֵּה.

《 and Who 〈 and inad- 〈 willful 〈 of 〈 Forgiver 《 for thousands 〈 of 〈 Preserver
absolves. vertent sin, sin, iniquity,   [of generations], kindness

וְסָלַחְתָּ לַעֲוֹנֵנוּ וּלְחַטָּאתֵנוּ וּנְחַלְתָּנוּ. סְלַח לָנוּ אָבִינוּ כִּי

〈 for 《 our 〈 us, 〈 Forgive 《 and make us 《 and our sins, 〈 our 〈 May You
Father,   Your heritage.   iniquities forgive

חָטָאנוּ, מְחַל לָנוּ מַלְכֵּנוּ כִּי פָשָׁעְנוּ. כִּי אַתָּה אֲדֹנָי טוֹב

〈 are 〈 O Lord, 〈 You, 〈 For 《 we have 〈 for 《 our King, 〈 us, 〈 pardon 《 we have
good   willfully sinned.   sinned;

וְסַלָּח, וְרַב חֶסֶד לְכָל קֹרְאֶיךָ.

《 who call 〈 to all 〈 kind 〈 and 《 and
upon You.   abundantly forgiving,

כִּי עִמְּךָ מְקוֹר חַיִּים, בְּאוֹרְךָ נִרְאֶה אוֹר.¹ בְּקָרְאֵנוּ עֲנֵנוּ

〈 answer 〈 When we 《 light. 〈 may we 〈 by Your 《 of life; 〈 is the 〈 with 〈 For
us, call,   see light   source You

אֱלֹהֵי צִדְקֵנוּ, בַּצַּר הִרְחַבְתָּ לָנוּ, חָנֵּנוּ וּשְׁמַע תְּפִלָּתֵנוּ.²

《 our prayer. 〈 and hear 〈 be gracious 《 us; 〈 You have 〈 In [our] 《 of our 〈 O God
to us   relieved distress vindication.

וְעַתָּה יִגְדַּל נָא כֹּחַ אֲדֹנָי, כַּאֲשֶׁר דִּבַּרְתָּ לֵאמֹר.³

《 saying. 〈 You have 〈 as 《 of the 〈 the 〈 please, 〈 let become 〈 And
spoken,   Lord, power   great, now

כְּרַחֵם אָב עַל בָּנִים, כֵּן תְּרַחֵם יהוה עָלֵינוּ. לַיהוה

〈 To 《 on us. 〈 Hashem, 〈 have 〈 so 《 his 〈 towards 〈 a 〈 As merciful
Hashem   mercy, children, father is as

הַיְשׁוּעָה, עַל עַמְּךָ בִרְכָתֶךָ סֶּלָה. יהוה צְבָאוֹת עִמָּנוּ,

《 is with 〈 Master of 〈 Hashem, 《 Selah. 《 is Your 〈 Your 〈 upon 《 is salvation,
us, Legions,   blessing, people

מִשְׂגָּב לָנוּ אֱלֹהֵי יַעֲקֹב סֶלָה. יהוה צְבָאוֹת, אַשְׁרֵי אָדָם

〈 is the 〈 – praise- 《 Master of 〈 Hashem, 《 Selah. 《 of 〈 is the 〈 for 〈 a
man worthy Legions   Jacob, God us stronghold

(1) *Psalms* 36:10. (2) Cf. 4:2. (3) *Numbers* 14:17.

בְּטֵחַ בָּךְ. יהוה הוֹשִׁיעָה, הַמֶּלֶךְ יַעֲנֵנוּ בְיוֹם קָרְאֵנוּ.

《 we call. 〈 on the 〈 answer 〈 May the 《 save! 〈 HASHEM, 《 in You. 〈 who
　　　　　　day　　us　　King　　　　　　　　　　　　　　　　trusts

אֱלֹהֵינוּ וֵאלֹהֵי אֲבוֹתֵינוּ

《 of our forefathers: 〈 and the God 〈 Our God

אַתָּה* הָאֵל עוֹשֵׂה פְלָאוֹת,[1]

《 wonders; 〈 Who works 〈 are the God 〈 You*

בָּעַמִּים הוֹדַעְתָּ עוֹז[2] נוֹרָאוֹת,

《 of [Your] awe- 〈 the 〈 You made 〈 among
　some deeds.　power　known　the nations

גָּאַלְתָּ בִּזְרוֹעַ עַמְּךָ[3] מִתְּלָאוֹת,

《 from 〈 Your 〈 with Your 〈 You
　hardships;　people powerful arm redeemed

דִּכִּיתָ צָרֵיהֶם בְּמוֹתֵי תַחֲלוּאוֹת.[4]

《 from diseases. 〈 with deaths 〈 their foes 〈 You crushed

הָאוֹיֵב בְּקוּמוֹ לְעוֹרֵר מְדָנִים,[5]

《 strife, 〈 to arouse 〈 when 〈 The enemy
　　　　he arose　he arose　[Haman],

וְדִמָּה לְהַכְרִית פִּרְחֵי שׁוֹשַׁנִּים,

《 of the rosebush [Israel], 〈 the flowers 〈 to cut down 〈 and plotted

זָמַם לִשְׁקוֹל לְגִנְזֵי אֲדוֹנִים,

《 of his 〈 for the 〈 to weigh 〈 conspired
　master,　treasury　out

חֲלִיפֵי מֵאַת כִּכְּרֵי אֲדָנִים.[6]

《 of the sockets 〈 kikar- 〈 the 〈 [silver]
[of the Tabernacle]. weights hundred to counter

טְלָאֶיךָ הִזְהַרְתָּ שִׁקְלֵיהֶם לְהַקְדִּים,

《 to advance; 〈 their own shekels 《 You exhorted, 〈 Your flock

יָדַעְתָּ הָעֲתִידוֹת[7] וְדָרַשְׁתָּ נִשְׁקָדִים,

《 [their] diligence, 〈 so You demanded 《 the future, 〈 You knew

כִּבּוּי לְהַמְצִיא לְלַהַב יוֹקְדִים,

《 that blazes, 〈 for the flame 〈 to provide 〈 extinguish-
[of Your anger]　　　　　　　　　ment

---

(1) Cf. *Exodus* 15:11. (2) *Psalms* 77:15. (3) Cf. 77:16. (4) Cf. *Jeremiah* 16:4.
(5) Cf. *Proverbs* 10:12. (6) Cf. *Exodus* 38:27. (7) See *Megillah* 13b.

◆§ אַתָּה — *You.* The author's name שִׁמְעוֹן בַּר
יִצְחָק, *Shimon bar Yitzchak,* and the blessing חֲזַק
וֶאֱמָץ, *may he be strong and persevere,* appear

after the alphabet in the acrostic. Also known as
Rabbi Shimon HaGadol (the Great), he lived in
Mainz, Germany (about 950-1020) where he

לְקוּחִים לַמָּוֶת לִתְחִי נִפְקָדִים. מַסֵּכָה צָרָה¹ בְּעָבְדָם לְפָנִים,²

<< outwardly, < they [Because < be counted. < would < for death < so that those
worshiped Nebuchadnezzar's] [instead] designated
molten idol for life

נִמְסְרוּ לְהַתֵּז קְנוֹקְנוֹת³ וּגְפָנִים, סְבָבוּם מוֹקְשִׁים בְּכָל דְּפָנִים,

<< side. < on < were snares < Surrounding << and the < – both the << for < they were
every them [fruitful] worthless chopping handed
vine. tendrils down over

עֵינֵיהֶם לְךָ תוֹלִים וּבְסִתְרְךָ נִצְפָּנִים.

<< they took < and in Your << they < upon < Their eyes
shelter. refuge raised, You

פּוּר נֶהְפַּךְ בְּאוֹיְבִים לִשְׁלוֹט, צְלִיבָה הוּכַן אֲגָגִי לִקְלוֹט,⁴

<< to receive, < the Agagite < was < the << [the Jews] < and [over] << was < The
[Haman] readied, gallows ruled; their enemies reversed, lot

קָלַע וּבַלַּע פְּנֵי הַלּוֹט הַלּוֹט,⁵ רִיבֵי עָם⁶ בְּאַשְׁמַנִּים לַעֲלוֹט.

<< to < in dark < of [the Jew- < the << that were hidden < the < and < casting
blacken. desolation ish] people opponents behind veils, faces destroying away

שָׁלוֹם וֶאֱמֶת נִכְתָּב מִכָּל צַד, תְּקֶף⁷ יֵשַׁע סֶלַע וּמְצַד,⁸

<< and < of the < salvation < about the << direction, < from < were < and < [Words of]
Fortress. Rock mighty every inscribed truth peace

שׁוֹדֵד הֻשְׁדַד וּבְרִשְׁתּוֹ נוֹצַד, מַלְשִׁנִי נִסְחַף נִצְמַת וְנִרְצַד.

<< and < cut < was swept < the << was < and in his < was < The
ambushed. down, away, slanderer captured; own net plundered plunderer

עָשׂוּ שְׂמָחוֹת וְלַדּוֹרוֹת קְבָעוּם, וּמִקְרָאוֹת שְׁלֹשׁוֹם וְלֹא רִבְּעוּם,⁹

<< four. < not < allowed [Amalek] < though << established < and for all < celebrations < [The
to be mentioned Scripture them, generations Jews]
three times, made

נִסְכְּמוּ מִמַּעַל וּלְמַטָּה טְבָעוּם,⁹ בַּסֵּפֶר נֶחֱקַק עַל מַה קְבָעוּם.

<< they es- < what < for < was < In the << they < and << up Above, < It was
tablished it. purpose inscribed Megillah formulated it. below accepted

רָמָה יָדְךָ¹⁰ לִסְלוֹחַ לַפּוֹשְׁעִים,

<< the sinners. < to forgive < was Your hand < Raised

יְהוּדִי וַהֲדַסָּה הֲקַמְתָּ מוֹשִׁיעִים,

<< as saviors. < You < and Hadassah < The Jew
established [Esther] [Mordechai]

---

(1) Cf. Isaiah 28:20. (2) See Megillah 12a. (3) See Chullin 92a. (4) Cf. Esther 9:1.
(5) Cf. Isaiah 25:7. (6) Cf. Psalms 18:44. (7) Cf. Esther 9:29-30. (8) Cf. Isaiah 33:16.
(9) See Megillah 7a. (10) Isaiah 26:11.

served on the rabbinical court alongside Rabbeinu Gershom *Meor HaGolah*. More than a dozen of his liturgical compositions have en-tered the *Siddur* and *Machzor*, among them בְּרַח דּוֹדִי, and בָּרוּךְ ה' יוֹם יוֹם, recited on Chol HaMoed Pesach.

צִדְקָתָם עוֹמֶדֶת לָעַד¹ לְשַׁעֲשׁוּעִים,

for [Israel's] delight; ⟪ forever ⟨ endures ⟨ Their righteousness

חֵקֶר כְּבוֹדָם² לְהִזָּכֵר לְנוֹשָׁעִים.

by those who ⟨ should be ⟨ of their ⟨ the inves-
were saved. remembered honor tigation

קַנֵּא לְשִׁמְךָ נוֹרָא וְנִקְדָּשׁ, חֲזֵה כַרְמְךָ נֶהֱרַס וְנִדְרָשׁ,

⟪ and ⟨ shattered ⟨ Your ⟨ See ⟪ and Sancti- ⟨ O ⟨ Your ⟨ Avenge
trampled. vineyard, fied One. Awesome Name,

זְרוּיֵּינוּ קַבֵּץ וְשִׁיר לְךָ יְחַדֵּשׁ,³

⟪ be sung ⟨ to ⟨ and let ⟪ gather ⟨ Our scattered
anew; You a song in, ones

קַיְּמֵם וְהַחֲיֵם בְּבִנְיַן בֵּית הַמִּקְדָּשׁ.

⟪ of the Temple. ⟨ with the ⟨ and give ⟨ preserve
rebuilding them life, them

❖ וְכַעֲשׂוֹתְךָ נוֹרָאוֹת בְּאוֹתָן הַיָּמִים,

⟪ days, ⟨ in those ⟨ awesome deeds ⟨ As you did

אִתָּנוּ הַפְלֵא תְּשׁוּעַת עוֹלָמִים,

⟪ that is eternal, ⟨ a salvation ⟪ do wonders, ⟨ with us

מְצוֹא לְפָנֶיךָ כְּפֶר וְתַנְחוּמִים,

⟨ and comfort ⟨ atonement ⟨ before ⟨ that we
You may find

אֵל מֶלֶךְ יוֹשֵׁב עַל כִּסֵּא רַחֲמִים.

⟪ of mercy. ⟨ the ⟨ on ⟨ Who ⟨ King, ⟨ — O
throne sits God,

AN INDIVIDUAL PRAYING WITHOUT A *MINYAN* OMITS THE NEXT TWO PARAGRAPHS, BEGINNING אֵל מֶלֶךְ, *O GOD, KING,* AND ה', *HASHEM.*

אֵל מֶלֶךְ יוֹשֵׁב עַל כִּסֵּא רַחֲמִים, מִתְנַהֵג בַּחֲסִידוּת, מוֹחֵל

⟨ Who ⟪ with ⟨ Who acts ⟪ of mercy, ⟨ the ⟨ on ⟨ Who ⟨ King ⟨ O God,
pardons kindness, throne sits

עֲוֹנוֹת עַמּוֹ, מַעֲבִיר רִאשׁוֹן רִאשׁוֹן, מַרְבֶּה מְחִילָה לַחַטָּאִים

⟨ to uninten- ⟨ pardon ⟨ Who abun- ⟪ by one, ⟨ [sins] one ⟨ Who ⟪ of His ⟨ the sins
tional sinners dantly grants removes people,

וּסְלִיחָה לַפּוֹשְׁעִים, עֹשֶׂה צְדָקוֹת עִם כָּל בָּשָׂר וָרוּחַ, לֹא

⟨ — not ⟪ and ⟨ [beings ⟨ all ⟨ with ⟨ acts of ⟨ Who ⟪ to willful ⟨ and
spirit of] flesh generosity performs sinners, forgiveness

כְּרָעָתָם תִּגְמוֹל. ❖ אֵל הוֹרֵיתָ לָּנוּ לוֹמַר שְׁלֹשׁ עֶשְׂרֵה, וּזְכוֹר

⟨ remember ⟪ the Thirteen ⟨ to recite ⟨ us ⟨ O ⟪ do You ⟨ in accord with
[Attributes of Mercy]; You taught God, repay them! their wickedness

---

(1) Cf. *Psalms* 112:9. (2) Cf. *Proverbs* 25:27. (3) Cf. *Psalms* 149:1.

לָנוּ הַיּוֹם בְּרִית שְׁלֹשׁ עֶשְׂרֵה, כְּמוֹ שֶׁהוֹדַעְתָּ לֶעָנָיו מִקֶּדֶם, כְּמוֹ

‹ as ‹‹ in ancient ‹ to the humble ‹ You made ‹ as ‹‹ of [these] Thirteen, ‹ the ‹ today ‹ for us
　　times,　　one [Moses]　　known　　　　　　　covenant

שֶׁכָּתוּב, וַיֵּרֶד יהוה בֶּעָנָן וַיִּתְיַצֵּב עִמּוֹ שָׁם, וַיִּקְרָא בְשֵׁם יהוה.

‹‹ of ‹ with the ‹ and He ‹‹ there, ‹ with ‹ and stood ‹ in a ‹ And HASHEM ‹‹ it is written:
HASHEM.　Name　called out　　　him　　　　cloud　descended

CONGREGATION AND *CHAZZAN* RECITE LOUDLY AND IN UNISON:

וַיַּעֲבֹר יהוה עַל פָּנָיו וַיִּקְרָא:

‹‹ and proclaimed: ‹‹ [Moses'] face,‹ before ‹ And HASHEM passed

יהוה, יהוה, אֵל, רַחוּם, וְחַנּוּן, אֶרֶךְ אַפַּיִם, וְרַב חֶסֶד, וֶאֱמֶת,

‹‹ and ‹ in ‹ and ‹ to anger, ‹ Slow ‹‹ and ‹ Compas- ‹ God, ‹ HASHEM, ‹ HASHEM,
Truth, Kindness Abundant　　　　　　　Gracious, sionate

נֹצֵר חֶסֶד לָאֲלָפִים, נֹשֵׂא עָוֹן, וָפֶשַׁע, וְחַטָּאָה, וְנַקֵּה.

‹‹ and Who ‹ and inad- ‹ willful ‹ of ‹ Forgiver ‹‹ for thousands ‹ of ‹ Preserver
absolves. vertent sin,　sin,　iniquity,　　　[of generations], kindness

וְסָלַחְתָּ לַעֲוֹנֵנוּ וּלְחַטָּאתֵנוּ וּנְחַלְתָּנוּ. סְלַח לָנוּ אָבִינוּ כִּי

‹ for ‹‹ our ‹ us, ‹ Forgive ‹‹ and make us ‹‹ and our sins, ‹ our ‹ May You
Father,　　　　　Your heritage.　　iniquities　forgive

חָטָאנוּ, מְחַל לָנוּ מַלְכֵּנוּ כִּי פָשָׁעְנוּ. כִּי אַתָּה אֲדֹנָי טוֹב

‹ are ‹ O Lord, ‹ You, ‹ For ‹‹ we have ‹ for ‹‹ our King, ‹ us, ‹ pardon ‹‹ we have
good　　　　　　　willfully sinned.　　　　　　　　　sinned;

וְסַלָּח, וְרַב חֶסֶד לְכָל קֹרְאֶיךָ.

‹‹ who call ‹ to all ‹ kind ‹ and ‹‹ and
upon You.　　　　　abundantly forgiving,

THE FOLLOWING PRAYER IS RECITED ALOUD RESPONSIVELY.
(IN SOME COMMUNITIES *HASHEM, HASHEM* . . . IS SAID AS A REFRAIN.)

***CHAZZAN,* THEN CONGREGATION:**

בְּמָתַי* מִסְפָּר[1] חִלֵּינוּ פָנֶיךָ,[2]

‹‹ before You; ‹ we plead ‹‹ in number, ‹　Few*

לְשַׁוְעַת נִכְאִים אַל תַּעְלֵם אָזְנֶךָ,

‹‹ Your ear. ‹ turn away ‹ do ‹ of the ‹ to the cry
not afflicted ones

הַקְשֵׁב תְּחִנָּתָם מִשְּׁמֵי מְעוֹנֶךָ,[3]

‹‹ of Your ‹ from the ‹ their ‹ Heed
abode,　heavens　supplication

---

(1) Cf. *Psalms* 105:12. (2) Cf. *Exodus* 32:11. (3) Cf. *Deuteronomy* 26:15.

בְּמָתַי ∙§ — *Few.* Rabbi Meshullam ben Klonimos (Lucca, Italy, about 950-1020) signed his name, מְשֻׁלָּם, after a reverse alphabetical acrostic. Among his other compositions that have entered the *Siddur* is בְּרַח דּוֹדִי, recited on the second day of Pesach.

כְּבִימֵי מוֹר וַהֲדַס¹ הוֹשַׁעְתָּ בָּנֶיךָ.

» Your ‹ You saved ‹‹ and *myrtle* ‹ of *myrrh* ‹ as in
children.   [Esther] [Mordechai] the days

CONGREGATION, THEN *CHAZZAN:*

תְּהִלּוֹת יִשְׂרָאֵל⁴ אַתָּה יוֹשֵׁב,² שַׁוְעָתָם מַאֲזִין³ וְרִנָּתָם קוֹשֵׁב,

» You ‹ and to their ‹ You give ‹ to their ‹‹ are ‹ You ‹ of Israel ‹ [Upon]
hearken. prayer   ear,   outcry enthroned;   the praises

רְפֻאוֹת לְמַחַץ⁵ מַקְדִּים וּמְחַשֵּׁב,⁶

» and ‹ You prepare ‹ to the ‹ The cure
determine, in advance wound

קִנְוֶיךָ לְהֵיטִיב וְנָוֵיהֶם לְיַשֵּׁב.

» to resettle. ‹ and their ‹‹ to do ‹ for [the
       homeland good, people] You
                   have acquired

CONGREGATION, THEN *CHAZZAN:*

צַר וְאוֹיֵב⁷ הִלְטִישׁ עֵינָיו,⁸ פִּיהוּ פָּעַר⁹ לִשְׁאוֹף עָנָיו,¹⁰

» the humble ‹ to swallow ‹ he opened ‹ his ‹‹ his glare; ‹ sharpened ‹ and foe ‹ The
[Mordechai].   up   wide   mouth   [Haman] oppressor

עָשֵׁת בִּשְׁלוֹ לְהַשְׁמִיד קְהַל הֲמוֹנָיו,¹¹

» of his ‹ the [entire] ‹ to ‹ because of him ‹ He
multitudes, congregation destroy [Mordechai] schemed

סְגֻל לְאַבֵּד חָרַת בְּנִשְׁתְּוָנָיו.

» in his edicts. ‹ he ‹ to ‹ the treasured
       inscribed destroy, [people]

CONGREGATION, THEN *CHAZZAN:*

נוֹקֵם לְצָרִים וְנוֹטֵר לְאוֹיְבִים,¹² מָדַדְתָּ מִדָּתָם כְּזֵדוּ לַאֲהוּבִים,

» against the ‹ equal ‹ their ‹ — You ‹‹ against ‹ and ‹ on ‹ [You] Who
beloved to their measure of measured enemies remembers oppressors wreaks
    ones. scheming punishment out   hostility   vengeance

לוֹחֵם וּבָנָיו הֻתְלוּ מִצְלָבִים, בְּבַחֲרֹזֶת דָּגִים חוֹרְזוּ תְּחוּבִים.

» threaded ‹ they were ‹ of fish ‹ as with ‹‹ upon the ‹ were ‹ and his ‹ The
together. strung up,   a string   gallows,   hung offspring aggressor

CONGREGATION, THEN *CHAZZAN:*

יוֹם אֲשֶׁר שִׂבְּרוּ¹³ צוֹרְרִים, טִבְחָה לַעֲשִׂית בְּעַם נְצוּרִים,

» who are ‹ upon the ‹ to inflict ‹ a slaughter ‹‹ — the ‹‹ they had ‹ on ‹ The
guarded [by God], people   oppressors — hoped   which   day

---

(1) See *Megillah* 10b. (2) Cf. *Psalms* 22:4. (3) Cf. 39:13. (4) Cf. 17:1.
(5) Cf. *Isaiah* 30:26. (6) Cf. *Psalms* 77:6. (7) *Esther* 7:6. (8) Cf. *Job* 16:9.
(9) Cf. 16:10. (10) Cf. *Amos* 2:7. (11) Cf. *Esther* 3:6. (12) *Nahum* 1:2. (13) Cf. *Esther* 9:1.

חֻלְּפָה הַדָּת וְנָפְלוּ פְגָרִים, זֻלְעֲפוּ זוֹעֲמוּ מוּבָסִים מֻגְרִים.

❮ dragged ❮ trampled, ❮ scorned ❮ they were ❮❮ dead; ❮ and they ❮❮ was the ❮ inverted
about.   terrified,   fell down   decree,

CONGREGATION, THEN *CHAZZAN*:

וּבְכֵן יִתְעַלֶּה שִׁמְךָ וְיִתְנַשֵּׂא, הוֹדְךָ שְׁמֵי שָׁמַיִם כִּסָּה,[1]

❮❮ covers. ❮ heavens ❮ the ❮❮ Your ❮❮ and ❮ may Your Name ❮ And
       loftiest   glory,   upraised;   be elevated   so too

דַּכִּים בְּרוֹמְמְךָ נְתוּנִים לִמְשִׁסָּה,[2]

❮❮ to plunder; ❮ — those who ❮❮ when You ❮❮ The
       are consigned   raise up   oppressed
                             ones,

גֵּיא וַאֲפָסֶיהָ תְּהִלָּתְךָ מְכַסָּה.

❮❮ will cover. ❮ Your praise ❮ to its very ❮ the
                      ends   earth

CONGREGATION, THEN *CHAZZAN*:

בִּינָה הֲגִיגֵנוּ[3] עַתָּה וּרְאֵה בַצָּר,

❮❮ [our] ❮ and ❮❮ now, ❮ our ❮ Under-
   distress;   look at   thoughts   stand

הֲשִׁיבֵנוּ לִמְנוּחָתֶךָ כִּי יָדְךָ לֹא תִקְצָר,[4]

❮❮ limited. ❮ is not ❮ Your ❮ for ❮ to Your ❮ return us
       power   resting place,

אָדוֹן, קְרָאנְוּךָ מִן הַמֵּצָר,[5]

❮❮ the straits; ❮ from ❮ we ❮❮ O Lord,
           called You

אָנָּא הוֹצִיאֵנוּ לַמֶּרְחָב[6] וְחַלְּצֵנוּ מִצָּר.[7]

❮❮ from ❮ and release ❮ into ❮ remove us ❮ please
distress.   us   expansiveness

CONGREGATION, THEN *CHAZZAN*:

מְאֹד תַּרְבֶּה לָנוּ מְחִילָה, שְׁמַע תְּפִלָּה וְהַעֲבֵר תִּפְלָה,

❮❮ [our] ❮ and ❮ [our] ❮ hear ❮❮ forgiveness; ❮ for us ❮ make ❮ Greatly
impropriety. remove   prayer   abundant

לוֹחֲצֵינוּ יַשְׁלִימוּ אִתָּנוּ וַעֲווֹנוֹתֵינוּ תַשְׁלִיךְ בִּמְצוּלָה,[8]

❮❮ into the ❮ may You ❮ and our ❮❮ with us, ❮ make ❮ May our
shadowy depths;   cast   iniquities   peace   oppressors

מִמֶּנּוּ רַחֲמֶיךָ לֹא תִכְלָא.[9]

❮❮ withhold. ❮ do not ❮ Your mercy ❮ from us,

TURN TO PAGE 684 FOR אֵל מֶלֶךְ, **AND CONTINUE UNTIL THE CONCLUSION OF** *SELICHOS*.

(1) Cf. *Habakkuk* 3:3. (2) Cf. *Isaiah* 42:24. (3) Cf. *Psalms* 5:2. (4) Cf. *Numbers* 11:23.
(5) Cf. *Psalms* 118:5. (6) Cf. 18:20. (7) Cf. *Proverbs* 11:8. (8) Cf. *Micah* 7:19. (9) Cf. *Psalms* 40:12.

❧ סליחות לשבעה עשר בתמוז ❧
❧ SELICHOS — SEVENTEENTH OF TAMMUZ ❧

ALL BEGIN HERE:

סְלַח לָנוּ אָבִינוּ, כִּי בְרוֹב אִוַּלְתֵּנוּ שָׁגִינוּ,

《 we have 〈 of our folly 〈 in the 〈 for 〈 our 〈 us, 〈 Forgive
erred; abundance Father,

מְחַל לָנוּ מַלְכֵּנוּ, כִּי רַבּוּ עֲוֹנֵינוּ.

《 our iniquities. 〈many are 〈 for 〈 our King, 〈 us, 〈 pardon

אֵל אֶרֶךְ אַפַּיִם אַתָּה, וּבַעַל הָרַחֲמִים נִקְרֵאתָ, וְדֶרֶךְ

〈 and 《 are You 〈 of Mercy 〈 and 《 are You, 〈 to anger,〈 Who 〈 God,
the way called; Master is slow

תְּשׁוּבָה הוֹרֵיתָ. גְּדֻלַּת רַחֲמֶיךָ וַחֲסָדֶיךָ, תִּזְכּוֹר הַיּוֹם וּבְכָל

〈 and 〈 this 〈 may You 〈 and Your 〈 of Your 〈 The 《 have You 〈 of
every day remember, kindness mercy greatness taught. repentance

יוֹם לְזֶרַע יְדִידֶיךָ. תֵּפֶן אֵלֵינוּ בְּרַחֲמִים, כִּי אַתָּה הוּא בַּעַל

〈 the 〈 are 〈 You 〈 for 《 in mercy, 〈 to us 〈 Turn 《 of Your 〈 for the 《 day,
Master beloved ones. offspring

הָרַחֲמִים. בְּתַחֲנוּן וּבִתְפִלָּה פָּנֶיךָ נְקַדֵּם, כְּהוֹדַעְתָּ לֶעָנָיו

〈 to the 〈 in the man- 《 we 〈 Your 〈 and prayer 〈 With 《 of Mercy.
humble one ner that You approach, Presence supplication
[Moses] made known

מִקֶּדֶם. מֵחֲרוֹן אַפְּךָ שׁוּב, כְּמוֹ בְתוֹרָתְךָ כָּתוּב.[1] וּבְצֵל כְּנָפֶיךָ

〈 of Your 〈 In the 《 it is 〈 in Your Torah 〈 as 《 turn 〈 of Your 〈 From the 《 in ancient
wings shadow written. back, anger fierceness times.

נֶחֱסֶה וְנִתְלוֹנָן, כְּיוֹם וַיֵּרֶד יהוה בֶּעָנָן.[2] ❖ תַּעֲבוֹר עַל פֶּשַׁע

〈 sin 〈 Overlook 《 in a 〈 when HASHEM 〈 as on 《 and may 〈 may we
cloud. descended the day we dwell, find shelter

וְתִמְחֶה אָשָׁם, כְּיוֹם וַיִּתְיַצֵּב עִמּוֹ שָׁם.[2] תַּאֲזִין שַׁוְעָתֵנוּ

〈 to our cry 〈 Give 《 there. 〈 with him 〈 when He 〈 as on 《 guilt, 〈 and erase
heed [Moses] [God] stood the day

---

(1) Cf. *Exodus* 32:12. (2) 34:5.

שִׁבְעָה עָשָׂר בְּתַמּוּז / Seventeenth of Tammuz ❧

The Seventeenth of Tammuz is second only to Tishah B'Av as a day of national tragedy. Although the prophets ordained it as a fast day to commemorate its role in the destruction of the Temple, it simultaneously recalls four other sad events, all of which are mentioned in the *Selichos*. The five tragedies of this day are:

1. In the Wilderness, Moses broke the first Tablets of the Covenant when he came down from Mount Sinai and found the people worshiping the Golden Calf.

2. During the siege of the First Temple, the Babylonians breached the wall of Jerusalem in Tammuz, but could not break into the Temple until 7 Av. However, on 17 Tammuz, the *Kohanim* no longer had any sheep for the daily continual [*tamid*] offering.

וְתַקְשִׁיב מֶנּוּ מַאֲמַר, כְּיוֹם וַיִּקְרָא בְשֵׁם יהוה,¹ וְשָׁם נֶאֱמַר:

《 it was said: 《 and 《 of 《 with the 《 when He 《 as on 《 [our] 《 from 《 and hear
there HASHEM, Name called out the day declaration, us

CONGREGATION AND *CHAZZAN* **RECITE LOUDLY AND IN UNISON:**

וַיַּעֲבֹר יהוה עַל פָּנָיו וַיִּקְרָא:

《 and 《 [Moses'] 《 before 《 And HASHEM passed
proclaimed: face,

יהוה, יהוה, אֵל, רַחוּם, וְחַנּוּן, אֶרֶךְ אַפַּיִם, וְרַב חֶסֶד, וֶאֱמֶת,

《 and 《 in 《 and 《 to anger, 《 Slow 《 and 《 Compas- 《 God, 《 HASHEM, 《 HASHEM,
Truth, Kindness Abundant Gracious, sionate

נֹצֵר חֶסֶד לָאֲלָפִים, נֹשֵׂא עָוֹן, וָפֶשַׁע, וְחַטָאָה, וְנַקֵּה,²

《 and Who 《 and inad- 《 willful 《 of 《 Forgiver 《 for thousands 《 of 《 Preserver
absolves. vertent sin, sin, iniquity, [of generations], kindness

וְסָלַחְתָּ לַעֲוֹנֵנוּ וּלְחַטָּאתֵנוּ וּנְחַלְתָּנוּ.³ סְלַח לָנוּ אָבִינוּ כִּי

《 for 《 our 《 us, 《 Forgive 《 and make us 《 and our sins, 《 our 《 May You
Father, Your heritage. iniquities forgive

חָטָאנוּ, מְחַל לָנוּ מַלְכֵּנוּ כִּי פָשָׁעְנוּ.⁴ כִּי אַתָּה אֲדֹנָי טוֹב

《 are 《 O Lord, 《 You, 《 For 《 we have 《 for 《 our King, 《 us, 《 pardon 《 we have
good willfully sinned. sinned;

וְסַלָּח, וְרַב חֶסֶד לְכָל קֹרְאֶיךָ.⁵

《 who call 《 to all 《 kind 《 and 《 and
upon You. abundantly forgiving,

אַל תִּתְּנוּ דֳמִי לוֹ, עַד יְכוֹנֵן וְעַד יָשִׂים אֶת יְרוּשָׁלַיִם תְּהִלָּה

《 a source 《 Jerusalem 《 He 《 and 《 He re- 《 until 《 for 《 silence 《 allow 《 Do
of praise makes until establishes Him, not

בָּאָרֶץ.⁶ כִּי עִמְּךָ מְקוֹר חַיִּים, בְּאוֹרְךָ נִרְאֶה אוֹר.⁷ אֱלֹהֵינוּ,

《 Our God, 《 light. 《 may we 《 by Your 《 of life; 《 is the 《 with 《 For 《 in the
see light source You Land.

בּוֹשְׁנוּ בְמַעֲשֵׂינוּ וְנִכְלַמְנוּ בַּעֲוֹנֵינוּ.⁸

《 by our 《 and 《 by our deeds 《 we are
iniquities. humiliated shamed

---

(1) *Exodus* 34:5. (2) 34:6-7. (3) 34:9. (4) From the weekday *Shemoneh Esrei*.
(5) *Psalms* 86:5. (6) *Isaiah* 62:7. (7) *Psalms* 36:10. (8) Cf. *Ezra* 9:6.

3. During the siege of the Second Temple, the Romans breached Jerusalem's defenses on 17 Tammuz and began their bloody carnage in the city. According to *Yerushalmi* (*Taanis* 4) this was the anniversary of the breaching in the First Temple period as well.

4. During the terror-filled years before the destruction of the Second Temple, a Roman officer named Apostomos shocked the Jewish people by publicly burning a Torah scroll, the first atrocity of this sort.

5. An idol was placed in the Temple. According to some, this was part of the desecration perpetrated by Apostomos; others say it was done by Menasheh, the idol-worshiping king of Judah during the time of the First Temple.

כְּרַחֵם אָב עַל בָּנִים, כֵּן תְּרַחֵם יהוה עָלֵינוּ. לַיהוה

To Hashem › ‹‹ on us. ‹ Hashem, ‹ have › so ‹‹ his ‹ toward › a ‹ As merciful mercy, children, father is as

הַיְשׁוּעָה, עַל עַמְּךָ בִרְכָתֶךָ סֶּלָה. יהוה צְבָאוֹת עִמָּנוּ,

‹‹ is with ‹ Master of ‹ Hashem, ‹‹ Selah. ‹ is Your ‹ Your ‹ upon ‹‹ is salvation, us, Legions, blessing, people

מִשְׂגָּב לָנוּ אֱלֹהֵי יַעֲקֹב סֶלָה. יהוה צְבָאוֹת, אַשְׁרֵי אָדָם

‹ is the ‹ — praise-‹‹ Master of ‹ Hashem, ‹‹ Selah. ‹‹ of ‹ is the ‹ for ‹ a man worthy Legions Jacob, God us stronghold

בֹּטֵחַ בָּךְ. יהוה הוֹשִׁיעָה, הַמֶּלֶךְ יַעֲנֵנוּ בְיוֹם קָרְאֵנוּ.

‹‹ we call. ‹ on the ‹ answer ‹ May the ‹‹ save! ‹ Hashem, ‹‹ in ‹ who day us King You. trusts

❖ סְלַח נָא לַעֲוֹן הָעָם הַזֶּה כְּגֹדֶל חַסְדֶּךָ, וְכַאֲשֶׁר נָשָׂאתָה

‹ You have ‹ and as ‹‹ of Your ‹ according to ‹ of this people ‹ the ‹ please, ‹ Forgive, forgiven kindness, the greatness iniquity

לָעָם הַזֶּה מִמִּצְרַיִם וְעַד הֵנָּה, וְשָׁם נֶאֱמַר:

‹‹ it was said: ‹ And there ‹‹ now. ‹ until ‹ from Egypt ‹ this people

ALL, ALOUD AND IN UNISON:

וַיֹּאמֶר יהוה סָלַחְתִּי כִּדְבָרֶךָ.

‹‹ according to your word! ‹ I have forgiven ‹‹ And Hashem said:

ALL CONTINUE:

הַטֵּה אֱלֹהַי אָזְנְךָ וּשֲׁמָע, פְּקַח עֵינֶיךָ וּרְאֵה שֹׁמְמֹתֵינוּ,

‹‹ our desolation, ‹ and see ‹ Your eyes ‹ open ‹‹ and listen; ‹ Your ear, ‹ my God, ‹ Incline,

וְהָעִיר אֲשֶׁר נִקְרָא שִׁמְךָ עָלֶיהָ, כִּי לֹא עַל צִדְקֹתֵינוּ אֲנַחְנוּ

‹ do we ‹ of our ‹ because ‹ not ‹ for ‹‹ upon; ‹ Your Name is ‹ which ‹ and [that of] the city righteousness proclaimed

מַפִּילִים תַּחֲנוּנֵינוּ לְפָנֶיךָ, כִּי עַל רַחֲמֶיךָ הָרַבִּים. אֲדֹנָי

‹ O Lord, ‹‹ which is ‹ of Your ‹ because ‹ but ‹‹ before ‹ our ‹ cast abundant. compassion, You; supplications

שְׁמָעָה, אֲדֹנָי סְלָחָה, אֲדֹנָי הַקְשִׁיבָה, וַעֲשֵׂה אַל תְּאַחַר,

‹‹ delay; ‹ do not ‹‹ and act, ‹ be attentive, ‹ O Lord, ‹‹ forgive; ‹ O Lord, ‹‹ heed;

לְמַעַנְךָ אֱלֹהַי, כִּי שִׁמְךָ נִקְרָא עַל עִירְךָ וְעַל עַמֶּךָ.

‹‹ Your ‹ and ‹ Your ‹ upon ‹ is ‹ Your ‹ for ‹‹ my God, ‹ for Your people. upon City proclaimed Name sake,

אֱלֹהֵינוּ וֵאלֹהֵי אֲבוֹתֵינוּ

‹‹ of our forefathers: ‹ and the God ‹ Our God

---

(1) Cf. *Psalms* 103:13. (2) 3:9. (3) Cf. 46:8. (4) 84:13.
(5) 20:10. (6) *Numbers* 14:19. (7) 14:20. (8) *Daniel* 9:18-19.

אֲתָאנוּ לְךָ יוֹצֵר רוּחוֹת,

‹‹ of spirits. ‹ O Molder ‹ to You, ‹ We have come

בְּרוֹב עֲוֺנֵינוּ כָּבְדוּ אֲנָחוֹת, גְּזֵרוֹת עָצְמוּ וְרַבּוּ צְרִיחוֹת,

‹‹ are the ‹ and ‹‹ have become ‹ the evil ‹‹ our ‹ intensified ‹‹ iniquities, ‹ Because
outcries many   severe,   decrees   groans; have been   of our abundant

כִּי בְּשִׁבְעָה עָשָׂר בְּתַמּוּז נִשְׁתַּבְּרוּ הַלּוּחוֹת.

‹‹ were the ‹ smashed ‹‹ of ‹ on the seventeenth ‹ – for
Tablets.   Tammuz,

גָּלִינוּ מִבֵּית הַבְּחִירָה,

‹‹ of [Your] ‹ from the ‹ We were
choosing; House exiled

דִּינֵנוּ נֶחְתַּם וְנִגְזְרָה גְזֵרָה, וְחָשַׁךְ בַּעֲדֵנוּ אוֹרָה,

‹‹ was [our] ‹ for us ‹ and ‹‹ was the ‹ and ‹ was ‹ our
light darkened decree, issued sealed, judgment

כִּי בְּשִׁבְעָה עָשָׂר בְּתַמּוּז נִשְׂרְפָה הַתּוֹרָה.

‹‹ was the ‹ burned ‹‹ of ‹ on the seventeenth ‹ – for
Torah.   Tammuz,

הָרְסוּ אוֹיְבֵינוּ הַהֵיכָל, וּבָרְחָה שְׁכִינָה מִזָּוִית הֵיכָל,

‹‹ of the ‹ from the ‹ did God's ‹ and flee ‹‹ the ‹ did our ‹ Destroy
Sanctuary. corner Presence   Sanctuary, enemies

וְנִמְסַרְנוּ בְּיַד זֵדִים לְהִתְאַכָּל,

‹‹ to be ‹ of wicked ‹ to the ‹ We were
consumed people, hands consigned

כִּי בְּשִׁבְעָה עָשָׂר בְּתַמּוּז הָעֳמַד צֶלֶם בַּהֵיכָל.

‹‹ in the ‹ was ‹ set up ‹‹ of ‹ on the seventeenth ‹ – for
Sanctuary. an idol   Tammuz,

זֵרוּנוּ מֵעִיר אֶל עִיר, וְנִלְכַּד מֶנּוּ רַב וְצָעִיר,[1]

‹‹ and the ‹ were [both] ‹ from ‹ and ‹‹ city, ‹ to ‹ from ‹ They scat-
young. the old us captured city tered us

חָרְבָה מְשׂוֹשֵׂנוּ וְאֵשׁ בָּהּ הִבְעִיר,

‹‹ did [the ‹ in it ‹ and a ‹ was [Jerusalem,] ‹ Destroyed
enemy] ignite fire our joy

כִּי בְּשִׁבְעָה עָשָׂר בְּתַמּוּז הָבְקְעָה הָעִיר.[2]

‹‹ was the City. ‹ breached ‹ of Tammuz ‹ on the seventeenth ‹ – for

טָפַשׁ מִקְדָּשֵׁנוּ צָר הַמַּשְׁמִיד,

‹‹ who ‹ – the ‹‹ in the ‹ He acted
destroyed, oppressor Temple foolishly

---

(1) Cf. *Genesis* 25:23. (2) *Jeremiah* 39:2.

וְנִטַּל מֵחֲתָן וְכַלָּה אֶצְעָדָה וְצָמִיד,¹

» and ‹ were [their ‹ and ‹ from ‹ and taken
bracelets. festive] armbands brides grooms away

יַעַן כְּעַסְנוּךְ נִתַּנּוּ לְהַשְׁמִיד,

« to destruction ‹ we were ‹ we angered ‹ Because
delivered You

כִּי בְּשִׁבְעָה עָשָׂר בְּתַמּוּז בָּטֵל הַתָּמִיד.

« was the continual ‹ can- ‹ of ‹ on the seventeenth ‹ — for
[daily] offering. celed Tammuz

כָּלָה מֶנּוּ כָּל הוֹד וָשֶׁבַח, חַרְבּוֹ שָׁלַף אוֹיֵב עָלֵינוּ לָאֱבַח,²

« to massacre ‹ against ‹ did the ‹ unsheathe ‹ his « and ‹ splendor ‹ was ‹ from ‹ Elimin-
[us], us foe sword praise; all us ated

לִהְיוֹת עוֹלְלִים וְיוֹנְקִים מוּכָנִים לַטֶּבַח,

« for the ‹ should be ‹ and ‹ babies ‹ that
slaughter prepared sucklings

כִּי בְּשִׁבְעָה עָשָׂר בְּתַמּוּז בָּטְלוּ עוֹלָה וָזֶבַח.

« and ‹ were ‹ canceled ‹ of ‹ on the seventeenth ‹ — for
[peace-] elevation- Tammuz
offerings. offerings

מָרַדְנוּ לְשׁוֹכֵן מְעוֹנוֹת, לָכֵן נִתְפַּזַּרְנוּ בְּכָל פִּנוֹת,

« corners. ‹ to all ‹ we were « in the loftiest ‹ against Him ‹ We
scattered there- heavens; Who dwells rebelled
fore

נֶהְפַּךְ מְחוֹלֵנוּ לְקִינוֹת,

« into dirges. ‹ were our dances ‹ Transformed

כִּי בְּשִׁבְעָה עָשָׂר בְּתַמּוּז בָּטְלוּ קָרְבָּנוֹת.

« were the ‹ canceled ‹ of ‹ on the seventeenth ‹ for
sacrifices. Tammuz

סָרַרְנוּ לְפָנֶיךָ מֵרִיב לְשׁוֹנוֹת, לָכֵן לָמְדָה לְשׁוֹנֵנוּ לוֹמַר קִינוֹת,

« lament- ‹ to ‹ did our ‹ learn ‹ there- « speech, ‹ through ‹ before ‹ We
ations. recite tongues fore contentious You strayed

עֻזַּבְנוּ בְּלִי לְהִמָּנוֹת,³

« being ‹ without ‹ We were
numbered forsaken,

כִּי בְּשִׁבְעָה עָשָׂר בְּתַמּוּז גָּרְמוּ לָנוּ עֲוֹנוֹת.

« by [our] ‹ for ‹ [the consequences] ‹ of ‹ on the seventeenth ‹ — for
iniquities. us were caused Tammuz,

פֻּזַּרְנוּ בְּלִי מְצוֹא רְוָחָה, לָכֵן רָבְתָה בָּנוּ אֲנָחָה,

« was ‹ among ‹ increased ‹ there- « relief; ‹ finding ‹ without ‹ We were
groaning. us fore scattered

_____

(1) *Numbers* 31:50. (2) Cf. *Ezekiel* 21:20. (3) Cf. *Ecclesiastes* 1:15.

צוּר רְאֵה נַפְשֵׁנוּ כִּי שָׁחָה,[1]

《 it is prostrate 《 that 《 our soul, 《 see 《 O Rock,

וְשִׁבְעָה עָשָׂר בְּתַמּוּז הֲפָךְ לָנוּ לְשָׂשׂוֹן וּלְשִׂמְחָה.[2]

《 and gladness. 《 into joy 《 for us 《 transform 《 of Tammuz 《— and the seventeenth

קָשִׁינוּ עְרֶף וְרֻבְּתָה בָּנוּ אָסוֹן, לָכֵן נִתַּנּוּ לִמְשִׁסָּה וְרִפְשׁוֹן,

《 and mired 《 to be 《 we were 《 there- 《《 did ca- 《 among 《 therefore 《《 our 《 We
in muck.　trampled consigned fore, tastrophe; us increase necks, stiffened

רְאֵה יהוה וְחַלְּצֵנוּ מֵאָסוֹן,

《《 from 《 and 《 HASHEM, 《 See
catastrophe extricate us [this],

וְשִׁבְעָה עָשָׂר בְּתַמּוּז הֲפָךְ לָנוּ לְשִׂמְחָה וּלְשָׂשׂוֹן.[2]

《《 and joy. 《 into gladness 《 for us 《 transform 《 of Tammuz 《— and the seventeenth

❖ שַׁעֲנוּ שׁוֹכֵן רוּמָה, וְקַבֵּץ נְפוּצוֹתֵינוּ מִקְצְווֹת אֲדָמָה,

《《 of the 《 from the 《 our dispersed 《 gather 《《 on high; 《 You Who 《《 Turn
earth.　ends　ones　in　dwells　to us,

תּוֹסִיף יָדְךָ שֵׁנִית לִקְנוֹת אֲיוּמָה, וְתֹאמַר לְצִיּוֹן קוּמָה,

《《 Arise! 《《 to Zion, 《 and say 《《 the awe-struck 《 acquire 《 once 《 Your 《 May
nation,　more　hand　again

וְשִׁבְעָה עָשָׂר בְּתַמּוּז הֲפָךְ לָנוּ לְיוֹם יְשׁוּעָה וְנֶחָמָה.

《《 and 《 of 《 into 《 for us 《 transform 《 of 《 And the seventeenth
consolation. salvation a day　　Tammuz

AN INDIVIDUAL PRAYING WITHOUT A *MINYAN* OMITS THE NEXT TWO PARAGRAPHS,
BEGINNING אֵל מֶלֶךְ, *O GOD, KING,* AND 'ה, *HASHEM.*

אֵל מֶלֶךְ יוֹשֵׁב עַל כִּסֵּא רַחֲמִים, מִתְנַהֵג בַּחֲסִידוּת, מוֹחֵל

《 Who 《《 with 《 Who acts 《《 of mercy, 《 the 《 on 《 Who 《 King 《 O God,
pardons kindness,　　throne　sits

עֲווֹנוֹת עַמּוֹ, מַעֲבִיר רִאשׁוֹן רִאשׁוֹן, מַרְבֶּה מְחִילָה לַחַטָּאִים

《 to uninten- 《 pardon 《 Who abun- 《《 by one, 《 [sins] one 《 Who 《《 of His 《 the sins
tional sinners　　dantly grants　　removes　people,

וּסְלִיחָה לַפּוֹשְׁעִים, עֹשֶׂה צְדָקוֹת עִם כָּל בָּשָׂר וָרוּחַ, לֹא

《— not 《《 and 《 [beings 《 all 《 with 《 acts of 《 Who 《《 to willful 《 and
spirit of] flesh　　generosity performs　sinners,　forgiveness

כְרָעָתָם תִּגְמוֹל. ❖ אֵל הוֹרֵיתָ לָּנוּ לוֹמַר שְׁלֹשׁ עֶשְׂרֵה,

《《 the Thirteen 《 to recite 《 us 《 You 《 O 《《 do You repay 《 in accord with
[Attributes of Mercy];　　taught　God,　them!　their wickedness

וּזְכוֹר לָנוּ הַיּוֹם בְּרִית שְׁלֹשׁ עֶשְׂרֵה, כְּמוֹ שֶׁהוֹדַעְתָּ לֶעָנָיו

《 to the humble 《 You made 《 as 《《 of [these] Thirteen, 《 the 《 today 《 for us 《 remember
one [Moses]　known　　covenant

---

(1) Cf. *Psalms* 44:26. (2) Cf. *Zechariah* 8:19.

מִקֶּדֶם, כְּמוֹ שֶׁכָּתוּב, וַיֵּרֶד יהוה בֶּעָנָן וַיִּתְיַצֵּב עִמּוֹ שָׁם,

in ancient times, ⟪ *as* ⟩ *it is written:* ⟩ *And Hashem descended* ⟩ *in a cloud* ⟩ *and stood with him* ⟩ *there,* ⟩

וַיִּקְרָא בְשֵׁם יהוה.

⟪ *of Hashem.* ⟩ *with the Name* ⟩ *and He called out* ⟩

CONGREGATION AND *CHAZZAN* RECITE LOUDLY AND IN UNISON:

וַיַּעֲבֹר יהוה עַל פָּנָיו וַיִּקְרָא:

⟪ *and proclaimed:* ⟪ *[Moses'] face,* ⟩ *before* ⟩ *And Hashem passed* ⟩

יהוה, יהוה, אֵל, רַחוּם, וְחַנּוּן, אֶרֶךְ אַפַּיִם, וְרַב חֶסֶד, וֶאֱמֶת,

⟪ *and Truth,* ⟩ *in Kindness* ⟩ *and Abundant* ⟩ *to anger,* ⟩ *Slow* ⟪ *and Gracious,* ⟩ *Compassionate* ⟩ *God,* ⟩ *Hashem,* ⟩ *Hashem,*

נֹצֵר חֶסֶד לָאֲלָפִים, נֹשֵׂא עָוֹן, וָפֶשַׁע, וְחַטָּאָה, וְנַקֵּה.

⟪ *and Who absolves.* ⟩ *and inadvertent sin,* ⟩ *willful sin,* ⟩ *of iniquity,* ⟩ *Forgiver* ⟪ *for thousands [of generations],* ⟩ *of kindness* ⟩ *Preserver*

וְסָלַחְתָּ לַעֲוֹנֵנוּ וּלְחַטָּאתֵנוּ וּנְחַלְתָּנוּ. סְלַח לָנוּ אָבִינוּ כִּי

⟩ *for* ⟪ *our Father,* ⟩ *us,* ⟩ *Forgive* ⟪ *and make us Your heritage.* ⟪ *and our sins,* ⟩ *our iniquities* ⟩ *May You forgive*

חָטָאנוּ, מְחַל לָנוּ מַלְכֵּנוּ כִּי פָשָׁעְנוּ. כִּי אַתָּה אֲדֹנָי טוֹב

⟩ *are good* ⟩ *O Lord,* ⟩ *You,* ⟩ *For* ⟪ *we have willfully sinned.* ⟩ *for* ⟪ *our King,* ⟩ *us,* ⟩ *pardon* ⟪ *we have sinned;*

וְסַלָּח, וְרַב חֶסֶד לְכָל קֹרְאֶיךָ.

⟪ *who call upon You.* ⟩ *to all* ⟩ *kind* ⟩ *and* ⟪ *and abundantly forgiving,*

אֱלֹהִים אַל דֳּמִי לָךְ, אַל תֶּחֱרַשׁ וְאַל תִּשְׁקֹט אֵל. כִּי הִנֵּה[1]

⟩ *behold,* ⟩ *For* ⟪ *O God.* ⟩ *still,* ⟩ *and be not* ⟩ *deaf* ⟩ *be not* ⟪ *hold Yourself silent;* ⟩ *do not* ⟩ *O God,*

אוֹיְבֶיךָ יֶהֱמָיוּן, וּמְשַׂנְאֶיךָ נָשְׂאוּ רֹאשׁ.[1] אֵל נְקָמוֹת יהוה,

⟪ *Hashem;* ⟩ *of vengeance,* ⟩ *O God* ⟪ *their head.* ⟩ *have raised* ⟩ *and those who hate You* ⟩ *are in uproar* ⟩ *Your enemies*

אֵל נְקָמוֹת הוֹפִיעַ.[2]

⟪ *appear!* ⟩ *of vengeance,* ⟩ *O God*

כְּרַחֵם אָב עַל בָּנִים, כֵּן תְּרַחֵם יהוה עָלֵינוּ. לַיהוה

⟩ *To Hashem* ⟪ *on us.* ⟩ *Hashem,* ⟩ *have mercy,* ⟩ *so* ⟪ *his children,* ⟩ *toward* ⟩ *a father is* ⟩ *As merciful as*

הַיְשׁוּעָה, עַל עַמְּךָ בִרְכָתֶךָ סֶּלָה. יהוה צְבָאוֹת עִמָּנוּ,

⟪ *is with us,* ⟩ *Master of Legions,* ⟩ *Hashem,* ⟪ *Selah.* ⟩ *is Your blessing,* ⟩ *Your people* ⟩ *upon* ⟪ *is salvation,*

---

(1) *Psalms* 83:2-3. (2) 94:1.

מִשְׂגָּב לָנוּ אֱלֹהֵי יַעֲקֹב סֶלָה. יהוה צְבָאוֹת, אַשְׁרֵי אָדָם

a / for / is the / stronghold / us / — praise- / Master of / Hashem, / Selah. / of / is the / for / a
man / worthy / Legions / / / Jacob, / God / us / stronghold

בְּטֵחַ בָּךְ. יהוה הוֹשִׁיעָה, הַמֶּלֶךְ יַעֲנֵנוּ בְיוֹם קָרְאֵנוּ.

we call. / on the day / answer us / May the King / save! / Hashem, / in You. / who trusts

אֱלֹהֵינוּ וֵאלֹהֵי אֲבוֹתֵינוּ

of our forefathers: / and the God / Our God

אָמֵר* בְּבֶכִי¹ מִפְּנֵי יָד שְׁלוּחָה בִּי,²

in / that was / the / because / with / I make
destruction. stretched out hand of weeping [myself] bitter*

בְּנַאֲצִי בְּתוֹךְ בֵּיתוֹ בִּבְגָדִי וְקָבְעִי,

and my / through my / His / inside / When I
robbery, treachery Temple scorned [God]

גָּח וּבָרַח וְנָסַע עֶשֶׂר³ וְעָלָה לַשְּׁבִיעִי,

to the seventh / and / in ten / and / and fled / He
[heaven]; ascended [stages], departed left

דְּמַנִּי הִצִּיקַנִי הִסִּיקַנִי בַּחֹדֶשׁ הָרְבִיעִי.

in the fourth month. / He set me / He oppressed / He cut
ablaze me, me down,

הֵבִיא מוֹעֵד בִּמְלֹאתוֹ⁴ לִשְׁבֹּר בַּחוּרֵי⁵ גְּמוּז,

who were / [my] / to break / in its / the appointed / He brought
blossoming; youths fullness time about

וְרִבָּה בוֹ פַעֲמַיִם⁶ בְּמַסְמוּס וּמִזְמוּז,⁷

and crushing. / crippling / twice / in it [the / He mul-
month] tiplied

זְבוּלוֹ כְּשֶׁר שַׁאֲנַנּוֹת מְבַכּוֹת אֶת הַתַּמּוּז,⁸

the Tammuz / over / weeping / complacent / He / When in
idol, women saw His Temple

חִיְּבַנִי אֹיְבַנִי אֲזַי בְּיֶרַח תַּמּוּז.

of / in the / then, / and made / He found
Tammuz. month me an enemy, me guilty

טָמְנוּ פַחִים חֲמִשָּׁה⁹ בְּמִקְרָא תְּלָאוֹת מְשֻׁלָּחוֹת,

are being / that [these] / proclaiming / five traps, / [Our ene-
dispatched; calamities mies] laid

---

(1) Cf. *Isaiah* 22:4. (2) Cf. *Job* 30:24. (3) See *Rosh Hashanah* 31a. (4) See *Taanis* 29a.
(5) Cf. *Lamentations* 1:15. (6) See *Taanis* 28b. (7) Cf. *Chullin* 45b. (8) *Ezekiel* 8:14. (9) See *Taanis* 26a.

◆§ אָמֵר — *I make [myself] bitter.* The first twenty-two verses follow an alphabetical scheme. The second letters of these verses along with the initial letters of the remaining verses spell מְנַחֵם בְּרַבִּי מָכִיר יִגְדַּל וְיִחְי לָנֶצַח חַיֵּי עַד סֶלָה אָמֵן, *Menachem, son of Rabbi Machir, may he become great and live triumphantly, an everlasting life. Selah. Amen* (see page 737).

יְבְלוּ   לִי   בְּשִׁבְעָה עָשָׂר בּוֹ בַּאֲלִיחוֹת,

because of [my] ⟨ of it ⟨ on the ⟨ me ⟨ they over-
depravities.   [Tammuz], seventeenth   powered

כִּי נוֹקַשְׁתִּי כְּכַלָּה עֲלוּבָה   בְּחֻפַּת   שַׁלְוָה וְהַצְלָחוֹת,

and   ⟨ which ⟨ [caught unfaithful] ⟨ who is ⟨ like a ⟨ I was ⟨ For
auspicious;   was calm in her bridal chamber disgraceful,   bride   ensnared

לְרוֹעִי   לֹא הִמְתַּנְתִּי שֵׁשׁ וְנִשְׁתַּבְּרוּ הַלֻחוֹת.

were the ⟨ and shattered ⟨ until the ⟨ wait ⟨ I did ⟨ for my shep-
Tablets.   sixth [hour]   not herd [Moses],

מִיָּדוֹ עָדִיתִי חֲלִי וָכֶתֶם אֶצְעָדָה וְצָמִיד,

and ⟨ armbands ⟨ and ⟨ with ⟨ I was ⟨ From
bracelets;   gold, ornaments adorned His hand

נִגְרוֹת בְּיוֹם אַפּוֹ כְּשֶׁחַתִּי דְרָכַי לְהַשְׁמִיד,

bringing about ⟨ my ⟨ when I ⟨ of His ⟨ on the ⟨ they were
destruction.   ways, corrupted wrath,   day swept away

סֵדֶר   עֲבוֹדָתוֹ   וְקֵיץ   מִזְבְּחוֹ קַצְתִּי לְהַעֲמִיד,

to maintain; ⟨ I ⟨ on His ⟨ and the extra ⟨ of His [Tem- ⟨ The pro-
disdained   Altar   elevation-offerings ple] service cedures

עַל כֵּן מִלִּשְׁכַּת הַטְּלָאִים בָּטַל הַתָּמִיד.

was the ⟨ canceled ⟨ where the sheep ⟨ from the ⟨ therefore
daily offering.   [were kept],   chamber

פּוּר הִתְפּוֹרָרָה וְנִתְפַּזֵּרָה סוֹעֲרָה עֲנִיָּה,

afflicted one ⟨ was the ⟨ and dispersed ⟨ Completely crumbled
[Israel];   storm-tossed

צִיָּה נִמְשְׁלָה מִבְּלִי חוֹבֵל וְנִטְרְפָה כָאֳנִיָּה,

like a boat. ⟨ and it was ⟨ a captain, ⟨ without ⟨ was it ⟨ to a
tossed about   likened,   ship

קָחְתָּה בְּחַטָּאתָהּ בְּרֹאשָׁהּ, וּבְכֶפֶל תַּאֲנִיָּה וַאֲנִיָּה,

and grief; ⟨ agony ⟨ and with ⟨ on her head, ⟨ [punishment] ⟨ She [Israel]
doubled   for her sin   received

רִיבוּהָ צָרֶיהָ כְּהַיּוֹם וְהִבְקְעָה הָעִיר בַּשְּׁנִיָּה.

in the Second ⟨ was the ⟨ and breached ⟨ on this ⟨ did her ⟨ attack
[Commonwealth].   City   day, tormentors   her

שְׁלוּחָה כַּצְּבִי מֻדָּח מֵאֵין דּוֹרֵשׁ לְהַסְתִּירָהּ,

to shelter her; ⟨ caring ⟨ with ⟨ that is ⟨ like a ⟨ She was
no one   chased away, deer   exiled

---

(1) See *Shabbos* 88b. (2) See 89a. (3) See 88a. (4) Cf. *Proverbs* 25:12.
(5) *Numbers* 31:50. (6) *Job* 20:28. (7) See *Succah* 56a. (8) *Isaiah* 24:19.
(9) Cf. 54:11. (10) *Lamentations* 2:5. (11) Cf. *Isaiah* 13:14.

שָׁנְנוּ לְשׁוֹנָם וּנְתָנוּהָ כְּשֶׂה צַמְרָה וְחֶלְבָּה לְהַתִּירָה,

have been 〈 and fat 〈 whose wool 〈 like a 〈 and con- 〈 their 〈 they
made available. sheep sidered her tongues sharpened

תִּצְעַק עַל כְּלִי חֶמְדָּה שֶׁבּוֹ נִכְתָּרָה,

she had been 〈 with 〈 the precious vessel 〈 over 〈 She
crowned, which [the Torah] cries out

תַּחֲמוֹד עֵינֶיהָ¹ נִצַּל כְּשָׂרַף אַפּוֹסְטְמוֹס הַתּוֹרָה.²

the Torah. 〈 when Apostomos burned 〈 was taken away 〈 of her eyes 〈 the darling

חֵרֵף עֲשׁוּקִים וּרְצוּצִים בַּעֲבוּר הַרְעִימָה³ סָכָל,

— [so did] the foolish 〈 to provoke 〈 in order 〈 and crushed 〈 the 〈 He
[Nebuchadnezzar] — them ones oppressed reviled

יְרוּדִים בּוְהָיָה לֶאֱכוֹל וּבְהַסְתֵּר פָּנִים⁴ מִלְּהִסְתַּכָּל,

— His not looking 〈〈 of [God's] 〈 and through 〈〈 *devoured*, 〈 through 〈 those
at them. face the concealment [the curses of] who were
They will be subjugated

יַד הַשָּׁלֵים⁵ מִבְּנַף שִׁקּוּצִים⁶ נֶאֱכָל,

that was consumed 〈 of the abomi- 〈 from the 〈 was broken off 〈 A
[that Menasheh placed in the Temple], nable idol arm [as punishment] hand

עֵת צָרָה כְּהִתְכַּנֵּס⁷ וְהָעֲמַד צֶלֶם בְּהֵיכָל.⁸

in the 〈 an idol 〈 and 〈 when there 〈 of 〈 at the
Sanctuary. erected was brought in distress, time

דְּוְוִים סְגוּפִים בָּנִים הֶהָיוּ מִקֶּדֶם רִאשׁוֹנִים,

foremost, 〈 previously 〈 who were 〈 were the children 〈 and afflicted 〈 Miserable

סְמוּכוֹת צָרוֹתֵיהֶם זוֹ לָזוֹ כַּמָּה שָׁנִים,

years. 〈 for many 〈 after the other, 〈 one 〈 came their troubles, 〈 consecutively

לוֹקִים כַּאֲשֶׁר תַּעֲשֶׂינָה הַדְּבוֹרִים⁹ וְהָעַקְרַבִּים שׁוֹנִים,

of all sorts; 〈 and scorpions 〈 bees 〈 do 〈 as 〈 They are stricken

הוֹגִים אָבַד שִׂבְרָם וּבָטֵל סִכּוּיָם¹⁰ בְּאִישׁוֹנִים.

in the darkness 〈 is their 〈 and 〈 is their 〈 that 〈 they think
[of exile]. aspiration nullified hope lost

❖ אֵל קַנָּא, בְּהִתְאַפֵּק בְּמַקְנִיאֶיךָ דְּשֵׁנִים רְטוּבִים,

and thriving, 〈 who 〈 from [punishing] those 〈 as You restrain 〈〈 Who is 〈 O
are fat who provoke You, Yourself Jealous, God

מְחַכִּים תָּקִים עוֹמְדִים לְעוֹלָמִים,

forever, 〈 [and] that they 〈 You should 〈 [the time has
remain standing raise up, arrived that]
those who await,

---

(1) Cf. *I Kings* 20:6. (2) See *Taanis* 26b. (3) *I Samuel* 1:6. (4) Cf. *Deuteronomy* 31:17.
(5) See *Taanis* 28b-29a. (6) Cf. *Daniel* 19:27. (7) Cf. *Isaiah* 28:20.
(8) See *Sanhedrin* 103b. (9) *Deuteronomy* 1:44. (10) Cf. *Yoma* 72a.

כִּנְטִיעִים מְחֻטָּבִים¹ בַּאֲהָבִים,

≪ lovingly. ⟨ crafted ⟨ like saplings

הָאֱמֶת וְהַשָּׁלוֹם² בְּצוֹמוֹת חֲטוּבִים,

≪ hewn, ⟨are from the fasts⟨ and peace ⟨ Truth

נֵצַח הֱיוֹתָם לְשִׂמְחָה וּלְשָׂשׂוֹן וּלְמוֹעֲדִים טוֹבִים.²

≪ and happy occasions. ⟨ and joy, ⟨[times for] gladness ⟨ to become ⟨ forever

**AN INDIVIDUAL PRAYING WITHOUT A *MINYAN* OMITS THE NEXT TWO PARAGRAPHS,
BEGINNING אֵל מֶלֶךְ, *O GOD, KING,* AND ה', *HASHEM.*

אֵל מֶלֶךְ יוֹשֵׁב עַל כִּסֵּא רַחֲמִים, מִתְנַהֵג בַּחֲסִידוּת, מוֹחֵל

⟨ Who ≪ with ⟨ Who acts ≪ of mercy, ⟨ the ⟨ on ⟨ Who ⟨ King ⟨ O God,
pardons kindness, throne sits

עֲוֹנוֹת עַמּוֹ, מַעֲבִיר רִאשׁוֹן רִאשׁוֹן, מַרְבֶּה מְחִילָה לְחַטָּאִים

⟨ to uninten- ⟨ pardon ⟨ Who abun- ⟨ by one, ⟨ [sins] one ⟨ Who ≪ of His ⟨ the sins
tional sinners dantly grants removes people,

וּסְלִיחָה לַפּוֹשְׁעִים, עֹשֶׂה צְדָקוֹת עִם כָּל בָּשָׂר וָרוּחַ, לֹא

⟨—not ≪ and ⟨ [beings ⟨ all ⟨ with ⟨ acts of ⟨ Who ≪ to willful ⟨ and
spirit generosity performs sinners, forgiveness
of] flesh

כְרָעָתָם תִּגְמוֹל. ❖ אֵל הוֹרֵיתָ לָּנוּ לוֹמַר שְׁלֹשׁ עֶשְׂרֵה, וּזְכוֹר

⟨ remember ≪ the Thirteen ⟨ to recite ⟨ us ⟨ You ⟨ O ≪ do You ⟨ in accord with
[Attributes of Mercy]; taught God, repay them! their wickedness

לָנוּ הַיּוֹם בְּרִית שְׁלֹשׁ עֶשְׂרֵה, כְּמוֹ שֶׁהוֹדַעְתָּ לֶעָנָיו מִקֶּדֶם, כְּמוֹ

⟨ as ≪ in ancient⟨ to the humble ⟨ You made ⟨ as ≪ of [these] Thirteen, ⟨ the ⟨ today ⟨ for us
times, one [Moses] known covenant

שֶׁכָּתוּב, וַיֵּרֶד יהוה בֶּעָנָן וַיִּתְיַצֵּב עִמּוֹ שָׁם, וַיִּקְרָא בְשֵׁם יהוה.

≪ of ⟨ with the ⟨ and He ≪ there, ⟨ with ⟨ and stood ⟨ in a ⟨ *And HASHEM* ≪ it is written:
HASHEM. Name called out him cloud descended

CONGREGATION AND *CHAZZAN* RECITE LOUDLY AND IN UNISON:

וַיַּעֲבֹר יהוה עַל פָּנָיו וַיִּקְרָא:

≪ and proclaimed: ≪ [Moses'] face, ⟨ before ⟨ *And HASHEM* passed

יהוה, יהוה, אֵל, רַחוּם, וְחַנּוּן, אֶרֶךְ אַפַּיִם, וְרַב חֶסֶד, וֶאֱמֶת,

≪ and ⟨ in ⟨ and ⟨ to anger, ⟨ Slow ≪ and ⟨ Compas- ⟨ God, ⟨ *HASHEM,* ⟨ *HASHEM,*
Truth, Kindness Abundant Gracious, sionate

נֹצֵר חֶסֶד לָאֲלָפִים, נֹשֵׂא עָוֹן, וָפֶשַׁע, וְחַטָּאָה, וְנַקֵּה.

≪ and Who ⟨ and inad- ⟨ willful ⟨ of ⟨ Forgiver ≪ for thousands ⟨ of ⟨ Preserver
absolves. vertent sin, sin, iniquity, [of generations], kindness

וְסָלַחְתָּ לַעֲוֹנֵנוּ וּלְחַטָּאתֵנוּ וּנְחַלְתָּנוּ. סְלַח לָנוּ אָבִינוּ כִּי

⟨ for ≪ our ⟨ us, ⟨ Forgive ≪ and make us ≪ and our sins, ⟨ our ⟨ May You
Father, Your heritage. iniquities forgive

---

(1) Cf. *Psalms* 144:12. (2) Cf. *Zechariah* 8:19.

חָטָאנוּ, מְחַל לָנוּ מַלְכֵּנוּ כִּי פָשָׁעְנוּ. כִּי אַתָּה אֲדֹנָי טוֹב

‹‹ we have ‹ pardon ‹‹ us, ‹ our King, ‹‹ for ‹ we have ‹‹ For ‹ You, ‹ O Lord, ‹ are
sinned; willfully sinned. good

וְסַלָּח, וְרַב חֶסֶד לְכָל קֹרְאֶיךָ.

‹‹ and ‹‹ and ‹ kind ‹ and ‹ to all ‹ who call
abundantly forgiving, upon You.

THE FOLLOWING PRAYER IS RECITED ALOUD RESPONSIVELY.

CHAZZAN, THEN CONGREGATION:

שְׁעֵה* נֶאֱסָר, אֲשֶׁר נִמְסַר, בְּיַד בָּבֶל וְגַם שֵׂעִיר,

‹‹ of Seir; ‹ and ‹ of ‹ into the ‹ was ‹ that ‹ the captive ‹ Turn to*
also Babylon hand delivered [nation]

לְךָ יֶהֱמֶה, זֶה כַּמֶּה, וְיִתְחַנֵן כְּבֶן צָעִיר,

‹‹ like a young child ‹ and supplicates ‹ for so long now, ‹ it yearns ‹ for You

יוֹם גָּבַר הָאוֹיֵב וַתִּבָּקַע הָעִיר.

‹‹ was ‹ and ‹ when the enemy ‹ — on
the City. breached prevailed, the day

CONGREGATION, THEN *CHAZZAN*:

לְזֹאת אֶכַּף, וְאֶסְפּוֹק כַּף,[1] בְּיוֹם חֲמֵשׁ[2] פְּזָרוֹנִי,

‹‹ dispersed me. ‹ when five ‹ on the ‹ my ‹ and I clap ‹ I am bowed ‹ For this
[tragedies] day hands [in grief] over,

וְעַל רֶגֶל, הָעֵגֶל, הַלוּחוֹת יְצָאוּנִי,

‹‹ went away ‹ the Tablets ‹ of the ‹ a con- ‹ As
from me; [Golden] Calf, sequence

וְגַם הִשְׁמִיד, הַתָּמִיד, וּבַסוּגַר הֱבִיאַנִי,[3]

‹‹ he took me; ‹ and in ‹‹ the daily ‹ [the enemy] ‹ also
chains offering, abolished

וְהוּשַׁם אֱלִיל, בְּהֵיכַל כְּלִיל, וּמֵעֲצָתוֹ,[4] כְּלָאַנִי,

‹‹ he imprisoned ‹ and through His coun- ‹‹ of consum- ‹ in the ‹ was an ‹ placed
me; sel [to the enemy] mate [beauty], Sanctuary idol

וְהַמִּנְחָה הוּנָחָה, וְדָתְךָ צָר בָּאֵשׁ הִבְעִיר.

‹‹ burned ‹ in flames ‹ the ‹ and Your ‹‹ came to ‹ the meal-
enemy Law a stop, offering

יוֹם גָּבַר הָאוֹיֵב וַתִּבָּקַע הָעִיר.

‹‹ was ‹ and ‹ when the enemy ‹ — on
the City. breached prevailed, the day

(1) Cf. *Lamentations* 1:15. (2) See *Taanis* 26b. (3) Cf. *Ezekiel* 19:9. (4) See *Sanhedrin* 97b.

❧§ שְׁעֵה — *Turn to.* The acrostic spells the author's name שְׁלֹמֹה, *Shlomo.*

CONGREGATION, THEN *CHAZZAN:*

מְאֹד אֶתְחַל, וָאֶתְחַלְחָל, בְּיוֹם שַׁדַּי דְּחָפָנִי,

Exceed- ⟩ I grow ill ⟩ and I become ⟩ on the ⟩ the ⟩ pushed ⟨⟨
ingly distraught day Almighty me away.

מְאוֹר חָשַׁךְ, וְגַם שֵׁשַׁךְ, כְּמוֹ כַדּוּר צְנָפָנִי,¹

The light ⟩ grew ⟩ and ⟩ Sheshach ⟩ like ⟩ a ball ⟩ wrapped around ⟨⟨
dark, also [Babylon] my [head].

וְהַשְּׁפִיפוֹן, מִצָּפוֹן, כְּשִׁבֹּלֶת שְׁטָפָנִי,²

The serpent ⟩ from the ⟩ like a rushing ⟩ swept me ⟨⟨
[Nebuchadnezzar] north current away.

וְהַצַּיִּד, שָׁלַח יָד, וְהַצָּפִיר וְהַשָּׂעִיר,³

The hunter ⟩ sent ⟩ his hand ⟩ as did the he-goat ⟨⟨
[Edom/Rome] forth [against me], [Greece]

יוֹם גָּבַר הָאוֹיֵב וַתִּבָּקַע הָעִיר.

— on ⟩ when the enemy ⟩ and ⟩ was ⟨⟨
the day prevailed, breached the City.

CONGREGATION, THEN *CHAZZAN:*

הוֹד לִבִּי, וּמִשְׂגַּבִּי, הֲלָעַד אַפְּךָ יֶעְשַׁן,⁴

O ⟩ Glory ⟩ of my ⟩ my Fortress, ⟨⟨ will ⟩ Your ⟩ fume? ⟨⟨
heart, wrath forever

הֲלֹא תִרְאֶה, עַם נִלְאָה, אֲשֶׁר הֻשְׁחַר כְּמוֹ כִבְשָׁן,

Do You not ⟩ see ⟩ the ⟩ that is ⟩ that ⟩ has become ⟩ like ⟩ a furnace? ⟨⟨
nation weary, blackened

גְּדוֹר פִּרְצִי, בְּבֶן פַּרְצִי, וּמֵחֶדֶק לְקֹט שׁוֹשָׁן,

Repair ⟩ my ⟩ breach ⟩ through ⟩ of Peretz ⟨⟨ and from among ⟩ pluck ⟩ the rose ⟨⟨
[the Messiah], the offspring the thorns [Israel].

בְּנֵה בֵית זְבוּל,⁵ לְהָשִׁיב גְּבוּל,⁶ הַכַּרְמֶל וְהַבָּשָׁן,⁷

Build ⟩ [Your] ⟩ dwelling, place ⟨⟨ and ⟩ restore ⟩ the ⟩ borders ⟩ of the ⟩ Carmel ⟩ and ⟩ Bashan.

וְעַיִן פְּקַח, וְנָקָם קַח, מֵאָצֶר וּמִדִּישָׁן,⁸

Your ⟩ eyes ⟩ open, ⟨⟨ and ⟩ take ⟩ revenge ⟩ from ⟩ Ezer ⟩ and from Dishan ⟨
[the Edomites].

שְׁפוֹט אִלֵּם, וְאָז יְשַׁלֵּם, הַמַּבְעֶה וְהַמַּבְעִיר,⁹

Bring ⟩ justice ⟩ to the mute ⟩ one [Israel], ⟨⟨ then ⟩ he will ⟨ pay ⟩ — the [nation] ⟨⟨ that consumes ⟩ and sets fire ⟨
[to Israel].

יוֹם גָּבַר הָאוֹיֵב וַתִּבָּקַע הָעִיר.

— on ⟩ when the enemy ⟩ and ⟩ was ⟨⟨
the day prevailed, breached the City.

TURN TO PAGE 684 FOR אֵל מֶלֶךְ, AND CONTINUE UNTIL THE CONCLUSION OF *SELICHOS.*

(1) Cf. *Isaiah* 22:18. (2) Cf. *Psalms* 69:3. (3) Cf. *Daniel* 8:21. (4) Cf. *Psalms* 74:1. (5) Cf. *I Kings* 8:13.
(6) Cf. *II Kings* 14:25. (7) *Jeremiah* 50:19. (8) Cf. *Genesis* 36:21. (9) Cf. *Bava Kamma* 2a.

﹖ PRAYER ON LACK OF RAIN / תפלה על עצירת גשמים ﹖

WHEN THE RABBIS OF *ERETZ YISRAEL* CALL FOR SPECIAL PRAYERS TO BE SAID BECAUSE OF A LACK OF RAIN, THIS PRAYER IS ADDED IN THE BLESSING FOR ACCEPTANCE OF PRAYER (שְׁמַע קוֹלֵנוּ) BEFORE כִּי אַתָּה . . . SOME AUTHORITIES HOLD THAT IT IS SAID BY THE *CHAZZAN* ONLY.

וַעֲנֵנוּ בּוֹרֵא עוֹלָם בְּמִדַּת הָרַחֲמִים בָּחַר בְּעַמּוֹ יִשְׂרָאֵל
‹ Israel ‹ His ‹ He Who ≪ of Mercy, ‹ with the ≪ of the ‹ O ≪ Answer
people chose Attribute universe, Creator us,

לְהוֹדִיעַ גָּדְלוֹ וְהַדְרַת כְּבוֹדוֹ. שׁוֹמֵעַ תְּפִלָּה, תֵּן טַל וּמָטָר עַל
‹ on ‹ and ‹ dew ‹ give ≪ prayer, ‹ He Who ≪ of His ‹ and the ‹ His ‹ to make
rain hears glory. splendor greatness known

פְּנֵי הָאֲדָמָה, וְשַׂבַּע אֶת הָעוֹלָם כֻּלּוֹ מִטּוּבֶךָ, וּמַלֵּא יָדֵינוּ
‹ our ‹ and fill ‹ from Your ‹ all ‹ the world, ‹ and satisfy ≪ of the earth, ‹ the
hands bounty, of it, face

מִבִּרְכוֹתֶיךָ וּמֵעֹשֶׁר מַתְּנַת יָדֶךָ. שְׁמֹר וְהַצֵּל שָׁנָה זוֹ מִכָּל דָּבָר
‹ thing ‹ from ‹ this year ‹ and ‹ Protect ≪ of Your ‹ of the ‹ and from ‹ from Your
every rescue hands. gift the richness blessings

רַע, וּמִכָּל מִינֵי מַשְׁחִית וּמִכָּל מִינֵי פֻּרְעָנִיּוֹת, וַעֲשֵׂה לָהּ תִּקְוָה
‹ hope ‹ for it ‹ Create ≪ of ‹ manner ‹ and ≪ of ‹ manner ‹ from ≪ evil,
misfortunes. from all destruction all

וְאַחֲרִית שָׁלוֹם. חוּס וְרַחֵם עָלֵינוּ וְעַל כָּל תְּבוּאָתָהּ
‹ its crops ‹ all ‹ and on ‹ on us ‹ and have ‹ Have ≪ [in] peace. ‹ and a
compassion pity culmination

וּפֵרוֹתֶיהָ, וּבָרְכָהּ בְּגִשְׁמֵי רָצוֹן בְּרָכָה וּנְדָבָה וְחַיִּים וְשֹׂבַע וְשָׁלוֹם
≪ and ‹ satis- ‹ life, ‹ generosity, ‹ blessing, ‹ of ‹ with ‹ bless it ≪ and its fruit;
peace, faction, favor, rains

כַּשָּׁנִים הַטּוֹבוֹת. וְהָסֵר מִמֶּנּוּ דֶּבֶר וְחֶרֶב וְרָעָב, וְחַיָּה רָעָה
‹ that are ‹ animals ≪ and ‹ sword, ‹ plague, ‹ from ‹ Remove ≪ that were ‹ like the
harmful, famine, us good. years

וּשְׁבִי וּבִזָּה, וְיֵצֶר הָרַע וַחֲלָיִים רָעִים וְקָשִׁים וּמְאֹרָעוֹת
‹ and ≪ and ‹ that are ‹ diseases ≪ for ‹ the ≪ and ‹ captivity,
incidents harsh, severe Evil, Inclination plundering,

רָעִים וְקָשִׁים. וּגְזֹר עָלֵינוּ גְּזֵרוֹת טוֹבוֹת מִלְּפָנֶיךָ, וְיִגָּלוּ
‹ Over- ≪ before You. ‹ that are ‹ decrees ‹ for us ‹ Decree ≪ and harsh. ‹ that are
whelm good severe

רַחֲמֶיךָ עַל מִדּוֹתֶיךָ וְתִתְנַהֵג עִם בָּנֶיךָ בְּמִדַּת רַחֲמִים,
≪ of Mercy. ‹ with the ‹ Your ‹ with ‹ and may You ‹ Your Attributes, ‹ may Your
Attribute children conduct Yourself Mercy

וְקַבֵּל בְּרַחֲמִים וּבְרָצוֹן אֶת תְּפִלָּתֵנוּ.
≪ our prayer. ‹ and favor ‹ with ‹ Accept
compassion

❧ VERSES FOR PEOPLE'S NAMES / פסוקים לשמות אנשים ❧

Kitzur Sh'lah teaches that it is a source of merit to recite a Scriptural verse representing one's name before יִהְיוּ לְרָצוֹן at the end of *Shemoneh Esrei*. The verse should either contain the person's name, or else begin and end with the first and last letters of the name.

Following is a selection of first and last letters of names, with appropriate verses:

א...א אָנָּא יהוה הוֹשִׁיעָה נָּא, אָנָּא יהוה הַצְלִיחָה נָּא.[1]

א...ה אַשְׁרֵי מַשְׂכִּיל אֶל דָּל, בְּיוֹם רָעָה יְמַלְּטֵהוּ יהוה.[2]

א...ו אַשְׁרֵי שֶׁאֵל יַעֲקֹב בְּעֶזְרוֹ, שִׂבְרוֹ עַל יהוה אֱלֹהָיו.[3]

א...י אֲמָרַי הַאֲזִינָה יהוה, בִּינָה הֲגִיגִי.[4]

א...ך אָמַרְתְּ לַיהוה, אֲדֹנָי אָתָּה, טוֹבָתִי בַּל עָלֶיךָ.[5]

א...ל אֶרֶץ רָעָשָׁה, אַף שָׁמַיִם נָטְפוּ מִפְּנֵי אֱלֹהִים; זֶה סִינַי, מִפְּנֵי אֱלֹהִים אֱלֹהֵי יִשְׂרָאֵל.[6]

א...ם אַתָּה הוּא יהוה הָאֱלֹהִים, אֲשֶׁר בָּחַרְתָּ בְּאַבְרָם, וְהוֹצֵאתוֹ מֵאוּר כַּשְׂדִּים, וְשַׂמְתָּ שְּׁמוֹ אַבְרָהָם.[7]

א...ן אֵלֶיךָ יהוה אֶקְרָא, וְאֶל אֲדֹנָי אֶתְחַנָּן.[8]

א...ע אָמַר בְּלִבּוֹ בַּל אֶמּוֹט, לְדֹר וָדֹר אֲשֶׁר לֹא בְרָע.[9]

א...ר אֵלֶּה בָרֶכֶב וְאֵלֶּה בַסּוּסִים, וַאֲנַחְנוּ בְּשֵׁם יהוה אֱלֹהֵינוּ נַזְכִּיר.[10]

ב...א בְּרִיתִי הָיְתָה אִתּוֹ הַחַיִּים וְהַשָּׁלוֹם, וָאֶתְּנֵם לוֹ מוֹרָא וַיִּירָאֵנִי, וּמִפְּנֵי שְׁמִי נִחַת הוּא.[11]

ב...ה בַּעֲבוּר יִשְׁמְרוּ חֻקָּיו, וְתוֹרֹתָיו יִנְצֹרוּ, הַלְלוּיָהּ.[12]

ב...ז בְּיוֹם קָרָאתִי וַתַּעֲנֵנִי, תַּרְהִבֵנִי בְנַפְשִׁי עֹז.[13]

ב...ך בָּרוּךְ אַתָּה יהוה, לַמְּדֵנִי חֻקֶּיךָ.[14]

ב...ל בְּמַקְהֵלוֹת בָּרְכוּ אֱלֹהִים, אֲדֹנָי מִמְּקוֹר יִשְׂרָאֵל.[15]

ב...ם בְּךָ יהוה חָסִיתִי, אַל אֵבוֹשָׁה לְעוֹלָם.[16]

ב...ן בָּרוּךְ יהוה אֱלֹהֵי יִשְׂרָאֵל מֵהָעוֹלָם וְעַד הָעוֹלָם, אָמֵן וְאָמֵן.[17]

ב...ע בְּחֶסֶד וֶאֱמֶת יְכֻפַּר עָוֹן, וּבְיִרְאַת יהוה סוּר מֵרָע.[18]

ג...ה גּוֹל עַל יהוה דַּרְכֶּךָ, וּבְטַח עָלָיו וְהוּא יַעֲשֶׂה.[19]

ג...ל גַּם אֲנִי אוֹדְךָ בִכְלִי נֶבֶל אֲמִתְּךָ אֱלֹהָי, אֲזַמְּרָה לְךָ בְכִנּוֹר, קְדוֹשׁ יִשְׂרָאֵל.[20]

ג...ן גַּם בְּנֵי אָדָם גַּם בְּנֵי אִישׁ, יַחַד עָשִׁיר וְאֶבְיוֹן.[21]

ד...א דִּרְשׁוּ יהוה בְּהִמָּצְאוֹ, קְרָאֻהוּ בִּהְיוֹתוֹ קָרוֹב.[22]

ד...ד דִּרְשׁוּ יהוה וְעֻזּוֹ, בַּקְּשׁוּ פָנָיו תָּמִיד.[23]

ד...ה דְּאָגָה בְלֶב אִישׁ יַשְׁחֶנָּה, וְדָבָר טוֹב יְשַׂמְּחֶנָּה.[24]

ד...ל דָּן יָדִין עַמּוֹ, כְּאַחַד שִׁבְטֵי יִשְׂרָאֵל.[25]

ה...א הַצּוּר תָּמִים פָּעֳלוֹ, כִּי כָל דְּרָכָיו מִשְׁפָּט, אֵל אֱמוּנָה וְאֵין עָוֶל, צַדִּיק וְיָשָׁר הוּא.[26]

ה...ה הַסְתֵּר פָּנֶיךָ מֵחֲטָאָי, וְכָל עֲוֹנֹתַי מְחֵה.[27]

ה...ל הַקְשִׁיבָה לְקוֹל שַׁוְעִי מַלְכִּי וֵאלֹהָי, כִּי אֵלֶיךָ אֶתְפַּלָּל.[28]

ז...ב זֵכֶר צַדִּיק לִבְרָכָה, וְשֵׁם רְשָׁעִים יִרְקָב.[29]

ז...ה זֹאת מְנוּחָתִי עֲדֵי עַד, פֹּה אֵשֵׁב כִּי אִוִּתִיהָ.[30]

ז...ח זָכַרְתִּי יָמִים מִקֶּדֶם, הָגִיתִי בְכָל פָּעֳלֶךָ, בְּמַעֲשֵׂה יָדֶיךָ אֲשׂוֹחֵחַ.[31]

ז...ן זְבוּלֻן לְחוֹף יַמִּים יִשְׁכֹּן, וְהוּא לְחוֹף אֳנִיּוֹת, וְיַרְכָתוֹ עַל צִידֹן.[32]

ח...ה חָגְרָה בְעוֹז מָתְנֶיהָ, וַתְּאַמֵּץ זְרוֹעֹתֶיהָ.[33]

ח...ך חֲצוֹת לַיְלָה אָקוּם לְהוֹדוֹת לָךְ, עַל מִשְׁפְּטֵי צִדְקֶךָ.[34]

---

(1) *Psalms* 118:25. (2) 41:2. (3) 146:5. (4) 5:2. (5) 16:2. (6) 68:9. (7) *Nehemiah* 9:7. (8) *Psalms* 30:9. (9) 10:6. (10) 20:8. (11) *Malachi* 2:5. (12) *Psalms* 105:45. (13) 138:3. (14) 119:12. (15) 68:27. (16) 71:1. (17) 41:14. (18) *Proverbs* 16:6. (19) *Psalms* 37:5. (20) 71:22. (21) 49:3. (22) *Isaiah* 55:6. (23) *Psalms* 105:4. (24) *Proverbs* 12:25. (25) *Genesis* 49:16. (26) *Deuteronomy* 32:4. (27) *Psalms* 51:11. (28) 5:3. (29) *Proverbs* 10:7. (30) *Psalms* 132:14. (31) 143:5. (32) *Genesis* 49:13. (33) *Proverbs* 31:17. (34) *Psalms* 119:62.

ח...ל חָדְלוּ פְרָזוֹן בְּיִשְׂרָאֵל חָדֵלוּ, עַד שַׁקַּמְתִּי דְּבוֹרָה, שַׁקַּמְתִּי אֵם בְּיִשְׂרָאֵל.[1]

ח...ם חֹנֶה מַלְאַךְ יהוה סָבִיב לִירֵאָיו, וַיְחַלְּצֵם.[2]

ט...א טוֹב יַנְחִיל בְּנֵי בָנִים, וְצָפוּן לַצַּדִּיק חֵיל חוֹטֵא.[3]

ט...ה טָמְנוּ גֵאִים פַּח לִי וַחֲבָלִים, פָּרְשׂוּ רֶשֶׁת לְיַד מַעְגָּל, מֹקְשִׁים שָׁתוּ לִי סֶלָה.[4]

י...א יִשְׂרָאֵל בְּטַח בַּיהוה, עֶזְרָם וּמָגִנָּם הוּא.[5]

י...ב יַעַנְךָ יהוה בְּיוֹם צָרָה, יְשַׂגֶּבְךָ שֵׁם אֱלֹהֵי יַעֲקֹב.[6]

י...ד יָסַד אֶרֶץ עַל מְכוֹנֶיהָ, בַּל תִּמּוֹט עוֹלָם וָעֶד.[7]

י...ה יהוה הַצִּילָה נַפְשִׁי מִשְּׂפַת שֶׁקֶר, מִלָּשׁוֹן רְמִיָּה.[8]

י...י יהוה לִי בְּעֹזְרָי, וַאֲנִי אֶרְאֶה בְשֹׂנְאָי.[9]

י...ל יְמִין יהוה רוֹמֵמָה, יְמִין יהוה עֹשָׂה חָיִל.[10]

י...ם יַעְלְזוּ חֲסִידִים בְּכָבוֹד, יְרַנְּנוּ עַל מִשְׁכְּבוֹתָם.[11]

י...ן יָשֵׂם נְהָרוֹת לְמִדְבָּר, וּמֹצָאֵי מַיִם לְצִמָּאוֹן.[12]

י...ע יָחֹס עַל דַּל וְאֶבְיוֹן, וְנַפְשׁוֹת אֶבְיוֹנִים יוֹשִׁיעַ.[13]

י...ף יהוה יִגְמֹר בַּעֲדִי, יהוה חַסְדְּךָ לְעוֹלָם, מַעֲשֵׂי יָדֶיךָ אַל תֶּרֶף.[14]

י...ץ יְבָרְכֵנוּ אֱלֹהִים, וְיִירְאוּ אֹתוֹ כָּל אַפְסֵי אָרֶץ.[15]

י...ק יוֹצִיאֵם מֵחֹשֶׁךְ וְצַלְמָוֶת, וּמוֹסְרוֹתֵיהֶם יְנַתֵּק.[16]

י...ר יהוה שִׁמְךָ לְעוֹלָם, יהוה זִכְרְךָ לְדֹר וָדֹר.[17]

י...ת יהוה שֹׁמֵר אֶת גֵּרִים, יָתוֹם וְאַלְמָנָה יְעוֹדֵד, וְדֶרֶךְ רְשָׁעִים יְעַוֵּת.[18]

כ...ב כִּי לֹא יִטֹּשׁ יהוה עַמּוֹ, וְנַחֲלָתוֹ לֹא יַעֲזֹב.[19]

כ...ל כִּי מֶלֶךְ כָּל הָאָרֶץ אֱלֹהִים זַמְּרוּ מַשְׂכִּיל.[20]

ל...א לֹא תִהְיֶה מְשַׁכֵּלָה וַעֲקָרָה בְּאַרְצֶךָ, אֶת מִסְפַּר יָמֶיךָ אֲמַלֵּא.[21]

ל...ה לְדָוִד, בָּרוּךְ יהוה צוּרִי, הַמְלַמֵּד יָדַי לַקְרָב, אֶצְבְּעוֹתַי לַמִּלְחָמָה.[22]

ל...י לוּלֵי תוֹרָתְךָ שַׁעֲשֻׁעָי, אָז אָבַדְתִּי בְעָנְיִי.[23]

ל...ת לַמְנַצֵּחַ עַל שֹׁשַׁנִּים לִבְנֵי קֹרַח, מַשְׂכִּיל שִׁיר יְדִידֹת.[24]

מ...א מִי כָמֹכָה בָּאֵלִם יהוה, מִי כָּמֹכָה נֶאְדָּר בַּקֹּדֶשׁ, נוֹרָא תְהִלֹּת עֹשֵׂה פֶלֶא.[25]

מ...ה מַחֲשָׁבוֹת בְּעֵצָה תִכּוֹן, וּבְתַחְבֻּלוֹת עֲשֵׂה מִלְחָמָה.[26]

מ...ו מַה דּוֹדֵךְ מִדּוֹד הַיָּפָה בַּנָּשִׁים, מַה דּוֹדֵךְ מִדּוֹד שֶׁכָּכָה הִשְׁבַּעְתָּנוּ.[27]

מ...י מָה אָהַבְתִּי תוֹרָתֶךָ, כָּל הַיּוֹם הִיא שִׂיחָתִי.[28]

מ...ל מַה טֹּבוּ אֹהָלֶיךָ יַעֲקֹב, מִשְׁכְּנֹתֶיךָ יִשְׂרָאֵל.[29]

מ...ם מְאוֹר עֵינַיִם יְשַׂמַּח לֵב, שְׁמוּעָה טוֹבָה תְּדַשֶּׁן עָצֶם.[30]

מ...ר מִי זֶה הָאִישׁ יְרֵא יהוה, יוֹרֶנּוּ בְּדֶרֶךְ יִבְחָר.[31]

נ...א נַפְשֵׁנוּ חִכְּתָה לַיהוה עֶזְרֵנוּ וּמָגִנֵּנוּ הוּא.[32]

נ...ה נָחַלְתִּי עֵדְוֹתֶיךָ לְעוֹלָם, כִּי שְׂשׂוֹן לִבִּי הֵמָּה.[33]

נ...ח נָסוּ וְאֵין רֹדֵף רָשָׁע, וְצַדִּיקִים כִּכְפִיר יִבְטָח.[34]

נ...י נִדְבוֹת פִּי רְצֵה נָא יהוה, וּמִשְׁפָּטֶיךָ לַמְּדֵנִי.[35]

נ...ל נֶחְשַׁבְתִּי עִם יוֹרְדֵי בוֹר, הָיִיתִי כְּגֶבֶר אֵין אֱיָל.[36]

נ...ם נַחֲמוּ נַחֲמוּ עַמִּי, יֹאמַר אֱלֹהֵיכֶם.[37]

נ...ן נֵר יהוה נִשְׁמַת אָדָם, חֹפֵשׂ כָּל חַדְרֵי בָטֶן.[38]

---

(1) *Judges* 5:7. (2) *Psalms* 34:8. (3) *Proverbs* 13:22. (4) *Psalms* 140:6. (5) 115:9. (6) 20:2. (7) 104:5.
(8) 120:2. (9) 118:7. (10) 118:16. (11) 149:5. (12) 107:33. (13) 72:13. (14) 138:8. (15) 67:8. (16) 107:14.
(17) 135:13. (18) 146:9. (19) 94:14. (20) 47:8. (21) *Exodus* 23:26. (22) *Psalms* 144:1. (23) 119:92.
(24) 45:1. (25) *Exodus* 15:11. (26) *Proverbs* 20:18. (27) *Song of Songs* 5:9. (28) *Psalms* 119:97.
(29) *Numbers* 24:5. (30) *Proverbs* 15:30. (31) *Psalms* 25:12. (32) 33:20. (33) 119:111.
(34) *Proverbs* 28:1 (35) *Psalms* 119:108. (36) 88:5. (37) *Isaiah* 40:1. (38) *Proverbs* 20:27.

ס...ה סֹבּוּ צִיּוֹן וְהַקִּיפוּהָ, סִפְרוּ מִגְדָּלֶיהָ.[1]

ס...י סְעַפִּים שָׂנֵאתִי, וְתוֹרָתְךָ אָהָבְתִּי.[2]

ע...א עַתָּה אָקוּם, יֹאמַר יהוה, עַתָּה אֵרוֹמָם, עַתָּה אֶנָּשֵׂא.[3]

ע...ב עַד אֶמְצָא מָקוֹם לַיהוה, מִשְׁכָּנוֹת לַאֲבִיר יַעֲקֹב.[4]

ע...ה עָזִּי וְזִמְרָת יָהּ, וַיְהִי לִי לִישׁוּעָה.[5]

ע...ל עַל דַּעְתְּךָ כִּי לֹא אֶרְשָׁע, וְאֵין מִיָּדְךָ מַצִּיל.[6]

ע...ם עֲרֹב עַבְדְּךָ לְטוֹב, אַל יַעַשְׁקֻנִי זֵדִים.[7]

ע...ר עֹשֶׂה גְדֹלוֹת וְאֵין חֵקֶר, נִפְלָאוֹת עַד אֵין מִסְפָּר.[8]

פ...א פָּתוֹת אֹתָהּ פִּתִּים וְיָצַקְתָּ עָלֶיהָ שָׁמֶן, מִנְחָה הִיא.[9]

פ...ה פִּתְחוּ לִי שַׁעֲרֵי צֶדֶק, אָבֹא בָם אוֹדֶה יָהּ.[10]

פ...ל פֶּן יִטְרֹף כְּאַרְיֵה נַפְשִׁי, פֹּרֵק וְאֵין מַצִּיל.[11]

פ...ס פֶּלֶס וּמֹאזְנֵי מִשְׁפָּט לַיהוה, מַעֲשֵׂהוּ כָּל אַבְנֵי כִיס.[12]

פ...ץ פָּנִיתָ לְפָנֶיהָ, וַתַּשְׁרֵשׁ שָׁרָשֶׁיהָ, וַתְּמַלֵּא אָרֶץ.[13]

צ...ה צִיּוֹן בְּמִשְׁפָּט תִּפָּדֶה, וְשָׁבֶיהָ בִּצְדָקָה.[14]

צ...ח צִיּוֹן יִשְׁאָלוּ דֶּרֶךְ הֵנָּה פְנֵיהֶם, בֹּאוּ וְנִלְווּ אֶל יהוה, בְּרִית עוֹלָם לֹא תִשָּׁכֵחַ.[15]

צ...י צַר וּמָצוֹק מְצָאוּנִי, מִצְוֹתֶיךָ שַׁעֲשֻׁעָי.[16]

צ...ל צַהֲלִי וָרֹנִּי יוֹשֶׁבֶת צִיּוֹן, כִּי גָדוֹל בְּקִרְבֵּךְ קְדוֹשׁ יִשְׂרָאֵל.[17]

ק...א קָרַבְתָּ בְּיוֹם אֶקְרָאֶךָּ, אָמַרְתָּ אַל תִּירָא.[18]

ק...ל קַמְתִּי אֲנִי לִפְתֹּחַ לְדוֹדִי, וְיָדַי נָטְפוּ מוֹר, וְאֶצְבְּעֹתַי מוֹר עֹבֵר עַל כַּפּוֹת הַמַּנְעוּל.[19]

ק...ן קוֹלִי אֶל יהוה אֶזְעָק, קוֹלִי אֶל יהוה אֶתְחַנָּן.[20]

ק...ת קָרוֹב אַתָּה יהוה, וְכָל מִצְוֹתֶיךָ אֱמֶת.[21]

ר...ה רִגְזוּ וְאַל תֶּחֱטָאוּ, אִמְרוּ בִלְבַבְכֶם עַל מִשְׁכַּבְכֶם, וְדֹמּוּ סֶלָה.[22]

ר...ל רְאוּ עַתָּה כִּי אֲנִי אֲנִי הוּא, וְאֵין אֱלֹהִים עִמָּדִי, אֲנִי אָמִית וַאֲחַיֶּה, מָחַצְתִּי וַאֲנִי אֶרְפָּא, וְאֵין מִיָּדִי מַצִּיל.[23]

ר...ן רְאֵה זֶה מָצָאתִי, אָמְרָה קֹהֶלֶת, אַחַת לְאַחַת לִמְצֹא חֶשְׁבּוֹן.[24]

ר...ת רָאוּךָ מַּיִם אֱלֹהִים, רָאוּךָ מַּיִם יָחִילוּ, אַף יִרְגְּזוּ תְהֹמוֹת.[25]

ש...א שַׂמֵּחַ נֶפֶשׁ עַבְדֶּךָ, כִּי אֵלֶיךָ אֲדֹנָי נַפְשִׁי אֶשָּׂא.[26]

ש...ה שְׂאוּ יְדֵכֶם קֹדֶשׁ, וּבָרְכוּ אֶת יהוה.[27]

ש...ח שָׁמַע יהוה תְּחִנָּתִי, יהוה תְּפִלָּתִי יִקָּח.[28]

ש...י שָׂנֵאתִי הַשֹּׁמְרִים הַבְלֵי שָׁוְא, וַאֲנִי אֶל יהוה בָּטָחְתִּי.[29]

ש...ל שָׁלוֹם רָב לְאֹהֲבֵי תוֹרָתֶךָ, וְאֵין לָמוֹ מִכְשׁוֹל.[30]

ש...ם שְׁמָר תָּם וּרְאֵה יָשָׁר, כִּי אַחֲרִית לְאִישׁ שָׁלוֹם.[31]

ש...ן שִׁיתוּ לִבְּכֶם לְחֵילָה, פַּסְּגוּ אַרְמְנוֹתֶיהָ, לְמַעַן תְּסַפְּרוּ לְדוֹר אַחֲרוֹן.[32]

ש...ר שְׂפַת אֱמֶת תִּכּוֹן לָעַד, וְעַד אַרְגִּיעָה לְשׁוֹן שָׁקֶר.[33]

ש...ת שִׁיר הַמַּעֲלוֹת, הִנֵּה בָּרְכוּ אֶת יהוה כָּל עַבְדֵי יהוה, הָעֹמְדִים בְּבֵית יהוה בַּלֵּילוֹת.[34]

ת...ה תַּעֲרֹךְ לְפָנַי שֻׁלְחָן נֶגֶד צֹרְרָי, דִּשַּׁנְתָּ בַשֶּׁמֶן רֹאשִׁי, כּוֹסִי רְוָיָה.[35]

ת...י תּוֹצִיאֵנִי מֵרֶשֶׁת זוּ, טָמְנוּ לִי, כִּי אַתָּה מָעוּזִּי.[36]

ת...ם תְּנוּ עֹז לֵאלֹהִים, עַל יִשְׂרָאֵל גַּאֲוָתוֹ, וְעֻזּוֹ בַּשְּׁחָקִים.[37]

(1) Psalms 48:13. (2) 119:113. (3) Isaiah 33:10. (4) Psalms 132:5. (5) 118:14. (6) Job 10:7. (7) Psalms 119:122.
(8) Job 5:9. (9) Leviticus 2:6. (10) Psalms 118:19. (11) 7:3. (12) Proverbs 16:11. (13) Psalms 80:10.
(14) Isaiah 1:27. (15) Jeremiah 50:5. (16) Psalms 119:143. (17) Isaiah 12:6. (18) Lamentations 3:57.
(19) Song of Songs 5:5. (20) Psalms 142:2. (21) 119:151. (22) 4:5. (23) Deuteronomy 32:39.
(24) Ecclesiastes 7:27. (25) Psalms 77:17. (26) 86:4. (27) 134:2. (28) 6:10. (29) 31:7. (30) 119:165.
(31) 37:37. (32) 48:14. (33) Proverbs 12:19. (34) Psalms 134:1. (35) 23:5. (36) 31:5. (37) 68:35.

‌﴾ סדר הפרשיות / **TORAH READINGS** ﴿‌

TORAH READINGS

‌﴾ פ׳ בראשית / BEREISHIS ﴿‌

(Genesis 1:1-13)

כהו: בְּרֵאשִׁית בָּרָא אֱלֹהִים אֵת הַשָּׁמַיִם וְאֵת הָאָרֶץ: וְהָאָרֶץ הָיְתָה תֹהוּ וָבֹהוּ וְחֹשֶׁךְ עַל־פְּנֵי תְהוֹם וְרוּחַ אֱלֹהִים מְרַחֶפֶת עַל־פְּנֵי הַמָּיִם: וַיֹּאמֶר אֱלֹהִים יְהִי אוֹר וַיְהִי־אוֹר: וַיַּרְא אֱלֹהִים אֶת־הָאוֹר כִּי־טוֹב וַיַּבְדֵּל אֱלֹהִים בֵּין הָאוֹר וּבֵין הַחֹשֶׁךְ: וַיִּקְרָא אֱלֹהִים ׀ לָאוֹר יוֹם וְלַחֹשֶׁךְ קָרָא לָיְלָה וַיְהִי־עֶרֶב וַיְהִי־בֹקֶר יוֹם אֶחָד:

לוי: וַיֹּאמֶר אֱלֹהִים יְהִי רָקִיעַ בְּתוֹךְ הַמָּיִם וִיהִי מַבְדִּיל בֵּין מַיִם לָמָיִם: וַיַּעַשׂ אֱלֹהִים אֶת־הָרָקִיעַ וַיַּבְדֵּל בֵּין הַמַּיִם אֲשֶׁר מִתַּחַת לָרָקִיעַ וּבֵין הַמַּיִם אֲשֶׁר מֵעַל לָרָקִיעַ וַיְהִי־כֵן: וַיִּקְרָא אֱלֹהִים לָרָקִיעַ שָׁמָיִם וַיְהִי־עֶרֶב וַיְהִי־בֹקֶר יוֹם שֵׁנִי:

ישראל: וַיֹּאמֶר אֱלֹהִים יִקָּווּ הַמַּיִם מִתַּחַת הַשָּׁמַיִם אֶל־מָקוֹם אֶחָד וְתֵרָאֶה הַיַּבָּשָׁה וַיְהִי־כֵן: וַיִּקְרָא אֱלֹהִים ׀ לַיַּבָּשָׁה אֶרֶץ וּלְמִקְוֵה הַמַּיִם קָרָא יַמִּים וַיַּרְא אֱלֹהִים כִּי־טוֹב: וַיֹּאמֶר אֱלֹהִים תַּדְשֵׁא הָאָרֶץ דֶּשֶׁא עֵשֶׂב מַזְרִיעַ זֶרַע עֵץ פְּרִי עֹשֶׂה פְּרִי לְמִינוֹ אֲשֶׁר זַרְעוֹ־בוֹ עַל־הָאָרֶץ וַיְהִי־כֵן: וַתּוֹצֵא הָאָרֶץ דֶּשֶׁא עֵשֶׂב מַזְרִיעַ זֶרַע לְמִינֵהוּ וְעֵץ עֹשֶׂה־פְּרִי אֲשֶׁר זַרְעוֹ־בוֹ לְמִינֵהוּ וַיַּרְא אֱלֹהִים כִּי־טוֹב: וַיְהִי־עֶרֶב וַיְהִי־בֹקֶר יוֹם שְׁלִישִׁי:

‌﴾ פ׳ נֹחַ / NOACH ﴿‌

(Genesis 6:9-22)

כהו: אֵלֶּה תּוֹלְדֹת נֹחַ נֹחַ אִישׁ צַדִּיק תָּמִים הָיָה בְּדֹרֹתָיו אֶת־הָאֱלֹהִים הִתְהַלֶּךְ־נֹחַ: וַיּוֹלֶד נֹחַ שְׁלֹשָׁה בָנִים אֶת־שֵׁם אֶת־חָם וְאֶת־יָפֶת: וַתִּשָּׁחֵת הָאָרֶץ לִפְנֵי הָאֱלֹהִים וַתִּמָּלֵא הָאָרֶץ חָמָס: וַיַּרְא אֱלֹהִים אֶת־הָאָרֶץ וְהִנֵּה נִשְׁחָתָה כִּי־הִשְׁחִית כָּל־בָּשָׂר אֶת־דַּרְכּוֹ עַל־הָאָרֶץ: וַיֹּאמֶר אֱלֹהִים לְנֹחַ קֵץ כָּל־בָּשָׂר בָּא לְפָנַי כִּי־מָלְאָה הָאָרֶץ חָמָס מִפְּנֵיהֶם וְהִנְנִי מַשְׁחִיתָם אֶת־הָאָרֶץ: עֲשֵׂה

לְךָ תֵּבַת עֲצֵי־גֹפֶר קִנִּים תַּעֲשֶׂה אֶת־הַתֵּבָה וְכָפַרְתָּ אֹתָהּ מִבַּיִת וּמִחוּץ בַּכֹּפֶר: וְזֶה אֲשֶׁר תַּעֲשֶׂה אֹתָהּ שְׁלֹשׁ מֵאוֹת אַמָּה אֹרֶךְ הַתֵּבָה חֲמִשִּׁים אַמָּה רָחְבָּהּ וּשְׁלֹשִׁים אַמָּה קוֹמָתָהּ: צֹהַר ׀ תַּעֲשֶׂה לַתֵּבָה וְאֶל־אַמָּה תְּכַלֶּנָּה מִלְמַעְלָה וּפֶתַח הַתֵּבָה בְּצִדָּהּ תָּשִׂים תַּחְתִּיִּם שְׁנִיִּם וּשְׁלִשִׁים תַּעֲשֶׂהָ:

לוי: וַאֲנִי הִנְנִי מֵבִיא אֶת־הַמַּבּוּל מַיִם עַל־הָאָרֶץ לְשַׁחֵת כָּל־בָּשָׂר אֲשֶׁר־בּוֹ רוּחַ חַיִּים מִתַּחַת הַשָּׁמָיִם כֹּל אֲשֶׁר־בָּאָרֶץ יִגְוָע: וַהֲקִמֹתִי אֶת־בְּרִיתִי אִתָּךְ וּבָאתָ אֶל־הַתֵּבָה אַתָּה וּבָנֶיךָ וְאִשְׁתְּךָ וּנְשֵׁי־בָנֶיךָ אִתָּךְ: וּמִכָּל־הָחַי מִכָּל־בָּשָׂר שְׁנַיִם מִכֹּל תָּבִיא אֶל־הַתֵּבָה לְהַחֲיֹת אִתָּךְ זָכָר וּנְקֵבָה יִהְיוּ: מֵהָעוֹף לְמִינֵהוּ וּמִן־הַבְּהֵמָה לְמִינָהּ מִכֹּל רֶמֶשׂ הָאֲדָמָה לְמִינֵהוּ שְׁנַיִם מִכֹּל יָבֹאוּ אֵלֶיךָ לְהַחֲיוֹת: וְאַתָּה קַח־לְךָ מִכָּל־מַאֲכָל אֲשֶׁר יֵאָכֵל וְאָסַפְתָּ אֵלֶיךָ וְהָיָה לְךָ וְלָהֶם לְאָכְלָה: וַיַּעַשׂ נֹחַ כְּכֹל אֲשֶׁר צִוָּה אֹתוֹ אֱלֹהִים כֵּן עָשָׂה:

‌﴾ פ׳ לֶךְ לְךָ / LECH LECHA ﴿‌

(Genesis 12:1-13)

כהו: וַיֹּאמֶר יהוה אֶל־אַבְרָם לֶךְ־לְךָ מֵאַרְצְךָ וּמִמּוֹלַדְתְּךָ וּמִבֵּית אָבִיךָ אֶל־הָאָרֶץ אֲשֶׁר אַרְאֶךָּ: וְאֶעֶשְׂךָ לְגוֹי גָּדוֹל וַאֲבָרֶכְךָ וַאֲגַדְּלָה שְׁמֶךָ וֶהְיֵה בְּרָכָה: וַאֲבָרֲכָה מְבָרֲכֶיךָ וּמְקַלֶּלְךָ אָאֹר וְנִבְרְכוּ בְךָ כֹּל מִשְׁפְּחֹת הָאֲדָמָה:

לוי: וַיֵּלֶךְ אַבְרָם כַּאֲשֶׁר דִּבֶּר אֵלָיו יהוה וַיֵּלֶךְ אִתּוֹ לוֹט וְאַבְרָם בֶּן־חָמֵשׁ שָׁנִים וְשִׁבְעִים שָׁנָה בְּצֵאתוֹ מֵחָרָן: וַיִּקַּח אַבְרָם אֶת־שָׂרַי אִשְׁתּוֹ וְאֶת־לוֹט בֶּן־אָחִיו וְאֶת־כָּל־רְכוּשָׁם אֲשֶׁר רָכָשׁוּ וְאֶת־הַנֶּפֶשׁ אֲשֶׁר־עָשׂוּ בְחָרָן וַיֵּצְאוּ לָלֶכֶת אַרְצָה כְּנַעַן וַיָּבֹאוּ אַרְצָה כְּנָעַן: וַיַּעֲבֹר אַבְרָם בָּאָרֶץ עַד מְקוֹם שְׁכֶם עַד אֵלוֹן מוֹרֶה וְהַכְּנַעֲנִי אָז בָּאָרֶץ: וַיֵּרָא יהוה אֶל־אַבְרָם וַיֹּאמֶר לְזַרְעֲךָ אֶתֵּן אֶת־הָאָרֶץ הַזֹּאת

וַיִּבֶן שָׁם מִזְבֵּחַ לַיהוה הַנִּרְאֶה אֵלָיו: וַיַּעְתֵּק
מִשָּׁם הָהָרָה מִקֶּדֶם לְבֵית־אֵל וַיֵּט אׇהֳלֹה
בֵּית־אֵל מִיָּם וְהָעַי מִקֶּדֶם וַיִּבֶן־שָׁם מִזְבֵּחַ
לַיהוה וַיִּקְרָא בְּשֵׁם יהוה: וַיִּסַּע אַבְרָם הָלוֹךְ
וְנָסוֹעַ הַנֶּגְבָּה:

ישראל: וַיְהִי רָעָב בָּאָרֶץ וַיֵּרֶד אַבְרָם מִצְרַיְמָה
לָגוּר שָׁם כִּי־כָבֵד הָרָעָב בָּאָרֶץ: וַיְהִי כַּאֲשֶׁר
הִקְרִיב לָבוֹא מִצְרָיְמָה וַיֹּאמֶר אֶל־שָׂרַי
אִשְׁתּוֹ הִנֵּה־נָא יָדַעְתִּי כִּי אִשָּׁה יְפַת־מַרְאֶה
אָתְּ: וְהָיָה כִּי־יִרְאוּ אֹתָךְ הַמִּצְרִים וְאָמְרוּ
אִשְׁתּוֹ זֹאת וְהָרְגוּ אֹתִי וְאֹתָךְ יְחַיּוּ: אִמְרִי־נָא
אֲחֹתִי אָתְּ לְמַעַן יִיטַב־לִי בַעֲבוּרֵךְ וְחָיְתָה
נַפְשִׁי בִּגְלָלֵךְ:

◈ פ׳ וַיֵּרָא / VAYEIRA ▷
(Genesis 18:1-14)

כח: וַיֵּרָא אֵלָיו יהוה בְּאֵלֹנֵי מַמְרֵא וְהוּא
יֹשֵׁב פֶּתַח־הָאֹהֶל כְּחֹם הַיּוֹם: וַיִּשָּׂא עֵינָיו
וַיַּרְא וְהִנֵּה שְׁלֹשָׁה אֲנָשִׁים נִצָּבִים עָלָיו וַיַּרְא
וַיָּרׇץ לִקְרָאתָם מִפֶּתַח הָאֹהֶל וַיִּשְׁתַּחוּ
אָרְצָה: וַיֹּאמַר אֲדֹנָי אִם־נָא מָצָאתִי חֵן
בְּעֵינֶיךָ אַל־נָא תַעֲבֹר מֵעַל עַבְדֶּךָ: יֻקַּח־נָא
מְעַט־מַיִם וְרַחֲצוּ רַגְלֵיכֶם וְהִשָּׁעֲנוּ תַּחַת
הָעֵץ: וְאֶקְחָה פַת־לֶחֶם וְסַעֲדוּ לִבְּכֶם אַחַר
תַּעֲבֹרוּ כִּי־עַל־כֵּן עֲבַרְתֶּם עַל־עַבְדְּכֶם
וַיֹּאמְרוּ כֵּן תַּעֲשֶׂה כַּאֲשֶׁר דִּבַּרְתָּ:

לוי: וַיְמַהֵר אַבְרָהָם הָאֹהֱלָה אֶל־שָׂרָה וַיֹּאמֶר
מַהֲרִי שְׁלֹשׁ סְאִים קֶמַח סֹלֶת לוּשִׁי וַעֲשִׂי
עֻגוֹת: וְאֶל־הַבָּקָר רָץ אַבְרָהָם וַיִּקַּח בֶּן־בָּקָר
רַךְ וָטוֹב וַיִּתֵּן אֶל־הַנַּעַר וַיְמַהֵר לַעֲשׂוֹת אֹתוֹ:
וַיִּקַּח חֶמְאָה וְחָלָב וּבֶן־הַבָּקָר אֲשֶׁר עָשָׂה
וַיִּתֵּן לִפְנֵיהֶם וְהוּא עֹמֵד עֲלֵיהֶם תַּחַת הָעֵץ
וַיֹּאכֵלוּ:

ישראל: וַיֹּאמְרוּ אֵלָיו אַיֵּה שָׂרָה אִשְׁתֶּךָ
וַיֹּאמֶר הִנֵּה בָאֹהֶל: וַיֹּאמֶר שׁוֹב אָשׁוּב אֵלֶיךָ
כָּעֵת חַיָּה וְהִנֵּה־בֵן לְשָׂרָה אִשְׁתֶּךָ וְשָׂרָה
שֹׁמַעַת פֶּתַח הָאֹהֶל וְהוּא אַחֲרָיו: וְאַבְרָהָם
וְשָׂרָה זְקֵנִים בָּאִים בַּיָּמִים חָדַל לִהְיוֹת
לְשָׂרָה אֹרַח כַּנָּשִׁים: וַתִּצְחַק שָׂרָה בְּקִרְבָּהּ
לֵאמֹר אַחֲרֵי בְלֹתִי הָיְתָה־לִּי עֶדְנָה וַאדֹנִי
זָקֵן: וַיֹּאמֶר יהוה אֶל־אַבְרָהָם לָמָּה זֶּה

צָחֲקָה שָׂרָה לֵאמֹר הַאַף אֻמְנָם אֵלֵד וַאֲנִי
זָקַנְתִּי: הֲיִפָּלֵא מֵיהוה דָּבָר לַמּוֹעֵד אָשׁוּב
אֵלֶיךָ כָּעֵת חַיָּה וּלְשָׂרָה בֵן:

◈ פ׳ חַיֵּי שָׂרָה / CHAYEI SARAH ▷
(Genesis 23:1-16)

כח: וַיִּהְיוּ חַיֵּי שָׂרָה מֵאָה שָׁנָה וְעֶשְׂרִים שָׁנָה
וְשֶׁבַע שָׁנִים שְׁנֵי חַיֵּי שָׂרָה: וַתָּמׇת שָׂרָה
בְּקִרְיַת אַרְבַּע הִוא חֶבְרוֹן בְּאֶרֶץ כְּנָעַן וַיָּבֹא
אַבְרָהָם לִסְפֹּד לְשָׂרָה וְלִבְכֹּתָהּ: וַיָּקׇם
אַבְרָהָם מֵעַל פְּנֵי מֵתוֹ וַיְדַבֵּר אֶל־בְּנֵי־חֵת
לֵאמֹר: גֵּר־וְתוֹשָׁב אָנֹכִי עִמָּכֶם תְּנוּ לִי
אֲחֻזַּת־קֶבֶר עִמָּכֶם וְאֶקְבְּרָה מֵתִי מִלְּפָנָי:
וַיַּעֲנוּ בְנֵי־חֵת אֶת־אַבְרָהָם לֵאמֹר לוֹ:
שְׁמָעֵנוּ ׀ אֲדֹנִי נְשִׂיא אֱלֹהִים אַתָּה בְּתוֹכֵנוּ
בְּמִבְחַר קְבָרֵינוּ קְבֹר אֶת־מֵתֶךָ אִישׁ מִמֶּנּוּ
אֶת־קִבְרוֹ לֹא־יִכְלֶה מִמְּךָ מִקְּבֹר מֵתֶךָ: וַיָּקׇם
אַבְרָהָם וַיִּשְׁתַּחוּ לְעַם־הָאָרֶץ לִבְנֵי־חֵת:

לוי: וַיְדַבֵּר אִתָּם לֵאמֹר אִם־יֵשׁ אֶת־נַפְשְׁכֶם
לִקְבֹּר אֶת־מֵתִי מִלְּפָנַי שְׁמָעוּנִי וּפִגְעוּ־לִי
בְּעֶפְרוֹן בֶּן־צֹחַר: וְיִתֶּן־לִי אֶת־מְעָרַת
הַמַּכְפֵּלָה אֲשֶׁר־לוֹ אֲשֶׁר בִּקְצֵה שָׂדֵהוּ בְּכֶסֶף
מָלֵא יִתְּנֶנָּה לִּי בְּתוֹכְכֶם לַאֲחֻזַּת־קָבֶר:
וְעֶפְרוֹן יֹשֵׁב בְּתוֹךְ בְּנֵי־חֵת וַיַּעַן עֶפְרוֹן הַחִתִּי
אֶת־אַבְרָהָם בְּאׇזְנֵי בְנֵי־חֵת לְכֹל בָּאֵי שַׁעַר־
עִירוֹ לֵאמֹר: לֹא־אֲדֹנִי שְׁמָעֵנִי הַשָּׂדֶה נָתַתִּי
לָךְ וְהַמְּעָרָה אֲשֶׁר־בּוֹ לְךָ נְתַתִּיהָ לְעֵינֵי בְנֵי־
עַמִּי נְתַתִּיהָ לָּךְ קְבֹר מֵתֶךָ: וַיִּשְׁתַּחוּ אַבְרָהָם
לִפְנֵי עַם־הָאָרֶץ:

ישראל: וַיְדַבֵּר אֶל־עֶפְרוֹן בְּאׇזְנֵי עַם־הָאָרֶץ
לֵאמֹר אַךְ אִם־אַתָּה לוּ שְׁמָעֵנִי נָתַתִּי כֶּסֶף
הַשָּׂדֶה קַח מִמֶּנִּי וְאֶקְבְּרָה אֶת־מֵתִי שָׁמָּה:
וַיַּעַן עֶפְרוֹן אֶת־אַבְרָהָם לֵאמֹר לוֹ: אֲדֹנִי
שְׁמָעֵנִי אֶרֶץ אַרְבַּע מֵאֹת שֶׁקֶל־כֶּסֶף בֵּינִי
וּבֵינְךָ מַה־הִוא וְאֶת־מֵתְךָ קְבֹר: וַיִּשְׁמַע
אַבְרָהָם אֶל־עֶפְרוֹן וַיִּשְׁקֹל אַבְרָהָם לְעֶפְרֹן
אֶת־הַכֶּסֶף אֲשֶׁר דִּבֶּר בְּאׇזְנֵי בְנֵי־חֵת אַרְבַּע
מֵאוֹת שֶׁקֶל כֶּסֶף עֹבֵר לַסֹּחֵר:

◈ פ׳ תּוֹלְדוֹת / TOLDOS ▷
(Genesis 25:19 — 26:5)

כח: וְאֵלֶּה תּוֹלְדֹת יִצְחָק בֶּן־אַבְרָהָם אַבְרָהָם

פ׳ ויצא / VAYEITZEI

(Genesis 28:10-22)

כהן: וַיֵּצֵא יַעֲקֹב מִבְּאֵר שֶׁבַע וַיֵּלֶךְ חָרָנָה: וַיִּפְגַּע בַּמָּקוֹם וַיָּלֶן שָׁם כִּי־בָא הַשֶּׁמֶשׁ וַיִּקַּח מֵאַבְנֵי הַמָּקוֹם וַיָּשֶׂם מְרַאֲשֹׁתָיו וַיִּשְׁכַּב בַּמָּקוֹם הַהוּא: וַיַּחֲלֹם וְהִנֵּה סֻלָּם מֻצָּב אַרְצָה וְרֹאשׁוֹ מַגִּיעַ הַשָּׁמָיְמָה וְהִנֵּה מַלְאֲכֵי אֱלֹהִים עֹלִים וְיֹרְדִים בּוֹ:

לוי: וְהִנֵּה יְהוָה נִצָּב עָלָיו וַיֹּאמַר אֲנִי יְהוָה אֱלֹהֵי אַבְרָהָם אָבִיךָ וֵאלֹהֵי יִצְחָק הָאָרֶץ אֲשֶׁר אַתָּה שֹׁכֵב עָלֶיהָ לְךָ אֶתְּנֶנָּה וּלְזַרְעֶךָ: וְהָיָה זַרְעֲךָ כַּעֲפַר הָאָרֶץ וּפָרַצְתָּ יָמָּה וָקֵדְמָה וְצָפֹנָה וָנֶגְבָּה וְנִבְרְכוּ בְךָ כָּל־מִשְׁפְּחֹת הָאֲדָמָה וּבְזַרְעֶךָ: וְהִנֵּה אָנֹכִי עִמָּךְ וּשְׁמַרְתִּיךָ בְּכֹל אֲשֶׁר־תֵּלֵךְ וַהֲשִׁבֹתִיךָ אֶל־הָאֲדָמָה הַזֹּאת כִּי לֹא אֶעֱזָבְךָ עַד אֲשֶׁר אִם־עָשִׂיתִי אֵת אֲשֶׁר־דִּבַּרְתִּי לָךְ: וַיִּיקַץ יַעֲקֹב מִשְּׁנָתוֹ וַיֹּאמֶר אָכֵן יֵשׁ יְהוָה בַּמָּקוֹם הַזֶּה וְאָנֹכִי לֹא יָדָעְתִּי: וַיִּירָא וַיֹּאמַר מַה־נּוֹרָא הַמָּקוֹם הַזֶּה אֵין זֶה כִּי אִם־בֵּית אֱלֹהִים וְזֶה שַׁעַר הַשָּׁמָיִם:

ישראל: וַיַּשְׁכֵּם יַעֲקֹב בַּבֹּקֶר וַיִּקַּח אֶת־הָאֶבֶן אֲשֶׁר־שָׂם מְרַאֲשֹׁתָיו וַיָּשֶׂם אֹתָהּ מַצֵּבָה וַיִּצֹק שֶׁמֶן עַל־רֹאשָׁהּ: וַיִּקְרָא אֶת־שֵׁם־הַמָּקוֹם הַהוּא בֵּית־אֵל וְאוּלָם לוּז שֵׁם־הָעִיר לָרִאשֹׁנָה: וַיִּדַּר יַעֲקֹב נֶדֶר לֵאמֹר אִם־יִהְיֶה אֱלֹהִים עִמָּדִי וּשְׁמָרַנִי בַּדֶּרֶךְ הַזֶּה אֲשֶׁר אָנֹכִי הוֹלֵךְ וְנָתַן־לִי לֶחֶם לֶאֱכֹל וּבֶגֶד לִלְבֹּשׁ: וְשַׁבְתִּי בְשָׁלוֹם אֶל־בֵּית אָבִי וְהָיָה יְהוָה לִי לֵאלֹהִים: וְהָאֶבֶן הַזֹּאת אֲשֶׁר־שַׂמְתִּי מַצֵּבָה יִהְיֶה בֵּית אֱלֹהִים וְכֹל אֲשֶׁר תִּתֶּן־לִי עַשֵּׂר אֲעַשְּׂרֶנּוּ לָךְ:

פ׳ וישלח / VAYISHLACH

(Genesis 32:4-13)

כהן: וַיִּשְׁלַח יַעֲקֹב מַלְאָכִים לְפָנָיו אֶל־עֵשָׂו אָחִיו אַרְצָה שֵׂעִיר שְׂדֵה אֱדוֹם: וַיְצַו אֹתָם לֵאמֹר כֹּה תֹאמְרוּן לַאדֹנִי לְעֵשָׂו כֹּה אָמַר עַבְדְּךָ יַעֲקֹב עִם־לָבָן גַּרְתִּי וָאֵחַר עַד־עָתָּה: וַיְהִי־לִי שׁוֹר וַחֲמוֹר צֹאן וְעֶבֶד וְשִׁפְחָה וָאֶשְׁלְחָה לְהַגִּיד לַאדֹנִי לִמְצֹא־חֵן בְּעֵינֶיךָ: לוי: וַיָּשֻׁבוּ הַמַּלְאָכִים אֶל־יַעֲקֹב לֵאמֹר בָּאנוּ

הוֹלִיד אֶת־יִצְחָק: וַיְהִי יִצְחָק בֶּן־אַרְבָּעִים שָׁנָה בְּקַחְתּוֹ אֶת־רִבְקָה בַּת־בְּתוּאֵל הָאֲרַמִּי מִפַּדַּן אֲרָם אֲחוֹת לָבָן הָאֲרַמִּי לוֹ לְאִשָּׁה: וַיֶּעְתַּר יִצְחָק לַיהוָה לְנֹכַח אִשְׁתּוֹ כִּי עֲקָרָה הִוא וַיֵּעָתֶר לוֹ יְהוָה וַתַּהַר רִבְקָה אִשְׁתּוֹ: וַיִּתְרֹצְצוּ הַבָּנִים בְּקִרְבָּהּ וַתֹּאמֶר אִם־כֵּן לָמָּה זֶּה אָנֹכִי וַתֵּלֶךְ לִדְרֹשׁ אֶת־יְהוָה:

לוי: וַיֹּאמֶר יְהוָה לָהּ שְׁנֵי גוֹיִם בְּבִטְנֵךְ וּשְׁנֵי לְאֻמִּים מִמֵּעַיִךְ יִפָּרֵדוּ וּלְאֹם מִלְאֹם יֶאֱמָץ וְרַב יַעֲבֹד צָעִיר: וַיִּמְלְאוּ יָמֶיהָ לָלֶדֶת וְהִנֵּה תוֹמִם בְּבִטְנָהּ: וַיֵּצֵא הָרִאשׁוֹן אַדְמוֹנִי כֻּלּוֹ כְּאַדֶּרֶת שֵׂעָר וַיִּקְרְאוּ שְׁמוֹ עֵשָׂו: וְאַחֲרֵי־כֵן יָצָא אָחִיו וְיָדוֹ אֹחֶזֶת בַּעֲקֵב עֵשָׂו וַיִּקְרָא שְׁמוֹ יַעֲקֹב וְיִצְחָק בֶּן־שִׁשִּׁים שָׁנָה בְּלֶדֶת אֹתָם:

ישראל: וַיִּגְדְּלוּ הַנְּעָרִים וַיְהִי עֵשָׂו אִישׁ יֹדֵעַ צַיִד אִישׁ שָׂדֶה וְיַעֲקֹב אִישׁ תָּם יֹשֵׁב אֹהָלִים: וַיֶּאֱהַב יִצְחָק אֶת־עֵשָׂו כִּי־צַיִד בְּפִיו וְרִבְקָה אֹהֶבֶת אֶת־יַעֲקֹב: וַיָּזֶד יַעֲקֹב נָזִיד וַיָּבֹא עֵשָׂו מִן־הַשָּׂדֶה וְהוּא עָיֵף: וַיֹּאמֶר עֵשָׂו אֶל־יַעֲקֹב הַלְעִיטֵנִי נָא מִן־הָאָדֹם הָאָדֹם הַזֶּה כִּי עָיֵף אָנֹכִי עַל־כֵּן קָרָא־שְׁמוֹ אֱדוֹם: וַיֹּאמֶר יַעֲקֹב מִכְרָה כַיּוֹם אֶת־בְּכֹרָתְךָ לִי: וַיֹּאמֶר עֵשָׂו הִנֵּה אָנֹכִי הוֹלֵךְ לָמוּת וְלָמָּה־זֶּה לִי בְּכֹרָה: וַיֹּאמֶר יַעֲקֹב הִשָּׁבְעָה לִּי כַּיּוֹם וַיִּשָּׁבַע לוֹ וַיִּמְכֹּר אֶת־בְּכֹרָתוֹ לְיַעֲקֹב: וְיַעֲקֹב נָתַן לְעֵשָׂו לֶחֶם וּנְזִיד עֲדָשִׁים וַיֹּאכַל וַיֵּשְׁתְּ וַיָּקָם וַיֵּלַךְ וַיִּבֶז עֵשָׂו אֶת־הַבְּכֹרָה: וַיְהִי רָעָב בָּאָרֶץ מִלְּבַד הָרָעָב הָרִאשׁוֹן אֲשֶׁר הָיָה בִּימֵי אַבְרָהָם וַיֵּלֶךְ יִצְחָק אֶל־אֲבִימֶלֶךְ מֶלֶךְ־פְּלִשְׁתִּים גְּרָרָה: וַיֵּרָא אֵלָיו יְהוָה וַיֹּאמֶר אַל־תֵּרֵד מִצְרָיְמָה שְׁכֹן בָּאָרֶץ אֲשֶׁר אֹמַר אֵלֶיךָ: גּוּר בָּאָרֶץ הַזֹּאת וְאֶהְיֶה עִמְּךָ וַאֲבָרְכֶךָּ כִּי־לְךָ וּלְזַרְעֲךָ אֶתֵּן אֶת־כָּל־הָאֲרָצֹת הָאֵל וַהֲקִמֹתִי אֶת־הַשְּׁבֻעָה אֲשֶׁר נִשְׁבַּעְתִּי לְאַבְרָהָם אָבִיךָ: וְהִרְבֵּיתִי אֶת־זַרְעֲךָ כְּכוֹכְבֵי הַשָּׁמַיִם וְנָתַתִּי לְזַרְעֲךָ אֵת כָּל־הָאֲרָצֹת הָאֵל וְהִתְבָּרֲכוּ בְזַרְעֲךָ כֹּל גּוֹיֵי הָאָרֶץ: עֵקֶב אֲשֶׁר־שָׁמַע אַבְרָהָם בְּקֹלִי וַיִּשְׁמֹר מִשְׁמַרְתִּי מִצְוֹתַי חֻקּוֹתַי וְתוֹרֹתָי:

אֶל־אָחִיךָ אֶל־עֵשָׂו וְגַם הֹלֵךְ לִקְרָאתְךָ וְאַרְבַּע־מֵאוֹת אִישׁ עִמּוֹ: וַיִּירָא יַעֲקֹב מְאֹד וַיֵּצֶר לוֹ וַיַּחַץ אֶת־הָעָם אֲשֶׁר־אִתּוֹ וְאֶת־הַצֹּאן וְאֶת־הַבָּקָר וְהַגְּמַלִּים לִשְׁנֵי מַחֲנוֹת: וַיֹּאמֶר אִם־יָבוֹא עֵשָׂו אֶל־הַמַּחֲנֶה הָאַחַת וְהִכָּהוּ וְהָיָה הַמַּחֲנֶה הַנִּשְׁאָר לִפְלֵיטָה:

ישראל: וַיֹּאמֶר יַעֲקֹב אֱלֹהֵי אָבִי אַבְרָהָם וֵאלֹהֵי אָבִי יִצְחָק יהוה הָאֹמֵר אֵלַי שׁוּב לְאַרְצְךָ וּלְמוֹלַדְתְּךָ וְאֵיטִיבָה עִמָּךְ: קָטֹנְתִּי מִכֹּל הַחֲסָדִים וּמִכָּל־הָאֱמֶת אֲשֶׁר עָשִׂיתָ אֶת־עַבְדֶּךָ כִּי בְמַקְלִי עָבַרְתִּי אֶת־הַיַּרְדֵּן הַזֶּה וְעַתָּה הָיִיתִי לִשְׁנֵי מַחֲנוֹת: הַצִּילֵנִי נָא מִיַּד אָחִי מִיַּד עֵשָׂו כִּי־יָרֵא אָנֹכִי אֹתוֹ פֶּן־יָבוֹא וְהִכַּנִי אֵם עַל־בָּנִים: וְאַתָּה אָמַרְתָּ הֵיטֵב אֵיטִיב עִמָּךְ וְשַׂמְתִּי אֶת־זַרְעֲךָ כְּחוֹל הַיָּם אֲשֶׁר לֹא־יִסָּפֵר מֵרֹב:

﴾ פ׳ וישב / VAYEISHEV ﴿

(Genesis 37:1-11)

כז: וַיֵּשֶׁב יַעֲקֹב בְּאֶרֶץ מְגוּרֵי אָבִיו בְּאֶרֶץ כְּנָעַן: אֵלֶּה ׀ תֹּלְדוֹת יַעֲקֹב יוֹסֵף בֶּן־שְׁבַע־עֶשְׂרֵה שָׁנָה הָיָה רֹעֶה אֶת־אֶחָיו בַּצֹּאן וְהוּא נַעַר אֶת־בְּנֵי בִלְהָה וְאֶת־בְּנֵי זִלְפָּה נְשֵׁי אָבִיו וַיָּבֵא יוֹסֵף אֶת־דִּבָּתָם רָעָה אֶל־אֲבִיהֶם: וְיִשְׂרָאֵל אָהַב אֶת־יוֹסֵף מִכָּל־בָּנָיו כִּי־בֶן־זְקֻנִים הוּא לוֹ וְעָשָׂה לוֹ כְּתֹנֶת פַּסִּים:

לוי: וַיִּרְאוּ אֶחָיו כִּי־אֹתוֹ אָהַב אֲבִיהֶם מִכָּל־אֶחָיו וַיִּשְׂנְאוּ אֹתוֹ וְלֹא יָכְלוּ דַּבְּרוֹ לְשָׁלֹם: וַיַּחֲלֹם יוֹסֵף חֲלוֹם וַיַּגֵּד לְאֶחָיו וַיּוֹסִפוּ עוֹד שְׂנֹא אֹתוֹ: וַיֹּאמֶר אֲלֵיהֶם שִׁמְעוּ־נָא הַחֲלוֹם הַזֶּה אֲשֶׁר חָלָמְתִּי: וְהִנֵּה אֲנַחְנוּ מְאַלְּמִים אֲלֻמִּים בְּתוֹךְ הַשָּׂדֶה וְהִנֵּה קָמָה אֲלֻמָּתִי וְגַם־נִצָּבָה וְהִנֵּה תְסֻבֶּינָה אֲלֻמֹּתֵיכֶם וַתִּשְׁתַּחֲוֶיןָ לַאֲלֻמָּתִי:

ישראל: וַיֹּאמְרוּ לוֹ אֶחָיו הֲמָלֹךְ תִּמְלֹךְ עָלֵינוּ אִם־מָשׁוֹל תִּמְשֹׁל בָּנוּ וַיּוֹסִפוּ עוֹד שְׂנֹא אֹתוֹ עַל־חֲלֹמֹתָיו וְעַל־דְּבָרָיו: וַיַּחֲלֹם עוֹד חֲלוֹם אַחֵר וַיְסַפֵּר אֹתוֹ לְאֶחָיו וַיֹּאמֶר הִנֵּה חָלַמְתִּי חֲלוֹם עוֹד וְהִנֵּה הַשֶּׁמֶשׁ וְהַיָּרֵחַ וְאַחַד עָשָׂר כּוֹכָבִים מִשְׁתַּחֲוִים לִי: וַיְסַפֵּר אֶל־אָבִיו וְאֶל־אֶחָיו וַיִּגְעַר־בּוֹ אָבִיו וַיֹּאמֶר לוֹ מָה הַחֲלוֹם

הַזֶּה אֲשֶׁר חָלָמְתָּ הֲבוֹא נָבוֹא אֲנִי וְאִמְּךָ וְאַחֶיךָ לְהִשְׁתַּחֲוֹת לְךָ אָרְצָה: וַיְקַנְאוּ־בוֹ אֶחָיו וְאָבִיו שָׁמַר אֶת־הַדָּבָר:

﴾ פ׳ מקץ / MIKEITZ ﴿

(Genesis 41:1-14)

כח: וַיְהִי מִקֵּץ שְׁנָתַיִם יָמִים וּפַרְעֹה חֹלֵם וְהִנֵּה עֹמֵד עַל־הַיְאֹר: וְהִנֵּה מִן־הַיְאֹר עֹלֹת שֶׁבַע פָּרוֹת יְפוֹת מַרְאֶה וּבְרִיאֹת בָּשָׂר וַתִּרְעֶינָה בָּאָחוּ: וְהִנֵּה שֶׁבַע פָּרוֹת אֲחֵרוֹת עֹלוֹת אַחֲרֵיהֶן מִן־הַיְאֹר רָעוֹת מַרְאֶה וְדַקּוֹת בָּשָׂר וַתַּעֲמֹדְנָה אֵצֶל הַפָּרוֹת עַל־שְׂפַת הַיְאֹר: וַתֹּאכַלְנָה הַפָּרוֹת רָעוֹת הַמַּרְאֶה וְדַקֹּת הַבָּשָׂר אֵת שֶׁבַע הַפָּרוֹת יְפֹת הַמַּרְאֶה וְהַבְּרִיאֹת וַיִּיקַץ פַּרְעֹה:

לוי: וַיִּישָׁן וַיַּחֲלֹם שֵׁנִית וְהִנֵּה ׀ שֶׁבַע שִׁבֳּלִים עֹלוֹת בְּקָנֶה אֶחָד בְּרִיאוֹת וְטֹבוֹת: וְהִנֵּה שֶׁבַע שִׁבֳּלִים דַּקּוֹת וּשְׁדוּפֹת קָדִים צֹמְחוֹת אַחֲרֵיהֶן: וַתִּבְלַעְנָה הַשִּׁבֳּלִים הַדַּקּוֹת אֵת שֶׁבַע הַשִּׁבֳּלִים הַבְּרִיאוֹת וְהַמְּלֵאוֹת וַיִּיקַץ פַּרְעֹה וְהִנֵּה חֲלוֹם:

ישראל: וַיְהִי בַבֹּקֶר וַתִּפָּעֶם רוּחוֹ וַיִּשְׁלַח וַיִּקְרָא אֶת־כָּל־חַרְטֻמֵּי מִצְרַיִם וְאֶת־כָּל־חֲכָמֶיהָ וַיְסַפֵּר פַּרְעֹה לָהֶם אֶת־חֲלֹמוֹ וְאֵין־פּוֹתֵר אוֹתָם לְפַרְעֹה: וַיְדַבֵּר שַׂר הַמַּשְׁקִים אֶת־פַּרְעֹה לֵאמֹר אֶת־חֲטָאַי אֲנִי מַזְכִּיר הַיּוֹם: פַּרְעֹה קָצַף עַל־עֲבָדָיו וַיִּתֵּן אֹתִי בְּמִשְׁמַר בֵּית שַׂר הַטַּבָּחִים אֹתִי וְאֵת שַׂר הָאֹפִים: וַנַּחַלְמָה חֲלוֹם בְּלַיְלָה אֶחָד אֲנִי וָהוּא אִישׁ כְּפִתְרוֹן חֲלֹמוֹ חָלָמְנוּ: וְשָׁם אִתָּנוּ נַעַר עִבְרִי עֶבֶד לְשַׂר הַטַּבָּחִים וַנְּסַפֶּר־לוֹ וַיִּפְתָּר־לָנוּ אֶת־חֲלֹמֹתֵינוּ אִישׁ כַּחֲלֹמוֹ פָּתָר: וַיְהִי כַּאֲשֶׁר פָּתַר־לָנוּ כֵּן הָיָה אֹתִי הֵשִׁיב עַל־כַּנִּי וְאֹתוֹ תָלָה: וַיִּשְׁלַח פַּרְעֹה וַיִּקְרָא אֶת־יוֹסֵף וַיְרִיצֻהוּ מִן־הַבּוֹר וַיְגַלַּח וַיְחַלֵּף שִׂמְלֹתָיו וַיָּבֹא אֶל־פַּרְעֹה:

﴾ פ׳ ויגש / VAYIGASH ﴿

(Genesis 44:18-30)

כח: וַיִּגַּשׁ אֵלָיו יְהוּדָה וַיֹּאמֶר בִּי אֲדֹנִי יְדַבֶּר־נָא עַבְדְּךָ דָבָר בְּאָזְנֵי אֲדֹנִי וְאַל־יִחַר אַפְּךָ בְּעַבְדֶּךָ כִּי כָמוֹךָ כְּפַרְעֹה: אֲדֹנִי שָׁאַל אֶת־

עֲבָדָיו לֵאמֹר הֲיֵשׁ-לָכֶם אָב אוֹ-אָח: וַנֹּאמֶר
אֶל-אֲדֹנִי יֶשׁ-לָנוּ אָב זָקֵן וְיֶלֶד זְקֻנִים קָטָן
וְאָחִיו מֵת וַיִּוָּתֵר הוּא לְבַדּוֹ לְאִמּוֹ וְאָבִיו
אֲהֵבוֹ:

לוי: וַתֹּאמֶר אֶל-עֲבָדֶיךָ הוֹרִדֻהוּ אֵלָי וְאָשִׂימָה
עֵינִי עָלָיו: וַנֹּאמֶר אֶל-אֲדֹנִי לֹא-יוּכַל הַנַּעַר
לַעֲזֹב אֶת-אָבִיו וְעָזַב אֶת-אָבִיו וָמֵת: וַתֹּאמֶר
אֶל-עֲבָדֶיךָ אִם-לֹא יֵרֵד אֲחִיכֶם הַקָּטֹן
אִתְּכֶם לֹא תֹסִפוּן לִרְאוֹת פָּנָי: וַיְהִי כִּי עָלִינוּ
אֶל-עַבְדְּךָ אָבִי וַנַּגֶּד-לוֹ אֵת דִּבְרֵי אֲדֹנִי:

ישראל: וַיֹּאמֶר אָבִינוּ שֻׁבוּ שִׁבְרוּ-לָנוּ מְעַט-
אֹכֶל: וַנֹּאמֶר לֹא נוּכַל לָרֶדֶת אִם-יֵשׁ אָחִינוּ
הַקָּטֹן אִתָּנוּ וְיָרַדְנוּ כִּי-לֹא נוּכַל לִרְאוֹת פְּנֵי
הָאִישׁ וְאָחִינוּ הַקָּטֹן אֵינֶנּוּ אִתָּנוּ: וַיֹּאמֶר
עַבְדְּךָ אָבִי אֵלֵינוּ אַתֶּם יְדַעְתֶּם כִּי שְׁנַיִם
יָלְדָה-לִי אִשְׁתִּי: וַיֵּצֵא הָאֶחָד מֵאִתִּי
וָאֹמַר אַךְ טָרֹף טֹרָף וְלֹא רְאִיתִיו עַד-הֵנָּה:
וּלְקַחְתֶּם גַּם-אֶת-זֶה מֵעִם פָּנַי וְקָרָהוּ אָסוֹן
וְהוֹרַדְתֶּם אֶת-שֵׂיבָתִי בְּרָעָה שְׁאֹלָה: וְעַתָּה
כְּבֹאִי אֶל-עַבְדְּךָ אָבִי וְהַנַּעַר אֵינֶנּוּ אִתָּנוּ
וְנַפְשׁוֹ קְשׁוּרָה בְנַפְשׁוֹ:

פ׳ וַיְחִי / VAYECHI

(Genesis 47:28 — 48:9)

כח: וַיְחִי יַעֲקֹב בְּאֶרֶץ מִצְרַיִם שְׁבַע עֶשְׂרֵה
שָׁנָה וַיְהִי יְמֵי-יַעֲקֹב שְׁנֵי חַיָּיו שֶׁבַע שָׁנִים
וְאַרְבָּעִים וּמְאַת שָׁנָה: וַיִּקְרְבוּ יְמֵי-יִשְׂרָאֵל
לָמוּת וַיִּקְרָא לִבְנוֹ לְיוֹסֵף וַיֹּאמֶר לוֹ אִם-נָא
מָצָאתִי חֵן בְּעֵינֶיךָ שִׂים-נָא יָדְךָ תַּחַת יְרֵכִי
וְעָשִׂיתָ עִמָּדִי חֶסֶד וֶאֱמֶת אַל-נָא תִקְבְּרֵנִי
בְּמִצְרָיִם: וְשָׁכַבְתִּי עִם-אֲבֹתַי וּנְשָׂאתַנִי
מִמִּצְרַיִם וּקְבַרְתַּנִי בִּקְבֻרָתָם וַיֹּאמַר אָנֹכִי
אֶעֱשֶׂה כִדְבָרֶךָ: וַיֹּאמֶר הִשָּׁבְעָה לִי וַיִּשָּׁבַע לוֹ
וַיִּשְׁתַּחוּ יִשְׂרָאֵל עַל-רֹאשׁ הַמִּטָּה:

לוי: וַיְהִי אַחֲרֵי הַדְּבָרִים הָאֵלֶּה וַיֹּאמֶר לְיוֹסֵף
הִנֵּה אָבִיךָ חֹלֶה וַיִּקַּח אֶת-שְׁנֵי בָנָיו עִמּוֹ
אֶת-מְנַשֶּׁה וְאֶת-אֶפְרָיִם: וַיַּגֵּד לְיַעֲקֹב
וַיֹּאמֶר הִנֵּה בִּנְךָ יוֹסֵף בָּא אֵלֶיךָ וַיִּתְחַזֵּק
יִשְׂרָאֵל וַיֵּשֶׁב עַל-הַמִּטָּה: וַיֹּאמֶר יַעֲקֹב אֶל-
יוֹסֵף אֵל שַׁדַּי נִרְאָה-אֵלַי בְּלוּז בְּאֶרֶץ כְּנָעַן
וַיְבָרֶךְ אֹתִי:

ישראל: וַיֹּאמֶר אֵלַי הִנְנִי מַפְרְךָ וְהִרְבִּיתִךָ
וּנְתַתִּיךָ לִקְהַל עַמִּים וְנָתַתִּי אֶת-הָאָרֶץ
הַזֹּאת לְזַרְעֲךָ אַחֲרֶיךָ אֲחֻזַּת עוֹלָם: וְעַתָּה
שְׁנֵי-בָנֶיךָ הַנּוֹלָדִים לְךָ בְּאֶרֶץ מִצְרַיִם עַד-
בֹּאִי אֵלֶיךָ מִצְרַיְמָה לִי-הֵם אֶפְרַיִם וּמְנַשֶּׁה
כִּרְאוּבֵן וְשִׁמְעוֹן יִהְיוּ-לִי: וּמוֹלַדְתְּךָ אֲשֶׁר-
הוֹלַדְתָּ אַחֲרֵיהֶם לְךָ יִהְיוּ עַל שֵׁם אֲחֵיהֶם
יִקָּרְאוּ בְּנַחֲלָתָם: וַאֲנִי בְּבֹאִי מִפַּדָּן מֵתָה עָלַי
רָחֵל בְּאֶרֶץ כְּנַעַן בַּדֶּרֶךְ בְּעוֹד כִּבְרַת-אֶרֶץ
לָבֹא אֶפְרָתָה וָאֶקְבְּרֶהָ שָּׁם בְּדֶרֶךְ אֶפְרָת
הִוא בֵּית לָחֶם: וַיַּרְא יִשְׂרָאֵל אֶת-בְּנֵי יוֹסֵף
וַיֹּאמֶר מִי-אֵלֶּה: וַיֹּאמֶר יוֹסֵף אֶל-אָבִיו בָּנַי
הֵם אֲשֶׁר-נָתַן-לִי אֱלֹהִים בָּזֶה וַיֹּאמַר קָחֶם-
נָא אֵלַי וַאֲבָרֲכֵם:

פ׳ שְׁמוֹת / SHEMOS

(Exodus 1:1-17)

כה: וְאֵלֶּה שְׁמוֹת בְּנֵי יִשְׂרָאֵל הַבָּאִים
מִצְרַיְמָה אֵת יַעֲקֹב אִישׁ וּבֵיתוֹ בָּאוּ: רְאוּבֵן
שִׁמְעוֹן לֵוִי וִיהוּדָה: יִשָּׂשכָר זְבוּלֻן וּבִנְיָמִן: דָּן
וְנַפְתָּלִי גָּד וְאָשֵׁר: וַיְהִי כָּל-נֶפֶשׁ יֹצְאֵי יֶרֶךְ-
יַעֲקֹב שִׁבְעִים נָפֶשׁ וְיוֹסֵף הָיָה בְמִצְרָיִם: וַיָּמָת
יוֹסֵף וְכָל-אֶחָיו וְכֹל הַדּוֹר הַהוּא: וּבְנֵי
יִשְׂרָאֵל פָּרוּ וַיִּשְׁרְצוּ וַיִּרְבּוּ וַיַּעַצְמוּ בִּמְאֹד
מְאֹד וַתִּמָּלֵא הָאָרֶץ אֹתָם:

לוי: וַיָּקָם מֶלֶךְ-חָדָשׁ עַל-מִצְרָיִם אֲשֶׁר לֹא-
יָדַע אֶת-יוֹסֵף: וַיֹּאמֶר אֶל-עַמּוֹ הִנֵּה עַם בְּנֵי
יִשְׂרָאֵל רַב וְעָצוּם מִמֶּנּוּ: הָבָה נִתְחַכְּמָה לוֹ
פֶּן-יִרְבֶּה וְהָיָה כִּי-תִקְרֶאנָה מִלְחָמָה וְנוֹסַף
גַּם-הוּא עַל-שֹׂנְאֵינוּ וְנִלְחַם-בָּנוּ וְעָלָה מִן-
הָאָרֶץ: וַיָּשִׂימוּ עָלָיו שָׂרֵי מִסִּים לְמַעַן עַנֹּתוֹ
בְּסִבְלֹתָם וַיִּבֶן עָרֵי מִסְכְּנוֹת לְפַרְעֹה אֶת-
פִּתֹם וְאֶת-רַעַמְסֵס: וְכַאֲשֶׁר יְעַנּוּ אֹתוֹ כֵּן
יִרְבֶּה וְכֵן יִפְרֹץ וַיָּקֻצוּ מִפְּנֵי בְּנֵי יִשְׂרָאֵל:

ישראל: וַיַּעֲבִדוּ מִצְרַיִם אֶת-בְּנֵי יִשְׂרָאֵל בְּפָרֶךְ:
וַיְמָרְרוּ אֶת-חַיֵּיהֶם בַּעֲבֹדָה קָשָׁה בְּחֹמֶר
וּבִלְבֵנִים וּבְכָל-עֲבֹדָה בַּשָּׂדֶה אֵת כָּל-
עֲבֹדָתָם אֲשֶׁר-עָבְדוּ בָהֶם בְּפָרֶךְ: וַיֹּאמֶר
מֶלֶךְ מִצְרַיִם לַמְיַלְּדֹת הָעִבְרִיֹּת אֲשֶׁר שֵׁם
הָאַחַת שִׁפְרָה וְשֵׁם הַשֵּׁנִית פּוּעָה: וַיֹּאמֶר
בְּיַלֶּדְכֶן אֶת-הָעִבְרִיּוֹת וּרְאִיתֶן עַל-הָאָבְנַיִם

אִם־בֵּן הוּא וַהֲמִתֶּן אֹתוֹ וְאִם־בַּת הִוא וָחָיָה: וַתִּירֶאןָ הַמְיַלְּדֹת אֶת־הָאֱלֹהִים וְלֹא עָשׂוּ כַּאֲשֶׁר דִּבֶּר אֲלֵיהֶן מֶלֶךְ מִצְרָיִם וַתְּחַיֶּיןָ אֶת־הַיְלָדִים:

פ׳ וארא / VAEIRA
(Exodus 6:2-13)

כח: וַיְדַבֵּר אֱלֹהִים אֶל־מֹשֶׁה וַיֹּאמֶר אֵלָיו אֲנִי יְהוָה: וָאֵרָא אֶל־אַבְרָהָם אֶל־יִצְחָק וְאֶל־יַעֲקֹב בְּאֵל שַׁדָּי וּשְׁמִי יְהוָה לֹא נוֹדַעְתִּי לָהֶם: וְגַם הֲקִמֹתִי אֶת־בְּרִיתִי אִתָּם לָתֵת לָהֶם אֶת־אֶרֶץ כְּנָעַן אֵת אֶרֶץ מְגֻרֵיהֶם אֲשֶׁר־גָּרוּ בָהּ: וְגַם | אֲנִי שָׁמַעְתִּי אֶת־נַאֲקַת בְּנֵי יִשְׂרָאֵל אֲשֶׁר מִצְרַיִם מַעֲבִדִים אֹתָם וָאֶזְכֹּר אֶת־בְּרִיתִי:

לוי: לָכֵן אֱמֹר לִבְנֵי־יִשְׂרָאֵל אֲנִי יְהוָה וְהוֹצֵאתִי אֶתְכֶם מִתַּחַת סִבְלֹת מִצְרַיִם וְהִצַּלְתִּי אֶתְכֶם מֵעֲבֹדָתָם וְגָאַלְתִּי אֶתְכֶם בִּזְרוֹעַ נְטוּיָה וּבִשְׁפָטִים גְּדֹלִים: וְלָקַחְתִּי אֶתְכֶם לִי לְעָם וְהָיִיתִי לָכֶם לֵאלֹהִים וִידַעְתֶּם כִּי אֲנִי יְהוָה אֱלֹהֵיכֶם הַמּוֹצִיא אֶתְכֶם מִתַּחַת סִבְלוֹת מִצְרָיִם: וְהֵבֵאתִי אֶתְכֶם אֶל־הָאָרֶץ אֲשֶׁר נָשָׂאתִי אֶת־יָדִי לָתֵת אֹתָהּ לְאַבְרָהָם לְיִצְחָק וּלְיַעֲקֹב וְנָתַתִּי אֹתָהּ לָכֶם מוֹרָשָׁה אֲנִי יְהוָה: וַיְדַבֵּר מֹשֶׁה כֵּן אֶל־בְּנֵי יִשְׂרָאֵל וְלֹא שָׁמְעוּ אֶל־מֹשֶׁה מִקֹּצֶר רוּחַ וּמֵעֲבֹדָה קָשָׁה:

ישראל: וַיְדַבֵּר יְהוָה אֶל־מֹשֶׁה לֵּאמֹר: בֹּא דַבֵּר אֶל־פַּרְעֹה מֶלֶךְ מִצְרָיִם וִישַׁלַּח אֶת־בְּנֵי־יִשְׂרָאֵל מֵאַרְצוֹ: וַיְדַבֵּר מֹשֶׁה לִפְנֵי יְהוָה לֵאמֹר הֵן בְּנֵי־יִשְׂרָאֵל לֹא־שָׁמְעוּ אֵלַי וְאֵיךְ יִשְׁמָעֵנִי פַרְעֹה וַאֲנִי עֲרַל שְׂפָתָיִם: וַיְדַבֵּר יְהוָה אֶל־מֹשֶׁה וְאֶל־אַהֲרֹן וַיְצַוֵּם אֶל־בְּנֵי יִשְׂרָאֵל וְאֶל־פַּרְעֹה מֶלֶךְ מִצְרָיִם לְהוֹצִיא אֶת־בְּנֵי־יִשְׂרָאֵל מֵאֶרֶץ מִצְרָיִם:

פ׳ בא / BO
(Exodus 10:1-11)

כח: וַיֹּאמֶר יְהוָה אֶל־מֹשֶׁה בֹּא אֶל־פַּרְעֹה כִּי־אֲנִי הִכְבַּדְתִּי אֶת־לִבּוֹ וְאֶת־לֵב עֲבָדָיו לְמַעַן שִׁתִי אֹתֹתַי אֵלֶּה בְּקִרְבּוֹ: וּלְמַעַן תְּסַפֵּר בְּאָזְנֵי בִנְךָ וּבֶן־בִּנְךָ אֵת אֲשֶׁר הִתְעַלַּלְתִּי בְּמִצְרַיִם וְאֶת־אֹתֹתַי אֲשֶׁר־שַׂמְתִּי בָם וִידַעְתֶּם כִּי־אֲנִי יְהוָה: וַיָּבֹא מֹשֶׁה וְאַהֲרֹן אֶל־פַּרְעֹה וַיֹּאמְרוּ אֵלָיו כֹּה־אָמַר יְהוָה אֱלֹהֵי הָעִבְרִים עַד־מָתַי מֵאַנְתָּ לֵעָנֹת מִפָּנָי שַׁלַּח עַמִּי וְיַעַבְדֻנִי:

לוי: כִּי אִם־מָאֵן אַתָּה לְשַׁלֵּחַ אֶת־עַמִּי הִנְנִי מֵבִיא מָחָר אַרְבֶּה בִּגְבֻלֶךָ: וְכִסָּה אֶת־עֵין הָאָרֶץ וְלֹא יוּכַל לִרְאֹת אֶת־הָאָרֶץ וְאָכַל | אֶת־יֶתֶר הַפְּלֵטָה הַנִּשְׁאֶרֶת לָכֶם מִן־הַבָּרָד וְאָכַל אֶת־כָּל־הָעֵץ הַצֹּמֵחַ לָכֶם מִן־הַשָּׂדֶה: וּמָלְאוּ בָתֶּיךָ וּבָתֵּי כָל־עֲבָדֶיךָ וּבָתֵּי כָל־מִצְרַיִם אֲשֶׁר לֹא־רָאוּ אֲבֹתֶיךָ וַאֲבוֹת אֲבֹתֶיךָ מִיּוֹם הֱיוֹתָם עַל־הָאֲדָמָה עַד הַיּוֹם הַזֶּה וַיִּפֶן וַיֵּצֵא מֵעִם פַּרְעֹה:

ישראל: וַיֹּאמְרוּ עַבְדֵי פַרְעֹה אֵלָיו עַד־מָתַי יִהְיֶה זֶה לָנוּ לְמוֹקֵשׁ שַׁלַּח אֶת־הָאֲנָשִׁים וְיַעַבְדוּ אֶת־יְהוָה אֱלֹהֵיהֶם הֲטֶרֶם תֵּדַע כִּי אָבְדָה מִצְרָיִם: וַיּוּשַׁב אֶת־מֹשֶׁה וְאֶת־אַהֲרֹן אֶל־פַּרְעֹה וַיֹּאמֶר אֲלֵהֶם לְכוּ עִבְדוּ אֶת־יְהוָה אֱלֹהֵיכֶם מִי וָמִי הַהֹלְכִים: וַיֹּאמֶר מֹשֶׁה בִּנְעָרֵינוּ וּבִזְקֵנֵינוּ נֵלֵךְ בְּבָנֵינוּ וּבִבְנוֹתֵנוּ בְּצֹאנֵנוּ וּבִבְקָרֵנוּ נֵלֵךְ כִּי חַג־יְהוָה לָנוּ: וַיֹּאמֶר אֲלֵהֶם יְהִי כֵן יְהוָה עִמָּכֶם כַּאֲשֶׁר אֲשַׁלַּח אֶתְכֶם וְאֶת־טַפְּכֶם רְאוּ כִּי רָעָה נֶגֶד פְּנֵיכֶם: לֹא כֵן לְכוּ נָא הַגְּבָרִים וְעִבְדוּ אֶת־יְהוָה כִּי אֹתָהּ אַתֶּם מְבַקְשִׁים וַיְגָרֶשׁ אֹתָם מֵאֵת פְּנֵי פַרְעֹה:

פ׳ בשלח / BESHALACH
(Exodus 13:17 — 14:8)

כח: וַיְהִי בְּשַׁלַּח פַּרְעֹה אֶת־הָעָם וְלֹא־נָחָם אֱלֹהִים דֶּרֶךְ אֶרֶץ פְּלִשְׁתִּים כִּי קָרוֹב הוּא כִּי | אָמַר אֱלֹהִים פֶּן־יִנָּחֵם הָעָם בִּרְאֹתָם מִלְחָמָה וְשָׁבוּ מִצְרָיְמָה: וַיַּסֵּב אֱלֹהִים | אֶת־הָעָם דֶּרֶךְ הַמִּדְבָּר יַם־סוּף וַחֲמֻשִׁים עָלוּ בְנֵי־יִשְׂרָאֵל מֵאֶרֶץ מִצְרָיִם: וַיִּקַּח מֹשֶׁה אֶת־עַצְמוֹת יוֹסֵף עִמּוֹ כִּי הַשְׁבֵּעַ הִשְׁבִּיעַ אֶת־בְּנֵי יִשְׂרָאֵל לֵאמֹר פָּקֹד יִפְקֹד אֱלֹהִים אֶתְכֶם וְהַעֲלִיתֶם אֶת־עַצְמֹתַי מִזֶּה אִתְּכֶם: וַיִּסְעוּ מִסֻּכֹּת וַיַּחֲנוּ בְאֵתָם בִּקְצֵה הַמִּדְבָּר: וַיהוָה הֹלֵךְ לִפְנֵיהֶם יוֹמָם בְּעַמּוּד עָנָן

לְנַחְתָם הַדֶּרֶךְ וְלַיְלָה בְּעַמּוּד אֵשׁ לְהָאִיר
לָהֶם לָלֶכֶת יוֹמָם וָלָיְלָה: לֹא־יָמִישׁ עַמּוּד
הֶעָנָן יוֹמָם וְעַמּוּד הָאֵשׁ לָיְלָה לִפְנֵי הָעָם:

לוי: וַיְדַבֵּר יהוה אֶל־מֹשֶׁה לֵּאמֹר: דַּבֵּר אֶל־
בְּנֵי יִשְׂרָאֵל וְיָשֻׁבוּ וְיַחֲנוּ לִפְנֵי פִּי הַחִירֹת בֵּין
מִגְדֹּל וּבֵין הַיָּם לִפְנֵי בַּעַל צְפֹן נִכְחוֹ תַחֲנוּ
עַל־הַיָּם: וְאָמַר פַּרְעֹה לִבְנֵי יִשְׂרָאֵל נְבֻכִים
הֵם בָּאָרֶץ סָגַר עֲלֵיהֶם הַמִּדְבָּר: וְחִזַּקְתִּי
אֶת־לֵב־פַּרְעֹה וְרָדַף אַחֲרֵיהֶם וְאִכָּבְדָה
בְּפַרְעֹה וּבְכָל־חֵילוֹ וְיָדְעוּ מִצְרַיִם כִּי־אֲנִי
יהוה וַיַּעֲשׂוּ־כֵן:

ישראל: וַיֻּגַּד לְמֶלֶךְ מִצְרַיִם כִּי בָרַח הָעָם
וַיֵּהָפֵךְ לְבַב פַּרְעֹה וַעֲבָדָיו אֶל־הָעָם וַיֹּאמְרוּ
מַה־זֹּאת עָשִׂינוּ כִּי־שִׁלַּחְנוּ אֶת־יִשְׂרָאֵל
מֵעָבְדֵנוּ: וַיֶּאְסֹר אֶת־רִכְבּוֹ וְאֶת־עַמּוֹ לָקַח
עִמּוֹ: וַיִּקַּח שֵׁשׁ־מֵאוֹת רֶכֶב בָּחוּר וְכֹל רֶכֶב
מִצְרָיִם וְשָׁלִשִׁם עַל־כֻּלּוֹ: וַיְחַזֵּק יהוה אֶת־
לֵב פַּרְעֹה מֶלֶךְ מִצְרַיִם וַיִּרְדֹּף אַחֲרֵי בְּנֵי
יִשְׂרָאֵל וּבְנֵי יִשְׂרָאֵל יֹצְאִים בְּיָד רָמָה:

‎ פ׳ יתרו / YISRO ‎
(Exodus 18:1-12)

כח: וַיִּשְׁמַע יִתְרוֹ כֹהֵן מִדְיָן חֹתֵן מֹשֶׁה אֵת
כָּל־אֲשֶׁר עָשָׂה אֱלֹהִים לְמֹשֶׁה וּלְיִשְׂרָאֵל
עַמּוֹ כִּי־הוֹצִיא יהוה אֶת־יִשְׂרָאֵל מִמִּצְרָיִם:
וַיִּקַּח יִתְרוֹ חֹתֵן מֹשֶׁה אֶת־צִפֹּרָה אֵשֶׁת
מֹשֶׁה אַחַר שִׁלּוּחֶיהָ: וְאֵת שְׁנֵי בָנֶיהָ אֲשֶׁר
שֵׁם הָאֶחָד גֵּרְשֹׁם כִּי אָמַר גֵּר הָיִיתִי בְּאֶרֶץ
נָכְרִיָּה: וְשֵׁם הָאֶחָד אֱלִיעֶזֶר כִּי־אֱלֹהֵי אָבִי
בְּעֶזְרִי וַיַּצִּלֵנִי מֵחֶרֶב פַּרְעֹה:

לוי: וַיָּבֹא יִתְרוֹ חֹתֵן מֹשֶׁה וּבָנָיו וְאִשְׁתּוֹ
אֶל־מֹשֶׁה אֶל־הַמִּדְבָּר אֲשֶׁר־הוּא חֹנֶה שָׁם
הַר הָאֱלֹהִים: וַיֹּאמֶר אֶל־מֹשֶׁה אֲנִי חֹתֶנְךָ
יִתְרוֹ בָּא אֵלֶיךָ וְאִשְׁתְּךָ וּשְׁנֵי בָנֶיהָ עִמָּהּ:
וַיֵּצֵא מֹשֶׁה לִקְרַאת חֹתְנוֹ וַיִּשְׁתַּחוּ וַיִּשַּׁק־לוֹ
וַיִּשְׁאֲלוּ אִישׁ־לְרֵעֵהוּ לְשָׁלוֹם וַיָּבֹאוּ הָאֹהֱלָה:
וַיְסַפֵּר מֹשֶׁה לְחֹתְנוֹ אֵת כָּל־אֲשֶׁר עָשָׂה
יהוה לְפַרְעֹה וּלְמִצְרַיִם עַל אוֹדֹת יִשְׂרָאֵל
אֵת כָּל־הַתְּלָאָה אֲשֶׁר מְצָאָתַם בַּדֶּרֶךְ
וַיַּצִּלֵם יהוה:

ישראל: וַיִּחַדְּ יִתְרוֹ עַל כָּל־הַטּוֹבָה אֲשֶׁר־עָשָׂה

יהוה לְיִשְׂרָאֵל אֲשֶׁר הִצִּילוֹ מִיַּד מִצְרָיִם:
וַיֹּאמֶר יִתְרוֹ בָּרוּךְ יהוה אֲשֶׁר הִצִּיל אֶתְכֶם
מִיַּד מִצְרַיִם וּמִיַּד פַּרְעֹה אֲשֶׁר הִצִּיל אֶת־
הָעָם מִתַּחַת יַד־מִצְרָיִם: עַתָּה יָדַעְתִּי כִּי־
גָדוֹל יהוה מִכָּל־הָאֱלֹהִים כִּי בַדָּבָר אֲשֶׁר זָדוּ
עֲלֵיהֶם: וַיִּקַּח יִתְרוֹ חֹתֵן מֹשֶׁה עֹלָה וּזְבָחִים
לֵאלֹהִים וַיָּבֹא אַהֲרֹן וְכֹל ׀ זִקְנֵי יִשְׂרָאֵל
לֶאֱכָל־לֶחֶם עִם־חֹתֵן מֹשֶׁה לִפְנֵי הָאֱלֹהִים:

‎ פ׳ משפטים / MISHPATIM ‎
(Exodus 21:1-19)

כח: וְאֵלֶּה הַמִּשְׁפָּטִים אֲשֶׁר תָּשִׂים לִפְנֵיהֶם:
כִּי תִקְנֶה עֶבֶד עִבְרִי שֵׁשׁ שָׁנִים יַעֲבֹד
וּבַשְּׁבִעִת יֵצֵא לַחָפְשִׁי חִנָּם: אִם־בְּגַפּוֹ יָבֹא
בְּגַפּוֹ יֵצֵא אִם־בַּעַל אִשָּׁה הוּא וְיָצְאָה אִשְׁתּוֹ
עִמּוֹ: אִם־אֲדֹנָיו יִתֶּן־לוֹ אִשָּׁה וְיָלְדָה־לוֹ
בָנִים אוֹ בָנוֹת הָאִשָּׁה וִילָדֶיהָ תִּהְיֶה לַאדֹנֶיהָ
וְהוּא יֵצֵא בְגַפּוֹ: וְאִם־אָמֹר יֹאמַר הָעֶבֶד
אָהַבְתִּי אֶת־אֲדֹנִי אֶת־אִשְׁתִּי וְאֶת־בָּנָי לֹא
אֵצֵא חָפְשִׁי: וְהִגִּישׁוֹ אֲדֹנָיו אֶל־הָאֱלֹהִים
וְהִגִּישׁוֹ אֶל־הַדֶּלֶת אוֹ אֶל־הַמְּזוּזָה וְרָצַע
אֲדֹנָיו אֶת־אָזְנוֹ בַּמַּרְצֵעַ וַעֲבָדוֹ לְעֹלָם:

לוי: וְכִי־יִמְכֹּר אִישׁ אֶת־בִּתּוֹ לְאָמָה לֹא תֵצֵא
כְּצֵאת הָעֲבָדִים: אִם־רָעָה בְּעֵינֵי אֲדֹנֶיהָ
אֲשֶׁר־לוֹ יְעָדָהּ וְהֶפְדָּהּ לְעַם נָכְרִי לֹא־יִמְשֹׁל
לְמָכְרָהּ בְּבִגְדוֹ־בָהּ: וְאִם־לִבְנוֹ יִיעָדֶנָּה
כְּמִשְׁפַּט הַבָּנוֹת יַעֲשֶׂה־לָּהּ: אִם־אַחֶרֶת
יִקַּח־לוֹ שְׁאֵרָהּ כְּסוּתָהּ וְעֹנָתָהּ לֹא יִגְרָע:
וְאִם־שְׁלָשׁ־אֵלֶּה לֹא יַעֲשֶׂה לָהּ וְיָצְאָה חִנָּם
אֵין כָּסֶף:

ישראל: מַכֵּה אִישׁ וָמֵת מוֹת יוּמָת: וַאֲשֶׁר לֹא
צָדָה וְהָאֱלֹהִים אִנָּה לְיָדוֹ וְשַׂמְתִּי לְךָ מָקוֹם
אֲשֶׁר יָנוּס שָׁמָּה: וְכִי־יָזִד אִישׁ עַל־רֵעֵהוּ
לְהָרְגוֹ בְעָרְמָה מֵעִם מִזְבְּחִי תִּקָּחֶנּוּ לָמוּת:
וּמַכֵּה אָבִיו וְאִמּוֹ מוֹת יוּמָת: וְגֹנֵב אִישׁ
וּמְכָרוֹ וְנִמְצָא בְיָדוֹ מוֹת יוּמָת: וּמְקַלֵּל אָבִיו
וְאִמּוֹ מוֹת יוּמָת: וְכִי־יְרִיבֻן אֲנָשִׁים וְהִכָּה־
אִישׁ אֶת־רֵעֵהוּ בְּאֶבֶן אוֹ בְאֶגְרֹף וְלֹא יָמוּת
וְנָפַל לְמִשְׁכָּב: אִם־יָקוּם וְהִתְהַלֵּךְ בַּחוּץ
עַל־מִשְׁעַנְתּוֹ וְנִקָּה הַמַּכֶּה רַק שִׁבְתּוֹ יִתֵּן
וְרַפֹּא יְרַפֵּא:

פ׳ תרומה / TERUMAH
(Exodus 25:1-16)

כה: וַיְדַבֵּ֥ר יְהֹוָ֖ה אֶל־מֹשֶׁ֥ה לֵּאמֹֽר: דַּבֵּר֙ אֶל־בְּנֵ֣י יִשְׂרָאֵ֔ל וְיִקְחוּ־לִ֖י תְּרוּמָ֑ה מֵאֵ֤ת כָּל־אִישׁ֙ אֲשֶׁ֣ר יִדְּבֶ֣נּוּ לִבּ֔וֹ תִּקְח֖וּ אֶת־תְּרוּמָתִֽי: וְזֹאת֙ הַתְּרוּמָ֔ה אֲשֶׁ֥ר תִּקְח֖וּ מֵאִתָּ֑ם זָהָ֥ב וָכֶ֖סֶף וּנְחֹֽשֶׁת: וּתְכֵ֧לֶת וְאַרְגָּמָ֛ן וְתוֹלַ֥עַת שָׁנִ֖י וְשֵׁ֥שׁ וְעִזִּֽים: וְעֹרֹ֨ת אֵילִ֧ם מְאׇדָּמִ֛ים וְעֹרֹ֥ת תְּחָשִׁ֖ים וַעֲצֵ֥י שִׁטִּֽים:

לוי: שֶׁ֖מֶן לַמָּאֹ֑ר בְּשָׂמִים֙ לְשֶׁ֣מֶן הַמִּשְׁחָ֔ה וְלִקְטֹ֖רֶת הַסַּמִּֽים: אַבְנֵי־שֹׁ֕הַם וְאַבְנֵ֖י מִלֻּאִ֑ים לָאֵפֹ֖ד וְלַחֹֽשֶׁן: וְעָ֥שׂוּ לִ֖י מִקְדָּ֑שׁ וְשָׁכַנְתִּ֖י בְּתוֹכָֽם: כְּכֹ֗ל אֲשֶׁ֤ר אֲנִי֙ מַרְאֶ֣ה אוֹתְךָ֔ אֵ֚ת תַּבְנִ֣ית הַמִּשְׁכָּ֔ן וְאֵ֖ת תַּבְנִ֣ית כָּל־כֵּלָ֑יו וְכֵ֖ן תַּעֲשֽׂוּ:

ישראל: וְעָשׂ֥וּ אֲר֖וֹן עֲצֵ֣י שִׁטִּ֑ים אַמָּתַ֨יִם וָחֵ֜צִי אׇרְכּ֗וֹ וְאַמָּ֤ה וָחֵ֨צִי֙ רׇחְבּ֔וֹ וְאַמָּ֥ה וָחֵ֖צִי קֹמָתֽוֹ: וְצִפִּיתָ֤ אֹתוֹ֙ זָהָ֣ב טָה֔וֹר מִבַּ֥יִת וּמִח֖וּץ תְּצַפֶּ֑נּוּ וְעָשִׂ֧יתָ עָלָ֛יו זֵ֥ר זָהָ֖ב סָבִֽיב: וְיָצַ֣קְתָּ לּ֗וֹ אַרְבַּע֙ טַבְּעֹ֣ת זָהָ֔ב וְנָ֣תַתָּ֔ה עַ֖ל אַרְבַּ֣ע פַּעֲמֹתָ֑יו וּשְׁתֵּ֣י טַבָּעֹ֗ת עַל־צַלְעוֹ֙ הָֽאֶחָ֔ת וּשְׁתֵּי֙ טַבָּעֹ֔ת עַל־צַלְע֖וֹ הַשֵּׁנִֽית: וְעָשִׂ֥יתָ בַדֵּ֖י עֲצֵ֣י שִׁטִּ֑ים וְצִפִּיתָ֥ אֹתָ֖ם זָהָֽב: וְהֵֽבֵאתָ֤ אֶת־הַבַּדִּים֙ בַּטַּבָּעֹ֔ת עַ֖ל צַלְעֹ֣ת הָאָרֹ֑ן לָשֵׂ֥את אֶת־הָאָרֹ֖ן בָּהֶֽם: בְּטַבְּעֹת֙ הָאָרֹ֔ן יִהְי֖וּ הַבַּדִּ֑ים לֹ֥א יָסֻ֖רוּ מִמֶּֽנּוּ: וְנָתַתָּ֖ אֶל־הָאָרֹ֑ן אֵ֚ת הָעֵדֻ֔ת אֲשֶׁ֥ר אֶתֵּ֖ן אֵלֶֽיךָ:

פ׳ תצוה / TETZAVEH
(Exodus 27:20—28:12)

כה: וְאַתָּ֞ה תְּצַוֶּ֣ה ׀ אֶת־בְּנֵ֣י יִשְׂרָאֵ֗ל וְיִקְח֨וּ אֵלֶ֜יךָ שֶׁ֣מֶן זַ֥יִת זָ֛ךְ כָּתִ֖ית לַמָּא֑וֹר לְהַעֲלֹ֥ת נֵ֖ר תָּמִֽיד: בְּאֹ֣הֶל מוֹעֵ֗ד מִחוּץ֩ לַפָּרֹ֨כֶת אֲשֶׁ֣ר עַל־הָעֵדֻ֗ת יַעֲרֹךְ֩ אֹת֨וֹ אַהֲרֹ֧ן וּבָנָ֛יו מֵעֶ֥רֶב עַד־בֹּ֖קֶר לִפְנֵ֣י יְהֹוָ֑ה חֻקַּ֤ת עוֹלָם֙ לְדֹ֣רֹתָ֔ם מֵאֵ֖ת בְּנֵ֥י יִשְׂרָאֵֽל: וְאַתָּ֡ה הַקְרֵ֣ב אֵלֶ֩יךָ֩ אֶת־אַהֲרֹ֨ן אָחִ֜יךָ וְאֶת־בָּנָ֣יו אִתּ֗וֹ מִתּ֛וֹךְ בְּנֵ֥י יִשְׂרָאֵ֖ל לְכַהֲנוֹ־לִ֑י אַהֲרֹ֕ן נָדָ֧ב וַאֲבִיה֛וּא אֶלְעָזָ֥ר וְאִיתָמָ֖ר בְּנֵ֥י אַהֲרֹֽן: וְעָשִׂ֥יתָ בִגְדֵי־קֹ֖דֶשׁ לְאַהֲרֹ֣ן אָחִ֑יךָ לְכָב֖וֹד וּלְתִפְאָֽרֶת: וְאַתָּ֗ה תְּדַבֵּר֙ אֶל־כָּל־חַכְמֵי־לֵ֔ב אֲשֶׁ֥ר מִלֵּאתִ֖יו ר֣וּחַ חָכְמָ֑ה וְעָשׂ֞וּ אֶת־בִּגְדֵ֧י אַהֲרֹ֛ן לְקַדְּשׁ֖וֹ לְכַהֲנוֹ־

לִֽי: וְאֵ֨לֶּה הַבְּגָדִ֜ים אֲשֶׁ֣ר יַעֲשׂ֗וּ חֹ֤שֶׁן וְאֵפוֹד֙ וּמְעִ֔יל וּכְתֹ֥נֶת תַּשְׁבֵּ֖ץ מִצְנֶ֣פֶת וְאַבְנֵ֑ט וְעָשׂ֨וּ בִגְדֵי־קֹ֜דֶשׁ לְאַהֲרֹ֥ן אָחִ֛יךָ וּלְבָנָ֖יו לְכַהֲנוֹ־לִֽי: וְהֵם֙ יִקְח֣וּ אֶת־הַזָּהָ֔ב וְאֶת־הַתְּכֵ֖לֶת וְאֶת־הָֽאַרְגָּמָ֑ן וְאֶת־תּוֹלַ֥עַת הַשָּׁנִ֖י וְאֶת־הַשֵּֽׁשׁ:

לוי: וְעָשׂ֖וּ אֶת־הָאֵפֹ֑ד זָ֠הָ֠ב תְּכֵ֨לֶת וְאַרְגָּמָ֜ן תּוֹלַ֧עַת שָׁנִ֛י וְשֵׁ֥שׁ מָשְׁזָ֖ר מַעֲשֵׂ֥ה חֹשֵֽׁב: שְׁתֵּ֧י כְתֵפֹ֣ת חֹֽבְרֹ֗ת יִֽהְיֶה־לּ֛וֹ אֶל־שְׁנֵ֥י קְצוֹתָ֖יו וְחֻבָּֽר: וְחֵ֨שֶׁב אֲפֻדָּת֜וֹ אֲשֶׁ֣ר עָלָ֗יו כְּמַעֲשֵׂ֙הוּ֙ מִמֶּ֣נּוּ יִהְיֶ֔ה זָהָ֗ב תְּכֵ֧לֶת וְאַרְגָּמָ֛ן וְתוֹלַ֥עַת שָׁנִ֖י וְשֵׁ֥שׁ מָשְׁזָֽר: וְלָ֣קַחְתָּ֔ אֶת־שְׁתֵּ֖י אַבְנֵי־שֹׁ֑הַם וּפִתַּחְתָּ֣ עֲלֵיהֶ֔ם שְׁמ֖וֹת בְּנֵ֥י יִשְׂרָאֵֽל:

ישראל: שִׁשָּׁה֙ מִשְּׁמֹתָ֔ם עַ֖ל הָאֶ֣בֶן הָאֶחָ֑ת וְאֶת־שְׁמ֞וֹת הַשִּׁשָּׁ֧ה הַנּוֹתָרִ֛ים עַל־הָאֶ֥בֶן הַשֵּׁנִ֖ית כְּתוֹלְדֹתָֽם: מַעֲשֵׂ֣ה חָרַשׁ֮ אֶבֶן֒ פִּתּוּחֵ֣י חֹתָ֗ם תְּפַתַּח֙ אֶת־שְׁתֵּ֣י הָאֲבָנִ֔ים עַל־שְׁמֹ֖ת בְּנֵ֣י יִשְׂרָאֵ֑ל מֻסַבֹּ֛ת מִשְׁבְּצ֥וֹת זָהָ֖ב תַּעֲשֶׂ֥ה אֹתָֽם: וְשַׂמְתָּ֞ אֶת־שְׁתֵּ֣י הָאֲבָנִ֗ים עַ֚ל כִּתְפֹ֣ת הָאֵפֹ֔ד אַבְנֵ֥י זִכָּרֹ֖ן לִבְנֵ֣י יִשְׂרָאֵ֑ל וְנָשָׂא֩ אַהֲרֹ֨ן אֶת־שְׁמוֹתָ֜ם לִפְנֵ֧י יְהֹוָ֛ה עַל־שְׁתֵּ֥י כְתֵפָ֖יו לְזִכָּרֹֽן:

פ׳ כי תשא / KI SISA
(Exodus 30:11-21)

כה: וַיְדַבֵּ֥ר יְהֹוָ֖ה אֶל־מֹשֶׁ֥ה לֵּאמֹֽר: כִּ֣י תִשָּׂ֞א אֶת־רֹ֥אשׁ בְּנֵֽי־יִשְׂרָאֵל֮ לִפְקֻדֵיהֶם֒ וְנָ֨תְנ֜וּ אִ֣ישׁ כֹּ֧פֶר נַפְשׁ֛וֹ לַיהֹוָ֖ה בִּפְקֹ֣ד אֹתָ֑ם וְלֹא־יִהְיֶ֥ה בָהֶ֛ם נֶ֖גֶף בִּפְקֹ֥ד אֹתָֽם: זֶ֣ה ׀ יִתְּנ֗וּ כָּל־הָעֹבֵר֙ עַל־הַפְּקֻדִ֔ים מַחֲצִ֥ית הַשֶּׁ֖קֶל בְּשֶׁ֣קֶל הַקֹּ֑דֶשׁ עֶשְׂרִ֤ים גֵּרָה֙ הַשֶּׁ֔קֶל מַחֲצִ֣ית הַשֶּׁ֔קֶל תְּרוּמָ֖ה לַֽיהֹוָֽה:

לוי: כֹּ֗ל הָעֹבֵר֙ עַל־הַפְּקֻדִ֔ים מִבֶּ֛ן עֶשְׂרִ֥ים שָׁנָ֖ה וָמָ֑עְלָה יִתֵּ֖ן תְּרוּמַ֥ת יְהֹוָֽה: הֶֽעָשִׁ֣יר לֹֽא־יַרְבֶּ֗ה וְהַדַּל֙ לֹ֣א יַמְעִ֔יט מִֽמַּחֲצִ֖ית הַשָּׁ֑קֶל לָתֵת֙ אֶת־תְּרוּמַ֣ת יְהֹוָ֔ה לְכַפֵּ֖ר עַל־נַפְשֹׁתֵיכֶֽם: וְלָקַחְתָּ֞ אֶת־כֶּ֣סֶף הַכִּפֻּרִ֗ים מֵאֵת֙ בְּנֵ֣י יִשְׂרָאֵ֔ל וְנָתַתָּ֣ אֹת֔וֹ עַל־עֲבֹדַ֖ת אֹ֣הֶל מוֹעֵ֑ד וְהָיָה֩ לִבְנֵ֨י יִשְׂרָאֵ֤ל לְזִכָּרוֹן֙ לִפְנֵ֣י יְהֹוָ֔ה לְכַפֵּ֖ר עַל־נַפְשֹׁתֵיכֶֽם:

ישראל: וַיְדַבֵּ֥ר יְהֹוָ֖ה אֶל־מֹשֶׁ֥ה לֵּאמֹֽר: וְעָשִׂ֜יתָ כִּיּ֥וֹר נְחֹ֛שֶׁת וְכַנּ֥וֹ נְחֹ֖שֶׁת לְרָחְצָ֑ה וְנָתַתָּ֣ אֹת֗וֹ

בֵּין־אֹהֶל מוֹעֵד וּבֵין הַמִּזְבֵּחַ וַיִּתֵּן שָׁמָּה
מָיִם: וְרָחֲצוּ אַהֲרֹן וּבָנָיו מִמֶּנּוּ אֶת־יְדֵיהֶם
וְאֶת־רַגְלֵיהֶם: בְּבֹאָם אֶל־אֹהֶל מוֹעֵד
יִרְחֲצוּ־מַיִם וְלֹא יָמֻתוּ אוֹ בְגִשְׁתָּם אֶל־
הַמִּזְבֵּחַ לְשָׁרֵת לְהַקְטִיר אִשֶּׁה לַיהוָה:
וְרָחֲצוּ יְדֵיהֶם וְרַגְלֵיהֶם וְלֹא יָמֻתוּ וְהָיְתָה
לָהֶם חָק־עוֹלָם לוֹ וּלְזַרְעוֹ לְדֹרֹתָם:

פ׳ וַיַּקְהֵל / VAYAKHEL
(Exodus 35:1-20)

לה: וַיַּקְהֵל מֹשֶׁה אֶת־כָּל־עֲדַת בְּנֵי יִשְׂרָאֵל
וַיֹּאמֶר אֲלֵהֶם אֵלֶּה הַדְּבָרִים אֲשֶׁר־צִוָּה יהוה
לַעֲשֹׂת אֹתָם: שֵׁשֶׁת יָמִים תֵּעָשֶׂה מְלָאכָה
וּבַיּוֹם הַשְּׁבִיעִי יִהְיֶה לָכֶם קֹדֶשׁ שַׁבַּת שַׁבָּתוֹן
לַיהוָה כָּל־הָעֹשֶׂה בוֹ מְלָאכָה יוּמָת: לֹא־
תְבַעֲרוּ אֵשׁ בְּכֹל מֹשְׁבֹתֵיכֶם בְּיוֹם הַשַּׁבָּת:
לוי: וַיֹּאמֶר מֹשֶׁה אֶל־כָּל־עֲדַת בְּנֵי־יִשְׂרָאֵל
לֵאמֹר זֶה הַדָּבָר אֲשֶׁר־צִוָּה יהוה לֵאמֹר:
קְחוּ מֵאִתְּכֶם תְּרוּמָה לַיהוָה כֹּל נְדִיב לִבּוֹ
יְבִיאֶהָ אֵת תְּרוּמַת יהוה זָהָב וָכֶסֶף וּנְחֹשֶׁת:
וּתְכֵלֶת וְאַרְגָּמָן וְתוֹלַעַת שָׁנִי וְשֵׁשׁ וְעִזִּים:
וְעֹרֹת אֵילִם מְאָדָּמִים וְעֹרֹת תְּחָשִׁים וַעֲצֵי
שִׁטִּים: וְשֶׁמֶן לַמָּאוֹר וּבְשָׂמִים לְשֶׁמֶן
הַמִּשְׁחָה וְלִקְטֹרֶת הַסַּמִּים: וְאַבְנֵי־שֹׁהַם
וְאַבְנֵי מִלֻּאִים לָאֵפוֹד וְלַחֹשֶׁן: וְכָל־חֲכַם־לֵב
בָּכֶם יָבֹאוּ וְיַעֲשׂוּ אֵת כָּל־אֲשֶׁר צִוָּה יהוה:
ישראל: אֶת־הַמִּשְׁכָּן אֶת־אָהֳלוֹ וְאֶת־מִכְסֵהוּ
אֶת־קְרָסָיו וְאֶת־קְרָשָׁיו אֶת־בְּרִיחָו אֶת־
עַמֻּדָיו וְאֶת־אֲדָנָיו: אֶת־הָאָרֹן וְאֶת־בַּדָּיו
אֶת־הַכַּפֹּרֶת וְאֵת פָּרֹכֶת הַמָּסָךְ: אֶת־
הַשֻּׁלְחָן וְאֶת־בַּדָּיו וְאֶת־כָּל־כֵּלָיו וְאֵת לֶחֶם
הַפָּנִים: וְאֶת־מְנֹרַת הַמָּאוֹר וְאֶת־כֵּלֶיהָ
וְאֶת־נֵרֹתֶיהָ וְאֵת שֶׁמֶן הַמָּאוֹר: וְאֶת־מִזְבַּח
הַקְּטֹרֶת וְאֶת־בַּדָּיו וְאֵת שֶׁמֶן הַמִּשְׁחָה וְאֵת
קְטֹרֶת הַסַּמִּים וְאֶת־מָסַךְ הַפֶּתַח לְפֶתַח
הַמִּשְׁכָּן: אֵת ו מִזְבַּח הָעֹלָה וְאֶת־מִכְבַּר
הַנְּחֹשֶׁת אֲשֶׁר־לוֹ אֶת־בַּדָּיו וְאֶת־כָּל־כֵּלָיו
אֶת־הַכִּיֹּר וְאֶת־כַּנּוֹ: אֵת קַלְעֵי הֶחָצֵר אֶת־
עַמֻּדָיו וְאֶת־אֲדָנֶיהָ וְאֵת מָסַךְ שַׁעַר הֶחָצֵר:
אֶת־יִתְדֹת הַמִּשְׁכָּן וְאֶת־יִתְדֹת הֶחָצֵר וְאֶת־
מֵיתְרֵיהֶם: אֶת־בִּגְדֵי הַשְּׂרָד לְשָׁרֵת בַּקֹּדֶשׁ

אֶת־בִּגְדֵי הַקֹּדֶשׁ לְאַהֲרֹן הַכֹּהֵן וְאֶת־בִּגְדֵי
בָנָיו לְכַהֵן: וַיֵּצְאוּ כָּל־עֲדַת בְּנֵי־יִשְׂרָאֵל
מִלִּפְנֵי מֹשֶׁה:

פ׳ פְּקוּדֵי / PEKUDEI
(Exodus 38:21 — 39:1)

לח: אֵלֶּה פְקוּדֵי הַמִּשְׁכָּן מִשְׁכַּן הָעֵדֻת אֲשֶׁר
פֻּקַּד עַל־פִּי מֹשֶׁה עֲבֹדַת הַלְוִיִּם בְּיַד אִיתָמָר
בֶּן־אַהֲרֹן הַכֹּהֵן: וּבְצַלְאֵל בֶּן־אוּרִי בֶן־חוּר
לְמַטֵּה יְהוּדָה עָשָׂה אֵת כָּל־אֲשֶׁר־צִוָּה יהוה
אֶת־מֹשֶׁה: וְאִתּוֹ אָהֳלִיאָב בֶּן־אֲחִיסָמָךְ
לְמַטֵּה־דָן חָרָשׁ וְחֹשֵׁב וְרֹקֵם בַּתְּכֵלֶת
וּבָאַרְגָּמָן וּבְתוֹלַעַת הַשָּׁנִי וּבַשֵּׁשׁ:
לוי: כָּל־הַזָּהָב הֶעָשׂוּי לַמְּלָאכָה בְּכֹל מְלֶאכֶת
הַקֹּדֶשׁ וַיְהִי ו זְהַב הַתְּנוּפָה תֵּשַׁע וְעֶשְׂרִים כִּכָּר
וּשְׁבַע מֵאוֹת וּשְׁלֹשִׁים שֶׁקֶל בְּשֶׁקֶל הַקֹּדֶשׁ:
וְכֶסֶף פְּקוּדֵי הָעֵדָה מְאַת כִּכָּר וְאֶלֶף וּשְׁבַע
מֵאוֹת וַחֲמִשָּׁה וְשִׁבְעִים שֶׁקֶל בְּשֶׁקֶל הַקֹּדֶשׁ:
בֶּקַע לַגֻּלְגֹּלֶת מַחֲצִית הַשֶּׁקֶל בְּשֶׁקֶל הַקֹּדֶשׁ
לְכֹל הָעֹבֵר עַל־הַפְּקֻדִים מִבֶּן עֶשְׂרִים שָׁנָה
וָמַעְלָה לְשֵׁשׁ־מֵאוֹת אֶלֶף וּשְׁלֹשֶׁת אֲלָפִים
וַחֲמֵשׁ מֵאוֹת וַחֲמִשִּׁים: וַיְהִי מְאַת כִּכַּר הַכֶּסֶף
לָצֶקֶת אֵת אַדְנֵי הַקֹּדֶשׁ וְאֵת אַדְנֵי הַפָּרֹכֶת
מְאַת אֲדָנִים לִמְאַת הַכִּכָּר כִּכָּר לָאָדֶן:
ישראל: וְאֶת־הָאֶלֶף וּשְׁבַע הַמֵּאוֹת וַחֲמִשָּׁה
וְשִׁבְעִים עָשָׂה וָוִים לָעַמּוּדִים וְצִפָּה
רָאשֵׁיהֶם וְחִשַּׁק אֹתָם: וּנְחֹשֶׁת הַתְּנוּפָה
שִׁבְעִים כִּכָּר וְאַלְפַּיִם וְאַרְבַּע־מֵאוֹת שָׁקֶל:
וַיַּעַשׂ בָּהּ אֶת־אַדְנֵי פֶּתַח אֹהֶל מוֹעֵד וְאֵת
מִזְבַּח הַנְּחֹשֶׁת וְאֶת־מִכְבַּר הַנְּחֹשֶׁת אֲשֶׁר־לוֹ
וְאֵת כָּל־כְּלֵי הַמִּזְבֵּחַ: וְאֶת־אַדְנֵי הֶחָצֵר
סָבִיב וְאֶת־אַדְנֵי שַׁעַר הֶחָצֵר וְאֵת כָּל־יִתְדֹת
הַמִּשְׁכָּן וְאֶת־כָּל־יִתְדֹת הֶחָצֵר סָבִיב: וּמִן־
הַתְּכֵלֶת וְהָאַרְגָּמָן וְתוֹלַעַת הַשָּׁנִי עָשׂוּ בִגְדֵי־
שְׂרָד לְשָׁרֵת בַּקֹּדֶשׁ וַיַּעֲשׂוּ אֶת־בִּגְדֵי הַקֹּדֶשׁ
אֲשֶׁר לְאַהֲרֹן כַּאֲשֶׁר צִוָּה יהוה אֶת־מֹשֶׁה:

פ׳ וַיִּקְרָא / VAYIKRA
(Leviticus 1:1-13)

א: וַיִּקְרָא אֶל־מֹשֶׁה וַיְדַבֵּר יהוה אֵלָיו
מֵאֹהֶל מוֹעֵד לֵאמֹר: דַּבֵּר אֶל־בְּנֵי יִשְׂרָאֵל
וְאָמַרְתָּ אֲלֵהֶם אָדָם כִּי־יַקְרִיב מִכֶּם קָרְבָּן

לַיהוָה מִן־הַבְּהֵמָה מִן־הַבָּקָר וּמִן־הַצֹּאן
תַּקְרִיבוּ אֶת־קָרְבַּנְכֶם: אִם־עֹלָה קָרְבָּנוֹ מִן־
הַבָּקָר זָכָר תָּמִים יַקְרִיבֶנּוּ אֶל־פֶּתַח אֹהֶל
מוֹעֵד יַקְרִיב אֹתוֹ לִרְצֹנוֹ לִפְנֵי יְהוָה: וְסָמַךְ
יָדוֹ עַל רֹאשׁ הָעֹלָה וְנִרְצָה לוֹ לְכַפֵּר עָלָיו:
לוי: וְשָׁחַט אֶת־בֶּן הַבָּקָר לִפְנֵי יְהוָה וְהִקְרִיבוּ
בְּנֵי אַהֲרֹן הַכֹּהֲנִים אֶת־הַדָּם וְזָרְקוּ אֶת־הַדָּם
עַל־הַמִּזְבֵּחַ סָבִיב אֲשֶׁר־פֶּתַח אֹהֶל מוֹעֵד:
וְהִפְשִׁיט אֶת־הָעֹלָה וְנִתַּח אֹתָהּ לִנְתָחֶיהָ:
וְנָתְנוּ בְּנֵי אַהֲרֹן הַכֹּהֵן אֵשׁ עַל־הַמִּזְבֵּחַ
וְעָרְכוּ עֵצִים עַל־הָאֵשׁ: וְעָרְכוּ בְּנֵי אַהֲרֹן
הַכֹּהֲנִים אֵת הַנְּתָחִים אֶת־הָרֹאשׁ וְאֶת־
הַפָּדֶר עַל־הָעֵצִים אֲשֶׁר עַל־הָאֵשׁ אֲשֶׁר
עַל־הַמִּזְבֵּחַ: וְקִרְבּוֹ וּכְרָעָיו יִרְחַץ בַּמָּיִם
וְהִקְטִיר הַכֹּהֵן אֶת־הַכֹּל הַמִּזְבֵּחָה עֹלָה
אִשֵּׁה רֵיחַ־נִיחוֹחַ לַיהוָה:
ישראל: וְאִם־מִן־הַצֹּאן קָרְבָּנוֹ מִן־הַכְּשָׂבִים אוֹ
מִן־הָעִזִּים לְעֹלָה זָכָר תָּמִים יַקְרִיבֶנּוּ: וְשָׁחַט
אֹתוֹ עַל יֶרֶךְ הַמִּזְבֵּחַ צָפֹנָה לִפְנֵי יְהוָה וְזָרְקוּ
בְּנֵי אַהֲרֹן הַכֹּהֲנִים אֶת־דָּמוֹ עַל־הַמִּזְבֵּחַ
סָבִיב: וְנִתַּח אֹתוֹ לִנְתָחָיו וְאֶת־רֹאשׁוֹ וְאֶת־
פִּדְרוֹ וְעָרַךְ הַכֹּהֵן אֹתָם עַל־הָעֵצִים אֲשֶׁר
עַל־הָאֵשׁ אֲשֶׁר עַל־הַמִּזְבֵּחַ: וְהַקֶּרֶב
וְהַכְּרָעַיִם יִרְחַץ בַּמָּיִם וְהִקְרִיב הַכֹּהֵן אֶת־
הַכֹּל וְהִקְטִיר הַמִּזְבֵּחָה עֹלָה הוּא אִשֵּׁה רֵיחַ
נִיחֹחַ לַיהוָה:

⟪ פ' צו / TZAV

(Leviticus 6:1-11)

כו: וַיְדַבֵּר יְהוָה אֶל־מֹשֶׁה לֵּאמֹר: צַו אֶת־
אַהֲרֹן וְאֶת־בָּנָיו לֵאמֹר זֹאת תּוֹרַת הָעֹלָה
הִוא הָעֹלָה עַל מוֹקְדָה עַל־הַמִּזְבֵּחַ כָּל־
הַלַּיְלָה עַד־הַבֹּקֶר וְאֵשׁ הַמִּזְבֵּחַ תּוּקַד בּוֹ:
וְלָבַשׁ הַכֹּהֵן מִדּוֹ בַד וּמִכְנְסֵי־בַד יִלְבַּשׁ עַל־
בְּשָׂרוֹ וְהֵרִים אֶת־הַדֶּשֶׁן אֲשֶׁר תֹּאכַל הָאֵשׁ
אֶת־הָעֹלָה עַל־הַמִּזְבֵּחַ וְשָׂמוֹ אֵצֶל הַמִּזְבֵּחַ:
לוי: וּפָשַׁט אֶת־בְּגָדָיו וְלָבַשׁ בְּגָדִים אֲחֵרִים
וְהוֹצִיא אֶת־הַדֶּשֶׁן אֶל־מִחוּץ לַמַּחֲנֶה אֶל־
מָקוֹם טָהוֹר: וְהָאֵשׁ עַל־הַמִּזְבֵּחַ תּוּקַד־בּוֹ
לֹא תִכְבֶּה וּבִעֵר עָלֶיהָ הַכֹּהֵן עֵצִים בַּבֹּקֶר
בַּבֹּקֶר וְעָרַךְ עָלֶיהָ הָעֹלָה וְהִקְטִיר עָלֶיהָ

חֶלְבֵי הַשְּׁלָמִים: אֵשׁ תָּמִיד תּוּקַד עַל־
הַמִּזְבֵּחַ לֹא תִכְבֶּה:
ישראל: וְזֹאת תּוֹרַת הַמִּנְחָה הַקְרֵב אֹתָהּ
בְּנֵי־אַהֲרֹן לִפְנֵי יְהוָה אֶל־פְּנֵי הַמִּזְבֵּחַ: וְהֵרִים
מִמֶּנּוּ בְּקֻמְצוֹ מִסֹּלֶת הַמִּנְחָה וּמִשַּׁמְנָהּ וְאֵת
כָּל־הַלְּבֹנָה אֲשֶׁר עַל־הַמִּנְחָה וְהִקְטִיר
הַמִּזְבֵּחַ רֵיחַ נִיחֹחַ אַזְכָּרָתָהּ לַיהוָה: וְהַנּוֹתֶרֶת
מִמֶּנָּה יֹאכְלוּ אַהֲרֹן וּבָנָיו מַצּוֹת תֵּאָכֵל
בְּמָקוֹם קָדֹשׁ בַּחֲצַר אֹהֶל־מוֹעֵד יֹאכְלוּהָ:
לֹא תֵאָפֶה חָמֵץ חֶלְקָם נָתַתִּי אֹתָהּ מֵאִשָּׁי
קֹדֶשׁ קָדָשִׁים הִוא כַּחַטָּאת וְכָאָשָׁם: כָּל־זָכָר
בִּבְנֵי אַהֲרֹן יֹאכְלֶנָּה חָק־עוֹלָם לְדֹרֹתֵיכֶם
מֵאִשֵּׁי יְהוָה כֹּל אֲשֶׁר־יִגַּע בָּהֶם יִקְדָּשׁ:

⟪ פ' שמיני / SHEMINI

(Leviticus 9:1-16)

כו: וַיְהִי בַּיּוֹם הַשְּׁמִינִי קָרָא מֹשֶׁה לְאַהֲרֹן
וּלְבָנָיו וּלְזִקְנֵי יִשְׂרָאֵל: וַיֹּאמֶר אֶל־אַהֲרֹן
קַח־לְךָ עֵגֶל בֶּן־בָּקָר לְחַטָּאת וְאַיִל לְעֹלָה
תְּמִימִם וְהַקְרֵב לִפְנֵי יְהוָה: וְאֶל־בְּנֵי יִשְׂרָאֵל
תְּדַבֵּר לֵאמֹר קְחוּ שְׂעִיר־עִזִּים לְחַטָּאת
וְעֵגֶל וָכֶבֶשׂ בְּנֵי־שָׁנָה תְּמִימִם לְעֹלָה: וְשׁוֹר
וָאַיִל לִשְׁלָמִים לִזְבֹּחַ לִפְנֵי יְהוָה וּמִנְחָה
בְלוּלָה בַשָּׁמֶן כִּי הַיּוֹם יְהוָה נִרְאָה אֲלֵיכֶם:
וַיִּקְחוּ אֵת אֲשֶׁר צִוָּה מֹשֶׁה אֶל־פְּנֵי אֹהֶל
מוֹעֵד וַיִּקְרְבוּ כָּל־הָעֵדָה וַיַּעַמְדוּ לִפְנֵי יְהוָה:
וַיֹּאמֶר מֹשֶׁה זֶה הַדָּבָר אֲשֶׁר־צִוָּה יְהוָה
תַּעֲשׂוּ וְיֵרָא אֲלֵיכֶם כְּבוֹד יְהוָה:
לוי: וַיֹּאמֶר מֹשֶׁה אֶל־אַהֲרֹן קְרַב אֶל־הַמִּזְבֵּחַ
וַעֲשֵׂה אֶת־חַטָּאתְךָ וְאֶת־עֹלָתֶךָ וְכַפֵּר
בַּעַדְךָ וּבְעַד הָעָם וַעֲשֵׂה אֶת־קָרְבַּן הָעָם
וְכַפֵּר בַּעֲדָם כַּאֲשֶׁר צִוָּה יְהוָה: וַיִּקְרַב אַהֲרֹן
אֶל־הַמִּזְבֵּחַ וַיִּשְׁחַט אֶת־עֵגֶל הַחַטָּאת
אֲשֶׁר־לוֹ: וַיַּקְרִבוּ בְּנֵי אַהֲרֹן אֶת־הַדָּם אֵלָיו
וַיִּטְבֹּל אֶצְבָּעוֹ בַּדָּם וַיִּתֵּן עַל־קַרְנוֹת הַמִּזְבֵּחַ
וְאֶת־הַדָּם יָצַק אֶל־יְסוֹד הַמִּזְבֵּחַ: וְאֶת־
הַחֵלֶב וְאֶת־הַכְּלָיֹת וְאֶת־הַיֹּתֶרֶת מִן־הַכָּבֵד
מִן־הַחַטָּאת הִקְטִיר הַמִּזְבֵּחָה כַּאֲשֶׁר צִוָּה
יְהוָה אֶת־מֹשֶׁה:
ישראל: וְאֶת־הַבָּשָׂר וְאֶת־הָעוֹר שָׂרַף בָּאֵשׁ
מִחוּץ לַמַּחֲנֶה: וַיִּשְׁחַט אֶת־הָעֹלָה וַיַּמְצִאוּ

פָּשָׂה הַנֶּגַע בָּעוֹר וְהִסְגִּירוֹ הַכֹּהֵן שִׁבְעַת יָמִים שֵׁנִית:

﴾ פ׳ מצורע / METZORA ﴿
(Leviticus 14:1-12)

כח: וַיְדַבֵּר יהוה אֶל־מֹשֶׁה לֵּאמֹר: זֹאת תִּהְיֶה תּוֹרַת הַמְּצֹרָע בְּיוֹם טָהֳרָתוֹ וְהוּבָא אֶל־הַכֹּהֵן: וְיָצָא הַכֹּהֵן אֶל־מִחוּץ לַמַּחֲנֶה וְרָאָה הַכֹּהֵן וְהִנֵּה נִרְפָּא נֶגַע־הַצָּרַעַת מִן־הַצָּרוּעַ: וְצִוָּה הַכֹּהֵן וְלָקַח לַמִּטַּהֵר שְׁתֵּי־צִפֳּרִים חַיּוֹת טְהֹרוֹת וְעֵץ אֶרֶז וּשְׁנִי תוֹלַעַת וְאֵזֹב: וְצִוָּה הַכֹּהֵן וְשָׁחַט אֶת־הַצִּפּוֹר הָאֶחָת אֶל־כְּלִי־חֶרֶשׂ עַל־מַיִם חַיִּים:

לוי: אֶת־הַצִּפֹּר הַחַיָּה יִקַּח אֹתָהּ וְאֶת־עֵץ הָאֶרֶז וְאֶת־שְׁנִי הַתּוֹלַעַת וְאֶת־הָאֵזֹב וְטָבַל אוֹתָם וְאֵת ׀ הַצִּפֹּר הַחַיָּה בְּדַם הַצִּפֹּר הַשְּׁחֻטָה עַל הַמַּיִם הַחַיִּים: וְהִזָּה עַל הַמִּטַּהֵר מִן־הַצָּרַעַת שֶׁבַע פְּעָמִים וְטִהֲרוֹ וְשִׁלַּח אֶת־הַצִּפֹּר הַחַיָּה עַל־פְּנֵי הַשָּׂדֶה: וְכִבֶּס הַמִּטַּהֵר אֶת־בְּגָדָיו וְגִלַּח אֶת־כָּל־שְׂעָרוֹ וְרָחַץ בַּמַּיִם וְטָהֵר וְאַחַר יָבוֹא אֶל־הַמַּחֲנֶה וְיָשַׁב מִחוּץ לְאָהֳלוֹ שִׁבְעַת יָמִים: וְהָיָה בַיּוֹם הַשְּׁבִיעִי יְגַלַּח אֶת־כָּל־שְׂעָרוֹ אֶת־רֹאשׁוֹ וְאֶת־זְקָנוֹ וְאֵת גַּבֹּת עֵינָיו וְאֶת־כָּל־שְׂעָרוֹ יְגַלֵּחַ וְכִבֶּס אֶת־בְּגָדָיו וְרָחַץ אֶת־בְּשָׂרוֹ בַּמַּיִם וְטָהֵר:

ישראל: וּבַיּוֹם הַשְּׁמִינִי יִקַּח שְׁנֵי־כְבָשִׂים תְּמִימִם וְכַבְשָׂה אַחַת בַּת־שְׁנָתָהּ תְּמִימָה וּשְׁלֹשָׁה עֶשְׂרֹנִים סֹלֶת מִנְחָה בְּלוּלָה בַשֶּׁמֶן וְלֹג אֶחָד שָׁמֶן: וְהֶעֱמִיד הַכֹּהֵן הַמְטַהֵר אֵת הָאִישׁ הַמִּטַּהֵר וְאֹתָם לִפְנֵי יהוה פֶּתַח אֹהֶל מוֹעֵד: וְלָקַח הַכֹּהֵן אֶת־הַכֶּבֶשׂ הָאֶחָד וְהִקְרִיב אֹתוֹ לְאָשָׁם וְאֶת־לֹג הַשָּׁמֶן וְהֵנִיף אֹתָם תְּנוּפָה לִפְנֵי יהוה:

﴾ פ׳ אחרי מות / ACHAREI MOS ﴿
(Leviticus 16:1-17)

כח: וַיְדַבֵּר יהוה אֶל־מֹשֶׁה אַחֲרֵי מוֹת שְׁנֵי בְּנֵי אַהֲרֹן בְּקָרְבָתָם לִפְנֵי־יהוה וַיָּמֻתוּ: וַיֹּאמֶר יהוה אֶל־מֹשֶׁה דַּבֵּר אֶל־אַהֲרֹן אָחִיךָ וְאַל־יָבֹא בְכָל־עֵת אֶל־הַקֹּדֶשׁ מִבֵּית לַפָּרֹכֶת אֶל־פְּנֵי הַכַּפֹּרֶת אֲשֶׁר עַל־הָאָרֹן וְלֹא יָמוּת כִּי בֶּעָנָן אֵרָאֶה עַל־הַכַּפֹּרֶת:

בְּנֵי אַהֲרֹן אֵלָיו אֶת־הַדָּם וַיִּזְרְקֵהוּ עַל־הַמִּזְבֵּחַ סָבִיב: וְאֶת־הָעֹלָה הִמְצִיאוּ אֵלָיו לִנְתָחֶיהָ וְאֶת־הָרֹאשׁ וַיַּקְטֵר עַל־הַמִּזְבֵּחַ: וַיִּרְחַץ אֶת־הַקֶּרֶב וְאֶת־הַכְּרָעַיִם וַיַּקְטֵר עַל־הָעֹלָה הַמִּזְבֵּחָה: וַיַּקְרֵב אֵת קָרְבַּן הָעָם וַיִּקַּח אֶת־שְׂעִיר הַחַטָּאת אֲשֶׁר לָעָם וַיִּשְׁחָטֵהוּ וַיְחַטְּאֵהוּ כָּרִאשׁוֹן: וַיַּקְרֵב אֶת־הָעֹלָה וַיַּעֲשֶׂהָ כַּמִּשְׁפָּט:

﴾ פ׳ תזריע / TAZRIA ﴿
(Leviticus 12:1—13:5)

כח: וַיְדַבֵּר יהוה אֶל־מֹשֶׁה לֵּאמֹר: דַּבֵּר אֶל־בְּנֵי יִשְׂרָאֵל לֵאמֹר אִשָּׁה כִּי תַזְרִיעַ וְיָלְדָה זָכָר וְטָמְאָה שִׁבְעַת יָמִים כִּימֵי נִדַּת דְּוֹתָהּ תִּטְמָא: וּבַיּוֹם הַשְּׁמִינִי יִמּוֹל בְּשַׂר עָרְלָתוֹ: וּשְׁלֹשִׁים יוֹם וּשְׁלֹשֶׁת יָמִים תֵּשֵׁב בִּדְמֵי טָהֳרָה בְּכָל־קֹדֶשׁ לֹא־תִגָּע וְאֶל־הַמִּקְדָּשׁ לֹא תָבֹא עַד־מְלֹאת יְמֵי טָהֳרָהּ:

לוי: וְאִם־נְקֵבָה תֵלֵד וְטָמְאָה שְׁבֻעַיִם כְּנִדָּתָהּ וְשִׁשִּׁים יוֹם וְשֵׁשֶׁת יָמִים תֵּשֵׁב עַל־דְּמֵי טָהֳרָה: וּבִמְלֹאת ׀ יְמֵי טָהֳרָהּ לְבֵן אוֹ לְבַת תָּבִיא כֶּבֶשׂ בֶּן־שְׁנָתוֹ לְעֹלָה וּבֶן־יוֹנָה אוֹ־תֹר לְחַטָּאת אֶל־פֶּתַח אֹהֶל־מוֹעֵד אֶל־הַכֹּהֵן: וְהִקְרִיבוֹ לִפְנֵי יהוה וְכִפֶּר עָלֶיהָ וְטָהֲרָה מִמְּקֹר דָּמֶיהָ זֹאת תּוֹרַת הַיֹּלֶדֶת לַזָּכָר אוֹ לַנְּקֵבָה: וְאִם־לֹא תִמְצָא יָדָהּ דֵּי שֶׂה וְלָקְחָה שְׁתֵּי־תֹרִים אוֹ שְׁנֵי בְּנֵי יוֹנָה אֶחָד לְעֹלָה וְאֶחָד לְחַטָּאת וְכִפֶּר עָלֶיהָ הַכֹּהֵן וְטָהֵרָה:

ישראל: וַיְדַבֵּר יהוה אֶל־מֹשֶׁה וְאֶל־אַהֲרֹן לֵאמֹר: אָדָם כִּי־יִהְיֶה בְעוֹר־בְּשָׂרוֹ שְׂאֵת אוֹ־סַפַּחַת אוֹ בַהֶרֶת וְהָיָה בְעוֹר־בְּשָׂרוֹ לְנֶגַע צָרָעַת וְהוּבָא אֶל־אַהֲרֹן הַכֹּהֵן אוֹ אֶל־אַחַד מִבָּנָיו הַכֹּהֲנִים: וְרָאָה הַכֹּהֵן אֶת־הַנֶּגַע בְּעוֹר־הַבָּשָׂר וְשֵׂעָר בַּנֶּגַע הָפַךְ ׀ לָבָן וּמַרְאֵה הַנֶּגַע עָמֹק מֵעוֹר בְּשָׂרוֹ נֶגַע צָרַעַת הוּא וְרָאָהוּ הַכֹּהֵן וְטִמֵּא אֹתוֹ: וְאִם־בַּהֶרֶת לְבָנָה הִוא בְּעוֹר בְּשָׂרוֹ וְעָמֹק אֵין־מַרְאֶהָ מִן־הָעוֹר וּשְׂעָרָה לֹא־הָפַךְ לָבָן וְהִסְגִּיר הַכֹּהֵן אֶת־הַנֶּגַע שִׁבְעַת יָמִים: וְרָאָהוּ הַכֹּהֵן בַּיּוֹם הַשְּׁבִיעִי וְהִנֵּה הַנֶּגַע עָמַד בְּעֵינָיו לֹא־

בְּזֹאת יָבֹא אַהֲרֹן אֶל־הַקֹּדֶשׁ בְּפַר בֶּן־בָּקָר לְחַטָּאת וְאַיִל לְעֹלָה: כְּתֹנֶת־בַּד קֹדֶשׁ יִלְבָּשׁ וּמִכְנְסֵי־בַד יִהְיוּ עַל־בְּשָׂרוֹ וּבְאַבְנֵט בַּד יַחְגֹּר וּבְמִצְנֶפֶת בַּד יִצְנֹף בִּגְדֵי־קֹדֶשׁ הֵם וְרָחַץ בַּמַּיִם אֶת־בְּשָׂרוֹ וּלְבֵשָׁם: וּמֵאֵת עֲדַת בְּנֵי יִשְׂרָאֵל יִקַּח שְׁנֵי שְׂעִירֵי עִזִּים לְחַטָּאת וְאַיִל אֶחָד לְעֹלָה: וְהִקְרִיב אַהֲרֹן אֶת־פַּר הַחַטָּאת אֲשֶׁר־לוֹ וְכִפֶּר בַּעֲדוֹ וּבְעַד בֵּיתוֹ:

לוי: וְלָקַח אֶת־שְׁנֵי הַשְּׂעִירִם וְהֶעֱמִיד אֹתָם לִפְנֵי יהוה פֶּתַח אֹהֶל מוֹעֵד: וְנָתַן אַהֲרֹן עַל־שְׁנֵי הַשְּׂעִירִם גֹּרָלוֹת גּוֹרָל אֶחָד לַיהוה וְגוֹרָל אֶחָד לַעֲזָאזֵל: וְהִקְרִיב אַהֲרֹן אֶת־הַשָּׂעִיר אֲשֶׁר עָלָה עָלָיו הַגּוֹרָל לַיהוה וְעָשָׂהוּ חַטָּאת: וְהַשָּׂעִיר אֲשֶׁר עָלָה עָלָיו הַגּוֹרָל לַעֲזָאזֵל יָעֳמַד־חַי לִפְנֵי יהוה לְכַפֵּר עָלָיו לְשַׁלַּח אֹתוֹ לַעֲזָאזֵל הַמִּדְבָּרָה: וְהִקְרִיב אַהֲרֹן אֶת־פַּר הַחַטָּאת אֲשֶׁר־לוֹ וְכִפֶּר בַּעֲדוֹ וּבְעַד בֵּיתוֹ וְשָׁחַט אֶת־פַּר הַחַטָּאת אֲשֶׁר־לוֹ:

ישראל: וְלָקַח מְלֹא־הַמַּחְתָּה גַּחֲלֵי־אֵשׁ מֵעַל הַמִּזְבֵּחַ מִלִּפְנֵי יהוה וּמְלֹא חָפְנָיו קְטֹרֶת סַמִּים דַּקָּה וְהֵבִיא מִבֵּית לַפָּרֹכֶת: וְנָתַן אֶת־הַקְּטֹרֶת עַל־הָאֵשׁ לִפְנֵי יהוה וְכִסָּה | עֲנַן הַקְּטֹרֶת אֶת־הַכַּפֹּרֶת אֲשֶׁר עַל־הָעֵדוּת וְלֹא יָמוּת: וְלָקַח מִדַּם הַפָּר וְהִזָּה בְאֶצְבָּעוֹ עַל־פְּנֵי הַכַּפֹּרֶת קֵדְמָה וְלִפְנֵי הַכַּפֹּרֶת יַזֶּה שֶׁבַע־פְּעָמִים מִן־הַדָּם בְּאֶצְבָּעוֹ: וְשָׁחַט אֶת־שְׂעִיר הַחַטָּאת אֲשֶׁר לָעָם וְהֵבִיא אֶת־דָּמוֹ אֶל־מִבֵּית לַפָּרֹכֶת וְעָשָׂה אֶת־דָּמוֹ כַּאֲשֶׁר עָשָׂה לְדַם הַפָּר וְהִזָּה אֹתוֹ עַל־הַכַּפֹּרֶת וְלִפְנֵי הַכַּפֹּרֶת: וְכִפֶּר עַל־הַקֹּדֶשׁ מִטֻּמְאֹת בְּנֵי יִשְׂרָאֵל וּמִפִּשְׁעֵיהֶם לְכָל־חַטֹּאתָם וְכֵן יַעֲשֶׂה לְאֹהֶל מוֹעֵד הַשֹּׁכֵן אִתָּם בְּתוֹךְ טֻמְאֹתָם: וְכָל־אָדָם לֹא־יִהְיֶה | בְּאֹהֶל מוֹעֵד בְּבֹאוֹ לְכַפֵּר בַּקֹּדֶשׁ עַד־צֵאתוֹ וְכִפֶּר בַּעֲדוֹ וּבְעַד בֵּיתוֹ וּבְעַד כָּל־קְהַל יִשְׂרָאֵל:

◆ פ' קדשים / KEDOSHIM ◆
(Leviticus 19:1-14)

כחו: וַיְדַבֵּר יהוה אֶל־מֹשֶׁה לֵּאמֹר: דַּבֵּר אֶל־כָּל־עֲדַת בְּנֵי־יִשְׂרָאֵל וְאָמַרְתָּ אֲלֵהֶם קְדֹשִׁים תִּהְיוּ כִּי קָדוֹשׁ אֲנִי יהוה אֱלֹהֵיכֶם:

אִישׁ אִמּוֹ וְאָבִיו תִּירָאוּ וְאֶת־שַׁבְּתֹתַי תִּשְׁמֹרוּ אֲנִי יהוה אֱלֹהֵיכֶם: אַל־תִּפְנוּ אֶל־הָאֱלִילִם וֵאלֹהֵי מַסֵּכָה לֹא תַעֲשׂוּ לָכֶם אֲנִי יהוה אֱלֹהֵיכֶם:

לוי: וְכִי תִזְבְּחוּ זֶבַח שְׁלָמִים לַיהוה לִרְצֹנְכֶם תִּזְבָּחֻהוּ: בְּיוֹם זִבְחֲכֶם יֵאָכֵל וּמִמָּחֳרָת וְהַנּוֹתָר עַד־יוֹם הַשְּׁלִישִׁי בָּאֵשׁ יִשָּׂרֵף: וְאִם הֵאָכֹל יֵאָכֵל בַּיּוֹם הַשְּׁלִישִׁי פִּגּוּל הוּא לֹא יֵרָצֶה: וְאֹכְלָיו עֲוֹנוֹ יִשָּׂא כִּי־אֶת־קֹדֶשׁ יהוה חִלֵּל וְנִכְרְתָה הַנֶּפֶשׁ הַהִוא מֵעַמֶּיהָ: וּבְקֻצְרְכֶם אֶת־קְצִיר אַרְצְכֶם לֹא תְכַלֶּה פְּאַת שָׂדְךָ לִקְצֹר וְלֶקֶט קְצִירְךָ לֹא תְלַקֵּט: וְכַרְמְךָ לֹא תְעוֹלֵל וּפֶרֶט כַּרְמְךָ לֹא תְלַקֵּט לֶעָנִי וְלַגֵּר תַּעֲזֹב אֹתָם אֲנִי יהוה אֱלֹהֵיכֶם:

ישראל: לֹא תִּגְנֹבוּ וְלֹא־תְכַחֲשׁוּ וְלֹא־תְשַׁקְּרוּ אִישׁ בַּעֲמִיתוֹ: וְלֹא־תִשָּׁבְעוּ בִשְׁמִי לַשָּׁקֶר וְחִלַּלְתָּ אֶת־שֵׁם אֱלֹהֶיךָ אֲנִי יהוה: לֹא־תַעֲשֹׁק אֶת־רֵעֲךָ וְלֹא תִגְזֹל לֹא־תָלִין פְּעֻלַּת שָׂכִיר אִתְּךָ עַד־בֹּקֶר: לֹא־תְקַלֵּל חֵרֵשׁ וְלִפְנֵי עִוֵּר לֹא תִתֵּן מִכְשֹׁל וְיָרֵאתָ מֵּאֱלֹהֶיךָ אֲנִי יהוה:

◆ פ' אמור / EMOR ◆
(Leviticus 21:1-15)

כחו: וַיֹּאמֶר יהוה אֶל־מֹשֶׁה אֱמֹר אֶל־הַכֹּהֲנִים בְּנֵי אַהֲרֹן וְאָמַרְתָּ אֲלֵהֶם לְנֶפֶשׁ לֹא־יִטַּמָּא בְּעַמָּיו: כִּי אִם־לִשְׁאֵרוֹ הַקָּרֹב אֵלָיו לְאִמּוֹ וּלְאָבִיו וְלִבְנוֹ וּלְבִתּוֹ וּלְאָחִיו: וְלַאֲחֹתוֹ הַבְּתוּלָה הַקְּרוֹבָה אֵלָיו אֲשֶׁר לֹא־הָיְתָה לְאִישׁ לָהּ יִטַּמָּא: לֹא יִטַּמָּא בַּעַל בְּעַמָּיו לְהֵחַלּוֹ: לֹא־יִקְרְחֻה קָרְחָה בְּרֹאשָׁם וּפְאַת זְקָנָם לֹא יְגַלֵּחוּ וּבִבְשָׂרָם לֹא יִשְׂרְטוּ שָׂרָטֶת: קְדֹשִׁים יִהְיוּ לֵאלֹהֵיהֶם וְלֹא יְחַלְּלוּ שֵׁם אֱלֹהֵיהֶם כִּי אֶת־אִשֵּׁי יהוה לֶחֶם אֱלֹהֵיהֶם הֵם מַקְרִיבִם וְהָיוּ קֹדֶשׁ:

לוי: אִשָּׁה זֹנָה וַחֲלָלָה לֹא יִקָּחוּ וְאִשָּׁה גְּרוּשָׁה מֵאִישָׁהּ לֹא יִקָּחוּ כִּי־קָדֹשׁ הוּא לֵאלֹהָיו: וְקִדַּשְׁתּוֹ כִּי־אֶת־לֶחֶם אֱלֹהֶיךָ הוּא מַקְרִיב קָדֹשׁ יִהְיֶה־לָּךְ כִּי קָדוֹשׁ אֲנִי יהוה מְקַדִּשְׁכֶם: וּבַת אִישׁ כֹּהֵן כִּי תֵחֵל לִזְנוֹת אֶת־אָבִיהָ הִיא מְחַלֶּלֶת בָּאֵשׁ תִּשָּׂרֵף: וְהַכֹּהֵן הַגָּדוֹל מֵאֶחָיו

פ׳ בחקתי / BECHUKOSAI

(Leviticus 26:3-13)

כו: אִם־בְּחֻקֹּתַי תֵּלֵכוּ וְאֶת־מִצְוֹתַי תִּשְׁמְרוּ
וַעֲשִׂיתֶם אֹתָם: וְנָתַתִּי גִשְׁמֵיכֶם בְּעִתָּם וְנָתְנָה
הָאָרֶץ יְבוּלָהּ וְעֵץ הַשָּׂדֶה יִתֵּן פִּרְיוֹ: וְהִשִּׂיג
לָכֶם דַּיִשׁ אֶת־בָּצִיר וּבָצִיר יַשִּׂיג אֶת־זֶרַע
וַאֲכַלְתֶּם לַחְמְכֶם לָשֹׂבַע וִישַׁבְתֶּם לָבֶטַח
בְּאַרְצְכֶם:

לוי: וְנָתַתִּי שָׁלוֹם בָּאָרֶץ וּשְׁכַבְתֶּם וְאֵין
מַחֲרִיד וְהִשְׁבַּתִּי חַיָּה רָעָה מִן־הָאָרֶץ וְחֶרֶב
לֹא־תַעֲבֹר בְּאַרְצְכֶם: וּרְדַפְתֶּם אֶת־אֹיְבֵיכֶם
וְנָפְלוּ לִפְנֵיכֶם לֶחָרֶב: וְרָדְפוּ מִכֶּם חֲמִשָּׁה
מֵאָה וּמֵאָה מִכֶּם רְבָבָה יִרְדֹּפוּ וְנָפְלוּ
אֹיְבֵיכֶם לִפְנֵיכֶם לֶחָרֶב: וּפָנִיתִי אֲלֵיכֶם
וְהִפְרֵיתִי אֶתְכֶם וְהִרְבֵּיתִי אֶתְכֶם וַהֲקִימֹתִי
אֶת־בְּרִיתִי אִתְּכֶם:

ישראל: וַאֲכַלְתֶּם יָשָׁן נוֹשָׁן וְיָשָׁן מִפְּנֵי חָדָשׁ
תּוֹצִיאוּ: וְנָתַתִּי מִשְׁכָּנִי בְּתוֹכְכֶם וְלֹא־תִגְעַל
נַפְשִׁי אֶתְכֶם: וְהִתְהַלַּכְתִּי בְּתוֹכְכֶם וְהָיִיתִי
לָכֶם לֵאלֹהִים וְאַתֶּם תִּהְיוּ־לִי לְעָם: אֲנִי
יְהוָה אֱלֹהֵיכֶם אֲשֶׁר הוֹצֵאתִי אֶתְכֶם מֵאֶרֶץ
מִצְרַיִם מִהְיֹת לָהֶם עֲבָדִים וָאֶשְׁבֹּר מֹטֹת
עֻלְּכֶם וָאוֹלֵךְ אֶתְכֶם קוֹמְמִיּוּת:

פ׳ במדבר / BAMIDBAR

(Numbers 1:1-19)

כו: וַיְדַבֵּר יְהוָה אֶל־מֹשֶׁה בְּמִדְבַּר סִינַי
בְּאֹהֶל מוֹעֵד בְּאֶחָד לַחֹדֶשׁ הַשֵּׁנִי בַּשָּׁנָה
הַשֵּׁנִית לְצֵאתָם מֵאֶרֶץ מִצְרַיִם לֵאמֹר:
שְׂאוּ אֶת־רֹאשׁ כָּל־עֲדַת בְּנֵי־יִשְׂרָאֵל
לְמִשְׁפְּחֹתָם לְבֵית אֲבֹתָם בְּמִסְפַּר שֵׁמוֹת
כָּל־זָכָר לְגֻלְגְּלֹתָם: מִבֶּן עֶשְׂרִים שָׁנָה
וָמַעְלָה כָּל־יֹצֵא צָבָא בְּיִשְׂרָאֵל תִּפְקְדוּ אֹתָם
לְצִבְאֹתָם אַתָּה וְאַהֲרֹן: וְאִתְּכֶם יִהְיוּ אִישׁ
אִישׁ לַמַּטֶּה אִישׁ רֹאשׁ לְבֵית־אֲבֹתָיו הוּא:

לוי: וְאֵלֶּה שְׁמוֹת הָאֲנָשִׁים אֲשֶׁר יַעַמְדוּ
אִתְּכֶם לִרְאוּבֵן אֱלִיצוּר בֶּן־שְׁדֵיאוּר:
לְשִׁמְעוֹן שְׁלֻמִיאֵל בֶּן־צוּרִישַׁדָּי: לִיהוּדָה
נַחְשׁוֹן בֶּן־עַמִּינָדָב: לְיִשָּׂשׂכָר נְתַנְאֵל בֶּן־
צוּעָר: לִזְבוּלֻן אֱלִיאָב בֶּן־חֵלֹן: לִבְנֵי יוֹסֵף
לְאֶפְרַיִם אֱלִישָׁמָע בֶּן־עַמִּיהוּד לִמְנַשֶּׁה

אֲשֶׁר־יוּצַק עַל־רֹאשׁוֹ ׀ שֶׁמֶן הַמִּשְׁחָה וּמִלֵּא
אֶת־יָדוֹ לִלְבֹּשׁ אֶת־הַבְּגָדִים אֶת־רֹאשׁוֹ לֹא
יִפְרָע וּבְגָדָיו לֹא יִפְרֹם: וְעַל כָּל־נַפְשֹׁת מֵת לֹא
יָבֹא לְאָבִיו וּלְאִמּוֹ לֹא יִטַּמָּא: וּמִן־הַמִּקְדָּשׁ
לֹא יֵצֵא וְלֹא יְחַלֵּל אֵת מִקְדַּשׁ אֱלֹהָיו כִּי נֵזֶר
שֶׁמֶן מִשְׁחַת אֱלֹהָיו עָלָיו אֲנִי יְהוָה:

ישראל: וְהוּא אִשָּׁה בִבְתוּלֶיהָ יִקָּח: אַלְמָנָה
וּגְרוּשָׁה וַחֲלָלָה זֹנָה אֶת־אֵלֶּה לֹא יִקָּח כִּי
אִם־בְּתוּלָה מֵעַמָּיו יִקַּח אִשָּׁה: וְלֹא־יְחַלֵּל
זַרְעוֹ בְּעַמָּיו כִּי אֲנִי יְהוָה מְקַדְּשׁוֹ:

פ׳ בהר / BEHAR

(Leviticus 25:1-13)

כו: וַיְדַבֵּר יְהוָה אֶל־מֹשֶׁה בְּהַר סִינַי לֵאמֹר:
דַּבֵּר אֶל־בְּנֵי יִשְׂרָאֵל וְאָמַרְתָּ אֲלֵהֶם כִּי
תָבֹאוּ אֶל־הָאָרֶץ אֲשֶׁר אֲנִי נֹתֵן לָכֶם
וְשָׁבְתָה הָאָרֶץ שַׁבָּת לַיהוָה: שֵׁשׁ שָׁנִים
תִּזְרַע שָׂדֶךָ וְשֵׁשׁ שָׁנִים תִּזְמֹר כַּרְמֶךָ וְאָסַפְתָּ
אֶת־תְּבוּאָתָהּ:

לוי: וּבַשָּׁנָה הַשְּׁבִיעִת שַׁבַּת שַׁבָּתוֹן יִהְיֶה
לָאָרֶץ שַׁבָּת לַיהוָה שָׂדְךָ לֹא תִזְרָע וְכַרְמְךָ
לֹא תִזְמֹר: אֵת סְפִיחַ קְצִירְךָ לֹא תִקְצוֹר
וְאֶת־עִנְּבֵי נְזִירֶךָ לֹא תִבְצֹר שְׁנַת שַׁבָּתוֹן
יִהְיֶה לָאָרֶץ: וְהָיְתָה שַׁבַּת הָאָרֶץ לָכֶם
לְאָכְלָה לְךָ וּלְעַבְדְּךָ וְלַאֲמָתֶךָ וְלִשְׂכִירְךָ
וּלְתוֹשָׁבְךָ הַגָּרִים עִמָּךְ: וְלִבְהֶמְתְּךָ וְלַחַיָּה
אֲשֶׁר בְּאַרְצֶךָ תִּהְיֶה כָל־תְּבוּאָתָהּ לֶאֱכֹל:

ישראל: וְסָפַרְתָּ לְךָ שֶׁבַע שַׁבְּתֹת שָׁנִים שֶׁבַע
שָׁנִים שֶׁבַע פְּעָמִים וְהָיוּ לְךָ יְמֵי שֶׁבַע שַׁבְּתֹת
הַשָּׁנִים תֵּשַׁע וְאַרְבָּעִים שָׁנָה: וְהַעֲבַרְתָּ שׁוֹפַר
תְּרוּעָה בַּחֹדֶשׁ הַשְּׁבִעִי בֶּעָשׂוֹר לַחֹדֶשׁ בְּיוֹם
הַכִּפֻּרִים תַּעֲבִירוּ שׁוֹפָר בְּכָל־אַרְצְכֶם:
וְקִדַּשְׁתֶּם אֵת שְׁנַת הַחֲמִשִּׁים שָׁנָה וּקְרָאתֶם
דְּרוֹר בָּאָרֶץ לְכָל־יֹשְׁבֶיהָ יוֹבֵל הִוא תִּהְיֶה
לָכֶם וְשַׁבְתֶּם אִישׁ אֶל־אֲחֻזָּתוֹ וְאִישׁ אֶל־
מִשְׁפַּחְתּוֹ תָּשֻׁבוּ: יוֹבֵל הִוא שְׁנַת הַחֲמִשִּׁים
שָׁנָה תִּהְיֶה לָכֶם לֹא תִזְרָעוּ וְלֹא תִקְצְרוּ
אֶת־סְפִיחֶיהָ וְלֹא תִבְצְרוּ אֶת־נְזִרֶיהָ: כִּי
יוֹבֵל הִוא קֹדֶשׁ תִּהְיֶה לָכֶם מִן־הַשָּׂדֶה
תֹּאכְלוּ אֶת־תְּבוּאָתָהּ: בִּשְׁנַת הַיּוֹבֵל הַזֹּאת
תָּשֻׁבוּ אִישׁ אֶל־אֲחֻזָּתוֹ:

גַּמְלִיאֵל בֶּן־פְּדָהצֽוּר: לְבִנְיָמִן אֲבִידָן בֶּן־גִּדְעֹנִי: לְדָן אֲחִיעֶזֶר בֶּן־עַמִּישַׁדָּי: לְאָשֵׁר פַּגְעִיאֵל בֶּן־עׇכְרָן: לְגָד אֶלְיָסָף בֶּן־דְּעוּאֵל: לְנַפְתָּלִי אֲחִירַע בֶּן־עֵינָן: אֵלֶּה קְרוּאֵי הָעֵדָה נְשִׂיאֵי מַטּוֹת אֲבוֹתָם רָאשֵׁי אַלְפֵי יִשְׂרָאֵל הֵם:

ישראל: וַיִּקַּח מֹשֶׁה וְאַהֲרֹן אֵת הָאֲנָשִׁים הָאֵלֶּה אֲשֶׁר נִקְּבוּ בְּשֵׁמוֹת: וְאֵת כׇּל־הָעֵדָה הִקְהִילוּ בְּאֶחָד לַחֹדֶשׁ הַשֵּׁנִי וַיִּתְיַלְדוּ עַל־מִשְׁפְּחֹתָם לְבֵית אֲבֹתָם בְּמִסְפַּר שֵׁמוֹת מִבֶּן עֶשְׂרִים שָׁנָה וָמַעְלָה לְגֻלְגְּלֹתָם: כַּאֲשֶׁר צִוָּה יְהֹוָה אֶת־מֹשֶׁה וַיִּפְקְדֵם בְּמִדְבַּר סִינָי:

פ' נשא / NASSO
(Numbers 4:21-37)

כהן: וַיְדַבֵּר יְהֹוָה אֶל־מֹשֶׁה לֵּאמֹר: נָשֹׂא אֶת־רֹאשׁ בְּנֵי גֵרְשׁוֹן גַּם־הֵם לְבֵית אֲבֹתָם לְמִשְׁפְּחֹתָם: מִבֶּן שְׁלֹשִׁים שָׁנָה וָמַעְלָה עַד בֶּן־חֲמִשִּׁים שָׁנָה תִּפְקֹד אוֹתָם כׇּל־הַבָּא לִצְבֹא צָבָא לַעֲבֹד עֲבֹדָה בְּאֹהֶל מוֹעֵד: זֹאת עֲבֹדַת מִשְׁפְּחֹת הַגֵּרְשֻׁנִּי לַעֲבֹד וּלְמַשָּׂא:

לוי: וְנָשְׂאוּ אֶת־יְרִיעֹת הַמִּשְׁכָּן וְאֶת־אֹהֶל מוֹעֵד מִכְסֵהוּ וּמִכְסֵה הַתַּחַשׁ אֲשֶׁר־עָלָיו מִלְמָעְלָה וְאֶת־מָסַךְ פֶּתַח אֹהֶל מוֹעֵד: וְאֵת קַלְעֵי הֶחָצֵר וְאֶת־מָסַךְ ׀ פֶּתַח ׀ שַׁעַר הֶחָצֵר אֲשֶׁר עַל־הַמִּשְׁכָּן וְעַל־הַמִּזְבֵּחַ סָבִיב וְאֵת מֵיתְרֵיהֶם וְאֶת־כׇּל־כְּלֵי עֲבֹדָתָם וְאֵת כׇּל־אֲשֶׁר יֵעָשֶׂה לָהֶם וְעָבָדוּ: עַל־פִּי אַהֲרֹן וּבָנָיו תִּהְיֶה כׇּל־עֲבֹדַת בְּנֵי הַגֵּרְשֻׁנִּי לְכׇל־מַשָּׂאָם וּלְכֹל עֲבֹדָתָם וּפְקַדְתֶּם עֲלֵהֶם בְּמִשְׁמֶרֶת אֵת כׇּל־מַשָּׂאָם: זֹאת עֲבֹדַת מִשְׁפְּחֹת בְּנֵי הַגֵּרְשֻׁנִּי בְּאֹהֶל מוֹעֵד וּמִשְׁמַרְתָּם בְּיַד אִיתָמָר בֶּן־אַהֲרֹן הַכֹּהֵן:

ישראל: בְּנֵי מְרָרִי לְמִשְׁפְּחֹתָם לְבֵית־אֲבֹתָם תִּפְקֹד אֹתָם: מִבֶּן שְׁלֹשִׁים שָׁנָה וָמַעְלָה וְעַד בֶּן־חֲמִשִּׁים שָׁנָה תִּפְקְדֵם כׇּל־הַבָּא לַצָּבָא לַעֲבֹד אֶת־עֲבֹדַת אֹהֶל מוֹעֵד: וְזֹאת מִשְׁמֶרֶת מַשָּׂאָם לְכׇל־עֲבֹדָתָם בְּאֹהֶל מוֹעֵד קַרְשֵׁי הַמִּשְׁכָּן וּבְרִיחָיו וְעַמּוּדָיו וַאֲדָנָיו: וְעַמּוּדֵי הֶחָצֵר סָבִיב וְאַדְנֵיהֶם וִיתֵדֹתָם וּמֵיתְרֵיהֶם לְכׇל־כְּלֵיהֶם וּלְכֹל עֲבֹדָתָם

וּבְשֵׂמֹת תִּפְקְדוּ אֶת־כְּלֵי מִשְׁמֶרֶת מַשָּׂאָם: זֹאת עֲבֹדַת מִשְׁפְּחֹת בְּנֵי מְרָרִי לְכׇל־עֲבֹדָתָם בְּאֹהֶל מוֹעֵד בְּיַד אִיתָמָר בֶּן־אַהֲרֹן הַכֹּהֵן:

Some end the reading at this point.

וַיִּפְקֹד מֹשֶׁה וְאַהֲרֹן וּנְשִׂיאֵי הָעֵדָה אֶת־בְּנֵי הַקְּהָתִי לְמִשְׁפְּחֹתָם וּלְבֵית אֲבֹתָם: מִבֶּן שְׁלֹשִׁים שָׁנָה וָמַעְלָה וְעַד בֶּן־חֲמִשִּׁים שָׁנָה כׇּל־הַבָּא לַצָּבָא לַעֲבֹדָה בְּאֹהֶל מוֹעֵד: וַיִּהְיוּ פְקֻדֵיהֶם לְמִשְׁפְּחֹתָם אַלְפַּיִם שְׁבַע מֵאוֹת וַחֲמִשִּׁים: אֵלֶּה פְקוּדֵי מִשְׁפְּחֹת הַקְּהָתִי כׇּל־הָעֹבֵד בְּאֹהֶל מוֹעֵד אֲשֶׁר פָּקַד מֹשֶׁה וְאַהֲרֹן עַל־פִּי יְהֹוָה בְּיַד־מֹשֶׁה:

פ' בהעלתך / BEHA'ALOSCHA
(Numbers 8:1-14)

כהן: וַיְדַבֵּר יְהֹוָה אֶל־מֹשֶׁה לֵּאמֹר: דַּבֵּר אֶל־אַהֲרֹן וְאָמַרְתָּ אֵלָיו בְּהַעֲלֹתְךָ אֶת־הַנֵּרֹת אֶל־מוּל פְּנֵי הַמְּנוֹרָה יָאִירוּ שִׁבְעַת הַנֵּרוֹת: וַיַּעַשׂ כֵּן אַהֲרֹן אֶל־מוּל פְּנֵי הַמְּנוֹרָה הֶעֱלָה נֵרֹתֶיהָ כַּאֲשֶׁר צִוָּה יְהֹוָה אֶת־מֹשֶׁה: וְזֶה מַעֲשֵׂה הַמְּנֹרָה מִקְשָׁה זָהָב עַד־יְרֵכָהּ עַד־פִּרְחָהּ מִקְשָׁה הִוא כַּמַּרְאֶה אֲשֶׁר הֶרְאָה יְהֹוָה אֶת־מֹשֶׁה כֵּן עָשָׂה אֶת־הַמְּנֹרָה:

לוי: וַיְדַבֵּר יְהֹוָה אֶל־מֹשֶׁה לֵּאמֹר: קַח אֶת־הַלְוִיִּם מִתּוֹךְ בְּנֵי יִשְׂרָאֵל וְטִהַרְתָּ אֹתָם: וְכֹה־תַעֲשֶׂה לָהֶם לְטַהֲרָם הַזֵּה עֲלֵיהֶם מֵי חַטָּאת וְהֶעֱבִירוּ תַעַר עַל־כׇּל־בְּשָׂרָם וְכִבְּסוּ בִגְדֵיהֶם וְהִטֶּהָרוּ: וְלָקְחוּ פַּר בֶּן־בָּקָר וּמִנְחָתוֹ סֹלֶת בְּלוּלָה בַשָּׁמֶן וּפַר־שֵׁנִי בֶן־בָּקָר תִּקַּח לְחַטָּאת: וְהִקְרַבְתָּ אֶת־הַלְוִיִּם לִפְנֵי אֹהֶל מוֹעֵד וְהִקְהַלְתָּ אֶת־כׇּל־עֲדַת בְּנֵי יִשְׂרָאֵל:

ישראל: וְהִקְרַבְתָּ אֶת־הַלְוִיִּם לִפְנֵי יְהֹוָה וְסָמְכוּ בְנֵי־יִשְׂרָאֵל אֶת־יְדֵיהֶם עַל־הַלְוִיִּם: וְהֵנִיף אַהֲרֹן אֶת־הַלְוִיִּם תְּנוּפָה לִפְנֵי יְהֹוָה מֵאֵת בְּנֵי יִשְׂרָאֵל וְהָיוּ לַעֲבֹד אֶת־עֲבֹדַת יְהֹוָה: וְהַלְוִיִּם יִסְמְכוּ אֶת־יְדֵיהֶם עַל רֹאשׁ הַפָּרִים וַעֲשֵׂה אֶת־הָאֶחָד חַטָּאת וְאֶת־הָאֶחָד עֹלָה לַיהֹוָה לְכַפֵּר עַל־הַלְוִיִּם: וְהַעֲמַדְתָּ אֶת־הַלְוִיִּם לִפְנֵי אַהֲרֹן וְלִפְנֵי בָנָיו וְהֵנַפְתָּ אֹתָם תְּנוּפָה לַיהֹוָה: וְהִבְדַּלְתָּ אֶת־הַלְוִיִּם מִתּוֹךְ בְּנֵי יִשְׂרָאֵל וְהָיוּ לִי הַלְוִיִּם:

◀ SHELACH / שלח ׳פ ▸

(Numbers 13:1-20)

כו: וַיְדַבֵּר יהוה אֶל־מֹשֶׁה לֵּאמֹר: שְׁלַח־לְךָ
אֲנָשִׁים וְיָתֻרוּ אֶת־אֶרֶץ כְּנַעַן אֲשֶׁר־אֲנִי נֹתֵן
לִבְנֵי יִשְׂרָאֵל אִישׁ אֶחָד אִישׁ אֶחָד לְמַטֵּה
אֲבֹתָיו תִּשְׁלָחוּ כֹּל נָשִׂיא בָהֶם: וַיִּשְׁלַח אֹתָם
מֹשֶׁה מִמִּדְבַּר פָּארָן עַל־פִּי יהוה כֻּלָּם
אֲנָשִׁים רָאשֵׁי בְנֵי־יִשְׂרָאֵל הֵמָּה:

לוי: וְאֵלֶּה שְׁמוֹתָם לְמַטֵּה רְאוּבֵן שַׁמּוּעַ בֶּן־
זַכּוּר: לְמַטֵּה שִׁמְעוֹן שָׁפָט בֶּן־חוֹרִי: לְמַטֵּה
יְהוּדָה כָּלֵב בֶּן־יְפֻנֶּה: לְמַטֵּה יִשָּׂשכָר יִגְאָל
בֶּן־יוֹסֵף: לְמַטֵּה אֶפְרָיִם הוֹשֵׁעַ בִּן־נוּן: לְמַטֵּה
בִנְיָמִן פַּלְטִי בֶּן־רָפוּא: לְמַטֵּה זְבוּלֻן גַּדִּיאֵל
בֶּן־סוֹדִי: לְמַטֵּה יוֹסֵף לְמַטֵּה מְנַשֶּׁה גַּדִּי בֶּן־
סוּסִי: לְמַטֵּה דָן עַמִּיאֵל בֶּן־גְּמַלִּי: לְמַטֵּה אָשֵׁר
סְתוּר בֶּן־מִיכָאֵל: לְמַטֵּה נַפְתָּלִי נַחְבִּי בֶּן־
וָפְסִי: לְמַטֵּה גָד גְּאוּאֵל בֶּן־מָכִי: אֵלֶּה שְׁמוֹת
הָאֲנָשִׁים אֲשֶׁר־שָׁלַח מֹשֶׁה לָתוּר אֶת־הָאָרֶץ
וַיִּקְרָא מֹשֶׁה לְהוֹשֵׁעַ בִּן־נוּן יְהוֹשֻׁעַ:

ישראל: וַיִּשְׁלַח אֹתָם מֹשֶׁה לָתוּר אֶת־אֶרֶץ
כְּנָעַן וַיֹּאמֶר אֲלֵהֶם עֲלוּ זֶה בַּנֶּגֶב וַעֲלִיתֶם
אֶת־הָהָר: וּרְאִיתֶם אֶת־הָאָרֶץ מַה־הִוא וְאֶת־
הָעָם הַיֹּשֵׁב עָלֶיהָ הֶחָזָק הוּא הֲרָפֶה הַמְעַט
הוּא אִם־רָב: וּמָה הָאָרֶץ אֲשֶׁר־הוּא יֹשֵׁב בָּהּ
הֲטוֹבָה הִוא אִם־רָעָה וּמָה הֶעָרִים אֲשֶׁר־הוּא
יוֹשֵׁב בָּהֵנָּה הַבְּמַחֲנִים אִם בְּמִבְצָרִים: וּמָה
הָאָרֶץ הַשְּׁמֵנָה הִוא אִם־רָזָה הֲיֵשׁ־בָּהּ עֵץ
אִם־אַיִן וְהִתְחַזַּקְתֶּם וּלְקַחְתֶּם מִפְּרִי הָאָרֶץ
וְהַיָּמִים יְמֵי בִּכּוּרֵי עֲנָבִים:

◀ KORACH / קרח ׳פ ▸

(Numbers 16:1-13)

כו: וַיִּקַּח קֹרַח בֶּן־יִצְהָר בֶּן־קְהָת בֶּן־לֵוִי
וְדָתָן וַאֲבִירָם בְּנֵי אֱלִיאָב וְאוֹן בֶּן־פֶּלֶת בְּנֵי
רְאוּבֵן: וַיָּקֻמוּ לִפְנֵי מֹשֶׁה וַאֲנָשִׁים מִבְּנֵי־
יִשְׂרָאֵל חֲמִשִּׁים וּמָאתָיִם נְשִׂיאֵי עֵדָה קְרִאֵי
מוֹעֵד אַנְשֵׁי־שֵׁם: וַיִּקָּהֲלוּ עַל־מֹשֶׁה וְעַל־
אַהֲרֹן וַיֹּאמְרוּ אֲלֵהֶם רַב־לָכֶם כִּי כָל־הָעֵדָה
כֻּלָּם קְדֹשִׁים וּבְתוֹכָם יהוה וּמַדּוּעַ תִּתְנַשְּׂאוּ
עַל־קְהַל יהוה:

לוי: וַיִּשְׁמַע מֹשֶׁה וַיִּפֹּל עַל־פָּנָיו: וַיְדַבֵּר אֶל־

קֹרַח וְאֶל־כָּל־עֲדָתוֹ לֵאמֹר בֹּקֶר וְיֹדַע יהוה
אֶת־אֲשֶׁר־לוֹ וְאֶת־הַקָּדוֹשׁ וְהִקְרִיב אֵלָיו
וְאֵת אֲשֶׁר יִבְחַר־בּוֹ יַקְרִיב אֵלָיו: זֹאת עֲשׂוּ
קְחוּ־לָכֶם מַחְתּוֹת קֹרַח וְכָל־עֲדָתוֹ: וּתְנוּ
בָהֶן ׀ אֵשׁ וְשִׂימוּ עֲלֵיהֶן ׀ קְטֹרֶת לִפְנֵי יהוה
מָחָר וְהָיָה הָאִישׁ אֲשֶׁר־יִבְחַר יהוה הוּא
הַקָּדוֹשׁ רַב־לָכֶם בְּנֵי לֵוִי:

ישראל: וַיֹּאמֶר מֹשֶׁה אֶל־קֹרַח שִׁמְעוּ־נָא בְּנֵי
לֵוִי: הַמְעַט מִכֶּם כִּי־הִבְדִּיל אֱלֹהֵי יִשְׂרָאֵל
אֶתְכֶם מֵעֲדַת יִשְׂרָאֵל לְהַקְרִיב אֶתְכֶם אֵלָיו
לַעֲבֹד אֶת־עֲבֹדַת מִשְׁכַּן יהוה וְלַעֲמֹד לִפְנֵי
הָעֵדָה לְשָׁרְתָם: וַיַּקְרֵב אֹתְךָ וְאֶת־כָּל־אַחֶיךָ
בְנֵי־לֵוִי אִתָּךְ וּבִקַּשְׁתֶּם גַּם־כְּהֻנָּה: לָכֵן אַתָּה
וְכָל־עֲדָתְךָ הַנֹּעָדִים עַל־יהוה וְאַהֲרֹן מַה־
הוּא כִּי תַלִּינוּ עָלָיו: וַיִּשְׁלַח מֹשֶׁה לִקְרֹא
לְדָתָן וְלַאֲבִירָם בְּנֵי אֱלִיאָב וַיֹּאמְרוּ לֹא
נַעֲלֶה: הַמְעַט כִּי הֶעֱלִיתָנוּ מֵאֶרֶץ זָבַת חָלָב
וּדְבַשׁ לַהֲמִיתֵנוּ בַּמִּדְבָּר כִּי־תִשְׂתָּרֵר עָלֵינוּ
גַּם־הִשְׂתָּרֵר:

◀ CHUKAS / חקת ׳פ ▸

(Numbers 19:1-17)

כו: וַיְדַבֵּר יהוה אֶל־מֹשֶׁה וְאֶל־אַהֲרֹן לֵאמֹר:
זֹאת חֻקַּת הַתּוֹרָה אֲשֶׁר־צִוָּה יהוה לֵאמֹר
דַּבֵּר ׀ אֶל־בְּנֵי יִשְׂרָאֵל וְיִקְחוּ אֵלֶיךָ פָרָה
אֲדֻמָּה תְּמִימָה אֲשֶׁר אֵין־בָּהּ מוּם אֲשֶׁר
לֹא־עָלָה עָלֶיהָ עֹל: וּנְתַתֶּם אֹתָהּ אֶל־אֶלְעָזָר
הַכֹּהֵן וְהוֹצִיא אֹתָהּ אֶל־מִחוּץ לַמַּחֲנֶה וְשָׁחַט
אֹתָהּ לְפָנָיו: וְלָקַח אֶלְעָזָר הַכֹּהֵן מִדָּמָהּ
בְּאֶצְבָּעוֹ וְהִזָּה אֶל־נֹכַח פְּנֵי אֹהֶל־מוֹעֵד
מִדָּמָהּ שֶׁבַע פְּעָמִים: וְשָׂרַף אֶת־הַפָּרָה לְעֵינָיו
אֶת־עֹרָהּ וְאֶת־בְּשָׂרָהּ וְאֶת־דָּמָהּ עַל־פִּרְשָׁהּ
יִשְׂרֹף: וְלָקַח הַכֹּהֵן עֵץ אֶרֶז וְאֵזוֹב וּשְׁנִי
תוֹלָעַת וְהִשְׁלִיךְ אֶל־תּוֹךְ שְׂרֵפַת הַפָּרָה:

לוי: וְכִבֶּס בְּגָדָיו הַכֹּהֵן וְרָחַץ בְּשָׂרוֹ בַּמַּיִם
וְאַחַר יָבֹא אֶל־הַמַּחֲנֶה וְטָמֵא הַכֹּהֵן עַד־
הָעָרֶב: וְהַשֹּׂרֵף אֹתָהּ יְכַבֵּס בְּגָדָיו בַּמַּיִם
וְרָחַץ בְּשָׂרוֹ בַּמָּיִם וְטָמֵא עַד־הָעָרֶב: וְאָסַף ׀
אִישׁ טָהוֹר אֵת אֵפֶר הַפָּרָה וְהִנִּיחַ מִחוּץ
לַמַּחֲנֶה בְּמָקוֹם טָהוֹר וְהָיְתָה לַעֲדַת בְּנֵי־
יִשְׂרָאֵל לְמִשְׁמֶרֶת לְמֵי נִדָּה חַטָּאת הִוא:

יִשְׂרָאֵל: וְכִבֶּס הָאֹסֵף אֶת־אֵפֶר הַפָּרָה אֶת־
בְּגָדָיו וְטָמֵא עַד־הָעָרֶב וְהָיְתָה לִבְנֵי יִשְׂרָאֵל
וְלַגֵּר הַגָּר בְּתוֹכָם לְחֻקַּת עוֹלָם: הַנֹּגֵעַ בְּמֵת
לְכָל־נֶפֶשׁ אָדָם וְטָמֵא שִׁבְעַת יָמִים: הוּא
יִתְחַטָּא־בוֹ בַּיּוֹם הַשְּׁלִישִׁי וּבַיּוֹם הַשְּׁבִיעִי
יִטְהָר וְאִם־לֹא יִתְחַטָּא בַּיּוֹם הַשְּׁלִישִׁי וּבַיּוֹם
הַשְּׁבִיעִי לֹא יִטְהָר: כָּל־הַנֹּגֵעַ בְּמֵת בְּנֶפֶשׁ
הָאָדָם אֲשֶׁר־יָמוּת וְלֹא יִתְחַטָּא אֶת־מִשְׁכַּן
יהוה טִמֵּא וְנִכְרְתָה הַנֶּפֶשׁ הַהִוא מִיִּשְׂרָאֵל
כִּי מֵי נִדָּה לֹא־זֹרַק עָלָיו טָמֵא יִהְיֶה עוֹד
טֻמְאָתוֹ בוֹ: זֹאת הַתּוֹרָה אָדָם כִּי־יָמוּת בְּאֹהֶל
כָּל־הַבָּא אֶל־הָאֹהֶל וְכָל־אֲשֶׁר בָּאֹהֶל יִטְמָא
שִׁבְעַת יָמִים: וְכֹל כְּלִי פָתוּחַ אֲשֶׁר אֵין־צָמִיד
פָּתִיל עָלָיו טָמֵא הוּא: וְכֹל אֲשֶׁר־יִגַּע עַל־פְּנֵי
הַשָּׂדֶה בַּחֲלַל־חֶרֶב אוֹ בְמֵת אוֹ־בְעֶצֶם אָדָם
אוֹ בְקָבֶר יִטְמָא שִׁבְעַת יָמִים: וְלָקְחוּ לַטָּמֵא
מֵעֲפַר שְׂרֵפַת הַחַטָּאת וְנָתַן עָלָיו מַיִם חַיִּים
אֶל־כֶּלִי:

◄§ פ׳ בלק / BALAK ◄§

(Numbers 22:2-12)

כב: וַיַּרְא בָּלָק בֶּן־צִפּוֹר אֵת כָּל־אֲשֶׁר־עָשָׂה
יִשְׂרָאֵל לָאֱמֹרִי: וַיָּגָר מוֹאָב מִפְּנֵי הָעָם מְאֹד
כִּי רַב־הוּא וַיָּקָץ מוֹאָב מִפְּנֵי בְּנֵי יִשְׂרָאֵל:
וַיֹּאמֶר מוֹאָב אֶל־זִקְנֵי מִדְיָן עַתָּה יְלַחֲכוּ
הַקָּהָל אֶת־כָּל־סְבִיבֹתֵינוּ כִּלְחֹךְ הַשּׁוֹר אֵת
יֶרֶק הַשָּׂדֶה וּבָלָק בֶּן־צִפּוֹר מֶלֶךְ לְמוֹאָב בָּעֵת
הַהִוא:

לוי: וַיִּשְׁלַח מַלְאָכִים אֶל־בִּלְעָם בֶּן־בְּעֹר
פְּתוֹרָה אֲשֶׁר עַל־הַנָּהָר אֶרֶץ בְּנֵי־עַמּוֹ
לִקְרֹא־לוֹ לֵאמֹר הִנֵּה עַם יָצָא מִמִּצְרַיִם הִנֵּה
כִסָּה אֶת־עֵין הָאָרֶץ וְהוּא יֹשֵׁב מִמֻּלִי: וְעַתָּה
לְכָה־נָּא אָרָה־לִּי אֶת־הָעָם הַזֶּה כִּי־עָצוּם
הוּא מִמֶּנִּי אוּלַי אוּכַל נַכֶּה־בּוֹ וַאֲגָרְשֶׁנּוּ
מִן־הָאָרֶץ כִּי יָדַעְתִּי אֵת אֲשֶׁר־תְּבָרֵךְ מְבֹרָךְ
וַאֲשֶׁר תָּאֹר יוּאָר: וַיֵּלְכוּ זִקְנֵי מוֹאָב וְזִקְנֵי
מִדְיָן וּקְסָמִים בְּיָדָם וַיָּבֹאוּ אֶל־בִּלְעָם וַיְדַבְּרוּ
אֵלָיו דִּבְרֵי בָלָק:

יִשְׂרָאֵל: וַיֹּאמֶר אֲלֵיהֶם לִינוּ פֹה הַלַּיְלָה
וַהֲשִׁבֹתִי אֶתְכֶם דָּבָר כַּאֲשֶׁר יְדַבֵּר יהוה אֵלָי
וַיֵּשְׁבוּ שָׂרֵי־מוֹאָב עִם־בִּלְעָם: וַיָּבֹא אֱלֹהִים

אֶל־בִּלְעָם וַיֹּאמֶר מִי הָאֲנָשִׁים הָאֵלֶּה עִמָּךְ:
וַיֹּאמֶר בִּלְעָם אֶל־הָאֱלֹהִים בָּלָק בֶּן־צִפֹּר
מֶלֶךְ מוֹאָב שָׁלַח אֵלָי: הִנֵּה הָעָם הַיֹּצֵא
מִמִּצְרַיִם וַיְכַס אֶת־עֵין הָאָרֶץ עַתָּה לְכָה
קָבָה־לִּי אֹתוֹ אוּלַי אוּכַל לְהִלָּחֶם בּוֹ וְגֵרַשְׁתִּיו:
וַיֹּאמֶר אֱלֹהִים אֶל־בִּלְעָם לֹא תֵלֵךְ עִמָּהֶם
לֹא תָאֹר אֶת־הָעָם כִּי בָרוּךְ הוּא:

◄§ פ׳ פנחס / PINCHAS ◄§

(Numbers 25:10—26:4)

כה: וַיְדַבֵּר יהוה אֶל־מֹשֶׁה לֵּאמֹר: פִּינְחָס
בֶּן־אֶלְעָזָר בֶּן־אַהֲרֹן הַכֹּהֵן הֵשִׁיב אֶת־חֲמָתִי
מֵעַל בְּנֵי־יִשְׂרָאֵל בְּקַנְאוֹ אֶת־קִנְאָתִי בְּתוֹכָם
וְלֹא־כִלִּיתִי אֶת־בְּנֵי־יִשְׂרָאֵל בְּקִנְאָתִי: לָכֵן
אֱמֹר הִנְנִי נֹתֵן לוֹ אֶת־בְּרִיתִי שָׁלוֹם:

לוי: וְהָיְתָה לּוֹ וּלְזַרְעוֹ אַחֲרָיו בְּרִית כְּהֻנַּת
עוֹלָם תַּחַת אֲשֶׁר קִנֵּא לֵאלֹהָיו וַיְכַפֵּר עַל־
בְּנֵי יִשְׂרָאֵל: וְשֵׁם אִישׁ יִשְׂרָאֵל הַמֻּכֶּה אֲשֶׁר
הֻכָּה אֶת־הַמִּדְיָנִית זִמְרִי בֶּן־סָלוּא נְשִׂיא
בֵית־אָב לַשִּׁמְעֹנִי: וְשֵׁם הָאִשָּׁה הַמֻּכָּה
הַמִּדְיָנִית כָּזְבִּי בַת־צוּר רֹאשׁ אֻמּוֹת בֵּית־
אָב בְּמִדְיָן הוּא:

יִשְׂרָאֵל: וַיְדַבֵּר יהוה אֶל־מֹשֶׁה לֵּאמֹר: צָרוֹר
אֶת־הַמִּדְיָנִים וְהִכִּיתֶם אוֹתָם: כִּי צֹרְרִים הֵם
לָכֶם בְּנִכְלֵיהֶם אֲשֶׁר־נִכְּלוּ לָכֶם עַל־דְּבַר
פְּעוֹר וְעַל־דְּבַר כָּזְבִּי בַת־נְשִׂיא מִדְיָן אֲחֹתָם
הַמֻּכָּה בְיוֹם־הַמַּגֵּפָה עַל־דְּבַר־פְּעוֹר: וַיְהִי
אַחֲרֵי הַמַּגֵּפָה וַיֹּאמֶר יהוה אֶל־מֹשֶׁה וְאֶל
אֶלְעָזָר בֶּן־אַהֲרֹן הַכֹּהֵן לֵאמֹר: שְׂאוּ אֶת־
רֹאשׁ ׀ כָּל־עֲדַת בְּנֵי־יִשְׂרָאֵל מִבֶּן עֶשְׂרִים
שָׁנָה וָמַעְלָה לְבֵית אֲבֹתָם כָּל־יֹצֵא צָבָא
בְּיִשְׂרָאֵל: וַיְדַבֵּר מֹשֶׁה וְאֶלְעָזָר הַכֹּהֵן אֹתָם
בְּעַרְבֹת מוֹאָב עַל־יַרְדֵּן יְרֵחוֹ לֵאמֹר: מִבֶּן
עֶשְׂרִים שָׁנָה וָמַעְלָה כַּאֲשֶׁר צִוָּה יהוה אֶת־
מֹשֶׁה וּבְנֵי יִשְׂרָאֵל הַיֹּצְאִים מֵאֶרֶץ מִצְרָיִם:

◄§ פ׳ מטות / MATOS ◄§

(Numbers 30:2-17)

ל: וַיְדַבֵּר מֹשֶׁה אֶל־רָאשֵׁי הַמַּטּוֹת לִבְנֵי
יִשְׂרָאֵל לֵאמֹר זֶה הַדָּבָר אֲשֶׁר צִוָּה יהוה:
אִישׁ כִּי־יִדֹּר נֶדֶר לַיהוה אוֹ־הִשָּׁבַע שְׁבֻעָה
לֶאְסֹר אִסָּר עַל־נַפְשׁוֹ לֹא יַחֵל דְּבָרוֹ כְּכָל־

הַיֹּצֵא מִפִּיו יַעֲשֶׂה: וְאִשָּׁה כִּי־תִדֹּר נֶדֶר
לַיהוָה וְאָסְרָה אִסָּר בְּבֵית אָבִיהָ בִּנְעֻרֶיהָ:
וְשָׁמַע אָבִיהָ אֶת־נִדְרָהּ וֶאֱסָרָהּ אֲשֶׁר אָסְרָה
עַל־נַפְשָׁהּ וְהֶחֱרִישׁ לָהּ אָבִיהָ וְקָמוּ כָּל־
נְדָרֶיהָ וְכָל־אִסָּר אֲשֶׁר אָסְרָה עַל־נַפְשָׁהּ
יָקוּם: וְאִם־הֵנִיא אָבִיהָ אֹתָהּ בְּיוֹם שָׁמְעוֹ
כָּל־נְדָרֶיהָ וֶאֱסָרֶיהָ אֲשֶׁר אָסְרָה עַל־נַפְשָׁהּ
לֹא יָקוּם וַיהוָה יִסְלַח־לָהּ כִּי־הֵנִיא אָבִיהָ
אֹתָהּ: וְאִם־הָיוֹ תִהְיֶה לְאִישׁ וּנְדָרֶיהָ עָלֶיהָ אוֹ
מִבְטָא שְׂפָתֶיהָ אֲשֶׁר אָסְרָה עַל־נַפְשָׁהּ:
וְשָׁמַע אִישָׁהּ בְּיוֹם שָׁמְעוֹ וְהֶחֱרִישׁ לָהּ וְקָמוּ
נְדָרֶיהָ וֶאֱסָרֶהָ אֲשֶׁר אָסְרָה עַל־נַפְשָׁהּ יָקֻמוּ:
וְאִם בְּיוֹם שְׁמֹעַ אִישָׁהּ יָנִיא אוֹתָהּ וְהֵפֵר
אֶת־נִדְרָהּ אֲשֶׁר עָלֶיהָ וְאֵת מִבְטָא שְׂפָתֶיהָ
אֲשֶׁר אָסְרָה עַל־נַפְשָׁהּ וַיהוָה יִסְלַח־לָהּ:

לוי: וְנֶדֶר אַלְמָנָה וּגְרוּשָׁה כֹּל אֲשֶׁר־אָסְרָה
עַל־נַפְשָׁהּ יָקוּם עָלֶיהָ: וְאִם־בֵּית אִישָׁהּ
נָדָרָה אוֹ־אָסְרָה אִסָּר עַל־נַפְשָׁהּ בִּשְׁבֻעָה:
וְשָׁמַע אִישָׁהּ וְהֶחֱרִשׁ לָהּ לֹא הֵנִיא אֹתָהּ
וְקָמוּ כָּל־נְדָרֶיהָ וְכָל־אִסָּר אֲשֶׁר־אָסְרָה עַל־
נַפְשָׁהּ יָקוּם: וְאִם־הָפֵר יָפֵר אֹתָם ׀ אִישָׁהּ
בְּיוֹם שָׁמְעוֹ כָּל־מוֹצָא שְׂפָתֶיהָ לִנְדָרֶיהָ
וּלְאִסַּר נַפְשָׁהּ לֹא יָקוּם אִישָׁהּ הֲפֵרָם וַיהוָה
יִסְלַח־לָהּ:

ישראל: כָּל־נֶדֶר וְכָל־שְׁבֻעַת אִסָּר לְעַנֹּת נֶפֶשׁ
אִישָׁהּ יְקִימֶנּוּ וְאִישָׁהּ יְפֵרֶנּוּ: וְאִם־הַחֲרֵשׁ
יַחֲרִישׁ לָהּ אִישָׁהּ מִיּוֹם אֶל־יוֹם וְהֵקִים אֶת־
כָּל־נְדָרֶיהָ אוֹ אֶת־כָּל־אֱסָרֶיהָ אֲשֶׁר עָלֶיהָ
הֵקִים אֹתָם כִּי־הֶחֱרִשׁ לָהּ בְּיוֹם שָׁמְעוֹ:
וְאִם־הָפֵר יָפֵר אֹתָם אַחֲרֵי שָׁמְעוֹ וְנָשָׂא
אֶת־עֲוֹנָהּ: אֵלֶּה הַחֻקִּים אֲשֶׁר צִוָּה יְהוָה
אֶת־מֹשֶׁה בֵּין אִישׁ לְאִשְׁתּוֹ בֵּין־אָב לְבִתּוֹ
בִּנְעֻרֶיהָ בֵּית אָבִיהָ:

פ׳ מסעי / MASEI
(Numbers 33:1-10)

לה: אֵלֶּה מַסְעֵי בְנֵי־יִשְׂרָאֵל אֲשֶׁר יָצְאוּ
מֵאֶרֶץ מִצְרַיִם לְצִבְאֹתָם בְּיַד־מֹשֶׁה וְאַהֲרֹן:
וַיִּכְתֹּב מֹשֶׁה אֶת־מוֹצָאֵיהֶם לְמַסְעֵיהֶם עַל־
פִּי יְהוָה וְאֵלֶּה מַסְעֵיהֶם לְמוֹצָאֵיהֶם: וַיִּסְעוּ
מֵרַעְמְסֵס בַּחֹדֶשׁ הָרִאשׁוֹן בַּחֲמִשָּׁה עָשָׂר

יוֹם לַחֹדֶשׁ הָרִאשׁוֹן מִמָּחֳרַת הַפֶּסַח יָצְאוּ
בְנֵי־יִשְׂרָאֵל בְּיָד רָמָה לְעֵינֵי כָּל־מִצְרָיִם:
לוי: וּמִצְרַיִם מְקַבְּרִים אֵת אֲשֶׁר הִכָּה יְהוָה
בָּהֶם כָּל־בְּכוֹר וּבֵאלֹהֵיהֶם עָשָׂה יְהוָה
שְׁפָטִים: וַיִּסְעוּ בְנֵי־יִשְׂרָאֵל מֵרַעְמְסֵס וַיַּחֲנוּ
בְּסֻכֹּת: וַיִּסְעוּ מִסֻּכֹּת וַיַּחֲנוּ בְאֵתָם אֲשֶׁר
בִּקְצֵה הַמִּדְבָּר:

ישראל: וַיִּסְעוּ מֵאֵתָם וַיָּשָׁב עַל־פִּי הַחִירֹת
אֲשֶׁר עַל־פְּנֵי בַּעַל צְפוֹן וַיַּחֲנוּ לִפְנֵי מִגְדֹּל:
וַיִּסְעוּ מִפְּנֵי הַחִירֹת וַיַּעַבְרוּ בְתוֹךְ־הַיָּם
הַמִּדְבָּרָה וַיֵּלְכוּ דֶּרֶךְ שְׁלֹשֶׁת יָמִים בְּמִדְבַּר
אֵתָם וַיַּחֲנוּ בְּמָרָה: וַיִּסְעוּ מִמָּרָה וַיָּבֹאוּ
אֵילִמָה וּבְאֵילִם שְׁתֵּים עֶשְׂרֵה עֵינֹת מַיִם
וְשִׁבְעִים תְּמָרִים וַיַּחֲנוּ־שָׁם: וַיִּסְעוּ מֵאֵילִם
וַיַּחֲנוּ עַל־יַם־סוּף:

פ׳ דברים / DEVARIM
(Deuteronomy 1:1-11)

כה: אֵלֶּה הַדְּבָרִים אֲשֶׁר דִּבֶּר מֹשֶׁה אֶל־כָּל־
יִשְׂרָאֵל בְּעֵבֶר הַיַּרְדֵּן בַּמִּדְבָּר בָּעֲרָבָה מוֹל
סוּף בֵּין־פָּארָן וּבֵין־תֹּפֶל וְלָבָן וַחֲצֵרֹת וְדִי
זָהָב: אַחַד עָשָׂר יוֹם מֵחֹרֵב דֶּרֶךְ הַר־שֵׂעִיר
עַד קָדֵשׁ בַּרְנֵעַ: וַיְהִי בְּאַרְבָּעִים שָׁנָה
בְּעַשְׁתֵּי־עָשָׂר חֹדֶשׁ בְּאֶחָד לַחֹדֶשׁ דִּבֶּר
מֹשֶׁה אֶל־בְּנֵי יִשְׂרָאֵל כְּכֹל אֲשֶׁר צִוָּה יְהוָה
אֹתוֹ אֲלֵהֶם:

לוי: אַחֲרֵי הַכֹּתוֹ אֵת סִיחֹן מֶלֶךְ הָאֱמֹרִי אֲשֶׁר
יוֹשֵׁב בְּחֶשְׁבּוֹן וְאֵת עוֹג מֶלֶךְ הַבָּשָׁן אֲשֶׁר־
יוֹשֵׁב בְּעַשְׁתָּרֹת בְּאֶדְרֶעִי: בְּעֵבֶר הַיַּרְדֵּן
בְּאֶרֶץ מוֹאָב הוֹאִיל מֹשֶׁה בֵּאֵר אֶת־הַתּוֹרָה
הַזֹּאת לֵאמֹר: יְהוָה אֱלֹהֵינוּ דִּבֶּר אֵלֵינוּ
בְּחֹרֵב לֵאמֹר רַב־לָכֶם שֶׁבֶת בָּהָר הַזֶּה: פְּנוּ ׀
וּסְעוּ לָכֶם וּבֹאוּ הַר הָאֱמֹרִי וְאֶל־כָּל־שְׁכֵנָיו
בָּעֲרָבָה בָהָר וּבַשְּׁפֵלָה וּבַנֶּגֶב וּבְחוֹף הַיָּם
אֶרֶץ הַכְּנַעֲנִי וְהַלְּבָנוֹן עַד־הַנָּהָר הַגָּדֹל נְהַר־
פְּרָת:

ישראל: רְאֵה נָתַתִּי לִפְנֵיכֶם אֶת־הָאָרֶץ בֹּאוּ
וּרְשׁוּ אֶת־הָאָרֶץ אֲשֶׁר נִשְׁבַּע יְהוָה
לַאֲבֹתֵיכֶם לְאַבְרָהָם לְיִצְחָק וּלְיַעֲקֹב לָתֵת
לָהֶם וּלְזַרְעָם אַחֲרֵיהֶם: וָאֹמַר אֲלֵכֶם בָּעֵת
הַהִוא לֵאמֹר לֹא־אוּכַל לְבַדִּי שְׂאֵת אֶתְכֶם:

יהוה אֱלֹהֵיכֶם הִרְבָּה אֶתְכֶם וְהִנְּכֶם הַיּוֹם
כְּכוֹכְבֵי הַשָּׁמַיִם לָרֹב: יהוה אֱלֹהֵי אֲבוֹתֵכֶם
יֹסֵף עֲלֵיכֶם כָּכֶם אֶלֶף פְּעָמִים וִיבָרֵךְ אֶתְכֶם
כַּאֲשֶׁר דִּבֶּר לָכֶם:

‹ פ' ואתחנן / VA'ESCHANAN ›
(Deuteronomy 3:23 – 4:8)

כג: וָאֶתְחַנַּן אֶל־יהוה בָּעֵת הַהִוא לֵאמֹר:
אֲדֹנָי יֱהוִה אַתָּה הַחִלּוֹתָ לְהַרְאוֹת אֶת־
עַבְדְּךָ אֶת־גָּדְלְךָ וְאֶת־יָדְךָ הַחֲזָקָה אֲשֶׁר
מִי־אֵל בַּשָּׁמַיִם וּבָאָרֶץ אֲשֶׁר־יַעֲשֶׂה
כְמַעֲשֶׂיךָ וְכִגְבוּרֹתֶךָ: אֶעְבְּרָה־נָּא וְאֶרְאֶה
אֶת־הָאָרֶץ הַטּוֹבָה אֲשֶׁר בְּעֵבֶר הַיַּרְדֵּן הָהָר
הַטּוֹב הַזֶּה וְהַלְּבָנֹן:

לו: וַיִּתְעַבֵּר יהוה בִּי לְמַעַנְכֶם וְלֹא שָׁמַע אֵלָי
וַיֹּאמֶר יהוה אֵלַי רַב־לָךְ אַל־תּוֹסֶף דַּבֵּר אֵלַי
עוֹד בַּדָּבָר הַזֶּה: עֲלֵה | רֹאשׁ הַפִּסְגָּה וְשָׂא
עֵינֶיךָ יָמָּה וְצָפֹנָה וְתֵימָנָה וּמִזְרָחָה וּרְאֵה
בְעֵינֶיךָ כִּי־לֹא תַעֲבֹר אֶת־הַיַּרְדֵּן הַזֶּה: וְצַו
אֶת־יְהוֹשֻׁעַ וְחַזְּקֵהוּ וְאַמְּצֵהוּ כִּי־הוּא יַעֲבֹר
לִפְנֵי הָעָם הַזֶּה וְהוּא יַנְחִיל אוֹתָם אֶת־
הָאָרֶץ אֲשֶׁר תִּרְאֶה: וַנֵּשֶׁב בַּגָּיְא מוּל בֵּית
פְּעוֹר: וְעַתָּה יִשְׂרָאֵל שְׁמַע אֶל־הַחֻקִּים
וְאֶל־הַמִּשְׁפָּטִים אֲשֶׁר אָנֹכִי מְלַמֵּד אֶתְכֶם
לַעֲשׂוֹת לְמַעַן תִּחְיוּ וּבָאתֶם וִירִשְׁתֶּם אֶת־
הָאָרֶץ אֲשֶׁר יהוה אֱלֹהֵי אֲבֹתֵיכֶם נֹתֵן לָכֶם:
לֹא תֹסִפוּ עַל־הַדָּבָר אֲשֶׁר אָנֹכִי מְצַוֶּה
אֶתְכֶם וְלֹא תִגְרְעוּ מִמֶּנּוּ לִשְׁמֹר אֶת־מִצְוֹת
יהוה אֱלֹהֵיכֶם אֲשֶׁר אָנֹכִי מְצַוֶּה אֶתְכֶם:
עֵינֵיכֶם הָרֹאֹת אֵת אֲשֶׁר־עָשָׂה יהוה בְּבַעַל
פְּעוֹר כִּי כָל־הָאִישׁ אֲשֶׁר הָלַךְ אַחֲרֵי בַעַל־
פְּעוֹר הִשְׁמִידוֹ יהוה אֱלֹהֶיךָ מִקִּרְבֶּךָ: וְאַתֶּם
הַדְּבֵקִים בַּיהוה אֱלֹהֵיכֶם חַיִּים כֻּלְּכֶם הַיּוֹם:
ישראל: רְאֵה | לִמַּדְתִּי אֶתְכֶם חֻקִּים וּמִשְׁפָּטִים
כַּאֲשֶׁר צִוַּנִי יהוה אֱלֹהָי לַעֲשׂוֹת כֵּן בְּקֶרֶב
הָאָרֶץ אֲשֶׁר אַתֶּם בָּאִים שָׁמָּה לְרִשְׁתָּהּ:
וּשְׁמַרְתֶּם וַעֲשִׂיתֶם כִּי הִוא חָכְמַתְכֶם
וּבִינַתְכֶם לְעֵינֵי הָעַמִּים אֲשֶׁר יִשְׁמְעוּן אֵת
כָּל־הַחֻקִּים הָאֵלֶּה וְאָמְרוּ רַק עַם־חָכָם
וְנָבוֹן הַגּוֹי הַגָּדוֹל הַזֶּה: כִּי מִי־גוֹי גָּדוֹל
אֲשֶׁר־לוֹ אֱלֹהִים קְרֹבִים אֵלָיו כַּיהוה

אֱלֹהֵינוּ בְּכָל־קָרְאֵנוּ אֵלָיו: וּמִי גּוֹי גָּדוֹל
אֲשֶׁר־לוֹ חֻקִּים וּמִשְׁפָּטִים צַדִּיקִם כְּכֹל
הַתּוֹרָה הַזֹּאת אֲשֶׁר אָנֹכִי נֹתֵן לִפְנֵיכֶם הַיּוֹם:

‹ פ' עקב / EIKEV ›
(Deuteronomy 7:12 – 8:10)

כח: וְהָיָה | עֵקֶב תִּשְׁמְעוּן אֵת הַמִּשְׁפָּטִים
הָאֵלֶּה וּשְׁמַרְתֶּם וַעֲשִׂיתֶם אֹתָם וְשָׁמַר יהוה
אֱלֹהֶיךָ לְךָ אֶת־הַבְּרִית וְאֶת־הַחֶסֶד אֲשֶׁר
נִשְׁבַּע לַאֲבֹתֶיךָ: וַאֲהֵבְךָ וּבֵרַכְךָ וְהִרְבֶּךָ וּבֵרַךְ
פְּרִי־בִטְנְךָ וּפְרִי־אַדְמָתֶךָ דְּגָנְךָ וְתִירֹשְׁךָ
וְיִצְהָרֶךָ שְׁגַר־אֲלָפֶיךָ וְעַשְׁתְּרֹת צֹאנֶךָ עַל
הָאֲדָמָה אֲשֶׁר־נִשְׁבַּע לַאֲבֹתֶיךָ לָתֶת לָךְ:
בָּרוּךְ תִּהְיֶה מִכָּל־הָעַמִּים לֹא־יִהְיֶה בְךָ עָקָר
וַעֲקָרָה וּבִבְהֶמְתֶּךָ: וְהֵסִיר יהוה מִמְּךָ כָּל־
חֹלִי וְכָל־מַדְוֵי מִצְרַיִם הָרָעִים אֲשֶׁר יָדַעְתָּ
לֹא יְשִׂימָם בָּךְ וּנְתָנָם בְּכָל־שֹׂנְאֶיךָ: וְאָכַלְתָּ
אֶת־כָּל־הָעַמִּים אֲשֶׁר יהוה אֱלֹהֶיךָ נֹתֵן לָךְ
לֹא־תָחוֹס עֵינְךָ עֲלֵיהֶם וְלֹא תַעֲבֹד אֶת־
אֱלֹהֵיהֶם כִּי־מוֹקֵשׁ הוּא לָךְ: כִּי תֹאמַר
בִּלְבָבְךָ רַבִּים הַגּוֹיִם הָאֵלֶּה מִמֶּנִּי אֵיכָה
אוּכַל לְהוֹרִישָׁם: לֹא תִירָא מֵהֶם זָכֹר תִּזְכֹּר
אֵת אֲשֶׁר־עָשָׂה יהוה אֱלֹהֶיךָ לְפַרְעֹה וּלְכָל־
מִצְרָיִם: הַמַּסֹּת הַגְּדֹלֹת אֲשֶׁר־רָאוּ עֵינֶיךָ
וְהָאֹתֹת וְהַמֹּפְתִים וְהַיָּד הַחֲזָקָה וְהַזְּרֹעַ
הַנְּטוּיָה אֲשֶׁר הוֹצִאֲךָ יהוה אֱלֹהֶיךָ כֵּן־יַעֲשֶׂה
יהוה אֱלֹהֶיךָ לְכָל־הָעַמִּים אֲשֶׁר־אַתָּה יָרֵא
מִפְּנֵיהֶם: וְגַם אֶת־הַצִּרְעָה יְשַׁלַּח יהוה
אֱלֹהֶיךָ בָּם עַד־אֲבֹד הַנִּשְׁאָרִים וְהַנִּסְתָּרִים
מִפָּנֶיךָ: לֹא תַעֲרֹץ מִפְּנֵיהֶם כִּי־יהוה אֱלֹהֶיךָ
בְּקִרְבֶּךָ אֵל גָּדוֹל וְנוֹרָא:

לו: וְנָשַׁל יהוה אֱלֹהֶיךָ אֶת־הַגּוֹיִם הָאֵל
מִפָּנֶיךָ מְעַט מְעָט לֹא תוּכַל כַּלֹּתָם מַהֵר
פֶּן־תִּרְבֶּה עָלֶיךָ חַיַּת הַשָּׂדֶה: וּנְתָנָם יהוה
אֱלֹהֶיךָ לְפָנֶיךָ וְהָמָם מְהוּמָה גְדֹלָה עַד
הִשָּׁמְדָם: וְנָתַן מַלְכֵיהֶם בְּיָדֶךָ וְהַאֲבַדְתָּ אֶת־
שְׁמָם מִתַּחַת הַשָּׁמָיִם לֹא־יִתְיַצֵּב אִישׁ
בְּפָנֶיךָ עַד הִשְׁמִדְךָ אֹתָם: פְּסִילֵי אֱלֹהֵיהֶם
תִּשְׂרְפוּן בָּאֵשׁ לֹא־תַחְמֹד כֶּסֶף וְזָהָב עֲלֵיהֶם
וְלָקַחְתָּ לָךְ פֶּן תִּוָּקֵשׁ בּוֹ כִּי תוֹעֲבַת יהוה
אֱלֹהֶיךָ הוּא: וְלֹא־תָבִיא תוֹעֵבָה אֶל־בֵּיתֶךָ

וְהָיִ֥יתָ חֵ֖רֶם כָּמֹ֑הוּ שַׁקֵּ֧ץ ׀ תְּשַׁקְּצֶ֣נּוּ וְתַעֵ֣ב ׀
תְּתַעֲבֶ֗נּוּ כִּי־חֵ֖רֶם הֽוּא׃ כָּל־הַמִּצְוָ֗ה אֲשֶׁ֨ר
אָנֹכִ֧י מְצַוְּךָ֛ הַיֹּ֖ום תִּשְׁמְר֣וּן לַעֲשֹׂ֑ות לְמַ֨עַן
תִּֽחְי֜וּן וּרְבִיתֶ֗ם וּבָאתֶם֙ וִֽירִשְׁתֶּ֣ם אֶת־הָאָ֔רֶץ
אֲשֶׁר־נִשְׁבַּ֥ע יְהֹוָ֖ה לַאֲבֹֽתֵיכֶֽם׃ וְזָכַרְתָּ֣ אֶת־
כָּל־הַדֶּ֗רֶךְ אֲשֶׁ֨ר הֹולִֽיכְךָ֜ יְהֹוָ֧ה אֱלֹהֶ֛יךָ זֶ֛ה
אַרְבָּעִ֥ים שָׁנָ֖ה בַּמִּדְבָּ֑ר לְמַ֨עַן עַנֹּֽתְךָ֜ לְנַסֹּֽתְךָ֗
לָדַ֜עַת אֶת־אֲשֶׁ֧ר בִּֽלְבָבְךָ֛ הֲתִשְׁמֹ֥ר מִצְוֺתָ֖ו
אִם־לֹֽא׃ וַֽיְעַנְּךָ֮ וַיַּרְעִבֶךָ֒ וַיַּֽאֲכִֽלְךָ֤ אֶת־הַמָּן֙
אֲשֶׁ֣ר לֹא־יָדַ֔עְתָּ וְלֹ֥א יָדְע֖וּן אֲבֹתֶ֑יךָ לְמַ֣עַן
הֹודִֽעֲךָ֗ כִּ֠י לֹ֣א עַל־הַלֶּ֤חֶם לְבַדֹּו֙ יִֽחְיֶ֣ה הָֽאָדָ֔ם
כִּ֛י עַל־כָּל־מֹוצָ֥א פִֽי־יְהֹוָ֖ה יִֽחְיֶ֥ה הָאָדָֽם׃

ישראל: שִׂמְלָ֨תְךָ֜ לֹ֤א בָֽלְתָה֙ מֵֽעָלֶ֔יךָ וְרַגְלְךָ֖ לֹ֣א
בָצֵ֑קָה זֶ֖ה אַרְבָּעִ֥ים שָׁנָֽה׃ וְיָדַעְתָּ֖ עִם־לְבָבֶ֑ךָ
כִּ֗י כַּאֲשֶׁ֨ר יְיַסֵּ֥ר אִישׁ֙ אֶת־בְּנֹ֔ו יְהֹוָ֥ה אֱלֹהֶ֖יךָ
מְיַסְּרֶֽךָּ׃ וְשָׁ֣מַרְתָּ֔ אֶת־מִצְוֺ֖ת יְהֹוָ֣ה אֱלֹהֶ֑יךָ
לָלֶ֥כֶת בִּדְרָכָ֖יו וּלְיִרְאָ֥ה אֹתֹֽו׃ כִּ֚י יְהֹוָ֣ה
אֱלֹהֶ֔יךָ מְבִֽיאֲךָ֖ אֶל־אֶ֣רֶץ טֹובָ֑ה אֶ֚רֶץ נַ֣חֲלֵי
מָ֔יִם עֲיָנֹת֙ וּתְהֹמֹ֔ת יֹֽצְאִ֥ים בַּבִּקְעָ֖ה וּבָהָֽר׃
אֶ֤רֶץ חִטָּה֙ וּשְׂעֹרָ֔ה וְגֶ֥פֶן וּתְאֵנָ֖ה וְרִמֹּ֑ון אֶֽרֶץ־
זֵ֥ית שֶׁ֖מֶן וּדְבָֽשׁ׃ אֶ֗רֶץ אֲשֶׁ֨ר לֹ֤א בְמִסְכֵּנֻת֙
תֹּֽאכַל־בָּ֣הּ לֶ֔חֶם לֹֽא־תֶחְסַ֥ר כֹּ֖ל בָּ֑הּ אֶ֚רֶץ
אֲשֶׁ֤ר אֲבָנֶ֨יהָ֙ בַרְזֶ֔ל וּמֵהֲרָרֶ֖יהָ תַּחְצֹ֥ב נְחֹֽשֶׁת׃
וְאָכַלְתָּ֖ וְשָׂבָ֑עְתָּ וּבֵֽרַכְתָּ֙ אֶת־יְהֹוָ֣ה אֱלֹהֶ֔יךָ
עַל־הָאָ֥רֶץ הַטֹּבָ֖ה אֲשֶׁ֥ר נָֽתַן־לָֽךְ׃

פ' ראה / RE'EH
(Deuteronomy 11:26 — 12:10)

כו רְאֵ֗ה אָנֹכִ֛י נֹתֵ֥ן לִפְנֵיכֶ֖ם הַיֹּ֑ום בְּרָכָ֖ה
וּקְלָלָֽה׃ אֶֽת־הַבְּרָכָ֑ה אֲשֶׁ֣ר תִּשְׁמְע֔וּ אֶל־
מִצְוֺת֙ יְהֹוָ֣ה אֱלֹֽהֵיכֶ֔ם אֲשֶׁ֧ר אָנֹכִ֛י מְצַוֶּ֥ה
אֶתְכֶ֖ם הַיֹּֽום׃ וְהַקְּלָלָ֗ה אִם־לֹ֤א תִשְׁמְעוּ֙
אֶל־מִצְוֺת֙ יְהֹוָ֣ה אֱלֹֽהֵיכֶ֔ם וְסַרְתֶּ֣ם מִן־הַדֶּ֔רֶךְ
אֲשֶׁ֧ר אָנֹכִ֛י מְצַוֶּ֥ה אֶתְכֶ֖ם הַיֹּ֑ום לָלֶ֗כֶת אַחֲרֵ֛י
אֱלֹהִ֥ים אֲחֵרִ֖ים אֲשֶׁ֥ר לֹֽא־יְדַעְתֶּֽם׃ וְהָיָ֗ה כִּ֤י
יְבִֽיאֲךָ֙ יְהֹוָ֣ה אֱלֹהֶ֔יךָ אֶל־הָאָ֕רֶץ אֲשֶׁר־אַתָּ֥ה
בָא־שָׁ֖מָּה לְרִשְׁתָּ֑הּ וְנָתַתָּ֤ה אֶת־הַבְּרָכָה֙ עַל־
הַ֣ר גְּרִזִ֔ים וְאֶת־הַקְּלָלָ֖ה עַל־הַ֥ר עֵיבָֽל׃ הֲלֹא־
הֵ֜מָּה בְּעֵ֣בֶר הַיַּרְדֵּ֗ן אַֽחֲרֵי֙ דֶּ֣רֶךְ מְבֹ֣וא
הַשֶּׁ֔מֶשׁ בְּאֶ֨רֶץ֙ הַֽכְּנַעֲנִ֔י הַיֹּשֵׁ֖ב בָּעֲרָבָ֑ה מֹ֚ול
הַגִּלְגָּ֔ל אֵ֖צֶל אֵלֹונֵ֣י מֹרֶ֑ה כִּ֤י אַתֶּם֙ עֹֽבְרִים

אֶת־הַיַּרְדֵּ֗ן לָבֹא֙ לָרֶ֣שֶׁת אֶת־הָאָ֔רֶץ אֲשֶׁר־
יְהֹוָ֥ה אֱלֹֽהֵיכֶ֖ם נֹתֵ֣ן לָכֶ֑ם וִֽירִשְׁתֶּ֥ם אֹתָ֖הּ
וִֽישַׁבְתֶּם־בָּֽהּ׃ לו וּשְׁמַרְתֶּ֣ם לַעֲשֹׂ֗ות אֵ֤ת כָּל־הַֽחֻקִּים֙ וְאֶת־
הַמִּשְׁפָּטִ֔ים אֲשֶׁ֧ר אָנֹכִ֛י נֹתֵ֥ן לִפְנֵיכֶ֖ם הַיֹּֽום׃
אֵ֣לֶּה הַֽחֻקִּ֣ים וְהַמִּשְׁפָּטִים֮ אֲשֶׁ֣ר תִּשְׁמְרוּן֒
לַעֲשֹׂ֗ות בָּאָ֨רֶץ֙ אֲשֶׁר֩ נָתַ֨ן יְהֹוָ֜ה אֱלֹהֵ֧י אֲבֹתֶ֛יךָ
לְךָ֖ לְרִשְׁתָּ֑הּ כָּל־הַיָּמִ֔ים אֲשֶׁר־אַתֶּ֥ם חַיִּ֖ים
עַל־הָאֲדָמָֽה׃ אַבֵּ֣ד תְּאַבְּד֠וּן אֶֽת־כָּל־הַ֠מְּקֹמֹות
אֲשֶׁ֨ר עָֽבְדוּ־שָׁ֜ם הַגֹּויִ֗ם אֲשֶׁ֥ר אַתֶּ֛ם
יֹֽרְשִׁ֥ים אֹתָ֖ם אֶת־אֱלֹֽהֵיהֶ֑ם עַל־הֶהָרִ֣ים
הָֽרָמִ֗ים וְעַל־הַגְּבָעֹ֔ות וְתַ֖חַת כָּל־עֵ֥ץ רַֽעֲנָֽן׃
וְנִתַּצְתֶּ֣ם אֶת־מִֽזְבְּחֹתָ֗ם וְשִׁבַּרְתֶּם֙ אֶת־
מַצֵּֽבֹתָ֔ם וַאֲשֵֽׁרֵיהֶם֙ תִּשְׂרְפ֣וּן בָּאֵ֔שׁ וּפְסִילֵ֥י
אֱלֹֽהֵיהֶ֖ם תְּגַדֵּע֑וּן וְאִבַּדְתֶּ֣ם אֶת־שְׁמָ֔ם מִן־
הַמָּקֹ֖ום הַהֽוּא׃ לֹֽא־תַעֲשׂ֣וּן כֵּ֔ן לַיהֹוָ֖ה
אֱלֹֽהֵיכֶֽם׃ כִּ֠י אִֽם־אֶל־הַמָּקֹ֞ום אֲשֶׁר־יִבְחַ֨ר
יְהֹוָ֤ה אֱלֹֽהֵיכֶם֙ מִכָּל־שִׁבְטֵיכֶ֔ם לָשׂ֥וּם אֶת־
שְׁמֹ֖ו שָׁ֑ם לְשִׁכְנֹ֥ו תִדְרְשׁ֖וּ וּבָ֥אתָ שָּֽׁמָּה׃

ישראל: וַֽהֲבֵאתֶ֣ם שָׁ֗מָּה עֹלֹֽתֵיכֶם֙ וְזִבְחֵיכֶ֔ם
וְאֵת֙ מַעְשְׂרֹ֣תֵיכֶ֔ם וְאֵ֖ת תְּרוּמַ֣ת יֶדְכֶ֑ם
וְנִדְרֵיכֶם֙ וְנִדְבֹ֣תֵיכֶ֔ם וּבְכֹרֹ֥ת בְּקַרְכֶ֖ם
וְצֹאנְכֶֽם׃ וַאֲכַלְתֶּם־שָׁ֗ם לִפְנֵי֙ יְהֹוָ֣ה אֱלֹֽהֵיכֶ֔ם
וּשְׂמַחְתֶּ֗ם בְּכֹל֙ מִשְׁלַ֣ח יֶדְכֶ֔ם אַתֶּ֖ם וּבָתֵּיכֶ֑ם
אֲשֶׁ֥ר בֵּֽרַכְךָ֖ יְהֹוָ֥ה אֱלֹהֶֽיךָ׃ לֹ֣א תַעֲשׂ֔וּן כְּ֠כֹל
אֲשֶׁ֨ר אֲנַ֧חְנוּ עֹשִׂ֛ים פֹּ֖ה הַיֹּ֑ום אִ֖ישׁ כָּל־הַיָּשָׁ֥ר
בְּעֵינָֽיו׃ כִּ֥י לֹֽא־בָאתֶ֖ם עַד־עָ֑תָּה אֶל־הַמְּנוּחָה֙
וְאֶל־הַֽנַּחֲלָ֔ה אֲשֶׁר־יְהֹוָ֥ה אֱלֹהֶ֖יךָ
נֹתֵ֥ן לָֽךְ׃ וַעֲבַרְתֶּם֮ אֶת־הַיַּרְדֵּן֒ וִישַׁבְתֶּ֣ם בָּאָ֔רֶץ
אֲשֶׁר־יְהֹוָ֥ה אֱלֹֽהֵיכֶ֖ם מַנְחִ֣יל אֶתְכֶ֑ם וְהֵנִ֨יחַ
לָכֶ֧ם מִכָּל־אֹיְבֵיכֶ֛ם מִסָּבִ֖יב וִֽישַׁבְתֶּם־בֶּֽטַח׃

פ' שופטים / SHOFTIM
(Deuteronomy 16:18—17:13)

כו שֹׁפְטִ֣ים וְשֹֽׁטְרִ֗ים תִּֽתֶּן־לְךָ֙ בְּכָל־שְׁעָרֶ֔יךָ
אֲשֶׁ֨ר יְהֹוָ֧ה אֱלֹהֶ֛יךָ נֹתֵ֥ן לְךָ֖ לִשְׁבָטֶ֑יךָ וְשָׁפְט֥וּ
אֶת־הָעָ֖ם מִשְׁפַּט־צֶֽדֶק׃ לֹֽא־תַטֶּ֣ה מִשְׁפָּ֔ט
לֹ֥א תַכִּ֖יר פָּנִ֑ים וְלֹֽא־תִקַּ֣ח שֹׁ֔חַד כִּ֣י הַשֹּׁ֗חַד
יְעַוֵּר֙ עֵינֵ֣י חֲכָמִ֔ים וִֽיסַלֵּ֖ף דִּבְרֵ֥י צַדִּיקִֽם׃ צֶ֥דֶק
צֶ֖דֶק תִּרְדֹּ֑ף לְמַ֤עַן תִּֽחְיֶה֙ וְיָרַשְׁתָּ֣ אֶת־הָאָ֔רֶץ
אֲשֶׁר־יְהֹוָ֥ה אֱלֹהֶ֖יךָ נֹתֵ֥ן לָֽךְ׃

לוי׳ לֹא־תִטַּע לְךָ אֲשֵׁרָה כָּל־עֵץ אֵצֶל מִזְבַּח יהוה אֱלֹהֶיךָ אֲשֶׁר תַּעֲשֶׂה־לָּךְ: וְלֹא־תָקִים לְךָ מַצֵּבָה אֲשֶׁר שָׂנֵא יהוה אֱלֹהֶיךָ: לֹא־תִזְבַּח לַיהוה אֱלֹהֶיךָ שׁוֹר וָשֶׂה אֲשֶׁר יִהְיֶה בוֹ מוּם כֹּל דָּבָר רָע כִּי תוֹעֲבַת יהוה אֱלֹהֶיךָ הוּא: כִּי־יִמָּצֵא בְקִרְבְּךָ בְּאַחַד שְׁעָרֶיךָ אֲשֶׁר־יהוה אֱלֹהֶיךָ נֹתֵן לָךְ אִישׁ אוֹ־אִשָּׁה אֲשֶׁר יַעֲשֶׂה אֶת־הָרַע בְּעֵינֵי יהוה־אֱלֹהֶיךָ לַעֲבֹר בְּרִיתוֹ: וַיֵּלֶךְ וַיַּעֲבֹד אֱלֹהִים אֲחֵרִים וַיִּשְׁתַּחוּ לָהֶם וְלַשֶּׁמֶשׁ ׀ אוֹ לַיָּרֵחַ אוֹ לְכָל־צְבָא הַשָּׁמַיִם אֲשֶׁר לֹא־צִוִּיתִי: וְהֻגַּד־לְךָ וְשָׁמָעְתָּ וְדָרַשְׁתָּ הֵיטֵב וְהִנֵּה אֱמֶת נָכוֹן הַדָּבָר נֶעֶשְׂתָה הַתּוֹעֵבָה הַזֹּאת בְּיִשְׂרָאֵל: וְהוֹצֵאתָ אֶת־הָאִישׁ הַהוּא אוֹ אֶת־הָאִשָּׁה הַהִוא אֲשֶׁר עָשׂוּ אֶת־הַדָּבָר הָרָע הַזֶּה אֶל־שְׁעָרֶיךָ אֶת־הָאִישׁ אוֹ אֶת־הָאִשָּׁה וּסְקַלְתָּם בָּאֲבָנִים וָמֵתוּ: עַל־פִּי ׀ שְׁנַיִם עֵדִים אוֹ שְׁלֹשָׁה עֵדִים יוּמַת הַמֵּת לֹא יוּמַת עַל־פִּי עֵד אֶחָד: יַד הָעֵדִים תִּהְיֶה־בּוֹ בָרִאשֹׁנָה לַהֲמִיתוֹ וְיַד כָּל־הָעָם בָּאַחֲרֹנָה וּבִעַרְתָּ הָרָע מִקִּרְבֶּךָ: כִּי יִפָּלֵא מִמְּךָ דָבָר לַמִּשְׁפָּט בֵּין־דָּם ׀ לְדָם בֵּין־דִּין לְדִין וּבֵין נֶגַע לָנֶגַע דִּבְרֵי רִיבֹת בִּשְׁעָרֶיךָ וְקַמְתָּ וְעָלִיתָ אֶל־הַמָּקוֹם אֲשֶׁר יִבְחַר יהוה אֱלֹהֶיךָ בּוֹ: וּבָאתָ אֶל־הַכֹּהֲנִים הַלְוִיִּם וְאֶל־הַשֹּׁפֵט אֲשֶׁר יִהְיֶה בַּיָּמִים הָהֵם וְדָרַשְׁתָּ וְהִגִּידוּ לְךָ אֵת דְּבַר הַמִּשְׁפָּט: וְעָשִׂיתָ עַל־פִּי הַדָּבָר אֲשֶׁר יַגִּידוּ לְךָ מִן־הַמָּקוֹם הַהוּא אֲשֶׁר יִבְחַר יהוה וְשָׁמַרְתָּ לַעֲשׂוֹת כְּכֹל אֲשֶׁר יוֹרוּךָ:

ישראל: עַל־פִּי הַתּוֹרָה אֲשֶׁר יוֹרוּךָ וְעַל־הַמִּשְׁפָּט אֲשֶׁר־יֹאמְרוּ לְךָ תַּעֲשֶׂה לֹא תָסוּר מִן־הַדָּבָר אֲשֶׁר־יַגִּידוּ לְךָ יָמִין וּשְׂמֹאל: וְהָאִישׁ אֲשֶׁר־יַעֲשֶׂה בְזָדוֹן לְבִלְתִּי שְׁמֹעַ אֶל־הַכֹּהֵן הָעֹמֵד לְשָׁרֶת שָׁם אֶת־יהוה אֱלֹהֶיךָ אוֹ אֶל־הַשֹּׁפֵט וּמֵת הָאִישׁ הַהוּא וּבִעַרְתָּ הָרָע מִיִּשְׂרָאֵל: וְכָל־הָעָם יִשְׁמְעוּ וְיִרָאוּ וְלֹא יְזִידוּן עוֹד:

פ׳ כי תצא / KI SEITZEI
(Deuteronomy 21:10-21)

כה: כִּי־תֵצֵא לַמִּלְחָמָה עַל־אֹיְבֶיךָ וּנְתָנוֹ יהוה אֱלֹהֶיךָ בְּיָדֶךָ וְשָׁבִיתָ שִׁבְיוֹ: וְרָאִיתָ

בַּשִּׁבְיָה אֵשֶׁת יְפַת־תֹּאַר וְחָשַׁקְתָּ בָהּ וְלָקַחְתָּ לְךָ לְאִשָּׁה: וַהֲבֵאתָהּ אֶל־תּוֹךְ בֵּיתֶךָ וְגִלְּחָה אֶת־רֹאשָׁהּ וְעָשְׂתָה אֶת־צִפָּרְנֶיהָ: וְהֵסִירָה אֶת־שִׂמְלַת שִׁבְיָהּ מֵעָלֶיהָ וְיָשְׁבָה בְּבֵיתֶךָ וּבָכְתָה אֶת־אָבִיהָ וְאֶת־אִמָּהּ יֶרַח יָמִים וְאַחַר כֵּן תָּבוֹא אֵלֶיהָ וּבְעַלְתָּהּ וְהָיְתָה לְךָ לְאִשָּׁה: וְהָיָה אִם־לֹא חָפַצְתָּ בָּהּ וְשִׁלַּחְתָּהּ לְנַפְשָׁהּ וּמָכֹר לֹא־תִמְכְּרֶנָּה בַּכָּסֶף לֹא־תִתְעַמֵּר בָּהּ תַּחַת אֲשֶׁר עִנִּיתָהּ:

לוי: כִּי־תִהְיֶיןָ לְאִישׁ שְׁתֵּי נָשִׁים הָאַחַת אֲהוּבָה וְהָאַחַת שְׂנוּאָה וְיָלְדוּ־לוֹ בָנִים הָאֲהוּבָה וְהַשְּׂנוּאָה וְהָיָה הַבֵּן הַבְּכֹר לַשְּׂנִיאָה: וְהָיָה בְּיוֹם הַנְחִילוֹ אֶת־בָּנָיו אֵת אֲשֶׁר־יִהְיֶה לוֹ לֹא יוּכַל לְבַכֵּר אֶת־בֶּן־הָאֲהוּבָה עַל־פְּנֵי בֶן־הַשְּׂנוּאָה הַבְּכֹר: כִּי אֶת־הַבְּכֹר בֶּן־הַשְּׂנוּאָה יַכִּיר לָתֶת לוֹ פִּי שְׁנַיִם בְּכֹל אֲשֶׁר־יִמָּצֵא לוֹ כִּי־הוּא רֵאשִׁית אֹנוֹ לוֹ מִשְׁפַּט הַבְּכֹרָה:

ישראל: כִּי־יִהְיֶה לְאִישׁ בֵּן סוֹרֵר וּמוֹרֶה אֵינֶנּוּ שֹׁמֵעַ בְּקוֹל אָבִיו וּבְקוֹל אִמּוֹ וְיִסְּרוּ אֹתוֹ וְלֹא יִשְׁמַע אֲלֵיהֶם: וְתָפְשׂוּ בוֹ אָבִיו וְאִמּוֹ וְהוֹצִיאוּ אֹתוֹ אֶל־זִקְנֵי עִירוֹ וְאֶל־שַׁעַר מְקֹמוֹ: וְאָמְרוּ אֶל־זִקְנֵי עִירוֹ בְּנֵנוּ זֶה סוֹרֵר וּמֹרֶה אֵינֶנּוּ שֹׁמֵעַ בְּקֹלֵנוּ זוֹלֵל וְסֹבֵא: וּרְגָמֻהוּ כָּל־אַנְשֵׁי עִירוֹ בָאֲבָנִים וָמֵת וּבִעַרְתָּ הָרָע מִקִּרְבֶּךָ וְכָל־יִשְׂרָאֵל יִשְׁמְעוּ וְיִרָאוּ:

פ׳ כי תבוא / KI SAVO
(Deuteronomy 26:1-15)

כו: וְהָיָה כִּי־תָבוֹא אֶל־הָאָרֶץ אֲשֶׁר יהוה אֱלֹהֶיךָ נֹתֵן לְךָ נַחֲלָה וִירִשְׁתָּהּ וְיָשַׁבְתָּ בָּהּ: וְלָקַחְתָּ מֵרֵאשִׁית ׀ כָּל־פְּרִי הָאֲדָמָה אֲשֶׁר תָּבִיא מֵאַרְצְךָ אֲשֶׁר יהוה אֱלֹהֶיךָ נֹתֵן לָךְ וְשַׂמְתָּ בַטֶּנֶא וְהָלַכְתָּ אֶל־הַמָּקוֹם אֲשֶׁר יִבְחַר יהוה אֱלֹהֶיךָ לְשַׁכֵּן שְׁמוֹ שָׁם: וּבָאתָ אֶל־הַכֹּהֵן אֲשֶׁר יִהְיֶה בַּיָּמִים הָהֵם וְאָמַרְתָּ אֵלָיו הִגַּדְתִּי הַיּוֹם לַיהוה אֱלֹהֶיךָ כִּי־בָאתִי אֶל־הָאָרֶץ אֲשֶׁר נִשְׁבַּע יהוה לַאֲבֹתֵינוּ לָתֶת לָנוּ:

לוי: וְלָקַח הַכֹּהֵן הַטֶּנֶא מִיָּדֶךָ וְהִנִּיחוֹ לִפְנֵי מִזְבַּח יהוה אֱלֹהֶיךָ: וְעָנִיתָ וְאָמַרְתָּ לִפְנֵי ׀ יהוה אֱלֹהֶיךָ אֲרַמִּי אֹבֵד אָבִי וַיֵּרֶד מִצְרַיְמָה

וַיָּגָר שָׁם בִּמְתֵי מְעָט וַיְהִי־שָׁם לְגוֹי גָּדוֹל
עָצוּם וָרָב: וַיָּרֵעוּ אֹתָנוּ הַמִּצְרִים וַיְעַנּוּנוּ
וַיִּתְּנוּ עָלֵינוּ עֲבֹדָה קָשָׁה: וַנִּצְעַק אֶל־יהוה
אֱלֹהֵי אֲבֹתֵינוּ וַיִּשְׁמַע יהוה אֶת־קֹלֵנוּ וַיַּרְא
אֶת־עָנְיֵנוּ וְאֶת־עֲמָלֵנוּ וְאֶת־לַחֲצֵנוּ: וַיּוֹצִאֵנוּ
יהוה מִמִּצְרַיִם בְּיָד חֲזָקָה וּבִזְרֹעַ נְטוּיָה
וּבְמֹרָא גָּדֹל וּבְאֹתוֹת וּבְמֹפְתִים: וַיְבִאֵנוּ
אֶל־הַמָּקוֹם הַזֶּה וַיִּתֶּן־לָנוּ אֶת־הָאָרֶץ הַזֹּאת
אֶרֶץ זָבַת חָלָב וּדְבָשׁ: וְעַתָּה הִנֵּה הֵבֵאתִי
אֶת־רֵאשִׁית פְּרִי הָאֲדָמָה אֲשֶׁר־נָתַתָּה לִּי
יהוה וְהִנַּחְתּוֹ לִפְנֵי יהוה אֱלֹהֶיךָ וְהִשְׁתַּחֲוִיתָ
לִפְנֵי יהוה אֱלֹהֶיךָ: וְשָׂמַחְתָּ בְכָל־הַטּוֹב
אֲשֶׁר נָתַן־לְךָ יהוה אֱלֹהֶיךָ וּלְבֵיתֶךָ אַתָּה
וְהַלֵּוִי וְהַגֵּר אֲשֶׁר בְּקִרְבֶּךָ:

ישראל: כִּי תְכַלֶּה לַעְשֵׂר אֶת־כָּל־מַעְשַׂר
תְּבוּאָתְךָ בַּשָּׁנָה הַשְּׁלִישִׁת שְׁנַת הַמַּעֲשֵׂר
וְנָתַתָּה לַלֵּוִי לַגֵּר לַיָּתוֹם וְלָאַלְמָנָה וְאָכְלוּ
בִשְׁעָרֶיךָ וְשָׂבֵעוּ: וְאָמַרְתָּ לִפְנֵי יהוה אֱלֹהֶיךָ
בִּעַרְתִּי הַקֹּדֶשׁ מִן־הַבַּיִת וְגַם נְתַתִּיו לַלֵּוִי
וְלַגֵּר לַיָּתוֹם וְלָאַלְמָנָה כְּכָל־מִצְוָתְךָ אֲשֶׁר
צִוִּיתָנִי לֹא־עָבַרְתִּי מִמִּצְוֹתֶיךָ וְלֹא שָׁכָחְתִּי:
לֹא־אָכַלְתִּי בְאֹנִי מִמֶּנּוּ וְלֹא־בִעַרְתִּי מִמֶּנּוּ
בְּטָמֵא וְלֹא־נָתַתִּי מִמֶּנּוּ לְמֵת שָׁמַעְתִּי בְּקוֹל
יהוה אֱלֹהָי עָשִׂיתִי כְּכֹל אֲשֶׁר צִוִּיתָנִי:
הַשְׁקִיפָה מִמְּעוֹן קָדְשְׁךָ מִן־הַשָּׁמַיִם וּבָרֵךְ
אֶת־עַמְּךָ אֶת־יִשְׂרָאֵל וְאֵת הָאֲדָמָה אֲשֶׁר
נָתַתָּה לָנוּ כַּאֲשֶׁר נִשְׁבַּעְתָּ לַאֲבֹתֵינוּ אֶרֶץ
זָבַת חָלָב וּדְבָשׁ:

◄§ פ׳ נצבים / NITZAVIM §►
(Deuteronomy 29:9-28)

כט: אַתֶּם נִצָּבִים הַיּוֹם כֻּלְּכֶם לִפְנֵי יהוה
אֱלֹהֵיכֶם רָאשֵׁיכֶם שִׁבְטֵיכֶם זִקְנֵיכֶם
וְשֹׁטְרֵיכֶם כֹּל אִישׁ יִשְׂרָאֵל: טַפְּכֶם נְשֵׁיכֶם
וְגֵרְךָ אֲשֶׁר בְּקֶרֶב מַחֲנֶיךָ מֵחֹטֵב עֵצֶיךָ עַד
שֹׁאֵב מֵימֶיךָ: לְעָבְרְךָ בִּבְרִית יהוה אֱלֹהֶיךָ
וּבְאָלָתוֹ אֲשֶׁר יהוה אֱלֹהֶיךָ כֹּרֵת עִמְּךָ הַיּוֹם:
לוי: לְמַעַן הָקִים־אֹתְךָ הַיּוֹם לוֹ לְעָם וְהוּא
יִהְיֶה־לְּךָ לֵאלֹהִים כַּאֲשֶׁר דִּבֶּר־לָךְ וְכַאֲשֶׁר
נִשְׁבַּע לַאֲבֹתֶיךָ לְאַבְרָהָם לְיִצְחָק וּלְיַעֲקֹב:
וְלֹא אִתְּכֶם לְבַדְּכֶם אָנֹכִי כֹּרֵת אֶת־הַבְּרִית

הַזֹּאת וְאֶת־הָאָלָה הַזֹּאת: כִּי אֶת־אֲשֶׁר יֶשְׁנוֹ
פֹּה עִמָּנוּ עֹמֵד הַיּוֹם לִפְנֵי יהוה אֱלֹהֵינוּ וְאֵת
אֲשֶׁר אֵינֶנּוּ פֹּה עִמָּנוּ הַיּוֹם:

ישראל: כִּי־אַתֶּם יְדַעְתֶּם אֵת אֲשֶׁר־יָשַׁבְנוּ
בְּאֶרֶץ מִצְרָיִם וְאֵת אֲשֶׁר־עָבַרְנוּ בְּקֶרֶב
הַגּוֹיִם אֲשֶׁר עֲבַרְתֶּם: וַתִּרְאוּ אֶת־שִׁקּוּצֵיהֶם
וְאֵת גִּלֻּלֵיהֶם עֵץ וָאֶבֶן כֶּסֶף וְזָהָב אֲשֶׁר
עִמָּהֶם: פֶּן־יֵשׁ בָּכֶם אִישׁ אוֹ־אִשָּׁה אוֹ
מִשְׁפָּחָה אוֹ־שֵׁבֶט אֲשֶׁר לְבָבוֹ פֹנֶה הַיּוֹם
מֵעִם יהוה אֱלֹהֵינוּ לָלֶכֶת לַעֲבֹד אֶת־אֱלֹהֵי
הַגּוֹיִם הָהֵם פֶּן־יֵשׁ בָּכֶם שֹׁרֶשׁ פֹּרֶה רֹאשׁ
וְלַעֲנָה: וְהָיָה בְּשָׁמְעוֹ אֶת־דִּבְרֵי הָאָלָה
הַזֹּאת וְהִתְבָּרֵךְ בִּלְבָבוֹ לֵאמֹר שָׁלוֹם יִהְיֶה־
לִּי כִּי בִּשְׁרִרוּת לִבִּי אֵלֵךְ לְמַעַן סְפוֹת הָרָוָה
אֶת־הַצְּמֵאָה: לֹא־יֹאבֶה יהוה סְלֹחַ לוֹ כִּי
אָז יֶעְשַׁן אַף־יהוה וְקִנְאָתוֹ בָּאִישׁ הַהוּא
וְרָבְצָה בּוֹ כָּל־הָאָלָה הַכְּתוּבָה בַּסֵּפֶר הַזֶּה
וּמָחָה יהוה אֶת־שְׁמוֹ מִתַּחַת הַשָּׁמָיִם:
וְהִבְדִּילוֹ יהוה לְרָעָה מִכֹּל שִׁבְטֵי יִשְׂרָאֵל
כְּכֹל אָלוֹת הַבְּרִית הַכְּתוּבָה בְּסֵפֶר הַתּוֹרָה
הַזֶּה: וְאָמַר הַדּוֹר הָאַחֲרוֹן בְּנֵיכֶם אֲשֶׁר
יָקוּמוּ מֵאַחֲרֵיכֶם וְהַנָּכְרִי אֲשֶׁר יָבֹא מֵאֶרֶץ
רְחוֹקָה וְרָאוּ אֶת־מַכּוֹת הָאָרֶץ הַהִוא וְאֶת־
תַּחֲלֻאֶיהָ אֲשֶׁר־חִלָּה יהוה בָּהּ: גָּפְרִית וָמֶלַח
שְׂרֵפָה כָל־אַרְצָהּ לֹא תִזָּרַע וְלֹא תַצְמִחַ
וְלֹא־יַעֲלֶה בָהּ כָּל־עֵשֶׂב כְּמַהְפֵּכַת סְדֹם
וַעֲמֹרָה אַדְמָה וּצְבוֹיִם אֲשֶׁר הָפַךְ יהוה בְּאַפּוֹ
וּבַחֲמָתוֹ: וְאָמְרוּ כָּל־הַגּוֹיִם עַל־מֶה עָשָׂה
יהוה כָּכָה לָאָרֶץ הַזֹּאת מֶה חֳרִי הָאַף הַגָּדוֹל
הַזֶּה: וְאָמְרוּ עַל אֲשֶׁר עָזְבוּ אֶת־בְּרִית יהוה
אֱלֹהֵי אֲבֹתָם אֲשֶׁר כָּרַת עִמָּם בְּהוֹצִיאוֹ
אֹתָם מֵאֶרֶץ מִצְרָיִם: וַיֵּלְכוּ וַיַּעַבְדוּ אֱלֹהִים
אֲחֵרִים וַיִּשְׁתַּחֲווּ לָהֶם אֱלֹהִים אֲשֶׁר לֹא־
יְדָעוּם וְלֹא חָלַק לָהֶם: וַיִּחַר אַף־יהוה בָּאָרֶץ
הַהִוא לְהָבִיא עָלֶיהָ אֶת־כָּל־הַקְּלָלָה
הַכְּתוּבָה בַּסֵּפֶר הַזֶּה: וַיִּתְּשֵׁם יהוה מֵעַל
אַדְמָתָם בְּאַף וּבְחֵמָה וּבְקֶצֶף גָּדוֹל וַיַּשְׁלִכֵם
אֶל־אֶרֶץ אַחֶרֶת כַּיּוֹם הַזֶּה: הַנִּסְתָּרֹת לַיהוה
אֱלֹהֵינוּ וְהַנִּגְלֹת לָנוּ וּלְבָנֵינוּ עַד־עוֹלָם
לַעֲשׂוֹת אֶת־כָּל־דִּבְרֵי הַתּוֹרָה הַזֹּאת:

פ׳ וילך / VAYEILECH

(Deuteronomy 31:1-13)

כהן: וַיֵּלֶךְ מֹשֶׁה וַיְדַבֵּר אֶת־הַדְּבָרִים הָאֵלֶּה אֶל־כָּל־יִשְׂרָאֵל: וַיֹּאמֶר אֲלֵהֶם בֶּן־מֵאָה וְעֶשְׂרִים שָׁנָה אָנֹכִי הַיּוֹם לֹא־אוּכַל עוֹד לָצֵאת וְלָבוֹא וַיהוה אָמַר אֵלַי לֹא תַעֲבֹר אֶת־הַיַּרְדֵּן הַזֶּה: יהוה אֱלֹהֶיךָ הוּא ׀ עֹבֵר לְפָנֶיךָ הוּא־יַשְׁמִיד אֶת־הַגּוֹיִם הָאֵלֶּה מִלְּפָנֶיךָ וִירִשְׁתָּם יְהוֹשֻׁעַ הוּא עֹבֵר לְפָנֶיךָ כַּאֲשֶׁר דִּבֶּר יהוה:

לוי: וְעָשָׂה יהוה לָהֶם כַּאֲשֶׁר עָשָׂה לְסִיחוֹן וּלְעוֹג מַלְכֵי הָאֱמֹרִי וּלְאַרְצָם אֲשֶׁר הִשְׁמִיד אֹתָם: וּנְתָנָם יהוה לִפְנֵיכֶם וַעֲשִׂיתֶם לָהֶם כְּכָל־הַמִּצְוָה אֲשֶׁר צִוִּיתִי אֶתְכֶם: חִזְקוּ וְאִמְצוּ אַל־תִּירְאוּ וְאַל־תַּעַרְצוּ מִפְּנֵיהֶם כִּי ׀ יהוה אֱלֹהֶיךָ הוּא הַהֹלֵךְ עִמָּךְ לֹא יַרְפְּךָ וְלֹא יַעַזְבֶךָּ:

ישראל: וַיִּקְרָא מֹשֶׁה לִיהוֹשֻׁעַ וַיֹּאמֶר אֵלָיו לְעֵינֵי כָל־יִשְׂרָאֵל חֲזַק וֶאֱמָץ כִּי אַתָּה תָּבוֹא אֶת־הָעָם הַזֶּה אֶל־הָאָרֶץ אֲשֶׁר נִשְׁבַּע יהוה לַאֲבֹתָם לָתֵת לָהֶם וְאַתָּה תַּנְחִילֶנָּה אוֹתָם: וַיהוה הוּא ׀ הַהֹלֵךְ לְפָנֶיךָ הוּא יִהְיֶה עִמָּךְ לֹא יַרְפְּךָ וְלֹא יַעַזְבֶךָּ לֹא תִירָא וְלֹא תֵחָת: וַיִּכְתֹּב מֹשֶׁה אֶת־הַתּוֹרָה הַזֹּאת וַיִּתְּנָהּ אֶל־הַכֹּהֲנִים בְּנֵי לֵוִי הַנֹּשְׂאִים אֶת־אֲרוֹן בְּרִית יהוה וְאֶל־כָּל־זִקְנֵי יִשְׂרָאֵל: וַיְצַו מֹשֶׁה אוֹתָם לֵאמֹר מִקֵּץ ׀ שֶׁבַע שָׁנִים בְּמֹעֵד שְׁנַת הַשְּׁמִטָּה בְּחַג הַסֻּכּוֹת: בְּבוֹא כָל־יִשְׂרָאֵל לֵרָאוֹת אֶת־פְּנֵי יהוה אֱלֹהֶיךָ בַּמָּקוֹם אֲשֶׁר יִבְחָר תִּקְרָא אֶת־הַתּוֹרָה הַזֹּאת נֶגֶד כָּל־יִשְׂרָאֵל בְּאָזְנֵיהֶם: הַקְהֵל אֶת־הָעָם הָאֲנָשִׁים וְהַנָּשִׁים וְהַטַּף וְגֵרְךָ אֲשֶׁר בִּשְׁעָרֶיךָ לְמַעַן יִשְׁמְעוּ וּלְמַעַן יִלְמְדוּ וְיָרְאוּ אֶת־יהוה אֱלֹהֵיכֶם וְשָׁמְרוּ לַעֲשׂוֹת אֶת־כָּל־דִּבְרֵי הַתּוֹרָה הַזֹּאת: וּבְנֵיהֶם אֲשֶׁר לֹא־יָדְעוּ יִשְׁמְעוּ וְלָמְדוּ לְיִרְאָה אֶת־יהוה אֱלֹהֵיכֶם כָּל־הַיָּמִים אֲשֶׁר אַתֶּם חַיִּים עַל־הָאֲדָמָה אֲשֶׁר אַתֶּם עֹבְרִים אֶת־הַיַּרְדֵּן שָׁמָּה לְרִשְׁתָּהּ:

פ׳ האזינו / HA'AZINU

(Deuteronomy 32:1-12)

כהן: הַאֲזִינוּ הַשָּׁמַיִם וַאֲדַבֵּרָה וְתִשְׁמַע הָאָרֶץ אִמְרֵי־פִי: יַעֲרֹף כַּמָּטָר לִקְחִי תִּזַּל כַּטַּל אִמְרָתִי כִּשְׂעִירִם עֲלֵי־דֶשֶׁא וְכִרְבִיבִים עֲלֵי־עֵשֶׂב: כִּי שֵׁם יהוה אֶקְרָא הָבוּ גֹדֶל לֵאלֹהֵינוּ: הַצּוּר תָּמִים פָּעֳלוֹ כִּי כָל־דְּרָכָיו מִשְׁפָּט אֵל אֱמוּנָה וְאֵין עָוֶל צַדִּיק וְיָשָׁר הוּא: שִׁחֵת לוֹ לֹא בָּנָיו מוּמָם דּוֹר עִקֵּשׁ וּפְתַלְתֹּל: הֲ־לַיהוה תִּגְמְלוּ־זֹאת עַם נָבָל וְלֹא חָכָם הֲלוֹא־הוּא אָבִיךָ קָּנֶךָ הוּא עָשְׂךָ וַיְכֹנְנֶךָ:

ישראל: זְכֹר יְמוֹת עוֹלָם בִּינוּ שְׁנוֹת דֹּר־וָדֹר שְׁאַל אָבִיךָ וְיַגֵּדְךָ זְקֵנֶיךָ וְיֹאמְרוּ לָךְ: בְּהַנְחֵל עֶלְיוֹן גּוֹיִם בְּהַפְרִידוֹ בְּנֵי אָדָם יַצֵּב גְּבֻלֹת עַמִּים לְמִסְפַּר בְּנֵי יִשְׂרָאֵל: כִּי חֵלֶק יהוה עַמּוֹ יַעֲקֹב חֶבֶל נַחֲלָתוֹ: יִמְצָאֵהוּ בְּאֶרֶץ מִדְבָּר וּבְתֹהוּ יְלֵל יְשִׁמֹן יְסֹבְבֶנְהוּ יְבוֹנְנֵהוּ יִצְּרֶנְהוּ כְּאִישׁוֹן עֵינוֹ: כְּנֶשֶׁר יָעִיר קִנּוֹ עַל־גּוֹזָלָיו יְרַחֵף יִפְרֹשׂ כְּנָפָיו יִקָּחֵהוּ יִשָּׂאֵהוּ עַל־אֶבְרָתוֹ: יהוה בָּדָד יַנְחֶנּוּ וְאֵין עִמּוֹ אֵל נֵכָר:

פ׳ ברכה / BERACHAH

(Deuteronomy 33:1-17)

כהן: וְזֹאת הַבְּרָכָה אֲשֶׁר בֵּרַךְ מֹשֶׁה אִישׁ הָאֱלֹהִים אֶת־בְּנֵי יִשְׂרָאֵל לִפְנֵי מוֹתוֹ: וַיֹּאמַר יהוה מִסִּינַי בָּא וְזָרַח מִשֵּׂעִיר לָמוֹ הוֹפִיעַ מֵהַר פָּארָן וְאָתָה מֵרִבְבֹת קֹדֶשׁ מִימִינוֹ אֵשׁ דָּת לָמוֹ: אַף חֹבֵב עַמִּים כָּל־קְדֹשָׁיו בְּיָדֶךָ וְהֵם תֻּכּוּ לְרַגְלֶךָ יִשָּׂא מִדַּבְּרֹתֶיךָ: תּוֹרָה צִוָּה־לָנוּ מֹשֶׁה מוֹרָשָׁה קְהִלַּת יַעֲקֹב: וַיְהִי בִישֻׁרוּן מֶלֶךְ בְּהִתְאַסֵּף רָאשֵׁי עָם יַחַד שִׁבְטֵי יִשְׂרָאֵל: יְחִי רְאוּבֵן וְאַל־יָמֹת וִיהִי מְתָיו מִסְפָּר: וְזֹאת לִיהוּדָה וַיֹּאמַר שְׁמַע יהוה קוֹל יְהוּדָה וְאֶל־עַמּוֹ תְּבִיאֶנּוּ יָדָיו רָב לוֹ וְעֵזֶר מִצָּרָיו תִּהְיֶה:

לוי: וּלְלֵוִי אָמַר תֻּמֶּיךָ וְאוּרֶיךָ לְאִישׁ חֲסִידֶךָ אֲשֶׁר נִסִּיתוֹ בְּמַסָּה תְּרִיבֵהוּ עַל־מֵי מְרִיבָה: הָאֹמֵר לְאָבִיו וּלְאִמּוֹ לֹא רְאִיתִיו וְאֶת־אֶחָיו לֹא הִכִּיר וְאֶת־בָּנָו לֹא יָדָע כִּי שָׁמְרוּ אִמְרָתֶךָ וּבְרִיתְךָ יִנְצֹרוּ: יוֹרוּ מִשְׁפָּטֶיךָ לְיַעֲקֹב וְתוֹרָתְךָ לְיִשְׂרָאֵל יָשִׂימוּ קְטוֹרָה בְּאַפֶּךָ וְכָלִיל עַל־מִזְבְּחֶךָ: בָּרֵךְ יהוה חֵילוֹ וּפֹעַל יָדָיו תִּרְצֶה מְחַץ מָתְנַיִם קָמָיו וּמְשַׂנְאָיו מִן־יְקוּמוּן: לְבִנְיָמִן אָמַר יְדִיד יהוה יִשְׁכֹּן לָבֶטַח עָלָיו חֹפֵף עָלָיו כָּל־הַיּוֹם וּבֵין כְּתֵפָיו שָׁכֵן:

ישראל: וּלְיוֹסֵף אָמַר מְבֹרֶכֶת יְהוָה אַרְצוֹ מִמֶּגֶד שָׁמַיִם מִטָּל וּמִתְּהוֹם רֹבֶצֶת תָּחַת: וּמִמֶּגֶד תְּבוּאֹת שָׁמֶשׁ וּמִמֶּגֶד גֶּרֶשׁ יְרָחִים: וּמֵרֹאשׁ הַרְרֵי־קֶדֶם וּמִמֶּגֶד גִּבְעוֹת עוֹלָם: וּמִמֶּגֶד אֶרֶץ וּמְלֹאָהּ וּרְצוֹן שֹׁכְנִי סְנֶה תָּבוֹאתָה לְרֹאשׁ יוֹסֵף וּלְקָדְקֹד נְזִיר אֶחָיו: בְּכוֹר שׁוֹרוֹ הָדָר לוֹ וְקַרְנֵי רְאֵם קַרְנָיו בָּהֶם עַמִּים יְנַגַּח יַחְדָּו אַפְסֵי־אָרֶץ וְהֵם רִבְבוֹת אֶפְרַיִם וְהֵם אַלְפֵי מְנַשֶּׁה:

ROSH CHODESH

(*Numbers 28:1-15*)

כֹּהֵן: וַיְדַבֵּר יְהוָה אֶל־מֹשֶׁה לֵּאמֹר: צַו אֶת־בְּנֵי יִשְׂרָאֵל וְאָמַרְתָּ אֲלֵהֶם אֶת־קָרְבָּנִי לַחְמִי לְאִשַּׁי רֵיחַ נִיחֹחִי תִּשְׁמְרוּ לְהַקְרִיב לִי בְּמוֹעֲדוֹ: וְאָמַרְתָּ לָהֶם זֶה הָאִשֶּׁה אֲשֶׁר תַּקְרִיבוּ לַיהוָה כְּבָשִׂים בְּנֵי־שָׁנָה תְמִימִם שְׁנַיִם לַיּוֹם עֹלָה תָמִיד:

לוי: וְאָמַרְתָּ לָהֶם זֶה הָאִשֶּׁה אֲשֶׁר תַּקְרִיבוּ לַיהוָה כְּבָשִׂים בְּנֵי־שָׁנָה תְמִימִם שְׁנַיִם לַיּוֹם עֹלָה תָמִיד: אֶת־הַכֶּבֶשׂ אֶחָד תַּעֲשֶׂה בַבֹּקֶר וְאֵת הַכֶּבֶשׂ הַשֵּׁנִי תַּעֲשֶׂה בֵּין הָעַרְבָּיִם: וַעֲשִׂירִית הָאֵיפָה סֹלֶת לְמִנְחָה בְּלוּלָה בְּשֶׁמֶן כָּתִית רְבִיעִת הַהִין:

ישראל: עֹלַת תָּמִיד הָעֲשֻׂיָה בְּהַר סִינַי לְרֵיחַ נִיחֹחַ אִשֶּׁה לַיהוָה: וְנִסְכּוֹ רְבִיעִת הַהִין לַכֶּבֶשׂ הָאֶחָד בַּקֹּדֶשׁ הַסֵּךְ נֶסֶךְ שֵׁכָר לַיהוָה: וְאֵת הַכֶּבֶשׂ הַשֵּׁנִי תַּעֲשֶׂה בֵּין הָעַרְבָּיִם כְּמִנְחַת הַבֹּקֶר וּכְנִסְכּוֹ תַּעֲשֶׂה אִשֵּׁה רֵיחַ נִיחֹחַ לַיהוָה: וּבְיוֹם הַשַּׁבָּת שְׁנֵי־כְבָשִׂים בְּנֵי־שָׁנָה תְּמִימִם וּשְׁנֵי עֶשְׂרֹנִים סֹלֶת מִנְחָה בְּלוּלָה בַשֶּׁמֶן וְנִסְכּוֹ: עֹלַת שַׁבַּת בְּשַׁבַּתּוֹ עַל־עֹלַת הַתָּמִיד וְנִסְכָּהּ:

רביעי: וּבְרָאשֵׁי חָדְשֵׁיכֶם תַּקְרִיבוּ עֹלָה לַיהוָה פָּרִים בְּנֵי־בָקָר שְׁנַיִם וְאַיִל אֶחָד כְּבָשִׂים בְּנֵי־שָׁנָה שִׁבְעָה תְּמִימִם: וּשְׁלֹשָׁה עֶשְׂרֹנִים סֹלֶת מִנְחָה בְּלוּלָה בַשֶּׁמֶן לַפָּר הָאֶחָד וּשְׁנֵי עֶשְׂרֹנִים סֹלֶת מִנְחָה בְּלוּלָה בַשֶּׁמֶן לָאַיִל הָאֶחָד: וְעִשָּׂרֹן עִשָּׂרוֹן סֹלֶת מִנְחָה בְּלוּלָה בַשֶּׁמֶן לַכֶּבֶשׂ הָאֶחָד עֹלָה רֵיחַ נִיחֹחַ אִשֶּׁה לַיהוָה: וְנִסְכֵּיהֶם חֲצִי הַהִין

יִהְיֶה לַפָּר וּשְׁלִישִׁת הַהִין לָאַיִל וּרְבִיעִת הַהִין לַכֶּבֶשׂ יָיִן זֹאת עֹלַת חֹדֶשׁ בְּחָדְשׁוֹ לְחָדְשֵׁי הַשָּׁנָה: וּשְׂעִיר עִזִּים אֶחָד לְחַטָּאת לַיהוָה עַל־עֹלַת הַתָּמִיד יֵעָשֶׂה וְנִסְכּוֹ:

FIRST DAY CHANUKAH

(*Numbers 6:22-27; 7:1-17*)

SOME BEGIN THE READING HERE:

כֹּהֵן: וַיְדַבֵּר יְהוָה אֶל־מֹשֶׁה לֵּאמֹר: דַּבֵּר אֶל־אַהֲרֹן וְאֶל־בָּנָיו לֵאמֹר כֹּה תְבָרֲכוּ אֶת־בְּנֵי יִשְׂרָאֵל אָמוֹר לָהֶם: יְבָרֶכְךָ יְהוָה וְיִשְׁמְרֶךָ: יָאֵר יְהוָה פָּנָיו אֵלֶיךָ וִיחֻנֶּךָּ: יִשָּׂא יְהוָה פָּנָיו אֵלֶיךָ וְיָשֵׂם לְךָ שָׁלוֹם: וְשָׂמוּ אֶת־שְׁמִי עַל־בְּנֵי יִשְׂרָאֵל וַאֲנִי אֲבָרֲכֵם:

OTHERS BEGIN THE READING HERE:

וַיְהִי בְּיוֹם כַּלּוֹת מֹשֶׁה לְהָקִים אֶת־הַמִּשְׁכָּן וַיִּמְשַׁח אֹתוֹ וַיְקַדֵּשׁ אֹתוֹ וְאֶת־כָּל־כֵּלָיו וְאֶת־הַמִּזְבֵּחַ וְאֶת־כָּל־כֵּלָיו וַיִּמְשָׁחֵם וַיְקַדֵּשׁ אֹתָם: וַיַּקְרִיבוּ נְשִׂיאֵי יִשְׂרָאֵל רָאשֵׁי בֵּית אֲבֹתָם הֵם נְשִׂיאֵי הַמַּטֹּת הֵם הָעֹמְדִים עַל־הַפְּקֻדִים: וַיָּבִיאוּ אֶת־קָרְבָּנָם לִפְנֵי יְהוָה שֵׁשׁ־עֶגְלֹת צָב וּשְׁנֵי עָשָׂר בָּקָר עֲגָלָה עַל־שְׁנֵי הַנְּשִׂאִים וְשׁוֹר לְאֶחָד וַיַּקְרִיבוּ אוֹתָם לִפְנֵי הַמִּשְׁכָּן: וַיֹּאמֶר יְהוָה אֶל־מֹשֶׁה לֵּאמֹר: קַח מֵאִתָּם וְהָיוּ לַעֲבֹד אֶת־עֲבֹדַת אֹהֶל מוֹעֵד וְנָתַתָּה אוֹתָם אֶל־הַלְוִיִּם אִישׁ כְּפִי עֲבֹדָתוֹ: וַיִּקַּח מֹשֶׁה אֶת־הָעֲגָלֹת וְאֶת־הַבָּקָר וַיִּתֵּן אוֹתָם אֶל־הַלְוִיִּם: אֵת שְׁתֵּי הָעֲגָלוֹת וְאֵת אַרְבַּעַת הַבָּקָר נָתַן לִבְנֵי גֵרְשׁוֹן כְּפִי עֲבֹדָתָם: וְאֵת אַרְבַּע הָעֲגָלֹת וְאֵת שְׁמֹנַת הַבָּקָר נָתַן לִבְנֵי מְרָרִי כְּפִי עֲבֹדָתָם בְּיַד אִיתָמָר בֶּן־אַהֲרֹן הַכֹּהֵן: וְלִבְנֵי קְהָת לֹא נָתָן כִּי־עֲבֹדַת הַקֹּדֶשׁ עֲלֵהֶם בַּכָּתֵף יִשָּׂאוּ: וַיַּקְרִיבוּ הַנְּשִׂאִים אֵת חֲנֻכַּת הַמִּזְבֵּחַ בְּיוֹם הִמָּשַׁח אֹתוֹ וַיַּקְרִיבוּ הַנְּשִׂיאִם אֶת־קָרְבָּנָם לִפְנֵי הַמִּזְבֵּחַ: וַיֹּאמֶר יְהוָה אֶל־מֹשֶׁה נָשִׂיא אֶחָד לַיּוֹם נָשִׂיא אֶחָד לַיּוֹם יַקְרִיבוּ אֶת־קָרְבָּנָם לַחֲנֻכַּת הַמִּזְבֵּחַ:

לוי: וַיְהִי הַמַּקְרִיב בַּיּוֹם הָרִאשׁוֹן אֶת־קָרְבָּנוֹ נַחְשׁוֹן בֶּן־עַמִּינָדָב לְמַטֵּה יְהוּדָה: וְקָרְבָּנוֹ קַעֲרַת־כֶּסֶף אַחַת שְׁלֹשִׁים וּמֵאָה מִשְׁקָלָהּ

מִזְרָק אֶחָד כֶּסֶף שִׁבְעִים שֶׁקֶל בְּשֶׁקֶל הַקֹּדֶשׁ שְׁנֵיהֶם ו מְלֵאִים סֹלֶת בְּלוּלָה בַשֶּׁמֶן לְמִנְחָה: כַּף אַחַת עֲשָׂרָה זָהָב מְלֵאָה קְטֹרֶת:

ישראל: פַּר אֶחָד בֶּן־בָּקָר אַיִל אֶחָד כֶּבֶשׂ־אֶחָד בֶּן־שְׁנָתוֹ לְעֹלָה: שְׂעִיר־עִזִּים אֶחָד לְחַטָּאת: וּלְזֶבַח הַשְּׁלָמִים בָּקָר שְׁנַיִם אֵילִם חֲמִשָּׁה עַתּוּדִים חֲמִשָּׁה כְּבָשִׂים בְּנֵי־שָׁנָה חֲמִשָּׁה זֶה קָרְבַּן נַחְשׁוֹן בֶּן־עַמִּינָדָב:

SECOND DAY CHANUKAH

(Numbers 7:18-29)

כח: בַּיּוֹם הַשֵּׁנִי הִקְרִיב נְתַנְאֵל בֶּן־צוּעָר נְשִׂיא יִשָּׂשכָר: הִקְרִב אֶת־קָרְבָּנוֹ קַעֲרַת־כֶּסֶף אַחַת שְׁלֹשִׁים וּמֵאָה מִשְׁקָלָהּ מִזְרָק אֶחָד כֶּסֶף שִׁבְעִים שֶׁקֶל בְּשֶׁקֶל הַקֹּדֶשׁ שְׁנֵיהֶם ו מְלֵאִים סֹלֶת בְּלוּלָה בַשֶּׁמֶן לְמִנְחָה: כַּף אַחַת עֲשָׂרָה זָהָב מְלֵאָה קְטֹרֶת:

לוי: פַּר אֶחָד בֶּן־בָּקָר אַיִל אֶחָד כֶּבֶשׂ־אֶחָד בֶּן־שְׁנָתוֹ לְעֹלָה: שְׂעִיר־עִזִּים אֶחָד לְחַטָּאת: וּלְזֶבַח הַשְּׁלָמִים בָּקָר שְׁנַיִם אֵילִם חֲמִשָּׁה עַתּוּדִים חֲמִשָּׁה כְּבָשִׂים בְּנֵי־שָׁנָה חֲמִשָּׁה זֶה קָרְבַּן נְתַנְאֵל בֶּן־צוּעָר:

ישראל: בַּיּוֹם הַשְּׁלִישִׁי נָשִׂיא לִבְנֵי זְבוּלֻן אֱלִיאָב בֶּן־חֵלֹן: קָרְבָּנוֹ קַעֲרַת־כֶּסֶף אַחַת שְׁלֹשִׁים וּמֵאָה מִשְׁקָלָה מִזְרָק אֶחָד כֶּסֶף שִׁבְעִים שֶׁקֶל בְּשֶׁקֶל הַקֹּדֶשׁ שְׁנֵיהֶם ו מְלֵאִים סֹלֶת בְּלוּלָה בַשֶּׁמֶן לְמִנְחָה: כַּף אַחַת עֲשָׂרָה זָהָב מְלֵאָה קְטֹרֶת: פַּר אֶחָד בֶּן־בָּקָר אַיִל אֶחָד כֶּבֶשׂ־אֶחָד בֶּן־שְׁנָתוֹ לְעֹלָה: שְׂעִיר־עִזִּים אֶחָד לְחַטָּאת: וּלְזֶבַח הַשְּׁלָמִים בָּקָר שְׁנַיִם אֵילִם חֲמִשָּׁה עַתּוּדִים חֲמִשָּׁה כְּבָשִׂים בְּנֵי־שָׁנָה חֲמִשָּׁה זֶה קָרְבַּן אֱלִיאָב בֶּן־חֵלֹן:

THIRD DAY CHANUKAH

(Numbers 7:24-35)

כח: בַּיּוֹם הַשְּׁלִישִׁי נָשִׂיא לִבְנֵי זְבוּלֻן אֱלִיאָב בֶּן־חֵלֹן: קָרְבָּנוֹ קַעֲרַת־כֶּסֶף אַחַת שְׁלֹשִׁים וּמֵאָה מִשְׁקָלָהּ מִזְרָק אֶחָד מִשְׁקָלָהּ מִזְרָק אֶחָד כֶּסֶף שִׁבְעִים שֶׁקֶל בְּשֶׁקֶל הַקֹּדֶשׁ שְׁנֵיהֶם ו מְלֵאִים סֹלֶת בְּלוּלָה בַשֶּׁמֶן לְמִנְחָה: כַּף אַחַת עֲשָׂרָה זָהָב מְלֵאָה קְטֹרֶת:

לוי: פַּר אֶחָד בֶּן־בָּקָר אַיִל אֶחָד כֶּבֶשׂ־אֶחָד בֶּן־שְׁנָתוֹ לְעֹלָה: שְׂעִיר־עִזִּים אֶחָד לְחַטָּאת: וּלְזֶבַח הַשְּׁלָמִים בָּקָר שְׁנַיִם אֵילִם חֲמִשָּׁה עַתּוּדִים חֲמִשָּׁה כְּבָשִׂים בְּנֵי־שָׁנָה חֲמִשָּׁה זֶה קָרְבַּן אֱלִיאָב בֶּן־חֵלֹן:

ישראל: בַּיּוֹם הָרְבִיעִי נָשִׂיא לִבְנֵי רְאוּבֵן אֱלִיצוּר בֶּן־שְׁדֵיאוּר: קָרְבָּנוֹ קַעֲרַת־כֶּסֶף אַחַת שְׁלֹשִׁים וּמֵאָה מִשְׁקָלָהּ מִזְרָק אֶחָד כֶּסֶף שִׁבְעִים שֶׁקֶל בְּשֶׁקֶל הַקֹּדֶשׁ שְׁנֵיהֶם ו מְלֵאִים סֹלֶת בְּלוּלָה בַשֶּׁמֶן לְמִנְחָה: כַּף אַחַת עֲשָׂרָה זָהָב מְלֵאָה קְטֹרֶת: פַּר אֶחָד בֶּן־בָּקָר אַיִל אֶחָד כֶּבֶשׂ־אֶחָד בֶּן־שְׁנָתוֹ לְעֹלָה: שְׂעִיר־עִזִּים אֶחָד לְחַטָּאת: וּלְזֶבַח הַשְּׁלָמִים בָּקָר שְׁנַיִם אֵילִם חֲמִשָּׁה עַתּוּדִים חֲמִשָּׁה כְּבָשִׂים בְּנֵי־שָׁנָה חֲמִשָּׁה זֶה קָרְבַּן אֱלִיצוּר בֶּן־שְׁדֵיאוּר:

FOURTH DAY CHANUKAH

(Numbers 7:30-41)

כח: בַּיּוֹם הָרְבִיעִי נָשִׂיא לִבְנֵי רְאוּבֵן אֱלִיצוּר בֶּן־שְׁדֵיאוּר: קָרְבָּנוֹ קַעֲרַת־כֶּסֶף אַחַת שְׁלֹשִׁים וּמֵאָה מִשְׁקָלָהּ מִזְרָק אֶחָד כֶּסֶף שִׁבְעִים שֶׁקֶל בְּשֶׁקֶל הַקֹּדֶשׁ שְׁנֵיהֶם ו מְלֵאִים סֹלֶת בְּלוּלָה בַשֶּׁמֶן לְמִנְחָה: כַּף אַחַת עֲשָׂרָה זָהָב מְלֵאָה קְטֹרֶת:

לוי: פַּר אֶחָד בֶּן־בָּקָר אַיִל אֶחָד כֶּבֶשׂ־אֶחָד בֶּן־שְׁנָתוֹ לְעֹלָה: שְׂעִיר־עִזִּים אֶחָד לְחַטָּאת: וּלְזֶבַח הַשְּׁלָמִים בָּקָר שְׁנַיִם אֵילִם חֲמִשָּׁה עַתּוּדִים חֲמִשָּׁה כְּבָשִׂים בְּנֵי־שָׁנָה חֲמִשָּׁה זֶה קָרְבַּן אֱלִיצוּר בֶּן־שְׁדֵיאוּר:

ישראל: בַּיּוֹם הַחֲמִישִׁי נָשִׂיא לִבְנֵי שִׁמְעוֹן שְׁלֻמִיאֵל בֶּן־צוּרִישַׁדָּי: קָרְבָּנוֹ קַעֲרַת־כֶּסֶף אַחַת שְׁלֹשִׁים וּמֵאָה מִשְׁקָלָהּ מִזְרָק אֶחָד כֶּסֶף שִׁבְעִים שֶׁקֶל בְּשֶׁקֶל הַקֹּדֶשׁ שְׁנֵיהֶם ו מְלֵאִים סֹלֶת בְּלוּלָה בַשֶּׁמֶן לְמִנְחָה: כַּף אַחַת עֲשָׂרָה זָהָב מְלֵאָה קְטֹרֶת: פַּר אֶחָד בֶּן־בָּקָר אַיִל אֶחָד כֶּבֶשׂ־אֶחָד בֶּן־שְׁנָתוֹ לְעֹלָה: שְׂעִיר־עִזִּים אֶחָד לְחַטָּאת: וּלְזֶבַח הַשְּׁלָמִים בָּקָר שְׁנַיִם אֵילִם חֲמִשָּׁה עַתּוּדִים חֲמִשָּׁה כְּבָשִׂים בְּנֵי־שָׁנָה חֲמִשָּׁה זֶה קָרְבַּן שְׁלֻמִיאֵל בֶּן־צוּרִישַׁדָּי:

FIFTH DAY CHANUKAH

(*Numbers 7:36-47*)

כח: בַּיּוֹם הַחֲמִישִׁי נָשִׂיא לִבְנֵי שִׁמְעוֹן שְׁלֻמִיאֵל בֶּן־צוּרִישַׁדָּי: קָרְבָּנוֹ קַעֲרַת־כֶּסֶף אַחַת שְׁלֹשִׁים וּמֵאָה מִשְׁקָלָהּ מִזְרָק אֶחָד כֶּסֶף שִׁבְעִים שֶׁקֶל בְּשֶׁקֶל הַקֹּדֶשׁ שְׁנֵיהֶם ׀ מְלֵאִים סֹלֶת בְּלוּלָה בַשֶּׁמֶן לְמִנְחָה: כַּף אַחַת עֲשָׂרָה זָהָב מְלֵאָה קְטֹרֶת:

לוי: פַּר אֶחָד בֶּן־בָּקָר אַיִל אֶחָד כֶּבֶשׂ־אֶחָד בֶּן־שְׁנָתוֹ לְעֹלָה: שְׂעִיר־עִזִּים אֶחָד לְחַטָּאת: וּלְזֶבַח הַשְּׁלָמִים בָּקָר שְׁנַיִם אֵילִם חֲמִשָּׁה עַתֻּדִים חֲמִשָּׁה כְּבָשִׂים בְּנֵי־שָׁנָה חֲמִשָּׁה זֶה קָרְבַּן שְׁלֻמִיאֵל בֶּן־צוּרִישַׁדָּי:

ישראל: בַּיּוֹם הַשִּׁשִּׁי נָשִׂיא לִבְנֵי גָד אֶלְיָסָף בֶּן־דְּעוּאֵל: קָרְבָּנוֹ קַעֲרַת־כֶּסֶף אַחַת שְׁלֹשִׁים וּמֵאָה מִשְׁקָלָהּ מִזְרָק אֶחָד כֶּסֶף שִׁבְעִים שֶׁקֶל בְּשֶׁקֶל הַקֹּדֶשׁ שְׁנֵיהֶם ׀ מְלֵאִים סֹלֶת בְּלוּלָה בַשֶּׁמֶן לְמִנְחָה: כַּף אַחַת עֲשָׂרָה זָהָב מְלֵאָה קְטֹרֶת: פַּר אֶחָד בֶּן־בָּקָר אַיִל אֶחָד כֶּבֶשׂ־אֶחָד בֶּן־שְׁנָתוֹ לְעֹלָה: שְׂעִיר־עִזִּים אֶחָד לְחַטָּאת: וּלְזֶבַח הַשְּׁלָמִים בָּקָר שְׁנַיִם אֵילִם חֲמִשָּׁה עַתֻּדִים חֲמִשָּׁה כְּבָשִׂים בְּנֵי־שָׁנָה חֲמִשָּׁה זֶה קָרְבַּן אֶלְיָסָף בֶּן־דְּעוּאֵל:

SIXTH DAY CHANUKAH

Two Torah scrolls are removed from the Ark. Three *olim* are called to the first Torah for the Rosh Chodesh reading (*Numbers 28:1-15*). A fourth *oleh* is called to the second Torah for the Chanukah reading (*Numbers 7:42-47*).

כח: וַיְדַבֵּר יהוה אֶל־מֹשֶׁה לֵּאמֹר: צַו אֶת־בְּנֵי יִשְׂרָאֵל וְאָמַרְתָּ אֲלֵהֶם אֶת־קָרְבָּנִי לַחְמִי לְאִשַּׁי רֵיחַ נִיחֹחִי תִּשְׁמְרוּ לְהַקְרִיב לִי בְּמוֹעֲדוֹ: וְאָמַרְתָּ לָהֶם זֶה הָאִשֶּׁה אֲשֶׁר תַּקְרִיבוּ לַיהוה כְּבָשִׂים בְּנֵי־שָׁנָה תְמִימִם שְׁנַיִם לַיּוֹם עֹלָה תָמִיד: אֶת־הַכֶּבֶשׂ אֶחָד תַּעֲשֶׂה בַבֹּקֶר וְאֵת הַכֶּבֶשׂ הַשֵּׁנִי תַּעֲשֶׂה בֵּין הָעַרְבָּיִם: וַעֲשִׂירִית הָאֵיפָה סֹלֶת לְמִנְחָה בְּלוּלָה בְשֶׁמֶן כָּתִית רְבִיעִת הַהִין:

לוי: עֹלַת תָּמִיד הָעֲשֻׂיָה בְּהַר סִינַי לְרֵיחַ

ניחֹחַ אִשֶּׁה לַיהוה וְנִסְכּוֹ רְבִיעִת הַהִין לַכֶּבֶשׂ הָאֶחָד בַּקֹּדֶשׁ הַסֵּךְ נֶסֶךְ שֵׁכָר לַיהוה: וְאֵת הַכֶּבֶשׂ הַשֵּׁנִי תַּעֲשֶׂה בֵּין הָעַרְבָּיִם כְּמִנְחַת הַבֹּקֶר וּכְנִסְכּוֹ תַּעֲשֶׂה אִשֵּׁה רֵיחַ נִיחֹחַ לַיהוה: וּבְיוֹם הַשַּׁבָּת שְׁנֵי־כְבָשִׂים בְּנֵי־שָׁנָה תְּמִימִם וּשְׁנֵי עֶשְׂרֹנִים סֹלֶת מִנְחָה בְּלוּלָה בַשֶּׁמֶן וְנִסְכּוֹ: עֹלַת שַׁבַּת בְּשַׁבַּתּוֹ עַל־עֹלַת הַתָּמִיד וְנִסְכָּהּ:

ישראל: וּבְרָאשֵׁי חָדְשֵׁיכֶם תַּקְרִיבוּ עֹלָה לַיהוה פָּרִים בְּנֵי־בָקָר שְׁנַיִם וְאַיִל אֶחָד כְּבָשִׂים בְּנֵי־שָׁנָה שִׁבְעָה תְּמִימִם: וּשְׁלֹשָׁה עֶשְׂרֹנִים סֹלֶת מִנְחָה בְּלוּלָה בַשֶּׁמֶן לַפָּר הָאֶחָד וּשְׁנֵי עֶשְׂרֹנִים סֹלֶת מִנְחָה בְּלוּלָה בַשֶּׁמֶן לָאַיִל הָאֶחָד: וְעִשָּׂרֹן עִשָּׂרוֹן סֹלֶת מִנְחָה בְּלוּלָה בַשֶּׁמֶן לַכֶּבֶשׂ הָאֶחָד עֹלָה רֵיחַ נִיחֹחַ אִשֶּׁה לַיהוה: וְנִסְכֵּיהֶם חֲצִי הַהִין יִהְיֶה לַפָּר וּשְׁלִישִׁת הַהִין לָאַיִל וּרְבִיעִת הַהִין לַכֶּבֶשׂ יָיִן זֹאת עֹלַת חֹדֶשׁ בְּחָדְשׁוֹ לְחָדְשֵׁי הַשָּׁנָה: וּשְׂעִיר עִזִּים אֶחָד לְחַטָּאת לַיהוה עַל־עֹלַת הַתָּמִיד יֵעָשֶׂה וְנִסְכּוֹ:

רביעי: בַּיּוֹם הַשִּׁשִּׁי נָשִׂיא לִבְנֵי גָד אֶלְיָסָף בֶּן־דְּעוּאֵל: קָרְבָּנוֹ קַעֲרַת־כֶּסֶף אַחַת שְׁלֹשִׁים וּמֵאָה מִשְׁקָלָהּ מִזְרָק אֶחָד כֶּסֶף שִׁבְעִים שֶׁקֶל בְּשֶׁקֶל הַקֹּדֶשׁ שְׁנֵיהֶם ׀ מְלֵאִים סֹלֶת בְּלוּלָה בַשֶּׁמֶן לְמִנְחָה: כַּף אַחַת עֲשָׂרָה זָהָב מְלֵאָה קְטֹרֶת: פַּר אֶחָד בֶּן־בָּקָר אַיִל אֶחָד כֶּבֶשׂ־אֶחָד בֶּן־שְׁנָתוֹ לְעֹלָה: שְׂעִיר־עִזִּים אֶחָד לְחַטָּאת: וּלְזֶבַח הַשְּׁלָמִים בָּקָר שְׁנַיִם אֵילִם חֲמִשָּׁה עַתֻּדִים חֲמִשָּׁה כְּבָשִׂים בְּנֵי־שָׁנָה חֲמִשָּׁה זֶה קָרְבַּן אֶלְיָסָף בֶּן־דְּעוּאֵל:

SEVENTH DAY CHANUKAH

In most years the seventh day of Chanukah is also Rosh Chodesh. The Rosh Chodesh reading is the same as that of the sixth day. The following (*Numbers 7:48-53*) is the Chanukah reading for the fourth *oleh*:

רביעי: בַּיּוֹם הַשְּׁבִיעִי נָשִׂיא לִבְנֵי אֶפְרָיִם אֱלִישָׁמָע בֶּן־עַמִּיהוּד: קָרְבָּנוֹ קַעֲרַת־כֶּסֶף אַחַת שְׁלֹשִׁים וּמֵאָה מִשְׁקָלָהּ מִזְרָק אֶחָד כֶּסֶף שִׁבְעִים שֶׁקֶל בְּשֶׁקֶל הַקֹּדֶשׁ שְׁנֵיהֶם ׀ מְלֵאִים סֹלֶת בְּלוּלָה בַשֶּׁמֶן לְמִנְחָה: כַּף

אַחַת עֲשָׂרָה זָהָב מְלֵאָה קְטֹרֶת: פַּר אֶחָד בֶּן־בָּקָר אַיִל אֶחָד כֶּבֶשׂ־אֶחָד בֶּן־שְׁנָתוֹ לְעֹלָה: שְׂעִיר־עִזִּים אֶחָד לְחַטָּאת: וּלְזֶבַח הַשְּׁלָמִים בָּקָר שְׁנַיִם אֵילִם חֲמִשָּׁה עַתֻּדִים חֲמִשָּׁה כְּבָשִׂים בְּנֵי־שָׁנָה חֲמִשָּׁה זֶה קָרְבַּן אֱלִישָׁמָע בֶּן־עַמִּיהוּד:

In years when only the sixth day of Chanukah is Rosh Chodesh, the following (*Numbers* 7:48-59) is the Torah reading for the seventh day.

כהן: בַּיּוֹם הַשְּׁבִיעִי נָשִׂיא לִבְנֵי אֶפְרָיִם אֱלִישָׁמָע בֶּן־עַמִּיהוּד: קָרְבָּנוֹ קַעֲרַת־כֶּסֶף אַחַת שְׁלֹשִׁים וּמֵאָה מִשְׁקָלָהּ מִזְרָק אֶחָד כֶּסֶף שִׁבְעִים שֶׁקֶל בְּשֶׁקֶל הַקֹּדֶשׁ שְׁנֵיהֶם | מְלֵאִים סֹלֶת בְּלוּלָה בַשֶּׁמֶן לְמִנְחָה: כַּף אַחַת עֲשָׂרָה זָהָב מְלֵאָה קְטֹרֶת:

לוי: פַּר אֶחָד בֶּן־בָּקָר אַיִל אֶחָד כֶּבֶשׂ־אֶחָד בֶּן־שְׁנָתוֹ לְעֹלָה: שְׂעִיר־עִזִּים אֶחָד לְחַטָּאת: וּלְזֶבַח הַשְּׁלָמִים בָּקָר שְׁנַיִם אֵילִם חֲמִשָּׁה עַתֻּדִים חֲמִשָּׁה כְּבָשִׂים בְּנֵי־שָׁנָה חֲמִשָּׁה זֶה קָרְבַּן אֱלִישָׁמָע בֶּן־עַמִּיהוּד:

ישראל: בַּיּוֹם הַשְּׁמִינִי נָשִׂיא לִבְנֵי מְנַשֶּׁה גַּמְלִיאֵל בֶּן־פְּדָהצוּר: קָרְבָּנוֹ קַעֲרַת־כֶּסֶף אַחַת שְׁלֹשִׁים וּמֵאָה מִשְׁקָלָהּ מִזְרָק אֶחָד כֶּסֶף שִׁבְעִים שֶׁקֶל בְּשֶׁקֶל הַקֹּדֶשׁ שְׁנֵיהֶם | מְלֵאִים סֹלֶת בְּלוּלָה בַשֶּׁמֶן לְמִנְחָה: כַּף אַחַת עֲשָׂרָה זָהָב מְלֵאָה קְטֹרֶת: פַּר אֶחָד בֶּן־בָּקָר אַיִל אֶחָד כֶּבֶשׂ־אֶחָד בֶּן־שְׁנָתוֹ לְעֹלָה: שְׂעִיר־עִזִּים אֶחָד לְחַטָּאת: וּלְזֶבַח הַשְּׁלָמִים בָּקָר שְׁנַיִם אֵילִם חֲמִשָּׁה עַתֻּדִים חֲמִשָּׁה כְּבָשִׂים בְּנֵי־שָׁנָה חֲמִשָּׁה זֶה קָרְבַּן גַּמְלִיאֵל בֶּן־פְּדָהצוּר:

EIGHTH DAY CHANUKAH

(*Numbers* 7:54-89; 8:1-4)

כהן: בַּיּוֹם הַשְּׁמִינִי נָשִׂיא לִבְנֵי מְנַשֶּׁה גַּמְלִיאֵל בֶּן־פְּדָהצוּר: קָרְבָּנוֹ קַעֲרַת־כֶּסֶף אַחַת שְׁלֹשִׁים וּמֵאָה מִשְׁקָלָהּ מִזְרָק אֶחָד כֶּסֶף שִׁבְעִים שֶׁקֶל בְּשֶׁקֶל הַקֹּדֶשׁ שְׁנֵיהֶם | מְלֵאִים סֹלֶת בְּלוּלָה בַשֶּׁמֶן לְמִנְחָה: כַּף אַחַת עֲשָׂרָה זָהָב מְלֵאָה קְטֹרֶת:

לוי: פַּר אֶחָד בֶּן־בָּקָר אַיִל אֶחָד כֶּבֶשׂ־אֶחָד בֶּן־שְׁנָתוֹ לְעֹלָה: שְׂעִיר־עִזִּים אֶחָד לְחַטָּאת:

וּלְזֶבַח הַשְּׁלָמִים בָּקָר שְׁנַיִם אֵילִם חֲמִשָּׁה עַתֻּדִים חֲמִשָּׁה כְּבָשִׂים בְּנֵי־שָׁנָה חֲמִשָּׁה זֶה קָרְבַּן גַּמְלִיאֵל בֶּן־פְּדָהצוּר:

ישראל: בַּיּוֹם הַתְּשִׁיעִי נָשִׂיא לִבְנֵי בִנְיָמִן אֲבִידָן בֶּן־גִּדְעֹנִי: קָרְבָּנוֹ קַעֲרַת־כֶּסֶף אַחַת שְׁלֹשִׁים וּמֵאָה מִשְׁקָלָהּ מִזְרָק אֶחָד כֶּסֶף שִׁבְעִים שֶׁקֶל בְּשֶׁקֶל הַקֹּדֶשׁ שְׁנֵיהֶם | מְלֵאִים סֹלֶת בְּלוּלָה בַשֶּׁמֶן לְמִנְחָה: כַּף אַחַת עֲשָׂרָה זָהָב מְלֵאָה קְטֹרֶת: פַּר אֶחָד בֶּן־בָּקָר אַיִל אֶחָד כֶּבֶשׂ־אֶחָד בֶּן־שְׁנָתוֹ לְעֹלָה: שְׂעִיר־עִזִּים אֶחָד לְחַטָּאת: וּלְזֶבַח הַשְּׁלָמִים בָּקָר שְׁנַיִם אֵילִם חֲמִשָּׁה עַתֻּדִים חֲמִשָּׁה כְּבָשִׂים בְּנֵי־שָׁנָה חֲמִשָּׁה זֶה קָרְבַּן אֲבִידָן בֶּן־גִּדְעֹנִי: בַּיּוֹם הָעֲשִׂירִי נָשִׂיא לִבְנֵי דָן אֲחִיעֶזֶר בֶּן־עַמִּישַׁדָּי: קָרְבָּנוֹ קַעֲרַת־כֶּסֶף אַחַת שְׁלֹשִׁים וּמֵאָה מִשְׁקָלָהּ מִזְרָק אֶחָד כֶּסֶף שִׁבְעִים שֶׁקֶל בְּשֶׁקֶל הַקֹּדֶשׁ שְׁנֵיהֶם | מְלֵאִים סֹלֶת בְּלוּלָה בַשֶּׁמֶן לְמִנְחָה: כַּף אַחַת עֲשָׂרָה זָהָב מְלֵאָה קְטֹרֶת: פַּר אֶחָד בֶּן־בָּקָר אַיִל אֶחָד כֶּבֶשׂ־אֶחָד בֶּן־שְׁנָתוֹ לְעֹלָה: שְׂעִיר־עִזִּים אֶחָד לְחַטָּאת: וּלְזֶבַח הַשְּׁלָמִים בָּקָר שְׁנַיִם אֵילִם חֲמִשָּׁה עַתֻּדִים חֲמִשָּׁה כְּבָשִׂים בְּנֵי־שָׁנָה חֲמִשָּׁה זֶה קָרְבַּן אֲחִיעֶזֶר בֶּן־עַמִּישַׁדָּי: בְּיוֹם עַשְׁתֵּי עָשָׂר יוֹם נָשִׂיא לִבְנֵי אָשֵׁר פַּגְעִיאֵל בֶּן־עָכְרָן: קָרְבָּנוֹ קַעֲרַת־כֶּסֶף אַחַת שְׁלֹשִׁים וּמֵאָה מִשְׁקָלָהּ מִזְרָק אֶחָד כֶּסֶף שִׁבְעִים שֶׁקֶל בְּשֶׁקֶל הַקֹּדֶשׁ שְׁנֵיהֶם | מְלֵאִים סֹלֶת בְּלוּלָה בַשֶּׁמֶן לְמִנְחָה: כַּף אַחַת עֲשָׂרָה זָהָב מְלֵאָה קְטֹרֶת: פַּר אֶחָד בֶּן־בָּקָר אַיִל אֶחָד כֶּבֶשׂ־אֶחָד בֶּן־שְׁנָתוֹ לְעֹלָה: שְׂעִיר־עִזִּים אֶחָד לְחַטָּאת: וּלְזֶבַח הַשְּׁלָמִים בָּקָר שְׁנַיִם אֵילִם חֲמִשָּׁה עַתֻּדִים חֲמִשָּׁה כְּבָשִׂים בְּנֵי־שָׁנָה חֲמִשָּׁה זֶה קָרְבַּן פַּגְעִיאֵל בֶּן־עָכְרָן: בְּיוֹם שְׁנֵים עָשָׂר יוֹם נָשִׂיא לִבְנֵי נַפְתָּלִי אֲחִירַע בֶּן־עֵינָן: קָרְבָּנוֹ קַעֲרַת־כֶּסֶף אַחַת שְׁלֹשִׁים וּמֵאָה מִשְׁקָלָהּ מִזְרָק אֶחָד כֶּסֶף שִׁבְעִים שֶׁקֶל בְּשֶׁקֶל הַקֹּדֶשׁ שְׁנֵיהֶם | מְלֵאִים סֹלֶת בְּלוּלָה בַשֶּׁמֶן לְמִנְחָה: כַּף אַחַת עֲשָׂרָה זָהָב מְלֵאָה קְטֹרֶת: פַּר אֶחָד אַיִל אֶחָד כֶּבֶשׂ־אֶחָד בֶּן־שְׁנָתוֹ לְעֹלָה: שְׂעִיר־עִזִּים אֶחָד לְחַטָּאת: וּלְזֶבַח הַשְּׁלָמִים בָּקָר

שְׁנַ֨יִם אֵילִ֜ם חֲמִשָּׁ֗ה עַתּוּדִ֤ים חֲמִשָּׁה֙ כְּבָשִׂ֣ים
בְּנֵֽי־שָׁנָ֣ה חֲמִשָּׁ֔ה זֶ֛ה קָרְבַּ֥ן נַחְשׁ֖וֹן בֶּן־עַמִּינָדָ֑ב׃
זֹ֣את ׀ חֲנֻכַּ֣ת הַמִּזְבֵּ֗חַ בְּי֤וֹם הִמָּשַׁח֙ אֹת֔וֹ מֵאֵ֖ת
נְשִׂיאֵ֣י יִשְׂרָאֵ֑ל קַעֲרֹ֨ת כֶּ֜סֶף שְׁתֵּ֣ים עֶשְׂרֵ֗ה
מִֽזְרְקֵי־כֶ֙סֶף֙ שְׁנֵ֣ים עָשָׂ֔ר כַּפּ֥וֹת זָהָ֖ב שְׁתֵּ֥ים
עֶשְׂרֵֽה׃ שְׁלֹשִׁ֣ים וּמֵאָ֗ה הַקְּעָרָ֤ה הָֽאַחַת֙ כֶּ֔סֶף
וְשִׁבְעִ֖ים הַמִּזְרָ֣ק הָאֶחָ֑ד כֹּ֚ל כֶּ֣סֶף הַכֵּלִ֔ים
אַלְפַּ֥יִם וְאַרְבַּע־מֵא֖וֹת בְּשֶׁ֥קֶל הַקֹּֽדֶשׁ׃ כַּפּ֨וֹת
זָהָ֤ב שְׁתֵּים־עֶשְׂרֵה֙ מְלֵאֹ֣ת קְטֹ֔רֶת עֲשָׂרָ֧ה
עֲשָׂרָ֛ה הַכַּ֖ף בְּשֶׁ֣קֶל הַקֹּ֑דֶשׁ כָּל־זְהַ֥ב הַכַּפּ֖וֹת
עֶשְׂרִ֥ים וּמֵאָֽה׃ כָּל־הַבָּקָ֨ר לָעֹלָ֜ה שְׁנֵ֧ים עָשָׂ֣ר
פָּרִ֗ים אֵילִ֤ם שְׁנֵֽים־עָשָׂר֙ כְּבָשִׂ֧ים בְּנֵֽי־שָׁנָ֛ה
שְׁנֵ֥ים עָשָׂ֖ר וּמִנְחָתָ֑ם וּשְׂעִירֵ֥י עִזִּ֛ים שְׁנֵ֥ים עָשָׂ֖ר
לְחַטָּֽאת׃ וְכֹ֞ל בְּקַ֣ר ׀ זֶ֣בַח הַשְּׁלָמִ֗ים עֶשְׂרִ֤ים
וְאַרְבָּעָה֙ פָּרִ֔ים אֵילִ֤ם שִׁשִּׁים֙ עַתּוּדִ֣ים שִׁשִּׁ֔ים
כְּבָשִׂ֥ים בְּנֵֽי־שָׁנָ֖ה שִׁשִּׁ֑ים זֹ֚את חֲנֻכַּ֣ת הַמִּזְבֵּ֔חַ
אַחֲרֵ֖י הִמָּשַׁ֥ח אֹתֽוֹ׃ וּבְבֹ֨א מֹשֶׁ֜ה אֶל־אֹ֣הֶל
מוֹעֵד֮ לְדַבֵּ֣ר אִתּוֹ֒ וַיִּשְׁמַ֨ע אֶת־הַקּ֜וֹל מִדַּבֵּ֣ר
אֵלָ֗יו מֵעַ֤ל הַכַּפֹּ֙רֶת֙ אֲשֶׁר֙ עַל־אֲרֹ֣ן הָעֵדֻ֔ת מִבֵּ֖ין
שְׁנֵ֣י הַכְּרֻבִ֑ים וַיְדַבֵּ֖ר אֵלָֽיו׃ וַיְדַבֵּ֥ר יְהֹוָ֖ה אֶל־
מֹשֶׁ֥ה לֵּאמֹֽר׃ דַּבֵּר֙ אֶֽל־אַהֲרֹ֔ן וְאָמַרְתָּ֖ אֵלָ֑יו
בְּהַעֲלֹֽתְךָ֙ אֶת־הַנֵּרֹ֔ת אֶל־מוּל֙ פְּנֵ֣י הַמְּנוֹרָ֔ה
יָאִ֖ירוּ שִׁבְעַ֥ת הַנֵּרֽוֹת׃ וַיַּ֤עַשׂ כֵּן֙ אַֽהֲרֹ֔ן אֶל־מוּל֙
פְּנֵ֣י הַמְּנוֹרָ֔ה הֶעֱלָ֖ה נֵֽרֹתֶ֑יהָ כַּֽאֲשֶׁ֛ר צִוָּ֥ה יְהֹוָ֖ה
אֶת־מֹשֶֽׁה׃ וְזֶ֨ה מַעֲשֵׂ֤ה הַמְּנֹרָה֙ מִקְשָׁ֣ה זָהָ֔ב עַד־
יְרֵכָ֥הּ עַד־פִּרְחָ֖הּ מִקְשָׁ֣ה הִ֑וא כַּמַּרְאֶ֗ה אֲשֶׁ֨ר
הֶרְאָ֤ה יְהֹוָה֙ אֶת־מֹשֶׁ֔ה כֵּ֥ן עָשָׂ֖ה אֶת־הַמְּנֹרָֽה׃

יְהוֹשֻׁ֖עַ אֶת־עֲמָלֵ֣ק וְאֶת־עַמּ֑וֹ לְפִי־חָֽרֶב׃
ישראל׃ וַיֹּ֨אמֶר יְהֹוָ֜ה אֶל־מֹשֶׁ֗ה כְּתֹ֨ב זֹ֤את זִכָּרוֹן֙
בַּסֵּ֔פֶר וְשִׂ֖ים בְּאָזְנֵ֣י יְהוֹשֻׁ֑עַ כִּֽי־מָחֹ֤ה אֶמְחֶה֙
אֶת־זֵ֣כֶר עֲמָלֵ֔ק מִתַּ֖חַת הַשָּׁמָֽיִם׃ וַיִּ֥בֶן מֹשֶׁ֖ה
מִזְבֵּ֑חַ וַיִּקְרָ֥א שְׁמ֖וֹ יְהֹוָ֥ה ׀ נִסִּֽי׃ וַיֹּ֗אמֶר כִּֽי־יָד֙
עַל־כֵּ֣ס יָ֔הּ מִלְחָמָ֥ה לַיהֹוָ֖ה בַּֽעֲמָלֵ֑ק מִדֹּ֖ר דֹּֽר׃

PUBLIC FAST DAY

During *Shacharis* of public fast days (except Tishah
B'Av (see p. 796), three *olim* are called to the
Torah. At *Minchah*, the same Torah reading is re-
peated, but the third *oleh* also reads the *Haftarah*.

Upon reaching the words in bold type, the reader
pauses. The congregation recites these verses,
which are then repeated by the reader.

(*Exodus 32:11-14; 34:1-10*)

כהן׃ וַיְחַ֣ל מֹשֶׁ֔ה אֶת־פְּנֵ֖י יְהֹוָ֣ה אֱלֹהָ֑יו וַיֹּ֗אמֶר
לָמָ֤ה יְהֹוָה֙ יֶחֱרֶ֤ה אַפְּךָ֙ בְּעַמֶּ֔ךָ אֲשֶׁ֤ר הוֹצֵ֙אתָ֙
מֵאֶ֣רֶץ מִצְרַ֔יִם בְּכֹ֥חַ גָּד֖וֹל וּבְיָ֥ד חֲזָקָֽה׃ לָ֣מָּה
יֹאמְר֣וּ מִצְרַ֗יִם לֵאמֹר֒ בְּרָעָ֤ה הֽוֹצִיאָם֙ לַהֲרֹ֤ג
אֹתָם֙ בֶּֽהָרִ֔ים וּֽלְכַלֹּתָ֔ם מֵעַ֖ל פְּנֵ֣י הָֽאֲדָמָ֑ה **שׁ֤וּב**
מֵֽחֲרוֹן֙ אַפֶּ֔ךָ וְהִנָּחֵ֥ם עַל־הָֽרָעָ֖ה לְעַמֶּֽךָ׃ זְכֹ֡ר
לְאַבְרָהָם֩ לְיִצְחָ֨ק וּלְיִשְׂרָאֵ֜ל עֲבָדֶ֗יךָ אֲשֶׁ֨ר
נִשְׁבַּ֣עְתָּ לָהֶם֮ בָּךְ֒ וַתְּדַבֵּ֣ר אֲלֵהֶ֔ם אַרְבֶּה֙ אֶֽת־
זַרְעֲכֶ֔ם כְּכוֹכְבֵ֖י הַשָּׁמָ֑יִם וְכָל־הָאָ֣רֶץ הַזֹּ֗את
אֲשֶׁ֤ר אָמַ֙רְתִּי֙ אֶתֵּ֣ן לְזַרְעֲכֶ֔ם וְנָחֲל֖וּ לְעֹלָֽם׃
וַיִּנָּ֖חֶם יְהֹוָ֑ה עַל־הָ֣רָעָ֔ה אֲשֶׁ֥ר דִּבֶּ֖ר לַעֲשׂ֥וֹת
לְעַמּֽוֹ׃

לוי׃ וַיֹּ֤אמֶר יְהֹוָה֙ אֶל־מֹשֶׁ֔ה פְּסָל־לְךָ֛ שְׁנֵֽי־לֻחֹ֥ת
אֲבָנִ֖ים כָּרִאשֹׁנִ֑ים וְכָתַבְתִּי֙ עַל־הַלֻּחֹ֔ת אֶת־
הַדְּבָרִ֔ים אֲשֶׁ֥ר הָי֛וּ עַל־הַלֻּחֹ֥ת הָרִאשֹׁנִ֖ים
אֲשֶׁ֥ר שִׁבַּֽרְתָּ׃ וֶהְיֵ֥ה נָכ֖וֹן לַבֹּ֑קֶר וְעָלִ֤יתָ בַבֹּ֙קֶר֙
אֶל־הַ֣ר סִינַ֔י וְנִצַּבְתָּ֥ לִ֛י שָׁ֖ם עַל־רֹ֥אשׁ הָהָֽר׃
וְאִישׁ֙ לֹֽא־יַעֲלֶ֣ה עִמָּ֔ךְ וְגַם־אִ֥ישׁ אַל־יֵרָ֖א
בְּכָל־הָהָ֑ר גַּם־הַצֹּ֤אן וְהַבָּקָר֙ אַל־יִרְע֔וּ אֶל־
מ֖וּל הָהָ֥ר הַהֽוּא׃

ישראל (ובמנחה מפטיר)׃ וַיִּפְסֹ֡ל שְׁנֵֽי־לֻחֹ֨ת אֲבָנִ֜ים
כָּרִאשֹׁנִ֗ים וַיַּשְׁכֵּ֨ם מֹשֶׁ֤ה בַבֹּ֙קֶר֙ וַיַּ֣עַל אֶל־הַ֣ר
סִינַ֔י כַּאֲשֶׁ֛ר צִוָּ֥ה יְהֹוָ֖ה אֹת֑וֹ וַיִּקַּ֣ח בְּיָד֔וֹ שְׁנֵ֖י
לֻחֹ֥ת אֲבָנִֽים׃ וַיֵּ֤רֶד יְהֹוָה֙ בֶּֽעָנָ֔ן וַיִּתְיַצֵּ֥ב עִמּ֖וֹ שָׁ֑ם
וַיִּקְרָ֥א בְשֵׁ֖ם יְהֹוָֽה׃ וַיַּעֲבֹ֨ר יְהֹוָ֥ה ׀ עַל־פָּנָיו֮
וַיִּקְרָא֒ **יְהֹוָ֣ה ׀ יְהֹוָ֔ה אֵ֥ל רַח֖וּם וְחַנּ֑וּן אֶ֥רֶךְ**

PURIM

(*Exodus 17:8-16*)

כהן׃ וַיָּבֹ֖א עֲמָלֵ֑ק וַיִּלָּ֥חֶם עִם־יִשְׂרָאֵ֖ל בִּרְפִידִֽם׃
וַיֹּ֨אמֶר מֹשֶׁ֤ה אֶל־יְהוֹשֻׁ֙עַ֙ בְּחַר־לָ֣נוּ אֲנָשִׁ֔ים
וְצֵ֖א הִלָּחֵ֣ם בַּעֲמָלֵ֑ק מָחָ֗ר אָנֹכִ֤י נִצָּב֙ עַל־רֹ֣אשׁ
הַגִּבְעָ֔ה וּמַטֵּ֥ה הָאֱלֹהִ֖ים בְּיָדִֽי׃ וַיַּ֣עַשׂ יְהוֹשֻׁ֗עַ
כַּֽאֲשֶׁ֤ר אָֽמַר־לוֹ֙ מֹשֶׁ֔ה לְהִלָּחֵ֖ם בַּעֲמָלֵ֑ק וּמֹשֶׁה֙
אַהֲרֹ֣ן וְח֔וּר עָל֖וּ רֹ֥אשׁ הַגִּבְעָֽה׃

לוי׃ וְהָיָ֗ה כַּאֲשֶׁ֨ר יָרִ֥ים מֹשֶׁ֛ה יָד֖וֹ וְגָבַ֣ר יִשְׂרָאֵ֑ל
וְכַאֲשֶׁ֥ר יָנִ֛יחַ יָד֖וֹ וְגָבַ֥ר עֲמָלֵֽק׃ וִידֵ֤י מֹשֶׁה֙
כְּבֵדִ֔ים וַיִּקְחוּ־אֶ֛בֶן וַיָּשִׂ֥ימוּ תַחְתָּ֖יו וַיֵּ֣שֶׁב עָלֶ֑יהָ
וְאַהֲרֹ֣ן וְח֗וּר תָּֽמְכ֤וּ בְיָדָיו֙ מִזֶּ֣ה אֶחָ֔ד וּמִזֶּ֣ה אֶחָ֔ד
וַיְהִ֥י יָדָ֛יו אֱמוּנָ֖ה עַד־בֹּ֥א הַשָּֽׁמֶשׁ׃ וַיַּחֲלֹ֧שׁ

הוּא וְסָלַחְתָּ לַעֲוֹנֵנוּ וּלְחַטָּאתֵנוּ וּנְחַלְתָּנוּ: וַיֹּאמֶר הִנֵּה אָנֹכִי כֹּרֵת בְּרִית נֶגֶד כָּל־עַמְּךָ אֶעֱשֶׂה נִפְלָאֹת אֲשֶׁר לֹא־נִבְרְאוּ בְכָל־הָאָרֶץ וּבְכָל־הַגּוֹיִם וְרָאָה כָל־הָעָם אֲשֶׁר־אַתָּה בְקִרְבּוֹ אֶת־מַעֲשֵׂה יהוה כִּי־נוֹרָא הוּא אֲשֶׁר אֲנִי עֹשֶׂה עִמָּךְ:

אַפַּיִם וְרַב־חֶסֶד וֶאֱמֶת: נֹצֵר חֶסֶד לָאֲלָפִים נֹשֵׂא עָוֹן וָפֶשַׁע וְחַטָּאָה וְנַקֵּה לֹא יְנַקֶּה פֹּקֵד עֲוֹן אָבוֹת עַל־בָּנִים וְעַל־בְּנֵי בָנִים עַל־שִׁלֵּשִׁים וְעַל־רִבֵּעִים: וַיְמַהֵר מֹשֶׁה וַיִּקֹּד אַרְצָה וַיִּשְׁתָּחוּ: וַיֹּאמֶר אִם־נָא מָצָאתִי חֵן בְּעֵינֶיךָ אֲדֹנָי יֵלֶךְ־נָא אֲדֹנָי בְּקִרְבֵּנוּ כִּי עַם־קְשֵׁה־עֹרֶף

BLESSING BEFORE THE HAFTARAH / ברכה קודם ההפטרה

THE TORAH IS RAISED FOR ALL TO SEE (P. 211). AFTER THE TORAH HAS BEEN TIED AND COVERED,
THE *OLEH* FOR *MAFTIR* RECITES THE BLESSING BEFORE THE *HAFTARAH*.

בָּרוּךְ אַתָּה יהוה אֱלֹהֵינוּ מֶלֶךְ הָעוֹלָם, אֲשֶׁר בָּחַר
⟨ has ⟨ Who ⟪ of the ⟨ King ⟨ our God, ⟨ HASHEM, ⟨ are You, ⟨ Blessed
chosen universe,

בִּנְבִיאִים טוֹבִים, וְרָצָה בְדִבְרֵיהֶם הַנֶּאֱמָרִים בֶּאֱמֶת,
⟪ with truth. ⟨ that were uttered ⟨ with their words ⟨ and was ⟨ good prophets
pleased

בָּרוּךְ אַתָּה יהוה, הַבּוֹחֵר בַּתּוֹרָה וּבְמֹשֶׁה עַבְדּוֹ, וּבְיִשְׂרָאֵל
⟨ and Israel, ⟨ His ⟨ and Moses, ⟨ the Torah ⟨ Who ⟨ HASHEM, ⟨ are You, ⟨ Blessed
servant, chooses

עַמּוֹ, וּבִנְבִיאֵי הָאֱמֶת וָצֶדֶק:
⟪ and ⟨ of truth ⟨ and the ⟨ His
righteousness. prophets people,

אָמֵן.) –Cong.)
⟪ Amen.

HAFTARAH FOR A FAST DAY

(Isaiah 55:6-56:8)

דִּרְשׁוּ יהוה בְּהִמָּצְאוֹ קְרָאֻהוּ בִּהְיוֹתוֹ קָרוֹב: יַעֲזֹב רָשָׁע דַּרְכּוֹ וְאִישׁ אָוֶן מַחְשְׁבֹתָיו וְיָשֹׁב אֶל־יהוה וִירַחֲמֵהוּ וְאֶל־אֱלֹהֵינוּ כִּי־יַרְבֶּה לִסְלוֹחַ: כִּי לֹא מַחְשְׁבוֹתַי מַחְשְׁבוֹתֵיכֶם וְלֹא דַרְכֵיכֶם דְּרָכָי נְאֻם יהוה: כִּי־גָבְהוּ שָׁמַיִם מֵאָרֶץ כֵּן גָּבְהוּ דְרָכַי מִדַּרְכֵיכֶם וּמַחְשְׁבֹתַי מִמַּחְשְׁבֹתֵיכֶם: כִּי כַּאֲשֶׁר יֵרֵד הַגֶּשֶׁם וְהַשֶּׁלֶג מִן־הַשָּׁמַיִם וְשָׁמָּה לֹא יָשׁוּב כִּי אִם־הִרְוָה אֶת־הָאָרֶץ וְהוֹלִידָהּ וְהִצְמִיחָהּ וְנָתַן זֶרַע לַזֹּרֵעַ וְלֶחֶם לָאֹכֵל: כֵּן יִהְיֶה דְבָרִי אֲשֶׁר יֵצֵא מִפִּי לֹא־יָשׁוּב אֵלַי רֵיקָם כִּי אִם־עָשָׂה אֶת־אֲשֶׁר חָפַצְתִּי וְהִצְלִיחַ אֲשֶׁר שְׁלַחְתִּיו: כִּי־בְשִׂמְחָה תֵצֵאוּ וּבְשָׁלוֹם תּוּבָלוּן הֶהָרִים וְהַגְּבָעוֹת יִפְצְחוּ לִפְנֵיכֶם רִנָּה וְכָל־עֲצֵי הַשָּׂדֶה יִמְחֲאוּ־כָף: תַּחַת הַנַּעֲצוּץ יַעֲלֶה בְרוֹשׁ וְתַחַת הַסִּרְפַּד יַעֲלֶה הֲדַס וְהָיָה לַיהוה לְשֵׁם לְאוֹת עוֹלָם לֹא

יִכָּרֵת: כֹּה אָמַר יהוה שִׁמְרוּ מִשְׁפָּט וַעֲשׂוּ צְדָקָה כִּי־קְרוֹבָה יְשׁוּעָתִי לָבוֹא וְצִדְקָתִי לְהִגָּלוֹת: אַשְׁרֵי אֱנוֹשׁ יַעֲשֶׂה־זֹּאת וּבֶן־אָדָם יַחֲזִיק בָּהּ שֹׁמֵר שַׁבָּת מֵחַלְּלוֹ וְשֹׁמֵר יָדוֹ מֵעֲשׂוֹת כָּל־רָע: וְאַל־יֹאמַר בֶּן־הַנֵּכָר הַנִּלְוָה אֶל־יהוה לֵאמֹר הַבְדֵּל יַבְדִּילַנִי יהוה מֵעַל עַמּוֹ וְאַל־יֹאמַר הַסָּרִיס הֵן אֲנִי עֵץ יָבֵשׁ: כִּי־כֹה ׀ אָמַר יהוה לַסָּרִיסִים אֲשֶׁר יִשְׁמְרוּ אֶת־שַׁבְּתוֹתַי וּבָחֲרוּ בַּאֲשֶׁר חָפָצְתִּי וּמַחֲזִיקִים בִּבְרִיתִי: וְנָתַתִּי לָהֶם בְּבֵיתִי וּבְחוֹמֹתַי יָד וָשֵׁם טוֹב מִבָּנִים וּמִבָּנוֹת שֵׁם עוֹלָם אֶתֶּן־לוֹ אֲשֶׁר לֹא יִכָּרֵת: וּבְנֵי הַנֵּכָר הַנִּלְוִים עַל־יהוה לְשָׁרְתוֹ וּלְאַהֲבָה אֶת־שֵׁם יהוה לִהְיוֹת לוֹ לַעֲבָדִים כָּל־שֹׁמֵר שַׁבָּת מֵחַלְּלוֹ וּמַחֲזִיקִים בִּבְרִיתִי: וַהֲבִיאוֹתִים אֶל־הַר קָדְשִׁי וְשִׂמַּחְתִּים בְּבֵית תְּפִלָּתִי עוֹלֹתֵיהֶם וְזִבְחֵיהֶם לְרָצוֹן עַל־מִזְבְּחִי כִּי בֵיתִי בֵּית־תְּפִלָּה יִקָּרֵא לְכָל־הָעַמִּים: נְאֻם ׀ אֲדֹנָי יֱהוִֹה מְקַבֵּץ נִדְחֵי יִשְׂרָאֵל עוֹד אֲקַבֵּץ עָלָיו לְנִקְבָּצָיו:

BLESSINGS AFTER THE HAFTARAH / ברכות אחרי ההפטרה

AFTER THE HAFTARAH IS READ, THE *OLEH* RECITES THE FOLLOWING BLESSINGS:

בָּרוּךְ אַתָּה יהוה אֱלֹהֵינוּ מֶלֶךְ הָעוֹלָם, צוּר כָּל

‹ of all ‹ Rock ‹‹ of the universe, ‹ King ‹ our God, ‹ Hashem, ‹ are You, ‹ Blessed

הָעוֹלָמִים, צַדִּיק בְּכָל הַדּוֹרוֹת, הָאֵל הַנֶּאֱמָן הָאוֹמֵר

‹ Who says ‹‹ Who is trustworthy, ‹ the God ‹‹ generations, ‹ in all ‹ Righteous ‹ eternities,

וְעֹשֶׂה, הַמְדַבֵּר וּמְקַיֵּם, שֶׁכָּל דְּבָרָיו אֱמֶת וָצֶדֶק. נֶאֱמָן

‹ Trust- ‹‹ and ‹ are true ‹ of His ‹ for all ‹‹ and fulfills, ‹ Who declares ‹‹ and does,
worthy   righteous.   words

אַתָּה הוּא יהוה אֱלֹהֵינוּ, וְנֶאֱמָנִים דְּבָרֶיךָ, וְדָבָר אֶחָד

‹ [even] one word ‹‹ are Your words; ‹ and trustworthy ‹ our God, ‹ Hashem, ‹ are You

מִדְּבָרֶיךָ אָחוֹר לֹא יָשׁוּב רֵיקָם, כִּי אֵל מֶלֶךְ נֶאֱמָן (וְרַחֲמָן)

‹ and com- ‹ trust- ‹ King, ‹ a ‹ for ‹‹ unfulfilled, ‹ returns ‹ never ‹ back ‹‹ of Your
passionate worthy God,   [to its source] words

אָתָּה. בָּרוּךְ אַתָּה יהוה, הָאֵל הַנֶּאֱמָן בְּכָל דְּבָרָיו. (–Cong. אָמֵן.)

‹‹ (Amen.) ‹‹ His words. ‹ in all ‹ Who is ‹ the ‹‹ Hashem, ‹ are ‹ Blessed ‹‹ are You.
                        trustworthy God   You,

רַחֵם עַל צִיּוֹן כִּי הִיא בֵּית חַיֵּינוּ, וְלַעֲלוּבַת נֶפֶשׁ תּוֹשִׁיעַ

‹ bring ‹ [to her ‹ and to ‹‹ [that is the ‹ is the ‹ it ‹ for ‹ Zion, ‹ on ‹ Have
salvation very] soul, [Israel,] who focus of] place   mercy
              is humiliated our life;

בִּמְהֵרָה בְיָמֵינוּ. בָּרוּךְ אַתָּה יהוה, מְשַׂמֵּחַ צִיּוֹן בְּבָנֶיהָ.

‹‹ through her children. ‹ Zion ‹‹ Who gladdens ‹‹ Hashem, ‹ are You, ‹ Blessed ‹‹ in our days. ‹ speedily

(–Cong. אָמֵן.)

‹‹ (Amen.)

שַׂמְּחֵנוּ יהוה אֱלֹהֵינוּ בְּאֵלִיָּהוּ הַנָּבִיא עַבְדֶּךָ, וּבְמַלְכוּת

‹ and with the ‹‹ Your ‹ the ‹ with Elijah ‹ our God, ‹ Hashem, ‹ Gladden us,
kingdom   servant, prophet,

בֵּית דָּוִד מְשִׁיחֶךָ, בִּמְהֵרָה יָבֹא וְיָגֵל לִבֵּנוּ, עַל כִּסְאוֹ לֹא

‹ may there ‹ his ‹ On ‹‹ and then our ‹ may he ‹ speedily ‹ Your anointed ‹ of ‹ of the
never throne   hearts will exult. come,   one;   David, House

יֵשֶׁב זָר וְלֹא יִנְחֲלוּ עוֹד אֲחֵרִים אֶת כְּבוֹדוֹ, כִּי בְשֵׁם קָדְשְׁךָ

‹ of Your ‹ by the ‹ for ‹‹ his honor, ‹ others ‹ any ‹ and do not ‹‹ any ‹ sit
Holiness Name   longer [allow to] inherit stranger,

נִשְׁבַּעְתָּ לּוֹ, שֶׁלֹּא יִכְבֶּה נֵרוֹ לְעוֹלָם וָעֶד. בָּרוּךְ אַתָּה יהוה,

‹‹ Hashem, ‹ are ‹ Blessed ‹‹ and ‹ forever ‹ would his ‹ extin- ‹ that ‹‹ to ‹ You swore
         You, ever.   lamp be guished not him

(–Cong. אָמֵן.)   מָגֵן דָּוִד.

‹‹ (Amen.)   ‹‹ of David. ‹ Shield

THE SERVICE CONTINUES ON PAGE 225.

TISHAH B'AV – SHACHARIS

(*Deuteronomy* 4:25-40)

כהן: כִּי־תוֹלִיד בָּנִים וּבְנֵי בָנִים וְנוֹשַׁנְתֶּם בָּאָרֶץ וְהִשְׁחַתֶּם וַעֲשִׂיתֶם פֶּסֶל תְּמוּנַת כֹּל וַעֲשִׂיתֶם הָרַע בְּעֵינֵי־יהוה אֱלֹהֶיךָ לְהַכְעִיסוֹ: הַעִידֹתִי בָכֶם הַיּוֹם אֶת־הַשָּׁמַיִם וְאֶת־הָאָרֶץ כִּי־אָבֹד תֹּאבֵדוּן מַהֵר מֵעַל הָאָרֶץ אֲשֶׁר אַתֶּם עֹבְרִים אֶת־הַיַּרְדֵּן שָׁמָּה לְרִשְׁתָּהּ לֹא־תַאֲרִיכֻן יָמִים עָלֶיהָ כִּי הִשָּׁמֵד תִּשָּׁמֵדוּן: וְהֵפִיץ יהוה אֶתְכֶם בָּעַמִּים וְנִשְׁאַרְתֶּם מְתֵי מִסְפָּר בַּגּוֹיִם אֲשֶׁר יְנַהֵג יהוה אֶתְכֶם שָׁמָּה: וַעֲבַדְתֶּם־שָׁם אֱלֹהִים מַעֲשֵׂה יְדֵי אָדָם עֵץ וָאֶבֶן אֲשֶׁר לֹא־יִרְאוּן וְלֹא יִשְׁמְעוּן וְלֹא יֹאכְלוּן וְלֹא יְרִיחֻן: וּבִקַּשְׁתֶּם מִשָּׁם אֶת־יהוה אֱלֹהֶיךָ וּמָצָאתָ כִּי תִדְרְשֶׁנּוּ בְּכָל־לְבָבְךָ וּבְכָל־נַפְשֶׁךָ:

לוי: בַּצַּר לְךָ וּמְצָאוּךָ כֹּל הַדְּבָרִים הָאֵלֶּה בְּאַחֲרִית הַיָּמִים וְשַׁבְתָּ עַד־יהוה אֱלֹהֶיךָ וְשָׁמַעְתָּ בְּקֹלוֹ: כִּי אֵל רַחוּם יהוה אֱלֹהֶיךָ לֹא יַרְפְּךָ וְלֹא יַשְׁחִיתֶךָ וְלֹא יִשְׁכַּח אֶת־בְּרִית אֲבֹתֶיךָ אֲשֶׁר נִשְׁבַּע לָהֶם: כִּי שְׁאַל־נָא לְיָמִים רִאשֹׁנִים אֲשֶׁר־הָיוּ לְפָנֶיךָ לְמִן־הַיּוֹם אֲשֶׁר בָּרָא אֱלֹהִים | אָדָם עַל־הָאָרֶץ וּלְמִקְצֵה הַשָּׁמַיִם וְעַד־קְצֵה הַשָּׁמָיִם הֲנִהְיָה כַּדָּבָר הַגָּדוֹל הַזֶּה אוֹ הֲנִשְׁמַע כָּמֹהוּ: הֲשָׁמַע עָם קוֹל אֱלֹהִים מְדַבֵּר מִתּוֹךְ־הָאֵשׁ כַּאֲשֶׁר־שָׁמַעְתָּ אַתָּה וַיֶּחִי: אוֹ | הֲנִסָּה אֱלֹהִים לָבוֹא לָקַחַת לוֹ גוֹי מִקֶּרֶב גּוֹי בְּמַסֹּת בְּאֹתֹת וּבְמוֹפְתִים וּבְמִלְחָמָה וּבְיָד חֲזָקָה וּבִזְרוֹעַ נְטוּיָה וּבְמוֹרָאִים גְּדֹלִים כְּכֹל אֲשֶׁר־עָשָׂה לָכֶם יהוה אֱלֹהֵיכֶם בְּמִצְרַיִם לְעֵינֶיךָ: אַתָּה הָרְאֵתָ לָדַעַת כִּי יהוה הוּא הָאֱלֹהִים אֵין עוֹד מִלְּבַדּוֹ:

מפטיר: מִן־הַשָּׁמַיִם הִשְׁמִיעֲךָ אֶת־קֹלוֹ לְיַסְּרֶךָּ וְעַל־הָאָרֶץ הֶרְאֲךָ אֶת־אִשּׁוֹ הַגְּדוֹלָה וּדְבָרָיו שָׁמַעְתָּ מִתּוֹךְ הָאֵשׁ: וְתַחַת כִּי אָהַב אֶת־אֲבֹתֶיךָ וַיִּבְחַר בְּזַרְעוֹ אַחֲרָיו וַיּוֹצִאֲךָ בְּפָנָיו בְּכֹחוֹ הַגָּדֹל מִמִּצְרָיִם: לְהוֹרִישׁ גּוֹיִם גְּדֹלִים וַעֲצֻמִים מִמְּךָ מִפָּנֶיךָ לַהֲבִיאֲךָ לָתֶת־לְךָ אֶת־אַרְצָם נַחֲלָה כַּיּוֹם הַזֶּה: וְיָדַעְתָּ הַיּוֹם וַהֲשֵׁבֹתָ אֶל־לְבָבֶךָ כִּי יהוה הוּא הָאֱלֹהִים בַּשָּׁמַיִם מִמַּעַל וְעַל־הָאָרֶץ מִתָּחַת אֵין עוֹד: וְשָׁמַרְתָּ אֶת־חֻקָּיו וְאֶת־מִצְוֹתָיו אֲשֶׁר אָנֹכִי מְצַוְּךָ הַיּוֹם אֲשֶׁר יִיטַב לְךָ וּלְבָנֶיךָ אַחֲרֶיךָ וּלְמַעַן תַּאֲרִיךְ יָמִים עַל־הָאֲדָמָה אֲשֶׁר יהוה אֱלֹהֶיךָ נֹתֵן לְךָ כָּל־הַיָּמִים:

HAFTARAH

The blessing before the *Haftarah* may be found on page 794.

(*Jeremiah* 8:13-9:23)

אָסֹף אֲסִיפֵם נְאֻם־יהוה אֵין עֲנָבִים בַּגֶּפֶן וְאֵין תְּאֵנִים בַּתְּאֵנָה וְהֶעָלֶה נָבֵל וָאֶתֵּן לָהֶם יַעַבְרוּם: עַל־מָה אֲנַחְנוּ יֹשְׁבִים הֵאָסְפוּ וְנָבוֹא אֶל־עָרֵי הַמִּבְצָר וְנִדְּמָה־שָּׁם כִּי יהוה אֱלֹהֵינוּ הֲדִמָּנוּ וַיַּשְׁקֵנוּ מֵי־רֹאשׁ כִּי חָטָאנוּ לַיהוה: קַוֵּה לְשָׁלוֹם וְאֵין טוֹב לְעֵת מַרְפֵּה וְהִנֵּה בְעָתָה: מִדָּן נִשְׁמַע נַחְרַת סוּסָיו מִקּוֹל מִצְהֲלוֹת אַבִּירָיו רָעֲשָׁה כָּל־הָאָרֶץ וַיָּבוֹאוּ וַיֹּאכְלוּ אֶרֶץ וּמְלוֹאָהּ עִיר וְיֹשְׁבֵי בָהּ: כִּי הִנְנִי מְשַׁלֵּחַ בָּכֶם נְחָשִׁים צִפְעֹנִים אֲשֶׁר אֵין־לָהֶם לָחַשׁ וְנִשְּׁכוּ אֶתְכֶם נְאֻם־יהוה: מַבְלִיגִיתִי עֲלֵי יָגוֹן עָלַי לִבִּי דַוָּי: הִנֵּה־קוֹל שַׁוְעַת בַּת־עַמִּי מֵאֶרֶץ מַרְחַקִּים הַיהוה אֵין בְּצִיּוֹן אִם־מַלְכָּהּ אֵין בָּהּ מַדּוּעַ הִכְעִסוּנִי בִּפְסִלֵיהֶם בְּהַבְלֵי נֵכָר: עָבַר קָצִיר כָּלָה קָיִץ וַאֲנַחְנוּ לוֹא נוֹשָׁעְנוּ: עַל־שֶׁבֶר בַּת־עַמִּי הָשְׁבָּרְתִּי קָדַרְתִּי שַׁמָּה הֶחֱזִקָתְנִי: הַצֳרִי אֵין בְּגִלְעָד אִם־רֹפֵא אֵין שָׁם כִּי מַדּוּעַ לֹא עָלְתָה אֲרֻכַת בַּת־עַמִּי: מִי־יִתֵּן רֹאשִׁי מַיִם וְעֵינִי מְקוֹר דִּמְעָה וְאֶבְכֶּה יוֹמָם וָלַיְלָה אֵת חַלְלֵי בַת־עַמִּי: מִי־יִתְּנֵנִי בַמִּדְבָּר מְלוֹן אֹרְחִים וְאֶעֶזְבָה אֶת־עַמִּי וְאֵלְכָה מֵאִתָּם כִּי כֻלָּם מְנָאֲפִים עֲצֶרֶת בֹּגְדִים: וַיַּדְרְכוּ אֶת־לְשׁוֹנָם קַשְׁתָּם שֶׁקֶר וְלֹא לֶאֱמוּנָה גָּבְרוּ בָאָרֶץ כִּי מֵרָעָה אֶל־רָעָה | יָצָאוּ וְאֹתִי לֹא־יָדָעוּ נְאֻם־יהוה: אִישׁ מֵרֵעֵהוּ הִשָּׁמֵרוּ וְעַל־כָּל־אָח אַל־תִּבְטָחוּ כִּי כָל־אָח עָקוֹב יַעְקֹב וְכָל־רֵעַ רָכִיל יַהֲלֹךְ: וְאִישׁ בְּרֵעֵהוּ יְהָתֵלּוּ וֶאֱמֶת לֹא יְדַבֵּרוּ לִמְּדוּ לְשׁוֹנָם דַּבֶּר־שֶׁקֶר הַעֲוֵה נִלְאוּ: שִׁבְתְּךָ בְּתוֹךְ מִרְמָה בְּמִרְמָה מֵאֲנוּ דַעַת־אוֹתִי נְאֻם־יהוה: לָכֵן כֹּה אָמַר יהוה צְבָאוֹת הִנְנִי צוֹרְפָם וּבְחַנְתִּים כִּי־אֵיךְ

TORAH READING FOR CHOL HAMOED PESACH

Each day two Torahs are removed from the Ark. Three *olim* are called to the first Torah, and a fourth *oleh* to the second Torah. When the first day of Chol HaMoed falls on the Sabbath, the readings for the first two days are each postponed one day and the third day's reading is omitted.

FIRST DAY CHOL HAMOED PESACH

(*Exodus* 13:1-16)

כה: וַיְדַבֵּר יהוה אֶל־מֹשֶׁה לֵּאמֹר: קַדֶּשׁ־לִי כָל־בְּכוֹר פֶּטֶר כָּל־רֶחֶם בִּבְנֵי יִשְׂרָאֵל בָּאָדָם וּבַבְּהֵמָה לִי הוּא: וַיֹּאמֶר מֹשֶׁה אֶל־הָעָם זָכוֹר אֶת־הַיּוֹם הַזֶּה אֲשֶׁר יְצָאתֶם מִמִּצְרַיִם מִבֵּית עֲבָדִים כִּי בְּחֹזֶק יָד הוֹצִיא יהוה אֶתְכֶם מִזֶּה וְלֹא יֵאָכֵל חָמֵץ: הַיּוֹם אַתֶּם יֹצְאִים בְּחֹדֶשׁ הָאָבִיב:

לוי: וְהָיָה כִּי־יְבִיאֲךָ יהוה אֶל־אֶרֶץ הַכְּנַעֲנִי וְהַחִתִּי וְהָאֱמֹרִי וְהַחִוִּי וְהַיְבוּסִי אֲשֶׁר נִשְׁבַּע לַאֲבֹתֶיךָ לָתֶת לָךְ אֶרֶץ זָבַת חָלָב וּדְבָשׁ וְעָבַדְתָּ אֶת־הָעֲבֹדָה הַזֹּאת בַּחֹדֶשׁ הַזֶּה: שִׁבְעַת יָמִים תֹּאכַל מַצֹּת וּבַיּוֹם הַשְּׁבִיעִי חַג לַיהוה: מַצּוֹת יֵאָכֵל אֵת שִׁבְעַת הַיָּמִים וְלֹא־יֵרָאֶה לְךָ חָמֵץ וְלֹא־יֵרָאֶה לְךָ שְׂאֹר בְּכָל־גְּבֻלֶךָ: וְהִגַּדְתָּ לְבִנְךָ בַּיּוֹם הַהוּא לֵאמֹר בַּעֲבוּר זֶה עָשָׂה יהוה לִי בְּצֵאתִי מִמִּצְרָיִם: וְהָיָה לְךָ לְאוֹת עַל־יָדְךָ וּלְזִכָּרוֹן בֵּין עֵינֶיךָ לְמַעַן תִּהְיֶה תּוֹרַת יהוה בְּפִיךָ כִּי בְּיָד חֲזָקָה הוֹצִאֲךָ יהוה מִמִּצְרָיִם: וְשָׁמַרְתָּ אֶת־הַחֻקָּה הַזֹּאת לְמוֹעֲדָהּ מִיָּמִים יָמִימָה:

שלישי: וְהָיָה כִּי־יְבִיאֲךָ יהוה אֶל־אֶרֶץ הַכְּנַעֲנִי כַּאֲשֶׁר נִשְׁבַּע לְךָ וְלַאֲבֹתֶיךָ וּנְתָנָהּ לָךְ: וְהַעֲבַרְתָּ כָל־פֶּטֶר־רֶחֶם לַיהוה וְכָל־פֶּטֶר שֶׁגֶר בְּהֵמָה אֲשֶׁר יִהְיֶה לְךָ הַזְּכָרִים לַיהוה: וְכָל־פֶּטֶר חֲמֹר תִּפְדֶּה בְשֶׂה וְאִם־לֹא תִפְדֶּה וַעֲרַפְתּוֹ וְכֹל בְּכוֹר אָדָם בְּבָנֶיךָ תִּפְדֶּה: וְהָיָה כִּי־יִשְׁאָלְךָ בִנְךָ מָחָר לֵאמֹר מַה־זֹּאת וְאָמַרְתָּ אֵלָיו בְּחֹזֶק יָד הוֹצִיאָנוּ יהוה מִמִּצְרַיִם מִבֵּית עֲבָדִים: וַיְהִי כִּי־הִקְשָׁה פַרְעֹה לְשַׁלְּחֵנוּ וַיַּהֲרֹג יהוה כָּל־בְּכוֹר בְּאֶרֶץ מִצְרַיִם מִבְּכֹר אָדָם וְעַד־בְּכוֹר בְּהֵמָה עַל־כֵּן אֲנִי זֹבֵחַ לַיהוה כָּל־פֶּטֶר רֶחֶם הַזְּכָרִים

אֶעֱשֶׂה מִפְּנֵי בַת־עַמִּי: חֵץ שָׁחוּט לְשׁוֹנָם מִרְמָה דִּבֵּר בְּפִיו שָׁלוֹם אֶת־רֵעֵהוּ יְדַבֵּר וּבְקִרְבּוֹ יָשִׂים אָרְבּוֹ: הַעַל־אֵלֶּה לֹא־אֶפְקָד־בָּם נְאֻם־יהוה אִם בְּגוֹי אֲשֶׁר־כָּזֶה לֹא תִתְנַקֵּם נַפְשִׁי: עַל־הֶהָרִים אֶשָּׂא בְכִי וָנֶהִי וְעַל־נְאוֹת מִדְבָּר קִינָה כִּי נִצְּתוּ מִבְּלִי־אִישׁ עֹבֵר וְלֹא שָׁמְעוּ קוֹל מִקְנֶה מֵעוֹף הַשָּׁמַיִם וְעַד־בְּהֵמָה נָדְדוּ הָלָכוּ: וְנָתַתִּי אֶת־יְרוּשָׁלַ͏ִם לְגַלִּים מְעוֹן תַּנִּים וְאֶת־עָרֵי יְהוּדָה אֶתֵּן שְׁמָמָה מִבְּלִי יוֹשֵׁב: מִי־הָאִישׁ הֶחָכָם וְיָבֵן אֶת־זֹאת וַאֲשֶׁר דִּבֶּר פִּי־יהוה אֵלָיו וְיַגִּדָהּ עַל־מָה אָבְדָה הָאָרֶץ נִצְּתָה כַמִּדְבָּר מִבְּלִי עֹבֵר: וַיֹּאמֶר יהוה עַל־עָזְבָם אֶת־תּוֹרָתִי אֲשֶׁר נָתַתִּי לִפְנֵיהֶם וְלֹא־שָׁמְעוּ בְקוֹלִי וְלֹא־הָלְכוּ בָהּ: וַיֵּלְכוּ אַחֲרֵי שְׁרִרוּת לִבָּם וְאַחֲרֵי הַבְּעָלִים אֲשֶׁר לִמְּדוּם אֲבוֹתָם: לָכֵן כֹּה־אָמַר יהוה צְבָאוֹת אֱלֹהֵי יִשְׂרָאֵל הִנְנִי מַאֲכִילָם אֶת־הָעָם הַזֶּה לַעֲנָה וְהִשְׁקִיתִים מֵי־רֹאשׁ: וַהֲפִצוֹתִים בַּגּוֹיִם אֲשֶׁר לֹא יָדְעוּ הֵמָּה וַאֲבוֹתָם וְשִׁלַּחְתִּי אַחֲרֵיהֶם אֶת־הַחֶרֶב עַד כַּלּוֹתִי אוֹתָם: כֹּה אָמַר יהוה צְבָאוֹת הִתְבּוֹנְנוּ וְקִרְאוּ לַמְקוֹנְנוֹת וּתְבוֹאֶינָה וְאֶל־הַחֲכָמוֹת שִׁלְחוּ וְתָבוֹאנָה: וּתְמַהֵרְנָה וְתִשֶּׂנָה עָלֵינוּ נֶהִי וְתֵרַדְנָה עֵינֵינוּ דִּמְעָה וְעַפְעַפֵּינוּ יִזְּלוּ־מָיִם: כִּי קוֹל נְהִי נִשְׁמַע מִצִּיּוֹן אֵיךְ שֻׁדָּדְנוּ בֹּשְׁנוּ מְאֹד כִּי־עָזַבְנוּ אָרֶץ כִּי הִשְׁלִיכוּ מִשְׁכְּנוֹתֵינוּ: כִּי־שְׁמַעְנָה נָשִׁים דְּבַר־יהוה וְתִקַּח אָזְנְכֶם דְּבַר־פִּיו וְלַמֵּדְנָה בְנוֹתֵיכֶם נֶהִי וְאִשָּׁה רְעוּתָהּ קִינָה: כִּי־עָלָה מָוֶת בְּחַלּוֹנֵינוּ בָּא בְּאַרְמְנוֹתֵינוּ לְהַכְרִית עוֹלָל מִחוּץ בַּחוּרִים מֵרְחֹבוֹת: דַּבֵּר כֹּה נְאֻם־יהוה וְנָפְלָה נִבְלַת הָאָדָם כְּדֹמֶן עַל־פְּנֵי הַשָּׂדֶה וּכְעָמִיר מֵאַחֲרֵי הַקֹּצֵר וְאֵין מְאַסֵּף: כֹּה אָמַר יהוה אַל־יִתְהַלֵּל חָכָם בְּחָכְמָתוֹ וְאַל־יִתְהַלֵּל הַגִּבּוֹר בִּגְבוּרָתוֹ אַל־יִתְהַלֵּל עָשִׁיר בְּעָשְׁרוֹ: כִּי אִם־בְּזֹאת יִתְהַלֵּל הַמִּתְהַלֵּל הַשְׂכֵּל וְיָדֹעַ אוֹתִי כִּי אֲנִי יהוה עֹשֶׂה חֶסֶד מִשְׁפָּט וּצְדָקָה בָּאָרֶץ כִּי־בְאֵלֶּה חָפַצְתִּי נְאֻם־יהוה:

The blessings following the *Haftarah* may be found on page 795.

וְכָל־בְּכוֹר בָּנֶיךָ תִּפְדֶּה: וְהָיָה לְאוֹת עַל־יָדְכָה וּלְטוֹטָפֹת בֵּין עֵינֶיךָ כִּי בְּחֹזֶק יָד הוֹצִיאָנוּ יהוה מִמִּצְרָיִם:

(Numbers 28:19-25)

רביעי: וְהִקְרַבְתֶּם אִשֶּׁה עֹלָה לַיהוה פָּרִים בְּנֵי־בָקָר שְׁנַיִם וְאַיִל אֶחָד וְשִׁבְעָה כְבָשִׂים בְּנֵי שָׁנָה תְּמִימִם יִהְיוּ לָכֶם: וּמִנְחָתָם סֹלֶת בְּלוּלָה בַשָּׁמֶן שְׁלֹשָׁה עֶשְׂרֹנִים לַפָּר וּשְׁנֵי עֶשְׂרֹנִים לָאַיִל תַּעֲשׂוּ: עִשָּׂרוֹן עִשָּׂרוֹן תַּעֲשֶׂה לַכֶּבֶשׂ הָאֶחָד לְשִׁבְעַת הַכְּבָשִׂים: וּשְׂעִיר חַטָּאת אֶחָד לְכַפֵּר עֲלֵיכֶם: מִלְּבַד עֹלַת הַבֹּקֶר אֲשֶׁר לְעֹלַת הַתָּמִיד תַּעֲשׂוּ אֶת־אֵלֶּה: כָּאֵלֶּה תַּעֲשׂוּ לַיּוֹם שִׁבְעַת יָמִים לֶחֶם אִשֵּׁה רֵיחַ־נִיחֹחַ לַיהוה עַל־עוֹלַת הַתָּמִיד יֵעָשֶׂה וְנִסְכּוֹ: וּבַיּוֹם הַשְּׁבִיעִי מִקְרָא־קֹדֶשׁ יִהְיֶה לָכֶם כָּל־מְלֶאכֶת עֲבֹדָה לֹא תַעֲשׂוּ:

SECOND DAY CHOL HAMOED PESACH

(Exodus 22:24-23:19)

כד: אִם־כֶּסֶף | תַּלְוֶה אֶת־עַמִּי אֶת־הֶעָנִי עִמָּךְ לֹא־תִהְיֶה לוֹ כְּנֹשֶׁה לֹא־תְשִׂימוּן עָלָיו נֶשֶׁךְ: אִם־חָבֹל תַּחְבֹּל שַׂלְמַת רֵעֶךָ עַד־בֹּא הַשֶּׁמֶשׁ תְּשִׁיבֶנּוּ לוֹ: כִּי הִוא כְסוּתֹה לְבַדָּהּ הִוא שִׂמְלָתוֹ לְעֹרוֹ בַּמֶּה יִשְׁכָּב וְהָיָה כִּי־יִצְעַק אֵלַי וְשָׁמַעְתִּי כִּי־חַנּוּן אָנִי:

כז: אֱלֹהִים לֹא תְקַלֵּל וְנָשִׂיא בְעַמְּךָ לֹא תָאֹר: מְלֵאָתְךָ וְדִמְעֲךָ לֹא תְאַחֵר בְּכוֹר בָּנֶיךָ תִּתֶּן־לִי: כֵּן־תַּעֲשֶׂה לְשֹׁרְךָ לְצֹאנֶךָ שִׁבְעַת יָמִים יִהְיֶה עִם־אִמּוֹ בַּיּוֹם הַשְּׁמִינִי תִּתְּנוֹ־לִי: וְאַנְשֵׁי־קֹדֶשׁ תִּהְיוּן לִי וּבָשָׂר בַּשָּׂדֶה טְרֵפָה לֹא תֹאכֵלוּ לַכֶּלֶב תַּשְׁלִכוּן אֹתוֹ: לֹא תִשָּׂא שֵׁמַע שָׁוְא אַל־תָּשֶׁת יָדְךָ עִם־רָשָׁע לִהְיֹת עֵד חָמָס: לֹא־תִהְיֶה אַחֲרֵי־רַבִּים לְרָעֹת וְלֹא־תַעֲנֶה עַל־רִב לִנְטֹת אַחֲרֵי רַבִּים לְהַטֹּת: וְדָל לֹא תֶהְדַּר בְּרִיבוֹ: כִּי תִפְגַּע שׁוֹר אֹיִבְךָ אוֹ חֲמֹרוֹ תֹּעֶה הָשֵׁב תְּשִׁיבֶנּוּ לוֹ: כִּי־תִרְאֶה חֲמוֹר שֹׂנַאֲךָ רֹבֵץ תַּחַת מַשָּׂאוֹ וְחָדַלְתָּ מֵעֲזֹב לוֹ עָזֹב תַּעֲזֹב עִמּוֹ:

שלישי: לֹא תַטֶּה מִשְׁפַּט אֶבְיֹנְךָ בְּרִיבוֹ: מִדְּבַר־שֶׁקֶר תִּרְחָק וְנָקִי וְצַדִּיק אַל־תַּהֲרֹג כִּי לֹא־אַצְדִּיק רָשָׁע: וְשֹׁחַד לֹא תִקָּח כִּי

הַשֹּׁחַד יְעַוֵּר פִּקְחִים וִיסַלֵּף דִּבְרֵי צַדִּיקִים: וְגֵר לֹא תִלְחָץ וְאַתֶּם יְדַעְתֶּם אֶת־נֶפֶשׁ הַגֵּר כִּי־גֵרִים הֱיִיתֶם בְּאֶרֶץ מִצְרָיִם: וְשֵׁשׁ שָׁנִים תִּזְרַע אֶת־אַרְצֶךָ וְאָסַפְתָּ אֶת־תְּבוּאָתָהּ: וְהַשְּׁבִיעִת תִּשְׁמְטֶנָּה וּנְטַשְׁתָּהּ וְאָכְלוּ אֶבְיֹנֵי עַמֶּךָ וְיִתְרָם תֹּאכַל חַיַּת הַשָּׂדֶה כֵּן־תַּעֲשֶׂה לְכַרְמְךָ לְזֵיתֶךָ: שֵׁשֶׁת יָמִים תַּעֲשֶׂה מַעֲשֶׂיךָ וּבַיּוֹם הַשְּׁבִיעִי תִּשְׁבֹּת לְמַעַן יָנוּחַ שׁוֹרְךָ וַחֲמֹרֶךָ וְיִנָּפֵשׁ בֶּן־אֲמָתְךָ וְהַגֵּר: וּבְכֹל אֲשֶׁר־אָמַרְתִּי אֲלֵיכֶם תִּשָּׁמֵרוּ וְשֵׁם אֱלֹהִים אֲחֵרִים לֹא תַזְכִּירוּ לֹא יִשָּׁמַע עַל־פִּיךָ: שָׁלֹשׁ רְגָלִים תָּחֹג לִי בַּשָּׁנָה: אֶת־חַג הַמַּצּוֹת תִּשְׁמֹר שִׁבְעַת יָמִים תֹּאכַל מַצּוֹת כַּאֲשֶׁר צִוִּיתִךָ לְמוֹעֵד חֹדֶשׁ הָאָבִיב כִּי־בוֹ יָצָאתָ מִמִּצְרָיִם וְלֹא־יֵרָאוּ פָנַי רֵיקָם: וְחַג הַקָּצִיר בִּכּוּרֵי מַעֲשֶׂיךָ אֲשֶׁר תִּזְרַע בַּשָּׂדֶה וְחַג הָאָסִף בְּצֵאת הַשָּׁנָה בְּאָסְפְּךָ אֶת־מַעֲשֶׂיךָ מִן־הַשָּׂדֶה: שָׁלֹשׁ פְּעָמִים בַּשָּׁנָה יֵרָאֶה כָּל־זְכוּרְךָ אֶל־פְּנֵי הָאָדֹן | יהוה: לֹא־תִזְבַּח עַל־חָמֵץ דַּם־זִבְחִי וְלֹא־יָלִין חֵלֶב־חַגִּי עַד־בֹּקֶר: רֵאשִׁית בִּכּוּרֵי אַדְמָתְךָ תָּבִיא בֵּית יהוה אֱלֹהֶיךָ לֹא־תְבַשֵּׁל גְּדִי בַּחֲלֵב אִמּוֹ:

(Numbers 28:19-25)

רביעי: וְהִקְרַבְתֶּם אִשֶּׁה עֹלָה לַיהוה פָּרִים בְּנֵי־בָקָר שְׁנַיִם וְאַיִל אֶחָד וְשִׁבְעָה כְבָשִׂים בְּנֵי שָׁנָה תְּמִימִם יִהְיוּ לָכֶם: וּמִנְחָתָם סֹלֶת בְּלוּלָה בַשָּׁמֶן שְׁלֹשָׁה עֶשְׂרֹנִים לַפָּר וּשְׁנֵי עֶשְׂרֹנִים לָאַיִל תַּעֲשׂוּ: עִשָּׂרוֹן עִשָּׂרוֹן תַּעֲשֶׂה לַכֶּבֶשׂ הָאֶחָד לְשִׁבְעַת הַכְּבָשִׂים: וּשְׂעִיר חַטָּאת אֶחָד לְכַפֵּר עֲלֵיכֶם: מִלְּבַד עֹלַת הַבֹּקֶר אֲשֶׁר לְעֹלַת הַתָּמִיד תַּעֲשׂוּ אֶת־אֵלֶּה: כָּאֵלֶּה תַּעֲשׂוּ לַיּוֹם שִׁבְעַת יָמִים לֶחֶם אִשֵּׁה רֵיחַ־נִיחֹחַ לַיהוה עַל־עוֹלַת הַתָּמִיד יֵעָשֶׂה וְנִסְכּוֹ: וּבַיּוֹם הַשְּׁבִיעִי מִקְרָא־קֹדֶשׁ יִהְיֶה לָכֶם כָּל־מְלֶאכֶת עֲבֹדָה לֹא תַעֲשׂוּ:

THIRD DAY CHOL HAMOED PESACH

(Exodus 34:1-26)

כד: וַיֹּאמֶר יהוה אֶל־מֹשֶׁה פְּסָל־לְךָ שְׁנֵי־לֻחֹת אֲבָנִים כָּרִאשֹׁנִים וְכָתַבְתִּי עַל־

הַלֻּחֹת אֶת־הַדְּבָרִים אֲשֶׁר הָיוּ עַל־הַלֻּחֹת
הָרִאשֹׁנִים אֲשֶׁר שִׁבַּרְתָּ: וֶהְיֵה נָכוֹן לַבֹּקֶר
וְעָלִיתָ בַבֹּקֶר אֶל־הַר סִינַי וְנִצַּבְתָּ לִי שָׁם
עַל־רֹאשׁ הָהָר: וְאִישׁ לֹא־יַעֲלֶה עִמָּךְ וְגַם־
אִישׁ אַל־יֵרָא בְּכָל־הָהָר גַּם־הַצֹּאן וְהַבָּקָר
אַל־יִרְעוּ אֶל־מוּל הָהָר הַהוּא:

לוי: וַיִּפְסֹל שְׁנֵי־לֻחֹת אֲבָנִים כָּרִאשֹׁנִים
וַיַּשְׁכֵּם מֹשֶׁה בַבֹּקֶר וַיַּעַל אֶל־הַר סִינַי
כַּאֲשֶׁר צִוָּה יהוה אֹתוֹ וַיִּקַּח בְּיָדוֹ שְׁנֵי לֻחֹת
אֲבָנִים: וַיֵּרֶד יהוה בֶּעָנָן וַיִּתְיַצֵּב עִמּוֹ שָׁם
וַיִּקְרָא בְשֵׁם יהוה: וַיַּעֲבֹר יהוה ׀ עַל־פָּנָיו
וַיִּקְרָא יהוה ׀ יהוה אֵל רַחוּם וְחַנּוּן אֶרֶךְ
אַפַּיִם וְרַב־חֶסֶד וֶאֱמֶת: נֹצֵר חֶסֶד לָאֲלָפִים
נֹשֵׂא עָוֹן וָפֶשַׁע וְחַטָּאָה וְנַקֵּה לֹא יְנַקֶּה
פֹּקֵד ׀ עֲוֹן אָבוֹת עַל־בָּנִים וְעַל־בְּנֵי בָנִים
עַל־שִׁלֵּשִׁים וְעַל־רִבֵּעִים: וַיְמַהֵר מֹשֶׁה וַיִּקֹּד
אַרְצָה וַיִּשְׁתָּחוּ: וַיֹּאמֶר אִם־נָא מָצָאתִי חֵן
בְּעֵינֶיךָ אֲדֹנָי יֵלֶךְ־נָא אֲדֹנָי בְּקִרְבֵּנוּ כִּי עַם־
קְשֵׁה־עֹרֶף הוּא וְסָלַחְתָּ לַעֲוֹנֵנוּ וּלְחַטָּאתֵנוּ
וּנְחַלְתָּנוּ: וַיֹּאמֶר הִנֵּה אָנֹכִי כֹּרֵת בְּרִית
נֶגֶד כָּל־עַמְּךָ אֶעֱשֶׂה נִפְלָאֹת אֲשֶׁר לֹא־
נִבְרְאוּ בְכָל־הָאָרֶץ וּבְכָל־הַגּוֹיִם וְרָאָה
כָל־הָעָם אֲשֶׁר־אַתָּה בְקִרְבּוֹ אֶת־מַעֲשֵׂה
יהוה כִּי־נוֹרָא הוּא אֲשֶׁר אֲנִי עֹשֶׂה
עִמָּךְ: שְׁמָר־לְךָ אֵת אֲשֶׁר אָנֹכִי מְצַוְּךָ הַיּוֹם
הִנְנִי גֹרֵשׁ מִפָּנֶיךָ אֶת־הָאֱמֹרִי וְהַכְּנַעֲנִי
וְהַחִתִּי וְהַפְּרִזִּי וְהַחִוִּי וְהַיְבוּסִי: הִשָּׁמֶר לְךָ
פֶּן־תִּכְרֹת בְּרִית לְיוֹשֵׁב הָאָרֶץ אֲשֶׁר אַתָּה
בָּא עָלֶיהָ פֶּן־יִהְיֶה לְמוֹקֵשׁ בְּקִרְבֶּךָ: כִּי אֶת־
מִזְבְּחֹתָם תִּתֹּצוּן וְאֶת־מַצֵּבֹתָם תְּשַׁבֵּרוּן
וְאֶת־אֲשֵׁרָיו תִּכְרֹתוּן: כִּי לֹא תִשְׁתַּחֲוֶה
לְאֵל אַחֵר כִּי יהוה קַנָּא שְׁמוֹ אֵל קַנָּא
הוּא: פֶּן־תִּכְרֹת בְּרִית לְיוֹשֵׁב הָאָרֶץ וְזָנוּ ׀
אַחֲרֵי אֱלֹהֵיהֶם וְזָבְחוּ לֵאלֹהֵיהֶם וְקָרָא לְךָ
וְאָכַלְתָּ מִזִּבְחוֹ: וְלָקַחְתָּ מִבְּנֹתָיו לְבָנֶיךָ
וְזָנוּ בְנֹתָיו אַחֲרֵי אֱלֹהֵיהֶן וְהִזְנוּ אֶת־בָּנֶיךָ
אַחֲרֵי אֱלֹהֵיהֶן: אֱלֹהֵי מַסֵּכָה לֹא תַעֲשֶׂה־
לָךְ:

שלישי: אֶת־חַג הַמַּצּוֹת תִּשְׁמֹר שִׁבְעַת יָמִים
תֹּאכַל מַצּוֹת אֲשֶׁר צִוִּיתִךָ לְמוֹעֵד חֹדֶשׁ

הָאָבִיב כִּי בְּחֹדֶשׁ הָאָבִיב יָצָאתָ מִמִּצְרָיִם:
כָּל־פֶּטֶר רֶחֶם לִי וְכָל־מִקְנְךָ תִּזָּכָר פֶּטֶר
שׁוֹר וָשֶׂה: וּפֶטֶר חֲמוֹר תִּפְדֶּה בְשֶׂה וְאִם־
לֹא תִפְדֶּה וַעֲרַפְתּוֹ כֹּל בְּכוֹר בָּנֶיךָ תִּפְדֶּה
וְלֹא־יֵרָאוּ פָנַי רֵיקָם: שֵׁשֶׁת יָמִים תַּעֲבֹד
וּבַיּוֹם הַשְּׁבִיעִי תִּשְׁבֹּת בֶּחָרִישׁ וּבַקָּצִיר
תִּשְׁבֹּת: וְחַג שָׁבֻעֹת תַּעֲשֶׂה לְךָ בִּכּוּרֵי קְצִיר
חִטִּים וְחַג הָאָסִיף תְּקוּפַת הַשָּׁנָה: שָׁלֹשׁ
פְּעָמִים בַּשָּׁנָה יֵרָאֶה כָּל־זְכוּרְךָ אֶת־פְּנֵי
הָאָדֹן ׀ יהוה אֱלֹהֵי יִשְׂרָאֵל: כִּי־אוֹרִישׁ גּוֹיִם
מִפָּנֶיךָ וְהִרְחַבְתִּי אֶת־גְּבֻלֶךָ וְלֹא־יַחְמֹד אִישׁ
אֶת־אַרְצְךָ בַּעֲלֹתְךָ לֵרָאוֹת אֶת־פְּנֵי יהוה
אֱלֹהֶיךָ שָׁלֹשׁ פְּעָמִים בַּשָּׁנָה: לֹא־תִשְׁחַט
עַל־חָמֵץ דַּם־זִבְחִי וְלֹא־יָלִין לַבֹּקֶר זֶבַח
חַג הַפָּסַח: רֵאשִׁית בִּכּוּרֵי אַדְמָתְךָ תָּבִיא
בֵּית יהוה אֱלֹהֶיךָ לֹא־תְבַשֵּׁל גְּדִי בַּחֲלֵב
אִמּוֹ:

(Numbers 28:19-25)

רביעי: וְהִקְרַבְתֶּם אִשֶּׁה עֹלָה לַיהוָה פָּרִים
בְּנֵי־בָקָר שְׁנַיִם וְאַיִל אֶחָד וְשִׁבְעָה כְבָשִׂים
בְּנֵי שָׁנָה תְּמִימִם יִהְיוּ לָכֶם: וּמִנְחָתָם סֹלֶת
בְּלוּלָה בַשָּׁמֶן שְׁלֹשָׁה עֶשְׂרֹנִים לַפָּר וּשְׁנֵי
עֶשְׂרֹנִים לָאַיִל תַּעֲשׂוּ: עִשָּׂרוֹן עִשָּׂרוֹן תַּעֲשֶׂה
לַכֶּבֶשׂ הָאֶחָד לְשִׁבְעַת הַכְּבָשִׂים: וּשְׂעִיר
חַטָּאת אֶחָד לְכַפֵּר עֲלֵיכֶם: מִלְּבַד עֹלַת
הַבֹּקֶר אֲשֶׁר לְעֹלַת הַתָּמִיד תַּעֲשׂוּ אֶת־
אֵלֶּה: כָּאֵלֶּה תַּעֲשׂוּ לַיּוֹם שִׁבְעַת יָמִים
לֶחֶם אִשֵּׁה רֵיחַ־נִיחֹחַ לַיהוָה עַל־עוֹלַת
הַתָּמִיד יֵעָשֶׂה וְנִסְכּוֹ: וּבַיּוֹם הַשְּׁבִיעִי מִקְרָא־
קֹדֶשׁ יִהְיֶה לָכֶם כָּל־מְלֶאכֶת עֲבֹדָה לֹא
תַעֲשׂוּ:

FOURTH DAY CHOL HAMOED PESACH

(Numbers 9:1-14)

כהן: וַיְדַבֵּר יהוה אֶל־מֹשֶׁה בְמִדְבַּר־סִינַי
בַּשָּׁנָה הַשֵּׁנִית לְצֵאתָם מֵאֶרֶץ מִצְרַיִם
בַּחֹדֶשׁ הָרִאשׁוֹן לֵאמֹר: וְיַעֲשׂוּ בְנֵי־יִשְׂרָאֵל
אֶת־הַפָּסַח בְּמוֹעֲדוֹ: בְּאַרְבָּעָה עָשָׂר־יוֹם
בַּחֹדֶשׁ הַזֶּה בֵּין הָעַרְבַּיִם תַּעֲשׂוּ אֹתוֹ בְּמֹעֲדוֹ
כְּכָל־חֻקֹּתָיו וּכְכָל־מִשְׁפָּטָיו תַּעֲשׂוּ אֹתוֹ:
וַיְדַבֵּר מֹשֶׁה אֶל־בְּנֵי יִשְׂרָאֵל לַעֲשֹׂת הַפָּסַח:

וַיַּעֲשׂוּ אֶת־הַפֶּסַח בָּרִאשׁוֹן בְּאַרְבָּעָה עָשָׂר יוֹם לַחֹדֶשׁ בֵּין הָעַרְבָּיִם בְּמִדְבַּר סִינָי כְּכֹל אֲשֶׁר צִוָּה יהוה אֶת־מֹשֶׁה כֵּן עָשׂוּ בְּנֵי יִשְׂרָאֵל:

לֵוִי: וַיְהִי אֲנָשִׁים אֲשֶׁר הָיוּ טְמֵאִים לְנֶפֶשׁ אָדָם וְלֹא־יָכְלוּ לַעֲשֹׂת־הַפֶּסַח בַּיּוֹם הַהוּא וַיִּקְרְבוּ לִפְנֵי מֹשֶׁה וְלִפְנֵי אַהֲרֹן בַּיּוֹם הַהוּא: וַיֹּאמְרוּ הָאֲנָשִׁים הָהֵמָּה אֵלָיו אֲנַחְנוּ טְמֵאִים לְנֶפֶשׁ אָדָם לָמָּה נִגָּרַע לְבִלְתִּי הַקְרִיב אֶת־קָרְבַּן יהוה בְּמֹעֲדוֹ בְּתוֹךְ בְּנֵי יִשְׂרָאֵל: וַיֹּאמֶר אֲלֵהֶם מֹשֶׁה עִמְדוּ וְאֶשְׁמְעָה מַה־יְצַוֶּה יהוה לָכֶם:

שְׁלִישִׁי: וַיְדַבֵּר יהוה אֶל־מֹשֶׁה לֵּאמֹר: דַּבֵּר אֶל־בְּנֵי יִשְׂרָאֵל לֵאמֹר אִישׁ אִישׁ כִּי־יִהְיֶה טָמֵא | לָנֶפֶשׁ אוֹ בְדֶרֶךְ רְחֹקָה לָכֶם אוֹ לְדֹרֹתֵיכֶם וְעָשָׂה פֶסַח לַיהוה: בַּחֹדֶשׁ הַשֵּׁנִי בְּאַרְבָּעָה עָשָׂר יוֹם בֵּין הָעַרְבָּיִם יַעֲשׂוּ אֹתוֹ עַל־מַצּוֹת וּמְרֹרִים יֹאכְלֻהוּ: לֹא־יַשְׁאִירוּ מִמֶּנּוּ עַד־בֹּקֶר וְעֶצֶם לֹא יִשְׁבְּרוּ־בוֹ כְּכָל־חֻקַּת הַפֶּסַח יַעֲשׂוּ אֹתוֹ: וְהָאִישׁ אֲשֶׁר־הוּא טָהוֹר וּבְדֶרֶךְ לֹא־הָיָה וְחָדַל לַעֲשׂוֹת הַפֶּסַח וְנִכְרְתָה הַנֶּפֶשׁ הַהִוא מֵעַמֶּיהָ כִּי | קָרְבַּן יהוה לֹא הִקְרִיב בְּמֹעֲדוֹ חֶטְאוֹ יִשָּׂא הָאִישׁ הַהוּא: וְכִי־יָגוּר אִתְּכֶם גֵּר וְעָשָׂה פֶסַח לַיהוה כְּחֻקַּת הַפֶּסַח וּכְמִשְׁפָּטוֹ כֵּן יַעֲשֶׂה חֻקָּה אַחַת יִהְיֶה לָכֶם וְלַגֵּר וּלְאֶזְרַח הָאָרֶץ:

(Numbers 28:19-25)

רְבִיעִי: וְהִקְרַבְתֶּם אִשֶּׁה עֹלָה לַיהוה פָּרִים בְּנֵי־בָקָר שְׁנַיִם וְאַיִל אֶחָד וְשִׁבְעָה כְבָשִׂים בְּנֵי שָׁנָה תְּמִימִם יִהְיוּ לָכֶם: וּמִנְחָתָם סֹלֶת בְּלוּלָה בַשָּׁמֶן שְׁלֹשָׁה עֶשְׂרֹנִים לַפָּר וּשְׁנֵי עֶשְׂרֹנִים לָאַיִל תַּעֲשׂוּ: עִשָּׂרוֹן עִשָּׂרוֹן תַּעֲשֶׂה לַכֶּבֶשׂ הָאֶחָד לְשִׁבְעַת הַכְּבָשִׂים: וּשְׂעִיר חַטָּאת אֶחָד לְכַפֵּר עֲלֵיכֶם: מִלְּבַד עֹלַת הַבֹּקֶר אֲשֶׁר לְעֹלַת הַתָּמִיד תַּעֲשׂוּ אֶת־אֵלֶּה: כָּאֵלֶּה תַּעֲשׂוּ לַיּוֹם שִׁבְעַת יָמִים לֶחֶם אִשֵּׁה רֵיחַ־נִיחֹחַ לַיהוה עַל־עוֹלַת הַתָּמִיד יֵעָשֶׂה וְנִסְכּוֹ: וּבַיּוֹם הַשְּׁבִיעִי מִקְרָא־קֹדֶשׁ יִהְיֶה לָכֶם כָּל־מְלֶאכֶת

עֲבֹדָה לֹא תַעֲשׂוּ:

TORAH READING FOR CHOL HAMOED SUCCOS

On each day of Chol HaMoed Succos (except on the Sabbath) one Torah is removed from the Ark and four *olim* are called to the Torah.
FOR HOSHANA RABBAH, SEE THE INTERLINEAR SIDDUR FOR THE SABBATH AND FESTIVALS.

FIRST DAY CHOL HAMOED SUCCOS

(Numbers 29:17-25)

כֹּהֵן: וּבַיּוֹם הַשֵּׁנִי פָּרִים בְּנֵי־בָקָר שְׁנֵים עָשָׂר אֵילִם שְׁנָיִם כְּבָשִׂים בְּנֵי־שָׁנָה אַרְבָּעָה עָשָׂר תְּמִימִם: וּמִנְחָתָם וְנִסְכֵּיהֶם לַפָּרִים לָאֵילִם וְלַכְּבָשִׂים בְּמִסְפָּרָם כַּמִּשְׁפָּט: וּשְׂעִיר־עִזִּים אֶחָד חַטָּאת מִלְּבַד עֹלַת הַתָּמִיד וּמִנְחָתָהּ וְנִסְכֵּיהֶם:

לֵוִי: וּבַיּוֹם הַשְּׁלִישִׁי פָּרִים עַשְׁתֵּי־עָשָׂר אֵילִם שְׁנָיִם כְּבָשִׂים בְּנֵי־שָׁנָה אַרְבָּעָה עָשָׂר תְּמִימִם: וּמִנְחָתָם וְנִסְכֵּיהֶם לַפָּרִים לָאֵילִם וְלַכְּבָשִׂים בְּמִסְפָּרָם כַּמִּשְׁפָּט: וּשְׂעִיר חַטָּאת אֶחָד מִלְּבַד עֹלַת הַתָּמִיד וּמִנְחָתָהּ וְנִסְכָּהּ:

שְׁלִישִׁי: וּבַיּוֹם הָרְבִיעִי פָּרִים עֲשָׂרָה אֵילִם שְׁנָיִם כְּבָשִׂים בְּנֵי־שָׁנָה אַרְבָּעָה עָשָׂר תְּמִימִם: מִנְחָתָם וְנִסְכֵּיהֶם לַפָּרִים לָאֵילִם וְלַכְּבָשִׂים בְּמִסְפָּרָם כַּמִּשְׁפָּט: וּשְׂעִיר־עִזִּים אֶחָד חַטָּאת מִלְּבַד עֹלַת הַתָּמִיד מִנְחָתָהּ וְנִסְכָּהּ:

רְבִיעִי: וּבַיּוֹם הַשֵּׁנִי פָּרִים בְּנֵי־בָקָר שְׁנֵים עָשָׂר אֵילִם שְׁנָיִם כְּבָשִׂים בְּנֵי־שָׁנָה אַרְבָּעָה עָשָׂר תְּמִימִם: וּמִנְחָתָם וְנִסְכֵּיהֶם לַפָּרִים לָאֵילִם וְלַכְּבָשִׂים בְּמִסְפָּרָם כַּמִּשְׁפָּט: וּבַיּוֹם הַשְּׁלִישִׁי פָּרִים עַשְׁתֵּי־עָשָׂר אֵילִם שְׁנָיִם כְּבָשִׂים בְּנֵי־שָׁנָה אַרְבָּעָה עָשָׂר תְּמִימִם: וּמִנְחָתָם וְנִסְכֵּיהֶם לָאֵילִם וְלַכְּבָשִׂים בְּמִסְפָּרָם כַּמִּשְׁפָּט: וּשְׂעִיר חַטָּאת אֶחָד מִלְּבַד עֹלַת הַתָּמִיד וּמִנְחָתָהּ וְנִסְכָּהּ:

SECOND DAY CHOL HAMOED SUCCOS

(Numbers 29:20-28)

כֹּהֵן: וּבַיּוֹם הַשְּׁלִישִׁי פָּרִים עַשְׁתֵּי־עָשָׂר אֵילִם שְׁנָיִם כְּבָשִׂים בְּנֵי־שָׁנָה אַרְבָּעָה עָשָׂר

מִלְּבַד עֹלַת הַתָּמִיד מִנְחָתָהּ וְנִסְכֶּיהָ:
רביעי: וּבַיּוֹם הָרְבִיעִי פָּרִים עֲשָׂרָה אֵילִם שְׁנָיִם
כְּבָשִׂים בְּנֵי־שָׁנָה אַרְבָּעָה עָשָׂר תְּמִימִם:
מִנְחָתָם וְנִסְכֵּיהֶם ׀ לַפָּרִים לָאֵילִם וְלַכְּבָשִׂים
בְּמִסְפָּרָם כַּמִּשְׁפָּט: וּשְׂעִיר־עִזִּים אֶחָד
חַטָּאת מִלְּבַד עֹלַת הַתָּמִיד מִנְחָתָהּ וְנִסְכָּהּ:
וּבַיּוֹם הַחֲמִישִׁי פָּרִים תִּשְׁעָה אֵילִם שְׁנָיִם
כְּבָשִׂים בְּנֵי־שָׁנָה אַרְבָּעָה עָשָׂר תְּמִימִם:
וּמִנְחָתָם וְנִסְכֵּיהֶם ׀ לַפָּרִים לָאֵילִם וְלַכְּבָשִׂים
בְּמִסְפָּרָם כַּמִּשְׁפָּט: וּשְׂעִיר חַטָּאת אֶחָד
מִלְּבַד עֹלַת הַתָּמִיד וּמִנְחָתָהּ וְנִסְכָּהּ:

(Numbers 29:26-34)

כח: וּבַיּוֹם הַחֲמִישִׁי פָּרִים תִּשְׁעָה אֵילִם שְׁנָיִם
כְּבָשִׂים בְּנֵי־שָׁנָה אַרְבָּעָה עָשָׂר תְּמִימִם:
וּמִנְחָתָם וְנִסְכֵּיהֶם ׀ לַפָּרִים לָאֵילִם וְלַכְּבָשִׂים
בְּמִסְפָּרָם כַּמִּשְׁפָּט: וּשְׂעִיר חַטָּאת אֶחָד
מִלְּבַד עֹלַת הַתָּמִיד וּמִנְחָתָהּ וְנִסְכָּהּ:
לוי: וּבַיּוֹם הַשִּׁשִּׁי פָּרִים שְׁמֹנָה אֵילִם שְׁנָיִם
כְּבָשִׂים בְּנֵי־שָׁנָה אַרְבָּעָה עָשָׂר תְּמִימִם:
וּמִנְחָתָם וְנִסְכֵּיהֶם ׀ לַפָּרִים לָאֵילִם וְלַכְּבָשִׂים
בְּמִסְפָּרָם כַּמִּשְׁפָּט: וּשְׂעִיר חַטָּאת אֶחָד
מִלְּבַד עֹלַת הַתָּמִיד מִנְחָתָהּ וּנְסָכֶיהָ:
שלישי: וּבַיּוֹם הַשְּׁבִיעִי פָּרִים שִׁבְעָה אֵילִם
שְׁנָיִם כְּבָשִׂים בְּנֵי־שָׁנָה אַרְבָּעָה עָשָׂר
תְּמִימִם: וּמִנְחָתָם וְנִסְכֵּהֶם ׀ לַפָּרִים לָאֵילִם
וְלַכְּבָשִׂים בְּמִסְפָּרָם כְּמִשְׁפָּטָם: וּשְׂעִיר
חַטָּאת אֶחָד מִלְּבַד עֹלַת הַתָּמִיד מִנְחָתָהּ
וְנִסְכָּהּ:
רביעי: וּבַיּוֹם הַחֲמִישִׁי פָּרִים תִּשְׁעָה אֵילִם
שְׁנָיִם כְּבָשִׂים בְּנֵי־שָׁנָה אַרְבָּעָה עָשָׂר
תְּמִימִם: וּמִנְחָתָם וְנִסְכֵּיהֶם ׀ לַפָּרִים לָאֵילִם
וְלַכְּבָשִׂים בְּמִסְפָּרָם כַּמִּשְׁפָּט: וּשְׂעִיר חַטָּאת
אֶחָד מִלְּבַד עֹלַת הַתָּמִיד וּמִנְחָתָהּ וְנִסְכָּהּ:
וּבַיּוֹם הַשִּׁשִּׁי פָּרִים שְׁמֹנָה אֵילִם שְׁנָיִם
כְּבָשִׂים בְּנֵי־שָׁנָה אַרְבָּעָה עָשָׂר תְּמִימִם:
וּמִנְחָתָם וְנִסְכֵּיהֶם ׀ לַפָּרִים לָאֵילִם וְלַכְּבָשִׂים
בְּמִסְפָּרָם כַּמִּשְׁפָּט: וּשְׂעִיר חַטָּאת אֶחָד
מִלְּבַד עֹלַת הַתָּמִיד מִנְחָתָה וְנִסְכֶּיהָ:

תְּמִימִם: וּמִנְחָתָם וְנִסְכֵּיהֶם ׀ לַפָּרִים לָאֵילִם
וְלַכְּבָשִׂים בְּמִסְפָּרָם כַּמִּשְׁפָּט: וּשְׂעִיר חַטָּאת
אֶחָד מִלְּבַד עֹלַת הַתָּמִיד וּמִנְחָתָהּ וְנִסְכָּהּ:
לוי: וּבַיּוֹם הָרְבִיעִי פָּרִים עֲשָׂרָה אֵילִם שְׁנָיִם
כְּבָשִׂים בְּנֵי־שָׁנָה אַרְבָּעָה עָשָׂר תְּמִימִם:
מִנְחָתָם וְנִסְכֵּיהֶם ׀ לַפָּרִים לָאֵילִם וְלַכְּבָשִׂים
בְּמִסְפָּרָם כַּמִּשְׁפָּט: וּשְׂעִיר־עִזִּים אֶחָד
חַטָּאת מִלְּבַד עֹלַת הַתָּמִיד מִנְחָתָהּ וְנִסְכָּהּ:
שלישי: וּבַיּוֹם הַחֲמִישִׁי פָּרִים תִּשְׁעָה אֵילִם
שְׁנָיִם כְּבָשִׂים בְּנֵי־שָׁנָה אַרְבָּעָה עָשָׂר
תְּמִימִם: וּמִנְחָתָם וְנִסְכֵּיהֶם ׀ לַפָּרִים לָאֵילִם
וְלַכְּבָשִׂים בְּמִסְפָּרָם כַּמִּשְׁפָּט: וּשְׂעִיר חַטָּאת
אֶחָד מִלְּבַד עֹלַת הַתָּמִיד וּמִנְחָתָהּ וְנִסְכָּהּ:
רביעי: וּבַיּוֹם הַשְּׁלִישִׁי פָּרִים עַשְׁתֵּי־עָשָׂר
אֵילִם שְׁנָיִם כְּבָשִׂים בְּנֵי־שָׁנָה אַרְבָּעָה עָשָׂר
תְּמִימִם: וּמִנְחָתָם וְנִסְכֵּיהֶם ׀ לַפָּרִים לָאֵילִם
וְלַכְּבָשִׂים בְּמִסְפָּרָם כַּמִּשְׁפָּט: וּשְׂעִיר חַטָּאת
אֶחָד מִלְּבַד עֹלַת הַתָּמִיד וּמִנְחָתָהּ וְנִסְכָּהּ:
וּבַיּוֹם הָרְבִיעִי פָּרִים עֲשָׂרָה אֵילִם שְׁנָיִם
כְּבָשִׂים בְּנֵי־שָׁנָה אַרְבָּעָה עָשָׂר תְּמִימִם:
מִנְחָתָם וְנִסְכֵּיהֶם ׀ לַפָּרִים לָאֵילִם וְלַכְּבָשִׂים
בְּמִסְפָּרָם כַּמִּשְׁפָּט: וּשְׂעִיר־עִזִּים אֶחָד
חַטָּאת מִלְּבַד עֹלַת הַתָּמִיד מִנְחָתָהּ וְנִסְכָּהּ:

(Numbers 29:23-31)

כח: וּבַיּוֹם הָרְבִיעִי פָּרִים עֲשָׂרָה אֵילִם שְׁנָיִם
כְּבָשִׂים בְּנֵי־שָׁנָה אַרְבָּעָה עָשָׂר תְּמִימִם:
מִנְחָתָם וְנִסְכֵּיהֶם ׀ לַפָּרִים לָאֵילִם וְלַכְּבָשִׂים
בְּמִסְפָּרָם כַּמִּשְׁפָּט: וּשְׂעִיר־עִזִּים אֶחָד
חַטָּאת מִלְּבַד עֹלַת הַתָּמִיד מִנְחָתָהּ וְנִסְכָּהּ:
לוי: וּבַיּוֹם הַחֲמִישִׁי פָּרִים תִּשְׁעָה אֵילִם שְׁנָיִם
כְּבָשִׂים בְּנֵי־שָׁנָה אַרְבָּעָה עָשָׂר תְּמִימִם:
וּמִנְחָתָם וְנִסְכֵּיהֶם ׀ לַפָּרִים לָאֵילִם וְלַכְּבָשִׂים
בְּמִסְפָּרָם כַּמִּשְׁפָּט: וּשְׂעִיר חַטָּאת אֶחָד
מִלְּבַד עֹלַת הַתָּמִיד וּמִנְחָתָהּ וְנִסְכָּהּ:
שלישי: וּבַיּוֹם הַשִּׁשִּׁי פָּרִים שְׁמֹנָה אֵילִם שְׁנָיִם
כְּבָשִׂים בְּנֵי־שָׁנָה אַרְבָּעָה עָשָׂר תְּמִימִם:
וּמִנְחָתָם וְנִסְכֵּיהֶם ׀ לַפָּרִים לָאֵילִם וְלַכְּבָשִׂים
בְּמִסְפָּרָם כַּמִּשְׁפָּט: וּשְׂעִיר חַטָּאת אֶחָד

❧ THE READING OF THE PRINCES' GIFTS / פרשת הנשיאים ❧

THE *SH'LAH* TEACHES THAT STARTING ON ROSH CHODESH NISSAN, ONE SHOULD RECITE EVERY DAY, THE PORTION OF פָּרָשַׁת הַנְּשִׂאִים (P. 789), THAT CORRESPONDS TO THAT DAY: ON THE FIRST OF NISSAN, ONE STARTS — AS ON THE FIRST DAY OF CHANUKAH — EITHER WITH בִּרְכַּת כֹּהֲנִים OR WITH וַיְהִי בְּיוֹם כַּלּוֹת מֹשֶׁה. ON THE THIRTEENTH DAY OF NISSAN ONE READS FROM THE BEGINNING OF *PARSHAS BEHA'ALOSCHA* UNTIL כֵּן עָשָׂה אֶת הַמְּנוֹרָה. MANY CONGREGATIONS READ UNTIL כֵּן עָשָׂה אֶת הַמְּנוֹרָה ON THE TWELFTH AND DO NOT RECITE AT ALL ON THE THIRTEENTH. MOST SOURCES SUGGEST THAT THE READINGS BE RECITED AT THE END OF *SHACHARIS*, AND ON ROSH CHODESH AFTER *MUSSAF*. SOME CONGREGATIONS READ FROM A PRINTED TEXT WHILE OTHERS READ FROM A SEFER TORAH (BUT WITHOUT RECITING A BLESSSING).

ON EVERY DAY AFTER THE READING, ONE RECITES THE FOLLOWING PRAYER:

יְהִי רָצוֹן מִלְּפָנֶיךָ יהוה אֱלֹהַי וֵאלֹהֵי אֲבוֹתַי, שֶׁתָּאִיר הַיּוֹם

⟨ today ⟩ that You shine ⟨⟨ of my forefathers, ⟩ and the God ⟩ my God ⟨ HASHEM, ⟨⟨ before You, ⟩ the will ⟨ May it be

בְּחַסְדְּךָ הַגָּדוֹל עַל נִשְׁמָתִין קַדִּישִׁין דְּמִתְרַחֲשִׁין כְּצִפְּרִין

⟨⟨ like birds, ⟨ that twitter ⟨⟨ that are holy, ⟨ the souls ⟨ on ⟨ with Your great kindness

וּמְצַפְצְפִין וּמְשַׁבְּחִין וּמְצַלְּאִין עַל עַמָּא קַדִּישָׁא יִשְׂרָאֵל.

⟨⟨ Israel. ⟨ the holy nation ⟨ for ⟨ and pray ⟨ and praise ⟨ and chirp

רִבּוֹנוֹ שֶׁל עוֹלָם, תַּכְנִיס וּתְעַיֵּיל הַנָּךְ צִיפְּרָא קַדִּישָׁא לַאֲתַר

⟨ to the place ⟨ that are holy ⟨ birds ⟨ these ⟨ and bring in ⟨ insert ⟨⟨ of the universe, ⟨ Master

קַדִּישָׁא דְּאִתְּמַר עֲלַיְיהוּ עַיִן לֹא רָאֲתָה אֱלֹהִים זוּלָתֶךָ.[1]

⟨⟨ besides You. ⟨ O God, ⟨ has seen [it], ⟨ No eye ⟨⟨ about it: ⟨ that it is said ⟨⟨ that is holy,

יְהִי רָצוֹן מִלְּפָנֶיךָ, יהוה אֱלֹהַי וֵאלֹהֵי אֲבוֹתַי, שֶׁבְּאָם אֲנִי עַבְדְּךָ

⟨ Your servant, ⟨ I, ⟨ that if ⟨⟨ of my forefathers, ⟨ and the God ⟨ My God ⟨ HASHEM, ⟨⟨ before You, ⟨ the will ⟨ May it be

מִשֵּׁבֶט (SPECIFY TRIBE OF THE DAY) שֶׁקָּרָאתִי בְּתוֹרָתֶךָ פָּרָשָׁה שֶׁל

⟨ of ⟨ the section ⟨ in Your Torah ⟨ that I read ⟨ [am] from the tribe

הַנָּשִׂיא הַיּוֹם, אֲזַי יָאִירוּ נָא עָלַי כָּל נִיצוֹצִין קַדִּישִׁין וְכָל

⟨ and all ⟨ of holiness ⟨ the sparks ⟨— all ⟨ upon me ⟨ may they please be illuminated ⟨ then ⟨⟨ today, ⟨ [its] prince

הָאוֹרוֹת הַקְּדוֹשׁוֹת הַכְּלוּלוֹת בִּקְדֻשַׁת זֶה הַשֵּׁבֶט, לְהָבִין

⟨ so that I understand ⟨⟨ of this tribe — ⟨ by the sanctity ⟨ that are encompassed ⟨ that are holy ⟨ the illuminations

וּלְהַשְׂכִּיל בְּתוֹרָתֶךָ וּבְיִרְאָתֶךָ, לַעֲשׂוֹת רְצוֹנָךְ כָּל יְמֵי חַיַּי,

⟨⟨ of my life ⟨ the days ⟨ all ⟨⟨ Your will, ⟨ in order that ⟨⟨ and the fear due You, ⟨ Your Torah ⟨ and comprehend I fulfill

אֲנִי וְזַרְעִי וְזֶרַע זַרְעִי, מֵעַתָּה וְעַד עוֹלָם, אָמֵן. סֶלָה.

⟨⟨ Selah! ⟨ Amen, ⟨⟨ eternity. ⟨ until ⟨ from this time ⟨⟨ of my children — ⟨ and the children ⟨ my children, ⟨ — I,

---

(1) *Isaiah* 64:3; see *Rashi*.

תְּהִלִּים ❧
Psalms

הֲלָכוֹת ❧
Laws

﴾ תפלה קודם אמירת תהלים ﴿
﴾ PRAYER BEFORE RECITING TEHILLIM ﴿

ON THE SABBATH AND ON FESTIVALS BEGIN WITH לְכוּ נְרַנְּנָה, *COME! LET US SING* . . . (PAGE 805).

יְהִי רָצוֹן מִלְּפָנֶיךָ יהוה אֱלֹהֵינוּ וֵאלֹהֵי אֲבוֹתֵינוּ
‹ of our forefathers ‹ and the God ‹ our God ‹ HASHEM, ‹ before You, ‹ the will ‹ May it be

הַבּוֹחֵר בְּדָוִד עַבְדּוֹ וּבְזַרְעוֹ אַחֲרָיו, וְהַבּוֹחֵר בְּשִׁירוֹת —
‹ songs ‹ and Who chose ‹‹ after him, ‹ and his offspring ‹ His servant ‹ David ‹ — Who chose

וְתִשְׁבָּחוֹת — שֶׁתֵּפֶן בְּרַחֲמִים אֶל קְרִיאַת מִזְמוֹרֵי תְהִלִּים
‹ of psalms ‹ the recitation ‹ to ‹ with mercy ‹ that you attend ‹‹ and praises —

שֶׁאֶקְרָא כְּאִלּוּ אֲמָרָם דָּוִד הַמֶּלֶךְ עָלָיו הַשָּׁלוֹם בְּעַצְמוֹ,
‹‹ himself, ‹ of blessed memory, ‹‹ by King David, ‹ they were recited ‹ [and consider it] as if ‹ that I shall recite

זְכוּתוֹ יָגֵן עָלֵינוּ. וְתַעֲמוֹד לָנוּ זְכוּת פְּסוּקֵי תְהִלִּים — וּזְכוּת
‹ — [together with] the merit ‹‹ of the psalms ‹ of the verses ‹ may the merit ‹ in our favor ‹ And stand ‹‹ over us. ‹ be a shield ‹ may his merit

תֵּבוֹתֵיהֶם וְאוֹתִיּוֹתֵיהֶם וּנְקוּדוֹתֵיהֶם וְטַעֲמֵיהֶם וְהַשֵּׁמוֹת
‹ and [together with] the Holy Names ‹‹ and their cantillations, ‹ and their vowels ‹ and their letters ‹ of their words

הַיּוֹצְאִים מֵהֶם מֵרָאשֵׁי תֵבוֹת וּמִסּוֹפֵי תֵבוֹת — לְכַפֵּר
‹ — [may their merit serve] to bring atonement ‹‹ of the words ‹ and from the final [letters] ‹ of the words ‹ from the initial [letters] ‹‹ from them, ‹ that are formed

פְּשָׁעֵינוּ וַעֲוֹנוֹתֵינוּ וְחַטֹּאתֵינוּ; וּלְזַמֵּר עָרִיצִים וּלְהַכְרִית כָּל
‹ all ‹ and slash away ‹ ruthless men, ‹ and to cut down ‹‹ and sins; ‹ iniquities, ‹ for our transgressions,

הַחוֹחִים וְהַקּוֹצִים הַסּוֹבְבִים אֶת הַשּׁוֹשַׁנָּה הָעֶלְיוֹנָה; וּלְחַבֵּר
‹ and to unite ‹‹ Celestial; ‹ the Rose, ‹ which surround ‹ and briars ‹ the thorns

אֵשֶׁת נְעוּרִים עִם דּוֹדָהּ בְּאַהֲבָה וְאַחֲוָה וְרֵעוּת. וּמִשָּׁם יִמָּשֵׁךְ
‹ may be drawn ‹ And from that ‹‹ and com- panionship. ‹ brother- hood, ‹ in love, ‹ her Beloved ‹ with ‹ of Youth ‹ the Bride

לָנוּ שֶׁפַע לְנֶפֶשׁ רוּחַ וּנְשָׁמָה, לְטַהֲרֵנוּ מֵעֲוֹנוֹתֵינוּ וְלִסְלוֹחַ
‹ to forgive ‹ of our iniquities, ‹ to purify us ‹‹ and soul, ‹ breath ‹ to our spirit, ‹ an abundant blessing ‹ to us

חַטֹּאתֵינוּ וּלְכַפֵּר פְּשָׁעֵינוּ. כְּמוֹ שֶׁסָּלַחְתָּ לְדָוִד שֶׁאָמַר
‹ Who recited ‹ David ‹ You forgave ‹ just as ‹ for our transgressions, ‹ and to atone ‹ our sins

מִזְמוֹרִים אֵלּוּ לְפָנֶיךָ — כְּמוֹ שֶׁנֶּאֱמַר: גַּם יהוה הֶעֱבִיר
‹ has forgiven ‹ HASHEM also ‹‹ it is said: ‹ — as ‹‹ before You ‹ these very same psalms

חֲטָאתְךָ לֹא תָמוּת. וְאַל תִּקָּחֵנוּ מֵהָעוֹלָם הַזֶּה קוֹדֶם זְמַנֵּנוּ

your sin, you shall not die. May You not take us from This World before our time,

עַד מְלֹאת שְׁנוֹתֵינוּ (בָּהֶם שִׁבְעִים שָׁנָה)[1] בְּאוֹפָן שֶׁנּוּכַל

until the completion of our years, (among them are seventy years,) in a manner that we be able

לְתַקֵּן אֶת אֲשֶׁר שִׁחַתְנוּ. וּזְכוּת דָּוִד הַמֶּלֶךְ עָלָיו הַשָּׁלוֹם יָגֵן

to rectify anything that we have ruined. May the merit of King David, of blessed memory, shield

עָלֵינוּ וּבַעֲדֵנוּ, שֶׁתַּאֲרִיךְ אַפְּךָ עַד שׁוּבֵנוּ אֵלֶיךָ בִּתְשׁוּבָה

over us and for us; that You may be patient [with us], [and wait] until we return to You in repentance

שְׁלֵמָה לְפָנֶיךָ. וּמֵאוֹצַר מַתְּנַת חִנָּם חָנֵּנוּ, כְּדִכְתִיב: וְחַנֹּתִי

complete before You. From Your treasury of grace that is undeserved, be gracious to us, as it is written: — I am Compassionate

אֶת אֲשֶׁר אָחֹן וְרִחַמְתִּי אֶת אֲשֶׁר אֲרַחֵם. וּכְשֵׁם שֶׁאָנוּ

to those upon whom I favor, and I am Merciful to those upon whom I have mercy. And just as we

אוֹמְרִים לְפָנֶיךָ שִׁירָה בָּעוֹלָם הַזֶּה, כַּךְ נִזְכֶּה לוֹמַר לְפָנֶיךָ,

recite before You a song in This World, so let us merit to recite before You,

יהוה אֱלֹהֵינוּ, שִׁיר וּשְׁבָחָה לָעוֹלָם הַבָּא. וְעַל יְדֵי אֲמִירַת

O Hashem, our God — songs and praises in the World to Come. And through the recitation

תְּהִלִּים תִּתְעוֹרֵר חֲבַצֶּלֶת הַשָּׁרוֹן לָשִׁיר בְּקוֹל נָעִים בְּגִילַת

of the psalms arouse the Rose of Sharon to sing with a pleasant voice, with ecstasy that is

וְרַנֵּן, כְּבוֹד הַלְּבָנוֹן נִתַּן לָהּ, הוֹד וְהָדָר בְּבֵית אֱלֹהֵינוּ, בִּמְהֵרָה

and joy. May the glory of Lebanon be given to her, majesty and splendor in the House of our God, speedily

בְּיָמֵינוּ, אָמֵן סֶלָה.

in our days. Amen. Selah!

לְכוּ נְרַנְּנָה לַיהוה, נָרִיעָה לְצוּר יִשְׁעֵנוּ. נְקַדְּמָה פָנָיו

Come! Let us sing joyfully to Hashem, let us call out to the Rock of our Salvation. Let us greet Him

בְּתוֹדָה, בִּזְמִרוֹת נָרִיעַ לוֹ. כִּי אֵל גָּדוֹל יהוה, וּמֶלֶךְ גָּדוֹל עַל

with thanksgiving, with praiseful songs let us call out to Him. For Hashem is a great God, and a great King above

כָּל אֱלֹהִים.

all heavenly powers.

---

1. Although this phrase appears in most editions, *Mishnah Berurah* (581:3) deletes it.

‭﷽‬ ספר ראשון / BOOK ONE ‭﷽‬

‭﷽‬ יום ראשון / SUNDAY ‭﷽‬

DAY 1 — יום א' לחודש

א אַשְׁרֵי הָאִישׁ אֲשֶׁר לֹא הָלַךְ בַּעֲצַת רְשָׁעִים, וּבְדֶרֶךְ חַטָּאִים לֹא עָמָד, וּבְמוֹשַׁב לֵצִים לֹא יָשָׁב. כִּי אִם בְּתוֹרַת יהוה חֶפְצוֹ, וּבְתוֹרָתוֹ יֶהְגֶּה יוֹמָם וָלָיְלָה. וְהָיָה כְּעֵץ שָׁתוּל עַל פַּלְגֵי מָיִם; אֲשֶׁר פִּרְיוֹ יִתֵּן בְּעִתּוֹ, וְעָלֵהוּ לֹא יִבּוֹל, וְכֹל אֲשֶׁר יַעֲשֶׂה יַצְלִיחַ. לֹא כֵן הָרְשָׁעִים, כִּי אִם כַּמֹּץ אֲשֶׁר תִּדְּפֶנּוּ רוּחַ. עַל כֵּן לֹא יָקֻמוּ רְשָׁעִים בַּמִּשְׁפָּט, וְחַטָּאִים בַּעֲדַת צַדִּיקִים. כִּי יוֹדֵעַ יהוה דֶּרֶךְ צַדִּיקִים, וְדֶרֶךְ רְשָׁעִים תֹּאבֵד.

ב לָמָּה רָגְשׁוּ גוֹיִם, וּלְאֻמִּים יֶהְגּוּ רִיק. יִתְיַצְּבוּ מַלְכֵי אֶרֶץ, וְרוֹזְנִים נוֹסְדוּ יָחַד, עַל יהוה וְעַל מְשִׁיחוֹ. נְנַתְּקָה אֶת מוֹסְרוֹתֵימוֹ, וְנַשְׁלִיכָה מִמֶּנּוּ עֲבֹתֵימוֹ. יוֹשֵׁב בַּשָּׁמַיִם יִשְׂחָק, אֲדֹנָי יִלְעַג לָמוֹ. אָז יְדַבֵּר אֵלֵימוֹ בְאַפּוֹ, וּבַחֲרוֹנוֹ יְבַהֲלֵמוֹ. וַאֲנִי נָסַכְתִּי מַלְכִּי, עַל צִיּוֹן הַר קָדְשִׁי. אֲסַפְּרָה אֶל חֹק, יהוה אָמַר אֵלַי בְּנִי אַתָּה, אֲנִי הַיּוֹם יְלִדְתִּיךָ. שְׁאַל מִמֶּנִּי וְאֶתְּנָה גוֹיִם נַחֲלָתֶךָ, וַאֲחֻזָּתְךָ אַפְסֵי אָרֶץ. תְּרֹעֵם בְּשֵׁבֶט בַּרְזֶל, כִּכְלִי יוֹצֵר תְּנַפְּצֵם. וְעַתָּה מְלָכִים הַשְׂכִּילוּ, הִוָּסְרוּ שֹׁפְטֵי אָרֶץ. עִבְדוּ אֶת יהוה בְּיִרְאָה, וְגִילוּ בִּרְעָדָה. נַשְּׁקוּ בַר, פֶּן יֶאֱנַף וְתֹאבְדוּ דֶרֶךְ, כִּי יִבְעַר כִּמְעַט אַפּוֹ; אַשְׁרֵי כָּל חוֹסֵי בוֹ.

ג מִזְמוֹר לְדָוִד, בְּבָרְחוֹ מִפְּנֵי אַבְשָׁלוֹם בְּנוֹ. יהוה, מָה רַבּוּ צָרָי, רַבִּים קָמִים עָלָי. רַבִּים אֹמְרִים לְנַפְשִׁי, אֵין יְשׁוּעָתָה לּוֹ בֵאלֹהִים סֶלָה. וְאַתָּה יהוה מָגֵן בַּעֲדִי, כְּבוֹדִי וּמֵרִים רֹאשִׁי. קוֹלִי אֶל יהוה אֶקְרָא, וַיַּעֲנֵנִי מֵהַר קָדְשׁוֹ סֶלָה. אֲנִי שָׁכַבְתִּי וָאִישָׁנָה, הֱקִיצוֹתִי, כִּי יהוה

יִסְמְכֵנִי. לֹא אִירָא מֵרִבְבוֹת עָם, אֲשֶׁר סָבִיב שָׁתוּ עָלָי. קוּמָה יהוה, הוֹשִׁיעֵנִי אֱלֹהַי, כִּי הִכִּיתָ אֶת כָּל אֹיְבַי לֶחִי, שִׁנֵּי רְשָׁעִים שִׁבַּרְתָּ. לַיהוה הַיְשׁוּעָה, עַל עַמְּךָ בִרְכָתֶךָ סֶּלָה.

ד לַמְנַצֵּחַ בִּנְגִינוֹת מִזְמוֹר לְדָוִד. בְּקָרְאִי עֲנֵנִי אֱלֹהֵי צִדְקִי, בַּצָּר הִרְחַבְתָּ לִּי, חָנֵּנִי וּשְׁמַע תְּפִלָּתִי. בְּנֵי אִישׁ, עַד מֶה כְבוֹדִי לִכְלִמָּה, תֶּאֱהָבוּן רִיק, תְּבַקְשׁוּ כָזָב סֶלָה. וּדְעוּ כִּי הִפְלָה יהוה חָסִיד לוֹ, יהוה יִשְׁמַע בְּקָרְאִי אֵלָיו. רִגְזוּ וְאַל תֶּחֱטָאוּ; אִמְרוּ בִלְבַבְכֶם עַל מִשְׁכַּבְכֶם, וְדֹמּוּ סֶלָה. זִבְחוּ זִבְחֵי צֶדֶק, וּבִטְחוּ אֶל יהוה. רַבִּים אֹמְרִים: מִי יַרְאֵנוּ טוֹב, נְסָה עָלֵינוּ אוֹר פָּנֶיךָ, יהוה. נָתַתָּה שִׂמְחָה בְלִבִּי, מֵעֵת דְּגָנָם וְתִירוֹשָׁם רָבּוּ. בְּשָׁלוֹם יַחְדָּו אֶשְׁכְּבָה וְאִישָׁן, כִּי אַתָּה יהוה לְבָדָד לָבֶטַח תּוֹשִׁיבֵנִי.

ה לַמְנַצֵּחַ, אֶל הַנְּחִילוֹת, מִזְמוֹר לְדָוִד. אֲמָרַי הַאֲזִינָה | יהוה, בִּינָה הֲגִיגִי. הַקְשִׁיבָה לְקוֹל שַׁוְעִי, מַלְכִּי וֵאלֹהָי, כִּי אֵלֶיךָ אֶתְפַּלָּל. יהוה, בֹּקֶר תִּשְׁמַע קוֹלִי, בֹּקֶר אֶעֱרָךְ לְךָ, וַאֲצַפֶּה. כִּי לֹא אֵל חָפֵץ רֶשַׁע | אָתָּה, לֹא יְגֻרְךָ רָע. לֹא יִתְיַצְּבוּ הוֹלְלִים לְנֶגֶד עֵינֶיךָ, שָׂנֵאתָ כָּל פֹּעֲלֵי אָוֶן. תְּאַבֵּד דֹּבְרֵי כָזָב, אִישׁ דָּמִים וּמִרְמָה יְתָעֵב | יהוה. וַאֲנִי בְּרֹב חַסְדְּךָ אָבוֹא בֵיתֶךָ, אֶשְׁתַּחֲוֶה אֶל הֵיכַל קָדְשְׁךָ בְּיִרְאָתֶךָ. יהוה, נְחֵנִי בְצִדְקָתֶךָ לְמַעַן שׁוֹרְרָי, הַיְשַׁר לְפָנַי דַּרְכֶּךָ. כִּי אֵין בְּפִיהוּ נְכוֹנָה, קִרְבָּם הַוּוֹת; קֶבֶר פָּתוּחַ גְּרֹנָם, לְשׁוֹנָם יַחֲלִיקוּן. הַאֲשִׁימֵם אֱלֹהִים; בְּרֹב פִּשְׁעֵיהֶם הַדִּיחֵמוֹ, כִּי מָרוּ בָךְ. וְיִשְׂמְחוּ כָל חוֹסֵי בָךְ, לְעוֹלָם יְרַנֵּנוּ, וְתָסֵךְ עָלֵימוֹ, וְיַעְלְצוּ בְךָ אֹהֲבֵי שְׁמֶךָ. כִּי אַתָּה תְּבָרֵךְ צַדִּיק; יהוה, כַּצִּנָּה רָצוֹן תַּעְטְרֶנּוּ.

ו לַמְנַצֵּחַ בִּנְגִינוֹת עַל הַשְּׁמִינִית, מִזְמוֹר לְדָוִד. יהוה, אַל בְּאַפְּךָ תוֹכִיחֵנִי, וְאַל בַּחֲמָתְךָ תְיַסְּרֵנִי. חָנֵּנִי יהוה כִּי אֻמְלַל אָנִי, רְפָאֵנִי יהוה כִּי נִבְהֲלוּ עֲצָמָי. וְנַפְשִׁי נִבְהֲלָה מְאֹד, וְאַתָּה יהוה עַד מָתָי. שׁוּבָה יהוה חַלְּצָה נַפְשִׁי, הוֹשִׁיעֵנִי לְמַעַן חַסְדֶּךָ. כִּי אֵין בַּמָּוֶת זִכְרֶךָ, בִּשְׁאוֹל מִי יוֹדֶה לָּךְ. יָגַעְתִּי בְּאַנְחָתִי, אַשְׂחֶה בְכָל לַיְלָה מִטָּתִי, בְּדִמְעָתִי עַרְשִׂי אַמְסֶה. עָשְׁשָׁה מִכַּעַס עֵינִי, עָתְקָה בְּכָל צוֹרְרָי. סוּרוּ מִמֶּנִּי כָּל פֹּעֲלֵי אָוֶן, כִּי שָׁמַע יהוה קוֹל בִּכְיִי. שָׁמַע יהוה תְּחִנָּתִי, יהוה תְּפִלָּתִי יִקָּח. יֵבֹשׁוּ וְיִבָּהֲלוּ מְאֹד כָּל אֹיְבָי, יָשֻׁבוּ יֵבֹשׁוּ רָגַע.

ז שִׁגָּיוֹן לְדָוִד, אֲשֶׁר שָׁר לַיהוה, עַל דִּבְרֵי כוּשׁ בֶּן יְמִינִי. יהוה אֱלֹהַי בְּךָ חָסִיתִי, הוֹשִׁיעֵנִי מִכָּל רֹדְפַי וְהַצִּילֵנִי. פֶּן יִטְרֹף כְּאַרְיֵה נַפְשִׁי, פֹּרֵק וְאֵין מַצִּיל. יהוה אֱלֹהַי, אִם עָשִׂיתִי זֹאת, אִם יֶשׁ עָוֶל בְּכַפָּי. אִם גָּמַלְתִּי שׁוֹלְמִי רָע, וָאֲחַלְּצָה צוֹרְרִי רֵיקָם. יִרַדֹּף אוֹיֵב נַפְשִׁי וְיַשֵּׂג, וְיִרְמֹס לָאָרֶץ חַיָּי, וּכְבוֹדִי לֶעָפָר יַשְׁכֵּן סֶלָה. קוּמָה יהוה בְּאַפֶּךָ, הִנָּשֵׂא בְּעַבְרוֹת צוֹרְרָי, וְעוּרָה אֵלַי מִשְׁפָּט צִוִּיתָ. וַעֲדַת לְאֻמִּים תְּסוֹבְבֶךָּ, וְעָלֶיהָ לַמָּרוֹם שׁוּבָה. יהוה יָדִין עַמִּים; שָׁפְטֵנִי יהוה, כְּצִדְקִי וּכְתֻמִּי עָלָי. יִגְמָר נָא רַע רְשָׁעִים, וּתְכוֹנֵן צַדִּיק, וּבֹחֵן לִבּוֹת וּכְלָיוֹת אֱלֹהִים צַדִּיק. מָגִנִּי עַל אֱלֹהִים, מוֹשִׁיעַ יִשְׁרֵי לֵב. אֱלֹהִים שׁוֹפֵט צַדִּיק, וְאֵל זֹעֵם בְּכָל יוֹם. אִם לֹא יָשׁוּב, חַרְבּוֹ יִלְטוֹשׁ, קַשְׁתּוֹ דָרַךְ וַיְכוֹנְנֶהָ. וְלוֹ הֵכִין כְּלֵי מָוֶת, חִצָּיו לְדֹלְקִים יִפְעָל. הִנֵּה יְחַבֶּל אָוֶן, וְהָרָה עָמָל וְיָלַד שָׁקֶר. בּוֹר כָּרָה וַיַּחְפְּרֵהוּ, וַיִּפֹּל בְּשַׁחַת יִפְעָל. יָשׁוּב עֲמָלוֹ בְרֹאשׁוֹ, וְעַל קָדְקֳדוֹ חֲמָסוֹ יֵרֵד. אוֹדֶה יהוה כְּצִדְקוֹ, וַאֲזַמְּרָה שֵׁם יהוה עֶלְיוֹן.

ח לַמְנַצֵּחַ עַל הַגִּתִּית, מִזְמוֹר לְדָוִד. יהוה אֲדֹנֵינוּ, מָה אַדִּיר שִׁמְךָ בְּכָל הָאָרֶץ, אֲשֶׁר תְּנָה הוֹדְךָ עַל הַשָּׁמָיִם. מִפִּי עוֹלְלִים וְיֹנְקִים יִסַּדְתָּ עֹז, לְמַעַן צוֹרְרֶיךָ, לְהַשְׁבִּית אוֹיֵב וּמִתְנַקֵּם. כִּי אֶרְאֶה שָׁמֶיךָ, מַעֲשֵׂי אֶצְבְּעֹתֶיךָ, יָרֵחַ וְכוֹכָבִים אֲשֶׁר כּוֹנָנְתָּה. מָה אֱנוֹשׁ כִּי תִזְכְּרֶנּוּ, וּבֶן אָדָם כִּי תִפְקְדֶנּוּ. וַתְּחַסְּרֵהוּ מְּעַט מֵאֱלֹהִים, וְכָבוֹד וְהָדָר תְּעַטְּרֵהוּ. תַּמְשִׁילֵהוּ בְּמַעֲשֵׂי יָדֶיךָ, כֹּל שַׁתָּה תַחַת רַגְלָיו. צֹנֶה וַאֲלָפִים כֻּלָּם, וְגַם בַּהֲמוֹת שָׂדָי. צִפּוֹר שָׁמַיִם וּדְגֵי הַיָּם, עֹבֵר אָרְחוֹת יַמִּים. יהוה אֲדֹנֵינוּ, מָה אַדִּיר שִׁמְךָ בְּכָל הָאָרֶץ.

ט לַמְנַצֵּחַ עַל מוּת לַבֵּן, מִזְמוֹר לְדָוִד. אוֹדֶה יהוה בְּכָל לִבִּי, אֲסַפְּרָה כָּל נִפְלְאוֹתֶיךָ. אֶשְׂמְחָה וְאֶעֶלְצָה בָךְ, אֲזַמְּרָה שִׁמְךָ עֶלְיוֹן. בְּשׁוּב אוֹיְבַי אָחוֹר, יִכָּשְׁלוּ וְיֹאבְדוּ מִפָּנֶיךָ. כִּי עָשִׂיתָ מִשְׁפָּטִי וְדִינִי, יָשַׁבְתָּ לְכִסֵּא שׁוֹפֵט צֶדֶק. גָּעַרְתָּ גוֹיִם, אִבַּדְתָּ רָשָׁע, שְׁמָם מָחִיתָ לְעוֹלָם וָעֶד. הָאוֹיֵב תַּמּוּ חֳרָבוֹת לָנֶצַח; וְעָרִים נָתַשְׁתָּ, אָבַד זִכְרָם הֵמָּה. וַיהוה לְעוֹלָם יֵשֵׁב, כּוֹנֵן לַמִּשְׁפָּט כִּסְאוֹ. וְהוּא יִשְׁפֹּט תֵּבֵל בְּצֶדֶק, יָדִין לְאֻמִּים בְּמֵישָׁרִים. וִיהִי יהוה מִשְׂגָּב לַדָּךְ, מִשְׂגָּב לְעִתּוֹת בַּצָּרָה. וְיִבְטְחוּ בְךָ יוֹדְעֵי שְׁמֶךָ, כִּי לֹא עָזַבְתָּ דֹרְשֶׁיךָ, יהוה. זַמְּרוּ לַיהוה יֹשֵׁב צִיּוֹן, הַגִּידוּ בָעַמִּים עֲלִילוֹתָיו. כִּי דֹרֵשׁ דָּמִים אוֹתָם זָכָר, לֹא שָׁכַח צַעֲקַת עֲנָוִים. חָנְנֵנִי יהוה, רְאֵה עָנְיִי מִשֹּׂנְאָי, מְרוֹמְמִי מִשַּׁעֲרֵי מָוֶת. לְמַעַן אֲסַפְּרָה כָּל תְּהִלָּתֶיךָ, בְּשַׁעֲרֵי בַת צִיּוֹן אָגִילָה בִּישׁוּעָתֶךָ. טָבְעוּ גוֹיִם בְּשַׁחַת עָשׂוּ, בְּרֶשֶׁת זוּ טָמָנוּ נִלְכְּדָה רַגְלָם. נוֹדַע יהוה מִשְׁפָּט עָשָׂה; בְּפֹעַל כַּפָּיו נוֹקֵשׁ רָשָׁע, הִגָּיוֹן סֶלָה. יָשׁוּבוּ רְשָׁעִים לִשְׁאוֹלָה, כָּל גּוֹיִם שְׁכֵחֵי אֱלֹהִים. כִּי לֹא לָנֶצַח יִשָּׁכַח אֶבְיוֹן, תִּקְוַת עֲנָוִים תֹּאבַד לָעַד. קוּמָה יהוה אַל יָעֹז אֱנוֹשׁ, יִשָּׁפְטוּ גוֹיִם עַל פָּנֶיךָ. שִׁיתָה יהוה מוֹרָה לָהֶם, יֵדְעוּ גוֹיִם אֱנוֹשׁ הֵמָּה סֶּלָה.

יב לַמְנַצֵּחַ עַל הַשְּׁמִינִית, מִזְמוֹר לְדָוִד. הוֹשִׁיעָה יהוה כִּי גָמַר חָסִיד, כִּי פַסּוּ אֱמוּנִים מִבְּנֵי אָדָם. שָׁוְא יְדַבְּרוּ אִישׁ אֶת רֵעֵהוּ; שְׂפַת חֲלָקוֹת, בְּלֵב וָלֵב יְדַבֵּרוּ. יַכְרֵת יהוה כָּל שִׂפְתֵי חֲלָקוֹת, לָשׁוֹן מְדַבֶּרֶת גְּדֹלוֹת. אֲשֶׁר אָמְרוּ: לִלְשֹׁנֵנוּ נַגְבִּיר, שְׂפָתֵינוּ אִתָּנוּ, מִי אָדוֹן לָנוּ. מִשֹּׁד עֲנִיִּים, מֵאַנְקַת אֶבְיוֹנִים; עַתָּה אָקוּם יֹאמַר יהוה, אָשִׁית בְּיֵשַׁע יָפִיחַ לוֹ. אִמְרוֹת יהוה אֲמָרוֹת טְהֹרוֹת, כֶּסֶף צָרוּף, בַּעֲלִיל לָאָרֶץ, מְזֻקָּק שִׁבְעָתָיִם. אַתָּה יהוה תִּשְׁמְרֵם, תִּצְּרֶנּוּ מִן הַדּוֹר זוּ לְעוֹלָם. סָבִיב רְשָׁעִים יִתְהַלָּכוּן, כְּרֻם זֻלּוּת לִבְנֵי אָדָם.

יג לַמְנַצֵּחַ מִזְמוֹר לְדָוִד. עַד אָנָה יהוה תִּשְׁכָּחֵנִי נֶצַח, עַד אָנָה תַּסְתִּיר אֶת פָּנֶיךָ מִמֶּנִּי. עַד אָנָה אָשִׁית עֵצוֹת בְּנַפְשִׁי, יָגוֹן בִּלְבָבִי יוֹמָם; עַד אָנָה יָרוּם אֹיְבִי עָלָי. הַבִּיטָה עֲנֵנִי יהוה אֱלֹהָי, הָאִירָה עֵינַי פֶּן אִישַׁן הַמָּוֶת. פֶּן יֹאמַר אֹיְבִי: יְכָלְתִּיו, צָרַי יָגִילוּ כִּי אֶמּוֹט. וַאֲנִי בְּחַסְדְּךָ בָטַחְתִּי, יָגֵל לִבִּי בִּישׁוּעָתֶךָ; אָשִׁירָה לַיהוה, כִּי גָמַל עָלָי.

יד לַמְנַצֵּחַ לְדָוִד. אָמַר נָבָל בְּלִבּוֹ אֵין אֱלֹהִים, הִשְׁחִיתוּ הִתְעִיבוּ עֲלִילָה, אֵין עֹשֵׂה טוֹב. יהוה מִשָּׁמַיִם הִשְׁקִיף עַל בְּנֵי אָדָם, לִרְאוֹת הֲיֵשׁ מַשְׂכִּיל דֹּרֵשׁ אֶת אֱלֹהִים. הַכֹּל סָר, יַחְדָּו נֶאֱלָחוּ; אֵין עֹשֵׂה טוֹב, אֵין גַּם אֶחָד. הֲלֹא יָדְעוּ כָּל פֹּעֲלֵי אָוֶן; אֹכְלֵי עַמִּי אָכְלוּ לֶחֶם, יהוה לֹא קָרָאוּ. שָׁם פָּחֲדוּ פָחַד, כִּי אֱלֹהִים בְּדוֹר צַדִּיק. עֲצַת עָנִי תָבִישׁוּ, כִּי יהוה מַחְסֵהוּ. מִי יִתֵּן מִצִּיּוֹן יְשׁוּעַת יִשְׂרָאֵל; בְּשׁוּב יהוה שְׁבוּת עַמּוֹ, יָגֵל יַעֲקֹב יִשְׂמַח יִשְׂרָאֵל.

טו מִזְמוֹר לְדָוִד; יהוה, מִי יָגוּר בְּאָהֳלֶךָ, מִי יִשְׁכֹּן בְּהַר קָדְשֶׁךָ. הוֹלֵךְ תָּמִים וּפֹעֵל צֶדֶק, וְדֹבֵר אֱמֶת בִּלְבָבוֹ. לֹא רָגַל עַל לְשֹׁנוֹ, לֹא עָשָׂה לְרֵעֵהוּ רָעָה, וְחֶרְפָּה לֹא נָשָׂא עַל קְרֹבוֹ.

י לָמָה יהוה תַּעֲמֹד בְּרָחוֹק, תַּעְלִים לְעִתּוֹת בַּצָּרָה. בְּגַאֲוַת רָשָׁע יִדְלַק עָנִי, יִתָּפְשׂוּ בִּמְזִמּוֹת זוּ חָשָׁבוּ. כִּי הִלֵּל רָשָׁע עַל תַּאֲוַת נַפְשׁוֹ, וּבֹצֵעַ בֵּרֵךְ נִאֵץ | יהוה. רָשָׁע, כְּגֹבַהּ אַפּוֹ בַּל יִדְרֹשׁ, אֵין אֱלֹהִים כָּל מְזִמּוֹתָיו. יָחִילוּ דְרָכָיו בְּכָל עֵת, מָרוֹם מִשְׁפָּטֶיךָ מִנֶּגְדּוֹ; כָּל צוֹרְרָיו יָפִיחַ בָּהֶם. אָמַר בְּלִבּוֹ: בַּל אֶמּוֹט, לְדֹר וָדֹר אֲשֶׁר לֹא בְרָע. אָלָה פִּיהוּ מָלֵא וּמִרְמוֹת וָתֹךְ, תַּחַת לְשׁוֹנוֹ עָמָל וָאָוֶן. יֵשֵׁב בְּמַאְרַב חֲצֵרִים, בַּמִּסְתָּרִים יַהֲרֹג נָקִי, עֵינָיו לְחֵלְכָה יִצְפֹּנוּ. יֶאֱרֹב בַּמִּסְתָּר כְּאַרְיֵה בְסֻכֹּה, יֶאֱרֹב לַחֲטוֹף עָנִי; יַחְטֹף עָנִי בְּמָשְׁכוֹ בְרִשְׁתּוֹ. יִדְכֶּה יָשֹׁחַ, וְנָפַל בַּעֲצוּמָיו חֵל כָּאִים. אָמַר בְּלִבּוֹ שָׁכַח אֵל, הִסְתִּיר פָּנָיו בַּל רָאָה לָנֶצַח. קוּמָה יהוה, אֵל נְשָׂא יָדֶךָ, אַל תִּשְׁכַּח עֲנָוִים. עַל מֶה נִאֵץ רָשָׁע | אֱלֹהִים, אָמַר בְּלִבּוֹ לֹא תִדְרֹשׁ. רָאִתָה, כִּי אַתָּה עָמָל וָכַעַס תַּבִּיט, לָתֵת בְּיָדֶךָ; עָלֶיךָ יַעֲזֹב חֵלְכָה, יָתוֹם אַתָּה הָיִיתָ עוֹזֵר. שְׁבֹר זְרוֹעַ רָשָׁע; וָרָע, תִּדְרוֹשׁ רִשְׁעוֹ בַל תִּמְצָא. יהוה מֶלֶךְ עוֹלָם וָעֶד, אָבְדוּ גוֹיִם מֵאַרְצוֹ. תַּאֲוַת עֲנָוִים שָׁמַעְתָּ, יהוה; תָּכִין לִבָּם תַּקְשִׁיב אָזְנֶךָ. לִשְׁפֹּט יָתוֹם וָדָךְ; בַּל יוֹסִיף עוֹד, לַעֲרֹץ אֱנוֹשׁ מִן הָאָרֶץ.

יא לַמְנַצֵּחַ לְדָוִד; בַּיהוה חָסִיתִי, אֵיךְ תֹּאמְרוּ לְנַפְשִׁי, נוּדִי הַרְכֶם צִפּוֹר. כִּי הִנֵּה הָרְשָׁעִים יִדְרְכוּן קֶשֶׁת, כּוֹנְנוּ חִצָּם עַל יֶתֶר, לִירוֹת בְּמוֹ אֹפֶל לְיִשְׁרֵי לֵב. כִּי הַשָּׁתוֹת יֵהָרֵסוּן, צַדִּיק מַה פָּעָל. יהוה בְּהֵיכַל קָדְשׁוֹ, יהוה בַּשָּׁמַיִם כִּסְאוֹ; עֵינָיו יֶחֱזוּ, עַפְעַפָּיו יִבְחֲנוּ בְּנֵי אָדָם. יהוה צַדִּיק יִבְחָן, וְרָשָׁע וְאֹהֵב חָמָס שָׂנְאָה נַפְשׁוֹ. יַמְטֵר עַל רְשָׁעִים פַּחִים; אֵשׁ וְגָפְרִית וְרוּחַ זִלְעָפוֹת מְנָת כּוֹסָם. כִּי צַדִּיק יהוה, צְדָקוֹת אָהֵב, יָשָׁר יֶחֱזוּ פָנֵימוֹ.

מִמְתִים מֵחֶלֶד, חֶלְקָם בַּחַיִּים, וּצְפוּנְךָ
תְּמַלֵּא בִטְנָם; יִשְׂבְּעוּ בָנִים, וְהִנִּיחוּ יִתְרָם
לְעוֹלְלֵיהֶם. אֲנִי בְּצֶדֶק אֶחֱזֶה פָנֶיךָ,
אֶשְׂבְּעָה בְהָקִיץ תְּמוּנָתֶךָ.

<hr>

— DAY 3 — יוֹם ג' לַחֹדֶשׁ

יח לַמְנַצֵּחַ לְעֶבֶד יהוה לְדָוִד; אֲשֶׁר
דִּבֶּר לַיהוה אֶת דִּבְרֵי הַשִּׁירָה
הַזֹּאת, בְּיוֹם הִצִּיל יהוה אוֹתוֹ מִכַּף כָּל
אֹיְבָיו, וּמִיַּד שָׁאוּל. וַיֹּאמַר, אֶרְחָמְךָ יהוה
חִזְקִי. יהוה סַלְעִי וּמְצוּדָתִי וּמְפַלְטִי; אֵלִי
צוּרִי אֶחֱסֶה בּוֹ, מָגִנִּי וְקֶרֶן יִשְׁעִי, מִשְׂגַּבִּי.
מְהֻלָּל אֶקְרָא יהוה, וּמִן אֹיְבַי אִוָּשֵׁעַ.
אֲפָפוּנִי חֶבְלֵי מָוֶת, וְנַחֲלֵי בְלִיַּעַל
יְבַעֲתוּנִי. חֶבְלֵי שְׁאוֹל סְבָבוּנִי, קִדְּמוּנִי
מוֹקְשֵׁי מָוֶת. בַּצַּר לִי אֶקְרָא יהוה, וְאֶל
אֱלֹהַי אֲשַׁוֵּעַ; יִשְׁמַע מֵהֵיכָלוֹ קוֹלִי,
וְשַׁוְעָתִי לְפָנָיו תָּבוֹא בְאָזְנָיו. וַתִּגְעַשׁ
וַתִּרְעַשׁ הָאָרֶץ, וּמוֹסְדֵי הָרִים יִרְגָּזוּ;
וַיִּתְגָּעֲשׁוּ כִּי חָרָה לוֹ. עָלָה עָשָׁן בְּאַפּוֹ,
וְאֵשׁ מִפִּיו תֹּאכֵל, גֶּחָלִים בָּעֲרוּ מִמֶּנּוּ.
וַיֵּט שָׁמַיִם וַיֵּרַד, וַעֲרָפֶל תַּחַת רַגְלָיו.
וַיִּרְכַּב עַל כְּרוּב וַיָּעֹף, וַיֵּדֶא עַל כַּנְפֵי
רוּחַ. יָשֶׁת חֹשֶׁךְ סִתְרוֹ, סְבִיבוֹתָיו סֻכָּתוֹ,
חֶשְׁכַת מַיִם עָבֵי שְׁחָקִים. מִנֹּגַהּ נֶגְדּוֹ,
עָבָיו עָבְרוּ, בָּרָד וְגַחֲלֵי אֵשׁ. וַיַּרְעֵם
בַּשָּׁמַיִם יהוה, וְעֶלְיוֹן יִתֵּן קֹלוֹ, בָּרָד
וְגַחֲלֵי אֵשׁ. וַיִּשְׁלַח חִצָּיו וַיְפִיצֵם, וּבְרָקִים
רָב וַיְהֻמֵּם. וַיֵּרָאוּ אֲפִיקֵי מַיִם, וַיִּגָּלוּ
מוֹסְדוֹת תֵּבֵל; מִגַּעֲרָתְךָ יהוה, מִנִּשְׁמַת
רוּחַ אַפֶּךָ. יִשְׁלַח מִמָּרוֹם יִקָּחֵנִי, יַמְשֵׁנִי
מִמַּיִם רַבִּים. יַצִּילֵנִי מֵאֹיְבִי עָז, וּמִשֹּׂנְאַי
כִּי אָמְצוּ מִמֶּנִּי. יְקַדְּמוּנִי בְיוֹם אֵידִי, וַיְהִי
יהוה לְמִשְׁעָן לִי. וַיּוֹצִיאֵנִי לַמֶּרְחָב,
יְחַלְּצֵנִי כִּי חָפֵץ בִּי. יִגְמְלֵנִי יהוה כְּצִדְקִי,
כְּבֹר יָדַי יָשִׁיב לִי. כִּי שָׁמַרְתִּי דַּרְכֵי יהוה,
וְלֹא רָשַׁעְתִּי מֵאֱלֹהָי. כִּי כָל מִשְׁפָּטָיו
לְנֶגְדִּי, וְחֻקֹּתָיו לֹא אָסִיר מֶנִּי. וָאֱהִי
תָמִים עִמּוֹ, וָאֶשְׁתַּמֵּר מֵעֲוֹנִי. וַיָּשֶׁב יהוה

נִבְזֶה בְּעֵינָיו נִמְאָס, וְאֶת יִרְאֵי יהוה
יְכַבֵּד, נִשְׁבַּע לְהָרַע וְלֹא יָמִר. כַּסְפּוֹ לֹא
נָתַן בְּנֶשֶׁךְ, וְשֹׁחַד עַל נָקִי לֹא לָקָח; עֹשֵׂה
אֵלֶּה לֹא יִמּוֹט לְעוֹלָם.

טז מִכְתָּם לְדָוִד, שָׁמְרֵנִי אֵל כִּי חָסִיתִי
בָךְ. אָמַרְתְּ לַיהוה, אֲדֹנָי אָתָּה,
טוֹבָתִי בַּל עָלֶיךָ. לִקְדוֹשִׁים אֲשֶׁר בָּאָרֶץ
הֵמָּה, וְאַדִּירֵי כָּל חֶפְצִי בָם. יִרְבּוּ
עַצְּבוֹתָם אַחֵר מָהָרוּ; בַּל אַסִּיךְ נִסְכֵּיהֶם
מִדָּם, וּבַל אֶשָּׂא אֶת שְׁמוֹתָם עַל שְׂפָתָי.
יהוה מְנָת חֶלְקִי וְכוֹסִי, אַתָּה תּוֹמִיךְ
גּוֹרָלִי. חֲבָלִים נָפְלוּ לִי בַּנְּעִמִים, אַף
נַחֲלָת שָׁפְרָה עָלָי. אֲבָרֵךְ אֶת יהוה אֲשֶׁר
יְעָצָנִי, אַף לֵילוֹת יִסְּרוּנִי כִלְיוֹתָי. שִׁוִּיתִי
יהוה לְנֶגְדִּי תָמִיד, כִּי מִימִינִי בַּל אֶמּוֹט.
לָכֵן שָׂמַח לִבִּי וַיָּגֶל כְּבוֹדִי, אַף בְּשָׂרִי
יִשְׁכֹּן לָבֶטַח. כִּי לֹא תַעֲזֹב נַפְשִׁי לִשְׁאוֹל,
לֹא תִתֵּן חֲסִידְךָ לִרְאוֹת שָׁחַת. תּוֹדִיעֵנִי
אֹרַח חַיִּים, שֹׂבַע שְׂמָחוֹת אֶת פָּנֶיךָ,
נְעִמוֹת בִּימִינְךָ נֶצַח.

יז תְּפִלָּה לְדָוִד; שִׁמְעָה יהוה צֶדֶק,
הַקְשִׁיבָה רִנָּתִי, הַאֲזִינָה תְפִלָּתִי,
בְּלֹא שִׂפְתֵי מִרְמָה. מִלְּפָנֶיךָ מִשְׁפָּטִי יֵצֵא,
עֵינֶיךָ תֶּחֱזֶינָה מֵישָׁרִים. בָּחַנְתָּ לִבִּי,
פָּקַדְתָּ לַּיְלָה, צְרַפְתַּנִי בַל תִּמְצָא; זַמֹּתִי
בַּל יַעֲבָר פִּי. לִפְעֻלּוֹת אָדָם בִּדְבַר
שְׂפָתֶיךָ, אֲנִי שָׁמַרְתִּי אָרְחוֹת פָּרִיץ. תָּמֹךְ
אֲשֻׁרַי בְּמַעְגְּלוֹתֶיךָ, בַּל נָמוֹטּוּ פְעָמָי.
אֲנִי קְרָאתִיךָ כִי תַעֲנֵנִי, אֵל; הַט אָזְנְךָ לִי,
שְׁמַע אִמְרָתִי. הַפְלֵה חֲסָדֶיךָ, מוֹשִׁיעַ
חוֹסִים, מִמִּתְקוֹמְמִים בִּימִינֶךָ. שָׁמְרֵנִי
כְּאִישׁוֹן בַּת עָיִן, בְּצֵל כְּנָפֶיךָ תַּסְתִּירֵנִי.
מִפְּנֵי רְשָׁעִים זוּ שַׁדּוּנִי, אֹיְבַי בְּנֶפֶשׁ יַקִּיפוּ
עָלָי. חֶלְבָּמוֹ סָגְרוּ, פִּימוֹ דִּבְּרוּ בְגֵאוּת.
אַשֻּׁרֵינוּ עַתָּה סְבָבוּנוּ, עֵינֵיהֶם יָשִׁיתוּ
לִנְטוֹת בָּאָרֶץ. דִּמְיֹנוֹ כְּאַרְיֵה יִכְסוֹף
לִטְרֹף, וְכִכְפִיר יֹשֵׁב בְּמִסְתָּרִים. קוּמָה
יהוה, קַדְּמָה פָנָיו הַכְרִיעֵהוּ, פַּלְּטָה נַפְשִׁי
מֵרָשָׁע חַרְבֶּךָ. מִמְתִים יָדְךָ | יהוה,

לִי כְצִדְקִי, כְּבֹר יָדַי לְנֶגֶד עֵינָיו. עִם חָסִיד תִּתְחַסָּד, עִם גְּבַר תָּמִים תִּתַּמָּם. עִם נָבָר תִּתְבָּרָר, וְעִם עִקֵּשׁ תִּתְפַּתָּל. כִּי אַתָּה עַם עָנִי תוֹשִׁיעַ, וְעֵינַיִם רָמוֹת תַּשְׁפִּיל. כִּי אַתָּה תָּאִיר נֵרִי, יהוה אֱלֹהַי יַגִּיהַּ חָשְׁכִּי. כִּי בְךָ אָרֻץ גְּדוּד, וּבֵאלֹהַי אֲדַלֶּג שׁוּר. הָאֵל תָּמִים דַּרְכּוֹ; אִמְרַת יהוה צְרוּפָה, מָגֵן הוּא לְכֹל הַחוֹסִים בּוֹ. כִּי מִי אֱלוֹהַּ מִבַּלְעֲדֵי יהוה, וּמִי צוּר זוּלָתִי אֱלֹהֵינוּ. הָאֵל הַמְאַזְּרֵנִי חָיִל, וַיִּתֵּן תָּמִים דַּרְכִּי. מְשַׁוֶּה רַגְלַי כָּאַיָּלוֹת, וְעַל בָּמֹתַי יַעֲמִידֵנִי. מְלַמֵּד יָדַי לַמִּלְחָמָה, וְנִחֲתָה קֶשֶׁת נְחוּשָׁה זְרוֹעֹתָי. וַתִּתֶּן לִי מָגֵן יִשְׁעֶךָ; וִימִינְךָ תִסְעָדֵנִי, וְעַנְוַתְךָ תַרְבֵּנִי. תַּרְחִיב צַעֲדִי תַחְתָּי, וְלֹא מָעֲדוּ קַרְסֻלָּי. אֶרְדּוֹף אוֹיְבַי וְאַשִּׂיגֵם, וְלֹא אָשׁוּב עַד כַּלּוֹתָם. אֶמְחָצֵם וְלֹא יֻכְלוּ קוּם, יִפְּלוּ תַּחַת רַגְלָי. וַתְּאַזְּרֵנִי חַיִל לַמִּלְחָמָה, תַּכְרִיעַ קָמַי תַּחְתָּי. וְאֹיְבַי נָתַתָּה לִּי עֹרֶף, וּמְשַׂנְאַי אַצְמִיתֵם. יְשַׁוְּעוּ וְאֵין מוֹשִׁיעַ, עַל יהוה וְלֹא עָנָם. וְאֶשְׁחָקֵם כְּעָפָר עַל פְּנֵי רוּחַ, כְּטִיט חוּצוֹת אֲרִיקֵם. תְּפַלְּטֵנִי מֵרִיבֵי עָם; תְּשִׂימֵנִי לְרֹאשׁ גּוֹיִם, עַם לֹא יָדַעְתִּי יַעַבְדוּנִי. לְשֵׁמַע אֹזֶן יִשָּׁמְעוּ לִי, בְּנֵי נֵכָר יְכַחֲשׁוּ לִי. בְּנֵי נֵכָר יִבֹּלוּ, וְיַחְרְגוּ מִמִּסְגְּרוֹתֵיהֶם. חַי יהוה וּבָרוּךְ צוּרִי, וְיָרוּם אֱלוֹהֵי יִשְׁעִי. הָאֵל הַנּוֹתֵן נְקָמוֹת לִי, וַיַּדְבֵּר עַמִּים תַּחְתָּי. מְפַלְּטִי מֵאֹיְבָי; אַף מִן קָמַי תְּרוֹמְמֵנִי, מֵאִישׁ חָמָס תַּצִּילֵנִי. עַל כֵּן אוֹדְךָ בַגּוֹיִם | יהוה, וּלְשִׁמְךָ אֲזַמֵּרָה. מַגְדִּיל יְשׁוּעוֹת מַלְכּוֹ; וְעֹשֶׂה חֶסֶד לִמְשִׁיחוֹ, לְדָוִד וּלְזַרְעוֹ עַד עוֹלָם.

יט לַמְנַצֵּחַ מִזְמוֹר לְדָוִד. הַשָּׁמַיִם מְסַפְּרִים כְּבוֹד אֵל, וּמַעֲשֵׂה יָדָיו מַגִּיד הָרָקִיעַ. יוֹם לְיוֹם יַבִּיעַ אֹמֶר, וְלַיְלָה לְּלַיְלָה יְחַוֶּה דָּעַת. אֵין אֹמֶר וְאֵין דְּבָרִים, בְּלִי נִשְׁמָע קוֹלָם. בְּכָל הָאָרֶץ יָצָא קַוָּם, וּבִקְצֵה תֵבֵל מִלֵּיהֶם; לַשֶּׁמֶשׁ שָׂם אֹהֶל

בָּהֶם. וְהוּא כְּחָתָן יֹצֵא מֵחֻפָּתוֹ, יָשִׂישׂ כְּגִבּוֹר לָרוּץ אֹרַח. מִקְצֵה הַשָּׁמַיִם מוֹצָאוֹ, וּתְקוּפָתוֹ עַל קְצוֹתָם; וְאֵין נִסְתָּר מֵחַמָּתוֹ. תּוֹרַת יהוה תְּמִימָה, מְשִׁיבַת נָפֶשׁ; עֵדוּת יהוה נֶאֱמָנָה, מַחְכִּימַת פֶּתִי. פִּקּוּדֵי יהוה יְשָׁרִים, מְשַׂמְּחֵי לֵב; מִצְוַת יהוה בָּרָה, מְאִירַת עֵינָיִם. יִרְאַת יהוה טְהוֹרָה, עוֹמֶדֶת לָעַד; מִשְׁפְּטֵי יהוה אֱמֶת, צָדְקוּ יַחְדָּו. הַנֶּחֱמָדִים מִזָּהָב וּמִפַּז רָב, וּמְתוּקִים מִדְּבַשׁ וְנֹפֶת צוּפִים. גַּם עַבְדְּךָ נִזְהָר בָּהֶם, בְּשָׁמְרָם עֵקֶב רָב. שְׁגִיאוֹת מִי יָבִין, מִנִּסְתָּרוֹת נַקֵּנִי. גַּם מִזֵּדִים חֲשֹׂךְ עַבְדֶּךָ, אַל יִמְשְׁלוּ בִי, אָז אֵיתָם; וְנִקֵּיתִי מִפֶּשַׁע רָב. יִהְיוּ לְרָצוֹן אִמְרֵי פִי וְהֶגְיוֹן לִבִּי לְפָנֶיךָ, יהוה צוּרִי וְגֹאֲלִי.

כ לַמְנַצֵּחַ מִזְמוֹר לְדָוִד. יַעַנְךָ יהוה בְּיוֹם צָרָה; יְשַׂגֶּבְךָ שֵׁם אֱלֹהֵי יַעֲקֹב. יִשְׁלַח עֶזְרְךָ מִקֹּדֶשׁ, וּמִצִּיּוֹן יִסְעָדֶךָּ. יִזְכֹּר כָּל מִנְחֹתֶךָ, וְעוֹלָתְךָ יְדַשְּׁנֶה סֶלָה. יִתֶּן לְךָ כִלְבָבֶךָ, וְכָל עֲצָתְךָ יְמַלֵּא. נְרַנְּנָה בִּישׁוּעָתֶךָ, וּבְשֵׁם אֱלֹהֵינוּ נִדְגֹּל; יְמַלֵּא יהוה כָּל מִשְׁאֲלוֹתֶיךָ. עַתָּה יָדַעְתִּי כִּי הוֹשִׁיעַ יהוה מְשִׁיחוֹ; יַעֲנֵהוּ מִשְּׁמֵי קָדְשׁוֹ, בִּגְבֻרוֹת יֵשַׁע יְמִינוֹ. אֵלֶּה בָרֶכֶב וְאֵלֶּה בַסּוּסִים, וַאֲנַחְנוּ בְּשֵׁם יהוה אֱלֹהֵינוּ נַזְכִּיר. הֵמָּה כָּרְעוּ וְנָפָלוּ, וַאֲנַחְנוּ קַּמְנוּ וַנִּתְעוֹדָד. יהוה הוֹשִׁיעָה, הַמֶּלֶךְ יַעֲנֵנוּ בְיוֹם קָרְאֵנוּ.

כא לַמְנַצֵּחַ מִזְמוֹר לְדָוִד. יהוה בְּעָזְּךָ יִשְׂמַח מֶלֶךְ, וּבִישׁוּעָתְךָ מַה יָּגֶל מְאֹד. תַּאֲוַת לִבּוֹ נָתַתָּה לּוֹ, וַאֲרֶשֶׁת שְׂפָתָיו בַּל מָנַעְתָּ סֶּלָה. כִּי תְקַדְּמֶנּוּ בִּרְכוֹת טוֹב, תָּשִׁית לְרֹאשׁוֹ עֲטֶרֶת פָּז. חַיִּים שָׁאַל מִמְּךָ נָתַתָּה לּוֹ, אֹרֶךְ יָמִים עוֹלָם וָעֶד. גָּדוֹל כְּבוֹדוֹ בִּישׁוּעָתֶךָ, הוֹד וְהָדָר תְּשַׁוֶּה עָלָיו. כִּי תְשִׁיתֵהוּ בְרָכוֹת לָעַד, תְּחַדֵּהוּ בְשִׂמְחָה אֶת פָּנֶיךָ. כִּי הַמֶּלֶךְ בֹּטֵחַ בַּיהוה, וּבְחֶסֶד עֶלְיוֹן בַּל

וּבְשַׁוְּעוֹ אֵלָיו שָׁמֵעַ. מֵאִתְּךָ תְהִלָּתִי בְּקָהָל רָב, נְדָרַי אֲשַׁלֵּם נֶגֶד יְרֵאָיו. יֹאכְלוּ עֲנָוִים וְיִשְׂבָּעוּ, יְהַלְלוּ יהוה דֹּרְשָׁיו; יְחִי לְבַבְכֶם לָעַד. יִזְכְּרוּ וְיָשֻׁבוּ אֶל יהוה כָּל אַפְסֵי אָרֶץ, וְיִשְׁתַּחֲווּ לְפָנֶיךָ כָּל מִשְׁפְּחוֹת גּוֹיִם. כִּי לַיהוה הַמְּלוּכָה, וּמֹשֵׁל בַּגּוֹיִם. אָכְלוּ וַיִּשְׁתַּחֲווּ כָּל דִּשְׁנֵי אֶרֶץ, לְפָנָיו יִכְרְעוּ כָּל יוֹרְדֵי עָפָר, וְנַפְשׁוֹ לֹא חִיָּה. זֶרַע יַעַבְדֶנּוּ, יְסֻפַּר לַאדֹנָי לַדּוֹר. יָבֹאוּ וְיַגִּידוּ צִדְקָתוֹ, לְעַם נוֹלָד כִּי עָשָׂה.

יום ד' לחודש — DAY 4

כג מִזְמוֹר לְדָוִד; יהוה רֹעִי, לֹא אֶחְסָר. בִּנְאוֹת דֶּשֶׁא יַרְבִּיצֵנִי, עַל מֵי מְנֻחוֹת יְנַהֲלֵנִי. נַפְשִׁי יְשׁוֹבֵב, יַנְחֵנִי בְמַעְגְּלֵי צֶדֶק לְמַעַן שְׁמוֹ. גַּם כִּי אֵלֵךְ בְּגֵיא צַלְמָוֶת, לֹא אִירָא רָע כִּי אַתָּה עִמָּדִי; שִׁבְטְךָ וּמִשְׁעַנְתֶּךָ הֵמָּה יְנַחֲמֻנִי. תַּעֲרֹךְ לְפָנַי שֻׁלְחָן נֶגֶד צֹרְרָי; דִּשַּׁנְתָּ בַשֶּׁמֶן רֹאשִׁי, כּוֹסִי רְוָיָה. אַךְ טוֹב וָחֶסֶד יִרְדְּפוּנִי כָּל יְמֵי חַיָּי, וְשַׁבְתִּי בְּבֵית יהוה לְאֹרֶךְ יָמִים.

כד לְדָוִד מִזְמוֹר; לַיהוה הָאָרֶץ וּמְלוֹאָהּ, תֵּבֵל וְיֹשְׁבֵי בָהּ. כִּי הוּא עַל יַמִּים יְסָדָהּ, וְעַל נְהָרוֹת יְכוֹנְנֶהָ. מִי יַעֲלֶה בְהַר יהוה, וּמִי יָקוּם בִּמְקוֹם קָדְשׁוֹ. נְקִי כַפַּיִם וּבַר לֵבָב; אֲשֶׁר לֹא נָשָׂא לַשָּׁוְא נַפְשִׁי, וְלֹא נִשְׁבַּע לְמִרְמָה. יִשָּׂא בְרָכָה מֵאֵת יהוה, וּצְדָקָה מֵאֱלֹהֵי יִשְׁעוֹ. זֶה דּוֹר דֹּרְשָׁיו, מְבַקְשֵׁי פָנֶיךָ יַעֲקֹב סֶלָה. שְׂאוּ שְׁעָרִים רָאשֵׁיכֶם, וְהִנָּשְׂאוּ פִּתְחֵי עוֹלָם, וְיָבוֹא מֶלֶךְ הַכָּבוֹד. מִי זֶה מֶלֶךְ הַכָּבוֹד, יהוה עִזּוּז וְגִבּוֹר, יהוה גִּבּוֹר מִלְחָמָה. שְׂאוּ שְׁעָרִים רָאשֵׁיכֶם, וּשְׂאוּ פִּתְחֵי עוֹלָם, וְיָבֹא מֶלֶךְ הַכָּבוֹד. מִי הוּא זֶה מֶלֶךְ הַכָּבוֹד, יהוה צְבָאוֹת הוּא מֶלֶךְ הַכָּבוֹד סֶלָה.

כה לְדָוִד, אֵלֶיךָ יהוה נַפְשִׁי אֶשָּׂא. אֱלֹהַי, בְּךָ בָטַחְתִּי, אַל אֵבוֹשָׁה, אַל

יָמוּט. תִּמְצָא יָדְךָ לְכָל אֹיְבֶיךָ, יְמִינְךָ תִּמְצָא שֹׂנְאֶיךָ. תְּשִׁיתֵמוֹ כְּתַנּוּר אֵשׁ לְעֵת פָּנֶיךָ; יהוה בְּאַפּוֹ יְבַלְּעֵם, וְתֹאכְלֵם אֵשׁ. פִּרְיָמוֹ מֵאֶרֶץ תְּאַבֵּד, וְזַרְעָם מִבְּנֵי אָדָם. כִּי נָטוּ עָלֶיךָ רָעָה, חָשְׁבוּ מְזִמָּה בַּל יוּכָלוּ. כִּי תְּשִׁיתֵמוֹ שֶׁכֶם, בְּמֵיתָרֶיךָ תְּכוֹנֵן עַל פְּנֵיהֶם. רוּמָה יהוה בְעֻזֶּךָ, נָשִׁירָה וּנְזַמְּרָה גְבוּרָתֶךָ.

כב לַמְנַצֵּחַ עַל אַיֶּלֶת הַשַּׁחַר, מִזְמוֹר לְדָוִד. אֵלִי אֵלִי לָמָה עֲזַבְתָּנִי, רָחוֹק מִישׁוּעָתִי דִּבְרֵי שַׁאֲגָתִי. אֱלֹהַי, אֶקְרָא יוֹמָם וְלֹא תַעֲנֶה, וְלַיְלָה וְלֹא דוּמִיָּה לִי. וְאַתָּה קָדוֹשׁ, יוֹשֵׁב תְּהִלּוֹת יִשְׂרָאֵל. בְּךָ בָּטְחוּ אֲבֹתֵינוּ, בָּטְחוּ וַתְּפַלְּטֵמוֹ. אֵלֶיךָ זָעֲקוּ וְנִמְלָטוּ, בְּךָ בָטְחוּ וְלֹא בוֹשׁוּ. וְאָנֹכִי תוֹלַעַת וְלֹא אִישׁ, חֶרְפַּת אָדָם וּבְזוּי עָם. כָּל רֹאַי יַלְעִגוּ לִי, יַפְטִירוּ בְשָׂפָה, יָנִיעוּ רֹאשׁ. גֹּל אֶל יהוה יְפַלְּטֵהוּ, יַצִּילֵהוּ כִּי חָפֵץ בּוֹ. כִּי אַתָּה גֹחִי מִבָּטֶן, מַבְטִיחִי עַל שְׁדֵי אִמִּי. עָלֶיךָ הָשְׁלַכְתִּי מֵרָחֶם, מִבֶּטֶן אִמִּי אֵלִי אָתָּה. אַל תִּרְחַק מִמֶּנִּי כִּי צָרָה קְרוֹבָה, כִּי אֵין עוֹזֵר. סְבָבוּנִי פָּרִים רַבִּים, אַבִּירֵי בָשָׁן כִּתְּרוּנִי. פָּצוּ עָלַי פִּיהֶם, אַרְיֵה טֹרֵף וְשֹׁאֵג. כַּמַּיִם נִשְׁפַּכְתִּי, וְהִתְפָּרְדוּ כָּל עַצְמוֹתָי; הָיָה לִבִּי כַּדּוֹנָג, נָמֵס בְּתוֹךְ מֵעָי. יָבֵשׁ כַּחֶרֶשׂ כֹּחִי, וּלְשׁוֹנִי מֻדְבָּק מַלְקוֹחָי; וְלַעֲפַר מָוֶת תִּשְׁפְּתֵנִי. כִּי סְבָבוּנִי כְּלָבִים, עֲדַת מְרֵעִים הִקִּיפוּנִי, כָּאֲרִי יָדַי וְרַגְלָי. אֲסַפֵּר כָּל עַצְמוֹתָי, הֵמָּה יַבִּיטוּ יִרְאוּ בִי. יְחַלְּקוּ בְגָדַי לָהֶם, וְעַל לְבוּשִׁי יַפִּילוּ גוֹרָל. וְאַתָּה יהוה אַל תִּרְחָק, אֱיָלוּתִי לְעֶזְרָתִי חוּשָׁה. הַצִּילָה מֵחֶרֶב נַפְשִׁי, מִיַּד כֶּלֶב יְחִידָתִי. הוֹשִׁיעֵנִי מִפִּי אַרְיֵה, וּמִקַּרְנֵי רֵמִים עֲנִיתָנִי. אֲסַפְּרָה שִׁמְךָ לְאֶחָי, בְּתוֹךְ קָהָל אֲהַלְלֶךָּ. יִרְאֵי יהוה הַלְלוּהוּ, כָּל זֶרַע יַעֲקֹב כַּבְּדוּהוּ, וְגוּרוּ מִמֶּנּוּ כָּל זֶרַע יִשְׂרָאֵל. כִּי לֹא בָזָה וְלֹא שִׁקַּץ עֱנוּת עָנִי, וְלֹא הִסְתִּיר פָּנָיו מִמֶּנּוּ;

יַעַלְצוּ אוֹיְבַי לִי. גַּם כָּל קֹוֶיךָ לֹא יֵבֹשׁוּ, יֵבֹשׁוּ הַבּוֹגְדִים רֵיקָם. דְּרָכֶיךָ יהוה הוֹדִיעֵנִי, אֹרְחוֹתֶיךָ לַמְּדֵנִי. הַדְרִיכֵנִי בַאֲמִתֶּךָ וְלַמְּדֵנִי, כִּי אַתָּה אֱלֹהֵי יִשְׁעִי, אוֹתְךָ קִוִּיתִי כָּל הַיּוֹם. זְכֹר רַחֲמֶיךָ יהוה וַחֲסָדֶיךָ, כִּי מֵעוֹלָם הֵמָּה. חַטֹּאות נְעוּרַי וּפְשָׁעַי אַל תִּזְכֹּר; כְּחַסְדְּךָ זְכָר לִי אַתָּה, לְמַעַן טוּבְךָ, יהוה. טוֹב וְיָשָׁר יהוה, עַל כֵּן יוֹרֶה חַטָּאִים בַּדָּרֶךְ. יַדְרֵךְ עֲנָוִים בַּמִּשְׁפָּט, וִילַמֵּד עֲנָוִים דַּרְכּוֹ. כָּל אָרְחוֹת יהוה חֶסֶד וֶאֱמֶת, לְנֹצְרֵי בְרִיתוֹ וְעֵדֹתָיו. לְמַעַן שִׁמְךָ יהוה, וְסָלַחְתָּ לַעֲוֹנִי כִּי רַב הוּא. מִי זֶה הָאִישׁ יְרֵא יהוה, יוֹרֶנּוּ בְּדֶרֶךְ יִבְחָר. נַפְשׁוֹ בְּטוֹב תָּלִין, וְזַרְעוֹ יִירַשׁ אָרֶץ. סוֹד יהוה לִירֵאָיו, וּבְרִיתוֹ לְהוֹדִיעָם. עֵינַי תָּמִיד אֶל יהוה, כִּי הוּא יוֹצִיא מֵרֶשֶׁת רַגְלָי. פְּנֵה אֵלַי וְחָנֵּנִי, כִּי יָחִיד וְעָנִי אָנִי. צָרוֹת לְבָבִי הִרְחִיבוּ, מִמְּצוּקוֹתַי הוֹצִיאֵנִי. רְאֵה עָנְיִי וַעֲמָלִי, וְשָׂא לְכָל חַטֹּאותָי. רְאֵה אֹיְבַי כִּי רָבּוּ, וְשִׂנְאַת חָמָס שְׂנֵאוּנִי. שָׁמְרָה נַפְשִׁי וְהַצִּילֵנִי, אַל אֵבוֹשׁ כִּי חָסִיתִי בָךְ. תֹּם וָיֹשֶׁר יִצְּרוּנִי, כִּי קִוִּיתִיךָ. פְּדֵה אֱלֹהִים אֶת יִשְׂרָאֵל מִכֹּל צָרוֹתָיו.

כו לְדָוִד; שָׁפְטֵנִי יהוה, כִּי אֲנִי בְּתֻמִּי הָלַכְתִּי; וּבַיהוה בָּטַחְתִּי, לֹא אֶמְעָד. בְּחָנֵנִי יהוה וְנַסֵּנִי, צָרְפָה כִלְיוֹתַי וְלִבִּי. כִּי חַסְדְּךָ לְנֶגֶד עֵינָי, וְהִתְהַלַּכְתִּי בַּאֲמִתֶּךָ. לֹא יָשַׁבְתִּי עִם מְתֵי שָׁוְא, וְעִם נַעֲלָמִים לֹא אָבוֹא. שָׂנֵאתִי קְהַל מְרֵעִים, וְעִם רְשָׁעִים לֹא אֵשֵׁב. אֶרְחַץ בְּנִקָּיוֹן כַּפָּי, וַאֲסֹבְבָה אֶת מִזְבַּחֲךָ, יהוה. לַשְׁמִעַ בְּקוֹל תּוֹדָה, וּלְסַפֵּר כָּל נִפְלְאוֹתֶיךָ. יהוה, אָהַבְתִּי מְעוֹן בֵּיתֶךָ, וּמְקוֹם מִשְׁכַּן כְּבוֹדֶךָ. אַל תֶּאֱסֹף עִם חַטָּאִים נַפְשִׁי, וְעִם אַנְשֵׁי דָמִים חַיָּי. אֲשֶׁר בִּידֵיהֶם זִמָּה, וִימִינָם מָלְאָה שֹּׁחַד. וַאֲנִי בְּתֻמִּי אֵלֵךְ, פְּדֵנִי וְחָנֵּנִי. רַגְלִי עָמְדָה בְמִישׁוֹר, בְּמַקְהֵלִים אֲבָרֵךְ יהוה.

כז לְדָוִד; יהוה אוֹרִי וְיִשְׁעִי, מִמִּי אִירָא; יהוה מָעוֹז חַיַּי, מִמִּי אֶפְחָד. בִּקְרֹב עָלַי מְרֵעִים לֶאֱכֹל אֶת בְּשָׂרִי, צָרַי וְאֹיְבַי לִי, הֵמָּה כָשְׁלוּ וְנָפָלוּ. אִם תַּחֲנֶה עָלַי מַחֲנֶה, לֹא יִירָא לִבִּי; אִם תָּקוּם עָלַי מִלְחָמָה, בְּזֹאת אֲנִי בוֹטֵחַ. אַחַת שָׁאַלְתִּי מֵאֵת יהוה, אוֹתָהּ אֲבַקֵּשׁ; שִׁבְתִּי בְּבֵית יהוה כָּל יְמֵי חַיַּי, לַחֲזוֹת בְּנֹעַם יהוה, וּלְבַקֵּר בְּהֵיכָלוֹ. כִּי יִצְפְּנֵנִי בְּסֻכֹּה בְּיוֹם רָעָה; יַסְתִּרֵנִי בְּסֵתֶר אָהֳלוֹ, בְּצוּר יְרוֹמְמֵנִי. וְעַתָּה יָרוּם רֹאשִׁי עַל אֹיְבַי סְבִיבוֹתַי, וְאֶזְבְּחָה בְאָהֳלוֹ זִבְחֵי תְרוּעָה; אָשִׁירָה וַאֲזַמְּרָה לַיהוה. שְׁמַע יהוה קוֹלִי אֶקְרָא, וְחָנֵּנִי וַעֲנֵנִי. לְךָ אָמַר לִבִּי בַּקְּשׁוּ פָנָי, אֶת פָּנֶיךָ יהוה אֲבַקֵּשׁ. אַל תַּסְתֵּר פָּנֶיךָ מִמֶּנִּי, אַל תַּט בְּאַף עַבְדֶּךָ; עֶזְרָתִי הָיִיתָ, אַל תִּטְּשֵׁנִי וְאַל תַּעַזְבֵנִי, אֱלֹהֵי יִשְׁעִי. כִּי אָבִי וְאִמִּי עֲזָבוּנִי, וַיהוה יַאַסְפֵנִי. הוֹרֵנִי יהוה דַּרְכֶּךָ; וּנְחֵנִי בְּאֹרַח מִישׁוֹר, לְמַעַן שׁוֹרְרָי. אַל תִּתְּנֵנִי בְּנֶפֶשׁ צָרָי, כִּי קָמוּ בִי עֵדֵי שֶׁקֶר, וִיפֵחַ חָמָס. לוּלֵא הֶאֱמַנְתִּי לִרְאוֹת בְּטוּב יהוה בְּאֶרֶץ חַיִּים. קַוֵּה אֶל יהוה, חֲזַק וְיַאֲמֵץ לִבֶּךָ, וְקַוֵּה אֶל יהוה.

כח לְךָ יהוה אֶקְרָא, צוּרִי אַל תֶּחֱרַשׁ מִמֶּנִּי; פֶּן תֶּחֱשֶׁה מִמֶּנִּי, וְנִמְשַׁלְתִּי עִם יוֹרְדֵי בוֹר. שְׁמַע קוֹל תַּחֲנוּנַי בְּשַׁוְּעִי אֵלֶיךָ, בְּנָשְׂאִי יָדַי אֶל דְּבִיר קָדְשֶׁךָ. אַל תִּמְשְׁכֵנִי עִם רְשָׁעִים וְעִם פֹּעֲלֵי אָוֶן, דֹּבְרֵי שָׁלוֹם עִם רֵעֵיהֶם, וְרָעָה בִּלְבָבָם. תֶּן לָהֶם כְּפָעֳלָם וּכְרֹעַ מַעַלְלֵיהֶם; כְּמַעֲשֵׂה יְדֵיהֶם תֵּן לָהֶם, הָשֵׁב גְּמוּלָם לָהֶם. כִּי לֹא יָבִינוּ אֶל פְּעֻלֹּת יהוה וְאֶל מַעֲשֵׂה יָדָיו, יֶהֶרְסֵם וְלֹא יִבְנֵם. בָּרוּךְ יהוה, כִּי שָׁמַע קוֹל תַּחֲנוּנָי. יהוה עֻזִּי וּמָגִנִּי, בּוֹ בָטַח לִבִּי וְנֶעֱזָרְתִּי; וַיַּעֲלֹז לִבִּי, וּמִשִּׁירִי אֲהוֹדֶנּוּ. יהוה עֹז לָמוֹ; וּמָעוֹז יְשׁוּעוֹת מְשִׁיחוֹ הוּא. הוֹשִׁיעָה אֶת עַמֶּךָ, וּבָרֵךְ אֶת נַחֲלָתֶךָ; וּרְעֵם וְנַשְּׂאֵם עַד הָעוֹלָם.

מְצוּדוֹת לְהוֹשִׁיעֵנִי. כִּי סַלְעִי וּמְצוּדָתִי
אַתָּה, וּלְמַעַן שִׁמְךָ תַּנְחֵנִי וּתְנַהֲלֵנִי.
תּוֹצִיאֵנִי מֵרֶשֶׁת זוּ טָמְנוּ לִי, כִּי אַתָּה
מָעוּזִּי. בְּיָדְךָ אַפְקִיד רוּחִי, פָּדִיתָה אוֹתִי
יהוה, אֵל אֱמֶת. שָׂנֵאתִי הַשֹּׁמְרִים הַבְלֵי
שָׁוְא, וַאֲנִי אֶל יהוה בָּטֶחְתִּי. אָגִילָה
וְאֶשְׂמְחָה בְּחַסְדֶּךָ; אֲשֶׁר רָאִיתָ אֶת עָנְיִי,
יָדַעְתָּ בְּצָרוֹת נַפְשִׁי. וְלֹא הִסְגַּרְתַּנִי בְּיַד
אוֹיֵב, הֶעֱמַדְתָּ בַמֶּרְחָב רַגְלָי. חָנֵּנִי יהוה
כִּי צַר לִי, עָשְׁשָׁה בְכַעַס עֵינִי נַפְשִׁי
וּבִטְנִי. כִּי כָלוּ בְיָגוֹן חַיַּי, וּשְׁנוֹתַי בַּאֲנָחָה;
כָּשַׁל בַּעֲוֹנִי כֹחִי, וַעֲצָמַי עָשֵׁשׁוּ. מִכָּל
צֹרְרַי הָיִיתִי חֶרְפָּה, וְלִשְׁכֵנַי מְאֹד, וּפַחַד
לִמְיֻדָּעָי, רֹאַי בַּחוּץ נָדְדוּ מִמֶּנִּי. נִשְׁכַּחְתִּי
כְּמֵת מִלֵּב, הָיִיתִי כִּכְלִי אֹבֵד. כִּי שָׁמַעְתִּי
דִּבַּת רַבִּים, מָגוֹר מִסָּבִיב; בְּהִוָּסְדָם יַחַד
עָלַי, לָקַחַת נַפְשִׁי זָמָמוּ. וַאֲנִי, עָלֶיךָ
בָטַחְתִּי יהוה, אָמַרְתִּי: אֱלֹהַי אָתָּה. בְּיָדְךָ
עִתֹּתָי, הַצִּילֵנִי מִיַּד אוֹיְבַי וּמֵרֹדְפָי.
הָאִירָה פָנֶיךָ עַל עַבְדֶּךָ, הוֹשִׁיעֵנִי
בְחַסְדֶּךָ. יהוה, אַל אֵבוֹשָׁה כִּי קְרָאתִיךָ;
יֵבֹשׁוּ רְשָׁעִים, יִדְּמוּ לִשְׁאוֹל. תֵּאָלַמְנָה
שִׂפְתֵי שָׁקֶר, הַדֹּבְרוֹת עַל צַדִּיק עָתָק
בְּגַאֲוָה וָבוּז. מָה רַב טוּבְךָ אֲשֶׁר צָפַנְתָּ
לִּירֵאֶיךָ, פָּעַלְתָּ לַחֹסִים בָּךְ נֶגֶד בְּנֵי
אָדָם. תַּסְתִּירֵם בְּסֵתֶר פָּנֶיךָ מֵרֻכְסֵי אִישׁ,
תִּצְפְּנֵם בְּסֻכָּה מֵרִיב לְשֹׁנוֹת. בָּרוּךְ יהוה,
כִּי הִפְלִיא חַסְדּוֹ לִי בְּעִיר מָצוֹר. וַאֲנִי
אָמַרְתִּי בְחָפְזִי נִגְרַזְתִּי מִנֶּגֶד עֵינֶיךָ, אָכֵן
שָׁמַעְתָּ קוֹל תַּחֲנוּנַי בְּשַׁוְּעִי אֵלֶיךָ. אֶהֱבוּ
אֶת יהוה כָּל חֲסִידָיו; אֱמוּנִים נֹצֵר יהוה,
וּמְשַׁלֵּם עַל יֶתֶר עֹשֵׂה גַאֲוָה. חִזְקוּ וְיַאֲמֵץ
לְבַבְכֶם, כָּל הַמְיַחֲלִים לַיהוה.

לב לְדָוִד מַשְׂכִּיל, אַשְׁרֵי נְשׂוּי פֶּשַׁע,
כְּסוּי חֲטָאָה. אַשְׁרֵי אָדָם לֹא
יַחְשֹׁב יהוה לוֹ עָוֹן, וְאֵין בְּרוּחוֹ רְמִיָּה. כִּי
הֶחֱרַשְׁתִּי בָּלוּ עֲצָמָי, בְּשַׁאֲגָתִי כָּל הַיּוֹם.
כִּי יוֹמָם וָלַיְלָה תִּכְבַּד עָלַי יָדֶךָ, נֶהְפַּךְ
לְשַׁדִּי בְּחַרְבֹנֵי קַיִץ סֶלָה. חַטָּאתִי

כט מִזְמוֹר לְדָוִד; הָבוּ לַיהוה בְּנֵי
אֵלִים, הָבוּ לַיהוה כָּבוֹד וָעֹז. הָבוּ
לַיהוה כְּבוֹד שְׁמוֹ, הִשְׁתַּחֲווּ לַיהוה
בְּהַדְרַת קֹדֶשׁ. קוֹל יהוה עַל הַמָּיִם, אֵל
הַכָּבוֹד הִרְעִים, יהוה עַל מַיִם רַבִּים. קוֹל
יהוה בַּכֹּחַ, קוֹל יהוה בֶּהָדָר. קוֹל יהוה
שֹׁבֵר אֲרָזִים, וַיְשַׁבֵּר יהוה אֶת אַרְזֵי
הַלְּבָנוֹן. וַיַּרְקִידֵם כְּמוֹ עֵגֶל, לְבָנוֹן וְשִׂרְיוֹן
כְּמוֹ בֶן רְאֵמִים. קוֹל יהוה חֹצֵב לַהֲבוֹת
אֵשׁ. קוֹל יהוה יָחִיל מִדְבָּר, יָחִיל יהוה
מִדְבַּר קָדֵשׁ. קוֹל יהוה יְחוֹלֵל אַיָּלוֹת,
וַיֶּחֱשֹׂף יְעָרוֹת; וּבְהֵיכָלוֹ כֻּלּוֹ אֹמֵר כָּבוֹד.
יהוה לַמַּבּוּל יָשָׁב, וַיֵּשֶׁב יהוה מֶלֶךְ
לְעוֹלָם. יהוה עֹז לְעַמּוֹ יִתֵּן, יהוה יְבָרֵךְ
אֶת עַמּוֹ בַשָּׁלוֹם.

◆§ MONDAY / יוֹם שֵׁנִי ◆

ל מִזְמוֹר שִׁיר חֲנֻכַּת הַבַּיִת לְדָוִד.
אֲרוֹמִמְךָ יהוה כִּי דִלִּיתָנִי, וְלֹא
שִׂמַּחְתָּ אֹיְבַי לִי. יהוה אֱלֹהָי, שִׁוַּעְתִּי
אֵלֶיךָ וַתִּרְפָּאֵנִי. יהוה, הֶעֱלִיתָ מִן שְׁאוֹל
נַפְשִׁי, חִיִּיתַנִי מִיָּרְדִי בוֹר. זַמְּרוּ לַיהוה
חֲסִידָיו, וְהוֹדוּ לְזֵכֶר קָדְשׁוֹ. כִּי רֶגַע
בְּאַפּוֹ, חַיִּים בִּרְצוֹנוֹ; בָּעֶרֶב יָלִין בֶּכִי
וְלַבֹּקֶר רִנָּה. וַאֲנִי אָמַרְתִּי בְשַׁלְוִי, בַּל
אֶמּוֹט לְעוֹלָם. יהוה, בִּרְצוֹנְךָ הֶעֱמַדְתָּה
לְהַרְרִי עֹז, הִסְתַּרְתָּ פָנֶיךָ הָיִיתִי נִבְהָל.
אֵלֶיךָ יהוה אֶקְרָא, וְאֶל אֲדֹנָי אֶתְחַנָּן. מַה
בֶּצַע בְּדָמִי, בְּרִדְתִּי אֶל שָׁחַת; הֲיוֹדְךָ
עָפָר, הֲיַגִּיד אֲמִתֶּךָ. שְׁמַע יהוה וְחָנֵּנִי,
יהוה הֱיֵה עֹזֵר לִי. הָפַכְתָּ מִסְפְּדִי לְמָחוֹל
לִי, פִּתַּחְתָּ שַׂקִּי וַתְּאַזְּרֵנִי שִׂמְחָה. לְמַעַן
יְזַמֶּרְךָ כָבוֹד וְלֹא יִדֹּם, יהוה אֱלֹהַי
לְעוֹלָם אוֹדֶךָּ.

לא לַמְנַצֵּחַ מִזְמוֹר לְדָוִד. בְּךָ יהוה
חָסִיתִי, אַל אֵבוֹשָׁה לְעוֹלָם;
בְּצִדְקָתְךָ פַלְּטֵנִי. הַטֵּה אֵלַי אָזְנְךָ, מְהֵרָה
הַצִּילֵנִי; הֱיֵה לִי לְצוּר מָעוֹז, לְבֵית

אֶת יהוה בְּכָל עֵת, תָּמִיד תְּהִלָּתוֹ בְּפִי. בַּיהוה תִּתְהַלֵּל נַפְשִׁי, יִשְׁמְעוּ עֲנָוִים וְיִשְׂמָחוּ. גַּדְּלוּ לַיהוה אִתִּי, וּנְרוֹמְמָה שְׁמוֹ יַחְדָּו. דָּרַשְׁתִּי אֶת יהוה וְעָנָנִי, וּמִכָּל מְגוּרוֹתַי הִצִּילָנִי. הִבִּיטוּ אֵלָיו וְנָהָרוּ, וּפְנֵיהֶם אַל יֶחְפָּרוּ. זֶה עָנִי קָרָא וַיהוה שָׁמֵעַ, וּמִכָּל צָרוֹתָיו הוֹשִׁיעוֹ. חֹנֶה מַלְאַךְ יהוה סָבִיב לִירֵאָיו, וַיְחַלְּצֵם. טַעֲמוּ וּרְאוּ כִּי טוֹב יהוה, אַשְׁרֵי הַגֶּבֶר יֶחֱסֶה בּוֹ. יְראוּ אֶת יהוה קְדֹשָׁיו, כִּי אֵין מַחְסוֹר לִירֵאָיו. כְּפִירִים רָשׁוּ וְרָעֵבוּ, וְדֹרְשֵׁי יהוה לֹא יַחְסְרוּ כָל טוֹב. לְכוּ בָנִים שִׁמְעוּ לִי, יִרְאַת יהוה אֲלַמֶּדְכֶם. מִי הָאִישׁ הֶחָפֵץ חַיִּים, אֹהֵב יָמִים לִרְאוֹת טוֹב. נְצֹר לְשׁוֹנְךָ מֵרָע, וּשְׂפָתֶיךָ מִדַּבֵּר מִרְמָה. סוּר מֵרָע וַעֲשֵׂה טוֹב, בַּקֵּשׁ שָׁלוֹם וְרָדְפֵהוּ. עֵינֵי יהוה אֶל צַדִּיקִים, וְאָזְנָיו אֶל שַׁוְעָתָם. פְּנֵי יהוה בְּעֹשֵׂי רָע, לְהַכְרִית מֵאֶרֶץ זִכְרָם. צָעֲקוּ וַיהוה שָׁמֵעַ, וּמִכָּל צָרוֹתָם הִצִּילָם. קָרוֹב יהוה לְנִשְׁבְּרֵי לֵב, וְאֶת דַּכְּאֵי רוּחַ יוֹשִׁיעַ. רַבּוֹת רָעוֹת צַדִּיק, וּמִכֻּלָּם יַצִּילֶנּוּ יהוה. שֹׁמֵר כָּל עַצְמוֹתָיו, אַחַת מֵהֵנָּה לֹא נִשְׁבָּרָה. תְּמוֹתֵת רָשָׁע רָעָה, וְשֹׂנְאֵי צַדִּיק יֶאְשָׁמוּ. פּוֹדֶה יהוה נֶפֶשׁ עֲבָדָיו, וְלֹא יֶאְשְׁמוּ כָּל הַחֹסִים בּוֹ.

— DAY 6 —   יום ו' לחודש

לה לְדָוִד; רִיבָה יהוה אֶת יְרִיבַי, לְחַם אֶת לֹחֲמָי. הַחֲזֵק מָגֵן וְצִנָּה, וְקוּמָה בְּעֶזְרָתִי. וְהָרֵק חֲנִית וּסְגֹר לִקְרַאת רֹדְפָי, אֱמֹר לְנַפְשִׁי יְשֻׁעָתֵךְ אָנִי. יֵבֹשׁוּ וְיִכָּלְמוּ מְבַקְשֵׁי נַפְשִׁי, יִסֹּגוּ אָחוֹר וְיַחְפְּרוּ, חֹשְׁבֵי רָעָתִי. יִהְיוּ כְּמֹץ לִפְנֵי רוּחַ, וּמַלְאַךְ יהוה דּוֹחֶה. יְהִי דַרְכָּם חֹשֶׁךְ וַחֲלַקְלַקֹּת, וּמַלְאַךְ יהוה רֹדְפָם. כִּי חִנָּם טָמְנוּ לִי שַׁחַת רִשְׁתָּם, חִנָּם חָפְרוּ לְנַפְשִׁי. תְּבוֹאֵהוּ שׁוֹאָה לֹא יֵדָע, וְרִשְׁתּוֹ אֲשֶׁר טָמַן תִּלְכְּדוֹ, בְּשׁוֹאָה יִפָּל בָּהּ. וְנַפְשִׁי תָּגִיל בַּיהוה, תָּשִׂישׂ בִּישׁוּעָתוֹ. כָּל

אוֹדִיעֲךָ, וַעֲוֹנִי לֹא כִסִּיתִי, אָמַרְתִּי אוֹדֶה עֲלֵי פְשָׁעַי לַיהוה; וְאַתָּה נָשָׂאתָ עֲוֹן חַטָּאתִי סֶלָה. עַל זֹאת יִתְפַּלֵּל כָּל חָסִיד אֵלֶיךָ לְעֵת מְצֹא, רַק לְשֵׁטֶף מַיִם רַבִּים אֵלָיו לֹא יַגִּיעוּ. אַתָּה סֵתֶר לִי, מִצַּר תִּצְּרֵנִי; רָנֵּי פַלֵּט תְּסוֹבְבֵנִי סֶלָה. אַשְׂכִּילְךָ וְאוֹרְךָ בְּדֶרֶךְ זוּ תֵלֵךְ, אִיעֲצָה עָלֶיךָ עֵינִי. אַל תִּהְיוּ כְּסוּס כְּפֶרֶד אֵין הָבִין; בְּמֶתֶג וָרֶסֶן עֶדְיוֹ לִבְלוֹם, בַּל קְרֹב אֵלֶיךָ. רַבִּים מַכְאוֹבִים לָרָשָׁע, וְהַבּוֹטֵחַ בַּיהוה חֶסֶד יְסוֹבְבֶנּוּ. שִׂמְחוּ בַיהוה וְגִילוּ צַדִּיקִים, וְהַרְנִינוּ כָּל יִשְׁרֵי לֵב.

לג רַנְּנוּ צַדִּיקִים בַּיהוה, לַיְשָׁרִים נָאוָה תְהִלָּה. הוֹדוּ לַיהוה בְּכִנּוֹר, בְּנֵבֶל עָשׂוֹר זַמְּרוּ לוֹ. שִׁירוּ לוֹ שִׁיר חָדָשׁ, הֵיטִיבוּ נַגֵּן בִּתְרוּעָה. כִּי יָשָׁר דְּבַר יהוה, וְכָל מַעֲשֵׂהוּ בֶּאֱמוּנָה. אֹהֵב צְדָקָה וּמִשְׁפָּט, חֶסֶד יהוה מָלְאָה הָאָרֶץ. בִּדְבַר יהוה שָׁמַיִם נַעֲשׂוּ, וּבְרוּחַ פִּיו כָּל צְבָאָם. כֹּנֵס כַּנֵּד מֵי הַיָּם, נֹתֵן בְּאוֹצָרוֹת תְּהוֹמוֹת. יִירְאוּ מֵיהוה כָּל הָאָרֶץ, מִמֶּנּוּ יָגוּרוּ כָּל יֹשְׁבֵי תֵבֵל. כִּי הוּא אָמַר וַיֶּהִי, הוּא צִוָּה וַיַּעֲמֹד. יהוה הֵפִיר עֲצַת גּוֹיִם, הֵנִיא מַחְשְׁבוֹת עַמִּים. עֲצַת יהוה לְעוֹלָם תַּעֲמֹד, מַחְשְׁבוֹת לִבּוֹ לְדֹר וָדֹר. אַשְׁרֵי הַגּוֹי אֲשֶׁר יהוה אֱלֹהָיו, הָעָם בָּחַר לְנַחֲלָה לוֹ. מִשָּׁמַיִם הִבִּיט יהוה, רָאָה אֶת כָּל בְּנֵי הָאָדָם. מִמְּכוֹן שִׁבְתּוֹ הִשְׁגִּיחַ, אֶל כָּל יֹשְׁבֵי הָאָרֶץ. הַיֹּצֵר יַחַד לִבָּם, הַמֵּבִין אֶל כָּל מַעֲשֵׂיהֶם. אֵין הַמֶּלֶךְ נוֹשָׁע בְּרָב חָיִל, גִּבּוֹר לֹא יִנָּצֵל בְּרָב כֹּחַ. שֶׁקֶר הַסּוּס לִתְשׁוּעָה, וּבְרֹב חֵילוֹ לֹא יְמַלֵּט. הִנֵּה עֵין יהוה אֶל יְרֵאָיו, לַמְיַחֲלִים לְחַסְדּוֹ. לְהַצִּיל מִמָּוֶת נַפְשָׁם, וּלְחַיּוֹתָם בָּרָעָב. נַפְשֵׁנוּ חִכְּתָה לַיהוה, עֶזְרֵנוּ וּמָגִנֵּנוּ הוּא. כִּי בוֹ יִשְׂמַח לִבֵּנוּ, כִּי בְשֵׁם קָדְשׁוֹ בָטָחְנוּ. יְהִי חַסְדְּךָ יהוה עָלֵינוּ, כַּאֲשֶׁר יִחַלְנוּ לָךְ.

לד לְדָוִד, בְּשַׁנּוֹתוֹ אֶת טַעְמוֹ לִפְנֵי אֲבִימֶלֶךְ, וַיְגָרְשֵׁהוּ וַיֵּלַךְ. אֲבָרְכָה

עֲצָמֹתַי תֹּאמַרְנָה: יהוה, מִי כָמְוֹךָ; מַצִּיל
עָנִי מֵחָזָק מִמֶּנּוּ, וְעָנִי וְאֶבְיוֹן מִגֹּזְלוֹ.
יְקוּמוּן עֵדֵי חָמָס, אֲשֶׁר לֹא יָדַעְתִּי
יִשְׁאָלְוּנִי. יְשַׁלְּמְוּנִי רָעָה תַּחַת טוֹבָה,
שְׁכוֹל לְנַפְשִׁי. וַאֲנִי בַּחֲלוֹתָם לְבוּשִׁי שָׂק,
עִנֵּיתִי בַצּוֹם נַפְשִׁי; וּתְפִלָּתִי עַל חֵיקִי
תָשׁוּב. כְּרֵעַ כְּאָח לִי הִתְהַלָּכְתִּי, כַּאֲבֶל
אֵם קֹדֵר שַׁחְוֹתִי. וּבְצַלְעִי שָׂמְחוּ וְנֶאֱסָפוּ,
נֶאֶסְפוּ עָלַי נֵכִים וְלֹא יָדַעְתִּי, קָרְעוּ וְלֹא
דָמּוּ. בְּחַנְפֵי לַעֲגֵי מָעוֹג, חָרֹק עָלַי
שִׁנֵּימוֹ. אֲדֹנָי, כַּמָּה תִּרְאֶה, הָשִׁיבָה נַפְשִׁי
מִשֹּׁאֵיהֶם, מִכְּפִירִים יְחִידָתִי. אוֹדְךָ
בְּקָהָל רָב, בְּעַם עָצוּם אֲהַלְלֶךָּ. אַל
יִשְׂמְחוּ לִי אֹיְבַי שֶׁקֶר, שֹׂנְאַי חִנָּם יִקְרְצוּ
עָיִן. כִּי לֹא שָׁלוֹם יְדַבֵּרוּ; וְעַל רִגְעֵי אֶרֶץ,
דִּבְרֵי מִרְמוֹת יַחֲשֹׁבוּן. וַיַּרְחִיבוּ עָלַי
פִּיהֶם; אָמְרוּ: הֶאָח הֶאָח, רָאֲתָה עֵינֵנוּ.
רָאִיתָה, יהוה, אַל תֶּחֱרַשׁ; אֲדֹנָי, אַל
תִּרְחַק מִמֶּנִּי. הָעִירָה וְהָקִיצָה לְמִשְׁפָּטִי,
אֱלֹהַי וַאדֹנָי לְרִיבִי. שָׁפְטֵנִי כְצִדְקְךָ יהוה
אֱלֹהָי, וְאַל יִשְׂמְחוּ לִי. אַל יֹאמְרוּ בְלִבָּם
הֶאָח נַפְשֵׁנוּ, אַל יֹאמְרוּ בִּלַּעֲנוּהוּ. יֵבֹשׁוּ
וְיַחְפְּרוּ יַחְדָּו שְׂמֵחֵי רָעָתִי; יִלְבְּשׁוּ בֹשֶׁת
וּכְלִמָּה, הַמַּגְדִּילִים עָלָי. יָרֹנּוּ וְיִשְׂמְחוּ
חֲפֵצֵי צִדְקִי; וְיֹאמְרוּ תָמִיד: יִגְדַּל יהוה,
הֶחָפֵץ שְׁלוֹם עַבְדּוֹ. וּלְשׁוֹנִי תֶּהְגֶּה צִדְקֶךָ,
כָּל הַיּוֹם תְּהִלָּתֶךָ.

לו לַמְנַצֵּחַ לְעֶבֶד יהוה לְדָוִד. נְאֻם
פֶּשַׁע לָרָשָׁע בְּקֶרֶב לִבִּי, אֵין פַּחַד
אֱלֹהִים לְנֶגֶד עֵינָיו. כִּי הֶחֱלִיק אֵלָיו
בְּעֵינָיו, לִמְצֹא עֲוֹנוֹ לִשְׂנֹא. דִּבְרֵי פִיו אָוֶן
וּמִרְמָה, חָדַל לְהַשְׂכִּיל לְהֵיטִיב. אָוֶן
יַחְשֹׁב עַל מִשְׁכָּבוֹ; יִתְיַצֵּב עַל דֶּרֶךְ לֹא
טוֹב, רָע לֹא יִמְאָס. יהוה, בְּהַשָּׁמַיִם
חַסְדֶּךָ, אֱמוּנָתְךָ עַד שְׁחָקִים. צִדְקָתְךָ
כְּהַרְרֵי אֵל, מִשְׁפָּטֶיךָ תְּהוֹם רַבָּה; אָדָם
וּבְהֵמָה תוֹשִׁיעַ | יהוה. מַה יָּקָר חַסְדְּךָ,
אֱלֹהִים; וּבְנֵי אָדָם בְּצֵל כְּנָפֶיךָ יֶחֱסָיוּן.
יִרְוְיֻן מִדֶּשֶׁן בֵּיתֶךָ, וְנַחַל עֲדָנֶיךָ תַשְׁקֵם.

כִּי עִמְּךָ מְקוֹר חַיִּים, בְּאוֹרְךָ נִרְאֶה אוֹר.
מְשֹׁךְ חַסְדְּךָ לְיֹדְעֶיךָ, וְצִדְקָתְךָ לְיִשְׁרֵי
לֵב. אַל תְּבוֹאֵנִי רֶגֶל גַּאֲוָה, וְיַד רְשָׁעִים
אַל תְּנִדֵנִי. שָׁם נָפְלוּ פֹּעֲלֵי אָוֶן, דֹּחוּ וְלֹא
יָכְלוּ קוּם.

לז לְדָוִד; אַל תִּתְחַר בַּמְּרֵעִים, אַל
תְּקַנֵּא בְּעֹשֵׂי עַוְלָה. כִּי כֶחָצִיר
מְהֵרָה יִמָּלוּ, וּכְיֶרֶק דֶּשֶׁא יִבּוֹלוּן. בְּטַח
בַּיהוה וַעֲשֵׂה טוֹב, שְׁכָן אֶרֶץ וּרְעֵה
אֱמוּנָה. וְהִתְעַנַּג עַל יהוה, וְיִתֶּן לְךָ
מִשְׁאֲלֹת לִבֶּךָ. גּוֹל עַל יהוה דַּרְכֶּךָ, וּבְטַח
עָלָיו וְהוּא יַעֲשֶׂה. וְהוֹצִיא כָאוֹר צִדְקֶךָ,
וּמִשְׁפָּטֶךָ כַּצָּהֳרָיִם. דּוֹם לַיהוה וְהִתְחוֹלֵל
לוֹ; אַל תִּתְחַר בְּמַצְלִיחַ דַּרְכּוֹ, בְּאִישׁ
עֹשֶׂה מְזִמּוֹת. הֶרֶף מֵאַף וַעֲזֹב חֵמָה; אַל
תִּתְחַר, אַךְ לְהָרֵעַ. כִּי מְרֵעִים יִכָּרֵתוּן,
וְקֹוֵי יהוה הֵמָּה יִירְשׁוּ אָרֶץ. וְעוֹד מְעַט
וְאֵין רָשָׁע, וְהִתְבּוֹנַנְתָּ עַל מְקוֹמוֹ וְאֵינֶנּוּ.
וַעֲנָוִים יִירְשׁוּ אָרֶץ, וְהִתְעַנְּגוּ עַל רֹב
שָׁלוֹם. זֹמֵם רָשָׁע לַצַּדִּיק, וְחֹרֵק עָלָיו
שִׁנָּיו. אֲדֹנָי יִשְׂחַק לוֹ, כִּי רָאָה כִּי יָבֹא
יוֹמוֹ. חֶרֶב פָּתְחוּ רְשָׁעִים וְדָרְכוּ קַשְׁתָּם,
לְהַפִּיל עָנִי וְאֶבְיוֹן, לִטְבוֹחַ יִשְׁרֵי דָרֶךְ.
חַרְבָּם תָּבוֹא בְלִבָּם, וְקַשְּׁתוֹתָם תִּשָּׁבַרְנָה.
טוֹב מְעַט לַצַּדִּיק, מֵהֲמוֹן רְשָׁעִים רַבִּים.
כִּי זְרוֹעוֹת רְשָׁעִים תִּשָּׁבַרְנָה, וְסוֹמֵךְ
צַדִּיקִים יהוה. יוֹדֵעַ יהוה יְמֵי תְמִימִם,
וְנַחֲלָתָם לְעוֹלָם תִּהְיֶה. לֹא יֵבֹשׁוּ בְּעֵת
רָעָה, וּבִימֵי רְעָבוֹן יִשְׂבָּעוּ. כִּי רְשָׁעִים
יֹאבֵדוּ, וְאֹיְבֵי יהוה כִּיקַר כָּרִים, כָּלוּ
בֶעָשָׁן כָּלוּ. לֹוֶה רָשָׁע וְלֹא יְשַׁלֵּם, וְצַדִּיק
חוֹנֵן וְנוֹתֵן. כִּי מְבֹרָכָיו יִירְשׁוּ אָרֶץ,
וּמְקֻלָּלָיו יִכָּרֵתוּ. מֵיהוה מִצְעֲדֵי גֶבֶר
כּוֹנָנוּ, וְדַרְכּוֹ יֶחְפָּץ. כִּי יִפֹּל לֹא יוּטָל, כִּי
יהוה סוֹמֵךְ יָדוֹ. נַעַר הָיִיתִי גַּם זָקַנְתִּי;
וְלֹא רָאִיתִי צַדִּיק נֶעֱזָב, וְזַרְעוֹ מְבַקֶּשׁ
לָחֶם. כָּל הַיּוֹם חוֹנֵן וּמַלְוֶה, וְזַרְעוֹ
לִבְרָכָה. סוּר מֵרָע וַעֲשֵׂה טוֹב, וּשְׁכֹן
לְעוֹלָם. כִּי יהוה אֹהֵב מִשְׁפָּט, וְלֹא יַעֲזֹב

אֶת חֲסִידָיו, לְעוֹלָם נִשְׁמָרוּ; וְזֶרַע רְשָׁעִים
נִכְרָת. צַדִּיקִים יִירְשׁוּ אָרֶץ, וְיִשְׁכְּנוּ לָעַד
עָלֶיהָ. פִּי צַדִּיק יֶהְגֶּה חָכְמָה, וּלְשׁוֹנוֹ
תְּדַבֵּר מִשְׁפָּט. תּוֹרַת אֱלֹהָיו בְּלִבּוֹ, לֹא
תִמְעַד אֲשֻׁרָיו. צוֹפֶה רָשָׁע לַצַּדִּיק,
וּמְבַקֵּשׁ לַהֲמִיתוֹ. יהוה לֹא יַעַזְבֶנּוּ בְיָדוֹ,
וְלֹא יַרְשִׁיעֶנּוּ בְּהִשָּׁפְטוֹ. קַוֵּה אֶל יהוה
וּשְׁמֹר דַּרְכּוֹ, וִירוֹמִמְךָ לָרֶשֶׁת אָרֶץ;
בְּהִכָּרֵת רְשָׁעִים תִּרְאֶה. רָאִיתִי רָשָׁע
עָרִיץ, וּמִתְעָרֶה כְּאֶזְרָח רַעֲנָן. וַיַּעֲבֹר
וְהִנֵּה אֵינֶנּוּ, וָאֲבַקְשֵׁהוּ וְלֹא נִמְצָא. שְׁמָר
תָּם וּרְאֵה יָשָׁר, כִּי אַחֲרִית לְאִישׁ שָׁלוֹם.
וּפֹשְׁעִים נִשְׁמְדוּ יַחְדָּו, אַחֲרִית רְשָׁעִים
נִכְרָתָה. וּתְשׁוּעַת צַדִּיקִים מֵיהוה, מָעוּזָּם
בְּעֵת צָרָה. וַיַּעְזְרֵם יהוה וַיְפַלְּטֵם; יְפַלְּטֵם
מֵרְשָׁעִים וְיוֹשִׁיעֵם, כִּי חָסוּ בוֹ.

לח מִזְמוֹר לְדָוִד לְהַזְכִּיר. יהוה, אַל
בְּקֶצְפְּךָ תוֹכִיחֵנִי, וּבַחֲמָתְךָ
תְיַסְּרֵנִי. כִּי חִצֶּיךָ נִחֲתוּ בִי, וַתִּנְחַת עָלַי
יָדֶךָ. אֵין מְתֹם בִּבְשָׂרִי מִפְּנֵי זַעְמֶךָ, אֵין
שָׁלוֹם בַּעֲצָמַי מִפְּנֵי חַטָּאתִי. כִּי עֲוֹנֹתַי
עָבְרוּ רֹאשִׁי, כְּמַשָּׂא כָבֵד יִכְבְּדוּ מִמֶּנִּי.
הִבְאִישׁוּ נָמַקּוּ חַבּוּרֹתָי, מִפְּנֵי אִוַּלְתִּי.
נַעֲוֵיתִי שַׁחֹתִי עַד מְאֹד, כָּל הַיּוֹם קֹדֵר
הִלָּכְתִּי. כִּי כְסָלַי מָלְאוּ נִקְלֶה, וְאֵין מְתֹם
בִּבְשָׂרִי. נְפוּגוֹתִי וְנִדְכֵּיתִי עַד מְאֹד,
שָׁאַגְתִּי מִנַּהֲמַת לִבִּי. אֲדֹנָי, נֶגְדְּךָ כָל
תַּאֲוָתִי, וְאַנְחָתִי מִמְּךָ לֹא נִסְתָּרָה. לִבִּי
סְחַרְחַר, עֲזָבַנִי כֹחִי; וְאוֹר עֵינַי גַּם הֵם
אֵין אִתִּי. אֹהֲבַי וְרֵעַי מִנֶּגֶד נִגְעִי יַעֲמֹדוּ,
וּקְרוֹבַי מֵרָחֹק עָמָדוּ. וַיְנַקְשׁוּ מְבַקְשֵׁי
נַפְשִׁי, וְדֹרְשֵׁי רָעָתִי דִּבְּרוּ הַוּוֹת, וּמִרְמוֹת
כָּל הַיּוֹם יֶהְגּוּ. וַאֲנִי כְחֵרֵשׁ לֹא אֶשְׁמָע,
וּכְאִלֵּם לֹא יִפְתַּח פִּיו. וָאֱהִי כְּאִישׁ אֲשֶׁר
לֹא שֹׁמֵעַ, וְאֵין בְּפִיו תּוֹכָחוֹת. כִּי לְךָ יהוה
הוֹחָלְתִּי; אַתָּה תַעֲנֶה, אֲדֹנָי אֱלֹהָי. כִּי
אָמַרְתִּי פֶּן יִשְׂמְחוּ לִי, בְּמוֹט רַגְלִי עָלַי
הִגְדִּילוּ. כִּי אֲנִי לְצֶלַע נָכוֹן, וּמַכְאוֹבִי
נֶגְדִּי תָמִיד. כִּי עֲוֹנִי אַגִּיד, אֶדְאַג

מֵחַטָּאתִי. וְאֹיְבַי חַיִּים עָצֵמוּ, וְרַבּוּ שֹׂנְאַי
שָׁקֶר. וּמְשַׁלְּמֵי רָעָה תַּחַת טוֹבָה יִשְׂטְנוּנִי,
תַּחַת רָדְפִי טוֹב. אַל תַּעַזְבֵנִי יהוה, אֱלֹהַי
אַל תִּרְחַק מִמֶּנִּי. חוּשָׁה לְעֶזְרָתִי, אֲדֹנָי
תְּשׁוּעָתִי.

לט לַמְנַצֵּחַ לִידוּתוּן, מִזְמוֹר לְדָוִד.
אָמַרְתִּי: אֶשְׁמְרָה דְרָכַי מֵחֲטוֹא
בִלְשׁוֹנִי, אֶשְׁמְרָה לְפִי מַחְסוֹם בְּעֹד רָשָׁע
לְנֶגְדִּי. נֶאֱלַמְתִּי דוּמִיָּה, הֶחֱשֵׁיתִי מִטּוֹב
וּכְאֵבִי נֶעְכָּר. חַם לִבִּי בְּקִרְבִּי, בַּהֲגִיגִי
תִבְעַר אֵשׁ; דִּבַּרְתִּי בִּלְשׁוֹנִי. הוֹדִיעֵנִי
יהוה | קִצִּי, וּמִדַּת יָמַי מַה הִיא; אֵדְעָה מֶה
חָדֵל אָנִי. הִנֵּה טְפָחוֹת נָתַתָּה יָמַי, וְחֶלְדִּי
כְאַיִן נֶגְדֶּךָ; אַךְ כָּל הֶבֶל כָּל אָדָם נִצָּב
סֶלָה. אַךְ בְּצֶלֶם יִתְהַלֶּךְ אִישׁ, אַךְ הֶבֶל
יֶהֱמָיוּן; יִצְבֹּר, וְלֹא יֵדַע מִי אֹסְפָם. וְעַתָּה
מַה קִּוִּיתִי אֲדֹנָי, תּוֹחַלְתִּי לְךָ הִיא. מִכָּל
פְּשָׁעַי הַצִּילֵנִי, חֶרְפַּת נָבָל אַל תְּשִׂימֵנִי.
נֶאֱלַמְתִּי לֹא אֶפְתַּח פִּי, כִּי אַתָּה עָשִׂיתָ.
הָסֵר מֵעָלַי נִגְעֶךָ, מִתִּגְרַת יָדְךָ אֲנִי
כָלִיתִי. בְּתוֹכָחוֹת עַל עָוֹן יִסַּרְתָּ אִישׁ,
וַתֶּמֶס כָּעָשׁ חֲמוּדוֹ; אַךְ הֶבֶל כָּל אָדָם
סֶלָה. שִׁמְעָה תְפִלָּתִי | יהוה, וְשַׁוְעָתִי
הַאֲזִינָה, אֶל דִּמְעָתִי אַל תֶּחֱרַשׁ; כִּי גֵר
אָנֹכִי עִמָּךְ, תּוֹשָׁב כְּכָל אֲבוֹתָי. הָשַׁע
מִמֶּנִּי וְאַבְלִיגָה, בְּטֶרֶם אֵלֵךְ וְאֵינֶנִּי.

מ לַמְנַצֵּחַ לְדָוִד מִזְמוֹר. קַוֹּה קִוִּיתִי
יהוה, וַיֵּט אֵלַי וַיִּשְׁמַע שַׁוְעָתִי.
וַיַּעֲלֵנִי מִבּוֹר שָׁאוֹן מִטִּיט הַיָּוֵן, וַיָּקֶם עַל
סֶלַע רַגְלַי, כּוֹנֵן אֲשֻׁרָי. וַיִּתֵּן בְּפִי שִׁיר
חָדָשׁ, תְּהִלָּה לֵאלֹהֵינוּ; יִרְאוּ רַבִּים
וְיִירָאוּ, וְיִבְטְחוּ בַּיהוה. אַשְׁרֵי הַגֶּבֶר
אֲשֶׁר שָׂם יהוה מִבְטַחוֹ, וְלֹא פָנָה אֶל
רְהָבִים וְשָׂטֵי כָזָב. רַבּוֹת עָשִׂיתָ אַתָּה
יהוה אֱלֹהַי, נִפְלְאֹתֶיךָ וּמַחְשְׁבֹתֶיךָ
אֵלֵינוּ; אֵין עֲרֹךְ אֵלֶיךָ, אַגִּידָה וַאֲדַבֵּרָה,
עָצְמוּ מִסַּפֵּר. זֶבַח וּמִנְחָה לֹא חָפַצְתָּ,

אָזְנַיִם כָּרִיתָ לִּי; עוֹלָה וַחֲטָאָה לֹא שָׁאָלְתָּ. אָז אָמַרְתִּי הִנֵּה בָאתִי, בִּמְגִלַּת סֵפֶר כָּתוּב עָלָי. לַעֲשׂוֹת רְצוֹנְךָ, אֱלֹהַי, חָפָצְתִּי; וְתוֹרָתְךָ בְּתוֹךְ מֵעָי. בִּשַּׂרְתִּי צֶדֶק בְּקָהָל רָב, הִנֵּה שְׂפָתַי לֹא אֶכְלָא; יהוה, אַתָּה יָדָעְתָּ. צִדְקָתְךָ לֹא כִסִּיתִי בְּתוֹךְ לִבִּי, אֱמוּנָתְךָ וּתְשׁוּעָתְךָ אָמָרְתִּי; לֹא כִחַדְתִּי חַסְדְּךָ וַאֲמִתְּךָ לְקָהָל רָב. אַתָּה יהוה לֹא תִכְלָא רַחֲמֶיךָ מִמֶּנִּי, חַסְדְּךָ וַאֲמִתְּךָ תָּמִיד יִצְּרוּנִי. כִּי אָפְפוּ עָלַי רָעוֹת עַד אֵין מִסְפָּר, הִשִּׂיגוּנִי עֲוֹנֹתַי וְלֹא יָכֹלְתִּי לִרְאוֹת; עָצְמוּ מִשַּׂעֲרוֹת רֹאשִׁי, וְלִבִּי עֲזָבָנִי. רְצֵה יהוה לְהַצִּילֵנִי, יהוה לְעֶזְרָתִי חוּשָׁה. יֵבֹשׁוּ וְיַחְפְּרוּ יַחַד מְבַקְשֵׁי נַפְשִׁי לִסְפּוֹתָהּ, יִסֹּגוּ אָחוֹר וְיִכָּלְמוּ חֲפֵצֵי רָעָתִי. יָשֹׁמּוּ עַל עֵקֶב בָּשְׁתָּם, הָאֹמְרִים לִי הֶאָח הֶאָח. יָשִׂישׂוּ וְיִשְׂמְחוּ בְּךָ כָּל מְבַקְשֶׁיךָ; יֹאמְרוּ תָמִיד יִגְדַּל יהוה, אֹהֲבֵי תְּשׁוּעָתֶךָ. וַאֲנִי עָנִי וְאֶבְיוֹן, אֲדֹנָי יַחֲשָׁב לִי; עֶזְרָתִי וּמְפַלְטִי

אַתָּה, אֱלֹהַי אַל תְּאַחַר.

מא לַמְנַצֵּחַ מִזְמוֹר לְדָוִד. אַשְׁרֵי מַשְׂכִּיל אֶל דָּל, בְּיוֹם רָעָה יְמַלְּטֵהוּ יהוה. יהוה יִשְׁמְרֵהוּ וִיחַיֵּהוּ, וְאֻשַּׁר בָּאָרֶץ, וְאַל תִּתְּנֵהוּ בְּנֶפֶשׁ אֹיְבָיו. יהוה יִסְעָדֶנּוּ עַל עֶרֶשׂ דְּוָי, כָּל מִשְׁכָּבוֹ הָפַכְתָּ בְחָלְיוֹ. אֲנִי אָמַרְתִּי: יהוה חָנֵּנִי, רְפָאָה נַפְשִׁי, כִּי חָטָאתִי לָךְ. אוֹיְבַי יֹאמְרוּ רַע לִי, מָתַי יָמוּת וְאָבַד שְׁמוֹ. וְאִם בָּא לִרְאוֹת שָׁוְא יְדַבֵּר, לִבּוֹ יִקְבָּץ אָוֶן לוֹ; יֵצֵא לַחוּץ יְדַבֵּר. יַחַד עָלַי יִתְלַחֲשׁוּ כָּל שֹׂנְאָי, עָלַי יַחְשְׁבוּ רָעָה לִי. דְּבַר בְּלִיַּעַל יָצוּק בּוֹ, וַאֲשֶׁר שָׁכַב לֹא יוֹסִיף לָקוּם. גַּם אִישׁ שְׁלוֹמִי אֲשֶׁר בָּטַחְתִּי בוֹ, אוֹכֵל לַחְמִי, הִגְדִּיל עָלַי עָקֵב. וְאַתָּה יהוה חָנֵּנִי וַהֲקִימֵנִי, וַאֲשַׁלְּמָה לָהֶם. בְּזֹאת יָדַעְתִּי כִּי חָפַצְתָּ בִּי, כִּי לֹא יָרִיעַ אֹיְבִי עָלָי. וַאֲנִי בְּתֻמִּי תָּמַכְתָּ בִּי, וַתַּצִּיבֵנִי לְפָנֶיךָ לְעוֹלָם. בָּרוּךְ יהוה אֱלֹהֵי יִשְׂרָאֵל מֵהָעוֹלָם וְעַד הָעוֹלָם, אָמֵן וְאָמֵן.

❧ סֵפֶר שֵׁנִי / BOOK TWO ❧

מב לַמְנַצֵּחַ מַשְׂכִּיל לִבְנֵי קֹרַח. כְּאַיָּל תַּעֲרֹג עַל אֲפִיקֵי מָיִם, כֵּן נַפְשִׁי תַעֲרֹג אֵלֶיךָ אֱלֹהִים. צָמְאָה נַפְשִׁי לֵאלֹהִים, לְאֵל חָי, מָתַי אָבוֹא וְאֵרָאֶה פְּנֵי אֱלֹהִים. הָיְתָה לִּי דִמְעָתִי לֶחֶם יוֹמָם וָלָיְלָה, בֶּאֱמֹר אֵלַי כָּל הַיּוֹם: אַיֵּה אֱלֹהֶיךָ. אֵלֶּה אֶזְכְּרָה וְאֶשְׁפְּכָה עָלַי נַפְשִׁי, כִּי אֶעֱבֹר בַּסָּךְ, אֶדַּדֵּם עַד בֵּית אֱלֹהִים; בְּקוֹל רִנָּה וְתוֹדָה הָמוֹן חוֹגֵג. מַה תִּשְׁתּוֹחֲחִי נַפְשִׁי, וַתֶּהֱמִי עָלָי; הוֹחִילִי לֵאלֹהִים, כִּי עוֹד אוֹדֶנּוּ יְשׁוּעוֹת פָּנָיו. אֱלֹהַי, עָלַי נַפְשִׁי תִשְׁתּוֹחָח, עַל כֵּן אֶזְכָּרְךָ מֵאֶרֶץ יַרְדֵּן וְחֶרְמוֹנִים, מֵהַר מִצְעָר. תְּהוֹם אֶל תְּהוֹם קוֹרֵא לְקוֹל צִנּוֹרֶיךָ, כָּל מִשְׁבָּרֶיךָ וְגַלֶּיךָ עָלַי עָבָרוּ. יוֹמָם יְצַוֶּה יהוה חַסְדּוֹ, וּבַלַּיְלָה שִׁירֹה עִמִּי; תְּפִלָּה לְאֵל חַיָּי. אוֹמְרָה לְאֵל

מג שָׁפְטֵנִי אֱלֹהִים וְרִיבָה רִיבִי מִגּוֹי לֹא חָסִיד, מֵאִישׁ מִרְמָה וְעַוְלָה תְפַלְּטֵנִי. כִּי אַתָּה אֱלֹהֵי מָעוּזִי, לָמָה זְנַחְתָּנִי; לָמָה קֹדֵר אֶתְהַלֵּךְ בְּלַחַץ אוֹיֵב. שְׁלַח אוֹרְךָ וַאֲמִתְּךָ, הֵמָּה יַנְחוּנִי, יְבִיאוּנִי אֶל הַר קָדְשְׁךָ וְאֶל מִשְׁכְּנוֹתֶיךָ. וְאָבוֹאָה אֶל מִזְבַּח אֱלֹהִים, אֶל אֵל שִׂמְחַת גִּילִי; וְאוֹדְךָ בְכִנּוֹר, אֱלֹהִים אֱלֹהָי. מַה תִּשְׁתּוֹחֲחִי נַפְשִׁי, וּמַה תֶּהֱמִי עָלָי; הוֹחִילִי לֵאלֹהִים, כִּי עוֹד אוֹדֶנּוּ יְשׁוּעֹת פָּנַי וֵאלֹהָי.

סַלְעִי, לָמָה שְׁכַחְתָּנִי, לָמָה קֹדֵר אֵלֵךְ בְּלַחַץ אוֹיֵב. בְּרֶצַח בְּעַצְמוֹתַי חֵרְפוּנִי צוֹרְרָי, בְּאָמְרָם אֵלַי כָּל הַיּוֹם: אַיֵּה אֱלֹהֶיךָ. מַה תִּשְׁתּוֹחֲחִי נַפְשִׁי, וּמַה תֶּהֱמִי עָלָי; הוֹחִילִי לֵאלֹהִים, כִּי עוֹד אוֹדֶנּוּ יְשׁוּעֹת פָּנַי וֵאלֹהָי.

חֵן בְּשִׂפְתוֹתֶיךָ, עַל כֵּן בֵּרַכְךָ אֱלֹהִים לְעוֹלָם. חֲגוֹר חַרְבְּךָ עַל יָרֵךְ, גִּבּוֹר, הוֹדְךָ וַהֲדָרֶךָ. וַהֲדָרְךָ, צְלַח רְכַב עַל דְּבַר אֱמֶת וְעַנְוָה צֶדֶק, וְתוֹרְךָ נוֹרָאוֹת יְמִינֶךָ. חִצֶּיךָ שְׁנוּנִים, עַמִּים תַּחְתֶּיךָ יִפְּלוּ, בְּלֵב אוֹיְבֵי הַמֶּלֶךְ. כִּסְאֲךָ אֱלֹהִים עוֹלָם וָעֶד, שֵׁבֶט מִישֹׁר שֵׁבֶט מַלְכוּתֶךָ. אָהַבְתָּ צֶּדֶק וַתִּשְׂנָא רֶשַׁע; עַל כֵּן מְשָׁחֲךָ אֱלֹהִים אֱלֹהֶיךָ, שֶׁמֶן שָׂשׂוֹן מֵחֲבֵרֶיךָ. מֹר וַאֲהָלוֹת קְצִיעוֹת כָּל בִּגְדֹתֶיךָ, מִן הֵיכְלֵי שֵׁן מִנִּי שִׂמְּחוּךָ. בְּנוֹת מְלָכִים בְּיִקְּרוֹתֶיךָ, נִצְּבָה שֵׁגַל לִימִינְךָ בְּכֶתֶם אוֹפִיר. שִׁמְעִי בַת וּרְאִי, וְהַטִּי אָזְנֵךְ; וְשִׁכְחִי עַמֵּךְ וּבֵית אָבִיךְ. וְיִתְאָו הַמֶּלֶךְ יָפְיֵךְ; כִּי הוּא אֲדֹנַיִךְ, וְהִשְׁתַּחֲוִי לוֹ. וּבַת צֹר, בְּמִנְחָה פָּנַיִךְ יְחַלּוּ עֲשִׁירֵי עָם. כָּל כְּבוּדָּה בַת מֶלֶךְ פְּנִימָה, מִמִּשְׁבְּצוֹת זָהָב לְבוּשָׁהּ. לִרְקָמוֹת תּוּבַל לַמֶּלֶךְ; בְּתוּלוֹת אַחֲרֶיהָ רֵעוֹתֶיהָ, מוּבָאוֹת לָךְ. תּוּבַלְנָה בִּשְׂמָחֹת וָגִיל, תְּבֹאֶינָה בְּהֵיכַל מֶלֶךְ. תַּחַת אֲבֹתֶיךָ יִהְיוּ בָנֶיךָ, תְּשִׁיתֵמוֹ לְשָׂרִים בְּכָל הָאָרֶץ. אַזְכִּירָה שִׁמְךָ בְּכָל דֹּר וָדֹר, עַל כֵּן עַמִּים יְהוֹדֻךָ לְעֹלָם וָעֶד.

מו לַמְנַצֵּחַ לִבְנֵי קֹרַח, עַל עֲלָמוֹת שִׁיר. אֱלֹהִים לָנוּ מַחֲסֶה וָעֹז, עֶזְרָה בְצָרוֹת, נִמְצָא מְאֹד. עַל כֵּן לֹא נִירָא בְּהָמִיר אָרֶץ, וּבְמוֹט הָרִים בְּלֵב יַמִּים. יֶהֱמוּ יֶחְמְרוּ מֵימָיו, יִרְעֲשׁוּ הָרִים בְּגַאֲוָתוֹ סֶלָה. נָהָר, פְּלָגָיו יְשַׂמְּחוּ עִיר אֱלֹהִים, קְדֹשׁ מִשְׁכְּנֵי עֶלְיוֹן. אֱלֹהִים בְּקִרְבָּהּ, בַּל תִּמּוֹט, יַעְזְרֶהָ אֱלֹהִים לִפְנוֹת בֹּקֶר. הָמוּ גוֹיִם מָטוּ מַמְלָכוֹת, נָתַן בְּקוֹלוֹ תָּמוּג אָרֶץ. יהוה צְבָאוֹת עִמָּנוּ, מִשְׂגָּב לָנוּ אֱלֹהֵי יַעֲקֹב סֶלָה. לְכוּ חֲזוּ מִפְעֲלוֹת יהוה, אֲשֶׁר שָׂם שַׁמּוֹת בָּאָרֶץ. מַשְׁבִּית מִלְחָמוֹת עַד קְצֵה הָאָרֶץ; קֶשֶׁת יְשַׁבֵּר וְקִצֵּץ חֲנִית, עֲגָלוֹת יִשְׂרֹף בָּאֵשׁ. הַרְפּוּ וּדְעוּ כִּי אָנֹכִי אֱלֹהִים; אָרוּם בַּגּוֹיִם, אָרוּם בָּאָרֶץ. יהוה צְבָאוֹת עִמָּנוּ, מִשְׂגָּב לָנוּ אֱלֹהֵי יַעֲקֹב סֶלָה.

מד לַמְנַצֵּחַ לִבְנֵי קֹרַח מַשְׂכִּיל. אֱלֹהִים | בְּאָזְנֵינוּ שָׁמַעְנוּ, אֲבוֹתֵינוּ סִפְּרוּ לָנוּ, פֹּעַל פָּעַלְתָּ בִימֵיהֶם בִּימֵי קֶדֶם. אַתָּה, יָדְךָ גּוֹיִם הוֹרַשְׁתָּ וַתִּטָּעֵם, תָּרַע לְאֻמִּים וַתְּשַׁלְּחֵם. כִּי לֹא בְחַרְבָּם יָרְשׁוּ אָרֶץ, וּזְרוֹעָם לֹא הוֹשִׁיעָה לָּמוֹ; כִּי יְמִינְךָ וּזְרוֹעֲךָ וְאוֹר פָּנֶיךָ כִּי רְצִיתָם. אַתָּה הוּא מַלְכִּי אֱלֹהִים, צַוֵּה יְשׁוּעוֹת יַעֲקֹב. בְּךָ צָרֵינוּ נְנַגֵּחַ, בְּשִׁמְךָ נָבוּס קָמֵינוּ. כִּי לֹא בְקַשְׁתִּי אֶבְטָח, וְחַרְבִּי לֹא תוֹשִׁיעֵנִי. כִּי הוֹשַׁעְתָּנוּ מִצָּרֵינוּ, וּמְשַׂנְאֵינוּ הֱבִישׁוֹתָ. בֵּאלֹהִים הִלַּלְנוּ כָל הַיּוֹם, וְשִׁמְךָ לְעוֹלָם נוֹדֶה סֶלָה. אַף זָנַחְתָּ וַתַּכְלִימֵנוּ, וְלֹא תֵצֵא בְּצִבְאוֹתֵינוּ. תְּשִׁיבֵנוּ אָחוֹר מִנִּי צָר, וּמְשַׂנְאֵינוּ שָׁסוּ לָמוֹ. תִּתְּנֵנוּ כְּצֹאן מַאֲכָל, וּבַגּוֹיִם זֵרִיתָנוּ. תִּמְכֹּר עַמְּךָ בְלֹא הוֹן, וְלֹא רִבִּיתָ בִּמְחִירֵיהֶם. תְּשִׂימֵנוּ חֶרְפָּה לִשְׁכֵנֵינוּ, לַעַג וָקֶלֶס לִסְבִיבוֹתֵינוּ. תְּשִׂימֵנוּ מָשָׁל בַּגּוֹיִם, מְנוֹד רֹאשׁ בַּלְאֻמִּים. כָּל הַיּוֹם כְּלִמָּתִי נֶגְדִּי, וּבֹשֶׁת פָּנַי כִּסָּתְנִי. מִקּוֹל מְחָרֵף וּמְגַדֵּף, מִפְּנֵי אוֹיֵב וּמִתְנַקֵּם. כָּל זֹאת בָּאַתְנוּ וְלֹא שְׁכַחֲנוּךָ, וְלֹא שִׁקַּרְנוּ בִּבְרִיתֶךָ. לֹא נָסוֹג אָחוֹר לִבֵּנוּ, וַתֵּט אֲשֻׁרֵינוּ מִנִּי אָרְחֶךָ. כִּי דִכִּיתָנוּ בִּמְקוֹם תַּנִּים, וַתְּכַס עָלֵינוּ בְצַלְמָוֶת. אִם שָׁכַחְנוּ שֵׁם אֱלֹהֵינוּ, וַנִּפְרֹשׂ כַּפֵּינוּ לְאֵל זָר. הֲלֹא אֱלֹהִים יַחֲקָר זֹאת, כִּי הוּא יֹדֵעַ תַּעֲלֻמוֹת לֵב. כִּי עָלֶיךָ הֹרַגְנוּ כָל הַיּוֹם, נֶחְשַׁבְנוּ כְּצֹאן טִבְחָה. עוּרָה לָמָּה תִישַׁן | אֲדֹנָי; הָקִיצָה, אַל תִּזְנַח לָנֶצַח. לָמָּה פָנֶיךָ תַסְתִּיר, תִּשְׁכַּח עָנְיֵנוּ וְלַחֲצֵנוּ. כִּי שָׁחָה לֶעָפָר נַפְשֵׁנוּ, דָּבְקָה לָאָרֶץ בִּטְנֵנוּ. קוּמָה עֶזְרָתָה לָּנוּ, וּפְדֵנוּ לְמַעַן חַסְדֶּךָ.

מה לַמְנַצֵּחַ עַל שֹׁשַׁנִּים לִבְנֵי קֹרַח, מַשְׂכִּיל שִׁיר יְדִידֹת. רָחַשׁ לִבִּי דָּבָר טוֹב, אֹמֵר אָנִי מַעֲשַׂי לְמֶלֶךְ, לְשׁוֹנִי עֵט סוֹפֵר מָהִיר. יָפְיָפִיתָ מִבְּנֵי אָדָם, הוּצַק

מז לַמְנַצֵּחַ לִבְנֵי קֹרַח מִזְמוֹר. כָּל הָעַמִּים תִּקְעוּ כָף, הָרִיעוּ לֵאלֹהִים בְּקוֹל רִנָּה. כִּי יהוה עֶלְיוֹן נוֹרָא, מֶלֶךְ גָּדוֹל עַל כָּל הָאָרֶץ. יַדְבֵּר עַמִּים תַּחְתֵּינוּ, וּלְאֻמִּים תַּחַת רַגְלֵינוּ. יִבְחַר לָנוּ אֶת נַחֲלָתֵנוּ, אֶת גְּאוֹן יַעֲקֹב אֲשֶׁר אָהֵב סֶלָה. עָלָה אֱלֹהִים בִּתְרוּעָה, יהוה בְּקוֹל שׁוֹפָר. זַמְּרוּ אֱלֹהִים זַמֵּרוּ, זַמְּרוּ לְמַלְכֵּנוּ זַמֵּרוּ. כִּי מֶלֶךְ כָּל הָאָרֶץ אֱלֹהִים, זַמְּרוּ מַשְׂכִּיל. מָלַךְ אֱלֹהִים עַל גּוֹיִם, אֱלֹהִים יָשַׁב עַל כִּסֵּא קָדְשׁוֹ. נְדִיבֵי עַמִּים נֶאֱסָפוּ, עַם אֱלֹהֵי אַבְרָהָם; כִּי לֵאלֹהִים מָגִנֵּי אֶרֶץ, מְאֹד נַעֲלָה.

מח שִׁיר מִזְמוֹר לִבְנֵי קֹרַח. גָּדוֹל יהוה וּמְהֻלָּל מְאֹד, בְּעִיר אֱלֹהֵינוּ, הַר קָדְשׁוֹ. יְפֵה נוֹף, מְשׂוֹשׂ כָּל הָאָרֶץ, הַר צִיּוֹן יַרְכְּתֵי צָפוֹן, קִרְיַת מֶלֶךְ רָב. אֱלֹהִים בְּאַרְמְנוֹתֶיהָ נוֹדַע לְמִשְׂגָּב. כִּי הִנֵּה הַמְּלָכִים נוֹעֲדוּ, עָבְרוּ יַחְדָּו. הֵמָּה רָאוּ כֵּן תָּמָהוּ, נִבְהֲלוּ נֶחְפָּזוּ. רְעָדָה אֲחָזָתַם שָׁם, חִיל כַּיּוֹלֵדָה. בְּרוּחַ קָדִים תְּשַׁבֵּר אֳנִיּוֹת תַּרְשִׁישׁ. כַּאֲשֶׁר שָׁמַעְנוּ כֵּן רָאִינוּ בְּעִיר יהוה צְבָאוֹת, בְּעִיר אֱלֹהֵינוּ, אֱלֹהִים יְכוֹנְנֶהָ עַד עוֹלָם סֶלָה. דִּמִּינוּ אֱלֹהִים חַסְדֶּךָ, בְּקֶרֶב הֵיכָלֶךָ. כְּשִׁמְךָ אֱלֹהִים, כֵּן תְּהִלָּתְךָ עַל קַצְוֵי אֶרֶץ; צֶדֶק מָלְאָה יְמִינֶךָ. יִשְׂמַח הַר צִיּוֹן, תָּגֵלְנָה בְּנוֹת יְהוּדָה, לְמַעַן מִשְׁפָּטֶיךָ. סֹבּוּ צִיּוֹן וְהַקִּיפוּהָ, סִפְרוּ מִגְדָּלֶיהָ. שִׁיתוּ לִבְּכֶם לְחֵילָה, פַּסְּגוּ אַרְמְנוֹתֶיהָ, לְמַעַן תְּסַפְּרוּ לְדוֹר אַחֲרוֹן. כִּי זֶה אֱלֹהִים אֱלֹהֵינוּ עוֹלָם וָעֶד, הוּא יְנַהֲגֵנוּ עַל מוּת.

DAY 9 — יום ט' לחודש

מט לַמְנַצֵּחַ לִבְנֵי קֹרַח מִזְמוֹר. שִׁמְעוּ זֹאת כָּל הָעַמִּים, הַאֲזִינוּ כָּל יֹשְׁבֵי חָלֶד. גַּם בְּנֵי אָדָם, גַּם בְּנֵי אִישׁ; יַחַד עָשִׁיר וְאֶבְיוֹן. פִּי יְדַבֵּר חָכְמוֹת, וְהָגוּת לִבִּי תְבוּנוֹת. אַטֶּה לְמָשָׁל אָזְנִי, אֶפְתַּח בְּכִנּוֹר חִידָתִי. לָמָּה אִירָא בִּימֵי רָע, עֲוֹן עֲקֵבַי יְסוּבֵּנִי. הַבֹּטְחִים עַל חֵילָם, וּבְרֹב עָשְׁרָם יִתְהַלָּלוּ. אָח לֹא פָדֹה יִפְדֶּה אִישׁ, לֹא יִתֵּן לֵאלֹהִים כָּפְרוֹ. וְיֵקַר פִּדְיוֹן נַפְשָׁם, וְחָדַל לְעוֹלָם. וִיחִי עוֹד לָנֶצַח, לֹא יִרְאֶה הַשָּׁחַת. כִּי יִרְאֶה חֲכָמִים יָמוּתוּ, יַחַד כְּסִיל וָבַעַר יֹאבֵדוּ, וְעָזְבוּ לַאֲחֵרִים חֵילָם. קִרְבָּם בָּתֵּימוֹ לְעוֹלָם, מִשְׁכְּנֹתָם לְדוֹר וָדֹר; קָרְאוּ בִשְׁמוֹתָם עֲלֵי אֲדָמוֹת. וְאָדָם בִּיקָר בַּל יָלִין, נִמְשַׁל כַּבְּהֵמוֹת נִדְמוּ. זֶה דַרְכָּם כֵּסֶל לָמוֹ, וְאַחֲרֵיהֶם בְּפִיהֶם יִרְצוּ סֶלָה. כַּצֹּאן לִשְׁאוֹל שַׁתּוּ, מָוֶת יִרְעֵם; וַיִּרְדּוּ בָם יְשָׁרִים לַבֹּקֶר, וְצוּרָם לְבַלּוֹת שְׁאוֹל מִזְּבֻל לוֹ. אַךְ אֱלֹהִים יִפְדֶּה נַפְשִׁי מִיַּד שְׁאוֹל, כִּי יִקָּחֵנִי סֶלָה. אַל תִּירָא כִּי יַעֲשִׁר אִישׁ, כִּי יִרְבֶּה כְּבוֹד בֵּיתוֹ. כִּי לֹא בְמוֹתוֹ יִקַּח הַכֹּל, לֹא יֵרֵד אַחֲרָיו כְּבוֹדוֹ. כִּי נַפְשׁוֹ בְּחַיָּיו יְבָרֵךְ, וְיוֹדֻךָ כִּי תֵיטִיב לָךְ. תָּבוֹא עַד דּוֹר אֲבוֹתָיו, עַד נֵצַח לֹא יִרְאוּ אוֹר. אָדָם בִּיקָר וְלֹא יָבִין, נִמְשַׁל כַּבְּהֵמוֹת נִדְמוּ.

נ מִזְמוֹר לְאָסָף; אֵל אֱלֹהִים יהוה דִּבֶּר וַיִּקְרָא אָרֶץ, מִמִּזְרַח שֶׁמֶשׁ עַד מְבֹאוֹ. מִצִּיּוֹן מִכְלַל יֹפִי, אֱלֹהִים הוֹפִיעַ. יָבֹא אֱלֹהֵינוּ וְאַל יֶחֱרַשׁ; אֵשׁ לְפָנָיו תֹּאכֵל, וּסְבִיבָיו נִשְׂעֲרָה מְאֹד. יִקְרָא אֶל הַשָּׁמַיִם מֵעָל, וְאֶל הָאָרֶץ לָדִין עַמּוֹ. אִסְפוּ לִי חֲסִידָי, כֹּרְתֵי בְרִיתִי עֲלֵי זָבַח. וַיַּגִּידוּ שָׁמַיִם צִדְקוֹ, כִּי אֱלֹהִים שֹׁפֵט הוּא סֶלָה. שִׁמְעָה עַמִּי וַאֲדַבֵּרָה, יִשְׂרָאֵל וְאָעִידָה בָּךְ, אֱלֹהִים אֱלֹהֶיךָ אָנֹכִי. לֹא עַל זְבָחֶיךָ אוֹכִיחֶךָ, וְעוֹלֹתֶיךָ לְנֶגְדִּי תָמִיד. לֹא אֶקַּח מִבֵּיתְךָ פָר, מִמִּכְלְאֹתֶיךָ עַתּוּדִים. כִּי לִי כָל חַיְתוֹ יָעַר, בְּהֵמוֹת בְּהַרְרֵי אָלֶף. יָדַעְתִּי כָּל עוֹף הָרִים, וְזִיז שָׂדַי עִמָּדִי. אִם אֶרְעַב לֹא אֹמַר לָךְ, כִּי לִי תֵבֵל וּמְלֹאָהּ. הַאוֹכַל בְּשַׂר אַבִּירִים, וְדַם עַתּוּדִים אֶשְׁתֶּה. זְבַח לֵאלֹהִים תּוֹדָה, וְשַׁלֵּם לְעֶלְיוֹן נְדָרֶיךָ. וּקְרָאֵנִי בְּיוֹם צָרָה, אֲחַלֶּצְךָ וּתְכַבְּדֵנִי.

נב לַמְנַצֵּחַ מַשְׂכִּיל לְדָוִד. בְּבוֹא דּוֹאֵג הָאֲדֹמִי וַיַּגֵּד לְשָׁאוּל, וַיֹּאמֶר לוֹ: בָּא דָוִד אֶל בֵּית אֲחִימֶלֶךְ. מַה תִּתְהַלֵּל בְּרָעָה, הַגִּבּוֹר, חֶסֶד אֵל כָּל הַיּוֹם. הַוּוֹת תַּחְשֹׁב לְשׁוֹנֶךָ, כְּתַעַר מְלֻטָּשׁ עֹשֵׂה רְמִיָּה. אָהַבְתָּ רָּע מִטּוֹב, שֶׁקֶר מִדַּבֵּר צֶדֶק סֶלָה. אָהַבְתָּ כָל דִּבְרֵי בָלַע, לְשׁוֹן מִרְמָה. גַּם אֵל יִתָּצְךָ לָנֶצַח, יַחְתְּךָ וְיִסָּחֲךָ מֵאֹהֶל, וְשֵׁרֶשְׁךָ מֵאֶרֶץ חַיִּים סֶלָה. וְיִרְאוּ צַדִּיקִים וְיִירָאוּ, וְעָלָיו יִשְׂחָקוּ. הִנֵּה הַגֶּבֶר לֹא יָשִׂים אֱלֹהִים מָעוּזּוֹ; וַיִּבְטַח בְּרֹב עָשְׁרוֹ, יָעֹז בְּהַוָּתוֹ. וַאֲנִי כְּזַיִת רַעֲנָן בְּבֵית אֱלֹהִים, בָּטַחְתִּי בְחֶסֶד אֱלֹהִים עוֹלָם וָעֶד. אוֹדְךָ לְעוֹלָם כִּי עָשִׂיתָ, וַאֲקַוֶּה שִׁמְךָ כִי טוֹב נֶגֶד חֲסִידֶיךָ.

נג לַמְנַצֵּחַ עַל מָחֲלַת מַשְׂכִּיל לְדָוִד. אָמַר נָבָל בְּלִבּוֹ אֵין אֱלֹהִים, הִשְׁחִיתוּ וְהִתְעִיבוּ עָוֶל, אֵין עֹשֵׂה טוֹב. אֱלֹהִים מִשָּׁמַיִם הִשְׁקִיף עַל בְּנֵי אָדָם, לִרְאוֹת הֲיֵשׁ מַשְׂכִּיל דֹּרֵשׁ אֶת אֱלֹהִים. כֻּלּוֹ סָג, יַחְדָּו נֶאֱלָחוּ; אֵין עֹשֵׂה טוֹב, אֵין גַּם אֶחָד. הֲלֹא יָדְעוּ פֹּעֲלֵי אָוֶן, אֹכְלֵי עַמִּי אָכְלוּ לֶחֶם, אֱלֹהִים לֹא קָרָאוּ. שָׁם פָּחֲדוּ פַחַד לֹא הָיָה פָחַד; כִּי אֱלֹהִים פִּזַּר עַצְמוֹת חֹנָךְ, הֱבִישֹׁתָה, כִּי אֱלֹהִים מְאָסָם. מִי יִתֵּן מִצִּיּוֹן יְשֻׁעוֹת יִשְׂרָאֵל; בְּשׁוּב אֱלֹהִים שְׁבוּת עַמּוֹ, יָגֵל יַעֲקֹב יִשְׂמַח יִשְׂרָאֵל.

נד לַמְנַצֵּחַ בִּנְגִינֹת מַשְׂכִּיל לְדָוִד. בְּבוֹא הַזִּיפִים וַיֹּאמְרוּ לְשָׁאוּל: הֲלֹא דָוִד מִסְתַּתֵּר עִמָּנוּ. אֱלֹהִים, בְּשִׁמְךָ הוֹשִׁיעֵנִי, וּבִגְבוּרָתְךָ תְדִינֵנִי. אֱלֹהִים, שְׁמַע תְּפִלָּתִי, הַאֲזִינָה לְאִמְרֵי פִי. כִּי זָרִים קָמוּ עָלַי, וְעָרִיצִים בִּקְשׁוּ נַפְשִׁי, לֹא שָׂמוּ אֱלֹהִים לְנֶגְדָּם סֶלָה. הִנֵּה אֱלֹהִים עֹזֵר לִי, אֲדֹנָי בְּסֹמְכֵי נַפְשִׁי. יָשִׁיב הָרַע לְשֹׁרְרָי, בַּאֲמִתְּךָ הַצְמִיתֵם. בִּנְדָבָה אֶזְבְּחָה לָּךְ, אוֹדֶה שִּׁמְךָ יהוה כִּי טוֹב. כִּי מִכָּל צָרָה הִצִּילָנִי, וּבְאֹיְבַי רָאֲתָה עֵינִי.

וְלָרָשָׁע אָמַר אֱלֹהִים: מַה לְּךָ לְסַפֵּר חֻקָּי, וַתִּשָּׂא בְרִיתִי עֲלֵי פִיךָ. וְאַתָּה שָׂנֵאתָ מוּסָר, וַתַּשְׁלֵךְ דְּבָרַי אַחֲרֶיךָ. אִם רָאִיתָ גַנָּב וַתִּרֶץ עִמּוֹ, וְעִם מְנָאֲפִים חֶלְקֶךָ. פִּיךָ שָׁלַחְתָּ בְרָעָה, וּלְשׁוֹנְךָ תַּצְמִיד מִרְמָה. תֵּשֵׁב בְּאָחִיךָ תְדַבֵּר, בְּבֶן אִמְּךָ תִּתֶּן דֹּפִי. אֵלֶּה עָשִׂיתָ וְהֶחֱרַשְׁתִּי, דִּמִּיתָ הֱיוֹת אֶהְיֶה כָמוֹךָ, אוֹכִיחֲךָ וְאֶעֶרְכָה לְעֵינֶיךָ. בִּינוּ נָא זֹאת שֹׁכְחֵי אֱלוֹהַּ, פֶּן אֶטְרֹף וְאֵין מַצִּיל. זֹבֵחַ תּוֹדָה יְכַבְּדָנְנִי; וְשָׂם דֶּרֶךְ, אַרְאֶנּוּ בְּיֵשַׁע אֱלֹהִים.

❧ יום שלישי / TUESDAY ❧

נא לַמְנַצֵּחַ מִזְמוֹר לְדָוִד. בְּבוֹא אֵלָיו נָתָן הַנָּבִיא, כַּאֲשֶׁר בָּא אֶל בַּת שָׁבַע. חָנֵּנִי אֱלֹהִים כְּחַסְדֶּךָ, כְּרֹב רַחֲמֶיךָ מְחֵה פְשָׁעָי. הֶרֶב כַּבְּסֵנִי מֵעֲוֹנִי, וּמֵחַטָּאתִי טַהֲרֵנִי. כִּי פְשָׁעַי אֲנִי אֵדָע, וְחַטָּאתִי נֶגְדִּי תָמִיד. לְךָ לְבַדְּךָ חָטָאתִי, וְהָרַע בְּעֵינֶיךָ עָשִׂיתִי; לְמַעַן תִּצְדַּק בְּדָבְרֶךָ, תִּזְכֶּה בְשָׁפְטֶךָ. הֵן בְּעָווֹן חוֹלָלְתִּי, וּבְחֵטְא יֶחֱמַתְנִי אִמִּי. הֵן אֱמֶת חָפַצְתָּ בַטֻּחוֹת, וּבְסָתֻם חָכְמָה תוֹדִיעֵנִי. תְּחַטְּאֵנִי בְאֵזוֹב וְאֶטְהָר, תְּכַבְּסֵנִי וּמִשֶּׁלֶג אַלְבִּין. תַּשְׁמִיעֵנִי שָׂשׂוֹן וְשִׂמְחָה, תָּגֵלְנָה עֲצָמוֹת דִּכִּיתָ. הַסְתֵּר פָּנֶיךָ מֵחֲטָאָי, וְכָל עֲוֹנֹתַי מְחֵה. לֵב טָהוֹר בְּרָא לִי אֱלֹהִים, וְרוּחַ נָכוֹן חַדֵּשׁ בְּקִרְבִּי. אַל תַּשְׁלִיכֵנִי מִלְּפָנֶיךָ, וְרוּחַ קָדְשְׁךָ אַל תִּקַּח מִמֶּנִּי. הָשִׁיבָה לִּי שְׂשׂוֹן יִשְׁעֶךָ, וְרוּחַ נְדִיבָה תִסְמְכֵנִי. אֲלַמְּדָה פֹשְׁעִים דְּרָכֶיךָ, וְחַטָּאִים אֵלֶיךָ יָשׁוּבוּ. הַצִּילֵנִי מִדָּמִים, אֱלֹהִים, אֱלֹהֵי תְּשׁוּעָתִי, תְּרַנֵּן לְשׁוֹנִי צִדְקָתֶךָ. אֲדֹנָי שְׂפָתַי תִּפְתָּח, וּפִי יַגִּיד תְּהִלָּתֶךָ. כִּי לֹא תַחְפֹּץ זֶבַח וְאֶתֵּנָה, עוֹלָה לֹא תִרְצֶה. זִבְחֵי אֱלֹהִים רוּחַ נִשְׁבָּרָה; לֵב נִשְׁבָּר וְנִדְכֶּה, אֱלֹהִים לֹא תִבְזֶה. הֵיטִיבָה בִרְצוֹנְךָ אֶת צִיּוֹן, תִּבְנֶה חוֹמוֹת יְרוּשָׁלָיִם. אָז תַּחְפֹּץ זִבְחֵי צֶדֶק, עוֹלָה וְכָלִיל; אָז יַעֲלוּ עַל מִזְבַּחֲךָ פָרִים.

נה לַמְנַצֵּחַ בִּנְגִינֹת מַשְׂכִּיל לְדָוִד. הַאֲזִינָה אֱלֹהִים תְּפִלָּתִי, וְאַל תִּתְעַלַּם מִתְּחִנָּתִי. הַקְשִׁיבָה לִּי וַעֲנֵנִי, אָרִיד בְּשִׂיחִי וְאָהִימָה. מִקּוֹל אוֹיֵב, מִפְּנֵי עָקַת רָשָׁע; כִּי יָמִיטוּ עָלַי אָוֶן, וּבְאַף יִשְׂטְמוּנִי. לִבִּי יָחִיל בְּקִרְבִּי, וְאֵימוֹת מָוֶת נָפְלוּ עָלָי. יִרְאָה וָרַעַד יָבֹא בִי, וַתְּכַסֵּנִי פַּלָּצוּת. וָאֹמַר, מִי יִתֶּן לִי אֵבֶר כַּיּוֹנָה, אָעוּפָה וְאֶשְׁכֹּנָה. הִנֵּה אַרְחִיק נְדֹד, אָלִין בַּמִּדְבָּר סֶלָה. אָחִישָׁה מִפְלָט לִי, מֵרוּחַ סֹעָה מִסָּעַר. בַּלַּע אֲדֹנָי, פַּלַּג לְשׁוֹנָם; כִּי רָאִיתִי חָמָס וְרִיב בָּעִיר. יוֹמָם וָלַיְלָה יְסוֹבְבֻהָ עַל חוֹמֹתֶיהָ, וְאָוֶן וְעָמָל בְּקִרְבָּהּ. הַוּוֹת בְּקִרְבָּהּ, וְלֹא יָמִישׁ מֵרְחֹבָהּ תֹּךְ וּמִרְמָה. כִּי לֹא אוֹיֵב יְחָרְפֵנִי וְאֶשָּׂא, לֹא מְשַׂנְאִי עָלַי הִגְדִּיל וְאֶסָּתֵר מִמֶּנּוּ. וְאַתָּה, אֱנוֹשׁ כְּעֶרְכִּי, אַלּוּפִי וּמְיֻדָּעִי. אֲשֶׁר יַחְדָּו נַמְתִּיק סוֹד, בְּבֵית אֱלֹהִים נְהַלֵּךְ בְּרָגֶשׁ. יַשִּׁי מָוֶת עָלֵימוֹ, יֵרְדוּ שְׁאוֹל חַיִּים; כִּי רָעוֹת בִּמְגוּרָם בְּקִרְבָּם. אֲנִי אֶל אֱלֹהִים אֶקְרָא, וַיהוה יוֹשִׁיעֵנִי. עֶרֶב וָבֹקֶר וְצָהֳרַיִם אָשִׂיחָה וְאֶהֱמֶה, וַיִּשְׁמַע קוֹלִי. פָּדָה בְשָׁלוֹם נַפְשִׁי מִקְּרָב לִי, כִּי בְרַבִּים הָיוּ עִמָּדִי. יִשְׁמַע אֵל וְיַעֲנֵם, וְיֹשֵׁב קֶדֶם סֶלָה; אֲשֶׁר אֵין חֲלִיפוֹת לָמוֹ, וְלֹא יָרְאוּ אֱלֹהִים. שָׁלַח יָדָיו בִּשְׁלֹמָיו, חִלֵּל בְּרִיתוֹ. חָלְקוּ מַחְמָאֹת פִּיו וּקְרָב לִבּוֹ; רַכּוּ דְבָרָיו מִשֶּׁמֶן, וְהֵמָּה פְתִחוֹת. הַשְׁלֵךְ עַל יהוה יְהָבְךָ, וְהוּא יְכַלְכְּלֶךָ; לֹא יִתֵּן לְעוֹלָם מוֹט לַצַּדִּיק. וְאַתָּה אֱלֹהִים, תּוֹרִדֵם לִבְאֵר שַׁחַת, אַנְשֵׁי דָמִים וּמִרְמָה לֹא יֶחֱצוּ יְמֵיהֶם; וַאֲנִי אֶבְטַח בָּךְ.

נו לַמְנַצֵּחַ עַל יוֹנַת אֵלֶם רְחֹקִים, לְדָוִד מִכְתָּם, בֶּאֱחֹז אֹתוֹ פְלִשְׁתִּים בְּגַת. חָנֵּנִי אֱלֹהִים כִּי שְׁאָפַנִי אֱנוֹשׁ, כָּל הַיּוֹם לֹחֵם יִלְחָצֵנִי. שָׁאֲפוּ שׁוֹרְרַי כָּל הַיּוֹם; כִּי רַבִּים לֹחֲמִים לִי, מָרוֹם. יוֹם אִירָא, אֲנִי

אֵלֶיךָ אֶבְטָח; בֵּאלֹהִים אֲהַלֵּל דְּבָרוֹ. בֵּאלֹהִים בָּטַחְתִּי לֹא אִירָא, מַה יַּעֲשֶׂה בָשָׂר לִי. כָּל הַיּוֹם דְּבָרַי יְעַצֵּבוּ, עָלַי כָּל מַחְשְׁבֹתָם לָרָע. יָגוּרוּ יִצְפּוֹנוּ, הֵמָּה עֲקֵבַי יִשְׁמֹרוּ, כַּאֲשֶׁר קִוּוּ נַפְשִׁי. עַל אָוֶן פַּלֶּט לָמוֹ; בְּאַף עַמִּים הוֹרֵד, אֱלֹהִים. נֹדִי סָפַרְתָּה אָתָּה, שִׂימָה דִמְעָתִי בְנֹאדֶךָ, הֲלֹא בְּסִפְרָתֶךָ. אָז יָשׁוּבוּ אוֹיְבַי אָחוֹר בְּיוֹם אֶקְרָא; זֶה יָדַעְתִּי כִּי אֱלֹהִים לִי. בֵּאלֹהִים אֲהַלֵּל דָּבָר, בַּיהוה אֲהַלֵּל דָּבָר. בֵּאלֹהִים בָּטַחְתִּי לֹא אִירָא, מַה יַּעֲשֶׂה אָדָם לִי. עָלַי אֱלֹהִים נְדָרֶיךָ, אֲשַׁלֵּם תּוֹדֹת לָךְ. כִּי הִצַּלְתָּ נַפְשִׁי מִמָּוֶת, הֲלֹא רַגְלַי מִדֶּחִי; לְהִתְהַלֵּךְ לִפְנֵי אֱלֹהִים בְּאוֹר הַחַיִּים.

נז לַמְנַצֵּחַ אַל תַּשְׁחֵת, לְדָוִד מִכְתָּם, בְּבָרְחוֹ מִפְּנֵי שָׁאוּל בַּמְּעָרָה. חָנֵּנִי אֱלֹהִים חָנֵּנִי, כִּי בְךָ חָסָיָה נַפְשִׁי; וּבְצֵל כְּנָפֶיךָ אֶחְסֶה עַד יַעֲבֹר הַוּוֹת. אֶקְרָא לֵאלֹהִים עֶלְיוֹן, לָאֵל גֹּמֵר עָלָי. יִשְׁלַח מִשָּׁמַיִם וְיוֹשִׁיעֵנִי חֵרֵף שֹׁאֲפִי סֶלָה, יִשְׁלַח אֱלֹהִים חַסְדּוֹ וַאֲמִתּוֹ. נַפְשִׁי בְּתוֹךְ לְבָאִם, אֶשְׁכְּבָה לֹהֲטִים; בְּנֵי אָדָם שִׁנֵּיהֶם חֲנִית וְחִצִּים, וּלְשׁוֹנָם חֶרֶב חַדָּה. רוּמָה עַל הַשָּׁמַיִם אֱלֹהִים, עַל כָּל הָאָרֶץ כְּבוֹדֶךָ. רֶשֶׁת הֵכִינוּ לִפְעָמַי, כָּפַף נַפְשִׁי; כָּרוּ לְפָנַי שִׁיחָה, נָפְלוּ בְתוֹכָהּ סֶלָה. נָכוֹן לִבִּי, אֱלֹהִים, נָכוֹן לִבִּי; אָשִׁירָה וַאֲזַמֵּרָה. עוּרָה כְבוֹדִי, עוּרָה הַנֵּבֶל וְכִנּוֹר, אָעִירָה שָּׁחַר. אוֹדְךָ בָעַמִּים, אֲדֹנָי; אֲזַמֶּרְךָ בַּלְאֻמִּים. כִּי גָדֹל עַד שָׁמַיִם חַסְדֶּךָ, וְעַד שְׁחָקִים אֲמִתֶּךָ. רוּמָה עַל שָׁמַיִם, אֱלֹהִים; עַל כָּל הָאָרֶץ כְּבוֹדֶךָ.

נח לַמְנַצֵּחַ אַל תַּשְׁחֵת, לְדָוִד מִכְתָּם. הַאֻמְנָם אֵלֶם צֶדֶק תְּדַבֵּרוּן, מֵישָׁרִים תִּשְׁפְּטוּ בְּנֵי אָדָם. אַף בְּלֵב עוֹלֹת תִּפְעָלוּן, בָּאָרֶץ חֲמַס יְדֵיכֶם תְּפַלֵּסוּן. זֹרוּ רְשָׁעִים מֵרָחֶם, תָּעוּ מִבֶּטֶן דֹּבְרֵי כָזָב. חֲמַת לָמוֹ כִּדְמוּת חֲמַת נָחָשׁ, כְּמוֹ פֶתֶן

ס לַמְנַצֵּחַ עַל שׁוּשַׁן עֵדוּת, מִכְתָּם לְדָוִד
לְלַמֵּד. בְּהַצּוֹתוֹ אֶת אֲרַם נַהֲרַיִם וְאֶת
אֲרַם צוֹבָה; וַיָּשָׁב יוֹאָב וַיַּךְ אֶת אֱדוֹם
בְּגֵיא מֶלַח, שְׁנֵים עָשָׂר אָלֶף. אֱלֹהִים,
זְנַחְתָּנוּ פְרַצְתָּנוּ; אָנַפְתָּ, תְּשׁוֹבֵב לָנוּ.
הִרְעַשְׁתָּה אֶרֶץ פְּצַמְתָּהּ, רְפָה שְׁבָרֶיהָ כִי
מָטָה. הִרְאִיתָ עַמְּךָ קָשָׁה, הִשְׁקִיתָנוּ יַיִן
תַּרְעֵלָה. נָתַתָּה לִּירֵאֶיךָ נֵּס לְהִתְנוֹסֵס,
מִפְּנֵי קֹשֶׁט סֶלָה. לְמַעַן יֵחָלְצוּן יְדִידֶיךָ,
הוֹשִׁיעָה יְמִינְךָ וַעֲנֵנִי. אֱלֹהִים דִּבֶּר
בְּקָדְשׁוֹ אֶעְלֹזָה; אֲחַלְּקָה שְׁכֶם, וְעֵמֶק
סֻכּוֹת אֲמַדֵּד. לִי גִלְעָד וְלִי מְנַשֶּׁה,
וְאֶפְרַיִם מָעוֹז רֹאשִׁי, יְהוּדָה מְחֹקְקִי.
מוֹאָב סִיר רַחְצִי, עַל אֱדוֹם אַשְׁלִיךְ נַעֲלִי,
עָלַי פְּלֶשֶׁת הִתְרוֹעָעִי. מִי יֹבִלֵנִי עִיר
מָצוֹר, מִי נָחַנִי עַד אֱדוֹם. הֲלֹא אַתָּה
אֱלֹהִים זְנַחְתָּנוּ, וְלֹא תֵצֵא אֱלֹהִים
בְּצִבְאוֹתֵינוּ. הָבָה לָּנוּ עֶזְרָת מִצָּר, וְשָׁוְא
תְּשׁוּעַת אָדָם. בֵּאלֹהִים נַעֲשֶׂה חָיִל, וְהוּא
יָבוּס צָרֵינוּ.

סא לַמְנַצֵּחַ עַל נְגִינַת לְדָוִד. שִׁמְעָה
אֱלֹהִים רִנָּתִי, הַקְשִׁיבָה תְּפִלָּתִי.
מִקְצֵה הָאָרֶץ אֵלֶיךָ אֶקְרָא בַּעֲטֹף לִבִּי,
בְּצוּר יָרוּם מִמֶּנִּי תַנְחֵנִי. כִּי הָיִיתָ מַחְסֶה
לִי, מִגְדַּל עֹז מִפְּנֵי אוֹיֵב. אָגוּרָה בְאָהָלְךָ
עוֹלָמִים, אֶחֱסֶה בְסֵתֶר כְּנָפֶיךָ סֶּלָה. כִּי
אַתָּה אֱלֹהִים שָׁמַעְתָּ לִנְדָרָי, נָתַתָּ יְרֻשַּׁת
יִרְאֵי שְׁמֶךָ. יָמִים עַל יְמֵי מֶלֶךְ תּוֹסִיף,
שְׁנוֹתָיו כְּמוֹ דֹר וָדֹר. יֵשֵׁב עוֹלָם לִפְנֵי
אֱלֹהִים, חֶסֶד וֶאֱמֶת מַן יִנְצְרֻהוּ. כֵּן
אֲזַמְּרָה שִׁמְךָ לָעַד, לְשַׁלְּמִי נְדָרַי יוֹם יוֹם.

סב לַמְנַצֵּחַ עַל יְדוּתוּן מִזְמוֹר לְדָוִד.
אַךְ אֶל אֱלֹהִים דּוּמִיָּה נַפְשִׁי, מִמֶּנּוּ
יְשׁוּעָתִי. אַךְ הוּא צוּרִי וִישׁוּעָתִי, מִשְׂגַּבִּי,
לֹא אֶמּוֹט רַבָּה. עַד אָנָה תְּהוֹתְתוּ עַל
אִישׁ, תְּרָצְּחוּ כֻלְּכֶם; כְּקִיר נָטוּי, גָּדֵר
הַדְּחוּיָה. אַךְ מִשְּׂאֵתוֹ יָעֲצוּ לְהַדִּיחַ, יִרְצוּ

חֵרֵשׁ יַאְטֵם אָזְנוֹ. אֲשֶׁר לֹא יִשְׁמַע לְקוֹל
מְלַחֲשִׁים, חוֹבֵר חֲבָרִים מְחֻכָּם. אֱלֹהִים,
הֲרָס שִׁנֵּימוֹ בְּפִימוֹ; מַלְתְּעוֹת כְּפִירִים
נְתֹץ, יְהוָה. יִמָּאֲסוּ כְמוֹ מַיִם יִתְהַלְּכוּ לָמוֹ,
יִדְרֹךְ חִצָּו כְּמוֹ יִתְמֹלָלוּ. כְּמוֹ שַׁבְּלוּל
תֶּמֶס יַהֲלֹךְ, נֵפֶל אֵשֶׁת בַּל חָזוּ שָׁמֶשׁ.
בְּטֶרֶם יָבִינוּ סִּירֹתֵיכֶם אָטָד, כְּמוֹ חַי כְּמוֹ
חָרוֹן יִשְׂעָרֶנּוּ. יִשְׂמַח צַדִּיק כִּי חָזָה נָקָם,
פְּעָמָיו יִרְחַץ בְּדַם הָרָשָׁע. וְיֹאמַר אָדָם,
אַךְ פְּרִי לַצַּדִּיק, אַךְ יֵשׁ אֱלֹהִים שֹׁפְטִים
בָּאָרֶץ.

נט לַמְנַצֵּחַ אַל תַּשְׁחֵת, לְדָוִד מִכְתָּם;
בִּשְׁלֹחַ שָׁאוּל, וַיִּשְׁמְרוּ אֶת הַבַּיִת
לַהֲמִיתוֹ. הַצִּילֵנִי מֵאֹיְבַי, אֱלֹהָי;
מִמִּתְקוֹמְמַי תְּשַׂגְּבֵנִי. הַצִּילֵנִי מִפֹּעֲלֵי אָוֶן,
וּמֵאַנְשֵׁי דָמִים הוֹשִׁיעֵנִי. כִּי הִנֵּה אָרְבוּ
לְנַפְשִׁי, יָגוּרוּ עָלַי עַזִּים; לֹא פִשְׁעִי וְלֹא
חַטָּאתִי, יְהוָה. בְּלִי עָוֹן יְרֻצוּן וְיִכּוֹנָנוּ,
עוּרָה לִקְרָאתִי וּרְאֵה. וְאַתָּה יְהוָה
אֱלֹהִים צְבָאוֹת אֱלֹהֵי יִשְׂרָאֵל, הָקִיצָה
לִפְקֹד כָּל הַגּוֹיִם, אַל תָּחֹן כָּל בֹּגְדֵי אָוֶן
סֶלָה. יָשׁוּבוּ לָעֶרֶב, יֶהֱמוּ כַכָּלֶב, וִיסוֹבְבוּ
עִיר. הִנֵּה יַבִּיעוּן בְּפִיהֶם, חֲרָבוֹת
בְּשִׂפְתוֹתֵיהֶם, כִּי מִי שֹׁמֵעַ. וְאַתָּה יְהוָה
תִּשְׂחַק לָמוֹ, תִּלְעַג לְכָל גּוֹיִם. עֻזּוֹ, אֵלֶיךָ
אֶשְׁמֹרָה, כִּי אֱלֹהִים מִשְׂגַּבִּי. אֱלֹהֵי חַסְדִּי
יְקַדְּמֵנִי, אֱלֹהִים יַרְאֵנִי בְשֹׁרְרָי. אַל
תַּהַרְגֵם פֶּן יִשְׁכְּחוּ עַמִּי, הֲנִיעֵמוֹ בְחֵילְךָ
וְהוֹרִידֵמוֹ, מָגִנֵּנוּ אֲדֹנָי. חַטַּאת פִּימוֹ דְּבַר
שְׂפָתֵימוֹ; וְיִלָּכְדוּ בִגְאוֹנָם, וּמֵאָלָה
וּמִכַּחַשׁ יְסַפֵּרוּ. כַּלֵּה בְחֵמָה, כַּלֵּה
וְאֵינֵמוֹ; וְיֵדְעוּ כִּי אֱלֹהִים מֹשֵׁל בְּיַעֲקֹב
לְאַפְסֵי הָאָרֶץ סֶלָה. וְיָשֻׁבוּ לָעֶרֶב,
יֶהֱמוּ כַכָּלֶב, וִיסוֹבְבוּ עִיר. הֵמָּה יְנִיעוּן
לֶאֱכֹל, אִם לֹא יִשְׂבְּעוּ וַיָּלִינוּ. וַאֲנִי
אָשִׁיר עֻזֶּךָ, וַאֲרַנֵּן לַבֹּקֶר חַסְדֶּךָ; כִּי
הָיִיתָ מִשְׂגָּב לִי, וּמָנוֹס בְּיוֹם צַר לִי. עֻזִּי
אֵלֶיךָ אֲזַמֵּרָה; כִּי אֱלֹהִים מִשְׂגַּבִּי, אֱלֹהֵי
חַסְדִּי.

וַיְכַשִּׁילֻהוּ עָלֵימוֹ לְשׁוֹנָם, יִתְנֹדֲדוּ כָּל
רֹאֵה בָם. וַיִּירְאוּ כָּל אָדָם, וַיַּגִּידוּ פֹּעַל
אֱלֹהִים, וּמַעֲשֵׂהוּ הִשְׂכִּילוּ. יִשְׂמַח צַדִּיק
בַּיהוה וְחָסָה בוֹ, וְיִתְהַלְלוּ כָּל יִשְׁרֵי לֵב.

סה לַמְנַצֵּחַ מִזְמוֹר לְדָוִד שִׁיר. לְךָ
דֻמִיָּה תְהִלָּה, אֱלֹהִים בְּצִיּוֹן; וּלְךָ
יְשֻׁלַּם נֶדֶר. שֹׁמֵעַ תְּפִלָּה, עָדֶיךָ כָּל בָּשָׂר
יָבֹאוּ. דִּבְרֵי עֲוֹנֹת גָּבְרוּ מֶנִּי, פְּשָׁעֵינוּ אַתָּה
תְכַפְּרֵם. אַשְׁרֵי תִּבְחַר וּתְקָרֵב יִשְׁכֹּן
חֲצֵרֶיךָ; נִשְׂבְּעָה בְּטוּב בֵּיתֶךָ, קְדֹשׁ
הֵיכָלֶךָ. נוֹרָאוֹת בְּצֶדֶק תַּעֲנֵנוּ, אֱלֹהֵי
יִשְׁעֵנוּ; מִבְטָח כָּל קַצְוֵי אֶרֶץ וְיָם רְחֹקִים.
מֵכִין הָרִים בְּכֹחוֹ, נֶאְזָר בִּגְבוּרָה. מַשְׁבִּיחַ
שְׁאוֹן יַמִּים, שְׁאוֹן גַּלֵּיהֶם, וַהֲמוֹן לְאֻמִּים.
וַיִּירְאוּ יֹשְׁבֵי קְצָוֹת מֵאוֹתֹתֶיךָ, מוֹצָאֵי
בֹקֶר וָעֶרֶב תַּרְנִין. פָּקַדְתָּ הָאָרֶץ
וַתְּשֹׁקְקֶהָ, רַבַּת תַּעְשְׁרֶנָּה פֶּלֶג אֱלֹהִים
מָלֵא מָיִם, תָּכִין דְּגָנָם כִּי כֵן תְּכִינֶהָ.
תְּלָמֶיהָ רַוֵּה, נַחֵת גְּדוּדֶהָ; בִּרְבִיבִים
תְּמֹגְגֶנָּה, צִמְחָהּ תְּבָרֵךְ. עִטַּרְתָּ שְׁנַת
טוֹבָתֶךָ, וּמַעְגָּלֶיךָ יִרְעֲפוּן דָּשֶׁן. יִרְעֲפוּ
נְאוֹת מִדְבָּר, וְגִיל גְּבָעוֹת תַּחְגֹּרְנָה. לָבְשׁוּ
כָרִים הַצֹּאן, וַעֲמָקִים יַעַטְפוּ בָר,
יִתְרוֹעֲעוּ אַף יָשִׁירוּ.

סו לַמְנַצֵּחַ שִׁיר מִזְמוֹר, הָרִיעוּ
לֵאלֹהִים כָּל הָאָרֶץ. זַמְּרוּ כְבוֹד
שְׁמוֹ, שִׂימוּ כָבוֹד תְּהִלָּתוֹ. אִמְרוּ
לֵאלֹהִים: מַה נּוֹרָא מַעֲשֶׂיךָ, בְּרֹב עֻזְּךָ
יְכַחֲשׁוּ לְךָ אֹיְבֶיךָ. כָּל הָאָרֶץ יִשְׁתַּחֲווּ לְךָ
וִיזַמְּרוּ לָךְ, יְזַמְּרוּ שִׁמְךָ סֶלָה. לְכוּ וּרְאוּ
מִפְעֲלוֹת אֱלֹהִים, נוֹרָא עֲלִילָה עַל בְּנֵי
אָדָם. הָפַךְ יָם לְיַבָּשָׁה, בַּנָּהָר יַעַבְרוּ
בְרָגֶל; שָׁם נִשְׂמְחָה בּוֹ. מֹשֵׁל בִּגְבוּרָתוֹ
עוֹלָם, עֵינָיו בַּגּוֹיִם תִּצְפֶּינָה; הַסּוֹרְרִים
אַל יָרוּמוּ לָמוֹ סֶלָה. בָּרְכוּ עַמִּים |
אֱלֹהֵינוּ, וְהַשְׁמִיעוּ קוֹל תְּהִלָּתוֹ. הַשָּׂם
נַפְשֵׁנוּ בַּחַיִּים, וְלֹא נָתַן לַמּוֹט רַגְלֵנוּ. כִּי

כָזָב; בְּפִיו יְבָרֵכוּ, וּבְקִרְבָּם יְקַלְלוּ סֶלָה.
אַךְ לֵאלֹהִים דּוֹמִּי נַפְשִׁי, כִּי מִמֶּנּוּ תִּקְוָתִי.
אַךְ הוּא צוּרִי וִישׁוּעָתִי; מִשְׂגַּבִּי, לֹא
אֶמּוֹט. עַל אֱלֹהִים יִשְׁעִי וּכְבוֹדִי; צוּר עֻזִּי
מַחְסִי בֵּאלֹהִים. בִּטְחוּ בוֹ בְכָל עֵת, עָם;
שִׁפְכוּ לְפָנָיו לְבַבְכֶם; אֱלֹהִים מַחֲסֶה לָנוּ
סֶלָה. אַךְ הֶבֶל בְּנֵי אָדָם, כָּזָב בְּנֵי אִישׁ;
בְּמֹאזְנַיִם לַעֲלוֹת, הֵמָּה מֵהֶבֶל יָחַד. אַל
תִּבְטְחוּ בְעֹשֶׁק, וּבְגָזֵל אַל תֶּהְבָּלוּ; חַיִל
כִּי יָנוּב, אַל תָּשִׁיתוּ לֵב. אַחַת דִּבֶּר
אֱלֹהִים, שְׁתַּיִם זוּ שָׁמָעְתִּי, כִּי עֹז
לֵאלֹהִים. וּלְךָ אֲדֹנָי חָסֶד, כִּי אַתָּה תְשַׁלֵּם
לְאִישׁ כְּמַעֲשֵׂהוּ.

סג מִזְמוֹר לְדָוִד, בִּהְיוֹתוֹ בְּמִדְבַּר
יְהוּדָה. אֱלֹהִים | אֵלִי אַתָּה,
אֲשַׁחֲרֶךָּ; צָמְאָה לְךָ נַפְשִׁי, כָּמַהּ לְךָ
בְשָׂרִי, בְּאֶרֶץ צִיָּה וְעָיֵף בְּלִי מָיִם. כֵּן
בַּקֹּדֶשׁ חֲזִיתִךָ, לִרְאוֹת עֻזְּךָ וּכְבוֹדֶךָ. כִּי
טוֹב חַסְדְּךָ מֵחַיִּים, שְׂפָתַי יְשַׁבְּחוּנְךָ. כֵּן
אֲבָרֶכְךָ בְחַיָּי, בְּשִׁמְךָ אֶשָּׂא כַפָּי. כְּמוֹ
חֵלֶב וָדֶשֶׁן תִּשְׂבַּע נַפְשִׁי, וְשִׂפְתֵי רְנָנוֹת
יְהַלֶּל פִּי. אִם זְכַרְתִּיךָ עַל יְצוּעָי,
בְּאַשְׁמֻרוֹת אֶהְגֶּה בָּךְ. כִּי הָיִיתָ עֶזְרָתָה לִּי,
וּבְצֵל כְּנָפֶיךָ אֲרַנֵּן. דָּבְקָה נַפְשִׁי אַחֲרֶיךָ,
בִּי תָּמְכָה יְמִינֶךָ. וְהֵמָּה לְשׁוֹאָה יְבַקְשׁוּ
נַפְשִׁי, יָבֹאוּ בְּתַחְתִּיּוֹת הָאָרֶץ. יַגִּירֻהוּ עַל
יְדֵי חָרֶב, מְנָת שֻׁעָלִים יִהְיוּ. וְהַמֶּלֶךְ
יִשְׂמַח בֵּאלֹהִים; יִתְהַלֵּל כָּל הַנִּשְׁבָּע בּוֹ,
כִּי יִסָּכֵר פִּי דוֹבְרֵי שָׁקֶר.

סד לַמְנַצֵּחַ מִזְמוֹר לְדָוִד. שְׁמַע אֱלֹהִים
קוֹלִי בְשִׂיחִי, מִפַּחַד אוֹיֵב תִּצֹּר
חַיָּי. תַּסְתִּירֵנִי מִסּוֹד מְרֵעִים, מֵרִגְשַׁת
פֹּעֲלֵי אָוֶן. אֲשֶׁר שָׁנְנוּ כַחֶרֶב לְשׁוֹנָם,
דָּרְכוּ חִצָּם דָּבָר מָר. לִירוֹת בַּמִּסְתָּרִים
תָּם, פִּתְאֹם יֹרֻהוּ וְלֹא יִירָאוּ. יְחַזְּקוּ לָמוֹ
דָּבָר רָע, יְסַפְּרוּ לִטְמוֹן מוֹקְשִׁים; אָמְרוּ
מִי יִרְאֶה לָּמוֹ. יַחְפְּשׂוּ עוֹלֹת, תַּמְנוּ חֵפֶשׂ
מְחֻפָּשׂ, וְקֶרֶב אִישׁ וְלֵב עָמֹק. וַיֹּרֵם
אֱלֹהִים; חֵץ פִּתְאוֹם הָיוּ מַכּוֹתָם.

נַחֲלָתְךָ וְנִלְאָה אַתָּה כוֹנַנְתָּהּ. חַיָּתְךָ יָשְׁבוּ
בָהּ, תָּכִין בְּטוֹבָתְךָ לֶעָנִי, אֱלֹהִים. אֲדֹנָי
יִתֶּן אֹמֶר, הַמְבַשְּׂרוֹת צָבָא רָב. מַלְכֵי
צְבָאוֹת יִדֹּדוּן יִדֹּדוּן, וּנְוַת בַּיִת תְּחַלֵּק
שָׁלָל. אִם תִּשְׁכְּבוּן בֵּין שְׁפַתָּיִם, כַּנְפֵי יוֹנָה
נֶחְפָּה בַכֶּסֶף, וְאֶבְרוֹתֶיהָ בִּירַקְרַק חָרוּץ.
בְּפָרֵשׂ שַׁדַּי מְלָכִים בָּהּ, תַּשְׁלֵג בְּצַלְמוֹן.
הַר אֱלֹהִים הַר בָּשָׁן, הַר גַּבְנֻנִּים הַר בָּשָׁן.
לָמָּה תְּרַצְּדוּן הָרִים גַּבְנֻנִּים, הָהָר חָמַד
אֱלֹהִים לְשִׁבְתּוֹ, אַף יְהוָה יִשְׁכֹּן לָנֶצַח.
רֶכֶב אֱלֹהִים רִבֹּתַיִם אַלְפֵי שִׁנְאָן, אֲדֹנָי
בָם סִינַי בַּקֹּדֶשׁ. עָלִיתָ לַמָּרוֹם שָׁבִיתָ
שֶּׁבִי, לָקַחְתָּ מַתָּנוֹת בָּאָדָם; וְאַף סוֹרְרִים
לִשְׁכֹּן | יָהּ אֱלֹהִים. בָּרוּךְ אֲדֹנָי, יוֹם יוֹם
יַעֲמָס לָנוּ, הָאֵל יְשׁוּעָתֵנוּ סֶלָה. הָאֵל לָנוּ
אֵל לְמוֹשָׁעוֹת; וְלֵיהוִֹה אֲדֹנָי, לַמָּוֶת
תּוֹצָאוֹת. אַךְ אֱלֹהִים יִמְחַץ רֹאשׁ אֹיְבָיו,
קָדְקֹד שֵׂעָר מִתְהַלֵּךְ בַּאֲשָׁמָיו. אָמַר
אֲדֹנָי: מִבָּשָׁן אָשִׁיב, אָשִׁיב מִמְּצֻלוֹת יָם.
לְמַעַן תִּמְחַץ רַגְלְךָ בְּדָם; לְשׁוֹן כְּלָבֶיךָ,
מֵאֹיְבִים מִנֵּהוּ. רָאוּ הֲלִיכוֹתֶיךָ, אֱלֹהִים;
הֲלִיכוֹת אֵלִי, מַלְכִּי בַקֹּדֶשׁ. קִדְּמוּ שָׁרִים
אַחַר נֹגְנִים, בְּתוֹךְ עֲלָמוֹת תּוֹפֵפוֹת.
בְּמַקְהֵלוֹת בָּרְכוּ אֱלֹהִים, אֲדֹנָי, מִמְּקוֹר
יִשְׂרָאֵל. שָׁם בִּנְיָמִן צָעִיר רֹדֵם, שָׂרֵי
יְהוּדָה רִגְמָתָם, שָׂרֵי זְבֻלוּן שָׂרֵי נַפְתָּלִי.
צִוָּה אֱלֹהֶיךָ עֻזֶּךָ; עוּזָּה אֱלֹהִים, זוּ
פָּעַלְתָּ לָּנוּ. מֵהֵיכָלֶךָ עַל יְרוּשָׁלָיִם, לְךָ
יוֹבִילוּ מְלָכִים שָׁי. גְּעַר חַיַּת קָנֶה, עֲדַת
אַבִּירִים בְּעֶגְלֵי עַמִּים, מִתְרַפֵּס בְּרַצֵּי
כָסֶף; בִּזַּר עַמִּים קְרָבוֹת יֶחְפָּצוּ. יֶאֱתָיוּ
חַשְׁמַנִּים מִנִּי מִצְרָיִם, כּוּשׁ תָּרִיץ יָדָיו
לֵאלֹהִים. מַמְלְכוֹת הָאָרֶץ שִׁירוּ
לֵאלֹהִים, זַמְּרוּ אֲדֹנָי סֶלָה. לָרֹכֵב בִּשְׁמֵי
שְׁמֵי קֶדֶם, הֵן יִתֵּן בְּקוֹלוֹ קוֹל עֹז. תְּנוּ עֹז
לֵאלֹהִים; עַל יִשְׂרָאֵל גַּאֲוָתוֹ, וְעֻזּוֹ
בַּשְּׁחָקִים. נוֹרָא אֱלֹהִים, מִמִּקְדָּשֶׁיךָ; אֵל
יִשְׂרָאֵל הוּא נֹתֵן עֹז וְתַעֲצֻמוֹת לָעָם,
בָּרוּךְ אֱלֹהִים.

בְּחַנְתָּנוּ, אֱלֹהִים; צְרַפְתָּנוּ כִּצְרָף כָּסֶף.
הֲבֵאתָנוּ בַמְּצוּדָה, שַׂמְתָּ מוּעָקָה
בְמָתְנֵינוּ. הִרְכַּבְתָּ אֱנוֹשׁ לְרֹאשֵׁנוּ; בָּאנוּ
בָאֵשׁ וּבַמַּיִם, וַתּוֹצִיאֵנוּ לָרְוָיָה. אָבוֹא
בֵיתְךָ בְעוֹלוֹת, אֲשַׁלֵּם לְךָ נְדָרָי. אֲשֶׁר
פָּצוּ שְׂפָתָי, וְדִבֶּר פִּי בַּצַּר לִי. עֹלוֹת מֵחִים
אַעֲלֶה לָּךְ עִם קְטֹרֶת אֵילִים, אֶעֱשֶׂה בָקָר
עִם עַתּוּדִים סֶלָה. לְכוּ שִׁמְעוּ וַאֲסַפְּרָה כָּל
יִרְאֵי אֱלֹהִים, אֲשֶׁר עָשָׂה לְנַפְשִׁי. אֵלָיו פִּי
קָרָאתִי; וְרוֹמַם תַּחַת לְשׁוֹנִי. אָוֶן אִם
רָאִיתִי בְלִבִּי, לֹא יִשְׁמַע | אֲדֹנָי. אָכֵן שָׁמַע
אֱלֹהִים, הִקְשִׁיב בְּקוֹל תְּפִלָּתִי. בָּרוּךְ
אֱלֹהִים, אֲשֶׁר לֹא הֵסִיר תְּפִלָּתִי וְחַסְדּוֹ
מֵאִתִּי.

סז לַמְנַצֵּחַ בִּנְגִינֹת מִזְמוֹר שִׁיר.
אֱלֹהִים יְחָנֵּנוּ וִיבָרְכֵנוּ, יָאֵר פָּנָיו
אִתָּנוּ סֶלָה. לָדַעַת בָּאָרֶץ דַּרְכֶּךָ, בְּכָל
גּוֹיִם יְשׁוּעָתֶךָ. יוֹדוּךָ עַמִּים, אֱלֹהִים;
יוֹדוּךָ עַמִּים כֻּלָּם. יִשְׂמְחוּ וִירַנְּנוּ לְאֻמִּים,
כִּי תִשְׁפֹּט עַמִּים מִישֹׁר, וּלְאֻמִּים בָּאָרֶץ
תַּנְחֵם סֶלָה. יוֹדוּךָ עַמִּים, אֱלֹהִים; יוֹדוּךָ
עַמִּים כֻּלָּם. אֶרֶץ נָתְנָה יְבוּלָהּ, יְבָרְכֵנוּ
אֱלֹהִים אֱלֹהֵינוּ. יְבָרְכֵנוּ אֱלֹהִים, וְיִירְאוּ
אֹתוֹ כָּל אַפְסֵי אָרֶץ.

סח לַמְנַצֵּחַ לְדָוִד מִזְמוֹר שִׁיר. יָקוּם
אֱלֹהִים, יָפוּצוּ אוֹיְבָיו, וְיָנוּסוּ
מְשַׂנְאָיו מִפָּנָיו. כְּהִנְדֹּף עָשָׁן תִּנְדֹּף;
כְּהִמֵּס דּוֹנַג מִפְּנֵי אֵשׁ, יֹאבְדוּ רְשָׁעִים
מִפְּנֵי אֱלֹהִים. וְצַדִּיקִים יִשְׂמְחוּ, יַעַלְצוּ
לִפְנֵי אֱלֹהִים; וְיָשִׂישׂוּ בְשִׂמְחָה. שִׁירוּ
לֵאלֹהִים, זַמְּרוּ שְׁמוֹ; סֹלּוּ לָרֹכֵב בָּעֲרָבוֹת
בְּיָהּ שְׁמוֹ, וְעִלְזוּ לְפָנָיו. אֲבִי יְתוֹמִים וְדַיַּן
אַלְמָנוֹת, אֱלֹהִים בִּמְעוֹן קָדְשׁוֹ. אֱלֹהִים
מוֹשִׁיב יְחִידִים בַּיְתָה, מוֹצִיא אֲסִירִים
בַּכּוֹשָׁרוֹת; אַךְ סוֹרְרִים שָׁכְנוּ צְחִיחָה.
אֱלֹהִים בְּצֵאתְךָ לִפְנֵי עַמֶּךָ, בְּצַעְדְּךָ
בִישִׁימוֹן סֶלָה. אֶרֶץ רָעָשָׁה, אַף שָׁמַיִם
נָטְפוּ מִפְּנֵי אֱלֹהִים; זֶה סִינַי, מִפְּנֵי אֱלֹהִים
אֱלֹהֵי יִשְׂרָאֵל. גֶּשֶׁם נְדָבוֹת תָּנִיף אֱלֹהִים,

סט לַמְנַצֵּחַ עַל שׁוֹשַׁנִּים לְדָוִד. הוֹשִׁיעֵנִי אֱלֹהִים, כִּי בָאוּ מַיִם עַד נָפֶשׁ. טָבַעְתִּי בִּיוֵן מְצוּלָה וְאֵין מָעֳמָד; בָּאתִי בְמַעֲמַקֵּי מַיִם, וְשִׁבֹּלֶת שְׁטָפָתְנִי. יָגַעְתִּי בְקָרְאִי, נִחַר גְּרוֹנִי; כָּלוּ עֵינַי מְיַחֵל לֵאלֹהָי. רַבּוּ מִשַּׂעֲרוֹת רֹאשִׁי שֹׂנְאַי חִנָּם; עָצְמוּ מַצְמִיתַי אֹיְבַי שֶׁקֶר, אֲשֶׁר לֹא גָזַלְתִּי אָז אָשִׁיב. אֱלֹהִים, אַתָּה יָדַעְתָּ לְאִוַּלְתִּי, וְאַשְׁמוֹתַי מִמְּךָ לֹא נִכְחָדוּ. אַל יֵבֹשׁוּ בִי קֹוֶיךָ, אֲדֹנָי יֱהֹוִה צְבָאוֹת; אַל יִכָּלְמוּ בִי מְבַקְשֶׁיךָ, אֱלֹהֵי יִשְׂרָאֵל. כִּי עָלֶיךָ נָשָׂאתִי חֶרְפָּה, כִּסְּתָה כְלִמָּה פָנָי. מוּזָר הָיִיתִי לְאֶחָי, וְנָכְרִי לִבְנֵי אִמִּי. כִּי קִנְאַת בֵּיתְךָ אֲכָלָתְנִי, וְחֶרְפּוֹת חוֹרְפֶיךָ נָפְלוּ עָלָי. וָאֶבְכֶּה בַצּוֹם נַפְשִׁי, וַתְּהִי לַחֲרָפוֹת לִי. וָאֶתְּנָה לְבוּשִׁי שָׂק, וָאֱהִי לָהֶם לְמָשָׁל. יָשִׂיחוּ בִי יֹשְׁבֵי שָׁעַר, וּנְגִינוֹת שׁוֹתֵי שֵׁכָר. וַאֲנִי, תְפִלָּתִי לְךָ יהוה, עֵת רָצוֹן; אֱלֹהִים, בְּרָב חַסְדֶּךָ, עֲנֵנִי בֶּאֱמֶת יִשְׁעֶךָ. הַצִּילֵנִי מִטִּיט וְאַל אֶטְבָּעָה, אִנָּצְלָה מִשֹּׂנְאַי וּמִמַּעֲמַקֵּי מָיִם. אַל תִּשְׁטְפֵנִי שִׁבֹּלֶת מַיִם, וְאַל תִּבְלָעֵנִי מְצוּלָה; וְאַל תֶּאְטַר עָלַי בְּאֵר פִּיהָ. עֲנֵנִי יהוה כִּי טוֹב חַסְדֶּךָ, כְּרֹב רַחֲמֶיךָ פְּנֵה אֵלָי. וְאַל תַּסְתֵּר פָּנֶיךָ מֵעַבְדֶּךָ; כִּי צַר לִי, מַהֵר עֲנֵנִי. קָרְבָה אֶל נַפְשִׁי גְאָלָהּ, לְמַעַן אֹיְבַי פְּדֵנִי. אַתָּה יָדַעְתָּ חֶרְפָּתִי וּבָשְׁתִּי וּכְלִמָּתִי, נֶגְדְּךָ כָּל צוֹרְרָי. חֶרְפָּה שָׁבְרָה לִבִּי וָאָנוּשָׁה, וָאֲקַוֶּה לָנוּד וָאַיִן, וְלַמְנַחֲמִים וְלֹא מָצָאתִי. וַיִּתְּנוּ בְּבָרוּתִי רֹאשׁ, וְלִצְמָאִי יַשְׁקוּנִי חֹמֶץ. יְהִי שֻׁלְחָנָם לִפְנֵיהֶם לְפָח, וְלִשְׁלוֹמִים לְמוֹקֵשׁ. תֶּחְשַׁכְנָה עֵינֵיהֶם מֵרְאוֹת, וּמָתְנֵיהֶם תָּמִיד הַמְעַד. שְׁפָךְ עֲלֵיהֶם זַעְמֶךָ, וַחֲרוֹן אַפְּךָ יַשִּׂיגֵם. תְּהִי טִירָתָם נְשַׁמָּה, בְּאָהֳלֵיהֶם אַל יְהִי יֹשֵׁב. כִּי אַתָּה אֲשֶׁר הִכִּיתָ רָדָפוּ, וְאֶל מַכְאוֹב חֲלָלֶיךָ יְסַפֵּרוּ.

תְּנָה עָוֹן עַל עֲוֹנָם, וְאַל יָבֹאוּ בְּצִדְקָתֶךָ. יִמָּחוּ מִסֵּפֶר חַיִּים, וְעִם צַדִּיקִים אַל יִכָּתֵבוּ. וַאֲנִי עָנִי וְכוֹאֵב, יְשׁוּעָתְךָ אֱלֹהִים תְּשַׂגְּבֵנִי. אֲהַלְלָה שֵׁם אֱלֹהִים בְּשִׁיר, וַאֲגַדְּלֶנּוּ בְתוֹדָה. וְתִיטַב לַיהוה מִשּׁוֹר פָּר מַקְרִן מַפְרִיס. רָאוּ עֲנָוִים יִשְׂמָחוּ, דֹּרְשֵׁי אֱלֹהִים, וִיחִי לְבַבְכֶם. כִּי שֹׁמֵעַ אֶל אֶבְיוֹנִים, יהוה, וְאֶת אֲסִירָיו לֹא בָזָה. יְהַלְלוּהוּ שָׁמַיִם וָאָרֶץ, יַמִּים וְכָל רֹמֵשׂ בָּם. כִּי אֱלֹהִים יוֹשִׁיעַ צִיּוֹן, וְיִבְנֶה עָרֵי יְהוּדָה, וְיָשְׁבוּ שָׁם וִירֵשׁוּהָ. וְזֶרַע עֲבָדָיו יִנְחָלוּהָ, וְאֹהֲבֵי שְׁמוֹ יִשְׁכְּנוּ בָהּ.

ע לַמְנַצֵּחַ לְדָוִד לְהַזְכִּיר. אֱלֹהִים לְהַצִּילֵנִי; יהוה, לְעֶזְרָתִי חוּשָׁה. יֵבֹשׁוּ וְיַחְפְּרוּ מְבַקְשֵׁי נַפְשִׁי, יִסֹּגוּ אָחוֹר וְיִכָּלְמוּ חֲפֵצֵי רָעָתִי. יָשׁוּבוּ עַל עֵקֶב בָּשְׁתָּם, הָאֹמְרִים הֶאָח הֶאָח. יָשִׂישׂוּ וְיִשְׂמְחוּ בְּךָ כָּל מְבַקְשֶׁיךָ; וְיֹאמְרוּ תָמִיד יִגְדַּל אֱלֹהִים, אֹהֲבֵי יְשׁוּעָתֶךָ. וַאֲנִי עָנִי וְאֶבְיוֹן, אֱלֹהִים חוּשָׁה לִּי; עֶזְרִי וּמְפַלְטִי אַתָּה, יהוה, אַל תְּאַחַר.

עא בְּךָ יהוה חָסִיתִי, אַל אֵבוֹשָׁה לְעוֹלָם. בְּצִדְקָתְךָ תַּצִּילֵנִי וּתְפַלְּטֵנִי, הַטֵּה אֵלַי אָזְנְךָ וְהוֹשִׁיעֵנִי. הֱיֵה לִי לְצוּר מָעוֹן לָבוֹא תָּמִיד, צִוִּיתָ לְהוֹשִׁיעֵנִי; כִּי סַלְעִי וּמְצוּדָתִי אָתָּה. אֱלֹהַי, פַּלְּטֵנִי מִיַּד רָשָׁע, מִכַּף מְעַוֵּל וְחוֹמֵץ. כִּי אַתָּה תִקְוָתִי; אֲדֹנָי יֱהֹוִה, מִבְטַחִי מִנְּעוּרָי. עָלֶיךָ נִסְמַכְתִּי מִבֶּטֶן, מִמְּעֵי אִמִּי אַתָּה גוֹזִי; בְּךָ תְהִלָּתִי תָמִיד. כְּמוֹפֵת הָיִיתִי לְרַבִּים, וְאַתָּה מַחֲסִי עֹז. יִמָּלֵא פִי תְּהִלָּתֶךָ, כָּל הַיּוֹם תִּפְאַרְתֶּךָ. אַל תַּשְׁלִיכֵנִי לְעֵת זִקְנָה, כִּכְלוֹת כֹּחִי אַל תַּעַזְבֵנִי. כִּי אָמְרוּ אוֹיְבַי לִי, וְשֹׁמְרֵי נַפְשִׁי נוֹעֲצוּ יַחְדָּו. לֵאמֹר אֱלֹהִים עֲזָבוֹ, רִדְפוּ וְתִפְשׂוּהוּ כִּי אֵין מַצִּיל. אֱלֹהִים, אַל תִּרְחַק מִמֶּנִּי; אֱלֹהַי, לְעֶזְרָתִי חֻשָׁה. יֵבֹשׁוּ יִכְלוּ שֹׂטְנֵי נַפְשִׁי; יַעֲטוּ חֶרְפָּה וּכְלִמָּה, מְבַקְשֵׁי רָעָתִי. וַאֲנִי תָּמִיד אֲיַחֵל, וְהוֹסַפְתִּי עַל כָּל תְּהִלָּתֶךָ. פִּי

יְסַפֵּר צִדְקָתֶךָ, כָּל הַיּוֹם תְּשׁוּעָתֶךָ, כִּי לֹא יָדַעְתִּי סְפֹרוֹת. אָבוֹא בִּגְבֻרוֹת אֲדֹנָי יֱהֹוִה, אַזְכִּיר צִדְקָתְךָ לְבַדֶּךָ. אֱלֹהִים, לִמַּדְתַּנִי מִנְּעוּרָי; וְעַד הֵנָּה אַגִּיד נִפְלְאוֹתֶיךָ. וְגַם עַד זִקְנָה וְשֵׂיבָה, אֱלֹהִים אַל תַּעַזְבֵנִי; עַד אַגִּיד זְרוֹעֲךָ לְדוֹר, לְכָל יָבוֹא גְּבוּרָתֶךָ. וְצִדְקָתְךָ אֱלֹהִים עַד מָרוֹם; אֲשֶׁר עָשִׂיתָ גְדֹלוֹת, אֱלֹהִים מִי כָמוֹךָ. אֲשֶׁר הִרְאִיתַנִי צָרוֹת רַבּוֹת וְרָעוֹת, תָּשׁוּב תְּחַיֵּינִי, וּמִתְּהֹמוֹת הָאָרֶץ תָּשׁוּב תַּעֲלֵנִי. תֶּרֶב גְּדֻלָּתִי, וְתִסֹּב תְּנַחֲמֵנִי. גַּם אֲנִי אוֹדְךָ בִכְלִי נֶבֶל אֲמִתְּךָ, אֱלֹהָי; אֲזַמְּרָה לְךָ בְכִנּוֹר, קְדוֹשׁ יִשְׂרָאֵל. תְּרַנֵּנָּה שְׂפָתַי כִּי אֲזַמְּרָה לָּךְ, וְנַפְשִׁי אֲשֶׁר פָּדִיתָ. גַּם לְשׁוֹנִי כָּל הַיּוֹם תֶּהְגֶּה צִדְקָתֶךָ, כִּי בֹשׁוּ כִי חָפְרוּ מְבַקְשֵׁי רָעָתִי.

עב לִשְׁלֹמֹה; אֱלֹהִים, מִשְׁפָּטֶיךָ לְמֶלֶךְ תֵּן, וְצִדְקָתְךָ לְבֶן מֶלֶךְ. יָדִין עַמְּךָ בְצֶדֶק, וַעֲנִיֶּיךָ בְמִשְׁפָּט. יִשְׂאוּ הָרִים שָׁלוֹם לָעָם, וּגְבָעוֹת בִּצְדָקָה. יִשְׁפֹּט עֲנִיֵּי

עָם, יוֹשִׁיעַ לִבְנֵי אֶבְיוֹן, וִידַכֵּא עוֹשֵׁק. יִירָאוּךָ עִם שָׁמֶשׁ, וְלִפְנֵי יָרֵחַ, דּוֹר דּוֹרִים. יֵרֵד כְּמָטָר עַל גֵּז, כִּרְבִיבִים זַרְזִיף אָרֶץ. יִפְרַח בְּיָמָיו צַדִּיק, וְרֹב שָׁלוֹם עַד בְּלִי יָרֵחַ. וְיֵרְדְּ מִיָּם עַד יָם, וּמִנָּהָר עַד אַפְסֵי אָרֶץ. לְפָנָיו יִכְרְעוּ צִיִּים, וְאֹיְבָיו עָפָר יְלַחֵכוּ. מַלְכֵי תַרְשִׁישׁ וְאִיִּים מִנְחָה יָשִׁיבוּ, מַלְכֵי שְׁבָא וּסְבָא אֶשְׁכָּר יַקְרִיבוּ. וְיִשְׁתַּחֲווּ לוֹ כָל מְלָכִים, כָּל גּוֹיִם יַעַבְדוּהוּ. כִּי יַצִּיל אֶבְיוֹן מְשַׁוֵּעַ, וְעָנִי וְאֵין עֹזֵר לוֹ. יָחֹס עַל דַּל וְאֶבְיוֹן, וְנַפְשׁוֹת אֶבְיוֹנִים יוֹשִׁיעַ. מִתּוֹךְ וּמֵחָמָס יִגְאַל נַפְשָׁם, וְיֵיקַר דָּמָם בְּעֵינָיו. וִיחִי, וְיִתֶּן לוֹ מִזְּהַב שְׁבָא, וְיִתְפַּלֵּל בַּעֲדוֹ תָמִיד, כָּל הַיּוֹם יְבָרְכֶנְהוּ. יְהִי פִסַּת בַּר בָּאָרֶץ בְּרֹאשׁ הָרִים, יִרְעַשׁ כַּלְּבָנוֹן פִּרְיוֹ, וְיָצִיצוּ מֵעִיר כְּעֵשֶׂב הָאָרֶץ. יְהִי שְׁמוֹ לְעוֹלָם, לִפְנֵי שֶׁמֶשׁ יִנּוֹן שְׁמוֹ; וְיִתְבָּרְכוּ בוֹ, כָּל גּוֹיִם יְאַשְּׁרוּהוּ. בָּרוּךְ יְהֹוָה אֱלֹהִים אֱלֹהֵי יִשְׂרָאֵל, עֹשֵׂה נִפְלָאוֹת לְבַדּוֹ. וּבָרוּךְ שֵׁם כְּבוֹדוֹ לְעוֹלָם, וְיִמָּלֵא כְבוֹדוֹ אֶת כָּל הָאָרֶץ, אָמֵן וְאָמֵן. כָּלּוּ תְפִלּוֹת דָּוִד בֶּן יִשָׁי.

ספר שלישי / BOOK THREE

WEDNESDAY / יום רביעי

עג מִזְמוֹר לְאָסָף; אַךְ טוֹב לְיִשְׂרָאֵל אֱלֹהִים, לְבָרֵי לֵבָב. וַאֲנִי כִּמְעַט נָטָיוּ רַגְלָי, כְּאַיִן שֻׁפְּכוּ אֲשֻׁרָי. כִּי קִנֵּאתִי בַּהוֹלְלִים, שְׁלוֹם רְשָׁעִים אֶרְאֶה. כִּי אֵין חַרְצֻבּוֹת לְמוֹתָם, וּבָרִיא אוּלָם. בַּעֲמַל אֱנוֹשׁ אֵינֵמוֹ, וְעִם אָדָם לֹא יְנֻגָּעוּ. לָכֵן עֲנָקַתְמוֹ גַאֲוָה, יַעֲטָף שִׁית חָמָס לָמוֹ. יָצָא מֵחֵלֶב עֵינֵמוֹ, עָבְרוּ מַשְׂכִּיּוֹת לֵבָב. יָמִיקוּ וִידַבְּרוּ בְרָע עֹשֶׁק, מִמָּרוֹם יְדַבֵּרוּ. שַׁתּוּ בַשָּׁמַיִם פִּיהֶם, וּלְשׁוֹנָם תִּהֲלַךְ בָּאָרֶץ. לָכֵן יָשׁוּב עַמּוֹ הֲלֹם, וּמֵי מָלֵא יִמָּצוּ לָמוֹ. וְאָמְרוּ: אֵיכָה יָדַע אֵל, וְיֵשׁ דֵּעָה בְעֶלְיוֹן. הִנֵּה אֵלֶּה רְשָׁעִים, וְשַׁלְוֵי עוֹלָם הִשְׂגּוּ חָיִל. אַךְ רִיק זִכִּיתִי לְבָבִי, וָאֶרְחַץ בְּנִקָּיוֹן

כַּפָּי. וָאֱהִי נָגוּעַ כָּל הַיּוֹם, וְתוֹכַחְתִּי לַבְּקָרִים. אִם אָמַרְתִּי אֲסַפְּרָה כְמוֹ, הִנֵּה דוֹר בָּנֶיךָ בָגָדְתִּי. וָאֲחַשְּׁבָה לָדַעַת זֹאת, עָמָל הוּא בְעֵינָי. עַד אָבוֹא אֶל מִקְדְּשֵׁי אֵל, אָבִינָה לְאַחֲרִיתָם. אַךְ בַּחֲלָקוֹת תָּשִׁית לָמוֹ, הִפַּלְתָּם לְמַשּׁוּאוֹת. אֵיךְ הָיוּ לְשַׁמָּה כְרָגַע, סָפוּ תַמּוּ מִן בַּלָּהוֹת. כַּחֲלוֹם מֵהָקִיץ; אֲדֹנָי, בָּעִיר צַלְמָם תִּבְזֶה. כִּי יִתְחַמֵּץ לְבָבִי, וְכִלְיוֹתַי אֶשְׁתּוֹנָן. וַאֲנִי בַעַר וְלֹא אֵדַע, בְּהֵמוֹת הָיִיתִי עִמָּךְ. וַאֲנִי תָמִיד עִמָּךְ, אָחַזְתָּ בְּיַד יְמִינִי. בַּעֲצָתְךָ תַנְחֵנִי, וְאַחַר כָּבוֹד תִּקָּחֵנִי. מִי לִי בַשָּׁמַיִם, וְעִמְּךָ לֹא חָפַצְתִּי בָאָרֶץ. כָּלָה שְׁאֵרִי וּלְבָבִי, צוּר לְבָבִי וְחֶלְקִי אֱלֹהִים לְעוֹלָם. כִּי הִנֵּה רְחֵקֶיךָ

יֹאבֵדוּ, הִצְמַתָּה כָּל זוֹנֶה מִמֶּךָּ. וַאֲנִי, קִרֲבַת אֱלֹהִים לִי טוֹב; שַׁתִּי בַּאדֹנָי יֱהֹוִה מַחְסִי, לְסַפֵּר כָּל מַלְאֲכוֹתֶיךָ.

עד מַשְׂכִּיל לְאָסָף; לָמָה אֱלֹהִים זָנַחְתָּ לָנֶצַח, יֶעְשַׁן אַפְּךָ בְּצֹאן מַרְעִיתֶךָ. זְכֹר עֲדָתְךָ קָנִיתָ קֶּדֶם, גָּאַלְתָּ שֵׁבֶט נַחֲלָתֶךָ; הַר צִיּוֹן זֶה שָׁכַנְתָּ בּוֹ. הָרִימָה פְעָמֶיךָ לְמַשֻּׁאוֹת נֶצַח, כָּל הֵרַע אוֹיֵב בַּקֹּדֶשׁ. שָׁאֲגוּ צֹרְרֶיךָ בְּקֶרֶב מוֹעֲדֶךָ, שָׂמוּ אוֹתֹתָם אֹתוֹת. יִוָּדַע כְּמֵבִיא לְמָעְלָה, בִּסְבָךְ עֵץ קַרְדֻּמּוֹת. וְעַתָּה פִּתּוּחֶיהָ יָּחַד, בְּכַשִּׁיל וְכֵילַפּוֹת יַהֲלֹמוּן. שִׁלְחוּ בָאֵשׁ מִקְדָּשֶׁךָ, לָאָרֶץ חִלְּלוּ מִשְׁכַּן שְׁמֶךָ. אָמְרוּ בְלִבָּם, נִינָם יָחַד, שָׂרְפוּ כָל מוֹעֲדֵי אֵל בָּאָרֶץ. אוֹתֹתֵינוּ לֹא רָאִינוּ; אֵין עוֹד נָבִיא, וְלֹא אִתָּנוּ יֹדֵעַ עַד מָה. עַד מָתַי אֱלֹהִים יְחָרֶף צָר, יְנָאֵץ אוֹיֵב שִׁמְךָ לָנֶצַח. לָמָּה תָשִׁיב יָדְךָ וִימִינֶךָ, מִקֶּרֶב חֵיקְךָ כַלֵּה. וֵאלֹהִים מַלְכִּי מִקֶּדֶם, פֹּעֵל יְשׁוּעוֹת בְּקֶרֶב הָאָרֶץ. אַתָּה פוֹרַרְתָּ בְעָזְּךָ יָם, שִׁבַּרְתָּ רָאשֵׁי תַנִּינִים עַל הַמָּיִם. אַתָּה רִצַּצְתָּ רָאשֵׁי לִוְיָתָן, תִּתְּנֶנּוּ מַאֲכָל לְעָם לְצִיִּים. אַתָּה בָקַעְתָּ מַעְיָן וָנָחַל, אַתָּה הוֹבַשְׁתָּ נַהֲרוֹת אֵיתָן. לְךָ יוֹם אַף לְךָ לָיְלָה, אַתָּה הֲכִינוֹתָ מָאוֹר וָשָׁמֶשׁ. אַתָּה הִצַּבְתָּ כָּל גְּבוּלוֹת אָרֶץ, קַיִץ וָחֹרֶף אַתָּה יְצַרְתָּם. זְכָר זֹאת, אוֹיֵב חֵרֵף | יהוה, וְעַם נָבָל נִאֲצוּ שְׁמֶךָ. אַל תִּתֵּן לְחַיַּת נֶפֶשׁ תּוֹרֶךָ, חַיַּת עֲנִיֶּיךָ אַל תִּשְׁכַּח לָנֶצַח. הַבֵּט לַבְּרִית, כִּי מָלְאוּ מַחֲשַׁכֵּי אֶרֶץ נְאוֹת חָמָס. אַל יָשֹׁב דַּךְ נִכְלָם, עָנִי וְאֶבְיוֹן יְהַלְלוּ שְׁמֶךָ. קוּמָה אֱלֹהִים רִיבָה רִיבֶךָ, זְכֹר חֶרְפָּתְךָ מִנִּי נָבָל כָּל הַיּוֹם. אַל תִּשְׁכַּח קוֹל צֹרְרֶיךָ, שְׁאוֹן קָמֶיךָ עֹלֶה תָמִיד.

עה לַמְנַצֵּחַ אַל תַּשְׁחֵת, מִזְמוֹר לְאָסָף שִׁיר. הוֹדִינוּ לְּךָ אֱלֹהִים, הוֹדִינוּ וְקָרוֹב שְׁמֶךָ, סִפְּרוּ נִפְלְאוֹתֶיךָ. כִּי אֶקַּח מוֹעֵד, אֲנִי מֵישָׁרִים אֶשְׁפֹּט. נְמֹגִים אֶרֶץ

וְכָל יֹשְׁבֶיהָ, אָנֹכִי תִכַּנְתִּי עַמּוּדֶיהָ סֶּלָה. אָמַרְתִּי לַהוֹלְלִים: אַל תָּהֹלּוּ, וְלָרְשָׁעִים: אַל תָּרִימוּ קָרֶן. אַל תָּרִימוּ לַמָּרוֹם קַרְנְכֶם, תְּדַבְּרוּ בְצַוָּאר עָתָק. כִּי לֹא מִמּוֹצָא וּמִמַּעֲרָב, וְלֹא מִמִּדְבַּר הָרִים. כִּי אֱלֹהִים שֹׁפֵט, זֶה יַשְׁפִּיל וְזֶה יָרִים. כִּי כוֹס בְּיַד יהוה, וְיַיִן חָמַר מָלֵא מֶסֶךְ, וַיַּגֵּר מִזֶּה; אַךְ שְׁמָרֶיהָ יִמְצוּ יִשְׁתּוּ כֹּל רִשְׁעֵי אָרֶץ. וַאֲנִי אַגִּיד לְעֹלָם, אֲזַמְּרָה לֵאלֹהֵי יַעֲקֹב. וְכָל קַרְנֵי רְשָׁעִים אֲגַדֵּעַ, תְּרוֹמַמְנָה קַרְנוֹת צַדִּיק.

עו לַמְנַצֵּחַ בִּנְגִינֹת, מִזְמוֹר לְאָסָף שִׁיר. נוֹדָע בִּיהוּדָה אֱלֹהִים, בְּיִשְׂרָאֵל גָּדוֹל שְׁמוֹ. וַיְהִי בְשָׁלֵם סוּכּוֹ, וּמְעוֹנָתוֹ בְצִיּוֹן. שָׁמָּה שִׁבַּר רִשְׁפֵי קָשֶׁת, מָגֵן וְחֶרֶב וּמִלְחָמָה סֶלָה. נָאוֹר אַתָּה, אַדִּיר מֵהַרְרֵי טָרֶף. אֶשְׁתּוֹלְלוּ אַבִּירֵי לֵב, נָמוּ שְׁנָתָם, וְלֹא מָצְאוּ כָל אַנְשֵׁי חַיִל יְדֵיהֶם. מִגַּעֲרָתְךָ אֱלֹהֵי יַעֲקֹב, נִרְדָּם וְרֶכֶב וָסוּס. אַתָּה | נוֹרָא אַתָּה, וּמִי יַעֲמֹד לְפָנֶיךָ מֵאָז אַפֶּךָ. מִשָּׁמַיִם הִשְׁמַעְתָּ דִּין, אֶרֶץ יָרְאָה וְשָׁקָטָה. בְּקוּם לַמִּשְׁפָּט אֱלֹהִים, לְהוֹשִׁיעַ כָּל עַנְוֵי אֶרֶץ סֶלָה. כִּי חֲמַת אָדָם תּוֹדֶךָּ, שְׁאֵרִית חֵמֹת תַּחְגֹּר. נִדְרוּ וְשַׁלְּמוּ לַיהוה אֱלֹהֵיכֶם; כָּל סְבִיבָיו, יֹבִילוּ שַׁי לַמּוֹרָא. יִבְצֹר רוּחַ נְגִידִים, נוֹרָא לְמַלְכֵי אָרֶץ.

יוֹם ט"ו לַחֹדֶשׁ — DAY 15

עז לַמְנַצֵּחַ עַל יְדוּתוּן לְאָסָף מִזְמוֹר. קוֹלִי אֶל אֱלֹהִים וְאֶצְעָקָה; קוֹלִי אֶל אֱלֹהִים, וְהַאֲזִין אֵלָי. בְּיוֹם צָרָתִי אֲדֹנָי דָּרָשְׁתִּי; יָדִי לַיְלָה נִגְּרָה וְלֹא תָפוּג, מֵאֲנָה הִנָּחֵם נַפְשִׁי. אֶזְכְּרָה אֱלֹהִים וְאֶהֱמָיָה, אָשִׂיחָה וְתִתְעַטֵּף רוּחִי סֶלָה. אָחַזְתָּ שְׁמֻרוֹת עֵינָי, נִפְעַמְתִּי וְלֹא אֲדַבֵּר. חִשַּׁבְתִּי יָמִים מִקֶּדֶם, שְׁנוֹת עוֹלָמִים. אֶזְכְּרָה נְגִינָתִי בַּלָּיְלָה; עִם לְבָבִי אָשִׂיחָה, וַיְחַפֵּשׂ רוּחִי. הַלְעוֹלָמִים יִזְנַח | אֲדֹנָי, וְלֹא יֹסִיף לִרְצוֹת עוֹד. הֶאָפֵס לָנֶצַח

חַסְדּוֹ, גָּמַר אֹמֶר לְדֹר וָדֹר. הֲשָׁכַח חַנּוֹת
אֵל, אִם קָפַץ בְּאַף רַחֲמָיו סֶלָה. וָאֹמַר:
חַלּוֹתִי הִיא, שְׁנוֹת יְמִין עֶלְיוֹן. אֶזְכּוֹר
מַעַלְלֵי יָהּ, כִּי אֶזְכְּרָה מִקֶּדֶם פִּלְאֶךָ.
וְהָגִיתִי בְכָל פָּעֳלֶךָ, וּבַעֲלִילוֹתֶיךָ
אָשִׂיחָה. אֱלֹהִים בַּקֹּדֶשׁ דַּרְכֶּךָ, מִי אֵל
גָּדוֹל כֵּאלֹהִים. אַתָּה הָאֵל עֹשֵׂה פֶלֶא,
הוֹדַעְתָּ בָעַמִּים עֻזֶּךָ. גָּאַלְתָּ בִּזְרוֹעַ עַמֶּךָ,
בְּנֵי יַעֲקֹב וְיוֹסֵף סֶלָה. רָאוּךָ מַּיִם אֱלֹהִים,
רָאוּךָ מַּיִם יָחִילוּ, אַף יִרְגְּזוּ תְהֹמוֹת. זֹרְמוּ
מַיִם עָבוֹת, קוֹל נָתְנוּ שְׁחָקִים, אַף חֲצָצֶיךָ
יִתְהַלָּכוּ. קוֹל רַעַמְךָ בַּגַּלְגַּל, הֵאִירוּ
בְרָקִים תֵּבֵל, רָגְזָה וַתִּרְעַשׁ הָאָרֶץ. בַּיָּם
דַּרְכֶּךָ, וּשְׁבִילְךָ בְּמַיִם רַבִּים; וְעִקְּבוֹתֶיךָ
לֹא נֹדָעוּ. נָחִיתָ כַצֹּאן עַמֶּךָ, בְּיַד מֹשֶׁה
וְאַהֲרֹן.

עח מַשְׂכִּיל לְאָסָף; הַאֲזִינָה עַמִּי
תוֹרָתִי, הַטּוּ אָזְנְכֶם לְאִמְרֵי פִי.
אֶפְתְּחָה בְמָשָׁל פִּי, אַבִּיעָה חִידוֹת מִנִּי
קֶדֶם. אֲשֶׁר שָׁמַעְנוּ וַנֵּדָעֵם, וַאֲבוֹתֵינוּ
סִפְּרוּ לָנוּ. לֹא נְכַחֵד מִבְּנֵיהֶם, לְדוֹר
אַחֲרוֹן מְסַפְּרִים תְּהִלּוֹת יהוה, וֶעֱזוּזוֹ
וְנִפְלְאֹתָיו אֲשֶׁר עָשָׂה. וַיָּקֶם עֵדוּת
בְּיַעֲקֹב, וְתוֹרָה שָׂם בְּיִשְׂרָאֵל, אֲשֶׁר צִוָּה
אֶת אֲבוֹתֵינוּ לְהוֹדִיעָם לִבְנֵיהֶם. לְמַעַן
יֵדְעוּ דּוֹר אַחֲרוֹן, בָּנִים יִוָּלֵדוּ, יָקֻמוּ
וִיסַפְּרוּ לִבְנֵיהֶם. וְיָשִׂימוּ בֵאלֹהִים כִּסְלָם,
וְלֹא יִשְׁכְּחוּ מַעַלְלֵי אֵל, וּמִצְוֹתָיו יִנְצֹרוּ.
וְלֹא יִהְיוּ כַּאֲבוֹתָם, דּוֹר סוֹרֵר וּמֹרֶה; דּוֹר
לֹא הֵכִין לִבּוֹ, וְלֹא נֶאֶמְנָה אֶת אֵל רוּחוֹ.
בְּנֵי אֶפְרַיִם נוֹשְׁקֵי רוֹמֵי קָשֶׁת, הָפְכוּ בְּיוֹם
קְרָב. לֹא שָׁמְרוּ בְּרִית אֱלֹהִים, וּבְתוֹרָתוֹ
מֵאֲנוּ לָלֶכֶת. וַיִּשְׁכְּחוּ עֲלִילוֹתָיו,
וְנִפְלְאוֹתָיו אֲשֶׁר הֶרְאָם. נֶגֶד אֲבוֹתָם
עָשָׂה פֶלֶא, בְּאֶרֶץ מִצְרַיִם שְׂדֵה צֹעַן.
בָּקַע יָם וַיַּעֲבִירֵם, וַיַּצֶּב מַיִם כְּמוֹ נֵד.
וַיַּנְחֵם בֶּעָנָן יוֹמָם, וְכָל הַלַּיְלָה בְּאוֹר אֵשׁ.
יְבַקַּע צֻרִים בַּמִּדְבָּר, וַיַּשְׁקְ כִּתְהֹמוֹת
רַבָּה. וַיּוֹצִא נוֹזְלִים מִסָּלַע, וַיּוֹרֶד כַּנְּהָרוֹת

מָיִם. וַיּוֹסִיפוּ עוֹד לַחֲטֹא לוֹ, לַמְרוֹת
עֶלְיוֹן בַּצִּיָּה. וַיְנַסּוּ אֵל בִּלְבָבָם, לִשְׁאָל
אֹכֶל לְנַפְשָׁם. וַיְדַבְּרוּ בֵּאלֹהִים; אָמְרוּ:
הֲיוּכַל אֵל לַעֲרֹךְ שֻׁלְחָן בַּמִּדְבָּר. הֵן הִכָּה
צוּר וַיָּזוּבוּ מַיִם, וּנְחָלִים יִשְׁטֹפוּ; הֲגַם
לֶחֶם יוּכַל תֵּת, אִם יָכִין שְׁאֵר לְעַמּוֹ. לָכֵן
שָׁמַע יהוה וַיִּתְעַבָּר; וְאֵשׁ נִשְּׂקָה בְיַעֲקֹב,
וְגַם אַף עָלָה בְיִשְׂרָאֵל. כִּי לֹא הֶאֱמִינוּ
בֵּאלֹהִים, וְלֹא בָטְחוּ בִּישׁוּעָתוֹ. וַיְצַו
שְׁחָקִים מִמָּעַל, וְדַלְתֵי שָׁמַיִם פָּתָח.
וַיַּמְטֵר עֲלֵיהֶם מָן לֶאֱכֹל, וּדְגַן שָׁמַיִם נָתַן
לָמוֹ. לֶחֶם אַבִּירִים אָכַל אִישׁ, צֵידָה
שָׁלַח לָהֶם לָשֹׂבַע. יַסַּע קָדִים בַּשָּׁמָיִם,
וַיְנַהֵג בְּעֻזּוֹ תֵימָן. וַיַּמְטֵר עֲלֵיהֶם כֶּעָפָר
שְׁאֵר, וּכְחוֹל יַמִּים עוֹף כָּנָף. וַיַּפֵּל בְּקֶרֶב
מַחֲנֵהוּ, סָבִיב לְמִשְׁכְּנֹתָיו. וַיֹּאכְלוּ
וַיִּשְׂבְּעוּ מְאֹד, וְתַאֲוָתָם יָבִא לָהֶם. לֹא זָרוּ
מִתַּאֲוָתָם, עוֹד אָכְלָם בְּפִיהֶם. וְאַף
אֱלֹהִים עָלָה בָהֶם, וַיַּהֲרֹג בְּמִשְׁמַנֵּיהֶם,
וּבַחוּרֵי יִשְׂרָאֵל הִכְרִיעַ. בְּכָל זֹאת חָטְאוּ
עוֹד, וְלֹא הֶאֱמִינוּ בְּנִפְלְאוֹתָיו. וַיְכַל
בַּהֶבֶל יְמֵיהֶם, וּשְׁנוֹתָם בַּבֶּהָלָה. אִם
הֲרָגָם וּדְרָשׁוּהוּ, וְשָׁבוּ וְשִׁחֲרוּ אֵל. וַיִּזְכְּרוּ
כִּי אֱלֹהִים צוּרָם, וְאֵל עֶלְיוֹן גֹּאֲלָם.
וַיְפַתּוּהוּ בְּפִיהֶם, וּבִלְשׁוֹנָם יְכַזְּבוּ לוֹ.
וְלִבָּם לֹא נָכוֹן עִמּוֹ, וְלֹא נֶאֶמְנוּ בִּבְרִיתוֹ.
וְהוּא רַחוּם, יְכַפֵּר עָוֹן וְלֹא יַשְׁחִית;
וְהִרְבָּה לְהָשִׁיב אַפּוֹ, וְלֹא יָעִיר כָּל חֲמָתוֹ.
וַיִּזְכֹּר כִּי בָשָׂר הֵמָּה, רוּחַ הוֹלֵךְ וְלֹא
יָשׁוּב. כַּמָּה יַמְרוּהוּ בַמִּדְבָּר, יַעֲצִיבוּהוּ
בִּישִׁימוֹן. וַיָּשׁוּבוּ וַיְנַסּוּ אֵל, וּקְדוֹשׁ
יִשְׂרָאֵל הִתְווּ. לֹא זָכְרוּ אֶת יָדוֹ, יוֹם אֲשֶׁר
פָּדָם מִנִּי צָר. אֲשֶׁר שָׂם בְּמִצְרַיִם אֹתוֹתָיו,
וּמוֹפְתָיו בִּשְׂדֵה צֹעַן. וַיַּהֲפֹךְ לְדָם
יְאֹרֵיהֶם, וְנֹזְלֵיהֶם בַּל יִשְׁתָּיוּן. יְשַׁלַּח בָּהֶם
עָרֹב וַיֹּאכְלֵם, וּצְפַרְדֵּעַ וַתַּשְׁחִיתֵם. וַיִּתֵּן
לֶחָסִיל יְבוּלָם, וִיגִיעָם לָאַרְבֶּה. יַהֲרֹג
בַּבָּרָד גַּפְנָם, וְשִׁקְמוֹתָם בַּחֲנָמַל. וַיַּסְגֵּר
לַבָּרָד בְּעִירָם, וּמִקְנֵיהֶם לָרְשָׁפִים. יְשַׁלַּח

עַד מָה יהוה תֶּאֱנַף לָנֶצַח, תִּבְעַר כְּמוֹ אֵשׁ קִנְאָתֶךָ. שְׁפֹךְ חֲמָתְךָ אֶל הַגּוֹיִם אֲשֶׁר לֹא יְדָעוּךָ, וְעַל מַמְלָכוֹת, אֲשֶׁר בְּשִׁמְךָ לֹא קָרָאוּ. כִּי אָכַל אֶת יַעֲקֹב, וְאֶת נָוֵהוּ הֵשַׁמּוּ. אַל תִּזְכָּר לָנוּ עֲוֹנֹת רִאשֹׁנִים; מַהֵר יְקַדְּמוּנוּ רַחֲמֶיךָ, כִּי דַלּוֹנוּ מְאֹד. עָזְרֵנוּ אֱלֹהֵי יִשְׁעֵנוּ עַל דְּבַר כְּבוֹד שְׁמֶךָ, וְהַצִּילֵנוּ וְכַפֵּר עַל חַטֹּאתֵינוּ לְמַעַן שְׁמֶךָ. לָמָּה יֹאמְרוּ הַגּוֹיִם: אַיֵּה אֱלֹהֵיהֶם; יִוָּדַע בַּגּוֹיִם לְעֵינֵינוּ, נִקְמַת דַּם עֲבָדֶיךָ הַשָּׁפוּךְ. תָּבוֹא לְפָנֶיךָ אֶנְקַת אָסִיר; כְּגֹדֶל זְרוֹעֲךָ, הוֹתֵר בְּנֵי תְמוּתָה. וְהָשֵׁב לִשְׁכֵנֵינוּ שִׁבְעָתַיִם אֶל חֵיקָם, חֶרְפָּתָם אֲשֶׁר חֵרְפוּךָ, אֲדֹנָי. וַאֲנַחְנוּ עַמְּךָ וְצֹאן מַרְעִיתֶךָ, נוֹדֶה לְּךָ לְעוֹלָם; לְדוֹר וָדֹר נְסַפֵּר תְּהִלָּתֶךָ.

פ לַמְנַצֵּחַ אֶל שֹׁשַׁנִּים, עֵדוּת לְאָסָף מִזְמוֹר. רֹעֵה יִשְׂרָאֵל הַאֲזִינָה, נֹהֵג כַּצֹּאן יוֹסֵף; יֹשֵׁב הַכְּרוּבִים הוֹפִיעָה. לִפְנֵי אֶפְרַיִם וּבִנְיָמִן וּמְנַשֶּׁה עוֹרְרָה אֶת גְּבוּרָתֶךָ, וּלְכָה לִישֻׁעָתָה לָּנוּ. אֱלֹהִים הֲשִׁיבֵנוּ, וְהָאֵר פָּנֶיךָ וְנִוָּשֵׁעָה. יהוה אֱלֹהִים צְבָאוֹת, עַד מָתַי עָשַׁנְתָּ בִּתְפִלַּת עַמֶּךָ. הֶאֱכַלְתָּם לֶחֶם דִּמְעָה, וַתַּשְׁקֵמוֹ בִּדְמָעוֹת שָׁלִישׁ. תְּשִׂימֵנוּ מָדוֹן לִשְׁכֵנֵינוּ, וְאֹיְבֵינוּ יִלְעֲגוּ לָמוֹ. אֱלֹהִים צְבָאוֹת הֲשִׁיבֵנוּ, וְהָאֵר פָּנֶיךָ וְנִוָּשֵׁעָה. גֶּפֶן מִמִּצְרַיִם תַּסִּיעַ, תְּגָרֵשׁ גּוֹיִם וַתִּטָּעֶהָ. פִּנִּיתָ לְפָנֶיהָ, וַתַּשְׁרֵשׁ שָׁרָשֶׁיהָ, וַתְּמַלֵּא אָרֶץ. כָּסּוּ הָרִים צִלָּהּ, וַעֲנָפֶיהָ אַרְזֵי אֵל. תְּשַׁלַּח קְצִירֶהָ עַד יָם, וְאֶל נָהָר יוֹנְקוֹתֶיהָ. לָמָּה פָּרַצְתָּ גְדֵרֶיהָ, וְאָרוּהָ כָּל עֹבְרֵי דָרֶךְ. יְכַרְסְמֶנָּה חֲזִיר מִיָּעַר, וְזִיז שָׂדַי יִרְעֶנָּה. אֱלֹהִים צְבָאוֹת שׁוּב נָא; הַבֵּט מִשָּׁמַיִם וּרְאֵה, וּפְקֹד גֶּפֶן זֹאת. וְכַנָּה אֲשֶׁר נָטְעָה יְמִינֶךָ, וְעַל בֵּן אִמַּצְתָּה לָּךְ. שְׂרֻפָה בָאֵשׁ כְּסוּחָה, מִגַּעֲרַת פָּנֶיךָ יֹאבֵדוּ. תְּהִי יָדְךָ עַל אִישׁ יְמִינֶךָ, עַל בֶּן אָדָם אִמַּצְתָּ לָּךְ. וְלֹא נָסוֹג מִמֶּךָּ, תְּחַיֵּנוּ וּבְשִׁמְךָ

בָּם חֲרוֹן אַפּוֹ, עֶבְרָה וָזַעַם וְצָרָה, מִשְׁלַחַת מַלְאֲכֵי רָעִים. יְפַלֵּס נָתִיב לְאַפּוֹ; לֹא חָשַׂךְ מִמָּוֶת נַפְשָׁם, וְחַיָּתָם לַדֶּבֶר הִסְגִּיר. וַיַּךְ כָּל בְּכוֹר בְּמִצְרָיִם, רֵאשִׁית אוֹנִים בְּאָהֳלֵי חָם. וַיַּסַּע כַּצֹּאן עַמּוֹ, וַיְנַהֲגֵם כָּעֵדֶר בַּמִּדְבָּר. וַיַּנְחֵם לָבֶטַח וְלֹא פָחָדוּ, וְאֶת אוֹיְבֵיהֶם כִּסָּה הַיָּם. וַיְבִיאֵם אֶל גְּבוּל קָדְשׁוֹ, הַר זֶה קָנְתָה יְמִינוֹ. וַיְגָרֶשׁ מִפְּנֵיהֶם גּוֹיִם, וַיַּפִּילֵם בְּחֶבֶל נַחֲלָה, וַיַּשְׁכֵּן בְּאָהֳלֵיהֶם שִׁבְטֵי יִשְׂרָאֵל. וַיְנַסּוּ וַיַּמְרוּ אֶת אֱלֹהִים עֶלְיוֹן, וְעֵדוֹתָיו לֹא שָׁמָרוּ. וַיִּסֹּגוּ וַיִּבְגְּדוּ כַּאֲבוֹתָם, נֶהְפְּכוּ כְּקֶשֶׁת רְמִיָּה. וַיַּכְעִיסוּהוּ בְּבָמוֹתָם, וּבִפְסִילֵיהֶם יַקְנִיאוּהוּ. שָׁמַע אֱלֹהִים וַיִּתְעַבָּר, וַיִּמְאַס מְאֹד בְּיִשְׂרָאֵל. וַיִּטֹּשׁ מִשְׁכַּן שִׁלוֹ, אֹהֶל שִׁכֵּן בָּאָדָם. וַיִּתֵּן לַשְּׁבִי עֻזּוֹ, וְתִפְאַרְתּוֹ בְיַד צָר. וַיַּסְגֵּר לַחֶרֶב עַמּוֹ, וּבְנַחֲלָתוֹ הִתְעַבָּר. בַּחוּרָיו אָכְלָה אֵשׁ, וּבְתוּלֹתָיו לֹא הוּלָּלוּ. כֹּהֲנָיו בַּחֶרֶב נָפָלוּ, וְאַלְמְנֹתָיו לֹא תִבְכֶּינָה. וַיִּקַץ כְּיָשֵׁן | אֲדֹנָי, כְּגִבּוֹר מִתְרוֹנֵן מִיָּיִן. וַיַּךְ צָרָיו אָחוֹר, חֶרְפַּת עוֹלָם נָתַן לָמוֹ. וַיִּמְאַס בְּאֹהֶל יוֹסֵף, וּבְשֵׁבֶט אֶפְרַיִם לֹא בָחָר. וַיִּבְחַר אֶת שֵׁבֶט יְהוּדָה, אֶת הַר צִיּוֹן אֲשֶׁר אָהֵב. וַיִּבֶן כְּמוֹ רָמִים מִקְדָּשׁוֹ, כְּאֶרֶץ יְסָדָהּ לְעוֹלָם. וַיִּבְחַר בְּדָוִד עַבְדּוֹ, וַיִּקָּחֵהוּ מִמִּכְלְאֹת צֹאן. מֵאַחַר עָלוֹת הֱבִיאוֹ; לִרְעוֹת בְּיַעֲקֹב עַמּוֹ, וּבְיִשְׂרָאֵל נַחֲלָתוֹ. וַיִּרְעֵם כְּתֹם לְבָבוֹ, וּבִתְבוּנוֹת כַּפָּיו יַנְחֵם.

עט מִזְמוֹר לְאָסָף; אֱלֹהִים בָּאוּ גוֹיִם בְּנַחֲלָתֶךָ, טִמְּאוּ אֶת הֵיכַל קָדְשֶׁךָ, שָׂמוּ אֶת יְרוּשָׁלַיִם לְעִיִּים. נָתְנוּ אֶת נִבְלַת עֲבָדֶיךָ מַאֲכָל לְעוֹף הַשָּׁמָיִם, בְּשַׂר חֲסִידֶיךָ לְחַיְתוֹ אָרֶץ. שָׁפְכוּ דָמָם כַּמַּיִם, סְבִיבוֹת יְרוּשָׁלַיִם, וְאֵין קוֹבֵר. הָיִינוּ חֶרְפָּה לִשְׁכֵנֵינוּ, לַעַג וָקֶלֶס לִסְבִיבוֹתֵינוּ.

נִקְרָא. יהוה אֱלֹהִים צְבָאוֹת הֲשִׁיבֵנוּ, הָאֵר פָּנֶיךָ וְנִוָּשֵׁעָה.

פא לַמְנַצֵּחַ עַל הַגִּתִּית לְאָסָף. הַרְנִינוּ לֵאלֹהִים עוּזֵּנוּ, הָרִיעוּ לֵאלֹהֵי יַעֲקֹב. שְׂאוּ זִמְרָה וּתְנוּ תֹף, כִּנּוֹר נָעִים עִם נָבֶל. תִּקְעוּ בַחֹדֶשׁ שׁוֹפָר, בַּכֶּסֶה לְיוֹם חַגֵּנוּ. כִּי חֹק לְיִשְׂרָאֵל הוּא, מִשְׁפָּט לֵאלֹהֵי יַעֲקֹב. עֵדוּת בִּיהוֹסֵף שָׂמוֹ, בְּצֵאתוֹ עַל אֶרֶץ מִצְרָיִם, שְׂפַת לֹא יָדַעְתִּי אֶשְׁמָע. הֲסִירוֹתִי מִסֵּבֶל שִׁכְמוֹ, כַּפָּיו מִדּוּד תַּעֲבֹרְנָה. בַּצָּרָה קָרָאתָ וָאֲחַלְּצֶךָּ, אֶעֶנְךָ בְּסֵתֶר רַעַם, אֶבְחָנְךָ עַל מֵי מְרִיבָה סֶלָה. שְׁמַע עַמִּי וְאָעִידָה בָּךְ, יִשְׂרָאֵל אִם תִּשְׁמַע לִי. לֹא יִהְיֶה בְךָ אֵל זָר, וְלֹא תִשְׁתַּחֲוֶה לְאֵל נֵכָר. אָנֹכִי יהוה אֱלֹהֶיךָ הַמַּעַלְךָ מֵאֶרֶץ מִצְרָיִם, הַרְחֶב פִּיךָ וַאֲמַלְאֵהוּ. וְלֹא שָׁמַע עַמִּי לְקוֹלִי, וְיִשְׂרָאֵל לֹא אָבָה לִי. וָאֲשַׁלְּחֵהוּ בִּשְׁרִירוּת לִבָּם, יֵלְכוּ בְּמוֹעֲצוֹתֵיהֶם. לוּ עַמִּי שֹׁמֵעַ לִי, יִשְׂרָאֵל בִּדְרָכַי יְהַלֵּכוּ. כִּמְעַט אוֹיְבֵיהֶם אַכְנִיעַ, וְעַל צָרֵיהֶם אָשִׁיב יָדִי. מְשַׂנְאֵי יהוה יְכַחֲשׁוּ לוֹ, וִיהִי עִתָּם לְעוֹלָם. וַיַּאֲכִילֵהוּ מֵחֵלֶב חִטָּה; וּמִצּוּר, דְּבַשׁ אַשְׂבִּיעֶךָ.

פב מִזְמוֹר לְאָסָף; אֱלֹהִים נִצָּב בַּעֲדַת אֵל, בְּקֶרֶב אֱלֹהִים יִשְׁפֹּט. עַד מָתַי תִּשְׁפְּטוּ עָוֶל, וּפְנֵי רְשָׁעִים תִּשְׂאוּ סֶלָה. שִׁפְטוּ דַל וְיָתוֹם, עָנִי וָרָשׁ הַצְדִּיקוּ. פַּלְּטוּ דַל וְאֶבְיוֹן, מִיַּד רְשָׁעִים הַצִּילוּ. לֹא יָדְעוּ וְלֹא יָבִינוּ, בַּחֲשֵׁכָה יִתְהַלָּכוּ; יִמּוֹטוּ כָּל מוֹסְדֵי אָרֶץ. אֲנִי אָמַרְתִּי אֱלֹהִים אַתֶּם, וּבְנֵי עֶלְיוֹן כֻּלְּכֶם. אָכֵן כְּאָדָם תְּמוּתוּן, וּכְאַחַד הַשָּׂרִים תִּפֹּלוּ. קוּמָה אֱלֹהִים שָׁפְטָה הָאָרֶץ, כִּי אַתָּה תִנְחַל בְּכָל הַגּוֹיִם.

פג שִׁיר מִזְמוֹר לְאָסָף. אֱלֹהִים, אַל דֳּמִי לָךְ; אַל תֶּחֱרַשׁ וְאַל תִּשְׁקֹט, אֵל. כִּי הִנֵּה אוֹיְבֶיךָ יֶהֱמָיוּן, וּמְשַׂנְאֶיךָ

נָשְׂאוּ רֹאשׁ. עַל עַמְּךָ יַעֲרִימוּ סוֹד, וְיִתְיָעֲצוּ עַל צְפוּנֶיךָ. אָמְרוּ: לְכוּ וְנַכְחִידֵם מִגּוֹי, וְלֹא יִזָּכֵר שֵׁם יִשְׂרָאֵל עוֹד. כִּי נוֹעֲצוּ לֵב יַחְדָּו, עָלֶיךָ בְּרִית יִכְרֹתוּ. אָהֳלֵי אֱדוֹם וְיִשְׁמְעֵאלִים, מוֹאָב וְהַגְרִים. גְּבָל וְעַמּוֹן וַעֲמָלֵק, פְּלֶשֶׁת עִם יֹשְׁבֵי צוֹר. גַּם אַשּׁוּר נִלְוָה עִמָּם, הָיוּ זְרוֹעַ לִבְנֵי לוֹט סֶלָה. עֲשֵׂה לָהֶם כְּמִדְיָן, כְּסִיסְרָא כְיָבִין בְּנַחַל קִישׁוֹן. נִשְׁמְדוּ בְעֵין דֹּאר, הָיוּ דֹּמֶן לָאֲדָמָה. שִׁיתֵמוֹ נְדִיבֵמוֹ כְּעֹרֵב וְכִזְאֵב, וּכְזֶבַח וּכְצַלְמֻנָּע כָּל נְסִיכֵמוֹ. אֲשֶׁר אָמְרוּ: נִירֲשָׁה לָּנוּ, אֵת נְאוֹת אֱלֹהִים. אֱלֹהַי, שִׁיתֵמוֹ כַגַּלְגַּל, כְּקַשׁ לִפְנֵי רוּחַ. כְּאֵשׁ תִּבְעַר יָעַר, וּכְלֶהָבָה תְּלַהֵט הָרִים. כֵּן תִּרְדְּפֵם בְּסַעֲרֶךָ, וּבְסוּפָתְךָ תְבַהֲלֵם. מַלֵּא פְנֵיהֶם קָלוֹן, וִיבַקְשׁוּ שִׁמְךָ יהוה. יֵבֹשׁוּ וְיִבָּהֲלוּ עֲדֵי עַד, וְיַחְפְּרוּ וְיֹאבֵדוּ. וְיֵדְעוּ כִּי אַתָּה שִׁמְךָ יהוה לְבַדֶּךָ, עֶלְיוֹן עַל כָּל הָאָרֶץ.

פד לַמְנַצֵּחַ עַל הַגִּתִּית, לִבְנֵי קֹרַח מִזְמוֹר. מַה יְּדִידוֹת מִשְׁכְּנוֹתֶיךָ, יהוה צְבָאוֹת. נִכְסְפָה וְגַם כָּלְתָה נַפְשִׁי לְחַצְרוֹת יהוה; לִבִּי וּבְשָׂרִי יְרַנְּנוּ אֶל אֵל חָי. גַּם צִפּוֹר מָצְאָה בַיִת, וּדְרוֹר קֵן לָהּ אֲשֶׁר שָׁתָה אֶפְרֹחֶיהָ; אֶת מִזְבְּחוֹתֶיךָ יהוה צְבָאוֹת, מַלְכִּי וֵאלֹהָי. אַשְׁרֵי יוֹשְׁבֵי בֵיתֶךָ, עוֹד יְהַלְלוּךָ סֶּלָה. אַשְׁרֵי אָדָם עוֹז לוֹ בָךְ, מְסִלּוֹת בִּלְבָבָם. עֹבְרֵי בְּעֵמֶק הַבָּכָא מַעְיָן יְשִׁיתוּהוּ, גַּם בְּרָכוֹת יַעְטֶה מוֹרֶה. יֵלְכוּ מֵחַיִל אֶל חָיִל, יֵרָאֶה אֶל אֱלֹהִים בְּצִיּוֹן. יהוה אֱלֹהִים צְבָאוֹת שִׁמְעָה תְפִלָּתִי, הַאֲזִינָה אֱלֹהֵי יַעֲקֹב סֶלָה. מָגִנֵּנוּ רְאֵה, אֱלֹהִים; וְהַבֵּט פְּנֵי מְשִׁיחֶךָ. כִּי טוֹב יוֹם בַּחֲצֵרֶיךָ מֵאָלֶף, בָּחַרְתִּי הִסְתּוֹפֵף בְּבֵית אֱלֹהַי, מִדּוּר בְּאָהֳלֵי רֶשַׁע. כִּי שֶׁמֶשׁ וּמָגֵן יהוה אֱלֹהִים; חֵן וְכָבוֹד יִתֵּן יהוה, לֹא יִמְנַע טוֹב לַהֹלְכִים בְּתָמִים. יהוה צְבָאוֹת, אַשְׁרֵי אָדָם בֹּטֵחַ בָּךְ.

אַתָּה יהוה עֲזַרְתַּנִי וְנִחַמְתָּנִי.

פז לִבְנֵי קֹרַח מִזְמוֹר שִׁיר, יְסוּדָתוֹ
בְּהַרְרֵי קֹדֶשׁ. אֹהֵב יהוה שַׁעֲרֵי צִיּוֹן,
מִכֹּל מִשְׁכְּנוֹת יַעֲקֹב. נִכְבָּדוֹת מְדֻבָּר בָּךְ,
עִיר הָאֱלֹהִים סֶלָה. אַזְכִּיר רַהַב וּבָבֶל
לְיֹדְעָי, הִנֵּה פְלֶשֶׁת וְצוֹר עִם כּוּשׁ, זֶה יֻלַּד
שָׁם. וּלְצִיּוֹן יֵאָמַר: אִישׁ וְאִישׁ יֻלַּד בָּהּ,
וְהוּא יְכוֹנְנֶהָ עֶלְיוֹן. יהוה יִסְפֹּר בִּכְתוֹב
עַמִּים, זֶה יֻלַּד שָׁם סֶלָה. וְשָׁרִים כְּחֹלְלִים,
כָּל מַעְיָנַי בָּךְ.

פח שִׁיר מִזְמוֹר לִבְנֵי קֹרַח, לַמְנַצֵּחַ עַל
מָחֲלַת לְעַנּוֹת, מַשְׂכִּיל לְהֵימָן
הָאֶזְרָחִי. יהוה אֱלֹהֵי יְשׁוּעָתִי, יוֹם
צָעַקְתִּי, בַלַּיְלָה נֶגְדֶּךָ. תָּבוֹא לְפָנֶיךָ
תְּפִלָּתִי, הַטֵּה אָזְנְךָ לְרִנָּתִי. כִּי שָׂבְעָה
בְרָעוֹת נַפְשִׁי, וְחַיַּי לִשְׁאוֹל הִגִּיעוּ.
נֶחְשַׁבְתִּי עִם יוֹרְדֵי בוֹר, הָיִיתִי כְּגֶבֶר אֵין
אֱיָל. בַּמֵּתִים חָפְשִׁי; כְּמוֹ חֲלָלִים שֹׁכְבֵי
קֶבֶר אֲשֶׁר לֹא זְכַרְתָּם עוֹד, וְהֵמָּה מִיָּדְךָ
נִגְזָרוּ. שַׁתַּנִי בְּבוֹר תַּחְתִּיּוֹת, בְּמַחֲשַׁכִּים
בִּמְצֹלוֹת. עָלַי סָמְכָה חֲמָתֶךָ, וְכָל
מִשְׁבָּרֶיךָ עִנִּיתָ סֶּלָה. הִרְחַקְתָּ מְיֻדָּעַי
מִמֶּנִּי; שַׁתַּנִי תוֹעֵבוֹת לָמוֹ, כָּלֻא וְלֹא
אֵצֵא. עֵינִי דָאֲבָה מִנִּי עֹנִי; קְרָאתִיךָ יהוה
בְּכָל יוֹם, שִׁטַּחְתִּי אֵלֶיךָ כַפָּי. הֲלַמֵּתִים
תַּעֲשֶׂה פֶּלֶא, אִם רְפָאִים יָקוּמוּ יוֹדוּךָ
סֶּלָה. הַיְסֻפַּר בַּקֶּבֶר חַסְדֶּךָ, אֱמוּנָתְךָ
בָּאֲבַדּוֹן. הֲיִוָּדַע בַּחֹשֶׁךְ פִּלְאֶךָ, וְצִדְקָתְךָ
בְּאֶרֶץ נְשִׁיָּה. וַאֲנִי אֵלֶיךָ יהוה שִׁוַּעְתִּי,
וּבַבֹּקֶר תְּפִלָּתִי תְקַדְּמֶךָּ. לָמָה יהוה תִּזְנַח
נַפְשִׁי, תַּסְתִּיר פָּנֶיךָ מִמֶּנִּי. עָנִי אֲנִי וְגֹוֵעַ
מִנֹּעַר, נָשָׂאתִי אֵמֶיךָ אָפוּנָה. עָלַי עָבְרוּ
חֲרוֹנֶיךָ, בִּעוּתֶיךָ צִמְּתוּתֻנִי. סַבּוּנִי כַמַּיִם
כָּל הַיּוֹם, הִקִּיפוּ עָלַי יָחַד. הִרְחַקְתָּ מִמֶּנִּי
אֹהֵב וָרֵעַ, מְיֻדָּעַי מַחְשָׁךְ.

פט מַשְׂכִּיל לְאֵיתָן הָאֶזְרָחִי. חַסְדֵי
יהוה עוֹלָם אָשִׁירָה, לְדֹר וָדֹר

פה לַמְנַצֵּחַ לִבְנֵי קֹרַח מִזְמוֹר. רָצִיתָ
יהוה אַרְצֶךָ, שַׁבְתָּ שְׁבִית יַעֲקֹב. נָשָׂאתָ
עֲוֹן עַמֶּךָ, כִּסִּיתָ כָל חַטָּאתָם סֶלָה. אָסַפְתָּ
כָל עֶבְרָתֶךָ, הֱשִׁיבוֹתָ מֵחֲרוֹן אַפֶּךָ. שׁוּבֵנוּ
אֱלֹהֵי יִשְׁעֵנוּ, וְהָפֵר כַּעַסְךָ עִמָּנוּ.
הַלְעוֹלָם תֶּאֱנַף בָּנוּ, תִּמְשֹׁךְ אַפְּךָ לְדֹר
וָדֹר. הֲלֹא אַתָּה תָּשׁוּב תְּחַיֵּינוּ, וְעַמְּךָ
יִשְׂמְחוּ בָךְ. הַרְאֵנוּ יהוה חַסְדֶּךָ, וְיֶשְׁעֲךָ
תִּתֶּן לָנוּ. אֶשְׁמְעָה מַה יְדַבֵּר הָאֵל יהוה;
כִּי יְדַבֵּר שָׁלוֹם אֶל עַמּוֹ וְאֶל חֲסִידָיו, וְאַל
יָשׁוּבוּ לְכִסְלָה. אַךְ קָרוֹב לִירֵאָיו יִשְׁעוֹ,
לִשְׁכֹּן כָּבוֹד בְּאַרְצֵנוּ. חֶסֶד וֶאֱמֶת נִפְגָּשׁוּ,
צֶדֶק וְשָׁלוֹם נָשָׁקוּ. אֱמֶת מֵאֶרֶץ תִּצְמָח,
וְצֶדֶק מִשָּׁמַיִם נִשְׁקָף. גַּם יהוה יִתֵּן הַטּוֹב,
וְאַרְצֵנוּ תִּתֵּן יְבוּלָהּ. צֶדֶק לְפָנָיו יְהַלֵּךְ,
וְיָשֵׂם לְדֶרֶךְ פְּעָמָיו.

פו תְּפִלָּה לְדָוִד; הַטֵּה יהוה אָזְנְךָ, עֲנֵנִי,
כִּי עָנִי וְאֶבְיוֹן אָנִי. שָׁמְרָה נַפְשִׁי כִּי
חָסִיד אָנִי; הוֹשַׁע עַבְדְּךָ, אַתָּה אֱלֹהַי,
הַבּוֹטֵחַ אֵלֶיךָ. חָנֵּנִי אֲדֹנָי, כִּי אֵלֶיךָ אֶקְרָא
כָּל הַיּוֹם. שַׂמֵּחַ נֶפֶשׁ עַבְדֶּךָ, כִּי אֵלֶיךָ
אֲדֹנָי נַפְשִׁי אֶשָּׂא. כִּי אַתָּה אֲדֹנָי טוֹב
וְסַלָּח, וְרַב חֶסֶד לְכָל קֹרְאֶיךָ. הַאֲזִינָה
יהוה תְּפִלָּתִי, וְהַקְשִׁיבָה בְּקוֹל תַּחֲנוּנוֹתָי.
בְּיוֹם צָרָתִי אֶקְרָאֶךָּ כִּי תַעֲנֵנִי. אֵין כָּמוֹךָ
בָאֱלֹהִים | אֲדֹנָי, וְאֵין כְּמַעֲשֶׂיךָ. כָּל גּוֹיִם
אֲשֶׁר עָשִׂיתָ יָבוֹאוּ וְיִשְׁתַּחֲווּ לְפָנֶיךָ,
אֲדֹנָי; וִיכַבְּדוּ לִשְׁמֶךָ. כִּי גָדוֹל אַתָּה
וְעֹשֵׂה נִפְלָאוֹת, אַתָּה אֱלֹהִים לְבַדֶּךָ.
הוֹרֵנִי יהוה דַּרְכֶּךָ, אֲהַלֵּךְ בַּאֲמִתֶּךָ; יַחֵד
לְבָבִי לְיִרְאָה שְׁמֶךָ. אוֹדְךָ אֲדֹנָי אֱלֹהַי
בְּכָל לְבָבִי, וַאֲכַבְּדָה שִׁמְךָ לְעוֹלָם. כִּי
חַסְדְּךָ גָּדוֹל עָלָי, וְהִצַּלְתָּ נַפְשִׁי מִשְּׁאוֹל
תַּחְתִּיָּה. אֱלֹהִים, זֵדִים קָמוּ עָלַי, וַעֲדַת
עָרִיצִים בִּקְשׁוּ נַפְשִׁי; וְלֹא שָׂמוּךָ לְנֶגְדָּם.
וְאַתָּה אֲדֹנָי אֵל רַחוּם וְחַנּוּן, אֶרֶךְ אַפַּיִם
וְרַב חֶסֶד וֶאֱמֶת. פְּנֵה אֵלַי וְחָנֵּנִי; תְּנָה
עֻזְּךָ לְעַבְדֶּךָ, וְהוֹשִׁיעָה לְבֶן אֲמָתֶךָ. עֲשֵׂה
עִמִּי אוֹת לְטוֹבָה, וְיִרְאוּ שֹׂנְאַי וְיֵבֹשׁוּ, כִּי

אֵלִי וְצוּר יְשׁוּעָתִי. אַף אֲנִי בְּכוֹר אֶתְּנֵהוּ, עֶלְיוֹן לְמַלְכֵי אָרֶץ. לְעוֹלָם אֶשְׁמָר לוֹ חַסְדִּי, וּבְרִיתִי נֶאֱמֶנֶת לוֹ. וְשַׂמְתִּי לָעַד זַרְעוֹ, וְכִסְאוֹ כִּימֵי שָׁמָיִם. אִם יַעַזְבוּ בָנָיו תּוֹרָתִי, וּבְמִשְׁפָּטַי לֹא יֵלֵכוּן. אִם חֻקֹּתַי יְחַלֵּלוּ, וּמִצְוֹתַי לֹא יִשְׁמֹרוּ. וּפָקַדְתִּי בְשֵׁבֶט פִּשְׁעָם, וּבִנְגָעִים עֲוֹנָם. וְחַסְדִּי לֹא אָפִיר מֵעִמּוֹ, וְלֹא אֲשַׁקֵּר בֶּאֱמוּנָתִי. לֹא אֲחַלֵּל בְּרִיתִי, וּמוֹצָא שְׂפָתַי לֹא אֲשַׁנֶּה. אַחַת נִשְׁבַּעְתִּי בְקָדְשִׁי, אִם לְדָוִד אֲכַזֵּב. זַרְעוֹ לְעוֹלָם יִהְיֶה, וְכִסְאוֹ כַשֶּׁמֶשׁ נֶגְדִּי. כְּיָרֵחַ יִכּוֹן עוֹלָם, וְעֵד בַּשַּׁחַק נֶאֱמָן סֶלָה. וְאַתָּה זָנַחְתָּ וַתִּמְאָס, הִתְעַבַּרְתָּ עִם מְשִׁיחֶךָ. נֵאַרְתָּה בְּרִית עַבְדֶּךָ, חִלַּלְתָּ לָאָרֶץ נִזְרוֹ. פָּרַצְתָּ כָל גְּדֵרֹתָיו, שַׂמְתָּ מִבְצָרָיו מְחִתָּה. שַׁסֻּהוּ כָּל עֹבְרֵי דָרֶךְ, הָיָה חֶרְפָּה לִשְׁכֵנָיו. הֲרִימוֹתָ יְמִין צָרָיו, הִשְׂמַחְתָּ כָּל אוֹיְבָיו. אַף תָּשִׁיב צוּר חַרְבּוֹ, וְלֹא הֲקֵמֹתוֹ בַּמִּלְחָמָה. הִשְׁבַּתָּ מִטְּהָרוֹ, וְכִסְאוֹ לָאָרֶץ מִגַּרְתָּה. הִקְצַרְתָּ יְמֵי עֲלוּמָיו, הֶעֱטִיתָ עָלָיו בּוּשָׁה סֶלָה. עַד מָה יהוה תִּסָּתֵר לָנֶצַח, תִּבְעַר כְּמוֹ אֵשׁ חֲמָתֶךָ. זְכָר אֲנִי מֶה חָלֶד, עַל מַה שָּׁוְא בָּרָאתָ כָל בְּנֵי אָדָם. מִי גֶבֶר יִחְיֶה וְלֹא יִרְאֶה מָּוֶת, יְמַלֵּט נַפְשׁוֹ מִיַּד שְׁאוֹל סֶלָה. אַיֵּה חֲסָדֶיךָ הָרִאשֹׁנִים | אֲדֹנָי, נִשְׁבַּעְתָּ לְדָוִד בֶּאֱמוּנָתֶךָ. זְכֹר אֲדֹנָי חֶרְפַּת עֲבָדֶיךָ, שְׂאֵתִי בְחֵיקִי כָּל רַבִּים עַמִּים. אֲשֶׁר חֵרְפוּ אוֹיְבֶיךָ | יהוה, אֲשֶׁר חֵרְפוּ עִקְּבוֹת מְשִׁיחֶךָ. בָּרוּךְ יהוה לְעוֹלָם, אָמֵן וְאָמֵן:

אוֹדִיעַ אֱמוּנָתְךָ בְּפִי. כִּי אָמַרְתִּי: עוֹלָם חֶסֶד יִבָּנֶה, שָׁמַיִם תָּכִן אֱמוּנָתְךָ בָהֶם. כָּרַתִּי בְרִית לִבְחִירִי, נִשְׁבַּעְתִּי לְדָוִד עַבְדִּי. עַד עוֹלָם אָכִין זַרְעֶךָ, וּבָנִיתִי לְדֹר וָדוֹר כִּסְאֲךָ סֶלָה. וְיוֹדוּ שָׁמַיִם פִּלְאֲךָ, יהוה, אַף אֱמוּנָתְךָ בִּקְהַל קְדֹשִׁים. כִּי מִי בַשַּׁחַק יַעֲרֹךְ לַיהוה, יִדְמֶה לַיהוה בִּבְנֵי אֵלִים. אֵל נַעֲרָץ בְּסוֹד קְדֹשִׁים רַבָּה, וְנוֹרָא עַל כָּל סְבִיבָיו. יהוה אֱלֹהֵי צְבָאוֹת, מִי כָמוֹךָ, חֲסִין יָהּ; וֶאֱמוּנָתְךָ סְבִיבוֹתֶיךָ. אַתָּה מוֹשֵׁל בְּגֵאוּת הַיָּם, בְּשׂוֹא גַלָּיו אַתָּה תְשַׁבְּחֵם. אַתָּה דִכִּאתָ כֶחָלָל רָהַב, בִּזְרוֹעַ עֻזְּךָ פִּזַּרְתָּ אוֹיְבֶיךָ. לְךָ שָׁמַיִם אַף לְךָ אָרֶץ, תֵּבֵל וּמְלֹאָהּ אַתָּה יְסַדְתָּם. צָפוֹן וְיָמִין אַתָּה בְרָאתָם, תָּבוֹר וְחֶרְמוֹן בְּשִׁמְךָ יְרַנֵּנוּ. לְךָ זְרוֹעַ עִם גְּבוּרָה, תָּעֹז יָדְךָ, תָּרוּם יְמִינֶךָ. צֶדֶק וּמִשְׁפָּט מְכוֹן כִּסְאֶךָ, חֶסֶד וֶאֱמֶת יְקַדְּמוּ פָנֶיךָ. אַשְׁרֵי הָעָם יוֹדְעֵי תְרוּעָה, יהוה בְּאוֹר פָּנֶיךָ יְהַלֵּכוּן. בְּשִׁמְךָ יְגִילוּן כָּל הַיּוֹם, וּבְצִדְקָתְךָ יָרוּמוּ. כִּי תִפְאֶרֶת עֻזָּמוֹ אָתָּה, וּבִרְצוֹנְךָ תָּרוּם קַרְנֵנוּ. כִּי לַיהוה מָגִנֵּנוּ, וְלִקְדוֹשׁ יִשְׂרָאֵל מַלְכֵּנוּ. אָז דִּבַּרְתָּ בְחָזוֹן לַחֲסִידֶיךָ, וַתֹּאמֶר שִׁוִּיתִי עֵזֶר עַל גִּבּוֹר, הֲרִימוֹתִי בָחוּר מֵעָם. מָצָאתִי דָּוִד עַבְדִּי, בְּשֶׁמֶן קָדְשִׁי מְשַׁחְתִּיו. אֲשֶׁר יָדִי תִּכּוֹן עִמּוֹ, אַף זְרוֹעִי תְאַמְּצֶנּוּ. לֹא יַשִּׁיא אוֹיֵב בּוֹ, וּבֶן עַוְלָה לֹא יְעַנֶּנּוּ. וְכַתּוֹתִי מִפָּנָיו צָרָיו, וּמְשַׂנְאָיו אֶגּוֹף. וֶאֱמוּנָתִי וְחַסְדִּי עִמּוֹ, וּבִשְׁמִי תָּרוּם קַרְנוֹ. וְשַׂמְתִּי בַיָּם יָדוֹ, וּבַנְּהָרוֹת יְמִינוֹ. הוּא יִקְרָאֵנִי אָבִי אָתָּה,

❧ ספר רביעי / BOOK FOUR ❧

עַד עוֹלָם אַתָּה אֵל. תָּשֵׁב אֱנוֹשׁ עַד דַּכָּא, וַתֹּאמֶר: שׁוּבוּ בְנֵי אָדָם. כִּי אֶלֶף שָׁנִים בְּעֵינֶיךָ כְּיוֹם אֶתְמוֹל כִּי יַעֲבֹר, וְאַשְׁמוּרָה בַלָּיְלָה. זְרַמְתָּם, שֵׁנָה יִהְיוּ, בַּבֹּקֶר כֶּחָצִיר יַחֲלֹף. בַּבֹּקֶר יָצִיץ וְחָלָף, לָעֶרֶב יְמוֹלֵל וְיָבֵשׁ. כִּי כָלִינוּ בְאַפֶּךָ, וּבַחֲמָתְךָ נִבְהָלְנוּ.

❧ יום חמישי / THURSDAY ❧

צ תְּפִלָּה לְמֹשֶׁה אִישׁ הָאֱלֹהִים, אֲדֹנָי, מָעוֹן אַתָּה הָיִיתָ לָּנוּ בְּדֹר וָדֹר. בְּטֶרֶם הָרִים יֻלָּדוּ, וַתְּחוֹלֵל אֶרֶץ וְתֵבֵל, וּמֵעוֹלָם

יהוה; מְאֹד עָמְקוּ מַחְשְׁבֹתֶיךָ. אִישׁ בַּעַר
לֹא יֵדָע, וּכְסִיל לֹא יָבִין אֶת זֹאת. בִּפְרֹחַ
רְשָׁעִים כְּמוֹ עֵשֶׂב, וַיָּצִיצוּ כָּל פֹּעֲלֵי אָוֶן,
לְהִשָּׁמְדָם עֲדֵי עַד. וְאַתָּה מָרוֹם לְעֹלָם,
יהוה. כִּי הִנֵּה אֹיְבֶיךָ | יהוה, כִּי הִנֵּה
אֹיְבֶיךָ יֹאבֵדוּ, יִתְפָּרְדוּ כָּל פֹּעֲלֵי אָוֶן.
וַתָּרֶם כִּרְאֵים קַרְנִי, בַּלֹּתִי בְּשֶׁמֶן רַעֲנָן.
וַתַּבֵּט עֵינִי בְּשׁוּרָי; בַּקָּמִים עָלַי מְרֵעִים,
תִּשְׁמַעְנָה אָזְנָי. צַדִּיק כַּתָּמָר יִפְרָח, כְּאֶרֶז
בַּלְּבָנוֹן יִשְׂגֶּה. שְׁתוּלִים בְּבֵית יהוה,
בְּחַצְרוֹת אֱלֹהֵינוּ יַפְרִיחוּ. עוֹד יְנוּבוּן
בְּשֵׂיבָה, דְּשֵׁנִים וְרַעֲנַנִּים יִהְיוּ. לְהַגִּיד כִּי
יָשָׁר יהוה, צוּרִי וְלֹא עַוְלָתָה בּוֹ.

צג יהוה מָלָךְ גֵּאוּת לָבֵשׁ, לָבֵשׁ יהוה
עֹז הִתְאַזָּר, אַף תִּכּוֹן תֵּבֵל בַּל
תִּמּוֹט. נָכוֹן כִּסְאֲךָ מֵאָז, מֵעוֹלָם אָתָּה.
נָשְׂאוּ נְהָרוֹת, יהוה, נָשְׂאוּ נְהָרוֹת קוֹלָם;
יִשְׂאוּ נְהָרוֹת דָּכְיָם. מִקֹּלוֹת מַיִם רַבִּים
אַדִּירִים מִשְׁבְּרֵי יָם, אַדִּיר בַּמָּרוֹם יהוה.
עֵדֹתֶיךָ נֶאֶמְנוּ מְאֹד לְבֵיתְךָ נַאֲוָה קֹדֶשׁ;
יהוה, לְאֹרֶךְ יָמִים.

צד אֵל נְקָמוֹת יהוה, אֵל נְקָמוֹת הוֹפִיעַ.
הִנָּשֵׂא שֹׁפֵט הָאָרֶץ, הָשֵׁב גְּמוּל עַל
גֵּאִים. עַד מָתַי רְשָׁעִים | יהוה, עַד מָתַי
רְשָׁעִים יַעֲלֹזוּ. יַבִּיעוּ יְדַבְּרוּ עָתָק,
יִתְאַמְּרוּ כָּל פֹּעֲלֵי אָוֶן. עַמְּךָ יהוה יְדַכְּאוּ,
וְנַחֲלָתְךָ יְעַנּוּ. אַלְמָנָה וְגֵר יַהֲרֹגוּ,
וִיתוֹמִים יְרַצֵּחוּ. וַיֹּאמְרוּ: לֹא יִרְאֶה יָּהּ,
וְלֹא יָבִין אֱלֹהֵי יַעֲקֹב. בִּינוּ בֹּעֲרִים בָּעָם,
וּכְסִילִים מָתַי תַּשְׂכִּילוּ. הֲנֹטַע אֹזֶן הֲלֹא
יִשְׁמָע, אִם יֹצֵר עַיִן הֲלֹא יַבִּיט. הֲיֹסֵר גּוֹיִם
הֲלֹא יוֹכִיחַ, הַמְלַמֵּד אָדָם דָּעַת. יהוה
יֹדֵעַ מַחְשְׁבוֹת אָדָם, כִּי הֵמָּה הָבֶל. אַשְׁרֵי
הַגֶּבֶר אֲשֶׁר תְּיַסְּרֶנּוּ יָּהּ, וּמִתּוֹרָתְךָ
תְלַמְּדֶנּוּ. לְהַשְׁקִיט לוֹ מִימֵי רָע, עַד יִכָּרֶה
לָרָשָׁע שָׁחַת. כִּי לֹא יִטֹּשׁ יהוה עַמּוֹ,
וְנַחֲלָתוֹ לֹא יַעֲזֹב. כִּי עַד צֶדֶק יָשׁוּב
מִשְׁפָּט, וְאַחֲרָיו כָּל יִשְׁרֵי לֵב. מִי יָקוּם לִי
עִם מְרֵעִים, מִי יִתְיַצֵּב לִי עִם פֹּעֲלֵי אָוֶן

שַׁתָּה עֲוֺנֹתֵינוּ לְנֶגְדֶּךָ, עֲלֻמֵנוּ לִמְאוֹר
פָּנֶיךָ. כִּי כָל יָמֵינוּ פָּנוּ בְעֶבְרָתֶךָ, כִּלִּינוּ
שָׁנֵינוּ כְמוֹ הֶגֶה. יְמֵי שְׁנוֹתֵינוּ בָהֶם
שִׁבְעִים שָׁנָה, וְאִם בִּגְבוּרֹת שְׁמוֹנִים שָׁנָה,
וְרָהְבָּם עָמָל וָאָוֶן, כִּי גָז חִישׁ וַנָּעֻפָה. מִי
יוֹדֵעַ עֹז אַפֶּךָ, וּכְיִרְאָתְךָ עֶבְרָתֶךָ. לִמְנוֹת
יָמֵינוּ כֵּן הוֹדַע, וְנָבִא לְבַב חָכְמָה. שׁוּבָה
יהוה עַד מָתָי, וְהִנָּחֵם עַל עֲבָדֶיךָ. שַׂבְּעֵנוּ
בַבֹּקֶר חַסְדֶּךָ, וּנְרַנְּנָה וְנִשְׂמְחָה בְּכָל
יָמֵינוּ. שַׂמְּחֵנוּ כִּימוֹת עִנִּיתָנוּ, שְׁנוֹת
רָאִינוּ רָעָה. יֵרָאֶה אֶל עֲבָדֶיךָ פָעֳלֶךָ,
וַהֲדָרְךָ עַל בְּנֵיהֶם. וִיהִי נֹעַם אֲדֹנָי אֱלֹהֵינוּ
עָלֵינוּ; וּמַעֲשֵׂה יָדֵינוּ כּוֹנְנָה עָלֵינוּ,
וּמַעֲשֵׂה יָדֵינוּ כּוֹנְנֵהוּ.

צא יֹשֵׁב בְּסֵתֶר עֶלְיוֹן, בְּצֵל שַׁדַּי
יִתְלוֹנָן. אֹמַר לַיהוה: מַחְסִי
וּמְצוּדָתִי, אֱלֹהַי אֶבְטַח בּוֹ. כִּי הוּא יַצִּילְךָ
מִפַּח יָקוּשׁ, מִדֶּבֶר הַוּוֹת. בְּאֶבְרָתוֹ יָסֶךְ
לָךְ, וְתַחַת כְּנָפָיו תֶּחְסֶה; צִנָּה וְסֹחֵרָה
אֲמִתּוֹ. לֹא תִירָא מִפַּחַד לָיְלָה, מֵחֵץ יָעוּף
יוֹמָם. מִדֶּבֶר בָּאֹפֶל יַהֲלֹךְ, מִקֶּטֶב יָשׁוּד
צָהֳרָיִם. יִפֹּל מִצִּדְּךָ אֶלֶף, וּרְבָבָה מִימִינֶךָ,
אֵלֶיךָ לֹא יִגָּשׁ. רַק בְּעֵינֶיךָ תַבִּיט, וְשִׁלֻּמַת
רְשָׁעִים תִּרְאֶה. כִּי אַתָּה יהוה מַחְסִי,
עֶלְיוֹן שַׂמְתָּ מְעוֹנֶךָ. לֹא תְאֻנֶּה אֵלֶיךָ
רָעָה, וְנֶגַע לֹא יִקְרַב בְּאָהֳלֶךָ. כִּי מַלְאָכָיו
יְצַוֶּה לָּךְ, לִשְׁמָרְךָ בְּכָל דְּרָכֶיךָ. עַל כַּפַּיִם
יִשָּׂאוּנְךָ, פֶּן תִּגֹּף בָּאֶבֶן רַגְלֶךָ. עַל שַׁחַל
וָפֶתֶן תִּדְרֹךְ, תִּרְמֹס כְּפִיר וְתַנִּין. כִּי בִי
חָשַׁק וַאֲפַלְּטֵהוּ, אֲשַׂגְּבֵהוּ כִּי יָדַע שְׁמִי.
יִקְרָאֵנִי וְאֶעֱנֵהוּ, עִמּוֹ אָנֹכִי בְצָרָה;
אֲחַלְּצֵהוּ וַאֲכַבְּדֵהוּ. אֹרֶךְ יָמִים
אַשְׂבִּיעֵהוּ, וְאַרְאֵהוּ בִּישׁוּעָתִי.

צב מִזְמוֹר שִׁיר לְיוֹם הַשַּׁבָּת. טוֹב
לְהֹדוֹת לַיהוה, וּלְזַמֵּר לְשִׁמְךָ
עֶלְיוֹן. לְהַגִּיד בַּבֹּקֶר חַסְדֶּךָ, וֶאֱמוּנָתְךָ
בַּלֵּילוֹת. עֲלֵי עָשׂוֹר וַעֲלֵי נָבֶל, עֲלֵי הִגָּיוֹן
בְּכִנּוֹר. כִּי שִׂמַּחְתַּנִי יהוה בְּפָעֳלֶךָ,
בְּמַעֲשֵׂי יָדֶיךָ אֲרַנֵּן. מַה גָּדְלוּ מַעֲשֶׂיךָ,

לוּלֵי יהוה עֶזְרָתָה לִּי, כִּמְעַט שָׁכְנָה דוּמָה נַפְשִׁי. אִם אָמַרְתִּי מָטָה רַגְלִי, חַסְדְּךָ יהוה יִסְעָדֵנִי. בְּרֹב שַׂרְעַפַּי בְּקִרְבִּי, תַּנְחוּמֶיךָ יְשַׁעַשְׁעוּ נַפְשִׁי. הַיְחָבְרְךָ כִּסֵּא הַוּוֹת, יֹצֵר עָמָל עֲלֵי חֹק. יָגוֹדּוּ עַל נֶפֶשׁ צַדִּיק, וְדָם נָקִי יַרְשִׁיעוּ. וַיְהִי יהוה לִי לְמִשְׂגָּב, וֵאלֹהַי לְצוּר מַחְסִי. וַיָּשֶׁב עֲלֵיהֶם אֶת אוֹנָם, וּבְרָעָתָם יַצְמִיתֵם; יַצְמִיתֵם יהוה אֱלֹהֵינוּ.

צה לְכוּ נְרַנְּנָה לַיהוה, נָרִיעָה לְצוּר יִשְׁעֵנוּ. נְקַדְּמָה פָנָיו בְּתוֹדָה, בִּזְמִרוֹת נָרִיעַ לוֹ. כִּי אֵל גָּדוֹל יהוה, וּמֶלֶךְ גָּדוֹל עַל כָּל אֱלֹהִים. אֲשֶׁר בְּיָדוֹ מֶחְקְרֵי אָרֶץ, וְתוֹעֲפוֹת הָרִים לוֹ. אֲשֶׁר לוֹ הַיָּם וְהוּא עָשָׂהוּ, וְיַבֶּשֶׁת יָדָיו יָצָרוּ. בֹּאוּ נִשְׁתַּחֲוֶה וְנִכְרָעָה, נִבְרְכָה לִפְנֵי יהוה עֹשֵׂנוּ. כִּי הוּא אֱלֹהֵינוּ, וַאֲנַחְנוּ עַם מַרְעִיתוֹ וְצֹאן יָדוֹ, הַיּוֹם אִם בְּקֹלוֹ תִשְׁמָעוּ. אַל תַּקְשׁוּ לְבַבְכֶם כִּמְרִיבָה, כְּיוֹם מַסָּה בַּמִּדְבָּר. אֲשֶׁר נִסּוּנִי אֲבוֹתֵיכֶם, בְּחָנוּנִי גַּם רָאוּ פָעֳלִי. אַרְבָּעִים שָׁנָה אָקוּט בְּדוֹר, וָאֹמַר: עַם תֹּעֵי לֵבָב הֵם, וְהֵם לֹא יָדְעוּ דְרָכָי. אֲשֶׁר נִשְׁבַּעְתִּי בְאַפִּי, אִם יְבֹאוּן אֶל מְנוּחָתִי.

צו שִׁירוּ לַיהוה שִׁיר חָדָשׁ, שִׁירוּ לַיהוה כָּל הָאָרֶץ. שִׁירוּ לַיהוה בָּרְכוּ שְׁמוֹ, בַּשְּׂרוּ מִיּוֹם לְיוֹם יְשׁוּעָתוֹ. סַפְּרוּ בַגּוֹיִם כְּבוֹדוֹ, בְּכָל הָעַמִּים נִפְלְאוֹתָיו. כִּי גָדוֹל יהוה וּמְהֻלָּל מְאֹד, נוֹרָא הוּא עַל כָּל אֱלֹהִים. כִּי כָּל אֱלֹהֵי הָעַמִּים אֱלִילִים, וַיהוה שָׁמַיִם עָשָׂה. הוֹד וְהָדָר לְפָנָיו, עֹז וְתִפְאֶרֶת בְּמִקְדָּשׁוֹ. הָבוּ לַיהוה מִשְׁפְּחוֹת עַמִּים, הָבוּ לַיהוה כָּבוֹד וָעֹז. הָבוּ לַיהוה כְּבוֹד שְׁמוֹ, שְׂאוּ מִנְחָה וּבֹאוּ לְחַצְרוֹתָיו. הִשְׁתַּחֲווּ לַיהוה בְּהַדְרַת קֹדֶשׁ, חִילוּ מִפָּנָיו כָּל הָאָרֶץ. אִמְרוּ בַגּוֹיִם יהוה מָלָךְ, אַף תִּכּוֹן תֵּבֵל בַּל תִּמּוֹט, יָדִין עַמִּים בְּמֵישָׁרִים. יִשְׂמְחוּ הַשָּׁמַיִם וְתָגֵל הָאָרֶץ, יִרְעַם הַיָּם וּמְלֹאוֹ. יַעֲלֹז שָׂדַי וְכָל אֲשֶׁר

בּוֹ, אָז יְרַנְּנוּ כָּל עֲצֵי יָעַר. לִפְנֵי יהוה כִּי בָא, כִּי בָא לִשְׁפֹּט הָאָרֶץ; יִשְׁפֹּט תֵּבֵל בְּצֶדֶק, וְעַמִּים בֶּאֱמוּנָתוֹ.

DAY 20 — יום כ' לחודש

צז יהוה מָלָךְ תָּגֵל הָאָרֶץ, יִשְׂמְחוּ אִיִּים רַבִּים. עָנָן וַעֲרָפֶל סְבִיבָיו, צֶדֶק וּמִשְׁפָּט מְכוֹן כִּסְאוֹ. אֵשׁ לְפָנָיו תֵּלֵךְ, וּתְלַהֵט סָבִיב צָרָיו. הֵאִירוּ בְרָקָיו תֵּבֵל, רָאֲתָה וַתָּחֵל הָאָרֶץ. הָרִים כַּדּוֹנַג נָמַסּוּ מִלִּפְנֵי יהוה, מִלִּפְנֵי אֲדוֹן כָּל הָאָרֶץ. הִגִּידוּ הַשָּׁמַיִם צִדְקוֹ, וְרָאוּ כָל הָעַמִּים כְּבוֹדוֹ. יֵבֹשׁוּ כָּל עֹבְדֵי פֶסֶל, הַמִּתְהַלְלִים בָּאֱלִילִים; הִשְׁתַּחֲווּ לוֹ כָּל אֱלֹהִים. שָׁמְעָה וַתִּשְׂמַח צִיּוֹן, וַתָּגֵלְנָה בְּנוֹת יְהוּדָה, לְמַעַן מִשְׁפָּטֶיךָ, יהוה. כִּי אַתָּה יהוה עֶלְיוֹן עַל כָּל הָאָרֶץ, מְאֹד נַעֲלֵיתָ עַל כָּל אֱלֹהִים. אֹהֲבֵי יהוה שִׂנְאוּ רָע; שֹׁמֵר נַפְשׁוֹת חֲסִידָיו, מִיַּד רְשָׁעִים יַצִּילֵם. אוֹר זָרֻעַ לַצַּדִּיק, וּלְיִשְׁרֵי לֵב שִׂמְחָה. שִׂמְחוּ צַדִּיקִים בַּיהוה, וְהוֹדוּ לְזֵכֶר קָדְשׁוֹ.

צח מִזְמוֹר, שִׁירוּ לַיהוה שִׁיר חָדָשׁ, כִּי נִפְלָאוֹת עָשָׂה; הוֹשִׁיעָה לּוֹ יְמִינוֹ וּזְרוֹעַ קָדְשׁוֹ. הוֹדִיעַ יהוה יְשׁוּעָתוֹ, לְעֵינֵי הַגּוֹיִם גִּלָּה צִדְקָתוֹ. זָכַר חַסְדּוֹ וֶאֱמוּנָתוֹ לְבֵית יִשְׂרָאֵל, רָאוּ כָל אַפְסֵי אָרֶץ אֵת יְשׁוּעַת אֱלֹהֵינוּ. הָרִיעוּ לַיהוה כָּל הָאָרֶץ, פִּצְחוּ וְרַנְּנוּ וְזַמֵּרוּ. זַמְּרוּ לַיהוה בְּכִנּוֹר, בְּכִנּוֹר וְקוֹל זִמְרָה. בַּחֲצֹצְרוֹת וְקוֹל שׁוֹפָר, הָרִיעוּ לִפְנֵי הַמֶּלֶךְ יהוה. יִרְעַם הַיָּם וּמְלֹאוֹ, תֵּבֵל וְיֹשְׁבֵי בָהּ. נְהָרוֹת יִמְחֲאוּ כָף, יַחַד הָרִים יְרַנֵּנוּ. לִפְנֵי יהוה כִּי בָא לִשְׁפֹּט הָאָרֶץ; יִשְׁפֹּט תֵּבֵל בְּצֶדֶק, וְעַמִּים בְּמֵישָׁרִים.

צט יהוה מָלָךְ יִרְגְּזוּ עַמִּים, יֹשֵׁב כְּרוּבִים תָּנוּט הָאָרֶץ. יהוה בְּצִיּוֹן גָּדוֹל, וְרָם הוּא עַל כָּל הָעַמִּים. יוֹדוּ שִׁמְךָ גָּדוֹל וְנוֹרָא, קָדוֹשׁ הוּא. וְעֹז מֶלֶךְ מִשְׁפָּט

וַיִּבַשׁ לִבִּי, כִּי שָׁכַחְתִּי מֵאֲכֹל לַחְמִי. מִקּוֹל אַנְחָתִי, דָּבְקָה עַצְמִי לִבְשָׂרִי. דָּמִיתִי לִקְאַת מִדְבָּר, הָיִיתִי כְּכוֹס חֳרָבוֹת. שָׁקַדְתִּי וָאֶהְיֶה כְּצִפּוֹר בּוֹדֵד עַל גָּג. כָּל הַיּוֹם חֵרְפוּנִי אוֹיְבָי, מְהוֹלָלַי בִּי נִשְׁבָּעוּ. כִּי אֵפֶר כַּלֶּחֶם אָכָלְתִּי, וְשִׁקֻּוַי בִּבְכִי מָסָכְתִּי. מִפְּנֵי זַעַמְךָ וְקִצְפֶּךָ, כִּי נְשָׂאתַנִי וַתַּשְׁלִיכֵנִי. יָמַי כְּצֵל נָטוּי, וַאֲנִי כָּעֵשֶׂב אִיבָשׁ. וְאַתָּה יהוה לְעוֹלָם תֵּשֵׁב, וְזִכְרְךָ לְדֹר וָדֹר. אַתָּה תָקוּם תְּרַחֵם צִיּוֹן, כִּי עֵת לְחֶנְנָהּ כִּי בָא מוֹעֵד. כִּי רָצוּ עֲבָדֶיךָ אֶת אֲבָנֶיהָ, וְאֶת עֲפָרָהּ יְחֹנֵנוּ. וְיִירְאוּ גוֹיִם אֶת שֵׁם יהוה, וְכָל מַלְכֵי הָאָרֶץ אֶת כְּבוֹדֶךָ. כִּי בָנָה יהוה צִיּוֹן, נִרְאָה בִּכְבוֹדוֹ. פָּנָה אֶל תְּפִלַּת הָעַרְעָר, וְלֹא בָזָה אֶת תְּפִלָּתָם. תִּכָּתֶב זֹאת לְדוֹר אַחֲרוֹן, וְעַם נִבְרָא יְהַלֶּל יָהּ. כִּי הִשְׁקִיף מִמְּרוֹם קָדְשׁוֹ, יהוה מִשָּׁמַיִם אֶל אֶרֶץ הִבִּיט. לִשְׁמֹעַ אֶנְקַת אָסִיר, לְפַתֵּחַ בְּנֵי תְמוּתָה. לְסַפֵּר בְּצִיּוֹן שֵׁם יהוה, וּתְהִלָּתוֹ בִּירוּשָׁלָֽםִ. בְּהִקָּבֵץ עַמִּים יַחְדָּו, וּמַמְלָכוֹת לַעֲבֹד אֶת יהוה. עִנָּה בַדֶּרֶךְ כֹּחִי, קִצַּר יָמָי. אֹמַר: אֵלִי, אַל תַּעֲלֵנִי בַּחֲצִי יָמָי, בְּדוֹר דּוֹרִים שְׁנוֹתֶֽיךָ. לְפָנִים הָאָרֶץ יָסַדְתָּ, וּמַעֲשֵׂה יָדֶיךָ שָׁמָיִם. הֵמָּה יֹאבֵדוּ, וְאַתָּה תַעֲמֹד; וְכֻלָּם כַּבֶּגֶד יִבְלוּ, כַּלְּבוּשׁ תַּחֲלִיפֵם וְיַחֲלֹֽפוּ. וְאַתָּה הוּא, וּשְׁנוֹתֶיךָ לֹא יִתָּמּוּ. בְּנֵי עֲבָדֶיךָ יִשְׁכּוֹנוּ, וְזַרְעָם לְפָנֶיךָ יִכּוֹן.

קג לְדָוִד, בָּרְכִי נַפְשִׁי אֶת יהוה, וְכָל קְרָבַי אֶת שֵׁם קָדְשׁוֹ. בָּרְכִי נַפְשִׁי אֶת יהוה, וְאַל תִּשְׁכְּחִי כָּל גְּמוּלָיו. הַסֹּלֵחַ לְכָל עֲוֺנֵכִי, הָרֹפֵא לְכָל תַּחֲלֻאָיְכִי. הַגּוֹאֵל מִשַּׁחַת חַיָּיְכִי, הַמְעַטְּרֵכִי חֶסֶד וְרַחֲמִים. הַמַּשְׂבִּיעַ בַּטּוֹב עֶדְיֵךְ, תִּתְחַדֵּשׁ כַּנֶּשֶׁר נְעוּרָיְכִי. עֹשֵׂה צְדָקוֹת יהוה, וּמִשְׁפָּטִים לְכָל עֲשׁוּקִים. יוֹדִיעַ דְּרָכָיו לְמֹשֶׁה, לִבְנֵי יִשְׂרָאֵל עֲלִילוֹתָיו. רַחוּם וְחַנּוּן יהוה, אֶרֶךְ אַפַּיִם וְרַב חָסֶד. לֹא לָנֶצַח יָרִיב, וְלֹא לְעוֹלָם יִטּוֹר. לֹא

אָהֵב; אַתָּה כּוֹנַנְתָּ מֵישָׁרִים, מִשְׁפָּט וּצְדָקָה בְּיַעֲקֹב אַתָּה עָשִׂיתָ. רוֹמְמוּ יהוה אֱלֹהֵינוּ, וְהִשְׁתַּחֲווּ לַהֲדֹם רַגְלָיו, קָדוֹשׁ הוּא. מֹשֶׁה וְאַהֲרֹן בְּכֹהֲנָיו, וּשְׁמוּאֵל בְּקֹרְאֵי שְׁמוֹ, קֹרִאים אֶל יהוה וְהוּא יַעֲנֵם. בְּעַמּוּד עָנָן יְדַבֵּר אֲלֵיהֶם, שָׁמְרוּ עֵדֹתָיו וְחֹק נָתַן לָמוֹ. יהוה אֱלֹהֵינוּ , אַתָּה עֲנִיתָם; אֵל נֹשֵׂא הָיִיתָ לָהֶם, וְנֹקֵם עַל עֲלִילוֹתָם. רוֹמְמוּ יהוה אֱלֹהֵינוּ, וְהִשְׁתַּחֲווּ לְהַר קָדְשׁוֹ; כִּי קָדוֹשׁ יהוה אֱלֹהֵינוּ.

ק מִזְמוֹר לְתוֹדָה; הָרִיעוּ לַיהוה כָּל הָאָרֶץ. עִבְדוּ אֶת יהוה בְּשִׂמְחָה, בֹּאוּ לְפָנָיו בִּרְנָנָה. דְּעוּ כִּי יהוה הוּא אֱלֹהִים; הוּא עָשָׂנוּ, וְלוֹ אֲנַחְנוּ, עַמּוֹ וְצֹאן מַרְעִיתוֹ. בֹּאוּ שְׁעָרָיו בְּתוֹדָה, חֲצֵרֹתָיו בִּתְהִלָּה; הוֹדוּ לוֹ, בָּרְכוּ שְׁמוֹ. כִּי טוֹב יהוה, לְעוֹלָם חַסְדּוֹ, וְעַד דֹּר וָדֹר אֱמוּנָתוֹ.

קא לְדָוִד מִזְמוֹר; חֶסֶד וּמִשְׁפָּט אָשִׁירָה, לְךָ יהוה אֲזַמֵּרָה. אַשְׂכִּֽילָה בְּדֶרֶךְ תָּמִים, מָתַי תָּבוֹא אֵלָי; אֶתְהַלֵּךְ בְּתָם לְבָבִי בְּקֶרֶב בֵּיתִי. לֹא אָשִׁית לְנֶגֶד עֵינַי דְּבַר בְּלִיָּעַל; עֲשֹׂה סֵטִים שָׂנֵאתִי, לֹא יִדְבַּק בִּי. לֵבָב עִקֵּשׁ יָסוּר מִמֶּֽנִּי, רָע לֹא אֵדָע. מְלָשְׁנִי בַסֵּתֶר רֵעֵהוּ, אוֹתוֹ אַצְמִית; גְּבַהּ עֵינַיִם וּרְחַב לֵבָב, אֹתוֹ לֹא אוּכָל. עֵינַי בְּנֶאֶמְנֵי אֶרֶץ לָשֶׁבֶת עִמָּדִי; הֹלֵךְ בְּדֶרֶךְ תָּמִים, הוּא יְשָׁרְתֵֽנִי. לֹא יֵשֵׁב בְּקֶרֶב בֵּיתִי עֹשֵׂה רְמִיָּה; דֹּבֵר שְׁקָרִים, לֹא יִכּוֹן לְנֶגֶד עֵינָי. לַבְּקָרִים אַצְמִית כָּל רִשְׁעֵי אָרֶץ, לְהַכְרִית מֵעִיר יהוה כָּל פֹּעֲלֵי אָוֶן.

קב תְּפִלָּה לְעָנִי כִי יַעֲטֹף, וְלִפְנֵי יהוה יִשְׁפֹּךְ שִׂיחוֹ. יהוה שִׁמְעָה תְפִלָּתִי, וְשַׁוְעָתִי אֵלֶיךָ תָבוֹא. אַל תַּסְתֵּר פָּנֶיךָ מִמֶּנִּי בְּיוֹם צַר לִי; הַטֵּה אֵלַי אָזְנֶךָ, בְּיוֹם אֶקְרָא, מַהֵר עֲנֵנִי. כִּי כָלוּ בְעָשָׁן יָמָי, וְעַצְמוֹתַי כְּמוֹקֵד נִחָרוּ. הוּכָּה כָעֵשֶׂב

כְּחֲטָאֵינוּ עָשָׂה לָּנוּ, וְלֹא כַעֲוֹנֹתֵינוּ גָּמַל עָלֵינוּ. כִּי כִגְבֹהַּ שָׁמַיִם עַל הָאָרֶץ, גָּבַר חַסְדּוֹ עַל יְרֵאָיו. כִּרְחֹק מִזְרָח מִמַּעֲרָב, הִרְחִיק מִמֶּנּוּ אֶת פְּשָׁעֵינוּ. כְּרַחֵם אָב עַל בָּנִים, רִחַם יהוה עַל יְרֵאָיו. כִּי הוּא יָדַע יִצְרֵנוּ, זָכוּר כִּי עָפָר אֲנָחְנוּ. אֱנוֹשׁ כֶּחָצִיר יָמָיו, כְּצִיץ הַשָּׂדֶה כֵּן יָצִיץ. כִּי רוּחַ עָבְרָה בּוֹ וְאֵינֶנּוּ, וְלֹא יַכִּירֶנּוּ עוֹד מְקוֹמוֹ. וְחֶסֶד יהוה מֵעוֹלָם וְעַד עוֹלָם עַל יְרֵאָיו, וְצִדְקָתוֹ לִבְנֵי בָנִים. לְשֹׁמְרֵי בְרִיתוֹ, וּלְזֹכְרֵי פִקֻּדָיו לַעֲשׂוֹתָם. יהוה בַּשָּׁמַיִם הֵכִין כִּסְאוֹ, וּמַלְכוּתוֹ בַּכֹּל מָשָׁלָה. בָּרְכוּ יהוה, מַלְאָכָיו; גִּבֹּרֵי כֹחַ עֹשֵׂי דְבָרוֹ, לִשְׁמֹעַ בְּקוֹל דְּבָרוֹ. בָּרְכוּ יהוה, כָּל צְבָאָיו, מְשָׁרְתָיו עֹשֵׂי רְצוֹנוֹ. בָּרְכוּ יהוה, כָּל מַעֲשָׂיו, בְּכָל מְקֹמוֹת מֶמְשַׁלְתּוֹ; בָּרְכִי נַפְשִׁי אֶת יהוה.

יום כ"א לחודש — DAY 21

קד בָּרְכִי נַפְשִׁי אֶת יהוה; יהוה אֱלֹהַי, גָּדַלְתָּ מְּאֹד, הוֹד וְהָדָר לָבָשְׁתָּ. עֹטֶה אוֹר כַּשַּׂלְמָה, נוֹטֶה שָׁמַיִם כַּיְרִיעָה. הַמְקָרֶה בַמַּיִם עֲלִיּוֹתָיו; הַשָּׂם עָבִים רְכוּבוֹ, הַמְהַלֵּךְ עַל כַּנְפֵי רוּחַ. עֹשֶׂה מַלְאָכָיו רוּחוֹת, מְשָׁרְתָיו אֵשׁ לֹהֵט. יָסַד אֶרֶץ עַל מְכוֹנֶיהָ, בַּל תִּמּוֹט עוֹלָם וָעֶד. תְּהוֹם כַּלְּבוּשׁ כִּסִּיתוֹ, עַל הָרִים יַעַמְדוּ מָיִם. מִן גַּעֲרָתְךָ יְנוּסוּן, מִן קוֹל רַעַמְךָ יֵחָפֵזוּן. יַעֲלוּ הָרִים, יֵרְדוּ בְקָעוֹת, אֶל מְקוֹם זֶה יָסַדְתָּ לָהֶם. גְּבוּל שַׂמְתָּ בַּל יַעֲבֹרוּן, בַּל יְשֻׁבוּן לְכַסּוֹת הָאָרֶץ. הַמְשַׁלֵּחַ מַעְיָנִים בַּנְּחָלִים, בֵּין הָרִים יְהַלֵּכוּן. יַשְׁקוּ כָּל חַיְתוֹ שָׂדָי, יִשְׁבְּרוּ פְרָאִים צְמָאָם. עֲלֵיהֶם עוֹף הַשָּׁמַיִם יִשְׁכּוֹן, מִבֵּין עֳפָאיִם יִתְּנוּ קוֹל. מַשְׁקֶה הָרִים מֵעֲלִיּוֹתָיו, מִפְּרִי מַעֲשֶׂיךָ תִּשְׂבַּע הָאָרֶץ. מַצְמִיחַ חָצִיר לַבְּהֵמָה, וְעֵשֶׂב לַעֲבֹדַת הָאָדָם; לְהוֹצִיא לֶחֶם מִן הָאָרֶץ. וְיַיִן יְשַׂמַּח לְבַב אֱנוֹשׁ, לְהַצְהִיל פָּנִים מִשָּׁמֶן, וְלֶחֶם לְבַב אֱנוֹשׁ יִסְעָד. יִשְׂבְּעוּ

עֲצֵי יהוה, אַרְזֵי לְבָנוֹן אֲשֶׁר נָטָע. אֲשֶׁר שָׁם צִפֳּרִים יְקַנֵּנוּ, חֲסִידָה בְּרוֹשִׁים בֵּיתָהּ. הָרִים הַגְּבֹהִים לַיְּעֵלִים, סְלָעִים מַחְסֶה לַשְׁפַנִּים. עָשָׂה יָרֵחַ לְמוֹעֲדִים, שֶׁמֶשׁ יָדַע מְבוֹאוֹ. תָּשֶׁת חֹשֶׁךְ וִיהִי לָיְלָה, בּוֹ תִרְמֹשׂ כָּל חַיְתוֹ יָעַר. הַכְּפִירִים שֹׁאֲגִים לַטָּרֶף, וּלְבַקֵּשׁ מֵאֵל אָכְלָם. תִּזְרַח הַשֶּׁמֶשׁ יֵאָסֵפוּן, וְאֶל מְעוֹנֹתָם יִרְבָּצוּן. יֵצֵא אָדָם לְפָעֳלוֹ, וְלַעֲבֹדָתוֹ עֲדֵי עָרֶב. מָה רַבּוּ מַעֲשֶׂיךָ | יהוה, כֻּלָּם בְּחָכְמָה עָשִׂיתָ, מָלְאָה הָאָרֶץ קִנְיָנֶךָ. זֶה הַיָּם, גָּדוֹל וּרְחַב יָדָיִם; שָׁם רֶמֶשׂ וְאֵין מִסְפָּר, חַיּוֹת קְטַנּוֹת עִם גְּדֹלוֹת. שָׁם אֳנִיּוֹת יְהַלֵּכוּן, לִוְיָתָן זֶה יָצַרְתָּ לְשַׂחֶק בּוֹ. כֻּלָּם אֵלֶיךָ יְשַׂבֵּרוּן, לָתֵת אָכְלָם בְּעִתּוֹ. תִּתֵּן לָהֶם, יִלְקֹטוּן; תִּפְתַּח יָדְךָ, יִשְׂבְּעוּן טוֹב. תַּסְתִּיר פָּנֶיךָ, יִבָּהֵלוּן; תֹּסֵף רוּחָם, יִגְוָעוּן, וְאֶל עֲפָרָם יְשׁוּבוּן. תְּשַׁלַּח רוּחֲךָ יִבָּרֵאוּן, וּתְחַדֵּשׁ פְּנֵי אֲדָמָה. יְהִי כְבוֹד יהוה לְעוֹלָם, יִשְׂמַח יהוה בְּמַעֲשָׂיו. הַמַּבִּיט לָאָרֶץ וַתִּרְעָד, יִגַּע בֶּהָרִים וְיֶעֱשָׁנוּ. אָשִׁירָה לַיהוה בְּחַיָּי, אֲזַמְּרָה לֵאלֹהַי בְּעוֹדִי. יֶעֱרַב עָלָיו שִׂיחִי, אָנֹכִי אֶשְׂמַח בַּיהוה. יִתַּמּוּ חַטָּאִים מִן הָאָרֶץ, וּרְשָׁעִים עוֹד אֵינָם, בָּרְכִי נַפְשִׁי אֶת יהוה; הַלְלוּיָהּ.

קה הוֹדוּ לַיהוה קִרְאוּ בִשְׁמוֹ, הוֹדִיעוּ בָעַמִּים עֲלִילוֹתָיו. שִׁירוּ לוֹ זַמְּרוּ לוֹ, שִׂיחוּ בְּכָל נִפְלְאוֹתָיו. הִתְהַלְלוּ בְּשֵׁם קָדְשׁוֹ, יִשְׂמַח לֵב מְבַקְשֵׁי יהוה. דִּרְשׁוּ יהוה וְעֻזּוֹ, בַּקְּשׁוּ פָנָיו תָּמִיד. זִכְרוּ נִפְלְאוֹתָיו אֲשֶׁר עָשָׂה, מֹפְתָיו וּמִשְׁפְּטֵי פִיו. זֶרַע אַבְרָהָם עַבְדּוֹ, בְּנֵי יַעֲקֹב בְּחִירָיו. הוּא יהוה אֱלֹהֵינוּ, בְּכָל הָאָרֶץ מִשְׁפָּטָיו. זָכַר לְעוֹלָם בְּרִיתוֹ, דָּבָר צִוָּה לְאֶלֶף דּוֹר. אֲשֶׁר כָּרַת אֶת אַבְרָהָם, וּשְׁבוּעָתוֹ לְיִשְׂחָק. וַיַּעֲמִידֶהָ לְיַעֲקֹב לְחֹק, לְיִשְׂרָאֵל בְּרִית עוֹלָם. לֵאמֹר: לְךָ אֶתֵּן אֶת אֶרֶץ כְּנָעַן, חֶבֶל נַחֲלַתְכֶם. בִּהְיוֹתָם מְתֵי מִסְפָּר, כִּמְעַט וְגָרִים בָּהּ. וַיִּתְהַלְּכוּ

מִגּוֹיֵ אֶל גּוֹי, מִמַּמְלָכָה אֶל עַם אַחֵר. לֹא
הִנִּיחַ אָדָם לְעָשְׁקָם, וַיּוֹכַח עֲלֵיהֶם
מְלָכִים. אַל תִּגְּעוּ בִמְשִׁיחָי, וְלִנְבִיאַי אַל
תָּרֵעוּ. וַיִּקְרָא רָעָב עַל הָאָרֶץ, כָּל מַטֵּה
לֶחֶם שָׁבָר. שָׁלַח לִפְנֵיהֶם אִישׁ, לְעֶבֶד
נִמְכַּר יוֹסֵף. עִנּוּ בַכֶּבֶל רַגְלוֹ, בַּרְזֶל בָּאָה
נַפְשׁוֹ. עַד עֵת בֹּא דְבָרוֹ, אִמְרַת יהוה
צְרָפָתְהוּ. שָׁלַח מֶלֶךְ וַיַּתִּירֵהוּ, מֹשֵׁל
עַמִּים וַיְפַתְּחֵהוּ. שָׂמוֹ אָדוֹן לְבֵיתוֹ, וּמֹשֵׁל
בְּכָל קִנְיָנוֹ. לֶאְסֹר שָׂרָיו בְּנַפְשׁוֹ, וּזְקֵנָיו
יְחַכֵּם. וַיָּבֹא יִשְׂרָאֵל מִצְרָיִם, וְיַעֲקֹב גָּר
בְּאֶרֶץ חָם. וַיֶּפֶר אֶת עַמּוֹ מְאֹד, וַיַּעֲצִמֵהוּ
מִצָּרָיו. הָפַךְ לִבָּם לִשְׂנֹא עַמּוֹ, לְהִתְנַכֵּל
בַּעֲבָדָיו. שָׁלַח מֹשֶׁה עַבְדּוֹ, אַהֲרֹן אֲשֶׁר
בָּחַר בּוֹ. שָׂמוּ בָם דִּבְרֵי אֹתוֹתָיו, וּמֹפְתִים
בְּאֶרֶץ חָם. שָׁלַח חֹשֶׁךְ וַיַּחְשִׁךְ, וְלֹא מָרוּ
אֶת דְּבָרוֹ. הָפַךְ אֶת מֵימֵיהֶם לְדָם, וַיָּמֶת
אֶת דְּגָתָם. שָׁרַץ אַרְצָם צְפַרְדְּעִים,
בְּחַדְרֵי מַלְכֵיהֶם. אָמַר וַיָּבֹא עָרֹב, כִּנִּים
בְּכָל גְּבוּלָם. נָתַן גִּשְׁמֵיהֶם בָּרָד, אֵשׁ
לֶהָבוֹת בְּאַרְצָם. וַיַּךְ גַּפְנָם וּתְאֵנָתָם,
וַיְשַׁבֵּר עֵץ גְּבוּלָם. אָמַר וַיָּבֹא אַרְבֶּה,
וְיֶלֶק וְאֵין מִסְפָּר. וַיֹּאכַל כָּל עֵשֶׂב
בְּאַרְצָם, וַיֹּאכַל פְּרִי אַדְמָתָם. וַיַּךְ כָּל
בְּכוֹר בְּאַרְצָם, רֵאשִׁית לְכָל אוֹנָם.
וַיּוֹצִיאֵם בְּכֶסֶף וְזָהָב, וְאֵין בִּשְׁבָטָיו כּוֹשֵׁל.
שָׂמַח מִצְרַיִם בְּצֵאתָם, כִּי נָפַל פַּחְדָּם
עֲלֵיהֶם. פָּרַשׂ עָנָן לְמָסָךְ, וְאֵשׁ לְהָאִיר
לָיְלָה. שָׁאַל וַיָּבֵא שְׂלָו, וְלֶחֶם שָׁמַיִם
יַשְׂבִּיעֵם. פָּתַח צוּר וַיָּזוּבוּ מָיִם, הָלְכוּ
בַּצִּיּוֹת נָהָר. כִּי זָכַר אֶת דְּבַר קָדְשׁוֹ, אֶת
אַבְרָהָם עַבְדּוֹ. וַיּוֹצִא עַמּוֹ בְשָׂשׂוֹן, בְּרִנָּה
אֶת בְּחִירָיו. וַיִּתֵּן לָהֶם אַרְצוֹת גּוֹיִם,
וַעֲמַל לְאֻמִּים יִירָשׁוּ. בַּעֲבוּר יִשְׁמְרוּ
חֻקָּיו, וְתוֹרֹתָיו יִנְצֹרוּ; הַלְלוּיָהּ.

יוֹם כ"ב לַחֹדֶשׁ — DAY 22

קו הַלְלוּיָהּ, הוֹדוּ לַיהוה כִּי טוֹב, כִּי
לְעוֹלָם חַסְדּוֹ. מִי יְמַלֵּל גְּבוּרוֹת
יהוה, יַשְׁמִיעַ כָּל תְּהִלָּתוֹ. אַשְׁרֵי שֹׁמְרֵי

מִשְׁפָּט, עֹשֵׂה צְדָקָה בְכָל עֵת. זָכְרֵנִי יהוה
בִּרְצוֹן עַמֶּךָ, פָּקְדֵנִי בִּישׁוּעָתֶךָ. לִרְאוֹת
בְּטוֹבַת בְּחִירֶיךָ, לִשְׂמֹחַ בְּשִׂמְחַת גּוֹיֶךָ;
לְהִתְהַלֵּל עִם נַחֲלָתֶךָ. חָטָאנוּ עִם אֲבוֹתֵינוּ,
הֶעֱוִינוּ הִרְשָׁעְנוּ. אֲבוֹתֵינוּ בְמִצְרַיִם לֹא
הִשְׂכִּילוּ נִפְלְאוֹתֶיךָ, לֹא זָכְרוּ אֶת רֹב
חֲסָדֶיךָ, וַיַּמְרוּ עַל יָם בְּיַם סוּף. וַיּוֹשִׁיעֵם
לְמַעַן שְׁמוֹ, לְהוֹדִיעַ אֶת גְּבוּרָתוֹ. וַיִּגְעַר
בְּיַם סוּף וַיֶּחֱרָב, וַיּוֹלִיכֵם בַּתְּהֹמוֹת
כַּמִּדְבָּר. וַיּוֹשִׁיעֵם מִיַּד שׂוֹנֵא, וַיִּגְאָלֵם
מִיַּד אוֹיֵב. וַיְכַסּוּ מַיִם צָרֵיהֶם, אֶחָד מֵהֶם
לֹא נוֹתָר. וַיַּאֲמִינוּ בִדְבָרָיו, יָשִׁירוּ
תְּהִלָּתוֹ. מִהֲרוּ שָׁכְחוּ מַעֲשָׂיו, לֹא חִכּוּ
לַעֲצָתוֹ. וַיִּתְאַוּוּ תַאֲוָה בַּמִּדְבָּר, וַיְנַסּוּ אֵל
בִּישִׁימוֹן. וַיִּתֵּן לָהֶם שֶׁאֱלָתָם, וַיְשַׁלַּח רָזוֹן
בְּנַפְשָׁם. וַיְקַנְאוּ לְמֹשֶׁה בַּמַּחֲנֶה, לְאַהֲרֹן
קְדוֹשׁ יהוה. תִּפְתַּח אֶרֶץ וַתִּבְלַע דָּתָן,
וַתְּכַס עַל עֲדַת אֲבִירָם. וַתִּבְעַר אֵשׁ
בַּעֲדָתָם, לֶהָבָה תְּלַהֵט רְשָׁעִים. יַעֲשׂוּ
עֵגֶל בְּחֹרֵב, וַיִּשְׁתַּחֲווּ לְמַסֵּכָה. וַיָּמִירוּ אֶת
כְּבוֹדָם, בְּתַבְנִית שׁוֹר אֹכֵל עֵשֶׂב. שָׁכְחוּ
אֵל מוֹשִׁיעָם, עֹשֶׂה גְדֹלוֹת בְּמִצְרָיִם.
נִפְלָאוֹת בְּאֶרֶץ חָם, נוֹרָאוֹת עַל יַם סוּף.
וַיֹּאמֶר לְהַשְׁמִידָם; לוּלֵי מֹשֶׁה בְחִירוֹ
עָמַד בַּפֶּרֶץ לְפָנָיו, לְהָשִׁיב חֲמָתוֹ
מֵהַשְׁחִית. וַיִּמְאֲסוּ בְּאֶרֶץ חֶמְדָּה, לֹא
הֶאֱמִינוּ לִדְבָרוֹ. וַיֵּרָגְנוּ בְאָהֳלֵיהֶם, לֹא
שָׁמְעוּ בְּקוֹל יהוה. וַיִּשָּׂא יָדוֹ לָהֶם, לְהַפִּיל
אוֹתָם בַּמִּדְבָּר. וּלְהַפִּיל זַרְעָם בַּגּוֹיִם,
וּלְזָרוֹתָם בָּאֲרָצוֹת. וַיִּצָּמְדוּ לְבַעַל פְּעוֹר,
וַיֹּאכְלוּ זִבְחֵי מֵתִים. וַיַּכְעִיסוּ
בְּמַעַלְלֵיהֶם, וַתִּפְרָץ בָּם מַגֵּפָה. וַיַּעֲמֹד
פִּינְחָס וַיְפַלֵּל, וַתֵּעָצַר הַמַּגֵּפָה. וַתֵּחָשֶׁב
לוֹ לִצְדָקָה, לְדֹר וָדֹר עַד עוֹלָם. וַיַּקְצִיפוּ
עַל מֵי מְרִיבָה, וַיֵּרַע לְמֹשֶׁה בַּעֲבוּרָם. כִּי
הִמְרוּ אֶת רוּחוֹ, וַיְבַטֵּא בִּשְׂפָתָיו. לֹא
הִשְׁמִידוּ אֶת הָעַמִּים, אֲשֶׁר אָמַר יהוה
לָהֶם. וַיִּתְעָרְבוּ בַגּוֹיִם, וַיִּלְמְדוּ מַעֲשֵׂיהֶם.
וַיַּעַבְדוּ אֶת עֲצַבֵּיהֶם, וַיִּהְיוּ לָהֶם לְמוֹקֵשׁ.

וַיִּזְבְּחוּ אֶת בְּנֵיהֶם וְאֶת בְּנוֹתֵיהֶם לַשֵּׁדִים. וַיִּשְׁפְּכוּ דָם נָקִי, דַּם בְּנֵיהֶם וּבְנוֹתֵיהֶם, אֲשֶׁר זִבְּחוּ לַעֲצַבֵּי כְנָעַן; וַתֶּחֱנַף הָאָרֶץ בַּדָּמִים. וַיִּטְמְאוּ בְמַעֲשֵׂיהֶם, וַיִּזְנוּ בְּמַעַלְלֵיהֶם. וַיִּחַר אַף יהוה בְּעַמּוֹ, וַיְתָעֵב אֶת נַחֲלָתוֹ. וַיִּתְּנֵם בְּיַד גּוֹיִם, וַיִּמְשְׁלוּ בָהֶם שֹׂנְאֵיהֶם. וַיִּלְחָצוּם אוֹיְבֵיהֶם, וַיִּכָּנְעוּ תַּחַת יָדָם. פְּעָמִים רַבּוֹת יַצִּילֵם; וְהֵמָּה יַמְרוּ בַעֲצָתָם, וַיָּמֹכּוּ בַּעֲוֺנָם. וַיַּרְא בַּצַּר לָהֶם, בְּשָׁמְעוֹ אֶת רִנָּתָם. וַיִּזְכֹּר לָהֶם בְּרִיתוֹ, וַיִּנָּחֵם כְּרֹב חֲסָדָיו. וַיִּתֵּן אוֹתָם לְרַחֲמִים, לִפְנֵי כָּל שׁוֹבֵיהֶם. הוֹשִׁיעֵנוּ יהוה אֱלֹהֵינוּ, וְקַבְּצֵנוּ מִן הַגּוֹיִם; לְהֹדוֹת לְשֵׁם קָדְשֶׁךָ, לְהִשְׁתַּבֵּחַ בִּתְהִלָּתֶךָ. בָּרוּךְ יהוה אֱלֹהֵי יִשְׂרָאֵל מִן הָעוֹלָם וְעַד הָעוֹלָם, וְאָמַר כָּל הָעָם אָמֵן; הַלְלוּיָהּ.

ספר חמישי / BOOK FIVE

FRIDAY / יום ששי

קז הֹדוּ לַיהוה כִּי טוֹב, כִּי לְעוֹלָם חַסְדּוֹ. יֹאמְרוּ גְּאוּלֵי יהוה, אֲשֶׁר גְּאָלָם מִיַּד צָר. וּמֵאֲרָצוֹת קִבְּצָם; מִמִּזְרָח וּמִמַּעֲרָב, מִצָּפוֹן וּמִיָּם. תָּעוּ בַמִּדְבָּר בִּישִׁימוֹן דָּרֶךְ, עִיר מוֹשָׁב לֹא מָצָאוּ. רְעֵבִים גַּם צְמֵאִים, נַפְשָׁם בָּהֶם תִּתְעַטָּף. וַיִּצְעֲקוּ אֶל יהוה בַּצַּר לָהֶם, מִמְּצוּקוֹתֵיהֶם יַצִּילֵם. וַיַּדְרִיכֵם בְּדֶרֶךְ יְשָׁרָה, לָלֶכֶת אֶל עִיר מוֹשָׁב. יוֹדוּ לַיהוה חַסְדּוֹ, וְנִפְלְאוֹתָיו לִבְנֵי אָדָם. כִּי הִשְׂבִּיעַ נֶפֶשׁ שֹׁקֵקָה, וְנֶפֶשׁ רְעֵבָה מִלֵּא טוֹב. יֹשְׁבֵי חֹשֶׁךְ וְצַלְמָוֶת, אֲסִירֵי עֳנִי וּבַרְזֶל. כִּי הִמְרוּ אִמְרֵי אֵל, וַעֲצַת עֶלְיוֹן נָאָצוּ. וַיַּכְנַע בֶּעָמָל לִבָּם, כָּשְׁלוּ וְאֵין עֹזֵר. וַיִּזְעֲקוּ אֶל יהוה בַּצַּר לָהֶם, מִמְּצֻקוֹתֵיהֶם יוֹשִׁיעֵם. יוֹצִיאֵם מֵחֹשֶׁךְ וְצַלְמָוֶת, וּמוֹסְרוֹתֵיהֶם יְנַתֵּק. יוֹדוּ לַיהוה חַסְדּוֹ, וְנִפְלְאוֹתָיו לִבְנֵי אָדָם. כִּי שִׁבַּר דַּלְתוֹת נְחֹשֶׁת, וּבְרִיחֵי בַרְזֶל גִּדֵּעַ. אֱוִלִים מִדֶּרֶךְ פִּשְׁעָם, וּמֵעֲוֺנֹתֵיהֶם יִתְעַנּוּ. כָּל אֹכֶל תְּתַעֵב נַפְשָׁם, וַיַּגִּיעוּ עַד שַׁעֲרֵי מָוֶת. וַיִּזְעֲקוּ אֶל יהוה בַּצַּר לָהֶם, מִמְּצֻקוֹתֵיהֶם יוֹשִׁיעֵם. יִשְׁלַח דְּבָרוֹ וְיִרְפָּאֵם, וִימַלֵּט מִשְּׁחִיתוֹתָם. יוֹדוּ לַיהוה חַסְדּוֹ, וְנִפְלְאוֹתָיו לִבְנֵי אָדָם. וְיִזְבְּחוּ זִבְחֵי תוֹדָה, וִיסַפְּרוּ מַעֲשָׂיו בְּרִנָּה. יוֹרְדֵי הַיָּם בָּאֳנִיּוֹת, עֹשֵׂי מְלָאכָה בְּמַיִם רַבִּים. הֵמָּה רָאוּ מַעֲשֵׂי יהוה, וְנִפְלְאוֹתָיו בִּמְצוּלָה. וַיֹּאמֶר וַיַּעֲמֵד רוּחַ סְעָרָה, וַתְּרוֹמֵם גַּלָּיו. יַעֲלוּ שָׁמַיִם יֵרְדוּ תְהוֹמוֹת, נַפְשָׁם בְּרָעָה תִתְמוֹגָג. יָחוֹגּוּ וְיָנוּעוּ כַּשִּׁכּוֹר, וְכָל חָכְמָתָם תִּתְבַּלָּע. וַיִּצְעֲקוּ אֶל יהוה בַּצַּר לָהֶם, וּמִמְּצוּקֹתֵיהֶם יוֹצִיאֵם. יָקֵם סְעָרָה לִדְמָמָה, וַיֶּחֱשׁוּ גַּלֵּיהֶם. וַיִּשְׂמְחוּ כִי יִשְׁתֹּקוּ, וַיַּנְחֵם אֶל מְחוֹז חֶפְצָם. יוֹדוּ לַיהוה חַסְדּוֹ, וְנִפְלְאוֹתָיו לִבְנֵי אָדָם. וִירֹמְמוּהוּ בִּקְהַל עָם, וּבְמוֹשַׁב זְקֵנִים יְהַלְלוּהוּ. יָשֵׂם נְהָרוֹת לְמִדְבָּר, וּמֹצָאֵי מַיִם לְצִמָּאוֹן. אֶרֶץ פְּרִי לִמְלֵחָה, מֵרָעַת יֹשְׁבֵי בָהּ. יָשֵׂם מִדְבָּר לַאֲגַם מַיִם, וְאֶרֶץ צִיָּה לְמֹצָאֵי מָיִם. וַיּוֹשֶׁב שָׁם רְעֵבִים, וַיְכוֹנְנוּ עִיר מוֹשָׁב. וַיִּזְרְעוּ שָׂדוֹת, וַיִּטְּעוּ כְרָמִים, וַיַּעֲשׂוּ פְּרִי תְבוּאָה. וַיְבָרֲכֵם וַיִּרְבּוּ מְאֹד, וּבְהֶמְתָּם לֹא יַמְעִיט. וַיִּמְעֲטוּ וַיָּשֹׁחוּ, מֵעֹצֶר רָעָה וְיָגוֹן. שֹׁפֵךְ בּוּז עַל נְדִיבִים, וַיַּתְעֵם בְּתֹהוּ לֹא דָרֶךְ. וַיְשַׂגֵּב אֶבְיוֹן מֵעוֹנִי, וַיָּשֶׂם כַּצֹּאן מִשְׁפָּחוֹת. יִרְאוּ יְשָׁרִים וְיִשְׂמָחוּ, וְכָל עַוְלָה קָפְצָה פִּיהָ. מִי חָכָם וְיִשְׁמָר אֵלֶּה, וְיִתְבּוֹנְנוּ חַסְדֵי יהוה.

יום כ"ג לחודש — DAY 23

קח שִׁיר מִזְמוֹר לְדָוִד. נָכוֹן לִבִּי אֱלֹהִים, אָשִׁירָה וַאֲזַמְּרָה אַף כְּבוֹדִי. עוּרָה הַנֵּבֶל וְכִנּוֹר, אָעִירָה שָּׁחַר. אוֹדְךָ בָעַמִּים, יהוה, וַאֲזַמֶּרְךָ בַּלְאֻמִּים. כִּי גָדֹל מֵעַל שָׁמַיִם חַסְדֶּךָ, וְעַד שְׁחָקִים

אֲמִתֶּךָ. רוּמָה עַל שָׁמַיִם, אֱלֹהִים; וְעַל כָּל הָאָרֶץ כְּבוֹדֶךָ. לְמַעַן יֵחָלְצוּן יְדִידֶיךָ, הוֹשִׁיעָה יְמִינְךָ וַעֲנֵנִי. אֱלֹהִים דִּבֶּר בְּקָדְשׁוֹ אֶעְלֹזָה; אֲחַלְּקָה שְׁכֶם, וְעֵמֶק סֻכּוֹת אֲמַדֵּד. לִי גִלְעָד, לִי מְנַשֶּׁה, וְאֶפְרַיִם מָעוֹז רֹאשִׁי, יְהוּדָה מְחֹקְקִי. מוֹאָב סִיר רַחְצִי, עַל אֱדוֹם אַשְׁלִיךְ נַעֲלִי, עָלַי פְּלֶשֶׁת אֶתְרוֹעָע. מִי יֹבִלֵנִי עִיר מִבְצָר, מִי נָחַנִי עַד אֱדוֹם. הֲלֹא אֱלֹהִים זְנַחְתָּנוּ, וְלֹא תֵצֵא אֱלֹהִים בְּצִבְאוֹתֵינוּ. הָבָה לָּנוּ עֶזְרָת מִצָּר, וְשָׁוְא תְּשׁוּעַת אָדָם. בֵּאלֹהִים נַעֲשֶׂה חָיִל, וְהוּא יָבוּס צָרֵינוּ.

קט לַמְנַצֵּחַ לְדָוִד מִזְמוֹר; אֱלֹהֵי תְהִלָּתִי, אַל תֶּחֱרַשׁ. כִּי פִי רָשָׁע וּפִי מִרְמָה עָלַי פָּתָחוּ, דִּבְּרוּ אִתִּי לְשׁוֹן שָׁקֶר. וְדִבְרֵי שִׂנְאָה סְבָבוּנִי, וַיִּלָּחֲמוּנִי חִנָּם. תַּחַת אַהֲבָתִי יִשְׂטְנוּנִי, וַאֲנִי תְפִלָּה. וַיָּשִׂימוּ עָלַי רָעָה תַּחַת טוֹבָה, וְשִׂנְאָה תַּחַת אַהֲבָתִי. הַפְקֵד עָלָיו רָשָׁע, וְשָׂטָן יַעֲמֹד עַל יְמִינוֹ. בְּהִשָּׁפְטוֹ יֵצֵא רָשָׁע, וּתְפִלָּתוֹ תִּהְיֶה לַחֲטָאָה. יִהְיוּ יָמָיו מְעַטִּים, פְּקֻדָּתוֹ יִקַּח אַחֵר. יִהְיוּ בָנָיו יְתוֹמִים, וְאִשְׁתּוֹ אַלְמָנָה. וְנוֹעַ יָנוּעוּ בָנָיו וְשִׁאֵלוּ, וְדָרְשׁוּ מֵחָרְבוֹתֵיהֶם. יְנַקֵּשׁ נוֹשֶׁה לְכָל אֲשֶׁר לוֹ, וְיָבֹזּוּ זָרִים יְגִיעוֹ. אַל יְהִי לוֹ מֹשֵׁךְ חָסֶד, וְאַל יְהִי חוֹנֵן לִיתוֹמָיו. יְהִי אַחֲרִיתוֹ לְהַכְרִית, בְּדוֹר אַחֵר יִמַּח שְׁמָם. יִזָּכֵר עֲוֹן אֲבֹתָיו אֶל יְהוָה, וְחַטַּאת אִמּוֹ אַל תִּמָּח. יִהְיוּ נֶגֶד יְהוָה תָּמִיד, וְיַכְרֵת מֵאֶרֶץ זִכְרָם. יַעַן אֲשֶׁר לֹא זָכַר עֲשׂוֹת חָסֶד; וַיִּרְדֹּף אִישׁ עָנִי וְאֶבְיוֹן, וְנִכְאֵה לֵבָב לְמוֹתֵת. וַיֶּאֱהַב קְלָלָה וַתְּבוֹאֵהוּ; וְלֹא חָפֵץ בִּבְרָכָה, וַתִּרְחַק מִמֶּנּוּ. וַיִּלְבַּשׁ קְלָלָה כְּמַדּוֹ; וַתָּבֹא כַמַּיִם בְּקִרְבּוֹ, וְכַשֶּׁמֶן בְּעַצְמוֹתָיו. תְּהִי לוֹ כְּבֶגֶד יַעְטֶה, וּלְמֵזַח תָּמִיד יַחְגְּרֶהָ. זֹאת פְּעֻלַּת שֹׂטְנַי מֵאֵת יְהוָה, וְהַדֹּבְרִים רָע עַל נַפְשִׁי. וְאַתָּה יְהוִה אֲדֹנָי, עֲשֵׂה אִתִּי לְמַעַן שְׁמֶךָ; כִּי טוֹב חַסְדְּךָ הַצִּילֵנִי. כִּי עָנִי וְאֶבְיוֹן אָנֹכִי, וְלִבִּי חָלַל בְּקִרְבִּי. כְּצֵל

כִּנְטוֹתוֹ נֶהֱלָכְתִּי, נִנְעַרְתִּי כָּאַרְבֶּה. בִּרְכַּי כָּשְׁלוּ מִצּוֹם, וּבְשָׂרִי כָּחַשׁ מִשָּׁמֶן. וַאֲנִי הָיִיתִי חֶרְפָּה לָהֶם, יִרְאוּנִי יְנִיעוּן רֹאשָׁם. עָזְרֵנִי יְהוָה אֱלֹהָי, הוֹשִׁיעֵנִי כְחַסְדֶּךָ. וְיֵדְעוּ כִּי יָדְךָ זֹּאת, אַתָּה יְהוָה עֲשִׂיתָהּ. יְקַלְלוּ הֵמָּה וְאַתָּה תְבָרֵךְ; קָמוּ וַיֵּבֹשׁוּ, וְעַבְדְּךָ יִשְׂמָח. יִלְבְּשׁוּ שׂוֹטְנַי כְּלִמָּה, וְיַעֲטוּ כַמְעִיל בָּשְׁתָּם. אוֹדֶה יְהוָה מְאֹד בְּפִי, וּבְתוֹךְ רַבִּים אֲהַלְלֶנּוּ. כִּי יַעֲמֹד לִימִין אֶבְיוֹן, לְהוֹשִׁיעַ מִשֹּׁפְטֵי נַפְשׁוֹ.

קי לְדָוִד מִזְמוֹר; נְאֻם יְהוָה | לַאדֹנִי: שֵׁב לִימִינִי, עַד אָשִׁית אֹיְבֶיךָ הֲדֹם לְרַגְלֶיךָ. מַטֵּה עֻזְּךָ יִשְׁלַח יְהוָה מִצִּיּוֹן, רְדֵה בְּקֶרֶב אֹיְבֶיךָ. עַמְּךָ נְדָבֹת בְּיוֹם חֵילֶךָ; בְּהַדְרֵי קֹדֶשׁ מֵרֶחֶם מִשְׁחָר, לְךָ טַל יַלְדֻתֶיךָ. נִשְׁבַּע יְהוָה וְלֹא יִנָּחֵם, אַתָּה כֹהֵן לְעוֹלָם, עַל דִּבְרָתִי מַלְכִּי צֶדֶק. אֲדֹנָי עַל יְמִינְךָ, מָחַץ בְּיוֹם אַפּוֹ מְלָכִים. יָדִין בַּגּוֹיִם מָלֵא גְוִיּוֹת, מָחַץ רֹאשׁ עַל אֶרֶץ רַבָּה. מִנַּחַל בַּדֶּרֶךְ יִשְׁתֶּה, עַל כֵּן יָרִים רֹאשׁ.

קיא הַלְלוּיָהּ, אוֹדֶה יְהוָה בְּכָל לֵבָב, בְּסוֹד יְשָׁרִים וְעֵדָה. גְּדֹלִים מַעֲשֵׂי יְהוָה, דְּרוּשִׁים לְכָל חֶפְצֵיהֶם. הוֹד וְהָדָר פָּעֳלוֹ, וְצִדְקָתוֹ עֹמֶדֶת לָעַד. זֵכֶר עָשָׂה לְנִפְלְאֹתָיו, חַנּוּן וְרַחוּם יְהוָה. טֶרֶף נָתַן לִירֵאָיו, יִזְכֹּר לְעוֹלָם בְּרִיתוֹ. כֹּחַ מַעֲשָׂיו הִגִּיד לְעַמּוֹ, לָתֵת לָהֶם נַחֲלַת גּוֹיִם. מַעֲשֵׂי יָדָיו אֱמֶת וּמִשְׁפָּט, נֶאֱמָנִים כָּל פִּקּוּדָיו. סְמוּכִים לָעַד לְעוֹלָם, עֲשׂוּיִם בֶּאֱמֶת וְיָשָׁר. פְּדוּת שָׁלַח לְעַמּוֹ, צִוָּה לְעוֹלָם בְּרִיתוֹ; קָדוֹשׁ וְנוֹרָא שְׁמוֹ. רֵאשִׁית חָכְמָה יִרְאַת יְהוָה, שֵׂכֶל טוֹב לְכָל עֹשֵׂיהֶם; תְּהִלָּתוֹ עֹמֶדֶת לָעַד.

קיב הַלְלוּיָהּ, אַשְׁרֵי אִישׁ יָרֵא אֶת יְהוָה, בְּמִצְוֹתָיו חָפֵץ מְאֹד. גִּבּוֹר בָּאָרֶץ יִהְיֶה זַרְעוֹ, דּוֹר יְשָׁרִים יְבֹרָךְ. הוֹן וָעֹשֶׁר בְּבֵיתוֹ, וְצִדְקָתוֹ עֹמֶדֶת לָעַד. זָרַח בַּחֹשֶׁךְ אוֹר לַיְשָׁרִים, חַנּוּן וְרַחוּם וְצַדִּיק.

טוֹב אִישׁ חוֹנֵן וּמַלְוֶה, יְכַלְכֵּל דְּבָרָיו בְּמִשְׁפָּט. כִּי לְעוֹלָם לֹא יִמּוֹט, לְזֵכֶר עוֹלָם יִהְיֶה צַדִּיק. מִשְּׁמוּעָה רָעָה לֹא יִירָא, נָכוֹן לִבּוֹ בָּטֻחַ בַּיהוה. סָמוּךְ לִבּוֹ לֹא יִירָא, עַד אֲשֶׁר יִרְאֶה בְצָרָיו. פִּזַּר נָתַן לָאֶבְיוֹנִים, צִדְקָתוֹ עֹמֶדֶת לָעַד; קַרְנוֹ תָּרוּם בְּכָבוֹד. רָשָׁע יִרְאֶה וְכָעָס, שִׁנָּיו יַחֲרֹק וְנָמָס; תַּאֲוַת רְשָׁעִים תֹּאבֵד.

יום כ"ד לחודש — DAY 24

קיג הַלְלוּיָהּ, הַלְלוּ עַבְדֵי יהוה, הַלְלוּ אֶת שֵׁם יהוה. יְהִי שֵׁם יהוה מְבֹרָךְ מֵעַתָּה וְעַד עוֹלָם. מִמִּזְרַח שֶׁמֶשׁ עַד מְבוֹאוֹ, מְהֻלָּל שֵׁם יהוה. רָם עַל כָּל גּוֹיִם | יהוה, עַל הַשָּׁמַיִם כְּבוֹדוֹ. מִי כַּיהוה אֱלֹהֵינוּ, הַמַּגְבִּיהִי לָשָׁבֶת. הַמַּשְׁפִּילִי לִרְאוֹת, בַּשָּׁמַיִם וּבָאָרֶץ. מְקִימִי מֵעָפָר דָּל, מֵאַשְׁפֹּת יָרִים אֶבְיוֹן. לְהוֹשִׁיבִי עִם נְדִיבִים, עִם נְדִיבֵי עַמּוֹ. מוֹשִׁיבִי עֲקֶרֶת הַבַּיִת, אֵם הַבָּנִים שְׂמֵחָה; הַלְלוּיָהּ.

קיד בְּצֵאת יִשְׂרָאֵל מִמִּצְרָיִם, בֵּית יַעֲקֹב מֵעַם לֹעֵז. הָיְתָה יְהוּדָה לְקָדְשׁוֹ, יִשְׂרָאֵל מַמְשְׁלוֹתָיו. הַיָּם רָאָה וַיָּנֹס, הַיַּרְדֵּן יִסֹּב לְאָחוֹר. הֶהָרִים רָקְדוּ כְאֵילִים, גְּבָעוֹת כִּבְנֵי צֹאן. מַה לְּךָ הַיָּם כִּי תָנוּס, הַיַּרְדֵּן תִּסֹּב לְאָחוֹר. הֶהָרִים תִּרְקְדוּ כְאֵילִים, גְּבָעוֹת כִּבְנֵי צֹאן. מִלִּפְנֵי אָדוֹן חוּלִי אָרֶץ, מִלִּפְנֵי אֱלוֹהַּ יַעֲקֹב. הַהֹפְכִי הַצּוּר אֲגַם מָיִם, חַלָּמִישׁ לְמַעְיְנוֹ מָיִם.

קטו לֹא לָנוּ, יהוה, לֹא לָנוּ; כִּי לְשִׁמְךָ תֵּן כָּבוֹד, עַל חַסְדְּךָ עַל אֲמִתֶּךָ. לָמָּה יֹאמְרוּ הַגּוֹיִם, אַיֵּה נָא אֱלֹהֵיהֶם. וֵאלֹהֵינוּ בַשָּׁמָיִם, כֹּל אֲשֶׁר חָפֵץ עָשָׂה. עֲצַבֵּיהֶם כֶּסֶף וְזָהָב, מַעֲשֵׂה יְדֵי אָדָם. פֶּה לָהֶם וְלֹא יְדַבֵּרוּ, עֵינַיִם לָהֶם וְלֹא יִרְאוּ. אָזְנַיִם לָהֶם וְלֹא יִשְׁמָעוּ, אַף לָהֶם וְלֹא יְרִיחוּן. יְדֵיהֶם וְלֹא יְמִישׁוּן, רַגְלֵיהֶם וְלֹא

יְהַלֵּכוּ, לֹא יֶהְגּוּ בִּגְרוֹנָם. כְּמוֹהֶם יִהְיוּ עֹשֵׂיהֶם, כֹּל אֲשֶׁר בֹּטֵחַ בָּהֶם. יִשְׂרָאֵל בְּטַח בַּיהוה, עֶזְרָם וּמָגִנָּם הוּא. בֵּית אַהֲרֹן בִּטְחוּ בַיהוה, עֶזְרָם וּמָגִנָּם הוּא. יִרְאֵי יהוה בִּטְחוּ בַיהוה, עֶזְרָם וּמָגִנָּם הוּא. יהוה זְכָרָנוּ יְבָרֵךְ; יְבָרֵךְ אֶת בֵּית יִשְׂרָאֵל, יְבָרֵךְ אֶת בֵּית אַהֲרֹן. יְבָרֵךְ יִרְאֵי יהוה, הַקְּטַנִּים עִם הַגְּדֹלִים. יֹסֵף יהוה עֲלֵיכֶם, עֲלֵיכֶם וְעַל בְּנֵיכֶם. בְּרוּכִים אַתֶּם לַיהוה, עֹשֵׂה שָׁמַיִם וָאָרֶץ. הַשָּׁמַיִם שָׁמַיִם לַיהוה, וְהָאָרֶץ נָתַן לִבְנֵי אָדָם. לֹא הַמֵּתִים יְהַלְלוּ יָהּ, וְלֹא כָּל יֹרְדֵי דוּמָה. וַאֲנַחְנוּ נְבָרֵךְ יָהּ, מֵעַתָּה וְעַד עוֹלָם; הַלְלוּיָהּ.

קטז אָהַבְתִּי כִּי יִשְׁמַע | יהוה, אֶת קוֹלִי תַּחֲנוּנָי. כִּי הִטָּה אָזְנוֹ לִי, וּבְיָמַי אֶקְרָא. אֲפָפוּנִי חֶבְלֵי מָוֶת, וּמְצָרֵי שְׁאוֹל מְצָאוּנִי, צָרָה וְיָגוֹן אֶמְצָא. וּבְשֵׁם יהוה אֶקְרָא: אָנָּה יהוה מַלְּטָה נַפְשִׁי. חַנּוּן יהוה וְצַדִּיק, וֵאלֹהֵינוּ מְרַחֵם. שֹׁמֵר פְּתָאיִם יהוה, דַּלּוֹתִי וְלִי יְהוֹשִׁיעַ. שׁוּבִי נַפְשִׁי לִמְנוּחָיְכִי, כִּי יהוה גָּמַל עָלָיְכִי. כִּי חִלַּצְתָּ נַפְשִׁי מִמָּוֶת; אֶת עֵינִי מִן דִּמְעָה, אֶת רַגְלִי מִדֶּחִי. אֶתְהַלֵּךְ לִפְנֵי יהוה, בְּאַרְצוֹת הַחַיִּים. הֶאֱמַנְתִּי כִּי אֲדַבֵּר, אֲנִי עָנִיתִי מְאֹד. אֲנִי אָמַרְתִּי בְחָפְזִי: כָּל הָאָדָם כֹּזֵב. מָה אָשִׁיב לַיהוה, כָּל תַּגְמוּלוֹהִי עָלָי. כּוֹס יְשׁוּעוֹת אֶשָּׂא, וּבְשֵׁם יהוה אֶקְרָא. נְדָרַי לַיהוה אֲשַׁלֵּם, נֶגְדָה נָּא לְכָל עַמּוֹ. יָקָר בְּעֵינֵי יהוה, הַמָּוְתָה לַחֲסִידָיו. אָנָּה יהוה כִּי אֲנִי עַבְדֶּךָ; אֲנִי עַבְדְּךָ בֶּן אֲמָתֶךָ, פִּתַּחְתָּ לְמוֹסֵרָי. לְךָ אֶזְבַּח זֶבַח תּוֹדָה, וּבְשֵׁם יהוה אֶקְרָא. נְדָרַי לַיהוה אֲשַׁלֵּם, נֶגְדָה נָּא לְכָל עַמּוֹ. בְּחַצְרוֹת בֵּית יהוה, בְּתוֹכֵכִי יְרוּשָׁלָיִם; הַלְלוּיָהּ.

קיז הַלְלוּ אֶת יהוה, כָּל גּוֹיִם, שַׁבְּחוּהוּ כָּל הָאֻמִּים. כִּי גָבַר עָלֵינוּ חַסְדּוֹ, וֶאֱמֶת יהוה לְעוֹלָם; הַלְלוּיָהּ.

מִשְׁפְּטֵי צִדְקֶךָ. אֶת חֻקֶּיךָ אֶשְׁמֹר, אַל תַּעַזְבֵנִי עַד מְאֹד.

בַּמֶּה יְזַכֶּה נַּעַר אֶת אָרְחוֹ, לִשְׁמֹר כִּדְבָרֶךָ. בְּכָל לִבִּי דְרַשְׁתִּיךָ, אַל תַּשְׁגֵּנִי מִמִּצְוֹתֶיךָ. בְּלִבִּי צָפַנְתִּי אִמְרָתֶךָ, לְמַעַן לֹא אֶחֱטָא לָךְ. בָּרוּךְ אַתָּה יהוה, לַמְּדֵנִי חֻקֶּיךָ. בִּשְׂפָתַי סִפַּרְתִּי, כֹּל מִשְׁפְּטֵי פִיךָ. בְּדֶרֶךְ עֵדְוֹתֶיךָ שַׂשְׂתִּי, כְּעַל כָּל הוֹן. בְּפִקּוּדֶיךָ אָשִׂיחָה, וְאַבִּיטָה אֹרְחֹתֶיךָ. בְּחֻקֹּתֶיךָ אֶשְׁתַּעֲשָׁע, לֹא אֶשְׁכַּח דְּבָרֶךָ.

גְּמֹל עַל עַבְדְּךָ, אֶחְיֶה, וְאֶשְׁמְרָה דְבָרֶךָ. גַּל עֵינַי, וְאַבִּיטָה נִפְלָאוֹת מִתּוֹרָתֶךָ. גֵּר אָנֹכִי בָאָרֶץ, אַל תַּסְתֵּר מִמֶּנִּי מִצְוֹתֶיךָ. גָּרְסָה נַפְשִׁי לְתַאֲבָה, אֶל מִשְׁפָּטֶיךָ בְכָל עֵת. גָּעַרְתָּ זֵדִים אֲרוּרִים, הַשֹּׁגִים מִמִּצְוֹתֶיךָ. גַּל מֵעָלַי חֶרְפָּה וָבוּז, כִּי עֵדֹתֶיךָ נָצָרְתִּי. גַּם יָשְׁבוּ שָׂרִים בִּי נִדְבָּרוּ, עַבְדְּךָ יָשִׂיחַ בְּחֻקֶּיךָ. גַּם עֵדֹתֶיךָ שַׁעֲשֻׁעָי, אַנְשֵׁי עֲצָתִי.

דָּבְקָה לֶעָפָר נַפְשִׁי, חַיֵּנִי כִּדְבָרֶךָ. דְּרָכַי סִפַּרְתִּי וַתַּעֲנֵנִי, לַמְּדֵנִי חֻקֶּיךָ. דֶּרֶךְ פִּקּוּדֶיךָ הֲבִינֵנִי, וְאָשִׂיחָה בְּנִפְלְאוֹתֶיךָ. דָּלְפָה נַפְשִׁי מִתּוּגָה, קַיְּמֵנִי כִּדְבָרֶךָ. דֶּרֶךְ שֶׁקֶר הָסֵר מִמֶּנִּי, וְתוֹרָתְךָ חָנֵּנִי. דֶּרֶךְ אֱמוּנָה בָחָרְתִּי, מִשְׁפָּטֶיךָ שִׁוִּיתִי. דָּבַקְתִּי בְעֵדְוֹתֶיךָ, יהוה אַל תְּבִישֵׁנִי. דֶּרֶךְ מִצְוֹתֶיךָ אָרוּץ, כִּי תַרְחִיב לִבִּי.

הוֹרֵנִי יהוה דֶּרֶךְ חֻקֶּיךָ, וְאֶצְּרֶנָּה עֵקֶב. הֲבִינֵנִי וְאֶצְּרָה תוֹרָתֶךָ, וְאֶשְׁמְרֶנָּה בְכָל לֵב. הַדְרִיכֵנִי בִּנְתִיב מִצְוֹתֶיךָ, כִּי בוֹ חָפָצְתִּי. הַט לִבִּי אֶל עֵדְוֹתֶיךָ, וְאַל אֶל בָּצַע. הַעֲבֵר עֵינַי מֵרְאוֹת שָׁוְא, בִּדְרָכֶךָ חַיֵּנִי. הָקֵם לְעַבְדְּךָ אִמְרָתֶךָ, אֲשֶׁר לְיִרְאָתֶךָ. הַעֲבֵר חֶרְפָּתִי אֲשֶׁר יָגֹרְתִּי, כִּי מִשְׁפָּטֶיךָ טוֹבִים. הִנֵּה תָּאַבְתִּי לְפִקֻּדֶיךָ, בְּצִדְקָתְךָ חַיֵּנִי.

וִיבֹאֻנִי חֲסָדֶךָ, יהוה, תְּשׁוּעָתְךָ כְּאִמְרָתֶךָ. וְאֶעֱנֶה חֹרְפִי דָבָר, כִּי בָטַחְתִּי בִּדְבָרֶךָ. וְאַל תַּצֵּל מִפִּי דְבַר אֱמֶת עַד

קיח הוֹדוּ לַיהוה כִּי טוֹב, כִּי לְעוֹלָם חַסְדּוֹ. יֹאמַר נָא יִשְׂרָאֵל, כִּי לְעוֹלָם חַסְדּוֹ. יֹאמְרוּ נָא בֵית אַהֲרֹן, כִּי לְעוֹלָם חַסְדּוֹ. יֹאמְרוּ נָא יִרְאֵי יהוה, כִּי לְעוֹלָם חַסְדּוֹ. מִן הַמֵּצַר קָרָאתִי יָּהּ, עָנָנִי בַמֶּרְחָב יָהּ. יהוה לִי לֹא אִירָא, מַה יַּעֲשֶׂה לִי אָדָם. יהוה לִי בְּעֹזְרָי, וַאֲנִי אֶרְאֶה בְשֹׂנְאָי. טוֹב לַחֲסוֹת בַּיהוה, מִבְּטֹחַ בָּאָדָם. טוֹב לַחֲסוֹת בַּיהוה, מִבְּטֹחַ בִּנְדִיבִים. כָּל גּוֹיִם סְבָבוּנִי, בְּשֵׁם יהוה כִּי אֲמִילַם. סַבְּוּנִי גַם סְבָבוּנִי, בְּשֵׁם יהוה כִּי אֲמִילַם. סַבְּוּנִי כִדְבֹרִים, דֹּעֲכוּ כְּאֵשׁ קוֹצִים; בְּשֵׁם יהוה כִּי אֲמִילַם. דָּחֹה דְחִיתַנִי לִנְפֹּל, וַיהוה עֲזָרָנִי. עָזִּי וְזִמְרָת יָהּ, וַיְהִי לִי לִישׁוּעָה. קוֹל רִנָּה וִישׁוּעָה בְּאָהֳלֵי צַדִּיקִים, יְמִין יהוה עֹשָׂה חָיִל. יְמִין יהוה רוֹמֵמָה, יְמִין יהוה עֹשָׂה חָיִל. לֹא אָמוּת כִּי אֶחְיֶה, וַאֲסַפֵּר מַעֲשֵׂי יָהּ. יַסֹּר יִסְּרַנִּי יָּהּ, וְלַמָּוֶת לֹא נְתָנָנִי. פִּתְחוּ לִי שַׁעֲרֵי צֶדֶק, אָבֹא בָם אוֹדֶה יָהּ. זֶה הַשַּׁעַר לַיהוה, צַדִּיקִים יָבֹאוּ בוֹ. אוֹדְךָ כִּי עֲנִיתָנִי, וַתְּהִי לִי לִישׁוּעָה. אֶבֶן מָאֲסוּ הַבּוֹנִים, הָיְתָה לְרֹאשׁ פִּנָּה. מֵאֵת יהוה הָיְתָה זֹּאת, הִיא נִפְלָאת בְּעֵינֵינוּ. זֶה הַיּוֹם עָשָׂה יהוה, נָגִילָה וְנִשְׂמְחָה בוֹ. אָנָּא יהוה, הוֹשִׁיעָה נָּא; אָנָּא יהוה, הַצְלִיחָה נָּא. בָּרוּךְ הַבָּא בְּשֵׁם יהוה, בֵּרַכְנוּכֶם מִבֵּית יהוה. אֵל יהוה וַיָּאֶר לָנוּ, אִסְרוּ חַג בַּעֲבֹתִים עַד קַרְנוֹת הַמִּזְבֵּחַ. אֵלִי אַתָּה וְאוֹדֶךָּ, אֱלֹהַי אֲרוֹמְמֶךָּ. הוֹדוּ לַיהוה כִּי טוֹב, כִּי לְעוֹלָם חַסְדּוֹ.

קיט אַשְׁרֵי תְמִימֵי דָרֶךְ, הַהֹלְכִים בְּתוֹרַת יהוה. אַשְׁרֵי נֹצְרֵי עֵדֹתָיו, בְּכָל לֵב יִדְרְשׁוּהוּ. אַף לֹא פָעֲלוּ עַוְלָה, בִּדְרָכָיו הָלָכוּ. אַתָּה צִוִּיתָה פִקֻּדֶיךָ, לִשְׁמֹר מְאֹד. אַחֲלַי, יִכֹּנוּ דְרָכָי לִשְׁמֹר חֻקֶּיךָ. אָז לֹא אֵבוֹשׁ, בְּהַבִּיטִי אֶל כָּל מִצְוֹתֶיךָ. אוֹדְךָ בְּיֹשֶׁר לֵבָב, בְּלָמְדִי

מְאֹד, כִּי לְמִשְׁפָּטֶךָ יִחָלְתִּי. וְאֶשְׁמְרָה תוֹרָתְךָ תָמִיד לְעוֹלָם וָעֶד. וְאֶתְהַלְּכָה בָרְחָבָה, כִּי פִקֻּדֶיךָ דָרָשְׁתִּי. וַאֲדַבְּרָה בְעֵדֹתֶיךָ נֶגֶד מְלָכִים, וְלֹא אֵבוֹשׁ. וְאֶשְׁתַּעֲשַׁע בְּמִצְוֹתֶיךָ אֲשֶׁר אָהָבְתִּי. וְאֶשָּׂא כַפַּי אֶל מִצְוֹתֶיךָ אֲשֶׁר אָהָבְתִּי, וְאָשִׂיחָה בְחֻקֶּיךָ.

זְכֹר דָּבָר לְעַבְדֶּךָ, עַל אֲשֶׁר יִחַלְתָּנִי. זֹאת נֶחָמָתִי בְעָנְיִי, כִּי אִמְרָתְךָ חִיָּתְנִי. זֵדִים הֱלִיצֻנִי עַד מְאֹד, מִתּוֹרָתְךָ לֹא נָטִיתִי. זָכַרְתִּי מִשְׁפָּטֶיךָ מֵעוֹלָם | יהוה, וָאֶתְנֶחָם. זַלְעָפָה אֲחָזַתְנִי מֵרְשָׁעִים, עֹזְבֵי תוֹרָתֶךָ. זְמִרוֹת הָיוּ לִי חֻקֶּיךָ, בְּבֵית מְגוּרָי. זָכַרְתִּי בַלַּיְלָה שִׁמְךָ, יהוה, וָאֶשְׁמְרָה תוֹרָתֶךָ. זֹאת הָיְתָה לִּי, כִּי פִקֻּדֶיךָ נָצָרְתִּי.

חֶלְקִי יהוה, אָמַרְתִּי לִשְׁמֹר דְּבָרֶיךָ. חִלִּיתִי פָנֶיךָ בְכָל לֵב, חָנֵּנִי כְּאִמְרָתֶךָ. חִשַּׁבְתִּי דְרָכָי, וָאָשִׁיבָה רַגְלַי אֶל עֵדֹתֶיךָ. חַשְׁתִּי וְלֹא הִתְמַהְמָהְתִּי, לִשְׁמֹר מִצְוֹתֶיךָ. חֶבְלֵי רְשָׁעִים עִוְּדֻנִי, תּוֹרָתְךָ לֹא שָׁכָחְתִּי. חֲצוֹת לַיְלָה אָקוּם לְהוֹדוֹת לָךְ, עַל מִשְׁפְּטֵי צִדְקֶךָ. חָבֵר אָנִי לְכָל אֲשֶׁר יְרֵאוּךָ, וּלְשֹׁמְרֵי פִּקּוּדֶיךָ. חַסְדְּךָ יהוה מָלְאָה הָאָרֶץ, חֻקֶּיךָ לַמְּדֵנִי.

טוֹב עָשִׂיתָ עִם עַבְדְּךָ, יהוה, כִּדְבָרֶךָ. טוּב טַעַם וָדַעַת לַמְּדֵנִי, כִּי בְמִצְוֹתֶיךָ הֶאֱמָנְתִּי. טֶרֶם אֶעֱנֶה אֲנִי שֹׁגֵג, וְעַתָּה אִמְרָתְךָ שָׁמָרְתִּי. טוֹב אַתָּה וּמֵטִיב, לַמְּדֵנִי חֻקֶּיךָ. טָפְלוּ עָלַי שֶׁקֶר זֵדִים, אֲנִי בְּכָל לֵב אֶצֹּר פִּקּוּדֶיךָ. טָפַשׁ כַּחֵלֶב לִבָּם, אֲנִי תּוֹרָתְךָ שִׁעֲשָׁעְתִּי. טוֹב לִי כִי עֻנֵּיתִי, לְמַעַן אֶלְמַד חֻקֶּיךָ. טוֹב לִי תוֹרַת פִּיךָ, מֵאַלְפֵי זָהָב וָכָסֶף.

יָדֶיךָ עָשׂוּנִי וַיְכוֹנְנוּנִי, הֲבִינֵנִי וְאֶלְמְדָה מִצְוֹתֶיךָ. יְרֵאֶיךָ יִרְאוּנִי וְיִשְׂמָחוּ, כִּי לִדְבָרְךָ יִחָלְתִּי. יָדַעְתִּי יהוה כִּי צֶדֶק מִשְׁפָּטֶיךָ, וֶאֱמוּנָה עִנִּיתָנִי. יְהִי נָא חַסְדְּךָ לְנַחֲמֵנִי, כְּאִמְרָתְךָ לְעַבְדֶּךָ. יְבֹאוּנִי

רַחֲמֶיךָ וְאֶחְיֶה, כִּי תוֹרָתְךָ שַׁעֲשֻׁעָי. יֵבֹשׁוּ זֵדִים כִּי שֶׁקֶר עִוְּתוּנִי, אֲנִי אָשִׂיחַ בְּפִקּוּדֶיךָ. יָשׁוּבוּ לִי יְרֵאֶיךָ, וְיֹדְעֵי עֵדֹתֶיךָ. יְהִי לִבִּי תָמִים בְּחֻקֶּיךָ, לְמַעַן לֹא אֵבוֹשׁ.

כָּלְתָה לִתְשׁוּעָתְךָ נַפְשִׁי, לִדְבָרְךָ יִחָלְתִּי. כָּלוּ עֵינַי לְאִמְרָתֶךָ, לֵאמֹר: מָתַי תְּנַחֲמֵנִי. כִּי הָיִיתִי כְּנֹאד בְּקִיטוֹר, חֻקֶּיךָ לֹא שָׁכָחְתִּי. כַּמָּה יְמֵי עַבְדֶּךָ, מָתַי תַּעֲשֶׂה בְרֹדְפַי מִשְׁפָּט. כָּרוּ לִי זֵדִים שִׁיחוֹת, אֲשֶׁר לֹא כְתוֹרָתֶךָ. כָּל מִצְוֹתֶיךָ אֱמוּנָה; שֶׁקֶר רְדָפוּנִי, עָזְרֵנִי. כִּמְעַט כִּלּוּנִי בָאָרֶץ, וַאֲנִי לֹא עָזַבְתִּי פִקֻּדֶיךָ. כְּחַסְדְּךָ חַיֵּנִי, וְאֶשְׁמְרָה עֵדוּת פִּיךָ.

לְעוֹלָם, יהוה, דְּבָרְךָ נִצָּב בַּשָּׁמָיִם. לְדֹר וָדֹר אֱמוּנָתֶךָ, כּוֹנַנְתָּ אֶרֶץ וַתַּעֲמֹד. לְמִשְׁפָּטֶיךָ עָמְדוּ הַיּוֹם, כִּי הַכֹּל עֲבָדֶיךָ. לוּלֵי תוֹרָתְךָ שַׁעֲשֻׁעָי, אָז אָבַדְתִּי בְעָנְיִי. לְעוֹלָם לֹא אֶשְׁכַּח פִּקּוּדֶיךָ, כִּי בָם חִיִּיתָנִי. לְךָ אֲנִי, הוֹשִׁיעֵנִי, כִּי פִקּוּדֶיךָ דָרָשְׁתִּי. לִי קִוּוּ רְשָׁעִים לְאַבְּדֵנִי, עֵדֹתֶיךָ אֶתְבּוֹנָן. לְכָל תִּכְלָה רָאִיתִי קֵץ, רְחָבָה מִצְוָתְךָ מְאֹד.

מָה אָהַבְתִּי תוֹרָתֶךָ, כָּל הַיּוֹם הִיא שִׂיחָתִי. מֵאֹיְבַי תְּחַכְּמֵנִי מִצְוֹתֶךָ, כִּי לְעוֹלָם הִיא לִי. מִכָּל מְלַמְּדַי הִשְׂכַּלְתִּי, כִּי עֵדְוֹתֶיךָ שִׂיחָה לִי. מִזְּקֵנִים אֶתְבּוֹנָן, כִּי פִקּוּדֶיךָ נָצָרְתִּי. מִכָּל אֹרַח רָע כָּלִאתִי רַגְלָי, לְמַעַן אֶשְׁמֹר דְּבָרֶךָ. מִמִּשְׁפָּטֶיךָ לֹא סָרְתִּי, כִּי אַתָּה הוֹרֵתָנִי. מַה נִּמְלְצוּ לְחִכִּי אִמְרָתֶךָ, מִדְּבַשׁ לְפִי. מִפִּקּוּדֶיךָ אֶתְבּוֹנָן, עַל כֵּן שָׂנֵאתִי כָּל אֹרַח שָׁקֶר.

נֵר לְרַגְלִי דְבָרֶךָ, וְאוֹר לִנְתִיבָתִי. נִשְׁבַּעְתִּי וָאֲקַיֵּמָה, לִשְׁמֹר מִשְׁפְּטֵי צִדְקֶךָ. נַעֲנֵיתִי עַד מְאֹד; יהוה, חַיֵּנִי כִדְבָרֶךָ. נִדְבוֹת פִּי רְצֵה נָא, יהוה, וּמִשְׁפָּטֶיךָ

לַמֵּדֵנִי. נַפְשִׁי בְכַפִּי תָמִיד, וְתוֹרָתְךָ לֹא שָׁכָחְתִּי. נָתְנוּ רְשָׁעִים פַּח לִי, וּמִפִּקּוּדֶיךָ לֹא תָעִיתִי. נָחַלְתִּי עֵדְוֹתֶיךָ לְעוֹלָם, כִּי שְׂשׂוֹן לִבִּי הֵמָּה. נָטִיתִי לִבִּי לַעֲשׂוֹת חֻקֶּיךָ לְעוֹלָם עֵקֶב.

סֵעֲפִים שָׂנֵאתִי, וְתוֹרָתְךָ אָהָבְתִּי. סִתְרִי וּמָגִנִּי אָתָּה, לִדְבָרְךָ יִחָלְתִּי. סוּרוּ מִמֶּנִּי מְרֵעִים, וְאֶצְּרָה מִצְוֹת אֱלֹהָי. סָמְכֵנִי כְאִמְרָתְךָ וְאֶחְיֶה, וְאַל תְּבִישֵׁנִי מִשִּׂבְרִי. סְעָדֵנִי וְאִוָּשֵׁעָה, וְאֶשְׁעָה בְחֻקֶּיךָ תָמִיד. סָלִיתָ כָּל שׁוֹגִים מֵחֻקֶּיךָ, כִּי שֶׁקֶר תַּרְמִיתָם. סִגִים הִשְׁבַּתָּ כָל רִשְׁעֵי אָרֶץ, לָכֵן אָהַבְתִּי עֵדֹתֶיךָ. סָמַר מִפַּחְדְּךָ בְשָׂרִי, וּמִמִּשְׁפָּטֶיךָ יָרֵאתִי.

עָשִׂיתִי מִשְׁפָּט וָצֶדֶק, בַּל תַּנִּיחֵנִי לְעֹשְׁקָי. עֲרֹב עַבְדְּךָ לְטוֹב, אַל יַעַשְׁקֻנִי זֵדִים. עֵינַי כָּלוּ לִישׁוּעָתֶךָ, וּלְאִמְרַת צִדְקֶךָ. עֲשֵׂה עִם עַבְדְּךָ כְחַסְדֶּךָ, וְחֻקֶּיךָ לַמְּדֵנִי. עַבְדְּךָ אָנִי, הֲבִינֵנִי, וְאֵדְעָה עֵדֹתֶיךָ. עֵת לַעֲשׂוֹת לַיהוה, הֵפֵרוּ תוֹרָתֶךָ. עַל כֵּן אָהַבְתִּי מִצְוֹתֶיךָ, מִזָּהָב וּמִפָּז. עַל כֵּן כָּל פִּקּוּדֵי כֹל יִשָּׁרְתִּי, כָּל אֹרַח שֶׁקֶר שָׂנֵאתִי.

פְּלָאוֹת עֵדְוֹתֶיךָ, עַל כֵּן נְצָרָתַם נַפְשִׁי. פֵּתַח דְּבָרֶיךָ יָאִיר, מֵבִין פְּתָיִים. פִּי פָעַרְתִּי וָאֶשְׁאָפָה, כִּי לְמִצְוֹתֶיךָ יָאָבְתִּי. פְּנֵה אֵלַי וְחָנֵּנִי, כְּמִשְׁפָּט לְאֹהֲבֵי שְׁמֶךָ. פְּעָמַי הָכֵן בְּאִמְרָתֶךָ, וְאַל תַּשְׁלֶט בִּי כָל אָוֶן. פְּדֵנִי מֵעֹשֶׁק אָדָם, וְאֶשְׁמְרָה פִּקּוּדֶיךָ. פָּנֶיךָ הָאֵר בְּעַבְדֶּךָ, וְלַמְּדֵנִי אֶת חֻקֶּיךָ. פַּלְגֵי מַיִם יָרְדוּ עֵינָי, עַל לֹא שָׁמְרוּ תוֹרָתֶךָ.

צַדִּיק אַתָּה יהוה, וְיָשָׁר מִשְׁפָּטֶיךָ. צִוִּיתָ צֶדֶק עֵדֹתֶיךָ, וֶאֱמוּנָה מְאֹד. צִמְּתַתְנִי קִנְאָתִי, כִּי שָׁכְחוּ דְבָרֶיךָ צָרָי. צְרוּפָה אִמְרָתְךָ מְאֹד, וְעַבְדְּךָ אֲהֵבָהּ. צָעִיר אָנֹכִי וְנִבְזֶה, פִּקֻּדֶיךָ לֹא שָׁכָחְתִּי. צִדְקָתְךָ צֶדֶק לְעוֹלָם, וְתוֹרָתְךָ אֱמֶת. צַר וּמָצוֹק מְצָאוּנִי, מִצְוֹתֶיךָ שַׁעֲשֻׁעָי. צֶדֶק

עֵדְוֹתֶיךָ לְעוֹלָם, הֲבִינֵנִי וְאֶחְיֶה.

קָרָאתִי בְכָל לֵב, עֲנֵנִי יהוה, חֻקֶּיךָ אֶצֹּרָה. קְרָאתִיךָ, הוֹשִׁיעֵנִי, וְאֶשְׁמְרָה עֵדֹתֶיךָ. קִדַּמְתִּי בַנֶּשֶׁף וָאֲשַׁוֵּעָה, לִדְבָרְךָ יִחָלְתִּי. קִדְּמוּ עֵינַי אַשְׁמֻרוֹת, לָשִׂיחַ בְּאִמְרָתֶךָ. קוֹלִי שִׁמְעָה כְחַסְדֶּךָ, יהוה, כְּמִשְׁפָּטֶךָ חַיֵּנִי. קָרְבוּ רֹדְפֵי זִמָּה, מִתּוֹרָתְךָ רָחָקוּ. קָרוֹב אַתָּה יהוה, וְכָל מִצְוֹתֶיךָ אֱמֶת. קֶדֶם יָדַעְתִּי מֵעֵדֹתֶיךָ, כִּי לְעוֹלָם יְסַדְתָּם.

רְאֵה עָנְיִי וְחַלְּצֵנִי, כִּי תוֹרָתְךָ לֹא שָׁכָחְתִּי. רִיבָה רִיבִי וּגְאָלֵנִי, לְאִמְרָתְךָ חַיֵּנִי. רָחוֹק מֵרְשָׁעִים יְשׁוּעָה, כִּי חֻקֶּיךָ לֹא דָרָשׁוּ. רַחֲמֶיךָ רַבִּים | יהוה, כְּמִשְׁפָּטֶיךָ חַיֵּנִי. רַבִּים רֹדְפַי וְצָרָי, מֵעֵדְוֹתֶיךָ לֹא נָטִיתִי. רָאִיתִי בֹגְדִים וָאֶתְקוֹטָטָה, אֲשֶׁר אִמְרָתְךָ לֹא שָׁמָרוּ. רְאֵה כִּי פִקּוּדֶיךָ אָהָבְתִּי, יהוה, כְּחַסְדְּךָ חַיֵּנִי. רֹאשׁ דְּבָרְךָ אֱמֶת, וּלְעוֹלָם כָּל מִשְׁפַּט צִדְקֶךָ.

שָׂרִים רְדָפוּנִי חִנָּם, וּמִדְּבָרְךָ פָּחַד לִבִּי. שָׂשׂ אָנֹכִי עַל אִמְרָתֶךָ, כְּמוֹצֵא שָׁלָל רָב. שֶׁקֶר שָׂנֵאתִי וַאֲתַעֵבָה, תּוֹרָתְךָ אָהָבְתִּי. שֶׁבַע בַּיּוֹם הִלַּלְתִּיךָ, עַל מִשְׁפְּטֵי צִדְקֶךָ. שָׁלוֹם רָב לְאֹהֲבֵי תוֹרָתֶךָ, וְאֵין לָמוֹ מִכְשׁוֹל. שִׂבַּרְתִּי לִישׁוּעָתְךָ יהוה, וּמִצְוֹתֶיךָ עָשִׂיתִי. שָׁמְרָה נַפְשִׁי עֵדֹתֶיךָ, וָאֹהֲבֵם מְאֹד. שָׁמַרְתִּי פִקּוּדֶיךָ וְעֵדֹתֶיךָ, כִּי כָל דְּרָכַי נֶגְדֶּךָ.

תִּקְרַב רִנָּתִי לְפָנֶיךָ, יהוה, כִּדְבָרְךָ הֲבִינֵנִי. תָּבוֹא תְחִנָּתִי לְפָנֶיךָ, כְּאִמְרָתְךָ הַצִּילֵנִי. תַּבַּעְנָה שְׂפָתַי תְּהִלָּה, כִּי תְלַמְּדֵנִי חֻקֶּיךָ. תַּעַן לְשׁוֹנִי אִמְרָתֶךָ, כִּי כָל מִצְוֹתֶיךָ צֶּדֶק. תְּהִי יָדְךָ לְעָזְרֵנִי, כִּי פִקּוּדֶיךָ בָחָרְתִּי. תָּאַבְתִּי לִישׁוּעָתְךָ יהוה, וְתוֹרָתְךָ שַׁעֲשֻׁעָי. תְּחִי נַפְשִׁי וּתְהַלְלֶךָּ, וּמִשְׁפָּטֶךָ יַעְזְרֻנִי. תָּעִיתִי כְּשֶׂה אֹבֵד, בַּקֵּשׁ עַבְדֶּךָ, כִּי מִצְוֹתֶיךָ לֹא שָׁכָחְתִּי.

קב שִׁיר הַמַּעֲלוֹת אֶל יהוה בַּצָּרָתָה לִי קָרָאתִי, וַיַּעֲנֵנִי. יהוה, הַצִּילָה נַפְשִׁי מִשְּׂפַת שֶׁקֶר, מִלָּשׁוֹן רְמִיָּה. מַה יִּתֵּן לְךָ, וּמַה יֹּסִיף לָךְ, לָשׁוֹן רְמִיָּה. חִצֵּי גִבּוֹר שְׁנוּנִים, עִם גַּחֲלֵי רְתָמִים. אוֹיָה לִי כִּי גַרְתִּי מֶשֶׁךְ, שָׁכַנְתִּי עִם אָהֳלֵי קֵדָר. רַבַּת שָׁכְנָה לָּהּ נַפְשִׁי, עִם שׂוֹנֵא שָׁלוֹם. אֲנִי שָׁלוֹם, וְכִי אֲדַבֵּר, הֵמָּה לַמִּלְחָמָה.

קכא שִׁיר לַמַּעֲלוֹת אֶשָּׂא עֵינַי אֶל הֶהָרִים, מֵאַיִן יָבֹא עֶזְרִי. עֶזְרִי מֵעִם יהוה, עֹשֵׂה שָׁמַיִם וָאָרֶץ. אַל יִתֵּן לַמּוֹט רַגְלֶךָ, אַל יָנוּם שֹׁמְרֶךָ. הִנֵּה לֹא יָנוּם וְלֹא יִישָׁן, שׁוֹמֵר יִשְׂרָאֵל. יהוה שֹׁמְרֶךָ, יהוה צִלְּךָ עַל יַד יְמִינֶךָ. יוֹמָם הַשֶּׁמֶשׁ לֹא יַכֶּכָּה, וְיָרֵחַ בַּלָּיְלָה. יהוה יִשְׁמָרְךָ מִכָּל רָע, יִשְׁמֹר אֶת נַפְשֶׁךָ. יהוה יִשְׁמָר צֵאתְךָ וּבוֹאֶךָ, מֵעַתָּה וְעַד עוֹלָם.

קכב שִׁיר הַמַּעֲלוֹת לְדָוִד שָׂמַחְתִּי בְּאֹמְרִים לִי, בֵּית יהוה נֵלֵךְ. עֹמְדוֹת הָיוּ רַגְלֵינוּ, בִּשְׁעָרַיִךְ יְרוּשָׁלָ͏ִם. יְרוּשָׁלַיִם הַבְּנוּיָה, כְּעִיר שֶׁחֻבְּרָה לָּהּ יַחְדָּו. שֶׁשָּׁם עָלוּ שְׁבָטִים, שִׁבְטֵי יָהּ, עֵדוּת לְיִשְׂרָאֵל, לְהֹדוֹת לְשֵׁם יהוה. כִּי שָׁמָּה יָשְׁבוּ כִסְאוֹת לְמִשְׁפָּט, כִּסְאוֹת לְבֵית דָּוִד. שַׁאֲלוּ שְׁלוֹם יְרוּשָׁלָ͏ִם, יִשְׁלָיוּ אֹהֲבָיִךְ. יְהִי שָׁלוֹם בְּחֵילֵךְ, שַׁלְוָה בְּאַרְמְנוֹתָיִךְ. לְמַעַן אַחַי וְרֵעָי, אֲדַבְּרָה נָּא שָׁלוֹם בָּךְ. לְמַעַן בֵּית יהוה אֱלֹהֵינוּ, אֲבַקְשָׁה טוֹב לָךְ.

קכג שִׁיר הַמַּעֲלוֹת אֵלֶיךָ נָשָׂאתִי אֶת עֵינַי, הַיֹּשְׁבִי בַּשָּׁמָיִם. הִנֵּה כְעֵינֵי עֲבָדִים אֶל יַד אֲדוֹנֵיהֶם, כְּעֵינֵי שִׁפְחָה אֶל יַד גְּבִרְתָּהּ; כֵּן עֵינֵינוּ אֶל יהוה אֱלֹהֵינוּ, עַד שֶׁיְּחָנֵּנוּ. חָנֵּנוּ יהוה חָנֵּנוּ, כִּי רַב שָׂבַעְנוּ בוּז. רַבַּת שָׂבְעָה לָּהּ נַפְשֵׁנוּ, הַלַּעַג הַשַּׁאֲנַנִּים, הַבּוּז לִגְאֵי יוֹנִים.

קכד שִׁיר הַמַּעֲלוֹת לְדָוִד לוּלֵי יהוה שֶׁהָיָה לָנוּ, יֹאמַר נָא יִשְׂרָאֵל. לוּלֵי יהוה שֶׁהָיָה לָנוּ, בְּקוּם עָלֵינוּ אָדָם. אֲזַי חַיִּים בְּלָעוּנוּ, בַּחֲרוֹת אַפָּם בָּנוּ. אֲזַי הַמַּיִם שְׁטָפוּנוּ, נַחְלָה עָבַר עַל נַפְשֵׁנוּ. אֲזַי עָבַר עַל נַפְשֵׁנוּ, הַמַּיִם הַזֵּידוֹנִים. בָּרוּךְ יהוה, שֶׁלֹּא נְתָנָנוּ טֶרֶף לְשִׁנֵּיהֶם. נַפְשֵׁנוּ כְּצִפּוֹר נִמְלְטָה מִפַּח יוֹקְשִׁים; הַפַּח נִשְׁבָּר וַאֲנַחְנוּ נִמְלָטְנוּ. עֶזְרֵנוּ בְּשֵׁם יהוה, עֹשֵׂה שָׁמַיִם וָאָרֶץ.

קכה שִׁיר הַמַּעֲלוֹת הַבֹּטְחִים בַּיהוה, כְּהַר צִיּוֹן לֹא יִמּוֹט, לְעוֹלָם יֵשֵׁב. יְרוּשָׁלַיִם הָרִים סָבִיב לָהּ; וַיהוה סָבִיב לְעַמּוֹ, מֵעַתָּה וְעַד עוֹלָם. כִּי לֹא יָנוּחַ שֵׁבֶט הָרֶשַׁע עַל גּוֹרַל הַצַּדִּיקִים, לְמַעַן לֹא יִשְׁלְחוּ הַצַּדִּיקִים בְּעַוְלָתָה יְדֵיהֶם. הֵיטִיבָה יהוה לַטּוֹבִים, וְלִישָׁרִים בְּלִבּוֹתָם. וְהַמַּטִּים עֲקַלְקַלּוֹתָם, יוֹלִיכֵם יהוה אֶת פֹּעֲלֵי הָאָוֶן, שָׁלוֹם עַל יִשְׂרָאֵל.

קכו שִׁיר הַמַּעֲלוֹת בְּשׁוּב יהוה אֶת שִׁיבַת צִיּוֹן, הָיִינוּ כְּחֹלְמִים. אָז יִמָּלֵא שְׂחוֹק פִּינוּ, וּלְשׁוֹנֵנוּ רִנָּה; אָז יֹאמְרוּ בַגּוֹיִם, הִגְדִּיל יהוה לַעֲשׂוֹת עִם אֵלֶּה. הִגְדִּיל יהוה לַעֲשׂוֹת עִמָּנוּ, הָיִינוּ שְׂמֵחִים. שׁוּבָה יהוה אֶת שְׁבִיתֵנוּ, כַּאֲפִיקִים בַּנֶּגֶב. הַזֹּרְעִים בְּדִמְעָה, בְּרִנָּה יִקְצֹרוּ. הָלוֹךְ יֵלֵךְ וּבָכֹה נֹשֵׂא מֶשֶׁךְ הַזָּרַע; בֹּא יָבֹא בְרִנָּה, נֹשֵׂא אֲלֻמֹּתָיו.

קכז שִׁיר הַמַּעֲלוֹת לִשְׁלֹמֹה אִם יהוה לֹא יִבְנֶה בַיִת, שָׁוְא עָמְלוּ בוֹנָיו בּוֹ; אִם יהוה לֹא יִשְׁמָר עִיר, שָׁוְא שָׁקַד שׁוֹמֵר. שָׁוְא לָכֶם מַשְׁכִּימֵי קוּם, מְאַחֲרֵי שֶׁבֶת, אֹכְלֵי לֶחֶם הָעֲצָבִים, כֵּן יִתֵּן לִידִידוֹ שֵׁנָא. הִנֵּה נַחֲלַת יהוה בָּנִים, שָׂכָר פְּרִי הַבָּטֶן. כְּחִצִּים בְּיַד גִּבּוֹר, כֵּן בְּנֵי הַנְּעוּרִים. אַשְׁרֵי הַגֶּבֶר אֲשֶׁר מִלֵּא אֶת אַשְׁפָּתוֹ מֵהֶם; לֹא יֵבֹשׁוּ, כִּי יְדַבְּרוּ אֶת אוֹיְבִים בַּשָּׁעַר.

קכח שִׁיר הַמַּעֲלוֹת; אַשְׁרֵי כָּל יְרֵא יהוה, הַהֹלֵךְ בִּדְרָכָיו. יְגִיעַ כַּפֶּיךָ כִּי תֹאכֵל, אַשְׁרֶיךָ וְטוֹב לָךְ. אֶשְׁתְּךָ כְּגֶפֶן פֹּרִיָּה בְּיַרְכְּתֵי בֵיתֶךָ; בָּנֶיךָ כִּשְׁתִלֵי זֵיתִים סָבִיב לְשֻׁלְחָנֶךָ. הִנֵּה כִי כֵן יְבֹרַךְ גָּבֶר יְרֵא יהוה. יְבָרֶכְךָ יהוה מִצִּיּוֹן, וּרְאֵה בְּטוּב יְרוּשָׁלָ͏ִם כֹּל יְמֵי חַיֶּיךָ. וּרְאֵה בָנִים לְבָנֶיךָ, שָׁלוֹם עַל יִשְׂרָאֵל.

קכט שִׁיר הַמַּעֲלוֹת; רַבַּת צְרָרוּנִי מִנְּעוּרַי, יֹאמַר נָא יִשְׂרָאֵל. רַבַּת צְרָרוּנִי מִנְּעוּרָי, גַּם לֹא יָכְלוּ לִי. עַל גַּבִּי חָרְשׁוּ חֹרְשִׁים, הֶאֱרִיכוּ לְמַעֲנִיתָם. יהוה צַדִּיק, קִצֵּץ עֲבוֹת רְשָׁעִים. יֵבֹשׁוּ וְיִסֹּגוּ אָחוֹר, כֹּל שֹׂנְאֵי צִיּוֹן. יִהְיוּ כַּחֲצִיר גַּגּוֹת, שֶׁקַּדְמַת שָׁלַף יָבֵשׁ. שֶׁלֹּא מִלֵּא כַפּוֹ קוֹצֵר, וְחִצְנוֹ מְעַמֵּר. וְלֹא אָמְרוּ הָעֹבְרִים: בִּרְכַּת יהוה אֲלֵיכֶם, בֵּרַכְנוּ אֶתְכֶם בְּשֵׁם יהוה.

קל שִׁיר הַמַּעֲלוֹת; מִמַּעֲמַקִּים קְרָאתִיךָ, יהוה. אֲדֹנָי, שִׁמְעָה בְקוֹלִי, תִּהְיֶינָה אָזְנֶיךָ קַשֻּׁבוֹת לְקוֹל תַּחֲנוּנָי. אִם עֲוֹנוֹת תִּשְׁמָר, יָהּ; אֲדֹנָי, מִי יַעֲמֹד. כִּי עִמְּךָ הַסְּלִיחָה, לְמַעַן תִּוָּרֵא. קִוִּיתִי יהוה, קִוְּתָה נַפְשִׁי, וְלִדְבָרוֹ הוֹחָלְתִּי. נַפְשִׁי לַאדֹנָי, מִשֹּׁמְרִים לַבֹּקֶר, שֹׁמְרִים לַבֹּקֶר. יַחֵל יִשְׂרָאֵל אֶל יהוה; כִּי עִם יהוה הַחֶסֶד, וְהַרְבֵּה עִמּוֹ פְדוּת. וְהוּא יִפְדֶּה אֶת יִשְׂרָאֵל, מִכֹּל עֲוֹנוֹתָיו.

קלא שִׁיר הַמַּעֲלוֹת לְדָוִד; יהוה | לֹא גָבַהּ לִבִּי, וְלֹא רָמוּ עֵינַי, וְלֹא הִלַּכְתִּי בִּגְדֹלוֹת וּבְנִפְלָאוֹת מִמֶּנִּי. אִם לֹא שִׁוִּיתִי וְדוֹמַמְתִּי נַפְשִׁי; כְּגָמֻל עֲלֵי אִמּוֹ, כַּגָּמֻל עָלַי נַפְשִׁי. יַחֵל יִשְׂרָאֵל אֶל יהוה, מֵעַתָּה וְעַד עוֹלָם.

קלב שִׁיר הַמַּעֲלוֹת; זְכוֹר יהוה לְדָוִד, אֵת כָּל עֻנּוֹתוֹ. אֲשֶׁר נִשְׁבַּע לַיהוה, נָדַר לַאֲבִיר יַעֲקֹב. אִם אָבֹא בְּאֹהֶל בֵּיתִי, אִם אֶעֱלֶה עַל עֶרֶשׂ יְצוּעָי.

אִם אֶתֵּן שְׁנַת לְעֵינָי, לְעַפְעַפַּי תְּנוּמָה. עַד אֶמְצָא מָקוֹם לַיהוה, מִשְׁכָּנוֹת לַאֲבִיר יַעֲקֹב. הִנֵּה שְׁמַעֲנוּהָ בְאֶפְרָתָה, מְצָאנוּהָ בִּשְׂדֵי יָעַר. נָבוֹאָה לְמִשְׁכְּנוֹתָיו, נִשְׁתַּחֲוֶה לַהֲדֹם רַגְלָיו. קוּמָה יהוה לִמְנוּחָתֶךָ, אַתָּה וַאֲרוֹן עֻזֶּךָ. כֹּהֲנֶיךָ יִלְבְּשׁוּ צֶדֶק, וַחֲסִידֶיךָ יְרַנֵּנוּ. בַּעֲבוּר דָּוִד עַבְדֶּךָ, אַל תָּשֵׁב פְּנֵי מְשִׁיחֶךָ. נִשְׁבַּע יהוה לְדָוִד, אֱמֶת לֹא יָשׁוּב מִמֶּנָּה: מִפְּרִי בִטְנְךָ אָשִׁית לְכִסֵּא לָךְ. אִם יִשְׁמְרוּ בָנֶיךָ בְּרִיתִי, וְעֵדֹתִי זוֹ אֲלַמְּדֵם; גַּם בְּנֵיהֶם עֲדֵי עַד, יֵשְׁבוּ לְכִסֵּא לָךְ. כִּי בָחַר יהוה בְּצִיּוֹן, אִוָּהּ לְמוֹשָׁב לוֹ. זֹאת מְנוּחָתִי עֲדֵי עַד, פֹּה אֵשֵׁב כִּי אִוִּתִיהָ. צֵידָהּ בָּרֵךְ אֲבָרֵךְ, אֶבְיוֹנֶיהָ אַשְׂבִּיעַ לָחֶם. וְכֹהֲנֶיהָ אַלְבִּישׁ יֶשַׁע, וַחֲסִידֶיהָ רַנֵּן יְרַנֵּנוּ. שָׁם אַצְמִיחַ קֶרֶן לְדָוִד, עָרַכְתִּי נֵר לִמְשִׁיחִי. אוֹיְבָיו אַלְבִּישׁ בֹּשֶׁת, וְעָלָיו יָצִיץ נִזְרוֹ.

קלג שִׁיר הַמַּעֲלוֹת לְדָוִד; הִנֵּה מַה טּוֹב וּמַה נָּעִים, שֶׁבֶת אַחִים גַּם יָחַד. כַּשֶּׁמֶן הַטּוֹב עַל הָרֹאשׁ, יֹרֵד עַל הַזָּקָן, זְקַן אַהֲרֹן, שֶׁיֹּרֵד עַל פִּי מִדּוֹתָיו. כְּטַל חֶרְמוֹן שֶׁיֹּרֵד עַל הַרְרֵי צִיּוֹן; כִּי שָׁם צִוָּה יהוה אֶת הַבְּרָכָה, חַיִּים עַד הָעוֹלָם.

קלד שִׁיר הַמַּעֲלוֹת; הִנֵּה בָּרְכוּ אֶת יהוה כָּל עַבְדֵי יהוה, הָעֹמְדִים בְּבֵית יהוה בַּלֵּילוֹת. שְׂאוּ יְדֵכֶם קֹדֶשׁ, וּבָרְכוּ אֶת יהוה. יְבָרֶכְךָ יהוה מִצִּיּוֹן, עֹשֵׂה שָׁמַיִם וָאָרֶץ.

יום כ"ח לחודש — DAY 28

קלה הַלְלוּיָהּ; הַלְלוּ אֶת שֵׁם יהוה, הַלְלוּ עַבְדֵי יהוה. שֶׁעֹמְדִים בְּבֵית יהוה, בְּחַצְרוֹת בֵּית אֱלֹהֵינוּ. הַלְלוּיָהּ, כִּי טוֹב יהוה, זַמְּרוּ לִשְׁמוֹ כִּי נָעִים. כִּי יַעֲקֹב בָּחַר לוֹ יָהּ, יִשְׂרָאֵל לִסְגֻלָּתוֹ. כִּי אֲנִי יָדַעְתִּי כִּי גָדוֹל יהוה, וַאֲדֹנֵינוּ מִכָּל אֱלֹהִים. כֹּל אֲשֶׁר חָפֵץ יהוה עָשָׂה; בַּשָּׁמַיִם וּבָאָרֶץ, בַּיַּמִּים וְכָל

תְּהֹמוֹת. מַעֲלֶה נְשִׂאִים מִקְצֵה הָאָרֶץ; בְּרָקִים לַמָּטָר עָשָׂה, מוֹצֵא רוּחַ מֵאוֹצְרוֹתָיו. שֶׁהִכָּה בְּכוֹרֵי מִצְרָיִם, מֵאָדָם עַד בְּהֵמָה. שָׁלַח אוֹתֹת וּמֹפְתִים בְּתוֹכֵכִי מִצְרָיִם, בְּפַרְעֹה וּבְכָל עֲבָדָיו. שֶׁהִכָּה גּוֹיִם רַבִּים, וְהָרַג מְלָכִים עֲצוּמִים. לְסִיחוֹן מֶלֶךְ הָאֱמֹרִי, וּלְעוֹג מֶלֶךְ הַבָּשָׁן, וּלְכֹל מַמְלְכוֹת כְּנָעַן. וְנָתַן אַרְצָם נַחֲלָה, נַחֲלָה לְיִשְׂרָאֵל עַמּוֹ. יהוה, שִׁמְךָ לְעוֹלָם; יהוה, זִכְרְךָ לְדֹר וָדֹר. כִּי יָדִין יהוה עַמּוֹ, וְעַל עֲבָדָיו יִתְנֶחָם. עֲצַבֵּי הַגּוֹיִם כֶּסֶף וְזָהָב, מַעֲשֵׂה יְדֵי אָדָם. פֶּה לָהֶם וְלֹא יְדַבֵּרוּ, עֵינַיִם לָהֶם וְלֹא יִרְאוּ. אָזְנַיִם לָהֶם וְלֹא יַאֲזִינוּ, אַף אֵין יֶשׁ רוּחַ בְּפִיהֶם. כְּמוֹהֶם יִהְיוּ עֹשֵׂיהֶם, כֹּל אֲשֶׁר בֹּטֵחַ בָּהֶם. בֵּית יִשְׂרָאֵל בָּרְכוּ אֶת יהוה, בֵּית אַהֲרֹן בָּרְכוּ אֶת יהוה. בֵּית הַלֵּוִי בָּרְכוּ אֶת יהוה, יִרְאֵי יהוה בָּרְכוּ אֶת יהוה. בָּרוּךְ יהוה מִצִּיּוֹן, שֹׁכֵן יְרוּשָׁלָיִם; הַלְלוּיָהּ.

קלו הוֹדוּ לַיהוה כִּי טוֹב, כִּי לְעוֹלָם חַסְדּוֹ. הוֹדוּ לֵאלֹהֵי הָאֱלֹהִים, כִּי לְעוֹלָם חַסְדּוֹ. הוֹדוּ לַאֲדֹנֵי הָאֲדֹנִים, כִּי לְעוֹלָם חַסְדּוֹ. לְעֹשֵׂה נִפְלָאוֹת גְּדֹלוֹת לְבַדּוֹ, כִּי לְעוֹלָם חַסְדּוֹ. לְעֹשֵׂה הַשָּׁמַיִם בִּתְבוּנָה, כִּי לְעוֹלָם חַסְדּוֹ. לְרֹקַע הָאָרֶץ עַל הַמָּיִם, כִּי לְעוֹלָם חַסְדּוֹ. לְעֹשֵׂה אוֹרִים גְּדֹלִים, כִּי לְעוֹלָם חַסְדּוֹ. אֶת הַשֶּׁמֶשׁ לְמֶמְשֶׁלֶת בַּיּוֹם, כִּי לְעוֹלָם חַסְדּוֹ. אֶת הַיָּרֵחַ וְכוֹכָבִים לְמֶמְשְׁלוֹת בַּלָּיְלָה, כִּי לְעוֹלָם חַסְדּוֹ. לְמַכֵּה מִצְרַיִם בִּבְכוֹרֵיהֶם, כִּי לְעוֹלָם חַסְדּוֹ. וַיּוֹצֵא יִשְׂרָאֵל מִתּוֹכָם, כִּי לְעוֹלָם חַסְדּוֹ. בְּיָד חֲזָקָה וּבִזְרוֹעַ נְטוּיָה, כִּי לְעוֹלָם חַסְדּוֹ. לְגֹזֵר יַם סוּף לִגְזָרִים, כִּי לְעוֹלָם חַסְדּוֹ. וְהֶעֱבִיר יִשְׂרָאֵל בְּתוֹכוֹ, כִּי לְעוֹלָם חַסְדּוֹ. וְנִעֵר פַּרְעֹה וְחֵילוֹ בְיַם סוּף, כִּי לְעוֹלָם חַסְדּוֹ. לְמוֹלִיךְ עַמּוֹ בַּמִּדְבָּר, כִּי לְעוֹלָם חַסְדּוֹ. לְמַכֵּה מְלָכִים גְּדֹלִים, כִּי לְעוֹלָם

חַסְדּוֹ. וַיַּהֲרֹג מְלָכִים אַדִּירִים, כִּי לְעוֹלָם חַסְדּוֹ. לְסִיחוֹן מֶלֶךְ הָאֱמֹרִי, כִּי לְעוֹלָם חַסְדּוֹ. וּלְעוֹג מֶלֶךְ הַבָּשָׁן, כִּי לְעוֹלָם חַסְדּוֹ. וְנָתַן אַרְצָם לְנַחֲלָה, כִּי לְעוֹלָם חַסְדּוֹ. נַחֲלָה לְיִשְׂרָאֵל עַבְדּוֹ, כִּי לְעוֹלָם חַסְדּוֹ. שֶׁבְּשִׁפְלֵנוּ זָכַר לָנוּ, כִּי לְעוֹלָם חַסְדּוֹ. וַיִּפְרְקֵנוּ מִצָּרֵינוּ, כִּי לְעוֹלָם חַסְדּוֹ. נֹתֵן לֶחֶם לְכָל בָּשָׂר, כִּי לְעוֹלָם חַסְדּוֹ. הוֹדוּ לְאֵל הַשָּׁמָיִם, כִּי לְעוֹלָם חַסְדּוֹ.

קלז עַל נַהֲרוֹת בָּבֶל, שָׁם יָשַׁבְנוּ, גַּם בָּכִינוּ, בְּזָכְרֵנוּ אֶת צִיּוֹן. עַל עֲרָבִים בְּתוֹכָהּ, תָּלִינוּ כִּנֹּרוֹתֵינוּ. כִּי שָׁם שְׁאֵלוּנוּ שׁוֹבֵינוּ דִּבְרֵי שִׁיר וְתוֹלָלֵינוּ שִׂמְחָה, שִׁירוּ לָנוּ מִשִּׁיר צִיּוֹן. אֵיךְ נָשִׁיר אֶת שִׁיר יהוה, עַל אַדְמַת נֵכָר. אִם אֶשְׁכָּחֵךְ יְרוּשָׁלָיִם, תִּשְׁכַּח יְמִינִי. תִּדְבַּק לְשׁוֹנִי לְחִכִּי, אִם לֹא אֶזְכְּרֵכִי; אִם לֹא אַעֲלֶה אֶת יְרוּשָׁלַיִם עַל רֹאשׁ שִׂמְחָתִי. זְכֹר יהוה לִבְנֵי אֱדוֹם אֵת יוֹם יְרוּשָׁלָיִם; הָאֹמְרִים עָרוּ עָרוּ, עַד הַיְסוֹד בָּהּ. בַּת בָּבֶל הַשְּׁדוּדָה, אַשְׁרֵי שֶׁיְשַׁלֶּם לָךְ אֶת גְּמוּלֵךְ שֶׁגָּמַלְתְּ לָנוּ. אַשְׁרֵי שֶׁיֹּאחֵז וְנִפֵּץ אֶת עֹלָלַיִךְ אֶל הַסָּלַע.

קלח לְדָוִד; אוֹדְךָ בְכָל לִבִּי, נֶגֶד אֱלֹהִים אֲזַמְּרֶךָּ. אֶשְׁתַּחֲוֶה אֶל הֵיכַל קָדְשְׁךָ וְאוֹדֶה אֶת שְׁמֶךָ, עַל חַסְדְּךָ וְעַל אֲמִתֶּךָ; כִּי הִגְדַּלְתָּ עַל כָּל שִׁמְךָ אִמְרָתֶךָ. בְּיוֹם קָרָאתִי וַתַּעֲנֵנִי, תַּרְהִבֵנִי בְנַפְשִׁי עֹז. יוֹדוּךָ יהוה כָּל מַלְכֵי אָרֶץ, כִּי שָׁמְעוּ אִמְרֵי פִיךָ. וְיָשִׁירוּ בְּדַרְכֵי יהוה, כִּי גָדוֹל כְּבוֹד יהוה. כִּי רָם יהוה, וְשָׁפָל יִרְאֶה, וְגָבֹהַּ מִמֶּרְחָק יְיֵדָע. אִם אֵלֵךְ בְּקֶרֶב צָרָה, תְּחַיֵּנִי; עַל אַף אֹיְבַי תִּשְׁלַח יָדֶךָ, וְתוֹשִׁיעֵנִי יְמִינֶךָ. יהוה יִגְמֹר בַּעֲדִי; יהוה, חַסְדְּךָ לְעוֹלָם, מַעֲשֵׂי יָדֶיךָ אַל תֶּרֶף.

קלט לַמְנַצֵּחַ לְדָוִד מִזְמוֹר; יהוה, חֲקַרְתַּנִי וַתֵּדָע. אַתָּה יָדַעְתָּ

שַׁבְתִּי וְקוּמִי, בַּנְתָּה לְרֵעִי מֵרָחוֹק. אָרְחִי וְרִבְעִי זֵרִיתָ, וְכָל דְּרָכַי הִסְכַּנְתָּה. כִּי אֵין מִלָּה בִּלְשׁוֹנִי, הֵן יהוה יָדַעְתָּ כֻלָּהּ. אָחוֹר וָקֶדֶם צַרְתָּנִי, וַתָּשֶׁת עָלַי כַּפֶּכָה. פְּלִיאָה דַעַת מִמֶּנִּי, נִשְׂגְּבָה לֹא אוּכַל לָהּ. אָנָה אֵלֵךְ מֵרוּחֶךָ, וְאָנָה מִפָּנֶיךָ אֶבְרָח. אִם אֶסַּק שָׁמַיִם שָׁם אָתָּה, וְאַצִּיעָה שְּׁאוֹל הִנֶּךָ. אֶשָּׂא כַנְפֵי שָׁחַר, אֶשְׁכְּנָה בְּאַחֲרִית יָם. גַּם שָׁם יָדְךָ תַנְחֵנִי, וְתֹאחֲזֵנִי יְמִינֶךָ. וָאֹמַר: אַךְ חֹשֶׁךְ יְשׁוּפֵנִי, וְלַיְלָה אוֹר בַּעֲדֵנִי. גַּם חֹשֶׁךְ לֹא יַחְשִׁיךְ מִמֶּךָ; וְלַיְלָה כַּיּוֹם יָאִיר, כַּחֲשֵׁיכָה כָּאוֹרָה. כִּי אַתָּה קָנִיתָ כִלְיֹתָי, תְּסֻכֵּנִי בְּבֶטֶן אִמִּי. אוֹדְךָ עַל כִּי נוֹרָאוֹת נִפְלֵיתִי; נִפְלָאִים מַעֲשֶׂיךָ, וְנַפְשִׁי יֹדַעַת מְאֹד. לֹא נִכְחַד עָצְמִי מִמֶּךָ; אֲשֶׁר עֻשֵּׂיתִי בַסֵּתֶר, רֻקַּמְתִּי בְּתַחְתִּיּוֹת אָרֶץ. גָּלְמִי רָאוּ עֵינֶיךָ, וְעַל סִפְרְךָ כֻּלָּם יִכָּתֵבוּ; יָמִים יֻצָּרוּ, וְלוֹ אֶחָד בָּהֶם. וְלִי מַה יָּקְרוּ רֵעֶיךָ, אֵל; מֶה עָצְמוּ רָאשֵׁיהֶם. אֶסְפְּרֵם, מֵחוֹל יִרְבּוּן; הֱקִיצֹתִי וְעוֹדִי עִמָּךְ. אִם תִּקְטֹל אֱלוֹהַּ | רָשָׁע, וְאַנְשֵׁי דָמִים סוּרוּ מֶנִּי. אֲשֶׁר יֹאמְרֻךָ לִמְזִמָּה, נָשֻׂא לַשָּׁוְא עָרֶיךָ. הֲלוֹא מְשַׂנְאֶיךָ יהוה | אֶשְׂנָא, וּבִתְקוֹמְמֶיךָ אֶתְקוֹטָט. תַּכְלִית שִׂנְאָה שְׂנֵאתִים, לְאוֹיְבִים הָיוּ לִי. חָקְרֵנִי אֵל וְדַע לְבָבִי, בְּחָנֵנִי וְדַע שַׂרְעַפָּי. וּרְאֵה אִם דֶּרֶךְ עֹצֶב בִּי, וּנְחֵנִי בְּדֶרֶךְ עוֹלָם.

יום כ"ט לחודש — DAY 29

קם לַמְנַצֵּחַ מִזְמוֹר לְדָוִד. חַלְּצֵנִי יהוה מֵאָדָם רָע, מֵאִישׁ חֲמָסִים תִּנְצְרֵנִי. אֲשֶׁר חָשְׁבוּ רָעוֹת בְּלֵב, כָּל יוֹם יָגוּרוּ מִלְחָמוֹת. שָׁנְנוּ לְשׁוֹנָם כְּמוֹ נָחָשׁ, חֲמַת עַכְשׁוּב תַּחַת שְׂפָתֵימוֹ סֶלָה. שָׁמְרֵנִי יהוה | מִידֵי רָשָׁע, מֵאִישׁ חֲמָסִים תִּנְצְרֵנִי, אֲשֶׁר חָשְׁבוּ לִדְחוֹת פְּעָמָי. טָמְנוּ גֵאִים פַּח לִי וַחֲבָלִים, פָּרְשׂוּ רֶשֶׁת לְיַד מַעְגָּל, מֹקְשִׁים שָׁתוּ לִי סֶלָה. אָמַרְתִּי לַיהוה: אֵלִי אָתָּה, הַאֲזִינָה יהוה קוֹל תַּחֲנוּנָי. יְהוִה אֲדֹנָי עֹז יְשׁוּעָתִי, סַכֹּתָה לְרֹאשִׁי בְּיוֹם נָשֶׁק. אַל תִּתֵּן יהוה מַאֲוַיֵּי רָשָׁע, זְמָמוֹ אַל תָּפֵק יָרוּמוּ סֶלָה. רֹאשׁ מְסִבָּי, עֲמַל שְׂפָתֵימוֹ יְכַסֵּמוֹ. יִמּוֹטוּ עֲלֵיהֶם גֶּחָלִים, בָּאֵשׁ יַפִּלֵם, בְּמַהֲמֹרוֹת בַּל יָקוּמוּ. אִישׁ לָשׁוֹן בַּל יִכּוֹן בָּאָרֶץ; אִישׁ חָמָס רָע, יְצוּדֶנּוּ לְמַדְחֵפֹת. יָדַעְתִּי כִּי יַעֲשֶׂה יהוה דִּין עָנִי, מִשְׁפַּט אֶבְיֹנִים. אַךְ צַדִּיקִים יוֹדוּ לִשְׁמֶךָ, יֵשְׁבוּ יְשָׁרִים אֶת פָּנֶיךָ.

קמא מִזְמוֹר לְדָוִד; יהוה, קְרָאתִיךָ, חוּשָׁה לִי, הַאֲזִינָה קוֹלִי בְּקָרְאִי לָךְ. תִּכּוֹן תְּפִלָּתִי קְטֹרֶת לְפָנֶיךָ, מַשְׂאַת כַּפַּי מִנְחַת עָרֶב. שִׁיתָה יהוה שָׁמְרָה לְפִי, נִצְרָה עַל דַּל שְׂפָתָי. אַל תַּט לִבִּי לְדָבָר רָע, לְהִתְעוֹלֵל עֲלִלוֹת בְּרֶשַׁע אֶת אִישִׁים פֹּעֲלֵי אָוֶן, וּבַל אֶלְחַם בְּמַנְעַמֵּיהֶם. יֶהֶלְמֵנִי צַדִּיק חֶסֶד וְיוֹכִיחֵנִי, שֶׁמֶן רֹאשׁ אַל יָנִי רֹאשִׁי, כִּי עוֹד וּתְפִלָּתִי בְּרָעוֹתֵיהֶם. נִשְׁמְטוּ בִידֵי סֶלַע שֹׁפְטֵיהֶם, וְשָׁמְעוּ אֲמָרַי כִּי נָעֵמוּ. כְּמוֹ פֹלֵחַ וּבֹקֵעַ בָּאָרֶץ, נִפְזְרוּ עֲצָמֵינוּ לְפִי שְׁאוֹל. כִּי אֵלֶיךָ יְהוִה אֲדֹנָי עֵינָי, בְּכָה חָסִיתִי אַל תְּעַר נַפְשִׁי. שָׁמְרֵנִי מִידֵי פַח יָקְשׁוּ לִי, וּמֹקְשׁוֹת פֹּעֲלֵי אָוֶן. יִפְּלוּ בְמַכְמֹרָיו רְשָׁעִים יַחַד אָנֹכִי עַד אֶעֱבוֹר.

קמב מַשְׂכִּיל לְדָוִד, בִּהְיוֹתוֹ בַמְּעָרָה תְפִלָּה. קוֹלִי אֶל יהוה אֶזְעָק, קוֹלִי אֶל יהוה אֶתְחַנָּן. אֶשְׁפֹּךְ לְפָנָיו שִׂיחִי, צָרָתִי לְפָנָיו אַגִּיד. בְּהִתְעַטֵּף עָלַי רוּחִי, וְאַתָּה יָדַעְתָּ נְתִיבָתִי; בְּאֹרַח זוּ אֲהַלֵּךְ טָמְנוּ פַח לִי. הַבֵּיט יָמִין וּרְאֵה וְאֵין לִי מַכִּיר; אָבַד מָנוֹס מִמֶּנִּי, אֵין דּוֹרֵשׁ לְנַפְשִׁי. זָעַקְתִּי אֵלֶיךָ יהוה; אָמַרְתִּי אַתָּה מַחְסִי, חֶלְקִי בְּאֶרֶץ הַחַיִּים. הַקְשִׁיבָה אֶל רִנָּתִי כִּי דַלּוֹתִי

מְאֹד, הַצִּילֵנִי מֵרֹדְפַי כִּי אָמְצוּ מִמֶּנִּי. הוֹצִיאָה מִמַּסְגֵּר נַפְשִׁי, לְהוֹדוֹת אֶת שְׁמֶךָ; בִּי יַכְתִּרוּ צַדִּיקִים, כִּי תִגְמֹל עָלָי.

קמג מִזְמוֹר לְדָוִד; יהוה | שְׁמַע תְּפִלָּתִי, הַאֲזִינָה אֶל תַּחֲנוּנַי, בֶּאֱמֻנָתְךָ עֲנֵנִי בְּצִדְקָתֶךָ. וְאַל תָּבוֹא בְמִשְׁפָּט אֶת עַבְדֶּךָ, כִּי לֹא יִצְדַּק לְפָנֶיךָ כָל חָי. כִּי רָדַף אוֹיֵב נַפְשִׁי, דִּכָּא לָאָרֶץ חַיָּתִי, הוֹשִׁיבַנִי בְמַחֲשַׁכִּים כְּמֵתֵי עוֹלָם. וַתִּתְעַטֵּף עָלַי רוּחִי, בְּתוֹכִי יִשְׁתּוֹמֵם לִבִּי. זָכַרְתִּי יָמִים מִקֶּדֶם, הָגִיתִי בְכָל פָּעֳלֶךָ, בְּמַעֲשֵׂה יָדֶיךָ אֲשׂוֹחֵחַ. פֵּרַשְׂתִּי יָדַי אֵלֶיךָ, נַפְשִׁי כְּאֶרֶץ עֲיֵפָה לְךָ סֶלָה. מַהֵר עֲנֵנִי יהוה, כָּלְתָה רוּחִי; אַל תַּסְתֵּר פָּנֶיךָ מִמֶּנִּי, וְנִמְשַׁלְתִּי עִם יֹרְדֵי בוֹר. הַשְׁמִיעֵנִי בַבֹּקֶר חַסְדֶּךָ, כִּי בְךָ בָטָחְתִּי; הוֹדִיעֵנִי דֶּרֶךְ זוּ אֵלֵךְ, כִּי אֵלֶיךָ נָשָׂאתִי נַפְשִׁי. הַצִּילֵנִי מֵאֹיְבַי | יהוה, אֵלֶיךָ כִסִּתִי. לַמְּדֵנִי לַעֲשׂוֹת רְצוֹנֶךָ כִּי אַתָּה אֱלוֹהָי; רוּחֲךָ טוֹבָה תַּנְחֵנִי בְּאֶרֶץ מִישׁוֹר. לְמַעַן שִׁמְךָ יהוה תְּחַיֵּנִי, בְּצִדְקָתְךָ תּוֹצִיא מִצָּרָה נַפְשִׁי. וּבְחַסְדְּךָ תַּצְמִית אֹיְבָי; וְהַאֲבַדְתָּ כָּל צֹרְרֵי נַפְשִׁי, כִּי אֲנִי עַבְדֶּךָ.

קמד לְדָוִד; בָּרוּךְ יהוה צוּרִי, הַמְלַמֵּד יָדַי לַקְרָב, אֶצְבְּעוֹתַי לַמִּלְחָמָה. חַסְדִּי וּמְצוּדָתִי מִשְׂגַּבִּי וּמְפַלְטִי לִי, מָגִנִּי וּבוֹ חָסִיתִי, הָרוֹדֵד עַמִּי תַחְתָּי. יהוה, מָה אָדָם וַתֵּדָעֵהוּ, בֶּן אֱנוֹשׁ וַתְּחַשְּׁבֵהוּ. אָדָם לַהֶבֶל דָּמָה, יָמָיו כְּצֵל עוֹבֵר. יהוה, הַט שָׁמֶיךָ וְתֵרֵד, גַּע בֶּהָרִים וְיֶעֱשָׁנוּ. בְּרוֹק בָּרָק וּתְפִיצֵם, שְׁלַח חִצֶּיךָ וּתְהֻמֵּם. שְׁלַח יָדֶיךָ מִמָּרוֹם; פְּצֵנִי וְהַצִּילֵנִי מִמַּיִם רַבִּים, מִיַּד בְּנֵי נֵכָר. אֲשֶׁר פִּיהֶם דִּבֶּר שָׁוְא, וִימִינָם יְמִין שָׁקֶר. אֱלֹהִים, שִׁיר חָדָשׁ אָשִׁירָה לָּךְ, בְּנֵבֶל עָשׂוֹר אֲזַמְּרָה לָּךְ. הַנּוֹתֵן תְּשׁוּעָה לַמְּלָכִים, הַפּוֹצֶה אֶת דָּוִד עַבְדּוֹ מֵחֶרֶב רָעָה. פְּצֵנִי וְהַצִּילֵנִי מִיַּד בְּנֵי

נֵכָר; אֲשֶׁר פִּיהֶם דִּבֶּר שָׁוְא, וִימִינָם יְמִין שָׁקֶר. אֲשֶׁר בָּנֵינוּ כִּנְטִעִים, מְגֻדָּלִים בִּנְעוּרֵיהֶם; בְּנוֹתֵינוּ כְזָוִיֹּת, מְחֻטָּבוֹת תַּבְנִית הֵיכָל. מְזָוֵינוּ מְלֵאִים, מְפִיקִים מִזַּן אֶל זַן; צֹאונֵנוּ מַאֲלִיפוֹת, מְרֻבָּבוֹת בְּחוּצוֹתֵינוּ. אַלּוּפֵינוּ מְסֻבָּלִים, אֵין פֶּרֶץ וְאֵין יוֹצֵאת, וְאֵין צְוָחָה בִּרְחֹבֹתֵינוּ. אַשְׁרֵי הָעָם שֶׁכָּכָה לּוֹ, אַשְׁרֵי הָעָם שֶׁיהוה אֱלֹהָיו.

— יום ל' לחודש / DAY 30 —

קמה תְּהִלָּה לְדָוִד; אֲרוֹמִמְךָ אֱלוֹהַי הַמֶּלֶךְ, וַאֲבָרְכָה שִׁמְךָ לְעוֹלָם וָעֶד. בְּכָל יוֹם אֲבָרְכֶךָּ, וַאֲהַלְלָה שִׁמְךָ לְעוֹלָם וָעֶד. גָּדוֹל יהוה וּמְהֻלָּל מְאֹד, וְלִגְדֻלָּתוֹ אֵין חֵקֶר. דּוֹר לְדוֹר יְשַׁבַּח מַעֲשֶׂיךָ, וּגְבוּרֹתֶיךָ יַגִּידוּ. הֲדַר כְּבוֹד הוֹדֶךָ, וְדִבְרֵי נִפְלְאֹתֶיךָ אָשִׂיחָה. וֶעֱזוּז נוֹרְאֹתֶיךָ יֹאמֵרוּ, וּגְדוּלָּתְךָ אֲסַפְּרֶנָּה. זֵכֶר רַב טוּבְךָ יַבִּיעוּ, וְצִדְקָתְךָ יְרַנֵּנוּ. חַנּוּן וְרַחוּם יהוה, אֶרֶךְ אַפַּיִם וּגְדָל חָסֶד. טוֹב יהוה לַכֹּל, וְרַחֲמָיו עַל כָּל מַעֲשָׂיו. יוֹדוּךָ יהוה כָּל מַעֲשֶׂיךָ, וַחֲסִידֶיךָ יְבָרְכוּכָה. כְּבוֹד מַלְכוּתְךָ יֹאמֵרוּ, וּגְבוּרָתְךָ יְדַבֵּרוּ. לְהוֹדִיעַ לִבְנֵי הָאָדָם גְּבוּרֹתָיו, וּכְבוֹד הֲדַר מַלְכוּתוֹ. מַלְכוּתְךָ מַלְכוּת כָּל עֹלָמִים, וּמֶמְשַׁלְתְּךָ בְּכָל דּוֹר וָדֹר. סוֹמֵךְ יהוה לְכָל הַנֹּפְלִים, וְזוֹקֵף לְכָל הַכְּפוּפִים. עֵינֵי כֹל אֵלֶיךָ יְשַׂבֵּרוּ, וְאַתָּה נוֹתֵן לָהֶם אֶת אָכְלָם בְּעִתּוֹ. פּוֹתֵחַ אֶת יָדֶךָ, וּמַשְׂבִּיעַ לְכָל חַי רָצוֹן. צַדִּיק יהוה בְּכָל דְּרָכָיו, וְחָסִיד בְּכָל מַעֲשָׂיו. קָרוֹב יהוה לְכָל קֹרְאָיו, לְכֹל אֲשֶׁר יִקְרָאֻהוּ בֶאֱמֶת. רְצוֹן יְרֵאָיו יַעֲשֶׂה, וְאֶת שַׁוְעָתָם יִשְׁמַע וְיוֹשִׁיעֵם. שׁוֹמֵר יהוה אֶת כָּל אֹהֲבָיו, וְאֵת כָּל הָרְשָׁעִים יַשְׁמִיד. תְּהִלַּת יהוה יְדַבֶּר פִּי, וִיבָרֵךְ כָּל בָּשָׂר שֵׁם קָדְשׁוֹ לְעוֹלָם וָעֶד.

קמו הַלְלוּיָהּ; הַלְלִי נַפְשִׁי אֶת יהוה.

אֲהַלְלָה יהוה בְּחַיָּי, אֲזַמְּרָה לֵאלֹהַי בְּעוֹדִי. אַל תִּבְטְחוּ בִנְדִיבִים, בְּבֶן אָדָם שֶׁאֵין לוֹ תְשׁוּעָה. תֵּצֵא רוּחוֹ יָשֻׁב לְאַדְמָתוֹ, בַּיּוֹם הַהוּא אָבְדוּ עֶשְׁתֹּנֹתָיו. אַשְׁרֵי שֶׁאֵל יַעֲקֹב בְּעֶזְרוֹ, שִׂבְרוֹ עַל יהוה אֱלֹהָיו. עֹשֶׂה שָׁמַיִם וָאָרֶץ, אֶת הַיָּם וְאֶת כָּל אֲשֶׁר בָּם; הַשֹּׁמֵר אֱמֶת לְעוֹלָם. עֹשֶׂה מִשְׁפָּט לַעֲשׁוּקִים, נֹתֵן לֶחֶם לָרְעֵבִים; יהוה מַתִּיר אֲסוּרִים. יהוה פֹּקֵחַ עִוְרִים, יהוה זֹקֵף כְּפוּפִים; יהוה אֹהֵב צַדִּיקִים. יהוה שֹׁמֵר אֶת גֵּרִים, יָתוֹם וְאַלְמָנָה יְעוֹדֵד; וְדֶרֶךְ רְשָׁעִים יְעַוֵּת. יִמְלֹךְ יהוה לְעוֹלָם, אֱלֹהַיִךְ צִיּוֹן לְדֹר וָדֹר; הַלְלוּיָהּ.

קמז הַלְלוּיָהּ; כִּי טוֹב זַמְּרָה אֱלֹהֵינוּ, כִּי נָעִים נָאוָה תְהִלָּה. בּוֹנֵה יְרוּשָׁלַיִם יהוה, נִדְחֵי יִשְׂרָאֵל יְכַנֵּס. הָרֹפֵא לִשְׁבוּרֵי לֵב, וּמְחַבֵּשׁ לְעַצְּבוֹתָם. מוֹנֶה מִסְפָּר לַכּוֹכָבִים, לְכֻלָּם שֵׁמוֹת יִקְרָא. גָּדוֹל אֲדוֹנֵינוּ וְרַב כֹּחַ, לִתְבוּנָתוֹ אֵין מִסְפָּר. מְעוֹדֵד עֲנָוִים יהוה, מַשְׁפִּיל רְשָׁעִים עֲדֵי אָרֶץ. עֱנוּ לַיהוה בְּתוֹדָה, זַמְּרוּ לֵאלֹהֵינוּ בְכִנּוֹר. הַמְכַסֶּה שָׁמַיִם בְּעָבִים, הַמֵּכִין לָאָרֶץ מָטָר; הַמַּצְמִיחַ הָרִים חָצִיר. נוֹתֵן לִבְהֵמָה לַחְמָהּ, לִבְנֵי עֹרֵב אֲשֶׁר יִקְרָאוּ. לֹא בִגְבוּרַת הַסּוּס יֶחְפָּץ, לֹא בְשׁוֹקֵי הָאִישׁ יִרְצֶה. רוֹצֶה יהוה אֶת יְרֵאָיו, אֶת הַמְיַחֲלִים לְחַסְדּוֹ. שַׁבְּחִי יְרוּשָׁלַיִם אֶת יהוה; הַלְלִי אֱלֹהַיִךְ, צִיּוֹן. כִּי חִזַּק בְּרִיחֵי שְׁעָרָיִךְ, בֵּרַךְ בָּנַיִךְ בְּקִרְבֵּךְ. הַשָּׂם גְּבוּלֵךְ שָׁלוֹם, חֵלֶב חִטִּים יַשְׂבִּיעֵךְ. הַשֹּׁלֵחַ אִמְרָתוֹ אָרֶץ, עַד מְהֵרָה יָרוּץ דְּבָרוֹ. הַנֹּתֵן שֶׁלֶג כַּצָּמֶר, כְּפוֹר כָּאֵפֶר יְפַזֵּר. מַשְׁלִיךְ קַרְחוֹ כְפִתִּים, לִפְנֵי קָרָתוֹ מִי יַעֲמֹד. יִשְׁלַח דְּבָרוֹ וְיַמְסֵם, יַשֵּׁב רוּחוֹ יִזְּלוּ מָיִם. מַגִּיד דְּבָרָיו לְיַעֲקֹב, חֻקָּיו וּמִשְׁפָּטָיו לְיִשְׂרָאֵל. לֹא עָשָׂה כֵן לְכָל גּוֹי, וּמִשְׁפָּטִים בַּל יְדָעוּם; הַלְלוּיָהּ.

קמח הַלְלוּיָהּ; הַלְלוּ אֶת יהוה מִן הַשָּׁמַיִם, הַלְלוּהוּ בַּמְּרוֹמִים. הַלְלוּהוּ כָל מַלְאָכָיו, הַלְלוּהוּ כָּל צְבָאָיו. הַלְלוּהוּ שֶׁמֶשׁ וְיָרֵחַ, הַלְלוּהוּ כָּל כּוֹכְבֵי אוֹר. הַלְלוּהוּ שְׁמֵי הַשָּׁמָיִם, וְהַמַּיִם אֲשֶׁר מֵעַל הַשָּׁמָיִם. יְהַלְלוּ אֶת שֵׁם יהוה, כִּי הוּא צִוָּה וְנִבְרָאוּ. וַיַּעֲמִידֵם לָעַד לְעוֹלָם, חָק נָתַן וְלֹא יַעֲבוֹר. הַלְלוּ אֶת יהוה מִן הָאָרֶץ, תַּנִּינִים וְכָל תְּהֹמוֹת. אֵשׁ וּבָרָד, שֶׁלֶג וְקִיטוֹר, רוּחַ סְעָרָה עֹשָׂה דְבָרוֹ. הֶהָרִים וְכָל גְּבָעוֹת, עֵץ פְּרִי וְכָל אֲרָזִים. הַחַיָּה וְכָל בְּהֵמָה, רֶמֶשׂ וְצִפּוֹר כָּנָף. מַלְכֵי אֶרֶץ וְכָל לְאֻמִּים, שָׂרִים וְכָל שֹׁפְטֵי אָרֶץ. בַּחוּרִים וְגַם בְּתוּלוֹת, זְקֵנִים עִם נְעָרִים. יְהַלְלוּ אֶת שֵׁם יהוה, כִּי נִשְׂגָּב שְׁמוֹ לְבַדּוֹ; הוֹדוֹ עַל אֶרֶץ וְשָׁמָיִם. וַיָּרֶם קֶרֶן לְעַמּוֹ, תְּהִלָּה לְכָל חֲסִידָיו, לִבְנֵי יִשְׂרָאֵל עַם קְרֹבוֹ; הַלְלוּיָהּ.

קמט הַלְלוּיָהּ; שִׁירוּ לַיהוה שִׁיר חָדָשׁ, תְּהִלָּתוֹ בִּקְהַל חֲסִידִים. יִשְׂמַח יִשְׂרָאֵל בְּעֹשָׂיו, בְּנֵי צִיּוֹן יָגִילוּ בְמַלְכָּם. יְהַלְלוּ שְׁמוֹ בְמָחוֹל, בְּתֹף וְכִנּוֹר יְזַמְּרוּ לוֹ. כִּי רוֹצֶה יהוה בְּעַמּוֹ, יְפָאֵר עֲנָוִים בִּישׁוּעָה. יַעְלְזוּ חֲסִידִים בְּכָבוֹד, יְרַנְּנוּ עַל מִשְׁכְּבוֹתָם. רוֹמְמוֹת אֵל בִּגְרוֹנָם, וְחֶרֶב פִּיפִיּוֹת בְּיָדָם. לַעֲשׂוֹת נְקָמָה בַּגּוֹיִם, תּוֹכֵחוֹת בַּלְאֻמִּים. לֶאְסֹר מַלְכֵיהֶם בְּזִקִּים, וְנִכְבְּדֵיהֶם בְּכַבְלֵי בַרְזֶל. לַעֲשׂוֹת בָּהֶם מִשְׁפָּט כָּתוּב, הָדָר הוּא לְכָל חֲסִידָיו; הַלְלוּיָהּ.

קנ הַלְלוּיָהּ; הַלְלוּ אֵל בְּקָדְשׁוֹ, הַלְלוּהוּ בִּרְקִיעַ עֻזּוֹ. הַלְלוּהוּ בִגְבוּרֹתָיו, הַלְלוּהוּ כְּרֹב גֻּדְלוֹ. הַלְלוּהוּ בְּתֵקַע שׁוֹפָר, הַלְלוּהוּ בְּנֵבֶל וְכִנּוֹר. הַלְלוּהוּ בְּתֹף וּמָחוֹל, הַלְלוּהוּ בְּמִנִּים וְעֻגָב. הַלְלוּהוּ בְּצִלְצְלֵי שָׁמַע, הַלְלוּהוּ בְּצִלְצְלֵי תְרוּעָה. כֹּל הַנְּשָׁמָה תְּהַלֵּל יָהּ; הַלְלוּיָהּ.

﴾ תפלה אחר אמירת תהלים ﴿
﴾ PRAYER AFTER RECITING TEHILLIM ﴿

מִי יִתֵּן מִצִּיּוֹן יְשׁוּעַת יִשְׂרָאֵל; בְּשׁוּב יהוה שְׁבוּת עַמּוֹ,

‹ of His ‹ the ‹ When Hashem ‹‹ of Israel! ‹ the ‹ out of ‹ If only He
people, captivity brings back salvation Zion would grant

יָגֵל יַעֲקֹב יִשְׂמַח יִשְׂרָאֵל.[1] וּתְשׁוּעַת צַדִּיקִים מֵיהוה, מָעוּזָּם

‹ their ‹‹ is from ‹ of the ‹ And the ‹‹ Israel will rejoice. ‹ Jacob will exult,
Might Hashem, righteous salvation

בְּעֵת צָרָה. וַיַּעְזְרֵם יהוה וַיְפַלְּטֵם; יְפַלְּטֵם מֵרְשָׁעִים וְיוֹשִׁיעֵם,

‹‹ and He will ‹ from the ‹ He will cause ‹‹ and caused ‹ Hashem helped ‹‹ of ‹ in time
save them, wicked them to escape them to escape; them distress.

כִּי חָסוּ בוֹ.[2]

‹‹ in ‹ they took ‹ for
Him. refuge

יְהִי רָצוֹן מִלְּפָנֶיךָ, יהוה אֱלֹהֵינוּ וֵאלֹהֵי אֲבוֹתֵינוּ, בִּזְכוּת

‹ in the ‹‹ of our ‹ and the ‹ our God ‹ Hashem, ‹‹ before You, ‹ the will ‹ May
merit forefathers, God it be

UPON COMPLETING THE ENTIRE FIRST BOOK OF *TEHILLIM* (PSALMS 1-41):

סֵפֶר רִאשׁוֹן שֶׁבַּתְּהִלִּים שֶׁקָּרָאנוּ לְפָנֶיךָ, שֶׁהוּא כְּנֶגֶד סֵפֶר

‹ with the ‹ corre- ‹ which ‹‹ before You, ‹ that we have ‹ of *Tehillim* ‹ of the First Book
Book sponds recited

בְּרֵאשִׁית, בִּזְכוּת מִזְמוֹרָיו וּבִזְכוּת פְּסוּקָיו וּבִזְכוּת תֵּבוֹתָיו

‹ of its ‹ and in ‹ of its ‹ and in ‹ of its psalms ‹ in the ‹‹ of Genesis,
words the merit verses the merit merit

UPON COMPLETING THE ENTIRE SECOND BOOK OF *TEHILLIM* (PSALMS 42-72):

סֵפֶר שֵׁנִי שֶׁבַּתְּהִלִּים שֶׁקָּרָאנוּ לְפָנֶיךָ, שֶׁהוּא כְּנֶגֶד סֵפֶר

‹ with the ‹ corre- ‹ which ‹‹ before You, ‹ that we have ‹ of *Tehillim* ‹ of the Second
Book sponds recited Book

שְׁמוֹת, בִּזְכוּת מִזְמוֹרָיו וּבִזְכוּת פְּסוּקָיו וּבִזְכוּת תֵּבוֹתָיו

‹ of its ‹ and in ‹ of its ‹ and in ‹ of its psalms ‹ in the ‹‹ of Exodus,
words the merit verses the merit merit

UPON COMPLETING THE ENTIRE THIRD BOOK OF *TEHILLIM* (PSALMS 73-89):

סֵפֶר שְׁלִישִׁי שֶׁבַּתְּהִלִּים שֶׁקָּרָאנוּ לְפָנֶיךָ, שֶׁהוּא כְּנֶגֶד סֵפֶר

‹ with the ‹ corre- ‹ which ‹‹ before You, ‹ that we have ‹ of *Tehillim* ‹ of the Third Book
Book sponds recited

---

(1) *Psalms* 14:7. (2) 37:39-40.

וַיִּקְרָא, בִּזְכוּת מִזְמוֹרָיו וּבִזְכוּת פְּסוּקָיו וּבִזְכוּת תֵּבוֹתָיו

‹ of its ‹ and in ‹ of its ‹ and in ‹ of its psalms ‹ in the ‹‹ of Leviticus,
words the merit verses the merit merit

UPON COMPLETING THE ENTIRE FOURTH BOOK OF *TEHILLIM* (PSALMS 90-106):

סֵפֶר רְבִיעִי שֶׁבַּתְּהִלִּים שֶׁקְּרָאנוּ לְפָנֶיךָ, שֶׁהוּא כְּנֶגֶד סֵפֶר

‹ with the ‹ corre- ‹ which ‹‹ before You, ‹ that we have ‹ of Tehillim ‹ of the Fourth Book
Book sponds recited

בַּמִּדְבָּר, בִּזְכוּת מִזְמוֹרָיו וּבִזְכוּת פְּסוּקָיו וּבִזְכוּת תֵּבוֹתָיו

‹ of its ‹ and in ‹ of its ‹ and in ‹ of its psalms ‹ in the ‹‹ of Numbers,
words the merit verses the merit merit

UPON COMPLETING THE ENTIRE FIFTH BOOK OF *TEHILLIM* (PSALMS 107-150):

סֵפֶר חֲמִישִׁי שֶׁבַּתְּהִלִּים שֶׁקְּרָאנוּ לְפָנֶיךָ, שֶׁהוּא כְּנֶגֶד סֵפֶר

‹ with the ‹ corre- ‹ which ‹‹ before You, ‹ that we have ‹ of Tehillim ‹ of the Fifth Book
Book sponds recited

דְּבָרִים, בִּזְכוּת מִזְמוֹרָיו וּבִזְכוּת פְּסוּקָיו וּבִזְכוּת תֵּבוֹתָיו

‹ of its ‹ and in ‹ of its ‹ and in ‹ of its psalms ‹ in the ‹‹ of
words the merit verses the merit merit Deuteronomy,

UPON COMPLETING LESS THAN AN ENTIRE BOOK SUBSTITUTE:

מִזְמוֹרֵי תְהִלִּים שֶׁקְּרָאנוּ לְפָנֶיךָ, וּבִזְכוּת פְּסוּקֵיהֶם וּבִזְכוּת

‹ and in ‹ of their ‹ and in ‹‹ before You, ‹ that we have ‹ of Tehillim ‹ of the
the merit verses the merit recited psalms

תֵּבוֹתֵיהֶם

‹ of their words

ON WEEKDAYS CONTINUE HERE
(ON THE SABBATH AND FESTIVALS CONTINUE ON PAGE 854.)

וּבִזְכוּת שְׁמוֹתֶיךָ הַקְּדוֹשִׁים וְהַטְּהוֹרִים הַיּוֹצְאִים מֵהֶם,

‹‹ from ‹ that emanate ‹ and that are pure ‹ that are holy ‹ of Your ‹ and in
them, [Divine] Names the merit

שֶׁתְּכַפֶּר לָנוּ עַל כָּל חַטֹּאתֵינוּ וְתִמְחָל לָנוּ עַל כָּל עֲוֹנוֹתֵינוּ,

‹‹ our ‹ all ‹ for ‹ us ‹ pardon ‹‹ our ‹ all ‹ for ‹ to us ‹ that you grant
iniquities, transgressions, atonement

וְתִסְלַח לָנוּ עַל כָּל פְּשָׁעֵינוּ, שֶׁחָטָאנוּ וְשֶׁעָוִינוּ וְשֶׁפָּשַׁעְנוּ

‹ and that we ‹ that we have ‹ that we have ‹‹ our willful ‹ all ‹ for ‹ us ‹ and forgive
have sinned been iniquitous, transgressed, sins,

לְפָנֶיךָ; וְתַחֲזִירֵנוּ בִּתְשׁוּבָה שְׁלֵמָה לְפָנֶיךָ; וְתַדְרִיכֵנוּ

‹ Guide us ‹‹ before You. ‹ that is complete ‹ in repentance ‹ Return us ‹‹ before You.

לַעֲבוֹדָתֶךָ; וְתִפְתַּח לִבֵּנוּ בְּתַלְמוּד תּוֹרָתֶךָ; וְתִשְׁלַח רְפוּאָה

⟨ a healing ⟨ Send ⟪ of Your Torah. ⟨ to the study ⟨ our hearts ⟨ and open ⟪ in Your service

שְׁלֵמָה לְחוֹלֵי עַמֶּךָ,

⟪ of Your ⟨ to the ⟨ that is
nation. sick people complete

ONE WHO RECITES *TEHILLIM* ON BEHALF OF A PARTICULAR SICK WOMAN ADDS:	**ONE WHO RECITES *TEHILLIM* ON BEHALF OF A PARTICULAR SICK MAN ADDS:**
MOTHER'S HEBREW NAME בַּת **PATIENT'S HEBREW NAME** וְלַחוֹלָה	**MOTHER'S HEBREW NAME** בֶּן **PATIENT'S HEBREW NAME** וְלַחוֹלֶה
⟪ daughter of ⟨ and particularly to the patient	⟪ son of ⟨ and particularly to the patient

---

וְתִקְרָא לִשְׁבוּיִם דְּרוֹר וְלַאֲסוּרִים פְּקַח קוֹחַ;[1] וּלְכָל הוֹלְכֵי

⟨ who walk ⟨ For all ⟪ from ⟨ release ⟨ and for those ⟪ liberty, ⟨ for captives ⟨ Proclaim
bondage. imprisoned

דְּרָכִים וְעוֹבְרֵי יַמִּים וּנְהָרוֹת מֵעַמְּךָ יִשְׂרָאֵל, תַּצִּילֵם

⟨ — rescue ⟪ Israel ⟨ who are of ⟪ and rivers, ⟨ over the ⟨ and ⟪ the roads
them Your people, seas voyagers

מִכָּל צַעַר וָנֶזֶק, וְתַגִּיעֵם לִמְחוֹז חֶפְצָם לְחַיִּים וּלְשָׁלוֹם;

⟪ and for ⟨ for life ⟨ they desire ⟨ to the ⟨ and bring ⟨ and ⟨ pain ⟨ from any
peace. destination them injury

וְתִפְקוֹד לְכָל חֲשׂוּכֵי בָנִים בְּזֶרַע שֶׁל קַיָּמָא לַעֲבוֹדָתֶךָ

⟨ to serve You ⟨ who are ⟨ [to grant them] ⟨ who are childless, ⟨ all ⟨ May You
healthy children remember

וּלְיִרְאָתֶךָ; וְעֻבָּרוֹת שֶׁל עַמְּךָ בֵּית יִשְׂרָאֵל תַּצִּילֵן שֶׁלֹּא

⟨ that ⟨ protect ⟨ of Israel, ⟨ the ⟨ Your ⟨ of ⟨ The pregnant ⟪ and to fear You.
they not family nation, women

תַּפֵּלְנָה וְלַדוֹתֵיהֶן; וְהַיּוֹשְׁבוֹת עַל הַמַּשְׁבֵּר בְּרַחֲמֶיךָ הָרַבִּים

⟨ that is ⟨ with Your ⟪ the ⟨ upon ⟨ and those now ⟪ their babies; ⟨ miscarry
abundant, mercy birthstool, found

תַּצִּילֵן מִכָּל רָע; וְאֶל הַמֵּינִיקוֹת תַּשְׁפִּיעַ שֶׁלֹּא יֶחְסַר חָלָב

⟨ milk ⟨ lack ⟨ that ⟨ cause ⟨ the nursing ⟨ And for ⟪ evil. ⟨ from ⟨ protect
they not mothers all them

מִדַּדֵּיהֶן; וְאַל יִמְשׁוֹל אַסְכָּרָה וְשֵׁדִין וְכָל פְּגָעִים וּמַרְעִין

⟨ and ⟪ of evil ⟨ nor all ⟨ nor ⟨ diphtheria, ⟨ hold sway ⟨ And let ⟪ in their
occurrences spirits forms demons not breasts.

בִּישִׁין בְּכָל יַלְדֵי עַמְּךָ בֵּית יִשְׂרָאֵל, וּתְגַדְּלֵם לְתוֹרָתֶךָ

⟪ to Your ⟨ Raise them ⟪ of Israel. ⟨ the ⟨ of Your ⟨ children ⟨ over ⟨ of evil
Torah, family people, any

---

(1) Cf. *Isaiah* 61:1.

לִלְמוֹד תּוֹרָה לִשְׁמָהּ, וְתַצִּילֵם מֵעַיִן הָרָע וּמִדֶּבֶר וּמִמַּגֵּפָה

‹ to study ‹ the ‹ for its ›› Protect ‹ from the evil eye, ‹ from ‹ from plague,
Torah own sake. them pestilence,

וּמִשָּׂטָן וּמִיֵּצֶר הָרָע; וּתְבַטֵּל מֵעָלֵינוּ וּמִכָּל עַמְּךָ בֵּית

‹ from Satan ‹ and from the ›› Nullify the ‹ against us ‹ and against Your ‹ the
Evil Inclination. threat entire nation, family

יִשְׂרָאֵל בְּכָל מָקוֹם שֶׁהֵם כָּל גְּזֵרוֹת קָשׁוֹת וְרָעוֹת; וְתַטֶּה לֵב

‹ of Israel, ‹ wherever ‹‹ they are, ‹ of ‹‹ decrees ‹ that are ›› and evil. ‹ Sway ‹ the
all harsh hearts

הַמַּלְכוּת עָלֵינוּ לְטוֹבָה, וְתִגְזוֹר עָלֵינוּ גְּזֵרוֹת טוֹבוֹת;

of the ‹ regarding ‹‹ for the good, ‹ that they ‹ upon us ‹ laws ‹ that are ››
government us may decree favorable.

וְתִשְׁלַח בְּרָכָה וְהַצְלָחָה בְּכָל מַעֲשֵׂה יָדֵינוּ; וְהָכֵן פַּרְנָסָתֵנוּ

‹ Dispatch ‹ blessing ‹ and success ‹ upon ‹ the work ‹ of our ›› Prepare ‹ our
all hands. livelihood

מִיָּדְךָ הָרְחָבָה וְהַמְּלֵאָה, וְלֹא יִצְטָרְכוּ עַמְּךָ יִשְׂרָאֵל זֶה לָזֶה

‹ from ‹ that is ‹ open ‹ and ›› generous, ‹ and let ‹ be forced ‹‹ — Your ‹ Israel — ‹‹ one ‹ upon
Your hand to rely [them] not people another

וְלֹא לְעַם אַחֵר; וְתֵן לְכָל אִישׁ וְאִישׁ דֵּי פַּרְנָסָתוֹ, וּלְכָל

‹ nor ‹ upon another ›› Give ‹ every ‹ single person ‹ an ‹ livelihood, ‹‹ and [grant]
nation. ample every

גּוּיָה וּגְוִיָּה דֵּי מַחְסוֹרָהּ; וּתְמַהֵר וְתָחִישׁ לְגָאֲלֵנוּ וְתִבְנֶה

‹ single body ‹ enough ‹ whatever ›› Speedily, ‹ hurry ‹ to redeem ‹‹ and build
to satisfy it lacks. us,

בֵּית מִקְדָּשֵׁנוּ וּתְפָאַרְתֵּנוּ;

‹ our ‹ of ‹ and our ››
Temple holiness splendor.

THE FOLLOWING IS RECITED ONLY IN THE PRESENCE OF A *MINYAN*:

וּבִזְכוּת שְׁלֹשׁ עֶשְׂרֵה מִדּוֹתֶיךָ שֶׁל רַחֲמִים הַכְּתוּבוֹת

‹ recorded ‹ Mercy ‹ of ‹ of Your Attributes ‹ of the Thirteen ‹ In the merit

בְּתוֹרָתֶךָ — כְּמוֹ שֶׁנֶּאֱמַר: יהוה יהוה אֵל רַחוּם וְחַנּוּן

‹ and ‹ Compas- ‹ God, ‹ HASHEM, ‹ HASHEM, ‹ it is said: ‹ — as ‹‹ in Your
Gracious, sionate Torah

אֶרֶךְ אַפַּיִם וְרַב חֶסֶד וֶאֱמֶת נֹצֵר חֶסֶד לָאֲלָפִים נֹשֵׂא

‹ For- ‹‹ for thousands ‹ of ‹ Preserver ‹‹ and ‹ in ‹ and ‹ to ‹ Slow
giver [of generations], kindness Truth, Kindness Abundant anger,

עָוֹן וָפֶשַׁע וְחַטָּאָה וְנַקֵּה,[1] שֶׁאֵינָן חוֹזְרוֹת רֵיקָם מִלְּפָנֶיךָ.

‹‹ from Your ‹ empty- ‹ turned ‹ — which [when ‹‹ and Who ‹ and inad- ‹ willful ‹ of
presence. handed away invoked] are never absolves vertent sin, sin, iniquity,

---

(1) *Exodus* 34:6-7.

עָזְרֵנוּ אֱלֹהֵי יִשְׁעֵנוּ עַל דְּבַר כְּבוֹד שְׁמֶךָ, וְהַצִּילֵנוּ וְכַפֵּר עַל

⟨ for ⟩ and grant ⟨ rescue us ⟨⟨ of Your ⟨ of the ⟨ the ⟨ for ⟨ of our ⟨ O God ⟨ Assist
atonement · · · Name; · glory · sake · · salvation, · · us,

חַטֹּאתֵינוּ לְמַעַן שְׁמֶךָ.¹ בָּרוּךְ יהוה לְעוֹלָם, אָמֵן וְאָמֵן.²

⟨⟨ and Amen. ⟨ Amen ⟨ forever, ⟨ is ⟨ Blessed ⟨⟨ of Your ⟨ for the ⟨ our sins
· · · · HASHEM · · Name. · sake

ON THE SABBATH AND FESTIVALS CONTINUE:

וּבִזְכוּת שְׁמוֹתֶיךָ הַקְּדוֹשִׁים וְהַטְּהוֹרִים הַיּוֹצְאִים מֵהֶם,

שֶׁתְּהֵא נֶחְשֶׁבֶת לָנוּ אֲמִירַת מִזְמוֹרֵי תְהִלִּים אֵלּוּ, כְּאִלּוּ

אֲמָרָם דָּוִד מֶלֶךְ יִשְׂרָאֵל עָלָיו הַשָּׁלוֹם בְּעַצְמוֹ, זְכוּתוֹ

יָגֵן עָלֵינוּ; וְיַעֲמוֹד לָנוּ לְחַבֵּר אֵשֶׁת נְעוּרִים עִם דּוֹדָהּ,

בְּאַהֲבָה וְאַחֲוָה וְרֵעוּת. וּמִשָּׁם יִמָּשֵׁךְ לָנוּ שֶׁפַע לְנֶפֶשׁ רוּחַ

וּנְשָׁמָה. וּכְשֵׁם שֶׁאָנוּ אוֹמְרִים לְפָנֶיךָ שִׁירָה בָּעוֹלָם הַזֶּה, כָּךְ

נִזְכֶּה לוֹמַר לְפָנֶיךָ, יהוה אֱלֹהֵינוּ וֵאלֹהֵי אֲבוֹתֵינוּ, שִׁיר

וּשְׁבָחָה לָעוֹלָם הַבָּא. וְעַל יְדֵי אֲמִירַת תְּהִלִּים תִּתְעוֹרֵר

חֲבַצֶּלֶת הַשָּׁרוֹן³ לָשִׁיר בְּקוֹל נָעִים גִּילַת וְרַנֵּן, כְּבוֹד הַלְּבָנוֹן

נִתַּן לָהּ,⁴ הוֹד וְהָדָר בְּבֵית אֱלֹהֵינוּ, בִּמְהֵרָה בְיָמֵינוּ, אָמֵן. סֶלָה.

(1) *Psalms* 79:9. (2) 89:53. (3) *Song of Songs* 2:1. (4) *Isaiah* 35:2.

‏תפלה בעד החולה‎ / PRAYER FOR THE SICK ‏‎

Among the psalms commonly recited for the sick are: 20, 6, 9, 13, 16, 17, 18, 22, 23, 28, 30, 31, 32, 33, 37, 38, 39, 41, 49, 55, 56, 69, 86, 88, 89, 90, 91, 102, 103, 104, 107, 116, 118, 142, 143, 148.

(Alternatively, some or all of the following psalms are recited: 20, 30, 121, 130, 142.)

Afterwards, verses whose initial letters spell the patient's Hebrew name are recited. Psalm 119 is customarily used for this purpose because it consists of twenty-two sets of eight verses, where all the verses in each set begin with the same Hebrew letter and the sets are arranged in alphabetical order. If, for example, the sick person's name is ‏יַעֲקֹב‎, the eight verses (73-80) which begin with the letter ‏י‎ are said first, then the verses which begin with the letters ‏ע, ק,‎ and ‏ב‎. Some continue the same pattern spelling out ‏בֵּן/בַּת‎, son/daughter, and the name of the patient's mother. Following this the words ‏קְרַע שָׂטָן‎, Tear away Satan, are spelled out by the same method of reciting the eight verses which correspond to the respective letters. Some add the following supplication.

THIS PASSAGE MAY ONLY BE RECITED IN THE PRESENCE OF A *MINYAN*:

‏יהוה יהוה אֵל רַחוּם וְחַנּוּן אֶרֶךְ אַפַּיִם וְרַב חֶסֶד וֶאֱמֶת‎

⟨⟨ and ⟨	in ⟨	and ⟨	to ⟨	Slow ⟨	and ⟨	Com- ⟨	God, ⟨	HASHEM, ⟨	HASHEM,
Truth,	Kindness	Abundant	anger,			Gracious, passionate			

‏נֹצֵר חֶסֶד לָאֲלָפִים נֹשֵׂא עָוֹן וָפֶשַׁע וְחַטָּאָה וְנַקֵּה.‎ [1]

⟨⟨ and Who ⟨	and inad- ⟨	willful ⟨	of ⟨	Forgiver ⟨⟨	for thousands ⟨	of ⟨	Preserver
absolves.	vertent sin,	sin,	iniquity,		[of generations],	kindness	

‏לְךָ יהוה‎ הַגְּדֻלָּה וְהַגְּבוּרָה וְהַתִּפְאֶרֶת וְהַנֵּצַח וְהַהוֹד כִּי

⟨ for ⟨⟨ and the ⟨	the ⟨		the glory, ⟨	the strength, ⟨	is the ⟨		HASHEM, ⟨	Yours,
majesty;	triumph,				greatness,			

‏כֹל בַּשָּׁמַיִם וּבָאָרֶץ, לְךָ יהוה הַמַּמְלָכָה וְהַמִּתְנַשֵּׂא לְכֹל

⟨ over ⟨	and the ⟨	is the kingdom ⟨	HASHEM, ⟨	Yours, ⟨⟨	and on ⟨	in heaven ⟨	every-
every	sovereignty				earth [is Yours];		thing

‏לְרֹאשׁ.‎ [2] ‏וְאַתָּה בְּיָדְךָ נֶפֶשׁ כָּל חָי וְרוּחַ כָּל בְּשַׂר אִישׁ,‎ [3]

⟨⟨	mankind. ⟨	of ⟨	and the ⟨	living ⟨	of ⟨	is the ⟨	in Your ⟨⟨	And You, ⟨⟨	leader.
		all	spirit	thing	every	soul	hands		

‏וּבְיָדְךָ כֹּחַ וּגְבוּרָה לְגַדֵּל וּלְחַזֵּק וּלְרַפְּאוֹת אֱנוֹשׁ עַד דַּכָּא,‎ [4]

⟨⟨ he who ⟨	even ⟨⟨	[every] ⟨	and to cure ⟨	to ⟨	to make ⟨	and the ⟨	is the ⟨	And in
is crushed,	human,			strengthen,	great,	power	strength	Your hands

‏עַד דִּכְדּוּכָה שֶׁל נֶפֶשׁ. וְלֹא יִפָּלֵא מִמְּךָ כָּל דָּבָר‎ [6] ‏וּבְיָדְךָ נֶפֶשׁ

⟨ is the ⟨	and in ⟨⟨	anything, ⟨	from ⟨	be ⟨	There ⟨⟨	[his] ⟨	of ⟨	the very ⟨	[crushed]
soul	Your hands		You	hidden	cannot	soul.		depths	to

‏כָּל חָי.‎ [7] ‏לָכֵן יְהִי רָצוֹן מִלְּפָנֶיךָ הָאֵל הַנֶּאֱמָן, אַב הָרַחֲמִים,‎

⟨⟨ of ⟨	Father ⟨⟨	Who is ⟨	O God ⟨⟨	before You, ⟨	the ⟨	may ⟨	There- ⟨⟨	living ⟨	of
Mercy,		trustworthy,			will	it be	fore	thing.	every

---

(1) *Exodus* 34:6-7. (2) *I Chronicles* 29:11. (3) Cf. *Job* 12:10. (4) Cf. *I Chronicles* 29:12. (5) *Psalms* 90:3. (6) *Jeremiah* 32:17. (7) Cf. *Job* 12:10.

הָרוֹפֵא לְכָל תַּחֲלוּאֵי¹ עַמְּךָ יִשְׂרָאֵל הַקְּרוֹבִים עַד שַׁעֲרֵי

⟨ the very ⟨ unto ⟨ [even] those ⟨⟨ Israel, ⟨ of Your ⟨ illnesses ⟨ of all ⟨ Healer
gates near people,

מָוֶת, וְהַמְחַבֵּשׁ מָזוֹר וּתְעָלָה לִידִידָיו, וְהַגּוֹאֵל מִשַּׁחַת³

⟨ from the pit ⟨ and Who ⟨⟨ His beloved ⟨ and healing ⟨ [with] ⟨ the One ⟨⟨ of
of destruction redeems ones, [medications] curing Who binds death;

חֲסִידָיו, וְהַמַּצִּיל מִמָּוֶת נֶפֶשׁ מְרוּדָיו. אַתָּה רוֹפֵא נֶאֱמָן שְׁלַח

⟨ send ⟨⟨ Who is ⟨ O Healer ⟨⟨ You, ⟨⟨ of His ⟨ the souls ⟨ from ⟨ and Who ⟨⟨ His devout
trustworthy, sorrowful ones. death delivers ones,

מַרְפֵּא וַאֲרוּכָה וּתְעָלָה בְּרוֹב חֶסֶד וַחֲנִינָה וְחֶמְלָה לְנֶפֶשׁ

⟨ to the ⟨ and ⟨ gracious- ⟨ kindness, ⟨ with ⟨ and remedy, ⟨ cure, ⟨ healing,
soul compassion ness, abundant

FOR A MALE PATIENT:

[PATIENT'S HEBREW NAME] בֶּן [PATIENT'S MOTHER'S HEBREW NAME] לְרוּחוֹ וְנַפְשׁוֹ

⟨ and his soul ⟨ to his spirit ⟨ the son

הָאוּמְלָלָה, וְלֹא תֵרֵד נַפְשׁוֹ לִשְׁאוֹלָה, וְהִמָּלֵא רַחֲמִים עָלָיו

⟨ upon ⟨ with mercy ⟨ May You ⟨⟨ to the grave. ⟨ his soul descend ⟨ Let not ⟨⟨ that are
him be filled unfortunate.

לְהַחֲלִימוֹ וּלְרַפְּאתוֹ לְהַחֲזִיקוֹ וּלְהַחֲיוֹתוֹ, כִּרְצוֹן כָּל קְרוֹבָיו

⟨ of his ⟨ of ⟨ as is the ⟨⟨ and to revitalize ⟨ to strengthen ⟨ to cure him, ⟨ to restore
relatives all wish him, him, him to health,

וְאוֹהֲבָיו. וְיֵרָאוּ לְפָנֶיךָ זְכִיּוֹתָיו וְצִדְקוֹתָיו, וְתַשְׁלִיךְ בִּמְצוּלוֹת

⟨ into the ⟨ and may ⟨⟨ and charitable ⟨ [all] his ⟨ before ⟨ May there ⟨⟨ and friends.
depths You cast deeds, merits You appear

יָם כָּל חַטֹּאתָיו,⁴ וְיִכְבְּשׁוּ רַחֲמֶיךָ אֶת כַּעַסְךָ מֵעָלָיו,

⟨⟨ from ⟨ Your anger ⟨ May Your mercy suppress ⟨⟨ of his sins. ⟨ all ⟨ of
upon him, the sea

וְתִשְׁלַח לוֹ רְפוּאָה שְׁלֵמָה, רְפוּאַת הַנֶּפֶשׁ וּרְפוּאַת הַגּוּף,

⟨⟨ of the ⟨ and a healing ⟨ of the ⟨ a healing ⟨ that is ⟨ a healing ⟨ him ⟨ and may
body. spirit, complete, You send

וּתְחַדֵּשׁ כַּנֶּשֶׁר נְעוּרָיו, וְתִשְׁלַח לוֹ וּלְכָל חוֹלֵי יִשְׂרָאֵל⁵

⟨⟨ of Israel, ⟨ the sick ⟨ and ⟨ to him ⟨ send ⟨⟨ his youth; ⟨ like the ⟨ Renew
people to all eagle

מַרְפֵּא אֲרוּכָה, מַרְפֵּא בְרָכָה, מַרְפֵּא תְרוּפָה וּתְעָלָה, מַרְפֵּא

⟨ a cure ⟨ and remedial, ⟨ that is ⟨ a cure ⟨⟨ that is ⟨ a cure ⟨⟨ that is ⟨ a cure
healing blessed, lasting,

---

(1) Cf. *Psalms* 103:3. (2) Cf. *Jeremiah* 30:13.
(3) *Psalms* 103:4. (4) Cf. *Micah* 7:19. (5) Cf. *Psalms* 103:5.

חֲנִינָה וְחֶמְלָה, מַרְפֵּא יְדוּעִים וּגְלוּיִם, מַרְפֵּא רַחֲמִים וְשָׁלוֹם

⟨ peace, ⟨ that is with ⟨ a cure ⟪ and clear, ⟨ that is ⟨ a cure ⟪ and com- ⟨ that is
mercy, understood passionate, gracious

וְחַיִּים, מַרְפֵּא אֹרֶךְ יָמִים וְשָׁנִים טוֹבִים. וִיקַיֵּם בּוֹ

⟨ for ⟨ May there ⟪ and good years. ⟨ days ⟨ that is ⟨ a cure ⟪ and life,
him be fulfilled for lengthy

CONTINUE ON PAGE 858.

FOR A FEMALE PATIENT:

[PATIENT'S MOTHER'S HEBREW NAME] לְרוּחָהּ וְנַפְשָׁהּ בַּת [PATIENT'S HEBREW NAME]

⟨ and her soul ⟨ to her spirit ⟨ the daughter

הָאוּמְלָלָה, וְלֹא תֵרֵד נַפְשָׁהּ לִשְׁאוֹלָה, וְהַמָּלֵא רַחֲמִים

⟨ with mercy ⟨ May You be filled ⟪ to the grave. ⟨ her soul descend ⟨ Let not ⟪ that are unfortunate.

עָלֶיהָ לְהַחֲלִימָהּ וּלְרַפֹּאתָהּ לְהַחֲזִיקָהּ וּלְהַחֲיוֹתָהּ, כִּרְצוֹן

⟨ as is ⟪ and to ⟨ to strengthen her, ⟨ to cure her, ⟨ to restore her ⟨ upon her
the wish revitalize her, to health,

כָּל קְרוֹבֶיהָ וְאוֹהֲבֶיהָ. וְיֵרָאוּ לְפָנֶיךָ זְכִיּוֹתֶיהָ וְצִדְקוֹתֶיהָ,

⟪ and charitable ⟨ [all] her ⟨ before ⟨ May there ⟪ and friends. ⟨ of her ⟨ of all
deeds, merits You appear relatives

וְתַשְׁלִיךְ בִּמְצוּלוֹת יָם כָּל חַטֹּאתֶיהָ, וְיִכְבְּשׁוּ רַחֲמֶיךָ

⟨ May Your mercy suppress ⟪ of her sins. ⟨ all ⟨ of the sea ⟨ into the depths ⟨ and may You cast

אֶת כַּעַסְךָ מֵעָלֶיהָ, וְתִשְׁלַח לָהּ רְפוּאָה שְׁלֵמָה, רְפוּאַת

⟨ a healing ⟨ that is ⟨ a healing ⟨ her ⟨ and may ⟪ from upon her, ⟨ Your anger
complete,

הַנֶּפֶשׁ וּרְפוּאַת הַגּוּף, וּתְחַדֵּשׁ כַּנֶּשֶׁר נְעוּרֶיהָ, וְתִשְׁלַח לָהּ

⟨ to her ⟨ send ⟪ her youth; ⟨ like the ⟨ Renew ⟪ of the ⟨ and a healing ⟨ of the
eagle body. spirit,

וּלְכָל חוֹלֵי יִשְׂרָאֵל מַרְפֵּא אֲרוּכָה, מַרְפֵּא בְּרָכָה, מַרְפֵּא

⟨ a cure ⟪ that is ⟨ a cure ⟪ that is lasting, ⟨ a cure ⟪ of Israel, ⟨ the sick ⟨ and to all
blessed, people

תְּרוּפָה וּתְעָלָה, מַרְפֵּא חֲנִינָה וְחֶמְלָה, מַרְפֵּא יְדוּעִים

⟨ that is ⟨ a cure ⟪ and ⟨ that is ⟨ a cure ⟨ and remedial, ⟨ that is
understood compassionate, gracious healing

וּגְלוּיִם, מַרְפֵּא רַחֲמִים וְשָׁלוֹם וְחַיִּים, מַרְפֵּא אֹרֶךְ יָמִים

⟨ days ⟨ that is ⟨ a cure ⟪ and life, ⟨ peace, ⟨ that is ⟨ a cure ⟪ and clear,
for lengthy with mercy,

וְשָׁנִים טוֹבִים. וִיקַיֵּם בָּהּ

⟨ for her ⟨ May there ⟪ and good years.
be fulfilled

FOR ALL PATIENTS CONTINUE HERE:

וּבְכָל חוֹלֵי יִשְׂרָאֵל מִקְרָא שֶׁכָּתוּב עַל יְדֵי מֹשֶׁה עַבְדְּךָ
and · for all · the sick · of Israel, · the verse · recorded · by · Moses · Your servant,

נֶאֱמָן בֵּיתֶךָ: וַיֹּאמֶר אִם שָׁמוֹעַ תִּשְׁמַע לְקוֹל יהוה אֱלֹהֶיךָ,
the most trustworthy · House: · And he [Moses] said: · If · you diligently listen · to the · voice · of · Hashem, · your God,

וְהַיָּשָׁר בְּעֵינָיו תַּעֲשֶׂה, וְהַאֲזַנְתָּ לְמִצְוֹתָיו, וְשָׁמַרְתָּ כָּל חֻקָּיו,
and what is proper · in His eyes · you do, · and you · give ear · to His commandments · and you · observe · all · His statutes,

כָּל הַמַּחֲלָה אֲשֶׁר שַׂמְתִּי בְמִצְרַיִם לֹא אָשִׂים עָלֶיךָ, כִּי אֲנִי
any · sickness · that · I have brought · upon Egypt, · not · I will · bring · upon you, · for · I am

יהוה רֹפְאֶךָ.[1] וַעֲבַדְתֶּם אֵת יהוה אֱלֹהֵיכֶם, וּבֵרַךְ אֶת לַחְמְךָ
Hashem · your healer. · And you · shall serve · Hashem, · your God, · and He · shall bless · your · bread

וְאֶת מֵימֶיךָ, וַהֲסִרֹתִי מַחֲלָה מִקִּרְבֶּךָ. לֹא תִהְיֶה מְשַׁכֵּלָה
and your water · and I shall remove · sickness · from your midst. · not be · There shall · [a woman] who miscarries

וַעֲקָרָה בְּאַרְצֶךָ, אֶת מִסְפַּר יָמֶיךָ אֲמַלֵּא.[2] וְהֵסִיר יהוה מִמְּךָ
or is barren · in your land; · the number · of your · days · I will fill out. · And Hashem · will remove · from you

כָּל חֹלִי, וְכָל מַדְוֵי מִצְרַיִם הָרָעִים אֲשֶׁר יָדַעְתָּ, לֹא יְשִׂימָם
all · sickness, · and · any · diseases · of Egypt · of the · that are evil · which · you · know — · will not · place them

בָּךְ, וּנְתָנָם בְּכָל שֹׂנְאֶיךָ.[3] וְעַל יְדֵי עֲבָדֶיךָ הַנְּבִיאִים כָּתוּב
upon you, · but He will · place them · upon · all · your · enemies. · And through · Your · servants, · the prophets, · it is written

לֵאמֹר: וַאֲכַלְתֶּם אָכוֹל וְשָׂבוֹעַ, וְהִלַּלְתֶּם אֶת שֵׁם יהוה
saying: · And you will eat, · eating · and being satisfied, · and you will · praise · the Name · of Hashem,

אֱלֹהֵיכֶם אֲשֶׁר עָשָׂה עִמָּכֶם לְהַפְלִיא, וְלֹא יֵבֹשׁוּ עַמִּי
your God, · Who has acted · with you · wondrously, · and not · ashamed · be · My people

לְעוֹלָם.[4] דְּרָכָיו רָאִיתִי וְאֶרְפָּאֵהוּ, וְאַנְחֵהוּ וַאֲשַׁלֵּם נִחֻמִים
evermore. · His ways · I have seen · and I will heal him, · and I will guide him · and bestow · consolations [of contrition]

(1) *Exodus* 15:26. (2) 23:25-26. (3) *Deuteronomy* 7:15. (4) *Joel* 2:26.

לוֹ וְלַאֲבֵלָיו. בּוֹרֵא נִיב שְׂפָתָיִם, שָׁלוֹם שָׁלוֹם לָרָחוֹק וְלַקָּרוֹב,

and for / for the far / peace, / Peace, / of the / a [new] / I create / and upon / upon
the near, / lips: / expression / his mourners. him

אָמַר יְהוָה, וּרְפָאתִיו. ¹ וְזָרְחָה לָכֶם יִרְאֵי שְׁמִי שֶׁמֶשׁ צְדָקָה

of / a sun / My / who / for you / There will / And I will / says Hashem,
righteousness, / Name, / fear / shine / heal him.

וּמַרְפֵּא בִּכְנָפֶיהָ. ² אָז יִבָּקַע כַּשַּׁחַר אוֹרֶךָ וַאֲרֻכָתְךָ מְהֵרָה

shall / and your / your light, / like the / shall / Then / in its wings. / with healing
speedily / healing / dawn / burst out

תִצְמָח. ³ רְפָאֵנוּ יְהוָה וְנֵרָפֵא, הוֹשִׁיעֵנוּ וְנִוָּשֵׁעָה, כִּי תְהִלָּתֵנוּ

our praise / for / then we / save us / then we / Hashem / Heal us, / sprout.
will be saved, / will be healed;

אָתָּה. ⁴ וְהַעֲלֵה רְפוּאָה שְׁלֵמָה לְכָל מַכּוֹת עַמְּךָ יִשְׂרָאֵל,

Israel, / of Your / the / for all / that is / healing / Bring / are You.
people, / ailments / complete

FOR A MALE PATIENT:

וּבִפְרָט לְ [PATIENT'S HEBREW NAME] בֶּן [PATIENT'S MOTHER'S HEBREW NAME] רְפוּאָה

a healing / the son of / to / and
particularly

שְׁלֵמָה לִרְמַ"ח אֵבָרָיו וּשְׁסַ"ה גִּידָיו, לְרַפֵּא אוֹתוֹ כְּחִזְקִיָּהוּ

like Hezekiah, / him / Cure / and to his 365 sinews. / to his 248 organs / that is
complete

מֶלֶךְ יְהוּדָה מֵחָלְיוֹ, ⁵ וּכְמִרְיָם הַנְּבִיאָה מִצָּרַעְתָּהּ, ⁶

King / of Judah, / from his sickness, / and like Miriam / the prophetess / from her leprosy.

[בְּשֵׁמוֹת הַקְּדוֹשִׁים הַיּוֹצְאִים מִפְּסוּקִים שֶׁל שָׁלֹשׁ עֶשְׂרֵה

the Thirteen / containing / from the / which / Employ the [Divine] Names
verses / emanate / that are sacred

מִדּוֹתֶיךָ] אֵל נָא רְפָא נָא ⁷ לְ [PATIENT'S HEBREW NAME] בֶּן

son of / now / heal / please, / O God, / of Your
Attributes.

[PATIENT'S MOTHER'S HEBREW NAME] לְהָקִים אוֹתוֹ מֵחָלְיוֹ וּלְהַאֲרִיךְ עוֹד

further / Lengthen / from his / him / and raise
sickbed.

יְמֵי חַיָּיו כְּדֵי שֶׁיַּעֲבוֹד לְךָ בְּאַהֲבָה וּבְיִרְאָה, וְתִתֶּן לוֹ

him / And / and fear. / with love / You / he may serve / so / of his life / the
grant / that / days

CONTINUE AT THE BOTTOM OF PAGE 860.

(1) *Isaiah* 57:18-19. (2) *Malachi* 3:20. (3) *Isaiah* 58:8. (4) Cf. *Jeremiah* 17:14.
(5) See *II Kings* 20:2-6. (6) See *Numbers* 12:10-15. (7) Cf. 12:13.

FOR A FEMALE PATIENT:

רְפוּאָה [PATIENT'S MOTHER'S HEBREW NAME], בַּת [PATIENT'S HEBREW NAME] וּבִפְרָט לְ

⟨ a healing   ⟨ the daughter of   ⟨ to ⟨ and particularly

שְׁלֵמָה לְכָל אֵבָרֶיהָ וּלְכָל גִּידֶיהָ, לְרַפֵּא אוֹתָהּ כְּחִזְקִיָּהוּ

⟨ like Hezekiah, ⟨ her ⟨ Cure ≪ her sinews. ⟨ and to all ⟨ her organs ⟨ to all ⟨ that is complete

מֶלֶךְ יְהוּדָה מֵחָלְיוֹ,[1] וּכְמִרְיָם הַנְּבִיאָה מִצָּרַעְתָּהּ,[2]

≪ from her leprosy. ⟨ the prophetess ⟨ and like Miriam ≪ from his sickness, ⟨ of Judah, ⟨ King

[בְּשֵׁמוֹת הַקְּדוֹשִׁים הַיּוֹצְאִים מִפְּסוּקִים שֶׁל שָׁלֹשׁ עֶשְׂרֵה

⟨ the Thirteen ⟨ containing ⟨ from the verses ⟨ which emanate ⟨ Employ the [Divine] Names that are sacred

מִדּוֹתֶיךָ] אֵל נָא רְפָא נָא לְ[3] [PATIENT'S HEBREW NAME] בַּת

⟨ daughter of   ⟨ now ⟨ heal ⟨ please, ⟨ O God, ≪ of Your Attributes.

[PATIENT'S MOTHER'S HEBREW NAME] לְהָקִים אוֹתָהּ מֵחָלְיָהּ וּלְהַאֲרִיךְ עוֹד

⟨ further ⟨ Lengthen ≪ from her sickbed. ⟨ her ⟨ and raise

יְמֵי חַיֶּיהָ כְּדֵי שֶׁתַּעֲבוֹד לָךְ בְּאַהֲבָה וּבְיִרְאָה, וְתִתֵּן לָהּ

⟨ her ⟨ And grant ≪ and fear. ⟨ with love ⟨ You ⟨ she may serve ⟨ so that ⟨ of her life ⟨ the days

FOR ALL PATIENTS CONTINUE HERE:

חַיִּים שֶׁל רַחֲמִים, חַיִּים שֶׁל בְּרִיאוּת, חַיִּים שֶׁל שָׁלוֹם,

≪ peace, ⟨ of ⟨ a life ≪ health, ⟨ of ⟨ a life ≪ mercy, ⟨ of ⟨ a life

חַיִּים שֶׁל בְּרָכָה, כְּדִכְתִיב: כִּי אֹרֶךְ יָמִים וּשְׁנוֹת חַיִּים

⟨ of life ⟨ and years ≪ of days, ⟨ length ⟨ For ≪ as it is written: ≪ blessing, ⟨ of ⟨ a life

וְשָׁלוֹם יוֹסִיפוּ לָךְ.[4] אָמֵן סֶלָה.

≪ Selah. ≪ Amen. ≪ to you. ⟨ shall they add ⟨ and peace

---

(1) See *II Kings* 20:2-6. (2) See *Numbers* 12:10-15. (3) Cf. 12:13. (4) *Proverbs* 3:2.

◄{ הלכות תפלה / GENERAL LAWS OF PRAYER }►

Although most of the laws appear in the course of the *siddur* where they are applicable, in some cases they are too involved or they apply to many areas. A selection of such laws are compiled in this section.

The reader should be aware that this digest cannot cover all eventualities and in many cases it should be regarded merely as a guide as to when to consult a competent halachic authority. As a general rule, when a particular *halachah* is in dispute, we follow the ruling of *Mishnah Berurah*. On occasion, however (usually when *Mishnah Berurah* does not give a definitive ruling), we cite more than one opinion. In such cases, each congregation is bound by its tradition and the ruling of its authorities.

Throughout this digest, *Orach Chaim* is abbreviated as O.C. and *Mishnah Berurah* as M.B.

compiled by *Rabbi Hersh Goldwurm zt"l*

GENERAL INSTRUCTIONS

◄§ The Obligation

1. The Torah commands us to pray every day, as it is said (*Ex.* 23:25): *And you shall serve* HASHEM *your God* . . . The Oral Tradition teaches that the service referred to is the service of the heart — prayer (*Rambam, Hil. Tefillah* 1:1).

2. Before praying, one should set aside a few minutes to collect his thoughts and to prepare himself mentally to stand before his Maker. One should also not rush away immediately after ending his prayer so as not to give the impression that praying is a burdensome task (O.C. 93:1).

Before beginning to pray, one should meditate upon God's infinite greatness and man's insignificance, and thereby remove from his heart any thoughts of physical pleasure (O.C. 98:1). By pondering God's works, man recognizes His infinite wisdom and comes to love and laud Him. This makes man cognizant of his own puny intelligence and flawed nature and puts him in a proper frame of mind to plead for God's mercy (*Rambam, Yesodei HaTorah* 2:2).

3. The prayers should be said with a feeling of awe and humility and surely not in an atmosphere of levity, frivolity, or mundane concerns, nor should one pray while under the influence of anger. Rather, one should pray with the feeling of happiness brought on by the knowledge of God's historic kindness to Israel and His mercy to all creatures (O.C. 93:2).

◄§ The Place

4. Ideally, one should pray in a building and not in an open place, for a private place is more conducive to both personal humility and the awe of the King (O.C. 90:5). The room where one prays should have windows or doors facing east toward Jerusalem (O.C. 90:4).

5. One who is traveling and cannot pray in a house should, if possible, stand among trees for they provide a modicum of privacy (M.B. 90:11). It is very important to choose a place where one is reasonably sure not to be interrupted (ibid.).

◄§ Concentration on the Prayers

6. During *Shemoneh Esrei* one's eyes should be directed downward (O.C. 95:2). His eyes should either be closed or reading from the *siddur* and not looking around (M.B. 95:5). One should not look up during *Shemoneh Esrei*, but when he feels his concentration failing he should raise his eyes heavenward to renew his inspiration (M.B. 90:8). One should imagine that he is in the Holy Temple and concentrate his feelings and thoughts toward Heaven (O.C. 95:2).

7. One must clear his mind of distractions and concentrate on his prayers, recognizing that he is in the Divine Presence. It is important that one should know the meaning of his prayers. If he had an audience with a human ruler he would take the utmost care in his choice of words and be aware of their meaning. Surely, therefore, when one speaks before the King of kings Who knows one's innermost thoughts, he must be careful how he speaks (O.C. 98:1). This concentration is stressed especially in regard to the

benedictions of *Shemoneh Esrei* (O.C. 101:1). If one finds it difficult to concentrate throughout the *Shemoneh Esrei* he should at least meditate on the concluding sentence of each benediction, which summarizes its theme (e.g., בָּרוּךְ . . . מְבָרֵךְ הַשָּׁנִים, *Blessed . . . Who blesses the years;* M.B. §1). The first benediction of the *Shemoneh Esrei* is treated with special stringency in this regard. This benediction must be repeated if it was said without concentration on its meaning (O.C. 101:1). However, *Rama* (loc. cit.) rules that it is best *not* to repeat it because it is likely that one will not concentrate properly even during the repetition. *Chayei Adam* (cited in M.B. 101:4) advises that if one realized his inattentiveness before saying the word HASHEM in the concluding formula (. . . בָּרוּךְ מָגֵן אַבְרָהָם), he should start over from אֱלֹהֵי אַבְרָהָם. Thus it is of utmost importance that one learn the meaning of the prayers in order to develop his power of concentration (M.B. 101:2).

◄§ Women's Obligation to Pray

8. Women are obligated to pray, and according to *Rambam* and *Shulchan Aruch* (O.C. 106:1) this obligation has Scriptural status. However, there are various opinions regarding the extent of their obligation.

According to the views preferred by M.B. (106:4), women are required to recite the *Shemoneh Esrei* of *Shacharis* and *Minchah,* they must recall the Exodus by reciting אֱמֶת וְיַצִּיב, *true and certain* (following the *Shacharis* recitation of *Shema* , p. 138), and אֱמֶת וֶאֱמוּנָה, *true and faithful* (following the *Maariv* recitation of *Shema* , p. 413), because they recall the Exodus (M.B. 70:2); and it is urged that they recite at least the first verse of *Shema* because it constitutes קַבָּלַת עוֹל מַלְכוּת שָׁמַיִם, *acceptance of God's sovereignty* (O.C. 70:1).

Some authorities rule that women should also recite all the morning benedictions (p. 23). According to one view, *Pesukei D'Zimrah* is introductory to *Shemoneh Esrei*

and, consequently, is obligatory upon women too (M.B. 70:2).

Women should recite בִּרְכוֹת הַתּוֹרָה, *blessings of the Torah* [p. 24] (O.C. 47:14, see *Be'ur Halachah*).

According to *Magen Avraham* (O.C. 106:2), women are required by the Torah to pray once a day and they may formulate the prayer as they wish. In many countries, this ruling became the basis for the custom that women recite a brief prayer early in the morning and do not recite any of the formal prayers from the *siddur.*

◄§ Miscellaneous Laws

9. One should not eat nor drink before praying (O.C. 89:3). However, it is permitted to drink water, tea, or coffee (M.B. 89:22), with milk (*Daas Torah* 89:5).

10. One must take care that the place where he prays be clean. It is prohibited to pray in an area where there are traces of feces or urine, or where one can smell them (see O.C. 76 and 79 for details). This is especially relevant in a home where there may be soiled diapers.

11. One may not pray in the presence of immodestly clad women or facing a window through which they can be observed (see O.C. 75 for details).

12. It is forbidden to pray while one feels the need to discharge his bodily functions (O.C. 92:1-3).

13. One must wash his hands before praying, but no benediction is recited (O.C. 92:4).

14. It is meritorious to give to charity before praying (O.C. 92:10), for this will facilitate the acceptance of the prayer (see M.B. 92:36, *Yoreh Deah* 247:3-4). In some congregations it is customary to collect for charity (or for individuals to set aside some coins for charity) when reciting (in וַיְבָרֶךְ דָּוִיד, p. 111) וְהָעֹשֶׁר וְהַכָּבוֹד מִלְּפָנֶיךָ וְאַתָּה מוֹשֵׁל בַּכֹּל, *wealth and honor come from before You, and You rule over everything. . .* (M.B. 92:36).

THE TIMES FOR PRAYER AND RECITAL OF SHEMA

◄§ The Morning Prayer – Shacharis

15. Ideally, one should recite the *Shemoneh Esrei* of the morning prayer after sunrise, but if one cannot wait that long (e.g., he must hurry to work or to perform a *mitzvah* that cannot be postponed) he may pray after

dawn, before sunrise, when light appears on the horizon (O.C. 89:1; see *Be'ur Halachah* s.v. ואם). However, if at all possible one should wait at least until the eastern horizon is fully lit up. According to all views it is not permissible to put on *tefillin* until there is sufficient daylight to recognize a casual acquaintance at a distance of four cubits (O.C. 30:1; see O.C. 19:3 in regard to donning a *tallis*). Since these times vary, competent authorities should be consulted on the exact time for each place and season (ibid.). For example, in the northern United States it varies from approximately fifty minutes before sunrise in March and September to as much as sixty-eight minutes (according to some) in June.

16. The *Shema* may be recited before sunrise (indeed, ideally it *should* be recited just before sunrise), but not before one can recognize a casual acquaintance at a distance of four cubits (O.C. 58:1). Nevertheless if one recited the *Shema* after dawn, he has discharged his obligation (O.C. 58:4).

17. The period allowed for the recitation of the *Shema* ends at the end of the first quarter of the day. Thereafter it is no longer possible to fulfill the *mitzvah*. If one suspects that the congregation will recite the *Shema* after the prescribed time, he should recite the *Shema* (without the benedictions preceding and following it) before the communal prayers, and should do so even before donning the *tallis* and *tefillin* if donning them would deter him from a timely recital (O.C. 58:1 with M.B. §5).

18. *Shacharis* should not be recited after a third of the day is gone. However, if one has failed to pray in time, he is permitted to recite *Shacharis* up to midday (O.C. 89:1; cf. O.C. 58:6 with M.B. and *Be'ur Halachah* regarding whether it is permitted to recite the Blessings of the *Shema* after a third of the day has passed).

19. There are two views on how to calculate one fourth and one third of the day for the purposes of *Shema* and *Shacharis*: (1) By calculating the hours and the minutes from sunrise to sunset; and (2) by calculating from dawn to dark (see M.B. 58:4). Each congregation should follow its own tradition

in this regard. "Midday" is determined by calculating the exact midpoint between the above times. It should be noted that midday is almost never exactly at noon.

⋙ The Afternoon Prayer — Minchah

20. A person should be very careful to recite *Minchah*, because the prophet Elijah was answered on Mount Carmel precisely during the time assigned for this prayer (*Berachos* 6b).

21. The beginning of the *Minchah* prayer period is one half-hour after midday (O.C. 233:1). The end of this period is nightfall, the emergence of (three medium-sized) stars (*Rama*, O.C. 233:1).

However, *Mishnah Berurah* (§14) contends that the permissible period for *Minchah* ends approximately one quarter-hour before nightfall. Furthermore, he points out that according to many authorities the *Minchah* period ends with sundown and concludes that this view should be followed if at all possible.

Regarding the time of nightfall, some hold that it is the visual sighting of three stars; others hold that it is always the same number of minutes after sundown. Still others hold that it varies according to latitude, since nightfall comes sooner near the equator than it does as one goes further north or south away from the equator.

22. For purposes of *Minchah*, the afternoon is divided into two parts: מִנְחָה גְדֹלָה, the *Greater Minchah Period*, and מִנְחָה קְטַנָּה, the *Lesser Minchah Period*. The first of these periods begins half an hour after midday and extends for three hours. The second begins three and a half hours after midday. (For this and all similar halachic times, an "hour" is $^1/_{12}$ of the daylight hours; see §19.)

23. Preferably, one should recite *Minchah* during the second, later, period (O.C. 233:1). However, if one recites *Minchah* any time after one half-hour after midday he has discharged his obligation (ibid.). Indeed, some congregations, following the view of *Tur* and others, prefer the first half of the afternoon for the *Minchah* prayer.

⋙ The Evening Prayer — Maariv

24. The evening prayer is composed of

three parts — the *Shema*, the benedictions preceding and following it, and the *Shemoneh Esrei*. The time requirements for these parts differ in some details, as will be explained below.

25. The time for the recitation of the *Shema* begins with the emergence of three small stars. [According to *Mishnah Berurah* 235:4, one should wait until at least 72 minutes after sundown.] If *Maariv* was recited before this time, all three paragraphs of the *Shema* should be repeated at night (O.C. 235:1; M.B. §11). Thus, if the congregation prays *Maariv* before this time, one should pray with them, then repeat only the *Shema* at the appropriate time (O.C. 235:1).

26. There are two views in the Mishnah (*Berachos* 26a) regarding the times of *Minchah* and *Maariv*. According to R' Yehudah, the deadline for *Minchah* is an hour and a quarter before sunset; and according to the Sages, the deadline is nightfall. According to both, the time for *Maariv* begins after that of *Minchah*. The *halachah* rules that one may rely on either R' Yehudah or the Sages, provided he follows the same view all the time. Thus, e.g., one may not recite *Minchah* half an hour before sunset (following the Sages) and then recite *Maariv* immediately (following R' Yehudah), since this is a contradiction (O.C. 233:1, M.B. §11). However, this prohibition applies only to an individual. A congregation is permitted to recite *Minchah* and *Maariv* in the same time period if it would be difficult or impossible to reassemble a *minyan* later on (ibid.).

27. The status of the *Shema* benedictions is a matter of dispute: Are they like the *Shema*, which must be recited after dark, or are they like *Shemoneh Esrei* which may be recited earlier? Most of the early authorities conclude that the benedictions before and after the *Maariv Shema* may not be recited before nightfall. However, *Rabbeinu Tam* defends the prevalent custom that the blessings are like *Shemoneh Esrei*, meaning that it is permissible to recite the full *Maariv,* including the blessings, before dark. This custom has been followed for centuries and has the tacit approval of the *poskim*, because if the benedictions were to be said only after nightfall, the communal *Maariv* prayer might be abandoned and many unlearned people might even omit this prayer altogether (O.C. 235:1; M.B. §8 with *Shaar HaTziyun*). Of course this reasoning does not extend to the Scriptural obligation to recite the *Shema*, which must be repeated at night, as explained above in §25.

28. Ideally one should recite the *Shema* as soon as possible after nightfall, and at the latest, before midnight. Nevertheless, the obligation is discharged as long as one recited the *Shema* (and the entire *Maariv* prayer) before the next dawn (O.C. 235:3). Where one could not recite *Maariv* and the delay was not due to neglect, he may discharge his obligation to recite *Shema* even after dawn (but before sunrise). However, in such an instance the fourth (הַשְׁכִּיבֵנוּ) and fifth (בָּרוּךְ ה') blessings are omitted, and the *Shemoneh Esrei* may no longer be recited (O.C. 235:4; M.B. §34).

<hr/>

PRAYER WITH THE CONGREGATION

◈ Prayer With a Minyan of Ten

29. One should try his utmost to pray in the synagogue together with the congregation (O.C. 90:9), for the Almighty does not reject the prayer of the many (M.B. §28). Contrary to the popular misconception that it is sufficient to respond to בָּרְכוּ and קְדוּשָׁה, the main objective of prayer with a *minyan* is to recite *Shemoneh Esrei* with a *minyan*. Therefore, one must arrive at the synagogue early enough so that he can keep up with the congregation.

◈ Instructions for Latecomers

30. If one arrived at the synagogue too late to recite the entire order of the prayers and still recite the *Shemoneh Esrei* together with the congregation, he may omit certain parts of the service and recite them after the end of *Shacharis*. If time is extremely short, it suffices to put on the *tallis* (and *tefillin*) and to say the benedictions עַל נְטִילַת יָדַיִם, אֱלֹהַי נְשָׁמָה, אֲשֶׁר יָצַר, and the benedictions over the Torah (pp. 23-27); בָּרוּךְ שֶׁאָמַר (p. 94); אַשְׁרֵי (p. 99); and from יִשְׁתַּבַּח (p. 119)

through *Shemoneh Esrei*.

31. If time permits, the following sections (listed in descending order of importance) should be recited:

(1) הַלְלוּיָהּ הַלְלוּ אֵל בְּקָדְשׁוֹ (p. 109);

(2) הַלְלוּיָהּ הַלְלוּ אֶת ה' מִן הַשָּׁמַיִם (p. 106);

(3) the other three הַלְלוּיָהּ psalms (pp. 103-108);

(4) לְשֵׁם תִּפְאַרְתֶּךָ until וַיָּבָרֶךְ (pp. 111-112);

(5) וְהוּא רַחוּם until הוֹדוּ (pp. 83-87);

(6) מִזְמוֹר לְתוֹדָה (p. 96);

(7) the rest of *Pesukei D'Zimrah* (O.C. 52:1, M.B. §4, *Ba'er Heitev* §3).

32. The above is only an emergency solution. One should not rely on this to arrive late for the *Pesukei D'Zimrah*, because the proper order of the prayers is of utmost importance. Indeed, some authorities contend that recitation of the prayers in their proper order takes priority over the obligation to recite *Shemoneh Esrei* together with the congregation (M.B. 52:1).

RESPONSES DURING THE PRAYERS

❧ During Pesukei D'Zimrah

33. Other than the exceptions noted below, it is prohibited to interrupt from the beginning of בָּרוּךְ שֶׁאָמַר (see §38) until the conclusion of the *Shemoneh Esrei* (O.C. 51:4). Furthermore, it is not proper to speak until after *Tachanun* (M.B. 51:9; see O.C. 131:1). Wherever one may not talk, it is forbidden to do so even in Hebrew (M.B. 51:7).

34. With the exception of *Shemoneh Esrei*, parts of *Shacharis* may be interrupted for certain responses to the *chazzan* or for certain blessings; but the rules vary widely, depending on the section of *Shacharis* and the response. In this regard, the most lenient part of *Shacharis* is *Pesukei D'Zimrah*, the unit that includes the verses between בָּרוּךְ שֶׁאָמַר and יִשְׁתַּבַּח (pp. 94-119). There, one may respond with *Amen* to any benediction, but may not say the customary בָּרוּךְ הוּא וּבָרוּךְ שְׁמוֹ. It is permitted to respond to *Kedushah* and מוֹדִים (in the repetition of *Shemoneh Esrei*), בָּרְכוּ, and *Kaddish*. If the congregation is reciting the *Shema*, one should recite the first verse (*Shema Yisrael* . . .) together with them. If one discharged his bodily functions, he may recite the benediction אֲשֶׁר יָצַר (M.B. 51:8).

35. For an aliyah: One saying *Pesukei D'Zimrah* should not be called up to the Torah unless he is the only *Kohen* or Levite present. If called, however, he may recite the benedictions and read along quietly with the reader (as usual) but he may not instruct the *gabbai* in regard to a מִי שֶׁבֵּרַךְ (M.B. 51:10).

36. For reciting the Shema: If one did not yet recite the *Shema* and calculates that he will miss the requisite time (see §17 above) if he waits until he reaches it in the prayers, or

if he forgot to say the daily *berachos* on the Torah (p. 24), he should say them in the *Pesukei D'Zimrah* (M.B. 51:10).

37. For reciting Hallel: On days when "half" *Hallel* is recited, one who is in the middle of *Pesukei D'Zimrah* when the congregation reaches *Hallel* should join with them, but should omit the blessings before and after *Hallel*, because his own blessings bracketing *Pesukei D'Zimrah* are in lieu of the blessings of *Hallel*. However, on days when "whole" *Hallel* is recited, one should forgo saying *Hallel* with the congregation and recite it after *Shemoneh Esrei* with its own blessings (M.B. 422:16).

❧ During the Pesukei D'Zimrah Blessings

38. The second level of stringency regarding interruptions includes the two benedictions of *Pesukei D'Zimrah* — בָּרוּךְ שֶׁאָמַר and יִשְׁתַּבַּח.

❏ בָּרוּךְ שֶׁאָמַר is composed of three parts:

(a) From בָּרוּךְ שֶׁאָמַר until the first בָּרוּךְ אַתָּה ה' is merely a preamble and all responses are permitted.

(b) From the first בָּרוּךְ אַתָּה ה' until the final one, all the interruptions permitted in §34 (with the exception of אֲשֶׁר יָצַר) for the rest of *Pesukei D'Zimrah* are also permitted here. The *Amen* after the benedictions בָּרוּךְ שֶׁאָמַר and יִשְׁתַּבַּח are exceptions to this rule; they may not be said.

(c) The last, brief blessing, בָּרוּךְ . . . בְּתִשְׁבָּחוֹת, during which no interruption at all is permitted (M.B. 51:2).

❏ יִשְׁתַּבַּח is composed of two parts:

(a) From the beginning (יִשְׁתַּבַּח) to בָּרוּךְ אַתָּה ה',

which corresponds to (b) above.

(b) From בָּרוּךְ אַתָּה ה' to the end, which corresponds to (c) above (M.B. 51:2, 65:11, 54:11).

✥ Between the Shema Blessings

39. The third level of stringency concerns the "intervals" between the various sections of the *Shema* and the benedictions bracketing it. In *Shacharis*, the intervals are as follows: After יוֹצֵר הַמְּאוֹרוֹת . . . בָּרוּךְ; after בָּרוּךְ וְאַהֲבָה . . .; and after the first and second sections of the *Shema*. [The end of the *Shema* is immediately followed by the first word of the following benediction (אֱמֶת) so that there is no "interval" there, and similarly the end of the benediction גָּאַל יִשְׂרָאֵל must be followed immediately by *Shemoneh Esrei* (O.C. 66:5,9).]

Corresponding "intervals" exist in *Maariv* following each blessing and after the first and second sections of the *Shema* (M.B. 66:27; *Be'ur Halachah* there).

40. Regarding the *Amen* after גָּאַל יִשְׂרָאֵל of *Shacharis*, *Rama*, followed by most Ashkenazi congregations, rules that it may be said, while others, particularly Chassidic congregations, follow R' Yosef Caro's ruling against *Amen* at this point. To avoid the controversy, many individuals recite the blessing in unison with the *chazzan*. In some congregations, the *chazzan* concludes the blessing silently (O.C. 66:7).

41. During the "intervals" one may respond with *Amen* to all benedictions (M.B. 66:23). Regarding קַדִּישׁ, קְדוּשָׁה, בָּרְכוּ, and other interruptions, the "intervals" are treated in the same way as are interruptions in the fourth level (see below §42). During the interval between בְּאַהֲבָה and שְׁמַע, however, only the *Amen* after בְּאַהֲבָה is permitted (*Derech HaChaim*; see M.B. 59:25).

✥ During the Shema and Its Blessings

42. The fourth level concerns the *Shema* itself and the benedictions bracketing it. The benedictions may be separated into two parts for this purpose: During the concluding, brief blessing, and during the verses of *Shema* and בָּרוּךְ שֵׁם, no interruption whatsoever is permitted (O.C. 66:1; M.B. §11,12). During the rest of the fourth level, one may respond with *Amen* only to the two blessings הָאֵל

שׁוֹמֵעַ תְּפִלָּה and הַקָּדוֹשׁ in *Shemoneh Esrei*. It is permitted to respond to בָּרְכוּ of both the *chazzan* and one who is called up to the Torah. In *Kaddish* one may respond with אָמֵן יֵהֵא שְׁמֵיהּ רַבָּא and with the *Amen* to דַּאֲמִירָן . . . בְּעָלְמָא. In *Kedushah* one may say only the verses קָדוֹשׁ . . . and . . . בָּרוּךְ. To *Modim,* one may respond only with the three words מוֹדִים אֲנַחְנוּ לָךְ.

A person who is in the midst of the recitation of the benediction of *Shema* should not be called up to the Torah even if he is the only *Kohen* or Levite present; in such a case it is preferable that he leave the room. However, if someone was called up to the Torah, he may recite the benedictions, but should not read along with the reader; if possible, he should attempt to get to an "interval" in his prayers before doing so (M.B. 66:26). All other responses are prohibited.

If one had to discharge his bodily functions he should merely wash his hands and defer the recitation of אֲשֶׁר יָצַר until after *Shemoneh Esrei* (M.B. 66:23).

43. If one has not yet responded to בָּרְכוּ, קְדוּשָׁה (or מוֹדִים) and he is holding shortly before *Shemoneh Esrei*, he should stop before שִׁירָה חֲדָשָׁה (p. 142) in order to make the responses. If he has already said שִׁירָה חֲדָשָׁה, but has not yet concluded the benediction, he may respond, but after the response he should start again from שִׁירָה חֲדָשָׁה (M.B. 66:52).

44. The fifth level concerns the *Shemoneh Esrei* prayer. Here, all interruptions are forbidden. Even motioning to someone is prohibited (O.C. 104:1; M.B. §1). If the *chazzan* is up to בָּרְכוּ, קְדוּשָׁה, or קַדִּישׁ, one should stop and listen to the *chazzan's* recitation; his own silent concentration is considered as if he had responded (O.C. 104:7; M.B. §26,27).

45. From the time one has concluded the last benediction of *Shemoneh Esrei* with בַּשָּׁלוֹם until the end of the standard prayers (אֱלֹהַי נְצוֹר at the end of יִהְיוּ לְרָצוֹן), one is restricted to the responses listed in level four. However, whenever possible, one should hurry to say the verse יִהְיוּ לְרָצוֹן . . . וְגוֹאֲלִי before any response. It is preferable to take the usual three steps backward before making the responses (O.C. 122:1; M.B. §2-4).

LAWS OF RECITING THE SHEMA

46. It is a Scriptural precept to recite the *Shema* twice daily, once in the morning and again in the evening (see above §16-17, 24-28). It is essential that one bears in mind that he is thereby fulfilling a Scriptural precept; otherwise it must be repeated (O.C. 60:4). However, if the circumstances make it obvious that the intention was present — e.g., he recited it during the prayer with the benedictions preceding and following it — he need not repeat the *Shema* even if he did not make a mental declaration of purpose (M.B. 60:10).

47. The third section of *Shema*, whose recitation is Rabbinical in origin according to almost all authorities, contains a verse whose recitation fulfills the Scriptural obligation to commemorate the Exodus from Egypt twice daily (see *Berachos* 12b; *Rambam, Hil. Kerias Shema* 1:3). The rule regarding a mental declaration of intent outlined in §46 applies here, too.

48. One should concentrate on the meaning of all the words, and read them with awe and trepidation (O.C. 61:1). He should read the *Shema* as if it were a new proclamation containing instructions never yet revealed (O.C. 61:2). The first verse of *Shema* is the essential profession of our faith. Therefore, the utmost concentration on its meaning is necessary. If one said it without such concentration, he has not fulfilled his obligation and must repeat it (O.C. 60:5, 63:4), but he should repeat the verse quietly, for one may not (publicly) say the first verse of *Shema* repeatedly (ibid.).

49. While reciting the first verse, it is customary to cover the eyes with the right hand to avoid distraction and enhance concentration (O.C. 61:5).

50. Although *Shema* may be recited quietly, one should recite it loudly enough to hear himself. However, one has discharged his obligation even if he does not hear himself, as long as he has enunciated the words (O.C. 62:3).

51. The last word of the first verse, אֶחָד, must be pronounced with special emphasis while one meditates on God's sole sovereignty over the seven heavens and the earth,

and the four directions — east, south, west, and north (O.C. 61:6).

52. Some consider it preferable to recite the entire *Shema* aloud (except for the passage בָּרוּךְ שֵׁם) while others say it quietly; our custom follows the latter usage. However, the first verse should be said aloud in order to arouse one's full concentration (O.C. 61:4,26). It is customary for the *chazzan* to lead the congregation in the recitation of the first verse so that they all proclaim God's sovereignty together (*Kol Bo* cited in *Darkei Moshe* to O.C. 61; *Levush*).

53. Every word must be enunciated clearly and uttered with the correct grammatical pronunciation (O.C. 61:15-21,23; 62:1). It is especially important to pause briefly between words ending and beginning with the same consonant, such as וַאֲבַדְתֶּם מְהֵרָה or בְּכָל לְבַבְכֶם, and to pause between a word that ends with a consonant and the next one that begins with a silent letter [א or ע], such as אֲשֶׁר אָנֹכִי, הַיּוֹם עַל, וּרְאִיתֶם אֹתוֹ (O.C. 61:20,21).

54. Although it is not the universal custom to chant the *Shema* with the cantillation melody used during the Torah reading, it is laudable to do so, unless one finds that such chanting interferes with his concentration. In any event, the proper punctuation must be followed so that words are grouped into the proper phrases in accordance with the syntax of each word-group and verse (O.C. 61:24; M.B. §37,38).

55. While reciting the first two portions of the *Shema*, one may not communicate with someone else by winking or motioning with his lips or fingers (O.C. 63:6; M.B. §18).

56. It is incumbent that each paragraph of the *Shema* be read word for word as it appears in the Torah. If one erred and skipped a word, he must return to the place of his error and continue the section from there (O.C. 64:1-2).

57. The *Shema* should be said in one uninterrupted recitation. If one interrupted, whether by talking or waiting silently, he does not have to repeat the *Shema*. However, if the interruption was involuntary in nature, e.g. one was forbidden to finish the

Shema because he had to relieve himself, and the interruption was long enough for him to recite all three paragraphs of the *Shema* at his own normal speed, he must repeat the entire *Shema* (*Rama*, O.C. 65:1). Multiple interruptions interspersed in the recitation of *Shema* are not added together to constitute one long, invalidating interruption (M.B. 65:4).

58. If one is present in the synagogue when the congregation recites the *Shema,* he must recite at least the first verse and the verse שָׁם בָּרוּךְ together with them. If he is in the midst of a prayer that he may not interrupt (see above §38, 39, 41, 42, 45), he should at least give the appearance of saying *Shema* by praying loudly in the tune the congregation uses for the *Shema* (O.C. 65:2,3; M.B. §10).

59. During morning services, it is the custom to gather the four *tzitzis* when one says the words הָאָרֶץ כַּנְפוֹת מֵאַרְבַּע . . . וַהֲבִיאֵנוּ מַהֵר,

Hurry and bring . . . from the four corners of the world, in the paragraph preceding the *Shema* (p. 131). From then on and throughout the *Shema,* the *tzitzis* are held — according to some customs, between the fourth finger and the little finger of the left hand — against the heart (*Ba'er Heitev*, O.C. 59:3; *Derech HaChaim*).

60. When reciting the third portion, 'ה וַיֹּאמֶר, *And* HASHEM *said,* during the morning services, one should also grasp the *tzitzis* with the right hand and look at them, until after he has said the words לָעַד וְנֶחֱמָדִים נֶאֱמָנִים in the וְיַצִּיב אֱמֶת prayer following *Shema.* At that point one should kiss the *tzitzis* and release them from his hand (ibid.). [According to the prevalent custom, one also kisses the *tzitzis* every time he says the word צִיצִית, the אֱמֶת at the end of the *Shema ,* and at לָעַד קַיֶּמֶת. Some kiss them also at הוּא שָׁאַתָּה אֱמֶת.]

ADJUSTMENTS IN THE SHEMONEH ESREI

⸰§ During the Ten Days of Awe

61. During the Ten Days of Repentance, the period between Rosh Hashanah and Yom Kippur, a number of insertions and adjustments are made in the *Shemoneh Esrei.* One group of inserts consists of the verses זָכְרֵנוּ (in the first benediction), כָמוֹךְ מִי (in the second benediction), וּכְתוֹב (in the second to last benediction), and בְּסֵפֶר (in the last benediction). If one omitted any of these inserts he need not (and may not) repeat the whole prayer. However, if he has not yet said the word HASHEM in the formula concluding that benediction, he may return to the insertion and repeat the rest of the benediction following the insert (O.C. 582:5; M.B. §16).

62. The end of the third benediction is changed from הַקָּדוֹשׁ הָאֵל (*the holy God*) to הַקָּדוֹשׁ הַמֶּלֶךְ (*the holy King*). If one forgot and concluded the benediction as usual, he must start again from the beginning of the *Shemoneh Esrei.* However, if he realized his oversight *immediately* and before he began the next benediction, he can rectify the error by saying the words הַקָּדוֹשׁ הַמֶּלֶךְ. In this context, ''immediately'' is defined as no longer than the interval needed to say the three words רַבִּי עָלֶיךָ שָׁלוֹם, *peace upon you, my rebbi* (O.C. 582:1,2; M.B. §7).

If one erred and said הַקָּדוֹשׁ הַמֶּלֶךְ during the rest of the year, he need not repeat the *Shemoneh Esrei* (*Ba'er Heitev* and *Shaarei Teshuvah* to O.C. 118:1).

63. If one is not sure whether he has completed the blessing properly, it is assumed that he said the usual formula הָאֵל הַקָּדוֹשׁ and he must repeat *Shemoneh Esrei* (O.C. 582:1; M.B. §3).

64. At the conclusion of the eleventh benediction, הַמִּשְׁפָּט הַמֶּלֶךְ (*the King of judgment*) is substituted for וּמִשְׁפָּט צְדָקָה אוֹהֵב מֶלֶךְ (*the King Who loves righteousness and judgment*). If one forgot to make this change, he does not have to repeat the prayer. However, if he realized the error immediately (see §62), he should rectify the error (O.C. 118:1; M.B. §3).

65. In some Ashkenazic congregations עוֹשֶׂה הַשָּׁלוֹם is substituted for עַמּוֹ אֶת הַמְבָרֵךְ בַּשָּׁלוֹם יִשְׂרָאֵל in the last benediction (see *Levush* O.C. 582:5; *Likutei Maharich* , et al.). if one concluded with the usual formula need not correct his error.

Many authorities oppose this change in the liturgy. *Mateh Ephraim* (582:22) rules that a chazzan should conform to the congregation's custom in his repetition of the *Shemoneh Esrei.* However, in the formula עוֹשֶׂה בִּמְרוֹמָיו שָׁלוֹם which is recited when stepping

out of *Shemoneh Esrei* and *Kaddish,* עֹשֶׂה הַשָּׁלוֹם should be substituted for עֹשֶׂה שָׁלוֹם (ibid.).

◄§ The End of the Sabbath or Yom Tov — אַתָּה חוֹנַנְתָּנוּ

66. In the first weekday *Maariv* prayer following the Sabbath or a *Yom Tov*, a special prayer, אַתָּה חוֹנַנְתָּנוּ, *You have graciously endowed us,* is inserted in the fourth benediction of *Shemoneh Esrei*. The function of this prayer is to declare the distinction between the higher holiness of the Sabbath and Festivals and the mundane nature of the weekdays. If one forgets to insert this prayer he may not repeat the benediction, nor should he insert this prayer in the benediction שְׁמַע קוֹלֵנוּ. Rather, he should rely on the *Havdalah* which will be recited over wine after *Maariv* (O.C. 294:1; M.B. §6).

Even after the Sabbath has departed, it is prohibited to do any forbidden work before reciting אַתָּה חוֹנַנְתָּנוּ or *Havdalah*. Therefore, if one has not yet recited either, one should be very careful not to do any work even after dark. This should be especially stressed in regard to women: Since they generally do not recite *Maariv*, they should not do any work before hearing *Havdalah*. However, by saying the words בָּרוּךְ הַמַּבְדִּיל בֵּין קֹדֶשׁ לְחוֹל, *Blessed is He Who separates between holy and secular,* one becomes permitted to do work (O.C. 299:10; see *Shaar HaTziyun* §47).

◄§ Seasonal Additions

67. Several insertions in the *Shemoneh Esrei* — the prayers regarding rain and dew — are related to the seasonal needs of agriculture. These prayers were fixed in Talmudic times according to the seasonal rain requirements of *Eretz Yisrael* and Babylonia. The Diaspora follows the practice of Babylonia as established in the Talmud.

◄§ מַשִּׁיב הָרוּחַ וּמוֹרִיד הַגֶּשֶׁם

68. The first of these insertions is in the second benediction. Beginning with the *Mussaf* prayer of *Shemini Atzeres*, מַשִּׁיב הָרוּחַ וּמוֹרִיד הַגֶּשֶׁם, *Who makes the wind blow and makes the rain descend,* is inserted (both in *Eretz Yisrael* and in the Diaspora). This formula is said until the *Mussaf* prayer of the first day of Pesach (see below §71). This is not an actual prayer for rain but merely a mention of God's rain-giving power.

69. If the insertion was omitted, one must start again from the beginning of the *Shemoneh Esrei*. Many congregations recite מוֹרִיד הַטָּל, *Who makes the dew descend,* in place of מַשִּׁיב הָרוּחַ between Pesach and *Shemini Atzeres* (see §71). If one said מוֹרִיד הַטָּל instead of מַשִּׁיב הָרוּחַ, the prayer need not be repeated since he has mentioned God's role in one form of needed precipitation (O.C. 114:5).

70. One is not considered to have omitted this insertion unless he has begun the word אַתָּה of the next benediction, אַתָּה קָדוֹשׁ. Thus, if one realizes his omission after having concluded the word מְחַיֶּה הַמֵּתִים (or said the word *Hashem* in the concluding formula) but has not yet begun אַתָּה קָדוֹשׁ (or in the case of the *chazzan's Shemoneh Esrei*, the *Kedushah*), he says the words מַשִּׁיב הָרוּחַ וּמוֹרִיד הַגֶּשֶׁם and continues with אַתָּה קָדוֹשׁ. If he has not even begun the concluding formula of the benediction (בָּרוּךְ . . . מְחַיֵּה הַמֵּתִים) or has at least not yet said the word *Hashem* in that formula, he should recite מַשִּׁיב הָרוּחַ וּמוֹרִיד הַגֶּשֶׁם between phrases and conclude the benediction (O.C. 114:6 with *Be'ur Halachah*). [However, if he realized his error after saying the word וְנֶאֱמָן, he should say מַשִּׁיב הָרוּחַ וּמוֹרִיד הַגֶּשֶׁם, and start over from וְנֶאֱמָן (see M.B. 114:29).]

71. The insertion of מַשִּׁיב הָרוּחַ וּמוֹרִיד הַגֶּשֶׁם is discontinued after the *Mussaf* prayer of the first day of Pesach. Most Ashkenazic congregations follow the old custom and do not recite מוֹרִיד הַטָּל in place of מוֹרִיד הַגֶּשֶׁם, while others, especially in *Eretz Yisrael*, practice the Sephardic custom to recite מוֹרִיד הַטָּל until *Shemini Atzeres*. But even those who adopt the latter custom agree that the omission of מוֹרִיד הַטָּל does not require that *Shemoneh Esrei* be repeated (O.C. 114:3).

72. Just as the omission of מוֹרִיד הַגֶּשֶׁם in the appropriate season necessitates repetition of the *Shemoneh Esrei*, so must one repeat the entire prayer if he has recited מוֹרִיד הַגֶּשֶׁם at the wrong time, because rain in the wrong season is an omen of bad times. If one realizes his error before concluding the benediction (מְחַיֵּה הַמֵּתִים), he should return to the beginning of the benediction (אַתָּה גִבּוֹר). If he has already concluded the benediction, he must start again from the beginning of the *Shemoneh Esrei*. This is so even if he said both מוֹרִיד הַטָּל and מוֹרִיד הַגֶּשֶׁם (O.C. 114:4).

73. If one is not sure whether he recited מוֹרִיד הַגֶּשֶׁם, it is assumed that someone recited whatever he has been accustomed to, until a different recitation becomes habitual. The Sages set down the presumption that until someone has recited a new addition for thirty days, it has not yet become habitual with him. Consequently, until thirty days after Pesach began, it is assumed that someone recited מַשִּׁיב הָרוּחַ, and until thirty days after *Shemini Atzeres* it is assumed that he said either nothing or מוֹרִיד הַטָּל (O.C. 114:8).

74. One can spare himself the necessity to repeat the *Shemoneh Esrei* in cases of the doubtful omission of מוֹרִיד הַגֶּשֶׁם. On Shemini Atzeres he may repeat the passage מְחַיֵּה מֵתִים ,,אַתָּה, רַב לְהוֹשִׁיעַ. מַשִּׁיב . . ." one hundred and one times [if he said this only ninety times it is sufficient *ex post facto*], thereby assuring that he will henceforth insert the מוֹרִיד הַגֶּשֶׁם. The same is true for those who say מוֹרִיד הַטָּל in the summer; they may repeat הַטָּל . . . מְחַיֵּה the same amount of times on the first day of Pesach. Some authorities rule that the same is true for those who practice the Ashkenazic custom and do not say מוֹרִיד הַטָּל in the summer. They, too, may repeat מְחַיֵּה . . . לְהוֹשִׁיעַ, מְבַלְכֵּל חַיִּים, omitting הַגֶּשֶׁם . . . מַשִּׁיב for the required amount of times, and be assured of saying the correct formula henceforth. However, *Derech HaChaim* disputes this analogy and cautions that it not be relied upon. Similarly the repetition of וְאֵת כָּל מִינֵי תְבוּאָתָהּ לְטוֹבָה, or of וְתֵן בְּרָכָה . . . וְאֵת, or וְתֵן טַל וּמָטָר לִבְרָכָה (see below), is efficacious to remove doubts of incorrect recitation (O.C. 114:9, M.B. there).

וְתֵן טַל וּמָטָר ﷼

75. A request for rain — וְתֵן טַל וּמָטָר — is inserted in the benediction בָּרֵךְ עָלֵינוּ, *Bless on our behalf*, in the appropriate season. The time for this request is fixed according to the usual need for rain in *Eretz Yisrael* and Babylonia in Talmudic times (O.C. 117:2).

76. In *Eretz Yisrael* the insertion is begun in the *Maariv* prayer of 7 Cheshvan and continued until the *Minchah* prayer immediately before Pesach. In the Diaspora, this recitation is begun on the sixtieth day after the autumnal equinox as computed according to the method of Shmuel. [See *Eruvin* 56a; ArtScroll *Bircas HaChammah* pp. 45-56.]

77. Thus, the recitation of טַל וּמָטָר is begun in the Diaspora on a fixed day on the solar calendar and its position in the Jewish calendar varies from year to year. Generally, the recitation is begun in the *Maariv* of December 4, but in the December preceding a civil leap year, it is begun in the *Maariv* of December 5.

A resident of the Diaspora who will be in *Eretz Yisrael* during the entire period from 7 Cheshvan through December 4, should conform to the local practice and recite וְתֵן טַל וּמָטָר in the benediction בָּרֵךְ עָלֵינוּ. However, a visitor to *Eretz Yisrael* who will be returning before December 4 should continue to say וְתֵן בְּרָכָה, but should insert the words וְתֵן טַל וּמָטָר לִבְרָכָה before the words כִּי אַתָּה שׁוֹמֵעַ, *for You hear*, in the benediction שׁוֹמֵעַ תְּפִלָּה.

A resident of *Eretz Yisrael* who is in the Diaspora on 7 Cheshvan and who intends to return within the year, should start reciting וְתֵן טַל וּמָטָר לִבְרָכָה in the benediction שׁוֹמֵעַ תְּפִלָּה on 7 Cheshvan. If he left *Eretz Yisrael* after 7 Cheshvan when he began reciting וְתֵן טַל וּמָטָר in the benediction בָּרֵךְ עָלֵינוּ, he should continue reciting it there.

Note that if one is serving as the *chazzan* he should conform to the local custom for the repetition of the *Shemoneh Esrei*. (See *Ishei Yisrael* 23:37-39; *Halichos Shlomo* 8:19-21).

78. If one forgot to say וְתֵן טַל וּמָטָר at the appropriate time, but has not yet said the word HASHEM in the concluding formula (בָּרוּךְ . . . מְבָרֵךְ הַשָּׁנִים.), he should say וְתֵן טַל וּמָטָר and continue from wherever he was up to (O.C. 117:4 with M.B.). However, the last portion of the בָּרֵךְ עָלֵינוּ formula [from וּבָרֵךְ שְׁנָתֵנוּ . . . and further] must always be said immediately before 'בָּרוּךְ אַתָּה ה. Thus, if one forgot וְתֵן טַל וּמָטָר, but had already begun the phrase וּבָרֵךְ שְׁנָתֵנוּ before realizing his oversight, he must recite וְתֵן טַל וּמָטָר and continue from וּבָרֵךְ שְׁנָתֵנוּ (M.B. 117:15).

79. If one had already concluded the benediction when he realized his error (even if he had not yet begun the following benediction; M.B. 15; cf. *Aruch HaShulchan* 117:6), he should continue his *Shemoneh Esrei* and insert the words וְתֵן טַל וּמָטָר לִבְרָכָה before the words כִּי אַתָּה שׁוֹמֵעַ, *for You hear*, in the benediction שׁוֹמֵעַ תְּפִלָּה. On a fast day, the insertion of טַל וּמָטָר at this point will precede עֲנֵנוּ (O.C. 117:5 with M.B.).

80. If one realized his error after he had already begun the benediction רְצֵה, he must return to בָּרֵךְ עָלֵינוּ. If he had already concluded the *Shemoneh Esrei* he must start again from the beginning. The conclusion of *Shemoneh Esrei* is defined as the recitation of the verse יִהְיוּ לְרָצוֹן, just before stepping out of *Shemoneh Esrei* (O.C. 117:5 with M.B.).

81. If טַל וּמָטָר was said in the wrong season of the year, one must go back to the beginning of בָּרֵךְ עָלֵינוּ and continue from there. If he has concluded the *Shemoneh Esrei* he must begin again from the beginning. Conclusion of *Shemoneh Esrei* is defined here as in §80 (O.C. 114:8).

82. When one is not sure what he said, the same laws apply as in §73 and §74 above.

83. If an entire country experienced a drought and was in special need of rain during a period when טַל וּמָטָר is not recited, but someone erred and *did* recite טַל וּמָטָר, he need not repeat the *Shemoneh Esrei* (O.C. 117:2; see *Be'ur Halachah* s.v. ושאל, and *Shoneh Halachos*). [For some of the refinements of this rule in regard to a country not in a state of drought but in which rain is not unwelcome during this period, see *Be'ur Halachah* to O.C. 117:2, s.v. הצריכין; M.B. §10.]

◆§ Fast Days — עֲנֵנוּ

84. On fast days a special prayer — עֲנֵנוּ — is interjected both in the silent *Shemoneh Esrei* and in the *chazzan's* repetition. This prayer may be said only by one who is fasting; for someone not fasting, to recite this prayer would be deceitful (see O.C. 565:3 and *Rama*). This insertion is made by the *chazzan* in the loud *Shemoneh Esrei* of both *Shacharis* and *Minchah,* but in the silent *Shemoneh Esrei* it is said only during *Minchah* (ibid.). The *chazzan's* prayer is placed between . . . בָּרוּךְ גּוֹאֵל יִשְׂרָאֵל and רְפָאֵנוּ and takes the form of a complete benediction, concluding with בָּרוּךְ . . . , *Blessed . . . Who responds to His people, Israel, in time of distress* (O.C. 566:1). The individual's recitation is said as part of the benediction שְׁמַע קוֹלֵנוּ (O.C. 565:1). In order for the *chazzan* to recite עֲנֵנוּ as a separate benediction in his repetition of the *Shemoneh Esrei* there should be ten congregants who are fasting. Some authori-

ties rule that in the four fasts which are of Biblical origin (Fast of Gedalyah; Tenth of Teves; Seventeenth of Tammuz; Ninth of Av) it is sufficient that there be seven fasting individuals (O.C. 566:3; M.B. §14). [On other fasts, e.g., the Fast of Esther, a full quorum of ten fasting individuals is required.]

85. If an individual forgot to insert עֲנֵנוּ in its proper place and has already said the word HASHEM in the concluding formula of שְׁמַע קוֹלֵנוּ, he must conclude with שׁוֹמֵעַ תְּפִלָּה and continue with רְצֵה. He may insert עֲנֵנוּ at the end of the *Shemoneh Esrei* before אֱלֹהַי. If he finished his prayer before realizing his error, he should not repeat the *Shemoneh Esrei* (M.B. 119:16,19).

86. If the *chazzan* forgot to insert עֲנֵנוּ in its proper place but has not yet said the word HASHEM of the concluding formula of the benediction רְפָאֵנוּ, he should interrupt his recitation, return to עֲנֵנוּ, and when he has concluded it, he should again say רְפָאֵנוּ. If he has already uttered the word HASHEM he must conclude with . . . רוֹפֵא חוֹלֵי and continue his prayer as usual. In this case, the *chazzan* inserts עֲנֵנוּ in the benediction שְׁמַע קוֹלֵנוּ as do individuals in the silent prayer, but the concluding formula בָּרוּךְ . . . הָעוֹנֶה לְעַמּוֹ יִשְׂרָאֵל בְּעֵת צָרָה is deleted. If he realized his error after he uttered the word HASHEM in the concluding formula of שְׁמַע קוֹלֵנוּ he must continue with הַמְבָרֵךְ אֶת עַמּוֹ; he may add עֲנֵנוּ after שׁוֹמֵעַ תְּפִלָּה; יִשְׂרָאֵל בַּשָּׁלוֹם, omitting the concluding formula (O.C. 119:4; M.B. §16,19).

◆§ Tishah B'Av — נַחֵם

87. In the *Minchah* prayer of Tishah B'Av, in addition to עֲנֵנוּ, yet another prayer (נַחֵם, *Console*), marking the destruction of the Holy Temple and supplicating for its rebuilding, is inserted in the benediction וְלִירוּשָׁלַיִם, *And to Jerusalem* (both in the silent and loud *Shemoneh Esrei*). The concluding formula is changed to בָּרוּךְ . . . מְנַחֵם צִיּוֹן וּבוֹנֶה יְרוּשָׁלַיִם, *Blessed . . . Who consoles Zion and rebuilds Jerusalem* (both for the individual and *chazzan*). If one forgot to recite this prayer in its appropriate place he should say it in the benediction רְצֵה before the words וְתֶחֱזֶינָה with the deletion of the concluding formula מְנַחֵם צִיּוֹן . . . (O.C. 557:1; M.B. §2). However, if it was said erroneously in the benediction

שְׁמַע קוֹלֵנוּ it need not be repeated in רְצֵה (Be'ur Halachah). If one has already concluded the רְצֵה benediction with לְצִיּוֹן . . . הַמַּחֲזִיר (or even said the word HASHEM), he continues the prayer and need not repeat it because of the deletion (O.C. 557).

◆§ Rosh Chodesh and Festivals — יַעֲלֶה וְיָבֹא

88. On Rosh Chodesh, the prayer יַעֲלֶה וְיָבֹא is inserted in the benediction רְצֵה, *Be favorable*. If it is forgotten in the *Maariv* prayer (of either the first or second night of Rosh Chodesh), one need not repeat the prayer (O.C. 422:1). If the omission occurred during the *Shacharis* or *Minchah* prayers, *Shemoneh Esrei* must be repeated. Thus, if one realized his error before uttering the word HASHEM in the formula concluding the benediction, he returns to יַעֲלֶה וְיָבֹא. If he has already concluded with לְצִיּוֹן שְׁכִינָתוֹ הַמַּחֲזִיר but not yet begun the benediction מוֹדִים, he should recite יַעֲלֶה וְיָבֹא there (till מֶלֶךְ חַנּוּן וְרַחוּם אַתָּה) and continue with מוֹדִים. If he had already begun to say מוֹדִים, he must return to the beginning of the benediction רְצֵה. If he had concluded *Shemoneh Esrei*, he must repeat it in its entirety (ibid.).

One is considered to have ''concluded'' in this context when one has recited the verse יִהְיוּ לְרָצוֹן at the conclusion of the prayer אֱלֹהַי (before עֹשֶׂה שָׁלוֹם; see M.B. 422:9).

If one is in doubt whether he has said יַעֲלֶה וְיָבֹא he must assume he has not said it. However, if he knows that while praying he was aware that he had to recite יַעֲלֶה וְיָבֹא, but is in doubt some time after concluding the prayer, he may assume that he fulfilled his intention and recited יַעֲלֶה וְיָבֹא (M.B. 422:10).

The rules for יַעֲלֶה וְיָבֹא on the intermediate days of the Festivals are the same as on Rosh Chodesh with the following exception: If יַעֲלֶה וְיָבֹא is forgotten even in the *Maariv* prayer, the *Shemoneh Esrei* must be repeated (O.C. 490:2).

◆§ Purim and Chanukah — עַל הַנִּסִּים

89. On Purim and Chanukah special prayers, beginning with the words וְעַל הַנִּסִּים, (And) for the miracles, commemorating the events of the Festival, are inserted in the benediction of מוֹדִים, *We thank*. If these prayers were omitted one must not repeat

the prayer. However, if one realized his error prior to saying the word HASHEM in the concluding formula of the benediction (בָּרוּךְ . . . וּלְךָ נָאֶה לְהוֹדוֹת) he should return to עַל הַנִּסִּים and proceed from there. If the word HASHEM has already been said, the benediction should be concluded and one should proceed until the end of *Shemoneh Esrei*. Then, before the verse יִהְיוּ לְרָצוֹן at the end of the prayer אֱלֹהַי which is said at the conclusion of the *Shemoneh Esrei*, he should add the introductory request הָרַחֲמָן (p. 308) followed by בִּימֵי (O.C. 682:1; M.B. §4).

◆§ The Chazzan's Repetition of the Shemoneh Esrei

90. According to a Rabbinic enactment dating back to Mishnaic times, *Shemoneh Esrei* must be repeated whenever at least six individuals of a quorum of ten (*minyan*) have prayed the silent *Shemoneh Esrei* together (O.C. 124:1; M.B. 69:8).

91. There must be a quorum (of ten, including the *chazzan*) present and listening to the recitation. If the congregants do not pay attention it is almost as if the *chazzan* were taking God's Name in vain. Every person should imagine that there are only ten congregants present and that he is one of the nine whose attentive listening is vital to the recitation (O.C. 124:4).

92. One must respond with *Amen* to every benediction he hears, and should teach his young children to do so (O.C. 124:6,7).

93. When saying *Amen*, one must enunciate all the vowels and consonants distinctly. One should not respond before the *chazzan* has concluded the benediction, and then the response should be immediate (O.C. 124:8).

94. It is absolutely forbidden to talk during the *Shemoneh Esrei* even if one makes sure to respond with *Amen* at the conclusion of the benediction (O.C. 124:7). *Mishnah Berurah* (§17) cautions even against Torah study or recitation of psalms or prayers during the *chazzan's* recitation of the *Shemoneh Esrei*.

95. On most days *Shemoneh Esrei* is followed with the *Tachanun* prayer. One should be careful not to engage in idle talk between *Shemoneh Esrei* and *Tachanun* (O.C. 131:1).

THE READING OF THE TORAH

◆§ The Aliyos

96. The Torah is read in public during *Sha-charis* and *Minchah* of the Sabbath and of fast days, and during *Shacharis* of *Yom Tov*, Chol HaMoed, Rosh Chodesh, Chanukah, Purim, and every Monday and Thursday. On most of these occasions, three people are called to the Torah; Rosh Chodesh and Chol HaMoed, four; Festivals, five; Yom Kippur *Shacharis*, six; Sabbath *Shacharis*, seven. On the Sabbath morning, more people may be called, although some authorities prefer not to do so. It is customary not to add to the *aliyos* on Yom Tov (with the exception of Simchas Torah). On other occasions of Torah reading it is forbidden to add *aliyos* (O.C. 135:1,10, 282:1, 423:1; *Mishnah, Megillah* 21a).

97. The first *aliyah* belongs to a *Kohen* and the second to a *Levi* (if any are present). If no *Kohen* is present, there is no obligation to call a *Levi* in his place, but if no *Levi* is present the same *Kohen* who has been called for his own *aliyah* is called again to replace the *Levi*. He recites both blessings again. According to the prevalent custom, a *Kohen* or *Levi* may not be called up for any other *aliyah* except *maftir* or *acharon*, the last *aliyah* of the weekly Sabbath portion (*sidra*). However, they may be called for *acharon* only after the prescribed number of seven *aliyos* has been completed (O.C. 135:10).

◆§ Entitlements to Aliyos

98. Time-honored custom has established that certain occasions entitle one to an *aliyah*. These are listed in *Levush* and *Magen Avraham* to *Orach Chaim* 282, and in *Be'ur Halachah* to O.C. 136. Below is a list of these entitlements in descending order of importance. If there are not enough *aliyos* to go around, then the *aliyos* are given according to the importance of the entitlement. If more than one individual are equally entitled, lots should be drawn for the *aliyah*. However, if one of the individuals is an acknowledged Torah scholar (*talmid chacham*), he should be given preference.

(a) **A bridegroom** on the day of his wedding has preference over any other entitled person.

(b) **A bridegroom** on the Sabbath before his wedding; however a widower or divorced man is not entitled to an *aliyah* before he remarries and has no preference over any entitled person. Nonetheless, *Shaarei Ephraim* advises that he should be given an *aliyah* if possible. [The bridegroom's father should also be given an *aliyah* if possible (*Shaarei Ephraim* 2:3).]

(c) **A bar mitzvah** on the Sabbath after his birthday. A *bar mitzvah* is equal to a bridegroom whose marriage will take place the following week. If there is a conflict, lots should be drawn.

[It can be inferred from the *poskim* that a *bar mitzvah* is not entitled to an *aliyah* the Sabbath preceding his *bar mitzvah*. Nevertheless, it is customary in many congregations to award him *maftir*. If he had an *aliyah*, even in the weekdays, he is no longer entitled to an *aliyah* on the Sabbath after his birthday (*Shaarei Ephraim* 2:10).

(d) **A husband** whose wife has given birth is entitled to an *aliyah* the first Sabbath his wife attends the synagogue. Even if she is not in the synagogue, he is entitled to an *aliyah* when forty days have elapsed after the birth of a son or eighty days after the birth of a daughter, even if the child was stillborn.

(e) **A bridegroom** whose marriage has taken place within the three days before the Sabbath, but only if it is the first marriage for either the groom or bride. [Although a bridegroom who was married earlier in the week is not entitled to have an *aliyah*, it is nevertheless customary to give him one (*Shaarei Epharim*).]

(f) **Someone observing yahrzeit** for a parent. If the *yahrzeit* is on the day of the Torah reading, there is no absolute obligation to give him an *aliyah*, but it is customary to give *maftir* or an *aliyah* on the Sabbath preceding a *yahrzeit*.

(g) **The father** of a newborn child on the Sabbath before the circumcision. In some places the *sandak* and *mohel* [if he performs the *mitzvah* gratis; cf. *Shaarei Ephraim* 2:15] are also awarded *aliyos*, whereas in some congregations they are honored with picking up (*hagbahah*) and rolling together (*gelilah*)

the Torah. [If the child is sick and his *bris* will surely be deferred the father is not entitled to an *aliyah* (*Shaarei Ephraim* 2:8).]

(h) **On Rosh Hashanah and Yom Kippur** some congregations award *aliyos* to the *chazzan* of *Mussaf* and the one who sounds the *shofar* on Rosh Hashanah. However, if they are paid for their services they forfeit their entitlement.

99. In addition to the above, whose priorities are established by a well-defined order of importance, there are other individuals to whom it is customary to award *aliyos*. A person who must recite the benediction הַגּוֹמֵל, e.g., he had been gravely ill and has recovered, or gone through another dangerous situation (see p. 193) should be given an *aliyah*. If it is not possible to give him an *aliyah* because of the presence of genuinely entitled individuals, he should go before the congregation and recite the benediction הַגּוֹמֵל without an *aliyah*.

100. It is customary to award an *aliyah* to the father of a newborn daughter on the occasion when she is given a name;

to one who will leave on a prolonged trip which will require his absence from the synagogue for longer than a week;

to one who has just returned from such a trip; and to a distinguished guest.

◄§ Close Relatives in Successive Aliyos

101. Two brothers, or a father and a son, should not be called up to the Torah in succession. Some authorities feel that this stringency be adhered to even in regard to a grandfather and his grandson (O.C. 141:6; M.B. there). However, when *maftir* is read from a second Torah Scroll, as on Yom Tov, even brothers or a father and a son may be called up in succession (*Ba'er Heitev* 141:6).

◄§ Procedure of the Aliyah

102. Before the *oleh* — the person called to the Torah for an *aliyah* — recites the benediction, he must open the Torah and find the passage that will be read for him (O.C. 139:4). In order to dispel any notion that he is reading the benedictions from the Torah, one should avert his face while reciting them; it is preferable to turn to the left side (*Rama* there). Some authorities maintain that it is better to face the Torah while saying the benedictions

but to close one's eyes to dispel the above-mentioned notion (M.B. §19). Others say that it is better to close the Torah during the recitation of the benedictions (*Be'ur Halachah* there). All three modes are practiced today in various congregations.

103. In many congregations it is customary to touch the Torah with the *tallis* (or the Torah's mantle or girdle) at the place in the Torah where the passage to be read begins, and to kiss the edge which touched the Torah. One should be careful not to rub on the Torah script forcefully for this can cause words to become erased and thus invalidate the Torah.

104. It is extremely important that the benedictions be said loud enough for the congregation to hear (O.C. 139:6). If the congregation did not hear the recitation of בָּרְכוּ they may not respond with וְעַד . . . בָּרוּךְ (*Be'ur Halachah* to O.C. 57:1). However, if the congregation (or at least a *minyan*) heard בָּרְכוּ, then even someone who has not heard בָּרְכוּ may respond with בָּרוּךְ . . וְעַד along with the congregation (M.B. 57:2).

105. While reciting the benedictions, one should hold the poles (*atzei chaim*) upon which the Torah is rolled (O.C. 139:11). According to *Arizal* (cited in *Magen Avraham* 139:13), the *oleh* holds the *atzei chaim* in both hands before reciting the benedictions, and only the right one in his right hand during the benedictions. The *oleh* should also hold the *eitz chaim* during the Torah reading (M.B. 139:35). However, the custom is that the *oleh* holds the *atzei chaim* in both hands while reciting the benedictions, and during the reading the *oleh* holds the right *eitz chaim* while the reader holds the left one.

106. Upon completion of the reading it is customary for the *oleh* to touch the Torah with his *tallis* (or the Torah's mantle or girdle) and to kiss the edge that has touched the Torah (see M.B. 139:35).

107. After the Torah passage has been read, the Torah scroll is closed and then the benediction is said (*Rama* O.C. 139:5). If the Torah reading will not be resumed immediately (e.g., a מִי שֶׁבֵּרַךְ is said), then a covering should be spread over the Torah (M.B. 139:21).

108. In Talmudic times the *oleh* would also read aloud from the Torah. This practice was still followed in Greek and Turkish communities up to the 16th century (see *Beis Yosef* to *Tur* O.C. 141), and the tradition persists to this day in Yemenite communities. However, since ancient times the Ashkenazic custom has been for a designated reader (*baal korei*) to read the Torah aloud to the congregation (see *Rosh* cited in *Tur* loc. cit.). Nevertheless, the person who recites the benedictions should read quietly along with the reader (O.C. 141:2).

109. The reader and *oleh* must stand while reading the Torah in public. It is forbidden even to lean upon something (O.C. 141:1).

110. When the *oleh* goes up to the *bimah*, he should pick the shortest route possible, and when returning to his place he should take the longer route. If two routes are equidistant, one should go to the *bimah* via the route which is to his right and descend via the opposite route (O.C. 141:7).

111. After reciting the concluding benediction, one should not return to his place until the next *oleh* has come to the *bimah* (O.C. 141:7). However, it is customary to wait until the reading for the next *oleh* has been completed (M.B. §26).

112. It is forbidden to talk or even to discuss Torah topics while the Torah is being read (O.C. 146:2).

113. It is forbidden to leave the synagogue while the Torah is being read (O.C. 146:1), even if one has already heard the reading of the passage elsewhere (M.B. §1). However, if necessary, one may leave during the pause between two portions (O.C. 146:1), provided that a *minyan* remains (M.B. §2).

KADDISH

114. The conclusion of a segment of prayer is usually signified by the recitation of the *Kaddish*. Many of these *Kaddish* recitations are the privilege of mourners (within the eleven months following the death or burial of a parent, or in some instances, of other close relatives), or of those observing *yahrzeit*, i.e., the anniversary of the death of a parent (and in some congregations, of a grandparent who has no living sons; see *Mateh Ephraim, Dinei Kaddish* 3:14). However, many recitations of *Kaddish* are exclusively the prerogative of the *chazzan*.

115. Basically, there are four types of *Kaddish*:

(a) חֲצִי קַדִּיש, Half-*Kaddish*, which ends with דַּאֲמִירָן בְּעָלְמָא וְאִמְרוּ אָמֵן;

(b) קַדִּיש יָתוֹם, the *Mourner's Kaddish*, which consists of Half-*Kaddish*, with the addition of יְהֵא שְׁלָמָא and עוֹשֶׂה שָׁלוֹם;

(c) קַדִּיש שָׁלֵם, the *Full Kaddish*, the same as the *Mourner's Kaddish* with the addition of תִּתְקַבֵּל before יְהֵא שְׁלָמָא; and

(d) קַדִּיש דְּרַבָּנָן, the *Rabbis' Kaddish*, the same as the *Mourner's Kaddish* with the addition of עַל יִשְׂרָאֵל.

116. The function of the Half-*Kaddish* is to link different segments of the prayer, e.g., it is recited between *Pesukei D'Zimrah* and the *Shema* benedictions, between *Shemoneh Esrei* (or *Tachanun*) and the prayers that conclude the service (*Pri Megadim* in *Mishbetzos Zahav, Orach Chaim* 55:1). Thus, it is recited by the *chazzan*.

Nevertheless, in some congregations it is customary for a mourner to recite the *Kaddish* following the reading of the Torah if he has been called to the Torah for the concluding segment (*Shaarei Ephraim* 10:9). The rationale for the latter custom is that the person called to the Torah is also a *chazzan* of sorts, since he too must read from the Torah, albeit quietly. In some congregations, a mourner recites this *Kaddish* even if he was not called to the Torah.

117. The Full *Kaddish* is recited only after the communal recitation of *Shemoneh Esrei* (or *Selichos*). It includes the *chazzan's* prayer that the just-concluded service be accepted by God. Consequently, it must be recited by the *chazzan*. In congregations where one *chazzan* recited *Shemoneh Esrei* and a different *chazzan* recited *Hallel*, the *Kaddish* should be recited by the *chazzan* who recited *Shemoneh Esrei*.

118. The Mourner's *Kaddish* is said after the

recital of Scriptural verses that supplement the main body of prayer. The recital of Kaddish after this portion of the service is not obligatory, and is not recited if there are no mourners present. If a mourner had served as chazzan, he would have fulfilled his Kaddish obligation with the four times Kaddish appears in the service. However, because there are mourners who cannot serve as chazzan, e.g., minors or when many mourners are present, it was necessary to reserve the Kaddish following the supplemental prayers for them (see Aruch HaShulchan O.C. 133:2). Since Kaddish in these parts of the service is recited exclusively by mourners, it has become customary that one whose parents are alive should not recite it, since this would be a mark of disrespect to his parents (see Pischei Teshuvah, Yoreh Deah 376:4).

If there are no mourners present, the Mourner's Kaddish is not recited, with one exception. After Aleinu, which also contains Scriptural verses, Kaddish should be recited even if there is no mourner present. In such a case, it should be recited by one of the congregants, preferably by one whose parents are no longer alive, or by one whose parents have not explicitly expressed their opposition to his recitation of Kaddish (Orach Chaim 132:2 with M.B. §11).

119. Ideally, each Mourner's Kaddish should be recited by only one person. Where more than one mourner is present, the poskim developed a system of rules establishing an order of priorities for those who must recite Kaddish (see M.B. in Be'ur Halachah to O.C. 132, et al.). However, since adherence to these rules can often cause discord in the congregation, it has become widely ac-

cepted for all the mourners to recite the Kaddish simultaneously (see Aruch HaShulchan O.C. 132:8; Siddur R' Yaakov Emden; Teshuvos Chasam Sofer, O.C. 159).

120. In many congregations it is customary that someone observing a yahrzeit is given the exclusive privilege of reciting a Kaddish, usually the one after Aleinu. In that case, an additional psalm (usually Psalm 24) is recited at the conclusion of the services so that the mourners can all recite Kaddish thereafter.

121. The Rabbis' Kaddish (Kaddish D'Rabbanan) is recited after segments of the Oral Torah (e.g., Talmud) have been studied or recited by a quorum of ten adult males (Rambam, Seder Tefillos Kol HaShanah). The Talmud (Sotah 49a) refers to the great significance of יְהֵא שְׁמֵהּ רַבָּא (a reference to Kaddish) that is said after Aggadah, indicating that this Kaddish has a special relevance to the Midrashic portion of the Torah. Therefore, it is customary to append a brief Aggadic selection to Torah study before reciting the Rabbis' Kaddish. Similarly, an Aggadic passage should be recited prior to Kaddish that is recited after the study of Mishnah (Magen Avraham 54:3).

122. Although Kaddish D'Rabbanan is not reserved for mourners and may be recited even by one whose parents are alive (Pischei Teshuvah, Yoreh Deah 376:4), it is customarily recited by mourners. However, when one celebrates the completion of a tractate of the Talmud, or when the rabbi delivers a derashah (homiletical discourse), it is customary for the celebrant or the rabbi to recite the Kaddish himself.

MINYAN

123. A minyan (quorum of ten adult males) must be present during Borchu; the chazzan's repetition of Shemoneh Esrei; Kaddish; and the Torah reading. Therefore, it is a grave sin (cf. Isaiah 1:28) to leave the synagogue during any of these recitations if one's presence is necessary to complete the minyan (O.C. 55:2).

124. Nonetheless, if any of these recitations began with a minyan, but some indi-

viduals left and a minyan is no longer present, the recitation may continue, if at least six individuals remain.

125. Thus, if the chazzan began his repetition of the Shemoneh Esrei, he may conclude it — including Kedushah — even if a minyan is no longer present. (If this happened at Mussaf of a Festival, the Kohanim may not ascend the duchan.) Moreover, the chazzan may even recite the Half-Kaddish after Tachanun and

the Full *Kaddish* after וּבָא לְצִיּוֹן, and the Full *Kaddish* after *Minchah,* since these prayers are considered contiguous with *Shemoneh Esrei*. It is, however, not permissible to read the Torah or to recite any other *Kaddish* (O.C. 55:3; M.B. §18-20).

126. At *Maariv,* the *chazzan* may recite the *Kaddish* preceding *Shemoneh Esrei* if a *minyan* was present for the recital of *Borchu*. The Full *Kaddish* may be recited after *Shemoneh Esrei* if a *minyan* was present at the beginning of *Shemoneh Esrei* (M.B. 55:22).

SERVICES ON SPECIAL DAYS

◆§ Taanis Esther

127. (a) *Maariv* on the eve of Taanis Esther follows the regular weekday service.

(b) *Shacharis* of Taanis Esther is the same as on other fast days (see below, §133).

(c) Before [in some congregations after] *Minchah,* the *machtzis hashekel* donation — based on the Torah-ordained annual contribution for the purchase of communal Temple sacrifices — is given. For every adult, male or female, three half-*shekels* (see below) are placed into a charity box or place designated for that purpose [many also donate for each child, some even for an unborn child]. The money is usually used for the upkeep of the synagogue or for another charity. Since half-*shekels* are not used today, a coin valued at half the basic currency (in the United States a half-dollar coin) is used to represent the half-*shekel*.

(d) *Minchah* of Taanis Esther is the same as that of other fast days (see below, §133) except that *Tachanun* and *Avinu Malkeinu* are not recited. When Purim falls on Sunday, Taanis Esther is moved back to the previous Thursday and *Tachanun* and *Avinu Malkeinu* are recited.

◆§ Purim — Maariv

128. (a) During every *Shemoneh Esrei* and *Bircas HaMazon* of Purim, עַל הַנִּסִּים is recited. If forgotten in *Shemoneh Esrei,* see *Laws* §89; during *Bircas HaMazon,* see page 273.

(b) The regular weekday *Maariv* (pp. 358-390) is recited, and then the Full *Kaddish* (p. 390); the *Megillah* is then read (see below).

(c) Before reading the *Megillah*, the reader recites three blessings. After the reading, the concluding blessing and the *piyut* אֲשֶׁר הֵנִיא are recited.

(d) On weekday nights, *Maariv* continues with וְאַתָּה קָדוֹשׁ (p. 430); the Full *Kaddish* (p. 434) with the omission of the verse תִּתְקַבֵּל;

עָלֵינוּ (p. 392) and the Mourner's *Kaddish* (p. 395).

On Saturday night, *Maariv* continues with the regular service for the conclusion of the Sabbath (p. 427), but with the omission in the Full *Kaddish* of the verse beginning תִּתְקַבֵּל.

◆§ Purim — Shacharis

129. (a) The weekday *Shacharis* is recited (with עַל הַנִּסִּים) until after the silent *Shemoneh Esrei*.

(b) During the *chazzan's* repetition many congregations recite *Krovetz*.

(c) One Torah scroll is removed from the Ark; the Purim portion is read; Half-*Kaddish* is recited; the Torah is raised; wrapped; and returned to the Ark.

(d) Before reading the *Megillah,* the reader recites three blessings. Each member of the congregation should declare mentally that the blessings also apply to the *mitzvos* of *mishloach manos,* gifts to the poor, and the Purim feast.

(e) After the reading, the concluding blessing and שׁוֹשַׁנַּת יַעֲקֹב are recited.

(f) The regular *Shacharis* service continues with אַשְׁרֵי, but לַמְנַצֵּחַ is omitted.

◆§ Tishah B'Av — Maariv

130. (a) Although other fasts begin in the morning and prohibit only eating/drinking, the fast of Tishah B'Av begins at sunset of the previous day and prohibits eating/drinking, bathing, anointing, wearing leather shoes, and cohabitation.

(b) *Maariv* begins in the usual manner (p. 358). After בָּרְכוּ the congregation sits on the floor or on low stools and the lights are dimmed. The regular *Maariv* service is followed [on Saturday night with the addition of אַתָּה חוֹנַנְתָּנוּ (p. 376)] until after the *Shemoneh Esrei* (p. 390), and then the Full *Kaddish* (p. 390) is recited.

(c) On Saturday night, although *Havdalah*

is not recited, the blessing בּוֹרֵא מְאוֹרֵי הָאֵשׁ is recited over a multiwicked candle.

(d) *Eichah* (the Book of *Lamentations*) is chanted aloud by the reader (in some congregations each individual reads along in an undertone). The evening *Kinnos* are then recited.

(e) *Kinnos* are followed by וְאַתָּה קָדוֹשׁ (p. 430); the Full *Kaddish* (p. 434) with the omission of the verse עָלֵינוּ; תִּתְקַבַּל (p. 392) and the Mourner's *Kaddish* (p. 395). [On Saturday night וַיְהִי נֹעַם and וְיִתֵּן לְךָ are omitted, and *Havdalah* is postponed until Sunday night.]

◄§ Tishah B'Av — Shacharis

131. (a) The *tallis kattan (tzitzis)* is worn but he accompanying blessing is omitted. Donning of the *tallis* and *tefillin* is postponed until *Minchah*.

(b) The morning blessings are recited as usual; however, the blessing שֶׁעָשָׂה לִי כָּל צָרְכִּי is recited by some, but omitted entirely or postponed until after the fast by others.

(c) The weekday service continues until after *Shemoneh Esrei*. [Some omit קָרְבָּנוֹת.]

(d) During his repetition the *chazzan* recites עֲנֵנוּ [see §133 rule (b) below]; and he omits בִּרְכַּת כֹּהֲנִים. After his repetition, the *chazzan* recites Half-*Kaddish*.

(e) One Torah scroll is removed from the Ark; the Tishah B'Av portion is read; Half-*Kaddish* is recited; the Torah is raised and wrapped; the *Haftarah* is read; and the Torah is returned to the Ark.

(f) *Kinnos* are recited, each congregation according to its custom. It is preferable that their recitation be extended until just before noon.

(g) After *Kinnos*, אַשְׁרֵי and וּבָא לְצִיוֹן with the omission of the second verse (וַאֲנִי זֹאת) are recited, followed by the Full *Kaddish* with the omission of the verse עָלֵינוּ; תִּתְקַבַּל, and the Mourner's *Kaddish*. The Song of the Day and other readings are postponed until *Minchah*.

◄§ Tishah B'Av — Minchah/Maariv

132. (a) The *tallis* and *tefillin* are donned and whatever passages were omitted from the *Shacharis* service are recited.

(b) The *Minchah* service is the same as for other fast days (see below) with two exceptions: The prayer נַחֵם is inserted into the Rebuilding Jerusalem blessing; and *Avinu Malkeinu* and *Tachanun* are omitted.

(c) The regular weekday *Maariv* is recited.

On Sunday night, an abridged form of *Havdalah* — omitting the first paragraph, spices, and flame — is recited.

(d) *Kiddush Levanah* (p. 406) is customarily postponed until after Tishah B'Av. However, since this blessing should be recited joyfully, one should break the fast before its recitation.

◄§ Other Fast Days

133. The fasts of 10 Teves, 3 Tishrei (Fast of Gedaliah), 17 Tammuz and 13 Adar (Fast of Esther) all begin at dawn. On the eve of these fasts, the regular *Maariv* (p. 358) is recited. At *Shacharis* and *Minchah* the service includes special prayers, as follows:

(a) The regular weekday *Shacharis* is recited until after *Shemoneh Esrei*.

(b) If ten members of the *minyan* [some authorities require only seven] are fasting, the *chazzan* recites עֲנֵנוּ between the blessings for Redemption and Health. If less than the required number are fasting, the *chazzan* inserts עֲנֵנוּ into the Acceptance of Prayer blessing and omits the closing sentence.

(c) After the *chazzan's* repetition, *Selichos* are recited.

(d) After *Selichos*, *Avinu Malkeinu* and *Tachanun* are recited.

(e) One Torah scroll is removed from the Ark, the fast day portion is read, and the regular weekday *Shacharis* is followed until its conclusion.

(f) *Minchah* begins with *Ashrei* and Half-*Kaddish*.

(g) If at least seven members of the *minyan* are fasting, one Torah scroll is removed from the Ark; the fast day portion is read; the Torah is raised and wrapped; the *Haftarah* is read; the Torah is returned to the Ark and Half-*Kaddish* is recited.

(h) *Shemoneh Esrei* is recited with the addition of עֲנֵנוּ [both in the silent *Shemoneh Esrei* and in the *chazzan's* repetition, but see (b) above] by those who are fasting.

(i) After the *chazzan's* repetition, *Avinu Malkeinu* and *Tachanun* are recited, followed by עָלֵינוּ, קַדִּישׁ שָׁלֵם and the Mourner's *Kaddish*.

For the practice on *Taanis Esther*, see above §127(d). When the fast of 10 *Teves* falls on Friday, *Tachanun* and *Avinu Malkeinu* are not recited at *Minchah*, due to the approaching Sabbath.

❖{ THE MOURNER'S KADDISH TRANSLITERATED }❖

TRANSLITERATED WITH ASHKENAZIC PRONUNCIATION

Yisgadal v'yiskadash Sh'mei rabbaw (Cong.– Amein.)
b'allmaw dee v'raw chir'usei v'yamlich malchusei,
v'yatzmach purkanei veekareiv M'shichei (Cong.– Amein.)
b'chayei'chon, uv'yomei'chon, uv'chayei d'chawl Beis Yisrawel,
ba'agawlaw u'vizman kawriv. V'imru: Amein.
(Cong. – Amein. Y'hei Sh'mei rabbaw m'vawrach l'allam ul'allmei allmayaw.)
Y'hei Sh'mei rabbaw m'vawrach, l'allam ul'allmei allmayaw.

Yisbawrach, v'yishtabach, v'yispaw'ar, v'yisromam, v'yisnasei,
v'yis'hadar, v'yis'aleh, v'yis'halawl
Sh'mei d'Kudshaw B'rich Hu (Cong. – B'rich Hu)
°l'aylaw min kawl
(°from Rosh Hashanah to Yom Kippur substitute: *l'aylaw [u]l'aylaw mikawl)*
bir'chawsaw v'shi'rawsaw,
tushb'chawsaw v'ne'che'mawsaw
da'ami'rawn b'allmaw. V'imru: Amein. (Cong. – Amein.)

Y'hei sh'lawmaw rabbaw min Sh'mayaw v'chayim tovim
awleinu v'al kawl Yisrawel. V'imru: Amein. (Cong. – Amein.)

Bow. Take three steps back.

[bow left] Oseh shawlom bimromawv,
[bow right] Hu ya'aseh shawlom awleinu,
[bow forward] v'al kawl Yisrawel. V'imru: Amein. (Cong. – Amein.)

Remain standing in place for a few moments, then take three steps forward.

◄◄ THE RABBIS' KADDISH / KADDISH D'RABBANAN ►►

TRANSLITERATED WITH ASHKENAZIC PRONUNCIATION

Yisgadal v'yiskadash Sh'mei rabbaw (Cong.– Amein.)
b'allmaw dee v'raw chir'usei v'yamlich malchusei,
v'yatzmach purkanei veekareiv M'shichei (Cong.– Amein.)
b'chayei'chon, uv'yomei'chon, uv'chayei d'chawl Beis Yisrawel,
ba'agawlaw u'vizman kawriv. V'imru: Amein.

(Cong. – Amein. Y'hei Sh'mei rabbaw m'vawrach l'allam ul'allmei allmayaw.)
Y'hei Sh'mei rabbaw m'vawrach, l'allam ul'allmei allmayaw.

Yisbawrach, v'yishtabach, v'yispaw'ar, v'yisromam, v'yisnasei,
v'yis'hadar, v'yis'aleh, v'yis'halawl
Sh'mei d'Kudshaw B'rich Hu (Cong. – B'rich Hu)
°l'aylaw min kawl

(°from Rosh Hashanah to Yom Kippur substitute: l'aylaw [u]l'aylaw mikawl)
bir'chawsaw v'shi'rawsaw,
tushb'chawsaw v'ne'che'mawsaw
da'ami'rawn b'allmaw. V'imru: Amein. (Cong. – Amein.)

Al Yisrawel v'al Rabaw'nawn v'al talmidei'hon,
v'al kawl talmidei salmidei'hon,
v'al kawl mawn d'awskin b'Oraysaw,
dee v'asraw (In Israel: kadishaw) hawdain, v'dee b'chol asar va'asar.
Y'hei l'hon ul'chon sh'lawmaw rabbaw,
cheenaw v'chisdaw v'rachamin,
v'chayin arichin, u'm'zonei r'vichei,
u'furkawnaw min kawdawm Avuhone dee viShmayaw (v'Araw.)
V'imru: Amein. (Cong. – Amein.)

Y'hei sh'lawmaw rabbaw min Sh'mayaw v'chayim tovim
awleinu v'al kawl Yisrawel. V'imru: Amein. (Cong. – Amein.)

Bow. Take three steps back.
[bow left] Oseh shawlom bimromawv,
[bow right] Hu b'rachamawv ya'aseh shawlom awleinu,
[bow forward] v'al kawl Yisrawel. V'imru: Amein. (Cong. – Amein.)

Remain standing in place for a few moments, then take three steps forward.